1st FULL TIME DEALER - STARTING May 1, 19... ...k!

1991 BASEBA...

1991 sets postpaid.
(All other items see shipping & insura...

TOPPS	FLEE...	SCORE
792 cards	660 card...	900 cards
Factory collated	Factory collate...	Factory collated
$29.75	$27.75	$28.50

PARTIAL LIST OF SETS AVAILABLE

(All sets are in NrMT-Mint condition)
See shipping and insurance table below.
NOTE: All prices subject to change without notice.

BASEBALL SETS

1990 Upper Deck (800) factory	$55.75
1990 Upper Deck High Number Series	
(701-800) factory	14.50
(701-800) hand	10.00
1990 Topps Traded (132)	13.75
1990 Fleer Update (132)	14.25
1990 Score Traded (110)	14.00
1990 Donruss Rookie (56)	13.50
1990 Topps (792) factory	28.75
1990 Fleer (660) factory	26.75
1990 Score (714) factory	call
1990 Donruss (715 plus puzzle) factory	
	29.75
1989 Topps (792) factory	27.50
1989 Topps (792)	25.50
1989 Fleer (660)	31.50
1989 Score (660)	27.50
1989 Donruss (660) factory	37.50
1989 Bowman (484) factory	32.95
1989 Topps Traded (132)	18.75
1989 Fleer Update (132)	24.00
1989 Score Traded (110)	17.50
1989 Donruss Traded (56)	18.50
1989 Donruss Rookies (56)	35.00
1989 Topps Glossy (792)	195.00
1989 Bowman Glossy (484)	169.95
1989 Bowman Wax Box (468)	12.00
1988 Topps (792)	35.00
1988 Fleer (660) factory	50.00
1988 Score (660) factory	27.50
1989 Donruss (660) factory	32.50
1988 Topps Traded (132)	37.50
1988 Fleer Update (132)	17.50
1988 Fleer Glossy Update (132)	22.95
1988 Score Traded (110)	85.00
1988 Donruss Rookies (56)	17.50
1988 Donruss Best	24.95
1988 Fleer Glossy (660)	44.95
1988 Topps Glossy (792)	135.00
1987 Topps (792)	53.50
1987 Fleer (660) factory	135.00
1987 Sportflics (200 plus trivia)	42.50
1987 Sportflics Rookies #2 (25 plus trivia)	17.00
1987 Fleer Glossy (660 in collectors tin)	
	99.95
1987 Topps Glossy (792)	125.00
1987 Topps Traded (132)	20.00
1987 Fleer Update (132)	25.00
1987 Fleer Glossy Update (132 plus tin)	
	94.95

1987 Donruss Opening Day (272)	25.00
1987 Donruss Rookies (56)	25.00
1986 Topps (792)	60.00
1986 Topps Traded (132)	50.00
1986 Fleer (660)	150.00
1986 Fleer Update (132)	45.00
1986 Donruss (660)	250.00
1986 Donruss Rookies (56)	125.00
1986 Donruss Highlights (56)	7.00
1986 Sportflics (200)	48.00
1986 SF Decade Greats (75)	24.75
1986 SF Rookies (50)	25.00
1985 Topps (792)	125.00
1985 Topps Traded (132)	23.00
1985 Fleer (660)	155.00
1985 Fleer Traded (132)	20.00
1985 Donruss (660)	190.00
1985 Donruss Leaf (264)	60.00
1984 Topps (792)	130.00
1984 Topps Traded (132)	125.00
1984 Fleer (660)	175.00
1984 Fleer Update (132)	700.00
1984 Donruss (656)	400.00
1983 Topps (792)	170.00
1983 Topps Traded (132)	115.00
1983 Fleer (660)	130.00
1983 Donruss (660)	160.00
1982 Topps (792)	105.00
1982 Topps Traded (132)	52.50
1982 Fleer (660)	65.00
1982 Donruss (660)	65.00
1981 Topps (726)	130.00
1981 Topps Traded (132)	37.50
1981 Fleer (660)	62.50
1981 Donruss (605)	65.00
1980 Topps (726)	325.00
1979 Topps (726) (Wills-Blue Jays)	
	250.00
1978 Topps (726)	300.00
1977 Topps (660)	400.00
1976 Topps (660)	425.00
1975 Topps (660)	725.00
1974 Topps (660)	575.00
1973 Topps (660)	1100.00

FOOTBALL SETS

1990 Topps (528) factory	23.95
1990 Topps Update (132)	14.50
1990 Score (665) factory	24.95
1990 Score Supplement (110)	14.75
1990 Score Young Superstars (40)	12.50

FOOTBALL SETS

1990 CFL Series 1 (110)	21.50
1990 CFL Series 2 (110)	20.50
1990 Action Packed Rookie/Update (84)	
	38.95
1990 Score Unopened Box	
Series 1 (5)	18.75
Series 2 (576)	18.25
1990 Pro-Set Unopened Box	
Series 1 (540)	18.00
Series 2 (540)	18.50
1989 Topps (396)	24.50
1989 Topps Football Update (132)	14.95
1989 Score (330)	75.75
1989 Score Football Supplement (110 plus 10 trivia)	30.95
1989 Pro Set Unopened Box 1st Series (540)	29.50
1988 Topps (396)	35.00
1987 Topps (396)	45.00
1986 Topps (396)	95.00
1985 Topps USFL (132)	90.00
1985 Topps USFL (132)	550.00
1985 Topps (396)	60.00
1985 Topps (396)	155.00
1983 Topps (396)	60.00
1982 Topps (528)	105.00
1981 Topps (528)	250.00
1980 Topps (528)	100.00
1979 Topps (528)	100.00
1978 Topps (528)	110.00
1977 Topps (528)	300.00
1976 Topps (528)	425.00
1975 Topps (528)	275.00
1974 Topps (528)	275.00
1973 Topps (528)	450.00
1972 Topps (351)	1,325.00
1971 Topps (263)	425.00
1970 Topps (263)	450.00
1970 Topps Super (35)	200.00
1968 Topps (219)	475.00

BASKETBALL SETS

1990-91 Fleer (198)	18.50
1990-91 Hoops Unopened Box (540)	21.00
1990 Star Pics (70)	29.95
1989-90 Fleer Basketball (168)	42.50
1989-90 Fleer Basketball Sticker Cards (11)	
	6.00
1988-89 Fleer (132)	100.00
1988-89 Fleer NBA Sticker Cards (11)	15.00

BASKETBALL SETS

1987-88 Fleer (132)	245.00
1987-88 Fleer NBA Sticker Cards (11)	25.00
1986-87 Fleer (132)	950.00
1986-87 Fleer NBA Sticker Cards (11)	75.00
1981-82 Topps (198)	115.00
1980-81 Topps (88) Bird & Johnson Same Cards	400.00
1980-81 Topps (88)	250.00
1979-80 Topps (132)	50.00
1978-79 Topps (132)	60.00
1977-78 Topps (132)	75.00
1976-77 Topps (144)	110.00
1975-76 Topps (330)	600.00
1974-75 Topps (264)	225.00
1973-74 Topps (264)	275.00
1972-73 Topps (264)	700.00

HOCKEY SETS

1990 Topps (396)	17.95
1990 Score-USA (445)	18.50
1990 Score-Canada (445)	19.50
1990 Bowman (264)	13.50
1990 Pro-Set Unopened Box (540)	18.95
1990 Upper Deck Unopened Box (432)	31.95
1990-91 O-Pee-Chee (528)	28.75
1989-90 O-Pee-Chee (330)	30.00
1989-90 Topps Hockey (198)	25.00
1989-90 Topps Hockey Sticker Cards (33)	
	10.00
1988-89 Topps (264)	90.00
1988-89 Topps NHL Sticker Cards (12)	7.50
1987-88 Topps (198)	POR
1987-88 OPC (264)	100.00
1987-88 OPC Leader Minis (42)	6.25
1987-88 Topps NHL Sticker Cards (12)	6.25
1985-86 Topps NHL Sticker Cards (33)	7.00
1984-85 Topps (165)	62.50
1983-84 OPC (396)	170.00
1982-83 OPC (396)	180.00
1981-82 Topps (198)	110.00
1980-81 Topps (264)	225.00
1978-79 Topps (264)	75.00
1977-78 Topps (265)	85.00
1976-77 Topps (264)	100.00
1975-76 Topps (330)	275.00
1974-75 Topps (264)	225.00
1973-74 Topps (198)	235.00
1972-73 Topps (176)	225.00
1971-72 Topps (132)	230.00
1968-69 Topps (132)	450.00

SHIPPING AND INSURANCE TABLE

$.01 to $25.00	add $3.50
$25.01 to $50.00	add $4.50
$50.01 And Over	add $5.50

All prices subject to change. Call to verify prices.

CHECK POLICY:
All personal checks will be held 15 working days for clearance. For faster service, please send postal money orders.

CANADA CUSTOMERS:
Please send Postal Money Order in U.S. Funds only, and an additional $6.00 per set for sets over 250 cards, $3.00 per set for sets under 250 cards for shipping your sets.

ALASKA, HAWAII, PUERTO RICO, APO, FPO & P.O. CUSTOMERS:
Add an additional $4.00 per set for sets over 250 cards and $2.50 per set for sets under 250 cards for shipping your set (if you have a P.O. Box and want your order shipped via UPS, please include your UPS shipping address).

OUR 44TH YEAR IN CARDS

735 Old Wausau Road
P.O. Box 863, Dept. 977
Stevens Point, WI 54481

(715) 344-8687 • FAX # (715) 344-1778

LARRY FRITSCH CARDS, INC.

See our inside back cover ad for other items in stock.

WITH OVER 50 MILLION CARDS IN STOCK. WE HAVE AMERICA'S MOST COMPLETE STOCK OF SPORTS TRADING CARDS. Full money back guarantee if you are not completely satisfied with our service and products. YOU, the customers are always NO. 1 to us!
To receive Super Service it is necessary to send a POSTAL MONEY ORDER with your order. (All personal checks are held 15 days for clearance) (Charge orders add 5% to total). Minimum charge order $20.00. WI residents add 5.5% sales tax.

Fifth Edition — 1991

Baseball Card Price Guide

Jeff Kurowski, Editor

Library of Congress Catalog Number: 87-80033
ISBN: 0-87341-155-2

Krause Publications, Inc.
700 E. State St.
Iola, WI 54990

Printed in the United States of America

ACKNOWLEDGEMENTS

Dozens of individuals have made countless valuable contributions which have been incorporated into the *Sports Collectors Digest Baseball Card Price Guide* While all cannot be acknowledged, special appreciation is extended to the following principal contributors who have exhibited a special dedication by creating, revising or verifying listings and technical data, reviewing market valuations or loaning cards for photography.

Johnny Adams, Jr.
Ken Agona
  (Sports Cards Plus)
Gary Agostino
Lisa Albano
Dan Albaugh
Mark Anker
Steve Applebaum
John Beisiegel
Karen Bell
Cathy Black
Mike Bodner
Bill Bossert
  (Mid-Atlantic Coin Exchange)
Brian Boston
Mike Boyd
Jon Brecka
John Brigandi
  (Brigandi Coin Co.)Lou Brown
Dan Bruner
  (The Card King)
Greg Bussineau
  (Superior Sports Cards)
Billy Caldwell
  (Packman)
Len Caprisecca
Tony Carrafiell
  (Delco Sports Cards)
Lee Champion
Dwight Chapin
Chriss Christiansen
Shane Cohen
  (Grand Slam Sports Collectibles)
Rich Cole
Charles Conlon
Eric Cooper
  (All Star Cards)
Bryan Couling
Clyde Cripe
Jim Cumpton
Robert Curtiss
Tom Daniels
  (T&J Sports Cards)
Tom Day
Dick DeCourcy
  (Georgia Music & Sports)
Mike Del Gado
  (All American Sportscards)
Larry Dluhy
  (Texas Trading Cards)
John Dorsey
Curtis Earl
Steve Ellingboe

Joe Esposito
  (B&E Collectibles)
Doak Ewing
Shirley Eross
  (Hobbyrama Sports By Eross)
David Festberg
  (Baseball and Hobby Shop)
Jay Finglass
Nick Flaviano
Jeff Fritsch
Larry Fritsch
Richard Galasso
Tom Galic
Tony Galovich
  (American Card Exchange)
Frank Giffune
Richard Gilkeson
Dick Goddard
Jack Goodman
Bill Goodwin
  (St. Louis Baseball Cards)
Audre Gold
  (Au Sports Memorabilia)
Mike Gordon
Howard Gordon
Bob Gray
Paul Green
Wayne Grove
  (First Base)
Gerry Guenther
Don Guilbert
Tom Guilfoile
David, Joel & Walter Hall
  (Hall's Nostalgia)
Gary Hamilton
Tom Harbin
Don Harrison
Rick Hawksley
Herbert Hecht
Bill Henderson
Gregg Hitesman
Jack Horkan
Jim Horne
Ron Hosmer
Marvin Huck
Robert Jacobsen
Donn Jennings
Scott Jensen
Jim Johnston
Stewart Jones
Larry Jordon
Judy Kay
  (Kay's Baseball Cards)
Allan Kaye
Michael Keedy

Mark Kemmerle
Rick Keplinger
John King
John Kittleson
  (Sports Collectibles)
Bob Koehler
David Kohler
John Kurowski
Steve Lacasse
Lee Lasseigne
William Lawrence
Morley Leeking
Don Lepore
Rod Lethbridge
Paul Lewicki
Neil Lewis
Howie Levy
  (Blue Chip Sportscard)
Rob Lifson
Ken & Norman Liss
Jeff Litteral
Mark MacRae
Ken Magee
Paul Marchant
Bill Mastro
Jay McCracken
Tony McLaughlin
Don McPherson
John Mehlin
Bill Mendel
Blake Meyer
  (Lone Star Sportcard Co.)
Dick Millerd
Minnesota Sports Collectibles
Keith Mitchell
J.A. Monaco
Joe Morano
Brian Morris
Mike Mowery
Peter Muldavin
Mark Murphy
  (The Baseball Card "Kid")
Vincent Murray
David Musser
  (D.M.B.'s Baseball Cards)
Frank Nagy
Chuck Nobriga
Mark Nochta
Wayne Nochta
Keith Olbermann
Joe Pasternack
  (Card Collectors Co.)
Marty Perry
Tom Pfirrman
  (Baseball Card Corner)
Dan Piepenbrok

Stan Pietruska
  (Pro Sports Investments)
Paul Pollard
Ed Ransom
Tom Reid
Bob Richardson
Gavin Riley
Ron Ritzler
Mike Rodell
Mike Rogers
Chris Ronan
Rocky Rosato
Alan Rosen
John Rumierz
Bob Rund
Jon Sands
  (Howard's Coin Shop)
Kevin Savage
  (The Sports Gallery)
Stephen Schauer
Robert Scott
Corey Shanus
Dan Shedrick
Max Silberman
Barry Sloate
Joe Smith
Mark Soltan
John Spalding
Kevin Spears
Gene Speranza
David Spivack
Don Steinbach
Dan Stickney
Larry Stone
Doug Stultz
Joe Szeremet
Erik Teller
K.J. Terplak
Dick Tinsley
Bud Tompkins
  (Minnesota Connection)
Scott Torrey
Rich Unruh
Jack Urban
Joe Valle
  (Cardboard Dreams)
Pete Waldman
Eric Waller
Gary Walter
Ken Weimer
Dale Weselowski
E.C. Wharton-Tigar
Chris Williams
Charles Williamson
Kit Young
Ted Zanidakis

ROOKIE/FIRST CARD DESIGNATIONS

A player's name in italic type indicates a rookie card. An (FC) designation indicates a player's first card for that particular company. FCs will be found in 1981-90 Donruss, Fleer, Score and Topps sets. They will also be located in the Donruss Rookies, Fleer Update, Topps Traded and Score Traded sets.

BASEBALL CARD HISTORY

In 1887 - over 100 years ago - the first nationally distributed baseball cards were issued by Goodwin & Co. of New York City. The 1½" x 2½" cards featured posed studio photographs glued to stiff cardboard. They were inserted into cigarette packages with such exotic brand names as Old Judge, Gypsy Queen and Dog's Head. Poses were formal, with artificial backgrounds and bare-handed players fielding balls suspended on strings to simulate action.

Then, as now, baseball cards were intended to stimulate product sales. What could be more American than using the diamond heroes of the national pastime to gain an edge on the competition? It is a tradition that has continued virtually unbroken for a century.

Following Goodwin's lead a year later, competitors began issuing baseball cards with their cigarettes, using full-color lithography to bring to life painted portraits of the era's top players.

After a few short years of intense competition, the cigarette industry's leading firms formed a monopoly and cornered the market. By the mid-1890's, there was little competition, and no reason to issue baseball cards. The first great period of baseball card issues came to an end.

The importing of Turkish tobaccos in the years just prior to 1910 created a revolution in American smoking habits. With dozens of new firms entering the market, the idea of using baseball cards to boost sales was revived.

In the years from 1909-1912, dozens of different sets of cards were produced to be given away in cigarette packages. There was a greater than ever variety in sizes, shapes and designs, from the extremely popular 1½" x 2⅝" color lithographed set of 500+ players which collectors call T206, to the large (5" x 8") Turkey Red brand cards. There were double folders, featuring two players on the same card, and triple folders; which had two player portraits and an action scene. Gold ink and embossed designs were also tried to make each competing company's cards attractive and popular.

It was this era that saw the issue of the "King of Baseball cards", the T206 Honus Wagner card, worth $200,000.

The zeal with which America's youngsters pursued their fathers, uncles, and neighbors for cigarette cards in the years just prior to World War I convinced the nation's confectioners that baseball cards could also be used to boost candy sales.

While baseball cards had been produced by candy companies on a limited basis as far back as the 1880s, by the early 1920s the concept was being widely used in the industry. The highly competitive caramel business was a major force in this new marketing strategy, offering a baseball card in each package of candy. Not to be outdone, Cracker Jack began including baseball cards in each box. The 1914-1915 Cracker Jack cards are important because they were the most popular of the candy cards to include players form a short-lived third major league, the Federal League.

Generally, candy cards of the era were not as colorful or well-printed as the earlier tobacco cards, due to a shortage of paper and ink-making ingredients caused by World War I.

The association of bubble gum and baseball cards is a phenomenon of only the past half-century. In the early 1930s techniques were developed using rubber tree products to give the elasticity necessary for blowing bubbles.

During this era the standard method of selling a slab of bubble gum and a baseball card in a colorfully wax-wrapped 1¢ package was developed. Bubble gum - and baseball cards - production in this era was centered in Massachusetts, where National Chicle Company (Cambridge) and Goudey Gum Company (Boston) were headquartered.

Most bubble gum cards produced in the early 1930s featured a roughly square (about 2½") format, with players depicted in colorful paintings. For the first time, considerable attention was paid to the backs of the cards, where biographical details, career highlights and past season statistics were presented.

In 1939, a new company entered the baseball card market - Gum, Inc., of Philadelphia. Its "Play Ball" gum was the major supplier of baseball cards until 1941, when World War II caused a shortage of the materials necessary both for the production of bubble gum and the printing of baseball cards.

Three years after the end of World War II baseball cards returned on a national scale, with two companies competing for the bubble gum market. In Philadelphia, the former Gum, Inc., reappeared on the market as Bowman Gum, Inc.

Bowman's first baseball card set appeared in 1948, very similar in format to the cards which had existed prior to the war, black and white player photos on nearly square (2" x 2½") cardboard. The 1948 Bowman effort was modest, with only 48 cards. The following year, color was added to the photos. For 1950, Bowman replaced the re-rouched photos with original color painting of players, many of which were repeated a year later in the 1951 issue. Also new for 1951 was a larger card size, 2" x 3⅛".

Bowman had little national competition in this era. In 1948-1949, Leaf Gum in Chicago produced a 98-card set that is the only bubble gum issue of the era to include a Joe DiMaggio card.

While Bowman dominated the post-war era through 1951, in that year Topps began production of its first baseball cards, issuing three different small sets of cards and serving warning that it was going to become a major force in the baseball card field.

In 1952, Brooklyn-based Topps entered the baseball card market in a big way. Not only was its 407-card set the largest single-year issue ever produced, but its 2⅝" x 3¾" format was the largest-size baseball card ever offered for over-the-counter sale. Other innovations in Topps' premiere issue for 1952 included the first-ever use of team logos in card design, and on the back of the card, the first use of line statistics to document the player's previous year and career performance. By contrast, Bowman's set for 1952 remained in the smaller format, had 72 fewer cards and showed little change in design from 1951.

Just as clearly as Topps won the 1952 baseball card battle, Bowman came back in 1953 with what is often considered the finest baseball card set ever produced. For the first time ever, actual color photographs were reproduced on baseball cards in Bowman's 160-card set. To allow the full impact of the new technology, there were no other design elements on the front of the card and Bowman adopted a larger format, 2½" x 3¾".

And so the competition went for five years, each company trying to gain an edge by signing players to exclusive contracts and creating new and exciting card designs each year. Gradually, Topps became the dominant force in the baseball card market. In late 1955, Bowman admitted defeat and the company was sold to Topps.

Baseball cards entered a new era in 1957. After years of intense competition, Topps enjoyed a virtual monopoly that was rarely seriously challenged in the next 25 years. One such challenge in the opening years of the 1960s came from Post cereal, which from 1961-1963 issued 200-card sets on the backs of its cereal boxes.

In 1957, Topps' baseball cards were issued in a new size - 2½" x 3½" - that would become the industry-wide standard that prevails to this day. It was also that year that Topps first used full-color photographs for its cards, rather than paintings or re-touched black and white photos. Another innovation in the 1957 set was the introduction of complete major and/or minor league statistics on the card backs. This feature quickly became a favorite with youngsters and provided fuel for endless schoolyard debates about whether one player was better than another.

In the ensuing five years, major league baseball underwent monumental changes. In 1958, the Giants and Dodgers left New York for California. In 1961-1962 expansion came to the major leagues, with new teams springing up from coast to coast and border to border.

The Topps baseball cards of the era preserve those days when modern baseball was in its formative stages.

In 1963, for the first time in seven years, it looked as if there might once again be two baseball card issues to choose from. After three years of issuing "old-timers" cards sets, Fleer issued a 66-card set of current players. Topps took Fleer to court, where the validity of Topps' exclusive contracts with baseball players to appear on bubble gum cards was upheld. It was the last major challenge to Topps for nearly 20 years.

The 1960's offered baseball card collecting at its traditional finest. Youngsters would wait and worry through the long winter, watching candy store shelves for the first appearance of the brightly colored 5¢ card packs in the spring. A cry of "They're in!" could empty a playground in seconds as youngsters rushed to the corner store to see what design innovations Topps had come up with for the new year. Then, periodically through the summer, new series would be released, offering a new challenge to complete. As the season wore down, fewer and fewer stores carried the final few series, and it became a real struggle to complete the "high numbers" from a given year's set. But is was all part of the fun of buying baseball cards in the 1960s.

The early 1970s brought some important changes to the baseball card scene. The decade's first two Topps issues were stunning in that the traditional white border was dropped in favor of gray in 1970, and black in 1971. In 1972, Topps' card design was absolutely psychedelic, with brightly colored frames around the player photos, and comic book typography popping out all over. The design for the 1973 cards was more traditional, but the photos were not. Instead of close-up portraits or posed "action" shots, many cards in the 1973 Topps set featured actual game action photos. Unfortunately, too many of those photos made it hard to tell which player was which, and the set was roundly panned by collectors.

But most significantly, 1973 marked the last year in which baseball cards were issued by series through the course of the summer. On the positive side, this eliminated the traditionally scarce "high numbers" produced toward the end of the season. On the negative side, it meant players who had been traded in the pre-season could no longer be shown in their "correct" uniforms, and outstanding new players had to wait a full year before their rookie cards would debut.

This marketing change made a significant impact on the hobby and helped spur a tremendous growth period in the late 1970s. By offering all of its cards at once, Topps made it easy for baseball card dealers to offer complete sets early in the year. Previously, collectors had to either assemble their sets by buying packs of cards, or wait until all series had been issued to buy a set from a dealer. It was in this era that many of today's top baseball card dealers got their start or made the switch to baseball cards as a full-time business.

During this era, the first significant national competition to Topps' baseball card monopoly in many years was introduced. Hostess, a bakery products company, began distributing baseball cards printed on the bottoms of packages of its snack cakes, while the Kellogg's company distributed simulated 3-D cards in boxes of its cereals. The eagerness with which collectors gobbled up these issues showed that the hobby was ready for a period of unprecedented growth.

The baseball card hobby literally boomed in 1981. A Federal court broke Topps' monopoly on the issue of baseball cards with bubble gum and Fleer of Philadelphia and Donruss of Memphis, entered the field as the first meaningful competition in nearly 20 years.

That same year also marked a beginning of the resurgence in the number of regional baseball card issues. Over the next few years, dozens of such sets came onto the market, helping to boost sales of everything from snack cakes to soda pop and police public relations. By 1984, more than half of the teams in the major leagues were issueing some type of baseball cards on a regional basis. The hobby had not enjoyed such diversity of issue since the mid-1950s.

While yet another court decision cost Fleer and Donruss the right to sell their baseball cards with bubble gum, both companies remained in the market and gained strength.

Topps' major contribution in this era was the introduction of annual "Traded" sets which offered cards of the year's new rookies as well as cards of traded players in their "correct" uniforms.

The mid-1980s showed continued strong growth in the number of active baseball card collectors, as well as the number of new baseball card issues. Topps, still the industry's leader, expanded the number and variety of its baseball issues with many different test issues and on-going specialty sets, including oversize cards, 3-D plastic cards, metal "cards" and much more.

After three years of over-production of its baseball card sets, Donruss, in 1984, significantly limited the number of cards printed, creating a situation in which demand exceeded supply, causing the value of Donruss cards to rise above Topps for the first time.

In 1984, Fleer followed Topps' lead and produced a season's-end "Update" set. Because the quantitiy of sets printed was extremely limited, and because it contains many of today's hottest young players, the 1984 Fleer Update set has become the most valuable baseball card issue produced in recent times.

In 1986, a fourth company joined the baseball "card wars." Called "Sprotflics," the cards were produced by a subsidiary of the Wrigley Gum company, and featured three different photos on each card in a simulated 3-D effect. For 1987, a fourth national baseball card set called Score entered the scene. A fifth national baseball card set (Upper Deck) was created for 1989.

HOW TO USE THIS CATALOG

This catalog has been uniquely designed to serve the needs of both beginning and advanced collectors. It provides a comprehensive guide to more than 100 years of baseball card issues, arranged so that even the most novice collector can consult it with confidence and erase.

The following explanations summarize the general practices used in preparing this catalog's listings. However, because of specialized requirements which may vary from card set to card set, these must not be considered ironclad. Where these standards have been set aside, appropriate notations are incorporated.

ARRANGEMENT

Because the most important feature in identifying, and pricing, a baseball card is its set of origin, this catalog has been alphabetically arranged according to the name by which the set is mostly popularly known to collectors.

Those sets that were issued for more than one year are then listed chronologically, from earliest to most recent.

Within each set, the cards are lsited by their designated card number, or in the absence of card numbers, alphabetically according to the last name of the player pictured.

IDENTIFICATION

While most modern baseball cards are well identified on front, back or both, as to date and issue, such has not always been the case. In general, the back of the card is more usefull in identifying the set of origin than the front. The issuer or sponsor's name will usually appera on the back since, after all, baseball cards were first issued as a promotional item to stimulate sales of other products. As often as not, that issuer's name is the name by which the set is known to collectors and under which it will be found listed in this catalog.

Virtually every set listed in this catalog is accompanied by a photograph of a representative card. If all else fails, a comparison of an unknown card with the photos in this book will usually produce a match.

As a special feature, each set listed in this catalog has been cross-indexed by its date of issue. This will allow identification in some difficult cases since a baseball card's general age, if not specific year of issue, can usually be fixed by studying the biographical or statistical information on the back of the card. The last year mentioned in either the biography or stats is usually the year which preceded the year of issue.

PHOTOGRAPHS

A photograph of the front and back of at least one representative card from virtually every set listed in this catalog has been incorporated into the listings to aid in identification.

Photographs have been printed in reduced size. The actual size of cards in each set is given in the introductory text preceding its listing.

DATING

The dating of baseball cards by year of issue on the front of back of the card itself is a relatively new phenomenon. In most cases, to accurately determine a date of issue for an unidentified card, it must be studied for clues. As mentioned, the biography, career summary or statistics on the back of the card are the best way to pinpoint a year of issue. In most cases, the year of issue will be the year after the last season mentioned on the card.

Luckily for today's collector, earlier generations have done much of the research in deter- mining year of issue for those cards which bear no clues. the painstaking task of matching players' listed and/or pictured team against their career records often allowed an issue date to be determined.

In some cases, particular card sets were issued over a period of more than one calendar year, but since they are collected together as a single set, their specific year of issue is not important. Such sets will be listed with their complete known range of issue years.

NUMBERING

While many baseball card issues as far back as the 1880s have contained card numbers assigned by the issuer, to facilitate the collecting of a complete set, the practice has by no means been universal. Even today, not every set bears card numbers.

Logically, those baseball cards which were numbered by their manufacturer are presented in that numerical order within the listings of this catalog. The many unnumbered issues, however, have been assigned *Sports Collectors Digest Baseball Card Price Guide* numbers to facilitate their universal identification within the hobby, especially when buying and selling by mail. In all cases, numbers which have been assigned, or which otherwise do not appear on the card through error or by design, are shown in this catalog within parenthesis. In virtually all cases, unless a more natural system suggested itself by the unique nature of a particular set, the assignment of *Sports Collectors Digest Baseball Card Price Guide* numbers by the cataloging staff has been done by alphabetical arrangement of the player's last names or the card's principal title.

Significant collectible variations of any particular card are noted within the listings by the application of a suffix letter within parentheses. In instances of variations, the suffix "a" is assigned to the variation which was created first.

NAMES

The identification of a player by full name on the front of his baseball card has been a common practice only since the 1920s. Prior to that, the player's last name and team were the more usual information found on the card front.

As a standard practice, the listings in the *Sports Collectors Digest Baseball Card Price Guide* present the player's name exactly as it appears on the front of the card, if his full name is given there. If the player's full name only appears on the back, rather than the front, of the card, the listing corresponds to that designation.

In cases where only the player's last name is given on the card, the cataloging staff has included the first name by which he was most often known for ease of identification.

Cards which contain misspelled first or last name, or even wrong initials, will have included in their listings the incorrect information, with a correction accompanying in parentheses. This extends, also, to cases where the name on the card does not correspond to the player actually picured.

THIS IS THE MOST VALUABLE CARD YOU'LL EVER FIND...

When your sports collectible dealer can show you this card you'll be assured you're getting the best product available from a reputable firm.

Sports collectible dealers who carry a Sports Collectibles Association International membership card have pledged to uphold a professional code of ethics and deal with you, the collector, in a fair and equitable manner.

An SCAI membership card means honesty and integrity in the industry. It's probably the most important card you'll ever see.

If you're a sports collectibles dealer who hasn't yet joined SCAI, call us at 305-892-2841 to see how you can add this card to your collection.

Sports Collectibles Association International

A Professional Trade Group • 1450 N.E. 123 Street, N. Miami, FL 33161

GRADING

It is necessary that some sort of card grading standard be used so that buyer and seller (especially when dealing by mail) may reach an informed agreement on the value of a card. Each card set's listings are priced in the three grades of preservation in which those cards are most commonly encountered in the day to day buying and selling of the hobby marketplace.

Older cards are listed in grades of Near Mint (NR MT), Excellent (EX) and Very Good (VG), reflecting the basic fact that few cards were able to survive for 25, 50 or even 100 years in a close semblance to the condition of their issue. The pricing of cards in these three conditions will allow readers to accurately price cards which fall in intermediate grades, such as EX-MT, or VG-EX.

More recent issues, which have been preserved in top condition in considerable number, are listed in the grades of Mint (MT), Near Mint and Excellent, reflective of the fact that there exists in the current market little or no demand for cards of the recent past in grades below Excellent.

In general, although grades below Very Good are not priced in this catalog, close approximations of low-grade card values may figured on the following formula; Good condition cards are valued at about 50% of VG price, with Fair cads priced about 50% of Good. Cards in Poor condition have no market value except in the cases of the rarest and most expensive cards. In such cases, value has to be negotiated individually.

For the benefit of the reader, we present herewith the grading guide which was originally formulated by *Baseball Cards* magazine and *Sports Collectors Digest* in 1981, and has been continually refined since that time. These grading definitions have been used in the pricing of cards in this catalog, but they are by no means a universally accepted grading standard. The potential buyer of a basebll card should keep that in mind when encountering cards of nominally the same grade, but at a price which differs widely from that quoted in this book. Ultimately, the collector himself, must formulate his own personal grading standards in deciding whether cards available for purchase meet the needs of his own collection.

No collector or dealer is required to adhere to the grading standards presented herewith - or to any other published grading standards - but all are invited to do so. The editors of the *Sports Collectors Digest Baseball Card Price Guide* are eager to work toward the development of a standardized system of card grading that will be consistent with the realities of the hobby marketplace. Contact the editors.

Mint (MT): A perfect card. Well-centered, with parallel borders which appear equal to the naked eye. Four sharp, square corners. No creases, edge dents, surface scratches, paper flaws, loss of luster, yellowing or fading, regardless of age. No imperfectly printed card - out of register, badly cut or ink flawed - or card stained by contact with gum, wax or other substances can be considered truly Mint, even if new out of the pack.

Near Mint (NR MT): A nearly perfect card. At first glance, a Near Mint card appears perfect; upon closer examination, however, a minor flaw will be discovered. On well-centered cards, three of the four corners must be perfectly sharp; only one corner showing a minor imperfection upon close inspection. A slightly off-cente card with one or more borders being noticeable unequal - but still present - would also fit this grade.

Excellent (EX): Corners are still fairly sharp with only moderate wear. Card borders may be off center. No creases. May have very minor gum, wax or product stains, front or back. Surfaces may show slight loss of luster from rubbing across other cards.

Very Good (VG): Shows obvious handling. Corners rounded and/or perhaps showing minor creases. Other minor creases may be visible. Surfaces may exhibit loss of luster, but all printing is intact. May show major gum, wax or other packaging stains. No major creases, tape marks or extraneous markings or writing. Exhibits honest wear.

Good (G): A well-worn card, but exhibits no intentional damage or abuse. May have major or multiple creases. Corners rounded well beyond the border.

Fair: Shows excessive wear, along with damage or abuse. Will show all of the wear characteristics of a Good card, along with such damage as thumb tack holes in or near margins, evidence of having been taped or pasted, perhaps small tears around the edges, or creases so heavy as to break the cardboard. Backs may show minor added pen or pencil writing, or be missing small bits of paper. Still, a basically complete card.

Poor: A card that has been tortured to death. Corners or other areas may be torn off. Card may have been trimmed, show holes from paper punch or have been used for BB gun practice. Front may have extraneous pen or pencil writing, or other defacement. Major portions of front or back design may be missing. Not a pretty sight.

In addition to these seven widely-used grading terms, collectors will often encounter intermediate grades, such as VG-EX (Very Good to Excellent), EX-MT (Excellent to Mint), or NR MT-MT (Near Mint to Mint). Persons who describe a card with such grades are usually trying to convey that the card has all the characteristics of the lower grade, with enough of the higher grade to merit mention. Such cards are usually priced at a point midway between the two grades.

VALUATIONS

Values quoted in this book represent the current retail market and are compiled from recommendations provided and verified through the author's day to day involvement in the publication of the hobby's leading advertising periodicals, as well as the input of specialized consultants.

It should be stressed, however, that this book is intended to serve only as an aid in evaluating cards; actual market conditions are constantly changing. This is especially true of the cards of current players, whose on-field performance during the course of a season can greatly affect the value of their cards - upwards or downwards.

Publication of this catalog is not intended as a solicitation to buy or sell the listed cards by the editors, publishers or contributors.

Again, the values listed here are retail prices; what a collector can expect to pay when buying a card from a dealer. The wholesale price; that which a collector can expect to receive from a dealer when selling cards will be significantly lower. Most dealers operate on a 100% mark-up, generally paying about 50% of a card's retail value. On some high-demand cards, dealers will pay up to 75% or even 100% or more of retail value, anticipating continued price increases. Conversely, for many low-demand cards, such as common players' cards of recent years, dealers may pay 25% or even less of retail.

It should also be noted that with several hundred thousand valuations quoted in this book, there are bound to be a few compilations or typographical errors which will creep into the final product; a fact readers should remember if they encounter a listing at a fraction of, or several times, the card's actual current retail price. The editors welcome the correction of any such errors discovered. Write: *Sports Collectors Digest Baseball Card Price Guide,* 700 E. State St., Iola, WI 54990.

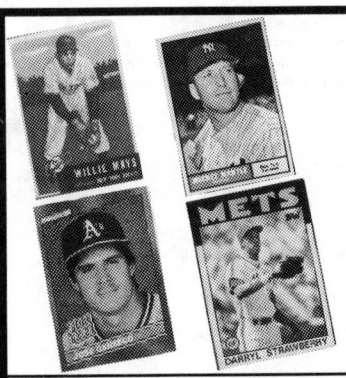

Mid-Atlantic Coin Exchange

In Swarthmore, PA 19081

(10 miles west of Philadelphia)

BUYING ● SELLING ● TRADING

One of the East's largest buyers & dealers in buying ...

COLLECTIONS

SUPERSTARS ● RARE ITEMS

at competitive prices

BRING CARDS TO OUR RETAIL STORE
FOR FREE APPRAISAL AND SALE

Selling Near Mint Sets SMALL SET PRICES ARE RISING!

This is your opportunity to own many of the inexpensive sets available today. Compare the prices to similar sets from the 1950's to 1970's.

1979 Burger King Yankees (23)	$12.00
1979 Burger King Phillies (23)	7.00
1980 Burger King Phillies (23)	7.00
1980 Burger King Pitch, Hit Run (34)	30.00
1986 Burger King set (20)	7.00
1987 Burger King set (20)	6.00
1981 Topps Coca Cola (132)	40.00
1985 Coca Cola White Sox	12.00
1986 Coca Cola White Sox	11.00
1988 Coca Cola White Sox	8.00
1989 Coca Cola White Sox	8.00
All Four White Sox sets	35.00
1983 Donruss Hall of Fame (44)	8.00
1982 Donruss Diamond Kings (27)	15.00
1983 Donruss Diamond Kings (27)	12.00
1986 Donruss Highlights (50)	8.00
1987 Donruss Highlights (56)	7.00
1986 Donruss Pop-ups (18)	7.00
1987 Donruss Pop-ups (20)	6.00
1988 Donruss Pop-ups (20)	5.00
Special: All three Pop-ups	15.00
1981 Drake's Topps (33)	8.00
1981 Fleer Stickers (128)	40.00
1984 Fleer Sticker set	15.00
1986 Fleer Sticker set (132)	25.00
1987 Fleer Sticker set (132)	25.00
1988 Fleer Sticker set (132)	25.00
1984 Gardner's Brewers (22)	12.00
1985 Gardner's Brewers (22)	12.00
1955 General Mills Stickers (28)	15.00
1985 Hostess Braves/Topps (23)	10.00
1980 Hostess Expos/Blue Jays (24)	8.00
1989 Marathon Tigers set	10.00
1987 M&M set (24)	15.00
1984 Topps/Milton Bradley (30)	10.00
1986 Meadow Gold star back set (20)	35.00
1971 Safety Washington Senators (10)	12.00
1981 Seattle Mariner set (16)	7.00
1981 Police Dodgers (32)	12.00
1982 Police Dodgers	10.00
1983 Police Dodgers (30)	8.00
1981 Police Braves (30)	15.00
1983 Police Braves (30)	15.00
1984 Police Braves (30)	15.00
1985 Police Braves (30)	16.00
1984 Police Brewers (30)	8.00

1984 Police/Dodgers (30)	7.00
1985 Police Blue Jays (30)	10.00
1985 Police Phillies (18)	7.00
1986 Police Astros (26)	8.00
1986 Police Blue Jays (30)	6.00
1986 Police Braves (30)	15.00
1986 Police Brewers (30)	6.00
1986 Police Dodgers (30)	6.00
1986 Police/Fire Safety Phillies (10)	8.00
1987 Police Astros	7.00
1987 Police Blue Jays (36)	10.00
1987 Police Brewers (30)	6.00
1987 Police Columbus Clippers (25)	10.00
1987 Iced Tea BB Superstars	5.00
1987 Police Dodgers (30)	6.00
1988 Police Brewers (30)	5.00
1988 Police Columbus Clippers	10.00
1988 Police Dodgers (30) World Champions	
	5.00
1988 Hardees Coke (6)	5.00
1989 Police Dodgers	7.00
1990 Police Dodger (30)	5.00
1986 Provigio Expos (panel set) (28)	5.00
1984 Ralston Purina (33)	5.00
1984 Smokey Bear Padres	15.00
1985 Smokey Bear Angels	10.00
1987 Smokey Bear A.L. All-Stars (16)	5.00
1987 Smokey Bear N.L. All-Stars	7.00
1987 Smokey Bear A's (12)	7.00
1983 Stuart Expos (30)	10.00
1989 Ralston Purina Superstars, MSA (12)	
	8.00
1985 Tastykake Phillies	8.00
1985 Topps Glossy All-Stars (22)	6.00
1986 Topps Glossy All-Stars (22)	6.00
1987 Topps Glossy All-Stars (22)	6.00
1988 Topps Glossy All-Stars (22)	5.00
1989 Topps Glossy All-Stars (22)	5.00
1990 Fleer League Standouts (6)	4.00
1991 Fleer Pro-Visions (12)	9.00
1982-88 Topps Sticker Set. Eacy year $19.00;	
All seven sticker sets (1982-88)	119.00
1989 Kahn's Weiners Mets (31)	10.00
1990 Kahn's Weiners Mets	7.00

WE ALSO TRADE OUR TRADING POLICY

We like to trade Police/safety and other small sets for greater variety. We will take a large quantity of one item and offer you a great variety. Advise what you have available and we will send our trade list with an offer. Minimum trade $50.00 value. We need most Police and small sets, yearbooks, posters, pins, Surf books, etc. Let's hear your deal! We have over 400 items on our trade list.

SELLING 1984 ● TOPPS/NESTLES
MINT COMPLETE ● SETS/SINGLES

Only 4,000 sets made. Pretty scarce. Mint/Singles

Mattingly #8	250.00
Strawberry #182	95.00
Brett #500	25.00
Boggs #30	60.00
Carew #600	10.00
Carter #450	10.00
Carlton #780	9.00
Garvey #380	15.00
Guerrero #90	5.00
Gwynn #251	25.00
Henderson #230	35.00
Hernandez #120	7.00
Hrbek #315	7.00
Jackson #100	15.00
Morgan #210	7.00
Murphy #150	25.00
Murray #240	15.00
Palmer #750	10.00
Raines #370	12.00
Rice #550	8.00
Ripken #490	25.00
Rose #300	30.00
Ryan #470	35.00
Sandberg #596	35.00
Schmidt #700	25.00
Seaver #740	20.00
Valenzuela #220	7.00
Winfield #460	8.00
Yount #10	20.00
650 different commons, our choice	75.00
50 different commons, our choice	10.00
100	17.00

Save by purchasing complete sets.

Complete set (792) mint cond. 625.00

Order Instuctions:
$3.00 Postage & Handling.
Minimum order $15.00.
MasterCard & VISA on orders over $25.00
PA residents add 6% sales tax.
Outside Continental US and PO boxes full
cost of postage to be paid by buyer.

Send SASE for catalogue

Fax: (215) 544-4770

MID-ATLANTIC
COIN EXCHANGE
Dept. PG-4
411 Dartmouth Avenue
Swarthmore, PA 19081
Phone: (215) 544-2171

Same Location Since 1972

SETS

Collectors may note that the complete set prices for newer issues quoted in htese listings are usually significantly lower than the total of the value of the individula cards which comprise the set.

This reflects two factors in the baseball card market. First, a seller is often willing to take a lower composite price for a complete set as a "volume discount," and to avoid inventorying a large number of common player or other lower-demand cards.

Second, to a degree, the value of common cards can be said to be inflated as a result of having built-in overhead charge to justify the dealer's time in sorting cards, carrying them in stock and filling orders. This accounts for the fact that even brand new baseball cards, which cost the dealer around 1¢ each when bought in bulk, carry individual price tags of 3¢ or higher.

ERRORS/VARIATIONS

It is often hard for the beginning collector to understand that an error on a baseball card, in and of itself, does not usually add premium value to that card. It is usually only when the correcting of an error in a subsequent printing

Minor errors such as wrong stats or personal data creates a variation that premium value attaches to an error. misspellings, inconsistencies, etc. - usually affecting the back of the card - are very common, especially in recent years. Unless a corrected variation was also printed, these errors are not noted in the listings of this book because they are not generally perceived by collectors to have premium value.

On the other hand, major effort has been expended to include the most complete listings ever for collectible variation cards. Many scarce and valuable variations - dozens of them never before cataloged - are included in these listings because they are widely collected and often have significant premium value.

COUNTERFEITS/REPRINTS

As the value of baseball cards has risen in the past 10-20 years, certain cards and sets have become too expensive for the average collector to obtain. This, along with changes in the technology of color printing, have given rise to increasing numbers of counterfeit and reprint cards.

While both terms describe essentially the same thing - a modern copy which attempts to duplicate as closely as possible an original baseball card - there are differences which are important to the collector.

Generally, a counterfeit is made with the intention of deceiving somebody into believing it is genuine, and thus paying large amounts of money for it. The counterfeiter takes every pain to try to make his fakes look as authentic as possible. In recent years, the 1963 Pete Rose, 1984 Donruss Don Mattingly and more than 30 superstar cards of the late 1960s-early 1980s have been counterfeited - all were quickly detected because of the differences in quality of cardboard on which they were printed.

A reprint, on the other hand, while it may have been made to look as close as possible to an original card, is made with the intention of allowing collectors to buy them as substitutes for cards they may never be otherwise able to afford. The big difference is that a reprint is generally marked as such, usually on the back of the card. In other cases, like the Topps 1952 reprint set, the replicas are printed in a size markedly different from the originals.

Collectors should be aware, however, that unscrupulous persons will sometimes cut off or otherwise obliterate the distinguishing word - "Reprint," "Copy", - or modern copyright date on the back of a reprint card in an attempt to pass it as genuine.

A collector's best defense against reprints and counterfeits is to acquire a knowledge of the "look" and "feel" of genuine baseball cards of various eras and issues.

UNLISTED CARDS

Readers who have cards or sets which are not covered in this edition are invited to correspond with the editor for purposes of adding to the compilation work now in progress.

Address: *Sports Collectors Digest Baseball Card Price Guide,* 700 E. State St., Iola, WI 54990.

Contributions will be acknowledged in future editions.

COLLECTOR ISSUES

There exists within the hobby a great body of cards which do not fall under the scope of this catalog by virtue of their nature of having been issued solely for the collector market. Known as "collector issues," these cards and sets are distinguished from "legitimate" issues in not having been created as a sales promotional item for another product or service — bubble gum, soda, snack cakes, dog food, cigarettes, gasoline, etc.

By their nature, and principally because the person issuing them is always free to print and distribute more of the same if they should ever attain any real value, collector issues are generally regarded by collectors as having little or no premium value.

NEW ISSUES

Because new baseball cards are being issued all the time, the cataloging of them remains an on-going challenge. The editor will attempt to keep abreast of new issues so that they may be added to future editions of this book.

Readers are invited to submit news of new issues, especially limited-edition or regionally issued cards to the editors. Address: *Sports Collectors Digest Baseball Card Price Guide,* 700 E. State St., Iola, WI 54990.

Table of Contents

BILL HENDERSON'S CARDS
"King of the Commons"

2320 RUGER AVE. - KG
JANESVILLE, WISCONSIN 53545
1-608-755-0922

"ALWAYS BUYING" Call or Write for Quote • "ALWAYS BUYING" Call or Write for Quote

Set	HI # OR SCARCE SERIES	PRICE PER COMMON CARD	COMMONS EACH	Commons (range/price)	50 Diff.	100 Diff.	300 Asst.	500 Asst.	VG+ 50 Diff.	VG+ 100 Diff.	VG+ 200 Diff.
1948 BOWMAN	(37-48)	25.00	18.00								
1949 BOWMAN	(145-240)	80.00	16.00		720.				430.		
50-51 BOWMAN	50 (1-72) 51 (253-324)	60.00	16.00	51 (2-36) 20.00	720.				430.		
1952 TOPPS	(311-407)	P.O.R.	30.00	(2-80) 60.00	1350.				800.		
1952 BOWMAN	(217-252)	30.00	16.00	(2-36) 20.00	720.				430.		
1953 TOPPS	(220-280)	80.00	20.00	(2-165) 30.00	900.				600.		
1953 BOWMAN	(129-160)	40.00	30.00	(113-128) 50.00	1350.				800.		
1954 TOPPS			14.00	(51-75) 30.00	630.				400.		
1954 BOWMAN			8.00	(129-224) 10.00	360.	685.			240.		
1955 TOPPS	(161-210)	20.00	7.00	(151-160) 15.00	360.				210.		
1955 BOWMAN	(225-320)	15.-20. Umps	6.00	(2-96) 8.00	270.	500.			180.	350.	
1956 TOPPS	(261-340)	10.00	8.00	(181-260) 15.00	360.				240.	460.	
1957 TOPPS	(1-80) 7.00	(265-352) 17.50	5.00	(353-407) 5.00	220.	420.			155.	300.	
1958 TOPPS	(111-198)	5.00	3.50	(1-110) 6.00	155.	300.	850.		105.	200.	
1959 TOPPS	(507-572)	12.50	3.00	(1-110) 4.00	135.	260.	750.		90.	175.	385.
1960 TOPPS	(523-572)	12.50	2.00	(441-506) 4.50	90.	175.	500.	800.	60.	115.	220.
1961 TOPPS	(523-589)	30.00	1.50	(371-522) 2.50	65.	125.	360.	700.	45.	80.	155.
1962 TOPPS	(523-590)	12.50	1.50	(371-522) 3.50	65.	125.	360.		45.	80.	155.
1963 TOPPS	(447-522) 10.00	(523-573) 6.00	1.50	(197-446) 2.00	65.	125.			45.	80.	
1964 TOPPS	(523-587)	7.50	1.25	(371-522) 2.50	55.	105.			32.	60.	115.
1965 TOPPS	(447-522) 4.00	(523-598) 6.00	1.00	(284-446) 2.50	45.	90.			32.	60.	115.
1966 TOPPS	(371-446) 2.50	(523-598) 15.00	1.00	(447-522) 5.00	45.	90.			32.	60.	115.
1967 TOPPS	(371-457) 2.00	(534-609) 15.00	1.00	(458-533) 5.00	45.	90.			32.	60.	115.
1968 TOPPS	(534-598)	2.00	1.00	(458-533) 1.50	45.	90.			32.	60.	115.
1969 TOPPS	(589-664)	1.00	.75	(219-327) 1.50	34.	65.	185.		22.	42.	80.
1970 TOPPS	(634-720)	3.50	.45	(547-633) 1.50	22.	42.	120.	190.	14.	26.	50.
1971 TOPPS	(394-523) .75	(644-752) 4.50	.45	(524-643) 1.50	22.	42.	120.	190.	14.	26.	50.
1972 TOPPS	(395-525) .60	(657-787) 4.50	.45	(526-656) 1.50	22.	42.	★120.	190.	14.	26.	50.
1973 TOPPS	(528-660)	2.00	.35	(397-528) .60	16.	32.	★90.		12.	22.	40.
1974 TOPPS			.35		16.	32.	★90.	★150.		22.	40.
1975 TOPPS		(8-132.50)	.35		16.	32.	★90.			22.	40.
1976-77			.20		18.	★50.	★85.			10.	18.
1978-1980			.15		13.	★38.	★65.			8.	15.
1981 thru 1991 Topps, Fleer, or Donruss; Specify Year & Company except below			.10		8.	★22.	★35.			5.	10.
					Per Yr.	Per Yr.	Per Yr.				
1984-86 DONRUSS			.15		7.	13.	★38.	★60.			

★ These lots are all different.

SPECIAL IN VG+ to EX CONDITION-POSTPAID

Qty	Years	Price
250	58-62	300.00
500	58-62	550.00
250	60-69	170.00
500	60-69	320.00
1000	60-69	600.00
250	70-79	50.00
500	70-79	90.00
1000	70-79	160.00
250	80-84	15.00
500	80-84	28.00
1000	80-84	55.00

Special 1 Different from each year 1949-80 EX/MT - $140.00, VG-EX $100.00
Special 100 Different from each year 1956-80 EX/MT - $2900.00, VG-EX $2000.00
Special 10 Different from each year 1956-80 EX/MT - $300.00, VG-EX $210.00

All lot groups are my choice only.
All assorted lots will contain as many different as possible.
Please list alternates whenever possible.
Send your want list and I will fill them at the above price for commons. High numbers, specials, scarce series, and stars extra.
You can use your Master Card or VISA to charge your purchases.
Minimum order $7.50 - Postage and handling $.50 per 100 cards (minimum $1.75)

Also interested in purchasing your collection.
Groups include various years of my choice.
ANY CARD NOT LISTED ON PRICE SHEET IS PRICED AT BECKETT-SPORTS AMERICANA PRICE GUIDE XIII

Topps Sets Available
1988, 1989, 1990, 1991
$20.95 + $2.50 UPS
6 for $20.75 + $9.00 UPS
18 for $20.25 + $20.00 UPS
54 for $19.75 + $60.00 UPS
mix or match

The MINNESOTA CONNECTION

The Scarcest Set Of The 1980's

1981-1989 Louisville Slugger Set
(17) EX-MT
$199.95 ppd

Singles

Graig Nettles (Yankee) 1981	$19.95 ppd
Steve Garvey (Dodgers) 1981	49.95 ppd
Fred Lynn (Angels) 1982	19.95 ppd
Pedro Guerrero (Dodgers) 1982	19.95 ppd
Ray Knight (Astros) 1984	39.95 ppd
Graig Nettles (Padres) 1984	19.95 ppd
Ray Knight (Mets) 1984	19.95 ppd
Gary Mathews (Cubs) 1985	29.95 ppd
Steve Garvey (Padres) 1985	19.95 ppd
Rick Rhoden (Pirates) 1985	29.95 ppd
Orel Hershiser (Dodgers) 1986	39.95 ppd
Eric Davis (Reds) 1988	19.95 ppd
Mike Pagilarulo (Yankees) 1988	19.95 ppd
Lou Whitaker (Tigers) 1989	19.95 ppd
Andy Van Slyke (Pirates) 1989	19.95 ppd
Orel Hershiser (Dodgers) 1988	19.95 ppd
Orel Hershiser (Dodgers) 1988 with 1988 stats	29.95 ppd

Louisville Slugger Baseball Cards
"Rare & Beautiful"

1981 1981 1982 1982 1984 1984 1984 1985 1985

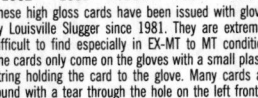

These high gloss cards have been issued with gloves by Louisville Slugger since 1981. They are extremely difficult to find especially in EX-MT to MT condition. The cards only come on the gloves with a small plastic string holding the card to the glove. Many cards are found with a tear through the hole on the left front of the card. NONE of our cards have a tear and are all EX-MT to MT.

              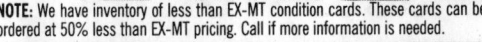

1981 1981   1986 1986   1988 1988

NOTE: We have inventory of less than EX-MT condition cards. These cards can be ordered at 50% less than EX-MT pricing. Call if more information is needed.

BASEBALL BOX SETS

TOPPS (33)   **FLEER (44)**

1982-1990 CHAIN STORE BOX SETS

YR	STORE	MAKER	SET NAME	PRICE
1989	Ames	Topps	20/20 Club (33)	$12.95 ppd
1990	Ames	Topps	Baseball All-Stars	9.95
1987	Ben Franklin	Fleer	Baseball All-Stars (44)	8.95 ppd
1988	Ben Franklin	Fleer	Baseball All-Stars (44)	6.95 ppd
1989	Ben Franklin	Fleer	Baseball All-Stars (44)	5.95 ppd
1990	Baseball All-Stars	Fleer	Baseball All-Stars (44)	5.95 ppd
1990	Ben Franklin	Fleer	Baseball All-Stars	5.95 ppd
1987	Boardwalk & Baseball	Topps	Run Producers (33)	5.95 ppd
1985	Circle-K	Topps	Collector's Series (33)	7.95 ppd
1987	Cumberland Farms	Fleer	Exciting Stars (44)	14.95 ppd
1988	Cumberland Farms	Fleer	Exciting Stars (44)	9.95 ppd
1989	Cumberland Farms	Fleer	Exciting Stars (44)	12.95 ppd
1987	Eckerd	Fleer	Record Setters (44)	6.95 ppd
1988	Eckerd	Fleer	Record Setters (44)	5.95 ppd
1986	Kay-Bee	Topps	Young Superstars (33)	6.95 ppd
1987	Kay-Bee	Topps	Superstars Of Baseball (33)	6.95 ppd
1988	Kay-Bee	Fleer	Team Leaders (44)	12.95 ppd
1988	Kay-Bee	Topps	Superstars (33)	6.95 ppd
1989	Kay-Bee	Topps	Superstars (33)	6.95 ppd
1990	Kay-Bee	—	Kings of Baseball	5.95 ppd
1989	Hills	Topps	Teams MVPS (33)	6.95 ppd
1990	Hills	Topps	Hitman	12.95 ppd
1990	Kay-Bee	—	Hitman Superstar	12.95 ppd
1982	K-Mart	Topps	Most Valuable Players (44)	4.95 ppd
1987	K-Mart	Topps	Topps Stars of the Decade (33)	6.95 ppd
1988	K-Mart	Topps	Topps Stars of the Decade (33)	5.95 ppd
1989	K-Mart	Topps	Topps Dream Team (33)	5.95 ppd
1990	K-Mart	Topps	Superstar	12.95 ppd
1985	McCrory's	Fleer	Baseball Superstars (44)	9.95 ppd
1986	McCrory's	Fleer	Baseball Superstars (44)	7.95 ppd
1986	McCrory's	Fleer	Sluggers vs. Pitchers (44)	9.95 ppd
1987	McCrory's	Fleer	Baseball Superstars (44)	6.95 ppd
1987	McCrory's	Fleer	Sluggers vs. Pitchers (44)	8.95 ppd
1988	McCrory's	Fleer	Baseball Superstars (44)	6.95 ppd
1988	McCrory's	Fleer	Sluggers vs. Pitchers (44)	7.95 ppd
1989	McCrory's	Fleer	Baseball Superstars (44)	8.95 ppd
1987	Pay 'N Save	Fleer	Game Winners (44)	8.95 ppd
1987	Revco	Fleer	Hottest Stars (44)	8.95 ppd
1988	Revco	Fleer	Hottest Stars (44)	7.95 ppd
1988	Revco	Topps	League Leaders (33)	6.95 ppd
1988	Rite Aid	Topps	Team MVP Set (33)	6.95 ppd
1987	Toys R Us	Topps	Rookies (33)	14.95 ppd
1988	Toys R Us	Topps	Rookies (33)	8.95 ppd
1989	Toys R Us	Topps	Rookies (33)	5.95 ppd
1989	Toys R Us	Fleer	Baseball's MVPs (44)	8.95 ppd
1989	Toys R Us	Fleer	Baseball's MVPs (44)	12.95 ppd
1990	Toys R Us	Topps	Rookies	5.95 ppd
1990	Toys R Us	Fleer	Baseball's MVP's	9.95 ppd
1986	Walgreens	Fleer	League Leaders (44)	9.95 ppd
1987	Walgreens	Fleer	League Leaders (44)	8.95 ppd
1988	Walgreens	Fleer	League Leaders (44)	8.95 ppd
1989	Walgreens	Fleer	League Leaders (44)	6.95 ppd
1990	Walgreens	Fleer	League Leaders (44)	5.95 ppd
1985	Woolworth's	Topps	All Time Record Holders (44)	9.95 ppd
1986	Woolworth's	Topps	Collectors Series (33)	8.95 ppd
1987	Woolworth's	Topps	Baseball Highlights (33)	7.95 ppd
1986	Woolworth's	Topps	Baseball Highlights (33)	6.95 ppd
1989	Woolworth's	Topps	Baseball Highlights (33)	5.95 ppd
1989	Woolworth's	Fleer	Heroes of Baseball (44)	12.95 ppd
1990	Woolworth's	Topps	Baseball Highlights (33)	5.95 ppd
1987	7/11	Fleer	Award Winners Set (44)	5.95 ppd
1988	7/11	Fleer	Award Winners Set (44)	14.95 ppd

1982-1990 Chain Store Box Set "Special" all 60 sets $349.95 ppd.

Hershiser Update (1988 Stats on back) added to Louisville Slugger Set 1981-1989
Louisville Slugger Set (17) EX/MT ....199.95 ppd

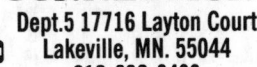  

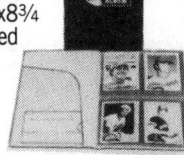

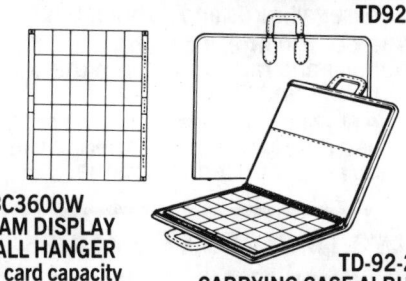

1983 Affiliated Food Rangers

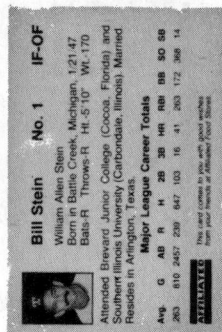

This 28-card set, featuring the Texas Rangers, was issued as a promotion by the Affiliated Food Stores chain of Arlington, Texas, late during the 1983 baseball season. Complete sets were given out free to youngsters 13 and under at the 9/3/83 Rangers game. The cards measure 2-3/8" by 3-1/2" and feature a full-color photo on the front. Also on the front, located inside a blue box, is the player's name, uniform number, and the words "1983 Rangers." The card backs contain a small player photo plus biographical and statistical information, along with the Affiliated logo and a brief promotional message. A total of 10,000 sets were reportedly printed. Cards are numbered by the players' uniform numbers in the checklist that follows.

		MT	NR MT	EX
Complete Set:		7.00	5.25	2.75
Common Player:		.10	.08	.04
1	Bill Stein	.10	.08	.04
2	Mike Richardt	.10	.08	.04
3	Wayne Tolleson	.10	.08	.04
5	Billy Sample	.10	.08	.04
6	Bobby Jones	.10	.08	.04
7	Bucky Dent	.30	.25	.12
8	Bobby Johnson	.10	.08	.04
9	Pete O'Brien	.70	.50	.30
10	Jim Sundberg	.20	.15	.08
11	Doug Rader	.10	.08	.04
12	Dave Hostetler	.10	.08	.04
14	Larry Biittner	.10	.08	.04
15	Larry Parrish	.35	.25	.14
17	Mickey Rivers	.20	.15	.08
21	Odell Jones	.10	.08	.04
24	Dave Schmidt	.15	.11	.06
25	Buddy Bell	.50	.40	.20
26	George Wright	.10	.08	.04
28	Frank Tanana	.20	.15	.08
29	John Butcher	.10	.08	.04
32	Jon Matlack	.15	.11	.06
40	Rick Honeycutt	.15	.11	.06
41	Dave Tobik	.10	.08	.04
44	Danny Darwin	.15	.11	.06
46	Jim Anderson	.10	.08	.04
48	Mike Smithson	.10	.08	.04
49	Charlie Hough	.35	.25	.14
-----	Coaching Staff (Rich Donnelly, Glenn Ezell, Merv Rettenmund, Dick Such, Wayne Terwilliger)	.10	.08	.04

1989 Ames 20/20 Club

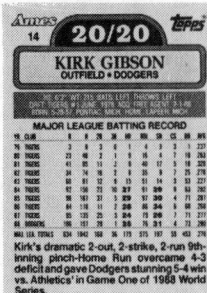

This 33-card set was produced by Topps for the Ames toy store chain. As its name implies, the special boxed set highlights members of the 20/20 club, players who have recorded 20 home runs and 20 stolen bases in the same season. The glossy cards feature action or posed photos on the front with the player's name at the top and "Ames 20/20 Club" along the bottom. The Topps logo appears in the upper right corner.

		MT	NR MT	EX
Complete Set:		5.00	3.75	2.00
Common Player:		.09	.07	.04
1	Jesse Barfield	.09	.07	.04
2	Kevin Bass	.09	.07	.04
3	Don Baylor	.09	.07	.04
4	George Bell	.12	.09	.05
5	Barry Bonds	.12	.09	.05
6	Phil Bradley	.09	.07	.04
7	Ellis Burks	.40	.30	.15
8	Jose Canseco	.70	.50	.30
9	Joe Carter	.15	.11	.06
10	Kal Daniels	.09	.07	.04
11	Eric Davis	.40	.30	.15
12	Mike Davis	.09	.07	.04
13	Andre Dawson	.12	.09	.05
14	Kirk Gibson	.09	.07	.04
15	Pedro Guerrero	.12	.09	.05
16	Rickey Henderson	.50	.40	.20
17	Bo Jackson	.80	.60	.30
18	Howard Johnson	.20	.15	.08
19	Jeffrey Leonard	.09	.07	.04
20	Kevin McReynolds	.12	.09	.05
21	Dale Murphy	.09	.07	.04
22	Dwayne Murphy	.09	.07	.04
23	Dave Parker	.12	.09	.05
24	Kirby Puckett	.50	.40	.20
25	Juan Samuel	.09	.07	.04
26	Ryne Sandberg	.20	.15	.08
27	Mike Schmidt	.80	.60	.30
28	Darryl Strawberry	.25	.20	.10
29	Alan Trammell	.09	.07	.04
30	Andy Van Slyke	.09	.07	.04
31	Devon White	.09	.07	.04
32	Dave Winfield	.12	.09	.05
33	Robin Yount	.30	.25	.12

1986 Ault Foods Blue Jays

The Ault Foods Blue Jays set is comprised of 24 full-color stickers. Designed to be placed in a special album, the stickers measure 2" by 3" in size. The attractive album measures 9" by 12" and is printed on glossy stock. While the stickers carry no information except for the player's last name and uniform number, the 20-page album contains extensive personal and statistical information about each of the 24 players.

	MT	NR MT	EX
Complete Set:	40.00	30.00	15.00

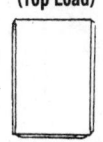
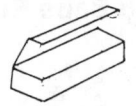

BELL

Common Player:	.60	.45	.25
Album:	5.00	3.75	2.00

1	Tony Fernandez	4.00	3.00	1.50
5	Rance Mulliniks	.60	.45	.25
7	Damaso Garcia	.60	.45	.25
11	George Bell	5.00	3.75	2.00
12	Ernie Whitt	.90	.70	.35
13	Buck Martinez	.60	.45	.25
15	Lloyd Moseby	1.25	.90	.50
16	Garth Iorg	.60	.45	.25
17	Kelly Gruber	2.00	1.50	.80
18	Jim Clancy	.90	.70	.35
22	Jimmy Key	2.00	1.50	.80
23	Cecil Fielder	2.00	1.50	.80
25	Steve Davis	.60	.45	.25
26	Willie Upshaw	.90	.70	.35
29	Jesse Barfield	1.75	1.25	.70
31	Jim Acker	.60	.45	.25
33	Doyle Alexander	.90	.70	.35
36	Bill Caudill	.60	.45	.25
37	Dave Stieb	2.50	2.00	1.00
39	Don Gordon	.60	.45	.25
44	Cliff Johnson	.60	.45	.25
46	Gary Lavelle	.60	.45	.25
50	Tom Henke	1.25	.90	.50
53	Dennis Lamp	.60	.45	.25

1948 Babe Ruth Story

The Philadelphia Gum Co., in 1948, created a card set about the movie "The Babe Ruth Story", which starred William Bendix and Claire Trevor. The set, whose American Card Catalog designation is R421, contains 28 black and white, numbered cards which measure 2" by 2-1/2". The Babe Ruth Story set was originally intended to consist of sixteen cards. Twelve additional cards (#'s 17-28) were added when Ruth died before the release of the film. The card backs include a offer for an autographed photo of William Bendix, starring as the Babe, for five Swell Bubble Gum wrappers and five cents.

		NR MT	EX	VG
Complete Set:		1000.00	500.00	300.00
Common Player: 1-16		12.00	6.00	3.50
Common Player: 17-28		35.00	17.50	10.50
1	"The Babe Ruth Story" In The Making	75.00	38.00	23.00
2	Bat Boy Becomes the Babe... William Bendix	12.00	6.00	3.50
3	Claire Hodgson...Claire Trevor	12.00	6.00	3.50
4	Babe Ruth and Claire Hodgson	12.00	6.00	3.50
5	Brother Matthias...Charles Bickford	12.00	6.00	3.50
6	Phil Conrad...Sam Levene	12.00	6.00	3.50
7	Night Club Singer...Gertrude Niesen	12.00	6.00	3.50
8	Baseball's Famous Deal...Jack Dunn (William Frawley)	12.00	6.00	3.50
9	Mr. & Mrs. Babe Ruth	12.00	6.00	3.50
10	Babe Ruth, Claire Ruth, and Brother Matthias	12.00	6.00	3.50
11	Babe Ruth and Miller Huggins (Fred Lightner)	12.00	6.00	3.50
12	Babe Ruth At Bed Of Ill Boy Johnny Sylvester (Gregory Marshall)	12.00	6.00	3.50
13	Sylvester Family Listening To Game	12.00	6.00	3.50
14	"When A Feller Needs a Friend" (With Dog At Police Station)	12.00	6.00	3.50
15	Dramatic Home Run	12.00	6.00	3.50
16	The Homer That Set the Record (#60)	12.00	6.00	3.50
17	"The Slap That Started Baseball's Famous Career"	35.00	17.50	10.50
18	The Babe Plays Santa Claus	35.00	17.50	10.50
19	Meeting Of Owner And Manager	35.00	17.50	10.50
20	"Broken Window Paid Off"	35.00	17.50	10.50
21	Babe In A Crowd Of Autograph Collectors	35.00	17.50	10.50
22	Charley Grimm And William Bendix	35.00	17.50	10.50
23	Ted Lyons And William Bendix	50.00	25.00	15.00
24	Lefty Gomez, William Bendix, And Bucky Harris	50.00	25.00	15.00
25	Babe Ruth and William Bendix	100.00	50.00	30.00
26	Babe Ruth And William Bendix	100.00	50.00	30.00
27	Babe Ruth And Claire Trevor	100.00	50.00	30.00
28	William Bendix, Babe Ruth, And Claire Trevor	100.00	50.00	30.00

1986 Baltimore Orioles Team Issue

CAL RIPKEN, JR.

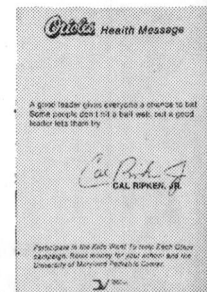

		MT	NR MT	EX
Complete Set:		10.00	7.50	4.00
Common Player:		.15	.11	.06
(1)	Don Aase	.15	.11	.06
(2a)	Mike Boddicker (message begins "I always...")	.40	.30	.15
(2b)	Mike Boddicker (message begins "They call...")	.40	.30	.15
(3)	Storm Davis	.20	.15	.08
(4a)	Rick Dempsey (message begins "I always...")	.15	.11	.06

 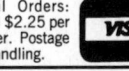

		MT	NR MT	EX
(4b)	Rick Dempsey (message begins "In baseball...")	.15	.11	.06
(5)	Ken Dixon	.15	.11	.06
(6)	Jim Dwyer	.15	.11	.06
(7a)	Mike Flanagan (message begins "I know...")	.20	.15	.08
(7b)	Mike Flanagan (message begins "It's a...")	.20	.15	.08
(8)	Lee Lacy	.15	.11	.06
(9a)	Fred Lynn (message begins "I need...")	.35	.25	.14
(9b)	Fred Lynn (message begins "There are...")	.35	.25	.14
(10a)	Dennis Martinez	.30	.25	.12
(11)	Tippy Martinez	.15	.11	.06
(12)	Scott McGregor	.20	.15	.08
(13a)	Eddie Murray (message begins "Do you...")	.90	.70	.35
(13b)	Eddie Murray (message begins "During my...")	.90	.70	.35
(13c)	Eddie Murray (message begins "You can't...")	.90	.70	.35
(14a)	Floyd Rayford (message begins "I always...")	.15	.11	.06
(14b)	Floyd Rayford (message begins "I had...")	.15	.11	.06
(15)	Cal Ripken, Jr. (message begins "A good...")	1.25	.90	.50
(15b)	Cal Ripken, Jr. (message begins "Drinking ...")	1.25	.90	.50
(15c)	Cal Ripken, Jr. (message begins "To hit...")	1.25	.90	.50
(16a)	Larry Sheets (message begins "As a...")	.25	.20	.10
(16b)	Larry Sheets (message begins "There is...")	.25	.20	.10
(17)	John Shelby	.15	.11	.06
(18)	Earl Weaver	.35	.25	.14
(19)	Alan Wiggins	.15	.11	.06
(20)	Mike Young	.20	.15	.08

1988 Baseball Immortals

 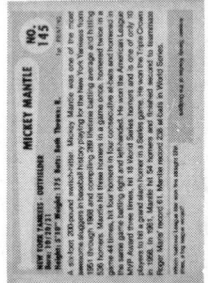

One of the most popular of the "collectors' issues", this set is produced with the permission of Major League Baseball by Renata Galasso Inc. and TCMA. The set features players in the Baseball Hall of Fame and was first issued in 1980. Each year since 1980 the set has been updated to include new inductees. The cards measure 2-1/2" by 3-1/2" and have colorful borders. The card fronts include the player's name, position and year of induction. The backs feature a short biography and a trivia question. The photos used are color; most players who were active before 1950 have colored black and white photos. The designation "first printing" appears on all cards issued 1981 and after.

		MT	NR MT	EX
Complete Set:		18.00	13.50	7.25
Common Player:		.05	.04	.02
1	Babe Ruth	.35	.25	.14
2	Ty Cobb	.25	.20	.10
3	Walter Johnson	.10	.08	.04
4	Christy Mathewson	.10	.08	.04
5	Honus Wagner	.10	.08	.04

		MT	NR MT	EX
6	Morgan Bulkeley	.05	.04	.02
7	Ban Johnson	.05	.04	.02
8	Larry Lajoie	.07	.05	.03
9	Connie Mack	.07	.05	.03
10	John McGraw	.07	.05	.03
11	Tris Speaker	.07	.05	.03
12	George Wright	.05	.04	.02
13	Cy Young	.08	.06	.04
14	Grover Alexander	.07	.05	.03
15	Alexander Cartwright	.05	.04	.02
16	Henry Chadwick	.05	.04	.02
17	Cap Anson	.07	.05	.03
18	Eddie Collins	.07	.05	.03
19	Charles Comiskey	.05	.04	.02
20	Candy Cummings	.05	.04	.02
21	Buck Ewing	.05	.04	.02
22	Lou Gehrig	.25	.20	.10
23	Willie Keeler	.05	.04	.02
24	Hoss Radbourne	.05	.04	.02
25	George Sisler	.07	.05	.03
26	Albert Spalding	.05	.04	.02
27	Rogers Hornsby	.10	.08	.04
28	Judge Landis	.05	.04	.02
29	Roger Bresnahan	.05	.04	.02
30	Dan Brouthers	.05	.04	.02
31	Fred Clarke	.05	.04	.02
32	James Collins	.05	.04	.02
33	Ed Delahanty	.05	.04	.02
34	Hugh Duffy	.05	.04	.02
35	Hughie Jennings	.05	.04	.02
36	Mike "King" Kelly	.05	.04	.02
37	James O'Rourke	.05	.04	.02
38	Wilbert Robinson	.05	.04	.02
39	Jesse Burkett	.05	.04	.02
40	Frank Chance	.05	.04	.02
41	Jack Chesbro	.05	.04	.02
42	John Evers	.05	.04	.02
43	Clark Griffith	.05	.04	.02
44	Thomas McCarthy	.05	.04	.02
45	Joe McGinnity	.05	.04	.02
46	Eddie Plank	.05	.04	.02
47	Joe Tinker	.05	.04	.02
48	Rube Waddell	.05	.04	.02
49	Ed Walsh	.05	.04	.02
50	Mickey Cochrane	.07	.05	.03
51	Frankie Frisch	.05	.04	.02
52	Lefty Grove	.07	.05	.03
53	Carl Hubbell	.07	.05	.03
54	Herb Pennock	.05	.04	.02
55	Pie Traynor	.05	.04	.02
56	Three Finger Brown	.05	.04	.02
57	Charlie Gehringer	.07	.05	.03
58	Kid Nichols	.05	.04	.02
59	Jimmie Foxx	.10	.08	.04
60	Mel Ott	.07	.05	.03
61	Harry Heilmann	.05	.04	.02
62	Paul Waner	.05	.04	.02
63	Ed Barrow	.05	.04	.02
64	Chief Bender	.05	.04	.02
65	Tom Connolly	.05	.04	.02
66	Dizzy Dean	.10	.08	.04
67	Bill Klem	.05	.04	.02
68	Al Simmons	.05	.04	.02
69	Bobby Wallace	.05	.04	.02
70	Harry Wright	.05	.04	.02
71	Bill Dickey	.07	.05	.03
72	Rabbit Maranville	.05	.04	.02
73	Bill Terry	.07	.05	.03
74	Home Run Baker	.05	.04	.02
75	Joe DiMaggio	.15	.11	.06
76	Gabby Hartnett	.05	.04	.02
77	Ted Lyons	.05	.04	.02
78	Ray Schalk	.05	.04	.02
79	Dazzy Vance	.05	.04	.02
80	Joe Cronin	.07	.05	.03
81	Hank Greenberg	.07	.05	.03
82	Sam Crawford	.05	.04	.02
83	Joe McCarthy	.05	.04	.02
84	Zack Wheat	.05	.04	.02
85	Max Carey	.05	.04	.02
86	Billy Hamilton	.05	.04	.02
87	Bob Feller	.10	.08	.04
88	Bill McKechnie	.05	.04	.02
89	Jackie Robinson	.15	.11	.06
90	Edd Roush	.05	.04	.02
91	John Clarkson	.05	.04	.02
92	Elmer Flick	.05	.04	.02
93	Sam Rice	.05	.04	.02
94	Eppa Rixey	.05	.04	.02
95	Luke Appling	.05	.04	.02
96	Red Faber	.05	.04	.02

		MT	NR MT	EX
97	Burleigh Grimes	.05	.04	.02
98	Miller Huggins	.05	.04	.02
99	Tim Keefe	.05	.04	.02
100	Heinie Manush	.05	.04	.02
101	John Ward	.05	.04	.02
102	Pud Galvin	.05	.04	.02
103	Casey Stengel	.10	.08	.04
104	Ted Williams	.15	.11	.06
105	Branch Rickey	.05	.04	.02
106	Red Ruffing	.05	.04	.02
107	Lloyd Waner	.05	.04	.02
108	Kiki Cuyler	.05	.04	.02
109	Goose Goslin	.05	.04	.02
110	Joe (Ducky) Medwick	.05	.04	.02
111	Roy Campanella	.10	.08	.04
112	Stan Coveleski	.05	.04	.02
113	Waite Hoyt	.05	.04	.02
114	Stan Musial	.15	.11	.06
115	Lou Boudreau	.05	.04	.02
116	Earle Combs	.05	.04	.02
117	Ford Frick	.05	.04	.02
118	Jesse Haines	.05	.04	.02
119	Dave Bancroft	.05	.04	.02
120	Jake Beckley	.05	.04	.02
121	Chick Hafey	.05	.04	.02
122	Harry Hooper	.05	.04	.02
123	Joe Kelley	.05	.04	.02
124	Rube Marquard	.05	.04	.02
125	Satchel Paige	.07	.05	.03
126	George Weiss	.05	.04	.02
127	Yogi Berra	.10	.08	.04
128	Josh Gibson	.05	.04	.02
129	Lefty Gomez	.07	.05	.03
130	Will Harridge	.05	.04	.02
131	Sandy Koufax	.10	.08	.04
132	Buck Leonard	.05	.04	.02
133	Early Wynn	.05	.04	.02
134	Ross Youngs	.05	.04	.02
135	Roberto Clemente	.15	.11	.06
136	Billy Evans	.05	.04	.02
137	Monte Irvin	.05	.04	.02
138	George Kelly	.05	.04	.02
139	Warren Spahn	.10	.08	.04
140	Mickey Welch	.05	.04	.02
141	Cool Papa Bell	.05	.04	.02
142	Jim Bottomley	.05	.04	.02
143	Jocko Conlan	.05	.04	.02
144	Whitey Ford	.05	.04	.02
145	Mickey Mantle	.25	.20	.10
146	Sam Thompson	.05	.04	.02
147	Earl Averill	.05	.04	.02
148	Bucky Harris	.05	.04	.02
149	Billy Herman	.05	.04	.02
150	Judy Johnson	.05	.04	.02
151	Ralph Kiner	.07	.05	.03
152	Oscar Charleston	.05	.04	.02
153	Roger Connor	.05	.04	.02
154	Cal Hubbard	.05	.04	.02
155	Bob Lemon	.05	.04	.02
156	Fred Lindstrom	.05	.04	.02
157	Robin Roberts	.05	.04	.02
158	Ernie Banks	.07	.05	.03
159	Martin Dihigo	.05	.04	.02
160	John Henry Lloyd	.05	.04	.02
161	Al Lopez	.05	.04	.02
162	Amos Rusie	.05	.04	.02
163	Joe Sewell	.05	.04	.02
164	Addie Joss	.05	.04	.02
165	Larry MacPhail	.05	.04	.02
166	Eddie Mathews	.05	.04	.02
167	Warren Giles	.05	.04	.02
168	Willie Mays	.25	.20	.10
169	Hack Wilson	.05	.04	.02
170	Duke Snider	.10	.08	.04
171	Al Kaline	.07	.05	.03
172	Chuck Klein	.05	.04	.02
173	Tom Yawkey	.05	.04	.02
174	Bob Gibson	.07	.05	.03
175	Rube Foster	.05	.04	.02
176	Johnny Mize	.05	.04	.02
177	Hank Aaron	.25	.20	.10
178	Frank Robinson	.07	.05	.03
179	Happy Chandler	.05	.04	.02
180	Travis Jackson	.05	.04	.02
181	Brooks Robinson	.07	.05	.03
182	Juan Marichal	.05	.04	.02
183	George Kell	.05	.04	.02
184	Walter Alston	.05	.04	.02
185	Harmon Killebrew	.07	.05	.03
186	Luis Aparicio	.05	.04	.02
187	Don Drysdale	.07	.05	.03

		MT	NR MT	EX
188	Pee Wee Reese	.07	.05	.03
189	Rick Ferrell	.05	.04	.02
190	Willie McCovey	.07	.05	.03
191	Ernie Lombardi	.05	.04	.02
192	Bobby Doerr	.05	.04	.02
193	Arky Vaughan	.05	.04	.02
194	Enos Slaughter	.05	.04	.02
195	Lou Brock	.07	.05	.03
196	Hoyt Wilhelm	.05	.04	.02
197	Billy Williams	.05	.04	.02
198	"Catfish" Hunter	.05	.04	.02
199	Ray Dandridge	.05	.04	.02

1987 Baseball Super Stars Discs

 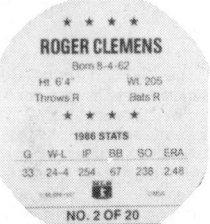

Produced by Mike Schecter and Associates, the "Baseball Super Stars" disc set was released as part of a promotion for various brands of iced tea mixes in many parts of the country. Among the brands participating in the promotion were Acme, Alpha Beta, Bustelo, Key, King Kullen, Lady Lee, Our Own and Weis. The discs were issued in three-part folding panels with each disc measuring 2-1/2" in diameter. The disc fronts feature a full-color photo inside a bright yellow border. Two player discs were included in each panel along with a coupon disc offering either an uncut press sheet of the set or a facsimile autographed ball.

		MT	NR MT	EX
Complete Panel Set:		9.00	6.75	3.50
Complete Singles Set:		4.00	3.00	1.50
Common Panel:		.25	.20	.10
Common Single Player:		.05	.04	.02
	Panel	.90	.70	.35
1	Darryl Strawberry	.20	.15	.08
2	Roger Clemens	.30	.25	.12
	Panel	.35	.25	.14
3	Ron Darling	.05	.04	.02
4	Keith Hernandez	.10	.08	.04
	Panel	1.25	.90	.50
5	Tony Pena	.05	.04	.02
6	Don Mattingly	.70	.50	.30
	Panel	.90	.70	.35
7	Eric Davis	.35	.25	.14
8	Gary Carter	.08	.06	.03
	Panel	.80	.60	.30
9	Dave Winfield	.12	.09	.05
10	Wally Joyner	.20	.15	.08
	Panel	.50	.40	.20
11	Mike Schmidt	.25	.20	.10
12	Robby Thompson	.05	.04	.02
	Panel	.90	.70	.35
13	Wade Boggs	.35	.25	.14
14	Cal Ripken Jr.	.15	.11	.06
	Panel	.90	.70	.35
15	Dale Murphy	.15	.11	.06
16	Tony Gwynn	.15	.11	.06
	Panel	1.75	1.25	.70
17	Jose Canseco	.70	.50	.30
18	Rickey Henderson	.30	.25	.12
	Panel	.25	.20	.10
19	Lance Parrish	.08	.06	.03
20	Dave Righetti	.08	.06	.03

1988 Baseball Superstars Discs

The "Second Annual Collector's Edition" of Baseball Super Stars Discs is very similar to the 1987 issue. A set of 20 discs (2-1/2" diameter) featuring full-color baseball player photos was inserted in specially marked cannisters of iced tea and fruit drinks. Each triple-fold insert consists of 2 player discs and one redemption card. Player discs are bright blue, yellow, red and green with a diamond design framing the player closeup. The player name appears upper left, the set logo appears upper right. Personalized disc series were issued for Tetley, Weis, Key Food and A&P supermarkets (untitled series were also sold at Lucky, Skaggs, Alpha Beta, Acme King Kullen, Laneco and Krasdale stores). The series name (i.e. Weis Winners) is printed below the player photo.

		MT	NR MT	EX
Complete Panel Set:		8.00	6.00	3.25
Complete Singles Set:		3.00	2.25	1.25
Common Panel:		.60	.45	.25
Common Single Player:		.05	.04	.02
	Panel	1.00	.70	.40
1	Wade Boggs	.35	.25	.14
2	Ellis Burks	.20	.15	.08
	Panel	1.25	.90	.50
3	Don Mattingly	.70	.50	.30
4	Mark McGwire	.25	.20	.10
	Panel	.70	.50	.30
5	Matt Nokes	.10	.08	.04
6	Kirby Puckett	.30	.25	.12
	Panel	.80	.60	.30
7	Billy Ripken	.05	.04	.02
8	Kevin Seitzer	.15	.11	.06
	Panel	.90	.70	.35
9	Roger Clemens	.30	.25	.12
10	Will Clark	.50	.40	.20
	Panel	.80	.60	.30
11	Vince Coleman	.10	.08	.04
12	Eric Davis	.30	.25	.12
	Panel	.70	.50	.30
13	Dave Magadan	.05	.04	.02
14	Dale Murphy	.15	.11	.06
	Panel	.80	.60	.30
15	Benito Santiago	.15	.11	.06
16	Mike Schmidt	.30	.25	.12
	Panel	.60	.45	.25
17	Darryl Strawberry	.20	.15	.08
18	Steve Bedrosian	.05	.04	.02
	Panel	.80	.60	.30
19	Dwight Gooden	.20	.15	.08
20	Fernando Valenzuela	.08	.06	.03

1959 Bazooka

The 1959 Bazooka set, consisting of 23 full-color, unnumbered cards, was issued on boxes of Bazooka one-cent bubble gum. The individually wrapped pieces of Bazooka gum were produced by Topps

Chewing Gum. The blank-backed cards measure 2-13/16" by 4-15/16" Nine cards were first issued, with 14 being added to the set later. The nine more plentiful cards are #'s 1, 5, 8, 9, 14, 15, 16, 17 and 22. Complete boxes would command 75 percent over the prices in the checklist that follows.

		NR MT	EX	VG
Complete Set:		8000.00	4000.00	2500.
Common Player:		125.00	62.00	37.00
(1a)	Hank Aaron (name in white)	600.00	300.00	180.00
(1b)	Hank Aaron (name in yellow)	600.00	300.00	180.00
(2)	Richie Ashburn	400.00	200.00	120.00
(3)	Ernie Banks	600.00	300.00	180.00
(4)	Ken Boyer	300.00	150.00	90.00
(5)	Orlando Cepeda	200.00	100.00	60.00
(6)	Bob Cerv	200.00	100.00	60.00
(7)	Rocco Colavito	450.00	225.00	135.00
(8)	Del Crandall	125.00	62.00	37.00
(9)	Jim Davenport	125.00	62.00	37.00
(10)	Don Drysdale	650.00	325.00	210.00
(11)	Nellie Fox	350.00	175.00	105.00
(12)	Jackie Jensen	250.00	125.00	75.00
(13)	Harvey Kuenn	250.00	125.00	75.00
(14)	Mickey Mantle	1800.00	900.00	550.00
(15)	Willie Mays	450.00	225.00	135.00
(16)	Bill Mazeroski	150.00	75.00	45.00
(17)	Roy McMillan	125.00	62.00	37.00
(18)	Billy Pierce	200.00	100.00	60.00
(19)	Roy Sievers	200.00	100.00	60.00
(20)	Duke Snider	800.00	400.00	250.00
(21)	Gus Triandos	200.00	100.00	60.00
(22)	Bob Turley	125.00	62.00	37.00
(23)	Vic Wertz	200.00	100.00	60.00

1960 Bazooka

Three-card panels were found on the bottoms of Bazooka bubble gum boxes in 1960. The blank-backed set is comprised of 36 cards with the card number located at the bottom of each full-color card. The individual cards measure 1-13/16" by 2-3/4"; the panels measure 2-3/4" by 5-1/2" in size. Prices, in the checklist that follows, are given for complete panels and individual cards.

		NR MT	EX	VG
	Complete Panel Set:	1500.00	750.00	450.00
	Complete Singles Set:	1000.00	500.00	300.00
	Common Panel:	75.00	37.00	22.00
	Common Single Player:	5.00	2.50	1.50
	Panel	90.00	45.00	27.00
1	Ernie Banks	50.00	25.00	15.00
2	Bud Daley	5.00	2.50	1.50
3	Wally Moon	5.00	2.50	1.50
	Panel	125.00	62.00	37.00
4	Hank Aaron	80.00	40.00	25.00
5	Milt Pappas	10.00	5.00	3.00
6	Dick Stuart	10.00	5.00	3.00
	Panel	200.00	100.00	60.00
7	Bob Clemente	90.00	45.00	27.00
8	Yogi Berra	50.00	25.00	15.00
9	Ken Boyer	12.00	6.00	3.50
	Panel	75.00	38.00	23.00
10	Orlando Cepeda	15.00	7.50	4.50
11	Gus Triandos	10.00	5.00	3.00
12	Frank Malzone	10.00	5.00	3.00
	Panel	80.00	40.00	25.00
13	Willie Mays	60.00	30.00	18.00
14	Camilo Pascual	5.00	2.50	1.50
15	Bob Cerv	5.00	2.50	1.50
	Panel	90.00	45.00	27.00
16	Vic Power	5.00	2.50	1.50
17	Larry Sherry	5.00	2.50	1.50
18	Al Kaline	50.00	25.00	15.00
	Panel	100.00	50.00	30.00
19	Warren Spahn	40.00	20.00	12.50
20	Harmon Killebrew	30.00	15.00	9.00
21	Jackie Jensen	12.00	6.00	3.50
	Panel	115.00	57.00	34.00
22	Luis Aparicio	25.00	12.50	7.50
23	Gil Hodges	30.00	15.00	9.00
24	Richie Ashburn	30.00	15.00	9.00
	Panel	100.00	50.00	30.00
25	Nellie Fox	30.00	15.00	9.00
26	Robin Roberts	30.00	15.00	9.00
27	Joe Cunningham	5.00	2.50	1.50
	Panel	100.00	50.00	30.00
28	Early Wynn	25.00	12.50	7.50
29	Frank Robinson	50.00	25.00	15.00
30	Rocky Colavito	15.00	7.50	4.50
	Panel	450.00	225.00	135.00
31	Mickey Mantle	250.00	125.00	75.00
32	Glen Hobbie	5.00	2.50	1.50
33	Roy McMillan	5.00	2.50	1.50
	Panel	75.00	37.00	22.00
34	Harvey Kuenn	12.00	6.00	3.50
35	Johnny Antonelli	5.00	2.50	1.50
36	Del Crandall	10.00	5.00	3.00

		NR MT	EX	VG
	Panel	400.00	200.00	120.00
1	Art Mahaffey	10.00	5.00	3.00
2	Mickey Mantle	250.00	125.00	75.00
3	Ron Santo	12.00	6.00	3.50
	Panel	80.00	40.00	24.00
4	Bud Daley	5.00	2.50	1.50
5	Roger Maris	70.00	35.00	21.00
6	Eddie Yost	5.00	2.50	1.50
	Panel	65.00	32.00	19.50
7	Minnie Minoso	12.00	6.00	3.50
8	Dick Groat	12.00	6.00	3.50
9	Frank Malzone	10.00	5.00	3.00
	Panel	70.00	35.00	21.00
10	Dick Donovan	5.00	2.50	1.50
11	Ed Mathews	30.00	15.00	9.00
12	Jim Lemon	5.00	2.50	1.50
	Panel	60.00	30.00	18.00
13	Chuck Estrada	5.00	2.50	1.50
14	Ken Boyer	12.00	6.00	3.50
15	Harvey Kuenn	12.00	6.00	3.50
	Panel	60.00	30.00	18.00
16	Ernie Broglio	5.00	2.50	1.50
17	Rocky Colavito	15.00	7.50	4.50
18	Ted Kluszewski	15.00	7.50	4.50
	Panel	250.00	125.00	75.00
19	Ernie Banks	75.00	38.00	23.00
20	Al Kaline	75.00	38.00	23.00
21	Ed Bailey	5.00	2.50	1.50
	Panel	75.00	37.00	22.00
22	Jim Perry	5.00	2.50	1.50
23	Willie Mays	70.00	35.00	21.00
24	Bill Mazeroski	12.00	6.00	3.50
	Panel	70.00	35.00	21.00
25	Gus Triandos	5.00	2.50	1.50
26	Don Drysdale	25.00	12.50	7.50
27	Frank Herrera	10.00	5.00	3.00
	Panel	70.00	35.00	21.00
28	Earl Battey	5.00	2.50	1.50
29	Warren Spahn	35.00	17.50	10.50
30	Gene Woodling	10.00	5.00	3.00
	Panel	60.00	30.00	18.00
31	Frank Robinson	35.00	17.50	10.50
32	Pete Runnels	10.00	5.00	3.00
33	Woodie Held	5.00	2.50	1.50
	Panel	65.00	32.00	19.50
34	Norm Larker	5.00	2.50	1.50
35	Luis Aparicio	20.00	10.00	6.00
36	Bill Tuttle	5.00	2.50	1.50

1961 Bazooka

TED KLUSZEWSKI

LOS ANGELES ANGELS 1st base

NO. 18 OF 36 CARDS

Similar in design to the 1960 Bazooka set, the 1961 edition consists of 36 cards issued in panels of three on the bottom of Bazooka bubble gum boxes. The full-color cards, which measure 1-13/16" by 2-3/4" individually and 2-3/4" by 5-1/2" as panels, are numbered 1 through 36. The backs are blank.

	NR MT	EX	VG
Complete Panel Set:	1200.00	600.00	350.00
Complete Singles Set:	700.00	350.00	200.00
Common Panel:	60.00	30.00	18.00
Common Single Player:	5.00	2.50	1.50

1962 Bazooka

KEN BOYER

ST. LOUIS CARDINALS   3rd base

In 1962, Bazooka increased the size of its set to 45 full-color cards. The set is unnumbered and was issued in panels of three on the bottoms of bubble gum boxes. The individual cards measure 1-13/16" by 2-3/4" in size, whereas the panels are 2-3/4" by 5-1/2". In the checklist that follows the cards have been numbered by panel using the name of the player who appears on the left side of the panel. Panel #'s 1-3, 31-33 and 43-45 were issued in much shorter supply and command a higher price.

	NR MT	EX	VG
Complete Panel Set:	3000.00	1500.00	900.00
Complete Singles Set:	1500.00	750.00	450.00
Common Panel:	30.00	15.00	9.00
Common Single Player:	8.00	4.00	2.50

		NR MT	EX	VG
	Panel	1000.00	500.00	300.00
(1)	Bob Allison	150.00	75.00	45.00
(2)	Ed Mathews	350.00	175.00	105.00
(3)	Vada Pinson	150.00	75.00	45.00
	Panel	50.00	25.00	15.00
(4)	Earl Battey	8.00	4.00	2.50
(5)	Warren Spahn	30.00	15.00	9.00
(6)	Lee Thomas	8.00	4.00	2.50
	Panel	40.00	20.00	12.00
(7)	Orlando Cepeda	15.00	7.50	4.50
(8)	Woodie Held	8.00	4.00	2.50
(9)	Bob Aspromonte	8.00	4.00	2.50
	Panel	100.00	50.00	30.00
(10)	Dick Howser	10.00	5.00	3.00
(11)	Bob Clemente	50.00	25.00	15.00
(12)	Al Kaline	30.00	15.00	9.00
	Panel	80.00	40.00	24.00
(13)	Joey Jay	8.00	4.00	2.50
(14)	Roger Maris	40.00	20.00	12.00
(15)	Frank Howard	15.00	7.50	4.50
	Panel	70.00	35.00	21.00
(16)	Sandy Koufax	50.00	25.00	15.00
(17)	Jim Gentile	8.00	4.00	2.50
(18)	Johnny Callison	10.00	5.00	3.00
	Panel	30.00	15.00	9.00
(19)	Jim Landis	8.00	4.00	2.50
(20)	Ken Boyer	12.00	6.00	3.50
(21)	Chuck Schilling	8.00	4.00	2.50
	Panel	450.00	225.00	135.00
(22)	Art Mahaffey	10.00	5.00	3.00
(23)	Mickey Mantle	200.00	100.00	60.00
(24)	Dick Stuart	10.00	5.00	3.00
	Panel	80.00	40.00	24.00
(25)	Ken McBride	8.00	4.00	2.50
(26)	Frank Robinson	35.00	17.50	10.50
(27)	Gil Hodges	25.00	12.50	7.50
	Panel	100.00	50.00	30.00
(28)	Milt Pappas	10.00	5.00	3.00
(29)	Hank Aaron	70.00	35.00	21.00
(30)	Luis Aparicio	20.00	10.00	6.00
	Panel	1000.00	500.00	300.00
(31)	Johnny Romano	150.00	75.00	45.00
(32)	Ernie Banks	450.00	225.00	135.00
(33)	Norm Siebern	150.00	75.00	45.00
	Panel	40.00	20.00	12.00
(34)	Ron Santo	12.00	6.00	3.50
(35)	Norm Cash	10.00	5.00	3.00
(36)	Jim Piersall	10.00	5.00	3.00
	Panel	70.00	35.00	21.00
(37)	Don Schwall	8.00	4.00	2.50
(38)	Willie Mays	50.00	25.00	15.00
(39)	Norm Larker	8.00	4.00	2.50
	Panel	70.00	35.00	21.00
(40)	Bill White	10.00	5.00	3.00
(41)	Whitey Ford	30.00	15.00	9.00
(42)	Rocky Colavito	15.00	7.50	4.50
	Panel	1000.00	500.00	300.00
(43)	Don Zimmer	200.00	100.00	60.00
(44)	Harmon Killebrew	300.00	150.00	90.00
(45)	Gene Woodling	150.00	75.00	45.00

1963 Bazooka

The 1963 Bazooka issue reverted back to a 12-panel, 36-card set, but saw a change in the size of the cards. Individual cards measure 1-9/16" by 2-1/2", while panels are 2-1/2" by 4-11/16" in size. The card design was altered also, with the player's name, team and position situated in a white oval space at the bottom of the card. The full-color, blank-backed set is numbered 1-36. Five Bazooka All-Time Greats cards were inserted in each box of bubble gum.

		NR MT	EX	VG
		1200.00	600.00	350.00
Complete Panel Set:				
Complete Singles Set:		650.00	325.00	200.00
Common Panel:		30.00	15.00	9.00
Common Single Player:		5.00	2.50	1.50
	Panel	400.00	200.00	120.00
1	Mickey Mantle (batting righty)	250.00	125.00	75.00
2	Bob Rodgers	5.00	2.50	1.50
3	Ernie Banks	40.00	20.00	12.50
	Panel	50.00	25.00	15.00
4	Norm Siebern	5.00	2.50	1.50
5	Warren Spahn (portrait)	30.00	15.00	9.00
6	Bill Mazeroski	10.00	5.00	3.00
	Panel	115.00	57.00	34.00
7	Harmon Killebrew (batting)	30.00	15.00	9.00
8	Dick Farrell (portrait)	5.00	2.50	1.50
9	Hank Aaron (glove in front)	60.00	30.00	17.50
	Panel	150.00	75.00	45.00
10	Dick Donovan	5.00	2.50	1.50
11	Jim Gentile (batting)	5.00	2.50	1.50
12	Willie Mays (bat in front)	75.00	38.00	23.00
	Panel	70.00	35.00	21.00
13	Camilo Pascual (hands at waist)	5.00	2.50	1.50
14	Bob Clemente (portrait)	50.00	25.00	15.00
15	Johnny Callison (wearing pinstripe uniform)	8.00	4.00	2.50
	Panel	175.00	87.00	52.00
16	Carl Yastrzemski (kneeling)	90.00	45.00	27.00
17	Don Drysdale	70.00	35.00	20.00
18	Johnny Romano (portrait)	5.00	2.50	1.50
	Panel	30.00	15.00	9.00
19	Al Jackson	8.00	4.00	2.50
20	Ralph Terry	8.00	4.00	2.50
21	Bill Monbouquette	5.00	2.50	1.50
	Panel	95.00	47.00	28.00
22	Orlando Cepeda	15.00	7.50	4.50
23	Stan Musial	50.00	25.00	15.00
24	Floyd Robinson (no pinstripes on uniform)	5.00	2.50	1.50
	Panel	30.00	15.00	9.00
25	Chuck Hinton (batting)	5.00	2.50	1.50
26	Bob Purkey	5.00	2.50	1.50
27	Ken Hubbs	12.00	6.00	3.50
	Panel	60.00	30.00	18.00
28	Bill White	8.00	4.00	2.50
29	Ray Herbert	5.00	2.50	1.50
30	Brooks Robinson (glove in front)	35.00	17.50	10.50
	Panel	60.00	30.00	18.00
31	Frank Robinson (batting, uniform number doesn't show)	50.00	25.00	15.00
32	Lee Thomas	5.00	2.50	1.50
33	Rocky Colavito (Detroit)	10.00	5.00	3.00
	Panel	60.00	30.00	18.00
34	Al Kaline (kneeling)	35.00	17.50	10.50
35	Art Mahaffey	5.00	2.50	1.50
36	Tommy Davis (batting follow-thru)	8.00	4.00	2.50

1963 Bazooka All-Time Greats

Consisting of 41 cards, the Bazooka All-Time Greats set was issued as inserts (5 per box) in boxes of Bazooka bubble gum. A black and white head-shot of the player is placed inside a gold plaque within a white border. The card backs have black print on white and white and yellow and contain a brief biography of the player. The numbered cards measure 1-9/16" by 2-1/2" in size. The cards can be found with silver fronts instead of gold. The silver are worth double the values listed in the following checklist.

		NR MT	EX	VG
Complete Set:		200.00	100.00	60.00
Common Player:		2.50	1.25	.70
1	Joe Tinker	3.50	1.75	1.00
2	Harry Heilmann	2.50	1.25	.70
3	Jack Chesbro	3.00	1.50	.90
4	Christy Mathewson	5.00	2.50	1.50
5	Herb Pennock	3.00	1.50	.90
6	Cy Young	6.00	3.00	1.75
7	Big Ed Walsh	2.50	1.25	.70
8	Nap Lajoie	3.50	1.75	1.00
9	Eddie Plank	2.50	1.25	.70
10	Honus Wagner	8.00	4.00	2.50
11	Chief Bender	3.00	1.50	.90
12	Walter Johnson	8.00	4.00	2.50
13	Three-Fingered Brown	2.50	1.25	.70
14	Rabbit Maranville	3.00	1.50	.90
15	Lou Gehrig	25.00	12.50	7.50
16	Ban Johnson	2.50	1.25	.70
17	Babe Ruth	40.00	20.00	12.00
18	Connie Mack	5.00	2.50	1.50
19	Hank Greenberg	3.50	1.75	1.00
20	John McGraw	3.50	1.75	1.00
21	Johnny Evers	2.50	1.25	.70
22	Al Simmons	2.50	1.25	.70
23	Jimmy Collins	2.50	1.25	.70
24	Tris Speaker	3.50	1.75	1.00
25	Frank Chance	2.50	1.25	.70
26	Fred Clarke	2.50	1.25	.70
27	Wilbert Robinson	2.50	1.25	.70
28	Dazzy Vance	2.50	1.25	.70
29	Pete Alexander	3.50	1.75	1.00
30	Judge Landis	2.50	1.25	.70
31	Wee Willie Keeler	2.50	1.25	.70
32	Rogers Hornsby	5.00	2.50	1.50
33	Hugh Duffy	2.50	1.25	.70
34	Mickey Cochrane	3.50	1.75	1.00
35	Ty Cobb	25.00	12.50	7.50
36	Mel Ott	3.50	1.75	1.00
37	Clark Griffith	2.50	1.25	.70
38	Ted Lyons	2.50	1.25	.70
39	Cap Anson	3.50	1.75	1.00
40	Bill Dickey	3.50	1.75	1.00
41	Eddie Collins	3.50	1.75	1.00

1964 Bazooka

WILLIE McCOVEY
S. F. GIANTS   OF

NO. 31 OF 36 CARDS

The 1964 Bazooka set is identical in design and size to the previous year's effort. However, different photographs were used from year to year by Topps, issuer of Bazooka bubble gum. The 1964 set consists of 36 full-color, blank-backed cards numbered 1 through 36. Individual cards measure 1-9/16" by 2-1/2"; three-card panels measure 2-1/2" by 4-11/16". Sheets of ten full-color baseball stamps were inserted in each box of bubble gum.

	NR MT	EX	VG
Complete Panel Set:	1200.00	600.00	350.00

		NR MT	EX	VG
Complete Singles Set:		600.00	300.00	180.00
Common Panel:		25.00	12.50	7.50
Common Single Player:		5.00	2.50	1.50
	Panel	220.00	110.00	66.00
1	Mickey Mantle (portrait)	175.00	87.00	52.00
2	Dick Groat	8.00	4.00	2.50
3	Steve Barber	5.00	2.50	1.50
	Panel	40.00	20.00	12.00
4	Ken McBride	5.00	2.50	1.50
5	Warren Spahn (head to waist shot)			
		30.00	15.00	9.00
6	Bob Friend	6.00	3.00	1.75
	Panel	115.00	57.00	34.00
7	Harmon Killebrew (portrait)	30.00	15.00	9.00
8	Dick Farrell (hands above head)	5.00	2.50	1.50
9	Hank Aaron (glove to left)	70.00	35.00	20.00
	Panel	70.00	35.00	21.00
10	Rich Rollins	5.00	2.50	1.50
11	Jim Gentile (portrait)	5.00	2.50	1.50
12	Willie Mays (looking to left)	50.00	25.00	15.00
	Panel	70.00	35.00	21.00
13	Camilo Pascual (pitching follow-thru)			
		5.00	2.50	1.50
14	Bob Clemente (throwing)	50.00	25.00	15.00
15	Johnny Callison (batting, screen showing)			
		8.00	4.00	2.50
	Panel	75.00	37.00	22.00
16	Carl Yastrzemski (batting)	50.00	25.00	15.00
17	Billy Williams (kneeling)	25.00	12.50	7.50
18	Johnny Romano (batting)	5.00	2.50	1.50
	Panel	55.00	27.00	16.50
19	Jim Maloney	5.00	2.50	1.50
20	Norm Cash	8.00	4.00	2.50
21	Willie McCovey	30.00	15.00	9.00
	Panel	25.00	12.50	7.50
22	Jim Fregosi (batting)	6.00	3.00	1.75
23	George Altman	5.00	2.50	1.50
24	Floyd Robinson (wearing pinstripe uniform)			
		5.00	2.50	1.50
	Panel	25.00	12.50	7.50
25	Chuck Hinton (portrait)	5.00	2.50	1.50
26	Ron Hunt (batting)	8.00	4.00	2.50
27	Gary Peters (pitching)	5.00	2.50	1.50
	Panel	60.00	30.00	18.00
28	Dick Ellsworth	5.00	2.50	1.50
29	Elston Howard (holding bat)	12.00	6.00	3.50
30	Brooks Robinson (kneeling with glove)			
		30.00	15.00	9.00
	Panel	110.00	55.00	33.00
31	Frank Robinson (uniform number shows)			
		40.00	20.00	12.00
32	Sandy Koufax (glove in front)	50.00	25.00	15.00
33	Rocky Colavito (Kansas City)	10.00	5.00	3.00
	Panel	65.00	32.00	19.50
34	Al Kaline (holding two bats)	30.00	15.00	9.00
35	Ken Boyer (head to waist shot)	10.00	5.00	3.00
36	Tommy Davis (batting)	8.00	4.00	2.50

1964 Bazooka Stamps

45

RUSTY STAUB
HOUSTON COLTS   1ST BASE

Occasionally mislabeled "Topps Stamps," the 1964 Bazooka Stamps set was produced by Topps, but was found only in boxes of 1¢ Bazooka bubble gum. Issued in sheets of ten, 100 color stamps make up the set. Each stamp measures 1" by 1-1/2" in size. While the stamps are not individually numbered, the sheets are numbered one through ten. The stamps are commonly found as complete sheets of ten and are priced in that fashion in the checklist that follows.

		NR MT	EX	VG
	Complete Sheet Set:	400.00	200.00	125.00
	Common Sheet:	15.00	7.50	4.50
1	Max Alvis, Ed Charles, Dick Ellsworth, Jimmie Hall, Frank Malzone, Milt Pappas, Vada Pinson, Tony Taylor, Pete Ward, Bill White	15.00	7.50	4.50
2	Bob Aspromonte, Larry Jackson, Willie Mays, Al McBean, Bill Monbouquette, Bobby Richardson, Floyd Robinson, Frank Robinson, Norm Siebern, Don Zimmer	20.00		12.00
3	Ernie Banks, Bob Clemente, Curt Flood, Jesse Gonder, Woody Held, Don Lock, Dave Nicholson, Joe Pepitone, Brooks Robinson, Carl Yastrzemski	60.00	30.00	18.00
4	Hank Aguirre, Jim Grant, Harmon Killebrew, Jim Maloney, Juan Marichal, Bill Mazeroski, Juan Pizarro, Boog Powell, Ed Roebuck, Ron Santo	30.00	15.00	9.00
5	Jim Bouton, Norm Cash, Orlando Cepeda, Tommy Harper, Chuck Hinton, Albie Pearson, Ron Perranoski, Dick Radatz, Johnny Romano, Carl Willey	18.00	9.00	5.50
6	Steve Barber, Jim Fregosi, Tony Gonzalez, Mickey Mantle, Jim O'Toole, Gary Peters, Rich Rollins, Warren Spahn, Dick Stuart, Joe Torre	125.00	62.00	37.00
7	Felipe Alou, George Altman, Ken Boyer, Rocky Colavito, Jim Davenport, Tommy Davis, Bill Freehan, Bob Friend, Ken Johnson, Billy Moran	18.00	9.00	5.50
8	Earl Battey, Ernie Broglio, Johnny Callison, Donn Clendenon, Don Drysdale, Jim Gentile, Elston Howard, Claude Osteen, Billy Williams, Hal Woodeshick	25.00	12.50	7.50
9	Hank Aaron, Jack Baldschun, Wayne Causey, Moe Drabowsky, Dick Groat, Frank Howard, Al Jackson, Jerry Lumpe, Ken McBride, Rusty Staub	40.00	20.00	12.00
10	Ray Culp, Vic Davalillo, Dick Farrell, Ron Hunt, Al Kaline, Sandy Koufax, Ed Mathews, Willie McCovey, Camilo Pascual, Lee Thomas	50.00	25.00	15.00

		NR MT	EX	VG
1	Mickey Mantle (batting lefty)	175.00	87.00	52.00
2	Larry Jackson	5.00	2.50	1.50
3	Chuck Hinton	5.00	2.50	1.50
	Panel	30.00	15.00	9.00
4	Tony Oliva	10.00	5.00	3.00
5	Dean Chance	5.00	2.50	1.50
6	Jim O'Toole	5.00	2.50	1.50
	Panel	95.00	47.00	28.00
7	Harmon Killebrew (bat on shoulder)	25.00	12.50	7.50
8	Pete Ward	5.00	2.50	1.50
9	Hank Aaron (batting)	50.00	25.00	15.00
	Panel	70.00	35.00	21.00
10	Dick Radatz	5.00	2.50	1.50
11	Boog Powell	10.00	5.00	3.00
12	Willie Mays (looking down)	40.00	20.00	12.00
	Panel	65.00	32.00	19.50
13	Bob Veale	5.00	2.50	1.50
14	Bob Clemente (batting)	40.00	20.00	12.00
15	Johnny Callison (batting, no screen in background)	8.00	4.00	2.50
	Panel	45.00	22.00	13.50
16	Joe Torre	8.00	4.00	2.50
17	Billy Williams (batting)	20.00	10.00	6.00
18	Bob Chance	5.00	2.50	1.50
	Panel	30.00	15.00	9.00
19	Bob Aspromonte	5.00	2.50	1.50
20	Joe Christopher	5.00	2.50	1.50
21	Jim Bunning	12.00	6.00	3.50
	Panel	70.00	35.00	21.00
22	Jim Fregosi (portrait)	8.00	4.00	2.50
23	Bob Gibson	25.00	12.50	7.50
24	Juan Marichal	20.00	10.00	6.00
	Panel	25.00	12.50	7.50
25	Dave Wickersham	5.00	2.50	1.50
26	Ron Hunt (throwing)	8.00	4.00	2.50
27	Gary Peters (portrait)	5.00	2.50	1.50
	Panel	70.00	35.00	21.00
28	Ron Santo	10.00	5.00	3.00
29	Elston Howard (with glove)	12.00	6.00	3.50
30	Brooks Robinson (portrait)	30.00	15.00	9.00
	Panel	95.00	47.00	28.00
31	Frank Robinson (portrait)	35.00	17.50	10.50
32	Sandy Koufax (hands over head)	40.00	20.00	12.00
33	Rocky Colavito (Cleveland)	10.00	5.00	3.00
	Panel	60.00	30.00	18.00
34	Al Kaline (portrait)	30.00	15.00	9.00
35	Ken Boyer (portrait)	10.00	5.00	3.00
36	Tommy Davis (fielding)	8.00	4.00	2.50

1965 Bazooka

The 1965 Bazooka set is identical to the 1963 and 1964 sets. Different players were added each year and different photographs were used for those players being included again. Individual cards cut from the boxes measure 1-9/16" by 2-1/2". Complete three-card panels measure 2-1/2" by 4-11/16". Thirty-six full-color, blank-backed, numbered cards comprise the set. Prices are given for individual cards and complete panels in the checklist that follows.

	NR MT	EX	VG
Complete Panel Set:	1100.00	550.00	325.00
Complete Singles Set:	600.00	300.00	180.00
Common Panel:	25.00	12.50	7.50
Common Single Player:	5.00	2.50	1.50
Panel	225.00	115.00	70.00

1966 Bazooka

The 1966 Bazooka set was increased to 48 cards. Issued in panels of three on the bottoms of boxes of bubble gum, the full-color cards are blank-backed and numbered. Individual cards measure 1-9/16" by 2-1/2", whereas panels measure 2-1/2" by 4-11/16".

		NR MT	EX	VG
	Complete Panel Set:	1500.00	750.00	450.00
	Complete Singles Set:	800.00	400.00	250.00
	Common Panel:	25.00	12.50	7.50
	Common Single Player:	5.00	2.50	1.50
	Panel	65.00	32.00	19.50
1	Sandy Koufax	40.00	20.00	12.00
2	Willie Horton	6.00	3.00	1.75

		NR MT	EX	VG
3	Frank Howard	8.00	4.00	2.50
	Panel	40.00	20.00	12.00
4	Richie Allen	10.00	5.00	3.00
5	Mel Stottlemyre	8.00	4.00	2.50
6	Tony Conigliaro	15.00	7.50	4.50
	Panel	250.00	125.00	70.00
7	Mickey Mantle	175.00	87.00	52.00
8	Leon Wagner	5.00	2.50	1.50
9	Ed Kranepool	6.00	3.00	1.75
	Panel	70.00	35.00	21.00
10	Juan Marichal	20.00	10.00	6.00
11	Harmon Killebrew	25.00	12.50	7.50
12	Johnny Callison	6.00	3.00	1.75
	Panel	55.00	27.00	16.50
13	Roy McMillan	5.00	2.50	1.50
14	Willie McCovey	25.00	12.50	7.50
15	Rocky Colavito	10.00	5.00	3.00
	Panel	65.00	32.00	19.50
16	Willie Mays	40.00	20.00	12.00
17	Sam McDowell	8.00	4.00	2.50
18	Vern Law	6.00	3.00	1.75
	Panel	50.00	25.00	15.00
19	Jim Fregosi	6.00	3.00	1.75
20	Ron Fairly	6.00	3.00	1.75
21	Bob Gibson	25.00	12.50	7.50
	Panel	70.00	35.00	21.00
22	Carl Yastrzemski	40.00	20.00	12.00
23	Bill White	8.00	4.00	2.50
24	Bob Aspromonte	5.00	2.50	1.50
	Panel	55.00	27.00	16.50
25	Dean Chance (California)	5.00	2.50	1.50
26	Bob Clemente	40.00	20.00	12.00
27	Tony Cloninger	5.00	2.50	1.50
	Panel	70.00	35.00	21.00
28	Curt Blefary	5.00	2.50	1.50
29	Milt Pappas	5.00	2.50	1.50
30	Hank Aaron	50.00	25.00	15.00
	Panel	60.00	30.00	18.00
31	Jim Bunning	12.00	6.00	3.50
32	Frank Robinson (portrait)	30.00	15.00	9.00
33	Bill Skowron	8.00	4.00	2.50
	Panel	60.00	30.00	18.00
34	Brooks Robinson	30.00	15.00	9.00
35	Jim Wynn	6.00	3.00	1.75
36	Joe Torre	8.00	4.00	2.50
	Panel	145.00	72.00	43.00
37	Jim Grant	5.00	2.50	1.50
38	Pete Rose	90.00	45.00	27.50
39	Ron Santo	10.00	5.00	3.00
	Panel	60.00	30.00	18.00
40	Tom Tresh	8.00	4.00	2.50
41	Tony Oliva	10.00	5.00	3.00
42	Don Drysdale	25.00	12.50	7.50
	Panel	25.00	12.50	7.50
43	Pete Richert	5.00	2.50	1.50
44	Bert Campaneris	8.00	4.00	2.50
45	Jim Maloney	5.00	2.50	1.50
	Panel	70.00	35.00	21.00
46	Al Kaline	30.00	15.00	9.00
47	Eddie Fisher	5.00	2.50	1.50
48	Billy Williams	20.00	10.00	6.00

1967 Bazooka

KEN BOYER
NEW YORK METS 3B

NO. 33 OF 48 CARDS

The 1967 Bazooka set is identical in design to the Bazooka sets of 1964-1966. Issued in panels of three on the bottoms of bubble gum boxes, the set is made up of 48 full-color, blank-backed, numbered cards. Individual cards measure 1-9/16" by 2-1/2";

complete panels measure 2-1/2" by 4-11/16" in size.

		NR MT	EX	VG
	Complete Panel Set:	1400.00	700.00	425.00
	Complete Singles Set:	775.00	387.00	232.00
	Common Panel:	25.00	12.50	7.50
	Common Single Player:	5.00	2.50	1.50
	Panel	25.00	12.50	7.50
1	Rick Reichardt	5.00	2.50	1.50
2	Tommy Agee	5.00	2.50	1.50
3	Frank Howard	8.00	4.00	2.50
	Panel	35.00	17.50	10.50
4	Richie Allen	10.00	5.00	3.00
5	Mel Stottlemyre	8.00	4.00	2.50
6	Tony Conigliaro	15.00	7.50	4.50
	Panel	225.00	110.00	70.00
7	Mickey Mantle	175.00	87.00	52.00
8	Leon Wagner	5.00	2.50	1.50
9	Gary Peters	5.00	2.50	1.50
	Panel	70.00	35.00	21.00
10	Juan Marichal	20.00	10.00	6.00
11	Harmon Killebrew	25.00	12.50	7.50
12	Johnny Callison	6.00	3.00	1.75
	Panel	50.00	25.00	15.00
13	Denny McLain	12.00	6.00	3.50
14	Willie McCovey	25.00	12.50	7.50
15	Rocky Colavito	10.00	5.00	3.00
	Panel	65.00	32.00	19.50
16	Willie Mays	40.00	20.00	12.00
17	Sam McDowell	6.00	3.00	1.75
18	Jim Kaat	12.00	6.00	3.50
	Panel	50.00	25.00	15.00
19	Jim Fregosi	6.00	3.00	1.75
20	Ron Fairly	6.00	3.00	1.75
21	Bob Gibson	25.00	12.50	7.50
	Panel	70.00	35.00	21.00
22	Carl Yastrzemski	40.00	20.00	12.00
23	Bill White	6.00	3.00	1.75
24	Bob Aspromonte	5.00	2.50	1.50
	Panel	60.00	30.00	18.00
25	Dean Chance (Minnesota)	5.00	2.50	1.50
26	Bob Clemente	40.00	20.00	12.00
27	Tony Cloninger	5.00	2.50	1.50
	Panel	70.00	35.00	21.00
28	Curt Blefary	5.00	2.50	1.50
29	Phil Regan	5.00	2.50	1.50
30	Hank Aaron	50.00	25.00	15.00
	Panel	60.00	30.00	18.00
31	Jim Bunning	12.00	6.00	3.50
32	Frank Robinson (batting)	25.00	12.50	7.50
33	Ken Boyer	10.00	5.00	3.00
	Panel	60.00	30.00	18.00
34	Brooks Robinson	30.00	15.00	9.00
35	Jim Wynn	6.00	3.00	1.75
36	Joe Torre	8.00	4.00	2.50
	Panel	140.00	70.00	42.00
37	Tommy Davis	6.00	3.00	1.75
38	Pete Rose	90.00	45.00	27.00
39	Ron Santo	10.00	5.00	3.00
	Panel	60.00	30.00	18.00
40	Tom Tresh	8.00	4.00	2.50
41	Tony Oliva	10.00	5.00	3.00
42	Don Drysdale	25.00	12.50	7.50
	Panel	25.00	12.50	7.50
43	Pete Richert	5.00	2.50	1.50
44	Bert Campaneris	6.00	3.00	1.75
45	Jim Maloney	5.00	2.50	1.50
	Panel	70.00	35.00	21.00
46	Al Kaline	30.00	15.00	9.00
47	Matty Alou	6.00	3.00	1.75
48	Billy Williams	20.00	10.00	6.00

1968 Bazooka

The design of the 1968 Bazooka set is radically different from previous years. The player cards are situated on the sides of the boxes with the box back containing "Tipps From The Topps." Four unnumbered player cards, measuring 1-1/4" by 3-1/8", are featured on each box. The box back includes a small player photo plus illustrated tips on various aspects of the game of baseball. The boxes are numbered 1-15 on the top panels. There are 56 different player cards in the set, with four of the cards (Agee, Drysdale, Rose, Santo) being used twice to round out the set of fifteen boxes.

		NR MT	EX	VG
	Complete Box Set:	3000.00	1500.00	900.00
	Complete Singles Set:	1800.00	900.00	550.00
	Common Box:	110.00	55.00	33.00
	Common Single Player:	5.00	2.50	1.50
	Box	175.00	87.00	52.00
	Maury Wills (Bunting)	20.00	10.00	6.00
(1)	Clete Boyer	9.00	4.50	2.75
(2)	Paul Casanova	7.00	3.50	2.00
(3)	Al Kaline	30.00	15.00	9.00
(4)	Tom Seaver	70.00	35.00	21.00
	Box	150.00	75.00	45.00
2	Carl Yastrzemski (Batting)	50.00	25.00	15.00
(5)	Matty Alou	9.00	4.50	2.75
(6)	Bill Freehan	9.00	4.50	2.75
(7)	Jim Hunter	20.00	10.00	6.00
(8)	Jim Lefebvre	7.00	3.50	2.00
	Box	110.00	55.00	33.00
3	Bert Campaneris (Stealing bases)	20.00	10.00	6.00
(9)	Bobby Knoop	7.00	3.50	2.00
(10)	Tim McCarver	12.00	6.00	3.50
(11)	Frank Robinson	25.00	12.50	7.50
(12)	Bob Veale	7.00	3.50	2.00
	Box	90.00	45.00	27.00
4	Maury Wills (Sliding)	20.00	10.00	6.00
(13)	Joe Azcue	7.00	3.50	2.00
(14)	Tony Conigliaro	15.00	7.50	4.50
(15)	Ken Holtzman	9.00	4.50	2.75
(16)	Bill White	9.00	4.50	2.75
	Box	150.00	75.00	45.00
5	Julian Javier (The Double Play)	20.00	10.00	6.00
(17)	Hank Aaron	50.00	25.00	15.00
(18)	Juan Marichal	20.00	10.00	6.00
(19)	Joe Pepitone	12.00	6.00	3.50
(20)	Rico Petrocelli	9.00	4.50	2.75
	Box	175.00	87.00	52.00
6	Orlando Cepeda (Playing 1st Base)	25.00	12.50	7.50
(21)	Tommie Agee	5.00	2.50	1.50
(22)	Don Drysdale	10.00	5.00	3.00
(23)	Pete Rose	70.00	35.00	21.00
(24)	Ron Santo	5.00	2.50	1.50
	Box	110.00	55.00	33.00
7	Bill Mazeroski (Playing 2nd Base)	20.00	10.00	6.00
(25)	Jim Bunning	12.00	6.00	3.50
(26)	Frank Howard	12.00	6.00	3.50
(27)	John Roseboro	9.00	4.50	2.75
(28)	George Scott	9.00	4.50	2.75
	Box	150.00	75.00	45.00
8	Brooks Robinson (Playing 3rd Base)	50.00	25.00	15.00
(29)	Tony Gonzalez	7.00	3.50	2.00
(30)	Willie Horton	9.00	4.50	2.75
(31)	Harmon Killebrew	25.00	12.50	7.50
(32)	Jim McGlothlin	7.00	3.50	2.00
	Box	110.00	55.00	33.00
9	Jim Fregosi (Playing Shortstop)	20.00	10.00	6.00
(33)	Max Alvis	7.00	3.50	2.00
(34)	Bob Gibson	20.00	10.00	6.00
(35)	Tony Oliva	12.00	6.00	3.50
(36)	Vada Pinson	12.00	6.00	3.50
	Box	110.00	55.00	33.00
10	Joe Torre (Catching)	25.00	12.50	7.50
(37)	Dean Chance	7.00	3.50	2.00
(38)	Tommy Davis	9.00	4.50	2.75
(39)	Ferguson Jenkins	15.00	7.50	4.50

		NR MT	EX	VG
(40)	Rick Monday	9.00	4.50	2.75
	Box	275.00	137.00	82.00
11	Jim Lonborg (Pitching)	25.00	12.50	7.50
(41)	Curt Flood	9.00	4.50	2.75
(42)	Joel Horlen	7.00	3.50	2.00
(43)	Mickey Mantle	125.00	62.00	37.00
(44)	Jim Wynn	7.00	3.50	2.00
	Box	150.00	75.00	45.00
12	Mike McCormick (Fielding the Pitcher's Position)	20.00	10.00	6.00
(45)	Bob Clemente	40.00	20.00	12.00
(46)	Al Downing	9.00	4.50	2.75
(47)	Don Mincher	7.00	3.50	2.00
(48)	Tony Perez	15.00	7.50	4.50
	Box	175.00	87.00	52.00
13	Frank Crosetti (Coaching)	35.00	17.50	10.50
(49)	Rod Carew	40.00	20.00	12.00
(50)	Willie McCovey	25.00	12.50	7.50
(51)	Ron Swoboda	7.00	3.50	2.00
(52)	Earl Wilson	7.00	3.50	2.00
	Box	150.00	75.00	45.00
14	Willie Mays (Playing the Outfield)	50.00	25.00	15.00
(53)	Richie Allen	12.00	6.00	3.50
(54)	Gary Peters	7.00	3.50	2.00
(55)	Rusty Staub	10.00	5.00	3.00
(56)	Billy Williams	20.00	10.00	6.00
	Box	175.00	87.00	52.00
15	Lou Brock (Base Running)	40.00	20.00	12.00
(57)	Tommie Agee	5.00	2.50	1.50
(58)	Don Drysdale	10.00	5.00	3.00
(59)	Pete Rose	70.00	35.00	21.00
(60)	Ron Santo	5.00	2.50	1.50

1969 Bazooka

Issued over a two-year span, the 1969-70 Bazooka set utilized the box bottom and sides. The box bottom, entitled "Baseball Extra," features an historic event in baseball. The bottom panels are numbered 1 through 12. Two "All-Time Great" cards were located on each side of the box. These cards are not numbered and have no distinct borders. Individual cards measure 1-1/4" by 3-1/8"; the "Baseball Extra" panels measure 3" by 6-1/4". The prices in the checklist that follows are for complete boxes only. Cards/panels cut from the boxes have a greatly reduced value - 25 per cent of the complete box prices for all cut pieces.

		NR MT	EX	VG
	Complete Box Set:	200.00	100.00	60.00
	Common Box:	10.00	5.00	3.00
1	No-Hit Duel By Toney And Vaughn (Mordecai Brown, Ty Cobb, Willie Keeler, Eddie Plank)	15.00	7.50	4.50
2	Alexander Conquers Yanks (Rogers Hornsby, Ban Johnson, Walter Johnson, Al Simmons)	10.00	5.00	3.00
3	Yanks Lazzeri Sets A.L. Hit Record (Hugh Duffy, Lou Gehrig, Tris Speaker, Joe Tinker)	15.00	7.50	4.50
4	Home Run Almost Hit Out Of Stadium (Grover Alexander, Chief Bender, Christy Mathewson, Cy Young)	10.00	5.00	3.00
5	Four Consecutive Homers By Gehrig (Frank Chance, Mickey Cochrane, John McGraw, Babe Ruth)	30.00	15.00	9.00

		NR MT	EX	VG
6	No-Hit Game By Walter Johnson (Johnny Evers, Walter Johnson, John McGraw, Cy Young)	10.00	5.00	3.00
7	Twelve RBI's By Bottomley (Ty Cobb, Eddie Collins, Johnny Evers, Lou Gehrig)	20.00	10.00	6.00
8	Ty Ties Record (Mickey Cochrane, Eddie Collins, Met Ott, Honus Wagner)	10.00	5.00	3.00
9	Babe Ruth Hits Three Homers In Game (Cap Anson, Jack Chesbro, Al Simmons, Tris Speaker)	25.00	12.50	7.50
10	Calls Shot In Series Game (Nap Lajoie, Connie Mack, Rabbit Maranville, Ed Walsh)	25.00	12.50	7.50
11	Ruth's 60th Homer Sets New Record (Frank Chance, Nap Lajoie, Mel Ott, Joe Tinker)	25.00	12.50	7.50
12	Double Shutout By Ed Reulbach (Rogers Hornsby, Rabbit Maranville, Christy Mathewson, Honus Wagner)	10.00	5.00	3.00

		NR MT	EX	VG
(17)	Willie Mays	20.00	10.00	4.50
(18)	Jim Hunter	6.00	3.00	1.75
(19)	Juan Marichal	6.00	3.00	1.75
(20)	Frank Howard	3.00	1.50	.90
(21)	Bill Melton	1.25	.60	.40
(22)	Willie McCovey	7.00	3.50	2.00
(23)	Carl Yastrzemski	12.00	6.00	3.50
(24)	Clyde Wright	1.25	.60	.40
(25)	Jim Merritt	1.25	.60	.40
(26)	Luis Aparicio	6.00	3.00	1.75
(27)	Bobby Murcer	3.00	1.50	.90
(28)	Rico Petrocelli	2.00	1.00	.60
(29)	Sam McDowell	2.00	1.00	.60
(30)	Clarence Gaston	1.25	.60	.40
(31)	Brooks Robinson	6.50	3.25	2.00
(32)	Hank Aaron	20.00	10.00	4.50
(33)	Larry Dierker	1.25	.60	.40
(34)	Rusty Staub	2.00	1.00	.60
(35)	Bob Gibson	7.00	3.50	2.00
(36)	Amos Otis	1.25	.60	.40

1971 Bazooka Unnumbered Set

This Bazooka set was issued in 1971, consisting of 36 full-color, blank-backed, unnumbered cards. Issued in panels of three on the bottoms of Bazooka bubble gum boxes, individual cards measure 2" by 2-5/8" whereas complete panels measure 2-5/8" by 5-5/16". In the checklist that follows, the cards have been numbered by panel using the name of the player who appears on the left portion of the panel.

		NR MT	EX	VG
Complete Panel Set:		325.00	162.00	97.00
Complete Singles Set:		190.00	95.00	57.00
Common Panel:		10.00	5.00	3.00
Common Single Player:		1.25	.60	.40
1	Panel	30.00	15.00	9.00
(1)	Tommie Agee	1.25	.60	.40
(2)	Harmon Killebrew	7.00	3.50	2.00
2	Panel	40.00	20.00	12.00
(3)	Reggie Jackson	20.00	10.00	6.00
3	Panel	25.00	12.50	7.50
(4)	Bert Campaneris	1.25	.60	.40
4	Panel	25.00	12.50	7.50
(5)	Pete Rose	25.00	12.50	7.50
5	Panel	15.00	7.50	4.50
(6)	Orlando Cepeda	3.00	1.50	.90
6	Panel	30.00	15.00	9.00
(7)	Rico Carty	2.00	1.00	.60
7	Panel	15.00	7.50	4.50
(8)	Johnny Bench	20.00	10.00	6.00
8	Panel	30.00	15.00	9.00
(9)	Tommy Harper	1.25	.60	.40
9	Panel	15.00	7.50	4.50
(10)	Bill Freehan	2.00	1.00	.60
10	Panel	10.00	5.00	3.00
(11)	Roberto Clemente	20.00	10.00	6.00
11	Panel	30.00	15.00	9.00
(12)	Claude Osteen	1.25	.60	.40
12	Panel	15.00	7.50	4.50
(13)	Jim Fregosi	2.00	1.00	.60
(14)	Billy Williams	6.00	3.00	1.75
(15)	Dave McNally	1.25	.60	.40
(16)	Randy Hundley	1.25	.60	.40

A player's name in *italic* indicates a rookie card. An (FC) indicates a player's first card for that particular card company.

1971 Bazooka Numbered Set

The 1971 Bazooka numbered set is a proof set produced by the company after the unnumbered set was released. The set is comprised of 48 cards as opposed to the 36 cards which make up the unnumbered set. Issued in panels of three, the nine cards not found in the unnumbered set are #'s 1-3, 13-15 and 43-45. All other cards are identical to those found in the unnumbered set. The cards, which measure 2" by 2-5/8", contain full-color photos and are blank-backed.

		NR MT	EX	VG
Complete Panel Set:		1000.00	500.00	300.00
Complete Singles Set:		550.00	275.00	165.00
Common Panel:		10.00	5.00	3.00
Common Single Player:		2.00	1.00	.60
	Panel	150.00	75.00	45.00
1	Tim McCarver	15.00	7.50	4.50
2	Frank Robinson	45.00	23.00	13.50
3	Bill Mazeroski	15.00	7.50	4.50
	Panel	45.00	22.00	13.50
4	Willie McCovey	12.00	6.00	3.50
5	Carl Yastrzemski	20.00	10.00	6.00
6	Clyde Wright	2.00	1.00	.60
	Panel	20.00	10.00	6.00
7	Jim Merritt	2.00	1.00	.60
8	Luis Aparicio	9.00	4.50	2.75
9	Bobby Murcer	5.00	2.50	1.50
	Panel	10.00	5.00	3.00
10	Rico Petrocelli	3.00	1.50	.90
11	Sam McDowell	3.00	1.50	.90
12	Clarence Gaston	2.00	1.00	.60
	Panel	150.00	75.00	45.00
13	Ferguson Jenkins	20.00	10.00	6.00
14	Al Kaline	45.00	23.00	13.50
15	Ken Harrelson	15.00	7.50	4.50
	Panel	45.00	22.00	13.50
16	Tommie Agee	2.00	1.00	.60
17	Harmon Killebrew	12.00	6.00	3.50
18	Reggie Jackson	20.00	10.00	6.00
	Panel	20.00	10.00	6.00
19	Juan Marichal	9.00	4.50	2.75
20	Frank Howard	5.00	2.50	1.50

		NR MT	EX	VG
21	Bill Melton	2.00	1.00	.60
	Panel	55.00	27.00	16.50
22	Brooks Robinson	15.00	7.50	4.50
23	Hank Aaron	30.00	15.00	9.00
24	Larry Dierker	2.00	1.00	.60
	Panel	20.00	10.00	6.00
25	Jim Fregosi	3.00	1.50	.90
26	Billy Williams	10.00	5.00	3.00
27	Dave McNally	2.00	1.00	.60
	Panel	30.00	15.00	9.00
28	Rico Carty	3.00	1.50	.90
29	Johnny Bench	18.00	9.00	5.50
30	Tommy Harper	2.00	1.00	.60
	Panel	60.00	30.00	18.00
31	Bert Campaneris	2.00	1.00	.60
32	Pete Rose	35.00	17.50	10.50
33	Orlando Cepeda	6.00	3.00	1.75
	Panel	45.00	22.00	13.50
34	Maury Wills	6.00	3.00	1.75
35	Tom Seaver	20.00	10.00	6.00
36	Tony Oliva	6.00	3.00	1.75
	Panel	30.00	15.00	9.00
37	Bill Freehan	3.00	1.50	.90
38	Roberto Clemente	25.00	12.50	7.50
39	Claude Osteen	2.00	1.00	.60
	Panel	20.00	10.00	6.00
40	Rusty Staub	3.00	1.50	.90
41	Bob Gibson	10.00	5.00	3.00
42	Amos Otis	2.00	1.00	.60
	Panel	125.00	62.00	37.00
43	Jim Wynn	10.00	5.00	3.00
44	Rich Allen	18.00	9.00	5.50
45	Tony Conigliaro	10.00	5.00	3.00
	Panel	40.00	20.00	12.00
46	Randy Hundley	2.00	1.00	.60
47	Willie Mays	30.00	15.00	9.00
48	Jim Hunter	9.00	4.50	2.75

1988 Bazooka

 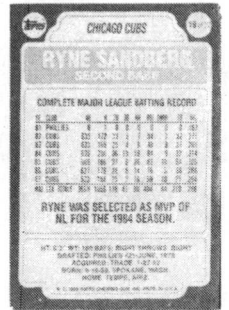

This 22-card set from Topps marks the first Bazooka issue since 1971. Full-color player photos are bordered in white, with the player name printed on a red, white and blue bubble gum box in the lower right corner. Flip sides are also red, white and blue, printed vertically. A large, but faint, Bazooka logo backs the Topps baseball logo, team name, card number, player's name and position, followed by batting records, personal information and brief career highlights. Cards were sold inside specially marked 59¢ and 79¢ Bazooka gum and candy boxes, one card per box.

		MT	NR MT	EX
Complete Set:		10.00	7.50	4.00
Common Player:		.20	.15	.08
1	George Bell	.25	.20	.10
2	Wade Boggs	.90	.70	.35
3	Jose Canseco	1.25	.90	.50
4	Roger Clemens	.60	.45	.25
5	Vince Coleman	.20	.15	.08
6	Eric Davis	.60	.45	.25
7	Tony Fernandez	.20	.15	.08
8	Dwight Gooden	.60	.45	.25
9	Tony Gwynn	.40	.30	.15
10	Wally Joyner	.40	.30	.15

		MT	NR MT	EX
11	Don Mattingly	2.00	1.50	.80
12	Willie McGee	.20	.15	.08
13	Mark McGwire	.90	.70	.35
14	Kirby Puckett	.50	.40	.20
15	Tim Raines	.30	.25	.12
16	Dave Righetti	.20	.15	.08
17	Cal Ripken	.35	.25	.14
18	Juan Samuel	.20	.15	.08
19	Ryne Sandberg	.30	.25	.12
20	Benny Santiago	.20	.15	.08
21	Darryl Strawberry	.60	.45	.25
22	Todd Worrell	.20	.15	.08

1989 Bazooka

This 22-card set marks the second consecutive year Bazooka has issued following a 17-year absence. Full color action and posed player shots are bordered by a white frame. Other features of this standard-size includes a "Shining Stars" logo across the top, a yellow stripe enclosing the player's name at the bottom, and the Topps/Bazooka logo in the bottom right corner. Flip sides are printed in red and blue, and contain a large but faint Bazooka logo, the Topps baseball logo, card number, team name, player's name and position, followed by batting or pitching records, personal information and brief highlights. Topps produced this 22-card set in 1989 to be included (one card per box) in specially-marked boxes of its Bazooka brand bubblegum. The player photos have the words "Shining Star" along the top, while the player's name appears along the bottom of the card, along with the Topps Bazooka logo in the lower right corner. The cards are numbered alphabetically.

		MT	NR MT	EX
Complete Set:		7.00	5.25	2.75
Common Player:		.15	.11	.06
1	Tim Belcher	.20	.15	.08
2	Damon Berryhill	.15	.11	.06
3	Wade Boggs	.80	.60	.30
4	Jay Buhner	.15	.11	.06
5	Jose Canseco	.80	.60	.30
6	Vince Coleman	.15	.11	.06
7	Cecil Espy	.15	.11	.06
8	Dave Gallagher	.15	.11	.06
9	Ron Gant	.15	.11	.06
10	Kirk Gibson	.15	.11	.06
11	Paul Gibson	.15	.11	.06
12	Mark Grace	.60	.45	.25
13	Tony Gwynn	.35	.25	.14
14	Rickey Henderson	.40	.30	.15
15	Orel Hershiser	.25	.20	.10
16	Gregg Jefferies	.50	.40	.20
17	Ricky Jordan	.25	.20	.10
18	Chris Sabo	.15	.11	.06
19	Gary Sheffield	.50	.40	.20
20	Darryl Strawberry	.50	.40	.20
21	Frank Viola	.20	.15	.08
22	Walt Weiss	.15	.11	.06

1990 Bazooka

For the second consecutive year, Bazooka entitled its set "Shining Stars." Full color action and posed player shots are featured on the card fronts. The flip sides feature player statistics in a style much like the cards from the previous two Bazooka issues. Unlike the past two releases, the cards are not numbered alphabetically. The cards measure 2-1/2" by 3-1/2" in size and 22 cards complete the set.

		MT	NR MT	EX
Complete Set:		7.00	5.25	2.75
Common Player:		.15	.11	.06
1	Kevin Mitchell	.50	.40	.20
2	Robin Yount	.20	.15	.08
3	Mark Davis	.15	.11	.06
4	Bret Saberhagen	.15	.11	.06
5	Fred McGriff	.20	.15	.08
6	Tony Gwynn	.20	.15	.08
7	Kirby Puckett	.30	.25	.12
8	Vince Coleman	.15	.11	.06
9	Rickey Henderson	.40	.30	.15
10	Ben McDonald	1.00	.70	.40
11	Gregg Olson	.20	.15	.08
12	Todd Zeile	.50	.40	.20
13	Carlos Martinez	.20	.15	.08
14	Gregg Jefferies	.40	.30	.15
15	Craig Worthington	.15	.11	.06
16	Gary Sheffield	.40	.30	.15
17	Greg Briley	.15	.11	.06
18	Ken Griffey, Jr.	1.00	.70	.40
19	Jerome Walton	.20	.15	.08
20	Bob Geren	.15	.11	.06
21	Tom Gordon	.20	.15	.08
22	Jim Abbott	.20	.15	.08

1958 Bell Brand Dodgers

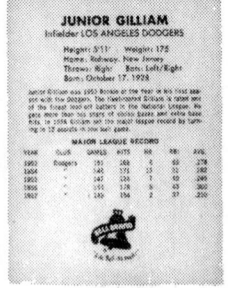

Celebrating the Dodgers first year of play in Los

Angeles, Bell Brand inserted ten different unnumbered cards in their bags of potato chips and corn chips. The cards, which measure 3" by 4", have a sepia-colored photo inside a 1/4" green woodgrain border. The card backs feature statistical and biographical information and include the Bell Brand logo. Roy Campanella is included in the set despite a career-ending car wreck that prevented him from ever playing in Los Angeles.

		NR MT	EX	VG
Complete Set:		1000.00	500.00	300.00
Common Player:		35.00	17.50	10.50
1	Roy Campanella	125.00	56.00	35.00
2	Gino Cimoli	100.00	50.00	30.00
3	Don Drysdale	90.00	45.00	27.00
4	Junior Gilliam	35.00	17.50	10.50
5	Gil Hodges	90.00	45.00	27.00
6	Sandy Koufax	125.00	56.00	35.00
7	Johnny Podres	100.00	50.00	30.00
8	Pee Wee Reese	90.00	45.00	27.00
9	Duke Snider	250.00	125.00	75.00
10	Don Zimmer	35.00	17.50	10.50

1960 Bell Brand Dodgers

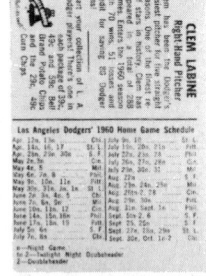

Bell Brand returned with a baseball card set in 1960 that was entirely different in style to their previous effort. The cards, which measure 2-1/2" by 3-1/2", feature beautiful, full-color photos. The backs carry a short player biography, the 1960 Dodgers home schedule, and the Bell Brand logo. Twenty different numbered cards were inserted in various size bags of potato chips and corn chips. Although sealed in cellophane, the cards were still subject to grease stains. Cards #'s 6, 12 and 18 are the scarcest in the set.

		NR MT	EX	VG
Complete Set:		700.00	350.00	210.00
Common Player:		15.00	7.50	4.50
1	Norm Larker	15.00	7.50	4.50
2	Duke Snider	70.00	35.00	21.00
3	Danny McDevitt	15.00	7.50	4.50
4	Jim Gilliam	18.00	9.00	5.50
5	Rip Repulski	15.00	7.50	4.50
6	Clem Labine	90.00	45.00	27.00
7	John Roseboro	15.00	7.50	4.50
8	Carl Furillo	18.00	9.00	5.50
9	Sandy Koufax	100.00	50.00	30.00
10	Joe Pignatano	15.00	7.50	4.50
11	Chuck Essegian	15.00	7.50	4.50
12	John Klippstein	80.00	40.00	25.00
13	Ed Roebuck	15.00	7.50	4.50
14	Don Demeter	15.00	7.50	4.50
15	Roger Craig	30.00	15.00	9.00
16	Stan Williams	15.00	7.50	4.50
17	Don Zimmer	18.00	9.00	5.50
18	Walter Alston	100.00	50.00	30.00
19	Johnny Podres	18.00	9.00	5.50
20	Maury Wills	30.00	15.00	9.00

1961 Bell Brand Dodgers

NORM LARKER
INFIELDER   L.A. DODGERS

The 1961 Bell Brand set is identical in format to the previous year, although printed on thinner stock. Cards can be distinguished from the 1960 set by the 1961 schedule on the backs. The cards, which measure 2-7/16" by 3-1/2", are numbered by the player's uniform number. Twenty different cards were inserted into various size potato chip and corn chip packages, each card being sealed in a cellophane wrapper.

		NR MT	EX	VG
Complete Set:		375.00	185.00	110.00
Common Player:		12.00	6.00	3.50
3	Willie Davis	15.00	7.50	4.50
4	Duke Snider	50.00	30.00	15.00
5	Norm Larker	12.00	6.00	3.50
8	John Roseboro	12.00	6.00	3.50
9	Wally Moon	12.00	6.00	3.50
11	Bob Lillis	12.00	6.00	3.50
12	Tom Davis	12.00	6.00	3.50
14	Gil Hodges	25.00	12.50	7.50
16	Don Demeter	12.00	6.00	3.50
19	Jim Gilliam	15.00	7.50	4.50
22	John Podres	15.00	7.50	4.50
24	Walter Alston	25.00	12.50	7.50
30	Maury Wills	25.00	12.50	7.50
32	Sandy Koufax	80.00	40.00	25.00
34	Norm Sherry	12.00	6.00	3.50
37	Ed Roebuck	12.00	6.00	3.50
38	Roger Craig	15.00	7.50	4.50
40	Stan Williams	12.00	6.00	3.50
43	Charlie Neal	12.00	6.00	3.50
51	Larry Sherry	12.00	6.00	3.50

1962 Bell Brand Dodgers

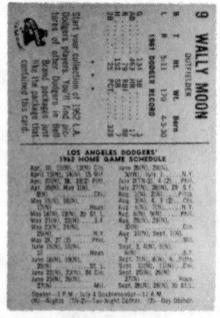

WALLY MOON
OUTFIELDER   L.A. DODGERS

The 1962 Bell Brand set is identical in style to the previous two years and cards can be distinguished by the 1962 Dodgers schedule on the back. The set consists of 20 cards, each measuring 2-7/16" by 3-1/2" and numbered by the player's uniform number. Printed on glossy stock, the 1962 set was less susceptible to grease stains.

		NR MT	EX	VG
Complete Set:		375.00	185.00	110.00
Common Player:		12.00	6.00	3.50
3	Willie Davis	15.00	7.50	4.50
4	Duke Snider	50.00	30.00	15.00
6	Ron Fairly	12.00	6.00	3.50
8	John Roseboro	12.00	6.00	3.50
9	Wally Moon	12.00	6.00	3.50
12	Tom Davis	12.00	6.00	3.50
16	Ron Perranoski	12.00	6.00	3.50
19	Jim Gilliam	15.00	7.50	4.50
20	Daryl Spencer	12.00	6.00	3.50
22	John Podres	15.00	7.50	4.50
24	Walter Alston	25.00	12.50	7.50
25	Frank Howard	15.00	7.50	4.50
30	Maury Wills	25.00	12.50	7.50
32	Sandy Koufax	80.00	40.00	25.00
34	Norm Sherry	12.00	6.00	3.50
37	Ed Roebuck	12.00	6.00	3.50
40	Stan Williams	12.00	6.00	3.50
51	Larry Sherry	12.00	6.00	3.50
53	Don Drysdale	35.00	17.50	10.50
56	Lee Walls	12.00	6.00	3.50

1951 Berk Ross

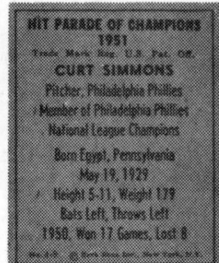

Entitled "Hit Parade of Champions," the 1951 Berk Ross set features 72 stars of various sports. The cards, which measure 2-1/16" by 2-1/2" and have tinted color photographs, were issued in boxes containing two-card panels. The issue is divided into four subsets with the first ten players of each series being baseball players. Only the baseball players are listed in the checklist that follows. Complete panels are valued 50 per cent higher than the sum of the individual cards.

		NR MT	EX	VG
Complete Set:		1100.00	550.00	330.00
Common Player:		12.00	6.00	3.50
1-1	Al Rosen	20.00	10.00	6.00
1-2	Bob Lemon	20.00	10.00	6.00
1-3	Phil Rizzuto	50.00	25.00	15.00
1-4	Hank Bauer	25.00	12.50	7.50
1-5	Billy Johnson	13.00	6.50	4.00
1-6	Jerry Coleman	13.00	6.50	4.00
1-7	Johnny Mize	30.00	15.00	7.50
1-8	Dom DiMaggio	25.00	12.50	7.50
1-9	Richie Ashburn	15.00	7.50	4.50
1-10	Del Ennis	13.00	6.50	4.00
2-1	Stan Musial	300.00	150.00	90.00
2-2	Warren Spahn	25.00	12.50	7.50
2-3	Tommy Henrich	15.00	7.50	4.50
2-4	Larry "Yogi" Berra	200.00	100.00	60.00
2-5	Joe DiMaggio	400.00	200.00	120.00
2-6	Bobby Brown	15.00	7.50	4.50
2-7	Granville Hamner	12.00	6.00	3.50
2-8	Willie Jones	12.00	6.00	3.50
2-9	Stanley Lopata	12.00	6.00	3.50
2-10	Mike Goliat	12.00	6.00	3.50
3-1	Ralph Kiner	30.00	15.00	9.00
3-2	Billy Goodman	12.00	6.00	3.50
3-3	Allie Reynolds	15.00	7.50	4.50
3-4	Vic Raschi	15.00	7.50	4.50
3-5	Joe Page	13.00	6.50	4.00
3-6	Eddie Lopat	15.00	7.50	4.50
3-7	Andy Seminick	12.00	6.00	3.50
3-8	Dick Sisler	12.00	6.00	3.50

		NR MT	EX	VG
3-9	Eddie Waitkus	12.00	6.00	3.50
3-10	Ken Heintzelman	12.00	6.00	3.50
4-1	Gene Woodling	15.00	7.50	4.50
4-2	Cliff Mapes	13.00	6.50	4.00
4-3	Fred Sanford	13.00	6.50	4.00
4-4	Tommy Bryne	13.00	6.50	4.00
4-5	Eddie (Whitey) Ford	125.00	62.00	37.00
4-6	Jim Konstanty	13.00	6.50	4.00
4-7	Russ Meyer	12.00	6.00	3.50
4-8	Robin Roberts	30.00	15.00	9.00
4-9	Curt Simmons	13.00	6.50	4.00
4-10	Sam Jethroe	30.00	15.00	9.00

1952 Berk Ross

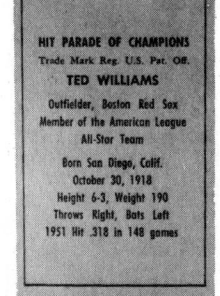

HIT PARADE OF CHAMPIONS
Trade Mark Reg. U.S. Pat. Off.

TED WILLIAMS

Outfielder, Boston Red Sox
Member of the American League
All-Star Team

Born San Diego, Calif.
October 30, 1918
Height 6-3, Weight 190
Throws Right, Bats Left
1951 Hit .318 in 148 games

Although the card size is different (2" by 3"), the style of the fronts and backs of the 1952 Berk Ross set is similar to the previous year's effort. Seventy-two unnumbered cards make up the set. Rizzuto is included twice in the set and the Blackwell and Fox cards have transposed backs. The cards were issued individually rather than as two-card panels like in 1951.

		NR MT	EX	VG
Complete Set:		4000.00	2000.00	1175.
Common Player:		12.00	6.00	3.50
(1)	Richie Ashburn	30.00	15.00	9.00
(2)	Hank Bauer	18.00	9.00	5.50
(3)	Larry "Yogi" Berra	100.00	50.00	30.00
(4)	Ewell Blackwell (photo actually Nelson Fox)	18.00	9.00	5.50
(5)	Bobby Brown	18.00	9.00	5.50
(6)	Jim Busby	12.00	6.00	3.50
(7)	Roy Campanella	125.00	56.00	35.00
(8)	Chico Carrasquel	12.00	6.00	3.50
(9)	Jerry Coleman	15.00	7.50	4.50
(10)	Joe Collins	15.00	7.50	4.50
(11)	Alvin Dark	15.00	7.50	4.50
(12)	Dom DiMaggio	18.00	9.00	5.50
(13)	Joe DiMaggio	700.00	350.00	200.00
(14)	Larry Doby	18.00	9.00	5.50
(15)	Bobby Doerr	35.00	17.50	10.50
(16)	Bob Elliot (Elliott)	12.00	6.00	3.50
(17)	Del Ennis	10.00	5.00	3.00
(18)	Ferris Fain	12.00	6.00	3.50
(19)	Bob Feller	75.00	38.00	23.00
(20)	Nelson Fox (photo actually Ewell Blackwell)	18.00	9.00	5.50
(21)	Ned Garver	12.00	6.00	3.50
(22)	Clint Hartung	12.00	6.00	3.50
(23)	Jim Hearn	12.00	6.00	3.50
(24)	Gil Hodges	50.00	30.00	15.00
(25)	Monte Irvin	30.00	15.00	9.00
(26)	Larry Jansen	12.00	6.00	3.50
(27)	George Kell	25.00	12.50	7.50
(28)	Sheldon Jones	12.00	6.00	3.50
(29)	Monte Kennedy	12.00	6.00	3.50
(30)	Ralph Kiner	40.00	20.00	12.00
(31)	Dave Koslo	12.00	6.00	3.50
(32)	Bob Kuzava	15.00	7.50	4.50
(33)	Bob Lemon	30.00	15.00	9.00
(34)	Whitey Lockman	12.00	6.00	3.50
(35)	Eddie Lopat	18.00	9.00	5.50
(36)	Sal Maglie	15.00	7.50	4.50
(37)	Mickey Mantle	1000.00	500.00	300.00
(38)	Billy Martin	50.00	30.00	15.00

		NR MT	EX	VG
(39)	Willie Mays	500.00	250.00	150.00
(40)	Gil McDougal (McDougald)	18.00	9.00	5.50
(41)	Orestes Minoso	15.00	7.50	4.50
(42)	Johnny Mize	40.00	20.00	12.00
(43)	Tom Morgan	15.00	7.50	4.50
(44)	Don Mueller	12.00	6.00	3.50
(45)	Stan Musial	400.00	200.00	120.00
(46)	Don Newcombe	18.00	9.00	5.50
(47)	Ray Noble	12.00	6.00	3.50
(48)	Joe Ostrowski	15.00	7.50	4.50
(49)	Mel Parnell	12.00	6.00	3.50
(50)	Vic Raschi	18.00	9.00	5.50
(51)	Pee Wee Reese	65.00	33.00	20.00
(52)	Allie Reynolds	18.00	9.00	5.50
(53)	Bill Rigney	10.00	5.00	3.00
(54)	Phil Rizzuto (bunting)	55.00	28.00	16.50
(55)	Phil Rizzuto (swinging)	55.00	28.00	16.50
(56)	Robin Roberts	30.00	15.00	9.00
(57)	Eddie Robinson	12.00	6.00	3.50
(58)	Jackie Robinson	200.00	100.00	60.00
(59)	Elwin "Preacher" Roe	15.00	7.50	4.50
(60)	Johnny Sain	15.00	7.50	4.50
(61)	Albert "Red" Schoendienst	30.00	15.00	9.00
(62)	Duke Snider	125.00	56.00	35.00
(63)	George Spencer	12.00	6.00	3.50
(64)	Eddie Stanky	15.00	7.50	4.50
(65)	Henry Thompson	12.00	6.00	3.50
(66)	Bobby Thomson	18.00	9.00	5.50
(67)	Vic Wertz	10.00	5.00	3.00
(68)	Waldon Westlake	12.00	6.00	3.50
(69)	Wes Westrum	10.00	5.00	3.00
(70)	Ted Williams	400.00	200.00	120.00
(71)	Gene Woodling	18.00	9.00	5.50
(72)	Gus Zernial	12.00	6.00	3.50

1986 Big League Chew

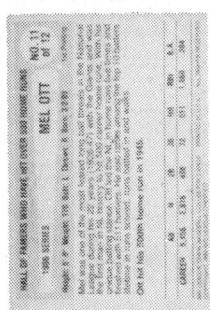

The 1986 Big Leauge Chew set consists of 12 cards featuring the players who have hit 500 or more career home runs. The cards, which measure 2-1/2" by 3-1/2", were inserted in specially marked packages of Big League Chew, the shredded bubble gum developed by former major leaguer Jim Bouton. The set is entitled "Home Run Legends" and was available through a write-in offer on the package. Recent-day players in the set are shown in color photos, while the older sluggers are pictured in black and white.

		MT	NR MT	EX
Complete Set:		6.00	4.50	2.50
Common Player:		.35	.25	.14
1	Hank Aaron	.60	.45	.25
2	Babe Ruth	.80	.60	.30
3	Willie Mays	.60	.45	.25
4	Frank Robinson	.35	.25	.14
5	Harmon Killebrew	.35	.25	.14
6	Mickey Mantle	1.25	.90	.50
7	Jimmie Foxx	.35	.25	.14
8	Ted Williams	.70	.50	.30
9	Ernie Banks	.35	.25	.14
10	Eddie Mathews	.35	.25	.14
11	Mel Ott	.35	.25	.14
12	500-HR Group Card	.50	.40	.20

1987 Boardwalk And Baseball

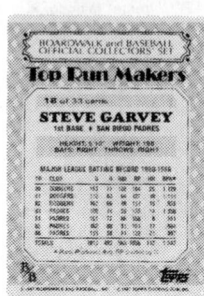

The 33-card "Top Run Makers" set was produced by Topps for distribution by the recreation amusement park "Boardwalk and Baseball," located near Orlando, Fla. The cards, which measure 2-1/2" by 3-1/2", feature fronts which contain full-color player photos and the park's logo (B/B). The card backs are printed in black and pink on white stock and offer personal data and career statistics. The set was issued in a specially designed box.

		MT	NR MT	EX
Complete Set:		7.00	5.25	2.75
Common Player:		.09	.07	.04
1	Mike Schmidt	.50	.40	.20
2	Eddie Murray	.35	.25	.14
3	Dale Murphy	.40	.30	.15
4	Dave Winfield	.30	.25	.12
5	Jim Rice	.30	.25	.12
6	Cecil Cooper	.12	.09	.05
7	Dwight Evans	.15	.11	.06
8	Rickey Henderson	.40	.30	.15
9	Robin Yount	.35	.25	.14
10	Andre Dawson	.25	.20	.10
11	Gary Carter	.35	.25	.14
12	Keith Hernandez	.30	.25	.12
13	George Brett	.40	.30	.15
14	Bill Buckner	.09	.07	.04
15	Tony Armas	.09	.07	.04
16	Harold Baines	.15	.11	.06
17	Don Baylor	.12	.09	.05
18	Steve Garvey	.35	.25	.14
19	Lance Parrish	.20	.15	.08
20	Dave Parker	.15	.11	.06
21	Buddy Bell	.09	.07	.04
22	Cal Ripken	.40	.30	.15
23	Bob Horner	.12	.09	.05
24	Tim Raines	.30	.25	.12
25	Jack Clark	.15	.11	.06
26	Leon Durham	.09	.07	.04
27	Pedro Guerrero	.15	.11	.06
28	Kent Hrbek	.15	.11	.06
29	Kirk Gibson	.20	.15	.08
30	Ryne Sandberg	.40	.30	.15
31	Wade Boggs	1.00	.70	.40
32	Don Mattingly	1.75	1.25	.70
33	Darryl Strawberry	.60	.45	.25

1987 Bohemian Hearth Bread Padres

Bohemian Hearth Bread Company of San Diego issued a 22-card set highlighting the San Diego Padres. Produced in conjunction with Mike Schechter Associates, the cards are the standard 2-1/2" by 3-1/2" size. The card fronts contain a full-color photo encompassed by a yellow border. The Bohemian Hearth Bread logo is located in the upper left corner of the card. The card backs are printed in light brown ink on a cream color card stock and carry player personal and statistical information.

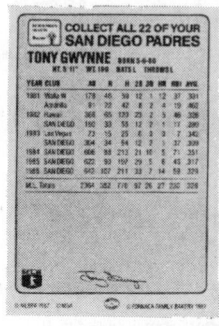

		MT	NR MT	EX
Complete Set:		50.00	37.50	20.00
Common Player:		.50	.40	.20
1	Garry Templeton	1.25	.90	.50
4	Jose Cora	.60	.45	.25
5	Randy Ready	.50	.40	.20
6	Steve Garvey	5.00	3.75	2.00
7	Kevin Mitchell	6.00	4.50	2.50
8	John Kruk	3.75	2.75	1.50
9	Benito Santiago	8.00	6.00	3.25
10	Larry Bowa	1.00	.70	.40
11	Tim Flannery	.50	.40	.20
14	Carmelo Martinez	.80	.60	.30
16	Marvell Wynne	.50	.40	.20
19	Tony Gwynn	12.00	9.00	4.75
21	James Steels	.50	.40	.20
22	Stan Jefferson	1.00	.70	.40
30	Eric Show	1.00	.70	.40
31	Ed Whitson	1.00	.70	.40
34	Storm Davis	1.00	.70	.40
37	Craig Lefferts	.80	.60	.30
40	Andy Hawkins	1.00	.70	.40
41	Lance McCullers	.80	.60	.30
43	Dave Dravecky	1.75	1.25	.70
54	Rich Gossage	2.25	1.75	.90

1948 Bowman

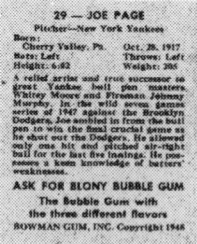

Bowman Gum Co.'s premiere set was produced in 1948, making it one of the first major issues of the post-war period. Forty-eight black and white cards comprise the set, with each card measuring 2-1/16" by 2-1/2" in size. The card backs, printed in black ink on grey stock, include the card number and the player's name, team, position, and a short biography. Twelve cards (#'s 7, 8, 13, 16, 20, 22, 24, 26, 29, 30 and 34) were printed in short supply when they were removed from the 36-card printing sheet to make room for the set's high numbers (#'s 37-48). These 24 cards command a higher price than the remaining cards in the set.

		NR MT	EX	VG
Complete Set:		2900.00	1450.00	875.00
Common Player: 1-36		18.00	9.00	5.50
Common Player: 37-48		25.00	12.50	7.50
1	Bob Elliott	70.00	9.00	5.00

		NR MT	EX	VG
2	Ewell (The Whip) Blackwell	25.00	12.50	7.50
3	Ralph Kiner	125.00	60.00	40.00
4	Johnny Mize	75.00	38.00	23.00
5	Bob Feller	150.00	75.00	45.00
6	*Larry (Yogi) Berra*	450.00	225.00	135.00
7	Pete (Pistol Pete) Reiser	40.00	20.00	12.00
8	Phil (Scooter) Rizzuto	225.00	112.00	67.00
9	Walker Cooper	18.00	9.00	5.50
10	Buddy Rosar	18.00	9.00	5.50
11	Johnny Lindell	18.00	9.00	5.50
12	Johnny Sain	25.00	12.50	7.50
13	Willard Marshall	30.00	15.00	9.00
14	Allie Reynolds	30.00	15.00	9.00
15	Eddie Joost	18.00	9.00	5.50
16	Jack Lohrke	30.00	15.00	9.00
17	Enos (Country) Slaughter	90.00	45.00	25.00
18	Warren Spahn	225.00	112.00	70.00
19	Tommy (The Clutch) Henrich	25.00	12.50	7.50
20	Buddy Kerr	30.00	15.00	9.00
21	Ferris Fain	15.00	7.50	4.50
22	Floyd (Bill) Bevins (Bevens)	40.00	20.00	12.00
23	Larry Jansen	18.00	9.00	5.50
24	Emil (Dutch) Leonard	30.00	15.00	9.00
25	Barney McCoskey (McCosky)	18.00	9.00	5.50
26	Frank Shea	40.00	20.00	12.00
27	Sid Gordon	18.00	9.00	5.50
28	Emil (The Antelope) Verban	30.00	15.00	9.00
29	Joe Page	40.00	20.00	12.00
30	"Whitey" Lockman	30.00	15.00	9.00
31	Bill McCahan	18.00	9.00	5.50
32	Bill Rigney	15.00	7.50	4.50
33	Bill (The Bull) Johnson	18.00	9.00	5.50
34	Sheldon (Available) Jones	30.00	15.00	9.00
35	George (Snuffy) Stirnweiss	18.00	9.00	5.50
36	Stan Musial	700.00	350.00	200.00
37	Clint Hartung	25.00	12.50	7.50
38	Al "Red" Schoendienst	100.00	50.00	30.00
39	Augie Galan	25.00	12.50	7.50
40	Marty Marion	60.00	30.00	18.00
41	Rex Barney	25.00	12.50	7.50
42	Ray Poat	25.00	12.50	7.50
43	Bruce Edwards	25.00	12.50	7.50
44	Johnny Wyrostek	25.00	12.50	7.50
45	Hank Sauer	25.00	12.50	7.50
46	Herman Wehmeier	25.00	12.50	7.50
47	Bobby Thomson	60.00	30.00	18.00
48	George "Dave" Koslo	50.00	8.00	5.00

1949 Bowman

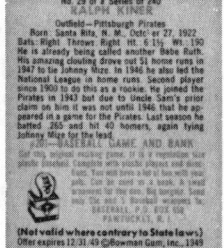

In 1949, Bowman increased the size of its issue to 240 numbered cards. The cards, which measure 2-1/16" by 2-1/2", are black and white photos overprinted with various pastel colors. Beginning with card #109 in the set, Bowman inserted the player's names on the card fronts. Twelve cards (#'s 4, 78, 83, 85, 88, 98, 109, 124, 127, 132 and 143), which were produced in the first four series of printings, were reprinted in the seventh series with either a card front or back modification. These variations are noted in the checklist that follows. Card #'s 1-3 and 5-73 can be found with either white or grey backs. The complete set of value in the following checklist does not include the higher priced variation cards.

	NR MT	EX	VG
Complete Set:	15000.00	7500.00	4500.

		NR MT	EX	VG
	Common Player: 1-36	10.00	5.00	3.00
	Common Player: 37-73	12.00	6.00	3.50
	Common Player: 74-144	10.00	5.00	3.00
	Common Player: 145-240	75.00	37.00	22.00
1	Vernon Bickford	75.00	7.50	3.00
2	Carroll "Whitey" Lockman	15.00	5.00	3.00
3	Bob Porterfield	15.00	7.50	4.50
4a	Jerry Priddy (no name on front)	12.00	6.00	3.50
4b	Jerry Priddy (name on front)	40.00	20.00	12.00
5	Hank Sauer	10.00	5.00	3.00
6	Phil Cavarretta	12.00	6.00	3.50
7	Joe Dobson	10.00	5.00	3.00
8	Murry Dickson	10.00	5.00	3.00
9	Ferris Fain	12.00	6.00	3.50
10	Ted Gray	10.00	5.00	3.00
11	Lou Boudreau	50.00	25.00	15.00
12	Cass Michaels	10.00	5.00	3.00
13	Bob Chesnes	10.00	5.00	3.00
14	*Curt Simmons*	25.00	12.50	7.50
15	Ned Garver	10.00	5.00	3.00
16	Al Kozar	10.00	5.00	3.00
17	Earl Torgeson	10.00	5.00	3.00
18	Bobby Thomson	25.00	12.50	7.50
19	*Bobby Brown*	35.00	17.50	10.50
20	Gene Hermanski	12.00	6.00	3.50
21	Frank Baumholtz	10.00	5.00	3.00
22	Harry "P-Nuts" Lowrey	10.00	5.00	3.00
23	Bobby Doerr	75.00	37.00	22.00
24	Stan Musial	500.00	250.00	150.00
25	Carl Scheib	10.00	5.00	3.00
26	George Kell	50.00	25.00	15.00
27	Bob Feller	125.00	60.00	40.00
28	Don Kolloway	10.00	5.00	3.00
29	Ralph Kiner	75.00	37.00	22.00
30	Andy Seminick	10.00	5.00	3.00
31	Dick Kokos	10.00	5.00	3.00
32	Eddie Yost	10.00	5.00	3.00
33	Warren Spahn	150.00	75.00	45.00
34	Dave Koslo	10.00	5.00	3.00
35	Vic Raschi	20.00	10.00	6.00
36	Harold "Peewee" Reese	150.00	60.00	38.00
37	John Wyrostek	12.00	6.00	3.50
38	Emil "The Antelope" Verban	12.00	6.00	3.50
39	Bill Goodman	12.00	6.00	3.50
40	George "Red" Munger	12.00	6.00	3.50
41	Lou Brissie	12.00	6.00	3.50
42	Walter "Hoot" Evers	12.00	6.00	3.50
43	Dale Mitchell	12.00	6.00	3.50
44	Dave Philley	12.00	6.00	3.50
45	Wally Westlake	12.00	6.00	3.50
46	*Robin Roberts*	200.00	100.00	60.00
47	Johnny Sain	18.00	9.00	5.50
48	Willard Marshall	12.00	6.00	3.50
49	Frank Shea	18.00	9.00	5.50
50	Jackie Robinson	700.00	350.00	200.00
51	Herman Wehmeier	12.00	6.00	3.50
52	Johnny Schmitz	12.00	6.00	3.50
53	Jack Kramer	12.00	6.00	3.50
54	Marty "Slats" Marion	16.00	8.00	4.75
55	Eddie Joost	12.00	6.00	3.50
56	Pat Mullin	12.00	6.00	3.50
57	Gene Bearden	12.00	6.00	3.50
58	Bob Elliott	12.00	6.00	3.50
59	Jack "Lucky" Lohrke	12.00	6.00	3.50
60	Larry "Yogi" Berra	300.00	150.00	90.00
61	Rex Barney	14.00	7.00	4.25
62	Grady Hatton	12.00	6.00	3.50
63	Andy Pafko	14.00	7.00	4.25
64	Dom "The Little Professor" DiMaggio	25.00	12.50	7.50
65	Enos "Country" Slaughter	75.00	37.00	22.00
66	Elmer Valo	12.00	6.00	3.50
67	Alvin Dark	25.00	12.50	7.50
68	Sheldon "Available" Jones	12.00	6.00	3.50
69	Tommy "The Clutch" Henrich	25.00	12.50	7.50
70	Carl Furillo	50.00	25.00	15.00
71	Vern "Junior" Stephens	12.00	6.00	3.50
72	Tommy Holmes	14.00	7.00	4.25
73	Billy Cox	14.00	7.00	4.25
74	Tom McBride	10.00	5.00	3.00
75	Eddie Mayo	10.00	5.00	3.00
76	Bill Nicholson	10.00	5.00	3.00
77	Ernie (Jumbo and Tiny) Bonham	10.00	5.00	3.00
78a	Sam Zoldak (no name on front)	12.00	6.00	3.50
78b	Sam Zoldak (name on front)	40.00	20.00	12.00
79	Ron Northey	10.00	5.00	3.00
80	Bill McCahan	10.00	5.00	3.00
81	Virgil "Red" Stallcup	10.00	5.00	3.00
82	Joe Page	16.00	8.00	4.75
83a	Bob Scheffing (no name on front)	12.00	6.00	3.50

		NR MT	EX	VG
83b	Bob Scheffing (name on front)	40.00	20.00	12.00
84	*Roy Campanella*	600.00	300.00	175.00
85a	Johnny "Big John" Mize (no name on front)	75.00	37.00	22.00
85b	Johnny "Big John" Mize (name on front)	110.00	50.00	28.00
86	Johnny Pesky	12.00	6.00	3.50
87	Randy Gumpert	10.00	5.00	3.00
88a	Bill Salkeld (no name on front)	12.00	6.00	3.50
88b	Bill Salkeld (name on front)	40.00	20.00	12.00
89	Mizell "Whitey" Platt	10.00	5.00	3.00
90	Gil Coan	10.00	5.00	3.00
91	Dick Wakefield	10.00	5.00	3.00
92	Willie "Puddin-Head" Jones	10.00	5.00	3.00
93	Ed Stevens	10.00	5.00	3.00
94	James "Mickey" Vernon	12.00	6.00	3.50
95	Howie Pollett	10.00	5.00	3.00
96	Taft Wright	10.00	5.00	3.00
97	Danny Litwhiler	10.00	5.00	3.00
98a	Phil Rizzuto (no name on front)	80.00	40.00	24.00
98b	Phil Rizzuto (name on front)	200.00	100.00	60.00
99	Frank Gustine	10.00	5.00	3.00
100	Gil Hodges	175.00	87.00	52.00
101	Sid Gordon	10.00	5.00	3.00
102	Stan Spence	10.00	5.00	3.00
103	Joe Tipton	10.00	5.00	3.00
104	Ed Stanky	12.00	6.00	3.50
105	Bill Kennedy	10.00	5.00	3.00
106	Jake Early	10.00	5.00	3.00
107	Eddie Lake	10.00	5.00	3.00
108	Ken Heintzelman	10.00	5.00	3.00
109a	Ed Fitzgerald (Fitz Gerald) (script name on back)	12.00	6.00	3.50
109b	Ed Fitzgerald (Fitz Gerald) (printed name on back)	40.00	20.00	12.00
110	Early Wynn	110.00	55.00	33.00
111	Al "Red" Schoendienst	75.00	37.00	22.00
112	Sam Chapman	10.00	5.00	3.00
113	Ray Lamanno	10.00	5.00	3.00
114	Allie Reynolds	30.00	15.00	9.00
115	Emil "Dutch" Leonard	10.00	5.00	3.00
116	Joe Hatten	12.00	6.00	3.50
117	Walker Cooper	10.00	5.00	3.00
118	Sam Mele	10.00	5.00	3.00
119	Floyd Baker	10.00	5.00	3.00
120	Cliff Fannin	10.00	5.00	3.00
121	Mark Christman	10.00	5.00	3.00
122	George Vico	10.00	5.00	3.00
123	Johnny Blatnick	10.00	5.00	3.00
124a	Danny Murtaugh (script name on back)	12.00	6.00	3.50
124b	Danny Murtaugh (printed name on back)	40.00	20.00	12.00
125	Ken Keltner	12.00	6.00	3.50
126a	Al Brazle (script name on back)	12.00	6.00	3.50
126b	Al Brazle (printed name on back)	40.00	20.00	12.00
127a	Henry "Heeney" Majeski (script name on back)	12.00	6.00	3.50
127b	Henry "Heeney" Majeski (printed name on back)	40.00	20.00	12.00
128	Johnny Vander Meer	16.00	8.00	4.75
129	Bill "The Bull" Johnson	16.00	8.00	4.75
130	Harry "The Hat" Walker	12.00	6.00	3.50
131	Paul Lehner	10.00	5.00	3.00
132a	Al Evans (script name on back)	12.00	6.00	3.50
132b	Al Evans (printed name on back)	40.00	20.00	12.00
133	Aaron Robinson	10.00	5.00	3.00
134	Hank Borowy	10.00	5.00	3.00
135	Stan Rojek	10.00	5.00	3.00
136	Henry "Hank" Edwards	10.00	5.00	3.00
137	Ted Wilks	10.00	5.00	3.00
138	Warren "Buddy" Rosar	10.00	5.00	3.00
139	Hank "Bow-Wow" Arft	10.00	5.00	3.00
140	Rae Scarborough (Ray)	10.00	5.00	3.00
141	Ulysses "Tony" Lupien	10.00	5.00	3.00
142	Eddie Waitkus	10.00	5.00	3.00
143a	Bob Dillinger (script name on back)	12.00	6.00	3.50
143b	Bob Dillinger (printed name on back)	40.00	20.00	12.00
144	Milton "Mickey" Haefner	10.00	5.00	3.00
145	Sylvester "Blix" Donnelly	75.00	37.00	22.00
146	Myron "Mike" McCormick	55.00	27.00	16.50
147	Elmer "Bert" Singleton	75.00	37.00	22.00
148	Bob Swift	75.00	37.00	22.00
149	Roy Partee	55.00	27.00	16.50
150	Alfred "Allie" Clark	75.00	37.00	22.00
151	Maurice "Mickey" Harris	75.00	37.00	22.00
152	Clarence Maddern	75.00	37.00	22.00
153	Phil Masi	75.00	37.00	22.00
154	Clint Hartung	75.00	37.00	22.00
155	Fermin "Mickey" Guerra	75.00	37.00	22.00
156	Al "Zeke" Zarilla	75.00	37.00	22.00
157	Walt Masterson	75.00	37.00	22.00
158	Harry "The Cat" Brecheen	75.00	37.00	22.00
159	Glen Moulder	75.00	37.00	22.00
160	Jim Blackburn	75.00	37.00	22.00
161	John "Jocko" Thompson	75.00	37.00	22.00
162	Elwin "Preacher" Roe	125.00	56.00	35.00
163	Clyde McCullough	75.00	37.00	22.00
164	Vic Wertz	55.00	27.00	16.50
165	George "Snuffy" Stirnweiss	75.00	37.00	22.00
166	Mike Tresh	75.00	37.00	22.00
167	Boris "Babe" Martin	75.00	37.00	22.00
168	Doyle Lade	75.00	37.00	22.00
169	Jeff Heath	75.00	37.00	22.00
170	Bill Rigney	55.00	27.00	16.50
171	Dick Fowler	75.00	37.00	22.00
172	Eddie Pellagrini	75.00	37.00	22.00
173	Eddie Stewart	75.00	37.00	22.00
174	Terry Moore	55.00	27.00	16.50
175	Luke Appling	125.00	62.00	37.00
176	Ken Raffensberger	75.00	37.00	22.00
177	Stan Lopata	75.00	37.00	22.00
178	Tommy Brown	55.00	27.00	16.50
179	Hugh Casey	55.00	27.00	16.50
180	Connie Berry	75.00	37.00	22.00
181	Gus Niarhos	75.00	37.00	22.00
182	Hal Peck	75.00	37.00	22.00
183	Lou Stringer	75.00	37.00	22.00
184	Bob Chipman	75.00	37.00	22.00
185	Pete Reiser	55.00	27.00	16.50
186	John "Buddy" Kerr	75.00	37.00	22.00
187	Phil Marchildon	75.00	37.00	22.00
188	Karl Drews	75.00	37.00	22.00
189	Earl Wooten	75.00	37.00	22.00
190	Jim Hearn	75.00	37.00	22.00
191	Joe Haynes	75.00	37.00	22.00
192	Harry Gumbert	75.00	37.00	22.00
193	Ken Trinkle	75.00	37.00	22.00
194	Ralph Branca	100.00	45.00	27.00
195	Eddie Bockman	75.00	37.00	22.00
196	Fred Hutchinson	55.00	27.00	16.50
197	Johnny Lindell	75.00	37.00	22.00
198	Steve Gromek	75.00	37.00	22.00
199	Cecil "Tex" Hughson	75.00	37.00	22.00
200	Jess Dobernic	75.00	37.00	22.00
201	Sibby Sisti	75.00	37.00	22.00
202	Larry Jansen	75.00	37.00	22.00
203	Barney McCosky	75.00	37.00	22.00
204	Bob Savage	75.00	37.00	22.00
205	Dick Sisler	75.00	37.00	22.00
206	Bruce Edwards	55.00	27.00	16.50
207	Johnny "Hippity" Hopp	75.00	37.00	22.00
208	Paul "Dizzy" Trout	55.00	27.00	16.50
209	Charlie "King Kong" Keller	100.00	50.00	30.00
210	Joe "Flash" Gordon	55.00	27.00	16.50
211	Dave "Boo" Ferris	75.00	37.00	22.00
212	Ralph Hamner	75.00	37.00	22.00
213	Charles "Red" Barrett	75.00	37.00	22.00
214	*Richie Ashburn*	500.00	250.00	150.00
215	Kirby Higbe	75.00	37.00	22.00
216	Lynwood "Schoolboy" Rowe	75.00	37.00	22.00
217	Marino Pieretti	75.00	37.00	22.00
218	Dick Kryhoski	75.00	37.00	22.00
219	Virgil "Fire" Trucks	55.00	27.00	16.50
220	Johnny McCarthy	75.00	37.00	22.00
221	Bob Muncrief	75.00	37.00	22.00
222	Alex Kellner	75.00	37.00	22.00
223	Bob Hoffman (Hofman)	75.00	37.00	22.00
224	*Leroy "Satchel" Paige*	1100.00	440.00	275.00
225	*Gerry Coleman*	90.00	45.00	27.00
226	Edwin "Duke" Snider	900.00	360.00	225.00
227	Fritz Ostermueller	75.00	37.00	22.00
228	Jackie Mayo	75.00	37.00	22.00
229	Ed Lopat	125.00	60.00	40.00
230	Augie Galan	75.00	37.00	22.00
231	Earl Johnson	75.00	37.00	22.00
232	George McQuinn	75.00	37.00	22.00
233	*Larry Doby*	150.00	75.00	45.00
234	Truett "Rip" Sewell	55.00	27.00	16.50
235	Jim Russell	75.00	37.00	22.00
236	Fred Sanford	75.00	37.00	22.00
237	Monte Kennedy	75.00	37.00	22.00
238	Bob Lemon	225.00	112.00	67.00
239	Frank McCormick	75.00	37.00	22.00
240	Norman "Babe" Young (photo actually Bobby Young)	100.00	45.00	27.00

1949 Bowman
Pacific Coast League

 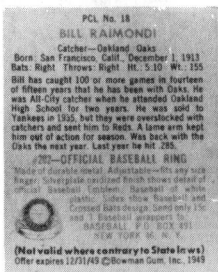

 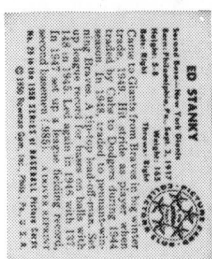

in the set (#'s 181-252) can be found with or without the copyright line at the bottom of the card, the "without" version being the less common.

One of the scarcest issues of the post-war period, the 1949 Bowman PCL set was issued only on the West Coast. Like the 1949 Bowman regular issue, the cards contain black and white photos overprinted with various pastel colors. Thirty-six cards, which measure 2-1/16" by 2-1/2", make up the set. It is believed that the cards may have been issued only in sheets and not sold in gum packs.

		NR MT	EX	VG
Complete Set:		6000.00	3000.00	1750.
Common Player:		150.00	75.00	45.00
1	Lee Anthony	150.00	75.00	45.00
2	George Metkovich	150.00	75.00	45.00
3	Ralph Hodgin	150.00	75.00	45.00
4	George Woods	150.00	75.00	45.00
5	Xavier Rescigno	150.00	75.00	45.00
6	Mickey Grasso	150.00	75.00	45.00
7	Johnny Rucker	150.00	75.00	45.00
8	Jack Brewer	150.00	75.00	45.00
9	Dom D'Allessandro	150.00	75.00	45.00
10	Charlie Gassaway	150.00	75.00	45.00
11	Tony Freitas	150.00	75.00	45.00
12	Gordon Maltzberger	150.00	75.00	45.00
13	John Jensen	150.00	75.00	45.00
14	Joyner White	150.00	75.00	45.00
15	Harvey Storey	150.00	75.00	45.00
16	Dick Lajeski	150.00	75.00	45.00
17	Albie Glossop	150.00	75.00	45.00
18	Bill Raimondi	150.00	75.00	45.00
19	Ken Holcombe	150.00	75.00	45.00
20	Don Ross	150.00	75.00	45.00
21	Pete Coscarart	150.00	75.00	45.00
22	Tony York	150.00	75.00	45.00
23	Jake Mooty	150.00	75.00	45.00
24	Charles Adams	150.00	75.00	45.00
25	Les Scarsella	150.00	75.00	45.00
26	Joe Marty	150.00	75.00	45.00
27	Frank Kelleher	150.00	75.00	45.00
28	Lee Handley	150.00	75.00	45.00
29	Herman Besse	150.00	75.00	45.00
30	John Lazor	150.00	75.00	45.00
31	Eddie Malone	150.00	75.00	45.00
32	Maurice Van Robays	150.00	75.00	45.00
33	Jim Tabor	150.00	75.00	45.00
34	Gene Handley	150.00	75.00	45.00
35	Tom Seats	150.00	75.00	45.00
36	Ora Burnett	150.00	75.00	45.00

1950 Bowman

The quality of the 1950 Bowman issue showed a marked improvement over the company's previous efforts. The cards are beautiful color art reproductions of actual photographs and measure 2-1/16" by 2-1/2" in size. The card backs include the same type of information as found in the previous year's issue but are designed in a horizontal format. Cards found in the first two series of the set (#'s 1-72) are the scarcest in the issue. The backs of the final 72 cards

		NR MT	EX	VG
Complete Set:		8000.00	4000.00	2500.
Common Player: 1-72		45.00	22.00	13.50
Common Player: 73-252		15.00	7.50	4.50
1	Mel Parnell	225.00	25.00	8.00
2	Vern Stephens	40.00	20.00	12.50
3	Dom DiMaggio	50.00	25.00	15.00
4	Gus Zernial	45.00	22.00	13.50
5	Bob Kuzava	45.00	22.00	13.50
6	Bob Feller	150.00	75.00	45.00
7	Jim Hegan	45.00	22.00	13.50
8	George Kell	70.00	35.00	21.00
9	Vic Wertz	45.00	22.00	13.50
10	Tommy Henrich	40.00	20.00	12.00
11	Phil Rizzuto	125.00	60.00	35.00
12	Joe Page	30.00	15.00	9.00
13	Ferris Fain	45.00	22.00	13.50
14	Alex Kellner	45.00	22.00	13.50
15	Al Kozar	45.00	22.00	13.50
16	*Roy Sievers*	30.00	15.00	9.00
17	Sid Hudson	45.00	22.00	13.50
18	Eddie Robinson	45.00	22.00	13.50
19	Warren Spahn	150.00	75.00	45.00
20	Bob Elliott	45.00	22.00	13.50
21	Harold Reese	150.00	60.00	38.00
22	Jackie Robinson	600.00	300.00	175.00
23	*Don Newcombe*	100.00	50.00	30.00
24	Johnny Schmitz	45.00	22.00	13.50
25	Hank Sauer	45.00	22.00	13.50
26	Grady Hatton	45.00	22.00	13.50
27	Herman Wehmeier	45.00	22.00	13.50
28	Bobby Thomson	50.00	25.00	15.00
29	Ed Stanky	45.00	22.00	13.50
30	Eddie Waitkus	45.00	22.00	13.50
31	Del Ennis	45.00	22.00	13.50
32	Robin Roberts	100.00	50.00	30.00
33	Ralph Kiner	100.00	50.00	30.00
34	Murry Dickson	45.00	22.00	13.50
35	Enos Slaughter	100.00	50.00	30.00
36	Eddie Kazak	45.00	22.00	13.50
37	Luke Appling	60.00	30.00	18.00
38	Bill Wight	45.00	22.00	13.50
39	Larry Doby	50.00	25.00	15.00
40	Bob Lemon	70.00	35.00	21.00
41	Walter "Hoot" Evers	45.00	22.00	13.50
42	Art Houtteman	45.00	22.00	13.50
43	Bobby Doerr	50.00	25.00	15.00
44	Joe Dobson	45.00	22.00	13.50
45	Al "Zeke" Zarilla	45.00	22.00	13.50
46	Larry "Yogi" Berra	350.00	175.00	100.00
47	Jerry Coleman	35.00	17.50	10.50
48	Leland "Lou" Brissie	45.00	22.00	13.50
49	Elmer Valo	45.00	22.00	13.50
50	Dick Kokos	45.00	22.00	13.50
51	Ned Garver	45.00	22.00	13.50
52	Sam Mele	45.00	22.00	13.50
53	Clyde Vollmer	45.00	22.00	13.50
54	Gil Coan	45.00	22.00	13.50
55	John "Buddy" Kerr	45.00	22.00	13.50
56	*Del Crandell (Crandall)*	50.00	25.00	15.00
57	Vernon Bickford	45.00	22.00	13.50
58	Carl Furillo	45.00	23.00	13.50
59	Ralph Branca	45.00	23.00	13.50
60	Andy Pafko	22.00	11.00	6.50
61	Bob Rush	45.00	22.00	13.50
62	Ted Kluszewski	50.00	25.00	15.00

		NR MT	EX	VG
63	Ewell Blackwell	22.00	11.00	6.50
64	Alvin Dark	45.00	23.00	13.50
65	Dave Koslo	45.00	22.00	13.50
66	Larry Jansen	45.00	22.00	13.50
67	Willie Jones	45.00	22.00	13.50
68	Curt Simmons	45.00	22.00	13.50
69	Wally Westlake	45.00	22.00	13.50
70	Bob Chesnes	45.00	22.00	13.50
71	Al Schoendienst	75.00	38.00	23.00
72	Howie Pollet	45.00	22.00	13.50
73	Willard Marshall	15.00	7.50	4.50
74	*Johnny Antonelli*	15.00	7.50	4.50
75	Roy Campanella	300.00	150.00	90.00
76	Rex Barney	12.00	6.00	3.50
77	Edwin "Duke" Snider	275.00	137.00	80.00
78	Mickey Owen	15.00	7.50	4.50
79	Johnny Vander Meer	12.00	6.00	3.50
80	Howard Fox	15.00	7.50	4.50
81	Ron Northey	15.00	7.50	4.50
82	Carroll Lockman	15.00	7.50	4.50
83	Sheldon Jones	15.00	7.50	4.50
84	Richie Ashburn	75.00	38.00	23.00
85	Ken Heintzelman	15.00	7.50	4.50
86	Stan Rojek	15.00	7.50	4.50
87	Bill Werle	15.00	7.50	4.50
88	Marty Marion	12.00	6.00	3.50
89	George Munger	15.00	7.50	4.50
90	Harry Brecheen	12.00	6.00	3.50
91	Cass Michaels	15.00	7.50	4.50
92	Hank Majeski	15.00	7.50	4.50
93	Gene Bearden	15.00	7.50	4.50
94	Lou Boudreau	40.00	20.00	12.00
95	Aaron Robinson	15.00	7.50	4.50
96	Virgil "Fire" Trucks	12.00	6.00	3.50
97	Maurice McDermott	15.00	7.50	4.50
98	Ted Williams	600.00	300.00	175.00
99	Billy Goodman	15.00	7.50	4.50
100	Vic Raschi	20.00	10.00	6.00
101	Bobby Brown	20.00	10.00	6.00
102	Billy Johnson	15.00	7.50	4.50
103	Eddie Joost	15.00	7.50	4.50
104	Sam Chapman	15.00	7.50	4.50
105	Bob Dillinger	15.00	7.50	4.50
106	Cliff Fannin	15.00	7.50	4.50
107	Sam Dente	15.00	7.50	4.50
108	Rae Scarborough (Ray)	15.00	7.50	4.50
109	Sid Gordon	15.00	7.50	4.50
110	Tommy Holmes	12.00	6.00	3.50
111	Walker Cooper	15.00	7.50	4.50
112	Gil Hodges	80.00	40.00	24.00
113	Gene Hermanski	12.00	6.00	3.50
114	Wayne Terwilliger	15.00	7.50	4.50
115	Roy Smalley	15.00	7.50	4.50
116	Virgil "Red" Stallcup	15.00	7.50	4.50
117	Bill Rigney	12.00	6.00	3.50
118	Clint Hartung	15.00	7.50	4.50
119	Dick Sisler	15.00	7.50	4.50
120	John Thompson	15.00	7.50	4.50
121	Andy Seminick	15.00	7.50	4.50
122	Johnny Hopp	15.00	7.50	4.50
123	Dino Restelli	15.00	7.50	4.50
124	Clyde McCullough	15.00	7.50	4.50
125	Del Rice	15.00	7.50	4.50
126	Al Brazle	15.00	7.50	4.50
127	Dave Philley	15.00	7.50	4.50
128	Phil Masi	15.00	7.50	4.50
129	Joe "Flash" Gordon	12.00	6.00	3.50
130	Dale Mitchell	15.00	7.50	4.50
131	Steve Gromek	15.00	7.50	4.50
132	James Vernon	12.00	6.00	3.50
133	Don Kolloway	15.00	7.50	4.50
134	Paul "Dizzy" Trout	12.00	6.00	3.50
135	Pat Mullin	15.00	7.50	4.50
136	Warren Rosar	15.00	7.50	4.50
137	Johnny Pesky	12.00	6.00	3.50
138	Allie Reynolds	45.00	22.00	13.50
139	Johnny Mize	60.00	30.00	18.00
140	Pete Suder	15.00	7.50	4.50
141	Joe Coleman	15.00	7.50	4.50
142	*Sherman Lollar*	12.00	6.00	3.50
143	Eddie Stewart	15.00	7.50	4.50
144	Al Evans	15.00	7.50	4.50
145	Jack Graham	15.00	7.50	4.50
146	Floyd Baker	15.00	7.50	4.50
147	*Mike Garcia*	12.00	6.00	3.50
148	Early Wynn	60.00	30.00	18.00
149	Bob Swift	15.00	7.50	4.50
150	George Vico	15.00	7.50	4.50
151	Fred Hutchinson	12.00	6.00	3.50
152	Ellis Kinder	15.00	7.50	4.50
153	Walt Masterson	15.00	7.50	4.50

		NR MT	EX	VG
154	Gus Niarhos	15.00	7.50	4.50
155	Frank "Spec" Shea	15.00	7.50	4.50
156	Fred Sanford	15.00	7.50	4.50
157	Mike Guerra	15.00	7.50	4.50
158	Paul Lehner	15.00	7.50	4.50
159	Joe Tipton	15.00	7.50	4.50
160	Mickey Harris	15.00	7.50	4.50
161	Sherry Robertson	15.00	7.50	4.50
162	Eddie Yost	15.00	7.50	4.50
163	Earl Torgeson	15.00	7.50	4.50
164	Sibby Sisti	15.00	7.50	4.50
165	Bruce Edwards	12.00	6.00	3.50
166	Joe Hatten	12.00	6.00	3.50
167	Elwin Roe	45.00	22.00	13.50
168	Bob Scheffing	15.00	7.50	4.50
169	Hank Edwards	15.00	7.50	4.50
170	Emil Leonard	15.00	7.50	4.50
171	Harry Gumbert	15.00	7.50	4.50
172	Harry Lowrey	15.00	7.50	4.50
173	Lloyd Merriman	15.00	7.50	4.50
174	Henry Thompson	15.00	7.50	4.50
175	Monte Kennedy	15.00	7.50	4.50
176	Sylvester Donnelly	15.00	7.50	4.50
177	Hank Borowy	15.00	7.50	4.50
178	Eddy Fitzgerald (Fitz Gerald)	15.00	7.50	4.50
179	Charles Diering	15.00	7.50	4.50
180	Harry Walker	12.00	6.00	3.50
181	Marino Pieretti	15.00	7.50	4.50
182	Sam Zoldak	15.00	7.50	4.50
183	Mickey Haefner	15.00	7.50	4.50
184	Randy Gumpert	15.00	7.50	4.50
185	Howie Judson	15.00	7.50	4.50
186	Ken Keltner	12.00	6.00	3.50
187	Lou Stringer	15.00	7.50	4.50
188	Earl Johnson	15.00	7.50	4.50
189	Owen Friend	15.00	7.50	4.50
190	Ken Wood	15.00	7.50	4.50
191	Dick Starr	15.00	7.50	4.50
192	Bob Chipman	15.00	7.50	4.50
193	Harold "Pete" Reiser	12.00	6.00	3.50
194	Billy Cox	15.00	7.50	4.50
195	Phil Cavaretta (Cavarretta)	12.00	6.00	3.50
196	Doyle Lade	15.00	7.50	4.50
197	Johnny Wyrostek	15.00	7.50	4.50
198	Danny Litwhiler	15.00	7.50	4.50
199	Jack Kramer	15.00	7.50	4.50
200	Kirby Higbe	15.00	7.50	4.50
201	Pete Castiglione	15.00	7.50	4.50
202	Cliff Chambers	15.00	7.50	4.50
203	Danny Murtaugh	12.00	6.00	3.50
204	Granville Hamner	15.00	7.50	4.50
205	Mike Goliat	15.00	7.50	4.50
206	Stan Lopata	15.00	7.50	4.50
207	Max Lanier	15.00	7.50	4.50
208	Jim Hearn	15.00	7.50	4.50
209	Johnny Lindell	15.00	7.50	4.50
210	Ted Gray	15.00	7.50	4.50
211	Charlie Keller	15.00	7.50	4.50
212	Gerry Priddy	15.00	7.50	4.50
213	Carl Scheib	15.00	7.50	4.50
214	Dick Fowler	15.00	7.50	4.50
215	Ed Lopat	20.00	10.00	6.00
216	Bob Porterfield	15.00	7.50	4.50
217	Casey Stengel	110.00	55.00	30.00
218	Cliff Mapes	15.00	7.50	4.50
219	*Hank Bauer*	60.00	30.00	17.50
220	Leo Durocher	50.00	25.00	15.00
221	Don Mueller	15.00	7.50	4.50
222	Bobby Morgan	12.00	6.00	3.50
223	Jimmy Russell	12.00	6.00	3.50
224	Jack Banta	12.00	6.00	3.50
225	Eddie Sawyer	15.00	7.50	4.50
226	Jim Konstanty	12.00	6.00	3.50
227	Bob Miller	15.00	7.50	4.50
228	Bill Nicholson	15.00	7.50	4.50
229	Frank Frisch	40.00	20.00	12.00
230	Bill Serena	15.00	7.50	4.50
231	Preston Ward	15.00	7.50	4.50
232	Al "Flip" Rosen	40.00	20.00	12.00
233	Allie Clark	15.00	7.50	4.50
234	*Bobby Shantz*	25.00	12.50	7.50
235	Harold Gilbert	15.00	7.50	4.50
236	Bob Cain	15.00	7.50	4.50
237	Bill Salkeld	15.00	7.50	4.50
238	Vernal Jones	15.00	7.50	4.50
239	Bill Howerton	15.00	7.50	4.50
240	Eddie Lake	15.00	7.50	4.50
241	Neil Berry	15.00	7.50	4.50
242	Dick Kryhoski	15.00	7.50	4.50
243	Johnny Groth	15.00	7.50	4.50
244	Dale Coogan	15.00	7.50	4.50

		NR MT	EX	VG
245	Al Papai	15.00	7.50	4.50
246	*Walt Dropo*	25.00	12.50	7.50
247	Irv Noren	15.00	7.50	4.50
248	*Sam Jethroe*	12.00	6.00	3.50
249	George Stirnweiss	15.00	7.50	4.50
250	Ray Coleman	15.00	7.50	4.50
251	John Lester Moss	15.00	5.00	3.00
252	Billy DeMars	100.00	15.00	9.00

1951 Bowman

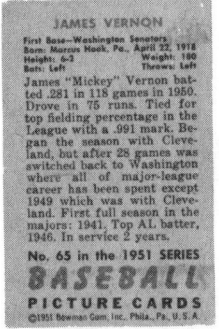

In 1951, Bowman increased the numbers of cards in its set for the third consecutive year when it issued 324 cards. The cards are, like 1950, color art reproductions of actual photographs but now measured 2-1/16" by 3-1/8" in size. The player's name is situated in a small, black box on the card front. Several of the card fronts are enlargements of the 1950 version. The high-numbered series of the set (#'s 253-324), which includes the rookie cards of Mantle and Mays, are the scarcest of the issue.

		NR MT	EX	VG
Complete Set:		17000.00	8500.00	4300.
Common Player: 1-36		12.00	6.00	3.50
Common Player: 37-252		10.00	5.00	3.00
Common Player: 253-324		40.00	20.00	12.00
1	*Ed Ford*	1500.00	500.00	300.00
2	Larry "Yogi" Berra	450.00	225.00	135.00
3	Robin Roberts	70.00	35.00	20.00
4	Del Ennis	12.00	6.00	3.50
5	Dale Mitchell	12.00	6.00	3.50
6	Don Newcombe	30.00	15.00	9.00
7	Gil Hodges	70.00	35.00	20.00
8	Paul Lehner	12.00	6.00	3.50
9	Sam Chapman	12.00	6.00	3.50
10	Al "Red" Schoendienst	60.00	30.00	18.00
11	George "Red" Munger	12.00	6.00	3.50
12	Hank Majeski	12.00	6.00	3.50
13	Ed Stanky	15.00	7.50	4.50
14	Alvin Dark	18.00	9.00	5.50
15	Johnny Pesky	15.00	7.50	4.50
16	Maurice McDermott	12.00	6.00	3.50
17	Pete Castiglione	12.00	6.00	3.50
18	Gil Coan	12.00	6.00	3.50
19	Sid Gordon	12.00	6.00	3.50
20	Del Crandall	15.00	7.50	4.50
21	George "Snuffy" Stirnweiss	12.00	6.00	3.50
22	Hank Sauer	12.00	6.00	3.50
23	Walter "Hoot" Evers	12.00	6.00	3.50
24	Ewell Blackwell	15.00	7.50	4.50
25	Vic Raschi	20.00	10.00	6.00
26	Phil Rizzuto	75.00	38.00	23.00
27	Jim Konstanty	12.00	6.00	3.50
28	Eddie Waitkus	12.00	6.00	3.50
29	Allie Clark	12.00	6.00	3.50
30	Bob Feller	100.00	50.00	30.00
31	Roy Campanella	275.00	137.00	82.00
32	Duke Snider	225.00	100.00	60.00
33	Bob Hooper	12.00	6.00	3.50
34	Marty Marion	15.00	7.50	4.50
35	Al Zarilla	12.00	6.00	3.50
36	Joe Dobson	12.00	6.00	3.50
37	Whitey Lockman	10.00	5.00	3.00
38	Al Evans	10.00	5.00	3.00
39	Ray Scarborough	10.00	5.00	3.00

		NR MT	EX	VG
40	Dave "Gus" Bell	12.00	6.00	3.50
41	Eddie Yost	12.00	6.00	3.50
42	Vern Bickford	10.00	5.00	3.00
43	Billy DeMars	10.00	5.00	3.00
44	Roy Smalley	10.00	5.00	3.00
45	Art Houtteman	10.00	5.00	3.00
46	George Kell	50.00	25.00	15.00
47	Grady Hatton	10.00	5.00	3.00
48	Ken Raffensberger	10.00	5.00	3.00
49	Jerry Coleman	15.00	7.50	4.50
50	Johnny Mize	50.00	25.00	15.00
51	Andy Seminick	10.00	5.00	3.00
52	Dick Sisler	10.00	5.00	3.00
53	Bob Lemon	40.00	20.00	12.00
54	Ray Boone	12.00	6.00	3.50
55	Gene Hermanski	12.00	6.00	3.50
56	Ralph Branca	30.00	15.00	9.00
57	Alex Kellner	10.00	5.00	3.00
58	Enos Slaughter	50.00	25.00	15.00
59	Randy Gumpert	10.00	5.00	3.00
60	Alfonso Carrasquel	10.00	5.00	3.00
61	Jim Hearn	10.00	5.00	3.00
62	Lou Boudreau	50.00	25.00	15.00
63	Bob Dillinger	10.00	5.00	3.00
64	Bill Werle	10.00	5.00	3.00
65	Mickey Vernon	12.00	6.00	3.50
66	Bob Elliott	10.00	5.00	3.00
67	Roy Sievers	12.00	6.00	3.50
68	Dick Kokos	10.00	5.00	3.00
69	Johnny Schmitz	10.00	5.00	3.00
70	Ron Northey	10.00	5.00	3.00
71	Jerry Priddy	10.00	5.00	3.00
72	Lloyd Merriman	10.00	5.00	3.00
73	Tommy Byrne	15.00	7.50	4.50
74	Billy Johnson	15.00	7.50	4.50
75	Russ Meyer	10.00	5.00	3.00
76	Stan Lopata	10.00	5.00	3.00
77	Mike Goliat	10.00	5.00	3.00
78	Early Wynn	50.00	25.00	15.00
79	Jim Hegan	10.00	5.00	3.00
80	Harold "Peewee" Reese	125.00	56.00	35.00
81	Carl Furillo	30.00	15.00	9.00
82	Joe Tipton	10.00	5.00	3.00
83	Carl Scheib	10.00	5.00	3.00
84	Barney McCosky	10.00	5.00	3.00
85	Eddie Kazak	10.00	5.00	3.00
86	Harry Brecheen	12.00	6.00	3.50
87	Floyd Baker	10.00	5.00	3.00
88	Eddie Robinson	10.00	5.00	3.00
89	Henry Thompson	10.00	5.00	3.00
90	Dave Koslo	10.00	5.00	3.00
91	Clyde Vollmer	10.00	5.00	3.00
92	Vern "Junior" Stephens	12.00	6.00	3.50
93	Danny O'Connell	10.00	5.00	3.00
94	Clyde McCullough	10.00	5.00	3.00
95	Sherry Robertson	10.00	5.00	3.00
96	Sandalio Consuegra	10.00	5.00	3.00
97	Bob Kuzava	10.00	5.00	3.00
98	Willard Marshall	10.00	5.00	3.00
99	Earl Torgeson	10.00	5.00	3.00
100	Sherman Lollar	12.00	6.00	3.50
101	Owen Friend	10.00	5.00	3.00
102	Emil "Dutch" Leonard	10.00	5.00	3.00
103	Andy Pafko	12.00	6.00	3.50
104	Virgil "Fire" Trucks	12.00	6.00	3.50
105	Don Kolloway	10.00	5.00	3.00
106	Pat Mullin	10.00	5.00	3.00
107	Johnny Wyrostek	10.00	5.00	3.00
108	Virgil Stallcup	10.00	5.00	3.00
109	Allie Reynolds	25.00	12.50	7.50
110	Bobby Brown	25.00	12.50	7.50
111	Curt Simmons	12.00	6.00	3.50
112	Willie Jones	10.00	5.00	3.00
113	Bill "Swish" Nicholson	10.00	5.00	3.00
114	Sam Zoldak	10.00	5.00	3.00
115	Steve Gromek	10.00	5.00	3.00
116	Bruce Edwards	12.00	6.00	3.50
117	Eddie Miksis	12.00	6.00	3.50
118	Preacher Roe	25.00	12.50	7.50
119	Eddie Joost	10.00	5.00	3.00
120	Joe Coleman	10.00	5.00	3.00
121	Gerry Staley	10.00	5.00	3.00
122	Joe Garagiola	125.00	62.00	37.00
123	Howie Judson	10.00	5.00	3.00
124	Gus Niarhos	10.00	5.00	3.00
125	Bill Rigney	12.00	6.00	3.50
126	Bobby Thomson	25.00	12.50	7.50
127	Sal Maglie	40.00	20.00	12.00
128	Ellis Kinder	10.00	5.00	3.00
129	Matt Batts	10.00	5.00	3.00
130	Tom Saffell	10.00	5.00	3.00

		NR MT	EX	VG
131	Cliff Chambers	10.00	5.00	3.00
132	Cass Michaels	10.00	5.00	3.00
133	Sam Dente	10.00	5.00	3.00
134	Warren Spahn	90.00	45.00	27.00
135	Walker Cooper	10.00	5.00	3.00
136	Ray Coleman	10.00	5.00	3.00
137	Dick Starr	10.00	5.00	3.00
138	Phil Cavarretta	12.00	6.00	3.50
139	Doyle Lade	10.00	5.00	3.00
140	Eddie Lake	10.00	5.00	3.00
141	Fred Hutchinson	12.00	6.00	3.50
142	Aaron Robinson	10.00	5.00	3.00
143	Ted Kluszewski	25.00	12.50	7.50
144	Herman Wehmeier	10.00	5.00	3.00
145	Fred Sanford	15.00	7.50	4.50
146	Johnny Hopp	15.00	7.50	4.50
147	Ken Heintzelman	10.00	5.00	3.00
148	Granny Hamner	10.00	5.00	3.00
149	Emory "Bubba" Church	10.00	5.00	3.00
150	Mike Garcia	12.00	6.00	3.50
151	Larry Doby	20.00	10.00	6.00
152	Cal Abrams	12.00	6.00	3.50
153	Rex Barney	12.00	6.00	3.50
154	Pete Suder	10.00	5.00	3.00
155	Lou Brissie	10.00	5.00	3.00
156	Del Rice	10.00	5.00	3.00
157	Al Brazle	10.00	5.00	3.00
158	Chuck Diering	10.00	5.00	3.00
159	Eddie Stewart	10.00	5.00	3.00
160	Phil Masi	10.00	5.00	3.00
161	Wes Westrum	12.00	6.00	3.50
162	Larry Jansen	10.00	5.00	3.00
163	Monte Kennedy	10.00	5.00	3.00
164	Bill Wight	10.00	5.00	3.00
165	Ted Williams	550.00	275.00	165.00
166	Stan Rojek	10.00	5.00	3.00
167	Murry Dickson	10.00	5.00	3.00
168	Sam Mele	10.00	5.00	3.00
169	Sid Hudson	10.00	5.00	3.00
170	Sibby Sisti	10.00	5.00	3.00
171	Buddy Kerr	10.00	5.00	3.00
172	Ned Garver	10.00	5.00	3.00
173	Hank Arft	10.00	5.00	3.00
174	Mickey Owen	10.00	5.00	3.00
175	Wayne Terwilliger	10.00	5.00	3.00
176	Vic Wertz	12.00	6.00	3.50
177	Charlie Keller	12.00	6.00	3.50
178	Ted Gray	10.00	5.00	3.00
179	Danny Litwhiler	10.00	5.00	3.00
180	Howie Fox	10.00	5.00	3.00
181	Casey Stengel	90.00	45.00	27.00
182	Tom Ferrick	15.00	7.50	4.50
183	Hank Bauer	25.00	12.50	7.50
184	Eddie Sawyer	10.00	5.00	3.00
185	Jimmy Bloodworth	10.00	5.00	3.00
186	Richie Ashburn	50.00	25.00	15.00
187	Al "Flip" Rosen	20.00	10.00	6.00
188	*Roberto Avila*	12.00	6.00	3.50
189	Erv Palica	12.00	6.00	3.50
190	Joe Hatten	12.00	6.00	3.50
191	Billy Hitchcock	10.00	5.00	3.00
192	Hank Wyse	10.00	5.00	3.00
193	Ted Wilks	10.00	5.00	3.00
194	Harry "Peanuts" Lowrey	10.00	5.00	3.00
195	Paul Richards	30.00	15.00	9.00
196	Bill Pierce	15.00	7.50	4.50
197	Bob Cain	10.00	5.00	3.00
198	*Monte Irvin*	100.00	50.00	30.00
199	Sheldon Jones	10.00	5.00	3.00
200	Jack Kramer	10.00	5.00	3.00
201	Steve O'Neill	10.00	5.00	3.00
202	Mike Guerra	10.00	5.00	3.00
203	*Vernon Law*	15.00	7.50	4.50
204	Vic Lombardi	10.00	5.00	3.00
205	Mickey Grasso	10.00	5.00	3.00
206	Conrado Marrero	10.00	5.00	3.00
207	Billy Southworth	10.00	5.00	3.00
208	Blix Donnelly	10.00	5.00	3.00
209	Ken Wood	10.00	5.00	3.00
210	Les Moss	10.00	5.00	3.00
211	Hal Jeffcoat	10.00	5.00	3.00
212	Bob Rush	10.00	5.00	3.00
213	Neil Berry	10.00	5.00	3.00
214	Bob Swift	10.00	5.00	3.00
215	Kent Peterson	10.00	5.00	3.00
216	Connie Ryan	10.00	5.00	3.00
217	Joe Page	15.00	7.50	4.50
218	Ed Lopat	25.00	12.50	7.50
219	Gene Woodling	25.00	12.50	7.50
220	Bob Miller	10.00	5.00	3.00
221	Dick Whitman	10.00	5.00	3.00

		NR MT	EX	VG
222	Thurman Tucker	10.00	5.00	3.00
223	Johnny Vander Meer	20.00	10.00	6.00
224	Billy Cox	15.00	7.50	4.50
225	Dan Bankhead	15.00	7.50	4.50
226	Jimmy Dykes	15.00	7.50	4.50
227	Bobby Schantz (Shantz)	15.00	7.50	4.50
228	Cloyd Boyer	10.00	5.00	3.00
229	Bill Howerton	10.00	5.00	3.00
230	Max Lanier	10.00	5.00	3.00
231	Luis Aloma	10.00	5.00	3.00
232	Nelson Fox	80.00	40.00	25.00
233	Leo Durocher	50.00	25.00	15.00
234	Clint Hartung	10.00	5.00	3.00
235	Jack "Lucky" Lohrke	10.00	5.00	3.00
236	Warren "Buddy" Rosar	10.00	5.00	3.00
237	Billy Goodman	10.00	5.00	3.00
238	Pete Reiser	15.00	7.50	4.50
239	Bill MacDonald	10.00	5.00	3.00
240	Joe Haynes	10.00	5.00	3.00
241	Irv Noren	10.00	5.00	3.00
242	Sam Jethroe	15.00	7.50	4.50
243	John Antonelli	15.00	7.50	4.50
244	Cliff Fannin	10.00	5.00	3.00
245	John Berardino	15.00	7.50	4.50
246	Bill Serena	10.00	5.00	3.00
247	Bob Ramazotti	10.00	5.00	3.00
248	*Johnny Klippstein*	15.00	7.50	4.50
249	Johnny Groth	10.00	5.00	3.00
250	Hank Borowy	10.00	5.00	3.00
251	Willard Ramsdell	10.00	5.00	3.00
252	Homer "Dixie" Howell	10.00	5.00	3.00
253	*Mickey Mantle*	4500.00	2300.00	1350.
254	*Jackie Jensen*	70.00	35.00	21.00
255	Milo Candini	40.00	20.00	12.00
256	Ken Silvestri	40.00	20.00	12.00
257	Birdie Tebbetts	40.00	20.00	12.00
258	*Luke Easter*	45.00	22.00	13.50
259	Charlie Dressen	45.00	22.00	13.50
260	Carl Erskine	90.00	45.00	27.00
261	Wally Moses	40.00	20.00	12.00
262	Gus Zernial	40.00	20.00	12.00
263	Howie Pollett (Pollet)	40.00	20.00	12.00
264	Don Richmond	40.00	20.00	12.00
265	Steve Bilko	40.00	20.00	12.00
266	Harry Dorish	40.00	20.00	12.00
267	Ken Holcombe	40.00	20.00	12.00
268	Don Mueller	40.00	20.00	12.00
269	Ray Noble	40.00	20.00	12.00
270	Willard Nixon	40.00	20.00	12.00
271	Tommy Wright	40.00	20.00	12.00
272	Billy Meyer	40.00	20.00	12.00
273	Danny Murtaugh	45.00	22.00	13.50
274	George Metkovich	40.00	20.00	12.00
275	Bucky Harris	80.00	40.00	25.00
276	Frank Quinn	40.00	20.00	12.00
277	Roy Hartsfield	40.00	20.00	12.00
278	Norman Roy	40.00	20.00	12.00
279	Jim Delsing	40.00	20.00	12.00
280	Frank Overmire	40.00	20.00	12.00
281	Al Widmar	40.00	20.00	12.00
282	Frank Frisch	80.00	40.00	25.00
283	Walt Dubiel	40.00	20.00	12.00
284	Gene Bearden	40.00	20.00	12.00
285	Johnny Lipon	40.00	20.00	12.00
286	Bob Usher	40.00	20.00	12.00
287	Jim Blackburn	40.00	20.00	12.00
288	Bobby Adams	40.00	20.00	12.00
289	Cliff Mapes	45.00	22.00	13.50
290	Bill Dickey	175.00	70.00	44.00
291	Tommy Henrich	60.00	30.00	18.00
292	Eddie Pellagrini	40.00	20.00	12.00
293	Ken Johnson	40.00	20.00	12.00
294	Jocko Thompson	40.00	20.00	12.00
295	Al Lopez	90.00	45.00	25.00
296	Bob Kennedy	40.00	20.00	12.00
297	Dave Philley	40.00	20.00	12.00
298	Joe Astroth	40.00	20.00	12.00
299	Clyde King	45.00	22.00	13.50
300	Hal Rice	40.00	20.00	12.00
301	Tommy Glaviano	40.00	20.00	12.00
302	Jim Busby	40.00	20.00	12.00
303	Marv Rotblatt	40.00	20.00	12.00
304	Allen Gettel	40.00	20.00	12.00
305	Willie Mays	1800.00	900.00	550.00
306	*Jim Piersall*	80.00	40.00	24.00
307	Walt Masterson	40.00	20.00	12.00
308	Ted Beard	40.00	20.00	12.00
309	Mel Queen	40.00	20.00	12.00
310	Erv Dusak	40.00	20.00	12.00
311	Mickey Harris	40.00	20.00	12.00
312	Gene Mauch	50.00	30.00	15.00

		NR MT	EX	VG
313	Ray Mueller	40.00	20.00	12.00
314	Johnny Sain	50.00	25.00	15.00
315	Zack Taylor	40.00	20.00	12.00
316	Duane Pillette	40.00	20.00	12.00
317	*Forrest Burgess*	50.00	25.00	15.00
318	Warren Hacker	40.00	20.00	12.00
319	Red Rolfe	40.00	20.00	12.00
320	Hal White	40.00	20.00	12.00
321	Earl Johnson	40.00	20.00	12.00
322	Luke Sewell	40.00	20.00	12.00
323	*Joe Adcock*	80.00	40.00	25.00
324	Johnny Pramesa	90.00	20.00	12.00

1952 Bowman

Bowman reverted back to a 252-card set in 1952, but retained the card size (2-1/16" by 3-1/8") employed the preceding year. The cards, which are color art reproductions of actual photographs, feature a facsimile autograph on the fronts. Artwork for 15 cards that were never issued was uncovered several years ago and a set featuring those cards was subsequently made available to the collecting public.

		NR MT	EX	VG
Complete Set:		8000.00	4000.00	2500.
Common Player: 1-36		12.00	6.00	3.50
Common Player: 37-216		10.00	5.00	3.00
Common Player: 217-252		20.00	10.00	6.00
1	Larry "Yogi" Berra	600.00	85.00	38.00
2	Bobby Thomson	30.00	10.00	6.00
3	Fred Hutchinson	14.00	7.00	4.25
4	Robin Roberts	50.00	25.00	15.00
5	*Orestes Minoso*	60.00	30.00	18.00
6	Virgil "Red" Stallcup	12.00	6.00	3.50
7	Mike Garcia	14.00	7.00	4.25
8	Harold "Pee Wee" Reese	150.00	60.00	38.00
9	Vern Stephens	12.00	6.00	3.50
10	Bob Hooper	12.00	6.00	3.50
11	Ralph Kiner	45.00	23.00	13.50
12	Max Surkont	12.00	6.00	3.50
13	Cliff Mapes	12.00	6.00	3.50
14	Cliff Chambers	12.00	6.00	3.50
15	Sam Mele	12.00	6.00	3.50
16	Omar Lown	12.00	6.00	3.50
17	Ed Lopat	25.00	12.50	7.50
18	Don Mueller	12.00	6.00	3.50
19	Bob Cain	12.00	6.00	3.50
20	Willie Jones	12.00	6.00	3.50
21	Nelson Fox	40.00	20.00	12.00
22	Willard Ramsdell	12.00	6.00	3.50
23	Bob Lemon	50.00	25.00	15.00
24	Carl Furillo	20.00	10.00	6.00
25	Maurice McDermott	12.00	6.00	3.50
26	Eddie Joost	12.00	6.00	3.50
27	Joe Garagiola	70.00	35.00	20.00
28	Roy Hartsfield	12.00	6.00	3.50
29	Ned Garver	12.00	6.00	3.50
30	Al "Red" Schoendienst	50.00	30.00	15.00
31	Eddie Yost	12.00	6.00	3.50
32	Eddie Miksis	12.00	6.00	3.50
33	*Gil McDougald*	40.00	20.00	12.00
34	Al Dark	16.00	8.00	4.75
35	Gran Hamner	12.00	6.00	3.50
36	Cass Michaels	12.00	6.00	3.50
37	Vic Raschi	18.00	9.00	5.50
38	Whitey Lockman	10.00	5.00	3.00

		NR MT	EX	VG
39	Vic Wertz	12.00	6.00	3.50
40	Emory Church	10.00	5.00	3.00
41	Chico Carrasquel	10.00	5.00	3.00
42	Johnny Wyrostek	10.00	5.00	3.00
43	Bob Feller	80.00	40.00	25.00
44	Roy Campanella	175.00	70.00	44.00
45	Johnny Pesky	12.00	6.00	3.50
46	Carl Scheib	10.00	5.00	3.00
47	Pete Castiglione	10.00	5.00	3.00
48	Vern Bickford	10.00	5.00	3.00
49	Jim Hearn	10.00	5.00	3.00
50	Gerry Staley	10.00	5.00	3.00
51	Gil Coan	10.00	5.00	3.00
52	Phil Rizzuto	80.00	40.00	25.00
53	Richie Ashburn	50.00	25.00	15.00
54	Billy Pierce	12.00	6.00	3.50
55	Ken Raffensberger	10.00	5.00	3.00
56	Clyde King	12.00	6.00	3.50
57	Clyde Vollmer	10.00	5.00	3.00
58	Hank Majeski	10.00	5.00	3.00
59	Murray Dickson (Murry)	10.00	5.00	3.00
60	Sid Gordon	10.00	5.00	3.00
61	Tommy Byrne	10.00	5.00	3.00
62	Joe Presko	10.00	5.00	3.00
63	Irv Noren	10.00	5.00	3.00
64	Roy Smalley	10.00	5.00	3.00
65	Hank Bauer	20.00	10.00	6.00
66	Sal Maglie	20.00	10.00	6.00
67	Johnny Groth	10.00	5.00	3.00
68	Jim Busby	10.00	5.00	3.00
69	Joe Adcock	12.00	6.00	3.50
70	Carl Erskine	18.00	9.00	5.50
71	Vernon Law	12.00	6.00	3.50
72	Earl Torgeson	10.00	5.00	3.00
73	Jerry Coleman	18.00	9.00	5.50
74	Wes Westrum	12.00	6.00	3.50
75	George Kell	40.00	20.00	12.00
76	Del Ennis	12.00	6.00	3.50
77	Eddie Robinson	10.00	5.00	3.00
78	Lloyd Merriman	10.00	5.00	3.00
79	Lou Brissie	10.00	5.00	3.00
80	Gil Hodges	60.00	30.00	15.00
81	Billy Goodman	10.00	5.00	3.00
82	Gus Zernial	10.00	5.00	3.00
83	Howie Pollet	10.00	5.00	3.00
84	Sam Jethroe	10.00	5.00	3.00
85	Marty Marion	12.00	6.00	3.50
86	Cal Abrams	12.00	6.00	3.50
87	Mickey Vernon	12.00	6.00	3.50
88	Bruce Edwards	10.00	5.00	3.00
89	Billy Hitchcock	10.00	5.00	3.00
90	Larry Jansen	10.00	5.00	3.00
91	Don Kolloway	10.00	5.00	3.00
92	Eddie Waitkus	10.00	5.00	3.00
93	Paul Richards	12.00	6.00	3.50
94	Luke Sewell	10.00	5.00	3.00
95	Luke Easter	12.00	6.00	3.50
96	Ralph Branca	18.00	9.00	5.50
97	Willard Marshall	10.00	5.00	3.00
98	Jimmy Dykes	12.00	6.00	3.50
99	Clyde McCullough	10.00	5.00	3.00
100	Sibby Sisti	10.00	5.00	3.00
101	Mickey Mantle	1400.00	560.00	280.00
102	Peanuts Lowrey	10.00	5.00	3.00
103	Joe Haynes	10.00	5.00	3.00
104	Hal Jeffcoat	10.00	5.00	3.00
105	Bobby Brown	18.00	9.00	5.50
106	Randy Gumpert	10.00	5.00	3.00
107	Del Rice	10.00	5.00	3.00
108	George Metkovich	10.00	5.00	3.00
109	Tom Morgan	15.00	7.50	4.50
110	Max Lanier	10.00	5.00	3.00
111	Walter "Hoot" Evers	10.00	5.00	3.00
112	Forrest "Smokey" Burgess	12.00	6.00	3.50
113	Al Zarilla	10.00	5.00	3.00
114	Frank Hiller	10.00	5.00	3.00
115	Larry Doby	20.00	10.00	6.00
116	Duke Snider	150.00	75.00	45.00
117	Bill Wight	10.00	5.00	3.00
118	Ray Murray	10.00	5.00	3.00
119	Bill Howerton	10.00	5.00	3.00
120	Chet Nichols	10.00	5.00	3.00
121	Al Corwin	10.00	5.00	3.00
122	Billy Johnson	10.00	5.00	3.00
123	Sid Hudson	10.00	5.00	3.00
124	George Tebbetts	10.00	5.00	3.00
125	Howie Fox	10.00	5.00	3.00
126	Phil Cavarretta	12.00	6.00	3.50
127	Dick Sisler	10.00	5.00	3.00
128	Don Newcombe	30.00	15.00	9.00
129	Gus Niarhos	10.00	5.00	3.00

		NR MT	EX	VG
130	Allie Clark	10.00	5.00	3.00
131	Bob Swift	10.00	5.00	3.00
132	Dave Cole	10.00	5.00	3.00
133	Dick Kryhoski	10.00	5.00	3.00
134	Al Brazle	10.00	5.00	3.00
135	Mickey Harris	10.00	5.00	3.00
136	Gene Hermanski	10.00	5.00	3.00
137	Stan Rojek	10.00	5.00	3.00
138	Ted Wilks	10.00	5.00	3.00
139	Jerry Priddy	10.00	5.00	3.00
140	Ray Scarborough	10.00	5.00	3.00
141	Hank Edwards	10.00	5.00	3.00
142	Early Wynn	45.00	23.00	13.50
143	Sandalio Consuegra	10.00	5.00	3.00
144	Joe Hatten	10.00	5.00	3.00
145	Johnny Mize	50.00	30.00	15.00
146	Leo Durocher	40.00	20.00	12.00
147	Marlin Stuart	10.00	5.00	3.00
148	Ken Heintzelman	10.00	5.00	3.00
149	Howie Judson	10.00	5.00	3.00
150	Herman Wehmeier	10.00	5.00	3.00
151	Al "Flip" Rosen	18.00	9.00	5.50
152	Billy Cox	12.00	6.00	3.50
153	Fred Hatfield	10.00	5.00	3.00
154	Ferris Fain	12.00	6.00	3.50
155	Billy Meyer	10.00	5.00	3.00
156	Warren Spahn	80.00	40.00	24.00
157	Jim Delsing	10.00	5.00	3.00
158	Bucky Harris	30.00	15.00	9.00
159	Dutch Leonard	10.00	5.00	3.00
160	Eddie Stanky	12.00	6.00	3.50
161	Jackie Jensen	25.00	12.50	7.50
162	Monte Irvin	40.00	20.00	12.00
163	Johnny Lipon	10.00	5.00	3.00
164	Connie Ryan	10.00	5.00	3.00
165	Saul Rogovin	10.00	5.00	3.00
166	Bobby Adams	10.00	5.00	3.00
167	Bob Avila	10.00	5.00	3.00
168	Preacher Roe	25.00	12.50	7.50
169	Walt Dropo	10.00	5.00	3.00
170	Joe Astroth	10.00	5.00	3.00
171	Mel Queen	10.00	5.00	3.00
172	Ebba St. Claire	10.00	5.00	3.00
173	Gene Bearden	10.00	5.00	3.00
174	Mickey Grasso	10.00	5.00	3.00
175	Ransom Jackson	10.00	5.00	3.00
176	Harry Brecheen	12.00	6.00	3.50
177	Gene Woodling	18.00	9.00	5.50
178	Dave Williams	10.00	5.00	3.00
179	Pete Suder	10.00	5.00	3.00
180	Eddie Fitzgerald (Fitz Gerald)	10.00	5.00	3.00
181	Joe Collins	15.00	7.50	4.50
182	Dave Koslo	10.00	5.00	3.00
183	Pat Mullin	10.00	5.00	3.00
184	Curt Simmons	12.00	6.00	3.50
185	Eddie Stewart	10.00	5.00	3.00
186	Frank Smith	10.00	5.00	3.00
187	Jim Hegan	10.00	5.00	3.00
188	Charlie Dressen	15.00	7.50	4.50
189	Jim Piersall	18.00	9.00	5.50
190	Dick Fowler	10.00	5.00	3.00
191	*Bob Friend*	15.00	7.50	4.50
192	John Cusick	10.00	5.00	3.00
193	Bobby Young	10.00	5.00	3.00
194	Bob Porterfield	10.00	5.00	3.00
195	Frank Baumholtz	10.00	5.00	3.00
196	Stan Musial	450.00	225.00	135.00
197	Charlie Silvera	15.00	7.50	4.50
198	Chuck Diering	10.00	5.00	3.00
199	Ted Gray	10.00	5.00	3.00
200	Ken Silvestri	10.00	5.00	3.00
201	Ray Coleman	10.00	5.00	3.00
202	Harry Perkowski	10.00	5.00	3.00
203	Steve Gromek	10.00	5.00	3.00
204	Andy Pafko	12.00	6.00	3.50
205	Walt Masterson	10.00	5.00	3.00
206	Elmer Valo	10.00	5.00	3.00
207	George Strickland	10.00	5.00	3.00
208	Walker Cooper	10.00	5.00	3.00
209	Dick Littlefield	10.00	5.00	3.00
210	Archie Wilson	10.00	5.00	3.00
211	Paul Minner	10.00	5.00	3.00
212	Solly Hemus	10.00	5.00	3.00
213	Monte Kennedy	10.00	5.00	3.00
214	Ray Boone	12.00	6.00	3.50
215	Sheldon Jones	10.00	5.00	3.00
216	Matt Batts	10.00	5.00	3.00
217	Casey Stengel	150.00	75.00	45.00
218	Willie Mays	800.00	400.00	250.00
219	Neil Berry	25.00	12.50	7.50
220	Russ Meyer	25.00	12.50	7.50

		NR MT	EX	VG
221	Lou Kretlow	25.00	12.50	7.50
222	Homer "Dixie" Howell	25.00	12.50	7.50
223	Harry Simpson	25.00	12.50	7.50
224	Johnny Schmitz	27.00	13.50	8.00
225	Del Wilber	25.00	12.50	7.50
226	Alex Kellner	25.00	12.50	7.50
227	Clyde Sukeforth	25.00	12.50	7.50
228	Bob Chipman	25.00	12.50	7.50
229	Hank Arft	25.00	12.50	7.50
230	Frank Shea	25.00	12.50	7.50
231	Dee Fondy	25.00	12.50	7.50
232	Enos Slaughter	70.00	35.00	21.00
233	Bob Kuzava	32.00	16.00	9.50
234	Fred Fitzsimmons	25.00	12.50	7.50
235	Steve Souchock	25.00	12.50	7.50
236	Tommy Brown	25.00	12.50	7.50
237	Sherman Lollar	27.00	13.50	8.00
238	*Roy McMillan*	27.00	13.50	8.00
239	Dale Mitchell	25.00	12.50	7.50
240	*Billy Loes*	35.00	17.50	10.50
241	Mel Parnell	27.00	13.50	8.00
242	Everett Kell	25.00	12.50	7.50
243	George "Red" Munger	25.00	12.50	7.50
244	*Lew Burdette*	60.00	30.00	18.00
245	George Schmees	25.00	12.50	7.50
246	Jerry Snyder	25.00	12.50	7.50
247	John Pramesa	25.00	12.50	7.50
248	Bill Werle	25.00	12.50	7.50
249	Henry Thompson	25.00	12.50	7.50
250	Ivan Delock	25.00	12.50	7.50
251	Jack Lohrke	32.00	12.50	7.50
252	Frank Crosetti	125.00	30.00	15.00

1953 Bowman Color

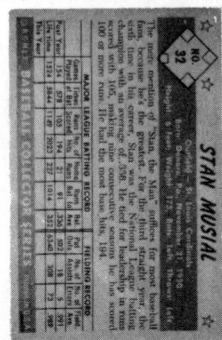

The first set of current major league players featuring actual color photographs, the 160-card 1953 Bowman Color set remains one of the most popular issues of the post-war era. The set is greatly appreciated for its uncluttered look; card fronts that contain no names, teams or facsimile autographs. Bowman increased the size of their cards to a 2-1/2" by 3-3/4" size in order to better compete with Topps Chewing Gum. Bowman copied an idea from the 1952 Topps set and developed card backs that gave player career and previous year statistics. The high-numbered cards (#'s 113-160) are the scarcest of the set, with #'s 113-128 being exceptionally difficult to find.

		NR MT	EX	VG
Complete Set:		12000.00	6000.00	3500.
Common Player: 1-112		35.00	17.50	10.50
Common Player: 113-128		50.00	25.00	15.00
Common Player: 129-160		35.00	17.50	10.50
1	Davey Williams	110.00	15.00	9.00
2	Vic Wertz	50.00	25.00	15.00
3	Sam Jethroe	35.00	17.50	10.50
4	Art Houtteman	35.00	17.50	10.50
5	Sid Gordon	35.00	17.50	10.50
6	Joe Ginsberg	35.00	17.50	10.50
7	Harry Chiti	35.00	17.50	10.50
8	Al Rosen	50.00	25.00	15.00
9	Phil Rizzuto	80.00	40.00	24.00
10	Richie Ashburn	70.00	35.00	21.00
11	Bobby Shantz	35.00	17.50	10.50

		NR MT	EX	VG
12	Carl Erskine	50.00	25.00	15.00
13	Gus Zernial	35.00	17.50	10.50
14	Billy Loes	35.00	17.50	10.50
15	Jim Busby	35.00	17.50	10.50
16	Bob Friend	35.00	17.50	10.50
17	Gerry Staley	35.00	17.50	10.50
18	Nelson Fox	60.00	30.00	18.00
19	Al Dark	35.00	17.50	10.50
20	Don Lenhardt	35.00	17.50	10.50
21	Joe Garagiola	60.00	30.00	18.00
22	Bob Porterfield	35.00	17.50	10.50
23	Herman Wehmeier	35.00	17.50	10.50
24	Jackie Jensen	35.00	17.50	10.50
25	Walter "Hoot" Evers	35.00	17.50	10.50
26	Roy McMillan	35.00	17.50	10.50
27	Vic Raschi	50.00	25.00	15.00
28	Forrest "Smoky" Burgess	35.00	17.50	10.50
29	Roberto Avila	35.00	17.50	10.50
30	Phil Cavarretta	35.00	17.50	10.50
31	Jimmy Dykes	35.00	17.50	10.50
32	Stan Musial	400.00	160.00	100.00
33	Harold "Peewee" Reese	275.00	137.00	82.00
34	Gil Coan	35.00	17.50	10.50
35	Maury McDermott	35.00	17.50	10.50
36	Orestes Minoso	50.00	25.00	15.00
37	Jim Wilson	35.00	17.50	10.50
38	Harry Byrd	35.00	17.50	10.50
39	Paul Richards	35.00	17.50	10.50
40	Larry Doby	50.00	25.00	15.00
41	Sammy White	35.00	17.50	10.50
42	Tommy Brown	35.00	17.50	10.50
43	Mike Garcia	35.00	17.50	10.50
44	Hank Bauer, Yogi Berra, Mickey Mantle	400.00	200.00	120.00
45	Walt Dropo	35.00	17.50	10.50
46	Roy Campanella	275.00	137.00	82.00
47	Ned Garver	35.00	17.50	10.50
48	Hank Sauer	35.00	17.50	10.50
49	Eddie Stanky	35.00	17.50	10.50
50	Lou Kretlow	35.00	17.50	10.50
51	Monte Irvin	45.00	23.00	13.50
52	Marty Marion	35.00	17.50	10.50
53	Del Rice	35.00	17.50	10.50
54	Chico Carrasquel	35.00	17.50	10.50
55	Leo Durocher	65.00	33.00	20.00
56	Bob Cain	35.00	17.50	10.50
57	Lou Boudreau	50.00	25.00	15.00
58	Willard Marshall	35.00	17.50	10.50
59	Mickey Mantle	1200.00	500.00	300.00
60	Granny Hamner	35.00	17.50	10.50
61	George Kell	50.00	25.00	15.00
62	Ted Kluszewski	50.00	25.00	15.00
63	Gil McDougald	50.00	25.00	15.00
64	Curt Simmons	35.00	17.50	10.50
65	Robin Roberts	70.00	35.00	21.00
66	Mel Parnell	35.00	17.50	10.50
67	Mel Clark	35.00	17.50	10.50
68	Allie Reynolds	50.00	25.00	15.00
69	Charlie Grimm	35.00	17.50	10.50
70	Clint Courtney	35.00	17.50	10.50
71	Paul Minner	35.00	17.50	10.50
72	Ted Gray	35.00	17.50	10.50
73	Billy Pierce	35.00	17.50	10.50
74	Don Mueller	35.00	17.50	10.50
75	Saul Rogovin	35.00	17.50	10.50
76	Jim Hearn	35.00	17.50	10.50
77	Mickey Grasso	35.00	17.50	10.50
78	Carl Furillo	40.00	20.00	12.00
79	Ray Boone	35.00	17.50	10.50
80	Ralph Kiner	70.00	35.00	21.00
81	Enos Slaughter	70.00	35.00	21.00
82	Joe Astroth	35.00	17.50	10.50
83	Jack Daniels	35.00	17.50	10.50
84	Hank Bauer	50.00	25.00	15.00
85	Solly Hemus	35.00	17.50	10.50
86	Harry Simpson	35.00	17.50	10.50
87	Harry Perkowski	35.00	17.50	10.50
88	Joe Dobson	35.00	17.50	10.50
89	Sandalio Consuegra	35.00	17.50	10.50
90	Joe Nuxhall	35.00	17.50	10.50
91	Steve Souchock	35.00	17.50	10.50
92	Gil Hodges	100.00	45.00	27.00
93	Billy Martin, Phil Rizzuto	200.00	100.00	60.00
94	Bob Addis	35.00	17.50	10.50
95	Wally Moses	35.00	17.50	10.50
96	Sal Maglie	35.00	17.50	10.50
97	Eddie Mathews	150.00	75.00	45.00
98	Hector Rodriquez	35.00	17.50	10.50
99	Warren Spahn	125.00	62.00	37.00
100	Bill Wight	35.00	17.50	10.50
101	Al "Red" Schoendienst	70.00	35.00	21.00

		NR MT	EX	VG
102	Jim Hegan	35.00	17.50	10.50
103	Del Ennis	35.00	17.50	10.50
104	Luke Easter	35.00	17.50	10.50
105	Eddie Joost	35.00	17.50	10.50
106	Ken Raffensberger	35.00	17.50	10.50
107	Alex Kellner	35.00	17.50	10.50
108	Bobby Adams	35.00	17.50	10.50
109	Ken Wood	35.00	17.50	10.50
110	Bob Rush	35.00	17.50	10.50
111	Jim Dyck	35.00	17.50	10.50
112	Toby Atwell	35.00	17.50	10.50
113	Karl Drews	50.00	25.00	15.00
114	Bob Feller	250.00	100.00	63.00
115	Cloyd Boyer	50.00	25.00	15.00
116	Eddie Yost	50.00	25.00	15.00
117	Duke Snider	500.00	225.00	150.00
118	Billy Martin	300.00	150.00	90.00
119	Dale Mitchell	50.00	25.00	15.00
120	Marlin Stuart	50.00	25.00	15.00
121	Yogi Berra	475.00	190.00	119.00
122	Bill Serena	50.00	25.00	15.00
123	Johnny Lipon	50.00	25.00	15.00
124	Charlie Dressen	45.00	23.00	13.50
125	Fred Hatfield	50.00	25.00	15.00
126	Al Corwin	50.00	25.00	15.00
127	Dick Kryhoski	50.00	25.00	15.00
128	Whitey Lockman	50.00	25.00	15.00
129	Russ Meyer	50.00	25.00	15.00
130	Cass Michaels	35.00	17.50	10.50
131	Connie Ryan	35.00	17.50	10.50
132	Fred Hutchinson	50.00	25.00	15.00
133	Willie Jones	35.00	17.50	10.50
134	Johnny Pesky	50.00	25.00	15.00
135	Bobby Morgan	50.00	25.00	15.00
136	Jim Brideweser	40.00	20.00	12.00
137	Sam Dente	35.00	17.50	10.50
138	Bubba Church	35.00	17.50	10.50
139	Pete Runnels	50.00	25.00	15.00
140	Alpha Brazle	35.00	17.50	10.50
141	Frank "Spec" Shea	35.00	17.50	10.50
142	Larry Miggins	35.00	17.50	10.50
143	Al Lopez	60.00	30.00	18.00
144	Warren Hacker	35.00	17.50	10.50
145	George Shuba	50.00	25.00	15.00
146	Early Wynn	125.00	62.00	40.00
147	Clem Koshorek	35.00	17.50	10.50
148	Billy Goodman	35.00	17.50	10.50
149	Al Corwin	35.00	17.50	10.50
150	Carl Scheib	35.00	17.50	10.50
151	Joe Adcock	40.00	20.00	12.00
152	Clyde Vollmer	35.00	17.50	10.50
153	Ed "Whitey" Ford	500.00	225.00	150.00
154	Omar "Turk" Lown	35.00	17.50	10.50
155	Allie Clark	35.00	17.50	10.50
156	Max Surkont	35.00	17.50	10.50
157	Sherman Lollar	50.00	25.00	15.00
158	Howard Fox	35.00	17.50	10.50
159	Mickey Vernon (Photo actually Floyd Baker)	40.00	17.50	10.50
160	Cal Abrams	100.00	17.50	9.00

1953 Bowman
Black & White

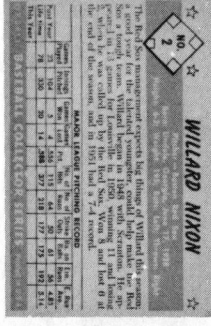

The 1953 Bowman Black and White set is similar in all respects to the 1953 Bowman Color set, except that it lacks color. Purportedly, high costs in producing the color series forced Bowman to issue the set in black and white. Sixty-four cards, which measure 2-1/2" by 3-3/4", comprise the set.

		NR MT	EX	VG
	Complete Set:	2200.00	880.00	440.00
	Common Player:	30.00	15.00	9.00
1	Gus Bell	100.00	45.00	27.00
2	Willard Nixon	32.00	11.00	6.50
3	Bill Rigney	27.00	13.50	8.00
4	Pat Mullin	30.00	15.00	9.00
5	Dee Fondy	30.00	15.00	9.00
6	Ray Murray	30.00	15.00	9.00
7	Andy Seminick	30.00	15.00	9.00
8	Pete Suder	30.00	15.00	9.00
9	Walt Masterson	30.00	15.00	9.00
10	Dick Sisler	30.00	15.00	9.00
11	Dick Gernert	30.00	15.00	9.00
12	Randy Jackson	30.00	15.00	9.00
13	Joe Tipton	30.00	15.00	9.00
14	Bill Nicholson	30.00	15.00	9.00
15	Johnny Mize	110.00	50.00	28.00
16	Stu Miller	30.00	15.00	9.00
17	Virgil Trucks	27.00	13.50	8.00
18	Billy Hoeft	30.00	15.00	9.00
19	Paul LaPalme	30.00	15.00	9.00
20	Eddie Robinson	30.00	15.00	9.00
21	Clarence "Bud" Podbielan	30.00	15.00	9.00
22	Matt Batts	30.00	15.00	9.00
23	Wilmer Mizell	30.00	15.00	9.00
24	Del Wilber	30.00	15.00	9.00
25	John Sain	50.00	25.00	15.00
26	Preacher Roe	50.00	25.00	15.00
27	Bob Lemon	100.00	50.00	30.00
28	Hoyt Wilhelm	100.00	50.00	28.00
29	Sid Hudson	30.00	15.00	9.00
30	Walker Cooper	30.00	15.00	9.00
31	Gene Woodling	40.00	20.00	12.00
32	Rocky Bridges	30.00	15.00	9.00
33	Bob Kuzava	32.00	16.00	9.50
34	Ebba St. Clair (St. Claire)	30.00	15.00	9.00
35	Johnny Wyrostek	30.00	15.00	9.00
36	Jim Piersall	40.00	20.00	12.00
37	Hal Jeffcoat	30.00	15.00	9.00
38	Dave Cole	30.00	15.00	9.00
39	Casey Stengel	300.00	150.00	90.00
40	Larry Jansen	30.00	15.00	9.00
41	Bob Ramazotti	30.00	15.00	9.00
42	Howie Judson	30.00	15.00	9.00
43	Hal Bevan	30.00	15.00	9.00
44	Jim Delsing	30.00	15.00	9.00
45	Irv Noren	32.00	16.00	9.50
46	Bucky Harris	60.00	30.00	18.00
47	Jack Lohrke	30.00	15.00	9.00
48	Steve Ridzik	30.00	15.00	9.00
49	Floyd Baker	30.00	15.00	9.00
50	Emil "Dutch" Leonard	30.00	15.00	9.00
51	Lou Burdette	50.00	25.00	15.00
52	Ralph Branca	40.00	20.00	12.00
53	Morris Martin	30.00	15.00	9.00
54	Bill Miller	32.00	16.00	9.50
55	Don Johnson	30.00	15.00	9.00
56	Roy Smalley	30.00	15.00	9.00
57	Andy Pafko	30.00	15.00	9.00
58	Jim Konstanty	30.00	15.00	9.00
59	Duane Pillette	30.00	15.00	9.00
60	Billy Cox	30.00	15.00	9.00
61	Tom Gorman	32.00	16.00	9.50
62	Keith Thomas	30.00	15.00	9.00
63	Steve Gromek	27.00	11.00	6.50
64	Andy Hansen	45.00	13.50	6.50

1954 Bowman

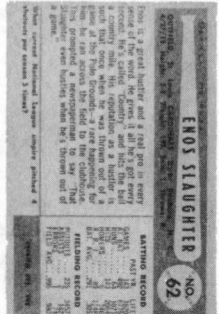

Bowman's 1954 set consists of 224 full-color cards that measure 2-1/2" by 3-3/4". It is believed that contractual problems caused the pulling of card #66 (Ted Williams) from the set, creating one of the most sought-after scarcities of the post-war era. The Williams card was replaced by Jim Piersall (who is also #210) in subsequent print runs. The set contains over 40 variations, most involving statistical errors on the card backs that were corrected. Neither variation carries a premium value as both varieties appear to have been printed in equal amounts. The complete set price that follows does not include all variations or #66 Williams.

		NR MT	EX	VG
	Complete Set:	4000.00	2000.00	1200.
	Common Player: 1-224	7.00	3.50	2.00
1	Phil Rizzuto	150.00	60.00	38.00
2	Jack Jensen	15.00	7.50	4.50
3	Marion Fricano	7.00	3.50	2.00
4	Bob Hooper	7.00	3.50	2.00
5	William Hunter	7.00	3.50	2.00
6	Nelson Fox	20.00	10.00	6.00
7	Walter Dropo	7.00	3.50	2.00
8	James F. Busby	7.00	3.50	2.00
9	Dave Williams	7.00	3.50	2.00
10	Carl Daniel Erskine	10.00	5.00	3.00
11	Sid Gordon	7.00	3.50	2.00
12a	Roy McMillan (551/1290 At Bat)	6.00	3.00	1.75
12b	Roy McMillan (557/1296 At Bat)	6.00	3.00	1.75
13	Paul Minner	7.00	3.50	2.00
14	Gerald Staley	7.00	3.50	2.00
15	Richie Ashburn	25.00	12.50	7.50
16	Jim Wilson	7.00	3.50	2.00
17	Tom Gorman	8.00	4.00	2.50
18	Walter "Hoot" Evers	7.00	3.50	2.00
19	Bobby Shantz	7.00	3.50	2.00
20	Artie Houtteman	7.00	3.50	2.00
21	Victor Wertz	6.00	3.00	1.75
22a	Sam Mele (213/1661 Putouts)	6.00	3.00	1.75
22b	Sam Mele (217/1665 Putouts)	6.00	3.00	1.75
23	*Harvey Kuenn*	25.00	12.50	7.50
24	Bob Porterfield	7.00	3.50	2.00
25a	Wes Westrum (1.000/.987 Field Avg.)	6.00	3.00	1.75
25b	Wes Westrum (.982/.986 Field Avg.)	6.00	3.00	1.75
26a	Billy Cox (1.000/.960 Field Avg.)	7.00	3.50	2.00
26b	Billy Cox (.972/.960 Field Avg.)	7.00	3.50	2.00
27	Richard Roy Cole	7.00	3.50	2.00
28a	Jim Greengrass (Birthplace Addison, N.J.)	6.00	3.00	1.75
28b	Jim Greengrass (Birthplace Addison, N.Y.)	6.00	3.00	1.75
29	Johnny Klippstein	7.00	3.50	2.00
30	Delbert Rice Jr.	7.00	3.50	2.00
31	"Smoky" Burgess	6.00	3.00	1.75
32	Del Crandall	6.00	3.00	1.75
33a	Victor Raschi (no traded line)	10.00	5.00	3.00
33b	Victor Raschi (with traded line)	25.00	12.50	7.50
34	Sammy White	7.00	3.50	2.00
35a	Eddie Joost (quiz answer is 8)	6.00	3.00	1.75
35b	Eddie Joost (quiz answer is 33)	6.00	3.00	1.75
36	George Strickland	7.00	3.50	2.00
37	Dick Kokos	7.00	3.50	2.00
38a	Orestes Minoso (.895/.961 Field Avg.)	8.00	4.00	2.50
38b	Orestes Minoso (.963/.963 Field Avg.)	8.00	4.00	2.50
39	Ned Garver	7.00	3.50	2.00
40	Gil Coan	7.00	3.50	2.00
41a	Alvin Dark (.986/.960 Field Avg.)	8.00	4.00	2.50
41b	Alvin Dark (.968/.960 Field Avg.)	8.00	4.00	2.50
42	Billy Loes	7.00	3.50	2.00
43a	Robert B. Friend (20 shutouts in quiz question)	7.00	3.50	2.00
43b	Robert B. Friend (16 shutouts in quiz question)	7.00	3.50	2.00
44	Harry Perkowski	7.00	3.50	2.00
45	Ralph Kiner	40.00	20.00	12.00
46	Eldon Repulski	7.00	3.50	2.00
47a	Granville Hamner (.970/.953 Field Avg.)	6.00	3.00	1.75
47b	Granville Hamner (.953/.951 Field Avg.)	6.00	3.00	1.75
48	Jack Dittmer	7.00	3.50	2.00
49	Harry Byrd	8.00	4.00	2.50
50	George Kell	25.00	12.50	7.50

		NR MT	EX	VG
51	Alex Kellner	7.00	3.50	2.00
52	Myron N. Ginsberg	7.00	3.50	2.00
53a	Don Lenhardt (.969/.984 Field Avg.)			
		6.00	3.00	1.75
53b	Don Lenhardt (.966/.983 Field Avg.)			
		6.00	3.00	1.75
54	Alfonso Carrasquel	7.00	3.50	2.00
55	Jim Delsing	7.00	3.50	2.00
56	Maurice M. McDermott	7.00	3.50	2.00
57	Hoyt Wilhelm	25.00	12.50	7.50
58	"Pee Wee" Reese	60.00	30.00	18.00
59	Robert D. Schultz	7.00	3.50	2.00
60	Fred Baczewski	7.00	3.50	2.00
61a	Eddie Miksis (.954/.962 Field Avg.)			
		6.00	3.00	1.75
61b	Eddie Miksis (.954/.961 Field Avg.)			
		6.00	3.00	1.75
62	Enos Slaughter	25.00	12.50	7.50
63	Earl Torgeson	7.00	3.50	2.00
64	Ed Mathews	50.00	25.00	15.00
65	Mickey Mantle	675.00	325.00	175.00
66a	Ted Williams	2750.00	1370.00	825.00
66b	Jimmy Piersall	90.00	45.00	27.00
67a	Carl Scheib (.306 Pct. with two lines under bio)	6.00	3.00	1.75
67b	Carl Scheib (.306 Pct. with one line under bio)	6.00	3.00	1.75
67c	Carl Scheib (.300 Pct.)	6.00	3.00	1.75
68	Bob Avila	6.00	3.00	1.75
69	Clinton Courtney	7.00	3.50	2.00
70	Willard Marshall	7.00	3.50	2.00
71	Ted Gray	7.00	3.50	2.00
72	Ed Yost	7.00	3.50	2.00
73	Don Mueller	7.00	3.50	2.00
74	James Gilliam	12.00	6.00	3.50
75	Max Surkont	7.00	3.50	2.00
76	Joe Nuxhall	6.00	3.00	1.75
77	Bob Rush	7.00	3.50	2.00
78	Sal A. Yvars	7.00	3.50	2.00
79	Curt Simmons	6.00	3.00	1.75
80a	John Logan (106 Runs)	6.00	3.00	1.75
80b	John Logan (100 Runs)	6.00	3.00	1.75
81a	Jerry Coleman (1.000/.975 Field Avg.)	8.00	4.00	2.50
81b	Jerry Coleman (.952/.975 Field Avg.)	8.00	4.00	2.50
82a	Bill Goodman (.965/.986 Field Avg.)			
		6.00	3.00	1.75
82b	Bill Goodman (.972/.985 Field Avg.)			
		6.00	3.00	1.75
83	Ray Murray	7.00	3.50	2.00
84	Larry Doby	8.00	4.00	2.50
85a	Jim Dyck (.926/.956 Field Avg.)	6.00	3.00	1.75
85b	Jim Dyck (.947/.960 Field Avg.)	6.00	3.00	1.75
86	Harry Dorish	7.00	3.50	2.00
87	Don Lund	7.00	3.50	2.00
88	Tommy Umphlett	7.00	3.50	2.00
89	Willie May (Mays)	300.00	120.00	75.00
90	Roy Campanella	150.00	60.00	38.00
91	Cal Abrams	7.00	3.50	2.00
92	Kenneth David Raffensberger	7.00	3.50	2.00
93a	Bill Serena (.983/.966 Field Avg.)	6.00	3.00	1.75
93b	Bill Serena (.977/.966 Field Avg.)	6.00	3.00	1.75
94a	Solly Hemus (476/1343 Assists)	6.00	3.00	1.75
94b	Solly Hemus (477/1343 Assists)	6.00	3.00	1.75
95	Robin Roberts	25.00	12.50	7.50
96	Joe Adcock	7.00	3.50	2.00
97	Gil McDougald	12.00	6.00	3.50
98	Ellis Kinder	7.00	3.50	2.00
99a	Peter Suder (.985/.974 Field Avg.)			
		6.00	3.00	1.75
99b	Peter Suder (.978/.974 Field Avg.)			
		6.00	3.00	1.75
100	Mike Garcia	6.00	3.00	1.75
101	*Don James Larsen*	30.00	15.00	9.00
102	Bill Pierce	6.00	3.00	1.75
103a	Stephen Souchock (144/1192 Putouts)	6.00	3.00	1.75
103b	Stephen Souchock (147/1195 Putouts)	6.00	3.00	1.75
104	Frank Spec Shea	7.00	3.50	2.00
105a	Sal Maglie (quiz answer is 8)	7.00	3.50	2.00
105b	Sal Maglie (quiz answer is 1904)	7.00	3.50	2.00
106	"Clem" Labine	7.00	3.50	2.00
107	Paul E. LaPalme	7.00	3.50	2.00
108	Bobby Adams	7.00	3.50	2.00
109	Roy Smalley	7.00	3.50	2.00
110	Al Schoendienst	30.00	15.00	9.00
111	Murry Monroe Dickson	7.00	3.50	2.00
112	Andy Pafko	6.00	3.00	1.75
113	Allie Reynolds	12.00	6.00	3.50

		NR MT	EX	VG
114	Willard Nixon	7.00	3.50	2.00
115	Don Bollweg	7.00	3.50	2.00
116	Luscious Luke Easter	7.00	3.50	2.00
117	Dick Kryhoski	7.00	3.50	2.00
118	Robert R. Boyd	7.00	3.50	2.00
119	Fred Hatfield	7.00	3.50	2.00
120	Mel Hoderlein	7.00	3.50	2.00
121	Ray Katt	7.00	3.50	2.00
122	Carl Furillo	15.00	7.50	4.50
123	Toby Atwell	7.00	3.50	2.00
124a	Gus Bell (15/27 Errors)	6.00	3.00	1.75
124b	Gus Bell (11/26 Errors)	6.00	3.00	1.75
125	Warren Hacker	7.00	3.50	2.00
126	Cliff Chambers	7.00	3.50	2.00
127	Del Ennis	6.00	3.00	1.75
128	Ebba St Claire	7.00	3.50	2.00
129	Hank Bauer	15.00	7.50	4.50
130	Milt Bolling	7.00	3.50	2.00
131	Joe Astroth	7.00	3.50	2.00
132	Bob Feller	70.00	35.00	21.00
133	Duane Pillette	7.00	3.50	2.00
134	Luis Aloma	7.00	3.50	2.00
135	Johnny Pesky	6.00	3.00	1.75
136	Clyde Vollmer	7.00	3.50	2.00
137	Elmer N. Corwin Jr.	7.00	3.50	2.00
138a	Gil Hodges (.993/.991 Field Avg.)			
		50.00	25.00	15.00
138b	Gil Hodges (.992/.991 Field Avg.)			
		55.00	28.00	16.50
139a	Preston Ward (.961/.992 Field Avg.)			
		6.00	3.00	1.75
139b	Preston Ward (.990/.992 Field Avg.)			
		6.00	3.00	1.75
140a	Saul Rogovin (7-12 Won/Lost with 2 Strikeouts)	6.00	3.00	1.75
140b	Saul Rogovin (7-12 Won/Lost with 62 Strikeouts)	6.00	3.00	1.75
140c	Saul Rogovin (8-12 Won/Lost)	6.00	3.00	1.75
141	Joe Garagiola	35.00	17.50	10.50
142	Al Brazle	7.00	3.50	2.00
143	Puddin Head Jones	7.00	3.50	2.00
144	Ernie Johnson	7.00	3.50	2.00
145a	Billy Martin (.985/.983 Field Avg.)			
		50.00	25.00	15.00
145b	Billy Martin (.983/.982 Field Avg.)			
		50.00	25.00	15.00
146	Dick Gernert	7.00	3.50	2.00
147	Joe DeMaestri	7.00	3.50	2.00
148	Dale Mitchell	7.00	3.50	2.00
149	Bob Young	7.00	3.50	2.00
150	Cass Michaels	7.00	3.50	2.00
151	Patrick J. Mullin	7.00	3.50	2.00
152	Mickey Vernon	6.00	3.00	1.75
153a	Whitey Lockman (100/331 Assists)			
		6.00	3.00	1.75
153b	Whitey Lockman (102/333 Assists)			
		6.00	3.00	1.75
154	Don Newcombe	15.00	7.50	4.50
155	*Frank J. Thomas*	6.00	3.00	1.75
156a	Everett Lamar Bridges (320/467 Assists)	6.00	3.00	1.75
156b	Everett Lamar Bridges (328/475 Assists)	6.00	3.00	1.75
157	Omar Lown	7.00	3.50	2.00
158	Stu Miller	7.00	3.50	2.00
159	John Lindell	7.00	3.50	2.00
160	Danny O'Connell	7.00	3.50	2.00
161	Yogi Berra	125.00	62.00	37.00
162	Ted Lepcio	7.00	3.50	2.00
163a	Dave Philley (152 Games with no traded line)	7.00	3.50	2.00
163b	Dave Philley (152 Games with traded line)	25.00	12.50	7.50
163c	Dave Philley (157 Games with traded line)	7.00	3.50	2.00
164	Early "Gus" Wynn	35.00	17.50	10.50
165	Johnny Groth	7.00	3.50	2.00
166	Sandalio Consuegra	7.00	3.50	2.00
167	Bill Hoeft	7.00	3.50	2.00
168	Edward Fitzgerald (Fitz Gerald)	7.00	3.50	2.00
169	Larry Jansen	7.00	3.50	2.00
170	Edwin D. Snider	125.00	62.00	40.00
171	Carlos Bernier	7.00	3.50	2.00
172	Andy Seminick	7.00	3.50	2.00
173	Dee V. Fondy Jr.	7.00	3.50	2.00
174a	Peter Paul Castiglione (.966/.959 Field Avg.)	6.00	3.00	1.75
174b	Peter Paul Castiglione (.970/.959 Field Avg.)	6.00	3.00	1.75
175	Melvin E. Clark	7.00	3.50	2.00
176	Vernon Bickford	7.00	3.50	2.00

		NR MT	EX	VG
177	Edward Ford	75.00	38.00	23.00
178	Del Wilber	7.00	3.50	2.00
179a	Morris Martin (44 ERA)	6.00	3.00	1.75
179b	Morris Martin (4.44 ERA)	6.00	3.00	1.75
180	Joe Tipton	7.00	3.50	2.00
181	Lester Moss	7.00	3.50	2.00
182	Sherman Lollar	6.00	3.00	1.75
183	Matt Batts	7.00	3.50	2.00
184	Mickey Grasso	7.00	3.50	2.00
185a	*Daryl Spencer* (.941/.944 Field Avg.)			
		6.00	3.00	1.75
185b	*Daryl Spencer* (.933/.936 Field Avg.)			
		6.00	3.00	1.75
186	Russell Meyer	7.00	3.50	2.00
187	Verne Law (Vern)	6.00	3.00	1.75
188	Frank Smith	7.00	3.50	2.00
189	Ransom Jackson	7.00	3.50	2.00
190	Joe Presko	7.00	3.50	2.00
191	Karl A. Drews	7.00	3.50	2.00
192	Selva L. Burdette	7.00	3.50	2.00
193	Eddie Robinson	8.00	4.00	2.50
194	Sid Hudson	7.00	3.50	2.00
195	Bob Cain	7.00	3.50	2.00
196	Bob Lemon	30.00	15.00	9.00
197	Lou Kretlow	7.00	3.50	2.00
198	Virgil Trucks	6.00	3.00	1.75
199	Steve Gromek	7.00	3.50	2.00
200	C. Marrero	7.00	3.50	2.00
201	Bob Thomson	7.00	3.50	2.00
202	George Shuba	7.00	3.50	2.00
203	Vic Janowicz	7.00	3.50	2.00
204	Jack Collum	7.00	3.50	2.00
205	Hal Jeffcoat	7.00	3.50	2.00
206	Steve Bilko	7.00	3.50	2.00
207	Stan Lopata	7.00	3.50	2.00
208	Johnny Antonelli	6.00	3.00	1.75
209	Gene Woodling (photo reversed)	10.00	5.00	3.00
210	Jimmy Piersall	12.00	6.00	3.50
211	Alfred James Robertson Jr.	7.00	3.50	2.00
212a	Owen L. Friend (.964/.957 Field Avg.)			
		6.00	3.00	1.75
212b	Owen L. Friend (.967/.958 Field Avg.)			
		6.00	3.00	1.75
213	Dick Littlefield	7.00	3.50	2.00
214	Ferris Fain	6.00	3.00	1.75
215	Johnny Bucha	7.00	3.50	2.00
216a	Jerry Snyder (.988/.988 Field Avg.)			
		6.00	3.00	1.75
216b	Jerry Snyder (.968/.968 Field Avg.)			
		6.00	3.00	1.75
217a	Henry Thompson (.956/.951 Field Avg.)			
		6.00	3.00	1.75
217b	Henry Thompson (.958/.952 Field Avg.)			
		6.00	3.00	1.75
218	Preacher Roe	12.00	6.00	3.50
219	Hal Rice	7.00	3.50	2.00
220	Hobie Landrith	7.00	3.50	2.00
221	Frank Baumholtz	7.00	3.50	2.00
222	Memo Luna	7.00	3.50	2.00
223	Steve Ridzik	7.00	2.50	1.50
224	William Bruton	30.00	9.00	4.00

1955 Bowman

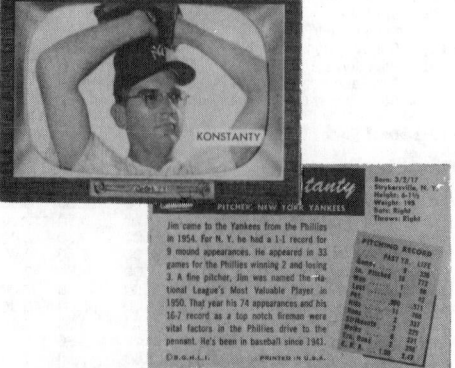

Bowman produced its final baseball card set in 1955, a popular issue which has player photographs placed inside a television set design. The set consists of 320 cards that measure 2-1/2" by 3-3/4" in size. The high-numbered cards (#'s 225-320) are scarcest in the set and include 31 umpire cards.

		NR MT	EX	VG
Complete Set:		4500.00	2300.00	1350.
Common Player: 1-224		5.00	2.50	1.50
Common Player: 225-320		15.00	7.50	4.50
1	Hoyt Wilhelm	100.00	20.00	6.00
2	Al Dark	15.00	7.50	4.50
3	Joe Coleman	5.00	2.50	1.50
4	Eddie Waitkus	5.00	2.50	1.50
5	Jim Robertson	5.00	2.50	1.50
6	Pete Suder	5.00	2.50	1.50
7	Gene Baker	5.00	2.50	1.50
8	Warren Hacker	5.00	2.50	1.50
9	Gil McDougald	10.00	5.00	3.00
10	Phil Rizzuto	40.00	20.00	12.00
11	Billy Bruton	5.00	2.50	1.50
12	Andy Pafko	6.00	3.00	1.75
13	Clyde Vollmer	5.00	2.50	1.50
14	Gus Keriazakos	5.00	2.50	1.50
15	*Frank Sullivan*	6.00	3.00	1.75
16	Jim Piersall	7.00	3.50	2.00
17	Del Ennis	6.00	3.00	1.75
18	Stan Lopata	5.00	2.50	1.50
19	Bobby Avila	5.00	2.50	1.50
20	Al Smith	5.00	2.50	1.50
21	Don Hoak	7.00	3.50	2.00
22	Roy Campanella	100.00	50.00	30.00
23	Al Kaline	100.00	50.00	30.00
24	Al Aber	5.00	2.50	1.50
25	Orestes "Minnie" Minoso	10.00	5.00	3.00
26	Virgil Trucks	6.00	3.00	1.75
27	Preston Ward	5.00	2.50	1.50
28	Dick Cole	5.00	2.50	1.50
29	Al "Red" Schoendienst	30.00	15.00	10.50
30	Bill Sarni	5.00	2.50	1.50
31	Johnny Temple	5.00	2.50	1.50
32	Wally Post	5.00	2.50	1.50
33	Nelson Fox	18.00	9.00	5.50
34	Clint Courtney	5.00	2.50	1.50
35	Bill Tuttle	5.00	2.50	1.50
36	Wayne Belardi	5.00	2.50	1.50
37	Harold "Pee Wee" Reese	60.00	30.00	18.00
38	Early Wynn	20.00	10.00	6.00
39	Bob Darnell	6.00	3.00	1.75
40	Vic Wertz	6.00	3.00	1.75
41	Mel Clark	5.00	2.50	1.50
42	Bob Greenwood	5.00	2.50	1.50
43	Bob Buhl	6.00	3.00	1.75
44	Danny O'Connell	5.00	2.50	1.50
45	Tom Umphlett	5.00	2.50	1.50
46	Mickey Vernon	6.00	3.00	1.75
47	Sammy White	5.00	2.50	1.50
48a	Milt Bolling (Frank Bolling back)	6.00	3.00	1.75
48b	Milt Bolling (Milt Bolling back)	15.00	7.50	4.50
49	Jim Greengrass	5.00	2.50	1.50
50	Hobie Landrith	5.00	2.50	1.50
51	Elvin Tappe	5.00	2.50	1.50
52	Hal Rice	5.00	2.50	1.50
53	Alex Kellner	5.00	2.50	1.50
54	Don Bollweg	5.00	2.50	1.50
55	Cal Abrams	5.00	2.50	1.50
56	Billy Cox	5.00	2.50	1.50
57	Bob Friend	6.00	3.00	1.75
58	Frank Thomas	5.00	2.50	1.50
59	Ed "Whitey" Ford	60.00	30.00	18.00
60	Enos Slaughter	20.00	10.00	6.00
61	Paul LaPalme	5.00	2.50	1.50
62	Royce Lint	5.00	2.50	1.50
63	Irv Noren	8.00	4.00	2.50
64	Curt Simmons	6.00	3.00	1.75
65	*Don Zimmer*	25.00	12.50	7.50
66	George Shuba	6.00	3.00	1.75
67	Don Larsen	15.00	7.50	4.50
68	*Elston Howard*	30.00	15.00	9.00
69	Bill Hunter	8.00	4.00	2.50
70	Lou Burdette	7.00	3.50	2.00
71	Dave Jolly	5.00	2.50	1.50
72	Chet Nichols	5.00	2.50	1.50
73	Eddie Yost	5.00	2.50	1.50
74	Jerry Snyder	5.00	2.50	1.50
75	Brooks Lawrence	5.00	2.50	1.50
76	Tom Poholsky	5.00	2.50	1.50
77	Jim McDonald	5.00	2.50	1.50
78	Gil Coan	5.00	2.50	1.50
79	Willie Miranda	5.00	2.50	1.50
80	Lou Limmer	5.00	2.50	1.50
81	Bob Morgan	5.00	2.50	1.50
82	Lee Walls	5.00	2.50	1.50
83	Max Surkont	5.00	2.50	1.50

		NR MT	EX	VG			NR MT	EX	VG
84	George Freese	5.00	2.50	1.50	166	Jim Busby	5.00	2.50	1.50
85	Cass Michaels	5.00	2.50	1.50	167	Bob Grim	8.00	4.00	2.50
86	Ted Gray	5.00	2.50	1.50	168	Larry "Yogi" Berra	80.00	40.00	25.00
87	Randy Jackson	5.00	2.50	1.50	169	Carl Furillo	15.00	7.50	4.50
88	Steve Bilko	5.00	2.50	1.50	170	Carl Erskine	10.00	5.00	3.00
89	Lou Boudreau	20.00	10.00	6.00	171	Robin Roberts	20.00	10.00	6.00
90	Art Ditmar	5.00	2.50	1.50	172	Willie Jones	5.00	2.50	1.50
91	Dick Marlowe	5.00	2.50	1.50	173	Al "Chico" Carrasquel	5.00	2.50	1.50
92	George Zuverink	5.00	2.50	1.50	174	Sherman Lollar	6.00	3.00	1.75
93	Andy Seminick	5.00	2.50	1.50	175	Wilmer Shantz	5.00	2.50	1.50
94	Hank Thompson	5.00	2.50	1.50	176	Joe DeMaestri	5.00	2.50	1.50
95	Sal Maglie	10.00	5.00	3.00	177	Willard Nixon	5.00	2.50	1.50
96	Ray Narleski	5.00	2.50	1.50	178	Tom Brewer	5.00	2.50	1.50
97	John Podres	15.00	7.50	4.50	179	Hank Aaron	200.00	100.00	60.00
98	James "Junior" Gilliam	15.00	7.50	4.50	180	Johnny Logan	5.00	2.50	1.50
99	Jerry Coleman	8.00	4.00	2.50	181	Eddie Miksis	5.00	2.50	1.50
100	Tom Morgan	8.00	4.00	2.50	182	Bob Rush	5.00	2.50	1.50
101a	Don Johnson (Ernie Johnson (Braves) on front)	6.00	3.00	1.75	183	Ray Katt	5.00	2.50	1.50
101b	Don Johnson (Don Johnson (Orioles) on front)	15.00	7.50	4.50	184	Willie Mays	200.00	100.00	60.00
					185	Vic Raschi	6.00	3.00	1.75
102	Bobby Thomson	10.00	5.00	3.00	186	Alex Grammas	5.00	2.50	1.50
103	Eddie Mathews	60.00	30.00	18.00	187	Fred Hatfield	5.00	2.50	1.50
104	Bob Porterfield	5.00	2.50	1.50	188	Ned Garver	5.00	2.50	1.50
105	Johnny Schmitz	5.00	2.50	1.50	189	Jack Collum	5.00	2.50	1.50
106	Del Rice	5.00	2.50	1.50	190	Fred Baczewski	5.00	2.50	1.50
107	Solly Hemus	5.00	2.50	1.50	191	Bob Lemon	25.00	12.50	7.50
108	Lou Kretlow	5.00	2.50	1.50	192	George Strickland	5.00	2.50	1.50
109	Vern Stephens	5.00	2.50	1.50	193	Howie Judson	5.00	2.50	1.50
110	Bob Miller	5.00	2.50	1.50	194	Joe Nuxhall	6.00	3.00	1.75
111	Steve Ridzik	5.00	2.50	1.50	195a	Erv Palica (no traded line on back)	7.00	3.50	2.00
112	Gran Hamner	5.00	2.50	1.50	195b	Erv Palica (traded line on back)	25.00	12.50	7.50
113	Bob Hall	5.00	2.50	1.50	196	Russ Meyer	6.00	3.00	1.75
114	Vic Janowicz	5.00	2.50	1.50	197	Ralph Kiner	30.00	15.00	9.00
115	Roger Bowman	5.00	2.50	1.50	198	Dave Pope	5.00	2.50	1.50
116	Sandalio Consuegra	5.00	2.50	1.50	199	Vernon Law	6.00	3.00	1.75
117	Johnny Groth	5.00	2.50	1.50	200	Dick Littlefield	5.00	2.50	1.50
118	Bobby Adams	5.00	2.50	1.50	201	Allie Reynolds	15.00	7.50	4.50
119	Joe Astroth	5.00	2.50	1.50	202	Mickey Mantle	400.00	175.00	100.00
120	Ed Burtschy	5.00	2.50	1.50	203	Steve Gromek	5.00	2.50	1.50
121	Rufus Crawford	5.00	2.50	1.50	204a	*Frank Bolling* (Milt Bolling back)	6.00	3.00	1.75
122	Al Corwin	5.00	2.50	1.50	204b	*Frank Bolling* (Frank Bolling back)			
123	Marv Grissom	5.00	2.50	1.50			20.00	10.00	6.00
124	Johnny Antonelli	6.00	3.00	1.75	205	Eldon "Rip" Repulski	5.00	2.50	1.50
125	Paul Giel	5.00	2.50	1.50	206	Ralph Beard	5.00	2.50	1.50
126	Billy Goodman	5.00	2.50	1.50	207	Frank Shea	5.00	2.50	1.50
127	Hank Majeski	5.00	2.50	1.50	208	Eddy Fitzgerald (Fitz Gerald)	5.00	2.50	1.50
128	Mike Garcia	6.00	3.00	1.75	209	Forrest "Smoky" Burgess	6.00	3.00	1.75
129	Hal Naragon	5.00	2.50	1.50	210	Earl Torgeson	5.00	2.50	1.50
130	Richie Ashburn	15.00	7.50	4.50	211	John "Sonny" Dixon	5.00	2.50	1.50
131	Willard Marshall	5.00	2.50	1.50	212	Jack Dittmer	5.00	2.50	1.50
132a	Harvey Kueen (incorrect spelling on back)	7.00	3.50	2.00	213	George Kell	25.00	12.50	7.50
					214	Billy Pierce	6.00	3.00	1.75
132b	Harvey Kuenn (correct spelling on back)	30.00	15.00	9.00	215	Bob Kuzava	5.00	2.50	1.50
					216	Preacher Roe	6.00	3.00	1.75
133	Charles King	5.00	2.50	1.50	217	Del Crandall	6.00	3.00	1.75
134	Bob Feller	55.00	28.00	16.50	218	Joe Adcock	6.00	3.00	1.75
135	Lloyd Merriman	5.00	2.50	1.50	219	Whitey Lockman	5.00	2.50	1.50
136	Rocky Bridges	5.00	2.50	1.50	220	Jim Hearn	5.00	2.50	1.50
137	Bob Talbot	5.00	2.50	1.50	221	Hector "Skinny" Brown	5.00	2.50	1.50
138	Davey Williams	5.00	2.50	1.50	222	Russ Kemmerer	5.00	2.50	1.50
139	Billy & Bobby Shantz	7.00	3.50	2.00	223	Hal Jeffcoat	5.00	2.50	1.50
140	Bobby Shantz	6.00	3.00	1.75	224	Dee Fondy	5.00	2.50	1.50
141	Wes Westrum	6.00	3.00	1.75	225	Paul Richards	11.00	5.50	3.25
142	Rudy Regalado	5.00	2.50	1.50	226	W.F. McKinley (umpire)	15.00	7.50	4.50
143	Don Newcombe	10.00	5.00	3.00	227	Frank Baumholtz	10.00	5.00	3.00
144	Art Houtteman	5.00	2.50	1.50	228	John M. Phillips	10.00	5.00	3.00
145	Bob Nieman	5.00	2.50	1.50	229	Jim Brosnan	11.00	5.50	3.25
146	Don Liddle	5.00	2.50	1.50	230	Al Brazle	10.00	5.00	3.00
147	Sam Mele	5.00	2.50	1.50	231	Jim Konstanty	15.00	7.50	4.50
148	Bob Chakales	5.00	2.50	1.50	232	Birdie Tebbetts	10.00	5.00	3.00
149	Cloyd Boyer	5.00	2.50	1.50	233	Bill Serena	10.00	5.00	3.00
150	Bill Klaus	5.00	2.50	1.50	234	Dick Bartell	10.00	5.00	3.00
151	Jim Brideweser	5.00	2.50	1.50	235	J.A. Paparella (umpire)	15.00	7.50	4.50
152	Johnny Klippstein	5.00	2.50	1.50	236	Murray Dickson (Murry)	10.00	5.00	3.00
153	Eddie Robinson	8.00	4.00	2.50	237	Johnny Wyrostek	10.00	5.00	3.00
154	*Frank Lary*	7.00	3.50	2.00	238	Eddie Stanky	11.00	5.50	3.25
155	Gerry Staley	5.00	2.50	1.50	239	Edwin A. Rommel (umpire)	15.00	7.50	4.50
156	Jim Hughes	6.00	3.00	1.75	240	Billy Loes	11.00	5.50	3.25
157a	Ernie Johnson (Don Johnson (Orioles) picture on front)	6.00	3.00	1.75	241	John Pesky	11.00	5.50	3.25
					242	Ernie Banks	350.00	175.00	100.00
157b	Ernie Johnson (Ernie Johnson (Braves) picture on front)	15.00	7.50	4.50	243	Gus Bell	11.00	5.50	3.25
					244	Duane Pillette	10.00	5.00	3.00
158	Gil Hodges	40.00	20.00	12.00	245	Bill Miller	10.00	5.00	3.00
159	Harry Byrd	5.00	2.50	1.50	246	Hank Bauer	25.00	12.50	7.50
160	Bill Skowron	15.00	7.50	4.50	247	Dutch Leonard	10.00	5.00	3.00
161	Matt Batts	5.00	2.50	1.50	248	Harry Dorish	10.00	5.00	3.00
162	Charlie Maxwell	5.00	2.50	1.50	249	Billy Gardner	10.00	5.00	3.00
163	Sid Gordon	5.00	2.50	1.50	250	Larry Napp (umpire)	15.00	7.50	4.50
164	Toby Atwell	5.00	2.50	1.50	251	Stan Jok	10.00	5.00	3.00
165	Maurice McDermott	5.00	2.50	1.50	252	Roy Smalley	10.00	5.00	3.00

		NR MT	EX	VG
253	Jim Wilson	10.00	5.00	3.00
254	Bennett Flowers	10.00	5.00	3.00
255	Pete Runnels	11.00	5.50	3.25
256	Owen Friend	10.00	5.00	3.00
257	Tom Alston	10.00	5.00	3.00
258	John W. Stevens (umpire)	15.00	7.50	4.50
259	*Don Mossi*	15.00	7.50	4.50
260	Edwin H. Hurley (umpire)	15.00	7.50	4.50
261	Walt Moryn	11.00	5.50	3.25
262	Jim Lemon	11.00	5.50	3.25
263	Eddie Joost	10.00	5.00	3.00
264	Bill Henry	10.00	5.00	3.00
265	Albert J. Barlick (umpire)	80.00	40.00	25.00
266	Mike Fornieles	10.00	5.00	3.00
267	George (Jim) Honochick (umpire)	60.00	30.00	18.00
268	Roy Lee Hawes	10.00	5.00	3.00
269	Joe Amalfitano	10.00	5.00	3.00
270	Chico Fernandez	11.00	5.50	3.25
271	Bob Hooper	10.00	5.00	3.00
272	John Flaherty (umpire)	15.00	7.50	4.50
273	Emory "Bubba" Church	10.00	5.00	3.00
274	Jim Delsing	10.00	5.00	3.00
275	William T. Grieve (umpire)	15.00	7.50	4.50
276	Ivan Delock	10.00	5.00	3.00
277	Ed Runge (umpire)	15.00	7.50	4.50
278	*Charles Neal*	15.00	7.50	4.50
279	Hank Soar (umpire)	15.00	7.50	4.50
280	Clyde McCullough	10.00	5.00	3.00
281	Charles Berry (umpire)	15.00	7.50	4.50
282	Phil Cavarretta	11.00	5.50	3.25
283	Nestor Chylak (umpire)	15.00	7.50	4.50
284	William A. Jackowski (umpire)	15.00	7.50	4.50
285	Walt Dropo	11.00	5.50	3.25
286	Frank E. Secory (umpire)	15.00	7.50	4.50
287	Ron Mrozinski	10.00	5.00	3.00
288	Dick Smith	10.00	5.00	3.00
289	Arthur J. Gore (umpire)	15.00	7.50	4.50
290	Hershell Freeman	10.00	5.00	3.00
291	Frank Dascoli (umpire)	15.00	7.50	4.50
292	Marv Blaylock	10.00	5.00	3.00
293	Thomas D. Gorman (umpire)	15.00	7.50	4.50
294	Wally Moses	10.00	5.00	3.00
295	E. Lee Ballanfant (umpire)	15.00	7.50	4.50
296	*Bill Virdon*	25.00	12.50	7.50
297	L.R. "Dusty" Boggess (umpire)	15.00	7.50	4.50
298	Charlie Grimm	15.00	7.50	4.50
299	Lonnie Warneke (umpire)	15.00	7.50	4.50
300	Tommy Byrne	14.00	7.00	4.25
301	William R. Engeln (umpire)	15.00	7.50	4.50
302	*Frank Malzone*	15.00	7.50	4.50
303	J.B. "Jocko" Conlan (umpire)	90.00	45.00	30.00
304	Harry Chiti	10.00	5.00	3.00
305	Frank Umont (umpire)	15.00	7.50	4.50
306	Bob Cerv	15.00	7.50	4.50
307	R.A. "Babe" Pinelli (umpire)	15.00	7.50	4.50
308	Al Lopez	35.00	17.50	10.50
309	Hal H. Dixon (umpire)	15.00	7.50	4.50
310	Ken Lehman	11.00	5.50	3.25
311	Lawrence J. Goetz (umpire)	15.00	7.50	4.50
312	Bill Wight	10.00	5.00	3.00
313	A.J. Donatelli (umpire)	15.00	7.50	4.50
314	Dale Mitchell	10.00	5.00	3.00
315	Cal Hubbard (umpire)	80.00	40.00	25.00
316	Marion Fricano	10.00	5.00	3.00
317	Wm. R. Summers (umpire)	15.00	7.50	4.50
318	Sid Hudson	10.00	5.00	3.00
319	Albert B. Schroll	15.00	7.50	4.50
320	George D. Susce, Jr.	70.00	35.00	21.00

1989 Bowman

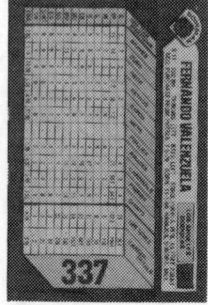

337

Topps, which purchased the Bowman Co. back in

1955, revived the Bowman name in 1989, issuing a 484-card set modeled after the 1953 Bowman cards. The cards are 2-1/2" by 3-3/4", slightly larger than a current standard-sized card. The fronts contain a full-color player photo, with facsimile autograph on the bottom and the Bowman logo in an upper corner. The unique card backs include a breakdown of the player's stats against each team in his league. A series of "Hot Rookie Stars" highlight the set. The cards were distributed in both wax packs and rack packs. Each pack included a special reproduction of a classic Bowman card with a sweepstakes on the back. The special cards said "reprint" on the front.

		MT	NR MT	EX
	Complete Set:	20.00	15.00	8.00
	Common Player:	.03	.02	.01
1	Oswald Peraza	.05	.04	.02
2	Brian Holton	.05	.04	.02
3	Jose Bautista	.05	.04	.02
4	Pete Harnisch	.10	.08	.04
5	Dave Schmidt	.03	.02	.01
6	Gregg Olson	.60	.45	.25
7	Jeff Ballard	.10	.08	.04
8	Bob Melvin	.03	.02	.01
9	Cal Ripken	.20	.15	.08
10	Randy Milligan	.08	.06	.03
11	Juan Bell	.15	.11	.06
12	Billy Ripken	.05	.04	.02
13	Jim Trabor	.03	.02	.01
14	Pete Stanicek	.03	.02	.01
15	Steve Finley	.20	.15	.08
16	Larry Sheets	.03	.02	.01
17	Phil Bradley	.05	.04	.02
18	Brady Anderson	.10	.08	.04
19	Lee Smith	.03	.02	.01
20	Tom Fischer	.15	.11	.06
21	Mike Boddicker	.03	.02	.01
22	Rob Murphy	.03	.02	.01
23	Wes Gardner	.03	.02	.01
24	John Dopson	.10	.08	.04
25	Bob Stanley	.03	.02	.01
26	Roger Clemens	.20	.15	.08
27	Rich Gedman	.03	.02	.01
28	Marty Barrett	.03	.02	.01
29	Luis Rivera	.03	.02	.01
30	Jody Reed	.05	.04	.02
31	Nick Esasky	.05	.04	.02
32	Wade Boggs	.40	.30	.15
33	Jim Rice	.10	.08	.04
34	Mike Greenwell	.40	.30	.15
35	Dwight Evans	.15	.11	.06
36	Ellis Burks	.25	.20	.10
37	Chuck Finley	.05	.04	.02
38	Kirk McCaskill	.05	.04	.02
39	Jim Abbott	1.00	.70	.40
40	Bryan Harvey	.05	.04	.02
41	Bert Blyleven	.08	.06	.03
42	Mike Witt	.03	.02	.01
43	Bob McClure	.03	.02	.01
44	Bill Schroeder	.03	.02	.01
45	Lance Parrish	.05	.04	.02
46	Dick Schofield	.03	.02	.01
47	Wally Joyner	.10	.08	.04
48	Jack Howell	.03	.02	.01
49	Johnny Ray	.03	.02	.01
50	Chili Davis	.05	.04	.02
51	Tony Armas	.03	.02	.01
52	Claudell Washington	.03	.02	.01
53	Brian Downing	.03	.02	.01
54	Devon White	.10	.08	.04
55	Bobby Thigpen	.08	.06	.03
56	Bill Long	.03	.02	.01
57	Jerry Reuss	.03	.02	.01
58	Shawn Hillegas	.03	.02	.01
59	Melido Perez	.05	.04	.02
60	Jeff Bittiger	.05	.04	.02
61	Jack McDowell	.03	.02	.01
62	Carlton Fisk	.10	.08	.04
63	Steve Lyons	.03	.02	.01
64	Ozzie Guillen	.05	.04	.02
65	Robin Ventura	.70	.50	.30
66	Fred Manrique	.03	.02	.01
67	Dan Pasqua	.03	.02	.01
68	Ivan Calderon	.03	.02	.01
69	Ron Kittle	.03	.02	.01
70	Daryl Boston	.03	.02	.01
71	Dave Gallagher	.05	.04	.02
72	Harold Baines	.08	.06	.03

		MT	NR MT	EX				MT	NR MT	EX
73	Charles Nagy	.20	.15	.08		164	Randy Bush	.03	.02	.01
74	John Farrell	.03	.02	.01		165	Dave LaPoint	.03	.02	.01
75	Kevin Wickander	.25	.20	.10		166	Andy Hawkins	.03	.02	.01
76	Greg Swindell	.15	.11	.06		167	Dave Righetti	.05	.04	.02
77	Mike Walker	.15	.11	.06		168	Lance McCullers	.03	.02	.01
78	Doug Jones	.05	.04	.02		169	Jimmy Jones	.03	.02	.01
79	Rich Yett	.03	.02	.01		170	Al Leiter	.03	.02	.01
80	Tom Candiotti	.03	.02	.01		171	John Candelaria	.03	.02	.01
81	Jesse Orosco	.03	.02	.01		172	Don Slaught	.03	.02	.01
82	Bud Black	.03	.02	.01		173	Jamie Quirk	.03	.02	.01
83	Andy Allanson	.03	.02	.01		174	Rafael Santana	.03	.02	.01
84	Pete O'Brien	.05	.04	.02		175	Mike Pagliarulo	.03	.02	.01
85	Jerry Browne	.05	.04	.02		176	Don Mattingly	.90	.70	.35
86	Brook Jacoby	.03	.02	.01		177	Ken Phelps	.03	.02	.01
87	Mark Lewis	.50	.40	.20		178	Steve Sax	.08	.06	.03
88	Luis Aguayo	.03	.02	.01		179	Dave Winfield	.20	.15	.08
89	Cory Snyder	.05	.04	.02		180	Stan Jefferson	.03	.02	.01
90	Oddibe McDowell	.05	.04	.02		181	Rickey Henderson	.40	.30	.15
91	Joe Carter	.15	.11	.06		182	Bob Brower	.03	.02	.01
92	Frank Tanana	.03	.02	.01		183	Roberto Kelly	.10	.08	.04
93	Jack Morris	.03	.02	.01		184	Curt Young	.03	.02	.01
94	Doyle Alexander	.03	.02	.01		185	Gene Nelson	.03	.02	.01
95	Steve Searcy	.08	.06	.03		186	Bob Welch	.03	.02	.01
96	Randy Bockus	.05	.04	.02		187	Rick Honeycutt	.03	.02	.01
97	Jeff Robinson	.05	.04	.02		188	Dave Stewart	.08	.06	.03
98	Mike Henneman	.05	.04	.02		189	Mike Moore	.08	.06	.03
99	Paul Gibson	.03	.02	.01		190	Dennis Eckersley	.08	.06	.03
100	Frank Williams	.03	.02	.01		191	Eric Plunk	.03	.02	.01
101	Matt Nokes	.05	.04	.02		192	Storm Davis	.03	.02	.01
102	Rico Brogna	.15	.11	.06		193	Terry Steinbach	.10	.08	.04
103	Lou Whitaker	.08	.06	.03		194	Ron Hassey	.03	.02	.01
104	Al Pedrique	.03	.02	.01		195	Stan Royer	.15	.11	.06
105	Alan Trammell	.05	.04	.02		196	Walt Weiss	.15	.11	.06
106	Chris Brown	.03	.02	.01		197	Mark McGwire	.40	.30	.15
107	Pat Sheridan	.03	.02	.01		198	Carney Lansford	.08	.06	.03
108	Gary Pettis	.03	.02	.01		199	Glenn Hubbard	.03	.02	.01
109	Keith Moreland	.03	.02	.01		200	Dave Henderson	.05	.04	.02
110	Mel Stottlemyre, Jr.	.15	.11	.06		201	Jose Canseco	1.00	.70	.40
111	Bret Saberhagen	.10	.08	.04		202	Dave Parker	.05	.04	.02
112	Floyd Bannister	.03	.02	.01		203	Scott Bankhead	.05	.04	.02
113	Jeff Montgomery	.05	.04	.02		204	Tom Niedenfuer	.03	.02	.01
114	Steve Farr	.05	.04	.02		205	Mark Langston	.15	.11	.06
115	Tom Gordon	.80	.60	.30		206	Erik Hanson	.15	.11	.06
116	Charlie Leibrandt	.03	.02	.01		207	Mike Jackson	.03	.02	.01
117	Mark Gubicza	.08	.06	.03		208	Dave Valle	.03	.02	.01
118	Mike MacFarlane	.03	.02	.01		209	Scott Bradley	.03	.02	.01
119	Bob Boone	.05	.04	.02		210	Harold Reynolds	.08	.06	.03
120	Kurt Stillwell	.05	.04	.02		211	Tino Martinez	1.25	.90	.50
121	George Brett	.15	.11	.06		212	Rich Renteria	.03	.02	.01
122	Frank White	.05	.04	.02		213	Rey Quinones	.03	.02	.01
123	Kevin Seitzer	.08	.06	.03		214	Jim Presley	.03	.02	.01
124	Willie Wilson	.03	.02	.01		215	Alvin Davis	.10	.08	.04
125	Pat Tabler	.03	.02	.01		216	Edgar Martinez	.03	.02	.01
126	Bo Jackson	.90	.70	.35		217	Darnell Coles	.03	.02	.01
127	Hugh Walker	.20	.15	.08		218	Jeffrey Leonard	.08	.06	.04
128	Danny Tartabull	.05	.04	.02		219	Jay Buhner	.03	.02	.01
129	Teddy Higuera	.08	.06	.03		220	Ken Griffey, Jr.	5.00	3.75	2.00
130	Don August	.03	.02	.01		221	Drew Hall	.03	.02	.01
131	Juan Nieves	.03	.02	.01		222	Bobby Witt	.03	.02	.01
132	Mike Birkbeck	.03	.02	.01		223	Jamie Moyer	.03	.02	.01
133	Dan Plesac	.05	.04	.02		224	Charlie Hough	.03	.02	.01
134	Chris Bosio	.05	.04	.02		225	Nolan Ryan	.70	.50	.30
135	Bill Wegman	.03	.02	.01		226	Jeff Russell	.05	.04	.02
136	Chuck Crim	.03	.02	.01		227	Jim Sundberg	.03	.02	.01
137	B.J. Surhoff	.05	.04	.02		228	Julio Franco	.15	.11	.06
138	Joey Meyer	.03	.02	.01		229	Buddy Bell	.03	.02	.01
139	Dale Sveum	.03	.02	.01		230	Scott Fletcher	.03	.02	.01
140	Paul Molitor	.08	.06	.03		231	Jeff Kunkel	.03	.02	.01
141	Jim Gantner	.03	.02	.01		232	Steve Buechele	.03	.02	.01
142	Gary Sheffield	1.25	.90	.50		233	Monty Fariss	.25	.20	.10
143	Greg Brock	.03	.02	.01		234	Rick Leach	.03	.02	.01
144	Robin Yount	.25	.20	.10		235	Ruben Sierra	.40	.30	.15
145	Glenn Braggs	.03	.02	.01		236	Cecil Espy	.05	.04	.02
146	Rob Deer	.03	.02	.01		237	Rafael Palmeiro	.10	.08	.04
147	Fred Toliver	.03	.02	.01		238	Pete Incaviglia	.03	.02	.01
148	Jeff Reardon	.03	.02	.01		239	Dave Steib	.05	.04	.02
149	Allan Anderson	.05	.04	.02		240	Jeff Musselman	.03	.02	.01
150	Frank Viola	.15	.11	.06		241	Mike Flanagan	.03	.02	.01
151	Shane Rawley	.03	.02	.01		242	Todd Stottlemyre	.05	.04	.02
152	Juan Berenguer	.03	.02	.01		243	Jimmy Key	.05	.04	.02
153	Johnny Ard	.20	.15	.08		244	Tony Castillo	.10	.08	.04
154	Tim Laudner	.03	.02	.01		245	Alex Sanchez	.05	.04	.02
155	Brian Harper	.03	.02	.01		246	Tom Henke	.03	.02	.01
156	Al Newman	.03	.02	.01		247	John Cerutti	.03	.02	.01
157	Kent Hrbek	.08	.06	.03		248	Ernie Whitt	.03	.02	.01
158	Gary Gaetti	.08	.06	.03		249	Bob Brenly	.03	.02	.01
159	Wally Backman	.03	.02	.01		250	Rance Mulliniks	.03	.02	.01
160	Gene Larkin	.03	.02	.01		251	Kelly Gruber	.10	.08	.04
161	Greg Gagne	.03	.02	.01		252	Ed Sprague	.20	.15	.08
162	Kirby Puckett	.35	.25	.14		253	Fred McGriff	.40	.30	.15
163	Danny Gladden	.03	.02	.01		254	Tony Fernandez	.08	.06	.03

		MT	NR MT	EX			MT	NR MT	EX
255	Tom Lawless	.03	.02	.01	346	Eddie Murray	.08	.06	.03
256	George Bell	.10	.08	.04	347	Mickey Hatcher	.03	.02	.01
257	Jesse Barfield	.05	.04	.02	348	Mike Sharperson	.03	.02	.01
258	Sandy Alomar	.20	.15	.08	349	John Shelby	.03	.02	.01
259	Ken Griffey	.30	.25	.12	350	Mike Marshall	.03	.02	.01
260	Cal Ripken, Sr.	.15	.11	.06	351	Kirk Gibson	.05	.04	.02
261	Mel Stottlemyre	.15	.11	.06	352	Mike Davis	.03	.02	.01
262	Zane Smith	.03	.02	.01	353	Bryn Smith	.03	.02	.01
263	Charlie Puleo	.03	.02	.01	354	Pascual Perez	.03	.02	.01
264	Derek Lilliquist	.15	.11	.06	355	Kevin Gross	.03	.02	.01
265	Paul Assenmacher	.03	.02	.01	356	Andy McGaffigan	.03	.02	.01
266	John Smoltz	.60	.45	.25	357	Brian Holman	.05	.04	.02
267	Tom Glavine	.10	.08	.04	358	Dave Wainhouse	.20	.15	.08
268	Steve Avery	1.00	.70	.40	359	Denny Martinez	.03	.02	.01
269	Pete Smith	.05	.04	.02	360	Tim Burke	.03	.02	.01
270	Jody Davis	.03	.02	.01	361	Nelson Santovenia	.08	.06	.04
271	Bruce Benedict	.03	.02	.01	362	Tim Wallach	.05	.04	.02
272	Andres Thomas	.03	.02	.01	363	Spike Owen	.03	.02	.01
273	Gerald Perry	.05	.04	.02	364	Rex Hudler	.03	.02	.01
274	Ron Gant	.05	.04	.02	365	Andres Galarraga	.08	.06	.03
275	Darrell Evans	.03	.02	.01	366	Otis Nixon	.03	.02	.01
276	Dale Murphy	.08	.06	.03	367	Hubie Brooks	.03	.02	.01
277	Dion James	.03	.02	.01	368	Mike Aldrete	.03	.02	.01
278	Lonnie Smith	.08	.06	.03	369	Rock Raines	.08	.06	.03
279	Geronimo Berroa	.05	.04	.02	370	Dave Martinez	.03	.02	.01
280	Steve Wilson	.20	.15	.08	371	Bob Ojeda	.03	.02	.01
281	Rick Suctcliffe	.05	.04	.02	372	Ron Darling	.05	.04	.02
282	Kevin Coffman	.03	.02	.01	373	Wally Whitehurst	.20	.15	.08
283	Mitch Williams	.10	.08	.04	374	Randy Myers	.05	.04	.02
284	Greg Maddux	.05	.04	.02	375	David Cone	.05	.04	.02
285	Paul Kilgus	.03	.02	.01	376	Doc Gooden	.25	.20	.10
286	Mike Harkey	.10	.08	.04	377	Sid Fernandez	.05	.04	.02
287	Lloyd McClendon	.05	.04	.02	378	Dave Proctor	.20	.15	.08
288	Damon Berryhill	.05	.04	.02	379	Gary Carter	.03	.02	.01
289	Ty Griffin	.60	.45	.25	380	Keith Miller	.05	.04	.02
290	Ryne Sandberg	.15	.11	.06	381	Gregg Jefferies	1.50	1.25	.60
291	Mark Grace	1.00	.70	.40	382	Tim Teufel	.03	.02	.01
292	Curt Wilkerson	.03	.02	.01	383	Kevin Elster	.03	.02	.01
293	Vance Law	.03	.02	.01	384	Dave Magadan	.03	.02	.01
294	Shawon Dunston	.08	.06	.04	385	Keith Hernandez	.05	.04	.02
295	Jerome Walton	1.25	.90	.50	386	Mookie Wilson	.05	.04	.02
296	Mitch Webster	.03	.02	.01	387	Darryl Strawberry	.40	.30	.15
297	Dwight Smith	.70	.50	.30	388	Kevin McReynolds	.10	.08	.04
298	Andre Dawson	.15	.11	.06	389	Mark Carreon	.05	.04	.02
299	Jeff Sellers	.03	.02	.01	390	Jeff Parrett	.05	.04	.02
300	Jose Rijo	.05	.04	.02	391	Mike Maddux	.03	.02	.01
301	John Franco	.05	.04	.02	392	Don Carman	.03	.02	.01
302	Rick Mahler	.03	.02	.01	393	Bruce Ruffin	.03	.02	.01
303	Ron Robinson	.03	.02	.01	394	Ken Howell	.03	.02	.01
304	Danny Jackson	.03	.02	.01	395	Steve Bedrosian	.05	.04	.02
305	Rob Dibble	.08	.06	.04	396	Floyd Youmans	.03	.02	.01
306	Tom Browning	.03	.02	.01	397	Larry McWilliams	.03	.02	.01
307	Bo Diaz	.03	.02	.01	398	Pat Combs	.40	.30	.15
308	Manny Trillo	.03	.02	.01	399	Steve Lake	.03	.02	.01
309	Chris Sabo	.15	.11	.06	400	Dickie Thon	.03	.02	.01
310	Ron Oester	.03	.02	.01	401	Ricky Jordan	.35	.25	.14
311	Barry Larkin	.15	.11	.06	402	Mike Schmidt	.60	.45	.25
312	Todd Benzinger	.05	.04	.02	403	Tom Herr	.03	.02	.01
313	Paul O'Neil	.05	.04	.02	404	Chris James	.03	.02	.01
314	Kal Daniels	.05	.04	.02	405	Juan Samuel	.08	.06	.03
315	Joel Youngblood	.03	.02	.01	406	Von Hayes	.08	.06	.03
316	Eric Davis	.25	.20	.10	407	Ron Jones	.15	.11	.06
317	Dave Smith	.05	.04	.03	408	Curt Ford	.03	.02	.01
318	Mark Portugal	.03	.02	.01	409	Bob Walk	.03	.02	.01
319	Brian Meyer	.03	.02	.01	410	Jeff Robinson	.03	.02	.01
320	Jim Deshaies	.05	.04	.02	411	Jim Gott	.03	.02	.01
321	Juan Agosto	.03	.02	.01	412	Scott Medvin	.03	.02	.01
322	Mike Scott	.10	.08	.04	413	John Smiley	.03	.02	.01
323	Rick Rhoden	.03	.02	.01	414	Bob Kipper	.03	.02	.01
324	Jim Clancy	.03	.02	.01	415	Brian Fisher	.03	.02	.01
325	Larry Andersen	.03	.02	.01	416	Doug Drabek	.03	.02	.01
326	Alex Trevino	.03	.02	.01	417	Mike Lavalliere	.03	.02	.01
327	Alan Ashby	.03	.02	.01	418	Ken Oberkfell	.03	.02	.01
328	Craig Reynolds	.03	.02	.01	419	Sid Bream	.03	.02	.01
329	Bill Doran	.03	.02	.01	420	Austin Manahan	.20	.15	.08
330	Rafael Ramirez	.03	.02	.01	421	Jose Lind	.03	.02	.01
331	Glenn Davis	.10	.08	.04	422	Bobby Bonilla	.10	.08	.04
332	Willie Ansley	.35	.25	.14	423	Glenn Wilson	.03	.02	.01
333	Gerald Young	.03	.02	.01	424	Andy Van Slyke	.10	.08	.04
334	Cameron Drew	.10	.08	.04	425	Gary Redus	.03	.02	.01
335	Jay Howell	.05	.04	.03	426	Barry Bonds	.10	.08	.04
336	Tim Belcher	.05	.04	.03	427	Don Heinkel	.03	.02	.01
337	Fernando Valenzuela	.05	.04	.03	428	Ken Dayley	.03	.02	.01
338	Ricky Horton	.03	.02	.01	429	Todd Worrell	.05	.04	.02
339	Tim Leary	.03	.02	.01	430	Brad DuVall	.20	.15	.08
340	Bill Bene	.15	.11	.06	431	Jose DeLeon	.03	.02	.01
341	Orel Hershiser	.20	.15	.08	432	Joe Magrane	.10	.08	.04
342	Mike Scioscia	.05	.04	.02	433	John Ericks	.20	.15	.08
343	Rick Dempsey	.03	.02	.01	434	Frank DiPino	.03	.02	.01
344	Willie Randolph	.03	.02	.01	435	Tony Pena	.05	.04	.02
345	Alfredo Griffin	.03	.02	.01	436	Ozzie Smith	.08	.06	.03

		MT	NR MT	EX
437	Terry Pendleton	.03	.02	.01
438	Jose Oquendo	.03	.02	.01
439	Tim Jones	.05	.04	.02
440	Pedro Guerrero	.10	.08	.04
441	Milt Thompson	.03	.02	.01
442	Willie McGee	.05	.04	.02
443	Vince Coleman	.05	.04	.02
444	Tom Brunansky	.05	.04	.02
445	Walt Terrell	.03	.02	.01
446	Eric Show	.03	.02	.01
447	Mark Davis	.10	.08	.04
448	Andy Benes	.70	.50	.30
449	Eddie Whitson	.03	.02	.01
450	Dennis Rasmussen	.03	.02	.01
451	Bruce Hurst	.03	.02	.01
452	Pat Clements	.03	.02	.01
453	Benito Santiago	.10	.08	.04
454	Sandy Alomar, Jr.	.60	.45	.25
455	Garry Templeton	.03	.02	.01
456	Jack Clark	.05	.04	.02
457	Tim Flannery	.03	.02	.01
458	Roberto Alomar	.80	.60	.30
459	Carmelo Martinez	.03	.02	.01
460	John Kruk	.03	.02	.01
461	Tony Gwynn	.20	.15	.08
462	Jerald Clark	.05	.04	.02
463	Don Robinson	.03	.02	.01
464	Craig Lefferts	.03	.02	.01
465	Kelly Downs	.03	.02	.01
466	Rick Rueschel	.05	.04	.02
467	Scott Garrelts	.03	.02	.01
468	Wil Tejada	.03	.02	.01
469	Kirt Manwaring	.10	.08	.04
470	Terry Kennedy	.03	.02	.01
471	Jose Uribe	.03	.02	.01
472	Royce Clayton	.20	.15	.08
473	Robby Thompson	.05	.04	.02
474	Kevin Mitchell	.80	.60	.30
475	Ernie Riles	.03	.02	.01
476	Will Clark	.80	.60	.30
477	Donnell Nixon	.03	.02	.01
478	Candy Maldonado	.03	.02	.01
479	Tracy Jones	.03	.02	.01
480	Brett Butler	.05	.04	.02
481	Checklist	.05	.04	.02
482	Checklist	.05	.04	.02
483	Checklist	.05	.04	.02
484	Checklist	.05	.04	.02

		MT	NR MT	EX
Complete Set:		25.00	18.00	9.00
Common Player:		.05	.04	.02
1	Tommy Greene	.25	.20	.10
2	Tom Glavine	.06	.05	.02
3	Andy Nezelek	.08	.06	.03
4	Mike Stanton	.20	.15	.08
5	Rick Lueken	.08	.06	.03
6	Kent Mercker	.25	.20	.10
7	Derek Lilliquist	.06	.05	.02
8	Charlie Liebrandt	.05	.04	.02
9	Steve Avery	.35	.25	.14
10	John Smoltz	.15	.11	.06
11	Mark Lemke	.08	.06	.03
12	Lonnie Smith	.06	.05	.02
13	Oddibe McDowell	.05	.04	.02
14	Tyler Houston	.30	.25	.12
15	Jeff Blauser	.05	.04	.02
16	Ernie Whitt	.05	.04	.02
17	Alexis Infante	.10	.08	.04
18	Jim Presley	.06	.05	.02
19	Dale Murphy	.10	.08	.04
20	Nick Esasky	.06	.05	.02
21	Rick Sutcliffe	.06	.05	.02
22	Mike Bielecki	.06	.05	.02
23	Steve Wilson	.10	.08	.04
24	Kevin Blankenship	.10	.08	.04
25	Mitch Williams	.10	.08	.04
26	Dean Wilkins	.10	.08	.04
27	Greg Maddux	.12	.09	.05
28	Mike Harkey	.20	.15	.08
29	Mark Grace	.20	.15	.08
30	Ryne Sandberg	.20	.15	.08
31	Greg Smith	.20	.15	.08
32	Dwight Smith	.15	.11	.06
33	Damon Berryhill	.05	.04	.02
34	Earl Cunningham	.60	.45	.25
35	Jerome Walton	.25	.20	.10
36	Lloyd McClendon	.05	.04	.02
37	Ty Griffin	.20	.15	.08
38	Shawon Dunston	.10	.08	.04
39	Andre Dawson	.10	.08	.04
40	Luis Salazar	.05	.04	.02
41	Tim Layana	.20	.15	.08
42	Rob Dibble	.10	.08	.04
43	Tom Browning	.05	.04	.02
44	Danny Jackson	.05	.04	.02
45	Jose Rijo	.06	.05	.02
46	Scott Scudder	.20	.15	.08
47	Randy Myers	.06	.05	.02
48	Brian Lane	.15	.11	.06
49	Paul O'Neill	.05	.04	.02
50	Barry Larkin	.10	.08	.04
51	Reggie Jefferson	.20	.15	.08
52	Jeff Branson	.20	.15	.08
53	Chris Sabo	.08	.06	.03
54	Joe Oliver	.10	.08	.04
55	Todd Benzinger	.05	.04	.02
56	Rolando Roomes	.05	.04	.02
57	Hal Morris	.20	.15	.08
58	Eric Davis	.15	.11	.06
59	Scott Bryant	.20	.15	.08
60	Ken Griffey	.06	.05	.02
61	Darryl Kile	.15	.11	.06
62	Dave Smith	.05	.04	.02
63	Mark Portugal	.05	.04	.02
64	Jeff Juden	.25	.20	.10
65	Bill Guullickson	.05	.04	.02
66	Danny Darwin	.05	.04	.02
67	Larry Andersen	.05	.04	.02
68	Jose Cano	.10	.08	.04
69	Dan Schatzeder	.05	.04	.02
70	Jim Deshaies	.05	.04	.02
71	Mike Scott	.06	.05	.02
72	Gerald Young	.05	.04	.02
73	Ken Caminiti	.05	.04	.02
74	Ken Oberkfell	.05	.04	.02
75	Dave Rhode	.20	.15	.08
76	Bill Doran	.06	.05	.02
77	Andujar Cedeno	.20	.15	.08
78	Craig Biggio	.08	.06	.03
79	Karl Rhodes	.15	.11	.06
80	Glenn Davis	.10	.08	.04
81	Eric Anthony	.60	.45	.25
82	John Wetteland	.20	.15	.08
83	Jay Howell	.06	.05	.02
84	Orel Hershiser	.10	.08	.04
85	Tim Belcher	.08	.06	.03
86	Kiki Jones	.25	.20	.10
87	Mike Hartley	.20	.15	.08
88	Ramon Martinez	.60	.45	.25
89	Mike Scioscia	.06	.05	.02

1990 Bowman

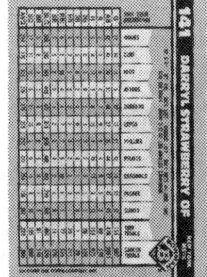

Bowman followed up its 1989 release with 528-card set in 1990. The 1990 cards follow the classic Bowman style featuring a full color photo bordered in white. The Bowman logo appears in the upper left corner. The player's team nickname and name appear on the bottom border of the card photo. Unlike the 1989 set, the 1990 cards measure 2-1/2" by 3-1/2" in size. The card backs are horizontal and display the player's statistics against the teams in his respective league. Included in the set are special insert cards that feature a reproduction of a painting of a modern-day superstar done in the style of the 1951 Bowman cards. The paintings were produced for Bowman by artist Craig Pursley. The card backs contain a sweepstakes offer with a chance to win a complete set of 11 lithographs made from these paintings.

#	Name	MT	NR MT	EX
90	Willie Randolph	.06	.05	.02
91	Juan Samuel	.06	.05	.02
92	Jose Offerman	1.00	.70	.40
93	Dave Hansen	.30	.25	.12
94	Jeff Hamilton	.05	.04	.02
95	Alfredo Griffin	.05	.04	.02
96	Tom Goodwin	.35	.25	.14
97	Kirk Gibson	.06	.05	.02
98	Jose Vizcaino	.20	.15	.08
99	Kal Daniels	.06	.05	.02
100	Hubie Brooks	.06	.05	.02
101	Eddie Murray	.08	.06	.03
102	Dennis Boyd	.05	.04	.02
103	Tim Burke	.06	.05	.02
104	Bill Sampen	.20	.15	.08
105	Brett Gideon	.06	.05	.02
106	Mark Gardner	.20	.15	.08
107	Howard Farmer	.15	.11	.06
108	Mel Rojas	.15	.11	.06
109	Kevin Gross	.05	.04	.02
110	Dave Schmidt	.05	.04	.02
111	Denny Martinez	.06	.05	.02
112	Jerry Goff	.10	.08	.04
113	Andres Galarraga	.08	.06	.03
114	Tim Welch	.12	.09	.05
115	Marquis Grissom	.40	.30	.15
116	Spike Owen	.05	.04	.02
117	Larry Walker	.30	.25	.12
118	Rock Raines	.08	.06	.03
119	Delino DeShields	.60	.45	.25
120	Tom Foley	.05	.04	.02
121	Dave Martinez	.05	.04	.02
122	Frank Viola	.10	.08	.04
123	Julio Valera	.15	.11	.06
124	Alejandro Pena	.05	.04	.02
125	David Cone	.08	.06	.03
126	Doc Gooden	.20	.15	.08
127	Kevin Brown	.20	.15	.08
128	John Franco	.08	.06	.03
129	Terry Bross	.25	.20	.10
130	Blaine Beatty	.20	.15	.08
131	Sid Fernandez	.08	.06	.03
132	Mike Marshall	.05	.04	.02
133	Howard Johnson	.10	.08	.04
134	Jaime Roseboro	.20	.15	.08
135	Alan Zinter	.20	.15	.08
136	Keith Miller	.06	.05	.02
137	Kevin Elster	.05	.04	.02
138	Kevin McReynolds	.06	.05	.02
139	Barry Lyons	.05	.04	.02
140	Gregg Jefferies	.25	.20	.10
141	Darryl Strawberry	.25	.20	.10
142	Todd Hundley	.25	.20	.10
143	Scott Service	.15	.11	.06
144	Chuck Malone	.15	.11	.06
145	Steve Ontiveros	.05	.04	.02
146	Roger McDowell	.06	.05	.02
147	Ken Howell	.05	.04	.02
148	Pat Combs	.15	.11	.06
149	Jeff Parrett	.05	.04	.02
150	Chuck McElroy	.15	.11	.06
151	Jason Grimsley	.15	.11	.06
152	Len Dykstra	.08	.06	.03
153	Mickey Morandini	.15	.11	.06
154	John Kruk	.05	.04	.02
155	Dickie Thon	.05	.04	.02
156	Ricky Jordan	.10	.08	.04
157	Jeff Jackson	.10	.08	.04
158	Darren Daulton	.05	.04	.02
159	Tom Herr	.05	.04	.02
160	Von Hayes	.06	.05	.02
161	Dave Hollins	.35	.25	.14
162	Carmelo Martinez	.05	.04	.02
163	Bob Walk	.05	.04	.02
164	Doug Drabek	.08	.06	.03
165	Walt Terrell	.05	.04	.02
166	Bill Landrum	.05	.04	.02
167	Scott Ruskin	.08	.06	.03
168	Bob Patterson	.05	.04	.02
169	Bobby Bonilla	.10	.08	.04
170	Jose Lind	.05	.04	.02
171	Andy Van Slyke	.08	.06	.03
172	Mike LaValliere	.05	.04	.02
173	Willie Greene	.20	.15	.08
174	Jay Bell	.06	.05	.02
175	Sid Bream	.05	.04	.02
176	Tom Prince	.05	.04	.02
177	Wally Backman	.05	.04	.02
178	Moises Alou	.25	.20	.10
179	Steve Carter	.08	.06	.03
180	Gary Redus	.05	.04	.02
181	Barry Bonds	.10	.08	.04
182	Don Slaught	.05	.04	.02
183	Joe Magrane	.06	.05	.02
184	Bryn Smith	.05	.04	.02
185	Todd Worrell	.06	.05	.02
186	Jose Deleon	.05	.04	.02
187	Frank DiPino	.05	.04	.02
188	John Tudor	.05	.04	.02
189	Howard Hilton	.10	.08	.04
190	John Ericks	.10	.08	.04
191	Ken Dayley	.05	.04	.02
192	Ray Lankford	1.25	.90	.50
193	Todd Zeile	.80	.60	.30
194	Willie McGee	.06	.05	.02
195	Ozzie Smith	.06	.05	.02
196	Milt Thompson	.05	.04	.02
197	Terry Pendleton	.05	.04	.02
198	Vince Coleman	.06	.05	.02
199	Paul Coleman	.25	.20	.10
200	Jose Oquendo	.05	.04	.02
201	Pedro Guerrero	.06	.05	.02
202	Tom Brunansky	.06	.05	.02
203	Roger Smithberg	.10	.08	.04
204	Eddie Whitson	.05	.04	.02
205	Dennis Rasmussen	.05	.04	.02
206	Craig Lefferts	.05	.04	.02
207	Andy Benes	.15	.11	.06
208	Bruce Hurst	.06	.05	.02
209	Eric Show	.05	.04	.02
210	Rafael Valdez	.10	.08	.04
211	Joey Cora	.05	.04	.02
212	Thomas Howard	.20	.15	.08
213	Rob Nelson	.05	.04	.02
214	Jack Clark	.06	.05	.02
215	Garry Templeton	.05	.04	.02
216	Fred Lynn	.05	.04	.02
217	Tony Gwynn	.08	.06	.03
218	Benny Santiago	.08	.06	.03
219	Mike Pagliarulo	.05	.04	.02
220	Joe Carter	.08	.06	.03
221	Roberto Alomar	.08	.06	.03
222	Bip Roberts	.05	.04	.02
223	Rick Reuschel	.05	.04	.02
224	Russ Swan	.20	.15	.08
225	Eric Gunderson	.20	.15	.08
226	Steve Bedrosian	.05	.04	.02
227	Mike Remlinger	.20	.15	.08
228	Scott Garrelts	.05	.04	.02
229	Ernie Camacho	.05	.04	.02
230	Andres Santana	.25	.20	.10
231	Will Clark	.35	.25	.14
232	Kevin Mitchell	.25	.20	.10
233	Robby Thompson	.05	.04	.02
234	Bill Bathe	.06	.05	.02
235	Tony Perezchica	.08	.06	.03
236	Gary Carter	.05	.04	.02
237	Brett Butler	.05	.04	.02
238	Matt Williams	.15	.11	.06
239	Ernie Riles	.05	.04	.02
240	Kevin Bass	.05	.04	.02
241	Terry Kennedy	.05	.04	.02
242	Steve Hosey	.30	.25	.12
243	Ben McDonald	1.00	.70	.40
244	Jeff Ballard	.05	.04	.02
245	Joe Price	.05	.04	.02
246	Curt Schilling	.05	.04	.02
247	Pete Harnisch	.06	.05	.02
248	Mark Williamson	.05	.04	.02
249	Gregg Olson	.15	.11	.06
250	Chris Myers	.15	.11	.06
251	David Segui	.40	.30	.15
252	Joe Orsulak	.05	.04	.02
253	Craig Worthington	.05	.04	.02
254	Mickey Tettleton	.06	.05	.02
255	Cal Ripken	.08	.06	.03
256	Billy Ripken	.05	.04	.02
257	Randy Milligan	.06	.05	.02
258	Brady Anderson	.05	.04	.02
259	Chris Hoiles	.20	.15	.08
260	Mike Devereaux	.05	.04	.02
261	Phil Bradley	.05	.04	.02
262	Leo Gomez	.30	.25	.12
263	Lee Smith	.06	.05	.02
264	Mike Rochford	.06	.05	.02
265	Jeff Reardon	.06	.05	.02
266	Wes Gardner	.05	.04	.02
267	Mike Boddicker	.05	.04	.02
268	Roger Clemens	.25	.20	.10
269	Rob Murphy	.05	.04	.02
270	Mickey Pina	.25	.20	.10
271	Tony Pena	.06	.05	.02

	MT	NR MT	EX			MT	NR MT	EX
272 Jody Reed	.06	.05	.02	363 Mark Gubicza	.08	.06	.03
273 Kevin Romine	.05	.04	.02	364 Bret Saberhagen	.10	.08	.04
274 Mike Greenwell	.08	.06	.03	365 Tom Gordon	.15	.11	.06
275 Maurice Vaughn	.35	.25	.14	366 Steve Farr	.05	.04	.02
276 Danny Heep	.05	.04	.02	367 Kevin Appier	.30	.25	.12
277 Scott Cooper	.25	.20	.10	368 Storm Davis	.05	.04	.02
278 Greg Blosser	.25	.20	.10	369 Mark Davis	.05	.04	.02
279 Dwight Evans	.06	.05	.02	370 Jeff Montgomery	.06	.05	.02
280 Ellis Burks	.08	.06	.03	371 Frank White	.06	.05	.02
281 Wade Boggs	.10	.08	.04	372 Brent Mayne	.20	.15	.08
282 Marty Barrett	.05	.04	.02	373 Bob Boone	.06	.05	.02
283 Kirk McCaskill	.06	.05	.02	374 Jim Eisenreich	.05	.04	.02
284 Mark Langston	.06	.05	.02	375 Danny Tartabull	.08	.06	.03
285 Bert Blyleven	.06	.05	.02	376 Kurt Stillwell	.05	.04	.02
286 Mike Fetters	.08	.06	.03	377 Bill Pecota	.05	.04	.02
287 Kyle Abbott	.20	.15	.08	378 Bo Jackson	.40	.30	.15
288 Jim Abbott	.10	.08	.04	379 Bob Hamelin	.20	.15	.08
289 Chuck Finley	.06	.05	.02	380 Kevin Seitzer	.08	.06	.03
290 Gary DiSarcina	.15	.11	.06	381 Rey Palacios	.05	.04	.02
291 Dick Schofield	.05	.04	.02	382 George Brett	.12	.09	.05
292 Devon White	.06	.05	.02	383 Gerald Perry	.05	.04	.02
293 Bobby Rose	.15	.11	.06	384 Teddy Higuera	.08	.06	.03
294 Brian Downing	.05	.04	.02	385 Tom Filer	.05	.04	.02
295 Lance Parrish	.06	.05	.02	386 Dan Plesac	.06	.05	.02
296 Jack Howell	.05	.04	.02	387 Cal Eldred	.20	.15	.08
297 Claudell Washington	.05	.04	.02	388 Jaime Navarro	.06	.05	.02
298 John Orton	.06	.05	.02	389 Chris Bosio	.05	.04	.02
299 Wally Joyner	.08	.06	.03	390 Randy Veres	.05	.04	.02
300 Lee Stevens	.30	.25	.12	391 Gary Sheffield	.20	.15	.08
301 Chili Davis	.05	.04	.02	392 George Canale	.10	.08	.04
302 Johnny Ray	.05	.04	.02	393 B.J. Surhoff	.06	.05	.02
303 Greg Hibbard	.15	.11	.06	394 Tim McIntosh	.15	.11	.06
304 Eric King	.06	.05	.02	395 Greg Brock	.05	.04	.02
305 Jack McDowell	.08	.06	.03	396 Greg Vaughn	.50	.40	.20
306 Bobby Thigpen	.08	.06	.03	397 Darryl Hamilton	.10	.08	.04
307 Adam Peterson	.05	.04	.02	398 Dave Parker	.10	.08	.04
308 Scott Radinsky	.20	.15	.08	399 Paul Molitor	.08	.06	.03
309 Wayne Edwards	.06	.05	.02	400 Jim Gantner	.05	.04	.02
310 Melido Perez	.06	.05	.02	401 Rob Deer	.05	.04	.02
311 Robin Ventura	.30	.25	.12	402 Billy Spiers	.15	.11	.06
312 Sammy Sosa	.30	.25	.12	403 Glenn Braggs	.06	.05	.02
313 Dan Pasqua	.05	.04	.02	404 Robin Yount	.15	.11	.06
314 Carlton Fisk	.08	.06	.03	405 Rick Aguilera	.05	.04	.02
315 Ozzie Guillen	.08	.06	.03	406 Johnny Ard	.15	.11	.06
316 Ivan Calderon	.08	.06	.03	407 Kevin Tapani	.25	.20	.10
317 Daryl Boston	.05	.04	.02	408 Park Pittman	.20	.15	.08
318 Craig Grebeck	.15	.11	.06	409 Allan Anderson	.05	.04	.02
319 Scott Fletcher	.05	.04	.02	410 Juan Berenguer	.05	.04	.02
320 Frank Thomas	1.50	1.25	.60	411 Willie Banks	.30	.25	.12
321 Steve Lyons	.05	.04	.02	412 Rich Yett	.05	.04	.02
322 Carlos Martinez	.10	.08	.04	413 Dave West	.08	.06	.03
323 Joe Skalski	.08	.06	.03	414 Greg Gagne	.05	.04	.02
324 Tom Candiotti	.05	.04	.02	415 Chuck Knoblauch	.25	.20	.10
325 Greg Swindell	.06	.05	.02	416 Randy Bush	.05	.04	.02
326 Steve Olin	.15	.11	.06	417 Gary Gaetti	.08	.06	.03
327 Kevin Wickander	.08	.06	.03	418 Kent Hrbek	.08	.06	.03
328 Doug Jones	.06	.05	.02	419 Al Newman	.05	.04	.02
329 Jeff Shaw	.10	.08	.04	420 Danny Gladden	.05	.04	.02
330 Kevin Bearse	.10	.08	.04	421 Paul Sorrento	.15	.11	.06
331 Dion James	.05	.04	.02	422 Derek Parks	.25	.20	.10
332 Jerry Browne	.06	.05	.02	423 Scott Leius	.20	.15	.08
333 Joey Belle	.15	.11	.06	424 Kirby Puckett	.20	.15	.08
334 Felix Fermin	.05	.04	.02	425 Willie Smith	.20	.15	.08
335 Candy Maldonado	.06	.05	.02	426 Dave Righetti	.08	.06	.02
336 Cory Snyder	.06	.05	.02	427 Jeff Robinson	.05	.04	.02
337 Sandy Alomar	.30	.25	.12	428 Alan Mills	.20	.15	.08
338 Mark Lewis	.12	.09	.05	429 Tim Leary	.05	.04	.02
339 Carlos Baerga	.40	.30	.15	430 Pascual Perez	.05	.04	.02
340 Chris James	.05	.04	.02	431 Alvaro Espinoza	.05	.04	.02
341 Brook Jacoby	.06	.05	.02	432 Dave Winfield	.12	.09	.05
342 Keith Hernandez	.06	.05	.02	433 Jesse Barfield	.06	.05	.02
343 Frank Tanana	.05	.04	.02	434 Randy Velarde	.05	.04	.02
344 Scott Aldred	.15	.11	.06	435 Rick Cerone	.05	.04	.02
345 Mike Henneman	.06	.05	.02	436 Steve Balboni	.05	.04	.02
346 Steve Wapnick	.15	.11	.06	437 Mel Hall	.05	.04	.02
347 Greg Gohr	.15	.11	.06	438 Bob Geren	.06	.05	.02
348 Eric Stone	.15	.11	.06	439 Bernie Williams	.40	.30	.15
349 Brian DuBois	.10	.08	.04	440 Kevin Maas	2.00	1.50	.80
350 Kevin Ritz	.10	.08	.04	441 Mike Blowers	.15	.11	.06
351 Rico Brogna	.10	.08	.04	442 Steve Sax	.08	.06	.03
352 Mike Heath	.05	.04	.02	443 Don Mattingly	.35	.25	.14
353 Alan Trammell	.08	.06	.03	444 Roberto Kelly	.08	.06	.03
354 Chet Lemon	.06	.05	.02	445 Mike Moore	.06	.05	.02
355 Dave Bergman	.05	.04	.02	446 Reggie Harris	.15	.11	.06
356 Lou Whitaker	.08	.06	.03	447 Scott Sanderson	.05	.04	.02
357 Cecil Fielder	.40	.30	.15	448 Dave Otto	.05	.04	.02
358 Milt Cuyler	.20	.15	.08	449 Dave Stewart	.08	.06	.03
359 Tony Phillips	.06	.05	.02	450 Rick Honeycutt	.05	.04	.02
360 Travis Fryman	.80	.60	.30	451 Dennis Eckersley	.08	.06	.03
361 Ed Romero	.05	.04	.02	452 Carney Lansford	.06	.05	.02
362 Lloyd Moseby	.06	.05	.02	453 Scott Hemond	.15	.11	.06

		MT	NR MT	EX
454	Mark McGwire	.20	.15	.08
455	Felix Jose	.15	.11	.06
456	Terry Steinbach	.06	.05	.02
457	Rickey Henderson	.25	.20	.10
458	Dave Henderson	.06	.05	.02
459	Mike Gallego	.05	.04	.02
460	Jose Canseco	.40	.30	.15
461	Walt Weiss	.06	.05	.02
462	Ken Phelps	.05	.04	.02
463	Darren Lewis	.30	.25	.12
464	Ron Hassey	.05	.04	.02
465	Roger Salkeld	.30	.25	.12
466	Scott Bankhead	.06	.05	.02
467	Keith Comstock	.05	.04	.02
468	Randy Johnson	.10	.08	.04
469	Erik Hanson	.10	.08	.04
470	Mike Schooler	.06	.05	.04
471	Gary Eave	.15	.11	.06
472	Jeffrey Leonard	.06	.05	.02
473	Dave Valle	.05	.04	.02
474	Omar Vizquel	.05	.04	.02
475	Pete O'Brien	.05	.04	.02
476	Henry Cotto	.05	.04	.02
477	Jay Buhner	.06	.05	.02
478	Harold Reynolds	.06	.05	.02
479	Alvin Davis	.08	.06	.03
480	Darnell Coles	.05	.04	.02
481	Ken Griffey, Jr.	2.50	2.00	1.00
482	Greg Briley	.12	.09	.05
483	Scott Bradley	.05	.04	.02
484	Tino Martinez	.40	.30	.15
485	Jeff Russell	.06	.05	.02
486	Nolan Ryan	.40	.30	.15
487	Robb Nen	.20	.15	.08
488	Kevin Brown	.06	.05	.02
489	Brian Bohanon	.20	.15	.08
490	Ruben Sierra	.15	.11	.06
491	Pete Incaviglia	.06	.05	.02
492	Juan Gonzalez	1.25	.90	.50
493	Steve Buechele	.05	.04	.02
494	Scott Coolbaugh	.15	.11	.06
495	Geno Petralli	.05	.04	.02
496	Rafael Palmeiro	.08	.06	.03
497	Julio Franco	.08	.06	.03
498	Gary Pettis	.05	.04	.02
499	Donald Harris	.20	.15	.08
500	Monty Fariss	.20	.15	.08
501	Harold Baines	.08	.06	.03
502	Cecil Espy	.05	.04	.02
503	Jack Daugherty	.08	.06	.03
504	Willie Blair	.15	.11	.06
505	Dave Steib	.06	.05	.02
506	Tom Henke	.06	.05	.02
507	John Cerutti	.05	.04	.02
508	Paul Kilgus	.05	.04	.02
509	Jimmy Key	.06	.05	.02
510	John Olerud	2.00	1.50	.80
511	Ed Sprague	.20	.15	.08
512	Manny Lee	.05	.04	.02
513	Fred McGriff	.08	.06	.03
514	Glenallen Hill	.10	.08	.04
515	George Bell	.08	.06	.03
516	Mookie Wilson	.06	.05	.02
517	Luis Sojo	.15	.11	.06
518	Nelson Liriano	.05	.04	.02
519	Kelly Gruber	.08	.06	.03
520	Greg Myers	.06	.05	.02
521	Pat Borders	.06	.05	.02
522	Junior Felix	.25	.20	.10
523	Eddie Zosky	.25	.20	.10
524	Tony Fernandez	.06	.05	.02
525	Checklist	.05	.04	.02
526	Checklist	.05	.04	.02
527	Checklist	.05	.04	.02
528	Checklist	.05	.04	.02

1977 Burger King Yankees

The first Topps-produced set for Burger King restaurants was issued in the New York area in 1977 and featured the A.L. champion New York Yankees. Twenty-two players plus an unnumbered checklist were issued at the beginning of the promotion with card #23 (Lou Piniella) being added to the set at a later date. The Piniella card was issued in limited

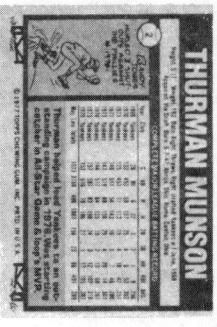

quantities. The cards, numbered 1 through 23, are 2-1/2" by 3-1/2" in size and have fronts identical to the regular 1977 Topps set except for the following numbers: 2, 6, 7, 13, 14, 15, 17, 20 and 21. These cards feature different poses or major picture-cropping variations. It should be noted that very minor cropping variations between the regular Topps sets and the Burger King issues exist throughout the years the sets were produced.

		NR MT	EX	VG
	Complete Set:	50.00	25.00	15.00
	Common Player:	.30	.15	.09
1	Yankees Team (Billy Martin)	1.25	.60	.40
2	Thurman Munson	7.00	3.50	2.00
3	Fran Healy	.30	.15	.09
4	Jim Hunter	2.00	1.00	.60
5	Ed Figueroa	.30	.15	.09
6	Don Gullett	.70	.35	.20
7	Mike Torrez	.70	.35	.20
8	Ken Holtzman	.50	.25	.15
9	Dick Tidrow	.30	.15	.09
10	Sparky Lyle	.50	.25	.15
11	Ron Guidry	1.25	.60	.40
12	Chris Chambliss	.50	.25	.15
13	Willie Randolph	.80	.40	.25
14	Bucky Dent	.80	.40	.25
15	Graig Nettles	1.25	.60	.40
16	Fred Stanley	.30	.15	.09
17	Reggie Jackson	8.00	4.00	2.50
18	Mickey Rivers	.50	.25	.15
19	Roy White	.50	.25	.15
20	Jim Wynn	.70	.35	.20
21	Paul Blair	.70	.35	.20
22	Carlos May	.30	.15	.09
23	Lou Piniella	25.00	12.50	7.50
-----	Checklist	.10	.05	.03

1978 Burger King Astros

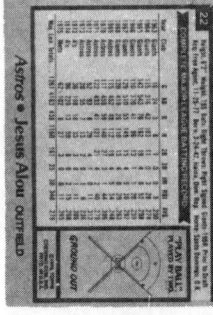

Burger King restaurants in the Houston area distributed a Topps-produced 23-card set showcasing the Astros in 1978. The cards are standard size (2-1/2" by 3-1/2") and are numbered 1 through 22.

The checklist card is unnumbered. The card fronts are identical to the regular 1978 Topps set with the exception of card numbers 21 and 22, which have different poses. Although not noted in the following checklist, it should be remembered that very minor picture-cropping variations between the regular Topps issues and the 1977-1980 Burger King sets do exist.

		NR MT	EX	VG
Complete Set:		12.00	6.00	3.50
Common Player:		.30	.15	.09
1	Bill Virdon	.50	.25	.15
2	Joe Ferguson	.30	.15	.09
3	Ed Herrmann	.30	.15	.09
4	J.R. Richard	.60	.30	.20
5	Joe Niekro	.60	.30	.20
6	Floyd Bannister	.70	.35	.20
7	Joaquin Andujar	.60	.30	.20
8	Ken Forsch	.40	.20	.12
9	Mark Lemongello	.30	.15	.09
10	Joe Sambito	.40	.20	.12
11	Gene Pentz	.30	.15	.09
12	Bob Watson	.40	.20	.12
13	Julio Gonzalez	.30	.15	.09
14	Enos Cabell	.40	.20	.12
15	Roger Metzger	.30	.15	.09
16	Art Howe	.60	.30	.20
17	Jose Cruz	.80	.40	.25
18	Cesar Cedeno	.80	.40	.25
19	Terry Puhl	.40	.20	.12
20	Wilbur Howard	.30	.15	.09
21	Dave Bergman	.60	.30	.20
22	Jesus Alou	.60	.30	.20
--—	Checklist	.04	.02	.01

1978 Burger King Rangers

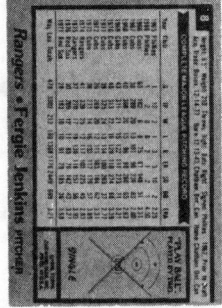

FERGIE JENKINS

Issued by Burger King restaurants in the Dallas-Fort Worth area, this 23-card Topps-produced set features the Texas Rangers. The cards are standard size (2-1/2" by 3-1/2") and are identical in style to the regular 1978 Topps set with the following exceptions: #'s 5, 8, 10, 12, 17, 21 and 22. An unnumbered checklist card was included with the set.

		NR MT	EX	VG
Complete Set:		12.00	6.00	3.50
Common Player:		.30	.15	.09
1	Billy Hunter	.30	.15	.09
2	Jim Sundberg	.50	.25	.15
3	John Ellis	.30	.15	.09
4	Doyle Alexander	.50	.25	.15
5	Jon Matlack	.60	.30	.20
6	Dock Ellis	.30	.15	.09
7	George Medich	.30	.15	.09
8	Fergie Jenkins	1.25	.60	.40
9	Len Barker	.30	.15	.09
10	Reggie Cleveland	.60	.30	.20
11	Mike Hargrove	.40	.20	.12
12	Bump Wills	.60	.30	.20
13	Toby Harrah	.50	.25	.15
14	Bert Campaneris	.50	.25	.15
15	Sandy Alomar	.30	.15	.09

		NR MT	EX	VG
16	Kurt Bevacqua	.30	.15	.09
17	Al Oliver	1.00	.50	.30
18	Juan Beniquez	.30	.15	.09
19	Claudell Washington	.50	.25	.15
20	Richie Zisk	.40	.20	.12
21	John Lowenstein	.60	.30	.20
22	Bobby Thompson	.60	.30	.20
--—	Checklist	.04	.02	.01

A player's name in *italic* indicates a rookie card. An (FC) indicates a player's first card for that particular card company.

1978 Burger King Tigers

Rookie cards of Morris, Trammell and Whitaker make the Topps-produced 1978 Burger King Detroit Tigers issue the most popular of the BK sets. Twenty-two player cards and an unnumbered checklist make up the set which was issued in the Detroit area. The cards measure 2-1/2" by 3-1/2", aruue ideuuntical to the regular 1978 Topps issue with the following exceptions - card #'s 6, 7, 8, 13, 15 and 16. Collectors are reminded that numerous minor picture-cropping variations between the regular Topps issues and the Burger King sets appear from the 1977 through 1980. These minor variations are not noted in the following checklist.

		NR MT	EX	VG
Complete Set:		60.00	30.00	18.00
Common Player:		.40	.20	.12
1	Ralph Houk	.40	.20	.12
2	Milt May	.40	.20	.12
3	John Wockenfuss	.40	.20	.12
4	Mark Fidrych	1.00	.50	.30
5	Dave Rozema	.40	.20	.12
6	Jack Billingham	.40	.20	.12
7	Jim Slaton	.40	.20	.12
8	Jack Morris	12.00	6.00	3.50
9	John Hiller	.50	.25	.15
10	Steve Foucault	.40	.20	.12
11	Milt Wilcox	.40	.20	.12
12	Jason Thompson	.50	.25	.15
13	Lou Whitaker	12.00	6.00	3.50
14	Aurelio Rodriguez	.40	.20	.12
15	Alan Trammell	20.00	10.00	6.00
16	Steve Dillard	.40	.20	.12
17	Phil Mankowski	.40	.20	.12
18	Steve Kemp	.50	.25	.15
19	Ron LeFlore	.50	.25	.15
20	Tim Corcoran	.40	.20	.12
21	Mickey Stanley	.40	.20	.12
22	Rusty Staub	1.00	.50	.30
---)	Checklist	.10	.05	.03

1978 Burger King Yankees

Produced by Topps for Burger King outlets in the New York area for the second year in a row, the 1978 Yankees set contains 22 cards plus an unnumbered checklist. The cards are numbered 1 through 22 and are the standard size of 2-1/2" by 3-1/2". The cards feature the same pictures found in the regular 1978 Topps set except for numbers 10, 11 and 16. Only

 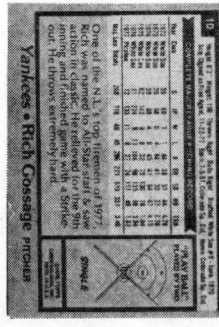

those variations containing different poses or major picture-cropping differences are noted. Numerous minor picture-cropping variations, that are very insignificant in nature, exist between the regular Topps sets and the Burger King issues of 1977-1980.

		NR MT	EX	VG
	Complete Set:	12.00	6.00	3.50
	Common Player:	.30	.15	.09
1	Billy Martin	.80	.40	.25
2	Thurman Munson	3.00	1.50	.90
3	Cliff Johnson	.30	.15	.09
4	Ron Guidry	1.25	.60	.40
5	Ed Figueroa	.30	.15	.09
6	Dick Tidrow	.30	.15	.09
7	Jim Hunter	1.00	.50	.30
8	Don Gullett	.30	.15	.09
9	Sparky Lyle	.50	.25	.15
10	Rich Gossage	1.25	.60	.40
11	Rawly Eastwick	.70	.35	.20
12	Chris Chambliss	.50	.25	.15
13	Willie Randolph	.50	.25	.15
14	Graig Nettles	.80	.40	.25
15	Bucky Dent	.50	.25	.15
16	Jim Spencer	.70	.35	.20
17	Fred Stanley	.30	.15	.09
18	Lou Piniella	.80	.40	.25
19	Roy White	.50	.25	.15
20	Mickey Rivers	.50	.25	.15
21	Reggie Jackson	4.00	2.00	1.25
22	Paul Blair	.30	.15	.09
----	Checklist	.04	.02	.01

1979 Burger King Phillies

 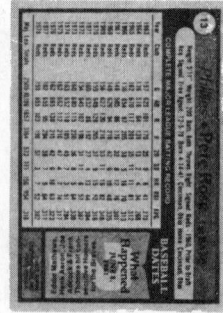

Twenty-two Philadelphia Phillies players are featured in the 1979 Burger King issue given out in the Philadelphia area. The Topps-produced set, whose cards measure 2-1/2" by 3-1/2", also includes an unnumbered checklist. The cards are identical to the regular 1979 Topps set except in seven instances. Card numbers 1, 11, 12, 13, 14, 17 and 22 have different poses. Very minor picture-cropping variations between the regular Topps issues

and the Burger King sets can be found throughout the four years the cards were produced, but only those variations featuring major changes are noted in the following checklist.

		NR MT	EX	VG
	Complete Set:	10.00	5.00	3.00
	Common Player:	.20	.10	.06
1	Danny Ozark	.60	.30	.20
2	Bob Boone	.60	.30	.20
3	Tim McCarver	.60	.30	.20
4	Steve Carlton	2.50	1.25	.70
5'	Larry Christenson	.20	.10	.06
6	Dick Ruthven	.20	.10	.06
7	Ron Reed	.20	.10	.06
8	Randy Lerch	.20	.10	.06
9	Warren Brusstar	.20	.10	.06
10	Tug McGraw	.40	.20	.12
11	Nino Espinosa	.60	.30	.20
12	Doug Bird	.20	.10	.06
13	Pete Rose	4.00	1.25	.90
14	Manny Trillo	.60	.30	.20
15	Larry Bowa	.50	.25	.15
16	Mike Schmidt	4.00	2.00	1.25
17	Pete Mackanin	.60	.30	.20
18	Jose Cardenal	.20	.10	.06
19	Greg Luzinski	.40	.20	.12
20	Garry Maddox	.30	.15	.09
21	Bake McBride	.20	.10	.06
22	Greg Gross	.20	.10	.06
----	Checklist	.04	.02	.01

1979 Burger King Yankees

 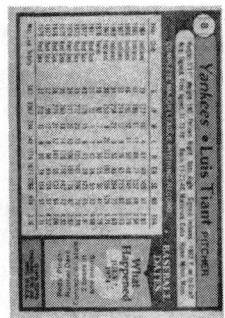

The New York Yankees were featured in a Topps-produced Burger King set for the third consecutive year in 1979. Once again, 22 numbered player cards and an unnumbered checklist made up the set. The cards, which measure 2-1/2" by 3-1/2", are identical to the 1979 Topps regular set except for card numbers 4, 8, 9 and 22 which included new poses. Only different poses or major picture-cropping variations between the regular Topps set and the Burger King issue are recognized in the checklist that follows. Numerous minor picture cropping variations between the regular Topps issue and the Burger King sets of 1977-1980 exist.

		NR MT	EX	VG
	Complete Set:	10.00	5.00	3.00
	Common Player:	.30	.15	.09
1	Yankees Team (Bob Lemon)	.50	.25	.15
2	Thurman Munson	2.00	1.00	.60
3	Cliff Johnson	.30	.15	.09
4	Ron Guidry	1.25	.60	.40
5	Jay Johnstone	.40	.20	.12
6	Jim Hunter	.90	.45	.25
7	Jim Beattie	.30	.15	.09
8	Luis Tiant	.80	.40	.25
9	Tommy John	1.00	.50	.30
10	Rich Gossage	.90	.45	.25
11	Ed Figueroa	.30	.15	.09
12	Chris Chambliss	.50	.25	.15

Here's your repli-card...

One of the classic baseball card sets of all time is the 1933 Goudey set. The first major "bubblegum" cards, the '33 Goudeys are revered by advanced collectors for their distinctive artwork and nostalgic style.

And while it may be impossible to improve on an original like the '33 Goudeys, we had the very talented sports artist Dan Gardiner give it a try with this very special Ryne Sandberg card that was inspired by the classic Goudey set. If Sandberg had played in 1933, this is what his baseball card might have looked like.

We hope you enjoy it. It's yours free for reading the Fifth Edition of the Sports Collectors Digest Baseball Card Price Guide.

FIFTH EDITION

BASEBALL CARD
price guide

Return this postcard for a

FREE ISSUE!

Your choice of Baseball Card Price Guide Monthly or Baseball Card News!

CHECK ONE: Please send an issue of

☐ **Baseball Card Price Guide Monthly**

☐ **Baseball Card News**
...to the following address:

Name _____

Address _____

City _____

State _____ Zip _____

Complete information above and drop in mail.

		NR MT	EX	VG
13	Willie Randolph	.50	.25	.15
14	Bucky Dent	.50	.25	.15
15	Graig Nettles	.70	.35	.20
16	Fred Stanley	.30	.15	.09
17	Jim Spencer	.30	.15	.09
18	Lou Piniella	.70	.35	.20
19	Roy White	.50	.25	.15
20	Mickey Rivers	.50	.25	.15
21	Reggie Jackson	3.00	1.50	.90
22	Juan Beniquez	.30	.15	.09
-----	Checklist	.04	.02	.01

1980 Burger King Phillies

 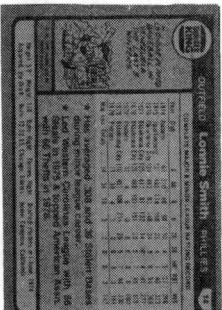

Philadelphia-area Burger King outlets issued a 23-card set featuring the Phillies for the second in a row in 1980. The Topps-produced set, whose cards measure 2-1/2" by 3-1/2", contains 22 player cards and an unnumbered checklist. The card fronts are identical in design to the regular 1980 Topps sets with the following exceptions - card numbers 1, 3, 8, 14 and 22 feature new poses. Collectors should note that very minor picture-cropping variations between the regular Topps issues and the Burger King sets exist in all years. Those minor differences are not noted in the checklist that follows. The 1980 Burger King sets were the first to include the Burger King logo on the card backs.

		NR MT	EX	VG
Complete Set:		7.00	3.50	2.00
Common Player:		.15	.08	.05
1	Dallas Green	.50	.25	.15
2	Bob Boone	.25	.13	.08
3	Keith Moreland	.60	.30	.20
4	Pete Rose	2.75	1.50	.80
5	Manny Trillo	.20	.10	.06
6	Mike Schmidt	2.75	1.50	.80
7	Larry Bowa	.40	.20	.12
8	John Vukovich	.50	.25	.15
9	Bake McBride	.15	.08	.05
10	Garry Maddox	.20	.10	.06
11	Greg Luzinski	.30	.15	.09
12	Greg Gross	.15	.08	.05
13	Del Unser	.15	.08	.05
14	Lonnie Smith	.50	.25	.15
15	Steve Carlton	1.25	.60	.40
16	Larry Christenson	.15	.08	.05
17	Nino Espinosa	.15	.08	.05
18	Randy Lerch	.15	.08	.05
19	Dick Ruthven	.15	.08	.05
20	Tug McGraw	.30	.15	.09
21	Ron Reed	.15	.08	.05
22	Kevin Saucier	.50	.25	.15
-----	Checklist	.04	.02	.01

1980 Burger King Pitch, Hit & Run

 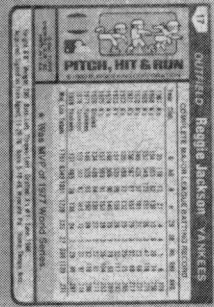

In 1980, Burger King issued, in conjunction with its "Pitch, Hit & Run" promotion, a Topps-produced 34-card set featuring pitchers (card #'s 1-11), hitters (#'s 12-22), and base stealers (#'s 23-33). The card fronts, which carry the Burger King logo, are identical in nature to the regular 1980 Topps set except for numbers 1, 4, 5, 7, 9, 10, 16, 17, 18, 22, 23, 27, 28, 29 and 30, which feature different poses. The cards, which are numbered 1 through 33, measure 2-1/2" by 3-1/2" in size. An unnumbered checklist was included with the set.

		NR MT	EX	VG
Complete Set:		18.00	9.00	5.50
Common Player:		.20	.10	.06
1	Vida Blue	.50	.25	.15
2	Steve Carlton	1.00	.50	.30
3	Rollie Fingers	.30	.15	.09
4	Ron Guidry	.70	.35	.20
5	Jerry Koosman	.40	.20	.12
6	Phil Niekro	.40	.20	.12
7	Jim Palmer	1.25	.60	.40
8	J.R. Richard	.20	.10	.06
9	Nolan Ryan	3.00	1.50	.90
10	Tom Seaver	1.25	.60	.40
11	Bruce Sutter	.25	.13	.08
12	Don Baylor	.25	.13	.08
13	George Brett	1.25	.60	.40
14	Rod Carew	.90	.45	.25
15	George Foster	.25	.13	.08
16	Keith Hernandez	.90	.45	.25
17	Reggie Jackson	2.25	1.25	.70
18	Fred Lynn	.70	.35	.20
19	Dave Parker	.40	.20	.12
20	Jim Rice	.80	.40	.25
21	Pete Rose	2.50	1.25	.70
22	Dave Winfield	1.25	.60	.40
23	Bobby Bonds	.40	.20	.12
24	Enos Cabell	.20	.10	.06
25	Cesar Cedeno	.20	.10	.06
26	Julio Cruz	.20	.10	.06
27	Ron LeFlore	.40	.20	.12
28	Dave Lopes	.40	.20	.12
29	Omar Moreno	.40	.20	.12
30	Joe Morgan	1.00	.50	.30
31	Bill North	.20	.10	.06
32	Frank Taveras	.20	.10	.06
33	Willie Wilson	.25	.13	.08
-----	Checklist	.04	.02	.01

1982 Burger King Braves

A set consisting of 27 "Collector Lids" featuring the Atlanta Braves was issued by Burger King restaurants in 1982. The lids, which measure 3-5/8" in diameter, were placed on a special Coca-Cola cup which listed the scores of the Braves' season-opening 13-game win streak. A black and white photo plus the player's

name, position, height, weight, and 1981 statistics are found on the lid front. The unnumbered, blank-backed lids also contain logos for Burger King, Coca-Cola, and the Major League Baseball Players Association.

		MT	NR MT	EX
Complete Set:		40.00	30.00	16.00
Common Player:		1.00	.70	.40
(1)	Steve Bedrosian	2.50	2.00	1.00
(2)	Bruce Benedict	1.00	.70	.40
(3)	Tommy Boggs	1.00	.70	.40
(4)	Brett Butler	2.50	2.00	1.00
(5)	Rick Camp	1.00	.70	.40
(6)	Chris Chambliss	1.25	.90	.50
(7)	Ken Dayley	1.00	.70	.40
(8)	Gene Garber	1.00	.70	.40
(9)	Preston Hanna	1.00	.70	.40
(10)	Terry Harper	1.00	.70	.40
(11)	Bob Horner	3.00	2.25	1.25
(12)	Al Hrabosky	1.25	.90	.50
(13)	Glenn Hubbard	1.00	.70	.40
(14)	Randy Johnson	1.00	.70	.40
(15)	Rufino Linares	1.00	.70	.40
(16)	Rick Mahler	1.50	1.25	.60
(17)	Larry McWilliams	1.00	.70	.40
(18)	Dale Murphy	12.00	9.00	4.75
(19)	Phil Niekro	5.00	3.75	2.00
(20)	Biff Pocoroba	1.00	.70	.40
(21)	Rafael Ramirez	1.00	.70	.40
(22)	Jerry Royster	1.00	.70	.40
(23)	Ken Smith	1.00	.70	.40
(24)	Bob Walk	1.00	.70	.40
(25)	Claudell Washington	1.25	.90	.50
(26)	Bob Watson	1.00	.70	.40
(27)	Larry Whisenton	1.00	.70	.40

1982 Burger King Indians

The 1982 Burger King Indians set was sponsored by WUAB-TV and Burger Kings in the Cleveland vicinity. The cards' green borders encompass a large yellow area which contains a black and white photo plus a baseball tip. Manager Dave Garcia and his four coaches provide the baseball hints. The cards, which measure 3" x 5", are unnumbered and blank-backed.

		MT	NR MT	EX
Complete Set:		10.00	7.50	4.00
Common Player:		.70	.50	.30
(1)	Dave Garcia (Be In The Game)	.70	.50	.30
(2)	Dave Garcia (Sportsmanship)	.70	.50	.30
(3)	Johnny Goryl (Rounding The Bases)	.70	.50	.30
(4)	Johnny Goryl (3rd Base Running)	.70	.50	.30
(5)	Tom McCraw (Follow Thru)	.70	.50	.30
(6)	Tom McCraw (Selecting A Bat)	.70	.50	.30
(7)	Tom McCraw (Watch The Ball)	.70	.50	.30
(8)	Mel Queen (Master One Pitch)	.70	.50	.30
(9)	Mel Queen (Warm Up)	.70	.50	.30
(10)	Dennis Sommers (Get Down On A Ground Ball)	.70	.50	.30
(11)	Dennis Sommers (Protect Your Fingers)	.70	.50	.30
(12)	Dennis Sommers (Tagging First Base)	.70	.50	.30

1986 Burger King

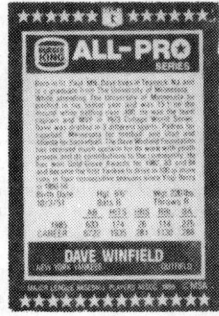

Burger King restaurants in the Pennsylvania and New Jersey areas issued a 20-card set entitled "All-Pro Series". The cards were issued with the purchase of a Whopper sandwich and came in folded panels of two cards each, along with a coupon card. The card fronts feature a color photo and contain the player's name, team and position plus the Burger King logo. Due to a licensing problem, the team insignias on the players' caps were airbrushed away. The card backs feature black print on white stock and contain brief biographical and statistical information.

		MT	NR MT	EX
Complete Panel Set		10.00	7.50	4.00
Complete Singles Set		6.00	4.50	2.50
Common Panel		.75	.60	.30
Common Single Player		.10	.08	.04
	Panel	.70	.50	.30
1	Tony Pena	.10	.08	.04
2	Dave Winfield	.20	.15	.08
	Panel	2.00	1.50	.80
3	Fernando Valenzuela	.20	.15	.08
4	Pete Rose	.50	.40	.20
	Panel	1.50	1.25	.60
5	Mike Schmidt	1.00	.70	.40
6	Steve Carlton	.30	.25	.12
	Panel	.70	.50	.30
7	Glenn Wilson	.10	.08	.04
8	Jim Rice	.20	.15	.08
	Panel	2.50	2.00	1.00
9	Wade Boggs	.80	.60	.30
10	Juan Samuel	.10	.08	.04
	Panel	1.50	1.25	.60
11	Dale Murphy	.40	.30	.15
12	Reggie Jackson	.30	.25	.12
	Panel	1.25	.90	.50
13	Kirk Gibson	.20	.15	.08
14	Eddie Murray	.30	.25	.12
	Panel	1.00	.70	.40
15	Cal Ripken, Jr.	.30	.25	.12
16	Willie McGee	.10	.08	.04

		MT	NR MT	EX
	Panel	1.75	1.25	.70
17	Dwight Gooden	.50	.40	.20
18	Steve Garvey	.25	.20	.10
	Panel	3.00	2.25	1.25
19	Don Mattingly	1.50	1.25	.60
20	George Brett	.40	.30	.15

1987 Burger King

 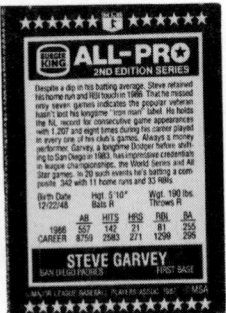

The 1987 Burger King "All-Pro 2nd Edition Series" set was part of a giveaway promotion at participating Burger King restaurants. The set is comprised of 20 players on ten different panels. The cards measure 2-1/2" by 3-1/2" each with a three-card panel (includes a coupon card) measuring 7-5/8" by 3-1/2". The card fronts feature a full-color photo and the Burger King logo surrounded by a blue stars-and-stripes border. The backs contain black print on white stock and carry a brief player biography and 1986 career statistics. The set was produced by Mike Schecter Associates and, as with many MSA issues, all team insignias were airbrushed away.

		MT	NR MT	EX
	Complete Panel Set:	7.00	5.25	2.75
	Complete Singles Set:	4.00	3.00	1.50
	Common Panel:	.25	.20	.10
	Common Single Player:	.05	.04	.02
	Panel	1.25	.90	.50
1	Wade Boggs	.40	.30	.15
2	Gary Carter	.15	.11	.06
	Panel	1.00	.70	.40
3	Will Clark	.50	.40	.20
4	Roger Clemens	.20	.15	.08
	Panel	.50	.40	.20
5	Steve Garvey	.15	.11	.06
6	Ron Darling	.08	.06	.03
	Panel	.25	.20	.10
7	Pedro Guerrero	.08	.06	.03
8	Von Hayes	.05	.04	.02
	Panel	.60	.45	.25
9	Rickey Henderson	.25	.20	.10
10	Keith Hernandez	.12	.09	.05
	Panel	.60	.45	.25
11	Wally Joyner	.20	.15	.08
12	Mike Krukow	.05	.04	.02
	Panel	1.75	1.25	.70
13	Don Mattingly	6.00	4.50	2.50
14	Ozzie Smith	.08	.06	.03
	Panel	.50	.40	.20
15	Tony Pena	.05	.04	.02
16	Jim Rice	.15	.11	.06
	Panel	.80	.60	.30
17	Ryne Sandberg	.25	.20	.10
18	Mike Schmidt	.40	.30	.15
	Panel	.80	.60	.30
19	Darryl Strawberry	.12	.09	.05
20	Fernando Valenzuela	.20	.15	.08

1985 Cain's Potato Chips Tigers

This 20-card set commemorating the 1984 World champion Tigers was issued by Cain's Potato Chips in the Michigan area in 1985. The yellow-bordered, unnumbered cards measure 2-3/4" in diameter and feature full-color oval photos inside a diamond. The word "Cain's" appears in the upper left corner, while the player's name appears in the lower left with his position directly below the photo. The words "1984 World Champions" are printed in the upper right corner. The backs include 1984 statistics. The cards were inserted in bags of potato chips.

		MT	NR MT	EX
	Complete Set:	40.00	30.00	16.00
	Common Player:	1.00	.70	.40
(1)	Doug Bair	1.00	.70	.40
(2)	Juan Berenguer	1.00	.70	.40
(3)	Dave Bergman	1.00	.70	.40
(4)	Tom Brookens	1.00	.70	.40
(5)	Marty Castillo	1.00	.70	.40
(6)	Darrell Evans	2.75	2.00	1.00
(7)	Barbaro Garbey	1.00	.70	.40
(8)	Kirk Gibson	3.50	2.75	1.50
(9)	John Grubb	1.00	.70	.40
(10)	Willie Hernandez	1.50	1.25	.60
(11)	Larry Herndon	1.50	1.25	.60
(12)	Chet Lemon	1.50	1.25	.60
(13)	Aurelio Lopez	1.00	.70	.40
(14)	Jack Morris	3.50	2.75	1.50
(15)	Lance Parrish	3.50	2.75	1.50
(16)	Dan Petry	1.50	1.25	.60
(17)	Bill Scherrer	1.00	.70	.40
(18)	Alan Trammell	4.00	3.00	1.50
(19)	Lou Whitaker	3.50	2.75	1.50
(20)	Milt Wilcox	1.00	.70	.40

1986 Cain's Potato Chips Tigers

For the second year in a row, player discs of the Detroit Tigers were found in boxes of Cain's Potato Chips sold in the Detroit area. Twenty discs make up the set which is branded as a "1986 Annual Collectors' Edition." The discs, which measure 2-3/4" in diameter, have fronts which contain a color photo plus the player's name, team and position. The Cain's logo and the Major League Baseball Players Association's logo also appear. The backs, which display black print on white stock, contain player information plus the card number.

		MT	NR MT	EX
Complete Set:		40.00	30.00	16.00
Common Player:		1.00	.70	.40
1	Tom Brookens	1.00	.70	.40
2	Willie Hernandez	1.50	1.25	.60
3	Dave Bergman	1.00	.70	.40
4	Lou Whitaker	3.50	2.75	1.50
5	Dave LaPoint	1.00	.70	.40
6	Lance Parrish	3.50	2.75	1.50
7	Randy O'Neal	1.00	.70	.40
8	Nelson Simmons	1.00	.70	.40
9	Larry Herndon	1.00	.70	.40
10	Doug Flynn	1.00	.70	.40
11	Jack Morris	3.50	2.75	1.50
12	Dan Petry	1.00	.70	.40
13	Walt Terrell	1.00	.70	.40
14	Chet Lemon	1.50	1.25	.60
15	Frank Tanana	1.50	1.25	.60
16	Kirk Gibson	4.00	3.00	1.50
17	Darrell Evans	2.75	2.00	1.00
18	Dave Collins	1.00	.70	.40
19	John Grubb	1.00	.70	.40
20	Alan Trammell	4.00	3.00	1.50

1987 Cain's Potato Chips Tigers

Player discs of the Detroit Tigers were inserted in boxes of Cain's Potato Chips for the third consecutive year. The 1987 edition is made up of 20 round cards, each measuring 2-3/4" in diameter. The discs, which were packaged in a cellophane wrapper, feature a full-color photo surrounded by an orange border. The backs are printed in red on white stock. The set was produced by Mike Schecter and Associates.

		MT	NR MT	EX
Complete Set:		20.00	15.00	8.00
Common Player:		.60	.45	.25
1	Tom Brookens	.60	.45	.25
2	Darnell Coles	.75	.60	.30
3	Mike Heath	.60	.45	.25
4	Dave Bergman	.60	.45	.25
5	Dwight Lowry	.60	.45	.25
6	Darrell Evans	1.25	.90	.50
7	Alan Trammell	2.75	2.00	1.00
8	Lou Whitaker	2.00	1.50	.80
9	Kirk Gibson	2.75	2.00	1.00
10	Chet Lemon	.75	.60	.30
11	Larry Herndon	.60	.45	.25
12	John Grubb	.60	.45	.25
13	Willie Hernandez	.75	.60	.30
14	Jack Morris	2.00	1.50	.80
15	Dan Petry	.60	.45	.25
16	Walt Terrell	.60	.45	.25

		MT	NR MT	EX
17	Mark Thurmond	.60	.45	.25
18	Pat Sheridan	.60	.45	.25
19	Eric King	.75	.60	.30
20	Frank Tanana	.75	.60	.30

1989 Cap'n Crunch

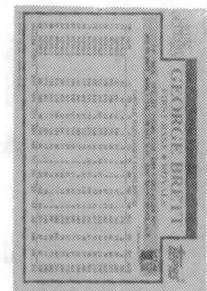

This 22-card set was produced by Topps for Cap'n Crunch cereal boxes. Two cards and a stick of gum were included in each cereal box while the offer was active. The fronts of these 2-1/2" by 3-1/2" cards feature red, white and blue borders. The card backs are horizontal and feature lifetime statistics. The set was not offered in any complete set deal.

		MT	NR MT	EX
Complete Set:		15.00	11.00	6.00
Common Player:		.50	.40	.20
1	Jose Canseco	1.00	.70	.40
2	Kirk Gibson	.50	.40	.20
3	Orel Hershiser	.60	.45	.35
4	Frank Viola	.70	.50	.30
5	Tony Gwynn	.60	.45	.35
6	Cal Ripken	.70	.50	.30
7	Darryl Strawberry	.80	.60	.30
8	Don Mattingly	.90	.70	.40
9	George Brett	.70	.50	.30
10	Andre Dawson	.60	.45	.25
11	Dale Murphy	.50	.40	.20
12	Alan Trammell	.50	.40	.20
13	Eric Davis	.80	.60	.30
14	Jack Clark	.50	.40	.20
15	Eddie Murray	.50	.40	.20
16	Mike Schmidt	1.00	.70	.40
17	Dwight Gooden	.80	.60	.30
18	Roger Clemens	.80	.60	.30
19	Will Clark	.80	.60	.30
20	Kirby Puckett	.70	.50	.30
21	Robin Yount	.60	.45	.25
22	Mark McGwire	.80	.60	.30

1984 Cereal Series

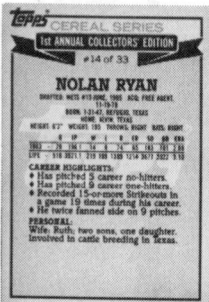

The Topps-produced 1984 Cereal Series set is identical to the Ralston Purina set from the same year in nearly all aspects. On the card fronts the words "Ralston Purina Company" were replaced by "Cereal Series" and Topps logos were substituted for Ralston checkerboard logos. The set is comprised of 33 cards, each measuring 2-1/2" by 3-1/2." The cards were inserted in unmarked boxes of Chex brand cereals.

		MT	NR MT	EX
	Complete Set	13.00	9.75	5.25
	Common Player	.20	.15	.08
1	Eddie Murray	.50	.40	.20
2	Ozzie Smith	.30	.25	.12
3	Ted Simmons	.20	.15	.08
4	Pete Rose	1.00	.70	.40
5	Greg Luzinski	.20	.15	.08
6	Andre Dawson	.50	.40	.20
7	Dave Winfield	.50	.40	.20
8	Tom Seaver	.50	.40	.20
9	Jim Rice	.50	.40	.20
10	Fernando Valenzuela	.40	.30	.15
11	Wade Boggs	1.75	1.25	.70
12	Dale Murphy	.90	.70	.35
13	George Brett	.90	.70	.35
14	Nolan Ryan	1.00	.70	.40
15	Rickey Henderson	.80	.60	.30
16	Steve Carlton	.50	.40	.20
17	Rod Carew	.60	.45	.25
18	Steve Garvey	.50	.40	.20
19	Reggie Jackson	.60	.45	.25
20	Dave Concepcion	.20	.15	.08
21	Robin Yount	.60	.45	.25
22	Mike Schmidt	1.00	.70	.40
23	Jim Palmer	1.00	.70	.40
24	Bruce Sutter	.20	.15	.08
25	Dan Quisenberry	.20	.15	.08
26	Bill Madlock	.20	.15	.08
27	Cecil Cooper	.20	.15	.08
28	Gary Carter	.30	.25	.12
29	Fred Lynn	.30	.25	.12
30	Pedro Guerrero	.30	.25	.12
31	Ron Guidry	.30	.25	.12
32	Keith Hernandez	.40	.30	.15
33	Carlton Fisk	.30	.25	.12

1987 Champion Phillies

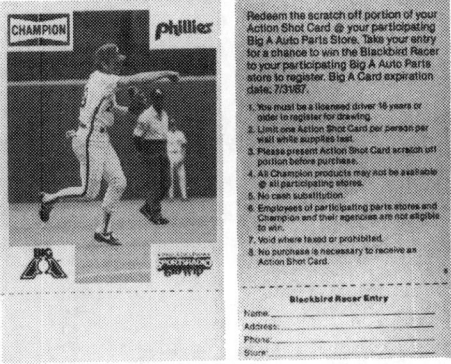

This four card set is interesting in that the players are not identified on the card fronts or backs. The full-color cards, which measure 2-3/4" by 4-5/16", were produced by the Champion Spark Plug Co. as part of a contest held at participating Big A, Car Quest and Pep Boys auto parts stores. Entrants were advised to return the scratch-off coupon portion of the card for a chance to win a Blackbird Racer. Each card contains a scratch-off portion which may have contained an instant prize. Each card can be found with either a Big A, Car Quest or Pep Boys logo in the lower left corner on the card front. The contest was also sponsored in part by the Philadelphia Phillies and radio station WIP.

		MT	NR MT	EX
	Complete Set:	18.00	13.50	7.25
	Common Player:	1.00	.70	.40
(1)	Von Hayes (glove on knee)	3.00	2.25	1.25
(2)	Steve Jeltz (#30 on uniform)	1.00	.70	.40
(3)	Juan Samuel (laying on base)	3.50	2.75	1.50
(4)	Mike Schmidt (making throw)	12.00	9.00	4.75

1988 Chef Boyardee

 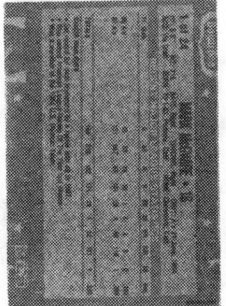

This uncut sheet of 24 cards highlights 12 American and 12 National League players. Full-color player closeup photos are printed beneath a red, white and blue "1988 1st Annual Collector's Edition" header. The player name, team and position appear beneath his photo. Card backs are printed in blue ink on a red background and include biographical information, stats and career highlights including acquisition date and draft date/choice number. The set was produced by American Home Food Products for exclusive distribution via a mail-in offer involving proofs of purchase from the company's Chef Boyardee products.

		MT	NR MT	EX
	Complete Uncut Sheet:	25.00	18.50	10.00
	Complete Singles Set:	20.00	15.00	8.00
	Common Single Player:	.50	.40	.20
1	Mark McGwire	2.50	2.00	1.00
2	Eric Davis	1.75	1.25	.70
3	Jack Morris	.50	.40	.20
4	George Bell	.75	.60	.30
5	Ozzie Smith	.50	.40	.20
6	Tony Gwynn	1.00	.70	.40
7	Cal Ripken, Jr.	1.00	.70	.40
8	Todd Worrell	.50	.40	.20
9	Larry Parrish	.50	.40	.20
10	Gary Carter	.70	.50	.30
11	Ryne Sandberg	.75	.60	.30
12	Keith Hernandez	.60	.45	.25
13	Kirby Puckett	1.25	.90	.50
14	Mike Schmidt	1.75	1.25	.70
15	Frank Viola	.50	.40	.20
16	Don Mattingly	3.00	2.25	1.25
17	Dale Murphy	.90	.70	.35
18a	Andre Dawson (1987 team is Expos)	.75	.60	.30
18b	Andre Dawson (1987 team is Cubs)	.75	.60	.30
19	Mike Scott	.50	.40	.20
20	Rickey Henderson	1.25	.90	.50
21	Jim Rice	.75	.60	.30
22	Wade Boggs	2.00	1.50	.80
23	Roger Clemens	1.75	1.25	.70
24	Fernando Valenzuela	.75	.60	.30

1985 Circle K

Produced by Topps for Circle K stores, this 33-card set is entitled "Baseball All Time Home Run Kings". The cards, which measure 2-1/2" by 3-1/2", are numbered on the back according to the player's position on the all-time career home run list. Joe DiMaggio, who ranked 31st, was not included in the set. The set is skip-numbered from 30 to 32. The glossy card fronts contain the player's name in the lower left corner and feature a color photo, although

set consists of 100 full-color cards which were used to play the game. Game participants were required to answer trivia questions found on the backs of the cards. The attractive cards measure 2 1/2" by 3 1/2" and are printed on glossy card stock. The card backs carry the player's career statistics besides the Classic Baseball Questions. The game was produced by Game Time, Ltd. of Marietta, Ga., and sold for $19.95 in most retail outlets.

black and white photos were utilized for a few of the homer kings who played before 1960. The card backs have blue and red print on white stock and contain the player's career batting statistics. The set was issued with a specially designed box.

		MT	NR MT	EX
Complete Set:		10.00	7.50	4.00
Common Player:		.15	.11	.06
1	Hank Aaron	.60	.45	.25
2	Babe Ruth	1.25	.90	.50
3	Willie Mays	.60	.45	.25
4	Frank Robinson	.25	.20	.10
5	Harmon Killebrew	.25	.20	.10
6	Mickey Mantle	2.00	1.50	.80
7	Jimmie Foxx	.25	.20	.10
8	Willie McCovey	.25	.20	.10
9	Ted Williams	.70	.50	.30
10	Ernie Banks	.25	.20	.10
11	Eddie Mathews	.25	.20	.10
12	Mel Ott	.20	.15	.08
13	Reggie Jackson	.40	.30	.15
14	Lou Gehrig	.70	.50	.30
15	Stan Musial	.60	.45	.25
16	Willie Stargell	.20	.15	.08
17	Carl Yastrzemski	.50	.40	.20
18	Billy Williams	.20	.15	.08
19	Mike Schmidt	.40	.30	.15
20	Duke Snider	.40	.30	.15
21	Al Kaline	.25	.20	.10
22	Johnny Bench	.35	.25	.14
23	Frank Howard	.15	.11	.06
24	Orlando Cepeda	.15	.11	.06
25	Norm Cash	.15	.11	.06
26	Dave Kingman	.15	.11	.06
27	Rocky Colavito	.15	.11	.06
28	Tony Perez	.15	.11	.06
29	Gil Hodges	.20	.15	.08
30	Ralph Kiner	.20	.15	.08
32	Johnny Mize	.20	.15	.08
33	Yogi Berra	.35	.25	.14
34	Lee May	.15	.11	.06

1987 Classic Major League Baseball Game

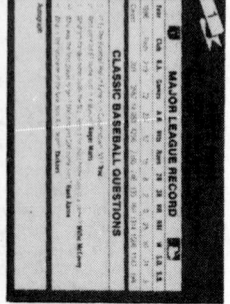

The "Classic Major League Baseball Board Game"

		MT	NR MT	EX
Complete Set:		200.00	150.00	80.00
Common Player:		.10	.08	.04
1	Pete Rose	1.00	.70	.40
2	Len Dykstra	2.00	1.50	.80
3	Darryl Strawberry	3.00	2.25	1.25
4	Keith Hernandez	.40	.30	.15
5	Gary Carter	.50	.40	.20
6	Wally Joyner	1.00	.70	.40
7	Andres Thomas	.15	.11	.06
8	Pat Dodson	.15	.11	.06
9	Kirk Gibson	.30	.25	.12
10	Don Mattingly	6.00	4.50	2.50
11	Dave Winfield	.40	.30	.15
12	Rickey Henderson	5.00	3.75	2.50
13	Dan Pasqua	.15	.11	.06
14	Don Baylor	.15	.11	.06
15	Bo Jackson	80.00	60.00	32.00
16	Pete Incaviglia	.60	.45	.25
17	Kevin Bass	.10	.08	.04
18	Barry Larkin	.80	.60	.30
19	Dave Magadan	.70	.50	.30
20	Steve Sax	.20	.15	.08
21	Eric Davis	1.25	.90	.50
22	Mike Pagliarulo	.15	.11	.06
23	Fred Lynn	.20	.15	.08
24	Reggie Jackson	.50	.40	.20
25	Larry Parrish	.10	.08	.04
26	Tony Gwynn	2.00	1.50	.80
27	Steve Garvey	.40	.30	.15
28	Glenn Davis	.20	.15	.08
29	Tim Raines	.40	.30	.15
30	Vince Coleman	.20	.15	.08
31	Willie McGee	.15	.11	.06
32	Ozzie Smith	.80	.60	.30
33	Dave Parker	.20	.15	.08
34	Tony Pena	.10	.08	.04
35	Ryne Sandberg	5.00	3.75	2.00
36	Brett Butler	.10	.08	.04
37	Dale Murphy	.70	.50	.30
38	Bob Horner	.15	.11	.06
39	Pedro Guerrero	.25	.20	.10
40	Brook Jacoby	.15	.11	.06
41	Carlton Fisk	.20	.15	.08
42	Harold Baines	.15	.11	.06
43	Rob Deer	.10	.08	.04
44	Robin Yount	1.00	.70	.40
45	Paul Molitor	.20	.15	.08
46	Jose Canseco	40.00	30.00	15.00
47	George Brett	.70	.50	.30
48	Jim Presley	.15	.11	.06
49	Rich Gedman	.10	.08	.04
50	Lance Parrish	.20	.15	.08
51	Eddie Murray	.50	.40	.20
52	Cal Ripken, Jr.	.60	.45	.25
53	Kent Hrbek	.25	.20	.10
54	Gary Gaetti	.20	.15	.08
55	Kirby Puckett	4.00	3.00	1.50
56	George Bell	.40	.30	.15
57	Tony Fernandez	.20	.15	.08
58	Jesse Barfield	.15	.11	.06
59	Jim Rice	.40	.30	.15
60	Wade Boggs	1.75	1.25	.70
61	Marty Barrett	.10	.08	.04
62	Mike Schmidt	5.00	3.75	2.00
63	Von Hayes	.15	.11	.06
64	Jeff Leonard	.10	.08	.04
65	Chris Brown	.15	.11	.06
66	Dave Smith	.10	.08	.04
67	Mike Krukow	.10	.08	.04
68	Ron Guidry	.20	.15	.08
69	Rob Woodward	.15	.11	.06
70	Rob Murphy	.15	.11	.06
71	Andres Galarraga	.25	.20	.10
72	Dwight Gooden	1.25	.90	.50
73	Bob Ojeda	.10	.08	.04
74	Sid Fernandez	.15	.11	.06
75	Jesse Orosco	.10	.08	.04
76	Roger McDowell	.15	.11	.06

		MT	NR MT	EX
77	John Tutor (Tudor)	.15	.11	.06
78	Tom Browning	.15	.11	.06
79	Rick Aguilera	.10	.08	.04
80	Lance McCullers	.15	.11	.06
81	Mike Scott	.20	.15	.08
82	Nolan Ryan	8.00	6.00	3.25
83	Bruce Hurst	.15	.11	.06
84	Roger Clemens	2.00	1.50	.80
85	Oil Can Boyd	.10	.08	.04
86	Dave Righetti	.20	.15	.08
87	Dennis Rasmussen	.10	.08	.04
88	Bret Saberhagan (Saberhagen)	.35	.25	.14
89	Mark Langston	.35	.25	.14
90	Jack Morris	.15	.11	.06
91	Fernando Valenzuela	.25	.20	.10
92	Orel Hershiser	.35	.25	.14
93	Rick Honeycutt	.10	.08	.04
94	Jeff Reardon	.15	.11	.06
95	John Habyan	.10	.08	.04
96	Goose Gossage	.15	.11	.06
97	Todd Worrell	.20	.15	.08
98	Floyd Youmans	.10	.08	.04
99	Don Aase	.10	.08	.04
100	John Franco	.15	.11	.06

		MT	NR MT	EX
123	Mike Scott	.20	.15	.08
124	Andre Dawson	.50	.40	.20
125	Jose Canseco	4.00	3.00	1.50
126	Kevin McReynolds	.25	.20	.10
127	Joe Carter	.20	.15	.08
128	Casey Candaele	.08	.06	.03
129	Matt Nokes	.30	.25	.12
130	Kal Daniels	.60	.45	.25
131	Pete Incaviglia	.60	.45	.25
132	Benito Santiago	.60	.45	.25
133	Barry Larkin	.60	.45	.25
134	Gary Pettis	.08	.06	.03
135	B.J. Surhoff	.60	.45	.25
136	Juan Nieves	.15	.11	.06
137	Jim Deshaies	.15	.11	.06
138	Pete O'Brien	.15	.11	.06
139	Kevin Seitzer	.50	.40	.20
140	Devon White	.50	.40	.20
141	Rob Deer	.08	.06	.03
142	Kurt Stillwell	.25	.20	.10
143	Edwin Correa	.08	.06	.03
144	Dion James	.08	.06	.03
145	Danny Tartabull	.40	.30	.15
146	Jerry Browne	.08	.06	.03
147	Ted Higuera	.15	.11	.06
148	Jack Clark	.20	.15	.08
149	Ruben Sierra	2.00	1.50	.80
150	McGwire/Davis (Eric Davis, Mark McGwire)	1.25	.90	.50

1987 Classic Baseball Travel Edition

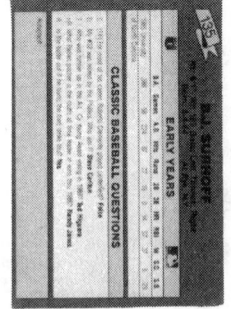

B.J. Surhoff

Game Time, Ltd. of Marietta, Ga., issued as an update to their Classic Baseball Board Game a 50-card set entitled "Travel Edition." The cards measure 2-1/2" by 3-1/2" and feature the same outstanding quality characteristic of the first release. Numbered from 101 to 150, the "Travel Edition" is an extension of the original set. Besides updating player trades and showcasing rookies, the set offers several highlights from the 1987 season, including Andre Dawson's beaning. All new trivia questions are contained on the card backs.

		MT	NR MT	EX
Complete Set:		30.00	22.00	12.00
Common Player:		.08	.06	.03
101	Mike Schmidt	1.25	.90	.50
102	Eric Davis	1.00	.70	.40
103	Pete Rose	.70	.50	.30
104	Don Mattingly	2.75	2.00	1.00
105	Wade Boggs	1.50	1.25	.60
106	Dale Murphy	.70	.50	.30
107	Glenn Davis	.20	.15	.08
108	Wally Joyner	1.00	.70	.40
109	Bo Jackson	5.00	3.75	2.50
110	Cory Snyder	.60	.45	.25
111	Jim Lindeman	.15	.11	.06
112	Kirby Puckett	.90	.70	.35
113	Barry Bonds	3.00	2.25	1.25
114	Roger Clemens	1.00	.70	.40
115	Oddibe McDowell	.08	.06	.03
116	Bret Saberhagen	.30	.25	.12
117	Joe Magrane	.30	.25	.12
118	Scott Fletcher	.08	.06	.03
119	Mark McLemore	.08	.06	.03
120	Who Me? (Joe Niekro)	.25	.20	.10
121	Mark McGwire	2.00	1.50	.80
122	Darryl Strawberry	1.00	.70	.40

1988 Classic Baseball Travel Edition - Red

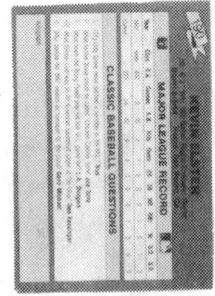

Kevin Elster

This 50-card set, numbered 151-200, was produced for use with the travel edition of Game Time's Classic Baseball Board Game. Special cards in the set include a McGwire/Mattingly, an instruction card with McGwire/Canseco, and three different cards featuring Phil Niekro (in different uniforms). A follow-up to the first edition in 1987, the 1988 Red Series was designed for use with the 1988 Blue Series (#'s 201-250). Red Series card fronts have red borders, a yellow Classic logo in the upper left corner and a black and beige player name banner beneath the photo. The card backs are printed in red and pink on white and include the player name, personal info, major league records, a baseball question and space for the player autograph. Classic card series were sold via hobby dealers and retail toy stores nationwide. Game Time Ltd., the set's producer, was purchased by Scoreboard of Cherry Hill, N.J. in 1988.

		MT	NR MT	EX
Complete Set:		12.00	9.00	4.75
Common Player:		.08	.06	.03
151	Don Mattingly, Mark McGwire,	2.00	1.50	.80
152	Don Mattingly	2.00	1.50	.80
153	Mark McGwire	.50	.40	.20
154	Eric Davis	.50	.40	.20
155	Wade Boggs	1.25	.90	.50
156	Dale Murphy	.50	.40	.20
157	Andre Dawson	.25	.20	.10
158	Roger Clemens	.50	.40	.20
159	Kevin Seitzer	.25	.20	.10

		MT	NR MT	EX
160	Benito Santiago	.25	.20	.10
161	Kal Daniels	.25	.20	.10
162	John Kruk	.25	.20	.10
163	Bill Ripken	.08	.06	.03
164	Kirby Puckett	.50	.40	.20
165	Jose Canseco	1.50	1.25	.60
166	Matt Nokes	.25	.20	.10
167	Mike Schmidt	1.00	.70	.40
168	Tim Raines	.25	.20	.10
169	Ryne Sandberg	.70	.50	.30
170	Dave Winfield	.25	.20	.10
171	Dwight Gooden	.70	.50	.30
172	Bret Saberhagen	.20	.15	.08
173	Willie McGee	.08	.06	.03
174	Jack Morris	.08	.06	.03
175	Jeff Leonard	.08	.06	.03
176	Cal Ripken, Jr.	.25	.20	.10
177	Pete Incaviglia	.08	.06	.03
178	Devon White	.10	.08	.04
179	Nolan Ryan	3.00	2.25	1.25
180	Ruben Sierra	.70	.50	.25
181	Todd Worrell	.08	.06	.03
182	Glenn Davis	.25	.20	.10
183	Frank Viola	.25	.20	.10
184	Cory Snyder	.40	.30	.15
185	Tracy Jones	.08	.06	.03
186	Terry Steinbach	.50	.40	.20
187	Julio Franco	.30	.25	.12
188	Larry Sheets	.08	.06	.03
189	John Marzano	.08	.06	.03
190	Kevin Elster	.08	.06	.03
191	Vincente Palacios	.08	.06	.03
192	Kent Hrbek	.25	.20	.10
193	Eric Bell	.25	.20	.10
194	Kelly Downs	.08	.06	.03
195	Jose Lind	.10	.08	.04
196	Dave Stewart	.30	.25	.12
197	Jose Canseco, Mark McGwire,	2.00	1.50	.80
198	Phil Niekro	.25	.20	.10
199	Phil Niekro	.25	.20	.10
200	Phil Niekro	.25	.20	.10

			MT	NR MT	EX
201	Davis/Murphy (Eric Davis, Dale Murphy)		.40	.30	.15
202	B.J. Surhoff		.15	.11	.06
203	John Kruk		.20	.15	.08
204	Sam Horn		.15	.11	.06
205	Jack Clark		.25	.20	.10
206	Wally Joyner		.35	.25	.14
207	Matt Nokes		.30	.25	.12
208	Bo Jackson		4.00	3.00	1.50
209	Darryl Strawberry		1.00	.70	.40
210	Ozzie Smith		.25	.20	.10
211	Don Mattingly		2.00	1.50	.80
212	Mark McGwire		1.25	.90	.50
213	Eric Davis		1.00	.70	.40
214	Wade Boggs		1.50	1.25	.60
215	Dale Murphy		.30	.25	.12
216	Andre Dawson		.30	.25	.12
217	Roger Clemens		.50	.40	.20
218	Kevin Seitzer		.30	.25	.12
219	Benito Santiago		.30	.25	.12
220	Tony Gwynn		.50	.40	.20
221	Mike Scott		.20	.15	.08
222	Steve Bedrosian		.15	.11	.06
223	Vince Coleman		.25	.20	.10
224	Rick Sutcliffe		.15	.11	.06
225	Will Clark		7.00	5.25	2.75
226	Pete Rose		.80	.60	.30
227	Mike Greenwell		1.50	1.25	.60
228	Ken Caminiti		.15	.11	.06
229	Ellis Burks		.80	.60	.30
230	Dave Magadan		.15	.11	.06
231	Alan Trammell		.30	.25	.12
232	Paul Molitor		.25	.20	.10
233	Gary Gaetti		.25	.20	.10
234	Rickey Henderson		.80	.60	.30
235	Danny Tartabull		.40	.30	.15
236	Bobby Bonilla		.50	.40	.20
237	Mike Dunne		.20	.15	.08
238	Al Leiter		.15	.11	.06
239	John Farrell		.15	.11	.06
240	Joe Magrane		.15	.11	.06
241	Mike Henneman		.15	.11	.06
242	George Bell		.40	.30	.15
243	Gregg Jefferies		2.25	1.75	.90
244	Jay Buhner		.40	.30	.15
245	Todd Benzinger		.30	.25	.12
246	Matt Williams		1.00	.70	.40
247	McGwire/Mattingly (Don Mattingly, Mark McGwire) (no card number on back)		1.50	1.25	.60
248	George Brett		.40	.30	.15
249	Jimmy Key		.20	.15	.08
250	Mark Langston		.20	.15	.08

1988 Classic Baseball Travel Edition - Blue

Darryl Strawberry

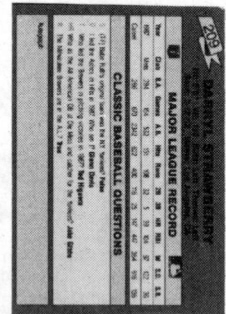

This 50-card set, numbered 201-250, was produced for use with the travel edition of Game Time's Classic Baseball Board Game. Two cards in the set feature two players: Davis/Murphy and McGwire/Mattingly. A follow-up to the first edition in 1987, the 1988 Blue was designed for use with the 1988 Red Series (151-200). Blue Series card fronts have blue borders, a yellow classic logo in the upper left corner and a black and beige player name banner beneath the photo. The card backs are printed in blue on white and include the player name, personal info, major league records, a baseball question and space for the player autograph. Classic card series are sold via hobby dealers and retail toy stores nationwide. Game Time Ltd., the set's producer, was purchased by Scoreboard of Cherry Hill, N.J. in 1988.

	MT	NR MT	EX
Complete Set:	20.00	15.00	8.00
Common Player:	.15	.11	.06

1989 Classic Baseball

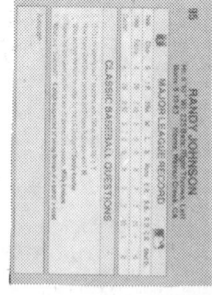

This 100-card set was released by The Score Board to accompany trivia board games. Cards numbered 1-100 correlate with the 1989 Classic Baseball Game, while cards numbered 101-150 belong to the 1989 Classic Travel Series No. 1. The card fronts display full-color photos with the Classic Baseball logo in the upper left corner. The player's name appears beneath the photo. The flip side includes the card number in the upper left, personal information, and the player's major league record in a boxed area. Another boxed area below the record presents five trivia questions. The lower border of the flip side provides an autograph space. The Classic card series was sold by retail stores and hobby dealers nationwide.

		MT	NR MT	EX
	Complete Set:	30.00	22.50	12.00
	Common Player:	.08	.06	.03
1	Orel Hershiser	.30	.25	.12
2	Wade Boggs	.60	.45	.25
3	Jose Canseco	1.75	1.25	.70
4	Mark McGwire	.60	.45	.25
5	Don Mattingly	.80	.60	.30
6	Gregg Jefferies	1.00	.70	.40
7	Dwight Gooden	.60	.45	.25
8	Darryl Strawberry	.40	.30	.15
9	Eric Davis	.50	.40	.20
10	Joey Meyer	.08	.06	.03
11	Joe Carter	.15	.11	.06
12	Paul Molitor	.15	.11	.06
13	Mark Grace	1.50	1.25	.60
14	Kurt Stillwell	.08	.06	.03
15	Kirby Puckett	.60	.45	.25
16	Keith Miller	.08	.06	.03
17	Glenn Davis	.15	.11	.06
18	Will Clark	1.50	1.25	.60
19	Cory Snyder	.15	.11	.06
20	Jose Lind	.08	.06	.03
21	Andres Thomas	.08	.06	.03
22	Dave Smith	.08	.06	.03
23	Mike Scott	.15	.11	.06
24	Kevin McReynolds	.20	.15	.08
25	B.J. Surhoff	.20	.15	.08
26	Mackey Sasser	.08	.06	.03
27	Chad Kreuter	.20	.15	.08
28	Hal Morris	.70	.50	.30
29	Wally Joyner	.20	.15	.08
30	Tony Gwynn	.40	.30	.15
31	Kevin Mitchell	1.75	1.25	.70
32	Dave Winfield	.25	.20	.10
33	Billy Bean	.08	.06	.03
34	Steve Bedrosian	.08	.06	.03
35	Ron Gant	.70	.50	.30
36	Len Dykstra	.20	.15	.08
37	Andre Dawson	.20	.15	.08
38	Brett Butler	.20	.15	.08
39	Rob Deer	.08	.06	.03
40	Tommy John	.08	.06	.03
41	Gary Gaetti	.20	.15	.08
42	Tim Raines	.20	.15	.08
43	George Bell	.20	.15	.08
44	Dwight Evans	.20	.15	.08
45	Denny Martinez	.08	.06	.03
46	Andres Galarraga	.20	.15	.08
47	George Brett	.40	.30	.15
48	Mike Schmidt	1.00	.70	.30
49	Dave Steib	.20	.15	.08
50	Rickey Henderson	.50	.40	.20
51	Craig Biggio	.80	.60	.30
52	Mark Lemke	.25	.20	.10
53	Chris Sabo	.60	.45	.25
54	Jeff Treadway	.15	.11	.06
55	Kent Hrbek	.15	.11	.06
56	Cal Ripken, Jr.	.25	.20	.10
57	Tim Belcher	.15	.11	.06
58	Ozzie Smith	.40	.30	.15
59	Keith Hernandez	.20	.15	.08
60	Pedro Guerrero	.20	.15	.08
61	Greg Swindell	.25	.20	.10
62	Bret Saberhagen	.40	.30	.15
63	John Tudor	.08	.06	.03
64	Gary Carter	.15	.11	.06
65	Kevin Seitzer	.20	.15	.08
66	Jesse Barfield	.20	.15	.08
67	Luis Medina	.20	.15	.08
68	Walt Weiss	.35	.25	.14
69	Terry Steinbach	.30	.25	.12
70	Barry Larkin	.30	.25	.12
71	Pete Rose	1.00	.70	.30
72	Luis Salazar	.08	.06	.03
73	Benito Santiago	.40	.30	.15
74	Kal Daniels	.20	.15	.08
75	Kevin Elster	.08	.06	.03
76	Rob Dibble	.50	.40	.20
77	Bobby Witt	.50	.40	.20
78	Steve Searcy	.25	.20	.10
79	Sandy Alomar	2.00	1.50	.80
80	Chili Davis	.20	.15	.08
81	Alvin Davis	.20	.15	.08
82	Charlie Leibrandt	.08	.06	.03
83	Robin Yount	1.00	.70	.30
84	Mark Carreon	.25	.20	.10

		MT	NR MT	EX
85	Pascual Perez	.08	.06	.03
86	Dennis Rasmussen	.08	.06	.03
87	Ernie Riles	.08	.06	.03
88	Melido Perez	.20	.15	.08
89	Doug Jones	.08	.06	.03
90	Dennis Eckersley	.15	.11	.06
91	Bob Welch	.15	.11	.06
92	Bob Milacki	.15	.11	.06
93	Jeff Robinson	.15	.11	.06
94	Mike Henneman	.15	.11	.06
95	Randy Johnson	.40	.30	.15
96	Ron Jones	.15	.11	.06
97	Jack Armstrong	.25	.20	.10
98	Willie McGee	.08	.06	.03
99	Ryne Sandberg	.40	.30	.15
100	David Cone / Danny Jackson	.70	.50	.25
101	Gary Sheffield	1.00	.70	.30
102	Wade Boggs	.60	.45	.25
103	Jose Canseco	1.25	.90	.50
104	Mark McGwire	1.25	.90	.50
105	Orel Hershiser	.30	.25	.12
106	Don Mattingly	1.25	.90	.50
107	Dwight Gooden	.70	.50	.30
108	Darryl Strawberry	.40	.30	.15
109	Eric Davis	.40	.30	.15
110	Bam Bam Meulens	.40	.30	.15
111	Andy Van Slyke	.20	.15	.08
112	Al Leiter	.08	.06	.03
113	Matt Nokes	.15	.11	.06
114	Mike Krukow	.08	.06	.03
115	Tony Fernandez	.25	.20	.10
116	Fred McGriff	.30	.25	.12
117	Barry Bonds	.50	.40	.20
118	Gerald Perry	.08	.06	.03
119	Roger Clemens	.40	.30	.15
120	Kirk Gibson	.12	.09	.05
121	Greg Maddux	.30	.25	.12
122	Bo Jackson	1.75	1.25	.70
123	Danny Jackson	.08	.06	.03
124	Dale Murphy	.20	.15	.08
125	David Cone	.35	.25	.14
126	Tom Browning	.15	.11	.06
127	Roberto Alomar	.50	.40	.20
128	Alan Trammell	.15	.11	.06
129	Rickey Jordan	.20	.15	.08
130	Ramon Martinez	1.00	.70	.40
131	Ken Griffey, Jr.	3.00	2.25	1.25
132	Gregg Olson	.50	.40	.20
133	Carlos Quintana	.35	.25	.14
134	Dave West	.30	.25	.12
135	Cameron Drew	.15	.11	.06
136	Ted Higuera	.25	.20	.20
137	Sil Campusano	.20	.15	.08
138	Mark Gubicza	.20	.15	.08
139	Mike Boddicker	.08	.06	.03
140	Paul Gibson	.08	.06	.03
141	Jose Rijo	.30	.25	.12
142	John Costello	.08	.06	.03
143	Cecil Espy	.08	.06	.03
144	Frank Viola	.25	.20	.10
145	Erik Hanson	.35	.25	.12
146	Juan Samuel	.08	.06	.03
147	Harold Reynolds	.15	.11	.06
148	Joe Magrane	.15	.11	.06
149	Mike Greenwell	.40	.20	.10
150	Darryl Strawberry / Will Clark	1.00	.70	.40

1989 Classic Update

Jim Abbott

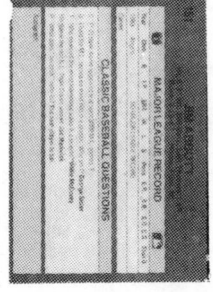

Numbered from 151-200, this 50-card set features

rookies and traded players with their new teams. The cards are purple and gray and were sold as part of a board game with baseball trivia questions.

		MT	NR MT	EX
Complete Set:		15.00	11.00	6.00
Common Player:		.05	.04	.02

151	Jim Abbott	.50	.40	.20
152	Ellis Burks	.30	.25	.12
153	Mike Schmidt	1.00	.70	.30
154	Gregg Jefferies	.50	.40	.20
155	Mark Grace	.30	.25	.12
156	Jerome Walton	.90	.70	.35
157	Bo Jackson	1.00	.70	.40
158	Jack Clark	.05	.04	.02
159	Tom Glavine	.10	.08	.04
160	Eddie Murray	.10	.08	.04
161	John Dopson	.05	.04	.02
162	Ruben Sierra	.35	.25	.14
163	Rafael Palmeiro	.20	.15	.08
164	Nolan Ryan	1.00	.70	.30
165	Barry Larkin	.20	.15	.08
166	Tommy Herr	.05	.04	.02
167	Roberto Kelly	.25	.20	.10
168	Glenn Davis	.10	.08	.04
169	Glenn Braggs	.05	.04	.02
170	Juan Bell	.30	.25	.12
171	Todd Burns	.05	.04	.02
172	Derek Lilliquist	.10	.08	.04
173	Orel Hershiser	.20	.15	.08
174	John Smoltz	.60	.45	.25
175	Ozzie Guillen / Ellis Burks	.30	.25	.12
176	Kirby Puckett	.50	.40	.20
177	Robin Ventura	.60	.45	.25
178	Allan Anderson	.05	.04	.02
179	Steve Sax	.05	.04	.02
180	Will Clark	.80	.60	.30
181	Mike Devereaux	.05	.04	.02
182	Tom Gordon	.60	.45	.25
183	Rob Murphy	.05	.04	.02
184	Pete O'Brien	.05	.04	.02
185	Cris Carpenter	.10	.08	.04
186	Tom Brunansky	.05	.04	.02
187	Bob Boone	.05	.04	.02
188	Lou Whitaker	.05	.04	.02
189	Dwight Gooden	.30	.25	.12
190	Mark McGwire	.40	.30	.15
191	John Smiley	.05	.04	.02
192	Tommy Gregg	.05	.04	.02
193	Ken Griffey, Jr.	2.50	2.00	1.00
194	Bruce Hurst	.05	.04	.02
195	Greg Swindell	.20	.15	.08
196	Nelson Liriano	.05	.04	.02
197	Randy Myers	.05	.04	.02
198	Kevin Mitchell	.70	.50	.30
199	Dante Bichette	.10	.08	.04
200	Deion Sanders	.25	.20	.10

1990 Classic Baseball

Mike Greenwell

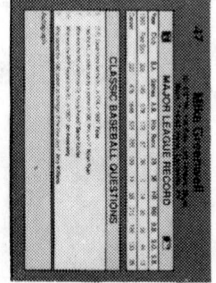

Classic Baseball returned in 1990 with another 150-card set. The cards were again sold as part of a baseball trivia game, and each game included a box designed to store all the cards in the set.

	MT	NR MT	EX
Complete Set:	18.00	13.50	7.25

		MT	NR MT	EX
Common Player:		.05	.04	.02
1	Nolan Ryan	1.00	.70	.40
2	Bo Jackson	.80	.60	.30
3	Gregg Olson	.30	.25	.12
4	Tom Gordon	.50	.40	.20
5	Robin Ventura	.60	.45	.25
6	Will Clark	.50	.40	.20
7	Ruben Sierra	.20	.15	.08
8	Mark Grace	.30	.25	.12
9	Luis de los Santos	.05	.04	.02
10	Bernie Williams	.40	.30	.15
11	Eric Davis	.10	.08	.04
12	Carney Lansford	.05	.04	.02
13	John Smoltz	.10	.08	.04
14	Gary Sheffield	.60	.45	.25
15	Kent Merker	.40	.30	.15
16	Don Mattingly	.50	.40	.20
17	Tony Gwynn	.15	.11	.06
18	Ozzie Smith	.05	.04	.02
19	Fred McGriff	.25	.20	.10
20	Ken Griffey, Jr.	2.00	1.50	.80
21a	Deion Sanders ("Prime Time")	10.00	7.50	4.00
21b	Deion Sanders (Deion "Prime Time" Sanders)	1.50	1.25	.60
22	Jose Canseco	.50	.40	.20
23	Mitch Williams	.20	.15	.08
24	Cal Ripken, Jr.	.10	.08	.04
25	Bob Geren	.20	.15	.08
26	Wade Boggs	.15	.11	.06
27	Ryne Sandberg	.25	.20	.10
28	Kirby Puckett	.25	.20	.10
29	Mike Scott	.05	.04	.02
30	Dwight Smith	.60	.45	.25
31	Craig Worthington	.10	.08	.04
32	Ricky Jordan	.15	.11	.06
33	Darryl Strawberry	.10	.08	.04
34	Jerome Walton	.70	.50	.30
35	John Olerud	2.50	2.00	1.00
36	Tom Glavine	.05	.04	.02
37	Rickey Henderson	.30	.25	.12
38	Rolando Roomes	.10	.08	.04
39	Mickey Tettleton	.10	.08	.04
40	Jim Abbott	.50	.40	.20
41	Dave Righetti	.05	.04	.02
42	Mike LaValliere	.05	.04	.02
43	Rob Dibble	.25	.20	.10
44	Pete Harnisch	.10	.08	.04
45	Jose Offerman	2.00	1.50	.80
46	Walt Weiss	.05	.04	.02
47	Mike Greenwell	.25	.20	.10
48	Barry Larkin	.10	.08	.04
49	Dave Gallagher	.05	.04	.02
50	Junior Felix	.60	.45	.25
51	Roger Clemens	.10	.08	.04
52	Lonnie Smith	.05	.04	.02
53	Jerry Browne	.05	.04	.02
54	Greg Briley	.25	.20	.10
55	Delino Desheilds	1.50	1.25	.70
56	Carmelo Martinez	.05	.04	.02
57	Craig Biggio	.20	.15	.08
58	Dwight Gooden	.15	.11	.06
59a	Bo Jackson, Ruben Sierra, Mark McGwire (Bo, Ruben, Mark)	6.00	4.50	2.50
59b	Bo Jackson, Ruben Sierra, Mark McGwire (A.L. Fence Busters)	.60	.45	.25
60	Greg Vaughn	.70	.50	.30
61	Roberto Alomar	.10	.08	.04
62	Steve Bedrosian	.05	.04	.02
63	Devon White	.05	.04	.02
64	Kevin Mitchell	.40	.30	.15
65	Marquis Grissom	.70	.50	.30
66	Brian Holman	.05	.04	.02
67	Julio Franco	.10	.08	.04
68	Dave West	.10	.08	.04
69	Harold Baines	.10	.08	.04
70	Eric Anthony	.70	.50	.30
71	Glenn Davis	.05	.04	.02
72	Mark Langston	.15	.11	.06
73	Matt Williams	.25	.20	.10
74	Rafael Palmeiro	.05	.04	.02
75	Pete Rose, Jr.	.70	.50	.30
76	Ramon Martinez	.50	.40	.20
77	Dwight Evans	.10	.08	.04
78	Mackey Sasser	.05	.04	.02
79	Mike Schooler	.05	.04	.02
80	Dennis Cook	.10	.08	.04
81	Orel Hershiser	.20	.15	.08
82	Barry Bonds	.30	.25	.12
83	Geronimo Berroa	.10	.08	.04
84	George Bell	.10	.08	.04

		MT	NR MT	EX
85	Andre Dawson	.10	.08	.04
86	John Franco	.05	.04	.02
87a	Will Clark, Tony Gwynn (Clark/Gwynn)			
		4.00	3.00	1.50
87b	Will Clark, Tony Gwynn (N.L. Hit Kings)			
		.40	.30	.15
88	Glenallen Hill	.35	.25	.14
89	Jeff Ballard	.10	.08	.04
90	Todd Zeile	1.25	.90	.50
91	Frank Viola	.15	.11	.06
92	Ozzie Guillen	.10	.08	.04
93	Jeff Leonard	.05	.04	.02
94	Dave Smith	.05	.04	.02
95	Dave Parker	.10	.08	.04
96	Jose Gonzalez	.20	.15	.08
97	Dave Steib	.05	.04	.02
98	Charlie Hayes	.15	.11	.06
99	Jesse Barfield	.05	.04	.02
100	Joey Belle	.30	.25	.12
101	Jeff Reardon	.05	.04	.02
102	Bruce Hurst	.05	.04	.02
103	Luis Medina	.05	.04	.02
104	Mike Moore	.10	.08	.04
105	Vince Coleman	.10	.08	.04
106	Alan Trammell	.10	.08	.04
107	Randy Myers	.05	.04	.02
108	Frank Tanana	.05	.04	.02
109	Craig Lefferts	.05	.04	.02
110	John Wetteland	.20	.15	.08
111	Chris Gwynn	.10	.08	.04
112	Mark Carreon	.10	.08	.04
113	Von Hayes	.05	.04	.02
114	Doug Jones	.05	.04	.02
115	Andres Galarraga	.10	.08	.04
116	Carlton Fisk	.10	.08	.04
117	Paul O'Neill	.05	.04	.02
118	Tim Raines	.10	.08	.04
119	Tom Brunansky	.05	.04	.02
120	Andy Benes	.50	.40	.20
121	Mark Portugal	.05	.04	.02
122	Willie Randolph	.05	.04	.02
123	Jeff Blauser	.05	.04	.02
124	Don August	.05	.04	.02
125	Chuck Cary	.05	.04	.02
126	John Smiley	.05	.04	.02
127	Terry Mullholland	.05	.04	.02
128	Harold Reynolds	.05	.04	.02
129	Hubie Brooks	.05	.04	.02
130	Ben McDonald	1.75	1.25	.70
131	Kevin Ritz	.20	.15	.08
132	Luis Quinones	.05	.04	.02
133	Bam Bam Meulens	.20	.15	.08
134	Bill Spiers	.20	.15	.08
135	Andy Hawkins	.05	.04	.02
136	Alvin Davis	.10	.08	.04
137	Lee Smith	.05	.04	.02
138	Joe Carter	.10	.08	.04
139	Bret Saberhagen	.10	.08	.04
140	Sammy Sosa	.50	.40	.20
141	Matt Nokes	.05	.04	.02
142	Bert Blyleven	.10	.08	.04
143	Bobby Bonilla	.20	.15	.08
144	Howard Johnson	.10	.08	.04
145	Joe Magrane	.05	.04	.02
146	Pedro Guerrero	.10	.08	.04
147	Robin Yount	.35	.25	.14
148	Dan Gladden	.05	.04	.02
149	Steve Sax	.10	.08	.04
150a	Will Clark, Kevin Mitchell (Clark/Mitchell)			
		4.00	3.00	1.50
150b	Will Clark, Kevin Mitchell (Bay Bombers)			
		.50	.40	.20

1990 Classic Series II

Like in previous years, Classic released a 50-card second series set for use with its baseball trivia game. Unlike the 1989 update set, the 1990 Classic Series II set is numbered 1-50 with a "T" designation accompanying the card number. The cards measure 2-1/2" by 3-1/2" and are designed after the original 1990 Classic cards. Series II cards have pink borders with a blue design, while the cards from the regular issue feature the opposite color combination. The cards are issued in a complete Series II set form.

		MT	NR MT	EX
	Complete Set:	10.00	7.50	4.00
	Common Player:	.05	.04	.02
1	Gregg Jefferies	.25	.20	.10
2	Steve Adkins	.30	.25	.12
3	Sandy Alomar, Jr.	.25	.20	.10
4	Steve Avery	.30	.25	.12
5	Mike Blowers	.20	.15	.08
6	George Brett	.05	.04	.02
7	Tom Browning	.05	.04	.02
8	Ellis Burks	.10	.08	.04
9	Joe Carter	.10	.08	.04
10	Jerald Clark	.10	.08	.04
11	"Hot Corners"	.40	.30	.15
12	Pat Combs	.25	.20	.10
13	Scott Cooper	.25	.20	.10
14	Mark Davis	.05	.04	.02
15	Storm Davis	.05	.04	.02
16	Larry Walker	.10	.08	.04
17	Brian DuBois	.10	.08	.04
18	Len Dykstra	.10	.08	.04
19	John Franco	.05	.04	.02
20	Kirk Gibson	.05	.04	.02
21	Juan Gonzalez	.80	.60	.30
22	Tommy Greene	.15	.11	.06
23	Kent Hrbek	.05	.04	.02
24	Mike Huff	.30	.25	.12
25	Bo Jackson	1.25	.90	.50
26	Nolan Knows Bo	3.50	2.75	1.50
27	Roberto Kelly	.05	.04	.02
28	Mark Langston	.10	.08	.04
29	Ray Lankford	.80	.60	.30
30	Kevin Maas	2.50	2.00	1.00
31	Julio Machado	.15	.11	.06
32	Greg Maddux	.05	.04	.02
33	Mark McGwire	.15	.11	.06
34	Paul Molitor	.05	.04	.02
35	Hal Morris	.30	.25	.12
36	Dale Murphy	.05	.04	.02
37	Eddie Murray	.05	.04	.02
38	Jaime Navarro	.10	.08	.04
39	Dean Palmer	.15	.11	.06
40	Derek Parks	.30	.25	.12
41	Bobby Rose	.20	.15	.08
42	Wally Joyner	.05	.04	.02
43	Chris Sabo	.05	.04	.02
44	Benito Santiago	.05	.04	.02
45	Mike Stanton	.10	.08	.04
46	Terry Steinbach	.05	.04	.02
47	Dave Stewart	.10	.08	.04
48	Greg Swindell	.05	.04	.02
49	Jose Vizcaino	.15	.11	.06
50	"Royal Flush"	.25	.20	.10

1990 Classic Series III

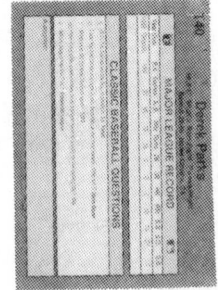

Derek Parks

Jim Leyritz

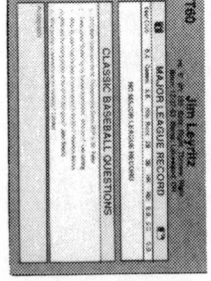

Classic's third series of 1990, features the same

style as the previous two releases. The only major difference is the border color. Series 3 features yellow borders with blue accent. 100 trivia playing cards are included in series 3. the cards are numbered 1T-100T. No card 51T or 57T exist. Two cards in the set are unnumbered. Like all other Classic issues, the cards are designed for use with the trivia board game.

		MT	NR MT	EX
Complete Set:		13.00	9.75	5.25
Common Player:		.05	.04	.02
1	Ken Griffey Jr.	1.00	.70	.40
2	John Tudor	.05	.04	.02
3	John Kruk	.05	.04	.02
4	Mark Gardner	.15	.11	.06
5	Scott Radinsky	.20	.15	.08
6	John Burkett	.20	.15	.08
7	Will Clark	.35	.25	.14
8	Gary Carter	.05	.04	.02
9	Ted Higuera	.05	.04	.02
10	Dave Parker	.10	.08	.04
11	Dante Bichette	.05	.04	.02
12	Don Mattingly	.35	.25	.14
13	Greg Harris	.05	.04	.02
14	David Hollins	.10	.08	.04
15	Matt Nokes	.05	.04	.02
16	Kevin Tapani	.15	.11	.06
17	Shane Mack	.05	.04	.02
18	Randy Myers	.05	.04	.02
19	Greg Olson	.15	.11	.06
20	Shawn Abner	.05	.04	.02
21	Jim Presley	.05	.04	.02
22	Randy Johnson	.05	.04	.02
23	Edgar Martinez	.05	.04	.02
24	Scott Coolbaugh	.15	.11	.06
25	Jeff Treadway	.05	.04	.02
26	Joe Klink	.05	.04	.02
27	Rickey Henderson	.25	.20	.10
28	Sam Horn	.05	.04	.02
29	Kurt Stillwell	.05	.04	.02
30	Andy Van Slyke	.05	.04	.02
31	Willie Banks	.35	.25	.14
32	Jose Canseco	.40	.30	.15
33	Felix Jose	.10	.08	.04
34	Candy Maldonado	.05	.04	.02
35	Carlos Baerga	.30	.25	.12
36	Keith Hernandez	.05	.04	.02
37	Frank Viola	.05	.04	.02
38	Pete O'Brien	.05	.04	.02
39	Pat Borders	.05	.04	.02
40	Mike Heath	.05	.04	.02
41	Kevin Brown	.10	.08	.04
42	Chris Bosio	.05	.04	.02
43	Shawn Boskie	.25	.20	.10
44	Carlos Quintana	.05	.04	.02
45	Juan Samuel	.05	.04	.02
46	Tim Layana	.15	.11	.06
47	Mike Harkey	.10	.08	.04
48	Gerald Perry	.05	.04	.02
49	Mike Witt	.05	.04	.02
50	Joe Orsulak	.05	.04	.02
52	Willie Blair	.10	.08	.04
53	Gene Larkin	.05	.04	.02
54	Jody Reed	.05	.04	.02
55	Jeff Reardon	.05	.04	.02
56	Kevin McReynolds	.05	.04	.02
58	Eric Yelding	.05	.04	.02
59	Fred Lynn	.05	.04	.02
60	Jim Leyritz	.35	.25	.14
61	John Orton	.05	.04	.02
62	Mike Lieberthal	.50	.40	.20
63	Mike Hartley	.10	.08	.04
64	Kal Daniels	.05	.04	.02
65	Terry Shumpert	.20	.15	.08
66	Sil Campusano	.05	.04	.02
67	Tony Pena	.05	.04	.02
68	Barry Bonds	.15	.11	.06
69	Oddibe McDowell	.05	.04	.02
70	Kelly Gruber	.10	.08	.04
71	Willie Randolph	.05	.04	.02
72	Rick Parker	.15	.11	.06
73	Bobby Bonilla	.10	.08	.04
74	Jack Armstrong	.10	.08	.04
75	Hubie Brooks	.05	.04	.02
76	Sandy Alomar, Jr.	.15	.11	.06
77	Ruben Sierra	.10	.08	.04
78	Erik Hanson	.08	.06	.03
79	Tony Phillips	.05	.04	.02
80	Rondell White	.25	.20	.10
81	Bobby Thigpen	.08	.06	.03
82	Ron Walden	.20	.15	.08
83	Don Peters	.20	.15	.08
84	#6 (Nolan Ryan)	1.00	.70	.40
85	Lance Dickson	.20	.15	.08
86	Ryne Sandberg	.10	.08	.04
87	Eric Christopherson	.20	.15	.08
88	Shane Andrews	.25	.20	.10
89	Marc Newfield	.30	.25	.12
90	Adam Hyzdu	.25	.20	.10
91	"Texas Heat" (Nolan Ryan, Reid Ryan)	1.50	1.25	.60
92	Chipper Jones	.50	.40	.20
93	Frank Thomas	1.00	.70	.40
94	Cecil Fielder	.40	.30	.15
95	Delino DeShields	.35	.25	.14
96	John Olerud	.80	.60	.30
97	Dave Justice	1.00	.70	.40
98	Joe Oliver	.10	.08	.04
99	Alex Fernandez	.80	.60	.30
100	Todd Hundley	.20	.15	.08
-----	Mike Marshall (Game Instructions On Back)	.05	.04	.02
-----	4 in 1 (Frank Viola)	.30	.25	.12
-----	4 in 1 ("Texas Heat")	.30	.25	.12
-----	4 in 1 (Chipper Jones)	.30	.25	.12
-----	4 in 1 (Don Mattingly)	.30	.25	.12

1990 Classic #1 Draft Picks

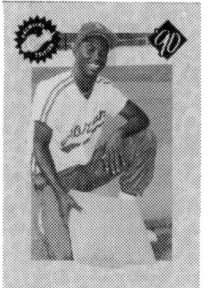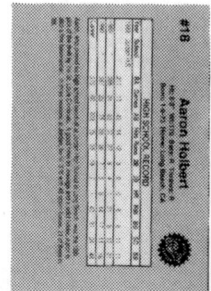

Todd Van Poppel and Alex Fernandez head up the 24- 1990 first round draft picks featured in this 25-card set. The set is limited with only 150,000 sets released to the hobby. A letter of authenticity accompanies each individually numbered set. Unlike other Classic issues, this set is not designed for use with the trivia board game.

		MT	NR MT	EX
Complete Set:		10.00	7.50	4.00
Common Player:		.20	.15	.08
1	Chipper Jones	.40	.30	.15
3	Mike Lieberthal	.35	.25	.14
4	Alex Fernandez	1.00	.70	.40
5	Kurt Miller	.30	.25	.12
6	Marc Newfield	.25	.20	.10
7	Dan Wilson	.20	.15	.08
8	Tim Costo	.70	.50	.30
9	Ron Walden	.25	.20	.10
10	Carl Everett	.25	.20	.10
11	Shane Andrews	.20	.15	.08
12	Todd Ritchie	.25	.20	.10
13	Donovan Osborne	.20	.15	.08
14	Todd Van Poppel	2.25	1.75	.90
15	Adam Hyzdu	.20	.15	.08
16	Dan Smith	.20	.15	.08
17	Jeromy Burnitz	.40	.30	.15
18	Aaron Holbert	.25	.20	.10
19	Eric Christopherson	.20	.15	.08
20	Mike Mussina	.60	.45	.25
21	Tom Nevers	.20	.15	.08
23	Lance Dickson	.30	.25	.12
24	Rondell White	.20	.15	.08
25	Robbie Beckett	.20	.15	.08
26	Don Peters	.20	.15	.08
-----	Future Stars-Checklist (Chipper Jones/ Rondell White)	.35	.25	.14

1991 Classic

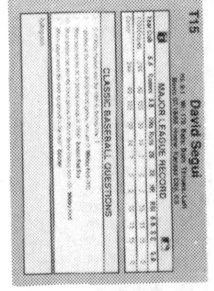

Top rookies and draft picks highlight this 99-card set from Classic. The cards come along with a boardgame and accessories designed for trivia game use. The card fronts feature fading blue borders with a touch of red. A "4-in-1" micro-player piece is included with each game set.

		MT	NR MT	EX
Complete Set:		12.00	9.00	4.75
Common Player:		.08	.06	.03
1	Ron Gant	.08	.06	.03
2	Dave Justice	.25	.20	.10
3	Leo Gomez	.30	.25	.12
4	Chris Hoiles	.20	.15	.08
5	Ben McDonald	.30	.25	.12
6	David Segui	.25	.20	.10
7	Anthony Telford	.25	.20	.10
8	Mike Mussina	.35	.25	.14
9	Wade Boggs	.10	.08	.04
10	Roger Clemens	.12	.09	.05
11	Tim Naehring	.30	.25	.12
12	Phil Plantier	.50	.40	.20
13	Maurice Vaughn	.40	.30	.15
14	Lee Stevens	.20	.15	.08
15	Mark Grace	.08	.06	.03
16	Derrick May	.60	.45	.25
17	Ryne Sandberg	.15	.11	.06
18	Matt Stark	.30	.25	.12
19	Frank Thomas	.50	.40	.20
20	Bobby Thigpen	.08	.06	.03
21	Reggie Jefferson	.25	.20	.10
22	Rob Dibble	.08	.06	.03
23	Hal Morris	.12	.09	.05
24	Chris Sabo	.08	.06	.03
25	Eric Davis	.10	.08	.04
26	Alex Cole	.20	.15	.08
27	Mark Lewis	.20	.15	.08
28	Tim Costo	.40	.30	.15
29	Sandy Alomar,Jr.	.15	.11	.06
30	Travis Fryman	.50	.40	.20
31	Cecil Fielder	.15	.11	.06
32	Milt Cuyler	.15	.11	.06
33	Andujar Cedeno	.30	.25	.12
34	Danny Darwin	.08	.06	.03
35	Randy Henis	.20	.15	.08
36	George Brett	.10	.08	.04
37	Jeff Conine	.70	.50	.30
38	Bo Jackson	.35	.25	.14
39	Brian McRae	.40	.30	.15
40	Brent Mayne	.20	.15	.08
41	Eddie Murray	.08	.06	.03
42	Ramon Martinez	.12	.09	.05
43	Jim Neidlinger	.15	.11	.06
44	Jim Poole	.30	.25	.12
45	Darryl Strawberry	.12	.09	.05
46	Tim McIntosh	.20	.15	.08
47	Randy Veres	.08	.06	.03
48	Kirby Puckett	.10	.08	.04
49	Todd Ritchie	.20	.15	.08
50	Rich Garces	.20	.15	.08
51	Moises Alou	.12	.09	.05
52	Delino DeShields	.15	.11	.06
53	Oscar Azocar	.30	.25	.12
54	Kevin Maas	.25	.20	.10
55	Alan Mills	.15	.11	.06

		MT	NR MT	EX
56	Don Mattingly	.15	.11	.06
57	Hensley Muelens	.10	.08	.04
58	John Franco	.08	.06	.03
59	Chris Jelic	.30	.25	.12
60	Dave Magadan	.08	.06	.03
61	Jeromy Burnitz	.35	.25	.14
62	Reggie Harris	.30	.25	.12
63	Rickey Henderson	.20	.15	.08
64	Mark McGwire	.15	.11	.06
65	Willie McGee	.08	.06	.03
66	Todd Van Poppel	2.00	1.50	.80
67	Bob Welch	.08	.06	.03
68	"Future Aces"	2.00	1.50	.80
69	Chuck Finley	.08	.06	.03
70	Lenny Dykstra	.08	.06	.03
71	Mickey Morandini	.20	.15	.08
72	Wes Chamberlain	.30	.25	.12
73	Dale Murphy	.08	.06	.03
74	Barry Bonds	.15	.11	.06
75	Doug Drabek	.08	.06	.03
76	Randy Tomlin	.20	.15	.08
77	Rod Brewer	.12	.09	.05
78	Bernard Gilkey	.35	.25	.14
79	Vince Coleman	.08	.06	.03
80	Roberto Alomar	.08	.06	.03
81	Joe Carter	.08	.06	.03
82	Kevin Mitchell	.10	.08	.04
83	Rafael Novoa	.20	.15	.08
84	Matt Williams	.10	.08	.04
85	Steve Decker	.20	.15	.08
86	Mike Benjamin	.15	.11	.06
87	Jose Rijo	.08	.06	.03
88	Ken Griffey,Jr.	.50	.40	.20
89	Tino Martinez	.30	.25	.12
90	Scott Chiamparino	.25	.20	.10
91	Rafael Palmeiro	.08	.06	.03
92	Nolan Ryan	.25	.20	.10
93	Bobby Witt	.08	.06	.03
94	Juan Gonzalez	.35	.25	.14
95	Fred McGriff	.08	.06	.03
96	Dave Steib	.08	.06	.03
97	Ed Sprague	.25	.20	.10
98	John Olerud	.25	.20	.10
99	Strawberry and Gooden	.10	.08	.04

1989 Cleveland Indians Team Set

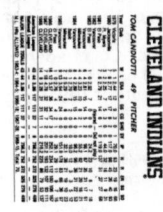

(49) Tom Candiotti, RHP

The Cleveland Indians released this oversized (2-3/4" by 4-1/2") 28-card set in 1989. The cards feature a full-color player photo on the front with the "Tribe" logo in the upper left corner. Card backs include major and minor league statistics and a facsimile autograph.

		MT	NR MT	EX
Complete Set:		6.00	4.50	2.50
Common Player:		.20	.15	.08
(1)	Doc Edwards	.20	.15	.08
(2)	Joel Skinner	.20	.15	.08
(3)	Andy Allanson	.20	.15	.08
(4)	Tom Candiotti	.20	.15	.08
(5)	Doug Jones	.20	.15	.08
(6)	Keith Atherton	.20	.15	.08
(7)	Rich Yett	.20	.15	.08
(8)	John Farrell	.20	.15	.08

		MT	NR MT	EX
(9)	Rod Nichols	.20	.15	.08
(10)	Joe Skalski	.30	.25	.12
(11)	Pete O'Brien	.30	.25	.12
(12)	Jerry Browne	.30	.25	.12
(13)	Brook Jacoby	.30	.25	.12
(14)	Felix Fermin	.20	.15	.08
(15)	Bud Black	.20	.15	.08
(16)	Brad Havens	.20	.15	.08
(17)	Greg Swindell	.40	.30	.15
(18)	Scott Bailes	.20	.15	.08
(19)	Jesse Orosco	.20	.15	.08
(20)	Oddibe McDowell	.30	.25	.12
(21)	Joe Carter	.50	.40	.20
(22)	Cory Snyder	.40	.30	.15
(23)	Louie Medina	.25	.20	.10
(24)	Dave Clark	.25	.20	.10
(25)	Brad Komminsk	.20	.15	.08
(26)	Luis Aguayo	.20	.15	.08
(27)	Pat Keedy	.25	.20	.10
(28)	Tribe Coaches	.20	.15	.08

1981 Coca-Cola

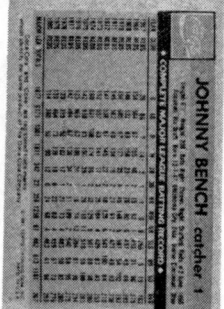

In 1981, Topps produced for Coca-Cola 12-card sets for 11 various American and National League teams. The sets include 11 player cards and one unnumbered header card. The card fronts, which measure 2-1/2" by 3-1/2", are identical in style to the 1981 Topps regular issue save for the Coca-Cola logo. The backs differ only from the '81 Topps regular set in that they are numbered 1-11 and carry the Coca-Cola trademark and copyright line. The backs of the header cards contain an offer for 132-card uncut sheets of 1981 Topps baseball cards.

		MT	NR MT	EX
Complete Set:		30.00	22.00	12.50
Common Player:		.06	.05	.02
1	Tom Burgmeier	.06	.05	.02
2	Dennis Eckersley	.15	.11	.06
3	Dwight Evans	.60	.45	.25
4	Bob Stanley	.10	.08	.04
5	Glenn Hoffman	.06	.05	.02
6	Carney Lansford	.20	.15	.08
7	Frank Tanana	.10	.08	.04
8	Tony Perez	.20	.15	.08
9	Jim Rice	.80	.60	.30
10	Dave Stapleton	.06	.05	.02
11	Carl Yastrzemski	2.00	1.50	.80
----	Header Card	.03	.02	.01
1	Tim Blackwell	.06	.05	.02
2	Bill Buckner	.15	.11	.06
3	Ivan DeJesus	.06	.05	.02
4	Leon Durham	.15	.11	.06
5	Steve Henderson	.06	.05	.02
6	Mike Krukow	.10	.08	.04
7	Ken Reitz	.06	.05	.02
8	Rick Reuschel	.15	.11	.06
9	Scot Thompson	.06	.05	.02
10	Dick Tidrow	.06	.05	.02
11	Mike Tyson	.06	.05	.02
----	Header Card	.03	.02	.01
1	Britt Burns	.10	.08	.04
2	Todd Cruz	.06	.05	.02
3	Rich Dotson	.20	.15	.08
4	Jim Essian	.06	.05	.02

		MT	NR MT	EX
5	Ed Farmer	.06	.05	.02
6	Lamar Johnson	.06	.05	.02
7	Ron LeFlore	.10	.08	.04
8	Chet Lemon	.10	.08	.04
9	Bob Molinaro	.06	.05	.02
10	Jim Morrison	.06	.05	.02
11	Wayne Nordhagen	.06	.05	.02
----	Header Card	.03	.02	.01
1	Johnny Bench	2.00	1.50	.80
2	Dave Collins	.10	.08	.04
3	Dave Concepcion	.15	.11	.06
4	Dan Driessen	.10	.08	.04
5	George Foster	.25	.20	.10
6	Ken Griffey	..15	.11	.06
7	Tom Hume	.06	.05	.02
8	Ray Knight	.10	.08	.04
9	Ron Oester	.06	.05	.02
10	Tom Seaver	1.25	.90	.50
11	Mario Soto	.10	.08	.04
----	Header Card	.03	.02	.01
1	Champ Summers	.06	.05	.02
2	Al Cowens	.06	.05	.02
3	Rich Hebner	.06	.05	.02
4	Steve Kemp	.10	.08	.04
5	Aurelio Lopez	.06	.05	.02
6	Jack Morris	.35	.25	.14
7	Lance Parrish	.35	.25	.14
8	Johnny Wockenfuss	.06	.05	.02
9	Alan Trammell	1.00	.70	.40
10	Lou Whitaker	1.00	.70	.40
11	Kirk Gibson	1.00	.70	.40
----	Header Card	.03	.02	.01
1	Alan Ashby	.06	.05	.02
2	Cesar Cedeno	.15	.11	.06
3	Jose Cruz	.15	.11	.06
4	Art Howe	.06	.05	.02
5	Rafael Landestoy	.06	.05	.02
6	Joe Niekro	.15	.11	.06
7	Terry Puhl	.06	.05	.02
8	J.R. Richard	.15	.11	.06
9	Nolan Ryan	3.00	2.25	1.25
10	Joe Sambito	.06	.05	.02
11	Don Sutton	.35	.25	.14
----	Header Card	.03	.02	.01
1	Willie Aikens	.06	.05	.02
2	George Brett	1.50	1.25	.60
3	Larry Gura	.06	.05	.02
4	Dennis Leonard	.06	.05	.02
5	Hal McRae	.15	.11	.06
6	Amos Otis	.10	.08	.04
7	Dan Quisenberry	.15	.11	.06
8	U.L. Washington	.06	.05	.02
9	John Wathan	.10	.08	.04
10	Frank White	.10	.08	.04
11	Willie Wilson	.15	.11	.06
----	Header Card	.03	.02	.01
1	Neil Allen	.06	.05	.02
2	Doug Flynn	.06	.05	.02
3	Dave Kingman	.15	.11	.06
4	Randy Jones	.06	.05	.02
5	Pat Zachry	.06	.05	.02
6	Lee Mazzilli	.10	.08	.04
7	Rusty Staub	.15	.11	.06
8	Craig Swan	.06	.05	.02
9	Frank Taveras	.06	.05	.02
10	Alex Trevino	.06	.05	.02
11	Joel Youngblood	.06	.05	.02
----	Header Card	.03	.02	.01
1	Bob Boone	.30	.25	.12
2	Larry Bowa	.15	.11	.06
3	Steve Carlton	1.00	.70	.40
4	Greg Luzinski	.15	.11	.06
5	Garry Maddox	.10	.08	.04
6	Bake McBride	.06	.05	.02
7	Tug McGraw	.15	.11	.06
8	Pete Rose	2.00	1.50	.80
9	Mike Schmidt	2.25	1.75	.90
10	Lonnie Smith	.15	.11	.06
11	Manny Trillo	.06	.05	.02
----	Header Card	.03	.02	.01
1	Jim Bibby	.06	.05	.02
2	John Candelaria	.10	.08	.04
3	Mike Easler	.10	.08	.04
4	Tim Foli	.06	.05	.02
5	Phil Garner	.06	.05	.02
6	Bill Madlock	.15	.11	.06
7	Omar Moreno	.06	.05	.02
8	Ed Ott	.06	.05	.02
9	Dave Parker	.35	.25	.14
10	Willie Stargell	1.00	.70	.40
11	Kent Tekulve	.10	.08	.04

		MT	NR MT	EX
----	Header Card	.03	.02	.01
1	Bob Forsch	.10	.08	.04
2	George Hendrick	.10	.08	.04
3	Keith Hernandez	.50	.40	.20
4	Tom Herr	.15	.11	.06
5	Sixto Lezcano	.06	.05	.02
6	Ken Oberkfell	.06	.05	.02
7	Darrell Porter	.10	.08	.04
8	Tony Scott	.06	.05	.02
9	Lary Sorensen	.06	.05	.02
10	Bruce Sutter	.15	.11	.06
11	Garry Templeton	.10	.08	.04
----	Header Card	.03	.02	.01

1982 Coca-Cola/Brigham's Red Sox

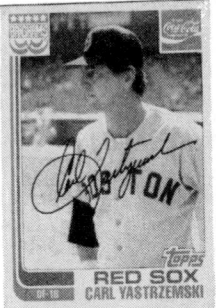
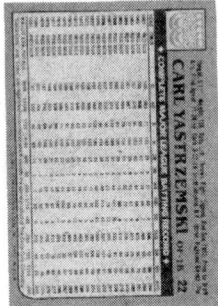

Coca-Cola, in conjunction with Brigham's Ice Cream stores, issued a 23-card set in the Boston area featuring Red Sox players. The Topps-produced cards, which measure 2-1/2" by 3-1/2", are identical in style to the regular 1982 Topps set but contain the Coca-Cola and Brigham's logos in the corners. The cards were distributed in three-card cello packs, including an unnumbered header card.

		MT	NR MT	EX
Complete Set:		6.00	4.50	2.50
Common Player:		.08	.06	.03
1	Gary Allenson	.08	.06	.03
2	Tom Burgmeier	.08	.06	.03
3	Mark Clear	.15	.11	.06
4	Steve Crawford	.08	.06	.03
5	Dennis Eckersley	.30	.25	.12
6	Dwight Evans	.80	.60	.30
7	Rich Gedman	.30	.25	.12
8	Garry Hancock	.08	.06	.03
9	Glen Hoffman (Glenn)	.08	.06	.03
10	Carney Lansford	.20	.15	.08
11	Rick Miller	.08	.06	.03
12	Reid Nichols	.08	.06	.03
13	Bob Ojeda	.20	.15	.08
14	Tony Perez	.30	.25	.12
15	Chuck Rainey	.08	.06	.03
16	Jerry Remy	.08	.06	.03
17	Jim Rice	.80	.60	.30
18	Bob Stanley	.15	.11	.06
19	Dave Stapleton	.08	.06	.03
20	Mike Torrez	.08	.06	.03
21	John Tudor	.30	.25	.12
22	Carl Yastrzemski	2.00	1.50	.80
----	Header Card	.05	.04	.02

1982 Coca-Cola Reds

Produced by Topps for Coca-Cola, the set consists of 23 cards featuring the Cincinnati Reds and was distributed in the Cincinnati area. The cards, which are 2-1/2" by 3-1/2" in size, are identical in design to the regular 1982 Topps set but have a Coca-Cola logo on the front and red backs. An unnumbered header

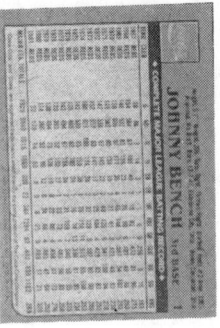

card is included in the set.

		MT	NR MT	EX
Complete Set:		7.00	5.25	2.75
Common Player:		.08	.06	.03
1	Johnny Bench	2.00	1.50	.80
2	Bruce Berenyi	.08	.06	.03
3	Larry Biittner	.08	.06	.03
4	Cesar Cedeno	.15	.11	.06
5	Dave Concepcion	.25	.20	.10
6	Dan Driessen	.15	.11	.06
7	Greg Harris	.08	.06	.03
8	Paul Householder	.08	.06	.03
9	Tom Hume	.08	.06	.03
10	Clint Hurdle	.08	.06	.03
11	Jim Kern	.08	.06	.03
12	Wayne Krenchicki	.08	.06	.03
13	Rafael Landestoy	.08	.06	.03
14	Charlie Leibrandt	.15	.11	.06
15	Mike O'Berry	.08	.06	.03
16	Ron Oester	.08	.06	.03
17	Frank Pastore	.08	.06	.03
18	Joe Price	.08	.06	.03
19	Tom Seaver	2.00	1.50	.80
20	Mario Soto	.15	.11	.06
21	Alex Trevino	.08	.06	.03
22	Mike Vail	.08	.06	.03
----	Header Card	.04	.03	.02

1985 Coca-Cola White Sox

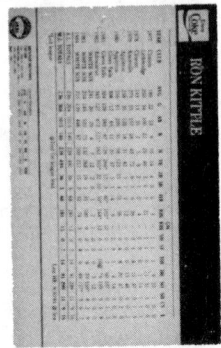

Featuring past and present White Sox players, the cards in this set were given out on Tuesday night home games. The cards, which measure 2-5/8" by 4-1/8", contain a color photo of a current Sox member. A red box at the bottom of the card carries the team logo, the player's name, uniform number and position, plus a small oval portrait of a past Sox player. The card backs contain the Coca-Cola logo and the lifetime hitting or pitching statistics for the current and past player. The set is numbered in the checklist that follows by the player's uniform number with the last three cards being unnumbered. Complete sets were available through a fan club offer found in White Sox programs.

		MT	NR MT	EX
Complete Set:		14.00	10.50	5.50
Common Player:		.25	.20	.10
	Oscar Gamble (Zeke Bonura)	.25	.20	.10
1	Scott Fletcher (Luke Appling)	.40	.30	.15
3	Harold Baines (Bill Melton)	.80	.60	.30
5	Luis Salazar (Chico Carrasquel)	.25	.20	.10
7	Marc Hill (Sherm Lollar)	.25	.20	.10
8	Daryl Boston (Jim Landis)	.25	.20	.10
10	Tony LaRussa (Al Lopez)	.40	.30	.15
12	Julio Cruz (Nellie Fox)	.40	.30	.15
13	Ozzie Guillen (Luis Aparicio)	.80	.60	.30
17	Jerry Hairston (Smoky Burgess)	.25	.20	.10
20	Joe DeSa (Carlos May)	.25	.20	.10
22	Joel Skinner (J.C. Martin)	.25	.20	.10
23	Rudy Law (Bill Skowron)	.25	.20	.10
24	Floyd Bannister (Red Faber)	.35	.25	.14
29	Greg Walker (Dick Allen)	.70	.50	.30
30	Gene Nelson (Early Wynn)	.35	.25	.14
32	Tim Hulett (Pete Ward)	.25	.20	.10
34	Richard Dotson (Ed Walsh)	.35	.25	.14
37	Dan Spillner (Thornton Lee)	.25	.20	.10
40	Britt Burns (Gary Peters)	.25	.20	.10
41	Tom Seaver (Ted Lyons)	.80	.60	.30
42	Ron Kittle (Minnie Minoso)	.40	.30	.15
43	Bob James (Hoyt Wilhelm)	.40	.30	.15
44	Tom Paciorek (Eddie Collins)	.35	.25	.14
46	Tim Lollar (Billy Pierce)	.25	.20	.10
50	Juan Agosto (Wilbur Wood)	.25	.20	.10
72	Carlton Fisk (Ray Schalk)	.70	.50	.30
----	Comiskey Park	.50	.40	.20
----	Ribbie and Roobarb (mascots)	.25	.20	.10
----	Nancy Faust (organist)	.25	.20	.10

		MT	NR MT	EX
12	Julio Cruz	.25	.20	.10
13	Ozzie Guillen	.45	.35	.20
17	Jerry Hairston	.25	.20	.10
19	Floyd Bannister	.35	.25	.14
20	Reid Nichols	.25	.20	.10
22	Joel Skinner	.25	.20	.10
24	Dave Schmidt	.25	.20	.10
26	Bobby Bonilla	.70	.50	.30
29	Greg Walker	.40	.30	.15
30	Gene Nelson	.25	.20	.10
32	Tim Hulett	.25	.20	.10
33	Neil Allen	.25	.20	.10
34	Richard Dotson	.35	.25	.14
40	Joe Cowley	.25	.20	.10
41	Tom Seaver	.70	.50	.30
42	Ron Kittle	.35	.25	.14
43	Bob James	.25	.20	.10
44	John Cangelosi	.35	.25	.14
50	Juan Agosto	.25	.20	.10
52	Joel Davis	.25	.20	.10
72	Carlton Fisk	.50	.40	.20
----	Ribbie & Roobarb (mascots)	.25	.20	.10
----	Nancy Faust (organist)	.25	.20	.10
----	Ken "Hawk" Harrelson	.30	.25	.12
----	Tony LaRussa	.30	.25	.12
----	Minnie Minoso	.30	.25	.12

1986 Coca-Cola White Sox

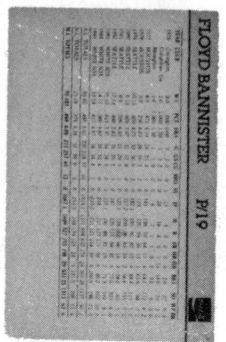

For the second year in a row, Coca-Cola, in conjunction with the Chicago White Sox, issued a 30-card set. As in 1985, cards were given out at the park on Tuesday night games. Full sets were again available through a fan club offer found in the White Sox program. The cards, which measure 2-5/8" by 4-1/8", feature 25 players plus other White Sox personnel. The card fronts feature a color photo (an action shot in most instances) and a white bar at the bottom. A black and white bat with "SOX" shown on the barrel is located within the white bar, along with the player's name, position and uniform number. The white and grey backs with black print include the Coca-Cola trademark. Lifetime statistics are shown on all player cards, but there is no personal information such as height, weight or age. The non-player cards are blank-backed save for the name and logo at the top. The cards in the checklist that follows are numbered by the players' uniform numbers, with the last five cards of the set being unnumbered.

		MT	NR MT	EX
Complete Set:		12.00	9.00	4.75
Common Player:		.25	.20	.10
1	Wayne Tolleson	.25	.20	.10
3	Harold Baines	.60	.45	.25
7	Marc Hill	.25	.20	.10
8	Daryl Boston	.25	.20	.10

1987 Coca-Cola Tigers

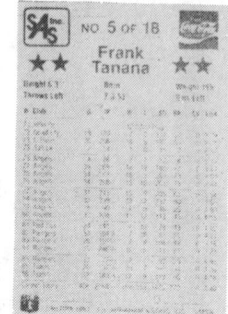

Coca-Cola and S. Abraham & Sons, Inc. issued a set of 18 baseball cards featuring members of the Detroit Tigers. The set is comprised of six four-part folding panels. Each panel includes three player cards (each 2-1/2" by 3-1/2") and one team logo card. A bright yellow border surrounds the full-color photo. The backs are designed on a vertical format and contain personal data and career statistics. The set was produced by Mike Schecter and Associates.

		MT	NR MT	EX
Complete Set:		6.00	4.50	2.50
Complete Singles Set:		2.00	1.50	.80
Common Panel:		.60	.45	.25
Common Single Player:		.05	.04	.02
	Panel	1.25	.90	.50
1	Kirk Gibson	.50	.40	.20
2	Larry Herndon	.08	.06	.03
3	Walt Terrell	.10	.08	.04
	Panel	1.25	.90	.50
4	Alan Trammell	.50	.40	.20
5	Frank Tanana	.10	.08	.04
6	Pat Sheridan	.05	.04	.02
	Panel	.90	.70	.35
7	Jack Morris	.30	.25	.12
8	Mike Heath	.05	.04	.02
9	Dave Bergman	.05	.04	.02
	Panel	.60	.45	.25
10	Chet Lemon	.10	.08	.04
11	Dwight Lowry	.08	.06	.04
12	Dan Petry	.10	.08	.04
	Panel	.80	.60	.30
13	Darrell Evans	.20	.15	.08
14	Darnell Coles	.10	.08	.04
15	Willie Hernandez	.10	.08	.04
	Panel	1.00	.70	.40
16	Lou Whitaker	.30	.25	.12
17	Tom Brookens	.05	.04	.02

18	John Grubb	MT .05	NR MT .04	EX .02

1987 Coca-Cola White Sox

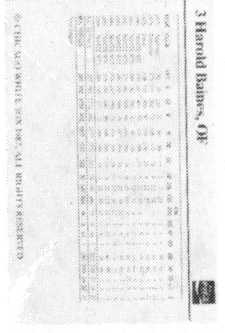

3 Harold Baines, OF

The Chicago White Sox Fan Club, in conjunction with Coca-Cola, offered members a set of 30 trading cards. For the $10 membership fee, fans received the set plus additional fan club gifts and privileges. The cards, which measure 2-5/8" by 4", feature full-color photos inside a blue and red border. The backs include the player's name, position, uniform number and statistics. The Coca-Cola logo is also included on the card backs.

		MT	NR MT	EX
	Complete Set:	12.00	9.00	4.75
	Common Player:	.25	.20	.10
1	Jerry Royster	.25	.20	.10
3	Harold Baines	.60	.45	.25
5	Ron Karkovice	.30	.25	.12
8	Daryl Boston	.25	.20	.10
10	Fred Manrique	.30	.25	.12
12	Steve Lyons	.25	.20	.10
13	Ozzie Guillen	.40	.30	.15
14	Russ Morman	.30	.25	.12
15	Donnie Hill	.25	.20	.10
16	Jim Fregosi	.30	.25	.12
17	Jerry Hairston	.25	.20	.10
19	Floyd Bannister	.35	.25	.14
21	Gary Redus	.25	.20	.10
22	Ivan Calderon	.40	.30	.15
25	Ron Hassey	.25	.20	.10
26	Jose DeLeon	.30	.25	.12
29	Greg Walker	.40	.30	.15
32	Tim Hulett	.25	.20	.10
33	Neil Allen	.25	.20	.10
34	Rich Dotson	.35	.25	.14
36	Ray Searage	.25	.20	.10
37	Bobby Thigpen	.40	.30	.15
40	Jim Winn	.25	.20	.10
43	Bob James	.25	.20	.10
50	Joel McKeon	.25	.20	.10
52	Joel Davis	.25	.20	.10
72	Carlton Fisk	.50	.40	.20
----	Ribbie & Roobarb (mascots)	.25	.20	.10
----	Nancy Faust (organist)	.25	.20	.10
----	Minnie Minoso	.30	.25	.12

1988 Coca-Cola Padres

A 20-card team set sponsored by Coca-Cola was designed as part of the San Diego Padres Junior Fan Club promotion for 1988. This set was distributed as a nine-card starter sheet, with 11 additional single cards handed out during the team's home games. The standard-size cards feature full-color player photos framed by a black and orange border. The player's name is printed above the photo; uniform number and position appear lower right. A large Padres logo curves upward from the lower left corner. Card backs are brown on white and include the Padres logo upper left opposite the player's name

and personal information. Career highlights and 1987 stats appear in the center of the card back above the Coca-Cola and Junior Padres Fan Club logos.

		MT	NR MT	EX
	Complete Set:	35.00	25.00	13.00
	Common Player:	.50	.40	.20
	Panel			
1	Garry Templeton	.75	.60	.30
5	Randy Ready	.50	.40	.20
10	Larry Bowa	.75	.60	.30
11	Tim Flannery	.50	.40	.20
35	Chris Brown	.75	.60	.30
45	Jimmy Jones	1.00	.70	.40
48	Mark Davis	.50	.40	.20
55	Mark Grant	.50	.40	.20
----	20th Anniversary Logo Card	.10	.08	.04
	Singles			
7	Keith Moreland	1.00	.70	.40
8	John Kruk	2.25	1.75	.90
9	Benito Santiago	3.25	2.50	1.25
14	Carmelo Martinez	1.00	.70	.40
15	Jack McKeon	1.00	.70	.40
19	Tony Gwynn	9.00	6.75	3.50
22	Stan Jefferson	1.00	.70	.40
27	Mark Parent	2.00	1.50	.80
30	Eric Show	1.50	1.25	.60
31	Ed Whitson	1.00	.70	.40
41	Lance McCullers	1.25	.90	.50
51	Greg Booker	1.00	.70	.40

1988 Coca-Cola White Sox

Part of a fan club membership package, this unnumbered 30-card set features full-color photos of 27 players, the team mascot, team organist and Comiskey Park. Cards have a bright red border, with the team logo in the lower left corner of the photo. A large player name fills the bottom border. Card backs are printed in black on grey and white and include player name, personal info and career summary. The set was included in the $10 membership package, with a portion of the cost going to the ChiSox Kids Charity.

		MT	NR MT	EX
Complete Set:		8.00	6.00	3.25
Common Player:		.20	.15	.08
(1)	Harold Baines	.50	.40	.20
(2)	Daryl Boston	.20	.15	.08
(3)	Ivan Calderon	.30	.25	.12
(4)	John Davis	.20	.15	.08
(5)	Jim Fregosi	.25	.20	.10
(6)	Carlton Fisk	.40	.30	.15
(7)	Ozzie Guillen	.30	.25	.12
(8)	Donnie Hill	.20	.15	.08
(9)	Rick Horton	.20	.15	.08
(10)	Lance Johnson	.30	.25	.12
(11)	Dave LaPoint	.20	.15	.08
(12)	Bill Long	.25	.20	.10
(13)	Steve Lyons	.20	.15	.08
(14)	Jack McDowell	.40	.30	.15
(15)	Fred Manrique	.20	.15	.08
(16)	Minnie Minoso	.25	.20	.10
(17)	Dan Pasqua	.30	.25	.12
(18)	John Pawlowski	.25	.20	.10
(19)	Melido Perez	.40	.30	.15
(20)	Billy Pierce	.25	.20	.10
(21)	Gary Redus	.20	.15	.08
(22)	Jerry Reuss	.25	.20	.10
(23)	Mark Salas	.20	.15	.08
(24)	Jose Segura	.30	.25	.12
(25)	Bobby Thigpen	.25	.20	.10
(26)	Greg Walker	.30	.25	.12
(27)	Kenny Williams	.30	.25	.12
(28)	Nancy Faust (organist)	.20	.15	.08
(29)	Ribbie & Roobarb (mascots)	.20	.15	.08
(30)	Comiskey Park	.40	.30	.15

1989 Coca-Cola Padres

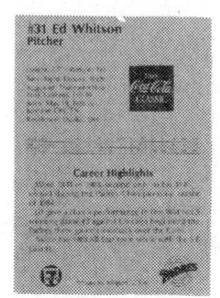

This 20-card set is part of the Junior Padres Fan Club membership package. Members receive a 9-card starter set printed on one large perforated sheet. Additional cards are distributed to kids at specially designated games (free admission for kids). Card fronts feature an orange-and-brown double border, with a bright orange Padres logo printed lower left. Player uniform number and position are printed diagonally across the upper right corner, with the player's name in large block letters along the bottom border.

		MT	NR MT	EX
Complete Set:		30.00	22.00	12.00
Common Player:		.50	.40	.30
	Panel			
1	Garry Templeton	.70	.50	.30
5	Randy Ready	.50	.40	.20
12	Roberto Alomar	1.00	.70	.40
14	Carmelo Martinez	.50	.40	.20
15	Jack McKeon	.50	.40	.20
30	Eric Show	.50	.40	.20
31	Ed Whitson	.50	.40	.20
43	Dennis Rasmussen	.50	.40	.20
----	Logo Card	.10	.08	.04
	Singles			
6	Luis Salazar	1.00	.70	.40
9	Benito Santiago	3.00	2.25	1.25
10	Leon Roberts	1.00	.70	.40
11	Tim Flannery	1.00	.70	.40
18	Chris James	2.00	1.50	.80

		MT	NR MT	EX
19	Tony Gwynn	7.00	5.25	2.75
25	Jack Clark	3.00	2.25	1.25
27	Mark Parent	2.00	1.50	.80
35	Walt Terrell	1.00	.70	.40
47	Bruce Hurst	2.00	1.50	.80
48	Mark Davis	3.00	2.25	1.25
55	Mark Grant	1.00	.70	.30

1989 Coca-Cola White Sox

For the fifth straight year, Coca-Cola sponsored a set of cards featuring the Chicago White Sox. The 30-card set was distributed to fans attending a special promotional day at Comiskey Park and was also available by mail to members of the ChiSox fan club. The fronts of the cards feature a red, white and blue color scheme and include a pair of crossed bats. "White Sox" appears along the top, while the name and position are in the lower right, and a pennant proclaiming "Chicago's American Pastime" is just below the photo. The horizontal backs include player biographies, other data, special facts about Comiskey Park and the Coca-Cola logo.

		MT	NR MT	EX
Complete Set:		7.00	5.25	2.75
Common Player:		.20	.15	.08
1	New Comiskey Park, 1991	.40	.30	.15
2	Comiskey Park	.40	.30	.15
3	Jeff Torborg	.20	.15	.08
4	Coaching Staff	.20	.15	.08
5	Harold Baines	.50	.40	.20
6	Daryl Boston	.20	.15	.08
7	Ivan Calderon	.30	.25	.12
8	Carlton Fisk	.40	.30	.15
9	Dave Gallagher	.30	.25	.12
10	Ozzie Guillen	.30	.25	.12
11	Shawn Hillegas	.20	.15	.08
12	Barry Jones	.20	.15	.08
13	Ron Karkovice	.20	.15	.08
14	Eric King	.20	.15	.08
15	Ron Kittle	.30	.25	.12
16	Bill Long	.20	.15	.08
17	Steve Lyons	.20	.15	.08
18	Donn Pall	.20	.15	.08
19	Dan Pasqua	.30	.25	.12
20	Ken Patterson	.20	.15	.08
21	Melido Perez	.30	.25	.12
22	Jerry Reuss	.25	.20	.10
23	Billy Jo Robidoux	.20	.15	.08
24	Steve Rosenberg	.20	.15	.08
25	Jeff Schaefer	.25	.20	.10
26	Bobby Thigpen	.25	.20	.10
27	Greg Walker	.25	.20	.10
28	Eddie Williams	.25	.20	.10
29	Nancy Faust, organist	.20	.15	.08
30	Minnie Minoso	.20	.15	.08

A player's name in *italic* type indicates a rookie card. An (FC) indicates a player's first card for that particular card company.

1990 Coca-Cola- Garry Templeton

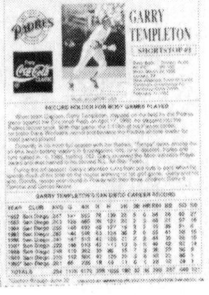

Coca-Cola, Vons stores and the San Diego Padres joined forces to release this special pin/baseball card collectible in honor of Garry Templeton becoming the club's all-time leader in games played. The card front features a full-color photo of Templeton and displays "Most Games Played" and "The Captain" in orange at the top of the photo. "Templeton" appears vertically in white along the left border. The Coca-Cola and Padre logos also appear on the card front. The bottom of the card features a perforated edge where the pin is attached as an extension of the card. The card back is printed in black and white and displays biographical information, career highlights and career statistics. The card was created by Imprinted Products Corporation of San Diego.

	MT	NR MT	EX
Complete Set:	2.25	1.75	.90
(1) Most Games Played card (Garry Templeton)	.50	.40	.20
(2) Most Games Played Pin (Garry Templeton)	1.75	1.25	.70

1990 Coca-Cola White Sox

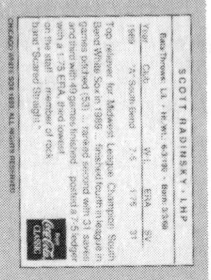

An attractive "Comiskey Park 1910-1990" logo is featured on the front of each of the 30 cards in this set. The card fronts feature full-color photos with a thin white inner border. The cards are numbered according to uniform number, with the exception of four special cards including Top Prospect Frank Thomas. The horizontal card backs feature black print on white and gray stock. 1989 statistics and career highlights are provided. The set was made available nationally through hobby dealers. The 1990 set marks the sixth straight year that Coca-Cola sponsored a White Sox set.

		MT	NR MT	EX
Complete Set:		6.00	4.50	2.50
Common Player:		.15	.11	.06
1	Lance Johnson	.20	.15	.08
7	Scott Fletcher	.15	.11	.06
10	Jeff Torborg	.15	.11	.06
12	Steve Lyons	.15	.11	.06
13	Ozzie Guillen	.25	.20	.10
14	Craig Grebeck	.20	.15	.08
17	Dave Gallagher	.15	.11	.06
20	Ron Karkovice	.15	.11	.06
22	Ivan Calderon	.25	.20	.10
23	Robin Ventura	.30	.25	.12
24	Carlos Martinez	.20	.15	.08
25	Sammy Sosa	.30	.25	.12
27	Greg Hibbard	.20	.15	.08
29	Jack McDowell	.20	.15	.08
30	Donn Pall	.15	.11	.06
31	Scott Radinsky	.25	.20	.10
33	Melido Perez	.15	.11	.06
34	Ken Patterson	.15	.11	.06
36	Eric King	.15	.11	.06
37	Bobby Thigpen	.20	.15	.08
42	Ron Kittle	.20	.15	.08
44	Dan Pasqua	.20	.15	.08
45	Wayne Edwards	.15	.11	.06
50	Barry Jones	.15	.11	.06
52	Jerry Kutzler	.15	.11	.06
72	Carlton Fisk	.35	.25	.14
----	Top Prospect (Frank Thomas)	1.00	.70	.40
----	Coaches	.15	.11	.06
----	Captains-Guillen, Fisk	.20	.15	.08
----	Rookies	.20	.15	.08

1982 Cracker Jack

The Topps-produced 1982 Cracker Jack set was issued to promote the first "Old Timers Baseball Classic," held in Washington, D.C. Sixteen cards comprise the set which was issued in two sheets of eight cards, plus an advertising card located in the center. The individual cards are 2-1/2" by 3-1/2" in size with the complete sheets measuring 7-1/2" by 10-1/2". Card #'s 1-8 feature American League players with #'s 9-16 being former National League stars. The card fronts feature a full-color photo inside a Cracker Jack border. The backs contain the Cracker Jack logo plus a short player biography and his lifetime pitching or batting record. Complete sheets were available through a write-in offer.

		MT	NR MT	EX
Complete Panel Set:		10.00	7.50	4.00
Complete Singles Set:		4.00	3.00	1.50
Common Single Player:		.05	.04	.02
	Panel	5.00	3.75	2.00
1	Larry Doby	.05	.04	.02
2	Bob Feller	.10	.08	.04
3	Whitey Ford	.10	.08	.04
4	Al Kaline	.10	.08	.04
5	Harmon Killebrew	.10	.08	.04
6	Mickey Mantle	1.75	1.25	.70

		MT	NR MT	EX
7	Tony Oliva	.05	.04	.02
8	Brooks Robinson	.10	.08	.04
	Panel	4.00	3.00	1.50
9	Hank Aaron	1.25	.90	.50
10	Ernie Banks	.10	.08	.04
11	Ralph Kiner	.10	.08	.04
12	Eddie Mathews	.10	.08	.04
13	Willie Mays	1.00	.70	.40
14	Robin Roberts	.10	.08	.04
15	Duke Snider	.10	.08	.04
16	Warren Spahn	.10	.08	.04
----	Advertising Card	.02	.02	.01

1976 Crane Potato Chips

This unnumbered 70-card set of player discs was issued with Crane Potato Chips in 1976. The front of the discs are designed to look like a baseball with the player's portrait in the center and his name, position and team beneath.

		NR MT	EX	VG
Complete Set:		20.00	15.00	8.00
Common Player:		.10	.05	.03
(1)	Henry Aaron	1.50	.70	.45
(2)	Johnny Bench	1.00	.50	.30
(3)	Vida Blue	.12	.06	.04
(4)	Larry Bowa	.12	.06	.04
(5)	Lou Brock	.60	.30	.20
(6)	Jeff Burroughs	.10	.05	.03
(7)	John Candelaria	.12	.06	.04
(8)	Jose Cardenal	.10	.05	.03
(9)	Rod Carew	1.00	.50	.30
(10)	Steve Carlton	1.00	.50	.30
(11)	Dave Cash	.10	.05	.03
(12)	Cesar Cedeno	.12	.06	.04
(13)	Ron Cey	.12	.06	.04
(14)	Carlton Fisk	.40	.20	.12
(15)	Tito Fuentes	.10	.05	.03
(16)	Steve Garvey	.70	.35	.20
(17)	Ken Griffey	.12	.06	.04
(18)	Don Gullett	.10	.05	.03
(19)	Willie Horton	.10	.05	.03
(20)	Al Hrabosky	.10	.05	.03
(21)	Catfish Hunter	.50	.25	.15
(22)	Reggie Jackson	1.25	.60	.40
(23)	Randy Jones	.10	.05	.03
(24)	Jim Kaat	.15	.08	.05
(25)	Don Kessinger	.10	.05	.03
(26)	Dave Kingman	.15	.08	.05
(27)	Jerry Koosman	.12	.06	.04
(28)	Mickey Lolich	.15	.08	.05
(29)	Greg Luzinski	.15	.08	.05
(30)	Fred Lynn	.20	.10	.06
(31)	Bill Madlock	.15	.08	.05
(32)	Carlos May	.10	.05	.03
(33)	John Mayberry	.10	.05	.03
(34)	Bake McBride	.10	.05	.03
(35)	Doc Medich	.10	.05	.03
(36)	Andy Messersmith	.10	.05	.03
(37)	Rick Monday	.12	.06	.04
(38)	John Montefusco	.10	.05	.03
(39)	Jerry Morales	.10	.05	.03
(40)	Joe Morgan	.40	.20	.12
(41)	Thurman Munson	.40	.20	.12
(42)	Bobby Murcer	.12	.06	.04
(43)	Al Oliver	.15	.08	.05
(44)	Jim Palmer	.60	.30	.20

		NR MT	EX	VG
(45)	Dave Parker	.20	.10	.06
(46)	Tony Perez	.20	.10	.06
(47)	Jerry Reuss	.12	.06	.04
(48)	Brooks Robinson	.70	.35	.20
(49)	Frank Robinson	.70	.35	.20
(50)	Steve Rogers	.10	.05	.03
(51)	Pete Rose	1.50	.70	.45
(52)	Nolan Ryan	1.50	.70	.45
(53)	Manny Sanguillen	.10	.05	.03
(54)	Mike Schmidt	1.25	.60	.40
(55)	Tom Seaver	1.25	.60	.40
(56)	Ted Simmons	.15	.08	.05
(57)	Reggie Smith	.12	.06	.04
(58)	Willie Stargell	.60	.30	.20
(59)	Rusty Staub	.15	.08	.05
(60)	Rennie Stennett	.10	.05	.03
(61)	Don Sutton	.20	.10	.06
(62)	Andy Thornton	.12	.06	.04
(63)	Luis Tiant	.15	.08	.05
(64)	Joe Torre	.12	.06	.04
(65)	Mike Tyson	.10	.05	.03
(66)	Bob Watson	.10	.05	.03
(67)	Wilbur Wood	.10	.05	.03
(68)	Jimmy Wynn	.10	.05	.03
(69)	Carl Yastrzemski	1.25	.60	.40
(70)	Richie Zisk	.10	.05	.03

1954 Dan-Dee Potato Chips

 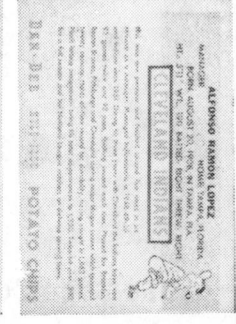

AL LOPEZ

Issued in bags of potato chips, the cards in this 29-card set are commonly found with grease stains despite their waxed surface. The unnumbered cards, which measure 2-1/2" by 3-5/8", feature full-color photos. The card backs contain player statistical and biographical information. The set consists mostly of players from the Indians and Pirates. Photos of the Yankees players were also used for the Briggs Meats and Stahl-Meyer Franks sets. Cooper and Smith are the scarcest cards in the set.

		NR MT	EX	VG
Complete Set		4500.00	2250.00	1350.
Common Player		60.00	30.00	18.00
(1)	Bob Avila	60.00	30.00	18.00
(2)	Hank Bauer	80.00	40.00	24.00
(3)	Walker Cooper	350.00	175.00	105.00
(4)	Larry Doby	90.00	45.00	27.00
(5)	Luke Easter	60.00	30.00	18.00
(6)	Bob Feller	200.00	100.00	60.00
(7)	Bob Friend	60.00	30.00	18.00
(8)	Mike Garcia	60.00	30.00	18.00
(9)	Sid Gordon	60.00	30.00	18.00
(10)	Jim Hegan	60.00	30.00	18.00
(11)	Gil Hodges	150.00	75.00	45.00
(12)	Art Houtteman	60.00	30.00	18.00
(13)	Monte Irvin	90.00	45.00	27.00
(14)	Paul LaPalm (LaPalme)	60.00	30.00	18.00
(15)	Bob Lemon	110.00	55.00	33.00
(16)	Al Lopez	90.00	45.00	27.00
(17)	Mickey Mantle	1500.00	750.00	450.00

		NR MT	EX	VG
(18)	Dale Mitchell	60.00	30.00	18.00
(19)	Phil Rizzuto	125.00	62.00	37.00
(20)	Curtis Roberts	60.00	30.00	18.00
(21)	Al Rosen	80.00	40.00	24.00
(22)	Red Schoendienst	110.00	55.00	33.00
(23)	Paul Smith	450.00	225.00	135.00
(24)	Duke Snider	225.00	112.00	67.00
(25)	George Strickland	60.00	30.00	18.00
(26)	Max Surkont	60.00	30.00	18.00
(27)	Frank Thomas	125.00	62.00	37.00
(28)	Wally Westlake	60.00	30.00	18.00
(29)	Early Wynn	110.00	55.00	33.00

1987 David Berg
Hot Dogs Cubs

Changing sponsors from Gatorade to David Berg Pure Beef Hot Dogs, the Chicago Cubs handed out a 26-card set of baseball cards to fans attending the July 29th game at Wrigley Field. The cards are printed in full-color on white stock and measure 2-7/8" by 4-1/4" in size. The set is numbered by the players' uniform numbers. The card backs contain player personal and statistical information, plus a full-color picture of a David Berg hot dog in a bun with all the garnishings. The set marked the sixth consecutive year the Cubs held a baseball card giveaway promotion.

		MT	NR MT	EX
	Complete Set:	10.00	7.50	4.00
	Common Player:	.15	.11	.06
1	Dave Martinez	.50	.40	.20
4	Gene Michael	.15	.11	.06
6	Keith Moreland	.30	.25	.12
7	Jody Davis	.30	.25	.12
8	Andre Dawson	1.00	.70	.40
10	Leon Durham	.30	.25	.12
11	Jim Sundberg	.15	.11	.06
12	Shawon Dunston	.60	.45	.25
19	Manny Trillo	.15	.11	.06
20	Bob Dernier	.15	.11	.06
21	Scott Sanderson	.15	.11	.06
22	Jerry Mumphrey	.15	.11	.06
23	Ryne Sandberg	2.00	1.50	.80
24	Brian Dayett	.15	.11	.06
29	Chico Walker	.15	.11	.06
31	Greg Maddux	.70	.50	.30
33	Frank DiPino	.15	.11	.06
34	Steve Trout	.20	.15	.08
36	Gary Matthews	.20	.15	.08
37	Ed Lynch	.15	.11	.06
39	Ron Davis	.15	.11	.06
40	Rick Sutcliffe	.70	.50	.30
46	Lee Smith	.30	.25	.12
47	Dickie Noles	.15	.11	.06
49	Jamie Moyer	.20	.15	.08
----	The Coaching Staff (Johnny Oates, Jim Snyder, Herm Starrette, John Vukovich, Billy Williams)	.15	.11	.06

1988 David Berg
Hot Dogs Cubs

 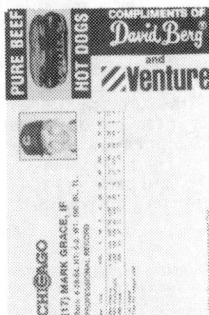

This oversized (2-7/8" by 4-1/2") set of 26 cards was distributed to fans at Wrigley Field on August 24th. The set includes cards for the manager and coaching staff, as well as players. Full-color action photos are framed in red and blue on a white background. The backs feature small black and white player close-ups, colorful team logos, statistics and sponsor logos (David Berg Hot Dogs and Venture Store Restaurants). The numbers in the following checklist refer to players' uniforms.

		MT	NR MT	EX
	Complete Set:	11.00	8.25	4.50
	Common Player:	.15	.11	.06
2	Vance Law	.15	.11	.06
4	Don Zimmer	.15	.11	.06
7	Jody Davis	.30	.25	.12
8	Andre Dawson	1.00	.70	.40
9	Damon Berryhill	.80	.60	.30
12	Shawon Dunston	.60	.45	.25
17	Mark Grace	3.00	2.25	1.25
18	Angel Salazar	.15	.11	.06
19	Manny Trillo	.15	.11	.06
21	Scott Sanderson	.15	.11	.06
22	Jerry Mumphrey	.15	.11	.06
23	Ryne Sandberg	2.00	1.50	.80
24	Gary Varsho	.40	.30	.15
25	Rafael Palmeiro	1.25	.90	.50
28	Mitch Webster	.15	.11	.06
30	Darrin Jackson	.40	.30	.15
31	Greg Maddux	.70	.50	.30
32	Calvin Schiraldi	.20	.15	.08
33	Frank DiPino	.15	.11	.06
37	Pat Perry	.15	.11	.06
40	Rick Sutcliffe	.70	.50	.30
41	Jeff Pico	.50	.40	.20
45	Al Nipper	.15	.11	.06
49	Jamie Moyer	.20	.15	.08
50	Les Lancaster	.15	.11	.06
54	Rich Gossage	.70	.50	.30
----	Joe Altobelli, Chuck Cottier, Larry Cox, Jose Martinez, Dick Pole	.15	.11	.06

1988 Domino's Pizza Tigers

 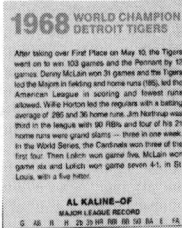

Domino's Pizza produced a 28-card set commemorating the 20th anniversary of the 1968 World Champion Detroit Tigers. The cards were given away at an Old Timers Game at Tiger Stadium in 1988. The cards, which measure 2-1/2" by 3-1/2", feature black and white photos semi-surrounded by a two-stripe band. The stripes on the card's left side are the same color (red and light blue) as the Domino's Pizza logo in the upper corner. The stripes on the card's right side match the colors of the Tigers logo (red and dark blue). The backs of all the cards (except for Ernie Harwell) contain a brief summary of the Tigers' 1968 season. Located at the bottom on the card backs are the players' major league records through 1968 plus their 1968 World Series statistics.

		MT	NR MT	EX
Complete Set:		11.00	8.25	4.50
Common Player:		.20	.15	.08
(1)	Gates Brown	.30	.25	.12
(2)	Norm Cash	.90	.70	.35
(3)	Wayne Comer	.20	.15	.08
(4)	Pat Dobson	.20	.15	.08
(5)	Bill Freehan	.60	.45	.25
(6)	John Hiller	.30	.25	.12
(7)	Ernie Harwell (announcer)	.30	.25	.12
(8)	Willie Horton	.60	.45	.25
(9)	Al Kaline	1.50	1.25	.60
(10)	Fred Lasher	.20	.15	.08
(11)	Mickey Lolich	.90	.70	.35
(12)	Tom Matchick	.20	.15	.08
(13)	Ed Mathews	1.00	.70	.40
(14)	Dick McAuliff (McAuliffe)	.40	.30	.15
(15)	Denny McLain	1.00	.70	.40
(16)	Don McMahon	.20	.15	.08
(17)	Jim Northrup	.40	.30	.15
(18)	Ray Oyler	.20	.15	.08
(19)	Daryl Patterson	.20	.15	.08
(20)	Jim Price	.20	.15	.08
(21)	Joe Sparma	.20	.15	.08
(22)	Mickey Stanley	.40	.30	.15
(23)	Dick Tracewski	.20	.15	.08
(24)	Jon Warden	.20	.15	.08
(25)	Don Wert	.20	.15	.08
(26)	Earl Wilson	.20	.15	.08
(27)	Header Card	.20	.15	.08
(28)	Coupon Card	.20	.15	.08

1981 Donruss

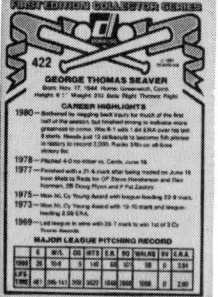

TOM SEAVER PITCHER

The Donruss Co. of Memphis, Tenn., produced its premiere baseball card issue in 1981 with a set that consisted of 600 numbered cards and five unnumbered checklists. The cards, which measure 2-1/2" by 3-1/2", are printed on thin stock. The card fronts contain the Donruss logo plus the year of issue. The card backs are designed on a vertical format and have black print on red and white. The set, entitled "First Edition Collector Series," contains nearly 40 variations, those being first-printing errors that were corrected in a subsequent print run. The cards were issued in gum wax packs, with hobby dealer sales being coordinated by TCMA of Amawalk, N.Y. The

complete set price does not include the higher priced variations.

		MT	NR MT	EX
Complete Set:		45.00	33.00	16.00
Common Player:		.06	.05	.02
1	Ozzie Smith	.90	.70	.35
2	Rollie Fingers	.25	.20	.10
3	Rick Wise	.08	.06	.03
4	Gene Richards	.06	.05	.02
5	Alan Trammell	.40	.30	.15
6	Tom Brookens	.08	.06	.03
7a	Duffy Dyer (1980 Avg. .185)	1.00	.70	.40
7b	Duffy Dyer (1980 Avg. 185)	.10	.08	.04
8	Mark Fidrych	.08	.06	.03
9	Dave Rozema	.06	.05	.02
10	Ricky Peters	.06	.05	.02
11	Mike Schmidt	2.50	2.00	1.00
12	Willie Stargell	.40	.30	.15
13	Tim Foli	.06	.05	.02
14	Manny Sanguillen	.06	.05	.02
15	Grant Jackson	.06	.05	.02
16	Eddie Solomon	.06	.05	.02
17	Omar Moreno	.06	.05	.02
18	Joe Morgan	.60	.45	.25
19	Rafael Landestoy	.06	.05	.02
20	Bruce Bochy	.06	.05	.02
21	Joe Sambito	.06	.05	.02
22	Manny Trillo	.08	.06	.03
23a	*Dave Smith (incomplete box around stats)*	1.00	.70	.40
23b	*Dave Smith (complete box around stats)*	.30	.25	.12
24	Terry Puhl	.06	.05	.02
25	Bump Wills	.06	.05	.02
26a	John Ellis (Danny Walton photo - with bat)	1.25	.90	.50
26b	John Ellis (John Ellis photo - with glove)	.10	.08	.04
27	Jim Kern	.06	.05	.02
28	Richie Zisk	.08	.06	.03
29	John Mayberry	.08	.06	.03
30	Bob Davis	.06	.05	.02
31	Jackson Todd	.06	.05	.02
32	Al Woods	.06	.05	.02
33	Steve Carlton	1.00	.70	.40
34	Lee Mazzilli	.08	.06	.03
35	John Stearns	.06	.05	.02
36	Roy Jackson	.06	.05	.02
37	Mike Scott	.70	.50	.30
38	Lamar Johnson	.06	.05	.02
39	Kevin Bell	.06	.05	.02
40	Ed Farmer	.06	.05	.02
41	Ross Baumgarten	.06	.05	.02
42	Leo Sutherland	.06	.05	.02
43	Dan Meyer	.06	.05	.02
44	Ron Reed	.06	.05	.02
45	Mario Mendoza	.06	.05	.02
46	Rick Honeycutt	.06	.05	.02
47	Glenn Abbott	.06	.05	.02
48	Leon Roberts	.06	.05	.02
49	Rod Carew	1.00	.70	.40
50	Bert Campaneris	.10	.08	.04
51a	Tom Donahue (incorrect spelling)	1.00	.70	.40
51b	Tom Donohue (Donohue on front)	.10	.08	.04
52	Dave Frost	.06	.05	.02
53	Ed Halicki	.06	.05	.02
54	Dan Ford	.06	.05	.02
55	Garry Maddox	.10	.08	.04
56a	Steve Garvey ("Surpassed 25 HR..." on back)	1.75	1.25	.70
56b	Steve Garvey ("Surpassed 21 HR..." on back)	.60	.45	.25
57	Bill Russell	.08	.06	.03
58	Don Sutton	.30	.25	.12
59	Reggie Smith	.10	.08	.04
60	Rick Monday	.10	.08	.04
61	Ray Knight	.10	.08	.04
62	Johnny Bench	1.00	.70	.40
63	Mario Soto	.08	.06	.03
64	Doug Bair	.06	.05	.02
65	George Foster	.20	.15	.08
66	Jeff Burroughs	.08	.06	.03
67	Keith Hernandez	.40	.30	.15
68	Tom Herr	.10	.08	.04
69	Bob Forsch	.08	.06	.03
70	John Fulgham	.06	.05	.02
71a	Bobby Bonds (lifetime HR 986)	1.00	.70	.40
71b	Bobby Bonds (lifetime HR 326)	.15	.11	.06
72a	Rennie Stennett ("...breaking broke leg..." on back)	1.00	.70	.40

#	Player	MT	NR MT	EX
72b	Rennie Stennett ("...breaking leg..." on back)	.10	.08	.04
73	Joe Strain	.06	.05	.02
74	Ed Whitson	.06	.05	.02
75	Tom Griffin	.06	.05	.02
76	Bill North	.06	.05	.02
77	Gene Garber	.06	.05	.02
78	Mike Hargrove	.06	.05	.02
79	Dave Rosello	.06	.05	.02
80	Ron Hassey	.06	.05	.02
81	Sid Monge	.06	.05	.02
82a	Joe Charboneau ("For some reason, Phillies..." on back)	1.00	.70	.40
82b	Joe Charboneau ("Phillies..." on back)	.12	.09	.05
83	Cecil Cooper	.15	.11	.06
84	Sal Bando	.10	.08	.04
85	Moose Haas	.06	.05	.02
86	Mike Caldwell	.06	.05	.02
87a	Larry Hisle ("...Twins with 28 RBI." on back)	1.00	.70	.40
87b	Larry Hisle ("...Twins with 28 HR" on back)	.10	.08	.04
88	Luis Gomez	.06	.05	.02
89	Larry Parrish	.10	.08	.04
90	Gary Carter	.40	.30	.15
91	*Bill Gullickson*	.15	.11	.06
92	Fred Norman	.06	.05	.02
93	Tommy Hutton	.06	.05	.02
94	Carl Yastrzemski	.80	.60	.30
95	Glenn Hoffman	.06	.05	.02
96	Dennis Eckersley	.12	.09	.05
97a	Tom Burgmeier (Throws: Right)	1.00	.70	.40
97b	Tom Burgmeier (Throws: Left)	.10	.08	.04
98	Win Remmerswaal	.06	.05	.02
99	Bob Horner	.12	.09	.05
100	George Brett	2.00	1.50	.80
101	Dave Chalk	.06	.05	.02
102	Dennis Leonard	.08	.06	.03
103	Renie Martin	.06	.05	.02
104	Amos Otis	.08	.06	.03
105	Graig Nettles	.15	.11	.06
106	Eric Soderholm	.06	.05	.02
107	Tommy John	.20	.15	.08
108	Tom Underwood	.06	.05	.02
109	Lou Piniella	.12	.09	.05
110	Mickey Klutts	.06	.05	.02
111	Bobby Murcer	.10	.08	.04
112	Eddie Murray	.70	.50	.30
113	Rick Dempsey	.08	.06	.03
114	Scott McGregor	.08	.06	.03
115	Ken Singleton	.10	.08	.04
116	Gary Roenicke	.06	.05	.02
117	Dave Revering	.06	.05	.02
118	Mike Norris	.06	.05	.02
119	Rickey Henderson	25.00	20.00	10.00
120	Mike Heath	.06	.05	.02
121	Dave Cash	.06	.05	.02
122	Randy Jones	.08	.06	.03
123	Eric Rasmussen	.06	.05	.02
124	Jerry Mumphrey	.06	.05	.02
125	Richie Hebner	.06	.05	.02
126	Mark Wagner	.06	.05	.02
127	Jack Morris	.30	.25	.12
128	Dan Petry	.08	.06	.03
129	Bruce Robbins	.06	.05	.02
130	Champ Summers	.06	.05	.02
131a	Pete Rose ("...see card 251." on back)	2.25	1.75	.90
131b	Pete Rose ("...see card 371." on back)	1.25	.90	.50
132	Willie Stargell	.40	.30	.15
133	Ed Ott	.06	.05	.02
134	Jim Bibby	.06	.05	.02
135	Bert Blyleven	.12	.09	.05
136	Dave Parker	.30	.25	.12
137	Bill Robinson	.06	.05	.02
138	Enos Cabell	.06	.05	.02
139	Dave Bergman	.06	.05	.02
140	J R Richard	.10	.08	.04
141	Ken Forsch	.06	.05	.02
142	Larry Bowa	.15	.11	.06
143	Frank LaCorte (photo actually Randy Niemann)	.06	.05	.02
144	Dennis Walling	.06	.05	.02
145	Buddy Bell	.12	.09	.05
146	Ferguson Jenkins	.20	.15	.08
147	Danny Darwin	.06	.05	.02
148	John Grubb	.06	.05	.02
149	Alfredo Griffin	.08	.06	.03
150	Jerry Garvin	.06	.05	.02
151	*Paul Mirabella*(FC)	.10	.08	.04
152	Rick Bosetti	.06	.05	.02
153	Dick Ruthven	.06	.05	.02
154	Frank Taveras	.06	.05	.02
155	Craig Swan	.06	.05	.02
156	*Jeff Reardon*	1.25	.90	.50
157	Steve Henderson	.06	.05	.02
158	Jim Morrison	.06	.05	.02
159	Glenn Borgmann	.06	.05	.02
160	*Lamarr Hoyt (LaMarr)*	.10	.08	.04
161	Rich Wortham	.06	.05	.02
162	Thad Bosley	.06	.05	.02
163	Julio Cruz	.06	.05	.02
164a	Del Unser (no 3B in stat heads)	1.00	.70	.40
164b	Del Unser (3B in stat heads)	.10	.08	.04
165	Jim Anderson	.06	.05	.02
166	Jim Beattie	.06	.05	.02
167	Shane Rawley	.10	.08	.04
168	Joe Simpson	.06	.05	.02
169	Rod Carew	1.00	.70	.40
170	Fred Patek	.06	.05	.02
171	Frank Tanana	.10	.08	.04
172	Alfredo Martinez	.06	.05	.02
173	Chris Knapp	.06	.05	.02
174	Joe Rudi	.10	.08	.04
175	Greg Luzinski	.15	.11	.06
176	Steve Garvey	.50	.40	.20
177	Joe Ferguson	.06	.05	.02
178	Bob Welch	.12	.09	.05
179	Dusty Baker	.10	.08	.04
180	Rudy Law	.06	.05	.02
181	Dave Concepcion	.15	.11	.06
182	Johnny Bench	.50	.40	.20
183	Mike LaCoss	.06	.05	.02
184	Ken Griffey	.12	.09	.05
185	Dave Collins	.08	.06	.03
186	Brian Asselstine	.06	.05	.02
187	Garry Templeton	.10	.08	.04
188	Mike Phillips	.06	.05	.02
189	Pete Vukovich	.08	.06	.03
190	John Urrea	.06	.05	.02
191	Tony Scott	.06	.05	.02
192	Darrell Evans	.12	.09	.05
193	Milt May	.06	.05	.02
194	Bob Knepper	.08	.06	.03
195	Randy Moffitt	.06	.05	.02
196	Larry Herndon	.08	.06	.03
197	Rick Camp	.06	.05	.02
198	Andre Thornton	.10	.08	.04
199	Tom Veryzer	.06	.05	.02
200	Gary Alexander	.06	.05	.02
201	Rick Waits	.06	.05	.02
202	Rick Manning	.06	.05	.02
203	Paul Molitor	.20	.15	.08
204	Jim Gantner	.08	.06	.03
205	Paul Mitchell	.06	.05	.02
206	Reggie Cleveland	.06	.05	.02
207	Sixto Lezcano	.06	.05	.02
208	Bruce Benedict	.06	.05	.02
209	Rodney Scott	.06	.05	.02
210	John Tamargo	.06	.05	.02
211	Bill Lee	.08	.06	.03
212	Andre Dawson	.80	.60	.30
213	Rowland Office	.06	.05	.02
214	Carl Yastrzemski	1.00	.70	.40
215	Jerry Remy	.06	.05	.02
216	Mike Torrez	.08	.06	.03
217	Skip Lockwood	.06	.05	.02
218	Fred Lynn	.20	.15	.08
219	Chris Chambliss	.08	.06	.03
220	Willie Aikens	.08	.06	.03
221	John Wathan	.08	.06	.03
222	Dan Quisenberry	.15	.11	.06
223	Willie Wilson	.15	.11	.06
224	Clint Hurdle	.06	.05	.02
225	Bob Watson	.08	.06	.03
226	Jim Spencer	.06	.05	.02
227	Ron Guidry	.25	.20	.10
228	Reggie Jackson	.90	.70	.35
229	Oscar Gamble	.08	.06	.03
230	Jeff Cox	.06	.05	.02
231	Luis Tiant	.12	.09	.05
232	Rich Dauer	.06	.05	.02
233	Dan Graham	.06	.05	.02
234	Mike Flanagan	.10	.08	.04
235	John Lowenstein	.06	.05	.02
236	Benny Ayala	.06	.05	.02
237	Wayne Gross	.06	.05	.02
238	Rick Langford	.06	.05	.02
239	Tony Armas	.10	.08	.04
240a	Bob Lacy (incorrect spelling)	1.00	.70	.40

		MT	NR MT	EX
240b	Bob Lacey (correct spelling)	.10	.08	.04
241	Gene Tenace	.08	.06	.03
242	Bob Shirley	.06	.05	.02
243	Gary Lucas	.08	.06	.03
244	Jerry Turner	.06	.05	.02
245	John Wockenfuss	.06	.05	.02
246	Stan Papi	.06	.05	.02
247	Milt Wilcox	.06	.05	.02
248	Dan Schatzeder	.06	.05	.02
249	Steve Kemp	.08	.06	.03
250	Jim Lentine	.06	.05	.02
251	Pete Rose	1.00	.70	.40
252	Bill Madlock	.12	.09	.05
253	Dale Berra	.06	.05	.02
254	Kent Tekulve	.08	.06	.03
255	Enrique Romo	.06	.05	.02
256	Mike Easler	.08	.06	.03
257	Chuck Tanner	.06	.05	.02
258	Art Howe	.06	.05	.02
259	Alan Ashby	.06	.05	.02
260	Nolan Ryan	3.50	2.75	1.50
261a	Vern Ruhle (Ken Forsch photo - head shot)	1.25	.90	.50
261b	Vern Ruhle (Vern Ruhle photo - waist to head shot)	.10	.08	.04
262	Bob Boone	.10	.08	.04
263	Cesar Cedeno	.12	.09	.05
264	Jeff Leonard	.12	.09	.05
265	Pat Putnam	.06	.05	.02
266	Jon Matlack	.08	.06	.03
267	Dave Rajsich	.06	.05	.02
268	Billy Sample	.06	.05	.02
269	*Damaso Garcia*	.10	.08	.04
270	Tom Buskey	.06	.05	.02
271	Joey McLaughlin	.06	.05	.02
272	Barry Bonnell	.06	.05	.02
273	Tug McGraw	.10	.08	.04
274	Mike Jorgensen	.06	.05	.02
275	Pat Zachry	.06	.05	.02
276	Neil Allen	.08	.06	.03
277	Joel Youngblood	.06	.05	.02
278	Greg Pryor	.06	.05	.02
279	*Britt Burns*	.10	.08	.04
280	*Rich Dotson*	.35	.25	.14
281	Chet Lemon	.08	.06	.03
282	Rusty Kuntz	.06	.05	.02
283	Ted Cox	.06	.05	.02
284	Sparky Lyle	.10	.08	.04
285	Larry Cox	.06	.05	.02
286	Floyd Bannister	.10	.08	.04
287	Byron McLaughlin	.06	.05	.02
288	Rodney Craig	.06	.05	.02
289	Bobby Grich	.10	.08	.04
290	Dickie Thon	.08	.06	.03
291	Mark Clear	.06	.05	.02
292	Dave Lemanczyk	.06	.05	.02
293	Jason Thompson	.06	.05	.02
294	Rick Miller	.06	.05	.02
295	Lonnie Smith	.08	.06	.03
296	Ron Cey	.12	.09	.05
297	Steve Yeager	.06	.05	.02
298	Bobby Castillo	.06	.05	.02
299	Manny Mota	.08	.06	.03
300	Jay Johnstone	.08	.06	.03
301	Dan Driessen	.08	.06	.03
302	Joe Nolan	.06	.05	.02
303	Paul Householder	.06	.05	.02
304	Harry Spilman	.06	.05	.02
305	Cesar Geronimo	.06	.05	.02
306a	Gary Mathews (Mathews on front)	1.25	.90	.50
306b	Gary Matthews (Matthews on front)	.10	.08	.04
307	Ken Reitz	.06	.05	.02
308	Ted Simmons	.12	.09	.05
309	John Littlefield	.06	.05	.02
310	George Frazier	.06	.05	.02
311	Dane Iorg	.06	.05	.02
312	Mike Ivie	.06	.05	.02
313	Dennis Littlejohn	.06	.05	.02
314	Gary LaVelle (Lavelle)	.06	.05	.02
315	Jack Clark	.25	.20	.10
316	Jim Wohlford	.06	.05	.02
317	Rick Matula	.06	.05	.02
318	Toby Harrah	.08	.06	.03
319a	Dwane Kuiper (Dwane on front)	1.00	.70	.40
319b	Duane Kuiper (Duane on front)	.10	.08	.04
320	Len Barker	.08	.06	.03
321	Victor Cruz	.06	.05	.02
322	Dell Alston	.06	.05	.02
323	Robin Yount	1.25	.90	.50

		MT	NR MT	EX
324	Charlie Moore	.06	.05	.02
325	Lary Sorensen	.06	.05	.02
326a	Gorman Thomas ("...30-HR mark 4th..." on back)	1.25	.90	.50
326b	Gorman Thomas ("...30-HR mark 3rd..." on back)	.10	.08	.04
327	Bob Rodgers	.08	.06	.03
328	Phil Niekro	.30	.25	.12
329	Chris Speier	.06	.05	.02
330a	Steve Rodgers (Rodgers on front)	1.00	.70	.40
330b	Steve Rogers (Rogers on front)	.10	.08	.04
331	Woodie Fryman	.08	.06	.03
332	Warren Cromartie	.06	.05	.02
333	Jerry White	.06	.05	.02
334	Tony Perez	.20	.15	.08
335	Carlton Fisk	.50	.40	.20
336	Dick Drago	.06	.05	.02
337	Steve Renko	.06	.05	.02
338	Jim Rice	.50	.40	.20
339	Jerry Royster	.06	.05	.02
340	Frank White	.10	.08	.04
341	Jamie Quirk	.06	.05	.02
342a	Paul Spittorff (Spittorff on front)	1.00	.70	.40
342b	Paul Splittorff (Splittorff on front)	.08	.06	.03
343	Marty Pattin	.06	.05	.02
344	Pete LaCock	.06	.05	.02
345	Willie Randolph	.10	.08	.04
346	Rick Cerone	.06	.05	.02
347	Rich Gossage	.20	.15	.08
348	Reggie Jackson	.70	.50	.30
349	Ruppert Jones	.06	.05	.02
350	Dave McKay	.06	.05	.02
351	Yogi Berra	.15	.11	.06
352	Doug Decinces (DeCinces)	.10	.08	.04
353	Jim Palmer	.70	.50	.30
354	Tippy Martinez	.06	.05	.02
355	Al Bumbry	.08	.06	.03
356	Earl Weaver	.10	.08	.04
357a	Bob Picciolo (Bob on front)	1.00	.70	.40
357b	Rob Picciolo (Rob on front)	.10	.08	.04
358	Matt Keough	.06	.05	.02
359	Dwayne Murphy	.08	.06	.03
360	Brian Kingman	.06	.05	.02
361	Bill Fahey	.06	.05	.02
362	Steve Mura	.06	.05	.02
363	Dennis Kinney	.06	.05	.02
364	Dave Winfield	.50	.40	.20
365	Lou Whitaker	.40	.30	.15
366	Lance Parrish	.35	.25	.14
367	Tim Corcoran	.06	.05	.02
368	Pat Underwood	.06	.05	.02
369	Al Cowens	.06	.05	.02
370	Sparky Anderson	.10	.08	.04
371	Pete Rose	1.00	.70	.40
372	Phil Garner	.08	.06	.03
373	Steve Nicosia	.06	.05	.02
374	John Candelaria	.10	.08	.04
375	Don Robinson	.08	.06	.03
376	Lee Lacy	.06	.05	.02
377	John Milner	.06	.05	.02
378	Craig Reynolds	.06	.05	.02
379a	Luis Pujois (Pujois on front)	1.00	.70	.40
379b	Luis Pujols (Pujols on front)	.10	.08	.04
380	Joe Niekro	.12	.09	.05
381	Joaquin Andujar	.10	.08	.04
382	*Keith Moreland*	.35	.25	.14
383	Jose Cruz	.12	.09	.05
384	Bill Virdon	.06	.05	.02
385	Jim Sundberg	.08	.06	.03
386	Doc Medich	.06	.05	.02
387	Al Oliver	.15	.11	.06
388	Jim Norris	.06	.05	.02
389	Bob Bailor	.06	.05	.02
390	Ernie Whitt	.08	.06	.03
391	Otto Velez	.06	.05	.02
392	Roy Howell	.06	.05	.02
393	*Bob Walk*	.35	.25	.14
394	Doug Flynn	.06	.05	.02
395	Pete Falcone	.06	.05	.02
396	Tom Hausman	.06	.05	.02
397	Elliott Maddox	.06	.05	.02
398	Mike Squires	.06	.05	.02
399	Marvis Foley	.06	.05	.02
400	Steve Trout	.06	.05	.02
401	Wayne Nordhagen	.06	.05	.02
402	Tony Larussa (LaRussa)	.08	.06	.03
403	Bruce Bochte	.06	.05	.02
404	Bake McBride	.06	.05	.02
405	Jerry Narron	.06	.05	.02
406	Rob Dressler	.06	.05	.02
407	Dave Heaverlo	.06	.05	.02

		MT	NR MT	EX
408	Tom Paciorek	.06	.05	.02
409	Carney Lansford	.10	.08	.04
410	Brian Downing	.10	.08	.04
411	Don Aase	.06	.05	.02
412	Jim Barr	.06	.05	.02
413	Don Baylor	.12	.09	.05
414	Jim Fregosi	.08	.06	.03
415	Dallas Green	.08	.06	.03
416	Dave Lopes	.10	.08	.04
417	Jerry Reuss	.10	.08	.04
418	Rick Sutcliffe	.20	.15	.08
419	Derrel Thomas	.06	.05	.02
420	Tommy LaSorda (Lasorda)	.10	.08	.04
421	*Charlie Leibrandt*	.30	.25	.12
422	Tom Seaver	1.00	.70	.40
423	Ron Oester	.06	.05	.02
424	Junior Kennedy	.06	.05	.02
425	Tom Seaver	1.00	.70	.40
426	Bobby Cox	.06	.05	.02
427	*Leon Durham*	.20	.15	.08
428	Terry Kennedy	.08	.06	.03
429	Silvio Martinez	.06	.05	.02
430	George Hendrick	.08	.06	.03
431	Red Schoendienst	.08	.06	.03
432	John LeMaster	.06	.05	.02
433	Vida Blue	.12	.09	.05
434	John Montefusco	.08	.06	.03
435	Terry Whitfield	.06	.05	.02
436	Dave Bristol	.06	.05	.02
437	Dale Murphy	.90	.70	.35
438	Jerry Dybzinski	.06	.05	.02
439	Jorge Orta	.06	.05	.02
440	Wayne Garland	.06	.05	.02
441	Miguel Dilone	.06	.05	.02
442	Dave Garcia	.06	.05	.02
443	Don Money	.06	.05	.02
444a	Buck Martinez (photo reversed)	1.00	.70	.40
444b	Buck Martinez (photo correct)	.10	.08	.04
445	Jerry Augustine	.06	.05	.02
446	Ben Oglivie	.08	.06	.03
447	Jim Slaton	.06	.05	.02
448	Doyle Alexander	.10	.08	.04
449	Tony Bernazard	.06	.05	.02
450	Scott Sanderson	.06	.05	.02
451	Dave Palmer	.06	.05	.02
452	Stan Bahnsen	.06	.05	.02
453	Dick Williams	.06	.05	.02
454	Rick Burleson	.08	.06	.03
455	Gary Allenson	.06	.05	.02
456	Bob Stanley	.06	.05	.02
457a	*John Tudor* (lifetime W/L 9.7)	1.50	1.25	.60
457b	*John Tudor* (lifetime W/L 9-7)	1.00	.70	.40
458	Dwight Evans	.15	.11	.06
459	Glenn Hubbard	.08	.06	.03
460	U L Washington	.06	.05	.02
461	Larry Gura	.06	.05	.02
462	Rich Gale	.06	.05	.02
463	Hal McRae	.10	.08	.04
464	Jim Frey	.06	.05	.02
465	Bucky Dent	.10	.08	.04
466	Dennis Werth	.06	.05	.02
467	Ron Davis	.08	.06	.03
468	Reggie Jackson	.70	.50	.30
469	Bobby Brown	.06	.05	.02
470	*Mike Davis*	.25	.20	.10
471	Gaylord Perry	.30	.25	.12
472	Mark Belanger	.08	.06	.03
473	Jim Palmer	.70	.50	.30
474	Sammy Stewart	.06	.05	.02
475	Tim Stoddard	.06	.05	.02
476	Steve Stone	.08	.06	.03
477	Jeff Newman	.06	.05	.02
478	Steve McCatty	.06	.05	.02
479	Billy Martin	.12	.09	.05
480	Mitchell Page	.06	.05	.02
481	Cy Young 1980 (Steve Carlton)	.40	.30	.15
482	Bill Buckner	.12	.09	.05
483a	Ivan DeJesus (lifetime hits 702)	1.00	.70	.40
483b	Ivan DeJesus (lifetime hits 642)	.10	.08	.04
484	Cliff Johnson	.06	.05	.02
485	Lenny Randle	.06	.05	.02
486	Larry Milbourne	.06	.05	.02
487	Roy Smalley	.06	.05	.02
488	John Castino	.06	.05	.02
489	Ron Jackson	.06	.05	.02
490a	Dave Roberts (1980 highlights begins "Showed pop...")	1.00	.70	.40
490b	Dave Roberts (1980 highlights begins "Declared himself...")	.10	.08	.04
491	MVP (George Brett)	.60	.45	.25
492	Mike Cubbage	.06	.05	.02

		MT	NR MT	EX
493	Rob Wilfong	.06	.05	.02
494	Danny Goodwin	.06	.05	.02
495	Jose Morales	.06	.05	.02
496	Mickey Rivers	.08	.06	.03
497	Mike Edwards	.06	.05	.02
498	Mike Sadek	.06	.05	.02
499	Lenn Sakata	.06	.05	.02
500	Gene Michael	.06	.05	.02
501	Dave Roberts	.06	.05	.02
502	Steve Dillard	.06	.05	.02
503	Jim Essian	.06	.05	.02
504	Rance Mulliniks	.06	.05	.02
505	Darrell Porter	.08	.06	.03
506	Joe Torre	.08	.06	.03
507	Terry Crowley	.06	.05	.02
508	Bill Travers	.06	.05	.02
509	Nelson Norman	.06	.05	.02
510	Bob McClure	.06	.05	.02
511	*Steve Howe*	.10	.08	.04
512	Dave Rader	.06	.05	.02
513	Mick Kelleher	.06	.05	.02
514	Kiko Garcia	.06	.05	.02
515	Larry Biittner	.06	.05	.02
516a	Willie Norwood (1980 highlights begins "Spent most...")	1.00	.70	.40
516b	Willie Norwood (1980 highlights begins "Traded to...")	.10	.08	.04
517	Bo Diaz	.08	.06	.03
518	Juan Beniquez	.06	.05	.02
519	Scot Thompson	.06	.05	.02
520	Jim Tracy	.06	.05	.02
521	Carlos Lezcano	.06	.05	.02
522	Joe Amalfitano	.06	.05	.02
523	Preston Hanna	.06	.05	.02
524a	Ray Burris (1980 highlights begins "Went on...")	1.00	.70	.40
524b	Ray Burris (1980 highlights begins "Drafted by...")	.10	.08	.04
525	Broderick Perkins	.06	.05	.02
526	Mickey Hatcher	.08	.06	.03
527	John Goryl	.06	.05	.02
528	Dick Davis	.06	.05	.02
529	Butch Wynegar	.06	.05	.02
530	Sal Butera	.06	.05	.02
531	Jerry Koosman	.10	.08	.04
532a	Jeff Zahn (Geoff) (1980 highlights begins "Was 2nd in...")	1.00	.70	.40
532b	Jeff Zahn (Geoff) (1980 highlights begins "Signed a 3 year...")	.10	.08	.04
533	Dennis Martinez	.08	.06	.03
534	Gary Thomasson	.06	.05	.02
535	Steve Macko	.06	.05	.02
536	Jim Kaat	.15	.11	.06
537	Best Hitters (George Brett, Rod Carew)	1.50	1.25	.60
538	*Tim Raines*	5.00	3.75	2.00
539	Keith Smith	.06	.05	.02
540	Ken Macha	.06	.05	.02
541	Burt Hooton	.08	.06	.03
542	Butch Hobson	.06	.05	.02
543	Bill Stein	.06	.05	.02
544	Dave Stapleton	.06	.05	.02
545	Bob Pate	.06	.05	.02
546	Doug Corbett	.06	.05	.02
547	Darrell Jackson	.06	.05	.02
548	Pete Redfern	.06	.05	.02
549	Roger Erickson	.06	.05	.02
550	Al Hrabosky	.08	.06	.03
551	Dick Tidrow	.06	.05	.02
552	Dave Ford	.06	.05	.02
553	Dave Kingman	.15	.11	.06
554a	Mike Vail (1980 highlights begins "After...")	1.00	.70	.40
554b	Mike Vail (1980 highlights begins "Traded...")	.10	.08	.04
555a	Jerry Martin (1980 highlights begins "Overcame...")	1.00	.70	.40
555b	Jerry Martin (1980 highlights begins "Traded...")	.10	.08	.04
556a	Jesus Figueroa (1980 highlights begins "Had...")	1.00	.70	.40
556b	Jesus Figueroa (1980 highlights begins "Traded...")	.10	.08	.04
557	Don Stanhouse	.06	.05	.02
558	Barry Foote	.06	.05	.02
559	Tim Blackwell	.06	.05	.02
560	Bruce Sutter	.15	.11	.06
561	Rick Reuschel	.10	.08	.04
562	Lynn McGlothen	.06	.05	.02
563a	Bob Owchinko (1980 highlights begins "Traded...")	1.00	.70	.40

		MT	NR MT	EX
563b	Bob Owchinko (1980 highlights begins "Involved...")	.10	.08	.04
564	John Verhoeven	.06	.05	.02
565	Ken Landreaux	.06	.05	.02
566a	Glen Adams (Glen on front)	1.00	.70	.40
566b	Glenn Adams (Glenn on front)	.10	.08	.04
567	Hosken Powell	.06	.05	.02
568	Dick Noles	.06	.05	.02
569	*Danny Ainge*	.25	.20	.10
570	Bobby Mattick	.06	.05	.02
571	Joe LeFebvre (Lefebvre)	.06	.05	.02
572	Bobby Clark	.06	.05	.02
573	Dennis Lamp	.06	.05	.02
574	Randy Lerch	.06	.05	.02
575	*Mookie Wilson*	.60	.45	.25
576	Ron LeFlore	.08	.06	.03
577	Jim Dwyer	.06	.05	.02
578	Bill Castro	.06	.05	.02
579	Greg Minton	.06	.05	.02
580	Mark Littell	.06	.05	.02
581	Andy Hassler	.06	.05	.02
582	Dave Stieb	.60	.45	.25
583	Ken Oberkfell	.06	.05	.02
584	Larry Bradford	.06	.05	.02
585	Fred Stanley	.06	.05	.02
586	Bill Caudill	.06	.05	.02
587	Doug Capilla	.06	.05	.02
588	George Riley	.06	.05	.02
589	Willie Hernandez	.10	.08	.04
590	MVP (Mike Schmidt)	.80	.60	.30
591	Cy Young 1980 (Steve Stone)	.08	.06	.03
592	Rick Sofield	.06	.05	.02
593	Bombo Rivera	.06	.05	.02
594	Gary Ward	.08	.06	.03
595a	Dave Edwards (1980 highlights begins "Sidelined...")	1.00	.70	.40
595b	Dave Edwards (1980 highlights begins "Traded...")	.10	.08	.04
596	Mike Proly	.06	.05	.02
597	Tommy Boggs	.06	.05	.02
598	Greg Gross	.06	.05	.02
599	Elias Sosa	.06	.05	.02
600	Pat Kelly	.06	.05	.02
---a	Checklist 1-120 (51 Tom Donohue)	2.00	1.50	.80
---b	Checklist 1-120 (51 Tom Donahue)	.10	.08	.04
----	Checklist 121-240	.06	.05	.02
---a	Checklist 241-360 (306 Gary Mathews)	.70	.50	.30
---b	Checklist 241-360 (306 Gary Matthews)	.10	.08	.04
---a	Checklist 361-480 (379 Luis Pujois)	.70	.50	.30
---b	Checklist 361-480 (379 Luis Pujols)	.10	.08	.04
---a	Checklist 481-600 (566 Glen Adams)	.70	.50	.30
---b	Checklist 481-600 (566 Glenn Adams)	.10	.08	.04

1982 Donruss

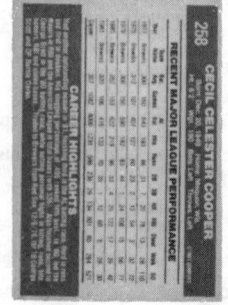

Using card stock thicker than the previous year, Donruss issued a 660-card set which includes 653 numbered cards and seven unnumbered checklists. The cards, which measure 2-1/2" by 3-1/2", were sold with puzzle pieces rather than gum as a result of a lawsuit by Topps. The puzzle pieces (three pieces on one card per pack) feature Babe Ruth. The first 26

cards of the set, entitled Diamond Kings, showcase the artwork of Dick Perez of Perez-Steele Galleries. The card fronts display the Donruss logo and the year of issue. The card backs have black and blue ink on white stock and include the player's career highlights. The complete set price does not include the higher priced variations.

		MT	NR MT	EX
	Complete Set:	45.00	33.00	18.00
	Common Player:	.06	.05	.02
1	Pete Rose (DK)	1.50	1.25	.60
2	Gary Carter (DK)	.50	.40	.20
3	Steve Garvey (DK)	.50	.40	.20
4	Vida Blue (DK)	.12	.09	.05
5a	Alan Trammel (DK) (name incorrect)	1.50	1.25	.60
5b	Alan Trammell (DK) (name correct)	.40	.30	.15
6	Len Barker (DK)	.08	.06	.03
7	Dwight Evans (DK)	.15	.11	.06
8	Rod Carew (DK)	.50	.40	.20
9	George Hendrick (DK)	.08	.06	.03
10	Phil Niekro (DK)	.30	.25	.12
11	Richie Zisk (DK)	.08	.06	.03
12	Dave Parker (DK)	.30	.25	.12
13	Nolan Ryan (DK)	1.25	.90	.50
14	Ivan DeJesus (DK)	.08	.06	.03
15	George Brett (DK)	.70	.50	.30
16	Tom Seaver (DK)	.50	.40	.20
17	Dave Kingman (DK)	.15	.11	.06
18	Dave Winfield (DK)	.50	.40	.20
19	Mike Norris (DK)	.08	.06	.03
20	Carlton Fisk (DK)	.25	.20	.10
21	Ozzie Smith (DK)	.20	.15	.08
22	Roy Smalley (DK)	.08	.06	.03
23	Buddy Bell (DK)	.12	.09	.05
24	Ken Singleton (DK)	.10	.08	.03
25	John Mayberry (DK)	.08	.06	.03
26	Gorman Thomas (DK)	.10	.08	.04
27	Earl Weaver	.10	.08	.04
28	Rollie Fingers	.20	.15	.08
29	Sparky Anderson	.10	.08	.04
30	Dennis Eckersley	.12	.09	.05
31	Dave Winfield	.50	.40	.20
32	Burt Hooton	.08	.06	.03
33	Rick Waits	.06	.05	.02
34	George Brett	1.00	.70	.40
35	Steve McCatty	.06	.05	.02
36	Steve Rogers	.08	.06	.03
37	Bill Stein	.06	.05	.02
38	Steve Renko	.06	.05	.02
39	Mike Squires	.06	.05	.02
40	George Hendrick	.08	.06	.03
41	Bob Knepper	.08	.06	.03
42	Steve Carlton	.50	.40	.20
43	Larry Biittner	.06	.05	.02
44	Chris Welsh	.06	.05	.02
45	Steve Nicosia	.06	.05	.02
46	Jack Clark	.25	.20	.10
47	Chris Chambliss	.08	.06	.03
48	Ivan DeJesus	.06	.05	.02
49	Lee Mazzilli	.08	.06	.03
50	Julio Cruz	.06	.05	.02
51	Pete Redfern	.06	.05	.02
52	Dave Stieb	.12	.09	.05
53	Doug Corbett	.06	.05	.02
54	*Jorge Bell*(FC)	7.00	5.25	2.75
55	Joe Simpson	.06	.05	.02
56	Rusty Staub	.10	.08	.04
57	Hector Cruz	.06	.05	.02
58	Claudell Washington(FC)	.10	.08	.04
59	Enrique Romo	.06	.05	.02
60	Gary Lavelle	.06	.05	.02
61	Tim Flannery	.06	.05	.02
62	Joe Nolan	.06	.05	.02
63	Larry Bowa	.15	.11	.06
64	Sixto Lezcano	.06	.05	.02
65	Joe Sambito	.06	.05	.02
66	Bruce Kison	.06	.05	.02
67	Wayne Nordhagen	.06	.05	.02
68	Woodie Fryman	.08	.06	.03
69	Billy Sample	.06	.05	.02
70	Amos Otis	.08	.06	.03
71	Matt Keough	.06	.05	.02
72	Toby Harrah	.08	.06	.03
73	*Dave Righetti*(FC)	2.00	1.50	.80
74	Carl Yastrzemski	.80	.60	.30
75	Bob Welch	.12	.09	.05

#	Name	MT	NR MT	EX
76a	Alan Trammel (name incorrect)	1.25	.90	.50
76b	Alan Trammel (name correct)	.40	.30	.15
77	Rick Dempsey	.08	.06	.03
78	Paul Molitor	.20	.15	.08
79	Dennis Martinez	.08	.06	.03
80	Jim Slaton	.06	.05	.02
81	Champ Summers	.06	.05	.02
82	Carney Lansford	.08	.06	.03
83	Barry Foote	.06	.05	.02
84	Steve Garvey	.50	.40	.20
85	Rick Manning	.06	.05	.02
86	John Wathan	.08	.06	.03
87	Brian Kingman	.06	.05	.02
88	Andre Dawson	.40	.30	.15
89	Jim Kern	.06	.05	.02
90	Bobby Grich	.10	.08	.04
91	Bob Forsch	.08	.06	.03
92	Art Howe	.06	.05	.02
93	Marty Bystrom	.06	.05	.02
94	Ozzie Smith	.20	.15	.08
95	Dave Parker	.30	.25	.12
96	Doyle Alexander	.10	.08	.04
97	Al Hrabosky	.08	.06	.03
98	Frank Taveras	.06	.05	.02
99	Tim Blackwell	.06	.05	.02
100	Floyd Bannister	.10	.08	.04
101	Alfredo Griffin	.08	.06	.03
102	Dave Engle	.06	.05	.02
103	Mario Soto	.08	.06	.03
104	Ross Baumgarten	.06	.05	.02
105	Ken Singleton	.10	.08	.04
106	Ted Simmons	.12	.09	.05
107	Jack Morris	.30	.25	.12
108	Bob Watson	.08	.06	.03
109	Dwight Evans	.15	.11	.06
110	Tom Lasorda	.10	.08	.04
111	Bert Blyleven	.12	.09	.05
112	Dan Quisenberry	.15	.11	.06
113	Rickey Henderson	5.00	3.75	2.00
114	Gary Carter	.35	.25	.14
115	Brian Downing	.10	.08	.04
116	Al Oliver	.15	.11	.06
117	LaMarr Hoyt	.06	.05	.02
118	Cesar Cedeno	.12	.09	.05
119	Keith Moreland	.10	.08	.04
120	Bob Shirley	.06	.05	.02
121	Terry Kennedy	.08	.06	.03
122	Frank Pastore	.06	.05	.02
123	Gene Garber	.06	.05	.02
124	Tony Pena(FC)	.25	.20	.10
125	Allen Ripley	.06	.05	.02
126	Randy Martz	.06	.05	.02
127	Richie Zisk	.08	.06	.03
128	Mike Scott	.15	.11	.06
129	Lloyd Moseby(FC)	.20	.15	.08
130	Rob Wilfong	.06	.05	.02
131	Tim Stoddard	.06	.05	.02
132	Gorman Thomas	.10	.08	.04
133	Dan Petry	.08	.06	.03
134	Bob Stanley	.06	.05	.02
135	Lou Piniella	.12	.09	.05
136	Pedro Guerrero(FC)	.70	.50	.30
137	Len Barker	.08	.06	.03
138	Richard Gale	.06	.05	.02
139	Wayne Gross	.06	.05	.02
140	*Tim Wallach*(FC)	2.50	2.00	1.00
141	Gene Mauch	.08	.06	.03
142	Doc Medich	.06	.05	.02
143	Tony Bernazard	.06	.05	.02
144	Bill Virdon	.06	.05	.02
145	John Littlefield	.06	.05	.02
146	Dave Bergman	.06	.05	.02
147	Dick Davis	.06	.05	.02
148	Tom Seaver	.60	.45	.25
149	Matt Sinatro	.06	.05	.02
150	Chuck Tanner	.06	.05	.02
151	Leon Durham	.08	.06	.03
152	Gene Tenace	.08	.06	.03
153	Al Bumbry	.08	.06	.03
154	Mark Brouhard	.06	.05	.02
155	Rick Peters	.06	.05	.02
156	Jerry Remy	.06	.05	.02
157	Rick Reuschel	.10	.08	.04
158	Steve Howe	.08	.06	.03
159	Alan Bannister	.06	.05	.02
160	U L Washington	.06	.05	.02
161	Rick Langford	.06	.05	.02
162	Bill Gullickson	.08	.06	.03
163	Mark Wagner	.06	.05	.02
164	Geoff Zahn	.06	.05	.02
165	Ron LeFlore	.08	.06	.03
166	Dane Iorg	.06	.05	.02
167	Joe Niekro	.12	.09	.05
168	Pete Rose	1.00	.70	.40
169	Dave Collins	.08	.06	.03
170	Rick Wise	.08	.06	.03
171	Jim Bibby	.06	.05	.02
172	Larry Herndon	.08	.06	.03
173	Bob Horner	.12	.09	.05
174	Steve Dillard	.06	.05	.02
175	Mookie Wilson	.12	.09	.05
176	Dan Meyer	.06	.05	.02
177	Fernando Arroyo	.06	.05	.02
178	Jackson Todd	.06	.05	.02
179	Darrell Jackson	.06	.05	.02
180	Al Woods	.06	.05	.02
181	Jim Anderson	.06	.05	.02
182	Dave Kingman	.15	.11	.06
183	Steve Henderson	.06	.05	.02
184	Brian Asselstine	.06	.05	.02
185	Rod Scurry	.06	.05	.02
186	Fred Breining	.06	.05	.02
187	Danny Boone	.06	.05	.02
188	Junior Kennedy	.06	.05	.02
189	Sparky Lyle	.10	.08	.04
190	Whitey Herzog	.08	.06	.03
191	Dave Smith	.10	.08	.04
192	Ed Ott	.06	.05	.02
193	Greg Luzinski	.15	.11	.06
194	Bill Lee	.08	.06	.03
195	Don Zimmer	.06	.05	.02
196	Hal McRae	.12	.09	.05
197	Mike Norris	.06	.05	.02
198	Duane Kuiper	.06	.05	.02
199	Rick Cerone	.06	.05	.02
200	Jim Rice	.40	.30	.15
201	Steve Yeager	.06	.05	.02
202	Tom Brookens	.06	.05	.02
203	Jose Morales	.06	.05	.02
204	Roy Howell	.06	.05	.02
205	Tippy Martinez	.06	.05	.02
206	Moose Haas	.06	.05	.02
207	Al Cowens	.06	.05	.02
208	Dave Stapleton	.06	.05	.02
209	Bucky Dent	.10	.08	.04
210	Ron Cey	.12	.09	.05
211	Jorge Orta	.06	.05	.02
212	Jamie Quirk	.06	.05	.02
213	Jeff Jones	.06	.05	.02
214	Tim Raines	1.00	.70	.40
215	Jon Matlack	.08	.06	.03
216	Rod Carew	.90	.70	.35
217	Jim Kaat	.15	.11	.06
218	Joe Pittman	.06	.05	.02
219	Larry Christenson	.06	.05	.02
220	Juan Bonilla	.06	.05	.02
221	Mike Easler	.08	.06	.03
222	Vida Blue	.12	.09	.05
223	Rick Camp	.06	.05	.02
224	Mike Jorgensen	.06	.05	.02
225	*Jody Davis*(FC)	.30	.25	.12
226	Mike Parrott	.06	.05	.02
227	Jim Clancy	.08	.06	.03
228	Hosken Powell	.06	.05	.02
229	Tom Hume	.06	.05	.02
230	Britt Burns	.06	.05	.02
231	Jim Palmer	.70	.50	.30
232	Bob Rodgers	.08	.06	.03
233	Milt Wilcox	.06	.05	.02
234	Dave Revering	.06	.05	.02
235	Mike Torrez	.08	.06	.03
236	Robert Castillo	.06	.05	.02
237	*Von Hayes*(FC)	1.25	.90	.50
238	Renie Martin	.06	.05	.02
239	Dwayne Murphy	.08	.06	.03
240	Rodney Scott	.06	.05	.02
241	Fred Patek	.06	.05	.02
242	Mickey Rivers	.08	.06	.03
243	Steve Trout	.06	.05	.02
244	Jose Cruz	.12	.09	.05
245	Manny Trillo	.08	.06	.03
246	Lary Sorensen	.06	.05	.02
247	Dave Edwards	.06	.05	.02
248	Dan Driessen	.08	.06	.03
249	Tommy Boggs	.06	.05	.02
250	Dale Berra	.06	.05	.02
251	Ed Whitson	.06	.05	.02
252	*Lee Smith*(FC)	.90	.70	.35
253	Tom Paciorek	.06	.05	.02
254	Pat Zachry	.06	.05	.02
255	Luis Leal	.06	.05	.02
256	John Castino	.06	.05	.02

		MT	NR MT	EX
257	Rich Dauer	.06	.05	.02
258	Cecil Cooper	.15	.11	.06
259	Dave Rozema	.06	.05	.02
260	John Tudor	.15	.11	.06
261	Jerry Mumphrey	.06	.05	.02
262	Jay Johnstone	.08	.06	.03
263	Bo Diaz	.08	.06	.03
264	Dennis Leonard	.08	.06	.03
265	Jim Spencer	.06	.05	.02
266	John Milner	.06	.05	.02
267	Don Aase	.06	.05	.02
268	Jim Sundberg	.08	.06	.03
269	Lamar Johnson	.06	.05	.02
270	Frank LaCorte	.06	.05	.02
271	Barry Evans	.06	.05	.02
272	Enos Cabell	.06	.05	.02
273	Del Unser	.06	.05	.02
274	George Foster	.20	.15	.08
275	Brett Butler(FC)	1.50	1.25	.70
276	Lee Lacy	.06	.05	.02
277	Ken Reitz	.06	.05	.02
278	Keith Hernandez	.40	.30	.15
279	Doug DeCinces	.10	.08	.04
280	Charlie Moore	.06	.05	.02
281	Lance Parrish	.35	.25	.14
282	Ralph Houk	.08	.06	.03
283	Rich Gossage	.20	.15	.08
284	Jerry Reuss	.10	.08	.04
285	Mike Stanton	.06	.05	.02
286	Frank White	.10	.08	.04
287	Bob Owchinko	.06	.05	.02
288	Scott Sanderson	.06	.05	.02
289	Bump Wills	.06	.05	.02
290	Dave Frost	.06	.05	.02
291	Chet Lemon	.08	.06	.03
292	Tito Landrum	.06	.05	.02
293	Vern Ruhle	.06	.05	.02
294	Mike Schmidt	1.00	.90	.50
295	Sam Mejias	.06	.05	.02
296	Gary Lucas	.06	.05	.02
297	John Candelaria	.10	.08	.04
298	Jerry Martin	.06	.05	.02
299	Dale Murphy	.90	.70	.35
300	Mike Lum	.06	.05	.02
301	Tom Hausman	.06	.05	.02
302	Glenn Abbott	.06	.05	.02
303	Roger Erickson	.06	.05	.02
304	Otto Velez	.06	.05	.02
305	Danny Goodwin	.06	.05	.02
306	John Mayberry	.08	.06	.03
307	Lenny Randle	.06	.05	.02
308	Bob Bailor	.06	.05	.02
309	Jerry Morales	.06	.05	.02
310	Rufino Linares	.06	.05	.02
311	Kent Tekulve	.08	.06	.03
312	Joe Morgan	.50	.40	.20
313	John Urrea	.06	.05	.02
314	Paul Householder	.06	.05	.02
315	Garry Maddox	.10	.08	.04
316	Mike Ramsey	.06	.05	.02
317	Alan Ashby	.06	.05	.02
318	Bob Clark	.06	.05	.02
319	Tony LaRussa	.08	.06	.03
320	Charlie Lea	.08	.06	.03
321	Danny Darwin	.06	.05	.02
322	Cesar Geronimo	.06	.05	.02
323	Tom Underwood	.06	.05	.02
324	Andre Thornton	.10	.08	.04
325	Rudy May	.06	.05	.02
326	Frank Tanana	.10	.08	.04
327	Davey Lopes	.10	.08	.04
328	Richie Hebner	.06	.05	.02
329	Mike Flanagan	.10	.08	.04
330	Mike Caldwell	.06	.05	.02
331	Scott McGregor	.08	.06	.03
332	Jerry Augustine	.06	.05	.02
333	Stan Papi	.06	.05	.02
334	Rick Miller	.06	.05	.02
335	Graig Nettles	.15	.11	.06
336	Dusty Baker	.10	.08	.04
337	Dave Garcia	.06	.05	.02
338	Larry Gura	.06	.05	.02
339	Cliff Johnson	.06	.05	.02
340	Warren Cromartie	.06	.05	.02
341	Steve Comer	.06	.05	.02
342	Rick Burleson	.08	.06	.03
343	John Martin	.06	.05	.02
344	Craig Reynolds	.06	.05	.02
345	Mike Proly	.06	.05	.02
346	Ruppert Jones	.06	.05	.02
347	Omar Moreno	.06	.05	.02

		MT	NR MT	EX
348	Greg Minton	.06	.05	.02
349	Rick Mahler(FC)	.25	.20	.10
350	Alex Trevino	.06	.05	.02
351	Mike Krukow	.08	.06	.03
352a	Shane Rawley (Jim Anderson photo — shaking hands)	1.25	.90	.50
352b	Shane Rawley (correct photo - kneeling)	.15	.11	.06
353	Garth Iorg	.06	.05	.02
354	Pete Mackanin	.06	.05	.02
355	Paul Moskau	.06	.05	.02
356	Richard Dotson	.10	.08	.04
357	Steve Stone	.08	.06	.03
358	Larry Hisle	.08	.06	.03
359	Aurelio Lopez	.06	.05	.02
360	Oscar Gamble	.08	.06	.03
361	Tom Burgmeier	.06	.05	.02
362	Terry Forster	.08	.06	.03
363	Joe Charboneau	.08	.06	.03
364	Ken Brett	.08	.06	.03
365	Tony Armas	.10	.08	.04
366	Chris Speier	.06	.05	.02
367	Fred Lynn	.20	.15	.08
368	Buddy Bell	.12	.09	.05
369	Jim Essian	.06	.05	.02
370	Terry Puhl	.06	.05	.02
371	Greg Gross	.06	.05	.02
372	Bruce Sutter	.15	.11	.06
373	Joe Lefebvre	.06	.05	.02
374	Ray Knight	.10	.08	.04
375	Bruce Benedict	.06	.05	.02
376	Tim Foli	.06	.05	.02
377	Al Holland	.06	.05	.02
378	Ken Kravec	.06	.05	.02
379	Jeff Burroughs	.08	.06	.03
380	Pete Falcone	.06	.05	.02
381	Ernie Whitt	.08	.06	.03
382	Brad Havens	.06	.05	.02
383	Terry Crowley	.06	.05	.02
384	Don Money	.06	.05	.02
385	Dan Schatzeder	.06	.05	.02
386	Gary Allenson	.06	.05	.02
387	Yogi Berra	.15	.11	.06
388	Ken Landreaux	.06	.05	.02
389	Mike Hargrove	.06	.05	.02
390	Darryl Motley	.06	.05	.02
391	Dave McKay	.06	.05	.02
392	Stan Bahnsen	.06	.05	.02
393	Ken Forsch	.06	.05	.02
394	Mario Mendoza	.06	.05	.02
395	Jim Morrison	.06	.05	.02
396	Mike Ivie	.06	.05	.02
397	Broderick Perkins	.06	.05	.02
398	Darrell Evans	.15	.11	.06
399	Ron Reed	.06	.05	.02
400	Johnny Bench	.60	.45	.25
401	Steve Bedrosian(FC)	1.00	.70	.40
402	Bill Robinson	.06	.05	.02
403	Bill Buckner	.12	.09	.05
404	Ken Oberkfell	.06	.05	.02
405	Cal Ripken, Jr.(FC)	18.00	13.50	7.25
406	Jim Gantner	.08	.06	.03
407	Kirk Gibson(FC)	1.50	1.25	.60
408	Tony Perez	.20	.15	.08
409	Tommy John	.20	.15	.08
410	Dave Stewart(FC)	7.00	5.25	2.75
411	Dan Spillner	.06	.05	.02
412	Willie Aikens	.06	.05	.02
413	Mike Heath	.06	.05	.02
414	Ray Burris	.06	.05	.02
415	Leon Roberts	.06	.05	.02
416	Mike Witt(FC)	.70	.50	.30
417	Bobby Molinaro	.06	.05	.02
418	Steve Braun	.06	.05	.02
419	Nolan Ryan	3.00	2.25	1.25
420	Tug McGraw	.12	.09	.05
421	Dave Concepcion	.12	.09	.05
422a	Juan Eichelberger (Gary Lucas photo — white player)	1.25	.90	.50
422b	Juan Eichelberger (correct photo - black player)	.08	.06	.03
423	Rick Rhoden	.10	.08	.04
424	Frank Robinson	.12	.09	.05
425	Eddie Miller	.06	.05	.02
426	Bill Caudill	.06	.05	.02
427	Doug Flynn	.06	.05	.02
428	Larry Anderson (Andersen)	.06	.05	.02
429	Al Williams	.06	.05	.02
430	Jerry Garvin	.06	.05	.02
431	Glenn Adams	.06	.05	.02
432	Barry Bonnell	.06	.05	.02

		MT	NR MT	EX
433	Jerry Narron	.06	.05	.02
434	John Stearns	.06	.05	.02
435	Mike Tyson	.06	.05	.02
436	Glenn Hubbard	.08	.06	.03
437	Eddie Solomon	.06	.05	.02
438	Jeff Leonard	.10	.08	.04
439	Randy Bass	.06	.05	.02
440	Mike LaCoss	.06	.05	.02
441	Gary Matthews	.10	.08	.04
442	Mark Littell	.06	.05	.02
443	Don Sutton	.30	.25	.12
444	John Harris	.06	.05	.02
445	Vada Pinson	.08	.06	.03
446	Elias Sosa	.06	.05	.02
447	Charlie Hough	.10	.08	.04
448	Willie Wilson	.15	.11	.06
449	Fred Stanley	.06	.05	.02
450	Tom Veryzer	.06	.05	.02
451	Ron Davis	.06	.05	.02
452	Mark Clear	.06	.05	.02
453	Bill Russell	.08	.06	.03
454	Lou Whitaker	.40	.30	.15
455	Dan Graham	.06	.05	.02
456	Reggie Cleveland	.06	.05	.02
457	Sammy Stewart	.06	.05	.02
458	Pete Vuckovich	.08	.06	.03
459	John Wockenfuss	.06	.05	.02
460	Glenn Hoffman	.06	.05	.02
461	Willie Randolph	.10	.08	.04
462	Fernando Valenzuela(FC)	.80	.60	.30
463	Ron Hassey	.06	.05	.02
464	Paul Splittorff	.06	.05	.02
465	Rob Picciolo	.06	.05	.02
466	Larry Parrish	.10	.08	.04
467	Johnny Grubb	.06	.05	.02
468	Dan Ford	.06	.05	.02
469	Silvio Martinez	.06	.05	.02
470	Kiko Garcia	.06	.05	.02
471	Bob Boone	.10	.08	.04
472	Luis Salazar	.08	.06	.03
473	Randy Niemann	.06	.05	.02
474	Tom Griffin	.06	.05	.02
475	Phil Niekro	.30	.25	.12
476	Hubie Brooks(FC)	.25	.20	.10
477	Dick Tidrow	.06	.05	.02
478	Jim Beattie	.06	.05	.02
479	Damaso Garcia	.06	.05	.02
480	Mickey Hatcher	.08	.06	.03
481	Joe Price	.06	.05	.02
482	Ed Farmer	.06	.05	.02
483	Eddie Murray	.60	.45	.25
484	Ben Oglivie	.08	.06	.03
485	Kevin Saucier	.06	.05	.02
486	Bobby Murcer	.10	.08	.04
487	Bill Campbell	.06	.05	.02
488	Reggie Smith	.10	.08	.04
489	Wayne Garland	.06	.05	.02
490	Jim Wright	.06	.05	.02
491	Billy Martin	.12	.09	.05
492	Jim Fanning	.06	.05	.02
493	Don Baylor	.12	.09	.05
494	Rick Honeycutt	.06	.05	.02
495	Carlton Fisk	.50	.40	.20
496	Denny Walling	.06	.05	.02
497	Bake McBride	.06	.05	.02
498	Darrell Porter	.08	.06	.03
499	Gene Richards	.06	.05	.02
500	Ron Oester	.06	.05	.02
501	*Ken Dayley*(FC)	.20	.15	.08
502	Jason Thompson	.06	.05	.02
503	Milt May	.06	.05	.02
504	Doug Bird	.06	.05	.02
505	Bruce Bochte	.06	.05	.02
506	Neil Allen	.06	.05	.02
507	Joey McLaughlin	.06	.05	.02
508	Butch Wynegar	.06	.05	.02
509	Gary Roenicke	.06	.05	.02
510	Robin Yount	1.50	1.25	.60
511	Dave Tobik	.06	.05	.02
512	*Rich Gedman*(FC)	.35	.25	.14
513	*Gene Nelson*(FC)	.12	.09	.05
514	Rick Monday	.10	.08	.04
515	Miguel Dilone	.06	.05	.02
516	Clint Hurdle	.06	.05	.02
517	Jeff Newman	.06	.05	.02
518	Grant Jackson	.06	.05	.02
519	Andy Hassler	.06	.05	.02
520	Pat Putnam	.06	.05	.02
521	Greg Pryor	.06	.05	.02
522	Tony Scott	.06	.05	.02
523	Steve Mura	.06	.05	.02
524	Johnnie LeMaster	.06	.05	.02
525	Dick Ruthven	.06	.05	.02
526	John McNamara	.06	.05	.02
527	Larry McWilliams	.06	.05	.02
528	*Johnny Ray*(FC)	.70	.50	.30
529	*Pat Tabler*(FC)	.60	.45	.25
530	Tom Herr	.10	.08	.04
531a	San Diego Chicken (trademark symbol on front)	1.25	.90	.50
531b	San Diego Chicken (no trademark symbol)	.50	.40	.20
532	Sal Butera	.06	.05	.02
533	Mike Griffin	.06	.05	.02
534	Kelvin Moore	.06	.05	.02
535	Reggie Jackson	.60	.45	.25
536	Ed Romero	.06	.05	.02
537	Derrel Thomas	.06	.05	.02
538	Mike O'Berry	.06	.05	.02
539	Jack O'Connor	.06	.05	.02
540	*Bob Ojeda*(FC)	.50	.40	.20
541	Roy Lee Jackson	.06	.05	.02
542	Lynn Jones	.06	.05	.02
543	Gaylord Perry	.30	.25	.12
544a	Phil Garner (photo reversed)	1.25	.90	.50
544b	Phil Garner (photo correct)	.10	.08	.04
545	Garry Templeton	.10	.08	.04
546	Rafael Ramirez(FC)	.10	.08	.04
547	Jeff Reardon	.20	.15	.08
548	Ron Guidry	.25	.20	.10
549	*Tim Laudner*(FC)	.25	.20	.10
550	John Henry Johnson	.06	.05	.02
551	Chris Bando	.06	.05	.02
552	Bobby Brown	.06	.05	.02
553	Larry Bradford	.06	.05	.02
554	*Scott Fletcher*(FC)	.30	.25	.12
555	Jerry Royster	.06	.05	.02
556	Shooty Babbitt	.06	.05	.02
557	Kent Hrbek(FC)	3.00	2.25	1.25
558	Yankee Winners (Ron Guidry, Tommy John)	.15	.11	.06
559	Mark Bomback	.06	.05	.02
560	Julio Valdez	.06	.05	.02
561	Buck Martinez	.06	.05	.02
562	*Mike Marshall*(FC)	.80	.60	.30
563	Rennie Stennett	.06	.05	.02
564	Steve Crawford	.06	.05	.02
565	Bob Babcock	.06	.05	.02
566	Johnny Podres	.08	.06	.03
567	Paul Serna	.06	.05	.02
568	Harold Baines(FC)	1.00	.70	.40
569	Dave LaRoche	.06	.05	.02
570	Lee May	.08	.06	.03
571	Gary Ward(FC)	.10	.08	.04
572	John Denny	.06	.05	.02
573	Roy Smalley	.06	.05	.02
574	*Bob Brenly*(FC)	.20	.15	.08
575	Bronx Bombers (Reggie Jackson, Dave Winfield)	.40	.30	.15
576	Luis Pujols	.06	.05	.02
577	Butch Hobson	.06	.05	.02
578	Harvey Kuenn	.08	.06	.03
579	Cal Ripken, Sr.	.08	.06	.03
580	Juan Berenguer	.08	.06	.03
581	Benny Ayala	.06	.05	.02
582	Vance Law(FC)	.15	.11	.06
583	*Rick Leach*(FC)	.12	.09	.05
584	George Frazier	.06	.05	.02
585	Phillies Finest (Pete Rose, Mike Schmidt)	.70	.50	.30
586	Joe Rudi	.10	.08	.04
587	Juan Beniquez	.06	.05	.02
588	*Luis DeLeon*(FC)	.08	.06	.03
589	Craig Swan	.06	.05	.02
590	Dave Chalk	.06	.05	.02
591	Billy Gardner	.06	.05	.02
592	Sal Bando	.08	.06	.03
593	Bert Campaneris	.10	.08	.04
594	Steve Kemp	.08	.06	.03
595a	Randy Lerch (Braves)	1.25	.90	.50
595b	Randy Lerch (Brewers)	.08	.06	.03
596	Bryan Clark	.06	.05	.02
597	Dave Ford	.06	.05	.02
598	Mike Scioscia(FC)	.20	.15	.08
599	John Lowenstein	.06	.05	.02
600	Rene Lachmann (Lachemann)	.06	.05	.02
601	Mick Kelleher	.06	.05	.02
602	Ron Jackson	.06	.05	.02
603	Jerry Koosman	.10	.08	.04
604	Dave Goltz	.08	.06	.03
605	Ellis Valentine	.06	.05	.02
606	Lonnie Smith	.08	.06	.03

		MT	NR MT	EX
607	Joaquin Andujar	.08	.06	.03
608	Garry Hancock	.06	.05	.02
609	Jerry Turner	.06	.05	.02
610	Bob Bonner	.06	.05	.02
611	Jim Dwyer	.06	.05	.02
612	Terry Bulling	.06	.05	.02
613	Joel Youngblood	.06	.05	.02
614	Larry Milbourne	.06	.05	.02
615	Phil Roof (Gene)	.06	.05	.02
616	Keith Drumright	.06	.05	.02
617	Dave Rosello	.06	.05	.02
618	Rickey Keeton	.06	.05	.02
619	Dennis Lamp	.06	.05	.02
620	Sid Monge	.06	.05	.02
621	Jerry White	.06	.05	.02
622	*Luis Aguayo*(FC)	.10	.08	.04
623	Jamie Easterly	.06	.05	.02
624	*Steve Sax*(FC)	3.00	2.25	1.25
625	Dave Roberts	.06	.05	.02
626	Rick Bosetti	.06	.05	.02
627	*Terry Francona*(FC)	.10	.08	.04
628	Pride of the Reds (Johnny Bench, Tom Seaver)	.35	.25	.14
629	Paul Mirabella	.06	.05	.02
630	Rance Mulliniks	.06	.05	.02
631	Kevin Hickey	.06	.05	.02
632	Reid Nichols	.06	.05	.02
633	Dave Geisel	.06	.05	.02
634	Ken Griffey	.12	.09	.05
635	Bob Lemon	.10	.08	.04
636	Orlando Sanchez	.06	.05	.02
637	Bill Almon	.06	.05	.02
638	Danny Ainge	.12	.09	.05
639	Willie Stargell	.40	.30	.15
640	Bob Sykes	.06	.05	.02
641	Ed Lynch	.06	.05	.02
642	John Ellis	.06	.05	.02
643	Fergie Jenkins	.15	.11	.06
644	Lenn Sakata	.06	.05	.02
645	Julio Gonzales	.06	.05	.02
646	Jesse Orosco(FC)	.15	.11	.06
647	Jerry Dybzinski	.06	.05	.02
648	Tommy Davis	.08	.06	.03
649	Ron Gardenhire	.06	.05	.02
650	Felipe Alou	.08	.06	.03
651	Harvey Haddix	.08	.06	.03
652	Willie Upshaw(FC)	.15	.11	.06
653	Bill Madlock	.12	.09	.05
---a	Checklist 1-26 DK (5 Trammel)	.70	.50	.30
---b	Checklist 1-26 DK (5 Trammell)	.08	.06	.03
-----	Checklist 27-130	.06	.05	.02
-----	Checklist 131-234	.06	.05	.02
-----	Checklist 235-338	.06	.05	.02
-----	Checklist 339-442	.06	.05	.02
-----	Checklist 443-544	.06	.05	.02
-----	Checklist 545-653	.06	.05	.02

1983 Donruss

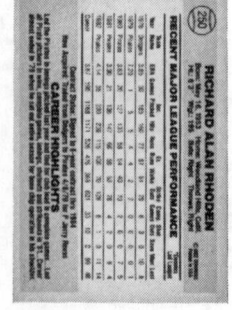

The 1983 Donruss set consists of 653 numbered cards plus seven unnumbered checklists. The cards, which measure 2-1/2" by 3-1/2", were issued with puzzle pieces (three pieces on one card per pack) that feature Ty Cobb. The first 26 cards in the set were once again the Diamond Kings series. The card fronts display the Donruss logo and the year of issue. The card backs have black print on yellow and white and include statistics, career highlights, and the

player's contract status. (DK) in the checklist that follows indicates cards which belong to the Diamond Kings series.

		MT	NR MT	EX
Complete Set:		100.00	75.00	40.00
Common Player:		.06	.05	.02
1	Fernando Valenzuela (DK)	.40	.30	.15
2	Rollie Fingers (DK)	.20	.15	.08
3	Reggie Jackson (DK)	.50	.40	.20
4	Jim Palmer (DK)	.40	.30	.15
5	Jack Morris (DK)	.30	.25	.12
6	George Foster (DK)	.20	.15	.08
7	Jim Sundberg (DK)	.08	.06	.03
8	Willie Stargell (DK)	.40	.30	.15
9	Dave Stieb (DK)	.12	.09	.05
10	Joe Niekro (DK)	.12	.09	.05
11	Rickey Henderson (DK)	1.00	.70	.40
12	Dale Murphy (DK)	.80	.60	.30
13	Toby Harrah (DK)	.08	.06	.03
14	Bill Buckner (DK)	.12	.09	.05
15	Willie Wilson (DK)	.15	.11	.06
16	Steve Carlton (DK)	.40	.30	.15
17	Ron Guidry (DK)	.25	.20	.10
18	Steve Rogers (DK)	.08	.06	.03
19	Kent Hrbek (DK)	.40	.30	.15
20	Keith Hernandez (DK)	.40	.30	.15
21	Floyd Bannister (DK)	.10	.08	.04
22	Johnny Bench (DK)	.40	.30	.15
23	Britt Burns (DK)	.08	.06	.03
24	Joe Morgan (DK)	.30	.25	.12
25	Carl Yastrzemski (DK)	.80	.60	.30
26	Terry Kennedy (DK)	.08	.06	.03
27	Gary Roenicke	.06	.05	.02
28	Dwight Bernard	.06	.05	.02
29	Pat Underwood	.06	.05	.02
30	Gary Allenson	.06	.05	.02
31	Ron Guidry	.25	.20	.10
32	Burt Hooton	.08	.06	.03
33	Chris Bando	.06	.05	.02
34	Vida Blue	.12	.09	.05
35	Rickey Henderson	4.00	3.00	1.50
36	Ray Burris	.06	.05	.02
37	John Butcher	.06	.05	.02
38	Don Aase	.06	.05	.02
39	Jerry Koosman	.10	.08	.04
40	Bruce Sutter	.15	.11	.06
41	Jose Cruz	.12	.09	.05
42	Pete Rose	1.00	.70	.40
43	Cesar Cedeno	.12	.09	.05
44	Floyd Chiffer	.06	.05	.02
45	Larry McWilliams	.06	.05	.02
46	Alan Fowlkes	.06	.05	.02
47	Dale Murphy	.90	.70	.35
48	Doug Bird	.06	.05	.02
49	Hubie Brooks	.12	.09	.05
50	Floyd Bannister	.10	.08	.04
51	Jack O'Connor	.06	.05	.02
52	Steve Senteney	.06	.05	.02
53	*Gary Gaetti*(FC)	4.00	3.00	1.50
54	Damaso Garcia	.06	.05	.02
55	Gene Nelson	.06	.05	.02
56	Mookie Wilson	.10	.08	.04
57	Allen Ripley	.06	.05	.02
58	Bob Horner	.12	.09	.05
59	Tony Pena	.10	.08	.04
60	Gary Lavelle	.06	.05	.02
61	Tim Lollar	.06	.05	.02
62	Frank Pastore	.06	.05	.02
63	Garry Maddox	.10	.08	.04
64	Bob Forsch	.08	.06	.03
65	Harry Spilman	.06	.05	.02
66	Geoff Zahn	.06	.05	.02
67	Salome Barojas	.06	.05	.02
68	David Palmer	.06	.05	.02
69	Charlie Hough	.10	.08	.04
70	Dan Quisenberry	.15	.11	.06
71	Tony Armas	.10	.08	.04
72	Rick Sutcliffe	.12	.09	.05
73	Steve Balboni(FC)	.15	.11	.06
74	Jerry Remy	.06	.05	.02
75	Mike Scioscia	.08	.06	.03
76	John Wockenfuss	.06	.05	.02
77	Jim Palmer	.70	.50	.30
78	Rollie Fingers	.20	.15	.08
79	Joe Nolan	.06	.05	.02
80	Pete Vuckovich	.08	.06	.03
81	Rick Leach	.06	.05	.02
82	Rick Miller	.06	.05	.02
83	Graig Nettles	.15	.11	.06

		MT	NR MT	EX			MT	NR MT	EX
84	Ron Cey	.12	.09	.05	172	Richard Gale	.06	.05	.02
85	Miguel Dilone	.06	.05	.02	173	Steve Bedrosian	.12	.09	.05
86	John Wathan	.08	.06	.03	174	Willie Hernandez	.08	.06	.03
87	Kelvin Moore	.06	.05	.02	175	Ron Gardenhire	.06	.05	.02
88a	Bryn Smith (first name incorrect)	.90	.70	.35	176	Jim Beattie	.06	.05	.02
88b	Bryn Smith (first name correct)	.08	.06	.03	177	Tim Laudner	.08	.06	.03
89	Dave Hostetler	.06	.05	.02	178	Buck Martinez	.06	.05	.02
90	Rod Carew	.50	.40	.20	179	Kent Hrbek	1.25	.90	.50
91	Lonnie Smith	.08	.06	.03	180	Alfredo Griffin	.08	.06	.03
92	Bob Knepper	.08	.06	.03	181	Larry Andersen	.06	.05	.02
93	Marty Bystrom	.06	.05	.02	182	Pete Falcone	.06	.05	.02
94	Chris Welsh	.06	.05	.02	183	Jody Davis	.10	.08	.04
95	Jason Thompson	.06	.05	.02	184	Glenn Hubbard	.08	.06	.03
96	Tom O'Malley	.06	.05	.02	185	Dale Berra	.06	.05	.02
97	Phil Niekro	.30	.25	.12	186	Greg Minton	.06	.05	.02
98	Neil Allen	.06	.05	.02	187	Gary Lucas	.06	.05	.02
99	Bill Buckner	.12	.09	.05	188	Dave Van Gorder	.06	.05	.02
100	*Ed VandeBerg (Vande Berg)(FC)*				189	Bob Dernier(FC)	.10	.08	.04
		.10	.08	.04	190	*Willie McGee(FC)*	3.00	2.25	1.25
101	Jim Clancy	.08	.06	.03	191	Dickie Thon	.08	.06	.03
102	Robert Castillo	.06	.05	.02	192	Bob Boone	.10	.08	.04
103	Bruce Berenyi	.06	.05	.02	193	Britt Burns	.06	.05	.02
104	Carlton Fisk	.40	.30	.15	194	Jeff Reardon	.12	.09	.05
105	Mike Flanagan	.10	.08	.04	195	Jon Matlack	.08	.06	.03
106	Cecil Cooper	.15	.11	.06	196	*Don Slaught(FC)*	.20	.15	.08
107	Jack Morris	.30	.25	.12	197	Fred Stanley	.06	.05	.02
108	Mike Morgan(FC)	.12	.09	.05	198	Rick Manning	.06	.05	.02
109	Luis Aponte	.06	.05	.02	199	Dave Righetti	.25	.20	.10
110	Pedro Guerrero	.25	.20	.10	200	Dave Stapleton	.06	.05	.02
111	Len Barker	.08	.06	.03	201	Steve Yeager	.06	.05	.02
112	Willie Wilson	.15	.11	.06	202	Enos Cabell	.06	.05	.02
113	Dave Beard	.06	.05	.02	203	Sammy Stewart	.06	.05	.02
114	Mike Gates	.06	.05	.02	204	Moose Haas	.06	.05	.02
115	Reggie Jackson	.50	.40	.20	205	Lenn Sakata	.06	.05	.02
116	George Wright	.06	.05	.02	206	Charlie Moore	.06	.05	.02
117	Vance Law	.08	.06	.03	207	Alan Trammell	.40	.30	.15
118	Nolan Ryan	3.00	2.25	1.25	208	Jim Rice	.40	.30	.15
119	Mike Krukow	.08	.06	.03	209	Roy Smalley	.06	.05	.02
120	Ozzie Smith	.20	.15	.08	210	Bill Russell	.08	.06	.03
121	Broderick Perkins	.06	.05	.02	211	Andre Thornton	.10	.08	.04
122	Tom Seaver	.50	.40	.20	212	Willie Aikens	.06	.05	.02
123	Chris Chambliss	.08	.06	.03	213	Dave McKay	.06	.05	.02
124	Chuck Tanner	.06	.05	.02	214	Tim Blackwell	.06	.05	.02
125	Johnnie LeMaster	.06	.05	.02	215	Buddy Bell	.12	.09	.05
126	*Mel Hall(FC)*	.50	.40	.20	216	Doug DeCinces	.10	.08	.04
127	Bruce Bochte	.06	.05	.02	217	Tom Herr	.10	.08	.04
128	*Charlie Puleo(FC)*	.12	.09	.05	218	Frank LaCorte	.06	.05	.02
129	Luis Leal	.06	.05	.02	219	Steve Carlton	.50	.40	.20
130	John Pacella	.06	.05	.02	220	Terry Kennedy	.08	.06	.03
131	Glenn Gulliver	.06	.05	.02	221	Mike Easler	.08	.06	.03
132	Don Money	.06	.05	.02	222	Jack Clark	.25	.20	.10
133	Dave Rozema	.06	.05	.02	223	Gene Garber	.06	.05	.02
134	Bruce Hurst(FC)	.25	.20	.10	224	Scott Holman	.06	.05	.02
135	Rudy May	.06	.05	.02	225	Mike Proly	.06	.05	.02
136	Tom LaSorda (Lasorda)	.10	.08	.04	226	Terry Bulling	.06	.05	.02
137	Dan Spillner (photo actually Ed Whitson)				227	Jerry Garvin	.06	.05	.02
		.06	.05	.02	228	Ron Davis	.06	.05	.02
138	Jerry Martin	.06	.05	.02	229	Tom Hume	.06	.05	.02
139	Mike Norris	.06	.05	.02	230	Marc Hill	.06	.05	.02
140	Al Oliver	.15	.11	.06	231	Dennis Martinez	.08	.06	.03
141	Daryl Sconiers	.06	.05	.02	232	Jim Gantner	.08	.06	.03
142	Lamar Johnson	.06	.05	.02	233	Larry Pashnick	.06	.05	.02
143	Harold Baines	.15	.11	.06	234	Dave Collins	.08	.06	.03
144	Alan Ashby	.06	.05	.02	235	Tom Burgmeier	.06	.05	.02
145	Garry Templeton	.10	.08	.04	236	Ken Landreaux	.06	.05	.02
146	Al Holland	.06	.05	.02	237	John Denny	.06	.05	.02
147	Bo Diaz	.08	.06	.03	238	Hal McRae	.12	.09	.05
148	Dave Concepcion	.12	.09	.05	239	Matt Keough	.06	.05	.02
149	Rick Camp	.06	.05	.02	240	Doug Flynn	.06	.05	.02
150	Jim Morrison	.06	.05	.02	241	Fred Lynn	.20	.15	.08
151	Randy Martz	.06	.05	.02	242	Billy Sample	.06	.05	.02
152	Keith Hernandez	.40	.30	.15	243	Tom Paciorek	.06	.05	.02
153	John Lowenstein	.06	.05	.02	244	Joe Sambito	.06	.05	.02
154	Mike Caldwell	.06	.05	.02	245	Sid Monge	.06	.05	.02
155	Milt Wilcox	.06	.05	.02	246	Ken Oberkfell	.06	.05	.02
156	Rich Gedman	.08	.06	.03	247	Joe Pittman (photo actually Juan			
157	Rich Gossage	.20	.15	.08		Eichelberger)	.06	.05	.02
158	Jerry Reuss	.10	.08	.04	248	Mario Soto	.08	.06	.03
159	Ron Hassey	.06	.05	.02	249	Claudell Washington	.08	.06	.03
160	Larry Gura	.06	.05	.02	250	Rick Rhoden	.10	.08	.04
161	Dwayne Murphy	.08	.06	.03	251	Darrell Evans	.15	.11	.06
162	Woodie Fryman	.08	.06	.03	252	Steve Henderson	.06	.05	.02
163	Steve Comer	.06	.05	.02	253	Manny Castillo	.06	.05	.02
164	Ken Forsch	.06	.05	.02	254	Craig Swan	.06	.05	.02
165	Dennis Lamp	.06	.05	.02	255	Joey McLaughlin	.06	.05	.02
166	David Green	.06	.05	.02	256	Pete Redfern	.06	.05	.02
167	Terry Puhl	.06	.05	.02	257	Ken Singleton	.10	.08	.04
168	Mike Schmidt	1.25	.90	.50	258	Robin Yount	.80	.60	.30
169	*Eddie Milner(FC)*	.10	.08	.04	259	Elias Sosa	.06	.05	.02
170	John Curtis	.06	.05	.02	260	Bob Ojeda	.12	.09	.05
171	Don Robinson	.08	.06	.03	261	Bobby Murcer	.10	.08	.04

	MT	NR MT	EX
262 Candy Maldonado(FC)	1.00	.70	.40
263 Rick Waits	.06	.05	.02
264 Greg Pryor	.06	.05	.02
265 Bob Owchinko	.06	.05	.02
266 Chris Speier	.06	.05	.02
267 Bruce Kison	.06	.05	.02
268 Mark Wagner	.06	.05	.02
269 Steve Kemp	.10	.08	.04
270 Phil Garner	.08	.06	.03
271 Gene Richards	.06	.05	.02
272 Renie Martin	.06	.05	.02
273 Dave Roberts	.06	.05	.02
274 Dan Driessen	.08	.06	.03
275 Rufino Linares	.06	.05	.02
276 Lee Lacy	.06	.05	.02
277 Ryne Sandberg(FC)	30.00	22.00	12.00
278 Darrell Porter	.08	.06	.03
279 Cal Ripken	3.00	2.25	1.25
280 Jamie Easterly	.06	.05	.02
281 Bill Fahey	.06	.05	.02
282 Glenn Hoffman	.06	.05	.02
283 Willie Randolph	.10	.08	.04
284 Fernando Valenzuela	.30	.25	.12
285 Alan Bannister	.06	.05	.02
286 Paul Splittorff	.06	.05	.02
287 Joe Rudi	.10	.08	.04
288 Bill Gullickson	.06	.05	.02
289 Danny Darwin	.06	.05	.02
290 Andy Hassler	.06	.05	.02
291 Ernesto Escarrega	.06	.05	.02
292 Steve Mura	.06	.05	.02
293 Tony Scott	.06	.05	.02
294 Manny Trillo	.08	.06	.03
295 Greg Harris(FC)	.08	.06	.03
296 Luis DeLeon	.06	.05	.02
297 Kent Tekulve	.08	.06	.03
298 Atlee Hammaker(FC)	.12	.09	.05
299 Bruce Benedict	.06	.05	.02
300 Fergie Jenkins	.15	.11	.06
301 Dave Kingman	.15	.11	.06
302 Bill Caudill	.06	.05	.02
303 John Castino	.06	.05	.02
304 Ernie Whitt	.08	.06	.03
305 Randy Johnson	.06	.05	.02
306 Garth Iorg	.06	.05	.02
307 Gaylord Perry	.30	.25	.12
308 Ed Lynch	.06	.05	.02
309 Keith Moreland	.08	.06	.03
310 Rafael Ramirez	.06	.05	.02
311 Bill Madlock	.12	.09	.05
312 Milt May	.06	.05	.02
313 John Montefusco	.06	.05	.02
314 Wayne Krenchicki	.06	.05	.02
315 George Vukovich	.06	.05	.02
316 Joaquin Andujar	.08	.06	.03
317 Craig Reynolds	.06	.05	.02
318 Rick Burleson	.08	.06	.03
319 Richard Dotson	.10	.08	.04
320 Steve Rogers	.08	.06	.03
321 Dave Schmidt(FC)	.10	.08	.04
322 Bud Black(FC)	.20	.15	.08
323 Jeff Burroughs	.08	.06	.03
324 Von Hayes	.15	.11	.06
325 Butch Wynegar	.06	.05	.02
326 Carl Yastrzemski	.80	.60	.30
327 Ron Roenicke	.06	.05	.02
328 Howard Johnson(FC)	10.00	7.50	4.00
329 Rick Dempsey	.08	.06	.03
330a Jim Slaton (one yellow box on back)			
	.70	.50	.30
330b Jim Slaton (two yellow boxes on back)			
	.08	.06	.03
331 Benny Ayala	.06	.05	.02
332 Ted Simmons	.12	.09	.05
333 Lou Whitaker	.40	.30	.15
334 Chuck Rainey	.06	.05	.02
335 Lou Piniella	.12	.09	.05
336 Steve Sax	.30	.25	.12
337 Toby Harrah	.08	.06	.03
338 George Brett	.70	.50	.30
339 Davey Lopes	.10	.08	.04
340 Gary Carter	.40	.30	.15
341 John Grubb	.06	.05	.02
342 Tim Foli	.06	.05	.02
343 Jim Kaat	.15	.11	.06
344 Mike LaCoss	.06	.05	.02
345 Larry Christenson	.06	.05	.02
346 Juan Bonilla	.06	.05	.02
347 Omar Moreno	.06	.05	.02
348 Charles Davis(FC)	.20	.15	.08
349 Tommy Boggs	.06	.05	.02

	MT	NR MT	EX
350 Rusty Staub	.10	.08	.04
351 Bump Wills	.06	.05	.02
352 Rick Sweet	.06	.05	.02
353 Jim Gott(FC)	.20	.15	.08
354 Terry Felton	.06	.05	.02
355 Jim Kern	.06	.05	.02
356 Bill Almon	.06	.05	.02
357 Tippy Martinez	.06	.05	.02
358 Roy Howell	.06	.05	.02
359 Dan Petry	.08	.06	.03
360 Jerry Mumphrey	.06	.05	.02
361 Mark Clear	.06	.05	.02
362 Mike Marshall	.20	.15	.08
363 Lary Sorensen	.06	.05	.02
364 Amos Otis	.08	.06	.03
365 Rick Langford	.06	.05	.02
366 Brad Mills	.06	.05	.02
367 Brian Downing	.10	.08	.04
368 Mike Richardt	.06	.05	.02
369 Aurelio Rodriguez	.08	.06	.03
370 Dave Smith	.08	.06	.03
371 Tug McGraw	.12	.09	.05
372 Doug Bair	.06	.05	.02
373 Ruppert Jones	.06	.05	.02
374 Alex Trevino	.06	.05	.02
375 Ken Dayley	.06	.05	.02
376 Rod Scurry	.06	.05	.02
377 Bob Brenly(FC)	.08	.06	.03
378 Scot Thompson	.06	.05	.02
379 Julio Cruz	.06	.05	.02
380 John Stearns	.06	.05	.02
381 Dale Murray	.06	.05	.02
382 Frank Viola(FC)	7.00	5.25	2.75
383 Al Bumbry	.08	.06	.03
384 Ben Oglivie	.08	.06	.03
385 Dave Tobik	.06	.05	.02
386 Bob Stanley	.06	.05	.02
387 Andre Robertson	.06	.05	.02
388 Jorge Orta	.06	.05	.02
389 Ed Whitson	.06	.05	.02
390 Don Hood	.06	.05	.02
391 Tom Underwood	.06	.05	.02
392 Tim Wallach	.20	.15	.08
393 Steve Renko	.06	.05	.02
394 Mickey Rivers	.08	.06	.03
395 Greg Luzinski	.12	.09	.05
396 Art Howe	.06	.05	.02
397 Alan Wiggins	.06	.05	.02
398 Jim Barr	.06	.05	.02
399 Ivan DeJesus	.06	.05	.02
400 Tom Lawless(FC)	.08	.06	.03
401 Bob Walk	.08	.06	.03
402 Jimmy Smith	.06	.05	.02
403 Lee Smith	.15	.11	.06
404 George Hendrick	.08	.06	.03
405 Eddie Murray	.60	.45	.25
406 Marshall Edwards	.06	.05	.02
407 Lance Parrish	.35	.25	.14
408 Carney Lansford	.08	.06	.03
409 Dave Winfield	.40	.30	.15
410 Bob Welch	.12	.09	.05
411 Larry Milbourne	.06	.05	.02
412 Dennis Leonard	.08	.06	.03
413 Dan Meyer	.06	.05	.02
414 Charlie Lea	.06	.05	.02
415 Rick Honeycutt	.06	.05	.02
416 Mike Witt	.15	.11	.06
417 Steve Trout	.06	.05	.02
418 Glenn Brummer	.06	.05	.02
419 Denny Walling	.06	.05	.02
420 Gary Matthews	.10	.08	.04
421 Charlie Liebrandt (Leibrandt)	.08	.06	.03
422 Juan Eichelberger	.06	.05	.02
423 Matt Guante (Cecilio)(FC)	.15	.11	.06
424 Bill Laskey	.06	.05	.02
425 Jerry Royster	.06	.05	.02
426 Dickie Noles	.06	.05	.02
427 George Foster	.15	.11	.06
428 Mike Moore(FC)	1.50	1.25	.60
429 Gary Ward	.08	.06	.03
430 Barry Bonnell	.06	.05	.02
431 Ron Washington	.06	.05	.02
432 Rance Mulliniks	.06	.05	.02
433 Mike Stanton	.06	.05	.02
434 Jesse Orosco	.10	.08	.04
435 Larry Bowa	.12	.09	.05
436 Biff Pocoroba	.06	.05	.02
437 Johnny Ray	.12	.09	.05
438 Joe Morgan	.30	.25	.12
439 Eric Show(FC)	.30	.25	.12
440 Larry Biittner	.06	.05	.02

		MT	NR MT	EX
441	Greg Gross	.06	.05	.02
442	Gene Tenace	.08	.06	.03
443	Danny Heep	.06	.05	.02
444	Bobby Clark	.06	.05	.02
445	Kevin Hickey	.06	.05	.02
446	Scott Sanderson	.06	.05	.02
447	Frank Tanana	.10	.08	.04
448	Cesar Geronimo	.06	.05	.02
449	Jimmy Sexton	.06	.05	.02
450	Mike Hargrove	.06	.05	.02
451	Doyle Alexander	.10	.08	.04
452	Dwight Evans	.15	.11	.06
453	Terry Forster	.08	.06	.03
454	Tom Brookens	.06	.05	.02
455	Rich Dauer	.06	.05	.02
456	Rob Picciolo	.06	.05	.02
457	Terry Crowley	.06	.05	.02
458	Ned Yost	.06	.05	.02
459	Kirk Gibson	.40	.30	.15
460	Reid Nichols	.06	.05	.02
461	Oscar Gamble	.08	.06	.03
462	Dusty Baker	.10	.08	.04
463	Jack Perconte	.06	.05	.02
464	Frank White	.10	.08	.04
465	Mickey Klutts	.06	.05	.02
466	Warren Cromartie	.06	.05	.02
467	Larry Parrish	.10	.08	.04
468	Bobby Grich	.10	.08	.04
469	Dane Iorg	.06	.05	.02
470	Joe Niekro	.12	.09	.05
471	Ed Farmer	.06	.05	.02
472	Tim Flannery	.06	.05	.02
473	Dave Parker	.30	.25	.12
474	Jeff Leonard	.10	.08	.04
475	Al Hrabosky	.08	.06	.03
476	Ron Hodges	.06	.05	.02
477	Leon Durham	.08	.06	.03
478	Jim Essian	.06	.05	.02
479	Roy Lee Jackson	.06	.05	.02
480	Brad Havens	.06	.05	.02
481	Joe Price	.06	.05	.02
482	Tony Bernazard	.06	.05	.02
483	Scott McGregor	.08	.06	.03
484	Paul Molitor	.20	.15	.08
485	Mike Ivie	.06	.05	.02
486	Ken Griffey	.12	.09	.05
487	Dennis Eckersley	.12	.09	.05
488	Steve Garvey	.40	.30	.15
489	Mike Fischlin	.06	.05	.02
490	U.L. Washington	.06	.05	.02
491	Steve McCatty	.06	.05	.02
492	Roy Johnson	.06	.05	.02
493	Don Baylor	.12	.09	.05
494	Bobby Johnson	.06	.05	.02
495	Mike Squires	.06	.05	.02
496	Bert Roberge	.06	.05	.02
497	Dick Ruthven	.06	.05	.02
498	Tito Landrum	.06	.05	.02
499	Sixto Lezcano	.06	.05	.02
500	Johnny Bench	.40	.30	.15
501	Larry Whisenton	.06	.05	.02
502	Manny Sarmiento	.06	.05	.02
503	Fred Breining	.06	.05	.02
504	Bill Campbell	.06	.05	.02
505	Todd Cruz	.06	.05	.02
506	Bob Bailor	.06	.05	.02
507	Dave Stieb	.12	.09	.05
508	Al Williams	.06	.05	.02
509	Dan Ford	.06	.05	.02
510	Gorman Thomas	.10	.08	.04
511	Chet Lemon	.08	.06	.03
512	Mike Torrez	.08	.06	.03
513	Shane Rawley	.10	.08	.04
514	Mark Belanger	.08	.06	.03
515	Rodney Craig	.06	.05	.02
516	Onix Concepcion	.06	.05	.02
517	Mike Heath	.06	.05	.02
518	Andre Dawson	.35	.25	.14
519	Luis Sanchez	.06	.05	.02
520	Terry Bogener	.06	.05	.02
521	Rudy Law	.06	.05	.02
522	Ray Knight	.10	.08	.04
523	Joe Lefebvre	.06	.05	.02
524	Jim Wohlford	.06	.05	.02
525	*Julio Franco*(FC)	6.00	4.50	2.50
526	Ron Oester	.06	.05	.02
527	Rick Mahler	.08	.06	.03
528	Steve Nicosia	.06	.05	.02
529	Junior Kennedy	.06	.05	.02
530a	Whitey Herzog (one yellow box on back)			
		.70	.50	.30

		MT	NR MT	EX
530b	Whitey Herzog (two yellow boxes on back)			
		.10	.08	.04
531a	Don Sutton (blue frame around photo)			
		1.00	.70	.40
531b	Don Sutton (green frame around photo)			
		.30	.25	.12
532	Mark Brouhard	.06	.05	.02
533a	Sparky Anderson (one yellow box on back)			
		.70	.50	.30
533b	Sparky Anderson (two yellow boxes on back)			
		.10	.08	.04
534	Roger LaFrancois	.06	.05	.02
535	George Frazier	.06	.05	.02
536	Tom Niedenfuer	.08	.06	.03
537	Ed Glynn	.06	.05	.02
538	Lee May	.08	.06	.03
539	Bob Kearney	.06	.05	.02
540	Tim Raines	.35	.25	.14
541	Paul Mirabella	.06	.05	.02
542	Luis Tiant	.12	.09	.05
543	Ron LeFlore	.08	.06	.03
544	*Dave LaPoint*(FC)	.30	.25	.12
545	Randy Moffitt	.06	.05	.02
546	Luis Aguayo	.06	.05	.02
547	Brad Lesley	.06	.05	.02
548	Luis Salazar	.06	.05	.02
549	John Candelaria	.10	.08	.04
550	Dave Bergman	.06	.05	.02
551	Bob Watson	.08	.06	.03
552	Pat Tabler	.10	.08	.04
553	Brent Gaff	.06	.05	.02
554	Al Cowens	.06	.05	.02
555	Tom Brunansky(FC)	.25	.20	.10
556	Lloyd Moseby	.12	.09	.05
557a	Pascual Perez (Twins)(FC)	.90	.70	.35
557b	Pascual Perez (Braves)(FC)	.15	.11	.06
558	Willie Upshaw	.08	.06	.03
559	Richie Zisk	.08	.06	.03
560	Pat Zachry	.06	.05	.02
561	Jay Johnstone	.08	.06	.03
562	Carlos Diaz	.06	.05	.02
563	John Tudor	.10	.08	.04
564	Frank Robinson	.12	.09	.05
565	Dave Edwards	.06	.05	.02
566	Paul Householder	.06	.05	.02
567	Ron Reed	.06	.05	.02
568	Mike Ramsey	.06	.05	.02
569	Kiko Garcia	.06	.05	.02
570	Tommy John	.20	.15	.08
571	Tony LaRussa	.08	.06	.03
572	Joel Youngblood	.06	.05	.02
573	*Wayne Tolleson*(FC)	.12	.09	.05
574	Keith Creel	.06	.05	.02
575	Billy Martin	.12	.09	.05
576	Jerry Dybzinski	.06	.05	.02
577	Rick Cerone	.06	.05	.02
578	Tony Perez	.20	.15	.08
579	*Greg Brock*(FC)	.35	.25	.14
580	*Glen Wilson (Glenn)*(FC)	.35	.25	.14
581	Tim Stoddard	.06	.05	.02
582	Bob McClure	.06	.05	.02
583	Jim Dwyer	.06	.05	.02
584	Ed Romero	.06	.05	.02
585	Larry Herndon	.08	.06	.03
586	*Wade Boggs*(FC)	25.00	18.00	9.00
587	Jay Howell(FC)	.15	.11	.06
588	Dave Stewart	1.25	.90	.50
589	Bert Blyleven	.12	.09	.05
590	Dick Howser	.06	.05	.02
591	Wayne Gross	.06	.05	.02
592	Terry Francona	.06	.05	.02
593	Don Werner	.06	.05	.02
594	Bill Stein	.06	.05	.02
595	Jesse Barfield(FC)	.70	.50	.30
596	Bobby Molinaro	.06	.05	.02
597	Mike Vail	.06	.05	.02
598	*Tony Gwynn*(FC)	16.00	12.00	6.50
599	Gary Rajsich	.06	.05	.02
600	Jerry Ujdur	.06	.05	.02
601	Cliff Johnson	.06	.05	.02
602	Jerry White	.06	.05	.02
603	Bryan Clark	.06	.05	.02
604	Joe Ferguson	.06	.05	.02
605	Guy Sularz	.06	.05	.02
606a	Ozzie Virgil (green frame around photo)(FC)	.90	.70	.35
606b	Ozzie Virgil (orange frame around photo)(FC)	.08	.06	.03
607	Terry Harper(FC)	.06	.05	.02
608	Harvey Kuenn	.08	.06	.03
609	Jim Sundberg	.08	.06	.03

		MT	NR MT	EX
610	Willie Stargell	.40	.30	.15
611	Reggie Smith	.10	.08	.04
612	Rob Wilfong	.06	.05	.02
613	Niekro Brothers (Joe Niekro, Phil Niekro)	.15	.11	.06
614	Lee Elia	.06	.05	.02
615	Mickey Hatcher	.08	.06	.03
616	Jerry Hairston	.06	.05	.02
617	John Martin	.06	.05	.02
618	Wally Backman(FC)	.15	.11	.06
619	*Storm Davis*(FC)	.50	.40	.20
620	Alan Knicely	.06	.05	.02
621	John Stuper	.06	.05	.02
622	Matt Sinatro	.06	.05	.02
623	*Gene Petralli*(FC)	.15	.11	.06
624	Duane Walker	.06	.05	.02
625	Dick Williams	.06	.05	.02
626	Pat Corrales	.06	.05	.02
627	Vern Ruhle	.06	.05	.02
628	Joe Torre	.08	.06	.03
629	Anthony Johnson	.06	.05	.02
630	Steve Howe	.08	.06	.03
631	Gary Woods	.06	.05	.02
632	Lamarr Hoyt (LaMarr)	.06	.05	.02
633	Steve Swisher	.06	.05	.02
634	Terry Leach(FC)	.12	.09	.05
635	Jeff Newman	.06	.05	.02
636	Brett Butler	.10	.08	.04
637	Gary Gray	.06	.05	.02
638	Lee Mazzilli	.08	.06	.03
639a	Ron Jackson (A's)	13.00	9.75	5.25
639b	Ron Jackson (Angels - green frame around photo)	.90	.70	.35
639c	Ron Jackson (Angels - red frame around photo)	.20	.15	.08
640	Juan Beniquez	.06	.05	.02
641	Dave Rucker	.06	.05	.02
642	Luis Pujols	.06	.05	.02
643	Rick Monday	.10	.08	.04
644	Hosken Powell	.06	.05	.02
645	San Diego Chicken	.20	.15	.08
646	Dave Engle	.06	.05	.02
647	Dick Davis	.06	.05	.02
648	MVP's (Vida Blue, Joe Morgan, Frank Robinson)	.15	.11	.06
649	Al Chambers	.06	.05	.02
650	Jesus Vega	.06	.05	.02
651	Jeff Jones	.06	.05	.02
652	Marvis Foley	.06	.05	.02
653	Ty Cobb Puzzle	.06	.05	.02
---a	Dick Perez/DK Checklist (no word "Checklist" on back)	.70	.50	.30
---b	Dick Perez/DK Checklist (word "Checklist" on back)	.08	.06	.03
----	Checklist 27-130	.06	.05	.02
----	Checklist 131-234	.06	.05	.02
----	Checklist 235-338	.06	.05	.02
----	Checklist 339-442	.06	.05	.02
----	Checklist 443-546	.06	.05	.02
----	Checklist 547-653	.06	.05	.02

1983 Donruss Action All-Stars

The cards in this 60-card set are designed on a horizontal format and contain a large close-up photo of the player on the left and a smaller action photo on the right. The cards, which measure 3-1/2" by 5",

have deep red borders and contain the Donruss logo and the year of issue. The card backs have black print on red and white and contain various statistical and biographical information. The cards were sold with puzzle pieces (three pieces on one card per pack) that feature Mickey Mantle.

		MT	NR MT	EX
	Complete Set:	8.00	6.00	3.25
	Common Player:	.10	.08	.04
1	Eddie Murray	.30	.25	.12
2	Dwight Evans	.15	.11	.06
3a	Reggie Jackson (red covers part of statistics on back)	.35	.25	.14
3b	Reggie Jackson (red does not cover any statistics on back)	.35	.25	.14
4	Greg Luzinski	.12	.09	.05
5	Larry Herndon	.10	.08	.04
6	Al Oliver	.12	.09	.05
7	Bill Buckner	.10	.08	.04
8	Jason Thompson	.10	.08	.04
9	Andre Dawson	.20	.15	.08
10	Greg Minton	.10	.08	.04
11	Terry Kennedy	.10	.08	.04
12	Phil Niekro	.20	.15	.08
13	Willie Wilson	.12	.09	.05
14	Johnny Bench	.35	.25	.14
15	Ron Guidry	.15	.11	.06
16	Hal McRae	.10	.08	.04
17	Damaso Garcia	.10	.08	.04
18	Gary Ward	.10	.08	.04
19	Cecil Cooper	.12	.09	.05
20	Keith Hernandez	.25	.20	.10
21	Ron Cey	.12	.09	.05
22	Rickey Henderson	.70	.50	.30
23	Nolan Ryan	1.00	.70	.40
24	Steve Carlton	.30	.25	.12
25	John Stearns	.10	.08	.04
26	Jim Sundberg	.10	.08	.04
27	Joaquin Andujar	.10	.08	.04
28	Gaylord Perry	.15	.11	.06
29	Jack Clark	.15	.11	.06
30	Bill Madlock	.12	.09	.05
31	Pete Rose	.35	.25	.14
32	Mookie Wilson	.10	.08	.04
33	Rollie Fingers	.15	.11	.06
34	Lonnie Smith	.10	.08	.04
35	Tony Pena	.10	.08	.04
36	Dave Winfield	.30	.25	.12
37	Tim Lollar	.10	.08	.04
38	Rod Carew	.35	.25	.14
39	Toby Harrah	.10	.08	.04
40	Buddy Bell	.10	.08	.04
41	Bruce Sutter	.12	.09	.05
42	George Brett	.40	.30	.15
43	Carlton Fisk	.35	.25	.14
44	Carl Yastrzemski	.40	.30	.15
45	Dale Murphy	.25	.20	.10
46	Bob Horner	.12	.09	.05
47	Dave Concepcion	.12	.09	.05
48	Dave Stieb	.12	.09	.05
49	Kent Hrbek	.20	.15	.08
50	Lance Parrish	.15	.11	.06
51	Joe Niekro	.12	.09	.05
52	Cal Ripken Jr.	.35	.25	.14
53	Fernando Valenzuela	.12	.09	.05
54	Rickie Zisk	.10	.08	.04
55	Leon Durham	.10	.08	.04
56	Robin Yount	.40	.30	.15
57	Mike Schmidt	.80	.60	.30
58	Gary Carter	.15	.11	.06
59	Fred Lynn	.15	.11	.06
60	Checklist	.10	.08	.04

1983 Donruss Hall Of Fame Heroes

The artwork of Dick Perez is featured in the 44-card Donruss Hall of Fame Heroes set issued in 1983. The standard-size cards (2-1/2" by 3-1/2") are available in wax packs that contained eight cards plus a Mickey Mantle puzzle piece card (three pieces on one card per pack). The backs, which display red and blue print on white stock, contain a short player

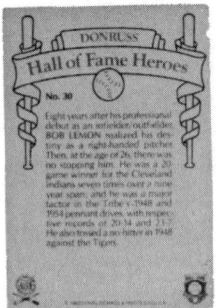

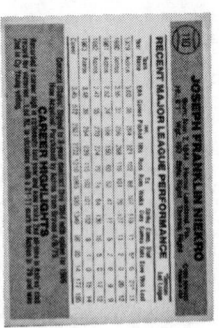

biograpical sketch derived from the Hall of Fame yearbook. The numbered set consists of 44 player cards, a Mantle puzzle card, and a checklist.

		MT	NR MT	EX
Complete Set:		8.00	6.00	3.25
Common Player:		.05	.04	.02
1	Ty Cobb	.70	.50	.30
2	Walter Johnson	.15	.11	.06
3	Christy Mathewson	.15	.11	.06
4	Josh Gibson	.10	.08	.04
5	Honus Wagner	.15	.11	.06
6	Jackie Robinson	.50	.40	.20
7	Mickey Mantle	1.00	.70	.40
8	Luke Appling	.05	.04	.02
9	Ted Williams	.70	.50	.30
10	Johnny Mize	.15	.11	.06
11	Satchel Paige	.15	.11	.06
12	Lou Boudreau	.15	.11	.06
13	Jimmie Foxx	.15	.11	.06
14	Duke Snider	.70	.50	.30
15	Monte Irvin	.15	.11	.06
16	Hank Greenberg	.15	.11	.06
17	Roberto Clemente	.40	.30	.15
18	Al Kaline	.50	.40	.20
19	Frank Robinson	.50	.40	.20
20	Joe Cronin	.09	.07	.04
21	Burleigh Grimes	.05	.04	.02
22	The Waner Brothers (Lloyd Waner, Paul Waner)	.09	.07	.04
23	Grover Alexander	.09	.07	.04
24	Yogi Berra	.50	.40	.20
25	James Bell	.05	.04	.02
26	Bill Dickey	.09	.07	.04
27	Cy Young	.15	.11	.06
28	Charlie Gehringer	.09	.07	.04
29	Dizzy Dean	.15	.11	.06
30	Bob Lemon	.15	.11	.06
31	Red Ruffing	.05	.04	.02
32	Stan Musial	.70	.50	.30
33	Carl Hubbell	.15	.11	.06
34	Hank Aaron	.70	.50	.30
35	John McGraw	.09	.07	.04
36	Bob Feller	.50	.40	.20
37	Casey Stengel	.15	.11	.06
38	Ralph Kiner	.15	.11	.06
39	Roy Campanella	.15	.11	.06
40	Mel Ott	.09	.07	.04
41	Robin Roberts	.15	.11	.06
42	Early Wynn	.15	.11	.06
43	Mickey Mantle Puzzle Card	.09	.07	.04
----	Checklist	.09	.07	.04

1984 Donruss

The 1984 Donruss set consists of 651 numbered cards, seven unnumbered checklists and two "Living Legends" cards (designated A and B). The A and B cards were issued only in wax packs and not available to hobby dealers purchasing vending sets. The card fronts differ in style from the previous years, however the Donruss logo and year of issue are still included. The card backs have black print on green and white and are identical in format to the preceding year. The standard-size cards (2-1/2" by 3-1/2") were issued

with a 63-piece puzzle of Duke Snider. A limited print run of the issue by Donruss has caused the set to escalate in price in recent years. The complete set price in the checklist that follows does not include the higher priced variations. Cards marked with (DK) or (RR) in the checklist refer to the Diamond Kings and Rated Rookies subsets.

		MT	NR MT	EX
Complete Set:		350.00	275.00	150.00
Common Player:		.10	.08	.04
1a	Robin Yount (DK) (Perez-Steel on back)	.80	.60	.30
1b	Robin Yount (DK) (Perez-Steele on back)	1.50	1.25	.60
2a	Dave Concepcion (DK) (Perez-Steel on back)	.30	.25	.12
2b	Dave Concepcion (DK) (Perez-Steel on back)	.60	.45	.25
3a	Dwayne Murphy (DK) (Perez-Steel on back)	.25	.20	.10
3b	Dwayne Murphy (DK) (Perez-Steel on back)	.60	.45	.25
4a	John Castino (DK) (Perez-Steel on back)	.20	.15	.08
4b	John Castino (DK) (Perez-Steel on back)	.60	.45	.25
5a	Leon Durham (DK) (Perez-Steel on back)	.25	.20	.10
5b	Leon Durham (DK) (Perez-Steel on back)	.60	.45	.25
6a	Rusty Staub (DK) (Perez-Steel on back)	.30	.25	.12
6b	Rusty Staub (DK) (Perez-Steel on back)	.60	.45	.25
7a	Jack Clark (DK) (Perez-Steel on back)	.40	.30	.15
7b	Jack Clark (DK) (Perez-Steel on back)	.80	.60	.30
8a	Dave Dravecky (DK) (Perez-Steel on back)	.25	.20	.10
8b	Dave Dravecky (DK) (Perez-Steele on back)	.60	.45	.25
9a	Al Oliver (DK) (Perez-Steel on back)	.35	.25	.14
9b	Al Oliver (DK) (Perez-Steel on back)	.70	.50	.30
10a	Dave Righetti (DK) (Perez-Steel on back)	.40	.30	.15
10b	Dave Righetti (DK) (Perez-Steel on back)	.80	.60	.30
11a	Hal McRae (DK) (Perez-Steel on back)	.30	.25	.12
11b	Hal McRae (DK) (Perez-Steel on back)	.60	.45	.25
12a	Ray Knight (DK) (Perez-Steel on back)	.25	.20	.10
12b	Ray Knight (DK) (Perez-Steele on back)	.60	.45	.25
13a	Bruce Sutter (DK) (Perez-Steel on back)	.35	.25	.14
13b	Bruce Sutter (DK) (Perez-Steel on back)	.70	.50	.30
14a	Bob Horner (DK) (Perez-Steel on back)	.40	.30	.15
14b	Bob Horner (DK) (Perez-Steel on back)	.80	.60	.30
15a	Lance Parrish (DK) (Perez-Steel on back)	.60	.45	.25

		MT	NR MT	EX
15b	Lance Parrish (DK) (Perez-Steele on back)	1.25	.90	.50
16a	Matt Young (DK) (Perez-Steel on back)	.25	.20	.10
16b	Matt Young (DK) (Perez-Steele on back)	.60	.45	.25
17a	Fred Lynn (DK) (Perez-Steel on back)	.35	.25	.14
17b	Fred Lynn (DK) (Perez-Steele on back)	.70	.50	.30
18a	Ron Kittle (DK) (Perez-Steel on back)(FC)	.35	.25	.14
18b	Ron Kittle (DK) (Perez-Steele on back)(FC)	.70	.50	.30
19a	Jim Clancy (DK) (Perez-Steel on back)	.25	.20	.10
19b	Jim Clancy (DK) (Perez-Steel on back)	.60	.45	.25
20a	Bill Madlock (DK) (Perez-Steel on back)	.30	.25	.12
20b	Bill Madlock (DK) (Perez-Steel on back)	.60	.45	.25
21a	Larry Parrish (DK) (Perez-Steel on back)	.30	.25	.12
21b	Larry Parrish (DK) (Perez-Steel on back)	.60	.45	.25
22a	Eddie Murray (DK) (Perez-Steel on back)	1.25	.90	.50
22b	Eddie Murray (DK) (Perez-Steele on back)	2.50	2.00	1.00
23a	Mike Schmidt (DK) (Perez-Steel on back)	1.25	.90	.50
23b	Mike Schmidt (DK) (Perez-Steel on back)	2.50	2.00	1.00
24a	Pedro Guerrero (DK) (Perez-Steel on back)	.50	.40	.20
24b	Pedro Guerrero (DK) (Perez-Steele on back)	1.00	.70	.40
25a	Andre Thornton (DK) (Perez-Steele on back)	.30	.25	.12
25b	Andre Thornton (DK) (Perez-Steele on back)	.60	.45	.25
26a	Wade Boggs (DK) (Perez-Steel on back)	3.75	2.75	1.50
26b	Wade Boggs (DK) (Perez-Steel on back)	5.00	3.75	2.00
27	Joel Skinner (RR)(FC)	.20	.15	.08
28	Tom Dunbar (RR)	.10	.08	.04
29a	Mike Stenhouse (RR) (no number on back)	.15	.11	.06
29b	Mike Stenhouse (RR) (29 on back)	5.00	3.75	2.00
30a	Ron Darling (no number on back)(FC)	5.00	3.75	2.00
30b	Ron Darling (30 on back)(FC)	18.00	13.50	7.25
31	Dion James (RR)(FC)	.40	.30	.15
32	Tony Fernandez (RR)(FC)	8.00	6.00	3.25
33	Angel Salazar (RR)	.10	.08	.04
34	Kevin McReynolds (RR)(FC)	12.00	9.00	4.75
35	Dick Schofield (RR)(FC)	.40	.30	.15
36	Brad Komminsk (RR)(FC)	.15	.11	.06
37	Tim Teufel (RR)(FC)	.40	.30	.15
38	Doug Frobel (RR)	.10	.08	.04
39	Greg Gagne (RR)(FC)	.80	.60	.30
40	Mike Fuentes (RR)	.10	.08	.04
41	Joe Carter (RR)(FC)	15.00	11.00	6.00
42	Mike Brown (RR)	.10	.08	.04
43	Mike Jeffcoat (RR)	.10	.08	.04
44	Sid Fernandez (RR)(FC)	6.00	4.50	2.50
45	Brian Dayett (RR)	.10	.08	.04
46	Chris Smith (RR)	.10	.08	.04
47	Eddie Murray	1.50	1.25	.70
48	Robin Yount	2.00	1.50	.80
49	Lance Parrish	.50	.40	.20
50	Jim Rice	.90	.70	.35
51	Dave Winfield	.90	.70	.35
52	Fernando Valenzuela	.70	.50	.30
53	George Brett	3.00	2.50	1.25
54	Rickey Henderson	12.00	9.00	4.75
55	Gary Carter	.80	.60	.30
56	Buddy Bell	.20	.15	.08
57	Reggie Jackson	2.00	1.50	.80
58	Harold Baines	.25	.20	.10
59	Ozzie Smith	.25	.20	.10
60	Nolan Ryan	8.00	6.00	3.25
61	Pete Rose	2.50	2.00	1.00
62	Ron Oester	.10	.08	.04
63	Steve Garvey	.90	.70	.35
64	Jason Thompson	.10	.08	.04
65	Jack Clark	.35	.25	.14
66	Dale Murphy	1.50	1.25	.60

		MT	NR MT	EX
67	Leon Durham	.12	.09	.05
68	Darryl Strawberry(FC)	40.00	30.00	15.00
69	Richie Zisk	.12	.09	.05
70	Kent Hrbek	.60	.45	.25
71	Dave Stieb	.25	.20	.10
72	Ken Schrom	.10	.08	.04
73	George Bell	1.75	1.25	.70
74	John Moses	.15	.11	.06
75	Ed Lynch	.10	.08	.04
76	Chuck Rainey	.10	.08	.04
77	Biff Pocoroba	.10	.08	.04
78	Cecilio Guante	.10	.08	.04
79	Jim Barr	.10	.08	.04
80	Kurt Bevacqua	.10	.08	.04
81	Tom Foley	.10	.08	.04
82	Joe Lefebvre	.10	.08	.04
83	Andy Van Slyke(FC)	8.00	6.00	3.25
84	Bob Lillis	.10	.08	.04
85	Rick Adams	.10	.08	.04
86	Jerry Hairston	.10	.08	.04
87	Bob James	.10	.08	.04
88	Joe Altobelli	.10	.08	.04
89	Ed Romero	.10	.08	.04
90	John Grubb	.10	.08	.04
91	John Henry Johnson	.10	.08	.04
92	Juan Espino	.10	.08	.04
93	Candy Maldonado	.20	.15	.08
94	Andre Thornton	.20	.15	.08
95	Onix Concepcion	.10	.08	.04
96	Don Hill(FC)	.20	.15	.08
97	Andre Dawson	1.00	.70	.40
98	Frank Tanana	.15	.11	.06
99	Curt Wilkerson(FC)	.15	.11	.06
100	Larry Gura	.10	.08	.04
101	Dwayne Murphy	.12	.09	.05
102	Tom Brennan	.10	.08	.04
103	Dave Righetti	.40	.30	.15
104	Steve Sax	.30	.25	.12
105	Dan Petry	.12	.09	.05
106	Cal Ripken	1.50	1.25	.60
107	Paul Molitor	.35	.25	.14
108	Fred Lynn	.35	.25	.14
109	Neil Allen	.10	.08	.04
110	Joe Niekro	.20	.15	.08
111	Steve Carlton	1.00	.70	.40
112	Terry Kennedy	.15	.11	.06
113	Bill Madlock	.20	.15	.08
114	Chili Davis	.15	.11	.06
115	Jim Gantner	.12	.09	.05
116	Tom Seaver	1.00	.70	.40
117	Bill Buckner	.20	.15	.08
118	Bill Caudill	.10	.08	.04
119	Jim Clancy	.15	.11	.06
120	John Castino	.10	.08	.04
121	Dave Concepcion	.20	.15	.08
122	Greg Luzinski	.20	.15	.08
123	Mike Boddicker(FC)	.20	.15	.08
124	Pete Ladd	.10	.08	.04
125	Juan Berenguer	.10	.08	.04
126	John Montefusco	.10	.08	.04
127	Ed Jurak	.10	.08	.04
128	Tom Niedenfuer	.12	.09	.05
129	Bert Blyleven	.30	.25	.14
130	Bud Black	.12	.09	.05
131	Gorman Heimueller	.10	.08	.04
132	Dan Schatzeder	.10	.08	.04
133	Ron Jackson	.10	.08	.04
134	Tom Henke(FC)	1.25	.90	.50
135	Kevin Hickey	.10	.08	.04
136	Mike Scott	.30	.25	.12
137	Bo Diaz	.12	.09	.05
138	Glenn Brummer	.10	.08	.04
139	Sid Monge	.10	.08	.04
140	Rich Gale	.10	.08	.04
141	Brett Butler	.15	.11	.06
142	Brian Harper	.10	.08	.04
143	John Rabb	.10	.08	.04
144	Gary Woods	.10	.08	.04
145	Pat Putnam	.10	.08	.04
146	Jim Acker(FC)	.15	.11	.06
147	Mickey Hatcher	.12	.09	.05
148	Todd Cruz	.10	.08	.04
149	Tom Tellmann	.10	.08	.04
150	John Wockenfuss	.10	.08	.04
151	Wade Boggs	12.00	9.00	4.75
152	Don Baylor	.20	.15	.08
153	Bob Welch	.20	.15	.08
154	Alan Bannister	.10	.08	.04
155	Willie Aikens	.10	.08	.04
156	Jeff Burroughs	.12	.09	.05
157	Bryan Little	.10	.08	.04

		MT	NR MT	EX			MT	NR MT	EX
158	Bob Boone	.15	.11	.06	249	Jeff Newman	.10	.08	.04
159	Dave Hostetler	.10	.08	.04	250	Alejandro Pena(FC)	.40	.30	.15
160	Jerry Dybzinski	.10	.08	.04	251	Toby Harrah	.12	.09	.05
161	Mike Madden	.10	.08	.04	252	Cesar Geronimo	.10	.08	.04
162	Luis DeLeon	.10	.08	.04	253	Tom Underwood	.10	.08	.04
163	Willie Hernandez	.15	.11	.06	254	Doug Flynn	.10	.08	.04
164	Frank Pastore	.10	.08	.04	255	Andy Hassler	.10	.08	.04
165	Rick Camp	.10	.08	.04	256	Odell Jones	.10	.08	.04
166	Lee Mazzilli	.12	.09	.05	257	Rudy Law	.10	.08	.04
167	Scot Thompson	.10	.08	.04	258	Harry Spilman	.10	.08	.04
168	Bob Forsch	.12	.09	.05	259	Marty Bystrom	.10	.08	.04
169	Mike Flanagan	.15	.11	.06	260	Dave Rucker	.10	.08	.04
170	Rick Manning	.10	.08	.04	261	Ruppert Jones	.10	.08	.04
171	Chet Lemon	.12	.09	.05	262	Jeff Jones	.10	.08	.04
172	Jerry Remy	.10	.08	.04	263	Gerald Perry(FC)	1.50	1.25	.60
173	Ron Guidry	.35	.25	.14	264	Gene Tenace	.12	.09	.05
174	Pedro Guerrero	.50	.40	.20	265	Brad Wellman	.10	.08	.04
175	Willie Wilson	.25	.20	.10	266	Dickie Noles	.10	.08	.04
176	Carney Lansford	.20	.15	.08	267	Jamie Allen	.10	.08	.04
177	Al Oliver	.30	.25	.12	268	Jim Gott	.15	.11	.06
178	Jim Sundberg	.12	.09	.05	269	Ron Davis	.10	.08	.04
179	Bobby Grich	.20	.15	.08	270	Benny Ayala	.10	.08	.04
180	Richard Dotson	.20	.15	.08	271	Ned Yost	.10	.08	.04
181	Joaquin Andujar	.12	.09	.05	272	Dave Rozema	.10	.08	.04
182	Jose Cruz	.20	.15	.08	273	Dave Stapleton	.10	.08	.04
183	Mike Schmidt	10.00	7.50	4.00	274	Lou Piniella	.20	.15	.08
184	Gary Redus(FC)	.30	.25	.12	275	Jose Morales	.10	.08	.04
185	Garry Templeton	.15	.11	.06	276	Brod Perkins	.10	.08	.04
186	Tony Pena	.20	.15	.08	277	Butch Davis	.10	.08	.04
187	Greg Minton	.10	.08	.04	278	Tony Phillips(FC)	.20	.15	.08
188	Phil Niekro	.50	.40	.20	279	Jeff Reardon	.25	.20	.10
189	Ferguson Jenkins	.30	.25	.12	280	Ken Forsch	.10	.08	.04
190	Mookie Wilson	.15	.11	.06	281	Pete O'Brien(FC)	1.00	.70	.40
191	Jim Beattie	.10	.08	.04	282	Tom Paciorek	.10	.08	.04
192	Gary Ward	.12	.09	.05	283	Frank LaCorte	.10	.08	.04
193	Jesse Barfield	.40	.30	.15	284	Tim Lollar	.10	.08	.04
194	Pete Filson	.10	.08	.04	285	Greg Gross	.10	.08	.04
195	Roy Lee Jackson	.10	.08	.04	286	Alex Trevino	.10	.08	.04
196	Rick Sweet	.10	.08	.04	287	Gene Garber	.10	.08	.04
197	Jesse Orosco	.15	.11	.06	288	Dave Parker	.50	.40	.20
198	Steve Lake(FC)	.12	.09	.05	289	Lee Smith	.20	.15	.08
199	Ken Dayley	.10	.08	.04	290	Dave LaPoint	.15	.11	.06
200	Manny Sarmiento	.10	.08	.04	291	John Shelby(FC)	.35	.25	.14
201	Mark Davis(FC)	.25	.20	.10	292	Charlie Moore	.10	.08	.04
202	Tim Flannery	.10	.08	.04	293	Alan Trammell	.60	.45	.25
203	Bill Scherrer	.10	.08	.04	294	Tony Armas	.20	.15	.08
204	Al Holland	.10	.08	.04	295	Shane Rawley	.20	.15	.08
205	David Von Ohlen	.10	.08	.04	296	Greg Brock	.15	.11	.06
206	Mike LaCoss	.10	.08	.04	297	Hal McRae	.20	.15	.08
207	Juan Beniquez	.10	.08	.04	298	Mike Davis	.12	.09	.05
208	Juan Agosto(FC)	.20	.15	.08	299	Tim Raines	.80	.60	.30
209	Bobby Ramos	.10	.08	.04	300	Bucky Dent	.15	.11	.06
210	Al Bumbry	.12	.09	.05	301	Tommy John	.35	.25	.14
211	Mark Brouhard	.10	.08	.04	302	Carlton Fisk	1.00	.70	.40
212	Howard Bailey	.10	.08	.04	303	Darrell Porter	.12	.09	.05
213	Bruce Hurst	.20	.15	.08	304	Dickie Thon	.12	.09	.05
214	Bob Shirley	.10	.08	.04	305	Garry Maddox	.12	.09	.05
215	Pat Zachry	.10	.08	.04	306	Cesar Cedeno	.20	.15	.08
216	Julio Franco	.25	.20	.10	307	Gary Lucas	.10	.08	.04
217	Mike Armstrong	.10	.08	.04	308	Johnny Ray	.20	.15	.08
218	Dave Beard	.10	.08	.04	309	Andy McGaffigan	.10	.08	.04
219	Steve Rogers	.12	.09	.05	310	Claudell Washington	.12	.09	.05
220	John Butcher	.10	.08	.04	311	Ryne Sandberg	15.00	11.00	6.00
221	Mike Smithson(FC)	.20	.15	.08	312	George Foster	.30	.25	.12
222	Frank White	.20	.15	.08	313	Spike Owen(FC)	.70	.50	.30
223	Mike Heath	.10	.08	.04	314	Gary Gaetti	.90	.70	.35
224	Chris Bando	.10	.08	.04	315	Willie Upshaw	.12	.09	.05
225	Roy Smalley	.10	.08	.04	316	Al Williams	.10	.08	.04
226	Dusty Baker	.20	.15	.08	317	Jorge Orta	.10	.08	.04
227	Lou Whitaker	.60	.45	.25	318	Orlando Mercado	.10	.08	.04
228	John Lowenstein	.10	.08	.04	319	Junior Ortiz(FC)	.12	.09	.05
229	Ben Oglivie	.12	.09	.05	320	Mike Proly	.10	.08	.04
230	Doug DeCinces	.15	.11	.06	321	Randy Johnson	.10	.08	.04
231	Lonnie Smith	.12	.09	.05	322	Jim Morrison	.10	.08	.04
232	Ray Knight	.15	.11	.06	323	Max Venable	.10	.08	.04
233	Gary Matthews	.20	.15	.08	324	Tony Gwynn	6.00	4.50	2.50
234	Juan Bonilla	.10	.08	.04	325	Duane Walker	.10	.08	.04
235	Rod Scurry	.10	.08	.04	326	Ozzie Virgil	.10	.08	.04
236	Atlee Hammaker	.10	.08	.04	327	Jeff Lahti	.10	.08	.04
237	Mike Caldwell	.10	.08	.04	328	Bill Dawley(FC)	.12	.09	.05
238	Keith Hernandez	.80	.60	.30	329	Rob Wilfong	.10	.08	.04
239	Larry Bowa	.25	.20	.10	330	Marc Hill	.10	.08	.04
240	Tony Bernazard	.10	.08	.04	331	Ray Burris	.10	.08	.04
241	Damaso Garcia	.10	.08	.04	332	Allan Ramirez	.10	.08	.04
242	Tom Brunansky	.35	.25	.14	333	Chuck Porter	.10	.08	.04
243	Dan Driessen	.12	.09	.05	334	Wayne Krenchicki	.10	.08	.04
244	Ron Kittle(FC)	.30	.25	.12	335	Gary Allenson	.10	.08	.04
245	Tim Stoddard	.10	.08	.04	336	Bob Meacham(FC)	.20	.15	.08
246	Bob Gibson	.10	.08	.04	337	Joe Beckwith	.10	.08	.04
247	Marty Castillo	.10	.08	.04	338	Rick Sutcliffe	.25	.20	.10
248	Don Mattingly(FC)	100.00	75.00	40.00	339	Mark Huismann(FC)	.15	.11	.06

		MT	NR MT	EX
340	Tim Conroy(FC)	.15	.11	.06
341	Scott Sanderson	.10	.08	.04
342	Larry Biittner	.10	.08	.04
343	Dave Stewart	1.50	1.25	.60
344	Darryl Motley	.10	.08	.04
345	Chris Codiroli(FC)	.12	.09	.05
346	Rick Behenna	.10	.08	.04
347	Andre Robertson	.10	.08	.04
348	Mike Marshall	.25	.20	.10
349	Larry Herndon	.12	.09	.05
350	Rich Dauer	.10	.08	.04
351	Cecil Cooper	.25	.20	.10
352	Rod Carew	.90	.70	.35
353	Willie McGee	.40	.30	.15
354	Phil Garner	.12	.09	.05
355	Joe Morgan	.60	.45	.25
356	Luis Salazar	.10	.08	.04
357	John Candelaria	.20	.15	.08
358	Bill Laskey	.10	.08	.04
359	Bob McClure	.10	.08	.04
360	Dave Kingman	.30	.25	.12
361	Ron Cey	.20	.15	.08
362	Matt Young(FC)	.20	.15	.08
363	Lloyd Moseby	.20	.15	.08
364	Frank Viola	1.25	.90	.50
365	Eddie Milner	.10	.08	.04
366	Floyd Bannister	.20	.15	.08
367	Dan Ford	.10	.08	.04
368	Moose Haas	.10	.08	.04
369	Doug Bair	.10	.08	.04
370	Ray Fontenot(FC)	.12	.09	.05
371	Luis Aponte	.10	.08	.04
372	Jack Fimple	.10	.08	.04
373	Neal Heaton(FC)	.20	.15	.08
374	Greg Pryor	.10	.08	.04
375	Wayne Gross	.10	.08	.04
376	Charlie Lea	.10	.08	.04
377	Steve Lubratich	.10	.08	.04
378	Jon Matlack	.12	.09	.05
379	Julio Cruz	.10	.08	.04
380	John Mizerock	.10	.08	.04
381	Kevin Gross(FC)	.40	.30	.15
382	Mike Ramsey	.10	.08	.04
383	Doug Gwosdz	.10	.08	.04
384	Kelly Paris	.10	.08	.04
385	Pete Falcone	.10	.08	.04
386	Milt May	.10	.08	.04
387	Fred Breining	.10	.08	.04
388	Craig Lefferts(FC)	.25	.20	.10
389	Steve Henderson	.10	.08	.04
390	Randy Moffitt	.10	.08	.04
391	Ron Washington	.10	.08	.04
392	Gary Roenicke	.10	.08	.04
393	Tom Candiotti(FC)	.30	.25	.12
394	Larry Pashnick	.10	.08	.04
395	Dwight Evans	.30	.25	.12
396	Goose Gossage	.40	.30	.15
397	Derrel Thomas	.10	.08	.04
398	Juan Eichelberger	.10	.08	.04
399	Leon Roberts	.10	.08	.04
400	Davey Lopes	.15	.11	.06
401	Bill Gullickson	.10	.08	.04
402	Geoff Zahn	.10	.08	.04
403	Billy Sample	.10	.08	.04
404	Mike Squires	.10	.08	.04
405	Craig Reynolds	.10	.08	.04
406	Eric Show	.15	.11	.06
407	John Denny	.10	.08	.04
408	Dann Bilardello	.10	.08	.04
409	Bruce Benedict	.10	.08	.04
410	Kent Tekulve	.12	.09	.05
411	Mel Hall	.20	.15	.08
412	John Stuper	.10	.08	.04
413	Rick Dempsey	.12	.09	.05
414	Don Sutton	.50	.40	.20
415	Jack Morris	.50	.40	.20
416	John Tudor	.20	.15	.08
417	Willie Randolph	.20	.15	.08
418	Jerry Reuss	.15	.11	.06
419	Don Slaught	.10	.08	.04
420	Steve McCatty	.10	.08	.04
421	Tim Wallach	.25	.20	.10
422	Larry Parrish	.20	.15	.08
423	Brian Downing	.20	.15	.08
424	Britt Burns	.10	.08	.04
425	David Green	.10	.08	.04
426	Jerry Mumphrey	.12	.09	.05
427	Ivan DeJesus	.10	.08	.04
428	Mario Soto	.12	.09	.05
429	Gene Richards	.10	.08	.04
430	Dale Berra	.10	.08	.04

		MT	NR MT	EX
431	Darrell Evans	.25	.20	.10
432	Glenn Hubbard	.12	.09	.05
433	Jody Davis	.15	.11	.06
434	Danny Heep	.10	.08	.04
435	Ed Nunez(FC)	.20	.15	.08
436	Bobby Castillo	.10	.08	.04
437	Ernie Whitt	.12	.09	.05
438	Scott Ullger	.10	.08	.04
439	Doyle Alexander	.15	.11	.06
440	Domingo Ramos	.10	.08	.04
441	Craig Swan	.10	.08	.04
442	Warren Brusstar	.10	.08	.04
443	Len Barker	.12	.09	.05
444	Mike Easler	.12	.09	.05
445	Renie Martin	.10	.08	.04
446	Dennis Rasmussen(FC)	.70	.50	.30
447	Ted Power(FC)	.15	.11	.06
448	Charlie Hudson(FC)	.25	.20	.10
449	Danny Cox(FC)	.70	.50	.30
450	Kevin Bass(FC)	.30	.25	.12
451	Daryl Sconiers	.10	.08	.04
452	Scott Fletcher	.12	.09	.05
453	Bryn Smith	.10	.08	.04
454	Jim Dwyer	.10	.08	.04
455	Rob Picciolo	.10	.08	.04
456	Enos Cabell	.10	.08	.04
457	Dennis "Oil Can" Boyd(FC)	.80	.60	.30
458	Butch Wynegar	.10	.08	.04
459	Burt Hooton	.12	.09	.05
460	Ron Hassey	.10	.08	.04
461	Danny Jackson(FC)	2.50	2.00	1.00
462	Bob Kearney	.10	.08	.04
463	Terry Francona	.10	.08	.04
464	Wayne Tolleson	.10	.08	.04
465	Mickey Rivers	.12	.09	.05
466	John Wathan	.12	.09	.05
467	Bill Almon	.10	.08	.04
468	George Vukovich	.10	.08	.04
469	Steve Kemp	.15	.11	.06
470	Ken Landreaux	.10	.08	.04
471	Milt Wilcox	.10	.08	.04
472	Tippy Martinez	.10	.08	.04
473	Ted Simmons	.20	.15	.08
474	Tim Foli	.10	.08	.04
475	George Hendrick	.12	.09	.05
476	Terry Puhl	.10	.08	.04
477	Von Hayes	.25	.20	.10
478	Bobby Brown	.10	.08	.04
479	Lee Lacy	.10	.08	.04
480	Joel Youngblood	.10	.08	.04
481	Jim Slaton	.10	.08	.04
482	Mike Fitzgerald(FC)	.20	.15	.08
483	Keith Moreland	.12	.09	.05
484	Ron Roenicke	.10	.08	.04
485	Luis Leal	.10	.08	.04
486	Bryan Oelkers	.10	.08	.04
487	Bruce Berenyi	.10	.08	.04
488	LaMarr Hoyt	.10	.08	.04
489	Joe Nolan	.10	.08	.04
490	Marshall Edwards	.10	.08	.04
491	Mike Laga(FC)	.12	.09	.05
492	Rick Cerone	.10	.08	.04
493	Mike Miller (Rick)	.10	.08	.04
494	Rick Honeycutt	.10	.08	.04
495	Mike Hargrove	.10	.08	.04
496	Joe Simpson	.10	.08	.04
497	Keith Atherton(FC)	.25	.20	.10
498	Chris Welsh	.10	.08	.04
499	Bruce Kison	.10	.08	.04
500	Bob Johnson	.10	.08	.04
501	Jerry Koosman	.15	.11	.06
502	Frank DiPino	.10	.08	.04
503	Tony Perez	.40	.30	.15
504	Ken Oberkfell	.10	.08	.04
505	Mark Thurmond(FC)	.12	.09	.05
506	Joe Price	.10	.08	.04
507	Pascual Perez	.15	.11	.06
508	Marvell Wynne(FC)	.25	.20	.10
509	Mike Krukow	.12	.09	.05
510	Dick Ruthven	.10	.08	.04
511	Al Cowens	.10	.08	.04
512	Cliff Johnson	.10	.08	.04
513	Randy Bush(FC)	.20	.15	.08
514	Sammy Stewart	.10	.08	.04
515	Bill Schroeder(FC)	.25	.20	.10
516	Aurelio Lopez	.10	.08	.04
517	Mike Brown	.10	.08	.04
518	Graig Nettles	.35	.25	.14
519	Dave Sax	.10	.08	.04
520	Gerry Willard	.10	.08	.04
521	Paul Splittorff	.10	.08	.04

		MT	NR MT	EX
522	Tom Burgmeier	.10	.08	.04
523	Chris Speier	.10	.08	.04
524	Bobby Clark	.10	.08	.04
525	George Wright	.10	.08	.04
526	Dennis Lamp	.10	.08	.04
527	Tony Scott	.10	.08	.04
528	Ed Whitson	.10	.08	.04
529	Ron Reed	.10	.08	.04
530	Charlie Puleo	.10	.08	.04
531	Jerry Royster	.10	.08	.04
532	Don Robinson	.12	.09	.05
533	Steve Trout	.10	.08	.04
534	Bruce Sutter	.30	.25	.12
535	Bob Horner	.20	.15	.08
536	Pat Tabler	.15	.11	.06
537	Chris Chambliss	.12	.09	.05
538	Bob Ojeda	.15	.11	.06
539	Alan Ashby	.10	.08	.04
540	Jay Johnstone	.12	.09	.05
541	Bob Dernier	.10	.08	.04
542	*Brook Jacoby*(FC)	3.00	2.25	1.25
543	U.L. Washington	.10	.08	.04
544	Danny Darwin	.10	.08	.04
545	Kiko Garcia	.10	.08	.04
546	Vance Law	.12	.09	.05
547	Tug McGraw	.20	.15	.08
548	Dave Smith	.12	.09	.05
549	Len Matuszek	.10	.08	.04
550	Tom Hume	.10	.08	.04
551	Dave Dravecky	.15	.11	.06
552	Rick Rhoden	.15	.11	.06
553	Duane Kuiper	.10	.08	.04
554	Rusty Staub	.20	.15	.08
555	Bill Campbell	.10	.08	.04
556	Mike Torrez	.12	.09	.05
557	Dave Henderson(FC)	.25	.20	.10
558	Len Whitehouse	.10	.08	.04
559	Barry Bonnell	.10	.08	.04
560	Rick Lysander	.10	.08	.04
561	Garth Iorg	.10	.08	.04
562	Bryan Clark	.10	.08	.04
563	Brian Giles	.10	.08	.04
564	Vern Ruhle	.10	.08	.04
565	Steve Bedrosian	.20	.15	.08
566	Larry McWilliams	.10	.08	.04
567	Jeff Leonard	.15	.11	.06
568	Alan Wiggins	.10	.08	.04
569	*Jeff Russell*(FC)	.25	.20	.10
570	Salome Barojas	.10	.08	.04
571	Dane Iorg	.10	.08	.04
572	Bob Knepper	.15	.11	.06
573	Gary Lavelle	.10	.08	.04
574	Gorman Thomas	.15	.11	.06
575	Manny Trillo	.12	.09	.05
576	Jim Palmer	1.00	.70	.40
577	Dale Murray	.10	.08	.04
578	Tom Brookens	.10	.08	.04
579	Rich Gedman	.15	.11	.06
580	*Bill Doran*(FC)	1.25	.90	.50
581	Steve Yeager	.10	.08	.04
582	Dan Spillner	.10	.08	.04
583	Dan Quisenberry	.15	.11	.06
584	Rance Mulliniks	.10	.08	.04
585	Storm Davis	.15	.11	.06
586	Dave Schmidt	.10	.08	.04
587	Bill Russell	.12	.09	.05
588	*Pat Sheridan*(FC)	.20	.15	.08
589	Rafael Ramirez	.10	.08	.04
590	Bud Anderson	.10	.08	.04
591	George Frazier	.10	.08	.04
592	*Lee Tunnell*(FC)	.12	.09	.05
593	Kirk Gibson	.60	.45	.25
594	Scott McGregor	.12	.09	.05
595	Bob Bailor	.10	.08	.04
596	Tom Herr	.20	.15	.08
597	Luis Sanchez	.10	.08	.04
598	Dave Engle	.10	.08	.04
599	*Craig McMurtry*(FC)	.15	.11	.06
600	Carlos Diaz	.10	.08	.04
601	Tom O'Malley	.10	.08	.04
602	*Nick Esasky*(FC)	1.75	1.25	.70
603	Ron Hodges	.10	.08	.04
604	Ed Vande Berg	.10	.08	.04
605	Alfredo Griffin	.12	.09	.05
606	Glenn Hoffman	.10	.08	.04
607	Hubie Brooks	.20	.15	.08
608	Richard Barnes (photo actually Neal Heaton)	.10	.08	.04
609	*Greg Walker*(FC)	.60	.45	.25
610	Ken Singleton	.20	.15	.08
611	Mark Clear	.10	.08	.04

		MT	NR MT	EX
612	Buck Martinez	.10	.08	.04
613	Ken Griffey	.15	.11	.06
614	Reid Nichols	.10	.08	.04
615	*Doug Sisk*(FC)	.12	.09	.05
616	Bob Brenly	.10	.08	.04
617	Joey McLaughlin	.10	.08	.04
618	Glenn Wilson	.12	.09	.05
619	Bob Stoddard	.10	.08	.04
620	Len Sakata (Lenn)	.10	.08	.04
621	*Mike Young*(FC)	.25	.20	.10
622	John Stefero	.10	.08	.04
623	*Carmelo Martinez*(FC)	.30	.25	.12
624	Dave Bergman	.10	.08	.04
625	Runnin' Reds (David Green, Willie McGee, Lonnie Smith, Ozzie Smith)	.30	.25	.12
626	Rudy May	.10	.08	.04
627	Matt Keough	.10	.08	.04
628	*Jose DeLeon*(FC)	.80	.60	.30
629	Jim Essian	.10	.08	.04
630	*Darnell Coles*(FC)	.35	.25	.14
631	Mike Warren	.10	.08	.04
632	Del Crandall	.10	.08	.04
633	Dennis Martinez	.12	.09	.05
634	Mike Moore	.12	.09	.05
635	Lary Sorensen	.10	.08	.04
636	Ricky Nelson	.10	.08	.04
637	Omar Moreno	.10	.08	.04
638	Charlie Hough	.15	.11	.06
639	Dennis Eckersley	.25	.20	.10
640	*Walt Terrell*(FC)	.40	.30	.15
641	Denny Walling	.10	.08	.04
642	*Dave Anderson*(FC)	.20	.15	.08
643	*Jose Oquendo*(FC)	.25	.20	.10
644	Bob Stanley	.10	.08	.04
645	Dave Geisel	.10	.08	.04
646	*Scott Garrelts*(FC)	.90	.70	.35
647	*Gary Pettis*(FC)	.40	.30	.15
648	Duke Snider Puzzle Card	.10	.08	.04
649	Johnnie LeMaster	.10	.08	.04
650	Dave Collins	.12	.09	.05
651	San Diego Chicken	.25	.20	.10
---a	Checklist 1-26 DK (Perez-Steel on back)	.12	.09	.05
---b	Checklist 1-26 DK (Perez-Steele on back)	.40	.30	.15
----	Checklist 27-130	.10	.08	.04
----	Checklist 131-234	.10	.08	.04
----	Checklist 235-338	.10	.08	.04
----	Checklist 339-442	.10	.08	.04
----	Checklist 443-546	.10	.08	.04
----	Checklist 547-651	.10	.08	.04
---A	Living Legends (Rollie Fingers, Gaylord Perry)	2.75	2.00	1.00
---B	Living Legends (Johnny Bench, Carl Yastrzemski)	5.00	3.75	2.00

1984 Donruss Action All-Stars

Full-color photos on the card fronts and backs make the 1984 Donruss Action All-Stars set somewhat unusual. The fronts contain a large action photo plus the Donruss logo and year of issue inside a deep red border. The top half of the card backs feature a close-up photo with the bottom portion containing biographical and statistical information. The cards, which measure 3-1/2" by 5", were sold with Ted Williams puzzle pieces.

		MT	NR MT	EX
	Complete Set:	8.00	6.00	3.25
	Common Player:	.09	.07	.04
1	Gary Lavelle	.09	.07	.04
2	Willie McGee	.15	.11	.06
3	Tony Pena	.09	.07	.04
4	Lou Whitaker	.15	.11	.06
5	Robin Yount	.35	.25	.14
6	Doug DeCinces	.09	.07	.04
7	John Castino	.09	.07	.04
8	Terry Kennedy	.09	.07	.04
9	Rickey Henderson	.50	.40	.20
10	Bob Horner	.12	.09	.05
11	Harold Baines	.15	.11	.06
12	Buddy Bell	.09	.07	.04
13	Fernando Valenzuela	.12	.09	.05
14	Nolan Ryan	1.00	.70	.40
15	Andre Thornton	.09	.07	.04
16	Gary Redus	.09	.07	.04
17	Pedro Guerrero	.15	.11	.06
18	Andre Dawson	.20	.15	.08
19	Dave Stieb	.12	.09	.05
20	Cal Ripken	.35	.25	.14
21	Ken Griffey	.12	.09	.05
22	Wade Boggs	1.00	.70	.40
23	Keith Hernandez	.25	.20	.10
24	Steve Carlton	.30	.25	.12
25	Hal McRae	.12	.09	.05
26	John Lowenstein	.09	.07	.04
27	Fred Lynn	.15	.11	.06
28	Bill Buckner	.09	.07	.04
29	Chris Chambliss	.09	.07	.04
30	Richie Zisk	.09	.07	.04
31	Jack Clark	.15	.11	.06
32	George Hendrick	.09	.07	.04
33	Bill Madlock	.12	.09	.05
34	Lance Parrish	.15	.11	.06
35	Paul Molitor	.15	.11	.06
36	Reggie Jackson	.35	.25	.14
37	Kent Hrbek	.20	.15	.08
38	Steve Garvey	.20	.15	.08
39	Carney Lansford	.09	.07	.04
40	Dale Murphy	.30	.25	.12
41	Greg Luzinski	.12	.09	.05
42	Larry Parrish	.09	.07	.04
43	Ryne Sandberg	.25	.20	.10
44	Dickie Thon	.09	.07	.04
45	Bert Blyleven	.12	.09	.05
46	Ron Oester	.09	.07	.04
47	Dusty Baker	.09	.07	.04
48	Steve Rogers	.09	.07	.04
49	Jim Clancy	.09	.07	.04
50	Eddie Murray	.15	.11	.06
51	Ron Guidry	.15	.11	.06
52	Jim Rice	.15	.11	.06
53	Tom Seaver	.30	.25	.12
54	Pete Rose	.30	.25	.12
55	George Brett	.40	.30	.15
56	Dan Quisenberry	.09	.07	.04
57	Mike Schmidt	.60	.45	.25
58	Ted Simmons	.12	.09	.05
59	Dave Righetti	.15	.11	.06
60	Checklist	.09	.07	.04

1984 Donruss Champions

The 60-card Donruss Champions set includes ten Hall of Famers, forty-nine current players and one numbered checklist. The ten Hall of Famers' cards (called Grand Champions) feature the artwork of Dick Perez, while cards of the current players (called Champions) are color photos. The cards measure 3-1/2" by 5". The Grand Champions represent hallmarks of excellence in various statistical categories, while the Champions are the leaders among active players in each category. The ten Grand Champion cards are #'s 1, 8, 14, 20, 26, 31, 37, 43, 50 and 55. The cards were issued with Duke Snider puzzle pieces.

		MT	NR MT	EX
	Complete Set:	7.00	5.25	275.00
	Common Player:	.07	.05	.03
1	Babe Ruth	.80	.60	.30
2	George Foster	.10	.08	.04
3	Dave Kingman	.10	.08	.04
4	Jim Rice	.10	.08	.04
5	Gorman Thomas	.10	.08	.04
6	Ben Oglivie	.07	.05	.03
7	Jeff Burroughs	.07	.05	.03
8	Hank Aaron	.35	.25	.14
9	Reggie Jackson	.30	.25	.12
10	Carl Yastrzemski	.50	.40	.20
11	Mike Schmidt	.50	.40	.20
12	Graig Nettles	.14	.11	.06
13	Greg Luzinski	.10	.08	.04
14	Ted Williams	1.00	.70	.40
15	George Brett	.35	.25	.14
16	Wade Boggs	.50	.40	.20
17	Hal McRae	.10	.08	.04
18	Bill Buckner	.10	.08	.04
19	Eddie Murray	.10	.08	.04
20	Rogers Hornsby	.14	.11	.06
21	Rod Carew	.20	.15	.08
22	Bill Madlock	.10	.08	.04
23	Lonnie Smith	.07	.05	.03
24	Cecil Cooper	.10	.08	.04
25	Ken Griffey	.10	.08	.04
26	Ty Cobb	.40	.30	.15
27	Pete Rose	.40	.30	.15
28	Rusty Staub	.10	.08	.04
29	Tony Perez	.10	.08	.04
30	Al Oliver	.10	.08	.04
31	Cy Young	.14	.11	.06
32	Gaylord Perry	.14	.11	.06
33	Ferguson Jenkins	.10	.08	.04
34	Phil Niekro	.14	.11	.06
35	Jim Palmer	.30	.25	.12
36	Tommy John	.10	.08	.04
37	Walter Johnson	.20	.15	.08
38	Steve Carlton	.25	.20	.10
39	Nolan Ryan	.50	.40	.20
40	Tom Seaver	.25	.20	.10
41	Don Sutton	.14	.11	.06
42	Bert Blyleven	.10	.08	.04
43	Frank Robinson	.35	.25	.14
44	Joe Morgan	.25	.20	.10
45	Rollie Fingers	.14	.11	.06
46	Keith Hernandez	.10	.08	.04
47	Robin Yount	.50	.40	.20
48	Cal Ripken	.25	.20	.10
49	Dale Murphy	.35	.25	.14
50	Mickey Mantle	1.00	.70	.40
51	Johnny Bench	.50	.40	.20
52	Carlton Fisk	.30	.25	.12
53	Tug McGraw	.10	.08	.04
54	Paul Molitor	.10	.08	.04
55	Carl Hubbell	.14	.11	.06
56	Steve Garvey	.15	.11	.06
57	Dave Parker	.14	.11	.06
58	Gary Carter	.15	.11	.06
59	Fred Lynn	.14	.11	.06
60	Checklist	.10	.08	.04

1985 Donruss

The black-bordered 1985 Donruss set includes 653 numbered cards and seven unnumbered checklists. Displaying the artwork of Dick Perez for the fourth consecutive year, card #'s 1-26 feature the Diamond Kings series. Donruss, realizing the hobby craze over rookie cards, included a Rated Rookies subset (card

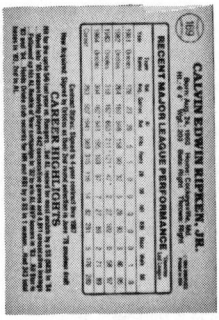

#'s 27-46). The cards, which are the standard size of 2-1/2" by 3-1/2", were issued with a Lou Gehrig puzzle. The backs of the cards have black print on yellow and white. The complete set price does not include the higher priced variations. (DK) and (RR) refer to the Diamond Kings and Rated Rookies subsets.

		MT	NR MT	EX
	Complete Set:	150.00	125.00	60.00
	Common Player:	.08	.06	.03
1	Ryne Sandberg (DK)	2.00	1.50	.80
2	Doug DeCinces (DK)	.10	.08	.04
3	Rich Dotson (DK)	.12	.09	.05
4	Bert Blyleven (DK)	.15	.11	.06
5	Lou Whitaker (DK)	.30	.25	.12
6	Dan Quisenberry (DK)	.15	.11	.06
7	Don Mattingly (DK)	6.00	4.50	2.50
8	Carney Lansford (DK)	.10	.08	.04
9	Frank Tanana (DK)	.12	.09	.05
10	Willie Upshaw (DK)	.10	.08	.04
11	Claudell Washington (DK)	.10	.08	.04
12	Mike Marshall (DK)	.20	.15	.08
13	Joaquin Andujar (DK)	.10	.08	.04
14	Cal Ripken, Jr. (DK)	.60	.45	.25
15	Jim Rice (DK)	.50	.40	.20
16	Don Sutton (DK)	.30	.25	.12
17	Frank Viola (DK)	.15	.11	.06
18	Alvin Davis (DK)(FC)	.60	.45	.25
19	Mario Soto (DK)	.10	.08	.04
20	Jose Cruz (DK)	.12	.09	.05
21	Charlie Lea (DK)	.10	.08	.04
22	Jesse Orosco (DK)	.10	.08	.04
23	Juan Samuel (DK)(FC)	.40	.30	.15
24	Tony Pena (DK)	.12	.09	.05
25	Tony Gwynn (DK)	.50	.40	.20
26	Bob Brenly (DK)	.10	.08	.04
27	Danny Tartabull (RR)(FC)	6.00	4.50	2.50
28	Mike Bielecki (RR)(FC)	.15	.11	.06
29	Steve Lyons (RR)(FC)	.20	.15	.08
30	Jeff Reed (RR)(FC)	.15	.11	.06
31	Tony Brewer (RR)	.08	.06	.03
32	John Morris (RR)(FC)	.15	.11	.06
33	Daryl Boston (RR)(FC)	.25	.20	.10
34	Alfonso Pulido (RR)	.08	.06	.03
35	Steve Kiefer (RR)(FC)	.10	.08	.04
36	Larry Sheets (RR)(FC)	.50	.40	.20
37	Scott Bradley (RR)(FC)	.25	.20	.10
38	Calvin Schiraldi (RR)(FC)	.30	.25	.12
39	Shawon Dunston (RR)(FC)	6.00	4.50	2.50
40	Charlie Mitchell (RR)	.08	.06	.03
41	Billy Hatcher (RR)(FC)	1.00	.70	.40
42	Russ Stephans (RR)	.08	.06	.03
43	Alejandro Sanchez (RR)	.08	.06	.03
44	Steve Jeltz (RR)(FC)	.15	.11	.06
45	Jim Traber (RR)(FC)	.30	.25	.12
46	Doug Loman (RR)	.08	.06	.03
47	Eddie Murray	.60	.45	.25
48	Robin Yount	.80	.60	.30
49	Lance Parrish	.30	.25	.12
50	Jim Rice	.50	.40	.20
51	Dave Winfield	.50	.40	.20
52	Fernando Valenzuela	.35	.25	.14
53	George Brett	.70	.50	.30
54	Dave Kingman	.15	.11	.06
55	Gary Carter	.40	.30	.15
56	Buddy Bell	.12	.09	.05
57	Reggie Jackson	.60	.45	.25
58	Harold Baines	.20	.15	.08
59	Ozzie Smith	.20	.15	.08
60	Nolan Ryan	4.00	3.00	1.50
61	Mike Schmidt	2.75	2.00	1.00
62	Dave Parker	.35	.25	.14
63	Tony Gwynn	2.00	1.50	.80
64	Tony Pena	.12	.09	.05
65	Jack Clark	.25	.20	.10
66	Dale Murphy	.80	.60	.30
67	Ryne Sandberg	4.00	3.00	1.50
68	Keith Hernandez	.40	.30	.15
69	Alvin Davis(FC)	4.00	3.00	1.50
70	Kent Hrbek	.30	.25	.12
71	Willie Upshaw	.10	.08	.04
72	Dave Engle	.08	.06	.03
73	Alfredo Griffin	.10	.08	.04
74a	Jack Perconte (last line of highlights begins "Batted .346...")	.10	.08	.04
74b	Jack Perconte (last line of highlights begins "Led the...")	1.25	.90	.50
75	Jesse Orosco	.10	.08	.04
76	Jody Davis	.12	.09	.05
77	Bob Horner	.12	.09	.05
78	Larry McWilliams	.08	.06	.03
79	Joel Youngblood	.08	.06	.03
80	Alan Wiggins	.08	.06	.03
81	Ron Oester	.08	.06	.03
82	Ozzie Virgil	.08	.06	.03
83	Ricky Horton(FC)	.35	.25	.14
84	Bill Doran	.12	.09	.05
85	Rod Carew	.50	.40	.20
86	LaMarr Hoyt	.08	.06	.03
87	Tim Wallach	.15	.11	.06
88	Mike Flanagan	.12	.09	.05
89	Jim Sundberg	.10	.08	.04
90	Chet Lemon	.10	.08	.04
91	Bob Stanley	.08	.06	.03
92	Willie Randolph	.12	.09	.05
93	Bill Russell	.10	.08	.04
94	Julio Franco	.15	.11	.06
95	Dan Quisenberry	.12	.09	.05
96	Bill Caudill	.08	.06	.03
97	Bill Gullickson	.08	.06	.03
98	Danny Darwin	.08	.06	.03
99	Curtis Wilkerson	.08	.06	.03
100	Bud Black	.08	.06	.03
101	Tony Phillips	.08	.06	.03
102	Tony Bernazard	.08	.06	.03
103	Jay Howell	.10	.08	.04
104	Burt Hooton	.10	.08	.04
105	Milt Wilcox	.08	.06	.03
106	Rich Dauer	.08	.06	.03
107	Don Sutton	.35	.25	.14
108	Mike Witt	.15	.11	.06
109	Bruce Sutter	.15	.11	.06
110	Enos Cabell	.08	.06	.03
111	John Denny	.08	.06	.03
112	Dave Dravecky	.10	.08	.04
113	Marvell Wynne	.08	.06	.03
114	Johnnie LeMaster	.08	.06	.03
115	Chuck Porter	.08	.06	.03
116	John Gibbons	.08	.06	.03
117	Keith Moreland	.10	.08	.04
118	Darnell Coles	.12	.09	.05
119	Dennis Lamp	.08	.06	.03
120	Ron Davis	.08	.06	.03
121	Nick Esasky	.10	.08	.04
122	Vance Law	.10	.08	.04
123	Gary Roenicke	.08	.06	.03
124	Bill Schroeder	.08	.06	.03
125	Dave Rozema	.08	.06	.03
126	Bobby Meacham	.08	.06	.03
127	Marty Barrett(FC)	.25	.20	.10
128	R.J. Reynolds(FC)	.30	.25	.12
129	Ernie Camacho	.08	.06	.03
130	Jorge Orta	.08	.06	.03
131	Lary Sorensen	.08	.06	.03
132	Terry Francona	.08	.06	.03
133	Fred Lynn	.25	.20	.10
134	Bobby Jones	.08	.06	.03
135	Jerry Hairston	.08	.06	.03
136	Kevin Bass	.12	.09	.05
137	Garry Maddox	.08	.06	.03
138	Dave LaPoint	.10	.08	.04
139	Kevin McReynolds	1.00	.70	.40
140	Wayne Krenchicki	.08	.06	.03
141	Rafael Ramirez	.08	.06	.03
142	Rod Scurry	.08	.06	.03
143	Greg Minton	.08	.06	.03
144	Tim Stoddard	.08	.06	.03
145	Steve Henderson	.08	.06	.03
146	George Bell	.50	.40	.20

	MT	NR MT	EX			MT	NR MT	EX
147 Dave Meier	.08	.06	.03	238 Mike Fitzgerald	.08	.06	.03
148 Sammy Stewart	.08	.06	.03	239 Gary Matthews	.12	.09	.05
149 Mark Brouhard	.08	.06	.03	240 Jim Presley(FC)	1.00	.70	.40
150 Larry Herndon	.10	.08	.04	241 Dave Collins	.10	.08	.04
151 Oil Can Boyd	.10	.08	.04	242 Gary Gaetti	.30	.25	.12
152 Brian Dayett	.08	.06	.03	243 Dann Bilardello	.08	.06	.03
153 Tom Niedenfuer	.10	.08	.04	244 Rudy Law	.08	.06	.03
154 Brook Jacoby	.15	.11	.06	245 John Lowenstein	.08	.06	.03
155 Onix Concepcion	.08	.06	.03	246 Tom Tellmann	.08	.06	.03
156 Tim Conroy	.08	.06	.03	247 Howard Johnson	1.75	1.25	.70
157 Joe Hesketh(FC)	.15	.11	.06	248 Ray Fontenot	.08	.06	.03
158 Brian Downing	.12	.09	.05	249 Tony Armas	.12	.09	.05
159 Tommy Dunbar	.08	.06	.03	250 Candy Maldonado	.12	.09	.05
160 Marc Hill	.08	.06	.03	251 Mike Jeffcoat(FC)	.10	.08	.04
161 Phil Garner	.10	.08	.04	252 Dane Iorg	.08	.06	.03
162 Jerry Davis	.08	.06	.03	253 Bruce Bochte	.08	.06	.03
163 Bill Campbell	.08	.06	.03	254 Pete Rose	1.25	.90	.50
164 John Franco(FC)	2.00	1.50	.80	255 Don Aase	.08	.06	.03
165 Len Barker	.10	.08	.04	256 George Wright	.08	.06	.03
166 Benny Distefano(FC)	.10	.08	.04	257 Britt Burns	.08	.06	.03
167 George Frazier	.08	.06	.03	258 Mike Scott	.20	.15	.08
168 Tito Landrum	.08	.06	.03	259 Len Matuszek	.08	.06	.03
169 Cal Ripken	.80	.60	.30	260 Dave Rucker	.08	.06	.03
170 Cecil Cooper	.15	.11	.06	261 Craig Lefferts	.10	.08	.04
171 Alan Trammell	.40	.30	.15	262 Jay Tibbs(FC)	.20	.15	.08
172 Wade Boggs	5.00	3.75	2.00	263 Bruce Benedict	.08	.06	.03
173 Don Baylor	.15	.11	.06	264 Don Robinson	.10	.08	.04
174 Pedro Guerrero	.30	.25	.12	265 Gary Lavelle	.08	.06	.03
175 Frank White	.12	.09	.05	266 Scott Sanderson	.08	.06	.03
176 Rickey Henderson	3.00	2.25	1.25	267 Matt Young	.08	.06	.03
177 Charlie Lea	.08	.06	.03	268 Ernie Whitt	.10	.08	.04
178 Pete O'Brien	.20	.15	.08	269 Houston Jimenez	.08	.06	.03
179 Doug DeCinces	.12	.09	.05	270 Ken Dixon(FC)	.12	.09	.05
180 Ron Kittle	.12	.09	.05	271 Peter Ladd	.08	.06	.03
181 George Hendrick	.10	.08	.04	272 Juan Berenguer	.08	.06	.03
182 Joe Niekro	.12	.09	.05	273 Roger Clemens(FC)	25.00	18.00	9.00
183 Juan Samuel(FC)	.60	.45	.25	274 Rick Cerone	.08	.06	.03
184 Mario Soto	.10	.08	.04	275 Dave Anderson	.08	.06	.03
185 Goose Gossage	.25	.20	.10	276 George Vukovich	.08	.06	.03
186 Johnny Ray	.15	.11	.06	277 Greg Pryor	.08	.06	.03
187 Bob Brenly	.08	.06	.03	278 Mike Warren	.08	.06	.03
188 Craig McMurtry	.08	.06	.03	279 Bob James	.08	.06	.03
189 Leon Durham	.10	.08	.04	280 Bobby Grich	.12	.09	.05
190 Dwight Gooden(FC)	15.00	11.00	6.00	281 Mike Mason(FC)	.12	.09	.05
191 Barry Bonnell	.08	.06	.03	282 Ron Reed	.08	.06	.03
192 Tim Teufel	.12	.09	.05	283 Alan Ashby	.08	.06	.03
193 Dave Stieb	.15	.11	.06	284 Mark Thurmond	.08	.06	.03
194 Mickey Hatcher	.08	.06	.03	285 Joe Lefebvre	.08	.06	.03
195 Jesse Barfield	.25	.20	.10	286 Ted Power	.08	.06	.03
196 Al Cowens	.08	.06	.03	287 Chris Chambliss	.10	.08	.04
197 Hubie Brooks	.12	.09	.05	288 Lee Tunnell	.08	.06	.03
198 Steve Trout	.08	.06	.03	289 Rich Bordi	.08	.06	.03
199 Glenn Hubbard	.08	.06	.03	290 Glenn Brummer	.08	.06	.03
200 Bill Madlock	.15	.11	.06	291 Mike Boddicker	.12	.09	.05
201 Jeff Robinson(FC)	.35	.25	.14	292 Rollie Fingers	.25	.20	.10
202 Eric Show	.10	.08	.04	293 Lou Whitaker	.40	.30	.15
203 Dave Concepcion	.15	.11	.06	294 Dwight Evans	.15	.11	.06
204 Ivan DeJesus	.08	.06	.03	295 Don Mattingly	16.00	12.00	6.50
205 Neil Allen	.08	.06	.03	296 Mike Marshall	.15	.11	.06
206 Jerry Mumphrey	.08	.06	.03	297 Willie Wilson	.15	.11	.06
207 Mike Brown	.08	.06	.03	298 Mike Heath	.08	.06	.03
208 Carlton Fisk	.40	.30	.15	299 Tim Raines	.50	.40	.20
209 Bryn Smith	.08	.06	.03	300 Larry Parrish	.12	.09	.05
210 Tippy Martinez	.08	.06	.03	301 Geoff Zahn	.08	.06	.03
211 Dion James	.10	.08	.04	302 Rich Dotson	.12	.09	.05
212 Willie Hernandez	.10	.08	.04	303 David Green	.08	.06	.03
213 Mike Easler	.10	.08	.04	304 Jose Cruz	.12	.09	.05
214 Ron Guidry	.30	.25	.12	305 Steve Carlton	.50	.40	.20
215 Rick Honeycutt	.08	.06	.03	306 Gary Redus	.10	.08	.04
216 Brett Butler	.12	.09	.05	307 Steve Garvey	.50	.40	.20
217 Larry Gura	.08	.06	.03	308 Jose DeLeon	.10	.08	.04
218 Ray Burris	.08	.06	.03	309 Randy Lerch	.08	.06	.03
219 Steve Rogers	.10	.08	.04	310 Claudell Washington	.10	.08	.04
220 Frank Tanana	.12	.09	.05	311 Lee Smith	.12	.09	.05
221 Ned Yost	.08	.06	.03	312 Darryl Strawberry	4.00	3.00	1.50
222 Bret Saberhagen	10.00	7.50	4.00	313 Jim Beattie	.08	.06	.03
223 Mike Davis	.10	.08	.04	314 John Butcher	.08	.06	.03
224 Bert Blyleven	.15	.11	.06	315 Damaso Garcia	.10	.08	.04
225 Steve Kemp	.10	.08	.04	316 Mike Smithson	.08	.06	.03
226 Jerry Reuss	.10	.08	.04	317 Luis Leal	.08	.06	.03
227 Darrell Evans	.15	.11	.06	318 Ken Phelps(FC)	.25	.20	.10
228 Wayne Gross	.08	.06	.03	319 Wally Backman	.10	.08	.04
229 Jim Gantner	.10	.08	.04	320 Ron Cey	.12	.09	.05
230 Bob Boone	.10	.08	.04	321 Brad Komminsk	.08	.06	.03
231 Lonnie Smith	.10	.08	.04	322 Jason Thompson	.08	.06	.03
232 Frank DiPino	.08	.06	.03	323 Frank Williams(FC)	.20	.15	.08
233 Jerry Koosman	.12	.09	.05	324 Tim Lollar	.08	.06	.03
234 Graig Nettles	.20	.15	.08	325 Eric Davis(FC)	20.00	15.00	8.00
235 John Tudor	.12	.09	.05	326 Von Hayes	.12	.09	.05
236 John Rabb	.08	.06	.03	327 Andy Van Slyke	.40	.30	.15
237 Rick Manning	.08	.06	.03	328 Craig Reynolds	.08	.06	.03

	MT	NR MT	EX
329 Dick Schofield	.10	.08	.04
330 Scott Fletcher	.10	.08	.04
331 Jeff Reardon	.15	.11	.06
332 Rick Dempsey	.10	.08	.04
333 Ben Oglivie	.10	.08	.04
334 Dan Petry	.10	.08	.04
335 Jackie Gutierrez	.08	.06	.03
336 Dave Righetti	.25	.20	.10
337 Alejandro Pena	.10	.08	.04
338 Mel Hall	.10	.08	.04
339 Pat Sheridan	.08	.06	.03
340 Keith Atherton	.08	.06	.03
341 David Palmer	.08	.06	.03
342 Gary Ward	.10	.08	.04
343 Dave Stewart	.15	.11	.06
344 *Mark Gubicza*(FC)	2.00	1.50	.80
345 Carney Lansford	.12	.09	.05
346 Jerry Willard	.08	.06	.03
347 Ken Griffey	.12	.09	.05
348 *Franklin Stubbs*(FC)	.80	.60	.30
349 Aurelio Lopez	.08	.06	.03
350 Al Bumbry	.10	.08	.04
351 Charlie Moore	.08	.06	.03
352 Luis Sanchez	.08	.06	.03
353 Darrell Porter	.10	.08	.04
354 Bill Dawley	.08	.06	.03
355 Charlie Hudson	.10	.08	.04
356 Garry Templeton	.10	.08	.04
357 Cecilio Guante	.08	.06	.03
358 Jeff Leonard	.12	.09	.05
359 Paul Molitor	.20	.15	.08
360 Ron Gardenhire	.08	.06	.03
361 Larry Bowa	.12	.09	.05
362 Bob Kearney	.08	.06	.03
363 Garth Iorg	.08	.06	.03
364 Tom Brunansky	.15	.11	.06
365 Brad Gulden	.08	.06	.03
366 Greg Walker	.12	.09	.05
367 Mike Young	.10	.08	.04
368 Rick Waits	.08	.06	.03
369 Doug Bair	.08	.06	.03
370 Bob Shirley	.08	.06	.03
371 Bob Ojeda	.12	.09	.05
372 Bob Welch	.15	.11	.06
373 Neal Heaton	.08	.06	.03
374 Danny Jackson (photo actually Steve Farr)	.80	.60	.30
375 Donnie Hill	.08	.06	.03
376 Mike Stenhouse	.08	.06	.03
377 Bruce Kison	.08	.06	.03
378 Wayne Tolleson	.08	.06	.03
379 Floyd Bannister	.12	.09	.05
380 Vern Ruhle	.08	.06	.03
381 Tim Corcoran	.08	.06	.03
382 Kurt Kepshire	.08	.06	.03
383 Bobby Brown	.08	.06	.03
384 Dave Van Gorder	.08	.06	.03
385 Rick Mahler	.08	.06	.03
386 Lee Mazzilli	.10	.08	.04
387 Bill Laskey	.08	.06	.03
388 Thad Bosley	.08	.06	.03
389 Al Chambers	.08	.06	.03
390 Tony Fernandez	.50	.40	.20
391 Ron Washington	.08	.06	.03
392 Bill Swaggerty	.08	.06	.03
393 Bob Gibson	.08	.06	.03
394 Marty Castillo	.08	.06	.03
395 Steve Crawford	.08	.06	.03
396 Clay Christiansen	.08	.06	.03
397 Bob Bailor	.08	.06	.03
398 Mike Hargrove	.08	.06	.03
399 Charlie Leibrandt	.10	.08	.04
400 Tom Burgmeier	.08	.06	.03
401 Razor Shines	.08	.06	.03
402 Rob Wilfong	.08	.06	.03
403 Tom Henke	.12	.09	.05
404 Al Jones	.08	.06	.03
405 Mike LaCoss	.08	.06	.03
406 Luis DeLeon	.08	.06	.03
407 Greg Gross	.08	.06	.03
408 Tom Hume	.08	.06	.03
409 Rick Camp	.08	.06	.03
410 Milt May	.08	.06	.03
411 *Henry Cotto*(FC)	.20	.15	.08
412 Dave Von Ohlen	.08	.06	.03
413 Scott McGregor	.10	.08	.04
414 Ted Simmons	.15	.11	.06
415 Jack Morris	.30	.25	.12
416 Bill Buckner	.15	.11	.06
417 Butch Wynegar	.08	.06	.03
418 Steve Sax	.25	.20	.10

	MT	NR MT	EX
419 Steve Balboni	.10	.08	.04
420 Dwayne Murphy	.10	.08	.04
421 Andre Dawson	.30	.25	.12
422 Charlie Hough	.10	.08	.04
423 Tommy John	.25	.20	.10
424a Tom Seaver (Floyd Bannister photo — throwing left)	.80	.60	.30
424b Tom Seaver (correct photo - throwing right)	12.00	9.00	4.75
425 Tom Herr	.12	.09	.05
426 Terry Puhl	.08	.06	.03
427 Al Holland	.08	.06	.03
428 Eddie Milner	.08	.06	.03
429 Terry Kennedy	.10	.08	.04
430 John Candelaria	.12	.09	.05
431 Manny Trillo	.10	.08	.04
432 Ken Oberkfell	.08	.06	.03
433 Rick Sutcliffe	.15	.11	.06
434 Ron Darling	.70	.50	.30
435 Spike Owen	.10	.08	.04
436 Frank Viola	.25	.20	.10
437 Lloyd Moseby	.12	.09	.05
438 *Kirby Puckett*(FC)	25.00	20.00	10.00
439 Jim Clancy	.10	.08	.04
440 Mike Moore	.08	.06	.03
441 Doug Sisk	.08	.06	.03
442 Dennis Eckersley	.15	.11	.06
443 Gerald Perry	.25	.20	.10
444 Dale Berra	.08	.06	.03
445 Dusty Baker	.10	.08	.04
446 Ed Whitson	.08	.06	.03
447 Cesar Cedeno	.12	.09	.05
448 *Rick Schu*(FC)	.20	.15	.08
449 Joaquin Andujar	.10	.08	.04
450 *Mark Bailey*(FC)	.12	.09	.05
451 *Ron Romanick*(FC)	.12	.09	.05
452 Julio Cruz	.08	.06	.03
453 Miguel Dilone	.08	.06	.03
454 Storm Davis	.12	.09	.05
455 Jaime Cocanower	.08	.06	.03
456 Barbaro Garbey	.12	.09	.05
457 Rich Gedman	.12	.09	.05
458 Phil Niekro	.30	.25	.12
459 Mike Scioscia	.10	.08	.04
460 Pat Tabler	.10	.08	.04
461 Darryl Motley	.08	.06	.03
462 Chris Codoroli (Codiroli)	.08	.06	.03
463 Doug Flynn	.08	.06	.03
464 Billy Sample	.08	.06	.03
465 Mickey Rivers	.10	.08	.04
466 John Wathan	.10	.08	.04
467 Bill Krueger	.08	.06	.03
468 Andre Thornton	.12	.09	.05
469 Rex Hudler	.12	.09	.05
470 *Sid Bream*(FC)	.50	.40	.20
471 Kirk Gibson	.40	.30	.15
472 John Shelby	.10	.08	.04
473 Moose Haas	.08	.06	.03
474 Doug Corbett	.08	.06	.03
475 Willie McGee	.35	.25	.14
476 Bob Knepper	.10	.08	.04
477 Kevin Gross	.12	.09	.05
478 Carmelo Martinez	.10	.08	.04
479 Kent Tekulve	.10	.08	.04
480 Chili Davis	.12	.09	.05
481 Bobby Clark	.08	.06	.03
482 Mookie Wilson	.12	.09	.05
483 Dave Owen	.08	.06	.03
484 Ed Nunez	.08	.06	.03
485 Rance Mulliniks	.08	.06	.03
486 Ken Schrom	.08	.06	.03
487 Jeff Russell	.08	.06	.03
488 Tom Paciorek	.08	.06	.03
489 Dan Ford	.08	.06	.03
490 Mike Caldwell	.08	.06	.03
491 Scottie Earl	.08	.06	.03
492 *Jose Rijo*(FC)	2.00	1.50	.80
493 Bruce Hurst	.15	.11	.06
494 Ken Landreaux	.08	.06	.03
495 Mike Fischlin	.08	.06	.03
496 Don Slaught	.08	.06	.03
497 Steve McCatty	.08	.06	.03
498 Gary Lucas	.08	.06	.03
499 Gary Pettis	.10	.08	.04
500 Marvis Foley	.08	.06	.03
501 Mike Squires	.08	.06	.03
502 *Jim Pankovitz*(FC)	.15	.11	.06
503 Luis Aguayo	.08	.06	.03
504 Ralph Citarella	.08	.06	.03
505 Bruce Bochy	.08	.06	.03
506 Bob Owchinko	.08	.06	.03

		MT	NR MT	EX
507	Pascual Perez	.10	.08	.04
508	Lee Lacy	.08	.06	.03
509	Atlee Hammaker	.08	.06	.03
510	Bob Dernier	.08	.06	.03
511	Ed Vande Berg	.08	.06	.03
512	Cliff Johnson	.08	.06	.03
513	Len Whitehouse	.08	.06	.03
514	Dennis Martinez	.10	.08	.04
515	Ed Romero	.08	.06	.03
516	Rusty Kuntz	.08	.06	.03
517	Rick Miller	.08	.06	.03
518	Dennis Rasmussen	.15	.11	.06
519	Steve Yeager	.08	.06	.03
520	Chris Bando	.08	.06	.03
521	U.L. Washington	.08	.06	.03
522	*Curt Young*(FC)	.40	.30	.15
523	Angel Salazar	.08	.06	.03
524	Curt Kaufman	.08	.06	.03
525	Odell Jones	.08	.06	.03
526	Juan Agosto	.08	.06	.03
527	Denny Walling	.08	.06	.03
528	Andy Hawkins(FC)	.20	.15	.08
529	Sixto Lezcano	.08	.06	.03
530	Skeeter Barnes	.08	.06	.03
531	Randy Johnson	.08	.06	.03
532	Jim Morrison	.08	.06	.03
533	Warren Brusstar	.08	.06	.03
534a	*Jeff Pendleton* (first name incorrect)(FC)	.85	.60	.35
534b	*Terry Pendleton* (first name correct)(FC)	3.00	2.25	1.25
535	Vic Rodriguez	.08	.06	.03
536	Bob McClure	.08	.06	.03
537	Dave Bergman	.08	.06	.03
538	Mark Clear	.08	.06	.03
539	*Mike Pagliarulo*(FC)	1.00	.70	.40
540	Terry Whitfield	.08	.06	.03
541	Joe Beckwith	.08	.06	.03
542	Jeff Burroughs	.10	.08	.04
543	Dan Schatzeder	.08	.06	.03
544	Donnie Scott	.08	.06	.03
545	Jim Slaton	.08	.06	.03
546	Greg Luzinski	.12	.09	.05
547	*Mark Salas*(FC)	.15	.11	.06
548	Dave Smith	.10	.08	.04
549	John Wockenfuss	.08	.06	.03
550	Frank Pastore	.08	.06	.03
551	Tim Flannery	.08	.06	.03
552	Rick Rhoden	.12	.09	.05
553	Mark Davis	.08	.06	.03
554	*Jeff Dedmon*(FC)	.15	.11	.06
555	Gary Woods	.08	.06	.03
556	Danny Heep	.08	.06	.03
557	*Mark Langston*(FC)	6.00	4.50	2.50
558	Darrell Brown	.08	.06	.03
559	*Jimmy Key*(FC)	1.50	1.25	.60
560	Rick Lysander	.08	.06	.03
561	Doyle Alexander	.12	.09	.05
562	Mike Stanton	.08	.06	.03
563	Sid Fernandez	.50	.40	.20
564	Richie Hebner	.08	.06	.03
565	Alex Trevino	.08	.06	.03
566	Brian Harper	.08	.06	.03
567	*Dan Gladden*(FC)	.60	.45	.25
568	Luis Salazar	.08	.06	.03
569	Tom Foley	.08	.06	.03
570	Larry Andersen	.08	.06	.03
571	Danny Cox	.12	.09	.05
572	Joe Sambito	.08	.06	.03
573	Juan Beniquez	.08	.06	.03
574	Joel Skinner	.08	.06	.03
575	*Randy St. Claire*(FC)	.15	.11	.06
576	Floyd Rayford	.08	.06	.03
577	Roy Howell	.08	.06	.03
578	John Grubb	.08	.06	.03
579	Ed Jurak	.08	.06	.03
580	John Montefusco	.08	.06	.03
581	*Orel Hershiser*(FC)	12.00	9.00	4.75
582	*Tom Waddell*(FC)	.08	.06	.03
583	Mark Huismann	.08	.06	.03
584	Joe Morgan	.30	.25	.12
585	Jim Wohlford	.08	.06	.03
586	Dave Schmidt	.08	.06	.03
587	*Jeff Kunkel*(FC)	.12	.09	.05
588	Hal McRae	.12	.09	.05
589	Bill Almon	.08	.06	.03
590	Carmen Castillo(FC)	.10	.08	.04
591	Omar Moreno	.08	.06	.03
592	*Ken Howell*(FC)	.20	.15	.08
593	Tom Brookens	.08	.06	.03
594	Joe Nolan	.08	.06	.03

		MT	NR MT	EX
595	Willie Lozado	.08	.06	.03
596	*Tom Nieto*(FC)	.12	.09	.05
597	Walt Terrell	.10	.08	.04
598	Al Oliver	.15	.11	.06
599	Shane Rawley	.12	.09	.05
600	*Denny Gonzalez*(FC)	.10	.08	.04
601	*Mark Grant*(FC)	.15	.11	.06
602	Mike Armstrong	.08	.06	.03
603	George Foster	.15	.11	.06
604	Davey Lopes	.10	.08	.04
605	Salome Barojas	.08	.06	.03
606	Roy Lee Jackson	.08	.06	.03
607	Pete Filson	.08	.06	.03
608	Duane Walker	.08	.06	.03
609	Glenn Wilson	.10	.08	.04
610	*Rafael Santana*(FC)	.20	.15	.08
611	Roy Smith	.08	.06	.03
612	Ruppert Jones	.08	.06	.03
613	*Joe Cowley*(FC)	.08	.06	.03
614	*Al Nipper* (photo actually Mike Brown)(FC)	.20	.15	.08
615	Gene Nelson	.08	.06	.03
616	Joe Carter	1.50	1.25	.60
617	Ray Knight	.12	.09	.05
618	Chuck Rainey	.08	.06	.03
619	Dan Driessen	.10	.08	.04
620	Daryl Sconiers	.08	.06	.03
621	Bill Stein	.08	.06	.03
622	Roy Smalley	.08	.06	.03
623	Ed Lynch	.08	.06	.03
624	*Jeff Stone*(FC)	.15	.11	.06
625	Bruce Berenyi	.08	.06	.03
626	Kelvin Chapman	.08	.06	.03
627	Joe Price	.08	.06	.03
628	Steve Bedrosian	.12	.09	.05
629	Vic Mata	.08	.06	.03
630	Mike Krukow	.10	.08	.04
631	*Phil Bradley*(FC)	.90	.70	.35
632	Jim Gott	.08	.06	.03
633	Randy Bush	.08	.06	.03
634	*Tom Browning*(FC)	2.00	1.50	.80
635	Lou Gehrig Puzzle Card	.08	.06	.03
636	Reid Nichols	.08	.06	.03
637	*Dan Pasqua*(FC)	.60	.45	.25
638	German Rivera	.08	.06	.03
639	*Don Schulze*(FC)	.10	.08	.04
640a	Mike Jones (last line of highlights begins "Was 11-7...")	.10	.08	.04
640b	Mike Jones (last line of highlights begins "Spent some ...")	1.25	.90	.50
641	Pete Rose	1.25	.90	.50
642	*Wade Rowdon*(FC)	.10	.08	.04
643	Jerry Narron	.08	.06	.03
644	*Darrell Miller*(FC)	.15	.11	.06
645	*Tim Hulett*(FC)	.15	.11	.06
646	Andy McGaffigan	.08	.06	.03
647	Kurt Bevacqua	.08	.06	.03
648	*John Russell*(FC)	.20	.15	.08
649	*Ron Robinson*(FC)	.25	.20	.10
650	Donnie Moore(FC)	.08	.06	.03
651a	Two for the Title (Don Mattingly, Dave Winfield) (player names in yellow)	8.00	6.00	3.25
651b	Two for the Title (Don Mattingly, Dave Winfield) (player names in white)	6.00	4.50	2.50
652	Tim Laudner	.08	.06	.03
653	*Steve Farr*(FC)	.35	.25	.14
----	Checklist 1-26 DK	.08	.06	.03
----	Checklist 27-130	.08	.06	.03
----	Checklist 131-234	.08	.06	.03
----	Checklist 235-338	.08	.06	.03
----	Checklist 339-442	.08	.06	.03
----	Checklist 443-546	.08	.06	.03
----	Checklist 547-653	.08	.06	.03

1985 Donruss
Action All-Stars

In 1985, Donruss issued an Action All-Stars set for the third consecutive year. The card fronts feature an action photo with an inset head-shot of the player inside a black border with grey boxes through it. The card backs have black print on blue and white and include statistical and biographical information. The cards were issued with a Lou Gehrig puzzle.

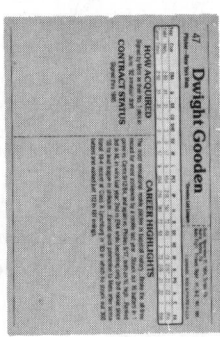

		MT	NR MT	EX
	Complete Set:	8.00	6.00	3.25
	Common Player:	.09	.07	.04
1	Tim Raines	.35	.25	.14
2	Jim Gantner	.09	.07	.04
3	Mario Soto	.09	.07	.04
4	Spike Owen	.09	.07	.04
5	Lloyd Moseby	.12	.09	.05
6	Damaso Garcia	.09	.07	.04
7	Cal Ripken	.35	.25	.14
8	Dan Quisenberry	.09	.07	.04
9	Eddie Murray	.12	.09	.05
10	Tony Pena	.09	.07	.04
11	Buddy Bell	.09	.07	.04
12	Dave Winfield	.30	.25	.12
13	Ron Kittle	.12	.09	.05
14	Rich Gossage	.12	.09	.05
15	Dwight Evans	.15	.11	.06
16	Al Davis	.15	.11	.06
17	Mike Schmidt	.40	.30	.15
18	Pascual Perez	.09	.07	.04
19	Tony Gwynn	.30	.25	.12
20	Nolan Ryan	.70	.50	.30
21	Robin Yount	.50	.40	.20
22	Mike Marshall	.12	.09	.05
23	Brett Butler	.09	.07	.04
24	Ryne Sandberg	.25	.20	.10
25	Dale Murphy	.40	.30	.15
26	George Brett	.40	.30	.15
27	Jim Rice	.15	.11	.06
28	Ozzie Smith	.15	.11	.06
29	Larry Parrish	.09	.07	.04
30	Jack Clark	.15	.11	.06
31	Manny Trillo	.09	.07	.04
32	Dave Kingman	.12	.09	.05
33	Geoff Zahn	.09	.07	.04
34	Pedro Guerrero	.15	.11	.06
35	Dave Parker	.20	.15	.08
36	Rollie Fingers	.15	.11	.06
37	Fernando Valenzuela	.12	.09	.05
38	Wade Boggs	1.00	.70	.40
39	Reggie Jackson	.30	.25	.12
40	Kent Hrbek	.20	.15	.08
41	Keith Hernandez	.25	.20	.10
42	Lou Whitaker	.15	.11	.06
43	Tom Herr	.09	.07	.04
44	Alan Trammell	.20	.15	.08
45	Butch Wynegar	.09	.07	.04
46	Leon Durham	.09	.07	.04
47	Dwight Gooden	1.50	1.25	.60
48	Don Mattingly	2.00	1.50	.80
49	Phil Niekro	.20	.15	.08
50	Johnny Ray	.09	.07	.04
51	Doug DeCinces	.09	.07	.04
52	Willie Upshaw	.09	.07	.04
53	Lance Parrish	.15	.11	.06
54	Jody Davis	.09	.07	.04
55	Steve Carlton	.30	.25	.12
56	Juan Samuel	.09	.07	.04
57	Gary Carter	.12	.09	.05
58	Harold Baines	.15	.11	.06
59	Eric Show	.09	.07	.04
60	Checklist	.09	.07	.04

1985 Donruss Box Panels

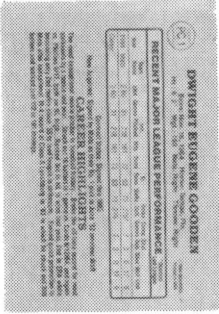

In 1985, Donruss placed on the bottoms of their wax pack boxes a four-card panel which included three player cards and a Lou Gehrig puzzle card. The player cards, numbered PC 1 through PC 3, have backs identical to the regular 1985 Donruss issue. The card fronts are identical in design to the regular issue, but carry different picture poses.

		MT	NR MT	EX
	Complete Panel Set:	7.00	5.25	2.75
	Complete Singles Set:	5.00	3.75	2.00
	Common Single Player:	.10	.08	.04
	Panel	7.00	5.25	2.75
1	Dwight Gooden	4.00	3.00	1.50
2	Ryne Sanberg	1.00	.70	.40
3	Ron Kittle	.10	.08	.04
----	Lou Gehrig Puzzle Card	.05	.04	.02

1985 Donruss Diamond Kings Supers

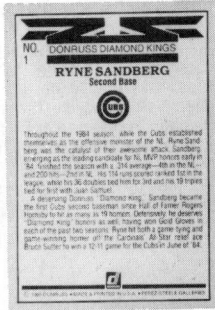

The 1985 Donruss Diamond Kings Supers are enlarged versions of the Diamond Kings card (#'s 1-26) in the regular 1985 Donruss set. The cards measure 4-15/16" by 6-3/4". The Diamond Kings series features the artwork of Dick Perez. Twenty-eight cards make up the set - 26 DK cards, an unnumbered checklist, and an unnumbered Dick Perez card. The back of the Perez card contains a brief history of Dick Perez and the Perez-Steele Galleries. The set could be obtained through a write-in offer found on the wrappers of the regular issue wax packs.

		MT	NR MT	EX
	Complete Set:	12.00	9.00	4.75
	Common Player:	.20	.15	.08
1	Ryne Sandberg	1.00	.70	.40
2	Doug DeCinces	.20	.15	.08
3	Richard Dotson	.20	.15	.08

		MT	NR MT	EX
4	Bert Blyleven	.25	.20	.10
5	Lou Whitaker	.30	.25	.12
6	Dan Quisenberry	.20	.15	.08
7	Don Mattingly	3.50	2.75	1.50
8	Carney Lansford	.20	.15	.08
9	Frank Tanana	.20	.15	.08
10	Willie Upshaw	.20	.15	.08
11	Claudell Washington	.20	.15	.08
12	Mike Marshall	.25	.20	.10
13	Joaquin Andujar	.20	.15	.08
14	Cal Ripken, Jr.	.50	.40	.20
15	Jim Rice	.35	.25	.14
16	Don Sutton	.30	.25	.12
17	Frank Viola	.35	.25	.14
18	Alvin Davis	.30	.25	.12
19	Mario Soto	.20	.15	.08
20	Jose Cruz	.20	.15	.08
21	Charlie Lea	.20	.15	.08
22	Jesse Orosco	.20	.15	.08
23	Juan Samuel	.20	.15	.08
24	Tony Pena	.20	.15	.08
25	Tony Gwynn	.40	.30	.15
26	Bob Brenly	.20	.15	.08
-----	Checklist	.12	.09	.05
-----	Dick Perez (DK artist)	.12	.09	.05

1985 Donruss Highlights

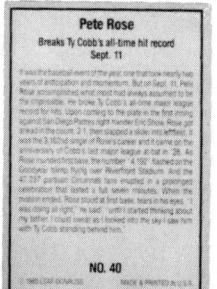

Designed in the style of the regular 1985 Donruss set, this issue features the Player of the Month in the major leagues plus highlight cards of special baseball events and milestones that occurred during the 1985 season. Fifty-six cards, including an unnumbered checklist, comprise the set which was available only through hobby dealers. The cards measure 2-1/2" by 3-1/2" and have glossy fronts. The last two cards in the set feature Donruss' picks for the A.L. and N.L. Rookies of the Year. The set was issued in a specially designed box.

		MT	NR MT	EX
Complete Set:		20.00	15.00	8.00
Common Player:		.12	.09	.05
1	Sets Opening Day Record (Tom Seaver) .40		.30	.15
2	Establishes A.L. Save Mark (Rollie Fingers) .15		.11	.06
3	A.L. Player of the Month - April (Mike Davis) .12		.09	.05
4	A.L. Pitcher of the Month - April (Charlie Leibrandt) .12		.09	.05
5	N.L. Player of the Month - April (Dale Murphy) .40		.30	.15
6	N.L. Pitcher of the Month - April (Fernando Valenzuela) .12		.09	.05
7	N.L. Shortstop Record (Larry Bowa) .12		.09	.05
8	Joins Reds 2000 Hit Club (Dave Concepcion) .12		.09	.05
9	Eldest Grand Slammer (Tony Perez) .15		.11	.06
10	N.L. Career Run Leader (Pete Rose) 1.25		.90	.50
11	A.L. Player of the Month - May (George Brett) .90		.70	.35
12	A.L. Pitcher of the Month - May (Dave Stieb) .12		.09	.05

		MT	NR MT	EX
13	N.L. Player of the Month - May (Dave Parker) .20		.15	.08
14	N.L. Pitcher of the Month - May (Andy Hawkins) .12		.09	.05
15	Records 11th Straight Win (Andy Hawkins) .12		.09	.05
16	Two Homers In First Inning (Von Hayes) .15		.11	.06
17	A.L. Player of the Month - June (Rickey Henderson) 1.00		.70	.40
18	A.L. Pitcher of the Month - June (Jay Howell) .12		.09	.05
19	N.L. Player of the Month - June (Pedro Guerrero) .20		.15	.08
20	N.L. Pitcher of the Month - June (John Tudor) .12		.09	.05
21	Marathon Game Iron Men (Gary Carter, Keith Hernandez) .35		.25	.14
22	Records 4000th K (Nolan Ryan) 1.25		.90	.50
23	All-Star Game MVP (LaMarr Hoyt) .12		.09	.05
24	1st Ranger To Hit For Cycle (Oddibe McDowell) .40		.30	.15
25	A.L. Player of the Month - July (George Brett) .90		.70	.35
26	A.L. Pitcher of the Month - July (Bret Saberhagen) 1.50		1.25	.60
27	N.L. Player of the Month - July (Keith Hernandez) .35		.25	.14
28	N.L. Pitcher of the Month - July (Fernando Valenzuela) .12		.09	.05
29	Record Setting Base Stealers (Vince Coleman, Willie McGee) .80		.60	.30
30	Notches 300th Career Win (Tom Seaver) .35		.25	.14
31	Strokes 3000th Hit (Rod Carew) .40		.30	.15
32	Establishes Met Record (Dwight Gooden) 2.25		1.75	.90
33	Achieves Strikeout Milestone (Dwight Gooden) 2.25		1.75	.90
34	Explodes For 9 RBI (Eddie Murray) .70		.50	.30
35	A.L. Career Hbp Leader (Don Baylor) .15		.11	.06
36	A.L. Player of the Month - August (Don Mattingly) 3.25		2.50	1.25
37	A.L. Pitcher of the Month - August (Dave Righetti) .20		.15	.08
38	N.L. Player of the Month (Willie McGee) .20		.15	.08
39	N.L. Pitcher of the Month - August (Shane Rawley) .12		.09	.05
40	Ty-Breaking Hit (Pete Rose) .90		.70	.35
41	Hits 3 Hrs Drives In 8 Runs (Andre Dawson) .20		.15	.08
42	Sets Yankee Theft Mark (Rickey Henderson) 1.00		.70	.40
43	20 Wins In Rookie Season (Tom Browning) .35		.25	.14
44	Yankee Milestone For Hits (Don Mattingly) 3.25		2.50	1.25
45	A.L. Player of the Month - September (Don Mattingly) 3.25		2.50	1.25
46	A.L. Pitcher of the Month - September (Charlie Leibrandt) .12		.09	.05
47	N.L. Player of the Month - September (Gary Carter) .12		.09	.05
48	N.L. Pitcher of the Month - September (Dwight Gooden) 2.25		1.75	.90
49	Major League Record Setter (Wade Boggs) 2.00		1.50	.80
50	Hurls Shutout For 300th Win (Phil Niekro) .30		.25	.12
51	Venerable HR King (Darrell Evans) .15		.11	.06
52	N.L. Switch-hitting Record (Willie McGee) .20		.15	.08
53	Equals DiMaggio Feat (Dave Winfield) .30		.25	.12
54	Donruss N.L. Rookie of the Year (Vince Coleman) 2.25		1.75	.90
55	Donruss A.L. Rookie of the Year (Ozzie Guillen) .50		.40	.20
-----	Checklist	.20	.15	.08

1985 Donruss Sluggers
of the Hall of Fame

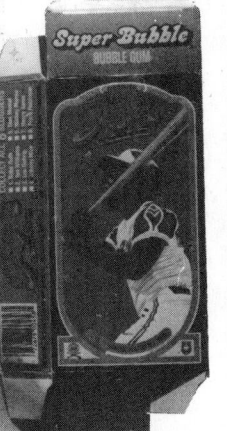

In much the same manner as the first Bazooka cards were issued in 1959, this eight-player set from Donruss consists of cards which formed the bottom panel of a box of bubble gum. When cut off the box, cards measure 3-1/2" by 6-1/2", with blank backs. Players are pictured on the cards in paintings done by Dick Perez.

		MT	NR MT	EX
Complete Set:		10.00	7.50	4.00
Common Player:		.60	.45	.25
1	Babe Ruth	1.75	1.25	.70
2	Ted Williams	1.00	.70	.40
3	Lou Gehrig	1.25	.90	.50
4	Johnny Mize	.60	.45	.25
5	Stan Musial	1.00	.70	.40
6	Mickey Mantle	3.00	2.25	1.25
7	Hank Aaron	1.50	1.25	.60
8	Frank Robinson	.90	.70	.35

1986 Donruss

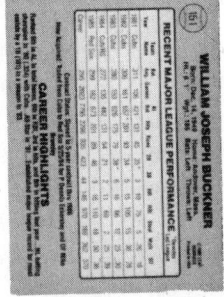

In 1986, Donruss issued a 660-card set which included 653 numbered cards and seven unnumbered checklists. The cards, which measure 2-1/2" by 3-1/2", have fronts that feature blue borders and backs that have black print on blue and white. For the fifth year in a row, the first 26 cards in the set are Diamond Kings. The Rated Rookies subset (card #'s 27-46) appears once again. The cards were distributed with a Hank Aaron puzzle. The complete set price does not include the higher priced variations. In the checklist that follows, (DK) and (RR) refer to the Diamond Kings and Rated Rookies series.

		MT	NR MT	EX
Complete Set:		175.00	125.00	70.00
Common Player:		.06	.05	.02
1	Kirk Gibson (DK)	.30	.25	.12

		MT	NR MT	EX
2	Goose Gossage (DK)	.20	.15	.08
3	Willie McGee (DK)	.15	.11	.06
4	George Bell (DK)	.30	.25	.12
5	Tony Armas (DK)	.10	.08	.04
6	Chili Davis (DK)	.10	.08	.04
7	Cecil Cooper (DK)	.12	.09	.05
8	Mike Boddicker (DK)	.10	.08	.04
9	Davey Lopes (DK)	.10	.08	.04
10	Bill Doran (DK)	.12	.09	.05
11	Bret Saberhagen (DK)	.25	.20	.10
12	Brett Butler (DK)	.10	.08	.04
13	Harold Baines (DK)	.15	.11	.06
14	Mike Davis (DK)	.10	.08	.04
15	Tony Perez (DK)	.15	.11	.06
16	Willie Randolph (DK)	.12	.09	.05
17	Bob Boone (DK)	.10	.08	.04
18	Orel Hershiser (DK)	1.00	.70	.40
19	Johnny Ray (DK)	.12	.09	.05
20	Gary Ward (DK)	.10	.08	.04
21	Rick Mahler (DK)	.08	.06	.03
22	Phil Bradley (DK)	.20	.15	.08
23	Jerry Koosman (DK)	.12	.09	.05
24	Tom Brunansky (DK)	.15	.11	.06
25	Andre Dawson (DK)	.30	.25	.12
26	Dwight Gooden (DK)	1.00	.70	.40
27	*Kal Daniels (RR)(FC)*	4.00	3.00	1.50
28	*Fred McGriff (RR)(FC)*	16.00	12.00	6.50
29	*Cory Snyder (RR)(FC)*	2.25	1.75	.90
30	*Jose Guzman (RR)(FC)*	.30	.25	.12
31	*Ty Gainey (RR)(FC)*	.10	.08	.04
32	*Johnny Abrego (RR)(FC)*	.08	.06	.03
33a	*Andres Galarraga (RR) (no accent mark above "e" in Andres on back)(FC)*	4.00	3.00	1.50
33b	*Andres Galarraga (RR) (accent mark above "e" in Andres on back)(FC)*	5.00	3.75	2.00
34	*Dave Shipanoff (RR)(FC)*	.08	.06	.03
35	*Mark McLemore (RR)(FC)*	.20	.15	.08
36	*Marty Clary (RR)(FC)*	.08	.06	.03
37	*Paul O'Neill (RR)(FC)*	3.00	2.25	1.25
38	*Danny Tartabull (RR)*	.80	.60	.30
39	*Jose Canseco (RR)(FC)*	110.00	82.00	45.00
40	*Juan Nieves (RR)(FC)*	.30	.25	.12
41	*Lance McCullers (RR)(FC)*	.35	.25	.14
42	*Rick Surhoff (RR)(FC)*	.08	.06	.03
43	*Todd Worrell (RR)(FC)*	1.00	.70	.40
44	*Bob Kipper (RR)(FC)*	.20	.15	.08
45	*John Habyan (RR)(FC)*	.15	.11	.06
46	*Mike Woodard (RR)(FC)*	.10	.08	.04
47	Mike Boddicker	.10	.08	.04
48	Robin Yount	.90	.70	.35
49	Lou Whitaker	.30	.25	.12
50	"Oil Can" Boyd	.08	.06	.03
51	Rickey Henderson	1.50	1.25	.70
52	Mike Marshall	.15	.11	.06
53	George Brett	.50	.40	.20
54	Dave Kingman	.15	.11	.06
55	Hubie Brooks	.10	.08	.04
56	*Oddibe McDowell(FC)*	.35	.25	.14
57	Doug DeCinces	.10	.08	.04
58	Britt Burns	.06	.05	.02
59	Ozzie Smith	.15	.11	.06
60	Jose Cruz	.10	.08	.04
61	Mike Schmidt	1.00	.70	.40
62	Pete Rose	.80	.60	.30
63	Steve Garvey	.40	.30	.15
64	Tony Pena	.10	.08	.04
65	Chili Davis	.10	.08	.04
66	Dale Murphy	.60	.45	.25
67	Ryne Sandberg	2.00	1.50	.80
68	Gary Carter	.35	.25	.14
69	Alvin Davis	.30	.25	.12
70	Kent Hrbek	.25	.20	.10
71	George Bell	.30	.25	.12
72	Kirby Puckett	4.50	3.25	1.50
73	Lloyd Moseby	.10	.08	.04
74	Bob Kearney	.06	.05	.02
75	Dwight Gooden	3.00	2.25	1.25
76	Gary Matthews	.10	.08	.04
77	Rick Mahler	.06	.05	.02
78	Benny Distefano	.06	.05	.02
79	Jeff Leonard	.08	.06	.03
80	Kevin McReynolds	.30	.25	.12
81	Ron Oester	.06	.05	.02
82	John Russell	.06	.05	.02
83	Tommy Herr	.10	.08	.04
84	Jerry Mumphrey	.06	.05	.02
85	Ron Romanick	.06	.05	.02
86	Daryl Boston	.08	.06	.03
87	Andre Dawson	.30	.25	.12
88	Eddie Murray	.40	.30	.15
89	Dion James	.08	.06	.03
90	Chet Lemon	.08	.06	.03

		MT	NR MT	EX
91	Bob Stanley	.06	.05	.02
92	Willie Randolph	.10	.08	.04
93	Mike Scioscia	.08	.06	.03
94	Tom Waddell	.06	.05	.02
95	Danny Jackson	.30	.25	.12
96	Mike Davis	.08	.06	.03
97	Mike Fitzgerald	.06	.05	.02
98	Gary Ward	.08	.06	.03
99	Pete O'Brien	.10	.08	.04
100	Bret Saberhagen	.60	.45	.25
101	Alfredo Griffin	.08	.06	.03
102	Brett Butler	.08	.06	.03
103	Ron Guidry	.20	.15	.08
104	Jerry Reuss	.08	.06	.03
105	Jack Morris	.30	.25	.12
106	Rick Dempsey	.08	.06	.03
107	Ray Burris	.06	.05	.02
108	Brian Downing	.10	.08	.04
109	Willie McGee	.15	.11	.06
110	Bill Doran	.10	.08	.04
111	Kent Tekulve	.08	.06	.03
112	Tony Gwynn	.40	.30	.15
113	Marvell Wynne	.06	.05	.02
114	David Green	.06	.05	.02
115	Jim Gantner	.08	.06	.03
116	George Foster	.15	.11	.06
117	Steve Trout	.06	.05	.02
118	Mark Langston	.30	.25	.12
119	Tony Fernandez	.20	.15	.08
120	John Butcher	.06	.05	.02
121	Ron Robinson	.08	.06	.03
122	Dan Spillner	.06	.05	.02
123	Mike Young	.06	.05	.02
124	Paul Molitor	.15	.11	.06
125	Kirk Gibson	.35	.25	.14
126	Ken Griffey	.12	.09	.05
127	Tony Armas	.08	.06	.03
128	*Mariano Duncan*(FC)	.15	.11	.06
129	Mr. Clutch (Pat Tabler)	.08	.06	.03
130	Frank White	.10	.08	.04
131	Carney Lansford	.10	.08	.04
132	Vance Law	.08	.06	.03
133	Dick Schofield	.06	.05	.02
134	Wayne Tolleson	.06	.05	.02
135	Greg Walker	.10	.08	.04
136	Denny Walling	.06	.05	.02
137	Ozzie Virgil	.06	.05	.02
138	Ricky Horton	.08	.06	.03
139	LaMarr Hoyt	.06	.05	.02
140	Wayne Krenchicki	.06	.05	.02
141	Glenn Hubbard	.06	.05	.02
142	Cecilio Guante	.06	.05	.02
143	Mike Krukow	.08	.06	.03
144	Lee Smith	.10	.08	.04
145	Edwin Nunez	.06	.05	.02
146	Dave Stieb	.12	.09	.05
147	Mike Smithson	.06	.05	.02
148	Ken Dixon	.06	.05	.02
149	Danny Darwin	.06	.05	.02
150	Chris Pittaro	.06	.05	.02
151	Bill Buckner	.12	.09	.05
152	Mike Pagliarulo	.20	.15	.08
153	Bill Russell	.08	.06	.03
154	Brook Jacoby	.10	.08	.04
155	Pat Sheridan	.06	.05	.02
156	*Mike Gallego*(FC)	.15	.11	.06
157	Jim Wohlford	.06	.05	.02
158	Gary Pettis	.06	.05	.02
159	Toby Harrah	.08	.06	.03
160	Richard Dotson	.10	.08	.04
161	Bob Knepper	.08	.06	.03
162	Dave Dravecky	.08	.06	.03
163	Greg Gross	.06	.05	.02
164	Eric Davis	3.50	2.75	1.50
165	Gerald Perry	.15	.11	.06
166	Rick Rhoden	.10	.08	.04
167	Keith Moreland	.08	.06	.03
168	Jack Clark	.20	.15	.08
169	Storm Davis	.10	.08	.04
170	Cecil Cooper	.12	.09	.05
171	Alan Trammell	.35	.25	.14
172	Roger Clemens	4.00	3.00	1.50
173	Don Mattingly	6.00	4.50	2.50
174	Pedro Guerrero	.20	.15	.08
175	Willie Wilson	.12	.09	.05
176	Dwayne Murphy	.08	.06	.03
177	Tim Raines	.40	.30	.15
178	Larry Parrish	.10	.08	.04
179	Mike Witt	.10	.08	.04
180	Harold Baines	.15	.11	.06
181	*Vince Coleman*(FC)	2.50	2.00	1.00

		MT	NR MT	EX
182	*Jeff Heathcock*(FC)	.10	.08	.04
183	Steve Carlton	.40	.30	.15
184	Mario Soto	.08	.06	.03
185	Goose Gossage	.20	.15	.08
186	Johnny Ray	.12	.09	.05
187	Dan Gladden	.08	.06	.03
188	Bob Horner	.12	.09	.05
189	Rick Sutcliffe	.12	.09	.05
190	Keith Hernandez	.35	.25	.14
191	Phil Bradley	.20	.15	.08
192	Tom Brunansky	.12	.09	.05
193	Jesse Barfield	.20	.15	.08
194	Frank Viola	.20	.15	.08
195	Willie Upshaw	.08	.06	.03
196	Jim Beattie	.06	.05	.02
197	Darryl Strawberry	3.00	2.25	1.25
198	Ron Cey	.10	.08	.04
199	Steve Bedrosian	.12	.09	.05
200	Steve Kemp	.08	.06	.03
201	Manny Trillo	.08	.06	.03
202	Garry Templeton	.08	.06	.03
203	Dave Parker	.25	.20	.10
204	John Denny	.06	.05	.02
205	Terry Pendleton	.15	.11	.06
206	Terry Puhl	.06	.05	.02
207	Bobby Grich	.10	.08	.04
208	*Ozzie Guillen*(FC)	1.25	.90	.50
209	Jeff Reardon	.12	.09	.05
210	Cal Ripken Jr.	.50	.40	.20
211	Bill Schroeder	.06	.05	.02
212	Dan Petry	.08	.06	.03
213	Jim Rice	.40	.30	.15
214	Dave Righetti	.20	.15	.08
215	Fernando Valenzuela	.35	.25	.14
216	Julio Franco	.12	.09	.05
217	Darryl Motley	.06	.05	.02
218	Dave Collins	.08	.06	.03
219	Tim Wallach	.12	.09	.05
220	George Wright	.06	.05	.02
221	Tommy Dunbar	.06	.05	.02
222	Steve Balboni	.08	.06	.03
223	Jay Howell	.08	.06	.03
224	Joe Carter	.25	.20	.10
225	Ed Whitson	.06	.05	.02
226	Orel Hershiser	1.25	.90	.50
227	Willie Hernandez	.08	.06	.03
228	Lee Lacy	.06	.05	.02
229	Rollie Fingers	.20	.15	.08
230	Bob Boone	.08	.06	.03
231	Joaquin Andujar	.08	.06	.03
232	Craig Reynolds	.06	.05	.02
233	Shane Rawley	.10	.08	.04
234	Eric Show	.08	.06	.03
235	Jose DeLeon	.08	.06	.03
236	*Jose Uribe*(FC)	.25	.20	.10
237	Moose Haas	.06	.05	.02
238	Wally Backman	.08	.06	.03
239	Dennis Eckersley	.12	.09	.05
240	Mike Moore	.06	.05	.02
241	Damaso Garcia	.06	.05	.02
242	Tim Teufel	.06	.05	.02
243	Dave Concepcion	.12	.09	.05
244	Floyd Bannister	.10	.08	.04
245	Fred Lynn	.20	.15	.08
246	Charlie Moore	.06	.05	.02
247	Walt Terrell	.08	.06	.03
248	Dave Winfield	.40	.30	.15
249	Dwight Evans	.12	.09	.05
250	*Dennis Powell*(FC)	.10	.08	.04
251	Andre Thornton	.10	.08	.04
252	Onix Concepcion	.06	.05	.02
253	Mike Heath	.06	.05	.02
254a	David Palmer (2B on front)	.06	.05	.02
254b	David Palmer (P on front)	1.00	.70	.40
255	Donnie Moore	.06	.05	.02
256	Curtis Wilkerson	.06	.05	.02
257	Julio Cruz	.06	.05	.02
258	Nolan Ryan	1.50	1.25	.60
259	Jeff Stone	.06	.05	.02
260a	John Tudor (1981 Games is .18)	.10	.08	.04
260b	John Tudor (1981 Games is 18)	1.00	.70	.40
261	Mark Thurmond	.06	.05	.02
262	Jay Tibbs	.06	.05	.02
263	Rafael Ramirez	.06	.05	.02
264	Larry McWilliams	.06	.05	.02
265	Mark Davis	.06	.05	.02
266	Bob Dernier	.06	.05	.02
267	Matt Young	.06	.05	.02
268	Jim Clancy	.08	.06	.03
269	Mickey Hatcher	.06	.05	.02
270	Sammy Stewart	.06	.05	.02

#	Player	MT	NR MT	EX
271	Bob Gibson	.06	.05	.02
272	Nelson Simmons	.06	.05	.02
273	Rich Gedman	.10	.08	.04
274	Butch Wynegar	.06	.05	.02
275	Ken Howell	.06	.05	.02
276	Mel Hall	.08	.06	.03
277	Jim Sundberg	.08	.06	.03
278	Chris Codiroli	.06	.05	.02
279	*Herman Winningham*(FC)	.15	.11	.06
280	Rod Carew	.40	.30	.15
281	Don Slaught	.06	.05	.02
282	Scott Fletcher	.08	.06	.03
283	Bill Dawley	.06	.05	.02
284	Andy Hawkins	.06	.05	.02
285	Glenn Wilson	.08	.06	.03
286	Nick Esasky	.08	.06	.03
287	Claudell Washington	.08	.06	.03
288	Lee Mazzilli	.08	.06	.03
289	Jody Davis	.10	.08	.04
290	Darrell Porter	.08	.06	.03
291	Scott McGregor	.08	.06	.03
292	Ted Simmons	.12	.09	.05
293	Aurelio Lopez	.06	.05	.02
294	Marty Barrett	.10	.08	.04
295	Dale Berra	.06	.05	.02
296	Greg Brock	.08	.06	.03
297	Charlie Leibrandt	.08	.06	.03
298	Bill Krueger	.06	.05	.02
299	Bryn Smith	.06	.05	.02
300	Burt Hooton	.08	.06	.03
301	*Stu Cliburn*(FC)	.12	.09	.05
302	Luis Salazar	.06	.05	.02
303	Ken Dayley	.06	.05	.02
304	Frank DiPino	.06	.05	.02
305	Von Hayes	.10	.08	.04
306a	Gary Redus (1983 2B is .20)	.08	.06	.03
306b	Gary Redus (1983 2B is 20)	1.00	.70	.40
307	Craig Lefferts	.06	.05	.02
308	Sam Khalifa	.06	.05	.02
309	Scott Garrelts	.06	.05	.02
310	Rick Cerone	.06	.05	.02
311	Shawon Dunston	.20	.15	.08
312	Howard Johnson	.12	.09	.05
313	Jim Presley	.15	.11	.06
314	Gary Gaetti	.25	.20	.10
315	Luis Leal	.06	.05	.02
316	Mark Salas	.06	.05	.02
317	Bill Caudill	.06	.05	.02
318	Dave Henderson	.10	.08	.04
319	Rafael Santana	.06	.05	.02
320	Leon Durham	.08	.06	.03
321	Bruce Sutter	.15	.11	.06
322	Jason Thompson	.06	.05	.02
323	Bob Brenly	.06	.05	.02
324	Carmelo Martinez	.08	.06	.03
325	Eddie Milner	.06	.05	.02
326	Juan Samuel	.15	.11	.06
327	Tom Nieto	.06	.05	.02
328	Dave Smith	.08	.06	.03
329	*Urbano Lugo*(FC)	.08	.06	.03
330	Joel Skinner	.06	.05	.02
331	Bill Gullickson	.06	.05	.02
332	Floyd Rayford	.06	.05	.02
333	Ben Oglivie	.08	.06	.03
334	Lance Parrish	.30	.25	.12
335	Jackie Gutierrez	.06	.05	.02
336	Dennis Rasmussen	.12	.09	.05
337	Terry Whitfield	.06	.05	.02
338	Neal Heaton	.06	.05	.02
339	Jorge Orta	.06	.05	.02
340	Donnie Hill	.06	.05	.02
341	Joe Hesketh	.06	.05	.02
342	Charlie Hough	.10	.08	.04
343	Dave Rozema	.06	.05	.02
344	Greg Pryor	.06	.05	.02
345	*Mickey Tettleton*(FC)	.80	.60	.30
346	George Vukovich	.06	.05	.02
347	Don Baylor	.12	.09	.05
348	Carlos Diaz	.06	.05	.02
349	Barbaro Garbey	.06	.05	.02
350	Larry Sheets	.12	.09	.05
351	*Ted Higuera*(FC)	1.25	.90	.50
352	Juan Beniquez	.06	.05	.02
353	Bob Forsch	.08	.06	.03
354	Mark Bailey	.06	.05	.02
355	Larry Andersen	.06	.05	.02
356	Terry Kennedy	.08	.06	.03
357	Don Robinson	.08	.06	.03
358	Jim Gott	.06	.05	.02
359	*Earnest Riles*(FC)	.20	.15	.08
360	*John Christensen*(FC)	.10	.08	.04
361	Ray Fontenot	.06	.05	.02
362	Spike Owen	.06	.05	.02
363	Jim Acker	.06	.05	.02
364a	Ron Davis (last line in highlights ends with "...in May.")	.08	.06	.03
364b	Ron Davis (last line in highlights ends with "...relievers (9).")	1.00	.70	.40
365	Tom Hume	.06	.05	.02
366	Carlton Fisk	.25	.20	.10
367	Nate Snell	.06	.05	.02
368	Rick Manning	.06	.05	.02
369	Darrell Evans	.15	.11	.06
370	Ron Hassey	.06	.05	.02
371	Wade Boggs	2.50	2.00	1.00
372	Rick Honeycutt	.06	.05	.02
373	Chris Bando	.06	.05	.02
374	Bud Black	.06	.05	.02
375	Steve Henderson	.06	.05	.02
376	Charlie Lea	.06	.05	.02
377	Reggie Jackson	.40	.30	.15
378	Dave Schmidt	.06	.05	.02
379	Bob James	.06	.05	.02
380	Glenn Davis(FC)	4.00	3.00	1.50
381	Tim Corcoran	.06	.05	.02
382	Danny Cox	.10	.08	.04
383	Tim Flannery	.06	.05	.02
384	Tom Browning	.20	.15	.08
385	Rick Camp	.06	.05	.02
386	Jim Morrison	.06	.05	.02
387	Dave LaPoint	.08	.06	.03
388	Davey Lopes	.08	.06	.03
389	Al Cowens	.06	.05	.02
390	Doyle Alexander	.10	.08	.04
391	Tim Laudner	.06	.05	.02
392	Don Aase	.06	.05	.02
393	Jaime Cocanower	.06	.05	.02
394	Randy O'Neal(FC)	.08	.06	.03
395	Mike Easler	.08	.06	.03
396	Scott Bradley	.06	.05	.02
397	Tom Niedenfuer	.08	.06	.03
398	Jerry Willard	.06	.05	.02
399	Lonnie Smith	.08	.06	.03
400	Bruce Bochte	.06	.05	.02
401	Terry Francona	.06	.05	.02
402	Jim Slaton	.06	.05	.02
403	Bill Stein	.06	.05	.02
404	Tim Hulett	.06	.05	.02
405	Alan Ashby	.06	.05	.02
406	Tim Stoddard	.06	.05	.02
407	Garry Maddox	.08	.06	.03
408	Ted Power	.06	.05	.02
409	Len Barker	.08	.06	.03
410	Denny Gonzalez	.06	.05	.02
411	George Frazier	.06	.05	.02
412	Andy Van Slyke	.15	.11	.06
413	Jim Dwyer	.06	.05	.02
414	Paul Householder	.06	.05	.02
415	Alejandro Sanchez	.06	.05	.02
416	Steve Crawford	.06	.05	.02
417	Dan Pasqua	.15	.11	.06
418	Enos Cabell	.06	.05	.02
419	Mike Jones	.06	.05	.02
420	Steve Kiefer	.06	.05	.02
421	*Tim Burke*(FC)	.30	.25	.12
422	Mike Mason	.06	.05	.02
423	Ruppert Jones	.06	.05	.02
424	Jerry Hairston	.06	.05	.02
425	Tito Landrum	.06	.05	.02
426	Jeff Calhoun	.06	.05	.02
427	*Don Carman*(FC)	.30	.25	.12
428	Tony Perez	.15	.11	.06
429	Jerry Davis	.06	.05	.02
430	Bob Walk	.06	.05	.02
431	Brad Wellman	.06	.05	.02
432	Terry Forster	.08	.06	.03
433	Billy Hatcher	.10	.08	.04
434	Clint Hurdle	.06	.05	.02
435	*Ivan Calderon*(FC)	1.00	.70	.40
436	Pete Filson	.06	.05	.02
437	Tom Henke	.08	.06	.03
438	Dave Engle	.06	.05	.02
439	Tom Filer	.06	.05	.02
440	Gorman Thomas	.10	.08	.04
441	*Rick Aguilera*(FC)	.25	.20	.10
442	Scott Sanderson	.06	.05	.02
443	Jeff Dedmon	.06	.05	.02
444	*Joe Orsulak*(FC)	.15	.11	.06
445	Atlee Hammaker	.06	.05	.02
446	Jerry Royster	.06	.05	.02
447	Buddy Bell	.10	.08	.04
448	Dave Rucker	.06	.05	.02

#	Player	MT	NR MT	EX
449	Ivan DeJesus	.06	.05	.02
450	Jim Pankovits	.06	.05	.02
451	Jerry Narron	.06	.05	.02
452	Bryan Little	.06	.05	.02
453	Gary Lucas	.06	.05	.02
454	Dennis Martinez	.08	.06	.03
455	Ed Romero	.06	.05	.02
456	*Bob Melvin*(FC)	.12	.09	.05
457	Glenn Hoffman	.06	.05	.02
458	Bob Shirley	.06	.05	.02
459	Bob Welch	.12	.09	.05
460	Carmen Castillo	.06	.05	.02
461	Dave Leeper	.06	.05	.02
462	*Tim Birtsas*(FC)	.12	.09	.05
463	Randy St. Claire	.06	.05	.02
464	Chris Welsh	.06	.05	.02
465	Greg Harris	.06	.05	.02
466	Lynn Jones	.06	.05	.02
467	Dusty Baker	.08	.06	.03
468	Roy Smith	.06	.05	.02
469	Andre Robertson	.06	.05	.02
470	Ken Landreaux	.06	.05	.02
471	Dave Bergman	.06	.05	.02
472	Gary Roenicke	.06	.05	.02
473	Pete Vuckovich	.08	.06	.03
474	*Kirk McCaskill*(FC)	.35	.25	.14
475	Jeff Lahti	.06	.05	.02
476	Mike Scott	.20	.15	.08
477	*Darren Daulton*(FC)	.12	.09	.05
478	Graig Nettles	.15	.11	.06
479	Bill Almon	.06	.05	.02
480	Greg Minton	.06	.05	.02
481	Randy Ready(FC)	.10	.08	.04
482	*Lenny Dykstra*(FC)	4.00	3.00	1.50
483	Thad Bosley	.06	.05	.02
484	*Harold Reynolds*(FC)	.60	.45	.25
485	Al Oliver	.12	.09	.05
486	Roy Smalley	.06	.05	.02
487	John Franco	.15	.11	.06
488	Juan Agosto	.06	.05	.02
489	Al Pardo	.06	.05	.02
490	*Bill Wegman*(FC)	.25	.20	.10
491	Frank Tanana	.10	.08	.04
492	*Brian Fisher*(FC)	.30	.25	.12
493	Mark Clear	.06	.05	.02
494	Len Matuszek	.06	.05	.02
495	Ramon Romero	.06	.05	.02
496	John Wathan	.08	.06	.03
497	Rob Picciolo	.06	.05	.02
498	U.L. Washington	.06	.05	.02
499	John Candelaria	.10	.08	.04
500	Duane Walker	.06	.05	.02
501	Gene Nelson	.06	.05	.02
502	John Mizerock	.06	.05	.02
503	Luis Aguayo	.06	.05	.02
504	Kurt Kepshire	.06	.05	.02
505	Ed Wojna	.06	.05	.02
506	Joe Price	.06	.05	.02
507	*Milt Thompson*(FC)	.30	.25	.12
508	Junior Ortiz	.06	.05	.02
509	Vida Blue	.10	.08	.04
510	Steve Engel	.06	.05	.02
511	Karl Best	.06	.05	.02
512	*Cecil Fielder*(FC)	15.00	11.00	6.00
513	Frank Eufemia	.06	.05	.02
514	Tippy Martinez	.06	.05	.02
515	*Billy Robidoux*(FC)	.10	.08	.04
516	Bill Scherrer	.06	.05	.02
517	Bruce Hurst	.12	.09	.05
518	Rich Bordi	.06	.05	.02
519	Steve Yeager	.06	.05	.02
520	Tony Bernazard	.06	.05	.02
521	Hal McRae	.10	.08	.04
522	Jose Rijo	.10	.08	.04
523	*Mitch Webster*(FC)	.25	.20	.10
524	*Jack Howell*(FC)	.35	.25	.14
525	Alan Bannister	.06	.05	.02
526	Ron Kittle	.10	.08	.04
527	Phil Garner	.08	.06	.03
528	Kurt Bevacqua	.06	.05	.02
529	Kevin Gross	.08	.06	.03
530	Bo Diaz	.08	.06	.03
531	Ken Oberkfell	.06	.05	.02
532	Rick Reuschel	.10	.08	.04
533	Ron Meridith	.06	.05	.02
534	Steve Braun	.06	.05	.02
535	Wayne Gross	.06	.05	.02
536	Ray Searage	.06	.05	.02
537	Tom Brookens	.06	.05	.02
538	Al Nipper	.06	.05	.02
539	Billy Sample	.06	.05	.02
540	Steve Sax	.20	.15	.08
541	Dan Quisenberry	.10	.08	.04
542	Tony Phillips	.06	.05	.02
543	*Floyd Youmans*(FC)	.30	.25	.12
544	*Steve Buechele*(FC)	.25	.20	.10
545	Craig Gerber	.06	.05	.02
546	Joe DeSa	.06	.05	.02
547	Brian Harper	.06	.05	.02
548	Kevin Bass	.10	.08	.04
549	Tom Foley	.06	.05	.02
550	Dave Van Gorder	.06	.05	.02
551	Bruce Bochy	.06	.05	.02
552	R.J. Reynolds	.08	.06	.03
553	*Chris Brown*(FC)	.20	.15	.08
554	Bruce Benedict	.06	.05	.02
555	Warren Brusstar	.06	.05	.02
556	Danny Heep	.06	.05	.02
557	Darnell Coles	.08	.06	.03
558	Greg Gagne	.08	.06	.03
559	Ernie Whitt	.08	.06	.03
560	Ron Washington	.06	.05	.02
561	Jimmy Key	.15	.11	.06
562	Billy Swift(FC)	.15	.11	.06
563	Ron Darling	.15	.11	.06
564	Dick Ruthven	.06	.05	.02
565	Zane Smith(FC)	.15	.11	.06
566	Sid Bream	.10	.08	.04
567a	Joel Youngblood (P on front)	.08	.06	.03
567b	Joel Youngblood (IF on front)	1.00	.70	.40
568	Mario Ramirez	.06	.05	.02
569	Tom Runnells	.06	.05	.02
570	Rick Schu	.06	.05	.02
571	Bill Campbell	.06	.05	.02
572	Dickie Thon	.08	.06	.03
573	Al Holland	.06	.05	.02
574	Reid Nichols	.06	.05	.02
575	Bert Roberge	.06	.05	.02
576	Mike Flanagan	.10	.08	.04
577	Tim Leary(FC)	.35	.25	.14
578	Mike Laga	.06	.05	.02
579	Steve Lyons	.06	.05	.02
580	Phil Niekro	.30	.25	.12
581	Gilberto Reyes	.06	.05	.02
582	Jamie Easterly	.06	.05	.02
583	Mark Gubicza	.12	.09	.05
584	*Stan Javier*(FC)	.15	.11	.06
585	Bill Laskey	.06	.05	.02
586	Jeff Russell	.06	.05	.02
587	Dickie Noles	.06	.05	.02
588	Steve Farr	.08	.06	.03
589	*Steve Ontiveros*(FC)	.15	.11	.06
590	Mike Hargrove	.06	.05	.02
591	Marty Bystrom	.06	.05	.02
592	Franklin Stubbs	.08	.06	.03
593	Larry Herndon	.08	.06	.03
594	Bill Swaggerty	.06	.05	.02
595	Carlos Ponce	.06	.05	.02
596	*Pat Perry*(FC)	.12	.09	.05
597	Ray Knight	.08	.06	.03
598	*Steve Lombardozzi*(FC)	.15	.11	.06
599	Brad Havens	.06	.05	.02
600	*Pat Clements*(FC)	.12	.09	.05
601	Joe Niekro	.12	.09	.05
602	Hank Aaron Puzzle Card	.06	.05	.02
603	*Dwayne Henry*(FC)	.10	.08	.04
604	Mookie Wilson	.10	.08	.04
605	Buddy Biancalana	.06	.05	.02
606	Rance Mulliniks	.06	.05	.02
607	Alan Wiggins	.06	.05	.02
608	Joe Cowley	.06	.05	.02
609a	Tom Seaver (green stripes around name)	.40	.30	.15
609b	Tom Seaver (yellow stripes around name)	2.00	1.50	.80
610	Neil Allen	.06	.05	.02
611	Don Sutton	.30	.25	.12
612	*Fred Toliver*(FC)	.15	.11	.06
613	Jay Baller	.06	.05	.02
614	Marc Sullivan	.06	.05	.02
615	John Grubb	.06	.05	.02
616	Bruce Kison	.06	.05	.02
617	Bill Madlock	.12	.09	.05
618	Chris Chambliss	.08	.06	.03
619	Dave Stewart	.12	.09	.05
620	Tim Lollar	.06	.05	.02
621	Gary Lavelle	.06	.05	.02
622	Charles Hudson	.06	.05	.02
623	*Joel Davis*(FC)	.08	.06	.03
624	*Joe Johnson*(FC)	.08	.06	.03
625	Sid Fernandez	.12	.09	.05
626	Dennis Lamp	.06	.05	.02

		MT	NR MT	EX
627	Terry Harper	.06	.05	.02
628	Jack Lazorko	.06	.05	.02
629	Roger McDowell(FC)	.60	.45	.25
630	Mark Funderburk	.06	.05	.02
631	Ed Lynch	.06	.05	.02
632	Rudy Law	.06	.05	.02
633	Roger Mason(FC)	.08	.06	.03
634	Mike Felder(FC)	.15	.11	.06
635	Ken Schrom	.06	.05	.02
636	Bob Ojeda	.08	.06	.03
637	Ed Vande Berg	.06	.05	.02
638	Bobby Meacham	.06	.05	.02
639	Cliff Johnson	.06	.05	.02
640	Garth Iorg	.06	.05	.02
641	Dan Driessen	.08	.06	.03
642	Mike Brown	.06	.05	.02
643	John Shelby	.06	.05	.02
644	Ty-Breaking Hit (Pete Rose)	.50	.40	.20
645	Knuckle Brothers (Joe Niekro, Phil Niekro)	.15	.11	.06
646	Jesse Orosco	.08	.06	.03
647	Billy Beane(FC)	.06	.05	.02
648	Cesar Cedeno	.10	.08	.04
649	Bert Blyleven	.15	.11	.06
650	Max Venable	.06	.05	.02
651	Fleet Feet (Vince Coleman, Willie McGee)	.35	.25	.14
652	Calvin Schiraldi	.08	.06	.03
653	King of Kings (Pete Rose)	.70	.50	.30
----	Checklist 1-26 DK	.06	.05	.02
---a	Checklist 27-130 (45 is Beane)	.08	.06	.03
---b	Checklist 27-130 (45 is Habyan)	.60	.45	.25
----	Checklist 131-234	.06	.05	.02
----	Checklist 235-338	.06	.05	.02
----	Checklist 339-442	.06	.05	.02
----	Checklist 443-546	.06	.05	.02
----	Checklist 547-653	.06	.05	.02

		MT	NR MT	EX
15	Dave Winfield	.25	.20	.10
16	Jim Rice	.12	.09	.05
17	Carlton Fisk	.15	.11	.06
18	Jack Morris	.15	.11	.06
19	Jose Cruz	.09	.07	.04
20	Tim Raines	.25	.20	.10
21	Nolan Ryan	.50	.40	.20
22	Tony Pena	.09	.07	.04
23	Jack Clark	.15	.11	.06
24	Dave Parker	.15	.11	.06
25	Tim Wallach	.12	.09	.05
26	Ozzie Virgil	.09	.07	.04
27	Fernando Valenzuela	.12	.09	.05
28	Dwight Gooden	.60	.45	.25
29	Glenn Wilson	.09	.07	.04
30	Garry Templeton	.09	.07	.04
31	Goose Gossage	.12	.09	.05
32	Ryne Sandberg	.25	.20	.10
33	Jeff Reardon	.12	.09	.05
34	Pete Rose	.35	.25	.14
35	Scott Garrelts	.09	.07	.04
36	Willie McGee	.12	.09	.05
37	Ron Darling	.12	.09	.05
38	Dick Williams	.09	.07	.04
39	Paul Molitor	.15	.11	.06
40	Damaso Garcia	.09	.07	.04
41	Phil Bradley	.12	.09	.05
42	Dan Petry	.09	.07	.04
43	Willie Hernandez	.09	.07	.04
44	Tom Brunansky	.12	.09	.05
45	Alan Trammell	.20	.15	.08
46	Donnie Moore	.09	.07	.04
47	Wade Boggs	.90	.70	.35
48	Ernie Whitt	.09	.07	.04
49	Harold Baines	.15	.11	.06
50	Don Mattingly	2.00	1.50	.80
51	Gary Ward	.09	.07	.04
52	Bert Blyleven	.12	.09	.05
53	Jimmy Key	.12	.09	.05
54	Cecil Cooper	.12	.09	.05
55	Dave Stieb	.12	.09	.05
56	Rich Gedman	.09	.07	.04
57	Jay Howell	.09	.07	.04
58	Sparky Anderson	.09	.07	.04
59	Minneapolis Metrodome	.09	.07	.04
----	Checklist	.09	.07	.04

1986 Donruss All-Stars

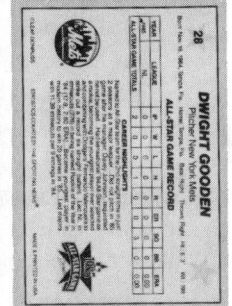

Issued in conjunction with the 1986 Donruss Pop-Ups set, the Donruss All-Stars set consists of 60 cards that measure 3-1/2" by 5". Fifty-nine players involved in the 1985 All-Star game plus an unnumbered checklist comprise the set. The card fronts have the same blue border found on the regular 1986 Donruss issue. Retail packs included one Pop-up card, three All-Star cards and one Hank Aaron puzzle card.

		MT	NR MT	EX
Complete Set:		6.00	4.50	2.50
Common Player:		.09	.07	.04
1	Tony Gwynn	.30	.25	.12
2	Tommy Herr	.09	.07	.04
3	Steve Garvey	.30	.25	.12
4	Dale Murphy	.40	.30	.15
5	Darryl Strawberry	.50	.40	.20
6	Graig Nettles	.12	.09	.05
7	Terry Kennedy	.09	.07	.04
8	Ozzie Smith	.15	.11	.06
9	LaMarr Hoyt	.09	.07	.04
10	Rickey Henderson	.50	.40	.20
11	Lou Whitaker	.15	.11	.06
12	George Brett	.40	.30	.15
13	Eddie Murray	.12	.09	.05
14	Cal Ripken, Jr.	.35	.25	.14

1986 Donruss Box Panels

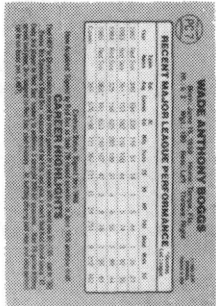

For the second year in a row, Donruss placed baseball cards on the bottom of their wax and cello pack boxes. The cards, which come four to a panel, are the standard 2-1/2" by 3-1/2" in size. With numbering that begins where Donruss left off in 1985, cards PC 4 through PC 6 were found on boxes of regular Donruss issue wax packs. Cards PC 7 through PC 9 were found on boxes of the 1986 All-Star/Pop-up packs. An unnumbered Hank Aaron puzzle card was included on each box.

		MT	NR MT	EX
Complete Panel Set:		5.00	3.75	2.00
Complete Singles Set:		3.00	2.25	1.25
Common Single Player:		.15	.11	.06
	Panel	1.00	.70	.40
4	Kirk Gibson	.35	.25	.14
5	Willie Hernandez	.15	.11	.06

		MT	NR MT	EX
6	Doug DeCinces	.15	.11	.06
----	Aaron Puzzle Card	.04	.03	.02
	Panel	4.00	3.00	1.50
7	Wade Boggs	2.00	1.50	.80
8	Lee Smith	.15	.11	.06
9	Cecil Cooper	.20	.15	.08
----	Aaron Puzzle Card	.04	.03	.02

1986 Donruss Diamond Kings Supers

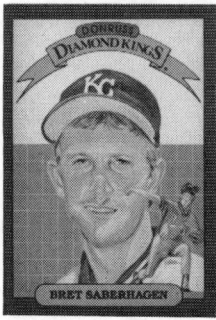
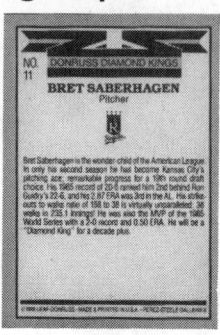

Donruss produced a set of giant-size Diamond Kings in 1986 for the second year in a row. The cards, which measure 4-11/6" by 6-3/4", are enlarged versions of the 26 Diamond Kings cards found in the regular 1986 Donruss set. Featuring the artwork of Dick Perez, the set consists of 28 cards - 26 DKs, an unnumbered checklist and an unnumbered Pete Rose "King of Kings" card.

		MT	NR MT	EX
	Complete Set:	10.00	7.50	4.00
	Common Player:	.20	.15	.08
1	Kirk Gibson	.50	.40	.20
2	Goose Gossage	.30	.25	.12
3	Willie McGee	.30	.25	.12
4	George Bell	.30	.25	.12
5	Tony Armas	.20	.15	.08
6	Chili Davis	.20	.15	.08
7	Cecil Cooper	.25	.20	.10
8	Mike Boddicker	.20	.15	.08
9	Davey Lopes	.20	.15	.08
10	Bill Doran	.25	.20	.10
11	Bret Saberhagen	.70	.50	.30
12	Brett Butler	.20	.15	.08
13	Harold Baines	.30	.25	.12
14	Mike Davis	.20	.15	.08
15	Tony Perez	.25	.20	.10
16	Willie Randolph	.25	.20	.10
18	Orel Hershiser	.70	.50	.30
19	Johnny Ray	.25	.20	.10
20	Gary Ward	.20	.15	.08
21	Rick Mahler	.20	.15	.08
22	Phil Bradley	.30	.25	.12
23	Jerry Koosman	.20	.15	.08
24	Tom Brunansky	.25	.20	.10
25	Andre Dawson	.35	.25	.14
26	Dwight Gooden	1.50	1.25	.60
----	Checklist	.15	.11	.06
----	King of Kings (Pete Rose)	1.50	1.25	.60

1986 Donruss Highlights

Donruss, for the second year in a row, issued a 56-card highlights set which featured cards of the A.L. and N.L. Player of the Month plus significant events that took place during the 1986 season. The cards, which measure 2-1/2" by 3-1/2" in size, are similar in design to the regular 1986 Donruss set but have a gold border instead of blue. A "Highlights" logo appears in the lower left corner of each card front.

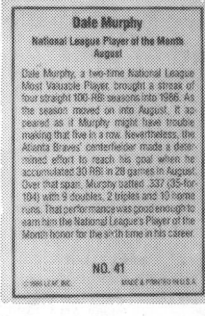

The card backs are designed on a vertical format and feature black print on a yellow background. As in 1985, the set includes Donruss' picks for the Rookies of the Year awards. A new feature was three cards honoring the 1986 Hall of Fame inductees. The set, available only through hobby dealers, was issued in a specially designed box.

		MT	NR MT	EX
	Complete Set:	10.00	7.50	4.00
	Common Player:	.10	.08	.04
1	Homers In First At-Bat (Will Clark)	2.00	1.50	.80
2	Oakland Milestone For Strikeouts (Jose Rijo)	.10	.08	.04
3	Royals' All-Time Hit Man (George Brett)	.20	.15	.08
4	Phillies RBI Leader (Mike Schmidt)	.30	.25	.12
5	KKKKKKKKKKKKKKKKKKKKKK (Roger Clemens)	.75	.55	.20
6	A.L. Pitcher of the Month-April (Roger Clemens)	.50	.40	.20
7	A.L. Player of the Month-April (Kirby Puckett)	.50	.40	.20
8	N.L. Pitcher of the Month-April (Dwight Gooden)	.50	.40	.20
9	N.L. Player of the Month-April (Johnny Ray)	.10	.08	.04
10	Eclipses Mantle HR Record (Reggie Jackson)	.25	.20	.10
11	First Five Hit Game of Career (Wade Boggs)	.50	.40	.20
12	A.L. Pitcher of the Month-May (Don Aase)	.10	.08	.04
13	A.L. Player of the Month-May (Wade Boggs)	.50	.40	.20
14	N.L. Pitcher of the Month-May (Jeff Reardon)	.15	.11	.06
15	N.L. Player of the Month-May (Hubie Brooks)	.10	.08	.04
16	Notches 300th Career Win (Don Sutton)	.10	.08	.04
17	Starts Season 14-0 (Roger Clemens)	.50	.40	.20
18	A.L. Pitcher of the Month-June (Roger Clemens)	.50	.40	.20
19	A.L. Player of the Month-June (Kent Hrbek)	.10	.08	.04
20	N.L. Pitcher of the Month-June (Rick Rhoden)	.10	.08	.04
21	N.L. Player of the Month-June (Kevin Bass)	.10	.08	.04
22	Blasts 4 HRS in 1 Game (Bob Horner)	.10	.08	.04
23	Starting All Star Rookie (Wally Joyner)	.50	.40	.20
24	Starts 3rd Straight All Star Game (Darryl Strawberry)	.25	.20	.10
25	Ties All Star Game Record (Fernando Valenzuela)	.10	.08	.04
26	All Star Game MVP (Roger Clemens)	.50	.40	.20
27	A.L. Pitcher of the Month-July (Jack Morris)	.10	.08	.04
28	A.L. Player of the Month-July (Scott Fletcher)	.10	.08	.04
29	N.L. Pitcher of the Month-July (Todd Worrell)	.25	.20	.10
30	N.L. PLayer of the Month-July (Eric Davis)	.40	.30	.15

		MT	NR MT	EX
31	Records 3000th Strikeout (Bert Blyleven) .15		.11	.06
32	1986 Hall of Fame Inductee (Bobby Doerr) .15		.11	.06
33	1986 Hall of Fame Inductee (Ernie Lombardi) .15		.11	.06
34	1986 Hall of Fame Inductee (Willie McCovey) .20		.15	.08
35	Notches 4000th K (Steve Carlton) .25		.20	.10
36	Surpasses DiMaggio Record (Mike Schmidt) .40		.30	.15
37	Records 3rd "Quadruple Double" (Juan Samuel) .10		.08	.04
38	A.L. Pitcher of the Month-August (Mike Witt) .10		.08	.04
39	A.L. Player of the Month-August (Doug DeCinces) .10		.08	.04
40	N.L. Pitcher of the Month-August (Bill Gullickson) .10		.08	.04
41	N.L. Player of the Month-August (Dale Murphy) .20		.15	.08
42	Sets Tribe Offensive Record (Joe Carter) .25		.20	.10
43	Longest HR In Royals Stadium (Bo Jackson) 2.00		1.50	.80
44	Majors 1st No-Hitter In 2 Years (Joe Cowley) .10		.08	.04
45	Sets M.L. Strikeout Record (Jim Deshaies) .15		.11	.06
46	No Hitter Clinches Division (Mike Scott) .10		.08	.04
47	A.L. Pitcher of the Month-September (Bruce Hurst) .10		.08	.04
48	A.L. Player of the Month-September (Don Mattingly) 1.00		.70	.40
49	N.L. Pitcher of the Month-September (Mike Krukow) .10		.08	.04
50	N.L. Player of the Month-September (Steve Sax) .10		.08	.04
51	A.L. Record For Steals By A Rookie (John Cangelosi) .10		.08	.04
52	Shatters M.L. Save Mark (Dave Righetti) .10		.08	.04
53	Yankee Record For Hits & Doubles (Don Mattingly) 1.00		.70	.40
54	Donruss N.L. Rookie of the Year (Todd Worrell) .25		.20	.10
55	Donruss A.L. Rookie of the Year (Jose Canseco) 3.00		2.25	1.25
56	Highlight Checklist .10		.08	.04

1986 Donruss Pop-Ups

Issued in conjunction with the 1986 Donruss All-Stars set, the Donruss Pop-Ups (18 unnumbered cards) feature the 1985 All-Star Game starting lineups. The cards, which measure 2-1/2" by 5", are die-cut and fold out to form a three-dimensional stand-up card. The background for the cards is the Minneapolis Metrodome, site of the 1985 All-Star Game. Retail packs included one Pop-Up card, three All-Star cards and one Hank Aaron puzzle card.

		MT	NR MT	EX
	Complete Set:	6.00	4.50	2.50
	Common Player:	.20	.15	.08
(1)	George Brett	.60	.45	.25
(2)	Carlton Fisk	.30	.25	.12
(3)	Steve Garvey	.20	.15	.08
(4)	Tony Gwynn	.50	.40	.20
(5)	Rickey Henderson	.70	.50	.30
(6)	Tommy Herr	.20	.15	.08
(7)	LaMarr Hoyt	.20	.15	.08
(8)	Terry Kennedy	.20	.15	.08
(9)	Jack Morris	.20	.15	.08
(10)	Dale Murphy	.30	.25	.12
(11)	Eddie Murray	.30	.25	.12
(12)	Graig Nettles	.20	.15	.08
(13)	Jim Rice	.20	.15	.08
(14)	Cal Ripken Jr.	.50	.40	.20
(15)	Ozzie Smith	.30	.25	.12
(16)	Darryl Strawberry	.70	.50	.30
(17)	Lou Whitaker	.30	.25	.12
(18)	Dave Winfield	.30	.25	.12

1986 Donruss Rookies

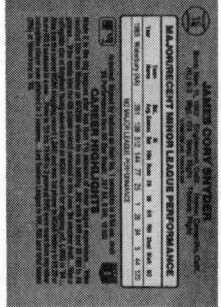

Entitled "The Rookies," this 56-card set includes the top 55 rookies of 1986 plus an unnumbered checklist. The cards, which measure 2-1/2" by 3-1/2", are similar to the format used for the 1986 Donruss regular issue, except that the borders are green rather than blue. Several of the rookies who had cards in the regular 1986 Donruss set appear again in "The Rookies" set. The sets, which were only available through hobby dealers, came in a specially designed box.

		MT	NR MT	EX
	Complete Set:	60.00	45.00	25.00
	Common Player:	.15	.11	.06
1	Wally Joyner(FC)	3.25	2.50	1.25
2	Tracy Jones(FC)	.50	.40	.20
3	Allan Anderson(FC)	.40	.30	.15
4	Ed Correa(FC)	.25	.20	.10
5	Reggie Williams	.20	.15	.08
6	Charlie Kerfeld(FC)	.15	.11	.06
7	Andres Galarraga(FC)	.80	.60	.30
8	Bob Tewksbury(FC)	.15	.11	.06
9	Al Newman	.15	.11	.06
10	Andres Thomas(FC)	.40	.30	.15
11	Barry Bonds(FC)	7.00	5.35	2.75
12	Juan Nieves	.15	.11	.06
13	Mark Eichhorn(FC)	.25	.20	.10
14	Dan Plesac(FC)	.40	.30	.15
15	Cory Snyder	1.00	.70	.40
16	Kelly Gruber	3.50	2.75	1.50
17	Kevin Mitchell(FC)	8.00	6.00	3.25
18	Steve Lombardozzi	.15	.11	.06
19	Mitch Williams	.60	.45	.25
20	John Cerutti(FC)	.25	.20	.10
21	Todd Worrell	.50	.40	.20
22	Jose Canseco	15.00	11.00	6.00
23	Pete Incaviglia(FC)	.80	.60	.30
24	Jose Guzman	.25	.20	.10
25	Scott Bailes(FC)	.25	.20	.10
26	Greg Mathews(FC)	.25	.20	.10
27	Eric King(FC)	.20	.15	.08
28	Paul Assenmacher(FC)	.20	.15	.08
29	Jeff Sellers	.25	.20	.10
30	Bobby Bonilla(FC)	6.00	4.50	2.50
31	Doug Drabek(FC)	1.25	.90	.50
32	Will Clark(FC)	15.00	11.00	6.00
33	Bip Roberts	.15	.11	.06

		MT	NR MT	EX
34	Jim Deshaies(FC)	.25	.20	.10
35	Mike Lavalliere (LaValliere)(FC)	.30	.25	.12
36	Scott Bankhead(FC)	.20	.15	.08
37	Dale Sveum(FC)	.25	.20	.10
38	Bo Jackson(FC)	12.00	9.00	4.75
39	Rob Thompson(FC)	.50	.40	.20
40	Eric Plunk(FC)	.20	.15	.08
41	Bill Bathe	.15	.11	.06
42	John Kruk(FC)	.40	.30	.15
43	Andy Allanson(FC)	.20	.15	.08
44	Mark Portugal	.15	.11	.06
45	Danny Tartabull	1.00	.70	.40
46	Bob Kipper	.15	.11	.06
47	Gene Walter	.15	.11	.06
48	Rey Quinonez	.15	.11	.06
49	Bobby Witt(FC)	1.25	.90	.50
50	Bill Mooneyham	.15	.11	.06
51	John Cangelosi(FC)	.20	.15	.08
52	Ruben Sierra(FC)	8.00	6.00	3.35
53	Rob Woodward	.15	.11	.06
54	Ed Hearn	.15	.11	.06
55	Joel McKeon	.15	.11	.06
56	Checklist 1-56	.05	.04	.02

1987 Donruss

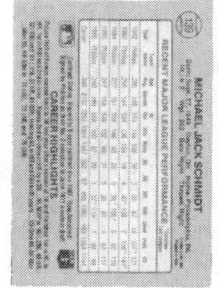

MIKE SCHMIDT 3B

The 1987 Donruss set consists of 660 numbered cards, each measuring 2-1/2" by 3-1/2" in size. Full color photos are surrounded by a bold black border separated by two narrow bands of yellow which enclose a brown area filled with baseballs. The player's name, team and team logo appear on the card fronts along with the words "Donruss '87." The card backs are designed on a horizontal format and contain black print on a yellow and white background. The backs are very similar to those in previous years' sets. Backs of cards issued in wax and rack packs face to the left when turned over, while those issued in vending sets face to the right.

		MT	NR MT	EX
Complete Set:		100.00	75.00	40.00
Common Player:		.05	.04	.02
1	Wally Joyner (DK)	.70	.50	.30
2	Roger Clemens (DK)	.70	.50	.30
3	Dale Murphy (DK)	.30	.25	.12
4	Darryl Strawberry (DK)	.40	.30	.15
5	Ozzie Smith (DK)	.12	.09	.05
6	Jose Canseco (DK)	2.00	1.50	.80
7	Charlie Hough (DK)	.07	.05	.03
8	Brook Jacoby (DK)	.10	.08	.04
9	Fred Lynn (DK)	.12	.09	.05
10	Rick Rhoden (DK)	.10	.08	.04
11	Chris Brown (DK)	.10	.08	.04
12	Von Hayes (DK)	.10	.08	.04
13	Jack Morris (DK)	.20	.15	.08
14a	Kevin McReynolds (DK) ("Donruss Diamond Kings" in white band on back)	1.25	.90	.50
14b	Kevin McReynolds (DK) ("Donruss Diamond Kings" in yellow band on back)	.20	.15	.08
15	George Brett (DK)	.40	.30	.15
16	Ted Higuera (DK)	.20	.15	.08
17	Hubie Brooks (DK)	.10	.08	.04
18	Mike Scott (DK)	.12	.09	.05

		MT	NR MT	EX
19	Kirby Puckett (DK)	.40	.30	.15
20	Dave Winfield (DK)	.25	.20	.10
21	Lloyd Moseby (DK)	.10	.08	.04
22a	Eric Davis (DK) ("Donruss Diamond Kings" in white band on back)	3.00	2.25	1.25
22b	Eric Davis (DK) ("Donruss Diamond Kings" in yellow band on back)	1.00	.70	.40
23	Jim Presley (DK)	.12	.09	.05
24	Keith Moreland (DK)	.07	.05	.03
25a	Greg Walker (DK) ("Donruss Diamond Kings" in white band on back)	1.00	.70	.40
25b	Greg Walker (DK) ("Donruss Diamond Kings" in yellow band on back)	.10	.08	.04
26	Steve Sax (DK)	.12	.09	.05
27	Checklist 1-27	.05	.04	.02
28	B.J. Surhoff (RR)(FC)	.70	.50	.30
29	Randy Myers (RR)(FC)	.90	.70	.35
30	Ken Gerhart (RR)(FC)	.15	.11	.06
31	Benito Santiago (RR)(FC)	3.00	2.25	1.25
32	Greg Swindell (RR)(FC)	1.25	.90	.50
33	Mike Birkbeck (RR)(FC)	.20	.15	.08
34	Terry Steinbach (RR)(FC)	1.00	.70	.40
35	Bo Jackson (RR)	12.00	9.00	4.75
36	Greg Maddux (RR)(FC)	2.00	1.50	.80
37	Jim Lindeman (RR)(FC)	.15	.11	.06
38	Devon White (RR)(FC)	1.00	.70	.40
39	Eric Bell (RR)(FC)	.12	.09	.05
40	Will Fraser (RR)(FC)	.20	.15	.08
41	Jerry Browne (RR)(FC)	.60	.45	.25
42	Chris James (RR)(FC)	.70	.50	.30
43	Rafael Palmeiro (RR)(FC)	3.50	2.75	1.50
44	Pat Dodson (RR)(FC)	.12	.09	.05
45	Duane Ward (RR)(FC)	.20	.15	.08
46	Mark McGwire (RR)(FC)	8.00	6.00	3.25
47	Bruce Fields (RR) (photo actually Darnell Coles)(FC)	.10	.08	.04
48	Eddie Murray	.35	.25	.14
49	Ted Higuera	.20	.15	.08
50	Kirk Gibson	.25	.20	.10
51	Oil Can Boyd	.07	.05	.03
52	Don Mattingly	2.50	2.00	1.00
53	Pedro Guerrero	.15	.11	.06
54	George Brett	.40	.30	.15
55	Jose Rijo	.07	.05	.03
56	Tim Raines	.30	.25	.12
57	Ed Correa	.15	.11	.06
58	Mike Witt	.10	.08	.04
59	Greg Walker	.10	.08	.04
60	Ozzie Smith	.15	.11	.06
61	Glenn Davis	.35	.25	.14
62	Glenn Wilson	.07	.05	.03
63	Tom Browning	.10	.08	.04
64	Tony Gwynn	.35	.25	.14
65	R.J. Reynolds	.07	.05	.03
66	Will Clark	12.00	9.00	4.75
67	Ozzie Virgil	.05	.04	.02
68	Rick Sutcliffe	.12	.09	.05
69	Gary Carter	.30	.25	.12
70	Mike Moore	.05	.04	.02
71	Bert Blyleven	.12	.09	.05
72	Tony Fernandez	.12	.09	.05
73	Kent Hrbek	.15	.11	.06
74	Lloyd Moseby	.10	.08	.04
75	Alvin Davis	.12	.09	.05
76	Keith Hernandez	.25	.20	.10
77	Ryne Sandberg	.60	.45	.25
78	Dale Murphy	.40	.30	.15
79	Sid Bream	.07	.05	.03
80	Chris Brown	.07	.05	.03
81	Steve Garvey	.25	.20	.10
82	Mario Soto	.07	.05	.03
83	Shane Rawley	.07	.05	.03
84	Willie McGee	.12	.09	.05
85	Jose Cruz	.10	.08	.04
86	Brian Downing	.07	.05	.03
87	Ozzie Guillen	.10	.08	.04
88	Hubie Brooks	.10	.08	.04
89	Cal Ripken	.35	.25	.14
90	Juan Nieves	.07	.05	.03
91	Lance Parrish	.20	.15	.08
92	Jim Rice	.30	.25	.12
93	Ron Guidry	.15	.11	.06
94	Fernando Valenzuela	.25	.20	.10
95	Andy Allanson	.15	.11	.06
96	Willie Wilson	.12	.09	.05
97	Jose Canseco	10.00	7.50	4.00
98	Jeff Reardon	.10	.08	.04
99	Bobby Witt	1.25	.90	.50
100	Checklist 28-133	.05	.04	.02
101	Jose Guzman	.10	.08	.04
102	Steve Balboni	.07	.05	.03

		MT	NR MT	EX
103	Tony Phillips	.05	.04	.02
104	Brook Jacoby	.10	.08	.04
105	Dave Winfield	.30	.25	.12
106	Orel Hershiser	.40	.30	.15
107	Lou Whitaker	.25	.20	.10
108	Fred Lynn	.15	.11	.06
109	Bill Wegman	.07	.05	.03
110	Donnie Moore	.05	.04	.02
111	Jack Clark	.15	.11	.06
112	Bob Knepper	.07	.05	.03
113	Von Hayes	.10	.08	.04
114	Leon "Bip" Roberts	.05	.04	.02
115	Tony Pena	.08	.06	.03
116	Scott Garrelts	.05	.04	.02
117	Paul Molitor	.15	.11	.06
118	Darryl Strawberry	.60	.45	.25
119	Shawon Dunston	.10	.08	.04
120	Jim Presley	.10	.08	.04
121	Jesse Barfield	.20	.15	.08
122	Gary Gaetti	.15	.11	.06
123	*Kurt Stillwell*	.50	.40	.20
124	Joel Davis	.05	.04	.02
125	Mike Boddicker	.07	.05	.03
126	Robin Yount	.50	.40	.20
127	Alan Trammell	.25	.20	.10
128	Dave Righetti	.15	.11	.06
129	Dwight Evans	.12	.09	.05
130	Mike Scioscia	.07	.05	.03
131	Julio Franco	.10	.08	.04
132	Bret Saberhagen	.25	.20	.10
133	Mike Davis	.07	.05	.03
134	Joe Hesketh	.05	.04	.02
135	*Wally Joyner*	1.25	.90	.50
136	Don Slaught	.05	.04	.02
137	Daryl Boston	.05	.04	.02
138	Nolan Ryan	.70	.50	.30
139	Mike Schmidt	.50	.40	.20
140	Tommy Herr	.10	.08	.04
141	Garry Templeton	.07	.05	.03
142	Kal Daniels	.80	.60	.30
143	Billy Sample	.05	.04	.02
144	Johnny Ray	.10	.08	.04
145	*Rob Thompson*	.30	.25	.12
146	Bob Dernier	.05	.04	.02
147	Danny Tartabull	.25	.20	.10
148	Ernie Whitt	.07	.05	.03
149	Kirby Puckett	1.50	1.25	.60
150	Mike Young	.05	.04	.02
151	Ernest Riles	.05	.04	.02
152	Frank Tanana	.07	.05	.03
153	Rich Gedman	.10	.08	.04
154	Willie Randolph	.10	.08	.04
155a	Bill Madlock (name in brown band)	.12	.09	.05
155b	Bill Madlock (name in red band)	.70	.50	.30
156a	Joe Carter (name in brown band)	.15	.11	.06
156b	Joe Carter (name in red band)	.70	.50	.30
157	Danny Jackson	.15	.11	.06
158	Carney Lansford	.10	.08	.04
159	Bryn Smith	.05	.04	.02
160	Gary Pettis	.05	.04	.02
161	Oddibe McDowell	.10	.08	.04
162	*John Cangelosi*	.12	.09	.05
163	Mike Scott	.15	.11	.06
164	Eric Show	.07	.05	.03
165	Juan Samuel	.12	.09	.05
166	Nick Esasky	.07	.05	.03
167	Zane Smith	.07	.05	.03
168	Mike Brown	.05	.04	.02
169	Keith Moreland	.07	.05	.03
170	John Tudor	.10	.08	.04
171	Ken Dixon	.05	.04	.02
172	Jim Gantner	.07	.05	.03
173	Jack Morris	.20	.15	.08
174	Bruce Hurst	.10	.08	.04
175	Dennis Rasmussen	.10	.08	.04
176	Mike Marshall	.12	.09	.05
177	Dan Quisenberry	.07	.05	.03
178	Eric Plunk(FC)	.10	.08	.04
179	Tim Wallach	.12	.09	.05
180	Steve Buechele	.07	.05	.03
181	Don Sutton	.20	.15	.08
182	Dave Schmidt	.05	.04	.02
183	Terry Pendleton	.10	.08	.04
184	*Jim Deshaies*	.35	.25	.14
185	Steve Bedrosian	.12	.09	.05
186	Pete Rose	.60	.45	.25
187	Dave Dravecky	.07	.05	.03
188	Rick Reuschel	.10	.08	.04
189	Dan Gladden	.05	.04	.02
190	Rick Mahler	.05	.04	.02
191	Thad Bosley	.05	.04	.02

		MT	NR MT	EX
192	Ron Darling	.15	.11	.06
193	Matt Young	.05	.04	.02
194	Tom Brunansky	.10	.08	.04
195	Dave Stieb	.12	.09	.05
196	Frank Viola	.15	.11	.06
197	Tom Henke	.07	.05	.03
198	Karl Best	.05	.04	.02
199	Dwight Gooden	.90	.70	.35
200	Checklist 134-239	.05	.04	.02
201	Steve Trout	.05	.04	.02
202	Rafael Ramirez	.05	.04	.02
203	Bob Walk	.05	.04	.02
204	Roger Mason	.05	.04	.02
205	Terry Kennedy	.07	.05	.03
206	Ron Oester	.05	.04	.02
207	John Russell	.05	.04	.02
208	*Greg Mathews*	.20	.15	.08
209	Charlie Kerfeld	.10	.08	.04
210	Reggie Jackson	.35	.25	.14
211	Floyd Bannister	.10	.08	.04
212	Vance Law	.07	.05	.03
213	Rich Bordi	.05	.04	.02
214	*Dan Plesac*	.35	.25	.14
215	Dave Collins	.07	.05	.03
216	Bob Stanley	.05	.04	.02
217	Joe Niekro	.10	.08	.04
218	Tom Niedenfuer	.07	.05	.03
219	Brett Butler	.07	.05	.03
220	Charlie Leibrandt	.07	.05	.03
221	Steve Ontiveros	.05	.04	.02
222	Tim Burke	.05	.04	.02
223	Curtis Wilkerson	.05	.04	.02
224	*Pete Incaviglia*	.60	.45	.25
225	Lonnie Smith	.07	.05	.03
226	Chris Codiroli	.05	.04	.02
227	*Scott Bailes*	.20	.15	.08
228	Rickey Henderson	.40	.30	.15
229	Ken Howell	.05	.04	.02
230	Darnell Coles	.07	.05	.03
231	Don Aase	.05	.04	.02
232	Tim Leary	.07	.05	.03
233	Bob Boone	.07	.05	.03
234	Ricky Horton	.07	.05	.03
235	Mark Bailey	.05	.04	.02
236	Kevin Gross	.07	.05	.03
237	Lance McCullers	.07	.05	.03
238	Cecilio Guante	.05	.04	.02
239	Bob Melvin	.05	.04	.02
240	Billy Jo Robidoux	.05	.04	.02
241	Roger McDowell	.12	.09	.05
242	Leon Durham	.07	.05	.03
243	Ed Nunez	.05	.04	.02
244	Jimmy Key	.12	.09	.05
245	Mike Smithson	.05	.04	.02
246	Bo Diaz	.07	.05	.03
247	Carlton Fisk	.20	.15	.08
248	Larry Sheets	.08	.06	.03
249	*Juan Castillo*(FC)	.10	.08	.04
250	*Eric King*	.25	.20	.10
251	Doug Drabek	1.75	1.25	.70
252	Wade Boggs	1.50	1.25	.60
253	Mariano Duncan	.05	.04	.02
254	Pat Tabler	.07	.05	.03
255	Frank White	.10	.08	.04
256	Alfredo Griffin	.07	.05	.03
257	Floyd Youmans	.07	.05	.03
258	Rob Wilfong	.05	.04	.02
259	Pete O'Brien	.10	.08	.04
260	Tim Hulett	.05	.04	.02
261	Dickie Thon	.07	.05	.03
262	Darren Daulton	.05	.04	.02
263	Vince Coleman	.25	.20	.10
264	Andy Hawkins	.05	.04	.02
265	Eric Davis	1.25	.90	.50
266	*Andres Thomas*	.25	.20	.10
267	*Mike Diaz*(FC)	.15	.11	.06
268	Chili Davis	.07	.05	.03
269	Jody Davis	.07	.05	.03
270	Phil Bradley	.12	.09	.05
271	George Bell	.25	.20	.10
272	Keith Atherton	.05	.04	.02
273	Storm Davis	.10	.08	.04
274	Rob Deer(FC)	.20	.15	.08
275	Walt Terrell	.07	.05	.03
276	Roger Clemens	1.75	1.25	.70
277	Mike Easler	.07	.05	.03
278	Steve Sax	.15	.11	.06
279	Andre Thornton	.07	.05	.03
280	Jim Sundberg	.07	.05	.03
281	Bill Bathe	.05	.04	.02
282	Jay Tibbs	.05	.04	.02

#	Player	MT	NR MT	EX
283	Dick Schofield	.05	.04	.02
284	Mike Mason	.05	.04	.02
285	Jerry Hairston	.05	.04	.02
286	Bill Doran	.10	.08	.04
287	Tim Flannery	.05	.04	.02
288	Gary Redus	.05	.04	.02
289	John Franco	.10	.08	.04
290	*Paul Assenmacher*	.15	.11	.06
291	Joe Orsulak	.05	.04	.02
292	Lee Smith	.10	.08	.04
293	Mike Laga	.05	.04	.02
294	Rick Dempsey	.07	.05	.03
295	Mike Felder	.05	.04	.02
296	Tom Brookens	.05	.04	.02
297	Al Nipper	.05	.04	.02
298	Mike Pagliarulo	.10	.08	.04
299	Franklin Stubbs	.07	.05	.03
300	Checklist 240-345	.05	.04	.02
301	Steve Farr	.05	.04	.02
302	*Bill Mooneyham*	.10	.08	.04
303	Andres Galarraga	.25	.20	.10
304	Scott Fletcher	.07	.05	.03
305	Jack Howell	.07	.05	.03
306	*Russ Morman*(FC)	.10	.08	.04
307	Todd Worrell	.20	.15	.08
308	Dave Smith	.07	.05	.03
309	Jeff Stone	.05	.04	.02
310	Ron Robinson	.05	.04	.02
311	Bruce Bochy	.05	.04	.02
312	Jim Winn	.05	.04	.02
313	Mark Davis	.05	.04	.02
314	Jeff Dedmon	.05	.04	.02
315	*Jamie Moyer*(FC)	.20	.15	.08
316	Wally Backman	.07	.05	.03
317	Ken Phelps	.07	.05	.03
318	Steve Lombardozzi	.05	.04	.02
319	Rance Mulliniks	.05	.04	.02
320	Tim Laudner	.05	.04	.02
321	*Mark Eichhorn*	.15	.11	.06
322	*Lee Guetterman*	.15	.11	.06
323	Sid Fernandez	.12	.09	.05
324	Jerry Mumphrey	.05	.04	.02
325	David Palmer	.05	.04	.02
326	Bill Almon	.05	.04	.02
327	Candy Maldonado	.07	.05	.03
328	*John Kruk*	.30	.25	.12
329	John Denny	.05	.04	.02
330	Milt Thompson	.07	.05	.03
331	*Mike LaValliere*	.25	.20	.10
332	Alan Ashby	.05	.04	.02
333	Doug Corbett	.05	.04	.02
334	*Ron Karkovice*(FC)	.10	.08	.04
335	Mitch Webster	.07	.05	.03
336	Lee Lacy	.05	.04	.02
337	*Glenn Braggs*(FC)	.30	.25	.12
338	Dwight Lowry	.05	.04	.02
339	Don Baylor	.12	.09	.05
340	Brian Fisher	.07	.05	.03
341	*Reggie Williams*	.10	.08	.04
342	Tom Candiotti	.05	.04	.02
343	Rudy Law	.05	.04	.02
344	Curt Young	.07	.05	.03
345	Mike Fitzgerald	.05	.04	.02
346	*Ruben Sierra*	7.00	5.25	2.75
347	*Mitch Williams*	.60	.45	.25
348	Jorge Orta	.05	.04	.02
349	Mickey Tettleton	.10	.08	.04
350	Ernie Camacho	.05	.04	.02
351	Ron Kittle	.10	.08	.04
352	Ken Landreaux	.05	.04	.02
353	Chet Lemon	.07	.05	.03
354	John Shelby	.05	.04	.02
355	Mark Clear	.05	.04	.02
356	Doug DeCinces	.07	.05	.03
357	Ken Dayley	.05	.04	.02
358	Phil Garner	.05	.04	.02
359	Steve Jeltz	.05	.04	.02
360	Ed Whitson	.05	.04	.02
361	*Barry Bonds*	9.00	6.75	3.50
362	Vida Blue	.10	.08	.04
363	Cecil Cooper	.12	.09	.05
364	Bob Ojeda	.07	.05	.03
365	Dennis Eckersley	.12	.09	.05
366	Mike Morgan	.05	.04	.02
367	Willie Upshaw	.07	.05	.03
368	*Allan Anderson*(FC)	.25	.20	.10
369	Bill Gullickson	.07	.05	.03
370	*Bobby Thigpen*(FC)	1.25	.90	.50
371	Juan Beniquez	.05	.04	.02
372	Charlie Moore	.05	.04	.02
373	Dan Petry	.07	.05	.03
374	Rod Scurry	.05	.04	.02
375	Tom Seaver	.40	.30	.15
376	Ed Vande Berg	.05	.04	.02
377	Tony Bernazard	.05	.04	.02
378	Greg Pryor	.05	.04	.02
379	Dwayne Murphy	.07	.05	.03
380	Andy McGaffigan	.05	.04	.02
381	Kirk McCaskill	.07	.05	.03
382	Greg Harris	.05	.04	.02
383	Rich Dotson	.07	.05	.03
384	Craig Reynolds	.05	.04	.02
385	Greg Gross	.05	.04	.02
386	Tito Landrum	.05	.04	.02
387	Craig Lefferts	.05	.04	.02
388	Dave Parker	.20	.15	.08
389	Bob Horner	.10	.08	.04
390	Pat Clements	.05	.04	.02
391	Jeff Leonard	.07	.05	.03
392	Chris Speier	.05	.04	.02
393	John Moses	.05	.04	.02
394	Garth Iorg	.05	.04	.02
395	Greg Gagne	.05	.04	.02
396	Nate Snell	.05	.04	.02
397	*Bryan Clutterbuck*(FC)	.10	.08	.04
398	Darrell Evans	.12	.09	.05
399	Steve Crawford	.05	.04	.02
400	Checklist 346-451	.05	.04	.02
401	*Phil Lombardi*(FC)	.10	.08	.04
402	Rick Honeycutt	.05	.04	.02
403	Ken Schrom	.05	.04	.02
404	Bud Black	.05	.04	.02
405	Donnie Hill	.05	.04	.02
406	Wayne Krenchicki	.05	.04	.02
407	*Chuck Finley*(FC)	1.50	1.25	.60
408	Toby Harrah	.07	.05	.03
409	Steve Lyons	.05	.04	.02
410	Kevin Bass	.10	.08	.04
411	Marvell Wynne	.05	.04	.02
412	Ron Roenicke	.05	.04	.02
413	*Tracy Jones*	.25	.20	.10
414	Gene Garber	.05	.04	.02
415	Mike Bielecki	.05	.04	.02
416	Frank DiPino	.05	.04	.02
417	Andy Van Slyke	.12	.09	.05
418	Jim Dwyer	.05	.04	.02
419	Ben Oglivie	.07	.05	.03
420	Dave Bergman	.05	.04	.02
421	Joe Sambito	.05	.04	.02
422	*Bob Tewksbury*	.12	.09	.05
423	Len Matuszek	.05	.04	.02
424	*Mike Kingery*(FC)	.15	.11	.06
425	Dave Kingman	.12	.09	.05
426	*Al Newman*	.07	.05	.03
427	Gary Ward	.07	.05	.03
428	Ruppert Jones	.05	.04	.02
429	Harold Baines	.15	.11	.06
430	Pat Perry	.05	.04	.02
431	Terry Puhl	.05	.04	.02
432	Don Carman	.07	.05	.03
433	Eddie Milner	.05	.04	.02
434	LaMarr Hoyt	.05	.04	.02
435	Rick Rhoden	.10	.08	.04
436	Jose Uribe	.07	.05	.03
437	Ken Oberkfell	.05	.04	.02
438	Ron Davis	.05	.04	.02
439	Jesse Orosco	.07	.05	.03
440	Scott Bradley	.05	.04	.02
441	Randy Bush	.05	.04	.02
442	*John Cerutti*	.20	.15	.08
443	Roy Smalley	.05	.04	.02
444	Kelly Gruber	1.25	.90	.50
445	Bob Kearney	.05	.04	.02
446	*Ed Hearn*	.10	.08	.04
447	Scott Sanderson	.05	.04	.02
448	Bruce Benedict	.05	.04	.02
449	Junior Ortiz	.05	.04	.02
450	*Mike Aldrete*	.25	.20	.10
451	Kevin McReynolds	.15	.11	.06
452	*Rob Murphy*(FC)	.20	.15	.08
453	Kent Tekulve	.07	.05	.03
454	*Curt Ford*(FC)	.07	.05	.03
455	Davey Lopes	.07	.05	.03
456	Bobby Grich	.10	.08	.04
457	Jose DeLeon	.07	.05	.03
458	Andre Dawson	.20	.15	.08
459	Mike Flanagan	.07	.05	.03
460	*Joey Meyer*(FC)	.25	.20	.10
461	*Chuck Cary*(FC)	.10	.08	.04
462	Bill Buckner	.10	.08	.04
463	Bob Shirley	.05	.04	.02
464	*Jeff Hamilton*(FC)	.30	.25	.12

	MT	NR MT	EX			MT	NR MT	EX
465 Phil Niekro	.20	.15	.08	556 Buddy Bell	.10	.08	.04
466 Mark Gubicza	.12	.09	.05	557 Jimmy Jones(FC)	.20	.15	.08
467 Jerry Willard	.05	.04	.02	558 Bobby Bonilla	7.00	5.25	2.75
468 Bob Sebra(FC)	.10	.08	.04	559 Jeff Robinson	.07	.05	.03
469 Larry Parrish	.10	.08	.04	560 Ed Olwine	.05	.04	.02
470 Charlie Hough	.07	.05	.03	561 Glenallen Hill(FC)	1.75	1.25	.70
471 Hal McRae	.10	.08	.04	562 Lee Mazzilli	.07	.05	.03
472 Dave Leiper(FC)	.10	.08	.04	563 Mike Brown	.05	.04	.02
473 Mel Hall	.07	.05	.03	564 George Frazier	.05	.04	.02
474 Dan Pasqua	.10	.08	.04	565 Mike Sharperson(FC)	.10	.08	.04
475 Bob Welch	.10	.08	.04	566 Mark Portugal	.10	.08	.04
476 Johnny Grubb	.05	.04	.02	567 Rick Leach	.05	.04	.02
477 Jim Traber	.07	.05	.03	568 Mark Langston	.12	.09	.05
478 Chris Bosio(FC)	.40	.30	.15	569 Rafael Santana	.05	.04	.02
479 Mark McLemore	.07	.05	.03	570 Manny Trillo	.07	.05	.03
480 John Morris	.05	.04	.02	571 Cliff Speck	.05	.04	.02
481 Billy Hatcher	.07	.05	.03	572 Bob Kipper	.05	.04	.02
482 Dan Schatzeder	.05	.04	.02	573 Kelly Downs(FC)	.30	.25	.12
483 Rich Gossage	.15	.11	.06	574 Randy Asadoor(FC)	.10	.08	.04
484 Jim Morrison	.05	.04	.02	575 Dave Magadan(FC)	2.00	1.50	.80
485 Bob Brenly	.05	.04	.02	576 Marvin Freeman(FC)	.12	.09	.05
486 Bill Schroeder	.05	.04	.02	577 Jeff Lahti	.05	.04	.02
487 Mookie Wilson	.10	.08	.04	578 Jeff Calhoun	.05	.04	.02
488 Dave Martinez(FC)	.25	.20	.10	579 Gus Polidor(FC)	.07	.05	.03
489 Harold Reynolds	.10	.08	.04	580 Gene Nelson	.05	.04	.02
490 Jeff Hearron	.05	.04	.02	581 Tim Teufel	.05	.04	.02
491 Mickey Hatcher	.05	.04	.02	582 Odell Jones	.05	.04	.02
492 Barry Larkin(FC)	6.00	4.50	2.50	583 Mark Ryal	.05	.04	.02
493 Bob James	.05	.04	.02	584 Randy O'Neal	.05	.04	.02
494 John Habyan	.05	.04	.02	585 Mike Greenwell(FC)	7.00	5.25	2.75
495 Jim Adduci(FC)	.07	.05	.03	586 Ray Knight	.07	.05	.03
496 Mike Heath	.05	.04	.02	587 Ralph Bryant(FC)	.12	.09	.05
497 Tim Stoddard	.05	.04	.02	588 Carmen Castillo	.05	.04	.02
498 Tony Armas	.07	.05	.03	589 Ed Wojna	.05	.04	.02
499 Dennis Powell	.05	.04	.02	590 Stan Javier	.05	.04	.02
500 Checklist 452-557	.05	.04	.02	591 Jeff Musselman(FC)	.20	.15	.08
501 Chris Bando	.05	.04	.02	592 Mike Stanley(FC)	.20	.15	.08
502 David Cone(FC)	2.75	2.00	1.00	593 Darrell Porter	.07	.05	.03
503 Jay Howell	.07	.05	.03	594 Drew Hall(FC)	.20	.15	.08
504 Tom Foley	.05	.04	.02	595 Rob Nelson(FC)	.10	.08	.04
505 Ray Chadwick(FC)	.10	.08	.04	596 Bryan Oelkers	.05	.04	.02
506 Mike Loynd(FC)	.15	.11	.06	597 Scott Nielsen(FC)	.10	.08	.04
507 Neil Allen	.05	.04	.02	598 Brian Holton(FC)	.20	.15	.08
508 Danny Darwin	.05	.04	.02	599 Kevin Mitchell	6.00	4.50	2.50
509 Rick Schu	.05	.04	.02	600 Checklist 558-660	.05	.04	.02
510 Jose Oquendo	.05	.04	.02	601 Jackie Gutierrez	.05	.04	.02
511 Gene Walter	.07	.05	.03	602 Barry Jones(FC)	.12	.09	.05
512 Terry McGriff(FC)	.12	.09	.05	603 Jerry Narron	.05	.04	.02
513 Ken Griffey	.10	.08	.04	604 Steve Lake	.05	.04	.02
514 Benny Distefano	.05	.04	.02	605 Jim Pankovits	.05	.04	.02
515 Terry Mulholland(FC)	.12	.09	.05	606 Ed Romero	.05	.04	.02
516 Ed Lynch	.05	.04	.02	607 Dave LaPoint	.07	.05	.03
517 Bill Swift	.05	.04	.02	608 Don Robinson	.07	.05	.03
518 Manny Lee(FC)	.07	.05	.03	609 Mike Krukow	.07	.05	.03
519 Andre David	.05	.04	.02	610 Dave Valle(FC)	.12	.09	.05
520 Scott McGregor	.07	.05	.03	611 Len Dykstra	.80	.60	.30
521 Rick Manning	.05	.04	.02	612 Roberto Clemente Puzzle Card	.05	.04	.02
522 Willie Hernandez	.07	.05	.03	613 Mike Trujillo(FC)	.05	.04	.02
523 Marty Barrett	.10	.08	.04	614 Damaso Garcia	.05	.04	.02
524 Wayne Tolleson	.05	.04	.02	615 Neal Heaton	.05	.04	.02
525 Jose Gonzalez(FC)	.15	.11	.06	616 Juan Berenguer	.05	.04	.02
526 Cory Snyder	.70	.50	.30	617 Steve Carlton	.25	.20	.10
527 Buddy Biancalana	.05	.04	.02	618 Gary Lucas	.05	.04	.02
528 Moose Haas	.05	.04	.02	619 Geno Petralli	.05	.04	.02
529 Wilfredo Tejada(FC)	.10	.08	.04	620 Rick Aguilera	.07	.05	.03
530 Stu Cliburn	.05	.04	.02	621 Fred McGriff	3.00	2.25	1.25
531 Dale Mohorcic(FC)	.20	.15	.08	622 Dave Henderson	.10	.08	.04
532 Ron Hassey	.05	.04	.02	623 Dave Clark(FC)	.20	.15	.08
533 Ty Gainey	.05	.04	.02	624 Angel Salazar	.05	.04	.02
534 Jerry Royster	.05	.04	.02	625 Randy Hunt	.05	.04	.02
535 Mike Maddux(FC)	.20	.15	.08	626 John Gibbons	.05	.04	.02
536 Ted Power	.05	.04	.02	627 Kevin Brown(FC)	.60	.45	.25
537 Ted Simmons	.12	.09	.05	628 Bill Dawley	.05	.04	.02
538 Rafael Belliard(FC)	.12	.09	.05	629 Aurelio Lopez	.05	.04	.02
539 Chico Walker	.05	.04	.02	630 Charlie Hudson	.05	.04	.02
540 Bob Forsch	.07	.05	.03	631 Ray Soff	.05	.04	.02
541 John Stefero	.05	.04	.02	632 Ray Hayward(FC)	.12	.09	.05
542 Dale Sveum	.20	.15	.08	633 Spike Owen	.05	.04	.02
543 Mark Thurmond	.05	.04	.02	634 Glenn Hubbard	.05	.04	.02
544 Jeff Sellers	.20	.15	.08	635 Kevin Elster(FC)	.40	.30	.15
545 Joel Skinner	.05	.04	.02	636 Mike LaCoss	.05	.04	.02
546 Alex Trevino	.05	.04	.02	637 Dwayne Henry	.05	.04	.02
547 Randy Kutcher(FC)	.10	.08	.04	638 Rey Quinones	.15	.11	.06
548 Joaquin Andujar	.07	.05	.03	639 Jim Clancy	.07	.05	.03
549 Casey Candaele(FC)	.15	.11	.06	640 Larry Andersen	.05	.04	.02
550 Jeff Russell	.05	.04	.02	641 Calvin Schiraldi	.05	.04	.02
551 John Candelaria	.10	.08	.04	642 Stan Jefferson(FC)	.15	.11	.06
552 Joe Cowley	.05	.04	.02	643 Marc Sullivan	.05	.04	.02
553 Danny Cox	.07	.05	.03	644 Mark Grant	.05	.04	.02
554 Denny Walling	.05	.04	.02	645 Cliff Johnson	.05	.04	.02
555 Bruce Ruffin(FC)	.20	.15	.08	646 Howard Johnson	.25	.20	.10

		MT	NR MT	EX
647	Dave Sax	.05	.04	.02
648	Dave Stewart	.25	.20	.10
649	Danny Heep	.05	.04	.02
650	Joe Johnson	.05	.04	.02
651	*Bob Brower*(FC)	.15	.11	.06
652	Rob Woodward	.07	.05	.03
653	John Mizerock	.05	.04	.02
654	*Tim Pyznarski*(FC)	.10	.08	.04
655	*Luis Aquino*(FC)	.10	.08	.04
656	Mickey Brantley(FC)	.10	.08	.04
657	Doyle Alexander	.07	.05	.03
658	Sammy Stewart	.05	.04	.02
659	Jim Acker	.05	.04	.02
660	Pete Ladd	.05	.04	.02

1987 Donruss All-Stars

Issued in conjunction with the Donruss Pop-Ups set for the second consecutive year, the 1987 Donruss All-Stars set consists of 59 players (plus a checklist) who were selected to the 1986 All-Star Game. Measuring 3-1/2" by 5" in size, the card fronts feature black borders and American or National League logos. Included on the backs are the player's career highlights and All-Star Game statistics. Retail packs included one pop-Up card, three All-Star cards and one Roberto Clemente puzzle.

		MT	NR MT	EX
Complete Set:		7.00	5.25	2.75
Common Player:		.09	.07	.04
1	Wally Joyner	.80	.60	.30
2	Dave Winfield	.25	.20	.10
3	Lou Whitaker	.15	.11	.06
4	Kirby Puckett	.50	.40	.20
5	Cal Ripken, Jr.	.30	.25	.12
6	Rickey Henderson	.50	.40	.20
7	Wade Boggs	.80	.60	.30
8	Roger Clemens	.50	.40	.20
9	Lance Parrish	.09	.07	.04
10	Dick Howser	.09	.07	.04
11	Keith Hernandez	.10	.08	.04
12	Darryl Strawberry	.50	.40	.20
13	Ryne Sandberg	.25	.20	.10
14	Dale Murphy	.40	.30	.15
15	Ozzie Smith	.15	.11	.06
16	Tony Gwynn	.30	.25	.12
17	Mike Schmidt	.40	.30	.15
18	Dwight Gooden	.60	.45	.25
19	Gary Carter	.15	.11	.06
20	Whitey Herzog	.09	.07	.04
21	Jose Canseco	1.50	1.25	.60
22	John Franco	.09	.07	.04
23	Jesse Barfield	.12	.09	.05
24	Rick Rhoden	.09	.07	.04
25	Harold Baines	.15	.11	.06
26	Sid Fernandez	.12	.09	.05
27	George Brett	.40	.30	.15
28	Steve Sax	.15	.11	.06
29	Jim Presley	.12	.09	.05
30	Dave Smith	.09	.07	.04
31	Eddie Murray	.10	.08	.04
32	Mike Scott	.12	.09	.05
33	Don Mattingly	2.00	1.50	.80
34	Dave Parker	.15	.11	.06
35	Tony Fernandez	.15	.11	.06

		MT	NR MT	EX
36	Tim Raines	.25	.20	.10
37	Brook Jacoby	.12	.09	.05
38	Chili Davis	.09	.07	.04
39	Rich Gedman	.09	.07	.04
40	Kevin Bass	.09	.07	.04
41	Frank White	.09	.07	.04
42	Glenn Davis	.15	.11	.06
43	Willie Hernandez	.09	.07	.04
44	Chris Brown	.09	.07	.04
45	Jim Rice	.10	.08	.04
46	Tony Pena	.09	.07	.04
47	Don Aase	.09	.07	.04
48	Hubie Brooks	.09	.07	.04
49	Charlie Hough	.09	.07	.04
50	Jody Davis	.09	.07	.04
51	Mike Witt	.09	.07	.04
52	Jeff Reardon	.12	.09	.05
53	Ken Schrom	.09	.07	.04
54	Fernando Valenzuela	.10	.08	.04
55	Dave Righetti	.15	.11	.06
56	Shane Rawley	.09	.07	.04
57	Ted Higuera	.12	.09	.05
58	Mike Krukow	.09	.07	.04
59	Lloyd Moseby	.09	.07	.04
60	Checklist	.09	.07	.04

1987 Donruss Box Panels

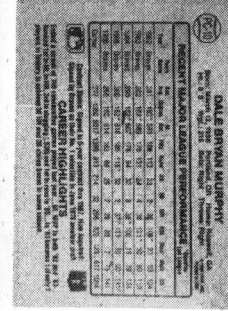

Continuing with an idea they initiated in 1985, Donruss once again placed baseball cards on the bottoms of their retail boxes. The cards, which are 2-1/2" by 3-1/2" in size, come four to a panel with each panel containing an unnumbered Roberto Clemente puzzle card. With numbering that begins where Donruss left off in 1986, cards PC 10 through PC 12 were found on boxes of Donruss regular issue wax packs. Cards PC 13 through PC 15 were located on boxes of the 1987 All-Star/Pop-Up packs.

		MT	NR MT	EX
Complete Panel Set:		6.00	4.50	2.50
Complete Singles Set:		3.00	2.25	1.25
Common Single Player:		.15	.11	.06
	Panel	4.00	3.00	1.50
10	Dale Murphy	.35	.25	.14
11	Jeff Reardon	.20	.15	.08
12	Jose Canseco	2.00	1.50	.80
——	Roberto Clemente Puzzle Card	.04	.03	.02
	Panel	2.25	1.75	.90
13	Mike Scott	.20	.15	.08
14	Roger Clemens	1.00	.70	.30
15	Mike Krukow	.15	.11	.06
——	Roberto Clemente Puzzle Card	.04	.03	.02

1987 Donruss Diamond Kings Supers

For a third straight baseball card season, Donruss produced a set of enlarged size Diamond Kings. The cards, which measure 4-11/16" by 6-3/4", are giant versions of the Diamond Kings subset found in the

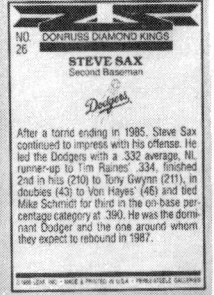

and include the date the event took place plus the particulars about it. As in the past, the set includes Donruss' picks for the A.L. and N.L. Rookies of the Year. The set was issued in a specially designed box and was available only through hobby dealers.

regular 1987 Donruss set. The 28-card set, which features the artwork of Dick Perez, contains 26 player cards, a checklist and a Roberto Clemente puzzle card. The set was available through a mail-in offer for $9.50 plus three wrappers.

		MT	NR MT	EX
	Complete Set:	9.00	6.75	3.50
	Common Player:	.20	.15	.08
1	Wally Joyner	.90	.70	.35
2	Roger Clemens	1.00	.70	.40
3	Dale Murphy	.40	.30	.15
4	Darryl Strawberry	.90	.70	.35
5	Ozzie Smith	.30	.25	.12
6	Jose Canseco	2.00	1.50	.80
7	Charlie Hough	.20	.15	.08
8	Brook Jacoby	.20	.15	.08
9	Fred Lynn	.20	.15	.08
10	Rick Rhoden	.20	.15	.08
11	Chris Brown	.25	.20	.10
12	Von Hayes	.25	.20	.10
13	Jack Morris	.20	.15	.08
14	Kevin McReynolds	.35	.25	.14
15	George Brett	.70	.50	.30
16	Ted Higuera	.20	.15	.08
17	Hubie Brooks	.20	.15	.08
18	Mike Scott	.20	.15	.08
19	Kirby Puckett	.90	.70	.35
20	Dave Winfield	.30	.25	.12
21	Lloyd Moseby	.20	.15	.08
22	Eric Davis	.90	.70	.35
23	Jim Presley	.25	.20	.10
24	Keith Moreland	.20	.15	.08
25	Greg Walker	.20	.15	.08
26	Steve Sax	.30	.25	.12
27	Checklist	.15	.11	.06
----	Roberto Clemente Puzzle Card	.15	.11	.06

1987 Donruss Highlights

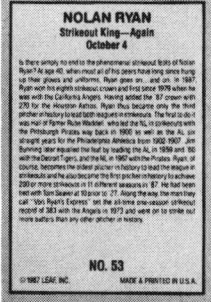

For a third consecutive year, Donruss produced a 56-card set which highlighted the special events of the 1987 baseball season. The cards, which measure 2-1/2" by 3-1/2", have a front design similar to the regular 1987 Donruss set. A blue border and the "Highlights" logo are the significant differences. The card backs feature black print on a white background

		MT	NR MT	EX
	Complete Set:	8.00	6.00	3.25
	Common Player:	.10	.08	.04
1	First No-Hitter For Brewers (Juan Nieves) .15		.11	.06
2	Hits 500th Homer (Mike Schmidt) .40		.30	.15
3	N.L. Player of the Month - April (Eric Davis) .50		.40	.20
4	N.L. Pitcher of the Month - April (Sid Fernandez) .10		.08	.04
5	A.L. Player of the Month - April (Brian Downing) .10		.08	.04
6	A.L. Pitcher of the Month - April (Bret Saberhagen) .30		.25	.12
7	Free Agent Holdout Returns (Tim Raines) .25		.20	.10
8	N.L. Player of the Month - May (Eric Davis) .50		.40	.20
9	N.L. Pitcher of the Month - May (Steve Bedrosian) .15		.11	.06
10	A.L. Player of the Month - May (Larry Parrish) .10		.08	.04
11	A.L. Pitcher of the Month - May (Jim Clancy) .10		.08	.04
12	N.L. Player of the Month - June (Tony Gwynn) .30		.25	.12
13	N.L. Pitcher of the Month - June (Orel Hershiser) .25		.20	.10
14	A.L. Player of the Month - June (Wade Boggs) .80		.60	.30
15	A.L. Pitcher of the Month - June (Steve Ontiveros) .10		.08	.04
16	All Star Game Hero (Tim Raines) .25		.20	.10
17	Consecutive Game Homer Streak (Don Mattingly) 1.00		.70	.40
18	1987 Hall of Fame Inductee (Jim "Catfish" Hunter) .20		.15	.08
19	1987 Hall of Fame Inductee (Ray Dandridge) .10		.08	.04
20	1987 Hall of Fame Inductee (Billy Williams) .20		.15	.08
21	N.L. Player of the Month - July (Bo Diaz) .10		.08	.04
22	N.L. Pitcher of the Month - July (Floyd Youmans) .10		.08	.04
23	A.L. Player of the Month - July (Don Mattingly) 1.00		.70	.40
24	A.L. Pitcher of the Month - July (Frank Viola) .20		.15	.08
25	Strikes Out 4 Batters In 1 Inning (Bobby Witt) .15		.11	.06
26	Ties A.L. 9-Inning Game Hit Mark (Kevin Seitzer) .50		.40	.20
27	Sets Rookie Home Run Record (Mark McGwire) 1.25		.90	.50
28	Sets Cubs' 1st Year Homer Mark (Andre Dawson) .20		.15	.08
29	Hits In 39 Straight Games (Paul Molitor) .15		.11	.06
30	Record Weekend (Kirby Puckett) .50		.40	.20
31	N.L. Player of the Month - August (Andre Dawson) .20		.15	.08
32	N.L. Pitcher of the Month - August (Doug Drabek) .10		.08	.04
33	A.L. Player of the Month - August (Dwight Evans) .15		.11	.06
34	A.L. Pitcher of the Month - August (Mark Langston) .25		.20	.10
35	100 RBI In 1st 2 Major League Seasons (Wally Joyner) .40		.30	.15
36	100 SB In 1st 3 Major League Seasons (Vince Coleman) .20		.15	.08
37	Orioles' All Time Homer King (Eddie Murray) .10		.08	.04
38	Ends Consecutive Innings Streak (Cal Ripken) .30		.25	.12
39	Blue Jays Hit Record 10 Homers In 1 Gamelers. (Rob Ducey, Fred McGriff, Ernie Whitt) .50		.40	.20
40	Equal A's RBI Marks (Jose Canseco, Mark McGwire) 2.50		2.00	1.00
41	Sets All-Time Catching Record (Bob Boone) .10		.08	.04
42	Sets Mets' One-Season HR Mark (Darryl Strawberry) .50		.40	.20

		MT	NR MT	EX
43	N.L.'s All-Time Switch Hit HR King			
	(Howard Johnson)	.15	.11	.06
44	Five Straight 200-Hit Seasons (Wade			
	Boggs)	.80	.60	.30
45	Eclipses Rookie Game Hitting Streak			
	(Benito Santiago)	.40	.30	.15
46	Eclipses Jackson's A's HR Record (Mark			
	McGwire)	1.25	.90	.50
47	13th Rookie To Collect 200 Hits (Kevin			
	Seitzer)	.50	.40	.20
48	Sets Slam Record (Don Mattingly)			
		1.00	.70	.40
49	N.L. Player of the Month - September			
	(Darryl Strawberry)	.50	.40	.20
50	N.L. Pitcher of the Month - September			
	(Pascual Perez)	.10	.08	.04
51	A.L. Player of the Month - September			
	(Alan Trammell)	.20	.15	.08
52	A.L. Pitcher of the Month - September			
	(Doyle Alexander)	.10	.08	.04
53	Strikeout King - Again (Nolan Ryan)			
		1.00	.70	.40
54	Donruss A.L. Rookie of the Year (Mark			
	McGwire)	1.25	.90	.50
55	Donruss N.L. Rookie of the Year (Benito			
	Santiago)	.40	.30	.15
56	Highlight Checklist	.10	.08	.04

1987 Donruss Opening Day

 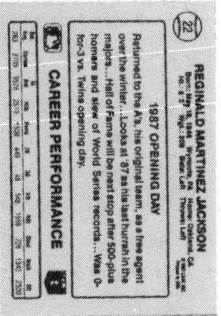

The Donruss Opening Day set includes all players in major league baseball's starting lineups on the opening day of the 1987 baseball season. Cards in the 272-piece set measure 2-1/2" by 3-1/2" and have a glossy coating. The card fronts are identical in design to the regular Donruss set, but new photos were utilized and the fronts contain maroon borders as opposed to black. The backs carry black printing on white and yellow and carry a brief player biography plus the player's career statistics. The set was packaged in a sturdy 15" by 5" by 2" box with a clear acetate lid.

		MT	NR MT	EX
	Complete Set:	20.00	15.00	8.00
	Common Player:	.05	.04	.02
1	Doug DeCinces	.07	.05	.03
2	Mike Witt	.12	.09	.05
3	George Hendrick	.07	.05	.03
4	Dick Schofield	.05	.04	.02
5	Devon White	.50	.40	.20
6	Butch Wynegar	.05	.04	.02
7	Wally Joyner	.75	.55	.30
8	Mark McLemore	.05	.04	.02
9	Brian Downing	.07	.05	.03
10	Gary Pettis	.05	.04	.02
11	Bill Doran	.07	.05	.03
12	Phil Garner	.05	.04	.02
13	Jose Cruz	.07	.05	.03
14	Kevin Bass	.07	.05	.03
15	Mike Scott	.12	.09	.05
16	Glenn Davis	.15	.11	.06
17	Alan Ashby	.05	.04	.02
18	Billy Hatcher	.07	.05	.03

		MT	NR MT	EX
19	Craig Reynolds	.05	.04	.02
20	Carney Lansford	.07	.05	.03
21	Mike Davis	.05	.04	.02
22	Reggie Jackson	.30	.25	.12
23	Mickey Tettleton	.07	.05	.03
24	Jose Canseco	1.75	1.25	.70
25	Rob Nelson	.05	.04	.02
26	Tony Phillips	.05	.04	.02
27	Dwayne Murphy	.05	.04	.02
28	Alfredo Griffin	.07	.05	.03
29	Curt Young	.05	.04	.02
30	Willie Upshaw	.05	.04	.02
31	Mike Sharperson	.05	.04	.02
32	Rance Mulliniks	.05	.04	.02
33	Ernie Whitt	.05	.04	.02
34	Jesse Barfield	.12	.09	.05
35	Tony Fernandez	.12	.09	.05
36	Lloyd Moseby	.07	.05	.03
37	Jimmy Key	.10	.08	.04
38	Fred McGriff	1.50	1.25	.60
39	George Bell	.25	.20	.10
40	Dale Murphy	.40	.30	.15
41	Rick Mahler	.05	.04	.02
42	Ken Griffey	.07	.05	.03
43	Andres Thomas	.10	.08	.04
44	Dion James	.05	.04	.02
45	Ozzie Virgil	.05	.04	.02
46	Ken Oberkfell	.05	.04	.02
47	Gary Roenicke	.05	.04	.02
48	Glenn Hubbard	.05	.04	.02
49	Bill Schroeder	.05	.04	.02
50	Greg Brock	.07	.05	.03
51	Billy Jo Robidoux	.05	.04	.02
52	Glenn Braggs	.12	.09	.05
53	Jim Gantner	.05	.04	.02
54	Paul Molitor	.15	.11	.06
55	Dale Sveum	.15	.11	.06
56	Ted Higuera	.12	.09	.05
57	Rob Deer	.07	.05	.03
58	Robin Yount	.35	.25	.14
59	Jim Lindeman	.10	.08	.04
60	Vince Coleman	.15	.11	.06
61	Tommy Herr	.07	.05	.03
62	Terry Pendleton	.07	.05	.03
63	John Tudor	.10	.08	.04
64	Tony Pena	.07	.05	.03
65	Ozzie Smith	.15	.11	.06
66	Tito Landrum	.05	.04	.02
67	Jack Clark	.15	.11	.06
68	Bob Dernier	.05	.04	.02
69	Rick Sutcliffe	.10	.08	.04
70	Andre Dawson	.20	.15	.08
71	Keith Moreland	.07	.05	.03
72	Jody Davis	.07	.05	.03
73	Brian Dayett	.05	.04	.02
74	Leon Durham	.07	.05	.03
75	Ryne Sandberg	.25	.20	.10
76	Shawon Dunston	.20	.15	.08
77	Mike Marshall	.10	.08	.04
78	Bill Madlock	.07	.05	.03
79	Orel Hershiser	.30	.25	.12
80	Mike Ramsey	.05	.04	.02
81	Ken Landreaux	.05	.04	.02
82	Mike Scioscia	.05	.04	.02
83	Franklin Stubbs	.07	.05	.03
84	Mariano Duncan	.05	.04	.02
85	Steve Sax	.15	.11	.06
86	Mitch Webster	.07	.05	.03
87	Reid Nichols	.05	.04	.02
88	Tim Wallach	.10	.08	.04
89	Floyd Youmans	.07	.05	.03
90	Andres Galarraga	.25	.20	.10
91	Hubie Brooks	.07	.05	.03
92	Jeff Reed	.05	.04	.02
93	Alonzo Powell	.05	.04	.02
94	Vance Law	.05	.04	.02
95	Bob Brenly	.05	.04	.02
96	Will Clark	2.00	1.50	.80
97	Chili Davis	.07	.05	.03
98	Mike Krukow	.05	.04	.02
99	Jose Uribe	.05	.04	.02
100	Chris Brown	.07	.05	.03
101	Rob Thompson	.10	.08	.04
102	Candy Maldonado	.07	.05	.03
103	Jeff Leonard	.07	.05	.03
104	Tom Candiotti	.05	.04	.02
105	Chris Bando	.05	.04	.02
106	Cory Snyder	.30	.25	.12
107	Pat Tabler	.07	.05	.03
108	Andre Thornton	.07	.05	.03
109	Joe Carter	.25	.20	.10

		MT	NR MT	EX
110	Tony Bernazard	.05	.04	.02
111	Julio Franco	.10	.08	.04
112	Brook Jacoby	.10	.08	.04
113	Brett Butler	.07	.05	.03
114	Donnell Nixon	.05	.04	.02
115	Alvin Davis	.12	.09	.05
116	Mark Langston	.25	.20	.10
117	Harold Reynolds	.07	.05	.03
118	Ken Phelps	.05	.04	.02
119	Mike Kingery	.10	.08	.04
120	Dave Valle	.07	.05	.03
121	Rey Quinones	.07	.05	.03
122	Phil Bradley	.12	.09	.05
123	Jim Presley	.12	.09	.05
124	Keith Hernandez	.12	.09	.05
125	Kevin McReynolds	.12	.09	.05
126	Rafael Santana	.05	.04	.02
127	Bob Ojeda	.07	.05	.03
128	Darryl Strawberry	.60	.45	.25
129	Mookie Wilson	.07	.05	.03
130	Gary Carter	.15	.11	.06
131	Tim Teufel	.05	.04	.02
132	Howard Johnson	.20	.15	.08
133	Cal Ripken	.30	.25	.12
134	Rick Burleson	.05	.04	.02
135	Fred Lynn	.12	.09	.05
136	Eddie Murray	.15	.11	.06
137	Ray Knight	.07	.05	.03
138	Alan Wiggins	.05	.04	.02
139	John Shelby	.05	.04	.02
140	Mike Boddicker	.07	.05	.03
141	Ken Gerhart	.07	.05	.03
142	Terry Kennedy	.07	.05	.03
143	Steve Garvey	.30	.25	.12
144	Marvell Wynne	.05	.04	.02
145	Kevin Mitchell	1.50	1.25	.60
146	Tony Gwynn	.35	.25	.14
147	Joey Cora	.10	.08	.04
148	Benito Santiago	.60	.45	.25
149	Eric Show	.07	.05	.03
150	Garry Templeton	.07	.05	.03
151	Carmelo Martinez	.05	.04	.02
152	Von Hayes	.10	.08	.04
153	Lance Parrish	.10	.08	.04
154	Milt Thompson	.07	.05	.03
155	Mike Easler	.05	.04	.02
156	Juan Samuel	.10	.08	.04
157	Steve Jeltz	.05	.04	.02
158	Glenn Wilson	.05	.04	.02
159	Shane Rawley	.07	.05	.03
160	Mike Schmidt	.40	.30	.15
161	Andy Van Slyke	.10	.08	.04
162	Johnny Ray	.07	.05	.03
163a	Barry Bonds (dark jersey, photo actually Johnny Ray)	125.00	94.00	50.00
163b	Barry Bonds (white jersey, correct photo)	.50	.40	.20
164	Junior Ortiz	.05	.04	.02
165	Rafael Belliard	.05	.04	.02
166	Bob Patterson	.05	.04	.02
167	Bobby Bonilla	.50	.40	.20
168	Sid Bream	.07	.05	.03
169	Jim Morrison	.05	.04	.02
170	Jerry Browne	.10	.08	.04
171	Scott Fletcher	.05	.04	.02
172	Ruben Sierra	1.50	1.25	.60
173	Larry Parrish	.07	.05	.03
174	Pete O'Brien	.07	.05	.03
175	Pete Incaviglia	.35	.25	.14
176	Don Slaught	.05	.04	.02
177	Oddibe McDowell	.10	.08	.04
178	Charlie Hough	.07	.05	.03
179	Steve Buechele	.05	.04	.02
180	Bob Stanley	.05	.04	.02
181	Wade Boggs	1.00	.70	.40
182	Jim Rice	.10	.08	.04
183	Bill Buckner	.07	.05	.03
184	Dwight Evans	.10	.08	.04
185	Spike Owen	.05	.04	.02
186	Don Baylor	.10	.08	.04
187	Marc Sullivan	.05	.04	.02
188	Marty Barrett	.07	.05	.03
189	Dave Henderson	.07	.05	.03
190	Bo Diaz	.05	.04	.02
191	Barry Larkin	.90	.70	.35
192	Kal Daniels	.25	.20	.10
193	Terry Francona	.05	.04	.02
194	Tom Browning	.07	.05	.03
195	Ron Oester	.05	.04	.02
196	Buddy Bell	.07	.05	.03
197	Eric Davis	.60	.45	.25

		MT	NR MT	EX
198	Dave Parker	.15	.11	.06
199	Steve Balboni	.05	.04	.02
200	Danny Tartabull	.30	.25	.12
201	Ed Hearn	.05	.04	.02
202	Buddy Biancalana	.05	.04	.02
203	Danny Jackson	.05	.04	.02
204	Frank White	.08	.06	.03
205	Bo Jackson	3.00	2.25	1.25
206	George Brett	.40	.30	.15
207	Kevin Seitzer	.90	.70	.35
208	Willie Wilson	.10	.08	.04
209	Orlando Mercado	.05	.04	.02
210	Darrell Evans	.07	.05	.03
211	Larry Herndon	.05	.04	.02
212	Jack Morris	.15	.11	.06
213	Chet Lemon	.07	.05	.03
214	Mike Heath	.05	.04	.02
215	Darnell Coles	.07	.05	.03
216	Alan Trammell	.20	.15	.08
217	Terry Harper	.05	.04	.02
218	Lou Whitaker	.15	.11	.06
219	Gary Gaetti	.15	.11	.06
220	Tom Nieto	.05	.04	.02
221	Kirby Puckett	.80	.60	.30
222	Tom Brunansky	.10	.08	.04
223	Greg Gagne	.05	.04	.02
224	Dan Gladden	.07	.05	.03
225	Mark Davidson	.07	.05	.03
226	Bert Blyleven	.10	.08	.04
227	Steve Lombardozzi	.05	.04	.02
228	Kent Hrbek	.15	.11	.06
229	Gary Redus	.05	.04	.02
230	Ivan Calderon	.10	.08	.04
231	Tim Hulett	.05	.04	.02
232	Carlton Fisk	.15	.11	.06
233	Greg Walker	.07	.05	.03
234	Ron Karkovice	.05	.04	.02
235	Ozzie Guillen	.07	.05	.03
236	Harold Baines	.12	.09	.05
237	Donnie Hill	.05	.04	.02
238	Rich Dotson	.07	.05	.03
239	Mike Pagliarulo	.10	.08	.04
240	Joel Skinner	.05	.04	.02
241	Don Mattingly	1.50	1.25	.60
242	Gary Ward	.05	.04	.02
243	Dave Winfield	.20	.15	.08
244	Dan Pasqua	.10	.08	.04
245	Wayne Tolleson	.05	.04	.02
246	Willie Randolph	.07	.05	.03
247	Dennis Rasmussen	.07	.05	.03
248	Rickey Henderson	.50	.40	.20
249	Angels Logo/Checklist	.05	.04	.02
250	Astros Logo/Checklist	.05	.04	.02
251	Athletics Logo/Checklist	.05	.04	.02
252	Blue Jays Logo/Checklist	.05	.04	.02
253	Braves Logo/Checklist	.05	.04	.02
254	Brewers Logo/Checklist	.05	.04	.02
255	Cardinals Logo/Checklist	.05	.04	.02
256	Dodgers Logo/Checklist	.05	.04	.02
257	Expos Logo/Checklist	.05	.04	.02
258	Giants Logo/Checklist	.05	.04	.02
259	Indians Logo/Checklist	.05	.04	.02
260	Mariners Logo/Checklist	.05	.04	.02
261	Orioles Logo/Checklist	.05	.04	.02
262	Padres Logo/Checklist	.05	.04	.02
263	Phillies Logo/Checklist	.05	.04	.02
264	Pirates Logo/Checklist	.05	.04	.02
265	Rangers Logo/Checklist	.05	.04	.02
266	Red Sox Logo/Checklist	.05	.04	.02
267	Reds Logo/Checklist	.05	.04	.02
268	Royals Logo/Checklist	.05	.04	.02
269	Tigers Logo/Checklist	.05	.04	.02
270	Twins Logo/Checklist	.05	.04	.02
271	White Sox-Cubs Logos/Checklist	.05	.04	.02
272	Yankees-Mets Logos/Checklist	.05	.04	.02

1987 Donruss Pop-Ups

For the second straight year, Donruss released in conjunction with its All-Stars issue a set of cards designed to fold out to form a three-dimensional stand-up card. Consisting of 20 cards, as opposed to the previous year's 18, the 1987 Donruss Pop-Ups set contains players selected to the 1986 All-Star Game. Background for the 2-1/2" by 5" cards is the Houston Astrodome, site of the 1986 mid-summer classic. Retail packs included one Pop-Up card, three

All-Star cards and one Roberto Clemente puzzle card.

		MT	NR MT	EX
Complete Set:		5.00	3.75	2.00
Common Player:		.20	.15	.08
(1)	Wade Boggs	1.00	.70	.40
(2)	Gary Carter	.25	.20	.10
(3)	Roger Clemens	.80	.60	.30
(4)	Dwight Gooden	.80	.60	.30
(5)	Tony Gwynn	.50	.40	.20
(6)	Rickey Henderson	.75	.55	.30
(7)	Keith Hernandez	.25	.20	.10
(8)	Whitey Herzog	.20	.15	.08
(9)	Dick Howser	.20	.15	.08
(10)	Wally Joyner	.40	.30	.15
(11)	Dale Murphy	.40	.30	.15
(12)	Lance Parrish	.20	.15	.08
(13)	Kirby Puckett	.75	.55	.30
(14)	Cal Ripken	.50	.40	.20
(15)	Ryne Sandberg	.80	.60	.30
(16)	Mike Schmidt	.60	.45	.25
(17)	Ozzie Smith	.30	.25	.12
(18)	Darryl Strawberry	.50	.40	.20
(19)	Lou Whitaker	.20	.15	.08
(20)	Dave Winfield	.30	.25	.12

1987 Donruss Rookies

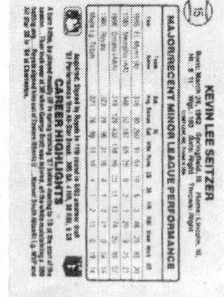

As they did in 1986, Donruss issued a 56-card set highlighting the major league's most promising rookies. The cards are the standard 2-1/2" by 3-1/2" size and are identical in design to the regular Donruss issue. The card fronts have green borders as opposed to the black found in the regular issue and carry the words "The Rookies" in the lower left portion of the card. The set came housed in a specially designed box and was available only through hobby dealers.

		MT	NR MT	EX
Complete Set:		20.00	15.00	8.00
Common Player:		.10	.08	.04
1	Mark McGwire	3.00	2.25	1.25
2	Eric Bell	.10	.08	.04
3	Mark Williamson(FC)	.15	.11	.06

		MT	NR MT	EX
4	Mike Greenwell	2.50	2.00	1.00
5	Ellis Burks(FC)	3.50	2.75	1.50
6	DeWayne Buice(FC)	.20	.15	.08
7	Mark Mclemore (McLemore)	.10	.08	.04
8	Devon White	.30	.25	.12
9	Willie Fraser	.15	.11	.06
10	Lester Lancaster(FC)	.15	.11	.06
11	Ken Williams(FC)	.20	.15	.08
12	Matt Nokes(FC)	.40	.30	.15
13	Jeff Robinson(FC)	.30	.25	.12
14	Bo Jackson	5.00	3.75	2.00
15	Kevin Seitzer(FC)	.80	.60	.30
16	Billy Ripken(FC)	.25	.20	.10
17	B.J. Surhoff	.20	.15	.08
18	Chuck Crim(FC)	.15	.11	.06
19	Mike Birbeck	.10	.08	.04
20	Chris Bosio	.10	.08	.04
21	Les Straker(FC)	.20	.15	.08
22	Mark Davidson(FC)	.15	.11	.06
23	Gene Larkin(FC)	.35	.25	.14
24	Ken Gerhart	.15	.11	.06
25	Luis Polonia(FC)	.35	.25	.14
26	Terry Steinbach	.25	.20	.10
27	Mickey Brantley	.10	.08	.04
28	Mike Stanley	.20	.15	.08
29	Jerry Browne	.10	.08	.04
30	Todd Benzinger(FC)	.50	.40	.20
31	Fred McGriff	2.00	1.50	.80
32	Mike Henneman(FC)	.30	.25	.12
33	Casey Candaele	.10	.08	.04
34	Dave Magadan	1.00	.70	.40
35	David Cone	1.00	.70	.40
36	Mike Jackson(FC)	.20	.15	.08
37	John Mitchell(FC)	.20	.15	.08
38	Mike Dunne(FC)	.25	.20	.10
39	John Smiley(FC)	.40	.30	.15
40	Joe Magrane(FC)	1.25	.90	.50
41	Jim Lindeman	.10	.08	.04
42	Shane Mack(FC)	.25	.20	.10
43	Stan Jefferson	.10	.08	.04
44	Benito Santiago	.60	.45	.25
45	Matt Williams(FC)	7.00	5.25	2.75
46	Dave Meads(FC)	.20	.15	.08
47	Rafael Palmeiro	1.50	1.25	.60
48	Bill Long(FC)	.20	.15	.08
49	Bob Brower	.10	.08	.04
50	James Steels(FC)	.15	.11	.06
51	Paul Noce(FC)	.15	.11	.06
52	Greg Maddux	.60	.45	.25
53	Jeff Musselman	.15	.11	.06
54	Brian Holton	.15	.11	.06
55	Chuck Jackson(FC)	.20	.15	.08
56	Checklist 1-56	.10	.08	.04

1988 Donruss

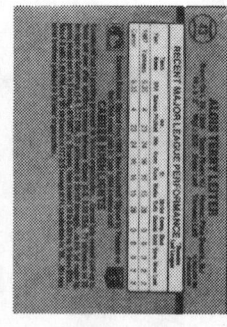

The 1988 Donruss set consists of 660 cards, each measuring 2-1/2" by 3-1/2" in size. The card fronts feature a full-color photo surrounded by a colorful border - alternating stripes of black, red, black, blue, black, blue, black, red and black (in that order), separated by soft-focus edges and airbrushed fades. The player's name and position appear in a red band at the bottom of the card. The Donruss logo is situated in the upper left corner of the card, while the team logo is located in the lower right corner. For the seventh consecutive season, Donruss included a subset of "Diamond Kings" cards (#'s 1-27) in the issue. And for the fifth straight year, Donruss incorporated their highly popular "Rated Rookies" (card #'s 28-47) with the set.

		MT	NR MT	EX
	Complete Set:	30.00	22.00	12.50
	Common Player	.05	.04	.02
1	Mark McGwire (DK)	.60	.45	.25
2	Tim Raines (DK)	.25	.20	.10
3	Benito Santiago (DK)	.30	.25	.12
4	Alan Trammell (DK)	.25	.20	.10
5	Danny Tartabull (DK)	.20	.15	.08
6	Ron Darling (DK)	.12	.09	.05
7	Paul Molitor (DK)	.12	.09	.05
8	Devon White (DK)	.20	.15	.08
9	Andre Dawson (DK)	.20	.15	.08
10	Julio Franco (DK)	.10	.08	.04
11	Scott Fletcher (DK)	.07	.05	.03
12	Tony Fernandez (DK)	.12	.09	.05
13	Shane Rawley (DK)	.07	.05	.03
14	Kal Daniels (DK)	.20	.15	.08
15	Jack Clark (DK)	.15	.11	.06
16	Dwight Evans (DK)	.12	.09	.05
17	Tommy John (DK)	.15	.11	.06
18	Andy Van Slyke (DK)	.15	.11	.06
19	Gary Gaetti (DK)	.12	.09	.05
20	Mark Langston (DK)	.10	.08	.04
21	Will Clark (DK)	.80	.60	.30
22	Glenn Hubbard (DK)	.07	.05	.03
23	Billy Hatcher (DK)	.07	.05	.03
24	Bob Welch (DK)	.10	.08	.04
25	Ivan Calderon (DK)	.10	.08	.04
26	Cal Ripken, Jr. (DK)	.35	.25	.14
27	Checklist 1-27	.05	.04	.02
28	*Mackey Sasser* (RR)(FC)	.40	.30	.15
29	*Jeff Treadway* (RR)(FC)	.30	.25	.12
30	*Mike Campbell* (RR)(FC)	.25	.20	.10
31	*Lance Johnson* (RR)(FC)	.40	.30	.15
32	*Nelson Liriano* (RR)(FC)	.25	.20	.10
33	*Shawn Abner* (RR)(FC)	.20	.15	.08
34	*Roberto Alomar* (RR)(FC)	2.50	2.00	1.00
35	*Shawn Hillegas* (RR)(FC)	.25	.20	.10
36	*Joey Meyer* (RR)	.20	.15	.08
37	Kevin Elster (RR)	.30	.25	.12
38	*Jose Lind* (RR)(FC)	.30	.25	.12
39	*Kirt Manwaring* (RR)(FC)	.35	.25	.14
40	*Mark Grace* (RR)(FC)	3.00	2.25	1.25
41	*Jody Reed* (RR)(FC)	.70	.50	.30
42	*John Farrell* (RR)(FC)	.35	.25	.14
43	*Al Leiter* (RR)(FC)	.20	.15	.08
44	*Gary Thurman* (RR)(FC)	.20	.15	.18
45	*Vicente Palacios* (RR)(FC)	.30	.25	.12
46	*Eddie Williams* (RR)(FC)	.25	.20	.10
47	*Jack McDowell* (RR)(FC)	.40	.30	.15
48	Ken Dixon	.05	.04	.02
49	Mike Birkbeck	.07	.05	.03
50	Eric King	.07	.05	.03
51	Roger Clemens	.80	.60	.30
52	Pat Clements	.05	.04	.02
53	Fernando Valenzuela	.25	.20	.10
54	Mark Gubicza	.12	.09	.05
55	Jay Howell	.07	.05	.03
56	Floyd Youmans	.05	.04	.02
57	Ed Correa	.05	.04	.02
58	*DeWayne Buice*	.15	.11	.06
59	Jose DeLeon	.07	.05	.03
60	Danny Cox	.07	.05	.03
61	Nolan Ryan	.50	.40	.20
62	Steve Bedrosian	.12	.09	.05
63	Tom Browning	.10	.08	.04
64	Mark Davis	.05	.04	.02
65	R.J. Reynolds	.05	.04	.02
66	Kevin Mitchell	.60	.45	.25
67	Ken Oberkfell	.05	.04	.02
68	Rick Sutcliffe	.10	.08	.04
69	Dwight Gooden	.60	.45	.25
70	Scott Bankhead	.07	.05	.03
71	Bert Blyleven	.12	.09	.05
72	Jimmy Key	.10	.08	.04
73	*Les Straker*	.15	.11	.06
74	Jim Clancy	.07	.05	.03
75	Mike Moore	.05	.04	.02
76	Ron Darling	.12	.09	.05
77	Ed Lynch	.05	.04	.02
78	Dale Murphy	.40	.30	.15
79	Doug Drabek	.07	.05	.03
80	Scott Garrelts	.05	.04	.02
81	Ed Whitson	.05	.04	.02
82	Rob Murphy	.07	.05	.03
83	Shane Rawley	.07	.05	.03

		MT	NR MT	EX
84	Greg Mathews	.07	.05	.03
85	Jim Deshaies	.07	.05	.03
86	Mike Witt	.07	.05	.03
87	Donnie Hill	.05	.04	.02
88	Jeff Reed	.05	.04	.02
89	Mike Boddicker	.07	.05	.03
90	Ted Higuera	.10	.08	.04
91	Walt Terrell	.07	.05	.03
92	Bob Stanley	.05	.04	.02
93	Dave Righetti	.15	.11	.06
94	Orel Hershiser	.25	.20	.10
95	Chris Bando	.05	.04	.02
96	Bret Saberhagen	.15	.11	.06
97	Curt Young	.07	.05	.03
98	Tim Burke	.05	.04	.02
99	Charlie Hough	.07	.05	.03
100a	Checklist 28-137	.05	.04	.02
100b	Checklist 28-133	.10	.08	.04
101	Bobby Witt	.10	.08	.04
102	George Brett	.40	.30	.15
103	Mickey Tettleton	.25	.20	.10
104	Scott Bailes	.07	.05	.03
105	Mike Pagliarulo	.10	.08	.04
106	Mike Scioscia	.07	.05	.03
107	Tom Brookens	.05	.04	.02
108	Ray Knight	.07	.05	.03
109	Dan Plesac	.10	.08	.04
110	Wally Joyner	.40	.30	.15
111	Bob Forsch	.07	.05	.03
112	Mike Scott	.12	.09	.05
113	Kevin Gross	.07	.05	.03
114	Benito Santiago	.35	.25	.14
115	Bob Kipper	.05	.04	.02
116	Mike Krukow	.07	.05	.03
117	Chris Bosio	.07	.05	.03
118	Sid Fernandez	.10	.08	.04
119	Jody Davis	.07	.05	.03
120	Mike Morgan	.05	.04	.02
121	Mark Eichhorn	.07	.05	.03
122	Jeff Reardon	.10	.08	.04
123	John Franco	.10	.08	.04
124	Richard Dotson	.07	.05	.03
125	Eric Bell	.05	.04	.02
126	Juan Nieves	.07	.05	.03
127	Jack Morris	.20	.15	.08
128	Rick Rhoden	.07	.05	.03
129	Rich Gedman	.07	.05	.03
130	Ken Howell	.05	.04	.02
131	Brook Jacoby	.10	.08	.04
132	Danny Jackson	.12	.09	.05
133	Gene Nelson	.05	.04	.02
134	Neal Heaton	.05	.04	.02
135	Willie Fraser	.05	.04	.02
136	Jose Guzman	.07	.05	.03
137	Ozzie Guillen	.07	.05	.03
138	Bob Knepper	.07	.05	.03
139	*Mike Jackson*	.20	.15	.08
140	*Joe Magrane*	.60	.45	.25
141	Jimmy Jones	.07	.05	.03
142	Ted Power	.05	.04	.02
143	Ozzie Virgil	.05	.04	.02
144	*Felix Fermin*(FC)	.15	.11	.06
145	Kelly Downs	.10	.08	.04
146	Shawon Dunston	.10	.08	.04
147	Scott Bradley	.05	.04	.02
148	Dave Stieb	.10	.08	.04
149	Frank Viola	.15	.11	.06
150	Terry Kennedy	.07	.05	.03
151	Bill Wegman	.05	.04	.02
152	*Matt Nokes*	.50	.40	.20
153	Wade Boggs	1.00	.70	.40
154	Wayne Tolleson	.05	.04	.02
155	Mariano Duncan	.05	.04	.02
156	Julio Franco	.10	.08	.04
157	Charlie Leibrandt	.07	.05	.03
158	Terry Steinbach	.10	.08	.04
159	Mike Fitzgerald	.05	.04	.02
160	Jack Lazorko	.05	.04	.02
161	Mitch Williams	.07	.05	.03
162	Greg Walker	.07	.05	.03
163	Alan Ashby	.05	.04	.02
164	Tony Gwynn	.35	.25	.14
165	Bruce Ruffin	.07	.05	.03
166	Ron Robinson	.05	.04	.02
167	Zane Smith	.07	.05	.03
168	Junior Ortiz	.05	.04	.02
169	Jamie Moyer	.07	.05	.03
170	Tony Pena	.07	.05	.03
171	Cal Ripken	.35	.25	.14
172	B.J. Surhoff	.12	.09	.05
173	Lou Whitaker	.25	.20	.10

		MT	NR MT	EX				MT	NR MT	EX
174	*Ellis Burks*	1.75	1.25	.70		264	Randy Ready	.05	.04	.02
175	Ron Guidry	.15	.11	.06		265	Kurt Stillwell	.10	.08	.04
176	Steve Sax	.15	.11	.06		266	David Palmer	.05	.04	.02
177	Danny Tartabull	.20	.15	.08		267	Mike Diaz	.07	.05	.03
178	Carney Lansford	.10	.08	.04		268	Rob Thompson	.07	.05	.03
179	Casey Candaele	.05	.04	.02		269	Andre Dawson	.20	.15	.08
180	Scott Fletcher	.07	.05	.03		270	Lee Guetterman	.05	.04	.02
181	Mark McLemore	.05	.04	.02		271	Willie Upshaw	.07	.05	.03
182	Ivan Calderon	.10	.08	.04		272	Randy Bush	.05	.04	.02
183	Jack Clark	.15	.11	.06		273	Larry Sheets	.07	.05	.03
184	Glenn Davis	.15	.11	.06		274	Rob Deer	.07	.05	.03
185	Luis Aguayo	.05	.04	.02		275	Kirk Gibson	.20	.15	.08
186	Bo Diaz	.07	.05	.03		276	Marty Barrett	.07	.05	.03
187	Stan Jefferson	.07	.05	.03		277	Rickey Henderson	.40	.30	.15
188	Sid Bream	.07	.05	.03		278	Pedro Guerrero	.15	.11	.06
189	Bob Brenly	.05	.04	.02		279	Brett Butler	.07	.05	.03
190	Dion James	.07	.05	.03		280	Kevin Seitzer	.80	.60	.30
191	Leon Durham	.07	.05	.03		281	Mike Davis	.07	.05	.03
192	Jesse Orosco	.07	.05	.03		282	Andres Galarraga	.15	.11	.06
193	Alvin Davis	.12	.09	.05		283	Devon White	.30	.25	.12
194	Gary Gaetti	.12	.09	.05		284	Pete O'Brien	.07	.05	.03
195	Fred McGriff	.40	.30	.15		285	Jerry Hairston	.05	.04	.02
196	Steve Lombardozzi	.05	.04	.02		286	Kevin Bass	.07	.05	.03
197	Rance Mulliniks	.05	.04	.02		287	Carmelo Martinez	.07	.05	.03
198	Rey Quinones	.05	.04	.02		288	Juan Samuel	.12	.09	.05
199	Gary Carter	.25	.20	.10		289	Kal Daniels	.20	.15	.08
200a	Checklist 138-247	.05	.04	.02		290	Albert Hall	.05	.04	.02
200b	Checklist 134-239	.10	.08	.04		291	Andy Van Slyke	.12	.09	.05
201	Keith Moreland	.07	.05	.03		292	Lee Smith	.10	.08	.04
202	Ken Griffey	.07	.05	.03		293	Vince Coleman	.20	.15	.08
203	*Tommy Gregg*(FC)	.25	.20	.10		294	Tom Niedenfuer	.07	.05	.03
204	Will Clark	1.25	.90	.50		295	Robin Yount	.30	.25	.12
205	John Kruk	.10	.08	.04		296	*Jeff Robinson*	.30	.25	.12
206	Buddy Bell	.07	.05	.03		297	*Todd Benzinger*	.40	.30	.15
207	Von Hayes	.07	.05	.03		298	Dave Winfield	.30	.25	.12
208	Tommy Herr	.07	.05	.03		299	Mickey Hatcher	.05	.04	.02
209	Craig Reynolds	.05	.04	.02		300a	Checklist 248-357	.05	.04	.02
210	Gary Pettis	.05	.04	.02		300b	Checklist 240-345	.10	.08	.04
211	Harold Baines	.12	.09	.05		301	Bud Black	.05	.04	.02
212	Vance Law	.07	.05	.03		302	Jose Canseco	1.75	1.25	.70
213	Ken Gerhart	.07	.05	.03		303	Tom Foley	.05	.04	.02
214	Jim Gantner	.05	.04	.02		304	Pete Incaviglia	.15	.11	.06
215	Chet Lemon	.07	.05	.03		305	Bob Boone	.07	.05	.03
216	Dwight Evans	.12	.09	.05		306	*Bill Long*	.20	.15	.08
217	Don Mattingly	1.25	.90	.50		307	Willie McGee	.12	.09	.05
218	Franklin Stubbs	.07	.05	.03		308	*Ken Caminiti*(FC)	.30	.25	.12
219	Pat Tabler	.07	.05	.03		309	Darren Daulton	.05	.04	.02
220	Bo Jackson	1.25	.90	.50		310	Tracy Jones	.12	.09	.05
221	Tony Phillips	.05	.04	.02		311	Greg Booker	.07	.05	.03
222	Tim Wallach	.10	.08	.04		312	Mike LaValliere	.07	.05	.03
223	Ruben Sierra	.60	.45	.25		313	Chili Davis	.07	.05	.03
224	Steve Buechele	.05	.04	.02		314	Glenn Hubbard	.05	.04	.02
225	Frank White	.07	.05	.03		315	*Paul Noce*	.10	.08	.04
226	Alfredo Griffin	.07	.05	.03		316	Keith Hernandez	.20	.15	.08
227	Greg Swindell	.20	.15	.08		317	Mark Langston	.12	.09	.05
228	Willie Randolph	.07	.05	.03		318	Keith Atherton	.05	.04	.02
229	Mike Marshall	.12	.09	.05		319	Tony Fernandez	.12	.09	.05
230	Alan Trammell	.25	.20	.10		320	Kent Hrbek	.15	.11	.06
231	Eddie Murray	.35	.25	.14		321	John Cerutti	.07	.05	.03
232	Dale Sveum	.07	.05	.03		322	Mike Kingery	.05	.04	.02
233	Dick Schofield	.05	.04	.02		323	Dave Magadan	.12	.09	.05
234	Jose Oquendo	.05	.04	.02		324	Rafael Palmeiro	.40	.30	.15
235	Bill Doran	.07	.05	.03		325	Jeff Dedmon	.05	.04	.02
236	Milt Thompson	.05	.04	.02		326	Barry Bonds	.12	.09	.05
237	Marvell Wynne	.05	.04	.02		327	Jeffrey Leonard	.07	.05	.03
238	Bobby Bonilla	.15	.11	.06		328	Tim Flannery	.05	.04	.02
239	Chris Speier	.05	.04	.02		329	Dave Concepcion	.07	.05	.03
240	Glenn Braggs	.10	.08	.04		330	Mike Schmidt	.50	.40	.20
241	Wally Backman	.07	.05	.03		331	Bill Dawley	.05	.04	.02
242	Ryne Sandberg	.50	.40	.20		332	Larry Andersen	.05	.04	.02
243	Phil Bradley	.10	.08	.04		333	Jack Howell	.07	.05	.03
244	Kelly Gruber	.05	.04	.02		334	*Ken Williams*	.20	.15	.08
245	Tom Brunansky	.10	.08	.04		335	Bryn Smith	.05	.04	.02
246	Ron Oester	.05	.04	.02		336	*Billy Ripken*	.25	.20	.10
247	Bobby Thigpen	.10	.08	.04		337	Greg Brock	.07	.05	.03
248	Fred Lynn	.15	.11	.06		338	Mike Heath	.05	.04	.02
249	Paul Molitor	.12	.09	.05		339	Mike Greenwell	1.25	.90	.50
250	Darrell Evans	.10	.08	.04		340	Claudell Washington	.07	.05	.03
251	Gary Ward	.07	.05	.03		341	Jose Gonzalez	.05	.04	.02
252	Bruce Hurst	.10	.08	.04		342	Mel Hall	.07	.05	.03
253	Bob Welch	.10	.08	.04		343	Jim Eisenreich	.07	.05	.03
254	Joe Carter	.12	.09	.05		344	Tony Bernazard	.05	.04	.02
255	Willie Wilson	.10	.08	.04		345	Tim Raines	.25	.20	.10
256	Mark McGwire	.80	.60	.30		346	Bob Brower	.07	.05	.03
257	Mitch Webster	.07	.05	.03		347	Larry Parrish	.07	.05	.03
258	Brian Downing	.07	.05	.03		348	Thad Bosley	.05	.04	.02
259	Mike Stanley	.10	.08	.04		349	Dennis Eckersley	.12	.09	.05
260	Carlton Fisk	.20	.15	.08		350	Cory Snyder	.20	.15	.08
261	Billy Hatcher	.07	.05	.03		351	Rick Cerone	.05	.04	.02
262	Glenn Wilson	.07	.05	.03		352	John Shelby	.05	.04	.02
263	Ozzie Smith	.15	.11	.06		353	Larry Herndon	.05	.04	.02

		MT	NR MT	EX			MT	NR MT	EX
354	John Habyan	.05	.04	.02	444	Garth Iorg	.05	.04	.02
355	*Chuck Crim*	.12	.09	.05	445	Ed Nunez	.05	.04	.02
356	Gus Polidor	.05	.04	.02	446	Rick Aguilera	.05	.04	.02
357	Ken Dayley	.05	.04	.02	447	Jerry Mumphrey	.05	.04	.02
358	Danny Darwin	.05	.04	.02	448	Rafael Ramirez	.05	.04	.02
359	Lance Parrish	.15	.11	.06	449	*John Smiley*	.35	.25	.14
360	*James Steels*	.12	.09	.05	450	Atlee Hammaker	.05	.04	.02
361	*Al Pedrique*(FC)	.15	.11	.06	451	Lance McCullers	.07	.05	.03
362	Mike Aldrete	.07	.05	.03	452	*Guy Hoffman*(FC)	.07	.05	.03
363	Juan Castillo	.05	.04	.02	453	Chris James	.12	.09	.05
364	Len Dykstra	.10	.08	.04	454	Terry Pendleton	.07	.05	.03
365	Luis Quinones	.05	.04	.02	455	*Dave Meads*	.15	.11	.06
366	Jim Presley	.10	.08	.04	456	Bill Buckner	.10	.08	.04
367	Lloyd Moseby	.07	.05	.03	457	*John Pawlowski*(FC)	.10	.08	.04
368	Kirby Puckett	.50	.40	.25	458	Bob Sebra	.05	.04	.02
369	Eric Davis	.80	.60	.30	459	Jim Dwyer	.05	.04	.02
370	Gary Redus	.05	.04	.02	460	*Jay Aldrich*(FC)	.12	.09	.05
371	Dave Schmidt	.05	.04	.02	461	Frank Tanana	.07	.05	.03
372	Mark Clear	.05	.04	.02	462	Oil Can Boyd	.07	.05	.03
373	Dave Bergman	.05	.04	.02	463	Dan Pasqua	.10	.08	.04
374	Charles Hudson	.05	.04	.02	464	*Tim Crews*(FC)	.15	.11	.06
375	Calvin Schiraldi	.05	.04	.02	465	Andy Allanson	.07	.05	.03
376	Alex Trevino	.05	.04	.02	466	*Bill Pecota*(FC)	.15	.11	.06
377	Tom Candiotti	.05	.04	.02	467	Steve Ontiveros	.05	.04	.02
378	Steve Farr	.05	.04	.02	468	Hubie Brooks	.10	.08	.04
379	Mike Gallego	.05	.04	.02	469	*Paul Kilgus*(FC)	.20	.15	.08
380	Andy McGaffigan	.05	.04	.02	470	Dale Mohorcic	.05	.04	.02
381	Kirk McCaskill	.07	.05	.03	471	Dan Quisenberry	.07	.05	.03
382	Oddibe McDowell	.07	.05	.03	472	Dave Stewart	.10	.08	.04
383	Floyd Bannister	.07	.05	.03	473	Dave Clark	.07	.05	.03
384	Denny Walling	.05	.04	.02	474	Joel Skinner	.05	.04	.02
385	Don Carman	.07	.05	.03	475	Dave Anderson	.05	.04	.02
386	Todd Worrell	.10	.08	.04	476	Dan Petry	.07	.05	.03
387	Eric Show	.07	.05	.03	477	*Carl Nichols*(FC)	.12	.09	.05
388	Dave Parker	.20	.15	.08	478	Ernest Riles	.05	.04	.02
389	Rick Mahler	.05	.04	.02	479	George Hendrick	.07	.05	.03
390	*Mike Dunne*	.25	.20	.08	480	John Morris	.05	.04	.02
391	Candy Maldonado	.07	.05	.03	481	*Manny Hernandez*(FC)	.10	.08	.04
392	Bob Dernier	.05	.04	.02	482	Jeff Stone	.05	.04	.02
393	Dave Valle	.05	.04	.02	483	Chris Brown	.07	.05	.03
394	Ernie Whitt	.07	.05	.03	484	Mike Bielecki	.05	.04	.02
395	Juan Berenguer	.05	.04	.02	485	Dave Dravecky	.07	.05	.03
396	Mike Young	.05	.04	.02	486	Rick Manning	.05	.04	.02
397	Mike Felder	.05	.04	.02	487	Bill Almon	.05	.04	.02
398	Willie Hernandez	.07	.05	.03	488	Jim Sundberg	.07	.05	.03
399	Jim Rice	.30	.25	.12	489	Ken Phelps	.07	.05	.03
400a	Checklist 358-467	.05	.04	.02	490	Tom Henke	.07	.05	.03
400b	Checklist 346-451	.10	.08	.04	491	Dan Gladden	.05	.04	.02
401	Tommy John	.15	.11	.06	492	Barry Larkin	.40	.30	.15
402	Brian Holton	.07	.05	.03	493	*Fred Manrique*(FC)	.15	.11	.06
403	Carmen Castillo	.05	.04	.02	494	Mike Griffin	.05	.04	.02
404	Jamie Quirk	.05	.04	.02	495	*Mark Knudson*(FC)	.10	.08	.04
405	Dwayne Murphy	.07	.05	.03	496	Bill Madlock	.10	.08	.04
406	*Jeff Parrett*(FC)	.25	.20	.10	497	Tim Stoddard	.05	.04	.02
407	Don Sutton	.20	.15	.08	498	*Sam Horn*(FC)	.30	.25	.12
408	Jerry Browne	.07	.05	.03	499	*Tracy Woodson*(FC)	.15	.11	.06
409	Jim Winn	.05	.04	.02	500a	Checklist 468-577	.05	.04	.02
410	Dave Smith	.07	.05	.03	500b	Checklist 452-557	.10	.08	.04
411	*Shane Mack*	.15	.11	.06	501	Ken Schrom	.05	.04	.02
412	Greg Gross	.05	.04	.02	502	Angel Salazar	.05	.04	.02
413	Nick Esasky	.07	.05	.03	503	Eric Plunk	.05	.04	.02
414	Damaso Garcia	.05	.04	.02	504	Joe Hesketh	.05	.04	.02
415	Brian Fisher	.07	.05	.03	505	Greg Minton	.05	.04	.02
416	Brian Dayett	.05	.04	.02	506	Geno Petralli	.05	.04	.02
417	Curt Ford	.05	.04	.02	507	Bob James	.05	.04	.02
418	*Mark Williamson*	.12	.09	.05	508	*Robbie Wine*(FC)	.12	.09	.05
419	Bill Schroeder	.05	.04	.02	509	Jeff Calhoun	.05	.04	.02
420	*Mike Henneman*	.25	.20	.10	510	Steve Lake	.05	.04	.02
421	*John Marzano*(FC)	.25	.20	.10	511	Mark Grant	.05	.04	.02
422	Ron Kittle	.07	.05	.03	512	Frank Williams	.05	.04	.02
423	Matt Young	.05	.04	.02	513	*Jeff Blauser*(FC)	.30	.25	.12
424	Steve Balboni	.07	.05	.03	514	Bob Walk	.05	.04	.02
425	*Luis Polonia*	.25	.20	.10	515	Craig Lefferts	.05	.04	.02
426	Randy St. Claire	.05	.04	.02	516	Manny Trillo	.07	.05	.03
427	Greg Harris	.05	.04	.02	517	Jerry Reed	.05	.04	.02
428	Johnny Ray	.07	.05	.03	518	Rick Leach	.05	.04	.02
429	Ray Searage	.05	.04	.02	519	*Mark Davidson*	.12	.09	.05
430	Ricky Horton	.07	.05	.03	520	*Jeff Ballard*(FC)	.25	.20	.10
431	*Gerald Young*(FC)	.35	.25	.14	521	*Dave Stapleton*(FC)	.10	.08	.04
432	Rick Schu	.05	.04	.02	522	Pat Sheridan	.05	.04	.02
433	Paul O'Neill	.07	.05	.03	523	Al Nipper	.05	.04	.02
434	Rich Gossage	.15	.11	.06	524	Steve Trout	.05	.04	.02
435	John Cangelosi	.05	.04	.02	525	Jeff Hamilton	.07	.05	.03
436	Mike LaCoss	.05	.04	.02	526	*Tommy Hinzo*(FC)	.15	.11	.06
437	Gerald Perry	.10	.08	.04	527	Lonnie Smith	.07	.05	.03
438	Dave Martinez	.07	.05	.03	528	*Greg Cadaret*(FC)	.20	.15	.08
439	Darryl Strawberry	.35	.25	.14	529	Rob McClure (Bob)	.05	.04	.02
440	John Moses	.05	.04	.02	530	Chuck Finley	.10	.08	.04
441	Greg Gagne	.05	.04	.02	531	Jeff Russell	.05	.04	.02
442	Jesse Barfield	.12	.09	.05	532	Steve Lyons	.05	.04	.02
443	George Frazier	.05	.04	.02	533	Terry Puhl	.05	.04	.02

		MT	NR MT	EX
534	*Eric Nolte*(FC)	.15	.11	.06
535	Kent Tekulve	.07	.05	.03
536	*Pat Pacillo*(FC)	.15	.11	.06
537	Charlie Puleo	.05	.04	.02
538	*Tom Prince*(FC)	.15	.11	.06
539	Greg Maddux	.15	.11	.06
540	Jim Lindeman	.07	.05	.03
541	*Pete Stanicek*(FC)	.15	.11	.06
542	Steve Kiefer	.05	.04	.02
543	Jim Morrison	.05	.04	.02
544	Spike Owen	.05	.04	.02
545	*Jay Buhner*(FC)	.30	.25	.12
546	*Mike Devereaux*(FC)	.30	.25	.12
547	Jerry Don Gleaton	.05	.04	.02
548	Jose Rijo	.07	.05	.03
549	Dennis Martinez	.05	.04	.02
550	Mike Loynd	.05	.04	.02
551	Darrell Miller	.05	.04	.02
552	Dave LaPoint	.07	.05	.03
553	John Tudor	.10	.08	.04
554	*Rocky Childress*(FC)	.12	.09	.05
555	*Wally Ritchie*(FC)	.15	.11	.06
556	Terry McGriff	.05	.04	.02
557	Dave Leiper	.05	.04	.02
558	Jeff Robinson	.07	.05	.03
559	Jose Uribe	.05	.04	.02
560	Ted Simmons	.10	.08	.04
561	*Lester Lancaster*	.15	.11	.06
562	*Keith Miller*(FC)	.25	.20	.10
563	Harold Reynolds	.07	.05	.03
564	*Gene Larkin*	.20	.15	.08
565	Cecil Fielder	.70	.50	.30
566	Roy Smalley	.05	.04	.02
567	Duane Ward	.07	.05	.03
568	*Bill Wilkinson*(FC)	.15	.11	.06
569	Howard Johnson	.10	.08	.04
570	Frank DiPino	.05	.04	.02
571	*Pete Smith*(FC)	.30	.25	.12
572	Darnell Coles	.07	.05	.03
573	Don Robinson	.07	.05	.03
574	Rob Nelson	.05	.04	.02
575	Dennis Rasmussen	.10	.08	.04
576	Steve Jeltz (photo actually Juan Samuel)			
		.05	.04	.02
577	*Tom Pagnozzi*(FC)	.15	.11	.06
578	Ty Gainey	.05	.04	.02
579	Gary Lucas	.05	.04	.02
580	Ron Hassey	.05	.04	.02
581	Herm Winningham	.05	.04	.02
582	*Rene Gonzales*(FC)	.15	.11	.06
583	Brad Komminsk	.05	.04	.02
584	Doyle Alexander	.07	.05	.03
585	Jeff Sellers	.07	.05	.03
586	Bill Gullickson	.05	.04	.02
587	Tim Belcher(FC)	.50	.40	.20
588	*Doug Jones*(FC)	.40	.30	.15
589	*Melido Perez*(FC)	.30	.25	.12
590	Rick Honeycutt	.05	.04	.02
591	Pascual Perez	.07	.05	.03
592	Curt Wilkerson	.05	.04	.02
593	Steve Howe	.07	.05	.03
594	*John Davis*(FC)	.20	.15	.08
595	Storm Davis	.10	.08	.04
596	Sammy Stewart	.05	.04	.02
597	Neil Allen	.05	.04	.02
598	Alejandro Pena	.07	.05	.03
599	Mark Thurmond	.05	.04	.02
600a	Checklist 578-BC26	.05	.04	.02
600b	Checklist 558-660	.10	.08	.04
601	*Jose Mesa*(FC)	.20	.15	.08
602	*Don August*(FC)	.15	.11	.06
603	Terry Leach	.10	.08	.04
604	*Tom Newell*(FC)	.20	.15	.08
605	*Randall Byers*(FC)	.20	.15	.08
606	Jim Gott	.05	.04	.02
607	Harry Spilman	.05	.04	.02
608	John Candelaria	.07	.05	.03
609	*Mike Brumley*(FC)	.20	.15	.08
610	Mickey Brantley	.07	.05	.03
611	*Jose Nunez*(FC)	.25	.20	.10
612	Tom Nieto	.05	.04	.02
613	Rick Reuschel	.10	.08	.04
614	Lee Mazzilli	.12	.09	.05
615	*Scott Lusader*(FC)	.20	.15	.08
616	Bobby Meacham	.05	.04	.02
617	Kevin McReynolds	.15	.11	.06
618	Gene Garber	.05	.04	.02
619	*Barry Lyons*(FC)	.15	.11	.06
620	Randy Myers	.10	.08	.04
621	Donnie Moore	.05	.04	.02
622	Domingo Ramos	.05	.04	.02

		MT	NR MT	EX
623	Ed Romero	.05	.04	.02
624	*Greg Myers*(FC)	.25	.20	.10
625	Ripken Baseball Family (Billy Ripken, Cal			
	Ripken, Jr., Cal Ripken, Sr.)	.15	.11	.06
626	Pat Perry	.05	.04	.02
627	Andres Thomas	.10	.08	.04
628	Matt Williams	3.00	2.25	1.25
629	*Dave Hengel*(FC)	.20	.15	.08
630	Jeff Musselman	.07	.05	.03
631	Tim Laudner	.05	.04	.02
632	Bob Ojeda	.07	.05	.03
633	Rafael Santana	.05	.04	.02
634	*Wes Gardner*(FC)	.25	.20	.10
635	*Roberto Kelly*(FC)	1.25	.90	.50
636	Mike Flanagan	.12	.09	.05
637	*Jay Bell*(FC)	.40	.30	.15
638	Bob Melvin	.05	.04	.02
639	*Damon Berryhill*(FC)	.40	.30	.15
640	*David Wells*(FC)	.25	.20	.10
641	Stan Musial Puzzle Card	.05	.04	.02
642	Doug Sisk	.05	.04	.02
643	*Keith Hughes*(FC)	.20	.15	.08
644	*Tom Glavine*(FC)	.40	.30	.15
645	Al Newman	.05	.04	.02
646	Scott Sanderson	.05	.04	.02
647	Scott Terry	.10	.08	.04
648	Tim Teufel	.12	.09	.05
649	Garry Templeton	.12	.09	.05
650	Manny Lee	.05	.04	.02
651	Roger McDowell	.10	.08	.04
652	Mookie Wilson	.15	.11	.06
653	David Cone	.70	.50	.30
654	*Ron Gant*(FC)	2.50	2.00	1.00
655	Joe Price	.12	.09	.05
656	George Bell	.25	.20	.10
657	*Gregg Jefferies*(FC)	5.00	3.75	2.00
658	*Todd Stottlemyre*(FC)	.50	.40	.20
659	*Geronimo Berroa*(FC)	.25	.20	.10
660	Jerry Royster	.12	.09	.05

1988 Donruss All-Stars

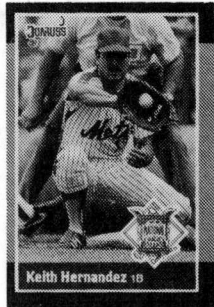 

For the third consecutive year, this set of 64 cards featuring major league All-Stars was marketed in conjunction with Donruss Pop-Ups. The 1988 issue included a major change - the cards were reduced in size from 3-1/2" x 5" to a standard 2-1/2" x 3-1/2". The set features players from the 1987 All-Star Game starting lineup. Card fronts feature full-color photos, framed in blue, black and white, with a Donruss logo upper left. Player name and position appear in a red banner below the photo, along with the appropriate National or American League logo. All-Stars card backs include player stats and All-Star Game record. In 1988, All-Stars cards were distributed in individual packages containing three All-Stars, one Pop-Up and three Donruss puzzle pieces.

		MT	NR MT	EX
	Complete Set:	8.00	6.00	3.25
	Common Player:	.09	.07	.04
1	Don Mattingly	2.00	1.50	.80
2	Dave Winfield	.25	.20	.10
3	Willie Randolph	.09	.07	.04
4	Rickey Henderson	.50	.40	.20
5	Cal Ripken, Jr.	.30	.25	.12

		MT	NR MT	EX
6	George Bell	.20	.15	.08
7	Wade Boggs	.80	.60	.30
8	Bret Saberhagen	.15	.11	.06
9	Terry Kennedy	.09	.07	.04
10	John McNamara	.09	.07	.04
11	Jay Howell	.09	.07	.04
12	Harold Baines	.12	.09	.05
13	Harold Reynolds	.09	.07	.04
14	Bruce Hurst	.09	.07	.04
15	Kirby Puckett	.50	.40	.20
16	Matt Nokes	.20	.15	.08
17	Pat Tabler	.09	.07	.04
18	Dan Plesac	.12	.09	.05
19	Mark McGwire	1.00	.70	.40
20	Mike Witt	.09	.07	.04
21	Larry Parrish	.09	.07	.04
22	Alan Trammell	.20	.15	.08
23	Dwight Evans	.12	.09	.05
24	Jack Morris	.12	.09	.05
25	Tony Fernandez	.12	.09	.05
26	Mark Langston	.20	.15	.08
27	Kevin Seitzer	.40	.30	.15
28	Tom Henke	.09	.07	.04
29	Dave Righetti	.12	.09	.05
30	Oakland Coliseum	.09	.07	.04
31	Top Vote Getter (Wade Boggs)	.60	.45	.25
32	Checklist 1-32	.09	.07	.04
33	Jack Clark	.15	.11	.06
34	Darryl Strawberry	.40	.30	.15
35	Ryne Sandberg	.20	.15	.08
36	Andre Dawson	.20	.15	.08
37	Ozzie Smith	.15	.11	.06
38	Eric Davis	.50	.40	.20
39	Mike Schmidt	.80	.60	.30
40	Mike Scott	.12	.09	.05
41	Gary Carter	.12	.09	.05
42	Davey Johnson	.09	.07	.04
43	Rick Sutcliffe	.12	.09	.05
44	Willie McGee	.12	.09	.05
45	Hubie Brooks	.09	.07	.04
46	Dale Murphy	.40	.30	.15
47	Bo Diaz	.09	.07	.04
48	Pedro Guerrero	.15	.11	.06
49	Keith Hernandez	.15	.11	.06
50	Ozzie Virgil	.09	.07	.04
51	Tony Gwynn	.25	.20	.10
52	Rick Reuschel	.12	.09	.05
53	John Franco	.12	.09	.05
54	Jeffrey Leonard	.09	.07	.04
55	Juan Samuel	.15	.11	.06
56	Orel Hershiser	.20	.15	.08
57	Tim Raines	.20	.15	.08
58	Sid Fernandez	.12	.09	.05
59	Tim Wallach	.12	.09	.05
60	Lee Smith	.09	.07	.04
61	Steve Bedrosian	.12	.09	.05
62	MVP (Tim Raines)	.20	.15	.08
63	Top Vote Getter (Ozzie Smith)	.15	.11	.06
64	Checklist 33-64	.09	.07	.04

1988 Donruss Baseball's Best

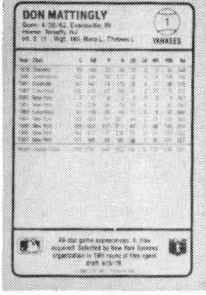

The design of this 336-card set (2-1/2" by 3-1/2") is similar to the regular 1988 Donruss issue with the exception of the borders which are orange, instead of blue. Full-color player photos are framed by the Donruss logo upper left, team logo lower right and a bright red and white player name that spans the bottom margin. The backs are black and white, framed by a yellow border, and include personal information, year-by-year stats and major league totals. This set was packaged in a bright red cardboard box (10" x 11" x 12") that contained six individually shrink-wrapped packs of 56 cards. Donruss marketed the set via retail chain outlets including Walgreens, Venture, Wall-Mart, Ben Franklin, Shopko, Super X, Target, McCrory's, Osco, Woolworth and J.C. Murphy.

		MT	NR MT	EX
	Complete Set:	20.00	15.00	8.00
	Common Player:	.05	.04	.02
1	Don Mattingly	1.50	1.25	.60
2	Ron Gant	.50	.40	.20
3	Bob Boone	.05	.04	.02
4	Mark Grace	1.50	1.25	.60
5	Andy Allanson	.05	.04	.02
6	Kal Daniels	.12	.09	.05
7	Floyd Bannister	.07	.05	.03
8	Alan Ashby	.05	.04	.02
9	Marty Barrett	.07	.05	.03
10	Tim Belcher	.10	.08	.04
11	Harold Baines	.12	.09	.05
12	Hubie Brooks	.07	.05	.03
13	Doyle Alexander	.07	.05	.03
14	Gary Carter	.15	.11	.06
15	Glenn Braggs	.07	.05	.03
16	Steve Bedrosian	.07	.05	.03
17	Barry Bonds	.30	.25	.12
18	Bert Blyleven	.10	.08	.04
19	Tom Brunansky	.10	.08	.04
20	John Candelaria	.07	.05	.03
21	Shawn Abner	.15	.11	.06
22	Jose Canseco	1.25	.90	.50
23	Brett Butler	.07	.05	.03
24	Scott Bradley	.05	.04	.02
25	Ivan Calderon	.10	.08	.04
26	Rich Gossage	.10	.08	.04
27	Brian Downing	.07	.05	.03
28	Jim Rice	.10	.08	.04
29	Dion James	.05	.04	.02
30	Terry Kennedy	.07	.05	.03
31	George Bell	.10	.08	.04
32	Scott Fletcher	.05	.04	.02
33	Bobby Bonilla	.30	.25	.12
34	Tim Burke	.05	.04	.02
35	Darrell Evans	.07	.05	.03
36	Mike Davis	.05	.04	.02
37	Shawon Dunston	.15	.11	.06
38	Kevin Bass	.07	.05	.03
39	George Brett	.40	.30	.15
40	David Cone	.25	.20	.10
41	Ron Darling	.10	.08	.04
42	Roberto Alomar	.20	.15	.08
43	Dennis Eckersley	.10	.08	.04
44	Vince Coleman	.15	.11	.06
45	Sid Bream	.07	.05	.03
46	Gary Gaetti	.12	.09	.05
47	Phil Bradley	.12	.09	.05
48	Jim Clancy	.05	.04	.02
49	Jack Clark	.15	.11	.06
50	Mike Krukow	.05	.04	.02
51	Henry Cotto	.05	.04	.02
52	Rich Dotson	.07	.05	.03
53	Jim Gantner	.05	.04	.02
54	John Franco	.07	.05	.03
55	Pete Incaviglia	.12	.09	.05
56	Joe Carter	.20	.15	.08
57	Roger Clemens	.70	.50	.30
58	Gerald Perry	.10	.08	.04
59	Jack Howell	.05	.04	.02
60	Vance Law	.05	.04	.02
61	Jay Bell	.07	.05	.03
62	Eric Davis	.70	.50	.30
63	Gene Garber	.05	.04	.02
64	Glenn Davis	.12	.09	.05
65	Wade Boggs	1.00	.70	.40
66	Kirk Gibson	.20	.15	.08
67	Carlton Fisk	.15	.11	.06
68	Casey Candaele	.05	.04	.02
69	Mike Heath	.05	.04	.02
70	Kevin Elster	.15	.11	.06
71	Greg Brock	.07	.05	.03
72	Don Carman	.05	.04	.02
73	Doug Drabek	.12	.09	.05
74	Greg Gagne	.05	.04	.02

#	Player	MT	NR MT	EX		#	Player	MT	NR MT	EX
75	Danny Cox	.07	.05	.03		166	Danny Jackson	.10	.08	.04
76	Rickey Henderson	.60	.45	.25		167	Pete O'Brien	.07	.05	.03
77	Chris Brown	.07	.05	.03		168	Julio Franco	.10	.08	.04
78	Terry Steinbach	.15	.11	.06		169	Mark McGwire	1.00	.70	.40
79	Will Clark	1.00	.70	.40		170	Zane Smith	.07	.05	.03
80	Mickey Brantley	.05	.04	.02		171	Johnny Ray	.07	.05	.03
81	Ozzie Guillen	.12	.09	.05		172	Lester Lancaster	.07	.05	.03
82	Greg Maddux	.12	.09	.05		173	Mel Hall	.05	.04	.02
83	Kirk McCaskill	.05	.04	.02		174	Tracy Jones	.12	.09	.05
84	Dwight Evans	.10	.08	.04		175	Kevin Seitzer	.35	.25	.14
85	Ozzie Virgil	.05	.04	.02		176	Bob Knepper	.07	.05	.03
86	Mike Morgan	.05	.04	.02		177	Mike Greenwell	.60	.45	.25
87	Tony Fernandez	.10	.08	.04		178	Mike Marshall	.10	.08	.04
88	Jose Guzman	.05	.04	.02		179	Melido Perez	.15	.11	.06
89	Mike Dunne	.12	.09	.05		180	Tim Raines	.30	.25	.12
90	Andres Galarraga	.15	.11	.06		181	Jack Morris	.12	.09	.05
91	Mike Henneman	.10	.08	.04		182	Darryl Strawberry	.60	.45	.25
92	Alfredo Griffin	.07	.05	.03		183	Robin Yount	.35	.25	.14
93	Rafael Palmeiro	.12	.09	.05		184	Lance Parrish	.15	.11	.06
94	Jim Deshaies	.07	.05	.03		185	Darnell Coles	.07	.05	.03
95	Mark Gubicza	.07	.05	.03		186	Kirby Puckett	.40	.30	.15
96	Dwight Gooden	.70	.50	.30		187	Terry Pendleton	.07	.05	.03
97	Howard Johnson	.25	.20	.10		188	Don Slaught	.05	.04	.02
98	Mark Davis	.05	.04	.02		189	Jimmy Jones	.07	.05	.03
99	Dave Stewart	.10	.08	.04		190	Dave Parker	.12	.09	.05
100	Joe Magrane	.12	.09	.05		191	Mike Aldrete	.07	.05	.03
101	Brian Fisher	.07	.05	.03		192	Mike Moore	.05	.04	.02
102	Kent Hrbek	.15	.11	.06		193	Greg Walker	.07	.05	.03
103	Kevin Gross	.05	.04	.02		194	Calvin Schiraldi	.07	.05	.03
104	Tom Henke	.07	.05	.03		195	Dick Schofield	.05	.04	.02
105	Mike Pagliarulo	.10	.08	.04		196	Jody Reed	.25	.20	.10
106	Kelly Downs	.10	.08	.04		197	Pete Smith	.10	.08	.04
107	Alvin Davis	.12	.09	.05		198	Cal Ripken	.30	.25	.12
108	Willie Randolph	.07	.05	.03		199	Lloyd Moseby	.07	.05	.03
109	Rob Deer	.07	.05	.03		200	Ruben Sierra	.25	.20	.10
110	Bo Diaz	.05	.04	.02		201	R.J. Reynolds	.07	.05	.03
111	Paul Kilgus	.10	.08	.04		202	Bryn Smith	.05	.04	.02
112	Tom Candiotti	.05	.04	.02		203	Gary Pettis	.05	.04	.02
113	Dale Murphy	.40	.30	.15		204	Steve Sax	.12	.09	.05
114	Rick Mahler	.05	.04	.02		205	Frank DiPino	.05	.04	.02
115	Wally Joyner	.40	.30	.15		206	Mike Scott	.12	.09	.05
116	Ryne Sandberg	.25	.20	.10		207	Kurt Stillwell	.12	.09	.05
117	John Farrell	.12	.09	.05		208	Mookie Wilson	.07	.05	.03
118	Nick Esasky	.05	.04	.02		209	Lee Mazzilli	.05	.04	.02
119	Bo Jackson	.90	.70	.35		210	Lance McCullers	.07	.05	.03
120	Bill Doran	.07	.05	.03		211	Rick Honeycutt	.05	.04	.02
121	Ellis Burks	.70	.50	.30		212	John Tudor	.10	.08	.04
122	Pedro Guerrero	.12	.09	.05		213	Jim Gott	.05	.04	.02
123	Dave LaPoint	.05	.04	.02		214	Frank Viola	.12	.09	.05
124	Neal Heaton	.05	.04	.02		215	Juan Samuel	.10	.08	.04
125	Willie Hernandez	.05	.04	.02		216	Jesse Barfield	.12	.09	.05
126	Roger McDowell	.07	.05	.03		217	Claudell Washington	.05	.04	.02
127	Ted Higuera	.10	.08	.04		218	Rick Reuschel	.07	.05	.03
128	Von Hayes	.10	.08	.04		219	Jim Presley	.10	.08	.04
129	Mike LaValliere	.07	.05	.03		220	Tommy John	.12	.09	.05
130	Dan Gladden	.07	.05	.03		221	Dan Plesac	.10	.08	.04
131	Willie McGee	.12	.09	.05		222	Barry Larkin	.20	.15	.08
132	Al Lieter	.20	.15	.08		223	Mike Stanley	.07	.05	.03
133	Mark Grant	.05	.04	.02		224	Cory Snyder	.25	.20	.10
134	Bob Welch	.07	.05	.03		225	Andre Dawson	.20	.15	.08
135	Dave Dravecky	.05	.04	.02		226	Ken Oberkfell	.05	.04	.02
136	Mark Langston	.10	.08	.04		227	Devon White	.20	.15	.08
137	Dan Pasqua	.10	.08	.04		228	Jamie Moyer	.05	.04	.02
138	Rick Sutcliffe	.12	.09	.05		229	Brook Jacoby	.10	.08	.04
139	Dan Petry	.05	.04	.02		230	Rob Murphy	.10	.08	.04
140	Rich Gedman	.07	.05	.03		231	Bret Saberhagen	.20	.15	.08
141	Ken Griffey	.07	.05	.03		232	Nolan Ryan	.50	.40	.20
142	Eddie Murray	.10	.08	.04		233	Bruce Hurst	.10	.08	.04
143	Jimmy Key	.10	.08	.04		234	Jesse Orosco	.07	.05	.03
144	Dale Mohoric	.05	.04	.02		235	Bobby Thigpen	.07	.05	.03
145	Jose Lind	.15	.11	.06		236	Pascual Perez	.05	.04	.02
146	Dennis Martinez	.05	.04	.02		237	Matt Nokes	.20	.15	.08
147	Chet Lemon	.07	.05	.03		238	Bob Ojeda	.07	.05	.03
148	Orel Hershiser	.20	.15	.08		239	Joey Meyer	.07	.05	.03
149	Dave Martinez	.07	.05	.03		240	Shane Rawley	.07	.05	.03
150	Billy Hatcher	.07	.05	.03		241	Jeff Robinson	.07	.05	.03
151	Charlie Leibrandt	.07	.05	.03		242	Jeff Reardon	.10	.08	.04
152	Keith Hernandez	.10	.08	.04		243	Ozzie Smith	.15	.11	.06
153	Kevin McReynolds	.12	.09	.05		244	Dave Winfield	.30	.25	.12
154	Tony Gwynn	.30	.25	.12		245	John Kruk	.12	.09	.05
155	Stan Javier	.05	.04	.02		246	Carney Lansford	.07	.05	.03
156	Tony Pena	.07	.05	.03		247	Candy Maldonado	.07	.05	.03
157	Andy Van Slyke	.10	.08	.04		248	Ken Phelps	.05	.04	.02
158	Gene Larkin	.07	.05	.03		249	Ken Williams	.10	.08	.04
159	Chris James	.10	.08	.04		250	Al Nipper	.05	.04	.02
160	Fred McGriff	.50	.40	.20		251	Mark McLemore	.05	.04	.02
161	Rick Rhoden	.07	.05	.03		252	Lee Smith	.07	.05	.03
162	Scott Garrelts	.05	.04	.02		253	Albert Hall	.05	.04	.02
163	Mike Campbell	.12	.09	.05		254	Billy Ripken	.15	.11	.06
164	Dave Righetti	.12	.09	.05		255	Kelly Gruber	.20	.15	.08
165	Paul Molitor	.15	.11	.06		256	Charlie Hough	.07	.05	.03

		MT	NR MT	EX
257	John Smiley	.07	.05	.03
258	Tim Wallach	.10	.08	.04
259	Frank Tanana	.07	.05	.03
260	Mike Scioscia	.05	.04	.02
261	Damon Berryhill	.10	.08	.04
262	Dave Smith	.07	.05	.03
263	Willie Wilson	.10	.08	.04
264	Len Dykstra	.07	.05	.03
265	Randy Myers	.10	.08	.04
266	Keith Moreland	.07	.05	.03
267	Eric Plunk	.05	.04	.02
268	Todd Worrell	.10	.08	.04
269	Bob Walk	.05	.04	.02
270	Keith Atherton	.05	.04	.02
271	Mike Schmidt	.40	.30	.15
272	Mike Flanagan	.07	.05	.03
273	Rafael Santana	.05	.04	.02
274	Rob Thompson	.10	.08	.04
275	Rey Quinones	.05	.04	.02
276	Cecilio Guante	.05	.04	.02
277	B.J. Surhoff	.15	.11	.06
278	Chris Sabo	.80	.60	.30
279	Mitch Williams	.07	.05	.03
280	Greg Swindell	.10	.08	.04
281	Alan Trammell	.20	.15	.08
282	Storm Davis	.07	.05	.03
283	Chuck Finley	.05	.04	.02
284	Dave Stieb	.10	.08	.04
285	Scott Bailes	.05	.04	.02
286	Larry Sheets	.07	.05	.03
287	Danny Tartabull	.20	.15	.08
288	Checklist	.05	.04	.02
289	Todd Benzinger	.15	.11	.06
290	John Shelby	.05	.04	.02
291	Steve Lyons	.05	.04	.02
292	Mitch Webster	.05	.04	.02
293	Walt Terrell	.05	.04	.02
294	Pete Stanicek	.12	.09	.05
295	Chris Bosio	.05	.04	.02
296	Milt Thompson	.07	.05	.03
297	Fred Lynn	.12	.09	.05
298	Juan Berenguer	.05	.04	.02
299	Ken Dayley	.05	.04	.02
300	Joel Skinner	.05	.04	.02
301	Benito Santiago	.30	.25	.12
302	Ron Hassey	.05	.04	.02
303	Jose Uribe	.05	.04	.02
304	Harold Reynolds	.07	.05	.03
305	Dale Sveum	.07	.05	.03
306	Glenn Wilson	.05	.04	.02
307	Mike Witt	.07	.05	.03
308	Ron Robinson	.05	.04	.02
309	Denny Walling	.05	.04	.02
310	Joe Orsulak	.05	.04	.02
311	David Wells	.10	.08	.04
312	Steve Buechele	.05	.04	.02
313	Jose Oquendo	.05	.04	.02
314	Floyd Youmans	.07	.05	.03
315	Lou Whitaker	.12	.09	.05
316	Fernando Valenzuela	.12	.09	.05
317	Mike Boddicker	.07	.05	.03
318	Gerald Young	.15	.11	.06
319	Frank White	.07	.05	.03
320	Bill Wegman	.05	.04	.02
321	Tom Niedenfuer	.05	.04	.02
322	Ed Whitson	.05	.04	.02
323	Curt Young	.05	.04	.02
324	Greg Mathews	.10	.08	.04
325	Doug Jones	.07	.05	.03
326	Tommy Herr	.07	.05	.03
327	Kent Tekulve	.07	.05	.03
328	Rance Mulliniks	.05	.04	.02
329	Checklist	.05	.04	.02
330	Craig Lefferts	.05	.04	.02
331	Franklin Stubbs	.07	.05	.03
332	Rick Cerone	.05	.04	.02
333	Dave Schmidt	.05	.04	.02
334	Larry Parrish	.07	.05	.03
335	Tom Browning	.07	.05	.03
336	Checklist	.05	.04	.02

1988 Donruss Boston Team Book

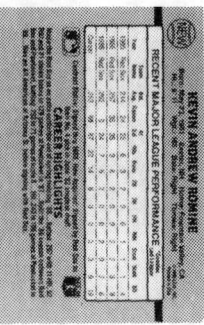

Kevin Romine OF

Three pages of cards and a Stan Musial puzzle highlight this special team collection book. The cards feature the same design as the regular 1988 Donruss cards, but contain a 1988 copyright date instead of 1987 like the regular set. The cards are numbered like the regular issue with the exception of eight new cards which were produced especially for the Red Sox collection book. The book is commonly found complete with the cards and puzzle. The puzzle pieces are perforated for removal, but the card sheet is not.

		MT	NR MT	EX
Complete Set:		6.00	4.50	2.50
Common Player:		.08	.06	.03
41	Jody Reed	.35	.25	.14
51	Roger Clemens	.80	.60	.30
92	Bob Stanley	.08	.06	.03
129	Rich Gedman	.08	.06	.03
153	Wade Boggs	.80	.60	.30
174	Ellis Burks	1.00	.70	.40
216	Dwight Evans	.25	.20	.10
252	Bruce Hurst	.25	.20	.10
276	Marty Barrett	.12	.09	.05
297	Todd Benzinger	.15	.11	.06
339	Mike Greenwell	.90	.70	.35
399	Jim Rice	.20	.15	.08
421	John Marzano	.12	.09	.05
462	Oil Can Boyd	.12	.09	.05
498	Sam Horn	.20	.15	.08
544	Spike Owen	.12	.09	.05
585	Jeff Sellers	.08	.06	.03
623	Ed Romero	.08	.06	.03
634	Wes Gardner	.12	.0c	.05
----	Brady Anderson	.20	.15	.08
----	Rick Cerone	.08	.06	.03
----	Steve Ellsworth	.08	.06	.03
----	Dennis Lamp	.08	.06	.03
----	Kevin Romine	.15	.11	.06
----	Lee Smith	.20	.15	.08
----	Mike Smithson	.08	.06	.03
----	John Trautwein	.08	.06	.03

1988 Donruss Chicago Cubs Team Book

Primarily sold intact, the 1988 Donruss Chicago Cubs team book features three pages of cards and a fourth page featuring a Stan Musial puzzle. The inside cover provides space for autographs and the back inside cover provides team and ballpark history. The card fronts feature the design of the regular Donruss set. Eight "New" players are included in the team book. The cards have a 1988 copyright on the back in contrast with the 1987 copyright on the regular Donruss cards.

A player's name in *italic* type indicates a rookie card. An (FC) indicates a player's first card for that particular card company.

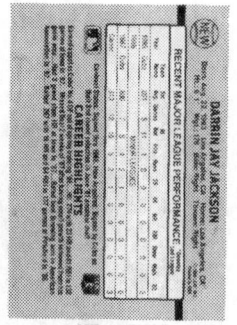

		MT	NR MT	EX
Complete Set:		7.00	5.25	2.75
Common Player:		.08	.06	.03
40	Mark Grace	1.75	1.25	.70
68	Rick Sutcliffe	.15	.11	.06
119	Jody Davis	.08	.06	.03
146	Shawon Dunston	.35	.25	.14
169	Jamie Moyer	.08	.06	.03
191	Leon Durham	.08	.06	.03
242	Ryne Sandberg	.70	.50	.30
269	Andre Dawson	.40	.30	.15
315	Paul Noce	.08	.06	.03
324	Rafael Palmeiro	.70	.50	.30
438	Dave Martinez	.15	.11	.06
447	Jerry Mumphrey	.08	.06	.03
488	Jim Sundberg	.08	.06	.03
516	Manny Trillo	.10	.08	.04
539	Greg Maddux	.50	.40	.20
561	Les Lancaster	.08	.06	.03
570	Frank DiPino	.08	.06	.03
639	Damon Berryhill	.30	.25	.12
646	Scott Sanderson	.08	.06	.03
----	Mike Bielecki	.20	.15	.08
----	Rich Gossage	.10	.08	.04
----	Drew Hall	.10	.08	.04
----	Darrin Jackson	.10	.08	.04
----	Vance Law	.08	.06	.03
----	Al Nipper	.08	.06	.03
----	Angel Salazar	.08	.06	.03
----	Calvin Schiraldi	.08	.06	.03

1988 Donruss Diamond Kings Supers

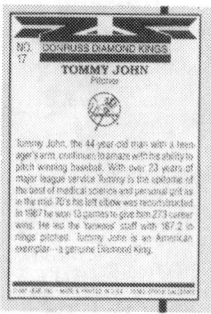

This 28-card set (including the checklist) marks the fourth edition of Donruss' super-size (5"x7") set. These cards, exact duplicates of the 1988 Diamond Kings that feature player portraits by Dick Perez, have a red, blue and black striped border. A gold Diamond Kings banner curves above the player portrait and a matching oval name banner is printed below. Each card features a large player closeup and a smaller full-figure inset on a split background that is white at the top and striped with multi-colors on the lower portion. Card backs are black and white with a blue border and contain the card number, DK logo, player name, team logo and a paragraph style career

summary. A 12-piece Stan Musial puzzle was also included with the purchase of the super-size set which was marketed via a mail-in offer printed on Donruss wrappers.

		MT	NR MT	EX
Complete Set:		9.00	6.75	3.50
Common Player:		.20	.15	.08
1	Mark McGwire	1.00	.70	.40
2	Tim Raines	.30	.25	.12
3	Benito Santiago	.30	.25	.12
4	Alan Trammell	.30	.25	.12
5	Danny Tartabull	.35	.25	.14
6	Ron Darling	.30	.25	.12
7	Paul Molitor	.30	.25	.12
8	Devon White	.35	.25	.14
9	Andre Dawson	.30	.25	.12
10	Julio Franco	.25	.20	.10
11	Scott Fletcher	.20	.15	.08
12	Tony Fernandez	.30	.25	.12
13	Shane Rawley	.20	.15	.08
14	Kal Daniels	.30	.25	.12
15	Jack Clark	.30	.25	.12
16	Dwight Evans	.25	.20	.10
17	Tommy John	.25	.20	.10
18	Andy Van Slyke	.25	.20	.10
19	Gary Gaetti	.30	.25	.12
20	Mark Langston	.35	.25	.14
21	Will Clark	1.25	.90	.50
22	Glenn Hubbard	.20	.15	.08
23	Billy Hatcher	.20	.15	.08
24	Bob Welch	.20	.15	.08
25	Ivan Calderon	.20	.15	.08
26	Cal Ripken, Jr.	.60	.45	.25
27	Checklist	.20	.15	.08
641	Stan Musial Puzzle Card	.20	.15	.08

1988 Donruss MVP

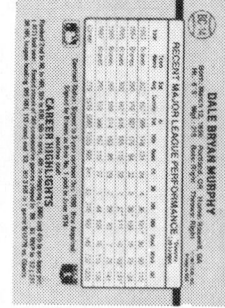

This 26-card set of standard-size player cards replaced the Donruss box-bottom cards in 1988. Instead of box-bottoms, the bonus cards (numbered BC-1 through BC-26) were randomly inserted in Donruss wax or rack packs. Cards feature the company's choice of Most Valuable Player for each major league team and are titled "Donruss MVP." The MVP cards were not included in the factory-collated sets. Card fronts carry the same basic red-blue-black flowing border design as the 1988 Donruss basic 660-card issue (with the exception of the Donruss MVP logo). Card backs are the same as the regular issue, except for the numbering system.

		MT	NR MT	EX
Complete Set:		8.00	6.00	3.25
Common Player:		.15	.11	.06
1	Cal Ripken	.30	.25	.12
2	Eric Davis	.50	.40	.20
3	Paul Molitor	.20	.15	.08
4	Mike Schmidt	.35	.25	.14
5	Ivan Calderon	.15	.11	.06
6	Tony Gwynn	.30	.25	.12
7	Wade Boggs	.75	.55	.30
8	Andy Van Slyke	.15	.11	.06

		MT	NR MT	EX
9	Joe Carter	.25	.20	.10
10	Andre Dawson	.25	.20	.10
11	Alan Trammell	.25	.20	.10
12	Mike Scott	.15	.11	.06
13	Wally Joyner	.25	.20	.10
14	Dale Murphy	.35	.25	.14
15	Kirby Puckett	.50	.40	.30
16	Pedro Guerrero	.20	.15	.08
17	Kevin Seitzer	.50	.40	.30
18	Tim Raines	.25	.20	.10
19	George Bell	.25	.20	.10
20	Darryl Strawberry	.50	.40	.30
21	Don Mattingly	1.50	1.25	.60
22	Ozzie Smith	.20	.15	.08
23	Mark McGwire	1.00	.70	.40
24	Will Clark	.90	.70	.35
25	Alvin Davis	.15	.11	.06
26	Ruben Sierra	.35	.25	.14

1988 Donruss New York Mets Team Book

 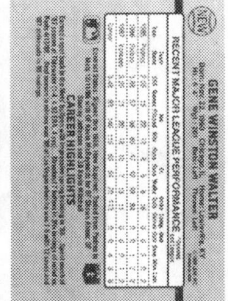

Distributed in book form, the 1988 Donruss New York Mets team book is still usually found intact. The team book features three pages of player cards, a full page featuring a perforated Stan Musial puzzle, space for autographs on the inside cover and team history information on the back inside cover. The outside covers of the Donruss team books are bright red. The player cards are the same as the regular Donruss issue with the exception of the copyright date. Three "New" Mets are featured in the team book.

		MT	NR MT	EX
Complete Set:		6.00	4.50	2.50
Common Player:		.08	.06	.03
37	Kevin Elster	.10	.08	.04
69	Dwight Gooden	.60	.45	.25
76	Ron Darling	.10	.08	.04
118	Sid Fernandez	.15	.11	.06
199	Gary Carter	.20	.15	.08
241	Wally Backman	.08	.06	.03
316	Keith Hernandez	.20	.15	.08
323	Dave Magadan	.30	.25	.12
364	Len Dykstra	.15	.11	.06
439	Darryl Strawberry	.70	.50	.30
446	Rick Aguilera	.10	.08	.04
562	Keith Miller	.10	.08	.04
569	Howard Johnson	.25	.20	.10
603	Terry Leach	.08	.06	.03
614	Lee Mazzilli	.08	.06	.03
617	Kevin McReynolds	.20	.15	.08
619	Barry Lyons	.08	.06	.03
620	Randy Myers	.20	.15	.08
632	Bob Ojeda	.08	.06	.03
648	Tim Teufel	.08	.06	.03
651	Roger McDowell	.15	.11	.06
652	Mookie Wilson	.10	.08	.04
653	David Cone	.30	.25	.12
657	Gregg Jefferies	2.00	1.50	.80
----	Jeff Innis	.15	.11	.06
----	Mackey Sasser	.30	.25	.12
----	Gene Walter	.08	.06	.03

1988 Donruss New York Yankees Team Book

 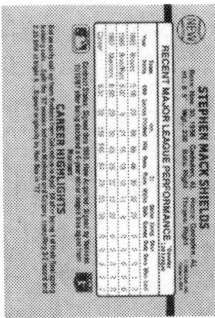

The 1988 Donruss New York Yankees team book includes the same features as the other team collection books. Three pages of cards, a Stan Musial puzzle, autograph space and team history information are provided. The team book is updated for 1988 trades. Nine "New" Yankees are included. The player cards are the same as the regular Donruss cards with the exception of the copyright dates. The team collection books are most often sold intact.

		MT	NR MT	EX
Complete Set:		6.00	4.50	2.50
Common Player:		.08	.06	.03
43	Al Leiter	.08	.06	.03
93	Dave Righetti	.15	.11	.06
105	Mike Pagliarulo	.10	.08	.04
128	Rick Rhoden	.08	.06	.03
175	Ron Guidry	.15	.11	.06
217	Don Mattingly	1.25	.90	.50
228	Willie Randolph	.15	.11	.06
251	Gary Ward	.08	.06	.03
277	Rickey Henderson	.70	.50	.30
278	Dave Winfield	.25	.20	.10
340	Claudell Washington	.08	.06	.03
374	Charles Hudson	.08	.06	.03
401	Tommy John	.15	.11	.06
474	Joel Skinner	.08	.06	.03
497	Tim Stoddard	.08	.06	.03
545	Jay Buhner	.30	.25	.12
616	Bobby Meacham	.08	.06	.03
635	Roberto Kelly	.90	.70	.35
----	John Candelaria	.10	.08	.04
----	Jack Clark	.25	.20	.10
----	Jose Cruz	.08	.06	.03
----	Richard Dotson	.08	.06	.03
----	Cecilio Guante	.08	.06	.03
----	Lee Guetterman	.08	.06	.03
----	Rafael Santana	.08	.06	.03
----	Steve Shields	.08	.06	.03
----	Don Slaught	.10	.08	.04

1988 Donruss Oakland Team Book

 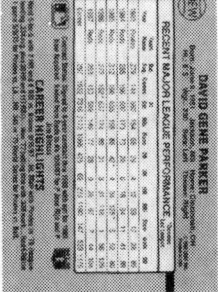

Eleven "New" players are among the featured cards in this unique collectible. The team book includes three pages of player cards, a Stan Musial puzzle, autograph space and team history infromation. The team books are most often sold intact. The player cards feature the same design as the regular Donruss cards.

		MT	NR MT	EX
	Complete Set:	7.00	5.25	2.75
	Common Player:	.08	.06	.03
97	Curt Young	.08	.06	.03
133	Gene Nelson	.08	.06	.03
158	Terry Steinbach	.20	.15	.08
178	Carney Lansford	.20	.15	.08
221	Tony Phillips	.08	.06	.03
256	Mark McGwire	1.25	.90	.50
302	Jose Canseco	1.75	1.25	.70
349	Dennis Eckersley	.40	.30	.15
379	Mike Gallego	.08	.06	.03
425	Luis Polonia	.08	.06	.03
467	Steve Ontiveros	.08	.06	.03
472	Dave Stewart	.40	.30	.15
503	Eric Plunk	.08	.06	.03
528	Greg Cadaret	.08	.06	.03
590	Rick Honeycutt	.08	.06	.03
595	Storm Davis	.08	.06	.03
9989	Don Baylor	.20	.15	.08
----	Ron Hassey	.12	.09	.05
----	Dave Henderson	.20	.15	.08
----	Glenn Hubbard	.08	.06	.03
----	Stan Javier	.10	.08	.04
----	Doug Jennings	.20	.15	.08
----	Edward Jurak	.08	.06	.03
----	Dave Parker	.35	.25	.14
----	Walt Weiss	.80	.60	.30
----	Bob Welch	.30	.25	.12
----	Matt Young	.08	.06	.03

1988 Donruss Pop-Ups

Donruss introduced its Pop-Up cards in 1986. The first two annual issues featured 2-1/2" x 5" cards. In 1988, Donruss reduced the size of the Pop-Ups cards to a standard 2-1/2"x 3-1/2". The 1988 set includes 20 cards that fold out so that the upper portion of the player stands upright, giving a three-dimensional effect. Pop-ups feature players from the All-Star Game starting lineup. Card fronts feature full-color photos, with the player's name, team and position printed in black on a yellow banner near the bottom of the card front. As in previous issues, the card backs contain only the player's name, league and position. Pop-Ups were distributed in individual packages containing one Pop-Up, three puzzle pieces and three All-Star cards.

		MT	NR MT	EX
	Complete Set:	4.00	3.00	1.50
	Common Player:	.15	.11	.06
(1)	George Bell	.20	.15	.08
(2)	Wade Boggs	.75	.55	.30
(3)	Gary Carter	.20	.15	.08
(4)	Jack Clark	.20	.15	.08

		MT	NR MT	EX
(5)	Eric Davis	.50	.40	.20
(6)	Andre Dawson	.20	.15	.08
(7)	Rickey Henderson	.50	.40	.20
(8)	Davey Johnson	.15	.11	.06
(9)	Don Mattingly	.80	.60	.30
(10)	Terry Kennedy	.15	.11	.06
(11)	John McNamara	.15	.11	.06
(12)	Willie Randolph	.15	.11	.06
(13)	Cal Ripken, Jr.	.50	.40	.20
(14)	Bret Saberhagen	.35	.25	.14
(15)	Ryne Sandberg	.50	.40	.20
(16)	Mike Schmidt	.60	.45	.25
(17)	Mike Scott	.15	.11	.06
(18)	Ozzie Smith	.20	.15	.08
(19)	Darryl Strawberry	.50	.40	.20
(20)	Dave Winfield	.25	.20	.10

1988 Donruss Rookies

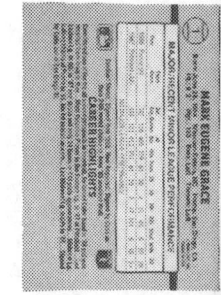

For the third consecutive year, Donruss issued this 56-card boxed set highlighting current rookies. The complete set includes a checklist and a 15-piece Stan Musial Diamond Kings puzzle. As in previous years, the set is similar to the company's basic issue, with the exception of the logo and border color. Card fronts feature red, green and black-striped borders, with a red-and-white player name printed in the lower left corner beneath the full-color photo. "The Rookies" logo is printed in red, white and black in the lower right corner. The card backs are printed in black on bright aqua and include personal data, recent performance stats and major league totals, as well as 1984-88 year-by-year minor league stats. The cards are the standard 2-1/2" by 3-1/2" size.

		MT	NR MT	EX
	Complete Set:	13.00	9.75	5.25
	Common Player:	.10	.08	.04
1	Mark Grace	4.00	3.00	1.50
2	Mike Campbell	.10	.08	.04
3	Todd Frowirth(FC)	.20	.15	.08
4	Dave Stapleton	.10	.08	.04
5	Shawn Abner	.15	.11	.06
6	Jose Cecena(FC)	.25	.20	.10
7	Dave Gallagher(FC)	.20	.15	.08
8	Mark Parent(FC)	.20	.15	.08
9	Cecil Espy(FC)	.15	.11	.06
10	Pete Smith	.10	.08	.04
11	Jay Buhner	.20	.15	.08
12	Pat Borders(FC)	.30	.25	.12
13	Doug Jennings(FC)	.25	.20	.10
14	Brady Anderson(FC)	.40	.30	.15
15	Pete Stanicek	.15	.11	.06
16	Roberto Kelly	.40	.30	.15
17	Jeff Treadway	.15	.11	.06
18	Walt Weiss(FC)	.90	.70	.35
19	Paul Gibson(FC)	.20	.15	.08
20	Tim Crews	.10	.08	.04
21	Melido Perez	.40	.30	.15
22	Steve Peters(FC)	.20	.15	.08
23	Craig Worthington(FC)	.50	.40	.20
24	John Trautwein(FC)	.15	.11	.06
25	DeWayne Vaughn(FC)	.15	.11	.06
26	David Wells	.10	.08	.04
27	Al Leiter	.30	.25	.12
28	Tim Belcher	.20	.15	.08

		MT	NR MT	EX
29	Johnny Paredes(FC)	.20	.15	.08
30	Chris Sabo(FC)	2.75	2.00	1.00
31	Damon Berryhill	.25	.20	.10
32	Randy Milligan(FC)	.40	.30	.15
33	Gary Thurman	.20	.15	.08
34	Kevin Elster	.20	.15	.08
35	Roberto Alomar	.80	.60	.30
36	Edgar Martinez(FC)	.50	.40	.20
37	Todd Stottlemyre	.15	.11	.06
38	Joey Meyer	.15	.11	.06
39	Carl Nichols	.10	.08	.04
40	Jack McDowell	.35	.25	.14
41	Jose Bautista(FC)	.20	.15	.08
42	Sil Campusano(FC)	.25	.20	.10
43	John Dopson(FC)	.20	.15	.08
44	Jody Reed	.35	.25	.14
45	Darrin Jackson(FC)	.20	.15	.08
46	Mike Capel(FC)	.20	.15	.08
47	Ron Gant	1.00	.70	.40
48	John Davis	.10	.08	.04
49	Kevin Coffman(FC)	.15	.11	.06
50	Cris Carpenter(FC)	.35	.25	.14
51	Mackey Sasser	.10	.08	.04
52	Luis Alicea(FC)	.25	.20	.10
53	Bryan Harvey(FC)	.30	.25	.12
54	Steve Ellsworth(FC)	.15	.11	.06
55	Mike Macfarlane(FC)	.25	.20	.10
56	Checklist 1-56	.10	.08	.04

1989 Donruss

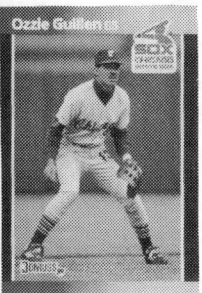
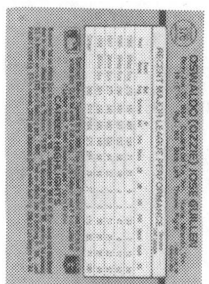

This basic annual issue consists of 660 standard-size (2-1/2" by 3-1/2") cards, including 26 Diamond Kings portrait cards and 20 Rated Rookies cards. Top and bottom borders of the cards are printed in a variety of colors that fade from dark to light (i.e. dark blue to light purple, bright red to pale yellow). A white-lettered player name is printed across the top margin. The team logo appears upper right and the Donruss logo lower left. A black stripe and thin white line make up the vertical side borders. The black outer stripe has a special varnish that gives a faintly visible filmstrip texture to the border. The backs (horizontal format) are printed in orange and black, similar to the 1988 design, with personal info, recent stats and major league totals. Team logo sticker cards (22 total) and Warren Spahn puzzle cards (63 total) are included in individual wax packs of cards.

		MT	NR MT	EX
Complete Set:		25.00	20.00	10.00
Common Player:		.04	.03	.02
1	Mike Greenwell (DK)	.40	.30	.15
2	Bobby Bonilla (DK)	.12	.09	.05
3	Pete Incaviglia (DK)	.12	.09	.05
4	Chris Sabo (DK)	.25	.20	.10
5	Robin Yount (DK)	.25	.20	.10
6	Tony Gwynn (DK)	.35	.25	.14
7	Carlton Fisk (DK)	.12	.09	.05
8	Cory Snyder (DK)	.15	.11	.06
9	David Cone (DK)	.35	.25	.14
10	Kevin Seitzer (DK)	.25	.20	.10
11	Rick Reuschel (DK)	.10	.08	.04
12	Johnny Ray (DK)	.10	.08	.04
13	Dave Schmidt (DK)	.08	.06	.03

		MT	NR MT	EX
14	Andres Galarraga (DK)	.15	.11	.06
15	Kirk Gibson (DK)	.20	.15	.08
16	Fred McGriff (DK)	.25	.20	.10
17	Mark Grace (DK)	.60	.45	.25
18	Jeff Robinson (DK)	.12	.09	.05
19	Vince Coleman (DK)	.20	.15	.08
20	Dave Henderson (DK)	.10	.08	.04
21	Harold Reynolds (DK)	.08	.06	.03
22	Gerald Perry (DK)	.10	.08	.04
23	Frank Viola (DK)	.15	.11	.06
24	Steve Bedrosian (DK)	.10	.08	.04
25	Glenn Davis (DK)	.15	.11	.06
26	Don Mattingly (DK)	1.25	.90	.50
27	Checklist 1-27	.04	.03	.02
28	Sandy Alomar, Jr. (RR)(FC)	2.00	1.50	.80
29	Steve Searcy (RR)(FC)	.20	.15	.08
30	Cameron Drew (RR)(FC)	.20	.15	.08
31	Gary Sheffield (RR)(FC)	2.00	1.50	.80
32	Erik Hanson (RR)(FC)	.50	.40	.20
33	Ken Griffey, Jr. (RR)(FC)	10.00	7.50	4.00
34	Greg Harris (RR)(FC)	.30	.25	.12
35	Gregg Jefferies (RR)	2.00	1.50	.80
36	Luis Medina (RR)(FC)	.30	.25	.12
37	Carlos Quintana (RR)	.50	.40	.20
38	Felix Jose (RR)(FC)	.50	.40	.20
39	Cris Carpenter (RR)(FC)	.25	.20	.10
40	Ron Jones (RR)(FC)	.35	.25	.14
41	Dave West (RR)(FC)	.30	.25	.12
42	Randy Johnson (RR)(FC)	.40	.30	.15
43	Mike Harkey (RR)(FC)	.60	.45	.25
44	Pete Harnisch (RR)(FC)	.30	.25	.12
45	Tom Gordon (RR)(FC)	.80	.60	.30
46	Gregg Olson (RR)(FC)	1.25	.90	.50
47	Alex Sanchez (RR)(FC)	.25	.20	.10
48	Ruben Sierra	.50	.40	.20
49	Rafael Palmeiro	.25	.20	.10
50	Ron Gant	.20	.15	.08
51	Cal Ripken, Jr.	.30	.25	.12
52	Wally Joyner	.20	.15	.08
53	Gary Carter	.20	.15	.08
54	Andy Van Slyke	.12	.09	.05
55	Robin Yount	.25	.20	.10
56	Pete Incaviglia	.10	.08	.04
57	Greg Brock	.06	.05	.02
58	Melido Perez	.08	.06	.03
59	Craig Lefferts	.04	.03	.02
60	Gary Pettis	.04	.03	.02
61	Danny Tartabull	.15	.11	.06
62	Guillermo Hernandez	.06	.05	.02
63	Ozzie Smith	.12	.09	.05
64	Gary Gaetti	.12	.09	.05
65	Mark Davis	.04	.03	.02
66	Lee Smith	.08	.06	.03
67	Dennis Eckersley	.10	.08	.04
68	Wade Boggs	.90	.70	.35
69	Mike Scott	.10	.08	.04
70	Fred McGriff	.50	.40	.20
71	Tom Browning	.08	.06	.03
72	Claudell Washington	.06	.05	.02
73	Mel Hall	.06	.05	.02
74	Don Mattingly	.80	.60	.30
75	Steve Bedrosian	.08	.06	.03
76	Juan Samuel	.10	.08	.04
77	Mike Scioscia	.06	.05	.02
78	Dave Righetti	.12	.09	.05
79	Alfredo Griffin	.06	.05	.02
80	Eric Davis	.40	.30	.15
81	Juan Berenguer	.04	.03	.02
82	Todd Worrell	.08	.06	.03
83	Joe Carter	.12	.09	.05
84	Steve Sax	.12	.09	.05
85	Frank White	.06	.05	.02
86	John Kruk	.06	.05	.02
87	Rance Mulliniks	.04	.03	.02
88	Alan Ashby	.04	.03	.02
89	Charlie Leibrandt	.06	.05	.02
90	Frank Tanana	.06	.05	.02
91	Jose Canseco	1.00	.70	.40
92	Barry Bonds	.12	.09	.05
93	Harold Reynolds	.06	.05	.02
94	Mark McLemore	.04	.03	.02
95	Mark McGwire	.60	.45	.25
96	Eddie Murray	.25	.20	.10
97	Tim Raines	.25	.20	.10
98	Rob Thompson	.06	.05	.02
99	Kevin McReynolds	.12	.09	.05
100	Checklist 28-137	.04	.03	.02
101	Carlton Fisk	.20	.15	.08
102	Dave Martinez	.06	.05	.02
103	Glenn Braggs	.06	.05	.02
104	Dale Murphy	.30	.25	.12

#	Player	MT	NR MT	EX
105	Ryne Sandberg	.25	.20	.10
106	Dennis Martinez	.06	.05	.02
107	Pete O'Brien	.06	.05	.02
108	Dick Schofield	.04	.03	.02
109	Henry Cotto	.04	.03	.02
110	Mike Marshall	.12	.09	.05
111	Keith Moreland	.06	.05	.02
112	Tom Brunansky	.10	.08	.04
113	Kelly Gruber	.04	.03	.02
114	Brook Jacoby	.08	.06	.03
115	Keith Brown(FC)	.20	.15	.08
116	Matt Nokes	.15	.11	.06
117	Keith Hernandez	.20	.15	.08
118	Bob Forsch	.06	.05	.02
119	Bert Blyleven	.10	.08	.04
120	Willie Wilson	.08	.06	.03
121	Tommy Gregg	.08	.06	.03
122	Jim Rice	.25	.20	.10
123	Bob Knepper	.06	.05	.02
124	Danny Jackson	.12	.09	.05
125	Eric Plunk	.04	.03	.02
126	Brian Fisher	.06	.05	.02
127	Mike Pagliarulo	.08	.06	.03
128	Tony Gwynn	.30	.25	.12
129	Lance McCullers	.06	.05	.02
130	Andres Galarraga	.15	.11	.06
131	Jose Uribe	.04	.03	.02
132	Kirk Gibson	.20	.15	.08
133	David Palmer	.04	.03	.02
134	R.J. Reynolds	.04	.03	.02
135	Greg Walker	.06	.05	.02
136	Kirk McCaskill	.06	.05	.02
137	Shawon Dunston	.08	.06	.03
138	Andy Allanson	.04	.03	.02
139	Rob Murphy	.04	.03	.02
140	Mike Aldrete	.06	.05	.02
141	Terry Kennedy	.06	.05	.02
142	Scott Fletcher	.06	.05	.02
143	Steve Balboni	.06	.05	.02
144	Bret Saberhagen	.12	.09	.05
145	Ozzie Virgil	.04	.03	.02
146	Dale Sveum	.06	.05	.02
147	Darryl Strawberry	.35	.25	.14
148	Harold Baines	.10	.08	.04
149	George Bell	.25	.20	.10
150	Dave Parker	.12	.09	.05
151	Bobby Bonilla	.12	.09	.05
152	Mookie Wilson	.06	.05	.02
153	Ted Power	.04	.03	.02
154	Nolan Ryan	.35	.25	.14
155	Jeff Reardon	.08	.06	.03
156	Tim Wallach	.08	.06	.03
157	Jamie Moyer	.04	.03	.02
158	Rich Gossage	.10	.08	.04
159	Dave Winfield	.25	.20	.10
160	Von Hayes	.08	.06	.03
161	Willie McGee	.10	.08	.04
162	Rich Gedman	.06	.05	.02
163	Tony Pena	.06	.05	.02
164	Mike Morgan	.04	.03	.02
165	Charlie Hough	.06	.05	.02
166	Mike Stanley	.04	.03	.02
167	Andre Dawson	.20	.15	.08
168	Joe Boever(FC)	.04	.03	.02
169	Pete Stanicek	.08	.06	.03
170	Bob Boone	.06	.05	.02
171	Ron Darling	.10	.08	.04
172	Bob Walk	.04	.03	.02
173	Rob Deer	.06	.05	.02
174	Steve Buechele	.04	.03	.02
175	Ted Higuera	.08	.06	.03
176	Ozzie Guillen	.06	.05	.02
177	Candy Maldonado	.06	.05	.02
178	Doyle Alexander	.06	.05	.02
179	Mark Gubicza	.10	.08	.04
180	Alan Trammell	.15	.11	.06
181	Vince Coleman	.15	.11	.06
182	Kirby Puckett	.30	.25	.12
183	Chris Brown	.06	.05	.02
184	Marty Barrett	.06	.05	.02
185	Stan Javier	.04	.03	.02
186	Mike Greenwell	.60	.45	.25
187	Billy Hatcher	.06	.05	.02
188	Jimmy Key	.08	.06	.03
189	Nick Esasky	.06	.05	.02
190	Don Slaught	.04	.03	.02
191	Cory Snyder	.15	.11	.06
192	John Candelaria	.06	.05	.02
193	Mike Schmidt	.40	.30	.15
194	Kevin Gross	.06	.05	.02
195	John Tudor	.08	.06	.03
196	Neil Allen	.04	.03	.02
197	Orel Hershiser	.25	.20	.10
198	Kal Daniels	.15	.11	.06
199	Kent Hrbek	.15	.11	.06
200	Checklist 138-247	.04	.03	.02
201	Joe Magrane	.08	.06	.03
202	Scott Bailes	.04	.03	.02
203	Tim Belcher	.10	.08	.04
204	George Brett	.30	.25	.12
205	Benito Santiago	.12	.09	.05
206	Tony Fernandez	.10	.08	.04
207	Gerald Young	.10	.08	.04
208	Bo Jackson	.80	.60	.30
209	Chet Lemon	.06	.05	.02
210	Storm Davis	.08	.06	.03
211	Doug Drabek	.06	.05	.02
212	Mickey Brantley (photo actually Nelson Simmons)	.04	.03	.02
213	Devon White	.10	.08	.04
214	Dave Stewart	.08	.06	.03
215	Dave Schmidt	.04	.03	.02
216	Bryn Smith	.04	.03	.02
217	Brett Butler	.06	.05	.02
218	Bob Ojeda	.06	.05	.02
219	Steve Rosenberg(FC)	.20	.15	.08
220	Hubie Brooks	.08	.06	.03
221	B.J. Surhoff	.08	.06	.03
222	Rick Mahler	.04	.03	.02
223	Rick Sutcliffe	.08	.06	.03
224	Neal Heaton	.04	.03	.02
225	Mitch Williams	.06	.05	.02
226	Chuck Finley	.08	.06	.03
227	Mark Langston	.10	.08	.04
228	Jesse Orosco	.06	.05	.02
229	Ed Whitson	.04	.03	.02
230	Terry Pendleton	.08	.06	.03
231	Lloyd Moseby	.06	.05	.02
232	Greg Swindell	.10	.08	.04
233	John Franco	.08	.06	.03
234	Jack Morris	.15	.11	.06
235	Howard Johnson	.08	.06	.03
236	Glenn Davis	.12	.09	.05
237	Frank Viola	.12	.09	.05
238	Kevin Seitzer	.25	.20	.10
239	Gerald Perry	.08	.06	.03
240	Dwight Evans	.10	.08	.04
241	Jim Deshaies	.04	.03	.02
242	Bo Diaz	.06	.05	.02
243	Carney Lansford	.06	.05	.02
244	Mike LaValliere	.06	.05	.02
245	Rickey Henderson	.35	.25	.14
246	Roberto Alomar	.25	.20	.10
247	Jimmy Jones	.04	.03	.02
248	Pascual Perez	.06	.05	.02
249	Will Clark	.80	.60	.30
250	Fernando Valenzuela	.15	.11	.06
251	Shane Rawley	.06	.05	.02
252	Sid Bream	.06	.05	.02
253	Steve Lyons	.04	.03	.02
254	Brian Downing	.06	.05	.02
255	Mark Grace	1.00	.70	.40
256	Tom Candiotti	.04	.03	.02
257	Barry Larkin	.20	.15	.08
258	Mike Krukow	.06	.05	.02
259	Billy Ripken	.06	.05	.02
260	Cecilio Guante	.04	.03	.02
261	Scott Bradley	.04	.03	.02
262	Floyd Bannister	.06	.05	.02
263	Pete Smith	.08	.06	.03
264	Jim Gantner	.04	.03	.02
265	Roger McDowell	.08	.06	.03
266	Bobby Thigpen	.08	.06	.03
267	Jim Clancy	.06	.05	.02
268	Terry Steinbach	.08	.06	.03
269	Mike Dunne	.08	.06	.03
270	Dwight Gooden	.50	.40	.20
271	Mike Heath	.04	.03	.02
272	Dave Smith	.06	.05	.02
273	Keith Atherton	.04	.03	.02
274	Tim Burke	.04	.03	.02
275	Damon Berryhill	.12	.09	.05
276	Vance Law	.06	.05	.02
277	Rich Dotson	.06	.05	.02
278	Lance Parrish	.15	.11	.06
279	Denny Walling	.04	.03	.02
280	Roger Clemens	.50	.40	.20
281	Greg Mathews	.06	.05	.02
282	Tom Niedenfuer	.06	.05	.02
283	Paul Kilgus	.10	.08	.04
284	Jose Guzman	.08	.06	.03
285	Calvin Schiraldi	.04	.03	.02

		MT	NR MT	EX
286	Charlie Puleo	.04	.03	.02
287	Joe Orsulak	.04	.03	.02
288	Jack Howell	.06	.05	.02
289	Kevin Elster	.08	.06	.03
290	Jose Lind	.10	.08	.04
291	Paul Molitor	.12	.09	.05
292	Cecil Espy	.08	.06	.03
293	Bill Wegman	.04	.03	.02
294	Dan Pasqua	.08	.06	.03
295	Scott Garrelts	.04	.03	.02
296	Walt Terrell	.06	.05	.02
297	Ed Hearn	.04	.03	.02
298	Lou Whitaker	.20	.15	.08
299	Ken Dayley	.04	.03	.02
300	Checklist 248-357	.04	.03	.02
301	Tommy Herr	.06	.05	.02
302	Mike Brumley	.06	.05	.02
303	Ellis Burks	.60	.45	.25
304	Curt Young	.06	.05	.02
305	Jody Reed	.10	.08	.04
306	Bill Doran	.06	.05	.02
307	David Wells	.06	.05	.02
308	Ron Robinson	.04	.03	.02
309	Rafael Santana	.04	.03	.02
310	Julio Franco	.10	.08	.04
311	Jack Clark	.15	.11	.06
312	Chris James	.08	.06	.03
313	Milt Thompson	.04	.03	.02
314	John Shelby	.04	.03	.02
315	Al Leiter	.15	.11	.06
316	Mike Davis	.06	.05	.02
317	*Chris Sabo*	1.00	.70	.40
318	Greg Gagne	.04	.03	.02
319	Jose Oquendo	.04	.03	.02
320	John Farrell	.10	.08	.04
321	Franklin Stubbs	.04	.03	.02
322	Kurt Stillwell	.06	.05	.02
323	Shawn Abner	.10	.08	.04
324	Mike Flanagan	.06	.05	.02
325	Kevin Bass	.06	.05	.02
326	Pat Tabler	.06	.05	.02
327	Mike Henneman	.08	.06	.03
328	Rick Honeycutt	.04	.03	.02
329	John Smiley	.10	.08	.04
330	Rey Quinones	.04	.03	.02
331	Johnny Ray	.06	.05	.02
332	Bob Welch	.08	.06	.03
333	Larry Sheets	.06	.05	.02
334	Jeff Parrett	.08	.06	.03
335	Rick Reuschel	.08	.06	.03
336	Randy Myers	.10	.08	.04
337	Ken Williams	.06	.05	.02
338	Andy McGaffigan	.04	.03	.02
339	Joey Meyer	.08	.06	.03
340	Dion James	.04	.03	.02
341	Les Lancaster	.06	.05	.02
342	Tom Foley	.04	.03	.02
343	Geno Petralli	.04	.03	.02
344	Dan Petry	.06	.05	.02
345	Alvin Davis	.12	.09	.05
346	Mickey Hatcher	.04	.03	.02
347	Marvell Wynne	.04	.03	.02
348	Danny Cox	.06	.05	.02
349	Dave Stieb	.08	.06	.03
350	Jay Bell	.06	.05	.02
351	Jeff Treadway	.10	.08	.04
352	Luis Salazar	.04	.03	.02
353	Lenny Dykstra	.08	.06	.03
354	Juan Agosto	.04	.03	.02
355	Gene Larkin	.10	.08	.04
356	Steve Farr	.04	.03	.02
357	Paul Assenmacher	.04	.03	.02
358	Todd Benzinger	.12	.09	.05
359	Larry Andersen	.04	.03	.02
360	Paul O'Neill	.04	.03	.02
361	Ron Hassey	.04	.03	.02
362	Jim Gott	.04	.03	.02
363	Ken Phelps	.06	.05	.02
364	Tim Flannery	.04	.03	.02
365	Randy Ready	.04	.03	.02
366	*Nelson Santovenia*(FC)	.30	.25	.12
367	Kelly Downs	.08	.06	.03
368	Danny Heep	.04	.03	.02
369	Phil Bradley	.08	.06	.03
370	Jeff Robinson	.06	.05	.02
371	Ivan Calderon	.06	.05	.02
372	Mike Witt	.06	.05	.02
373	Greg Maddux	.10	.08	.04
374	Carmen Castillo	.04	.03	.02
375	Jose Rijo	.06	.05	.02
376	Joe Price	.04	.03	.02
377	R.C. Gonzalez	.04	.03	.02
378	Oddibe McDowell	.06	.05	.02
379	Jim Presley	.06	.05	.02
380	Brad Wellman	.04	.03	.02
381	Tom Glavine	.10	.08	.04
382	Dan Plesac	.08	.06	.03
383	Wally Backman	.06	.05	.02
384	*Dave Gallagher*	.25	.20	.10
385	Tom Henke	.06	.05	.02
386	Luis Polonia	.06	.05	.02
387	Junior Ortiz	.04	.03	.02
388	David Cone	.35	.25	.14
389	Dave Bergman	.04	.03	.02
390	Danny Darwin	.04	.03	.02
391	Dan Gladden	.04	.03	.02
392	*John Dopson*	.25	.20	.10
393	Frank DiPino	.04	.03	.02
394	Al Nipper	.04	.03	.02
395	Willie Randolph	.06	.05	.02
396	Don Carman	.06	.05	.02
397	Scott Terry	.06	.05	.02
398	Rick Cerone	.04	.03	.02
399	Tom Pagnozzi	.06	.05	.02
400	Checklist 358-467	.04	.03	.02
401	Mickey Tettleton	.08	.06	.03
402	Curtis Wilkerson	.04	.03	.02
403	Jeff Russell	.04	.03	.02
404	Pat Perry	.04	.03	.02
405	*Jose Alvarez*(FC)	.15	.11	.06
406	Rick Schu	.04	.03	.02
407	*Sherman Corbett*(FC)	.15	.11	.06
408	Dave Magadan	.10	.08	.04
409	Bob Kipper	.04	.03	.02
410	Don August	.08	.06	.03
411	Bob Brower	.04	.03	.02
412	Chris Bosio	.04	.03	.02
413	Jerry Reuss	.06	.05	.02
414	Atlee Hammaker	.04	.03	.02
415	Jim Walewander(FC)	.06	.05	.02
416	*Mike Macfarlane*	.20	.15	.08
417	Pat Sheridan	.04	.03	.02
418	Pedro Guerrero	.15	.11	.06
419	Allan Anderson	.06	.05	.02
420	*Mark Parent*	.20	.15	.08
421	Bob Stanley	.04	.03	.02
422	Mike Gallego	.04	.03	.02
423	Bruce Hurst	.08	.06	.03
424	Dave Meads	.04	.03	.02
425	Jesse Barfield	.10	.08	.04
426	*Rob Dibble*(FC)	.70	.50	.30
427	Joel Skinner	.04	.03	.02
428	Ron Kittle	.06	.05	.02
429	Rick Rhoden	.08	.06	.03
430	Bob Dernier	.04	.03	.02
431	Steve Jeltz	.04	.03	.02
432	Rick Dempsey	.06	.05	.02
433	Roberto Kelly	.10	.08	.04
434	Dave Anderson	.04	.03	.02
435	Herm Winningham	.04	.03	.02
436	Al Newman	.04	.03	.02
437	Jose DeLeon	.06	.05	.02
438	Doug Jones	.10	.08	.04
439	Brian Holton	.06	.05	.02
440	Jeff Montgomery(FC)	.06	.05	.02
441	Dickie Thon	.04	.03	.02
442	Cecil Fielder	.04	.03	.02
443	*John Fishel*(FC)	.20	.15	.08
444	Jerry Don Gleaton	.04	.03	.02
445	*Paul Gibson*	.15	.11	.06
446	Walt Weiss	.40	.30	.15
447	Glenn Wilson	.06	.05	.02
448	Mike Moore	.04	.03	.02
449	Chili Davis	.06	.05	.02
450	Dave Henderson	.08	.06	.03
451	*Jose Bautista*	.20	.15	.08
452	Rex Hudler	.04	.03	.02
453	Bob Brenly	.04	.03	.02
454	Mackey Sasser	.06	.05	.02
455	Daryl Boston	.04	.03	.02
456	Mike Fitzgerald	.04	.03	.02
457	Jeffery Leonard	.06	.05	.02
458	Bruce Sutter	.08	.06	.03
459	Mitch Webster	.06	.05	.02
460	Joe Hesketh	.04	.03	.02
461	Bobby Witt	.08	.06	.03
462	Stew Cliburn	.04	.03	.02
463	Scott Bankhead	.04	.03	.02
464	Ramon Martinez(FC)	2.00	1.50	.80
465	Dave Leiper	.04	.03	.02
466	*Luis Alicea*	.20	.15	.08
467	John Cerutti	.06	.05	.02

#	Player	MT	NR MT	EX
468	Ron Washington	.04	.03	.02
469	Jeff Reed	.04	.03	.02
470	Jeff Robinson	.12	.09	.05
471	Sid Fernandez	.08	.06	.03
472	Terry Puhl	.04	.03	.02
473	Charlie Lea	.04	.03	.02
474	*Israel Sanchez*(FC)	.15	.11	.06
475	Bruce Benedict	.04	.03	.02
476	Oil Can Boyd	.06	.05	.02
477	Craig Reynolds	.04	.03	.02
478	Frank Williams	.04	.03	.02
479	Greg Cadaret	.10	.08	.04
480	*Randy Kramer*(FC)	.15	.11	.06
481	*Dave Eiland*(FC)	.20	.15	.08
482	Eric Show	.06	.05	.02
483	Garry Templeton	.06	.05	.02
484	Wallace Johnson(FC)	.04	.03	.02
485	Kevin Mitchell	.60	.45	.25
486	Tim Crews	.06	.05	.02
487	Mike Maddux	.04	.03	.02
488	Dave LaPoint	.06	.05	.02
489	Fred Manrique	.06	.05	.02
490	Greg Minton	.04	.03	.02
491	*Doug Dascenzo*(FC)	.25	.20	.10
492	Willie Upshaw	.06	.05	.02
493	*Jack Armstrong*(FC)	.40	.30	.15
494	Kirt Manwaring	.10	.08	.04
495	Jeff Ballard	.06	.05	.02
496	Jeff Kunkel	.04	.03	.02
497	Mike Campbell	.08	.06	.03
498	Gary Thurman	.10	.08	.04
499	Zane Smith	.06	.05	.02
500	Checklist 468-577	.04	.03	.02
501	Mike Birkbeck	.04	.03	.02
502	Terry Leach	.04	.03	.02
503	Shawn Hillegas	.06	.05	.02
504	Manny Lee	.04	.03	.02
505	*Doug Jennings*	.20	.15	.08
506	Ken Oberkfell	.04	.03	.02
507	Tim Teufel	.04	.03	.02
508	Tom Brookens	.04	.03	.02
509	Rafael Ramirez	.04	.03	.02
510	Fred Toliver	.04	.03	.02
511	*Brian Holman*(FC)	.40	.30	.15
512	Mike Bielecki	.04	.03	.02
513	*Jeff Pico*(FC)	.25	.20	.10
514	Charles Hudson	.04	.03	.02
515	Bruce Ruffin	.04	.03	.02
516	Larry McWilliams	.04	.03	.02
517	Jeff Sellers	.04	.03	.02
518	*John Costello*(FC)	.20	.15	.08
519	*Brady Anderson*	.35	.25	.14
520	Craig McMurtry	.04	.03	.02
521	Ray Hayward	.08	.06	.03
522	Drew Hall	.08	.06	.03
523	*Mark Lemke*(FC)	.20	.15	.08
524	*Oswald Peraza*(FC)	.20	.15	.08
525	*Bryan Harvey*	.25	.20	.10
526	Rick Aguilera	.04	.03	.02
527	Tom Prince	.06	.05	.02
528	Mark Clear	.04	.03	.02
529	Jerry Browne	.04	.03	.02
530	Juan Castillo	.04	.03	.02
531	Jack McDowell	.08	.06	.03
532	Chris Speier	.04	.03	.02
533	Darrell Evans	.08	.06	.03
534	Luis Aquino	.04	.03	.02
535	Eric King	.04	.03	.02
536	*Ken Hill*(FC)	.25	.20	.10
537	Randy Bush	.04	.03	.02
538	Shane Mack	.06	.05	.02
539	Tom Bolton(FC)	.06	.05	.02
540	Gene Nelson	.04	.03	.02
541	Wes Gardner	.06	.05	.02
542	Ken Caminiti	.06	.05	.02
543	Duane Ward	.04	.03	.02
544	*Norm Charlton*(FC)	.30	.25	.12
545	*Hal Morris*(FC)	.80	.60	.30
546	*Rich Yett*(FC)	.04	.03	.02
547	*Hensley Meulens*(FC)	.60	.45	.25
548	Greg Harris	.04	.03	.02
549	Darren Daulton	.04	.03	.02
550	Jeff Hamilton	.06	.05	.02
551	Luis Aguayo	.04	.03	.02
552	Tim Leary	.06	.05	.02
553	Ron Oester	.04	.03	.02
554	Steve Lombardozzi	.04	.03	.02
555	*Tim Jones*(FC)	.15	.11	.06
556	Bud Black	.04	.03	.02
557	Alejandro Pena	.04	.03	.02
558	*Jose DeJesus*(FC)	.15	.11	.06
559	Dennis Rasmussen	.08	.06	.03
560	*Pat Borders*	.20	.15	.08
561	*Craig Biggio*(FC)	.50	.40	.20
562	*Luis de los Santos*(FC)	.20	.15	.08
563	Fred Lynn	.10	.08	.04
564	*Todd Burns*(FC)	.30	.25	.12
565	Felix Fermin	.06	.05	.02
566	Darnell Coles	.06	.05	.02
567	Willie Fraser	.04	.03	.02
568	Glenn Hubbard	.04	.03	.02
569	*Craig Worthington*	.30	.25	.12
570	*Johnny Paredes*	.20	.15	.08
571	Don Robinson	.04	.03	.02
572	Barry Lyons	.04	.03	.02
573	Bill Long	.06	.05	.02
574	Tracy Jones	.10	.08	.04
575	Juan Nieves	.06	.05	.02
576	Andres Thomas	.06	.05	.02
577	*Rolando Roomes*(FC)	.25	.20	.10
578	*Luis Rivera*(FC)	.04	.03	.02
579	*Chad Kreuter*(FC)	.20	.15	.08
580	Tony Armas	.06	.05	.02
581	Jay Buhner	.10	.08	.04
582	Ricky Horton	.06	.05	.02
583	Andy Hawkins	.04	.03	.02
584	*Sil Campusano*	.20	.15	.08
585	Dave Clark	.06	.05	.02
586	*Van Snider*(FC)	.20	.15	.08
587	Todd Frohwirth(FC)	.06	.05	.02
588	Warren Spahn Puzzle Card	.04	.03	.02
589	*William Brennan*(FC)	.20	.15	.08
590	*German Gonzalez*(FC)	.20	.15	.08
591	Ernie Whitt	.06	.05	.02
592	Jeff Blauser	.08	.06	.03
593	Spike Owen	.04	.03	.02
594	Matt Williams	.40	.30	.15
595	Lloyd McClendon(FC)	.04	.03	.02
596	Steve Ontiveros	.04	.03	.02
597	*Scott Medvin*(FC)	.20	.15	.08
598	*Hipolito Pena*(FC)	.15	.11	.06
599	*Jerald Clark*(FC)	.25	.20	.10
600a	Checklist 578-BC26 (#635 is Kurt Schilling)	.15	.11	.06
600b	Checklist 578-BC26 (#635 is Curt Schilling)	.06	.05	.02
601	Carmelo Martinez	.04	.03	.02
602	Mike LaCoss	.04	.03	.02
603	Mike Devereaux	.15	.11	.06
604	*Alex Madrid*(FC)	.15	.11	.06
605	Gary Redus	.04	.03	.02
606	Lance Johnson	.06	.05	.02
607	*Terry Clark*(FC)	.15	.11	.06
608	Manny Trillo	.04	.03	.02
609	*Scott Jordan*(FC)	.15	.11	.06
610	Jay Howell	.06	.05	.02
611	*Francisco Melendez*(FC)	.25	.20	.10
612	Mike Boddicker	.06	.05	.02
613	Kevin Brown	.20	.15	.08
614	Dave Valle	.04	.03	.02
615	Tim Laudner	.04	.03	.02
616	*Andy Nezelek*(FC)	.20	.15	.08
617	Chuck Crim	.04	.03	.02
618	Jack Savage(FC)	.10	.08	.04
619	Adam Peterson(FC)	.10	.08	.04
620	Todd Stottlemyre	.10	.08	.04
621	Lance Blankenship(FC)	.25	.20	.10
622	*Miguel Garcia*(FC)	.15	.11	.06
623	Keith Miller	.06	.05	.02
624	*Ricky Jordan*(FC)	.40	.30	.15
625	Ernest Riles	.04	.03	.02
626	John Moses	.04	.03	.02
627	Nelson Liriano	.06	.05	.02
628	Mike Smithson	.04	.03	.02
629	Scott Sanderson	.04	.03	.02
630	Dale Mohorcic	.04	.03	.02
631	Marvin Freeman	.04	.03	.02
632	Mike Young	.04	.03	.02
633	Dennis Lamp	.04	.03	.02
634	*Dante Bichette*(FC)	.35	.25	.14
635	*Curt Schilling*(FC)	.15	.11	.06
636	*Scott May*(FC)	.15	.11	.06
637	*Mike Schooler*(FC)	.35	.25	.14
638	Rick Leach	.04	.03	.02
639	*Tom Lampkin*(FC)	.15	.11	.06
640	*Brian Meyer*(FC)	.15	.11	.06
641	Brian Harper	.04	.03	.02
642	*John Smoltz*(FC)	.80	.60	.30
643	40/40 Club (Jose Canseco)	.60	.45	.25
644	Bill Schroeder	.04	.03	.02
645	*Edgar Martinez*	.40	.30	.15
646	*Dennis Cook*(FC)	.40	.30	.15

		MT	NR MT	EX
647	Barry Jones	.04	.03	.02
648	59 and Counting (Orel Hershiser)	.15	.11	.06
649	Rod Nichols(FC)	.15	.11	.06
650	Jody Davis	.06	.05	.02
651	Bob Milacki(FC)	.25	.20	.10
652	Mike Jackson	.06	.05	.02
653	Derek Lilliquist(FC)	.35	.25	.14
654	Paul Mirabella	.04	.03	.02
655	Mike Diaz	.06	.05	.02
656	Jeff Musselman	.06	.05	.02
657	Jerry Reed	.04	.03	.02
658	Kevin Blankenship(FC)	.20	.15	.08
659	Wayne Tolleson	.04	.03	.02
660	Eric Hetzel(FC)	.20	.15	.08

1989 Donruss Grand Slammers

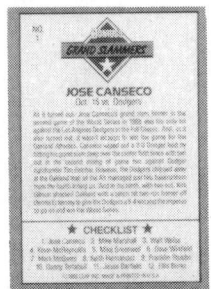

One card from this 12-card set was included in each Donruss cello pack. The featured players all hit grand slams in 1988. The 2-1/2" by 3-1/2" cards feature full color action photos. The card backs feature the story of the player's grand slam. Border variations on the front of the card have been discovered, but the prices are consistent with all forms of the cards.

		MT	NR MT	EX
	Complete Set:	5.00	3.75	2.00
	Common Player:	.12	.09	.05
1	Jose Canseco	1.25	.90	.50
2	Mike Marshall	.12	.09	.05
3	Walt Weiss	.12	.09	.05
4	Kevin McReynolds	.15	.11	.06
5	Mike Greenwell	.40	.30	.15
6	Dave Winfield	.40	.30	.15
7	Mark McGwire	.70	.50	.30
8	Keith Hernandez	.15	.11	.06
9	Franklin Stubbs	.12	.09	.05
10	Danny Tartabull	.25	.20	.10
11	Jesse Barfield	.15	.11	.06
12	Ellis Burks	.35	.25	.14

1989 Donruss Traded

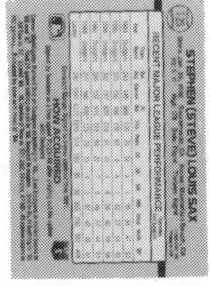

Donruss issued its first "Traded" set in 1989,

releasing a 56-card boxed set designed in the same style as the regular 1989 Donruss set. The set included a Stan Musial puzzle card and a checklist.

		MT	NR MT	EX
	Complete Set:	5.00	3.75	2.00
	Common Player:	.06	.05	.02
1	Jeffrey Leonard	.08	.06	.03
2	Jack Clark	.15	.11	.06
3	Kevin Gross	.06	.05	.02
4	Tommy Herr	.08	.06	.03
5	Bob Boone	.10	.08	.04
6	Rafael Palmeiro	.20	.15	.08
7	John Dopson	.15	.11	.06
8	Willie Randolph	.08	.06	.03
9	Chris Brown	.06	.05	.02
10	Wally Backman	.06	.05	.02
11	Steve Ontiveros	.06	.05	.02
12	Eddie Murray	.30	.25	.12
13	Lance McCullers	.08	.06	.03
14	Spike Owen	.06	.05	.02
15	Rob Murphy	.06	.05	.02
16	Pete O'Brien	.08	.06	.03
17	Ken Williams	.06	.05	.02
18	Nick Esasky	.06	.05	.02
19	Nolan Ryan	1.00	.70	.40
20	Brian Holton	.06	.05	.02
21	Mike Moore	.08	.06	.03
22	Joel Skinner	.06	.05	.02
23	Steve Sax	.15	.11	.06
24	Rick Mahler	.06	.05	.02
25	Mike Aldrete	.06	.05	.02
26	Jesse Orosco	.08	.06	.03
27	Dave LaPoint	.06	.05	.02
28	Walt Terrell	.08	.06	.03
29	Eddie Williams	.08	.06	.03
30	Mike Devereaux	.10	.08	.04
31	Julio Franco	.15	.11	.06
32	Jim Clancy	.06	.05	.02
33	Felix Fermin	.06	.05	.02
34	Curtis Wilkerson	.06	.05	.02
35	Bert Blyleven	.12	.09	.05
36	Mel Hall	.08	.06	.03
37	Eric King	.06	.05	.02
38	Mitch Williams	.12	.09	.05
39	Jamie Moyer	.06	.05	.02
40	Rick Rhoden	.08	.06	.03
41	Phil Bradley	.08	.06	.03
42	Paul Kilgus	.08	.06	.03
43	Milt Thompson	.06	.05	.02
44	Jerry Browne	.08	.06	.03
45	Bruce Hurst	.08	.06	.03
46	Claudell Washington	.08	.06	.03
47	Todd Benzinger	.12	.09	.05
48	Steve Balboni	.06	.05	.02
49	Oddibe McDowell	.08	.06	.03
50	Charles Hudson	.06	.05	.02
51	Ron Kittle	.08	.06	.03
52	Andy Hawkins	.06	.05	.02
53	Tom Brookens	.06	.05	.02
54	Tom Niedenfuer	.06	.05	.02
55	Jeff Parrett	.08	.06	.03
56	Checklist	.06	.05	.02

1989 Donruss Rookies

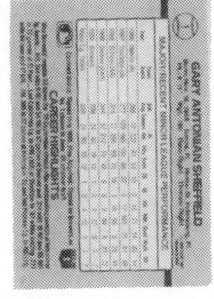

For the fourth straight year, Donruss issued a 56-card "Rookies" set in 1989. As in previous years, the set is similar in design to the regular Donruss set, except for a new "The Rookies" logo and a green and black border.

		MT	NR MT	EX
Complete Set:		20.00	15.00	8.00
Common Player:		.10	.08	.04
1	Gary Sheffield	1.50	1.25	.60
2	Gregg Jefferies	1.50	1.25	.60
3	Ken Griffey, Jr.	7.00	5.25	2.75
4	Tom Gordon	.90	.70	.35
5	Billy Spiers(FC)	.35	.25	.14
6	Deion Sanders(FC)	.80	.60	.30
7	Donn Pall(FC)	.20	.15	.08
8	Steve Carter(FC)	.20	.15	.08
9	Francisco Oliveras(FC)	.15	.11	.06
10	Steve Wilson(FC)	.25	.20	.10
11	Bob Geren(FC)	.30	.25	.12
12	Tony Castillo(FC)	.15	.11	.06
13	Kenny Rogers(FC)	.20	.15	.08
14	Carlos Martinez(FC)	.30	.25	.12
15	Edgar Martinez	.30	.25	.12
16	Jim Abbott(FC)	1.00	.70	.40
17	Torey Lovullo(FC)	.20	.15	.08
18	Mark Carreon(FC)	.15	.11	.06
19	Geronimo Berroa	.10	.08	.04
20	Luis Medina	.10	.08	.04
21	Sandy Alomar, Jr.	.70	.50	.30
22	Bob Milacki	.10	.08	.04
23	Joe Girardi(FC)	.30	.25	.12
24	German Gonzalez	.10	.08	.04
25	Craig Worthington	.15	.11	.06
26	Jerome Walton(FC)	1.50	1.25	.60
27	Gary Wayne(FC)	.20	.15	.08
28	Tim Jones	.10	.08	.04
29	Dante Bichette	.10	.08	.04
30	Alexis Infante(FC)	.15	.11	.06
31	Ken Hill	.10	.08	.04
32	Dwight Smith(FC)	.70	.50	.30
33	Luis de los Santos	.10	.08	.04
34	Eric Yelding(FC)	.35	.25	.14
35	Gregg Olson	1.00	.70	.40
36	Phil Stephenson(FC)	.15	.11	.06
37	Ken Patterson(FC)	.15	.11	.06
38	Rick Wrona(FC)	.15	.11	.06
39	Mike Brumley	.10	.08	.04
40	Cris Carpenter	.10	.08	.04
41	Jeff Brantley(FC)	.20	.15	.08
42	Ron Jones	.10	.08	.04
43	Randy Johnson	.10	.08	.04
44	Kevin Brown	.10	.08	.04
45	Ramon Martinez	1.50	1.25	.60
46	Greg Harris	.10	.08	.04
47	Steve Finley(FC)	.30	.25	.12
48	Randy Kramer	.10	.08	.04
49	Erik Hanson	.40	.30	.15
50	Matt Merullo(FC)	.15	.11	.06
51	Mike Devereaux	.10	.08	.04
52	Clay Parker(FC)	.15	.11	.06
53	Omar Vizquel(FC)	.20	.15	.08
54	Derek Lilliquist	.10	.08	.04
55	Junior Felix(FC)	1.25	.90	.50
56	Checklist	.10	.08	.04

1989 Donruss Pop-Ups

This set features the eighteen starters from the 1988 Major League All-Star game. The cards are designed with a perforated outline so each player can

be popped out and made to stand upright. On the front side, each player's name, team, and position is featured in an orange-and-yellow rectangle below the borderless full-color photo. Each Pop-Up includes a unique double card, folded over and glued together on the back. The flip side features a red, white, and blue "Cincinnati Reds All-Star Game" logo at the top, a blue-lettered league designation, and the player's name and position in red. The lower portion of the flip side displays illustrated instructions for creating the base of the Pop-Up. The Pop-Ups were marketed in conjunction with All-Star and Warren Spahn Puzzle Cards.

		MT	NR MT	EX
Complete Set:		6.00	4.50	2.50
Common Player:		.20	.15	.08
(1)	Mark McGwire	.70	.50	.30
(2)	Jose Canseco	1.00	.70	.40
(3)	Paul Molitor	.30	.25	.12
(4)	Rickey Henderson	.50	.40	.20
(5)	Cal Ripken, Jr.	.50	.40	.20
(6)	Dave Winfield	.40	.30	.15
(7)	Wade Boggs	.80	.60	.30
(8)	Frank Viola	.30	.25	.12
(9)	Terry Steinbach	.20	.15	.08
(10)	Tom Kelly	.20	.15	.08
(11)	Will Clark	1.00	.70	.40
(12)	Darryl Strawberry	.70	.50	.30
(13)	Ryne Sandberg	.40	.30	.15
(14)	Andre Dawson	.35	.25	.14
(15)	Ozzie Smith	.30	.25	.12
(16)	Vince Coleman	.30	.25	.12
(17)	Bobby Bonilla	.30	.25	.12
(18)	Dwight Gooden	.50	.40	.20
(19)	Gary Carter	.20	.15	.08
(20)	Whitey Herzog	.20	.15	.08

1989 Donruss All-Stars

For the fourth consecutive year in conjunction with the Pop-Ups, Donruss featured a 64-card set with players from the 1988 All-Star Game. The card fronts include a red- to-gold fade or gold-to-red fade border and blue vertical side borders. The top border features the player's name and position along with the "Donruss 89" logo. Each full-color player photo is highlighted by a thin white line and includes a league logo in the lower right corner. Card backs reveal an orange-gold border and black and white printing. The player's ID and personal information is displayed with a gold star on both sides. The star in the left corner includes the card number. 1988 All-Star game statistics and run totals follow along with a career highlights feature surrounded by the team, All-Star Game MLB, MLBPA, and Leaf Inc. logos. The All-Stars were distributed in wax packages containing five All-Stars, one Pop-Up, and one three-piece Warren Spahn puzzle card.

		MT	NR MT	EX
Complete Set:		8.00	6.00	3.25
Common Player:		.09	.07	.04

		MT	NR MT	EX
1	Mark McGwire	.80	.60	.30
2	Jose Canseco	1.00	.70	.40
3	Paul Molitor	.12	.09	.05
4	Rickey Henderson	.30	.25	.12
5	Cal Ripken, Jr.	.30	.25	.12
6	Dave Winfield	.20	.15	.08
7	Wade Boggs	.80	.60	.30
8	Frank Viola	.15	.11	.06
9	Terry Steinbach	.15	.11	.06
10	Tom Kelly	.09	.07	.04
11	George Brett	.12	.09	.05
12	Doyle Alexander	.09	.07	.04
13	Gary Gaetti	.12	.09	.05
14	Roger Clemens	.25	.20	.10
15	Mike Greenwell	.25	.20	.10
16	Dennis Eckersley	.12	.09	.05
17	Carney Lansford	.09	.07	.04
18	Mark Gubicza	.09	.07	.04
19	Tim Laudner	.09	.07	.04
20	Doug Jones	.09	.07	.04
21	Don Mattingly	1.50	1.25	.60
22	Dan Plesac	.12	.09	.05
23	Kirby Puckett	.30	.25	.12
24	Jeff Reardon	.09	.07	.04
25	Johnny Ray	.09	.07	.04
26	Jeff Russell	.09	.07	.04
27	Harold Reynolds	.09	.07	.04
28	Dave Stieb	.09	.07	.04
29	Kurt Stillwell	.09	.07	.04
30	Jose Canseco	1.25	.90	.50
31	Terry Steinbach	.15	.11	.06
32	AL Checklist	.09	.07	.05
33	Will Clark	1.25	.90	.50
34	Darryl Strawberry	.60	.45	.25
35	Ryne Sandberg	.20	.15	.08
36	Andre Dawson	.20	.15	.08
37	Ozzie Smith	.20	.15	.08
38	Vince Coleman	.15	.11	.06
39	Bobby Bonilla	.15	.11	.06
40	Dwight Gooden	.40	.30	.15
41	Gary Carter	.10	.08	.04
42	Whitey Herzog	.09	.07	.05
43	Shawon Dunston	.09	.07	.05
44	David Cone	.12	.09	.05
45	Andres Galarraga	.12	.09	.05
46	Mark Davis	.12	.09	.05
47	Barry Larkin	.12	.09	.05
48	Kevin Gross	.09	.07	.04
49	Vance Law	.09	.07	.04
50	Orel Hershiser	.20	.15	.08
51	Willie McGee	.09	.07	.04
52	Danny Jackson	.09	.07	.04
53	Rafael Palmeiro	.09	.07	.04
54	Bob Knepper	.09	.07	.04
55	Lance Parrish	.09	.07	.04
56	Greg Maddux	.20	.15	.08
57	Gerald Perry	.09	.07	.04
58	Bob Walk	.09	.07	.04
59	Chris Sabo	.12	.09	.04
60	Todd Worrell	.12	.09	.04
61	Andy Van Slyke	.12	.09	.04
62	Ozzie Smith	.20	.15	.08
63	Riverfront Stadium	.09	.07	.04
64	NL Checklist	.09	.07	.04

Players highlighted in this set are selected by Donruss, one player per team. MVP cards feature a variation of the design in the basic Donruss issue, with multi-color upper and lower borders and black side borders. The player name and Donruss '89 logos appear in the upper margin with the team logo appearing lower right. The "MVP" designation in large, bright letters serves as a backdrop for the full-color player photo. The cards measure 2-1/2" by 3-1/2" in size.

		MT	NR MT	EX
	Complete Set:	4.00	3.00	1.50
	Common Player:	.15	.11	.06
1	Kirby Puckett	.50	.40	.20
2	Mike Scott	.15	.11	.06
3	Joe Carter	.20	.15	.08
4	Orel Hershiser	.25	.20	.10
5	Jose Canseco	.75	.55	.30
6	Darryl Strawberry	.60	.45	.25
7	George Brett	.35	.25	.14
8	Andre Dawson	.25	.20	.10
9	Paul Molitor	.20	.15	.08
10	Andy Van Slyke	.15	.11	.06
11	Dave Winfield	.20	.15	.08
12	Kevin Gross	.15	.11	.06
13	Mike Greenwell	.60	.45	.25
14	Ozzie Smith	.20	.15	.08
15	Cal Ripken	.30	.25	.12
16	Andres Galarraga	.20	.15	.08
17	Alan Trammell	.25	.20	.10
18	Kal Daniels	.20	.15	.08
19	Fred McGriff	.35	.25	.14
20	Tony Gwynn	.30	.25	.12
21	Wally Joyner	.30	.25	.12
22	Will Clark	.75	.55	.30
23	Ozzie Guillen	.15	.11	.06
24	Gerald Perry	.15	.11	.06
25	Alvin Davis	.15	.11	.06
26	Ruben Sierra	.25	.20	.10

1989 Donruss Baseball's Best

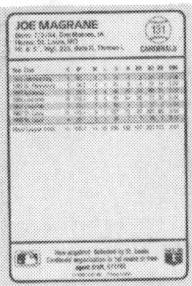

For the second consecutive year, Donruss issued a "Baseball's Best" set in 1989 to highlight the game's top players. The special 336-card set was packaged in a special box and was sold at various retail chains nationwide following the conclusion of the 1989 baseball season. The cards are styled after the regular 1989 Donruss set with green borders and a glossy finish. The set included a Warren Spahn puzzle.

		MT	NR MT	EX
	Complete Set:	18.00	13.50	7.25
	Common Player:	.05	.04	.02
1	Don Mattingly	2.00	1.50	.80
2	Tom Glavine	.08	.06	.03
3	Bert Blyleven	.08	.06	.03
4	Andre Dawson	.10	.08	.04
5	Pete O'Brien	.05	.04	.02
6	Eric Davis	.70	.50	.30
7	George Brett	.10	.08	.04

1989 Donruss MVP

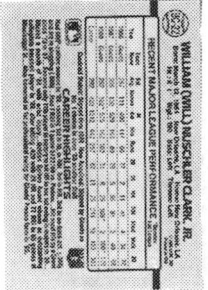

This 26-card set, numbered BC-1 through BC-26, was randomly packed in Donruss wax packs, but were not included in factory sets or other card packs.

		MT	NR MT	EX			MT	NR MT	EX
8	Glenn Davis	.10	.08	.04	99	Dave Stewart	.20	.15	.08
9	Ellis Burks	.50	.40	.20	100	Jose Oquendo	.06	.05	.02
10	Kirk Gibson	.08	.06	.03	101	Jose Lind	.05	.04	.02
11	Carlton Fisk	.08	.06	.03	102	Gary Gaetti	.12	.09	.05
12	Andres Galarraga	.08	.06	.03	103	Ricky Jordan	.25	.20	.10
13	Alan Trammell	.06	.05	.02	104	Fred McGriff	.50	.40	.20
14	Dwight Gooden	.60	.45	.25	105	Don Slaught	.05	.04	.02
15	Paul Molitor	.10	.08	.04	106	Jose Uribe	.05	.04	.02
16	Roger McDowell	.05	.04	.02	107	Jeffrey Leonard	.07	.05	.02
17	Doug Drabek	.05	.04	.02	108	Lee Guetterman	.05	.04	.02
18	Kent Hrbek	.08	.06	.03	109	Chris Bosio	.08	.06	.03
19	Vince Coleman	.08	.06	.03	110	Barry Larkin	.15	.11	.06
20	Steve Sax	.08	.06	.03	111	Ruben Sierra	.30	.25	.12
21	Roberto Alomar	.30	.25	.12	112	Greg Swindell	.12	.09	.05
22	Carney Lansford	.06	.05	.02	113	Gary Sheffield	.90	.70	.40
23	Will Clark	1.50	1.25	.60	114	Lonnie Smith	.10	.08	.04
24	Alvin Davis	.08	.06	.03	115	Chili Davis	.08	.06	.03
25	Bobby Thigpen	.08	.06	.03	116	Damon Berryhill	.08	.06	.03
26	Ryne Sandberg	.25	.20	.10	117	Tom Candiotti	.05	.04	.02
27	Devon White	.08	.06	.03	118	Kal Daniels	.10	.08	.04
28	Mike Greenwell	.40	.30	.15	119	Mark Gubicza	.10	.08	.04
29	Dale Murphy	.10	.08	.04	120	Jim Deshaies	.08	.06	.03
30	Jeff Ballard	.10	.08	.04	121	Dwight Evans	.10	.08	.04
31	Kelly Gruber	.08	.06	.03	122	Mike Morgan	.05	.04	.02
32	Julio Franco	.07	.05	.03	123	Dan Pasqua	.05	.04	.02
33	Bobby Bonilla	.15	.11	.06	124	Bryn Smith	.07	.05	.03
34	Tim Wallach	.05	.04	.02	125	Doyle Alexander	.07	.05	.03
35	Lou Whitaker	.07	.05	.03	126	Howard Johnson	.25	.20	.10
36	Jay Howell	.07	.05	.03	127	Chuck Crim	.07	.05	.03
37	Greg Maddux	.30	.25	.12	128	Darren Daulton	.05	.04	.02
38	Bill Doran	.07	.05	.03	129	Jeff Robinson	.08	.06	.03
39	Danny Tartabull	.12	.09	.05	130	Kirby Puckett	.50	.40	.20
40	Darryl Strawberry	.50	.40	.20	131	Joe Magrane	.10	.08	.04
41	Ron Darling	.10	.08	.06	132	Jesse Barfield	.07	.05	.03
42	Tony Gwynn	.30	.25	.12	133	Mark Davis (Photo actually Dave Leiper)			
43	Mark McGwire	.80	.60	.30			.25	.20	.10
44	Ozzie Smith	.15	.11	.06	134	Dennis Eckersley	.10	.08	.04
45	Andy Van Slyke	.12	.09	.05	135	Mike Krukow	.05	.04	.02
46	Juan Berenguer	.05	.04	.02	136	Jay Buhner	.10	.08	.04
47	Von Hayes	.08	.06	.03	137	Ozzie Guillen	.08	.06	.03
48	Tony Fernandez	.12	.09	.05	138	Rick Sutcliffe	.12	.09	.05
49	Eric Plunk	.05	.04	.02	139	Wally Joyner	.25	.20	.10
50	Ernest Riles	.05	.04	.02	140	Wade Boggs	1.00	.70	.40
51	Harold Reynolds	.07	.05	.03	141	Jeff Treadway	.08	.06	.05
52	Andy Hawkins	.06	.05	.02	142	Cal Ripken	.30	.25	.12
53	Robin Yount	.35	.25	.14	143	Dave Steib	.10	.08	.04
54	Danny Jackson	.06	.05	.02	144	Pete Incaviglia	.07	.05	.03
55	Nolan Ryan	.40	.30	.15	145	Bob Walk	.05	.04	.02
56	Joe Carter	.12	.09	.05	146	Nelson Santovenia	.10	.08	.04
57	Jose Canseco	1.00	.70	.40	147	Mike Heath	.05	.04	.02
58	Jody Davis	.05	.04	.02	148	Willie Randolph	.08	.06	.03
59	Lance Parrish	.06	.05	.02	149	Paul Kilgus	.05	.04	.02
60	Mitch Williams	.15	.11	.06	150	Billy Hatcher	.07	.05	.03
61	Brook Jacoby	.06	.05	.02	151	Steve Farr	.05	.04	.02
62	Tom Browning	.10	.08	.06	152	Gregg Jefferies	1.00	.70	.40
63	Kurt Stillwell	.06	.05	.02	153	Randy Myers	.06	.05	.02
64	Rafael Ramirez	.05	.04	.02	154	Garry Templeton	.06	.05	.02
65	Roger Clemens	.50	.40	.20	155	Walt Weiss	.10	.08	.04
66	Mike Scioscia	.07	.05	.02	156	Terry Pendleton	.10	.08	.04
67	Dave Gallagher	.07	.05	.02	157	John Smiley	.08	.06	.03
68	Mark Langston	.15	.11	.06	158	Greg Gagne	.05	.04	.02
69	Chet Lemon	.06	.05	.02	159	Lenny Dykstra	.08	.06	.03
70	Kevin McReynolds	.25	.20	.10	160	Nelson Liriano	.05	.04	.02
71	Rob Deer	.06	.05	.02	161	Alvaro Espinosa	.70	.50	.30
72	Tommy Herr	.07	.05	.03	162	Rick Reuschel	.08	.06	.03
73	Barry Bonds	.12	.09	.05	163	Omar Vizquel	.35	.25	.14
74	Frank Viola	.15	.11	.06	164	Clay Parker	.15	.11	.06
75	Pedro Guerrero	.15	.11	.06	165	Dan Plesac	.06	.05	.02
76	Dave Righetti	.07	.05	.03	166	John Franco	.06	.05	.02
77	Bruce Hurst	.08	.06	.03	167	Scott Fletcher	.06	.05	.02
78	Rickey Henderson	.40	.30	.15	168	Cory Snyder	.12	.09	.05
79	Robby Thompson	.08	.06	.03	169	Bo Jackson	1.00	.70	.40
80	Randy Johnson	.25	.20	.10	170	Tommy Gregg	.08	.06	.03
81	Harold Baines	.12	.09	.05	171	Jim Abbott	1.25	.90	.50
82	Calvin Schiraldi	.05	.04	.02	172	Jerome Walton	1.75	1.25	.70
83	Kirk McCaskill	.05	.04	.02	173	Doug Jones	.06	.05	.02
84	Lee Smith	.07	.05	.03	174	Todd Benzinger	.08	.06	.03
85	John Smoltz	.25	.20	.10	175	Frank White	.08	.06	.03
86	Mickey Tettleton	.20	.15	.08	176	Craig Biggio	.20	.15	.08
87	Jimmy Key	.08	.06	.03	177	John Dopson	.10	.08	.06
88	Rafael Palmeiro	.10	.08	.04	178	Alfredo Griffin	.06	.05	.02
89	Sid Bream	.05	.04	.02	179	Melido Perez	.06	.05	.02
90	Dennis Martinez	.05	.04	.02	180	Tim Burke	.06	.05	.02
91	Frank Tanana	.05	.04	.02	181	Matt Nokes	.10	.08	.04
92	Eddie Murray	.15	.11	.06	182	Gary Carter	.10	.08	.04
93	Shawon Dunston	.15	.11	.06	183	Ted Higuera	.08	.06	.03
94	Mike Scott	.10	.08	.04	184	Ken Howell	.05	.04	.02
95	Bret Saberhagen	.25	.20	.10	185	Rey Quinones	.05	.04	.02
96	David Cone	.20	.15	.08	186	Wally Backman	.07	.05	.02
97	Kevin Elster	.05	.04	.02	187	Tom Brunansky	.07	.05	.03
98	Jack Clark	.20	.15	.08	188	Steve Balboni	.05	.04	.02

		MT	NR MT	EX
189	Marvell Wynne	.05	.04	.02
190	Dave Henderson	.08	.06	.03
191	Don Robinson	.05	.04	.02
192	Ken Griffey, Jr.	1.50	1.25	.60
193	Ivan Calderon	.05	.04	.02
194	Mike Bielecki	.07	.05	.03
195	Johnny Ray	.07	.05	.03
196	Rob Murphy	.05	.04	.02
197	Andres Thomas	.05	.04	.02
198	Phil Bradley	.06	.05	.02
199	Junior Felix	.70	.50	.30
200	Jeff Russell	.08	.06	.03
201	Mike LaValliere	.05	.04	.02
202	Kevin Gross	.06	.05	.02
203	Keith Moreland	.06	.05	.02
204	Mike Marshall	.06	.05	.02
205	Dwight Smith	.90	.70	.40
206	Jim Clancy	.05	.04	.02
207	Kevin Seitzer	.10	.08	.04
208	Keith Hernandez	.10	.08	.04
209	Bob Ojeda	.06	.05	.02
210	Ed Whitson	.06	.05	.02
211	Tony Phillips	.06	.05	.02
212	Milt Thompson	.05	.04	.02
213	Randy Kramer	.05	.04	.02
214	Randy Bush	.05	.04	.02
215	Randy Ready	.05	.04	.02
216	Duane Ward	.05	.04	.02
217	Jimmy Jones	.05	.04	.02
218	Scott Garrelts	.08	.06	.03
219	Scott Bankhead	.10	.08	.04
220	Lance McCullers	.06	.05	.02
221	B.J. Surhoff	.06	.05	.02
222	Chris Sabo	.06	.05	.02
223	Steve Buechele	.06	.05	.02
224	Joel Skinner	.05	.04	.02
225	Orel Hershiser	.15	.11	.06
226	Derek Lilliquist	.10	.08	.06
227	Claudell Washington	.08	.06	.05
228	Lloyd McClendon	.10	.08	.04
229	Felix Fermin	.05	.04	.02
230	Paul O'Neill	.08	.06	.03
231	Charlie Leibrandt	.05	.04	.02
232	Dave Smith	.06	.05	.02
233	Bob Stanley	.05	.04	.02
234	Tim Belcher	.15	.11	.06
235	Eric King	.05	.04	.02
236	Spike Owen	.05	.04	.02
237	Mike Henneman	.05	.04	.02
238	Juan Samuel	.06	.05	.02
239	Greg Brock	.06	.05	.02
240	John Kruk	.06	.05	.02
241	Glenn Wilson	.06	.05	.02
242	Jeff Reardon	.06	.05	.02
243	Todd Worrell	.08	.06	.03
244	Dave LaPoint	.05	.04	.02
245	Walt Terrell	.05	.04	.02
246	Mike Moore	.08	.06	.03
247	Kelly Downs	.05	.04	.02
248	Dave Valle	.05	.04	.02
249	Ron Kittle	.06	.05	.04
250	Steve Wilson	.10	.08	.04
251	Dick Schofield	.05	.04	.02
252	Marty Barrett	.06	.05	.02
253	Dion James	.06	.05	.02
254	Bob Milacki	.10	.08	.04
255	Ernie Whitt	.06	.05	.02
256	Kevin Brown	.08	.06	.03
257	R.J. Reynolds	.05	.04	.02
258	Tim Raines	.10	.08	.04
259	Frank Williams	.05	.04	.02
260	Jose Gonzalez	.05	.04	.02
261	Mitch Webster	.05	.04	.02
262	Ken Caminiti	.07	.05	.03
263	Bob Boone	.07	.05	.03
264	Dave Magadan	.07	.05	.03
265	Rick Aguilera	.05	.04	.02
266	Chris James	.05	.04	.02
267	Bob Welch	.07	.05	.03
268	Ken Dayley	.05	.04	.02
269	Junior Ortiz	.05	.04	.02
270	Allan Anderson	.08	.06	.03
271	Steve Jeltz	.05	.04	.02
272	George Bell	.10	.08	.04
273	Roberto Kelly	.10	.08	.04
274	Brett Butler	.07	.05	.03
275	Mike Schooler	.07	.05	.02
276	Ken Phelps	.05	.04	.02
277	Glenn Braggs	.06	.05	.02
278	Jose Rijo	.06	.05	.02
279	Bobby Witt	.06	.05	.02

		MT	NR MT	EX
280	Jerry Browne	.06	.05	.02
281	Kevin Mitchell	.70	.50	.30
282	Craig Worthington	.30	.25	.12
283	Greg Minton	.05	.04	.02
284	Nick Esasky	.07	.05	.03
285	John Farrell	.05	.04	.02
286	Rick Mahler	.05	.04	.02
287	Tom Gordon	.60	.45	.25
288	Gerald Young	.05	.04	.02
289	Jody Reed	.08	.06	.03
290	Jeff Hamilton	.05	.04	.02
291	Gerald Perry	.05	.04	.02
292	Hubie Brooks	.05	.04	.02
293	Bo Diaz	.05	.04	.02
294	Terry Puhl	.05	.04	.02
295	Jim Gantner	.05	.04	.02
296	Jeff Parrett	.05	.04	.02
297	Mike Boddicker	.05	.04	.02
298	Dan Gladden	.05	.04	.02
299	Tony Pena	.07	.05	.03
300	Checklist	.05	.04	.02
301	Tom Henke	.05	.04	.02
302	Pascual Perez	.05	.04	.02
303	Steve Bedrosian	.05	.04	.02
304	Ken Hill	.10	.08	.04
305	Jerry Reuss	.07	.05	.03
306	Jim Eisenreich	.05	.04	.02
307	Jack Howell	.05	.04	.02
308	Rick Cerone	.05	.04	.02
309	Tim Leary	.05	.04	.02
310	Joe Orsulak	.05	.04	.02
311	Jim Dwyer	.05	.04	.02
312	Geno Petralli	.05	.04	.02
313	Rick Honeycutt	.05	.04	.02
314	Tom Foley	.05	.04	.02
315	Kenny Rogers	.10	.08	.04
316	Mike Flanagan	.06	.05	.02
317	Bryan Harvey	.06	.05	.02
318	Billy Ripken	.05	.04	.02
319	Jeff Montgomery	.05	.04	.02
320	Erik Hanson	.12	.09	.05
321	Brian Downing	.06	.05	.02
322	Gregg Olson	.60	.45	.25
323	Terry Steinbach	.12	.09	.05
324	Sammy Sosa	.90	.70	.40
325	Gene Harris	.05	.04	.02
326	Mike Devereaux	.10	.08	.04
327	Dennis Cook	.12	.09	.05
328	David Wells	.08	.06	.03
329	Checklist	.05	.04	.02
330	Kirt Manwaring	.10	.08	.04
331	Jim Presley	.05	.04	.02
332	Checklist	.05	.04	.02
333	Chuck Finley	.05	.04	.02
334	Rob Dibble	.08	.06	.03
335	Cecil Espy	.06	.05	.02
336	Dave Parker	.08	.06	.02

1990 Donruss MVP

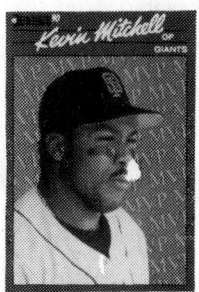
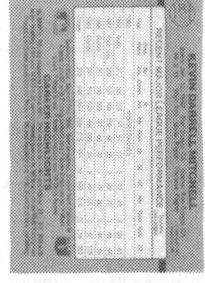

This special 26-card set includes one player from each Major League team. Numbered BC-1 (the "BC" stands for "Bonus Card") through BC-26, the cards from this set were randomly packed in 1990 Donruss wax packs and were not available in factory sets or other types of packaging. The red-bordered cards are similar in design to the regular 1990 Donruss set, except the player photos are set against a special background made up of the "MVP" logo.

	MT	NR MT	EX
Complete Set:	4.00	3.00	1.50
Common Player:	.08	.06	.03

		MT	NR MT	EX
1	Bo Jackson	.30	.25	.12
2	Howard Johnson	.10	.08	.04
3	Dave Stewart	.08	.06	.03
4	Tony Gwynn	.15	.11	.06
5	Orel Hershiser	.10	.08	.04
6	Pedro Guerrero	.10	.08	.04
7	Tim Raines	.10	.08	.04
8	Kirby Puckett	.30	.25	.12
9	Alvin Davis	.08	.06	.03
10	Ryne Sandberg	.10	.08	.04
11	Kevin Mitchell	.20	.15	.08
12a	John Smoltz (photo of Tom Glavine)			
		5.00	3.75	2.00
12b	John Smoltz (corrected)	.40	.30	.15
13	George Bell	.10	.08	.04
14	Julio Franco	.10	.08	.04
15	Paul Molitor	.10	.08	.04
16	Bobby Bonilla	.12	.09	.05
17	Mike Greenwell	.30	.25	.12
18	Cal Ripken	.30	.25	.12
19	Carlton Fisk	.12	.09	.05
20	Chili Davis	.08	.06	.03
21	Glenn Davis	.10	.08	.04
22	Steve Sax	.10	.08	.04
23	Eric Davis	.30	.25	.12
24	Greg Swindell	.08	.06	.03
25	Von Hayes	.08	.06	.03
26	Alan Trammell	.10	.08	.04

1990 Donruss

 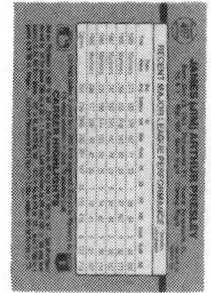

Donruss celebrated its 10th anniversary in the baseball card hobby with a 715-card set in 1990, up from the 660-card sets of previous years. The standard-size cards feature bright red borders with the player's name in script along the top. The 1990 set included 26 "Diamond Kings" and 20 "Rated Rookies," along with a Carl Yastrzemski puzzle.

	MT	NR MT	EX
Complete Set:	25.00	18.50	10.00
Common Player:	.04	.03	.02

		MT	NR MT	EX
1	Bo Jackson (DK)	.60	.45	.25
2	Steve Sax (DK)	.12	.09	.05
3a	Ruben Sierra (DK - missing line on top border)	1.25	.90	.50
3b	Ruben Sierra (DK)	.30	.25	.12
4	Ken Griffey, Jr. (DK)	2.00	1.50	.80
5	Mickey Tettleton (DK)	.12	.09	.05
6	Dave Stewart (DK)	.12	.09	.05
7	Jim Deshaies (DK)	.07	.05	.03
8	John Smoltz (DK)	.25	.20	.10
9	Mike Bielecki (DK)	.07	.05	.03
10a	Brian Downing DK (Reverse Negative)	1.75	1.25	.70
10b	Brian Downing DK (Corrected)	.25	.20	.10
11	Kevin Mitchell (DK)	.35	.25	.14
12	Kelly Gruber (DK)	.08	.06	.03
13	Joe Magrane (DK)	.08	.06	.03
14	John Franco (DK)	.08	.06	.03
15	Ozzie Guillen (DK)	.08	.06	.03
16	Lou Whitaker (DK)	.08	.06	.03

		MT	NR MT	EX
17	John Smiley (DK)	.08	.06	.03
18	Howard Johnson (DK)	.30	.25	.12
19	Willie Randolph (DK)	.08	.06	.03
20	Chris Bosio (DK)	.07	.05	.03
21	Tommy Herr (DK)	.07	.05	.03
22	Dan Gladden (DK)	.07	.05	.03
23	Ellis Burks (DK)	.20	.15	.08
24	Pete O'Brien (DK)	.08	.06	.03
25	Bryn Smith (DK)	.07	.05	.03
26	Ed Whitson (DK)	.07	.05	.03
27	Checklist 1-27	.04	.03	.02
28	Robin Ventura (RR)(FC)	.50	.40	.20
29	Todd Zeile (RR)(FC)	1.00	.70	.40
30	Sandy Alomar, Jr. (RR)	.30	.25	.12
31	Kent Mercker (RR)(FC)	.30	.25	.12
32	Ben McDonald (RR)(FC)	2.00	1.50	.80
33a	Juan Gonzalez RR (Reverse Negative)(FC)			
		4.00	3.00	1.50
33b	Juan Gonzalez RR (Corrected)(FC)			
		2.00	1.50	.80
34	Eric Anthony (RR)(FC)	.80	.60	.30
35	Mike Fetters (RR)(FC)	.20	.15	.08
36	Marquis Grissom (RR)(FC)	.60	.45	.25
37	Greg Vaughn (RR)(FC)	.60	.45	.25
38	Brian Dubois (RR)(FC)	.25	.20	.10
39	Steve Avery (RR)(FC)	.60	.45	.25
40	Mark Gardner (RR)(FC)	.20	.15	.08
41	Andy Benes (RR)(FC)	.40	.30	.15
42	Delino Deshields (RR)(FC)	1.00	.70	.40
43	Scott Coolbaugh (RR)(FC)	.30	.25	.12
44	Pat Combs (RR)(FC)	.25	.20	.10
45	Alex Sanchez (RR)	.15	.11	.06
46	Kelly Mann (RR)(FC)	.20	.15	.08
47	Julio Machado (RR)(FC)	.20	.15	.08
48	Pete Incaviglia	.05	.04	.02
49	Shawon Dunston	.07	.05	.03
50	Jeff Treadway	.05	.04	.02
51	Jeff Ballard	.10	.08	.04
52	Claudell Washington	.08	.06	.03
53	Juan Samuel	.10	.08	.04
54	John Smiley	.08	.06	.03
55	Rob Deer	.06	.05	.02
56	Geno Petralli	.04	.03	.02
57	Chris Bosio	.10	.08	.04
58	Carlton Fisk	.12	.09	.05
59	Kirt Manwaring	.10	.08	.04
60	Chet Lemon	.06	.05	.02
61	Bo Jackson	.60	.45	.25
62	Doyle Alexander	.05	.04	.02
63	Pedro Guerrero	.12	.09	.05
64	Allan Anderson	.07	.05	.03
65	Greg Harris	.07	.05	.03
66	Mike Greenwell	.25	.20	.10
67	Walt Weiss	.08	.06	.03
68	Wade Boggs	.30	.25	.12
69	Jim Clancy	.04	.03	.02
70	Junior Felix	.40	.30	.15
71	Barry Larkin	.12	.09	.05
72	Dave LaPoint	.05	.04	.02
73	Joel Skinner	.04	.03	.02
74	Jesse Barfield	.08	.06	.03
75	Tommy Herr	.08	.06	.03
76	Ricky Jordan	.20	.15	.08
77	Eddie Murray	.15	.11	.06
78	Steve Sax	.10	.08	.04
79	Tim Belcher	.10	.08	.04
80	Danny Jackson	.06	.05	.02
81	Kent Hrbek	.10	.08	.04
82	Milt Thompson	.05	.04	.02
83	Brook Jacoby	.07	.05	.03
84	Mike Marshall	.08	.06	.03
85	Kevin Seitzer	.12	.09	.05
86	Tony Gwynn	.15	.11	.06
87	Dave Steib	.08	.06	.03
88	Dave Smith	.06	.05	.02
89	Bret Saberhagen	.15	.11	.06
90	Alan Trammell	.10	.08	.04
91	Tony Phillips	.05	.04	.03
92	Doug Drabek	.05	.04	.03
93	Jeffrey Leonard	.09	.07	.04
94	Wally Joyner	.15	.11	.06
95	Carney Lansford	.09	.07	.04
96	Cal Ripken	.15	.11	.06
97	Andres Galarraga	.15	.11	.06
98	Kevin Mitchell	.30	.25	.12
99	Howard Johnson	.15	.11	.06
100	Checklist	.04	.03	.02
101	Melido Perez	.07	.05	.03
102	Spike Owen	.05	.04	.02
103	Paul Molitor	.10	.08	.04
104	Geronimo Berroa	.06	.05	.02

		MT	NR MT	EX			MT	NR MT	EX
105	Ryne Sandberg	.15	.11	.06	196	Eric Plunk	.05	.04	.02
106	Bryn Smith	.06	.05	.02	197	Orel Hershiser	.20	.15	.08
107	Steve Buechele	.04	.03	.02	198	Paul O'Neil	.07	.05	.03
108	Jim Abbott	.60	.45	.25	199	Randy Bush	.04	.03	.02
109	Alvin Davis	.10	.08	.04	200	Checklist	.04	.03	.02
110	Lee Smith	.05	.04	.02	201	Ozzie Smith	.10	.08	.04
111	Roberto Alomar	.15	.11	.06	202	Pete O'Brien	.06	.05	.02
112	Rick Reuschel	.09	.07	.04	203	Jay Howell	.06	.05	.02
113	Kelly Gruber	.09	.07	.04	204	Mark Gibicza	.08	.06	.03
114	Joe Carter	.09	.07	.04	205	Ed Whitson	.04	.03	.02
115	Jose Rijo	.06	.05	.02	206	George Bell	.09	.07	.04
116	Greg Minton	.04	.03	.02	207	Mike Scott	.09	.07	.04
117	Bob Ojeda	.04	.03	.02	208	Charlie Leibrandt	.04	.03	.02
118	Glenn Davis	.08	.06	.03	209	Mike Heath	.04	.03	.02
119	Jeff Reardon	.05	.04	.02	210	Dennis Eckersley	.09	.07	.04
120	Kurt Stillwell	.05	.04	.02	211	Mike LaValliere	.04	.03	.02
121	John Smoltz	.15	.11	.06	212	Darnell Coles	.04	.03	.02
122	Dwight Evans	.08	.06	.03	213	Lance Parrish	.07	.05	.03
123	Eric Yelding	.08	.06	.03	214	Mike Moore	.07	.05	.03
124	John Franco	.05	.04	.02	215	*Steve Finley*	.20	.15	.08
125	Jose Canseco	.70	.50	.30	216	Tim Raines	.09	.07	.04
126	Barry Bonds	.15	.11	.06	217	Scott Garrelts	.06	.05	.02
127	Lee Guetterman	.04	.03	.02	218	Kevin McReynolds	.09	.07	.04
128	Jack Clark	.10	.08	.04	219	Dave Gallagher	.08	.06	.03
129	Dave Valle	.04	.03	.02	220	Tim Wallach	.08	.06	.03
130	Hubie Brooks	.05	.04	.02	221	Chuck Crim	.04	.03	.02
131	Ernest Riles	.04	.03	.02	222	Lonnie Smith	.08	.06	.03
132	Mike Morgan	.04	.03	.02	223	Andre Dawson	.10	.08	.04
133	Steve Jeltz	.04	.03	.02	224	Nelson Santovenia	.07	.05	.03
134	Jeff Robinson	.05	.04	.02	225	Rafael Palmeiro	.07	.05	.03
135	Ozzie Guillen	.05	.04	.02	226	Devon White	.07	.05	.03
136	Chili Davis	.06	.05	.02	227	Harold Reynolds	.07	.05	.03
137	Mitch Webster	.04	.03	.02	228	Ellis Burks	.15	.11	.06
138	Jerry Browne	.06	.05	.02	229	Mark Parent	.04	.03	.02
139	Bo Diaz	.04	.03	.02	230	Will Clark	.60	.45	.25
140	Robby Thompson	.07	.05	.03	231	Jimmy Key	.08	.06	.03
141	Craig Worthington	.09	.07	.04	232	John Farrell	.04	.03	.02
142	Julio Franco	.09	.07	.04	233	Eric Davis	.30	.25	.12
143	Brian Holman	.05	.04	.02	234	Johnny Ray	.05	.04	.02
144	George Brett	.10	.08	.04	235	Darryl Strawberry	.30	.25	.12
145	Tom Glavine	.10	.08	.04	236	Bill Doran	.05	.04	.02
146	Robin Yount	.20	.15	.08	237	Greg Gagne	.05	.04	.02
147	Gary Carter	.06	.05	.02	238	Jim Eisenreich	.04	.03	.02
148	Ron Kittle	.06	.05	.02	239	Tommy Gregg	.06	.05	.02
149	Tony Fernandez	.07	.05	.03	240	Marty Barrett	.05	.04	.02
150	Dave Stewart	.07	.05	.03	241	Rafael Ramirez	.05	.04	.02
151	Gary Gaetti	.07	.05	.03	242	Chris Sabo	.07	.05	.03
152	Kevin Elster	.04	.03	.02	243	Dave Henderson	.07	.05	.03
153	Gerald Perry	.05	.04	.02	244	Andy Van Slyke	.07	.05	.03
154	Jesse Orosco	.05	.04	.02	245	Alvaro Espinoza	.10	.07	.04
155	Wally Backman	.05	.04	.02	246	Garry Templeton	.06	.05	.02
156	Dennis Martinez	.05	.04	.02	247	Gene Harris	.04	.03	.02
157	Rick Sutcliffe	.08	.06	.03	248	Kevin Gross	.05	.04	.02
158	Greg Maddux	.12	.09	.05	249	Brett Butler	.09	.07	.04
159	Andy Hawkins	.05	.04	.02	250	Willie Randolph	.07	.05	.03
160	John Kruk	.05	.04	.02	251	Roger McDowell	.05	.04	.02
161	Jose Oquendo	.05	.04	.02	252	Rafael Belliard	.04	.03	.02
162	John Dopson	.08	.06	.03	253	Steve Rosenberg	.04	.03	.02
163	Joe Magrane	.08	.06	.03	254	Jack Howell	.04	.03	.02
164	Billy Ripken	.04	.03	.02	255	Marvell Wynne	.04	.03	.02
165	Fred Manrique	.04	.03	.02	256	Tom Candiotti	.05	.04	.02
166	Nolan Ryan	.25	.20	.10	257	Todd Benzinger	.05	.04	.02
167	Damon Berryhill	.06	.05	.02	258	Don Robinson	.04	.03	.02
168	Dale Murphy	.09	.07	.04	259	Phil Bradley	.08	.06	.03
169	Mickey Tettleton	.08	.06	.03	260	Cecil Espy	.05	.04	.02
170	Kirk McCaskill	.05	.04	.02	261	Scott Bankhead	.05	.04	.02
171	Dwight Gooden	.15	.11	.06	262	Frank White	.07	.05	.03
172	Jose Lind	.04	.03	.02	263	Andres Thomas	.05	.04	.02
173	B.J. Surhoff	.07	.05	.03	264	Glenn Braggs	.05	.04	.02
174	Ruben Sierra	.15	.11	.06	265	David Cone	.10	.08	.04
175	Dan Plesac	.08	.06	.03	266	Bobby Thigpen	.07	.05	.03
176	Dan Pasqua	.05	.04	.02	267	Nelson Liriano	.04	.03	.02
177	Kelly Downs	.05	.04	.02	268	Terry Steinbach	.09	.07	.04
178	Matt Nokes	.08	.06	.03	269	Kirby Puckett	.30	.25	.12
179	Luis Aquino	.04	.03	.02	270	Gregg Jefferies	.40	.30	.15
180	Frank Tanana	.04	.03	.02	271	Jeff Blauser	.05	.04	.02
181	Tony Pena	.07	.05	.03	272	Cory Snyder	.07	.05	.03
182	Dan Gladden	.05	.04	.02	273	Roy Smith	.05	.04	.02
183	Bruce Hurst	.05	.04	.02	274	Tom Foley	.04	.03	.02
184	Roger Clemens	.20	.15	.08	275	Mitch Williams	.09	.07	.04
185	Mark McGwire	.30	.25	.12	276	Paul Kilgus	.04	.03	.02
186	Rob Murphy	.04	.03	.02	277	Don Slaught	.04	.03	.02
187	Jim Deshaies	.06	.05	.02	278	Von Hayes	.08	.06	.03
188	Fred McGriff	.20	.15	.08	279	Vince Coleman	.10	.08	.04
189	Rob Dibble	.06	.05	.02	280	Mike Boddicker	.05	.04	.02
190	Don Mattingly	.90	.70	.35	281	Ken Dayley	.04	.03	.02
191	Felix Fermin	.04	.03	.02	282	Mike Devereaux	.07	.05	.03
192	Roberto Kelly	.08	.06	.03	283	*Kenny Rogers*	.09	.07	.04
193	Dennis Cook	.08	.06	.03	284	Jeff Russell	.07	.05	.04
194	Darren Daulton	.04	.03	.02	285	*Jerome Walton*	.70	.50	.30
195	Alfredo Griffin	.05	.04	.02	286	*Derek Lilliquist*	.08	.06	.03

		MT	NR MT	EX
287	Joe Orsulak	.04	.03	.02
288	Dick Schofield	.04	.03	.02
289	Ron Darling	.09	.07	.04
290	Bobby Bonilla	.10	.07	.04
291	Jim Gantner	.05	.04	.02
292	Bobby Witt	.05	.04	.02
293	Greg Brock	.05	.04	.02
294	Ivan Calderon	.05	.04	.02
295	Steve Bedrosian	.06	.05	.02
296	Mike Henneman	.06	.05	.02
297	Tom Gordon	.25	.20	.10
298	Lou Whitaker	.08	.06	.03
299	Terry Pendleton	.07	.05	.03
300	Checklist	.04	.03	.02
301	Juan Berenguer	.04	.03	.02
302	Mark Davis	.09	.07	.05
303	Nick Esasky	.09	.07	.05
304	Rickey Henderson	.15	.11	.06
305	Rick Cerone	.04	.03	.02
306	Craig Biggio	.15	.11	.06
307	Duane Ward	.04	.03	.02
308	Tom Browning	.07	.05	.03
309	Walt Terrell	.05	.04	.02
310	Greg Swindell	.10	.08	.04
311	Dave Righetti	.07	.05	.03
312	Mike Maddux	.04	.03	.02
313	Lenny Dykstra	.07	.05	.03
314	Jose Gonzalez	.08	.06	.03
315	Steve Balboni	.04	.03	.02
316	Mike Scioscia	.07	.05	.02
317	Ron Oester	.04	.03	.02
318	*Gary Wayne*	.09	.07	.04
319	Todd Worrell	.06	.05	.02
320	Doug Jones	.05	.04	.02
321	Jeff Hamilton	.05	.04	.02
322	Danny Tartabull	.09	.07	.04
323	Chris James	.05	.04	.02
324	Mike Flanagan	.05	.04	.02
325	Gerald Young	.05	.04	.02
326	Bob Boone	.09	.07	.04
327	Frank Williams	.04	.03	.02
328	Dave Parker	.09	.07	.04
329	Sid Bream	.04	.03	.02
330	Mike Schooler	.06	.05	.02
331	Bert Blyleven	.08	.06	.03
332	Bob Welch	.07	.05	.03
333	Bob Milacki	.06	.05	.02
334	Tim Burke	.05	.04	.02
335	Jose Uribe	.05	.04	.02
336	Randy Myers	.05	.04	.02
337	Eric King	.04	.03	.02
338	Mark Langston	.12	.09	.05
339	Ted Higuera	.08	.06	.03
340	Oddibe McDowell	.06	.05	.02
341	Lloyd McClendon	.07	.05	.03
342	Pascual Perez	.05	.04	.02
343	Kevin Brown	.08	.06	.03
344	Chuck Finley	.05	.04	.02
345	Erik Hanson	.09	.07	.05
346	Rich Gedman	.05	.04	.02
347	Bip Roberts	.10	.08	.04
348	Matt Williams	.20	.15	.08
349	Tom Henke	.05	.04	.02
350	Brad Komminsk	.05	.04	.02
351	Jeff Reed	.04	.03	.02
352	Brian Downing	.05	.04	.02
353	Frank Viola	.09	.07	.04
354	Terry Puhl	.05	.04	.02
355	Brian Harper	.05	.04	.02
356	Steve Farr	.05	.04	.02
357	Joe Boever	.05	.04	.02
358	Danny Heep	.04	.03	.02
359	Larry Andersen	.04	.03	.02
360	Rolando Roomes	.10	.08	.04
361	Mike Gallego	.05	.04	.02
362	Bob Kipper	.04	.03	.02
363	Clay Parker	.07	.05	.03
364	Mike Pagliarulo	.05	.04	.02
365	Ken Griffey, Jr.	2.50	2.00	1.00
366	Rex Hudler	.04	.03	.02
367	Pat Sheridan	.04	.03	.02
368	Kirk Gibson	.09	.07	.04
369	Jeff Parrett	.05	.04	.02
370	Bob Walk	.05	.04	.02
371	Ken Patterson	.04	.03	.02
372	Bryan Harvey	.05	.04	.02
373	Mike Bielecki	.07	.05	.03
374	*Tom Magrann*(FC)	.20	.15	.08
375	Rick Mahler	.05	.04	.02
376	Craig Lefferts	.05	.04	.02
377	Gregg Olson	.20	.15	.08

		MT	NR MT	EX
378	Jamie Moyer	.04	.03	.02
379	Randy Johnson	.09	.07	.04
380	Jeff Montgomery	.06	.05	.02
381	Marty Clary	.06	.05	.02
382	*Bill Spiers*	.15	.11	.06
383	Dave Magadan	.06	.05	.02
384	*Greg Hibbard*(FC)	.20	.15	.08
385	Ernie Whitt	.05	.04	.02
386	Rick Honeycutt	.04	.03	.02
387	Dave West	.08	.06	.03
388	Keith Hernandez	.07	.05	.03
389	Jose Alvarez	.04	.03	.02
390	*Joey Belle*(FC)	.30	.25	.12
391	Rick Aguilera	.05	.04	.02
392	Mike Fitzgerald	.04	.03	.02
393	*Dwight Smith*	.50	.40	.20
394	*Steve Wilson*	.09	.07	.04
395	*Bob Geren*	.20	.15	.08
396	Randy Ready	.04	.03	.02
397	Ken Hill	.07	.05	.03
398	Jody Reed	.05	.04	.02
399	Tom Brunansky	.07	.05	.03
400	Checklist	.04	.03	.02
401	Rene Gonzales	.04	.03	.02
402	Harold Baines	.09	.07	.04
403	Cecilio Guante	.04	.03	.02
404	Joe Girardi	.15	.11	.06
405	*Sergio Valdez*(FC)	.20	.15	.08
406	Mark Williamson	.04	.03	.02
407	Glenn Hoffman	.04	.03	.02
408	*Jeff Innis*(FC)	.10	.08	.04
409	Randy Kramer	.04	.03	.02
410	Charlie O'Brien(FC)	.04	.03	.02
411	Charlie Hough	.06	.05	.02
412	Gus Polidor	.04	.03	.02
413	Ron Karkovice	.04	.03	.02
414	Trevor Wilson(FC)	.07	.05	.03
415	*Kevin Ritz*(FC)	.20	.15	.08
416	Gary Thurman	.04	.03	.02
417	Jeff Robinson	.04	.03	.02
418	Scott Terry	.05	.04	.02
419	Tim Laudner	.04	.03	.02
420	Dennis Rasmussen	.04	.03	.02
421	Luis Rivera	.04	.03	.02
422	Jim Corsi(FC)	.07	.05	.02
423	Dennis Lamp	.04	.03	.02
424	Ken Caminiti	.06	.05	.02
425	David Wells	.06	.05	.02
426	Norm Charlton	.09	.07	.04
427	*Deion Sanders*	.35	.25	.14
428	Dion James	.05	.04	.02
429	Chuck Cary	.05	.04	.02
430	Ken Howell	.04	.03	.02
431	Steve Lake	.04	.03	.02
432	Kal Daniels	.09	.07	.04
433	Lance McCullers	.05	.04	.02
434	Lenny Harris(FC)	.10	.08	.04
435	*Scott Scudder*(FC)	.20	.15	.08
436	Gene Larkin	.04	.03	.02
437	Dan Quisenberry	.05	.04	.02
438	*Steve Olin*(FC)	.15	.11	.06
439	Mickey Hatcher	.05	.04	.02
440	Willie Wilson	.05	.04	.02
441	Mark Grant	.05	.04	.02
442	Mookie Wilson	.07	.05	.03
443	Alex Trevino	.04	.03	.02
444	Pat Tabler	.05	.04	.02
445	Dave Bergman	.04	.03	.02
446	Todd Burns	.05	.04	.02
447	R.J. Reynolds	.04	.03	.02
448	Jay Buhner	.08	.06	.03
449	*Lee Stevens*(FC)	.20	.15	.08
450	Ron Hassey	.04	.03	.02
451	Bob Melvin	.04	.03	.02
452	Dave Martinez	.05	.04	.02
453	*Greg Litton*(FC)	.25	.20	.10
454	Mark Carreon	.10	.07	.04
455	Scott Fletcher	.05	.04	.02
456	Otis Nixon	.04	.03	.02
457	*Tony Fossas*(FC)	.10	.08	.04
458	John Russell	.04	.03	.02
459	Paul Assenmacher	.04	.03	.02
460	Zane Smith	.04	.03	.02
461	*Jack Daugherty*	.25	.20	.10
462	*Rich Monteleone*(FC)	.15	.11	.06
463	Greg Briley(FC)	.25	.20	.10
464	Mike Smithson	.04	.03	.02
465	Benito Santiago	.09	.07	.04
466	*Jeff Brantley*	.10	.08	.04
467	Jose Nunez	.07	.05	.03
468	Scott Bailes	.04	.03	.02

		MT	NR MT	EX
469	Ken Griffey	.06	.05	.02
470	Bob McClure	.04	.03	.02
471	Mackey Sasser	.04	.03	.02
472	Glenn Wilson	.04	.03	.02
473	*Kevin Tapani*(FC)	.30	.25	.15
474	Bill Buckner	.05	.04	.02
475	Ron Gant	.05	.04	.02
476	Kevin Romine(FC)	.05	.04	.02
477	Juan Agosto	.04	.03	.02
478	Herm Winningham	.04	.03	.02
479	Storm Davis	.05	.04	.02
480	Jeff King(FC)	.09	.07	.04
481	*Kevin Mmahat*(FC)	.25	.20	.10
482	Carmelo Martinez	.05	.04	.02
483	*Omar Vizquel*	.10	.08	.04
484	Jim Dwyer	.04	.03	.02
485	Bob Knepper	.04	.03	.02
486	Dave Anderson	.04	.03	.02
487	Ron Jones	.09	.07	.04
488	Jay Bell	.05	.04	.02
489	*Sammy Sosa*(FC)	.60	.45	.25
490	Kent Anderson(FC)	.15	.11	.06
491	Domingo Ramos	.04	.03	.02
492	Dave Clark	.05	.04	.02
493	Tim Birtsas	.04	.03	.02
494	Ken Oberkfell	.04	.03	.02
495	Larry Sheets	.04	.03	.02
496	Jeff Kunkel	.04	.03	.02
497	Jim Presley	.04	.03	.02
498	Mike Macfarlane	.04	.03	.02
499	Pete Smith	.05	.04	.02
500	Checklist	.04	.03	.02
501	Gary Sheffield	.40	.30	.15
502	*Terry Bross*(FC)	.20	.15	.08
503	*Jerry Kutzler*(FC)	.20	.15	.08
504	Lloyd Moseby	.05	.04	.02
505	Curt Young	.04	.03	.02
506	Al Newman	.04	.03	.02
507	Keith Miller	.04	.03	.02
508	*Mike Stanton*(FC)	.20	.15	.08
509	Rich Yett	.04	.03	.02
510	*Tim Drummond*(FC)	.20	.15	.08
511	Joe Hesketh	.04	.03	.02
512	*Rick Wrona*	.10	.08	.04
513	Luis Salazar	.04	.03	.02
514	Hal Morris	.06	.05	.02
515	Terry Mullholland	.07	.05	.03
516	John Morris	.05	.04	.02
517	Carlos Quintana	.08	.06	.03
518	Frank DiPino	.04	.03	.02
519	Randy Milligan	.06	.05	.02
520	Chad Kreuter	.07	.05	.03
521	Mike Jeffcoat	.04	.03	.02
522	Mike Harkey	.10	.08	.04
523	Andy Nezelek	.07	.05	.03
524	Dave Schmidt	.04	.03	.02
525	Tony Armas	.04	.03	.02
526	Barry Lyons	.04	.03	.02
527	*Rick Reed*(FC)	.20	.15	.08
528	Jerry Reuss	.06	.05	.02
529	Dean Palmer(FC)	.30	.25	.12
530	*Jeff Peterek*(FC)	.20	.15	.08
531	Carlos Martinez	.20	.15	.08
532	Atlee Hammaker	.05	.04	.02
533	Mike Brumley	.04	.03	.02
534	Terry Leach	.04	.03	.02
535	*Doug Strange*(FC)	.20	.15	.08
536	Jose DeLeon	.05	.04	.02
537	Shane Rawley	.05	.04	.02
538	Joey Cora(FC)	.10	.08	.04
539	Eric Hetzel	.08	.06	.03
540	Gene Nelson	.04	.03	.02
541	Wes Gardner	.04	.03	.02
542	Mark Portugal	.04	.03	.02
543	Al Leiter	.05	.04	.02
544	Jack Armstrong	.04	.03	.02
545	Greg Cadaret	.04	.03	.02
546	Rod Nichols	.04	.03	.02
547	Luis Polonia	.05	.04	.02
548	Charlie Hayes(FC)	.15	.11	.06
549	Dickie Thon	.04	.03	.02
550	Tim Crews	.04	.03	.02
551	Dave Winfield	.20	.15	.08
552	Mike Davis	.04	.03	.02
553	Ron Robinson	.04	.03	.02
554	Carmen Castillo	.04	.03	.02
555	John Costello	.04	.03	.02
556	Bud Black	.04	.03	.02
557	Rick Dempsey	.04	.03	.02
558	Jim Acker	.04	.03	.02
559	Eric Show	.06	.05	.02

		MT	NR MT	EX
560	Pat Borders	.06	.05	.02
561	Danny Darwin	.04	.03	.02
562	*Rick Luecken*(FC)	.20	.15	.08
563	Edwin Nunez	.05	.04	.02
564	Felix Jose	.09	.07	.04
565	John Cangelosi	.04	.03	.02
566	Billy Swift	.04	.03	.02
567	Bill Schroeder	.04	.03	.02
568	Stan Javier	.04	.03	.02
569	Jim Traber	.04	.03	.02
570	Wallace Johnson	.04	.03	.02
571	Donell Nixon	.04	.03	.02
572	Sid Fernandez	.08	.06	.03
573	Lance Johnson	.09	.07	.04
574	Andy McGaffigan	.04	.03	.02
575	Mark Knudson	.04	.03	.02
576	*Tommy Greene*(FC)	.25	.20	.10
577	Mark Grace	.25	.20	.10
578	*Larry Walker*(FC)	.35	.25	.14
579	Mike Stanley	.04	.03	.02
580	Mike Witt	.05	.04	.02
581	Scott Bradley	.04	.03	.02
582	Greg Harris	.07	.05	.03
583	Kevin Hickey	.04	.03	.02
584	Lee Mazzilli	.04	.03	.02
585	Jeff Pico	.04	.03	.02
586	*Joe Oliver*(FC)	.40	.30	.15
587	Willie Fraser	.04	.03	.02
588	Puzzle Card	.04	.03	.02
589	Kevin Bass	.06	.05	.03
590	John Moses	.04	.03	.02
591	Tom Pagnozzi	.04	.03	.02
592	*Tony Castillo*	.10	.08	.04
593	Jerald Clark	.06	.05	.03
594	Dan Schatzeder	.04	.03	.02
595	Luis Quinones	.04	.03	.02
596	Pete Harnisch	.08	.06	.03
597	Gary Redus	.04	.03	.02
598	Mel Hall	.05	.04	.02
599	Rick Schu	.04	.03	.02
600	Checklist	.04	.03	.02
601	Mike Kingery	.04	.03	.02
602	Terry Kennedy	.04	.03	.02
603	Mike Sharperson	.06	.05	.02
604	Don Carman	.04	.03	.02
605	Jim Gott	.05	.04	.03
606	Donn Pall	.05	.04	.03
607	Rance Mulliniks	.04	.03	.02
608	Curt Wilkerson	.04	.03	.02
609	Mike Felder	.04	.03	.02
610	Guillermo Hernandez	.04	.03	.02
611	Candy Maldonado	.05	.04	.02
612	Mark Thurmond	.04	.03	.02
613	Rick Leach	.04	.03	.02
614	Jerry Reed	.04	.03	.02
615	Franklin Stubbs	.05	.04	.02
616	Billy Hatcher	.05	.04	.02
617	Don August	.05	.04	.02
618	Tim Teufel	.04	.03	.02
619	Shawn Hillegas	.04	.03	.02
620	Manny Lee	.04	.03	.02
621	Gary Ward	.05	.04	.02
622	*Mark Guthrie*(FC)	.20	.15	.08
623	Jeff Musselman	.05	.04	.02
624	Mark Lemke	.07	.05	.03
625	Fernando Valenzuela	.07	.05	.03
626	*Paul Sorrento*(FC)	.25	.20	.10
627	Glenallen Hill	.20	.15	.08
628	Les Lancaster	.05	.04	.03
629	Vance Law	.04	.03	.02
630	Randy Velarde(FC)	.10	.08	.04
631	Todd Frohwirth	.04	.03	.02
632	Willie McGee	.06	.05	.02
633	Oil Can Boyd	.06	.05	.02
634	Cris Carpenter	.09	.07	.04
635	Brian Holton	.04	.03	.02
636	Tracy Jones	.05	.04	.02
637	Terry Steinbach (AS)	.09	.07	.04
638	Brady Anderson	.09	.07	.04
639	Jack Morris	.06	.05	.02
640	*Jaime Navarro*(FC)	.20	.15	.08
641	Darrin Jackson	.05	.04	.02
642	*Mike Dyer*(FC)	.20	.15	.08
643	Mike Schmidt	.40	.30	.15
644	Henry Cotto	.04	.03	.02
645	John Cerutti	.05	.04	.02
646	*Francisco Cabrera*(FC)	.40	.30	.15
647	Scott Sanderson	.05	.04	.02
648	Brian Meyer	.05	.04	.02
649	Ray Searage	.05	.04	.02
650a	Bo Jackson AS (Recent Major League Performance on back)	3.00	2.25	1.25

			MT	NR MT	EX
650b	Bo Jackson AS (Corrected)		.50	.40	.20
651	Steve Lyons		.04	.03	.02
652	Mike LaCoss		.04	.03	.02
653	Ted Power		.04	.03	.02
654	Howard Johnson (AS)		.20	.15	.08
655	*Mauro Gozzo*(FC)		.15	.11	.06
656	*Mike Blowers*(FC)		.30	.25	.12
657	Paul Gibson		.05	.04	.02
658	Neal Heaton		.05	.04	.02
659a	5000 K (Nolan Ryan) (King card number 665 back)		10.00	7.50	4.00
659b	5000 K (Nolan Ryan) (Corrected)		1.00	.70	.40
660a	Harold Baines (AS - recent major league performance on back)		5.00	3.75	2.00
660b	Harold Baines (AS - line through star on front-incorrect back)		10.00	7.50	4.00
660c	Harold Baines (AS - Incorrect front and back)		10.00	7.50	4.00
660d	Harold Baines (AS - Corrected)		.10	.08	.04
661	Gary Pettis		.05	.04	.02
662	*Clint Zavaras*(FC)		.20	.15	.08
663	Rick Reuschel		.08	.06	.03
664	Alejandro Pena		.05	.04	.02
665a	King of Kings (Nolan Ryan) (5000 K card number 659 back)		10.00	7.50	4.00
665b	King of Kings (Nolan Ryan) (Corrected)		1.00	.70	.40
666	Ricky Horton		.04	.03	.02
667	Curt Schilling		.06	.05	.02
668	Bill Landrum(FC)		.05	.04	.02
669	Todd Stottlemyre		.05	.04	.02
670	Tim Leary		.05	.04	.02
671	*John Wetteland*(FC)		.25	.20	.10
672	Calvin Schiraldi		.04	.03	.02
673	Ruben Sierra (AS)		.09	.07	.04
674	Pedro Guerrero (AS)		.09	.07	.04
675	Ken Phelps		.04	.03	.02
676	Cal Ripken (AS)		.09	.07	.04
677	Denny Walling		.04	.03	.02
678	Goose Gossage		.04	.03	.02
679	*Gary Mielke*(FC)		.20	.15	.08
680	Bill Bathe		.04	.03	.02
681	Tom Lawless		.04	.03	.02
682	*Xavier Hernandez*(FC)		.20	.15	.08
683	Kirby Puckett (AS)		.09	.07	.04
684	Mariano Duncan		.05	.04	.02
685	Ramon Martinez		.10	.08	.04
686	Tim Jones		.05	.04	.02
687	Tom Filer		.04	.03	.02
688	Steve Lombardozzi		.04	.03	.02
689	*Bernie Williams*(FC)		.50	.40	.20
690	Chip Hale(FC)		.25	.20	.10
691	*Beau Allred*(FC)		.40	.30	.15
692	Ryne Sandberg (AS)		.09	.07	.04
693	*Jeff Huson*(FC)		.25	.20	.10
694	Curt Ford		.04	.03	.02
695	Eric Davis (AS)		.09	.07	.04
696	Scott Lusader		.05	.04	.02
697	Mark McGwire (AS)		.09	.07	.04
698	*Steve Cummings*(FC)		.20	.15	.08
699	*George Canale*(FC)		.20	.15	.08
700	Checklist		.04	.03	.02
701	Julio Franco (AS)		.09	.07	.04
702	*Dave Johnson*(FC)		.10	.08	.04
703	Dave Stewart (AS)		.08	.06	.03
704	*Dave Justice*(FC)		3.75	2.75	1.50
705	Tony Gwynn (AS)		.09	.07	.04
706	Greg Myers		.06	.05	.02
707	Will Clark (AS)		.15	.11	.06
708	Benito Santiago (AS)		.08	.06	.03
709	Larry McWilliams		.04	.03	.02
710	Ozzie Smith (AS)		.08	.06	.03
711	*John Olerud*(FC)		2.75	2.00	1.00
712	Wade Boggs (AS)		.09	.07	.04
713	*Gary Eave*(FC)		.15	.11	.06
714	Bob Tewksbury		.05	.04	.02
715	Kevin Mitchell (AS)		.09	.07	.04
716	A. Bartlett Giamatti		1.25	.90	.50

1990 Donruss A.L. Best

This 144-card set features the top players of the American League. The cards measure 2-1/2" by 3-1/2" and feature the same card front design as the regular Donruss set with the exception of having blue borders instead of red. The card backs feature a yellow frame with complete statistics and biographical

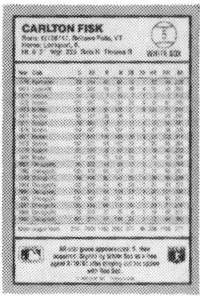

information provided. 1990 marks the first year that Donruss divided its baseball best issue into two sets designated by league.

		MT	NR MT	EX
Complete Set:		13.00	9.75	5.25
Common Player:		.04	.03	.02
1	Ken Griffey,Jr.	1.00	.70	.40
2	Bob Milacki	.04	.03	.02
3	Mike Boddicker	.06	.05	.02
4	Bert Blyleven	.08	.06	.03
5	Carlton Fisk	.10	.08	.04
6	Greg Swindell	.06	.05	.02
7	Alan Trammell	.10	.08	.04
8	Mark Davis	.05	.04	.02
9	Chris Bosio	.04	.03	.02
10	Gary Gaetti	.10	.08	.04
11	Matt Nokes	.06	.05	.02
12	Dennis Eckersley	.10	.08	.04
13	Kevin Brown	.08	.06	.03
14	Tom Henke	.06	.05	.02
15	Mickey Tettleton	.08	.06	.03
16	Jody Reed	.08	.06	.03
17	Mark Langston	.08	.06	.03
18	Melido Perez	.06	.05	.02
19	John Farrell	.04	.03	.02
20	Tony Phillips	.04	.03	.02
21	Bret Saberhagen	.10	.08	.04
22	Robin Yount	.10	.08	.04
23	Kirby Puckett	.15	.11	.06
24	Steve Sax	.10	.08	.04
25	Dave Stewart	.10	.08	.04
26	Alvin Davis	.08	.06	.03
27	Geno Petralli	.04	.03	.02
28	Mookie Wilson	.05	.04	.02
29	Jeff Ballard	.04	.03	.02
30	Ellis Burks	.10	.08	.04
31	Wally Joyner	.08	.06	.03
32	Bobby Thigpen	.10	.08	.04
33	Keith Hernandez	.06	.05	.02
34	Jack Morris	.06	.05	.02
35	George Brett	.10	.08	.04
36	Dan Plesac	.08	.06	.03
37	Brian Harper	.05	.04	.02
38	Don Mattingly	.40	.30	.15
39	Dave Henderson	.08	.06	.03
40	Scott Bankhead	.06	.05	.02
41	Rafael Palmeiro	.10	.08	.04
42	Jimmy Key	.06	.05	.02
43	Gregg Olson	.10	.08	.04
44	Tony Pena	.06	.05	.02
45	Jack Howell	.04	.03	.02
46	Eric King	.04	.03	.02
47	Cory Snyder	.06	.05	.02
48	Frank Tanana	.04	.03	.02
49	Nolan Ryan	.40	.30	.15
50	Bob Boone	.06	.05	.02
51	Dave Parker	.10	.08	.04
52	Allan Anderson	.04	.03	.02
53	Tim Leary	.05	.04	.02
54	Mark McGwire	.40	.30	.15
55	Dave Valle	.04	.03	.02
56	Fred McGriff	.25	.20	.10
57	Cal Ripken	.15	.11	.06
58	Roger Clemens	.30	.25	.12
59	Lance Parrish	.08	.06	.03
60	Robin Ventura	.30	.25	.12
61	Doug Jones	.08	.06	.03
62	Lloyd Moseby	.06	.05	.02
63	Bo Jackson	.80	.60	.30

		MT	NR MT	EX
64	Paul Molitor	.08	.06	.03
65	Kent Hrbek	.08	.06	.03
66	Mel Hall	.04	.03	.02
67	Bob Welch	.10	.08	.04
68	Erik Hanson	.10	.08	.04
69	Harold Baines	.08	.06	.03
70	Junior Felix	.10	.08	.04
71	Craig Worthington	.06	.05	.02
72	Jeff Reardon	.08	.06	.03
73	Johnny Ray	.05	.04	.02
74	Ozzie Guillen	.10	.08	.04
75	Brook Jacoby	.08	.06	.03
76	Chet Lemon	.05	.04	.02
77	Mark Gubicza	.08	.06	.03
78	B.J. Surhoff	.08	.06	.03
79	Rick Aguilera	.05	.04	.02
80	Pascual Perez	.04	.03	.02
81	Jose Canseco	.70	.50	.30
82	Mike Schooler	.08	.06	.03
83	Jeff Huson	.12	.09	.05
84	Kelly Gruber	.15	.11	.06
85	Randy Milligan	.08	.06	.03
86	Wade Boggs	.35	.25	.14
87	Dave Winfield	.20	.15	.08
88	Scott Fletcher	.04	.03	.02
89	Tom Candiotti	.04	.03	.02
90	Mike Heath	.04	.03	.02
91	Kevin Seitzer	.08	.06	.03
92	Ted Higuera	.08	.06	.03
93	Kevin Tapani	.15	.11	.06
94	Roberto Kelly	.08	.06	.03
95	Walt Weiss	.06	.05	.02
96	Checklist	.04	.03	.02
97	Sandy Alomar	.30	.25	.12
98	Pete O'Brien	.05	.04	.02
99	Jeff Russell	.06	.05	.02
100	John Olerud	1.00	.70	.40
101	Pete Harnisch	.05	.04	.02
102	Dwight Evans	.08	.06	.03
103	Chuck Finley	.08	.06	.03
104	Sammy Sosa	.25	.20	.10
105	Mike Henneman	.06	.05	.02
106	Kurt Stillwell	.06	.05	.02
107	Greg Vaughn	.30	.25	.12
108	Dan Gladden	.05	.04	.02
109	Jesse Barfield	.06	.05	.02
110	Willie Randolph	.06	.05	.02
111	Randy Johnson	.08	.06	.03
112	Julio Franco	.08	.06	.03
113	Tony Fernandez	.08	.06	.03
114	Ben McDonald	1.00	.70	.40
115	Mike Greenwell	.20	.15	.08
116	Luis Polonia	.04	.03	.02
117	Carney Lansford	.06	.05	.02
118	Bud Black	.05	.04	.02
119	Lou Whitaker	.08	.06	.03
120	Jim Eisenreich	.04	.03	.02
121	Gary Sheffield	.25	.20	.10
122	Shane Mack	.08	.06	.03
123	Alvaro Espinoza	.04	.03	.02
124	Rickey Henderson	.40	.30	.15
125	Jeffrey Leonard	.05	.04	.02
126	Gary Pettis	.04	.03	.02
127	Dave Steib	.08	.06	.03
128	Danny Tartabull	.08	.06	.03
129	Joe Orsulak	.04	.03	.02
130	Tom Brunansky	.06	.05	.02
131	Dick Schofield	.04	.03	.02
132	Candy Maldonado	.06	.05	.02
133	Cecil Fielder	.30	.25	.12
134	Terry Shumpert	.20	.15	.08
135	Greg Gagne	.05	.04	.02
136	Dave Righetti	.08	.06	.03
137	Terry Steinbach	.06	.05	.02
138	Harold Reynolds	.08	.06	.03
139	George Bell	.08	.06	.03
140	Carlos Quintana	.06	.05	.02
141	Ivan Calderon	.08	.06	.03
142	Greg Brock	.04	.03	.02
143	Ruben Sierra	.15	.11	.06
144	Checklist	.04	.03	.02

A player's name in *italic* type indicates a rookie card. An (FC) indicates a player's first card for that particular card company.

1990 Donruss Diamond Kings Supers

Donruss made this set available through a mail-in offer. Three wrappers, $10 and $2 for postage were necessary to obtain this set. The cards are exactly the same design as the regular Donruss Diamond Kings except they measure approximately 5" by 6-3/4" in size. The artwork of Dick Perez is featured.

		MT	NR MT	EX
Complete Set:		10.00	7.50	4.00
Common Player:		.10	.08	.04
1	Bo Jackson	1.25	.90	.50
2	Steve Sax	.15	.11	.06
3	Ruben Sierra	.35	.25	.12
4	Ken Griffey,Jr.	2.00	1.50	.80
5	Mickey Tettleton	.10	.08	.04
6	Dave Stewart	.25	.20	.10
7	Jim Deshaies	.10	.08	.04
8	John Smoltz	.20	.15	.08
9	Mike Bielecki	.10	.08	.04
10	Brian Downing	.10	.08	.04
11	Kevin Mitchell	.50	.40	.20
12	Kelly Gruber	.25	.20	.10
13	Joe Magrane	.15	.11	.06
14	John Franco	.15	.11	.06
15	Ozzie Guillen	.20	.15	.08
16	Lou Whitaker	.15	.11	.06
17	John Smiley	.10	.08	.04
18	Howard Johnson	.25	.20	.10
19	Willie Randolph	.10	.08	.04
20	Chris Bosio	.10	.08	.04
21	Tommy Herr	.10	.08	.04
22	Dan Gladden	.10	.08	.04
23	Ellis Burks	.40	.30	.15
24	Pete O'Brien	.10	.08	.04
25	Bryn Smith	.10	.08	.04
26	Ed Whitson	.10	.08	.04

1990 Donruss N.L. Best

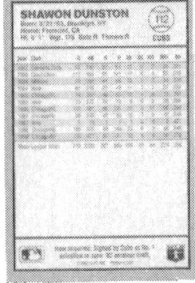

This 144-card set features the top players in the National League for 1990. The cards measure 2-1/2" by 3-1/2" and feature the same design as the regular Donruss cards. The only difference on the card fronts is the border color. The N.L. Best cards contain blue borders, while the regular cards featured red borders. Traded players are featured with their new teams. This set along with the A.L. Best set was available at select retail stores and within the hobby.

		MT	NR MT	EX
Complete Set:		13.00	9.75	5.25
Common Player:		.04	.03	.02
1	Eric Davis	.35	.25	.14
2	Tom Glavine	.06	.05	.02
3	Mike Bielecki	.05	.04	.02
4	Jim Deshaies	.05	.04	.02
5	Mike Scioscia	.05	.04	.02
6	Spike Owen	.05	.04	.02
7	Dwight Gooden	.20	.15	.08
8	Ricky Jordan	.08	.06	.03
9	Doug Drabek	.10	.08	.04
10	Bryn Smith	.04	.03	.02
11	Tony Gwynn	.10	.08	.04
12	John Burkett	.20	.15	.08
13	Nick Esasky	.06	.05	.02
14	Greg Maddux	.08	.06	.03
15	Joe Oliver	.08	.06	.03
16	Mike Scott	.08	.06	.03
17	Tim Belcher	.08	.06	.03
18	Kevin Gross	.06	.05	.02
19	Howard Johnson	.10	.08	.04
20	Darren Daulton	.06	.05	.02
21	John Smiley	.06	.05	.02
22	Ken Dayley	.05	.04	.02
23	Craig Lefferts	.05	.04	.02
24	Will Clark	.60	.45	.25
25	Greg Olson	.12	.09	.05
26	Ryne Sandberg	.50	.40	.20
27	Tom Browning	.06	.05	.02
28	Eric Anthony	.40	.30	.15
29	Juan Samuel	.06	.05	.02
30	Dennis Martinez	.06	.05	.02
31	Kevin Elster	.05	.04	.02
32	Tom Herr	.06	.05	.02
33	Sid Bream	.06	.05	.02
34	Terry Pendleton	.06	.05	.02
35	Roberto Alomar	.20	.15	.08
36	Kevin Bass	.06	.05	.02
37	Jim Presley	.06	.05	.02
38	Les Lancaster	.04	.03	.02
39	Paul O'Neill	.08	.06	.03
40	Dave Smith	.06	.05	.02
41	Kirk Gibson	.10	.08	.04
42	Tim Burke	.06	.05	.02
43	David Cone	.10	.08	.04
44	Ken Howell	.06	.05	.02
45	Barry Bonds	.15	.11	.06
46	Joe Magrane	.08	.06	.03
47	Andy Benes	.08	.06	.03
48	Gary Carter	.10	.08	.04
49	Pat Combs	.08	.06	.03
50	John Smoltz	.10	.08	.04
51	Mark Grace	.10	.08	.04
52	Barry Larkin	.10	.08	.04
53	Danny Darwin	.08	.06	.03
54	Orel Hershiser	.10	.08	.04
55	Tim Wallach	.08	.06	.03
56	Dave Magadan	.10	.08	.04
57	Roger McDowell	.08	.06	.03
58	Bill Landrum	.06	.05	.02
59	Jose DeLeon	.06	.05	.02
60	Bip Roberts	.06	.05	.02
61	Matt Williams	.10	.08	.04
62	Dale Murphy	.08	.06	.03
63	Dwight Smith	.08	.06	.03
64	Chris Sabo	.10	.08	.04
65	Glenn Davis	.10	.08	.04
66	Jay Howell	.06	.05	.02
67	Andres Galarraga	.08	.06	.03
68	Frank Viola	.10	.08	.04
69	John Kruk	.06	.05	.02
70	Bobby Bonilla	.15	.11	.06
71	Todd Zeile	.60	.45	.25
72	Joe Carter	.10	.08	.04
73	Robby Thompson	.06	.05	.02
74	Jeff Blauser	.04	.03	.02
75	Mitch Williams	.08	.06	.03
76	Rob Dibble	.10	.08	.04
77	Rafael Ramirez	.04	.03	.02
78	Eddie Murray	.10	.08	.04
79	Dave Martinez	.05	.04	.02
80	Darryl Strawberry	.50	.40	.20
		MT	**NR MT**	**EX**
81	Dickie Thon	.04	.03	.02
82	Jose Lind	.05	.04	.02
83	Ozzie Smith	.10	.08	.04
84	Bruce Hurst	.06	.05	.02
85	Kevin Mitchell	.20	.15	.08
86	Lonnie Smith	.05	.04	.02
87	Joe Girardi	.08	.06	.03
88	Randy Myers	.10	.08	.04
89	Craig Biggio	.08	.06	.03
90	Fernando Valenzuela	.06	.05	.02
91	Larry Walker	.20	.15	.08
92	John Franco	.10	.08	.04
93	Dennis Cook	.06	.05	.02
94	Bob Walk	.05	.04	.02
95	Pedro Guerrero	.08	.06	.03
96	Checklist	.04	.03	.02
97	Andre Dawson	.10	.08	.04
98	Ed Whitson	.06	.05	.02
99	Steve Bedrosian	.06	.05	.02
100	Oddibe McDowell	.06	.05	.02
101	Todd Benzinger	.06	.05	.02
102	Bill Doran	.08	.06	.03
103	Alfredo Griffin	.04	.03	.02
104	Tim Raines	.10	.08	.04
105	Sid Fernandez	.08	.06	.03
106	Charlie Hayes	.08	.06	.03
107	Mike LaValliere	.05	.04	.02
108	Jose Oquendo	.04	.03	.02
109	Jack Clark	.08	.06	.03
110	Scott Garrelts	.06	.05	.02
111	Ron Gant	.10	.08	.04
112	Shawon Dunston	.10	.08	.04
113	Mariano Duncan	.06	.05	.02
114	Eric Yelding	.10	.08	.04
115	Hubie Brooks	.08	.06	.03
116	Delino DeShields	.50	.40	.20
117	Gregg Jefferies	.20	.15	.08
118	Len Dykstra	.10	.08	.04
119	Andy Van Slyke	.10	.08	.04
120	Lee Smith	.08	.06	.03
121	Benito Santiago	.10	.08	.04
122	Jose Uribe	.04	.03	.02
123	Jeff Treadway	.05	.04	.02
124	Jerome Walton	.10	.08	.04
125	Billy Hatcher	.06	.05	.02
126	Ken Caminiti	.04	.03	.02
127	Kal Daniels	.08	.06	.03
128	Marquis Grissom	.30	.25	.12
129	Kevin McReynolds	.08	.06	.03
130	Wally Backman	.04	.03	.02
131	Willie McGee	.10	.08	.04
132	Terry Kennedy	.04	.03	.02
133	Garry Templeton	.04	.03	.02
134	Lloyd McClendon	.04	.03	.02
135	Daryl Boston	.04	.03	.02
136	Jay Bell	.08	.06	.03
137	Mike Pagliarulo	.06	.05	.02
138	Vince Coleman	.08	.06	.03
139	Brett Butler	.06	.05	.02
140	Von Hayes	.08	.06	.03
141	Ramon Martinez	.20	.15	.08
142	Jack Armstrong	.10	.08	.04
143	Franklin Stubbs	.05	.04	.02
144	Checklist	.04	.03	.02

1990 Donruss Rookies

 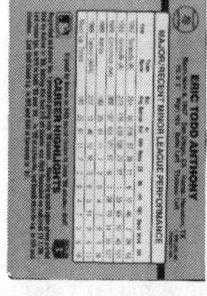

For the fifth straight year, Donruss issued a 56-card "Rookies" set in 1990. As in previous years, the set is similar in design to the regular Donruss set, except for a new "The Rookies" logo and green borders instead of red. The set is packaged in a special box and includes a special Carl Yastrzemski puzzle card.

		MT	NR MT	EX
Complete Set:		12.00	9.00	4.75
Common Player:		.10	.08	.04
1	Sandy Alomar	.25	.20	.10
2	John Olerud	1.25	.90	.50
3	Pat Combs	.20	.15	.08
4	Brian Dubois	.10	.08	.04
5	Felix Jose	.12	.09	.05
6	Delino DeShields	.70	.50	.30
7	Mike Stanton	.10	.08	.04
8	Mike Munoz(FC)	.10	.08	.04
9	Craig Grebeck(FC)	.15	.11	.06
10	Joe Kraemer(FC)	.10	.08	.04
11	Jeff Huson	.10	.08	.04
12	Bill Sampen(FC)	.30	.25	.12
13	Brian Bohanon(FC)	.12	.09	.05
14	Dave Justice	2.25	1.75	.90
15	Robin Ventura	.20	.15	.08
16	Greg Vaughn	.40	.30	.15
17	Wayne Edwards(FC)	.15	.11	.06
18	Shawn Boskie	.25	.20	.10
19	Carlos Baerga(FC)	.50	.40	.20
20	Mark Gardner	.20	.15	.08
21	Kevin Appier(FC)	.30	.25	.12
22	Mike Harkey	.25	.20	.10
23	Tim Layana(FC)	.30	.25	.12
24	Glenallen Hill	.20	.15	.08
25	Jerry Kutzler	.10	.08	.04
26	Mike Blowers	.15	.11	.06
27	Scott Ruskin(FC)	.25	.20	.10
28	Dana Kiecker(FC)	.15	.11	.06
29	Willie Blair(FC)	.10	.08	.04
30	Ben McDonald	1.00	.70	.40
31	Todd Zeile	.60	.45	.25
32	Scott Coolbaugh	.12	.09	.05
33	Xavier Hernandez	.10	.08	.04
34	Mike Hartley(FC)	.15	.11	.06
35	Kevin Tapani	.30	.25	.12
36	Kevin Wickander(FC)	.10	.08	.04
37	Carlos Hernandez(FC)	.15	.11	.06
38	Brian Traxler(FC)	.20	.15	.08
39	Marty Brown(FC)	.10	.08	.04
40	Scott Radinsky(FC)	.25	.20	.10
41	Julio Machado	.15	.11	.06
42	Steve Avery	.35	.25	.14
43	Mark Lemke	.12	.09	.05
44	Alan Mills(FC)	.25	.20	.10
45	Marquis Grissom	.40	.30	.15
46	Greg Olson(FC)	.15	.11	.06
47	Dave Hollins(FC)	.25	.20	.10
48	Jerald Clark	.10	.08	.04
49	Eric Anthony	.50	.40	.20
50	Tim Drummond	.10	.08	.04
51	John Burkett(FC)	.35	.25	.14
52	Brent Knackert(FC)	.12	.09	.05
53	Jeff Shaw(FC)	.12	.09	.05
54	John Orton(FC)	.10	.08	.04
55	Terry Shumpert(FC)	.30	.25	.12
56	Checklist	.10	.08	.04

1991 Donruss Series I

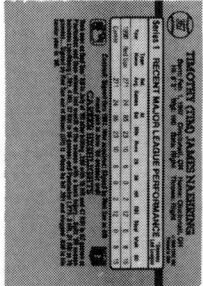

Tim Naehring   SHORTSTOP

Donruss decided to use a two series format in 1991. The first series was released in December and the second in February. The 1991 design is somewhat reminiscent of the 1986 set. Blue borders are used. Limited edition cards including an autographed Ryne Sandberg card (5,000) were randomly inserted in wax packs. Other features of the set include 40 Rated Rookies, a "Legends Series," Elite Series, and another Diamond King subset. Collectors could also take part in Donruss' Instant Win promotion.

		MT	NR MT	EX
Complete Set:		13.00	9.75	5.25
Common Player:		.04	.03	.02
1	Delino DeShields (DK)	.08	.06	.03
2	Barry Larkin (DK)	.06	.05	.02
3	Sandy Alomar (DK)	.12	.09	.05
4	Cecil Fielder (DK)	.15	.11	.06
5	Kurt Stillwell (DK)	.04	.03	.02
6	Roberto Alomar (DK)	.08	.06	.03
7	Gregg Olson (DK)	.05	.04	.02
8	Roger Clemens (DK)	.10	.08	.04
9	Gary Sheffield (DK)	.08	.06	.03
10	Brian Harper (DK)	.04	.03	.02
11	Bob Welch (DK)	.06	.05	.02
12	Ron Gant (DK)	.08	.06	.03
13	Ryne Sandberg (DK)	.15	.11	.06
14	Barry Bonds (DK)	.10	.08	.04
15	Kevin Maas (DK)	.15	.11	.06
16	Ramon Martinez (DK)	.06	.05	.02
17	Chuck Finley (DK)	.04	.03	.02
18	Bobby Thigpen (DK)	.08	.06	.03
19	Edgar Martinez (DK)	.04	.03	.02
20	Rafael Palmeiro (DK)	.05	.04	.02
21	Dave Steib (DK)	.05	.04	.02
22	Len Dykstra (DK)	.06	.05	.02
23	Pedro Guerrero (DK)	.05	.04	.02
24	Craig Biggio (DK)	.05	.04	.02
25	Matt Williams (DK)	.08	.06	.03
26	Dave Magadan (DK)	.08	.06	.03
27	DK Checklist	.04	.03	.02
28	Tino Martinez (RR)(FC)	.25	.20	.10
29	Mark Lewis (RR)(FC)	.20	.15	.08
30	*Bernard Gilkey* (RR)(FC)	.30	.25	.12
31	Hensley Meulens (RR)	.08	.06	.03
32	*Derek Bell* (RR)(FC)	.30	.25	.12
33	Jose Offerman (RR)(FC)	.25	.20	.10
34	Terry Bross (RR)	.10	.08	.04
35	*Leo Gomez* (RR)(FC)	.50	.40	.20
36	Derrick May (RR)(FC)	.25	.20	.10
37	*Kevin Morton* (RR)(FC)	.20	.15	.08
38	Moises Alou (RR)(FC)	.10	.08	.04
39	*Julio Valera* (RR)(FC)	.15	.11	.06
40	Milt Cuyler (RR)(FC)	.10	.08	.04
41	*Phil Plantier* (RR)(FC)	.50	.40	.20
42	Scott Chiamparino (RR)(FC)	.30	.25	.12
43	*Ray Lankford* (RR)(FC)	.40	.30	.15
44	Mickey Morandini (RR)(FC)	.20	.15	.08
45	Dave Hansen (RR)(FC)	.10	.08	.04
46	*Kevin Belcher* (RR)(FC)	.15	.11	.06
47	Darrin Fletcher (RR)(FC)	.10	.08	.04
48	Steve Sax (AS)	.05	.04	.02
49	Ken Griffey, Jr. (AS)	.25	.20	.10
50	Jose Canseco (AS)	.25	.20	.10
51	Sandy Alomar (AS)	.10	.08	.04
52	Cal Ripken (AS)	.05	.04	.02
53	Rickey Henderson (AS)	.15	.11	.06
54	Bob Welch (AS)	.05	.04	.02
55	Wade Boggs (AS)	.10	.08	.04
56	Mark McGwire (AS)	.10	.08	.04
57	Jack McDowell	.06	.05	.02
58	Jose Lind	.05	.04	.02
59	*Alex Fernandez*(FC)	1.00	.70	.40
60	Pat Combs	.08	.06	.03
61	*Mike Walker*(FC)	.15	.11	.06
62	Juan Samuel	.05	.04	.02
63	Mike Blowers	.05	.04	.02
64	Mark Guthrie	.05	.04	.02
65	Mark Salas	.04	.03	.02
66	Tim Jones	.04	.03	.02
67	Tim Leary	.05	.04	.02
68	Andres Galarraga	.08	.06	.03
69	Bob Milacki	.05	.04	.02
70	Tim Belcher	.08	.06	.03
71	Todd Zeile	.20	.15	.08
72	Jerome Walton	.08	.06	.03
73	Kevin Seitzer	.06	.05	.02
74	Jerald Clark	.06	.05	.02
75	John Smoltz	.08	.06	.03
76	Mike Henneman	.05	.04	.02
77	Ken Griffey, Jr.	.60	.45	.25

#	Player	MT	NR MT	EX	#	Player	MT	NR MT	EX
78	Jim Abbott	.06	.05	.02	169	Lee Smith	.08	.06	.03
79	Gregg Jefferies	.15	.11	.06	170	Matt Nokes	.06	.05	.02
80	Kevin Reimer(FC)	.15	.11	.06	171	Jesse Orosco	.05	.04	.02
81	Roger Clemens	.15	.11	.06	172	Rick Aguilera	.06	.05	.02
82	Mike Fitzgerald	.04	.03	.02	173	Jim Presley	.06	.05	.02
83	Bruce Hurst	.06	.05	.02	174	Lou Whitaker	.08	.06	.03
84	Eric Davis	.15	.11	.06	175	Harold Reynolds	.08	.06	.03
85	Paul Molitor	.08	.06	.03	176	Brook Jacoby	.06	.05	.02
86	Will Clark	.25	.20	.10	177	Wally Backman	.05	.04	.02
87	Mike Bielecki	.04	.03	.02	178	Wade Boggs	.20	.15	.08
88	Bret Saberhagen	.10	.08	.04	179	Chuck Cary	.04	.03	.02
89	Nolan Ryan	.25	.20	.10	180	Tom Foley	.04	.03	.02
90	Bobby Thigpen	.08	.06	.03	181	Pete Harnisch	.05	.04	.02
91	Dickie Thon	.04	.03	.02	182	Mike Morgan	.05	.04	.02
92	Duane Ward	.04	.03	.02	183	Bob Tewksbury	.05	.04	.02
93	Luis Polonia	.04	.03	.02	184	Joe Girardi	.06	.05	.02
94	Terry Kennedy	.04	.03	.02	185	Storm Davis	.05	.04	.02
95	Kent Hrbek	.08	.06	.03	186	Ed Whitson	.06	.05	.02
96	Danny Jackson	.06	.05	.02	187	Steve Avery	.20	.15	.08
97	Sid Fernandez	.08	.06	.03	188	Lloyd Moseby	.06	.05	.02
98	Jimmy Key	.06	.05	.02	189	Scott Bankhead	.06	.05	.02
99	Franklin Stubbs	.05	.04	.02	190	Mark Langston	.08	.06	.03
100	Checklist	.04	.03	.02	191	Kevin McReynolds	.06	.05	.02
101	R.J. Reynolds	.04	.03	.02	192	Julio Franco	.08	.06	.03
102	Dave Stewart	.08	.06	.03	193	John Dopson	.05	.04	.02
103	Dan Pasqua	.05	.04	.02	194	Oil Can Boyd	.05	.04	.02
104	Dan Plesac	.06	.05	.02	195	Bip Roberts	.06	.05	.02
105	Mark McGwire	.20	.15	.08	196	Billy Hatcher	.06	.05	.02
106	John Farrell	.04	.03	.02	197	Edgar Diaz(FC)	.08	.06	.02
107	Don Mattingly	.20	.15	.08	198	Greg Litton	.05	.04	.02
108	Carlton Fisk	.10	.08	.04	199	Mark Grace	.10	.08	.04
109	Ken Oberkfell	.04	.03	.02	200	Checklist	.04	.03	.02
110	Darrel Akerfelds	.04	.03	.02	201	George Brett	.10	.08	.04
111	Gregg Olson	.08	.06	.03	202	Jeff Russell	.06	.05	.02
112	Mike Scioscia	.06	.05	.02	203	Ivan Calderon	.08	.06	.03
113	Bryn Smith	.04	.03	.02	204	Ken Howell	.04	.03	.02
114	Bob Geren	.05	.04	.02	205	Tom Henke	.08	.06	.03
115	Tom Candiotti	.04	.03	.02	206	Bryan Harvey	.06	.05	.02
116	Kevin Tapani	.15	.11	.06	207	Steve Bedrosian	.08	.06	.03
117	Jeff Treadway	.05	.04	.02	208	Al Newman	.04	.03	.02
118	Alan Trammell	.08	.06	.03	209	Randy Myers	.08	.06	.03
119	Pete O'Brien	.04	.03	.02	210	Daryl Boston	.04	.03	.02
120	Joel Skinner	.04	.03	.02	211	Manny Lee	.06	.05	.02
121	Mike LaValliere	.05	.04	.02	212	Dave Smith	.06	.05	.02
122	Dwight Evans	.08	.06	.03	213	Don Slaught	.04	.03	.02
123	Jody Reed	.08	.06	.03	214	Walt Weiss	.06	.05	.02
124	Lee Guetterman	.04	.03	.02	215	Donn Pall	.04	.03	.02
125	Tim Burke	.05	.04	.02	216	Jamie Navarro	.06	.05	.02
126	Dave Johnson	.04	.03	.02	217	Willie Randolph	.06	.05	.02
127	Fernando Valenzuela	.08	.06	.03	218	Rudy Seanez(FC)	.08	.06	.03
128	Jose DeLeon	.06	.05	.02	219	Jim Leyritz(FC)	.20	.15	.08
129	Andre Dawson	.10	.08	.04	220	Ron Karkovice	.05	.04	.02
130	Gerald Perry	.05	.04	.02	221	Ken Caminiti	.05	.04	.02
131	Greg Harris	.04	.03	.02	222	Von Hayes	.08	.06	.03
132	Tom Glavine	.08	.06	.03	223	Cal Ripken	.10	.08	.04
133	Lance McCullers	.04	.03	.02	224	Lenny Harris	.06	.05	.02
134	Randy Johnson	.08	.06	.03	225	Milt Thompson	.05	.04	.02
135	Lance Parrish	.08	.06	.03	226	Alvaro Espinoza	.05	.04	.02
136	Mackey Sasser	.08	.06	.03	227	Chris James	.06	.05	.02
137	Geno Petralli	.04	.03	.02	228	Dan Gladden	.06	.05	.02
138	Dennis Lamp	.04	.03	.02	229	Jeff Blauser	.05	.04	.02
139	Dennis Martinez	.06	.05	.02	230	Mike Heath	.04	.03	.02
140	Mike Pagliarulo	.05	.04	.02	231	Omar Vizquel	.05	.04	.02
141	Hal Morris	.10	.08	.04	232	Doug Jones	.08	.06	.03
142	Dave Parker	.10	.08	.04	233	Jeff King	.06	.05	.02
143	Brett Butler	.06	.05	.02	234	Luis Rivera	.04	.03	.02
144	Paul Assenmacher	.04	.03	.02	235	Ellis Burks	.10	.08	.04
145	Mark Gubicza	.06	.05	.02	236	Greg Cadaret	.04	.03	.02
146	Charlie Hough	.05	.04	.02	237	Dave Martinez	.05	.04	.02
147	Sammy Sosa	.15	.11	.06	238	Mark Williamson	.04	.03	.02
148	Randy Ready	.04	.03	.02	239	Stan Javier	.05	.04	.02
149	Kelly Gruber	.08	.06	.03	240	Ozzie Smith	.10	.08	.04
150	Devon White	.06	.05	.02	241	Shawn Boskie	.15	.11	.02
151	Gary Carter	.08	.06	.03	242	Tom Gordon	.10	.08	.04
152	Gene Larkin	.05	.04	.02	243	Tony Gwynn	.10	.08	.04
153	Chris Sabo	.08	.06	.03	244	Tommy Gregg	.04	.03	.02
154	David Cone	.08	.06	.03	245	Jeff Robinson	.05	.04	.02
155	Todd Stottlemyre	.06	.05	.02	246	Keith Comstock	.04	.03	.02
156	Glenn Wilson	.05	.04	.02	247	Jack Howell	.05	.04	.02
157	Bob Walk	.05	.04	.02	248	Keith Miller	.05	.04	.02
158	Mike Gallego	.04	.03	.02	249	Bobby Witt	.08	.06	.03
159	Greg Hibbard	.06	.05	.02	250	Rob Murphy	.04	.03	.02
160	Chris Bosio	.05	.04	.02	251	Spike Owen	.06	.05	.02
161	Mike Moore	.06	.05	.02	252	Garry Templeton	.06	.05	.02
162	Jerry Browne	.06	.05	.02	253	Glenn Braggs	.06	.05	.02
163	Steve Sax	.08	.06	.03	254	Ron Robinson	.06	.05	.02
164	Melido Perez	.06	.05	.02	255	Kevin Mitchell	.20	.15	.08
165	Danny Darwin	.05	.04	.02	256	Les Lancaster	.04	.03	.02
166	Roger McDowell	.06	.05	.02	257	Mel Stottlemyre(FC)	.20	.15	.08
167	Bill Ripken	.04	.03	.02	258	Kenny Rogers	.06	.05	.02
168	Mike Sharperson	.05	.04	.02	259	Lance Johnson	.06	.05	.02

		MT	NR MT	EX
260	John Kruk	.06	.05	.02
261	Fred McGriff	.15	.11	.06
262	Dick Schofield	.04	.03	.02
263	Trevor Wilson	.05	.04	.02
264	Scott Scudder, David West	.05	.04	.02
266	Dwight Gooden	.20	.15	.08
267	*Willie Blair*(FC)	.15	.11	.06
268	Mark Portugal	.04	.03	.02
269	Doug Drabek	.10	.08	.04
270	Dennis Eckersley	.10	.08	.04
271	Eric King	.05	.04	.02
272	Robin Yount	.10	.08	.04
273	Carney Lansford	.08	.06	.02
274	*Carlos Baerga*	.25	.20	.10
275	Dave Righetti	.08	.06	.03
276	Scott Fletcher	.04	.03	.02
277	Eric Yelding	.08	.06	.03
278	Charlie Hayes	.08	.06	.03
279	Jeff Ballard	.05	.04	.02
280	Orel Hershiser	.10	.08	.04
281	Jose Oquendo	.04	.03	.02
282	Mike Witt	.05	.04	.02
283	Mitch Webster	.04	.03	.02
284	Greg Gagne	.05	.04	.02
285	*Greg Olson*	.10	.08	.04
286	Tony Phillips	.05	.04	.02
287	Scott Bradley	.04	.03	.02
288	Cory Snyder	.08	.06	.03
289	Jay Bell	.06	.05	.02
290	Kevin Romine	.04	.03	.02
291	Jeff Robinson	.05	.04	.02
292	Steve Frey(FC)	.06	.05	.02
293	Craig Worthington	.05	.04	.02
294	Tim Crews	.04	.03	.02
295	Joe Magrane	.08	.06	.03
296	Hector Villanueva(FC)	.20	.15	.08
297	*Terry Shumpert*	.10	.08	.04
298	Joe Carter	.10	.08	.04
299	Kent Mercker	.10	.08	.04
300	Checklist	.04	.03	.02
301	Chet Lemon	.05	.04	.02
302	Mike Schooler	.08	.06	.03
303	Dante Bichette	.06	.05	.02
304	Kevin Elster	.05	.04	.02
305	Jeff Huson	.06	.05	.02
306	Greg Harris	.05	.04	.02
307	Marquis Grissom	.10	.08	.04
308	Calvin Schiraldi	.04	.03	.02
309	Mariano Duncan	.06	.05	.02
310	Bill Spiers	.06	.05	.02
311	Scott Garrelts	.06	.05	.02
312	Mitch Williams	.08	.06	.03
313	Mike Macfarlane	.05	.04	.02
314	Kevin Brown	.06	.05	.02
315	Robin Ventura	.10	.08	.04
316	Darren Daulton	.06	.05	.02
317	PUuat Borders	.06	.05	.02
318	Mark Eichhorn	.04	.03	.02
319	Jeff Brantley	.08	.06	.03
320	Shane Mack	.05	.04	.02
321	Rob Dibble	.10	.08	.04
322	John Franco	.10	.08	.04
323	Junior Felix	.08	.06	.03
324	Casey Candaele	.04	.03	.02
325	Bobby Bonilla	.10	.08	.04
326	Dave Henderson	.06	.05	.02
327	Wayne Edwards	.06	.05	.02
328	Mark Knudson	.04	.03	.02
329	Terry Steinbach	.06	.05	.02
330	*Colby Ward*(FC)	.20	.15	.08
331	*Oscar Azocar*(FC)	.20	.15	.08
332	*Scott Radinsky*	.15	.11	.06
333	Eric Anthony	.10	.08	.04
334	Steve Lake	.04	.03	.02
335	Bob Melvin	.04	.03	.02
336	Kal Daniels	.08	.06	.03
337	Tom Pagnozzi	.05	.04	.02
338	*Alan Mills*	.15	.11	.06
339	Steve Olin	.06	.05	.02
340	Juan Berenguer	.04	.03	.02
341	Francisco Cabrera	.06	.05	.02
342	Dave Bergman	.04	.03	.02
343	Henry Cotto	.04	.03	.02
344	Sergio Valdez	.08	.06	.03
345	Bob Patterson	.04	.03	.02
346	John Marzano	.05	.04	.02
347	*Dana Kiecker*	.08	.06	.03
348	Dion James	.04	.03	.02
349	Hubie Brooks	.08	.06	.03
350	Bill Landrum	.05	.04	.02
351	*Bill Sampen*	.15	.11	.06

		MT	NR MT	EX
352	Greg Briley	.05	.04	.02
353	Paul Gibson	.04	.03	.02
354	Dave Eiland	.04	.03	.02
355	Steve Finley	.06	.05	.02
356	Bob Boone	.06	.05	.02
357	Steve Buechele	.06	.05	.02
358	*Chris Hoiles*(FC)	.20	.15	.08
359	Larry Walker	.10	.08	.04
360	Frank DiPino	.04	.03	.02
361	Mark Grant	.04	.03	.02
362	Dave Magadan	.08	.06	.03
363	Robby Thompson	.06	.05	.02
364	Lonnie Smith	.05	.04	.02
365	Steve Farr	.05	.04	.02
366	Dave Valle	.05	.04	.02
367	*Tim Naehring*(FC)	.30	.25	.12
368	Jim Acker	.04	.03	.02
369	Jeff Reardon	.08	.06	.04
370	Tim Teufel	.04	.03	.02
371	Juan Gonzales	.25	.20	.10
372	Luis Salazar	.04	.03	.02
373	Rick Honeycutt	.04	.03	.02
374	Greg Maddux	.08	.06	.03
375	Jose Uribe	.05	.04	.02
376	Donnie Hill	.04	.03	.02
377	Don Carman	.04	.03	.02
378	*Craig Grebeck*	.06	.05	.02
379	Willie Fraser	.05	.04	.02
380	Glenallen Hill	.08	.06	.03
381	Joe Oliver	.06	.05	.02
382	Randy Bush	.04	.03	.02
383	Alex Cole(FC)	.30	.25	.12
384	Norm Charlton	.08	.06	.03
385	Gene Nelson	.04	.03	.02
386	Checklist	.04	.03	.02

1986 Dorman's Cheese

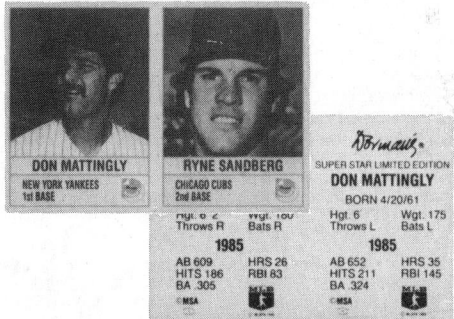

Found in specially-marked packages of Dorman's American Cheese Singles, the Dorman's set consists of ten two-card panels of baseball superstars. Labeled as a "Super Star Limited Edition" set, the panels measure 1-1/2" by 2" each and have a perforation line in the center. The fronts contain a color photo along with the Dorman's logo and the player's name, team and position. Due to a lack of proper licensing, all team insignias have been airbrushed from the players' caps. The backs of the cards contain brief player statistics.

		MT	NR MT	EX
Complete Panel Set:		30.00	22.00	12.00
Complete Singles Set:		15.00	11.00	6.00
Common Panel:		1.25	.90	.50
Common Single Player:		.15	.11	.06
( )	Panel	2.00	1.50	.80
(1)	George Brett	.50	.40	.20
(2)	Jack Morris	.15	.11	.06
( )	Panel	2.00	1.50	.80
(3)	Gary Carter	.30	.25	.12
(4)	Cal Ripken	.40	.30	.15
( )	Panel	2.00	1.50	.80
(5)	Dwight Gooden	.60	.45	.25
(6)	Kent Hrbek	.20	.15	.08
( )	Panel	3.00	1.50	.90
(7)	Rickey Henderson	.60	.45	.25

		MT	NR MT	EX
(8)	Mike Schmidt	.80	.60	.30
()	Panel	2.00	1.50	.80
(9)	Keith Hernandez	.30	.25	.12
(10)	Dale Murphy	.30	.25	.12
()	Panel	2.00	1.50	.80
(11)	Reggie Jackson	.40	.30	.15
(12)	Eddie Murray	.40	.30	.15
()	Panel	4.00	3.00	1.50
(13)	Don Mattingly	1.00	.70	.40
(14)	Ryne Sandberg	.60	.45	.25
()	Panel	1.25	.90	.50
(15)	Willie McGee	.15	.11	.06
(16)	Robin Yount	.30	.25	.12
()	Panel	2.25	1.75	.90
(17)	Rick Sutcliff (Sutcliffe)	.15	.11	.06
(18)	Wade Boggs	.80	.60	.30
()	Panel	1.50	1.25	.60
(19)	Dave Winfield	.40	.30	.15
(20)	Jim Rice	.20	.15	.10

1950 Drake's

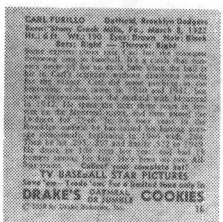

Entitled "TV Baseball Series", the 1950 Drake's Bakeries set pictures 36 different players on a television screen format. The cards, which measure 2-1/2" by 2-1/2", contain black and white photos surrounded by a black border. The card backs carry a player biography plus an advertisement advising collectors to look for the cards in packages of Oatmeal or Jumble cookies. The ACC designation for the set is D358.

		NR MT	EX	VG
Complete Set:		5000.00	3000.00	1500.
Common Player:		50.00	25.00	15.00
1	Elwin "Preacher" Roe	100.00	50.00	30.00
2	Clint Hartung	50.00	25.00	15.00
3	Earl Torgeson	50.00	25.00	15.00
4	Leland "Lou" Brissie	50.00	25.00	15.00
5	Edwin "Duke" Snider	350.00	175.00	100.00
6	Roy Campanella	400.00	200.00	125.00
7	Sheldon "Available" Jones	50.00	25.00	15.00
8	Carroll "Whitey" Lockman	50.00	25.00	15.00
9	Bobby Thomson	80.00	40.00	25.00
10	Dick Sisler	50.00	25.00	15.00
11	Gil Hodges	200.00	100.00	60.00
12	Eddie Waitkus	50.00	25.00	15.00
13	Bobby Doerr	150.00	75.00	45.00
14	Warren Spahn	225.00	125.00	70.00
15	John "Buddy" Kerr	50.00	25.00	15.00
16	Sid Gordon	50.00	25.00	15.00
17	Willard Marshall	50.00	25.00	15.00
18	Carl Furillo	90.00	45.00	25.00
19	Harold "Pee Wee" Reese	300.00	150.00	90.00
20	Alvin Dark	70.00	35.00	20.00
21	Del Ennis	50.00	25.00	15.00
22	Ed Stanky	70.00	35.00	20.00
23	Tommy "Old Reliable" Henrich	90.00	45.00	25.00
24	Larry "Yogi" Berra	400.00	200.00	125.00
25	Phil "Scooter" Rizzuto	275.00	150.00	100.00
26	Jerry Coleman	70.00	35.00	20.00
27	Joe Page	70.00	35.00	20.00
28	Allie Reynolds	90.00	45.00	25.00
29	Ray Scarborough	50.00	25.00	15.00
30	George "Birdie" Tebbetts	50.00	25.00	15.00
31	Maurice "Lefty" McDermott	50.00	25.00	15.00
32	Johnny Pesky	70.00	35.00	20.00

		NR MT	EX	VG
33	Dom "Little Professor" DiMaggio	80.00	40.00	25.00
34	Vern "Junior" Stephens	50.00	25.00	15.00
35	Bob Elliott	50.00	25.00	15.00
36	Enos "Country" Slaughter	225.00	112.00	70.00

1981 Drake's

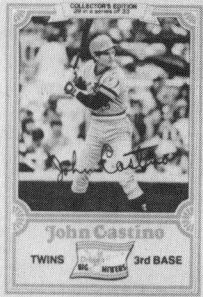
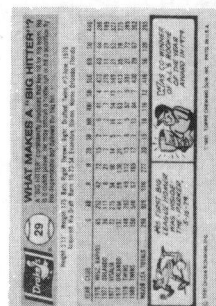

Producing their first baseball card set since 1950, Drake Bakeries, in conjunction with Topps, issued a 33-card set entitled "Big Hitters." The cards, which are the standard 2-1/2" by 3-1/2" in size, feature 19 American League and 14 National League sluggers. Full-color photos, containing a facsimile autograph, are positioned in red frames for A.L. players and blue frames for N.L. hitters. The player's name, team, position, and the Drake's logo are also included on the card fronts. The card backs, which are similar to the regular 1981 Topps issue, contain the card number (1-33), statistical and biographical information, and the Drake's logo.

		MT	NR MT	EX
Complete Set:		7.00	5.25	2.75
Common Player:		.12	.09	.05
1	Carl Yastrzemski	.70	.50	.30
2	Rod Carew	.50	.40	.20
3	Pete Rose	1.00	.70	.40
4	Dave Parker	.25	.20	.10
5	George Brett	.70	.50	.30
6	Eddie Murray	.50	.40	.20
7	Mike Schmidt	1.00	.70	.40
8	Jim Rice	.45	.35	.20
9	Fred Lynn	.25	.20	.10
10	Reggie Jackson	.60	.45	.25
11	Steve Garvey	.45	.35	.20
12	Ken Singleton	.12	.09	.05
13	Bill Buckner	.12	.09	.05
14	Dave Winfield	.50	.40	.20
15	Jack Clark	.30	.25	.12
16	Cecil Cooper	.20	.15	.08
17	Bob Horner	.20	.15	.08
18	George Foster	.20	.15	.08
19	Dave Kingman	.20	.15	.08
20	Cesar Cedeno	.12	.09	.05
21	Joe Charboneau	.12	.09	.05
22	George Hendrick	.12	.09	.05
23	Gary Carter	.45	.35	.20
24	Al Oliver	.20	.15	.08
25	Bruce Bochte	.12	.09	.05
26	Jerry Mumphrey	.12	.09	.05
27	Steve Kemp	.12	.09	.05
28	Bob Watson	.12	.09	.05
29	John Castino	.12	.09	.05
30	Tony Armas	.12	.09	.05
31	John Mayberry	.12	.09	.05
32	Carlton Fisk	.30	.25	.12
33	Lee Mazzilli	.12	.09	.05

A player's name in *italic* type indicates a rookie card. An (FC) indicates a player's first card for that particular card company.

1982 Drake's

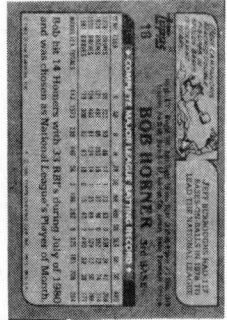

Drake Bakeries produced, in conjunction with Topps, a "2nd Annual Collectors' Edition" in 1982. Thirty-three standard-size cards (2-1/2" by 3-1/2") make up the set. Like the previous year, the set is entitled "Big Hitters" and is comprised of 19 American League players and 14 from the National League. The card fronts have a mounted photo appearance and contain a facsimile autograph. The player's name, team, position, and the Drake's logo also are located on the fronts. The card backs, other than being numbered 1-33 and containing a Drake's copyright line, are identical to the regular 1982 Topps issue.

		MT	NR MT	EX
Complete Set:		9.00	6.75	3.50
Common Player:		.12	.09	.05
1	Tony Armas	.12	.09	.05
2	Buddy Bell	.20	.15	.08
3	Johnny Bench	.50	.40	.20
4	George Brett	.70	.50	.30
5	Bill Buckner	.12	.09	.05
6	Rod Carew	.50	.40	.20
7	Gary Carter	.45	.35	.20
8	Jack Clark	.30	.25	.12
9	Cecil Cooper	.20	.15	.08
10	Jose Cruz	.12	.09	.05
11	Dwight Evans	.20	.15	.08
12	Carlton Fisk	.30	.25	.12
13	George Foster	.20	.15	.08
14	Steve Garvey	.45	.35	.20
15	Kirk Gibson	.40	.30	.15
16	Mike Hargrove	.12	.09	.05
17	George Hendrick	.12	.09	.05
18	Bob Horner	.20	.15	.08
19	Reggie Jackson	.60	.45	.25
20	Terry Kennedy	.12	.09	.05
21	Dave Kingman	.20	.15	.08
22	Greg Luzinski	.20	.15	.08
23	Bill Madlock	.20	.15	.08
24	John Mayberry	.12	.09	.05
25	Eddie Murray	.50	.40	.20
26	Graig Nettles	.20	.15	.08
27	Jim Rice	.45	.35	.20
28	Pete Rose	1.00	.70	.40
29	Mike Schmidt	1.00	.70	.40
30	Ken Singleton	.12	.09	.05
31	Dave Winfield	.50	.40	.20
32	Butch Wynegar	.12	.09	.05
33	Richie Zisk	.12	.09	.05

1983 Drake's

Seventeen American League and 16 National League "Big Hitters" make up the 33-card "3rd Annual Collectors' Edition" set issued by Drake Bakeries in 1983. The Topps-produced set contains 33 cards which measure 2-1/2" by 3-1/2" in size. The card fronts are somewhat similar in design to the previous year's set. The backs are identical to the 1983 Topps regular issue except for being numbered 1-33 and containing a Drake's logo and copyright line.

		MT	NR MT	EX
Complete Set:		7.00	5.25	2.75
Common Player:		.12	.09	.05
1	Don Baylor	.20	.15	.08
2	Bill Buckner	.12	.09	.05
3	Rod Carew	.50	.40	.20
4	Gary Carter	.45	.35	.20
5	Jack Clark	.25	.20	.10
6	Cecil Cooper	.20	.15	.08
7	Dwight Evans	.20	.15	.08
8	George Foster	.20	.15	.08
9	Pedro Guerrero	.25	.20	.10
10	George Hendrick	.12	.09	.05
11	Bob Horner	.20	.15	.08
12	Reggie Jackson	.60	.45	.25
13	Steve Kemp	.12	.09	.05
14	Dave Kingman	.20	.15	.08
15	Bill Madlock	.20	.15	.08
16	Gary Matthews	.12	.09	.05
17	Hal McRae	.12	.09	.05
18	Dale Murphy	.70	.50	.30
19	Eddie Murray	.50	.40	.20
20	Ben Oglivie	.12	.09	.05
21	Al Oliver	.20	.15	.08
22	Jim Rice	.45	.35	.20
23	Cal Ripken	.60	.45	.25
24	Pete Rose	1.00	.70	.40
25	Mike Schmidt	1.00	.70	.40
26	Ken Singleton	.12	.09	.05
27	Gorman Thomas	.12	.09	.05
28	Jason Thompson	.12	.09	.05
29	Mookie Wilson	.10	.08	.04
30	Willie Wilson	.20	.15	.08
31	Dave Winfield	.50	.40	.20
32	Carl Yastrzemski	.70	.50	.30
33	Robin Yount	.40	.30	.15

1984 Drake's

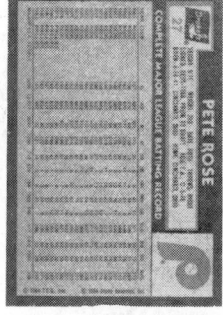

For the fourth year in a row, Drake Bakeries issued a 33-card "Big Hitters" set. The 1984 edition, produced again by Topps, includes 17 National League players and 16 from the American League. As in all previous years, the card fronts feature the player in a batting pose. The backs are identical to the 1984 Topps regular issue except for being numbered 1-33 and carrying the Drake's logo and copyright line. The cards are the standard size 2-1/2" by 3-1/2".

		MT	NR MT	EX
	Complete Set:	8.00	6.00	3.25
	Complete Set:	.12	.09	.05
1	Don Baylor	.20	.15	.08
2	Wade Boggs	1.25	.90	.50
3	George Brett	.70	.50	.30
4	Bill Buckner	.12	.09	.05
5	Rod Carew	.50	.40	.20
6	Gary Carter	.45	.35	.20
7	Ron Cey	.12	.09	.05
8	Cecil Cooper	.20	.15	.08
9	Andre Dawson	.35	.25	.14
10	Steve Garvey	.45	.35	.20
11	Pedro Guerrero	.25	.20	.10
12	George Hendrick	.12	.09	.05
13	Keith Hernandez	.40	.30	.15
14	Bob Horner	.20	.15	.08
15	Reggie Jackson	.60	.45	.25
16	Steve Kemp	.12	.09	.05
17	Ron Kittle	.20	.15	.08
18	Greg Luzinski	.20	.15	.08
19	Fred Lynn	.20	.15	.08
20	Bill Madlock	.20	.15	.08
21	Gary Matthews	.12	.09	.05
22	Dale Murphy	.70	.50	.30
23	Eddie Murray	.50	.40	.20
24	Al Oliver	.20	.15	.08
25	Jim Rice	.45	.35	.20
26	Cal Ripken	.60	.45	.25
27	Pete Rose	1.00	.70	.40
28	Mike Schmidt	1.00	.70	.40
29	Darryl Strawberry	1.25	.90	.50
30	Alan Trammell	.30	.25	.12
31	Mookie Wilson	.12	.09	.05
32	Dave Winfield	.50	.40	.20
33	Robin Yount	.40	.30	.15

		MT	NR MT	EX
11	Steve Garvey	.45	.35	.20
12	Kirk Gibson	.35	.25	.14
13	Pedro Guerrero	.25	.20	.10
14	Tony Gwynn	.60	.45	.25
15	Keith Hernandez	.40	.30	.15
16	Kent Hrbek	.35	.25	.14
17	Reggie Jackson	.60	.45	.25
18	Gary Matthews	.12	.09	.05
19	Don Mattingly	2.25	1.75	.90
20	Dale Murphy	.70	.50	.30
21	Eddie Murray	.45	.35	.20
22	Dave Parker	.20	.15	.08
23	Lance Parrish	.25	.20	.10
24	Tim Raines	.45	.35	.20
25	Jim Rice	.45	.35	.20
26	Cal Ripken	.60	.45	.25
27	Juan Samuel	.25	.20	.10
28	Ryne Sandberg	.40	.30	.15
29	Mike Schmidt	1.00	.70	.40
30	Darryl Strawberry	.90	.70	.35
31	Alan Trammell	.30	.25	.12
32	Dave Winfield	.50	.40	.20
33	Robin Yount	.40	.30	.15
34	Mike Boddicker	.12	.09	.05
35	Steve Carlton	.40	.30	.15
36	Dwight Gooden	1.50	1.25	.60
37	Willie Hernandez	.12	.09	.05
38	Mark Langston	.20	.15	.08
39	Dan Quisenberry	.12	.09	.05
40	Dave Righetti	.20	.15	.08
41	Tom Seaver	.40	.30	.15
42	Bob Stanley	.12	.09	.05
43	Rick Sutcliffe	.20	.15	.08
44	Bruce Sutter	.20	.15	.08

1986 Drake's

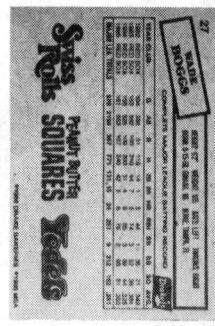

For the sixth year in a row, Drake Bakeries issued a baseball card set. Produced for Drake's by Topps in the past, the 1986 set was not and was available only by buying the actual products the cards were printed on. The cards, which measure 2-1/2" by 3-1/2", were issued in either two-, three-, or four-card panels. Fourteen panels, consisting of 37 different players, comprise the set. The players who make up the set are tabbed as either "Big Hitters" or "Super Pitchers." Logos of various Drake's products can be found on the panel backs. The value of the set is higher when collected in either panel or complete box form.

		MT	NR MT	EX
	Complete Panel Set:	40.00	30.00	16.00
	Complete Singles Set:	25.00	18.50	10.00
	Common Panel:	1.75	1.25	.70
	Common Single Player:	.20	.15	.08
	Panel	1.75	1.25	.70
1	Gary Carter	.50	.40	.20
2	Dwight Evans	.25	.20	.10
	Panel	2.00	1.50	.80
3	Reggie Jackson	.60	.45	.25
4	Dave Parker	.25	.20	.10
	Panel	2.00	1.50	.80
5	Rickey Henderson	1.00	.70	.40
6	Pedro Guerrero	.30	.25	.12
	Panel	5.00	3.75	2.00

1985 Drake's

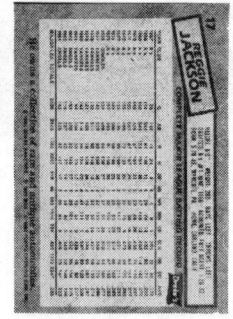

The "5th Annual Collectors' Edition" set produced by Topps for Drake Bakeries consists of 33 "Big Hitters" and 11 "Super Pitchers." The new "Super Pitchers" feature increased the set's size from the usual 33 cards to 44. The cards, which measure 2-1/2" by 3-1/2", show the player in either a batting or pitching pose. The backs differ only from the regular 1985 Topps issue in that they are numbered 1-44 and carry the Drake's logo.

		MT	NR MT	EX
	Complete Set:	13.00	9.75	5.25
	Commmon Player:	.12	.09	.05
1	Tony Armas	.12	.09	.05
2	Harold Baines	.20	.15	.08
3	Don Baylor	.20	.15	.08
4	George Brett	.70	.50	.30
5	Gary Carter	.45	.35	.20
6	Ron Cey	.12	.09	.05
7	Jose Cruz	.12	.09	.05
8	Alvin Davis	.25	.20	.10
9	Chili Davis	.12	.09	.05
10	Dwight Evans	.20	.15	.08

		MT	NR MT	EX
7	Don Mattingly	2.00	1.50	.80
8	Mike Marshall	.25	.20	.10
9	Keith Moreland	.20	.15	.08
	Panel	2.00	1.50	.80
10	Keith Hernandez	.40	.30	.15
11	Cal Ripken	.60	.45	.25
	Panel	2.25	1.75	.90
12	Dale Murphy	.60	.45	.25
13	Jim Rice	.40	.30	.15
	Panel	2.25	1.75	.90
14	George Brett	.60	.45	.25
15	Tim Raines	.50	.40	.20
	Panel	2.00	1.50	.80
16	Darryl Strawberry	.80	.60	.30
17	Bill Buckner	.20	.15	.08
	Panel	2.75	2.00	1.00
18	Dave Winfield	.50	.40	.20
19	Ryne Sandberg	.40	.30	.15
20	Steve Balboni	.20	.15	.08
21	Tom Herr	.25	.20	.10
	Panel	3.75	2.75	1.50
22	Pete Rose	.90	.70	.35
23	Willie McGee	.25	.20	.10
24	Harold Baines	.25	.20	.10
25	Eddie Murray	.50	.40	.20
	Panel	4.00	3.00	1.50
26	Mike Schmidt	1.00	.70	.40
27	Wade Boggs	1.25	.90	.50
28	Kirk Gibson	.35	.25	.14
	Panel	2.00	1.50	.80
29	Bret Saberhagen	.35	.25	.14
30	John Tudor	.20	.15	.08
31	Orel Hershiser	.40	.30	.15
	Panel	2.00	1.50	.80
32	Ron Guidry	.25	.20	.10
33	Nolan Ryan	1.00	.70	.40
34	Dave Stieb	.25	.20	.10
	Panel	2.75	2.00	1.00
35	Dwight Gooden	.80	.60	.30
36	Fernando Valenzuela	.35	.25	.14
37	Tom Browning	.25	.20	.10

		MT	NR MT	EX
4	Jose Canseco	1.75	1.25	.70
	Panel	2.00	1.50	.80
5	Dave Winfield	.50	.40	.20
6	Cal Ripken	.60	.45	.25
	Panel	4.50	3.50	1.75
7	Keith Moreland	.20	.15	.08
8	Don Mattingly	2.00	1.50	.80
9	Willie McGee	.25	.20	.10
	Panel	2.00	1.50	.80
10	Keith Hernandez	.40	.30	.15
11	Tony Gwynn	.60	.45	.25
	Panel	4.25	3.25	1.75
12	Rickey Henderson	1.00	.70	.40
13	Dale Murphy	.60	.45	.25
14	George Brett	.60	.45	.25
15	Jim Rice	.40	.30	.15
	Panel	4.00	3.00	1.50
16	Wade Boggs	1.25	.90	.50
17	Kevin Bass	.20	.15	.08
18	Dave Parker	.25	.20	.10
19	Kirby Puckett	.50	.40	.20
	Panel	2.00	1.50	.80
20	Gary Carter	.50	.40	.20
21	Ryne Sandberg	.40	.30	.15
22	Harold Baines	.25	.20	.10
	Panel	2.75	2.00	1.00
23	Mike Schmidt	1.00	.70	.40
24	Eddie Murray	.50	.40	.20
25	Steve Sax	.25	.20	.10
	Panel	1.75	1.25	.70
26	Dwight Gooden	.80	.60	.30
27	Jack Morris	.25	.20	.10
	Panel	1.75	1.25	.70
28	Ron Darling	.25	.20	.10
29	Fernando Valenzuela	.35	.25	.14
30	John Tudor	.20	.15	.08
	Panel	2.50	2.00	1.00
31	Roger Clemens	.80	.60	.30
32	Nolan Ryan	1.00	.70	.40
33	Mike Scott	.25	.20	.10

1987 Drake's

 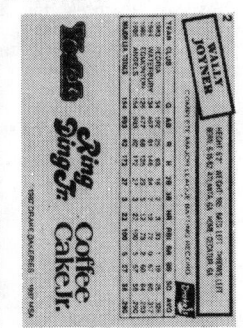

For the seventh consecutive season, Drake Bakeries produced a baseball card set. The cards, which measure 2-1/2" by 3-1/2", were included in either two-, three-, or four-card panels on boxes of various Drake's products distributed in the eastern United States. The set is comprised of 33 cards, with 25 players branded as "Big Hitters" and 8 as "Super Pitchers". The card fronts carry a full-color photo and the Drake's logo surrounded by a brown and yellow border. The backs contain the player's complete major league record.

		MT	NR MT	EX
	Complete Panel Set:	40.00	30.00	16.00
	Complete Singles Set:	25.00	18.50	10.00
	Common Panel:	1.75	1.25	.70
	Common Single Player:	.20	.15	.08
	Panel	4.00	3.00	1.50
1	Darryl Strawberry	.80	.60	.30
2	Wally Joyner	1.25	.90	.50
	Panel	3.75	2.75	1.50
3	Von Hayes	.25	.20	.10

1988 Drake's

 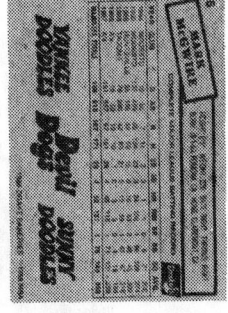

The 8th annual edition of this set includes 33 glossy full-color cards printed on cut-out panels of 2, 3 or 4 cards on Drake's dessert snack boxes. Card fronts have white borders with a large red and blue "Super Pitchers" (6 cards) or "Big Hitters" (27 cards) caption upper left, beside the "8th Annual Collector's Edition label. The Drake logo, player name and team logo are printed in black and include the card number, personal data, batting/pitching record and sponsor logos. Sets were available exclusively on 12 different Drake's packages. To complete the set, collectors had to purchase all 12 products.

		MT	NR MT	EX
	Complete Panel Set:	40.00	30.00	16.00
	Complete Singles Set:	25.00	18.50	10.00
	Common Panel:	1.75	1.25	.70
	Common Single Player:	.20	.15	.08
	Panel	4.25	3.25	1.75
1	Don Mattingly	2.00	1.50	.80
2	Tim Raines	.50	.40	.20
	Panel	3.75	2.75	1.50
3	Darryl Strawberry	.80	.60	.30

		MT	NR MT	EX
4	Wade Boggs	1.25	.90	.50
	Panel	3.25	2.50	1.25
5	Keith Hernandez	.40	.30	.15
6	Mark McGwire	1.25	.90	.50
	Panel	2.75	2.00	1.00
7	Rickey Henderson	1.00	.70	.40
8	Mike Schmidt	.60	.45	.25
9	Dwight Evans	.25	.20	.10
	Panel	1.75	1.25	.70
10	Gary Carter	.50	.40	.20
11	Paul Molitor	.30	.25	.12
	Panel	2.75	2.00	1.00
12	Dave Winfield	.50	.40	.20
13	Alan Trammell	.35	.25	.14
14	Tony Gwynn	.50	.40	.20
	Panel	2.50	2.00	1.00
15	Dale Murphy	.60	.45	.25
16	Andre Dawson	.30	.25	.12
17	Von Hayes	.20	.15	.08
18	Willie Randolph	.20	.15	.08
	Panel	2.00	1.50	.80
19	Kirby Puckett	.50	.40	.20
20	Juan Samuel	.25	.20	.10
21	Eddie Murray	.40	.30	.15
	Panel	3.00	2.25	1.25
22	George Bell	.35	.25	.14
23	Larry Sheets	.20	.15	.08
24	Eric Davis	.70	.50	.30
	Panel	2.25	1.75	.90
25	Cal Ripken	.60	.45	.25
26	Pedro Guerrero	.25	.20	.10
27	Will Clark	1.75	1.25	.70
	Panel	2.00	1.50	.80
28	Dwight Gooden	.80	.60	.30
29	Frank Viola	.25	.20	.10
	Panel	3.00	2.25	1.25
30	Roger Clemens	.80	.60	.30
31	Rick Sutcliffe	.20	.15	.08
32	Jack Morris	.25	.20	.10
33	John Tudor	.20	.15	.08

1966 East Hills Pirates

JESSE GONDER   (Catcher)

Stores in the East Hills Shopping Center, a large mall located in suburban Pittsburgh, distributed cards from this 25-card full-color set in 1966. The cards, which measure 3-1/4" by 4-1/4", are blank-backed and are numbered by the players' uniform numbers. The numbers appear in the lower right corners of the cards.

		NR MT	EX	VG
	Complete Set:	35.00	17.50	10.50
	Common Player:	.50	.25	.15
3	Harry Walker	.70	.35	.20
7	Bob Bailey	.50	.25	.15
8	Willie Stargell	8.00	4.00	2.50
9	Bill Mazeroski	2.00	1.00	.60
10	Jim Pagliaroni	.50	.25	.15
11	Jose Pagan	.50	.25	.15

		NR MT	EX	VG
12	Jerry May	.50	.25	.15
14	Gene Alley	.60	.30	.20
15	Manny Mota	.80	.40	.25
16	Andy Rodgers	.50	.25	.15
17	Donn Clendenon	.60	.30	.20
18	Matty Alou	.80	.40	.25
19	Pete Mikkelsen	.50	.25	.15
20	Jesse Gonder	.50	.25	.15
21	Bob Clemente	18.00	9.00	5.50
22	Woody Fryman	.60	.30	.20
24	Jerry Lynch	.50	.25	.15
25	Tommie Sisk	.50	.25	.15
26	Roy Face	1.25	.60	.40
28	Steve Blass	.60	.30	.20
32	Vernon Law	1.25	.60	.40
34	Al McBean	.50	.25	.15
39	Bob Veale	.60	.30	.20
43	Don Cardwell	.50	.25	.15
45	Gene Michael	.60	.30	.20

1954 Esskay Hot Dogs Orioles

VINICIO "CHICO" GARCIA, Infielder

Measuring 2-1/4" by 3-1/2", the 1954 Esskay Hot Dogs set features the Baltimore Orioles. The unnumbered color cards were issued in panels of two on packages of hot dogs and are usually found with grease stains. The cards have waxed fronts with blank backs on a white stock. Complete boxes of Esskay Hot Dogs are scarce and command a price of 2-3 times greater than the single card values.

		NR MT	EX	VG
	Complete Set:	3300.00	1650.00	990.00
	Common Player:	90.00	45.00	27.00
(1)	Neil Berry	90.00	45.00	27.00
(2)	Michael Blyzka	90.00	45.00	27.00
(3)	Harry Brecheen	90.00	45.00	27.00
(4)	Gil Coan	90.00	45.00	27.00
(5)	Joe Coleman	90.00	45.00	27.00
(6)	Clinton Courtney	90.00	45.00	27.00
(7)	Charles E. Diering	90.00	45.00	27.00
(8)	Jimmie Dykes	100.00	50.00	30.00
(9)	Frank J. Fanovich	90.00	45.00	27.00
(10)	Howard Fox	90.00	45.00	27.00
(11)	Jim Fridley	90.00	45.00	27.00
(12)	Vinicio "Chico" Garcia	90.00	45.00	27.00
(13)	Jehosie Heard	90.00	45.00	27.00
(14)	Darrell Johnson	90.00	45.00	27.00
(15)	Bob Kennedy	90.00	45.00	27.00
(16)	Dick Kokos	90.00	45.00	27.00
(17)	Dave Koslo	90.00	45.00	27.00
(18)	Lou Kretlow	90.00	45.00	27.00
(19)	Richard D. Kryhoski	90.00	45.00	27.00
(20)	Don Larsen	100.00	50.00	30.00
(21)	Donald E. Lenhardt	90.00	45.00	27.00
(22)	Richard Littlefield	90.00	45.00	27.00
(23)	Sam Mele	90.00	45.00	27.00
(24)	Les Moss	90.00	45.00	27.00
(25)	Ray L. Murray	90.00	45.00	27.00
(26a)	"Bobo" Newsom (no stadium lights in background)	125.00	62.00	37.00
(26b)	"Bobo" Newson (stadium lights in background)	125.00	62.00	37.00
(27)	Tom Oliver	90.00	45.00	27.00
(28)	Duane Pillette	90.00	45.00	27.00
(29)	Francis M. Skaff	90.00	45.00	27.00
(30)	Marlin Stuart	90.00	45.00	27.00

		NR MT	EX	VG
(31)	Robert L. Turley	150.00	75.00	45.00
(32)	Eddie Waitkus	90.00	45.00	27.00
(33)	Vic Wertz	110.00	55.00	33.00
(34)	Robert G. Young	90.00	45.00	27.00

1955 Esskay Hot Dogs Orioles

For the second consecutive year, Esskay Meats placed two baseball cards of Orioles players on their boxes of hot dogs. The unnumbered, color cards measure 2-1/4" by 3-1/2" and can be distinguished from the previous year by unwaxed fronts and grey backs. Many of the same photos from 1954 were used with only minor picture-cropping differences

		NR MT	EX	VG
Complete Set:		2400.00	1200.00	720.00
Common Player:		90.00	45.00	27.00
(1)	Cal Abrams	90.00	45.00	27.00
(2)	Robert S. Alexander	90.00	45.00	27.00
(3)	Harry Byrd	90.00	45.00	27.00
(4)	Gil Coan	90.00	45.00	27.00
(5)	Joseph P. Coleman	90.00	45.00	27.00
(6)	William R. Cox	90.00	45.00	27.00
(7)	Charles E. Diering	90.00	45.00	27.00
(8)	Walter A. Evers	90.00	45.00	27.00
(9)	Don Johnson	90.00	45.00	27.00
(10)	Robert D. Kennedy	90.00	45.00	27.00
(11)	Lou Kretlow	90.00	45.00	27.00
(12)	Robert L. Kuzava	90.00	45.00	27.00
(13)	Fred Marsh	90.00	45.00	27.00
(14)	Charles Maxwell	90.00	45.00	27.00
(15)	Jimmie McDonald	90.00	45.00	27.00
(16)	Bill Miller	90.00	45.00	27.00
(17)	Willy Miranda	90.00	45.00	27.00
(18)	Raymond L. Moore	90.00	45.00	27.00
(19)	John Lester Moss	90.00	45.00	27.00
(20)	"Bobo" Newsom	100.00	50.00	30.00
(21)	Duane Pillette	90.00	45.00	27.00
(22)	Edward S. Waitkus	90.00	45.00	27.00
(23)	Harold W. Smith	90.00	45.00	27.00
(24)	Gus Triandos	110.00	55.00	33.00
(25)	Eugene R. Woodling	110.00	55.00	33.00
(26)	Robert G. Young	90.00	45.00	27.00

A player's name in *italic* indicates a rookie card. An (FC) indicates a player's first card for that particular card company.

Exhibits - 1947-1966

Called "Exhibits" as they were produced by the Exhibit Supply Co. of Chicago, Ill., this group covers a span of twenty years. Each unnumbered, black and white card, printed on heavy stock, measures 3-3/8" by 5-3/8" and is blank-backed. The Exhibit Supply Co. issued new sets each year, with many players being repeated year after year. Other players appeared in only one or two years, thereby creating levels of scarcity. Many variations of the same basic pose are found in the group. Those cards are listed in the checklist that follows with an "a", "b", etc. following the assigned card number. The complete set includes all variations

		NR MT	EX	VG
Complete Set:		4500.00	2250.00	1350.
Common Player:		3.00	1.50	.90
(1)	Hank Aaron	25.00	12.50	7.50
(2a)	Joe Adcock (script signature)	3.00	1.50	.90
(2b)	Joe Adcock (plain signature)	5.00	2.50	1.50
(3)	Max Alvis	20.00	10.00	6.00
(4)	Johnny Antonelli (Braves)	3.00	1.50	.90
(5)	Johnny Antonelli (Giants)	5.00	2.50	1.50
(6)	Luis Aparicio (portrait)	7.00	3.50	2.00
(7)	Luis Aparicio (batting)	20.00	10.00	6.00
(8)	Luke Appling	7.00	3.50	2.00
(9a)	Ritchie Ashburn (Phillies, first-name incorrect)	5.00	2.50	1.50
(9b)	Richie Ashburn (Phillies, first name correct)	7.00	3.50	2.00
(10)	Richie Ashburn (Cubs)	13.00	6.50	4.00
(11)	Bob Aspromonte	3.00	1.50	.90
(12)	Toby Atwell	3.00	1.50	.90
(13)	Ed Bailey (with cap)	5.00	2.50	1.50
(14)	Ed Bailey (no cap)	3.00	1.50	.90
(15)	Gene Baker	3.00	1.50	.90
(16a)	Ernie Banks (bat on shoulder, script signature)	20.00	10.00	6.00
(16b)	Ernie Banks (bat on shoulder, plain signature)	10.00	5.00	3.00
(17)	Ernie Banks (portrait)	20.00	10.00	6.00
(18)	Steve Barber	3.00	1.50	.90
(19)	Earl Battey	5.00	2.50	1.50
(20)	Matt Batts	3.00	1.50	.90
(21a)	Hank Bauer (N.Y. cap)	5.00	2.50	1.50
(21b)	Hank Bauer (plain cap)	7.00	3.50	2.00
(22)	Frank Baumholtz	3.00	1.50	.90
(23)	Gene Bearden	3.00	1.50	.90
(24)	Joe Beggs	12.00	6.00	3.50
(25)	Larry "Yogi" Berra	30.00	15.00	9.00
(26)	Yogi Berra	10.00	5.00	3.00
(27)	Steve Bilko	5.00	2.50	1.50
(28)	Ewell Blackwell (pitching)	7.00	3.50	2.00
(29)	Ewell Blackwell (portrait)	3.00	1.50	.90
(30a)	Don Blasingame (St. Louis cap)	3.00	1.50	.90
(30b)	Don Blasingame (plain cap)	6.00	3.00	1.75
(31)	Ken Boyer	7.00	3.50	2.00
(32)	Ralph Branca	7.00	3.50	2.00
(33)	Jackie Brandt	50.00	25.00	15.00
(34)	Harry Brecheen	3.00	1.50	.90
(35)	Tom Brewer	12.00	6.00	3.50
(36)	Lou Brissie	5.00	2.50	1.50
(37)	Bill Bruton	3.00	1.50	.90
(38)	Lew Burdette (pitching, side view)	3.00	1.50	.90
(39)	Lew Burdette (pitching, front view)	6.00	3.00	1.75
(40)	Johnny Callison	7.00	3.50	2.00
(41)	Roy Campanella	13.00	6.50	4.00
(42)	Chico Carrasquel (portrait)	13.00	6.50	4.00
(43)	Chico Carrasquel (leaping)	3.00	1.50	.90
(44)	George Case	12.00	6.00	3.50
(45)	Hugh Casey	5.00	2.50	1.50
(46)	Norm Cash	7.00	3.50	2.00
(47)	Orlando Cepeda (portrait)	7.00	3.50	2.00
(48)	Orlando Cepeda (batting)	7.00	3.50	2.00
(49a)	Bob Cerv (A's cap)	7.00	3.50	2.00
(49b)	Bob Cerv (plain cap)	16.00	8.00	4.75
(50)	Dean Chance	3.00	1.50	.90
(51)	Spud Chandler	12.00	6.00	3.50
(52)	Tom Cheney	3.00	1.50	.90
(53)	Bubba Church	5.00	2.50	1.50
(54)	Roberto Clemente	25.00	12.50	7.50
(55)	Rocky Colavito (portrait)	25.00	12.50	7.50
(56)	Rocky Colavito (batting)	7.00	3.50	2.00
(57)	Choo Choo Coleman	13.00	6.50	4.00
(58)	Gordy Coleman	20.00	10.00	6.00
(59)	Jerry Coleman	5.00	2.50	1.50

	NR MT	EX	VG
(60) Mort Cooper	12.00	6.00	3.50
(61) Walker Cooper	3.00	1.50	.90
(62) Roger Craig	12.00	6.00	3.50
(63) Delmar Crandall	3.00	1.50	.90
(64) Joe Cunningham (batting)	25.00	12.50	7.50
(65) Joe Cunningham (portrait)	7.00	3.50	2.00
(66) Guy Curtwright (Curtright)	5.00	2.50	1.50
(67) Bud Daley	35.00	17.50	10.50
(68a) Alvin Dark (Braves)	7.00	3.50	2.00
(68b) Alvin Dark (Giants)	5.00	2.50	1.50
(69) Alvin Dark (Cubs)	7.00	3.50	2.00
(70) Murray Dickson (Murry)	5.00	2.50	1.50
(71) Bob Dillinger	7.00	3.50	2.00
(72) Dom DiMaggio	18.00	9.00	5.50
(73) Joe Dobson	7.00	3.50	2.00
(74) Larry Doby	3.00	1.50	.90
(75) Bobby Doerr	12.00	6.00	3.50
(76) Dick Donovan (plain cap)	7.00	3.50	2.00
(77) Dick Donovan (Sox cap)	4.00	2.00	1.25
(78) Walter Dropo	3.00	1.50	.90
(79) Don Drysdale (glove at waist)	25.00	12.50	7.50
(80) Don Drysdale (portrait)	25.00	12.50	7.50
(81) Luke Easter	5.00	2.50	1.50
(82) Bruce Edwards	5.00	2.50	1.50
(83) Del Ennis	3.00	1.50	.90
(84) Al Evans	4.50	2.25	1.25
(85) Walter Evers	3.00	1.50	.90
(86) Ferris Fain (fielding)	7.00	3.50	2.00
(87) Ferris Fain (portrait)	3.00	1.50	.90
(88) Dick Farrell	3.00	1.50	.90
(89) Ed "Whitey" Ford	15.00	7.50	4.50
(90) Whitey Ford (pitching)	10.00	5.00	3.00
(91) Whitey Ford (portrait)	60.00	30.00	17.50
(92) Dick Fowler	7.00	3.50	2.00
(93) Nelson Fox	5.00	2.50	1.50
(94) Tito Francona	3.00	1.50	.90
(95) Bob Friend	3.00	1.50	.90
(96) Carl Furillo	7.00	3.50	2.00
(97) Augie Galan	7.00	3.50	2.00
(98) Jim Gentile	3.00	1.50	.90
(99) Tony Gonzalez	3.00	1.50	.90
(100) Billy Goodman (leaping)	3.00	1.50	.90
(101) Billy Goodman (batting)	7.00	3.50	2.00
(102) Ted Greengrass (Jim)	3.00	1.50	.90
(103) Dick Groat	7.00	3.50	2.00
(104) Steve Gromek	3.00	1.50	.90
(105) Johnny Groth	3.00	1.50	.90
(106) Orval Grove	13.00	6.50	4.00
(107a) Frank Gustine (Pirates uniform)	5.00	2.50	1.50
(107b) Frank Gustine (plain uniform)	5.00	2.50	1.50
(108) Berthold Haas	13.00	6.50	4.00
(109) Grady Hatton	5.00	2.50	1.50
(110) Jim Hegan	3.00	1.50	.90
(111) Tom Henrich	7.00	3.50	2.00
(112) Ray Herbert	20.00	10.00	6.00
(113) Gene Hermanski	4.50	2.25	1.25
(114) Whitey Herzog	7.00	3.50	2.00
(115) Kirby Higbe	13.00	6.50	4.00
(116) Chuck Hinton	3.00	1.50	.90
(117) Don Hoak	13.00	6.50	4.00
(118a) Gil Hodges ("B" on cap)	9.00	4.50	2.75
(118b) Gil Hodges ("LA" on cap)	9.00	4.50	2.75
(119) Johnny Hopp	12.00	6.00	3.50
(120) Elston Howard	3.00	1.50	.90
(121) Frank Howard	7.00	3.50	2.00
(122) Ken Hubbs	35.00	17.50	10.50
(123) Tex Hughson	12.00	6.00	3.50
(124) Fred Hutchinson	4.50	2.25	1.25
(125) Monty Irvin	7.00	3.50	2.00
(126) Joey Jay	3.00	1.50	.90
(127) Jackie Jensen	25.00	12.50	7.50
(128) Sam Jethroe	5.00	2.50	1.50
(129) Bill Johnson	5.00	2.50	1.50
(130) Walter Judnich	12.00	6.00	3.50
(131) Al Kaline (kneeling)	25.00	12.50	7.50
(132) Al Kaline (portrait)	25.00	12.50	7.50
(133) George Kell	7.00	3.50	2.00
(134) Charley Keller	4.50	2.25	1.25
(135) Alex Kellner	3.00	1.50	.90
(136) Kenn Keltner (Ken)	5.00	2.50	1.50
(137) Harmon Killebrew (batting)	25.00	12.50	7.50
(138) Harmon Killebrew (throwing)	25.00	12.50	7.50
(139) Harmon Killibrew (Killebrew) (portrait)	25.00	12.50	7.50
(140) Ellis Kinder	3.00	1.50	.90
(141) Ralph Kiner	6.00	3.00	1.75
(142) Billy Klaus	20.00	10.00	6.00
(143) Ted Kluzewski (Kluszewski) (batting)	5.00	2.50	1.50
(144a) Ted Kluzewski (Kluszewski) (Pirates uniform)	5.00	2.50	1.50
(144b) Ted Kluzewski (Kluszewski) (plain uniform)	13.00	6.50	4.00
(145) Don Kolloway	7.00	3.50	2.00
(146) Jim Konstanty	5.00	2.50	1.50
(147) Sandy Koufax	20.00	10.00	6.00
(148) Ed Kranepool	50.00	25.00	15.00
(149a) Tony Kubek (light background)	7.00	3.50	2.00
(149b) Tony Kubek (dark background)	5.00	2.50	1.50
(150a) Harvey Kuenn ("D" on cap)	12.00	6.00	3.50
(150b) Harvey Kuenn (plain cap)	13.00	6.50	4.00
(151) Harvey Kuenn ("SF" on cap)	7.00	3.50	2.00
(152) Kurowski (Whitey)	4.50	2.25	1.25
(153) Eddie Lake	5.00	2.50	1.50
(154) Jim Landis	3.00	1.50	.90
(155) Don Larsen	3.00	1.50	.90
(156) Bob Lemon (glove not visible)	7.00	3.50	2.00
(157) Bob Lemon (glove partially visible)	25.00	12.50	7.50
(158) Buddy Lewis	12.00	6.00	3.50
(159) Johnny Lindell	20.00	10.00	6.00
(160) Phil Linz	20.00	10.00	6.00
(161) Don Lock	20.00	10.00	6.00
(162) Whitey Lockman	3.00	1.50	.90
(163) Johnny Logan	3.00	1.50	.90
(164) Dale Long ("P" on cap)	3.00	1.50	.90
(165) Dale Long ("C" on cap)	7.00	3.50	2.00
(166) Ed Lopat	5.00	2.50	1.50
(167a) Harry Lowery (name misspelled)	5.00	2.50	1.50
(167b) Harry Lowrey (name correct)	5.00	2.50	1.50
(168) Sal Maglie	3.00	1.50	.90
(169) Art Mahaffey	5.00	2.50	1.50
(170) Hank Majeski	3.00	1.50	.90
(171) Frank Malzone	3.00	1.50	.90
(172) Mickey Mantle (batting, pinstriped uniform)	100.00	50.00	30.00
(173a) Mickey Mantle (batting, no pinstripes, first name outlined in white)	75.00	38.00	23.00
(173b) Mickey Mantle (batting, no pinstripes, first name not outlined in white)	75.00	38.00	23.00
(174) Mickey Mantle (portrait)	300.00	120.00	75.00
(175) Martin Marion	7.00	3.50	2.00
(176) Roger Maris	20.00	10.00	6.00
(177) Willard Marshall	5.00	2.50	1.50
(178a) Eddie Matthews (name incorrect)	12.00	6.00	3.50
(178b) Eddie Mathews (name correct)	13.00	6.50	4.00
(179) Ed Mayo	5.00	2.50	1.50
(180) Willie Mays (batting)	18.00	9.00	5.50
(181) Willie Mays (portrait)	20.00	10.00	6.00
(182) Bill Mazeroski (portrait)	7.00	3.50	2.00
(183) Bill Mazeroski (batting)	7.00	3.50	2.00
(184) Ken McBride	3.00	1.50	.90
(185a) Barney McCaskey (McCosky)	13.00	6.50	4.00
(185b) Barney McCoskey (McCosky)	90.00	45.00	27.00
(186) Lindy McDaniel	3.00	1.50	.90
(187) Gil McDougald	3.00	1.50	.90
(188) Albert Mele	13.00	6.50	4.00
(189) Sam Mele	5.00	2.50	1.50
(190) Orestes Minoso ("C" on cap)	7.00	3.50	2.00
(191) Orestes Minoso (Sox on cap)	3.00	1.50	.90
(192) Dale Mitchell	3.00	1.50	.90
(193) Wally Moon	7.00	3.50	2.00
(194) Don Mueller	5.00	2.50	1.50
(195) Stan Musial (kneeling)	15.00	7.50	4.50
(196) Stan Musial (batting)	35.00	17.50	10.50
(197) Charley Neal	18.00	9.00	5.50
(198) Don Newcombe (shaking hands)	7.00	3.50	2.00
(199a) Don Newcombe (Dodgers on jacket)	5.00	2.50	1.50
(199b) Don Newcombe (plain jacket)	5.00	2.50	1.50
(200) Hal Newhouser	3.00	1.50	.90
(201) Ron Northey	12.00	6.00	3.50
(202) Bill O'Dell	3.00	1.50	.90
(203) Joe Page	12.00	6.00	3.50
(204) Satchel Paige	35.00	17.50	10.50
(205) Milt Pappas	3.00	1.50	.90
(206) Camilo Pascual	3.00	1.50	.90
(207) Albie Pearson	20.00	10.00	6.00
(208) Johnny Pesky	3.00	1.50	.90
(209) Gary Peters	20.00	10.00	6.00
(210) Dave Philley	3.00	1.50	.90
(211) Billy Pierce	3.00	1.50	.90
(212) Jimmy Piersall	16.00	8.00	4.75
(213) Vada Pinson	7.00	3.50	2.00
(214) Bob Porterfield	3.00	1.50	.90
(215) John "Boog" Powell	35.00	17.50	10.50
(216) Vic Raschi	4.50	2.25	1.25
(217a) Harold "Peewee" Reese (fielding, ball partially visible)	10.00	5.00	3.00
(217b) Harold "Peewee" Reese (fielding, ball not visible)	10.00	5.00	3.00

	NR MT	EX	VG
(218) Del Rice	3.00	1.50	.90
(219) Bobby Richardson	55.00	28.00	16.50
(220) Phil Rizzuto	6.00	3.00	1.75
(221a) Robin Roberts (script signature)	12.00	6.00	3.50
(221b) Robin Roberts (plain signature)	6.00	3.00	1.75
(222) Brooks Robinson	25.00	12.50	7.50
(223) Eddie Robinson	3.00	1.50	.90
(224) Floyd Robinson	20.00	10.00	6.00
(225) Frankie Robinson	18.00	9.00	5.50
(226) Jackie Robinson	30.00	15.00	9.00
(227) Preacher Roe	4.50	2.25	1.25
(228) Bob Rogers (Rodgers)	20.00	10.00	6.00
(229) Richard Rollins	20.00	10.00	6.00
(230) Pete Runnels	12.00	6.00	3.50
(231) John Sain	5.00	2.50	1.50
(232) Ron Santo	6.00	3.00	1.75
(233) Henry Sauer	5.00	2.50	1.50
(234a) Carl Sawatski ("M" on cap)	3.00	1.50	.90
(234b) Carl Sawatski ("P" on cap)	3.00	1.50	.90
(234c) Carl Sawatski (plain cap)	13.00	6.50	4.00
(235) Johnny Schmitz	5.00	2.50	1.50
(236a) Red Schoendeinst (Schoendienst) (fielding, name in white)	5.00	2.50	1.50
(236b) Red Schoendeinst (Schoendienst) (fielding, name in red-brown)	7.00	3.50	2.00
(237) Red Schoendinst (Schoendienst) (batting)	3.00	1.50	.90
(238a) Herb Score ("C" on cap)	5.00	2.50	1.50
(238b) Herb Score (plain cap)	12.00	6.00	3.50
(239) Andy Seminick	3.00	1.50	.90
(240) Rip Sewell	7.00	3.50	2.00
(241) Norm Siebern	3.00	1.50	.90
(242) Roy Sievers (batting)	5.00	2.50	1.50
(243a) Roy Sievers (portrait, "W" on cap, light background)	7.00	3.50	2.00
(243b) Roy Sievers (portrait, "W" on cap, dark background)	5.00	2.50	1.50
(243c) Roy Sievers (portrait, plain cap)	4.50	2.25	1.25
(244) Curt Simmons	5.00	2.50	1.50
(245) Dick Sisler	5.00	2.50	1.50
(246) Bill Skowron	5.00	2.50	1.50
(247) Bill "Moose" Skowron	55.00	28.00	16.50
(248) Enos Slaughter	7.00	3.50	2.00
(249a) Duke Snider ("B" on cap)	8.50	4.25	2.50
(249b) Duke Snider ("LA" on cap)	18.00	9.00	5.50
(250a) Warren Spahn ("B" on cap)	10.00	5.00	3.00
(250b) Warren Spahn ("M" on cap)	12.00	6.00	3.50
(251) Stanley Spence	13.00	6.50	4.00
(252) Ed Stanky (plain uniform)	5.00	2.50	1.50
(253) Ed Stanky (Giants uniform)	5.00	2.50	1.50
(254) Vern Stephens (batting)	5.00	2.50	1.50
(255) Vern Stephens (portrait)	5.00	2.50	1.50
(256) Ed Stewart	5.00	2.50	1.50
(257) Snuffy Stirnweiss	13.00	6.50	4.00
(258) George "Birdie" Tebbetts	12.00	6.00	3.50
(259) Frankie Thomas (photo actually Bob Skinner)	25.00	12.50	7.50
(260) Frank Thomas (portrait)	13.00	6.50	4.00
(261) Lee Thomas	3.00	1.50	.90
(262) Bobby Thomson	7.00	3.50	2.00
(263a) Earl Torgeson (Braves uniform)	3.00	1.50	.90
(263b) Earl Torgeson (plain uniform)	5.00	2.50	1.50
(264) Gus Triandos	7.00	3.50	2.00
(265) Virgil Trucks	3.00	1.50	.90
(266) Johnny Vandermeer (VanderMeer)	13.00	6.50	4.00
(267) Emil Verban	7.00	3.50	2.00
(268) Mickey Vernon (throwing)	3.00	1.50	.90
(269) Mickey Vernon (batting)	3.00	1.50	.90
(270) Bill Voiselle	7.00	3.50	2.00
(271) Leon Wagner	3.00	1.50	.90
(272a) Eddie Waitkus (throwing, Chicago uniform)	7.00	3.50	2.00
(272b) Eddie Waitkus (throwing, plain uniform)	5.00	2.50	1.50
(273) Eddie Waitkus (portrait)	13.00	6.50	4.00
(274) Dick Wakefield	5.00	2.50	1.50
(275) Harry Walker	7.00	3.50	2.00
(276) Bucky Walters	4.50	2.25	1.25
(277) Pete Ward	25.00	12.50	7.50
(278) Herman Wehmeier	5.00	2.50	1.50
(279) Vic Wertz (batting)	3.00	1.50	.90
(280) Vic Wertz (portrait)	3.00	1.50	.90
(281) Wally Westlake	5.00	2.50	1.50
(282) Wes Westrum	13.00	6.50	4.00
(283) Billy Williams	13.00	6.50	4.00
(284) Maurice Wills	12.00	6.00	3.50
(285a) Gene Woodling (script signature)	3.00	1.50	.90
(285b) Gene Woodling (plain signature)	7.00	3.50	2.00
(286) Taffy Wright	5.00	2.50	1.50
(287) Carl Yastrazemski (Yastrzemski)	175.00	90.00	50.00

	NR MT	EX	VG
(288) Al Zarilla	5.00	2.50	1.50
(289a) Gus Zernial (script signature)	3.00	1.50	.90
(289b) Gus Zernial (plain signature)	7.00	3.50	2.00
(290) Braves Team - 1948	18.00	9.00	5.50
(291) Dodgers Team - 1949	20.00	10.00	6.00
(292) Dodgers Team - 1952	20.00	10.00	6.00
(293) Dodgers Team - 1955	20.00	10.00	6.00
(294) Dodgers Team - 1956	20.00	10.00	6.00
(295) Giants Team - 1951	18.00	9.00	5.50
(296) Giants Team - 1954	18.00	9.00	5.50
(297) Indians Team - 1948	18.00	9.00	5.50
(298) Indians Team - 1954	18.00	9.00	5.50
(299) Phillies Team - 1950	18.00	9.00	5.50
(300) Yankees Team - 1949	25.00	12.50	7.50
(301) Yankees Team - 1950	25.00	12.50	7.50
(302) Yankees Team - 1951	25.00	12.50	7.50
(303) Yankees Team - 1952	25.00	12.50	7.50
(304) Yankees Team - 1955	25.00	12.50	7.50
(305) Yankees Team - 1956	25.00	12.50	7.50

1962 Exhibit Supply Co.
Statistic Backs

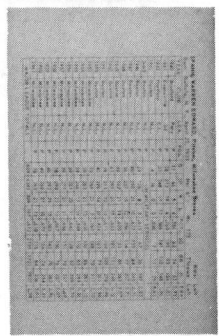

In 1962, the Exhibit Supply Co. added career statistics to the yearly set they produced. The black and white, unnumbered cards measure 3-3/8" by 5-3/8". The statistics found on the back are printed in black or red. The red backs are three times greater in value. The set is comprised of 32 cards.

	NR MT	EX	VG
Complete Set:	350.00	175.00	105.00
Common Player:	3.00	1.50	.90
(1) Hank Aaron	30.00	15.00	9.00
(2) Luis Aparicio	4.00	2.00	1.25
(3) Ernie Banks	7.00	3.50	2.00
(4) Larry "Yogi" Berra	10.00	5.00	3.00
(5) Ken Boyer	4.00	2.00	1.25
(6) Lew Burdette	3.50	1.75	1.00
(7) Norm Cash	3.50	1.75	1.00
(8) Orlando Cepeda	3.00	1.50	.90
(9) Roberto Clemente	30.00	15.00	9.00
(10) Rocky Colavito	4.00	2.00	1.25
(11) Ed "Whitey" Ford	7.00	3.50	2.00
(12) Nelson Fox	3.00	1.50	.90
(13) Tito Francona	3.00	1.50	.90
(14) Jim Gentile	3.00	1.50	.90
(15) Dick Groat	3.50	1.75	1.00
(16) Don Hoak	3.50	1.75	1.00
(17) Al Kaline	10.00	5.00	3.00
(18) Harmon Killebrew	10.00	5.00	3.00
(19) Sandy Koufax	25.00	12.50	7.50
(20) Jim Landis	3.00	1.50	.90
(21) Art Mahaffey	3.00	1.50	.90
(22) Frank Malzone	3.00	1.50	.90
(23) Mickey Mantle	60.00	30.00	18.00
(24) Roger Maris	10.00	5.00	3.00
(25) Eddie Mathews	5.00	2.50	1.50
(26) Willie Mays	30.00	15.00	9.00
(27) Wally Moon	3.50	1.75	1.00
(28) Stan Musial	30.00	15.00	9.00
(29) Milt Pappas	3.50	1.75	1.00
(30) Vada Pinson	4.00	2.00	1.25
(31) Norm Siebern	3.00	1.50	.90
(32) Warren Spahn	10.00	5.00	3.00

1963 Exhibit Supply Co.
Statistic Backs

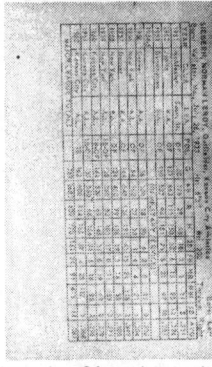

The Exhibit Supply Co. issued a 64-card set with career statistics on the backs of the cards in 1963. The unnumbered, black and white cards are printed on thick cardboard and measure 3-3/8" by 5-3/8" in size. The statistics on the back are printed in black.

		NR MT	EX	VG
Complete Set:		450.00	225.00	135.00
Common Player:		3.00	1.50	.90
(1)	Hank Aaron	30.00	15.00	9.00
(2)	Luis Aparicio	4.00	2.00	1.25
(3)	Bob Aspromonte	3.00	1.50	.90
(4)	Ernie Banks	18.00	9.00	5.50
(5)	Steve Barber	3.00	1.50	.90
(6)	Earl Battey	3.00	1.50	.90
(7)	Larry "Yogi" Berra	12.00	6.00	3.50
(8)	Ken Boyer	4.00	2.00	1.25
(9)	Lew Burdette	3.50	1.75	1.00
(10)	Johnny Callison	3.50	1.75	1.00
(11)	Norm Cash	3.50	1.75	1.00
(12)	Orlando Cepeda	3.00	1.50	.90
(13)	Dean Chance	3.00	1.50	.90
(14)	Tom Cheney	3.00	1.50	.90
(15)	Roberto Clemente	30.00	15.00	9.00
(16)	Rocky Colavito	4.00	2.00	1.25
(17)	Choo Choo Coleman	3.00	1.50	.90
(18)	Roger Craig	3.50	1.75	1.00
(19)	Joe Cunningham	3.00	1.50	.90
(20)	Don Drysdale	7.00	3.50	2.00
(21)	Dick Farrell	3.00	1.50	.90
(22)	Ed "Whitey" Ford	13.00	6.50	4.00
(23)	Nelson Fox	3.00	1.50	.90
(24)	Tito Francona	3.00	1.50	.90
(25)	Jim Gentile	3.00	1.50	.90
(26)	Tony Gonzalez	3.00	1.50	.90
(27)	Dick Groat	3.50	1.75	1.00
(28)	Ray Herbert	3.00	1.50	.90
(29)	Chuck Hinton	3.00	1.50	.90
(30)	Don Hoak	3.50	1.75	1.00
(31)	Frank Howard	4.00	2.00	1.25
(32)	Ken Hubbs	3.50	1.75	1.00
(33)	Joey Jay	3.00	1.50	.90
(34)	Al Kaline	13.00	6.50	4.00
(35)	Harmon Killebrew	13.00	6.50	4.00
(36)	Sandy Koufax	20.00	10.00	6.00
(37)	Harvey Kuenn	4.00	2.00	1.25
(38)	Jim Landis	3.00	1.50	.90
(39)	Art Mahaffey	3.00	1.50	.90
(40)	Frank Malzone	3.00	1.50	.90
(41)	Mickey Mantle	100.00	50.00	30.00
(42)	Roger Maris	13.00	6.50	4.00
(43)	Eddie Mathews	5.00	2.50	1.50
(44)	Willie Mays	30.00	15.00	9.00
(45)	Bill Mazeroski	4.00	2.00	1.25
(46)	Ken McBride	3.00	1.50	.90
(47)	Wally Moon	3.50	1.75	1.00
(48)	Stan Musial	30.00	15.00	9.00
(49)	Charlie Neal	3.00	1.50	.90
(50)	Bill O'Dell	3.00	1.50	.90
(51)	Milt Pappas	3.50	1.75	1.00
(52)	Camilo Pascual	3.50	1.75	1.00
(53)	Jimmy Piersall	4.00	2.00	1.25
(54)	Vada Pinson	4.00	2.00	1.25
(55)	Brooks Robinson	13.00	6.50	4.00
(56)	Frankie Robinson	13.00	6.50	4.00

		NR MT	EX	VG
(57)	Pete Runnels	3.50	1.75	1.00
(58)	Ron Santo	4.00	2.00	1.25
(59)	Norm Siebern	3.00	1.50	.90
(60)	Warren Spahn	10.00	5.00	3.00
(61)	Lee Thomas	3.00	1.50	.90
(62)	Leon Wagner	3.00	1.50	.90
(63)	Billy Williams	4.00	2.00	1.25
(64)	Maurice Wills	3.00	1.50	.90

1988 Fantastic Sam's

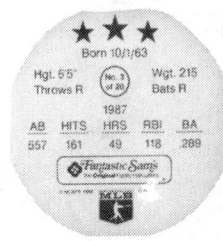

This set of 20 full-color player discs (2-1/2" diameter) was distributed during a Superstar Sweepstakes sponsored by Fantastic Sam's Family Haircutters' 1,800 stores nationwide. Each sweepstakes card consists of two connected discs (bright orange fronts, white backs) perforated for easy separation. One disc features the baseball player photo, the other carries the sweepstakes logo and a list of prizes. Player discs carry a Fantastic Sam's Baseball Superstars header curved above the photo, with his name, team and position printed in black. The disc backs are black and white and include personal info, card number and 1987 player stats. Sweepstakes discs list contest prizes (Grand Prize was 4 tickets to a 1988 Championship game) on the front and an entry form on the flipside. Below the prize list is a silver scratch-off rectangle which may reveal an instant prize.

		MT	NR MT	EX
Complete Set:		9.00	6.75	3.50
Common Player:		.20	.15	.08
1	Kirby Puckett	.75	.60	.30
2	George Brett	1.00	.70	.40
3	Mark McGwire	1.75	1.25	.70
4	Wally Joyner	1.25	.90	.50
5	Paul Molitor	.20	.15	.08
6	Alan Trammell	.40	.30	.15
7	George Bell	.50	.40	.20
8	Wade Boggs	1.75	1.25	.70
9	Don Mattingly	3.00	2.25	1.25
10	Julio Franco	.20	.15	.08
11	Ozzie Smith	.20	.15	.08
12	Will Clark	.75	.60	.30
13	Dale Murphy	1.00	.70	.40
14	Eric Davis	1.50	1.25	.60
15	Andre Dawson	.50	.40	.20
16	Tim Raines	.60	.45	.25
17	Darryl Strawberry	1.25	.90	.50
18	Tony Gwynn	.75	.60	.30
19	Mike Schmidt	1.50	1.25	.60
20	Pedro Guerrero	.20	.15	.08

Definitions for grading conditions are located in the introduction section at the front of this book.

1987 Farmland Dairies Mets

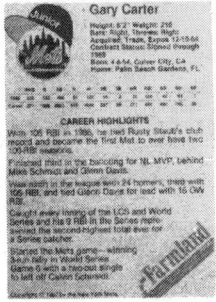

		MT	NR MT	EX
Complete Panel Set:		15.00	11.00	6.00
Complete Singles Set:		6.00	4.50	2.50
Common Single Player:		.25	.20	.10
	Panel	12.00	9.00	4.75
8	Gary Carter	.70	.50	.30
16	Dwight Gooden	1.25	.90	.50
17	Keith Hernandez	.60	.45	.25
18	Darryl Strawberry	1.25	.90	.50
20	Howard Johnson	.70	.50	.30
21	Kevin Elster	.35	.25	.14
42	Roger McDowell	.25	.20	.10
48	Randy Myers	.35	.25	.14

The New York Mets and Farmland Dairies produced a nine-card panel of baseball cards for members of the Junior Mets Club. Members of the club, kids 14 years of age and younger, received the perforated panel as part of a package featuring gifts and special privileges. The cards are the standard 2-1/2" by 3-1/2" with fronts containing a full-color photo encompassed by a blue border. The backs are designed on a vertical format and have player statistics and career highlights. The Farmland Dairies and Junior Mets Club logos are also carried on the card backs.

		MT	NR MT	EX
Complete Panel Set:		15.00	11.00	6.00
Complete Singles Set:		6.00	4.50	2.50
Common Single Player:		.25	.20	.10
	Panel	12.00	9.00	4.75
1	Mookie Wilson	.25	.20	.10
4	Len Dykstra	.50	.40	.20
8	Gary Carter	.70	.50	.30
12	Ron Darling	.40	.30	.15
18	Darryl Strawberry	1.25	.90	.50
19	Bob Ojeda	.25	.20	.10
22	Kevin McReynolds	.40	.30	.15
42	Roger McDowell	.35	.25	.14
-----	Team Card	.25	.20	.10

1988 Farmland Dairies Mets

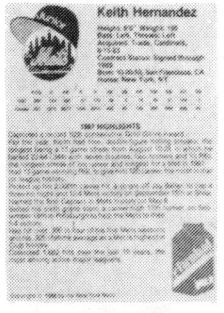

Part of the Junior Mets Fan Club membership package, this set of 9 standard size cards was printed on a single panel. Card fronts feature full-color action shots framed in orange and blue. A white player name runs across the top border, with a large team logo, uniform number and position printed below the photo. Card backs are blue on brown and include personal data, stats and 1987 season highlights. The set was offered to fans 14 years and younger for a $6 fan club membership fee, with a $1 discount for those who sent in two proofs of purchase from Farmland Dairies milk cartons.

1959 Fleer Ted Williams

This 80-card 1959 Fleer set tells of the life of baseball great Ted Williams, from his childhood years up to 1958. The full-color cards measure 2-1/2" by 3-1/2" in size and make use of both horizontal and vertical formats. The card backs, all designed horizontally, contain a continuing biography of Williams. Card #68 was withdrawn from the set early in production and is scarce. Counterfeit cards of #68 have been produced and can be distinguished by a cross-hatch pattern which appears over the photo on the card fronts.

		NR MT	EX	VG
Complete Set:		700.00	350.00	200.00
Common Player:		3.00	1.50	.90
1	The Early Years	15.00	7.50	4.50
2	Ted's Idol - Babe Ruth	15.00	7.50	4.50
3	Practice Makes Perfect	3.00	1.50	.90
4	1934 - Ted Learns The Fine Points			
		3.00	1.50	.90
5	Ted's Fame Spreads - 1935-36	3.00	1.50	.90
6	Ted Turns Professional	3.00	1.50	.90
7	1936 - From Mound To Plate	3.00	1.50	.90
8	1937 - First Full Season	3.00	1.50	.90
9	1937 - First Step To The Majors	3.00	1.50	.90
10	1938 - Gunning As A Pastime	3.00	1.50	.90
11	1938 - First Spring Training	4.00	2.00	1.25
12	1939 - Burning Up The Minors	3.00	1.50	.90
13	1939 - Ted Shows He Will Stay	3.00	1.50	.90
14	Outstanding Rookie of 1939	3.00	1.50	.90
15	1940 - Williams Licks Sophomore Jinx			
		3.00	1.50	.90
16	1941 - Williams' Greatest Year	3.00	1.50	.90
17	1941 - How Ted Hit .400	3.00	1.50	.90
18	1941 - All-Star Hero	3.00	1.50	.90
19	1942 - Ted Wins Triple Crown	3.00	1.50	.90
20	1942 - On To Naval Training	3.00	1.50	.90
21	1943 - Honors For Williams	3.00	1.50	.90
22	1944 - Ted Solos	3.00	1.50	.90
23	1944 - Williams Wins His Wings	3.00	1.50	.90
24	1945 - Sharpshooter	3.00	1.50	.90
25	1945 - Ted Is Discharged	3.00	1.50	.90
26	1946 - Off To A Flying Start	3.00	1.50	.90
27	July 9, 1946 - One Man Show	3.00	1.50	.90
28	July 14, 1946 - The Williams Shift	3.00	1.50	.90
29	July 21, 1946, Ted Hits For The Cycle			
		3.00	1.50	.90
30	1946 - Beating The Williams Shift	3.00	1.50	.90

		NR MT	EX	VG
31	Oct. 1946 - Sox Lose The Series	3.00	1.50	.90
32	1946 - Most Valuable Player	3.00	1.50	.90
33	1947 - Another Triple Crown For Ted			
		3.00	1.50	.90
34	1947 - Ted Sets Runs-Scored Record			
		3.00	1.50	.90
35	1948 - The Sox Miss The Pennant	3.00	1.50	.90
36	1948 - Banner Year For Ted	3.00	1.50	.90
37	1949 - Sox Miss Out Again	3.00	1.50	.90
38	1949 - Power Rampage	3.00	1.50	.90
39	1950 - Great Start	4.50	2.25	1.25
40	July 11, 1950 - Ted Crashes Into Wall			
		3.00	1.50	.90
41	1950 - Ted Recovers	3.00	1.50	.90
42	1951 - Williams Slowed By Injury	3.00	1.50	.90
43	1951 - Leads Outfielders In Double Plays			
		3.00	1.50	.90
44	1952 - Back To The Marines	3.00	1.50	.90
45	1952 - Farewell To Baseball?	3.00	1.50	.90
46	1952 - Ready For Combat	3.00	1.50	.90
47	1953 - Ted Crash Lands Jet	3.00	1.50	.90
48	July 14, 1953 - Ted Returns	3.00	1.50	.90
49	1953 - Smash Return	3.00	1.50	.90
50	March 1954 - Spring Injury	3.00	1.50	.90
51	May 16, 1954 - Ted Is Patched Up	3.00	1.50	.90
52	1954 - Ted's Comeback	3.00	1.50	.90
53	1954 - Ted's Comeback Is A Sucess			
		3.00	1.50	.90
54	Dec. 1954, Fisherman Ted Hooks a Big			
One		3.00	1.50	.90
55	1955 - Ted Decides Retirement Is "No Go"			
		3.00	1.50	.90
56	1956 - Ted Reaches 400th Homer,			
		3.00	1.50	.90
58	1957 - Williams Hits .388	3.00	1.50	.90
59	1957 - Hot September For Ted	3.00	1.50	.90
60	1957 - More Records For Ted	3.00	1.50	.90
61	1957 - Outfielder Ted	3.00	1.50	.90
62	1958 - 6th Batting Title For Ted	3.00	1.50	.90
63	Ted's All-Star Record	3.00	1.50	.90
64	1958 - Daughter And Famous Daddy			
		3.00	1.50	.90
65	August 30, 1958	3.00	1.50	.90
66	1958 - Powerhouse	3.00	1.50	.90
67	Two Famous Fisherman	4.50	2.25	1.25
68	Jan. 23, 1959 - Ted Signs For 1959			
		450.00	225.00	135.00
69	A Future Ted Williams?	3.00	1.50	.90
70	Ted Williams & Jim Thorpe	4.50	2.25	1.25
71	Ted's Hitting Fundamentals #1	3.00	1.50	.90
72	Ted's Hitting Fundamentals #2	3.00	1.50	.90
73	Ted's Hitting Fundamentals #3	3.00	1.50	.90
74	Here's How!	3.00	1.50	.90
75	Williams' Value To Red Sox	7.00	3.50	2.00
76	Ted's Remarkable "On Base" Record			
		3.00	1.50	.90
77	Ted Relaxes	3.00	1.50	.90
78	Honors For Williams	3.00	1.50	.90
79	Where Ted Stands	3.00	1.50	.90
80	Ted's Goals For 1959	7.00	3.50	2.00

1961 Fleer

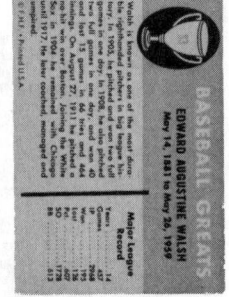

Over a two-year period, Fleer issued another set utilizing the Baseball Greats theme. The 154-card set was issued in two series and features a color player portrait against a color background. The player's name is located in a pennant set at the bottom of the card. The card backs feature orange and black on white stock and contain player biographical and statistical information. The cards measure 2-1/2" by 3-1/2" in size. The second series cards (#'s 89-154) were issued in 1962.

		NR MT	EX	VG
Complete Set:		550.00	275.00	165.00
Common Player: 1-88		1.75	.90	.50
Common Player: 89-154		3.00	1.50	.90
1	Baker, Cobb, Wheat/Checklist	20.00	10.00	6.00
2	G.C. Alexander	3.00	1.50	.90
3	Nick Altrock	1.75	.90	.50
4	Cap Anson	2.00	1.00	.60
5	Earl Averill	1.75	.90	.50
6	Home Run Baker	1.75	.90	.50
7	Dave Bancroft	1.75	.90	.50
8	Chief Bender	1.75	.90	.50
9	Jim Bottomley	1.75	.90	.50
10	Roger Bresnahan	1.75	.90	.50
11	Mordecai Brown	1.75	.90	.50
12	Max Carey	1.75	.90	.50
13	Jack Chesbro	1.75	.90	.50
14	Ty Cobb	20.00	10.00	6.00
15	Mickey Cochrane	2.00	1.00	.60
16	Eddie Collins	2.00	1.00	.60
17	Earle Combs	1.75	.90	.50
18	Charles Comiskey	1.75	.90	.50
19	Ki Ki Cuyler	1.75	.90	.50
20	Paul Derringer	1.75	.90	.50
21	Howard Ehmke	1.75	.90	.50
22	Billy Evans	1.75	.90	.50
23	Johnny Evers	1.75	.90	.50
24	Red Faber	1.75	.90	.50
25	Bob Feller	4.00	2.00	1.25
26	Wes Ferrell	1.75	.90	.50
27	Lew Fonseca	1.75	.90	.50
28	Jimmy Foxx	3.00	1.50	.90
29	Ford Frick	1.75	.90	.50
30	Frankie Frisch	2.00	1.00	.60
31	Lou Gehrig	20.00	10.00	6.00
32	Charlie Gehringer	2.00	1.00	.60
33	Warren Giles	1.75	.90	.50
34	Lefty Gomez	2.00	1.00	.60
35	Goose Goslin	1.75	.90	.50
36	Clark Griffith	1.75	.90	.50
37	Burleigh Grimes	1.75	.90	.50
38	Lefty Grove	1.50	.70	.45
39	Chick Hafey	1.75	.90	.50
40	Jesse Haines	1.75	.90	.50
41	Gabby Hartnett	1.75	.90	.50
42	Harry Heilmann	1.75	.90	.50
43	Rogers Hornsby	3.00	1.50	.90
44	Waite Hoyt	1.75	.90	.50
45	Carl Hubbell	1.50	.70	.45
46	Miller Huggins	1.75	.90	.50
47	Hughie Jennings	1.75	.90	.50
48	Ban Johnson	1.75	.90	.50
49	Walter Johnson	3.00	1.50	.90
50	Ralph Kiner	2.00	1.00	.60
51	Chuck Klein	1.75	.90	.50
52	Johnny Kling	1.75	.90	.50
53	Judge Landis	1.75	.90	.50
54	Tony Lazzeri	1.75	.90	.50
55	Ernie Lombardi	1.75	.90	.50
56	Dolf Luque	1.75	.90	.50
57	Heinie Manush	1.75	.90	.50
58	Marty Marion	1.75	.90	.50
59	Christy Mathewson	2.50	1.25	.70
60	John McGraw	2.00	1.00	.60
61	Joe Medwick	1.75	.90	.50
62	Bing Miller	1.75	.90	.50
63	Johnny Mize	2.00	1.00	.60
64	Johnny Mostil	1.75	.90	.50
65	Art Nehf	1.75	.90	.50
66	Hal Newhouser	1.75	.90	.50
67	Bobo Newsom	1.75	.90	.50
68	Mel Ott	1.50	.70	.45
69	Allie Reynolds	1.75	.90	.50
70	Sam Rice	1.75	.90	.50
71	Eppa Rixey	1.75	.90	.50
72	Edd Roush	1.75	.90	.50
73	Schoolboy Rowe	1.75	.90	.50
74	Red Ruffing	1.75	.90	.50
75	Babe Ruth	45.00	23.00	13.50
76	Joe Sewell	1.75	.90	.50
77	Al Simmons	1.75	.90	.50
78	George Sisler	2.00	1.00	.60
79	Tris Speaker	1.50	.70	.45
80	Fred Toney	1.75	.90	.50
81	Dazzy Vance	1.75	.90	.50

		NR MT	EX	VG
82	Jim Vaughn	1.75	.90	.50
83	Big Ed Walsh	1.75	.90	.50
84	Lloyd Waner	1.75	.90	.50
85	Paul Waner	1.75	.90	.50
86	Zach Wheat	1.75	.90	.50
87	Hack Wilson	1.75	.90	.50
88	Jimmy Wilson	1.75	.90	.50
89	Sisler & Traynor/Checklist	20.00	10.00	6.00
90	Babe Adams	3.00	1.50	.90
91	Dale Alexander	3.00	1.50	.90
92	Jim Bagby	3.00	1.50	.90
93	Ossie Bluege	3.00	1.50	.90
94	Lou Boudreau	4.00	2.00	1.25
95	Tommy Bridges	3.00	1.50	.90
96	Donnie Bush (Donie)	3.00	1.50	.90
97	Dolph Camilli	3.00	1.50	.90
98	Frank Chance	4.00	2.00	1.25
99	Jimmy Collins	3.00	1.50	.90
100	Stanley Coveleskie (Coveleski)	3.00	1.50	.90
101	Hughie Critz	3.00	1.50	.90
102	General Crowder	3.00	1.50	.90
103	Joe Dugan	3.00	1.50	.90
104	Bibb Falk	3.00	1.50	.90
105	Rick Ferrell	3.00	1.50	.90
106	Art Fletcher	3.00	1.50	.90
107	Dennis Galehouse	3.00	1.50	.90
108	Chick Galloway	3.00	1.50	.90
109	Mule Haas	3.00	1.50	.90
110	Stan Hack	3.00	1.50	.90
111	Bump Hadley	3.00	1.50	.90
112	Billy Hamilton	3.00	1.50	.90
113	Joe Hauser	3.00	1.50	.90
114	Babe Herman	3.00	1.50	.90
115	Travis Jackson	3.00	1.50	.90
116	Eddie Joost	3.00	1.50	.90
117	Addie Joss	3.00	1.50	.90
118	Joe Judge	3.00	1.50	.90
119	Joe Kuhel	3.00	1.50	.90
120	Nap Lajoie	6.00	3.00	1.75
121	Dutch Leonard	3.00	1.50	.90
122	Ted Lyons	3.00	1.50	.90
123	Connie Mack	6.00	3.00	1.75
124	Rabbit Maranville	3.00	1.50	.90
125	Fred Marberry	3.00	1.50	.90
126	Iron Man McGinnity	3.00	1.50	.90
127	Oscar Melillo	3.00	1.50	.90
128	Ray Mueller	3.00	1.50	.90
129	Kid Nichols	3.00	1.50	.90
130	Lefty O'Doul	3.00	1.50	.90
131	Bob O'Farrell	3.00	1.50	.90
132	Roger Peckinpaugh	3.00	1.50	.90
133	Herb Pennock	3.00	1.50	.90
134	George Pipgras	3.00	1.50	.90
135	Eddie Plank	3.00	1.50	.90
136	Ray Schalk	3.00	1.50	.90
137	Hal Schumacher	3.00	1.50	.90
138	Luke Sewell	3.00	1.50	.90
139	Bob Shawkey	3.00	1.50	.90
140	Riggs Stephenson	3.00	1.50	.90
141	Billy Sullivan	3.00	1.50	.90
142	Bill Terry	5.00	2.50	1.50
143	Joe Tinker	2.75	1.50	.80
144	Pie Traynor	4.00	2.00	1.25
145	George Uhle	3.00	1.50	.90
146	Hal Troskey (Trosky)	3.00	1.50	.90
147	Arky Vaughan	3.00	1.50	.90
148	Johnny Vander Meer	3.00	1.50	.90
149	Rube Waddell	3.00	1.50	.90
150	Honus Wagner	20.00	10.00	6.00
151	Dixie Walker	3.00	1.50	.90
152	Ted Williams	45.00	23.00	13.50
153	Cy Young	8.00	4.00	2.50
154	Ross Young (Youngs)	6.00	3.00	1.75

1963 Fleer

A lawsuit by Topps stopped Fleer's 1963 set at one series of 66 cards. Issued with a cookie rather than gum, the set features color photos of current players. The card backs include statistical information for 1962 and career plus a brief player biography. The cards, which measure 2-1/2" by 3-1/2", are numbered 1-66. An unnumbered checklist was issued with the set and is included in the complete set price in the checklist that follows. The checklist and #46 Adcock are scarce.

FRANK BOLLING
Milwaukee Braves—2nd Base

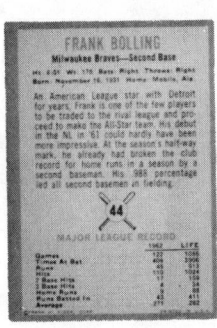

		NR MT	EX	VG
Complete Set:		850.00	425.00	255.00
Common Player:		5.00	2.50	1.50
1	Steve Barber	10.00	2.00	1.25
2	Ron Hansen	5.00	2.50	1.50
3	Milt Pappas	2.25	1.25	.70
4	Brooks Robinson	30.00	15.00	9.00
5	Willie Mays	75.00	38.00	23.00
6	Lou Clinton	5.00	2.50	1.50
7	Bill Monbouquette	5.00	2.50	1.50
8	Carl Yastrzemski	75.00	38.00	23.00
9	Ray Herbert	5.00	2.50	1.50
10	Jim Landis	5.00	2.50	1.50
11	Dick Donovan	5.00	2.50	1.50
12	Tito Francona	5.00	2.50	1.50
13	Jerry Kindall	5.00	2.50	1.50
14	Frank Lary	2.25	1.25	.70
15	Dick Howser	4.00	2.00	1.25
16	Jerry Lumpe	5.00	2.50	1.50
17	Norm Siebern	5.00	2.50	1.50
18	Don Lee	5.00	2.50	1.50
19	Albie Pearson	5.00	2.50	1.50
20	Bob Rodgers	2.25	1.25	.70
21	Leon Wagner	5.00	2.50	1.50
22	Jim Kaat	7.00	3.50	2.00
23	Vic Power	5.00	2.50	1.50
24	Rich Rollins	5.00	2.50	1.50
25	Bobby Richardson	5.00	2.50	1.50
26	Ralph Terry	2.50	1.25	.70
27	Tom Cheney	2.25	1.25	.70
28	Chuck Cottier	5.00	2.50	1.50
29	Jimmy Piersall	2.50	1.25	.70
30	Dave Stenhouse	5.00	2.50	1.50
31	Glen Hobbie	5.00	2.50	1.50
32	Ron Santo	6.00	3.00	1.75
33	Gene Freese	5.00	2.50	1.50
34	Vada Pinson	6.00	3.00	1.75
35	Bob Purkey	5.00	2.50	1.50
36	Joe Amalfitano	5.00	2.50	1.50
37	Bob Aspromonte	5.00	2.50	1.50
38	Dick Farrell	5.00	2.50	1.50
39	Al Spangler	5.00	2.50	1.50
40	Tommy Davis	2.50	1.25	.70
41	Don Drysdale	25.00	12.50	7.50
42	Sandy Koufax	80.00	40.00	24.00
43	Maury Wills	35.00	17.50	10.50
44	Frank Bolling	5.00	2.50	1.50
45	Warren Spahn	40.00	20.00	12.00
46	Joe Adcock	100.00	45.00	27.00
47	Roger Craig	10.00	5.00	3.00
48	Al Jackson	2.25	1.25	.70
49	Rod Kanehl	2.25	1.25	.70
50	Ruben Amaro	5.00	2.50	1.50
51	John Callison	2.25	1.25	.70
52	Clay Dalrymple	5.00	2.50	1.50
53	Don Demeter	5.00	2.50	1.50
54	Art Mahaffey	5.00	2.50	1.50
55	"Smoky" Burgess	2.25	1.25	.70
56	Roberto Clemente	75.00	38.00	23.00
57	Elroy Face	2.25	1.25	.70
58	Vernon Law	2.25	1.25	.70
59	Bill Mazeroski	6.00	3.00	1.75
60	Ken Boyer	6.00	3.00	1.75
61	Bob Gibson	25.00	12.50	7.50
62	Gene Oliver	5.00	2.50	1.50
63	Bill White	5.00	2.50	1.50
64	Orlando Cepeda	10.00	5.00	3.00
65	Jimmy Davenport	5.00	2.50	1.50
66	Billy O'Dell	6.00	3.00	1.75
----	Checklist 1-66	325.00	130.00	81.00

1981 Fleer

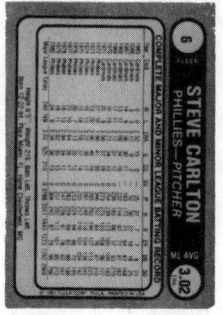

For the first time in 18 years, Fleer issued a baseball card set featuring current players. Fleer's 660-card effort included numerous errors in the first printing run which were subsequently corrected in additional runs. The cards, which measure 2-1/2" by 3-1/2", are numbered alphabetically by team. The card fronts feature a full-color photo inside a border which is color-coded by team. The card backs have black, grey and yellow ink on white stock and carry player statistical information. The player's batting average or earned run average is located in a circle in the upper right corner of the card. The complete set price in the checklist that follows does not include the higher priced variations.

		MT	NR MT	EX
Complete Set:		45.00	33.00	16.00
Common Player:		.06	.05	.02
1	Pete Rose	1.75	1.25	.70
2	Larry Bowa	.15	.11	.06
3	Manny Trillo	.08	.06	.03
4	Bob Boone	.10	.08	.04
5a	Mike Schmidt (portrait)	2.00	1.50	.80
5b	Mike Schmidt (batting)	2.00	1.50	.80
6a	Steve Carlton ("Lefty" on front)	1.00	.70	.40
6b	Steve Carlton (Pitcher of the Year on front, date 1066 on back)	2.00	1.50	.80
6c	Steve Carlton (Pitcher of the Year on front, date 1966 on back)	3.00	2.25	1.25
7a	Tug McGraw (Game Saver on front)	.50	.40	.20
7b	Tug McGraw (Pitcher on front)	.12	.09	.05
8	Larry Christenson	.06	.05	.02
9	Bake McBride	.06	.05	.02
10	Greg Luzinski	.15	.11	.06
11	Ron Reed	.06	.05	.02
12	Dickie Noles	.06	.05	.02
13	Keith Moreland	.35	.25	.14
14	Bob Walk	.25	.20	.10
15	Lonnie Smith	.08	.06	.03
16	Dick Ruthven	.06	.05	.02
17	Sparky Lyle	.10	.08	.04
18	Greg Gross	.06	.05	.02
19	Garry Maddox	.10	.08	.04
20	Nino Espinosa	.06	.05	.02
21	George Vukovich	.06	.05	.02
22	John Vukovich	.06	.05	.02
23	Ramon Aviles	.06	.05	.02
24a	Kevin Saucier (Ken Saucier on back)	.15	.11	.06
24b	Kevin Saucier (Kevin Saucier on back)	.70	.50	.30
25	Randy Lerch	.06	.05	.02
26	Del Unser	.06	.05	.02
27	Tim McCarver	.15	.11	.06
28a	George Brett (batting)	1.50	1.25	.60
28b	George Brett (portrait)	1.00	.70	.40
29a	Willie Wilson (portrait)	.60	.45	.25
29b	Willie Wilson (batting)	.15	.11	.06
30	Paul Splittorff	.06	.05	.02
31	Dan Quisenberry	.15	.11	.06
32a	Amos Otis (batting)	.50	.40	.20
32b	Amos Otis (portrait)	.10	.08	.04
33	Steve Busby	.08	.06	.03
34	U.L. Washington	.06	.05	.02
35	Dave Chalk	.06	.05	.02

		MT	NR MT	EX
36	Darrell Porter	.08	.06	.03
37	Marty Pattin	.06	.05	.02
38	Larry Gura	.06	.05	.02
39	Renie Martin	.06	.05	.02
40	Rich Gale	.06	.05	.02
41a	Hal McRae (dark blue "Royals" on front)	.40	.30	.15
41b	Hal McRae (light blue "Royals" on front)	.10	.08	.04
42	Dennis Leonard	.08	.06	.03
43	Willie Aikens	.06	.05	.02
44	Frank White	.10	.08	.04
45	Clint Hurdle	.06	.05	.02
46	John Wathan	.08	.06	.03
47	Pete LaCock	.06	.05	.02
48	Rance Mulliniks	.06	.05	.02
49	Jeff Twitty	.06	.05	.02
50	Jamie Quirk	.06	.05	.02
51	Art Howe	.06	.05	.02
52	Ken Forsch	.06	.05	.02
53	Vern Ruhle	.06	.05	.02
54	Joe Niekro	.12	.09	.05
55	Frank LaCorte	.06	.05	.02
56	J.R. Richard	.10	.08	.04
57	Nolan Ryan	7.00	5.25	2.75
58	Enos Cabell	.06	.05	.02
59	Cesar Cedeno	.12	.09	.05
60	Jose Cruz	.12	.09	.05
61	Bill Virdon	.06	.05	.02
62	Terry Puhl	.06	.05	.02
63	Joaquin Andujar	.10	.08	.04
64	Alan Ashby	.06	.05	.02
65	Joe Sambito	.06	.05	.02
66	Denny Walling	.06	.05	.02
67	Jeff Leonard	.12	.09	.05
68	Luis Pujols	.06	.05	.02
69	Bruce Bochy	.06	.05	.02
70	Rafael Landestoy	.06	.05	.02
71	Dave Smith	.30	.25	.12
72	Danny Heep	.10	.08	.04
73	Julio Gonzalez	.06	.05	.02
74	Craig Reynolds	.06	.05	.02
75	Gary Woods	.06	.05	.02
76	Dave Bergman	.06	.05	.02
77	Randy Niemann	.06	.05	.02
78	Joe Morgan	.60	.45	.25
79a	Reggie Jackson (portrait)	1.00	.70	.40
79b	Reggie Jackson (batting)	.75	.60	.30
80	Bucky Dent	.10	.08	.04
81	Tommy John	.20	.15	.08
82	Luis Tiant	.12	.09	.05
83	Rick Cerone	.06	.05	.02
84	Dick Howser	.06	.05	.02
85	Lou Piniella	.12	.09	.05
86	Ron Davis	.08	.06	.03
87a	Graig Nettles (Craig on back)	12.00	9.00	4.75
87b	Graig Nettles (Graig on back)	.30	.25	.12
88	Ron Guidry	.25	.20	.10
89	Rich Gossage	.20	.15	.08
90	Rudy May	.06	.05	.02
91	Gaylord Perry	1.00	.70	.40
92	Eric Soderholm	.06	.05	.02
93	Bob Watson	.08	.06	.03
94	Bobby Murcer	.10	.08	.04
95	Bobby Brown	.06	.05	.02
96	Jim Spencer	.06	.05	.02
97	Tom Underwood	.06	.05	.02
98	Oscar Gamble	.08	.06	.02
99	Johnny Oates	.06	.05	.02
100	Fred Stanley	.06	.05	.02
101	Ruppert Jones	.06	.05	.02
102	Dennis Werth	.06	.05	.02
103	Joe Lefebvre	.06	.05	.02
104	Brian Doyle	.06	.05	.02
105	Aurelio Rodriguez	.08	.06	.03
106	Doug Bird	.06	.05	.02
107	Mike Griffin	.06	.05	.02
108	Tim Lollar	.06	.05	.02
109	Willie Randolph	.10	.08	.04
110	Steve Garvey	.50	.40	.20
111	Reggie Smith	.10	.08	.04
112	Don Sutton	.30	.25	.12
113	Burt Hooton	.08	.06	.03
114a	Davy Lopes (Davey) (no finger on back)	.10	.08	.04
114b	Davy Lopes (Davey) (small finger on back)	1.00	.70	.40
115	Dusty Baker	.10	.08	.04
116	Tom Lasorda	.10	.08	.04
117	Bill Russell	.08	.06	.03
118	Jerry Reuss	.10	.08	.04
119	Terry Forster	.08	.06	.03

		MT	NR MT	EX
120a	Robert Welch (Bob Welch on back)	.20	.15	.08
120b	Robert Welch (Robert Welch on back)			
		1.00	.70	.40
121	Don Stanhouse	.06	.05	.02
122	Rick Monday	.10	.08	.04
123	Derrel Thomas	.06	.05	.02
124	Joe Ferguson	.06	.05	.02
125	Rick Sutcliffe	.20	.15	.08
126a	Ron Cey (no finger on back)	.12	.09	.05
126b	Ron Cey (small finger on back)	1.00	.70	.40
127	Dave Goltz	.08	.06	.03
128	Jay Johnstone	.08	.06	.03
129	Steve Yeager	.06	.05	.02
130	Gary Weiss	.06	.05	.02
131	*Mike Scioscia*	.60	.45	.25
132	Vic Davalillo	.08	.06	.03
133	Doug Rau	.06	.05	.02
134	Pepe Frias	.06	.05	.02
135	Mickey Hatcher	.08	.06	.03
136	*Steve Howe*	.10	.08	.04
137	Robert Castillo	.06	.05	.02
138	Gary Thomasson	.06	.05	.02
139	Rudy Law	.06	.05	.02
140	*Fernand Valenzuela (Fernando)*	4.00	3.00	1.50
141	Manny Mota	.08	.06	.03
142	Gary Carter	.40	.30	.15
143	Steve Rogers	.08	.06	.03
144	Warren Cromartie	.06	.05	.02
145	Andre Dawson	1.00	.70	.40
146	Larry Parrish	.10	.08	.04
147	Rowland Office	.06	.05	.02
148	Ellis Valentine	.06	.05	.02
149	Dick Williams	.06	.05	.02
150	*Bill Gullickson*	.15	.11	.06
151	Elias Sosa	.06	.05	.02
152	John Tamargo	.06	.05	.02
153	Chris Speier	.06	.05	.02
154	Ron LeFlore	.08	.06	.03
155	Rodney Scott	.06	.05	.02
156	Stan Bahnsen	.06	.05	.02
157	Bill Lee	.08	.06	.03
158	Fred Norman	.06	.05	.02
159	Woodie Fryman	.08	.06	.03
160	Dave Palmer	.06	.05	.02
161	Jerry White	.06	.05	.02
162	Roberto Ramos	.06	.05	.02
163	John D'Acquisto	.06	.05	.02
164	Tommy Hutton	.06	.05	.02
165	*Charlie Lea*	.12	.09	.05
166	Scott Sanderson	.06	.05	.02
167	Ken Macha	.06	.05	.02
168	Tony Bernazard	.06	.05	.02
169	Jim Palmer	.80	.60	.30
170	Steve Stone	.08	.06	.03
171	Mike Flanagan	.10	.08	.04
172	Al Bumbry	.08	.06	.03
173	Doug DeCinces	.10	.08	.04
174	Scott McGregor	.08	.06	.03
175	Mark Belanger	.08	.06	.03
176	Tim Stoddard	.06	.05	.02
177a	Rick Dempsey (no finger on front)	.10	.08	.04
177b	Rick Dempsey (small finger on front)			
		1.00	.70	.40
178	Earl Weaver	.10	.08	.04
179	Tippy Martinez	.06	.05	.02
180	Dennis Martinez	.08	.06	.03
181	Sammy Stewart	.06	.05	.02
182	Rich Dauer	.06	.05	.02
183	Lee May	.08	.06	.03
184	Eddie Murray	.80	.60	.30
185	Benny Ayala	.06	.05	.02
186	John Lowenstein	.06	.05	.02
187	Gary Roenicke	.06	.05	.02
188	Ken Singleton	.10	.08	.04
189	Dan Graham	.06	.05	.02
190	Terry Crowley	.06	.05	.02
191	Kiko Garcia	.06	.05	.02
192	Dave Ford	.06	.05	.02
193	Mark Corey	.06	.05	.02
194	Lenn Sakata	.06	.05	.02
195	Doug DeCinces	.10	.08	.04
196	Johnny Bench	1.00	.70	.40
197	Dave Concepcion	.15	.11	.06
198	Ray Knight	.10	.08	.04
199	Ken Griffey	.12	.09	.05
200	Tom Seaver	1.50	1.25	.60
201	Dave Collins	.08	.06	.03
202	George Foster	.20	.15	.08
203	Junior Kennedy	.06	.05	.02
204	Frank Pastore	.06	.05	.02
205	Dan Driessen	.08	.06	.03

		MT	NR MT	EX
206	Hector Cruz	.06	.05	.02
207	Paul Moskau	.06	.05	.02
208	*Charlie Leibrandt*	.30	.25	.12
209	Harry Spilman	.06	.05	.02
210	*Joe Price*	.12	.09	.05
211	Tom Hume	.06	.05	.02
212	Joe Nolan	.06	.05	.02
213	Doug Bair	.06	.05	.02
214	Mario Soto	.08	.06	.03
215a	Bill Bonham (no finger on back)	.08	.06	.03
215b	Bill Bonham (small finger on back)			
		1.00	.70	.40
216a	George Foster (Slugger on front)	.25	.20	.10
216b	George Foster (Outfield on front)	.20	.15	.08
217	Paul Householder	.06	.05	.02
218	Ron Oester	.06	.05	.02
219	Sam Mejias	.06	.05	.02
220	Sheldon Burnside	.06	.05	.02
221	Carl Yastrzemski	1.00	.70	.40
222	Jim Rice	.50	.40	.20
223	Fred Lynn	.20	.15	.08
224	Carlton Fisk	.50	.40	.20
225	Rick Burleson	.08	.06	.03
226	Dennis Eckersley	.12	.09	.05
227	Butch Hobson	.06	.05	.02
228	Tom Burgmeier	.06	.05	.02
229	Garry Hancock	.06	.05	.02
230	Don Zimmer	.06	.05	.02
231	Steve Renko	.06	.05	.02
232	Dwight Evans	.15	.11	.06
233	Mike Torrez	.08	.06	.03
234	Bob Stanley	.06	.05	.02
235	Jim Dwyer	.06	.05	.02
236	Dave Stapleton	.06	.05	.02
237	Glenn Hoffman	.06	.05	.02
238	Jerry Remy	.06	.05	.02
239	Dick Drago	.06	.05	.02
240	Bill Campbell	.06	.05	.02
241	Tony Perez	.20	.15	.08
242	Phil Niekro	.30	.25	.12
243	Dale Murphy	.90	.70	.35
244	Bob Horner	.12	.09	.05
245	Jeff Burroughs	.08	.06	.03
246	Rick Camp	.06	.05	.02
247	Bob Cox	.06	.05	.02
248	Bruce Benedict	.06	.05	.02
249	Gene Garber	.06	.05	.02
250	Jerry Royster	.06	.05	.02
251a	Gary Matthews (no finger on back)	.12	.09	.05
251b	Gary Matthews (small finger on back)			
		1.00	.70	.40
252	Chris Chambliss	.08	.06	.03
253	Luis Gomez	.06	.05	.02
254	Bill Nahorodny	.06	.05	.02
255	Doyle Alexander	.10	.08	.04
256	Brian Asselstine	.06	.05	.02
257	Biff Pocoroba	.06	.05	.02
258	Mike Lum	.06	.05	.02
259	Charlie Spikes	.06	.05	.02
260	Glenn Hubbard	.08	.06	.03
261	Tommy Boggs	.06	.05	.02
262	Al Hrabosky	.08	.06	.03
263	Rick Matula	.06	.05	.02
264	Preston Hanna	.06	.05	.02
265	Larry Bradford	.06	.05	.02
266	*Rafael Ramirez*	.20	.15	.08
267	Larry McWilliams	.06	.05	.02
268	Rod Carew	1.50	1.25	.60
269	Bobby Grich	.10	.08	.04
270	Carney Lansford	.10	.08	.04
271	Don Baylor	.12	.09	.05
272	Joe Rudi	.10	.08	.04
273	Dan Ford	.06	.05	.02
274	Jim Fregosi	.08	.06	.03
275	Dave Frost	.06	.05	.02
276	Frank Tanana	.10	.08	.04
277	Dickie Thon	.08	.06	.03
278	Jason Thompson	.06	.05	.02
279	Rick Miller	.06	.05	.02
280	Bert Campaneris	.10	.08	.04
281	Tom Donohue	.06	.05	.02
282	Brian Downing	.10	.08	.04
283	Fred Patek	.06	.05	.02
284	Bruce Kison	.06	.05	.02
285	Dave LaRoche	.06	.05	.02
286	Don Aase	.06	.05	.02
287	Jim Barr	.06	.05	.02
288	Alfredo Martinez	.06	.05	.02
289	Larry Harlow	.06	.05	.02
290	Andy Hassler	.06	.05	.02
291	Dave Kingman	.15	.11	.06

		MT	NR MT	EX
292	Bill Buckner	.12	.09	.05
293	Rick Reuschel	.10	.08	.04
294	Bruce Sutter	.15	.11	.06
295	Jerry Martin	.06	.05	.02
296	Scot Thompson	.06	.05	.02
297	Ivan DeJesus	.06	.05	.02
298	Steve Dillard	.06	.05	.02
299	Dick Tidrow	.06	.05	.02
300	Randy Martz	.06	.05	.02
301	Lenny Randle	.06	.05	.02
302	Lynn McGlothen	.06	.05	.02
303	Cliff Johnson	.06	.05	.02
304	Tim Blackwell	.06	.05	.02
305	Dennis Lamp	.06	.05	.02
306	Bill Caudill	.06	.05	.02
307	Carlos Lezcano	.06	.05	.02
308	Jim Tracy	.06	.05	.02
309	Doug Capilla	.06	.05	.02
310	Willie Hernandez	.10	.08	.04
311	Mike Vail	.06	.05	.02
312	Mike Krukow	.08	.06	.03
313	Barry Foote	.06	.05	.02
314	Larry Biittner	.06	.05	.02
315	Mike Tyson	.06	.05	.02
316	Lee Mazzilli	.08	.06	.03
317	John Stearns	.06	.05	.02
318	Alex Trevino	.06	.05	.02
319	Craig Swan	.06	.05	.02
320	Frank Taveras	.06	.05	.02
321	Steve Henderson	.06	.05	.02
322	Neil Allen	.08	.06	.03
323	Mark Bomback	.06	.05	.02
324	Mike Jorgensen	.06	.05	.02
325	Joe Torre	.08	.06	.03
326	Elliott Maddox	.06	.05	.02
327	Pete Falcone	.06	.05	.02
328	Ray Burris	.06	.05	.02
329	Claudell Washington	.08	.06	.03
330	Doug Flynn	.06	.05	.02
331	Joel Youngblood	.06	.05	.02
332	Bill Almon	.06	.05	.02
333	Tom Hausman	.06	.05	.02
334	Pat Zachry	.06	.05	.02
335	*Jeff Reardon*	.70	.50	.30
336	*Wally Backman*	.35	.25	.14
337	Dan Norman	.06	.05	.02
338	Jerry Morales	.06	.05	.02
339	Ed Farmer	.06	.05	.02
340	Bob Molinaro	.06	.05	.02
341	Todd Cruz	.06	.05	.02
342a	*Britt Burns (no finger on front)*	.20	.15	.08
342b	*Britt Burns (small finger on front)*	1.00	.70	.40
343	Kevin Bell	.06	.05	.02
344	Tony LaRussa	.08	.06	.03
345	Steve Trout	.06	.05	.02
346	*Harold Baines*	3.00	2.25	1.25
347	Richard Wortham	.06	.05	.02
348	Wayne Nordhagen	.06	.05	.02
349	Mike Squires	.06	.05	.02
350	Lamar Johnson	.06	.05	.02
351	Rickey Henderson	18.00	13.50	7.25
352	Francisco Barrios	.06	.05	.02
353	Thad Bosley	.06	.05	.02
354	Chet Lemon	.08	.06	.03
355	Bruce Kimm	.06	.05	.02
356	*Richard Dotson*	.35	.25	.14
357	Jim Morrison	.06	.05	.02
358	Mike Proly	.06	.05	.02
359	Greg Pryor	.06	.05	.02
360	Dave Parker	.30	.25	.12
361	Omar Moreno	.06	.05	.02
362a	Kent Tekulve (1071 Waterbury on back)	.15	.11	.06
362b	Kent Tekulve (1971 Waterbury on back)	.70	.50	.30
363	Willie Stargell	.40	.30	.15
364	Phil Garner	.08	.06	.03
365	Ed Ott	.06	.05	.02
366	Don Robinson	.08	.06	.03
367	Chuck Tanner	.06	.05	.02
368	Jim Rooker	.06	.05	.02
369	Dale Berra	.06	.05	.02
370	Jim Bibby	.06	.05	.02
371	Steve Nicosia	.06	.05	.02
372	Mike Easler	.08	.06	.03
373	Bill Robinson	.06	.05	.02
374	Lee Lacy	.06	.05	.02
375	John Candelaria	.10	.08	.04
376	Manny Sanguillen	.06	.05	.02
377	Rick Rhoden	.10	.08	.04
378	Grant Jackson	.06	.05	.02

		MT	NR MT	EX
379	Tim Foli	.06	.05	.02
380	*Rod Scurry*	.08	.06	.03
381	Bill Madlock	.12	.09	.05
382a	Kurt Bevacqua (photo reversed, backwards "P" on cap)	.15	.11	.06
382b	Kurt Bevacqua (correct photo)	.70	.50	.30
383	Bert Blyleven	.12	.09	.05
384	Eddie Solomon	.06	.05	.02
385	Enrique Romo	.06	.05	.02
386	John Milner	.06	.05	.02
387	Mike Hargrove	.06	.05	.02
388	Jorge Orta	.06	.05	.02
389	Toby Harrah	.08	.06	.03
390	Tom Veryzer	.06	.05	.02
391	Miguel Dilone	.06	.05	.02
392	Dan Spillner	.06	.05	.02
393	Jack Brohamer	.06	.05	.02
394	Wayne Garland	.06	.05	.02
395	Sid Monge	.06	.05	.02
396	Rick Waits	.06	.05	.02
397	*Joe Charboneau*	.10	.08	.04
398	Gary Alexander	.06	.05	.02
399	Jerry Dybzinski	.06	.05	.02
400	Mike Stanton	.06	.05	.02
401	Mike Paxton	.06	.05	.02
402	Gary Gray	.06	.05	.02
403	Rick Manning	.06	.05	.02
404	Bo Diaz	.08	.06	.03
405	Ron Hassey	.06	.05	.02
406	Ross Grimsley	.06	.05	.02
407	Victor Cruz	.06	.05	.02
408	Len Barker	.08	.06	.03
409	Bob Bailor	.06	.05	.02
410	Otto Velez	.06	.05	.02
411	Ernie Whitt	.08	.06	.03
412	Jim Clancy	.08	.06	.03
413	Barry Bonnell	.06	.05	.02
414	Dave Stieb	.60	.45	.25
415	*Damaso Garcia*	.10	.08	.04
416	John Mayberry	.08	.06	.03
417	Roy Howell	.06	.05	.02
418	*Dan Ainge*	.25	.20	.10
419a	Jesse Jefferson (Pirates on back)	.10	.08	.04
419b	Jesse Jefferson (Blue Jays on back)	.50	.40	.20
420	Joey McLaughlin	.06	.05	.02
421	*Lloyd Moseby*	1.00	.70	.02
422	Al Woods	.06	.05	.02
423	Garth Iorg	.06	.05	.02
424	Doug Ault	.06	.05	.02
425	*Ken Schrom*	.06	.05	.02
426	Mike Willis	.06	.05	.02
427	Steve Braun	.06	.05	.02
428	Bob Davis	.06	.05	.02
429	Jerry Garvin	.06	.05	.02
430	Alfredo Griffin	.08	.06	.03
431	Bob Mattick	.06	.05	.02
432	Vida Blue	.12	.09	.05
433	Jack Clark	.25	.20	.10
434	Willie McCovey	.40	.30	.15
435	Mike Ivie	.06	.05	.02
436a	Darrel Evans (Darrel on front)	.15	.11	.06
436b	Darrell Evans (Darrell on front)	.70	.50	.30
437	Terry Whitfield	.06	.05	.02
438	Rennie Stennett	.06	.05	.02
439	John Montefusco	.08	.06	.03
440	Jim Wohlford	.06	.05	.02
441	Bill North	.06	.05	.02
442	Milt May	.06	.05	.02
443	Max Venable	.06	.05	.02
444	Ed Whitson	.06	.05	.02
445	*Al Holland*	.08	.06	.03
446	Randy Moffitt	.06	.05	.02
447	Bob Knepper	.08	.06	.03
448	Gary Lavelle	.06	.05	.02
449	Greg Minton	.06	.05	.02
450	Johnnie LeMaster	.06	.05	.02
451	Larry Herndon	.08	.06	.03
452	Rich Murray	.06	.05	.02
453	Joe Pettini	.06	.05	.02
454	Allen Ripley	.06	.05	.02
455	Dennis Littlejohn	.06	.05	.02
456	Tom Griffin	.06	.05	.02
457	Alan Hargesheimer	.06	.05	.02
458	Joe Strain	.06	.05	.02
459	Steve Kemp	.08	.06	.03
460	Sparky Anderson	.10	.08	.04
461	Alan Trammell	.40	.30	.15
462	Mark Fidrych	.08	.06	.03
463	Lou Whitaker	.40	.30	.15
464	Dave Rozema	.06	.05	.02

		MT	NR MT	EX
465	Milt Wilcox	.06	.05	.02
466	Champ Summers	.06	.05	.02
467	Lance Parrish	.35	.25	.14
468	Dan Petry	.08	.06	.03
469	Pat Underwood	.06	.05	.02
470	Rick Peters	.06	.05	.02
471	Al Cowens	.06	.05	.02
472	John Wockenfuss	.06	.05	.02
473	Tom Brookens	.08	.06	.03
474	Richie Hebner	.06	.05	.02
475	Jack Morris	.30	.25	.12
476	Jim Lentine	.06	.05	.02
477	Bruce Robbins	.06	.05	.02
478	Mark Wagner	.06	.05	.02
479	Tim Corcoran	.06	.05	.02
480a	Stan Papi (Pitcher on front)	.15	.11	.06
480b	Stan Papi (Shortstop on front)	.70	.50	.30
481	*Kirk Gibson*	3.75	2.75	1.50
482	Dan Schatzeder	.06	.05	.02
483	Amos Otis	.70	.50	.30
484	Dave Winfield	.50	.40	.20
485	Rollie Fingers	1.00	.70	.40
486	Gene Richards	.06	.05	.02
487	Randy Jones	.08	.06	.03
488	Ozzie Smith	1.00	.70	.40
489	Gene Tenace	.08	.06	.03
490	Bill Fahey	.06	.05	.02
491	John Curtis	.06	.05	.02
492	Dave Cash	.06	.05	.02
493a	Tim Flannery (photo reversed, batting righty)	.15	.11	.06
493b	Tim Flannery (photo correct, batting lefty)	.70	.50	.30
494	Jerry Mumphrey	.06	.05	.02
495	Bob Shirley	.06	.05	.02
496	Steve Mura	.06	.05	.02
497	Eric Rasmussen	.06	.05	.02
498	Broderick Perkins	.06	.05	.02
499	Barry Evans	.06	.05	.02
500	Chuck Baker	.06	.05	.02
501	*Luis Salazar*	.15	.11	.06
502	Gary Lucas	.08	.06	.03
503	Mike Armstrong	.06	.05	.02
504	Jerry Turner	.06	.05	.02
505	Dennis Kinney	.06	.05	.02
506	Willy Montanez (Willie)	.06	.05	.02
507	Gorman Thomas	.10	.08	.04
508	Ben Oglivie	.08	.06	.03
509	Larry Hisle	.08	.06	.03
510	Sal Bando	.10	.08	.04
511	Robin Yount	5.00	3.75	2.00
512	Mike Caldwell	.06	.05	.02
513	Sixto Lezcano	.06	.05	.02
514a	Jerry Augustine (Billy Travers photo)	.15	.11	.06
514b	Billy Travers (correct name with photo)	.70	.50	.30
515	Paul Molitor	.20	.15	.08
516	Moose Haas	.06	.05	.02
517	Bill Castro	.06	.05	.02
518	Jim Slaton	.06	.05	.02
519	Lary Sorensen	.06	.05	.02
520	Bob McClure	.06	.05	.02
521	Charlie Moore	.06	.05	.02
522	Jim Gantner	.08	.06	.03
523	Reggie Cleveland	.06	.05	.02
524	Don Money	.06	.05	.02
525	Billy Travers	.06	.05	.02
526	Buck Martinez	.06	.05	.02
527	Dick Davis	.06	.05	.02
528	Ted Simmons	.12	.09	.05
529	Garry Templeton	.10	.08	.04
530	Ken Reitz	.06	.05	.02
531	Tony Scott	.06	.05	.02
532	Ken Oberkfell	.06	.05	.02
533	Bob Sykes	.06	.05	.02
534	Keith Smith	.06	.05	.02
535	John Littlefield	.06	.05	.02
536	Jim Kaat	.15	.11	.06
537	Bob Forsch	.08	.06	.03
538	Mike Phillips	.06	.05	.02
539	*Terry Landrum*	.10	.08	.04
540	*Leon Durham*	.20	.15	.08
541	Terry Kennedy	.08	.06	.03
542	George Hendrick	.08	.06	.03
543	Dane Iorg	.06	.05	.02
544	Mark Littell (photo actually Jeff Little)	.06	.05	.02
545	Keith Hernandez	.40	.30	.15
546	Silvio Martinez	.06	.05	.02
547a	Pete Vuckovich (photo actually Don Hood)	.15	.11	.06
547b	Don Hood (correct name with photo)	.70	.50	.30
548	Bobby Bonds	.10	.08	.04
549	Mike Ramsey	.06	.05	.02
550	Tom Herr	.10	.08	.04
551	Roy Smalley	.06	.05	.02
552	Jerry Koosman	.10	.08	.04
553	Ken Landreaux	.06	.05	.02
554	John Castino	.06	.05	.02
555	Doug Corbett	.06	.05	.02
556	Bombo Rivera	.06	.05	.02
557	Ron Jackson	.06	.05	.02
558	Butch Wynegar	.06	.05	.02
559	Hosken Powell	.06	.05	.02
560	Pete Redfern	.06	.05	.02
561	Roger Erickson	.06	.05	.02
562	Glenn Adams	.06	.05	.02
563	Rick Sofield	.06	.05	.02
564	Geoff Zahn	.06	.05	.02
565	Pete Mackanin	.06	.05	.02
566	Mike Cubbage	.06	.05	.02
567	Darrell Jackson	.06	.05	.02
568	Dave Edwards	.06	.05	.02
569	Rob Wilfong	.06	.05	.02
570	Sal Butera	.06	.05	.02
571	Jose Morales	.06	.05	.02
572	Rick Langford	.06	.05	.02
573	Mike Norris	.06	.05	.02
574	Rickey Henderson	20.00	15.00	8.00
575	Tony Armas	.10	.08	.04
576	Dave Revering	.06	.05	.02
577	Jeff Newman	.06	.05	.02
578	Bob Lacey	.06	.05	.02
579	Brian Kingman (photo actually Alan Wirth)	.06	.05	.02
580	Mitchell Page	.06	.05	.02
581	Billy Martin	.12	.09	.05
582	Rob Picciolo	.06	.05	.02
583	Mike Heath	.06	.05	.02
584	Mickey Klutts	.06	.05	.02
585	Orlando Gonzalez	.06	.05	.02
586	*Mike Davis*	.25	.20	.10
587	Wayne Gross	.06	.05	.02
588	Matt Keough	.06	.05	.02
589	Steve McCatty	.06	.05	.02
590	Dwayne Murphy	.08	.06	.03
591	Mario Guerrero	.06	.05	.02
592	Dave McKay	.06	.05	.02
593	Jim Essian	.06	.05	.02
594	Dave Heaverlo	.06	.05	.02
595	Maury Wills	.10	.08	.04
596	Juan Beniquez	.06	.05	.02
597	Rodney Craig	.06	.05	.02
598	Jim Anderson	.06	.05	.02
599	Floyd Bannister	.10	.08	.04
600	Bruce Bochte	.06	.05	.02
601	Julio Cruz	.06	.05	.02
602	Ted Cox	.06	.05	.02
603	Dan Meyer	.06	.05	.02
604	Larry Cox	.06	.05	.02
605	Bill Stein	.06	.05	.02
606	Steve Garvey	.50	.40	.20
607	Dave Roberts	.06	.05	.02
608	Leon Roberts	.06	.05	.02
609	Reggie Walton	.06	.05	.02
610	Dave Edler	.06	.05	.02
611	Larry Milbourne	.06	.05	.02
612	Kim Allen	.06	.05	.02
613	Mario Mendoza	.06	.05	.02
614	Tom Paciorek	.06	.05	.02
615	Glenn Abbott	.06	.05	.02
616	Joe Simpson	.06	.05	.02
617	Mickey Rivers	.08	.06	.03
618	Jim Kern	.06	.05	.02
619	Jim Sundberg	.08	.06	.03
620	Richie Zisk	.08	.06	.03
621	Jon Matlack	.08	.06	.03
622	Ferguson Jenkins	.20	.15	.08
623	Pat Corrales	.06	.05	.02
624	Ed Figueroa	.06	.05	.02
625	Buddy Bell	.12	.09	.05
626	Al Oliver	.15	.11	.06
627	Doc Medich	.06	.05	.02
628	Bump Wills	.06	.05	.02
629	Rusty Staub	.10	.08	.04
630	Pat Putnam	.06	.05	.02
631	John Grubb	.06	.05	.02
632	Danny Darwin	.06	.05	.02
633	Ken Clay	.06	.05	.02
634	Jim Norris	.06	.05	.02
635	John Butcher	.06	.05	.02

		MT	NR MT	EX
636	Dave Roberts	.06	.05	.02
637	Billy Sample	.06	.05	.02
638	Carl Yastrzemski	.80	.60	.30
639	Cecil Cooper	.15	.11	.06
640	Mike Schmidt	4.00	3.00	1.50
641a	Checklist 1-50 (41 Hal McRae)	.10	.08	.04
641b	Checklist 1-50 (41 Hal McRae Double Threat)	.40	.30	.15
642	Checklist 51-109	.06	.05	.02
643	Checklist 110-168	.06	.05	.02
644a	Checklist 169-220 (202 George Foster)	.10	.08	.04
644b	Checklist 169-220 (202 George Foster "Slugger")	.40	.30	.15
645a	Triple Threat (Larry Bowa, Pete Rose, Mike Schmidt) (no number on back)	1.00	.70	.40
645b	Triple Threat (Larry Bowa, Pete Rose, Mike Schmidt) (645 on back)	2.00	1.50	.80
646	Checklist 221-267	.06	.05	.02
647	Checklist 268-315	.06	.05	.02
648	Checklist 316-359	.06	.05	.02
649	Checklist 360-408	.06	.05	.02
650	Reggie Jackson	3.00	2.25	1.25
651	Checklist 409-458	.06	.05	.02
652a	Checklist 459-509 (483 Aurelio Lopez)	.10	.08	.04
652b	Checklist 459-506 (no 483)	.40	.30	.15
653	Willie Wilson	1.00	.70	.40
654a	Checklist 507-550 (514 Jerry Augustine)	.10	.08	.04
654b	Checklist 507-550 (514 Billy Travers)	.40	.30	.15
655	George Brett	2.00	1.50	.80
656	Checklist 551-593	.06	.05	.02
657	Tug McGraw	1.00	.70	.40
658	Checklist 594-637	.06	.05	.02
659a	Checklist 640-660 (last number on front is 551)	.10	.08	.04
659b	Checklist 640-660 (last number on front is 483)	.40	.30	.15
660a	Steve Carlton (date 1066 on back)	1.00	.70	.40
660b	Steve Carlton (date 1966 on back)	2.00	1.50	.80

1981 Fleer Star Stickers

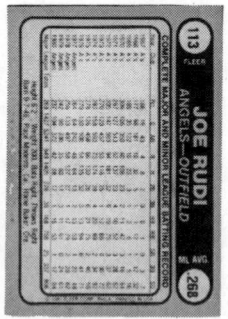

The 128-card 1981 Fleer Star Sticker set was designed for the card fronts to be peeled away from the cardboard backs. The card obverses feature color photos with blue and yellow trim. The card backs are identical in design to the regular 1981 Fleer set except for color and numbering. The set contains three unnumbered checklist cards whose fronts depict Reggie Jackson (#'s 1-42), George Brett (#'s 43-83) and Mike Schmidt (#'s 84-125). The cards, which are the standard 2-1/2" by 3-1/2", were issued in gum wax packs.

		MT	NR MT	EX
	Complete Set	50.00	37.00	20.00
	Common Player	.10	.08	.04
1	Steve Garvey	1.00	.70	.40
2	Ron LeFlore	.10	.08	.04
3	Ron Cey	.25	.20	.10
4	Dave Revering	.10	.08	.04

		MT	NR MT	EX
5	Tony Armas	.15	.11	.06
6	Mike Norris	.10	.08	.04
7	Steve Kemp	.15	.11	.06
8	Bruce Bochte	.10	.08	.04
9	Mike Schmidt	3.00	2.25	1.25
10	Scott McGregor	.10	.08	.04
11	Buddy Bell	.20	.15	.08
12	Carney Lansford	.20	.15	.08
13	Carl Yastrzemski	3.50	2.75	1.50
14	Ben Oglivie	.10	.08	.04
15	Willie Stargell	3.00	2.25	1.25
16	Cecil Cooper	.15	.11	.06
17	Gene Richards	.10	.08	.04
18	Jim Kern	.10	.08	.04
19	Jerry Koosman	.15	.11	.06
20	Larry Bowa	.20	.15	.08
21	Kent Tekulve	.15	.11	.06
22	Dan Driessen	.10	.08	.04
23	Phil Niekro	1.00	.70	.40
24	Dan Quisenberry	.30	.25	.12
25	Dave Winfield	1.00	.70	.40
26	Dave Parker	1.00	.70	.40
27	Rick Langford	.10	.08	.04
28	Amos Otis	.15	.11	.06
29	Bill Buckner	.15	.11	.06
30	Al Bumbry	.10	.08	.04
31	Bake McBride	.10	.08	.04
32	Mickey Rivers	.10	.08	.04
33	Rick Burleson	.10	.08	.04
34	Dennis Eckersley	.25	.20	.10
35	Cesar Cedeno	.20	.15	.08
36	Enos Cabell	.10	.08	.04
37	Johnny Bench	3.00	2.25	1.25
38	Robin Yount	3.00	2.25	1.25
39	Mark Belanger	.10	.08	.04
40	Rod Carew	1.00	.70	.40
41	George Foster	.40	.30	.15
42	Lee Mazzilli	.15	.11	.06
43	Triple Threat (Larry Bowa, Pete Rose, Mike Schmidt)	2.00	1.50	.80
44	J.R. Richard	.15	.11	.06
45	Lou Piniella	.30	.25	.12
46	Ken Landreaux	.10	.08	.04
47	Rollie Fingers	1.00	.70	.40
48	Joaquin Andujar	.10	.08	.04
49	Tom Seaver	3.00	2.25	1.25
50	Bobby Grich	.20	.15	.08
51	Jon Matlack	.10	.08	.04
52	Jack Clark	.25	.20	.10
53	Jim Rice	.25	.20	.10
54	Rickey Henderson	3.00	2.25	1.25
55	Roy Smalley	.10	.08	.04
56	Mike Flanagan	.15	.11	.06
57	Steve Rogers	.10	.08	.04
58	Carlton Fisk	.60	.45	.25
59	Don Sutton	1.00	.70	.40
60	Ken Griffey	.20	.15	.08
61	Burt Hooton	.10	.08	.04
62	Dusty Baker	.20	.15	.08
63	Vida Blue	.25	.20	.10
64	Al Oliver	.30	.25	.12
65	Jim Bibby	.10	.08	.04
66	Tony Perez	1.00	.70	.40
67	Davy Lopes (Davey)	.15	.11	.06
68	Bill Russell	.15	.11	.06
69	Larry Parrish	.20	.15	.08
70	Garry Maddox	.15	.11	.06
71	Phil Garner	.15	.11	.06
72	Graig Nettles	.35	.25	.14
73	Gary Carter	1.00	.70	.40
74	Pete Rose	3.00	2.25	1.25
75	Greg Luzinski	.30	.25	.12
76	Ron Guidry	.25	.20	.10
77	Gorman Thomas	.15	.11	.06
78	Jose Cruz	.20	.15	.08
79	Bob Boone	.15	.11	.06
80	Bruce Sutter	.35	.25	.14
81	Chris Chambliss	.15	.11	.06
82	Paul Molitor	.60	.45	.25
83	Tug McGraw	.25	.20	.10
84	Ferguson Jenkins	.40	.30	.15
85	Steve Carlton	1.25	.90	.50
86	Miguel Dilone	.10	.08	.04
87	Reggie Smith	.20	.15	.08
88	Rick Cerone	.10	.08	.04
89	Alan Trammell	1.00	.70	.40
90	Doug DeCinces	.20	.15	.08
91	Sparky Lyle	.15	.11	.06
92	Warren Cromartie	.10	.08	.04
93	Rick Reuschel	.25	.20	.10
94	Larry Hisle	.10	.08	.04

		MT	NR MT	EX
95	Paul Splittorff	.10	.08	.04
96	Manny Trillo	.10	.08	.04
97	Frank White	.20	.15	.08
98	Fred Lynn	.25	.20	.10
99	Bob Horner	.15	.11	.06
100	Omar Moreno	.10	.08	.04
101	Dave Concepcion	.20	.15	.08
102	Larry Gura	.10	.08	.04
103	Ken Singleton	.20	.15	.08
104	Steve Stone	.15	.11	.06
105	Richie Zisk	.10	.08	.04
106	Willie Wilson	.40	.30	.15
107	Willie Randolph	.20	.15	.08
108	Nolan Ryan	1.25	.90	.50
109	Joe Morgan	1.00	.70	.40
110	Bucky Dent	.20	.15	.08
111	Dave Kingman	.40	.30	.15
112	John Castino	.10	.08	.04
113	Joe Rudi	.20	.15	.08
114	Ed Farmer	.10	.08	.04
115	Reggie Jackson	3.00	2.25	1.25
116	George Brett	1.00	.70	.40
117	Eddie Murray	.25	.20	.10
118	Rich Gossage	.25	.20	.10
119	Dale Murphy	1.00	.70	.40
120	Ted Simmons	.15	.11	.06
121	Tommy John	.25	.20	.10
122	Don Baylor	.30	.25	.12
123	Andre Dawson	1.00	.70	.40
124	Jim Palmer	3.00	2.25	1.25
125	Garry Templeton	.20	.15	.08
——	Reggie Jackson/Checklist 1-42	3.00	2.25	1.25
——	George Brett/Checklist 43-83	3.00	2.25	1.25
——	Mike Schmidt/Checklist 84-125	3.00	2.25	1.25

1982 Fleer

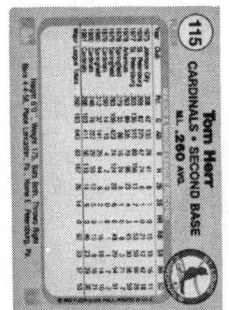

Fleer's 1982 set did not match the quality of the previous year's effort. Many of the photos in the set are blurred and have muddied backgrounds. The cards, which measure 2-1/2" by 3-1/2", feature color photos surrounded by a border frame which is color-coded by team. The card backs are blue, white, and yellow and contain the player's team logo plus the logos of Major League Baseball and the Major League Baseball Players Association. Due to a lawsuit by Topps, Fleer was forced to issue the set with team logo stickers rather than gum. The complete set price does not include the higher priced variations.

		MT	NR MT	EX
Complete Set:		45.00	33.00	18.00
Common Player:		.06	.05	.02
1	Dusty Baker	.10	.08	.04
2	Robert Castillo	.06	.05	.02
3	Ron Cey	.12	.09	.05
4	Terry Forster	.08	.06	.03
5	Steve Garvey	.50	.40	.20
6	Dave Goltz	.08	.06	.03
7	Pedro Guerrero(FC)	.60	.45	.25
8	Burt Hooton	.08	.06	.03
9	Steve Howe	.08	.06	.03
10	Jay Johnstone	.08	.06	.03
11	Ken Landreaux	.06	.05	.02
12	Davey Lopes	.10	.08	.04
13	*Mike Marshall*(FC)	.80	.60	.30

		MT	NR MT	EX
14	Bobby Mitchell	.06	.05	.02
15	Rick Monday	.10	.08	.04
16	*Tom Niedenfuer*(FC)	.20	.15	.08
17	*Ted Power*(FC)	.20	.15	.08
18	Jerry Reuss	.10	.08	.04
19	Ron Roenicke	.06	.05	.02
20	Bill Russell	.08	.06	.03
21	*Steve Sax*(FC)	3.00	2.25	1.25
22	Mike Scioscia	.08	.06	.03
23	Reggie Smith	.10	.08	.04
24	*Dave Stewart*(FC)	8.00	6.00	3.25
25	Rick Sutcliffe	.15	.11	.06
26	Derrel Thomas	.06	.05	.02
27	Fernando Valenzuela	.60	.45	.25
28	Bob Welch	.12	.09	.05
29	Steve Yeager	.06	.05	.02
30	Bobby Brown	.06	.05	.02
31	Rick Cerone	.06	.05	.02
32	Ron Davis	.06	.05	.02
33	Bucky Dent	.10	.08	.04
34	Barry Foote	.06	.05	.02
35	George Frazier	.06	.05	.02
36	Oscar Gamble	.08	.06	.03
37	Rich Gossage	.20	.15	.08
38	Ron Guidry	.25	.20	.10
39	Reggie Jackson	.60	.45	.25
40	Tommy John	.20	.15	.08
41	Rudy May	.06	.05	.02
42	Larry Milbourne	.06	.05	.02
43	Jerry Mumphrey	.06	.05	.02
44	Bobby Murcer	.10	.08	.04
45	*Gene Nelson*	.12	.09	.05
46	Graig Nettles	.15	.11	.06
47	Johnny Oates	.06	.05	.02
48	Lou Piniella	.12	.09	.05
49	Willie Randolph	.10	.08	.04
50	Rick Reuschel	.10	.08	.04
51	Dave Revering	.06	.05	.02
52	*Dave Righetti*(FC)	2.00	1.50	.80
53	Aurelio Rodriguez	.08	.06	.03
54	Bob Watson	.08	.06	.03
55	Dennis Werth	.06	.05	.02
56	Dave Winfield	.50	.40	.20
57	Johnny Bench	.60	.45	.25
58	Bruce Berenyi	.06	.05	.02
59	Larry Biittner	.06	.05	.02
60	Scott Brown	.06	.05	.02
61	Dave Collins	.08	.06	.03
62	Geoff Combe	.06	.05	.02
63	Dave Concepcion	.12	.09	.05
64	Dan Driessen	.08	.06	.03
65	Joe Edelen	.06	.05	.02
66	George Foster	.20	.15	.08
67	Ken Griffey	.12	.09	.05
68	Paul Householder	.06	.05	.02
69	Tom Hume	.06	.05	.02
70	Junior Kennedy	.06	.05	.02
71	Ray Knight	.10	.08	.04
72	Mike LaCoss	.06	.05	.02
73	Rafael Landestoy	.06	.05	.02
74	Charlie Leibrandt	.10	.08	.04
75	Sam Mejias	.06	.05	.02
76	Paul Moskau	.06	.05	.02
77	Joe Nolan	.06	.05	.02
78	Mike O'Berry	.06	.05	.02
79	Ron Oester	.06	.05	.02
80	Frank Pastore	.06	.05	.02
81	Joe Price	.06	.05	.02
82	Tom Seaver	.60	.45	.25
83	Mario Soto	.08	.06	.03
84	Mike Vail	.06	.05	.02
85	Tony Armas	.10	.08	.04
86	Shooty Babitt	.06	.05	.02
87	Dave Beard	.06	.05	.02
88	Rick Bosetti	.06	.05	.02
89	Keith Drumright	.06	.05	.02
90	Wayne Gross	.06	.05	.02
91	Mike Heath	.06	.05	.02
92	Rickey Henderson	5.00	3.75	2.00
93	Cliff Johnson	.06	.05	.02
94	Jeff Jones	.06	.05	.02
95	Matt Keough	.06	.05	.02
96	Brian Kingman	.06	.05	.02
97	Mickey Klutts	.06	.05	.02
98	Rick Langford	.06	.05	.02
99	Steve McCatty	.06	.05	.02
100	Dave McKay	.06	.05	.02
101	Dwayne Murphy	.08	.06	.03
102	Jeff Newman	.06	.05	.02
103	Mike Norris	.06	.05	.02
104	Bob Owchinko	.06	.05	.02

		MT	NR MT	EX
105	Mitchell Page	.06	.05	.02
106	Rob Picciolo	.06	.05	.02
107	Jim Spencer	.06	.05	.02
108	Fred Stanley	.06	.05	.02
109	Tom Underwood	.06	.05	.02
110	Joaquin Andujar	.08	.06	.03
111	Steve Braun	.06	.05	.02
112	Bob Forsch	.08	.06	.03
113	George Hendrick	.08	.06	.03
114	Keith Hernandez	.40	.30	.15
115	Tom Herr	.10	.08	.04
116	Dane Iorg	.06	.05	.02
117	Jim Kaat	.15	.11	.06
118	Tito Landrum	.06	.05	.02
119	Sixto Lezcano	.06	.05	.02
120	Mark Littell	.06	.05	.02
121	John Martin	.06	.05	.02
122	Silvio Martinez	.06	.05	.02
123	Ken Oberkfell	.06	.05	.02
124	Darrell Porter	.08	.06	.03
125	Mike Ramsey	.06	.05	.02
126	Orlando Sanchez	.06	.05	.02
127	Bob Shirley	.06	.05	.02
128	Lary Sorensen	.06	.05	.02
129	Bruce Sutter	.15	.11	.06
130	Bob Sykes	.06	.05	.02
131	Garry Templeton	.10	.08	.04
132	Gene Tenace	.08	.06	.03
133	Jerry Augustine	.06	.05	.02
134	Sal Bando	.08	.06	.03
135	Mark Brouhard	.06	.05	.02
136	Mike Caldwell	.06	.05	.02
137	Reggie Cleveland	.06	.05	.02
138	Cecil Cooper	.15	.11	.06
139	Jamie Easterly	.06	.05	.02
140	Marshall Edwards	.06	.05	.02
141	Rollie Fingers	.20	.15	.08
142	Jim Gantner	.08	.06	.03
143	Moose Haas	.06	.05	.02
144	Larry Hisle	.08	.06	.03
145	Roy Howell	.06	.05	.02
146	Rickey Keeton	.06	.05	.02
147	Randy Lerch	.06	.05	.02
148	Paul Molitor	.20	.15	.08
149	Don Money	.06	.05	.02
150	Charlie Moore	.06	.05	.02
151	Ben Oglivie	.08	.06	.03
152	Ted Simmons	.12	.09	.05
153	Jim Slaton	.06	.05	.02
154	Gorman Thomas	.10	.08	.04
155	Robin Yount	1.25	.90	.50
156	Pete Vukovich	.08	.06	.03
157	Benny Ayala	.06	.05	.02
158	Mark Belanger	.08	.06	.03
159	Al Bumbry	.08	.06	.03
160	Terry Crowley	.06	.05	.02
161	Rich Dauer	.06	.05	.02
162	Doug DeCinces	.10	.08	.04
163	Rick Dempsey	.08	.06	.03
164	Jim Dwyer	.06	.05	.02
165	Mike Flanagan	.10	.08	.04
166	Dave Ford	.06	.05	.02
167	Dan Graham	.06	.05	.02
168	Wayne Krenchicki	.06	.05	.02
169	John Lowenstein	.06	.05	.02
170	Dennis Martinez	.08	.06	.03
171	Tippy Martinez	.06	.05	.02
172	Scott McGregor	.08	.06	.03
173	Jose Morales	.06	.05	.02
174	Eddie Murray	.60	.45	.25
175	Jim Palmer	.40	.30	.15
176	*Cal Ripken, Jr.*(FC)	18.00	13.50	7.25
177	Gary Roenicke	.06	.05	.02
178	Lenn Sakata	.06	.05	.02
179	Ken Singleton	.10	.08	.04
180	Sammy Stewart	.06	.05	.02
181	Tim Stoddard	.06	.05	.02
182	Steve Stone	.08	.06	.03
183	Stan Bahnsen	.06	.05	.02
184	Ray Burris	.06	.05	.02
185	Gary Carter	.35	.25	.14
186	Warren Cromartie	.06	.05	.02
187	Andre Dawson	.40	.30	.15
188	*Terry Francona*(FC)	.10	.08	.04
189	Woodie Fryman	.08	.06	.03
190	Bill Gullickson	.08	.06	.03
191	Grant Jackson	.06	.05	.02
192	Wallace Johnson	.06	.05	.02
193	Charlie Lea	.06	.05	.02
194	Bill Lee	.08	.06	.03
195	Jerry Manuel	.06	.05	.02

		MT	NR MT	EX
196	Brad Mills	.06	.05	.02
197	John Milner	.06	.05	.02
198	Rowland Office	.06	.05	.02
199	David Palmer	.06	.05	.02
200	Larry Parrish	.10	.08	.04
201	Mike Phillips	.06	.05	.02
202	Tim Raines	1.50	1.25	.60
203	Bobby Ramos	.06	.05	.02
204	Jeff Reardon	.20	.15	.08
205	Steve Rogers	.08	.06	.03
206	Scott Sanderson	.06	.05	.02
207	Rodney Scott (photo actually Tim Raines)			
		.10	.08	.04
208	Elias Sosa	.06	.05	.02
209	Chris Speier	.06	.05	.02
210	*Tim Wallach*(FC)	2.50	2.00	1.00
211	Jerry White	.06	.05	.02
212	Alan Ashby	.06	.05	.02
213	Cesar Cedeno	.12	.09	.05
214	Jose Cruz	.12	.09	.05
215	Kiko Garcia	.06	.05	.02
216	Phil Garner	.08	.06	.03
217	Danny Heep	.06	.05	.02
218	Art Howe	.06	.05	.02
219	Bob Knepper	.08	.06	.03
220	Frank LaCorte	.06	.05	.02
221	Joe Niekro	.12	.09	.05
222	Joe Pittman	.06	.05	.02
223	Terry Puhl	.06	.05	.02
224	Luis Pujols	.06	.05	.02
225	Craig Reynolds	.06	.05	.02
226	J.R. Richard	.10	.08	.04
227	Dave Roberts	.06	.05	.02
228	Vern Ruhle	.06	.05	.02
229	Nolan Ryan	3.00	2.25	1.25
230	Joe Sambito	.06	.05	.02
231	Tony Scott	.06	.05	.02
232	Dave Smith	.10	.08	.04
233	Harry Spilman	.06	.05	.02
234	Don Sutton	.30	.25	.12
235	Dickie Thon	.08	.06	.03
236	Denny Walling	.06	.05	.02
237	Gary Woods	.06	.05	.02
238	*Luis Aguayo*(FC)	.10	.08	.04
239	Ramon Aviles	.06	.05	.02
240	Bob Boone	.10	.08	.04
241	Larry Bowa	.15	.11	.06
242	Warren Brusstar	.06	.05	.02
243	Steve Carlton	.50	.40	.20
244	Larry Christenson	.06	.05	.02
245	Dick Davis	.06	.05	.02
246	Greg Gross	.06	.05	.02
247	Sparky Lyle	.10	.08	.04
248	Garry Maddox	.10	.08	.04
249	Gary Matthews	.10	.08	.04
250	Bake McBride	.06	.05	.02
251	Tug McGraw	.12	.09	.05
252	Keith Moreland	.10	.08	.04
253	Dickie Noles	.06	.05	.02
254	Mike Proly	.06	.05	.02
255	Ron Reed	.06	.05	.02
256	Pete Rose	1.00	.70	.40
257	Dick Ruthven	.06	.05	.02
258	Mike Schmidt	1.00	.70	.40
259	Lonnie Smith	.08	.06	.03
260	Manny Trillo	.08	.06	.03
261	Del Unser	.06	.05	.02
262	George Vukovich	.06	.05	.02
263	Tom Brookens	.06	.05	.02
264	George Cappuzzello	.06	.05	.02
265	Marty Castillo	.06	.05	.02
266	Al Cowens	.06	.05	.02
267	Kirk Gibson	.70	.50	.30
268	Richie Hebner	.06	.05	.02
269	Ron Jackson	.06	.05	.02
270	Lynn Jones	.06	.05	.02
271	Steve Kemp	.08	.06	.03
272	*Rick Leach*(FC)	.12	.09	.05
273	Aurelio Lopez	.06	.05	.02
274	Jack Morris	.30	.25	.12
275	Kevin Saucier	.06	.05	.02
276	Lance Parrish	.35	.25	.14
277	Rick Peters	.06	.05	.02
278	Dan Petry	.08	.06	.03
279	David Rozema	.06	.05	.02
280	Stan Papi	.06	.05	.02
281	Dan Schatzeder	.06	.05	.02
282	Champ Summers	.06	.05	.02
283	Alan Trammell	.40	.30	.15
284	Lou Whitaker	.40	.30	.15
285	Milt Wilcox	.06	.05	.02

		MT	NR MT	EX			MT	NR MT	EX
286	John Wockenfuss	.06	.05	.02	377	Dave Rosello	.06	.05	.02
287	Gary Allenson	.06	.05	.02	378	Dan Spillner	.06	.05	.02
288	Tom Burgmeier	.06	.05	.02	379	Mike Stanton	.06	.05	.02
289	Bill Campbell	.06	.05	.02	380	Andre Thornton	.10	.08	.04
290	Mark Clear	.06	.05	.02	381	Tom Veryzer	.06	.05	.02
291	Steve Crawford	.06	.05	.02	382	Rick Waits	.06	.05	.02
292	Dennis Eckersley	.12	.09	.05	383	Doyle Alexander	.10	.08	.04
293	Dwight Evans	.15	.11	.06	384	Vida Blue	.12	.09	.05
294	*Rich Gedman*(FC)	.35	.25	.14	385	Fred Breining	.06	.05	.02
295	Garry Hancock	.06	.05	.02	386	Enos Cabell	.06	.05	.02
296	Glenn Hoffman	.06	.05	.02	387	Jack Clark	.25	.20	.10
297	Bruce Hurst(FC)	.30	.25	.12	388	Darrell Evans	.15	.11	.06
298	Carney Lansford	.08	.06	.03	389	Tom Griffin	.06	.05	.02
299	Rick Miller	.06	.05	.02	390	Larry Herndon	.08	.06	.03
300	Reid Nichols	.06	.05	.02	391	Al Holland	.06	.05	.02
301	*Bob Ojeda*(FC)	.50	.40	.20	392	Gary Lavelle	.06	.05	.02
302	Tony Perez	.20	.15	.08	393	Johnnie LeMaster	.06	.05	.02
303	Chuck Rainey	.06	.05	.02	394	Jerry Martin	.06	.05	.02
304	Jerry Remy	.06	.05	.02	395	Milt May	.06	.05	.02
305	Jim Rice	.40	.30	.15	396	Greg Minton	.06	.05	.02
306	Joe Rudi	.10	.08	.04	397	Joe Morgan	.50	.40	.20
307	Bob Stanley	.06	.05	.02	398	Joe Pettini	.06	.05	.02
308	Dave Stapleton	.06	.05	.02	399	Alan Ripley	.06	.05	.02
309	Frank Tanana	.10	.08	.04	400	Billy Smith	.06	.05	.02
310	Mike Torrez	.08	.06	.03	401	Rennie Stennett	.06	.05	.02
311	John Tudor(FC)	.25	.20	.10	402	Ed Whitson	.06	.05	.02
312	Carl Yastrzemski	.80	.60	.30	403	Jim Wohlford	.06	.05	.02
313	Buddy Bell	.12	.09	.05	404	Willie Aikens	.06	.05	.02
314	Steve Comer	.06	.05	.02	405	George Brett	1.00	.70	.40
315	Danny Darwin	.06	.05	.02	406	Ken Brett	.08	.06	.03
316	John Ellis	.06	.05	.02	407	Dave Chalk	.06	.05	.02
317	John Grubb	.06	.05	.02	408	Rich Gale	.06	.05	.02
318	Rick Honeycutt	.06	.05	.02	409	Cesar Geronimo	.06	.05	.02
319	Charlie Hough	.10	.08	.04	410	Larry Gura	.06	.05	.02
320	Ferguson Jenkins	.15	.11	.06	411	Clint Hurdle	.06	.05	.02
321	John Henry Johnson	.06	.05	.02	412	Mike Jones	.06	.05	.02
322	Jim Kern	.06	.05	.02	413	Dennis Leonard	.08	.06	.03
323	Jon Matlack	.08	.06	.03	414	Renie Martin	.06	.05	.02
324	Doc Medich	.06	.05	.02	415	Lee May	.08	.06	.03
325	Mario Mendoza	.06	.05	.02	416	Hal McRae	.12	.09	.05
326	Al Oliver	.15	.11	.06	417	Darryl Motley	.06	.05	.02
327	Pat Putnam	.06	.05	.02	418	Rance Mulliniks	.06	.05	.02
328	Mickey Rivers	.08	.06	.03	419	Amos Otis	.08	.06	.03
329	Leon Roberts	.06	.05	.02	420	*Ken Phelps*(FC)	.40	.30	.15
330	Billy Sample	.06	.05	.02	421	Jamie Quirk	.06	.05	.02
331	Bill Stein	.06	.05	.02	422	Dan Quisenberry	.15	.11	.06
332	Jim Sundberg	.08	.06	.03	423	Paul Splittorff	.06	.05	.02
333	Mark Wagner	.06	.05	.02	424	U.L. Washington	.06	.05	.02
334	Bump Wills	.06	.05	.02	425	John Wathan	.08	.06	.03
335	Bill Almon	.06	.05	.02	426	Frank White	.10	.08	.04
336	Harold Baines	.30	.25	.12	427	Willie Wilson	.15	.11	.06
337	Ross Baumgarten	.06	.05	.02	428	Brian Asselstine	.06	.05	.02
338	Tony Bernazard	.06	.05	.02	429	Bruce Benedict	.06	.05	.02
339	Britt Burns	.06	.05	.02	430	Tom Boggs	.06	.05	.02
340	Richard Dotson	.10	.08	.04	431	Larry Bradford	.06	.05	.02
341	Jim Essian	.06	.05	.02	432	Rick Camp	.06	.05	.02
342	Ed Farmer	.06	.05	.02	433	Chris Chambliss	.08	.06	.03
343	Carlton Fisk	.50	.40	.20	434	Gene Garber	.06	.05	.02
344	Kevin Hickey	.06	.05	.02	435	Preston Hanna	.06	.05	.02
345	Lamarr Hoyt (LaMarr)	.06	.05	.02	436	Bob Horner	.12	.09	.05
346	Lamar Johnson	.06	.05	.02	437	Glenn Hubbard	.08	.06	.03
347	Jerry Koosman	.10	.08	.04	438a	Al Hrabosky (All Hrabosky, 5'1" on back)			
348	Rusty Kuntz	.06	.05	.02			20.00	15.00	8.00
349	Dennis Lamp	.06	.05	.02	438b	Al Hrabosky (Al Hrabosky, 5'1" on back)			
350	Ron LeFlore	.08	.06	.03			1.25	.90	.50
351	Chet Lemon	.08	.06	.03	438c	Al Hrabosky (Al Hrabosky, 5'10" on back)			
352	Greg Luzinski	.15	.11	.06			.35	.25	.14
353	Bob Molinaro	.06	.05	.02	439	Rufino Linares	.06	.05	.02
354	Jim Morrison	.06	.05	.02	440	*Rick Mahler*(FC)	.25	.20	.10
355	Wayne Nordhagen	.06	.05	.02	441	Ed Miller	.06	.05	.02
356	Greg Pryor	.06	.05	.02	442	John Montefusco	.08	.06	.03
357	Mike Squires	.06	.05	.02	443	Dale Murphy	.90	.70	.35
358	Steve Trout	.06	.05	.02	444	Phil Niekro	.30	.25	.12
359	Alan Bannister	.06	.05	.02	445	Gaylord Perry	.30	.25	.12
360	Len Barker	.08	.06	.03	446	Biff Pocoroba	.06	.05	.02
361	Bert Blyleven	.12	.09	.05	447	Rafael Ramirez	.08	.06	.03
362	Joe Charboneau	.08	.06	.03	448	Jerry Royster	.06	.05	.02
363	John Denny	.06	.05	.02	449	Claudell Washington	.08	.06	.03
364	Bo Diaz	.08	.06	.03	450	Don Aase	.06	.05	.02
365	Miguel Dilone	.06	.05	.02	451	Don Baylor	.12	.09	.05
366	Jerry Dybzinski	.06	.05	.02	452	Juan Beniquez	.06	.05	.02
367	Wayne Garland	.06	.05	.02	453	Rick Burleson	.08	.06	.03
368	Mike Hargrove	.06	.05	.02	454	Bert Campaneris	.10	.08	.04
369	Toby Harrah	.08	.06	.03	455	Rod Carew	.50	.40	.20
370	Ron Hassey	.06	.05	.02	456	Bob Clark	.06	.05	.02
371	*Von Hayes*(FC)	1.25	.90	.50	457	Brian Downing	.10	.08	.04
372	Pat Kelly	.06	.05	.02	458	Dan Ford	.06	.05	.02
373	Duane Kuiper	.06	.05	.02	459	Ken Forsch	.06	.05	.02
374	Rick Manning	.06	.05	.02	460	Dave Frost	.06	.05	.02
375	Sid Monge	.06	.05	.02	461	Bobby Grich	.10	.08	.04
376	Jorge Orta	.06	.05	.02	462	Larry Harlow	.06	.05	.02

		MT	NR MT	EX
463	John Harris	.06	.05	.02
464	Andy Hassler	.06	.05	.02
465	Butch Hobson	.06	.05	.02
466	Jesse Jefferson	.06	.05	.02
467	Bruce Kison	.06	.05	.02
468	Fred Lynn	.20	.15	.08
469	Angel Moreno	.06	.05	.02
470	Ed Ott	.06	.05	.02
471	Fred Patek	.06	.05	.02
472	Steve Renko	.06	.05	.02
473	*Mike Witt*(FC)	.70	.50	.30
474	Geoff Zahn	.06	.05	.02
475	Gary Alexander	.06	.05	.02
476	Dale Berra	.06	.05	.02
477	Kurt Bevacqua	.06	.05	.02
478	Jim Bibby	.06	.05	.02
479	John Candelaria	.10	.08	.04
480	Victor Cruz	.06	.05	.02
481	Mike Easler	.08	.06	.03
482	Tim Foli	.06	.05	.02
483	Lee Lacy	.06	.05	.02
484	Vance Law(FC)	.12	.09	.05
485	Bill Madlock	.12	.09	.05
486	Willie Montanez	.06	.05	.02
487	Omar Moreno	.06	.05	.02
488	Steve Nicosia	.06	.05	.02
489	Dave Parker	.30	.25	.12
490	Tony Pena(FC)	.25	.20	.10
491	Pascual Perez(FC)	.15	.11	.06
492	*Johnny Ray*(FC)	.70	.50	.30
493	Rick Rhoden	.10	.08	.04
494	Bill Robinson	.06	.05	.02
495	Don Robinson	.08	.06	.03
496	Enrique Romo	.06	.05	.02
497	Rod Scurry	.06	.05	.02
498	Eddie Solomon	.06	.05	.02
499	Willie Stargell	.40	.30	.15
500	Kent Tekulve	.08	.06	.03
501	Jason Thompson	.06	.05	.02
502	Glenn Abbott	.06	.05	.02
503	Jim Anderson	.06	.05	.02
504	Floyd Bannister	.10	.08	.04
505	Bruce Bochte	.06	.05	.02
506	Jeff Burroughs	.08	.06	.03
507	Bryan Clark	.06	.05	.02
508	Ken Clay	.06	.05	.02
509	Julio Cruz	.06	.05	.02
510	Dick Drago	.06	.05	.02
511	Gary Gray	.06	.05	.02
512	Dan Meyer	.06	.05	.02
513	Jerry Narron	.06	.05	.02
514	Tom Paciorek	.06	.05	.02
515	Casey Parsons	.06	.05	.02
516	Lenny Randle	.06	.05	.02
517	Shane Rawley	.10	.08	.04
518	Joe Simpson	.06	.05	.02
519	Richie Zisk	.08	.06	.03
520	Neil Allen	.06	.05	.02
521	Bob Bailor	.06	.05	.02
522	Hubie Brooks(FC)	.25	.20	.10
523	Mike Cubbage	.06	.05	.02
524	Pete Falcone	.06	.05	.02
525	Doug Flynn	.06	.05	.02
526	Tom Hausman	.06	.05	.02
527	Ron Hodges	.06	.05	.02
528	Randy Jones	.08	.06	.03
529	Mike Jorgensen	.06	.05	.02
530	Dave Kingman	.15	.11	.06
531	Ed Lynch	.06	.05	.02
532	Mike Marshall	.10	.08	.04
533	Lee Mazzilli	.08	.06	.03
534	Dyar Miller	.06	.05	.02
535	Mike Scott(FC)	.60	.45	.25
536	Rusty Staub	.10	.08	.04
537	John Stearns	.06	.05	.02
538	Craig Swan	.06	.05	.02
539	Frank Taveras	.06	.05	.02
540	Alex Trevino	.06	.05	.02
541	Ellis Valentine	.06	.05	.02
542	Mookie Wilson(FC)	.15	.11	.06
543	Joel Youngblood	.06	.05	.02
544	Pat Zachry	.06	.05	.02
545	Glenn Adams	.06	.05	.02
546	Fernando Arroyo	.06	.05	.02
547	John Verhoeven	.06	.05	.02
548	Sal Butera	.06	.05	.02
549	John Castino	.06	.05	.02
550	Don Cooper	.06	.05	.02
551	Doug Corbett	.06	.05	.02
552	Dave Engle	.06	.05	.02
553	Roger Erickson	.06	.05	.02

		MT	NR MT	EX
554	Danny Goodwin	.06	.05	.02
555a	Darrell Jackson (black cap)	1.00	.70	.40
555b	Darrell Jackson (red cap with emblem)			
		.10	.08	.04
555c	Darrell Jackson (red cap, no emblem)			
		.25	.20	.10
556	Pete Mackanin	.06	.05	.02
557	Jack O'Connor	.06	.05	.02
558	Hosken Powell	.06	.05	.02
559	Pete Redfern	.06	.05	.02
560	Roy Smalley	.06	.05	.02
561	Chuck Baker	.06	.05	.02
562	Gary Ward	.08	.06	.03
563	Rob Wilfong	.06	.05	.02
564	Al Williams	.06	.05	.02
565	Butch Wynegar	.06	.05	.02
566	Randy Bass	.06	.05	.02
567	Juan Bonilla	.06	.05	.02
568	Danny Boone	.06	.05	.02
569	John Curtis	.06	.05	.02
570	Juan Eichelberger	.06	.05	.02
571	Barry Evans	.06	.05	.02
572	Tim Flannery	.06	.05	.02
573	Ruppert Jones	.06	.05	.02
574	Terry Kennedy	.08	.06	.03
575	Joe Lefebvre	.06	.05	.02
576a	*John Littlefield* (pitching lefty)	150.00	105.00	60.00
576b	John Littlefield (pitching righty)	.08	.06	.03
577	Gary Lucas	.06	.05	.02
578	Steve Mura	.06	.05	.02
579	Broderick Perkins	.06	.05	.02
580	Gene Richards	.06	.05	.02
581	Luis Salazar	.06	.05	.02
582	Ozzie Smith	.20	.15	.08
583	John Urrea	.06	.05	.02
584	Chris Welsh	.06	.05	.02
585	Rick Wise	.08	.06	.03
586	Doug Bird	.06	.05	.02
587	Tim Blackwell	.06	.05	.02
588	Bobby Bonds	.10	.08	.04
589	Bill Buckner	.12	.09	.05
590	Bill Caudill	.06	.05	.02
591	Hector Cruz	.06	.05	.02
592	*Jody Davis*(FC)	.30	.25	.12
593	Ivan DeJesus	.06	.05	.02
594	Steve Dillard	.06	.05	.02
595	Leon Durham	.08	.06	.03
596	Rawly Eastwick	.06	.05	.02
597	Steve Henderson	.06	.05	.02
598	Mike Krukow	.08	.06	.03
599	Mike Lum	.06	.05	.02
600	Randy Martz	.06	.05	.02
601	Jerry Morales	.06	.05	.02
602	Ken Reitz	.06	.05	.02
603a	*Lee Smith* (Cubs logo reversed on back)(FC)	2.00	1.50	.80
603b	*Lee Smith* (Cubs logo correct)(FC)	1.00	.70	.40
604	Dick Tidrow	.06	.05	.02
605	Jim Tracy	.06	.05	.02
606	Mike Tyson	.06	.05	.02
607	Ty Waller	.06	.05	.02
608	Danny Ainge	.12	.09	.05
609	*Jorge Bell*(FC)	7.00	5.25	2.75
610	Mark Bomback	.06	.05	.02
611	Barry Bonnell	.06	.05	.02
612	Jim Clancy	.08	.06	.03
613	Damaso Garcia	.06	.05	.02
614	Jerry Garvin	.06	.05	.02
615	Alfredo Griffin	.08	.06	.03
616	Garth Iorg	.06	.05	.02
617	Luis Leal	.06	.05	.02
618	Ken Macha	.06	.05	.02
619	John Mayberry	.08	.06	.03
620	Joey McLaughlin	.06	.05	.02
621	Lloyd Moseby	.12	.09	.05
622	Dave Stieb	.12	.09	.05
623	Jackson Todd	.06	.05	.02
624	Willie Upshaw(FC)	.15	.11	.06
625	Otto Velez	.06	.05	.02
626	Ernie Whitt	.08	.06	.03
627	Al Woods	.06	.05	.02
628	1981 All-Star Game	.08	.06	.03
629	All-Star Infielders (Bucky Dent, Frank White)	.10	.08	.04
630	Big Red Machine (Dave Concepcion, Dan Driessen, George Foster)	.15	.11	.06
631	Top N.L. Relief Pitcher (Bruce Sutter)	.15	.11	.06
632	Steve & Carlton (Steve Carlton, Carlton Fisk)	.25	.20	.10

		MT	NR MT	EX
633	3000th Game, May 25, 1981 (Carl Yastrzemski)	.35	.25	.14
634	Dynamic Duo (Johnny Bench, Tom Seaver)	.30	.25	.12
635	West Meets East (Gary Carter, Fernando Valenzuela)	.30	.25	.12
636a	N.L. Strikeout King (Fernando Valenzuela) ("...led he National League...")	1.00	.70	.40
636b	N.L. Strikeout King (Fernando Valenzuela) ("...led the National League...")	.50	.40	.20
637	1981 Home Run King (Mike Schmidt)	.40	.30	.15
638	N.L. All-Stars (Gary Carter, Dave Parker)	.25	.20	.10
639	Perfect Game! (Len Barker, Bo Diaz)	.08	.06	.03
640	Pete & Re-Pete (Pete Rose, Pete Rose, Jr.)	2.00	1.50	.80
641	Phillies' Finest (Steve Carlton, Mike Schmidt, Lonnie Smith)	.50	.40	.20
642	Red Sox Reunion (Dwight Evans, Fred Lynn)	.15	.11	.06
643	1981 Most Hits, Most Runs (Rickey Henderson)	.35	.25	.14
644	Most Saves 1981 A.L. (Rollie Fingers)	.15	.11	.06
645	Most 1981 Wins (Tom Seaver)	.25	.20	.10
646a	Yankee Powerhouse (Reggie Jackson, Dave Winfield) (comma after "outfielder" on back)	1.25	.90	.50
646b	Yankee Powerhouse (Reggie Jackson, Dave Winfield) (no comma after "oufielder")	.60	.45	.25
647	Checklist 1-56	.06	.05	.02
648	Checklist 57-109	.06	.05	.02
649	Checklist 110-156	.06	.05	.02
650	Checklist 157-211	.06	.05	.02
651	Checklist 212-262	.06	.05	.02
652	Checklist 263-312	.06	.05	.02
653	Checklist 313-358	.06	.05	.02
654	Checklist 359-403	.06	.05	.02
655	Checklist 404-449	.06	.05	.02
656	Checklist 450-501	.06	.05	.02
657	Checklist 502-544	.06	.05	.02
658	Checklist 545-585	.06	.05	.02
659	Checklist 586-627	.06	.05	.02
660	Checklist 628-646	.06	.05	.02

1983 Fleer

 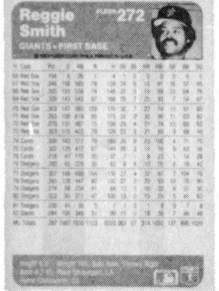

Reggie Smith
FIRST BASE

The 1983 Fleer set features color photos set inside a light brown border. The cards are the standard size of 2-1/2" by 3-1/2". A team logo is located at the card bottom and the word "Fleer" is found at the top. The card backs are designed on a vertical format and include a small black and white photo of the player along with biographical and statistical information. The reverses are done in two shades of brown on white stock. The set was issued with team logo stickers.

		MT	NR MT	EX
	Complete Set:	100.00	75.00	40.00
	Common Player:	.06	.05	.02
1	Joaquin Andujar	.08	.06	.03
2	Doug Bair	.06	.05	.02

		MT	NR MT	EX
3	Steve Braun	.06	.05	.02
4	Glenn Brummer	.06	.05	.02
5	Bob Forsch	.08	.06	.03
6	David Green	.06	.05	.02
7	George Hendrick	.08	.06	.03
8	Keith Hernandez	.40	.30	.15
9	Tom Herr	.10	.08	.04
10	Dane Iorg	.06	.05	.02
11	Jim Kaat	.15	.11	.06
12	Jeff Lahti	.06	.05	.02
13	Tito Landrum	.06	.05	.02
14	*Dave LaPoint*(FC)	.30	.25	.12
15	*Willie McGee*(FC)	3.00	2.25	1.25
16	Steve Mura	.06	.05	.02
17	Ken Oberkfell	.06	.05	.02
18	Darrell Porter	.08	.06	.03
19	Mike Ramsey	.06	.05	.02
20	Gene Roof	.06	.05	.02
21	Lonnie Smith	.08	.06	.03
22	Ozzie Smith	.20	.15	.08
23	John Stuper	.06	.05	.02
24	Bruce Sutter	.15	.11	.06
25	Gene Tenace	.08	.06	.03
26	Jerry Augustine	.06	.05	.02
27	Dwight Bernard	.06	.05	.02
28	Mark Brouhard	.06	.05	.02
29	Mike Caldwell	.06	.05	.02
30	Cecil Cooper	.15	.11	.06
31	Jamie Easterly	.06	.05	.02
32	Marshall Edwards	.06	.05	.02
33	Rollie Fingers	.20	.15	.08
34	Jim Gantner	.08	.06	.03
35	Moose Haas	.06	.05	.02
36	Roy Howell	.06	.05	.02
37	Peter Ladd	.06	.05	.02
38	Bob McClure	.06	.05	.02
39	Doc Medich	.06	.05	.02
40	Paul Molitor	.20	.15	.08
41	Don Money	.06	.05	.02
42	Charlie Moore	.06	.05	.02
43	Ben Oglivie	.08	.06	.03
44	Ed Romero	.06	.05	.02
45	Ted Simmons	.12	.09	.05
46	Jim Slaton	.06	.05	.02
47	Don Sutton	.30	.25	.12
48	Gorman Thomas	.10	.08	.04
49	Pete Vuckovich	.08	.06	.03
50	Ned Yost	.06	.05	.02
51	Robin Yount	.70	.50	.30
52	Benny Ayala	.06	.05	.02
53	Bob Bonner	.06	.05	.02
54	Al Bumbry	.08	.06	.03
55	Terry Crowley	.06	.05	.02
56	*Storm Davis*(FC)	.50	.40	.20
57	Rich Dauer	.06	.05	.02
58	Rick Dempsey	.08	.06	.03
59	Jim Dwyer	.06	.05	.02
60	Mike Flanagan	.10	.08	.04
61	Dan Ford	.06	.05	.02
62	Glenn Gulliver	.06	.05	.02
63	John Lowenstein	.06	.05	.02
64	Dennis Martinez	.08	.06	.03
65	Tippy Martinez	.06	.05	.02
66	Scott McGregor	.08	.06	.03
67	Eddie Murray	.60	.45	.25
68	Joe Nolan	.06	.05	.02
69	Jim Palmer	.50	.40	.20
70	Cal Ripken, Jr.	3.00	2.25	1.25
71	Gary Roenicke	.06	.05	.02
72	Lenn Sakata	.06	.05	.02
73	Ken Singleton	.10	.08	.04
74	Sammy Stewart	.06	.05	.02
75	Tim Stoddard	.06	.05	.02
76	Don Aase	.06	.05	.02
77	Don Baylor	.12	.09	.05
78	Juan Beniquez	.06	.05	.02
79	Bob Boone	.10	.08	.04
80	Rick Burleson	.08	.06	.03
81	Rod Carew	.50	.40	.20
82	Bobby Clark	.06	.05	.02
83	Doug Corbett	.06	.05	.02
84	John Curtis	.06	.05	.02
85	Doug DeCinces	.10	.08	.04
86	Brian Downing	.10	.08	.04
87	Joe Ferguson	.06	.05	.02
88	Tim Foli	.06	.05	.02
89	Ken Forsch	.06	.05	.02
90	Dave Goltz	.08	.06	.03
91	Bobby Grich	.10	.08	.04
92	Andy Hassler	.06	.05	.02
93	Reggie Jackson	.50	.40	.20

#	Name	MT	NR MT	EX
94	Ron Jackson	.06	.05	.02
95	Tommy John	.20	.15	.08
96	Bruce Kison	.06	.05	.02
97	Fred Lynn	.20	.15	.08
98	Ed Ott	.06	.05	.02
99	Steve Renko	.06	.05	.02
100	Luis Sanchez	.06	.05	.02
101	Rob Wilfong	.06	.05	.02
102	Mike Witt	.15	.11	.06
103	Geoff Zahn	.06	.05	.02
104	Willie Aikens	.06	.05	.02
105	Mike Armstrong	.06	.05	.02
106	Vida Blue	.12	.09	.05
107	*Bud Black*(FC)	.20	.15	.08
108	George Brett	.70	.50	.30
109	Bill Castro	.06	.05	.02
110	Onix Concepcion	.06	.05	.02
111	Dave Frost	.06	.05	.02
112	Cesar Geronimo	.06	.05	.02
113	Larry Gura	.06	.05	.02
114	Steve Hammond	.06	.05	.02
115	Don Hood	.06	.05	.02
116	Dennis Leonard	.08	.06	.03
117	Jerry Martin	.06	.05	.02
118	Lee May	.08	.06	.03
119	Hal McRae	.12	.09	.05
120	Amos Otis	.08	.06	.03
121	Greg Pryor	.06	.05	.02
122	Dan Quisenberry	.15	.11	.06
123	*Don Slaught*(FC)	.20	.15	.08
124	Paul Splittorff	.06	.05	.02
125	U.L. Washington	.06	.05	.02
126	John Wathan	.08	.06	.03
127	Frank White	.10	.08	.04
128	Willie Wilson	.15	.11	.06
129	Steve Bedrosian(FC)	.35	.25	.14
130	Bruce Benedict	.06	.05	.02
131	Tommy Boggs	.06	.05	.02
132	Brett Butler(FC)	.15	.11	.06
133	Rick Camp	.06	.05	.02
134	Chris Chambliss	.08	.06	.03
135	Ken Dayley(FC)	.10	.08	.04
136	Gene Garber	.06	.05	.02
137	Terry Harper	.06	.05	.02
138	Bob Horner	.12	.09	.05
139	Glenn Hubbard	.08	.06	.03
140	Rufino Linares	.06	.05	.02
141	Rick Mahler	.08	.06	.03
142	Dale Murphy	.90	.70	.35
143	Phil Niekro	.30	.25	.12
144	Pascual Perez	.08	.06	.03
145	Biff Pocoroba	.06	.05	.02
146	Rafael Ramirez	.06	.05	.02
147	Jerry Royster	.06	.05	.02
148	Ken Smith	.06	.05	.02
149	Bob Walk	.08	.06	.03
150	Claudell Washington	.08	.06	.03
151	Bob Watson	.08	.06	.03
152	Larry Whisenton	.06	.05	.02
153	Porfirio Altamirano	.06	.05	.02
154	Marty Bystrom	.06	.05	.02
155	Steve Carlton	.50	.40	.20
156	Larry Christenson	.06	.05	.02
157	Ivan DeJesus	.06	.05	.02
158	John Denny	.06	.05	.02
159	Bob Dernier(FC)	.10	.08	.04
160	Bo Diaz	.08	.06	.03
161	Ed Farmer	.06	.05	.02
162	Greg Gross	.06	.05	.02
163	Mike Krukow	.08	.06	.03
164	Garry Maddox	.10	.08	.04
165	Gary Matthews	.10	.08	.04
166	Tug McGraw	.12	.09	.05
167	Bob Molinaro	.06	.05	.02
168	Sid Monge	.06	.05	.02
169	Ron Reed	.06	.05	.02
170	Bill Robinson	.06	.05	.02
171	Pete Rose	1.00	.70	.40
172	Dick Ruthven	.06	.05	.02
173	Mike Schmidt	.80	.60	.30
174	Manny Trillo	.08	.06	.03
175	Ozzie Virgil(FC)	.10	.08	.04
176	George Vukovich	.06	.05	.02
177	Gary Allenson	.06	.05	.02
178	Luis Aponte	.06	.05	.02
179	*Wade Boggs*(FC)	25.00	18.00	9.00
180	Tom Burgmeier	.06	.05	.02
181	Mark Clear	.06	.05	.02
182	Dennis Eckersley	.12	.09	.05
183	Dwight Evans	.15	.11	.06
184	Rich Gedman	.08	.06	.03
185	Glenn Hoffman	.06	.05	.02
186	Bruce Hurst	.10	.08	.04
187	Carney Lansford	.08	.06	.03
188	Rick Miller	.06	.05	.02
189	Reid Nichols	.06	.05	.02
190	Bob Ojeda	.12	.09	.05
191	Tony Perez	.20	.15	.08
192	Chuck Rainey	.06	.05	.02
193	Jerry Remy	.06	.05	.02
194	Jim Rice	.40	.30	.15
195	Bob Stanley	.06	.05	.02
196	Dave Stapleton	.06	.05	.02
197	Mike Torrez	.08	.06	.03
198	John Tudor	.10	.08	.04
199	Julio Valdez	.06	.05	.02
200	Carl Yastrzemski	.70	.50	.30
201	Dusty Baker	.10	.08	.04
202	Joe Beckwith	.06	.05	.02
203	*Greg Brock*(FC)	.35	.25	.14
204	Ron Cey	.12	.09	.05
205	Terry Forster	.08	.06	.03
206	Steve Garvey	.40	.30	.15
207	Pedro Guerrero	.25	.20	.10
208	Burt Hooton	.08	.06	.03
209	Steve Howe	.08	.06	.03
210	Ken Landreaux	.06	.05	.02
211	Mike Marshall	.20	.15	.08
212	*Candy Maldonado*(FC)	1.00	.70	.40
213	Rick Monday	.10	.08	.04
214	Tom Niedenfuer	.10	.08	.04
215	Jorge Orta	.06	.05	.02
216	Jerry Reuss	.10	.08	.04
217	Ron Roenicke	.06	.05	.02
218	Vicente Romo	.06	.05	.02
219	Bill Russell	.08	.06	.03
220	Steve Sax	.30	.25	.12
221	Mike Scioscia	.08	.06	.03
222	Dave Stewart	1.00	.70	.40
223	Derrel Thomas	.06	.05	.02
224	Fernando Valenzuela	.30	.25	.12
225	Bob Welch	.12	.09	.05
226	Ricky Wright	.06	.05	.02
227	Steve Yeager	.06	.05	.02
228	Bill Almon	.06	.05	.02
229	Harold Baines	.15	.11	.06
230	Salome Barojas	.06	.05	.02
231	Tony Bernazard	.06	.05	.02
232	Britt Burns	.06	.05	.02
233	Richard Dotson	.10	.08	.04
234	Ernesto Escarrega	.06	.05	.02
235	Carlton Fisk	.50	.40	.20
236	Jerry Hairston	.06	.05	.02
237	Kevin Hickey	.06	.05	.02
238	LaMarr Hoyt	.06	.05	.02
239	Steve Kemp	.10	.08	.04
240	Jim Kern	.06	.05	.02
241	*Ron Kittle*(FC)	.70	.50	.30
242	Jerry Koosman	.10	.08	.04
243	Dennis Lamp	.06	.05	.02
244	Rudy Law	.06	.05	.02
245	Vance Law	.08	.06	.03
246	Ron LeFlore	.08	.06	.03
247	Greg Luzinski	.12	.09	.05
248	Tom Paciorek	.06	.05	.02
249	Aurelio Rodriguez	.08	.06	.03
250	Mike Squires	.06	.05	.02
251	Steve Trout	.06	.05	.02
252	Jim Barr	.06	.05	.02
253	Dave Bergman	.06	.05	.02
254	Fred Breining	.06	.05	.02
255	Bob Brenly(FC)	.08	.06	.03
256	Jack Clark	.25	.20	.10
257	Chili Davis(FC)	.20	.15	.08
258	Darrell Evans	.15	.11	.06
259	Alan Fowlkes	.06	.05	.02
260	Rich Gale	.06	.05	.02
261	Atlee Hammaker(FC)	.12	.09	.05
262	Al Holland	.06	.05	.02
263	Duane Kuiper	.06	.05	.02
264	Bill Laskey	.06	.05	.02
265	Gary Lavelle	.06	.05	.02
266	Johnnie LeMaster	.06	.05	.02
267	Renie Martin	.06	.05	.02
268	Milt May	.06	.05	.02
269	Greg Minton	.06	.05	.02
270	Joe Morgan	.40	.30	.15
271	Tom O'Malley	.06	.05	.02
272	Reggie Smith	.10	.08	.04
273	Guy Sularz	.06	.05	.02
274	Champ Summers	.06	.05	.02
275	Max Venable	.06	.05	.02

		MT	NR MT	EX			MT	NR MT	EX
276	Jim Wohlford	.06	.05	.02	364	Sixto Lezcano	.06	.05	.02
277	Ray Burris	.06	.05	.02	365	Tim Lollar	.06	.05	.02
278	Gary Carter	.35	.25	.14	366	Gary Lucas	.06	.05	.02
279	Warren Cromartie	.06	.05	.02	367	John Montefusco	.06	.05	.02
280	Andre Dawson	.35	.25	.14	368	Broderick Perkins	.06	.05	.02
281	Terry Francona	.06	.05	.02	369	Joe Pittman	.06	.05	.02
282	Doug Flynn	.06	.05	.02	370	Gene Richards	.06	.05	.02
283	Woody Fryman	.08	.06	.03	371	Luis Salazar	.06	.05	.02
284	Bill Gullickson	.06	.05	.02	372	*Eric Show*(FC)	.30	.25	.12
285	Wallace Johnson	.06	.05	.02	373	Garry Templeton	.10	.08	.04
286	Charlie Lea	.06	.05	.02	374	Chris Welsh	.06	.05	.02
287	Randy Lerch	.06	.05	.02	375	Alan Wiggins	.06	.05	.02
288	Brad Mills	.06	.05	.02	376	Rick Cerone	.06	.05	.02
289	Dan Norman	.06	.05	.02	377	Dave Collins	.08	.06	.03
290	Al Oliver	.15	.11	.06	378	Roger Erickson	.06	.05	.02
291	David Palmer	.06	.05	.02	379	George Frazier	.06	.05	.02
292	Tim Raines	.35	.25	.14	380	Oscar Gamble	.08	.06	.03
293	Jeff Reardon	.12	.09	.05	381	Goose Gossage	.20	.15	.08
294	Steve Rogers	.08	.06	.03	382	Ken Griffey	.12	.09	.05
295	Scott Sanderson	.06	.05	.02	383	Ron Guidry	.25	.20	.10
296	Dan Schatzeder	.06	.05	.02	384	Dave LaRoche	.06	.05	.02
297	Bryn Smith	.08	.06	.03	385	Rudy May	.06	.05	.02
298	Chris Speier	.06	.05	.02	386	John Mayberry	.08	.06	.03
299	Tim Wallach	.20	.15	.08	387	Lee Mazzilli	.08	.06	.03
300	Jerry White	.06	.05	.02	388	Mike Morgan(FC)	.12	.09	.05
301	Joel Youngblood	.06	.05	.02	389	Jerry Mumphrey	.06	.05	.02
302	Ross Baumgarten	.06	.05	.02	390	Bobby Murcer	.10	.08	.04
303	Dale Berra	.06	.05	.02	391	Graig Nettles	.15	.11	.06
304	John Candelaria	.10	.08	.04	392	Lou Piniella	.12	.09	.05
305	Dick Davis	.06	.05	.02	393	Willie Randolph	.10	.08	.04
306	Mike Easler	.08	.06	.03	394	Shane Rawley	.10	.08	.04
307	Richie Hebner	.06	.05	.02	395	Dave Righetti	.25	.20	.10
308	Lee Lacy	.06	.05	.02	396	Andre Robertson	.06	.05	.02
309	Bill Madlock	.12	.09	.05	397	Roy Smalley	.06	.05	.02
310	Larry McWilliams	.06	.05	.02	398	Dave Winfield	.40	.30	.15
311	John Milner	.06	.05	.02	399	Butch Wynegar	.06	.05	.02
312	Omar Moreno	.06	.05	.02	400	Chris Bando	.06	.05	.02
313	Jim Morrison	.06	.05	.02	401	Alan Bannister	.06	.05	.02
314	Steve Nicosia	.06	.05	.02	402	Len Barker	.08	.06	.03
315	Dave Parker	.30	.25	.12	403	Tom Brennan	.06	.05	.02
316	Tony Pena	.10	.08	.04	404	*Carmelo Castillo*(FC)	.12	.09	.05
317	Johnny Ray	.12	.09	.05	405	Miguel Dilone	.06	.05	.02
318	Rick Rhoden	.10	.08	.04	406	Jerry Dybzinski	.06	.05	.02
319	Don Robinson	.08	.06	.03	407	Mike Fischlin	.06	.05	.02
320	Enrique Romo	.06	.05	.02	408	Ed Glynn (photo actually Bud Anderson)			
321	Manny Sarmiento	.06	.05	.02			.06	.05	.02
322	Rod Scurry	.06	.05	.02	409	Mike Hargrove	.06	.05	.02
323	Jim Smith	.06	.05	.02	410	Toby Harrah	.08	.06	.03
324	Willie Stargell	.40	.30	.15	411	Ron Hassey	.06	.05	.02
325	Jason Thompson	.06	.05	.02	412	Von Hayes	.15	.11	.06
326	Kent Tekulve	.08	.06	.03	413	Rick Manning	.06	.05	.02
327a	Tom Brookens (narrow (1/4") brown box				414	Bake McBride	.06	.05	.02
	at bottom on back)	.30	.25	.12	415	Larry Milbourne	.06	.05	.02
327b	Tom Brookens (wide (1 1/4") brown box				416	Bill Nahorodny	.06	.05	.02
	at bottom on back)	.08	.06	.03	417	Jack Perconte	.06	.05	.02
328	Enos Cabell	.06	.05	.02	418	Lary Sorensen	.06	.05	.02
329	Kirk Gibson	.40	.30	.15	419	Dan Spillner	.06	.05	.02
330	Larry Herndon	.08	.06	.03	420	Rick Sutcliffe	.12	.09	.05
331	Mike Ivie	.06	.05	.02	421	Andre Thornton	.10	.08	.04
332	*Howard Johnson*(FC)	10.00	7.50	4.00	422	Rick Waits	.06	.05	.02
333	Lynn Jones	.06	.05	.02	423	Eddie Whitson	.06	.05	.02
334	Rick Leach	.06	.05	.02	424	Jesse Barfield(FC)	.60	.45	.25
335	Chet Lemon	.08	.06	.03	425	Barry Bonnell	.06	.05	.02
336	Jack Morris	.30	.25	.12	426	Jim Clancy	.08	.06	.03
337	Lance Parrish	.35	.25	.14	427	Damaso Garcia	.06	.05	.02
338	Larry Pashnick	.06	.05	.02	428	Jerry Garvin	.06	.05	.02
339	Dan Petry	.08	.06	.03	429	Alfredo Griffin	.08	.06	.03
340	Dave Rozema	.06	.05	.02	430	Garth Iorg	.06	.05	.02
341	Dave Rucker	.06	.05	.02	431	Roy Lee Jackson	.06	.05	.02
342	Elias Sosa	.06	.05	.02	432	Luis Leal	.06	.05	.02
343	Dave Tobik	.06	.05	.02	433	Buck Martinez	.06	.05	.02
344	Alan Trammell	.40	.30	.15	434	Joey McLaughlin	.06	.05	.02
345	Jerry Turner	.06	.05	.02	435	Lloyd Moseby	.12	.09	.05
346	Jerry Ujdur	.06	.05	.02	436	Rance Mulliniks	.06	.05	.02
347	Pat Underwood	.06	.05	.02	437	Dale Murray	.06	.05	.02
348	Lou Whitaker	.40	.30	.15	438	Wayne Nordhagen	.06	.05	.02
349	Milt Wilcox	.06	.05	.02	439	*Gene Petralli*(FC)	.15	.11	.06
350	*Glenn Wilson*(FC)	.35	.25	.14	440	Hosken Powell	.06	.05	.02
351	John Wockenfuss	.06	.05	.02	441	Dave Stieb	.12	.09	.05
352	Kurt Bevacqua	.06	.05	.02	442	Willie Upshaw	.08	.06	.03
353	Juan Bonilla	.06	.05	.02	443	Ernie Whitt	.08	.06	.03
354	Floyd Chiffer	.06	.05	.02	444	Al Woods	.06	.05	.02
355	Luis DeLeon	.06	.05	.02	445	Alan Ashby	.06	.05	.02
356	*Dave Dravecky*(FC)	.80	.60	.30	446	Jose Cruz	.12	.09	.05
357	Dave Edwards	.06	.05	.02	447	Kiko Garcia	.06	.05	.02
358	Juan Eichelberger	.06	.05	.02	448	Phil Garner	.08	.06	.03
359	Tim Flannery	.06	.05	.02	449	Danny Heep	.06	.05	.02
360	*Tony Gwynn*(FC)	16.00	12.00	6.50	450	Art Howe	.06	.05	.02
361	Ruppert Jones	.06	.05	.02	451	Bob Knepper	.08	.06	.03
362	Terry Kennedy	.08	.06	.03	452	Alan Knicely	.06	.05	.02
363	Joe Lefebvre	.06	.05	.02	453	Ray Knight	.10	.08	.04

		MT	NR MT	EX
454	Frank LaCorte	.06	.05	.02
455	Mike LaCoss	.06	.05	.02
456	Randy Moffitt	.06	.05	.02
457	Joe Niekro	.12	.09	.05
458	Terry Puhl	.06	.05	.02
459	Luis Pujols	.06	.05	.02
460	Craig Reynolds	.06	.05	.02
461	Bert Roberge	.06	.05	.02
462	Vern Ruhle	.06	.05	.02
463	Nolan Ryan	3.00	2.25	1.25
464	Joe Sambito	.06	.05	.02
465	Tony Scott	.06	.05	.02
466	Dave Smith	.08	.06	.03
467	Harry Spilman	.06	.05	.02
468	Dickie Thon	.08	.06	.03
469	Denny Walling	.06	.05	.02
470	Larry Andersen	.06	.05	.02
471	Floyd Bannister	.10	.08	.04
472	Jim Beattie	.06	.05	.02
473	Bruce Bochte	.06	.05	.02
474	Manny Castillo	.06	.05	.02
475	Bill Caudill	.06	.05	.02
476	Bryan Clark	.06	.05	.02
477	Al Cowens	.06	.05	.02
478	Julio Cruz	.06	.05	.02
479	Todd Cruz	.06	.05	.02
480	Gary Gray	.06	.05	.02
481	Dave Henderson(FC)	.20	.15	.08
482	*Mike Moore*(FC)	1.25	.90	.50
483	Gaylord Perry	.30	.25	.12
484	Dave Revering	.06	.05	.02
485	Joe Simpson	.06	.05	.02
486	Mike Stanton	.06	.05	.02
487	Rick Sweet	.06	.05	.02
488	*Ed Vande Berg*(FC)	.10	.08	.04
489	Richie Zisk	.08	.06	.03
490	Doug Bird	.06	.05	.02
491	Larry Bowa	.12	.09	.05
492	Bill Buckner	.12	.09	.05
493	Bill Campbell	.06	.05	.02
494	Jody Davis	.10	.08	.04
495	Leon Durham	.08	.06	.03
496	Steve Henderson	.06	.05	.02
497	Willie Hernandez	.08	.06	.03
498	Ferguson Jenkins	.15	.11	.06
499	Jay Johnstone	.08	.06	.03
500	Junior Kennedy	.06	.05	.02
501	Randy Martz	.06	.05	.02
502	Jerry Morales	.06	.05	.02
503	Keith Moreland	.08	.06	.03
504	Dickie Noles	.06	.05	.02
505	Mike Proly	.06	.05	.02
506	Allen Ripley	.06	.05	.02
507	*Ryne Sandberg*(FC)	30.00	22.00	12.00
508	Lee Smith	.15	.11	.06
509	Pat Tabler(FC)	.15	.11	.06
510	Dick Tidrow	.06	.05	.02
511	Bump Wills	.06	.05	.02
512	Gary Woods	.06	.05	.02
513	Tony Armas	.10	.08	.04
514	Dave Beard	.06	.05	.02
515	Jeff Burroughs	.08	.06	.03
516	John D'Acquisto	.06	.05	.02
517	Wayne Gross	.06	.05	.02
518	Mike Heath	.06	.05	.02
519	Rickey Henderson	3.00	2.25	1.25
520	Cliff Johnson	.06	.05	.02
521	Matt Keough	.06	.05	.02
522	Brian Kingman	.06	.05	.02
523	Rick Langford	.06	.05	.02
524	Davey Lopes	.10	.08	.04
525	Steve McCatty	.06	.05	.02
526	Dave McKay	.06	.05	.02
527	Dan Meyer	.06	.05	.02
528	Dwayne Murphy	.08	.06	.03
529	Jeff Newman	.06	.05	.02
530	Mike Norris	.06	.05	.02
531	Bob Owchinko	.06	.05	.02
532	Joe Rudi	.10	.08	.04
533	Jimmy Sexton	.06	.05	.02
534	Fred Stanley	.06	.05	.02
535	Tom Underwood	.06	.05	.02
536	Neil Allen	.06	.05	.02
537	Wally Backman	.08	.06	.03
538	Bob Bailor	.06	.05	.02
539	Hubie Brooks	.12	.09	.05
540	Carlos Diaz	.06	.05	.02
541	Pete Falcone	.06	.05	.02
542	George Foster	.15	.11	.06
543	Ron Gardenhire	.06	.05	.02
544	Brian Giles	.06	.05	.02

		MT	NR MT	EX
545	Ron Hodges	.06	.05	.02
546	Randy Jones	.08	.06	.03
547	Mike Jorgensen	.06	.05	.02
548	Dave Kingman	.15	.11	.06
549	Ed Lynch	.06	.05	.02
550	Jesse Orosco(FC)	.15	.11	.06
551	Rick Ownbey	.06	.05	.02
552	*Charlie Puleo*(FC)	.12	.09	.05
553	Gary Rajsich	.06	.05	.02
554	Mike Scott	.15	.11	.06
555	Rusty Staub	.10	.08	.04
556	John Stearns	.06	.05	.02
557	Craig Swan	.06	.05	.02
558	Ellis Valentine	.06	.05	.02
559	Tom Veryzer	.06	.05	.02
560	Mookie Wilson	.10	.08	.04
561	Pat Zachry	.06	.05	.02
562	Buddy Bell	.12	.09	.05
563	John Butcher	.06	.05	.02
564	Steve Comer	.06	.05	.02
565	Danny Darwin	.06	.05	.02
566	Bucky Dent	.10	.08	.04
567	John Grubb	.06	.05	.02
568	Rick Honeycutt	.06	.05	.02
569	Dave Hostetler	.06	.05	.02
570	Charlie Hough	.10	.08	.04
571	Lamar Johnson	.06	.05	.02
572	Jon Matlack	.08	.06	.03
573	Paul Mirabella	.06	.05	.02
574	Larry Parrish	.10	.08	.04
575	Mike Richardt	.06	.05	.02
576	Mickey Rivers	.08	.06	.03
577	Billy Sample	.06	.05	.02
578	*Dave Schmidt*(FC)	.10	.08	.04
579	Bill Stein	.06	.05	.02
580	Jim Sundberg	.08	.06	.03
581	Frank Tanana	.10	.08	.04
582	Mark Wagner	.06	.05	.02
583	George Wright	.06	.05	.02
584	Johnny Bench	.40	.30	.15
585	Bruce Berenyi	.06	.05	.02
586	Larry Biittner	.06	.05	.02
587	Cesar Cedeno	.12	.09	.05
588	Dave Concepcion	.12	.09	.05
589	Dan Driessen	.08	.06	.03
590	Greg Harris(FC)	.08	.06	.03
591	Ben Hayes	.06	.05	.02
592	Paul Householder	.06	.05	.02
593	Tom Hume	.06	.05	.02
594	Wayne Krenchicki	.06	.05	.02
595	Rafael Landestoy	.06	.05	.02
596	Charlie Leibrandt	.08	.06	.03
597	*Eddie Milner*(FC)	.10	.08	.04
598	Ron Oester	.06	.05	.02
599	Frank Pastore	.06	.05	.02
600	Joe Price	.06	.05	.02
601	Tom Seaver	.50	.40	.20
602	Bob Shirley	.06	.05	.02
603	Mario Soto	.08	.06	.03
604	Alex Trevino	.06	.05	.02
605	Mike Vail	.06	.05	.02
606	Duane Walker	.06	.05	.02
607	Tom Brunansky(FC)	.25	.20	.10
608	Bobby Castillo	.06	.05	.02
609	John Castino	.06	.05	.02
610	Ron Davis	.06	.05	.02
611	Lenny Faedo	.06	.05	.02
612	Terry Felton	.06	.05	.02
613	*Gary Gaetti*(FC)	4.00	3.00	1.50
614	Mickey Hatcher	.08	.06	.03
615	Brad Havens	.06	.05	.02
616	Kent Hrbek(FC)	1.50	1.25	.60
617	Randy Johnson	.06	.05	.02
618	Tim Laudner(FC)	.12	.09	.05
619	Jeff Little	.06	.05	.02
620	Bob Mitchell	.06	.05	.02
621	Jack O'Connor	.06	.05	.02
622	John Pacella	.06	.05	.02
623	Pete Redfern	.06	.05	.02
624	Jesus Vega	.06	.05	.02
625	*Frank Viola*(FC)	7.00	5.25	2.75
626	Ron Washington	.06	.05	.02
627	Gary Ward	.08	.06	.03
628	Al Williams	.06	.05	.02
629	Red Sox All-Stars (Mark Clear, Dennis Eckersley, Carl Yastrzemski)	.25	.20	.10
630	300 Career Wins (Terry Bulling, Gaylord Perry)	.15	.11	.06
631	Pride of Venezuela (Dave Concepcion, Manny Trillo)	.10	.08	.04
632	All-Star Infielders (Buddy Bell, Robin Yount)	.15	.11	.06

		MT	NR MT	EX
633	Mr. Vet & Mr. Rookie (Kent Hrbek, Dave Winfield)	.25	.20	.10
634	Fountain of Youth (Pete Rose, Willie Stargell)	.40	.30	.15
635	Big Chiefs (Toby Harrah, Andre Thornton)	.08	.06	.03
636	"Smith Bros." (Lonnie Smith, Ozzie Smith)	.10	.08	.04
637	Base Stealers' Threat (Gary Carter, Bo Diaz)	.15	.11	.06
638	All-Star Catchers (Gary Carter, Carlton Fisk)	.20	.15	.08
639	The Silver Shoe (Rickey Henderson)	.30	.25	.12
640	Home Run Threats (Reggie Jackson, Ben Oglivie)	.25	.20	.10
641	Two Teams - Same Day (Joel Youngblood)	.08	.06	.03
642	Last Perfect Game (Len Barker, Ron Hassey)	.08	.06	.03
643	Blue (Vida Blue)	.10	.08	.04
644	Black & (Bud Black)	.10	.08	.04
645	Power (Reggie Jackson)	.30	.25	.12
646	Speed & (Rickey Henderson)	.30	.25	.12
647	Checklist 1-51	.06	.05	.02
648	Checklist 52-103	.06	.05	.02
649	Checklist 104-152	.06	.05	.02
650	Checklist 153-200	.06	.05	.02
651	Checklist 201-251	.06	.05	.02
652	Checklist 252-301	.06	.05	.02
653	Checklist 302-351	.06	.05	.02
654	Checklist 352-399	.06	.05	.02
655	Checklist 400-444	.06	.05	.02
656	Checklist 445-489	.06	.05	.02
657	Checklist 490-535	.06	.05	.02
658	Checklist 536-583	.06	.05	.02
659	Checklist 584-628	.06	.05	.02
660	Checklist 629-646	.06	.05	.02

1984 Fleer

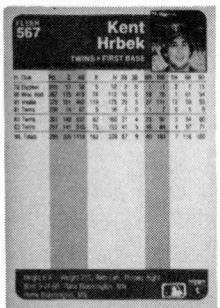

The 1984 Fleer set contained 660 cards for the fourth consecutive year. The cards, which measure 2-1/2" by 3-1/2", feature a color photo surrounded by four white borders and two blue stripes. The top stripe contains the word "Fleer" with the lower carrying the player's name. The card backs contain a small black and white photo of the player and are done in blue ink on white stock. The set was issued with team logo stickers.

		MT	NR MT	EX
Complete Set:		175.00	130.00	75.00
Common Player:		.08	.06	.03
1	Mike Boddicker(FC)	.20	.15	.08
2	Al Bumbry	.10	.08	.04
3	Todd Cruz	.08	.06	.03
4	Rich Dauer	.08	.06	.03
5	Storm Davis	.12	.09	.05
6	Rick Dempsey	.10	.08	.04
7	Jim Dwyer	.08	.06	.03
8	Mike Flanagan	.12	.09	.05
9	Dan Ford	.08	.06	.03
10	John Lowenstein	.08	.06	.03
11	Dennis Martinez	.10	.08	.04
12	Tippy Martinez	.08	.06	.03
13	Scott McGregor	.10	.08	.04

		MT	NR MT	EX
14	Eddie Murray	.60	.45	.25
15	Joe Nolan	.08	.06	.03
16	Jim Palmer	.40	.30	.15
17	Cal Ripken, Jr.	3.00	2.25	1.25
18	Gary Roenicke	.08	.06	.03
19	Lenn Sakata	.08	.06	.03
20	*John Shelby*(FC)	.25	.20	.10
21	Ken Singleton	.12	.09	.05
22	Sammy Stewart	.08	.06	.03
23	Tim Stoddard	.08	.06	.03
24	Marty Bystrom	.08	.06	.03
25	Steve Carlton	.70	.50	.30
26	Ivan DeJesus	.08	.06	.03
27	John Denny	.08	.06	.03
28	Bob Dernier	.08	.06	.03
29	Bo Diaz	.10	.08	.04
30	Kiko Garcia	.08	.06	.03
31	Greg Gross	.08	.06	.03
32	*Kevin Gross*(FC)	.35	.25	.14
33	Von Hayes	.15	.11	.06
34	Willie Hernandez	.12	.09	.05
35	Al Holland	.08	.06	.03
36	*Charles Hudson*(FC)	.20	.15	.08
37	Joe Lefebvre	.08	.06	.03
38	Sixto Lezcano	.08	.06	.03
39	Garry Maddox	.10	.08	.04
40	Gary Matthews	.12	.09	.05
41	Len Matuszek	.08	.06	.03
42	Tug McGraw	.12	.09	.05
43	Joe Morgan	.40	.30	.15
44	Tony Perez	.20	.15	.08
45	Ron Reed	.08	.06	.03
46	Pete Rose	1.00	.70	.40
47	*Juan Samuel*(FC)	3.50	2.75	1.50
48	Mike Schmidt	5.00	3.75	2.00
49	Ozzie Virgil	.08	.06	.03
50	*Juan Agosto*(FC)	.15	.11	.06
51	Harold Baines	.25	.20	.10
52	Floyd Bannister	.12	.09	.05
53	Salome Barojas	.08	.06	.03
54	Britt Burns	.08	.06	.03
55	Julio Cruz	.08	.06	.03
56	Richard Dotson	.12	.09	.05
57	Jerry Dybzinski	.08	.06	.03
58	Carlton Fisk	.30	.25	.12
59	Scott Fletcher(FC)	.15	.11	.06
60	Jerry Hairston	.08	.06	.03
61	Kevin Hickey	.08	.06	.03
62	Marc Hill	.08	.06	.03
63	LaMarr Hoyt	.08	.06	.03
64	Ron Kittle	.15	.11	.06
65	Jerry Koosman	.12	.09	.05
66	Dennis Lamp	.08	.06	.03
67	Rudy Law	.08	.06	.03
68	Vance Law	.10	.08	.04
69	Greg Luzinski	.12	.09	.05
70	Tom Paciorek	.08	.06	.03
71	Mike Squires	.08	.06	.03
72	Dick Tidrow	.08	.06	.03
73	*Greg Walker*(FC)	.45	.35	.20
74	Glenn Abbott	.08	.06	.03
75	Howard Bailey	.08	.06	.03
76	Doug Bair	.08	.06	.03
77	Juan Berenguer	.08	.06	.03
78	Tom Brookens	.08	.06	.03
79	Enos Cabell	.08	.06	.03
80	Kirk Gibson	.40	.30	.15
81	John Grubb	.08	.06	.03
82	Larry Herndon	.10	.08	.04
83	Wayne Krenchicki	.08	.06	.03
84	Rick Leach	.08	.06	.03
85	Chet Lemon	.10	.08	.04
86	Aurelio Lopez	.08	.06	.03
87	Jack Morris	.30	.25	.12
88	Lance Parrish	.35	.25	.14
89	Dan Petry	.10	.08	.04
90	Dave Rozema	.08	.06	.03
91	Alan Trammell	.40	.30	.15
92	Lou Whitaker	.40	.30	.15
93	Milt Wilcox	.08	.06	.03
94	Glenn Wilson	.10	.08	.04
95	John Wockenfuss	.08	.06	.03
96	Dusty Baker	.12	.09	.05
97	Joe Beckwith	.08	.06	.03
98	Greg Brock	.12	.09	.05
99	Jack Fimple	.08	.06	.03
100	Pedro Guerrero	.35	.25	.14
101	Rick Honeycutt	.08	.06	.03
102	Burt Hooton	.10	.08	.04
103	Steve Howe	.12	.09	.05
104	Ken Landreaux	.08	.06	.03
105	Mike Marshall	.15	.11	.06

		MT	NR MT	EX
106	Rick Monday	.10	.08	.04
107	Jose Morales	.08	.06	.03
108	Tom Niedenfuer	.10	.08	.04
109	*Alejandro Pena*(FC)	.30	.25	.12
110	Jerry Reuss	.12	.09	.05
111	Bill Russell	.10	.08	.04
112	Steve Sax	.20	.15	.08
113	Mike Scioscia	.10	.08	.04
114	Derrel Thomas	.08	.06	.03
115	Fernando Valenzuela	.40	.30	.15
116	Bob Welch	.15	.11	.06
117	Steve Yeager	.08	.06	.03
118	Pat Zachry	.08	.06	.03
119	Don Baylor	.15	.11	.06
120	Bert Campaneris	.12	.09	.05
121	Rick Cerone	.08	.06	.03
122	*Ray Fontenot*(FC)	.10	.08	.04
123	George Frazier	.08	.06	.03
124	Oscar Gamble	.10	.08	.04
125	Goose Gossage	.25	.20	.10
126	Ken Griffey	.12	.09	.05
127	Ron Guidry	.30	.25	.12
128	Jay Howell(FC)	.15	.11	.06
129	Steve Kemp	.10	.08	.04
130	Matt Keough	.08	.06	.03
131	*Don Mattingly*(FC)	50.00	37.50	20.00
132	John Montefusco	.08	.06	.03
133	Omar Moreno	.08	.06	.03
134	Dale Murray	.08	.06	.03
135	Graig Nettles	.20	.15	.08
136	Lou Piniella	.15	.11	.06
137	Willie Randolph	.12	.09	.05
138	Shane Rawley	.12	.09	.05
139	Dave Righetti	.25	.20	.10
140	Andre Robertson	.08	.06	.03
141	Bob Shirley	.08	.06	.03
142	Roy Smalley	.08	.06	.03
143	Dave Winfield	.40	.30	.15
144	Butch Wynegar	.08	.06	.03
145	*Jim Acker*(FC)	.12	.09	.05
146	Doyle Alexander	.12	.09	.05
147	Jesse Barfield	.25	.20	.10
148	Jorge Bell	1.00	.70	.40
149	Barry Bonnell	.08	.06	.03
150	Jim Clancy	.10	.08	.04
151	Dave Collins	.10	.08	.04
152	*Tony Fernandez*(FC)	6.00	4.50	2.50
153	Damaso Garcia	.08	.06	.03
154	Dave Geisel	.08	.06	.03
155	Jim Gott(FC)	.10	.08	.04
156	Alfredo Griffin	.10	.08	.04
157	Garth Iorg	.08	.06	.03
158	Roy Lee Jackson	.08	.06	.03
159	Cliff Johnson	.08	.06	.03
160	Luis Leal	.08	.06	.03
161	Buck Martinez	.08	.06	.03
162	Joey McLaughlin	.08	.06	.03
163	Randy Moffitt	.08	.06	.03
164	Lloyd Moseby	.12	.09	.05
165	Rance Mulliniks	.08	.06	.03
166	Jorge Orta	.08	.06	.03
167	Dave Stieb	.15	.11	.06
168	Willie Upshaw	.10	.08	.04
169	Ernie Whitt	.10	.08	.04
170	Len Barker	.10	.08	.04
171	Steve Bedrosian	.12	.09	.05
172	Bruce Benedict	.08	.06	.03
173	Brett Butler	.10	.08	.04
174	Rick Camp	.08	.06	.03
175	Chris Chambliss	.10	.08	.04
176	Ken Dayley	.08	.06	.03
177	Pete Falcone	.08	.06	.03
178	Terry Forster	.10	.08	.04
179	Gene Garber	.08	.06	.03
180	Terry Harper	.08	.06	.03
181	Bob Horner	.12	.09	.05
182	Glenn Hubbard	.10	.08	.04
183	Randy Johnson	.08	.06	.03
184	*Craig McMurtry*(FC)	.12	.09	.05
185	Donnie Moore(FC)	.10	.08	.04
186	Dale Murphy	1.00	.70	.40
187	Phil Niekro	.30	.25	.12
188	Pascual Perez	.10	.08	.04
189	Biff Pocoroba	.08	.06	.03
190	Rafael Ramirez	.08	.06	.03
191	Jerry Royster	.08	.06	.03
192	Claudell Washington	.10	.08	.04
193	Bob Watson	.10	.08	.04
194	Jerry Augustine	.08	.06	.03
195	Mark Brouhard	.08	.06	.03
196	Mike Caldwell	.08	.06	.03

		MT	NR MT	EX
197	*Tom Candiotti*(FC)	.25	.20	.10
198	Cecil Cooper	.15	.11	.06
199	Rollie Fingers	.25	.20	.10
200	Jim Gantner	.10	.08	.04
201	Bob Gibson	.08	.06	.03
202	Moose Haas	.08	.06	.03
203	Roy Howell	.08	.06	.03
204	Pete Ladd	.08	.06	.03
205	Rick Manning	.08	.06	.03
206	Bob McClure	.08	.06	.03
207	Paul Molitor	.20	.15	.08
208	Don Money	.08	.06	.03
209	Charlie Moore	.08	.06	.03
210	Ben Oglivie	.10	.08	.04
211	Chuck Porter	.08	.06	.03
212	Ed Romero	.08	.06	.03
213	Ted Simmons	.15	.11	.06
214	Jim Slaton	.08	.06	.03
215	Don Sutton	.30	.25	.12
216	Tom Tellmann	.08	.06	.03
217	Pete Vuckovich	.10	.08	.04
218	Ned Yost	.08	.06	.03
219	Robin Yount	1.25	.90	.50
220	Alan Ashby	.08	.06	.03
221	Kevin Bass(FC)	.20	.15	.08
222	Jose Cruz	.12	.09	.05
223	*Bill Dawley*(FC)	.10	.08	.04
224	Frank DiPino	.08	.06	.03
225	*Bill Doran*(FC)	1.00	.70	.50
226	Phil Garner	.10	.08	.04
227	Art Howe	.08	.06	.03
228	Bob Knepper	.10	.08	.04
229	Ray Knight	.12	.09	.05
230	Frank LaCorte	.08	.06	.03
231	Mike LaCoss	.08	.06	.03
232	Mike Madden	.08	.06	.03
233	Jerry Mumphrey	.08	.06	.03
235	Terry Puhl	.08	.06	.03
236	Luis Pujols	.08	.06	.03
237	Craig Reynolds	.08	.06	.03
238	Vern Ruhle	.08	.06	.03
239	Nolan Ryan	5.00	3.75	2.00
240	Mike Scott	.20	.15	.08
241	Tony Scott	.08	.06	.03
242	Dave Smith	.10	.08	.04
243	Dickie Thon	.10	.08	.04
244	Denny Walling	.08	.06	.03
245	Dale Berra	.08	.06	.03
246	Jim Bibby	.08	.06	.03
247	John Candelaria	.12	.09	.05
248	*Jose DeLeon*(FC)	.50	.40	.20
249	Mike Easler	.10	.08	.04
250	Cecilio Guante(FC)	.10	.08	.04
251	Richie Hebner	.08	.06	.03
252	Lee Lacy	.08	.06	.03
253	Bill Madlock	.12	.09	.05
254	Milt May	.08	.06	.03
255	Lee Mazzilli	.10	.08	.04
256	Larry McWilliams	.08	.06	.03
257	Jim Morrison	.08	.06	.03
258	Dave Parker	.30	.25	.12
259	Tony Pena	.12	.09	.05
260	Johnny Ray	.12	.09	.05
261	Rick Rhoden	.12	.09	.05
262	Don Robinson	.10	.08	.04
263	Manny Sarmiento	.08	.06	.03
264	Rod Scurry	.08	.06	.03
265	Kent Tekulve	.10	.08	.04
266	Gene Tenace	.10	.08	.04
267	Jason Thompson	.08	.06	.03
268	*Lee Tunnell*(FC)	.10	.08	.04
269	*Marvell Wynne*(FC)	.20	.15	.08
270	Ray Burris	.08	.06	.03
271	Gary Carter	.40	.30	.15
272	Warren Cromartie	.08	.06	.03
273	Andre Dawson	.35	.25	.14
274	Doug Flynn	.08	.06	.03
275	Terry Francona	.08	.06	.03
276	Bill Gullickson	.08	.06	.03
277	Bob James	.08	.06	.03
278	Charlie Lea	.08	.06	.03
279	Bryan Little	.08	.06	.03
280	Al Oliver	.20	.15	.08
281	Tim Raines	.40	.30	.15
282	Bobby Ramos	.08	.06	.03
283	Jeff Reardon	.15	.11	.06
284	Steve Rogers	.10	.08	.04
285	Scott Sanderson	.08	.06	.03
286	Dan Schatzeder	.08	.06	.03
287	Bryn Smith	.08	.06	.03
288	Chris Speier	.08	.06	.03

#	Player	MT	NR MT	EX
289	Manny Trillo	.10	.08	.04
290	Mike Vail	.08	.06	.03
291	Tim Wallach	.15	.11	.06
292	Chris Welsh	.08	.06	.03
293	Jim Wohlford	.08	.06	.03
294	Kurt Bevacqua	.08	.06	.03
295	Juan Bonilla	.08	.06	.03
296	Bobby Brown	.08	.06	.03
297	Luis DeLeon	.08	.06	.03
298	Dave Dravecky	.10	.08	.04
299	Tim Flannery	.08	.06	.03
300	Steve Garvey	.50	.40	.20
301	Tony Gwynn	2.00	1.50	.80
302	Andy Hawkins(FC)	.40	.30	.15
303	Ruppert Jones	.08	.06	.03
304	Terry Kennedy	.10	.08	.04
305	Tim Lollar	.08	.06	.03
306	Gary Lucas	.08	.06	.03
307	Kevin McReynolds(FC)	7.00	5.25	2.75
308	Sid Monge	.08	.06	.03
309	Mario Ramirez	.08	.06	.03
310	Gene Richards	.08	.06	.03
311	Luis Salazar	.08	.06	.03
312	Eric Show	.12	.09	.05
313	Elias Sosa	.08	.06	.03
314	Garry Templeton	.12	.09	.05
315	Mark Thurmond(FC)	.10	.08	.04
316	Ed Whitson	.08	.06	.03
317	Alan Wiggins	.08	.06	.03
318	Neil Allen	.08	.06	.03
319	Joaquin Andujar	.10	.08	.04
320	Steve Braun	.08	.06	.03
321	Glenn Brummer	.08	.06	.03
322	Bob Forsch	.10	.08	.04
323	David Green	.08	.06	.03
324	George Hendrick	.10	.08	.04
325	Tom Herr	.12	.09	.05
326	Dane Iorg	.08	.06	.03
327	Jeff Lahti	.08	.06	.03
328	Dave LaPoint	.10	.08	.04
329	Willie McGee	.35	.25	.14
330	Ken Oberkfell	.08	.06	.03
331	Darrell Porter	.10	.08	.04
332	Jamie Quirk	.08	.06	.03
333	Mike Ramsey	.08	.06	.03
334	Floyd Rayford	.08	.06	.03
335	Lonnie Smith	.10	.08	.04
336	Ozzie Smith	.20	.15	.08
337	John Stuper	.08	.06	.03
338	Bruce Sutter	.20	.15	.08
339	Andy Van Slyke(FC)	3.00	2.25	1.25
340	Dave Von Ohlen	.08	.06	.03
341	Willie Aikens	.08	.06	.03
342	Mike Armstrong	.08	.06	.03
343	Bud Black	.10	.08	.04
344	George Brett	.70	.50	.30
345	Onix Concepcion	.08	.06	.03
346	Keith Creel	.08	.06	.03
347	Larry Gura	.08	.06	.03
348	Don Hood	.08	.06	.03
349	Dennis Leonard	.10	.08	.04
350	Hal McRae	.12	.09	.05
351	Amos Otis	.12	.09	.05
352	Gaylord Perry	.30	.25	.12
353	Greg Pryor	.08	.06	.03
354	Dan Quisenberry	.12	.09	.05
355	Steve Renko	.08	.06	.03
356	Leon Roberts	.08	.06	.03
357	Pat Sheridan(FC)	.15	.11	.06
358	Joe Simpson	.08	.06	.03
359	Don Slaught	.08	.06	.03
360	Paul Splittorff	.08	.06	.03
361	U.L. Washington	.08	.06	.03
362	John Wathan	.10	.08	.04
363	Frank White	.12	.09	.05
364	Willie Wilson	.15	.11	.06
365	Jim Barr	.08	.06	.03
366	Dave Bergman	.08	.06	.03
367	Fred Breining	.08	.06	.03
368	Bob Brenly	.08	.06	.03
369	Jack Clark	.25	.20	.10
370	Chili Davis	.12	.09	.05
371	Mark Davis(FC)	.20	.15	.08
372	Darrell Evans	.15	.11	.06
373	Atlee Hammaker	.08	.06	.03
374	Mike Krukow	.10	.08	.04
375	Duane Kuiper	.08	.06	.03
376	Bill Laskey	.08	.06	.03
377	Gary Lavelle	.08	.06	.03
378	Johnnie LeMaster	.08	.06	.03
379	Jeff Leonard	.12	.09	.05
380	Randy Lerch	.08	.06	.03
381	Renie Martin	.08	.06	.03
382	Andy McGaffigan	.08	.06	.03
383	Greg Minton	.08	.06	.03
384	Tom O'Malley	.08	.06	.03
385	Max Venable	.08	.06	.03
386	Brad Wellman	.08	.06	.03
387	Joel Youngblood	.08	.06	.03
388	Gary Allenson	.08	.06	.03
389	Luis Aponte	.08	.06	.03
390	Tony Armas	.12	.09	.05
391	Doug Bird	.08	.06	.03
392	Wade Boggs	7.00	5.25	2.75
393	Dennis Boyd(FC)	.35	.25	.14
394	Mike Brown	.08	.06	.03
395	Mark Clear	.08	.06	.03
396	Dennis Eckersley	.15	.11	.06
397	Dwight Evans	.20	.15	.08
398	Rich Gedman	.10	.08	.04
399	Glenn Hoffman	.08	.06	.03
400	Bruce Hurst	.15	.11	.06
401	John Henry Johnson	.08	.06	.03
402	Ed Jurak	.08	.06	.03
403	Rick Miller	.08	.06	.03
404	Jeff Newman	.08	.06	.03
405	Reid Nichols	.08	.06	.03
406	Bob Ojeda	.12	.09	.05
407	Jerry Remy	.08	.06	.03
408	Jim Rice	.40	.30	.15
409	Bob Stanley	.08	.06	.03
410	Dave Stapleton	.08	.06	.03
411	John Tudor	.12	.09	.05
412	Carl Yastrzemski	.80	.60	.30
413	Buddy Bell	.12	.09	.05
414	Larry Biittner	.08	.06	.03
415	John Butcher	.08	.06	.03
416	Danny Darwin	.08	.06	.03
417	Bucky Dent	.12	.09	.05
418	Dave Hostetler	.08	.06	.03
419	Charlie Hough	.12	.09	.05
420	Bobby Johnson	.08	.06	.03
421	Odell Jones	.08	.06	.03
422	Jon Matlack	.10	.08	.04
423	Pete O'Brien(FC)	.80	.60	.30
424	Larry Parrish	.12	.09	.05
425	Mickey Rivers	.10	.08	.04
426	Billy Sample	.08	.06	.03
427	Dave Schmidt	.08	.06	.03
428	Mike Smithson(FC)	.15	.11	.06
429	Bill Stein	.08	.06	.03
430	Dave Stewart	.15	.11	.06
431	Jim Sundberg	.10	.08	.04
432	Frank Tanana	.12	.09	.05
433	Dave Tobik	.08	.06	.03
434	Wayne Tolleson(FC)	.10	.08	.04
435	George Wright	.08	.06	.03
436	Bill Almon	.08	.06	.03
437	Keith Atherton(FC)	.20	.15	.08
438	Dave Beard	.08	.06	.03
439	Tom Burgmeier	.08	.06	.03
440	Jeff Burroughs	.10	.08	.04
441	Chris Codiroli(FC)	.10	.08	.04
442	Tim Conroy(FC)	.12	.09	.05
443	Mike Davis	.10	.08	.04
444	Wayne Gross	.08	.06	.03
445	Garry Hancock	.08	.06	.03
446	Mike Heath	.08	.06	.03
447	Rickey Henderson	6.00	4.50	2.50
448	Don Hill(FC)	.15	.11	.06
449	Bob Kearney	.08	.06	.03
450	Bill Krueger	.08	.06	.03
451	Rick Langford	.08	.06	.03
452	Carney Lansford	.12	.09	.05
453	Davey Lopes	.10	.08	.04
454	Steve McCatty	.08	.06	.03
455	Dan Meyer	.08	.06	.03
456	Dwayne Murphy	.10	.08	.04
457	Mike Norris	.08	.06	.03
458	Ricky Peters	.08	.06	.03
459	Tony Phillips(FC)	.15	.11	.06
460	Tom Underwood	.08	.06	.03
461	Mike Warren	.08	.06	.03
462	Johnny Bench	.80	.60	.30
463	Bruce Berenyi	.08	.06	.03
464	Dann Bilardello	.08	.06	.03
465	Cesar Cedeno	.12	.09	.05
466	Dave Concepcion	.15	.11	.06
467	Dan Driessen	.10	.08	.04
468	Nick Esasky(FC)	1.50	1.25	.60
469	Rich Gale	.08	.06	.03
470	Ben Hayes	.08	.06	.03

#	Player	MT	NR MT	EX
471	Paul Householder	.08	.06	.03
472	Tom Hume	.08	.06	.03
473	Alan Knicely	.08	.06	.03
474	Eddie Milner	.08	.06	.03
475	Ron Oester	.08	.06	.03
476	Kelly Paris	.08	.06	.03
477	Frank Pastore	.08	.06	.03
478	Ted Power	.10	.08	.04
479	Joe Price	.08	.06	.03
480	Charlie Puleo	.08	.06	.03
481	*Gary Redus*(FC)	.25	.20	.10
482	Bill Scherrer	.08	.06	.03
483	Mario Soto	.10	.08	.04
484	Alex Trevino	.08	.06	.03
485	Duane Walker	.08	.06	.03
486	Larry Bowa	.15	.11	.06
487	Warren Brusstar	.08	.06	.03
488	Bill Buckner	.15	.11	.06
489	Bill Campbell	.08	.06	.03
490	Ron Cey	.12	.09	.05
491	Jody Davis	.10	.08	.04
492	Leon Durham	.10	.08	.04
493	Mel Hall(FC)	.20	.15	.08
494	Ferguson Jenkins	.20	.15	.08
495	Jay Johnstone	.10	.08	.04
496	*Craig Lefferts*(FC)	.20	.15	.08
497	*Carmelo Martinez*(FC)	.25	.20	.10
498	Jerry Morales	.08	.06	.03
499	Keith Moreland	.10	.08	.04
500	Dickie Noles	.08	.06	.03
501	Mike Proly	.08	.06	.03
502	Chuck Rainey	.08	.06	.03
503	Dick Ruthven	.08	.06	.03
504	Ryne Sandberg	7.00	5.25	2.75
505	Lee Smith	.15	.11	.06
506	Steve Trout	.08	.06	.03
507	Gary Woods	.08	.06	.03
508	Juan Beniquez	.08	.06	.03
509	Bob Boone	.10	.08	.04
510	Rick Burleson	.10	.08	.04
511	Rod Carew	.80	.60	.30
512	Bobby Clark	.08	.06	.03
513	John Curtis	.08	.06	.03
514	Doug DeCinces	.12	.09	.05
515	Brian Downing	.12	.09	.05
516	Tim Foli	.08	.06	.03
517	Ken Forsch	.08	.06	.03
518	Bobby Grich	.12	.09	.05
519	Andy Hassler	.08	.06	.03
520	Reggie Jackson	1.00	.70	.40
521	Ron Jackson	.08	.06	.03
522	Tommy John	.25	.20	.10
523	Bruce Kison	.08	.06	.03
524	Steve Lubratich	.08	.06	.03
525	Fred Lynn	.25	.20	.10
526	*Gary Pettis*(FC)	.25	.20	.10
527	Luis Sanchez	.08	.06	.03
528	Daryl Sconiers	.08	.06	.03
529	Ellis Valentine	.08	.06	.03
530	Rob Wilfong	.08	.06	.03
531	Mike Witt	.15	.11	.06
532	Geoff Zahn	.08	.06	.03
533	Bud Anderson	.08	.06	.03
534	Chris Bando	.08	.06	.03
535	Alan Bannister	.08	.06	.03
536	Bert Blyleven	.20	.15	.08
537	Tom Brennan	.08	.06	.03
538	Jamie Easterly	.08	.06	.03
539	Juan Eichelberger	.08	.06	.03
540	Jim Essian	.08	.06	.03
541	Mike Fischlin	.08	.06	.03
542	Julio Franco(FC)	2.50	2.00	1.00
543	Mike Hargrove	.08	.06	.03
544	Toby Harrah	.10	.08	.04
545	Ron Hassey	.08	.06	.03
546	*Neal Heaton*(FC)	.15	.11	.06
547	Bake McBride	.08	.06	.03
548	Broderick Perkins	.08	.06	.03
549	Lary Sorensen	.08	.06	.03
550	Dan Spillner	.08	.06	.03
551	Rick Sutcliffe	.15	.11	.06
552	Pat Tabler	.10	.08	.04
553	Gorman Thomas	.10	.08	.04
554	Andre Thornton	.12	.09	.05
555	George Vukovich	.08	.06	.03
556	Darrell Brown	.08	.06	.03
557	Tom Brunansky	.20	.15	.08
558	*Randy Bush*(FC)	.15	.11	.06
559	Bobby Castillo	.08	.06	.03
560	John Castino	.08	.06	.03
561	Ron Davis	.08	.06	.03

#	Player	MT	NR MT	EX
562	Dave Engle	.08	.06	.03
563	Lenny Faedo	.08	.06	.03
564	Pete Filson	.08	.06	.03
565	Gary Gaetti	.60	.45	.25
566	Mickey Hatcher	.10	.08	.04
567	Kent Hrbek	.40	.30	.15
568	Rusty Kuntz	.08	.06	.03
569	Tim Laudner	.08	.06	.03
570	Rick Lysander	.08	.06	.03
571	Bobby Mitchell	.08	.06	.03
572	Ken Schrom	.08	.06	.03
573	Ray Smith	.08	.06	.03
574	*Tim Teufel*(FC)	.30	.25	.12
575	Frank Viola	.80	.60	.30
576	Gary Ward	.10	.08	.04
577	Ron Washington	.08	.06	.03
578	Len Whitehouse	.08	.06	.03
579	Al Williams	.08	.06	.03
580	Bob Bailor	.08	.06	.03
581	Mark Bradley	.08	.06	.03
582	Hubie Brooks	.15	.11	.06
583	Carlos Diaz	.08	.06	.03
584	George Foster	.20	.15	.08
585	Brian Giles	.08	.06	.03
586	Danny Heep	.08	.06	.03
587	Keith Hernandez	.40	.30	.15
588	Ron Hodges	.08	.06	.03
589	Scott Holman	.08	.06	.03
590	Dave Kingman	.15	.11	.06
591	Ed Lynch	.08	.06	.03
592	*Jose Oquendo*(FC)	.15	.11	.06
593	Jesse Orosco	.10	.08	.04
594	*Junior Ortiz*(FC)	.10	.08	.04
595	Tom Seaver	1.50	1.25	.60
596	*Doug Sisk*(FC)	.10	.08	.04
597	Rusty Staub	.12	.09	.05
598	John Stearns	.08	.06	.03
599	*Darryl Strawberry*(FC)	30.00	22.00	12.00
600	Craig Swan	.08	.06	.03
601	*Walt Terrell*(FC)	.30	.25	.12
602	Mike Torrez	.10	.08	.04
603	Mookie Wilson	.12	.09	.05
604	Jamie Allen	.08	.06	.03
605	Jim Beattie	.08	.06	.03
606	Tony Bernazard	.08	.06	.03
607	Manny Castillo	.08	.06	.03
608	Bill Caudill	.08	.06	.03
609	Bryan Clark	.08	.06	.03
610	Al Cowens	.08	.06	.03
611	Dave Henderson	.12	.09	.05
612	Steve Henderson	.08	.06	.03
613	Orlando Mercado	.08	.06	.03
614	Mike Moore	.10	.08	.04
615	Ricky Nelson	.08	.06	.03
616	*Spike Owen*(FC)	.20	.15	.08
617	Pat Putnam	.08	.06	.03
618	Ron Roenicke	.08	.06	.03
619	Mike Stanton	.08	.06	.03
620	Bob Stoddard	.08	.06	.03
621	Rick Sweet	.08	.06	.03
622	Roy Thomas	.08	.06	.03
623	Ed Vande Berg	.08	.06	.03
624	*Matt Young*(FC)	.15	.11	.06
625	Richie Zisk	.10	.08	.04
626	'83 All-Star Game Record Breaker (Fred Lynn)	.12	.09	.05
627	'83 All-Star Game Record Breaker (Manny Trillo)	.10	.08	.04
628	N.L. Iron Man (Steve Garvey)	.20	.15	.08
629	A.L. Batting Runner-Up (Rod Carew)	.25	.20	.10
630	A.L. Batting Champion (Wade Boggs)	.60	.45	.25
631	Letting Go Of The Raines (Tim Raines)	.20	.15	.08
632	Double Trouble (Al Oliver)	.10	.08	.04
633	All-Star Second Base (Steve Sax)	.15	.11	.06
634	All-Star Shortstop (Dickie Thon)	.10	.08	.04
635	Ace Firemen (Tippy Martinez, Dan Quisenberry)	.10	.08	.04
636	Reds Reunited (Joe Morgan, Tony Perez, Pete Rose)	.50	.40	.20
637	Backstop Stars (Bob Boone, Lance Parrish)	.15	.11	.06
638	The Pine Tar Incident, 7/24/83 (George Brett, Gaylord Perry)	.30	.25	.12
639	1983 No-Hitters (Bob Forsch, Dave Righetti, Mike Warren)	.10	.08	.04
640	Retiring Superstars (Johnny Bench, Carl Yastrzemski)	1.00	.70	.40
641	Going Out In Style (Gaylord Perry)	.15	.11	.06

		MT	NR MT	EX
642	300 Club & Strikeout Record (Steve Carlton)	.20	.15	.08
643	The Managers (Joe Altobelli, Paul Owens)	.10	.08	.04
644	The MVP (Rick Dempsey)	.10	.08	.04
645	The Rookie Winner (Mike Boddicker)(FC)	.12	.09	.05
646	The Clincher (Scott McGregor)	.10	.08	.04
647	Checklist: Orioles/Royals (Joe Altobelli)	.08	.06	.03
648	Checklist: Phillies/Giants (Paul Owens)	.08	.06	.03
649	Checklist: White Sox/Red Sox (Tony LaRussa)	.08	.06	.03
650	Checklist: Tigers/Rangers (Sparky Anderson)	.08	.06	.03
651	Checklist: Dodgers/A's (Tom Lasorda)	.08	.06	.03
652	Checklist: Yankees/Reds (Billy Martin)	.08	.06	.03
653	Checklist: Blue Jays/Cubs (Bobby Cox)	.08	.06	.03
654	Checklist: Braves/Angels (Joe Torre)	.08	.06	.03
655	Checklist: Brewers/Indians (Rene Lachemann)	.08	.06	.03
656	Checklist: Astros/Twins (Bob Lillis)	.08	.06	.03
657	Checklist: Pirates/Mets (Chuck Tanner)	.08	.06	.03
658	Checklist: Expos/Mariners (Bill Virdon)	.08	.06	.03
659	Checklist: Padres/Specials (Dick Williams)	.08	.06	.03
660	Checklist: Cardinals/Specials (Whitey Herzog)	.08	.06	.03

1984 Fleer Update

 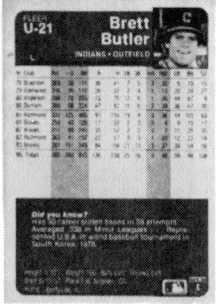

Brett Butler
OUTFIELD

Following the lead of Topps, Fleer issued near the end of the baseball season a 132-card set to update player trades and include rookies not depicted in the regular issue. The cards, which measure 2-1/2" by 3-1/2", are identical in design to the regular issue but are numbered U-1 through U-132. Available to the collecting public only through hobby dealers, the set was printed in limited quantities and has escalated in price quite rapidly the past several years. The set was issued with team logo stickers in a specially designed box.

		MT	NR MT	EX
Complete Set:		525.00	400.00	225.00
Common Player:		.15	.11	.06
1	Willie Aikens	.15	.11	.06
2	Luis Aponte	.15	.11	.06
3	Mark Bailey(FC)	.20	.15	.08
4	Bob Bailor	.15	.11	.06
5	Dusty Baker	.30	.25	.12
6	Steve Balboni(FC)	.40	.30	.15
7	Alan Bannister	.15	.11	.06
8	Marty Barrett(FC)	3.00	2.25	1.25
9	Dave Beard	.15	.11	.06
10	Joe Beckwith	.15	.11	.06
11	Dave Bergman	.15	.11	.06
12	Tony Bernazard	.15	.11	.06
13	Bruce Bochte	.15	.11	.06

		MT	NR MT	EX
14	Barry Bonnell	.15	.11	.06
15	Phil Bradley(FC)	4.00	3.00	1.50
16	Fred Breining	.15	.11	.06
17	Mike Brown	.15	.11	.06
18	Bill Buckner	.50	.40	.20
19	Ray Burris	.15	.11	.06
20	John Butcher	.15	.11	.06
21	Brett Butler	.30	.25	.12
22	Enos Cabell	.15	.11	.06
23	Bill Campbell	.15	.11	.06
24	Bill Caudill	.15	.11	.06
25	Bobby Clark	.15	.11	.06
26	Bryan Clark	.15	.11	.06
27	Roger Clemens(FC)	150.00	110.00	60.00
28	Jaime Cocanower	.15	.11	.06
29	Ron Darling(FC)	8.00	6.00	3.25
30	Alvin Davis(FC)	15.00	11.00	6.00
31	Bob Dernier	.15	.11	.06
32	Carlos Diaz	.15	.11	.06
33	Mike Easler	.20	.15	.08
34	Dennis Eckersley	2.00	1.50	.80
35	Jim Essian	.15	.11	.06
36	Darrell Evans	.60	.45	.25
37	Mike Fitzgerald(FC)	.20	.15	.08
38	Tim Foli	.15	.11	.06
39	John Franco(FC)	9.00	6.75	3.50
40	George Frazier	.15	.11	.06
41	Rich Gale	.15	.11	.06
42	Barbaro Garbey	.20	.15	.08
43	Dwight Gooden(FC)	100.00	75.00	40.00
44	Goose Gossage	1.00	.70	.40
45	Wayne Gross	.15	.11	.06
46	Mark Gubicza(FC)	7.00	5.25	2.75
47	Jackie Gutierrez	.15	.11	.06
48	Toby Harrah	.20	.15	.08
49	Ron Hassey	.15	.11	.06
50	Richie Hebner	.15	.11	.06
51	Willie Hernandez	.40	.30	.15
52	Ed Hodge	.15	.11	.06
53	Ricky Horton(FC)	.70	.50	.30
54	Art Howe	.15	.11	.06
55	Dane Iorg	.15	.11	.06
56	Brook Jacoby(FC)	4.00	3.00	1.50
57	Dion James(FC)	.40	.30	.15
58	Mike Jeffcoat(FC)	.20	.15	.08
59	Ruppert Jones	.15	.11	.06
60	Bob Kearney	.15	.11	.06
61	Jimmy Key(FC)	6.00	4.50	2.50
62	Dave Kingman	.70	.50	.30
63	Brad Komminsk(FC)	.20	.15	.08
64	Jerry Koosman	.50	.40	.20
65	Wayne Krenchicki	.15	.11	.06
66	Rusty Kuntz	.15	.11	.06
67	Frank LaCorte	.15	.11	.06
68	Dennis Lamp	.15	.11	.06
69	Tito Landrum	.15	.11	.06
70	Mark Langston(FC)	18.00	13.50	7.25
71	Rick Leach	.15	.11	.06
72	Craig Lefferts(FC)	.30	.25	.12
73	Gary Lucas	.15	.11	.06
74	Jerry Martin	.15	.11	.06
75	Carmelo Martinez	.30	.25	.12
76	Mike Mason(FC)	.20	.15	.08
77	Gary Matthews	.30	.25	.12
78	Andy McGaffigan	.15	.11	.06
79	Joey McLaughlin	.15	.11	.06
80	Joe Morgan	4.00	3.00	1.50
81	Darryl Motley	.15	.11	.06
82	Graig Nettles	1.50	1.25	.60
83	Phil Niekro	2.50	2.00	1.00
84	Ken Oberkfell	.15	.11	.06
85	Al Oliver	.80	.60	.30
86	Jorge Orta	.15	.11	.06
87	Amos Otis	.30	.25	.12
88	Bob Owchinko	.15	.11	.06
89	Dave Parker	3.00	2.25	1.25
90	Jack Perconte	.15	.11	.06
91	Tony Perez	1.50	1.25	.60
92	Gerald Perry(FC)	1.75	1.25	.70
93	Kirby Puckett(FC)	175.00	125.00	70.00
94	Shane Rawley	.35	.30	.14
95	Floyd Rayford	.15	.11	.06
96	Ron Reed	.20	.15	.08
97	R.J. Reynolds(FC)	.90	.70	.35
98	Gene Richards	.15	.11	.06
99	Jose Rijo(FC)	7.00	5.25	2.75
100	Jeff Robinson(FC)	1.00	.70	.40
101	Ron Romanick(FC)	.20	.15	.08
102	Pete Rose	25.00	18.50	10.00
103	Bret Saberhagen(FC)	30.00	22.00	12.00
104	Scott Sanderson	.15	.11	.06

		MT	NR MT	EX
105	Dick Schofield(FC)	.40	.30	.15
106	Tom Seaver	15.00	11.00	6.00
107	Jim Slaton	.15	.11	.06
108	Mike Smithson	.20	.15	.08
109	Lary Sorensen	.15	.11	.06
110	Tim Stoddard	.15	.11	.06
111	Jeff Stone(FC)	.30	.25	.12
112	Champ Summers	.15	.11	.06
113	Jim Sundberg	.20	.15	.08
114	Rick Sutcliffe	.80	.60	.30
115	Craig Swan	.15	.11	.06
116	Derrel Thomas	.15	.11	.06
117	Gorman Thomas	.35	.30	.14
118	Alex Trevino	.15	.11	.06
119	Manny Trillo	.20	.15	.08
120	John Tudor	.60	.45	.25
121	Tom Underwood	.15	.11	.06
122	Mike Vail	.15	.11	.06
123	Tom Waddell(FC)	.15	.11	.06
124	Gary Ward	.20	.15	.08
125	Terry Whitfield	.15	.11	.06
126	Curtis Wilkerson	.15	.11	.06
127	Frank Williams(FC)	.35	.25	.14
128	Glenn Wilson	.25	.20	.10
129	John Wockenfuss	.15	.11	.06
130	Ned Yost	.15	.11	.06
131	Mike Young(FC)	.35	.25	.14
132	Checklist 1-132	.15	.11	.06

1985 Fleer

 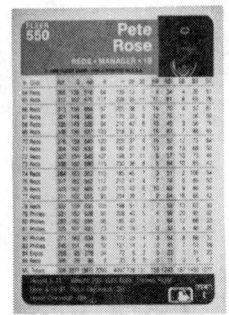

The 1985 Fleer set consists of 660 cards, each measuring 2-1/2" by 3-1/2" in size. The card fronts feature a color photo plus the player's team logo and the word "Fleer." The photos have a color-coded frame which corresponds to the player's team. A grey border surrounds the color-coded frame. The card backs are similar in design to the previous two years, but have two shades of red and black ink on white stock. For the fourth consecutive year, Fleer included special cards and team checklists in the set. Also incorporated in a set for the first time were ten "Major League Prospect" cards, each featuring two rookie hopefuls. The set was issued with team logo stickers.

		MT	NR MT	EX
Complete Set:		125.00	90.00	50.00
Common Player:		.06	.05	.02
1	Doug Bair	.06	.05	.02
2	Juan Berenguer	.06	.05	.02
3	Dave Bergman	.06	.05	.02
4	Tom Brookens	.06	.05	.02
5	Marty Castillo	.06	.05	.02
6	Darrell Evans	.12	.09	.05
7	Barbaro Garbey	.12	.09	.05
8	Kirk Gibson	.35	.25	.14
9	John Grubb	.06	.05	.02
10	Willie Hernandez	.08	.06	.03
11	Larry Herndon	.08	.06	.03
12	Howard Johnson	2.00	1.50	.80
13	Ruppert Jones	.06	.05	.02
14	Rusty Kuntz	.06	.05	.02
15	Chet Lemon	.08	.06	.03
16	Aurelio Lopez	.06	.05	.02
17	Sid Monge	.06	.05	.02

		MT	NR MT	EX
18	Jack Morris	.25	.20	.10
19	Lance Parrish	.30	.25	.12
20	Dan Petry	.08	.06	.03
21	Dave Rozema	.06	.05	.02
22	Bill Scherrer	.06	.05	.02
23	Alan Trammell	.35	.25	.14
24	Lou Whitaker	.35	.25	.14
25	Milt Wilcox	.06	.05	.02
26	Kurt Bevacqua	.06	.05	.02
27	*Greg Booker*(FC)	.15	.11	.06
28	Bobby Brown	.06	.05	.02
29	Luis DeLeon	.06	.05	.02
30	Dave Dravecky	.08	.06	.03
31	Tim Flannery	.06	.05	.02
32	Steve Garvey	.40	.30	.15
33	Goose Gossage	.20	.15	.08
34	Tony Gwynn	2.00	1.50	.80
35	Greg Harris	.06	.05	.02
36	Andy Hawkins	.08	.06	.03
37	Terry Kennedy	.08	.06	.03
38	Craig Lefferts	.08	.06	.03
39	Tim Lollar	.06	.05	.02
40	Carmelo Martinez	.08	.06	.03
41	Kevin McReynolds	1.00	.70	.40
42	Graig Nettles	.15	.11	.06
43	Luis Salazar	.06	.05	.02
44	Eric Show	.08	.06	.03
45	Garry Templeton	.08	.06	.03
46	Mark Thurmond	.06	.05	.02
47	Ed Whitson	.06	.05	.02
48	Alan Wiggins	.06	.05	.02
49	Rich Bordi	.06	.05	.02
50	Larry Bowa	.12	.09	.05
51	Warren Brusstar	.06	.05	.02
52	Ron Cey	.10	.08	.04
53	*Henry Cotto*(FC)	.15	.11	.06
54	Jody Davis	.10	.08	.04
55	Bob Dernier	.06	.05	.02
56	Leon Durham	.08	.06	.03
57	Dennis Eckersley	.12	.09	.05
58	George Frazier	.06	.05	.02
59	Richie Hebner	.06	.05	.02
60	Dave Lopes	.08	.06	.03
61	Gary Matthews	.10	.08	.04
62	Keith Moreland	.08	.06	.03
63	Rick Reuschel	.10	.08	.04
64	Dick Ruthven	.06	.05	.02
65	Ryne Sandberg	3.00	2.25	1.25
66	Scott Sanderson	.06	.05	.02
67	Lee Smith	.10	.08	.04
68	Tim Stoddard	.06	.05	.02
69	Rick Sutcliffe	.12	.09	.05
70	Steve Trout	.06	.05	.02
71	Gary Woods	.06	.05	.02
72	Wally Backman	.08	.06	.03
73	Bruce Berenyi	.06	.05	.02
74	Hubie Brooks	.10	.08	.04
75	Kelvin Chapman	.06	.05	.02
76	Ron Darling	1.25	.90	.50
77	Sid Fernandez(FC)	1.00	.70	.40
78	Mike Fitzgerald	.08	.06	.03
79	George Foster	.15	.11	.06
80	Brent Gaff	.06	.05	.02
81	Ron Gardenhire	.06	.05	.02
82	*Dwight Gooden*	12.00	9.00	4.75
83	Tom Gorman	.06	.05	.02
84	Danny Heep	.06	.05	.02
85	Keith Hernandez	.30	.25	.12
86	Ray Knight	.10	.08	.04
87	Ed Lynch	.06	.05	.02
88	Jose Oquendo	.08	.06	.03
89	Jesse Orosco	.08	.06	.03
90	*Rafael Santana*(FC)	.20	.15	.08
91	Doug Sisk	.06	.05	.02
92	Rusty Staub	.12	.09	.05
93	Darryl Strawberry	5.00	3.75	2.00
94	Walt Terrell	.08	.06	.03
95	Mookie Wilson	.10	.08	.04
96	Jim Acker	.06	.05	.02
97	Willie Aikens	.06	.05	.02
98	Doyle Alexander	.10	.08	.04
99	Jesse Barfield	.25	.20	.10
100	George Bell	.50	.40	.20
101	Jim Clancy	.08	.06	.03
102	Dave Collins	.08	.06	.03
103	Tony Fernandez	.35	.25	.14
104	Damaso Garcia	.06	.05	.02
105	Jim Gott	.06	.05	.02
106	Alfredo Griffin	.08	.06	.03
107	Garth Iorg	.06	.05	.02
108	Roy Lee Jackson	.06	.05	.02

		MT	NR MT	EX
109	Cliff Johnson	.06	.05	.02
110	*Jimmy Key*	1.00	.70	.40
111	Dennis Lamp	.06	.05	.02
112	Rick Leach	.06	.05	.02
113	Luis Leal	.06	.05	.02
114	Buck Martinez	.06	.05	.02
115	Lloyd Moseby	.10	.08	.04
116	Rance Mulliniks	.06	.05	.02
117	Dave Stieb	.12	.09	.05
118	Willie Upshaw	.08	.06	.03
119	Ernie Whitt	.08	.06	.03
120	Mike Armstrong	.06	.05	.02
121	Don Baylor	.12	.09	.05
122	Marty Bystrom	.06	.05	.02
123	Rick Cerone	.06	.05	.02
124	Joe Cowley(FC)	.06	.05	.02
125	Brian Dayett(FC)	.06	.05	.02
126	Tim Foli	.06	.05	.02
127	Ray Fontenot	.06	.05	.02
128	Ken Griffey	.10	.08	.04
129	Ron Guidry	.25	.20	.10
130	Toby Harrah	.08	.06	.03
131	Jay Howell	.08	.06	.03
132	Steve Kemp	.08	.06	.03
133	Don Mattingly	12.00	9.00	4.75
134	Bobby Meacham	.06	.05	.02
135	John Montefusco	.06	.05	.02
136	Omar Moreno	.06	.05	.02
137	Dale Murray	.06	.05	.02
138	Phil Niekro	.25	.20	.10
139	*Mike Pagliarulo*(FC)	.90	.70	.35
140	Willie Randolph	.10	.08	.04
141	Dennis Rasmussen(FC)	.30	.25	.12
142	Dave Righetti	.20	.15	.08
143	*Jose Rijo*	1.50	1.25	.60
144	Andre Robertson	.06	.05	.02
145	Bob Shirley	.06	.05	.02
146	Dave Winfield	.35	.25	.14
147	Butch Wynegar	.06	.05	.02
148	Gary Allenson	.06	.05	.02
149	Tony Armas	.10	.08	.04
150	Marty Barrett	.20	.15	.08
151	Wade Boggs	3.75	2.75	1.50
152	Dennis Boyd	.10	.08	.04
153	Bill Buckner	.12	.09	.05
154	Mark Clear	.06	.05	.02
155	Roger Clemens	20.00	15.00	8.00
156	Steve Crawford	.06	.05	.02
157	Mike Easler	.08	.06	.03
158	Dwight Evans	.12	.09	.05
159	Rich Gedman	.10	.08	.04
160	Jackie Gutierrez	.06	.05	.02
161	Bruce Hurst	.12	.09	.05
162	John Henry Johnson	.06	.05	.02
163	Rick Miller	.06	.05	.02
164	Reid Nichols	.06	.05	.02
165	*Al Nipper*(FC)	.15	.11	.06
166	Bob Ojeda	.10	.08	.04
167	Jerry Remy	.06	.05	.02
168	Jim Rice	.35	.25	.14
169	Bob Stanley	.06	.05	.02
170	Mike Boddicker	.10	.08	.04
171	Al Bumbry	.08	.06	.03
172	Todd Cruz	.06	.05	.02
173	Rich Dauer	.06	.05	.02
174	Storm Davis	.10	.08	.04
175	Rick Dempsey	.08	.06	.03
176	Jim Dwyer	.06	.05	.02
177	Mike Flanagan	.10	.08	.04
178	Dan Ford	.06	.05	.02
179	Wayne Gross	.06	.05	.02
180	John Lowenstein	.06	.05	.02
181	Dennis Martinez	.08	.06	.03
182	Tippy Martinez	.06	.05	.02
183	Scott McGregor	.08	.06	.03
184	Eddie Murray	.50	.40	.20
185	Joe Nolan	.06	.05	.02
186	Floyd Rayford	.06	.05	.02
187	Cal Ripken, Jr.	.50	.40	.20
188	Gary Roenicke	.06	.05	.02
189	Lenn Sakata	.06	.05	.02
190	John Shelby	.08	.06	.03
191	Ken Singleton	.08	.06	.03
192	Sammy Stewart	.06	.05	.02
193	Bill Swaggerty	.06	.05	.02
194	Tom Underwood	.06	.05	.02
195	Mike Young	.12	.09	.05
196	Steve Balboni	.08	.06	.03
197	Joe Beckwith	.06	.05	.02
198	Bud Black	.06	.05	.02
199	George Brett	.50	.40	.20
200	Onix Concepcion	.06	.05	.02
201	*Mark Gubicza*	1.75	1.25	.70
202	Larry Gura	.06	.05	.02
203	Mark Huismann(FC)	.06	.05	.02
204	Dane Iorg	.06	.05	.02
205	Danny Jackson(FC)	1.00	.70	.40
206	Charlie Leibrandt	.08	.06	.03
207	Hal McRae	.10	.08	.04
208	Darryl Motley	.06	.05	.02
209	Jorge Orta	.06	.05	.02
210	Greg Pryor	.06	.05	.02
211	Dan Quisenberry	.10	.08	.04
212	*Bret Saberhagen*	8.00	6.00	3.25
213	Pat Sheridan	.06	.05	.02
214	Don Slaught	.06	.05	.02
215	U.L. Washington	.06	.05	.02
216	John Wathan	.08	.06	.03
217	Frank White	.10	.08	.04
218	Willie Wilson	.12	.09	.05
219	Neil Allen	.06	.05	.02
220	Joaquin Andujar	.08	.06	.03
221	Steve Braun	.06	.05	.02
222	Danny Cox(FC)	.20	.20	.10
223	Bob Forsch	.08	.06	.03
224	David Green	.06	.05	.02
225	George Hendrick	.08	.06	.03
226	Tom Herr	.10	.08	.04
227	*Ricky Horton*	.30	.25	.12
228	Art Howe	.06	.05	.02
229	Mike Jorgensen	.06	.05	.02
230	Kurt Kepshire	.06	.05	.02
231	Jeff Lahti	.06	.05	.02
232	Tito Landrum	.06	.05	.02
233	Dave LaPoint	.08	.06	.03
234	Willie McGee	.30	.25	.12
235	*Tom Nieto*(FC)	.10	.08	.04
236	*Terry Pendleton*(FC)	.70	.50	.30
237	Darrell Porter	.08	.06	.03
238	Dave Rucker	.06	.05	.02
239	Lonnie Smith	.08	.06	.03
240	Ozzie Smith	.15	.11	.06
241	Bruce Sutter	.12	.09	.05
242	Andy Van Slyke	.35	.25	.14
243	Dave Von Ohlen	.06	.05	.02
244	Larry Andersen	.06	.05	.02
245	Bill Campbell	.06	.05	.02
246	Steve Carlton	.40	.30	.15
247	Tim Corcoran	.06	.05	.02
248	Ivan DeJesus	.06	.05	.02
249	John Denny	.06	.05	.02
250	Bo Diaz	.08	.06	.03
251	Greg Gross	.06	.05	.02
252	Kevin Gross	.10	.08	.04
253	Von Hayes	.12	.09	.05
254	Al Holland	.06	.05	.02
255	Charles Hudson	.08	.06	.03
256	Jerry Koosman	.10	.08	.04
257	Joe Lefebvre	.06	.05	.02
258	Sixto Lezcano	.06	.05	.02
259	Garry Maddox	.10	.08	.04
260	Len Matuszek	.06	.05	.02
261	Tug McGraw	.10	.08	.04
262	Al Oliver	.12	.09	.05
263	Shane Rawley	.10	.08	.04
264	Juan Samuel	.30	.25	.12
265	Mike Schmidt	2.00	1.50	.80
266	*Jeff Stone*	.12	.09	.05
267	Ozzie Virgil	.06	.05	.02
268	Glenn Wilson	.08	.06	.03
269	John Wockenfuss	.06	.05	.02
270	Darrell Brown	.06	.05	.02
271	Tom Brunansky	.12	.09	.05
272	Randy Bush	.06	.05	.02
273	John Butcher	.06	.05	.02
274	Bobby Castillo	.06	.05	.02
275	Ron Davis	.06	.05	.02
276	Dave Engle	.06	.05	.02
277	Pete Filson	.06	.05	.02
278	Gary Gaetti	.25	.20	.10
279	Mickey Hatcher	.06	.05	.02
280	Ed Hodge	.06	.05	.02
281	Kent Hrbek	.25	.20	.10
282	Houston Jimenez	.06	.05	.02
283	Tim Laudner	.06	.05	.02
284	Rick Lysander	.06	.05	.02
285	Dave Meier	.06	.05	.02
286	*Kirby Puckett*	20.00	15.00	8.00
287	Pat Putnam	.06	.05	.02
288	Ken Schrom	.06	.05	.02
289	Mike Smithson	.06	.05	.02
290	Tim Teufel	.08	.06	.03

	MT	NR MT	EX			MT	NR MT	EX
291 Frank Viola	.20	.15	.08	382 German Rivera	.06	.05	.02
292 Ron Washington	.06	.05	.02	383 Bill Russell	.08	.06	.03
293 Don Aase	.06	.05	.02	384 Steve Sax	.20	.15	.08
294 Juan Beniquez	.06	.05	.02	385 Mike Scioscia	.08	.06	.03
295 Bob Boone	.08	.06	.03	386 *Franklin Stubbs*(FC)	.60	.45	.25
296 Mike Brown	.06	.05	.02	387 Fernando Valenzuela	.35	.25	.14
297 Rod Carew	.40	.30	.15	388 Bob Welch	.12	.09	.05
298 Doug Corbett	.06	.05	.02	389 Terry Whitfield	.06	.05	.02
299 Doug DeCinces	.10	.08	.04	390 Steve Yeager	.06	.05	.02
300 Brian Downing	.10	.08	.04	391 Pat Zachry	.06	.05	.02
301 Ken Forsch	.06	.05	.02	392 Fred Breining	.06	.05	.02
302 Bobby Grich	.10	.08	.04	393 Gary Carter	.35	.25	.14
303 Reggie Jackson	.40	.30	.15	394 Andre Dawson	.30	.25	.12
304 Tommy John	.20	.15	.08	395 Miguel Dilone	.06	.05	.02
305 Curt Kaufman	.06	.05	.02	396 Dan Driessen	.08	.06	.03
306 Bruce Kison	.06	.05	.02	397 Doug Flynn	.06	.05	.02
307 Fred Lynn	.20	.15	.08	398 Terry Francona	.06	.05	.02
308 Gary Pettis	.08	.06	.03	399 Bill Gullickson	.06	.05	.02
309 *Ron Romanick*	.10	.08	.04	400 Bob James	.06	.05	.02
310 Luis Sanchez	.06	.05	.02	401 Charlie Lea	.06	.05	.02
311 Dick Schofield	.12	.09	.05	402 Bryan Little	.06	.05	.02
312 Daryl Sconiers	.06	.05	.02	403 Gary Lucas	.06	.05	.02
313 Jim Slaton	.06	.05	.02	404 David Palmer	.06	.05	.02
314 Derrel Thomas	.06	.05	.02	405 Tim Raines	.35	.25	.14
315 Rob Wilfong	.06	.05	.02	406 Mike Ramsey	.06	.05	.02
316 Mike Witt	.12	.09	.05	407 Jeff Reardon	.12	.09	.05
317 Geoff Zahn	.06	.05	.02	408 Steve Rogers	.08	.06	.03
318 Len Barker	.08	.06	.03	409 Dan Schatzeder	.06	.05	.02
319 Steve Bedrosian	.12	.09	.05	410 Bryn Smith	.06	.05	.02
320 Bruce Benedict	.06	.05	.02	411 Mike Stenhouse	.06	.05	.02
321 Rick Camp	.06	.05	.02	412 Tim Wallach	.12	.09	.05
322 Chris Chambliss	.08	.06	.03	413 Jim Wohlford	.06	.05	.02
323 *Jeff Dedmon*(FC)	.12	.09	.05	414 Bill Almon	.06	.05	.02
324 Terry Forster	.08	.06	.03	415 Keith Atherton	.06	.05	.02
325 Gene Garber	.06	.05	.02	416 Bruce Bochte	.06	.05	.02
326 *Albert Hall*(FC)	.15	.11	.06	417 Tom Burgmeier	.06	.05	.02
327 Terry Harper	.06	.05	.02	418 Ray Burris	.06	.05	.02
328 Bob Horner	.12	.09	.05	419 Bill Caudill	.06	.05	.02
329 Glenn Hubbard	.06	.05	.02	420 Chris Codiroli	.06	.05	.02
330 Randy Johnson	.06	.05	.02	421 Tim Conroy	.06	.05	.02
331 Brad Komminsk	.06	.05	.02	422 Mike Davis	.08	.06	.03
332 Rick Mahler	.06	.05	.02	423 Jim Essian	.06	.05	.02
333 Craig McMurtry	.06	.05	.02	424 Mike Heath	.06	.05	.02
334 Donnie Moore	.06	.05	.02	425 Rickey Henderson	3.00	2.25	1.25
335 Dale Murphy	.60	.45	.25	426 Donnie Hill	.06	.05	.02
336 Ken Oberkfell	.06	.05	.02	427 Dave Kingman	.15	.11	.06
337 Pascual Perez	.08	.06	.03	428 Bill Krueger	.06	.05	.02
338 Gerald Perry	.35	.25	.14	429 Carney Lansford	.10	.08	.04
339 Rafael Ramirez	.06	.05	.02	430 Steve McCatty	.06	.05	.02
340 Jerry Royster	.06	.05	.02	431 Joe Morgan	.30	.25	.12
341 Alex Trevino	.06	.05	.02	432 Dwayne Murphy	.08	.06	.03
342 Claudell Washington	.08	.06	.03	433 Tony Phillips	.06	.05	.02
343 Alan Ashby	.06	.05	.02	434 Lary Sorensen	.06	.05	.02
344 *Mark Bailey*	.10	.08	.04	435 Mike Warren	.06	.05	.02
345 Kevin Bass	.10	.08	.04	436 *Curt Young*(FC)	.35	.25	.14
346 Enos Cabell	.06	.05	.02	437 Luis Aponte	.06	.05	.02
347 Jose Cruz	.10	.08	.04	438 Chris Bando	.06	.05	.02
348 Bill Dawley	.06	.05	.02	439 Tony Bernazard	.06	.05	.02
349 Frank DiPino	.06	.05	.02	440 Bert Blyleven	.15	.11	.06
350 Bill Doran	.12	.09	.05	441 Brett Butler	.10	.08	.04
351 Phil Garner	.08	.06	.03	442 Ernie Camacho	.06	.05	.02
352 Bob Knepper	.08	.06	.03	443 Joe Carter(FC)	4.00	3.00	1.50
353 Mike LaCoss	.06	.05	.02	444 Carmelo Castillo	.06	.05	.02
354 Jerry Mumphrey	.06	.05	.02	445 Jamie Easterly	.06	.05	.02
355 Joe Niekro	.10	.08	.04	446 *Steve Farr*(FC)	.30	.25	.12
356 Terry Puhl	.06	.05	.02	447 Mike Fischlin	.06	.05	.02
357 Craig Reynolds	.06	.05	.02	448 Julio Franco	.12	.09	.05
358 Vern Ruhle	.06	.05	.02	449 Mel Hall	.08	.06	.03
359 Nolan Ryan	2.00	1.50	.80	450 Mike Hargrove	.06	.05	.02
360 Joe Sambito	.06	.05	.02	451 Neal Heaton	.06	.05	.02
361 Mike Scott	.15	.11	.06	452 Brook Jacoby	.30	.25	.12
362 Dave Smith	.08	.06	.03	453 *Mike Jeffcoat*	.08	.06	.03
363 *Julio Solano*(FC)	.08	.06	.03	454 *Don Schulze*(FC)	.08	.06	.03
364 Dickie Thon	.08	.06	.03	455 Roy Smith	.06	.05	.02
365 Denny Walling	.06	.05	.02	456 Pat Tabler	.08	.06	.03
366 Dave Anderson	.06	.05	.02	457 Andre Thornton	.10	.08	.04
367 Bob Bailor	.06	.05	.02	458 George Vukovich	.06	.05	.02
368 Greg Brock	.08	.06	.03	459 Tom Waddell	.06	.05	.02
369 Carlos Diaz	.06	.05	.02	460 Jerry Willard	.06	.05	.02
370 Pedro Guerrero	.25	.20	.10	461 Dale Berra	.06	.05	.02
371 *Orel Hershiser*(FC)	8.00	6.00	3.25	462 John Candelaria	.10	.08	.04
372 Rick Honeycutt	.06	.05	.02	463 Jose DeLeon	.08	.06	.03
373 Burt Hooton	.08	.06	.03	464 Doug Frobel	.06	.05	.02
374 *Ken Howell*(FC)	.15	.11	.06	465 Cecilio Guante	.06	.05	.02
375 Ken Landreaux	.08	.06	.03	466 Brian Harper	.06	.05	.02
376 Candy Maldonado	.10	.08	.04	467 Lee Lacy	.06	.05	.02
377 Mike Marshall	.15	.11	.06	468 Bill Madlock	.12	.09	.05
378 Tom Niedenfuer	.08	.06	.03	469 Lee Mazzilli	.08	.06	.03
379 Alejandro Pena	.08	.06	.03	470 Larry McWilliams	.06	.05	.02
380 Jerry Reuss	.08	.06	.03	471 Jim Morrison	.06	.05	.02
381 *R.J. Reynolds*	.25	.20	.10	472 Tony Pena	.10	.08	.04

	MT	NR MT	EX
473 Johnny Ray	.12	.09	.05
474 Rick Rhoden	.10	.08	.04
475 Don Robinson	.08	.06	.03
476 Rod Scurry	.06	.05	.02
477 Kent Tekulve	.08	.06	.03
478 Jason Thompson	.06	.05	.02
479 John Tudor	.10	.08	.04
480 Lee Tunnell	.06	.05	.02
481 Marvell Wynne	.06	.05	.02
482 Salome Barojas	.06	.05	.02
483 Dave Beard	.06	.05	.02
484 Jim Beattie	.06	.05	.02
485 Barry Bonnell	.06	.05	.02
486 *Phil Bradley*	.90	.70	.35
487 Al Cowens	.06	.05	.02
488 *Alvin Davis*	3.00	2.25	1.25
489 Dave Henderson	.10	.08	.04
490 Steve Henderson	.06	.05	.02
491 Bob Kearney	.06	.05	.02
492 *Mark Langston*	4.00	3.00	1.50
493 Larry Milbourne	.06	.05	.02
494 Paul Mirabella	.06	.05	.02
495 Mike Moore	.06	.05	.02
496 Edwin Nunez(FC)	.08	.06	.03
497 Spike Owen	.08	.06	.03
498 Jack Perconte	.06	.05	.02
499 Ken Phelps	.10	.08	.04
500 *Jim Presley*(FC)	1.00	.70	.40
501 Mike Stanton	.06	.05	.02
502 Bob Stoddard	.06	.05	.02
503 Gorman Thomas	.10	.08	.04
504 Ed Vande Berg	.06	.05	.02
505 Matt Young	.06	.05	.02
506 Juan Agosto	.06	.05	.02
507 Harold Baines	.15	.11	.06
508 Floyd Bannister	.10	.08	.04
509 Britt Burns	.06	.05	.02
510 Julio Cruz	.06	.05	.02
511 Richard Dotson	.10	.08	.04
512 Jerry Dybzinski	.06	.05	.02
513 Carlton Fisk	.30	.25	.12
514 Scott Fletcher	.08	.06	.03
515 Jerry Hairston	.06	.05	.02
516 Marc Hill	.06	.05	.02
517 LaMarr Hoyt	.06	.05	.02
518 Ron Kittle	.10	.08	.04
519 Rudy Law	.06	.05	.02
520 Vance Law	.08	.06	.03
521 Greg Luzinski	.10	.08	.04
522 Gene Nelson	.06	.05	.02
523 Tom Paciorek	.06	.05	.02
524 Ron Reed	.06	.05	.02
525 Bert Roberge	.06	.05	.02
526 Tom Seaver	.40	.30	.15
527 Roy Smalley	.06	.05	.02
528 Dan Spillner	.06	.05	.02
529 Mike Squires	.06	.05	.02
530 Greg Walker	.12	.09	.05
531 Cesar Cedeno	.10	.08	.04
532 Dave Concepcion	.12	.09	.05
533 *Eric Davis*(FC)	18.00	13.50	7.25
534 Nick Esasky	.08	.06	.03
535 Tom Foley	.06	.05	.02
536 *John Franco*	2.00	1.50	.80
537 Brad Gulden	.06	.05	.02
538 Tom Hume	.06	.05	.02
539 Wayne Krenchicki	.06	.05	.02
540 Andy McGaffigan	.06	.05	.02
541 Eddie Milner	.06	.05	.02
542 Ron Oester	.06	.05	.02
543 Bob Owchinko	.06	.05	.02
544 Dave Parker	.25	.20	.10
545 Frank Pastore	.06	.05	.02
546 Tony Perez	.15	.11	.06
547 Ted Power	.06	.05	.02
548 Joe Price	.06	.05	.02
549 Gary Redus	.08	.06	.03
550 Pete Rose	1.00	.70	.40
551 Jeff Russell(FC)	.10	.08	.04
552 Mario Soto	.08	.06	.03
553 *Jay Tibbs*(FC)	.15	.11	.06
554 Duane Walker	.06	.05	.02
555 Alan Bannister	.06	.05	.02
556 Buddy Bell	.12	.09	.05
557 Danny Darwin	.06	.05	.02
558 Charlie Hough	.08	.06	.03
559 Bobby Jones	.06	.05	.02
560 Odell Jones	.06	.05	.02
561 *Jeff Kunkel*(FC)	.10	.08	.04
562 *Mike Mason*	.10	.08	.04
563 Pete O'Brien	.12	.09	.05

	MT	NR MT	EX
564 Larry Parrish	.10	.08	.04
565 Mickey Rivers	.08	.06	.03
566 Billy Sample	.06	.05	.02
567 Dave Schmidt	.06	.05	.02
568 Donnie Scott	.06	.05	.02
569 Dave Stewart	.12	.09	.05
570 Frank Tanana	.10	.08	.04
571 Wayne Tolleson	.06	.05	.02
572 Gary Ward	.08	.06	.03
573 Curtis Wilkerson	.08	.06	.03
574 George Wright	.06	.05	.02
575 Ned Yost	.06	.05	.02
576 Mark Brouhard	.06	.05	.02
577 Mike Caldwell	.06	.05	.02
578 Bobby Clark	.06	.05	.02
579 Jaime Cocanower	.06	.05	.02
580 Cecil Cooper	.15	.11	.06
581 Rollie Fingers	.20	.15	.08
582 Jim Gantner	.08	.06	.03
583 Moose Haas	.06	.05	.02
584 Dion James	.12	.09	.05
585 Pete Ladd	.06	.05	.02
586 Rick Manning	.06	.05	.02
587 Bob McClure	.06	.05	.02
588 Paul Molitor	.15	.11	.06
589 Charlie Moore	.06	.05	.02
590 Ben Oglivie	.08	.06	.03
591 Chuck Porter	.06	.05	.02
592 *Randy Ready*(FC)	.20	.15	.08
593 Ed Romero	.06	.05	.02
594 Bill Schroeder(FC)	.10	.08	.04
595 Ray Searage	.06	.05	.02
596 Ted Simmons	.12	.09	.05
597 Jim Sundberg	.08	.06	.03
598 Don Sutton	.30	.25	.12
599 Tom Tellmann	.06	.05	.02
600 Rick Waits	.06	.05	.02
601 Robin Yount	.70	.50	.30
602 Dusty Baker	.08	.06	.03
603 Bob Brenly	.06	.05	.02
604 Jack Clark	.20	.15	.08
605 Chili Davis	.10	.08	.04
606 Mark Davis	.06	.05	.02
607 *Dan Gladden*(FC)	.50	.40	.20
608 Atlee Hammaker	.06	.05	.02
609 Mike Krukow	.08	.06	.03
610 Duane Kuiper	.06	.05	.02
611 Bob Lacey	.06	.05	.02
612 Bill Laskey	.06	.05	.02
613 Gary Lavelle	.06	.05	.02
614 Johnnie LeMaster	.06	.05	.02
615 Jeff Leonard	.10	.08	.04
616 Randy Lerch	.06	.05	.02
617 Greg Minton	.06	.05	.02
618 Steve Nicosia	.06	.05	.02
619 Gene Richards	.06	.05	.02
620 *Jeff Robinson*	.30	.25	.12
621 Scot Thompson	.06	.05	.02
622 Manny Trillo	.08	.06	.03
623 Brad Wellman	.06	.05	.02
624 *Frank Williams*	.15	.11	.06
625 Joel Youngblood	.06	.05	.02
626 Ripken-In-Action (Cal Ripken)	.30	.25	.12
627 Schmidt-In-Action (Mike Schmidt)	.30	.25	.12
628 Giving the Signs (Sparky Anderson)	.08	.06	.03
629 A.L. Pitcher's Nightmare (Rickey Henderson, Dave Winfield)	.30	.25	.12
630 N.L. Pitcher's Nightmare (Ryne Sandberg, Mike Schmidt)	.30	.25	.12
631 N.L. All-Stars (Gary Carter, Steve Garvey, Ozzie Smith, Darryl Strawberry)	.30	.25	.12
632 All-Star Game Winning Battery (Gary Carter, Charlie Lea)	.15	.11	.06
633 N.L. Pennant Clinchers (Steve Garvey, Goose Gossage)	.20	.15	.08
634 N.L. Rookie Phenoms (Dwight Gooden, Juan Samuel)	1.00	.70	.40
635 Toronto's Big Guns (Willie Upshaw)	.08	.06	.03
636 Toronto's Big Guns (Lloyd Moseby)	.08	.06	.03
637 Holland (Al Holland)	.08	.06	.03
638 Tunnell (Lee Tunnell)	.08	.06	.03
639 500th Homer (Reggie Jackson)	.30	.25	.12
640 4,000th Hit (Pete Rose)	.50	.40	.20
641 Father & Son (Cal Ripken, Jr., Cal Ripken, Sr.)	.30	.25	.12
642 Cubs Team	.08	.06	.03
643 1984's Two Perfect Games & One No Hitter (Jack Morris, David Palmer, Mike Witt)	.15	.11	.06
644 Major League Prospect (Willie Lozado, Vic Mata)	.06	.05	.02

		MT	NR MT	EX
645	Major League Prospect (Kelly Gruber, Randy O'Neal)(FC)	8.00	6.00	3.25
646	Major League Prospect (Jose Roman, Joel Skinner)(FC)	.12	.09	.05
647	Major League Prospect (Steve Kiefer, Danny Tartabull)(FC)	5.00	3.75	2.00
648	Major League Prospect (Rob Deer, Alejandro Sanchez)(FC)	1.50	1.25	.60
649	Major League Prospect (Shawon Dunston, Bill Hatcher)(FC)	6.00	4.50	2.50
650	Major League Prospect (Mike Bielecki, Ron Robinson)(FC)	.30	.25	.12
651	Major League Prospect (Zane Smith, Paul Zuvella)(FC)	.35	.25	.14
652	Major League Prospect (Glenn Davis, Joe Hesketh)(FC)	12.00	9.00	4.75
653	Major League Prospect (Steve Jeltz, John Russell)(FC)	.20	.15	.08
654	Checklist 1-95	.06	.05	.02
655	Checklist 96-195	.06	.05	.02
656	Checklist 196-292	.06	.05	.02
657	Checklist 293-391	.06	.05	.02
658	Checklist 392-481	.06	.05	.02
659	Checklist 482-575	.06	.05	.02
660	Checklist 576-660	.06	.05	.02

		MT	NR MT	EX
24	Tony Pena	.07	.05	.03
25	Dan Quisenberry	.07	.05	.03
26	Tim Raines	.25	.20	.10
27	Jim Rice	.25	.20	.10
28	Cal Ripken, Jr.	.30	.25	.12
29	Pete Rose	.60	.45	.25
30	Nolan Ryan	.70	.50	.30
31	Ryne Sandberg	.70	.50	.30
32	Steve Sax	.15	.11	.06
33	Mike Schmidt	.50	.40	.20
34	Tom Seaver	.50	.40	.20
35	Ozzie Smith	.12	.09	.05
36	Mario Soto	.05	.04	.02
37	Dave Stieb	.10	.08	.04
38	Darryl Strawberry	.60	.45	.25
39	Rick Sutcliffe	.10	.08	.04
40	Alan Trammell	.20	.15	.08
41	Willie Upshaw	.05	.04	.02
42	Fernando Valenzuela	.20	.15	.08
43	Dave Winfield	.25	.20	.10
44	Robin Yount	.50	.40	.20

1985 Fleer Update

For the second straight year, Fleer issued a 132-card update set. The cards, which measure 2-1/2" by 3-1/2", portray players on their new teams and also includes rookies not depicted in the regular issue. The cards are identical in design to the 1985 Fleer set but are numbered U-1 through U-132. The set was issued with team logo stickers in a specially designed box and was available only through hobby dealers.

		MT	NR MT	EX
	Complete Set:	18.00	13.50	7.25
	Common Player:	.10	.08	.04
1	Don Aase	.15	.11	.06
2	Bill Almon	.10	.08	.04
3	Dusty Baker	.15	.11	.06
4	Dale Berra	.10	.08	.04
5	Karl Best(FC)	.10	.08	.04
6	Tim Birtsas(FC)	.20	.15	.08
7	Vida Blue	.20	.15	.08
8	Rich Bordi	.10	.08	.04
9	Daryl Boston(FC)	.20	.15	.08
10	Hubie Brooks	.20	.15	.08
11	Chris Brown(FC)	.25	.20	.10
12	Tom Browning(FC)	1.25	.90	.50
13	Al Bumbry	.10	.08	.04
14	Tim Burke(FC)	.50	.40	.20
15	Ray Burris	.10	.08	.04
16	Jeff Burroughs	.15	.11	.06
17	Ivan Calderon(FC)	2.00	1.50	.80
18	Jeff Calhoun	.10	.08	.04
19	Bill Campbell	.10	.08	.04
20	Don Carman(FC)	.40	.30	.15
21	Gary Carter	.80	.60	.30
22	Bobby Castillo	.10	.08	.04
23	Bill Caudill	.10	.08	.04
24	Rick Cerone	.10	.08	.04
25	Jack Clark	.35	.25	.14
26	Pat Clements(FC)	.20	.15	.08
27	Stewart Cliburn(FC)	.15	.11	.06
28	Vince Coleman(FC)	6.00	4.50	2.50
29	Dave Collins	.15	.11	.06
30	Fritz Connally	.10	.08	.04
31	Henry Cotto(FC)	.20	.15	.08

1985 Fleer Limited Edition

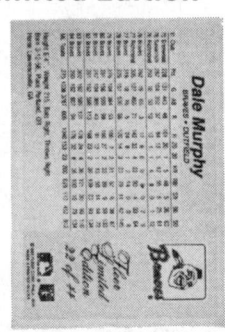

The 1985 Fleer Limited Edition 44-card set was distributed through McCrory's, J.J. Newbury, McClellan, Kress, YDC, and Green stores. The cards, which are the standard 2-1/2" by 3-1/2" size, have full-color photos inside a red and yellow frame. The card backs are set in black type against two different shades of yellow and contain the player's personal and statistical information. The set was issued in a specially designed box which carried the complete checklist for the set on the back. Six team logo stickers were also included with the set.

		MT	NR MT	EX
	Complete Set:	8.00	6.00	3.25
	Common Player:	.05	.04	.02
1	Buddy Bell	.07	.05	.03
2	Bert Blyleven	.10	.08	.04
3	Wade Boggs	.70	.50	.30
4	George Brett	.30	.25	.12
5	Rod Carew	.30	.25	.12
6	Steve Carlton	.25	.20	.10
7	Alvin Davis	.20	.15	.08
8	Andre Dawson	.15	.11	.06
9	Steve Garvey	.25	.20	.10
10	Goose Gossage	.12	.09	.05
11	Tony Gwynn	.40	.30	.15
12	Keith Hernandez	.20	.15	.08
13	Kent Hrbek	.15	.11	.06
14	Reggie Jackson	.30	.25	.12
15	Dave Kingman	.10	.08	.04
16	Ron Kittle	.07	.05	.03
17	Mark Langston	.25	.20	.10
18	Jeff Leonard	.05	.04	.02
19	Bill Madlock	.07	.05	.03
20	Don Mattingly	1.00	.70	.40
21	Jack Morris	.15	.11	.06
22	Dale Murphy	.30	.25	.12
23	Eddie Murray	.25	.20	.10

		MT	NR MT	EX
32	Danny Darwin	.15	.11	.06
33	Darren Daulton(FC)	.50	.40	.20
34	Jerry Davis	.10	.08	.04
35	Brian Dayett	.10	.08	.04
36	Ken Dixon(FC)	.10	.08	.04
37	Tommy Dunbar	.10	.08	.04
38	Mariano Duncan(FC)	1.00	.70	.40
39	Bob Fallon	.10	.08	.04
40	Brian Fisher(FC)	.30	.25	.12
41	Mike Fitzgerald	.10	.08	.04
42	Ray Fontenot	.10	.08	.04
43	Greg Gagne(FC)	.35	.25	.14
44	Oscar Gamble	.15	.11	.06
45	Jim Gott	.10	.08	.04
46	David Green	.10	.08	.04
47	Alfredo Griffin	.15	.11	.06
48	Ozzie Guillen(FC)	3.00	2.25	1.25
49	Toby Harrah	.15	.11	.06
50	Ron Hassey	.10	.08	.04
51	Rickey Henderson	3.00	2.25	1.25
52	Steve Henderson	.10	.08	.04
53	George Hendrick	.15	.11	.06
54	Teddy Higuera(FC)	2.25	1.75	.90
55	Al Holland	.10	.08	.04
56	Burt Hooton	.15	.11	.06
57	Jay Howell	.15	.11	.06
58	LaMarr Hoyt	.10	.08	.04
59	Tim Hulett(FC)	.20	.15	.08
60	Bob James	.10	.08	.04
61	Cliff Johnson	.10	.08	.04
62	Howard Johnson	2.25	1.75	.90
63	Ruppert Jones	.10	.08	.04
64	Steve Kemp	.15	.11	.06
65	Bruce Kison	.10	.08	.04
66	Mike LaCoss	.15	.11	.06
67	Lee Lacy	.15	.11	.06
68	Dave LaPoint	.20	.15	.08
69	Gary Lavelle	.10	.08	.04
70	Vance Law	.15	.11	.06
71	Manny Lee(FC)	.20	.15	.08
72	Sixto Lezcano	.10	.08	.04
73	Tim Lollar	.10	.08	.04
74	Urbano Lugo(FC)	.15	.11	.06
75	Fred Lynn	.30	.25	.12
76	Steve Lyons(FC)	.15	.11	.06
77	Mickey Mahler	.10	.08	.04
78	Ron Mathis(FC)	.10	.08	.04
79	Len Matuszek	.10	.08	.04
80	Oddibe McDowell(FC)	.70	.50	.30
81	Roger McDowell(FC)	.90	.70	.35
82	Donnie Moore	.10	.08	.04
83	Ron Musselman	.10	.08	.04
84	Al Oliver	.25	.20	.10
85	Joe Orsulak(FC)	.20	.15	.08
86	Dan Pasqua(FC)	.50	.40	.20
87	Chris Pittaro(FC)	.10	.08	.04
88	Rick Reuschel	.20	.15	.08
89	Earnie Riles(FC)	.20	.15	.08
90	Jerry Royster	.10	.08	.04
91	Dave Rozema	.10	.08	.04
92	Dave Rucker	.10	.08	.04
93	Vern Ruhle	.10	.08	.04
94	Mark Salas(FC)	.20	.15	.08
95	Luis Salazar	.10	.08	.04
96	Joe Sambito	.10	.08	.04
97	Billy Sample	.10	.08	.04
98	Alex Sanchez	.10	.08	.04
99	Calvin Schiraldi(FC)	.25	.20	.10
100	Rick Schu(FC)	.20	.15	.08
101	Larry Sheets(FC)	.50	.40	.20
102	Ron Shepherd	.10	.08	.04
103	Nelson Simmons(FC)	.10	.08	.04
104	Don Slaught	.10	.08	.04
105	Roy Smalley	.15	.11	.06
106	Lonnie Smith	.15	.11	.06
107	Nate Snell(FC)	.10	.08	.04
108	Lary Sorensen	.10	.08	.04
109	Chris Speier	.10	.08	.04
110	Mike Stenhouse	.10	.08	.04
111	Tim Stoddard	.10	.08	.04
112	John Stuper	.10	.08	.04
113	Jim Sundberg	.15	.11	.06
114	Bruce Sutter	.25	.20	.10
115	Don Sutton	.60	.45	.25
116	Bruce Tanner(FC)	.10	.08	.04
117	Kent Tekulve	.15	.11	.06
118	Walt Terrell	.15	.11	.06
119	Mickey Tettleton(FC)	1.00	.70	.40
120	Rich Thompson	.10	.08	.04
121	Louis Thornton(FC)	.10	.08	.04
122	Alex Trevino	.10	.08	.04

		MT	NR MT	EX
123	John Tudor	.30	.25	.12
124	Jose Uribe(FC)	.25	.20	.10
125	Dave Valle(FC)	.20	.15	.08
126	Dave Von Ohlen	.10	.08	.04
127	Curt Wardle	.10	.08	.04
128	U.L. Washington	.10	.08	.04
129	Ed Whitson	.10	.08	.04
130	Herm Winningham(FC)	.20	.15	.08
131	Rich Yett(FC)	.15	.11	.06
132	Checklist	.10	.08	.04

1986 Fleer

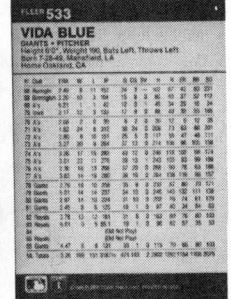

The 1986 Fleer set contains 660 color photos, with each card measuring 2-1/2" by 3-1/2" in size. The card fronts include the word "Fleer," the player's team logo, and a player picture enclosed by a dark blue border. The card reverses are minus the black and white photo that was included in past Fleer efforts. Player biographical and statistical information appear in black and yellow ink on white stock. As in 1985, Fleer devoted ten cards, entitled "Major League Prospects," to twenty promising rookie players. The 1986 set, as in the previous four years, was issued with team logo stickers.

		MT	NR MT	EX
Complete Set:		125.00	90.00	50.00
Common Player:		.06	.05	.02
1	Steve Balboni	.08	.06	.03
2	Joe Beckwith	.06	.05	.02
3	Buddy Biancalana	.06	.05	.02
4	Bud Black	.06	.05	.02
5	George Brett	.50	.40	.20
6	Onix Concepcion	.06	.05	.02
7	Steve Farr	.08	.06	.03
8	Mark Gubicza	.12	.09	.05
9	Dane Iorg	.06	.05	.02
10	Danny Jackson	.20	.15	.08
11	Lynn Jones	.06	.05	.02
12	Mike Jones	.06	.05	.02
13	Charlie Leibrandt	.08	.06	.03
14	Hal McRae	.10	.08	.04
15	Omar Moreno	.06	.05	.02
16	Darryl Motley	.06	.05	.02
17	Jorge Orta	.06	.05	.02
18	Dan Quisenberry	.08	.06	.03
19	Bret Saberhagen	1.50	1.25	.60
20	Pat Sheridan	.06	.05	.02
21	Lonnie Smith	.08	.06	.03
22	Jim Sundberg	.08	.06	.03
23	John Wathan	.08	.06	.03
24	Frank White	.10	.08	.04
25	Willie Wilson	.12	.09	.05
26	Joaquin Andujar	.08	.06	.03
27	Steve Braun	.06	.05	.02
28	Bill Campbell	.06	.05	.02
29	Cesar Cedeno	.10	.08	.04
30	Jack Clark	.20	.15	.08
31	*Vince Coleman*	3.00	2.25	1.25
32	Danny Cox	.10	.08	.04
33	Ken Dayley	.06	.05	.02
34	Ivan DeJesus	.06	.05	.02
35	Bob Forsch	.08	.06	.03
36	Brian Harper	.06	.05	.02
37	Tom Herr	.10	.08	.04

		MT	NR MT	EX				MT	NR MT	EX
38	Ricky Horton	.08	.06	.03		129	Mariano Duncan	.15	.11	.06
39	Kurt Kepshire	.06	.05	.02		130	Pedro Guerrero	.20	.15	.08
40	Jeff Lahti	.06	.05	.02		131	Orel Hershiser	1.25	.90	.50
41	Tito Landrum	.06	.05	.02		132	Rick Honeycutt	.06	.05	.02
42	Willie McGee	.15	.11	.06		133	Ken Howell	.06	.05	.02
43	Tom Nieto	.06	.05	.02		134	Ken Landreaux	.06	.05	.02
44	Terry Pendleton	.15	.11	.06		135	Bill Madlock	.12	.09	.05
45	Darrell Porter	.08	.06	.03		136	Candy Maldonado	.10	.08	.04
46	Ozzie Smith	.15	.11	.06		137	Mike Marshall	.15	.11	.06
47	John Tudor	.10	.08	.04		138	Len Matuszek	.06	.05	.02
48	Andy Van Slyke	.15	.11	.06		139	Tom Niedenfuer	.08	.06	.03
49	Todd Worrell(FC)	.90	.70	.35		140	Alejandro Pena	.08	.06	.03
50	Jim Acker	.06	.05	.02		141	Jerry Reuss	.08	.06	.03
51	Doyle Alexander	.10	.08	.04		142	Bill Russell	.08	.06	.03
52	Jesse Barfield	.20	.15	.08		143	Steve Sax	.20	.15	.08
53	George Bell	.30	.25	.12		144	Mike Scioscia	.08	.06	.03
54	Jeff Burroughs	.08	.06	.03		145	Fernando Valenzuela	.30	.25	.12
55	Bill Caudill	.06	.05	.02		146	Bob Welch	.12	.09	.05
56	Jim Clancy	.08	.06	.03		147	Terry Whitfield	.06	.05	.02
57	Tony Fernandez	.20	.15	.08		148	Juan Beniquez	.06	.05	.02
58	Tom Filer	.06	.05	.02		149	Bob Boone	.08	.06	.03
59	Damaso Garcia	.06	.05	.02		150	John Candelaria	.10	.08	.04
60	Tom Henke(FC)	.15	.11	.06		151	Rod Carew	.30	.25	.12
61	Garth Iorg	.06	.05	.02		152	Stewart Cliburn(FC)	.12	.09	.05
62	Cliff Johnson	.06	.05	.02		153	Doug DeCinces	.10	.08	.04
63	Jimmy Key	.15	.11	.06		154	Brian Downing	.08	.06	.03
64	Dennis Lamp	.06	.05	.02		155	Ken Forsch	.06	.05	.02
65	Gary Lavelle	.06	.05	.02		156	Craig Gerber	.06	.05	.02
66	Buck Martinez	.06	.05	.02		157	Bobby Grich	.10	.08	.04
67	Lloyd Moseby	.10	.08	.04		158	George Hendrick	.08	.06	.03
68	Rance Mulliniks	.06	.05	.02		159	Al Holland	.06	.05	.02
69	Al Oliver	.10	.08	.04		160	Reggie Jackson	.35	.25	.14
70	Dave Stieb	.12	.09	.05		161	Ruppert Jones	.06	.05	.02
71	Louis Thornton	.06	.05	.02		162	Urbano Lugo	.08	.06	.03
72	Willie Upshaw	.08	.06	.03		163	Kirk McCaskill(FC)	.35	.25	.14
73	Ernie Whitt	.08	.06	.03		164	Donnie Moore	.06	.05	.02
74	Rick Aguilera(FC)	.25	.20	.10		165	Gary Pettis	.06	.05	.02
75	Wally Backman	.08	.06	.03		166	Ron Romanick	.06	.05	.02
76	Gary Carter	.25	.20	.10		167	Dick Schofield	.06	.05	.02
77	Ron Darling	.15	.11	.06		168	Daryl Sconiers	.06	.05	.02
78	Len Dykstra(FC)	4.00	3.00	1.50		169	Jim Slaton	.06	.05	.02
79	Sid Fernandez	.12	.09	.05		170	Don Sutton	.25	.20	.10
80	George Foster	.15	.11	.06		171	Mike Witt	.10	.08	.04
81	Dwight Gooden	2.00	1.50	.80		172	Buddy Bell	.10	.08	.04
82	Tom Gorman	.06	.05	.02		173	Tom Browning	.30	.25	.12
83	Danny Heep	.06	.05	.02		174	Dave Concepcion	.12	.09	.05
84	Keith Hernandez	.30	.25	.12		175	Eric Davis	3.00	2.25	1.25
85	Howard Johnson	.12	.09	.05		176	Bo Diaz	.08	.06	.03
86	Ray Knight	.08	.06	.03		177	Nick Esasky	.08	.06	.03
87	Terry Leach	.08	.06	.03		178	John Franco	.12	.09	.05
88	Ed Lynch	.06	.05	.02		179	Tom Hume	.06	.05	.02
89	Roger McDowell(FC)	.60	.45	.25		180	Wayne Krenchicki	.06	.05	.02
90	Jesse Orosco	.08	.06	.03		181	Andy McGaffigan	.06	.05	.02
91	Tom Paciorek	.06	.05	.02		182	Eddie Milner	.06	.05	.02
92	Ronn Reynolds	.06	.05	.02		183	Ron Oester	.06	.05	.02
93	Rafael Santana	.06	.05	.02		184	Dave Parker	.20	.15	.08
94	Doug Sisk	.06	.05	.02		185	Frank Pastore	.06	.05	.02
95	Rusty Staub	.10	.08	.04		186	Tony Perez	.15	.11	.06
96	Darryl Strawberry	2.00	1.50	.80		187	Ted Power	.08	.06	.03
97	Mookie Wilson	.10	.08	.04		188	Joe Price	.06	.05	.02
98	Neil Allen	.06	.05	.02		189	Gary Redus	.06	.05	.02
99	Don Baylor	.12	.09	.05		190	Ron Robinson	.08	.06	.03
100	Dale Berra	.06	.05	.02		191	Pete Rose	.70	.50	.30
101	Rich Bordi	.06	.05	.02		192	Mario Soto	.08	.06	.03
102	Marty Bystrom	.06	.05	.02		193	John Stuper	.06	.05	.02
103	Joe Cowley	.06	.05	.02		194	Jay Tibbs	.06	.05	.02
104	Brian Fisher	.30	.25	.12		195	Dave Van Gorder	.06	.05	.02
105	Ken Griffey	.10	.08	.04		196	Max Venable	.06	.05	.02
106	Ron Guidry	.20	.15	.08		197	Juan Agosto	.06	.05	.02
107	Ron Hassey	.06	.05	.02		198	Harold Baines	.15	.11	.06
108	Rickey Henderson	.40	.30	.15		199	Floyd Bannister	.10	.08	.04
109	Don Mattingly	4.00	3.00	1.50		200	Britt Burns	.06	.05	.02
110	Bobby Meacham	.06	.05	.02		201	Julio Cruz	.06	.05	.02
111	John Montefusco	.06	.05	.02		202	Joel Davis(FC)	.08	.06	.03
112	Phil Niekro	.25	.20	.10		203	Richard Dotson	.10	.08	.04
113	Mike Pagliarulo	.20	.15	.08		204	Carlton Fisk	.30	.25	.12
114	Dan Pasqua	.20	.15	.08		205	Scott Fletcher	.08	.06	.03
115	Willie Randolph	.10	.08	.04		206	Ozzie Guillen	1.25	.90	.50
116	Dave Righetti	.20	.15	.08		207	Jerry Hairston	.06	.05	.02
117	Andre Robertson	.06	.05	.02		208	Tim Hulett	.08	.06	.03
118	Billy Sample	.06	.05	.02		209	Bob James	.06	.05	.02
119	Bob Shirley	.06	.05	.02		210	Ron Kittle	.10	.08	.04
120	Ed Whitson	.06	.05	.02		211	Rudy Law	.06	.05	.02
121	Dave Winfield	.30	.25	.12		212	Bryan Little	.06	.05	.02
122	Butch Wynegar	.06	.05	.02		213	Gene Nelson	.06	.05	.02
123	Dave Anderson	.06	.05	.02		214	Reid Nichols	.06	.05	.02
124	Bob Bailor	.06	.05	.02		215	Luis Salazar	.06	.05	.02
125	Greg Brock	.08	.06	.03		216	Tom Seaver	.40	.30	.15
126	Enos Cabell	.06	.05	.02		217	Dan Spillner	.06	.05	.02
127	Bobby Castillo	.06	.05	.02		218	Bruce Tanner	.06	.05	.02
128	Carlos Diaz	.06	.05	.02		219	Greg Walker	.10	.08	.04

		MT	NR MT	EX				MT	NR MT	EX
220	Dave Wehrmeister	.06	.05	.02		311	Mike Scott	.15	.11	.06
221	Juan Berenguer	.06	.05	.02		312	Dave Smith	.08	.06	.03
222	Dave Bergman	.06	.05	.02		313	Dickie Thon	.08	.06	.03
223	Tom Brookens	.06	.05	.02		314	Denny Walling	.06	.05	.02
224	Darrell Evans	.12	.09	.05		315	Kurt Bevacqua	.06	.05	.02
225	Barbaro Garbey	.06	.05	.02		316	Al Bumbry	.06	.05	.02
226	Kirk Gibson	.30	.25	.12		317	Jerry Davis	.06	.05	.02
227	John Grubb	.06	.05	.02		318	Luis DeLeon	.06	.05	.02
228	Willie Hernandez	.08	.06	.03		319	Dave Dravecky	.08	.06	.03
229	Larry Herndon	.08	.06	.03		320	Tim Flannery	.06	.05	.02
230	Chet Lemon	.08	.06	.03		321	Steve Garvey	.30	.25	.12
231	Aurelio Lopez	.06	.05	.02		322	Goose Gossage	.20	.15	.08
232	Jack Morris	.20	.15	.08		323	Tony Gwynn	.40	.30	.15
233	Randy O'Neal	.06	.05	.02		324	Andy Hawkins	.06	.05	.02
234	Lance Parrish	.20	.15	.08		325	LaMarr Hoyt	.06	.05	.02
235	Dan Petry	.08	.06	.03		326	Roy Lee Jackson	.06	.05	.02
236	Alex Sanchez	.06	.05	.02		327	Terry Kennedy	.08	.06	.03
237	Bill Scherrer	.06	.05	.02		328	Craig Lefferts	.06	.05	.02
238	Nelson Simmons	.06	.05	.02		329	Carmelo Martinez	.08	.06	.03
239	Frank Tanana	.10	.08	.04		330	*Lance McCullers*(FC)	.25	.20	.10
240	Walt Terrell	.08	.06	.03		331	Kevin McReynolds	.30	.25	.12
241	Alan Trammell	.30	.25	.12		332	Graig Nettles	.15	.11	.06
242	Lou Whitaker	.30	.25	.12		333	Jerry Royster	.06	.05	.02
243	Milt Wilcox	.06	.05	.02		334	Eric Show	.08	.06	.03
244	Hubie Brooks	.10	.08	.04		335	Tim Stoddard	.06	.05	.02
245	*Tim Burke*(FC)	.30	.25	.12		336	Garry Templeton	.08	.06	.03
246	Andre Dawson	.20	.15	.08		337	Mark Thurmond	.06	.05	.02
247	Mike Fitzgerald	.06	.05	.02		338	Ed Wojna	.06	.05	.02
248	Terry Francona	.06	.05	.02		339	Tony Armas	.08	.06	.03
249	Bill Gullickson	.06	.05	.02		340	Marty Barrett	.10	.08	.04
250	Joe Hesketh	.06	.05	.02		341	Wade Boggs	2.25	1.75	.90
251	Bill Laskey	.06	.05	.02		342	Dennis Boyd	.08	.06	.03
252	Vance Law	.08	.06	.03		343	Bill Buckner	.12	.09	.05
253	Charlie Lea	.06	.05	.02		344	Mark Clear	.06	.05	.02
254	Gary Lucas	.06	.05	.02		345	Roger Clemens	3.00	2.25	1.25
255	David Palmer	.06	.05	.02		346	Steve Crawford	.06	.05	.02
256	Tim Raines	.30	.25	.12		347	Mike Easler	.08	.06	.03
257	Jeff Reardon	.12	.09	.05		348	Dwight Evans	.12	.09	.05
258	Bert Roberge	.06	.05	.02		349	Rich Gedman	.10	.08	.04
259	Dan Schatzeder	.06	.05	.02		350	Jackie Gutierrez	.06	.05	.02
260	Bryn Smith	.06	.05	.02		351	Glenn Hoffman	.06	.05	.02
261	Randy St. Claire(FC)	.08	.06	.03		352	Bruce Hurst	.12	.09	.05
262	Scot Thompson	.06	.05	.02		353	Bruce Kison	.06	.05	.02
263	Tim Wallach	.12	.09	.05		354	Tim Lollar	.06	.05	.02
264	U.L. Washington	.06	.05	.02		355	Steve Lyons	.08	.06	.03
265	*Mitch Webster*(FC)	.25	.20	.10		356	Al Nipper	.08	.06	.03
266	*Herm Winningham*	.15	.11	.06		357	Bob Ojeda	.08	.06	.03
267	*Floyd Youmans*(FC)	.30	.25	.12		358	Jim Rice	.30	.25	.12
268	Don Aase	.06	.05	.02		359	Bob Stanley	.06	.05	.02
269	Mike Boddicker	.08	.06	.03		360	Mike Trujillo	.06	.05	.02
270	Rich Dauer	.06	.05	.02		361	Thad Bosley	.06	.05	.02
271	Storm Davis	.10	.08	.04		362	Warren Brusstar	.06	.05	.02
272	Rick Dempsey	.08	.06	.03		363	Ron Cey	.10	.08	.04
273	Ken Dixon	.06	.05	.02		364	Jody Davis	.10	.08	.04
274	Jim Dwyer	.06	.05	.02		365	Bob Dernier	.06	.05	.02
275	Mike Flanagan	.10	.08	.04		366	Shawon Dunston	.15	.11	.06
276	Wayne Gross	.06	.05	.02		367	Leon Durham	.08	.06	.03
277	Lee Lacy	.06	.05	.02		368	Dennis Eckersley	.12	.09	.05
278	Fred Lynn	.20	.15	.08		369	Ray Fontenot	.06	.05	.02
279	Tippy Martinez	.06	.05	.02		370	George Frazier	.06	.05	.02
280	Dennis Martinez	.08	.06	.03		371	Bill Hatcher	.10	.08	.04
281	Scott McGregor	.08	.06	.03		372	Dave Lopes	.08	.06	.03
282	Eddie Murray	.40	.30	.15		373	Gary Matthews	.10	.08	.04
283	Floyd Rayford	.06	.05	.02		374	Ron Meredith	.06	.05	.02
284	Cal Ripken, Jr.	.40	.30	.15		375	Keith Moreland	.08	.06	.03
285	Gary Roenicke	.06	.05	.02		376	Reggie Patterson	.06	.05	.02
286	Larry Sheets	.20	.15	.08		377	Dick Ruthven	.06	.05	.02
287	John Shelby	.06	.05	.02		378	Ryne Sandberg	1.50	1.25	.60
288	Nate Snell	.06	.05	.02		379	Scott Sanderson	.06	.05	.02
289	Sammy Stewart	.06	.05	.02		380	Lee Smith	.10	.08	.04
290	Alan Wiggins	.06	.05	.02		381	Lary Sorensen	.06	.05	.02
291	Mike Young	.06	.05	.02		382	Chris Speier	.06	.05	.02
292	Alan Ashby	.06	.05	.02		383	Rick Sutcliffe	.12	.09	.05
293	Mark Bailey	.06	.05	.02		384	Steve Trout	.06	.05	.02
294	Kevin Bass	.10	.08	.04		385	Gary Woods	.06	.05	.02
295	Jeff Calhoun	.06	.05	.02		386	Bert Blyleven	.15	.11	.06
296	Jose Cruz	.10	.08	.04		387	Tom Brunansky	.12	.09	.05
297	Glenn Davis	.70	.50	.30		388	Randy Bush	.06	.05	.02
298	Bill Dawley	.06	.05	.02		389	John Butcher	.06	.05	.02
299	Frank DiPino	.06	.05	.02		390	Ron Davis	.06	.05	.02
300	Bill Doran	.10	.08	.04		391	Dave Engle	.06	.05	.02
301	Phil Garner	.08	.06	.03		392	Frank Eufemia	.06	.05	.02
302	*Jeff Heathcock*(FC)	.10	.08	.04		393	Pete Filson	.06	.05	.02
303	*Charlie Kerfeld*(FC)	.15	.11	.06		394	Gary Gaetti	.20	.15	.08
304	Bob Knepper	.08	.06	.03		395	Greg Gagne	.10	.08	.04
305	Ron Mathis	.06	.05	.02		396	Mickey Hatcher	.06	.05	.02
306	Jerry Mumphrey	.06	.05	.02		397	Kent Hrbek	.20	.15	.08
307	Jim Pankovits	.06	.05	.02		398	Tim Laudner	.06	.05	.02
308	Terry Puhl	.06	.05	.02		399	Rick Lysander	.06	.05	.02
309	Craig Reynolds	.06	.05	.02		400	Dave Meier	.06	.05	.02
310	Nolan Ryan	.50	.40	.20		401	Kirby Puckett	4.00	3.00	1.50

	MT	NR MT	EX			MT	NR MT	EX
402	Mark Salas	.08	.06	.03	493	Rick Manning	.06	.05	.02
403	Ken Schrom	.06	.05	.02	494	Bob McClure	.06	.05	.02
404	Roy Smalley	.06	.05	.02	495	Paul Molitor	.15	.11	.06
405	Mike Smithson	.06	.05	.02	496	Charlie Moore	.06	.05	.02
406	Mike Stenhouse	.06	.05	.02	497	Ben Oglivie	.08	.06	.03
407	Tim Teufel	.06	.05	.02	498	Randy Ready	.06	.05	.02
408	Frank Viola	.15	.11	.06	499	*Earnie Riles*	.20	.15	.08
409	Ron Washington	.06	.05	.02	500	Ed Romero	.06	.05	.02
410	Keith Atherton	.06	.05	.02	501	Bill Schroeder	.06	.05	.02
411	Dusty Baker	.08	.06	.03	502	Ray Searage	.06	.05	.02
412	*Tim Birtsas*	.12	.09	.05	503	Ted Simmons	.12	.09	.05
413	Bruce Bochte	.06	.05	.02	504	Pete Vuckovich	.08	.06	.03
414	Chris Codiroli	.06	.05	.02	505	Rick Waits	.06	.05	.02
415	Dave Collins	.08	.06	.03	506	Robin Yount	.30	.25	.12
416	Mike Davis	.08	.06	.03	507	Len Barker	.08	.06	.03
417	Alfredo Griffin	.08	.06	.03	508	Steve Bedrosian	.12	.09	.05
418	Mike Heath	.06	.05	.02	509	Bruce Benedict	.06	.05	.02
419	Steve Henderson	.06	.05	.02	510	Rick Camp	.06	.05	.02
420	Donnie Hill	.06	.05	.02	511	Rick Cerone	.06	.05	.02
421	Jay Howell	.08	.06	.03	512	Chris Chambliss	.08	.06	.03
422	Tommy John	.20	.15	.08	513	Jeff Dedmon	.06	.05	.02
423	Dave Kingman	.15	.11	.06	514	Terry Forster	.08	.06	.03
424	Bill Krueger	.06	.05	.02	515	Gene Garber	.06	.05	.02
425	Rick Langford	.06	.05	.02	516	Terry Harper	.06	.05	.02
426	Carney Lansford	.10	.08	.04	517	Bob Horner	.12	.09	.05
427	Steve McCatty	.06	.05	.02	518	Glenn Hubbard	.06	.05	.02
428	Dwayne Murphy	.08	.06	.03	519	*Joe Johnson*(FC)	.08	.06	.03
429	*Steve Ontiveros*(FC)	.12	.09	.05	520	Brad Komminsk	.06	.05	.02
430	Tony Phillips	.06	.05	.02	521	Rick Mahler	.06	.05	.02
431	Jose Rijo	.10	.08	.04	522	Dale Murphy	.50	.40	.20
432	*Mickey Tettleton*	.90	.70	.35	523	Ken Oberkfell	.06	.05	.02
433	Luis Aguayo	.06	.05	.02	524	Pascual Perez	.08	.06	.03
434	Larry Andersen	.06	.05	.02	525	Gerald Perry	.12	.09	.05
435	Steve Carlton	.30	.25	.12	526	Rafael Ramirez	.06	.05	.02
436	*Don Carman*	.30	.25	.12	527	*Steve Shields*(FC)	.12	.09	.05
437	Tim Corcoran	.06	.05	.02	528	Zane Smith	.10	.08	.04
438	*Darren Daulton*	.12	.09	.05	529	Bruce Sutter	.12	.09	.05
439	John Denny	.06	.05	.02	530	*Milt Thompson*(FC)	.30	.25	.12
440	Tom Foley	.06	.05	.02	531	Claudell Washington	.08	.06	.03
441	Greg Gross	.06	.05	.02	532	Paul Zuvella	.06	.05	.02
442	Kevin Gross	.08	.06	.03	533	Vida Blue	.10	.08	.04
443	Von Hayes	.10	.08	.04	534	Bob Brenly	.06	.05	.02
444	Charles Hudson	.06	.05	.02	535	*Chris Brown*	.20	.15	.08
445	Garry Maddox	.08	.06	.03	536	Chili Davis	.10	.08	.04
446	Shane Rawley	.10	.08	.04	537	Mark Davis	.06	.05	.02
447	Dave Rucker	.06	.05	.02	538	Rob Deer	.12	.09	.05
448	John Russell	.06	.05	.02	539	Dan Driessen	.08	.06	.03
449	Juan Samuel	.12	.09	.05	540	Scott Garrelts	.08	.06	.03
450	Mike Schmidt	.50	.40	.20	541	Dan Gladden	.08	.06	.03
451	Rick Schu	.08	.06	.03	542	Jim Gott	.06	.05	.02
452	Dave Shipanoff	.06	.05	.02	543	David Green	.06	.05	.02
453	Dave Stewart	.12	.09	.05	544	Atlee Hammaker	.06	.05	.02
454	Jeff Stone	.06	.05	.02	545	Mike Jeffcoat	.06	.05	.02
455	Kent Tekulve	.08	.06	.03	546	Mike Krukow	.08	.06	.03
456	Ozzie Virgil	.06	.05	.02	547	Dave LaPoint	.08	.06	.03
457	Glenn Wilson	.08	.06	.03	548	Jeff Leonard	.08	.06	.03
458	Jim Beattie	.06	.05	.02	549	Greg Minton	.06	.05	.02
459	Karl Best	.06	.05	.02	550	Alex Trevino	.06	.05	.02
460	Barry Bonnell	.06	.05	.02	551	Manny Trillo	.08	.06	.03
461	Phil Bradley	.20	.15	.08	552	*Jose Uribe*	.20	.15	.08
462	*Ivan Calderon*	1.00	.70	.40	553	Brad Wellman	.06	.05	.02
463	Al Cowens	.06	.05	.02	554	Frank Williams	.06	.05	.02
464	Alvin Davis	.30	.25	.12	555	Joel Youngblood	.06	.05	.02
465	Dave Henderson	.10	.08	.04	556	Alan Bannister	.06	.05	.02
466	Bob Kearney	.06	.05	.02	557	Glenn Brummer	.06	.05	.02
467	Mark Langston	.30	.25	.12	558	*Steve Buechele*(FC)	.20	.15	.08
468	Bob Long	.06	.05	.02	559	*Jose Guzman*(FC)	.20	.15	.08
469	Mike Moore	.06	.05	.02	560	Toby Harrah	.08	.06	.03
470	Edwin Nunez	.06	.05	.02	561	Greg Harris	.06	.05	.02
471	Spike Owen	.06	.05	.02	562	*Dwayne Henry*(FC)	.10	.08	.04
472	Jack Perconte	.06	.05	.02	563	Burt Hooton	.08	.06	.03
473	Jim Presley	.15	.11	.06	564	Charlie Hough	.08	.06	.03
474	Donnie Scott	.06	.05	.02	565	Mike Mason	.06	.05	.02
475	Bill Swift(FC)	.12	.09	.05	566	*Oddibe McDowell*	.30	.25	.12
476	Danny Tartabull	.50	.40	.20	567	Dickie Noles	.06	.05	.02
477	Gorman Thomas	.10	.08	.04	568	Pete O'Brien	.10	.08	.04
478	Roy Thomas	.06	.05	.02	569	Larry Parrish	.10	.08	.04
479	Ed Vande Berg	.06	.05	.02	570	Dave Rozema	.06	.05	.02
480	Frank Wills	.06	.05	.02	571	Dave Schmidt	.06	.05	.02
481	Matt Young	.06	.05	.02	572	Don Slaught	.06	.05	.02
482	Ray Burris	.06	.05	.02	573	Wayne Tolleson	.06	.05	.02
483	Jaime Cocanower	.06	.05	.02	574	Duane Walker	.06	.05	.02
484	Cecil Cooper	.12	.09	.05	575	Gary Ward	.08	.06	.03
485	Danny Darwin	.06	.05	.02	576	Chris Welsh	.06	.05	.02
486	Rollie Fingers	.20	.15	.08	577	Curtis Wilkerson	.06	.05	.02
487	Jim Gantner	.08	.06	.03	578	George Wright	.06	.05	.02
488	Bob Gibson	.06	.05	.02	579	Chris Bando	.06	.05	.02
489	Moose Haas	.06	.05	.02	580	Tony Bernazard	.06	.05	.02
490	*Teddy Higuera*	1.00	.70	.40	581	Brett Butler	.08	.06	.03
491	Paul Householder	.06	.05	.02	582	Ernie Camacho	.06	.05	.02
492	Pete Ladd	.06	.05	.02	583	Joe Carter	.20	.15	.08

		MT	NR MT	EX
584	Carmello Castillo (Carmelo)	.06	.05	.02
585	Jamie Easterly	.06	.05	.02
586	Julio Franco	.10	.08	.04
587	Mel Hall	.08	.06	.03
588	Mike Hargrove	.06	.05	.02
589	Neal Heaton	.06	.05	.02
590	Brook Jacoby	.10	.08	.04
591	Otis Nixon(FC)	.12	.09	.05
592	Jerry Reed	.06	.05	.02
593	Vern Ruhle	.06	.05	.02
594	Pat Tabler	.08	.06	.03
595	Rich Thompson	.06	.05	.02
596	Andre Thornton	.08	.06	.03
597	Dave Von Ohlen	.06	.05	.02
598	George Vukovich	.06	.05	.02
599	Tom Waddell	.06	.05	.02
600	Curt Wardle	.06	.05	.02
601	Jerry Willard	.06	.05	.02
602	Bill Almon	.06	.05	.02
603	Mike Bielecki	.08	.06	.03
604	Sid Bream	.10	.08	.04
605	Mike Brown	.06	.05	.02
606	Pat Clements	.12	.09	.05
607	Jose DeLeon	.08	.06	.03
608	Denny Gonzalez	.06	.05	.02
609	Cecilio Guante	.06	.05	.02
610	Steve Kemp	.08	.06	.03
611	Sam Khalifa	.06	.05	.02
612	Lee Mazzilli	.08	.06	.03
613	Larry McWilliams	.06	.05	.02
614	Jim Morrison	.06	.05	.02
615	Joe Orsulak	.15	.11	.06
616	Tony Pena	.10	.08	.04
617	Johnny Ray	.10	.08	.04
618	Rick Reuschel	.10	.08	.04
619	R.J. Reynolds	.08	.06	.03
620	Rick Rhoden	.10	.08	.04
621	Don Robinson	.08	.06	.03
622	Jason Thompson	.06	.05	.02
623	Lee Tunnell	.06	.05	.02
624	Jim Winn	.06	.05	.02
625	Marvell Wynne	.06	.05	.02
626	Gooden In Action (Dwight Gooden)	.50	.40	.20
627	Mattingly In Action (Don Mattingly)	1.25	.90	.50
628	4,192! (Pete Rose)	.50	.40	.20
629	3,000 Career Hits (Rod Carew)	.20	.15	.08
630	300 Career Wins (Phil Niekro, Tom Seaver)	.20	.15	.08
631	Ouch! (Don Baylor)	.08	.06	.03
632	Instant Offense (Tim Raines, Darryl Strawberry)	.30	.25	.12
633	Shortstops Supreme (Cal Ripken, Jr., Alan Trammell)	.30	.25	.12
634	Boggs & "Hero" (Wade Boggs, George Brett)	.60	.45	.25
635	Braves Dynamic Duo (Bob Horner, Dale Murphy)	.30	.25	.12
636	Cardinal Ignitors (Vince Coleman, Willie McGee)	.35	.25	.14
637	Terror on the Basepaths (Vince Coleman)	.35	.25	.14
638	Charlie Hustle & Dr. K (Dwight Gooden, Pete Rose)	.70	.50	.30
639	1984 and 1985 A.L. Batting Champs (Wade Boggs, Don Mattingly)	1.75	1.25	.70
640	N.L. West Sluggers (Steve Garvey, Dale Murphy, Dave Parker)	.30	.25	.12
641	Staff Aces (Dwight Gooden, Fernando Valenzuela)	.40	.30	.15
642	Blue Jay Stoppers (Jimmy Key, Dave Stieb)	.10	.08	.04
643	A.L. All-Star Backstops (Carlton Fisk, Rich Gedman)	.10	.08	.04
644	Major League Prospect (Benito Santiago, Gene Walter)(FC)	6.00	4.50	2.50
645	Major League Prospect (Colin Ward, Mike Woodard)(FC)	.10	.08	.04
646	Major League Prospect (Kal Daniels, Paul O'Neill)(FC)	6.00	4.50	2.50
647	Major League Prospect (Andres Galarraga, Fred Toliver)(FC)	3.50	2.75	1.50
648	Major League Prospect (Curt Ford, Bob Kipper)(FC)	.25	.20	.10
649	Major League Prospect (Jose Canseco, Eric Plunk)(FC)	50.00	37.00	20.00
650	Major League Prospect (Mark McLemore, Gus Polidor)(FC)	.20	.15	.08
651	Major League Prospect (Mickey Brantley, Rob Woodward)(FC)	.35	.25	.14
652	Major League Prospect (Mark Funderburk, Billy Joe Robidoux)(FC)	.10	.08	.04

		MT	NR MT	EX
653	Major League Prospect (Cecil Fielder, Cory Snyder)(FC)	18.00	13.50	7.25
654	Checklist 1-97	.06	.05	.02
655	Checklist 98-196	.06	.05	.02
656	Checklist 197-291	.06	.05	.02
657	Checklist 292-385	.06	.05	.02
658	Checklist 386-482	.06	.05	.02
659	Checklist 483-578	.06	.05	.02
660	Checklist 579-660	.06	.05	.02

1986 Fleer
All Star Team

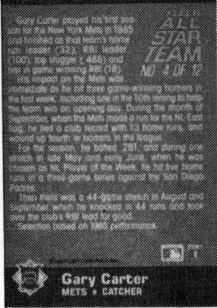

Fleer's choices for a major league All-Star team make up this 12-card set. The cards, which measure 2-1/2" by 3-1/2", were randomly inserted in 35¢ wax packs and 59¢ cello packs. The card fronts have a color photo set against a bright red background for A.L. players or a bright blue background for N.L. players. The card backs feature the player's career highlights set in white type against a red and blue background.

		MT	NR MT	EX
	Complete Set:	18.00	13.50	7.25
	Common Player:	.60	.45	.25
1	Don Mattingly	5.00	3.75	2.00
2	Tom Herr	.60	.45	.25
3	George Brett	2.00	1.50	.80
4	Gary Carter	1.00	.70	.40
5	Cal Ripken, Jr.	1.75	1.25	.70
6	Dave Parker	.75	.60	.30
7	Rickey Henderson	3.00	2.25	1.25
8	Pedro Guerrero	.75	.60	.30
9	Dan Quisenberry	.60	.45	.25
10	Dwight Gooden	4.00	3.00	1.50
11	Gorman Thomas	.60	.45	.25
12	John Tudor	.60	.45	.25

1986 Fleer
Baseball's Best

The 1986 Fleer Baseball's Best set consists of 44

cards and was produced for the McCrory's store chain and their affiliated stores. Subtitled "Sluggers vs. Pitchers," the set contains 22 each of the game's best hitters and pitchers. The cards, which measure 2-1/2" by 3-1/2", have color photos depicting an action pose. The backs are done in blue and red ink on white stock and carry the player's personal and statistical information. The sets were issued in a specially designed box with six team logo stickers.

		MT	NR MT	EX
Complete Set:		7.00	5.25	2.75
Common Player:		.05	.04	.02
1	Bert Blyleven	.10	.08	.04
2	Wade Boggs	1.00	.70	.40
3	George Brett	.30	.25	.12
4	Tom Browning	.15	.11	.06
5	Jose Canseco	3.50	2.75	1.50
6	Will Clark	1.50	1.25	.60
7	Roger Clemens	.70	.50	.30
8	Alvin Davis	.10	.08	.04
9	Julio Franco	.10	.08	.04
10	Kirk Gibson	.20	.15	.08
11	Dwight Gooden	1.00	.70	.40
12	Goose Gossage	.12	.09	.05
13	Pedro Guerrero	.15	.11	.06
14	Ron Guidry	.12	.09	.05
15	Tony Gwynn	.25	.20	.10
16	Orel Hershiser	.20	.15	.08
17	Kent Hrbek	.15	.11	.06
18	Reggie Jackson	.25	.20	.10
19	Wally Joyner	.50	.40	.20
20	Charlie Leibrandt	.05	.04	.02
21	Don Mattingly	1.50	1.25	.60
22	Willie McGee	.12	.09	.05
23	Jack Morris	.15	.11	.06
24	Dale Murphy	.30	.25	.12
25	Eddie Murray	.25	.20	.10
26	Jeff Reardon	.07	.05	.03
27	Rick Reuschel	.07	.05	.03
28	Cal Ripken, Jr	.30	.25	.12
29	Pete Rose	.60	.45	.25
30	Nolan Ryan	.50	.40	.20
31	Bret Saberhagen	.15	.11	.06
32	Ryne Sandberg	.60	.45	.25
33	Mike Schmidt	.30	.25	.12
34	Tom Seaver	.25	.20	.10
35	Bryn Smith	.05	.04	.02
36	Mario Soto	.05	.04	.02
37	Dave Stieb	.10	.08	.04
38	Darryl Strawberry	.40	.30	.15
39	Rick Sutcliffe	.10	.08	.04
40	John Tudor	.10	.08	.04
41	Fernando Valenzuela	.20	.15	.08
42	Bobby Witt	.15	.11	.06
43	Mike Witt	.07	.05	.03
44	Robin Yount	.35	.25	.14

1986 Fleer Box Panels

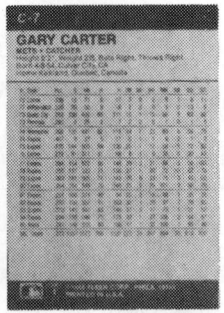

Picking up on a Donruss idea, Fleer issued eight cards in panels of four on the bottoms of the wax and cello pack boxes. The cards are numbered C-1 through C-8 and are 2-1/2" by 3-1/2", with a complete panel measuring 5" by 7-1/8" in size. Included in the eight cards are six player cards and two team logo/checklist cards.

		MT	NR MT	EX
Complete Panel Set:		4.00	3.00	1.50
Complete Singles Set:		1.75	1.25	.70
Common Single Player:		.20	.15	.08
	Panel	2.75	2.00	1.00
1	Royals Logo/Checklist	.05	.04	.02
2	George Brett	.60	.45	.25
3	Ozzie Guillen	.40	.30	.15
4	Dale Murphy	.40	.30	.15
	Panel	1.50	1.25	.60
5	Cardinals Logo/Checklist	.05	.04	.02
6	Tom Browning	.20	.15	.08
7	Gary Carter	.35	.25	.14
8	Carlton Fisk	.20	.15	.08

1986 Fleer Future Hall Of Famers

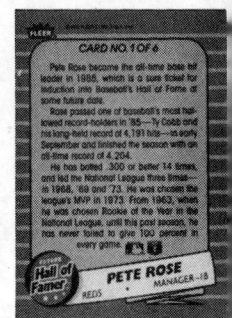

The 1986 Fleer Future Hall of Famers set is comprised of six players Fleer felt would gain eventual entrance into the Baseball Hall of Fame. The cards are the standard 2-1/2" by 3-1/2" in size and were randomly inserted in three-pack cello packs. The card fronts feature a player photo set against a blue background with horizontal light blue stripes. The card backs are printed in black on a blue background and feature player highlights in paragraph form.

		MT	NR MT	EX
Complete Set:		10.00	7.50	4.00
Common Player:		1.50	1.25	.60
1	Pete Rose	1.50	1.25	.60
2	Steve Carlton	1.50	1.25	.60
3	Tom Seaver	1.50	1.25	.60
4	Rod Carew	1.50	1.25	.60
5	Nolan Ryan	2.00	1.50	.80
6	Reggie Jackson	1.50	1.25	.60

1986 Fleer League Leaders

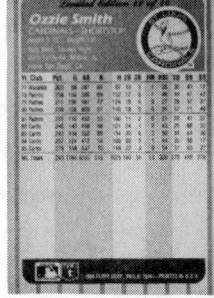

Fleer's 1986 "League Leaders" set features 44 of the game's top players and was issued through the Walgreens drug store chain. The card fronts contain a color photo and feature the player's name, team and postition in a blue band near the bottom of the card. The words "League Leaders" appear in a red band at the top of the card. The background for the card fronts is alternating blue and white stripes. The card backs are printed in blue, red and white and carry the player's statistical information and team logo. The cards are the standard 2-1/2" by 3-1/2" size. The set was issued in a special cardboard box, along with six team logo stickers.

		MT	NR MT	EX
	Complete Set:	9.00	6.75	3.50
	Common Player:	.05	.04	.02
1	Wade Boggs	1.00	.70	.40
2	George Brett	.30	.25	.12
3	Jose Canseco	3.50	2.75	1.50
4	Rod Carew	.30	.25	.12
5	Gary Carter	.25	.20	.10
6	Jack Clark	.12	.09	.05
7	Vince Coleman	.60	.45	.25
8	Jose Cruz	.05	.04	.02
9	Alvin Davis	.10	.08	.04
10	Mariano Duncan	.05	.04	.02
11	Leon Durham	.05	.04	.02
12	Carlton Fisk	.15	.11	.06
13	Julio Franco	.10	.08	.04
14	Scott Garrelts	.05	.04	.02
15	Steve Garvey	.25	.20	.10
16	Dwight Gooden	1.00	.70	.40
17	Ozzie Guillen	.10	.08	.04
18	Willie Hernandez	.05	.04	.02
19	Bob Horner	.07	.05	.03
20	Kent Hrbek	.15	.11	.06
21	Charlie Leibrandt	.05	.04	.02
22	Don Mattingly	1.50	1.25	.60
23	Oddibe McDowell	.12	.09	.05
24	Willie McGee	.10	.08	.04
25	Keith Moreland	.05	.04	.02
26	Lloyd Moseby	.07	.05	.03
27	Dale Murphy	.30	.25	.12
28	Phil Niekro	.15	.11	.06
29	Joe Orsulak	.05	.04	.02
30	Dave Parker	.12	.09	.05
31	Lance Parrish	.15	.11	.06
32	Kirby Puckett	.70	.50	.30
33	Tim Raines	.25	.20	.10
34	Earnie Riles	.07	.05	.03
35	Cal Ripken, Jr.	.30	.25	.12
36	Pete Rose	.60	.45	.25
37	Bret Saberhagen	.15	.11	.06
38	Juan Samuel	.10	.08	.04
39	Ryne Sandberg	.60	.45	.25
40	Tom Seaver	.25	.20	.10
41	Lee Smith	.07	.05	.03
42	Ozzie Smith	.12	.09	.05
43	Dave Stieb	.10	.08	.04
44	Robin Yount	.35	.25	.12

1986 Fleer Limited Edition

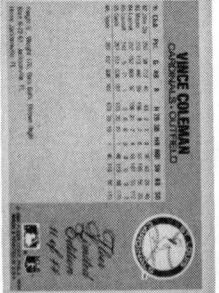

VINCE COLEMAN
CARDINALS-OUTFIELD

Produced for the McCrory's store chain and their

affiliates for the second year in a row, the 1986 Fleer Limited Edition set contains 44 cards. The cards, which are the standard 2-1/2" by 3-1/2" size, have color photos enclosed by green, red and yellow trim. The card backs carry black print on two shades of red. The set was issued in a special cardboard box, along with six team logo stickers.

		MT	NR MT	EX
	Complete Set:	6.00	4.50	2.50
	Common Player:	.05	.04	.02
1	Doyle Alexander	.05	.04	.02
2	Joaquin Andujar	.05	.04	.02
3	Harold Baines	.12	.09	.05
4	Wade Boggs	1.00	.70	.40
5	Phil Bradley	.12	.09	.05
6	George Brett	.30	.25	.12
7	Hubie Brooks	.07	.05	.03
8	Chris Brown	.12	.09	.05
9	Tom Brunansky	.10	.08	.04
10	Gary Carter	.25	.20	.10
11	Vince Coleman	.60	.45	.25
12	Cecil Cooper	.07	.05	.03
13	Jose Cruz	.05	.04	.02
14	Mike Davis	.05	.04	.02
15	Carlton Fisk	.15	.11	.06
16	Julio Franco	.10	.08	.04
17	Damaso Garcia	.05	.04	.02
18	Rich Gedman	.05	.04	.02
19	Kirk Gibson	.20	.15	.08
20	Dwight Gooden	1.00	.70	.40
21	Pedro Guerrero	.15	.11	.06
22	Tony Gwynn	.25	.20	.10
23	Rickey Henderson	.50	.40	.20
24	Orel Hershiser	.20	.15	.08
25	LaMarr Hoyt	.05	.04	.02
26	Reggie Jackson	.30	.25	.12
27	Don Mattingly	1.50	1.25	.60
28	Oddibe McDowell	.12	.09	.05
29	Willie McGee	.10	.08	.04
30	Paul Molitor	.12	.09	.05
31	Dale Murphy	.30	.25	.12
32	Eddie Murray	.25	.20	.10
33	Dave Parker	.12	.09	.05
34	Tony Pena	.07	.05	.03
35	Jeff Reardon	.07	.05	.03
36	Cal Ripken, Jr.	.30	.25	.12
37	Pete Rose	.60	.45	.25
38	Bret Saberhagen	.15	.11	.06
39	Juan Samuel	.10	.08	.04
40	Ryne Sandberg	.60	.45	.25
41	Mike Schmidt	.30	.25	.12
42	Lee Smith	.07	.05	.03
43	Don Sutton	.12	.09	.05
44	Lou Whitaker	.15	.11	.06

1986 Fleer Mini

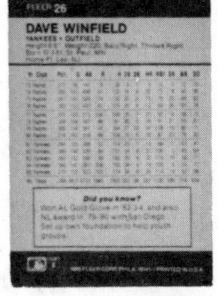

Fleer's 1986 "Classic Miniatures" set contains 120 cards that measure 1-13/16" by 2-9/16" in size. The design of the high-gloss cards is identical to the regular 1986 Fleer set but the player photos are entirely different. The set, which was issued in a specially designed box along with 18 team logo stickers, was available to the collecting public only through hobby dealers.

		MT	NR MT	EX
Complete Set:		15.00	11.00	6.00
Common Player:		.05	.04	.02
1	George Brett	.30	.25	.12
2	Dan Quisenberry	.07	.05	.03
3	Bret Saberhagen	.15	.11	.06
4	Lonnie Smith	.05	.04	.02
5	Willie Wilson	.10	.08	.04
6	Jack Clark	.12	.09	.05
7	Vince Coleman	.50	.40	.20
8	Tom Herr	.07	.05	.03
9	Willie McGee	.10	.08	.04
10	Ozzie Smith	.12	.09	.05
11	John Tudor	.07	.05	.03
12	Jesse Barfield	.12	.09	.05
13	George Bell	.20	.15	.08
14	Tony Fernandez	.10	.08	.04
15	Damaso Garcia	.05	.04	.02
16	Dave Stieb	.07	.05	.03
17	Gary Carter	.20	.15	.08
18	Ron Darling	.10	.08	.04
19	Dwight Gooden	.60	.45	.25
20	Keith Hernandez	.20	.15	.08
21	Darryl Strawberry	.50	.40	.20
22	Ron Guidry	.15	.11	.06
23	Rickey Henderson	.30	.25	.12
24	Don Mattingly	1.75	1.25	.70
25	Dave Righetti	.12	.09	.05
26	Dave Winfield	.20	.15	.08
27	Mariano Duncan	.07	.05	.03
28	Pedro Guerrero	.12	.09	.05
29	Bill Madlock	.10	.08	.04
30	Mike Marshall	.10	.08	.04
31	Fernando Valenzuela	.10	.08	.04
32	Reggie Jackson	.30	.25	.12
33	Gary Pettis	.05	.04	.02
34	Ron Romanick	.05	.04	.02
35	Don Sutton	.12	.09	.05
36	Mike Witt	.07	.05	.03
37	Buddy Bell	.07	.05	.03
38	Tom Browning	.10	.08	.04
39	Dave Parker	.12	.09	.05
40	Pete Rose	.60	.45	.25
41	Mario Soto	.05	.04	.02
42	Harold Baines	.12	.09	.05
43	Carlton Fisk	.15	.11	.06
44	Ozzie Guillen	.12	.09	.05
45	Ron Kittle	.07	.05	.03
46	Tom Seaver	.20	.15	.08
47	Kirk Gibson	.20	.15	.08
48	Jack Morris	.15	.11	.06
49	Lance Parrish	.15	.11	.06
50	Alan Trammell	.20	.15	.08
51	Lou Whitaker	.15	.11	.06
52	Hubie Brooks	.07	.05	.03
53	Andre Dawson	.15	.11	.06
54	Tim Raines	.20	.15	.08
55	Bryn Smith	.05	.04	.02
56	Tim Wallach	.10	.08	.04
57	Mike Boddicker	.05	.04	.02
58	Eddie Murray	.25	.20	.10
59	Cal Ripken	.30	.25	.12
60	John Shelby	.05	.04	.02
61	Mike Young	.05	.04	.02
62	Jose Cruz	.07	.05	.03
63	Glenn Davis	.15	.11	.06
64	Phil Garner	.05	.04	.02
65	Nolan Ryan	.50	.40	.20
66	Mike Scott	.12	.09	.05
67	Steve Garvey	.20	.15	.08
68	Goose Gossage	.12	.09	.05
69	Tony Gwynn	.25	.20	.10
70	Andy Hawkins	.05	.04	.02
71	Garry Templeton	.05	.04	.02
72	Wade Boggs	1.00	.70	.40
73	Roger Clemens	1.00	.70	.40
74	Dwight Evans	.12	.09	.05
75	Rich Gedman	.05	.04	.02
76	Jim Rice	.20	.15	.08
77	Shawon Dunston	.10	.08	.04
78	Leon Durham	.05	.04	.02
79	Keith Moreland	.05	.04	.02
80	Ryne Sandberg	.20	.15	.08
81	Rick Sutcliffe	.10	.08	.04
82	Bert Blyleven	.12	.09	.05
83	Tom Brunansky	.10	.08	.04
84	Kent Hrbek	.15	.11	.06
85	Kirby Puckett	.70	.50	.30
86	Bruce Bochte	.05	.04	.02
87	Jose Canseco	3.50	2.75	1.50
88	Mike Davis	.05	.04	.02
89	Jay Howell	.07	.05	.03

		MT	NR MT	EX
90	Dwayne Murphy	.05	.04	.02
91	Steve Carlton	.20	.15	.08
92	Von Hayes	.10	.08	.04
93	Juan Samuel	.12	.09	.05
94	Mike Schmidt	.30	.25	.12
95	Glenn Wilson	.05	.04	.02
96	Phil Bradley	.10	.08	.04
97	Alvin Davis	.10	.08	.04
98	Jim Presley	.10	.08	.04
99	Danny Tartabull	.15	.11	.06
100	Cecil Cooper	.10	.08	.04
101	Paul Molitor	.12	.09	.05
102	Earnie Riles	.07	.05	.03
103	Robin Yount	.30	.25	.12
104	Bob Horner	.10	.08	.04
105	Dale Murphy	.30	.25	.12
106	Bruce Sutter	.10	.08	.04
107	Claudell Washington	.05	.04	.02
108	Chris Brown	.12	.09	.05
109	Chili Davis	.05	.04	.02
110	Scott Garrelts	.05	.04	.02
111	Oddibe McDowell	.12	.09	.05
112	Pete O'Brien	.07	.05	.03
113	Gary Ward	.05	.04	.02
114	Brett Butler	.05	.04	.02
115	Julio Franco	.10	.08	.04
116	Brook Jacoby	.10	.08	.04
117	Mike Brown	.05	.04	.02
118	Joe Orsulak	.05	.04	.02
119	Tony Pena	.07	.05	.03
120	R.J. Reynolds	.05	.04	.02

1986 Fleer Star Stickers

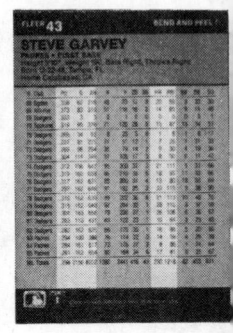

After a five-year layoff, Fleer once again produced a Star Sticker set. The cards, which measure 2-1/2" by 3-1/2", have color photos inside dark maroon borders. The card backs are identical to the 1986 regular issue except for the 1-132 numbering system and blue ink instead of yellow. The words "Bend and Peel" are found in the upper right corner of the card backs. Card #132 is a multi-player card featuring Dwight Gooden and Dale Murphy on the front and a complete checklist for the set on the reverse. The cards were sold in wax packs with team logo stickers.

		MT	NR MT	EX
Complete Set		25.00	20.00	10.00
Common Player		.05	.04	.02
1	Harold Baines	.20	.15	.08
2	Jesse Barfield	.20	.15	.08
3	Don Baylor	.12	.09	.05
4	Juan Beniquez	.05	.04	.02
5	Tim Birtsas	.08	.06	.03
6	Bert Blyleven	.15	.11	.06
7	Bruce Bochte	.05	.04	.02
8	Wade Boggs	1.00	.70	.40
9	Dennis Boyd	.12	.09	.05
10	Phil Bradley	.20	.15	.08
11	George Brett	.50	.40	.20
12	Hubie Brooks	.12	.09	.05
13	Chris Brown	.45	.35	.20
14	Tom Browning	.15	.11	.06
15	Tom Brunansky	.15	.11	.06
16	Bill Buckner	.10	.08	.04
17	Britt Burns	.05	.04	.02

		MT	NR MT	EX
18	Brett Butler	.08	.06	.03
19	Jose Canseco	3.50	2.75	1.50
20	Rod Carew	.40	.30	.15
21	Steve Carlton	.40	.30	.15
22	Don Carman	.20	.15	.08
23	Gary Carter	.40	.30	.15
24	Jack Clark	.20	.15	.08
25	Vince Coleman	.70	.50	.30
26	Cecil Cooper	.15	.11	.06
27	Jose Cruz	.10	.08	.04
28	Ron Darling	.20	.15	.08
29	Alvin Davis	.20	.15	.08
30	Jody Davis	.08	.06	.03
31	Mike Davis	.05	.04	.02
32	Andre Dawson	.25	.20	.10
33	Mariano Duncan	.10	.08	.04
34	Shawon Dunston	.15	.11	.06
35	Leon Durham	.08	.06	.03
36	Darrell Evans	.12	.09	.05
37	Tony Fernandez	.15	.11	.06
38	Carlton Fisk	.20	.15	.08
39	John Franco	.10	.08	.04
40	Julio Franco	.12	.09	.05
41	Damaso Garcia	.05	.04	.02
42	Scott Garrelts	.05	.04	.02
43	Steve Garvey	.25	.20	.10
44	Rich Gedman	.10	.08	.04
45	Kirk Gibson	.30	.25	.12
46	Dwight Gooden	.90	.70	.35
47	Pedro Guerrero	.20	.15	.08
48	Ron Guidry	.20	.15	.08
49	Ozzie Guillen	.30	.25	.12
50	Tony Gwynn	.40	.30	.15
51	Andy Hawkins	.08	.06	.03
52	Von Hayes	.12	.09	.05
53	Rickey Henderson	1.00	.70	.40
54	Tom Henke	.12	.09	.05
55	Keith Hernandez	.35	.25	.14
56	Willie Hernandez	.05	.04	.02
57	Tom Herr	.10	.08	.04
58	Orel Hershiser	.30	.25	.12
59	Teddy Higuera	.60	.45	.25
60	Bob Horner	.12	.09	.05
61	Charlie Hough	.08	.06	.03
62	Jay Howell	.08	.06	.03
63	LaMarr Hoyt	.05	.04	.02
64	Kent Hrbek	.30	.25	.12
65	Reggie Jackson	.50	.40	.20
66	Bob James	.05	.04	.02
67	Dave Kingman	.12	.09	.05
68	Ron Kittle	.12	.09	.05
69	Charlie Leibrandt	.08	.06	.03
70	Fred Lynn	.25	.20	.10
71	Mike Marshall	.20	.15	.08
72	Don Mattingly	2.25	1.75	.90
73	Oddibe McDowell	.25	.20	.10
74	Willie McGee	.20	.15	.08
75	Scott McGregor	.05	.04	.02
76	Paul Molitor	.20	.15	.08
77	Donnie Moore	.05	.04	.02
78	Keith Moreland	.08	.06	.03
79	Jack Morris	.25	.20	.10
80	Dale Murphy	.40	.30	.15
81	Eddie Murray	.50	.40	.20
82	Phil Niekro	.25	.20	.10
83	Joe Orsulak	.10	.08	.04
84	Dave Parker	.25	.20	.10
85	Lance Parrish	.25	.20	.10
86	Larry Parrish	.08	.06	.03
87	Tony Pena	.10	.08	.04
88	Gary Pettis	.05	.04	.02
89	Jim Presley	.15	.11	.06
90	Kirby Puckett	1.00	.70	.40
91	Dan Quisenberry	.12	.09	.05
92	Tim Raines	.35	.25	.14
93	Johnny Ray	.10	.08	.04
94	Jeff Reardon	.10	.08	.04
95	Rick Reuschel	.10	.08	.04
96	Jim Rice	.15	.11	.06
97	Dave Righetti	.20	.15	.08
98	Earnie Riles	.12	.09	.05
99	Cal Ripken, Jr.	.60	.45	.25
100	Ron Romanick	.05	.04	.02
101	Pete Rose	1.00	.70	.40
102	Nolan Ryan	1.00	.70	.40
103	Bret Saberhagen	.25	.20	.10
104	Mark Salas	.05	.04	.02
105	Juan Samuel	.15	.11	.06
106	Ryne Sandberg	.70	.50	.30
107	Mike Schmidt	1.00	.70	.40
108	Mike Scott	.15	.11	.06

		MT	NR MT	EX
109	Tom Seaver	.30	.25	.12
110	Bryn Smith	.05	.04	.02
111	Dave Smith	.05	.04	.02
112	Lee Smith	.10	.08	.04
113	Ozzie Smith	.20	.15	.08
114	Mario Soto	.05	.04	.02
115	Dave Stieb	.12	.09	.05
116	Darryl Strawberry	1.00	.70	.40
117	Bruce Sutter	.10	.08	.04
118	Garry Templeton	.08	.06	.03
119	Gorman Thomas	.08	.06	.03
120	Andre Thornton	.10	.08	.04
121	Allan Trammell	.20	.15	.08
122	John Tudor	.12	.09	.05
123	Fernando Valenzuela	.30	.25	.12
124	Frank Viola	.20	.15	.08
125	Gary Ward	.05	.04	.02
126	Lou Whitaker	.25	.20	.10
127	Frank White	.10	.08	.04
128	Glenn Wilson	.08	.06	.03
129	Willie Wilson	.15	.11	.06
130	Dave Winfield	.40	.30	.15
131	Robin Yount	.35	.25	.14
132	Dwight Gooden, Dale Murphy/Checklist			
		1.25	.90	.50

1986 Fleer
Star Stickers Box Panels

Four cards, numbered S-1 through S-4, were placed on the bottoms of 1986 Fleer Star Stickers wax pack boxes. The cards are nearly identical in format to the regular issue sticker cards. Individual cards measure 2-1/2" by 3-1/2" in size, while a complete panel of four measures 5" by 7-1/8".

		MT	NR MT	EX
Complete Panel Set:		3.00	2.25	1.25
Complete Singles Set:		1.50	1.25	.60
Common Single Player:		.30	.25	.12
	Panel	3.00	2.25	1.25
1	Dodgers Logo	.05	.04	.02
2	Wade Boggs	1.00	.70	.40
3	Steve Garvey	.30	.25	.12
4	Dave Winfield	.30	.25	.12

1986 Fleer Update

Issued near the end of the baseball season, the 1986 Fleer Update set consists of 132 cards numbered U-1 through U-132. The cards, which measure 2-1/2" by 3-1/2" in size, are identical in design to the regular 1986 Fleer set. The purpose of the set is to update player trades and include new players not depicted in the regular issue. The set was issued with team logo stickers in a specially designed box and was available only through hobby dealers.

	MT	NR MT	EX
Complete Set:	40.00	30.00	15.00
Common Player:	.08	.06	.03

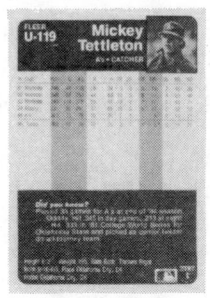

		MT	NR MT	EX
1	Mike Aldrete(FC)	.35	.25	.14
2	Andy Allanson(FC)	.20	.15	.08
3	Neil Allen	.08	.06	.03
4	Joaquin Andujar	.10	.08	.04
5	Paul Assenmacher(FC)	.20	.15	.08
6	Scott Bailes(FC)	.25	.20	.10
7	Jay Baller(FC)	.15	.11	.06
8	Scott Bankhead(FC)	.20	.15	.08
9	Bill Bathe(FC)	.08	.06	.03
10	Don Baylor	.15	.11	.06
11	Billy Beane(FC)	.08	.06	.03
12	Steve Bedrosian	.15	.11	.06
13	Juan Beniquez	.08	.06	.03
14	Barry Bonds(FC)	7.00	5.25	2.75
15	Bobby Bonilla(FC)	6.00	4.50	2.50
16	Rich Bordi	.08	.06	.03
17	Bill Campbell	.08	.06	.03
18	Tom Candiotti	.08	.06	.03
19	John Cangelosi(FC)	.20	.15	.08
20	Jose Canseco	12.00	9.00	4.75
21	Chuck Cary(FC)	.15	.11	.06
22	Juan Castillo(FC)	.10	.08	.04
23	Rick Cerone	.08	.06	.03
24	John Cerutti(FC)	.25	.20	.10
25	Will Clark(FC)	15.00	11.00	6.00
26	Mark Clear	.08	.06	.03
27	Darnell Coles(FC)	.15	.11	.06
28	Dave Collins	.10	.08	.04
29	Tim Conroy	.08	.06	.03
30	Ed Correa(FC)	.20	.15	.08
31	Joe Cowley	.08	.06	.03
32	Bill Dawley	.08	.06	.03
33	Rob Deer	.15	.11	.06
34	John Denny	.08	.06	.03
35	Jim DeShaies (Deshaies)(FC)	.25	.20	.10
36	Doug Drabek(FC)	1.25	.90	.50
37	Mike Easler	.12	.09	.05
38	Mark Eichhorn(FC)	.20	.15	.08
39	Dave Engle	.08	.06	.03
40	Mike Fischlin	.08	.06	.03
41	Scott Fletcher	.15	.11	.06
42	Terry Forster	.12	.09	.05
43	Terry Francona	.08	.06	.03
44	Andres Galarraga	.70	.50	.30
45	Lee Guetterman(FC)	.20	.15	.08
46	Bill Gullickson	.08	.06	.03
47	Jackie Gutierrez	.08	.06	.03
48	Moose Haas	.08	.06	.03
49	Billy Hatcher	.15	.11	.06
50	Mike Heath	.08	.06	.03
51	Guy Hoffman(FC)	.10	.08	.04
52	Tom Hume	.08	.06	.03
53	Pete Incaviglia(FC)	.50	.40	.20
54	Dane Iorg	.08	.06	.03
55	Chris James(FC)	.60	.45	.25
56	Stan Javier(FC)	.25	.20	.10
57	Tommy John	.20	.15	.08
58	Tracy Jones(FC)	.40	.30	.15
59	Wally Joyner(FC)	2.00	1.50	.80
60	Wayne Krenchicki	.08	.06	.03
61	John Kruk(FC)	.40	.30	.15
62	Mike LaCoss	.08	.06	.03
63	Pete Ladd	.08	.06	.03
64	Dave LaPoint	.15	.11	.06
65	Mike LaValliere(FC)	.30	.25	.12
66	Rudy Law	.08	.06	.03
67	Dennis Leonard	.10	.08	.04
68	Steve Lombardozzi(FC)	.20	.15	.08
69	Aurelio Lopez	.08	.06	.03
70	Mickey Mahler	.08	.06	.03
71	Candy Maldonado	.15	.11	.06
72	Roger Mason(FC)	.10	.08	.04
73	Greg Mathews(FC)	.25	.20	.10
74	Andy McGaffigan	.08	.06	.03
75	Joel McKeon(FC)	.12	.09	.05
76	Kevin Mitchell(FC)	7.00	5.25	2.75
77	Bill Mooneyham(FC)	.12	.09	.05
78	Omar Moreno	.08	.06	.03
79	Jerry Mumphrey	.08	.06	.03
80	Al Newman(FC)	.12	.09	.05
81	Phil Niekro	.40	.30	.15
82	Randy Niemann	.08	.06	.03
83	Juan Nieves(FC)	.20	.15	.08
84	Bob Ojeda	.12	.09	.05
85	Rick Ownbey	.08	.06	.03
86	Tom Paciorek	.08	.06	.03
87	David Palmer	.08	.06	.03
88	Jeff Parrett(FC)	.25	.20	.10
89	Pat Perry(FC)	.15	.11	.06
90	Dan Plesac(FC)	.35	.25	.14
91	Darrell Porter	.12	.09	.05
92	Luis Quinones(FC)	.12	.09	.05
93	Rey Quinonez(FC)	.20	.15	.08
94	Gary Redus	.10	.08	.04
95	Jeff Reed(FC)	.12	.09	.05
96	Bip Roberts(FC)	.08	.06	.03
97	Billy Joe Robidoux	.12	.09	.05
98	Gary Roenicke	.08	.06	.03
99	Ron Roenicke	.08	.06	.03
100	Angel Salazar	.08	.06	.03
101	Joe Sambito	.08	.06	.03
102	Billy Sample	.08	.06	.03
103	Dave Schmidt	.08	.06	.03
104	Ken Schrom	.08	.06	.03
105	Ruben Sierra(FC)	7.00	5.25	2.75
106	Ted Simmons	.20	.15	.08
107	Sammy Stewart	.08	.06	.03
108	Kurt Stillwell(FC)	.30	.25	.12
109	Dale Sveum(FC)	.25	.20	.10
110	Tim Teufel	.08	.06	.03
111	Bob Tewksbury(FC)	.12	.09	.05
112	Andres Thomas(FC)	.25	.20	.10
113	Jason Thompson	.08	.06	.03
114	Milt Thompson	.12	.09	.05
115	Rob Thompson(FC)	.40	.30	.15
116	Jay Tibbs	.08	.06	.03
117	Fred Toliver	.12	.09	.05
118	Wayne Tolleson	.08	.06	.03
119	Alex Trevino	.08	.06	.03
120	Manny Trillo	.10	.08	.04
121	Ed Vande Berg	.08	.06	.03
122	Ozzie Virgil	.08	.06	.03
123	Tony Walker(FC)	.08	.06	.03
124	Gene Walter	.12	.09	.05
125	Duane Ward(FC)	.20	.15	.08
126	Jerry Willard	.08	.06	.03
127	Mitch Williams(FC)	.60	.45	.25
128	Reggie Williams(FC)	.20	.15	.08
129	Bobby Witt(FC)	1.25	.90	.50
130	Marvell Wynne	.08	.06	.03
131	Steve Yeager	.08	.06	.03
132	Checklist	.08	.06	.03

1987 Fleer

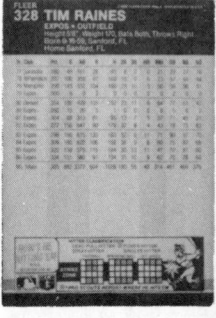

The 1987 Fleer set consists of 660 cards, each measuring 2-1/2" by 3-1/2". The card fronts feature an attractive blue and white border. The player's name and position appears in the upper left corner of the card. The player's team logo is located in the lower right corner. The card backs are done in blue, red and white and contain an innovative "Pro Scouts Report" feature which lists the hitter's or pitcher's batting and pitching strengths. For the third year in a row, Fleer included its "Major League Prospects" subset. Fleer produced a glossy-finish Collectors Edition set which came housed in a specially-designed tin box. It was speculated that 100,000 of the glossy sets were produced. After experiencing a dramatic drop in price during 1987, the glossy set now sells for only a few dollars more than the regular issue.

		MT	NR MT	EX
	Complete Set:	125.00	90.00	50.00
	Common Player:	.06	.05	.02
1	Rick Aguilera	.08	.06	.03
2	Richard Anderson	.06	.05	.02
3	Wally Backman	.08	.06	.03
4	Gary Carter	.25	.20	.10
5	Ron Darling	.15	.11	.06
6	Len Dykstra	1.00	.70	.40
7	Kevin Elster(FC)	.50	.40	.20
8	Sid Fernandez	.12	.09	.05
9	Dwight Gooden	.90	.70	.35
10	Ed Hearn(FC)	.10	.08	.04
11	Danny Heep	.06	.05	.02
12	Keith Hernandez	.25	.20	.10
13	Howard Johnson	.10	.08	.04
14	Ray Knight	.08	.06	.03
15	Lee Mazzilli	.08	.06	.03
16	Roger McDowell	.12	.09	.05
17	Kevin Mitchell	9.00	6.75	3.50
18	Randy Niemann	.06	.05	.02
19	Bob Ojeda	.08	.06	.03
20	Jesse Orosco	.08	.06	.03
21	Rafael Santana	.06	.05	.02
22	Doug Sisk	.06	.05	.02
23	Darryl Strawberry	1.00	.70	.40
24	Tim Teufel	.06	.05	.02
25	Mookie Wilson	.10	.08	.04
26	Tony Armas	.08	.06	.03
27	Marty Barrett	.10	.08	.04
28	Don Baylor	.12	.09	.05
29	Wade Boggs	1.50	1.25	.60
30	Oil Can Boyd	.08	.06	.03
31	Bill Buckner	.10	.08	.04
32	Roger Clemens	2.25	1.75	.90
33	Steve Crawford	.06	.05	.02
34	Dwight Evans	.12	.09	.05
35	Rich Gedman	.10	.08	.04
36	Dave Henderson	.10	.08	.04
37	Bruce Hurst	.10	.08	.04
38	Tim Lollar	.06	.05	.02
39	Al Nipper	.06	.05	.02
40	Spike Owen	.06	.05	.02
41	Jim Rice	.30	.25	.12
42	Ed Romero	.06	.05	.02
43	Joe Sambito	.06	.05	.02
44	Calvin Schiraldi	.10	.08	.04
45	Tom Seaver	.40	.30	.15
46	Jeff Sellers(FC)	.20	.15	.08
47	Bob Stanley	.06	.05	.02
48	Sammy Stewart	.06	.05	.02
49	Larry Andersen	.06	.05	.02
50	Alan Ashby	.06	.05	.02
51	Kevin Bass	.10	.08	.04
52	Jeff Calhoun	.06	.05	.02
53	Jose Cruz	.10	.08	.04
54	Danny Darwin	.06	.05	.02
55	Glenn Davis	.30	.25	.12
56	Jim Deshaies	.25	.20	.10
57	Bill Doran	.10	.08	.04
58	Phil Garner	.06	.05	.02
59	Billy Hatcher	.08	.06	.03
60	Charlie Kerfeld	.06	.05	.02
61	Bob Knepper	.08	.06	.03
62	Dave Lopes	.08	.06	.03
63	Aurelio Lopez	.06	.05	.02
64	Jim Pankovits	.06	.05	.02
65	Terry Puhl	.06	.05	.02
66	Craig Reynolds	.06	.05	.02
67	Nolan Ryan	1.00	.70	.40
68	Mike Scott	.15	.11	.06
69	Dave Smith	.08	.06	.03
70	Dickie Thon	.08	.06	.03
71	Tony Walker	.06	.05	.02
72	Denny Walling	.06	.05	.02
73	Bob Boone	.08	.06	.03
74	Rick Burleson	.08	.06	.03

		MT	NR MT	EX
75	John Candelaria	.10	.08	.04
76	Doug Corbett	.06	.05	.02
77	Doug DeCinces	.08	.06	.03
78	Brian Downing	.08	.06	.03
79	Chuck Finley(FC)	2.25	1.75	.90
80	Terry Forster	.08	.06	.03
81	Bobby Grich	.10	.08	.04
82	George Hendrick	.08	.06	.03
83	Jack Howell(FC)	.10	.08	.04
84	Reggie Jackson	.35	.25	.14
85	Ruppert Jones	.06	.05	.02
86	Wally Joyner	2.00	1.50	.80
87	Gary Lucas	.06	.05	.02
88	Kirk McCaskill	.08	.06	.03
89	Donnie Moore	.06	.05	.02
90	Gary Pettis	.06	.05	.02
91	Vern Ruhle	.06	.05	.02
92	Dick Schofield	.06	.05	.02
93	Don Sutton	.20	.15	.08
94	Rob Wilfong	.06	.05	.02
95	Mike Witt	.10	.08	.04
96	Doug Drabek	3.50	2.75	1.50
97	Mike Easler	.08	.06	.03
98	Mike Fischlin	.06	.05	.02
99	Brian Fisher	.08	.06	.03
100	Ron Guidry	.15	.11	.06
101	Rickey Henderson	1.50	1.25	.60
102	Tommy John	.20	.15	.08
103	Ron Kittle	.10	.08	.04
104	Don Mattingly	3.00	2.25	1.25
105	Bobby Meacham	.06	.05	.02
106	Joe Niekro	.10	.08	.04
107	Mike Pagliarulo	.10	.08	.04
108	Dan Pasqua	.10	.08	.04
109	Willie Randolph	.10	.08	.04
110	Dennis Rasmussen	.10	.08	.04
111	Dave Righetti	.15	.11	.06
112	Gary Roenicke	.06	.05	.02
113	Rod Scurry	.06	.05	.02
114	Bob Shirley	.06	.05	.02
115	Joel Skinner	.06	.05	.02
116	Tim Stoddard	.06	.05	.02
117	Bob Tewksbury	.12	.09	.05
118	Wayne Tolleson	.06	.05	.02
119	Claudell Washington	.08	.06	.03
120	Dave Winfield	.30	.25	.12
121	Steve Buechele	.08	.06	.03
122	Ed Correa	.15	.11	.06
123	Scott Fletcher	.08	.06	.03
124	Jose Guzman	.10	.08	.04
125	Toby Harrah	.08	.06	.03
126	Greg Harris	.06	.05	.02
127	Charlie Hough	.08	.06	.03
128	Pete Incaviglia	.60	.45	.25
129	Mike Mason	.06	.05	.02
130	Oddibe McDowell	.10	.08	.04
131	Dale Mohorcic(FC)	.20	.15	.08
132	Pete O'Brien	.10	.08	.04
133	Tom Paciorek	.06	.05	.02
134	Larry Parrish	.08	.06	.03
135	Geno Petralli	.06	.05	.02
136	Darrell Porter	.08	.06	.03
137	Jeff Russell	.06	.05	.02
138	Ruben Sierra	12.00	9.00	4.75
139	Don Slaught	.06	.05	.02
140	Gary Ward	.08	.06	.03
141	Curtis Wilkerson	.06	.05	.02
142	Mitch Williams	.60	.45	.25
143	Bobby Witt	1.50	1.25	.60
144	Dave Bergman	.06	.05	.02
145	Tom Brookens	.06	.05	.02
146	Bill Campbell	.06	.05	.02
147	Chuck Cary	.10	.08	.04
148	Darnell Coles	.08	.06	.03
149	Dave Collins	.08	.06	.03
150	Darrell Evans	.12	.09	.05
151	Kirk Gibson	.25	.20	.10
152	John Grubb	.06	.05	.02
153	Willie Hernandez	.08	.06	.03
154	Larry Herndon	.08	.06	.03
155	Eric King	.25	.20	.10
156	Chet Lemon	.08	.06	.03
157	Dwight Lowry	.06	.05	.02
158	Jack Morris	.20	.15	.08
159	Randy O'Neal	.06	.05	.02
160	Lance Parrish	.20	.15	.08
161	Dan Petry	.08	.06	.03
162	Pat Sheridan	.06	.05	.02
163	Jim Slaton	.06	.05	.02
164	Frank Tanana	.08	.06	.03
165	Walt Terrell	.08	.06	.03

		MT	NR MT	EX
166	Mark Thurmond	.06	.05	.02
167	Alan Trammell	.25	.20	.10
168	Lou Whitaker	.25	.20	.10
169	Luis Aguayo	.06	.05	.02
170	Steve Bedrosian	.12	.09	.05
171	Don Carman	.10	.08	.04
172	Darren Daulton	.06	.05	.02
173	Greg Gross	.06	.05	.02
174	Kevin Gross	.08	.06	.03
175	Von Hayes	.10	.08	.04
176	Charles Hudson	.06	.05	.02
177	Tom Hume	.06	.05	.02
178	Steve Jeltz	.06	.05	.02
179	*Mike Maddux*(FC)	.20	.15	.08
180	Shane Rawley	.08	.06	.03
181	Gary Redus	.06	.05	.02
182	Ron Roenicke	.06	.05	.02
183	*Bruce Ruffin*(FC)	.20	.15	.08
184	John Russell	.06	.05	.02
185	Juan Samuel	.12	.09	.05
186	Dan Schatzeder	.06	.05	.02
187	Mike Schmidt	.60	.45	.25
188	Rick Schu	.06	.05	.02
189	Jeff Stone	.06	.05	.02
190	Kent Tekulve	.08	.06	.03
191	Milt Thompson	.08	.06	.03
192	Glenn Wilson	.08	.06	.03
193	Buddy Bell	.10	.08	.04
194	Tom Browning	.10	.08	.04
195	Sal Butera	.06	.05	.02
196	Dave Concepcion	.12	.09	.05
197	Kal Daniels	.80	.60	.30
198	Eric Davis	1.50	1.25	.60
199	John Denny	.06	.05	.02
200	Bo Diaz	.08	.06	.03
201	Nick Esasky	.08	.06	.03
202	John Franco	.10	.08	.04
203	Bill Gullickson	.06	.05	.02
204	*Barry Larkin*(FC)	9.00	6.75	3.50
205	Eddie Milner	.06	.05	.02
206	*Rob Murphy*(FC)	.20	.15	.08
207	Ron Oester	.06	.05	.02
208	Dave Parker	.20	.15	.08
209	Tony Perez	.15	.11	.06
210	Ted Power	.06	.05	.02
211	Joe Price	.06	.05	.02
212	Ron Robinson	.06	.05	.02
213	Pete Rose	.60	.45	.25
214	Mario Soto	.08	.06	.03
215	*Kurt Stillwell*	.50	.40	.20
216	Max Venable	.06	.05	.02
217	Chris Welsh	.06	.05	.02
218	*Carl Willis*(FC)	.10	.08	.04
219	Jesse Barfield	.15	.11	.06
220	George Bell	.25	.20	.10
221	Bill Caudill	.06	.05	.02
222	*John Cerutti*	.20	.15	.08
223	Jim Clancy	.08	.06	.03
224	*Mark Eichhorn*	.15	.11	.06
225	Tony Fernandez	.12	.09	.05
226	Damaso Garcia	.06	.05	.02
227	Kelly Gruber	.70	.50	.30
228	Tom Henke	.08	.06	.03
229	Garth Iorg	.06	.05	.02
230	Cliff Johnson	.06	.05	.02
231	Joe Johnson	.06	.05	.02
232	Jimmy Key	.12	.09	.05
233	Dennis Lamp	.06	.05	.02
234	Rick Leach	.06	.05	.02
235	Buck Martinez	.06	.05	.02
236	Lloyd Moseby	.10	.08	.04
237	Rance Mulliniks	.06	.05	.02
238	Dave Stieb	.12	.09	.05
239	Willie Upshaw	.08	.06	.03
240	Ernie Whitt	.08	.06	.03
241	*Andy Allanson*	.15	.11	.06
242	*Scott Bailes*	.20	.15	.08
243	Chris Bando	.06	.05	.02
244	Tony Bernazard	.06	.05	.02
245	John Butcher	.06	.05	.02
246	Brett Butler	.08	.06	.03
247	Ernie Camacho	.06	.05	.02
248	Tom Candiotti	.06	.05	.02
249	Joe Carter	.25	.20	.10
250	Carmen Castillo	.06	.05	.02
251	Julio Franco	.10	.08	.04
252	Mel Hall	.08	.06	.03
253	Brook Jacoby	.10	.08	.04
254	Phil Niekro	.20	.15	.08
255	Otis Nixon	.06	.05	.02
256	Dickie Noles	.06	.05	.02

		MT	NR MT	EX
257	Bryan Oelkers	.06	.05	.02
258	Ken Schrom	.06	.05	.02
259	Don Schulze	.06	.05	.02
260	Cory Snyder	.70	.50	.30
261	Pat Tabler	.08	.06	.03
262	Andre Thornton	.08	.06	.03
263	*Rich Yett*(FC)	.12	.09	.05
264	*Mike Aldrete*	.25	.20	.10
265	Juan Berenguer	.06	.05	.02
266	Vida Blue	.10	.08	.04
267	Bob Brenly	.06	.05	.02
268	Chris Brown	.08	.06	.03
269	*Will Clark*	30.00	22.00	12.00
270	Chili Davis	.08	.06	.03
271	Mark Davis	.06	.05	.02
272	*Kelly Downs*(FC)	.30	.25	.12
273	Scott Garrelts	.06	.05	.02
274	Dan Gladden	.06	.05	.02
275	Mike Krukow	.08	.06	.03
276	*Randy Kutcher*(FC)	.10	.08	.04
277	Mike LaCoss	.06	.05	.02
278	Jeff Leonard	.08	.06	.03
279	Candy Maldonado	.08	.06	.03
280	Roger Mason	.06	.05	.02
281	Bob Melvin(FC)	.08	.06	.03
282	Greg Minton	.06	.05	.02
283	Jeff Robinson	.08	.06	.03
284	Harry Spilman	.06	.05	.02
285	*Rob Thompson*	.35	.25	.14
286	Jose Uribe	.08	.06	.03
287	Frank Williams	.06	.05	.02
288	Joel Youngblood	.06	.05	.02
289	Jack Clark	.15	.11	.06
290	Vince Coleman	.25	.20	.10
291	Tim Conroy	.06	.05	.02
292	Danny Cox	.08	.06	.03
293	Ken Dayley	.06	.05	.02
294	Curt Ford	.06	.05	.02
295	Bob Forsch	.08	.06	.03
296	Tom Herr	.10	.08	.04
297	Ricky Horton	.08	.06	.03
298	Clint Hurdle	.06	.05	.02
299	Jeff Lahti	.06	.05	.02
300	Steve Lake	.06	.05	.02
301	Tito Landrum	.06	.05	.02
302	*Mike LaValliere*	.25	.20	.10
303	*Greg Mathews*(FC)	.20	.15	.08
304	Willie McGee	.12	.09	.05
305	Jose Oquendo	.06	.05	.02
306	Terry Pendleton	.10	.08	.04
307	Pat Perry	.08	.06	.03
308	Ozzie Smith	.15	.11	.06
309	Ray Soff	.06	.05	.02
310	John Tudor	.10	.08	.04
311	Andy Van Slyke	.12	.09	.05
312	Todd Worrell	.20	.15	.08
313	Dann Bilardello	.06	.05	.02
314	Hubie Brooks	.10	.08	.04
315	Tim Burke	.06	.05	.02
316	Andre Dawson	.20	.15	.08
317	Mike Fitzgerald	.06	.05	.02
318	Tom Foley	.06	.05	.02
319	Andres Galarraga	.40	.30	.15
320	Joe Hesketh	.06	.05	.02
321	Wallace Johnson	.06	.05	.02
322	Wayne Krenchicki	.06	.05	.02
323	Vance Law	.08	.06	.03
324	Dennis Martinez	.08	.06	.03
325	Bob McClure	.06	.05	.02
326	Andy McGaffigan	.06	.05	.02
327	*Al Newman*	.08	.06	.03
328	Tim Raines	.30	.25	.12
329	Jeff Reardon	.10	.08	.04
330	*Luis Rivera*(FC)	.10	.08	.04
331	*Bob Sebra*(FC)	.10	.08	.04
332	Bryn Smith	.06	.05	.02
333	Jay Tibbs	.06	.05	.02
334	Tim Wallach	.12	.09	.05
335	Mitch Webster	.08	.06	.03
336	Jim Wohlford	.06	.05	.02
337	Floyd Youmans	.08	.06	.03
338	*Chris Bosio*(FC)	.40	.30	.15
339	*Glenn Braggs*(FC)	.40	.30	.15
340	Rick Cerone	.06	.05	.02
341	Mark Clear	.06	.05	.02
342	*Bryan Clutterbuck*(FC)	.10	.08	.04
343	Cecil Cooper	.12	.09	.05
344	Rob Deer	.10	.08	.04
345	Jim Gantner	.08	.06	.03
346	Ted Higuera	.20	.15	.08
347	John Henry Johnson	.06	.05	.02

		MT	NR MT	EX
348	Tim Leary(FC)	.30	.25	.12
349	Rick Manning	.06	.05	.02
350	Paul Molitor	.15	.11	.06
351	Charlie Moore	.06	.05	.02
352	Juan Nieves	.10	.08	.04
353	Ben Oglivie	.08	.06	.03
354	*Dan Plesac*	.35	.25	.14
355	Ernest Riles	.06	.05	.02
356	Billy Joe Robidoux	.06	.05	.02
357	Bill Schroeder	.06	.05	.02
358	*Dale Sveum*	.20	.15	.08
359	Gorman Thomas	.10	.08	.04
360	Bill Wegman(FC)	.10	.08	.04
361	Robin Yount	.40	.30	.15
362	Steve Balboni	.08	.06	.03
363	*Scott Bankhead*	.30	.25	.12
364	Buddy Biancalana	.06	.05	.02
365	Bud Black	.06	.05	.02
366	George Brett	.40	.30	.15
367	Steve Farr	.06	.05	.02
368	Mark Gubicza	.12	.09	.05
369	*Bo Jackson*	20.00	15.00	8.00
370	Danny Jackson	.15	.11	.06
371	*Mike Kingery*	.15	.11	.06
372	Rudy Law	.06	.05	.02
373	Charlie Leibrandt	.08	.06	.03
374	Dennis Leonard	.08	.06	.03
375	Hal McRae	.10	.08	.04
376	Jorge Orta	.06	.05	.02
377	Jamie Quirk	.06	.05	.02
378	Dan Quisenberry	.08	.06	.03
379	Bret Saberhagen	.30	.25	.12
380	Angel Salazar	.06	.05	.02
381	Lonnie Smith	.08	.06	.03
382	Jim Sundberg	.08	.06	.03
383	Frank White	.10	.08	.04
384	Willie Wilson	.12	.09	.05
385	Joaquin Andujar	.08	.06	.03
386	Doug Bair	.06	.05	.02
387	Dusty Baker	.08	.06	.03
388	Bruce Bochte	.06	.05	.02
389	Jose Canseco	12.00	9.00	4.75
390	Chris Codiroli	.06	.05	.02
391	Mike Davis	.08	.06	.03
392	Alfredo Griffin	.08	.06	.03
393	Moose Haas	.06	.05	.02
394	Donnie Hill	.06	.05	.02
395	Jay Howell	.08	.06	.03
396	Dave Kingman	.12	.09	.05
397	Carney Lansford	.10	.08	.04
398	*David Leiper*(FC)	.12	.09	.05
399	*Bill Mooneyham*	.10	.08	.04
400	Dwayne Murphy	.08	.06	.03
401	Steve Ontiveros	.06	.05	.02
402	Tony Phillips	.06	.05	.02
403	Eric Plunk	.08	.06	.03
404	Jose Rijo	.08	.06	.03
405	*Terry Steinbach*(FC)	.90	.70	.35
406	Dave Stewart	.12	.09	.05
407	Mickey Tettleton	.06	.05	.02
408	Dave Von Ohlen	.06	.05	.02
409	Jerry Willard	.06	.05	.02
410	Curt Young	.08	.06	.03
411	Bruce Bochy	.06	.05	.02
412	Dave Dravecky	.08	.06	.03
413	Tim Flannery	.06	.05	.02
414	Steve Garvey	.25	.20	.10
415	Goose Gossage	.15	.11	.06
416	Tony Gwynn	.35	.25	.14
417	Andy Hawkins	.06	.05	.02
418	LaMarr Hoyt	.06	.05	.02
419	Terry Kennedy	.08	.06	.03
420	*John Kruk*	.35	.25	.14
421	Dave LaPoint	.08	.06	.03
422	Craig Lefferts	.06	.05	.02
423	Carmelo Martinez	.08	.06	.03
424	Lance McCullers	.08	.06	.03
425	Kevin McReynolds	.15	.11	.06
426	Graig Nettles	.12	.09	.05
427	Bip Roberts	.06	.05	.02
428	Jerry Royster	.06	.05	.02
429	Benito Santiago	1.25	.90	.50
430	Eric Show	.08	.06	.03
431	Bob Stoddard	.06	.05	.02
432	Garry Templeton	.08	.06	.03
433	Gene Walter	.06	.05	.02
434	Ed Whitson	.06	.05	.02
435	Marvell Wynne	.06	.05	.02
436	Dave Anderson	.06	.05	.02
437	Greg Brock	.08	.06	.03
438	Enos Cabell	.06	.05	.02

		MT	NR MT	EX
439	Mariano Duncan	.06	.05	.02
440	Pedro Guerrero	.15	.11	.06
441	Orel Hershiser	.40	.30	.15
442	Rick Honeycutt	.06	.05	.02
443	Ken Howell	.06	.05	.02
444	Ken Landreaux	.06	.05	.02
445	Bill Madlock	.12	.09	.05
446	Mike Marshall	.12	.09	.05
447	Len Matuszek	.06	.05	.02
448	Tom Niedenfuer	.08	.06	.03
449	Alejandro Pena	.08	.06	.03
450	Dennis Powell(FC)	.08	.06	.03
451	Jerry Reuss	.08	.06	.03
452	Bill Russell	.08	.06	.03
453	Steve Sax	.15	.11	.06
454	Mike Scioscia	.08	.06	.03
455	Franklin Stubbs	.08	.06	.03
456	Alex Trevino	.06	.05	.02
457	Fernando Valenzuela	.25	.20	.10
458	Ed Vande Berg	.06	.05	.02
459	Bob Welch	.10	.08	.04
460	*Reggie Williams*	.10	.08	.04
461	Don Aase	.06	.05	.02
462	Juan Beniquez	.06	.05	.02
463	Mike Boddicker	.08	.06	.03
464	Juan Bonilla	.06	.05	.02
465	Rich Bordi	.06	.05	.02
466	Storm Davis	.10	.08	.04
467	Rick Dempsey	.08	.06	.03
468	Ken Dixon	.06	.05	.02
469	Jim Dwyer	.06	.05	.02
470	Mike Flanagan	.08	.06	.03
471	Jackie Gutierrez	.06	.05	.02
472	Brad Havens	.06	.05	.02
473	Lee Lacy	.06	.05	.02
474	Fred Lynn	.15	.11	.06
475	Scott McGregor	.08	.06	.03
476	Eddie Murray	.35	.25	.14
477	Tom O'Malley	.06	.05	.02
478	Cal Ripken, Jr.	.35	.25	.14
479	Larry Sheets	.08	.06	.03
480	John Shelby	.06	.05	.02
481	Nate Snell	.06	.05	.02
482	Jim Traber(FC)	.10	.08	.04
483	Mike Young	.06	.05	.02
484	Neil Allen	.06	.05	.02
485	Harold Baines	.15	.11	.06
486	Floyd Bannister	.10	.08	.04
487	Daryl Boston	.08	.06	.03
488	Ivan Calderon	.12	.09	.05
489	*John Cangelosi*	.12	.09	.05
490	Steve Carlton	.25	.20	.10
491	Joe Cowley	.06	.05	.02
492	Julio Cruz	.06	.05	.02
493	Bill Dawley	.06	.05	.02
494	Jose DeLeon	.08	.06	.03
495	Richard Dotson	.08	.06	.03
496	Carlton Fisk	.15	.11	.06
497	Ozzie Guillen	.10	.08	.04
498	Jerry Hairston	.06	.05	.02
499	Ron Hassey	.06	.05	.02
500	Tim Hulett	.06	.05	.02
501	Bob James	.06	.05	.02
502	Steve Lyons	.06	.05	.02
503	*Joel McKeon*	.10	.08	.04
504	Gene Nelson	.06	.05	.02
505	Dave Schmidt	.06	.05	.02
506	Ray Searage	.06	.05	.02
507	*Bobby Thigpen*(FC)	2.75	2.00	1.00
508	Greg Walker	.10	.08	.04
509	Jim Acker	.06	.05	.02
510	Doyle Alexander	.08	.06	.03
511	*Paul Assenmacher*	.15	.11	.06
512	Bruce Benedict	.06	.05	.02
513	Chris Chambliss	.08	.06	.03
514	Jeff Dedmon	.06	.05	.02
515	Gene Garber	.06	.05	.02
516	Ken Griffey	.10	.08	.04
517	Terry Harper	.06	.05	.02
518	Bob Horner	.10	.08	.04
519	Glenn Hubbard	.06	.05	.02
520	Rick Mahler	.06	.05	.02
521	Omar Moreno	.06	.05	.02
522	Dale Murphy	.40	.30	.15
523	Ken Oberkfell	.06	.05	.02
524	Ed Olwine	.06	.05	.02
525	David Palmer	.06	.05	.02
526	Rafael Ramirez	.06	.05	.02
527	Billy Sample	.06	.05	.02
528	Ted Simmons	.12	.09	.05
529	Zane Smith	.08	.06	.03

		MT	NR MT	EX
530	Bruce Sutter	.12	.09	.05
531	*Andres Thomas*	.25	.20	.10
532	Ozzie Virgil	.06	.05	.02
533	*Allan Anderson*(FC)	.25	.20	.10
534	Keith Atherton	.06	.05	.02
535	Billy Beane	.06	.05	.02
536	Bert Blyleven	.12	.09	.05
537	Tom Brunansky	.10	.08	.04
538	Randy Bush	.06	.05	.02
539	George Frazier	.06	.05	.02
540	Gary Gaetti	.15	.11	.06
541	Greg Gagne	.06	.05	.02
542	Mickey Hatcher	.06	.05	.02
543	Neal Heaton	.06	.05	.02
544	Kent Hrbek	.15	.11	.06
545	Roy Lee Jackson	.06	.05	.02
546	Tim Laudner	.06	.05	.02
547	Steve Lombardozzi	.10	.08	.04
548	*Mark Portugal*(FC)	.10	.08	.04
549	Kirby Puckett	2.25	1.75	.90
550	Jeff Reed	.08	.06	.03
551	Mark Salas	.06	.05	.02
552	Roy Smalley	.06	.05	.02
553	Mike Smithson	.06	.05	.02
554	Frank Viola	.15	.11	.06
555	Thad Bosley	.06	.05	.02
556	Ron Cey	.10	.08	.04
557	Jody Davis	.08	.06	.03
558	Ron Davis	.06	.05	.02
559	Bob Dernier	.06	.05	.02
560	Frank DiPino	.06	.05	.02
561	Shawon Dunston	.10	.08	.04
562	Leon Durham	.08	.06	.03
563	Dennis Eckersley	.12	.09	.05
564	Terry Francona	.06	.05	.02
565	Dave Gumpert	.06	.05	.02
566	Guy Hoffman	.08	.06	.03
567	Ed Lynch	.06	.05	.02
568	Gary Matthews	.10	.08	.04
569	Keith Moreland	.08	.06	.03
570	*Jamie Moyer*(FC)	.20	.15	.08
571	Jerry Mumphrey	.06	.05	.02
572	Ryne Sandberg	.90	.70	.35
573	Scott Sanderson	.06	.05	.02
574	Lee Smith	.10	.08	.04
575	Chris Speier	.06	.05	.02
576	Rick Sutcliffe	.12	.09	.05
577	Manny Trillo	.08	.06	.03
578	Steve Trout	.06	.05	.02
579	Karl Best	.06	.05	.02
580	Scott Bradley(FC)	.08	.06	.03
581	Phil Bradley	.12	.09	.05
582	Mickey Brantley	.08	.06	.03
583	Mike Brown	.06	.05	.02
584	Alvin Davis	.12	.09	.05
585	*Lee Guetterman*(FC)	.15	.11	.06
586	Mark Huismann	.06	.05	.02
587	Bob Kearney	.06	.05	.02
588	Pete Ladd	.06	.05	.02
589	Mark Langston	.12	.09	.05
590	Mike Moore	.06	.05	.02
591	Mike Morgan	.06	.05	.02
592	John Moses	.06	.05	.02
593	Ken Phelps	.08	.06	.03
594	Jim Presley	.10	.08	.04
595	*Rey Quinonez (Quinones)*	.15	.11	.06
596	Harold Reynolds	.15	.11	.06
597	Billy Swift	.06	.05	.02
598	Danny Tartabull	.25	.20	.10
599	Steve Yeager	.06	.05	.02
600	Matt Young	.06	.05	.02
601	Bill Almon	.06	.05	.02
602	*Rafael Belliard*(FC)	.12	.09	.05
603	Mike Bielecki	.06	.05	.02
604	*Barry Bonds*	13.00	9.75	5.25
605	*Bobby Bonilla*	11.00	8.25	4.50
606	Sid Bream	.08	.06	.03
607	Mike Brown	.06	.05	.02
608	Pat Clements	.06	.05	.02
609	*Mike Diaz*(FC)	.15	.11	.06
610	Cecilio Guante	.06	.05	.02
611	*Barry Jones*(FC)	.12	.09	.05
612	Bob Kipper	.06	.05	.02
613	Larry McWilliams	.06	.05	.02
614	Jim Morrison	.06	.05	.02
615	Joe Orsulak	.06	.05	.02
616	Junior Ortiz	.06	.05	.02
617	Tony Pena	.08	.06	.03
618	Johnny Ray	.10	.08	.04
619	Rick Reuschel	.10	.08	.04
620	R.J. Reynolds	.06	.05	.02

		MT	NR MT	EX
621	Rick Rhoden	.10	.08	.04
622	Don Robinson	.08	.06	.03
623	Bob Walk	.06	.05	.02
624	Jim Winn	.06	.05	.02
625	Youthful Power (Jose Canseco, Pete Incaviglia)	.70	.50	.30
626	300 Game Winners (Phil Niekro, Don Sutton)	.12	.09	.05
627	A.L. Firemen (Don Aase, Dave Righetti)	.08	.06	.03
628	Rookie All-Stars (Jose Canseco, Wally Joyner)	2.00	1.50	.80
629	Magic Mets (Gary Carter, Sid Fernandez, Dwight Gooden, Keith Hernandez, Darryl Strawberry)	.60	.45	.25
630	N.L. Best Righties (Mike Krukow, Mike Scott)	.08	.06	.03
631	Sensational Southpaws (John Franco, Fernando Valenzuela)	.10	.08	.04
632	Count 'Em (Bob Horner)	.08	.06	.03
633	A.L. Pitcher's Nightmare (Jose Canseco, Kirby Puckett, Jim Rice)	1.50	1.25	.60
634	All Star Battery (Gary Carter, Roger Clemens)	.25	.20	.10
635	4,000 Strikeouts (Steve Carlton)	.12	.09	.05
636	Big Bats At First Sack (Glenn Davis, Eddie Murray)	.20	.15	.08
637	On Base (Wade Boggs, Keith Hernandez)	.35	.25	.14
638	Sluggers From Left Side (Don Mattingly, Darryl Strawberry)	.90	.70	.35
639	Former MVP's (Dave Parker, Ryne Sandberg)	.12	.09	.05
640	Dr. K. & Super K (Roger Clemens, Dwight Gooden)	.50	.40	.20
641	A.L. West Stoppers (Charlie Hough, Mike Witt)	.08	.06	.03
642	Doubles & Triples (Tim Raines, Juan Samuel)	.12	.09	.05
643	Outfielders With Punch (Harold Baines, Jesse Barfield)	.10	.08	.04
644	Major League Prospects *(Dave Clark, Greg Swindell)*(FC)	1.75	1.25	.70
645	Major League Prospects *(Ron Karkovice, Russ Morman)*(FC)	.12	.09	.05
646	Major League Prospects *(Willie Fraser, Devon White)*(FC)	1.25	.90	.50
647	Major League Prospects *(Jerry Browne, Mike Stanley)*(FC)	.60	.45	.25
648	Major League Prospects *(Phil Lombardi, Dave Magadan)*(FC)	3.50	2.75	1.50
649	Major League Prospects *(Ralph Bryant, Jose Gonzalez)*(FC)	.20	.15	.08
650	Major League Prospects *(Randy Asadoor, Jimmy Jones)*(FC)	.20	.15	.08
651	Major League Prospects *(Marvin Freeman, Tracy Jones)*	.25	.20	.10
652	Major League Prospects *(Kevin Seitzer, John Stefero)*(FC)	5.00	3.75	2.00
653	Major League Prospects *(Steve Fireovid, Rob Nelson)*(FC)	.10	.08	.04
654	Checklist 1-95	.06	.05	.02
655	Checklist 96-192	.06	.05	.02
656	Checklist 193-288	.06	.05	.02
657	Checklist 289-384	.06	.05	.02
658	Checklist 385-483	.06	.05	.02
659	Checklist 484-578	.06	.05	.02
660	Checklist 579-660	.06	.05	.02

1987 Fleer
All Star Team

As in 1986, Fleer All Star Team cards were

randomly inserted in Fleer wax and cello packs. Twelve cards, each measuring the standard 2-1/2" by 3-1/2", comprise the set. The card fronts feature a full-color player photo set against a gray background for American League players and a black background for National Leaguers. Card backs are printed in black, red and white and feature a lengthy player biography. Fleer's choices for a major league All-Star team is once again the theme for the set.

		MT	NR MT	EX
Complete Set:		18.00	13.50	7.25
Common Player:		.60	.45	.25
1	Don Mattingly	5.00	3.75	2.00
2	Gary Carter	1.00	.70	.40
3	Tony Fernandez	.75	.60	.30
4	Steve Sax	.75	.60	.30
5	Kirby Puckett	3.00	2.25	1.25
6	Mike Schmidt	2.00	1.50	.80
7	Mike Easler	.60	.45	.25
8	Todd Worrell	.75	.60	.30
9	George Bell	1.00	.70	.40
10	Fernando Valenzuela	1.00	.70	.40
11	Roger Clemens	2.25	1.75	.90
12	Tim Raines	1.25	.90	.50

		MT	NR MT	EX
18	Bill Gullickson	.05	.04	.02
19	Tony Gwynn	.25	.20	.10
20	Bob Knepper	.05	.04	.02
21	Ray Knight	.05	.04	.02
22	Mark Langston	.20	.15	.08
23	Candy Maldonado	.05	.04	.02
24	Don Mattingly	1.25	.90	.50
25	Roger McDowell	.07	.05	.03
26	Dale Murphy	.30	.25	.12
27	Dave Parker	.12	.09	.05
28	Lance Parrish	.15	.11	.06
29	Gary Pettis	.05	.04	.02
30	Kirby Puckett	.70	.50	.40
31	Johnny Ray	.07	.05	.03
32	Dave Righetti	.12	.09	.05
33	Cal Ripken, Jr.	.30	.25	.12
34	Bret Saberhagen	.15	.11	.06
35	Ryne Sandberg	.20	.15	.08
36	Mike Schmidt	.30	.25	.12
37	Mike Scott	.12	.09	.05
38	Ozzie Smith	.12	.09	.05
39	Robbie Thompson	.10	.08	.04
40	Fernando Valenzuela	.20	.15	.08
41	Mitch Webster	.05	.04	.02
42	Frank White	.07	.05	.03
43	Mike Witt	.07	.05	.03
44	Todd Worrell	.15	.11	.06

1987 Fleer Baseball's Award Winners

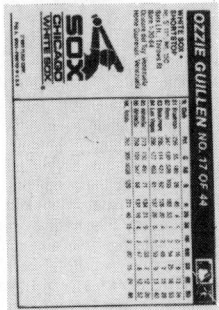

Rookie of the Year

The 1987 Fleer Award Winners boxed set was prepared by Fleer for distribution by 7-Eleven stores. The cards, which measure 2-1/2" by 3-1/2", feature players who have won various major league awards during their careers. The card fronts contain full-color photos surrounded by a yellow border. The name of the award the player won is printed at the bottom of the card in an oval-shaped band designed to resemble a metal nameplate on a trophy. Card backs, printed in black, yellow and white, include lifetime major and minor league statistics along with typical personal information. Each boxed set contained six team logo stickers.

		MT	NR MT	EX
Complete Set:		6.00	4.50	2.50
Common Player:		.05	.04	.02
1	Marty Barrett	.07	.05	.03
2	George Bell	.20	.15	.08
3	Bert Blyleven	.10	.08	.04
4	Bob Boone	.05	.04	.02
5	John Candelaria	.05	.04	.02
6	Jose Canseco	1.50	1.25	.60
7	Gary Carter	.25	.20	.10
8	Joe Carter	.25	.20	.10
9	Roger Clemens	.50	.40	.20
10	Cecil Cooper	.10	.08	.04
11	Eric Davis	.60	.45	.25
12	Tony Fernandez	.10	.08	.04
13	Scott Fletcher	.05	.04	.02
14	Bob Forsch	.05	.04	.02
15	Dwight Gooden	.50	.40	.20
16	Ron Guidry	.12	.09	.05
17	Ozzie Guillen	.07	.05	.03

1987 Fleer Baseball All Stars

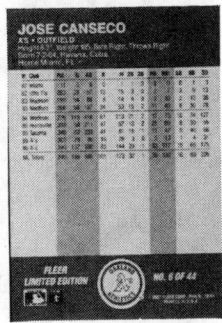

Produced by Fleer for exclusive distribution through Ben Franklin stores, the "Baseball All Stars" set is comprised of 44 cards which are the standard 2-1/2" by 3-1/2" size. The cards have full-color photos surrounded by a bright red border with white pinstripes at the top and bottom. The card backs are printed in blue, white and dark red and include complete major and minor league statistics. The set was issued in a special cardboard box.

		MT	NR MT	EX
Complete Set:		8.00	6.00	3.25
Common Player:		.05	.04	.02
1	Harold Baines	.10	.08	.04
2	Jesse Barfield	.12	.09	.05
3	Wade Boggs	1.00	.70	.40
4	Dennis "Oil Can" Boyd	.05	.04	.02
5	Scott Bradley	.05	.04	.02
6	Jose Canseco	1.50	1.25	.60
7	Gary Carter	.25	.20	.10
8	Joe Carter	.25	.20	.10
9	Mark Clear	.05	.04	.02
10	Roger Clemens	.50	.40	.20
11	Jose Cruz	.05	.04	.02
12	Chili Davis	.07	.05	.03
13	Jody Davis	.05	.04	.02
14	Rob Deer	.05	.04	.02
15	Brian Downing	.05	.04	.02
16	Sid Fernandez	.07	.05	.03
17	John Franco	.07	.05	.03
18	Andres Galarraga	.15	.11	.06
19	Dwight Gooden	.50	.40	.20
20	Tony Gwynn	.25	.20	.10
21	Charlie Hough	.05	.04	.02
22	Bruce Hurst	.10	.08	.04

		MT	NR MT	EX
23	Wally Joyner	.70	.50	.30
24	Carney Lansford	.05	.04	.02
25	Fred Lynn	.12	.09	.05
26	Don Mattingly	1.50	1.25	.60
27	Willie McGee	.10	.08	.04
28	Jack Morris	.15	.11	.06
29	Dale Murphy	.30	.25	.12
30	Bob Ojeda	.07	.05	.03
31	Tony Pena	.07	.05	.03
32	Kirby Puckett	.70	.50	.30
33	Dan Quisenberry	.07	.05	.03
34	Tim Raines	.25	.20	.10
35	Willie Randolph	.07	.05	.03
36	Cal Ripken, Jr.	.25	.20	.10
37	Pete Rose	.50	.40	.20
38	Nolan Ryan	.50	.40	.20
39	Juan Samuel	.10	.08	.04
40	Mike Schmidt	.30	.25	.12
41	Ozzie Smith	.12	.09	.05
42	Andres Thomas	.10	.08	.04
43	Fernando Valenzuela	.20	.15	.08
44	Mike Witt	.07	.05	.03

		MT	NR MT	EX
28	Dale Murphy	.30	.25	.12
29	Dave Parker	.12	.09	.05
30	Ken Phelps	.05	.04	.02
31	Kirby Puckett	.70	.50	.30
32	Tim Raines	.25	.20	.10
33	Jeff Reardon	.10	.08	.04
34	Dave Righetti	.12	.09	.05
35	Cal Ripken, Jr.	.30	.25	.12
36	Bret Saberhagen	.15	.11	.06
37	Mike Schmidt	.30	.25	.12
38	Mike Scott	.12	.09	.05
39	Kevin Seitzer	.50	.40	.20
40	Darryl Strawberry	.40	.30	.15
41	Rick Sutcliffe	.10	.08	.04
42	Pat Tabler	.05	.04	.02
43	Fernando Valenzuela	.10	.08	.04
44	Mike Witt	.07	.05	.03

1987 Fleer Baseball's Best

For a second straight baseball card season, Fleer produced for McCrory's stores and their affiliates a 44-card "Baseball's Best" set. Subtitled "Sluggers vs. Pitchers," 28 everyday players and 16 pitchers are featured. The card design is nearly identical to the previous year's effort. The cards, which measure 2-1/2" by 3-1/2", were housed in a specially designed box along with six team logo stickers.

		MT	NR MT	EX
Complete Set:		6.00	4.50	2.50
Common Player:		.05	.04	.02
1	Kevin Bass	.07	.05	.03
2	Jesse Barfield	.12	.09	.05
3	George Bell	.20	.15	.08
4	Wade Boggs	1.00	.70	.40
5	Sid Bream	.05	.04	.02
6	George Brett	.30	.25	.12
7	Ivan Calderon	.10	.08	.04
8	Jose Canseco	1.50	1.25	.60
9	Jack Clark	.12	.09	.05
10	Roger Clemens	.50	.40	.20
11	Eric Davis	.50	.40	.20
12	Andre Dawson	.15	.11	.06
13	Sid Fernandez	.07	.05	.03
14	John Franco	.07	.05	.03
15	Dwight Gooden	.50	.40	.20
16	Pedro Guerrero	.15	.11	.06
17	Tony Gwynn	.25	.20	.10
18	Rickey Henderson	.30	.25	.12
19	Tom Henke	.05	.04	.02
20	Ted Higuera	.10	.08	.04
21	Pete Incaviglia	.30	.25	.12
22	Wally Joyner	.50	.40	.20
23	Jeff Leonard	.05	.04	.02
24	Joe Magrane	.15	.11	.06
25	Don Mattingly	1.50	1.25	.60
26	Mark McGwire	1.50	1.25	.60
27	Jack Morris	.15	.11	.06

1987 Fleer Baseball's Exciting Stars

 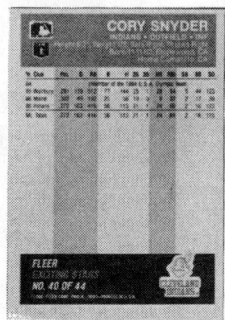

Another entry into the Fleer lineup of individual boxed sets, the "Baseball's Exciting Stars" set was produced by Fleer for Cumberland Farms stores. The card fronts feature a red, white and blue border with the words "Exciting Stars" printed in yellow at the top. The backs are printed in red and blue and carry complete major and minor league statistics. Included with the boxed set of 44 cards were six team logo stickers.

		MT	NR MT	EX
Complete Set:		7.00	5.25	2.75
Common Player:		.05	.04	.02
1	Don Aase	.05	.04	.02
2	Rick Aguilera	.07	.05	.03
3	Jesse Barfield	.12	.09	.05
4	Wade Boggs	1.00	.70	.40
5	Dennis "Oil Can" Boyd	.05	.04	.02
6	Sid Bream	.07	.05	.03
7	Jose Canseco	1.50	1.25	.60
8	Steve Carlton	.25	.20	.10
9	Gary Carter	.25	.20	.10
10	Will Clark	1.00	.70	.40
11	Roger Clemens	.40	.30	.15
12	Danny Cox	.07	.05	.03
13	Alvin Davis	.10	.08	.04
14	Eric Davis	.50	.40	.20
15	Rob Deer	.07	.05	.03
16	Brian Downing	.05	.04	.02
17	Gene Garber	.05	.04	.02
18	Steve Garvey	.25	.20	.10
19	Dwight Gooden	.50	.40	.20
20	Mark Gubicza	.10	.08	.04
21	Mel Hall	.05	.04	.02
22	Terry Harper	.05	.04	.02
23	Von Hayes	.10	.08	.04
24	Rickey Henderson	.60	.45	.25
25	Tom Henke	.05	.04	.02
26	Willie Hernandez	.05	.04	.02
27	Ted Higuera	.10	.08	.04
28	Rick Honeycutt	.05	.04	.02
29	Kent Hrbek	.15	.11	.06
30	Wally Joyner	.60	.45	.25
31	Charlie Kerfeld	.05	.04	.02

		MT	NR MT	EX
32	Fred Lynn	.12	.09	.05
33	Don Mattingly	1.50	1.25	.60
34	Tim Raines	.25	.20	.10
35	Dennis Rasmussen	.07	.05	.03
36	Johnny Ray	.07	.05	.03
37	Jim Rice	.20	.15	.08
38	Pete Rose	.50	.40	.20
39	Lee Smith	.07	.05	.03
40	Cory Snyder	.25	.20	.10
41	Darryl Strawberry	.40	.30	.15
42	Kent Tekulve	.05	.04	.02
43	Willie Wilson	.10	.08	.04
44	Bobby Witt	.12	.09	.05

		MT	NR MT	EX
35	Dennis Rasmussen	.07	.05	.03
36	Ernest Riles	.07	.05	.03
37	Cal Ripken, Jr.	.30	.25	.12
38	Ron Robinson	.05	.04	.02
39	Steve Sax	.15	.11	.06
40	Mike Schmidt	.30	.25	.12
41	John Tudor	.07	.05	.03
42	Fernando Valenzuela	.20	.15	.08
43	Mike Witt	.07	.05	.03
44	Curt Young	.05	.04	.02

1987 Fleer Baseball's Game Winners

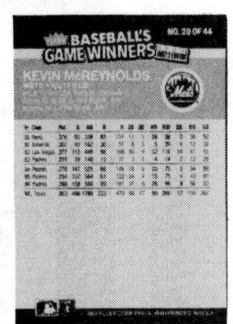

The 1987 Fleer "Baseball's Game Winners" boxed set of 44 cards was produced for distribution through Bi-Mart Discount Drug, Pay'n-Save, Mott's 5 & 10, M.E. Moses, and Winn's stores. The cards, which measure 2-1/2" by 3-1/2", have a light blue border with the player's name and game winning RBI or games won statistics in a yellow oval band at the top of the card. Below the full-color player photo is the name of the set in blue, yellow and red. Included with the boxed set were six team logo stickers.

		MT	NR MT	EX
Complete Set:		6.00	4.50	2.50
Common Player:		.05	.04	.02
1	Harold Baines	.10	.08	.04
2	Don Baylor	.10	.08	.04
3	George Bell	.20	.15	.08
4	Tony Bernazard	.05	.04	.02
5	Wade Boggs	1.00	.70	.40
6	George Brett	.40	.30	.15
7	Hubie Brooks	.07	.05	.03
8	Jose Canseco	1.00	.70	.40
9	Gary Carter	.20	.15	.08
10	Roger Clemens	.40	.30	.15
11	Eric Davis	.50	.40	.20
12	Glenn Davis	.15	.11	.06
13	Shawon Dunston	.07	.05	.03
14	Mark Eichhorn	.10	.08	.04
15	Gary Gaetti	.12	.09	.05
16	Steve Garvey	.25	.20	.10
17	Kirk Gibson	.20	.15	.08
18	Dwight Gooden	.50	.40	.20
19	Von Hayes	.07	.05	.03
20	Willie Hernandez	.07	.05	.03
21	Ted Higuera	.10	.08	.04
22	Wally Joyner	.80	.60	.30
23	Bob Knepper	.05	.04	.02
24	Mike Krukow	.05	.04	.02
25	Jeff Leonard	.05	.04	.02
26	Don Mattingly	1.50	1.25	.60
27	Kirk McCaskill	.07	.05	.03
28	Kevin McReynolds	.12	.09	.05
29	Jim Morrison	.05	.04	.02
30	Dale Murphy	.30	.25	.12
31	Pete O'Brien	.07	.05	.03
32	Bob Ojeda	.07	.05	.03
33	Larry Parrish	.05	.04	.02
34	Ken Phelps	.05	.04	.02

1987 Fleer Baseball's Hottest Stars

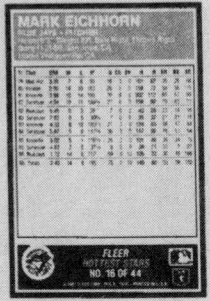

The "Baseball's Hottest Stars" 44-card set was produced by Fleer for the Revco Drug Store chain. Measuring the standard 2-1/2" by 3-1/2", the cards feature full-color photos surrounded by a red, white and blue border. The player's name, position and team appear in a blue band at the bottom of the card. Card backs are printed in red, white and black and contain the player's lifetime professional statistics. The set was housed in a special cardboard box with six team logo stickers.

		MT	NR MT	EX
Complete Set:		7.00	5.25	2.75
Common Player:		.05	.04	.02
1	Joaquin Andujar	.05	.04	.02
2	Harold Baines	.10	.08	.04
3	Kevin Bass	.07	.05	.03
4	Don Baylor	.10	.08	.04
5	Barry Bonds	.20	.15	.08
6	George Brett	.30	.25	.12
7	Tom Brunansky	.10	.08	.04
8	Brett Butler	.05	.04	.02
9	Jose Canseco	1.50	1.25	.60
10	Roger Clemens	.50	.40	.20
11	Ron Darling	.10	.08	.04
12	Eric Davis	.50	.40	.20
13	Andre Dawson	.15	.11	.06
14	Doug DeCinces	.05	.04	.02
15	Leon Durham	.07	.05	.03
16	Mark Eichhorn	.10	.08	.04
17	Scott Garrelts	.05	.04	.02
18	Dwight Gooden	.50	.40	.20
19	Dave Henderson	.05	.04	.02
20	Rickey Henderson	.50	.40	.20
21	Keith Hernandez	.15	.11	.06
22	Ted Higuera	.10	.08	.04
23	Bob Horner	.07	.05	.03
24	Pete Incaviglia	.40	.30	.15
25	Wally Joyner	.50	.40	.20
26	Mark Langston	.07	.05	.03
27	Don Mattingly	1.75	1.25	.70
28	Dale Murphy	.30	.25	.12
29	Kirk McCaskill	.07	.05	.03
30	Willie McGee	.10	.08	.04
31	Dave Righetti	.12	.09	.05
32	Pete Rose	.40	.30	.15
33	Bruce Ruffin	.15	.11	.06
34	Steve Sax	.15	.11	.06
35	Mike Schmidt	.30	.25	.12
36	Larry Sheets	.10	.08	.04
37	Eric Show	.07	.05	.03

		MT	NR MT	EX
38	Dave Smith	.05	.04	.02
39	Cory Snyder	.25	.20	.10
40	Frank Tanana	.05	.04	.02
41	Alan Trammell	.20	.15	.08
42	Reggie Williams	.07	.05	.03
43	Mookie Wilson	.07	.05	.03
44	Todd Worrell	.15	.11	.06

1987 Fleer Box Panels

 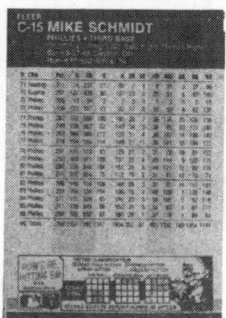

For the second straight year, Fleer produced a special set of cards designed to stimulate sales of their wax and cello pack boxes. In 1987, Fleer issued 16 cards in panels of four on the bottoms of retail boxes. The cards are numbered C-1 through C-16 and are 2-1/2" by 3-1/2" in size. The cards have the same design as the regular issue set with the player photos and card numbers being different.

		MT	NR MT	EX
Complete Panel Set:		8.00	6.00	3.25
Complete Singles Set:		3.50	2.75	1.50
Common Panel:		2.25	1.75	.90
Common Single Player:		.20	.15	.08
	Panel	2.50	2.00	1.00
1	Mets Logo	.05	.04	.02
6	Keith Hernandez	.30	.25	.12
8	Dale Murphy	.60	.45	.25
14	Ryne Sandberg	.30	.25	.12
	Panel	2.25	1.75	.90
2	Jesse Barfield	.20	.15	.08
3	George Brett	.60	.45	.25
5	Red Sox Logo	.05	.04	.02
11	Kirby Puckett	.30	.25	.12
	Panel	2.75	2.00	1.00
4	Dwight Gooden	.80	.60	.30
9	Astros Logo	.05	.04	.02
10	Dave Parker	.25	.20	.10
15	Mike Schmidt	.60	.45	.25
	Panel	2.75	2.00	1.00
7	Wally Joyner	1.00	.70	.40
12	Dave Righetti	.20	.15	.08
13	Angels Logo	.05	.04	.02
16	Robin Yount	.25	.20	.10

1987 Fleer '86 World Series

Fleer issued a set of 12 cards highlighting the 1986 World Series between the Boston Red Sox and New York Mets. The sets were available only with Fleer factory-packaged sets of 660 regular issue cards. The cards, which are the standard 2-1/2" by 3-1/2" size, have either horizontal or vertical formats. The fronts are bordered in red, white and blue stars and stripes with a thin gold frame around the photo. The backs are printed in red and blue ink on white stock and include information regarding the photo on the card fronts.

 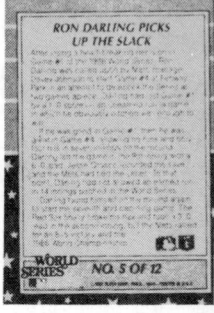

		MT	NR MT	EX
Complete Set:		5.00	3.75	2.00
Common Player:		.50	.40	.20
1	Left-Hand Finesse Beats Mets (Bruce Hurst)	.50	.40	.20
2	Hernandez And Boggs (Wade Boggs, Keith Hernandez)	1.00	.70	.40
3	Roger Clemens	.70	.50	.30
4	Clutch Hitting (Gary Carter)	.50	.40	.20
5	Darling Picks Up The Slack (Ron Darling)	.50	.40	.20
6	.433 Series Batting Average (Marty Barrett)	.50	.40	.20
7	Dwight Gooden	.70	.50	.30
8	Strategy At Work	.50	.40	.20
9	Dewey! (Dwight Evans)	.50	.40	.20
10	One Strike From Boston Victory (Dave Henderson, Spike Owen)	.50	.40	.20
11	Series Home Run Duo (Ray Knight, Darryl Strawberry)	.50	.40	.20
12	Series M.V.P. (Ray Knight)	.50	.40	.20

1987 Fleer Headliners

 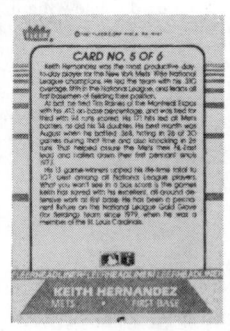

A continuation of the 1986 Future Hall of Famers idea, Fleer encountered legal problems with using the Hall of Fame name and abated them by entitling the set "Headliners." The cards, which are the standard 2-1/2" by 3-1/2" size, were randomly inserted in three-pack cello packs. Card fronts feature a player photo set against a beige background with bright red stripes. The card backs are printed in black, red and gray and offer a brief biography with an emphasis on the player's performance during the 1986 season.

		MT	NR MT	EX
Complete Set:		10.00	7.50	4.00
Common Player:		1.00	.70	.40
1	Wade Boggs	2.25	1.75	.90
2	Jose Canseco	3.00	2.25	1.25
3	Dwight Gooden	1.50	1.25	.60
4	Rickey Henderson	2.00	1.50	.80
5	Keith Hernandez	1.00	.70	.40
6	Jim Rice	1.00	.70	.40

1987 Fleer
League Leaders

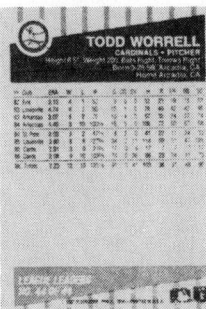

For the second year in a row, Fleer produced a 44-card "League Leaders" set for Walgreens. The card fronts feature a border style which is identical to that used in 1986. However, an elliptical shaped full-color player photo is placed diagonally on the front. "1987 Fleer League Leaders" appears in the upper left corner of the front although nowhere on the card does it state in which pitching, hitting or fielding department was the player a league leader. The card backs are printed in red and blue on white stock. The cards in the boxed set are the standard 2-1/2" by 3-1/2" size.

		MT	NR MT	EX
Complete Set:		5.00	3.75	2.00
Common Player:		.05	.04	.02
1	Jesse Barfield	.12	.09	.05
2	Mike Boddicker	.07	.05	.03
3	Wade Boggs	1.00	.70	.40
4	Phil Bradley	.10	.08	.04
5	George Brett	.30	.25	.12
6	Hubie Brooks	.07	.05	.03
7	Chris Brown	.07	.05	.03
8	Jose Canseco	.70	.50	.30
9	Joe Carter	.12	.09	.05
10	Roger Clemens	.40	.30	.15
11	Vince Coleman	.15	.11	.06
12	Joe Cowley	.05	.04	.02
13	Kal Daniels	.20	.15	.08
14	Glenn Davis	.15	.11	.06
15	Jody Davis	.07	.05	.03
16	Darrell Evans	.07	.05	.03
17	Dwight Evans	.10	.08	.04
18	John Franco	.07	.05	.03
19	Julio Franco	.10	.08	.04
20	Dwight Gooden	.40	.30	.15
21	Goose Gossage	.12	.09	.05
22	Tom Herr	.07	.05	.03
23	Ted Higuera	.10	.08	.04
24	Bob Horner	.07	.05	.03
25	Pete Incaviglia	.40	.30	.15
26	Wally Joyner	.40	.30	.15
27	Dave Kingman	.10	.08	.04
28	Don Mattingly	1.75	1.25	.70
29	Willie McGee	.10	.08	.04
30	Donnie Moore	.05	.04	.02
31	Keith Moreland	.05	.04	.02
32	Eddie Murray	.25	.20	.10
33	Mike Pagliarulo	.10	.08	.04
34	Larry Parrish	.05	.04	.02
35	Tony Pena	.07	.05	.03
36	Kirby Puckett	.50	.40	.20
37	Pete Rose	.50	.40	.20
38	Juan Samuel	.12	.09	.05
39	Ryne Sandberg	.20	.15	.08
40	Mike Schmidt	.30	.25	.12
41	Darryl Strawberry	.40	.30	.15
42	Greg Walker	.07	.05	.03
43	Bob Welch	.07	.05	.03
44	Todd Worrell	.12	.09	.05

1987 Fleer
Limited Edition

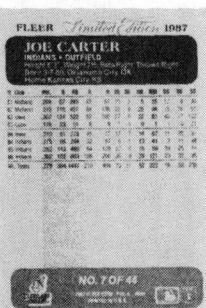

For the third straight year, Fleer produced a Limited Edition set for the McCrory's store chain and their affiliates. The cards are the standard 2-1/2" by 3-1/2" size and feature light blue borders at the top and bottom and a diagonal red and white border running along both sides. The set was issued in a specially prepared cardboard box, along with six team logo stickers.

		MT	NR MT	EX
Complete Set:		5.00	3.75	2.00
Common Player:		.05	.04	.02
1	Floyd Bannister	.05	.04	.02
2	Marty Barrett	.07	.05	.03
3	Steve Bedrosian	.10	.08	.04
4	George Bell	.20	.15	.08
5	George Brett	.30	.25	.12
6	Jose Canseco	1.00	.70	.40
7	Joe Carter	.12	.09	.05
8	Will Clark	1.00	.70	.40
9	Roger Clemens	.40	.30	.15
10	Vince Coleman	.15	.11	.06
11	Glenn Davis	.15	.11	.06
12	Mike Davis	.05	.04	.02
13	Len Dykstra	.07	.05	.03
14	John Franco	.07	.05	.03
15	Julio Franco	.10	.08	.04
16	Steve Garvey	.25	.20	.10
17	Kirk Gibson	.20	.15	.08
18	Dwight Gooden	.40	.30	.15
19	Tony Gwynn	.25	.20	.10
20	Keith Hernandez	.20	.15	.08
21	Teddy Higuera	.10	.08	.04
22	Kent Hrbek	.15	.11	.06
23	Wally Joyner	.50	.40	.20
24	Mike Krukow	.05	.04	.02
25	Mike Marshall	.10	.08	.04
26	Don Mattingly	1.00	.70	.40
27	Oddibe McDowell	.10	.08	.04
28	Jack Morris	.15	.11	.06
29	Lloyd Moseby	.07	.05	.03
30	Dale Murphy	.30	.25	.12
31	Eddie Murray	.25	.20	.10
32	Tony Pena	.07	.05	.03
33	Jim Presley	.10	.08	.04
34	Jeff Reardon	.10	.08	.04
35	Jim Rice	.20	.15	.08
36	Pete Rose	.40	.30	.15
37	Mike Schmidt	.30	.25	.12
38	Mike Scott	.12	.09	.05
39	Lee Smith	.07	.05	.03
40	Lonnie Smith	.05	.04	.02
41	Gary Ward	.05	.04	.02
42	Dave Winfield	.25	.20	.10
43	Todd Worrell	.12	.09	.05
44	Robin Yount	.20	.15	.08

Definitions for grading conditions are located in the introduction section at the front of this book.

1987 Fleer Mini

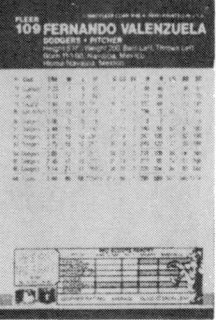

Continuing with an idea originated the previous year, the Fleer "Classic Miniatures" set consists of 120 cards that measure 1-13/16" by 2-9/16" in size. The cards are identical in design to the regular issue set produced by Fleer, but use completely different photos. The set was issued in a specially prepared collectors box along with 18 team logo stickers. The Fleer Mini set was available only through hobby dealers.

		MT	NR MT	EX
	Complete Set:	8.00	6.00	3.25
	Common Player:	.05	.04	.02
1	Don Aase	.05	.04	.02
2	Joaquin Andujar	.05	.04	.02
3	Harold Baines	.12	.09	.05
4	Jesse Barfield	.12	.09	.05
5	Kevin Bass	.05	.04	.02
6	Don Baylor	.10	.08	.04
7	George Bell	.20	.15	.08
8	Tony Bernazard	.05	.04	.02
9	Bert Blyleven	.12	.09	.05
10	Wade Boggs	1.00	.70	.40
11	Phil Bradley	.10	.08	.04
12	Sid Bream	.05	.04	.02
13	George Brett	.30	.25	.12
14	Hubie Brooks	.07	.05	.03
15	Chris Brown	.07	.05	.03
16	Tom Candiotti	.05	.04	.02
17	Jose Canseco	1.50	1.25	.60
18	Gary Carter	.20	.15	.08
19	Joe Carter	.12	.09	.05
20	Roger Clemens	.60	.45	.25
21	Vince Coleman	.15	.11	.06
22	Cecil Cooper	.10	.08	.04
23	Ron Darling	.10	.08	.04
24	Alvin Davis	.10	.08	.04
25	Chili Davis	.05	.04	.02
26	Eric Davis	.80	.60	.30
27	Glenn Davis	.15	.11	.06
28	Mike Davis	.05	.04	.02
29	Doug DeCinces	.05	.04	.02
30	Rob Deer	.07	.05	.03
31	Jim Deshaies	.10	.08	.04
32	Bo Diaz	.05	.04	.02
33	Richard Dotson	.07	.05	.03
34	Brian Downing	.05	.04	.02
35	Shawon Dunston	.07	.05	.03
36	Mark Eichhorn	.10	.08	.04
37	Dwight Evans	.12	.09	.05
38	Tony Fernandez	.10	.08	.04
39	Julio Franco	.10	.08	.04
40	Gary Gaetti	.12	.09	.05
41	Andres Galarraga	.15	.11	.06
42	Scott Garrelts	.05	.04	.02
43	Steve Garvey	.20	.15	.08
44	Kirk Gibson	.20	.15	.08
45	Dwight Gooden	.60	.45	.25
46	Ken Griffey	.07	.05	.03
47	Mark Gubicza	.10	.08	.04
48	Ozzie Guillen	.07	.05	.03
49	Bill Gullickson	.05	.04	.02
50	Tony Gwynn	.25	.20	.10
51	Von Hayes	.10	.08	.04
52	Rickey Henderson	.50	.40	.20
53	Keith Hernandez	.15	.11	.06

		MT	NR MT	EX
54	Willie Hernandez	.05	.04	.02
55	Ted Higuera	.10	.08	.04
56	Charlie Hough	.05	.04	.02
57	Kent Hrbek	.15	.11	.06
58	Pete Incaviglia	.40	.30	.15
59	Wally Joyner	.80	.60	.30
60	Bob Knepper	.07	.05	.03
61	Mike Krukow	.05	.04	.02
62	Mark Langston	.10	.08	.04
63	Carney Lansford	.07	.05	.03
64	Jim Lindeman	.12	.09	.05
65	Bill Madlock	.10	.08	.04
66	Don Mattingly	1.75	1.25	.70
67	Kirk McCaskill	.05	.04	.02
68	Lance McCullers	.10	.08	.04
69	Keith Moreland	.05	.04	.02
70	Jack Morris	.15	.11	.06
71	Jim Morrison	.05	.04	.02
72	Lloyd Moseby	.07	.05	.03
73	Jerry Mumphrey	.05	.04	.02
74	Dale Murphy	.30	.25	.12
75	Eddie Murray	.25	.20	.10
76	Pete O'Brien	.07	.05	.03
77	Bob Ojeda	.07	.05	.03
78	Jesse Orosco	.05	.04	.02
79	Dan Pasqua	.10	.08	.04
80	Dave Parker	.12	.09	.05
81	Larry Parrish	.05	.04	.02
82	Jim Presley	.10	.08	.04
83	Kirby Puckett	.50	.40	.20
84	Dan Quisenberry	.07	.05	.03
85	Tim Raines	.20	.15	.08
86	Dennis Rasmussen	.07	.05	.03
87	Johnny Ray	.07	.05	.03
88	Jeff Reardon	.07	.05	.03
89	Jim Rice	.20	.15	.08
90	Dave Righetti	.12	.09	.05
91	Earnest Riles	.05	.04	.02
92	Cal Ripken, Jr.	.30	.25	.12
93	Ron Robinson	.05	.04	.02
94	Juan Samuel	.12	.09	.05
95	Ryne Sandberg	.20	.15	.08
96	Steve Sax	.15	.11	.06
97	Mike Schmidt	.30	.25	.12
98	Ken Schrom	.05	.04	.02
99	Mike Scott	.12	.09	.05
100	Ruben Sierra	1.50	1.25	.60
101	Lee Smith	.07	.05	.03
102	Ozzie Smith	.12	.09	.05
103	Cory Snyder	.20	.15	.08
104	Kent Tekulve	.05	.04	.02
105	Andres Thomas	.10	.08	.04
106	Rob Thompson	.10	.08	.04
107	Alan Trammell	.20	.15	.08
108	John Tudor	.07	.05	.03
109	Fernando Valenzuela	.20	.15	.08
110	Greg Walker	.07	.05	.03
111	Mitch Webster	.05	.04	.02
112	Lou Whitaker	.15	.11	.06
113	Frank White	.07	.05	.03
114	Reggie Williams	.10	.08	.04
115	Glenn Wilson	.05	.04	.02
116	Willie Wilson	.10	.08	.04
117	Dave Winfield	.20	.15	.08
118	Mike Witt	.07	.05	.03
119	Todd Worrell	.12	.09	.05
120	Floyd Youmans	.05	.04	.02

1987 Fleer Baseball Record Setters

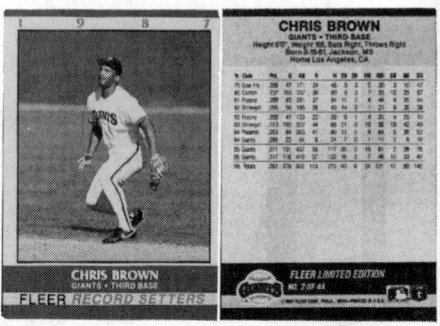

Produced by Fleer for the Eckerd Drug chain, the

1987 Fleer Record Setters set contains 44 cards that measure the standard 2-1/2" by 3-1/2" size. Although the set is titled "Record Setters," the actual records the players have set is not specified anywhere on the cards. Given that several players included in the set were young prospects, a better title for those cards might have been "Possible Record Setters." The set came housed in a special cardboard box with six team logo stickers.

		MT	NR MT	EX
	Complete Set:	5.00	3.75	2.00
	Common Player:	.05	.04	.02
1	George Brett	.30	.25	.12
2	Chris Brown	.07	.05	.03
3	Jose Canseco	1.00	.70	.40
4	Roger Clemens	.40	.30	.15
5	Alvin Davis	.10	.08	.04
6	Shawon Dunston	.07	.05	.03
7	Tony Fernandez	.10	.08	.04
8	Carlton Fisk	.12	.09	.05
9	Gary Gaetti	.10	.08	.04
10	Gene Garber	.05	.04	.02
11	Rich Gedman	.05	.04	.02
12	Dwight Gooden	.40	.30	.15
13	Ozzie Guillen	.07	.05	.03
14	Bill Gullickson	.05	.04	.02
15	Billy Hatcher	.07	.05	.03
16	Orel Hershiser	.20	.15	.08
17	Wally Joyner	.70	.50	.30
18	Ray Knight	.05	.04	.02
19	Craig Lefferts	.05	.04	.02
20	Don Mattingly	1.75	1.25	.70
21	Kevin Mitchell	.70	.50	.30
22	Lloyd Moseby	.07	.05	.03
23	Dale Murphy	.30	.25	.12
24	Eddie Murray	.25	.20	.10
25	Phil Niekro	.15	.11	.06
26	Ben Oglivie	.05	.04	.02
27	Jesse Orosco	.05	.04	.02
28	Joe Orsulak	.05	.04	.02
29	Larry Parrish	.05	.04	.02
30	Tim Raines	.25	.20	.10
31	Shane Rawley	.07	.05	.03
32	Dave Righetti	.12	.09	.05
33	Pete Rose	.40	.30	.15
34	Steve Sax	.15	.11	.06
35	Mike Schmidt	.30	.25	.12
36	Mike Scott	.12	.09	.05
37	Don Sutton	.12	.09	.05
38	Alan Trammell	.20	.15	.08
39	John Tudor	.10	.08	.04
40	Gary Ward	.05	.04	.02
41	Lou Whitaker	.15	.11	.06
42	Willie Wilson	.10	.08	.04
43	Todd Worrell	.15	.11	.06
44	Floyd Youmans	.10	.08	.04

1987 Fleer Star Stickers

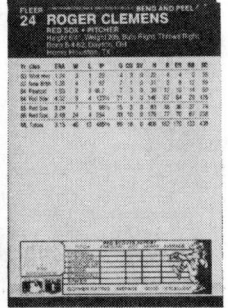

The 1987 Fleer Star Stickers set contains 132 cards which become stickers if the back is bent and peeled off. As in the previous year, the card backs are identical, save the numbering system, to the regular issue cards. The cards measure 2-1/2" by 3-1/2" and were sold in wax packs with team logo stickers. The fronts have a green border with a red and white banner wrapped across the upper left corner and the sides. The backs are printed in green and yellow.

		MT	NR MT	EX
	Complete Set:	23.00	17.00	9.25
	Common Player:	.05	.04	.02
1	Don Aase	.05	.04	.02
2	Harold Baines	.20	.15	.08
3	Floyd Bannister	.08	.06	.03
4	Jesse Barfield	.20	.15	.08
5	Marty Barrett	.10	.08	.04
6	Kevin Bass	.10	.08	.04
7	Don Baylor	.12	.09	.05
8	Steve Bedrosian	.15	.11	.06
9	George Bell	.35	.25	.14
10	Bert Blyleven	.15	.11	.06
11	Mike Boddicker	.08	.06	.03
12	Wade Boggs	1.75	1.25	.70
13	Phil Bradley	.15	.11	.06
14	Sid Bream	.08	.06	.03
15	George Brett	.70	.50	.30
16	Hubie Brooks	.10	.08	.04
17	Tom Brunansky	.15	.11	.06
18	Tom Candiotti	.05	.04	.02
19	Jose Canseco	2.00	1.50	.80
20	Gary Carter	.40	.30	.15
21	Joe Carter	.20	.15	.08
22	Will Clark	2.00	1.50	.80
23	Mark Clear	.05	.04	.02
24	Roger Clemens	.90	.70	.35
25	Vince Coleman	.25	.20	.10
26	Jose Cruz	.10	.08	.04
27	Ron Darling	.20	.15	.08
28	Alvin Davis	.20	.15	.08
29	Chili Davis	.10	.08	.04
30	Eric Davis	1.00	.70	.40
31	Glenn Davis	.20	.15	.08
32	Mike Davis	.05	.04	.02
33	Andre Dawson	.25	.20	.10
34	Doug DeCinces	.08	.06	.03
35	Brian Downing	.08	.06	.03
36	Shawon Dunston	.12	.09	.05
37	Mark Eichhorn	.12	.09	.05
38	Dwight Evans	.15	.11	.06
39	Tony Fernandez	.15	.11	.06
40	Bob Forsch	.05	.04	.02
41	John Franco	.10	.08	.04
42	Julio Franco	.12	.09	.05
43	Gary Gaetti	.20	.15	.08
44	Gene Garber	.05	.04	.02
45	Scott Garrelts	.05	.04	.02
46	Steve Garvey	.40	.30	.15
47	Kirk Gibson	.30	.25	.12
48	Dwight Gooden	.90	.70	.35
49	Ken Griffey	.10	.08	.04
50	Ozzie Guillen	.10	.08	.04
51	Bill Gullickson	.05	.04	.02
52	Tony Gwynn	.40	.30	.15
53	Mel Hall	.08	.06	.03
54	Greg Harris	.05	.04	.02
55	Von Hayes	.12	.09	.05
56	Rickey Henderson	.70	.50	.30
57	Tom Henke	.10	.08	.04
58	Keith Hernandez	.35	.25	.14
59	Willie Hernandez	.05	.04	.02
60	Ted Higuera	.20	.15	.08
61	Bob Horner	.12	.09	.05
62	Charlie Hough	.08	.06	.03
63	Jay Howell	.08	.06	.03
64	Kent Hrbek	.30	.25	.12
65	Bruce Hurst	.12	.09	.05
66	Pete Incaviglia	.60	.45	.25
67	Bob James	.05	.04	.02
68	Wally Joyner	.50	.40	.20
69	Mike Krukow	.05	.04	.02
70	Mark Langston	.15	.11	.06
71	Carney Lansford	.08	.06	.03
72	Fred Lynn	.25	.20	.10
73	Bill Madlock	.12	.09	.05
74	Don Mattingly	2.00	1.50	.80
75	Kirk McCaskill	.05	.04	.02
76	Lance McCullers	.12	.09	.05
77	Oddibe McDowell	.15	.11	.06
78	Paul Molitor	.20	.15	.08
79	Keith Moreland	.08	.06	.03
80	Jack Morris	.25	.20	.10
81	Jim Morrison	.05	.04	.02
82	Jerry Mumphrey	.05	.04	.02
83	Dale Murphy	.70	.50	.30
84	Eddie Murray	.50	.40	.20
85	Ben Oglivie	.05	.04	.02

		MT	NR MT	EX
86	Bob Ojeda	.10	.08	.04
87	Jesse Orosco	.08	.06	.03
88	Dave Parker	.25	.20	.10
89	Larry Parrish	.08	.06	.03
90	Tony Pena	.10	.08	.04
91	Jim Presley	.15	.11	.06
92	Kirby Puckett	.70	.50	.30
93	Dan Quisenberry	.12	.09	.05
94	Tim Raines	.35	.25	.14
95	Dennis Rasmussen	.10	.08	.04
96	Shane Rawley	.08	.06	.03
97	Johnny Ray	.10	.08	.04
98	Jeff Reardon	.10	.08	.04
99	Jim Rice	.35	.25	.14
100	Dave Righetti	.20	.15	.08
101	Cal Ripken, Jr.	.60	.45	.25
102	Pete Rose	1.00	.70	.40
103	Nolan Ryan	1.25	.90	.50
104	Juan Samuel	.15	.11	.06
105	Ryne Sandberg	.35	.25	.14
106	Steve Sax	.20	.15	.08
107	Mike Schmidt	1.25	.90	.50
108	Mike Scott	.15	.11	.06
109	Dave Smith	.05	.04	.02
110	Lee Smith	.10	.08	.04
111	Lonnie Smith	.05	.04	.02
112	Ozzie Smith	.20	.15	.08
113	Cory Snyder	.50	.40	.20
114	Darryl Strawberry	.70	.50	.30
115	Don Sutton	.25	.20	.10
116	Kent Tekulve	.08	.06	.03
117	Gorman Thomas	.08	.06	.03
118	Alan Trammell	.30	.25	.12
119	John Tudor	.12	.09	.05
120	Fernando Valenzuela	.12	.09	.05
121	Bob Welch	.12	.09	.05
122	Lou Whitaker	.25	.20	.10
123	Frank White	.10	.08	.04
124	Reggie Williams	.12	.09	.05
125	Willie Wilson	.15	.11	.06
126	Dave Winfield	.40	.30	.15
127	Mike Witt	.10	.08	.04
128	Todd Worrell	.25	.20	.10
129	Curt Young	.08	.06	.03
130	Robin Yount	.30	.25	.12
131	Jose Canseco, Don Mattingly/Checklist	2.50	2.00	1.00
132	Eric Davis, Bo Jackson/Checklist	1.25	.90	.50

1987 Fleer
Star Sticker Box Panels

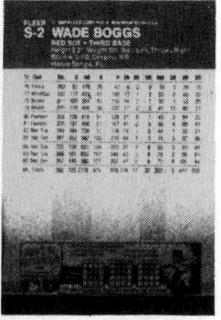

Fleer issued on the bottoms of their Fleer Star Stickers wax pack boxes six player cards plus two team logo/checklist cards. The cards, which measure 2-1/2" by 3-1/2", are numbered S-1 through S-8. The cards are identical in design to the Star Stickers.

		MT	NR MT	EX
Complete Panel Set:		6.50	5.00	2.50
Complete Singles Set:		3.25	2.50	1.25
Common Single Player:		.15	.11	.06
	Panel	5.75	4.25	2.25
2	Wade Boggs	1.00	.70	.40
3	Bert Blyleven	.20	.15	.08

		MT	NR MT	EX
6	Phillies Logo	.05	.04	.02
8	Don Mattingly	2.00	1.50	.80
	Panel	1.00	.70	.40
1	Tigers Logo	.05	.04	.02
4	Jose Cruz	.15	.11	.06
5	Glenn Davis	.20	.15	.08
7	Bob Horner	.15	.11	.06

1987 Fleer Update

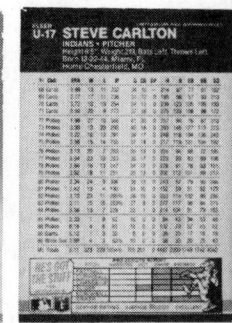

Fleer followed suit on a Topps idea in 1984 and began producing "Update" sets. The 1987 edition brings the regular Fleer set to date by including traded players and hot rookies. The cards measure 2-1/2" by 3-1/2" and are housed in a specially designed box with 25 team logo stickers. As a companion to the glossy-coated Fleer Collectors Edition set, Fleer produced a special edition Update set in its own tin box. Values of the glossy-coated cards are only a few dollars more than the regular Update cards.

		MT	NR MT	EX
Complete Set:		20.00	15.00	8.00
Common Player:		.06	.05	.02
1	Scott Bankhead	.08	.06	.03
2	Eric Bell(FC)	.15	.11	.06
3	Juan Beniquez	.06	.05	.02
4	Juan Berenguer	.06	.05	.02
5	Mike Birkbeck(FC)	.20	.15	.08
6	Randy Bockus(FC)	.15	.11	.06
7	Rod Booker(FC)	.15	.11	.06
8	Thad Bosley	.06	.05	.02
9	Greg Brock	.10	.08	.04
10	Bob Brower(FC)	.15	.11	.06
11	Chris Brown	.12	.09	.05
12	Jerry Browne	.15	.11	.06
13	Ralph Bryant	.10	.08	.04
14	DeWayne Buice(FC)	.20	.15	.08
15	Ellis Burks(FC)	3.50	2.75	1.50
16	Casey Candaele(FC)	.15	.11	.06
17	Steve Carlton	.30	.25	.12
18	Juan Castillo	.08	.06	.03
19	Chuck Crim(FC)	.15	.11	.06
20	Mark Davidson(FC)	.20	.15	.08
21	Mark Davis	.06	.05	.02
22	Storm Davis	.12	.09	.05
23	Bill Dawley	.06	.05	.02
24	Andre Dawson	.40	.30	.15
25	Brian Dayett	.06	.05	.02
26	Rick Dempsey	.08	.06	.03
27	Ken Dowell(FC)	.15	.11	.06
28	Dave Dravecky	.10	.08	.04
29	Mike Dunne(FC)	.35	.25	.14
30	Dennis Eckersley	.20	.15	.08
31	Cecil Fielder	2.50	2.00	1.00
32	Brian Fisher	.10	.08	.04
33	Willie Fraser	.10	.08	.04
34	Ken Gerhart(FC)	.15	.11	.06
35	Jim Gott	.06	.05	.02
36	Dan Gladden	.06	.05	.02
37	Mike Greenwell(FC)	3.00	2.25	1.25
38	Cecilio Guante	.06	.05	.02
39	Albert Hall	.06	.05	.02
40	Atlee Hammaker	.06	.05	.02
41	Mickey Hatcher	.06	.05	.02

		MT	NR MT	EX
42	Mike Heath	.06	.05	.02
43	Neal Heaton	.06	.05	.02
44	Mike Henneman(FC)	.30	.25	.12
45	Guy Hoffman	.06	.05	.02
46	Charles Hudson	.06	.05	.02
47	Chuck Jackson(FC)	.20	.15	.08
48	Mike Jackson(FC)	.20	.15	.08
49	Reggie Jackson	.50	.40	.20
50	Chris James	.35	.25	.14
51	Dion James	.12	.09	.05
52	Stan Javier	.06	.05	.02
53	Stan Jefferson(FC)	.20	.15	.08
54	Jimmy Jones	.10	.08	.04
55	Tracy Jones	.20	.15	.08
56	Terry Kennedy	.08	.06	.03
57	Mike Kingery	.08	.06	.03
58	Ray Knight	.10	.08	.04
59	Gene Larkin(FC)	.40	.30	.15
60	Mike LaValliere	.12	.09	.05
61	Jack Lazorko(FC)	.06	.05	.02
62	Terry Leach	.06	.05	.02
63	Rick Leach	.06	.05	.02
64	Craig Lefferts	.06	.05	.02
65	Jim Lindeman(FC)	.15	.11	.06
66	Bill Long(FC)	.20	.15	.08
67	Mike Loynd(FC)	.15	.11	.06
68	Greg Maddux(FC)	.90	.70	.35
69	Bill Madlock	.15	.11	.06
70	Dave Magadan	.80	.60	.30
71	Joe Magrane(FC)	1.00	.70	.40
72	Fred Manrique(FC)	.20	.15	.08
73	Mike Mason	.06	.05	.02
74	Lloyd McClendon(FC)	.15	.11	.06
75	Fred McGriff(FC)	2.50	2.00	1.00
76	Mark McGwire(FC)	3.00	2.25	1.25
77	Mark McLemore	.06	.05	.02
78	Kevin McReynolds	.30	.25	.12
79	Dave Meads(FC)	.15	.11	.06
80	Greg Minton	.06	.05	.02
81	John Mitchell(FC)	.15	.11	.06
82	Kevin Mitchell	2.00	1.50	.80
83	John Morris	.06	.05	.02
84	Jeff Musselman(FC)	.25	.20	.10
85	Randy Myers(FC)	.60	.45	.25
86	Gene Nelson	.06	.05	.02
87	Joe Niekro	.10	.08	.04
88	Tom Nieto	.06	.05	.02
89	Reid Nichols	.06	.05	.02
90	Matt Nokes(FC)	.40	.30	.15
91	Dickie Noles	.06	.05	.02
92	Edwin Nunez	.06	.05	.02
93	Jose Nunez(FC)	.25	.20	.10
94	Paul O'Neill	.10	.08	.04
95	Jim Paciorek(FC)	.06	.05	.02
96	Lance Parrish	.20	.15	.08
97	Bill Pecota(FC)	.20	.15	.08
98	Tony Pena	.12	.09	.05
99	Luis Polonia(FC)	.30	.25	.12
100	Randy Ready	.06	.05	.02
101	Jeff Reardon	.15	.11	.06
102	Gary Redus	.08	.06	.03
103	Rick Rhoden	.10	.08	.04
104	Wally Ritchie(FC)	.15	.11	.06
105	Jeff Robinson(FC)	.30	.25	.12
106	Mark Salas	.06	.05	.02
107	Dave Schmidt	.06	.05	.02
108	Kevin Seitzer	.80	.60	.30
109	John Shelby	.06	.05	.02
110	John Smiley(FC)	.40	.30	.15
111	Lary Sorenson	.06	.05	.02
112	Chris Speier	.06	.05	.02
113	Randy St. Claire	.06	.05	.02
114	Jim Sundberg	.08	.06	.03
115	B.J. Surhoff(FC)	.50	.40	.20
116	Greg Swindell	.50	.40	.20
117	Danny Tartabull	.35	.25	.14
118	Dorn Taylor(FC)	.12	.09	.05
119	Lee Tunnell	.06	.05	.02
120	Ed Vande Berg	.06	.05	.02
121	Andy Van Slyke	.20	.15	.08
122	Gary Ward	.06	.05	.02
123	Devon White	.30	.25	.12
124	Alan Wiggins	.06	.05	.02
125	Bill Wilkinson(FC)	.15	.11	.06
126	Jim Winn	.06	.05	.02
127	Frank Williams	.06	.05	.02
128	Ken Williams(FC)	.20	.15	.08
129	Matt Williams(FC)	7.00	5.25	2.75
130	Herm Winningham	.06	.05	.02
131	Matt Young	.06	.05	.02
132	Checklist 1-132	.06	.05	.02

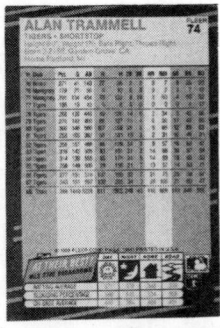

1988 Fleer

A clean, uncluttered look was the trademark of the 660-card 1988 Fleer set. The cards, which are the standard 2-1/2" by 3-1/2", feature blue and red diagonal lines set inside a white border. The player name and position are located on a slant in the upper left corner of the card. The player's team logo appears in the upper right corner. Below the player photo a blue and red band with the word "Fleer" appears. The backs of the cards include the card number, player personal information, and career statistics, plus a new feature called "At Their Best." This feature graphically shows a player's pitching or hitting statistics for home and road games and how he fared during day games as opposed to night contests. The set includes 19 special cards (#'s 622-640) and 12 "Major League Prospects" cards (#'s 641-653).

		MT	NR MT	EX
Complete Set:		50.00	37.00	20.00
Common Player:		.06	.05	.02
1	Keith Atherton	.06	.05	.02
2	Don Baylor	.10	.08	.04
3	Juan Berenguer	.06	.05	.02
4	Bert Blyleven	.12	.09	.05
5	Tom Brunansky	.10	.08	.04
6	Randy Bush	.06	.05	.02
7	Steve Carlton	.25	.20	.10
8	*Mark Davidson*(FC)	.12	.09	.05
9	George Frazier	.06	.05	.02
10	Gary Gaetti	.15	.11	.06
11	Greg Gagne	.06	.05	.02
12	Dan Gladden	.06	.05	.02
13	Kent Hrbek	.15	.11	.06
14	*Gene Larkin*	.20	.15	.08
15	Tim Laudner	.06	.05	.02
16	Steve Lombardozzi	.06	.05	.02
17	Al Newman	.06	.05	.02
18	Joe Niekro	.08	.06	.03
19	Kirby Puckett	.50	.40	.20
20	Jeff Reardon	.10	.08	.04
21a	Dan Schatzader (incorrect spelling)	.40	.30	.15
21b	Dan Schatzeder (correct spelling)	.06	.05	.02
22	Roy Smalley	.06	.05	.02
23	Mike Smithson	.06	.05	.02
24	*Les Straker*(FC)	.15	.11	.06
25	Frank Viola	.15	.11	.06
26	Jack Clark	.15	.11	.06
27	Vince Coleman	.20	.15	.08
28	Danny Cox	.08	.06	.03
29	Bill Dawley	.06	.05	.02
30	Ken Dayley	.06	.05	.02
31	Doug DeCinces	.08	.06	.03
32	Curt Ford	.06	.05	.02
33	Bob Forsch	.08	.06	.03
34	David Green	.06	.05	.02
35	Tom Herr	.08	.06	.03
36	Ricky Horton	.08	.06	.03
37	*Lance Johnson*(FC)	.40	.30	.15
38	Steve Lake	.06	.05	.02
39	Jim Lindeman	.10	.08	.04
40	*Joe Magrane*	.60	.45	.25

		MT	NR MT	EX
41	Greg Mathews	.08	.06	.03
42	Willie McGee	.12	.09	.05
43	John Morris	.06	.05	.02
44	Jose Oquendo	.06	.05	.02
45	Tony Pena	.08	.06	.03
46	Terry Pendleton	.08	.06	.03
47	Ozzie Smith	.15	.11	.06
48	John Tudor	.10	.08	.04
49	Lee Tunnell	.06	.05	.02
50	Todd Worrell	.10	.08	.04
51	Doyle Alexander	.08	.06	.03
52	Dave Bergman	.06	.05	.02
53	Tom Brookens	.06	.05	.02
54	Darrell Evans	.10	.08	.04
55	Kirk Gibson	.20	.15	.08
56	Mike Heath	.06	.05	.02
57	*Mike Henneman*	.25	.20	.10
58	Willie Hernandez	.08	.06	.03
59	Larry Herndon	.06	.05	.02
60	Eric King	.08	.06	.03
61	Chet Lemon	.08	.06	.03
62	*Scott Lusader*(FC)	.20	.15	.08
63	Bill Madlock	.10	.08	.04
64	Jack Morris	.20	.15	.08
65	Jim Morrison	.06	.05	.02
66	*Matt Nokes*	.50	.40	.20
67	Dan Petry	.08	.06	.03
68a	*Jeff Robinson* (Born 12-13-60 on back)			
		.80	.60	.30
68b	*Jeff Robinson* (Born 12/14/61 on back)			
		.30	.25	.12
69	Pat Sheridan	.06	.05	.02
70	Nate Snell	.06	.05	.02
71	Frank Tanana	.08	.06	.03
72	Walt Terrell	.08	.06	.03
73	Mark Thurmond	.06	.05	.02
74	Alan Trammell	.25	.20	.10
75	Lou Whitaker	.25	.20	.10
76	Mike Aldrete	.08	.06	.03
77	Bob Brenly	.06	.05	.02
78	Will Clark	4.00	3.00	1.50
79	Chili Davis	.08	.06	.03
80	Kelly Downs	.10	.08	.04
81	Dave Dravecky	.08	.06	.03
82	Scott Garrelts	.06	.05	.02
83	Atlee Hammaker	.06	.05	.02
84	Dave Henderson	.10	.08	.04
85	Mike Krukow	.08	.06	.03
86	Mike LaCoss	.06	.05	.02
87	Craig Lefferts	.06	.05	.02
88	Jeff Leonard	.08	.06	.03
89	Candy Maldonado	.08	.06	.03
90	Ed Milner	.06	.05	.02
91	Bob Melvin	.06	.05	.02
92	Kevin Mitchell	1.00	.70	.40
93	*Jon Perlman*(FC)	.12	.09	.05
94	Rick Reuschel	.10	.08	.04
95	Don Robinson	.08	.06	.03
96	Chris Speier	.06	.05	.02
97	Harry Spilman	.06	.05	.02
98	Robbie Thompson	.08	.06	.03
99	Jose Uribe	.06	.05	.02
100	*Mark Wasinger*(FC)	.15	.11	.06
101	*Matt Williams*	5.00	3.75	2.00
102	Jesse Barfield	.15	.11	.06
103	George Bell	.25	.20	.10
104	Juan Beniquez	.06	.05	.02
105	John Cerutti	.08	.06	.03
106	Jim Clancy	.08	.06	.03
107	*Rob Ducey*(FC)	.15	.11	.06
108	Mark Eichhorn	.08	.06	.03
109	Tony Fernandez	.12	.09	.05
110	Cecil Fielder	.70	.50	.30
111	Kelly Gruber	.50	.40	.20
112	Tom Henke	.08	.06	.03
113	Garth Iorg (Iorg)	.06	.05	.02
114	Jimmy Key	.10	.08	.04
115	Rick Leach	.06	.05	.02
116	Manny Lee	.08	.06	.03
117	*Nelson Liriano*(FC)	.25	.20	.10
118	*Fred McGriff*	2.00	1.50	.80
119	Lloyd Moseby	.08	.06	.03
120	Rance Mulliniks	.06	.05	.02
121	Jeff Musselman	.10	.08	.04
122	*Jose Nunez*	.25	.20	.10
123	Dave Stieb	.10	.08	.04
124	Willie Upshaw	.08	.06	.03
125	Duane Ward(FC)	.08	.06	.03
126	Ernie Whitt	.08	.06	.03
127	Rick Aguilera	.06	.05	.02
128	Wally Backman	.08	.06	.03

		MT	NR MT	EX
129	*Mark Carreon*(FC)	.12	.09	.05
130	Gary Carter	.25	.20	.10
131	David Cone(FC)	1.25	.90	.50
132	Ron Darling	.12	.09	.05
133	Len Dykstra	.10	.08	.04
134	Sid Fernandez	.10	.08	.04
135	Dwight Gooden	.60	.45	.25
136	Keith Hernandez	.20	.15	.08
137	*Gregg Jefferies*(FC)	8.00	6.00	3.25
138	Howard Johnson	.10	.08	.04
139	Terry Leach	.06	.05	.02
140	*Barry Lyons*(FC)	.15	.11	.06
141	Dave Magadan	.30	.25	.12
142	Roger McDowell	.10	.08	.04
143	Kevin McReynolds	.15	.11	.06
144	*Keith Miller*(FC)	.25	.20	.10
145	*John Mitchell*(FC)	.20	.15	.08
146	Randy Myers	.15	.11	.06
147	Bob Ojeda	.08	.06	.03
148	Jesse Orosco	.08	.06	.03
149	Rafael Santana	.06	.05	.02
150	Doug Sisk	.06	.05	.02
151	Darryl Strawberry	.35	.25	.14
152	Tim Teufel	.06	.05	.02
153	Gene Walter	.06	.05	.02
154	Mookie Wilson	.08	.06	.03
155	*Jay Aldrich*(FC)	.12	.09	.05
156	Chris Bosio	.08	.06	.03
157	Glenn Braggs	.10	.08	.04
158	Greg Brock	.08	.06	.03
159	Juan Castillo	.06	.05	.02
160	Mark Clear	.06	.05	.02
161	Cecil Cooper	.10	.08	.04
162	*Chuck Crim*	.12	.09	.05
163	Rob Deer	.08	.06	.03
164	Mike Felder	.06	.05	.02
165	Jim Gantner	.06	.05	.02
166	Ted Higuera	.10	.08	.04
167	Steve Kiefer	.06	.05	.02
168	Rick Manning	.06	.05	.02
169	Paul Molitor	.12	.09	.05
170	Juan Nieves	.08	.06	.03
171	Dan Plesac	.10	.08	.04
172	Earnest Riles	.06	.05	.02
173	Bill Schroeder	.06	.05	.02
174	*Steve Stanicek*(FC)	.15	.11	.06
175	B.J. Surhoff	.20	.15	.08
176	Dale Sveum	.08	.06	.03
177	Bill Wegman	.06	.05	.02
178	Robin Yount	.30	.25	.12
179	Hubie Brooks	.10	.08	.04
180	Tim Burke	.06	.05	.02
181	Casey Candaele	.06	.05	.02
182	Mike Fitzgerald	.06	.05	.02
183	Tom Foley	.06	.05	.02
184	Andres Galarraga	.15	.11	.06
185	Neal Heaton	.06	.05	.02
186	Wallace Johnson	.06	.05	.02
187	Vance Law	.08	.06	.03
188	Dennis Martinez	.08	.06	.03
189	Bob McClure	.06	.05	.02
190	Andy McGaffigan	.06	.05	.02
191	Reid Nichols	.06	.05	.02
192	Pascual Perez	.08	.06	.03
193	Tim Raines	.25	.20	.10
194	Jeff Reed	.06	.05	.02
195	Bob Sebra	.06	.05	.02
196	Bryn Smith	.06	.05	.02
197	Randy St. Claire	.06	.05	.02
198	Tim Wallach	.10	.08	.04
199	Mitch Webster	.08	.06	.03
200	Herm Winningham	.06	.05	.02
201	Floyd Youmans	.06	.05	.02
202	*Brad Arnsberg*(FC)	.20	.15	.08
203	Rick Cerone	.06	.05	.02
204	Pat Clements	.06	.05	.02
205	Henry Cotto	.06	.05	.02
206	Mike Easler	.08	.06	.03
207	Ron Guidry	.15	.11	.06
208	Bill Gullickson	.06	.05	.02
209	Rickey Henderson	.35	.25	.14
210	Charles Hudson	.06	.05	.02
211	Tommy John	.15	.11	.06
212	*Roberto Kelly*(FC)	1.50	1.25	.60
213	Ron Kittle	.08	.06	.03
214	Don Mattingly	1.50	1.25	.60
215	Bobby Meacham	.06	.05	.02
216	Mike Pagliarulo	.10	.08	.04
217	Dan Pasqua	.10	.08	.04
218	Willie Randolph	.08	.06	.03
219	Rick Rhoden	.08	.06	.03

		MT	NR MT	EX			MT	NR MT	EX
220	Dave Righetti	.15	.11	.06	311	Shane Rawley	.08	.06	.03
221	Jerry Royster	.06	.05	.02	312	*Wally Ritchie*	.15	.11	.06
222	Tim Stoddard	.06	.05	.02	313	Bruce Ruffin	.08	.06	.03
223	Wayne Tolleson	.06	.05	.02	314	Juan Samuel	.12	.09	.05
224	Gary Ward	.08	.06	.03	315	Mike Schmidt	.50	.40	.20
225	Claudell Washington	.08	.06	.03	316	Rick Schu	.06	.05	.02
226	Dave Winfield	.30	.25	.12	317	Jeff Stone	.06	.05	.02
227	Buddy Bell	.08	.06	.03	318	Kent Tekulve	.08	.06	.03
228	Tom Browning	.10	.08	.04	319	Milt Thompson	.06	.05	.02
229	Dave Concepcion	.08	.06	.03	320	Glenn Wilson	.08	.06	.03
230	Kal Daniels	.20	.15	.08	321	Rafael Belliard	.06	.05	.02
231	Eric Davis	.80	.60	.30	322	Barry Bonds	1.75	1.25	.70
232	Bo Diaz	.08	.06	.03	323	Bobby Bonilla	1.50	1.25	.60
233	Nick Esasky	.08	.06	.03	324	Sid Bream	.08	.06	.03
234	John Franco	.10	.08	.04	325	John Cangelosi	.06	.05	.02
235	Guy Hoffman	.06	.05	.02	326	Mike Diaz	.08	.06	.03
236	Tom Hume	.06	.05	.02	327	Doug Drabek	.08	.06	.03
237	Tracy Jones	.12	.09	.05	328	*Mike Dunne*	.25	.20	.10
238	Bill Landrum(FC)	.10	.08	.04	329	Brian Fisher	.08	.06	.03
239	Barry Larkin	1.00	.70	.40	330	*Brett Gideon*(FC)	.12	.09	.05
240	Terry McGriff(FC)	.06	.05	.02	331	Terry Harper	.06	.05	.02
241	Rob Murphy	.08	.06	.03	332	Bob Kipper	.06	.05	.02
242	Ron Oester	.06	.05	.02	333	Mike LaValliere	.08	.06	.03
243	Dave Parker	.20	.15	.08	334	*Jose Lind*(FC)	.30	.25	.12
244	Pat Perry	.06	.05	.02	335	Junior Ortiz	.06	.05	.02
245	Ted Power	.06	.05	.02	336	*Vicente Palacios*(FC)	.30	.25	.12
246	Dennis Rasmussen	.10	.08	.04	337	*Bob Patterson*(FC)	.12	.09	.05
247	Ron Robinson	.06	.05	.02	338	*Al Pedrique*(FC)	.15	.11	.06
248	Kurt Stillwell	.10	.08	.04	339	R.J. Reynolds	.06	.05	.02
249	*Jeff Treadway*(FC)	.40	.30	.15	340	*John Smiley*	.35	.25	.14
250	Frank Williams	.06	.05	.02	341	Andy Van Slyke	.12	.09	.05
251	Steve Balboni	.08	.06	.03	342	Bob Walk	.06	.05	.02
252	Bud Black	.06	.05	.02	343	Marty Barrett	.08	.06	.03
253	Thad Bosley	.06	.05	.02	344	*Todd Benzinger*(FC)	.40	.30	.15
254	George Brett	.40	.30	.15	345	Wade Boggs	1.00	.70	.40
255	*John Davis*(FC)	.20	.15	.08	346	*Tom Bolton*(FC)	.15	.11	.06
256	Steve Farr	.06	.05	.02	347	Oil Can Boyd	.08	.06	.03
257	Gene Garber	.06	.05	.02	348	*Ellis Burks*	3.00	2.25	1.25
258	Jerry Gleaton	.06	.05	.02	349	Roger Clemens	.60	.45	.25
259	Mark Gubicza	.12	.09	.05	350	Steve Crawford	.06	.05	.02
260	Bo Jackson	3.75	2.75	1.50	351	Dwight Evans	.12	.09	.05
261	Danny Jackson	.12	.09	.05	352	*Wes Gardner*(FC)	.25	.20	.10
262	Ross Jones(FC)	.12	.09	.05	353	Rich Gedman	.08	.06	.03
263	Charlie Leibrandt	.08	.06	.03	354	Mike Greenwell	2.00	1.50	.80
264	Bill Pecota	.15	.11	.06	355	*Sam Horn*(FC)	.30	.25	.12
265	*Melido Perez*(FC)	.30	.25	.12	356	Bruce Hurst	.10	.08	.04
266	Jamie Quirk	.06	.05	.02	357	*John Marzano*(FC)	.20	.15	.08
267	Dan Quisenberry	.08	.06	.03	358	Al Nipper	.06	.05	.02
268	Bret Saberhagen	.15	.11	.06	359	Spike Owen	.06	.05	.02
269	Angel Salazar	.06	.05	.02	360	*Jody Reed*(FC)	.80	.60	.30
270	Kevin Seitzer	.50	.40	.20	361	Jim Rice	.30	.25	.12
271	Danny Tartabull	.20	.15	.08	362	Ed Romero	.06	.05	.02
272	*Gary Thurman*(FC)	.20	.15	.08	363	Kevin Romine(FC)	.08	.06	.03
273	Frank White	.08	.06	.03	364	Joe Sambito	.06	.05	.02
274	Willie Wilson	.10	.08	.04	365	Calvin Schiraldi	.06	.05	.02
275	Tony Bernazard	.06	.05	.02	366	Jeff Sellers	.08	.06	.03
276	Jose Canseco	3.25	2.50	1.25	367	Bob Stanley	.06	.05	.02
277	Mike Davis	.08	.06	.03	368	Scott Bankhead	.06	.05	.02
278	Storm Davis	.10	.08	.04	369	Phil Bradley	.10	.08	.04
279	Dennis Eckersley	.12	.09	.05	370	Scott Bradley	.06	.05	.02
280	Alfredo Griffin	.08	.06	.03	371	Mickey Brantley	.06	.05	.02
281	Rick Honeycutt	.06	.05	.02	372	*Mike Campbell*(FC)	.25	.20	.10
282	Jay Howell	.08	.06	.03	373	Alvin Davis	.12	.09	.05
283	Reggie Jackson	.50	.40	.20	374	Lee Guetterman	.06	.05	.02
284	Dennis Lamp	.06	.05	.02	375	*Dave Hengel*(FC)	.20	.15	.08
285	Carney Lansford	.10	.08	.04	376	Mike Kingery	.06	.05	.02
286	Mark McGwire	2.75	2.00	1.00	377	Mark Langston	.12	.09	.05
287	Dwayne Murphy	.08	.06	.03	378	*Edgar Martinez*(FC)	1.25	.90	.50
288	Gene Nelson	.06	.05	.02	379	Mike Moore	.06	.05	.02
289	Steve Ontiveros	.06	.05	.02	380	Mike Morgan	.06	.05	.02
290	Tony Phillips	.06	.05	.02	381	John Moses	.06	.05	.02
291	Eric Plunk	.06	.05	.02	382	*Donnell Nixon*(FC)	.20	.15	.08
292	*Luis Polonia*	.25	.20	.10	383	Edwin Nunez	.06	.05	.02
293	*Rick Rodriguez*(FC)	.12	.09	.05	384	Ken Phelps	.08	.06	.03
294	Terry Steinbach	.10	.08	.04	385	Jim Presley	.10	.08	.04
295	Dave Stewart	.10	.08	.04	386	Rey Quinones	.06	.05	.02
296	Curt Young	.08	.06	.03	387	Jerry Reed	.06	.05	.02
297	Luis Aguayo	.06	.05	.02	388	Harold Reynolds	.08	.06	.03
298	Steve Bedrosian	.12	.09	.05	389	Dave Valle	.08	.06	.03
299	Jeff Calhoun	.06	.05	.02	390	*Bill Wilkinson*	.15	.11	.06
300	Don Carman	.08	.06	.03	391	Harold Baines	.12	.09	.05
301	*Todd Frohwirth*(FC)	.20	.15	.08	392	Floyd Bannister	.08	.06	.03
302	Greg Gross	.06	.05	.02	393	Daryl Boston	.06	.05	.02
303	Kevin Gross	.08	.06	.03	394	Ivan Calderon	.10	.08	.04
304	Von Hayes	.08	.06	.03	395	Jose DeLeon	.08	.06	.03
305	*Keith Hughes*(FC)	.20	.15	.08	396	Richard Dotson	.08	.06	.03
306	*Mike Jackson*	.20	.15	.08	397	Carlton Fisk	.20	.15	.08
307	Chris James	.20	.15	.08	398	Ozzie Guillen	.08	.06	.03
308	Steve Jeltz	.06	.05	.02	399	Ron Hassey	.06	.05	.02
309	Mike Maddux	.07	.05	.03	400	Donnie Hill	.06	.05	.02
310	Lance Parrish	.15	.11	.06	401	Bob James	.06	.05	.02

	MT	NR MT	EX			MT	NR MT	EX
402 Dave LaPoint	.08	.06	.03	487 *DeWayne Buice*	.15	.11	.06
403 *Bill Lindsey*(FC)	.12	.09	.05	488 Brian Downing	.08	.06	.03
404 *Bill Long*(FC)	.20	.15	.08	489 Chuck Finley	.06	.05	.02
405 Steve Lyons	.06	.05	.02	490 Willie Fraser	.06	.05	.02
406 *Fred Manrique*	.15	.11	.06	491 Jack Howell	.08	.06	.03
407 *Jack McDowell*(FC)	.25	.20	.10	492 Ruppert Jones	.06	.05	.02
408 Gary Redus	.06	.05	.02	493 Wally Joyner	.40	.30	.15
409 Ray Searage	.06	.05	.02	494 Jack Lazorko	.06	.05	.02
410 Bobby Thigpen	.10	.08	.04	495 Gary Lucas	.06	.05	.02
411 Greg Walker	.08	.06	.03	496 Kirk McCaskill	.08	.06	.03
412 *Kenny Williams*	.20	.15	.08	497 Mark McLemore	.06	.05	.02
413 Jim Winn	.06	.05	.02	498 Darrell Miller	.06	.05	.02
414 Jody Davis	.08	.06	.03	499 Greg Minton	.06	.05	.02
415 Andre Dawson	.20	.15	.08	500 Donnie Moore	.06	.05	.02
416 Brian Dayett	.06	.05	.02	501 Gus Polidor	.06	.05	.02
417 Bob Dernier	.06	.05	.02	502 Johnny Ray	.08	.06	.03
418 Frank DiPino	.06	.05	.02	503 Mark Ryal(FC)	.06	.05	.02
419 Shawon Dunston	.10	.08	.04	504 Dick Schofield	.06	.05	.02
420 Leon Durham	.08	.06	.03	505 Don Sutton	.20	.15	.08
421 *Les Lancaster*(FC)	.20	.15	.08	506 Devon White	.25	.20	.10
422 Ed Lynch	.06	.05	.02	507 Mike Witt	.08	.06	.03
423 Greg Maddux	.35	.25	.14	508 Dave Anderson	.06	.05	.02
424 Dave Martinez(FC)	.07	.05	.03	509 Tim Belcher(FC)	.60	.45	.25
425a Keith Moreland (bunting, photo actually				510 Ralph Bryant	.06	.05	.02
Jody Davis)	3.50	2.75	1.50	511 *Tim Crews*(FC)	.15	.11	.06
425b Keith Moreland (standing upright, correct				512 *Mike Devereaux*(FC)	.30	.25	.12
photo)	.08	.06	.03	513 Mariano Duncan	.06	.05	.02
426 Jamie Moyer	.08	.06	.03	514 Pedro Guerrero	.15	.11	.06
427 Jerry Mumphrey	.06	.05	.02	515 Jeff Hamilton(FC)	.12	.09	.05
428 *Paul Noce*(FC)	.10	.08	.04	516 Mickey Hatcher	.06	.05	.02
429 Rafael Palmeiro(FC)	1.50	1.25	.60	517 Brad Havens	.06	.05	.02
430 Wade Rowdon(FC)	.08	.06	.03	518 Orel Hershiser	.25	.20	.10
431 Ryne Sandberg	.50	.40	.20	519 *Shawn Hillegas*(FC)	.20	.15	.08
432 Scott Sanderson	.06	.05	.02	520 Ken Howell	.06	.05	.02
433 Lee Smith	.10	.08	.04	521 Tim Leary	.08	.06	.03
434 Jim Sundberg	.08	.06	.03	522 Mike Marshall	.12	.09	.05
435 Rick Sutcliffe	.10	.08	.04	523 Steve Sax	.15	.11	.06
436 Manny Trillo	.08	.06	.03	524 Mike Scioscia	.08	.06	.03
437 Juan Agosto	.06	.05	.02	525 Mike Sharperson(FC)	.06	.05	.02
438 Larry Andersen	.06	.05	.02	526 John Shelby	.06	.05	.02
439 Alan Ashby	.06	.05	.02	527 Franklin Stubbs	.08	.06	.03
440 Kevin Bass	.08	.06	.03	528 Fernando Valenzuela	.20	.15	.08
441 *Ken Caminiti*(FC)	.35	.25	.14	529 Bob Welch	.10	.08	.04
442 *Rocky Childress*(FC)	.12	.09	.05	530 Matt Young	.06	.05	.02
443 Jose Cruz	.08	.06	.03	531 Jim Acker	.06	.05	.02
444 Danny Darwin	.06	.05	.02	532 Paul Assenmacher	.06	.05	.02
445 Glenn Davis	.15	.11	.06	533 *Jeff Blauser*(FC)	.25	.20	.10
446 Jim Deshaies	.08	.06	.03	534 *Joe Boever*(FC)	.25	.20	.10
447 Bill Doran	.08	.06	.03	535 Martin Clary(FC)	.06	.05	.02
448 Ty Gainey	.06	.05	.02	536 *Kevin Coffman*(FC)	.12	.09	.05
449 Billy Hatcher	.08	.06	.03	537 Jeff Dedmon	.06	.05	.02
450 Jeff Heathcock	.06	.05	.02	538 *Ron Gant*(FC)	3.00	2.25	1.25
451 Bob Knepper	.08	.06	.03	539 *Tom Glavine*(FC)	.40	.30	.15
452 *Rob Mallicoat*(FC)	.12	.09	.05	540 Ken Griffey	.08	.06	.03
453 *Dave Meads*	.15	.11	.06	541 Al Hall	.06	.05	.02
454 Craig Reynolds	.06	.05	.02	542 Glenn Hubbard	.06	.05	.02
455 Nolan Ryan	.50	.40	.20	543 Dion James	.08	.06	.03
456 Mike Scott	.12	.09	.05	544 Dale Murphy	.40	.30	.15
457 Dave Smith	.08	.06	.03	545 Ken Oberkfell	.06	.05	.02
458 Denny Walling	.06	.05	.02	546 David Palmer	.06	.05	.02
459 *Robbie Wine*(FC)	.12	.09	.05	547 Gerald Perry	.10	.08	.04
460 *Gerald Young*(FC)	.25	.20	.10	548 Charlie Puleo	.06	.05	.02
461 Bob Brower	.08	.06	.03	549 Ted Simmons	.10	.08	.04
462a Jerry Browne (white player, photo				550 Zane Smith	.08	.06	.03
actually Bob Brower)	3.50	2.75	1.50	551 Andres Thomas	.08	.06	.03
462b Jerry Browne (black player, correct				552 Ozzie Virgil	.06	.05	.02
photo)	.08	.06	.03	553 Don Aase	.06	.05	.02
463 Steve Buechele	.06	.05	.02	554 *Jeff Ballard*(FC)	.35	.25	.14
464 Edwin Correa	.06	.05	.02	555 Eric Bell	.08	.06	.03
465 *Cecil Espy*(FC)	.30	.25	.12	556 Mike Boddicker	.08	.06	.03
466 Scott Fletcher	.08	.06	.03	557 Ken Dixon	.06	.05	.02
467 Jose Guzman	.08	.06	.03	558 Jim Dwyer	.06	.05	.02
468 Greg Harris	.06	.05	.02	559 Ken Gerhart	.08	.06	.03
469 Charlie Hough	.08	.06	.03	560 Rene Gonzales(FC)	.15	.11	.06
470 Pete Incaviglia	.15	.11	.06	561 Mike Griffin	.06	.05	.02
471 *Paul Kilgus*(FC)	.15	.11	.06	562 John Hayban (Habyan)	.06	.05	.02
472 Mike Loynd	.08	.06	.03	563 Terry Kennedy	.08	.06	.03
473 Oddibe McDowell	.08	.06	.03	564 Ray Knight	.08	.06	.03
474 Dale Mohorcic	.08	.06	.03	565 Lee Lacy	.06	.05	.02
475 Pete O'Brien	.08	.06	.03	566 Fred Lynn	.15	.11	.06
476 Larry Parrish	.08	.06	.03	567 Eddie Murray	.35	.25	.14
477 Geno Petralli	.06	.05	.02	568 Tom Niedenfuer	.08	.06	.03
478 Jeff Russell	.06	.05	.02	569 *Bill Ripken*(FC)	.25	.20	.10
479 Ruben Sierra	.70	.50	.30	570 Cal Ripken, Jr.	.35	.25	.14
480 Mike Stanley	.08	.06	.03	571 Dave Schmidt	.06	.05	.02
481 Curtis Wilkerson	.06	.05	.02	572 Larry Sheets	.08	.06	.03
482 Mitch Williams	.08	.06	.03	573 *Pete Stanicek*(FC)	.15	.11	.06
483 Bobby Witt	.10	.08	.04	574 *Mark Williamson*(FC)	.12	.09	.05
484 Tony Armas	.08	.06	.03	575 Mike Young	.06	.05	.02
485 Bob Boone	.08	.06	.03	576 Shawn Abner(FC)	.20	.15	.08
486 Bill Buckner	.10	.08	.04	577 Greg Booker	.06	.05	.02

		MT	NR MT	EX
578	Chris Brown	.08	.06	.03
579	*Keith Comstock*(FC)	.12	.09	.05
580	*Joey Cora*(FC)	.12	.09	.05
581	Mark Davis	.06	.05	.02
582	Tim Flannery	.06	.05	.02
583	Goose Gossage	.15	.11	.06
584	Mark Grant	.06	.05	.02
585	Tony Gwynn	.35	.25	.14
586	Andy Hawkins	.06	.05	.02
587	Stan Jefferson	.10	.08	.04
588	Jimmy Jones	.08	.06	.03
589	John Kruk	.10	.08	.04
590	*Shane Mack*(FC)	.20	.15	.08
591	Carmelo Martinez	.08	.06	.03
592	Lance McCullers	.08	.06	.03
593	*Eric Nolte*(FC)	.15	.11	.06
594	Randy Ready	.06	.05	.02
595	Luis Salazar	.06	.05	.02
596	Benito Santiago	.35	.25	.14
597	Eric Show	.08	.06	.03
598	Garry Templeton	.08	.06	.03
599	Ed Whitson	.06	.05	.02
600	Scott Bailes	.08	.06	.03
601	Chris Bando	.06	.05	.02
602	*Jay Bell*(FC)	.30	.25	.12
603	Brett Butler	.08	.06	.03
604	Tom Candiotti	.06	.05	.02
605	Joe Carter	.12	.09	.05
606	Carmen Castillo	.06	.05	.02
607	*Brian Dorsett*(FC)	.15	.11	.06
608	*John Farrell*(FC)	.35	.25	.14
609	Julio Franco	.10	.08	.04
610	Mel Hall	.08	.06	.03
611	*Tommy Hinzo*(FC)	.15	.11	.06
612	Brook Jacoby	.10	.08	.04
613	*Doug Jones*(FC)	.40	.30	.15
614	Ken Schrom	.06	.05	.02
615	Cory Snyder	.20	.15	.08
616	Sammy Stewart	.06	.05	.02
617	Greg Swindell	.25	.20	.10
618	Pat Tabler	.08	.06	.03
619	Ed Vande Berg	.06	.05	.02
620	*Eddie Williams*(FC)	.20	.15	.08
621	Rich Yett	.06	.05	.02
622	Slugging Sophomores (Wally Joyner, Cory Snyder)	.35	.25	.14
623	Dominican Dynamite (George Bell, Pedro Guerrero)	.12	.09	.05
624	Oakland's Power Team (Jose Canseco, Mark McGwire)	1.25	.90	.50
625	Classic Relief (Dan Plesac, Dave Righetti)	.08	.06	.03
626	All Star Righties (Jack Morris, Bret Saberhagen, Mike Witt)	.10	.08	.04
627	Game Closers (Steve Bedrosian, John Franco)	.08	.06	.03
628	Masters of the Double Play (Ryne Sandberg, Ozzie Smith)	.12	.09	.05
629	Rookie Record Setter (Mark McGwire)	1.00	.70	.40
630	Changing the Guard in Boston (Todd Benzinger, Ellis Burks, Mike Greenwell)	1.00	.70	.40
631	N.L. Batting Champs (Tony Gwynn, Tim Raines)	.15	.11	.06
632	Pitching Magic (Orel Hershiser, Mike Scott)	.12	.09	.05
633	Big Bats At First (Mark McGwire, Pat Tabler)	.60	.45	.25
634	Hitting King and the Thief (Vince Coleman, Tony Gwynn)	.12	.09	.05
635	A.L. Slugging Shortstops (Tony Fernandez, Cal Ripken, Jr., Alan Trammell)	.15	.11	.06
636	Tried and True Sluggers (Gary Carter, Mike Schmidt)	.20	.15	.08
637	Crunch Time (Eric Davis, Darryl Strawberry)	.70	.50	.30
638	A.L. All Stars (Matt Nokes, Kirby Puckett)	.20	.15	.08
639	N.L. All Stars (Keith Hernandez, Dale Murphy)	.20	.15	.08
640	The "O's" Brothers (Bill Ripken, Cal Ripken, Jr.)	.12	.09	.05
641	Major League Prospects (*Mark Grace, Darrin Jackson*)(FC)	7.00	5.25	2.75
642	Major League Prospects (*Damon Berryhill, Jeff Montgomery*)(FC)	.80	.60	.30
643	Major League Prospects (*Felix Fermin, Jessie Reid*)(FC)	.20	.15	.08
644	Major League Prospects (*Greg Myers, Greg Tabor*)(FC)	.20	.15	.08

		MT	NR MT	EX
645	Major League Prospects (*Jim Eppard, Joey Meyer*)(FC)	.20	.15	.08
646	Major League Prospects (*Adam Peterson, Randy Velarde*)(FC)	.30	.25	.12
647	Major League Prospects (*Chris Gwynn, Peter Smith*)(FC)	.40	.30	.15
648	Major League Prospects (*Greg Jelks, Tom Newell*)(FC)	.25	.20	.10
649	Major League Prospects (*Mario Diaz, Clay Parker*)(FC)	.25	.20	.10
650	Major League Prospects (*Jack Savage, Todd Simmons*)(FC)	.25	.20	.10
651	Major League Prospects (*John Burkett, Kirt Manwaring*)(FC)	.80	.60	.30
652	Major League Prospects (*Dave Otto, Walt Weiss*)(FC)	1.00	.70	.40
653	Major League Prospects (*Randell Byers (Randall), Jeff King*)(FC)	.60	.45	.25
654a	Checklist 1-101 (21 is Schatzeder)	.10	.08	.04
654b	Checklist 1-101 (21 is Schatzeder)	.06	.05	.02
655	Checklist 102-201	.06	.05	.02
656	Checklist 202-296	.06	.05	.02
657	Checklist 297-390	.06	.05	.02
658	Checklist 391-483	.06	.05	.02
659	Checklist 484-575	.06	.05	.02
660	Checklist 576-660	.06	.05	.02

1988 Fleer
All Star Team

 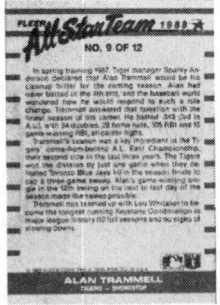

For the third consecutive year, Fleer randomly inserted All Star Team cards in their wax and cello packs. Twelve cards make up the set, each card measuring 2-1/2" by 3-1/2" in size. Players chosen for the set are Fleer's choices for a major league All-Star team.

		MT	NR MT	EX
	Complete Set:	16.00	12.00	6.50
	Common Player:	.60	.45	.25
1	Matt Nokes	.75	.60	.30
2	Tom Henke	.60	.45	.25
3	Ted Higuera	.60	.45	.25
4	Roger Clemens	2.25	1.75	.90
5	George Bell	1.00	.70	.40
6	Andre Dawson	1.00	.70	.40
7	Eric Davis	2.25	1.75	.90
8	Wade Boggs	3.25	2.50	1.25
9	Alan Trammell	1.00	.70	.40
10	Juan Samuel	.75	.60	.30
11	Jack Clark	.75	.60	.30
12	Paul Molitor	.75	.60	.30

1988 Fleer
Award Winners

This limited edition 44-card boxed set of 1987 award-winning player cards also includes six team logo sticker cards. Red, white, blue and yellow bands border the sharp, full-color player photos printed below a "Fleer Award Winners 1988" banner. The

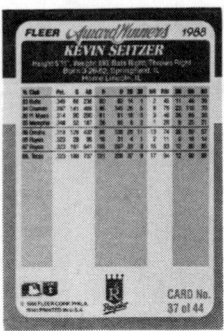

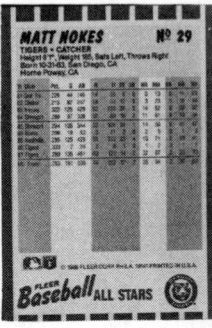

player's name and award are printed beneath the photo. Flip sides are red, white and blue and list personal information, career data, team logo and card number. This set was sold exclusively at 7-11 stores nationwide.

		MT	NR MT	EX
	Complete Set:	7.00	5.25	2.75
	Common Player:	.05	.04	.02
1	Steve Bedrosian	.10	.08	.04
2	George Bell	.20	.15	.08
3	Wade Boggs	1.25	.90	.50
4	Jose Canseco	1.25	.90	.50
5	Will Clark	.50	.40	.20
6	Roger Clemens	.40	.30	.15
7	Kal Daniels	.20	.15	.08
8	Eric Davis	.50	.40	.20
9	Andre Dawson	.15	.11	.06
10	Mike Dunne	.10	.08	.04
11	Dwight Evans	.10	.08	.04
12	Carlton Fisk	.15	.11	.06
13	Julio Franco	.07	.05	.03
14	Dwight Gooden	.40	.30	.15
15	Pedro Guerrero	.15	.11	.06
16	Tony Gwynn	.25	.20	.10
17	Orel Hershiser	.20	.15	.08
18	Tom Henke	.05	.04	.02
19	Ted Higuera	.10	.08	.04
20	Charlie Hough	.05	.04	.02
21	Wally Joyner	.30	.25	.12
22	Jimmy Key	.07	.05	.03
23	Don Mattingly	1.25	.90	.50
24	Mark McGwire	1.25	.90	.50
25	Paul Molitor	.12	.09	.05
26	Jack Morris	.12	.09	.05
27	Dale Murphy	.30	.25	.12
28	Terry Pendleton	.05	.04	.02
29	Kirby Puckett	.70	.50	.30
30	Tim Raines	.25	.20	.10
31	Jeff Reardon	.07	.05	.03
32	Harold Reynolds	.05	.04	.02
33	Dave Righetti	.12	.09	.05
34	Benito Santiago	.25	.20	.10
35	Mike Schmidt	.30	.25	.12
36	Mike Scott	.10	.08	.04
37	Kevin Seitzer	.60	.45	.25
38	Larry Sheets	.07	.05	.03
39	Ozzie Smith	.15	.11	.06
40	Darryl Strawberry	.40	.30	.15
41	Rick Sutcliffe	.10	.08	.04
42	Danny Tartabull	.12	.09	.05
43	Alan Trammell	.15	.11	.06
44	Tim Wallach	.10	.08	.04

1988 Fleer Baseball All Stars

This limited edition 44-card boxed set features excellent photography of major league All-Stars. The standard-size cards feature a sporty bright blue- and yellow-striped background. The player name is printed in white across the upper left front corner. "Fleer Baseball 88 All Stars" appears on a yellow band beneath the photo. Card backs feature a blue-

and white-striped design with a yellow highlighted section at the top that contains the player name, card number, team, position and personal data, followed by lifetime career stats. Fleer All Stars are cello-wrapped in blue and yellow striped boxes with checklist backs. The set includes six team logo sticker cards that feature black and white aerial shots of major league ballparks. The set was marketed exclusively by Ben Franklin stores.

		MT	NR MT	EX
	Complete Set:	6.00	4.50	2.50
	Common Player:	.05	.04	.02
1	George Bell	.20	.15	.08
2	Wade Boggs	1.00	.70	.40
3	Bobby Bonilla	.12	.09	.05
4	George Brett	.30	.25	.12
5	Jose Canseco	1.00	.70	.40
6	Jack Clark	.15	.11	.06
7	Will Clark	1.00	.70	.40
8	Roger Clemens	.40	.30	.15
9	Eric Davis	.50	.40	.20
10	Andre Dawson	.15	.11	.06
11	Julio Franco	.07	.05	.03
12	Dwight Gooden	.40	.30	.15
13	Tony Gwynn	.25	.20	.10
14	Orel Hershiser	.20	.15	.08
15	Teddy Higuera	.10	.08	.04
16	Charlie Hough	.05	.04	.02
17	Kent Hrbek	.15	.11	.06
18	Bruce Hurst	.10	.08	.04
19	Wally Joyner	.30	.25	.12
20	Mark Langston	.10	.08	.04
21	Dave LaPoint	.05	.04	.02
22	Candy Maldonado	.05	.04	.02
23	Don Mattingly	1.00	.70	.40
24	Roger McDowell	.07	.05	.03
25	Mark McGwire	1.00	.70	.40
26	Jack Morris	.12	.09	.05
27	Dale Murphy	.30	.25	.12
28	Eddie Murray	.20	.15	.08
29	Matt Nokes	.30	.25	.12
30	Kirby Puckett	.70	.50	.30
31	Tim Raines	.25	.20	.10
32	Willie Randolph	.07	.05	.03
33	Jeff Reardon	.07	.05	.03
34	Nolan Ryan	.50	.40	.20
35	Juan Samuel	.10	.08	.04
36	Mike Schmidt	.30	.25	.12
37	Mike Scott	.10	.08	.04
38	Kevin Seitzer	.60	.45	.25
39	Ozzie Smith	.15	.11	.06
40	Darryl Strawberry	.40	.30	.15
41	Rick Sutcliffe	.10	.08	.04
42	Alan Trammell	.15	.11	.06
43	Tim Wallach	.10	.08	.04
44	Dave Winfield	.20	.15	.08

A player's name in *italic* type indicates a rookie card. An (FC) indicates a player's first card for that particular card company.

1988 Fleer
Baseball MVP

 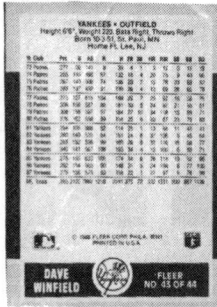

1988 Fleer
Baseball's Best

This boxed set of 44 standard-size cards and six team logo stickers was produced by Fleer for exclusive distribution at Toys "R" Us stores. This premiere edition features full-color player photos framed by a yellow and blue border. The player's name is printed in red below and to the left of the photo; team and position are printed in black in the lower right corner. The "Fleer Baseball MVP" logo appears bottom center. Card backs are yellow and blue on a white background. The player's team, position and personal data are followed by stats, logo and a blue banner bearing the player's name, team logo and card number. The six sticker cards feature black and white stadium photos on the backs.

		MT	NR MT	EX
Complete Set:		7.00	5.25	2.75
Common Player:		.05	.04	.02
1	George Bell	.20	.15	.08
2	Wade Boggs	1.00	.70	.40
3	Jose Canseco	1.00	.70	.40
4	Ivan Calderon	.07	.05	.03
5	Will Clark	1.00	.70	.40
6	Roger Clemens	.40	.30	.15
7	Vince Coleman	.15	.11	.06
8	Eric Davis	.50	.40	.20
9	Andre Dawson	.15	.11	.06
10	Dave Dravecky	.05	.04	.02
11	Mike Dunne	.10	.08	.04
12	Dwight Evans	.10	.08	.04
13	Sid Fernandez	.07	.05	.03
14	Tony Fernandez	.10	.08	.04
15	Julio Franco	.07	.05	.03
16	Dwight Gooden	.40	.30	.15
17	Tony Gwynn	.25	.20	.10
18	Ted Higuera	.10	.08	.04
19	Charlie Hough	.05	.04	.02
20	Wally Joyner	.30	.25	.12
21	Mark Langston	.10	.08	.04
22	Don Mattingly	1.25	.90	.50
23	Mark McGwire	1.00	.70	.40
24	Jack Morris	.12	.09	.05
25	Dale Murphy	.30	.25	.12
26	Kirby Puckett	.50	.40	.20
27	Tim Raines	.25	.20	.10
28	Willie Randolph	.07	.05	.03
29	Ryne Sandberg	.20	.15	.08
30	Benito Santiago	.25	.20	.10
31	Mike Schmidt	.30	.25	.12
32	Mike Scott	.10	.08	.04
33	Kevin Seitzer	.60	.45	.25
34	Larry Sheets	.07	.05	.03
35	Ozzie Smith	.15	.11	.06
36	Dave Stewart	.10	.08	.04
37	Darryl Strawberry	.40	.30	.15
38	Rick Sutcliffe	.10	.08	.04
39	Alan Trammell	.15	.11	.06
40	Fernando Valenzuela	.20	.15	.08
41	Frank Viola	.12	.09	.05
42	Tim Wallach	.10	.08	.04
43	Dave Winfield	.20	.15	.08
44	Robin Yount	.25	.20	.10

This boxed set of 44 standard-size cards (2-1/2" by 3-1/2") and six team logo stickers is the third annual issue from Fleer highlighting the best major league sluggers and pitchers. Five additional player cards were printed on retail display box bottoms, along with a checklist logo card (numbered C-1 through C-6). Full-color player photos are framed by a green border that fades to yellow. A red (slugger) or blue (pitcher) player name is printed beneath the photo. The card backs are printed in green on a white background with yellow highlights. Card number, player name and personal info appear in a green vertical box on the left-hand side of the card back with a yellow cartoon-style team logo overprinted across a stats chart on the right. This set was produced by Fleer for exclusive distribution by McCrory's stores (McCrory, McClellan, J.J. Newberry, H.L. Green, TG&Y).

		MT	NR MT	EX
Complete Set:		5.00	3.75	2.00
Common Player:		.05	.04	.02
1	George Bell	.20	.15	.08
2	Wade Boggs	1.00	.70	.40
3	Bobby Bonilla	.12	.09	.05
4	Tom Brunansky	.10	.08	.04
5	Ellis Burks	1.00	.70	.40
6	Jose Canseco	1.00	.70	.40
7	Joe Carter	.12	.09	.05
8	Will Clark	1.00	.70	.40
9	Roger Clemens	.40	.30	.15
10	Eric Davis	.50	.40	.20
11	Glenn Davis	.12	.09	.05
12	Andre Dawson	.15	.11	.06
13	Dennis Eckersley	.07	.05	.03
14	Andres Galarraga	.15	.11	.06
15	Dwight Gooden	.40	.30	.15
16	Pedro Guerrero	.15	.11	.06
17	Tony Gwynn	.25	.20	.10
18	Orel Hershiser	.20	.15	.08
19	Ted Higuera	.10	.08	.04
20	Pete Incaviglia	.12	.09	.05
21	Danny Jackson	.10	.08	.04
22	Doug Jennings	.07	.05	.03
23	Mark Langston	.10	.08	.04
24	Dave LaPoint	.05	.04	.02
25	Mike LaValliere	.07	.05	.03
26	Don Mattingly	1.00	.70	.40
27	Mark McGwire	1.00	.70	.40
28	Dale Murphy	.30	.25	.12
29	Ken Phelps	.05	.04	.02
30	Kirby Puckett	.50	.40	.20
31	Johnny Ray	.05	.04	.02
32	Jeff Reardon	.07	.05	.03
33	Dave Righetti	.12	.09	.05
34	Cal Ripkin, Jr. (Ripken)	.30	.25	.12
35	Chris Sabo	.90	.70	.35
36	Mike Schmidt	.30	.25	.12
37	Mike Scott	.10	.08	.04
38	Kevin Seitzer	.60	.45	.25
39	Dave Stewart	.10	.08	.04
40	Darryl Strawberry	.40	.30	.15
41	Greg Swindell	.10	.08	.04
42	Frank Tanana	.05	.04	.02

		MT	NR MT	EX
43	Dave Winfield	.20	.15	.08
44	Todd Worrell	.10	.08	.04

1988 Fleer
Baseball's Best Box Panel

Six cards were placed on the bottoms of retail boxes of the Fleer 44-card Baseball's Best boxed sets in 1988. The cards, which measure 2-1/2" by 3-1/2", are identical in design to cards found in the 44-card set. The cards are numbered C-1 through C-6 and were produced by Fleer for distribution by McCrory stores and its affiliates.

		MT	NR MT	EX
	Complete Panel Set:	1.50	1.25	.60
	Complete Singles Set:	.90	.70	.35
	Common Single Player:	.15	.11	.06
	Panel	1.50	1.25	.60
1	Ron Darling	.20	.15	.08
2	Rickey Henderson	.40	.30	.15
3	Carney Lansford	.15	.11	.06
4	Rafael Palmeiro	.20	.15	.08
5	Frank Viola	.20	.15	.08
6	Twins Logo	.05	.04	.02

1988 Fleer Baseball's
Exciting Stars

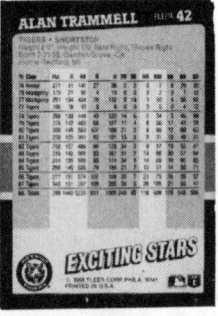

This 44-card limited-edition boxed set showcases star major leaguers. Player photos are slanted upwards to the right, framed by a blue border with a red and white bar stripe across the middle. The player's name is printed in white above the photo. "Baseball's Exciting Stars" is printed in red and yellow across the bottom margin, following the upward slant of the photo. Fleer's logo appears lower right intersecting a white baseball bearing the number "88." Card backs are numbered and printed in red, white and blue. The set was packaged in a checklist box, with six team logo sticker cards featuring black

and white stadium photos on the flip sides. Exciting Stars was distributed via Cumberland Farm stores throughout the northeastern U.S. and Florida.

		MT	NR MT	EX
	Complete Set:	6.00	4.50	2.50
	Common Player:	.05	.04	.02
1	Harold Baines	.10	.08	.04
2	Kevin Bass	.07	.05	.03
3	George Bell	.20	.15	.08
4	Wade Boggs	1.00	.70	.40
5	Mickey Brantley	.05	.04	.02
6	Sid Bream	.05	.04	.02
7	Jose Canseco	1.00	.70	.40
8	Jack Clark	.15	.11	.06
9	Will Clark	1.00	.70	.40
10	Roger Clemens	.40	.30	.15
11	Vince Coleman	.15	.11	.06
12	Eric Davis	.50	.40	.20
13	Andre Dawson	.15	.11	.06
14	Julio Franco	.07	.05	.03
15	Dwight Gooden	.40	.30	.15
16	Mike Greenwell	.70	.50	.30
17	Tony Gwynn	.25	.20	.10
18	Von Hayes	.07	.05	.03
19	Tom Henke	.05	.04	.02
20	Orel Hershiser	.20	.15	.08
21	Teddy Higuera	.10	.08	.04
22	Brook Jacoby	.07	.05	.03
23	Wally Joyner	.30	.25	.12
24	Jimmy Key	.07	.05	.03
25	Don Mattingly	1.00	.70	.40
26	Mark McGwire	1.00	.70	.40
27	Jack Morris	.12	.09	.05
28	Dale Murphy	.30	.25	.12
29	Matt Nokes	.30	.25	.12
30	Kirby Puckett	.50	.40	.20
31	Tim Raines	.25	.20	.10
32	Ryne Sandberg	.20	.15	.08
33	Benito Santiago	.25	.20	.10
34	Mike Schmidt	.30	.25	.12
35	Mike Scott	.10	.08	.04
36	Kevin Seitzer	.60	.45	.25
37	Larry Sheets	.07	.05	.03
38	Ruben Sierra	.12	.09	.05
39	Darryl Strawberry	.40	.30	.15
40	Ozzie Smith	.15	.11	.06
41	Danny Tartabull	.10	.08	.04
42	Alan Trammell	.15	.11	.06
43	Fernando Valenzuela	.20	.15	.08
44	Devon White	.20	.15	.08

1988 Fleer Baseball's
Hottest Stars

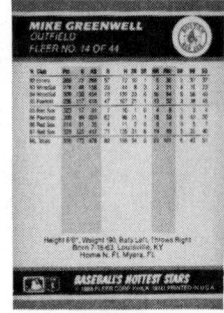

This boxed set of 44 standard-size player cards and six team logo sticker cards was produced by Fleer for exclusive distribution at Revco drug stores nationwide. Card fronts feature full-color photos of players representing every major league team. Photos are framed in red, orange and yellow, with a blue and white player name printed across the bottom of the card front. A flaming baseball logo bearing the words "Hottest Stars" appears in the lower left corner of the player photo. Card backs are red, white and blue. The player's name, position, card number and team logo are printed across the top section, followed by a stats box, personal data, batting and throwing preferences. The set also includes six team logo sticker cards with flipside stadium photos in black and white.

		MT	NR MT	EX
Complete Set:		6.00	4.50	2.50
Common Player:		.05	.04	.02
1	George Bell	.20	.15	.08
2	Wade Boggs	1.00	.70	.40
3	Bobby Bonilla	.12	.09	.05
4	George Brett	.30	.25	.12
5	Jose Canseco	1.00	.70	.40
6	Will Clark	1.00	.70	.40
7	Roger Clemens	.40	.30	.15
8	Eric Davis	.50	.40	.20
9	Andre Dawson	.15	.11	.06
10	Tony Fernandez	.10	.08	.04
11	Julio Franco	.07	.05	.03
12	Gary Gaetti	.10	.08	.04
13	Dwight Gooden	.40	.30	.15
14	Mike Greenwell	.70	.50	.30
15	Tony Gwynn	.25	.20	.10
16	Rickey Henderson	.50	.40	.20
17	Keith Hernandez	.15	.11	.06
18	Tom Herr	.07	.05	.03
19	Orel Hershiser	.20	.15	.08
20	Ted Higuera	.10	.08	.04
21	Wally Joyner	.30	.25	.12
22	Jimmy Key	.07	.05	.03
23	Mark Langston	.10	.08	.04
24	Don Mattingly	1.25	.90	.50
25	Jack McDowell	.20	.15	.08
26	Mark McGwire	1.00	.70	.40
27	Kevin Mitchell	.50	.40	.20
28	Jack Morris	.12	.09	.05
29	Dale Murphy	.30	.25	.12
30	Kirby Puckett	.50	.40	.20
31	Tim Raines	.25	.20	.10
32	Shane Rawley	.05	.04	.02
33	Benito Santiago	.25	.20	.10
34	Mike Schmidt	.30	.25	.12
35	Mike Scott	.10	.08	.04
36	Kevin Seitzer	.60	.45	.25
37	Larry Sheets	.07	.05	.03
38	Ruben Sierra	.50	.40	.20
39	Dave Smith	.05	.04	.02
41	Darryl Strawberry	.40	.30	.15
42	Rick Sutcliffe	.10	.08	.04
43	Pat Tabler	.05	.04	.02
44	Alan Trammell	.15	.11	.06

1988 Fleer Box Panels

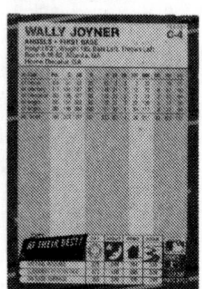

Fleer's third annual box-bottom issue once again included 16 full-color trading cards printed on the bottoms of four different wax and cello pack retail display boxes. Each box contains three player cards and one team logo card. Player cards follow the same design as the basic 1988 Fleer issue - full-color player photo, name upper left, team logo upper right, Fleer logo lower right. Card fronts feature a blue and red striped border, with a thin white line framing the photo. Card backs are printed in blue and red and include personal information and statistics. Standard-size, the cards are numbered C-1 through C-16.

		MT	NR MT	EX
Complete Panel Set:		6.25	4.75	2.50
Complete Singles Set:		2.50	2.00	1.00
Common Panel:		1.25	.90	.50
Common Single Player:		.15	.11	.06
	Panel	2.00	1.50	.80
1	Cardinals Logo	.05	.04	.02
11	Mike Schmidt	.60	.45	.25
14	Dave Stewart	.15	.11	.06
15	Tim Wallach	.20	.15	.08
	Panel	1.25	.90	.50
2	Dwight Evans	.15	.11	.06
8	Shane Rawley	.15	.11	.06
10	Ryne Sandberg	.30	.25	.12
13	Tigers Logo	.05	.04	.02
	Panel	2.75	2.00	1.00
3	Andres Galarraga	.25	.20	.10
6	Dale Murphy	.60	.45	.25
9	Giants Logo	.05	.04	.02
12	Kevin Seitzer	.80	.60	.30
	Panel	2.25	1.75	.90
4	Wally Joyner	.60	.45	.25
5	Twins Logo	.05	.04	.02
7	Kirby Puckett	.40	.30	.15
16	Todd Worrell	.20	.15	.08

1988 Fleer '87 World Series

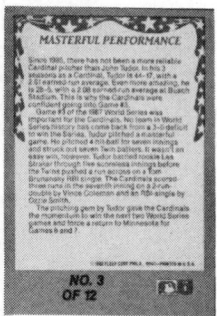

Highlights of the 1987 Series are captured in this full-color insert set found only in Fleer's regular 660-card factory sealed sets. This second World Series edition by Fleer features cards framed in red, with a blue and white starred bunting draped over the upper edges of the photo and a brief photo caption printed on a yellow band across the lower border. Numbered card backs are red, white and blue and include a description of the action pictured on the front, with stats for the Series.

		MT	NR MT	EX
Complete Set:		4.00	3.00	1.50
Common Player:		.30	.25	.12
1	"Grand" Hero In Game 1 (Dan Gladden)	.30	.25	.12
2	The Cardinals "Bush" Whacked (Randy Bush, Tony Pena)	.30	.25	.12
3	Masterful Performance Turns Momentum (John Tudor)	.30	.25	.12
4	The Wizard (Ozzie Smith)	.35	.25	.14
5	Throw Smoke! (Tony Pena, Todd Worrell)	.35	.25	.14
6	Cardinal Attack - Disruptive Speed (Vince Coleman)	.40	.30	.15
7	Herr's Wallop (Dan Driessen, Tom Herr)	.30	.25	.12
8	Kirby's Bat Comes Alive in Game 6 (Kirby Puckett)	1.00	.70	.40
9	Hrbek's Slam Forces Game 7 (Kent Hrbek)	.30	.25	.12
10	Herr, Out At First? (Rich Hacker (coach), Tom Herr, Lee Weyer (umpire))	.30	.25	.12
11	Game 7's Play At The Plate (Don Baylor, Dave Phillips (umpire))	.30	.25	.12

		MT	NR MT	EX
12	Series MVP with 16 K's (Frank Viola)	.35	.25	.14

1988 Fleer
Headliners

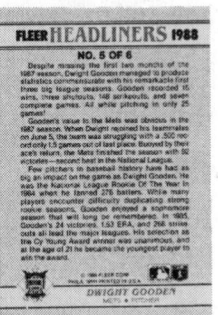

This six-card special set was inserted in Fleer three-packs, sold by retail outlets and hobby dealers nationwide. The card fronts feature crisp full-color player cut-outs printed on a grey and white USA Today-style sports page. "Fleer Headliners 1988" is printed in black and red on a white banner across the top of the card, both front and back. A similar white banner across the card bottom bears the black and white National or American League logo and a red player/team name. Card backs are black on grey with red accents and include the card number and a three-paragraph career summary.

		MT	NR MT	EX
Complete Set:		10.00	7.50	4.00
Common Player:		1.00	.70	.40
1	Don Mattingly	3.00	2.25	1.25
2	Mark McGwire	2.00	1.50	.80
3	Jack Morris	1.00	.70	.40
4	Darryl Strawberry	1.50	1.25	.60
5	Dwight Gooden	1.50	1.25	.60
6	Tim Raines	1.25	.90	.50

1988 Fleer
League Leaders

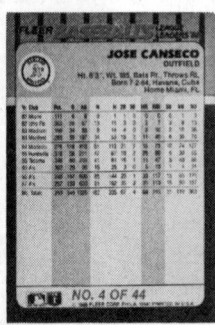

This 44-card boxed set is the third annual limited edition set from Fleer highlighting leading players. The 1988 edition contains the same type of information, front and back, as the previous sets, with a new color scheme and design. Card fronts have bright blue borders, solid on the lower portion, striped on the upper, with a gold bar separating the two sections. "Fleer's Baseball's League Leaders '88" headlines the card face. The full-color player photo is

centered above a yellow player name banner. The numbered card backs are blue, pink and white, and contain player stats and personal notes. Six team logo sticker cards, with flipside black and white photos of ballparks, accompany this set which was marketed exclusively by Walgreen drug stores.

		MT	NR MT	EX
Complete Set:		6.00	4.50	2.50
Common Player:		.05	.04	.02
1	George Bell	.20	.15	.08
2	Wade Boggs	1.00	.70	.40
3	Ivan Calderon	.07	.05	.03
4	Jose Canseco	1.00	.70	.40
5	Will Clark	1.00	.70	.40
6	Roger Clemens	.40	.30	.15
7	Vince Coleman	.15	.11	.06
8	Eric Davis	.50	.40	.20
9	Andre Dawson	.15	.11	.06
10	Bill Doran	.07	.05	.03
11	Dwight Evans	.10	.08	.04
12	Julio Franco	.07	.05	.03
13	Gary Gaetti	.10	.08	.04
14	Andres Galarraga	.15	.11	.06
15	Dwight Gooden	.40	.30	.15
16	Tony Gwynn	.25	.20	.10
17	Tom Henke	.05	.04	.02
18	Keith Hernandez	.20	.15	.08
19	Orel Hershiser	.20	.15	.08
20	Ted Higuera	.10	.08	.04
21	Kent Hrbek	.15	.11	.06
22	Wally Joyner	.30	.25	.12
23	Jimmy Key	.07	.05	.03
24	Mark Langston	.10	.08	.04
25	Don Mattingly	1.00	.70	.40
26	Mark McGwire	1.00	.70	.40
27	Paul Molitor	.12	.09	.05
28	Jack Morris	.12	.09	.05
29	Dale Murphy	.30	.25	.12
30	Kirby Puckett	.50	.40	.20
31	Tim Raines	.25	.20	.10
32	Rick Rueschel	.07	.05	.03
33	Bret Saberhagen	.15	.11	.06
34	Benito Santiago	.25	.20	.10
35	Mike Schmidt	.30	.25	.12
36	Mike Scott	.10	.08	.04
37	Kevin Seitzer	.60	.45	.25
38	Larry Sheets	.07	.05	.03
39	Ruben Sierra	.50	.40	.20
40	Darryl Strawberry	.40	.30	.15
41	Rick Sutcliffe	.10	.08	.04
42	Alan Trammell	.15	.11	.06
43	Andy Van Slyke	.10	.08	.04
44	Todd Worrell	.10	.08	.04

1988 Fleer Mini

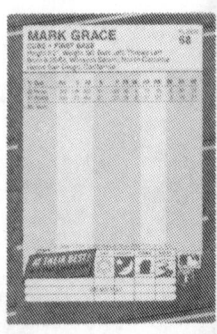

This third annual issue of miniatures (1-7/8" by 2-5/8") includes 120 high-gloss cards featuring new photos, not copies from the regular issue, although the card designs are identical. Card fronts have white borders, with red and blue striping and a bright color band beneath the photo leading to a blue Fleet logo lower right. The player name is printed upper left; the full-color team logo appears upper right. Card backs are red, white and blue and include personal data, yearly career stats and a stats breakdown of batting average, slugging percentage and on-base average, listed for day, night, home and road games. Card backs are numbered in alphabetical order by teams which are also listed alphabetically. The set includes 18 team logo stickers with black and white aerial stadium photos on the flip sides.

		MT	NR MT	EX
	Complete Set:	10.00	7.50	4.00
	Common Player:	.05	.04	.02
1	Eddie Murray	.25	.20	.10
2	Dave Schmidt	.05	.04	.02
3	Larry Sheets	.07	.05	.03
4	Wade Boggs	1.00	.70	.40
5	Roger Clemens	.60	.45	.25
6	Dwight Evans	.12	.09	.05
7	Mike Greenwell	1.00	.70	.40
8	Sam Horn	.20	.15	.08
9	Lee Smith	.07	.05	.03
10	Brian Downing	.05	.04	.02
11	Wally Joyner	.30	.25	.12
12	Devon White	.10	.08	.04
13	Mike Witt	.07	.05	.03
14	Ivan Calderon	.07	.05	.03
15	Ozzie Guillen	.07	.05	.03
16	Jack McDowell	.20	.15	.08
17	Kenny Williams	.12	.09	.05
18	Joe Carter	.20	.15	.08
19	Julio Franco	.10	.08	.04
20	Pat Tabler	.05	.04	.02
21	Doyle Alexander	.05	.04	.02
22	Jack Morris	.15	.11	.06
23	Matt Nokes	.30	.25	.12
24	Walt Terrell	.05	.04	.02
25	Alan Trammell	.20	.15	.08
26	Bret Saberhagen	.15	.11	.06
27	Kevin Seitzer	.60	.45	.25
28	Danny Tartabull	.15	.11	.06
29	Gary Thurman	.20	.15	.08
30	Ted Higuera	.10	.08	.04
31	Paul Molitor	.12	.09	.05
32	Dan Plesac	.10	.08	.04
33	Robin Yount	.25	.20	.10
34	Gary Gaetti	.12	.09	.05
35	Kent Hrbek	.15	.11	.06
36	Kirby Puckett	.50	.40	.20
37	Jeff Reardon	.07	.05	.03
38	Frank Viola	.12	.09	.05
39	Jack Clark	.12	.09	.05
40	Rickey Henderson	.50	.40	.20
41	Don Mattingly	1.75	1.25	.70
42	Willie Randolph	.05	.04	.02
43	Dave Righetti	.12	.09	.05
44	Dave Winfield	.20	.15	.08
45	Jose Canseco	1.50	1.25	.60
46	Mark McGwire	1.00	.70	.40
47	Dave Parker	.12	.09	.05
48	Dave Stewart	.07	.05	.03
49	Walt Weiss	.60	.45	.25
50	Bob Welch	.07	.05	.03
51	Mickey Brantley	.05	.04	.02
52	Mark Langston	.10	.08	.04
53	Harold Reynolds	.07	.05	.03
54	Scott Fletcher	.05	.04	.02
55	Charlie Hough	.05	.04	.02
56	Pete Incaviglia	.12	.09	.05
57	Larry Parrish	.05	.04	.02
58	Ruben Sierra	.35	.25	.14
59	George Bell	.20	.15	.08
60	Mark Eichhorn	.05	.04	.02
61	Tony Fernandez	.10	.08	.04
62	Tom Henke	.05	.04	.02
63	Jimmy Key	.07	.05	.03
64	Dion James	.05	.04	.02
65	Dale Murphy	.30	.25	.12
66	Zane Smith	.05	.04	.02
67	Andre Dawson	.15	.11	.06
68	Mark Grace	1.75	1.25	.70
69	Jerry Mumphrey	.05	.04	.02
70	Ryne Sandberg	.20	.15	.08
71	Rick Sutcliffe	.10	.08	.04
72	Kal Daniels	.12	.09	.05
73	Eric Davis	.70	.50	.30
74	John Franco	.07	.05	.03
75	Ron Robinson	.05	.04	.02
76	Jeff Treadway	.20	.15	.08
77	Kevin Bass	.07	.05	.03
78	Glenn Davis	.15	.11	.06
79	Nolan Ryan	.50	.40	.20
80	Mike Scott	.12	.09	.05
81	Dave Smith	.05	.04	.02

		MT	NR MT	EX
82	Kirk Gibson	.20	.15	.08
83	Pedro Guerrero	.12	.09	.05
84	Orel Hershiser	.20	.15	.08
85	Steve Sax	.15	.11	.06
86	Fernando Valenzuela	.15	.11	.06
87	Tim Burke	.05	.04	.02
88	Andres Galarraga	.15	.11	.06
89	Neal Heaton	.05	.04	.02
90	Tim Raines	.20	.15	.08
91	Tim Wallach	.10	.08	.04
92	Dwight Gooden	.60	.45	.25
93	Keith Hernandez	.15	.11	.06
94	Gregg Jefferies	2.00	1.50	.80
95	Howard Johnson	.10	.08	.04
96	Roger McDowell	.05	.04	.02
97	Darryl Strawberry	.50	.40	.20
98	Steve Bedrosian	.10	.08	.04
99	Von Hayes	.10	.08	.04
100	Shane Rawley	.05	.04	.02
101	Juan Samuel	.12	.09	.05
102	Mike Schmidt	.30	.25	.12
103	Bobby Bonilla	.15	.11	.06
104	Mike Dunne	.07	.05	.03
105	Andy Van Slyke	.10	.08	.04
106	Vince Coleman	.15	.11	.06
107	Bob Horner	.07	.05	.03
108	Willie McGee	.10	.08	.04
109	Ozzie Smith	.12	.09	.05
110	John Tudor	.07	.05	.03
111	Todd Worrell	.10	.08	.04
112	Tony Gwynn	.25	.20	.10
113	John Kruk	.12	.09	.05
114	Lance McCullers	.05	.04	.02
115	Benito Santiago	.15	.11	.06
116	Will Clark	.30	.25	.12
117	Jeff Leonard	.05	.04	.02
118	Candy Maldonado	.05	.04	.02
119	Rick Rueschel	.07	.05	.03
120	Don Robinson	.05	.04	.02

1988 Fleer Record Setters

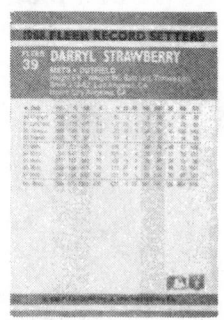

For the second consecutive year, Fleer Corp. issued this special limited-edition 44-card set for exclusive distribution by Eckerd Drug stores. Cards are standard-size with red and blue borders framing the full-color player photos. A "1988 Fleer Record Setters" headline is printed on a yellow strip above the player's photo. The player's name, team and position appear beneath the pose. Card backs list personal information and career stats in red and blue ink on a white background. Each 44-card set comes cello-wrapped in a checklist box that contains six additional cards with peel-off team logo stickers. The sticker cards feature black and white aerial photos of major league ballparks, along with stadium statistics such as field size, seating capacity and date of the first game played.

		MT	NR MT	EX
	Complete Set:	5.00	3.75	2.00
	Common Player:	.05	.04	.02
1	Jesse Barfield	.10	.08	.04

		MT	NR MT	EX
2	George Bell	.20	.15	.08
3	Wade Boggs	1.00	.70	.40
4	Jose Canseco	1.00	.70	.40
5	Jack Clark	.15	.11	.06
6	Will Clark	1.00	.70	.40
7	Roger Clemens	.40	.30	.15
8	Alvin Davis	.10	.08	.04
9	Eric Davis	.50	.40	.20
10	Andre Dawson	.15	.11	.06
11	Mike Dunne	.10	.08	.04
12	John Franco	.07	.05	.03
13	Julio Franco	.07	.05	.03
14	Dwight Gooden	.40	.30	.15
15	Mark Gubicza	.07	.05	.03
16	Ozzie Guillen	.07	.05	.03
17	Tony Gwynn	.25	.20	.10
18	Orel Hershiser	.20	.15	.08
19	Teddy Higuera	.10	.08	.04
20	Howard Johnson	.07	.05	.03
21	Wally Joyner	.30	.25	.12
22	Jimmy Key	.07	.05	.03
23	Jeff Leonard	.05	.04	.02
24	Don Mattingly	1.25	.90	.50
25	Mark McGwire	1.00	.70	.40
26	Jack Morris	.12	.09	.05
27	Dale Murphy	.30	.25	.12
28	Larry Parrish	.05	.04	.02
29	Kirby Puckett	.50	.40	.20
30	Tim Raines	.25	.20	.10
31	Harold Reynolds	.07	.05	.03
32	Dave Righetti	.12	.09	.05
33	Cal Ripken, Jr.	.30	.25	.12
34	Benito Santiago	.25	.20	.10
35	Mike Schmidt	.30	.25	.12
36	Mike Scott	.10	.08	.04
37	Kevin Seitzer	.60	.45	.25
38	Ozzie Smith	.12	.09	.05
39	Darryl Strawberry	.40	.30	.15
40	Rick Sutcliffe	.10	.08	.04
41	Alan Trammell	.15	.11	.06
42	Frank Viola	.12	.09	.05
43	Mitch Williams	.05	.04	.02
44	Todd Worrell	.10	.08	.04

1988 Fleer Star Stickers

 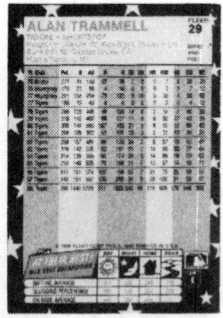

This set of 132 standard-size sticker cards (including a checklist card) features exclusive player photos, different from those in the Fleer regular issue. Card fronts have light gray borders sprinkled with multi-colored stars. The "Fleer Star Stickers" logo appears upper left, player names are printed beneath the photos. Card backs are printed in red, gray and black on white and include personal data and a breakdown of pitching and batting stats into day, night, home and road categories. Cards were marketed in two different display boxes that feature six players and two team logos from Fleer's 1988 Limited Edition box-bottom set.

		MT	NR MT	EX
Complete Set:		18.00	13.50	7.25
Common Player:		.05	.04	.02
1	Mike Boddicker	.08	.06	.03
2	Eddie Murray	.50	.40	.20
3	Cal Ripken, Jr.	.60	.45	.25

		MT	NR MT	EX
4	Larry Sheets	.15	.11	.06
5	Wade Boggs	1.75	1.25	.70
6	Ellis Burks	1.00	.70	.40
7	Roger Clemens	.90	.70	.35
8	Dwight Evans	.15	.11	.06
9	Mike Greenwell	1.00	.70	.40
10	Bruce Hurst	.12	.09	.05
11	Brian Downing	.08	.06	.03
12	Wally Joyner	.60	.45	.25
13	Mike Witt	.10	.08	.04
14	Ivan Calderon	.12	.09	.05
15	Jose DeLeon	.05	.04	.02
16	Ozzie Guillen	.15	.11	.06
17	Bobby Thigpen	.10	.08	.04
18	Joe Carter	.20	.15	.08
19	Julio Franco	.12	.09	.05
20	Brook Jacoby	.12	.09	.05
21	Cory Snyder	.40	.30	.15
22	Pat Tabler	.10	.08	.04
23	Doyle Alexander	.08	.06	.03
24	Kirk Gibson	.30	.25	.12
25	Mike Henneman	.20	.15	.08
26	Jack Morris	.25	.20	.10
27	Matt Nokes	.60	.45	.25
28	Walt Terrell	.05	.04	.02
29	Alan Trammell	.30	.25	.12
30	George Brett	.70	.50	.30
31	Charlie Leibrandt	.05	.04	.02
32	Bret Saberhagen	.25	.20	.10
33	Kevin Seitzer	.70	.50	.30
34	Danny Tartabull	.25	.20	.10
35	Frank White	.10	.08	.04
36	Rob Deer	.10	.08	.04
37	Ted Higuera	.15	.11	.06
38	Paul Molitor	.20	.15	.08
39	Dan Plesac	.12	.09	.05
40	Robin Yount	.30	.25	.12
41	Bert Blyleven	.15	.11	.06
42	Tom Brunansky	.15	.11	.06
43	Gary Gaetti	.20	.15	.08
44	Kent Hrbek	.30	.25	.12
45	Kirby Puckett	.50	.40	.20
46	Jeff Reardon	.10	.08	.04
47	Frank Viola	.15	.11	.06
48	Don Mattingly	2.00	1.50	.80
49	Mike Pagliarulo	.12	.09	.05
50	Willie Randolph	.08	.06	.03
51	Rick Rhoden	.08	.06	.03
52	Dave Righetti	.20	.15	.08
53	Dave Winfield	.40	.30	.15
54	Jose Canseco	2.00	1.50	.80
55	Carney Lansford	.08	.06	.03
56	Mark McGwire	1.25	.90	.50
57	Dave Stewart	.12	.09	.05
58	Curt Young	.08	.06	.03
59	Alvin Davis	.15	.11	.06
60	Mark Langston	.15	.11	.06
61	Ken Phelps	.05	.04	.02
62	Harold Reynolds	.10	.08	.04
63	Scott Fletcher	.05	.04	.02
64	Charlie Hough	.08	.06	.03
65	Pete Incaviglia	.25	.20	.10
66	Oddibe McDowell	.10	.08	.04
67	Pete O'Brien	.10	.08	.04
68	Larry Parrish	.08	.06	.03
69	Ruben Sierra	.25	.20	.10
70	Jesse Barfield	.12	.09	.05
71	George Bell	.25	.20	.10
72	Tony Fernandez	.12	.09	.05
73	Tom Henke	.10	.08	.04
74	Jimmy Key	.12	.09	.05
75	Lloyd Moseby	.10	.08	.04
76	Dion James	.05	.04	.02
77	Dale Murphy	.70	.50	.30
78	Zane Smith	.08	.06	.03
79	Andre Dawson	.25	.20	.10
80	Ryne Sandberg	.35	.25	.14
81	Rick Sutcliffe	.15	.11	.06
82	Kal Daniels	.25	.20	.10
83	Eric Davis	.80	.60	.30
84	John Franco	.10	.08	.04
85	Kevin Bass	.10	.08	.04
86	Glenn Davis	.20	.15	.08
87	Bill Doran	.10	.08	.04
88	Nolan Ryan	.50	.40	.20
89	Mike Scott	.15	.11	.06
90	Dave Smith	.05	.04	.02
91	Pedro Guerrero	.20	.15	.08
92	Orel Hershiser	.35	.25	.14
93	Steve Sax	.20	.15	.08
94	Fernando Valenzuela	.35	.25	.14

		MT	NR MT	EX
95	Tim Burke	.05	.04	.02
96	Andres Galarraga	.20	.15	.08
97	Tim Raines	.35	.25	.14
98	Tim Wallach	.12	.09	.05
99	Mitch Webster	.05	.04	.02
100	Ron Darling	.20	.15	.08
101	Sid Fernandez	.10	.08	.04
102	Dwight Gooden	.90	.70	.35
103	Keith Hernandez	.30	.25	.12
104	Howard Johnson	.12	.09	.05
105	Roger McDowell	.10	.08	.04
106	Darryl Strawberry	.70	.50	.30
107	Steve Bedrosian	.12	.09	.05
108	Von Hayes	.12	.09	.05
109	Shane Rawley	.08	.06	.03
110	Juan Samuel	.15	.11	.06
111	Mike Schmidt	.70	.50	.30
112	Milt Thompson	.05	.04	.02
113	Sid Bream	.08	.06	.03
114	Bobby Bonilla	.20	.15	.08
115	Mike Dunne	.15	.11	.06
116	Andy Van Slyke	.12	.09	.05
117	Vince Coleman	.25	.20	.10
118	Willie McGee	.15	.11	.06
119	Terry Pendleton	.10	.08	.04
120	Ozzie Smith	.20	.15	.08
121	John Tudor	.12	.09	.05
122	Todd Worrell	.20	.15	.08
123	Tony Gwynn	.40	.30	.15
124	John Kruk	.20	.15	.08
125	Benito Santiago	.30	.25	.12
126	Will Clark	1.00	.70	.40
127	Dave Dravecky	.05	.04	.02
128	Jeff Leonard	.05	.04	.02
129	Candy Maldonado	.05	.04	.02
130	Rick Rueschel	.10	.08	.04
131	Don Robinson	.05	.04	.02
132	Checklist	.05	.04	.02

1988 Fleer Star Stickers Box Panels

RON GUIDRY

This set of eight box-bottom cards was printed on two different retail display boxes. Six players and two team logo sticker cards are included in the set, three player photos and one team photo per box. The full-color player photos are exclusively limited to the Fleer Star Sticker set. The cards, which measure 2-1/2" by 3-1/2", have a light gray border sprinkled with multi-color stars. The backs are printed in navy blue and red.

		MT	NR MT	EX
Complete Panel Set:		3.50	2.75	1.50
Complete Singles Set:		1.75	1.25	.70
Common Singles Player:		.15	.11	.06
	Panel	2.50	2.00	1.00
1	Eric Davis, Mark McGwire	.70	.50	.30
3	Kevin Mitchell	.50	.40	.20
5	Rickey Henderson	.50	.40	.20
7	Tigers Logo	.05	.04	.02
	Panel	1.25	.90	.50
2	Gary Carter	.35	.25	.14
4	Ron Guidry	.20	.15	.08
6	Don Baylor	.15	.11	.06

		MT	NR MT	EX
8	Giants Logo	.05	.04	.02

1988 Fleer Superstars

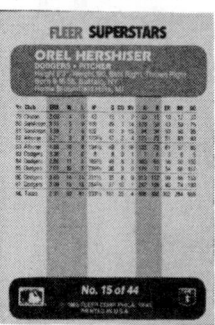

This is the fourth edition of Fleer's 44-card boxed set produced for distribution by McCrory's (1985-87 issues were simply titled "Fleer Limited Edition"). The Superstars standard-size card set features full-color player photos framed by red, white and blue striped top and bottom borders. "Fleer 1988" is printed in an elongated yellow oval banner above the photo. A pale yellow rectangle below the photo carries the player's name and team logo. Card fronts have a semi-glossy slightly textured finish. Card backs are red and blue on white and include card numbers, personal data and statistics. Six team logo sticker cards are also included in this set which was marketed in red, white and blue boxes with checklist backs. Boxed sets were sold exclusively at McCrory's stores and its affiliates.

		MT	NR MT	EX
Complete Set:		7.00	5.25	2.75
Common Player:		.05	.04	.02
1	Steve Bedrosian	.10	.08	.04
2	George Bell	.20	.15	.08
3	Wade Boggs	1.00	.70	.40
4	Barry Bonds	.12	.09	.05
5	Jose Canseco	1.00	.70	.40
6	Joe Carter	.12	.09	.05
7	Jack Clark	.15	.11	.06
8	Will Clark	1.00	.70	.40
9	Roger Clemens	.40	.30	.15
10	Alvin Davis	.10	.08	.04
11	Eric Davis	.50	.40	.20
12	Glenn Davis	.12	.09	.05
13	Andre Dawson	.15	.11	.06
14	Dwight Gooden	.40	.30	.15
15	Orel Hershiser	.20	.15	.08
16	Teddy Higuera	.10	.08	.04
17	Kent Hrbek	.15	.11	.06
18	Wally Joyner	.30	.25	.12
19	Jimmy Key	.07	.05	.03
20	John Kruk	.10	.08	.04
21	Jeff Leonard	.05	.04	.02
22	Don Mattingly	1.75	1.25	.70
23	Mark McGwire	1.00	.70	.40
24	Kevin McReynolds	.12	.09	.05
25	Dale Murphy	.30	.25	.12
26	Matt Nokes	.30	.25	.12
27	Terry Pendleton	.05	.04	.02
28	Kirby Puckett	.50	.40	.20
29	Tim Raines	.25	.20	.10
30	Rick Rhoden	.07	.05	.03
31	Cal Ripken, Jr.	.30	.25	.12
32	Benito Santiago	.25	.20	.10
33	Mike Schmidt	.30	.25	.12
34	Mike Scott	.10	.08	.04
35	Kevin Seitzer	.60	.45	.25
36	Ruben Sierra	.25	.20	.10
37	Cory Snyder	.12	.09	.05
38	Darryl Strawberry	.40	.30	.15
39	Rick Sutcliffe	.10	.08	.04
40	Danny Tartabull	.12	.09	.05
41	Alan Trammell	.15	.11	.06
42	Ken Williams	.07	.05	.03
43	Mike Witt	.07	.05	.03

		MT	NR MT	EX
44	Robin Yount	.15	.11	.06

1988 Fleer Update

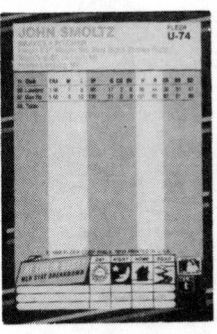

This 132-card update set (numbered U-1 through U-132 and 2-1/2" by 3-1/2") features traded veterans and rookies in a mixture of full-color action shots and close-ups, framed by white borders with red and blue stripes. Player name and position appear upper left, printed on an upward slant leading into the team logo, upper right. A bright stripe in a variety of colors (blue, red, green, yellow) edges the bottom of the photo and leads into the Fleer logo at lower right. The backs are red, white and blue-grey and include personal info, along with yearly and "At Their Best" (day, night, home, road) stats charts. The set was packaged in white cardboard boxes with red and blue stripes. A glossy-coated edition of the update set was issued in its own tin box and is valued at two times greater than the regular issue.

		MT	NR MT	EX
Complete Set:		12.00	9.00	4.75
Common Player:		.06	.05	.02
1	Jose Bautista(FC)	.20	.15	.08
2	Joe Orsulak	.06	.05	.02
3	Doug Sisk	.06	.05	.02
4	Craig Worthington(FC)	.50	.40	.20
5	Mike Boddicker	.08	.06	.03
6	Rick Cerone	.06	.05	.02
7	Larry Parrish	.08	.06	.03
8	Lee Smith	.10	.08	.04
9	Mike Smithson	.06	.05	.02
10	John Trautwein(FC)	.15	.11	.06
11	Sherman Corbett(FC)	.15	.11	.06
12	Chili Davis	.10	.08	.04
13	Jim Eppard	.08	.06	.03
14	Bryan Harvey(FC)	.30	.25	.12
15	John Davis	.08	.06	.03
16	Dave Gallagher(FC)	.20	.15	.08
17	Ricky Horton	.08	.06	.03
18	Dan Pasqua	.10	.08	.04
19	Melido Perez	.12	.09	.05
20	Jose Segura(FC)	.15	.11	.06
21	Andy Allanson	.08	.06	.03
22	Jon Perlman	.06	.05	.02
23	Domingo Ramos	.06	.05	.02
24	Rick Rodriguez	.08	.06	.03
25	Willie Upshaw	.10	.08	.04
26	Paul Gibson(FC)	.15	.11	.06
27	Don Heinkel(FC)	.15	.11	.06
28	Ray Knight	.08	.06	.03
29	Gary Pettis	.08	.06	.03
30	Luis Salazar	.06	.05	.02
31	Mike MacFarlane (Macfarlane)(FC)	.20	.15	.08
32	Jeff Montgomery	.08	.06	.03
33	Ted Power	.06	.05	.02
34	Israel Sanchez(FC)	.15	.11	.06
35	Kurt Stillwell	.10	.08	.04
36	Pat Tabler	.08	.06	.03
37	Don August(FC)	.15	.11	.06
38	Darryl Hamilton(FC)	.15	.11	.06
39	Jeff Leonard	.08	.06	.03
40	Joey Meyer	.15	.11	.06
41	Allan Anderson	.10	.08	.04
42	Brian Harper	.06	.05	.02

		MT	NR MT	EX
43	Tom Herr	.10	.08	.04
44	Charlie Lea	.06	.05	.02
45	John Moses	.06	.05	.02
46	John Candelaria	.10	.08	.04
47	Jack Clark	.15	.11	.06
48	Richard Dotson	.10	.08	.04
49	Al Leiter(FC)	.25	.20	.10
50	Rafael Santana	.06	.05	.02
51	Don Slaught	.06	.05	.02
52	Todd Burns(FC)	.25	.20	.10
53	Dave Henderson	.10	.08	.04
54	Doug Jennings(FC)	.15	.11	.06
55	Dave Parker	.12	.09	.05
56	Walt Weiss	.60	.45	.25
57	Bob Welch	.10	.08	.04
58	Henry Cotto	.06	.05	.02
59	Marion Diaz (Mario)	.08	.06	.03
60	Mike Jackson	.06	.05	.02
61	Bill Swift	.06	.05	.02
62	Jose Cecena(FC)	.15	.11	.06
63	Ray Hayward(FC)	.08	.06	.03
64	Jim Steels(FC)	.08	.06	.03
65	Pat Borders(FC)	.20	.15	.08
66	Sil Campusano(FC)	.25	.20	.10
67	Mike Flanagan	.10	.08	.04
68	Todd Stottlemyre(FC)	.30	.25	.12
69	David Wells(FC)	.08	.06	.03
70	Jose Alvarez(FC)	.15	.11	.06
71	Paul Runge	.06	.05	.02
72	Cesar Jimenez (German)(FC)	.15	.11	.06
73	Pete Smith	.08	.06	.03
74	John Smoltz(FC)	1.75	1.25	.70
75	Damon Berryhill	.10	.08	.04
76	Goose Gossage	.15	.11	.06
77	Mark Grace	3.00	2.25	1.25
78	Darrin Jackson	.08	.06	.03
79	Vance Law	.08	.06	.03
80	Jeff Pico(FC)	.20	.15	.08
81	Gary Varsho(FC)	.20	.15	.08
82	Tim Birtsas	.06	.05	.02
83	Rob Dibble(FC)	1.00	.70	.45
84	Danny Jackson	.15	.11	.06
85	Paul O'Neill	.08	.06	.03
86	Jose Rijo	.08	.06	.03
87	Chris Sabo(FC)	3.00	2.25	1.25
88	John Fishel(FC)	.15	.11	.06
89	Craig Biggio(FC)	1.25	.90	.50
90	Terry Puhl	.06	.05	.02
91	Rafael Ramirez	.06	.05	.02
92	Louie Meadows(FC)	.15	.11	.06
93	Kirk Gibson(FC)	.15	.11	.06
94	Alfredo Griffin	.08	.06	.03
95	Jay Howell	.08	.06	.03
96	Jesse Orosco	.08	.06	.03
97	Alejandro Pena	.08	.06	.03
98	Tracy Woodson(FC)	.10	.08	.04
99	John Dopson(FC)	.25	.20	.10
100	Brian Holman(FC)	.40	.30	.15
101	Rex Hudler(FC)	.08	.06	.03
102	Jeff Parrett(FC)	.10	.08	.04
103	Nelson Santovenia(FC)	.40	.30	.15
104	Kevin Elster	.12	.09	.05
105	Jeff Innis(FC)	.20	.15	.08
106	Mackey Sasser(FC)	.10	.08	.04
107	Phil Bradley	.10	.08	.04
108	Danny Clay(FC)	.15	.11	.06
109	Greg Harris	.06	.05	.02
110	Ricky Jordan(FC)	.80	.60	.30
111	David Palmer	.06	.05	.02
112	Jim Gott	.06	.05	.02
113	Tommy Gregg (photo actually Randy Milligan)(FC)	.10	.08	.04
114	Barry Jones	.06	.05	.02
115	Randy Milligan(FC)	.10	.08	.04
116	Luis Alicea(FC)	.15	.11	.06
117	Tom Brunansky	.12	.09	.05
118	John Costello(FC)	.15	.11	.06
119	Jose DeLeon	.08	.06	.03
120	Bob Horner	.10	.08	.04
121	Scott Terry(FC)	.10	.08	.04
122	Roberto Alomar(FC)	3.00	2.25	1.25
123	Dave Leiper	.06	.05	.02
124	Keith Moreland	.08	.06	.03
125	Mark Parent(FC)	.20	.15	.08
126	Dennis Rasmussen	.10	.08	.04
127	Randy Bockus	.06	.05	.02
128	Brett Butler	.08	.06	.03
129	Donell Nixon	.06	.05	.02
130	Earnest Riles	.06	.05	.02
131	Roger Samuels(FC)	.15	.11	.06
132	Checklist	.06	.05	.02

1989 Fleer

 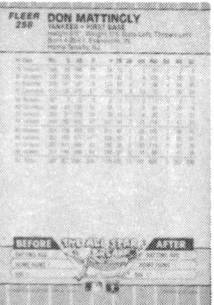

This set includes 660 standard-size cards and was issued with 45 team logo stickers. Individual card fronts feature a grey and white striped background with full-color player photos framed by a bright line of color that slants upward to the right. The set also includes two subsets: 15 Major League Prospects and 12 SuperStar Specials. A special bonus set of 12 All-Star Team cards was randomly inserted in individual wax packs of 15 cards. The last seven cards in the set are checklists, with players listed alphabetically by teams.

		MT	NR MT	EX
Complete Set:		28.00	21.00	12.00
Common Player:		.05	.04	.02

1	Don Baylor	.10	.08	.04
2	Lance Blankenship(FC)	.25	.20	.10
3	Todd Burns	.30	.25	.12
4	Greg Cadaret(FC)	.07	.05	.03
5	Jose Canseco	1.25	.90	.50
6	Storm Davis	.10	.08	.04
7	Dennis Eckersley	.12	.09	.05
8	Mike Gallego(FC)	.05	.04	.02
9	Ron Hassey	.05	.04	.02
10	Dave Henderson	.10	.08	.04
11	Rick Honeycutt	.05	.04	.02
12	Glenn Hubbard	.05	.04	.02
13	Stan Javier	.05	.04	.02
14	Doug Jennings	.20	.15	.08
15	Felix Jose(FC)	.50	.40	.20
16	Carney Lansford	.07	.05	.03
17	Mark McGwire	.70	.50	.30
18	Gene Nelson	.05	.04	.02
19	Dave Parker	.12	.09	.05
20	Eric Plunk	.05	.04	.02
21	Luis Polonia	.07	.05	.03
22	Terry Steinbach	.10	.08	.04
23	Dave Stewart	.10	.08	.04
24	Walt Weiss	.30	.25	.12
25	Bob Welch	.10	.08	.04
26	Curt Young	.07	.05	.03
27	Rick Aguilera	.05	.04	.02
28	Wally Backman	.07	.05	.03
29	Mark Carreon	.07	.05	.03
30	Gary Carter	.20	.15	.08
31	David Cone	.40	.30	.15
32	Ron Darling	.12	.09	.05
33	Len Dykstra	.10	.08	.04
34	Kevin Elster	.10	.08	.04
35	Sid Fernandez	.10	.08	.04
36	Dwight Gooden	.50	.40	.20
37	Keith Hernandez	.25	.20	.10
38	Gregg Jefferies	2.00	1.50	.80
39	Howard Johnson	.10	.08	.04
40	Terry Leach	.05	.04	.02
41	Dave Magadan	.10	.08	.04
42	Bob McClure	.05	.04	.02
43	Roger McDowell	.10	.08	.04
44	Kevin McReynolds	.15	.11	.06
45	Keith Miller	.10	.08	.04
46	Randy Myers	.10	.08	.04
47	Bob Ojeda	.07	.05	.03
48	Mackey Sasser	.07	.05	.03

		MT	NR MT	EX
49	Darryl Strawberry	.40	.30	.15
50	Tim Teufel	.05	.04	.02
51	Dave West(FC)	.30	.25	.12
52	Mookie Wilson	.07	.05	.03
53	Dave Anderson	.05	.04	.02
54	Tim Belcher	.10	.08	.04
55	Mike Davis	.07	.05	.03
56	Mike Devereaux	.15	.11	.06
57	Kirk Gibson	.20	.15	.08
58	Alfredo Griffin	.07	.05	.03
59	Chris Gwynn	.12	.09	.05
60	Jeff Hamilton	.07	.05	.03
61a	Danny Heep (Home: San Antonio, TX)	1.00	.70	.40
61b	Danny Heep (Home: Lake Hills, TX)	.05	.04	.02
62	Orel Hershiser	.25	.20	.10
63	Brian Holton(FC)	.07	.05	.03
64	Jay Howell	.07	.05	.03
65	Tim Leary	.07	.05	.03
66	Mike Marshall	.12	.09	.05
67	Ramon Martinez(FC)	2.25	1.75	.90
68	Jesse Orosco	.07	.05	.03
69	Alejandro Pena	.07	.05	.03
70	Steve Sax	.15	.11	.06
71	Mike Scioscia	.07	.05	.03
72	Mike Sharperson	.05	.04	.02
73	John Shelby	.05	.04	.02
74	Franklin Stubbs	.05	.04	.02
75	John Tudor	.10	.08	.04
76	Fernando Valenzuela	.20	.15	.08
77	Tracy Woodson	.10	.08	.04
78	Marty Barrett	.07	.05	.03
79	Todd Benzinger	.12	.09	.05
80	Mike Boddicker	.07	.05	.03
81	Wade Boggs	.60	.45	.25
82	"Oil Can" Boyd	.07	.05	.03
83	Ellis Burks	.60	.45	.25
84	Rick Cerone	.05	.04	.02
85	Roger Clemens	.50	.40	.20
86	Steve Curry(FC)	.20	.15	.08
87	Dwight Evans	.10	.08	.04
88	Wes Gardner	.07	.05	.03
89	Rich Gedman	.07	.05	.03
90	Mike Greenwell	.70	.50	.30
91	Bruce Hurst	.10	.08	.04
92	Dennis Lamp	.05	.04	.02
93	Spike Owen	.05	.04	.02
94	Larry Parrish	.07	.05	.03
95	Carlos Quintana(FC)	.50	.40	.20
96	Jody Reed	.12	.09	.05
97	Jim Rice	.25	.20	.10
98a	Kevin Romine (batting follow-thru, photo actually Randy Kutcher)	.50	.40	.20
98b	Kevin Romine (arms crossed on chest, correct photo)	.60	.45	.25
99	Lee Smith	.10	.08	.04
100	Mike Smithson	.05	.04	.02
101	Bob Stanley	.05	.04	.02
102	Allan Anderson	.07	.05	.03
103	Keith Atherton	.05	.04	.02
104	Juan Berenguer	.05	.04	.02
105	Bert Blyleven	.12	.09	.05
106	Eric Bullock(FC)	.15	.11	.06
107	Randy Bush	.05	.04	.02
108	John Christensen(FC)	.05	.04	.02
109	Mark Davidson	.07	.05	.03
110	Gary Gaetti	.15	.11	.06
111	Greg Gagne	.05	.04	.02
112	Dan Gladden	.05	.04	.02
113	German Gonzalez(FC)	.20	.15	.08
114	Brian Harper	.05	.04	.02
115	Tom Herr	.07	.05	.03
116	Kent Hrbek	.20	.15	.08
117	Gene Larkin	.10	.08	.04
118	Tim Laudner	.05	.04	.02
119	Charlie Lea	.05	.04	.02
120	Steve Lombardozzi	.05	.04	.02
121a	John Moses (Home: Phoenix, AZ)	1.00	.70	.40
121b	John Moses (Home: Tempe, AZ)	.05	.04	.02
122	Al Newman	.05	.04	.02
123	Mark Portugal	.05	.04	.02
124	Kirby Puckett	.35	.25	.14
125	Jeff Reardon	.10	.08	.04
126	Fred Toliver	.05	.04	.02
127	Frank Viola	.15	.11	.06
128	Doyle Alexander	.07	.05	.03
129	Dave Bergman	.05	.04	.02
130a	Tom Brookens (Mike Heath stats on back)	2.25	1.75	.90
130b	Tom Brookens (correct stats on back)	.30	.25	.12

		MT	NR MT	EX
131	*Paul Gibson*	.15	.11	.06
132a	Mike Heath (Tom Brookens stats on back)	2.25	1.75	.90
132b	Mike Heath (correct stats on back)	.30	.25	.12
133	*Don Heinkel*	.15	.11	.06
134	Mike Henneman	.10	.08	.04
135	Guillermo Hernandez	.07	.05	.03
136	Eric King	.05	.04	.02
137	Chet Lemon	.07	.05	.03
138	Fred Lynn	.10	.08	.04
139	Jack Morris	.15	.11	.06
140	Matt Nokes	.20	.15	.08
141	Gary Pettis	.05	.04	.02
142	Ted Power	.05	.04	.02
143	Jeff Robinson	.12	.09	.05
144	Luis Salazar	.05	.04	.02
145	*Steve Searcy*(FC)	.30	.25	.12
146	Pat Sheridan	.05	.04	.02
147	Frank Tanana	.07	.05	.03
148	Alan Trammell	.20	.15	.08
149	Walt Terrell	.07	.05	.03
150	Jim Walewander(FC)	.07	.05	.03
151	Lou Whitaker	.20	.15	.08
152	Tim Birtsas	.05	.04	.02
153	Tom Browning	.10	.08	.04
154	*Keith Brown*(FC)	.20	.15	.08
155	*Norm Charlton*(FC)	.30	.25	.12
156	Dave Concepcion	.10	.08	.04
157	Kal Daniels	.15	.11	.06
158	Eric Davis	.50	.40	.20
159	Bo Diaz	.07	.05	.03
160	*Rob Dibble*	.80	.60	.30
161	Nick Esasky	.07	.05	.03
162	John Franco	.10	.08	.04
163	Danny Jackson	.15	.11	.06
164	Barry Larkin	.25	.20	.10
165	Rob Murphy	.05	.04	.02
166	Paul O'Neill	.05	.04	.02
167	Jeff Reed	.05	.04	.02
168	Jose Rijo	.07	.05	.03
169	Ron Robinson	.05	.04	.02
170	*Chris Sabo*	1.00	.70	.40
171	*Candy Sierra*(FC)	.15	.11	.06
172	*Van Snider*(FC)	.20	.15	.08
173	Jeff Treadway	.12	.09	.05
174	Frank Williams	.05	.04	.02
175	Herm Winningham	.05	.04	.02
176	Jim Adduci(FC)	.05	.04	.02
177	Don August	.10	.08	.04
178	Mike Birkbeck	.05	.04	.02
179	Chris Bosio	.05	.04	.02
180	Glenn Braggs	.07	.05	.03
181	Greg Brock	.07	.05	.03
182	Mark Clear	.05	.04	.02
183	Chuck Crim	.05	.04	.02
184	Rob Deer	.07	.05	.03
185	Tom Filer	.05	.04	.02
186	Jim Gantner	.05	.04	.02
187	*Darryl Hamilton*	.15	.11	.06
188	Ted Higuera	.10	.08	.04
189	Odell Jones	.05	.04	.02
190	Jeffrey Leonard	.07	.05	.03
191	Joey Meyer	.10	.08	.04
192	Paul Mirabella	.05	.04	.02
193	Paul Molitor	.15	.11	.06
194	Charlie O'Brien(FC)	.07	.05	.03
195	Dan Plesac	.10	.08	.04
196	*Gary Sheffield*(FC)	2.00	1.50	.80
197	B.J. Surhoff	.10	.08	.04
198	Dale Sveum	.07	.05	.03
199	Bill Wegman	.05	.04	.02
200	Robin Yount	.25	.20	.10
201	Rafael Belliard	.05	.04	.02
202	Barry Bonds	.12	.09	.05
203	Bobby Bonilla	.12	.09	.05
204	Sid Bream	.07	.05	.03
205	Benny Distefano(FC)	.05	.04	.02
206	Doug Drabek	.07	.05	.03
207	Mike Dunne	.10	.08	.04
208	Felix Fermin	.07	.05	.03
209	Brian Fisher	.07	.05	.03
210	Jim Gott	.05	.04	.02
211	Bob Kipper	.05	.04	.02
212	Dave LaPoint	.07	.05	.03
213	Mike LaValliere	.07	.05	.03
214	Jose Lind	.10	.08	.04
215	Junior Ortiz	.05	.04	.02
216	Vicente Palacios	.07	.05	.03
217	Tom Prince(FC)	.10	.08	.04
218	Gary Redus	.05	.04	.02
219	R.J. Reynolds	.05	.04	.02
220	Jeff Robinson	.07	.05	.03
221	John Smiley	.12	.09	.05
222	Andy Van Slyke	.12	.09	.05
223	Bob Walk	.05	.04	.02
224	Glenn Wilson	.07	.05	.03
225	Jesse Barfield	.10	.08	.04
226	George Bell	.25	.20	.10
227	*Pat Borders*	.25	.20	.10
228	John Cerutti	.07	.05	.03
229	Jim Clancy	.07	.05	.03
230	Mark Eichhorn	.07	.05	.03
231	Tony Fernandez	.12	.09	.05
232	Cecil Fielder	.05	.04	.02
233	Mike Flanagan	.07	.05	.03
234	Kelly Gruber	.05	.04	.02
235	Tom Henke	.07	.05	.03
236	Jimmy Key	.10	.08	.04
237	Rick Leach	.05	.04	.02
238	Manny Lee	.05	.04	.02
239	Nelson Liriano	.07	.05	.03
240	Fred McGriff	.50	.40	.20
241	Lloyd Moseby	.07	.05	.03
242	Rance Mulliniks	.05	.04	.02
243	Jeff Musselman	.07	.05	.03
244	Dave Stieb	.10	.08	.04
245	Todd Stottlemyre	.10	.08	.04
246	Duane Ward	.05	.04	.02
247	David Wells	.10	.08	.04
248	Ernie Whitt	.07	.05	.03
249	Luis Aguayo	.05	.04	.02
250a	Neil Allen (Home: Sarasota, FL)	1.50	1.25	.60
250b	Neil Allen (Home: Syosset, NY)	.05	.04	.02
251	John Candelaria	.07	.05	.03
252	Jack Clark	.15	.11	.06
253	Richard Dotson	.07	.05	.03
254	Rickey Henderson	.35	.25	.14
255	Tommy John	.12	.09	.05
256	Roberto Kelly	.20	.15	.08
257	Al Leiter	.15	.11	.06
258	Don Mattingly	1.50	1.25	.60
259	Dale Mohorcic	.05	.04	.02
260	*Hal Morris*(FC)	1.75	1.25	.70
261	Scott Nielsen(FC)	.10	.08	.04
262	Mike Pagliarulo	.10	.08	.04
263	Hipolito Pena(FC)	.15	.11	.06
264	Ken Phelps	.07	.05	.03
265	Willie Randolph	.07	.05	.03
266	Rick Rhoden	.07	.05	.03
267	Dave Righetti	.12	.09	.05
268	Rafael Santana	.05	.04	.02
269	Steve Shields(FC)	.07	.05	.03
270	Joel Skinner	.05	.04	.02
271	Don Slaught	.05	.04	.02
272	Claudell Washington	.07	.05	.03
273	Gary Ward	.07	.05	.03
274	Dave Winfield	.30	.25	.12
275	Luis Aquino(FC)	.05	.04	.02
276	Floyd Bannister	.07	.05	.03
277	George Brett	.35	.25	.14
278	Bill Buckner	.10	.08	.04
279	*Nick Capra*(FC)	.20	.15	.08
280	*Jose DeJesus*(FC)	.15	.11	.06
281	Steve Farr	.05	.04	.02
282	Jerry Gleaton	.05	.04	.02
283	Mark Gubicza	.10	.08	.04
284	*Tom Gordon*(FC)	1.00	.70	.40
285	Bo Jackson	1.00	.70	.40
286	Charlie Leibrandt	.07	.05	.03
287	*Mike Macfarlane*	.20	.15	.08
288	Jeff Montgomery	.07	.05	.03
289	Bill Pecota	.07	.05	.03
290	Jamie Quirk	.05	.04	.02
291	Bret Saberhagen	.15	.11	.06
292	Kevin Seitzer	.30	.25	.12
293	Kurt Stillwell	.07	.05	.03
294	Pat Tabler	.07	.05	.03
295	Danny Tartabull	.20	.15	.08
296	Gary Thurman	.12	.09	.05
297	Frank White	.07	.05	.03
298	Willie Wilson	.10	.08	.04
299	Roberto Alomar	1.00	.70	.40
300	*Sandy Alomar, Jr.*(FC)	2.00	1.50	.80
301	Chris Brown	.07	.05	.03
302	Mike Brumley(FC)	.07	.05	.03
303	Mark Davis	.05	.04	.02
304	Mark Grant	.05	.04	.02
305	Tony Gwynn	.35	.25	.14
306	*Greg Harris*(FC)	.30	.25	.12
307	Andy Hawkins	.05	.04	.02
308	Jimmy Jones	.05	.04	.02
309	John Kruk	.07	.05	.03

		MT	NR MT	EX				MT	NR MT	EX
310	Dave Leiper	.05	.04	.02		401	Carmen Castillo	.05	.04	.02
311	Carmelo Martinez	.05	.04	.02		402	Dave Clark	.07	.05	.03
312	Lance McCullers	.07	.05	.03		403	John Farrell	.10	.08	.04
313	Keith Moreland	.07	.05	.03		404	Julio Franco	.10	.08	.04
314	Dennis Rasmussen	.10	.08	.04		405	Don Gordon	.05	.04	.02
315	Randy Ready	.05	.04	.02		406	Mel Hall	.07	.05	.03
316	Benito Santiago	.15	.11	.06		407	Brad Havens	.05	.04	.02
317	Eric Show	.07	.05	.03		408	Brook Jacoby	.10	.08	.04
318	Todd Simmons	.10	.08	.04		409	Doug Jones	.12	.09	.05
319	Garry Templeton	.07	.05	.03		410	*Jeff Kaiser*(FC)	.15	.11	.06
320	Dickie Thon	.05	.04	.02		411	*Luis Medina*(FC)	.30	.25	.12
321	Ed Whitson	.05	.04	.02		412	Cory Snyder	.15	.11	.06
322	Marvell Wynne	.05	.04	.02		413	Greg Swindell	.12	.09	.05
323	Mike Aldrete	.07	.05	.03		414	*Ron Tingley*(FC)	.15	.11	.06
324	Brett Butler	.07	.05	.03		415	Willie Upshaw	.07	.05	.03
325	Will Clark	.80	.60	.30		416	Ron Washington	.05	.04	.02
326	Kelly Downs	.10	.08	.04		417	Rich Yett	.05	.04	.02
327	Dave Dravecky	.07	.05	.03		418	Damon Berryhill	.12	.09	.05
328	Scott Garrelts	.05	.04	.02		419	Mike Bielecki	.05	.04	.02
329	Atlee Hammaker	.05	.04	.02		420	*Doug Dascenzo*(FC)	.30	.25	.12
330	*Charlie Hayes*(FC)	.30	.25	.12		421	Jody Davis	.07	.05	.03
331	Mike Krukow	.07	.05	.03		422	Andre Dawson	.20	.15	.08
332	Craig Lefferts	.05	.04	.02		423	Frank DiPino	.05	.04	.02
333	Candy Maldonado	.07	.05	.03		424	Shawon Dunston	.10	.08	.04
334	Kirt Manwaring	.10	.08	.04		425	"Goose" Gossage	.12	.09	.05
335	Bob Melvin	.05	.04	.02		426	Mark Grace	1.75	1.25	.70
336	Kevin Mitchell	.60	.45	.25		427	*Mike Harkey*(FC)	.50	.40	.20
337	Donell Nixon	.05	.04	.02		428	Darrin Jackson	.07	.05	.03
338	*Tony Perezchica*(FC)	.15	.11	.06		429	Les Lancaster	.07	.05	.03
339	Joe Price	.05	.04	.02		430	Vance Law	.07	.05	.03
340	Rick Reuschel	.10	.08	.04		431	Greg Maddux	.12	.09	.05
341	Earnest Riles	.05	.04	.02		432	Jamie Moyer	.05	.04	.02
342	Don Robinson	.05	.04	.02		433	Al Nipper	.05	.04	.02
343	Chris Speier	.05	.04	.02		434	Rafael Palmeiro	.15	.11	.06
344	Robby Thompson	.07	.05	.03		435	Pat Perry	.05	.04	.02
345	Jose Uribe	.05	.04	.02		436	*Jeff Pico*	.25	.20	.10
346	Matt Williams	.12	.09	.05		437	Ryne Sandberg	.25	.20	.10
347	*Trevor Wilson*(FC)	.15	.11	.06		438	Calvin Schiraldi	.05	.04	.02
348	Juan Agosto	.05	.04	.02		439	Rick Sutcliffe	.10	.08	.04
349	Larry Andersen	.05	.04	.02		440	Manny Trillo	.05	.04	.02
350	Alan Ashby	.05	.04	.02		441	*Gary Varsho*	.20	.15	.08
351	Kevin Bass	.07	.05	.03		442	Mitch Webster	.07	.05	.03
352	Buddy Bell	.07	.05	.03		443	*Luis Alicea*	.20	.15	.08
353	*Craig Biggio*	.90	.70	.35		444	Tom Brunansky	.12	.09	.05
354	Danny Darwin	.05	.04	.02		445	Vince Coleman	.15	.11	.06
355	Glenn Davis	.25	.20	.10		446	*John Costello*	.20	.15	.08
356	Jim Deshaies	.05	.04	.02		447	Danny Cox	.07	.05	.03
357	Bill Doran	.07	.05	.03		448	Ken Dayley	.05	.04	.02
358	*John Fishel*	.20	.15	.08		449	Jose DeLeon	.07	.05	.03
359	Billy Hatcher	.07	.05	.03		450	Curt Ford	.05	.04	.02
360	Bob Knepper	.07	.05	.03		451	Pedro Guerrero	.15	.11	.06
361	*Louie Meadows*	.15	.11	.06		452	Bob Horner	.10	.08	.04
362	Dave Meads	.05	.04	.02		453	*Tim Jones*(FC)	.15	.11	.06
363	Jim Pankovits	.05	.04	.02		454	Steve Lake	.05	.04	.02
364	Terry Puhl	.05	.04	.02		455	Joe Magrane	.10	.08	.04
365	Rafael Ramirez	.05	.04	.02		456	Greg Mathews	.07	.05	.03
366	Craig Reynolds	.05	.04	.02		457	Willie McGee	.12	.09	.05
367	Mike Scott	.12	.09	.05		458	Larry McWilliams	.05	.04	.02
368	Nolan Ryan	.40	.30	.15		459	Jose Oquendo	.05	.04	.02
369	Dave Smith	.07	.05	.03		460	Tony Pena	.07	.05	.03
370	Gerald Young	.12	.09	.05		461	Terry Pendleton	.10	.08	.04
371	Hubie Brooks	.10	.08	.04		462	*Steve Peters*(FC)	.15	.11	.06
372	Tim Burke	.05	.04	.02		463	Ozzie Smith	.15	.11	.06
373	*John Dopson*	.25	.20	.10		464	Scott Terry	.08	.06	.03
374	Mike Fitzgerald	.05	.04	.02		465	Denny Walling	.05	.04	.02
375	Tom Foley	.05	.04	.02		466	Todd Worrell	.10	.08	.04
376	Andres Galarraga	.15	.11	.06		467	Tony Armas	.07	.05	.03
377	Neal Heaton	.05	.04	.02		468	*Dante Bichette*(FC)	.30	.25	.12
378	Joe Hesketh	.05	.04	.02		469	Bob Boone	.07	.05	.03
379	*Brian Holman*	.35	.25	.14		470	*Terry Clark*(FC)	.15	.11	.06
380	Rex Hudler	.05	.04	.02		471	*Stew Cliburn*(FC)	.05	.04	.02
381	*Randy Johnson*(FC)	.50	.40	.20		472	*Mike Cook*(FC)	.15	.11	.06
382	Wallace Johnson	.05	.04	.02		473	*Sherman Corbett*	.15	.11	.06
383	Tracy Jones	.10	.08	.04		474	Chili Davis	.07	.05	.03
384	Dave Martinez	.07	.05	.03		475	Brian Downing	.07	.05	.03
385	Dennis Martinez	.07	.05	.03		476	Jim Eppard	.07	.05	.03
386	Andy McGaffigan	.05	.04	.02		477	Chuck Finley	.05	.04	.02
387	Otis Nixon	.05	.04	.02		478	Willie Fraser	.05	.04	.02
388	*Johnny Paredes*(FC)	.20	.15	.08		479	*Bryan Harvey*	.25	.20	.10
389	Jeff Parrett	.10	.08	.04		480	Jack Howell	.07	.05	.03
390	Pascual Perez	.07	.05	.03		481	Wally Joyner	.25	.20	.10
391	Tim Raines	.25	.20	.10		482	Jack Lazorko	.05	.04	.02
392	Luis Rivera	.05	.04	.02		483	Kirk McCaskill	.07	.05	.03
393	*Nelson Santovenia*	.25	.20	.10		484	Mark McLemore	.05	.04	.02
394	Bryn Smith	.05	.04	.02		485	Greg Minton	.05	.04	.02
395	Tim Wallach	.10	.08	.04		486	Dan Petry	.07	.05	.03
396	Andy Allanson	.05	.04	.02		487	Johnny Ray	.07	.05	.03
397	*Rod Allen*	.15	.11	.06		488	Dick Schofield	.05	.04	.02
398	Scott Bailes	.05	.04	.02		489	Devon White	.12	.09	.05
399	Tom Candiotti	.05	.04	.02		490	Mike Witt	.07	.05	.03
400	Joe Carter	.12	.09	.05		491	Harold Baines	.12	.09	.05

		MT	NR MT	EX
492	Daryl Boston	.05	.04	.02
493	Ivan Calderon	.07	.05	.03
494	Mike Diaz	.07	.05	.03
495	Carlton Fisk	.20	.15	.08
496	*Dave Gallagher*	.25	.20	.10
497	Ozzie Guillen	.07	.05	.03
498	Shawn Hillegas	.07	.05	.03
499	Lance Johnson	.07	.05	.03
500	Barry Jones	.05	.04	.02
501	Bill Long	.07	.05	.03
502	Steve Lyons	.05	.04	.02
503	Fred Manrique	.07	.05	.03
504	Jack McDowell	.10	.08	.04
505	*Donn Pall*	.20	.15	.08
506	Kelly Paris	.05	.04	.02
507	Dan Pasqua	.10	.08	.04
508	*Ken Patterson*	.20	.15	.08
509	Melido Perez	.10	.08	.04
510	Jerry Reuss	.07	.05	.03
511	Mark Salas	.05	.04	.02
512	Bobby Thigpen	.10	.08	.04
513	Mike Woodard	.05	.04	.02
514	Bob Brower	.05	.04	.02
515	Steve Buechele	.05	.04	.02
516	*Jose Cecena*	.15	.11	.06
517	Cecil Espy	.07	.05	.03
518	Scott Fletcher	.07	.05	.03
519	Cecilio Guante	.05	.04	.02
520	Jose Guzman	.10	.08	.04
521	Ray Hayward	.05	.04	.02
522	Charlie Hough	.07	.05	.03
523	Pete Incaviglia	.12	.09	.05
524	Mike Jeffcoat	.05	.04	.02
525	Paul Kilgus	.10	.08	.04
526	*Chad Kreuter*(FC)	.20	.15	.08
527	Jeff Kunkel	.05	.04	.02
528	Oddibe McDowell	.07	.05	.03
529	Pete O'Brien	.07	.05	.03
530	Geno Petralli	.05	.04	.02
531	Jeff Russell	.05	.04	.02
532	Ruben Sierra	.50	.40	.20
533	Mike Stanley	.05	.04	.02
534	Ed Vande Berg	.05	.04	.02
535	Curtis Wilkerson	.05	.04	.02
536	Mitch Williams	.07	.05	.03
537	Bobby Witt	.10	.08	.04
538	Steve Balboni	.07	.05	.03
539	Scott Bankhead	.05	.04	.02
540	Scott Bradley	.05	.04	.02
541	Mickey Brantley	.05	.04	.02
542	Jay Buhner(FC)	.10	.08	.04
543	Mike Campbell	.10	.08	.04
544	Darnell Coles	.07	.05	.03
545	Henry Cotto	.05	.04	.02
546	Alvin Davis	.12	.09	.05
547	Mario Diaz	.07	.05	.03
548	*Ken Griffey, Jr.*(FC)	12.00	9.00	4.75
549	*Erik Hanson*(FC)	.80	.60	.30
550	Mike Jackson	.07	.05	.03
551	Mark Langston	.10	.08	.04
552	Edgar Martinez	.20	.15	.08
553	*Bill McGuire*(FC)	.15	.11	.06
554	Mike Moore	.05	.04	.02
555	Jim Presley	.07	.05	.03
556	Rey Quinones	.05	.04	.02
557	Jerry Reed	.05	.04	.02
558	Harold Reynolds	.07	.05	.03
559	*Mike Schooler*(FC)	.35	.25	.14
560	Bill Swift	.05	.04	.02
561	Dave Valle	.05	.04	.02
562	Steve Bedrosian	.10	.08	.04
563	Phil Bradley	.10	.08	.04
564	Don Carman	.07	.05	.03
565	Bob Dernier	.05	.04	.02
566	Marvin Freeman	.05	.04	.02
567	Todd Frohwirth	.07	.05	.03
568	Greg Gross	.05	.04	.02
569	Kevin Gross	.07	.05	.03
570	Greg Harris	.05	.04	.02
571	Von Hayes	.10	.08	.04
572	Chris James	.10	.08	.04
573	Steve Jeltz	.05	.04	.02
574	*Ron Jones*(FC)	.35	.25	.14
575	*Ricky Jordan*	.80	.60	.30
576	Mike Maddux	.05	.04	.02
577	David Palmer	.05	.04	.02
578	Lance Parrish	.15	.11	.06
579	Shane Rawley	.07	.05	.03
580	Bruce Ruffin	.05	.04	.02
581	Juan Samuel	.12	.09	.05
582	Mike Schmidt	.50	.40	.20

		MT	NR MT	EX
583	Kent Tekulve	.07	.05	.03
584	Milt Thompson	.05	.04	.02
585	*Jose Alvarez*	.15	.11	.06
586	Paul Assenmacher	.05	.04	.02
587	Bruce Benedict	.05	.04	.02
588	Jeff Blauser	.10	.08	.04
589	*Terry Blocker*(FC)	.15	.11	.06
590	Ron Gant	.12	.09	.05
591	Tom Glavine	.10	.08	.04
592	Tommy Gregg	.10	.08	.04
593	Albert Hall	.05	.04	.02
594	Dion James	.05	.04	.02
595	Rick Mahler	.05	.04	.02
596	Dale Murphy	.40	.30	.15
597	Gerald Perry	.10	.08	.04
598	Charlie Puleo	.05	.04	.02
599	Ted Simmons	.10	.08	.04
600	Pete Smith	.10	.08	.04
601	Zane Smith	.07	.05	.03
602	*John Smoltz*	.90	.70	.35
603	Bruce Sutter	.10	.08	.04
604	Andres Thomas	.07	.05	.03
605	Ozzie Virgil	.05	.04	.02
606	*Brady Anderson*(FC)	.35	.25	.14
607	Jeff Ballard	.07	.05	.03
608	*Jose Bautista*	.20	.15	.08
609	Ken Gerhart	.07	.05	.03
610	Terry Kennedy	.07	.05	.03
611	Eddie Murray	.30	.25	.12
612	Carl Nichols(FC)	.10	.08	.04
613	Tom Niedenfuer	.07	.05	.03
614	Joe Orsulak	.05	.04	.02
615	*Oswaldo Peraza (Oswald)*(FC)	.20	.15	.08
616a	Bill Ripken (obscenity on bat)	18.00	13.50	7.25
616b	Bill Ripken (obscenity on bat scrawled out in black)	15.00	11.00	6.00
616c	Bill Ripken (obscenity on bat blocked out in black)	1.00	.70	.40
616d	Bill Ripken (obscenity on bat whiteout)	30.00	22.00	12.50
617	Cal Ripken, Jr.	.35	.25	.14
618	Dave Schmidt	.05	.04	.02
619	Rick Schu	.05	.04	.02
620	Larry Sheets	.07	.05	.03
621	Doug Sisk	.05	.04	.02
622	Pete Stanicek	.10	.08	.04
623	Mickey Tettleton	.05	.04	.02
624	Jay Tibbs	.05	.04	.02
625	Jim Traber	.07	.05	.03
626	Mark Williamson	.07	.05	.03
627	*Craig Worthington*	.40	.30	.15
628	Speed and Power (Jose Canseco)	.80	.60	.30
629	Pitcher Perfect (Tom Browning)	.10	.08	.04
630	Like Father - Like Sons (Roberto Alomar, Sandy Alomar, Jr.)	.40	.30	.15
631	N.L. All-Stars (Will Clark, Rafael Palmeiro)	.40	.30	.15
632	Homeruns Coast to Coast (Will Clark, Darryl Strawberry)	.30	.25	.12
633	Hot Corner's - Hot Hitters (Wade Boggs, Carney Lansford)	.40	.30	.15
634	Triple A's (Jose Canseco, Mark McGwire, Terry Steinbach)	.60	.45	.25
635	Dual Heat (Mark Davis, Dwight Gooden)	.20	.15	.08
636	N.L. Pitching Power (David Cone, Danny Jackson)	.15	.11	.06
637	Cannon Arms (Bobby Bonilla, Chris Sabo)	.20	.15	.08
638	Double Trouble (Andres Galarraga, Gerald Perry)	.10	.08	.04
639	Power Center (Eric Davis, Kirby Puckett)	.30	.25	.12
640	Major League Prospects (*Cameron Drew, Steve Wilson*)(FC)	.25	.20	.10
641	Major League Prospects (*Kevin Brown, Kevin Reimer*)(FC)	.40	.30	.15
642	Major League Prospects (*Jerald Clark, Brad Pounders*)(FC)	.30	.25	.12
643	Major League Prospects (*Mike Capel, Drew Hall*)(FC)	.25	.20	.10
644	Major League Prospects (*Joe Girardi, Rolando Roomes*)(FC)	.50	.40	.20
645	Major League Prospects (*Marty Brown, Lenny Harris*)(FC)	.40	.30	.15
646	Major League Prospects (*Luis de los Santos, Jim Campbell*)(FC)	.30	.15	.08
647	Major League Prospects (*Miguel Garcia, Randy Kramer*)(FC)	.25	.20	.10
648	Major League Prospects (*Torey Lovullo, Robert Palacios*)(FC)	.25	.20	.10

		MT	NR MT	EX
649	Major League Prospects (Jim Corsi, Bob Milacki)(FC)	.25	.20	.10
650	Major League Prospects (Grady Hall, Mike Rochford)(FC)	.25	.20	.10
651	Major League Prospects (Vance Lovelace, Terry Taylor)(FC)	.25	.20	.10
652	Major League Prospects (Dennis Cook, Ken Hill)(FC)	.40	.30	.15
653	Major League Prospects (Scott Service, Shane Turner)(FC)	.25	.20	.10
654	Checklist 1-101	.05	.04	.02
655	Checklist 102-200	.05	.04	.02
656	Checklist 201-298	.05	.04	.02
657	Checklist 299-395	.05	.04	.02
658	Checklist 396-490	.05	.04	.02
659	Checklist 491-584	.05	.04	.02
660	Checklist 585-660	.05	.04	.02

1989 Fleer All Star Team

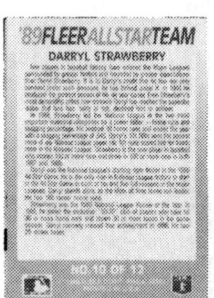

This special 12-card set represents Fleer's choices for its 1989 Major League All-Star Team. For the fourth consecutive year, Fleer inserted the special cards randomly inside their regular 1989 wax and cello packs. The cards feature two player photos set against a green background with the "1989 Fleer All Star Team" logo bannered across the top, and the player's name, position and team in the lower left corner. The backs contain a several-paragraph player profile.

		MT	NR MT	EX
Complete Set:		13.00	9.75	5.25
Common Player:		.50	.40	.20
1	Bobby Bonilla	.60	.45	.25
2	Jose Canseco	2.00	1.50	.80
3	Will Clark	2.50	2.00	1.00
4	Dennis Eckersley	.50	.40	.20
5	Julio Franco	.60	.45	.25
6	Mike Greenwell	1.00	.70	.40
7	Orel Hershiser	1.00	.70	.40
8	Paul Molitor	.70	.50	.30
9	Mike Scioscia	.50	.40	.20
10	Darryl Strawberry	1.25	.90	.50
11	Alan Trammell	1.00	.70	.40
12	Frank Viola	.80	.60	.30

1989 Fleer Baseball All Stars

This specially-boxed set was produced by Fleer for the Ben Franklin store chain. The full-color player photos are surrounded by a border of pink and yellow vertical bands. "Fleer Baseball All-Stars" appears along the top in red, white and blue. The set was sold in a box with a checklist on the back.

	MT	NR MT	EX
Complete Set:	4.00	3.00	1.50

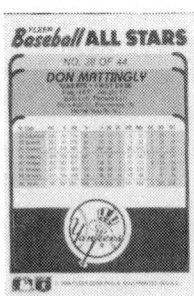

Common Player:		.05	.04	.02
1	Doyle Alexander	.05	.04	.02
2	George Bell	.12	.09	.05
3	Wade Boggs	.70	.50	.30
4	Bobby Bonilla	.08	.06	.04
5	Jose Canseco	.80	.60	.30
6	Will Clark	.90	.70	.35
7	Roger Clemens	.30	.25	.12
8	Vince Coleman	.15	.11	.06
9	David Cone	.15	.11	.06
10	Mark Davis	.08	.06	.03
11	Andre Dawson	.10	.08	.04
12	Dennis Eckersley	.08	.06	.03
13	Andres Galarraga	.12	.09	.05
14	Kirk Gibson	.12	.09	.05
15	Dwight Gooden	.30	.25	.12
16	Mike Greenwell	.70	.50	.30
17	Mark Gubicza	.08	.06	.03
18	Ozzie Guillen	.05	.04	.02
19	Tony Gwynn	.20	.15	.08
20	Rickey Henderson	.15	.08	.04
21	Orel Hershiser	.20	.15	.08
22	Danny Jackson	.05	.04	.02
23	Doug Jones	.05	.04	.02
24	Ricky Jordan	.50	.40	.20
25	Bob Knepper	.05	.04	.02
26	Barry Larkin	.20	.15	.08
27	Vance Law	.05	.04	.02
28	Don Mattingly	1.00	.70	.40
29	Mark McGwire	.80	.60	.30
30	Paul Molitor	.08	.06	.02
31	Gerald Perry	.05	.04	.02
32	Kirby Puckett	.35	.25	.12
33	Johnny Ray	.05	.04	.02
34	Harold Reynolds	.08	.06	.03
35	Cal Ripken, Jr.	.15	.11	.06
36	Don Robinson	.05	.04	.02
37	Ruben Sierra	.30	.25	.12
38	Dave Smith	.05	.04	.02
39	Darryl Strawberry	.35	.25	.14
40	Dave Steib	.08	.06	.03
41	Alan Trammell	.15	.11	.06
42	Andy Van Slyke	.10	.08	.04
43	Frank Viola	.15	.11	.06
44	Dave Winfield	.15	.11	.06

1989 Fleer Update

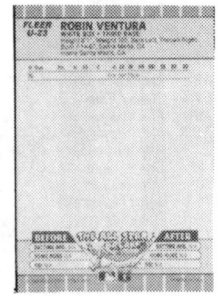

Fleer produced its sixth consecutive "Update"

set in 1989 to supplement the company's regular set. As in the past, the set consisted of 132 cards (numbered U-1 through U-132) that were sold by hobby dealers in special collector's boxes.

		MT	NR MT	EX
	Complete Set:	15.00	11.00	6.00
	Common Player:	.06	.05	.02
1	Phil Bradley	.06	.05	.02
2	Mike Devereaux	.10	.08	.04
3	Steve Finley(FC)	.30	.25	.12
4	Kevin Hickey	.06	.05	.02
5	Brian Holton	.06	.05	.02
6	Bob Milacki	.20	.15	.08
7	Randy Milligan	.10	.08	.04
8	John Dopson	.15	.11	.06
9	Nick Esasky	.10	.08	.04
10	Rob Murphy	.06	.05	.02
11	Jim Abbott(FC)	1.00	.70	.40
12	Bert Blyleven	.06	.05	.02
13	Jeff Manto(FC)	.30	.25	.12
14	Bob McClure	.06	.05	.02
15	Lance Parrish	.06	.05	.02
16	Lee Stevens(FC)	.50	.40	.20
17	Claudell Washington	.06	.05	.02
18	Mark Davis	.06	.05	.02
19	Eric King	.06	.05	.02
20	Ron Kittle	.06	.05	.02
21	Matt Merullo(FC)	.25	.20	.10
22	Steve Rosenberg(FC)	.08	.06	.03
23	Robin Ventura(FC)	1.00	.70	.40
24	Keith Atherton	.06	.05	.02
25	Joey Belle(FC)	.50	.40	.20
26	Jerry Browne	.06	.05	.02
27	Felix Fermin	.06	.05	.02
28	Brad Komminsk	.06	.05	.02
29	Pete O'Brien	.06	.05	.02
30	Mike Brumley	.06	.05	.02
31	Tracy Jones	.06	.05	.02
32	Mike Schwabe(FC)	.30	.25	.12
33	Gary Ward	.06	.05	.02
34	Frank Williams	.06	.05	.02
35	Kevin Appier(FC)	.60	.45	.25
36	Bob Boone	.06	.05	.02
37	Luis de los Santos	.10	.08	.04
38	Jim Eisenreich(FC)	.06	.05	.02
39	Jaime Navarro(FC)	.30	.25	.12
40	Bill Spiers(FC)	.40	.30	.15
41	Greg Vaughn(FC)	1.75	1.25	.70
42	Randy Veres(FC)	.20	.15	.08
43	Wally Backman	.06	.05	.02
44	Shane Rawley	.06	.05	.02
45	Steve Balboni	.06	.05	.02
46	Jesse Barfield	.06	.05	.02
47	Alvaro Espinosa(FC)	.30	.25	.12
48	Bob Geren(FC)	.40	.30	.15
49	Mel Hall	.06	.05	.02
50	Andy Hawkins	.06	.05	.02
51	Hensley Meulens(FC)	.50	.40	.20
52	Steve Sax	.15	.11	.06
53	Deion Sanders(FC)	.80	.60	.30
54	Rickey Henderson	.40	.30	.15
55	Mike Moore	.10	.08	.04
56	Tony Phillips	.06	.05	.02
57	Greg Briley(FC)	.50	.40	.20
58	Gene Harris	.10	.08	.04
59	Randy Johnson	.08	.06	.03
60	Jeffrey Leonard	.06	.05	.02
61	Dennis Powell	.06	.05	.02
62	Omar Vizquel(FC)	.30	.25	.12
63	Kevin Brown	.08	.06	.03
64	Julio Franco	.15	.11	.06
65	Jamie Moyer	.06	.05	.02
66	Rafael Palmeiro	.15	.11	.06
67	Nolan Ryan	1.75	1.25	.70
68	Francisco Cabrera(FC)	.30	.25	.12
69	Junior Felix(FC)	1.25	.90	.50
70	Al Leiter	.06	.05	.02
71	Alex Sanchez(FC)	.20	.15	.08
72	Geronimo Berroa(FC)	.08	.06	.03
73	Derek Lilliquist(FC)	.20	.15	.08
74	Lonnie Smith	.10	.08	.04
75	Jeff Treadway	.06	.05	.02
76	Paul Kilgus	.06	.05	.02
77	Lloyd McClendon	.15	.11	.06
78	Scott Sanderson	.06	.05	.02
79	Dwight Smith(FC)	.60	.45	.25
80	Jerome Walton(FC)	1.50	1.25	.60
81	Mitch Williams	.20	.15	.08
82	Steve Wilson	.25	.20	.10
83	Todd Benzinger	.06	.05	.02
84	Ken Griffey	.20	.15	.08
85	Rick Mahler	.06	.05	.02
86	Rolando Roomes	.20	.15	.08
87	Scott Scudder(FC)	.30	.25	.12
88	Jim Clancy	.06	.05	.02
89	Rick Rhoden	.06	.05	.02
90	Dan Schatzeder	.06	.05	.02
91	Mike Morgan	.06	.05	.02
92	Eddie Murray	.20	.15	.08
93	Willie Randolph	.06	.05	.02
94	Ray Searage	.06	.05	.02
95	Mike Aldrete	.06	.05	.02
96	Kevin Gross	.06	.05	.02
97	Mark Langston	.15	.11	.06
98	Spike Owen	.06	.05	.02
99	Zane Smith	.06	.05	.02
100	Don Aase	.06	.05	.02
101	Barry Lyons	.06	.05	.02
102	Juan Samuel	.06	.05	.02
103	Wally Whitehurst(FC)	.20	.15	.08
104	Dennis Cook	.25	.20	.10
105	Lenny Dykstra	.06	.05	.02
106	Charlie Hayes(FC)	.10	.08	.04
107	Tommy Herr	.06	.05	.02
108	Ken Howell	.06	.05	.02
109	John Kruk	.06	.05	.02
110	Roger McDowell	.06	.05	.02
111	Terry Mulholland(FC)	.06	.05	.02
112	Jeff Parrett	.06	.05	.02
113	Neal Heaton	.06	.05	.02
114	Jeff King	.10	.08	.04
115	Randy Kramer	.06	.05	.02
116	Bill Landrum	.06	.05	.02
117	Cris Carpenter(FC)	.25	.20	.10
118	Frank DiPino	.06	.05	.02
119	Ken Hill	.15	.11	.06
120	Dan Quisenberry	.06	.05	.02
121	Milt Thompson	.06	.05	.02
122	Todd Zeile(FC)	1.50	1.25	.60
123	Jack Clark	.10	.08	.04
124	Bruce Hurst	.06	.05	.02
125	Mark Parent	.06	.05	.02
126	Bip Roberts	.06	.05	.02
127	Jeff Brantley(FC)	.25	.20	.10
128	Terry Kennedy	.06	.05	.02
129	Mike LaCoss	.06	.05	.02
130	Greg Litton(FC)	.25	.20	.10
131	Mike Schmidt	2.00	1.50	.80
132	Checklist	.06	.05	.02

1989 Fleer Baseball MVP

Filled with superstars, this 44-card boxed set was produced by Fleer in 1989 for the Toys 'R' Us chain. The fronts of the cards are designed in a yellow and green color scheme and include a "Fleer Baseball MVP" logo above the color player photo. The backs are printed in shades of green and yellow and include biographical notes and stats. The set was issued in a special box with a checklist on the back.

		MT	NR MT	EX
	Complete Set:	3.75	2.75	1.50
	Common Player:	.05	.04	.02
1	Steve Bedrosian	.05	.04	.02

		MT	NR MT	EX				MT	NR MT	EX
2	George Bell	.12	.09	.05	8	David Cone		.15	.11	.06
3	Wade Boggs	.70	.50	.30	9	Eric Davis		.20	.15	.08
4	George Brett	.15	.11	.06	10	Glenn Davis		.15	.11	.06
5	Hubie Brooks	.05	.04	.02	11	Andre Dawson		.12	.09	.05
6	Jose Canseco	.90	.70	.35	12	Dwight Evans		.09	.07	.04
7	Will Clark	.90	.70	.35	13	Andres Galarraga		.12	.09	.05
8	Roger Clemens	.30	.25	.12	14	Kirk Gibson		.12	.09	.05
9	Eric Davis	.20	.15	.08	15	Dwight Gooden		.30	.25	.12
10	Glenn Davis	.12	.09	.05	16	Jim Gott		.05	.04	.02
11	Andre Dawson	.12	.09	.05	17	Mark Grace		.30	.25	.12
12	Andres Galarraga	.12	.09	.05	18	Mike Greenwell		.70	.50	.30
13	Kirk Gibson	.15	.11	.06	19	Mark Gibicza		.07	.05	.03
14	Dwight Gooden	.30	.25	.12	20	Tony Gwynn		.20	.15	.08
15	Mark Grace	.25	.20	.10	21	Rickey Henderson		.20	.15	.08
16	Mike Greenwell	.50	.40	.20	22	Tom Henke		.05	.04	.02
17	Tony Gwynn	.20	.15	.08	23	Mike Henneman		.05	.04	.02
18	Bryan Harvey	.05	.04	.02	24	Orel Hershiser		.25	.20	.10
19	Orel Hershiser	.25	.20	.10	25	Danny Jackson		.05	.04	.02
20	Ted Higuera	.07	.05	.03	26	Gregg Jefferies		.80	.60	.30
21	Danny Jackson	.05	.04	.02	27	Ricky Jordan		.60	.45	.25
22	Mike Jackson	.05	.04	.02	28	Wally Joyner		.15	.11	.06
23	Doug Jones	.05	.04	.02	29	Mark Langston		.15	.11	.06
24	Greg Maddux	.07	.05	.03	30	Tim Leary		.05	.04	.02
25	Mike Marshall	.05	.04	.02	31	Don Mattingly		1.00	.70	.40
26	Don Mattingly	1.00	.70	.40	32	Mark McGwire		.80	.60	.30
27	Fred McGriff	.30	.25	.12	33	Dale Murphy		.15	.11	.06
28	Mark McGwire	.80	.60	.30	34	Kirby Puckett		.35	.25	.14
29	Kevin McReynolds	.15	.11	.06	35	Chris Sabo		.30	.25	.12
30	Jack Morris	.05	.04	.02	36	Kevin Seitzer		.15	.11	.06
31	Gerald Perry	.05	.04	.02	37	Ruben Sierra		.30	.25	.12
32	Kirby Puckett	.35	.25	.12	38	Ozzie Smith		.15	.11	.06
33	Chris Sabo	.20	.15	.08	39	Dave Stewart		.07	.05	.03
34	Mike Scott	.12	.09	.05	40	Darryl Strawberry		.35	.25	.14
35	Ruben Sierra	.25	.20	.10	41	Alan Trammell		.15	.11	.06
36	Darryl Strawberry	.35	.25	.12	42	Frank Viola		.15	.11	.06
37	Danny Tartabull	.09	.07	.04	43	Dave Winfield		.15	.11	.06
38	Bobby Thigpen	.09	.07	.04	44	Robin Yount		.15	.11	.06
39	Alan Trammell	.15	.11	.06						
40	Andy Van Slyke	.12	.09	.05						
41	Frank Viola	.12	.09	.05						
42	Walt Weiss	.20	.15	.08						
43	Dave Winfield	.15	.11	.06						
44	Todd Worrell	.07	.05	.03						

1989 Fleer Baseball's Exciting Stars

Sold exclusively in Cumberland Farm stores, this 44-card boxed set pictures the game's top stars. The card fronts feature a color player photo surrounded by a blue border with "Baseball's Exciting Stars" along the top. The cards were were numbered alphabetically and packed in a special box with a complete checklist on the back.

		MT	NR MT	EX
Complete Set:		4.00	3.00	1.50
Common Player:		.05	.04	.02
1	Harold Baines	.07	.05	.03
2	Wade Boggs	.70	.50	.30
3	Jose Canseco	.90	.70	.35
4	Joe Carter	.12	.09	.05
5	Will Clark	.90	.70	.35
6	Roger Clemens	.30	.25	.12
7	Vince Coleman	.15	.11	.06

1989 Fleer Heroes of Baseball

Robin Yount

This 44-card boxed set was produced by Fleer for the Woolworth store chain. The fronts of the cards are designed in a red and blue color scheme and feature full-color photos that fade into a soft focus on all edges. "Fleer Heroes of Baseball" appears just above the player's name, team and position at the bottom of the card. The set is numbered alphabetically and was packaged in a special box with a checklist on the back.

		MT	NR MT	EX
Complete Set:		3.75	2.75	1.50
Common Player:		.05	.04	.02
1	George Bell	.12	.09	.05
2	Wade Boggs	.70	.50	.30
3	Barry Bonds	.12	.09	.05
4	Tom Brunansky	.08	.06	.03
5	Jose Canseco	.90	.70	.35
6	Joe Carter	.12	.09	.05
7	Will Clark	.90	.70	.35
8	Roger Clemens	.30	.25	.12
9	David Cone	.15	.11	.06
10	Eric Davis	.40	.30	.15
11	Glenn Davis	.12	.09	.05
12	Andre Dawson	.12	.09	.05
13	Dennis Eckersley	.07	.05	.03
14	John Franco	.05	.04	.02

		MT	NR MT	EX				MT	NR MT	EX
15	Gary Gaetti	.12	.09	.05		16	Dwight Gooden	.30	.25	.12
16	Andres Galarraga	.15	.11	.06		17	Mark Grace	.30	.25	.12
17	Kirk Gibson	.12	.09	.05		18	Mike Greenwell	.60	.45	.25
18	Dwight Gooden	.30	.25	.12		19	Tony Gwynn	.20	.15	.08
19	Mike Greenwell	.50	.40	.20		20	Orel Hershiser	.25	.20	.10
20	Tony Gwynn	.25	.20	.10		21	Pete Incaviglia	.05	.04	.02
21	Bryan Harvey	.05	.04	.02		22	Danny Jackson	.05	.04	.02
22	Orel Hershiser	.20	.15	.08		23	Gregg Jefferies	.90	.70	.35
23	Ted Higuera	.07	.05	.03		24	Joe Magrane	.09	.07	.05
24	Danny Jackson	.05	.04	.02		25	Don Mattingly	1.00	.70	.40
25	Ricky Jordan	.40	.30	.15		26	Fred McGriff	.30	.25	.12
26	Don Mattingly	1.00	.70	.40		27	Mark McGwire	.80	.60	.30
27	Fred McGriff	.30	.25	.12		28	Dale Murphy	.15	.11	.06
28	Mark McGwire	.60	.45	.25		29	Dan Plesac	.07	.05	.03
29	Kevin McReynolds	.15	.11	.06		30	Kirby Puckett	.40	.30	.15
30	Gerald Perry	.05	.04	.02		31	Harold Reynolds	.12	.09	.05
31	Kirby Puckett	.30	.25	.12		32	Cal Ripken, Jr.	.15	.11	.06
32	Johnny Ray	.05	.04	.02		33	Jeff Robinson	.05	.04	.02
33	Harold Reynolds	.05	.04	.02		34	Mike Scott	.12	.09	.05
34	Cal Ripken, Jr.	.15	.11	.06		35	Ozzie Smith	.15	.09	.05
35	Ryne Sandberg	.15	.11	.06		36	Dave Stewart	.07	.05	.03
36	Kevin Seitzer	.15	.11	.06		37	Darryl Strawberry	.30	.25	.12
37	Ruben Sierra	.30	.25	.12		38	Greg Swindell	.15	.11	.06
38	Darryl Strawberry	.30	.25	.12		39	Bobby Thigpen	.08	.06	.03
39	Bobby Thigpen	.05	.04	.02		40	Alan Trammell	.12	.09	.05
40	Alan Trammell	.12	.09	.05		41	Andy Van Slyke	.12	.09	.05
41	Andy Van Slyke	.10	.08	.04		42	Frank Viola	.12	.09	.05
42	Frank Viola	.15	.11	.06		43	Dave Winfield	.12	.09	.05
43	Dave Winfield	.15	.11	.06		44	Robin Yount	.20	.15	.08
44	Robin Yount	.20	.15	.08						

1989 Fleer League Leaders

Roger Clemens

Another of the various small, boxed sets issued by Fleer, the 44-card "League Leaders" set was produced for Walgreen stores. The standard-size cards feature color photos on the front surrounded by a red border with "Fleer League Leaders" across the top. The player's name, team and position appear in a yellow band at the bottom. The backs include player stats and data and the team logo. The cards are numbered alphabetically and packaged in a special box that includes the full checklist on the back.

		MT	NR MT	EX
Complete Set:		4.00	3.00	1.50
Common Player:		.05	.04	.02
1	Allan Anderson	.05	.04	.02
2	Wade Boggs	.70	.50	.30
3	Jose Canseco	.90	.70	.35
4	Will Clark	.90	.70	.35
5	Roger Clemens	.30	.25	.12
6	Vince Coleman	.15	.11	.06
7	David Cone	.15	.11	.06
8	Kal Daniels	.12	.09	.05
9	Chili Davis	.05	.04	.02
10	Eric Davis	.20	.15	.08
11	Glenn Davis	.15	.11	.06
12	Andre Dawson	.12	.09	.05
13	John Franco	.05	.04	.02
14	Andres Galarraga	.12	.09	.05
15	Kirk Gibson	.12	.09	.05

1989 Fleer Superstars

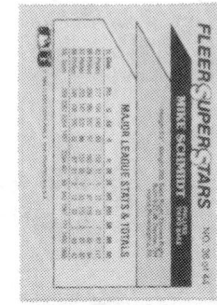

MIKE SCHMIDT THIRD BASE

This 44-card boxed set was produced by Fleer for the McCrory store chain. The cards are the standard 2-1/2" by 3-1/2" and the full-color player photos are outlined with a tan-and-white striped border. The player's name, position and team logo appear at the bottom of the card. The backs carry yellow and white stripes and include the Fleer "SuperStars" logo, player stats and biographical information. The cards are numbered alphabetically and packaged in a special box that includes a checklist on the back.

		MT	NR MT	EX
Complete Set:		4.00	3.00	1.50
Common Player:		.05	.04	.02
1	Roberto Alomar	.20	.15	.08
2	Harold Baines	.12	.09	.05
3	Tim Belcher	.12	.09	.05
4	Wade Boggs	.70	.50	.30
5	George Brett	.15	.11	.06
6	Jose Canseco	.90	.70	.35
7	Gary Carter	.05	.04	.02
8	Will Clark	.90	.70	.35
9	Roger Clemens	.30	.25	.12
10	Kal Daniels	.15	.11	.06
11	Eric Davis	.20	.15	.08
12	Andre Dawson	.12	.09	.05
13	Tony Fernandez	.12	.09	.05
14	Scott Fletcher	.05	.04	.02
15	Andres Galarraga	.15	.11	.06
16	Kirk Gibson	.15	.11	.06
17	Dwight Gooden	.30	.25	.12
18	Jim Gott	.05	.04	.02

		MT	NR MT	EX
19	Mark Grace	.30	.25	.12
20	Mike Greenwell	.50	.40	.20
21	Tony Gwynn	.20	.15	.08
22	Rickey Henderson	.20	.15	.08
23	Orel Hershiser	.20	.15	.08
24	Ted Higuera	.07	.05	.02
25	Gregg Jefferies	.90	.70	.35
26	Wally Joyner	.15	.11	.06
27	Mark Langston	.15	.11	.06
28	Greg Maddux	.15	.11	.06
29	Don Mattingly	1.00	.70	.40
30	Fred McGriff	.30	.25	.12
31	Mark McGwire	.80	.60	.30
32	Dan Plesac	.09	.07	.04
33	Kirby Puckett	.30	.25	.12
34	Jeff Reardon	.05	.04	.02
35	Chris Sabo	.12	.09	.05
36	Mike Schmidt	.25	.20	.10
37	Mike Scott	.10	.08	.04
38	Cory Snyder	.10	.08	.04
39	Darryl Strawberry	.30	.25	.12
40	Alan Trammell	.12	.09	.05
41	Frank Viola	.12	.09	.05
42	Walt Weiss	.12	.09	.05
43	Dave Winfield	.12	.09	.05
44	Todd Worrell	.05	.04	.02

		MT	NR MT	EX
25	Darryl Strawberry	.40	.30	.15
26	Alan Trammell	.20	.15	.08
27	Andy Van Slyke	.25	.20	.10
28	Frank Viola	.20	.15	.08

1989 Fleer For The Record

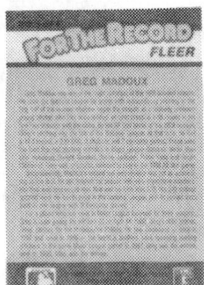

Fleer's "For the Record" set features six players and their achievements from 1988. Fronts of the standard 2-1/2" by 3-1/2" cards feature a full color photo of the player set against a red background. The words "For the Record" appear in blue script at the top of the card and the players name on the bottom, printed in white type. Card backs are grey and describe individual accomplishments. The cards were distributed randomly in rack packs.

		MT	NR MT	EX
Complete Set:		5.00	3.75	2.00
Common Player:		.80	.60	.30
1	Wade Boggs	1.25	.90	.60
2	Roger Clemens	1.00	.70	.40
3	Andres Galarraga	.80	.60	.30
4	Kirk Gibson	.80	.60	.30
5	Greg Maddux	1.00	.70	.40
6	Don Mattingly	1.75	1.25	.80

1989 Fleer Box Panels

For the fourth consecutive year, Fleer issued a series of cards on the bottom panels of its regular 1989 wax pack boxes. The 28-card set includes 20 players and eight team logo cards, all designed in the identical style of the regular 1989 Fleer set. The box-bottom cards were randomly printed, four cards (three player cards and one team logo) on each bottom panel. The cards were numbered from C-1 to C-28.

		MT	NR MT	EX
Complete Panel Set:		6.00	4.50	2.50
Complete Singles Set:		3.00	2.25	1.25
Common Single Player:		.15	.11	.06
1	Mets Logo	5.00	.04	.02
2	Wade Boggs	.40	.30	.15
3	George Brett	.25	.20	.10
4	Jose Canseco	.50	.40	.20
5	A's Logo	.05	.04	.02
6	Will Clark	.50	.40	.20
7	David Cone	.50	.40	.20
8	Andres Galarraga	.25	.20	.10
9	Dodgers Logo	.05	.04	.02
10	Kirk Gibson	.15	.11	.06
11	Mike Greenwell	.25	.20	.10
12	Tony Gwynn	.25	.20	.10
13	Tigers Logo	.05	.04	.02
14	Orel Hershiser	.20	.15	.08
15	Danny Jackson	.15	.11	.06
16	Wally Joyner	.50	.40	.20
17	Red Sox Logo	.05	.04	.02
18	Yankees Logo	.05	.04	.02
19	Fred McGriff	.60	.45	.25
20	Kirby Puckett	.30	.25	.12
21	Chris Sabo	.15	.11	.06
22	Kevin Seitzer	.30	.25	.12
23	Pirates Logo	.05	.04	.02
24	Astros Logo	.05	.04	.02

1989 Fleer '88 World Series

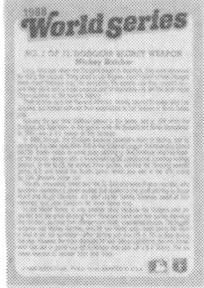

This 12-card set, which depicts highlights of the 1988 World Series, was included as a special sub-set with the regular factory-collated Fleer set. It was not available as individual cards in wax packs, cello packs or any other form.

	MT	NR MT	EX
Complete Set:	3.00	2.25	1.25
Common Player:	.25	.20	.10

		MT	NR MT	EX
1	Dodgers' Secret Weapon (Mickey Hatcher)	.25	.20	.10
2	Rookie Starts Series (Tim Belcher)	.35	.25	.14
3	Canseco Slams L.A. (Jose Canseco)	.40	.30	.20
4	Dramatic Comeback (Mike Scioscia)	.25	.20	.10
5	Gibson Steals The Show (Kirk Gibson)	.40	.30	.15
6	"Bulldog" (Orel Hershiser)	.30	.25	.12
7	One Swing, Three RBI's (Mike Marshall)	.25	.20	.10
8	Game-Winning Home Run (Mark McGwire)	.40	.30	.15
9	Sax's Speed Wins Game 4 (Steve Sax)	.25	.20	.10
10	Series Caps Award-Winning Year (Walt Weiss)	.25	.20	.10
11	The M.V.P. And His Shutout Magic (Orel Hershiser)	.35	.25	.14
12	Dodger Blue, World Champs	.25	.20	.10

1990 Fleer

Fleer's 1990 set, its 10th consecutive baseball card offering, again consisted of 660 cards numbered by team. The front of the cards feature mostly action photos surrounded by one of several different color bands and a white border. The "Fleer '90" logo appears in the upper left corner, while the team logo is the upper right. The player's name and position are printed in a flowing banner below the photo. The set includes various special cards, including a series of "Major League Prospects," Players of the Decade, team checklist cards and a series of multi-player cards. The backs include complete career stats, player data, and a special "Vital Signs" section showing on-base percentage, slugging percentage, etc. for batters; and strikeout and walk ratios, opposing batting averages, etc. for pitchers.

		MT	NR MT	EX
Complete Set:		22.00	16.50	8.75
Common Player:		.05	.04	.02
1	Lance Blankenship	.07	.05	.03
2	Todd Burns	.06	.05	.02
3	Jose Canseco	.60	.45	.25
4	Jim Corsi	.09	.07	.04
5	Storm Davis	.06	.05	.02
6	Dennis Eckersley	.12	.09	.05
7	Mike Gallego	.06	.05	.02
8	Ron Hassey	.05	.04	.02
9	Dave Henderson	.10	.08	.06
10	Rickey Henderson	.30	.25	.12
11	Rick Honeycutt	.05	.04	.02
12	Stan Javier	.05	.04	.02
13	Felix Jose	.12	.09	.05
14	Carney Lansford	.07	.05	.03
15	Mark McGwire	.35	.25	.12
16	Mike Moore	.10	.08	.04
17	Gene Nelson	.05	.04	.02
18	Dave Parker	.12	.09	.05
19	Tony Phillips	.05	.04	.02
20	Terry Steinbach	.10	.08	.06
21	Dave Stewart	.10	.08	.06

		MT	NR MT	EX
22	Walt Weiss	.10	.08	.06
23	Bob Welch	.06	.05	.03
24	Curt Young	.05	.04	.02
25	Paul Assenmacher	.05	.04	.02
26	Damon Berryhill	.10	.08	.04
27	Mike Bielecki	.10	.08	.04
28	Kevin Blankenship	.07	.05	.03
29	Andre Dawson	.12	.09	.05
30	Shawon Dunston	.09	.07	.04
31	Joe Girardi	.20	.15	.08
32	Mark Grace	.25	.20	.10
33	Mike Harkey	.12	.09	.05
34	Paul Kilgus	.05	.04	.02
35	Les Lancaster	.06	.05	.02
36	Vance Law	.05	.04	.02
37	Greg Maddux	.10	.08	.04
38	Lloyd McClendon	.10	.08	.04
39	Jeff Pico	.05	.04	.02
40	Ryne Sandberg	.15	.11	.06
41	Scott Sanderson	.05	.04	.02
42	Dwight Smith	.50	.40	.20
43	Rick Sutcliffe	.08	.06	.03
44	*Jerome Walton*	.80	.60	.30
45	Mitch Webster	.05	.04	.02
46	Curt Wilkerson	.05	.04	.02
47	*Dean Wilkins*(FC)	.25	.20	.10
48	Mitch Williams	.08	.06	.03
49	Steve Wilson	.15	.11	.06
50	Steve Bedrosian	.06	.05	.02
51	*Mike Benjamin*(FC)	.35	.25	.14
52	*Jeff Brantley*	.25	.20	.10
53	Brett Butler	.07	.05	.03
54	Will Clark	.50	.40	.20
55	Kelly Downs	.05	.04	.02
56	Scott Garrelts	.09	.07	.04
57	Atlee Hammaker	.05	.04	.02
58	Terry Kennedy	.05	.04	.02
59	Mike LaCoss	.05	.04	.02
60	Craig Lefferts	.06	.05	.02
61	*Greg Litton*	.25	.20	.10
62	Candy Maldonado	.06	.05	.02
63	Kirt Manwaring	.09	.07	.04
64	*Randy McCament*(FC)	.20	.15	.08
65	Kevin Mitchell	.30	.25	.12
66	Donell Nixon	.05	.04	.02
67	Ken Oberkfell	.05	.04	.02
68	Rick Reuschel	.09	.07	.04
69	Ernest Riles	.05	.04	.02
70	Don Robinson	.05	.04	.02
71	Pat Sheridan	.05	.04	.02
72	Chris Speier	.05	.04	.02
73	Robby Thompson	.07	.05	.03
74	Jose Uribe	.06	.05	.02
75	Matt Williams	.20	.15	.08
76	George Bell	.10	.08	.04
77	Pat Borders	.07	.05	.03
78	John Cerutti	.05	.04	.02
79	*Junior Felix*	.80	.60	.30
80	Tony Fernandez	.09	.07	.04
81	Mike Flanagan	.05	.04	.02
82	*Mauro Gozzo*(FC)	.20	.15	.08
83	Kelly Gruber	.07	.05	.03
84	Tom Henke	.05	.04	.02
85	Jimmy Key	.07	.05	.03
86	Manny Lee	.05	.04	.02
87	Nelson Liriano	.05	.04	.02
88	Lee Mazzilli	.05	.04	.02
89	Fred McGriff	.25	.20	.10
90	Lloyd Moseby	.06	.05	.02
91	Rance Mulliniks	.05	.04	.02
92	Alex Sanchez	.15	.11	.06
93	Dave Steib	.09	.07	.05
94	Todd Stottlemyre	.09	.07	.05
95	Duane Ward	.05	.04	.02
96	David Wells	.05	.04	.02
97	Ernie Whitt	.06	.05	.02
98	Frank Wills	.05	.04	.02
99	Mookie Wilson	.09	.07	.04
100	*Kevin Appier*(FC)	.35	.25	.14
101	Luis Aquino	.05	.04	.02
102	Bob Boone	.07	.05	.03
103	George Brett	.15	.11	.06
104	Jose DeJesus	.08	.06	.03
105	Luis de los Santos	.08	.06	.03
106	Jim Eisenreich	.05	.04	.02
107	Steve Farr	.05	.04	.02
108	Tom Gordon	.50	.40	.20
109	Mark Gubicza	.09	.07	.04
110	Bo Jackson	.35	.25	.14
111	Terry Leach	.05	.04	.02
112	Charlie Leibrandt	.05	.04	.02

	MT	NR MT	EX
113 Rick Luecken(FC)	.25	.20	.10
114 Mike Macfarlane	.05	.04	.02
115 Jeff Montgomery	.06	.05	.03
116 Bret Saberhagen	.10	.08	.04
117 Kevin Seitzer	.10	.08	.04
118 Kurt Stillwell	.06	.05	.02
119 Pat Tabler	.05	.04	.02
121 Gary Thurman	.05	.04	.02
122 Frank White	.07	.05	.03
123 Willie Wilson	.06	.05	.03
124 Matt Winters(FC)	.20	.15	.08
125 Jim Abbott	.90	.70	.35
126 Tony Armas	.05	.04	.02
127 Dante Bichette	.09	.07	.04
128 Bert Blyleven	.09	.07	.04
129 Chili Davis	.06	.05	.02
130 Brian Downing	.06	.05	.02
131 Mike Fetters(FC)	.35	.25	.12
132 Chuck Finley	.06	.05	.02
133 Willie Fraser	.05	.04	.02
134 Bryan Harvey	.05	.04	.02
135 Jack Howell	.05	.04	.02
136 Wally Joyner	.10	.08	.04
137 Jeff Manto	.20	.15	.08
138 Kirk McCaskill	.06	.05	.02
139 Bob McClure	.05	.04	.02
140 Greg Minton	.05	.04	.02
141 Lance Parrish	.07	.05	.02
142 Dan Petry	.05	.04	.02
143 Johnny Ray	.05	.04	.02
144 Dick Schofield	.06	.05	.02
145 Lee Stevens	.30	.25	.12
146 Claudell Washington	.06	.05	.02
147 Devon White	.08	.06	.03
148 Mike Witt	.06	.05	.02
149 Roberto Alomar	.10	.08	.04
150 Sandy Alomar, Jr.	.40	.30	.15
151 Andy Benes(FC)	.50	.40	.20
152 Jack Clark	.06	.05	.02
153 Pat Clements	.05	.04	.02
154 Joey Cora	.15	.11	.06
155 Mark Davis	.09	.07	.04
156 Mark Grant	.05	.04	.02
157 Tony Gwynn	.25	.20	.10
158 Greg Harris	.10	.08	.04
159 Bruce Hurst	.06	.05	.02
160 Darrin Jackson	.05	.04	.02
161 Chris James	.06	.05	.02
162 Carmelo Martinez	.06	.05	.02
163 Mike Pagliarulo	.06	.05	.02
164 Mark Parent	.05	.04	.02
165 Dennis Rasmussen	.05	.04	.02
166 Bip Roberts	.08	.06	.03
167 Benito Santiago	.12	.09	.05
168 Calvin Schiraldi	.05	.04	.02
169 Eric Show	.06	.05	.02
170 Garry Templeton	.06	.05	.02
171 Ed Whitson	.06	.05	.02
172 Brady Anderson	.07	.05	.03
173 Jeff Ballard	.07	.05	.03
174 Phil Bradley	.07	.05	.03
175 Mike Devereaux	.07	.05	.03
176 Steve Finley	.20	.15	.08
177 Pete Harnisch(FC)	.10	.08	.04
178 Kevin Hickey	.10	.08	.04
179 Brian Holton	.05	.04	.02
180 Ben McDonald(FC)	2.00	1.50	.80
181 Bob Melvin	.05	.04	.02
182 Bob Milacki	.07	.05	.03
183 Randy Milligan	.06	.05	.02
184 Gregg Olson(FC)	.60	.45	.25
185 Joe Orsulak	.05	.04	.02
186 Bill Ripken	.05	.04	.02
187 Cal Ripken, Jr.	.15	.11	.06
188 Dave Schmidt	.05	.04	.02
189 Larry Sheets	.05	.04	.02
190 Mickey Tettleton	.08	.06	.03
191 Mark Thurmond	.05	.04	.02
192 Jay Tibbs	.05	.04	.02
193 Jim Traber	.05	.04	.02
194 Mark Williamson	.05	.04	.02
195 Craig Worthington	.15	.11	.06
196 Don Aase	.05	.04	.02
197 Blaine Beatty(FC)	.35	.25	.12
198 Mark Carreon	.10	.08	.04
199 Gary Carter	.06	.05	.02
200 David Cone	.10	.08	.04
201 Ron Darling	.07	.05	.03
202 Kevin Elster	.05	.04	.02
203 Sid Fernandez	.09	.07	.04
204 Dwight Gooden	.20	.15	.08

	MT	NR MT	EX
205 Keith Hernandez	.06	.05	.02
206 Jeff Innis	.15	.11	.06
207 Gregg Jefferies	.50	.40	.20
208 Howard Johnson	.15	.11	.06
209 Barry Lyons	.05	.04	.02
210 Dave Magadan	.06	.05	.02
211 Kevin McReynolds	.07	.05	.03
212 Jeff Musselman	.05	.04	.02
213 Randy Myers	.06	.05	.02
214 Bob Ojeda	.06	.05	.02
215 Juan Samuel	.06	.05	.02
216 Mackey Sasser	.05	.04	.02
217 Darryl Strawberry	.25	.20	.10
218 Tim Teufel	.05	.04	.02
219 Frank Viola	.10	.08	.04
220 Juan Agosto	.05	.04	.02
221 Larry Anderson	.05	.04	.02
222 Eric Anthony(FC)	.80	.60	.30
223 Kevin Bass	.08	.06	.03
224 Craig Biggio	.10	.08	.04
225 Ken Caminiti	.06	.05	.02
226 Jim Clancy	.05	.04	.02
227 Danny Darwin	.05	.04	.02
228 Glenn Davis	.09	.07	.04
229 Jim Deshaies	.07	.05	.02
230 Bill Doran	.06	.05	.02
231 Bob Forsch	.05	.04	.02
233 Terry Puhl	.05	.04	.02
234 Rafael Ramirez	.05	.04	.02
235 Rick Rhoden	.05	.04	.02
236 Dan Schatzeder	.05	.04	.02
237 Mike Scott	.08	.06	.03
238 Dave Smith	.06	.05	.02
239 Alex Trevino	.05	.04	.02
240 Glenn Wilson	.05	.04	.02
241 Gerald Young	.05	.04	.02
242 Tom Brunansky	.07	.05	.03
243 Cris Carpenter	.10	.08	.04
244 Alex Cole(FC)	1.00	.70	.40
245 Vince Coleman	.10	.08	.04
246 John Costello	.05	.04	.02
247 Ken Dayley	.05	.04	.02
248 Jose DeLeon	.06	.05	.02
249 Frank DiPino	.05	.04	.02
250 Pedro Guerrero	.09	.07	.04
251 Ken Hill	.09	.07	.04
252 Joe Magrane	.09	.07	.04
253 Willie McGee	.06	.05	.02
254 John Morris	.05	.04	.02
255 Jose Oquendo	.06	.05	.02
256 Tony Pena	.06	.05	.02
257 Terry Pendleton	.06	.05	.02
258 Ted Power	.05	.04	.02
259 Dan Quisenberry	.05	.04	.02
260 Ozzie Smith	.09	.07	.04
261 Scott Terry	.06	.05	.02
262 Milt Thompson	.05	.04	.02
263 Denny Walling	.05	.04	.02
264 Todd Worrell	.06	.05	.02
265 Todd Zeile	2.00	1.50	.80
266 Marty Barrett	.05	.04	.02
267 Mike Boddicker	.05	.04	.02
268 Wade Boggs	.40	.30	.15
269 Ellis Burks	.35	.25	.12
270 Rick Cerone	.05	.04	.02
271 Roger Clemens	.25	.20	.10
272 John Dopson	.06	.05	.02
273 Nick Esasky	.07	.05	.03
274 Dwight Evans	.09	.07	.05
275 Wes Gardner	.05	.04	.02
276 Rich Gedman	.05	.04	.02
277 Mike Greenwell	.50	.40	.20
278 Danny Heep	.05	.04	.02
279 Eric Hetzel	.10	.08	.04
280 Dennis Lamp	.05	.04	.02
281 Rob Murphy	.05	.04	.02
282 Joe Price	.05	.04	.02
283 Carlos Quintana	.10	.07	.04
284 Jody Reed	.06	.05	.02
285 Luis Rivera	.05	.04	.02
286 Kevin Romine	.05	.04	.02
287 Lee Smith	.05	.04	.02
288 Mike Smithson	.05	.04	.02
289 Bob Stanley	.05	.04	.02
290 Harold Baines	.09	.07	.04
291 Kevin Brown	.09	.07	.04
292 Steve Buechele	.05	.04	.02
293 Scott Coolbaugh(FC)	.35	.25	.14
294 Jack Daugherty(FC)	.25	.20	.10
295 Cecil Espy	.06	.05	.02
296 Julio Franco	.07	.05	.03

		MT	NR MT	EX				MT	NR MT	EX
297	Juan Gonzalez(FC)	2.00	1.50	.80		388	Dave West	.25	.20	.10
298	Cecilio Guante	.05	.04	.02		389	Tim Belcher	.12	.09	.05
299	Drew Hall	.05	.04	.02		390	Tim Crews	.05	.04	.02
300	Charlie Hough	.06	.05	.02		391	Mike Davis	.05	.04	.02
301	Pete Incaviglia	.08	.06	.03		392	Rick Dempsey	.05	.04	.02
302	Mike Jeffcoat	.05	.04	.02		393	Kirk Gibson	.09	.07	.04
303	Chad Kreuter	.08	.06	.03		394	Jose Gonzalez	.05	.04	.02
304	Jeff Kunkel	.05	.04	.02		395	Alfredo Griffin	.06	.05	.02
305	Rick Leach	.05	.04	.02		396	Jeff Hamilton	.06	.05	.02
306	Fred Manrique	.05	.04	.02		397	Lenny Harris	.10	.08	.06
307	Jamie Moyer	.06	.05	.02		398	Mickey Hatcher	.05	.04	.02
308	Rafael Palmeiro	.07	.05	.02		399	Orel Hershiser	.12	.09	.05
309	Geno Petralli	.05	.04	.02		400	Jay Howell	.06	.05	.02
310	Kevin Reimer	.10	.08	.06		401	Mike Marshall	.06	.05	.02
311	Kenny Rogers(FC)	.20	.15	.08		402	Ramon Martinez	.20	.15	.08
312	Jeff Russell	.06	.05	.02		403	Mike Morgan	.05	.04	.02
313	Nolan Ryan	.50	.40	.20		404	Eddie Murray	.10	.08	.04
314	Ruben Sierra	.15	.11	.06		405	Alejandro Pena	.05	.04	.02
315	Bobby Witt	.05	.04	.02		406	Willie Randolph	.08	.06	.03
316	Chris Bosio	.07	.05	.02		407	Mike Scioscia	.06	.05	.02
317	Glenn Braggs	.07	.05	.02		408	Ray Searage	.05	.04	.02
318	Greg Brock	.05	.04	.02		409	Fernando Valenzuela	.07	.05	.03
319	Chuck Crim	.05	.04	.02		410	Jose Vizcaino(FC)	.30	.25	.12
320	Rob Deer	.06	.05	.02		411	John Wetteland(FC)	.25	.20	.10
321	Mike Felder	.05	.04	.02		412	Jack Armstrong	.05	.04	.02
322	Tom Filer	.05	.04	.02		413	Todd Benzinger	.07	.05	.03
323	Tony Fossas(FC)	.10	.08	.04		414	Tim Birtsas	.05	.04	.02
324	Jim Gantner	.06	.05	.02		415	Tom Browning	.07	.05	.03
325	Darryl Hamilton	.08	.06	.03		416	Norm Charlton	.08	.06	.03
326	Ted Higuera	.08	.06	.03		417	Eric Davis	.20	.15	.08
327	Mark Knudson(FC)	.10	.08	.04		418	Rob Dibble	.15	.11	.06
328	Bill Krueger	.05	.04	.02		419	John Franco	.07	.05	.03
329	Tim McIntosh(FC)	.25	.20	.10		420	Ken Griffey, Sr.	.07	.05	.03
330	Paul Molitor	.08	.06	.03		421	Chris Hammond(FC)	.25	.20	.10
331	Jaime Navarro	.20	.15	.08		422	Danny Jackson	.06	.05	.02
332	Charlie O'Brien	.05	.04	.02		423	Barry Larkin	.15	.11	.06
333	Jeff Peterek(FC)	.25	.20	.10		424	Tim Leary	.06	.05	.02
334	Dan Plesac	.07	.05	.03		425	Rick Mahler	.05	.04	.02
335	Jerry Reuss	.06	.05	.02		426	Joe Oliver(FC)	.30	.25	.12
336	Gary Sheffield	.40	.30	.15		427	Paul O'Neill	.07	.05	.03
337	Bill Spiers	.35	.25	.12		428	Luis Quinones	.05	.04	.02
338	B.J. Surhoff	.07	.05	.02		429	Jeff Reed	.05	.04	.02
339	Greg Vaughn	1.00	.70	.40		430	Jose Rijo	.07	.05	.03
340	Robin Yount	.20	.15	.08		431	Ron Robinson	.05	.04	.02
341	Hubie Brooks	.06	.05	.02		432	Rolando Roomes	.10	.08	.04
342	Tim Burke	.06	.05	.02		433	Chris Sabo	.15	.11	.06
343	Mike Fitzgerald	.05	.04	.02		434	Scott Scudder	.30	.25	.12
344	Tom Foley	.05	.04	.02		435	Herm Winningham	.05	.04	.02
345	Andres Galarraga	.15	.11	.06		436	Steve Balboni	.05	.04	.02
346	Damaso Garcia	.05	.04	.02		437	Jesse Barfield	.08	.06	.03
347	Marquis Grissom(FC)	1.00	.70	.40		438	Mike Blowers(FC)	.25	.20	.10
348	Kevin Gross	.06	.05	.02		439	Tom Brookens	.05	.04	.02
349	Joe Hesketh	.05	.04	.02		440	Greg Cadaret	.05	.04	.02
350	Jeff Huson(FC)	.25	.20	.10		441	Alvaro Espinoza	.25	.20	.10
351	Wallace Johnson	.05	.04	.02		442	Bob Geren	.25	.20	.10
352	Mark Langston	.15	.11	.06		443	Lee Guetterman	.05	.04	.02
353	Dave Martinez	.06	.05	.02		444	Mel Hall	.06	.05	.02
354	Dennis Martinez	.06	.05	.02		445	Andy Hawkins	.06	.05	.02
355	Andy McGaffigan	.05	.04	.02		446	Roberto Kelly	.15	.11	.06
356	Otis Nixon	.05	.04	.02		447	Don Mattingly	.80	.60	.30
357	Spike Owen	.05	.04	.02		448	Lance McCullers	.05	.04	.02
358	Pascual Perez	.06	.05	.02		449	Hensley Meulens	.35	.25	.14
359	Tim Raines	.10	.08	.04		450	Dale Mohorcic	.05	.04	.02
360	Nelson Santovenia	.10	.08	.04		451	Clay Parker	.10	.07	.04
361	Bryn Smith	.06	.05	.02		452	Eric Plunk	.05	.04	.02
362	Zane Smith	.05	.04	.02		453	Dave Righetti	.07	.05	.03
363	Larry Walker(FC)	.35	.25	.14		454	Deion Sanders	.40	.30	.15
364	Tim Wallach	.06	.05	.02		455	Steve Sax	.07	.05	.03
365	Rick Aguilera	.05	.04	.02		456	Don Slaught	.05	.04	.02
366	Allan Anderson	.06	.05	.02		457	Walt Terrell	.05	.04	.02
367	Wally Backman	.06	.05	.02		458	Dave Winfield	.15	.11	.06
368	Doug Baker(FC)	.08	.06	.03		459	Jay Bell	.05	.04	.02
369	Juan Berenguer	.05	.04	.02		460	Rafael Belliard	.05	.04	.02
370	Randy Bush	.05	.04	.02		461	Barry Bonds	.10	.08	.04
371	Carmen Castillo	.05	.04	.02		462	Bobby Bonilla	.10	.08	.04
372	Mike Dyer(FC)	.15	.11	.06		463	Sid Bream	.05	.04	.02
373	Gary Gaetti	.07	.05	.03		464	Benny Distefano	.06	.05	.02
374	Greg Gagne	.05	.04	.02		465	Doug Drabek	.06	.05	.02
375	Dan Gladden	.05	.04	.02		466	Jim Gott	.06	.05	.02
376	German Gonzalez	.05	.04	.02		467	Billy Hatcher	.06	.05	.02
377	Brian Harper	.06	.05	.02		468	Neal Heaton	.06	.05	.02
378	Kent Hrbek	.10	.08	.04		469	Jeff King	.20	.15	.08
379	Gene Larkin	.05	.04	.02		470	Bob Kipper	.05	.04	.02
380	Tim Laudner	.05	.04	.02		471	Randy Kramer	.05	.04	.02
381	John Moses	.05	.04	.02		472	Bill Landrum	.06	.05	.02
382	Al Newman	.05	.04	.02		473	Mike LaValliere	.06	.05	.02
383	Kirby Puckett	.40	.30	.15		474	Jose Lind	.06	.05	.02
384	Shane Rawley	.06	.05	.02		475	Junior Ortiz	.05	.04	.02
385	Jeff Reardon	.06	.05	.02		476	Gary Redus	.05	.04	.02
386	Roy Smith	.05	.04	.02		477	Rick Reed(FC)	.20	.15	.08
387	Gary Wayne(FC)	.15	.11	.06		478	R.J. Reynolds	.05	.04	.02

		MT	NR MT	EX
479	Jeff Robinson	.05	.04	.02
480	John Smiley	.07	.05	.03
481	Andy Van Slyke	.09	.07	.04
482	Bob Walk	.06	.05	.04
483	Andy Allanson	.05	.04	.02
484	Scott Bailes	.05	.04	.02
485	*Joey Belle*	.70	.50	.30
486	Bud Black	.05	.04	.02
487	Jerry Browne	.07	.05	.03
488	Tom Candiotti	.05	.04	.02
489	Joe Carter	.08	.06	.03
490	David Clark	.06	.05	.02
491	John Farrell	.06	.05	.02
492	Felix Fermin	.05	.04	.02
493	Brook Jacoby	.06	.05	.02
494	Dion James	.06	.05	.02
495	Doug Jones	.06	.05	.02
496	Brad Komminsk	.05	.04	.02
497	Rod Nichols	.05	.04	.02
498	Pete O'Brien	.07	.05	.03
499	*Steve Olin*(FC)	.35	.25	.12
500	Jesse Orosco	.05	.04	.02
501	Joel Skinner	.05	.04	.02
502	Cory Snyder	.09	.07	.04
503	Greg Swindell	.10	.08	.04
504	Rich Yett	.05	.04	.02
505	Scott Bankhead	.07	.05	.03
506	Scott Bradley	.05	.04	.02
507	Greg Briley	.20	.15	.08
508	Jay Buhner	.07	.05	.03
509	Darnell Coles	.05	.04	.02
510	Keith Comstock	.05	.04	.02
511	Henry Cotto	.05	.04	.02
512	Alvin Davis	.12	.09	.05
513	Ken Griffey, Jr.	2.50	2.00	1.00
514	Erik Hanson	.20	.15	.08
515	Gene Harris	.15	.11	.06
516	Brian Holman	.07	.05	.03
517	Mike Jackson	.05	.04	.02
518	Randy Johnson	.15	.11	.06
519	Jeffrey Leonard	.08	.06	.03
520	Edgar Martinez	.10	.08	.04
521	Dennis Powell	.05	.04	.02
522	Jim Presley	.06	.05	.02
523	Jerry Reed	.05	.04	.02
524	Harold Reynolds	.07	.05	.03
525	Mike Schooler	.06	.05	.04
526	Bill Swift	.05	.04	.02
527	David Valle	.05	.04	.02
528	*Omar Vizquel*	.20	.15	.08
529	Ivan Calderon	.06	.05	.02
530	Carlton Fisk	.10	.08	.04
531	Scott Fletcher	.06	.05	.02
532	Dave Gallagher	.09	.07	.04
533	Ozzie Guillen	.07	.05	.03
534	*Greg Hibbard*(FC)	.15	.11	.06
535	Shawn Hillegas	.05	.04	.02
536	Lance Johnson	.07	.05	.03
537	Eric King	.05	.04	.02
538	Ron Kittle	.07	.05	.02
539	Steve Lyons	.05	.04	.02
540	Carlos Martinez	.15	.11	.06
541	*Tom McCarthy*(FC)	.10	.07	.04
542	*Matt Merullo*	.25	.20	.10
543	Donn Pall	.05	.04	.02
544	Dan Pasqua	.06	.05	.02
545	Ken Patterson	.06	.05	.02
546	Melido Perez	.07	.05	.03
547	Steve Rosenberg	.07	.05	.03
548	*Sammy Sosa*(FC)	.50	.40	.20
549	Bobby Thigpen	.07	.05	.03
550	Robin Ventura	1.00	.90	.50
551	Greg Walker	.06	.05	.02
552	Don Carman	.05	.04	.02
553	*Pat Combs*(FC)	.50	.40	.20
554	Dennis Cook	.20	.15	.08
555	Darren Daulton	.05	.04	.02
556	Lenny Dykstra	.07	.05	.03
557	Curt Ford	.05	.04	.02
558	Charlie Hayes	.10	.08	.04
559	Von Hayes	.07	.05	.03
560	Tom Herr	.06	.05	.02
561	Ken Howell	.05	.04	.02
562	Steve Jeltz	.05	.04	.02
563	Ron Jones	.15	.11	.06
564	Ricky Jordan	.35	.25	.14
565	John Kruk	.07	.05	.03
566	Steve Lake	.05	.04	.02
567	Roger McDowell	.06	.05	.02
568	Terry Mulholland	.05	.04	.02
569	Dwayne Murphy	.05	.04	.02

		MT	NR MT	EX
570	Jeff Parrett	.06	.05	.02
571	Randy Ready	.05	.04	.02
572	Bruce Ruffin	.05	.04	.02
573	Dickie Thon	.05	.04	.02
574	Jose Alvarez	.05	.04	.02
575	Geronimo Berroa	.06	.05	.03
576	Jeff Blauser	.05	.04	.02
577	Joe Boever	.07	.05	.03
578	Marty Clary	.05	.04	.02
579	Jody Davis	.05	.04	.02
580	Mark Eichhorn	.05	.04	.02
581	Darrell Evans	.06	.05	.02
582	Ron Gant	.06	.05	.02
583	Tom Glavine	.09	.07	.04
584	*Tommy Greene*(FC)	.40	.30	.15
585	Tommy Gregg	.10	.07	.04
586	*David Justice*(FC)	3.00	2.25	1.25
587	Mark Lemke(FC)	.10	.08	.04
588	Derek Lilliquist	.10	.08	.04
589	Oddibe McDowell	.07	.05	.03
590	*Kent Mercker*(FC)	.40	.30	.15
591	Dale Murphy	.15	.11	.06
592	Gerald Perry	.06	.05	.02
593	Lonnie Smith	.06	.05	.02
594	Pete Smith	.07	.05	.03
595	John Smoltz	.15	.11	.06
596	*Mike Stanton*(FC)	.35	.25	.14
597	Andres Thomas	.06	.05	.02
598	Jeff Treadway	.06	.05	.02
599	Doyle Alexander	.06	.05	.02
600	Dave Bergman	.05	.04	.02
601	*Brian Dubois*(FC)	.35	.25	.14
602	Paul Gibson	.06	.05	.02
603	Mike Heath	.05	.04	.02
604	Mike Henneman	.07	.05	.03
605	Guillermo Hernandez	.05	.04	.02
606	*Shawn Holman*(FC)	.20	.15	.08
607	Tracy Jones	.09	.07	.04
608	Chet Lemon	.06	.05	.02
609	Fred Lynn	.06	.05	.02
610	Jack Morris	.07	.05	.02
611	Matt Nokes	.10	.08	.04
612	Gary Pettis	.05	.04	.02
613	*Kevin Ritz*(FC)	.15	.11	.06
614	Jeff Robinson	.07	.05	.03
615	Steve Searcy	.10	.08	.04
616	Frank Tanana	.06	.05	.02
617	Alan Trammell	.09	.07	.04
618	Gary Ward	.05	.04	.02
619	Lou Whitaker	.09	.07	.04
620	Frank Williams	.05	.04	.02
621a	Players Of The Decade - 1980 (George Brett) (10 .390 hitting seasons)	3.00	2.25	1.25
621b	Players Of The Decade - 1980 (George Brett) (10 .300 hitting seasons)	.50	.40	.20
622	Players Of The Decade - 1981 (Fernando Valenzuela)	.20	.15	.08
623	Players Of The Decade - 1982 (Dale Murphy)	.25	.20	.10
624a	Players Of The Decade - 1983 (Cal Ripkin, Jr.)	1.00	.70	.40
624b	Players Of The Decade - 1983 (Cal Ripkin, Jr.)	.25	.20	.10
625	Players Of The Decade - 1984 (Ryne Sandberg)	.25	.20	.10
626	Players Of The Decade - 1985 (Don Mattingly)	.50	.40	.20
627	Players Of The Decade - 1986 (Roger Clemens)	.25	.20	.10
628	Players Of The Decade - 1987 (George Bell)	.20	.15	.08
629	Players Of The Decade - (Jose Canseco)	.60	.45	.25
630a	Players Of The Decade - 1989 (Will Clark) (total bases (32))	5.00	3.75	2.00
630b	Players Of The Decade - 1989 (Will Clark) (total bases (321))	.60	.45	.25
631	Game Savers	.10	.08	.04
632	Boston Igniters	.10	.08	.04
633	The Starter & Stopper	.10	.08	.04
634	League's Best Shortstops	.10	.08	.04
635	Human Dynamos	.10	.08	.04
636	300 Strikeout Club	.10	.08	.04
637	The Dynamic Duo	.10	.08	.04
638	A.L. All Stars	.10	.08	.04
639	N.L. East Rivals	.10	.08	.04
640	*Rudy Seanez, Colin Charland*(FC)	.20	.15	.08
641	*George Canale, Kevin Maas*(FC)	4.00	3.00	1.50
642	*Kelly Mann, Dave Hansen*(FC)	.30	.25	.12

		MT	NR MT	EX
643	*Greg Smith, Stu Tate*(FC)	.20	.15	.08
644	*Tom Drees, Dan Howitt*(FC)	.20	.15	.08
645	*Mike Roesler, Derrick May*(FC)	.80	.60	.30
646	*Scott Hemond, Mark Gardner*(FC)	.35	.25	.14
647	*John Orton, Scott Leuis*(FC)	.20	.15	.08
648	*Rich Monteleone, Dana Williams*(FC)	.15	.11	.06
649	*Mike Huff, Steve Frey*(FC)	.20	.15	.08
650	*Chuck McElroy, Moises Alou*(FC)	.40	.30	.15
651	*Bobby Rose, Mike Hartley*(FC)	.25	.20	.10
652	*Matt Kinzer, Wayne Edwards*(FC)	.25	.20	.10
653	*Delino Deshields, Jason Grimsley*(FC)	1.00	.70	.40
654	Athletics, Cubs, Giants & Blue Jays (Checklist)	.05	.04	.03
655	Royals, Angels, Padres & Orioles (Checklist)	.05	.04	.03
656	Mets, Astros, Cardinals & Red Sox (Checklist)	.05	.04	.03
657	Rangers, Brewers, Expos & Twins (Checklist)	.05	.04	.03
658	Dodgers, Reds, Yankees & Pirates (Checklist)	.05	.04	.03
659	Indians, Mariners, White Sox & Phillies (Checklist)	.05	.04	.03
660	Braves, Tigers & Special Cards (Checklist)	.05	.04	.03

A player's name in *italic* indicates a rookie card. An (FC) indicates a player's first card for that particular card company.

1990 Fleer All-Star Team

The top players at each position, as selected by Fleer, are featured in this 12-card set. The cards were inserted in cello packs and some wax packs. The cards measure 2-1/2" by 3-1/2" and feature a unique two-photo format on the card fronts.

		MT	NR MT	EX
	Complete Set:	10.00	7.50	4.00
	Common Player:	.20	.15	.08
1	Harold Baines	.25	.20	.10
2	Will Clark	2.00	1.50	.80
3	Mark Davis	.20	.15	.08
4	Howard Johnson	.40	.30	.15
5	Joe Magrane	.25	.20	.10
6	Kevin Mitchell	.80	.60	.30
7	Kirby Puckett	.60	.45	.25
8	Cal Ripken	.70	.50	.30
9	Ryne Sandberg	2.00	1.50	.80
10	Mike Scott	.20	.15	.08
11	Ruben Sierra	.80	.60	.30
12	Mickey Tettleton	.20	.15	.08

1990 Fleer Award Winners

Hill's Department Stores and 7-Eleven Outlets are exclusively carrying the 1990 Fleer "Award Winners." This 44-card boxed set includes baseball's statistical leaders of 1989, six special cards that feature peel-off team logo stickers and a baseball trivia quiz. The card fronts feature a full-color player photo

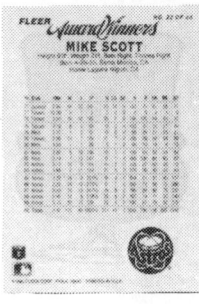

framed by a winner's cup design and a blue border. The card backs showcase player statistics in blue on a yellow and white background. The cards measure 2-1/2" by 3-1/2" in size. A complete checklist is provided on the back of each box. The checklist incorrectly lists Bob Boone's team as the Angels.

		MT	NR MT	EX
	Complete Set:	2.75	2.00	1.00
	Common Player:	.05	.04	.02
1	Jeff Ballard	.05	.04	.02
2	Tim Belcher	.08	.06	.03
3	Bert Blyleven	.08	.06	.03
4	Wade Boggs	.35	.25	.14
5	Bob Boone	.05	.04	.02
6	Jose Canseco	.60	.45	.25
7	Will Clark	.50	.40	.20
8	Jack Clark	.05	.04	.02
9	Vince Coleman	.05	.04	.02
10	Ron Darling	.05	.04	.02
11	Eric Davis	.40	.30	.15
12	Jose DeLeon	.05	.04	.02
13	Tony Fernandez	.05	.04	.02
14	Carlton Fisk	.10	.08	.04
15	Scott Garrelts	.05	.04	.02
16	Tom Gordon	.15	.11	.06
17	Ken Griffey,Jr.	1.00	.70	.40
18	Von Hayes	.05	.04	.02
19	Rickey Henderson	.35	.25	.14
20	Bo Jackson	.80	.60	.30
21	Howard Johnson	.15	.11	.06
22	Don Mattingly	.40	.30	.15
23	Fred McGriff	.25	.20	.10
24	Kevin Mitchell	.30	.25	.12
25	Gregg Olson	.15	.11	.06
26	Gary Pettis	.05	.04	.02
27	Kirby Puckett	.30	.25	.12
28	Harold Reynolds	.05	.04	.02
29	Jeff Russell	.05	.04	.02
30	Nolan Ryan	.50	.40	.20
31	Bret Saberhagen	.10	.08	.04
32	Ryne Sandberg	.25	.20	.10
33	Benito Santiago	.10	.08	.04
34	Mike Scott	.05	.04	.02
35	Ruben Sierra	.25	.20	.10
36	Lonnie Smith	.05	.04	.02
37	Ozzie Smith	.10	.08	.04
38	Dave Stewart	.10	.08	.04
39	Greg Swindell	.05	.04	.02
40	Andy Van Slyke	.08	.06	.03
41	Tim Wallach	.05	.04	.02
42	Jerome Walton	.20	.15	.08
43	Mitch Williams	.08	.06	.03
44	Robin Yount	.15	.11	.06

1990 Fleer Baseball All Stars

Sold Exclusively in Ben Franklin stores, this 44-card boxed set showcases the game's top players. The card fronts feature a full color player photo surrounded by a tan border. The flip side contains individual player statistics and data printed in red and black. The cards measure 2-1/2" by 3-1/2" in size and are packed in a special box with a complete checklist on the back. Like other Fleer boxed

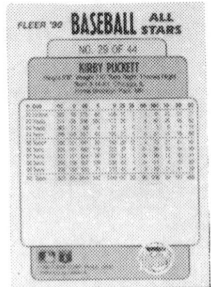

This 44-card boxed set was produced by Fleer for the Toys "R" Us chain. Card fronts are designed with graduating black-to-white borders, surrounding a color photo of each player. Card backs contain individual player data and career statistics. The back of each box carries a checklist of all the players in the set. Six peel-off team logo stickers featuring a baseball trivia quiz on the back are also included with each set. The cards are 2-1/2" by 3-1/2" in size and are numbered alphabetically.

		MT	NR MT	EX
Complete Set:		3.75	2.75	1.50
Common Player:		.05	.04	.02
1	George Bell	.10	.08	.04
2	Bert Blyleven	.10	.08	.04
3	Wade Boggs	.40	.30	.15
4	Bobby Bonilla	.15	.11	.06
5	George Brett	.15	.11	.06
6	Jose Canseco	.70	.50	.30
7	Will Clark	.60	.45	.25
8	Roger Clemens	.30	.25	.12
9	Eric Davis	.60	.45	.25
10	Glenn Davis	.15	.11	.06
11	Tony Fernandez	.08	.06	.03
12	Dwight Gooden	.25	.20	.10
13	Mike Greenwell	.20	.15	.08
14	Ken Griffey,Jr.	1.00	.70	.40
15	Pedro Guerrero	.08	.06	.03
16	Tony Gwynn	.15	.11	.06
17	Rickey Henderson	.40	.30	.15
18	Tom Herr	.05	.04	.02
19	Orel Hershiser	.10	.08	.04
20	Kent Hrbek	.05	.04	.02
21	Bo Jackson	.80	.60	.30
22	Howard Johnson	.25	.20	.10
23	Don Mattingly	.50	.40	.20
24	Fred McGriff	.25	.20	.10
25	Mark McGwire	.50	.40	.20
26	Kevin Mitchell	.35	.25	.14
27	Paul Molitor	.10	.08	.04
28	Dale Murphy	.10	.08	.04
29	Kirby Puckett	.40	.30	.15
30	Tim Raines	.10	.08	.04
31	Cal Riken,Jr.	.20	.15	.08
32	Bret Saberhagen	.10	.08	.04
33	Ryne Sandberg	.20	.15	.08
34	Ruben Sierra	.30	.25	.12
35	Dwight Smith	.08	.06	.03
36	Ozzie Smith	.10	.08	.04
37	Darryl Strawberry	.35	.25	.14
38	Dave Stewart	.10	.08	.04
39	Greg Swindell	.05	.04	.02
40	Bobby Thigpen	.08	.06	.03
41	Alan Trammell	.10	.08	.04
42	Jerome Walton	.25	.20	.10
43	Mitch Williams	.08	.06	.03
44	Robin Yount	.20	.15	.08

sets, the cards are numbered alphabetically.

		MT	NR MT	EX
Complete Set:		3.00	2.25	1.25
Common Player:		.05	.04	.02
1	Wade Boggs	.35	.25	.14
2	Bobby Bonilla	.20	.15	.08
3	Tim Burke	.05	.04	.02
4	Jose Canseco	.60	.45	.25
5	Will Clark	.50	.40	.20
6	Eric Davis	.40	.30	.15
7	Glenn Davis	.20	.15	.08
8	Julio Franco	.10	.08	.04
9	Tony Fernandez	.10	.08	.04
10	Gary Gaetti	.10	.08	.04
11	Scott Garrelts	.05	.04	.02
12	Mark Grace	.20	.15	.08
13	Mike Greenwell	.20	.15	.08
14	Ken Griffey,Jr.	1.00	.70	.40
15	Mark Gubicza	.05	.04	.02
16	Pedro Guerrero	.10	.08	.04
17	Von Hayes	.05	.04	.02
18	Orel Hershiser	.10	.08	.04
19	Bruce Hurst	.05	.04	.02
20	Bo Jackson	.80	.60	.30
21	Howard Johnson	.20	.15	.08
22	Doug Jones	.05	.04	.02
23	Barry Larkin	.30	.25	.12
24	Don Mattingly	.60	.45	.25
25	Mark McGwire	.50	.40	.20
26	Kevin McReynolds	.05	.04	.02
27	Kevin Mitchell	.40	.30	.15
28	Dan Plesac	.05	.04	.02
29	Kirby Puckett	.40	.30	.15
30	Cal Ripken,Jr.	.15	.11	.06
31	Bret Saberhagen	.10	.08	.04
32	Ryne Sandberg	.20	.15	.08
33	Steve Sax	.10	.08	.04
34	Ruben Sierra	.35	.25	.14
35	Ozzie Smith	.10	.08	.04
36	John Smoltz	.10	.08	.04
37	Darryl Strawberry	.30	.25	.12
38	Terry Steinbach	.05	.04	.02
39	Dave Stewart	.10	.08	.04
40	Bobby Thigpen	.10	.08	.04
41	Alan Trammell	.10	.08	.04
42	Devon White	.05	.04	.02
43	Mitch Williams	.05	.04	.02
44	Robin Yount	.15	.11	.06

1990 Fleer Baseball MVP

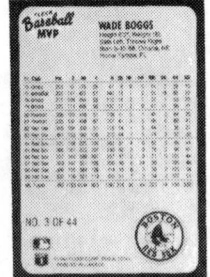

A player's name in *italic* indicates a rookie card. An (FC) indicates a player's first card for that particular card company.

1990 Fleer Box Panels

For the fifth consecutive year, Fleer issued a series of cards on the bottom panels of its regular 1990 wax pack boxes. This 28-card set features both players and team logo cards. The cards were numbered C-1 to C-28.

		MT	NR MT	EX
Complete Set:		5.00	3.75	2.00
Common Player:		.05	.04	.02
1	Giants Logo	.05	.04	.02
2	Tim Belcher	.06	.05	.02
3	Roger Clemens	.35	.25	.14
4	Eric Davis	.35	.25	.14
5	Glenn Davis	.10	.08	.04
6	Cubs Logo	.05	.04	.02
7	Jon Franco	.06	.05	.02
8	Mike Greenwell	.30	.25	.12
9	Athletics Logo	.05	.04	.02
10	Ken Griffey, Jr.	1.25	.90	.50
11	Pedro Guerrero	.05	.04	.02
12	Tony Gwynn	.20	.15	.08
13	Blue Jays Logo	.05	.04	.02
14	Orel Hershiser	.20	.15	.08
15	Bo Jackson	.70	.50	.30
16	Howard Johnson	.15	.11	.06
17	Mets Logo	.05	.04	.02
18	Cardinals Logo	.05	.04	.02
19	Don Mattingly	.60	.45	.25
20	Mark McGwire	.40	.30	.15
21	Kevin Mitchell	.25	.20	.10
22	Kirby Puckett	.35	.25	.14
23	Royals Logo	.05	.04	.02
24	Orioles Logo	.05	.04	.02
25	Ruben Sierra	.30	.25	.12
26	Dave Stewart	.20	.15	.08
27	Jerome Walton	.50	.40	.20
28	Robin Yount	.25	.20	.10

1990 Fleer '89 World Series

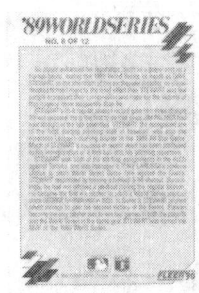

This 12-card set, which depicts highlights of the 1989 World Series, was included as a special sub-set with the regular factory-collated Fleer set. Ironically, single World·Series cards were discovered in cello and three-packs. This was not intended to happen. Fronts of the 2-1/2" by 3-1/2" cards feature full color photos set against a white background with a red and blue "'89 World Series" banner. The card backs are pink and white and describe the events of the 1989 FALL Classic.

		MT	NR MT	EX
Complete Set:		3.00	2.25	1.25
Common Player:		.20	.15	.08
1	The Final Piece To The Puzzle (Mike Moore)	.20	.15	.08
2	The National League M.V.P. (Kevin Mitchell)	.30	.25	.12
3	Game Two's Crushing Blow	.20	.15	.08
4	Clark Pwers The Giants Into The Series (Will Clark)	.35	.25	.14
5	Canseco Crushed World Series Slump (Jose Canseco)	.40	.30	.15
6	Great leather In The Field	.20	.15	.08
7	Game One And A's Break Out On Top	.20	.15	.08
8	Oakland's M.V.P. (Dave Stewart)	.25	.20	.10
9	Parker's Bat Produces Power (Dave Parker)	.20	.15	.08
10	World Series Record Book Game 3	.20	.15	.08
11	Swipes Championship Series Records (Rickey Henderson)	.35	.25	.14
12	Oakland A's - Baseball's Best In '89	.25	.20	.10

1990 Fleer League Leaders

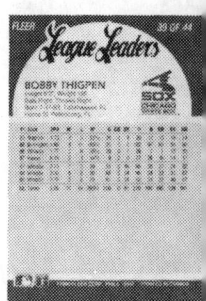

For the fifth consecutive year Fleer released a "League Leaders" trading card set. The set includes 44 top Major League players and features six special cards containing peel-off team logos and a baseball trivia quiz. Card number 42 (Jerome Walton) pictures a player other than Walton. The cards measure 2-1/2" by 3-1/2" in size. The card fronts display a full- color photo bordered by a blue frame. The card backs feature complete statistics. The cards are numbered alphabetically and a complete checklist is displayed on the back of the card box. The set is available at Walgreen Drug Stores.

		MT	NR MT	EX
Complete Set:		3.25	2.50	1.25
Common Player:		.05	.04	.02
1	Roberto Alomar	.25	.20	.10
2	Tim Belcher	.08	.06	.03
3	George Bell	.10	.08	.04
4	Wade Boggs	.35	.25	.14
5	Jose Canseco	.60	.45	.25
6	Will Clark	.50	.40	.20
7	David Cone	.08	.06	.03
8	Eric Davis	.40	.30	.15
9	Glenn Davis	.20	.15	.08
10	Nick Esasky	.10	.08	.04
11	Dennis Eckersley	.10	.08	.04
12	Mark Grace	.15	.11	.06
13	Mike Greenwell	.20	.15	.08
14	Ken Griffey,Jr.	1.00	.70	.40
15	Mark Gubicza	.05	.04	.02
16	Pedro Guerrero	.05	.04	.02
17	Tony Gwynn	.15	.11	.06
18	Rickey Henderson	.40	.30	.15
19	Bo Jackson	.80	.60	.30
20	Doug Jones	.05	.04	.02
21	Ricky Jordan	.08	.06	.03
22	Barry Larkin	.25	.20	.10
23	Don Mattingly	.40	.30	.15
24	Fred McGriff	.25	.20	.10
25	Mark McGwire	.40	.30	.15
26	Kevin Mitchell	.40	.30	.15
27	Jack Morris	.05	.04	.02
28	Gregg Olson	.15	.11	.06
29	Dan Plesac	.05	.04	.02
30	Kirby Puckett	.30	.25	.12
31	Nolan Ryan	.50	.40	.20
32	Bret Saberhagen	.10	.08	.04
33	Ryne Sandberg	.20	.15	.08
34	Steve Sax	.10	.08	.04
35	Mike Scott	.05	.04	.02
36	Ruben Sierra	.30	.25	.12
37	Lonnie Smith	.05	.04	.02
38	Darryl Strawberry	.30	.25	.12
39	Bobby Thigpen	.08	.06	.03
40	Andy Van Slyke	.10	.08	.04
41	Tim Wallach	.05	.04	.02
42	Jerome Walton	.20	.15	.08
43	Devon White	.05	.04	.02
44	Robin Yount	.15	.11	.06

1990 Fleer League Standouts

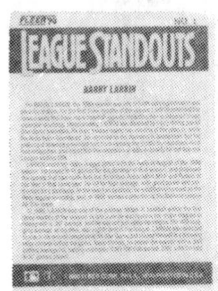

Fleer's "League Standouts" set features six of baseball's top players. The cards were distributed randomly in Fleer three-packs. The card fronts feature full color photos with a six dimensional effect. An attractive black and gold frame borders the photo. The card backs are yellow and describe the player's iuuuundividual accomplishments. The cards measure 2-1/2" by 3-1/2" in size.

	MT	NR MT	EX
Complete Set:	4.00	3.00	1.50
Common Player:	.50	.40	.20
1 Barry Larkin	.50	.40	.20
2 Mark Grace	.50	.40	.20
3 Don Mattingly	1.00	.70	.40
4 Darryl Strawberry	.60	.45	.25
5 Jose Canseco	1.00	.70	.40
6 Wade Boggs	.60	.45	.25

1990 Fleer Update

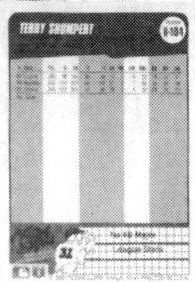

Fleer produced its seventh consecutive "Update" set in 1990 to supplement the company's regular set. As in the past, the set consists of 132 cards (numbered U-1 through U-132) that were sold by hobby dealers in special collectors boxes. The cards are designed in the exact same style as the regular issue. A special Nolan Ryan commemorative card is included in the 1990 Fleer Update set.

	MT	NR MT	EX
Complete Set:	12.00	9.00	4.75
Common Player:	.06	.05	.02
1 Steve Avery(FC)	.40	.30	.15
2 Francisco Cabrera	.20	.15	.08
3 Nick Esasky	.06	.05	.02
4 Jim Kremers(FC)	.20	.15	.08
5 Greg Olson(FC)	.12	.09	.05
6 Jim Presley	.06	.05	.02
7 Shawn Boskie(FC)	.25	.20	.10
8 Joe Kraemer(FC)	.08	.06	.03
9 Luis Salazar	.06	.05	.02

		MT	NR MT	EX
10	Hector Villanueva(FC)	.30	.25	.12
11	Glenn Braggs	.06	.05	.02
12	Mariano Duncan	.06	.05	.02
13	Billy Hatcher	.06	.05	.02
14	Tim Layana(FC)	.20	.15	.08
15	Hal Morris	.20	.15	.08
16	Javier Ortiz(FC)	.20	.15	.08
17	Dave Rohde(FC)	.15	.11	.06
18	Eric Yelding(FC)	.20	.15	.08
19	Hubie Brooks	.08	.06	.03
20	Kal Daniels	.08	.06	.03
21	Dave Hansen	.15	.11	.06
22	Mike Hartley	.15	.11	.06
23	Stan Javier	.06	.05	.02
24	Jose Offerman(FC)	1.50	1.25	.60
25	Juan Samuel	.06	.05	.02
26	Dennis Boyd	.06	.05	.02
27	Delino DeShields	.80	.60	.30
28	Steve Frey	.12	.09	.05
29	Mark Gardner	.15	.11	.06
30	Chris Nabholz(FC)	.40	.30	.15
31	Bill Sampen(FC)	.25	.20	.10
32	Dave Schmidt	.06	.05	.02
33	Daryl Boston	.06	.05	.02
34	Chuck Carr(FC)	.20	.15	.08
35	John Franco	.08	.06	.03
36	Todd Hundley(FC)	.20	.15	.08
37	Julio Machado(FC)	.15	.11	.06
38	Alejandro Pena	.06	.05	.02
39	Darren Reed(FC)	.25	.20	.10
40	Kelvin Torve(FC)	.12	.09	.05
41	Darrel Akerfelds(FC)	.12	.09	.05
42	Jose DeJesus	.20	.15	.08
43	Dave Hollins(FC)	.30	.25	.12
44	Carmelo Martinez	.06	.05	.02
45	Brad Moore(FC)	.15	.11	.06
46	Dale Murphy	.10	.08	.04
47	Wally Backman	.06	.05	.02
48	Stan Belinda(FC)	.20	.15	.08
49	Bob Patterson	.06	.05	.02
50	Ted Power	.06	.05	.02
51	Don Slaught	.06	.05	.02
52	Geronimo Pena(FC)	.25	.20	.10
53	Lee Smith	.08	.06	.03
54	John Tudor	.06	.05	.02
55	Joe Carter	.10	.08	.04
56	Tom Howard(FC)	.30	.25	.12
57	Craig Lefferts	.06	.05	.02
58	Rafael Valdez(FC)	.20	.15	.08
59	Dave Anderson	.06	.05	.02
60	Kevin Bass	.06	.05	.02
61	John Burkett	.35	.25	.12
62	Gary Carter	.10	.08	.04
63	Rick Parker(FC)	.10	.08	.04
64	Trevor Wilson	.10	.08	.04
65	Chris Hoiles(FC)	.25	.20	.10
66	Tim Hulett	.06	.05	.02
67	Dave Johnson(FC)	.10	.08	.04
68	Curt Schilling(FC)	.10	.08	.04
69	David Segui(FC)	.35	.25	.12
70	Tom Brunansky	.08	.06	.03
71	Greg Harris	.06	.05	.02
72	Dana Kiecker(FC)	.12	.09	.05
73	Tim Naehring(FC)	.40	.30	.15
74	Tony Pena	.06	.05	.02
75	Jeff Reardon	.08	.06	.03
76	Jerry Reed	.06	.05	.02
77	Mark Eichhorn	.06	.05	.02
78	Mark Langston	.08	.06	.03
79	John Orton	.12	.09	.05
80	Luis Polonia	.06	.05	.02
81	Dave Winfield	.12	.09	.05
82	Cliff Young(FC)	.20	.15	.08
83	Wayne Edwards	.10	.08	.04
84	Alex Fernandez(FC)	1.50	1.25	.60
85	Craig Grebeck(FC)	.15	.11	.06
86	Scott Radinsky(FC)	.25	.20	.10
87	Frank Thomas(FC)	2.00	1.50	.80
88	Beau Allred(FC)	.20	.15	.08
89	Sandy Alomar,Jr.	.35	.25	.14
90	Carlos Baerga(FC)	.50	.40	.20
91	Kevin Bearse(FC)	.25	.20	.10
92	Chris James	.06	.05	.02
93	Candy Maldonado	.06	.05	.02
94	Jeff Manto	.12	.09	.05
95	Cecil Fielder	.60	.45	.25
96	Travis Fryman(FC)	1.00	.70	.40
97	Lloyd Moseby	.06	.05	.02
98	Edwin Nunez	.06	.05	.02
99	Tony Phillips	.06	.05	.02
100	Larry Sheets	.06	.05	.02
101	Mark Davis	.06	.05	.02

		MT	NR MT	EX
102	Storm Davis	.06	.05	.02
103	Gerald Perry	.06	.05	.02
104	Terry Shumpert(FC)	.30	.25	.12
105	Edgar Diaz(FC)	.15	.11	.06
106	Dave Parker	.10	.08	.04
107	Tim Drummond(FC)	.15	.11	.06
108	Junior Ortiz	.06	.05	.02
109	Park Pittman(FC)	.25	.20	.10
110	Kevin Tapani(FC)	.25	.20	.10
111	Oscar Azocar(FC)	.50	.40	.20
112	Jim Leyritz(FC)	.50	.40	.20
113	Kevin Maas	2.00	1.50	.80
114	Alan Mills(FC)	.25	.20	.10
115	Matt Nokes	.06	.05	.02
116	Pascual Perez	.06	.05	.02
117	Ozzie Canseco(FC)	.60	.45	.25
118	Scott Sanderson	.06	.05	.02
119	Tino Martinez(FC)	1.00	.70	.40
120	Jeff Schaefer(FC)	.15	.11	.06
121	Matt Young	.06	.05	.02
122	Brian Bohanon(FC)	.20	.15	.08
123	Jeff Huson	.15	.11	.06
124	Ramon Manon(FC)	.20	.15	.08
125	Gary Mielke(FC)	.15	.11	.06
126	Willie Blair(FC)	.15	.11	.06
127	Glenallen Hill(FC)	.15	.11	.06
128	John Olerud(FC)	1.75	1.25	.70
129	Luis Sojo(FC)	.15	.11	.06
130	Mark Whiten(FC)	.50	.40	.20
131	Three Decades Of No Hitters (Nolan Ryan)	1.50	1.25	.60
132	Checklist	.06	.05	.02

1991 Fleer

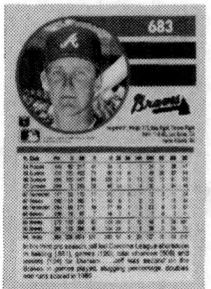

Fleer expanded its 1991 set to include 720 cards. The cards feature yellow boders surrounding full-color action photos. The player's name appears above the photo, while the team and position in displayed below. The "Fleer 91" logo appears in the lower right corner of the photo. The card backs feature a player photo in a circle design, biographical information, complete statistics, and career highlights. Five special Super Star cards are among the cards in the regular set. Once again the cards are numbered according to team.

		MT	NR MT	EX
Complete Set:		22.00	16.00	9.00
Common Player:		.05	.04	.02
1	Troy Afenir(FC)	.20	.15	.08
2	Harold Baines	.08	.06	.03
3	Lance Blankenship	.06	.05	.02
4	Todd Burns	.05	.04	.02
5	Jose Canseco	.30	.25	.12
6	Dennis Eckersley	.10	.08	.04
7	Mike Gallego	.05	.04	.02
8	Ron Hassey	.05	.04	.02
9	Dave Henderson	.08	.06	.03
10	Rickey Henderson	.20	.15	.08
11	Rick Honeycutt	.05	.04	.02
12	Doug Jennings	.06	.05	.02
13	Joe Klink(FC)	.10	.08	.04
14	Carney Lansford	.08	.06	.03
15	Darren Lewis(FC)	.35	.25	.14
16	Willie McGee	.08	.06	.03
17	Mark McGwire	.20	.15	.08

		MT	NR MT	EX
18	Mike Moore	.06	.05	.02
19	Gene Nelson	.05	.04	.02
20	Dave Otto	.05	.04	.02
21	Jamie Quirk	.05	.04	.02
22	Willie Randolph	.06	.05	.02
23	Scott Sanderson	.06	.05	.02
24	Terry Steinbach	.06	.05	.02
25	Dave Stewart	.10	.08	.04
26	Walt Weiss	.06	.05	.02
27	Bob Welch	.08	.06	.03
28	Curt Young	.05	.04	.02
29	Wally Backman	.05	.04	.02
30	Stan Belinda	.10	.08	.04
31	Jay Bell	.06	.05	.02
32	Rafael Belliard	.05	.04	.02
33	Barry Bonds	.20	.15	.08
34	Bobby Bonilla	.15	.11	.06
35	Sid Bream	.06	.05	.02
36	Doug Drabek	.10	.08	.04
37	Carlos Garcia(FC)	.25	.20	.10
38	Neal Heaton	.06	.05	.02
39	Jeff King	.08	.06	.03
40	Bob Kipper	.05	.04	.02
41	Bill Landrum	.06	.05	.02
42	Mike LaValliere	.06	.05	.02
43	Jose Lind	.06	.05	.02
44	Carmelo Martinez	.05	.04	.02
45	Bob Patterson	.05	.04	.02
46	Ted Power	.05	.04	.02
47	Gary Redus	.05	.04	.02
48	R.J. Reynolds	.05	.04	.02
49	Don Slaught	.05	.04	.02
50	John Smiley	.05	.04	.02
51	Zane Smith	.06	.05	.02
52	Randy Tomlin(FC)	.20	.15	.08
53	Andy Van Slyke	.08	.06	.03
54	Bob Walk	.05	.04	.02
55	Jack Armstrong	.08	.06	.03
56	Todd Benzinger	.06	.05	.02
57	Glenn Braggs	.06	.05	.02
58	Keith Brown	.06	.05	.02
59	Tom Browning	.08	.06	.03
60	Norm Charlton	.08	.06	.03
61	Eric Davis	.20	.15	.08
62	Rob Dibble	.10	.08	.04
63	Bill Doran	.08	.06	.03
64	Mariano Duncan	.06	.05	.02
65	Chris Hammond	.06	.05	.02
66	Billy Hatcher	.06	.05	.02
67	Danny Jackson	.06	.05	.02
68	Barry Larkin	.15	.11	.06
69	Tim Layana	.20	.15	.08
70	Terry Lee(FC)	.25	.20	.10
71	Rick Mahler	.05	.04	.02
72	Hal Morris	.12	.09	.05
73	Randy Myers	.08	.06	.03
74	Ron Oester	.05	.04	.02
75	Joe Oliver	.08	.06	.03
76	Paul O'Neill	.06	.05	.02
77	Luis Quinones	.05	.04	.02
78	Jeff Reed	.05	.04	.02
79	Jose Rijo	.08	.06	.03
80	Chris Sabo	.08	.06	.03
81	Scott Scudder	.06	.05	.02
82	Herm Winningham	.05	.04	.02
83	Larry Andersen	.05	.04	.02
84	Marty Barrett	.05	.04	.02
85	Mike Boddicker	.06	.05	.02
86	Wade Boggs	.20	.15	.08
87	Tom Bolton	.05	.04	.02
88	Tom Brunansky	.06	.05	.02
89	Ellis Burks	.15	.11	.06
90	Roger Clemens	.20	.15	.08
91	Scott Cooper(FC)	.15	.11	.06
92	John Dopson	.05	.04	.02
93	Dwight Evans	.06	.05	.02
94	Wes Gardner	.05	.04	.02
95	Jeff Gray(FC)	.15	.11	.06
96	Mike Greenwell	.10	.08	.04
97	Greg Harris	.05	.04	.02
98	Daryl Irvine(FC)	.20	.15	.08
99	Dana Kiecker	.10	.08	.04
100	Randy Kutcher	.05	.04	.02
101	Dennis Lamp	.05	.04	.02
102	Mike Marshall	.05	.04	.02
103	John Marzano	.05	.04	.02
104	Rob Murphy	.05	.04	.02
105	Tim Naehring	.25	.20	.10
106	Tony Pena	.06	.05	.02
107	Phil Plantier(FC)	.30	.25	.12
108	Carlos Quintana	.06	.05	.02

		MT	NR MT	EX			MT	NR MT	EX
109	Jeff Reardon	.06	.05	.02	200	Jim Gott	.05	.04	.02
110	Jerry Reed	.05	.04	.02	201	Alfredo Griffin	.05	.04	.02
111	Jody Reed	.06	.05	.02	202	Chris Gwynn	.06	.05	.02
112	Luis Rivera	.05	.04	.02	203	Dave Hansen	.20	.15	.08
113	Kevin Romine	.05	.04	.02	204	Lenny Harris	.06	.05	.02
114	Phil Bradley	.06	.05	.02	205	Mike Hartley	.10	.08	.04
115	Ivan Calderon	.06	.05	.02	206	Mickey Hatcher	.05	.04	.02
116	Wayne Edwards	.05	.04	.02	207	*Carlos Hernandez*(FC)	.20	.15	.08
117	*Alex Fernandez*	1.00	.70	.40	208	Orel Hershiser	.10	.08	.04
118	Carlton Fisk	.10	.08	.04	209	Jay Howell	.06	.05	.02
119	Scott Fletcher	.05	.04	.02	210	Mike Huff	.10	.08	.04
120	*Craig Grebeck*	.15	.11	.06	211	Stan Javier	.05	.04	.02
121	Ozzie Guillen	.08	.06	.03	212	Ramon Martinez	.20	.15	.08
122	Greg Hibbard	.06	.05	.02	213	Mike Morgan	.05	.04	.02
123	Lance Johnson	.06	.05	.02	214	Eddie Murray	.08	.06	.03
124	Barry Jones	.05	.04	.02	215	*Jim Neidlinger*(FC)	.20	.15	.08
125	Ron Karkovice	.05	.04	.02	216	Jose Offerman	.40	.30	.15
126	Eric King	.05	.04	.02	217	*Jim Poole*(FC)	.20	.15	.08
127	Steve Lyons	.05	.04	.02	218	Juan Samuel	.06	.05	.02
128	Carlos Martinez	.06	.05	.02	219	Mike Scioscia	.06	.05	.02
129	Jack McDowell	.06	.05	.02	220	Ray Searage	.05	.04	.02
130	Donn Pall	.05	.04	.02	221	Mike Sharperson	.06	.05	.02
131	Dan Pasqua	.05	.04	.02	222	Fernando Valenzuela	.06	.05	.02
132	Ken Patterson	.05	.04	.02	223	Jose Vizcaino	.10	.08	.04
133	Melido Perez	.06	.05	.02	224	Mike Aldrete	.05	.04	.02
134	Adam Peterson	.05	.04	.02	225	*Scott Anderson*(FC)	.20	.15	.08
135	*Scott Radinsky*	.15	.11	.06	226	Dennis Boyd	.06	.05	.02
136	Sammy Sosa	.15	.11	.06	227	Tim Burke	.06	.05	.02
137	Bobby Thigpen	.08	.06	.03	228	Delino DeShields	.30	.25	.12
138	Frank Thomas	1.00	.70	.40	229	Mike Fitzgerald	.05	.04	.02
139	Robin Ventura	.15	.11	.06	230	Tom Foley	.05	.04	.02
140	Daryl Boston	.05	.04	.02	231	Steve Frey	.05	.04	.02
141	*Chuck Carr*	.20	.15	.08	232	Andres Galarraga	.08	.06	.03
142	Mark Carreon	.05	.04	.02	233	Mark Gardner	.10	.08	.04
143	David Cone	.06	.05	.02	234	Marquis Grissom(FC)	.20	.15	.08
144	Ron Darling	.06	.05	.02	235	Kevin Gross	.06	.05	.02
145	Kevin Elster	.05	.04	.02	236	Drew Hall	.05	.04	.02
146	Sid Fernandez	.06	.05	.02	237	Dave Martinez	.06	.05	.02
147	John Franco	.08	.06	.03	238	Dennis Martinez	.06	.05	.02
148	Dwight Gooden	.20	.15	.08	239	Dale Mohorcic	.05	.04	.02
149	Tom Herr	.06	.05	.02	240	*Chris Nabholz*	.40	.30	.15
150	*Todd Hundley*	.20	.15	.08	241	Otis Nixon	.05	.04	.02
151	Gregg Jefferies	.15	.11	.06	242	Junior Noboa(FC)	.08	.06	.03
152	Howard Johnson	.08	.06	.03	243	Spike Owen	.05	.04	.02
153	Dave Magadan	.08	.06	.03	244	Tim Raines	.08	.06	.03
154	Kevin McReynolds	.08	.06	.03	245	*Mel Rojas*(FC)	.20	.15	.08
155	Keith Miller	.06	.05	.02	246	*Scott Ruskin*(FC)	.15	.11	.06
156	Bob Ojeda	.05	.04	.02	247	*Bill Sampen*	.25	.20	.10
157	Tom O'Malley	.05	.04	.02	248	Nelson Santovenia	.05	.04	.02
158	Alejandro Pena	.05	.04	.02	249	Dave Schmidt	.05	.04	.02
159	*Darren Reed*	.20	.15	.08	250	Larry Walker	.15	.11	.06
160	Mackey Sasser	.06	.05	.02	251	Tim Wallach	.08	.06	.03
161	Darryl Strawberry	.25	.20	.10	252	Dave Anderson	.05	.04	.02
162	Tim Teufel	.05	.04	.02	253	Kevin Bass	.06	.05	.02
163	Kelvin Torve	.08	.06	.03	254	Steve Bedrosian	.06	.05	.02
164	Julio Valera	.25	.20	.10	255	Jeff Brantley	.08	.06	.03
165	Frank Viola	.12	.09	.05	256	John Burkett	.12	.09	.05
166	Wally Whitehurst	.05	.04	.02	257	Brett Butler	.06	.05	.02
167	Jim Acker	.05	.04	.02	258	Gary Carter	.08	.06	.03
168	*Derek Bell*(FC)	.50	.40	.20	259	Will Clark	.25	.20	.10
169	George Bell	.08	.06	.03	260	*Steve Decker*(FC)	.30	.25	.12
170	*Willie Blair*	.15	.11	.06	261	Kelly Downs	.05	.04	.02
171	Pat Borders	.06	.05	.02	262	Scott Garrelts	.06	.05	.02
172	John Cerutti	.05	.04	.02	263	Terry Kennedy	.05	.04	.02
173	Juunior Felix	.12	.09	.05	264	Mike LaCoss	.05	.04	.02
174	Tony Fernandez	.08	.06	.03	265	*Mark Leonard*(FC)	.20	.15	.08
175	Kelly Gruber	.12	.09	.05	266	Greg Litton	.06	.05	.02
176	Tom Henke	.06	.05	.02	267	Kevin Mitchell	.20	.15	.08
177	Glenallen Hill	.08	.06	.03	268	Randy O'Neal(FC)	.05	.04	.02
178	Jimmy Key	.06	.05	.02	269	*Rick Parker*	.15	.11	.06
179	Manny Lee	.05	.04	.02	270	Rick Reuschel	.06	.05	.02
180	Fred McGriff	.15	.11	.06	271	Ernest Riles	.05	.04	.02
181	Rance Mulliniks	.05	.04	.02	272	Don Robinson	.05	.04	.02
182	Greg Myers	.05	.04	.02	273	Robby Thompson	.06	.05	.02
183	John Olerud	.50	.40	.20	274	Mark Thurmond	.05	.04	.02
184	Luis Sojo	.15	.11	.06	275	Jose Uribe	.05	.04	.02
185	Dave Steib	.08	.06	.03	276	Matt Williams	.15	.11	.06
186	Todd Stottlemyre	.06	.05	.02	277	Trevor Wilson	.06	.05	.02
187	Duane Ward	.05	.04	.02	278	Gerald Alexander(FC)	.20	.15	.08
188	David Wells	.05	.04	.02	279	Brad Arnsberg	.06	.05	.02
189	*Mark Whiten*	.50	.40	.20	280	*Kevin Belcher*(FC)	.30	.25	.12
190	Ken Williams	.05	.04	.02	281	*Joe Bitker*(FC)	.20	.15	.08
191	Frank Wills	.05	.04	.02	282	Kevin Brown	.06	.05	.02
192	Mookie Wilson	.05	.04	.02	283	Steve Buechele	.05	.04	.02
193	Don Aase	.05	.04	.02	284	Jack Daugherty	.06	.05	.02
194	Tim Belcher	.08	.06	.03	285	Julio Franco	.10	.08	.04
195	Hubie Brooks	.08	.06	.03	286	Juan Gonzalez	.20	.15	.08
196	Dennis Cook	.06	.05	.02	287	*Bill Haselman*(FC)	.25	.20	.10
197	Tim Crews	.05	.04	.02	288	Charlie Hough	.05	.04	.02
198	Kal Daniels	.06	.05	.02	289	Jeff Huson	.06	.05	.02
199	Kirk Gibson	.08	.06	.03	290	Pete Incaviglia	.06	.05	.02

		MT	NR MT	EX			MT	NR MT	EX
291	Mike Jeffcoat	.05	.04	.02	382	Colby Ward(FC)	.20	.15	.08
292	Jeff Kunkel	.05	.04	.02	383	Turner Ward(FC)	.25	.20	.10
293	Gary Mielke	.08	.06	.03	384	Mitch Webster	.05	.04	.02
294	Jamie Moyer	.05	.04	.02	385	Kevin Wickander(FC)	.15	.11	.06
295	Rafael Palmeiro	.08	.06	.03	386	Darrel Akerfelds	.06	.05	.02
296	Geno Petralli	.05	.04	.02	387	Joe Boever	.05	.04	.02
297	Gary Pettis	.06	.05	.02	388	Rod Booker	.05	.04	.02
298	Kevin Reimer	.10	.08	.04	389	Sil Campusano	.05	.04	.02
299	Kenny Rogers	.06	.05	.02	390	Don Carman	.05	.04	.02
300	Jeff Russell	.06	.05	.02	391	Wes Chamberlain(FC)	.30	.25	.12
301	John Russell	.05	.04	.02	392	Pat Combs	.06	.05	.02
302	Nolan Ryan	.25	.20	.10	393	Darren Daulton	.06	.05	.02
303	Ruben Sierra	.12	.09	.05	394	Jose DeJesus	.06	.05	.02
304	Bobby Witt	.08	.06	.03	395	Len Dykstra	.08	.06	.03
305	Jim Abbott	.08	.06	.03	396	Jason Grimsley	.06	.05	.02
306	Kent Anderson(FC)	.06	.05	.02	397	Charlie Hayes	.08	.06	.03
307	Dante Bichette	.06	.05	.02	398	Von Hayes	.08	.06	.03
308	Bert Blyleven	.08	.06	.03	399	David Hollins	.15	.11	.06
309	Chili Davis	.06	.05	.02	400	Ken Howell	.06	.05	.02
310	Brian Downing	.05	.04	.02	401	Ricky Jordan	.10	.08	.04
311	Mark Eichhorn	.05	.04	.02	402	John Kruk	.06	.05	.02
312	Mike Fetters	.08	.06	.03	403	Steve Lake	.05	.04	.02
313	Chuck Finley	.08	.06	.03	404	Chuck Malone(FC)	.15	.11	.06
314	Willie Fraser	.05	.04	.02	405	Roger McDowell	.08	.06	.03
315	Bryan Harvey	.06	.05	.02	406	Chuck McElroy	.15	.11	.06
316	Donnie Hill	.05	.04	.02	407	Mickey Morandini(FC)	.15	.11	.06
317	Wally Joyner	.10	.08	.04	408	Terry Mulholland	.06	.05	.02
318	Mark Langston	.10	.08	.04	409	Dale Murphy	.10	.08	.04
319	Kirk McCaskill	.06	.05	.02	410	Randy Ready	.05	.04	.02
320	John Orton	.06	.05	.02	411	Bruce Ruffin	.05	.04	.02
321	Lance Parrish	.08	.06	.03	412	Dickie Thon	.05	.04	.02
322	Luis Polonia	.05	.04	.02	413	Paul Assenmacher	.05	.04	.02
323	Johnny Ray	.05	.04	.02	414	Damon Berryhill	.06	.05	.02
324	Bobby Rose	.06	.05	.02	415	Mike Bielecki	.06	.05	.02
325	Dick Schofield	.05	.04	.02	416	Shawn Boskie	.15	.11	.06
326	Rick Schu	.05	.04	.02	417	Dave Clark	.05	.04	.02
327	Lee Stevens	.10	.08	.04	418	Doug Dascenzo	.05	.04	.02
328	Devon White	.06	.05	.02	419	Andre Dawson	.10	.08	.04
329	Dave Winfield	.12	.09	.05	420	Shawon Dunston	.10	.08	.04
330	Cliff Young	.15	.11	.06	421	Joe Girardi	.06	.05	.02
331	Dave Bergman	.05	.04	.02	422	Mark Grace	.15	.11	.06
332	Phil Clark(FC)	.25	.20	.10	423	Mike Harkey	.08	.06	.03
333	Darnell Coles	.05	.04	.02	424	Les Lancaster	.05	.04	.02
334	Milt Cuyler(FC)	.20	.15	.08	425	Bill Long	.05	.04	.02
335	Cecil Fielder	.30	.25	.12	426	Greg Maddux	.08	.06	.03
336	Travis Fryman	.80	.60	.30	427	Derrick May	.25	.20	.10
337	Paul Gibson	.05	.04	.02	428	Jeff Pico	.05	.04	.02
338	Jerry Don Gleaton	.05	.04	.02	429	Domingo Ramos	.05	.04	.02
339	Mike Heath	.05	.04	.02	430	Luis Salazar	.05	.04	.02
340	Mike Henneman	.06	.05	.02	431	Ryne Sandberg	.20	.15	.08
341	Chet Lemon	.06	.05	.02	432	Dwight Smith	.06	.05	.02
342	Lance McCullers	.05	.04	.02	433	Greg Smith	.08	.06	.03
343	Jack Morris	.08	.06	.03	434	Rick Sutcliffe	.08	.06	.03
344	lloyd Moseby	.06	.05	.02	435	Gary Varsho	.05	.04	.02
345	Edwin Nunez	.05	.04	.02	436	Hector Villanueva	.15	.11	.06
346	Clay Parker	.05	.04	.02	437	Jerome Walton	.08	.06	.03
347	Dan Petry	.05	.04	.02	438	Curtis Wilkerson	.05	.04	.02
348	Tony Phillips	.06	.05	.02	439	Mitch Williams	.08	.06	.03
349	Jeff Robinson	.06	.05	.02	440	Steve Wilson	.06	.05	.02
350	Mark Salas	.05	.04	.02	441	Marvell Wynne	.05	.04	.02
351	Mike Schwabe	.15	.11	.06	442	Scott Bankhead	.06	.05	.02
352	Larry Sheets	.05	.04	.02	443	Scott Bradley	.05	.04	.02
353	John Shelby	.05	.04	.02	444	Greg Briley	.06	.05	.02
354	Frank Tanana	.06	.05	.02	445	Mike Brumley	.05	.04	.02
355	Alan Trammell	.08	.06	.03	446	Jay Buhner	.06	.05	.02
356	Gary Ward	.05	.04	.02	447	Dave Burba(FC)	.15	.11	.06
357	Lou Whitaker	.08	.06	.03	448	Henry Cotto	.05	.04	.02
358	Beau Allred	.15	.11	.06	449	Alvin Davis	.08	.06	.03
359	Sandy Alomar,Jr.	.20	.15	.08	450	Ken Griffey,Jr.	.70	.50	.30
360	Carlos Baerga	.20	.15	.08	451	Erik Hanson	.12	.09	.05
361	Kevin Bearse	.12	.09	.05	452	Gene Harris	.05	.04	.02
362	Tom Brookens	.05	.04	.02	453	Brian Holman	.06	.05	.02
363	Jerry Browne	.06	.05	.02	454	Mike Jackson	.06	.05	.02
364	Tom Candiotti	.05	.04	.02	455	Randy Johnson	.10	.08	.04
365	Alex Cole	.25	.20	.10	456	Jeffrey Leonard	.06	.05	.02
366	John Farrell	.05	.04	.02	457	Edgar Martinez	.06	.05	.02
367	Felix Fermin	.05	.04	.02	458	Tino Martinez	.35	.25	.14
368	Keith Hernandez	.08	.06	.03	459	Pete O'Brien	.05	.04	.02
369	Brook Jacoby	.08	.06	.03	460	Harold Reynolds	.08	.06	.03
370	Chris James	.06	.05	.02	461	Mike Schooler	.08	.06	.03
371	Dion James	.05	.04	.02	462	Bill Swift	.06	.05	.02
372	Doug Jones	.08	.06	.03	463	David Valle	.05	.04	.02
373	Candy Maldonado	.08	.06	.03	464	Omar Vizquel	.06	.05	.02
374	Steve Olin	.06	.05	.02	465	Matt Young	.06	.05	.02
375	Jesse Orosco	.05	.04	.02	466	Brady Anderson	.05	.04	.02
376	Rudy Seanez	.06	.05	.02	467	Jeff Ballard	.06	.05	.02
377	Joel Skinner	.05	.04	.02	468	Juan Bell(FC)	.20	.15	.08
378	Cory Snyder	.08	.06	.03	469	Mike Devereaux	.06	.05	.02
379	Greg Swindell	.06	.05	.02	470	Steve Finley	.06	.05	.02
380	Sergio Valdez(FC)	.08	.06	.03	471	Dave Gallagher	.05	.04	.02
381	Mike Walker(FC)	.15	.11	.06	472	Leo Gomez(FC)	.40	.30	.15

		MT	NR MT	EX
473	Rene Gonzales	.05	.04	.02
474	Pete Harnisch	.06	.05	.02
475	Kevin Hickey	.05	.04	.02
476	Chris Hoiles	.20	.15	.08
477	Sam Horn	.06	.05	.02
478	Tim Hulett	.05	.04	.02
479	Dave Johnson	.05	.04	.02
480	Ron Kittle	.08	.06	.03
481	Ben McDonald	.40	.30	.15
482	Bob Melvin	.05	.04	.02
483	Bob Milacki	.06	.05	.02
484	Randy Milligan	.06	.05	.02
485	John Mitchell(FC)	.15	.11	.06
486	Gregg Olson	.08	.06	.03
487	Joe Orsulak	.05	.04	.02
488	Joe Price	.05	.04	.02
489	Bill Ripken	.05	.04	.02
490	Cal Ripken,Jr.	.15	.11	.06
491	Curt Schilling	.06	.05	.02
492	David Segui	.30	.25	.12
493	Anthony Telford(FC)	.20	.15	.08
494	Mickey Tettleton	.06	.05	.02
495	Mark Williamson	.05	.04	.02
496	Craig Worthington	.06	.05	.02
497	Juan Agosto	.05	.04	.02
498	Eric Anthony	.15	.11	.06
499	Craig Biggio	.08	.06	.03
500	Ken Caminiti	.06	.05	.02
501	Casey Candaele	.05	.04	.02
502	Andujar Cedeno(FC)	.40	.30	.15
503	Danny Darwin	.06	.05	.02
504	Mark Davidson	.05	.04	.02
505	Glenn Davis	.15	.11	.06
506	Jim Deshaies	.06	.05	.02
507	Luis Gonzalez(FC)	.30	.25	.12
508	Bill Gullickson	.05	.04	.02
509	Xavier Hernandez(FC)	.08	.06	.03
510	Brian Meyer	.06	.05	.02
511	Ken Oberkfell	.05	.04	.02
512	Mark Portugal	.05	.04	.02
513	Rafael Ramirez	.05	.04	.02
514	Karl Rhodes(FC)	.20	.15	.08
515	Mike Scott	.08	.06	.03
516	Mike Simms(FC)	.25	.20	.10
517	Dave Smith	.06	.05	.02
518	Franklin Stubbs	.06	.05	.02
519	Glenn Wilson	.06	.05	.02
520	Eric Yelding	.10	.08	.04
521	Gerald Young	.05	.04	.02
522	Shawn Abner	.05	.04	.02
523	Roberto Alomar	.10	.08	.04
524	Andy Benes	.15	.11	.06
525	Joe Carter	.10	.08	.04
526	Jack Clark	.08	.06	.03
527	Joey Cora	.06	.05	.02
528	Paul Faries(FC)	.20	.15	.08
529	Tony Gwynn	.15	.11	.06
530	Atlee Hammaker	.05	.04	.02
531	Greg Harris	.06	.05	.02
532	Thomas Howard	.20	.15	.08
533	Bruce Hurst	.06	.05	.02
534	Craig Lefferts	.06	.05	.02
535	Derek Lilliquist	.06	.05	.02
536	Fred Lynn	.06	.05	.02
537	Mike Pagliarulo	.06	.05	.02
538	Mark Parent	.05	.04	.02
539	Dennis Rasmussen	.05	.04	.02
540	Bip Roberts	.08	.06	.03
541	Richard Rodriguez(FC)	.20	.15	.08
542	Benito Santiago	.10	.08	.04
543	Calvin Schiraldi	.05	.04	.02
544	Eric Show	.06	.05	.02
545	Phil Stephenson	.05	.04	.02
546	Garry Templeton	.06	.05	.02
547	Ed Whitson	.06	.05	.02
548	Eddie Williams	.05	.04	.02
549	Kevin Appier	.10	.08	.04
550	Luis Aquino	.05	.04	.02
551	Bob Boone	.08	.06	.03
552	George Brett	.12	.09	.05
553	Jeff Conine(FC)	.35	.25	.14
554	Steve Crawford	.05	.04	.02
555	Mark Davis	.06	.05	.02
556	Storm Davis	.06	.05	.02
557	Jim Eisenreich	.06	.05	.02
558	Steve Farr	.05	.04	.02
559	Tom Gordon	.10	.08	.04
560	Mark Gubicza	.08	.06	.03
561	Bo Jackson	.30	.25	.12
562	Mike Macfarlane	.05	.04	.02
563	Brian McRae(FC)	.50	.40	.20
564	Jeff Montgomery	.06	.05	.02
565	Bill Pecota	.05	.04	.02
566	Gerald Perry	.06	.05	.02
567	Bret Saberhagen	.10	.08	.04
568	Jeff Schulz(FC)	.20	.15	.08
569	Kevin Seitzer	.08	.06	.03
570	Terry Shumpert	.25	.20	.10
571	Kurt Stillwell	.06	.05	.02
572	Danny Tartabull	.08	.06	.03
573	Gary Thurman	.05	.04	.02
574	Frank White	.06	.05	.02
575	Willie Wilson	.06	.05	.02
576	Chris Bosio	.06	.05	.02
577	Greg Brock	.06	.05	.02
578	George Canale	.06	.05	.02
579	Chuck Crim	.05	.04	.02
580	Rob Deer	.06	.05	.02
581	Edgar Diaz	.06	.05	.02
582	Tom Edens(FC)	.08	.06	.03
583	Mike Felder	.05	.04	.02
584	Jim Gantner	.06	.05	.02
585	Darryl Hamilton	.06	.05	.02
586	Ted Higuera	.08	.06	.03
587	Mark Knudson	.05	.04	.02
588	Bill Krueger	.05	.04	.02
589	Tim McIntosh	.08	.06	.03
590	Paul Mirabella	.05	.04	.02
591	Paul Molitor	.10	.08	.04
592	Jaime Navarro	.08	.06	.03
593	Dave Parker	.12	.09	.05
594	Dan Plesac	.06	.05	.02
595	Ron Robinson	.06	.05	.02
596	Gary Sheffield	.15	.11	.06
597	Bill Spiers	.06	.05	.02
598	B.J. Surhoff	.06	.05	.02
599	Greg Vaughn	.15	.11	.06
600	Randy Veres	.05	.04	.02
601	Robin Yount	.15	.11	.06
602	Rick Aguilera	.06	.05	.02
603	Allan Anderson	.05	.04	.02
604	Juan Berenguer	.05	.04	.02
605	Randy Bush	.05	.04	.02
606	Carmen Castillo	.05	.04	.02
607	Tim Drummond	.06	.05	.02
608	Scott Erickson(FC)	.25	.20	.10
609	Gary Gaetti	.08	.06	.03
610	Greg Gagne	.06	.05	.02
611	Dan Gladden	.06	.05	.02
612	Mark Guthrie(FC)	.06	.05	.02
613	Brian Harper	.06	.05	.02
614	Kent Hrbek	.08	.06	.03
615	Gene Larkin	.06	.05	.02
616	Terry Leach	.05	.04	.02
617	Nelson Liriano	.05	.04	.02
618	Shane Mack	.06	.05	.02
619	John Moses	.05	.04	.02
620	Pedro Munoz(FC)	.30	.25	.12
621	Al Newman	.05	.04	.02
622	Junior Ortiz	.05	.04	.02
623	Kirby Puckett	.15	.11	.06
624	Roy Smith	.05	.04	.02
625	Kevin Tapani	.10	.08	.04
626	Gary Wayne	.05	.04	.02
627	David West	.06	.05	.02
628	Cris Carpenter	.06	.05	.02
629	Vince Coleman	.08	.06	.03
630	Ken Dayley	.06	.05	.02
631	Jose DeLeon	.06	.05	.02
632	Frank DiPino	.05	.04	.02
633	Bernard Gilkey(FC)	.30	.25	.12
634	Pedro Guerrero	.08	.06	.03
635	Ken Hill	.06	.05	.02
636	Felix Jose	.08	.06	.03
637	Ray Lankford(FC)	.70	.50	.30
638	Joe Magrane	.08	.06	.03
639	Tom Niedenfuer	.05	.04	.02
640	Jose Oquendo	.05	.04	.02
641	Tom Pagnozzi	.05	.04	.02
642	Terry Pendleton	.06	.05	.02
643	Mike Perez(FC)	.20	.15	.08
644	Bryn Smith	.05	.04	.02
645	Lee Smith	.08	.06	.03
646	Ozzie Smith	.10	.08	.04
647	Scott Terry	.05	.04	.02
648	Bob Tewksbury	.05	.04	.02
649	Milt Thompson	.05	.04	.02
650	John Tudor	.06	.05	.02
651	Denny Walling	.05	.04	.02
652	Craig Wilson(FC)	.15	.11	.06
653	Todd Worrell	.06	.05	.02
654	Todd Zeile	.20	.15	.08

		MT	NR MT	EX
655	Oscar Azocar	.20	.15	.08
656	Steve Balboni	.05	.04	.02
657	Jesse Barfield	.08	.06	.03
658	Greg Cadaret	.05	.04	.02
659	Chuck Cary	.05	.04	.02
660	Rick Cerone	.05	.04	.02
661	Dave Eiland(FC)	.06	.05	.02
662	Alvaro Espinoza	.06	.05	.02
663	Bob Geren	.06	.05	.02
664	Lee Guettuerman	.05	.04	.02
665	Mel Hall	.06	.05	.02
666	Andy Hawkins	.06	.05	.02
667	Jimmy Jones	.05	.04	.02
668	Roberto Kelly	.10	.08	.04
669	Dave LaPoint	.05	.04	.02
670	Tim Leary	.06	.05	.02
671	Jim Leyritz	.20	.15	.08
672	Kevin Maas	.50	.40	.20
673	Don Mattingly	.40	.30	.15
674	Matt Nokes	.06	.05	.02
675	Pascual Perez	.06	.05	.02
676	Eric Plunk	.05	.04	.02
677	Dave Righetti	.08	.06	.03
678	Jeff Robinson	.05	.04	.02
679	Steve Sax	.10	.08	.04
680	Mike Witt	.06	.05	.02
681	Steve Avery	.15	.11	.06
682	Mike Bell	.20	.15	.08
683	Jeff Blauser	.06	.05	.02
684	Francisco Cabrera	.10	.08	.04
685	Tony Castillo(FC)	.08	.06	.03
686	Marty Clary	.05	.04	.02
687	Nick Esasky	.08	.06	.03
688	Ron Gant	.10	.08	.04
689	Tom Glavine	.06	.05	.02
690	Mark Grant	.05	.04	.02
691	Tommy Gregg	.06	.05	.02
692	Dwayne Henry	.05	.04	.02
693	Dave Justice	.60	.45	.25
694	Jimmy Kremers	.20	.15	.08
695	Charlie Leibrandt	.06	.05	.02
696	Mark Lemke	.06	.05	.02
697	Oddibe McDowell	.06	.05	.02
698	Greg Olson	.08	.06	.03
699	Jeff Parrett	.06	.05	.02
700	Jim Presley	.06	.05	.02
701	Victor Rosario(FC)	.20	.15	.08
702	Lonnie Smith	.06	.05	.02
703	Pete Smith	.06	.05	.02
704	John Smoltz	.08	.06	.03
705	Mike Stanton	.08	.06	.03
706	Andres Thomas	.05	.04	.02
707	Jeff Treadway	.06	.05	.02
708	Jim Vatcher(FC)	.15	.11	.06
709	Home Run Kings (Ryne Sandberg, Cecil Fielder)	.35	.25	.14
710	Second Generation Stars (Barry Bonds, Ken Griffey,Jr.)	.50	.40	.20
711	NLCS Team Leaders (Bobby Bonilla, Barry Larkin)	.25	.20	.10
712	Top Game Savers (Bobby Thigpen, John Franco)	.15	.11	.06
713	Chicago's 100 Club (Andre Dawson, Ryne Sandberg)	.25	.20	.10
714	Checklists (Athletics, Pirates, Reds, Red Sox)	.05	.04	.02
715	Checklists (White Sox, Mets Blue Jays, Dodgers)	.05	.04	.02
716	Checklists (Expos, Giants, Rangers, Angels)	.05	.04	.02
717	Checklists (Tigers, Indians, Phillies, Cubs)	.05	.04	.02
718	Checklists (Mariners, Orioles, Astros, Padres)	.05	.04	.02
719	Checklists (Royals, Brewers, Twins, Cardinals)	.05	.04	.02
720	Checklists (Yankees, Braves, Super Stars)	.05	.04	.02

1987 French/Bray Orioles

The Baltimore Orioles and French Bray, Inc. issued a baseball card set to be handed out to fans in attendance at Memorial Stadium on July 26th. Thirty perforated, detachable cards were printed within a three-panel fold-out piece measuring 9-1/2" by 11-1/4". The card fronts feature full-color player

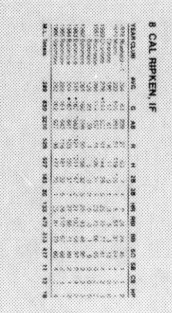

8 CAL RIPKEN, IF
Compliments of
FRENCH/BRAY, INC.

photos surrounded by an orange border. The French/Bray logo appears on the card front. The backs are of simple design, containing only the player's name, uniform number, position and professional record.

		MT	NR MT	EX
Complete Set:		10.00	7.50	4.00
Common Player:		.15	.11	.06
2	Alan Wiggins	.15	.11	.06
3	Bill Ripken	.80	.60	.30
6	Floyd Rayford	.15	.11	.06
7	Cal Ripken, Sr.	.15	.11	.06
8	Cal Ripken	1.75	1.25	.70
9	Jim Dwyer	.15	.11	.06
10	Terry Crowley	.15	.11	.06
15	Terry Kennedy	.20	.15	.08
16	Scott McGregor	.20	.15	.08
18	Larry Sheets	.50	.40	.20
19	Fred Lynn	.50	.40	.20
20	Frank Robinson	.40	.30	.15
24	Dave Schmidt	.15	.11	.06
25	Ray Knight	.20	.15	.08
27	Lee Lacy	.15	.11	.06
31	Mark Wiley	.15	.11	.06
32	Mark Williamson	.30	.25	.12
33	Eddie Murray	1.50	1.25	.60
38	Ken Gerhart	.50	.40	.20
39	Ken Dixon	.15	.11	.06
40	Jimmy Williams	.15	.11	.06
42	Mike Griffin	.15	.11	.06
43	Mike Young	.20	.15	.08
44	Elrod Hendricks	.15	.11	.06
45	Eric Bell	.30	.25	.12
46	Mike Flanagan	.25	.20	.10
49	Tom Niedenfuer	.20	.15	.08
52	Mike Boddicker	.25	.20	.10
54	John Habyan	.15	.11	.06
57	Tony Arnold	.15	.11	.06

1988 French/Bray Orioles

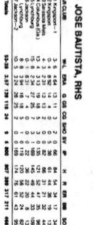

48 JOSE BAUTISTA, RHS
Compliments of
FRENCH BRAY, INC.

French-Bray sponsored a full-color brochure that was distributed to fans during an in-stadium promotion. A blue and orange front cover features inset photos of the Orioles in action on the upper left in a filmstrip motif. To the right is the Orioles logo and their 1988 slogan, "You Gotta Be There" above a baseball glove and ball. The 3-panel foldout measures approximately 9-1/2" by 11-1/4" and includes a team photo on the inside cover, with two perforated pages of individual cards featuring players, coaches and the team manager. Individual cards measure 2-1/4" by 3-1/8", with close-ups framed in white with an orange accent line. The player name and sponsor logo are printed beneath the photo. The black and white backs are numbered by player uniform number and provide career stats. Additional copies of the brochure were made available from the Orioles Baseball Store following the free giveaway.

	MT	NR MT	EX
Complete Set:	8.00	6.00	3.25
Common Player:	.15	.11	.06
2 Don Buford	.15	.11	.06
6 Joe Orsulak	.15	.11	.06
7 Bill Ripken	.40	.30	.15
8 Cal Ripken	1.75	1.25	.70
9 Jim Dwyer	.15	.11	.06
10 Terry Crowley	.15	.11	.06
12 Mike Morgan	.15	.11	.06
14 Mickey Tettleton	.15	.11	.06
15 Terry Kennedy	.20	.15	.08
17 Pete Stanicek	.60	.45	.25
18 Larry Sheets	.40	.30	.15
19 Fred Lynn	.50	.40	.20
20 Frank Robinson	.40	.30	.15
23 Ozzie Peraza	.40	.30	.15
24 Dave Schmidt	.15	.11	.06
25 Rich Schu	.15	.11	.06
28 Jim Traber	.25	.20	.10
31 Herm Starrette	.15	.11	.06
33 Eddie Murray	1.50	1.25	.60
34 Jeff Ballard	.30	.25	.12
38 Ken Gerhart	.30	.25	.12
40 Minnie Mendoza	.15	.11	.06
41 Don Aase	.20	.15	.08
44 Elrod Hendricks	.15	.11	.06
47 John Hart	.15	.11	.06
48 Jose Bautista	.30	.25	.12
49 Tom Niedenfuer	.20	.15	.08
52 Mike Boddicker	.25	.20	.10
53 Jay Tibbs	.15	.11	.06
88 Rene Gonzales	.30	.25	.12

1989 French/Bray Orioles

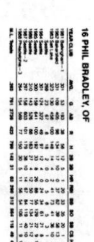

This 32-card Baltimore Orioles team set was co-sponsored by French-Bray and the Wilcox Walter Furlong Paper Co., and was distributed as an in-stadium promotion to fans attending the May 12, 1989, Orioles game. Smaller than standard size, the cards measure 2-1/4" by 3" and feature a full-color player photo with number, name and position below. The backs, done in black and white, include brief player data and complete major and minor league stats.

	MT	NR MT	EX
Complete Set:	8.00	6.00	3.25

	MT	NR MT	EX
Common Player:	.15	.11	.06
3 Bill Ripken	.30	.25	.12
6 Joe Orsulak	.15	.11	.06
7 Cal Ripken, Sr.	.15	.11	.06
8 Cal Ripken, Jr.	1.75	1.25	.70
9 Brady Anderson	.20	.15	.08
10 Steve Finley	.80	.60	.30
11 Craig Worthington	.50	.40	.20
12 Mike Devereaux	.20	.15	.08
14 Mickey Tettleton	.20	.15	.08
15 Randy Milligan	.15	.11	.06
16 Phil Bradley	.20	.15	.08
18 Bob Milacki	.20	.15	.08
19 Larry Sheets	.15	.11	.06
20 Frank Robinson	.40	.30	.15
21 Mark Thurmond	.15	.11	.06
23 Kevin Hickey	.15	.11	.06
24 Dave Schmidt	.15	.11	.06
28 Jim Traber	.20	.15	.08
29 Jeff Ballard	.30	.25	.12
30 Gregg Olson	1.50	1.25	.60
31 Al Jackson	.15	.11	.06
32 Mark Williamson	.15	.11	.06
36 Bob Melvin	.15	.11	.06
37 Brian Holton	.15	.11	.06
40 Tom McCraw	.15	.11	.06
42 Pete Harnisch	.35	.25	.14
43 Fransisco Melendez	.20	.15	.08
44 Elrod Hendricks	.15	.11	.06
46 Johnny Oates	.15	.11	.06
48 Jose Bautista	.20	.15	.08
88 Rene Gonzales	.25	.20	.10

1983 Gardner's Brewers

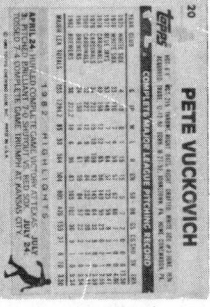

Topps produced in 1983 for Gardner's Bakery of Madison, Wisconsin, a 22-card set featuring the American League champion Milwaukee Brewers. The cards, which measure 2-1/2" by 3-1/2", have colorful fronts which contain the player's name, team and position plus the Brewers and Gardner's logos. The card backs are identical to the regular Topps issue but are numbered 1-22. The cards were inserted in specially marked packages of Gardner's bread products and were susceptible to grease stains.

	MT	NR MT	EX
Complete Set	25.00	18.50	10.00
Common Player	.50	.40	.20
1 Harvey Kuenn	.70	.50	.30
2 Dwight Bernard	.50	.40	.20
3 Mark Brouhard	.50	.40	.20
4 Mike Caldwell	.50	.40	.20
5 Cecil Cooper	1.25	.90	.50
6 Marshall Edwards	.50	.40	.20
7 Rollie Fingers	4.00	3.00	1.50
8 Jim Gantner	.70	.50	.30

		MT	NR MT	EX
9	Moose Haas	.50	.40	.20
10	Bob McClure	.50	.40	.20
11	Paul Molitor	4.00	3.00	1.50
12	Don Money	.50	.40	.20
13	Charlie Moore	.50	.40	.20
14	Ben Oglivie	.60	.45	.25
15	Ed Romero	.50	.40	.20
16	Ted Simmons	.90	.70	.35
17	Jim Slaton	.50	.40	.20
18	Don Sutton	2.00	1.50	.80
19	Gorman Thomas	.70	.50	.30
20	Pete Vuckovich	.70	.50	.30
21	Ned Yost	.50	.40	.20
22	Robin Yount	7.00	5.25	2.75

1984 Gardner's Brewers

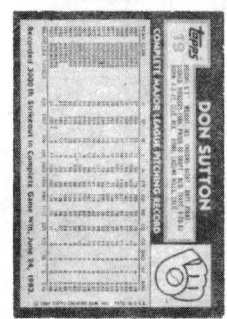

For the second straight year, Gardner's Bakery inserted baseball cards featuring the Milwaukee Brewers with their bread products. The 22-card set, entitled "1984 Series II," have multi-colored fronts that include the Brewers and Gardner's logos. The card backs are identical to the regular 1984 Topps issue except for the 1-22 numbering system. The Topps-produced cards are the standard 2-1/2" by 3-1/2" size. The cards are sometimes found with grease stains, resulting from contact with the bread.

		MT	NR MT	EX
Complete Set:		20.00	15.00	8.00
Common Player:		.50	.40	.20
1	Rene Lachemann	.50	.40	.20
2	Mark Brouhard	.50	.40	.20
3	Mike Caldwell	.50	.40	.20
4	Bobby Clark	.50	.40	.20
5	Cecil Cooper	1.00	.70	.40
6	Rollie Fingers	2.00	1.50	.80
7	Jim Gantner	.70	.50	.30
8	Moose Haas	.50	.40	.20
9	Roy Howell	.50	.40	.20
10	Pete Ladd	.50	.40	.20
11	Rick Manning	.50	.40	.20
12	Bob McClure	.50	.40	.20
13	Paul Molitor	2.00	1.50	.80
14	Charlie Moore	.50	.40	.20
15	Ben Oglivie	.60	.45	.25
16	Ed Romero	.50	.40	.20
17	Ted Simmons	.80	.60	.30
18	Jim Sundberg	.50	.40	.20
19	Don Sutton	1.25	.90	.50
20	Tom Tellmann	.50	.40	.20
21	Pete Vuckovich	.60	.45	.25
22	Robin Yount	5.00	3.75	2.00

1985 Gardner's Brewers

Gardner's Bakery issued a 22-card set featuring the Milwaukee Brewers for the third consecutive year in 1985. The set was produced by Topps and is designed in a horizontal format. The card fronts feature color photos inside blue, red and yellow frames. The player's name and position are placed in orange boxes to the right of the photo and are accompanied by the Brewers and Gardner's logos. The card backs are identical in design to the regular 1985 Topps set but are blue rather than green and are numbered 1-22. The cards, which were inserted in specially marked bread products, are often found with grease stains.

		MT	NR MT	EX
Complete Set:		15.00	11.00	6.00
Common Player:		.35	.25	.14
1	George Bamberger	.35	.25	.14
2	Mark Brouhard	.35	.25	.14
3	Bob Clark	.35	.25	.14
4	Jaime Cocanower	.35	.25	.14
5	Cecil Cooper	.90	.70	.35
6	Rollie Fingers	1.25	.90	.50
7	Jim Gantner	.50	.40	.20
8	Moose Haas	.35	.25	.14
9	Dion James	.70	.50	.30
10	Pete Ladd	.35	.25	.14
11	Rick Manning	.35	.25	.14
12	Bob McClure	.35	.25	.14
13	Paul Molitor	1.50	1.25	.60
14	Charlie Moore	.35	.25	.14
15	Ben Oglivie	.50	.40	.20
16	Chuck Porter	.35	.25	.14
17	Ed Romero	.35	.25	.14
18	Bill Schroeder	.35	.25	.14
19	Ted Simmons	.70	.50	.30
20	Tom Tellmann	.35	.25	.14
21	Pete Vuckovich	.50	.40	.20
22	Robin Yount	4.00	3.00	1.50

1989 Gardners Brewers

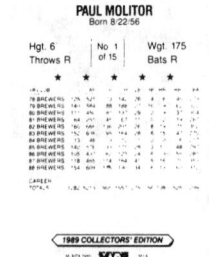

Returning after a three-year hiatus, Gardner's Bread of Madison, Wis., issued a 15-card Milwaukee Brewers set in 1989. The blue and white-bordered cards are the standard size and feature posed portrait photos with all Brewer logos airbrushed from the players' caps. The Gardner's logo appears at the top of the card, while the player's name is below the photo. The set, which was produced in conjunction with Mike Schechter Associates, was issued with loaves of bread or packages of buns, one card per package.

		MT	NR MT	EX
Complete Set:		5.00	3.75	2.00
Common Player:		.10	.08	.04
1	Paul Molitor	1.00	.70	.40
2	Robin Yount	1.25	.90	.50
3	Jim Gantner	.25	.20	.10
4	Rob Deer	.25	.20	.10
5	B.J. Surhoff	.25	.20	.10
6	Dale Sveum	.20	.15	.08
7	Ted Higuera	.25	.20	.10
8	Dan Plesac	.25	.20	.10
9	Bill Wegman	.15	.11	.06
10	Juan Nieves	.15	.11	.06
11	Greg Brock	.20	.15	.08
12	Glenn Braggs	.25	.20	.10
13	Joey Meyer	.15	.11	.06
14	Ernest Riles	.10	.08	.04
15	Don August	.15	.11	.06

1986 Gatorade Cubs

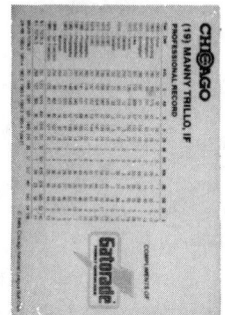

(19) MANNY TRILLO, IF

Gatorade sponsored this 28-card set which was given away at the July 17, 1986 Cubs game. The cards measure 2-7/8" by 4-1/4" and feature color photos set inside red and white frames. The Cubs logo appears at the top of the card in blue and red. The card backs include statistical information and the Gatorade logo. This set marked the fifth consecutive year the Cubs had held a baseball card giveaway promotion.

		MT	NR MT	EX
Complete Set:		10.00	7.50	4.00
Common Player:		.10	.08	.04
4	Gene Michael	.10	.08	.04
6	Keith Moreland	.30	.25	.12
7	Jody Davis	.30	.25	.12
10	Leon Durham	.30	.25	.12
11	Ron Cey	.30	.25	.12
12	Shawon Dunston	1.25	.90	.50
15	Davey Lopes	.25	.20	.10
16	Terry Francona	.10	.08	.04
18	Steve Christmas	.10	.08	.04
19	Manny Trillo	.15	.11	.06
20	Bob Dernier	.10	.08	.04
21	Scott Sanderson	.10	.08	.04
22	Jerry Mumphrey	.10	.08	.04
23	Ryne Sandberg	3.00	2.25	1.25
27	Thad Bosley	.10	.08	.04
28	Chris Speier	.10	.08	.04
29	Steve Lake	.10	.08	.04
31	Ray Fontenot	.10	.08	.04
34	Steve Trout	.20	.15	.08
36	Gary Matthews	.30	.25	.12
39	George Frazier	.10	.08	.04
40	Rick Sutcliffe	.70	.50	.30
43	Dennis Eckersley	.70	.50	.30
46	Lee Smith	.35	.25	.14
48	Jay Baller	.15	.11	.06
49	Jamie Moyer	.35	.25	.14
50	Guy Hoffman	.10	.08	.04
----	The Coaching Staff (Ruben Amaro, Billy Connors, Johnny Oates, John Vuckovich, Billy Williams)	.15	.11	.06

1987 Gatorade Indians

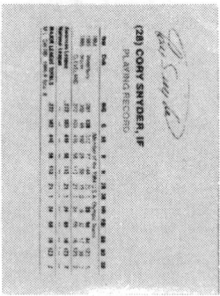

(28) CORY SNYDER, IF   COMPLIMENTS OF Gatorade

For the second year in a row, the Cleveland Indians gave out a perforated set of baseball cards to fans attending the Team Photo/Baseball Card Day promotion. Sponsored by Gatorade, the individual cards measure 2-1/2" by 3-1/8". The fronts contain a full-color photo surrounded by a red frame inside a white border. The player's name, uniform number and the Gatorade logo are also on the fronts. The card backs are printed in black, blue and red and carry a facsimile autograph and the player's playing record.

		MT	NR MT	EX
Complete Set:		8.00	5.00	2.50
Common Player:		.10	.05	.02
2	Brett Butler	.35	.25	.14
4	Tony Bernazard	.10	.09	.05
6	Andy Allanson	.15	.09	.05
7	Pat Corrales	.10	.09	.05
8	Carmen Castillo	.10	.05	.02
10	Pat Tabler	.20	.20	.10
11	Jamie Easterly	.10	.05	.02
12	Dave Clark	.20	.15	.08
13	Ernie Camacho	.10	.05	.02
14	Julio Franco	.60	.45	.25
17	Junior Noboa	.10	.15	.08
18	Ken Schrom	.10	.08	.04
20	Otis Nixon	.15	.05	.02
21	Greg Swindell	.80	.45	.25
22	Frank Wills	.10	.05	.02
23	Chris Bando	.10	.05	.02
24	Rick Dempsey	.15	.09	.05
26	Brook Jacoby	.60	.30	.15
27	Mel Hall	.30	.25	.12
28	Cory Snyder	.90	.70	.35
29	Andre Thornton	.30	.25	.12
30	Joe Carter	.80	.45	.25
35	Phil Niekro	.40	.30	.15
36	Ed Vande Berg	.10	.05	.02
42	Rich Yett	.10	.05	.02
43	Scott Bailes	.40	.30	.15
46	Doug Jones	.40	.15	.08
49	Tom Candiotti	.20	.09	.05
54	Tom Waddell	.10	.05	.02
----	Manager and Coaching Staff (Jack Aker, Bobby Bonds, Pat Corrales, Doc Edwards, Johnny Goryl)	.10	.05	.02

1988 Gatorade Indians

This 3-panel foldout was sponsored by Gatorade for distribution during an in-stadium giveaway. The white cover includes four game day photos. One panel of the 9-1/2" by 11-1/4" glossy full-color brochure features a team photo (with checklist), two panels consist of 30 perforated baseball cards (2-1/4" by 3") featuring team members. Posed close-up photos are framed in red on a white background. The player's name and uniform number are printed below the photo. The card backs are printed in red, blue and black on white. A facsimile autograph appears at the top right portion of the card back, opposite the player

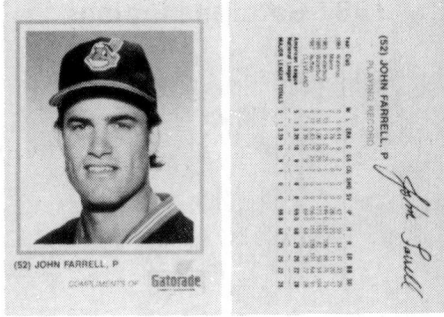

(52) JOHN FARRELL, P

COMPLIMENTS OF Gatorade

uniform number, name and position. Both major and minor league stats are listed.

		MT	NR MT	EX
Complete Set:		8.00	6.00	3.25
Common Player:		.10	.08	.04
2	Tom Spencer	.10	.08	.04
6	Andy Allanson	.15	.11	.06
7	Luis Issac	.10	.08	.04
8	Carmen Castillo	.10	.08	.04
9	Charlie Manuel	.10	.08	.04
10	Pat Tabler	.20	.15	.08
11	Doug Jones	.30	.25	.12
14	Julio Franco	.60	.45	.25
15	Ron Washington	.10	.08	.04
16	Jay Bell	.20	.15	.08
17	Bill Laskey	.10	.08	.04
20	Willie Upshaw	.20	.15	.08
21	Greg Swindell	.80	.60	.30
23	Chris Bando	.10	.08	.04
25	Dave Clark	.15	.11	.06
26	Brook Jacoby	.60	.45	.25
27	Mel Hall	.30	.25	.12
28	Cory Snyder	.80	.60	.30
30	Joe Carter	.80	.60	.30
31	Dan Schatzeder	.10	.08	.04
32	Doc Edwards	.10	.08	.04
33	Ron Kittle	.25	.20	.10
35	Mark Wiley	.10	.08	.04
42	Rich Yett	.10	.08	.04
43	Scott Bailes	.20	.15	.08
45	Johnny Goryl	.10	.08	.04
47	Jeff Kaiser	.10	.08	.04
49	Tom Candiotti	.20	.15	.08
50	Jeff Dedmon	.10	.08	.04
52	John Farrell	.40	.30	.15

1953 Glendale Hot Dogs Tigers

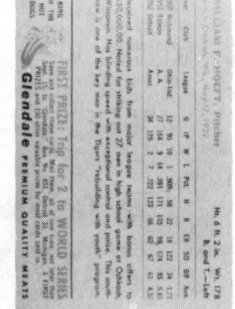

BILL HOEFT

Glendale Meats issued these unnumbered, full-color cards (2-5/8" by 3-3/4") in packages of hot dogs. Featuring Detroit Tigers players, the card fronts contain a player picture plus the player's name, a facsimile autograph, and the Tigers logo. The card reverses carry player statistical and biographical information plus an offer for a trip for two to the World Series. Collectors were advised to mail all the cards they had saved to Glendale Meats. The World

Series trip plus 150 other prizes were to be given to the individuals sending in the most cards. As with most cards issued with food products, quality-condition cards are tough to find because of the cards' susceptibilty to stains. The Houtteman card is extremely scarce.

		NR MT	EX	VG
Complete Set:		5500.00	2750.00	1650.
Common Player:		115.00	57.00	34.00
(1)	Matt Batts	115.00	57.00	34.00
(2)	Johnny Bucha	115.00	57.00	34.00
(3)	Frank Carswell	115.00	57.00	34.00
(4)	Jim Delsing	115.00	57.00	34.00
(5)	Walt Dropo	115.00	57.00	34.00
(6)	Hal Erickson	115.00	57.00	34.00
(7)	Paul Foytack	115.00	57.00	34.00
(8)	Owen Friend	125.00	62.00	37.00
(9)	Ned Garver	115.00	57.00	34.00
(10)	Joe Ginsberg	350.00	175.00	105.00
(11)	Ted Gray	115.00	57.00	34.00
(12)	Fred Hatfield	115.00	57.00	34.00
(13)	Ray Herbert	125.00	62.00	37.00
(14)	Bill Hitchcock	115.00	57.00	34.00
(15)	Bill Hoeft	275.00	137.00	82.00
(16)	Art Houtteman	2000.00	1000.00	600.00
(17)	Milt Jordan	200.00	100.00	60.00
(18)	Harvey Kuenn	225.00	112.00	67.00
(19)	Don Lund	115.00	57.00	34.00
(20)	Dave Madison	115.00	57.00	34.00
(21)	Dick Marlowe	115.00	57.00	34.00
(22)	Pat Mullin	115.00	57.00	34.00
(23)	Bob Neiman	115.00	57.00	34.00
(24)	Johnny Pesky	125.00	62.00	37.00
(25)	Jerry Priddy	115.00	57.00	34.00
(26)	Steve Souchock	115.00	57.00	34.00
(27)	Russ Sullivan	115.00	57.00	34.00
(28)	Bill Wight	200.00	100.00	60.00

1961 Golden Press

JOHN McGRAW
third base

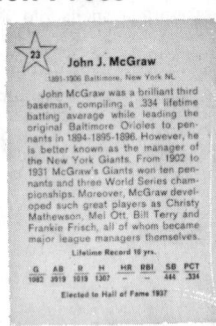

23
John J. McGraw
1891-1906 Baltimore, New York NL

John McGraw was a brilliant third baseman, compiling a .334 lifetime batting average while leading the original Baltimore Orioles to pennants in 1894-1895-1896. However, he is better known as the manager of the New York Giants. From 1902 to 1931 McGraw's Giants won ten pennants and three World Series championships. Moreover, McGraw developed such great players as Christy Mathewson, Mel Ott, Bill Terry and Frankie Frisch, all of whom became major league managers themselves.

Lifetime Record 10 yrs.

G	AB	R	H	RBI	SB	PCT
1082	3919	1019	1307	—	444	.334

Elected to Hall of Fame 1937.

The 1961 Golden Press set features 33 players, all enshrined in the Baseball Hall of Fame. The full color cards measure 2-1/2" by 3-1/2" and came in a booklet with perforations so that they could be easily removed. Full books with the cards intact would command 50 percent over the set price in the checklist that follows. Card numbers 1-3 and 28-33 are slightly higher in price as they were located on the book's front and back covers, making them more susceptible to scuffing and wear.

		NR MT	EX	VG
Complete Set:		65.00	33.00	20.00
Common Player:		.60	.30	.20
1	Mel Ott	1.50	.70	.45
2	Grover Cleveland Alexander	1.50	.70	.45
3	Babe Ruth	18.00	9.00	5.50
4	Hank Greenberg	1.25	.60	.40
5	Bill Terry	.75	.40	.25
6	Carl Hubbell	.75	.40	.25
7	Rogers Hornsby	1.75	.90	.50
8	Dizzy Dean	5.00	2.50	1.50
9	Joe DiMaggio	12.00	6.00	3.50
10	Charlie Gehringer	.75	.40	.25

		NR MT	EX	VG
11	Gabby Hartnett	.60	.30	.20
12	Mickey Cochrane	.75	.40	.25
13	George Sisler	.75	.40	.25
14	Joe Cronin	.75	.40	.25
15	Pie Traynor	.60	.30	.20
16	Lou Gehrig	12.00	6.00	3.50
17	Lefty Grove	.90	.45	.25
18	Chief Bender	.60	.30	.20
19	Frankie Frisch	.75	.40	.25
20	Al Simmons	.60	.30	.20
21	Home Run Baker	.60	.30	.20
22	Jimmy Foxx	1.75	.90	.50
23	John McGraw	.90	.45	.25
24	Christy Mathewson	2.50	1.25	.70
25	Ty Cobb	12.00	6.00	3.50
26	Dazzy Vance	.60	.30	.20
27	Bill Dickey	.90	.45	.25
28	Eddie Collins	.75	.40	.25
29	Walter Johnson	3.00	1.50	.90
30	Tris Speaker	1.50	.70	.45
31	Nap Lajoie	1.50	.70	.45
32	Honus Wagner	3.00	1.50	.90
33	Cy Young	3.00	1.50	.90

1981 Granny Goose Potato Chips A's

The 1981 Granny Goose set features the Oakland A's. The cards, which measure 2-1/2" by 3-1/2" in size, were issued in bags of potato chips and are sometimes found with grease stains. The cards have full color fronts with the print done in the team's green and yellow colors. The backs contain the A's logo and a short player biography. The Revering card was withdrawn from the set shortly after he was traded and is in shorter supply than the rest of the cards in the set. The cards are numbered in the checklist that follows by the player's uniform number.

		MT	NR MT	EX
Complete Set:		100.00	75.00	40.00
Common Player:		2.00	1.50	.80
1	Billy Martin	10.00	7.50	4.00
2	Mike Heath	2.00	1.50	.80
5	Jeff Newman	2.00	1.50	.80
6	Mitchell Page	2.00	1.50	.80
8	Rob Picciolo	2.00	1.50	.80
10	Wayne Gross	5.00	3.75	2.00
13	Dave Revering	45.00	34.00	18.00
17	Mike Norris	2.00	1.50	.80
20	Tony Armas	4.00	3.00	1.50
21	Dwayne Murphy	3.00	2.25	1.25
22	Rick Langford	2.00	1.50	.80
27	Matt Keough	2.00	1.50	.80
35	Rickey Henderson	30.00	22.00	12.00
39	Dave McKay	2.00	1.50	.80
54	Steve McCatty	2.00	1.50	.80

1982 Granny Goose Potato Chips A's

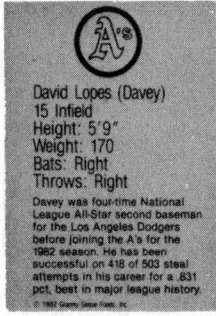

Granny Goose repeated its promotion from the previous year and issued another set featuring the Oakland A's. The cards, which measure 2-1/2" by 3-1/2", were distributed in two fashions - in bags of potato chips and at Fan Appreciation Day at Oakland-Alameda Coliseum. The cards are identical in design to the 1981 set and can be distinguished from it by the date on the copyright on the bottom of the card reverse. The cards are numbered in the checklist that follows by the player's uniform number.

		MT	NR MT	EX
Complete Set:		20.00	15.00	7.50
Common Player:		.40	.30	.15
1	Billy Martin	2.00	1.50	.80
2	Mike Heath	.40	.30	.15
5	Jeff Newman	.40	.30	.15
8	Rob Picciolo	.40	.30	.15
10	Wayne Gross	.40	.30	.15
11	Fred Stanley	.40	.30	.15
15	Davey Lopes	.80	.60	.30
17	Mike Norris	.40	.30	.15
20	Tony Armas	1.00	.70	.40
21	Dwayne Murphy	.60	.45	.25
22	Rick Langford	.40	.30	.15
27	Matt Keough	.40	.30	.15
35	Rickey Henderson	12.00	9.00	4.75
44	Cliff Johnson, Jr.	.40	.30	.15
54	Steve McCatty	.40	.30	.15

1983 Granny Goose Potato Chips A's

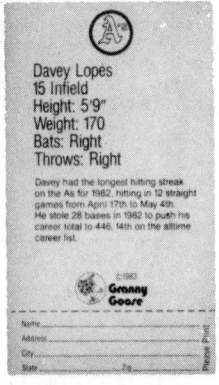

For the third consecutive year, Granny Goose issued a set of baseball cards featuring the Oakland A's. The cards were issued with or without a detachable coupon found at the bottom of each card. Issued in bags of potato chips were the coupon cards, which contain a scratch-off section offering prizes. The cards without the coupon section were given away to fans at Oakland-Alameda Coliseum on July 3, 1983. Cards with the detachable coupon command a 50 per cent premium over the coupon-less variety. The cards in the following checklist are numbered by the player's uniform number.

		MT	NR MT	EX
Complete Set		15.00	11.00	6.00
Common Player		.40	.30	.15
2	Mike Heath	.40	.30	.15
4	Carney Lansford	1.00	.70	.40
10	Wayne Gross	.40	.30	.15
14	Steve Boros	.40	.30	.15
15	Davey Lopes	.80	.60	.30
16	Mike Davis	.80	.60	.30
17	Mike Norris	.40	.30	.15
21	Dwayne Murphy	.60	.45	.25
22	Rick Langford	.40	.30	.15
27	Matt Keough	.40	.30	.15
31	Tom Underwood	.40	.30	.15
33	Dave Beard	.40	.30	.15
35	Rickey Henderson	10.00	7.50	4.00
39	Tom Burgmeier	.40	.30	.15
54	Steve McCatty	.40	.30	.15

1989 Hills Team MVP's

This high-gloss, 33-card boxed set of superstars was produced by Topps for the Hills department store chain. The words "Hills Team MVP's" appear above the player photos, while the player's name and team are printed below. The front of the card carries a red, white and blue color scheme with yellow and gold accents. The horizontal backs include player data set against a green playing field background.

		MT	NR MT	EX
Complete Set:		3.00	2.25	1.25
Common Player:		.05	.04	.02
1	Harold Baines	.05	.04	.02
2	Wade Boggs	.30	.25	.12
3	George Brett	.09	.07	.04
4	Tom Brunansky	.05	.04	.02
5	Jose Canseco	.35	.25	.14
6	Joe Carter	.05	.04	.02
7	Will Clark	.35	.25	.12
8	Roger Clemens	.10	.08	.04
9	Dave Cone	.05	.04	.02
10	Glenn Davis	.05	.04	.02
11	Andre Dawson	.09	.07	.04
12	Dennis Eckersley	.09	.07	.04
13	Andres Galarraga	.10	.08	.06
14	Kirk Gibson	.06	.05	.02
15	Mike Greenwell	.15	.11	.06
16	Tony Gwynn	.15	.11	.06
17	Orel Hershiser	.09	.07	.03
18	Danny Jackson	.05	.04	.02

		MT	NR MT	EX
19	Mark Langston	.09	.07	.04
20	Fred McGriff	.10	.08	.04
21	Dale Murphy	.06	.05	.04
22	Eddie Murray	.06	.05	.04
23	Kirby Puckett	.25	.20	.10
24	Johnny Ray	.05	.04	.02
25	Juan Samuel	.05	.04	.02
26	Ruben Sierra	.15	.11	.06
27	Dave Stewart	.05	.04	.02
28	Darryl Strawberry	.20	.15	.08
29	Allan Trammell	.06	.05	.02
30	Andy Van Slyke	.05	.04	.02
31	Frank Viola	.06	.05	.02
32	Dave Winfield	.06	.05	.02
33	Robin Yount	.09	.07	.03

1990 Hills Hit Men

The 33 slugging percentage leaders are featured in this high-gloss set. The cards were produced by Topps for the Hills department store chain. The card fronts feature "Hit Men" ina bat design above the photo. The player's name appears on a band below the photo. The horizontal backs feature a breakdown of the player's slugging percentage and also display career statistics.

		MT	NR MT	EX
Complete Set:		2.50	2.00	1.00
Common Player:		.05	.04	.02
1	Eric Davis	.15	.11	.06
2	Will Clark	.25	.20	.10
3	Don Mattingly	.25	.20	.10
4	Darryl Strawberry	.20	.15	.08
5	Kevin Mitchell	.15	.11	.06
6	Pedro Guerrero	.05	.04	.02
7	Jose Canseco	.30	.25	.12
8	Jim Rice	.05	.04	.02
9	Danny Tartabull	.05	.04	.02
10	Goerge Brett	.09	.07	.04
11	Kent Hrbek	.05	.04	.02
12	George Bell	.05	.04	.02
13	Eddie Murray	.08	.06	.03
14	Fred Lynn	.05	.04	.02
15	Andre Dawson	.09	.07	.04
16	Dale Murphy	.09	.07	.04
17	Dave Winfield	.09	.07	.04
18	Jack Clark	.05	.04	.02
19	Wade Boggs	.25	.20	.10
20	Ruben Sierra	.15	.11	.06
21	Dave Parker ( )	.10	.08	.04
22	Glenn Davis	.05	.04	.02
23	Dwight Evans	.05	.04	.02
24	Jesse Barfield	.05	.04	.02
25	Kirk Gibson	.06	.05	.02
26	Alvin Davis	.05	.04	.02
27	Kirby Puckett	.20	.15	.08
28	Joe Carter	.05	.04	.02
29	Carlton Fisk	.10	.08	.04
30	Harold Baines	.05	.04	.02
31	Andres Galarraga	.05	.04	.02
32	Cal Ripken	.10	.08	.04
33	Howard Johnson	.08	.06	.03

1958 Hires Root Beer Test Set

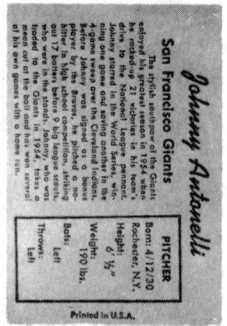

Among the scarcest of the regional issues of the late 1950s is the eight-card test issue which preceded the Hires Root Beer set of 66 cards. Probably issued in a very limited area in the Northeast, the test cards differ from the regular issue in that they have sepia-toned, rather than color pictures, which are set against plain yellow or orange backgrounds (much like the 1958 Topps), instead of viewed through a knothole. Like the regular Hires cards, the 2-5/16" by 3-1/2" cards were issued with an attached wedge-shaped tab of like size. The tab offered membership in Hires baseball fan club, and served to hold the card into the carton of bottled root beer with which it was given away. Values quoted here are for cards with tabs. Cards without tabs would be valued approximately 50 per cent lower.

		NR MT	EX	VG
Complete Set:		1500.00	750.00	450.00
Common Player:		125.00	60.00	40.00
(1)	Johnny Antonelli	150.00	75.00	45.00
(2)	Jim Busby	125.00	60.00	40.00
(3)	Chico Fernandez	125.00	60.00	40.00
(4)	Bob Friend	150.00	75.00	45.00
(5)	Vern Law	150.00	75.00	45.00
(6)	Stan Lopata	125.00	60.00	40.00
(7)	Willie Mays	550.00	280.00	165.00
(8)	Al Pilarcik	125.00	60.00	40.00

1958 Hires Root Beer

Like most baseball cards issued with a tab in the 1950s, the Hires cards are extremely scarce today in their original form. The basic card was attached to a wedge-shaped tab that served the dual purpose of offering a fan club membership and of holding the card into the cardboard carton of soda bottles with which it was distributed. The card itself measures 2-5/16" by 3-1/2". The tab extends for another 3-1/2". Numbering of the Hires set begins at 10 and goes through 76, with card #69 never issued, making a set complete at 66 cards. Values given below are

for cards with tabs. Cards without tabs would be valued approximately 50 per cent lower.

		NR MT	EX	VG
Complete Set:		2500.00	1250.00	700.00
Common Player:		25.00	12.50	7.50
10	Richie Ashburn	150.00	40.00	25.00
11	Chico Carrasquel	25.00	12.50	7.50
12	Dave Philley	25.00	12.50	7.50
13	Don Newcombe	28.00	14.00	8.50
14	Wally Post	25.00	12.50	7.50
15	Rip Repulski	25.00	12.50	7.50
16	Chico Fernandez	25.00	12.50	7.50
17	Larry Doby	28.00	14.00	8.50
18	Hector Brown	25.00	12.50	7.50
19	Danny O'Connell	25.00	12.50	7.50
20	Granny Hamner	25.00	12.50	7.50
21	Dick Groat	30.00	15.00	9.00
22	Ray Narleski	25.00	12.50	7.50
23	Pee Wee Reese	100.00	50.00	30.00
24	Bob Friend	30.00	15.00	9.00
25	Willie Mays	275.00	150.00	80.00
26	Bob Nieman	25.00	12.50	7.50
27	Frank Thomas	25.00	12.50	7.50
28	Curt Simmons	30.00	15.00	9.00
29	Stan Lopata	25.00	12.50	7.50
30	Bob Skinner	25.00	12.50	7.50
31	Ron Kline	25.00	12.50	7.50
32	Willie Miranda	25.00	12.50	7.50
33	Bob Avila	25.00	12.50	7.50
34	Clem Labine	30.00	15.00	9.00
35	Ray Jablonski	25.00	12.50	7.50
36	Bill Mazeroski	28.00	14.00	8.50
37	Billy Gardner	25.00	12.50	7.50
38	Pete Runnels	30.00	15.00	9.00
39	Jack Sanford	25.00	12.50	7.50
40	Dave Sisler	25.00	12.50	7.50
41	Don Zimmer	30.00	15.00	9.00
42	Johnny Podres	28.00	14.00	8.50
43	Dick Farrell	25.00	12.50	7.50
44	Hank Aaron	275.00	150.00	80.00
45	Bill Virdon	30.00	15.00	9.00
46	Bobby Thomson	30.00	15.00	9.00
47	Willard Nixon	25.00	12.50	7.50
48	Billy Loes	25.00	12.50	7.50
49	Hank Sauer	25.00	12.50	7.50
50	Johnny Antonelli	30.00	15.00	9.00
51	Daryl Spencer	25.00	12.50	7.50
52	Ken Lehman	25.00	12.50	7.50
53	Sammy White	25.00	12.50	7.50
54	Charley Neal	25.00	12.50	7.50
55	Don Drysdale	80.00	40.00	24.00
56	Jack Jensen	28.00	14.00	8.50
57	Ray Katt	25.00	12.50	7.50
58	Franklin Sullivan	25.00	12.50	7.50
59	Roy Face	30.00	15.00	9.00
60	Willie Jones	25.00	12.50	7.50
61	Duke Snider	125.00	62.00	37.00
62	Whitey Lockman	25.00	12.50	7.50
63	Gino Cimoli	30.00	15.00	9.00
64	Marv Grissom	25.00	12.50	7.50
65	Gene Baker	25.00	12.50	7.50
66	George Zuverink	25.00	12.50	7.50
67	Ted Kluszewski	28.00	14.00	8.50
68	Jim Busby	25.00	12.50	7.50
69	Not Issued			
70	Curt Barclay	25.00	12.50	7.50
71	Hank Foiles	25.00	12.50	7.50
72	Gene Stephens	25.00	12.50	7.50
73	Al Worthington	25.00	12.50	7.50
74	Al Walker	25.00	12.50	7.50
75	Bob Boyd	25.00	12.50	7.50
76	Al Pilarcik	30.00	9.00	5.50

1959 Home Run Derby

This 20-card unnumbered set was produced by American Motors to publicize the Home Run Derby television program. The cards measure approximately 3-1/4" by 5-1/4" and feature black and white player photos on black-backed white stock. The player name and team are printed beneath the photo. This set was reprinted (and marked as such) in 1988 by Card Collectors' Company of New York.

HANK AARON
MILWAUKEE BRAVES

	NR MT	EX	VG
Complete Set:	4500.00	2250.00	1350.
Common Player:	100.00	50.00	30.00

(1)	Hank Aaron	500.00	250.00	150.00
(2)	Bob Allison	100.00	50.00	30.00
(3)	Ernie Banks	350.00	175.00	105.00
(4)	Ken Boyer	175.00	87.00	52.00
(5)	Bob Cerv	100.00	50.00	30.00
(6)	Rocky Colavito	175.00	87.00	52.00
(7)	Gil Hodges	225.00	112.00	67.00
(8)	Jackie Jensen	175.00	87.00	52.00
(9)	Al Kaline	350.00	175.00	105.00
(10)	Harmon Killebrew	275.00	137.00	82.00
(11)	Jim Lemon	100.00	50.00	30.00
(12)	Mickey Mantle	1200.00	600.00	400.00
(13)	Ed Mathews	325.00	162.00	97.00
(14)	Willie Mays	550.00	275.00	165.00
(15)	Wally Post	100.00	50.00	30.00
(16)	Frank Robinson	325.00	162.00	97.00
(17)	Mark Scott (host)	175.00	87.00	52.00
(18)	Duke Snider	450.00	225.00	135.00
(19)	Dick Stuart	100.00	50.00	30.00
(20)	Gus Triandos	100.00	50.00	30.00

1975 Hostess

RENNIE STENNETT
INFIELD
Pittsburgh PIRATES

The first of what would become five annual issues, the 1975 Hostess set consists of 50 three-card panels which formed the bottom of boxes of family-size snack cake products. Unlike many similar issues, the Hostess cards do not share common borders, so it was possible to cut them neatly and evenly from the box. Well-cut single cards measure 2-1/4" by 3-1/4", while a three-card panel measures 7-1/4" by 3-1/4". Because some of the panels were issued on packages of less popular snack cakes, they are somewhat scarcer today. Since the hobby was quite well-developed when the Hostess cards were first issued, there is no lack of complete panels. Even unused complete boxes are available today. Some of the photos in this issue also appear on Topps cards of the era.

	NR MT	EX	VG
Complete Panel Set:	400.00	200.00	120.00
Complete Singles Set:	200.00	100.00	60.00
Common Panel:	2.50	1.25	.70
Common Single Player:	.40	.20	.12

	Panel 1	2.50	1.25	.70
1	Bobby Tolan	.40	.20	.12
2	Cookie Rojas	.40	.20	.12
3	Darrell Evans	.70	.35	.20
	Panel 2	5.50	2.75	1.75
4	Sal Bando	.50	.25	.15
5	Joe Morgan	2.00	1.00	.60
6	Mickey Lolich	.60	.30	.20
	Panel 3	4.00	2.00	1.25
7	Don Sutton	1.50	.70	.45
8	Bill Melton	.40	.20	.12
9	Tim Foli	.40	.20	.12
	Panel 4	5.00	2.50	1.50
10	Joe Lahoud	.40	.20	.12
11a	Bert Hooten (incorrect spelling)	1.50	.70	.45
11b	Burt Hooton (correct spelling)	1.50	.70	.45
12	Paul Blair	.40	.20	.12
	Panel 5	2.50	1.25	.70
13	Jim Barr	.40	.20	.12
14	Toby Harrah	.50	.25	.15
15	John Milner	.40	.20	.12
	Panel 6	3.50	1.75	1.00
16	Ken Holtzman	.50	.25	.15
17	Cesar Cedeno	.50	.25	.15
18	Dwight Evans	.90	.45	.25
	Panel 7	7.50	3.75	2.25
19	Willie McCovey	3.00	1.50	.90
20	Tony Oliva	.70	.35	.20
21	Manny Sanguillen	.40	.20	.12
	Panel 8	8.00	4.00	2.50
22	Mickey Rivers	.50	.25	.15
23	Lou Brock	3.00	1.50	.90
24	Craig Nettles	.90	.45	.25
	Panel 9	3.00	1.50	.90
25	Jimmy Wynn	.50	.25	.15
26	George Scott	.50	.25	.15
27	Greg Luzinski	.50	.25	.15
	Panel 10	20.00	10.00	6.00
28	Bert Campaneris	.50	.25	.15
29	Pete Rose	8.00	4.00	2.50
30	Buddy Bell	.50	.25	.15
	Panel 11	2.50	1.25	.70
31	Gary Matthews	.50	.25	.15
32	Fred Patek	.40	.20	.12
33	Mike Lum	.40	.20	.12
	Panel 12	2.50	1.25	.70
34	Ellie Rodriguez	.40	.20	.12
35	Milt May	.40	.20	.12
36	Willie Horton	.50	.25	.15
	Panel 13	10.00	5.00	3.00
37	Dave Winfield	4.50	2.25	1.25
38	Tom Grieve	.40	.20	.12
39	Barry Foote	.40	.20	.12
	Panel 14	2.50	1.25	.70
40	Joe Rudi	.50	.25	.15
41	Bake McBride	.40	.20	.12
42	Mike Cuellar	.50	.25	.15
	Panel 15	2.50	1.25	.70
43	Garry Maddox	.50	.25	.15
44	Carlos May	.40	.20	.12
45	Bud Harrelson	.40	.20	.12
	Panel 16	15.00	7.50	4.50
46	Dave Chalk	.40	.20	.12
47	Dave Concepcion	.50	.25	.15
48	Carl Yastrzemski	6.50	3.25	2.00
	Panel 17	9.00	4.50	2.75
49	Steve Garvey	4.00	2.00	1.25
50	Amos Otis	.50	.25	.15
51	Rickey Reuschel	.50	.25	.15
	Panel 18	3.75	2.00	1.25
52	Rollie Fingers	1.25	.60	.40
53	Bob Watson	.40	.20	.12
54	John Ellis	.40	.20	.12
	Panel 19	9.50	4.75	2.75
55	Bob Bailey	.40	.20	.12
56	Rod Carew	4.00	2.00	1.25
57	Richie Hebner	.40	.20	.12
	Panel 20	10.00	5.00	3.00
58	Nolan Ryan	4.00	2.00	1.25
59	Reggie Smith	.50	.25	.15
60	Joe Coleman	.40	.20	.12
	Panel 21	10.00	5.00	3.00
61	Ron Cey	.50	.25	.15
62	Darrell Porter	.50	.25	.15
63	Steve Carlton	4.00	2.00	1.25
	Panel 22	2.50	1.25	.70
64	Gene Tenace	.40	.20	.12
65	Jose Cardenal	.40	.20	.12
66	Bill Lee	.40	.20	.12
	Panel 23	2.50	1.25	.70
67	Dave Lopes	.50	.25	.15

		NR MT	EX	VG
68	Wilbur Wood	.50	.25	.15
69	Steve Renko	.40	.20	.12
	Panel 24	3.00	1.50	.90
70	Joe Torre	.50	.25	.15
71	Ted Sizemore	.40	.20	.12
72	Bobby Grich	.50	.25	.15
	Panel 25	11.00	5.50	3.25
73	Chris Speier	.40	.20	.12
74	Bert Blyleven	.70	.35	.20
75	Tom Seaver	4.50	2.25	1.25
	Panel 26	2.50	1.25	.70
76	Nate Colbert	.40	.20	.12
77	Don Kessinger	.40	.20	.12
78	George Medich	.40	.20	.12
	Panel 27	23.00	11.50	7.00
79	Andy Messersmith	.70	.35	.20
80	Robin Yount	9.00	4.50	2.75
81	Al Oliver	1.50	.70	.45
	Panel 28	18.00	9.00	5.50
82	Bill Singer	.50	.25	.15
83	Johnny Bench	6.00	3.00	1.75
84	Gaylord Perry	3.00	1.50	.90
	Panel 29	5.00	2.50	1.50
85	Dave Kingman	1.25	.60	.40
86	Ed Herrmann	.50	.25	.15
87	Ralph Garr	.60	.30	.20
	Panel 30	23.00	11.50	7.00
88	Reggie Jackson	9.00	4.50	2.75
89a	Doug Radar (incorrect spelling)	2.00	1.00	.60
89b	Doug Rader (correct spelling)	2.00	1.00	.60
90	Elliott Maddox	.50	.25	.15
	Panel 31	3.50	1.75	1.00
91	Bill Russell	.60	.30	.20
92	John Mayberry	.50	.25	.15
93	Dave Cash	.50	.25	.15
	Panel 32	5.00	2.50	1.50
94	Jeff Burroughs	.60	.30	.20
95	Ted Simmons	1.25	.60	.40
96	Joe Decker	.50	.25	.15
	Panel 33	10.00	5.00	3.00
97	Bill Buckner	1.00	.50	.30
98	Bobby Darwin	.50	.25	.15
99	Phil Niekro	3.50	1.75	1.00
	Panel 34	3.00	1.50	.90
100	Mike Sundberg (Jim)	.50	.25	.15
101	Greg Gross	.40	.20	.12
102	Luis Tiant	.70	.35	.20
	Panel 35	2.50	1.25	.70
103	Glenn Beckert	.40	.20	.12
104	Hal McRae	.50	.25	.15
105	Mike Jorgensen	.40	.20	.12
	Panel 36	2.50	1.25	.70
106	Mike Hargrove	.40	.20	.12
107	Don Gullett	.40	.20	.12
108	Tito Fuentes	.40	.20	.12
	Panel 37	3.50	1.75	1.00
109	John Grubb	.40	.20	.12
110	Jim Kaat	.90	.45	.25
111	Felix Millan	.40	.20	.12
	Panel 38	2.50	1.25	.70
112	Don Money	.40	.20	.12
113	Rick Monday	.50	.25	.15
114	Dick Bosman	.40	.20	.12
	Panel 39	3.50	1.75	1.00
115	Roger Metzger	.40	.20	.12
116	Fergie Jenkins	.90	.45	.25
117	Dusky Baker	.50	.25	.15
	Panel 40	10.00	5.00	3.00
118	Billy Champion	.50	.25	.15
119	Bob Gibson	3.50	1.75	1.00
120	Bill Freehan	.80	.40	.25
	Panel 41	2.50	1.25	.70
121	Cesar Geronimo	.40	.20	.12
122	Jorge Orta	.40	.20	.12
123	Cleon Jones	.40	.20	.12
	Panel 42	10.50	5.25	3.25
124	Steve Busby	.40	.20	.12
125a	Bill Madlock (Pitcher)	2.00	1.00	.60
125b	Bill Madlock (Third Base)	2.00	1.00	.60
126	Jim Palmer	2.75	1.50	.80
	Panel 43	4.25	2.25	1.25
127	Tony Perez	1.00	.50	.30
128	Larry Hisle	.40	.20	.12
129	Rusty Staub	.70	.35	.20
	Panel 44	20.00	10.00	6.00
130	Hank Aaron	9.00	4.50	2.75
131	Rennie Stennett	.50	.25	.15
132	Rico Petrocelli	.70	.35	.20
	Panel 45	16.00	8.00	4.75
133	Mike Schmidt	6.00	3.00	1.75
134	Sparky Lyle	.50	.25	.15

		NR MT	EX	VG
135	Willie Stargell	3.00	1.50	.90
	Panel 46	7.00	3.50	2.00
136	Ken Henderson	.40	.20	.12
137	Willie Montanez	.40	.20	.12
138	Thurman Munson	2.50	1.25	.70
	Panel 47	2.50	1.25	.70
139	Richie Zisk	.40	.20	.12
140	Geo. Hendricks (Hendrick)	.50	.25	.15
141	Bobby Murcer	.50	.25	.15
	Panel 48	10.00	5.00	3.00
142	Lee May	.50	.25	.15
143	Carlton Fisk	1.00	.50	.30
144	Brooks Robinson	3.50	1.75	1.00
	Panel 49	2.50	1.25	.70
145	Bobby Bonds	.50	.25	.15
146	Gary Sutherland	.40	.20	.12
147	Oscar Gamble	.40	.20	.12
	Panel 50	6.00	3.00	1.75
148	Jim Hunter	2.50	1.25	.70
149	Tug McGraw	.50	.25	.15
150	Dave McNally	.50	.25	.15

1975 Hostess Twinkies

HANK AARON
DESIGNATED HITTER
Milwaukee BREWERS

Believed to have been issued only in the Western states, and on a limited basis at that, the 1975 Hostess Twinkie set features 60 of the cards from the "regular" Hostess set of that year. The cards were issued one per pack with the popular snack cake. Card #'s 1-36 are a direct pick-up from the Hostess set, while the remaining 24 cards in the set were selected from the more popular names in the remainder of the Hostess issue - with an emphasis on West Coast players. Thus, after card #36, the '75 Twinkie cards are skip-numbered from 40-136. In identical 2-1/4" by 3-1/4" size, the Twinkie cards differ from the Hostess issue only in the presence of small black bars at top and bottom center of the back of the card. Values quoted are for full bottom panels.

		NR MT	EX	VG
Complete Set:		200.00	100.00	60.00
Common Player:		.90	.45	.25
1	Bobby Tolan	.90	.45	.25
2	Cookie Rojas	.90	.45	.25
3	Darrell Evans	2.00	1.00	.60
4	Sal Bando	1.25	.60	.40
5	Joe Morgan	5.00	2.50	1.50
6	Mickey Lolich	2.00	1.00	.60
7	Don Sutton	4.50	2.25	1.25
8	Bill Melton	.90	.45	.25
9	Tim Foli	.90	.45	.25
10	Joe Lahoud	.90	.45	.25
11	Bert Hooten (Burt Hooton)	1.25	.60	.40
12	Paul Blair	.90	.45	.25
13	Jim Barr	.90	.45	.25
14	Toby Harrah	.90	.45	.25
15	John Milner	.90	.45	.25
16	Ken Holtzman	1.00	.50	.30
17	Cesar Cedeno	1.25	.60	.40
18	Dwight Evans	3.00	1.50	.90
19	Willie McCovey	7.00	3.50	2.00
20	Tony Oliva	2.00	1.00	.60
21	Manny Sanguillen	.90	.45	.25
22	Mickey Rivers	.90	.45	.25
23	Lou Brock	6.50	3.25	2.00

		NR MT	EX	VG
24	Graig Nettles	3.00	1.50	.90
25	Jim Wynn	.90	.45	.25
26	George Scott	.90	.45	.25
27	Greg Luzinski	1.25	.60	.40
28	Bert Campaneris	1.25	.60	.40
29	Pete Rose	20.00	10.00	6.00
30	Buddy Bell	1.75	.90	.50
31	Gary Matthews	1.25	.60	.40
32	Fred Patek	.90	.45	.25
33	Mike Lum	.90	.45	.25
34	Ellie Rodriguez	.90	.45	.25
35	Milt May (photo actually Lee May)	1.25	.60	.40
36	Willie Horton	.90	.45	.25
40	Joe Rudi	1.25	.60	.40
43	Garry Maddox	.90	.45	.25
46	Dave Chalk	.90	.45	.25
49	Steve Garvey	10.00	5.00	3.00
52	Rollie Fingers	4.00	2.00	1.25
58	Nolan Ryan	10.00	5.00	3.00
61	Ron Cey	1.50	.70	.45
64	Gene Tenace	.90	.45	.25
65	Jose Cardenal	.90	.45	.25
67	Dave Lopes	1.25	.60	.40
68	Wilbur Wood	.90	.45	.25
73	Chris Speier	.90	.45	.25
77	Don Kessinger	.90	.45	.25
79	Andy Messersmith	.90	.45	.25
80	Robin Yount	15.00	7.50	4.50
82	Bill Singer	.90	.45	.25
103	Glenn Beckert	.90	.45	.25
110	Jim Kaat	2.50	1.25	.70
112	Don Money	.90	.45	.25
113	Rick Monday	1.25	.60	.40
122	Jorge Orta	.90	.45	.25
125	Bill Madlock	2.25	1.25	.70
130	Hank Aaron	15.00	7.50	4.50
136	Ken Henderson	.90	.45	.25

1976 Hostess

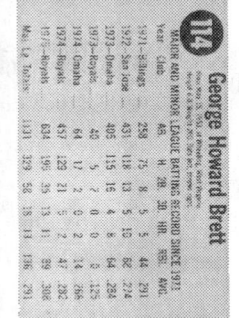

The second of five annual Hostess issues, the 1976 cards carried a "Bicentennial" color theme, with red, white and blue stripes at the bottom of the 2-1/4" by 3-1/4" cards. Like other Hostess issues, the cards were printed in panels of three as the bottom of family-size boxes of snack cake products. This leads to a degree of scarcity for some of the 150 cards in the set; those which were found on less-popular brands. A well-trimmed three-card panel measures 7-1/4" by 3-1/4" size. Some of the photos used in the 1976 Hostess set can also be found on Topps issues of the era.

		NR MT	EX	VG
	Complete Panel Set:	400.00	200.00	120.00
	Complete Singles Set:	225.00	112.00	67.00
	Common Panel:	2.50	1.25	.70
	Common Single Player:	.40	.20	.12
	Panel 1	11.75	6.00	3.50
1	Fred Lynn	1.25	.60	.40
2	Joe Morgan	2.00	1.00	.60
3	Phil Niekro	2.25	1.25	.70
	Panel 2	4.50	2.25	1.25
4	Gaylord Perry	1.75	.90	.50
5	Bob Watson	.40	.20	.12

		NR MT	EX	VG
6	Bill Freehan	.50	.25	.15
	Panel 3	6.50	3.25	2.00
7	Lou Brock	3.00	1.50	.90
8	Al Fitzmorris	.40	.20	.12
9	Rennie Stennett	.40	.20	.12
	Panel 4	9.00	4.50	2.75
10	Tony Oliva	.70	.35	.20
11	Robin Yount	4.00	2.00	1.25
12	Rick Manning	.40	.20	.12
	Panel 5	3.50	1.75	1.00
13	Bobby Grich	.50	.25	.15
14	Terry Forster	.40	.20	.12
15	Dave Kingman	.70	.35	.20
	Panel 6	7.00	3.50	2.00
16	Thurman Munson	2.50	1.25	.70
17	Rick Reuschel	.50	.25	.15
18	Bobby Bonds	.50	.25	.15
	Panel 7	9.50	4.75	2.75
19	Steve Garvey	4.00	2.00	1.25
20	Vida Blue	.50	.25	.15
21	Dave Rader	.40	.20	.12
	Panel 8	9.00	4.50	2.75
22	Johnny Bench	4.00	2.00	1.25
23	Luis Tiant	.50	.25	.15
24	Darrell Evans	.70	.35	.20
	Panel 9	2.50	1.25	.70
25	Larry Dierker	.40	.20	.12
26	Willie Horton	.50	.25	.15
27	John Ellis	.40	.20	.12
	Panel 10	3.00	1.50	.90
28	Al Cowens	.40	.20	.12
29	Jerry Reuss	.50	.25	.15
30	Reggie Smith	.50	.25	.15
	Panel 11	13.00	6.50	4.00
31	Bobby Darwin	.50	.25	.15
32	Fritz Peterson	.50	.25	.15
33	Rod Carew	6.00	3.00	1.75
	Panel 12	21.00	10.50	6.25
34	Carlos May	.50	.25	.15
35	Tom Seaver	6.00	3.00	1.75
36	Brooks Robinson	5.00	2.50	1.50
	Panel 13	2.50	1.25	.70
37	Jose Cardenal	.40	.20	.12
38	Ron Blomberg	.40	.20	.12
39	Lee Stanton	.40	.20	.12
	Panel 14	2.50	1.25	.70
40	Dave Cash	.40	.20	.12
41	John Montefusco	.40	.20	.12
42	Bob Tolan	.40	.20	.12
	Panel 15	2.50	1.25	.70
43	Carl Morton	.40	.20	.12
44	Rick Burleson	.50	.25	.15
45	Don Gullett	.40	.20	.12
	Panel 16	2.50	1.25	.70
46	Vern Ruhle	.40	.20	.12
47	Cesar Cedeno	.50	.25	.15
48	Toby Harrah	.50	.25	.15
	Panel 17	6.00	3.00	1.75
49	Willie Stargell	3.00	1.50	.90
50	Al Hrabosky	.40	.20	.12
51	Amos Otis	.50	.25	.15
	Panel 18	2.50	1.25	.70
52	Bud Harrelson	.50	.25	.15
53	Jim Hughes	.40	.20	.12
54	George Scott	.50	.25	.15
	Panel 19	9.50	4.75	2.75
55	Mike Vail	.50	.25	.15
56	Jim Palmer	4.00	2.00	1.25
57	Jorge Orta	.80	.40	.25
	Panel 20	3.50	1.75	1.00
58	Chris Chambliss	.80	.40	.25
59	Dave Chalk	.50	.25	.15
60	Ray Burris	.50	.25	.15
	Panel 21	14.00	7.00	4.25
61	Bert Campaneris	.80	.40	.25
62	Gary Carter	6.00	3.00	1.75
63	Ron Cey	.90	.45	.25
	Panel 22	28.00	14.00	8.50
64	Carlton Fisk	2.00	1.00	.60
65	Marty Perez	.50	.25	.15
66	Pete Rose	10.00	5.00	3.00
	Panel 23	3.50	1.75	1.00
67	Roger Metzger	.50	.25	.15
68	Jim Sundberg	.60	.30	.20
69	Ron LeFlore	.60	.30	.20
	Panel 24	3.50	1.75	1.00
70	Ted Sizemore	.50	.25	.15
71	Steve Busby	.50	.25	.15
72	Manny Sanguillen	.50	.25	.15
	Panel 25	5.00	2.50	1.50
73	Larry Hisle	.60	.30	.20

		NR MT	EX	VG
74	Pete Broberg	.50	.25	.15
75	Boog Powell	1.25	.60	.40
	Panel 26	6.50	3.25	2.00
76	Ken Singleton	.80	.40	.25
77	Rich Gossage	2.00	1.00	.60
78	Jerry Grote	.50	.25	.15
	Panel 27	16.00	8.00	4.75
79	Nolan Ryan	6.00	3.00	1.75
80	Rick Monday	.70	.35	.20
81	Graig Nettles	1.25	.60	.40
	Panel 28	18.00	9.00	5.50
82	Chris Speier	.40	.20	.12
83	Dave Winfield	4.00	2.00	1.25
84	Mike Schmidt	6.00	3.00	1.75
	Panel 29	4.00	2.00	1.25
85	Buzz Capra	.40	.20	.12
86	Tony Perez	1.00	.50	.30
87	Dwight Evans	.90	.45	.25
	Panel 30	2.50	1.25	.70
88	Mike Hargrove	.40	.20	.12
89	Joe Coleman	.40	.20	.12
90	Greg Gross	.40	.20	.12
	Panel 31	2.50	1.25	.70
91	John Mayberry	.40	.20	.12
92	John Candelaria	.50	.25	.15
93	Bake McBride	.40	.20	.12
	Panel 32	15.00	7.50	4.50
94	Hank Aaron	7.00	3.50	2.00
95	Buddy Bell	.50	.25	.15
96	Steve Braun	.40	.20	.12
	Panel 33	2.50	1.25	.70
97	Jon Matlack	.40	.20	.12
98	Lee May	.50	.25	.15
99	Wilbur Wood	.50	.25	.15
	Panel 34	4.00	2.00	1.25
100	Bill Madlock	.90	.45	.25
101	Frank Tanana	.50	.25	.15
102	Mickey Rivers	.50	.25	.15
	Panel 35	3.75	2.00	1.25
103	Mike Ivie	.40	.20	.12
104	Rollie Fingers	1.25	.60	.40
105	Dave Lopes	.50	.25	.15
	Panel 36	3.50	1.75	1.00
106	George Foster	.90	.45	.25
107	Denny Doyle	.40	.20	.12
108	Earl Williams	.40	.20	.12
	Panel 37	2.50	1.25	.70
109	Tom Veryzer	.40	.20	.12
110	J.R. Richard	.50	.25	.15
111	Jeff Burroughs	.40	.20	.12
	Panel 38	14.00	7.00	4.25
112	Al Oliver	.90	.45	.25
113	Ted Simmons	.80	.40	.25
114	Geroge Brett	5.00	2.50	1.50
	Panel 39	3.00	1.50	.90
115	Frank Duffy	.40	.20	.12
116	Bert Blyleven	.80	.40	.25
117	Darrell Porter	.50	.25	.15
	Panel 40	2.50	1.25	.70
118	Don Baylor	.70	.35	.20
119	Bucky Dent	.50	.25	.15
120	Felix Millan	.40	.20	.12
	Panel 41	2.50	1.25	.70
121	Mike Cuellar	.50	.25	.15
122	Gene Tenace	.40	.20	.12
123	Bobby Murcer	.50	.25	.15
	Panel 42	7.00	3.50	2.00
124	Willie McCovey	3.00	1.50	.90
125	Greg Luzinski	.50	.25	.15
126	Larry Parrish	.50	.25	.15
	Panel 43	10.00	5.00	3.00
127	Jim Rice	4.00	2.00	1.25
128	Dave Concepcion	.50	.25	.15
129	Jim Wynn	.50	.25	.15
	Panel 44	2.50	1.25	.70
130	Tom Grieve	.40	.20	.12
131	Mike Cosgrove	.40	.20	.12
132	Dan Meyer	.40	.20	.12
	Panel 45	5.00	2.50	1.50
133	Dave Parker	1.50	.70	.45
134	Don Kessinger	.40	.20	.12
135	Hal McRae	.50	.25	.15
	Panel 46	4.00	2.00	1.25
136	Don Money	.70	.35	.20
137	Dennis Eckersley	.90	.45	.25
138	Fergie Jenkins	.80	.40	.25
	Panel 47	4.00	2.00	1.25
139	Mike Torrez	.40	.20	.12
140	Jerry Morales	.40	.20	.12
141	Jim Hunter	1.25	.60	.40
	Panel 48	2.50	1.25	.70

		NR MT	EX	VG
142	Gary Matthews	.50	.25	.15
143	Randy Jones	.40	.20	.12
144	Mike Jorgensen	.40	.20	.12
	Panel 49	13.00	6.50	4.00
145	Larry Bowa	.60	.30	.20
146	Reggie Jackson	5.00	2.50	1.50
147	Steve Yeager	.40	.20	.12
	Panel 50	15.00	7.50	4.50
148	Dave May	.40	.20	.12
149	Carl Yastrzemski	6.50	3.25	2.00
150	Cesar Geronimo	.40	.20	.12

1976 Hostess Twinkies

 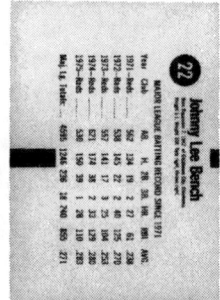

The 60 cards in this regionally-issued (West Coast only) set closely parallel the first 60 cards in the numerical sequence of the "regular" 1976 Hostess issue. The singular difference is the appearance on the back of a black band toward the center of the card at top and bottom. Also unlike the three-card panels of the regular Hostess issue, the 2-1/4" by 3-1/4" Twinkie cards were issued singly, as the cardboard stiffener for the cellophane-wrapped snack cakes. Values quoted are for complete bottom panels.

		NR MT	EX	VG
	Complete Set:	200.00	100.00	60.00
	Common Player:	.90	.45	.25
1	Fred Lynn	3.00	1.50	.90
2	Joe Morgan	5.00	2.50	1.50
3	Phil Niekro	4.50	2.25	1.25
4	Gaylord Perry	5.00	2.50	1.50
5	Bob Watson	.90	.45	.25
6	Bill Freehan	1.25	.60	.40
7	Lou Brock	7.00	3.50	2.00
8	Al Fitzmorris	.90	.45	.25
9	Rennie Stennett	.90	.45	.25
10	Tony Oliva	2.00	1.00	.60
11	Robin Yount	7.00	3.50	2.00
12	Rick Manning	.90	.45	.25
13	Bobby Grich	1.25	.60	.40
14	Terry Forster	.90	.45	.25
15	Dave Kingman	2.00	1.00	.60
16	Thurman Munson	6.50	3.25	2.00
17	Rick Reuschel	1.25	.60	.40
18	Bobby Bonds	1.25	.60	.40
19	Steve Garvey	10.00	5.00	3.00
20	Vida Blue	1.75	.90	.50
21	Dave Rader	.90	.45	.25
22	Johnny Bench	10.00	5.00	3.00
23	Luis Tiant	1.50	.70	.45
24	Darrell Evans	2.00	1.00	.60
25	Larry Dierker	.90	.45	.25
26	Willie Horton	.90	.45	.25
27	John Ellis	.90	.45	.25
28	Al Cowens	.90	.45	.25
29	Jerry Reuss	1.25	.60	.40
30	Reggie Smith	1.25	.60	.40
31	Bobby Darwin	.90	.45	.25
32	Fritz Peterson	.90	.45	.25
33	Rod Carew	10.00	5.00	3.00
34	Carlos May	.90	.45	.25
35	Tom Seaver	10.00	5.00	3.00
36	Brooks Robinson	9.00	4.50	2.75
37	Jose Cardenal	.90	.45	.25

		NR MT	EX	VG
38	Ron Blomberg	.90	.45	.25
39	Lee Stanton	.90	.45	.25
40	Dave Cash	.90	.45	.25
41	John Montefusco	.90	.45	.25
42	Bob Tolan	.90	.45	.25
43	Carl Morton	.90	.45	.25
44	Rick Burleson	.90	.45	.25
45	Don Gullett	.90	.45	.25
46	Vern Ruhle	.90	.45	.25
47	Cesar Cedeno	1.25	.60	.40
48	Toby Harrah	.90	.45	.25
49	Willie Stargell	7.00	3.50	2.00
50	Al Hrabosky	.90	.45	.25
51	Amos Otis	.90	.45	.25
52	Bud Harrelson	.90	.45	.25
53	Jim Hughes	.90	.45	.25
54	George Scott	.90	.45	.25
55	Mike Vail	.90	.45	.25
56	Jim Palmer	7.00	3.50	2.00
57	Jorge Orta	.90	.45	.25
58	Chris Chambliss	1.25	.60	.40
59	Dave Chalk	.90	.45	.25
60	Ray Burris	.90	.45	.25

1977 Hostess

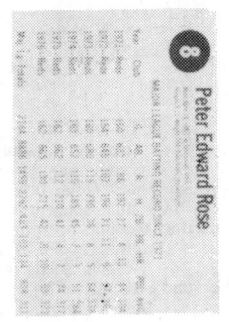

The third of five consecutive annual issues, the 1977 Hostess cards retained the same card size 2-1/4" by 3-1/4", set size - 150 cards, and mode of issue - three cards on a 7-1/4" by 3-1/4" panel, as the previous two efforts. Because they were issued as the bottom panel of snack cake boxes, and because some brands of Hostess products were more popular than others, certain cards in the set are scarcer than others.

		NR MT	EX	VG
Complete Panel Set:		350.00	175.00	105.00
Complete Singles Set:		200.00	100.00	60.00
Common Panel:		2.50	1.25	.70
Common Single Player:		.40	.20	.12
	Panel 1	18.00	9.00	5.50
1	Jim Palmer	2.75	1.50	.80
2	Joe Morgan	2.00	1.00	.60
3	Reggie Jackson	5.00	2.50	1.50
	Panel 2	23.00	11.50	7.00
4	Carl Yastrzemski	6.00	3.00	1.75
5	Thurman Munson	2.50	1.25	.70
6	Johnny Bench	4.00	2.00	1.25
	Panel 3	32.00	16.00	9.50
7	Tom Seaver	3.00	1.50	.90
8	Pete Rose	8.00	4.00	2.50
9	Rod Carew	4.00	2.00	1.25
	Panel 4	2.50	1.25	.70
10	Luis Tiant	.60	.30	.20
11	Phil Garner	.50	.25	.15
12	Sixto Lezcano	.40	.20	.12
	Panel 5	2.50	1.25	.70
13	Mike Torrez	.40	.20	.12
14	Dave Lopes	.50	.25	.15
15	Doug DeCinces	.50	.25	.15
	Panel 6	2.50	1.25	.70
16	Jim Spencer	.40	.20	.12
17	Hal McRae	.50	.25	.15
18	Mike Hargrove	.40	.20	.12
	Panel 7	4.50	2.25	1.25
19	Willie Montanez	.50	.25	.15

		NR MT	EX	VG
20	Roger Metzger	.50	.25	.15
21	Dwight Evans	1.50	.70	.45
	Panel 8	10.00	5.00	3.00
22	Steve Rogers	.50	.25	.15
23	Jim Rice	4.00	2.00	1.25
24	Pete Falcone	.50	.25	.15
	Panel 9	9.00	4.50	2.75
25	Greg Luzinski	.90	.45	.25
26	Randy Jones	.50	.25	.15
27	Willie Stargell	3.00	1.50	.90
	Panel 10	3.50	1.75	1.00
28	John Hiller	.50	.25	.15
29	Bobby Murcer	.70	.35	.20
30	Rick Monday	.70	.35	.20
	Panel 11	9.00	4.50	2.75
31	John Montefusco	.50	.25	.15
32	Lou Brock	4.00	2.00	1.25
33	Bill North	.50	.25	.15
	Panel 12	32.00	16.00	9.50
34	Robin Yount	4.00	2.00	1.25
35	Steve Garvey	5.00	2.50	1.50
36	George Brett	8.00	4.00	2.50
	Panel 13	3.50	1.75	1.00
37	Toby Harrah	.70	.35	.20
38	Jerry Royster	.50	.25	.15
39	Bob Watson	.60	.30	.20
	Panel 14	9.50	4.75	2.75
40	George Foster	.90	.45	.25
41	Gary Carter	3.50	1.75	1.00
42	John Denny	.40	.20	.12
	Panel 15	18.00	9.00	5.50
43	Mike Schmidt	5.00	2.50	1.50
44	Dave Winfield	3.75	2.00	1.25
45	Al Oliver	.90	.45	.25
	Panel 16	3.00	1.50	.90
46	Mark Fidrych	.60	.30	.20
47	Larry Herndon	.50	.25	.15
48	Dave Goltz	.40	.20	.12
	Panel 17	3.50	1.75	1.00
49	Jerry Morales	.40	.20	.12
50	Ron LeFlore	.50	.25	.15
51	Fred Lynn	.90	.45	.25
	Panel 18	3.50	1.75	1.00
52	Vida Blue	.50	.25	.15
53	Rick Manning	.40	.20	.12
54	Bill Buckner	.70	.35	.20
	Panel 19	2.50	1.25	.70
55	Lee May	.50	.25	.15
56	John Mayberry	.40	.20	.12
57	Darrel Chaney	.40	.20	.12
	Panel 20	3.50	1.75	1.00
58	Cesar Cedeno	.50	.25	.15
59	Ken Griffey	.50	.25	.15
60	Dave Kingman	.80	.40	.25
	Panel 21	3.50	1.75	1.00
61	Ted Simmons	.80	.40	.25
62	Larry Bowa	.50	.25	.15
63	Frank Tanana	.50	.25	.15
	Panel 22	2.50	1.25	.70
64	Jason Thompson	.40	.20	.12
65	Ken Brett	.40	.20	.12
66	Roy Smalley	.40	.20	.12
	Panel 23	2.50	1.25	.70
67	Ray Burris	.40	.20	.12
68	Rick Burleson	.40	.20	.12
69	Buddy Bell	.50	.25	.15
	Panel 24	5.00	2.50	1.50
70	Don Sutton	2.00	1.00	.60
71	Mark Belanger	.40	.20	.12
72	Dennis Leonard	.40	.20	.12
	Panel 25	5.00	2.50	1.50
73	Gaylord Perry	1.50	.70	.45
74	Dick Ruthven	.40	.20	.12
75	Jose Cruz	.50	.25	.15
	Panel 26	4.25	2.25	1.25
76	Cesar Geronimo	.40	.20	.12
77	Jerry Koosman	.50	.25	.15
78	Garry Templeton	.80	.40	.25
	Panel 27	10.00	5.00	3.00
79	Jim Hunter	1.25	.60	.40
80	John Candelaria	.50	.25	.15
81	Nolan Ryan	3.50	1.75	1.00
	Panel 28	2.50	1.25	.70
82	Rusty Staub	.50	.25	.15
83	Jim Barr	.40	.20	.12
84	Butch Wynegar	.50	.25	.15
	Panel 29	2.50	1.25	.70
85	Jose Cardenal	.40	.20	.12
86	Claudell Washington	.50	.25	.15
87	Bill Travers	.40	.20	.12
	Panel 30	2.50	1.25	.70
88	Rick Waits	.40	.20	.12

		NR MT	EX	VG
89	Ron Cey	.50	.25	.15
90	Al Bumbry	.40	.20	.12
	Panel 31	2.50	1.25	.70
91	Bucky Dent	.50	.25	.15
92	Amos Otis	.50	.25	.15
93	Tom Grieve	.40	.20	.12
	Panel 32	2.50	1.25	.70
94	Enos Cabell	.40	.20	.12
95	Dave Concepcion	.50	.25	.15
96	Felix Millan	.40	.20	.12
	Panel 33	2.50	1.25	.70
97	Bake McBride	.40	.20	.12
98	Chris Chambliss	.50	.25	.15
99	Butch Metzger	.40	.20	.12
	Panel 34	2.50	1.25	.70
100	Rennie Stennett	.40	.20	.12
101	Dave Roberts	.40	.20	.12
102	Lyman Bostock	.50	.25	.15
	Panel 35	3.50	1.75	1.00
103	Rick Reuschel	.50	.25	.15
104	Carlton Fisk	1.00	.50	.30
105	Jim Slaton	.40	.20	.12
	Panel 36	2.50	1.25	.70
106	Dennis Eckersley	.60	.30	.20
107	Ken Singleton	.50	.25	.15
108	Ralph Garr	.40	.20	.12
	Panel 37	8.00	4.00	2.50
109	Freddie Patek	.50	.25	.15
110	Jim Sundberg	.60	.30	.20
111	Phil Niekro	3.25	1.75	1.00
	Panel 38	3.50	1.75	1.00
112	J.R. Richard	.70	.35	.20
113	Gary Nolan	.50	.25	.15
114	Jon Matlack	.60	.30	.20
	Panel 39	20.00	10.00	6.00
115	Keith Hernandez	4.00	2.00	1.25
116	Graig Nettles	.70	.35	.20
117	Steve Carlton	4.50	2.25	1.25
	Panel 40	6.50	3.25	2.00
118	Bill Madlock	1.50	.70	.45
119	Jerry Reuss	.80	.40	.25
120	Aurelio Rodriguez	.50	.25	.15
	Panel 41	3.50	1.75	1.00
121	Dan Ford	.50	.25	.15
122	Ray Fosse	.50	.25	.15
123	George Hendrick	.70	.35	.20
	Panel 42	2.50	1.25	.70
124	Alan Ashby	.40	.20	.12
125	Joe Lis	.40	.20	.12
126	Sal Bando	.50	.25	.15
	Panel 43	4.00	2.00	1.25
127	Richie Zisk	.50	.25	.15
128	Rich Gossage	.90	.45	.25
129	Don Baylor	.60	.30	.20
	Panel 44	2.50	1.25	.70
130	Dave McKay	.40	.20	.12
131	Bob Grich	.50	.25	.15
132	Dave Pagan	.40	.20	.12
	Panel 45	2.50	1.25	.70
133	Dave Cash	.40	.20	.12
134	Steve Braun	.40	.20	.12
135	Dan Meyer	.40	.20	.12
	Panel 46	4.25	2.25	1.25
136	Bill Stein	.40	.20	.12
137	Rollie Fingers	1.50	.70	.45
138	Brian Downing	.50	.25	.15
	Panel 47	2.50	1.25	.70
139	Bill Singer	.40	.20	.12
140	Doyle Alexander	.50	.25	.15
141	Gene Tenace	.40	.20	.12
	Panel 48	2.50	1.25	.70
142	Gary Matthews	.50	.25	.15
143	Don Gullett	.40	.20	.12
144	Wayne Garland	.40	.20	.12
	Panel 49	2.50	1.25	.70
145	Pete Broberg	.40	.20	.12
146	Joe Rudi	.50	.25	.15
147	Glenn Abbott	.40	.20	.12
	Panel 50	2.50	1.25	.70
148	George Scott	.50	.25	.15
149	Bert Campaneris	.50	.25	.15
150	Andy Messersmith	.50	.25	.15

Definitions for grading conditions are located in the introduction section at the front of this book.

1977 Hostess Twinkies

The 1977 Hostess Twinkie issue, at 150 different cards, is the largest of the single-panel Twinkie sets. It is also the most obscure. The cards, which measure 2-1/4" by 3-1/4", but are part of a larger panel, were found not only with Twinkies, but with Hostess Cupcakes as well. Card #'s 1-30 and 111-150 are Twinkies panels and #'s 31-135 are Cupcakes panels. Complete Cupcakes panels are approximately 2-1/4" by 4-1/2" in size, while complete Twinkies panels measure 3-1/8" by 4-1/4". The photos used in the set are identical to those in the 1977 Hostess three-card panel set. The main difference is the appearance of a black band at the center of the card back. The values quoted in the checklist that follows are for complete bottom panels.

		NR MT	EX	VG
	Complete Set:	350.00	175.00	105.00
	Common Player:	.80	.40	.25
1	Jim Palmer	6.00	3.00	1.75
2	Joe Morgan	4.00	2.00	1.25
3	Reggie Jackson	10.00	5.00	3.00
4	Carl Yastrzemski	12.00	6.00	3.50
5	Thurman Munson	5.00	2.50	1.50
6	Johnny Bench	8.00	4.00	2.50
7	Tom Seaver	7.00	3.50	2.00
8	Pete Rose	15.00	7.50	4.50
9	Rod Carew	8.00	4.00	2.50
10	Luis Tiant	1.00	.50	.30
11	Phil Garner	.80	.40	.25
12	Sixto Lezcano	.80	.40	.25
13	Mike Torrez	.80	.40	.25
14	Dave Lopes	1.00	.50	.30
15	Doug DeCinces	1.00	.50	.30
16	Jim Spencer	.80	.40	.25
17	Hal McRae	1.00	.50	.30
18	Mike Hargrove	.80	.40	.25
19	Willie Montanez	.80	.40	.25
20	Roger Metzger	.80	.40	.25
21	Dwight Evans	2.00	1.00	.60
22	Steve Rogers	.80	.40	.25
23	Jim Rice	6.00	3.00	1.75
24	Pete Falcone	.80	.40	.25
25	Greg Luzinski	1.50	.70	.45
26	Randy Jones	.80	.40	.25
27	Willie Stargell	6.00	3.00	1.75
28	John Hiller	.80	.40	.25
29	Bobby Murcer	1.25	.60	.40
30	Rick Monday	1.00	.50	.30
31	John Montefusco	.80	.40	.25
32	Lou Brock	6.00	3.00	1.75
33	Bill North	.80	.40	.25
34	Robin Yount	6.00	3.00	1.75
35	Steve Garvey	7.00	3.50	2.00
36	George Brett	10.00	5.00	3.00
37	Toby Harrah	.80	.40	.25
38	Jerry Royster	.80	.40	.25
39	Bob Watson	1.00	.50	.30
40	George Foster	1.75	.90	.50
41	Gary Carter	7.00	3.50	2.00
42	John Denny	.80	.40	.25
43	Mike Schmidt	9.00	4.50	2.75
44	Dave Winfield	7.00	3.50	2.00
45	Al Oliver	1.75	.90	.50
46	Mark Fidrych	1.50	.70	.45
47	Larry Herndon	1.00	.50	.30

		NR MT	EX	VG
48	Dave Goltz	.80	.40	.25
49	Jerry Morales	.80	.40	.25
50	Ron LeFlore	1.00	.50	.30
51	Fred Lynn	1.75	.90	.50
52	Vida Blue	1.00	.50	.30
53	Rick Manning	.80	.40	.25
54	Bill Buckner	1.50	.70	.45
55	Lee May	1.00	.50	.30
56	John Mayberry	.80	.40	.25
57	Darrel Chaney	.80	.40	.25
58	Cesar Cedeno	1.25	.60	.40
59	Ken Griffey	1.25	.60	.40
60	Dave Kingman	1.75	.90	.50
61	Ted Simmons	1.50	.70	.45
62	Larry Bowa	1.25	.60	.40
63	Frank Tanana	1.00	.50	.30
64	Jason Thompson	.80	.40	.25
65	Ken Brett	.80	.40	.25
66	Roy Smalley	.80	.40	.25
67	Ray Burris	.80	.40	.25
68	Rick Burleson	.80	.40	.25
69	Buddy Bell	1.25	.60	.40
70	Don Sutton	3.50	1.75	1.00
71	Mark Belanger	.80	.40	.25
72	Dennis Leonard	.80	.40	.25
73	Gaylord Perry	4.00	2.00	1.25
74	Dick Ruthven	.80	.40	.25
75	Jose Cruz	1.25	.60	.40
76	Cesar Geronimo	.80	.40	.25
77	Jerry Koosman	1.25	.60	.40
78	Garry Templeton	2.50	1.25	.70
79	Jim Hunter	4.00	2.00	1.25
80	John Candelaria	1.00	.50	.30
81	Nolan Ryan	7.00	3.50	2.00
82	Rusty Staub	1.50	.70	.45
83	Jim Barr	.80	.40	.25
84	Butch Wynegar	1.00	.50	.30
85	Jose Cardenal	.80	.40	.25
86	Claudell Washington	1.00	.50	.30
87	Bill Travers	.80	.40	.25
88	Rick Waits	.80	.40	.25
89	Ron Cey	1.25	.60	.40
90	Al Bumbry	.80	.40	.25
91	Bucky Dent	1.00	.50	.30
92	Amos Otis	1.00	.50	.30
93	Tom Grieve	.80	.40	.25
94	Enos Cabell	.80	.40	.25
95	Dave Concepcion	1.25	.60	.40
96	Felix Millan	.80	.40	.25
97	Bake McBride	.80	.40	.25
98	Chris Chambliss	1.00	.50	.30
99	Butch Metzger	.80	.40	.25
100	Rennie Stennett	.80	.40	.25
101	Dave Roberts	.80	.40	.25
102	Lyman Bostock	1.00	.50	.30
103	Rick Reuschel	1.00	.50	.30
104	Carlton Fisk	2.25	1.25	.70
105	Jim Slaton	.80	.40	.25
106	Dennis Eckersley	1.25	.60	.40
107	Ken Singleton	1.00	.50	.30
108	Ralph Garr	.80	.40	.25
109	Freddie Patek	.80	.40	.25
110	Jim Sundberg	.80	.40	.25
111	Phil Niekro	3.50	1.75	1.00
112	J. R. Richard	1.00	.50	.30
113	Gary Nolan	.80	.40	.25
114	Jon Matlack	.80	.40	.25
115	Keith Hernandez	5.00	2.50	1.50
116	Graig Nettles	2.00	1.00	.60
117	Steve Carlton	7.00	3.50	2.00
118	Bill Madlock	1.50	.70	.45
119	Jerry Reuss	1.00	.50	.30
120	Aurelio Rodriguez	.80	.40	.25
121	Dan Ford	.80	.40	.25
122	Ray Fosse	.80	.40	.25
123	George Hendrick	1.00	.50	.30
124	Alan Ashby	.80	.40	.25
125	Joe Lis	.80	.40	.25
126	Sal Bando	1.00	.50	.30
127	Richie Zisk	1.00	.50	.30
128	Rich Gossage	1.75	.90	.50
129	Don Baylor	1.50	.70	.45
130	Dave McKay	.80	.40	.25
131	Bob Grich	1.00	.50	.30
132	Dave Pagan	.80	.40	.25
133	Dave Cash	.80	.40	.25
134	Steve Braun	.80	.40	.25
135	Dan Meyer	.80	.40	.25
136	Bill Stein	.80	.40	.25
137	Rollie Fingers	3.00	1.50	.90
138	Brian Downing	1.00	.50	.30
139	Bill Singer	.80	.40	.25

		NR MT	EX	VG
140	Doyle Alexander	1.00	.50	.30
141	Gene Tenace	1.00	.50	.30
142	Gary Matthews	1.00	.50	.30
143	Don Gullett	.80	.40	.25
144	Wayne Garland	.80	.40	.25
145	Pete Broberg	.80	.40	.25
146	Joe Rudi	1.00	.50	.30
147	Glenn Abbott	.80	.40	.25
148	George Scott	1.00	.50	.30
149	Bert Campaneris	1.25	.60	.40
150	Andy Messersmith	1.00	.50	.30

1978 Hostess

 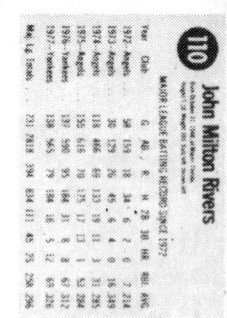

Other than the design on the front of the card, there was little different about the 1978 Hostess cards from the three years' issues which had preceded it, or the one which followed. The 2-1/4" by 3-1/4" cards were printed in panels of three (7-1/4" by 3-1/4") as the bottom of family-sized boxes of snake cakes. The 1978 set was again complete at 150 cards. Like other years of Hostess issues, there are scarcities within the 1978 set that are the result of those panels having been issued with less-popular brands of snack cakes.

		NR MT	EX	VG
Complete Panel:		325.00	162.00	97.00
Complete Singles Set:		200.00	100.00	60.00
Common Panel:		2.50	1.25	.70
Common Single Player:		.40	.20	.12
	Panel 1	4.00	2.00	1.25
1	Butch Hobson	.40	.20	.12
2	George Foster	.90	.45	.25
3	Bob Forsch	.50	.25	.15
	Panel 2	5.00	2.50	1.50
4	Tony Perez	1.00	.50	.30
5	Bruce Sutter	.90	.45	.25
6	Hal McRae	.50	.25	.15
	Panel 3	6.00	3.00	1.75
7	Tommy John	1.50	.70	.45
8	Greg Luzinski	.50	.25	.15
9	Enos Cabell	.40	.20	.12
	Panel 4	7.00	3.50	2.00
10	Doug DeCinces	.50	.25	.15
11	Willie Stargell	3.00	1.50	.90
12	Ed Halicki	.40	.20	.12
	Panel 5	2.50	1.25	.70
13	Larry Hisle	.40	.20	.12
14	Jim Slaton	.40	.20	.12
15	Buddy Bell	.50	.25	.15
	Panel 6	2.50	1.25	.70
16	Earl Williams	.40	.20	.12
17	Glenn Abbott	.40	.20	.12
18	Dan Ford	.40	.20	.12
	Panel 7	2.50	1.25	.70
19	Gary Mathews	.50	.25	.15
20	Eric Soderholm	.40	.20	.12
21	Bump Wills	.40	.20	.12
	Panel 8	7.00	3.50	2.00
22	Keith Hernandez	2.50	1.25	.70
23	Dave Cash	.40	.20	.12
24	George Scott	.50	.25	.15
	Panel 9	15.00	7.50	4.50
25	Ron Guidry	1.50	.70	.45
26	Dave Kingman	.80	.40	.25

		NR MT	EX	VG
27	George Brett	5.00	2.50	1.50
	Panel 10	3.50	1.75	1.00
28	Bob Watson	.50	.25	.15
29	Bob Boone	.70	.35	.20
30	Reggie Smith	.70	.35	.20
	Panel 11	20.00	10.00	6.00
31	Eddie Murray	10.00	5.00	3.00
32	Gary Lavelle	.50	.25	.15
33	Rennie Stennett	.50	.25	.15
	Panel 12	3.50	1.75	1.00
34	Duane Kuiper	.50	.25	.15
35	Sixto Lezcano	.50	.25	.15
36	Dave Rozema	.50	.25	.15
	Panel 13	3.50	1.75	1.00
37	Butch Wynegar	.50	.25	.15
38	Mitchell Page	.50	.25	.15
39	Bill Stein	.50	.25	.15
	Panel 14	2.50	1.25	.70
40	Elliott Maddox	.40	.20	.12
41	Mike Hargrove	.40	.20	.12
42	Bobby Bonds	.50	.25	.15
	Panel 15	15.00	7.50	4.50
43	Garry Templeton	.80	.40	.25
44	Johnny Bench	4.00	2.00	1.25
45	Jim Rice	4.00	2.00	1.25
	Panel 16	13.00	6.50	4.00
46	Bill Buckner	.80	.40	.25
47	Reggie Jackson	5.00	2.50	1.50
48	Freddie Patek	.40	.20	.12
	Panel 17	8.50	4.25	2.50
49	Steve Carlton	3.50	1.75	1.00
50	Cesar Cedeno	.50	.25	.15
51	Steve Yeager	.40	.20	.12
	Panel 18	3.50	1.75	1.00
52	Phil Garner	.50	.25	.15
53	Lee May	.50	.25	.15
54	Darrell Evans	.70	.35	.20
	Panel 19	2.50	1.25	.70
55	Steve Kemp	.50	.25	.15
56	Dusty Baker	.50	.25	.15
57	Ray Fosse	.40	.20	.12
	Panel 20	2.50	1.25	.70
58	Manny Sanguillen	.40	.20	.12
59	Tom Johnson	.40	.20	.12
60	Lee Stanton	.40	.20	.12
	Panel 21	10.00	5.00	3.00
61	Jeff Burroughs	.40	.20	.12
62	Bobby Grich	.50	.25	.15
63	Dave Winfield	4.00	2.00	1.25
	Panel 22	3.50	1.75	1.00
64	Dan Driessen	.50	.25	.15
65	Ted Simmons	.80	.40	.25
66	Jerry Remy	.40	.20	.12
	Panel 23	2.50	1.25	.70
67	Al Cowens	.40	.20	.12
68	Sparky Lyle	.50	.25	.15
69	Manny Trillo	.50	.25	.15
	Panel 24	5.00	2.50	1.50
70	Don Sutton	1.50	.70	.45
71	Larry Bowa	.50	.25	.15
72	Jose Cruz	.50	.25	.15
	Panel 25	8.00	4.00	2.50
73	Willie McCovey	3.00	1.50	.90
74	Bert Blyleven	.70	.35	.20
75	Ken Singleton	.50	.25	.15
	Panel 26	2.50	1.25	.70
76	Bill North	.40	.20	.12
77	Jason Thompson	.40	.20	.12
78	Dennis Eckersley	.50	.25	.15
	Panel 27	2.50	1.25	.70
79	Jim Sundberg	.50	.25	.15
80	Jerry Koosman	.50	.25	.15
81	Bruce Bochte	.40	.20	.12
	Panel 28	8.50	4.25	2.50
82	George Hendrick	.50	.25	.15
83	Nolan Ryan	3.50	1.75	1.00
84	Roy Howell	.40	.20	.12
	Panel 29	5.50	2.75	1.75
85	Butch Metzger	.40	.20	.12
86	George Medich	.40	.20	.12
87	Joe Morgan	2.00	1.00	.60
	Panel 30	3.00	1.50	.90
88	Dennis Leonard	.50	.25	.15
89	Willie Randolph	.50	.25	.15
90	Bobby Murcer	.50	.25	.15
	Panel 31	3.00	1.50	.90
91	Rick Manning	.40	.20	.12
92	J.R. Richard	.50	.25	.15
93	Ron Cey	.60	.30	.20
	Panel 32	2.50	1.25	.70
94	Sal Bando	.50	.25	.15

		NR MT	EX	VG
95	Ron LeFlore	.50	.25	.15
96	Dave Goltz	.40	.20	.12
	Panel 33	2.50	1.25	.70
97	Dan Meyer	.40	.20	.12
98	Chris Chambliss	.50	.25	.15
99	Biff Pocoroba	.40	.20	.12
	Panel 34	2.50	1.25	.70
100	Oscar Gamble	.40	.20	.12
101	Frank Tanana	.50	.25	.15
102	Lenny Randle	.40	.20	.12
	Panel 35	2.50	1.25	.70
103	Tommy Hutton	.40	.20	.12
104	John Candelaria	.50	.25	.15
105	Jorge Orta	.40	.20	.12
	Panel 36	3.00	1.50	.90
106	Ken Reitz	.40	.20	.12
107	Bill Campbell	.40	.20	.12
108	Dave Concepcion	.70	.35	.20
	Panel 37	2.50	1.25	.70
109	Joe Ferguson	.40	.20	.12
110	Mickey Rivers	.50	.25	.15
111	Paul Splittorff	.40	.20	.12
	Panel 38	12.00	6.00	3.50
112	Davey Lopes	.50	.25	.15
113	Mike Schmidt	5.00	2.50	1.50
114	Joe Rudi	.50	.25	.15
	Panel 39	7.00	3.50	2.00
115	Milt May	.40	.20	.12
116	Jim Palmer	3.00	1.50	.90
117	Bill Madlock	.70	.35	.20
	Panel 40	2.50	1.25	.70
118	Roy Smalley	.40	.20	.12
119	Cecil Cooper	.50	.25	.15
120	Rick Langford	.40	.20	.12
	Panel 41	5.75	3.00	1.75
121	Ruppert Jones	.40	.20	.12
122	Phil Niekro	2.25	1.25	.70
123	Toby Harrah	.50	.25	.15
	Panel 42	2.50	1.25	.70
124	Chet Lemon	.50	.25	.15
125	Gene Tenace	.40	.20	.12
126	Steve Henderson	.40	.20	.12
	Panel 43	20.00	10.00	6.00
127	Mike Torrez	.40	.20	.12
128	Pete Rose	8.00	4.00	2.50
129	John Denny	.50	.25	.15
	Panel 44	4.00	2.00	1.25
130	Darrell Porter	.50	.25	.15
131	Rick Reuschel	.50	.25	.15
132	Graig Nettles	.90	.45	.25
	Panel 45	4.50	2.25	1.25
133	Garry Maddox	.50	.25	.15
134	Mike Flanagan	.50	.25	.15
135	Dave Parker	1.25	.60	.40
	Panel 46	7.50	3.75	2.25
136	Terry Whitfield	.40	.20	.12
137	Wayne Garland	.40	.20	.12
138	Robin Yount	3.00	1.50	.90
	Panel 47	12.00	6.00	3.50
139	Gaylord Perry	2.50	1.25	.70
140	Rod Carew	4.00	2.00	1.25
141	Wayne Gross	.40	.20	.12
	Panel 48	5.00	2.50	1.50
142	Barry Bonnell	.40	.20	.12
143	Willie Montanez	.40	.20	.12
144	Rollie Fingers	1.75	.90	.50
	Panel 49	12.00	6.00	3.50
145	Bob Bailor	.40	.20	.12
146	Tom Seaver	3.50	1.75	1.00
147	Thurman Munson	2.50	1.25	.70
	Panel 50	8.00	4.00	2.50
148	Lyman Bostock	.50	.25	.15
149	Gary Carter	3.50	1.75	1.00
150	Ron Blomberg	.40	.20	.12

1979 Hostess

The last of five consecutive annual issues, the 1979 Hostess set retained the 150-card set size, 2-1/4" by 3-1/4" single-card size and 7-1/4" by 3-1/4" three-card panel format from the previous years. The cards were printed as the bottom panel on family-size boxes of Hostess snack cakes. Some panels, which were printed on less-popular brands, are somewhat scarcer today than the rest of the set. Like all Hostess issues, because the hobby was in a well-developed state at the time of issue, the 1979s

survive today in complete panels and complete unused boxes, for collectors who like original packaging.

		NR MT	EX	VG
	Complete Panel Set:	350.00	175.00	105.00
	Complete Singles Set:	200.00	100.00	60.00
	Common Panel:	2.50	1.25	.70
	Common Single Player:	.40	.20	.12
	Panel 1	9.50	4.75	2.75
1	John Denny	.40	.20	.12
2	Jim Rice	4.00	2.00	1.25
3	Doug Bair	.40	.20	.12
	Panel 2	2.50	1.25	.70
4	Darrell Porter	.50	.25	.15
5	Ross Grimsley	.40	.20	.12
6	Bobby Murcer	.50	.25	.15
	Panel 3	18.00	9.00	5.50
7	Lee Mazzilli	.50	.25	.15
8	Steve Garvey	4.00	2.00	1.25
9	Mike Schmidt	5.00	2.50	1.50
	Panel 4	6.50	3.25	2.00
10	Terry Whitfield	.40	.20	.12
11	Jim Palmer	3.00	1.50	.90
12	Omar Moreno	.40	.20	.12
	Panel 5	2.50	1.25	.70
13	Duane Kuiper	.40	.20	.12
14	Mike Caldwell	.40	.20	.12
15	Steve Kemp	.50	.25	.15
	Panel 6	2.50	1.25	.70
16	Dave Goltz	.40	.20	.12
17	Mitchell Page	.40	.20	.12
18	Bill Stein	.40	.20	.12
	Panel 7	2.50	1.25	.70
19	Gene Tenace	.40	.20	.12
20	Jeff Burroughs	.40	.20	.12
21	Francisco Barrios	.40	.20	.12
	Panel 8	8.00	4.00	2.50
22	Mike Torrez	.40	.20	.12
23	Ken Reitz	.40	.20	.12
24	Gary Carter	3.50	1.75	1.00
	Panel 9	8.00	4.00	2.50
25	Al Hrabosky	.50	.25	.15
26	Thurman Munson	2.50	1.25	.70
27	Bill Buckner	.80	.40	.25
	Panel 10	5.00	2.50	1.50
28	Ron Cey	.90	.45	.25
29	J.R. Richard	.70	.35	.20
30	Greg Luzinski	.90	.45	.25
	Panel 11	5.00	2.50	1.50
31	Ed Ott	.50	.25	.15
32	Denny Martinez	.50	.25	.15
33	Darrell Evans	1.25	.60	.40
	Panel 12	2.50	1.25	.70
34	Ron LeFlore	.50	.25	.15
35	Rick Waits	.40	.20	.12
36	Cecil Cooper	.50	.25	.15
	Panel 13	9.50	4.75	2.75
37	Leon Roberts	.40	.20	.12
38	Rod Carew	4.00	2.00	1.25
39	John Henry Johnson	.40	.20	.12
	Panel 14	2.50	1.25	.70
40	Chet Lemon	.50	.25	.15
41	Craig Swan	.40	.20	.12
42	Gary Matthews	.50	.25	.15
	Panel 15	3.50	1.75	1.00
43	Lamar Johnson	.40	.20	.12
44	Ted Simmons	.80	.40	.25
45	Ken Griffey	.50	.25	.15
	Panel 16	4.00	2.00	1.25

		NR MT	EX	VG
46	Freddie Patek	.40	.20	.12
47	Frank Tanana	.50	.25	.15
48	Rich Gossage	1.25	.60	.40
	Panel 17	2.50	1.25	.70
49	Burt Hooton	.40	.20	.12
50	Ellis Valentine	.40	.20	.12
51	Ken Forsch	.40	.20	.12
	Panel 18	5.00	2.50	1.50
52	Bob Knepper	.50	.25	.15
53	Dave Parker	1.50	.70	.45
54	Doug DeCinces	.50	.25	.15
	Panel 19	8.00	4.00	2.50
55	Robin Yount	3.00	1.50	.90
56	Rusty Staub	.80	.40	.25
57	Gary Alexander	.40	.20	.12
	Panel 20	2.50	1.25	.70
58	Julio Cruz	.40	.20	.12
59	Matt Keough	.40	.20	.12
60	Roy Smalley	.40	.20	.12
	Panel 21	10.00	5.00	3.00
61	Joe Morgan	2.50	1.25	.70
62	Phil Niekro	2.50	1.25	.70
63	Don Baylor	.80	.40	.25
	Panel 22	10.00	5.00	3.00
64	Dwight Evans	.90	.45	.25
65	Tom Seaver	4.00	2.00	1.25
66	George Hendrick	.50	.25	.15
	Panel 23	14.00	7.00	4.25
67	Rick Reuschel	.50	.25	.15
68	Geroge Brett	6.00	3.00	1.75
69	Lou Piniella	.80	.40	.25
	Panel 24	8.50	4.25	2.50
70	Enos Cabell	.40	.20	.12
71	Steve Carlton	3.50	1.75	1.00
72	Reggie Smith	.50	.25	.15
	Panel 25	4.00	2.00	1.25
73	Rick Dempsey	.50	.25	.15
74	Vida Blue	.80	.40	.25
75	Phil Garner	.70	.35	.20
	Panel 26	3.50	1.75	1.00
76	Rick Manning	.50	.25	.15
77	Mark Fidrych	.80	.40	.25
78	Mario Guerrero	.50	.25	.15
	Panel 27	5.00	2.50	1.50
79	Bob Stinson	.50	.25	.15
80	Al Oliver	1.25	.60	.40
81	Doug Flynn	.50	.25	.15
	Panel 28	6.00	3.00	1.75
82	John Mayberry	.40	.20	.12
83	Gaylord Perry	2.50	1.25	.70
84	Joe Rudi	.50	.25	.15
	Panel 29	3.50	1.75	1.00
85	Dave Concepcion	.70	.35	.20
86	John Candelaria	.50	.25	.15
87	Pete Vuckovich	.50	.25	.15
	Panel 30	5.00	2.50	1.50
88	Ivan DeJesus	.40	.20	.12
89	Ron Guidry	1.50	.70	.45
90	Hal McRae	.50	.25	.15
	Panel 31	5.50	2.75	1.75
91	Cesar Cedeno	.50	.25	.15
92	Don Sutton	2.00	1.00	.60
93	Andre Thornton	.50	.25	.15
	Panel 32	2.50	1.25	.70
94	Roger Erickson	.40	.20	.12
95	Larry Hisle	.40	.20	.12
96	Jason Thompson	.40	.20	.12
	Panel 33	7.50	3.75	2.25
97	Jim Sundberg	.50	.25	.15
98	Bob Horner	3.00	1.50	.90
99	Ruppert Jones	.40	.20	.12
	Panel 34	8.50	4.25	2.50
100	Willie Montanez	.40	.20	.12
101	Nolan Ryan	3.50	1.75	1.00
102	Ozzie Smith	.70	.35	.20
	Panel 35	7.50	3.75	2.25
103	Eric Soderholm	.40	.20	.12
104	Willie Stargell	3.00	1.50	.90
105	Bob Bailor	.40	.20	.12
	Panel 36	9.00	4.50	2.75
106	Carlton Fisk	1.25	.60	.40
107	George Foster	.90	.45	.25
108	Keith Hernandez	2.50	1.25	.70
	Panel 37	4.00	2.00	1.25
109	Dennis Leonard	.50	.25	.15
110	Graig Nettles	.90	.45	.25
111	Jose Cruz	.50	.25	.15
	Panel 38	3.50	1.75	1.00
112	Bobby Grich	.50	.25	.15
113	Bob Boone	.50	.25	.15
114	Dave Lopes	.50	.25	.15

		NR MT	EX	VG
	Panel 39	15.00	7.50	4.50
115	Eddie Murray	4.50	2.25	1.25
116	Jack Clark	.90	.45	.25
117	Lou Whitaker	.50	.25	.15
	Panel 40	10.00	5.00	3.00
118	Miguel Dilone	.40	.20	.12
119	Sal Bando	.50	.25	.15
120	Reggie Jackson	4.50	2.25	1.25
	Panel 41	14.00	7.00	4.25
121	Dale Murphy	7.00	3.50	2.00
122	Jon Matlack	.40	.20	.12
123	Bruce Bochte	.40	.20	.12
	Panel 42	9.00	4.50	2.75
124	John Stearns	.40	.20	.12
125	Dave Winfield	3.50	1.75	1.00
126	Jorge Orta	.40	.20	.12
	Panel 43	9.00	4.50	2.75
127	Garry Templeton	.70	.35	.20
128	Johnny Bench	4.00	2.00	1.25
129	Butch Hobson	.40	.20	.12
	Panel 44	4.50	2.25	1.25
130	Bruce Sutter	1.25	.60	.40
131	Bucky Dent	.50	.25	.15
132	Amos Otis	.50	.25	.15
	Panel 45	3.50	1.75	1.00
133	Bert Blyleven	.70	.35	.20
134	Larry Bowa	.50	.25	.15
135	Ken Singleton	.50	.25	.15
	Panel 46	3.50	1.75	1.00
136	Sixto Lezcano	.40	.20	.12
137	Roy Howell	.40	.20	.12
138	Bill Madlock	.80	.40	.25
	Panel 47	2.50	1.25	.70
139	Dave Revering	.40	.20	.12
140	Richie Zisk	.50	.25	.15
141	Butch Wynegar	.50	.25	.15
	Panel 48	18.00	9.00	5.50
142	Alan Ashby	.40	.20	.12
143	Sparky Lyle	.50	.25	.15
144	Pete Rose	8.00	4.00	2.50
	Panel 49	4.00	2.00	1.25
145	Dennis Eckersley	.60	.30	.20
146	Dave Kingman	.80	.40	.25
147	Buddy Bell	.60	.30	.20
	Panel 50	2.50	1.25	.70
148	Mike Hargrove	.40	.20	.12
149	Jerry Koosman	.50	.25	.15
150	Toby Harrah	.50	.25	.15

		MT	NR MT	EX
5	Rick Camp	.35	.25	.14
6	Rick Cerone	.35	.25	.14
7	Chris Chambliss	.40	.30	.15
8	Terry Forster	.35	.25	.14
9	Gene Garber	.35	.25	.14
10	Albert Hall	.50	.40	.20
11	Bob Horner	.50	.40	.20
12	Glenn Hubbard	.35	.25	.14
13	Brad Komminsk	.35	.25	.14
14	Rick Mahler	.40	.30	.15
15	Craig McMurtry	.35	.25	.14
16	Dale Murphy	2.00	1.50	.80
17	Ken Oberkfell	.40	.30	.15
18	Pascual Perez	.40	.30	.15
19	Gerald Perry	.80	.60	.30
20	Rafael Ramirez	.35	.25	.14
21	Bruce Sutter	.50	.40	.20
22	Claudell Washington	.40	.30	.15
----	Header Card	.10	.08	.04

1987 Hostess Stickers

Hostess of Canada issued a 30-card set of stickers in specially marked bags of potato chips. One sticker, measuring 1-3/4" by 1-3/8" in size, was found in each bag. The stickers have full-color fronts with the player's name appearing in black type in a white band. The Hostess logo and the sticker number are also included on the fronts. The backs are written in both English and French and contain the player's name, position and team.

		MT	NR MT	EX
	Complete Set:	30.00	22.00	12.00
	Common Player:	.20	.15	.08
1	Jesse Barfield	.35	.25	.14
2	Ernie Whitt	.20	.15	.08
3	George Bell	1.00	.70	.40
4	Hubie Brooks	.20	.15	.08
5	Tim Wallach	.35	.25	.14
6	Floyd Youmans	.20	.15	.08
7	Dale Murphy	1.50	1.25	.60
8	Ryne Sandberg	1.00	.70	.40
9	Eric Davis	2.00	1.50	.80
10	Mike Scott	.35	.25	.14
11	Fernando Valenzuela	.75	.60	.30
12	Gary Carter	1.00	.70	.40
13	Mike Schmidt	1.50	1.25	.60
14	Tony Pena	.20	.15	.08
15	Ozzie Smith	.60	.45	.25
16	Tony Gwynn	1.25	.90	.50
17	Mike Krukow	.20	.15	.08
18	Eddie Murray	1.25	.90	.50
19	Wade Boggs	2.25	1.75	.90
20	Wally Joyner	2.00	1.50	.80
21	Harold Baines	.35	.25	.14
22	Brook Jacoby	.35	.25	.14
23	Lou Whitaker	.50	.40	.20
24	George Brett	1.50	1.25	.60
25	Robin Yount	.75	.60	.30
26	Kirby Puckett	1.25	.90	.50
27	Don Mattingly	3.50	2.75	1.50
28	Jose Canseco	3.00	2.25	1.25
29	Phil Bradley	.35	.25	.14
30	Pete O'Brien	.20	.15	.08

1985 Hostess Braves

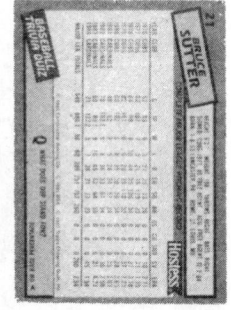

After a five-year hiatus, Hostess returned to the production of baseball cards in 1985 with an Atlanta Braves team set. The 22 cards in the set were printed by Topps and inserted into packages of snack cake products, three cello-wrapped player cards and a header card per box. The 2-1/2" by 3-1/2" cards share a common back design with the regular-issue Topps cards of 1985.

		MT	NR MT	EX
	Complete Set:	8.00	6.00	3.25
	Common Player:	.35	.25	.14
1	Eddie Haas	.35	.25	.14
2	Len Barker	.35	.25	.14
3	Steve Bedrosian	.90	.70	.35
4	Bruce Benedict	.35	.25	.14

1988 Hostess
Potato Chips Expos

The Expos and Blue Jays are showcased in this set of 24 discs (1-1/2" diameter). Full-color head shots are framed in white, surrounded by red stars. A yellow-banner "1988 Collectors Edition" label is printed (English and French) beneath the photo, followed by the player's name in black. Numbered disc backs are bilingual, blue and white, and include player name and stats. This set was distributed inside Hostess potato chip packages sold in Canada.

		MT	NR MT	EX
Complete Panel Set:		12.00	9.00	4.75
Complete Singles Set:		7.00	5.25	2.75
Common Panel:		.75	.60	.30
Common Single Player:		.25	.20	.10
	Panel	.90	.70	.35
1	Mitch Webster	.25	.20	.10
20	Lloyd Moseby	.40	.30	.15
	Panel	.90	.70	.35
2	Tim Burke	.25	.20	.10
23	Tom Henke	.40	.30	.15
	Panel	.80	.60	.30
3	Tom Foley	.25	.20	.10
13	Jim Clancy	.30	.25	.12
	Panel	.75	.60	.30
4	Herm Winningham	.25	.20	.10
14	Rance Mulliniks	.25	.20	.10
	Panel	1.25	.90	.50
5	Hubie Brooks	.40	.30	.15
24	Jimmy Key	.60	.45	.25
	Panel	1.00	.70	.40
6	Mike Fitzgerald	.25	.20	.10
17	Dave Stieb	.60	.45	.25
	Panel	2.25	1.75	.90
7	Tim Wallach	.70	.50	.30
15	Fred McGriff	1.00	.70	.40
	Panel	2.25	1.75	.90
8	Andres Galarraga	1.00	.70	.40
21	Tony Fernandez	.70	.50	.30
	Panel	.80	.60	.30
9	Floyd Youmans	.30	.25	.12
18	Mark Eichhorn	.30	.25	.12
	Panel	1.00	.70	.40
10	Neal Heaton	.25	.20	.10
19	Jesse Barfield	.70	.50	.30
	Panel	2.00	1.50	.80
11	Tim Raines	1.25	.90	.50
16	Ernie Whitt	.25	.20	.10
	Panel	1.75	1.25	.70
12	Casey Candaele	.25	.20	.10
22	George Bell	1.00	.70	.40

1953 Hunter
Wieners Cardinals

From the great era of the regionally issued hot dog cards in the mid-1950s, the 1953 Hunter wieners set of St. Louis Cardinals is certainly among the rarest today. Originally issued in two-card panels, the cards

are most often found as 2-1/4" by 3-1/4" singles today when they can be found at all. The cards feature a light blue facsimile autograph printed over the stat box at the bottom. They are blank-backed.

		NR MT	EX	VG
Complete Set:		2500.00	1250.00	750.00
Common Player:		60.00	30.00	18.00
(1)	Steve Bilko	60.00	30.00	18.00
(2)	Alpha Brazle	60.00	30.00	18.00
(3)	Cloyd Boyer	60.00	30.00	18.00
(4)	Cliff Chambers	60.00	30.00	18.00
(5)	Michael Clark	60.00	30.00	18.00
(6)	Jack Crimian	60.00	30.00	18.00
(7)	Lester Fusselman	60.00	30.00	18.00
(8)	Harvey Haddix	65.00	33.00	20.00
(9)	Solly Hemus	60.00	30.00	18.00
(10)	Ray Jablonski	60.00	30.00	18.00
(11)	William Johnson	60.00	30.00	18.00
(12)	Harry Lowrey	60.00	30.00	18.00
(13)	Lawrence Miggins	60.00	30.00	18.00
(14)	Stuart Miller	60.00	30.00	18.00
(15)	Wilmer Mizell	60.00	30.00	18.00
(16)	Stanley Musial	600.00	300.00	175.00
(17)	Joseph Presko	60.00	30.00	18.00
(18)	Delbert Rice	60.00	30.00	18.00
(19)	Harold Rice	60.00	30.00	18.00
(20)	Willard Schmidt	60.00	30.00	18.00
(21)	Albert Schoendienst	100.00	50.00	30.00
(22)	Richard Sisler	60.00	30.00	18.00
(23)	Enos Slaughter	150.00	75.00	45.00
(24)	Gerald Staley	60.00	30.00	18.00
(25)	Edward Stanky	70.00	35.00	21.00
(26)	John Yuhas	60.00	30.00	18.00

1954 Hunter
Wieners Cardinals

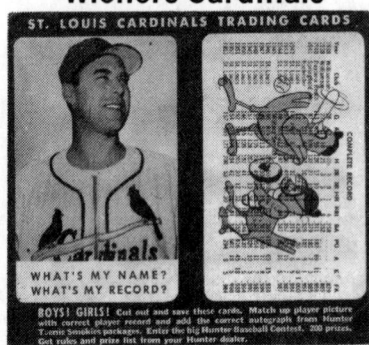

A nearly impossible set to complete today by virtue of the method of its issue, the 1954 Hunter hot dog set essentially features what would traditionally be the front and back of a normal baseball card on two different cards. The "front," containing a color photo of one of 30 St. Louis Cardinals has a box at bottom challenging the collector to name him and quote his stats. The "back" features cartoon Cardinals in action, and contains the answers. However, because both parts were printed on a single panel, and because most of the back (non-picture) panels were thrown away years ago, it is an impossible challenge to complete a '54 Hunter set today. There is no back printing on the 2-1/4" by 3-1/2" cards.

		NR MT	EX	VG
Complete Set:		4000.00	2000.00	1200.
Common Player:		60.00	30.00	18.00
(1)	Tom Alston	60.00	30.00	18.00
(2)	Steve Bilko	60.00	30.00	18.00
(3)	Al Brazle	60.00	30.00	18.00
(4)	Tom Burgess	60.00	30.00	18.00
(5)	Cot Deal	60.00	30.00	18.00
(6)	Alex Grammas	60.00	30.00	18.00
(7)	Harvey Haddix	60.00	30.00	18.00
(8)	Solly Hemus	60.00	30.00	18.00
(9)	Ray Jablonski	60.00	30.00	18.00
(10)	Royce Lint	60.00	30.00	18.00
(11)	Peanuts Lowrey	60.00	30.00	18.00
(12)	Memo Luna	60.00	30.00	18.00
(13)	Stu Miller	60.00	30.00	18.00
(14)	Stan Musial	600.00	300.00	180.00
(15)	Tom Poholsky	60.00	30.00	18.00
(16)	Bill Posedel	60.00	30.00	18.00
(17)	Joe Presko	60.00	30.00	18.00
(18)	Vic Raschi	60.00	30.00	18.00
(19)	Dick Rand	60.00	30.00	18.00
(20)	Rip Repulski	60.00	30.00	18.00
(21)	Del Rice	60.00	30.00	18.00
(22)	John Riddle	60.00	30.00	18.00
(23)	Mike Ryba	60.00	30.00	18.00
(24)	Red Schoendienst	100.00	50.00	30.00
(25)	Dick Schofield	100.00	50.00	30.00
(26)	Eddie Stanky	110.00	55.00	33.00
(27)	Enos Slaughter	150.00	75.00	45.00
(28)	Gerry Staley	60.00	30.00	18.00
(29)	Ed Yuhas	60.00	30.00	18.00
(30)	Sal Yvars	60.00	30.00	18.00

1955 Hunter Wieners Cardinals

The 1955 team set of St. Louis Cardinals, included with packages of Hunter hot dogs, features the third format change in three years of issue. For 1955, the cards were printed in a tall, narrow 2" by 4-3/4" format, two to a panel. The cards featured both a posed action photo and a portrait photo, along with a facsimile autograph and brief biographical data on the front. There is no back printing, as the cards were part of the wrapping for packages of hot dogs.

		NR MT	EX	VG
Complete Set:		3500.00	1750.00	1050.
Common Player:		75.00	37.00	22.00
(1)	Thomas Edison Alston	75.00	37.00	22.00
(2)	Kenton Lloyd Boyer	225.00	112.00	67.00
(3)	Harry Lewis Elliott	75.00	37.00	22.00
(4)	John Edward Faszholz	75.00	37.00	22.00
(5)	Joseph Filmore Frazier	75.00	37.00	22.00
(6)	Alexander Pete Grammas	75.00	37.00	22.00
(7)	Harvey Haddix	125.00	62.00	37.00

		NR MT	EX	VG
(8)	Solly Joseph Hemus	75.00	37.00	22.00
(9)	Lawrence Curtis Jackson	75.00	37.00	22.00
(10)	Tony R. Jacobs	75.00	37.00	22.00
(11)	Gordon Bassett Jones	75.00	37.00	22.00
(12)	Paul Edmore LaPalme	75.00	37.00	22.00
(13)	Brooks Ulysses Lawrence	75.00	37.00	22.00
(14)	Wallace Wade Moon	125.00	62.00	37.00
(15)	Stanley Frank Musial	1000.00	500.00	300.00
(16)	Thomas George Poholsky	75.00	37.00	22.00
(17)	William John Posedel	75.00	37.00	22.00
(18)	Victor Angelo John Raschi	75.00	37.00	22.00
(19)	Eldon John Repulski	75.00	37.00	22.00
(20)	Delbert Rice	75.00	37.00	22.00
(21)	John Ludy Riddle	75.00	37.00	22.00
(22)	William F. Sarni	75.00	37.00	22.00
(23)	Albert Fred Schoendienst	175.00	87.00	52.00
(24)	Richard John Schofield (actually John Richard)	75.00	37.00	22.00
(25)	Frank Thomas Smith	75.00	37.00	22.00
(26)	Edward R. Stanky	125.00	62.00	37.00
(27)	Bobby Gene Tiefenauer	75.00	37.00	22.00
(28)	William Charles Virdon	175.00	87.00	52.00
(29)	Frederick E. Walker	75.00	37.00	22.00
(30)	Floyd Lewis Woolridge	75.00	37.00	22.00

1982 Hygrade Expos

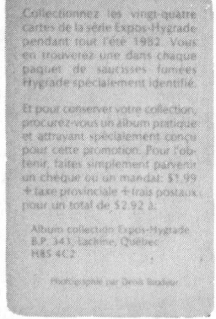

Gary Carter 8

This 24-card Montreal Expos team set was the object of intense collector speculation when it was first issued. Single cello-wrapped cards were included in packages of Hygrade luncheon meat in the province of Quebec only. Until a mail-in offer for the complete set appeared later in the season, the set was selling for as high as $50. It remains a relatively scarce issue today. The 2" by 3" cards are printed on heavy paper, with round corners. Backs are printed only in French, and contain an offer for an album to house the set.

		MT	NR MT	EX
Complete Set:		45.00	34.00	18.00
Common Player:		1.00	.70	.40
Album:		6.00	4.50	2.50
0	Al Oliver	2.25	1.75	.90
4	Chris Speier	1.00	.70	.40
5	John Milner	1.00	.70	.40
6	Jim Fanning	1.00	.70	.40
8	Gary Carter	7.00	5.25	2.75
10	Andre Dawson	5.00	3.75	2.00
11	Frank Tavaras (Taveras)	1.00	.70	.40
16	Terry Francona	1.25	.90	.50
17	Tim Blackwell	1.00	.70	.40
18	Jerry White	1.00	.70	.40
20	Bob James	1.25	.90	.50
21	Scott Sanderson	1.00	.70	.40
24	Brad Mills	1.00	.70	.40
29	Tim Wallach	3.00	2.25	1.25
30	Tim Raines	7.00	5.25	2.75
34	Bill Gullickson	1.25	.90	.50
35	Woodie Fryman	1.00	.70	.40
38	Bryn Smith	1.50	1.25	.60
41	Jeff Reardon	2.00	1.50	.80
44	Dan Norman	1.00	.70	.40
45	Steve Rogers	1.25	.90	.50
48	Ray Burris	1.00	.70	.40
49	Warren Cromartie	1.00	.70	.40

		MT	NR MT	EX
53	Charlie Lea	1.00	.70	.40

1984 Jarvis Press Rangers

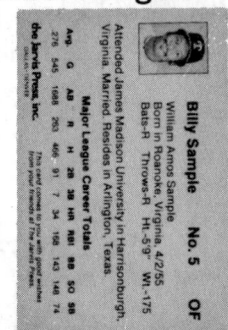

For its second annual "Baseball Card Day" game promotional set, the Rangers picked up a new sponsor, Jarvis Press of Dallas. The 30 cards in the set include 27 players, the manager, trainer and a group card of the coaches. Cards measure 2-3/8" by 3-1/2". Color game-action photos make up the card fronts. Backs, printed in black and white, include a portrait photo of the player. A source close to the promotion indicated 10,000 sets were produced.

		MT	NR MT	EX
Complete Set:		5.00	3.75	2.00
Common Player:		.12	.09	.05
1	Bill Stein	.12	.09	.05
2	Alan Bannister	.12	.09	.05
3	Wayne Tolleson	.12	.09	.05
5	Billy Sample	.12	.09	.05
6	Bobby Jones	.12	.09	.05
7	Ned Yost	.12	.09	.05
9	Pete O'Brien	.30	.25	.12
11	Doug Rader	.12	.09	.05
13	Tommy Dunbar	.12	.09	.05
14	Jim Anderson	.12	.09	.05
15	Larry Parrish	.20	.15	.08
16	Mike Mason	.12	.09	.05
17	Mickey Rivers	.20	.15	.08
19	Curtis Wilkerson	.12	.09	.05
20	Jeff Kunkel	.12	.09	.05
21	Odell Jones	.12	.09	.05
24	Dave Schmidt	.15	.11	.06
25	Buddy Bell	.35	.25	.14
26	George Wright	.12	.09	.05
28	Frank Tanana	.20	.15	.08
30	Marv Foley	.12	.09	.05
31	Dave Stewart	.70	.50	.30
32	Gary Ward	.20	.15	.08
36	Dickie Noles	.12	.09	.05
43	Donnie Scott	.12	.09	.05
44	Danny Darwin	.25	.20	.10
49	Charlie Hough	.30	.25	.12
53	Joey McLaughlin	.12	.09	.05
-----	Coaching Staff (Rich Donnelly, Glenn Ezell, Merv Rettenmund, Dick Such, Wayne Terwilliger)	.12	.09	.05
-----	Trainer (Bill Zeigler)	.12	.09	.05

A player's name in *italic* type indicates a rookie card. An (FC) indicates a player's first card for that particular card company.

1986 Jays Potato Chips

One of a handful of round baseball cards produced for inclusion in boxes of potato chips on a regional basis in 1986, the Jays set of 2-7/8" discs is believed to be the scarcest of the type. The 20 cards in the issue include the most popular Milwaukee Brewers and Chicago Cubs and White Sox players; the set having been distributed in the southern Wisconsin-northern Illinois area. Like many of the recent sets produced by Mike Schecter Associates, the '86 Jays cards feature player photos on which the team logos have been airbrushed off the caps.

		MT	NR MT	EX
Complete Set:		25.00	18.50	10.00
Common Player:		.60	.45	.25
(1)	Harold Baines	1.25	.90	.50
(2)	Cecil Cooper	.80	.60	.30
(3)	Jody Davis	.60	.45	.25
(4)	Bob Dernier	.60	.45	.25
(5)	Richard Dotson	.60	.45	.25
(6)	Shawon Dunston	1.00	.70	.40
(7)	Carlton Fisk	1.50	1.25	.60
(8)	Jim Gantner	.60	.45	.25
(9)	Ozzie Guillen	1.00	.70	.40
(10)	Teddy Higuera	1.75	1.25	.70
(11)	Ron Kittle	.75	.60	.30
(12)	Paul Molitor	1.50	1.25	.60
(13)	Keith Moreland	.60	.45	.25
(14)	Ernie Riles	.60	.45	.25
(15)	Ryne Sandberg	3.00	2.25	1.25
(16)	Tom Seaver	2.00	1.50	.80
(17)	Lee Smith	.90	.70	.35
(18)	Rick Sutcliffe	.90	.70	.35
(19)	Greg Walker	.60	.45	.25
(20)	Robin Yount	2.00	1.50	.80

1962 Jell-O

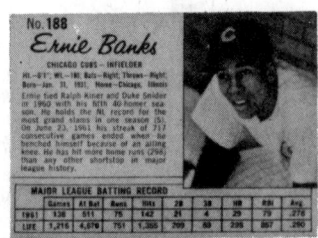

Virtually identical in content to the 1962 Post cereal cards, the '62 Jell-O set of 197 was only issued in the Midwest. Players and card numbers are identical in the two sets, except Brooks Robinson (#29), Ted Kluszewski (#82) and Smoky Burgess (#176) were not issued in the Jell-O version. The

Jell-O cards are easy to distinguish from the Post of that year by the absence of the red oval Post logo and red or blue border around the stat box. Cards which have been neatly trimmed from the box which they were printed will measure 3-1/2" by 2-1/2".

		NR MT	EX	VG
	Complete Set:	4000.00	2000.00	1200.
	Common Player:	5.00	2.50	1.50
1	Bill Skowron	20.00	10.00	6.00
2	Bobby Richardson	20.00	10.00	6.00
3	Cletis Boyer	10.00	5.00	3.00
4	Tony Kubek	15.00	7.50	4.50
5	Mickey Mantle	550.00	275.00	165.00
6	Roger Maris	100.00	50.00	30.00
7	Yogi Berra	60.00	30.00	18.00
8	Elston Howard	15.00	7.50	4.50
9	Whitey Ford	40.00	20.00	12.00
10	Ralph Terry	10.00	5.00	3.00
11	John Blanchard	6.00	3.00	1.75
12	Luis Arroyo	6.00	3.00	1.75
13	Bill Stafford	20.00	10.00	6.00
14	Norm Cash	10.00	5.00	3.00
15	Jake Wood	5.00	2.50	1.50
16	Steve Boros	5.00	2.50	1.50
17	Chico Fernandez	5.00	2.50	1.50
18	Billy Bruton	5.00	2.50	1.50
19	Ken Aspromonte	5.00	2.50	1.50
20	Al Kaline	40.00	20.00	12.00
21	Dick Brown	5.00	2.50	1.50
22	Frank Lary	6.00	3.00	1.75
23	Don Mossi	6.00	3.00	1.75
24	Phil Regan	5.00	2.50	1.50
25	Charley Maxwell	5.00	2.50	1.50
26	Jim Bunning	15.00	7.50	4.50
27	Jim Gentile	6.00	3.00	1.75
28	Marv Breeding	5.00	2.50	1.50
29	Not Issued			
30	Ron Hansen	5.00	2.50	1.50
31	Jackie Brandt	20.00	10.00	6.00
32	Dick Williams	6.00	3.00	1.75
33	Gus Triandos	6.00	3.00	1.75
34	Milt Pappas	6.00	3.00	1.75
35	Hoyt Wilhelm	25.00	12.50	7.50
36	Chuck Estrada	5.00	2.50	1.50
37	Vic Power	5.00	2.50	1.50
38	Johnny Temple	5.00	2.50	1.50
39	Bubba Phillips	20.00	10.00	6.00
40	Tito Francona	6.00	3.00	1.75
41	Willie Kirkland	5.00	2.50	1.50
42	John Romano	5.00	2.50	1.50
43	Jim Perry	10.00	5.00	3.00
44	Woodie Held	5.00	2.50	1.50
45	Chuck Essegian	5.00	2.50	1.50
46	Roy Sievers	6.00	3.00	1.75
47	Nellie Fox	15.00	7.50	4.50
48	Al Smith	5.00	2.50	1.50
49	Luis Aparicio	25.00	12.50	7.50
50	Jim Landis	5.00	2.50	1.50
51	Minnie Minoso	10.00	5.00	3.00
52	Andy Carey	20.00	10.00	6.00
53	Sherman Lollar	6.00	3.00	1.75
54	Bill Pierce	6.00	3.00	1.75
55	Early Wynn	25.00	12.50	7.50
56	Chuck Schilling	20.00	10.00	6.00
57	Pete Runnels	6.00	3.00	1.75
58	Frank Malzone	6.00	3.00	1.75
59	Don Buddin	10.00	5.00	3.00
60	Gary Geiger	5.00	2.50	1.50
61	Carl Yastrzemski	200.00	100.00	60.00
62	Jackie Jensen	20.00	10.00	6.00
63	Jim Pagliaroni	20.00	10.00	6.00
64	Don Schwall	5.00	2.50	1.50
65	Dale Long	6.00	3.00	1.75
66	Chuck Cottier	10.00	5.00	3.00
67	Billy Klaus	20.00	10.00	6.00
68	Coot Veal	5.00	2.50	1.50
69	Marty Keough	35.00	17.50	10.50
70	Willie Tasby	35.00	17.50	10.50
71	Gene Woodling	6.00	3.00	1.75
72	Gene Green	35.00	17.50	10.50
73	Dick Donovan	10.00	5.00	3.00
74	Steve Bilko	10.00	5.00	3.00
75	Rocky Bridges	20.00	10.00	6.00
76	Eddie Yost	10.00	5.00	3.00
77	Leon Wagner	10.00	5.00	3.00
78	Albie Pearson	10.00	5.00	3.00
79	Ken Hunt	10.00	5.00	3.00
80	Earl Averill	35.00	17.50	10.50
81	Ryne Duren	10.00	5.00	3.00
82	Not Issued			
83	Bob Allison	6.00	3.00	1.75
84	Billy Martin	15.00	7.50	4.50
85	Harmon Killebrew	35.00	17.50	10.50
86	Zorro Versalles	6.00	3.00	1.75
87	Lennie Green	20.00	10.00	6.00
88	Bill Tuttle	5.00	2.50	1.50
89	Jim Lemon	6.00	3.00	1.75
90	Earl Battey	20.00	10.00	6.00
91	Camilo Pascual	6.00	3.00	1.75
92	Norm Siebern	10.00	5.00	3.00
93	Jerry Lumpe	10.00	5.00	3.00
94	Dick Howser	10.00	5.00	3.00
95	Gene Stephens	35.00	17.50	10.50
96	Leo Posada	10.00	5.00	3.00
97	Joe Pignatano	10.00	5.00	3.00
98	Jim Archer	10.00	5.00	3.00
99	Haywood Sullivan	20.00	10.00	6.00
100	Art Ditmar	10.00	5.00	3.00
101	Gil Hodges	35.00	17.50	10.50
102	Charlie Neal	10.00	5.00	3.00
103	Daryl Spencer	10.00	5.00	3.00
104	Maury Wills	20.00	10.00	6.00
105	Tommy Davis	10.00	5.00	3.00
106	Willie Davis	10.00	5.00	3.00
107	John Roseboro	35.00	17.50	10.50
108	John Podres	10.00	5.00	3.00
109	Sandy Koufax	80.00	40.00	24.00
110	Don Drysdale	50.00	25.00	15.00
111	Larry Sherry	20.00	10.00	6.00
112	Jim Gilliam	20.00	10.00	6.00
113	Norm Larker	35.00	17.50	10.50
114	Duke Snider	70.00	35.00	21.00
115	Stan Williams	20.00	10.00	6.00
116	Gordon Coleman	70.00	35.00	21.00
117	Don Blasingame	20.00	10.00	6.00
118	Gene Freese	35.00	17.50	10.50
119	Ed Kasko	35.00	17.50	10.50
120	Gus Bell	20.00	10.00	6.00
121	Vada Pinson	10.00	5.00	3.00
122	Frank Robinson	35.00	17.50	10.50
123	Bob Purkey	10.00	5.00	3.00
124	Joey Jay	10.00	5.00	3.00
125	Jim Brosnan	10.00	5.00	3.00
126	Jim O'Toole	10.00	5.00	3.00
127	Jerry Lynch	10.00	5.00	3.00
128	Wally Post	10.00	5.00	3.00
129	Ken Hunt	10.00	5.00	3.00
130	Jerry Zimmerman	10.00	5.00	3.00
131	Willie McCovey	35.00	17.50	10.50
132	Jose Pagan	20.00	10.00	6.00
133	Felipe Alou	10.00	5.00	3.00
134	Jim Davenport	10.00	5.00	3.00
135	Harvey Kuenn	10.00	5.00	3.00
136	Orlando Cepeda	15.00	7.50	4.50
137	Ed Bailey	10.00	5.00	3.00
138	Sam Jones	10.00	5.00	3.00
139	Mike McCormick	10.00	5.00	3.00
140	Juan Marichal	40.00	20.00	12.00
141	Jack Sanford	10.00	5.00	3.00
142	Willie Mays	125.00	62.00	37.00
143	Stu Miller	70.00	35.00	21.00
144	Joe Amalfitano	10.00	5.00	3.00
145	Joe Adcock	10.00	5.00	3.00
146	Frank Bolling	5.00	2.50	1.50
147	Ed Mathews	35.00	17.50	10.50
148	Roy McMillan	6.00	3.00	1.75
149	Hank Aaron	125.00	62.00	37.00
150	Gino Cimoli	20.00	10.00	6.00
151	Frank Thomas	6.00	3.00	1.75
152	Joe Torre	10.00	5.00	3.00
153	Lou Burdette	10.00	5.00	3.00
154	Bob Buhl	6.00	3.00	1.75
155	Carlton Willey	5.00	2.50	1.50
156	Lee Maye	18.00	9.00	5.50
157	Al Spangler	35.00	17.50	10.50
158	Bill White	35.00	17.50	10.50
159	Ken Boyer	15.00	7.50	4.50
160	Joe Cunningham	10.00	5.00	3.00
161	Carl Warwick	10.00	5.00	3.00
162	Carl Sawatski	5.00	2.50	1.50
163	Lindy McDaniel	5.00	2.50	1.50
164	Ernie Broglio	10.00	5.00	3.00
165	Larry Jackson	5.00	2.50	1.50
166	Curt Flood	15.00	7.50	4.50
167	Curt Simmons	35.00	17.50	10.50
168	Alex Grammas	20.00	10.00	6.00
169	Dick Stuart	6.00	3.00	1.75
170	Bill Mazeroski	20.00	10.00	6.00
171	Don Hoak	10.00	5.00	3.00
172	Dick Groat	10.00	5.00	3.00

		NR MT	EX	VG
173	Roberto Clemente	125.00	62.00	37.00
174	Bob Skinner	20.00	10.00	6.00
175	Bill Virdon	35.00	17.50	10.50
176	Not Issued			
177	Elroy Face	10.00	5.00	3.00
178	Bob Friend	6.00	3.00	1.75
179	Vernon Law	20.00	10.00	6.00
180	Harvey Haddix	35.00	17.50	10.50
181	Hal Smith	20.00	10.00	6.00
182	Ed Bouchee	20.00	10.00	6.00
183	Don Zimmer	6.00	3.00	1.75
184	Ron Santo	10.00	5.00	3.00
185	Andre Rodgers	5.00	2.50	1.50
186	Richie Ashburn	15.00	7.50	4.50
187	George Altman	5.00	2.50	1.50
188	Ernie Banks	35.00	17.50	10.50
189	Sam Taylor	5.00	2.50	1.50
190	Don Elston	5.00	2.50	1.50
191	Jerry Kindall	20.00	10.00	6.00
192	Pancho Herrera	5.00	2.50	1.50
193	Tony Taylor	5.00	2.50	1.50
194	Ruben Amaro	20.00	10.00	6.00
195	Don Demeter	5.00	2.50	1.50
196	Bobby Gene Smith	5.00	2.50	1.50
197	Clay Dalrymple	5.00	2.50	1.50
198	Robin Roberts	25.00	12.50	7.50
199	Art Mahaffey	5.00	2.50	1.50
200	John Buzhardt	5.00	2.50	1.50

1963 Jell-O

Like the other Post and Jell-O issues of the era, the '63 Jell-O set includes many scarce cards; primarily those which were printed as the backs of less popular brands and sizes of the gelatin dessert. Slightly smaller than the virtually identical Post cereal cards of the same year, the 200 cards in the Jell-O issue measure 3-3/8" by 2-1/2". The easiest way to distinguish 1963 Jell-O cards from Post cards is by the red line that separates the 1962 stats from the lifetime stats. On Post cards, the line extends almost all the way to the side borders, on the Jell-O cards, the line begins and ends much closer to the stats.

		NR MT	EX	VG
Complete Set:		2500.00	1250.00	750.00
Common Player:		1.75	.90	.50
1	Vic Power	2.50	1.25	.70
2	Bernie Allen	20.00	10.00	6.00
3	Zoilo Versalles	20.00	10.00	6.00
4	Rich Rollins	1.75	.90	.50
5	Harmon Killebrew	8.00	4.00	2.50
6	Lenny Green	20.00	10.00	6.00
7	Bob Allison	3.00	1.50	.90
8	Earl Battey	15.00	7.50	4.50
9	Camilo Pascual	2.50	1.25	.70
10	Jim Kaat	35.00	17.50	10.50
11	Jack Kralick	1.75	.90	.50
12	Bill Skowron	20.00	10.00	6.00
13	Bobby Richardson	5.00	2.50	1.50
14	Cletis Boyer	2.50	1.25	.70
15	Mickey Mantle	175.00	87.00	52.00
16	Roger Maris	20.00	10.00	6.00
17	Yogi Berra	20.00	10.00	6.00
18	Elston Howard	20.00	10.00	6.00
19	Whitey Ford	10.00	5.00	3.00

		NR MT	EX	VG
20	Ralph Terry	2.00	1.00	.60
21	John Blanchard	15.00	7.50	4.50
22	Bill Stafford	20.00	10.00	6.00
23	Tom Tresh	2.50	1.25	.70
24	Steve Bilko	1.75	.90	.50
25	Bill Moran	1.75	.90	.50
26	Joe Koppe	1.75	.90	.50
27	Felix Torres	1.75	.90	.50
28	Leon Wagner	2.50	1.25	.70
29	Albie Pearson	1.75	.90	.50
30	Lee Thomas	1.75	.90	.50
31	Bob Rodgers	20.00	10.00	6.00
32	Dean Chance	1.50	.70	.45
33	Ken McBride	20.00	10.00	6.00
34	George Thomas	20.00	10.00	6.00
35	Joe Cunningham	20.00	10.00	6.00
36	Nelson Fox	5.00	2.50	1.50
37	Luis Aparicio	6.00	3.00	1.75
38	Al Smith	1.75	.90	.50
39	Floyd Robinson	1.75	.90	.50
40	Jim Landis	1.75	.90	.50
41	Charlie Maxwell	1.75	.90	.50
42	Sherman Lollar	2.00	1.00	.60
43	Early Wynn	6.00	3.00	1.75
44	Juan Pizarro	20.00	10.00	6.00
45	Ray Herbert	20.00	10.00	6.00
46	Norm Cash	3.50	1.75	1.00
47	Steve Boros	20.00	10.00	6.00
48	Dick McAuliffe	2.00	1.00	.60
49	Bill Bruton	2.00	1.00	.60
50	Rocky Colavito	5.00	2.50	1.50
51	Al Kaline	12.00	6.00	3.50
52	Dick Brown	20.00	10.00	6.00
53	Jim Bunning	5.00	2.50	1.50
54	Hank Aguirre	1.75	.90	.50
55	Frank Lary	20.00	10.00	6.00
56	Don Mossi	20.00	10.00	6.00
57	Jim Gentile	2.00	1.00	.60
58	Jackie Brandt	1.75	.90	.50
59	Brooks Robinson	15.00	7.50	4.50
60	Ron Hansen	1.75	.90	.50
61	Jerry Adair	55.00	27.00	16.50
62	John Powell	3.50	1.75	1.00
63	Russ Snyder	20.00	10.00	6.00
64	Steve Barber	1.75	.90	.50
65	Milt Pappas	20.00	10.00	6.00
66	Robin Roberts	6.00	3.00	1.75
67	Tito Francona	2.00	1.00	.60
68	Jerry Kindall	20.00	10.00	6.00
69	Woodie Held	2.00	1.00	.60
70	Bubba Phillips	1.75	.90	.50
71	Chuck Essegian	1.75	.90	.50
72	Willie Kirkland	20.00	10.00	6.00
73	Al Luplow	1.75	.90	.50
74	Ty Cline	20.00	10.00	6.00
75	Dick Donovan	1.75	.90	.50
76	John Romano	1.75	.90	.50
77	Pete Runnels	2.00	1.00	.60
78	Ed Bressoud	20.00	10.00	6.00
79	Frank Malzone	2.00	1.00	.60
80	Carl Yastrzemski	70.00	35.00	21.00
81	Gary Geiger	1.75	.90	.50
82	Lou Clinton	20.00	10.00	6.00
83	Earl Wilson	2.50	1.25	.70
84	Bill Monbouquette	2.50	1.25	.70
85	Norm Siebern	2.50	1.25	.70
86	Jerry Lumpe	2.50	1.25	.70
87	Manny Jimenez	1.75	.90	.50
88	Gino Cimoli	1.75	.90	.50
89	Ed Charles	55.00	27.00	16.50
90	Ed Rakow	1.75	.90	.50
91	Bob Del Greco	20.00	10.00	6.00
92	Haywood Sullivan	20.00	10.00	6.00
93	Chuck Hinton	1.75	.90	.50
94	Ken Retzer	20.00	10.00	6.00
95	Harry Bright	20.00	10.00	6.00
96	Bob Johnson	1.75	.90	.50
97	Dave Stenhouse	20.00	10.00	6.00
98	Chuck Cottier	2.00	1.00	.60
99	Tom Cheney	1.75	.90	.50
100	Claude Osteen	20.00	10.00	6.00
101	Orlando Cepeda	5.00	2.50	1.50
102	Charley Hiller	20.00	10.00	6.00
103	Jose Pagan	20.00	10.00	6.00
104	Jim Davenport	1.75	.90	.50
105	Harvey Kuenn	3.50	1.75	1.00
106	Willie Mays	60.00	30.00	18.00
107	Felipe Alou	3.00	1.50	.90
108	Tom Haller	2.00	1.00	.60
109	Juan Marichal	6.00	3.00	1.75
110	Jack Sanford	2.00	1.00	.60

		NR MT	EX	VG
111	Bill O'Dell	1.75	.90	.50
112	Willie McCovey	90.00	45.00	27.00
113	Lee Walls	20.00	10.00	6.00
114	Jim Gilliam	20.00	10.00	6.00
115	Maury Wills	5.00	2.50	1.50
116	Ron Fairly	2.00	1.00	.60
117	Tommy Davis	3.00	1.50	.90
118	Duke Snider	9.00	4.50	2.75
119	Willie Davis	3.00	1.50	.90
120	John Roseboro	2.00	1.00	.60
121	Sandy Koufax	20.00	10.00	6.00
122	Stan Williams	20.00	10.00	6.00
123	Don Drysdale	9.00	4.50	2.75
124	Daryl Spencer	1.75	.90	.50
125	Gordy Coleman	1.75	.90	.50
126	Don Blasingame	20.00	10.00	6.00
127	Leo Cardenas	1.75	.90	.50
128	Eddie Kasko	20.00	10.00	6.00
129	Jerry Lynch	1.75	.90	.50
130	Vada Pinson	4.00	2.00	1.25
131	Frank Robinson	9.00	4.50	2.75
132	John Edwards	20.00	10.00	6.00
133	Joey Jay	1.75	.90	.50
134	Bob Purkey	1.75	.90	.50
135	Marty Keough	55.00	27.00	16.50
136	Jim O'Toole	20.00	10.00	6.00
137	Dick Stuart	2.00	1.00	.60
138	Bill Mazeroski	3.50	1.75	1.00
139	Dick Groat	3.00	1.50	.90
140	Don Hoak	2.00	1.00	.60
141	Bob Skinner	2.00	1.00	.60
142	Bill Virdon	3.00	1.50	.90
143	Roberto Clemente	60.00	30.00	18.00
144	Smoky Burgess	3.00	1.50	.90
145	Bob Friend	2.00	1.00	.60
146	Al McBean	20.00	10.00	6.00
147	ElRoy Face	3.00	1.50	.90
148	Joe Adcock	3.50	1.75	1.00
149	Frank Bolling	1.75	.90	.50
150	Roy McMillan	1.75	.90	.50
151	Eddie Mathews	8.00	4.00	2.50
152	Hank Aaron	60.00	30.00	18.00
153	Del Crandall	20.00	10.00	6.00
154	Bob Shaw	1.75	.90	.50
155	Lew Burdette	3.50	1.75	1.00
156	Joe Torre	20.00	10.00	6.00
157	Tony Cloninger	35.00	17.50	10.50
158	Bill White	2.50	1.25	.70
159	Julian Javier	20.00	10.00	6.00
160	Ken Boyer	4.00	2.00	1.25
161	Julio Gotay	20.00	10.00	6.00
162	Curt Flood	3.00	1.50	.90
163	Charlie James	35.00	17.50	10.50
164	Gene Oliver	20.00	10.00	6.00
165	Ernie Broglio	1.75	.90	.50
166	Bob Gibson	60.00	30.00	18.00
167	Lindy McDaniel	20.00	10.00	6.00
168	Ray Washburn	1.75	.90	.50
169	Ernie Banks	12.00	6.00	3.50
170	Ron Santo	3.50	1.75	1.00
171	George Altman	1.75	.90	.50
172	Billy Williams	60.00	30.00	18.00
173	Andre Rodgers	20.00	10.00	6.00
174	Ken Hubbs	3.00	1.50	.90
175	Don Landrum	20.00	10.00	6.00
176	Dick Bertell	20.00	10.00	6.00
177	Roy Sievers	2.50	1.25	.70
178	Tony Taylor	20.00	10.00	6.00
179	John Callison	2.50	1.25	.70
180	Don Demeter	1.75	.90	.50
181	Tony Gonzalez	20.00	10.00	6.00
182	Wes Covington	20.00	10.00	6.00
183	Art Mahaffey	1.75	.90	.50
184	Clay Dalrymple	1.75	.90	.50
185	Al Spangler	1.75	.90	.50
186	Roman Mejias	1.75	.90	.50
187	Bob Aspromonte	50.00	25.00	15.00
188	Norm Larker	1.75	.90	.50
189	Johnny Temple	1.75	.90	.50
190	Carl Warwick	20.00	10.00	6.00
191	Bob Lillis	20.00	10.00	6.00
192	Dick Farrell	50.00	25.00	15.00
193	Gil Hodges	8.00	4.00	2.50
194	Marv Throneberry	3.00	1.50	.90
195	Charlie Neal	20.00	10.00	6.00
196	Frank Thomas	2.00	1.00	.60
197	Richie Ashburn	5.00	2.50	1.50
198	Felix Mantilla	20.00	10.00	6.00
199	Rod Kanehl	20.00	10.00	6.00
200	Roger Craig	20.00	10.00	6.00

1986 Jiffy Pop

One of the scarcer of the 1986 "regionals," the 20-card Jiffy Pop issue was inserted in packages of heat-and-eat popcorn. A production of Mike Schecter Associates, the 2-7/8" round discs feature 20 popular stars, many in the same pictures found in other '86 regionals. Like other MSA issues, caps have had the team logos erased, allowing Jiffy Pop to avoid having to pay a licensing fee to the teams.

		MT	NR MT	EX
Complete Set:		35.00	26.00	14.00
Common Player:		1.00	.70	.40
1	Jim Rice	1.75	1.25	.70
2	Wade Boggs	3.00	2.25	1.25
3	Lance Parrish	1.00	.70	.40
4	George Brett	2.50	2.00	1.00
5	Robin Yount	1.75	1.25	.70
6	Don Mattingly	5.00	3.75	2.00
7	Dave Winfield	2.00	1.50	.80
8	Reggie Jackson	2.50	2.00	1.00
9	Cal Ripken	2.50	2.00	1.00
10	Eddie Murray	2.00	1.50	.80
11	Pete Rose	3.00	2.25	1.25
12	Ryne Sandberg	1.75	1.25	.70
13	Nolan Ryan	1.50	1.25	.60
14	Fernando Valenzuela	1.25	.90	.50
15	Willie McGee	1.00	.70	.40
16	Dale Murphy	2.50	2.00	1.00
17	Mike Schmidt	2.50	2.00	1.00
18	Steve Garvey	2.00	1.50	.80
19	Gary Carter	2.00	1.50	.80
20	Dwight Gooden	3.00	2.25	1.25

1987 Jiffy Pop

For the second year in a row, Jiffy Pop inserted baseball discs in their packages of popcorn. The full-color discs measure 2-7/8" in diameter and were produced by Mike Schecter Associates of Cos Cob, Conn. Titled "2nd Annual Collectors' Edition," the card fronts feature player photos with all team insignias airbrushed away. Information on the backs of the discs are printed in bright red on white stock. Die-cut press sheets containing all 20 discs were available via a mail-in offer.

		MT	NR MT	EX
Complete Set:		35.00	26.00	14.00
Common Player:		1.00	.70	.40
1	Ryne Sandberg	2.50	2.00	1.00
2	Dale Murphy	2.50	2.00	1.00
3	Jack Morris	1.00	.70	.40
4	Keith Hernandez	1.50	1.25	.60
5	George Brett	2.50	2.00	1.00
6	Don Mattingly	5.00	3.75	2.00
7	Ozzie Smith	1.00	.70	.40
8	Cal Ripken	2.25	1.75	.90
9	Dwight Gooden	3.00	2.25	1.25
10	Pedro Guerrero	1.00	.70	.40
11	Lou Whitaker	1.00	.70	.40
12	Roger Clemens	3.00	2.25	1.25
13	Lance Parrish	1.00	.70	.40
14	Rickey Henderson	2.25	1.75	.90
15	Fernando Valenzuela	1.25	.90	.50
16	Mike Schmidt	2.50	2.00	1.00
17	Darryl Strawberry	2.75	2.00	1.00
18	Mike Scott	1.00	.70	.40
19	Jim Rice	2.75	2.00	1.00
20	Wade Boggs	2.50	2.00	1.00

1988 Jiffy Pop

This 20-disc set is the third Jiffy Pop issue spotlighting leading players. Discs are 2-/12" in diameter, with a semi-gloss finish, and feature full-color closeups on white stock. Team logos have been airbrushed off the player's caps. The Jiffy Pop logo appears in red at the top of the disc; a banner running across the bottom encloses a "1988" and player name, also in red. The circular border is blue, with two large baseballs streaking toward the top logo. A third baseball appears lower right under the curved label "3rd Annual Collector's Edition." Dsic backs are white, with dark blue lettering, and contain player information and disc number.

		MT	NR MT	EX
Complete Set:		20.00	15.00	8.00
Common Player:		.75	.60	.30
1	Buddy Bell	.75	.60	.30
2	Wade Boggs	2.25	1.75	.90
3	Gary Carter	1.50	1.25	.60
4	Jack Clark	.80	.60	.30
5	Will Clark	1.50	1.25	.60
6	Roger Clemens	2.25	1.75	.90
7	Vince Coleman	.80	.60	.30
8	Andre Dawson	1.25	.90	.50
9	Keith Hernandez	1.25	.90	.50
10	Kent Hrbek	1.25	.90	.50
11	Wally Joyner	1.50	1.25	.60
12	Paul Molitor	.80	.60	.30
13	Eddie Murray	1.50	1.25	.60
14	Tim Raines	1.50	1.25	.60
15	Bret Saberhagen	1.25	.90	.50
16	Alan Trammell	1.25	.90	.50
17	Ozzie Virgil	.75	.60	.30
18	Tim Wallach	.75	.60	.30
19	Dave Winfield	1.50	1.25	.60
20	Robin Yount	1.25	.90	.50

1953 Johnston Cookies Braves

 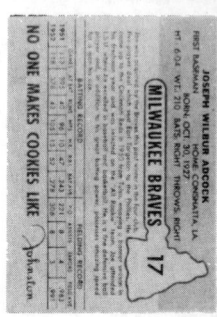

The first and most common of three annual issues, the '53 Johnston's were inserted into boxes of cookies on a regional basis. Complete sets were also available from the company, whose factory sits in the shadow of Milwaukee County Stadium. While at first glance appearing to be color photos, the pictures on the 25 cards in the set are actually well-done colorizations of black and white photos. Cards measure 2-9/16" by 3-5/8". Write-ups on the backs were "borrowed" from the Braves' 1953 yearbook.

		NR MT	EX	VG
Complete Set:		325.00	175.00	100.00
Common Player:		8.00	4.00	2.50
1	Charlie Grimm	10.00	5.00	3.00
2	John Antonelli	10.00	5.00	3.00
3	Vern Bickford	8.00	4.00	2.50
4	Bob Buhl	10.00	5.00	3.00
5	Lew Burdette	15.00	7.50	4.50
6	Dave Cole	8.00	4.00	2.50
7	Ernie Johnson	8.00	4.00	2.50
8	Dave Jolly	8.00	4.00	2.50
9	Don Liddle	8.00	4.00	2.50
10	Warren Spahn	45.00	23.00	13.50
11	Max Surkont	8.00	4.00	2.50
12	Jim Wilson	8.00	4.00	2.50
13	Sibby Sisti	8.00	4.00	2.50
14	Walker Cooper	8.00	4.00	2.50
15	Del Crandall	12.00	6.00	3.50
16	Ebba St. Claire	8.00	4.00	2.50
17	Joe Adcock	12.00	6.00	3.50
18	George Crowe	8.00	4.00	2.50
19	Jack Dittmer	8.00	4.00	2.50
20	Johnny Logan	10.00	5.00	3.00
21	Ed Mathews	45.00	23.00	13.50
22	Bill Bruton	10.00	5.00	3.00
23	Sid Gordon	8.00	4.00	2.50
24	Andy Pafko	10.00	5.00	3.00
25	Jim Pendleton	8.00	4.00	2.50

1954 Johnston Cookies Braves

 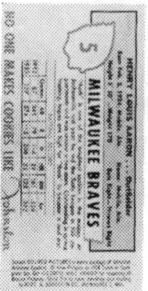

In its second of three annual issues, Johnston's increased the number of cards in its 1954 Braves issue to 35, and switched to an unusual size, a narrow format, 2" by 3-7/8". Besides the players and managers, the '54 set also includes unnumbered cards of the team trainer and equipment manager. Other cards are numbered by uniform number. After his early-season injury (which gave Hank Aaron a chance to play regularly), Bobby Thomson's card was withdrawn, accounting for its scarcity and high value. A cardboard wall-hanging display into which cards could be inserted was available as a premium offer.

		NR MT	EX	VG
	Complete Set:	1000.00	500.00	300.00
	Common Player:	10.00	5.00	3.00
1	Del Crandall	15.00	7.50	4.50
3	Jim Pendleton	10.00	5.00	3.00
4	Danny O'Connell	10.00	5.00	3.00
5	Henry Aaron	400.00	200.00	125.00
6	Jack Dittmer	10.00	5.00	3.00
9	Joe Adcock	15.00	7.50	4.50
10	Robert Buhl	15.00	7.50	4.50
11	Phillip Paine (Phillips)	10.00	5.00	3.00
12	Ben Johnson	10.00	5.00	3.00
13	Sibby Sisti	10.00	5.00	3.00
15	Charles Gorin	10.00	5.00	3.00
16	Chet Nichols	10.00	5.00	3.00
17	Dave Jolly	10.00	5.00	3.00
19	Jim Wilson	10.00	5.00	3.00
20	Ray Crone	10.00	5.00	3.00
21	Warren Spahn	55.00	28.00	16.50
22	Gene Conley	9.00	4.50	2.75
23	Johnny Logan	12.00	6.00	3.50
24	Charlie White	10.00	5.00	3.00
27	George Metkovich	10.00	5.00	3.00
28	John Cooney	10.00	5.00	3.00
29	Paul Burris	10.00	5.00	3.00
31	Wm. Walters	10.00	5.00	3.00
32	Ernest T. Johnson	10.00	5.00	3.00
33	Lew Burdette	18.00	9.00	5.50
34	Bob Thomson	175.00	87.00	52.00
35	Robert Keely	10.00	5.00	3.00
38	Billy Bruton	10.00	5.00	3.00
40	Charles Grimm	10.00	5.00	3.00
41	Ed Mathews	55.00	28.00	16.50
42	Sam Calderone	10.00	5.00	3.00
47	Joey Jay	10.00	5.00	3.00
48	Andy Pafko	12.00	6.00	3.50
----	Dr. Charles Lacks (trainer)	10.00	5.00	3.00
----	Joseph F. Taylor (asst. trainer)	10.00	5.00	3.00

1955 Johnston Cookies Braves

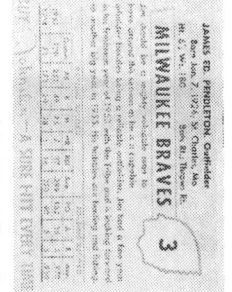

A third change in size and format was undertaken in the third and final year of Braves sets produced by Johnston's. The 35 cards in the 1955 set were issued in six fold-out panels of six cards each (Andy Pafko was double-printed). As in 1954, cards are numbered by uniform number, except those of the team equipment manager, trainer and road secretary (former Boston star Duffy Lewis). Single cards measure 2-7/8" by 4". Besides including panels in boxes of cookies, the '55 Johnston's could be ordered for 5¢ per panel by mail. The scarcest of the Johnston's issues, the 1955 set can be found today still in complete panels, or as single cards.

		NR MT	EX	VG
	Complete Folder Set:	1200.00	600.00	350.00
	Complete Singles Set:	750.00	375.00	225.00
	Common Player:	15.00	7.50	4.50
	Common Folder:	110.00	55.00	33.00
1	Del Crandall	20.00	10.00	6.00
3	Jim Pendleton	15.00	7.50	4.50
4	Danny O'Connell	15.00	7.50	4.50
6	Jack Dittmer	15.00	7.50	4.50
9	Joe Adcock	20.00	10.00	6.00
10	Bob Buhl	18.00	9.00	5.50
11	Phil Paine	15.00	7.50	4.50
12	Ray Crone	15.00	7.50	4.50
15	Charlie Gorin	15.00	7.50	4.50
16	Dave Jolly	15.00	7.50	4.50
17	Chet Nichols	15.00	7.50	4.50
18	Chuck Tanner	20.00	10.00	6.00
19	Jim Wilson	15.00	7.50	4.50
20	Dave Koslo	15.00	7.50	4.50
21	Warren Spahn	65.00	33.00	20.00
22	Gene Conley	18.00	9.00	5.50
23	John Logan	18.00	9.00	5.50
24	Charlie White	15.00	7.50	4.50
28	Johnny Cooney	15.00	7.50	4.50
30	Roy Smalley	15.00	7.50	4.50
31	Bucky Walters	15.00	7.50	4.50
32	Ernie Johnson	15.00	7.50	4.50
33	Lew Burdette	25.00	12.50	7.50
34	Bobby Thomson	20.00	10.00	6.00
35	Bob Keely	15.00	7.50	4.50
38	Billy Bruton	18.00	9.00	5.50
39	George Crowe	15.00	7.50	4.50
40	Charlie Grimm	18.00	9.00	5.50
41	Eddie Mathews	65.00	33.00	20.00
44	Hank Aaron	350.00	175.00	105.00
47	Joe Jay	15.00	7.50	4.50
48	Andy Pafko	18.00	9.00	5.50
----	Dr. Charles K. Lacks	15.00	7.50	4.50
----	Duffy Lewis	15.00	7.50	4.50
----	Joe Taylor	15.00	7.50	4.50
----	Series 1 Folder (Hank Aaron, Lew Burdette, Del Crandall, Charlie Gorin, Bob Keely, Danny O'Connell)	375.00	187.00	112.00
----	Series 2 Folder (Joe Adcock, Joe Jay, Dr. Charles K. Lacks, Chet Nichols, Andy Pafko, Charlie White)	125.00	62.00	37.00
----	Series 3 Folder (Gene Conley, George Crowe, Jim Pendleton, Roy Smalley, Warren Spahn, Joe Taylor)	175.00	87.00	52.00
----	Series 4 Folder (Billy Bruton, John Cooney, Dave Jolly, Dave Koslo, Johnny Logan, Andy Pafko)	125.00	62.00	37.00
----	Series 5 Folder (Ray Crone, Ernie Johnson, Duffy Lewis, Eddie Mathews, Phil Paine, Chuck Tanner)	200.00	100.00	60.00
----	Series 6 Folder (Bob Buhl, Jack Dittmer, Charlie Grimm, Bobby Thomson, Bucky Walters, Jim Wilson)	125.00	62.00	37.00

1982 K-Mart

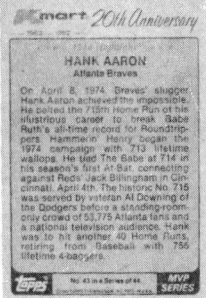

The first of what became dozens of boxed sets

specially produced for retail chain stores by the major card producers, the 1982 K-Mart set has not enjoyed any collector popularity. The theme of the set is Most Valuable Players and selected record-breaking performances of the 1962-1981 seasons. The design used miniature reproductions of Topps cards of the era, except in a few cases where designs had to be created because original cards were never issued (1962 Maury Wills, 1975 Fred Lynn.) Originally sold for about $2 per boxed set of 44, large quantities were bought up by speculators who got burned when over-production and lack of demand caused the set to drop as low as 10¢. The 2-1/2" by 3-1/2" cards were printed by Topps.

		MT	NR MT	EX
Complete Set:		1.00	.70	.40
Common Player:		.03	.02	.01
1	Mickey Mantle	.40	.30	.15
2	Maury Wills	.05	.04	.02
3	Elston Howard	.03	.02	.01
4	Sandy Koufax	.10	.08	.04
5	Brooks Robinson	.05	.04	.02
6	Ken Boyer	.03	.02	.01
7	Zoilo Versalles	.03	.02	.01
8	Willie Mays	.10	.08	.04
9	Frank Robinson	.05	.04	.02
10	Bob Clemente	.10	.08	.04
11	Carl Yastrzemski	.10	.08	.04
12	Orlando Cepeda	.03	.02	.01
13	Denny McLain	.03	.02	.01
14	Bob Gibson	.05	.04	.02
15	Harmon Killebrew	.05	.04	.02
16	Willie McCovey	.05	.04	.02
17	Boog Powell	.03	.02	.01
18	Johnny Bench	.07	.05	.03
19	Vida Blue	.03	.02	.01
20	Joe Torre	.03	.02	.01
21	Rich Allen	.03	.02	.01
22	Johnny Bench	.07	.05	.03
23	Reggie Jackson	.07	.05	.03
24	Pete Rose	.12	.09	.05
25	Jeff Burroughs	.03	.02	.01
26	Steve Garvey	.07	.05	.03
27	Fred Lynn	.03	.02	.01
28	Joe Morgan	.05	.04	.02
29	Thurman Munson	.05	.04	.02
30	Joe Morgan	.05	.04	.02
31	Rod Carew	.07	.05	.03
32	George Foster	.03	.02	.01
33	Jim Rice	.05	.04	.02
34	Dave Parker	.05	.04	.02
35	Don Baylor	.03	.02	.01
36	Keith Hernandez	.03	.02	.01
37	Willie Stargell	.05	.04	.02
38	George Brett	.07	.05	.03
39	Mike Schmidt	.07	.05	.03
40	Rollie Fingers	.05	.04	.02
41	Mike Schmidt	.07	.05	.03
42	Don Drysdale	.05	.04	.02
43	Hank Aaron	.10	.08	.04
44	Pete Rose	.12	.09	.05

1987 K-Mart

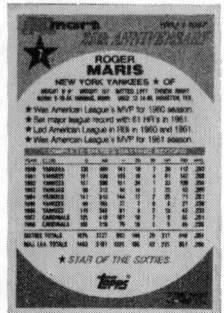

Produced by Topps for K-Mart, the 1987 K-Mart set was distributed by the department stores to celebrate their 25th anniversary. Entitled "Baseball's Stars of the Decades," the 33-card set was issued in a special cardboard box with one stick of bubblegum. The card fronts feature a full-color photo set diagonally against a red background. The backs contain career highlights plus pitching or batting statistics for the decade in which the player enjoyed his greatest success. Cards are the standard 2-1/2" by 3-1/2" size.

		MT	NR MT	EX
Complete Set:		5.00	3.75	2.00
Common Player:		.10	.08	.04
1	Hank Aaron	.50	.40	.20
2	Roberto Clemente	.40	.30	.15
3	Bob Gibson	.10	.08	.04
4	Harmon Killebrew	.10	.08	.04
5	Mickey Mantle	1.00	.70	.40
6	Juan Marichal	.10	.08	.04
7	Roger Maris	.30	.25	.12
8	Willie Mays	.50	.40	.20
9	Brooks Robinson	.30	.25	.12
10	Frank Robinson	.20	.15	.08
11	Carl Yastrzemski	.50	.40	.20
12	Johnny Bench	.30	.25	.12
13	Lou Brock	.20	.15	.08
14	Rod Carew	.30	.25	.12
15	Steve Carlton	.20	.15	.08
16	Reggie Jackson	.30	.25	.12
17	Jim Palmer	.10	.08	.04
18	Jim Rice	.10	.08	.04
19	Pete Rose	.60	.45	.25
20	Nolan Ryan	.20	.15	.08
21	Tom Seaver	.20	.15	.08
22	Willie Stargell	.10	.08	.04
23	Wade Boggs	.60	.45	.25
24	George Brett	.40	.30	.15
25	Gary Carter	.20	.15	.08
26	Dwight Gooden	.50	.40	.20
27	Rickey Henderson	.35	.25	.12
28	Don Mattingly	.70	.50	.30
29	Dale Murphy	.40	.30	.15
30	Eddie Murray	.20	.15	.08
31	Mike Schmidt	.30	.25	.12
32	Darryl Strawberry	.40	.30	.15
33	Fernando Valenzuela	.10	.08	.04

1988 K-Mart

This 33-card boxed set, titled "Memorable Moments," was produced by Topps for distribution via K-Mart. Two previous Topps K-Mart sets were issued: a 44-card set in 1982 in honor of K-Mart's 20th anniversary and a 33-card set in 1987 for the company's 25th anniversary. The 1988 cards are standard-size with red, white and blue borders and a super glossy coating. Numbered card backs are printed in red and blue on white and highlight special events in the featured players' careers. The set was marketed in a bright yellow and green checklist box (gum included).

	MT	NR MT	EX
Complete Set:	4.00	3.00	1.50
Common Player:	.10	.08	.04

		MT	NR MT	EX
1	George Bell	.20	.15	.08
2	Wade Boggs	.50	.40	.20
3	George Brett	.30	.25	.12
4	Jose Canseco	.50	.40	.20
5	Jack Clark	.15	.11	.06
6	Will Clark	.25	.20	.10
7	Roger Clemens	.40	.30	.15
8	Vince Coleman	.15	.11	.06
9	Andre Dawson	.15	.11	.06
10	Dwight Gooden	.40	.30	.15
11	Pedro Guerrero	.15	.11	.06
12	Tony Gwynn	.25	.20	.10
13	Rickey Henderson	.25	.20	.10
14	Keith Hernandez	.15	.11	.06
15	Don Mattingly	.80	.60	.30
16	Mark McGwire	.80	.60	.30
17	Paul Molitor	.12	.09	.05
18	Dale Murphy	.20	.15	.08
19	Tim Raines	.20	.15	.08
20	Dave Righetti	.12	.09	.05
21	Cal Ripken	.25	.20	.10
22	Pete Rose	.50	.40	.20
23	Nolan Ryan	.25	.20	.10
24	Benny Santiago	.25	.20	.10
25	Mike Schmidt	.30	.25	.12
26	Mike Scott	.10	.08	.04
27	Kevin Seitzer	.25	.20	.10
28	Ozzie Smith	.15	.11	.06
29	Darryl Strawberry	.30	.25	.12
30	Rick Sutcliffe	.10	.08	.04
31	Fernando Valenzuela	.15	.11	.06
32	Todd Worrell	.10	.08	.04
33	Robin Yount	.15	.11	.06

1989 K-Mart

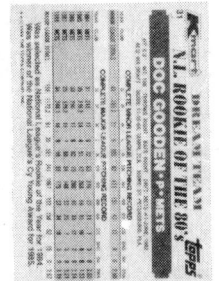

This 33-card, glossy set was produced by Topps for K-Mart, where it was sold in stores nationwide. The standard-size cards feature mostly action shots on the front, and include the Topps "Dream Team" logo at the top, with the K-Mart logo in the lower right corner. The first 11 cards in the set picture the top rookies of 1988, while next 11 picture the top A.L. rookies of the '80s, and the final 11 cards highlight the top N.L. rookies of the decade.

		MT	NR MT	EX
Complete Set:		5.00	3.75	2.00
Common Player:		.10	.08	.04
1	Mark Grace	.70	.50	.30
2	Ron Gant	.15	.11	.06
3	Chris Sabo	.15	.11	.06
4	Walt Weiss	.15	.11	.06
5	Jay Buhner	.15	.11	.06
6	Cecil Espy	.10	.08	.04
7	Dave Gallagher	.15	.11	.06
8	Damon Berryhill	.10	.08	.04
9	Tim Belcher	.20	.15	.08
10	Paul Gibson	.10	.08	.04
11	Gregg Jefferies	.90	.70	.40
12	Don Mattingly	1.50	1.25	.60
13	Harold Reynolds	.15	.11	.06
14	Wade Boggs	.80	.60	.30
15	Cal Ripken	.25	.20	.10
16	Kirby Puckett	.40	.30	.15

		MT	NR MT	EX
17	George Bell	.15	.11	.06
18	Jose Canseco	.50	.40	.20
19	Terry Steinbach	.20	.15	.08
20	Roger Clemens	.40	.30	.15
21	Mark Langston	.20	.15	.08
22	Harold Baines	.15	.11	.06
23	Will Clark	.50	.40	.20
24	Ryne Sanberg	.25	.20	.10
25	Tim Wallach	.10	.08	.04
26	Shawon Dunston	.10	.08	.04
27	Rock Raines	.15	.11	.06
28	Darryl Strawberry	.35	.25	.14
29	Tony Gwynn	.35	.25	.14
30	Tony Pena	.10	.08	.04
31	Doc Gooden	.35	.25	.12
32	Fernando Valenzuela	.15	.11	.06
33	Pedro Guerrero	.15	.11	.06

1990 K-Mart

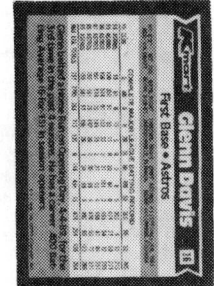

This 33-card, glossy set was produced by Topps for K-Mart, where it was available nationwide. The set is subtitled "Superstars" and features sixteen A.L. players, sixteen N.L. stars and a managers' card featuring both Tony LaRussa and Roger Craig. A special Superstars logo is featured on the card fronts. 1990 marks the fourth consecutive year that Topps has produced a set in cooperation with K-Mart.

		MT	NR MT	EX
Complete Set:		4.00	3.00	1.50
Common Player:		.08	.06	.03
1	Will Clark	.25	.20	.10
2	Ryne Sandberg	.25	.20	.10
3	Howard Johnson	.15	.11	.06
4	Ozzie Smith	.15	.11	.06
5	Tony Gwynn	.15	.11	.06
6	Kevin Mitchell	.20	.15	.08
7	Jerome Walton	.15	.11	.06
8	Craig Biggio	.08	.06	.03
9	Mike Scott	.08	.06	.03
10	Doc Gooden	.20	.15	.08
11	Sid Fernandez	.08	.06	.03
12	Joe Magrane	.08	.06	.03
13	Jay Howell	.08	.06	.03
14	Mark Davis	.08	.06	.03
15	Pedro Guerrero	.10	.08	.04
16	Glenn Davis	.15	.11	.06
17	Don Mattingly	.25	.20	.10
18	Julio Franco	.10	.08	.04
19	Wade Boggs	.20	.15	.08
20	Cal Ripken	.15	.11	.06
21	Jose Canseco	.40	.30	.15
22	Kirby Puckett	.20	.15	.08
23	Rickey Henderson	.25	.20	.10
24	Mickey Tettleton	.08	.06	.03
25	Nolan Ryan	.25	.20	.10
26	Bret Saberhagen	.10	.08	.04
27	Jeff Ballard	.08	.06	.03
28	Chuck Finley	.08	.06	.03
29	Dennis Eckersley	.15	.11	.06
30	Dan Plesac	.08	.06	.03
31	Fred McGriff	.15	.11	.06
32	Mark McGwire	.20	.15	.08
33	Managers (Tony LaRussa, Roger Craig)			
		.08	.06	.03

1955 Kahn's Wieners Reds

Compliments of Kahn's Wieners
"THE WIENER THE WORLD AWAITED"

The first of what would become 15 successive years of baseball card issues by the Kahn's meat company of Cincinnati is also the rarest. The set consists of six Cincinnati Redlegs player cards, 3-1/4" by 4". Printed in black and white, with blank backs, the '55 Kahn's cards were distributed at a one-day promotional event at a Cincinnati amusement park, where the featured players were on hand to sign autographs. Like the other Kahn's issues through 1963, the '55 cards have a 1/2" white panel containing an advertising message below the player photo. These cards are sometimes found with this portion cut off, greatly reducing the value of the card.

	NR MT	EX	VG
Complete Set:	2750.00	1375.00	800.00
Common Player:	400.00	200.00	120.00
(1) Gus Bell	750.00	375.00	230.00
(2) Ted Kluszewski	650.00	325.00	200.00
(3) Roy McMillan	400.00	200.00	120.00
(4) Joe Nuxhall	400.00	200.00	120.00
(5) Wally Post	400.00	200.00	120.00
(6) Johnny Temple	400.00	200.00	120.00

1956 Kahn's Wieners Reds

Compliments of Kahn's Wieners
"THE WIENER THE WORLD AWAITED"

In 1956, Kahn's expanded its baseball card program to include 15 Redlegs players, and began issuing the cards one per pack in packages of hot dogs. Because the cards were packaged in direct contact with the meat, they are often found today in stained condition. In 3-1/4" by 4" format, black and white with blank backs, the '56 Kahn's cards can be distinguished from later issues by the presence of full stadium photographic backgrounds behind the player photos. Like all Kahn's issues, the 1956 set is unnumbered; the checklists are arranged alphabe-

tically for convenience. The set features the first-ever baseball card of Hall of Famer Frank Robinson.

	NR MT	EX	VG
Complete Set:	1500.00	750.00	450.00
Common Player:	75.00	37.00	22.00
(1) Ed Bailey	75.00	37.00	22.00
(2) Gus Bell	100.00	50.00	30.00
(3) Joe Black	100.00	50.00	30.00
(4) "Smokey" Burgess	100.00	50.00	30.00
(5) Art Fowler	75.00	37.00	22.00
(6) Hershell Freeman	75.00	37.00	22.00
(7) Ray Jablonski	75.00	37.00	22.00
(8) John Klippstein	75.00	37.00	22.00
(9) Ted Kluszewski	125.00	62.00	37.00
(10) Brooks Lawrence	75.00	37.00	22.00
(11) Roy McMillan	75.00	37.00	22.00
(12) Joe Nuxhall	100.00	50.00	30.00
(13) Wally Post	75.00	37.00	22.00
(14) Frank Robinson	300.00	150.00	90.00
(15) Johnny Temple	100.00	50.00	30.00

1957 Kahn's Wieners

Compliments of Kahn's Wieners
"THE WIENER THE WORLD AWAITED"

In its third season of baseball card issue, Kahn's kept the basic 3-1/4" by 4" format, with black and white photos and blank backs. The issue was expanded to 28 players, all Pirates or Reds. The last of the blank-backed Kahn's sets, the 1957 Reds players can be distinguished from the 1956 issue by the general lack of background photo detail, in favor of a neutral light gray background. The Dick Groat card appears with two name variations, a facsimile autograph, "Richard Groat," and a printed "Dick Groat." Both Groat varieties are included in the complete set price.

	NR MT	EX	VG
Complete Set	2250.00	1125.00	700.00
Common Player	50.00	25.00	15.00
(1) Tom Acker	50.00	25.00	15.00
(2) Ed Bailey	50.00	25.00	15.00
(3) Gus Bell	70.00	35.00	21.00
(4) Smokey Burgess	70.00	35.00	21.00
(5) Roberto Clemente	450.00	225.00	135.00
(6) George Crowe	50.00	25.00	15.00
(7) Elroy Face	70.00	35.00	21.00
(8) Hershell Freeman	50.00	25.00	15.00
(9) Robert Friend	50.00	25.00	15.00
(10) Don Gross	50.00	25.00	15.00
(11a) Dick Groat	70.00	35.00	21.00
(11b) Richard Groat	175.00	87.00	52.00
(12) Warren Hacker	50.00	25.00	15.00
(13) Don Hoak	70.00	35.00	21.00
(14) Hal Jeffcoat	50.00	25.00	15.00
(15) Ron Kline	50.00	25.00	15.00
(16) John Klippstein	50.00	25.00	15.00
(17) Ted Kluszewski	100.00	50.00	30.00
(18) Brooks Lawrence	50.00	25.00	15.00
(19) Dale Long	50.00	25.00	15.00
(20) Wm. Mazeroski	100.00	50.00	30.00
(21) Roy McMillan	50.00	25.00	15.00
(22) Joe Nuxhall	50.00	25.00	15.00
(23) Wally Post	50.00	25.00	15.00
(24) Frank Robinson	200.00	100.00	60.00
(25) Johnny Temple	50.00	25.00	15.00
(26) Frank Thomas	50.00	25.00	15.00
(27) Bob Thurman	50.00	25.00	15.00
(28) Lee Walls	50.00	25.00	15.00

1958 Kahn's Wieners

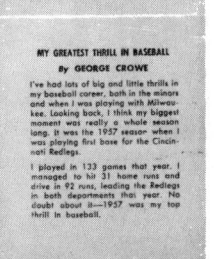

MY GREATEST THRILL IN BASEBALL
By GEORGE CROWE

I've had lots of big and little thrills in my baseball career, both in the minors and when I was playing with the Milwaukee. Looking back, I think my biggest moment was really a whole season long. It was the 1957 season when I was playing first base for the Cincinnati Redlegs.

I played in 133 games that year. I managed to hit 31 home runs and drive in 92 runs, leading the Redlegs in both departments that year. No doubt about it—1957 was my top thrill in baseball.

Compliments of Kahn's Wieners
"THE WIENER THE WORLD AWAITED"

Long-time Cincinnati favorite Wally Post became the only Philadelphia Phillies ballplayer to appear in the 15-year run of Kahn's issues when he was traded in 1958, but included as part of the otherwise exclusively Pirates-Reds set. Like previous years, the '58 Kahn's were 3-1/4" by 4", with black and white player photos. Unlike previous years, however, the cards had printing on the back, a story by the pictured player, titled "My Greatest Thrill in Baseball." Quite similar to the 1959 issue, the '58 Kahn's can be distinguished by the fact that the top line of the advertising panel at bottom has the word "Wieners" in 1958, but not in 1959.

		NR MT	EX	VG
Complete Set:		2500.00	1250.00	750.00
Common Player:		50.00	25.00	15.00
(1)	Ed Bailey	50.00	25.00	15.00
(2)	Gene Baker	50.00	25.00	15.00
(3)	Gus Bell	60.00	30.00	18.00
(4)	Smokey Burgess	60.00	30.00	18.00
(5)	Roberto Clemente	400.00	200.00	120.00
(6)	George Crowe	50.00	25.00	15.00
(7)	Elroy Face	60.00	30.00	18.00
(8)	Henry Foiles	50.00	25.00	15.00
(9)	Dee Fondy	50.00	25.00	15.00
(10)	Robert Friend	60.00	30.00	18.00
(11)	Richard Groat	60.00	30.00	18.00
(12)	Harvey Haddix	60.00	30.00	18.00
(13)	Don Hoak	60.00	30.00	18.00
(14)	Hal Jeffcoat	60.00	30.00	18.00
(15)	Ronald L. Kline	60.00	30.00	18.00
(16)	Ted Kluszewski	100.00	50.00	30.00
(17)	Vernon Law	60.00	30.00	18.00
(18)	Brooks Lawrence	50.00	25.00	15.00
(19)	William Mazeroski	100.00	50.00	30.00
(20)	Roy McMillan	50.00	25.00	15.00
(21)	Joe Nuxhall	60.00	30.00	18.00
(22)	Wally Post	275.00	137.00	80.00
(23)	John Powers	50.00	25.00	15.00
(24)	Robert T. Purkey	50.00	25.00	15.00
(25)	Charles Rabe	275.00	137.00	80.00
(26)	Frank Robinson	275.00	137.00	80.00
(27)	Robert Skinner	50.00	25.00	15.00
(28)	Johnny Temple	50.00	25.00	15.00
(29)	Frank Thomas	275.00	137.00	80.00

1959 Kahn's Wieners

A third team was added to the Kahn's lineup in 1959, the Cleveland Indians joining the Pirates and Reds, bringing the number of cards in the set to 38. Again printed in black and white in the 3-1/4" by 4" size, the 1959 Kahn's cards can be differentiated from the previous issue by the lack of the word "Wieners" on the top line of the advertising panel at bottom. Backs again featured a story written by the pictured player, titled "The Toughest Play I Had to Make," "My Most Difficult Moment in Baseball," or "The Toughest Batters I Have to Face."

THE MOST DIFFICULT PLAY I HAVE TO MAKE
by GARY BELL

"THE WIENER THE WORLD AWAITED"

		NR MT	EX	VG
Complete Set:		3750.00	1875.00	1150.
Common Player:		40.00	20.00	12.00
(1)	Ed Bailey	40.00	20.00	12.00
(2)	Gary Bell	40.00	20.00	12.00
(3)	Gus Bell	50.00	25.00	15.00
(4)	Richard Brodowski	450.00	225.00	135.00
(5)	Forrest Burgess	50.00	25.00	15.00
(6)	Roberto Clemente	400.00	200.00	120.00
(7)	Rocky Colavito	75.00	37.00	22.00
(8)	ElRoy Face	50.00	25.00	15.00
(9)	Robert Friend	50.00	25.00	15.00
(10)	Joe Gordon	50.00	25.00	15.00
(11)	Jim Grant	40.00	20.00	12.00
(12)	Richard M. Groat	60.00	30.00	18.00
(13)	Harvey Haddix	350.00	175.00	105.00
(14)	Woodie Held	350.00	175.00	105.00
(15)	Don Hoak	45.00	22.00	13.50
(16)	Ronald Kline	40.00	20.00	12.00
(17)	Ted Kluszewski	75.00	37.00	22.00
(18)	Vernon Law	50.00	25.00	15.00
(19)	Jerry Lynch	40.00	20.00	12.00
(20)	Billy Martin	75.00	37.00	22.00
(21)	William Mazeroski	50.00	25.00	15.00
(22)	Cal McLish	350.00	175.00	105.00
(23)	Roy McMillan	40.00	20.00	12.00
(24)	Minnie Minoso	60.00	30.00	18.00
(25)	Russell Nixon	40.00	20.00	12.00
(26)	Joe Nuxhall	50.00	25.00	15.00
(27)	Jim Perry	50.00	25.00	15.00
(28)	Vada Pinson	60.00	30.00	18.00
(29)	Vic Power	40.00	20.00	12.00
(30)	Robert Purkey	40.00	20.00	12.00
(31)	Frank Robinson	175.00	87.00	52.00
(32)	Herb Score	50.00	25.00	15.00
(33)	Robert Skinner	40.00	20.00	12.00
(34)	George Strickland	40.00	20.00	12.00
(35)	Richard L. Stuart	45.00	22.00	13.50
(36)	John Temple	40.00	20.00	12.00
(37)	Frank Thomas	45.00	22.00	13.50
(38)	George A. Witt	40.00	20.00	12.00

1960 Kahn's Wieners

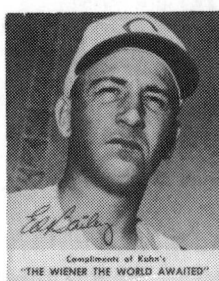

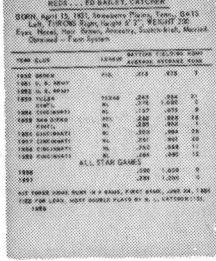

Compliments of Kahn's
"THE WIENER THE WORLD AWAITED"

Three more teams joined the Kahn's roster in 1960, the Chicago Cubs, Chicago White Sox and St. Louis Cardinals. A total of 42 different players are represented in the set. Again 3-1/4" by 4" with black and white photos, the 1960 Kahn's cards featured for the first time player stats and personal data on the back, except Harvey Kuenn, which was issued with blank back, probably because of the lateness of his trade to the Indians.

		NR MT	EX	VG
	Complete Set:	1900.00	950.00	570.00
	Common Player:	30.00	15.00	9.00
(1)	Ed Bailey	30.00	15.00	9.00
(2)	Gary Bell	30.00	15.00	9.00
(3)	Gus Bell	35.00	17.50	10.50
(4)	Forrest Burgess	35.00	17.50	10.50
(5)	Gino N. Cimoli	30.00	15.00	9.00
(6)	Roberto Clemente	250.00	125.00	75.00
(7)	ElRoy Face	35.00	17.50	10.50
(8)	Tito Francona	35.00	17.50	10.50
(9)	Robert Friend	35.00	17.50	10.50
(10)	Jim Grant	30.00	15.00	9.00
(11)	Richard Groat	40.00	20.00	12.00
(12)	Harvey Haddix	35.00	17.50	10.50
(13)	Woodie Held	30.00	15.00	9.00
(14)	Bill Henry	30.00	15.00	9.00
(15)	Don Hoak	35.00	17.50	10.50
(16)	Jay Hook	30.00	15.00	9.00
(17)	Eddie Kasko	30.00	15.00	9.00
(18)	Ronnie Kline	40.00	20.00	12.00
(19)	Ted Kluszewski	50.00	25.00	15.00
(20)	Harvey Kuenn	250.00	125.00	75.00
(21)	Vernon S. Law	35.00	17.50	10.50
(22)	Brooks Lawrence	30.00	15.00	9.00
(23)	Jerry Lynch	30.00	15.00	9.00
(24)	Billy Martin	60.00	30.00	18.00
(25)	William Mazeroski	40.00	20.00	12.00
(26)	Cal McLish	30.00	15.00	9.00
(27)	Roy McMillan	30.00	15.00	9.00
(28)	Don Newcombe	35.00	17.50	10.50
(29)	Russ Nixon	30.00	15.00	9.00
(30)	Joe Nuxhall	35.00	17.50	10.50
(31)	James J. O'Toole	30.00	15.00	9.00
(32)	Jim Perry	35.00	17.50	10.50
(33)	Vada Pinson	40.00	20.00	12.00
(34)	Vic Power	30.00	15.00	9.00
(35)	Robert T. Purkey	30.00	15.00	9.00
(36)	Frank Robinson	125.00	62.00	37.00
(37)	Herb Score	35.00	17.50	10.50
(38)	Robert R. Skinner	30.00	15.00	9.00
(39)	Richard L. Stuart	35.00	17.50	10.50
(40)	John Temple	30.00	15.00	9.00
(41)	Frank Thomas	40.00	20.00	12.00
(42)	Lee Walls	35.00	17.50	10.50

1961 Kahn's Wieners

Compliments of Kahn's
"THE WIENER THE WORLD AWAITED"

After a single season, the Chicago and St. Louis teams dropped out of the Kahn's program, but the 1961 set was larger than ever, at 43 cards. The same basic format - 3-1/4" by 4" size, black and white photos and statistical information on the back - was retained. For the first time in '61, the meat company made complete sets of the Kahn's cards available to collectors via a mail-in offer. This makes the 1961 and later Kahn's cards considerably easier to obtain than the earlier issues.

A player's name in *italic* type indicates a rookie card. An (FC) indicates a player's first card for that particular card company.

		NR MT	EX	VG
	Complete Set:	1200.00	600.00	360.00
	Common Player:	18.00	9.00	5.50
(1)	John A. Antonelli	20.00	10.00	6.00
(2)	Ed Bailey	18.00	9.00	5.50
(3)	Gary Bell	18.00	9.00	5.50
(4)	Gus Bell	20.00	10.00	6.00
(5)	James P. Brosnan	18.00	9.00	5.50
(6)	Forrest Burgess	20.00	10.00	6.00
(7)	Gino Cimoli	18.00	9.00	5.50
(8)	Roberto Clemente	175.00	87.00	52.00
(9)	Gordon Coleman	18.00	9.00	5.50
(10)	Jimmie Dykes	20.00	10.00	6.00
(11)	ElRoy Face	25.00	12.50	7.50
(12)	Tito Francona	20.00	10.00	6.00
(13)	Robert Friend	20.00	10.00	6.00
(14)	Gene L. Freese	18.00	9.00	5.50
(15)	Jim Grant	18.00	9.00	5.50
(16)	Richard M. Groat	30.00	15.00	9.00
(17)	Harvey Haddix	20.00	10.00	6.00
(18)	Woodie Held	18.00	9.00	5.50
(19)	Don Hoak	20.00	10.00	6.00
(20)	Jay Hook	18.00	9.00	5.50
(21)	Joe Jay	18.00	9.00	5.50
(22)	Eddie Kasko	18.00	9.00	5.50
(23)	Willie Kirkland	18.00	9.00	5.50
(24)	Vernon S. Law	25.00	12.50	7.50
(25)	Jerry Lynch	18.00	9.00	5.50
(26)	Jim Maloney	25.00	12.50	7.50
(27)	William Mazeroski	30.00	15.00	9.00
(28)	Wilmer D. Mizell	20.00	10.00	6.00
(29)	Glenn R. Nelson	18.00	9.00	5.50
(30)	James J. O'Toole	18.00	9.00	5.50
(31)	Jim Perry	20.00	10.00	6.00
(32)	John M. Phillips	18.00	9.00	5.50
(33)	Vada E. Pinson Jr.	30.00	15.00	9.00
(34)	Wally Post	18.00	9.00	5.50
(35)	Vic Power	18.00	9.00	5.50
(36)	Robert T. Purkey	18.00	9.00	5.50
(37)	Frank Robinson	125.00	62.00	37.00
(38)	John A. Romano Jr.	18.00	9.00	5.50
(39)	Dick Schofield	18.00	9.00	5.50
(40)	Robert Skinner	18.00	9.00	5.50
(41)	Hal Smith	18.00	9.00	5.50
(42)	Richard Stuart	20.00	10.00	6.00
(43)	John E. Temple	18.00	9.00	5.50

1962 Kahn's Wieners

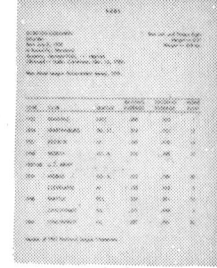

Compliments of Kahn's
"THE WIENER THE WORLD AWAITED"

Besides the familiar Reds, Pirates and Indians players in the 1962 Kahn's set, a fourth team was added, the Minnesota Twins, though the overall size of the set was decreased from the previous year, to 38 players in 1962. The cards retained the 3-1/4" by 4" black and white format of previous years. The '62 Kahn's set is awash in variations. Besides the photo and front design variations on the Bell, Purkey and Power cards, each Cleveland player can be found with two back variations, listing the team either as "Cleveland" or "Cleveland Indians." The complete set values listed below include all variations.

		NR MT	EX	VG
	Complete Set:	2400.00	1200.00	720.00
	Common Player:	15.00	7.50	4.50
(1a)	Gary Bell (fat man in background)			
		150.00	75.00	45.00

		NR MT	EX	VG
(1b)	Gary Bell (no fat man)	40.00	20.00	12.00
(2)	James P. Brosnan	15.00	7.50	4.50
(3)	Forrest Burgess	20.00	10.00	6.00
(4)	Leonardo Cardenas	15.00	7.50	4.50
(5)	Roberto Clemente	125.00	62.00	37.00
(6a)	Ty Cline (Cleveland Indians back)			
		75.00	37.00	22.00
(6b)	Ty Cline (Cleveland back)	30.00	15.00	9.00
(7)	Gordon Coleman	15.00	7.50	4.50
(8)	Dick Donovan	30.00	15.00	9.00
(9)	John Edwards	15.00	7.50	4.50
(10a)	Tito Francona (Cleveland Indians back)			
		75.00	37.00	22.00
(10b)	Tito Francona (Cleveland back)	30.00	15.00	9.00
(11)	Gene Freese	15.00	7.50	4.50
(12)	Robert B. Friend	20.00	10.00	6.00
(13)	Joe Gibbon	90.00	45.00	27.00
(14a)	Jim Grant (Cleveland Indians back)			
		75.00	37.00	22.00
(14b)	Jim Grant (Cleveland back)	30.00	15.00	9.00
(15)	Richard M. Groat	25.00	12.50	7.50
(16)	Harvey Haddix	20.00	10.00	6.00
(17a)	Woodie Held (Cleveland Indians back)			
		90.00	45.00	27.00
(17b)	Woodie Held (Cleveland back)	30.00	15.00	9.00
(18)	Bill Henry	15.00	7.50	4.50
(19)	Don Hoak	20.00	10.00	6.00
(20)	Ken Hunt	15.00	7.50	4.50
(21)	Joseph R. Jay	15.00	7.50	4.50
(22)	Eddie Kasko	15.00	7.50	4.50
(23a)	Willie Kirkland (Cleveland Indians back)			
		75.00	37.00	22.00
(23b)	Willie Kirkland (Cleveland back)	30.00	15.00	9.00
(24a)	Barry Latman (Cleveland Indians back)			
		75.00	37.00	22.00
(24b)	Barry Latman (Cleveland back)	30.00	15.00	9.00
(25)	Jerry Lynch	15.00	7.50	4.50
(26)	Jim Maloney	20.00	10.00	6.00
(27)	William Mazeroski	25.00	12.50	7.50
(28)	Jim O'Toole	15.00	7.50	4.50
(29a)	Jim Perry (Cleveland Indians back)			
		90.00	45.00	27.00
(29b)	Jim Perry (Cleveland back)	30.00	15.00	9.00
(30a)	John M. Phillips (Cleveland Indians back)			
		75.00	37.00	22.00
(30b)	John M. Phillips (Cleveland back)			
		30.00	15.00	9.00
(31)	Vada E. Pinson	25.00	12.50	7.50
(32)	Wally Post	15.00	7.50	4.50
(33a)	Vic Power (Cleveland Indians back)			
		75.00	37.00	22.00
(33b)	Vic Power (Cleveland back)	30.00	15.00	9.00
(33c)	Vic Power (Minnesota Twins back)			
		150.00	75.00	45.00
(34a)	Robert T. Purkey (no autograph)			
		150.00	75.00	45.00
(34b)	Robert T. Purkey (with autograph)			
		40.00	20.00	12.00
(35)	Frank Robinson	80.00	40.00	24.00
(36a)	John Romano (Cleveland Indians back)			
		75.00	37.00	22.00
(36b)	John Romano (Cleveland back)	30.00	15.00	9.00
(37)	Dick Stuart	20.00	10.00	6.00
(38)	Bill Virdon	20.00	10.00	6.00

1963 Kahn's Wieners

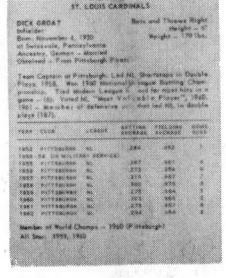

In 1963, for the first time since Kahn's began issuing baseball cards in 1955, the design underwent a significant change, white borders were added to the

top and sides of player photo. Also, the card size was changed to 3-3/16" by 4-1/4". Statistical and personal data continued to be printed on the card backs. Joining traditional Reds, Pirates and Indians personnel in the 30-card 1963 set were a handful of New York Yankees and Dick Groat, in his new identity as a St. Louis Cardinal.

		NR MT	EX	VG
Complete Set:		800.00	400.00	240.00
Common Player:		15.00	7.50	4.50
(1)	Robert Bailey	15.00	7.50	4.50
(2)	Don Blasingame	15.00	7.50	4.50
(3)	Clete Boyer	25.00	12.50	7.50
(4)	Forrest Burgess	20.00	10.00	6.00
(5)	Leonardo Cardenas	15.00	7.50	4.50
(6)	Roberto Clemente	125.00	62.00	37.00
(7)	Don Clendennon (Donn Clendenon)			
		15.00	7.50	4.50
(8)	Gordon Coleman	15.00	7.50	4.50
(9)	John A. Edwards	15.00	7.50	4.50
(10)	Gene Freese	15.00	7.50	4.50
(11)	Robert B. Friend	20.00	10.00	6.00
(12)	Joe Gibbon	15.00	7.50	4.50
(13)	Dick Groat	25.00	12.50	7.50
(14)	Harvey Haddix	20.00	10.00	6.00
(15)	Elston Howard	30.00	15.00	9.00
(16)	Joey Jay	15.00	7.50	4.50
(17)	Eddie Kasko	15.00	7.50	4.50
(18)	Tony Kubek	30.00	15.00	9.00
(19)	Jerry Lynch	15.00	7.50	4.50
(20)	Jim Maloney	20.00	10.00	6.00
(21)	William Mazeroski	25.00	12.50	7.50
(22)	Joe Nuxhall	20.00	10.00	6.00
(23)	Jim O'Toole	15.00	7.50	4.50
(24)	Vada E. Pinson	25.00	12.50	7.50
(25)	Robert T. Purkey	15.00	7.50	4.50
(26)	Bob Richardson	30.00	15.00	9.00
(27)	Frank Robinson	70.00	35.00	21.00
(28)	Bill Stafford	20.00	10.00	6.00
(29)	Ralph W. Terry	25.00	12.50	7.50
(30)	Bill Virdon	20.00	10.00	6.00

1964 Kahn's Wieners

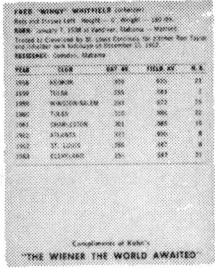

After nearly a decade of virtually identical card issues, the 1964 Kahn's issue was an abrupt change. In a new size, 3" by 3-1/2", the nearly square cards featured a borderless color photo. The only other design element on the front of the card was a facsimile autograph. The advertising slogan which had traditionally appeared on the front of the card was moved to the back, where it joined the player's stats and personal data. The teams in the 1964 issue once again reverted to the Reds, Pirates and Indians, for a total of 31 cards.

		NR MT	EX	VG
Complete Set:		925.00	462.00	277.00
Common Player:		9.00	4.50	2.75
(1)	Max Alvis	9.00	4.50	2.75
(2)	Bob Bailey	9.00	4.50	2.75
(3)	Leonardo Cardenas	9.00	4.50	2.75
(4)	Roberto Clemente	125.00	62.00	37.00

		NR MT	EX	VG
(5)	Donn A. Clendenon	9.00	4.50	2.75
(6)	Victor Davalillo	9.00	4.50	2.75
(7)	Dick Donovan	9.00	4.50	2.75
(8)	John A. Edwards	9.00	4.50	2.75
(9)	Robert Friend	15.00	7.50	4.50
(10)	Jim Grant	9.00	4.50	2.75
(11)	Tommy Harper	9.00	4.50	2.75
(12)	Woodie Held	9.00	4.50	2.75
(13)	Joey Jay	9.00	4.50	2.75
(14)	Jack Kralick	9.00	4.50	2.75
(15)	Jerry Lynch	9.00	4.50	2.75
(16)	Jim Maloney	15.00	7.50	4.50
(17)	William S. Mazeroski	20.00	10.00	6.00
(18)	Alvin McBean	9.00	4.50	2.75
(19)	Joe Nuxhall	15.00	7.50	4.50
(20)	Jim Pagliaroni	9.00	4.50	2.75
(21)	Vada E. Pinson Jr.	20.00	10.00	6.00
(22)	Robert T. Purkey	9.00	4.50	2.75
(23)	Pedro Ramos	9.00	4.50	2.75
(24)	Frank Robinson	70.00	35.00	21.00
(25)	John Romano	9.00	4.50	2.75
(26)	Pete Rose	400.00	200.00	120.00
(27)	John Tsitouris	9.00	4.50	2.75
(28)	Robert A. Veale Jr.	9.00	4.50	2.75
(29)	Bill Virdon	15.00	7.50	4.50
(30)	Leon Wagner	9.00	4.50	2.75
(31)	Fred Whitfield	9.00	4.50	2.75

		NR MT	EX	VG
(23)	Jim Maloney	15.00	7.50	4.50
(24)	Lee Maye	12.00	6.00	3.50
(25)	William S. Mazeroski	20.00	10.00	6.00
(26)	Alvin McBean	12.00	6.00	3.50
(27)	Bill McCool	12.00	6.00	3.50
(28)	Sam McDowell	15.00	7.50	4.50
(29)	Donald McMahon	12.00	6.00	3.50
(30)	Denis Menke	12.00	6.00	3.50
(31)	Joe Nuxhall	15.00	7.50	4.50
(32)	Gene Oliver	12.00	6.00	3.50
(33)	Jim O'Toole	12.00	6.00	3.50
(34)	Jim Pagliaroni	12.00	6.00	3.50
(35)	Vada E. Pinson Jr.	20.00	10.00	6.00
(36)	Frank Robinson	70.00	35.00	21.00
(37)	Pete Rose	250.00	125.00	75.00
(38)	Willie Stargell	70.00	35.00	21.00
(39)	Ralph W. Terry	12.00	6.00	3.50
(40)	Luis Tiant	20.00	10.00	6.00
(41)	Joe Torre	25.00	12.50	7.50
(42)	John Tsitouris	12.00	6.00	3.50
(43)	Robert A. Veale Jr.	12.00	6.00	3.50
(44)	Bill Virdon	15.00	7.50	4.50
(45)	Leon Wagner	12.00	6.00	3.50

1965 Kahn's Wieners

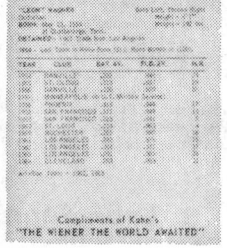

There was little change for the Kahn's issue in 1965 beyond the addition of Milwaukee Braves players to the Reds, Pirates and Indians traditionally included in the set. At 45 players, the 1965 issue was the largest of the Kahn's sets. Once again in 3" by 3-1/2" size, the 1965s retained the borderless color photo design of the previous season. A look at the stats on the back will confirm the year of issue, however, since the last year of statistics is the year prior to the card's issue.

		NR MT	EX	VG
Complete Set:		1100.00	550.00	330.00
Common Player:		12.00	6.00	3.50
(1)	Hank Aaron	125.00	62.00	37.00
(2)	Max Alvis	12.00	6.00	3.50
(3)	Jose Azcue	12.00	6.00	3.50
(4)	Bob Bailey	12.00	6.00	3.50
(5)	Frank Bolling	12.00	6.00	3.50
(6)	Leonardo Cardenas	12.00	6.00	3.50
(7)	Rico Ricardo Carty	15.00	7.50	4.50
(8)	Donn A. Clendenon	12.00	6.00	3.50
(9)	Tony Cloninger	12.00	6.00	3.50
(10)	Gordon Coleman	12.00	6.00	3.50
(11)	Victor Davalillo	12.00	6.00	3.50
(12)	John A. Edwards	12.00	6.00	3.50
(13)	Sam Ellis	12.00	6.00	3.50
(14)	Robert Friend	15.00	7.50	4.50
(15)	Tommy Harper	12.00	6.00	3.50
(16)	Chuck Hinton	12.00	6.00	3.50
(17)	Dick Howser	15.00	7.50	4.50
(18)	Joey Jay	12.00	6.00	3.50
(19)	Deron Johnson	12.00	6.00	3.50
(20)	Jack Kralick	12.00	6.00	3.50
(21)	Denny Lemaster	12.00	6.00	3.50
(22)	Jerry Lynch	12.00	6.00	3.50

1966 Kahn's Wieners

The fourth new format in five years greeted collector's with the introduction of Kahn's 1966 issue of 32 cards. The design consisted of a color photo bordered by white and yellow vertical stripes. The player's name was printed above the photo, and a facsimile autograph appeared across the photo. As printed, the cards were 2-13/16" by 4" in size. However, the top portion consisted of a 2-13/16" by 1-3/8" advertising panel with a red rose logo and the word "Kahn's," separated from the player portion of the card by a black dotted line. Naturally, many of the cards are found today with the top portion cut off. Values listed here are for cards with the top portion intact. Players from the Cincinnati Reds, Pittsburgh Pirates, Cleveland Indians and Atlanta Braves were included in the set. Since the cards are blank-backed, collectors must learn to differentiate player poses to determine year of issue for some cards.

		NR MT	EX	VG
Complete Set:		1200.00	600.00	360.00
Common Player:		18.00	9.00	5.50
(1)	Henry Aaron	125.00	62.00	37.00
(2)	Felipe Alou	24.00	12.00	7.25
(3)	Max Alvis	18.00	9.00	5.50
(4)	Robert Bailey	18.00	9.00	5.50
(5)	Wade Blasingame	18.00	9.00	5.50
(6)	Frank Bolling	18.00	9.00	5.50
(7)	Leo Cardenas	18.00	9.00	5.50
(8)	Roberto Clemente	125.00	62.00	37.00
(9)	Tony Cloninger	18.00	9.00	5.50
(10)	Vic Davalillo	18.00	9.00	5.50
(11)	John Edwards	18.00	9.00	5.50
(12)	Sam Ellis	18.00	9.00	5.50
(13)	Pedro Gonzalez	18.00	9.00	5.50
(14)	Tommy Harper	18.00	9.00	5.50
(15)	Deron Johnson	18.00	9.00	5.50
(16)	Mack Jones	18.00	9.00	5.50
(17)	Denny Lemaster	18.00	9.00	5.50

		NR MT	EX	VG
(18)	Jim Maloney	24.00	12.00	7.25
(19)	William Mazeroski	28.00	14.00	8.50
(20)	Bill McCool	18.00	9.00	5.50
(21)	Sam McDowell	24.00	12.00	7.25
(22)	Denis Menke	18.00	9.00	5.50
(23)	Joe Nuxhall	24.00	12.00	7.25
(24)	Jim Pagliaroni	18.00	9.00	5.50
(25)	Milt Pappas	24.00	12.00	7.25
(26)	Vada Pinson	28.00	14.00	8.50
(27)	Pete Rose	250.00	125.00	75.00
(28)	Sonny Siebert	18.00	9.00	5.50
(29)	Willie Stargell	80.00	40.00	24.00
(30)	Joe Torre	28.00	14.00	8.50
(31)	Bob Veale	18.00	9.00	5.50
(32)	Fred Whitfield	18.00	9.00	5.50

1967 Kahn's Wieners

Retaining the basic format of the 1966 set (see listing for description), the '67 Kahn's set was expanded to 41 players through the addition of several New York Mets players to the previous season's lineup of Reds, Pirates, Indians and Braves. Making the 1967 set especially challenging for collectors is the fact that some cards are found in a smaller size and/or with different colored stripes bordering the color player photo. On the majority of cards, the size remained 2-13/16" by 4" (with ad at top; 2-13/16" by 2-5/8"without ad at top). However, because of packing in different products, the Ellis, Helms and Torre cards can be found in 2-13/16" by 3-1/4" size (with ad; 2-13/16" by 2-1/8" without ad). The handful of known border stripe variations are listed below. Values quoted are for cards with the top ad panel intact. All variation cards are included in the valuations given below for complete sets.

		NR MT	EX	VG
Complete Set:		1400.00	700.00	420.00
Common Player:		18.00	9.00	5.50
(1)	Henry Aaron	125.00	62.00	37.00
(2)	Gene Alley	18.00	9.00	5.50
(3)	Felipe Alou	24.00	12.00	7.25
(4a)	Matty Alou (yellow & white striped border)	24.00	12.00	7.25
(4b)	Matty Alou (red & white striped border)	28.00	14.00	8.50
(5)	Max Alvis	18.00	9.00	5.50
(6a)	Ken Boyer (yellow & white striped border)	30.00	15.00	9.00
(6b)	Ken Boyer (red & white striped border)	35.00	17.50	10.50
(7)	Leo Cardenas	18.00	9.00	5.50
(8)	Rico Carty	24.00	12.00	7.25
(9)	Tony Cloninger	18.00	9.00	5.50
(10)	Tommy Davis	24.00	12.00	7.25
(11)	John Edwards	18.00	9.00	5.50
(12a)	Sam Ellis (large size)	18.00	9.00	5.50
(12b)	Sam Ellis (small size)	28.00	14.00	8.50
(13)	Jack Fisher	18.00	9.00	5.50
(14)	Steve Hargan	18.00	9.00	5.50
(15)	Tom Harper	18.00	9.00	5.50
(16a)	Tom Helms (large size)	18.00	9.00	5.50
(16b)	Tom Helms (small size)	28.00	14.00	8.50

		NR MT	EX	VG
(17)	Deron Johnson	18.00	9.00	5.50
(18)	Ken Johnson	18.00	9.00	5.50
(19)	Cleon Jones	18.00	9.00	5.50
(20a)	Ed Kranepool (yellow & white striped border)	18.00	9.00	5.50
(20b)	Ed Kranepool (red & white striped border)	25.00	12.50	7.50
(21a)	James Maloney (yellow & white striped border)	24.00	12.00	7.25
(21b)	James Maloney (red & white striped border)	28.00	14.00	8.50
(22)	Lee May	24.00	12.00	7.25
(23)	Wm. Mazeroski	28.00	14.00	8.50
(24)	Wm. McCool	18.00	9.00	5.50
(25)	Sam McDowell	24.00	12.00	7.25
(26)	Dennis Menke (Denis)	18.00	9.00	5.50
(27)	Jim Pagliaroni	18.00	9.00	5.50
(28)	Don Pavletich	18.00	9.00	5.50
(29)	Tony Perez	35.00	17.50	10.50
(30)	Vada Pinson	28.00	14.00	8.50
(31)	Dennis Ribant	18.00	9.00	5.50
(32)	Pete Rose	200.00	100.00	60.00
(33)	Art Shamsky	18.00	9.00	5.50
(34)	Bob Shaw	18.00	9.00	5.50
(35)	Sonny Siebert	18.00	9.00	5.50
(36)	Wm. Stargell (first name actually Wilver)	80.00	40.00	24.00
(37a)	Joe Torre (large size)	28.00	14.00	8.50
(37b)	Joe Torre (small size)	32.00	16.00	9.50
(38)	Bob Veale	18.00	9.00	5.50
(39)	Leon Wagner	18.00	9.00	5.50
(40)	Fred Whitfield	18.00	9.00	5.50
(41)	Woody Woodward	18.00	9.00	5.50

1968 Kahn's Wieners

The number of card size and stripe color variations increased with the 1968 Kahn's issue (see 1967 listing), though the basic card design was retained from the previous two seasons: 2-13/16" by 4" size (with ad panel at top; 2-13/16" by 2-5/8" with ad panel cut off), color photo bordered by yellow and white vertical stripes. In addition to the basic issue, a number of the cards appear in a smaller, 2-13/16" by 3-1/4", size, while some of them, and others, appear with variations in the color of border stripes. One card, Maloney, can be found with a top portion advertising Blue Mountain brand meats, as well as Kahn's. All in all, quite a challenge for the specialist. The 1968 set featured the largest number of teams represented in any Kahn's issue: Atlanta Braves, Chicago Cubs and White Sox, Cincinnati Reds, Cleveland Indians, Detroit Tigers, New York Mets and Pittsburgh Pirates. Values quoted below are for cards with the ad panel at top; complete set prices include all variations.

		NR MT	EX	VG
Complete Set:		2000.00	1000.00	600.00
Common Player:		18.00	9.00	5.50
(1a)	Hank Aaron (large size)	125.00	62.00	37.00
(1b)	Hank Aaron (small size)	150.00	75.00	45.00
(2)	Tommy Agee	18.00	9.00	5.50
(3a)	Gene Alley (large size)	18.00	9.00	5.50
(3b)	Gene Alley (small size)	24.00	12.00	7.25

		NR MT	EX	VG
(4)	Felipe Alou	24.00	12.00	7.25
(5a)	Matty Alou (yellow striped border)			
		24.00	12.00	7.25
(5b)	Matty Alou (red striped border)	28.00	14.00	8.50
(6a)	Max Alvis (large size)	18.00	9.00	5.50
(6b)	Max Alvis (small size)	24.00	12.00	7.25
(7)	Gerry Arrigo	18.00	9.00	5.50
(8)	John Bench	450.00	225.00	135.00
(9a)	Clete Boyer (large size)	18.00	9.00	5.50
(9b)	Clete Boyer (small size)	24.00	12.00	7.25
(10)	Larry Brown	18.00	9.00	5.50
(11a)	Leo Cardenas (large size)	18.00	9.00	5.50
(11b)	Leo Cardenas (small size)	24.00	12.00	7.25
(12a)	Bill Freehan (large size)	24.00	12.00	7.25
(12b)	Bill Freehan (small size)	28.00	14.00	8.50
(13)	Steve Hargan	18.00	9.00	5.50
(14)	Joel Horlen	18.00	9.00	5.50
(15)	Tony Horton	24.00	12.00	7.25
(16)	Willie Horton	24.00	12.00	7.25
(17)	Ferguson Jenkins	32.00	16.00	9.50
(18)	Deron Johnson	18.00	9.00	5.50
(19)	Mack Jones	18.00	9.00	5.50
(20)	Bob Lee	18.00	9.00	5.50
(21a)	Jim Maloney (large size, rose logo)			
		24.00	12.00	7.25
(21b)	Jim Maloney (large size, blue mountain logo)			
		28.00	14.00	8.50
(21c)	Jim Maloney (small size, yellow & white striped border)			
		28.00	14.00	8.50
(21d)	Jim Maloney (small size, yellow, white & green striped border)			
		28.00	14.00	8.50
(22a)	Lee May (large size)	24.00	12.00	7.25
(22b)	Lee May (small size)	28.00	14.00	8.50
(23a)	Wm. Mazeroski (large size)	24.00	12.00	7.25
(23b)	Wm. Mazeroski (small size)	28.00	14.00	8.50
(24)	Dick McAuliffe	18.00	9.00	5.50
(25)	Bill McCool	18.00	9.00	5.50
(26a)	Sam McDowell (yellow striped border)			
		24.00	12.00	7.25
(26b)	Sam McDowell (red striped border)			
		28.00	14.00	8.50
(27a)	Tony Perez (yellow striped border)			
		35.00	17.50	10.50
(27b)	Tony Perez (red striped border)	40.00	20.00	12.00
(28)	Gary Peters	18.00	9.00	5.50
(29a)	Vada Pinson (large size)	24.00	12.00	7.25
(29b)	Vada Pinson (small size)	28.00	14.00	8.50
(30)	Chico Ruiz	18.00	9.00	5.50
(31a)	Ron Santo (yellow striped border)			
		24.00	12.00	7.25
(31b)	Ron Santo (red striped border)	28.00	14.00	8.50
(32)	Art Shamsky	18.00	9.00	5.50
(33)	Luis Tiant	24.00	12.00	7.25
(34a)	Joe Torre (large size)	28.00	14.00	8.50
(34b)	Joe Torre (small size)	32.00	16.00	9.50
(35a)	Bob Veale (large size)	18.00	9.00	5.50
(35b)	Bob Veale (small size)	24.00	12.00	7.25
(36)	Leon Wagner	18.00	9.00	5.50
(37)	Billy Williams	50.00	25.00	15.00
(38)	Earl Wilson	18.00	9.00	5.50

1969 Kahn's Wieners

In its 15th consecutive year of baseball card issuing, Kahn's continued the basic format adopted in 1966. The basic card issue of 22 players was printed in 2-13/16" by 4" size (with ad panel at top; 2-13/16" by 2-5/8" without panel) and are blanked-backed. Teams represented in the set included

the Braves, Cubs, White Sox, Reds, Cardinals, Indians and Pirates. The cards featured a color photo and facsimile autograph bordered by yellow and white vertical stripes. At top was an ad panel consisting of the Kahn's red rose logo. However, because some cards were produced for inclusion in packages other than the standard hot dogs, a number of variations in card size and stripe color were created, as noted in the listings below. The smaller size cards, 2-13/16" by 3-1/4" with ad, 2-13/16" by 2-1/8" without ad, were created by more closely cropping the player photo at top and bottom. Values quoted below are for cards with the top logo panel intact. Complete set values include all the variations.

		NR MT	EX	VG
Complete Set:		1000.00	500.00	300.00
Common Player:		18.00	9.00	5.50
(1a)	Hank Aaron (large size)	125.00	62.00	37.00
(1b)	Hank Aaron (small size)	150.00	75.00	45.00
(2)	Matty Alou	24.00	12.00	7.25
(3)	Max Alvis	18.00	9.00	5.50
(4)	Gerry Arrigo	18.00	9.00	5.50
(5)	Steve Blass	18.00	9.00	5.50
(6)	Clay Carroll	18.00	9.00	5.50
(7)	Tony Cloninger	18.00	9.00	5.50
(8)	George Culver	18.00	9.00	5.50
(9)	Joel Horlen	18.00	9.00	5.50
(10)	Tony Horton	24.00	12.00	7.25
(11)	Alex Johnson	18.00	9.00	5.50
(12a)	Jim Maloney (large size)	24.00	12.00	7.25
(12b)	Jim Maloney (small size)	28.00	14.00	8.50
(13a)	Lee May (yellow striped border)	24.00	12.00	7.25
(13b)	Lee May (red striped border)	28.00	14.00	8.50
(14a)	Wm. Mazeroski (yellow striped border)			
		24.00	12.00	7.25
(14b)	Wm. Mazeroski (red striped border)			
		28.00	14.00	8.50
(15a)	Sam McDowell (yellow striped border)			
		24.00	12.00	7.25
(15b)	Sam McDowell (red striped border)			
		28.00	14.00	8.50
(16a)	Tony Perez (large size)	35.00	17.50	10.50
(16b)	Tony Perez (small size)	40.00	20.00	12.00
(17)	Gary Peters	18.00	9.00	5.50
(18a)	Ron Santo (yellow striped border)			
		24.00	12.00	7.25
(18b)	Ron Santo (red striped border)	28.00	14.00	8.50
(19)	Luis Tiant	24.00	12.00	7.25
(20)	Joe Torre	28.00	14.00	8.50
(21)	Bob Veale	18.00	9.00	5.50
(22)	Billy Williams	50.00	25.00	15.00

1987 Kahn's Wieners Reds

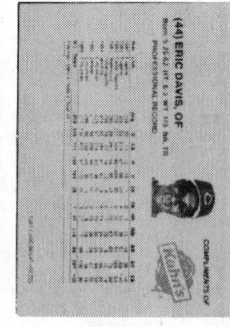

After a nearly 20-year layoff, Kahn's Wieners produced a baseball card set. Kahn's, who produced card sets between 1955 and 1968, sponsored a 28-card 9set that was distributed to fans attending the August 2nd game at Riverfront Stadium. The cards are the standard 2-1/2" by 3-1/2" size. The fronts offer a full-color player photo bordered in red and white. The backs carry the Kahn's logo and a head shot of the player.

		MT	NR MT	EX
Complete Set:		20.00	15.00	8.00
Common Player:		.20	.15	.08
6	Bo Diaz	.25	.20	.10
10	Terry Francona	.20	.15	.08
11	Kurt Stillwell	.70	.50	.30
12	Nick Esasky	.70	.50	.30
13	Dave Concepcion	.70	.50	.30
15	Barry Larkin	2.00	1.50	.80
16	Ron Oester	.20	.15	.08
21	Paul O'Neill	1.00	.70	.40
23	Lloyd McClendon	.40	.30	.15
25	Buddy Bell	.35	.25	.14
28	Kal Daniels	1.50	1.25	.60
29	Tracy Jones	.70	.50	.30
30	Guy Hoffman	.20	.15	.08
31	John Franco	.80	.60	.30
32	Tom Browning	.80	.60	.30
33	Ron Robinson	.25	.20	.10
34	Bill Gullickson	.20	.15	.08
35	Pat Pacillo	.30	.25	.12
39	Dave Parker	.80	.60	.30
43	Bill Landrum	.50	.40	.20
44	Eric Davis	4.00	3.00	1.50
46	Rob Murphy	.40	.30	.15
47	Frank Williams	.25	.20	.10
48	Ted Power	.20	.15	.08

		MT	NR MT	EX
21	Kevin Elster	.50	.40	.20
22	Kevin McReynolds	.60	.45	.25
26	Terry Leach	.20	.15	.08
28	Bill Robinson	.20	.15	.08
29	Dave Magadan	.40	.30	.15
30	Mel Stottlemyre	.20	.15	.08
31	Gene Walter	.20	.15	.08
33	Barry Lyons	.20	.15	.08
34	Sam Perlozzo	.20	.15	.08
42	Roger McDowell	.30	.25	.12
44	David Cone	.70	.50	.30
48	Randy Myers	.50	.40	.20
50	Sid Fernandez	.35	.25	.14
52	Greg Pavlick	.20	.15	.08
-----	Team Photo	.20	.15	.08

1988 Kahn's Wieners Reds

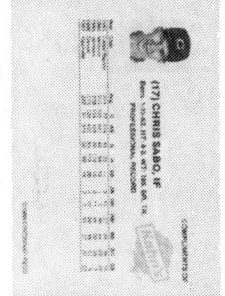

This 26-card set was a one-time giveaway during the August 14th, 1988 Cincinnati Reds game. The glossy cards (2-1/2" by 3-1/2") feature full-color action photos inside red and white borders. The Reds logo, player uniform number, name and position are printed below the photo. The backs are black and white, with small player close-ups and career stats. A promotional 25-cent coupon for Kahn's Wieners was included with each set.

		MT	NR MT	EX
Complete Set:		12.00	9.00	4.75
Common Player:		.20	.15	.08
6	Bo Diaz	.25	.20	.10
8	Terry McGriff	.20	.15	.08
9	Eddie Milner	.20	.15	.08
10	Leon Durham	.30	.25	.12
11	Barry Larkin	.70	.50	.30
12	Nick Esasky	.30	.25	.12
13	Dave Concepcion	.40	.30	.15
14	Pete Rose	1.25	.90	.50
15	Jeff Treadway	.50	.40	.20
17	Chris Sabo	1.50	1.25	.60
20	Danny Jackson	.60	.45	.25
21	Paul O'Neill	.30	.25	.12
22	Dave Collins	.20	.15	.08
27	Jose Rijo	.35	.25	.14
28	Kal Daniels	.70	.50	.30
29	Tracy Jones	.50	.40	.20
30	Lloyd McClendon	.20	.15	.08
31	John Franco	.50	.40	.20
32	Tom Browning	.50	.40	.20
33	Ron Robinson	.25	.20	.10
40	Jack Armstrong	.25	.20	.10
44	Eric Davis	2.00	1.50	.80
46	Rob Murphy	.25	.20	.10
47	Frank Williams	.20	.15	.08
48	Tim Birtsas	.20	.15	.08
-----	Coaches (Scott Breeden, Tommy Helms, Bruce Kimm, Jim Lett, Lee May, Tony Perez)			
		.20	.15	.08

1988 Kahn's Wieners Mets

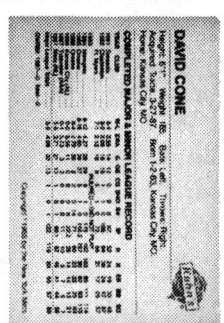

Approximately 50,000 Mets fans received this complimentary card set during a ballpark promotion sponsored by Kahn's Wieners. Twenty-five players are featured in the set, along with manager Davey Johnson, four coaches and a team photo. Card fronts have a dark blue border with an orange rectangle framing the full-color player photo. Card numbers reflecting the players' uniform numbers, are printed in white in the upper right corner of the card face, beside the team logo. The player name appears upper left and the player position is centered in the bottom margin. The card backs are black and white with red line accents. In addition to player acquisition date, birthday and residence, a paragraph-style career summary is included. The cards measure 2-1/2" by 3-1/2".

		MT	NR MT	EX
Complete Set:		14.00	10.50	5.50
Common Player:		.20	.15	.08
1	Mookie Wilson	.35	.25	.14
2	Mackey Sasser	.30	.25	.12
3	Bud Harrelson	.20	.15	.08
4	Lenny Dykstra	.40	.30	.15
5	Davey Johnson	.30	.25	.12
6	Wally Backman	.20	.15	.08
8	Gary Carter	.80	.60	.30
11	Tim Teufel	.20	.15	.08
12	Ron Darling	.60	.45	.25
13	Lee Mazzilli	.20	.15	.08
15	Rick Aguilera	.20	.15	.08
16	Dwight Gooden	2.00	1.50	.80
17	Keith Hernandez	.80	.60	.30
18	Darryl Strawberry	1.50	1.25	.60
19	Bob Ojeda	.35	.25	.14
20	Howard Johnson	.80	.60	.30

NOTE: A card number in parentheses ( ) indicates the set is unnumbered.

1989 Kahn's-Hillshire Farms

This 11-player card set was available through a mail-in offer. One dollar and three proofs of purchase from Hillshire Farms were needed to obtain the set. The card fronts feature paintings of recent Hall of Fame inductees. A coupon card was also included with each set.

	MT	NR MT	EX
Complete Set:	6.00	4.50	2.50
Common Player:	.40	.30	.10
(1) Cool Papa Bell	.40	.30	.15
(2) Johnny Bench	.80	.60	.30
(3) Lou Brock	.80	.60	.30
(4) Whitey Ford	.80	.60	.30
(5) Bob Gibson	.80	.60	.30
(6) Billy Herman	.40	.30	.15
(7) Harmon Killebrew	.80	.60	.30
(8) Eddie Mathews	.90	.70	.35
(9) Brooks Robinson	.90	.70	.35
(10) Willie Stargell	.80	.60	.30
(11) Carl Yastrzemski	.80	.60	.30

1989 Kahn's Wieners Mets

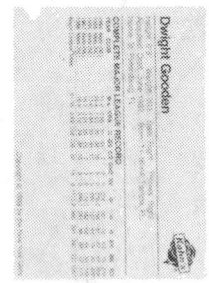

This 30-card New York Mets team set was sponsored by Kahn's Wieners and was given to fans attending the July 6, 1989 Mets game at Shea Stadium. The standard-size cards feature a full-color photo surrounded by a blue and orange border with the player's name and uniform number across the top. The backs include the Kahn's logo, along with player information and complete Major League stats. Four update cards were later added to the set.

	MT	NR MT	EX
Complete Set:	18.00	13.50	7.25
Common Player:	.20	.15	.08
1 Mookie Wilson	.35	.25	.14
2 Mackey Sasser	.25	.20	.10
3 Bud Harrelson	.20	.15	.08
5 Davey Johnson	.25	.20	.10
7 Juan Samuel	.40	.30	.15

	MT	NR MT	EX
8 Gary Carter	.50	.40	.20
9 Gregg Jefferies	2.00	1.50	.80
12 Ron Darling	.50	.40	.20
13 Lee Mazzilli	.20	.15	.08
16 Dwight Gooden	1.75	1.50	.70
17 Keith Hernandez	.60	.45	.25
18 Darryl Strawberry	1.25	.90	.50
19 Bob Ojeda	.25	.20	.10
20 Howard Johnson	.70	.50	.30
21 Kevin Elster	.35	.25	.14
22 Kevin McReynolds	.50	.40	.20
28 Bill Robinson	.20	.15	.08
29 Dave Magadan	.40	.30	.15
30 Mel Stottlemyre	.20	.15	.08
32 Mark Carreon	.40	.30	.15
33 Barry Lyons	.20	.15	.08
34 Sam Perlozzo	.20	.15	.08
38 Rick Aguilera	.20	.15	.08
44 David Cone	.50	.40	.20
46 Dave West	.60	.45	.25
48 Randy Myers	.35	.25	.14
50 Sid Fernandez	.35	.25	.14
51 Don Aase	.20	.15	.08
52 Greg Pavlick	.20	.15	.08
---- Team Card	.20	.15	.08
---- Jeff Innis	.90	.70	.50
---- Keith Miller	.70	.50	.30
---- Jeff Musselman	.70	.50	.30
---- Frank Viola	1.50	1.25	.60

1989 Kahn's Wieners Reds

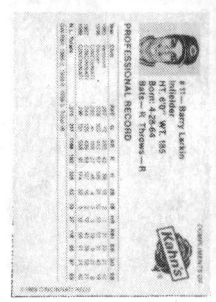

This 26-card Cincinnati Reds team set, sponsored by Kahn's Wieners, was distributed to fans attending the Aug. 6 Reds game at Riverfront Stadium. The standard-size, red-bordered cards feature action photos with the player's name in the upper left corner, his uniform number in the upper right and the Reds logo in the middle. The backs include a black-and-white head shot, player data and complete major and minor league stats. The Kahn's logo appears in the upper right corner of the back.

	MT	NR MT	EX
Complete Set:	10.00	7.50	4.00
Common Player:	.20	.15	.08
6 Bo Diaz	.20	.15	.08
7 Lenny Harris	.40	.30	.15
11 Barry Larkin	.50	.40	.20
12 Joel Youngblood	.20	.15	.08
14 Pete Rose	1.00	.70	.40
16 Ron Oester	.25	.20	.10
17 Chris Sabo	.40	.30	.15
20 Danny Jackson	.25	.20	.15
21 Paul O'Neill	.25	.20	.15
25 Todd Benzinger	.40	.30	.15
27 Jose Rijo	.25	.20	.10
28 Kal Daniels	.40	.30	.15
29 Herm Winningham	.20	.15	.08
30 Ken Griffey	.30	.25	.12
31 John Franco	.30	.25	.12
32 Tom Browning	.35	.25	.14
33 Ron Robinson	.20	.15	.08
34 Jeff Reed	.20	.15	.08
36 Rolando Roomes	.70	.50	.30
37 Norm Charlton	.50	.40	.20

		MT	NR MT	EX
42	Rick Mahler	.25	.20	.10
43	Kent Tekulve	.20	.15	.08
44	Eric Davis	2.00	1.50	.80
48	Tim Birtsas	.20	.15	.08
49	Rob Dibble	.60	.45	.25
----	Coaches Card	.20	.15	.08

1990 Kahn's Wieners Mets

 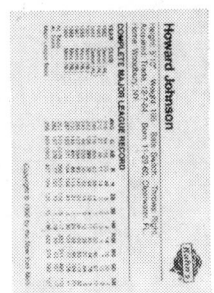

For the third consecutive year, Kahn's issued a set of baseball cards of members of the New York Mets. The sets were given out at Shea Stadium on May 3- prior to the Mets/Reds game. The cards feature blue and orange highlights like the team colors and are numbered according to uniform number. Two coupon cards were also included with each set.

		MT	NR MT	EX
Complete Set:		10.00	7.50	4.00
Common Player:		.20	.15	.08
1	Lou Thornton	.20	.15	.08
2	Mackey Sasser	.25	.20	.10
3	Bud Harrelson	.20	.15	.08
4	Mike Cubbage	.20	.15	.08
5	Davey Johnson	.20	.15	.08
6	Mike Marshall	.25	.20	.10
9	Gregg Jefferies	1.00	.70	.40
10	Dave Magadan	.40	.30	.15
11	Tim Teufel	.20	.15	.08
13	Jeff Musselman	.20	.15	.08
15	Ron Darling	.30	.25	.12
16	Dwight Gooden	1.00	.70	.40
18	Darryl Strawberry	1.00	.70	.40
19	Bob Ojeda	.20	.15	.08
20	Howard Johnson	.50	.40	.20
21	Kevin Elster	.25	.20	.10
22	Kevin McReynolds	.40	.30	.15
25	Keith Miller	.25	.20	.10
26	Alejandro Pena	.20	.15	.08
27	Tom O'Malley	.20	.15	.08
29	Frank Viola	.80	.60	.30
30	Mel Stottlemyre	.20	.15	.08
31	John Franco	.40	.30	.15
32	Doc Edwards	.20	.15	.08
33	Barry Lyons	.20	.15	.08
35	Orlando Mercado	.20	.15	.08
40	Jeff Innis	.25	.20	.15
44	David Cone	.40	.30	.15
45	Mark Carreon	.30	.25	.12
47	Wally Whitehurst	.30	.25	.12
48	Julio Machado	.30	.25	.12
50	Sid Fernandez	.35	.25	.14
52	Greg Pavlick	.20	.15	.08
----	Team Card	.20	.15	.08

1986 Kas Potato Chips Cardinals

One of a handful of 2-7/8" round baseball card "discs" created by Mike Schecter Associates for inclusion in boxes of potato chips, the 20-card Kas set features players of the defending National League Champion St. Louis Cardinals. Fronts feature color photo on which the team logos have been removed from the caps by airbrushing the photos, indicating Kas did not license with the Cardinals for use of its uniform logos. Card backs have minimal personal data and 1985 stats.

		MT	NR MT	EX
Complete Set:		15.00	11.00	6.00
Common Player:		.70	.50	.30
1	Vince Coleman	2.25	1.75	.90
2	Ken Dayley	.70	.50	.30
3	Tito Landrum	.70	.50	.30
4	Steve Braun	.70	.50	.30
5	Danny Cox	1.25	.90	.50
6	Bob Forsch	.80	.60	.30
7	Ozzie Smith	1.50	1.25	.60
8	Brian Harper	.70	.50	.30
9	Jack Clark	1.50	1.25	.60
10	Todd Worrell	2.25	1.75	.90
11	Joaquin Andujar	.70	.50	.30
12	Tom Nieto	.70	.50	.30
13	Kurt Kepshire	.70	.50	.30
14	Terry Pendleton	1.00	.70	.40
15	Tom Herr	1.00	.70	.40
16	Darrell Porter	.70	.50	.30
17	John Tudor	1.00	.70	.40
18	Jeff Lahti	.70	.50	.30
19	Andy Van Slyke	1.25	.90	.50
20	Willie McGee	1.50	1.25	.60

1986 Kay Bee

 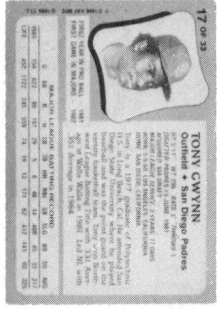

One of the most-widely distributed of the specialty boxed sets of 1986, the Kay Bee toy store chain sets of "Young Superstars of Baseball" was produced by Topps. The 2-1/2" by 3-1/2" cards are printed on white stock with a glossy surface finish. Backs,

Definitions for grading conditions are located in the introduction section at the front of this book.

printed in red and black, are strongly reminiscent of the 1971 Topps cards. While the set concentrated on "young" stars of the game, few of the year's top rookies were included.

		MT	NR MT	EX
Complete Set:		5.00	3.75	2.00
Common Player:		.05	.04	.02
1	Rick Aguilera	.12	.09	.05
2	Chris Brown	.15	.11	.06
3	Tom Browning	.07	.05	.03
4	Tom Brunansky	.07	.05	.03
5	Vince Coleman	.50	.40	.20
6	Ron Darling	.10	.08	.04
7	Alvin Davis	.10	.08	.04
8	Mariano Duncan	.07	.05	.03
9	Shawon Dunston	.07	.05	.03
10	Sid Fernandez	.10	.08	.04
11	Tony Fernandez	.10	.08	.04
12	Brian Fisher	.10	.08	.04
13	John Franco	.07	.05	.03
14	Julio Franco	.10	.08	.04
15	Dwight Gooden	.50	.40	.20
16	Ozzie Guillen	.15	.11	.06
17	Tony Gwynn	.30	.25	.12
18	Jimmy Key	.10	.08	.04
19	Don Mattingly	1.75	1.25	.70
20	Oddibe McDowell	.15	.11	.06
21	Roger McDowell	.15	.11	.06
22	Dan Pasqua	.10	.08	.04
23	Terry Pendleton	.07	.05	.03
24	Jim Presley	.10	.08	.04
25	Kirby Puckett	.25	.20	.10
26	Earnie Riles	.07	.05	.03
27	Bret Saberhagen	.15	.11	.06
28	Mark Salas	.05	.04	.02
29	Juan Samuel	.12	.09	.05
30	Jeff Stone	.05	.04	.02
31	Darryl Strawberry	.40	.30	.15
32	Andy Van Slyke	.10	.08	.04
33	Frank Viola	.12	.09	.05

1987 Kay Bee

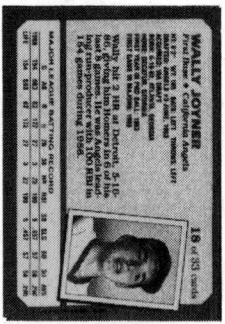

For a second straight year, Topps produced a 33-card set for the Kay Bee toy store chain. Called "Superstars of Baseball," the cards in the set measure the standard 2-1/2" by 3-1/2" size. The glossy-coated card fronts carry a full-color player photo plus the Kay Bee logo. The card backs, reminiscent of those found in the 1971 Topps set, offer a black and white head shot of the player along with his name, postion, personal information, playing record and a brief biography. The set was packaged in a specially designed box.

		MT	NR MT	EX
Complete Set:		5.00	3.75	2.00
Common Player:		.05	.04	.02
1	Harold Baines	.10	.08	.04
2	Jesse Barfield	.12	.09	.05
3	Don Baylor	.10	.08	.04
4	Wade Boggs	1.00	.70	.40
5	George Brett	.40	.30	.15
6	Hubie Brooks	.07	.05	.03

		MT	NR MT	EX
7	Jose Canseco	1.00	.70	.40
8	Gary Carter	.20	.15	.08
9	Joe Carter	.12	.09	.05
10	Roger Clemens	.40	.30	.15
11	Vince Coleman	.15	.11	.06
12	Glenn Davis	.15	.11	.06
13	Dwight Gooden	.40	.30	.15
14	Pedro Guerrero	.15	.11	.06
15	Tony Gwynn	.25	.20	.10
16	Rickey Henderson	.25	.20	.10
17	Keith Hernandez	.20	.15	.08
18	Wally Joyner	.50	.40	.20
19	Don Mattingly	1.75	1.25	.70
20	Jack Morris	.15	.11	.06
21	Dale Murphy	.30	.25	.12
22	Eddie Murray	.25	.20	.10
23	Dave Parker	.15	.11	.06
24	Kirby Puckett	.25	.20	.10
25	Tim Raines	.25	.20	.10
26	Jim Rice	.25	.20	.10
27	Dave Righetti	.12	.09	.05
28	Ryne Sandberg	.20	.15	.08
29	Mike Schmidt	.30	.25	.12
30	Mike Scott	.12	.09	.05
31	Darryl Strawberry	.40	.30	.15
32	Fernando Valenzuela	.20	.15	.08
33	Dave Winfield	.20	.15	.08

1988 Kay Bee Superstars Of Baseball

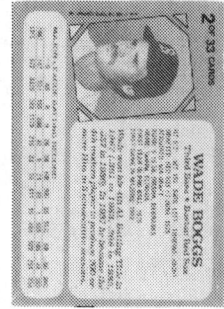

This 33-card boxed set was produced by Topps for exclusive distribution via Kay Bee toy stores nationwide. Card fronts are super glossy and feature full-color player action photos below a bright red and yellow player name banner. Photos are framed in green above a large, cartoon-style Kay Bee logo. Card backs feature player closeups in a horizontal layout in blue ink on a green and white background. Card backs are numbered and carry a player name section that includes biographical information, career data and major league batting stats.

		MT	NR MT	EX
Complete Set:		5.00	3.75	2.00
Common Player:		.10	.08	.04
1	George Bell	.20	.15	.08
2	Wade Boggs	1.00	.70	.40
3	Jose Canseco	1.00	.70	.40
4	Joe Carter	.12	.09	.05
5	Jack Clark	.15	.11	.06
6	Alvin Davis	.10	.08	.04
7	Eric Davis	.80	.60	.30
8	Andre Dawson	.15	.11	.06
9	Darrell Evans	.10	.08	.04
10	Dwight Evans	.10	.08	.04
11	Gary Gaetti	.12	.09	.05
12	Pedro Guerrero	.15	.11	.06
13	Tony Gwynn	.25	.20	.10
14	Howard Johnson	.12	.09	.05
15	Wally Joyner	.30	.25	.12
16	Don Mattingly	1.75	1.25	.70
17	Willie McGee	.10	.08	.04
18	Mark McGwire	1.00	.70	.40
19	Paul Molitor	.12	.09	.05

		MT	NR MT	EX
20	Dale Murphy	.30	.25	.12
21	Dave Parker	.15	.11	.06
22	Lance Parrish	.15	.11	.06
23	Kirby Puckett	.25	.20	.10
24	Tim Raines	.25	.20	.10
25	Cal Ripken	.30	.25	.12
26	Juan Samuel	.12	.09	.05
27	Mike Schmidt	.30	.25	.12
28	Ruben Sierra	.12	.09	.05
29	Darryl Strawberry	.40	.30	.15
30	Danny Tartabull	.12	.09	.05
31	Alan Trammell	.15	.11	.06
32	Tim Wallach	.10	.08	.04
33	Dave Winfield	.20	.15	.08

1988 Kay Bee Team Leaders

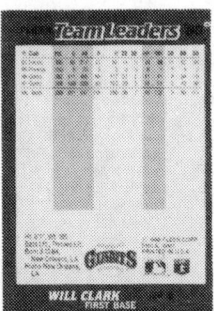

WILL CLARK
GIANTS • FIRST BASE

WILL CLARK
FIRST BASE

This first-year boxed edition of 44 player and 6 team logo cards was produced by Fleer for distribution by Kay Bee toy stores nationwide. Full-color player photos are framed in black against a bright red border. Lettering is blue, yellow and black. The "Fleer Team Leaders 1988" logo is printed vertically along the left side of the card front; the Kay Bee logo appears in the lower right corner of the photo; player's name, team and position are centered in the bottom margin. Card backs (red, white and pink) repeat the Team Leaders logo, followed by stats, personal data, team and major league baseball logos. The player's name, card number and position are listed on the lower border. The set includes six team logo sticker cards that feature black and white stadium photos on the backs.

		MT	NR MT	EX
Complete Set:		5.00	3.75	2.00
Common Player:		.05	.04	.02
1	George Bell	.20	.15	.08
2	Wade Boggs	1.00	.70	.40
3	Jose Canseco	1.00	.70	.40
4	Will Clark	.25	.20	.10
5	Roger Clemens	.40	.30	.15
6	Eric Davis	.80	.60	.30
7	Andre Dawson	.15	.11	.06
8	Julio Franco	.07	.05	.03
9	Andres Galarraga	.15	.11	.06
10	Dwight Gooden	.40	.30	.15
11	Tony Gwynn	.25	.20	.10
12	Tom Henke	.05	.04	.02
13	Orel Hershiser	.10	.08	.04
14	Kent Hrbek	.15	.11	.06
15	Ted Higuera	.10	.08	.04
16	Wally Joyner	.30	.25	.12
17	Jimmy Key	.07	.05	.03
18	Mark Langston	.10	.08	.04
19	Don Mattingly	1.75	1.25	.70
20	Willie McGee	.10	.08	.04
21	Mark McGwire	1.00	.70	.40
22	Paul Molitor	.12	.09	.05
23	Jack Morris	.12	.09	.05
24	Dale Murphy	.30	.25	.12
25	Larry Parrish	.05	.04	.02
26	Kirby Puckett	.20	.15	.08

		MT	NR MT	EX
27	Tim Raines	.20	.15	.08
28	Jeff Reardon	.07	.05	.03
29	Dave Righetti	.12	.09	.05
30	Cal Ripken, Jr.	.30	.25	.12
31	Don Robinson	.05	.04	.02
32	Bret Saberhagen	.15	.11	.06
33	Juan Samuel	.12	.09	.05
34	Mike Schmidt	.30	.25	.12
35	Mike Scott	.12	.09	.05
36	Kevin Seitzer	.60	.45	.25
37	Dave Smith	.05	.04	.02
38	Ozzie Smith	.15	.11	.06
39	Zane Smith	.05	.04	.02
40	Darryl Strawberry	.40	.30	.15
41	Rick Sutcliffe	.10	.08	.04
42	Bobby Thigpen	.07	.05	.03
43	Alan Trammell	.15	.11	.06
44	Andy Van Slyke	.10	.08	.04

1989 Kay-Bee Superstars

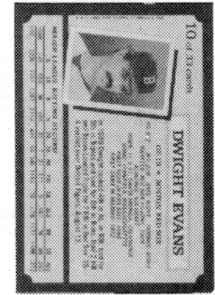

SUPERSTARS OF BASEBALL
DWIGHT EVANS

DWIGHT EVANS

The top stars of baseball were featured in this 33-card boxed set produced by Topps for the Kay-Bee Toy store chain. The glossy, standard-size cards display the Kee-Bee logo below the player photo on the front. The top of the card is headlined "Superstars of Baseball," with the player's name underneath. The backs of the cards include a small black-and-white player photo and personal data.

		MT	NR MT	EX
Complete Set:		5.00	3.75	2.00
Common Player:		.10	.08	.04
1	Wade Boggs	1.00	.70	.40
2	George Brett	.15	.11	.08
3	Jose Canseco	1.00	.70	.40
4	Gary Carter	.10	.08	.04
5	Jack Clark	.10	.08	.04
6	Will Clark	1.00	.70	.40
7	Roger Clemens	.25	.20	.10
8	Eric Davis	.60	.45	.25
9	Andre Dawson	.15	.11	.06
10	Dwight Evans	.10	.08	.04
11	Carlton Fisk	.10	.08	.04
12	Andres Galarraga	.10	.08	.04
13	Kirk Gibson	.10	.08	.04
14	Doc Gooden	.30	.25	.12
15	Mike Greenwell	.30	.25	.12
16	Pedro Guerrero	.15	.11	.08
17	Tony Gwynn	.25	.20	.10
18	Rickey Henderson	.25	.20	.10
19	Orel Hershiser	.15	.11	.06
20	Don Mattingly	1.25	.90	.50
21	Mark McGwire	.90	.70	.35
22	Dale Murphy	.20	.15	.08
23	Eddie Murray	.15	.11	.06
24	Kirby Puckett	.25	.20	.10
25	Rock Raines	.15	.11	.06
26	Ryne Sanberg	.15	.11	.06
27	Mike Schmidt	.30	.25	.12
28	Ozzie Smith	.10	.08	.04
29	Darryl Strawberry	.30	.25	.12
30	Alan Trammell	.12	.09	.05
31	Frank Viola	.12	.09	.05
32	Dave Winfield	.12	.09	.05
33	Robin Yount			

1970 Kellogg's

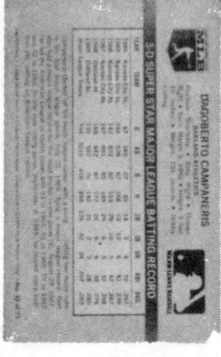

For 14 years in the 1970s and early 1980s, the Kellogg's cereal company provided Topps with virtually the only meaningful national competition in the baseball card market. Kellogg's kicked off its baseball card program in 1970 with a 75-player set of simulated 3-D cards. Single cards were available in selected brands of the company's cereal, while a mail-in program offered complete sets. The 3-D effect was achieved by the sandwiching of a clear color player photo between a purposely blurred stadium background scene and a layer of ribbed plastic. The relatively narrow dimension of the card, 2-1/4" by 3-1/2" and the nature of the plastic overlay seem to conspire to cause the cards to curl, often cracking the plastic layer, if not stored properly. Cards with major cracks in the plastic can be considered in Fair condition, at best.

		NR MT	EX	VG
Complete Set:		150.00	75.00	45.00
Common Player: 1-15		.80	.40	.25
Common Player: 16-30		.90	.45	.25
Common Player: 31-75		.80	.40	.25
1	Ed Kranepool	1.50	.70	.45
2	Pete Rose	20.00	10.00	6.00
3	Cleon Jones	.80	.40	.25
4	Willie McCovey	3.50	1.75	1.00
5	Mel Stottlemyre	1.00	.50	.30
6	Frank Howard	1.25	.60	.40
7	Tom Seaver	5.00	2.50	1.50
8	Don Sutton	2.50	1.25	.70
9	Jim Wynn	.80	.40	.25
10	Jim Maloney	.80	.40	.25
11	Tommie Agee	.80	.40	.25
12	Willie Mays	8.00	4.00	2.50
13	Juan Marichal	3.00	1.50	.90
14	Dave McNally	.90	.45	.25
15	Frank Robinson	3.50	1.75	1.00
16	Carlos May	1.00	.50	.30
17	Bill Singer	1.00	.50	.30
18	Rick Reichardt	1.00	.50	.30
19	Boog Powell	1.50	.70	.45
20	Gaylord Perry	3.50	1.75	1.00
21	Brooks Robinson	6.00	3.00	1.75
22	Luis Aparicio	3.50	1.75	1.00
23	Joel Horlen	1.00	.50	.30
24	Mike Epstein	1.00	.50	.30
25	Tom Haller	1.00	.50	.30
26	Willie Crawford	1.00	.50	.30
27	Roberto Clemente	10.00	5.00	3.00
28	Matty Alou	1.25	.60	.40
29	Willie Stargell	4.00	2.00	1.25
30	Tim Cullen	1.00	.50	.30
31	Randy Hundley	.80	.40	.25
32	Reggie Jackson	6.50	3.25	2.00
33	Rich Allen	1.25	.60	.40
34	Tim McCarver	1.00	.50	.30
35	Ray Culp	.80	.40	.25
36	Jim Fregosi	.90	.45	.25
37	Billy Williams	3.00	1.50	.90
38	Johnny Odom	.80	.40	.25
39	Bert Campaneris	.90	.45	.25
40	Ernie Banks	3.50	1.75	1.00
41	Chris Short	.80	.40	.25

		NR MT	EX	VG
42	Ron Santo	.90	.45	.25
43	Glenn Beckert	.80	.40	.25
44	Lou Brock	3.50	1.75	1.00
45	Larry Hisle	.80	.40	.25
46	Reggie Smith	.90	.45	.25
47	Rod Carew	4.00	2.00	1.25
48	Curt Flood	.90	.45	.25
49	Jim Lonborg	.80	.40	.25
50	Sam McDowell	.90	.45	.25
51	Sal Bando	.90	.45	.25
52	Al Kaline	4.00	2.00	1.25
53	Gary Nolan	.80	.40	.25
54	Rico Petrocelli	.80	.40	.25
55	Ollie Brown	.80	.40	.25
56	Luis Tiant	1.25	.60	.40
57	Bill Freehan	.90	.45	.25
58	Johnny Bench	5.00	2.50	1.50
59	Joe Pepitone	.90	.45	.25
60	Bobby Murcer	1.00	.50	.30
61	Harmon Killebrew	3.50	1.75	1.00
62	Don Wilson	.80	.40	.25
63	Tony Oliva	1.25	.60	.40
64	Jim Perry	.90	.45	.25
65	Mickey Lolich	1.25	.60	.40
66	Coco Laboy	.80	.40	.25
67	Dean Chance	.80	.40	.25
68	Ken Harrelson	.90	.45	.25
69	Willie Horton	.90	.45	.25
70	Wally Bunker	.80	.40	.25
71a	Bob Gibson (1959 IP blank)	5.00	2.50	1.50
71b	Bob Gibson (1959 IP 76)	3.00	1.50	.90
72	Joe Morgan	3.00	1.50	.90
73	Denny McLain	1.25	.60	.40
74	Tommy Harper	.80	.40	.25
75	Don Mincher	1.25	.60	.40

1971 Kellogg's

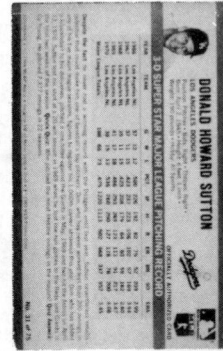

The scarcest and most valuable of the Kellogg's editions, the 75-card 1971 set was the only one not offered by the company on a mail-in basis; the only way to complete it was to buy ... and buy and buy ... boxes of cereal. Kellogg's again used the simulated 3-D effect in the cards' design, with the same result being many of the 2-1/4" by 3-1/2" cards are found today with cracks resulting from the cards' curling. A number of scarcer back variations are checklisted below. In addition, all 75 cards can be found with and without the 1970 date before the "Xograph" copyright line on the back; though there is no difference in value.

		NR MT	EX	VG
Complete Set:		800.00	400.00	240.00
Common Player:		8.00	4.00	2.50
1a	Wayne Simpson (SO 120)	12.00	6.00	3.50
1b	Wayne Simpson (SO 119)	15.00	7.50	4.50
2	Tom Seaver	30.00	15.00	9.00
3a	Jim Perry (IP 2238)	10.00	5.00	3.00
3b	Jim Perry (IP 2239)	15.00	7.50	4.50
4a	Bob Robertson (RBI 94)	8.00	4.00	2.50
4b	Bob Robertson (RBI 95)	12.00	6.00	3.50
5	Roberto Clemente	35.00	17.50	10.50
6a	Gaylord Perry (IP 2014)	15.00	7.50	4.50
6b	Gaylord Perry (IP 2015)	20.00	10.00	6.00
7a	Felipe Alou (1970 Oakland NL)	15.00	7.50	4.50

		NR MT	EX	VG
7b	Felipe Alou (1970 Oakland AL)	10.00	5.00	3.00
8	Denis Menke	8.00	4.00	2.50
9a	Don Kessinger (Hits 849)	10.00	5.00	3.00
9b	Don Kessinger (Hits 850)	15.00	7.50	4.50
10	Willie Mays	35.00	17.50	10.50
11	Jim Hickman	8.00	4.00	2.50
12	Tony Oliva	12.00	6.00	3.50
13	Manny Sanguillen	8.00	4.00	2.50
14a	Frank Howard (1968 Washington NL)	18.00	9.00	5.50
14b	Frank Howard (1968 Washington AL)	12.00	6.00	3.50
15	Frank Robinson	25.00	12.50	7.50
16	Willie Davis	10.00	5.00	3.00
17	Lou Brock	20.00	10.00	6.00
18	Cesar Tovar	8.00	4.00	2.50
19	Luis Aparicio	15.00	7.50	4.50
20	Boog Powell	12.00	6.00	3.50
21a	Dick Selma (SO 584)	8.00	4.00	2.50
21b	Dick Selma (SO 587)	12.00	6.00	3.50
22	Danny Walton	8.00	4.00	2.50
23	Carl Morton	8.00	4.00	2.50
24a	Sonny Siebert (SO 1054)	8.00	4.00	2.50
24b	Sonny Siebert (SO 1055)	12.00	6.00	3.50
25	Jim Merritt	8.00	4.00	2.50
26a	Jose Cardenal (Hits 828)	8.00	4.00	2.50
26b	Jose Cardenal (Hits 829)	12.00	6.00	3.50
27	Don Mincher	8.00	4.00	2.50
28a	Clyde Wright (California state logo)	8.00	4.00	2.50
28b	Clyde Wright (Angels crest logo)	12.00	6.00	3.50
29	Les Cain	8.00	4.00	2.50
30	Danny Cater	8.00	4.00	2.50
31	Don Sutton	15.00	7.50	4.50
32	Chuck Dobson	8.00	4.00	2.50
33	Willie McCovey	20.00	10.00	6.00
34	Mike Epstein	8.00	4.00	2.50
35a	Paul Blair (Runs 386)	8.00	4.00	2.50
35b	Paul Blair (Runs 385)	12.00	6.00	3.50
36a	Gary Nolan (SO 577)	8.00	4.00	2.50
36b	Gary Nolan (SO 581)	12.00	6.00	3.50
37	Sam McDowell	10.00	5.00	3.00
38	Amos Otis	10.00	5.00	3.00
39a	Ray Fosse (RBI 69)	8.00	4.00	2.50
39b	Ray Fosse (RBI 70)	12.00	6.00	3.50
40	Mel Stottlemyre	10.00	5.00	3.00
41	Cito Gaston	8.00	4.00	2.50
42	Dick Dietz	8.00	4.00	2.50
43	Roy White	10.00	5.00	3.00
44	Al Kaline	25.00	12.50	7.50
45	Carlos May	8.00	4.00	2.50
46a	Tommie Agee (RBI 313)	8.00	4.00	2.50
46b	Tommie Agee (RBI 314)	12.00	6.00	3.50
47	Tommy Harper	8.00	4.00	2.50
48	Larry Dierker	8.00	4.00	2.50
49	Mike Cuellar	10.00	5.00	3.00
50	Ernie Banks	25.00	12.50	7.50
51	Bob Gibson	20.00	10.00	6.00
52	Reggie Smith	10.00	5.00	3.00
53a	Matty Alou (RBI 273)	10.00	5.00	3.00
53b	Matty Alou (RBI 274)	15.00	7.50	4.50
54a	Alex Johnson (California state logo)	8.00	4.00	2.50
54b	Alex Johnson (Angels crest logo)	12.00	6.00	3.50
55	Harmon Killebrew	20.00	10.00	6.00
56	Billy Grabarkewitz	8.00	4.00	2.50
57	Rich Allen	12.00	6.00	3.50
58	Tony Perez	15.00	7.50	4.50
59a	Dave McNally (SO 1065)	10.00	5.00	3.00
59b	Dave McNally (SO 1067)	15.00	7.50	4.50
60a	Jim Palmer (SO 564)	15.00	7.50	4.50
60b	Jim Palmer (SO 567)	20.00	10.00	6.00
61	Billy Williams	15.00	7.50	4.50
62	Joe Torre	12.00	6.00	3.50
63a	Jim Northrup (AB 2773)	8.00	4.00	2.50
63b	Jim Northrup (AB 2772)	12.00	6.00	3.50
64a	Jim Fregosi (Calif. state logo - Hits 1326)	8.00	4.00	2.50
64b	Jim Fregosi (Calif. state logo - Hits 1327)	12.00	6.00	3.50
64c	Jim Fregosi (Angels crest logo)	12.00	6.00	3.50
65	Pete Rose	75.00	37.00	22.00
66a	Bud Harrelson (RBI 112)	8.00	4.00	2.50
66b	Bud Harrelson (RBI 113)	12.00	6.00	3.50
67	Tony Taylor	8.00	4.00	2.50
68	Willie Stargell	20.00	10.00	6.00
69	Tony Horton	8.50	4.25	2.50
70a	Claude Osteen (no number)	20.00	10.00	6.00
70b	Claude Osteen (#70 on back)	8.00	4.00	2.50
71	Glenn Beckert	10.00	5.00	3.00
72	Nate Colbert	8.00	4.00	2.50

		NR MT	EX	VG
73a	Rick Monday (AB 1705)	10.00	5.00	3.00
73b	Rick Monday (AB 1704)	15.00	7.50	4.50
74a	Tommy John (BB 444)	15.00	7.50	4.50
74b	Tommy John (BB 443)	20.00	10.00	6.00
75	Chris Short	12.00	6.00	3.50

1972 Kellogg's

 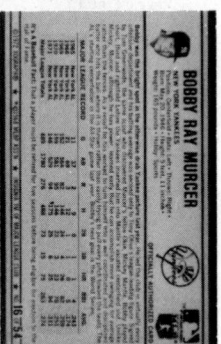

For 1972, Kellogg's reduced both the number of cards in its set and the dimensions of each card, moving to a 2-1/8" by 3-1/4" size and fixing the set at 54 cards. Once again, the cards were produced to simulate a 3-D effect (see description for 1970 Kellogg's). The set was available via a mail-in offer. The checklist includes variations which resulted from the correction of erroneous statistics on the backs of some cards. The complete set values quoted do not include the scarcer variations.

		NR MT	EX	VG
	Complete Set:	55.00	27.00	16.50
	Common Player:	.70	.35	.20
1a	Tom Seaver (1970 ERA 2.85)	9.00	4.50	2.75
1b	Tom Seaver (1970 ERA 2.81)	6.50	3.25	2.00
2	Amos Otis	.80	.40	.25
3a	Willie Davis (Runs 842)	1.25	.60	.40
3b	Willie Davis (Runs 841)	.80	.40	.25
4	Wilbur Wood	.80	.40	.25
5	Bill Parsons	.70	.35	.20
6	Pete Rose	20.00	10.00	6.00
7a	Willie McCovey (HR 360)	5.00	2.50	1.50
7b	Willie McCovey (HR 370)	3.50	1.75	1.00
8	Fergie Jenkins	1.25	.60	.40
9a	Vida Blue (ERA 2.35)	1.50	.70	.45
9b	Vida Blue (ERA 2.31)	.90	.45	.25
10	Joe Torre	.90	.45	.25
11	Merv Rettenmund	.70	.35	.20
12	Bill Melton	.70	.35	.20
13a	Jim Palmer (Games 170)	4.75	2.50	1.50
13b	Jim Palmer (Games 168)	3.00	1.50	.90
14	Doug Rader	.70	.35	.20
15a	Dave Roberts (...Seaver, the NL leader...)	1.25	.60	.40
15b	Dave Roberts (...Seaver, the league leader...)	.70	.35	.20
16	Bobby Murcer	.80	.40	.25
17	Wes Parker	.70	.35	.20
18a	Joe Coleman (BB 394)	1.25	.60	.40
18b	Joe Coleman (BB 393)	.70	.35	.20
19	Manny Sanguillen	.70	.35	.20
20	Reggie Jackson	4.50	2.25	1.25
21	Ralph Garr	.70	.35	.20
22	Jim "Catfish" Hunter	2.50	1.25	.70
23	Rick Wise	.70	.35	.20
24	Glenn Beckert	.70	.35	.20
25	Tony Oliva	.90	.45	.25
26a	Bob Gibson (SO 2577)	4.75	2.50	1.50
26b	Bob Gibson (SO 2578)	3.00	1.50	.90
27a	Mike Cuellar (1971 ERA 3.80)	1.25	.60	.40
27b	Mike Cuellar (1971 ERA 3.08)	.80	.40	.25
28	Chris Speier	.70	.35	.20
29a	Dave McNally (ERA 3.18)	1.25	.60	.40
29b	Dave McNally (ERA 3.15)	.80	.40	.25
30	Chico Cardenas	.70	.35	.20
31a	Bill Freehan (AVG. .263)	1.25	.60	.40
31b	Bill Freehan (AVG. .262)	.80	.40	.25

		NR MT	EX	VG
32a	Bud Harrelson (Hits 634)	1.25	.60	.40
32b	Bud Harrelson (Hits 624)	.70	.35	.20
33a	Sam McDowell (...less than 200 innings...)	1.25	.60	.40
33b	Sam McDowell (...less than 225 innings...)	.80	.40	.25
34a	Claude Osteen (1971 ERA 3.25)	1.25	.60	.40
34b	Claude Osteen (1971 ERA 3.51)	.70	.35	.20
35	Reggie Smith	.80	.40	.25
36	Sonny Siebert	.70	.35	.20
37	Lee May	.80	.40	.25
38	Mickey Lolich	.90	.45	.25
39a	Cookie Rojas (2B 149)	1.25	.60	.40
39b	Cookie Rojas (2B 150)	.70	.35	.20
40	Dick Drago	.70	.35	.20
41	Nate Colbert	.70	.35	.20
42	Andy Messersmith	.70	.35	.20
43a	Dave Johnson (AVG. .262)	1.50	.70	.45
43b	Dave Johnson (AVG. .264)	.90	.45	.25
44	Steve Blass	.70	.35	.20
45	Bob Robertson	.70	.35	.20
46a	Billy Williams (...missed only one last season...)	5.00	2.50	1.50
46b	Billy Williams (phrase omitted)	3.00	1.50	.90
47	Juan Marichal	3.00	1.50	.90
48	Lou Brock	3.50	1.75	1.00
49	Roberto Clemente	7.00	3.50	2.00
50	Mel Stottlemyre	.80	.40	.25
51	Don Wilson	.70	.35	.20
52a	Sal Bando (RBI 355)	1.25	.60	.40
52b	Sal Bando (RBI 356)	.80	.40	.25
53a	Willie Stargell (2B 197)	5.00	2.50	1.50
53b	Willie Stargell (2B 196)	3.00	1.50	.90
54a	Willie Mays (RBI 1855)	12.00	6.00	3.50
54b	Willie Mays (RBI 1856)	8.50	4.25	2.50

1972 Kellogg's All-Time Baseball Greats

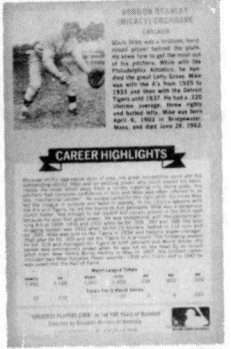

Kellogg's issued a second baseball card set in 1972, inserted into packages of breakfast rolls. The 2-1/4" by 3-1/2" cards also featured a simulated 3-D effect, but the 15 players in the set were "All-Time Baseball Greats", rather than current players. The set is virtually identical to a Rold Gold pretzel issue of 1970; the only difference being the 1972 copyright date on the back of the Kellog's cards, while the pretzel issue bears a 1970 date. The pretzel cards are considerably scarcer than the Kellogg's.

		NR MT	EX	VG
Complete Set:		15.00	7.50	4.50
Common Player:		.50	.25	.15
1	Walter Johnson	1.25	.60	.40
2	Rogers Hornsby	.80	.40	.25
3	John McGraw	.50	.25	.15
4	Mickey Cochrane	.50	.25	.15
5	George Sisler	.50	.25	.15
6	Babe Ruth	3.50	1.75	1.00
7	Robert "Lefty" Grove	.70	.35	.20
8	Harold "Pie" Traynor	.50	.25	.15
9	Honus Wagner	1.00	.50	.30
10	Eddie Collins	.50	.25	.15
11	Tris Speaker	.70	.35	.20
12	Cy Young	.80	.40	.25

		NR MT	EX	VG
13	Lou Gehrig	2.00	1.00	.60
14	Babe Ruth	3.50	1.75	1.00
15	Ty Cobb	2.00	1.00	.60

1973 Kellogg's

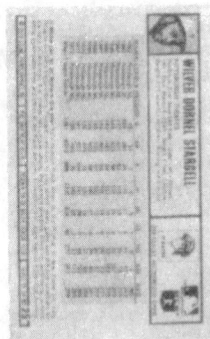

The lone exception to Kellogg's long run of simulated 3-D effect cards came in 1973, when the cereal company's 54-card set was produced by "normal" printing methods. In 2'1/4" by 3-1/2" size, the design was otherwise quite compatible with the issues which preceded and succeeded it. Because it was available via a mail-in offer, it is not as scarce as some other Kellogg's issues.

		NR MT	EX	VG
Complete Set:		55.00	28.00	16.50
Common Player:		.50	.25	.15
1	Amos Otis	.60	.30	.20
2	Ellie Rodriguez	.50	.25	.15
3	Mickey Lolich	.80	.40	.25
4	Tony Oliva	.80	.40	.25
5	Don Sutton	1.25	.60	.40
6	Pete Rose	11.00	5.50	3.25
7	Steve Carlton	4.00	2.00	1.25
8	Bobby Bonds	.70	.35	.20
9	Wilbur Wood	.60	.30	.20
10	Billy Williams	2.50	1.25	.70
11	Steve Blass	.50	.25	.15
12	Jon Matlack	.50	.25	.15
13	Cesar Cedeno	.70	.35	.20
14	Bob Gibson	2.50	1.25	.70
15	Sparky Lyle	.60	.30	.20
16	Nolan Ryan	3.50	1.75	1.00
17	Jim Palmer	2.50	1.25	.70
18	Ray Fosse	.50	.25	.15
19	Bobby Murcer	.60	.30	.20
20	Jim "Catfish" Hunter	2.50	1.25	.70
21	Tug McGraw	.80	.40	.25
22	Reggie Jackson	4.50	2.25	1.25
23	Bill Stoneman	.50	.25	.15
24	Lou Piniella	.80	.40	.25
25	Willie Stargell	2.50	1.25	.70
26	Dick Allen	.90	.45	.25
27	Carlton Fisk	1.25	.60	.40
28	Fergie Jenkins	.90	.45	.25
29	Phil Niekro	1.50	.70	.45
30	Gary Nolan	.50	.25	.15
31	Joe Torre	.80	.40	.25
32	Bobby Tolan	.50	.25	.15
33	Nate Colbert	.50	.25	.15
34	Joe Morgan	2.50	1.25	.70
35	Bert Blyleven	.90	.45	.25
36	Joe Rudi	.60	.30	.20
37	Ralph Garr	.50	.25	.15
38	Gaylord Perry	2.00	1.00	.60
39	Bobby Grich	.60	.30	.20
40	Lou Brock	2.50	1.25	.70
41	Pete Broberg	.50	.25	.15
42	Manny Sanguillen	.50	.25	.15
43	Willie Davis	.60	.30	.20
44	Dave Kingman	.90	.45	.25
45	Carlos May	.50	.25	.15
46	Tom Seaver	4.00	2.00	1.25
47	Mike Cuellar	.60	.30	.20
48	Joe Coleman	.50	.25	.15
49	Claude Osteen	.50	.25	.15

		NR MT	EX	VG
50	Steve Kline	.50	.25	.15
51	Rod Carew	4.00	2.00	1.25
52	Al Kaline	3.50	1.75	1.00
53	Larry Dierker	.50	.25	.15
54	Ron Santo	.70	.35	.20

		NR MT	EX	VG
48	Ken Singleton	.60	.30	.20
49	Manny Mota	.60	.30	.20
50	Dave Johnson	.90	.45	.25
51	Sal Bando	.60	.30	.20
52	Tom Seaver	3.50	1.75	1.00
53	Felix Millan	.50	.25	.15
54	Ron Blomberg	.80	.40	.25

1974 Kellogg's

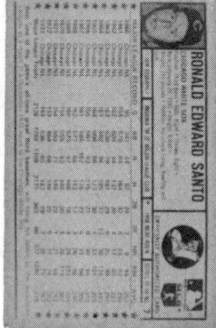

For 1974, Kellogg's returned to the use of simulated 3-D for its 54-player baseball card issue (see 1970 Kellogg's listing for description). In 2-1/8" by 3-1/4" size, the cards were available as a complete set via a mail-in offer.

		NR MT	EX	VG
Complete Set:		55.00	28.00	16.50
Common Player:		.50	.25	.15
1	Bob Gibson	3.50	1.75	1.00
2	Rick Monday	.70	.35	.20
3	Joe Coleman	.50	.25	.15
4	Bert Campaneris	.70	.35	.20
5	Carlton Fisk	1.25	.60	.40
6	Jim Palmer	2.50	1.25	.70
7a	Ron Santo (Chicago Cubs)	1.50	.70	.45
7b	Ron Santo (Chicago White Sox)	.80	.40	.25
8	Nolan Ryan	3.50	1.75	1.00
9	Greg Luzinski	.80	.40	.25
10a	Buddy Bell (Runs 134)	1.50	.70	.45
10b	Buddy Bell (Runs 135)	.80	.40	.25
11	Bob Watson	.50	.25	.15
12	Bill Singer	.50	.25	.15
13	Dave May	.50	.25	.15
14	Jim Brewer	.50	.25	.15
15	Manny Sanguillen	.50	.25	.15
16	Jeff Burroughs	.50	.25	.15
17	Amos Otis	.50	.25	.15
18	Ed Goodson	.50	.25	.15
19	Nate Colbert	.50	.25	.15
20	Reggie Jackson	4.00	2.00	1.25
21	Ted Simmons	.90	.45	.25
22	Bobby Murcer	.60	.30	.20
23	Willie Horton	.60	.30	.20
24	Orlando Cepeda	1.25	.60	.40
25	Ron Hunt	.50	.25	.15
26	Wayne Twitchell	.50	.25	.15
27	Ron Fairly	.50	.25	.15
28	Johnny Bench	3.50	1.75	1.00
29	John Mayberry	.50	.25	.15
30	Rod Carew	3.50	1.75	1.00
31	Ken Holtzman	.50	.25	.15
32	Billy Williams	2.50	1.25	.70
33	Dick Allen	.80	.40	.25
34a	Wilbur Wood (SO 959)	1.25	.60	.40
34b	Wilbur Wood (SO 960)	.70	.35	.20
35	Danny Thompson	.50	.25	.15
36	Joe Morgan	2.50	1.25	.70
37	Willie Stargell	3.00	1.50	.90
38	Pete Rose	13.00	6.50	4.00
39	Bobby Bonds	.70	.35	.20
40	Chris Speier	.50	.25	.15
41	Sparky Lyle	.60	.30	.20
42	Cookie Rojas	.50	.25	.15
43	Tommy Davis	.60	.30	.20
44	Jim "Catfish" Hunter	2.50	1.25	.70
45	Willie Davis	.60	.30	.20
46	Bert Blyleven	.90	.45	.25
47	Pat Kelly	.50	.25	.15

1975 Kellogg's

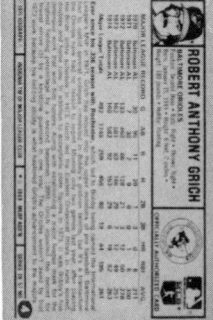

While the card size remained the same at 2-1/8" by 3-1/4", the size of the 1975 Kellogg's "3-D" set was increased by three, to 57 cards. Despite the fact cards could be obtained via a mail-in offer, as well as in cereal boxes, the '75 Kellogg's are noticeably scarcer than the company's other issues, with the exception of the 1971 set. Also helping to raise the value of the cards is the presence of an unusually large number of current and future Hall of Famers.

		NR MT	EX	VG
Complete Set:		150.00	75.00	45.00
Common Player:		2.00	1.00	.60
1	Roy White	3.50	1.75	1.00
2	Ross Grimsley	2.00	1.00	.60
3	Reggie Smith	2.50	1.25	.70
4a	Bob Grich ("...1973 work..." in last line)	4.00	2.00	1.25
4b	Bob Grich (no "...1973 work...")	2.50	1.25	.70
5	Greg Gross	2.00	1.00	.60
6	Bob Watson	2.00	1.00	.60
7	Johnny Bench	11.00	5.50	3.25
8	Jeff Burroughs	2.00	1.00	.60
9	Elliott Maddox	2.00	1.00	.60
10	Jon Matlack	2.00	1.00	.60
11	Pete Rose	24.00	12.00	7.25
12	Leroy Stanton	2.00	1.00	.60
13	Bake McBride	2.00	1.00	.60
14	Jorge Orta	2.00	1.00	.60
15	Al Oliver	2.50	1.25	.70
16	John Briggs	2.00	1.00	.60
17	Steve Garvey	9.00	4.50	2.75
18	Brooks Robinson	10.00	5.00	3.00
19	John Hiller	2.00	1.00	.60
20	Lynn McGlothen	2.00	1.00	.60
21	Cleon Jones	2.00	1.00	.60
22	Fergie Jenkins	2.50	1.25	.70
23	Bill North	2.00	1.00	.60
24	Steve Busby	2.00	1.00	.60
25	Richie Zisk	2.00	1.00	.60
26	Nolan Ryan	10.00	5.00	3.00
27	Joe Morgan	6.50	3.25	2.00
28	Joe Rudi	2.50	1.25	.70
29	Jose Cardenal	2.00	1.00	.60
30	Andy Messersmith	2.00	1.00	.60
31	Willie Montanez	2.00	1.00	.60
32	Bill Buckner	2.50	1.25	.70
33	Rod Carew	10.00	5.00	3.00
34	Lou Piniella	2.50	1.25	.70
35	Ralph Garr	2.00	1.00	.60
36	Mike Marshall	2.00	1.00	.60
37	Garry Maddox	2.00	1.00	.60
38	Dwight Evans	3.00	1.50	.90
39	Lou Brock	9.00	4.50	2.75
40	Ken Singleton	2.50	1.25	.70
41	Steve Braun	2.00	1.00	.60
42	Dick Allen	2.50	1.25	.70

		NR MT	EX	VG
43	Johnny Grubb	2.00	1.00	.60
44a	Jim Hunter (Oakland)	12.00	6.00	3.50
44b	Jim Hunter (New York)	8.00	4.00	2.50
45	Gaylord Perry	6.50	3.25	2.00
46	George Hendrick	2.00	1.00	.60
47	Sparky Lyle	2.50	1.25	.70
48	Dave Cash	2.00	1.00	.60
49	Luis Tiant	2.50	1.25	.70
50	Cesar Geronimo	2.00	1.00	.60
51	Carl Yastrzemski	16.00	8.00	4.75
52	Ken Brett	2.00	1.00	.60
53	Hal McRae	2.50	1.25	.70
54	Reggie Jackson	12.00	6.00	3.50
55	Rollie Fingers	3.50	1.75	1.00
56	Mike Schmidt	14.00	7.00	4.25
57	Richie Hebner	2.50	1.25	.70

1976 Kellogg's

 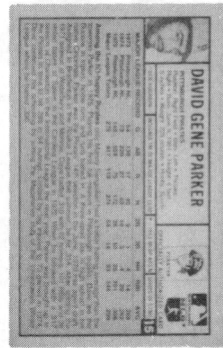

A sizeable list of corrected errors and other variation cards dots the checklist for the 57-card 1976 Kellogg's 3-D set. Again containing 57 cards, the first three cards in the set are found far less often than cards #4-57, indicating they were short-printed in relation to the rest of the set. The complete set values quoted below do not include the scarcer variation cards. Card size remained at 2-1/8" by 3-1/4".

		NR MT	EX	VG
Complete Set:		70.00	35.00	21.00
Common Player:		1.25	.60	.40
1	Steve Hargan	10.00	5.00	3.00
2	Claudell Washington	10.00	5.00	3.00
3	Don Gullett	10.00	5.00	3.00
4	Randy Jones	1.25	.60	.40
5	Jim "Catfish" Hunter	6.50	3.25	2.00
6a	Clay Carroll (Cincinnati)	3.00	1.50	.90
6b	Clay Carroll (Chicago)	1.50	.70	.45
7	Joe Rudi	1.50	.70	.45
8	Reggie Jackson	10.00	5.00	3.00
9	Felix Millan	1.25	.60	.40
10	Jim Rice	8.00	4.00	2.50
11	Bert Blyleven	2.50	1.25	.70
12	Ken Singleton	1.50	.70	.45
13	Don Sutton	2.50	1.25	.70
14	Joe Morgan	5.00	2.50	1.50
15	Dave Parker	4.00	2.00	1.25
16	Dave Cash	1.25	.60	.40
17	Ron LeFlore	1.25	.60	.40
18	Greg Luzinski	2.00	1.00	.60
19	Dennis Eckersley	2.25	1.25	.70
20	Bill Madlock	2.25	1.25	.70
21	George Scott	1.25	.60	.40
22	Willie Stargell	6.50	3.25	2.00
23	Al Hrabosky	1.25	.60	.40
24	Carl Yastrzemski	13.00	6.50	4.00
25	Jim Kaat	2.50	1.25	.70
26	Marty Perez	1.25	.60	.40
27	Bob Watson	1.25	.60	.40
28	Eric Soderholm	1.25	.60	.40
29	Bill Lee	1.25	.60	.40
30a	Frank Tanana (1975 ERA 2.63)	2.50	1.25	.70
30b	Frank Tanana (1975 ERA 2.62)	1.50	.70	.45
31	Fred Lynn	3.50	1.75	1.00
32a	Tom Seaver (1967 PCT. 552)	10.00	5.00	3.00
32b	Tom Seaver (1967 Pct. .552)	8.00	4.00	2.50

		NR MT	EX	VG
33	Steve Busby	1.25	.60	.40
34	Gary Carter	10.00	5.00	3.00
35	Rick Wise	1.25	.60	.40
36	Johnny Bench	10.00	5.00	3.00
37	Jim Palmer	8.00	4.00	2.50
38	Bobby Murcer	2.00	1.00	.60
39	Von Joshua	1.25	.60	.40
40	Lou Brock	8.00	4.00	2.50
41a	Mickey Rivers (last line begins "In three...")	2.75	1.50	.80
41b	Mickey Rivers (last line begins "The Yankees...")	1.25	.60	.40
42	Manny Sanguillen	1.25	.60	.40
43	Jerry Reuss	1.50	.70	.45
44	Ken Griffey	1.50	.70	.45
45a	Jorge Orta (AB 1616)	2.25	1.25	.70
45b	Jorge Orta (AB 1615)	1.25	.60	.40
46	John Mayberry	1.25	.60	.40
47a	Vida Blue (2nd line reads "...pitched more innings...")	3.00	1.50	.90
47b	Vida Blue (2nd line reads "...struck out more...")	2.00	1.00	.60
48	Rod Carew	10.00	5.00	3.00
49a	Jon Matlack (1975 ER 87)	2.25	1.25	.70
49b	Jon Matlack (1975 ER 86)	1.25	.60	.40
50	Boog Powell	2.50	1.25	.70
51a	Mike Hargrove (AB 935)	2.25	1.25	.70
51b	Mike Hargrove (AB 934)	1.25	.60	.40
52a	Paul Lindblad (1975 ERA 2.72)	2.25	1.25	.70
52b	Paul Lindblad (1975 ERA 2.73)	1.25	.60	.40
53	Thurman Munson	6.50	3.25	2.00
54	Steve Garvey	8.00	4.00	2.50
55	Pete Rose	18.00	9.00	5.50
56a	Greg Gross (Games 302)	2.25	1.25	.70
56b	Greg Gross (Games 334)	1.25	.60	.40
57	Ted Simmons	2.50	1.25	.70

1977 Kellogg's

 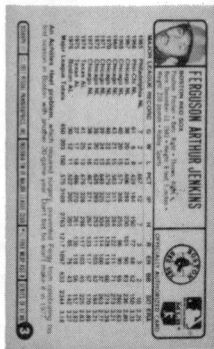

Other than another innovative card design to complement the simulated 3-D effect, there was little change in the 1977 Kellogg's issue. Set size remained at 57 cards, the set remained in the 2-1/8" by 3-1/4" format, and the cards were available either individually in boxes of cereal, or as a complete set via a mail-in box top offer. The 1977 set is the last in which Kellogg's used a player portrait photo on the back of the card.

		NR MT	EX	VG
Complete Set:		55.00	28.00	16.50
Common Player:		.40	.20	.12
1	George Foster	.90	.45	.25
2	Bert Campaneris	.60	.30	.20
3	Fergie Jenkins	.90	.45	.25
4	Dock Ellis	.40	.20	.12
5	John Montefusco	.40	.20	.12
6	George Brett	8.50	4.25	2.50
7	John Candelaria	.50	.25	.15
8	Fred Norman	.40	.20	.12
9	Bill Travers	.40	.20	.12
10	Hal McRae	.60	.30	.20
11	Doug Rau	.40	.20	.12
12	Greg Luzinski	.70	.35	.20
13	Ralph Garr	.40	.20	.12
14	Steve Garvey	4.50	2.25	1.25
15	Rick Manning	.40	.20	.12

		NR MT	EX	VG
16	Lyman Bostock	.50	.25	.15
17	Randy Jones	.40	.20	.12
18a	Ron Cey (58 homers in first sentence)	1.00	.50	.30
18b	Ron Cey (48 homers in first sentence)	.60	.30	.20
19	Dave Parker	1.25	.60	.40
20	Pete Rose	11.00	5.50	3.25
21a	Wayne Garland (last line begins "Prior to...")	.90	.45	.25
21b	Wayne Garland (last line begins "There he...")	.40	.20	.12
22	Bill North	.40	.20	.12
23	Thurman Munson	2.50	1.25	.70
24	Tom Poquette	.40	.20	.12
25	Ron LeFlore	.50	.25	.15
26	Mark Fidrych	.50	.25	.15
27	Sixto Lezcano	.40	.20	.12
28	Dave Winfield	4.00	2.00	1.25
29	Jerry Koosman	.50	.25	.15
30	Mike Hargrove	.40	.20	.12
31	Willie Montanez	.40	.20	.12
32	Don Stanhouse	.40	.20	.12
33	Jay Johnstone	.50	.25	.15
34	Bake McBride	.40	.20	.12
35	Dave Kingman	.70	.35	.20
36	Freddie Patek	.40	.20	.12
37	Garry Maddox	.50	.25	.15
38a	Ken Reitz (last line begins "The previous...")	.90	.45	.25
38b	Ken Reitz (last line begins "In late...")	.40	.20	.12
39	Bobby Grich	.60	.30	.20
40	Cesar Geronimo	.40	.20	.12
41	Jim Lonborg	.40	.20	.12
42	Ed Figueroa	.40	.20	.12
43	Bill Madlock	.80	.40	.25
44	Jerry Remy	.40	.20	.12
45	Frank Tanana	.50	.25	.15
46	Al Oliver	.90	.45	.25
47	Charlie Hough	.50	.25	.15
48	Lou Piniella	.70	.35	.20
49	Ken Griffey	.60	.30	.20
50	Jose Cruz	.60	.30	.20
51	Rollie Fingers	1.25	.60	.40
52	Chris Chambliss	.50	.25	.15
53	Rod Carew	4.00	2.00	1.25
54	Andy Messersmith	.40	.20	.12
55	Mickey Rivers	.40	.20	.12
56	Butch Wynegar	.40	.20	.12
57	Steve Carlton	5.00	2.50	1.50

		NR MT	EX	VG
1	Steve Carlton	4.00	2.00	1.25
2	Bucky Dent	.50	.25	.15
3	Mike Schmidt	4.00	2.00	1.25
4	Ken Griffey	.50	.25	.15
5	Al Cowens	.40	.20	.12
6	George Brett	5.00	2.50	1.50
7	Lou Brock	3.00	1.50	.90
8	Rich Gossage	1.25	.60	.40
9	Tom Johnson	.40	.20	.12
10	George Foster	.70	.35	.20
11	Dave Winfield	3.50	1.75	1.00
12	Dan Meyer	.40	.20	.12
13	Chris Chambliss	.50	.25	.15
14	Paul Dade	.40	.20	.12
15	Jeff Burroughs	.40	.20	.12
16	Jose Cruz	.60	.30	.20
17	Mickey Rivers	.40	.20	.12
18	John Candelaria	.50	.25	.15
19	Ellis Valentine	.40	.20	.12
20	Hal McRae	.50	.25	.15
21	Dave Rozema	.40	.20	.12
22	Lenny Randle	.40	.20	.12
23	Willie McCovey	3.00	1.50	.90
24	Ron Cey	.70	.35	.20
25	Eddie Murray	10.00	5.00	3.00
26	Larry Bowa	.60	.30	.20
27	Tom Seaver	3.50	1.75	1.00
28	Garry Maddox	.50	.25	.15
29	Rod Carew	4.00	2.00	1.25
30	Thurman Munson	2.50	1.25	.70
31	Garry Templeton	.60	.30	.20
32	Eric Soderholm	.40	.20	.12
33	Greg Luzinski	.70	.35	.20
34	Reggie Smith	.50	.25	.15
35	Dave Goltz	.40	.20	.12
36	Tommy John	1.25	.60	.40
37	Ralph Garr	.40	.20	.12
38	Alan Bannister	.40	.20	.12
39	Bob Bailor	.40	.20	.12
40	Reggie Jackson	4.00	2.00	1.25
41	Cecil Cooper	.80	.40	.25
42	Burt Hooton	.40	.20	.12
43	Sparky Lyle	.50	.25	.15
44	Steve Ontiveros	.40	.20	.12
45	Rick Reuschel	.60	.30	.20
46	Lyman Bostock	.50	.25	.15
47	Mitchell Page	.40	.20	.12
48	Bruce Sutter	.70	.35	.20
49	Jim Rice	3.50	1.75	1.00
50	Bob Forsch	.40	.20	.12
51	Nolan Ryan	3.50	1.75	1.00
52	Dave Parker	1.25	.60	.40
53	Bert Blyleven	.90	.45	.25
54	Frank Tanana	.50	.25	.15
55	Ken Singleton	.50	.25	.15
56	Mike Hargrove	.40	.20	.12
57	Don Sutton	2.50	1.25	.70

1978 Kellogg's

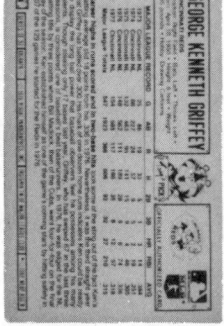

Besides the substitution of a Tony the Tiger drawing for a player portrait photo on the back of the card, the 1978 Kellogg's set offered no major changes from the previous few years issues. Cards were once again in the 2-1/8" by 3-1/4" format, with 57 cards comprising a complete set. Single cards were available in selected brands of the company's cereal, while complete sets could be obtained by a mail-in offer.

	NR MT	EX	VG
Complete Set:	40.00	20.00	12.00
Common Player:	.40	.20	.12

1979 Kellogg's

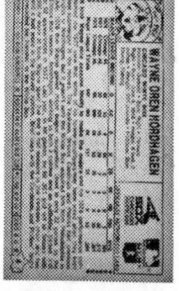

For its 1979 3-D issue, Kellogg's increased the size of the set to 60 cards, but reduced the width of the cards to 1-15/16". Depth stayed the same as in previous years, 3-1/4". The narrower card format seems to have compounded the problem of curling and subsequent cracking of the ribbed plastic surface which helps give the card a 3-D effect. Cards with major cracks can be graded no higher than VG. The complete set price in the checklist that follows does not include the scarcer variations. Numerous minor variations featuring copyright and trademark logos can be found in the set.

		NR MT	EX	VG
	Complete Set:	30.00	15.00	9.00
	Common Player:	.30	.15	.09
1	Bruce Sutter	.80	.40	.25
2	Ted Simmons	.70	.35	.20
3	Ross Grimsley	.30	.15	.09
4	Wayne Nordhagen	.30	.15	.09
5a	Jim Palmer (PCT. .649)	2.25	1.25	.70
5b	Jim Palmer (PCT. .650)	1.50	.70	.45
6	John Henry Johnson	.30	.15	.09
7	Jason Thompson	.30	.15	.09
8	Pat Zachry	.30	.15	.09
9	Dennis Eckersley	.60	.30	.20
10a	Paul Splittorff (IP 1665)	.60	.30	.20
10b	Paul Splittorff (IP 1666)	.30	.15	.09
11a	Ron Guidry (Hits 397)	2.00	1.00	.60
11b	Ron Guidry (Hits 396)	1.25	.60	.40
12	Jeff Burroughs	.30	.15	.09
13	Rod Carew	2.50	1.25	.70
14a	Buddy Bell (no trade line in bio)	1.25	.60	.40
14b	Buddy Bell (trade line in bio)	.60	.30	.20
15	Jim Rice	2.50	1.25	.70
16	Garry Maddox	.50	.25	.15
17	Willie McCovey	2.50	1.25	.70
18	Steve Carlton	2.50	1.25	.70
19a	J. R. Richard (stats begin with 1972)	.60	.30	.20
19b	J. R. Richard (stats begin with 1971)	.30	.15	.09
20	Paul Molitor	.90	.45	.25
21a	Dave Parker (AVG. .281)	2.00	1.00	.60
21b	Dave Parker (AVG. .318)	1.00	.50	.30
22a	Pete Rose (1978 3B 3)	12.00	6.00	3.50
22b	Pete Rose (1978 3B 33)	8.00	4.00	2.50
23a	Vida Blue (Runs 819)	1.25	.60	.40
23b	Vida Blue (Runs 818)	.60	.30	.20
24	Richie Zisk	.30	.15	.09
25a	Darrell Porter (2B 101)	.80	.40	.25
25b	Darrell Porter (2B 111)	.40	.20	.12
26a	Dan Driessen (Games 642)	.80	.40	.25
26b	Dan Driessen (Games 742)	.40	.20	.12
27a	Geoff Zahn (1978 Minnesota)	.60	.30	.20
27b	Geoff Zahn (1978 Minnesota)	.30	.15	.09
28	Phil Niekro	1.25	.60	.40
29	Tom Seaver	2.50	1.25	.70
30	Fred Lynn	1.00	.50	.30
31	Bill Bonham	.30	.15	.09
32	George Foster	.70	.35	.20
33a	Terry Puhl (last line of bio begins "Terry...")	.60	.30	.20
33b	Terry Puhl (last line of bio begins "His...")	.30	.15	.09
34a	John Candelaria (age is 24)	.90	.45	.25
34b	John Candelaria (age is 25)	.50	.25	.15
35	Bob Knepper	.40	.20	.12
36	Freddie Patek	.30	.15	.09
37	Chris Chambliss	.40	.20	.12
38a	Bob Forsch (1977 Games 86)	.80	.40	.25
38b	Bob Forsch (1977 Games 35)	.40	.20	.12
39a	Ken Griffey (1978 AB 674)	.90	.45	.25
39b	Ken Griffey (1978 AB 614)	.50	.25	.15
40	Jack Clark	.90	.45	.25
41a	Dwight Evans (1978 Hits 13)	1.50	.70	.45
41b	Dwight Evans (1978 Hits 123)	.90	.45	.25
42	Lee Mazzilli	.40	.20	.12
43	Mario Guerrero	.30	.15	.09
44	Larry Bowa	.50	.25	.15
45a	Carl Yastrzemski (Games 9930)	6.00	3.00	1.75
45b	Carl Yastrzemski (Games 9929)	4.00	2.00	1.25
46a	Reggie Jackson (1978 Games 162)	5.00	2.50	1.50
46b	Reggie Jackson (1978 Games 139)	3.00	1.50	.90
47	Rick Reuschel	.60	.30	.20
48a	Mike Flanagan (1976 SO 57)	.90	.45	.25
48b	Mike Flanagan (1976 SO 56)	.50	.25	.15
49a	Gaylord Perry (1973 Hits 325)	2.00	1.00	.60
49b	Gaylord Perry (1973 Hits 315)	1.25	.60	.40
50	George Brett	3.50	1.75	1.00
51a	Craig Reynolds (last line of bio begins "He spent...")	.60	.30	.20
51b	Craig Reynolds (last line of bio begins "In those...")	.30	.15	.09
52	Davey Lopes	.40	.20	.12
53a	Bill Almon (2B 31)	.60	.30	.20
53b	Bill Almon (2B 41)	.30	.15	.09

		NR MT	EX	VG
54	Roy Howell	.30	.15	.09
55	Frank Tanana	.50	.25	.15
56a	Doug Rau (1978 PCT. .577)	.60	.30	.20
56b	Doug Rau (1978 PCT. .625)	.30	.15	.09
57a	Rick Monday (1976 Runs 197)	.90	.45	.25
57b	Rick Monday (1976 Runs 107)	.50	.25	.15
58	Jon Matlack	.30	.15	.09
59a	Ron Jackson (last line of bio begins "His best...")	.60	.30	.20
59b	Ron Jackson (last line of bio begins "The Twins...")	.30	.15	.09
60	Jim Sundberg	.50	.25	.15

1980 Kellogg's

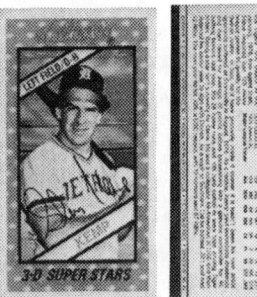

The 1980 cereal company issue featured the narrowest format of any Kellogg's card, 1-7/8" by 3-1/4". For the second straight year, set size remained at 60 cards, available either singly in boxes of cereal, or as complete sets by a mail-in offer.

		NR MT	EX	VG
	Complete Set:	20.00	10.00	6.00
	Common Player:	.30	.15	.09
1	Ross Grimsley	.30	.15	.09
2	Mike Schmidt	3.00	1.50	.90
3	Mike Flanagan	.40	.20	.12
4	Ron Guidry	.90	.45	.25
5	Bert Blyleven	.80	.40	.25
6	Dave Kingman	.70	.35	.20
7	Jeff Newman	.30	.15	.09
8	Steve Rogers	.30	.15	.09
9	George Brett	3.00	1.50	.90
10	Bruce Sutter	.70	.35	.20
11	Gorman Thomas	.40	.20	.12
12	Darrell Porter	.30	.15	.09
13	Roy Smalley	.30	.15	.09
14	Steve Carlton	1.75	.90	.50
15	Jim Palmer	1.50	.70	.45
16	Bob Bailor	.30	.15	.09
17	Jason Thompson	.30	.15	.09
18	Graig Nettles	.80	.40	.25
19	Ron Cey	.50	.25	.15
20	Nolan Ryan	1.75	.90	.50
21	Ellis Valentine	.30	.15	.09
22	Larry Hisle	.30	.15	.09
23	Dave Parker	.90	.45	.25
24	Eddie Murray	2.50	1.25	.70
25	Willie Stargell	1.75	.90	.50
26	Reggie Jackson	2.50	1.25	.70
27	Carl Yastrzemski	3.50	1.75	1.00
28	Andre Thornton	.40	.20	.12
29	Davey Lopes	.40	.20	.12
30	Ken Singleton	.40	.20	.12
31	Steve Garvey	2.50	1.25	.70
32	Dave Winfield	2.50	1.25	.70
33	Steve Kemp	.40	.20	.12
34	Claudell Washington	.40	.20	.12
35	Pete Rose	6.50	3.25	2.00
36	Cesar Cedeno	.40	.20	.12
37	John Stearns	.30	.15	.09
38	Lee Mazzilli	.30	.15	.09
39	Larry Bowa	.40	.20	.12
40	Fred Lynn	.80	.40	.25
41	Carlton Fisk	.90	.45	.25
42	Vida Blue	.50	.25	.15
43	Keith Hernandez	1.25	.60	.40

		NR MT	EX	VG
44	Jim Rice	1.75	.90	.50
45	Ted Simmons	.80	.40	.25
46	Chet Lemon	.30	.15	.09
47	Fergie Jenkins	.50	.25	.15
48	Gary Matthews	.40	.20	.12
49	Tom Seaver	2.50	1.25	.70
50	George Foster	.70	.35	.20
51	Phil Niekro	1.25	.60	.40
52	Johnny Bench	2.50	1.25	.70
53	Buddy Bell	.50	.25	.15
54	Lance Parrish	.90	.45	.25
55	Joaquin Andujar	.30	.15	.09
56	Don Baylor	.50	.25	.15
57	Jack Clark	.80	.40	.25
58	J.R. Richard	.30	.15	.09
59	Bruce Bochte	.30	.15	.09
60	Rod Carew	2.50	1.25	.70

		MT	NR MT	EX
34	Frank White	.10	.05	.03
35	George Hendrick	.08	.04	.02
36	Reggie Smith	.10	.05	.03
37	Tug McGraw	.10	.05	.03
38	Tom Seaver	.50	.25	.13
39	Ken Singleton	.10	.05	.03
40	Fred Lynn	.20	.10	.05
41	Rich "Goose" Gossage	.20	.10	.05
42	Terry Puhl	.08	.04	.02
43	Larry Bowa	.10	.05	.03
44	Phil Garner	.08	.04	.02
45	Ron Guidry	.20	.10	.05
46	Lee Mazzilli	.08	.04	.02
47	Dave Kingman	.15	.08	.04
48	Carl Yastrzemski	.80	.40	.20
49	Rick Burleson	.08	.04	.02
50	Steve Carlton	.40	.20	.10
51	Alan Trammell	.30	.15	.08
52	Tommy John	.20	.10	.05
53	Paul Molitor	.20	.10	.05
54	Joe Charboneau	.08	.04	.02
55	Rick Langford	.08	.04	.02
56	Bruce Sutter	.10	.05	.03
57	Robin Yount	.35	.20	.09
58	Steve Stone	.08	.04	.02
59	Larry Gura	.08	.04	.02
60	Mike Flanagan	.10	.05	.03
61	Bob Horner	.15	.08	.04
62	Bruce Bochte	.08	.04	.02
63	Pete Rose	1.00	.50	.25
64	Buddy Bell	.15	.08	.04
65	Johnny Bench	.60	.30	.15
66	Mike Hargrove	.08	.04	.02

1981 Kellogg's

"Bigger" is the word to best describe Kellogg's 1981 card set. Not only were the cards themselves larger than ever before (or since) at 2-1/2" by 3-1/2", but the size of the set was increased to 66, the largest since the 75-card issues of 1970-1971. The '81 Kellogg's set was available only as complete sets by mail. It is thought that the wider format of the 1981s may help prevent the problems of curling and cracking from which other years of Kellogg's issues suffer.

		MT	NR MT	EX
Complete Set:		8.00	4.00	2.00
Common Player:		.08	.04	.02
1	George Foster	.15	.08	.04
2	Jim Palmer	.30	.15	.08
3	Reggie Jackson	.60	.30	.15
4	Al Oliver	.15	.08	.04
5	Mike Schmidt	.70	.35	.20
6	Nolan Ryan	.40	.20	.10
7	Bucky Dent	.10	.05	.03
8	George Brett	.70	.35	.20
9	Jim Rice	.35	.20	.09
10	Steve Garvey	.40	.20	.10
11	Willie Stargell	.30	.15	.08
12	Phil Niekro	.25	.13	.06
13	Dave Parker	.20	.10	.05
14	Cesar Cedeno	.10	.05	.03
15	Don Baylor	.10	.05	.03
16	J.R. Richard	.08	.04	.02
17	Tony Perez	.15	.08	.04
18	Eddie Murray	.60	.30	.15
19	Chet Lemon	.08	.04	.02
20	Ben Oglivie	.08	.04	.02
21	Dave Winfield	.50	.25	.13
22	Joe Morgan	.20	.10	.05
23	Vida Blue	.10	.05	.03
24	Willie Wilson	.15	.08	.04
25	Steve Henderson	.08	.04	.02
26	Rod Carew	.50	.25	.13
27	Garry Templeton	.08	.04	.02
28	Dave Concepcion	.10	.05	.03
29	Davey Lopes	.08	.04	.02
30	Ken Landreaux	.08	.04	.02
31	Keith Hernandez	.40	.20	.10
32	Cecil Cooper	.10	.05	.03
33	Rickey Henderson	.60	.30	.15

1982 Kellogg's

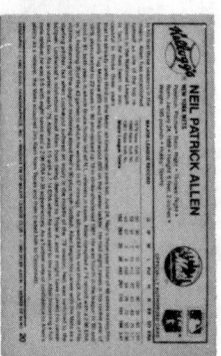

For the second straight year in 1982, Kellogg's cards were not inserted into cereal boxes, but had to be obtained by sending cash and box tops to the company for complete sets. The '82 cards were downsized both in number of cards in the set - 64 - and in physical dimensions, 2-1/8" by 3-1/4".

		MT	NR MT	EX
Complete Set:		12.00	6.00	3.00
Common Player:		.12	.06	.03
1	Richie Zisk	.12	.06	.03
2	Bill Buckner	.12	.06	.03
3	George Brett	.90	.45	.25
4	Rickey Henderson	.80	.40	.20
5	Jack Morris	.30	.15	.08
6	Ozzie Smith	.25	.13	.06
7	Rollie Fingers	.25	.13	.06
8	Tom Seaver	.50	.25	.13
9	Fernando Valenzuela	.60	.30	.15
10	Hubie Brooks	.12	.06	.03
11	Nolan Ryan	.50	.25	.13
12	Dave Winfield	.60	.30	.15
13	Bob Horner	.20	.10	.05
14	Reggie Jackson	.90	.45	.25
15	Burt Hooton	.12	.06	.03
16	Mike Schmidt	.90	.45	.25
17	Bruce Sutter	.20	.10	.05
18	Pete Rose	1.50	.70	.40
19	Dave Kingman	.20	.10	.05
20	Neil Allen	.12	.06	.03
21	Don Sutton	.25	.13	.06

		MT	NR MT	EX
22	Dave Concepcion	.20	.10	.05
23	Keith Hernandez	.50	.25	.13
24	Gary Carter	.70	.35	.20
25	Carlton Fisk	.30	.15	.08
26	Ron Guidry	.25	.13	.06
27	Steve Carlton	.50	.25	.13
28	Robin Yount	.40	.20	.10
29	John Castino	.12	.06	.03
30	Johnny Bench	.80	.40	.20
31	Bob Knepper	.12	.06	.03
32	Rich "Goose" Gossage	.20	.10	.05
33	Buddy Bell	.20	.10	.05
34	Art Howe	.12	.06	.03
35	Tony Armas	.12	.06	.03
36	Phil Niekro	.30	.15	.08
37	Len Barker	.12	.06	.03
38	Bobby Grich	.20	.10	.05
39	Steve Kemp	.12	.06	.03
40	Kirk Gibson	.35	.20	.09
41	Carney Lansford	.20	.10	.05
42	Jim Palmer	.40	.20	.10
43	Carl Yastrzemski	1.00	.50	.25
44	Rick Burleson	.12	.06	.03
45	Dwight Evans	.25	.13	.06
46	Ron Cey	.20	.10	.05
47	Steve Garvey	.70	.35	.20
48	Dave Parker	.30	.15	.08
49	Mike Easler	.12	.06	.03
50	Dusty Baker	.12	.06	.03
51	Rod Carew	.70	.35	.20
52	Chris Chambliss	.12	.06	.03
53	Tim Raines	.70	.35	.20
54	Chet Lemon	.12	.06	.03
55	Bill Madlock	.20	.10	.05
56	George Foster	.20	.10	.05
57	Dwayne Murphy	.12	.06	.03
58	Ken Singleton	.20	.10	.05
59	Mike Norris	.12	.06	.03
60	Cecil Cooper	.20	.10	.05
61	Al Oliver	.20	.10	.05
62	Willie Wilson	.25	.13	.06
63	Vida Blue	.20	.10	.05
64	Eddie Murray	.80	.40	.20

1983 Kellogg's

In its 14th and final year of baseball card issue, Kellogg's returned to the policy of inserting single cards into cereal boxes, as well as offering complete sets by a mail-in box top redemption offer. The 3-D cards themselves returned to a narrow - 1-7/8" by 3-1/4" format, while the set size was reduced to 60 cards.

		MT	NR MT	EX
Complete Set:		12.00	9.00	4.75
Common Player:		.10	.08	.04
1	Rod Carew	.50	.40	.20
2	Rollie Fingers	.20	.15	.08
3	Reggie Jackson	.50	.40	.20
4	George Brett	.70	.50	.30
5	Hal McRae	.15	.11	.06
6	Pete Rose	1.25	.90	.50
7	Fernando Valenzuela	.35	.25	.14
8	Rickey Henderson	.60	.45	.25
9	Carl Yastrzemski	.70	.50	.30
10	Rich "Goose" Gossage	.20	.15	.08

		MT	NR MT	EX
11	Eddie Murray	.50	.40	.20
12	Buddy Bell	.15	.11	.06
13	Jim Rice	.40	.30	.15
14	Robin Yount	.35	.25	.14
15	Dave Winfield	.50	.40	.20
16	Harold Baines	.20	.15	.08
17	Garry Templeton	.15	.11	.06
18	Bill Madlock	.25	.20	.10
19	Pete Vuckovich	.10	.08	.04
20	Pedro Guerrero	.25	.20	.10
21	Ozzie Smith	.20	.15	.08
22	George Foster	.20	.15	.08
23	Willie Wilson	.20	.15	.08
24	Johnny Ray	.15	.11	.06
25	George Hendrick	.10	.08	.04
26	Andre Thornton	.10	.08	.04
27	Leon Durham	.10	.08	.04
28	Cecil Cooper	.15	.11	.06
29	Don Baylor	.15	.11	.06
30	Lonnie Smith	.10	.08	.04
31	Nolan Ryan	.40	.30	.15
32	Dan Quiesenberry (Quisenberry)	.15	.11	.06
33	Len Barker	.10	.08	.04
34	Neil Allen	.10	.08	.04
35	Jack Morris	.30	.25	.12
36	Dave Stieb	.15	.11	.06
37	Bruce Sutter	.15	.11	.06
38	Jim Sundberg	.10	.08	.04
39	Jim Palmer	.35	.25	.14
40	Lance Parrish	.30	.25	.12
41	Floyd Bannister	.15	.11	.06
42	Larry Gura	.10	.08	.04
43	Britt Burns	.10	.08	.04
44	Toby Harrah	.10	.08	.04
45	Steve Carlton	.40	.30	.15
46	Greg Minton	.10	.08	.04
47	Gorman Thomas	.15	.11	.06
48	Jack Clark	.25	.20	.10
49	Keith Hernandez	.40	.30	.15
50	Greg Luzinski	.15	.11	.06
51	Fred Lynn	.25	.20	.10
52	Dale Murphy	.70	.50	.30
53	Kent Hrbek	.35	.25	.14
54	Bob Horner	.15	.11	.06
55	Gary Carter	.50	.40	.20
56	Carlton Fisk	.25	.20	.10
57	Dave Concepcion	.15	.11	.06
58	Mike Schmidt	.70	.50	.30
59	Bill Buckner	.15	.11	.06
60	Bobby Grich	.15	.11	.06

1988 Kenner Starting Lineup

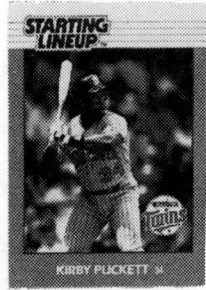
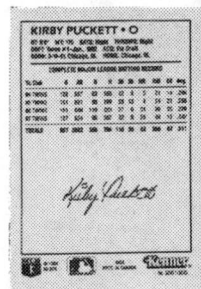

This massive three-sport set was distributed in conjunction with Kenner's Starting Lineup sports figurines, one card per statue. Cards were not sold separately. Baseball, football and basketball stars are included in the lineup of full-color figurines, with 123 cards devoted to baseball. Individual major league team assortments include one to seven players per team. The figurines are mildly reminiscent of the 1950s Hartland Statues, but Kenner's version features smaller (4" to 6") figures and a more extensive catalog which includes athletes other than baseball players. The Starting Lineup cards feature action photos framed in red and white, with the

"Starting Lineup" logo in the upper left corner and the player's name printed along the bottom border. Colorful team logos are superimposed in the lower right corner of the player photos. As an added incentive to collectors, five UPC codes from the sport statue packages could be redeemed for an autographed baseball. The values in the checklist that follows include both the statue and card for the 123 baseball players in the set. Several players which were included in the package's checklist were pulled before production.

		MT	NR MT	EX
Complete Set:		1300.00	975.00	520.00
Common Player:		9.00	6.75	3.50
(1)	Alan Ashby	13.00	9.75	5.25
(2)	Harold Baines	10.00	7.50	4.00
(3)	Kevin Bass	13.00	9.75	5.25
(4)	Steve Bedrosian	10.00	7.50	4.00
(5)	Buddy Bell	10.00	7.50	4.00
(6)	George Bell	12.00	9.00	4.75
(7)	Mike Boddicker	10.00	7.50	4.00
(8)	Wade Boggs	13.00	9.75	5.25
(9)	Barry Bonds	13.00	9.75	5.25
(10)	Bobby Bonilla	13.00	9.75	5.25
(11)	Sid Bream	20.00	15.00	8.00
(12)	George Brett	12.00	9.00	4.75
(13)	Chris Brown	13.00	9.75	5.25
(14)	Tom Brunansky	12.00	9.00	4.75
(15)	Ellis Burks	25.00	18.50	10.00
(16)	Jose Canseco	40.00	30.00	16.00
(17)	Gary Carter	9.00	6.75	3.50
(18)	Joe Carter	12.00	9.00	4.75
(19)	Jack Clark	20.00	15.00	8.00
(20)	Will Clark	13.00	9.75	5.25
(21)	Roger Clemens	12.00	9.00	4.75
(22)	Vince Coleman	10.00	7.50	4.00
(23)	Kal Daniels	12.00	9.00	4.75
(24)	Alvin Davis	10.00	7.50	4.00
(25)	Eric Davis	12.00	9.00	4.75
(26)	Glenn Davis	13.00	9.75	5.25
(27)	Jody Davis	12.00	9.00	4.75
(28)	Andre Dawson	10.00	7.50	4.00
(29)	Rob Deer	10.00	7.50	4.00
(30)	Brian Downing	10.00	7.50	4.00
(31)	Mike Dunne	10.00	7.50	4.00
(32)	Shawon Dunston	20.00	15.00	8.00
(33)	Leon Durham	9.00	6.75	3.50
(34)	Len Dykstra	12.00	9.00	4.75
(35)	Dwight Evans	12.00	9.00	4.75
(36)	Carlton Fisk	12.00	9.00	4.75
(37)	John Franco	12.00	9.00	4.75
(38)	Julio Franco	12.00	9.00	4.75
(39)	Gary Gaetti	10.00	7.50	4.00
(40)	Dwight Gooden	12.00	9.00	4.75
(41)	Ken Griffey	12.00	9.00	4.75
(42)	Pedro Guerrero	10.00	7.50	4.00
(43)	Ozzie Guillen	12.00	9.00	4.75
(44)	Tony Gwynn	10.00	7.50	4.00
(45)	Mel Hall	12.00	9.00	4.75
(46)	Billy Hatcher	12.00	9.00	4.75
(47)	Von Hayes	13.00	9.75	5.25
(48)	Rickey Henderson	10.00	7.50	4.00
(49)	Keith Hernandez	12.00	9.00	4.75
(50)	Willie Hernandez	13.00	9.75	5.25
(51)	Tom Herr	12.00	9.00	4.75
(52)	Ted Higuera	13.00	9.75	5.25
(53)	Charlie Hough	12.00	9.00	4.75
(54)	Kent Hrbek	10.00	7.50	4.00
(55)	Pete Incaviglia	10.00	7.50	4.00
(56)	Howard Johnson	13.00	9.75	5.25
(57)	Wally Joyner	12.00	9.00	4.75
(58)	Terry Kennedy	12.00	9.00	4.75
(59)	John Kruk	13.00	9.75	5.25
(60)	Mark Langston	13.00	9.75	5.25
(61)	Carney Lansford	20.00	15.00	8.00
(62)	Jeffrey Leonard	9.00	6.75	3.50
(63)	Fred Lynn	10.00	7.50	4.00
(64)	Candy Maldonado	13.00	9.75	5.25
(65)	Mike Marshall	20.00	15.00	8.00
(66)	Don Mattingly	13.00	9.75	5.25
(67)	Willie McGee	10.00	7.50	4.00
(68)	Mark McGwire	25.00	18.50	10.00
(69)	Kevin McReynolds	13.00	9.75	5.25
(70)	Paul Molitor	10.00	7.50	4.00
(71)	Donnie Moore	13.00	9.75	5.25
(72)	Jack Morris	12.00	9.00	4.75
(73)	Dale Murphy	10.00	7.50	4.00
(74)	Eddie Murray	10.00	7.50	4.00

		MT	NR MT	EX
(75)	Matt Nokes	12.00	9.00	4.75
(76)	Pete O'Brien	12.00	9.00	4.75
(77)	Ken Oberkfell	12.00	9.00	4.75
(78)	Dave Parker	20.00	15.00	8.00
(79)	Larry Parrish	10.00	7.50	4.00
(80)	Ken Phelps	20.00	15.00	8.00
(81)	Jim Presley	10.00	7.50	4.00
(82)	Kirby Puckett	12.00	9.00	4.75
(83)	Dan Quisenberry	10.00	7.50	4.00
(84)	Tim Raines	12.00	9.00	4.75
(85)	Willie Randolph	10.00	7.50	4.00
(86)	Shane Rawley	12.00	9.00	4.75
(87)	Jeff Reardon	12.00	9.00	4.75
(88)	Gary Redus	13.00	9.75	5.25
(89)	Rick Reuschel	12.00	9.00	4.75
(90)	Jim Rice	10.00	7.50	4.00
(91)	Dave Righetti	10.00	7.50	4.00
(92)	Cal Ripken	12.00	9.00	4.75
(93)	Pete Rose	20.00	15.00	8.00
(94)	Nolan Ryan	25.00	18.50	10.00
(95)	Bret Saberhagen	10.00	7.50	4.00
(96)	Juan Samuel	10.00	7.50	4.00
(97)	Ryne Sandberg	10.00	7.50	4.00
(98)	Benito Santiago	12.00	9.00	4.75
(99)	Steve Sax	10.00	7.50	4.00
(100)	Mike Schmidt	12.00	9.00	4.75
(101)	Mike Scott	10.00	7.50	4.00
(102)	Kevin Seitzer	20.00	15.00	8.00
(103)	Ruben Sierra	13.00	9.75	5.25
(104)	Ozzie Smith	10.00	7.50	4.00
(105)	Zane Smith	12.00	9.00	4.75
(106)	Cory Snyder	12.00	9.00	4.75
(107)	Darryl Strawberry	10.00	7.50	4.00
(108)	Franklin Stubbs	20.00	15.00	8.00
(109)	B.J. Surhoff	12.00	9.00	4.75
(110)	Rick Sutcliffe	12.00	9.00	4.75
(111)	Pat Tabler	12.00	9.00	4.75
(112)	Danny Tartabull	12.00	9.00	4.75
(113)	Alan Trammell	12.00	9.00	4.75
(114)	Fernando Valenzuela	10.00	7.50	4.00
(115)	Andy Van Slyke	18.00	13.50	7.25
(116)	Frank Viola	12.00	9.00	4.75
(117)	Ozzie Virgil	10.00	7.50	4.00
(118)	Greg Walker	10.00	7.50	4.00
(119)	Lou Whitaker	10.00	7.50	4.00
(120)	Devon White	12.00	9.00	4.75
(121)	Dave Winfield	10.00	7.50	4.00
(122)	Mike Witt	10.00	7.50	4.00
(123)	Todd Worrell	13.00	9.75	5.25
(124)	Robin Yount	10.00	7.50	4.00

1989 Kenner
Starting Lineup

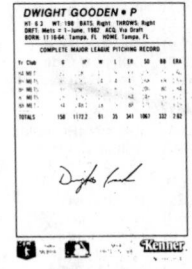

Kenner returned in 1989 with another set of sports figurines and accompanying trading cards. As in the previous year, the figurines were sold individually with one card packaged with each figure. No cards were sold separately. The cards have the "Starting Lineup" logo in the upper left, while the words "1989 Edition" appear in the lower right corner. The values listed below include both the figure and the card. The values are based on relative scarcity, resulting in some minor stars and common players being priced higher than superstars, whose cards and figures were produced in much greater numbers.

		MT	NR MT	EX
Complete Set:		1100.00	825.00	450.00
Common Player:		6.00	4.50	2.50
(1)	Ozzie Smith	8.00	6.00	3.25
(2)	Tom Brunansky	9.00	6.75	3.50
(3)	Vince Coleman	8.00	6.00	3.25
(4)	Willie McGee	8.00	6.00	3.25
(5)	Todd Worrell	7.00	5.25	2.75
(6)	Tony Pena	9.00	6.75	3.50
(7)	Terry Pendleton	9.00	6.75	3.50
(8)	Pedro Guerrero	10.00	7.50	4.00
(9)	Mike Schmidt	10.00	7.50	4.00
(10)	Von Hayes	6.00	4.50	2.50
(11)	Juan Samuel	7.00	5.25	2.75
(12)	Steve Bedrosian	7.00	5.25	2.75
(13)	Milt Thompson	7.00	5.25	2.75
(14)	Phil Bradley	7.00	5.25	2.75
(15)	Chris James	8.00	6.00	3.25
(16)	Dale Murphy	10.00	7.50	4.00
(17)	Zane Smith	6.00	4.50	2.50
(18)	Gerald Perry	8.00	6.00	3.25
(19)	Dion James	8.00	6.00	3.25
(20)	Albert Hall	6.00	4.50	2.50
(21)	Bruce Sutter	7.00	5.25	2.75
(22)	Ron Gant	8.00	6.00	3.25
(23)	Tony Gwynn	9.00	6.75	3.50
(24)	Benito Santiago	8.00	6.00	3.25
(25)	John Kruk	7.00	5.25	2.75
(26)	Marvell Wynne	7.00	5.25	2.75
(27)	Roberto Alomar	9.00	6.75	3.50
(28)	Mark Davis	8.00	6.00	3.25
(29)	Ryne Sandberg	8.00	6.00	3.25
(30)	Andre Dawson	8.00	6.00	3.25
(31)	Greg Maddux	9.00	6.75	3.50
(32)	Rick Sutcliffe	7.00	5.25	2.75
(33)	Mark Grace	10.00	7.50	4.00
(34)	Shawon Dunston	6.00	4.50	2.50
(35)	Damon Berryhill	7.00	5.25	2.75
(36)	Barry Bonds	8.00	6.00	3.25
(37)	Andy Van Slyke	7.00	5.25	2.75
(38)	Bob Walk	7.00	5.25	2.75
(39)	Bobby Bonilla	7.00	5.25	2.75
(40)	Mike LaValliere	7.00	5.25	2.75
(41)	Doug Drabek	8.00	6.00	3.25
(42)	Jose Lind	8.00	6.00	3.25
(43)	Fernando Valenzuela	7.00	5.25	2.75
(44)	Mike Marshall	6.00	4.50	2.50
(45)	Orel Hershiser	10.00	7.50	4.00
(46)	John Shelby	6.00	4.50	2.50
(47)	Kirk Gibson	8.00	6.00	3.25
(48)	Mike Scioscia	7.00	5.25	2.75
(49)	Eric Davis	10.00	7.50	4.00
(50)	Kal Daniels	8.00	6.00	3.25
(51)	John Franco	8.00	6.00	3.25
(52)	Danny Jackson	7.00	5.25	2.75
(53)	Bo Diaz	7.00	5.25	2.75
(54)	Barry Larkin	9.00	6.75	3.50
(55)	Jeff Treadway	8.00	6.00	3.25
(56)	Chris Sabo	9.00	6.75	3.50
(57)	Darryl Strawberry	10.00	7.50	4.00
(58)	Keith Hernandez	8.00	6.00	3.25
(59)	Gary Carter	8.00	6.00	3.25
(60)	Dwight Gooden	12.00	9.00	4.75
(61)	Len Dykstra	6.00	4.50	2.50
(62)	David Cone	9.00	6.75	3.50
(63)	Kevin Elster	8.00	6.00	3.25
(64)	Kevin McReynolds	8.00	6.00	3.25
(65)	Randy Myers	8.00	6.00	3.25
(66)	Gregg Jefferies	18.00	13.50	7.25
(67)	Mike Scott	7.00	5.25	2.75
(68)	Glenn Davis	8.00	6.00	3.25
(69)	Kevin Bass	6.00	4.50	2.50
(70)	Dave Smith	6.00	4.50	2.50
(71)	Bill Doran	8.00	6.00	3.25
(72)	Gerald Young	6.00	4.50	2.50
(73)	Billy Hatcher	6.00	4.50	2.50
(74)	Will Clark	13.00	9.75	5.25
(75)	Candy Maldonado	6.00	4.50	2.50
(76)	Brett Butler	8.00	6.00	3.25
(77)	Kevin Mitchell	12.00	9.00	4.75
(78)	Jose Uribe	7.00	5.25	2.75
(79)	Robby Thompson	8.00	6.00	3.25
(80)	Tim Raines	9.00	6.75	3.50
(81)	Joe Carter	8.00	6.00	3.25
(82)	Mel Hall	7.00	5.25	2.75
(83)	Cory Snyder	8.00	6.00	3.25
(84)	Brook Jacoby	8.00	6.00	3.25
(85)	Greg Swindell	10.00	7.50	4.00
(86)	Doug Jones	8.00	6.00	3.25
(87)	Jack Morris	8.00	6.00	3.25
(88)	Alan Trammell	9.00	6.75	3.50
(89)	Matt Nokes	9.00	6.75	3.50
90	Luis Salazar	6.00	4.50	2.50
(91)	Chet Lemon	6.00	4.50	2.50
(92)	Lou Whitaker	8.00	6.00	3.25
(93)	Tom Brookens	6.00	4.50	2.50
(94)	Mike Henneman	8.00	6.00	3.25
(95)	Jose Canseco	18.00	13.50	7.25
(96)	Mark McGwire	13.00	9.75	5.25
(97)	Dave Parker	8.00	6.00	3.25
(98)	Dave Stewart	9.00	6.75	3.50
(99)	Bob Welch	8.00	6.00	3.25
(100)	Terry Steinbach	10.00	7.50	4.00
(101)	Carney Lansford	7.00	5.25	2.75
(102)	Dennis Eckersley	8.00	6.00	3.25
(103)	Walt Weiss	9.00	6.75	3.50
(104)	George Brett	10.00	7.50	4.00
105	Bret Saberhagen	10.00	7.50	4.00
(106)	Danny Tartabull	8.00	6.00	3.25
(107)	Kevin Seitzer	13.00	9.75	5.25
(108)	Bo Jackson	18.00	13.50	7.25
(109)	Kurt Stillwell	8.00	6.00	3.25
(110)	Pat Tabler	8.00	6.00	3.25
(111)	Mark Gubicza	9.00	6.75	3.50
(112)	Robin Yount	9.00	6.75	3.50
(113)	Rob Deer	7.00	5.25	2.75
(114)	Paul Molitor	8.00	6.00	3.25
(115)	Ted Higuera	8.00	6.00	3.25
(116)	B.J. Surhoff	8.00	6.00	3.25
(117)	Dan Plesac	8.00	6.00	3.25
(118)	Glenn Braggs	8.00	6.00	3.25
(119)	Wade Boggs	13.00	9.75	5.25
(120)	Roger Clemens	13.00	9.75	5.25
(121)	Jim Rice	8.00	6.00	3.25
(122)	Ellis Burks	10.00	7.50	4.00
(123)	Mike Greenwell	10.00	7.50	4.00
(124)	Lee Smith	7.00	5.25	2.75
(125)	Marty Barrett	7.00	5.25	2.75
(126)	Wally Joyner	10.00	7.50	4.00
(127)	Mike Witt	6.00	4.50	2.50
(128)	Devon White	8.00	6.00	3.25
(129)	Johnny Ray	7.00	5.25	2.75
(130)	Chili Davis	7.00	5.25	2.75
(131)	Jack Howell	7.00	5.25	2.75
(132)	Dick Schofield	7.00	5.25	2.75
(133)	Rickey Henderson	10.00	7.50	4.00
(134)	Don Mattingly	13.00	9.75	5.25
(135)	Dave Winfield	9.00	6.75	3.50
(136)	Dave Righetti	9.00	6.75	3.50
(137)	Mike Pagliarulo	7.00	5.25	2.75
(138)	Don Slaught	6.00	4.50	2.50
(139)	Al Leiter	6.00	4.50	2.50
(140)	George Bell	9.00	6.75	3.50
(141)	Brady Anderson	8.00	6.00	3.25
(142)	Cal Ripken	9.00	6.75	3.50
(143)	Larry Sheets	6.00	4.50	2.50
(144)	Pete Stanicek	6.00	4.50	2.50
(145)	Kirby Puckett	10.00	7.50	4.00
(146)	Kent Hrbek	8.00	6.00	3.25
(147)	Gary Gaetti	8.00	6.00	3.25
(148)	Jeff Reardon	7.00	5.25	2.75
(149)	Dan Gladden	7.00	5.25	2.75
(150)	Frank Viola	7.00	5.25	2.75
(151)	Tim Laudner	6.00	4.50	2.50
(152)	Alvin Davis	8.00	6.00	3.25
(153)	Mark Langston	8.00	6.00	3.25
(154)	Harold Reynolds	8.00	6.00	3.25
(155)	Rey Quinones	6.00	4.50	2.50
(156)	Harold Baines	8.00	6.00	3.25
(157)	Ozzie Guillen	6.00	4.50	2.50
(158)	Greg Walker	6.00	4.50	2.50
(159)	Ivan Calderon	7.00	5.25	2.75
(160)	Melido Perez	7.00	5.25	2.75
(161)	Bobby Thigpen	9.00	6.75	3.50
(162)	Dan Pasqua	8.00	6.00	3.25
(163)	Pete Incaviglia	8.00	6.00	3.25
(164)	Ruben Sierra	12.00	9.00	4.75
(165)	Scott Fletcher	6.00	4.50	2.50
(166)	Steve Buechele	6.00	4.50	2.50
(167)	Jeff Russell	7.00	5.25	2.75

1989 Kenner Starting Lineup Baseball Greats

The "Baseball Greats" series of figurines and trading cards was an addition to the Kenner "Starting Lineup" series for 1989. The series features baseball greats of the past, and were packaged two figurines

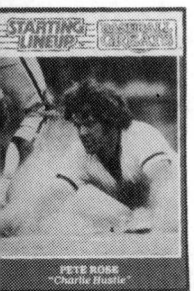

PETE ROSE · OF/1B

PETE ROSE
"Charlie Hustle"

and two collector cards per package. The collector cards that accompany the figures feature an original action photo of the player done in a sepia-tone to enhance the historic nature of the set. The Starting Lineup logo and "Baseball Greats' heading appear at the top of the card. The player's name and a descriptive nickname, such as "Sultan of Swat" appear below the photo. The backs of the cards carry a blue-and-white color scheme and include career stats. The values listed below include both the figure and the card.

	MT	NR MT	EX
Complete Set:	200.00	150.00	80.00
Common Player:	15.00	11.00	6.00
(1) Willie Mays/ Willie McCovey	15.00	11.00	6.00
(2) Johnny Bench/ Pete Rose	15.00	11.00	6.00
(3) Ernie Banks/ Billy Williams	15.00	11.00	6.00
(4) Stan Musial/ Bob Gibson	25.00	20.00	10.00
(5) Roberto Clemente/ Willie Stargell	15.00	11.00	6.00
(6) Babe Ruth/ Lou Gehrig	18.00	13.50	7.25
(7) Hank Aaron/ Eddie Mathews	25.00	20.00	10.00
(8) Mickey Mantle/ Joe DiMaggio	18.00	13.50	7.25
(9) Don Drysdale/ Reggie Jackson	18.00	13.50	7.25
(10) Carl Yastrzemski/ Hank Aaron	20.00	15.00	8.00

1990 Kenner Starting Lineup

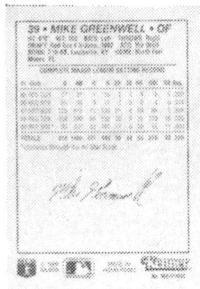

39 · MIKE GREENWELL · OF

MIKE GREENWELL
STARTING LINEUP

Kenner introduced special bonus rookie year cards with its regular card and statue in 1990. The card follow designs much like the Kenner cards of 1988 and 1989. The values are based on relative scarcity. Esasky, Backman and Pettis Kenners wer pulled when the players switched teams, thus making them rare. Five variations of figures are included in the 1990 set.

	MT	NR MT	EX
Complete Set:	600.00	450.00	250.00
Common Player:	6.00	4.50	2.50
(1a) Will Clark (bat held in one hand)	20.00	15.00	8.00
(1b) Will Clark (swinging)	20.00	15.00	8.00
(2) Kevin Mitchell	12.00	9.00	4.75

		MT	NR MT	EX
(3)	Steve Bedrosian	6.00	4.50	2.50
(4)	Rick Reuschel	8.00	6.00	3.25
(5)	Orel Hershiser	10.00	7.50	4.00
(6)	Eddie Murray	6.00	4.50	2.50
(7)	Willie Randolph	6.00	4.50	2.50
(8)	Kirk Gibson	6.00	4.50	2.50
(9)	Eric Davis	7.00	5.25	2.75
(10)	Barry Larkin	10.00	7.50	4.00
(11)	Chris Sabo	6.00	4.50	2.50
(12)	Paul O'Neill	8.00	6.00	3.25
(13)	Todd Benzinger	10.00	7.50	4.00
(14)	Rob Dibble	10.00	7.50	4.00
(15)	Barry Bonds	18.00	13.50	7.25
(16)	Andy Van Slyke	7.00	5.25	2.75
(17)	Bobby Bonilla	8.00	6.00	3.25
(18)	John Smiley	8.00	6.00	3.25
(19)	Von Hayes	7.00	5.25	2.75
(20)	Ricky Jordan	8.00	6.00	3.25
(21)	Tom Herr	6.00	4.50	2.50
(22)	Len Dykstra	15.00	11.00	6.00
(23a)	Darryl Strawberry (standing at bat)	18.00	13.50	7.25
(23b)	Darryl Strawberry (fielding)	18.00	13.50	7.25
(24)	Dwight Gooden	6.00	4.50	2.50
(25)	Kevin McReynolds	7.00	5.25	2.75
(26)	Gregg Jefferies	10.00	7.50	4.00
(27)	Ron Darling	7.00	5.25	2.75
(28)	Howard Johnson	10.00	7.50	4.00
(29)	Juan Samuel	10.00	7.50	4.00
(30)	Frank Viola	10.00	7.50	4.00
(31)	Ozzie Smith	6.00	4.50	2.50
(32)	Vince Coleman	6.00	4.50	2.50
(33)	Pedro Guerrero	7.00	5.25	2.75
(34)	Jose Oquendo	8.00	6.00	3.25
(35)	Joe Magrane	7.00	5.25	2.75
(36)	Mike Scott	10.00	7.50	4.00
(37)	Andres Gallarraga	12.00	9.00	4.75
(38)	Ryne Sandberg	10.00	7.50	4.00
(39)	Andre Dawson	7.00	5.25	2.75
(40)	Greg Maddux	10.00	7.50	4.00
(41)	Rick Sutcliffe	8.00	6.00	3.25
(42a)	Mark Grace (standing at bat)	20.00	15.00	8.00
(42b)	Mark Grace (swinging)	20.00	15.00	8.00
(43)	Damon Berryhill	8.00	6.00	3.25
(44)	Mitch Williams	10.00	7.50	4.00
(45)	Jerome Walton	15.00	11.00	6.00
(46)	Jose Canseco	18.00	13.50	7.25
(47)	Mark McGwire	10.00	7.50	4.00
(48)	Dave Stewart	10.00	7.50	4.00
(49)	Dennis Eckersley	10.00	7.50	4.00
(50)	Dave Henderson	8.00	6.00	3.25
(51)	Rickey Henderson	15.00	11.00	6.00
(52)	Kirby Puckett	6.00	4.50	2.50
(53)	Kent Hrbek	7.00	5.25	2.75
(54)	Gary Gaetti	7.00	5.25	2.75
(55)	Allan Anderson	7.00	5.25	2.75
(56)	Wally Backman	40.00	30.00	15.00
(57)	Wade Boggs	6.00	4.50	2.50
(58)	Roger Clemens	6.00	4.50	2.50
(59)	Ellis Burks	7.00	5.25	2.75
(60)	Mike Greenwell	6.00	4.50	2.50
(61)	Jody Reed	10.00	7.50	4.00
(62)	Nick Esasky	40.00	30.00	15.00
(63a)	Don Mattingly (Bat held in one hand)	18.00	13.50	7.25
(63b)	Don Mattingly (Swinging)	18.00	13.50	7.25
(64)	Dave Winfield	7.00	5.25	2.75
(65)	Dave Righetti	12.00	9.00	4.75
(66)	Steve Sax	6.00	4.50	2.50
(67)	Roberto Kelly	10.00	7.50	4.00
(68)	Jesse Barfield	10.00	7.50	4.00
(69)	Cal Ripken	6.00	4.50	2.50
(70)	Mickey Tettleton	6.00	4.50	2.50
(71)	Jeff Ballard	6.00	4.50	2.50
(72)	Ben McDonald	20.00	15.00	8.00
(73)	Robin Yount	10.00	7.50	4.00
(74)	Paul Molitor	6.00	4.50	2.50
(75)	Gary Sheffield	10.00	7.50	4.00
(76)	Chris Bosio	7.00	5.25	2.75
(77)	Alan Trammell	6.00	4.50	2.50
(78)	Matt Nokes	6.00	4.50	2.50
(79)	Gary Pettis	40.00	30.00	15.00
(80)	Lou Whitaker	6.00	4.50	2.50
(81a)	Ken Griffey, Jr. (sliding)	30.00	22.00	12.00
(81b)	Ken Griffey, Jr. (fielding)	25.00	18.00	10.00
(82)	Bo Jackson	15.00	11.00	6.00
(83)	Nolan Ryan	20.00	15.00	8.00
(84)	Fred McGriff	10.00	7.50	4.00
(85)	Jim Abbott	20.00	15.00	8.00
(86)	Sandy Alomar	15.00	7.50	4.00
(87)	Joe Carter	20.00	15.00	8.00

1988 King-B

Created by Mike Schechter Associates, the 1988 King-B set consists of 24 numbered discs that measure 2-3/4" in size. The cards were inserted in specially marked 7/16 ounce tubs of Jerky Stuff (shredded beef jerky). The card fronts feature full-color photos surrounded by a blue border. The King-B logo appears in the upper left portion of the disc. The disc backs are printed in blue on white stock and carry player personal and playing information. Team insignias have been airbrushed from the players' caps and jerseys.

		MT	NR MT	EX
Complete Set:		35.00	27.00	15.00
Common Player:		.75	.60	.30
1	Mike Schmidt	1.75	1.25	.70
2	Dale Murphy	1.75	1.25	.70
3	Kirby Puckett	1.50	1.25	.60
4	Ozzie Smith	1.00	.70	.40
5	Tony Gwynn	1.50	1.25	.60
6	Mark McGwire	2.50	2.00	1.00
7	George Brett	1.75	1.25	.70
8	Darryl Strawberry	1.75	1.25	.70
9	Wally Joyner	1.50	1.25	.60
10	Cory Snyder	1.00	.70	.40
11	Barry Bonds	1.00	.70	.40
12	Darrell Evans	.75	.60	.30
13	Mike Scott	.75	.60	.30
14	Andre Dawson	1.25	.90	.50
15	Don Mattingly	5.00	3.75	2.00
16	Candy Maldonado	.75	.60	.30
17	Alvin Davis	1.00	.70	.40
18	Carlton Fisk	1.00	.70	.40
19	Fernando Valenzuela	1.00	.70	.40
20	Roger Clemens	2.00	1.50	.80
21	Larry Parrish	.75	.60	.30
22	Eric Davis	2.00	1.50	.80
23	Paul Molitor	1.00	.70	.40
24	Cal Ripken, Jr.	1.75	1.25	.70

1989 King-B

The second King-B baseball card set created by Mike Schechter Associates also consists of 24

circular baseball cards measuring 2-3/4" across. The cards were inserted into specially-marked tubs of "Jerky Stuff." The card fronts feature full-color photos bordered in red. The King-B logo appears in the upper left portion of the disc. Like the 1988 set, the team insignias have airbrushed from uniforms and caps. The backs are printed in red and display personal information and stats.

		MT	NR MT	EX
Complete Set:		30.00	22.00	12.00
Common Player:		.75	.60	.30
1	Kirk Gibson	1.00	.70	.40
2	Eddie Murray	1.00	.70	.40
3	Wade Boggs	2.25	1.75	.90
4	Mark McGwire	2.25	1.75	.90
5	Ryne Sandberg	1.75	1.25	.70
6	Ozzie Guillen	.75	.60	.30
7	Chris Sabo	1.25	.90	.50
8	Joe Carter	1.00	.70	.40
9	Alan Trammell	1.00	.70	.40
10	Nolan Ryan	2.50	2.00	1.00
11	Bo Jackson	2.50	2.00	1.00
12	Orel Hershiser	1.00	.70	.40
13	Robin Yount	1.50	1.25	.60
14	Frank Viola	1.00	.70	.40
15	Darryl Strawberry	1.50	1.25	.60
16	Dave Winfield	1.00	.70	.40
17	Jose Canseco	3.50	2.75	1.50
18	Von Hayes	.75	.60	.30
19	Andy Van Slyke	.75	.60	.30
20	Pedro Guerrero	1.00	.70	.40
21	Tony Gwynn	1.75	1.25	.70
22	Will Clark	2.50	2.00	1.00
23	Danny Jackson	.75	.60	.30
24	Pete Incaviglia	.75	.60	.30

1986 Kitty Clover Potato Chips Royals

Twenty players of the 1985 World's Champion Kansas City Royals were featured in a round card set inserted into packages of potato chips in the K.C. area. The 2-7/8" discs were similar to a handful of snack issues produced by Mike Schecter Associates in that team logos have been airbrushed off the players' caps, and the photos of some of the players can be found on other regional issues of 1986.

		MT	NR MT	EX
Complete Set:		20.00	15.00	8.00
Common Player:		.70	.50	.30
1	Lonnie Smith	.70	.50	.30
2	Buddy Biancalana	.70	.50	.30
3	Bret Saberhagen	1.75	1.25	.70
4	Hal McRae	.90	.70	.35
5	Onix Concepcion	.70	.50	.30

		MT	NR MT	EX
6	Jorge Orta	.70	.50	.30
7	Bud Black	.70	.50	.30
8	Dan Quisenberry	1.00	.70	.40
9	Dane Iorg	.70	.50	.30
10	Charlie Leibrandt	.80	.60	.30
11	Pat Sheridan	.70	.50	.30
12	John Wathan	.80	.60	.30
13	Frank White	1.00	.70	.40
14	Darryl Motley	.70	.50	.30
15	Willie Wilson	1.25	.90	.50
16	Danny Jackson	1.25	.90	.50
17	Steve Balboni	.80	.60	.30
18	Jim Sundberg	.70	.50	.30
19	Mark Gubicza	1.25	.90	.50
20	George Brett	3.25	2.50	1.25

		MT	NR MT	EX
33	Dave Winfield	.60	.45	.25
34	Pete Rose	1.25	.90	.50
35	Jose Canseco	2.00	1.50	.80
36	Glenn Davis	.35	.25	.14
37	Alvin Davis	.35	.25	.14
38	Steve Sax	.35	.25	.14
39	Pete Incaviglia	.70	.50	.30
40	Jeff Reardon	.35	.25	.14
41	Jesse Barfield	.35	.25	.14
42	Hubie Brooks	.20	.15	.08
43	George Bell	.50	.40	.20
44	Tony Gwynn	.75	.60	.30
45	Roger Clemens	1.00	.70	.40
46	Chili Davis	.20	.15	.08
47	Mike Witt	.20	.15	.08
48	Nolan Ryan	1.00	.70	.40

1987 Kraft

Kraft Foods, Inc. issued a 48-card set on specially marked packages of their Macaroni & Cheese Dinners. Titled "Home Plate Heroes," 24 two-card panels measuring 3-1/2" by 7-1/8" make up the set. Individual cards measure 2-1/4" by 3-1/2" and are numbered 1 through 48. The blank-backed cards feature fronts with full-color photos, although all team insignias have been erased. In conjunction with the card set, Kraft offered a contest to "Win A Day With A Major Leaguer." Mike Schecter Associates produced the set for Kraft. 120 different panel combinatons can be found.

		MT	NR MT	EX
Complete Set:		35.00	27.50	15.00
Common Player:		.20	.15	.08
1	Eddie Murray	.75	.60	.30
2	Dale Murphy	1.00	.70	.40
3	Cal Ripken	.75	.60	.30
4	Mike Scott	.35	.25	.14
5	Jim Rice	.50	.40	.20
6	Jody Davis	.20	.15	.08
7	Wade Boggs	1.50	1.25	.60
8	Ryne Sandberg	.50	.40	.20
9	Wally Joyner	1.50	1.25	.60
10	Eric Davis	1.25	.90	.50
11	Ozzie Guillen	.20	.15	.08
12	Tony Pena	.20	.15	.08
13	Harold Baines	.35	.25	.14
14	Johnny Ray	.20	.15	.08
15	Joe Carter	.35	.25	.14
16	Ozzie Smith	.35	.25	.14
17	Cory Snyder	.60	.45	.25
18	Vince Coleman	.35	.25	.14
19	Kirk Gibson	.50	.40	.20
20	Steve Garvey	.75	.60	.30
21	George Brett	1.00	.70	.40
22	John Tudor	.20	.15	.08
23	Robin Yount	.70	.50	.30
24	Von Hayes	.35	.25	.14
25	Kent Hrbek	.50	.40	.20
26	Darryl Strawberry	1.00	.70	.40
27	Kirby Puckett	.75	.60	.30
28	Ron Darling	.35	.25	.14
29	Don Mattingly	2.50	2.00	1.00
30	Mike Schmidt	1.00	.70	.40
31	Rickey Henderson	.75	.60	.30
32	Fernando Valenzuela	.50	.40	.20

1960 Lake To Lake Dairy Braves

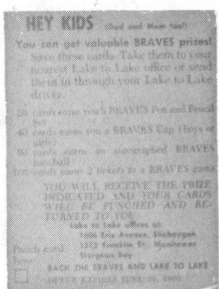

This 28-card set of unnumbered 2-1/2" by 3-1/4" cards offers a special challenge for the condition-conscious collector. Originally issued by being stapled to milk cartons, the cards were redeemable for prizes ranging from pen and pencil sets to Braves tickets. When sent in for redemption, the cards had a hole punched in the corner. Naturally, collectors most desire cards without the staple or punch holes. Cards are printed in blue ink on front, red ink on back. Because he was traded in May, and his card withdrawn, the Ray Boone card is scarce; the Billy Bruton card is unaccountably scarcer still.

		NR MT	EX	VG
Complete Set:		950.00	475.00	285.00
Common Player:		12.00	6.00	3.50
(1)	Henry Aaron	200.00	100.00	60.00
(2)	Joe Adcock	17.50	8.75	5.25
(3)	Ray Boone	125.00	62.00	37.00
(4)	Bill Bruton	200.00	100.00	60.00
(5)	Bob Buhl	17.50	8.75	5.25
(6)	Lou Burdette	20.00	10.00	6.00
(7)	Chuck Cottier	12.00	6.00	3.50
(8)	Wes Covington	15.00	7.50	4.50
(9)	Del Crandall	17.50	8.75	5.25
(10)	Charlie Dressen	15.00	7.50	4.50
(11)	Bob Giggie	12.00	6.00	3.50
(12)	Joey Jay	12.00	6.00	3.50
(13)	Johnny Logan	15.00	7.50	4.50
(14)	Felix Mantilla	12.00	6.00	3.50
(15)	Lee Maye	12.00	6.00	3.50
(16)	Don McMahon	12.00	6.00	3.50
(17)	George Myatt	12.00	6.00	3.50
(18)	Andy Pafko	15.00	7.50	4.50
(19)	Juan Pizarro	12.00	6.00	3.50
(20)	Mel Roach	12.00	6.00	3.50
(21)	Bob Rush	12.00	6.00	3.50

		NR MT	EX	VG
(22)	Bob Scheffing	12.00	6.00	3.50
(23)	Red Schoendienst	20.00	10.00	6.00
(24)	Warren Spahn	50.00	25.00	15.00
(25)	Al Spangler	12.00	6.00	3.50
(26)	Frank Torre	12.00	6.00	3.50
(27)	Carl Willey	12.00	6.00	3.50
(28)	Whitlow Wyatt	12.00	6.00	3.50

1948 Leaf

 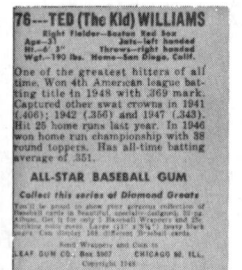

The first color baseball cards of the post-World War II era were the 98-card, 2-3/8" by 2-7/8", set produced by Chicago's Leaf Gum Company in 1948-1949. The color was crude, probably helping to make the set less popular than the Bowman issues of the same era. One of the toughest post-war sets to complete, exactly half of the Leaf issue - 49 of the cards - are significantly harder to find than the other 49. Probably intended to confound bubble gum buyers of the day, the set is skip-numbered between 1-168. Card backs contain offers of felt pennants, an album for the cards or 5-1/2" by 7-1/2" premium photos of Hall of Famers.

		NR MT	EX	VG
Complete Set:		30000.00	15000.00	9000.
Common Player:		20.00	10.00	6.00
Common Scarce Player:		300.00	150.00	90.00
1	Joe DiMaggio	1200.00	600.00	350.00
3	Babe Ruth	1500.00	750.00	450.00
4	Stan Musial	450.00	225.00	135.00
5	Virgil Trucks	300.00	150.00	90.00
8	Leroy Paige	2000.00	1000.00	600.00
10	Paul Trout	20.00	10.00	6.00
11	Phil Rizzuto	75.00	37.00	22.00
13	Casimer Michaels	300.00	150.00	90.00
14	Billy Johnson	18.00	9.00	5.50
17	Frank Overmire	20.00	10.00	6.00
19	John Wyrostek	300.00	150.00	90.00
20	Hank Sauer	300.00	150.00	90.00
22	Al Evans	20.00	10.00	6.00
26	Sam Chapman	20.00	10.00	6.00
27	Mickey Harris	20.00	10.00	6.00
28	Jim Hegan	20.00	10.00	6.00
29	Elmer Valo	20.00	10.00	6.00
30	Bill Goodman	300.00	150.00	90.00
31	Lou Brissie	20.00	10.00	6.00
32	Warren Spahn	200.00	100.00	60.00
33	Harry Lowrey	300.00	150.00	90.00
36	Al Zarilla	300.00	150.00	90.00
38	Ted Kluszewski	40.00	20.00	12.00
39	Ewell Blackwell	35.00	17.50	10.50
42	Kent Peterson	20.00	10.00	6.00
43	Eddie Stevens	300.00	150.00	90.00
45	Ken Keltner	300.00	150.00	90.00
46	Johnny Mize	90.00	45.00	27.00
47	George Vico	20.00	10.00	6.00
48	Johnny Schmitz	300.00	150.00	90.00
49	Del Ennis	20.00	10.00	6.00
50	Dick Wakefield	20.00	10.00	6.00
51	Alvin Dark	350.00	175.00	105.00
53	John Vandermeer (Vander Meer)			
		18.00	9.00	5.50
54	Bobby Adams	300.00	150.00	90.00
55	Tommy Henrich	350.00	175.00	105.00
56	Larry Jensen (Jansen)	20.00	10.00	6.00

		NR MT	EX	VG
57	Bob McCall	20.00	10.00	6.00
59	Lucius Appling	50.00	25.00	15.00
61	Jake Early	20.00	10.00	6.00
62	Eddie Joost	300.00	150.00	90.00
63	Barney McCosky	300.00	150.00	90.00
65	Bob Elliot (Elliott)	20.00	10.00	6.00
66	Orval Grove	300.00	150.00	90.00
68	Ed Miller	300.00	150.00	90.00
70	John Wagner	250.00	125.00	75.00
72	Hank Edwards	20.00	10.00	6.00
73	Pat Seerey	20.00	10.00	6.00
75	Dom DiMaggio	400.00	200.00	120.00
76	Ted Williams	900.00	450.00	275.00
77	Roy Smalley	20.00	10.00	6.00
78	Walter Evers	300.00	150.00	90.00
79	Jackie Robinson	550.00	225.00	165.00
81	George Kurowski	300.00	150.00	90.00
82	Johnny Lindell	20.00	10.00	6.00
83	Bobby Doerr	90.00	45.00	27.00
84	Sid Hudson	20.00	10.00	6.00
85	Dave Philley	300.00	150.00	90.00
86	Ralph Weigel	20.00	10.00	6.00
88	Frank Gustine	300.00	150.00	90.00
91	Ralph Kiner	90.00	45.00	27.00
93	Bob Feller	1200.00	600.00	350.00
95	George Stirnweiss	20.00	10.00	6.00
97	Martin Marion	20.00	10.00	6.00
98	Hal Newhouser	400.00	200.00	125.00
102a	Gene Hermansk (incorrect spelling)			
		300.00	150.00	90.00
102b	Gene Hermanski (correct spelling)			
		20.00	10.00	6.00
104	Edward Stewart	300.00	150.00	90.00
106	Lou Boudreau	80.00	40.00	25.00
108	Matthew Batts	300.00	150.00	90.00
111	Gerald Priddy	20.00	10.00	6.00
113	Emil Leonard	300.00	150.00	90.00
117	Joe Gordon	20.00	10.00	6.00
120	George Kell	550.00	275.00	165.00
121	John Pesky	300.00	150.00	90.00
123	Clifford Fannin	300.00	150.00	90.00
125	Andy Pafko	20.00	10.00	6.00
127	Enos Slaughter	600.00	300.00	180.00
128	Warren Rosar	20.00	10.00	6.00
129	Kirby Higbe	300.00	150.00	90.00
131	Sid Gordon	300.00	150.00	90.00
133	Tommy Holmes	300.00	150.00	90.00
136a	Cliff Aberson (full sleeve)	20.00	10.00	6.00
136b	Cliff Aberson (short sleeve)	175.00	87.00	52.00
137	Harry Walker	300.00	150.00	90.00
138	Larry Doby	400.00	200.00	120.00
139	Johnny Hopp	20.00	10.00	6.00
142	Danny Murtaugh	300.00	150.00	90.00
143	Dick Sisler	300.00	150.00	90.00
144	Bob Dillinger	300.00	150.00	90.00
146	Harold Reiser	400.00	200.00	120.00
149	Henry Majeski	300.00	150.00	90.00
153	Floyd Baker	300.00	150.00	90.00
158	Harry Brecheen	300.00	150.00	90.00
159	Mizell Platt	20.00	10.00	6.00
160	Bob Scheffing	300.00	150.00	90.00
161	Vernon Stephens	400.00	200.00	120.00
163	Freddy Hutchinson	400.00	200.00	120.00
165	Dale Mitchell	300.00	150.00	90.00
168	Phil Cavaretta (Cavarretta)	300.00	150.00	90.00

1960 Leaf

 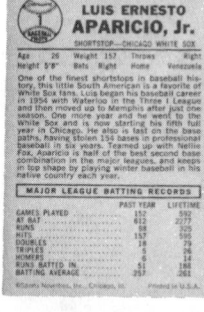

While known to the hobby as "Leaf" cards, this set of 144 cards carries the copyright of Sports Novelties

Inc., Chicago. The 2-1/2" by 3-1/2" cards feature black and white player portrait photos, with background airbrushed away. Cards were sold in 5¢ wax packs with a marble, rather than a piece of bubble gum. The second half of the set, cards #73-144, are very scarce and make the set a real challenge for the collector. Card #25, Jim Grant, is found in two versions, with his own picture (black cap) and with a photo of Brooks Lawrence (white cap). Eight cards (#'s 1, 12, 17, 23, 35, 58, 61 and 72) exist with close-up photos that are much rarer than the normal cap to chest photos. It is believed the scarce "face only" cards are proof cards prepared by Leaf as only a handful are known to exist.

		NR MT	EX	VG
	Complete Set:	1800.00	900.00	550.00
	Common Player: 1-72	4.00	2.00	1.25
	Common Player: 73-144	15.00	7.50	4.50
1	Luis Aparicio	25.00	12.50	7.50
2	Woody Held	4.00	2.00	1.25
3	Frank Lary	3.00	1.50	.90
4	Camilo Pascual	3.00	1.50	.90
5	Frank Herrera	4.00	2.00	1.25
6	Felipe Alou	3.00	1.50	.90
7	Bennie Daniels	4.00	2.00	1.25
8	Roger Craig	3.00	1.50	.90
9	Eddie Kasko	4.00	2.00	1.25
10	Bob Grim	4.00	2.00	1.25
11	Jim Busby	4.00	2.00	1.25
12	Ken Boyer	4.00	2.00	1.25
13	Bob Boyd	4.00	2.00	1.25
14	Sam Jones	4.00	2.00	1.25
15	Larry Jackson	4.00	2.00	1.25
16	Roy Face	4.00	2.00	1.25
17	Walt Moryn	4.00	2.00	1.25
18	Jim Gilliam	4.00	2.00	1.25
19	Don Newcombe	3.00	1.50	.90
20	Glen Hobbie	4.00	2.00	1.25
21	Pedro Ramos	4.00	2.00	1.25
22	Ryne Duren	4.00	2.00	1.25
23	Joe Jay	4.00	2.00	1.25
24	Lou Berberet	4.00	2.00	1.25
25a	Jim Grant (white cap, photo actually Brooks Lawrence)	25.00	12.50	7.50
25b	Jim Grant (dark cap, correct photo)	50.00	25.00	15.00
26	Tom Borland	4.00	2.00	1.25
27	Brooks Robinson	50.00	25.00	15.00
28	Jerry Adair	3.00	1.50	.90
29	Ron Jackson	4.00	2.00	1.25
30	George Strickland	4.00	2.00	1.25
31	Rocky Bridges	4.00	2.00	1.25
32	Bill Tuttle	4.00	2.00	1.25
33	Ken Hunt	3.00	1.50	.90
34	Hal Griggs	4.00	2.00	1.25
35	Jim Coates	3.00	1.50	.90
36	Brooks Lawrence	4.00	2.00	1.25
37	Duke Snider	50.00	25.00	15.00
38	Al Spangler	4.00	2.00	1.25
39	Jim Owens	4.00	2.00	1.25
40	Bill Virdon	4.00	2.00	1.25
41	Ernie Broglio	4.00	2.00	1.25
42	Andre Rodgers	4.00	2.00	1.25
43	Julio Becquer	4.00	2.00	1.25
44	Tony Taylor	4.00	2.00	1.25
45	Jerry Lynch	3.00	1.50	.90
46	Cletis Boyer	4.00	2.00	1.25
47	Jerry Lumpe	3.00	1.50	.90
48	Charlie Maxwell	4.00	2.00	1.25
49	Jim Perry	3.00	1.50	.90
50	Danny McDevitt	4.00	2.00	1.25
51	Juan Pizarro	4.00	2.00	1.25
52	Dallas Green	4.00	2.00	1.25
53	Bob Friend	3.00	1.50	.90
54	Jack Sanford	3.00	1.50	.90
55	Jim Rivera	4.00	2.00	1.25
56	Ted Wills	4.00	2.00	1.25
57	Milt Pappas	3.00	1.50	.90
58a	Hal Smith (team & position on back)	4.00	2.00	1.25
58b	Hal Smith (team blackened out on back)	50.00	25.00	15.00
58c	Hal Smith (team missing on back)	50.00	25.00	15.00
59	Bob Avila	4.00	2.00	1.25
60	Clem Labine	3.00	1.50	.90
61	Vic Rehm	3.00	1.50	.90

		NR MT	EX	VG
62	John Gabler	3.00	1.50	.90
63	John Tsitouris	4.00	2.00	1.25
64	Dave Sisler	4.00	2.00	1.25
65	Vic Power	3.00	1.50	.90
66	Earl Battey	3.00	1.50	.90
67	Bob Purkey	3.00	1.50	.90
68	Moe Drabowsky	4.00	2.00	1.25
69	Hoyt Wilhelm	6.00	3.00	1.75
70	Humberto Robinson	4.00	2.00	1.25
71	Whitey Herzog	4.00	2.00	1.25
72	Dick Donovan	3.00	1.50	.90
73	Gordon Jones	15.00	7.50	4.50
74	Joe Hicks	15.00	7.50	4.50
75	Ray Culp	18.00	9.00	5.50
76	Dick Drott	15.00	7.50	4.50
77	Bob Duliba	15.00	7.50	4.50
78	Art Ditmar	18.00	9.00	5.50
79	Steve Korcheck	15.00	7.50	4.50
80	Henry Mason	15.00	7.50	4.50
81	Harry Simpson	15.00	7.50	4.50
82	Gene Green	15.00	7.50	4.50
83	Bob Shaw	15.00	7.50	4.50
84	Howard Reed	15.00	7.50	4.50
85	Dick Stigman	15.00	7.50	4.50
86	Rip Repulski	15.00	7.50	4.50
87	Seth Morehead	15.00	7.50	4.50
88	Camilo Carreon	15.00	7.50	4.50
89	John Blanchard	18.00	9.00	5.50
90	Billy Hoeft	15.00	7.50	4.50
91	Fred Hopke	18.00	9.00	5.50
92	Joe Martin	15.00	7.50	4.50
93	Wally Shannon	18.00	9.00	5.50
94	Baseball's Two Hal Smiths (Harold Raymond Smith, Harold Wayne Smith)	20.00	10.00	6.00
95	Al Schroll	15.00	7.50	4.50
96	John Kucks	15.00	7.50	4.50
97	Tom Morgan	15.00	7.50	4.50
98	Willie Jones	15.00	7.50	4.50
99	Marshall Renfroe	18.00	9.00	5.50
100	Willie Tasby	15.00	7.50	4.50
101	Irv Noren	15.00	7.50	4.50
102	Russ Snyder	15.00	7.50	4.50
103	Bob Turley	30.00	15.00	9.00
104	Jim Woods	15.00	7.50	4.50
105	Ronnie Kline	15.00	7.50	4.50
106	Steve Bilko	15.00	7.50	4.50
107	Elmer Valo	18.00	9.00	5.50
108	Tom McAvoy	18.00	9.00	5.50
109	Stan Williams	15.00	7.50	4.50
110	Earl Averill	15.00	7.50	4.50
111	Lee Walls	15.00	7.50	4.50
112	Paul Richards	18.00	9.00	5.50
113	Ed Sadowski	15.00	7.50	4.50
114	Stover McIlwain	18.00	9.00	5.50
115	Chuck Tanner (photo actually Ken Kuhn)	20.00	10.00	6.00
116	Lou Klimchock	15.00	7.50	4.50
117	Neil Chrisley	15.00	7.50	4.50
118	John Callison	20.00	10.00	6.00
119	Hal Smith	15.00	7.50	4.50
120	Carl Sawatski	15.00	7.50	4.50
121	Frank Leja	18.00	9.00	5.50
122	Earl Torgeson	15.00	7.50	4.50
123	Art Schult	15.00	7.50	4.50
124	Jim Brosnan	18.00	9.00	5.50
125	George Anderson	40.00	20.00	12.00
126	Joe Pignatano	15.00	7.50	4.50
127	Rocky Nelson	15.00	7.50	4.50
128	Orlando Cepeda	50.00	25.00	15.00
129	Daryl Spencer	15.00	7.50	4.50
130	Ralph Lumenti	15.00	7.50	4.50
131	Sam Taylor	15.00	7.50	4.50
132	Harry Brecheen	18.00	9.00	5.50
133	Johnny Groth	15.00	7.50	4.50
134	Wayne Terwilliger	15.00	7.50	4.50
135	Kent Hadley	18.00	9.00	5.50
136	Faye Throneberry	15.00	7.50	4.50
137	Jack Meyer	15.00	7.50	4.50
138	Chuck Cottier	15.00	7.50	4.50
139	Joe DeMaestri	18.00	9.00	5.50
140	Gene Freese	15.00	7.50	4.50
141	Curt Flood	40.00	20.00	12.00
142	Gino Cimoli	15.00	7.50	4.50
143	Clay Dalrymple	15.00	7.50	4.50
144	Jim Bunning	75.00	38.00	23.00

NOTE: A card number in parentheses ( ) indicates the set is unnumbered.

1990 Leaf

ROBIN VENTURA 3B

This 528-card set was issued in two 264-card series. The cards were printed on heavy quality stock and both the card fronts and backs have full color player photos. Cards also have an ultra-glossy finish on both the fronts and the backs. A high-tech foil Hall of Fame puzzle featuring former Yankee great Yogi Berra.

		MT	NR MT	EX
Complete Set:		70.00	52.00	27.00
Common Player:		.06	.05	.02
1	Introductory Card	.06	.05	.02
2	Mike Henneman	.08	.06	.03
3	Steve Bedrosian	.08	.06	.03
4	Mike Scott	.10	.08	.04
5	Allan Anderson	.08	.06	.03
6	Rick Sutcliffe	.10	.08	.04
7	Gregg Olson	.25	.20	.10
8	Kevin Elster	.08	.06	.03
9	Pete O'Brien	.06	.05	.02
10	Carlton Fisk	.20	.15	.08
11	Joe Magrane	.12	.09	.05
12	Roger Clemens	.30	.25	.12
14	Tom Gordon	.30	.25	.12
15	Todd Benzinger	.08	.06	.03
16	Hubie Brooks	.10	.08	.04
17	Roberto Kelly	.20	.15	.08
18	Barry Larkin	.20	.15	.08
19	Mike Boddicker	.08	.06	.03
20	Roger McDowell	.08	.06	.03
21	Nolan Ryan	1.00	.70	.40
22	John Farrell	.06	.05	.02
23	Bruce Hurst	.08	.06	.03
24	Wally Joyner	.12	.09	.05
25	Greg Maddux	.10	.08	.04
26	Chris Bosio	.06	.05	.02
27	John Cerutti	.06	.05	.02
28	Tim Burke	.08	.06	.03
29	Dennis Eckersley	.15	.11	.06
30	Glenn Davis	.15	.11	.06
31	Jim Abbott	.30	.25	.12
32	Mike LaValliere	.08	.06	.03
33	Andres Thomas	.06	.05	.02
34	Lou Whitaker	.10	.08	.04
35	Alvin Davis	.10	.08	.04
36	Melido Perez	.08	.06	.03
37	Craig Biggio	.10	.08	.04
38	Rick Aguilera	.08	.06	.03
39	Pete Harnisch	.10	.08	.04
40	David Cone	.10	.08	.04
41	Scott Garrelts	.08	.06	.03
42	Jay Howell	.08	.06	.03
43	Eric King	.08	.06	.03
44	Pedro Guerrero	.10	.08	.04
45	Mike Bielecki	.08	.06	.03
46	Bob Boone	.08	.06	.03
47	Kevin Brown	.15	.11	.06
48	Jerry Browne	.08	.06	.03
49	Mike Scioscia	.08	.06	.03
50	Chuck Cary	.06	.05	.02
51	Wade Boggs	.30	.25	.12
52	Von Hayes	.08	.06	.03
53	Tony Fernandez	.10	.08	.04
54	Dennis Martinez	.08	.06	.03
55	Tom Candiotti	.06	.05	.02
56	Andy Benes	.25	.20	.10
57	Rob Dibble	.15	.11	.06
58	Chuck Crim	.06	.05	.02

		MT	NR MT	EX
59	John Smoltz	.15	.11	.06
60	Mike Heath	.06	.05	.02
61	Kevin Gross	.08	.06	.03
62	Mark McGwire	.35	.25	.14
63	Bert Blyleven	.10	.08	.04
64	Bob Walk	.06	.05	.02
65	Mickey Tettleton	.08	.06	.03
66	Sid Fernandez	.10	.08	.04
67	Terry Kennedy	.06	.05	.02
68	Fernando Valenzuela	.12	.09	.05
69	Don Mattingly	.50	.40	.20
70	Paul O'Neill	.08	.06	.03
71	Robin Yount	.20	.15	.08
72	Bret Saberhagen	.15	.11	.06
73	Geno Petralli	.06	.05	.02
74	Brook Jacoby	.08	.06	.03
75	Roberto Alomar	.15	.11	.06
76	Devon White	.08	.06	.03
77	Jose Lind	.06	.05	.02
78	Pat Combs	.10	.08	.04
79	Dave Steib	.10	.08	.04
80	Tim Wallach	.10	.08	.04
81	Dave Stewart	.15	.11	.06
82	Eric Anthony	.60	.45	.25
83	Randy Bush	.06	.05	.02
84	Checklist	.06	.05	.02
85	Jaime Navarro	.15	.11	.06
86	Tommy Gregg	.06	.05	.02
87	Frank Tanana	.08	.06	.03
88	Omar Vizquel	.06	.05	.02
89	Ivan Calderon	.08	.06	.03
90	Vince Coleman	.10	.08	.04
91	Barry Bonds	.30	.25	.12
92	Randy Milligan	.10	.08	.04
93	Frank Viola	.10	.08	.04
94	Matt Williams	.30	.25	.12
95	Alfredo Griffin	.06	.05	.02
96	Steve Sax	.10	.08	.04
97	Gary Gaetti	.10	.08	.04
98	Ryne Sandberg	.50	.40	.20
99	Danny Tartabull	.08	.06	.03
100	Rafael Palmeiro	.15	.11	.06
101	Jesse Orosco	.06	.05	.02
102	Garry Templeton	.08	.06	.03
103	Frank DiPino	.06	.05	.02
104	Tony Pena	.08	.06	.03
105	Dickie Thon	.06	.05	.02
106	Kelly Gruber	.20	.15	.08
107	Marquis Grissom	.60	.45	.25
108	Jose Canseco	1.00	.70	.40
109	Mike Blowers	.20	.15	.08
110	Tom Browning	.08	.06	.03
111	Greg Vaughn	.60	.45	.25
112	Oddibe McDowell	.06	.05	.02
113	Gary Ward	.06	.05	.02
114	Jay Buhner	.08	.06	.03
115	Eric Show	.06	.05	.02
116	Bryan Harvey	.08	.06	.03
117	Andy Van Slyke	.10	.08	.04
118	Jeff Ballard	.08	.06	.03
119	Barry Lyons	.06	.05	.02
120	Kevin Mitchell	.25	.20	.10
121	Mike Gallego	.06	.05	.02
122	Dave Smith	.08	.06	.03
123	Kirby Puckett	.25	.20	.10
124	Jerome Walton	.60	.45	.25
125	Bo Jackson	1.00	.70	.40
126	Harold Baines	.10	.08	.04
127	Scott Bankhead	.08	.06	.03
128	Ozzie Guillen	.10	.08	.04
129	Jose Oquendo	.06	.05	.02
130	John Dopson	.06	.05	.02
131	Charlie Hayes	.08	.06	.03
132	Fred McGriff	.20	.15	.08
133	Chet Lemon	.08	.06	.03
134	Gary Carter	.10	.08	.04
135	Rafael Ramirez	.06	.05	.02
136	Shane Mack	.08	.06	.03
137	Mark Grace	.20	.15	.08
138	Phil Bradley	.08	.06	.03
139	Dwight Gooden	.40	.30	.15
140	Harold Reynolds	.10	.08	.04
141	Scott Fletcher	.06	.05	.02
142	Ozzie Smith	.10	.08	.04
143	Mike Greenwell	.15	.11	.06
144	Pete Smith	.08	.06	.03
145	Mark Gibicza	.08	.06	.03
146	Chris Sabo	.12	.09	.05
147	Ramon Martinez	1.00	.70	.40
148	Dave Winfiled	.15	.11	.06
149	Randy Myers	.10	.08	.04

		MT	NR MT	EX			MT	NR MT	EX
150	Jody Reed	.08	.06	.03	241	Billy Hatcher	.08	.06	.03
151	Bruce Ruffin	.06	.05	.02	242	Paul Molitor	.10	.08	.04
152	Jeff Russell	.08	.06	.03	243	Dale Murphy	.10	.08	.04
153	Doug Jones	.08	.06	.03	244	Dave Bergman	.06	.05	.02
154	Tony Gwynn	.20	.15	.08	245	Ken Griffey,Jr.	5.00	3.75	2.00
155	Mark Langston	.10	.08	.04	246	Ed Whitson	.08	.06	.03
156	Mitch Williams	.08	.04	.02	247	Kirk McCaskill	.08	.06	.03
157	Gary Sheffield	.30	.25	.12	248	Jay Bell	.08	.06	.03
158	Tom Henke	.08	.06	.03	249	Ben McDonald	3.00	2.25	1.25
159	Oil Can Boyd	.08	.06	.03	250	Darryl Strawberry	.30	.25	.12
160	Rickey Henderson	.50	.40	.20	251	Brett Butler	.08	.06	.03
161	Bill Doran	.08	.06	.03	252	Terry Steinbach	.08	.06	.03
162	Chuck Finley	.08	.06	.03	253	Ken Caminiti	.08	.05	.02
163	Jeff King	.08	.06	.03	254	Dan Gladden	.08	.06	.03
164	Nick Esasky	.08	.06	.03	255	Dwight Smith	.10	.08	.04
165	Cecil Fielder	1.00	.70	.40	256	Kurt Stillwell	.08	.06	.03
166	Dave Valle	.06	.05	.02	257	Ruben Sierra	.20	.15	.08
167	Robin Ventura	.40	.30	.15	258	Mike Schooler	.08	.06	.03
168	Jim Deshaies	.08	.06	.03	259	Lance Johnson	.08	.06	.03
169	Juan Berenguer	.06	.05	.02	260	Terry Pendleton	.08	.06	.03
170	Craig Worthington	.10	.08	.04	261	Ellis Burks	.20	.15	.08
171	Gregg Jefferies	.35	.25	.14	262	Len Dykstra	.10	.08	.04
172	Will Clark	.50	.40	.20	263	Mookie Wilson	.08	.06	.03
173	Kirk Gibson	.10	.08	.04	264	Checklist	.06	.05	.02
174	Checklist	.06	.05	.02	265	No Hit King (Nolan Ryan)	1.25	.90	.50
175	Bobby Thigpen	.12	.09	.05	266	Brian DuBois	.10	.08	.04
176	John Tudor	.08	.06	.03	267	Don Robinson	.06	.05	.02
177	Andre Dawson	.15	.11	.06	268	Glenn Wilson	.06	.05	.02
178	George Brett	.15	.11	.06	269	Kevin Tapani	.40	.30	.15
179	Steve Buechele	.06	.05	.02	270	Marvell Wynne	.06	.05	.02
180	Joey Belle	.10	.08	.04	271	Billy Ripken	.06	.05	.02
181	Eddie Murray	.15	.11	.06	272	Howard Johnson	.10	.08	.04
182	Bob Geren	.08	.06	.03	273	Brian Holman	.10	.08	.04
183	Rob Murphy	.06	.05	.02	274	Dan Pasqua	.06	.05	.02
184	Tom Herr	.08	.06	.03	275	Ken Dayley	.06	.05	.02
185	George Bell	.15	.11	.06	276	Jeff Reardon	.08	.06	.03
186	Spike Owen	.08	.06	.03	277	Jim Presley	.08	.06	.03
187	Cory Snyder	.10	.08	.04	278	Jim Eisenreich	.06	.05	.02
188	Fred Lynn	.08	.06	.03	279	Danny Jackson	.08	.06	.03
189	Eric Davis	.30	.25	.12	280	Orel Hershiser	.10	.08	.04
190	Dave Parker	.15	.11	.06	281	Andy Hawkins	.06	.05	.02
191	Jeff Blauser	.06	.05	.02	282	Jose Rijo	.08	.06	.03
192	Matt Nokes	.08	.06	.03	283	Luis Rivera	.06	.05	.02
193	Delino DeShields	1.25	.90	.50	284	John Kruk	.08	.06	.03
194	Scott Sanderson	.08	.06	.03	285	Jeff Huson	.15	.11	.06
195	Lance Parrish	.08	.06	.03	286	Joel Skinner	.06	.05	.02
196	Bobby Bonilla	.20	.15	.08	287	Jack Clark	.10	.08	.04
197	Cal Ripken	.20	.15	.08	288	Chili Davis	.08	.06	.03
198	Kevin McReynolds	.10	.08	.04	289	Joe Girardi	.08	.06	.03
199	Robby Thompson	.08	.06	.03	290	B.J. Surhoff	.08	.06	.03
200	Tim Belcher	.08	.06	.03	291	Luis Sojo	.15	.11	.06
201	Jesse Barfield	.08	.06	.03	292	Tom Foley	.06	.05	.02
202	Mariano Duncan	.08	.06	.03	293	Mike Moore	.08	.06	.03
203	Bill Spiers	.12	.09	.05	294	Ken Oberkfell	.06	.05	.02
204	Frank White	.08	.06	.03	295	Luis Polonia	.06	.05	.02
205	Julio Franco	.10	.08	.04	296	Doug Drabek	.10	.08	.04
206	Greg Swindell	.08	.06	.03	297	Dave Justice	5.00	3.75	2.00
207	Benito Santiago	.15	.11	.06	298	Paul Gibson	.06	.05	.02
208	Johnny Ray	.06	.05	.02	299	Edgar Martinez	.08	.06	.03
209	Gary Redus	.06	.05	.02	300	Frank Thomas	5.00	3.75	2.00
210	Jeff Parrett	.06	.05	.02	301	Eric Yelding	.20	.15	.08
211	Jimmy Key	.08	.06	.03	302	Greg Gagne	.06	.05	.02
212	Tim Raines	.10	.08	.04	303	Brad Komminsk	.06	.05	.02
213	Carney Lansford	.08	.06	.03	304	Ron Darling	.08	.06	.03
214	Gerald Young	.06	.05	.02	305	Kevin Bass	.08	.06	.03
215	Gene Larkin	.06	.05	.02	306	Jeff Hamilton	.06	.05	.02
216	Dan Plesac	.08	.06	.03	307	Ron Karkovice	.06	.05	.02
217	Lonnie Smith	.08	.06	.03	308	Milt Thompson	.06	.05	.02
218	Alan Trammell	.12	.09	.05	309	Mike Harkey	.30	.25	.12
219	Jeffrey Leonard	.08	.06	.03	310	Mel Stottlemyre	.15	.11	.06
220	Sammy Sosa	.60	.45	.25	311	Kenny Rogers	.10	.08	.04
221	Todd Zeile	.60	.45	.25	312	Mitch Webster	.06	.05	.02
222	Bill Landrum	.08	.06	.03	313	Kal Daniels	.10	.08	.04
223	Mike Devereaux	.08	.06	.03	314	Matt Nokes	.08	.06	.03
224	Mike Marshall	.08	.06	.03	315	Dennis Lamp	.06	.05	.02
225	Jose Uribe	.06	.05	.02	316	Ken Howell	.06	.05	.02
226	Juan Samuel	.08	.06	.03	317	Glenallen Hill	.10	.08	.04
227	Mel Hall	.06	.05	.02	318	Dave Martinez	.08	.06	.03
228	Kent Hrbek	.12	.09	.05	319	Chris James	.08	.06	.03
229	Shawon Dunston	.12	.09	.05	320	Mike Pagliarulo	.08	.06	.03
230	Kevin Seitzer	.10	.08	.04	321	Hal Morris	.50	.40	.20
231	Pete Incaviglia	.08	.06	.03	322	Rob Deer	.06	.05	.02
232	Sandy Alomar	.40	.30	.15	323	Greg Olson	.20	.15	.08
233	Bip Roberts	.08	.06	.03	324	Tony Phillips	.06	.05	.02
234	Scott Terry	.06	.05	.02	325	Larry Walker	.50	.40	.20
235	Dwight Evans	.10	.08	.04	326	Ron Hassey	.06	.05	.02
236	Ricky Jordan	.10	.08	.04	327	Jack Howell	.06	.05	.02
237	John Olerud	2.75	2.00	1.00	328	John Smiley	.08	.06	.03
238	Zane Smith	.08	.06	.03	329	Steve Finley	.10	.08	.04
239	Walt Weiss	.08	.06	.03	330	Dave Magadan	.08	.06	.03
240	Alvaro Espinoza	.06	.05	.02	331	Greg Litton	.10	.08	.04

		MT	NR MT	EX			MT	NR MT	EX
332	Mickey Hatcher	.06	.05	.02	423	Drew Hall	.06	.05	.02
333	Lee Guetterman	.06	.05	.02	424	Curt Young	.06	.05	.02
334	Norm Charlton	.10	.08	.04	425	Franklin Stubbs	.08	.06	.03
335	Edgar Diaz	.08	.06	.03	426	Dave Winfield	.15	.11	.06
336	Willie Wilson	.08	.06	.03	427	Rick Reed	.06	.05	.02
337	Bobby Witt	.10	.08	.04	428	Charlie Leibrandt	.08	.06	.03
338	Candy Maldonado	.10	.08	.04	429	Jeff Robinson	.06	.05	.02
339	Craig Lefferts	.08	.06	.03	430	Erik Hanson	.30	.25	.12
340	Dante Bichette	.08	.06	.03	431	Barry Jones	.08	.06	.03
341	Wally Backman	.06	.05	.02	432	Alex Trevino	.06	.05	.02
342	Dennis Cook	.08	.06	.03	433	John Moses	.06	.05	.02
343	Pat Borders	.08	.06	.03	434	Dave Johnson	.06	.05	.02
344	Wallace Johnson	.06	.05	.02	435	Mackey Sasser	.08	.06	.03
345	Willie Randolph	.08	.06	.03	436	Rick Leach	.06	.05	.02
346	Danny Darwin	.08	.06	.03	437	Lenny Harris	.10	.08	.04
347	Al Newman	.06	.05	.02	438	Carlos Martinez	.08	.06	.03
348	Mark Knudson	.06	.05	.02	439	Rex Hudler	.06	.05	.02
349	Joe Boever	.06	.05	.02	440	Domingo Ramos	.06	.05	.02
350	Larry Sheets	.06	.05	.02	441	Gerald Perry	.06	.05	.02
351	Mike Jackson	.06	.05	.02	442	John Russell	.06	.05	.02
352	Wayne Edwards	.15	.11	.06	443	Carlos Baerga	.60	.45	.25
353	Bernard Gilkey	.40	.30	.15	444	Checklist	.06	.05	.02
354	Don Slaught	.06	.05	.02	445	Stan Javier	.06	.05	.02
355	Joe Orsulak	.06	.05	.02	446	Kevin Maas	4.00	3.00	1.50
356	John Franco	.10	.08	.04	447	Tom Brunansky	.08	.06	.03
357	Jeff Brantley	.08	.06	.03	448	Carmelo Martinez	.06	.05	.02
358	Mike Morgan	.06	.05	.02	449	Willie Blair	.15	.11	.06
359	Deion Sanders	.35	.25	.14	450	Andres Galarraga	.10	.08	.04
360	Terry Leach	.06	.05	.02	451	Bud Black	.06	.05	.02
361	Les Lancaster	.06	.05	.02	452	Greg Harris	.06	.05	.02
362	Storm Davis	.08	.06	.03	453	Joe Oliver	.15	.11	.06
363	Scott Coolbaugh	.20	.15	.08	454	Greg Brock	.06	.05	.02
364	Checklist	.06	.05	.02	455	Jeff Treadway	.08	.06	.03
365	Cecilio Guante	.06	.05	.02	456	Lance McCullers	.06	.05	.02
366	Joey Cora	.06	.05	.02	457	Dave Schmidt	.06	.05	.02
367	Willie McGee	.10	.08	.04	458	Todd Burns	.06	.05	.02
368	Jerry Reed	.06	.05	.02	459	Max Venable	.06	.05	.02
369	Darren Daulton	.08	.06	.03	460	Neal Heaton	.06	.05	.02
370	Manny Lee	.08	.06	.03	461	Mark Williamson	.06	.05	.02
371	Mark Gardner	.20	.15	.08	462	Keith Miller	.06	.05	.02
372	Rick Honeycutt	.06	.05	.02	463	Mike LaCoss	.06	.05	.02
373	Steve Balboni	.06	.05	.02	464	Jose Offerman	1.25	.90	.50
374	Jack Armstrong	.15	.11	.06	465	Jim Leyritz	.30	.25	.12
375	Charlie O'Brien	.06	.05	.02	466	Glenn Braggs	.06	.05	.02
376	Ron Gant	.25	.20	.10	467	Ron Robinson	.06	.05	.02
377	Lloyd Moseby	.08	.06	.03	468	Mark Davis	.06	.05	.02
378	Gene Harris	.06	.05	.02	469	Gary Pettis	.06	.05	.02
379	Joe Carter	.10	.08	.04	470	Keith Hernandez	.08	.06	.03
380	Scott Bailes	.06	.05	.02	471	Dennis Rasmussen	.05	.04	.02
381	R.J. Reynolds	.06	.05	.02	472	Mark Eichhorn	.05	.04	.02
382	Bob Melvin	.06	.05	.02	473	Ted Power	.05	.04	.02
383	Tim Teufel	.06	.05	.02	474	Terry Mulholland	.08	.06	.03
384	John Burkett	.25	.20	.10	475	Todd Stottlemyre	.08	.06	.03
385	Felix Jose	.10	.08	.04	476	Jerry Goff	.15	.11	.06
386	Larry Andersen	.06	.05	.02	477	Gene Nelson	.06	.05	.02
387	David West	.08	.06	.03	478	Rich Gedman	.06	.05	.02
388	Luis Salazar	.06	.05	.02	479	Brian Harper	.08	.06	.03
389	Mike Macfarlane	.06	.05	.02	480	Mike Felder	.06	.05	.02
390	Charlie Hough	.08	.06	.02	481	Steve Avery	.40	.30	.15
391	Greg Briley	.10	.08	.04	482	Jack Morris	.08	.06	.02
392	Donn Pall	.06	.05	.02	483	Randy Johnson	.10	.08	.04
393	Bryn Smith	.06	.05	.02	484	Scott Radinsky	.20	.15	.08
394	Carlos Quintana	.15	.11	.06	485	Jose DeLeon	.06	.05	.02
395	Steve Lake	.06	.05	.02	486	Stan Belinda	.20	.15	.08
396	Mark Whiten	.60	.45	.25	487	Brain Holton	.06	.05	.02
397	Edwin Nunez	.06	.05	.02	488	Mark Carreon	.08	.06	.03
398	Rick Parker	.10	.08	.04	489	Trevor Wilson	.15	.11	.06
399	Mark Portugal	.06	.05	.02	490	Mike Sharperson	.08	.06	.03
400	Roy Smith	.06	.05	.02	491	Alan Mills	.20	.15	.08
401	Hector Villanueva	.25	.20	.10	492	John Candelaria	.08	.06	.03
402	Bob Milacki	.08	.06	.03	493	Paul Assenmacher	.06	.05	.02
403	Alejandro Pena	.06	.05	.02	494	Steve Crawford	.06	.05	.02
404	Scott Bradley	.06	.05	.02	495	Brad Arnsberg	.08	.06	.03
405	Ron Kittle	.08	.06	.03	496	Sergio Valdez	.15	.11	.06
406	Bob Tewksbury	.06	.05	.02	497	Mark Parent	.06	.05	.02
407	Wes Gardner	.06	.05	.02	498	Tom Pagnozzi	.06	.05	.02
408	Ernie Whitt	.06	.05	.02	499	Greg Harris	.06	.05	.02
409	Terry Shumpert	.25	.20	.10	500	Randy Ready	.06	.05	.02
410	Tim Layana	.25	.20	.10	501	Duane Ward	.06	.05	.02
411	Chris Gwynn	.08	.06	.03	502	Nelson Santovenia	.06	.05	.02
412	Jeff Robinson	.06	.05	.02	503	Joe Klink	.08	.06	.03
413	Scott Scudder	.20	.15	.08	504	Eric Plunk	.06	.05	.02
414	Kevin Romine	.06	.05	.02	505	Jeff Reed	.06	.05	.02
415	Jose DeJesus	.15	.11	.06	506	Ted Higuera	.10	.08	.04
416	Mike Jeffcoat	.06	.05	.02	507	Joe Hesketh	.06	.05	.02
417	Rudy Seanez	.10	.08	.04	508	Dan Petry	.06	.05	.02
418	Mike Dunne	.06	.05	.02	509	Matt Young	.06	.05	.02
419	Dick Schofield	.06	.05	.02	510	Jerald Clark	.08	.06	.03
420	Steve Wilson	.10	.08	.04	511	John Orton	.10	.08	.04
421	Bill Krueger	.06	.05	.02	512	Scott Ruskin	.20	.15	.08
422	Junior Felix	.35	.25	.14	513	Chris Hoiles	.30	.25	.12

		MT	NR MT	EX
514	Daryl Boston	.06	.05	.02
515	Francisco Oliveras	.10	.08	.04
516	Ozzie Canseco	.50	.40	.20
517	Xavier Hernandez	.10	.08	.04
518	Fred Manrique	.06	.05	.02
519	Shawn Boskie	.30	.25	.12
520	Jeff Montgomery	.08	.06	.03
521	Jack Daugherty	.15	.11	.06
522	Keith Comstock	.06	.05	.02
523	Greg Hibbard	.25	.20	.10
524	Lee Smith	.08	.06	.03
525	Dana Kiecker	.20	.15	.08
526	Darrel Akerfelds	.06	.05	.02
527	Greg Myers	.08	.06	.03
528	Checklist	.06	.05	.02

1986 Lite Beer Astros

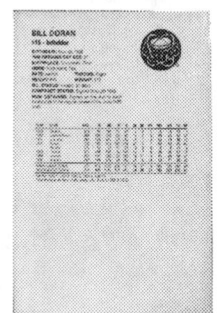

		MT	NR MT	EX
Complete Set:		60.00	45.00	24.00
Common Player:		1.50	1.25	.60
3	Phil Garner	1.50	1.25	.60
6	Mark Bailey	1.50	1.25	.60
10	Dickie Thon	2.00	1.50	.80
11	Frank DiPino	1.50	1.25	.60
12	Craig Reynolds	1.50	1.25	.60
14	Alan Ashby	1.50	1.25	.60
17	Kevin Bass	3.00	2.25	1.25
19	Bill Doran	3.00	2.25	1.25
20	Jim Pankovits	1.50	1.25	.60
21	Terry Puhl	1.50	1.25	.60
22	Hal Lanier	1.50	1.25	.60
25	Jose Cruz	3.00	2.25	1.25
27	Glenn Davis	7.00	5.25	2.75
28	Billy Hatcher	2.50	2.00	1.00
29	Denny Walling	1.50	1.25	.60
33	Mike Scott	4.00	3.00	1.50
34	Nolan Ryan	7.00	5.25	2.75
37	Charlie Kerfeld	2.00	1.50	.80
39	Bob Knepper	2.00	1.50	.80
43	Jim Deshaies	3.00	2.25	1.25
45	Dave Smith	2.00	1.50	.80
53	Mike Madden	1.50	1.25	.60

1986 Lite Beer Rangers

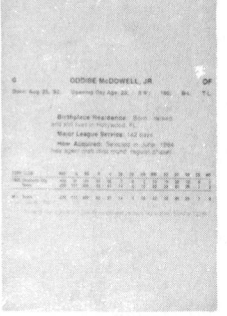

This postcard-size (approximately 4" by 6")

regional set of 28 Texas Rangers cards was sponsored by Lite Beer and was available by mail directly from the Rangers. The fronts featured full-color photos surrounded by a wide, white border with the player's name, uniform number and postion appearing below. The Rangers logo is displayed in the lower left corner, while the Lite Beer logo is in the lower right.

		MT	NR MT	EX
Complete Set:		60.00	45.00	24.00
Common Player:		1.50	1.25	.60
0	Oddibe McDowell	3.00	2.25	1.25
1	Scott Fletcher	2.00	1.50	.80
2	Bobby Valentine	2.00	1.50	.80
4	Don Slaught	1.50	1.25	.60
5	Pete Incaviglia	6.00	4.50	2.50
9	Pete O'Brien	3.00	2.25	1.25
10	Art Howe	1.50	1.25	.60
11	Toby Harrah	2.00	1.50	.80
12	Geno Petralli	1.50	1.25	.60
13	Joe Ferguson	1.50	1.25	.60
14	Tim Foli	1.50	1.25	.60
15	Larry Parrish	2.50	2.00	1.00
16	Mike Mason	1.50	1.25	.60
17	Darrell Porter	2.00	1.50	.80
18	Ed Correa	3.00	2.25	1.25
19	Curtis Wilkerson	1.50	1.25	.60
22	Steve Buechele	3.00	2.25	1.25
23	Jose Guzman	4.00	3.00	1.50
24	Ricky Wright	1.50	1.25	.60
27	Greg Harris	1.50	1.25	.60
31	Tom Robson	1.50	1.25	.60
32	Gary Ward	2.00	1.50	.80
35	Tom House	1.50	1.25	.60
44	Tom Paciorek	1.50	1.25	.60
45	Dwayne Henry	2.00	1.50	.80
48	Bobby Witt	5.00	3.75	2.00
49	Charlie Hough	3.00	2.25	1.25
-----	Arlington Stadium	1.50	1.25	.60

Definitions for grading conditions are located in the introduction section at the front of this book.

1987 M & M's

The M&M's "Star Lineup" set consists of 12 two card panels inserted in specially marked packages of large M&M's candy. The two-card panels measure 5"

by 3-1/2" with individual cards measuring 2-1/2" by 3-1/2" in size. The full-color photos are enclosed by a wavy blue frame and a white border. Card backs are printed in red ink on white stock and carry the player's career statistics and highlights. All team insignias have been airbrushed away. The set was designed and produced by Mike Schechter and Associates.

		MT	NR MT	EX
	Complete Panel Set:	18.00	13.50	7.25
	Complete Singles Set:	8.00	6.00	3.25
	Common Panel:	1.00	.70	.40
	Common Single Player:	.10	.08	.04
	Panel	1.50	1.25	.60
1	Wally Joyner	.50	.40	.20
2	Tony Pena	.10	.08	.04
	Panel	1.50	1.25	.60
3	Mike Schmidt	.30	.25	.12
4	Ryne Sandberg	.20	.15	.08
	Panel	2.25	1.75	.90
5	Wade Boggs	.70	.50	.30
6	Jack Morris	.20	.15	.08
	Panel	1.25	.90	.50
7	Roger Clemens	.30	.25	.12
8	Harold Baines	.15	.11	.06
	Panel	2.75	2.00	1.00
9	Dale Murphy	.30	.25	.12
10	Jose Canseco	1.00	.70	.40
	Panel	3.25	2.50	1.25
11	Don Mattingly	1.25	.90	.50
12	Gary Carter	.20	.15	.08
	Panel	1.50	1.25	.60
13	Cal Ripken, Jr.	.25	.20	.10
14	George Brett	.30	.25	.12
	Panel	1.00	.70	.40
15	Kirby Puckett	.20	.15	.08
16	Joe Carter	.15	.11	.06
	Panel	1.00	.70	.40
17	Mike Witt	.15	.11	.06
18	Mike Scott	.15	.11	.06
	Panel	1.25	.90	.50
19	Fernando Valenzuela	.20	.15	.08
20	Steve Garvey	.20	.15	.08
	Panel	1.00	.70	.40
21	Steve Sax	.15	.11	.06
22	Nolan Ryan	.20	.15	.08
	Panel	1.25	.90	.50
23	Tony Gwynn	.25	.20	.10
24	Ozzie Smith	.15	.11	.06

1989 Marathon Cubs

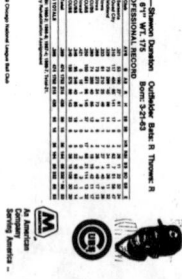

This colorful 25-card Cubs team set was sponsored by Marathon and was distributed as a stadium promotion to fans attending the August 10, 1989, game at Chicago's Wrigley Field. The oversize (2-3/4" by 4-1/4") feature an action photo inside a diagonal box on the card front, with the Chicago Cubs logo at the top and the player's uniform number, name and position along the bottom. The backs include a small black-and-white photo, player data and the Cubs and Marathon logos.

	MT	NR MT	EX
Complete Set:	10.00	7.50	4.00
Common Player:	.10	.08	.04

2	Vance Law	.10	.08	.04
4	Don Zimmer	.15	.11	.06
7	Joe Girardi	.50	.40	.20
8	Andre Dawson	.70	.50	.30
9	Damon Berryhill	.40	.30	.15
10	Lloyd McClendon	.50	.40	.20
12	Shawon Dunston	.50	.40	.20
15	Domingo Ramos	.10	.08	.04
17	Mark Grace	2.00	1.50	.80
18	Dwight Smith	2.00	1.50	.80
19	Curt Wilkerson	.10	.08	.04
20	Jerome Walton	2.50	2.00	1.00
21	Scott Sanderson	.10	.08	.04
23	Ryne Sandberg	3.00	2.25	1.25
28	Mitch Williams	1.00	.70	.40
31	Greg Maddux	.70	.50	.30
32	Calvin Schiraldi	.10	.08	.04
33	Mitch Webster	.10	.08	.04
36	Mike Bielecki	.40	.30	.15
39	Paul Kilgus	.10	.08	.04
40	Rick Sutcliffe	.40	.30	.15
41	Jeff Pico	.25	.20	.10
44	Steve Wilson	.50	.40	.20
50	Les Lancaster	.15	.11	.06
-----	Coaches Card	.10	.08	.04

1989 Marathon Tigers

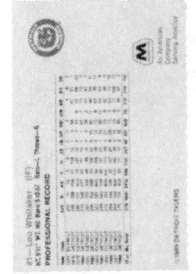

Marathon sponsored this give-away set for a 1989 Tigers home game. The oversized cards feature thin white stock and full-color player photos. The cards are numbered according to uniform number.

	MT	NR MT	EX
Complete Set:	7.00	5.25	2.75
Common Player:	.10	.08	.04

1	Lou Whitaker	.50	.40	.20
3	Alan Trammell	.60	.45	.25
8	Mike Heath	.10	.08	.04
9	Fred Lynn	.30	.25	.12
10	Keith Moreland	.15	.11	.06
11	Sparky Anderson	.40	.30	.15
12	Mike Brumley	.10	.08	.04
14	Dave Bergman	.10	.08	.04
15	Pat Sheridan	.10	.08	.04
17	Al Pedrique	.10	.08	.04
18	Ramon Pena	.15	.11	.06
19	Doyle Alexander	.20	.15	.08
21	Guillermo Hernandez	.20	.15	.08
23	Torey Lovullo	.30	.25	.12
24	Gary Pettis	.20	.15	.08
25	Ken Williams	.10	.08	.04
26	Frank Tanana	.20	.15	.08
27	Charles Hudson	.10	.08	.04
32	Gary Ward	.10	.08	.04
33	Matt Nokes	.40	.30	.15
34	Chet Lemon	.25	.20	.10
35	Rick Schu	.10	.08	.04
36	Frank Williams	.10	.08	.04
39	Mike Henneman	.30	.25	.12
44	Jeff Robinson	.20	.15	.08
47	Jack Morris	.40	.30	.15
48	Paul Gibson	.10	.08	.04
-----	Coaches	.10	.08	.04

1990 Marathon Cubs

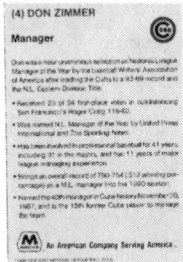

		MT	NR MT	EX
Complete Set:		8.00	6.00	3.25
Common Player:		.10	.08	.04
4	Don Zimmer	.15	.11	.06
7	Joe Girardi	.20	.15	.08
8	Andre Dawson	.60	.45	.25
10	Lloyd McClendon	.10	.08	.04
11	Luis Salazar	.10	.08	.04
12	Shawon Dunston	.50	.40	.20
15	Domingo Ramos	.10	.08	.04
17	Mark Grace	1.50	1.25	.60
18	Dwight Smith	.40	.30	.15
19	Curtis Wilkerson	.10	.08	.04
20	Jerome Walton	1.00	.70	.40
22	Mike Harkey	.70	.50	.30
23	Ryne Sandberg	2.00	1.50	.80
25	Marvell Wynne	.10	.08	.04
28	Mitch Williams	.40	.30	.15
29	Doug Dascenzo	.20	.15	.08
30	Dave Clark	.15	.11	.06
31	Greg Maddux	.60	.45	.25
32	Hector Villanueva	.40	.30	.15
36	Mike Bielecki	.20	.15	.08
37	Bill Long	.10	.08	.04
40	Rick Sutcliffe	.30	.25	.12
41	Jeff Pico	.10	.08	.04
44	Steve Wilson	.30	.25	.12
45	Paul Assenmacher	.10	.08	.04
47	Shawn Boskie	.80	.60	.30
50	Les Lancaster	.10	.08	.04
----	Coaches	.10	.08	.04

1988 Master Bread Twins

This set of 12 cardboard discs (2-3/4" diameter) features full-color photos of Minnesota Twins team members. Disc fronts have a bright blue background with red, yellow and black printing. A thin white line frames the player photo which is centered beneath a "Master Is Good Bread" headliner and a vivid yellow player/team name banner. Disc backs are black and white with five stars printed above the player's name, team, personal data, disc number, stats and "1988 Collector's Edition" banner. The discs were printed in

Canada and marketed exclusively in Minnesota in packages of Master Bread, one disc per loaf.

		MT	NR MT	EX
Complete Set:		15.00	11.00	6.00
Common Player:		.50	.40	.20
1	Bert Blyleven	1.00	.70	.40
2	Frank Viola	2.25	1.75	.90
3	Juan Berenguer	.50	.40	.20
4	Jeff Reardon	.80	.60	.30
5	Tim Laudner	.50	.40	.20
6	Steve Lombardozzi	.50	.40	.20
7	Randy Bush	.50	.40	.20
8	Kirby Puckett	4.00	3.00	1.50
9	Gary Gaetti	1.75	1.25	.70
10	Kent Hrbek	1.75	1.25	.70
11	Greg Gagne	.50	.40	.20
12	Tom Brunansky	1.25	.90	.50

1986 Meadow Gold Blank Back Set Of 16

This was the second set to be distributed by Meadow Gold Dairy (Beatrice Foods) in 1986. It was issued on Double Play ice cream cartons, one card per package. Full-color player photos have team logos and insignias airbrushed away. This 16-card set is very similar to the Meadow Gold popsicle set, but the photos are different in some instances. The cards measure 2-3/8" by 3-1/2". The Willie McGee card is reportedly tougher to find than other cards in the set.

		MT	NR MT	EX
Complete Set:		100.00	75.00	40.00
Common Player:		4.00	3.00	1.50
(1)	George Brett	7.00	5.25	2.75
(2)	Wade Boggs	10.00	7.50	4.00
(3)	Carlton Fisk	4.00	3.00	1.50
(4)	Steve Garvey	6.00	4.50	2.50
(5)	Dwight Gooden	7.50	5.75	3.00
(6)	Pedro Guerrero	4.00	3.00	1.50
(7)	Reggie Jackson	6.50	5.00	2.50
(8)	Don Mattingly	15.00	11.00	6.00
(9)	Willie McGee	4.00	3.00	1.50
(10)	Dale Murphy	7.00	5.25	2.75
(11)	Cal Ripken	6.50	5.00	2.50
(12)	Pete Rose	8.00	6.00	3.25
(13)	Ryne Sandberg	6.00	4.50	2.50
(14)	Mike Schmidt	7.00	5.25	2.75
(15)	Fernando Valenzuela	5.00	3.75	2.00
(16)	Dave Winfield	6.50	5.00	2.50

1986 Meadow Gold Statistic Back Set Of 20

Beatrice Foods produced this set of 20 cards on specially marked boxes of Meadow Gold Double Play popsicles, fudgesicles and bubble gum coolers. They came in two-card panels and have full-color player

pictures with player name, team and position printed below the photo. Card backs are printed in red ink and feature player career highlights. The cards measure 2-3/8" by 3-1/2" and were distributed in the West and Midwest. It is considered one of the toughest 1986 regional sets to complete.

		MT	NR MT	EX
Complete Panel Set:		40.00	30.00	15.00
Complete Singles Set:		20.00	15.00	8.00
Common Panel:		2.00	1.50	.80
Common Single Player:		.30	.25	.12
	Panel 1	5.00	3.75	2.00
1	George Brett	1.50	1.25	.60
2	Fernando Valenzuela	.70	.50	.30
	Panel 2	6.50	5.00	2.50
3	Dwight Gooden	2.00	1.50	.80
4	Dale Murphy	1.50	1.25	.60
	Panel 3	10.00	7.50	4.00
5	Don Mattingly	5.00	3.75	2.00
6	Reggie Jackson	2.00	1.50	.80
	Panel 4	6.50	5.00	2.50
7	Dave Winfield	1.00	.70	.40
8	Pete Rose	2.00	1.50	.80
	Panel 5	6.00	4.50	2.50
9	Wade Boggs	3.00	2.25	1.25
10	Willie McGee	.50	.40	.20
	Panel 6	5.50	4.25	2.25
11	Cal Ripkin (Ripken)	1.25	.90	.50
12	Ryne Sandberg	2.00	1.50	.80
	Panel 7	5.00	3.75	2.00
13	Carlton Fisk	.50	.40	.20
14	Jim Rice	1.00	.70	.40
	Panel 8	7.00	5.25	2.75
15	Steve Garvey	1.00	.70	.40
16	Mike Schmidt	2.00	1.50	.80
	Panel 9	4.00	3.00	1.50
17	Bruce Sutter	.60	.45	.25
18	Pedro Guerrero	.60	.45	.25
	Panel 10	4.00	3.00	1.50
19	Rick Sutcliff (Sutcliffe)	.60	.45	.25
20	Rich Gossage	.60	.45	.25

1986 Meadow Gold Milk

The third set from Meadow Gold from 1986 came on milk cartons; on pint, quart and half-gallon size

containers. The cards measure 2-1/2" by 3-1/2" and feature drawings instead of photographs. Different dairies distributed the cards in various colors of ink. The cards can be found printed in red, brown or black ink. The crude drawings have prevented this rare set from being higher in price. It was believed that Don Mattingly and Fernando Valenzuela were part of the original set, but it has since been proven they were not.

		MT	NR MT	EX
Complete Set:		50.00	37.00	20.00
Common Player:		2.00	1.50	.80
(1)	Wade Boggs	10.00	7.50	4.00
(2)	George Brett	5.00	3.75	2.00
(3)	Steve Carlton	3.00	2.25	1.25
(4)	Dwight Gooden	10.00	7.50	4.00
(5)	Willie McGee	2.00	1.50	.80
(6)	Dale Murphy	5.00	3.75	2.00
(7)	Cal Ripken, Jr.	4.00	3.00	1.50
(8)	Pete Rose	10.00	7.50	4.00
(9)	Ryne Sandberg	3.00	2.25	1.25
(10)	Mike Schmidt	5.00	3.75	2.00

1971 Milk Duds

These cards were issued on the backs of five-cent packages of Milk Duds candy. Most collectors prefer to collect complete boxes, rather than cut-out cards, which measure approximately 1-13/16" by 2-5/8" when trimmed tightly. Values quoted below are for complete boxes. The set includes 37 National League and 32 American League players. Card numbers appear on the box flap, with each number from 1 through 24 being shared by three different players. A suffix (a, b and c) has been added for the collector's convenience. Harmon Killebrew, Brooks Robinson and Pete Rose were double-printed.

		NR MT	EX	VG
Complete Set:		1200.00	600.00	350.00
Common Player:		7.00	3.50	2.00
1a	Frank Howard	11.00	5.50	3.25
1b	Fritz Peterson	7.00	3.50	2.00
1c	Pete Rose	80.00	40.00	24.00
2a	Johnny Bench	30.00	15.00	9.00
2b	Rico Carty	9.00	4.50	2.75
2c	Pete Rose	80.00	40.00	24.00
3a	Ken Holtzman	8.00	4.00	2.50
3b	Willie Mays	60.00	30.00	18.00
3c	Cesar Tovar	7.00	3.50	2.00
4a	Willie Davis	9.00	4.50	2.75
4b	Harmon Killebrew	20.00	10.00	6.00
4c	Felix Millan	7.00	3.50	2.00
5a	Billy Grabarkewitz	7.00	3.50	2.00
5b	Andy Messersmith	8.00	4.00	2.50
5c	Thurman Munson	20.00	10.00	6.00

		NR MT	EX	VG
6a	Luis Aparicio	18.00	9.00	5.50
6b	Lou Brock	25.00	12.50	7.50
6c	Bill Melton	7.00	3.50	2.00
7a	Ray Culp	7.00	3.50	2.00
7b	Willie McCovey	25.00	12.50	7.50
7c	Luke Walker	7.00	3.50	2.00
8a	Roberto Clemente	40.00	20.00	12.00
8b	Jim Merritt	7.00	3.50	2.00
8c	Claud Osteen (Claude)	8.00	4.00	2.50
9a	Stan Bahnsen	7.00	3.50	2.00
9b	Sam McDowell	9.00	4.50	2.75
9c	Billy Williams	18.00	9.00	5.50
10a	Jim Hickman	7.00	3.50	2.00
10b	Dave McNally	9.00	4.50	2.75
10c	Tony Perez	13.00	6.50	4.00
11a	Hank Aaron	60.00	30.00	18.00
11b	Glen Beckert (Glenn)	8.00	4.00	2.50
11c	Ray Fosse	7.00	3.50	2.00
12a	Alex Johnson	7.00	3.50	2.00
12b	Gaylord Perry	18.00	9.00	5.50
12c	Wayne Simpson	7.00	3.50	2.00
13a	Dave Johnson	9.00	4.50	2.75
13b	George Scott	8.00	4.00	2.50
13c	Tom Seaver	30.00	15.00	9.00
14a	Bill Freehan	9.00	4.50	2.75
14b	Bud Harrelson	8.00	4.00	2.50
14c	Manny Sanguillen	7.00	3.50	2.00
15a	Bob Gibson	25.00	12.50	7.50
15b	Rusty Staub	11.00	5.50	3.25
15c	Roy White	8.00	4.00	2.50
16a	Jim Fregosi	9.00	4.50	2.75
16b	Jim Hunter	18.00	9.00	5.50
16c	Mel Stottlemyer (Stottlemyre)	8.00	4.00	2.50
17a	Tommy Harper	7.00	3.50	2.00
17b	Frank Robinson	25.00	12.50	7.50
17c	Reggie Smith	9.00	4.50	2.75
18a	Orlando Cepeda	13.00	6.50	4.00
18b	Rico Petrocelli	8.00	4.00	2.50
18c	Brooks Robinson	25.00	12.50	7.50
19a	Tony Oliva	11.00	5.50	3.25
19b	Milt Pappas	8.00	4.00	2.50
19c	Bobby Tolan	7.00	3.50	2.00
20a	Ernie Banks	25.00	12.50	7.50
20b	Don Kessinger	8.00	4.00	2.50
20c	Joe Torre	9.00	4.50	2.75
21a	Fergie Jenkins	13.00	6.50	4.00
21b	Jim Palmer	18.00	9.00	5.50
21c	Ron Santo	9.00	4.50	2.75
22a	Randy Hundley	7.00	3.50	2.00
22b	Dennis Menke (Denis)	7.00	3.50	2.00
22c	Boog Powell	11.00	5.50	3.25
23a	Dick Dietz	7.00	3.50	2.00
23b	Tommy John	13.00	6.50	4.00
23c	Brooks Robinson	25.00	12.50	7.50
24a	Danny Cater	7.00	3.50	2.00
24b	Harmon Killebrew	18.00	9.00	5.50
24c	Jim Perry	8.00	4.00	2.50

		MT	NR MT	EX
Complete Set:		12.00	9.00	4.75
Common Player:		.25	.20	.10
(1)	Wade Boggs	1.50	1.25	.60
(2)	George Brett	1.00	.70	.40
(3)	Rod Carew	.50	.40	.20
(4)	Steve Carlton	.40	.30	.15
(5)	Gary Carter	.50	.40	.20
(6)	Dave Concepcion	.25	.20	.10
(7)	Cecil Cooper	.25	.20	.10
(8)	Andre Dawson	.50	.40	.20
(9)	Carlton Fisk	.40	.30	.15
(10)	Steve Garvey	.50	.40	.20
(11)	Pedro Guerrero	.35	.25	.14
(12)	Ron Guidry	.25	.20	.10
(13)	Rickey Henderson	1.00	.70	.40
(14)	Reggie Jackson	.50	.40	.20
(15)	Ron Kittle	.25	.20	.10
(16)	Bill Madlock	.25	.20	.10
(17)	Dale Murphy	.80	.60	.30
(18)	Al Oliver	.25	.20	.10
(19)	Darrell Porter	.25	.20	.10
(20)	Cal Ripken	.60	.45	.25
(21)	Pete Rose	1.25	.90	.50
(22)	Steve Sax	.35	.25	.14
(23)	Mike Schmidt	.80	.60	.30
(24)	Ted Simmons	.25	.20	.10
(25)	Ozzie Smith	.35	.25	.14
(26)	Dave Stieb	.25	.20	.10
(27)	Fernando Valenzuela	.35	.25	.14
(28)	Lou Whitaker	.35	.25	.14
(29)	Dave Winfield	.50	.40	.20
(30)	Robin Yount	.40	.30	.15

1983 Minnesota Twins Team Issue

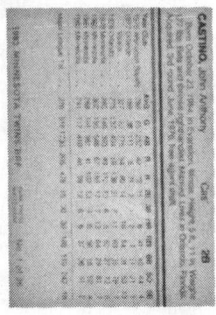

The Minnesota Twins produced a 36-card set in 1983 to be sold at concession stands and through the mail. The full-color borderless cards measure 2-1/2" by 3-1/2" and displayed the player's uniform number on a white Twins jersey at the bottom of the card. The backs contain full career statistics.

		MT	NR MT	EX
Complete Set:		9.00	6.75	3.50
Common Player:		.10	.08	.04
1	John Anthony Castino	.10	.08	.04
2	James Michael Eisenreich	.20	.15	.08
3	Raymond Edward Smith	.10	.08	.04
4	Scott Matthew Ullger	.10	.08	.04
5	Gary Joseph Gaetti	.50	.40	.20
6	Michael Vaughn Hatcher	.10	.08	.04
7	Robert Van Mitchell	.10	.08	.04
8	Leonardo Lago Faedo, Jr.	.10	.08	.04
9	Kent Alan Hrbek	.75	.60	.30
10	Timothy Jon Laudner	.15	.11	.06
11	Frank John Viola, Jr.	.50	.40	.20
12	Bryan Alois Oelkers	.10	.08	.04
13	Richard Eugene Lysander	.10	.08	.04
14	Ralph David Engle	.10	.08	.04
15	Leonard Joseph Whitehouse, Jr.	.10	.08	.04
16	William Peter Filson	.10	.08	.04
17	Thomas Andrew Brunansky	.50	.40	.20

1984 Milton Bradley

In 1984 Milton Bradley printed their baseball game cards in full-color and adopted the standard baseball card size of 2-1/2" by 3-1/2". A total of 30 cards were in the set. The card fronts show the player photos with the team insignias and logos airbrushed away. The game is called Championship Baseball. Card backs varied in style; some had player statistics plus game information, and others only game information.

		MT	NR MT	EX
18	Robert Randall Bush	.10	.08	.04
19	Bradley David Havens	.10	.08	.04
20	Albert Hamilton Williams	.10	.08	.04
21	Gary Lamell Ward	.10	.08	.04
22	Jack William O'Connor	.10	.08	.04
23	Robert Ernie Castillo, Jr.	.10	.08	.04
24	Ronald Washington	.10	.08	.04
25	Ronald Gene Davis	.10	.08	.04
26	Jay Thomas Kelly	.15	.11	.06
27	William Frederick Gardner	.10	.08	.04
28	Richard Francis Stelmaszek	.10	.08	.04
29	James Robert Lemon	.10	.08	.04
30	John Joseph Podres	.15	.11	.06
31	Minnesota's Native Sons (Jim Eisenreich, Kent Hrbek, Tim Laudner)	.25	.20	.10
32	Twins' Catchers (Dave Engle, Tim Laudner)	.10	.08	.04
33	The Lumber Company (Tom Brunansky, Gary Gaetti, Kent Hrbek, Gary Ward)	.35	.25	.14
34	Twins' Coaches (Billy Gardner, Tom Kelly, Jim Lemon, Johnny Podres, Rick Stelmaszek)	.10	.08	.04
35	Team Photo	.10	.08	.04
36	Metrodome/Checklist	.10	.08	.04

		MT	NR MT	EX
26	Ronald Gene Davis	.08	.06	.03
27	Jay Thomas Kelly	.15	.11	.06
28	William Frederick Gardner	.08	.06	.03
29	Richard Francis Stelmaszek	.08	.06	.03
30	James Robert Lemon	.08	.06	.03
31	John Joseph Podres	.10	.08	.04
32	Billy Mike Smithson	.08	.06	.03
33	Harmon Killebrew	.50	.40	.20
34	Team Photo	.08	.06	.03
35	Logo Card	.08	.06	.03
36	Metrodome/Checklist	.08	.06	.03

1985 Minnesota Twins Team Issue

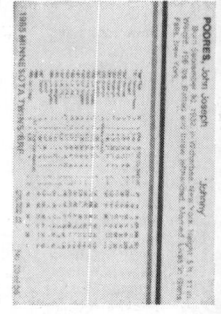

Similar in format to the previous two yers, this 36-card team-issued set features full-color, border-less cards. The player's uniform number is again displayed on a white Twins jersey in the lower right corner, and the 1985 All-Star Game logo is shown in the lower left. The All-Star Game logo also appears on a special card in the set that lists on the back all Twins who have been selected for previous All-Star Games. The set was sold at ballpark concession stands and through the mail.

		MT	NR MT	EX
Complete Set:		6.00	4.50	2.50
Common Player:		.08	.06	.03
1	Alvaro Alberto Espinoza	.08	.06	.03
2	Roy Frederick Smalley, III	.10	.08	.04
3	Pedro Oliva, Jr.	.15	.11	.06
4	David Keith Meier	.08	.06	.03
5	Gary Joseph Gaetti	.35	.25	.14
6	Michael Vaughn Hatcher	.08	.06	.03
7	Jeffrey Scott Reed	.08	.06	.03
8	Timothy Shawn Teufel	.10	.08	.04
9	Mark Bruce Salas	.08	.06	.03
10	Kent Alan Hrbek	.50	.40	.20
11	Timothy Jon Laudner	.15	.11	.06
12	Frank John Viola, Jr.	.35	.25	.14
13	Kenneth Marvin Schrom	.08	.06	.03
14	Richard Eugene Lysander	.08	.06	.03
15	Ralph David Engle	.08	.06	.03
16	Andre Anter David	.08	.06	.03
17	Leonard Joseph Whitehouse, Jr.	.08	.06	.03
18	William Peter Filson	.08	.06	.03
19	Thomas Andrew Brunansky	.35	.25	.14
20	Robert Randall Bush	.08	.06	.03
21	Gregory Carpenter Gagne	.08	.06	.03
22	John Daniel Butcher	.08	.06	.03
23	Michael Steven Stenhouse	.08	.06	.03
24	Kirby Puckett	.80	.60	.30
25	Thomas Carl Klawitter	.08	.06	.03
26	Curtis Ray Wardle	.08	.06	.03
27	Richard Martin Yett	.15	.11	.06
28	Ronald Washington	.08	.06	.03
29	Ronald Gene Davis	.08	.06	.03
30	Jay Thomas Kelly	.15	.11	.06
31	William Frederick Gardner	.08	.06	.03
32	Richard Francis Stelmaszek	.08	.06	.03
33	John Joseph Podres	.10	.08	.04
34	Billy Mike Smithson	.08	.06	.03
35	1985 All-Star Game Logo Card	.08	.06	.03
36	Twins Logo/Checklist	.08	.06	.03

1984 Minnesota Twins Team Issue

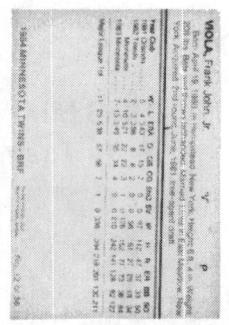

This team-issued set from the Minnesota Twins consists of 36 full-color, borderless cards, each measuring 2-1/2" by 3-1/2". As in the previous year, the player's uniform number appears on a white Twins jersey at the bottom of the card. The backs are printed in red and blue on white stock and include career stats. The set feaqtures several special cards, including one of Harmon Killebrew.

		MT	NR MT	EX
Complete Set:		6.00	4.50	2.50
Common Player:		.08	.06	.03
1	John Anthony Castino	.08	.06	.03
2	James Michael Eisenreich	.10	.08	.04
3	Alfonso Jimenez	.08	.06	.03
4	David Keith Meier	.08	.06	.03
5	Gary Joseph Gaetti	.35	.25	.14
6	Michael Vaughn Hatcher	.08	.06	.03
7	Jeffrey Scott Reed	.08	.06	.03
8	Timothy Shawn Teufel	.10	.08	.04
9	Leonardo Lago Faedo, Jr.	.08	.06	.03
10	Kent Alan Hrbek	.50	.40	.20
11	Timothy Jon Laudner	.15	.11	.06
12	Frank John Viola, Jr.	.35	.25	.14
13	Kenneth Marvin Schrom	.08	.06	.03
14	Larry John Pashnick	.08	.06	.03
15	Ralph David Engle	.08	.06	.03
16	Keith Martin Comstock	.10	.08	.04
17	William Peter Filson	.08	.06	.03
18	Thomas Andrew Brunansky	.35	.25	.14
19	Robert Randall Bush	.08	.06	.03
20	Darrell Wayne Brown	.08	.06	.03
21	Albert Hamilton Williams	.08	.06	.03
22	Michael Charles Walters	.08	.06	.03
23	John David Butcher	.08	.06	.03
24	Robert Ernie Castillo, Jr.	.08	.06	.03
25	Ronald Washington	.08	.06	.03

1986 Minnesota Twins Team Issue

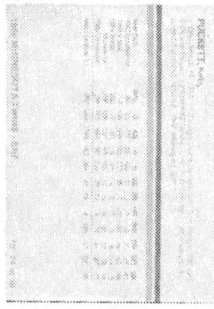

This team-issued set contains 36 2-9/16" by 3-1/2" full-color cards. Fronts feature the Twins 25th anniversary logo and a jersey at the bottom of each card with the player's uniform number. All cards, except an action shot of Bert Blyleven, are posed photos, with a facsimile autograph on each. The set also includes a checklist and a team photo.

		MT	NR MT	EX
Complete Set:		6.00	4.50	2.50
Common Player:		.08	.06	.03
1	Christopher Francis Pittaro	.08	.06	.03
2	Stephen Paul Lombardozzi	.15	.11	.06
3	Roy Frederick Smalley, III	.10	.08	.04
4	Pedro Oliva, Jr.	.15	.11	.06
5	Gary Joseph Gaetti	.50	.40	.20
6	Michael Vaughn Hatcher	.08	.06	.03
7	Jeffrey Scott Reed	.08	.06	.03
8	Mark Bruce Salas	.08	.06	.03
9	Kent Alan Hrbek	.60	.45	.25
10	Timothy Jon Laudner	.15	.11	.06
11	Frank John Viola, Jr.	.50	.40	.20
12	Dennis Allen Burtt	.08	.06	.03
13	Alejandro Sanchez	.08	.06	.03
14	LeRoy Purdy Smith, III	.08	.06	.03
15	William Lamar Beane, III	.08	.06	.03
16	William Peter Filson	.08	.06	.03
17	Thomas Andrew Brunansky	.35	.25	.14
18	Robert Randall Bush	.08	.06	.03
19	Frank Anthony Eufemia, III	.08	.06	.03
20	John Mark Davidson	.15	.11	.06
21	Rik Aalbert Blyleven	.25	.20	.10
22	Gregory Carpenter Gagne	.15	.11	.06
23	John Daniel Butcher	.08	.06	.03
24	Kirby Puckett	.80	.60	.30
25	William Carol Latham, Jr.	.08	.06	.03
26	Ronald Washington	.08	.06	.03
27	Ronald Gene Davis	.08	.06	.03
28	Jay Thomas Kelly	.15	.11	.06
29	Richard Stanley Such	.08	.06	.03
30	Richard Francis Stelmaszek	.08	.06	.03
31	Raymond Robert Miller	.08	.06	.03
32	Willard Wayne Terwilliger	.08	.06	.03
33	Billy Mike Smithson	.08	.06	.03
34	Alvis Woods	.08	.06	.03
35	Team Photo	.08	.06	.03
36	Twins Logo/Checklist	.08	.06	.03

1987 Minnesota Twins Team Issue

The Minnesota Twins produced a 32-card set of 2-1/2" by 3-1/2" full-color baseball cards to be sold at the ballpark and through their souvenir catalog. The card fronts are borderless, containing only the player photo. The backs are printed in blue and red on white card stock and carry the player's personal data and career record. The Twins also produced a post card set which was similar in design to the

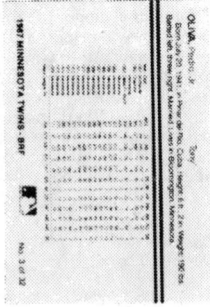

standard-size card set, but utilized different photos.

		MT	NR MT	EX
Complete Set:		6.00	4.50	2.50
Common Player:		.08	.06	.03
1	Stephen Paul Lombardozzi	.15	.11	.06
2	Roy Frederick Smalley III	.10	.08	.04
3	Pedro Oliva, Jr.	.15	.11	.06
4	Gregory Carpenter Gagne	.15	.11	.06
5	Gary Joseph Gaetti	.50	.40	.20
6	Jay Thomas Kelly	.15	.11	.06
7	Thomas Andrew Nieto	.08	.06	.03
8	Mark Bruce Salas	.08	.06	.03
9	Kent Alan Hrbek	.60	.45	.25
10	Timothy Jon Laudner	.15	.11	.06
11	Frank John Viola, Jr.	.50	.40	.20
12	Lester Paul Straker	.25	.20	.10
13	George Allen Frazier	.08	.06	.03
14	Keith Rowe Atherton	.08	.06	.03
15	Thomas Andrew Brunansky	.35	.25	.14
16	Robert Randall Bush	.08	.06	.03
17	Albert Dwayne Newman	.08	.06	.03
18	John Mark Davidson	.08	.06	.03
19	Rik Aalbert Blyleven	.25	.20	.10
20	Clinton Daniel Gladden III	.15	.11	.06
21	Kirby Puckett	.80	.60	.30
22	Mark Steven Portugal	.08	.06	.03
23	Juan Bautista Berenguer	.08	.06	.03
24	Jeffrey James Reardon	.30	.25	.12
25	Richard Stanley Such	.08	.06	.03
26	Richard Francis Stelmaszek	.08	.06	.03
27	Warren Richard Renick	.08	.06	.03
28	Willard Wayne Terwilliger	.08	.06	.03
29	Joseph Charles Klink	.08	.06	.03
30	Billy Mike Smithson	.08	.06	.03
31	Team Photo	.08	.06	.03
32	Twins Logo/Checklist	.08	.06	.03

1988 Minnesota Twins Team Issue

The Twins issued this 33-card set (including checklist) to commemorate the team's 1987 Series victory. The slightly oversized cards (2-5/8" x 3-7/16") feature deluxe player photos printed on heavy stock with a gold-embossed "1987 World

Champions" logo in the lower left corner. Many photos are duplicates of the regular season set but several new photos, including a group team shot, are included. Numbered card backs are red, white and blue and contain a player name, personal info and stats. A limited edition of 5000 sets were printed but only a few hundred were sold before the cards were taken off the market due to Major League Baseball licensing restrictions.

		MT	NR MT	EX
Complete Set:		150.00	110.00	60.00
Common Player:		1.25	.90	.50
1	Stephen Paul Lombardozzi	1.25	.90	.50
2	Roy Frederick Smalley, III	1.25	.90	.50
3	Pedro Oliva, Jr.	1.25	.90	.50
4	Gregory Carpenter Gagne	3.00	2.25	1.25
5	Gary Joseph Gaetti	12.00	9.00	4.75
6	Eugene Thomas Larkin	3.00	2.25	1.25
7	Jay Thomas Kelly	2.00	1.50	.80
8	Kent Alan Hrbek	12.00	9.00	4.75
9	Timothy Jon Laudner	2.00	1.50	.80
10	Frank John Viola, Jr.	15.00	11.00	6.00
11	Lester Paul Straker	1.25	.90	.50
12	Donald Edward Baylor	2.00	1.50	.80
13	George Allen Frazier	1.25	.90	.50
14	Keith Rowe Atherton	1.25	.90	.50
15	Thomas Andrew Brunansky	10.00	7.50	4.00
16	Robert Randall Bush	2.00	1.50	.80
17	Albert Dwayne Newman	1.25	.90	.50
18	John Mark Davidson	1.25	.90	.50
19	Rik Aalbert Blyleven	10.00	7.50	4.00
20	Daniel Ernest Schatzeder	1.25	.90	.50
21	Clinton Daniel Gladden III	3.00	2.25	1.25
22	Salvatore Philip Butera	1.25	.90	.50
23	Kirby Puckett	25.00	20.00	10.00
24	Joseph Franklin Niekro	2.00	1.50	.80
25	Juan Bautista Berenguer	1.25	.90	.50
26	Jeffrey James Reardon	4.00	3.00	1.50
27	Richard Stanley Such	1.25	.90	.50
28	Richard Francis Stelmaszek	1.25	.90	.50
29	Warren Richard Renick	1.25	.90	.50
30	Willard Wayne Terwilliger	1.25	.90	.50
31	Team Photo	1.25	.90	.50
32	World Champions Team Logo Card	1.25	.90	.50
33	Team Logo Card/Checklist	1.25	.90	.50

1959 Morrell Meats Dodgers

This popular set of Los Angeles Dodgers player cards was the first issue of a three-year run for the Southern California meat company. The 12 cards in this 2-1/2" by 3-1/2" set are unnumbered and feature fullframe, unbordered color photos. Card backs feature a company ad and list only the player's name, birthdate and birthplace. Two interesting errors exist in the set, as the cards for Clem Labine and Norm Larker show photos of Stan Williams and Joe Pignatano, respectively. Dodger greats Sandy Koufax and Duke Snider are key cards in the set.

	NR MT	EX	VG
Complete Set:	1200.00	600.00	350.00
Common Player:	50.00	25.00	15.00

(1)	Don Drysdale	100.00	50.00	30.00
(2)	Carl Furillo	65.00	32.00	19.50
(3)	Jim Gilliam	65.00	32.00	19.50
(4)	Gil Hodges	100.00	50.00	30.00
(5)	Sandy Koufax	225.00	112.00	70.00
(6)	Clem Labine (photo actually Stan Williams)	50.00	25.00	15.00
(7)	Norm Larker (photo actually Joe Pignatano)	50.00	25.00	15.00
(8)	Charlie Neal	50.00	25.00	15.00
(9)	Johnny Podres	65.00	32.00	19.50
(10)	John Roseboro	50.00	25.00	15.00
(11)	Duke Snider	225.00	112.00	70.00
(12)	Don Zimmer	80.00	40.00	25.00

1960 Morrell Meats Dodgers

 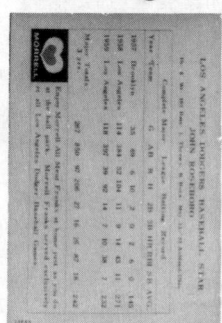

This 12-card set is the same 2-1/2" by 3-1/2" size as the 1959 set, and again features unbordered color card fronts. Five of the players included are new to the Morrell's sets. Card backs in 1960 list player statistics and brief personal data on each player. Cards for Gil Hodges, Carl Furillo and Duke Snider are apparently more scarce than others in the set. The 1960 set is again unnumbered.

	NR MT	EX	VG
Complete Set:	800.00	400.00	250.00
Common Player:	15.00	7.50	4.50

(1)	Walt Alston	25.00	12.50	7.50
(2)	Roger Craig	15.00	7.50	4.50
(3)	Don Drysdale	40.00	20.00	12.00
(4)	Carl Furillo	90.00	45.00	27.00
(5)	Gil Hodges	125.00	62.00	37.00
(6)	Sandy Koufax	125.00	62.00	37.00
(7)	Wally Moon	15.00	7.50	4.50
(8)	Charlie Neal	15.00	7.50	4.50
(9)	Johnny Podres	20.00	10.00	6.00
(10)	John Roseboro	15.00	7.50	4.50
(11)	Larry Sherry	15.00	7.50	4.50
(12)	Duke Snider	225.00	112.00	70.00

1961 Morrell Meats Dodgers

 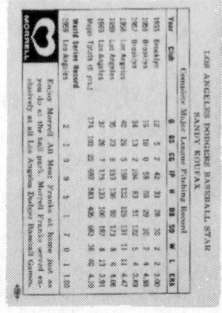

The Morrell set shrunk to just six cards in 1961,

with a format almost identical to the 1960 cards. Card fronts are again full-color, unbordered photos, with player statistics on the backs. The unnumbered cards measure a slightly smaller 2-1/4" by 3-1/4", and comparison of statistical information can also distinguish the cards from the 1960 version. Top cards in the set are Don Drysdale and Sandy Koufax, who are also the only two players to appear in all three years of the Morrell Meats sets.

	NR MT	EX	VG
Complete Set:	200.00	100.00	60.00
Common Player:	15.00	7.50	4.50
(1) Tommy Davis	20.00	10.00	6.00
(2) Don Drysdale	40.00	20.00	12.00
(3) Frank Howard	20.00	10.00	6.00
(4) Sandy Koufax	80.00	40.00	24.00
(5) Norm Larker	15.00	7.50	4.50
(6) Maury Wills	25.00	12.50	7.50

1983 Mother's Cookies Giants

After putting out Pacific Coast League sets in 1952 and 1953 Mother's Cookies distributed this full-color set of 20 San Francisco Giants cards three decades later. The 2-1/2" by 3-1/2" cards were produced by Barry Colla and included the Giants logo and player's name on the attractive card fronts. Card backs are numbered and contain biographical information, the Mother's Cookies logo, and a space for the player's autograph. Fifteen cards were given to every fan at the August 7, 1983 Giants game, with each fan also receiving a coupon good for five additional cards.

	MT	NR MT	EX
Complete Set:	18.00	13.50	7.25
Common Player:	.50	.40	.20
1 Frank Robinson	1.50	1.25	.60
2 Jack Clark	2.50	2.00	1.00
3 Chili Davis	1.50	1.25	.60
4 Johnnie LeMaster	.50	.40	.20
5 Greg Minton	.50	.40	.20
6 Bob Brenly	.70	.50	.30
7 Fred Breining	.50	.40	.20
8 Jeff Leonard	1.00	.70	.40
9 Darrell Evans	1.50	1.25	.60
10 Tom O'Malley	.50	.40	.20
11 Duane Kuiper	.50	.40	.20
12 Mike Krukow	.70	.50	.30
13 Atlee Hammaker	.70	.50	.30
14 Gary Lavelle	.50	.40	.20
15 Bill Laskey	.50	.40	.20
16 Max Venable	.50	.40	.20
17 Joel Youngblood	.50	.40	.20
18 Dave Bergman	.50	.40	.20
19 Mike Vail	.50	.40	.20
20 Andy McGaffigan	.50	.40	.20

Definitions for grading conditions are located in the introduction section at the front of this book.

1984 Mother's Cookies A's

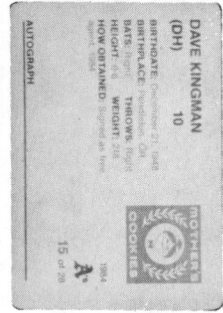

Following the success of their one set in 1983, Mother's Cookies issued five more team sets of cards in 1984. The A's set measures 2-1/2" by 3-1/2", and card fronts feature unbordered color photos with rounded corners. Card backs are quite similar in format to the 1983 Mother's Cookies Giants, with brief biographical information, card numbers, Mother's Cookies logo and space for player autograph. There are 28 cards in the A's set, with 20 of the cards distributed during a stadium promotion. Fans also received a coupon redeemable for eight additional cards. Since these additional cards do not necessarily complete collectors' sets, Mother's Cookies cards become very popular among card traders. The A's set includes cards for the manager, coaches and a checklist.

	MT	NR MT	EX
Complete Set:	15.00	11.00	6.00
Common Player:	.50	.40	.20
1 Steve Boros	.50	.40	.20
2 Rickey Henderson	3.00	2.25	1.25
3 Joe Morgan	1.50	1.25	.60
4 Dwayne Murphy	.70	.50	.30
5 Mike Davis	.70	.50	.30
6 Bruce Bochte	.50	.40	.20
7 Carney Lansford	.80	.60	.30
8 Steve McCatty	.50	.40	.20
9 Mike Heath	.50	.40	.20
10 Chris Codiroli	.50	.40	.20
11 Bill Almon	.50	.40	.20
12 Bill Caudill	.50	.40	.20
13 Donnie Hill	.50	.40	.20
14 Lary Sorenson	.50	.40	.20
15 Dave Kingman	.80	.60	.30
16 Garry Hancock	.50	.40	.20
17 Jeff Burroughs	.60	.45	.25
18 Tom Burgmeier	.50	.40	.20
19 Jim Essian	.50	.40	.20
20 Mike Warren	.50	.40	.20
21 Davey Lopes	.60	.45	.25
22 Ray Burris	.50	.40	.20
23 Tony Phillips	.50	.40	.20
24 Tim Conroy	.50	.40	.20
25 Jeff Bettendorf	.50	.40	.20
26 Keith Atherton	.60	.45	.25
27 A's Coaches (Clete Boyer, Bob Didier, Jackie Moore, Ron Schueler, Billy Williams)			
	.50	.40	.20
28 Oakland Coliseum/Checklist	.50	.40	.20

1984 Mother's Cookies Astros

Mother's Cookies also issued a full-color team set for the Houston Astros in 1984. The Astros set measures 2-1/2" by 3-1/2", and card fronts feature unbordered color photos with rounded corners. Card backs are quite similar in format to the 1983 Mother's Cookies Giants, with brief biographical information, card numbers, Mother's Cookies logo and space for player autograph. There are 28 cards

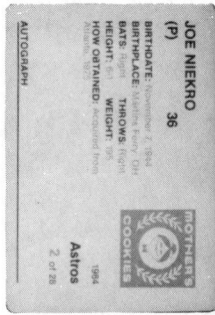

in the Astros set, with 20 of the cards distributed during a stadium promotion. Fans also received a coupon redeemable for eight additional cards. Since these additional cards do not necessarily complete collectors' sets, Mother's Cookies cards became very popular among card traders. The Astros set includes one card for the coaches and a checklist.

		MT	NR MT	EX
Complete Set:		15.00	11.00	6.00
Common Player:		.50	.40	.20
1	Nolan Ryan	2.50	2.00	1.00
2	Joe Niekro	.60	.45	.25
3	Alan Ashby	.50	.40	.20
4	Bill Doran	1.00	.70	.40
5	Phil Garner	.60	.45	.25
6	Ray Knight	.60	.45	.25
7	Dickie Thon	.60	.45	.25
8	Jose Cruz	.70	.50	.30
9	Jerry Mumphrey	.50	.40	.20
10	Terry Puhl	.50	.40	.20
11	Enos Cabell	.50	.40	.20
12	Harry Spilman	.50	.40	.20
13	Dave Smith	.60	.45	.25
14	Mike Scott	1.25	.90	.50
15	Bob Lillis	.50	.40	.20
16	Bob Knepper	.60	.45	.25
17	Frank DiPino	.50	.40	.20
18	Tom Wieghaus	.50	.40	.20
19	Denny Walling	.50	.40	.20
20	Tony Scott	.50	.40	.20
21	Alan Bannister	.50	.40	.20
22	Bill Dawley	.50	.40	.20
23	Vern Ruhle	.50	.40	.20
24	Mike LaCoss	.50	.40	.20
25	Mike Madden	.50	.40	.20
26	Craig Reynolds	.50	.40	.20
27	Astros Coaches (Cot Deal, Don Leppert, Denis Menke, Les Moss, Jerry Walker)	.50	.40	.20
28	Astros Logo/Checklist	.50	.40	.20

1984 Mother's Cookies Giants

Mother's Cookies issued a second annual full-color card set for the San Francisco Giants in 1984. The Giants set measures 2-1/2" by 3-1/2", and the round-cornered cards feature drawings of former Giant All-Star team selections. Card backs are quite similar in format to the 1983 Mother's Cookies Giants, with brief biographical information, card numbers and Mother's Cookies logo. No autograph space is included. There are 28 cards in the Giants set, with 20 of the cards distributed during a stadium promotion. Fans also received a coupon redeemable for eight additional cards. Since these additional cards do not necessarily complete collectors' sets, Mother's Cookies cards became very popular among card traders. Card number 28 is a checklist chart.

		MT	NR MT	EX
Complete Set:		15.00	11.00	6.00
Common Player:		.50	.40	.20
1	Willie Mays	2.50	2.00	1.00
2	Willie McCovey	2.00	1.50	.80
3	Juan Marichal	2.00	1.50	.80
4	Gaylord Perry	2.00	1.50	.80
5	Tom Haller	.60	.45	.25
6	Jim Davenport	.50	.40	.20
7	Jack Clark	1.25	.90	.50
8	Greg Minton	.50	.40	.20
9	Atlee Hammaker	.50	.40	.20
10	Gary Lavelle	.50	.40	.20
11	Orlando Cepeda	1.00	.70	.40
12	Bobby Bonds	.80	.60	.30
13	John Antonelli	.60	.45	.25
14	Bob Schmidt (photo actually Wes Westrum)	.50	.40	.20
15	Sam Jones	.50	.40	.20
16	Mike McCormick	.60	.45	.25
17	Ed Bailey	.50	.40	.20
18	Stu Miller	.50	.40	.20
19	Felipe Alou	.70	.50	.30
20	Jim Hart	.60	.45	.25
21	Dick Dietz	.50	.40	.20
22	Chris Speier	.50	.40	.20
23	Bobby Murcer	.70	.50	.30
24	John Montefusco	.50	.40	.20
25	Vida Blue	.70	.50	.30
26	Ed Whitson	.50	.40	.20
27	Darrell Evans	.70	.50	.30
28	All-Star Game Logo/Checklist	.50	.40	.20

1984 Mother's Cookies Mariners

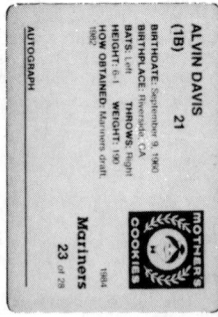

Mother's Cookies also issued a full-color set for the Seattle Mariners in 1984. The Mariners set measures 2-1/2" by 3-1/2", and card fronts feature unbordered color photos with rounded corners. Card backs are quite similar in format to the 1983 Mother's Cookies Giants, with brief biographical information, card numbers, Mother's Cookies logo and space for player autograph. There are 28 cards in the Mariners set, with 20 of the cards distributed during a stadium promotion. Fans also received a coupon redeemable for eight additional cards. Since these additional cards do not necessarily complete collectors' sets, Mother's Cookies cards became very popular among card traders. The Mariners set includes one card each for the manager, coaches and a checklist.

		MT	NR MT	EX
Complete Set:		15.00	11.00	6.00
Common Player:		.50	.40	.20
1	Del Crandall	.60	.45	.25
2	Barry Bonnell	.50	.40	.20
3	Dave Henderson	.70	.50	.30
4	Bob Kearney	.50	.40	.20
5	Mike Moore	.50	.40	.20
6	Spike Owen	.70	.50	.30
7	Gorman Thomas	.70	.50	.30
8	Ed Vande Berg	.50	.40	.20
9	Matt Young	.60	.45	.25
10	Larry Milbourne	.50	.40	.20
11	Dave Beard	.50	.40	.20
12	Jim Beattie	.50	.40	.20
13	Mark Langston	1.50	1.25	.60
14	Orlando Mercado	.50	.40	.20
15	Jack Perconte	.50	.40	.20
16	Pat Putnam	.50	.40	.20
17	Paul Mirabella	.50	.40	.20
18	Domingo Ramos	.50	.40	.20
19	Al Cowens	.50	.40	.20
20	Mike Stanton	.50	.40	.20
21	Steve Henderson	.50	.40	.20
22	Bob Stoddard	.50	.40	.20
23	Alvin Davis	1.75	1.25	.70
24	Phil Bradley	1.50	1.25	.60
25	Roy Thomas	.50	.40	.20
26	Darnell Coles	.80	.60	.30
27	Mariners Coaches (Chuck Cottier, Frank Funk, Ben Hines, Phil Roof, Rick Sweet)	.50	.40	.20
28	Seattle Kingdome/Checklist	.50	.40	.20

1984 Mother's Cookies Padres

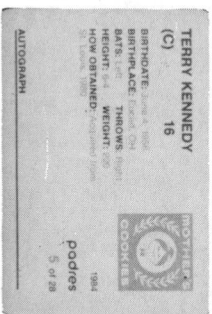

Mother's Cookies also issued a full-color set for the San Diego Padres in 1984. The Padres set measures 2-1/2" by 3-1/2", and card fronts feature unbordered color photos with rounded corners. Card backs are quite similar in format to the 1983 Mother's Cookies Giants, with brief biographical information, card numbers, Mother's Cookies logo and space for player autograph. There are 28 cards in the Padres set, with 20 of the cards distributed during a stadium promotion. Fans also received a coupon redeemable for eight additional cards. Since these additional cards do not necessarily complete collector's sets, Mother's Cookies cards became very popular among card traders. The Padres set includes one card each for the manager, coaches and a checklist.

		MT	NR MT	EX
Complete Set:		18.00	13.50	7.25
Common Player:		.50	.40	.20
1	Dick Williams	.50	.40	.20
2	Rich Gossage	1.00	.70	.40
3	Tim Lollar	.50	.40	.20
4	Eric Show	.70	.50	.30
5	Terry Kennedy	.60	.45	.25
6	Kurt Bevacqua	.50	.40	.20
7	Steve Garvey	2.00	1.50	.80
8	Garry Templeton	.70	.50	.30

		MT	NR MT	EX
9	Tony Gwynn	3.50	2.75	1.50
10	Alan Wiggins	.50	.40	.20
11	Dave Dravecky	.60	.45	.25
12	Tim Flannery	.50	.40	.20
13	Kevin McReynolds	2.25	1.75	.90
14	Bobby Brown	.50	.40	.20
15	Ed Whitson	.50	.40	.20
16	Doug Gwosdz	.50	.40	.20
17	Luis DeLeon	.50	.40	.20
18	Andy Hawkins	.60	.45	.25
19	Craig Lefferts	.50	.40	.20
20	Carmelo Martinez	.60	.45	.25
21	Sid Monge	.50	.40	.20
22	Graig Nettles	.80	.60	.30
23	Mario Ramirez	.50	.40	.20
24	Luis Salazar	.50	.40	.20
25	Champ Summers	.50	.40	.20
26	Mark Thurmond	.50	.40	.20
27	Padres Coaches (Harry Dunlop, Deacon Jones, Jack Krol, Norm Sherry, Ozzie Virgil)	.50	.40	.20
28	Jack Murphy Stadium/Checklist	.50	.40	.20

1985 Mother's Cookies A's

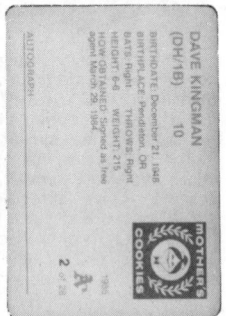

Mother's Cookies again issued five full-color sets for major league teams in 1985. The A's set measures 2-1/2" by 3-1/2", and card fronts feature unbordered color photos with rounded corners. Card backs are quite similar in format to the 1984 Mother's Cookies A's, with brief biographical information, card numbers, Mother's Cookies logo and space for player autograph. Card backs are dated 1985. There are 28 cards in the A's set, which was distributed in its entirety during a stadium promotion. The A's set includes one card each for the manager, coaches and a checklist.

		MT	NR MT	EX
Complete Set:		12.00	9.00	4.75
Common Player:		.40	.30	.15
1	Jackie Moore	.40	.30	.15
2	Dave Kingman	.70	.50	.30
3	Don Sutton	1.00	.70	.40
4	Mike Heath	.40	.30	.15
5	Alfredo Griffin	.60	.45	.25
6	Dwayne Murphy	.60	.45	.25
7	Mike Davis	.60	.45	.25
8	Carney Lansford	.70	.50	.30
9	Chris Codiroli	.40	.30	.15
10	Bruce Bochte	.40	.30	.15
11	Mickey Tettleton	.50	.40	.20
12	Donnie Hill	.40	.30	.15
13	Rob Picciolo	.40	.30	.15
14	Dave Collins	.50	.40	.20
15	Dusty Baker	.60	.45	.25
16	Tim Conroy	.40	.30	.15
17	Keith Atherton	.40	.30	.15
18	Jay Howell	.60	.45	.25
19	Mike Warren	.40	.30	.15
20	Steve McCatty	.40	.30	.15
21	Bill Krueger	.40	.30	.15
22	Curt Young	.70	.50	.30
23	Dan Meyer	.40	.30	.15
24	Mike Gallego	.50	.40	.20
25	Jeff Kaiser	.40	.30	.15

		MT	NR MT	EX
26	Steve Henderson	.40	.30	.15
27	A's Coaches (Clete Boyer, Bob Didier, Dave McKay, Wes Stock, Billy Williams)			
		.40	.30	.15
28	Oakland Coliseum/Checklist	.40	.30	.15

1985 Mother's Cookies Astros

Mother's Cookies issued a second annual full-color set for the Houston Astros in 1985. The Astros set measures 2-1/2" by 3-1/2", and card fronts feature unbordered color photos with rounded corners. Card backs are quite similar in format to the 1984 Mother's Cookies Astros, with brief biographical information, card number, Mother's Cookies logo and space for player autograph. Card backs are dated 1985. There are 28 cards in the Astros set, which was distributed in its entirety during a stadium promotion. The Astros set includes one card each for the manager, coaches and a checklist.

		MT	NR MT	EX
	Complete Set:	13.00	9.75	5.25
	Complete Player:	.40	.30	.15
1	Bob Lillis	.40	.30	.15
2	Nolan Ryan	3.00	2.25	1.25
3	Phil Garner	.50	.40	.20
4	Jose Cruz	.60	.45	.25
5	Denny Walling	.40	.30	.15
6	Joe Niekro	.60	.45	.25
7	Terry Puhl	.40	.30	.15
8	Bill Doran	.60	.45	.25
9	Dickie Thon	.40	.30	.15
10	Enos Cabell	.40	.30	.15
11	Frank Dipino (DiPino)	.40	.30	.15
12	Julio Solano	.40	.30	.15
13	Alan Ashby	.40	.30	.15
14	Craig Reynolds	.40	.30	.15
15	Jerry Mumphrey	.40	.30	.15
16	Bill Dawley	.40	.30	.15
17	Mark Bailey	.40	.30	.15
18	Mike Scott	1.00	.70	.40
19	Harry Spilman	.40	.30	.15
20	Bob Knepper	.50	.40	.20
21	Dave Smith	.50	.40	.20
22	Kevin Bass	.60	.45	.25
23	Tim Tolman	.40	.30	.15
24	Jeff Calhoun	.40	.30	.15
25	Jim Pankovits	.40	.30	.15
26	Ron Mathis	.40	.30	.15
27	Astros Coaches (Cot Deal, Matt Galante, Don Leppert, Denis Menke, Jerry Walker)			
		.40	.30	.15
28	Astros Logo/Checklist	.40	.30	.15

1985 Mother's Cookies Giants

Mother's Cookies issued a third annual full-color set for the San Francisco Giants in 1985. The Giants set measures 2-1/2" by 3-1/2", and card fronts feature unbordered color photos of current players with rounded corners. Card backs are quite similar in

format to the 1983 Mother's Cookies Giants, with brief biographical information, card numbers, Mother's Cookies logo and space for player autograph. Card backs are dated 1985. There are 28 cards in the Giants set, which was distributed in its entirety during a stadium promotion. The Giants set includes one card each for the manager, coaches and a checklist.

		MT	NR MT	EX
	Complete Set:	12.00	9.00	4.75
	Common Player:	.40	.30	.15
1	Jim Davenport	.40	.30	.15
2	Chili Davis	.60	.45	.25
3	Dan Gladden	.60	.45	.25
4	Jeff Leonard	.60	.45	.25
5	Manny Trillo	.50	.40	.20
6	Atlee Hammaker	.50	.40	.20
7	Bob Brenly	.50	.40	.20
8	Greg Minton	.40	.30	.15
9	Bill Laskey	.40	.30	.15
10	Vida Blue	.60	.45	.25
11	Mike Krukow	.50	.40	.20
12	Frank Williams	.60	.45	.25
13	Jose Uribe	.50	.40	.20
14	Johnnie LeMaster	.40	.30	.15
15	Scot Thompson	.40	.30	.15
16	Dave LaPoint	.50	.40	.20
17	David Green	.40	.30	.15
18	Chris Brown	1.00	.70	.40
19	Joel Youngblood	.40	.30	.15
20	Mark Davis	.40	.30	.15
21	Jim Gott	.40	.30	.15
22	Doug Gwosdz	.40	.30	.15
23	Scott Garrelts	.50	.40	.20
24	Gary Rajsich	.40	.30	.15
25	Rob Deer	1.00	.70	.40
26	Brad Wellman	.40	.30	.15
27	Coaches (Rocky Bridges, Chuck Hiller, Tom McCraw, Bob Miller, Jack Mull)			
		.40	.30	.15
28	Candlestick Park/Checklist	.40	.30	.15

1985 Mother's Cookies Mariners

 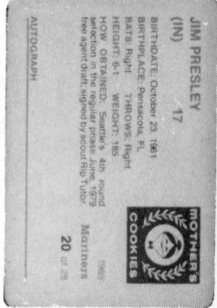

Mother's Cookies issued a second annual full-color

set for the Seattle Mariners in 1985. The Mariners set measures 2-1/2" by 3-1/2", and card fronts feature unbordered color photos with rounded corners. Card backs are quite similar in format to the 1984 Mother's Cookies Mariners, with brief biographical information, card numbers, Mother's Cookies logo and space for player autograph. Card backs are dated 1985. There are 28 cards in the Mariners set, which was distributed in its entirety during a stadium promotion. The Mariners set includes one card each for the coaches and a checklist.

		MT	NR MT	EX
Complete Set:		13.00	9.75	5.25
Common Player:		.40	.30	.15
1	Chuck Cottier	.40	.30	.15
2	Alvin Davis	1.25	.90	.50
3	Mark Langston	1.00	.70	.40
4	Dave Henderson	.40	.30	.15
5	Ed Vande Berg	.40	.30	.15
6	Al Cowens	.40	.30	.15
7	Spike Owen	.40	.30	.15
8	Mike Moore	.40	.30	.15
9	Gorman Thomas	.60	.45	.25
10	Barry Bonnell	.40	.30	.15
11	Jack Perconte	.40	.30	.15
12	Domingo Ramos	.40	.30	.15
13	Bob Kearney	.40	.30	.15
14	Matt Young	.40	.30	.15
15	Jim Beattie	.40	.30	.15
16	Mike Stanton	.40	.30	.15
17	David Valle	.50	.40	.20
18	Ken Phelps	.60	.45	.25
19	Salome Barojas	.40	.30	.15
20	Jim Presley	1.50	1.25	.60
21	Phil Bradley	1.00	.70	.40
22	Dave Geisel	.40	.30	.15
23	Harold Reynolds	.80	.60	.30
24	Edwin Nunez	.50	.40	.20
25	Mike Morgan	.40	.30	.15
26	Ivan Calderon	.80	.60	.30
27	Mariners Coaches (Deron Johnson, Jim Mahoney, Marty Martinez, Phil Regan, Phil Roof)	.40	.30	.15
28	Seattle Kingdome/Checklist	.40	.30	.15

1985 Mother's Cookies Padres

Mother's Cookies issued a second annual full-color set for the San Diego Padres in 1985. The Padres set measures 2-1/2" by 3-1/2", and card fronts feature unbordered color photos with rounded corners. Card backs are quite similar in format to the 1984 Mother's Cookies Padres, with brief biographical information, card numbers, Mother's Cookies logo and space for player autograph. Card backs are dated 1985. There are 28 cards in the Padres set, which was distributed in its entirety during a stadium promotion. The Padres set includes one card each for the manager, coaches and a checklist.

		MT	NR MT	EX
Complete Set:		12.00	9.00	4.75
Common Player:		.40	.30	.15

		MT	NR MT	EX
1	Dick Williams	.40	.30	.15
2	Tony Gwynn	3.00	2.25	1.25
3	Kevin McReynolds	1.50	1.25	.60
4	Graig Nettles	.70	.50	.30
5	Rich Gossage	.90	.70	.35
6	Steve Garvey	1.75	1.25	.70
7	Garry Templeton	.50	.40	.20
8	Dave Dravecky	.50	.40	.20
9	Eric Show	.60	.45	.25
10	Terry Kennedy	.50	.40	.20
11	Luis DeLeon	.40	.30	.15
12	Bruce Bochy	.40	.30	.15
13	Andy Hawkins	.50	.40	.20
14	Kurt Bevacqua	.40	.30	.15
15	Craig Lefferts	.40	.30	.15
16	Mario Ramirez	.40	.30	.15
17	LaMarr Hoyt	.40	.30	.15
18	Jerry Royster	.40	.30	.15
19	Tim Stoddard	.40	.30	.15
20	Tim Flannery	.40	.30	.15
21	Mark Thurmond	.40	.30	.15
22	Greg Booker	.50	.40	.20
23	Bobby Brown	.40	.30	.15
24	Carmelo Martinez	.50	.40	.20
25	Al Bumbry	.40	.30	.15
26	Jerry Davis	.40	.30	.15
27	Padres Coaches (Galen Cisco, Harry Dunlop, Deacon Jones, Jack Krol, Ozzie Virgil)	.40	.30	.15
28	Jack Murphy Stadium/Checklist	.40	.30	.15

1986 Mother's Cookies A's

Mother's Cookies produced four more full-color team card sets in 1986, with only the San Diego Padres not repeating from the 1985 group. The third annual set for the Oakland A's measures 2-1/2" by 3-1/2", and card fronts feature unbordered color photos with rounded corners. Card backs are quite similar in format to previous years, with brief biographical information, card numbers and the Mother's Cookies logo. Card backs are dated 1986. There are 28 cards in the A's set, with 20 of the cards distributed during a stadium promotion. Each fan also received a coupon redeemable for eight additional cards. The A's set includes one card each for the manager, coaches and a checklist.

		MT	NR MT	EX
Complete Set:		25.00	20.00	10.00
Common Player:		.30	.25	.12
1	Jackie Moore	.30	.25	.12
2	Dave Kingman	.60	.45	.25
3	Dusty Baker	.40	.30	.15
4	Joaquin Andujar	.40	.30	.15
5	Alfredo Griffin	.40	.30	.15
6	Dwayne Murphy	.40	.30	.15
7	Mike Davis	.40	.30	.15
8	Carney Lansford	.50	.40	.20
9	Jose Canseco	18.00	13.50	7.25
10	Bruce Bochte	.30	.25	.12
11	Mickey Tettleton	.30	.25	.12
12	Donnie Hill	.30	.25	.12
13	Jose Rijo	.60	.45	.25
14	Rick Langford	.30	.25	.12
15	Chris Codiroli	.30	.25	.12

		MT	NR MT	EX
16	Moose Haas	.30	.25	.12
17	Keith Atherton	.30	.25	.12
18	Jay Howell	.40	.30	.15
19	Tony Phillips	.30	.25	.12
20	Steve Henderson	.30	.25	.12
21	Bill Krueger	.30	.25	.12
22	Steve Ontiveros	.40	.30	.15
23	Bill Bathe	.30	.25	.12
24	Rickey Peters	.30	.25	.12
25	Tim Birtsas	.30	.25	.12
26	Trainers Card (Frank Ciensczyk, Larry Davis, Steve Vucinich, Barry Weinberg)	.30	.25	.12
27	Coaches Card (Bob Didier, Dave McKay, Jeff Newman, Ron Plaza, Wes Stock, Bob Watson)	.30	.25	.12
28	Oakland Coliseum/Checklist	.30	.25	.12

1986 Mother's Cookies Astros

Mother's Cookies produced a third annual set for the Houston Astros in 1985. The set measure 2-1/2" by 3-1/2", and card fronts feature unbordered color paintings of Houston's past All-Star Game performers. The round-cornered cards have backs quite similar in format to previous years, with brief biographical information, card numbers and the Mother's Cookies logo. Card backs are dated 1986. There are 28 cards in the Astros set, with 20 of the cards distributed during a stadium promotion. Each fan also received a coupon redeemable for eight additional cards. The Astros set also includes a checklist card.

		MT	NR MT	EX
	Complete Set:	10.00	7.50	4.00
	Common Player:	.30	.25	.12
1	Dick Farrell	.30	.25	.12
2	Hal Woodeschick (Woodeshick)	.30	.25	.12
3	Joe Morgan	1.00	.70	.40
4	Claude Raymond	.30	.25	.12
5	Mike Cuellar	.40	.30	.15
6	Rusty Staub	.60	.45	.25
7	Jimmy Wynn	.40	.30	.15
8	Larry Dierker	.40	.30	.15
9	Denis Menke	.30	.25	.12
10	Don Wilson	.30	.25	.12
11	Cesar Cedeno	.50	.40	.20
12	Lee May	.40	.30	.15
13	Bob Watson	.40	.30	.15
14	Ken Forsch	.40	.30	.15
15	Joaquin Andujar	.40	.30	.15
16	Terry Puhl	.30	.25	.12
17	Joe Niekro	.40	.30	.15
18	Craig Reynolds	.30	.25	.12
19	Joe Sambito	.30	.25	.12
20	Jose Cruz	.60	.45	.25
21	J.R. Richard	.40	.30	.15
22	Bob Knepper	.40	.30	.15
23	Nolan Ryan	1.50	1.25	.60
24	Ray Knight	.40	.30	.15
25	Bill Dawley	.30	.25	.12
26	Dickie Thon	.40	.30	.15
27	Jerry Mumphrey	.30	.25	.12
28	Astros Logo/Checklist	.30	.25	.12

1986 Mother's Cookies Giants

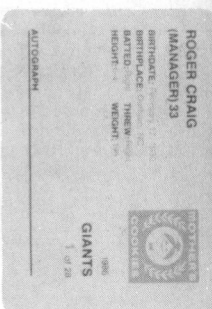

Mother's Cookies produced a fourth annual set for the San Francisco Giants in 1985. Cards in the set measure 2-1/2" by 3-1/2", and the fronts feature unbordered color photos with rounded corners. Card backs are quite similar in format to previous years, with brief biographical information, card numbers, and the Mother's Cookies logo. Card backs are dated 1986. There are 28 cards in the Giants set, with 20 of the cards distributed during a stadium promotion. Each fan also received a coupon redeemable for eight additional cards. The Giants set also includes a card for the manager and a checklist.

		MT	NR MT	EX
	Complete Set:	18.00	13.50	7.25
	Common Player:	.30	.25	.12
1	Roger Craig	.40	.30	.15
2	Chili Davis	.60	.45	.25
3	Dan Gladden	.40	.30	.15
4	Jeff Leonard	.60	.45	.25
5	Bob Brenly	.40	.30	.15
6	Atlee Hammaker	.40	.30	.15
7	Will Clark	10.00	7.50	4.00
8	Greg Minton	.30	.25	.12
9	Candy Maldonado	.40	.30	.15
10	Vida Blue	.50	.40	.20
11	Mike Krukow	.40	.30	.15
12	Bob Melvin	.40	.30	.15
13	Jose Uribe	.40	.30	.15
14	Dan Driessen	.40	.30	.15
15	Jeff Robinson	.50	.40	.20
16	Rob Thompson	.80	.60	.30
17	Mike LaCoss	.30	.25	.12
18	Chris Brown	.35	.25	.14
19	Scott Garrelts	.50	.40	.20
20	Mark Davis	.50	.40	.20
21	Jim Gott	.30	.25	.12
22	Brad Wellman	.30	.25	.12
23	Roger Mason	.30	.25	.12
24	Bill Laskey	.30	.25	.12
25	Brad Gulden	.30	.25	.12
26	Joel Youngblood	.30	.25	.12
27	Juan Berenguer	.30	.25	.12
28	Coaches/Checklist (Bill Fahey, Bob Lillis, Gordy MacKenzie, Jose Morales, Norm Sherry)	.30	.25	.12

1986 Mother's Cookies Mariners

Mother's Cookies produced a third annual set for the Seattle Mariners in 1985. The set measures 2-1/2" by 3-1/2", and card fronts feature unbordered color photos with rounded corners. Card backs are quite similar in format to previous years, with brief biographical information, card numbers and the Mother's Cookies logo. Card backs are dated 1986. There are 28 cards in the Mariners set, with 20 of the cards distributed during a stadium promotion. Each fan also received a coupon redeemable for eight

additional cards. The Mariners set also includes a card for the manager and a checklist.

		MT	NR MT	EX
	Complete Set:	12.00	9.00	4.75
	Common Player:	.30	.25	.12
1	Dick Williams	.30	.25	.12
2	Alvin Davis	1.00	.70	.40
3	Mark Langston	.80	.60	.30
4	Dave Henderson	.50	.40	.20
5	Steve Yeager	.30	.25	.12
6	Al Cowens	.30	.25	.12
7	Jim Presley	.70	.50	.30
8	Phil Bradley	.70	.50	.30
9	Gorman Thomas	.50	.40	.20
10	Barry Bonnell	.30	.25	.12
11	Milt Wilcox	.30	.25	.12
12	Domingo Ramos	.30	.25	.12
13	Paul Mirabella	.30	.25	.12
14	Matt Young	.30	.25	.12
15	Ivan Calderon	.60	.45	.25
16	Bill Swift	.40	.30	.15
17	Pete Ladd	.30	.25	.12
18	Ken Phelps	.40	.30	.15
19	Karl Best	.30	.25	.12
20	Spike Owen	.40	.30	.15
21	Mike Moore	.30	.25	.12
22	Danny Tartabull	1.75	1.25	.70
23	Bob Kearney	.30	.25	.12
24	Edwin Nunez	.30	.25	.12
25	Mike Morgan	.30	.25	.12
26	Roy Thomas	.30	.25	.12
27	Jim Beattie	.30	.25	.12
28	Coaches/Checklist (Deron Johnson, Marty Martinez, Phil Regan, Phil Roof, Ozzie Virgil)	.30	.25	.12

1987 Mother's Cookies A's

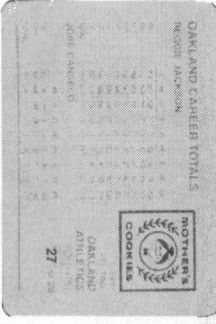

Continuing with a tradition of producing beautiful baseball cards, Mother's Cookies of Oakland, Calif. issued a 28-card set featuring every Oakland A's player to have been elected to the All-Star Game since 1968. The full-color photos came from the private collection of nationally known photographer Doug McWilliams. Twenty of the 28 cards were given out to fans attending the A's game of July 5th. An

additional eight cards were available by redeeming a mail-in certificate. The cards, which measure 2-1/2" by 3-1/2", feature rounded corners. The card backs carry the player's All-Star Game statistics.

		MT	NR MT	EX
	Complete Set:	18.00	13.50	7.25
	Common Player:	.30	.25	.12
1	Bert Campaneris	.40	.30	.15
2	Rick Monday	.40	.30	.15
3	John Odom	.30	.25	.12
4	Sal Bando	.40	.30	.15
5	Reggie Jackson	2.00	1.50	.80
6	Jim Hunter	1.00	.70	.40
7	Vida Blue	.50	.40	.20
8	Dave Duncan	.30	.25	.12
9	Joe Rudi	.40	.30	.15
10	Rollie Fingers	.70	.50	.30
11	Ken Holtzman	.40	.30	.15
12	Dick Williams	.40	.30	.15
13	Alvin Dark	.30	.25	.12
14	Gene Tenace	.40	.30	.15
15	Claudell Washington	.40	.30	.15
16	Phil Garner	.30	.25	.12
17	Wayne Gross	.30	.25	.12
18	Matt Keough	.30	.25	.12
19	Jeff Newman	.30	.25	.12
20	Rickey Henderson	2.00	1.50	.80
21	Tony Armas	.40	.30	.15
22	Mike Norris	.30	.25	.12
23	Billy Martin	.50	.40	.20
24	Bill Caudill	.30	.25	.12
25	Jay Howell	.40	.30	.15
26	Jose Canseco	3.00	2.25	1.25
27	Jose and Reggie (Jose Canseco, Reggie Jackson)	2.00	1.50	.80
28	A's Logo/Checklist	.30	.25	.12

1987 Mother's Cookies Astros

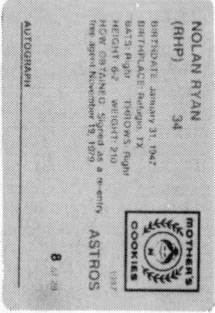

Twenty of 28 cards featuring Astros players were given out to the first 25,000 fans attending the July 17th game at the Astrodome. An additional eight cards (though not necessarily the exact eight needed to complete a set) were available from the card producer, Mother's Cookies, by redeeming a mail-in certificate. The cards have rounded corners and measure the standard 2-1/2" by 3-1/2". The backs are printed in purple and orange and contain personal player information, the Mother's Cookies logo, the card number and a spot for the player's autograph.

		MT	NR MT	EX
	Complete Set:	12.00	9.00	4.75
	Common Player:	.30	.25	.12
1	Hal Lanier	.30	.25	.12
2	Mike Scott	1.00	.70	.40
3	Jose Cruz	.50	.40	.20
4	Bill Doran	.50	.40	.20
5	Bob Knepper	.40	.30	.15
6	Phil Garner	.40	.30	.15
7	Terry Puhl	.30	.25	.12
8	Nolan Ryan	3.00	2.25	1.25
9	Kevin Bass	.50	.40	.20
10	Glenn Davis	1.00	.70	.40

		MT	NR MT	EX
11	Alan Ashby	.30	.25	.12
12	Charlie Kerfeld	.30	.25	.12
13	Denny Walling	.30	.25	.12
14	Danny Darwin	.30	.25	.12
15	Mark Bailey	.30	.25	.12
16	Davey Lopes	.40	.30	.15
17	Dave Meads	.40	.30	.15
18	Aurelio Lopez	.30	.25	.12
19	Craig Reynolds	.30	.25	.12
20	Dave Smith	.40	.30	.15
21	Larry Anderson (Andersen)	.30	.25	.12
22	Jim Pankovits	.30	.25	.12
23	Jim Deshaies	.50	.40	.20
24	Bert Pena	.30	.25	.12
25	Dickie Thon	.30	.25	.12
26	Billy Hatcher	.50	.40	.20
27	Astros Coaches (Yogi Berra, Matt Galante, Denis Menke, Les Moss, Gene Tenace)	.30	.25	.12
28	Houston Astrodome/Checklist	.30	.25	.12

1987 Mother's Cookies Dodgers

Mother's Cookies produced for the first time in 1987 a baseball card set featuring the Los Angeles Dodgers. Twenty of the 28 cards in the set were given out to youngsters 14 and under at Dodger Stadium on August 9th. An additional eight cards were available from Mother's Cookies via a mail-in coupon card. The borderless, full-color cards measure 2-1/2" by 3-1/2" and have rounded corners. A special album designed to house the set was available for $3.95 through a mail-in offer.

		MT	NR MT	EX
	Complete Set:	12.00	9.00	4.75
	Common Player:	.30	.25	.12
1	Tom Lasorda	.40	.30	.15
2	Pedro Guerrero	.80	.60	.30
3	Steve Sax	.80	.60	.30
4	Fernando Valenzuela	1.00	.70	.40
5	Mike Marshall	.70	.50	.30
6	Orel Hershiser	1.00	.70	.40
7	Mariano Duncan	.30	.25	.12
8	Bill Madlock	.40	.30	.15
9	Bob Welch	.60	.45	.25
10	Mike Scioscia	.40	.30	.15
11	Mike Ramsey	.30	.25	.12
12	Matt Young	.30	.25	.12
13	Franklin Stubbs	.40	.30	.15
14	Tom Niedenfuer	.40	.30	.15
15	Reggie Williams	.40	.30	.15
16	Rick Honeycutt	.30	.25	.12
17	Dave Anderson	.30	.25	.12
18	Alejandro Pena	.40	.30	.15
19	Ken Howell	.30	.25	.12
20	Len Matuszek	.30	.25	.12
21	Tim Leary	.40	.30	.15
22	Tracy Woodson	.40	.30	.15
23	Alex Trevino	.30	.25	.12
24	Ken Landreaux	.30	.25	.12
25	Mickey Hatcher	.30	.25	.12
26	Brian Holton	.40	.30	.15
27	Dodgers' Coaches (Joey Amalfitano, Mark Cresse, Don McMahon, Manny Mota, Ron Perranoski, Bill Russell)	.30	.25	.12

		MT	NR MT	EX
28	Dodger Stadium/Checklist	.30	.25	.12

1987 Mother's Cookies Giants

Distribution of the 1987 Mother's Cookies Giants, cards took place at Candlestick Park for the Giants' June 27th game. Twenty of the 28 cards in the set were given to the first 25,000 fans entering the park. The starter packet of 20 cards contained a mail-in coupon card which was good for an additional eight cards. The cards, which measure 2-1/2" by 3-1/2" in size have rounded corners. The card backs are printed in red and purple and contain personal and statistical information along with the Mother's Cookies logo.

		MT	NR MT	EX
	Complete Set:	12.00	9.00	4.75
	Common Player:	.30	.25	.12
1	Roger Craig	.40	.30	.15
2	Will Clark	4.50	3.50	1.75
3	Chili Davis	.40	.30	.15
4	Bob Brenly	.30	.25	.12
5	Chris Brown	.30	.25	.12
6	Mike Krukow	.40	.30	.15
7	Candy Maldonado	.40	.30	.15
8	Jeffrey Leonard	.50	.40	.20
9	Greg Minton	.30	.25	.12
10	Robby Thompson	.40	.30	.15
11	Scott Garrelts	.30	.25	.12
12	Bob Melvin	.30	.25	.12
13	Jose Uribe	.30	.25	.12
14	Mark Davis	.30	.25	.12
15	Eddie Milner	.30	.25	.12
16	Harry Spilman	.30	.25	.12
17	Kelly Downs	.60	.45	.25
18	Chris Speier	.30	.25	.12
19	Jim Gott	.30	.25	.12
20	Joel Youngblood	.30	.25	.12
21	Mike LaCoss	.30	.25	.12
22	Matt Williams	1.75	1.25	.70
23	Roger Mason	.30	.25	.12
24	Mike Aldrete	.60	.45	.25
25	Jeff Robinson	.40	.30	.15
26	Mark Grant	.30	.25	.12
27	Coaches (Bill Fahey, Bob Lillis, Gordon MacKenzie, Jose Morales, Norm Sherry, Don Zimmer)	.30	.25	.12
28	Candlestick Park/Checklist	.30	.25	.12

1987 Mother's Cookies Mariners

For the fourth consecutive year, Mother's Cookies issued a baseball card set featuring the Seattle Mariners. Twenty of the 28 cards in the set were distributed to the first 20,000 fans entering the Kingdome on August 9th. An additional eight cards (though not necessarily the eight cards needed to complete the set) were available by redeeming a mail-in certificate. Collectors were encouraged to

were handed out to the first 25,000 fans entering Arlington Stadium on July 17th. An additional eight cards (though not necessarily the eight needed to complete a set) were available by redeeming a mail-in certificate. The cards, which measure 2-1/2" by 3-1/2", have rounded corners and glossy finishes like all Mother's Cookies issued in 1987.

		MT	NR MT	EX
	Complete Set:	10.00	7.50	4.00
	Complete Set:	.30	.25	.12
1	Bobby Valentine	.40	.30	.15
2	Pete Incaviglia	1.00	.70	.40
3	Charlie Hough	.40	.30	.15
4	Oddibe McDowell	.50	.40	.20
5	Larry Parrish	.50	.40	.20
6	Scott Fletcher	.40	.30	.15
7	Steve Buechele	.30	.25	.12
8	Tom Paciorek	.30	.25	.12
9	Pete O'Brien	.60	.45	.25
10	Darrell Porter	.30	.25	.12
11	Greg Harris	.30	.25	.12
12	Don Slaught	.30	.25	.12
13	Ruben Sierra	1.75	1.25	.70
14	Curtis Wilkerson	.30	.25	.12
15	Dale Mohorcic	.40	.30	.15
16	Ron Meredith	.30	.25	.12
17	Mitch Williams	.40	.30	.15
18	Bob Brower	.40	.30	.15
19	Edwin Correa	.30	.25	.12
20	Geno Petralli	.30	.25	.12
21	Mike Loynd	.40	.30	.15
22	Jerry Browne	.40	.30	.15
23	Jose Guzman	.50	.40	.20
24	Jeff Kunkel	.30	.25	.12
25	Bobby Witt	.60	.45	.25
26	Jeff Russell	.30	.25	.12
27	Trainers (Danny Wheat, Bill Zeigler)			
		.30	.25	.12
28	Rangers' Coaches/Checklist (Joe Ferguson, Tim Foli, Tom House, Art Howe, Dave Oliver, Tom Robson)	.30	.25	.12

1987 Mother's Cookies
Mark McGwire

A four-card set featuring outstanding rookie Mark McGwire of the Oakland Athletics was produced by Mother's Cookies of Oakland, Calif. Cards are 2-1/2" by 3-1/2" and have rounded corners and glossy finishes like other Mother's issues. The four-card set was obtainable by two methods. A complete set could be received by sending in eight proof-of-purchase seals. Also, sets could be secured at the National Sports Collectors Convention held July 9-12 in San Francisco. Convention goers received one card as a bonus for each Mother's Cookies baseball card album purchased.

		MT	NR MT	EX
	Complete Set:	20.00	15.00	8.00
	Common Player:	4.00	3.00	1.50
1	Mark McGwire (portrait)	4.00	3.00	1.50

trade to complete a set. The 2-1/2" by 3-1/2" full-color cards feature glossy finishes and rounded corners. A specially designed album to house the set was available.

		MT	NR MT	EX
	Complete Set:	9.00	6.75	3.50
	Common Player:	.30	.25	.12
1	Dick Williams	.30	.25	.12
2	Alvin Davis	.80	.60	.30
3	Mike Moore	.30	.25	.12
4	Jim Presley	.60	.45	.25
5	Mark Langston	.70	.50	.30
6	Phil Bradley	.60	.45	.25
7	Ken Phelps	.40	.30	.15
8	Mike Morgan	.30	.25	.12
9	David Valle	.30	.25	.12
10	Harold Reynolds	.60	.45	.25
11	Edwin Nunez	.30	.25	.12
12	Bob Kearney	.30	.25	.12
13	Scott Bankhead	.40	.30	.15
14	Scott Bradley	.30	.25	.12
15	Mickey Brantley	.40	.30	.15
16	Mark Huismann	.30	.25	.12
17	Mike Kingery	.40	.30	.15
18	John Moses	.30	.25	.12
19	Donell Nixon	.40	.30	.15
20	Rey Quinones	.40	.30	.15
21	Domingo Ramos	.30	.25	.12
22	Jerry Reed	.30	.25	.12
23	Rich Renteria	.40	.30	.15
24	Rich Monteleone	.40	.30	.15
25	Mike Trujillo	.30	.25	.12
26	Bill Wilkinson	.40	.30	.15
27	John Christensen	.30	.25	.12
28	Coaches/Checklist (Billy Connors, Frank Howard, Phil Roof, Bobby Tolan, Ozzie Virgil)			
		.30	.25	.12

1987 Mother's Cookies
Rangers

While Mother's Cookies of Oakland, Calif., had been producing high-quality baseball card sets of various teams, the Texas Rangers were highlighted for the first time in 1987. Twenty cards from the 28-card set

		MT	NR MT	EX
2	Mark McGwire (leaning on bat rack)			
		4.00	3.00	1.50
3	Mark McGwire (beginning batting swing)			
		4.00	3.00	1.50
4	Mark McGwire (batting follow-through)			
		4.00	3.00	1.50

1988 Mother's Cookies A's

Complete at 28 cards (including checklist), the 1988 Mother's Cookies A's set features full-color, borderless cards with rounded corners in the standard 2-1/2" by 3-1/2" size. The backs are printed in red and purple on white and include biographical information, the Mother's Cookies logo and card number. Starter sets of 20 cards were distributed at the stadium along with a promotional card redeemable for another eights cards (not necessarily those needed to complete the set). An album to house the cards was also available.

		MT	NR MT	EX
Complete Set:		16.00	12.00	6.50
Common Player:		.30	.25	.12
1	Tony LaRussa	.30	.25	.12
2	Mark McGwire	3.00	2.25	1.25
3	Dave Stewart	.50	.40	.20
4	Mickey Tettleton	.30	.25	.12
5	Dave Parker	.70	.50	.30
6	Carney Lansford	.50	.40	.20
7	Jose Canseco	3.00	2.25	1.25
8	Don Baylor	.50	.40	.20
9	Bob Welch	.40	.30	.15
10	Dennis Eckersley	.40	.30	.15
11	Walt Weiss	1.50	1.25	.60
12	Tony Phillips	.30	.25	.12
13	Steve Ontiveros	.30	.25	.12
14	Dave Henderson	.30	.25	.12
15	Stan Javier	.30	.25	.12
16	Ron Hassey	.30	.25	.12
17	Curt Young	.40	.30	.15
18	Glenn Hubbard	.30	.25	.12
19	Storm Davis	.30	.25	.12
20	Eric Plunk	.30	.25	.12
21	Matt Young	.30	.25	.12
22	Mike Gallego	.30	.25	.12
23	Rick Honeycutt	.30	.25	.12
24	Doug Jennings	.50	.40	.20
25	Gene Nelson	.30	.25	.12
26	Greg Cadaret	.40	.30	.15
27	A's Coaches (Dave Duncan, Rene Lachemann, Jim Lefebvre, Dave McKay, Mike Paul, Bob Watson)	.30	.25	.12
28	Jose Canseco, Mark McGwire	3.00	2.25	1.25

1988 Mother's Cookies Astros

One of six team sets issued by Mother's Cookies in 1988, the 28-card Houston Astros set is similar in design to other Mother's Cookies sets. The cards are the standard 2-1/2" by 3-1/2" size with rounded corners and feature full-color, borderless photos on the fronts with the player's name in an upper or lower

corner. The backs feature red and purple printing on white and include brief biographical information, the Mother's logo and card number. Twenty of the cards were distributed in a stadium promotion, along with a redemption card that could be exchanged for an additional eight cards (but not necessarily the eight needed to complete the set.) An album was also available to house the set.

		MT	NR MT	EX
Complete Set:		10.00	7.50	4.00
Common Player:		.30	.25	.12
1	Hal Lanier	.30	.25	.12
2	Mike Scott	.90	.70	.35
3	Gerald Young	.70	.50	.30
4	Bill Doran	.50	.40	.20
5	Bob Knepper	.40	.30	.15
6	Billy Hatcher	.50	.40	.20
7	Terry Puhl	.30	.25	.12
8	Nolan Ryan	2.00	1.50	.80
9	Kevin Bass	.50	.40	.20
10	Glenn Davis	.90	.70	.35
11	Alan Ashby	.30	.25	.12
12	Steve Henderson	.30	.25	.12
13	Denny Walling	.30	.25	.12
14	Danny Darwin	.30	.25	.12
15	Mark Bailey	.30	.25	.12
16	Ernie Camacho	.30	.25	.12
17	Rafael Ramirez	.30	.25	.12
18	Jeff Heathcock	.30	.25	.12
19	Craig Reynolds	.30	.25	.12
20	Dave Smith	.40	.30	.15
21	Larry Andersen	.30	.25	.12
22	Jim Pankovits	.30	.25	.12
23	Jim Deshaies	.40	.30	.15
24	Juan Agosto	.30	.25	.12
25	Chuck Jackson	.40	.30	.15
26	Joaquin Andujar	.40	.30	.15
27	Astros Coaches (Yogi Berra, Gene Clines, Matt Galante, Marc Hill, Denis Menke, Les Moss)	.30	.25	.12
28	Trainers Card/Checklist (Doc Ewell, Dave Labossiere, Dennis Liborio)	.30	.25	.12

1988 Mother's Cookies Dodgers

 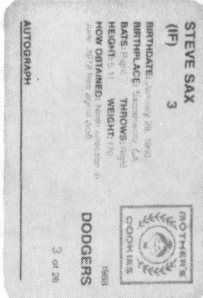

Similar in design to other Mother's Cookies sets,

the 1988 Dodgers issue featured full-color, borderless photos with backs printed in red and purple. The 28 cards in the set measure the standard 2-1/2" by 3-1/2" with rounded corners. Starter packs of 20 cards were distributed at a ballpark promotion along with a coupon card that could be exchanged for an additional eight cards at a local card show or through the mail. The backs of the cards include brief player information, the Mother's Cookies logo and card number. The promotion also included a special album to house the set.

		MT	NR MT	EX
	Complete Set:	12.00	9.00	4.75
	Common Player:	.30	.25	.12
1	Tom Lasorda	.40	.30	.15
2	Pedro Guerrero	.80	.60	.30
3	Steve Sax	.80	.60	.30
4	Fernando Valenzuela	1.00	.70	.40
5	Mike Marshall	.70	.50	.30
6	Orel Hershiser	1.00	.70	.40
7	Alfredo Griffin	.30	.25	.12
8	Kirk Gibson	1.00	.70	.40
9	Don Sutton	.50	.40	.20
10	Mike Scioscia	.40	.30	.15
11	Franklin Stubbs	.40	.30	.15
12	Mike Davis	.40	.30	.15
13	Jesse Orosco	.40	.30	.15
14	John Shelby	.30	.25	.12
15	Rick Dempsey	.40	.30	.15
16	Jay Howell	.40	.30	.15
17	Dave Anderson	.30	.25	.12
18	Alejandro Pena	.40	.30	.15
19	Jeff Hamilton	.40	.30	.15
20	Danny Heep	.30	.25	.12
21	Tim Leary	.40	.30	.15
22	Brad Havens	.30	.25	.12
23	Tim Belcher	.60	.45	.25
24	Ken Howell	.30	.25	.12
25	Mickey Hatcher	.30	.25	.12
26	Brian Holton	.30	.25	.12
27	Mike Devereaux	.60	.45	.25
28	Dodgers Coaches/Checklist (Joe Amalfitano, Mark Cresse, Joe Ferguson, Ben Hines, Manny Mota, Ron Perranoski, Bill Russell)	.30	.25	.12

1988 Mother's Cookies Giants

One of six team sets issued in 1988 by Mother's Cookies, this 28-card Giants set featured full-color borderless photos on a standard-size card with rounded corners. The backs, printed in red and purple, include brief player information, the Mother's Cookies logo and card number. Twenty different cards were distributed as a starter set at a stadium promotion along with a coupon card that could be redeemed for an additional eight cards (not necessarily those needed to complete the set). The redemption cards could be exchanged through the mail or redeemed at a local card show.

		MT	NR MT	EX
	Complete Set:	12.00	9.00	4.75
	Common Player:	.30	.25	.12

		MT	NR MT	EX
1	Roger Craig	.40	.30	.15
2	Will Clark	3.50	2.75	1.50
3	Kevin Mitchell	1.50	1.25	.60
4	Bob Brenly	.40	.30	.15
5	Mike Aldrete	.40	.30	.15
6	Mike Krukow	.40	.30	.15
7	Candy Maldonado	.40	.30	.15
8	Jeffrey Leonard	.40	.30	.15
9	Dave Dravecky	.40	.30	.15
10	Robby Thompson	.40	.30	.15
11	Scott Garrelts	.30	.25	.12
12	Bob Melvin	.30	.25	.12
13	Jose Uribe	.30	.25	.12
14	Brett Butler	.40	.30	.15
15	Rick Reuschel	.50	.40	.20
16	Harry Spilman	.30	.25	.12
17	Kelly Downs	.50	.40	.20
18	Chris Speier	.30	.25	.12
19	Atlee Hammaker	.30	.25	.12
20	Joel Youngblood	.30	.25	.12
21	Mike LaCoss	.30	.25	.12
22	Don Robinson	.30	.25	.12
23	Mark Wasinger	.40	.30	.15
24	Craig Lefferts	.30	.25	.12
25	Phil Garner	.30	.25	.12
26	Joe Price	.30	.25	.12
27	Giants Coaches (Dusty Baker, Bill Fahey, Bob Lillis, Gordie MacKenzie, Jose Morales, Norm Sherry)	.30	.25	.12
28	Logo Card/Checklist	.30	.25	.12

1988 Mother's Cookies Mariners

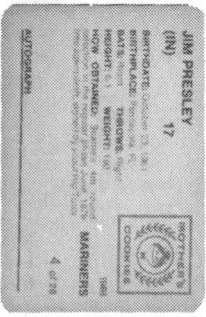

Similar in design to other Mother's Cookies sets, the 28-card Mariners issue featured full-color, borderless photos on a standard-size card with rounded corners. The backs, printed in red and purple, included brief biographical information, the Mother's Cookies logo and card number. Twenty-card starter packs were distributed at a stadium promotion, where fans also received a coupon card that could be exchanged for an additional eight cards (not necessarily those needed to complete the set). The coupon card could be redeemed through the mail or exchanged at a local baseball card show. As with the rest of the 1988 Mother's Cookies sets, an album was also available to house the cards.

		MT	NR MT	EX
	Complete Set:	10.00	7.50	4.00
	Common Player:	.30	.25	.12
1	Dick Williams	.30	.25	.12
2	Alvin Davis	.70	.50	.30
3	Mike Moore	.30	.25	.12
4	Jim Presley	.50	.40	.20
5	Mark Langston	.60	.45	.25
6	Henry Cotto	.30	.25	.12
7	Ken Phelps	.40	.30	.15
8	Steve Trout	.30	.25	.12
9	David Valle	.30	.25	.12
10	Harold Reynolds	.40	.30	.15
11	Edwin Nunez	.30	.25	.12
12	Glenn Wilson	.30	.25	.12
13	Scott Bankhead	.30	.25	.12

		MT	NR MT	EX
14	Scott Bradley	.30	.25	.12
15	Mickey Brantley	.30	.25	.12
16	Bruce Fields	.30	.25	.12
17	Mike Kingery	.30	.25	.12
18	Mike Campbell	.50	.40	.20
19	Mike Jackson	.40	.30	.15
20	Rey Quinones	.30	.25	.12
21	Mario Diaz	.30	.25	.12
22	Jerry Reed	.30	.25	.12
23	Rich Renteria	.30	.25	.12
24	Julio Solano	.30	.25	.12
25	Bill Swift	.30	.25	.12
26	Bill Wilkinson	.30	.25	.12
27	Mariners Coaches (Billy Connors, Frank Howard, Phil Roof, Jim Snyder, Ozzie Virgil)			
		.30	.25	.12
28	Trainers Card/Checklist (Henry Genzale, Rick Griffin)	.30	.25	.12

1988 Mother's Cookies
Rangers

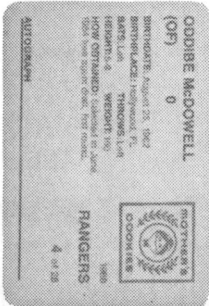

This 28-card set featuring the Texas Rangers was one of six team sets issued in 1988 by Mother's Cookies. Similar to other Mother's Cookies sets, the Rangers issue features full-color, borderless cards printed in the standard 2-1/2" by 3-1/2" format with rounded corners. The backs were printed in red and purple on white and included player information, the Mother's Cookies logo and card number. Twenty-card starter packs were distributed at a stadium promotion that included a redemption card good for another eight cards (not necessarily those needed to complete the set) either through the mail or at a local card show.

		MT	NR MT	EX
	Complete Set:	10.00	7.50	4.00
	Common Player:	.30	.25	.12
1	Bobby Valentine	.40	.30	.15
2	Pete Incaviglia	.70	.50	.30
3	Charlie Hough	.40	.30	.15
4	Oddibe McDowell	.50	.40	.20
5	Larry Parrish	.50	.40	.20
6	Scott Fletcher	.40	.30	.15
7	Steve Buechele	.40	.30	.15
8	Steve Kemp	.40	.30	.15
9	Pete O'Brien	.60	.45	.25
10	Ruben Sierra	.90	.70	.35
11	Mike Stanley	.50	.40	.20
12	Jose Cecena	.40	.30	.15
13	Cecil Espy	.40	.30	.15
14	Curtis Wilkerson	.30	.25	.12
15	Dale Mohorcic	.30	.25	.12
16	Ray Hayward	.30	.25	.12
17	Mitch Williams	.40	.30	.15
18	Bob Brower	.30	.25	.12
19	Paul Kilgus	.40	.30	.15
20	Geno Petralli	.30	.25	.12
21	James Steels	.30	.25	.12
22	Jerry Browne	.30	.25	.12
23	Jose Guzman	.40	.30	.15
24	DeWayne Vaughn	.40	.30	.15
25	Bobby Witt	.50	.40	.20
26	Jeff Russell	.30	.25	.12

		MT	NR MT	EX
27	Rangers Coaches (Richard Egan, Tom House, Art Howe, Davey Lopes, David Oliver, Tom Robson)	.30	.25	.12
28	Trainers Card/Checklist (Danny Wheat, Bill Zeigler)	.30	.25	.12

1988 Mother's Cookies
Will Clark

In a baseball spring training-related promotion, Mother's Cookies of Oakland, Calif. produced a full-color four-card set featuring San Francisco Giants first baseman Will Clark. The cards, which have glossy finishes and rounded corners, came cellophane-wrapped in specially marked 18-ounce packages of Mother's Cookies products. The cards are identical in style to the regular Mother's Cookies issues.

		MT	NR MT	EX
	Complete Set:	16.00	12.00	6.50
	Common Player:	4.00	3.00	1.50
1	Will Clark (bat on shoulder)	4.00	3.00	1.50
2	Will Clark (kneeling)	4.00	3.00	1.50
3	Will Clark (batting follow-thru)	4.00	3.00	1.50
4	Will Clark (heading for first base)	4.00	3.00	1.50

1988 Mother's Cookies
Mark McGwire

For the second consecutive year, Mother's Cookies devoted a four-card set to Oakland A's slugger Mark McGwire. The full-color cards have rounded corners and measure 2-1/2" by 3-1/2" in size. The cards were issued in specially marked 18-ounce packages of Mother's Cookies products in the northern California area. The cards are identical in design to the regular team issues produced by Mother's.

		MT	NR MT	EX
	Complete Set:	15.00	11.00	6.00
	Common Player:	3.00	2.25	1.25

1	Mark McGwire (holding oversized bat)			
		3.00	2.25	1.25
2	Mark McGwire (fielding)	3.00	2.25	1.25
3	Mark McGwire (kneeling)	3.00	2.25	1.25
4	Mark McGwire (bat in air)	3.00	2.25	1.25

1989 Mother's Cookies A's

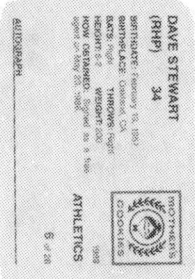

	MT	NR MT	EX
Complete Set:	10.00	7.50	4.00
Common Player:	2.00	1.50	.80

		MT	NR MT	EX
1	Jose Canseco	3.50	2.75	1.50
2	Mark McGwire	3.00	2.25	1.25
3	Walt Weiss	2.00	1.50	.80
4	Walt Weiss, Mark McGwire, & Jose Canseco	3.00	2.25	1.25

The 1989 Mother's Cookies A's set consists of 28 cards designed in the traditional style: a glossy card with a borderless photo and rounded corners. A starter set of the cards was used as a stadium promotion and distributed to fans attending the July 30 Oakland game.

		MT	NR MT	EX
	Complete Set:	12.00	9.00	4.75
	Common Player:	.30	.25	.12
1	Tony LaRussa	.30	.25	.12
2	Mark McGwire	2.75	2.00	1.00
3	Terry Steinbach	.60	.45	.25
4	Dave Parker	.60	.45	.25
5	Carney Lansford	.50	.40	.20
6	Dave Stewart	.50	.40	.20
7	Jose Canseco	3.00	2.25	1.25
8	Walt Weiss	.50	.40	.20
9	Bob Welch	.40	.30	.15
10	Dennis Eckersley	.40	.30	.15
11	Tony Phillips	.30	.25	.12
12	Mike Moore	.50	.40	.20
13	Dave Henderson	.30	.25	.12
14	Curt Young	.30	.25	.12
15	Ron Hassey	.30	.25	.12
16	Eric Plunk	.30	.25	.12
17	Luis Polonia	.30	.25	.12
18	Storm Davis	.30	.25	.12
19	Glenn Hubbard	.30	.25	.12
20	Greg Cadaret	.30	.25	.12
21	Stan Javier	.30	.25	.12
22	Felix Jose	.40	.30	.15
23	Mike Gallego	.30	.25	.12
24	Todd Burns	.30	.25	.12
25	Rick Honeycutt	.30	.25	.12
26	Gene Nelson	.30	.25	.12
27	A's Coaches (Dave Duncan, Rene Lachemann, Art Kusnyer, Tommie Reynolds, Merv Rettenmund)	.30	.25	.12
28	Walt Wiess, Mark McGwire & Jose Canseco	.70	.50	.30

1989 Mother's Cookies A's Rookies Of The Year

This four-card set features the American League Rookies of the Year for 1986, 1987 and 1988, all members of the Oakland A's. The 2-1/2" by 3-1/2" cards feature full color photos in the traditional Mother's Cookies style. One card was devoted to each player along with a special card showcasing all three players, Weiss, McGwire and Canseco, together. The cards were distributed one per box in Mother's Cookies.

1989 Mother's Cookies Astros

The 1989 Houston Astros team set issued by Mother's Cookies consisted of 28 cards designed in the traditional style of borderless photos and rounded corners. Partial sets were distributed to fans attending the July 22 Astros game at the Houston Astrodome. The cards feature the photography of Barry Colla and display the Mother's Cookies logo on the back.

		MT	NR MT	EX
	Complete Set:	10.00	7.50	4.00
	Common Player:	.30	.25	.12
1	Art Howe	.30	.25	.12
2	Mike Scott	.90	.70	.25
3	Gerald Young	.50	.40	.20
4	Bill Doran	.50	.40	.20
5	Billy Hatcher	.50	.40	.20
6	Terry Puhl	.30	.25	.12
7	Bob Knepper	.30	.25	.12
8	Kevin Bass	.50	.40	.20
9	Glenn Davis	.90	.70	.35
10	Alann Ashby	.30	.25	.12
11	Bob Forsch	.30	.25	.12
12	Greg Gross	.30	.25	.12
13	Danny Darwin	.30	.25	.12
14	Craig Biggio	1.00	.70	.40
15	Jim Clancy	.30	.25	.12
16	Rafael Ramirez	.30	.25	.12
17	Alex Trevino	.30	.25	.12
18	Craig Reynolds	.30	.25	.12
19	Dave Smith	.40	.30	.15
20	Larry Andersen	.30	.25	.12
21	Eric Yelding	.60	.45	.25
22	Jim Deshaies	.40	.30	.15
23	Juan Agosto	.30	.25	.12
24	Rick Rhoden	.30	.25	.12
25	Ken Caminiti	.60	.45	.25

		MT	NR MT	EX
26	Dave Meads	.30	.25	.12
27	Astro Coaches (Yogi Berra, Matt Galante, Phil Garner, Les Moss, Ed Napoleon, Ed Ott)	.30	.25	.12
28	Trainers Card/Checklist (Dave Labossiere, Doc Ewell Equip. Mgr.- Dennis Liborio)	.30	.25	.12

A player's name in *italic* indicates a rookie card. An (FC) indicates a player's first card for that particular card company.

		MT	NR MT	EX
Complete Set:		12.00	9.00	4.75
Common Player:		.30	.25	.12
1	Roger Craig	.40	.30	.15
2	Will Clark	1.25	.90	.50
3	Kevin Mitchell	1.00	.70	.40
4	Kelly Downs	.35	.25	.14
5	Brett Butler	.40	.30	.15
6	Mike Krukow	.30	.25	.12
7	Candy Maldonado	.30	.25	.12
8	Terry Kennedy	.30	.25	.12
9	Dave Dravecky	.40	.30	.15
10	Robby Thompson	.40	.30	.15
11	Scott Garrelts	.40	.30	.15
12	Matt Williams	.70	.50	.30
13	Jose Uribe	.30	.25	.12
14	Tracy Jones	.30	.25	.12
15	Rick Reuschel	.40	.30	.15
16	Ernest Riles	.30	.25	.12
17	Jeff Brantley	.50	.40	.20
18	Chris Speier	.30	.25	.12
19	Atlee Hammaker	.30	.25	.12
20	Ed Jurak	.30	.25	.12
21	Mike LaCoss	.30	.25	.12
22	Don Robinson	.30	.25	.12
23	Kirt Manwaring	.50	.40	.20
24	Craig Lefferts	.30	.25	.12
25	Donnell Nixon	.30	.25	.12
26	Joe Price	.30	.25	.12
27	Rich Gossage	.30	.25	.12
28	Coaches/Checklist (Bill Fahey, Dusty Baker, Bob Lillis, Wendell Kim, Norm Sherry)	.30	.25	.12

A player's name in *italic* indicates a rookie card. An (FC) indicates a player's first card for that particular card company.

1989 Mother's Cookies Mariners

For the sixth straight season Mother's Cookies released a set of the Seattle Mariners. The 1989 issue features 28 cards. Starter sets featuring 20 cards were distribted at a Mariner home game. The cards are 2-1/2" by 3-1/2" in size and feature borderless full color photos. The card backs are printed horizontally. Rookie sensation Ken Griffey Jr. was included in the 1989 issue.

	MT	NR MT	EX
Complete Set:	10.00	7.50	4.00

1989 Mother's Cookies Dodgers

This 28-card set features the players and coaching staff of the Los Angeles Dodgers. The cards follow the traditional Mother's Cookies style featuring rounded corners, borderless color photos, horizontal backs and are 2-1/2" by 3-1/2" in size. Initially twenty cards were given away as starter sets at Dodger Stadium.

		MT	NR MT	EX
Complete Set:		8.00	6.00	3.25
Common Player:		.30	.15	.03
1	Tom Lasorda	.40	.30	.15
2	Eddie Murray	.60	.45	.25
3	Mike Scioscia	.40	.30	.15
4	Fernando Valenzuela	.60	.45	.25
5	Mike Marshall	.50	.40	.20
6	Orel Hershiser	.80	.60	.30
7	Alfredo Griffin	.35	.25	.14
8	Kirk Gibson	.70	.50	.30
9	John Tudor	.40	.30	.15
10	Willie Randolph	.40	.30	.15
11	Franklin Stubbs	.30	.25	.12
12	Mike Davis	.30	.25	.12
13	Mike Morgan	.30	.25	.12
14	John Shelby	.30	.25	.12
15	Rick Dempsey	.30	.25	.12
16	Jay Howell	.40	.30	.15
17	Dave Anderson	.30	.25	.12
18	Alejandro Pena	.35	.25	.14
19	Jeff Hamilton	.35	.25	.14
20	Ricky Horton	.30	.25	.12
21	Tim Leary	.40	.30	.15
22	Ray Searage	.30	.25	.12
23	Tim Belcher	.70	.50	.30
24	Tim Crews	.30	.25	.12
25	Mickey Hatcher	.30	.25	.12
26	Mariano Duncan	.35	.25	.14
27	Coaches Card	.30	.25	.12
28	Checklist	.30	.25	.12

1989 Mother's Cookies Giants

The 1989 Mother's Cookies Giants set consists of 28 cards, all featuring borderless, color photos with rounded corners. Starter sets of the cards were distributed as a stadium promotion to fans attending the Aug. 6, 1989, Giants game at Candlestick Park.

Common Player:	MT	NR MT	EX
	.30	.25	.12
1 Jim Lefebvre	.30	.25	.12
2 Alvin Davis	.50	.40	.20
3 Ken Griffey, Jr.	5.00	3.75	2.00
4 Jim Presley	.50	.40	.20
5 Mark Langston	.70	.50	.30
6 Henry Cotto	.30	.25	.12
7 Mickey Brantley	.30	.25	.12
8 Jeffrey Leonard	.70	.50	.30
9 Dave Valle	.35	.25	.14
10 Harold Reynolds	.70	.50	.30
11 Edgar Martinez	.40	.30	.15
12 Tom Niedenfuer	.30	.25	.12
13 Scott Bankhead	.50	.40	.20
14 Scott Bradley	.35	.25	.14
15 Omar Vizquel	.40	.30	.15
16 Erik Hanson,			
17 Bill Swift	.40	.30	.15
18 Mike Campbell	.30	.25	.12
19 Mike Jackson	.35	.25	.14
20 Rich Renteria	.30	.25	.12
21 Mario Diaz	.30	.25	.12
22 Jerry Reed	.30	.25	.12
23 Darnell Coles	.35	.25	.14
24 Steve Trout	.30	.25	.12
25 Mike Schooler	.60	.45	.25
26 Julio Solano	.30	.25	.12
27 Coaches Card	.30	.25	.12
28 Checklist	.30	.25	.12

1989 Mother's Cookies Rangers

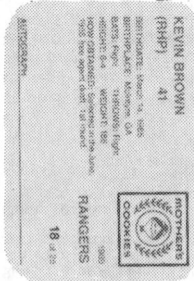

The 1989 Mother's Cookies Rangers team set featured the traditional borderless photos and rounded corners. The standard-size set consisted of 28 cards featuring the photography of Barry Colla. Partial sets were distributed to fans attending the July 30, 1989 game at Arlington Stadium.

	MT	NR MT	EX
Complete Set:	9.00	6.75	3.50
Common Player:	.30	.25	.12
1 Bobby Valentine	.40	.30	.15
2 Nolan Ryan	1.50	1.25	.60
3 Julio Franco	.70	.50	.30
4 Charlie Hough	.40	.30	.15
5 Rafael Palmeiro	.70	.50	.30
6 Jeff Russell	.30	.25	.12
7 Ruben Sierra	.90	.70	.35
8 Steve Buechele	.30	.25	.12
9 Buddy Bell	.40	.30	.15
10 Pete Incaviglia	.40	.30	.15
11 Geno Petralli	.30	.25	.12
12 Cecil Espy	.40	.30	.15
13 Scott Fletcher	.30	.25	.12
14 Bobby Witt	.30	.25	.12
15 Brad Arnsberg	.40	.30	.15
16 Rick Leach	.30	.25	.12
17 Jamie Moyer	.40	.30	.15
18 Kevin Brown	.50	.40	.20
19 Jeff Kunkel	.30	.25	.12
20 Craig McMurtry	.30	.25	.12
21 Kenny Rogers	.50	.40	.20
22 Mike Stanley	.30	.25	.12

	MT	NR MT	EX
23 Cecilio Guante	.50	.40	.20
24 Jim Sundberg	.50	.40	.20
25 Jose Guzman	.50	.40	.20
26 Jeff Stone	.50	.40	.20
27 Rangers Coaches (Dick Egan, Tom Robson, Toby Harrah, Dave Oliver, Tom House, Dave Lopes)	.30	.25	.12
28 Trainers Card/checklist (Bill Ziegler, Danny Wheat)	.30	.25	.12

1989 Mother's Cookies Jose Canseco

This special insert 4-card glossy set features Canseco in two posed (one standing, one kneeling) and two action (one batting, one running) shots. Full-color card fronts have rounded corners. Flip sides are numbered, printed in red and purple, and carry 1988 stats and career notes. Cards are individually cello-wrapped and inserted in Mother's Fudge 'N Chips, Oatmeal Raisin and Cocadas cookie bags.

	MT	NR MT	EX
Complete Set:	15.00	11.00	6.00
Common Player:	3.00	2.25	1.25
1 Jose Canseco (ball in hand)	3.00	2.25	1.25
2 Jose Canseco (on one knee grasping bat)	3.00	2.25	1.25
3 Jose Canseco (swinging-in action)	3.00	2.25	1.25
4 Jose Canseco (baserunning)	3.00	2.25	1.25

1989 Mother's Cookies Will Clark

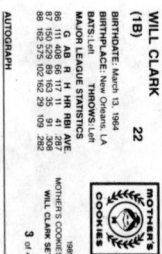

Will Clark is featured on a special-edition glossy 4-card set inserted in Mother's big bag chocolate chip cookies. The standard-size (2-1/2" by 3-1/2") cards feature Clark in two posed (batting and catching) and two action (batting and running) shots. Purple and red backs (numbered) list 1986-88 stats.

	MT	NR MT	EX
Complete Set:	10.00	7.50	4.00
Common Player:	2.00	1.50	.80
1 Will Clark (displaying ball in glove)	2.00	1.50	.80
2 Will Clark (batting stance)	2.00	1.50	.80
3 Will Clark (in action-after swing)	2.00	1.50	.80
4 Will Clark (heading towards first)	2.00	1.50	.80

1989 Mother's Cookies
Ken Griffey, Jr.

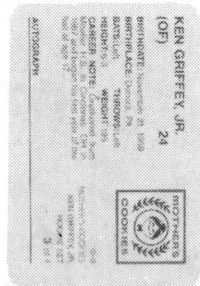

This four-card set featuring Ken Griffey, Jr. was issued by Mother's Cookies and was available only in cookie packages in the states of Washington and Oregon. The cards were also available at a Seattle Mariners Kingdome Baseball Card Show on Aug. 20, 1989, where the set was introduced. The cards were then packed inside specially-marked bags of cookies, one card per bag. The cards display the traditional Mother's Cookie's design: glossy, borderless cards with rounded corners.

	MT	NR MT	EX
Complete Set:	16.00	12.00	6.50
Common Player:	3.50	2.75	1.50
1 Ken Griffey, Jr. (arms folded)	3.50	2.75	1.50
2 Ken Griffey, Jr. (ball in hand)	3.50	2.75	1.50
3 Ken Griffey, Jr. (bat over left shoulder)	3.50	2.75	1.50
4 Ken Griffey, Jr. (back of jersey showing)	3.50	2.75	1.50

1989 Mother's Cookies
Mark McGwire

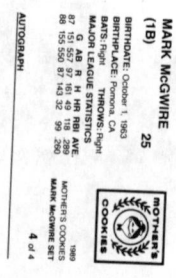

This special edition 4-card set features full-color glossy player photos by Barry Colla on standard-size (2-1/2" by 3-1/2") cards with rounded corners. Photos feature four different batting poses. Numbered flip sides, printed in purple and red, carry 1987 and 1988 statistics. Cards are individually cello-wrapped and inserted in

Mother's Cookie Parade variety cookie bags.

	MT	NR MT	EX
Complete Set:	15.00	11.00	6.00
Common Player:	3.00	2.25	1.25
1 Mark McGwire (bat on shoulder)	3.00	2.25	1.25
2 Mark McGwire (batting stance)	3.00	2.25	1.25
3 Mark McGwire (bat in front)	3.00	2.25	1.25
4 Mark McGwire (batting follow through)	3.00	2.25	1.25

1990 Mother's Cookies
Jose Canseco

This special insert 4-card glossy set features Canseco in four posed shots. Full-color card fronts have rounded corners. Flip sides are numbered, printed in red and purple and feature the Mother's Cookies logo. The cards are individually cello-wrapped and inserted one per Mother's Cookies bag.

	MT	NR MT	EX
Complete Set:	20.00	15.00	8.00
Common Player:	4.00	3.00	1.50
1 Jose Canseco (sitting, bat on shoulder)	4.00	3.00	1.50
2 Jose Canseco (bat behind neck)	4.00	3.00	1.50
3 Jose Canseco (batting stance)	4.00	3.00	1.50
4 Jose Canseco (on dugout step)	4.00	3.00	1.50

1990 Mother's Cookies
Will Clark

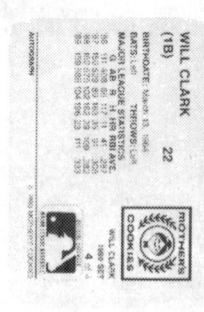

1990 marks the third consecutive year that Mother's Cookies devoted a set to Giant slugger Will Clark. This 4-card set features four posed full-color shots. The cards follow the same design as all recent Mother's Cookies cards.

	MT	NR MT	EX
Complete Set:	16.00	12.00	6.50
Common Player:	3.50	2.75	1.50

1	Will Clark (bat on shoulder)	3.50	2.75	1.50
2	Will Clark (closeup in stance)	3.50	2.75	1.50
3	Will Clark (open in stance)	3.50	2.75	1.50
4	Will Clark (bat behind neck)	3.50	2.75	1.50

1990 Mother's Cookies
Mark McGwire

1990 marks the fourth year that A's slugger Mark McGwire has been featured on a special 4-card Mother's Cookies set. The photos for the cards were once again by Barry Colla. Four different posed shots of McGwire are showcased.

		MT	NR MT	EX
Complete Set:		16.00	12.00	6.50
Common Player:		3.50	2.75	1.50
1	Mark McGwire (bat on shoulder)	3.50	2.75	1.50
2	Mark McGwire (leaning against bat rack)			
		3.50	2.75	1.50
3	Mark McGwire (glove in hand)	3.50	2.75	1.50
4	Mark McGwire (on dugout step)	3.50	2.75	1.50

1990 Mother's Cookies
Nolan Ryan

Unlike other special Mother's Cookies player sets, the Nolan Ryan cards feature 5000 K's along with his name and team on the card fronts. This 4-card set honors the strikout kings monumental feat. The cards follow the classic Mother's Cookies style.

		MT	NR MT	EX
Complete Set:		20.00	15.00	8.00
Common Player:		4.00	3.00	1.50
1	Nolan Ryan (facing with ball in hand)			
		4.00	3.00	1.50
2	Nolan Ryan (standing in dugout)	4.00	3.00	1.50
3	Nolan Ryan (gripping ball behind back)			
		4.00	3.00	1.50
4	Nolan Ryan (sitting on dugout step)			
		4.00	3.00	1.50

1990 Mother's Cookies
Matt Williams

Matt Williams made his Mother's Cookies single player card set debut in 1990. Four posed shots of the Giant third baseman are showcased. Williams is featured twice in batting related poses and also twice as a fielder.

		MT	NR MT	EX
Complete Set:		16.00	12.00	6.50
Common Player:		3.50	2.75	1.50
1	Matt Williams (bat on shoulder)	3.50	2.75	1.50
2	Matt Williams (in batting stance)	3.50	2.75	1.50
3	Matt Williams (glove in hand)	3.50	2.75	1.50
4	Matt Williams (fielding)	3.50	2.75	1.50

1969 Nabisco Team Flakes

Frank Robinson—OF
Baltimore Orioles

This set of cards is seen in two different sizes: 1-15/16" by 3" and 1-3/4" by 2-15/16". This is explained by the varying widths of the card borders on the backs of Nabisco cereal packages. Cards are action color photos bordered in yellow. Twenty-four of the top players in the game are included in the set, which was issued in three series of eight cards each. No team insignias are visible on any of the cards. Packages described the cards as "Mini Posters."

	NR MT	EX	VG
Complete Set:	600.00	300.00	180.00
Common Player:	4.00	2.00	1.25

		NR MT	EX	VG
(1)	Hank Aaron	60.00	30.00	18.00
(2)	Richie Allen	7.00	3.50	2.00
(3)	Lou Brock	40.00	20.00	12.00
(4)	Paul Casanova	4.00	2.00	1.25
(5)	Roberto Clemente	60.00	30.00	18.00
(6)	Al Ferrara	4.00	2.00	1.25
(7)	Bill Freehan	5.00	2.50	1.50
(8)	Jim Fregosi	5.00	2.50	1.50
(9)	Bob Gibson	20.00	10.00	6.00
(10)	Tony Horton	5.00	2.50	1.50
(11)	Tommy John	10.00	5.00	3.00
(12)	Al Kaline	40.00	20.00	12.00
(13)	Jim Lonborg	4.00	2.00	1.25
(14)	Juan Marichal	20.00	10.00	6.00
(15)	Willie Mays	60.00	30.00	18.00
(16)	Rick Monday	5.00	2.50	1.50
(17)	Tony Oliva	6.00	3.00	1.75
(18)	Brooks Robinson	45.00	22.00	13.50
(19)	Frank Robinson	40.00	20.00	12.00
(20)	Pete Rose	65.00	32.00	19.50
(21)	Ron Santo	6.00	3.00	1.75
(22)	Tom Seaver	50.00	25.00	15.00
(23)	Rusty Staub	6.00	3.00	1.75
(24)	Mel Stottlemyre	5.00	2.50	1.50

	MT	NR MT	EX
---- Discount Card	.25	.20	.10

1984 Nestle

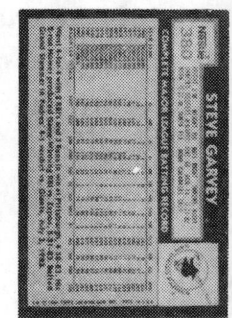

The 792 cards in the 1984 Nestle set are identical to those in the 1984 Topps regular issue set except for the Nestle logo which replaces the Topps logo in the upper right corner of the card front. The set was issued by Nestle as six sheets (24" by 48" each) of 132 cards. A few enterprising dealers bought up the major portion of the 5,000 sheet sets that were supposedly issued and had them professionally cut into individual cards. Due to the ease in handling single cards, sets of individual cards have a greater value than complete sheet sets.

	MT	NR MT	EX
Complete Singles Set:	500.00	375.00	200.00
Common Single Player:	.20	.15	.08
Complete Sheet Set:	350.00	262.00	140.00
Sheet A:	200.00	150.00	80.00
Sheet B:	20.00	15.00	8.00
Sheet C:	20.00	15.00	8.00
Sheet D:	20.00	15.00	8.00
Sheet E:	20.00	15.00	8.00
Sheet F:	20.00	15.00	8.00

#		MT	NR MT	EX
1	1983 Highlight (Steve Carlton)	1.75	1.25	.70
2	1983 Highlight (Rickey Henderson)	1.75	1.25	.70
3	1983 Highlight (Dan Quisenberry)	.30	.25	.12
4	1983 Highlight (Steve Carlton, Gaylord Perry, Nolan Ryan)	2.00	1.50	.80
5	1983 Highlight (Bob Forsch, Dave Righetti, Mike Warren)	.70	.50	.30
6	1983 Highlight (Johnny Bench, Gaylord Perry, Carl Yastrzemski)	2.00	1.50	.80
7	Gary Lucas	.20	.15	.08
8	Don Mattingly	275.00	200.00	100.00
9	Jim Gott	.20	.15	.08
10	Robin Yount	5.00	3.75	2.00
11	Twins Batting & Pitching Leaders (Kent Hrbek, Ken Schrom)	.70	.50	.30
12	Billy Sample	.20	.15	.08
13	Scott Holman	.20	.15	.08
14	Tom Brookens	.20	.15	.08
15	Burt Hooton	.30	.25	.12
16	Omar Moreno	.20	.15	.08
17	John Denny	.20	.15	.08
18	Dale Berra	.20	.15	.08
19	Ray Fontenot	.30	.25	.12
20	Greg Luzinski	.60	.45	.25
21	Joe Altobelli	.20	.15	.08
22	Bryan Clark	.20	.15	.08
23	Keith Moreland	.30	.25	.12
24	John Martin	.20	.15	.08
25	Glenn Hubbard	.30	.25	.12
26	Bud Black	.30	.25	.12
27	Daryl Sconiers	.20	.15	.08
28	Frank Viola	5.00	3.75	2.00
29	Danny Heep	.20	.15	.08
30	Wade Boggs	50.00	37.00	20.00
31	Andy McGaffigan	.20	.15	.08
32	Bobby Ramos	.20	.15	.08
33	Tom Burgmeier	.20	.15	.08
34	Eddie Milner	.20	.15	.08
35	Don Sutton	2.00	1.50	.80

1986 National Photo Royals

(5) GEORGE BRETT, 3B

These 2-7/8" by 4-1/4" cards were a team issue produced in conjunction with National Photo. The 24-card set includes 21 players, manager Dick Howser, a card commemorating the Royals' 1985 World Championship and a discount offer card from National Photo. Card fronts feature full-color action photos with a blue "Kansas City Royals" at the top of each card. Each player's name, number and position are also included. Card backs list complete professional career statistics, along with the National Photo logo.

		MT	NR MT	EX
	Complete Set:	12.00	9.00	4.75
	Common Player:	.25	.20	.10
1	Buddy Biancalana	.25	.20	.10
3	Jorge Orta	.25	.20	.10
4	Greg Pryor	.25	.20	.10
5	George Brett	3.00	2.25	1.25
6	Willie Wilson	.70	.50	.30
8	Jim Sundberg	.25	.20	.10
10	Dick Howser	.35	.25	.14
11	Hal McRae	.50	.40	.20
20	Frank White	.50	.40	.20
21	Lonnie Smith	.40	.30	.15
22	Dennis Leonard	.35	.25	.14
23	Mark Gubicza	.70	.50	.30
24	Darryl Motley	.25	.20	.10
25	Danny Jackson	.70	.50	.30
26	Steve Farr	.25	.20	.10
29	Dan Quisenberry	.50	.40	.20
31	Bret Saberhagen	1.00	.70	.40
35	Lynn Jones	.25	.20	.10
37	Charlie Leibrandt	.35	.25	.14
38	Mark Huismann	.25	.20	.10
40	Buddy Black	.35	.25	.14
45	Steve Balboni	.35	.25	.14
----	Header Card	.25	.20	.10

		MT	NR MT	EX
36	Denny Walling	.20	.15	.08
37	Rangers Batting & Pitching Leaders			
	(Buddy Bell, Rick Honeycutt)	.40	.30	.15
38	Luis DeLeon	.20	.15	.08
39	Garth Iorg	.20	.15	.08
40	Dusty Baker	.40	.30	.15
41	Tony Bernazard	.20	.15	.08
42	Johnny Grubb	.20	.15	.08
43	Ron Reed	.20	.15	.08
44	Jim Morrison	.20	.15	.08
45	Jerry Mumphrey	.20	.15	.08
46	Ray Smith	.20	.15	.08
47	Rudy Law	.20	.15	.08
48	Julio Franco	1.50	1.25	.60
49	John Stuper	.20	.15	.08
50	Chris Chambliss	.30	.25	.12
51	Jim Frey	.20	.15	.08
52	Paul Splittorff	.30	.25	.12
53	Juan Beniquez	.20	.15	.08
54	Jesse Orosco	.30	.25	.12
55	Dave Concepcion	.50	.40	.20
56	Gary Allenson	.20	.15	.08
57	Dan Schatzeder	.20	.15	.08
58	Max Venable	.20	.15	.08
59	Sammy Stewart	.20	.15	.08
60	Paul Molitor	1.25	.90	.50
61	Chris Codiroli	.30	.25	.12
62	Dave Hostetler	.20	.15	.08
63	Ed Vande Berg	.20	.15	.08
64	Mike Scioscia	.30	.25	.12
65	Kirk Gibson	4.00	3.00	1.50
66	Astros Batting & Pitching Leaders (Jose			
	Cruz, Nolan Ryan)	1.00	.70	.40
67	Gary Ward	.30	.25	.12
68	Luis Salazar	.20	.15	.08
69	Rod Scurry	.20	.15	.08
70	Gary Matthews	.30	.25	.12
71	Leo Hernandez	.20	.15	.08
72	Mike Squires	.20	.15	.08
73	Jody Davis	.30	.25	.12
74	Jerry Martin	.20	.15	.08
75	Bob Forsch	.30	.25	.12
76	Alfredo Griffin	.30	.25	.12
77	Brett Butler	.30	.25	.12
78	Mike Torrez	.30	.25	.12
79	Rob Wilfong	.20	.15	.08
80	Steve Rogers	.30	.25	.12
81	Billy Martin	.50	.40	.20
82	Doug Bird	.20	.15	.08
83	Richie Zisk	.30	.25	.12
84	Lenny Faedo	.20	.15	.08
85	Atlee Hammaker	.20	.15	.08
86	John Shelby	1.00	.70	.40
87	Frank Pastore	.20	.15	.08
88	Rob Picciolo	.20	.15	.08
89	Mike Smithson	.20	.15	.08
90	Pedro Guerrero	3.50	2.75	1.50
91	Dan Spillner	.20	.15	.08
92	Lloyd Moseby	.40	.30	.15
93	Bob Knepper	.30	.25	.12
94	Mario Ramirez	.20	.15	.08
95	Aurelio Lopez	.20	.15	.08
96	Royals Batting & Pitching Leaders (Larry			
	Gura, Hal McRae)	.40	.30	.15
97	LaMarr Hoyt	.20	.15	.08
98	Steve Nicosia	.20	.15	.08
99	Craig Lefferts	.70	.50	.30
100	Reggie Jackson	10.00	7.50	4.00
101	Porfirio Altamirano	.20	.15	.08
102	Ken Oberkfell	.20	.15	.08
103	Dwayne Murphy	.30	.25	.12
104	Ken Dayley	.30	.25	.12
105	Tony Armas	.30	.25	.12
106	Tim Stoddard	.20	.15	.08
107	Ned Yost	.20	.15	.08
108	Randy Moffitt	.20	.15	.08
109	Brad Wellman	.20	.15	.08
110	Ron Guidry	2.75	2.00	1.00
111	Bill Virdon	.30	.25	.12
112	Tom Niedenfuer	.30	.25	.12
113	Kelly Paris	.20	.15	.08
114	Checklist 1-132	.20	.15	.08
115	Andre Thornton	.30	.25	.12
116	George Bjorkman	.20	.15	.08
117	Tom Veryzer	.20	.15	.08
118	Charlie Hough	.30	.25	.12
119	Johnny Wockenfuss	.20	.15	.08
120	Keith Hernandez	5.00	3.75	2.00
121	Pat Sheridan	.70	.50	.30
122	Cecilio Guante	.30	.25	.12
123	Butch Wynegar	.30	.25	.12

		MT	NR MT	EX
124	Damaso Garcia	.20	.15	.08
125	Britt Burns	.20	.15	.08
126	Braves Batting & Pitching Leaders (Craig			
	McMurtry, Dale Murphy)	1.25	.90	.50
127	Mike Madden	.20	.15	.08
128	Rick Manning	.20	.15	.08
129	Bill Laskey	.20	.15	.08
130	Ozzie Smith	2.00	1.50	.80
131	Batting Leaders (Wade Boggs, Bill			
	Madlock)	2.50	2.00	1.00
132	Home Run Leaders (Jim Rice, Mike			
	Schmidt)	2.00	1.50	.80
133	Runs Batted in Leaders (Cecil Cooper,			
	Dale Murphy, Jim Rice)	2.00	1.50	.80
134	Stolen Base Leaders (Rickey Henderson,			
	Tim Raines)	1.75	1.25	.70
135	Victory Leaders (John Denny, LaMarr			
	Hoyt)	.30	.25	.12
136	Strikeout Leaders (Steve Carlton, Jack			
	Morris)	1.00	.70	.40
137	Earned Run Average Leaders (Atlee			
	Hammaker, Rick Honeycutt)	.30	.25	.12
138	Leading Firemen (Al Holland, Dan			
	Quisenberry)	.30	.25	.12
139	Bert Campaneris	.40	.30	.15
140	Storm Davis	.50	.40	.20
141	Pat Corrales	.20	.15	.08
142	Rich Gale	.20	.15	.08
143	Jose Morales	.20	.15	.08
144	Brian Harper	.20	.15	.08
145	Gary Lavelle	.20	.15	.08
146	Ed Romero	.20	.15	.08
147	Dan Petry	.30	.25	.12
148	Joe Lefebvre	.20	.15	.08
149	Jon Matlack	.30	.25	.12
150	Dale Murphy	15.00	11.00	6.00
151	Steve Trout	.20	.15	.08
152	Glenn Brummer	.20	.15	.08
153	Dick Tidrow	.20	.15	.08
154	Dave Henderson	.40	.30	.15
155	Frank White	.40	.30	.15
156	Athletics Batting & Pitching Leaders (Tim			
	Conroy, Rickey Henderson)	1.00	.70	.40
157	Gary Gaetti	2.50	2.00	1.00
158	John Curtis	.20	.15	.08
159	Darryl Cias	.20	.15	.08
160	Mario Soto	.30	.25	.12
161	Junior Ortiz	.20	.15	.08
162	Bob Ojeda	.40	.30	.15
163	Lorenzo Gray	.20	.15	.08
164	Scott Sanderson	.20	.15	.08
165	Ken Singleton	.40	.30	.15
166	Jamie Nelson	.20	.15	.08
167	Marshall Edwards	.20	.15	.08
168	Juan Bonilla	.20	.15	.08
169	Larry Parrish	.40	.30	.15
170	Jerry Reuss	.30	.25	.12
171	Frank Robinson	.40	.30	.15
172	Frank DiPino	.20	.15	.08
173	Marvell Wynne	.80	.60	.30
174	Juan Berenguer	.20	.15	.08
175	Graig Nettles	.80	.60	.30
176	Lee Smith	.60	.45	.25
177	Jerry Hairston	.20	.15	.08
178	Bill Krueger	.20	.15	.08
179	Buck Martinez	.20	.15	.08
180	Manny Trillo	.30	.25	.12
181	Roy Thomas	.20	.15	.08
182	Darryl Strawberry	70.00	52.00	27.00
183	Al Williams	.20	.15	.08
184	Mike O'Berry	.20	.15	.08
185	Sixto Lezcano	.20	.15	.08
186	Cardinals Batting & Pitching Leaders			
	(Lonnie Smith, John Stuper)	.20	.15	.08
187	Luis Aponte	.20	.15	.08
188	Bryan Little	.20	.15	.08
189	Tim Conroy	.30	.25	.12
190	Ben Oglivie	.30	.25	.12
191	Mike Boddicker	.30	.25	.12
192	Nick Esasky	1.25	.90	.50
193	Darrell Brown	.20	.15	.08
194	Domingo Ramos	.20	.15	.08
195	Jack Morris	3.50	2.75	1.50
196	Don Slaught	.40	.30	.15
197	Gary Hancock	.20	.15	.08
198	Bill Doran	1.50	1.25	.60
199	Willie Hernandez	.30	.25	.12
200	Andre Dawson	4.50	3.50	1.75
201	Bruce Kison	.20	.15	.08
202	Bobby Cox	.20	.15	.08
203	Matt Keough	.20	.15	.08

		MT	NR MT	EX
204	Bobby Meacham	.40	.30	.15
205	Greg Minton	.20	.15	.08
206	Andy Van Slyke	5.00	3.75	2.00
207	Donnie Moore	.20	.15	.08
208	Jose Oquendo	.20	.15	.08
209	Manny Sarmiento	.20	.15	.08
210	Joe Morgan	3.00	2.25	1.25
211	Rick Sweet	.20	.15	.08
212	Broderick Perkins	.20	.15	.08
213	Bruce Hurst	.60	.45	.25
214	Paul Householder	.20	.15	.08
215	Tippy Martinez	.20	.15	.08
216	White Sox Batting & Pitching Leaders (Richard Dotson, Carlton Fisk)	.40	.30	.15
217	Alan Ashby	.20	.15	.08
218	Rick Waits	.20	.15	.08
219	Joe Simpson	.20	.15	.08
220	Fernando Valenzuela	5.00	3.75	2.00
221	Cliff Johnson	.20	.15	.08
222	Rick Honeycutt	.20	.15	.08
223	Wayne Krenchicki	.20	.15	.08
224	Sid Monge	.20	.15	.08
225	Lee Mazzilli	.30	.25	.12
226	Juan Eichelberger	.20	.15	.08
227	Steve Braun	.20	.15	.08
228	John Rabb	.20	.15	.08
229	Paul Owens	.20	.15	.08
230	Rickey Henderson	10.00	7.50	4.00
231	Gary Woods	.20	.15	.08
232	Tim Wallach	.70	.50	.30
233	Checklist 133-264	.20	.15	.08
234	Rafael Ramirez	.20	.15	.08
235	Matt Young	.40	.30	.15
236	Ellis Valentine	.20	.15	.08
237	John Castino	.20	.15	.08
238	Reid Nichols	.20	.15	.08
239	Jay Howell	.30	.25	.12
240	Eddie Murray	8.00	6.00	3.25
241	Billy Almon	.20	.15	.08
242	Alex Trevino	.20	.15	.08
243	Pete Ladd	.20	.15	.08
244	Candy Maldonado	.60	.45	.25
245	Rick Sutcliffe	.70	.50	.30
246	Mets Batting & Pitching Leaders (Tom Seaver, Mookie Wilson)	.70	.50	.30
247	Onix Concepcion	.20	.15	.08
248	Bill Dawley	.20	.15	.08
249	Jay Johnstone	.30	.25	.12
250	Bill Madlock	.60	.45	.25
251	Tony Gwynn	12.00	9.00	4.75
252	Larry Christenson	.20	.15	.08
253	Jim Wohlford	.20	.15	.08
254	Shane Rawley	.30	.25	.12
255	Bruce Benedict	.20	.15	.08
256	Dave Geisel	.20	.15	.08
257	Julio Cruz	.20	.15	.08
258	Luis Sanchez	.20	.15	.08
259	Sparky Anderson	.30	.25	.12
260	Scott McGregor	.30	.25	.12
261	Bobby Brown	.20	.15	.08
262	Tom Candiotti	.80	.60	.30
263	Jack Fimple	.20	.15	.08
264	Doug Frobel	.20	.15	.08
265	Donnie Hill	.20	.15	.08
266	Steve Lubratich	.20	.15	.08
267	Carmelo Martinez	.60	.45	.25
268	Jack O'Connor	.20	.15	.08
269	Aurelio Rodriguez	.30	.25	.12
270	Jeff Russell	.40	.30	.15
271	Moose Haas	.20	.15	.08
272	Rick Dempsey	.30	.25	.12
273	Charlie Puleo	.20	.15	.08
274	Rick Monday	.30	.25	.12
275	Len Matuszek	.20	.15	.08
276	Angels Batting & Pitching Leaders (Rod Carew, Geoff Zahn)	.70	.50	.30
277	Eddie Whitson	.20	.15	.08
278	Jorge Bell	6.00	4.50	2.50
279	Ivan DeJesus	.20	.15	.08
280	Floyd Bannister	.30	.25	.12
281	Larry Milbourne	.20	.15	.08
282	Jim Barr	.20	.15	.08
283	Larry Biittner	.20	.15	.08
284	Howard Bailey	.20	.15	.08
285	Darrell Porter	.30	.25	.12
286	Lary Sorensen	.20	.15	.08
287	Warren Cromartie	.20	.15	.08
288	Jim Beattie	.20	.15	.08
289	Randy Johnson	.20	.15	.08
290	Dave Dravecky	.30	.25	.12
291	Chuck Tanner	.30	.25	.12

		MT	NR MT	EX
292	Tony Scott	.20	.15	.08
293	Ed Lynch	.20	.15	.08
294	U.L. Washington	.20	.15	.08
295	Mike Flanagan	.30	.25	.12
296	Jeff Newman	.20	.15	.08
297	Bruce Berenyi	.20	.15	.08
298	Jim Gantner	.30	.25	.12
299	John Butcher	.20	.15	.08
300	Pete Rose	25.00	18.50	10.00
301	Frank LaCorte	.20	.15	.08
302	Barry Bonnell	.20	.15	.08
303	Marty Castillo	.20	.15	.08
304	Warren Brusstar	.20	.15	.08
305	Roy Smalley	.20	.15	.08
306	Dodgers Batting & Pitching Leaders (Pedro Guerrero, Bob Welch)	.60	.45	.25
307	Bobby Mitchell	.20	.15	.08
308	Ron Hassey	.20	.15	.08
309	Tony Phillips	.30	.25	.12
310	Willie McGee	3.00	2.25	1.25
311	Jerry Koosman	.40	.30	.15
312	Jorge Orta	.20	.15	.08
313	Mike Jorgensen	.20	.15	.08
314	Orlando Mercado	.20	.15	.08
315	Bob Grich	.30	.25	.12
316	Mark Bradley	.20	.15	.08
317	Greg Pryor	.20	.15	.08
318	Bill Gullickson	.20	.15	.08
319	Al Bumbry	.20	.15	.08
320	Bob Stanley	.20	.15	.08
321	Harvey Kuenn	.20	.15	.08
322	Ken Schrom	.20	.15	.08
323	Alan Knicely	.20	.15	.08
324	Alejandro Pena	.80	.60	.30
325	Darrell Evans	.40	.30	.15
326	Bob Kearney	.20	.15	.08
327	Ruppert Jones	.20	.15	.08
328	Vern Ruhle	.20	.15	.08
329	Pat Tabler	.50	.40	.20
330	John Candelaria	.40	.30	.15
331	Bucky Dent	.30	.25	.12
332	Kevin Gross	1.00	.70	.40
333	Larry Herndon	.20	.15	.08
334	Chuck Rainey	.20	.15	.08
335	Don Baylor	.50	.40	.20
336	Mariners Batting & Pitching Leaders (Pat Putnam, Matt Young)	.20	.15	.08
337	Kevin Hagen	.20	.15	.08
338	Mike Warren	.20	.15	.08
339	Roy Lee Jackson	.20	.15	.08
340	Hal McRae	.40	.30	.15
341	Dave Tobik	.20	.15	.08
342	Tim Foli	.20	.15	.08
343	Mark Davis	.20	.15	.08
344	Rick Miller	.20	.15	.08
345	Kent Hrbek	4.00	3.00	1.50
346	Kurt Bevacqua	.20	.15	.08
347	Allan Ramirez	.20	.15	.08
348	Toby Harrah	.30	.25	.12
349	Bob Gibson	.20	.15	.08
350	George Foster	.80	.60	.30
351	Russ Nixon	.20	.15	.08
352	Dave Stewart	.60	.45	.25
353	Jim Anderson	.20	.15	.08
354	Jeff Burroughs	.20	.15	.08
355	Jason Thompson	.20	.15	.08
356	Glenn Abbott	.20	.15	.08
357	Ron Cey	.40	.30	.15
358	Bob Dernier	.20	.15	.08
359	Jim Acker	.30	.25	.12
360	Willie Randolph	.50	.40	.20
361	Dave Smith	.30	.25	.12
362	David Green	.20	.15	.08
363	Tim Laudner	.20	.15	.08
364	Scott Fletcher	.40	.30	.15
365	Steve Bedrosian	.40	.30	.15
366	Padres Batting & Pitching Leaders (Dave Dravecky, Terry Kennedy)	.20	.15	.08
367	Jamie Easterly	.20	.15	.08
368	Hubie Brooks	.30	.25	.12
369	Steve McCatty	.20	.15	.08
370	Tim Raines	5.00	3.75	2.00
371	Dave Gumpert	.20	.15	.08
372	Gary Roenicke	.20	.15	.08
373	Bill Scherrer	.20	.15	.08
374	Don Money	.20	.15	.08
375	Dennis Leonard	.30	.25	.12
376	Dave Anderson	.30	.25	.12
377	Danny Darwin	.30	.25	.12
378	Bob Brenly	.20	.15	.08
379	Checklist 265-396	.20	.15	.08

	MT	NR MT	EX
380 Steve Garvey	8.00	6.00	3.25
381 Ralph Houk	.20	.15	.08
382 Chris Nyman	.20	.15	.08
383 Terry Puhl	.20	.15	.08
384 Lee Tunnell	.20	.15	.08
385 Tony Perez	1.00	.70	.40
386 George Hendrick AS	.30	.25	.12
387 Johnny Ray AS	.30	.25	.12
388 Mike Schmidt AS	3.00	2.25	1.25
389 Ozzie Smith AS	1.25	.90	.50
390 Tim Raines AS	2.00	1.50	.80
391 Dale Murphy AS	3.00	2.25	1.25
392 Andre Dawson AS	1.75	1.25	.70
393 Gary Carter AS	2.00	1.50	.80
394 Steve Rogers AS	.30	.25	.12
395 Steve Carlton AS	2.00	1.50	.80
396 Jesse Orosco AS	.30	.25	.12
397 Eddie Murray AS	2.50	2.00	1.00
398 Lou Whitaker AS	1.25	.90	.50
399 George Brett AS	3.00	2.25	1.25
400 Cal Ripken AS	2.75	2.00	1.00
401 Jim Rice AS	2.00	1.50	.80
402 Dave Winfield AS	2.50	2.00	1.00
403 Lloyd Moseby AS	.30	.25	.12
404 Ted Simmons AS	.40	.30	.15
405 LaMarr Hoyt AS	.30	.25	.12
406 Ron Guidry AS	1.25	.90	.50
407 Dan Quisenberry AS	.30	.25	.12
408 Lou Piniella	.80	.60	.30
409 Juan Agosto	.40	.30	.15
410 Claudell Washington	.30	.25	.12
411 Houston Jimenez	.20	.15	.08
412 Doug Rader	.20	.15	.08
413 Spike Owen	.30	.25	.12
414 Mitchell Page	.20	.15	.08
415 Tommy John	1.25	.90	.50
416 Dane Iorg	.20	.15	.08
417 Mike Armstrong	.20	.15	.08
418 Ron Hodges	.20	.15	.08
419 John Henry Johnson	.20	.15	.08
420 Cecil Cooper	.60	.45	.25
421 Charlie Lea	.20	.15	.08
422 Jose Cruz	.30	.25	.12
423 Mike Morgan	.20	.15	.08
424 Dann Bilardello	.20	.15	.08
425 Steve Howe	.30	.25	.12
426 Orioles Batting & Pitching Leaders (Mike Boddicker, Cal Ripken)	.90	.70	.35
427 Rick Leach	.20	.15	.08
428 Fred Breining	.20	.15	.08
429 Randy Bush	.20	.15	.08
430 Rusty Staub	.50	.40	.20
431 Chris Bando	.20	.15	.08
432 Charlie Hudson	.80	.60	.30
433 Rich Hebner	.20	.15	.08
434 Harold Baines	1.75	1.25	.70
435 Neil Allen	.20	.15	.08
436 Rick Peters	.20	.15	.08
437 Mike Proly	.20	.15	.08
438 Biff Pocoroba	.20	.15	.08
439 Bob Stoddard	.20	.15	.08
440 Steve Kemp	.30	.25	.12
441 Bob Lillis	.20	.15	.08
442 Byron McLaughlin	.20	.15	.08
443 Benny Ayala	.20	.15	.08
444 Steve Renko	.20	.15	.08
445 Jerry Remy	.20	.15	.08
446 Luis Pujols	.20	.15	.08
447 Tom Brunansky	1.25	.90	.50
448 Ben Hayes	.20	.15	.08
449 Joe Pettini	.20	.15	.08
450 Gary Carter	6.00	4.50	2.50
451 Bob Jones	.20	.15	.08
452 Chuck Porter	.20	.15	.08
453 Willie Upshaw	.30	.25	.12
454 Joe Beckwith	.20	.15	.08
455 Terry Kennedy	.30	.25	.12
456 Cubs Batting & Pitching Leaders (Keith Moreland, Fergie Jenkins)	.50	.40	.20
457 Dave Rozema	.20	.15	.08
458 Kiko Garcia	.20	.15	.08
459 Kevin Hickey	.20	.15	.08
460 Dave Winfield	6.00	4.50	2.50
461 Jim Maler	.20	.15	.08
462 Lee Lacy	.20	.15	.08
463 Dave Engle	.20	.15	.08
464 Jeff Jones	.20	.15	.08
465 Mookie Wilson	.30	.25	.12
466 Gene Garber	.20	.15	.08
467 Mike Ramsey	.20	.15	.08
468 Geoff Zahn	.20	.15	.08

	MT	NR MT	EX
469 Tom O'Malley	.20	.15	.08
470 Nolan Ryan	10.00	7.50	4.00
471 Dick Howser	.30	.25	.12
472 Mike Brown	.20	.15	.08
473 Jim Dwyer	.20	.15	.08
474 Greg Bargar	.20	.15	.08
475 Gary Redus	.80	.60	.30
476 Tom Tellmann	.20	.15	.08
477 Rafael Landestoy	.20	.15	.08
478 Alan Bannister	.20	.15	.08
479 Frank Tanana	.30	.25	.12
480 Ron Kittle	.80	.60	.30
481 Mark Thurmond	.30	.25	.12
482 Enos Cabell	.20	.15	.08
483 Fergie Jenkins	1.75	1.25	.70
484 Ozzie Virgil	.20	.15	.08
485 Rick Rhoden	.40	.30	.15
486 Yankees Batting & Pitching Leaders (Don Baylor, Ron Guidry)	.60	.45	.25
487 Ricky Adams	.20	.15	.08
488 Jesse Barfield	1.50	1.25	.60
489 Dave Von Ohlen	.20	.15	.08
490 Cal Ripken	10.00	7.50	4.00
491 Bobby Castillo	.20	.15	.08
492 Tucker Ashford	.20	.15	.08
493 Mike Norris	.20	.15	.08
494 Chili Davis	.30	.25	.12
495 Rollie Fingers	2.50	2.00	1.00
496 Terry Francona	.20	.15	.08
497 Bud Anderson	.20	.15	.08
498 Rich Gedman	.30	.25	.12
499 Mike Witt	.70	.50	.30
500 George Brett	15.00	11.00	6.00
501 Steve Henderson	.20	.15	.08
502 Joe Torre	.30	.25	.12
503 Elias Sosa	.20	.15	.08
504 Mickey Rivers	.20	.15	.08
505 Pete Vuckovich	.20	.15	.08
506 Ernie Whitt	.20	.15	.08
507 Mike LaCoss	.20	.15	.08
508 Mel Hall	.30	.25	.12
509 Brad Havens	.20	.15	.08
510 Alan Trammell	5.00	3.75	2.00
511 Marty Bystrom	.20	.15	.08
512 Oscar Gamble	.20	.15	.08
513 Dave Beard	.20	.15	.08
514 Floyd Rayford	.20	.15	.08
515 Gorman Thomas	.30	.25	.12
516 Expos Batting & Pitching Leaders (Charlie Lea, Al Oliver)	.20	.15	.08
517 John Moses	.20	.15	.08
518 Greg Walker	1.25	.90	.50
519 Ron Davis	.20	.15	.08
520 Bob Boone	.30	.25	.12
521 Pete Falcone	.20	.15	.08
522 Dave Bergman	.20	.15	.08
523 Glenn Hoffman	.20	.15	.08
524 Carlos Diaz	.20	.15	.08
525 Willie Wilson	.60	.45	.25
526 Ron Oester	.20	.15	.08
527 Checklist 397-528	.20	.15	.08
528 Mark Brouhard	.20	.15	.08
529 Keith Atherton	.60	.45	.25
530 Dan Ford	.20	.15	.08
531 Steve Boros	.20	.15	.08
532 Eric Show	.40	.30	.15
533 Ken Landreaux	.20	.15	.08
534 Pete O'Brien	1.50	1.25	.60
535 Bo Diaz	.30	.25	.12
536 Doug Bair	.20	.15	.08
537 Johnny Ray	.40	.30	.15
538 Kevin Bass	.40	.30	.15
539 George Frazier	.20	.15	.08
540 George Hendrick	.30	.25	.12
541 Dennis Lamp	.20	.15	.08
542 Duane Kuiper	.20	.15	.08
543 Craig McMurtry	.40	.30	.15
544 Cesar Geronimo	.20	.15	.08
545 Bill Buckner	.60	.45	.25
546 Indians Batting & Pitching Leaders (Mike Hargrove, Lary Sorensen)	.20	.15	.08
547 Mike Moore	.20	.15	.08
548 Ron Jackson	.20	.15	.08
549 Walt Terrell	1.00	.70	.40
550 Jim Rice	6.00	4.50	2.50
551 Scott Ullger	.20	.15	.08
552 Ray Burris	.20	.15	.08
553 Joe Nolan	.20	.15	.08
554 Ted Power	.30	.25	.12
555 Greg Brock	.50	.40	.20
556 Joey McLaughlin	.20	.15	.08

#	Name	MT	NR MT	EX
557	Wayne Tolleson	.20	.15	.08
558	Mike Davis	.30	.25	.12
559	Mike Scott	1.50	1.25	.60
560	Carlton Fisk	2.00	1.50	.80
561	Whitey Herzog	.30	.25	.12
562	Manny Castillo	.20	.15	.08
563	Glenn Wilson	.30	.25	.12
564	Al Holland	.20	.15	.08
565	Leon Durham	.30	.25	.12
566	Jim Bibby	.20	.15	.08
567	Mike Heath	.20	.15	.08
568	Pete Filson	.20	.15	.08
569	Bake McBride	.20	.15	.08
570	Dan Quisenberry	.40	.30	.15
571	Bruce Bochy	.20	.15	.08
572	Jerry Royster	.20	.15	.08
573	Dave Kingman	.80	.60	.30
574	Brian Downing	.30	.25	.12
575	Jim Clancy	.30	.25	.12
576	Giants Batting & Pitching Leaders (Atlee Hammaker, Jeff Leonard)	.20	.15	.08
577	Mark Clear	.20	.15	.08
578	Lenn Sakata	.20	.15	.08
579	Bob James	.20	.15	.08
580	Lonnie Smith	.30	.25	.12
581	Jose DeLeon	1.00	.70	.40
582	Bob McClure	.20	.15	.08
583	Derrel Thomas	.20	.15	.08
584	Dave Schmidt	.20	.15	.08
585	Dan Driessen	.30	.25	.12
586	Joe Niekro	.40	.30	.15
587	Von Hayes	.40	.30	.15
588	Milt Wilcox	.20	.15	.08
589	Mike Easler	.30	.25	.12
590	Dave Stieb	.50	.40	.20
591	Tony LaRussa	.30	.25	.12
592	Andre Robertson	.20	.15	.08
593	Jeff Lahti	.20	.15	.08
594	Gene Richards	.20	.15	.08
595	Jeff Reardon	.50	.40	.20
596	Ryne Sandberg	18.00	13.50	7.25
597	Rick Camp	.20	.15	.08
598	Rusty Kuntz	.20	.15	.08
599	Doug Sisk	.20	.15	.08
600	Rod Carew	7.00	5.25	2.75
601	John Tudor	.60	.45	.25
602	John Wathan	.30	.25	.12
603	Renie Martin	.20	.15	.08
604	John Lowenstein	.20	.15	.08
605	Mike Caldwell	.20	.15	.08
606	Blue Jays Batting & Pitching Leaders (Lloyd Moseby, Dave Stieb)	.40	.30	.15
607	Tom Hume	.20	.15	.08
608	Bobby Johnson	.20	.15	.08
609	Dan Meyer	.20	.15	.08
610	Steve Sax	2.50	2.00	1.00
611	Chet Lemon	.30	.25	.12
612	Harry Spilman	.20	.15	.08
613	Greg Gross	.20	.15	.08
614	Len Barker	.20	.15	.08
615	Garry Templeton	.30	.25	.12
616	Don Robinson	.20	.15	.08
617	Rick Cerone	.20	.15	.08
618	Dickie Noles	.20	.15	.08
619	Jerry Dybzinski	.20	.15	.08
620	Al Oliver	.70	.50	.30
621	Frank Howard	.30	.25	.12
622	Al Cowens	.20	.15	.08
623	Ron Washington	.20	.15	.08
624	Terry Harper	.20	.15	.08
625	Larry Gura	.20	.15	.08
626	Bob Clark	.20	.15	.08
627	Dave LaPoint	.40	.30	.15
628	Ed Jurak	.20	.15	.08
629	Rick Langford	.20	.15	.08
630	Ted Simmons	.80	.60	.30
631	Denny Martinez	.30	.25	.12
632	Tom Foley	.20	.15	.08
633	Mike Krukow	.30	.25	.12
634	Mike Marshall	1.50	1.25	.60
635	Dave Righetti	2.75	2.00	1.00
636	Pat Putnam	.20	.15	.08
637	Phillies Batting & Pitching Leaders (John Denny, Gary Matthews)	.20	.15	.08
638	George Vukovich	.20	.15	.08
639	Rick Lysander	.20	.15	.08
640	Lance Parrish	3.00	2.25	1.25
641	Mike Richardt	.20	.15	.08
642	Tom Underwood	.20	.15	.08
643	Mike Brown	.20	.15	.08
644	Tim Lollar	.20	.15	.08
645	Tony Pena	.40	.30	.15
646	Checklist 529-660	.20	.15	.08
647	Ron Roenicke	.20	.15	.08
648	Len Whitehouse	.20	.15	.08
649	Tom Herr	.40	.30	.15
650	Phil Niekro	2.75	2.00	1.00
651	John McNamara	.20	.15	.08
652	Rudy May	.20	.15	.08
653	Dave Stapleton	.20	.15	.08
654	Bob Bailor	.20	.15	.08
655	Amos Otis	.30	.25	.12
656	Bryn Smith	.20	.15	.08
657	Thad Bosley	.20	.15	.08
658	Jerry Augustine	.20	.15	.08
659	Duane Walker	.20	.15	.08
660	Ray Knight	.30	.25	.12
661	Steve Yeager	.20	.15	.08
662	Tom Brennan	.20	.15	.08
663	Johnnie LeMaster	.20	.15	.08
664	Dave Stegman	.20	.15	.08
665	Buddy Bell	.40	.30	.15
666	Tigers Batting & Pitching Leaders (Jack Morris, Lou Whitaker)	.70		.30
667	Vance Law	.30	.25	.12
668	Larry McWilliams	.20	.15	.08
669	Dave Lopes	.20	.15	.08
670	Rich Gossage	2.00	1.50	.80
671	Jamie Quirk	.20	.15	.08
672	Ricky Nelson	.20	.15	.08
673	Mike Walters	.20	.15	.08
674	Tim Flannery	.20	.15	.08
675	Pascual Perez	.30	.25	.12
676	Brian Giles	.20	.15	.08
677	Doyle Alexander	.30	.25	.12
678	Chris Speier	.20	.15	.08
679	Art Howe	.20	.15	.08
680	Fred Lynn	2.25	1.75	.90
681	Tom Lasorda	.40	.30	.15
682	Dan Morogiello	.20	.15	.08
683	Marty Barrett	2.00	1.50	.80
684	Bob Shirley	.20	.15	.08
685	Willie Aikens	.20	.15	.08
686	Joe Price	.20	.15	.08
687	Roy Howell	.20	.15	.08
688	George Wright	.20	.15	.08
689	Mike Fischlin	.20	.15	.08
690	Jack Clark	3.50	2.75	1.50
691	Steve Lake	.20	.15	.08
692	Dickie Thon	.30	.25	.12
693	Alan Wiggins	.20	.15	.08
694	Mike Stanton	.20	.15	.08
695	Lou Whitaker	3.00	2.25	1.25
696	Pirates Batting & Pitching Leaders (Bill Madlock, Rick Rhoden)	.50	.40	.20
697	Dale Murray	.20	.15	.08
698	Marc Hill	.20	.15	.08
699	Dave Rucker	.20	.15	.08
700	Mike Schmidt	18.00	13.50	7.25
701	NL Active Career Batting Leaders (Bill Madlock, Dave Parker, Pete Rose)	2.00	1.50	.80
702	NL Active Career Hit Leaders (Tony Perez, Pete Rose, Rusty Staub)	2.00	1.50	.80
703	NL Active Career Home Run Leaders (Dave Kingman, Tony Perez, Mike Schmidt)	2.00	1.50	.80
704	NL Active Career RBI Leaders (Al Oliver, Tony Perez, Rusty Staub)	.60	.45	.25
705	NL Active Career Stolen Bases Leaders (Larry Bowa, Cesar Cedeno, Joe Morgan)	.70	.50	.30
706	NL Active Career Victory Leaders (Steve Carlton, Fergie Jenkins, Tom Seaver)	1.75	1.25	.70
707	NL Active Career Strikeout Leaders (Steve Carlton, Nolan Ryan, Tom Seaver)	2.00	1.50	.80
708	NL Active Career ERA Leaders (Steve Carlton, Steve Rogers, Tom Seaver)	1.75	1.25	.70
709	NL Active Career Save Leaders (Gene Garber, Tug McGraw, Bruce Sutter)	.50	.40	.20
710	AL Active Career Batting Leaders (George Brett, Rod Carew, Cecil Cooper)	2.00	1.50	.80
711	AL Active Career Hit Leaders (Bert Campaneris, Rod Carew, Reggie Jackson)	1.75	1.25	.70
712	AL Active Career Home Run Leaders (Reggie Jackson, Greg Luzinski, Graig Nettles)	1.50	1.25	.60
713	AL Active Career RBI Leaders (Reggie Jackson, Graig Nettles, Ted Simmons)	1.50	1.25	.60
714	AL Active Career Stolen Bases Leaders (Bert Campaneris, Dave Lopes, Omar Moreno)	.40	.30	.15

		MT	NR MT	EX
715	AL Active Career Victory Leaders (Tommy John, Jim Palmer, Don Sutton)	1.25	.90	.50
716	AL Active Strikeout Leaders (Bert Blyleven, Jerry Koosman, Don Sutton)	.70	.50	.30
717	AL Active Career ERA Leaders (Rollie Fingers, Ron Guidry, Jim Palmer)	1.25	.90	.50
718	AL Active Career Save Leaders (Rollie Fingers, Rich Gossage, Dan Quisenberry)	.90	.70	.35
719	Andy Hassler	.20	.15	.08
720	Dwight Evans	.80	.60	.30
721	Del Crandall	.20	.15	.08
722	Bob Welch	.40	.30	.15
723	Rich Dauer	.20	.15	.08
724	Eric Rasmussen	.20	.15	.08
725	Cesar Cedeno	.30	.25	.12
726	Brewers Batting & Pitching Leaders (Moose Haas, Ted Simmons)	.30	.25	.12
727	Joel Youngblood	.20	.15	.08
728	Tug McGraw	.30	.25	.12
729	Gene Tenace	.30	.25	.12
730	Bruce Sutter	1.25	.90	.50
731	Lynn Jones	.20	.15	.08
732	Terry Crowley	.20	.15	.08
733	Dave Collins	.30	.25	.12
734	Odell Jones	.20	.15	.08
735	Rick Burleson	.30	.25	.12
736	Dick Ruthven	.20	.15	.08
737	Jim Essian	.20	.15	.08
738	Bill Schroeder	.60	.45	.25
739	Bob Watson	.30	.25	.12
740	Tom Seaver	7.00	5.25	2.75
741	Wayne Gross	.20	.15	.08
742	Dick Williams	.20	.15	.08
743	Don Hood	.20	.15	.08
744	Jamie Allen	.20	.15	.08
745	Dennis Eckersley	.50	.40	.20
746	Mickey Hatcher	.20	.15	.08
747	Pat Zachry	.20	.15	.08
748	Jeff Leonard	.30	.25	.12
749	Doug Flynn	.20	.15	.08
750	Jim Palmer	5.00	3.75	2.00
751	Charlie Moore	.20	.15	.08
752	Phil Garner	.30	.25	.12
753	Doug Gwosdz	.20	.15	.08
754	Kent Tekulve	.30	.25	.12
755	Garry Maddox	.30	.25	.12
756	Reds Batting & Pitching Leaders (Ron Oester, Mario Soto)	.20	.15	.08
757	Larry Bowa	.40	.30	.15
758	Bill Stein	.20	.15	.08
759	Richard Dotson	.40	.30	.15
760	Bob Horner	.80	.60	.30
761	John Montefusco	.20	.15	.08
762	Rance Mulliniks	.20	.15	.08
763	Craig Swan	.20	.15	.08
764	Mike Hargrove	.20	.15	.08
765	Ken Forsch	.20	.15	.08
766	Mike Vail	.20	.15	.08
767	Carney Lansford	.40	.30	.15
768	Champ Summers	.20	.15	.08
769	Bill Caudill	.20	.15	.08
770	Ken Griffey	.30	.25	.12
771	Billy Gardner	.20	.15	.08
772	Jim Slaton	.20	.15	.08
773	Todd Cruz	.20	.15	.08
774	Tom Gorman	.20	.15	.08
775	Dave Parker	1.75	1.25	.70
776	Craig Reynolds	.20	.15	.08
777	Tom Paciorek	.20	.15	.08
778	Andy Hawkins	.80	.60	.30
779	Jim Sundberg	.20	.15	.08
780	Steve Carlton	6.00	4.50	2.50
781	Checklist 661-792	.20	.15	.08
782	Steve Balboni	.30	.25	.12
783	Luis Leal	.20	.15	.08
784	Leon Roberts	.20	.15	.08
785	Joaquin Andujar	.30	.25	.12
786	Red Sox Batting & Pitching Leaders (Wade Boggs, Bob Ojeda)	1.25	.90	.50
787	Bill Campbell	.20	.15	.08
788	Milt May	.20	.15	.08
789	Bert Blyleven	1.25	.90	.50
790	Doug DeCinces	.30	.25	.12
791	Terry Forster	.30	.25	.12
792	Bill Russell	.30	.25	.12

NOTE: A card number in parentheses ( ) indicates the set is unnumbered.

1984 Nestle Dream Team

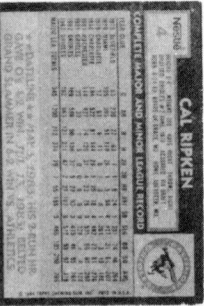

This set was issued by the Nestle candy company in conjunction with Topps. Cards are in standard 2-1/2" by 3-1/2" size and feature the top 22 players of 1984, 11 from each league. This full-color "Dream Team" includes one player at each position, plus right- and left-handed starting pitchers and one reliever. Card fronts have a Nestle logo in the upper-right corner and card backs have the candy company logo in the upper left. An unnumbered checklist was included with the set.

		MT	NR MT	EX
	Complete Set:	20.00	15.00	8.00
	Common Player:	.60	.45	.25
1	Eddie Murray	1.75	1.25	.70
2	Lou Whitaker	1.00	.70	.40
3	George Brett	2.25	1.75	.90
4	Cal Ripken	2.00	1.50	.80
5	Jim Rice	1.25	.90	.50
6	Dave Winfield	1.50	1.25	.60
7	Lloyd Moseby	.60	.45	.25
8	Lance Parrish	1.00	.70	.40
9	LaMarr Hoyt	.60	.45	.25
10	Ron Guidry	.80	.60	.30
11	Dan Quisenberry	.60	.45	.25
12	Steve Garvey	1.50	1.25	.60
13	Johnny Ray	.60	.45	.25
14	Mike Schmidt	2.75	2.00	1.00
15	Ozzie Smith	.80	.60	.30
16	Andre Dawson	1.00	.70	.40
17	Tim Raines	1.50	1.25	.60
18	Dale Murphy	2.25	1.75	.90
19	Tony Pena	.60	.45	.25
20	John Denny	.60	.45	.25
21	Steve Carlton	1.25	.90	.50
22	Al Holland	.60	.45	.25
----	Checklist	.30	.25	.12

1987 Nestle

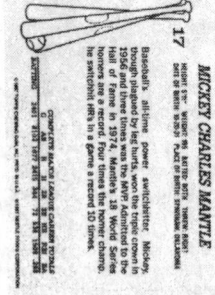

Nestle, in conjunction with Topps, issued a 33-card set in 1987. Card #'s 1-11 feature black and white photos of players from the "Golden Era." Card #'s 12-33 feature full-color photos of American

(12-22.00) and National League (23-33.00) players from the "Modern Era" of baseball. Interestingly, the Feller card is not a photo but rather a color rendering of his 1953 Topps card. The cards measure 2-1/2" by 3-1/2" and have all team emblems airbrushed away. Three cards were inserted in specially marked six-packs of various Nestle candy bars. Two complete sets were available through a mail-in offer for $1.50 and three proof of purchase seals.

		MT	NR MT	EX
Complete Set:		9.00	6.75	3.50
Common Player:		.12	.09	.05
1	Lou Gehrig	.50	.40	.20
2	Rogers Hornsby	.25	.20	.10
3	Pie Traynor	.12	.09	.05
4	Honus Wagner	.30	.25	.12
5	Babe Ruth	.80	.60	.30
6	Tris Speaker	.20	.15	.08
7	Ty Cobb	.60	.45	.25
8	Mickey Cochrane	.12	.09	.05
9	Walter Johnson	.30	.25	.12
10	Carl Hubbell	.12	.09	.05
11	Jimmie Foxx	.25	.20	.10
12	Rod Carew	.30	.25	.12
13	Nellie Fox	.12	.09	.05
14	Brooks Robinson	.30	.25	.12
15	Luis Aparicio	.12	.09	.05
16	Frank Robinson	.20	.15	.08
17	Mickey Mantle	1.00	.70	.40
18	Ted Williams	.50	.40	.20
19	Yogi Berra	.30	.25	.12
20	Bob Feller	.25	.20	.10
21	Whitey Ford	.25	.20	.10
22	Harmon Killebrew	.20	.15	.08
23	Stan Musial	.50	.40	.20
24	Jackie Robinson	.40	.30	.15
25	Eddie Mathews	.20	.15	.08
26	Ernie Banks	.20	.15	.08
27	Roberto Clemente	.40	.30	.15
28	Willie Mays	.50	.40	.20
29	Hank Aaron	.50	.40	.20
30	Johnny Bench	.30	.25	.12
31	Bob Gibson	.20	.15	.08
32	Warren Spahn	.20	.15	.08
33	Duke Snider	.25	.20	.10

autographed baseball.

		MT	NR MT	EX
Complete Set:		18.00	13.50	7.25
Common Player:		.25	.20	.10
1	Roger Clemens	.75	.60	.30
2	Dale Murphy	.60	.45	.25
3	Eric Davis	.60	.45	.25
4	Gary Gaetti	.30	.25	.12
5	Ozzie Smith	.35	.25	.14
6	Mike Schmidt	.60	.45	.25
7	Ozzie Guillen	.25	.20	.10
8	John Franco	.25	.20	.10
9	Andre Dawson	.40	.30	.15
10	Mark McGwire	1.00	.70	.40
11	Bret Saberhagen	.35	.25	.14
12	Benny Santiago	.35	.25	.14
13	Jose Uribe	.25	.20	.10
14	Will Clark	.50	.40	.20
15	Don Mattingly	1.75	1.25	.70
16	Juan Samuel	.30	.25	.12
17	Jack Clark	.35	.25	.14
18	Darryl Strawberry	.75	.60	.30
19	Bill Doran	.25	.20	.10
20	Pete Incaviglia	.30	.25	.12
21	Dwight Gooden	.75	.60	.30
22	Willie Randolph	.25	.20	.10
23	Tim Wallach	.25	.20	.10
24	Pedro Guerrero	.35	.25	.14
25	Steve Bedrosian	.25	.20	.10
26	Gary Carter	.50	.40	.20
27	Jeff Reardon	.25	.20	.10
28	Dave Righetti	.35	.25	.14
29	Frank White	.25	.20	.10
30	Buddy Bell	.25	.20	.10
31	Tim Raines	.50	.40	.20
32	Wade Boggs	1.00	.70	.40
33	Dave Winfield	.50	.40	.20
34	George Bell	.40	.30	.15
35	Alan Trammell	.40	.30	.15
36	Joe Carter	.30	.25	.14
37	Jose Canseco	1.50	1.25	.60
38	Carlton Fisk	.40	.30	.15
39	Kirby Puckett	.50	.40	.20
40	Tony Gwynn	.50	.40	.20
41	Matt Nokes	.40	.30	.15
42	Keith Hernandez	.40	.30	.15
43	Nolan Ryan	.40	.30	.15
44	Wally Joyner	.50	.40	.20

1988 Nestle

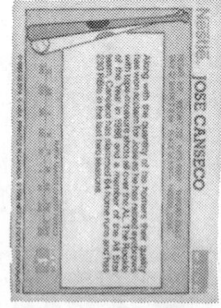

This 44-card set was produced by Mike Schechter Associates for Nestle. "Dream Team" packets of 3 player cards and one checklist card were inserted in 6-packs of Nestle's chocolate candy bars. The 1988 issue, similar to the 33-card Nestle set produced by Topps, features current players divided into four Dream Teams (East and West teams for each league). The "1988 Nestle" header appears at the top of the red and yellow-bordered cards. Below the player closeup (in a plain airbrushed cap) is a blue oval player name banner. Card backs are red, white and blue with card numbers printed upper right above personal stats, career highlights and major league totals. The bright red, blue and yellow checklist card outlines two special offers; one for an uncut sheet of all 44 player cards and one for a 1988 replica

1954 N.Y. Journal-American

Issued during the Golden Age of baseball in New York City, this 59-card set features only players from the three New York teams of the day - the Giants, Yankees and Dodgers. The 2" by 4" cards were issued at newsstands with the purchase of the now-extinct newspaper. Card fronts were promotional copy and a contest serial number in addition to the player's name and photo. Cards are black and white and unnumbered. Many of the game's top stars are included, such as Mickey Mantle, Willie Mays, Gil Hodges, Duke Snider, Jackie Robinson and Yogi Berra. Card backs featured team schedules. It has been theorized that a 60th Dodgers card should exist. Don Hoak and Bob Milliken have been suggested as the missing card, but the existence of either card has never been confirmed.

		NR MT	EX	VG
Complete Set:		2000.00	1000.00	600.00
Common Player:		10.00	5.00	3.00
(1)	Johnny Antonelli	12.00	6.00	3.50
(2)	Hank Bauer	20.00	10.00	6.00
(3)	Yogi Berra	75.00	37.00	22.00
(4)	Joe Black	12.00	6.00	3.50
(5)	Harry Byrd	10.00	5.00	3.00
(6)	Roy Campanella	65.00	32.00	19.50
(7)	Andy Carey	10.00	5.00	3.00
(8)	Jerry Coleman	10.00	5.00	3.00
(9)	Joe Collins	10.00	5.00	3.00
(10)	Billy Cox	10.00	5.00	3.00
(11)	Al Dark	12.00	6.00	3.50
(12)	Carl Erskine	20.00	10.00	6.00
(13)	Whitey Ford	40.00	20.00	12.00
(14)	Carl Furillo	20.00	10.00	6.00
(15)	Junior Gilliam	20.00	10.00	6.00
(16)	Ruben Gomez	10.00	5.00	3.00
(17)	Marv Grissom	10.00	5.00	3.00
(18)	Jim Hearn	10.00	5.00	3.00
(19)	Gil Hodges	35.00	17.50	10.50
(20)	Bobby Hofman	10.00	5.00	3.00
(21)	Jim Hughes	10.00	5.00	3.00
(22)	Monte Irvin	25.00	12.50	7.50
(23)	Larry Jansen	10.00	5.00	3.00
(24)	Ray Katt	10.00	5.00	3.00
(25)	Steve Kraly	10.00	5.00	3.00
(26)	Bob Kuzava	10.00	5.00	3.00
(27)	Clem Labine	12.00	6.00	3.50
(28)	Frank Leja	10.00	5.00	3.00
(29)	Don Liddle	10.00	5.00	3.00
(30)	Whitey Lockman	10.00	5.00	3.00
(31)	Billy Loes	10.00	5.00	3.00
(32)	Eddie Lopat	20.00	10.00	6.00
(33)	Gil McDougald	20.00	10.00	6.00
(34)	Sal Maglie	12.00	6.00	3.50
(35)	Mickey Mantle	450.00	225.00	135.00
(36)	Willie Mays	175.00	87.00	52.00
(37)	Russ Meyer	10.00	5.00	3.00
(38)	Bill Miller	10.00	5.00	3.00
(39)	Tom Morgan	10.00	5.00	3.00
(40)	Don Mueller	10.00	5.00	3.00
(41)	Don Newcombe	20.00	10.00	6.00
(42)	Irv Noren	10.00	5.00	3.00
(43)	Erv Palica	10.00	5.00	3.00
(44)	PeeWee Reese	55.00	27.00	16.50
(45)	Allie Reynolds	20.00	10.00	6.00
(46)	Dusty Rhodes	10.00	5.00	3.00
(47)	Phil Rizzuto	35.00	17.50	10.50
(48)	Ed Robinson	10.00	5.00	3.00
(49)	Jackie Robinson	225.00	112.00	67.00
(50)	Preacher Roe	20.00	10.00	6.00
(51)	George Shuba	10.00	5.00	3.00
(52)	Duke Snider	150.00	75.00	45.00
(53)	Hank Thompson	10.00	5.00	3.00
(54)	Wes Westrum	10.00	5.00	3.00
(55)	Hoyt Wilhelm	30.00	15.00	9.00
(56)	Davey Williams	10.00	5.00	3.00
(57)	Dick Williams	12.00	6.00	3.50
(58)	Gene Woodling	12.00	6.00	3.50
(59)	Al Worthington	10.00	5.00	3.00

1986 N.Y. Mets Super Fan Club

This special nine-card panel was issued by the fan

club of the 1986 World Champion New York Mets, along with other souvenir items gained with membership in the club. Included in the full-color set are eight top Mets players, with a promotional card in the center of the panel. Individual cards measure 2-1/2" by 3-1/2", and are perforated at the edges to facilitate separation. The full panel measures 70-1/2" by 10-1/2". Card fronts feature posed photos of each player, along with name, position and team logo. Backs feature career and personal data, and are printed in the team's blue and orange colors.

		MT	NR MT	EX
Complete Panel Set:		12.00	9.00	4.75
Complete Singles Set:		4.00	3.00	1.50
Common Single Player:		.15	.11	.06
	Panel	12.00	9.00	4.75
1	Wally Backman	.15	.11	.06
2	Gary Carter	.70	.50	.30
3	Ron Darling	.40	.30	.15
4	Dwight Gooden	1.25	.90	.50
5	Keith Hernandez	.60	.45	.25
6	Howard Johnson	.70	.50	.30
7	Roger McDowell	.40	.30	.15
8	Darryl Strawberry	1.25	.90	.50
-----	Membership Card	.05	.04	.02

1960 Nu-Card

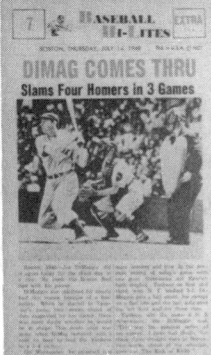
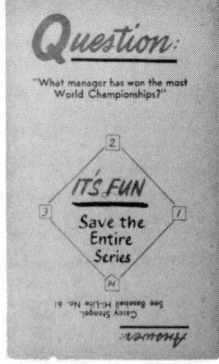

These large, 3-1/4" by 5-3/8" cards are printed in a mock newspaper format, with a headline, picture and story describing one of baseball's greatest events. There are 72 events featured in the set, which is printed in red and black. Each card is numbered in the upper left corner. The card backs offer a quiz question and answer. Certain cards in the set can be found with the fronts printed entirely in black. These cards may command a slight premium.

		NR MT	EX	VG
Complete Set:		175.00	87.00	52.00
Common Player:		1.00	.50	.30
1	Babe Hits 3 Homers In A Series Game	10.00	5.00	3.00
2	Podres Pitching Wins Series	.75	.40	.25
3	Bevans Pitches No Hitter, Almost	.75	.40	.25
4	Box Score Devised By Reporter	1.00	.50	.30
5	VanderMeer Pitches 2 No Hitters	1.00	.50	.30
6	Indians Take Bums	1.00	.50	.30
7	DiMag Comes Thru	10.00	5.00	3.00
8	Mathewson Pitches 3 W.S. Shutouts	1.75	.90	.50
9	Haddix Pitches 12 Perfect Innings	.75	.40	.25
10	Thomson's Homer Sinks Dodgers	1.75	.90	.50
11	Hubbell Strikes Out 5 A.L. Stars	1.50	.70	.45
12	Pickoff Ends Series (Marty Marion)	.75	.40	.25
13	Cards Take Series From Yanks (Grover Cleveland Alexander)	1.50	.70	.45
14	Dizzy And Daffy Win Series	3.50	1.75	1.00
15	Owen Drops 3rd Strike	.75	.40	.25
16	Ruth Calls His Shot	8.00	4.00	2.50
17	Merkle Pulls Boner	.75	.40	.25
18	Larsen Hurls Perfect World Series Game	1.50	.70	.45

	NR MT	EX	VG
19 Bean Ball Ends Career Of Mickey Cochranepremium. 1.25		.60	.40
20 Banks Belts 47 Homers, Earns MVP Honors premium. 2.00		1.00	.60
21 Stan Musial Hits 5 Homers In 1 Day 3.50		1.75	1.00
22 Mickey Mantle Hits Longest Homer 12.00		6.00	3.50
23 Sievers Captures Home Run Title .75		.40	.25
24 Gehrig Consecutive Game Record Ends 10.00		5.00	3.00
25 Red Schoendienst Key Player In Victory .75		.40	.25
26 Midget Pinch-Hits For St. Louis Browns (Eddie Gaedel) 1.25		.60	.40
27 Willie Mays Makes Greatest Catch 4.00		2.00	1.25
28 Homer By Berra Puts Yanks In 1st Place 3.00		1.50	.90
29 Campy National League's MVP 3.00		1.50	.90
30 Bob Turley Hurls Yanks To Championship .75		.40	.25
31 Dodgers Take Series From Sox In Six .75		.40	.25
32 Furillo Hero As Dodgers Beat Chicago .75		.40	.25
33 Adcock Gets Four Homers And A Double .75		.40	.25
34 Dickey Chosen All Star Catcher 1.25		.60	.40
35 Burdette Beats Yanks In 3 Series Games 1.00		.50	.30
36 Umpires Clear White Sox Bench 1.00		.50	.30
37 Reese Honored As Greatest Dodger S.S. 2.50		1.25	.70
38 Joe DiMaggio Hits In 56 Straight Games 10.00		5.00	3.00
39 Ted Williams Hits .406 For Season 5.00		2.50	1.50
40 Johnson Pitches 56 Scoreless Innings 2.25		1.25	.70
41 Hodges Hits 4 Home Runs In Nite Game 1.75		.90	.50
42 Greenberg Returns To Tigers From Army 1.25		.60	.40
43 Ty Cobb Named Best Player Of All Time 10.00		5.00	3.00
44 Robin Roberts Wins 28 Games 1.25		.60	.40
45 Rizzuto's 2 Runs Save 1st Place 1.50		.70	.45
46 Tigers Beat Out Senators For Pennant (Hal Newhouser) .75		.40	.25
47 Babe Ruth Hits 60th Home Run 9.00		4.50	2.75
48 Cy Young Honored 1.75		.90	.50
49 Killebrew Starts Spring Training 1.75		.90	.50
50 Mantle Hits Longest Homer At Stadium 12.00		6.00	3.50
51 Braves Take Pennant (Hank Aaron) 3.50		1.75	1.00
52 Ted Williams Hero Of All Star Game 5.00		2.50	1.50
53 Robinson Saves Dodgers For Playoffs (Jackie Robinson) 3.50		1.75	1.00
54 Snodgrass Muffs A Fly Ball .75		.40	.25
55 Snider Belts 2 Homers 2.25		1.25	.70
56 New York Giants Win 26 Straight Games (Christy Mathewson) 1.75		.90	.50
57 Ted Kluszewski Stars In 1st Game Win .75		.40	.25
58 Ott Walks 5 Times In A Single Game (Mel Ott) 1.25		.60	.40
59 Harvey Kuenn Takes Batting Title .75		.40	.25
60 Bob Feller Hurls 3rd No-Hitter Of Careerpremium. 2.25		1.25	.70
61 Yanks Champs Again! (Casey Stengel) 1.50		.70	.45
62 Aaron's Bat Beats Yankees In Series 4.00		2.00	1.25
63 Warren Spahn Beats Yanks In World Seriespremium. 1.50		.70	.45
64 Ump's Wrong Call Helps Dodgers .75		.40	.25
65 Kaline Hits 3 Homers, 2 In Same Inning 2.00		1.00	.60
66 Bob Allison Named A.L. Rookie of Year .75		.40	.25
67 McCovey Blasts Way Into Giant Lineup 1.75		.90	.50
68 Colavito Hits Four Homers In One Game 1.00		.50	.30
69 Erskine Sets Strike Out Record In W.S. .75		.40	.25
70 Sal Maglie Pitches No-Hit Game .75		.40	.25
71 Early Wynn Victory Crushes Yanks 1.25		.60	.40
72 Nellie Fox American League's M.V.P. 3.00		1.50	.90

1961 Nu-Card

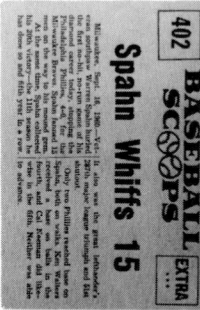

Very similar in style to their set of the year before, the Nu-Card Baseball Scoops were issued in a smaller 2-1/2" by 3-1/2" size, but still featured the mock newspaper card front. This 80-card set is numbered from 401 to 480, with numbers shown on both the card front and back. These cards, which commemorate great moments in individual players' careers, included only the headline and black and white photo on the fronts, with the descriptive story on the card backs. Cards are again printed in red and black. It appears the set may have been counterfeited, though when is not known. These cards can be determined by examining the card photo for unusual blurring and fuzziness.

	NR MT	EX	VG
Complete Set:	110.00	55.00	30.00
Common Player:	.30	.15	.09
401 Gentile Powers Birds Into 1st 1.00		.50	.30
402 Warren Spahn Hurls No-Hitter, Whiffs 15 1.00		.50	.30
403 Mazeroski's Homer Wins Series For Bucs .75		.40	.25
404 Willie Mays' 3 Triples Paces Giants 4.00		2.00	1.25
405 Woodie Held Slugs 2 Homers, 6 RBIs .30		.15	.09
406 Vern Law Winner Of Cy Young Award .40		.20	.12
407 Runnels Makes 9 Hits in Twin-Bill .30		.15	.09
408 Braves' Lew Burdette Wins No-Hitter, 1-0 .70		.35	.20
409 Dick Stuart Hits 3 Homers, Single .30		.15	.09
410 Don Cardwell Of Cubs Pitches No-Hit Game .30		.15	.09
411 Camilo Pascual Strikes Out 15 Bosox .30		.15	.09
412 Eddie Mathews Blasts 300th Big League HR 1.00		.50	.30
413 Groat, NL Bat King, Named Loop's MVP .70		.35	.20
414 AL Votes To Expand To 10 Teams (Gene Autry) 1.25		.60	.40
415 Bobby Richardson Sets Series Mark .75		.40	.25
416 Maris Nips Mantle For AL MVP Award 2.50		1.25	.70
417 Merkle Pulls Boner .30		.15	.09
418 Larsen Hurls Perefect World Series Game .75		.40	.25
419 Bean Ball Ends Career Of Mickey Cochrane .70		.35	.20
420 Banks Belts 47 Homers, Earns MVP Award 1.50		.70	.45
421 Stan Musial Hits 5 Homers In 1 Day 2.50		1.25	.70
422 Mickey Mantle Hits Longest Homer 10.00		5.00	3.00
423 Sievers Captures Home Run Title .30		.15	.09
424 Gehrig Consecutive Game Record Ends 2.50		1.50	
425 Red Schoendienst Key Player In Victory .70		.35	.20
426 Midget Pinch-Hits For St. Louis Browns (Eddie Gaedel) .75		.40	.25

		NR MT	EX	VG
427	Willie Mays Makes Greatest Catch	2.50	1.25	.70
428	Robinson Saves Dodgers For Playoffs	2.50	1.25	.70
429	Campy Most Valuable Player	2.50	1.25	.70
430	Turley Hurls Yanks To Championship	.40	.20	.12
431	Dodgers Take Series From Sox In Six (Larry Sherry)	.30	.15	.09
432	Furillo Hero In 3rd World Series Game	.70	.35	.20
433	Adcock Gets Four Homers, Double	.70	.35	.20
434	Dickey Chosen All Star Catcher	1.00	.50	.30
435	Burdette Beats Yanks In 3 Series Games	.75	.40	.25
436	Umpires Clear White Sox Bench	.30	.15	.09
437	Reese Honored As Greatest Dodgers S.S.	1.50	.70	.45
438	Joe DiMaggio Hits In 56 Straight Games	5.00	2.50	1.50
439	Ted Williams Hits .406 For Season	4.00	2.00	1.25
440	Johnson Pitches 56 Scoreless Innings	2.50	1.25	.70
441	Hodges Hits 4 Home Runs In Nite Game	1.50	.70	.45
442	Greenberg Returns To Tigers From Army	1.00	.50	.30
443	Ty Cobb Named Best Player Of All Time	4.00	2.00	1.25
444	Robin Roberts Wins 28 Games	1.00	.50	.30
445	Rizzuto's 2 Runs Save 1st Place	1.25	.60	.40
446	Tigers Beat Out Senators For Pennant (Hal Newhouser)	.30	.15	.09
447	Babe Ruth Hits 60th Home Run	6.00	3.00	1.75
448	Cy Young Honored	1.50	.70	.45
449	Killebrew Starts Spring Training	1.25	.60	.40
450	Mantle Hits Longest Homer At Stadium	9.00	4.50	2.75
451	Braves Take Pennant	.30	.15	.09
452	Ted Williams Hero Of All Star Game	2.50	1.25	.70
453	Homer By Berra Puts Yanks In 1st Place	2.50	1.25	.70
454	Snodgrass Muffs A Fly Ball	.30	.15	.09
455	Babe Hits 3 Homers In A Series Game	8.00	4.00	2.50
456	New York Wins 26 Straight Games	.30	.15	.09
457	Ted Kluszewski Stars In 1st Series Win	.40	.20	.12
458	Ott Walks 5 Times In A Single Game	1.00	.50	.30
459	Harvey Kuenn Takes Batting Title	.40	.20	.12
460	Bob Feller Hurls 3rd No-Hitter Of Career	2.50	1.25	.70
461	Yanks Champs Again! (Casey Stengel)	1.50	.70	.45
462	Aaron's Bat Beats Yankees In Series	2.50	1.25	.70
463	Warren Spahn Beats Yanks In World Series	1.00	.50	.30
464	Ump's Wrong Call Helps Dodgers	.30	.15	.09
465	Kaline Hits 3 Homers, 2 In Same Inning	1.50	.70	.45
466	Bob Allison Named A.L. Rookie Of Year	.40	.20	.12
467	DiMag Comes Thru	5.00	2.50	1.50
468	Colavito Hits Four Homers In One Game	.70	.35	.20
469	Erskine Sets Strike Out Record In W.S.	.70	.35	.20
470	Sal Maglie Pitches No-Hit Game	.70	.35	.20
471	Early Wynn Victory Crushes Yanks	1.00	.50	.30
472	Nellie Fox American League's MVP	.75	.40	.25
473	Pickoff Ends Series (Marty Marion)	.40	.20	.12
474	Podres Pitching Wins Series	.80	.40	.25
475	Owen Drops 3rd Strike	.30	.15	.09
476	Dizzy And Daffy Win Series	2.50	1.25	.70
477	Mathewson Pitches 3 W.S. Shutouts	1.50	.70	.45
478	Haddix Pitches 12 Perfect Innings	.40	.20	.12
479	Hubbell Strike Out 5 A.L. Stars	1.00	.50	.30
480	Homer Sinks Dodgers (Bobby Thomson)	1.25	.60	.40

1986 Oh Henry Indians

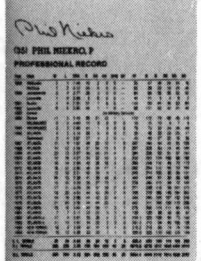

This 30-card set of Cleveland Indians players was distributed by the team at a special Photo/Baseball Card Day at Municipal Stadium. The cards were printed within a special three-panel, perforated fold-out piece which featured four action shots of the Indians on the cover. Unfolded, there are two panels containing the baseball cards and a third which contains a team photo. Cards measure 2-1/4" by 3-1/8" and are full-color studio portraits. Photos are framed in blue with a white border and list player name, number and position. Card fronts also include a picture of the sponsoring candy bar. Card backs include facsimile autograph and professional records. Each card is perforated for separation.

		MT	NR MT	EX
	Complete Set:	11.00	8.25	4.50
	Common Player:	.15	.11	.06
2	Brett Butler	.50	.40	.20
4	Tony Bernazard	.15	.11	.06
6	Andy Allanson	.25	.20	.10
7	Pat Corrales	.15	.11	.06
8	Carmen Castillo	.15	.11	.06
10	Pat Tabler	.30	.25	.12
13	Ernie Camacho	.15	.11	.06
14	Julio Franco	1.00	.70	.40
15	Dan Rohn	.15	.11	.06
18	Ken Schrom	.15	.11	.06
20	Otis Nixon	.20	.15	.08
22	Fran Mullins	.15	.11	.06
23	Chris Bando	.15	.11	.06
24	Ed Williams	.35	.25	.14
26	Brook Jacoby	.80	.60	.30
27	Mel Hall	.30	.25	.12
29	Andre Thornton	.30	.25	.12
30	Joe Carter	1.00	.70	.40
35	Phil Niekro	.80	.60	.30
36	Jamie Easterly	.15	.11	.06
37	Don Schulze	.15	.11	.06
42	Rich Yett	.20	.15	.08
43	Scott Bailes	.35	.25	.14
44	Neal Heaton	.15	.11	.06
46	Jim Kern	.15	.11	.06
48	Dickie Noles	.15	.11	.06
49	Tom Candiotti	.25	.20	.10
53	Reggie Ritter	.15	.11	.06
54	Tom Waddell	.15	.11	.06
----	Coaching Staff (Jack Aker, Bobby Bonds, Doc Edwards, Johnny Goryl)	.15	.11	.06

A player's name in *italic* type indicates a rookie card. An (FC) indicates a player's first card for that particular card company.

Definitions for grading conditions are located in the introduction section at the front of this book.

1988 Pacific Trading Cards Baseball Legends

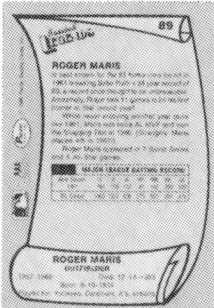

Pacific Trading Cards rounded up 110 photos of the greatest baseball players from the past 40 years for its 1988 "Baseball Legends" set. All players featured in the set are (or were) members of the Major League Baseball Alumni Association. Card fronts feature silver outer borders and large, clear full-color player photos outlined in black against colorful banner-style inner borders of red, blue, green, orange or gold. The player's name and position are printed in white letters on the lower portion of the banner. Card backs are numbered and carry the Baseball Legends logo, player biography, major league career stats, and personal information. The cards were sold in boxed sets via candy wholesalers, with emphasis on Midwest and New England states. Complete collector sets in clear plastic boxes were made available via dealers or directly from Pacific Trading Cards.

		MT	NR MT	EX
Complete Set:		12.00	9.00	4.75
Common Player:		.06	.05	.02
1	Hank Aaron	.50	.40	.20
2	Red Shoendienst (Schoendienst)	.10	.08	.04
3	Brooks Robinson	.30	.25	.12
4	Luke Appling	.15	.11	.06
5	Gene Woodling	.06	.05	.02
6	Stan Musial	.50	.40	.20
7	Mickey Mantle	1.00	.70	.40
8	Richie Ashburn	.10	.08	.04
9	Ralph Kiner	.20	.15	.08
10	Phil Rizzuto	.20	.15	.08
11	Harvey Haddix	.06	.05	.02
12	Ken Boyer	.10	.08	.04
13	Clete Boyer	.06	.05	.02
14	Ken Harrelson	.06	.05	.02
15	Robin Roberts	.20	.15	.08
16	Catfish Hunter	.20	.15	.08
17	Frank Howard	.10	.08	.04
18	Jim Perry	.06	.05	.02
19	Elston Howard	.10	.08	.04
20	Jim Bouton	.10	.08	.04
21	Pee Wee Reese	.25	.20	.10
22	Mel Stottlemyer (Stottlemyre)	.10	.08	.04
23	Hank Sauer	.06	.05	.02
24	Willie Mays	.50	.40	.20
25	Tom Tresh	.06	.05	.02
26	Roy Sievers	.06	.05	.02
27	Leo Durocher	.15	.11	.06
28	Al Dark	.10	.08	.04
29	Tony Kubek	.15	.11	.06
30	Johnny Vander Meer	.10	.08	.04
31	Joe Adcock	.10	.08	.04
32	Bob Lemon	.20	.15	.08
33	Don Newcombe	.15	.11	.06
34	Thurman Munson	.20	.15	.08
35	Earl Battey	.06	.05	.02

		MT	NR MT	EX
36	Ernie Banks	.30	.25	.12
37	Matty Alou	.06	.05	.02
38	Dave McNally	.06	.05	.02
39	Mickey Lolich	.10	.08	.04
40	Jackie Robinson	.50	.40	.20
41	Allie Reynolds	.15	.11	.06
42	Don Larson (Larsen)	.10	.08	.04
43	Fergie Jenkins	.15	.11	.06
44	Jim Gilliam	.10	.08	.04
45	Bobby Thomson	.10	.08	.04
46	Sparky Anderson	.10	.08	.04
47	Roy Campanella	.30	.25	.12
48	Marv Throneberry	.10	.08	.04
49	Bill Virdon	.06	.05	.02
50	Ted Williams	.50	.40	.20
51	Minnie Minoso	.10	.08	.04
52	Bob Turley	.10	.08	.04
53	Yogi Berra	.30	.25	.12
54	Juan Marichal	.20	.15	.08
55	Duke Snider	.30	.25	.12
56	Harvey Kuenn	.10	.08	.04
57	Nellie Fox	.15	.11	.06
58	Felipe Alou	.06	.05	.02
59	Tony Oliva	.10	.08	.04
60	Bill Mazeroski	.10	.08	.04
61	Bobby Shantz	.10	.08	.04
62	Mark Fidrych	.06	.05	.02
63	Johnny Mize	.15	.11	.06
64	Ralph Terry	.06	.05	.02
65	Gus Bell	.06	.05	.02
66	Jerry Koosman	.10	.08	.04
67	Mike McCormick	.06	.05	.02
68	Lou Burdette	.10	.08	.04
69	George Kell	.15	.11	.06
70	Vic Raschi	.10	.08	.04
71	Chuck Connors	.20	.15	.08
72	Ted Kluszewski	.10	.08	.04
73	Bobby Doerr	.15	.11	.06
74	Bobby Richardson	.15	.11	.06
75	Carl Erskine	.15	.11	.06
76	Hoyt Wilhelm	.20	.15	.08
77	Bob Purkey	.06	.05	.02
78	Bob Friend	.06	.05	.02
79	Monte Irvin	.15	.11	.06
80	Jim Longborg (Lonborg)	.06	.05	.02
81	Wally Moon	.06	.05	.02
82	Moose Skowron	.10	.08	.04
83	Tommy Davis	.10	.08	.04
84	Enos Slaughter	.20	.15	.08
85	Sal Maglie	.10	.08	.04
86	Harmon Killebrew	.25	.20	.10
87	Gil Hodges	.25	.20	.10
88	Jim Kaat	.10	.08	.04
89	Roger Maris	.30	.25	.12
90	Billy Williams	.20	.15	.08
91	Luis Aparicio	.15	.11	.06
92	Jim Bunning	.15	.11	.06
93	Bill Freehan	.06	.05	.02
94	Orlando Cepeda	.10	.08	.04
95	Early Wynn	.20	.15	.08
96	Tug McGraw	.10	.08	.04
97	Ron Santo	.10	.08	.04
98	Del Crandall	.06	.05	.02
99	Sal Bando	.06	.05	.02
100	Joe DiMaggio	.70	.50	.30
101	Bob Feller	.30	.25	.12
102	Larry Doby	.15	.11	.06
103	Rollie Fingers	.15	.11	.06
104	Al Kaline	.30	.25	.12
105	Johnny Podres	.10	.08	.04
106	Lou Boudreau	.15	.11	.06
107	Zoilo Versalles	.06	.05	.02
108	Dick Groat	.06	.05	.02
109	Warren Spahn	.25	.20	.10
110	Johnny Bench	.40	.30	.15

A player's name in *italic* indicates a rookie card. An (FC) indicates a player's first card for that particular card company.

1989 Pacific Trading Cards Legends II

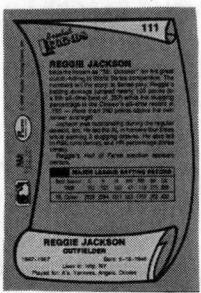

Pacific Trading Cards issued its Baseball Legends II set as a carry over of its initial set. The photos are printed on silver background and have colorful inner borders of red, blue, orange or gold. Players' names and positions are printed in white letters below the photos. The card backs once again present the "Baseball Legends" logo, player biography, major league career statistics, and personal information. The Baseball Legends II are numbered 110-220 and were available in wax packs at a limited number of retail chains. The complete set was also made available via dealers or could be ordered directly from Pacific Trading Cards.

		MT	NR MT	EX
Complete Set:		11.00	8.25	4.50
Common Player:		.06	.05	.02
111	Reggie Jackson	.30	.25	.12
112	Rich Reese	.06	.05	.02
113	Frankie Frisch	.15	.11	.06
114	Ed Kranepool	.06	.05	.02
115	Al Hrabosky	.06	.05	.02
116	Eddie Mathews	.25	.20	.10
117	Ty Cobb	.50	.40	.20
118	Jim Davenport	.06	.05	.02
119	Buddy Lewis	.06	.05	.02
120	Virgil Trucks	.10	.08	.04
121	Del Ennis	.06	.05	.02
122	Dick Radatz	.06	.05	.02
123	Andy Pafko	.12	.09	.05
124	Wilbur Wood	.10	.08	.04
125	Joe Sewell	.15	.11	.06
126	Herb Score	.06	.05	.02
127	Paul Waner	.06	.05	.02
128	Lloyd Waner	.06	.05	.02
129	Brooks Robinson	.30	.25	.12
130	Bo Belinsky	.10	.08	.04
131	Phil Cavaretta	.06	.05	.02
132	Claude Osteen	.06	.05	.02
133	Tito Francona	.06	.05	.02
134	Billy Pierce	.06	.05	.02
135	Roberto Clemente	.50	.40	.20
136	Spud Chandler	.06	.05	.02
137	Enos Slaughter	.25	.20	.10
138	Ken Holtzman	.06	.05	.02
139	John Hopp	.06	.05	.02
140	Tony LaRussa	.06	.05	.02
141	Ryne Duren	.06	.05	.02
142	Glenn Beckert	.06	.05	.02
143	Ken Keltner	.06	.05	.02
144	Hank Bauer	.15	.11	.06
145	Roger Craig	.10	.08	.04
146	Frank Baker	.10	.08	.04
147	Jim O'Toole	.06	.05	.02
148	Rogers Hornsby	.30	.25	.12
149	Jose Cardenal	.06	.05	.02
150	Bobby Doerr	.10	.08	.04
151	Mickey Cochrane	.10	.08	.04
152	Gaylord Perry	.10	.08	.04
153	Frank Thomas	.06	.05	.02
154	Ted Williams	.40	.30	.15
155	Sam McDowell	.10	.08	.04
156	Bob Feller	.20	.15	.08
157	Bert Campaneris	.06	.05	.02

		MT	NR MT	EX
158	Thornton Lee	.06	.05	.02
159	Gary Peters	.06	.05	.02
160	Joe Medwick	.10	.08	.04
161	Joe Nuxhall	.10	.08	.04
162	Joe Schultz	.06	.05	.02
163	Harmon Killebrew	.25	.20	.10
164	Bucky Walters	.06	.05	.02
165	Bobby Allison	.10	.08	.04
166	Lou Boudreau	.15	.11	.08
167	Joe Cronin	.10	.08	.04
168	Mike Torrez	.10	.08	.04
169	Rich Rollins	.06	.05	.02
170	Tony Cuccinello	.06	.05	.02
171	Hoyt Wilhelm	.20	.15	.08
172	Ernie Harwell	.10	.08	.04
173	George Foster	.06	.05	.02
174	Lou Gehrig	.80	.60	.30
175	Dave Kingman	.06	.05	.02
176	Babe Ruth	1.00	.70	.40
177	Joe Black	.10	.08	.04
178	Roy Face	.10	.08	.04
179	Earl Weaver	.06	.05	.02
180	Johnny Mize	.15	.11	.06
181	Roger Cramer	.06	.05	.02
182	Jim Piersall	.06	.05	.02
183	Ned Garver	.06	.05	.02
184	Billy Williams	.25	.20	.10
185	Lefty Grove	.15	.11	.06
186	Jim Grant	.06	.05	.02
187	Elmer Valo	.06	.05	.02
188	Ewell Blackwell	.10	.08	.04
189	Mel Ott	.20	.15	.08
190	Harry Walker	.06	.05	.02
191	Bill Campbell	.06	.05	.02
192	Walter Johnson	.30	.25	.12
193	Jim "Catfish" Hunter	.10	.08	.04
194	Charlie Keller	.10	.08	.04
195	Hank Greenberg	.15	.11	.06
196	Bobby Murcer	.06	.05	.02
197	Al Lopez	.06	.05	.02
198	Vida Blue	.10	.08	.04
199	Shag Crawford	.06	.05	.02
200	Arky Vaughan	.10	.08	.04
201	Smoky Burgess	.25	.20	.10
202	Rip Sewell	.06	.05	.02
203	Earl Avrerill	.10	.08	.04
204	Milt Pappas	.06	.05	.02
205	Mel Harder	.06	.05	.02
206	Sam Jethroe	.06	.05	.02
207	Randy Hundley	.06	.05	.02
208	Jessie Haines	.10	.08	.04
209	Jack Brickhouse	.10	.08	.04
210	Whitey Ford	.20	.15	.08
211	Honus Wagner	1.00	.70	.40
212	Phil Niekro	.10	.08	.04
213	Gary Bell	.06	.05	.02
214	Jon Matlack	.06	.05	.02
215	Moe Drabowsky	.06	.05	.02
216	Edd Roush	.10	.08	.04
217	Joel Horlen	.06	.05	.02
218	Casey Stengel	.30	.25	.12
219	Burt Hooton	.06	.05	.02
220	Joe Jackson	.80	.60	.30

1963 Pepsi-Cola Colt .45'S

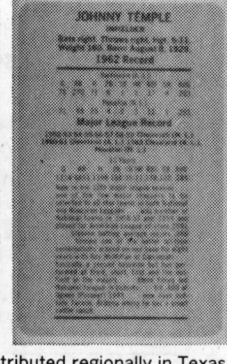

This 16-card set was distributed regionally in Texas in bottled six-packs of Pepsi. The cards were issued on panels 2-3/8" by 9-1/8", which were fit in between the bottles in each carton. Values quoted in the checklist below are for complete panels. A standard 2-3/8" by 3-3/4" card was printed on each panel, which also included promos for Pepsi and the Colt .45's, as well as a team schedule. Card fronts were black and white posed action photos with blue and red trim. Player name and position and Pepsi logo are also included. Card backs offer player statistics and career highlights. The John Bateman card, which was apparently never distributed publicly, is among the rarest collectible baseball cards of the 1960s. The complete set price does not include the Bateman card.

		NR MT	EX	VG
Complete Set:		200.00	100.00	60.00
Common Player:		7.00	3.50	2.00
1	Bob Aspromonte	7.00	3.50	2.00
2	John Bateman	500.00	250.00	150.00
3	Bob Bruce	7.00	3.50	2.00
4	Jim Campbell	7.00	3.50	2.00
5	Dick Farrell	7.00	3.50	2.00
6	Ernie Fazio	7.00	3.50	2.00
7	Carroll Hardy	7.00	3.50	2.00
8	J.C. Hartman	7.00	3.50	2.00
9	Ken Johnson	7.00	3.50	2.00
10	Bob Lillis	7.00	3.50	2.00
11	Don McMahon	7.00	3.50	2.00
12	Pete Runnels	10.00	5.00	3.00
13	Al Spangler	7.00	3.50	2.00
14	Rusty Staub	25.00	12.50	7.50
15	Johnny Temple	7.00	3.50	2.00
16	Carl Warwick	60.00	30.00	18.00

1988 Pepsi-Cola/Kroger Tigers

(41) DARRELL EVANS, IF

Approximately 38,000 sets of cards were given to fans at Tiger Stadium on July 30th, 1988. The set, sponsored by Pepsi-Cola and Kroger, includes 25 oversized (2-7/8" by 4-1/4") cards printed on glossy white stock with blue and orange borders. The card backs include small black and white close-up photos, the players' professional records and sponsor logos. The numbers in the following checklist refer to the players' uniform.

		MT	NR MT	EX
Complete Set:		9.00	6.75	3.50
Common Player:		.20	.15	.08
1	Lou Whitaker	.70	.50	.30
2	Alan Trammell	.90	.70	.35
8	Mike Heath	.20	.15	.08
11	Sparky Anderson	.40	.30	.15
12	Luis Salazar	.20	.15	.08
14	Dave Bergman	.20	.15	.08
15	Pat Sheridan	.20	.15	.08
16	Tom Brookens	.20	.15	.08
19	Doyle Alexander	.25	.20	.10
21	Guillermo Hernandez	.25	.20	.10
22	Ray Knight	.25	.20	.10
24	Gary Pettis	.20	.15	.08
25	Eric King	.30	.25	.12
26	Frank Tanana	.30	.25	.12

		MT	NR MT	EX
31	Larry Herndon	.20	.15	.08
32	Jim Walewander	.25	.20	.10
33	Matt Nokes	.90	.70	.35
34	Chet Lemon	.25	.20	.10
35	Walt Terrell	.25	.20	.10
39	Mike Henneman	.40	.30	.15
41	Darrell Evans	.40	.30	.15
44	Jeff Robinson	.50	.40	.20
47	Jack Morris	.70	.50	.30
48	Paul Gibson	.30	.25	.12
-----	Coaches (Billy Consolo, Alex Grammas, Billy Muffett, Vada Pinson, Dick Tracewski)			
		.20	.15	.08

1990 Pepsi-Cola Red Sox

 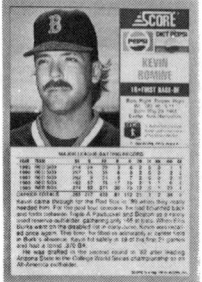

Pepsi combined with Score to produce this special 20-card Boston Red Sox team set. Cards were inserted regionally in 12-packs of Pepsi and Diet Pepsi. The card fronts feature full-color action photos with the team name across the top border and the player's name along the bottom border. The Pepsi and Diet Pepsi logos also appear on the bottom border. The card backs represent standard Score card backs, but are not numbered and also once again feature the Pepsi and Diet Pepsi logos.

		MT	NR MT	EX
Complete Set:		10.00	7.50	4.00
Common Player:		.25	.20	.10
(1)	Marty Barrett	.25	.20	.10
(2)	Mike Boddicker	.35	.25	.14
(3)	Wade Boggs	1.00	.70	.40
(4)	Bill Buckner	.25	.20	.10
(5)	Ellis Burks	1.00	.70	.40
(6)	Roger Clemens	1.00	.70	.40
(7)	John Dopson	.25	.20	.10
(8)	Dwight Evans	.50	.40	.20
(9)	Wes Gardner	.25	.20	.10
(10)	Rich Gedman	.25	.20	.10
(11)	Mike Greenwell	.80	.60	.30
(12)	Dennis Lamp	.25	.20	.10
(13)	Rob Murphy	.25	.20	.10
(14)	Tony Pena	.50	.40	.20
(15)	Carlos Quintana	.50	.40	.20
(16)	Jeff Reardon	.40	.30	.15
(17)	Jody Reed	.50	.40	.20
(18)	Luis Rivera	.25	.20	.10
(19)	Kevin Romine	.25	.20	.10
(20)	Lee Smith	.40	.30	.15

1985 Performance Printing Rangers

A local printing company sponsored this 28-card set of the Texas Rangers. The 2-3/8" by 3-1/2" cards are in full color and are numbered on the back by uniform number. Card fronts feature full-color, game-action photos. The 25 players on the Rangers' active roster at press time are included, along with manager Bobby Valentine and unnumbered coaches and trainer cards. The black and white card backs

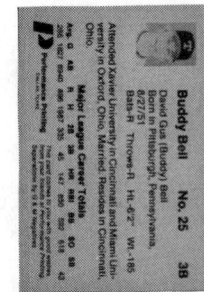

have a smaller portrait photo of each player, as well as biographical information and career statistics.

		MT	NR MT	EX
Complete Set:		6.00	4.50	2.50
Common Player:		.12	.09	.05
0	Oddibe McDowell	.50	.40	.20
1	Bill Stein	.12	.09	.05
2	Bobby Valentine	.15	.11	.06
3	Wayne Tolleson	.12	.09	.05
4	Don Slaught	.12	.09	.05
5	Alan Bannister	.12	.09	.05
6	Bobby Jones	.12	.09	.05
7	Glenn Brummer	.12	.09	.05
8	Luis Pujols	.12	.09	.05
9	Pete O'Brien	.50	.40	.20
11	Toby Harrah	.20	.15	.08
13	Tommy Dunbar	.12	.09	.05
15	Larry Parrish	.30	.25	.12
16	Mike Mason	.12	.09	.05
19	Curtis Wilkerson	.12	.09	.05
24	Dave Schmidt	.15	.11	.06
25	Buddy Bell	.50	.40	.20
27	Greg Harris	.15	.11	.06
30	Dave Rozema	.12	.09	.05
32	Gary Ward	.20	.15	.08
36	Dickie Noles	.12	.09	.05
41	Chris Welsh	.12	.09	.05
44	Cliff Johnson	.12	.09	.05
46	Burt Hooton	.20	.15	.08
48	Dave Stewart	.40	.30	.15
49	Charlie Hough	.30	.25	.12
----	Trainers (Danny Wheat, Bill Ziegler)			
		.12	.09	.05
----	Rangers Coaches (Rich Donnelly, Glenn Ezell, Tom House, Art Howe, Wayne Terwilliger)			
		.12	.09	.05

1986 Performance Printing Rangers

For the second time, the Texas Rangers issued a full-color card set in conjunction with this local printing company. Fronts of the 28-card set include player name, position and team logo beneath the color photo. Backs of the 2-3/8" by 3-1/2" cards are in black and white, with a small portrait photo of each

player along with personal and professional statistics. Cards were distributed at the August 23 Rangers home game, and the set includes all of the Rangers' fine rookies such as Bobby Witt, Pete Incaviglia, Edwin Correa and Ruben Sierra.

		MT	NR MT	EX
Complete Set:		10.00	7.50	4.00
Common Player:		.10	.08	.04
0	Oddibe McDowell	.50	.40	.20
1	Scott Fletcher	.20	.15	.08
2	Bobby Valentine	.15	.11	.06
3	Ruben Sierra	5.00	3.75	2.00
4	Don Slaught	.10	.08	.04
9	Pete O'Brien	.40	.30	.15
11	Toby Harrah	.20	.15	.08
12	Geno Petralli	.10	.08	.04
15	Larry Parrish	.25	.20	.10
16	Mike Mason	.10	.08	.04
17	Darrell Porter	.15	.11	.06
18	Edwin Correa	.40	.30	.15
19	Curtis Wilkerson	.10	.08	.04
22	Steve Buechele	.30	.25	.12
23	Jose Guzman	.40	.30	.15
24	Ricky Wright	.10	.08	.04
27	Greg Harris	.15	.11	.06
28	Mitch Williams	.30	.25	.12
29	Pete Incaviglia	1.25	.90	.50
32	Gary Ward	.15	.11	.06
34	Dale Mohorcic	.30	.25	.12
40	Jeff Russell	.10	.08	.04
44	Tom Paciorek	.10	.08	.04
46	Mike Loynd	.30	.25	.12
48	Bobby Witt	.60	.45	.25
49	Charlie Hough	.25	.20	.10
----	Coaching Staff (Joe Ferguson, Tim Foli, Tom House, Art Howe, Tom Robson)	.10	.08	.04
----	Trainers (Danny Wheat, Bill Zeigler)			
		.10	.08	.04

1961 Peters Meats Twins

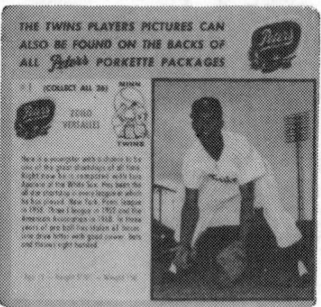

This set, featuring the first-year 1961 Minnesota Twins, is in a large, 4-5/8" by 3-1/2", format. Cards are on thick cardboard and heavily waxed, as they were used as partial packaging for the company's meat products. Card fronts feature full-color photos, team and Peters logos, and biographical information. The cards are blank-backed.

		NR MT	EX	VG
Complete Set:		600.00	300.00	175.00
Common Player:		12.00	6.00	3.50
1	Zoilo Versalles	20.00	10.00	6.00
2	Eddie Lopat	20.00	10.00	6.00
3	Pedro Ramos	12.00	6.00	3.50
4	Charles "Chuck" Stobbs	12.00	6.00	3.50
5	Don Mincher	20.00	10.00	6.00
6	Jack Kralick	12.00	6.00	3.50
7	Jim Kaat	50.00	25.00	15.00
8	Hal Naragon	12.00	6.00	3.50
9	Don Lee	12.00	6.00	3.50
10	Harry "Cookie" Lavagetto	15.00	7.50	4.50
11	Tom "Pete" Whisenant	12.00	6.00	3.50
12	Elmer Valo	12.00	6.00	3.50

		NR MT	EX	VG
13	Ray Moore	12.00	6.00	3.50
14	Billy Gardner	12.00	6.00	3.50
15	Lenny Green	12.00	6.00	3.50
16	Sam Mele	12.00	6.00	3.50
17	Jim Lemon	15.00	7.50	4.50
18	Harmon "Killer" Killebrew	150.00	75.00	45.00
19	Paul Giel	15.00	7.50	4.50
20	Reno Bertoia	12.00	6.00	3.50
21	Clyde McCullough	12.00	6.00	3.50
22	Earl Battey	20.00	10.00	6.00
23	Camilo Pascual	20.00	10.00	6.00
24	Dan Dobbek	12.00	6.00	3.50
25	Joe "Valvy" Valdivielso	12.00	6.00	3.50
26	Billy Consolo	12.00	6.00	3.50

1979 Police/Fire Safety Giants

3 Mike Sadek Catcher

Tips from the Giants

Each of the full-color cards measures 2-5/8" by 4-1/8" and is numbered by player uniform number. The set includes 20 Giants players and coaches. The player's name, position and facsimile autograph are on the card fronts, along with the Giants logo. Card backs have a "Tip from the Giants" and sponsor logos for the Giants and radio station KNBR, all printed the Giants' orange and black colors. Half of the set was distributed at a ballpark promotion during the 1979 season, while the other cards were available only from police agencies in several San Francisco Bay area counties.

		NR MT	EX	VG
Complete Set:		20.00	10.00	6.00
Common Player:		.40	.20	.12
1	Dave Bristol	.40	.20	.12
2	Marc Hill	.40	.20	.12
3	Mike Sadek	.50	.25	.15
5	Tom Haller	.40	.20	.12
6	Joe Altobelli	.50	.25	.15
8	Larry Shepard	.50	.25	.15
9	Heity Cruz	.40	.20	.12
10	Johnnie LeMaster	.40	.20	.12
12	Jim Davenport	.40	.20	.12
14	Vida Blue	.80	.40	.25
15	Mike Ivie	.40	.20	.12
16	Roger Metzger	.40	.20	.12
17	Randy Moffitt	.40	.20	.12
18	Bill Madlock	1.25	.60	.40
21	Rob Andrews	.50	.25	.15
22	Jack Clark	2.50	1.25	.70
24	Dave Roberts	.40	.20	.12
26	John Montefusco	.50	.25	.15
29	Ed Halicki	.50	.25	.15
30	John Tamargo	.40	.20	.12
31	Larry Herndon	.40	.20	.12
38	Bill North	.50	.25	.15
39	Bob Knepper	.70	.35	.20
40	John Curtis	.50	.25	.15
41	Darrell Evans	1.25	.60	.40
43	Tom Griffin	.50	.25	.15
44	Willie McCovey	3.00	1.50	.90
46	Gary Lavelle	.50	.25	.15
49	Max Venable	.50	.25	.15

1980 Police/Fire Safety Dodgers

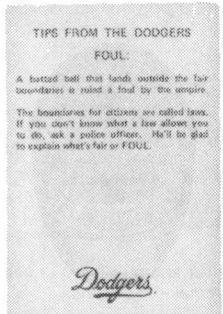

Producers of one of the most popular police and safety sets in baseball, the Los Angeles Dodgers began this successful promotion in 1980. The 2-13/16" by 4-1/8" cards feature attractive, full-color photos on the card fronts, along with brief personal statistics. Card backs include "Tips from the Dodgers" along with the team and Los Angeles Police Department logos. The 30 cards are numbered by player uniform number, with an unnumbered team card also included in the set.

		NR MT	EX	VG
Complete Set:		10.00	5.00	3.00
Common Player:		.30	.15	.09
5	Johnny Oates	.30	.15	.09
6	Steve Garvey	1.50	.70	.45
7	Steve Yeager	.30	.15	.09
8	Reggie Smith	.50	.25	.15
9	Gary Thomasson	.30	.15	.09
10	Ron Cey	.50	.25	.15
12	Dusty Baker	.40	.20	.12
13	Joe Ferguson	.30	.15	.09
15	Davey Lopes	.50	.25	.15
16	Rick Monday	.40	.20	.12
18	Bill Russell	.40	.20	.12
20	Don Sutton	.80	.40	.25
21	Jay Johnstone	.40	.20	.12
23	Teddy Martinez	.30	.15	.09
27	Joe Beckwith	.30	.15	.09
28	Pedro Guerrero	1.00	.50	.30
29	Don Stanhouse	.30	.15	.09
30	Derrel Thomas	.30	.15	.09
31	Doug Rau	.30	.15	.09
34	Ken Brett	.30	.15	.09
35	Bob Welch	.50	.25	.15
37	Robert Castillo	.30	.15	.09
38	Dave Goltz	.40	.20	.12
41	Jerry Reuss	.50	.25	.15
43	Rick Sutcliffe	.60	.30	.20
44	Mickey Hatcher	.40	.20	.12
46	Burt Hooton	.40	.20	.12
49	Charlie Hough	.40	.20	.12
51	Terry Forster	.40	.20	.12
----	Team Photo	.30	.15	.09

1980 Police/Fire Safety Giants

The 1980 Giants police set is virtually identical in format to its 1979 forerunner. Card design and colors are the same on both front and back, with radio station KNBR and the San Francisco Police Department once again co-sponsors. The 2-5/8" by 4-1/8" cards again feature fronts with full-color photos and facsimile autographs, while backs are in the team's orange and black colors. The set numbers 31 players and coaches, with each card numbered by uniform number. As in 1979, half the cards were

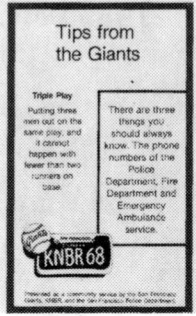

Tips from
the Giants

Triple Play
Putting three men out on the same play, and it cannot happen with fewer than two runners on base.

There are three things you should always know. The phone numbers of the Police Department, Fire Department and Emergency Ambulance service.

KNBR 68

Presented as a community service by the San Francisco Giants, KNBR, and the San Francisco Police Department.

distributed at a stadium promotion, with the remainder available only from police officers.

		NR MT	EX	VG
Complete Set:		12.00	9.00	4.75
Common Player:		.30	.15	.09
1	Dave Bristol	.30	.15	.09
2	Marc Hill	.30	.15	.09
3	Mike Sadek	.30	.15	.09
5	Jim Lefebvre	.30	.15	.09
6	Rennie Stennett	.30	.15	.09
7	Milt May	.30	.15	.09
8	Vern Benson	.30	.15	.09
9	Jim Wohlford	.30	.15	.09
10	Johnnie LeMaster	.30	.15	.09
12	Jim Davenport	.30	.15	.09
14	Vida Blue	.80	.40	.25
15	Mike Ivie	.30	.15	.09
16	Roger Metzger	.30	.15	.09
17	Randy Moffitt	.30	.15	.09
19	Al Holland	.30	.15	.09
20	Joe Strain	.30	.15	.09
22	Jack Clark	2.25	1.25	.70
26	John Montefusco	.40	.20	.12
28	Ed Halicki	.30	.15	.09
31	Larry Herndon	.40	.20	.12
32	Ed Whitson	.40	.20	.12
36	Bill North	.30	.15	.09
38	Greg Minton	.30	.15	.09
39	Bob Knepper	.50	.25	.15
41	Darrell Evans	.90	.45	.25
42	John Van Ornum	.30	.15	.09
43	Tom Griffin	.30	.15	.09
44	Willie McCovey	2.50	1.25	.70
45	Terry Whitfield	.30	.15	.09
46	Gary Lavelle	.30	.15	.09
47	Don McMahon	.30	.15	.09

1981 Police/Fire Safety
Braves

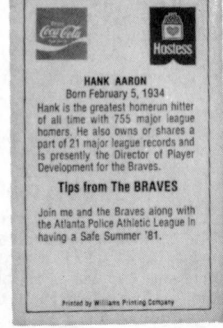

Coca-Cola   Hostess

HANK AARON
Born February 5, 1934
Hank is the greatest homerun hitter of all time with 755 major league homers. He also owns or shares a part of 21 major league records and is presently the Director of Player Development for the Braves.

Tips from The BRAVES
Join me and the Braves along with the Atlanta Police Athletic League in having a Safe Summer '81.

Printed by Williams Printing Company

The first Atlanta Braves police set was a cooperative effort of the team, Hostess, Coca-Cola and the Atlanta Police Department. Card fronts feature full-color photos of 27 different Braves and manager Bobby Cox. Police and team logos are on

the card backs. Card backs offer capsule biographies of the players, along with a tip for youngsters. The 2-5/8" by 4-1/8" cards are numbered by uniform number. Terry Harper (#19) appears to be somewhat scarcer than the other cards in the set. Reportedly, 33,000 sets were printed.

		MT	NR MT	EX
Complete Set:		12.00	9.00	4.75
Common Player:		.30	.25	.12
1	Jerry Royster	.30	.25	.12
3	Dale Murphy	2.50	2.00	1.00
4	Biff Pocoroba	.30	.25	.12
5	Bob Horner	1.00	.70	.40
6	Bob Cox	.30	.25	.12
9	Luis Gomez	.30	.25	.12
10	Chris Chambliss	.40	.30	.15
15	Bill Nahorodny	.30	.25	.12
16	Rafael Ramirez	.35	.25	.14
17	Glenn Hubbard	.35	.25	.14
18	Claudell Washington	.40	.30	.15
19	Terry Harper	.70	.50	.30
20	Bruce Benedict	.30	.25	.12
24	John Montefusco	.30	.25	.12
25	Rufino Linares	.30	.25	.12
26	Gene Garber	.30	.25	.12
30	Brian Asselstine	.30	.25	.12
34	Larry Bradford	.30	.25	.12
35	Phil Niekro	1.50	1.25	.60
37	Rick Camp	.30	.25	.12
39	Al Hrabosky	.35	.25	.14
40	Tommy Boggs	.30	.25	.12
42	Rick Mahler	.40	.30	.15
45	Ed Miller	.30	.25	.12
46	Gaylord Perry	1.50	1.25	.60
49	Preston Hanna	.30	.25	.12
-----	Hank Aaron	2.50	2.00	1.00

1981 Police/Fire Safety
Dodgers

A WORD FROM MANAGER
TOM LASORDA:
"Here's the difference between a gang and a team. Gangs have no rules. They believe that anything goes. They rob, cripple and even kill just to get rid of the opposition. But teams thrive on opposition and every member plays by the rules. Gangs make cowards. Teams make heroes. Don't let anyone force you into a gang. Be good to yourself and join a team."

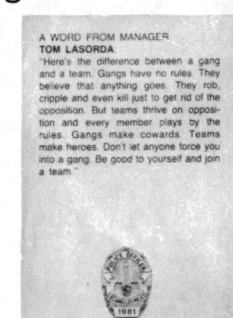

TOM LASORDA
No. 2 — Manager
LAPD SALUTES THE 1981
Dodgers

Very similar in format to their successful set of the year before, the Los Angeles Dodgers 1981 police set grew to 32 cards (from 30). This was due to the acquisitions of Ken Landreaux and Dave Stewart shortly before printing of the sets. These two cards may even have been added after the initial printing run, making them slightly more difficult to obtain. The full-color cards are again 2-13/16" by 4-1/8", with a safety tip on the card back. Each card front has the line "LAPD Salutes the 1981 Dodgers."

		NR MT	EX	
Complete Set:		12.00	9.00	
Common Player:		.20	.15	.08
2	Tom Lasorda	.40	.30	.15
3	Rudy Law	.20	.15	.08
6	Steve Garvey	1.25	.90	.50
7	Steve Yeager	.20	.15	.08
8	Reggie Smith	.40	.30	.15
10	Ron Cey	.40	.30	.15
12	Dusty Baker	.30	.25	.12
13	Joe Ferguson	.20	.15	.08

		NR MT	EX	
14	Mike Scioscia	.30	.25	.12
15	Davey Lopes	.35	.25	.14
16	Rick Monday	.30	.25	.12
18	Bill Russell	.30	.25	.12
21	Jay Johnstone	.25	.20	.10
26	Don Stanhouse	.20	.15	.08
27	Joe Beckwith	.20	.15	.08
28	Pete Guerrero	.70	.50	.30
30	Derrel Thomas	.20	.15	.08
34	Fernando Valenzuela	2.00	1.50	.80
35	Bob Welch	.40	.30	.15
36	Pepe Frias	.20	.15	.08
37	Robert Castillo	.20	.15	.08
38	Dave Goltz	.25	.20	.10
41	Jerry Reuss	.35	.25	.14
43	Rick Sutcliffe	.50	.40	.20
44a	Mickey Hatcher	.25	.20	.10
44b	Ken Landreaux	.70	.50	.30
46	Burt Hooton	.25	.20	.10
48	Dave Stewart	3.00	2.25	1.25
51	Terry Forster	.25	.20	.10
57	Steve Howe	.25	.20	.10
----	Coaching Staff (Monty Basgall, Mark Cresse, Tom Lasorda, Manny Mota, Danny Ozark, Ron Perranoski)	.20	.15	.08
----	Team Photo/Checklist	.20	.15	.08

1981 Police/Fire Safety Mariners

These 2-5/8" by 4-1/8" cards were co-sponsored by the Washington State Crime Prevention Assoc., Coca-Cola, Kiawanis and Ernst Home Centers. There are 16 players featured in this full-color set with each card numbered in the lower left of the card back. Card fronts list player name and position and have a team logo. Card backs are printed in blue and red and offer a "Tip from the Mariners" along with the four sponsor logos.

		MT	NR MT	EX
	Complete Set:	5.00	3.75	2.00
	Common Player:	.25	.20	.10
1	Jeff Burroughs	.35	.25	.14
2	Floyd Bannister	.60	.45	.25
3	Glenn Abbott	.25	.20	.10
4	Jim Anderson	.25	.20	.10
5	Danny Meyer	.25	.20	.10
6	Dave Edler	.25	.20	.10
7	Julio Cruz	.25	.20	.10
8	Kenny Clay	.25	.20	.10
9	Lenny Randle	.25	.20	.10
10	Mike Parrott	.25	.20	.10
11	Tom Paciorek	.25	.20	.10
12	Jerry Narron	.25	.20	.10
13	Richie Zisk	.35	.25	.14
14	Maury Wills	.50	.40	.20
15	Joe Simpson	.25	.20	.10
16	Shane Rawley	.60	.45	.25

NOTE: A card number in parentheses ( ) indicates the set is unnumbered.

1981 Police/Fire Safety Royals

Ten of the most popular 1981 Kansas City players are featured in this 2-1/2" by 4-1/8" card set. Card fronts feature full-color photos with player name, position, facsimile autograph and team logo. Backs include player statistics, a tip from the Royals and list the four sponsoring organizations. Surprisingly, the set was issued by the Ft. Myers, Fla., police department near the Royals' spring training headquarters.

		MT	NR MT	EX
	Complete Set:	35.00	26.00	14.00
	Common Player:	1.50	1.25	.60
(1)	Willie Mays Aikens	1.50	1.25	.60
(2)	George Brett	18.00	13.50	7.25
(3)	Rich Gale	1.50	1.25	.60
(4)	Clint Hurdle	1.50	1.25	.60
(5)	Dennis Leonard	2.00	1.50	.80
(6)	Hal McRae	2.25	1.75	.90
(7)	Amos Otis	2.00	1.50	.80
(8)	U.L. Washington	1.50	1.25	.60
(9)	Frank White	3.50	2.75	1.50
(10)	Willie Wilson	4.00	3.00	1.50

1982 Police/Fire Safety Braves

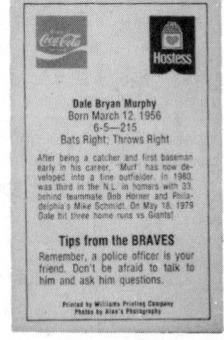

After their successful debut in 1981, the Atlanta Braves, the Atlanta Police Department, Coca-Cola and Hostess issued another card set in '82. This 30-card set is extremely close in format to the 1981 set and again measures 2-5/8" by 4-1/8". The full-color player photos are outstanding, and each card front also bears a statement marking the 1982 Braves' record-breaking 13-game win streak at the season's beginning. Card backs offer short biographies and "Tips from the Braves." Sponsors logos are also included. Reportedly, only 8,000 of these sets were printed.

		MT	NR MT	EX
Complete Set:		20.00	15.00	8.00
Common Player:		.30	.25	.12
1	Jerry Royster	.30	.25	.12
3	Dale Murphy	3.50	2.75	1.50
4	Biff Pocoroba	.30	.25	.12
5	Bob Horner	1.25	.90	.50
6	Randy Johnson	.30	.25	.12
8	Bob Watson	2.00	1.50	.80
9	Joe Torre	.40	.30	.15
10	Chris Chambliss	.40	.30	.15
15	C. Washington	.40	.30	.15
16	Rafael Ramirez	.35	.25	.14
17	Glenn Hubbard	.35	.25	.14
20	Bruce Benedict	.30	.25	.12
22	Brett Butler	.70	.50	.30
23	Tommie Aaron	.40	.30	.15
25	Rufino Linares	.30	.25	.12
26	Gene Garber	.30	.25	.12
27	Larry McWilliams	.30	.25	.12
28	Larry Whisenton	.30	.25	.12
32	Steve Bedrosian	1.00	.70	.40
35	Phil Niekro	2.00	1.50	.80
37	Rick Camp	.30	.25	.12
38	Joe Cowley	.30	.25	.12
39	Al Hrabosky	.35	.25	.14
42	Rick Mahler	.40	.30	.15
43	Bob Walk	.35	.25	.14
45	Bob Gibson	1.50	1.25	.60
49	Preston Hanna	.30	.25	.12
52	Joe Pignatano	.30	.25	.12
53	Dal Maxvill	.30	.25	.12
54	Rube Walker	.30	.25	.12

1982 Police/Fire Safety Brewers

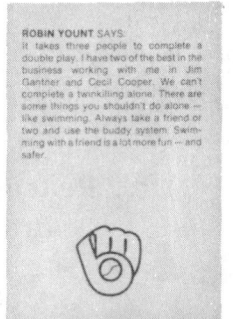

ROBIN YOUNT SAYS:
It takes three people to complete a double play. I have two of the best in the business working with me in Jim Gantner and Cecil Cooper. We can't complete a twinkling alone. There are some things you shouldn't do alone — like swimming. Always take a friend or two and use the buddy system. Swimming with a friend is a lot more fun — and safer.

ROBIN YOUNT
No. 19 – Shortstop
New Berlin Police Department
Salutes The 1982
Milwaukee Brewers

The inaugural Milwaukee Brewers police set contains 30 cards in a 2-13/16" by 4-1/8" format. There are 26 players included in the set, which is numbered by player uniform number. Unnumbered cards were also issued for general manager Harry Dalton, manager Buck Rodgers, the coaches and a team card with checklist. The full-color photos are especially attractive, printed on the cards' crisp white stock. A number of Wisconsin law enforcement agencies distributed the cards and credit lines on the card fronts were changed accordingly.

		MT	NR MT	EX
Complete Set:		15.00	11.00	6.00
Common Player:		.30	.25	.12
4	Paul Molitor	1.00	.70	.40
5	Ned Yost	.30	.25	.12
7	Don Money	.25	.20	.10
9	Larry Hisle	.25	.20	.10
10	Bob McClure	.30	.25	.12
11	Ed Romero	.30	.25	.12
13	Roy Howell	.30	.25	.12
15	Cecil Cooper	.50	.40	.20
17	Jim Gantner	.30	.25	.12
19	Robin Yount	1.50	1.25	.60
20	Gorman Thomas	.40	.30	.15

		MT	NR MT	EX
22	Charlie Moore	.30	.25	.12
23	Ted Simmons	.50	.40	.20
24	Ben Oglivie	.30	.25	.12
26	Kevin Bass	.60	.45	.25
28	Jamie Easterly	.30	.25	.12
29	Mark Brouhard	.30	.25	.12
30	Moose Haas	.30	.25	.12
34	Rollie Fingers	.70	.50	.30
35	Randy Lerch	.30	.25	.12
37	Buck Rodgers	.30	.25	.12
41	Jim Slaton	.30	.25	.12
45	Doug Jones	.30	.25	.12
46	Jerry Augustine	.30	.25	.12
47	Dwight Bernard	.30	.25	.12
48	Mike Caldwell	.25	.20	.10
50	Pete Vuckovich	.30	.25	.12
----	Team Photo/Checklist	.30	.25	.12
----	Harry Dalton (general mgr.)	.30	.25	.12
----	Coaches Card (Pat Dobson, Larry Haney, Ron Hansen, Cal McLish, Buck Rodgers, Harry Warner)	.30	.25	.12

1982 Police/Fire Safety Dodgers

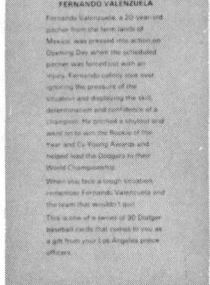

FERNANDO VALENZUELA

Fernando Valenzuela, a 20-year-old pitcher from the farm lands of Mexico, was pressed into action on Opening Day when the scheduled pitcher was forced out with an injury. Fernando calmly rose over ignoring the pressure of the situation and displaying the skill, determination and confidence of a champion. He pitched a shutout and went on to win the Rookie of the Year and Cy Young Awards and helped lead the Dodgers to their World Championship.

When you face a tough situation, remember Fernando Valenzuela and the team that wouldn't quit.

This is one of a series of 30 Dodger baseball cards that comes to you as a gift from your Los Angeles police officers.

FERNANDO VALENZUELA
No. 34 – PITCHER
The Los Angeles Police Department
presents the World Champion
Dodgers

Again issued in the same 2-13/16" by 4-1/8" size of the '80 and '81 sets, the 1982 Los Angeles set commemorates the team's 1981 World Championship. In addition to the 26 cards numbered by uniform for players and manager Tom Lasorda, there are four unnumbered cards which feature the team winning the division, league and World Series titles, plus one of the World Series trophy. The full-color card photos are once again vivid portraits on a clean white card stock. Card backs offer brief biographies and stadium information in addition to a safety tip.

		MT	NR MT	EX
Complete Set:		7.00	5.25	2.75
Common Player:		.15	.11	.06
2	Tom Lasorda	.30	.25	.12
6	Steve Garvey	1.00	.70	.40
7	Steve Yeager	.15	.11	.06
8	Mark Belanger	.20	.15	.08
10	Ron Cey	.30	.25	.12
12	Dusty Baker	.25	.20	.10
14	Mike Scioscia	.25	.20	.10
16	Rick Monday	.25	.20	.10
18	Bill Russell	.20	.15	.08
21	Jay Johnstone	.20	.15	.08
26	Alejandro Pena	.60	.45	.25
28	Pedro Guerrero	.80	.60	.30
30	Derrel Thomas	.15	.11	.06
31	Jorge Orta	.15	.11	.06
34	Fernando Valenzuela	1.00	.70	.40
35	Bob Welch	.35	.25	.14
38	Dave Goltz	.15	.11	.06
40	Ron Roenicke	.15	.11	.06
41	Jerry Reuss	.25	.20	.10
44	Ken Landreaux	.15	.11	.06
46	Burt Hooton	.20	.15	.08
48	Dave Stewart	.30	.25	.12
49	Tom Niedenfuer	.35	.25	.14
51	Terry Forster	.20	.15	.08
52	Steve Sax	.90	.70	.35

	MT	NR MT	EX
57 Steve Howe	.20	.15	.08
—— Division Championship	.15	.11	.06
-— League Championship	.15	.11	.06
-— World Series Championship	.15	.11	.06
-— Trophy Card/Checklist	.15	.11	.06

1983 Police/Fire Safety Braves

Brett Butler (22)
Outfielder

Brett M. Butler
Born June 15, 1957
5-10 — 160
Bats Left; Throws Left
Home: Atlanta, Georgia

Young Brett was the starting centerfielder and lead-off man during the Braves' 13-game winning streak last season. After spending considerable time at Richmond in '82, the speedy flychaser won back the centerfield job with another outstanding spring in 1983.

Tips from the BRAVES
Shoplifting is a crime not a game.
Are you willing to pay the price?

Printed by Williams Printing Company
Photos by Allen's Photography

An almost exact replica of their 1982 set, the 1983 Atlanta Braves police set includes 30 cards numbered by uniform. Sponsors Hostess, Coca-Cola and the Atlanta Police Department returned for the third year. The cards are again 2-5/8" by 4-1/8", with full-color photos and police and team logos on the card fronts. A statement noting the team's 1982 National League Western Division title in the upper right corner is the key difference on the card fronts. As in 1982, 8,000 sets were reportedly printed.

	MT	NR MT	EX
Complete Set:	15.00	11.00	6.00
Common Player:	.30	.25	.12
1 Jerry Royster	.30	.25	.12
3 Dale Murphy	3.50	2.75	1.50
4 Biff Pocoroba	.30	.25	.12
5 Bob Horner	1.00	.70	.40
6 Randy Johnson	.30	.25	.12
8 Bob Watson	.35	.25	.14
9 Joe Torre	.40	.30	.15
10 Chris Chambliss	.40	.30	.15
11 Ken Smith	.30	.25	.12
15 Claudell Washington	.40	.30	.15
16 Rafael Ramirez	.35	.25	.14
17 Glenn Hubbard	.35	.25	.14
19 Terry Harper	.30	.25	.12
20 Bruce Benedict	.30	.25	.12
22 Brett Butler	.40	.30	.15
24 Larry Owen	.30	.25	.12
26 Gene Garber	.30	.25	.12
27 Pascual Perez	.35	.25	.14
29 Craig McMurtry	.35	.25	.14
32 Steve Bedrosian	.60	.45	.25
33 Pete Falcone	.30	.25	.12
35 Phil Niekro	1.50	1.25	.60
36 Sonny Jackson	.30	.25	.12
37 Rick Camp	.30	.25	.12
45 Bob Gibson	1.25	.90	.50
49 Rick Behenna	.30	.25	.12
51 Terry Forster	.35	.25	.14
52 Joe Pignatano	.30	.25	.12
53 Dal Maxvill	.30	.25	.12
54 Rube Walker	.30	.25	.12

1983 Police/Fire Safety Brewers

Similar to 1982, a number of issuer variations exist for the 1983 Brewers police set, as law enforcement agencies throughout the state distributed the set

16 MARSHALL EDWARDS — OF
The Milwaukee Police Department
Presents The 1983
Milwaukee Brewers

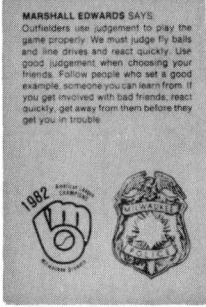

MARSHALL EDWARDS SAYS:
Outfielders use judgement to play the game properly. We must judge fly balls and line drives and react quickly. Use good judgement when choosing your friends. Follow people who set a good example, someone you can learn from. If you get involved with bad friends, react quickly, get away from them before they get you in trouble.

with their own credit lines on the cards. At least 28 variations are known to exist, with those issued by smaller agencies being scarcest. Prices quoted below are for the most common variations, generally the Milwaukee police department and a few small-town departments whose entire supply of police cards seem to have fallen into dealers' hands. Some specialists are willing to pay a premium for the scarcer departments' issues. The 30 2-13/16" by 4-1/8" cards include 29 players and coaches, along with a team card (with a checklist back). The team card and group coaches' card are unnumbered, while the others are numbered by uniform number.

	MT	NR MT	EX
Complete Set:	10.00	7.50	4.00
Common Player:	.20	.15	.08
4 Paul Molitor	1.00	.70	.40
5 Ned Yost	.20	.15	.08
7 Don Money	.25	.20	.10
8 Rob Picciolo	.20	.15	.08
10 Bob McClure	.20	.15	.08
11 Ed Romero	.20	.15	.08
13 Roy Howell	.20	.15	.08
15 Cecil Cooper	.50	.40	.20
16 Marshall Edwards	.20	.15	.08
17 Jim Gantner	.30	.25	.12
19 Robin Yount	2.00	1.50	.80
20 Gorman Thomas	.40	.30	.15
21 Don Sutton	.80	.60	.30
22 Charlie Moore	.20	.15	.08
23 Ted Simmons	.50	.40	.20
24 Ben Oglivie	.30	.25	.12
26 Bob Skube	.20	.15	.08
27 Pete Ladd	.20	.15	.08
28 Jamie Easterly	.20	.15	.08
30 Moose Haas	.20	.15	.08
32 Harvey Kuenn	.30	.25	.12
34 Rollie Fingers	.90	.70	.35
40 Bob Gibson	.20	.15	.08
41 Jim Slaton	.20	.15	.08
42 Tom Tellmann	.20	.15	.08
46 Jerry Augustine	.20	.15	.08
48 Mike Caldwell	.25	.20	.10
50 Pete Vuckovich	.30	.25	.12
—— Team Photo/Checklist	.20	.15	.08
—— Coaches Card (Pat Dobson, Dave Garcia, Larry Haney, Ron Hansen)	.20	.15	.08

1983 Police/Fire Safety Dodgers

While these full-color cards remained 2-13/16" by 4-1/8" and card fronts were similar to those of previous years, the card backs are quite different. Card backs are in a horizontal design for the first time, and include a small head portrait photo of the player in the upper left corner. Fairly complete player statistics are included but there is no safety tip. The 30 cards are numbered by uniform number, with an unnumbered coaches card also included. Fronts include the year, team logo, player name and

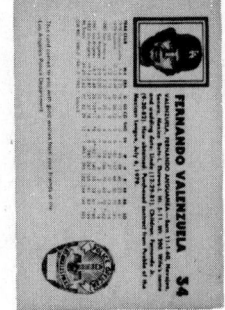

number.

		MT	NR MT	EX
Complete Set:		7.00	5.25	2.75
Common Player:		.15	.11	.06
2	Tom Lasorda	.30	.25	.12
3	Steve Sax	.60	.45	.25
5	Mike Marshall	.60	.45	.25
7	Steve Yeager	.15	.11	.06
12	Dusty Baker	.25	.20	.10
14	Mike Scioscia	.25	.20	.10
16	Rick Monday	.25	.20	.10
17	Greg Brock	.40	.30	.15
18	Bill Russell	.20	.15	.08
20	Candy Maldonado	.40	.30	.15
21	Ricky Wright	.15	.11	.06
22	Mark Bradley	.15	.11	.06
23	Dave Sax	.15	.11	.06
26	Alejandro Pena	.25	.20	.10
27	Joe Beckwith	.15	.11	.06
28	Pedro Guerrero	.60	.45	.25
30	Derrel Thomas	.15	.11	.06
34	Fernando Valenzuela	.70	.50	.30
35	Bob Welch	.30	.25	.12
38	Pat Zachry	.15	.11	.06
40	Ron Roenicke	.15	.11	.06
41	Jerry Reuss	.25	.20	.10
43	Jose Morales	.15	.11	.06
44	Ken Landreaux	.15	.11	.06
46	Burt Hooton	.20	.15	.08
47	Larry White	.15	.11	.06
48	Dave Stewart	.25	.20	.10
49	Tom Niedenfuer	.20	.15	.08
57	Steve Howe	.20	.15	.08
-----	Coaches Card (Joe Amalfitano, Monty Basgall, Mark Cresse, Manny Mota, Ron Perranoski)			
		.15	.11	.06

1983 Police/Fire Safety Royals

After skipping the 1982 season, the Ft. Myers, Fla., police department issued a Royals safety set in 1983 that is almost identical to their set of 1981. The set is again 2-1/2" by 4-1/8" and numbers just 10 players. Cards are unnumbered, with vertical fronts and

horizontal backs. Card fronts have team logos, player name and position and facsimile autographs. Backs list the four sponsoring organizations, a "Tip from the Royals" and a "Kids and Cops Fact" about each player.

		MT	NR MT	EX
Complete Set:		30.00	23.00	12.00
Common Player:		1.00	.70	.40
(1)	Willie Mays Aikens	1.00	.70	.40
(2)	George Brett	18.00	13.50	7.25
(3)	Dennis Leonard	2.00	1.50	.80
(4)	Hal McRae	2.00	1.50	.80
(5)	Amos Otis	2.00	1.50	.80
(6)	Dan Quisenberry	3.00	2.25	1.25
(7)	U.L. Washington	1.00	.70	.40
(8)	John Wathan	2.00	1.50	.80
(9)	Frank White	3.50	2.75	1.50
(10)	Willie Wilson	3.75	2.75	1.50

1984 Police/Fire Safety Blue Jays

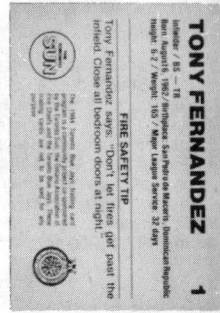

This 35-card set was issued in conjuction with the Toronto Sun newspaper and various Ontario area fire departments. The cards feature full-color action photos on the fronts, along with the player name, number and position. Rather than the customary wide white border on front, the Blue Jays fire safety set features bright blue borders. The card backs include brief player biographies and a fire safety tip. The 2-1/2" by 3-1/2" cards were distributed five at a time at two-week intervals during the summer of 1984.

		MT	NR MT	EX
Complete Set:		10.00	7.50	4.00
Common Player:		.20	.15	.08
1	Tony Fernandez	1.00	.70	.40
3	Jimy Williams	.20	.15	.08
4	Alfredo Griffin	.30	.25	.12
5	Rance Mulliniks	.20	.15	.08
6	Bobby Cox	.20	.15	.08
7	Damaso Garcia	.30	.25	.12
8	John Sullivan	.20	.15	.08
9	Rick Leach	.20	.15	.08
10	Dave Collins	.25	.20	.10
11	George Bell	1.50	1.25	.60
12	Ernie Whitt	.30	.25	.12
13	Buck Martinez	.20	.15	.08
15	Lloyd Moseby	.50	.40	.20
16	Garth Iorg	.20	.15	.08
17	Kelly Gruber	.25	.20	.10
18	Jim Clancy	.30	.25	.12
23	Mitch Webster	.50	.40	.20
24	Willie Aikens	.20	.15	.08
25	Roy Lee Jackson	.20	.15	.08
26	Willie Upshaw	.30	.25	.12
27	Jimmy Key	1.00	.70	.40
29	Jesse Barfield	.80	.60	.30
31	Jim Acker	.20	.15	.08
33	Doyle Alexander	.30	.25	.12
34	Stan Clarke	.20	.15	.08

		MT	NR MT	EX
35	Bryan Clark	.20	.15	.08
37	Dave Stieb	.60	.45	.25
38	Jim Gott	.20	.15	.08
41	Al Widmar	.20	.15	.08
42	Billy Smith	.20	.15	.08
43	Cito Gaston	.20	.15	.08
44	Cliff Johnson	.20	.15	.08
48	Luis Leal	.20	.15	.08
53	Dennis Lamp	.20	.15	.08
----	Team Logo/Checklist	.20	.15	.08

1984 Police/Fire Safety Braves

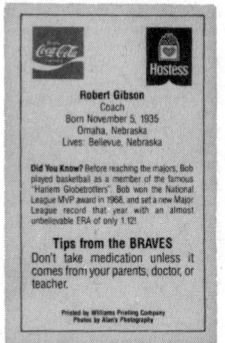

A fourth annual effort by the Braves, the Atlanta Police Department, Coca-Cola and Hostess. This 30-card set continued to be printed in a 2-5/8" by 4-1/8" format, with full-color photos plus team and police logos on the card fronts. For the first time, the cards also have a large logo and date in the upper right corner. Hostess and Coke logos again are on the card backs, with brief player information and a safety tip. Two cards in the set (Pascual Perez and Rafael Ramirez) were issued in Spanish. Cards were distributed two per week by Atlanta police officers. As in 1982 and 1983, a reported 8,000 sets were printed.

		MT	NR MT	EX
	Complete Set:	12.00	9.00	4.75
	Common Player:	.25	.20	.10
1	Jerry Royster	.25	.20	.10
3	Dale Murphy	3.50	2.75	1.50
5	Bob Horner	1.00	.70	.40
6	Randy Johnson	.25	.20	.10
8	Bob Watson	.30	.25	.12
9	Joe Torre	.40	.30	.15
10	Chris Chambliss	.40	.30	.15
11	Mike Jorgensen	.25	.20	.10
15	Claudell Washington	.40	.30	.15
16	Rafael Ramirez	.30	.25	.12
17	Glenn Hubbard	.30	.25	.12
19	Terry Harper	.25	.20	.10
20	Bruce Benedict	.25	.20	.10
25	Alex Trevino	.25	.20	.10
26	Gene Garber	.25	.20	.10
27	Pascual Perez	.30	.25	.12
28	Gerald Perry	1.50	1.25	.60
29	Craig McMurtry	.25	.20	.10
31	Donnie Moore	.25	.20	.10
32	Steve Bedrosian	.60	.45	.25
33	Pete Falcone	.25	.20	.10
37	Rick Camp	.25	.20	.10
39	Len Barker	.25	.20	.10
42	Rick Mahler	.40	.30	.15
45	Bob Gibson	1.25	.90	.50
51	Terry Forster	.30	.25	.12
52	Joe Pignatano	.25	.20	.10
53	Dal Maxvill	.25	.20	.10
54	Rube Walker	.25	.20	.10
55	Luke Appling	.60	.45	.25

1984 Police/Fire Safety Brewers

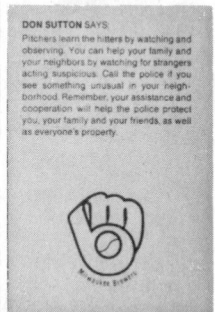

The king of the variations again in 1984, the Milwaukee Brewers set has been found with more than 50 different police agencies' credit lines on the front of the cards. Once again, law enforcement agencies statewide participated in distributing the sets. Some departments also include a badge of the participating agency on the card backs. The full-color cards measure 2-13/16" by 4-1/8". There are 28 numbered player and manager cards, along with an unnumbered coaches card and a team card. Player names, uniform numbers and positions are listed on each card front. Prices listed are for the most common variety (Milwaukee police department); sets issued by smaller departments may be worth a premium to specialists.

		MT	NR MT	EX
	Complete Set:	8.00	6.00	3.25
	Common Player:	.15	.11	.06
2	Randy Ready	.30	.25	.12
4	Paul Molitor	.80	.60	.30
8	Jim Sundberg	.15	.11	.06
9	Rene Lachemann	.15	.11	.06
10	Bob McClure	.15	.11	.06
11	Ed Romero	.15	.11	.06
13	Roy Howell	.15	.11	.06
14	Dion James	.50	.40	.20
15	Cecil Cooper	.40	.30	.15
17	Jim Gantner	.25	.20	.10
19	Robin Yount	1.50	1.25	.60
20	Don Sutton	.50	.40	.20
21	Bill Schroeder	.30	.25	.12
22	Charlie Moore	.15	.11	.06
23	Ted Simmons	.40	.30	.15
24	Ben Oglivie	.25	.20	.10
25	Bobby Clark	.15	.11	.06
27	Pete Ladd	.15	.11	.06
28	Rick Manning	.15	.11	.06
29	Mark Brouhard	.15	.11	.06
30	Moose Haas	.15	.11	.06
34	Rollie Fingers	.60	.45	.25
42	Tom Tellmann	.15	.11	.06
43	Chuck Porter	.15	.11	.06
46	Jerry Augustine	.15	.11	.06
47	Jaime Cocanower	.15	.11	.06
48	Mike Caldwell	.20	.15	.08
50	Pete Vuckovich	.25	.20	.10
----	Team Photo/Checklist	.15	.11	.06
----	Coaches Card (Pat Dobson, Dave Garcia, Larry Haney, Tom Trebelhorn)	.15	.11	.06

1984 Police/Fire Safety Dodgers

This was the fifth yearly effort of the Dodgers and the Los Angeles Police Department. There are 30 cards in the set, which remains 2-13/16" by 4-1/8". Card fronts are designed somewhat differently than

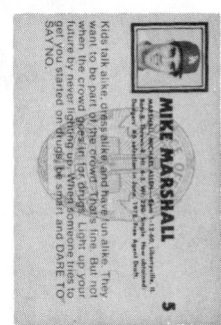

previous years, with more posed photos, bolder player names and numbers and a different team logo. Card backs again feature a small portrait photo in the upper left corner, along with brief biographical information and an anti-drug tip. Card backs are in Dodger blue. Cards are numbered by uniform number, with an unnumbered coaches card also included.

		MT	NR MT	EX
Complete Set:		8.00	6.00	3.25
Common Player:		.15	.11	.06
2	Tom Lasorda	.30	.25	.12
3	Steve Sax	.60	.45	.25
5	Mike Marshall	.50	.40	.20
7	Steve Yeager	.15	.11	.06
9	Greg Brock	.30	.25	.12
10	Dave Anderson	.20	.15	.08
14	Mike Scioscia	.25	.20	.10
16	Rick Monday	.25	.20	.10
17	Rafael Landestoy	.15	.11	.06
18	Bill Russell	.20	.15	.08
20	Candy Maldonado	.25	.20	.10
21	Bob Bailor	.15	.11	.06
25	German Rivera	.15	.11	.06
26	Alejandro Pena	.25	.20	.10
27	Carlos Diaz	.15	.11	.06
28	Pedro Guerrero	.70	.50	.30
31	Jack Fimple	.15	.11	.06
34	Fernando Valenzuela	.70	.50	.30
35	Bob Welch	.30	.25	.12
38	Pat Zachry	.15	.11	.06
40	Rick Honeycutt	.15	.11	.06
41	Jerry Reuss	.25	.20	.10
43	Jose Morales	.15	.11	.06
44	Ken Landreaux	.15	.11	.06
45	Terry Whitfield	.15	.11	.06
46	Burt Hooton	.20	.15	.08
49	Tom Niedenfuer	.20	.15	.08
55	Orel Hershiser	2.50	2.00	1.00
56	Richard Rodas	.15	.11	.06
-----	Coaches Card (Joe Amalfitano, Monty Basgall, Mark Cresse, Manny Mota, Ron Perranoski)	.15	.11	.06

1985 Police/Fire Safety Blue Jays

The Toronto Blue Jays issued a 35-card fire safety set for the second year in a row in 1985. Cards feature players, coaches, manager, checklist and team picture. The full-color photos are on the card fronts with a blue border. The backs feature player stats and a safety tip. The cards measure 2-1/2" by 3-1/2" and were distributed throughout the Province of Ontario, Canada.

		MT	NR MT	EX
Complete Set:		8.00	6.00	3.25
Common Player:		.20	.15	.08
1	Tony Fernandez	.70	.50	.30
3	Jimy Williams	.20	.15	.08
4	Manny Lee	.25	.20	.10
5	Rance Mulliniks	.20	.15	.08
6	Bobby Cox	.20	.15	.08
7	Damaso Garcia	.30	.25	.12
8	John Sullivan	.20	.15	.08
11	George Bell	1.25	.90	.50
12	Ernie Whitt	.30	.25	.12
13	Buck Martinez	.20	.15	.08
15	Lloyd Moseby	.40	.30	.15
16	Garth Iorg	.20	.15	.08
17	Kelly Gruber	.20	.15	.08
18	Jim Clancy	.30	.25	.12
22	Jimmy Key	.50	.40	.20
23	Mitch Webster	.25	.20	.10
24	Willie Aikens	.20	.15	.08
25	Len Matuszek	.20	.15	.08
26	Willie Upshaw	.30	.25	.12
28	Lou Thornton	.20	.15	.08
29	Jesse Barfield	.80	.60	.30
30	Ron Musselman	.20	.15	.08
31	Jim Acker	.20	.15	.08
33	Doyle Alexander	.30	.25	.12
36	Bill Caudill	.20	.15	.08
37	Dave Stieb	.50	.40	.20
41	Al Widmar	.20	.15	.08
42	Billy Smith	.20	.15	.08
43	Cito Gaston	.20	.15	.08
44	Jeff Burroughs	.20	.15	.08
46	Gary Lavelle	.20	.15	.08
48	Luis Leal	.20	.15	.08
50	Tom Henke	.40	.30	.15
53	Dennis Lamp	.20	.15	.08
-----	Team Logo/Checklist	.20	.15	.08
-----	Team Photo/Schedule	.20	.15	.08

1985 Police/Fire Safety Braves

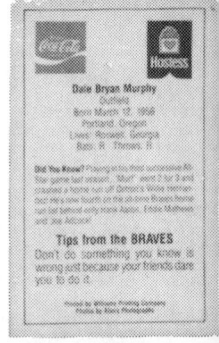

There are again 30 full-color cards in this fifth annual set. Hostess, Coca-Cola and the Atlanta Police Department joined the team as sponsors again for the 2-5/8" by 4-1/8" set. Card backs are similar to previous years, with the only difference on the fronts being a swap in position for the year and team logo. The cards are checklisted by uniform number.

	MT	NR MT	EX
Complete Set:	12.00	9.00	4.75
Common Player:	.25	.20	.10

		MT	NR MT	EX
2	Albert Hall	.40	.30	.15
3	Dale Murphy	3.25	2.50	1.25
5	Rick Cerone	.25	.20	.10
7	Bobby Wine	.25	.20	.10
10	Chris Chambliss	.35	.25	.14
11	Bob Horner	1.00	.70	.40
12	Paul Runge	.30	.25	.12
15	Claudell Washington	.35	.25	.14
16	Rafael Ramirez	.30	.25	.12
17	Glenn Hubbard	.30	.25	.12
18	Paul Zuvella	.30	.25	.12
19	Terry Harper	.25	.20	.10
20	Bruce Benedict	.25	.20	.10
22	Eddie Haas	.25	.20	.10
24	Ken Oberkfell	.30	.25	.12
26	Gene Garber	.25	.20	.10
27	Pascual Perez	.30	.25	.12
28	Gerald Perry	1.00	.70	.40
29	Craig McMurtry	.25	.20	.10
32	Steve Bedrosian	.50	.40	.20
33	Johnny Sain	.35	.25	.14
34	Zane Smith	.60	.45	.25
36	Brad Komminsk	.25	.20	.10
37	Rick Camp	.25	.20	.10
39	Len Barker	.25	.20	.10
40	Bruce Sutter	.70	.50	.30
42	Rick Mahler	.35	.25	.14
51	Terry Forster	.30	.25	.12
52	Leo Mazzone	.25	.20	.10
53	Bobby Dews	.25	.20	.10

1985 Police/Fire Safety Brewers

49   Ted Higuera   P
The Milwaukee Police Department and The Milwaukee Journal present the 1985
Milwaukee Brewers

Ted Higuera says:
When athletes graduate from high school, the best ones are drafted by the major-league teams. The rest pursue other careers.
It's important to learn a trade or profession. Be the best at what you do, and you'll be drafted for a good job when you graduate from school.

Watch the Thursday **Milwaukee Journal** Sports Weekend Section for the 2 players featured on next week's baseball cards. You could win free tickets to a Brewer game!

The Brewers changed the size of their annual police set in 1985, but almost imperceptibly. The full-color cards are 2-3/4" by 4-1/8", a slight 1/16" narrower than the four previous efforts. Player and team name on the card fronts are much bolder than in previous years. Once again, numerous area police groups distributed the sets, leading to nearly 60 variations, as each agency put their own credit line on the cards. Card backs include the Brewers logo, a safety tip and, in some cases, a badge of the participating law enforcement group. There are 27 numbered player cards (by uniform number) and three unnumbered cards - team roster, coaches and a newspaper carrier card. Prices are for the most common departments.

		MT	NR MT	EX
Complete Set:		8.00	6.00	3.25
Common Player:		.15	.11	.06
2	Randy Ready	.15	.11	.06
4	Paul Molitor	.70	.50	.30
5	Doug Loman	.15	.11	.06
7	Paul Householder	.15	.11	.06
10	Bob McClure	.15	.11	.06
11	Ed Romero	.15	.11	.06
14	Dion James	.25	.20	.10
15	Cecil Cooper	.40	.30	.15
17	Jim Gantner	.25	.20	.10
18	Danny Darwin	.20	.15	.08
19	Robin Yount	1.25	.90	.50
21	Bill Schroeder	.20	.15	.08
22	Charlie Moore	.15	.11	.06

		MT	NR MT	EX
23	Ted Simmons	.40	.30	.15
24	Ben Oglivie	.25	.20	.10
26	Brian Giles	.15	.11	.06
27	Pete Ladd	.15	.11	.06
28	Rick Manning	.15	.11	.06
29	Mark Brouhard	.15	.11	.06
30	Moose Haas	.15	.11	.06
31	George Bamberger	.15	.11	.06
34	Rollie Fingers	.60	.45	.25
40	Bob Gibson	.15	.11	.06
41	Ray Searage	.15	.11	.06
47	Jaime Cocanower	.15	.11	.06
48	Ray Burris	.15	.11	.06
49	Ted Higuera	1.25	.90	.50
50	Pete Vuckovich	.25	.20	.10
----	Coaches Card (Andy Etchebarren, Larry Haney, Frank Howard, Tony Muser, Herm Starrette)	.15	.11	.06
----	Team Photo	.15	.11	.06

1985 Police/Fire Safety Phillies

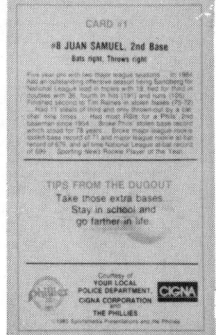

phillies   #8 JUAN SAMUEL 2ND BASE

CARD #1
#8 JUAN SAMUEL, 2nd Base
Bats right, Throws right

TIPS FROM THE DUGOUT
Take those extra bases.
Stay in school and go farther in life.

Courtesy of
YOUR LOCAL POLICE DEPARTMENT, CIGNA CORPORATION and THE PHILLIES

This is a brilliantly colored 2-5/8" by 4-1/8" set, co-sponsored by the Phillies and Cigna Corporation. Card fronts include the player name, number, position and team logo. The 16 cards are numbered on the back and include biographical information and a safety tip. The cards were distributed by several Philadelphia area police departments.

		MT	NR MT	EX
Complete Set:		8.00	6.00	3.25
Common Player:		.15	.11	.06
1	Juan Samuel	.50	.40	.20
2	Von Hayes	.35	.25	.14
3	Ozzie Virgil	.20	.15	.08
4	Mike Schmidt	1.75	1.25	.70
5	Greg Gross	.15	.11	.06
6	Tim Corcoran	.15	.11	.06
7	Jerry Koosman	.25	.20	.10
8	Jeff Stone	.20	.15	.08
9	Glenn Wilson	.25	.20	.10
10	Steve Jeltz	.20	.15	.08
11	Garry Maddox	.20	.15	.08
12	Steve Carlton	1.25	.90	.50
13	John Denny	.15	.11	.06
14	Kevin Gross	.30	.25	.12
15	Shane Rawley	.30	.25	.12
16	Charlie Hudson	.25	.20	.10

1986 Police/Fire Safety Astros

This full-color police safety set for the 1986 Houston Astros was issued by the Houston Police Department and sponsored by Kool-Aid. The 26-card set was distributed at the Astrodome on June 14, when 15,000 sets of the first 12 cards were given away. The balance of the set was distributed throughout the summer by the Houston police. The

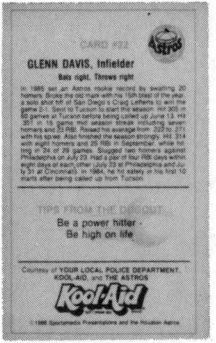

cards feature player photos on the fronts and a safety tip on the card backs. The cards measure 4-1/8" by 2-5/8".

	MT	NR MT	EX
Complete Set:	8.00	6.00	3.25
Common Player:	.20	.15	.08

		MT	NR MT	EX
1	Jim Pankovits	.20	.15	.08
2	Nolan Ryan	1.25	.90	.50
3	Mike Scott	.60	.45	.25
4	Kevin Bass	.40	.30	.15
5	Bill Doran	.40	.30	.15
6	Hal Lanier	.20	.15	.08
7	Denny Walling	.20	.15	.08
8	Alan Ashby	.20	.15	.08
9	Phil Garner	.25	.20	.10
10	Charlie Kerfeld	.25	.20	.10
11	Dave Smith	.30	.25	.12
12	Jose Cruz	.35	.25	.14
13	Craig Reynolds	.20	.15	.08
14	Mark Bailey	.20	.15	.08
15	Bob Knepper	.30	.25	.12
16	Julio Solano	.20	.15	.08
17	Dickie Thon	.25	.20	.10
18	Mike Madden	.20	.15	.08
19	Jeff Calhoun	.20	.15	.08
20	Tony Walker	.20	.15	.08
21	Terry Puhl	.20	.15	.08
22	Glenn Davis	1.00	.70	.40
23	Billy Hatcher	.40	.30	.15
24	Jim Deshaies	.40	.30	.15
25	Frank DiPino	.20	.15	.08
26	Coaching Staff (Yogi Berra, Matt Galante, Denis Menke, Les Moss, Gene Tenace)	.20	.15	.08

1986 Police/Fire Safety Blue Jays

This was the third consecutive year the Toronto Blue Jays issued a fire safety set of 36 baseball cards. The cards were given out at many fire stations in Ontario, Canada. The cards are printed in full color and include players and other personnel. The set was co-sponsored by the local fire departments, Bubble Yum and the Toronto Star. The cards measure 2-1/2" by 3-1/2".

	MT	NR MT	EX
Complete Set:	8.00	6.00	3.25
Common Player:	.20	.15	.08

		MT	NR MT	EX
1	Tony Fernandez	.70	.50	.30
3	Jimy Williams	.20	.15	.08
5	Rance Mulliniks	.20	.15	.08
7	Damaso Garcia	.30	.25	.12
8	John Sullivan	.20	.15	.08
9	Rick Leach	.20	.15	.08
11	George Bell	1.25	.90	.50
12	Ernie Whitt	.30	.25	.12
13	Buck Martinez	.20	.15	.08
15	Lloyd Moseby	.40	.30	.15
16	Garth Iorg	.20	.15	.08
17	Kelly Gruber	.20	.15	.08
18	Jim Clancy	.30	.25	.12
22	Jimmy Key	.50	.40	.20
23	Cecil Fielder	.20	.15	.08
24	John McLaren	.20	.15	.08
25	Steve Davis	.20	.15	.08
26	Willie Upshaw	.30	.25	.12
29	Jesse Barfield	.80	.60	.30
31	Jim Acker	.20	.15	.08
33	Doyle Alexander	.30	.25	.12
36	Bill Caudill	.20	.15	.08
37	Dave Stieb	.50	.40	.20
38	Mark Eichhorn	.40	.30	.15
39	Don Gordon	.25	.20	.10
41	Al Widmar	.20	.15	.08
42	Billy Smith	.20	.15	.08
43	Cito Gaston	.20	.15	.08
44	Cliff Johnson	.20	.15	.08
46	Gary Lavelle	.20	.15	.08
49	Tom Filer	.20	.15	.08
50	Tom Henke	.40	.30	.15
53	Dennis Lamp	.20	.15	.08
54	Jeff Hearron	.20	.15	.08
----	Team Photo	.20	.15	.08
----	10th Anniversary Logo Card	.20	.15	.08

1986 Police/Fire Safety Braves

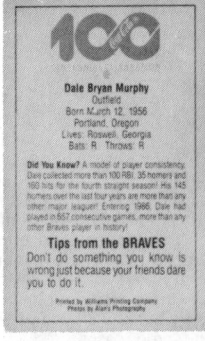

The Police Athletic League of Atlanta issued a 30-card full-color set featuring the Atlanta Braves players and personnel. The cards measure 2-5/8" by 4-1/8". Card fronts include player photos with name, uniform number and position below the photo. The cards backs offer the 100th Anniversary Coca-Cola logo, player information, statistics and a safety related tip. This was the sixth consecutive year that the Braves issued a safety set. The cards were available from police officers in Atlanta.

	MT	NR MT	EX
Complete Set:	11.00	8.25	4.50
Common Player:	.25	.20	.10

		MT	NR MT	EX
2	Russ Nixon	.25	.20	.10
3	Dale Murphy	2.75	2.00	1.00
4	Bob Skinner	.25	.20	.10
5	Billy Sample	.25	.20	.10
7	Chuck Tanner	.35	.25	.14
8	Willie Stargell	.80	.60	.30

		MT	NR MT	EX
9	Ozzie Virgil	.35	.25	.14
10	Chris Chambliss	.35	.25	.14
11	Bob Horner	.80	.60	.30
14	Andres Thomas	.50	.40	.20
15	Claudell Washington	.35	.25	.14
16	Rafael Ramirez	.30	.25	.12
17	Glenn Hubbard	.30	.25	.12
18	Omar Moreno	.25	.20	.10
19	Terry Harper	.25	.20	.10
20	Bruce Benedict	.25	.20	.10
23	Ted Simmons	.50	.40	.20
24	Ken Oberkfell	.30	.25	.12
26	Gene Garber	.25	.20	.10
29	Craig McMurtry	.25	.20	.10
30	Paul Assenmacher	.40	.30	.15
33	Johnny Sain	.30	.25	.12
34	Zane Smith	.40	.30	.15
38	Joe Johnson	.25	.20	.10
40	Bruce Sutter	.60	.45	.25
42	Rick Mahler	.35	.25	.14
46	David Palmer	.25	.20	.10
48	Duane Ward	.30	.25	.12
49	Jeff Dedmon	.25	.20	.10
52	Al Monchak	.25	.20	.10

1986 Police/Fire Safety Brewers

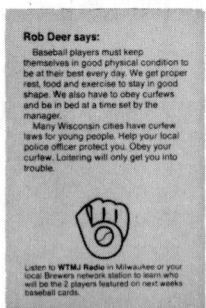

45   Rob Deer   OF
The Fond du Lac Police Dept., KFIZ Radio,
and National Exchange Bank & Trust
present the 1986
Milwaukee Brewers

Rob Deer says:
Baseball players must keep themselves in good physical condition to be at their best every day. We get proper rest, food and exercise to stay in good shape. We also have to obey curfews and be in bed at a time set by the manager.
Many Wisconsin cities have curfew laws for young people. Help your local police officer protect you. Obey your curfew. Loitering will only get you into trouble.

Listen to **WTMJ Radio** in Milwaukee or your local Brewers network station to learn who will be the 2 players featured on next weeks baseball cards.

The Milwaukee Brewers, in conjunction with the Milwaukee Police Department, WTMJ Radio and Kinney Shoes, produced this attractive police safety set of 30 cards. The cards measure 2-13/16" by 4-1/2". A thin black border encloses a full-color Player photo on the front. The card backs give a safety tip and promos for the sponsor. The cards were distributed throughout the state of Wisconsin by numerous police departments; those of the smaller departments generally being scarcer than those issued in the big cities. Prices quoted below are for the most common departments' issues.

		MT	NR MT	EX
	Complete Set:	7.00	5.25	2.75
	Common Player:	.15	.11	.06
1	Ernest Riles	.30	.25	.12
2	Randy Ready	.15	.11	.06
3	Juan Castillo	.20	.15	.08
4	Paul Molitor	.70	.50	.30
7	Paul Householder	.15	.11	.06
10	Bob McClure	.15	.11	.06
11	Rick Cerone	.15	.11	.06
13	Billy Jo Robidoux	.30	.25	.12
15	Cecil Cooper	.40	.30	.15
16	Mike Felder	.30	.25	.12
17	Jim Gantner	.25	.20	.10
18	Danny Darwin	.20	.15	.08
19	Robin Yount	1.00	.70	.40
20	Juan Nieves	.40	.30	.15
21	Bill Schroeder	.15	.11	.06
22	Charlie Moore	.15	.11	.06
24	Ben Oglivie	.25	.20	.10
25	Mark Clear	.15	.11	.06
28	Rick Manning	.15	.11	.06
31	George Bamberger	.15	.11	.06
37	Dan Plesac	.60	.45	.25

		MT	NR MT	EX
39	Tim Leary	.15	.11	.06
41	Ray Searage	.15	.11	.06
43	Chuck Porter	.15	.11	.06
45	Rob Deer	.40	.30	.15
46	Bill Wegman	.30	.25	.12
47	Jamie Cocanower	.15	.11	.06
49	Ted Higuera	.50	.40	.20
-----	Coaches Card (Andy Etchebarren, Larry Haney, Frank Howard, Tony Muser, Herm Starrette)	.15	.11	.06
-----	Team Photo/Roster	.15	.11	.06

1986 Police/Fire Safety Dodgers

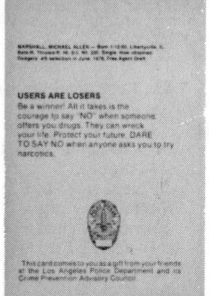

MIKE MARSHALL   5

After skipping the 1985 season, the Los Angeles Dodgers once again issued baseball cards related to police safety. The club had issued sets from 1980-84. The 1986 set features 30 full-color glossy cards measuring 2-1/4" by 4-1/8". The cards are numbered according to player uniforms. The backs feature brief player data and a safety tip from the Los Angeles Police Department. The sets were given away May 18 during Baseball Card Day at Dodger Stadium.

		MT	NR MT	EX
	Complete Set:	7.00	5.25	2.75
	Common Player:	.15	.11	.06
2	Tom Lasorda	.25	.20	.10
3	Steve Sax	.50	.40	.20
5	Mike Marshall	.40	.30	.15
9	Greg Brock	.25	.20	.10
10	Dave Anderson	.15	.11	.06
12	Bill Madlock	.30	.25	.12
14	Mike Scioscia	.25	.20	.10
17	Len Matuszek	.15	.11	.06
18	Bill Russell	.20	.15	.08
22	Franklin Stubbs	.25	.20	.10
23	Enos Cabell	.15	.11	.06
25	Mariano Duncan	.20	.15	.08
26	Alejandro Pena	.25	.20	.10
27	Carlos Diaz	.15	.11	.06
28	Pedro Guerrero	.60	.45	.25
29	Alex Trevino	.15	.11	.06
31	Ed Vande Berg	.15	.11	.06
34	Fernando Valenzuela	.60	.45	.25
35	Bob Welch	.30	.25	.12
40	Rick Honeycutt	.15	.11	.06
41	Jerry Reuss	.25	.20	.10
43	Ken Howell	.20	.15	.08
44	Ken Landreaux	.15	.11	.06
45	Terry Whitfield	.15	.11	.06
48	Dennis Powell	.20	.15	.08
49	Tom Niedenfuer	.20	.15	.08
51	Reggie Williams	.20	.15	.08
55	Orel Hershiser	1.00	.70	.40
-----	Team Photo/Checklist	.15	.11	.06
-----	Coaching Staff (Joe Amalfitano, Monty Basgall, Mark Cresse, Ben Hines, Don McMahon, Manny Mota, Ron Perranoski)	.15	.11	.06

1986 Police/Fire Safety Phillies

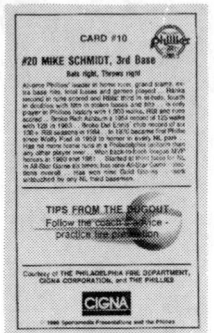

For the second straight year, the Philadelphia Phillies issued a 16-card safety set. However, in 1986 the set was issued in conjunction with the Philadelphia Fire Department rather than the police. Cigna Corporation remained a sponsor. The cards, which measure 2-5/8" by 4-1/8" in size, feature full color photos. Along with other pertinent information, the card backs contain a short player biography and a "Tips From The Dugout" fire safety hint.

		MT	NR MT	EX
Complete Set:		8.00	6.00	3.25
Common Player:		.15	.11	.06
1	Juan Samuel	.50	.40	.20
2	Don Carman	.35	.25	.14
3	Von Hayes	.30	.25	.12
4	Kent Tekulve	.20	.15	.08
5	Greg Gross	.15	.11	.06
6	Shane Rawley	.25	.20	.10
7	Darren Daulton	.20	.15	.08
8	Kevin Gross	.25	.20	.10
9	Steve Jeltz	.15	.11	.06
10	Mike Schmidt	1.25	.90	.50
11	Steve Bedrosian	.35	.25	.14
12	Gary Redus	.15	.11	.06
13	Charles Hudson	.15	.11	.06
14	John Russell	.20	.15	.08
15	Fred Toliver	.20	.15	.08
16	Glenn Wilson	.20	.15	.08

1987 Police/Fire Safety Astros

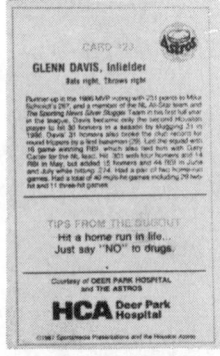

The 1987 Houston Astros safety set was produced through the combined efforts of the Astros, Deer Park Hospital and Sportsmedia Presentations. #'s 1-12 were handed out to youngsters 14 and under at the Astrodome on July 14th. The balance of the distribution was handled by Deer Park Hospital. The cards, which measure 2-5/8" by 4-1/8", contain

full-color photos. The backs offer a brief team/player history and a "Tips From The Dugout" anti-drug message.

		MT	NR MT	EX
Complete Set:		8.00	6.00	3.25
Common Player:		.20	.15	.08
1	Larry Andersen	.20	.15	.08
2	Mark Bailey	.20	.15	.08
3	Jose Cruz	.35	.25	.14
4	Danny Darwin	.25	.20	.10
5	Bill Doran	.40	.30	.15
6	Billy Hatcher	.40	.30	.15
7	Hal Lanier	.20	.15	.08
8	Davey Lopes	.30	.25	.12
9	Dave Meads	.30	.25	.12
10	Craig Reynolds	.20	.15	.08
11	Mike Scott	.60	.45	.25
12	Denny Walling	.20	.15	.08
13	Aurelio Lopez	.20	.15	.08
14	Dickie Thon	.25	.20	.10
15	Terry Puhl	.20	.15	.08
16	Nolan Ryan	1.25	.90	.50
17	Dave Smith	.30	.25	.12
18	Julio Solano	.20	.15	.08
19	Jim Deshaies	.30	.25	.12
20	Bob Knepper	.30	.25	.12
21	Alan Ashby	.20	.15	.08
22	Kevin Bass	.40	.30	.15
23	Glenn Davis	1.00	.70	.40
24	Phil Garner	.25	.20	.10
25	Jim Pankovits	.20	.15	.08
26	Coaching Staff (Yogi Berra, Matt Galante, Denis Menke, Les Moss, Gene Tenace)	.20	.15	.08

1987 Police/Fire Safety Blue Jays

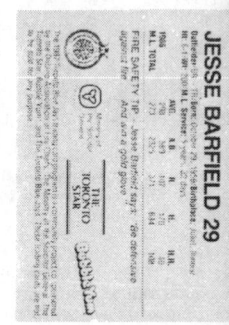

For the fourth consecutive year, the Toronto Blue Jays issued a fire safety set of 36 cards. As in 1986, the set was sponsored by the local fire departments and governing agencies, Bubble Yum and the Toronto Star. The card fronts feature a full-color photo surrounded by a white border. The backs carry a fire safety tip and logos of all sponsors, plus player personal data and statistics. Produced on thin stock, cards in the set are the standard 2-1/2" by 3-1/2" size.

		MT	NR MT	EX
Complete Set:		9.00	6.75	3.50
Common Player:		.15	.11	.06
1	Tony Fernandez	.50	.40	.20
3	Jimy Williams	.15	.11	.06
5	Rance Mulliniks	.15	.11	.06
8	John Sullivan	.15	.11	.06
9	Rick Leach	.15	.11	.06
10	Mike Sharperson	.20	.15	.08
11	George Bell	1.00	.70	.40
12	Ernie Whitt	.25	.20	.10
15	Lloyd Moseby	.35	.25	.14
16	Garth Iorg	.15	.11	.06
17	Kelly Gruber	.15	.11	.06
18	Jim Clancy	.25	.20	.10

		MT	NR MT	EX
19	Fred McGriff	2.00	1.50	.80
22	Jimmy Key	.40	.30	.15
23	Cecil Fielder	.15	.11	.06
24	John McLaren	.15	.11	.06
26	Willie Upshaw	.25	.20	.10
29	Jesse Barfield	.60	.45	.25
31	Duane Ward	.15	.11	.06
33	Joe Johnson	.15	.11	.06
35	Jeff Musselman	.35	.25	.14
37	Dave Stieb	.40	.30	.15
38	Mark Eichhorn	.20	.15	.08
40	Rob Ducey	.20	.15	.08
41	Al Widmar	.15	.11	.06
42	Billy Smith	.15	.11	.06
43	Cito Gaston	.15	.11	.06
45	Jose Nunez	.35	.25	.14
46	Gary Lavelle	.15	.11	.06
47	Matt Stark	.15	.11	.06
48	Craig McMurtry	.15	.11	.06
50	Tom Henke	.30	.25	.12
54	Jeff Hearron	.15	.11	.06
55	John Cerutti	.20	.15	.08
——	Logo/Won-Loss Record	.15	.11	.06
——	Team Photo/Checklist	.15	.11	.06

1987 Police/Fire Safety Brewers

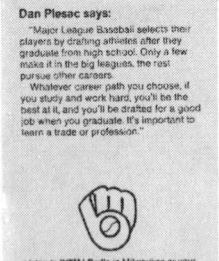

37   **Dan Plesac**   P
Iola, Manawa & Marion Police Departments
and Wisconsin Power and Light
present the 1987
Milwaukee Brewers

Dan Plesac says:
"Major League Baseball selects their players by drafting athletes after they graduate from high school. Only a few make it in the big leagues, the rest pursue other careers.
Whatever career path you choose, if you study and work hard, you'll be the best at it, and you'll be drafted for a good job when you graduate. It's important to learn a trade or profession."

Listen to **WTMJ Radio** in Milwaukee or your local Brewers network station to learn who will be the 2 players featured on next weeks baseball cards.

The Milwaukee Brewers issued a safety set in 1987 for the sixth consecutive year. As in the past, many local police departments throughout Wisconsin participated in the giveaway program. The Milwaukee version was sponsored by Kinney Shoe Stores and WTMJ Radio and was handed out to youngsters attending the Baseball Card Day at County Stadium on May 9th. The cards, which measure 2-1/4" by 4-1/8", feature full-color photos plus a safety tip on the backs. Chris Bosio can be found with a uniform number of 26 or 29. The card was corrected to #29 in later printings.

		MT	NR MT	EX
	Complete Set:	6.00	4.50	2.50
	Common Player:	.15	.11	.06
1	Ernest Riles	.15	.11	.06
2	Edgar Diaz	.20	.15	.08
3	Juan Castillo	.15	.11	.06
4	Paul Molitor	.60	.45	.25
5	B.J. Surhoff	.60	.45	.25
7	Dale Sveum	.35	.25	.14
9	Greg Brock	.25	.20	.10
13	Billy Jo Robidoux	.15	.11	.06
14	Jim Paciorek	.15	.11	.06
15	Cecil Cooper	.30	.25	.12
16	Mike Felder	.15	.11	.06
17	Jim Gantner	.20	.15	.08
19	Robin Yount	1.00	.70	.40
20	Juan Nieves	.30	.25	.12
21	Bill Schroeder	.15	.11	.06
25	Mark Clear	.15	.11	.06
26a	Glenn Braggs	.60	.45	.25
26b	Chris Bosio	1.00	.70	.40
28	Rick Manning	.15	.11	.06
29	Chris Bosio	.30	.25	.12
32	Chuck Crim	.25	.20	.10

		MT	NR MT	EX
34	Mark Ciardi	.20	.15	.08
37	Dan Plesac	.40	.30	.15
38	John Henry Johnson	.15	.11	.06
40	Mike Birbeck	.25	.20	.10
42	Tom Trebelhorn	.20	.15	.08
45	Rob Deer	.30	.25	.12
46	Bill Wegman	.20	.15	.08
49	Ted Higuera	.40	.30	.15
——	Coaches Card (Andy Etchebarren, Larry Haney, Chuck Hartenstein, Dave Hilton, Tony Muser)	.15	.11	.06
——	Team Photo/Roster	.15	.11	.06

1987 Police/Fire Safety Dodgers

JOSE GONZALEZ 47

Producing a police set for the seventh time in eight years, the 1987 edition contains 30 cards which measure 2-13/16" by 4-1/8". The set includes a special Dodger Stadium 25th Anniversary card. The card fronts contain a full-color photo plus the Dodger Stadium 25th Anniversary logo. The photos are a mix of action and posed shots. The backs contain personal player data plus a police safety tip. The cards were given out April 24th at Dodger Stadium and were distributed by the Los Angeles police department at a rate of two cards per week.

		MT	NR MT	EX
	Complete Set:	6.00	4.50	2.50
	Common Player:	.15	.11	.06
2	Tom Lasorda	.25	.20	.10
3	Steve Sax	.50	.40	.20
5	Mike Marshall	.40	.30	.15
10	Dave Anderson	.15	.11	.06
12	Bill Madlock	.30	.25	.12
14	Mike Scioscia	.25	.20	.10
15	Gilberto Reyes	.15	.11	.06
17	Len Matuszek	.15	.11	.06
21	Reggie Williams	.15	.11	.06
22	Franklin Stubbs	.25	.20	.10
23	Tim Leary	.15	.11	.06
25	Mariano Duncan	.15	.11	.06
26	Alejandro Pena	.25	.20	.10
28	Pedro Guerrero	.60	.45	.25
29	Alex Trevino	.15	.11	.06
33	Jeff Hamilton	.35	.25	.14
34	Fernando Valenzuela	.60	.45	.25
35	Bob Welch	.30	.25	.12
36	Matt Young	.15	.11	.06
40	Rick Honeycutt	.15	.11	.06
41	Jerry Reuss	.25	.20	.10
43	Ken Howell	.15	.11	.06
44	Ken Landreaux	.15	.11	.06
46	Ralph Bryant	.25	.20	.10
47	Jose Gonzalez	.30	.25	.12
49	Tom Niedenfuer	.20	.15	.08
51	Brian Holton	.30	.25	.12
55	Orel Hershiser	1.00	.70	.40
——	Coaching Staff (Joe Amalfitano, Mark Cresse, Tom Lasorda, Don McMahon, Manny Mota, Ron Perranoski, Bill Russell)	.15	.11	.06
——	Dodger Stadium/Checklist	.15	.11	.06

1988 Police/Fire Safety
Astros

This set of 26 full-color cards highlighting the Houston Astros was produced by the team, in conjunction with Deer Park Hospital and Sportsmedia Promotions for distribution to fans 14 years and younger at a ballpark giveaway. The 2-5/8" by 4-1/8" cards feature full-color player photos framed by a narrow blue border with an orange player/team name block below the photo. The blue and white card backs have orange borders and list card numbers, player information, career highlights and anti-drug tips.

		MT	NR MT	EX
Complete Set:		8.00	6.00	3.25
Common Player:		.20	.15	.08
1	Juan Agosto	.20	.15	.08
2	Larry Andersen	.20	.15	.08
3	Joaquin Andujar	.30	.25	.12
4	Alan Ashby	.20	.15	.08
5	Mark Bailey	.20	.15	.08
6	Kevin Bass	.40	.30	.15
7	Danny Darwin	.25	.20	.10
8	Glenn Davis	1.00	.70	.40
9	Jim Deshaies	.30	.25	.12
10	Bill Doran	.40	.30	.15
11	Billy Hatcher	.40	.30	.15
12	Jeff Heathcock	.20	.15	.08
13	Steve Henderson	.20	.15	.08
14	Chuck Jackson	.30	.25	.12
15	Bob Knepper	.30	.25	.12
16	Jim Pankovits	.20	.15	.08
17	Terry Puhl	.20	.15	.08
18	Rafael Ramirez	.20	.15	.08
19	Craig Reynolds	.20	.15	.08
20	Nolan Ryan	1.25	.90	.50
21	Mike Scott	.60	.45	.25
22	Dave Smith	.30	.25	.12
23	Denny Walling	.20	.15	.08
24	Gerald Young	.60	.45	.25
25	Hal Lanier	.20	.15	.08
26	Coaching Staff (Yogi Berra, Gene Clines, Matt Galante, Marc Hill, Denis Menke, Les Moss)	.20	.15	.08

1988 Police/Fire Safety
Blue Jays

This 36-card set features full-color action photos on 3-1/2" by 5" cards with white borders and a thin black line framing the photos. Card numbers (player's uniform #) appear lower left, team logo lower right; player's name and position are printed bottom center. Card backs are blue on white and include personal and career info, 1987 and career stats, sponsor logos and a fire safety tip. The set includes 34 player cards, a team photo checklist card and a team logo card with a year-by-year won/loss record. The set was sponsored by the Ontario Fire

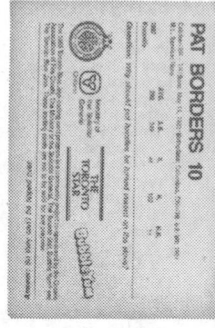

PAT BORDERS
catcher

Chief Association, Ontario's Solicitor General, The Toronto Star and Bubble Yum and was distributed free as part of a community service project.

		MT	NR MT	EX
Complete Set:		7.00	5.25	2.75
Common Player:		.15	.11	.06
1	Tony Fernandez	.60	.45	.25
2	Nelson Liriano	.25	.20	.10
3	Jimy Williams	.15	.11	.06
4	Manny Lee	.15	.11	.06
5	Rance Mulliniks	.15	.11	.06
6	Silvestre Campusuano	.40	.30	.15
7	John McLaren	.15	.11	.06
8	John Sullivan	.15	.11	.06
9	Rick Leach	.15	.11	.06
10	Pat Borders	.40	.30	.15
11	George Bell	1.00	.70	.40
12	Ernie Whitt	.25	.20	.10
13	Jeff Musselman	.20	.15	.08
15	Lloyd Moseby	.30	.25	.12
16	Todd Stottlemyre	.60	.45	.25
17	Kelly Gruber	.15	.11	.06
18	Jim Clancy	.25	.20	.10
19	Fred McGriff	1.00	.70	.40
21	Juan Beniquez	.15	.11	.06
22	Jimmy Key	.40	.30	.15
23	Cecil Fielder	.15	.11	.06
29	Jesse Barfield	.60	.45	.25
31	Duane Ward	.15	.11	.06
36	David Wells	.25	.20	.10
37	Dave Stieb	.40	.30	.15
38	Mark Eichhorn	.20	.15	.08
40	Rob Ducey	.15	.11	.06
41	Al Widmar	.15	.11	.06
42	Billy Smith	.15	.11	.06
43	Cito Gaston	.15	.11	.06
46	Mike Flanagan	.25	.20	.10
50	Tom Henke	.25	.20	.10
55	John Cerutti	.20	.15	.08
57	Winston Llenas	.15	.11	.06
----	Team Photo	.15	.11	.06
----	Team Logo	.15	.11	.06

1988 Police/Fire Safety
Brewers

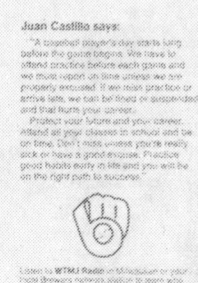

Juan Castillo says:

"A baseball player's day starts long before the game begins. We have to attend practice before each game and we must report on time unless we are properly excused. If we miss practice or arrive late, we can be fined or suspended and that hurts your career.

Protect your future and your career. Attend all your classes in school and be on time. Don't miss classes; you're really sick or have a good excuse. Practice good habits early in life and you will be on the right path to success."

Juan Castillo
The Marathon County Sheriff's Dept. and Brickner Chrysler Center Inc.
7525 Grand Avenue, Wausau, WI 54401
produced the 1988
Milwaukee Brewers

This 30-card set is the 7th annual issue sponsored

by the Milwaukee Police Department for local distribution during a crime prevention promotion. The full-color card fronts (2-3/4" by 4-1/8") feature the same design as the 1987 set with white borders and a black frame outling the player photo and name. Sponsor credits and the team name are listed below the photo. The vertical card backs are blue on white with messages from the player and sponsors. Two group photos - one of the team's five coaches and one of the team (with a checklist back) - are unnumbered and printed horizontally. Card numbers refer to the players uniform numbers.

		MT	NR MT	EX
Complete Set:		6.00	4.50	2.50
Common Player:		.15	.11	.06
1	Ernest Riles	.15	.11	.06
3	Juan Castillo	.15	.11	.06
4	Paul Molitor	.60	.45	.25
5	B.J. Surhoff	.30	.25	.12
7	Dale Sveum	.20	.15	.08
9	Greg Brock	.20	.15	.08
11	Charlie O'Brien	.20	.15	.08
14	Jim Adduci	.15	.11	.06
16	Mike Felder	.15	.11	.06
17	Jim Gantner	.20	.15	.08
19	Robin Yount	1.00	.70	.40
20	Juan Nieves	.25	.20	.10
21	Bill Schroeder	.15	.11	.06
23	Joey Meyer	.35	.25	.14
25	Mark Clear	.15	.11	.06
26	Glenn Braggs	.30	.25	.12
28	Odell Jones	.15	.11	.06
29	Chris Bosio	.15	.11	.06
30	Steve Kiefer	.15	.11	.06
32	Chuck Crim	.15	.11	.06
33	Jay Aldrich	.15	.11	.06
37	Dan Plesac	.40	.30	.15
40	Mike Birkbeck	.20	.15	.08
42	Tom Trebelhorn	.15	.11	.06
43	Dave Stapleton	.25	.20	.10
45	Rob Deer	.30	.25	.12
46	Bill Wegman	.20	.15	.08
49	Ted Higuera	.40	.30	.15
--	Coaches Card (Andy Etchebarren, Larry Haney, Chuck Hartenstein, Dave Hilton, Tony Muser)	.15	.11	.06
--	Team Photo	.15	.11	.06

1988 Police/Fire Safety Dodgers

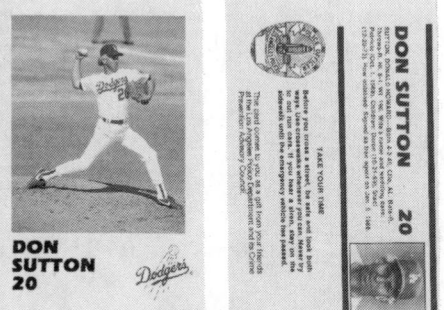

DON
SUTTON
20

The Los Angeles police department sponsored this 30-card set (2-3/4" by 4-1/8") for use in a local crime prevention promotion. The sets include an unnumbered manager/coaches photo and three double-photo cards. The double cards feature posed closeups; the rest are action photos. The card fronts have white borders, with the team logo lower right and a bold black player name lower left. Card backs are black and white with a small closeup photo of the player, followed by personal and career info, a crime prevention tip and a LAPD badge logo. Card numbers refer to players' uniform numbers (the double-photo

cards carry two numbers on both front and back).

		MT	NR MT	EX
Complete Set:		6.00	4.50	2.50
Common Player:		.15	.11	.06
2	Tom Lasorda	.25	.20	.10
3	Steve Sax	.50	.40	.20
5	Mike Marshall	.40	.30	.15
7	Alfredo Griffin	.20	.15	.08
9	Mickey Hatcher	.15	.11	.06
10	Dave Anderson	.15	.11	.06
12	Danny Heep	.15	.11	.06
14	Mike Scioscia	.20	.15	.08
17-21	Tito Landrum, Len Matuszek	.15	.11	.06
20	Don Sutton	.40	.30	.15
22	Franklin Stubbs	.20	.15	.08
23	Kirk Gibson	.60	.45	.25
25	Mariano Duncan	.15	.11	.06
26	Alejandro Pena	.20	.15	.08
27-52	Tim Crews, Mike Sharperson	.25	.20	.10
28	Pedro Guerrero	.50	.40	.20
29	Alex Trevino	.15	.11	.06
31	John Shelby	.15	.11	.06
33	Jeff Hamilton	.25	.20	.10
34	Fernando Valenzuela	.60	.45	.25
37	Mike Davis	.20	.15	.08
41	Brad Havens	.15	.11	.06
43	Ken Howell	.15	.11	.06
47	Jesse Orosco	.20	.15	.08
49-57	Tim Belcher, Shawn Hillegas	.30	.25	.12
50	Jay Howell	.20	.15	.08
51	Brian Holton	.20	.15	.08
54	Tim Leary	.25	.20	.10
55	Orel Hershiser	.80	.60	.30
	Manager/Coaches (Joe Amalfitano, Steve Boros, Mark Cresse, Joe Ferguson, Tom Lasorda, Manny Mota, Ron Perranoski, Bill Russell)	.15	.11	.06

1988 Police/Fire Safety Tigers

LOU WHITAKER   2B
B L T R HT:5'11" WT: 160 BORN: 5-12-57

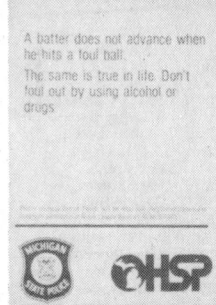

A batter does not advance when he hits a foul ball.

The same is true in life. Don't foul out by using alcohol or drugs.

This unnumbered issue, sponsored by the Michigan State Police features 13 players and manager Sparky Anderson in full-color standard-size (2-1/2" by 3-1/2") cards. Player photos are framed by a blue border, with the Detroit logo upper left and a large name block that lists the player's name, position batting/throwing preference, height, weight and birthday beneath the photo. The backs carry an anti-drug or anti-crime message.

		MT	NR MT	EX
Complete Set:		35.00	25.00	14.00
Common Player:		.50	.40	.20
(1)	Doyle Alexander	.50	.40	.20
(2)	Sparky Anderson	.50	.40	.20
(3)	Dave Bergman	.50	.40	.20
(4)	Tom Brookens	.50	.40	.20
(5)	Darrell Evans	.60	.45	.25
(6)	Larry Herndon	.50	.40	.20
(7)	Chet Lemon	.50	.40	.20
(8)	Jack Morris	.80	.60	.30
(9)	Matt Nokes	.80	.60	.30

		MT	NR MT	EX
(10)	Jeff Robinson	.60	.45	.25
(11)	Frank Tanana	.40	.30	.15
(12)	Walt Terrell	.50	.40	.20
(13)	Alan Trammell	1.00	.70	.40
(14)	Lou Whitaker	.80	.60	.30

1989 Police/Fire Safety
Blue Jays

The 1989 Toronto Blue Jays safety set consisted of 34 standard-size cards co-sponsored by the Ontario Association of Fire Chiefs, Oh Henry! candy bars and A&P supermarkets. The card fronts feature color photos with the player's uniform number in large type in the upper left corner. His name and position are to the right above the photo. The Blue Jays "On the Move" logo is centered at the bottom. The backs of the cards include fire safety messages.

		MT	NR MT	EX
Complete Set:		6.00	4.50	2.50
Common Player:		.15	.11	.06
1	Tony Fernandez	.50	.40	.20
2	Nelson Liriano	.15	.11	.06
3	Jimy Williams	.15	.11	.06
4	Manny Lee	.15	.11	.06
5	Rance Mulliniks	.15	.11	.06
6	Silvestre Campusano	.20	.15	.08
7	John McLaren	.15	.11	.06
8	John Sullivan	.15	.11	.06
9	Bob Brenly	.15	.11	.06
10	Pat Borders	.30	.25	.12
11	George Bell	.90	.70	.35
12	Ernie Whitt	.25	.20	.10
13	Jeff Musselman	.15	.11	.06
15	Lloyd Moseby	.25	.20	.10
16	Greg Myers	.40	.30	.15
17	Kelly Gruber	.30	.25	.12
18	Tom Lawless	.15	.11	.06
19	Fred McGriff	1.00	.70	.40
22	Jimmy Key	.25	.20	.10
25	Mike Squires	.15	.11	.06
26	Sal Butera	.15	.11	.06
29	Jesse Barfield	.40	.30	.15
30	Todd Stottlemyre	.40	.30	.15
31	Duane Ward	.15	.11	.06
36	David Wells	.20	.15	.08
37	Dave Steib	.40	.30	.20
40	Rob Ducey	.15	.11	.06
41	Al Widman	.15	.11	.06
43	Cito Gaston	.20	.15	.08
44	Frank Wills	.15	.11	.06
45	Jose Nunez	.20	.15	.08
46	Mike Flanagan	.20	.15	.08
50	Tom Henke	.20	.15	.08
55	John Cerutti	.20	.15	.08
	Team Photo, Team Logo	.15	.11	.06

Definitions for grading conditions are located in the introduction section at the front of this book.

1989 Police/Fire Safety
Brewers

Jim Gantner says:
"Teamwork is very important in baseball. We know that we can't do it alone. Baseball players work together with their teammates and help each other. We develop strong friendships which last after our playing days are over.
Your teammates are your family, your teachers, and your local police officers. They want to be your friends. Take advantage of their friendship and ask them for advice when needed. They'll work with you, help you, and be the friends you need to succeed in life."

Listen to **WTMJ** Radio in Milwaukee or your local Brewers network station to learn who will be the 2 players featured on next weeks baseball cards.

The Milwaukee Brewers, in conjunction with various corporate and civic sponsors, issued a 30-card police set in 1989, the eighth consecutive police set issued by the club. Some 95 law enforcement agencies in Wisconsin participated in the program, each releasing their own version of the same set. The cards measure 2-13/16" by 4-1/8" and feature full-color action photos with the player's name, uniform number and position below, along with the sponsoring agencies. The backs include the traditional safety messages. The cards were distributed in complete sets at a stadium promotion and also handed out individually over the course of the summer by uniformed police officers in various Wisconsin cities and counties.

		MT	NR MT	EX
Complete Set:		7.00	5.25	2.75
Common Player:		.15	.11	.06
1	Gary Sheffield	1.00	.70	.40
4	Paul Molitor	.60	.45	.25
5	B.J. Surhoff	.30	.25	.12
6	Bill Spiers	.80	.60	.30
7	Dale Sveum	.20	.15	.08
9	Greg Brock	.20	.15	.08
14	Gus Polidor	.15	.11	.06
16	Mike Felder	.15	.11	.06
17	Jim Gantner	.20	.15	.08
19	Robin Yount	1.00	.70	.40
20	Juan Nieves	.20	.15	.08
22	Charlie O'Brien	.20	.15	.08
23	Joey Meyer	.15	.11	.06
25	Dave Engle	.15	.11	.06
26	Glenn Braggs	.25	.20	.10
27	Paul Mirabella	.15	.11	.06
29	Chris Bosio	.20	.15	.08
30	Terry Francona	.15	.11	.06
32	Chuck Crim	.15	.11	.06
37	Dan Plesac	.35	.25	.14
40	Mike Birkbeck	.15	.11	.06
41	Mark Knudson	.20	.15	.08
42	Tom Trebelhorn	.15	.11	.06
45	Rob Deer	.30	.25	.12
46	Bill Wegman	.15	.11	.06
48	Bryan Clutterbuck	.15	.11	.06
49	Teddy Higuera	.40	.30	.15
	Team Photo, Coaching Staff	.15	.11	.06

1989 Police/Fire Safety
Dodgers

The Los Angeles Dodgers and the L.A. Police Department teamed up in 1989 to produce a 30-card police set. The cards, which measure 4-1/4" by 2-5/8", feature color action photos with the player's name and uniform number below. The Dodgers logo and "1989" appear in the upper left. The backs include player information plus a safety message.

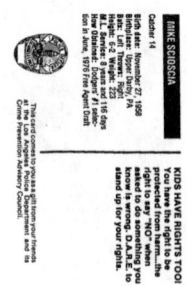

	MT	NR MT	EX
Complete Set:	9.00	6.75	3.50
Common Player:	.25	.20	.10
(1) Doyle Alexander	.35	.25	.14
(2) Sparky Anderson	.50	.40	.20
(3) Dave Bergman	.25	.20	.10
(4) Mike Henneman	.50	.40	.20
(5) Guillermo Hernandez	.35	.25	.14
(6) Chet Lemon	.35	.25	.14
(7) Fred Lynn	.40	.30	.15
(8) Jack Morris	.50	.40	.20
(9) Matt Nokes	.50	.40	.20
(10) Jeff Robinson	.40	.30	.15
(11) Pat Sheridan	.25	.20	.10
(12) Frank Tanana	.40	.30	.15
(13) Alan Trammell	.90	.70	.35
(14) Lou Whitaker	.60	.45	.25

1990 Police/Fire Safety Blue Jays

This 35-card set was co-sponsored by the Ontario Association of Fire Chiefs, The Ministry of the Solicitor General, A & P/Dominion, Oh Henry and the Toronto Blue Jays. The card fronts feature full-color photos on white stock and display a special Blue Jays fan club lougo in the upper left corner. The flip sides feature biographical information, statistics, and a fire fact. The cards are numbered according to the respective player or coaches' uniform number.

	MT	NR MT	EX
Complete Set:	8.00	6.00	3.25
Common Player:	.15	.11	.06
1 Tony Fernandez	.40	.30	.15
2 Nelson Liriano	.15	.11	.06
3 Mookie Wilson	.25	.20	.10
4 Manny Lee	.15	.11	.06
5 Rance Mulliniks	.15	.11	.06
7 John McLaren	.15	.11	.06
8 John Sullivan	.15	.11	.06
9 John Olerud	2.00	1.50	.80
10 Pat Borders	.20	.15	.08
11 George Bell	.60	.45	.25
15 Gene Tenace	.15	.11	.06
18 Tom Lawless	.15	.11	.06
19 Fred McGriff	.70	.50	.30
21 Greg Myers	.25	.20	.10
22 Jimmy Key	.25	.20	.10
23 Alex Sanchez	.30	.25	.12
24 Glenallen Hill	.50	.40	.20
25 Mike Squires	.15	.11	.06
26 Ozzie Virgil	.15	.11	.06
27 Willie Blair	.30	.25	.12
28 Al Leiter	.15	.11	.06
30 Todd Stottlemyre	.25	.20	.10
31 Duane Ward	.15	.11	.06
34 Jim Acker	.15	.11	.06
36 David Wells	.15	.11	.06
37 Dave Steib	.35	.25	.14
39 Paul Kilgus	.15	.11	.06
42 Galen Cisco	.15	.11	.06
43 Cito Gaston	.20	.15	.08
44 Frank Wills	.15	.11	.06
47 Junior Felix	.70	.50	.30

	MT	NR MT	EX
Complete Set:	7.00	5.25	2.75
Common Player:	.15	.11	.06
2 Tom Lasorda	.25	.20	.10
3 Jeff Hamilton	.25	.20	.10
5 Mike Marshall	.30	.25	.12
7 Alfredo Griffin	.15	.11	.06
9 Mickey Hatcher	.15	.11	.06
10 Dave Anderson	.15	.11	.06
12 Willie Randolph	.25	.20	.10
14 Mike Scioscia	.20	.15	.08
17 Rick Dempsey	.15	.11	.06
20 Mike Davis	.15	.11	.06
21 Tracy Woodson	.25	.20	.10
22 Franklin Stubbs	.15	.11	.06
23 Kirk Gibson	.40	.30	.15
25 Mariano Duncan	.20	.15	.08
26 Alejandro Pena	.15	.11	.06
27 Mike Sharperson	.20	.15	.08
29 Ricky Horton	.15	.11	.06
30 John Tudor	.25	.20	.10
31 John Shelby	.15	.11	.06
33 Eddie Murray	.60	.45	.25
34 Fernando Valenzuela	.40	.30	.15
36 Mike Morgan	.15	.11	.06
48 Ramon Martinez	2.00	1.50	.80
49 Tim Belcher	.30	.25	.12
50 Jay Howell	.20	.15	.08
52 Tim Crews	.15	.11	.06
54 Tim Leary	.20	.15	.08
55 Orel Hershiser	.80	.60	.30
57 Ray Searage	.15	.11	.06
—— Dodger Coaches	.15	.11	.06

NOTE: A card number in parentheses ( ) indicates the set is unnumbered.

1989 Police/Fire Safety Tigers

This unnumbered issue, distributed and sponsored by the Michigan State Police Department features 14 full-color 2-1/2" by 3-1/2" cards. Player photos are framed by a blue and orange border, with the team logo in the upper left and biographical information below the photo. The card backs featue anti-drug or anti-crime messages.

		MT	NR MT	EX
50	Tom Henke	.20	.15	.08
55	John Cerutti	.15	.11	.06
----	Skydome/checklist	.15	.11	.06
----	Logo/Schedule	.15	.11	.06

1990 Police/Fire Safety Dodgers

 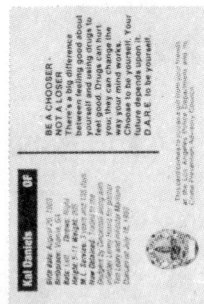

This set honors the centennial celebration of the Los Angeles Dodgers. A special 100 Anniversary logo appears on the card fronts. The cards measure 2-3/4" by 4-1/4" and feature full-color photos. The card backs are printed horizontally and contain a special safety tip or anti-drug message along with player information. The L.A.P.D. logo is featured on the bottom of the card back.

		MT	NR MT	EX
Complete Set:		6.00	4.50	2.50
Common Player:		.15	.11	.06
2	Tommy Lasorda	.25	.20	.10
3	Jeff Hamilton	.15	.11	.06
7	Alfredo Griffin	.15	.11	.06
9	Mickey Hatcher	.15	.11	.06
10	Juan Samuel	.25	.20	.10
12	Willie Randolph	.25	.20	.10
14	Mike Scioscia	.20	.15	.08
15	Chris Gwynn	.25	.20	.10
17	Rick Dempsey	.15	.11	.06
21	Hubie Brooks	.40	.30	.15
22	Franklin Stubbs	.15	.11	.06
23	Kirk Gibson	.35	.25	.14
27	Mike Sharperson	.25	.20	.10
28	Kal Daniels	.40	.30	.15
29	Lenny Harris	.25	.20	.10
31	John Shelby	.15	.11	.06
33	Eddie Murray	.60	.45	.25
34	Fernando Valenzuela	.35	.25	.14
35	Jim Gott	.15	.11	.06
36	Mike Morgan	.15	.11	.06
38	Jose Gonzalez	.25	.20	.10
46	Mike Hartley	.40	.30	.15
48	Ramon Martinez	1.00	.70	.40
49	Tim Belcher	.30	.25	.12
50	Jay Howell	.20	.15	.08
52	Tim Crews	.15	.11	.06
55	Orel Hershiser	.60	.45	.25
57	John Wetteland	.40	.30	.15
59	Ray Searage	.15	.11	.06
----	Coaches	.15	.11	.06

1960 Post Cereal

These cards were issued on the backs of Grape Nuts cereal and measure an oversized 7" by 8-3/4". The nine cards in the set include five baseball players (Al Kaline, Mickey Mantle, Don Drysdale, Harmon Killebrew and Ed Mathews) as well as two football and two basketball players. The full-color photos were placed on a color background and bordered by a wood frame design. The cards covered the entire

back of the cereal box and were blank backed. Card fronts also include the player's name and team and a facsimile autograph. A panel on the side of the box contains player biographical information. A scarce set, the cards are very difficult to obtain in mint condition.

		NR MT	EX	VG
Complete Set:		4000.00	2000.00	1200.
Common Player:		300.00	150.00	90.00
(1)	Bob Cousy	300.00	150.00	90.00
(2)	Don Drysdale	400.00	200.00	120.00
(3)	Frank Gifford	400.00	200.00	120.00
(4)	Al Kaline	450.00	225.00	135.00
(5)	Harmon Killebrew	400.00	200.00	120.00
(6)	Ed Mathews	400.00	200.00	120.00
(7)	Mickey Mantle	1200.00	600.00	360.00
(8)	Bob Pettit	300.00	150.00	90.00
(9)	John Unitas	300.00	150.00	90.00

1961 Post Cereal

Two hundred different players are included in this set, but with variations the number of different cards exceeds 350. This was the first large-scale card set by the cereal company and it proved very popular with fans. Cards were issued both singly and in various panel sizes on the thick cardboard stock of cereal boxes, as well on thinner stock, in team sheets issued directly by Post via a mail-in offer. About 10 cards in the set were issued in significantly smaller quantities, making their prices much higher than other comparable players in the set. Individual cards measure a 3-1/2" by 2-1/2", and all cards are numbered in the upper left corner. Card fronts have full-color portait photos of the player, along with biographical information and 1960 and career statistics. Card backs are blank. The complete set price includes does not include the scarcer variations.

		NR MT	EX	VG
Complete Set:		1400.00	700.00	420.00
Common Player:		1.50	.70	.45

		NR MT	EX	VG
1a	Yogi Berra (box)	20.00	10.00	6.00
1b	Yogi Berra (company)	15.00	7.50	4.50
2a	Elston Howard (box)	5.00	2.50	1.50
2b	Elston Howard (company)	3.00	1.50	.90
3a	Bill Skowron (box)	2.50	1.25	.70
3b	Bill Skowron (company)	2.50	1.25	.70
4a	Mickey Mantle (box)	75.00	37.00	22.00
4b	Mickey Mantle (company)	75.00	37.00	22.00
5	Bob Turley (company)	12.00	6.00	3.50
6a	Whitey Ford (box)	8.00	4.00	2.50
6b	Whitey Ford (company)	8.00	4.00	2.50
7a	Roger Maris (box)	12.00	6.00	3.50
7b	Roger Maris (company)	12.00	6.00	3.50
8a	Bobby Richardson (box)	3.00	1.50	.90
8b	Bobby Richardson (company)	3.00	1.50	.90
9a	Tony Kubek (box)	3.00	1.50	.90
9b	Tony Kubek (company)	3.00	1.50	.90
10	Gil McDougald (box)	25.00	12.50	7.50
11	Cletis Boyer (box)	2.00	1.00	.60
12a	Hector Lopez (box)	2.00	1.00	.60
12b	Hector Lopez (company)	2.00	1.00	.60
13	Bob Cerv (box)	2.00	1.00	.60
14	Ryne Duren (box)	2.00	1.00	.60
15	Bobby Shantz (box)	2.00	1.00	.60
16	Art Ditmar (box)	2.00	1.00	.60
17	Jim Coates (box)	2.00	1.00	.60
18	John Blanchard (box)	2.00	1.00	.60
19a	Luis Aparicio (box)	5.00	2.50	1.50
19b	Luis Aparicio (company)	5.00	2.50	1.50
20a	Nelson Fox (box)	4.00	2.00	1.25
20b	Nelson Fox (company)	4.00	2.00	1.25
21a	Bill Pierce (box)	6.00	3.00	1.75
21b	Bill Pierce (company)	3.50	1.75	1.00
22a	Early Wynn (box)	7.00	3.50	2.00
22b	Early Wynn (company)	12.00	6.00	3.50
23	Bob Shaw (box)	75.00	37.00	22.00
24a	Al Smith (box)	3.00	1.50	.90
24b	Al Smith (company)	1.50	.70	.45
25a	Minnie Minoso (box)	2.50	1.25	.70
25b	Minnie Minoso (company)	2.50	1.25	.70
26a	Roy Sievers (box)	1.75	.90	.50
26b	Roy Sievers (company)	1.75	.90	.50
27a	Jim Landis (box)	2.00	1.00	.60
27b	Jim Landis (company)	1.50	.70	.45
28a	Sherman Lollar (box)	3.00	1.50	.90
28b	Sherman Lollar (company)	1.50	.70	.45
29	Gerry Staley (box)	1.50	.70	.45
30a	Gene Freese (box, White Sox)	1.50	.70	.45
30b	Gene Freese (company, Reds)	6.00	3.00	1.75
31	Ted Kluszewski (box)	3.00	1.50	.90
32	Turk Lown (box)	1.50	.70	.45
33a	Jim Rivera (box)	1.50	.70	.45
33b	Jim Rivera (company)	1.50	.70	.45
34	Frank Baumann (box)	1.50	.70	.45
35a	Al Kaline (box)	12.00	6.00	3.50
35b	Al Kaline (company)	10.00	5.00	3.00
36a	Rocky Colavito (box)	6.00	3.00	1.75
36b	Rocky Colavito (company)	3.50	1.75	1.00
37a	Charley Maxwell (box)	4.00	2.00	1.25
37b	Charley Maxwell (company)	1.50	.70	.45
38a	Frank Lary (box)	1.50	.70	.45
38b	Frank Lary (company)	1.50	.70	.45
39a	Jim Bunning (box)	4.00	2.00	1.25
39b	Jim Bunning (company)	4.00	2.00	1.25
40a	Norm Cash (box)	2.00	1.00	.60
40b	Norm Cash (company)	2.00	1.00	.60
41a	Frank Bolling (box, Tigers)	8.00	4.00	2.50
41b	Frank Bolling (company, Braves)	5.00	2.50	1.50
42a	Don Mossi (box)	1.50	.70	.45
42b	Don Mossi (company)	1.50	.70	.45
43a	Lou Berberet (box)	1.50	.70	.45
43b	Lou Berberet (company)	1.50	.70	.45
44	Dave Sisler (box)	1.50	.70	.45
45	Ed Yost (box)	1.50	.70	.45
46	Pete Burnside (box)	1.50	.70	.45
47a	Pete Runnels (box)	3.00	1.50	.90
47b	Pete Runnnels (company)	1.75	.90	.50
48a	Frank Malzone (box)	1.50	.70	.45
48b	Frank Malzone (company)	1.50	.70	.45
49a	Vic Wertz (box)	5.00	2.50	1.50
49b	Vic Wertz (company)	3.00	1.50	.90
50a	Tom Brewer (box)	2.50	1.25	.70
50b	Tom Brewer (company)	1.50	.70	.45
51a	Willie Tasby (box, no sold line)	8.00	4.00	2.50
51b	Willie Tasby (company, sold line)	1.50	.70	.45
52a	Russ Nixon (box)	1.50	.70	.45
52b	Russ Nixon (company)	1.50	.70	.45
53a	Don Buddin (box)	1.50	.70	.45
53b	Don Buddin (company)	1.50	.70	.45
54a	Bill Monbouquette (box)	1.50	.70	.45
54b	Bill Monbouquette (company)	1.50	.70	.45
55a	Frank Sullivan (box, Red Sox)	1.50	.70	.45

		NR MT	EX	VG
55b	Frank Sullivan (company, Phillies)	18.00	9.00	5.50
56a	Haywood Sullivan (box)	1.50	.70	.45
56b	Haywood Sullivan (company)	1.50	.70	.45
57a	Harvey Kuenn (box, Indians)	3.00	1.50	.90
57b	Harvey Kuenn (company, Giants)	6.00	3.00	1.75
58a	Gary Bell (box)	5.00	2.50	1.50
58b	Gary Bell (company)	1.75	.90	.50
59a	Jim Perry (box)	1.75	.90	.50
59b	Jim Perry (company)	1.75	.90	.50
60a	Jim Grant (box)	3.00	1.50	.90
60b	Jim Grant (company)	1.75	.90	.50
61a	Johnny Temple (box)	1.50	.70	.45
61b	Johnny Temple (company)	1.50	.70	.45
62a	Paul Foytack (box)	1.50	.70	.45
62b	Paul Foytack (company)	1.50	.70	.45
63a	Vic Power (box)	1.50	.70	.45
63b	Vic Power (company)	1.50	.70	.45
64a	Tito Francona (box)	1.50	.70	.45
64b	Tito Francona (company)	1.50	.70	.45
65a	Ken Aspromonte (box, no sold line)	6.00	3.00	1.75
65b	Ken Aspromonte (company, sold line)	6.00	3.00	1.75
66	Bob Wilson (box)	1.50	.70	.45
67a	John Romano (box)	1.50	.70	.45
67b	John Romano (company)	1.50	.70	.45
68a	Jim Gentile (box)	2.50	1.25	.70
68b	Jim Gentile (company)	1.50	.70	.45
69a	Gus Triandos (box)	3.00	1.50	.90
69b	Gus Triandos (company)	1.50	.70	.45
70	Gene Woodling (box)	15.00	7.50	4.50
71a	Milt Pappas (box)	3.00	1.50	.90
71b	Milt Pappas (company)	1.50	.70	.45
72a	Ron Hansen (box)	3.00	1.50	.90
72b	Ron Hansen (company)	1.50	.70	.45
73	Chuck Estrada (company)	75.00	37.00	22.00
74a	Steve Barber (box)	1.50	.70	.45
74b	Steve Barber (company)	1.50	.70	.45
75a	Brooks Robinson (box)	12.00	6.00	3.50
75b	Brooks Robinson (company)	10.00	5.00	3.00
76a	Jackie Brandt (box)	1.50	.70	.45
76b	Jackie Brandt (company)	1.50	.70	.45
77a	Marv Breeding (box)	1.50	.70	.45
77b	Marv Breeding (company)	1.50	.70	.45
78	Hal Brown (box)	1.50	.70	.45
79	Billy Klaus (box)	1.50	.70	.45
80a	Hoyt Wilhelm (box)	5.00	2.50	1.50
80b	Hoyt Wilhelm (company)	6.00	3.00	1.75
81a	Jerry Lumpe (box)	6.00	3.00	1.75
81b	Jerry Lumpe (company)	4.00	2.00	1.25
82a	Norm Siebern (box)	1.50	.70	.45
82b	Norm Siebern (company)	1.50	.70	.45
83a	Bud Daley (box)	1.75	.90	.50
83b	Bud Daley (company)	2.50	1.25	.70
84a	Bill Tuttle (box)	1.50	.70	.45
84b	Bill Tuttle (company)	1.50	.70	.45
85a	Marv Throneberry (box)	2.50	1.25	.70
85b	Marv Throneberry (company)	2.50	1.25	.70
86a	Dick Williams (box)	1.75	.90	.50
86b	Dick Williams (company)	2.00	1.00	.60
87a	Ray Herbert (box)	1.50	.70	.45
87b	Ray Herbert (company)	2.00	1.00	.60
88a	Whitey Herzog (box)	2.00	1.00	.60
88b	Whitey Herzog (company)	2.00	1.00	.60
89a	Ken Hamlin (box, no sold line)	1.50	.70	.45
89b	Ken Hamlin (company, sold line)	8.00	4.00	2.50
90a	Hank Bauer (box)	2.00	1.00	.60
90b	Hank Bauer (company)	2.00	1.00	.60
91a	Bob Allison (box, Minneapolis)	4.00	2.00	1.25
91b	Bob Allison (company, Minnesota)	5.00	2.50	1.50
92a	Harmon Killebrew (box, Minneapolis)	12.00	6.00	3.50
92b	Harmon Killebrew (company, Minnesota)	10.00	5.00	3.00
93a	Jim Lemon (box, Minneapolis)	40.00	20.00	12.00
93b	Jim Lemon (company, Minnesota)	5.00	2.50	1.50
94	Chuck Stobbs (company)	125.00	62.00	37.00
95a	Reno Bertoia (box, Minneapolis)	1.50	.70	.45
95b	Reno Bertoia (company, Minnesota)	4.00	2.00	1.25
96a	Billy Gardner (box, Minneapolis)	1.50	.70	.45
96b	Billy Gardner (company, Minnesota)	4.00	2.00	1.25
97a	Earl Battey (box, Minneapolis)	4.00	2.00	1.25
97b	Earl Battey (company, Minnesota)	4.00	2.00	1.25
98a	Pedro Ramos (box, Minneapolis)	1.50	.70	.45
98b	Pedro Ramos (company, Minnesota)	4.00	2.00	1.25

		NR MT	EX	VG
99a	Camilio Pascual (Camilo) (box, Minneapolis)	1.50	.70	.45
99b	Camilio Pascual (Camilo) (company, Minnesota)	4.00	2.00	1.25
100a	Billy Consolo (box, Minneapolis)	1.50	.70	.45
100b	Billy Consolo (company, Minnesota)	4.00	2.00	1.25
101a	Warren Spahn (box)	15.00	7.50	4.50
101b	Warren Spahn (company)	8.00	4.00	2.50
102a	Lew Burdette (box)	2.50	1.25	.70
102b	Lew Burdette (company)	2.50	1.25	.70
103a	Bob Buhl (box)	1.50	.70	.45
103b	Bob Buhl (company)	1.50	.70	.45
104a	Joe Adcock (box)	4.00	2.00	1.25
104b	Joe Adcock (company)	2.50	1.25	.70
105a	John Logan (box)	4.00	2.00	1.25
105b	John Logan (company)	1.75	.90	.50
106	Ed Mathews (company)	25.00	12.50	7.50
107a	Hank Aaron (box)	18.00	9.00	5.50
107b	Hank Aaron (company)	18.00	9.00	5.50
108a	Wes Covington (box)	1.50	.70	.45
108b	Wes Covington (company)	1.50	.70	.45
109a	Bill Bruton (box, Braves)	6.00	3.00	1.75
109b	Bill Bruton (company, Tigers)	8.00	4.00	2.50
110a	Del Crandall (box)	4.00	2.00	1.25
110b	Del Crandall (company)	1.75	.90	.50
111	Red Schoendienst (box)	5.00	2.50	1.50
112	Juan Pizarro (box)	1.50	.70	.45
113	Chuck Cottier (box)	8.00	4.00	2.50
114	Al Spangler (box)	1.50	.70	.45
115a	Dick Farrell (box)	6.00	3.00	1.75
115b	Dick Farrell (company)	4.00	2.00	1.25
116a	Jim Owens (box)	6.00	3.00	1.75
116b	Jim Owens (company)	4.00	2.00	1.25
117a	Robin Roberts (box)	6.00	3.00	1.75
117b	Robin Roberts (company)	6.00	3.00	1.75
118a	Tony Taylor (box)	1.50	.70	.45
118b	Tony Taylor (company)	1.50	.70	.45
119a	Lee Walls (box)	1.50	.70	.45
119b	Lee Walls (company)	1.50	.70	.45
120a	Tony Curry (box)	1.50	.70	.45
120b	Tony Curry (company)	1.50	.70	.45
121a	Pancho Herrera (box)	1.50	.70	.45
121b	Pancho Herrera (company)	1.50	.70	.45
122a	Ken Walters (box)	1.50	.70	.45
122b	Ken Walters (company)	1.50	.70	.45
123a	John Callison (box)	1.50	.70	.45
123b	John Callison (company)	1.50	.70	.45
124a	Gene Conley (box, Phillies)	1.50	.70	.45
124b	Gene Conley (company, Red Sox)	15.00	7.50	4.50
125a	Bob Friend (box)	4.00	2.00	1.25
125b	Bob Friend (company)	2.00	1.00	.60
126a	Vernon Law (box)	4.00	2.00	1.25
126b	Vernon Law (company)	2.00	1.00	.60
127a	Dick Stuart (box)	1.50	.70	.45
127b	Dick Stuart (company)	1.50	.70	.45
128a	Bill Mazeroski (box)	2.50	1.25	.70
128b	Bill Mazeroski (company)	2.50	1.25	.70
129a	Dick Groat (box)	3.00	1.50	.90
129b	Dick Groat (company)	2.00	1.00	.60
130a	Don Hoak (box)	1.50	.70	.45
130b	Don Hoak (company)	1.50	.70	.45
131a	Bob Skinner (box)	1.50	.70	.45
131b	Bob Skinner (company)	1.50	.70	.45
132a	Bob Clemente (box)	20.00	10.00	6.00
132b	Bob Clemente (company)	18.00	9.00	5.50
133	Roy Face (box)	3.00	1.50	.90
134	Harvey Haddix (box)	1.75	.90	.50
135	Bill Virdon (box)	25.00	12.50	7.50
136a	Gino Cimoli (box)	1.50	.70	.45
136b	Gino Cimoli (company)	1.50	.70	.45
137	Rocky Nelson (box)	1.50	.70	.45
138a	Smoky Burgess (box)	1.75	.90	.50
138b	Smoky Burgess (company)	1.75	.90	.50
139	Hal Smith (box)	1.50	.70	.45
140	Wilmer Mizell (box)	1.50	.70	.45
141a	Mike McCormick (box)	1.50	.70	.45
141b	Mike McCormick (company)	1.50	.70	.45
142a	John Antonelli (box, Giants)	3.00	1.50	.90
142b	John Antonelli (company, Indians)	4.00	2.00	1.25
143a	Sam Jones (box)	4.00	2.00	1.25
143b	Sam Jones (company)	2.00	1.00	.60
144a	Orlando Cepeda (box)	5.00	2.50	1.50
144b	Orlando Cepeda (company)	5.00	2.50	1.50
145a	Willie Mays (box)	18.00	9.00	5.50
145b	Willie Mays (company)	18.00	9.00	5.50
146a	Willie Kirkland (box, Giants)	5.00	2.50	1.50
146b	Willie Kirkland (company, Indians)	5.00	2.50	1.50
147a	Willie McCovey (box)	7.00	3.50	2.00
147b	Willie McCovey (company)	10.00	5.00	3.00
148a	Don Blasingame (box)	1.50	.70	.45
148b	Don Blasingame (company)	1.50	.70	.45
149a	Jim Davenport (box)	1.50	.70	.45
149b	Jim Davenport (company)	1.50	.70	.45
150a	Hobie Landrith (box)	1.50	.70	.45
150b	Hobie Landrith (company)	1.50	.70	.45
151	Bob Schmidt (box)	1.50	.70	.45
152a	Ed Bressoud (box)	1.50	.70	.45
152b	Ed Bressoud (company)	1.50	.70	.45
153a	Andre Rodgers (box, no traded line)	6.00	3.00	1.75
153b	Andre Rodgers (box, traded line)	1.50	.70	.45
154	Jack Sanford (box)	1.50	.70	.45
155	Billy O'Dell (box)	1.50	.70	.45
156a	Norm Larker (box)	2.50	1.25	.70
156b	Norm Larker (company)	2.50	1.25	.70
157a	Charlie Neal (box)	1.50	.70	.45
157b	Charlie Neal (company)	1.50	.70	.45
158a	Jim Gilliam (box)	4.00	2.00	1.25
158b	Jim Gilliam (company)	2.50	1.25	.70
159a	Wally Moon (box)	1.50	.70	.45
159b	Wally Moon (company)	1.50	.70	.45
160a	Don Drysdale (box)	7.00	3.50	2.00
160b	Don Drysdale (company)	8.00	4.00	2.50
161a	Larry Sherry (box)	1.50	.70	.45
161b	Larry Sherry (company)	1.50	.70	.45
162	Stan Williams (box)	5.00	2.50	1.50
163	Mel Roach (box)	40.00	20.00	12.00
164a	Maury Wills (box)	4.00	2.00	1.25
164b	Maury Wills (company)	4.00	2.00	1.25
165	Tom Davis (box)	2.00	1.00	.60
166a	John Roseboro (box)	1.50	.70	.45
166b	John Roseboro (company)	1.50	.70	.45
167a	Duke Snider (box)	8.00	4.00	2.50
167b	Duke Snider (company)	10.00	5.00	3.00
168a	Gil Hodges (box)	5.00	2.50	1.50
168b	Gil Hodges (company)	6.00	3.00	1.75
169	John Podres (box)	2.50	1.25	.70
170	Ed Roebuck (box)	1.50	.70	.45
171a	Ken Boyer (box)	6.00	3.00	1.75
171b	Ken Boyer (company)	4.00	2.00	1.25
172a	Joe Cunningham (box)	1.50	.70	.45
172b	Joe Cunningham (company)	1.50	.70	.45
173a	Daryl Spencer (box)	1.50	.70	.45
173b	Daryl Spencer (company)	1.50	.70	.45
174a	Larry Jackson (box)	1.50	.70	.45
174b	Larry Jackson (company)	1.50	.70	.45
175a	Lindy McDaniel (box)	1.50	.70	.45
175b	Lindy McDaniel (company)	1.50	.70	.45
176a	Bill White (box)	1.75	.90	.50
176b	Bill White (company)	1.75	.90	.50
177a	Alex Grammas (box)	1.50	.70	.45
177b	Alex Grammas (company)	1.50	.70	.45
178a	Curt Flood (box)	2.00	1.00	.60
178b	Curt Flood (company)	2.00	1.00	.60
179a	Ernie Broglio (box)	1.50	.70	.45
179b	Ernie Broglio (company)	1.50	.70	.45
180a	Hal Smith (box)	1.50	.70	.45
180b	Hal Smith (company)	1.50	.70	.45
181a	Vada Pinson (box)	2.50	1.25	.70
181b	Vada Pinson (company)	2.50	1.25	.70
182a	Frank Robinson (box)	12.00	6.00	3.50
182b	Frank Robinson (company)	18.00	9.00	5.50
183	Roy McMillan (box)	55.00	27.00	16.50
184a	Bob Purkey (box)	1.50	.70	.45
184b	Bob Purkey (company)	1.50	.70	.45
185a	Ed Kasko (box)	1.50	.70	.45
185b	Ed Kasko (company)	1.50	.70	.45
186a	Gus Bell (box)	1.50	.70	.45
186b	Gus Bell (company)	1.50	.70	.45
187a	Jerry Lynch (box)	1.50	.70	.45
187b	Jerry Lynch (company)	1.50	.70	.45
188a	Ed Bailey (box)	1.50	.70	.45
188b	Ed Bailey (company)	1.50	.70	.45
189a	Jim O'Toole (box)	1.50	.70	.45
189b	Jim O'Toole (company)	1.50	.70	.45
190a	Billy Martin (box, no sold line)	3.00	1.50	.90
190b	Billy Martin (company, sold line)	9.00	4.50	2.75
191a	Ernie Banks (box)	9.00	4.50	2.75
191b	Ernie Banks (company)	9.00	4.50	2.75
192a	Richie Ashburn (box)	3.00	1.50	.90
192b	Richie Ashburn (company)	3.00	1.50	.90
193a	Frank Thomas (box)	35.00	17.50	10.50
193b	Frank Thomas (company)	5.00	2.50	1.50
194a	Don Cardwell (box)	1.50	.70	.45
194b	Don Cardwell (company)	2.00	1.00	.60
195a	George Altman (box)	1.50	.70	.45
195b	George Altman (company)	2.00	1.00	.60
196a	Ron Santo (box)	3.00	1.50	.90
196b	Ron Santo (company)	3.00	1.50	.90

		NR MT	EX	VG
197a	Glen Hobbie (box)	1.50	.70	.45
197b	Glen Hobbie (company)	2.00	1.00	.60
198a	Sam Taylor (box)	1.50	.70	.45
198b	Sam Taylor (company)	2.00	1.00	.60
199a	Jerry Kindall (box)	1.50	.70	.45
199b	Jerry Kindall (company)	2.00	1.00	.60
200a	Don Elston (box)	3.00	1.50	.90
200b	Don Elston (company)	3.00	1.50	.90

1962 Post Cereal

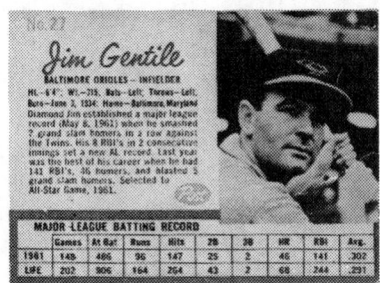

Like the 1961 Post set, there are 200 players pictured in the set of 3-1/2" by 2-1/2" cards. Differences include a Post logo on the card fronts and the player's name in script lettering. Cards are again blank backed and were issued in panels of five to seven cards on cereal boxes. American League players are numbered 1-100 and National League players 101-200. With variations there are 210 of the full-color cards known. A handful of the '62 cards were also issued in smaller quantities. The cards of Mickey Mantle and Roger Maris were reproduced in a special two-card panel for a Life magazine insert. the card stock for this insert is slightly thinner, with white margins. The 1962 Post Canadian and Jell-O sets have virtually the same checklist as this set. The complete set price does not include the scarcer variations.

		NR MT	EX	VG
Complete Set:		1200.00	600.00	350.00
Common Player:		1.50	.70	.45
1	Bill Skowron	4.00	2.00	1.25
2	Bobby Richardson	3.00	1.50	.90
3	Cletis Boyer	2.00	1.00	.60
4	Tony Kubek	3.00	1.50	.90
5a	Mickey Mantle (from box, no printing on back)	65.00	32.00	19.50
5b	Mickey Mantle (from ad, printing on back)	70.00	35.00	21.00
6a	Roger Maris (from box, no printing on back)	10.00	5.00	3.00
6b	Roger Maris (from ad, printing on back)	12.00	6.00	3.50
7	Yogi Berra	10.00	5.00	3.00
8	Elston Howard	3.00	1.50	.90
9	Whitey Ford	7.00	3.50	2.00
10	Ralph Terry	2.00	1.00	.60
11	John Blanchard	2.00	1.00	.60
12	Luis Arroyo	2.00	1.00	.60
13	Bill Stafford	2.00	1.00	.60
14a	Norm Cash (Throws: Right)	2.00	1.00	.60
14b	Norm Cash (Throws: Left)	5.00	2.50	1.50
15	Jake Wood	1.50	.70	.45
16	Steve Boros	1.50	.70	.45
17	Chico Fernandez	1.50	.70	.45
18	Bill Bruton	1.50	.70	.45
19	Rocky Colavito	3.00	1.50	.90
20	Al Kaline	8.00	4.00	2.50
21	Dick Brown	1.50	.70	.45
22	Frank Lary	1.50	.70	.45
23	Don Mossi	1.50	.70	.45
24	Phil Regan	1.50	.70	.45
25	Charley Maxwell	1.50	.70	.45
26	Jim Bunning	3.00	1.50	.90

		NR MT	EX	VG
27a	Jim Gentile (Home: Baltimore)	1.50	.70	.45
27b	Jim Gentile (Home: San Lorenzo)	5.00	2.50	1.50
28	Marv Breeding	1.50	.70	.45
29	Brooks Robinson	8.00	4.00	2.50
30	Ron Hansen	1.50	.70	.45
31	Jackie Brandt	1.50	.70	.45
32	Dick Williams	1.75	.90	.50
33	Gus Triandos	1.50	.70	.45
34	Milt Pappas	1.50	.70	.45
35	Hoyt Wilhelm	4.00	2.00	1.25
36	Chuck Estrada	5.00	2.50	1.50
37	Vic Power	1.50	.70	.45
38	Johnny Temple	1.50	.70	.45
39	Bubba Phillips	1.50	.70	.45
40	Tito Francona	1.50	.70	.45
41	Willie Kirkland	1.50	.70	.45
42	John Romano	1.50	.70	.45
43	Jim Perry	1.75	.90	.50
44	Woodie Held	1.50	.70	.45
45	Chuck Essegian	1.50	.70	.45
46	Roy Sievers	1.75	.90	.50
47	Nellie Fox	3.50	1.75	1.00
48	Al Smith	1.50	.70	.45
49	Luis Aparicio	4.00	2.00	1.25
50	Jim Landis	1.50	.70	.45
51	Minnie Minoso	2.00	1.00	.60
52	Andy Carey	1.50	.70	.45
53	Sherman Lollar	1.50	.70	.45
54	Bill Pierce	1.75	.90	.50
55	Early Wynn	25.00	12.50	7.50
56	Chuck Schilling	1.50	.70	.45
57	Pete Runnels	1.50	.70	.45
58	Frank Malzone	1.50	.70	.45
59	Don Buddin	1.50	.70	.45
60	Gary Geiger	1.50	.70	.45
61	Carl Yastrzemski	30.00	15.00	9.00
62	Jackie Jensen	2.00	1.00	.60
63	Jim Pagliaroni	1.50	.70	.45
64	Don Schwall	1.50	.70	.45
65	Dale Long	1.50	.70	.45
66	Chuck Cottier	1.50	.70	.45
67	Billy Klaus	1.50	.70	.45
68	Coot Veal	1.50	.70	.45
69	Marty Keough	25.00	12.50	7.50
70	Willie Tasby	1.50	.70	.45
71	Gene Woodling	1.50	.70	.45
72	Gene Green	1.50	.70	.45
73	Dick Donovan	1.50	.70	.45
74	Steve Bilko	1.50	.70	.45
75	Rocky Bridges	1.50	.70	.45
76	Eddie Yost	1.50	.70	.45
77	Leon Wagner	1.50	.70	.45
78	Albie Pearson	1.50	.70	.45
79	Ken Hunt	1.50	.70	.45
80	Earl Averill	1.50	.70	.45
81	Ryne Duren	1.50	.70	.45
82	Ted Kluszewski	2.50	1.25	.70
83	Bob Allison	20.00	10.00	6.00
84	Billy Martin	3.50	1.75	1.00
85	Harmon Killebrew	7.00	3.50	2.00
86	Zoilo Versalles	1.50	.70	.45
87	Lenny Green	1.50	.70	.45
88	Bill Tuttle	1.50	.70	.45
89	Jim Lemon	1.50	.70	.45
90	Earl Battey	1.50	.70	.45
91	Camilo Pascual	1.50	.70	.45
92	Norm Siebern	45.00	22.00	13.50
93	Jerry Lumpe	1.50	.70	.45
94	Dick Howser	2.00	1.00	.60
95a	Gene Stephens (Born: Jan. 5)	1.50	.70	.45
95b	Gene Stephens (Born: Jan. 20)	5.00	2.50	1.50
96	Leo Posada	1.50	.70	.45
97	Joe Pignatano	1.50	.70	.45
98	Jim Archer	1.50	.70	.45
99	Haywood Sullivan	1.50	.70	.45
100	Art Ditmar	1.50	.70	.45
101	Gil Hodges	50.00	25.00	15.00
102	Charlie Neal	1.50	.70	.45
103	Daryl Spencer	15.00	7.50	4.50
104	Maury Wills	4.00	2.00	1.25
105	Tommy Davis	2.00	1.00	.60
106	Willie Davis	1.75	.90	.50
107	John Roseboro	1.50	.70	.45
108	John Podres	2.50	1.25	.70
109a	Sandy Koufax (blue lines around stats)	25.00	12.50	7.50
109b	Sandy Koufax (red lines around stats)	15.00	7.50	4.50
110	Don Drysdale	7.00	3.50	2.00
111	Larry Sherry	1.50	.70	.45
112	Jim Gilliam	2.50	1.25	.70

		NR MT	EX	VG
113	Norm Larker	25.00	12.50	7.50
114	Duke Snider	8.00	4.00	2.50
115	Stan Williams	1.50	.70	.45
116	Gordy Coleman	60.00	30.00	18.00
117	Don Blasingame	1.50	.70	.45
118	Gene Freese	1.50	.70	.45
119	Ed Kasko	1.50	.70	.45
120	Gus Bell	1.50	.70	.45
121	Vada Pinson	2.50	1.25	.70
122	Frank Robinson	15.00	7.50	4.50
123	Bob Purkey	1.50	.70	.45
124a	Joey Jay (blue lines around stats)	8.00	4.00	2.50
124b	Joey Jay (red lines around stats)	1.50	.70	.45
125	Jim Brosnan	15.00	7.50	4.50
126	Jim O'Toole	1.50	.70	.45
127	Jerry Lynch	45.00	22.00	13.50
128	Wally Post	1.50	.70	.45
129	Ken Hunt	1.50	.70	.45
130	Jerry Zimmerman	1.50	.70	.45
131	Willie McCovey	60.00	30.00	18.00
132	Jose Pagan	1.50	.70	.45
133	Felipe Alou	1.75	.90	.50
134	Jim Davenport	1.50	.70	.45
135	Harvey Kuenn	2.00	1.00	.60
136	Orlando Cepeda	3.50	1.75	1.00
137	Ed Bailey	1.50	.70	.45
138	Sam Jones	1.50	.70	.45
139	Mike McCormick	1.50	.70	.45
140	Juan Marichal	60.00	30.00	18.00
141	Jack Sanford	1.50	.70	.45
142	Willie Mays	20.00	10.00	6.00
143	Stu Miller (photo actually Chuck Hiller)			
		6.00	3.00	1.75
144	Joe Amalfitano	10.00	5.00	3.00
145a	Joe Adock (name incorrect)	25.00	12.50	7.50
145b	Joe Adcock (name correct)	2.00	1.00	.60
146	Frank Bolling	1.50	.70	.45
147	Ed Mathews	7.00	3.50	2.00
148	Roy McMillan	1.50	.70	.45
149	Hank Aaron	30.00	15.00	9.00
150	Gino Cimoli	1.50	.70	.45
151	Frank Thomas	1.50	.70	.45
152	Joe Torre	3.00	1.50	.90
153	Lou Burdette	2.50	1.25	.70
154	Bob Buhl	1.50	.70	.45
155	Carlton Willey	1.50	.70	.45
156	Lee Maye	1.50	.70	.45
157	Al Spangler	1.50	.70	.45
158	Bill White	30.00	15.00	9.00
159	Ken Boyer	3.00	1.50	.90
160	Joe Cunningham	1.50	.70	.45
161	Carl Warwick	1.50	.70	.45
162	Carl Sawatski	1.50	.70	.45
163	Lindy McDaniel	1.50	.70	.45
164	Ernie Broglio	1.50	.70	.45
165	Larry Jackson	1.50	.70	.45
166	Curt Flood	2.00	1.00	.60
167	Curt Simmons	1.50	.70	.45
168	Alex Grammas	1.50	.70	.45
169	Dick Stuart	1.50	.70	.45
170	Bill Mazeroski	2.50	1.25	.70
171	Don Hoak	1.50	.70	.45
172	Dick Groat	2.00	1.00	.60
173a	Roberto Clemente (blue lines around stats)	25.00	12.50	7.50
173b	Roberto Clemente (red lines around stats)	15.00	7.50	4.50
174	Bob Skinner	1.50	.70	.45
175	Bill Virdon	1.75	.90	.50
176	Smoky Burgess	1.75	.90	.50
177	Elroy Face	1.75	.90	.50
178	Bob Friend	1.50	.70	.45
179	Vernon Law	1.50	.70	.45
180	Harvey Haddix	1.50	.70	.45
181	Hal Smith	1.50	.70	.45
182	Ed Bouchee	1.50	.70	.45
183	Don Zimmer	1.50	.70	.45
184	Ron Santo	2.50	1.25	.70
185	Andre Rodgers	1.50	.70	.45
186	Richie Ashburn	3.00	1.50	.90
187a	George Altman (last line is "...1955".)			
		1.50	.70	.45
187b	George Altman (last line is "...1955.")			
		3.00	1.50	.90
188	Ernie Banks	10.00	5.00	3.00
189	Sam Taylor	1.50	.70	.45
190	Don Elston	1.50	.70	.45
191	Jerry Kindall	1.50	.70	.45
192	Pancho Herrera	1.50	.70	.45
193	Tony Taylor	1.50	.70	.45
194	Ruben Amaro	1.50	.70	.45

		NR MT	EX	VG
195	Don Demeter	1.50	.70	.45
196	Bobby Gene Smith	1.50	.70	.45
197	Clay Dalrymple	1.50	.70	.45
198	Robin Roberts	5.00	2.50	1.50
199	Art Mahaffey	1.50	.70	.45
200	John Buzhardt	2.50	1.25	.70

1962 Post Cereal Canadian

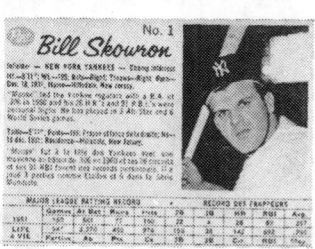

This Canadian set of cards is scarce due to the much more limited distribution in Canada. The cards were printed on the back of the cereal box itself and contains a full-color player photo with biography and statistics given in both French and English. The card backs are blank. Cards measure 3-1/2" by 2-1/2". This 200-card set is very similar to the Post Cereal cards printed in the United States. the Post logo appears at the upper left corner in the Canadian issue. Several cards are scarce because of limited distribution and there are two Whitey Ford cards, the corrected version being the most scarce. The complete set price does not include the scarcer variations.

		NR MT	EX	VG
Complete Set:		2000.00	1000.00	600.00
Common Player:		2.50	1.25	.70
1	Bill Skowron	8.00	4.00	2.50
2	Bobby Richardson	6.00	3.00	1.75
3	Cletis Boyer	3.50	1.75	1.00
4	Tony Kubek	6.00	3.00	1.75
5a	Mickey Mantle (script name large)			
		150.00	75.00	45.00
5b	Mickey Mantle (script name small)			
		90.00	45.00	27.00
6	Roger Maris	15.00	7.50	4.50
7	Yogi Berra	15.00	7.50	4.50
8	Elston Howard	4.00	2.00	1.25
9a	Whitey Ford (Dodgers)	20.00	10.00	6.00
9b	Whitey Ford (Yankees)	35.00	17.50	10.50
10	Ralph Terry	25.00	12.50	7.50
11	John Blanchard	3.00	1.50	.90
12	Luis Arroyo	3.00	1.50	.90
13	Bill Stafford	3.00	1.50	.90
14	Norm Cash	4.00	2.00	1.25
15	Jake Wood	2.50	1.25	.70
16	Steve Boros	2.50	1.25	.70
17	Chico Fernandez	2.50	1.25	.70
18	Bill Bruton	2.50	1.25	.70
19a	Rocky Colavito (script name large)			
		7.00	3.50	2.00
19b	Rocky Colavito (script name small)			
		7.00	3.50	2.00
20	Al Kaline	15.00	7.50	4.50
21	Dick Brown	7.00	3.50	2.00
22a	Frank Lary (French bio variation)	7.00	3.50	2.00
22b	Frank Lary (French bio variation)	7.00	3.50	2.00
23	Don Mossi	2.50	1.25	.70
24	Phil Regan	2.50	1.25	.70
25	Charley Maxwell	2.50	1.25	.70
26	Jim Bunning	6.00	3.00	1.75
27a	Jim Gentile (French bio variation)	5.00	2.50	1.50
27b	Jim Gentile (French bio variation)	5.00	2.50	1.50
28	Marv Breeding	2.50	1.25	.70
29	Brooks Robinson	25.00	12.50	7.50
30	Ron Hansen	2.50	1.25	.70

		NR MT	EX	VG			NR MT	EX	VG
31	Jackie Brandt	2.50	1.25	.70	122	Frank Robinson	15.00	7.50	4.50
32	Dick Williams	25.00	12.50	7.50	123	Bob Purkey	25.00	12.50	7.50
33	Gus Triandos	2.50	1.25	.70	124	Joey Jay	2.50	1.25	.70
34	Milt Pappas	3.00	1.50	.90	125	Jim Brosnan	3.00	1.50	.90
35	Hoyt Wilhelm	15.00	7.50	4.50	126	Jim O'Toole	2.50	1.25	.70
36	Chuck Estrada	2.50	1.25	.70	127	Jerry Lynch	2.50	1.25	.70
37	Vic Power	2.50	1.25	.70	128	Wally Post	55.00	27.00	16.50
38	Johnny Temple	2.50	1.25	.70	129	Ken Hunt	2.50	1.25	.70
39	Bubba Phillips	25.00	12.50	7.50	130	Jerry Zimmerman	2.50	1.25	.70
40	Tito Francona	2.50	1.25	.70	131	Willie McCovey	15.00	7.50	4.50
41	Willie Kirkland	7.00	3.50	2.00	132	Jose Pagan	2.50	1.25	.70
42	John Romano	7.00	3.50	2.00	133	Felipe Alou	3.50	1.75	1.00
43	Jim Perry	4.00	2.00	1.25	134	Jim Davenport	2.50	1.25	.70
44	Woodie Held	2.50	1.25	.70	135	Harvey Kuenn	4.00	2.00	1.25
45	Chuck Essegian	2.50	1.25	.70	136	Orlando Cepeda	6.00	3.00	1.75
46	Roy Sievers	3.50	1.75	1.00	137	Ed Bailey	25.00	12.50	7.50
47	Nellie Fox	6.00	3.00	1.75	138	Sam Jones	25.00	12.50	7.50
48	Al Smith	2.50	1.25	.70	139	Mike McCormick	2.50	1.25	.70
49	Luis Aparicio	15.00	7.50	4.50	140	Juan Marichal	15.00	7.50	4.50
50	Jim Landis	2.50	1.25	.70	141	Jack Sanford	2.50	1.25	.70
51	Minnie Minoso	25.00	12.50	7.50	142a	Willie Mays (big head)	35.00	17.50	10.50
52	Andy Carey	7.00	3.50	2.00	142b	Willie Mays (small head)	50.00	25.00	15.00
53	Sherman Lollar	2.50	1.25	.70	143	Stu Miller	2.50	1.25	.70
54	Bill Pierce	3.50	1.75	1.00	144	Joe Amalfitano	25.00	12.50	7.50
55	Early Wynn	12.00	6.00	3.50	145	Joe Adcock	4.00	2.00	1.25
56	Chuck Schilling	2.50	1.25	.70	146	Frank Bolling	2.50	1.25	.70
57	Pete Runnels	3.00	1.50	.90	147	Ed Mathews	12.00	6.00	3.50
58	Frank Malzone	2.50	1.25	.70	148	Roy McMillan	2.50	1.25	.70
59	Don Buddin	7.00	3.50	2.00	149a	Hank Aaron (script name large)	35.00	17.50	10.50
60	Gary Geiger	2.50	1.25	.70	149b	Hank Aaron (script name small)	35.00	17.50	10.50
61	Carl Yastrzemski	40.00	20.00	12.00	150	Gino Cimoli	2.50	1.25	.70
62	Jackie Jensen	9.00	4.50	2.75	151	Frank Thomas	2.50	1.25	.70
63	Jim Pagliaroni	2.50	1.25	.70	152	Joe Torre	5.00	2.50	1.50
64	Don Schwall	2.50	1.25	.70	153	Lou Burdette	5.00	2.50	1.50
65	Dale Long	2.50	1.25	.70	154	Bob Buhl	3.00	1.50	.90
66	Chuck Cottier	2.50	1.25	.70	155	Carlton Willey	2.50	1.25	.70
67	Billy Klaus	2.50	1.25	.70	156	Lee Maye	2.50	1.25	.70
68	Coot Veal	2.50	1.25	.70	157	Al Spangler	2.50	1.25	.70
69	Marty Keough	2.50	1.25	.70	158	Bill White	3.50	1.75	1.00
70	Willie Tasby	25.00	12.50	7.50	159	Ken Boyer	30.00	15.00	9.00
71	Gene Woodling (photo reversed)	3.00	1.50	.90	160	Joe Cunningham	2.50	1.25	.70
72	Gene Green	2.50	1.25	.70	161	Carl Warwick	7.00	3.50	2.00
73	Dick Donovan	2.50	1.25	.70	162	Carl Sawatski	2.50	1.25	.70
74	Steve Bilko	2.50	1.25	.70	163	Lindy McDaniel	2.50	1.25	.70
75	Rocky Bridges	6.00	3.00	1.75	164	Ernie Broglio	2.50	1.25	.70
76	Eddie Yost	2.50	1.25	.70	165	Larry Jackson	2.50	1.25	.70
77	Leon Wagner	25.00	12.50	7.50	166	Curt Flood	4.00	2.00	1.25
78	Albie Pearson	7.00	3.50	2.00	167	Curt Simmons	8.00	4.00	2.50
79	Ken Hunt	2.50	1.25	.70	168	Alex Grammas	2.50	1.25	.70
80	Earl Averill	2.50	1.25	.70	169	Dick Stuart	3.00	1.50	.90
81	Ryne Duren	4.00	2.00	1.25	170	Bill Mazeroski	25.00	12.50	7.50
82	Ted Kluszewski	4.00	2.00	1.25	171	Don Hoak	2.50	1.25	.70
83	Bob Allison	3.00	1.50	.90	172	Dick Groat	9.00	4.50	2.75
84	Billy Martin	6.00	3.00	1.75	173	Roberto Clemente	30.00	15.00	9.00
85	Harmon Killebrew	12.00	6.00	3.50	174	Bob Skinner	2.50	1.25	.70
86	Zoilo Versalles	2.50	1.25	.70	175	Bill Virdon	4.00	2.00	1.25
87	Lenny Green	2.50	1.25	.70	176	Smoky Burgess	8.00	4.00	2.50
88	Bill Tuttle	2.50	1.25	.70	177	Elroy Face	8.00	4.00	2.50
89	Jim Lemon	2.50	1.25	.70	178	Bob Friend	3.00	1.50	.90
90	Earl Battey	2.50	1.25	.70	179	Vernon Law	3.50	1.75	1.00
91	Camilo Pascual	3.00	1.50	.90	180	Harvey Haddix	3.00	1.50	.90
92	Norm Siebern	2.50	1.25	.70	181	Hal Smith	25.00	12.50	7.50
93	Jerry Lumpe	2.50	1.25	.70	182	Ed Bouchee	2.50	1.25	.70
94	Dick Howser	25.00	12.50	7.50	183	Don Zimmer	4.00	2.00	1.25
95	Gene Stephens	2.50	1.25	.70	184	Ron Santo	5.00	2.50	1.50
96	Leo Posada	2.50	1.25	.70	185	Andre Rodgers	2.50	1.25	.70
97	Joe Pignatano	2.50	1.25	.70	186	Richie Ashburn	6.00	3.00	1.75
98	Jim Archer	2.50	1.25	.70	187	George Altman	2.50	1.25	.70
99	Haywood Sullivan	25.00	12.50	7.50	188	Ernie Banks	25.00	12.50	7.50
100	Art Ditmar	25.00	12.50	7.50	189	Sam Taylor	2.50	1.25	.70
101	Gil Hodges	12.00	6.00	3.50	190	Don Elston	2.50	1.25	.70
102	Charlie Neal	2.50	1.25	.70	191	Jerry Kindall	2.50	1.25	.70
103	Daryl Spencer	2.50	1.25	.70	192	Pancho Herrera	2.50	1.25	.70
104	Maury Wills	5.00	2.50	1.50	193	Tony Taylor	2.50	1.25	.70
105	Tommy Davis	9.00	4.50	2.75	194	Ruben Amaro	2.50	1.25	.70
106	Willie Davis	4.00	2.00	1.25	195	Don Demeter	25.00	12.50	7.50
107	John Roseboro	3.00	1.50	.90	196	Bobby Gene Smith	2.50	1.25	.70
108	John Podres	4.00	2.00	1.25	197	Clay Dalrymple	2.50	1.25	.70
109	Sandy Koufax	30.00	15.00	9.00	198	Robin Roberts	12.00	6.00	3.50
110	Don Drysdale	15.00	7.50	4.50	199	Art Mahaffey	2.50	1.25	.70
111	Larry Sherry	25.00	12.50	7.50	200	John Buzhardt	5.00	2.50	1.50
112	Jim Gilliam	25.00	12.50	7.50					
113	Norm Larker	2.50	1.25	.70					
114	Duke Snider	25.00	12.50	7.50					
115	Stan Williams	2.50	1.25	.70					
116	Gordy Coleman	2.50	1.25	.70					
117	Don Blasingame	25.00	12.50	7.50					
118	Gene Freese	7.00	3.50	2.00					
119	Ed Kasko	2.50	1.25	.70					
120	Gus Bell	2.50	1.25	.70					
121	Vada Pinson	5.00	2.50	1.50					

1963 Post Cereal

Another 200-player, 3-1/2" by 2-1/2" set that, with variations, totals more than 205 cards. Numerous color variations also exist due to the different cereal boxes on which the cards were

printed. As many as 25 cards in the set are considered scarce, making it much more difficult to complete than the other major Post sets. Star cards also command higher prices than in the '61 or '62 Post cards. The 1963 Post cards are almost identical to the '63 Jell-O set, which is a slight 1/4" narrower. Cards are still blank backed, with a color player photo, biographies and statistics on the numbered card fronts. No Post logo appears on the '63 cards. The complete set price does not include the scarcer variations.

		NR MT	EX	VG
Complete Set:		3250.00	1625.00	975.00
Common Player:		1.50	.70	.45
1	Vic Power	3.50	1.75	1.00
2	Bernie Allen	1.50	.70	.45
3	Zoilo Versalles	1.50	.70	.45
4	Rich Rollins	1.50	.70	.45
5	Harmon Killebrew	12.00	6.00	3.50
6	Lenny Green	35.00	17.50	10.50
7	Bob Allison	1.75	.90	.50
8	Earl Battey	1.50	.70	.45
9	Camilo Pascual	1.50	.70	.45
10	Jim Kaat	3.00	1.50	.90
11	Jack Kralick	1.50	.70	.45
12	Bill Skowron	2.00	1.00	.60
13	Bobby Richardson	3.00	1.50	.90
14	Cletis Boyer	2.00	1.00	.60
15	Mickey Mantle	325.00	162.00	97.00
16	Roger Maris	150.00	75.00	45.00
17	Yogi Berra	15.00	7.50	4.50
18	Elston Howard	3.00	1.50	.90
19	Whitey Ford	8.00	4.00	2.50
20	Ralph Terry	2.00	1.00	.60
21	John Blanchard	2.00	1.00	.60
22	Bill Stafford	2.00	1.00	.60
23	Tom Tresh	2.00	1.00	.60
24	Steve Bilko	1.50	.70	.45
25	Bill Moran	1.50	.70	.45
26a	Joe Koppe (1962 Avg. is .277)	1.50	.70	.45
26b	Joe Koppe (1962 Avg. is .227)	12.00	6.00	3.50
27	Felix Torres	1.50	.70	.45
28a	Leon Wagner (lifetime Avg. is .278)			
		1.50	.70	.45
28b	Leon Wagner (lifetime Avg. is .272)			
		12.00	6.00	3.50
29	Albie Pearson	1.50	.70	.45
30	Lee Thomas (photo actually George Thomas)	70.00	35.00	21.00
31	Bob Rodgers	1.50	.70	.45
32	Dean Chance	1.50	.70	.45
33	Ken McBride	1.50	.70	.45
34	George Thomas (photo actually Lee Thomas)	1.50	.70	.45
35	Joe Cunningham	1.50	.70	.45
36a	Nelson Fox (no bat showing)	3.50	1.75	1.00
36b	Nelson Fox (part of bat showing)	10.00	5.00	3.00
37	Luis Aparicio	4.00	2.00	1.25
38	Al Smith	25.00	12.50	7.50
39	Floyd Robinson	80.00	40.00	24.00
40	Jim Landis	1.50	.70	.45
41	Charlie Maxwell	1.50	.70	.45
42	Sherman Lollar	1.50	.70	.45
43	Early Wynn	6.00	3.00	1.75
44	Juan Pizarro	1.50	.70	.45
45	Ray Herbert	1.50	.70	.45
46	Norm Cash	2.00	1.00	.60

		NR MT	EX	VG
47	Steve Boros	1.50	.70	.45
48	Dick McAuliffe	25.00	12.50	7.50
49	Bill Bruton	1.50	.70	.45
50	Rocky Colavito	3.00	1.50	.90
51	Al Kaline	10.00	5.00	3.00
52	Dick Brown	1.50	.70	.45
53	Jim Bunning	90.00	45.00	27.00
54	Hank Aguirre	1.50	.70	.45
55	Frank Lary	1.50	.70	.45
56	Don Mossi	1.50	.70	.45
57	Jim Gentile	1.50	.70	.45
58	Jackie Brandt	1.50	.70	.45
59	Brooks Robinson	10.00	5.00	3.00
60	Ron Hansen	1.50	.70	.45
61	Jerry Adair	150.00	75.00	45.00
62	John Powell	3.00	1.50	.90
63	Russ Snyder	1.50	.70	.45
64	Steve Barber	1.50	.70	.45
65	Milt Pappas	1.50	.70	.45
66	Robin Roberts	4.00	2.00	1.25
67	Tito Francona	1.50	.70	.45
68	Jerry Kindall	1.50	.70	.45
69	Woodie Held	1.50	.70	.45
70	Bubba Phillips	15.00	7.50	4.50
71	Chuck Essegian	1.50	.70	.45
72	Willie Kirkland	1.50	.70	.45
73	Al Luplow	1.50	.70	.45
74	Ty Cline	1.50	.70	.45
75	Dick Donovan	1.50	.70	.45
76	John Romano	1.50	.70	.45
77	Pete Runnels	1.50	.70	.45
78	Ed Bressoud	1.50	.70	.45
79	Frank Malzone	1.50	.70	.45
80	Carl Yastrzemski	275.00	137.00	82.00
81	Gary Geiger	1.50	.70	.45
82	Lou Clinton	1.50	.70	.45
83	Earl Wilson	1.50	.70	.45
84	Bill Monbouquette	1.50	.70	.45
85	Norm Siebern	1.50	.70	.45
86	Jerry Lumpe	80.00	40.00	24.00
87	Manny Jimenez	80.00	40.00	24.00
88	Gino Cimoli	1.50	.70	.45
89	Ed Charles	1.50	.70	.45
90	Ed Rakow	1.50	.70	.45
91	Bob Del Greco	1.50	.70	.45
92	Haywood Sullivan	1.50	.70	.45
93	Chuck Hinton	1.50	.70	.45
94	Ken Retzer	1.50	.70	.45
95	Harry Bright	1.50	.70	.45
96	Bob Johnson	1.50	.70	.45
97	Dave Stenhouse	15.00	7.50	4.50
98	Chuck Cottier	25.00	12.50	7.50
99	Tom Cheney	1.50	.70	.45
100	Claude Osteen	15.00	7.50	4.50
101	Orlando Cepeda	3.00	1.50	.90
102	Charley Hiller	1.50	.70	.45
103	Jose Pagan	1.50	.70	.45
104	Jim Davenport	1.50	.70	.45
105	Harvey Kuenn	2.00	1.00	.60
106	Willie Mays	25.00	12.50	7.50
107	Felipe Alou	1.75	.90	.50
108	Tom Haller	90.00	45.00	27.00
109	Juan Marichal	6.00	3.00	1.75
110	Jack Sanford	1.50	.70	.45
111	Bill O'Dell	1.50	.70	.45
112	Willie McCovey	7.00	3.50	2.00
113	Lee Walls	1.50	.70	.45
114	Jim Gilliam	3.00	1.50	.90
115	Maury Wills	3.00	1.50	.90
116	Ron Fairly	1.50	.70	.45
117	Tommy Davis	2.00	1.00	.60
118	Duke Snider	8.00	4.00	2.50
119	Willie Davis	150.00	75.00	45.00
120	John Roseboro	1.50	.70	.45
121	Sandy Koufax	15.00	7.50	4.50
122	Stan Williams	1.50	.70	.45
123	Don Drysdale	7.00	3.50	2.00
124a	Daryl Spencer (no arm showing)	1.50	.70	.45
124b	Daryl Spencer (part of arm showing)			
		10.00	5.00	3.00
125	Gordy Coleman	1.50	.70	.45
126	Don Blasingame	1.50	.70	.45
127	Leo Cardenas	1.50	.70	.45
128	Eddie Kasko	150.00	75.00	45.00
129	Jerry Lynch	15.00	7.50	4.50
130	Vada Pinson	2.00	1.00	.60
131a	Frank Robinson (no stripes on hat)	8.00	4.00	2.50
131b	Frank Robinson (stripes on hat)	15.00	7.50	4.50
132	John Edwards	1.50	.70	.45
133	Joey Jay	1.50	.70	.45

		NR MT	EX	VG
134	Bob Purkey	1.50	.70	.45
135	Marty Keough	15.00	7.50	4.50
136	Jim O'Toole	1.50	.70	.45
137	Dick Stuart	1.50	.70	.45
138	Bill Mazeroski	2.00	1.00	.60
139	Dick Groat	2.00	1.00	.60
140	Don Hoak	30.00	15.00	9.00
141	Bob Skinner	15.00	7.50	4.50
142	Bill Virdon	2.00	1.00	.60
143	Roberto Clemente	20.00	10.00	6.00
144	Smoky Burgess	1.75	.90	.50
145	Bob Friend	1.50	.70	.45
146	Al McBean	1.50	.70	.45
147	El Roy Face (Elroy)	2.00	1.00	.60
148	Joe Adcock	2.00	1.00	.60
149	Frank Bolling	1.50	.70	.45
150	Roy McMillan	1.50	.70	.45
151	Eddie Mathews	6.00	3.00	1.75
152	Hank Aaron	70.00	35.00	21.00
153	Del Crandall	30.00	15.00	9.00
154a	Bob Shaw (third sentence has "In 1959" twice)	10.00	5.00	3.00
154b	Bob Shaw (third sentence has "In 1959" once)	1.50	.70	.45
155	Lew Burdette	2.00	1.00	.60
156	Joe Torre	3.00	1.50	.90
157	Tony Cloninger	1.50	.70	.45
158	Bill White	2.00	1.00	.60
159	Julian Javier	1.50	.70	.45
160	Ken Boyer	3.00	1.50	.90
161	Julio Gotay	1.50	.70	.45
162	Curt Flood	90.00	45.00	27.00
163	Charlie James	1.50	.70	.45
164	Gene Oliver	1.50	.70	.45
165	Ernie Broglio	1.50	.70	.45
166	Bob Gibson	7.00	3.50	2.00
167a	Lindy McDaniel (asterisk before trade line)	1.50	.70	.45
167b	Lindy McDaniel (no asterisk before trade line)	5.00	2.50	1.50
168	Ray Washburn	1.50	.70	.45
169	Ernie Banks	8.00	4.00	2.50
170	Ron Santo	2.00	1.00	.60
171	George Altman	1.50	.70	.45
172	Billy Williams	90.00	45.00	27.00
173	Andre Rodgers	6.00	3.00	1.75
174	Ken Hubbs	20.00	10.00	6.00
175	Don Landrum	1.50	.70	.45
176	Dick Bertell	15.00	7.50	4.50
177	Roy Sievers	1.75	.90	.50
178	Tony Taylor	1.50	.70	.45
179	John Callison	1.75	.90	.50
180	Don Demeter	1.50	.70	.45
181	Tony Gonzalez	1.50	.70	.45
182	Wes Covington	20.00	10.00	6.00
183	Art Mahaffey	1.50	.70	.45
184	Clay Dalrymple	1.50	.70	.45
185	Al Spangler	1.50	.70	.45
186	Roman Mejias	1.50	.70	.45
187	Bob Aspromonte	275.00	137.00	82.00
188	Norm Larker	30.00	15.00	9.00
189	Johnny Temple	1.50	.70	.45
190	Carl Warwick	1.50	.70	.45
191	Bob Lillis	1.50	.70	.45
192	Dick Farrell	1.50	.70	.45
193	Gil Hodges	7.00	3.50	2.00
194	Marv Throneberry	3.00	1.50	.90
195	Charlie Neal	10.00	5.00	3.00
196	Frank Thomas	150.00	75.00	45.00
197	Richie Ashburn	20.00	10.00	6.00
198	Felix Mantilla	1.50	.70	.45
199	Rod Kanehl	20.00	10.00	6.00
200	Roger Craig	3.00	1.50	.90

1990 Post Cereal

Post Cereal returned in 1990 with a 30-card set. The card fronts feature borders in white, red and blue, with the post logo in the upper left and the Major League Baseball logo in the upper right. Below the full-color shot of the player is his name in red. Backs of the cards show complete major league statistics; underneath is a facsimile autograph. The player photos do not display team logos. Cards were included three per box, inside Alpha-Bits cereal. Considered a difficult set to complete, the insert offer was only available for a limited time.

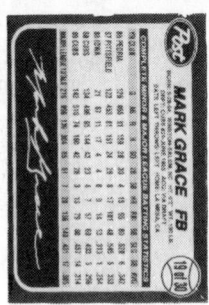

MARK GRACE
CHICAGO CUBS — FIRST BASE

		MT	NR MT	EX
Complete Set:		30.00	22.00	12.00
Common Player:		.30	.25	.12
1	Don Mattingly	.80	.60	.30
2	Roger Clemens	.80	.60	.30
3	Kirby Puckett	.60	.45	.25
4	George Brett	.60	.45	.25
5	Tony Gwynn	.50	.40	.20
6	Ozzie Smith	.50	.40	.20
7	Will Clark	.80	.60	.30
8	Orel Hershiser	.40	.30	.15
9	Ryne Sandberg	1.00	.70	.40
10	Darryl Strawberry	.80	.60	.30
11	Nolan Ryan	1.25	.90	.50
12	Mark McGwire	.80	.60	.30
13	Jim Abbott	.30	.25	.12
14	Bo Jackson	1.50	1.25	.60
15	Kevin Mitchell	.60	.45	.25
16	Jose Canseco	1.25	.90	.50
17	Wade Boggs	.70	.50	.30
18	Dale Murphy	.40	.30	.15
19	Mark Grace	.50	.40	.20
20	Mike Scott	.30	.25	.12
21	Cal Ripken, Jr.	.60	.45	.25
22	Pedro Guerrero	.30	.25	.12
23	Ken Griffey, Jr.	1.50	1.25	.60
24	Eric Davis	.60	.45	.25
25	Rickey Henderson	.80	.60	.30
26	Robin Yount	.40	.30	.15
27	Von Hayes	.30	.25	.12
28	Alan Trammell	.40	.30	.15
29	Dwight Gooden	.80	.60	.30
30	Joe Carter	.40	.30	.15

1986 Quaker Oats

RYNE SANDBERG
CHICAGO CUBS • 2B

The Quaker Company, in conjunction with Topps, produced this 33-card set of current baseball stars for packaging in groups of three in Chewy Granola Bars packages. The cards are noted as the "1st

Annual Collectors Edition." They are numbered and measure 2-1/2" by 3-1/2". Card fronts feature full-color player photos with the product name at the top and the player name, team and position below the photo. The complete set was offered via mail order by the Quaker Company.

		MT	NR MT	EX
	Complete Set:	10.00	7.50	4.00
	Common Player:	.15	.11	.06
1	Willie McGee	.15	.11	.06
2	Dwight Gooden	.60	.45	.25
3	Vince Coleman	.30	.25	.12
4	Gary Carter	.25	.20	.10
5	Jack Clark	.15	.11	.06
6	Steve Garvey	.25	.20	.10
7	Tony Gwynn	.35	.25	.14
8	Dale Murphy	.40	.30	.15
9	Dave Parker	.15	.11	.06
10	Tim Raines	.25	.20	.10
11	Pete Rose	.60	.45	.25
12	Nolan Ryan	.60	.45	.25
13	Ryne Sandberg	.60	.45	.25
14	Mike Schmidt	.40	.30	.15
15	Ozzie Smith	.15	.11	.06
16	Darryl Strawberry	.40	.30	.15
17	Fernando Valenzuela	.20	.15	.08
18	Don Mattingly	1.50	1.25	.60
19	Bret Saberhagen	.20	.15	.08
20	Ozzie Guillen	.15	.11	.06
21	Bert Blyleven	.15	.11	.06
22	Wade Boggs	.80	.60	.30
23	George Brett	.40	.30	.15
24	Darrell Evans	.15	.11	.06
25	Rickey Henderson	.60	.45	.25
26	Reggie Jackson	.30	.25	.12
27	Eddie Murray	.30	.25	.12
28	Phil Niekro	.20	.15	.08
29	Dan Quisenberry	.15	.11	.06
30	Jim Rice	.25	.20	.10
31	Cal Ripken	.30	.25	.12
32	Tom Seaver	.25	.20	.10
33	Dave Winfield	.25	.20	.10
----	Offer Card	.03	.02	.01

cereals, and the complete set was available via a mail-in offer.

		MT	NR MT	EX
	Complete Set:	5.00	3.75	2.00
	Common Player:	.10	.08	.04
1	Eddie Murray	.30	.25	.12
2	Ozzie Smith	.10	.08	.04
3	Ted Simmons	.10	.08	.04
4	Pete Rose	.50	.40	.20
5	Greg Luzinski	.10	.08	.04
6	Andre Dawson	.15	.11	.06
7	Dave Winfield	.25	.20	.10
8	Tom Seaver	.25	.20	.10
9	Jim Rice	.25	.20	.10
10	Fernando Valenzuela	.20	.15	.08
11	Wade Boggs	.60	.45	.25
12	Dale Murphy	.35	.25	.14
13	George Brett	.35	.25	.14
14	Nolan Ryan	.50	.40	.20
15	Rickey Henderson	.50	.40	.20
16	Steve Carlton	.30	.25	.12
17	Rod Carew	.30	.25	.12
18	Steve Garvey	.25	.20	.10
19	Reggie Jackson	.30	.25	.12
20	Dave Concepcion	.10	.08	.04
21	Robin Yount	.20	.15	.08
22	Mike Schmidt	.35	.25	.14
23	Jim Palmer	.20	.15	.08
24	Bruce Sutter	.10	.08	.04
25	Dan Quisenberry	.10	.08	.04
26	Bill Madlock	.10	.08	.04
27	Cecil Cooper	.10	.08	.04
28	Gary Carter	.25	.20	.10
29	Fred Lynn	.15	.11	.06
30	Pedro Guerrero	.15	.11	.06
31	Ron Guidry	.15	.11	.06
32	Keith Hernandez	.20	.15	.08
33	Carlton Fisk	.20	.15	.08

1984 Ralston Purina

This set, produced in conjunction with Topps, has 33 of the game's top players, and is titled "1st Annual Collector's Edition." The full-color photos on the 2-1/2" by 3-1/2" cards are all close-up poses. Topps' logo appears only on the card fronts, and the backs are completely different from Topps' regular issue of 1984. Card backs feature a checkerboard look, coinciding with the well-known Ralston Purina logo. Cards are numbered 1-33, with odd numbers for American Leaguers and even numbered cards for National League players. Four cards were packed in boxes of Cookie Crisp and Donkey Kong Junior brand

1987 Ralston Purina

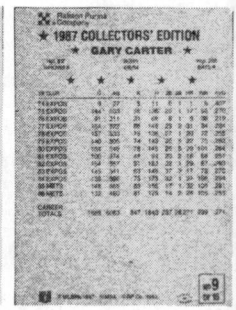

The Ralston Purina Company, in conjunction with Mike Schecter Associates, issued a 15-card set in specially marked boxes of Cookie Crisp and Honey Graham Chex brands of cereal. Three different cards, each measuring 2-1/2" by 3-1/2" and wrapped in cellophane, were inserted in each box. The card fronts contain a full-color photo with the team insignia airbrushed away. Above the photo are two yellow crossed bats and a star, with the player's uniform number inside the star. The card backs are grey with red printing and contain the set name, card number, player's name, personal information and career major league statistics. As part of the Ralston Purina promotion, the company advertised an uncut sheet of cards which was available by finding an "instant-winner" game card or sending $1 plus two non-winning cards. Cards on the uncut sheet are identical in design to the single cards, save the omission of the words "1987 Collectors Edition" in the upper right corner. A complete uncut sheet in mint condition is valued at $10.

	MT	NR MT	EX
Complete Set:	15.00	11.00	6.00
Common Player:	1.00	.70	.40
1 Nolan Ryan	1.25	.90	.50
2 Steve Garvey	1.25	.90	.50
3 Wade Boggs	1.25	.90	.50
4 Dave Winfield	1.25	.90	.50
5 Don Mattingly	3.00	2.25	1.25
6 Don Sutton	1.00	.70	.40
7 Dave Parker	1.00	.70	.40
8 Eddie Murray	1.25	.90	.50
9 Gary Carter	1.25	.90	.50
10 Roger Clemens	1.50	1.25	.60
11 Fernando Valenzuela	1.25	.90	.50
12 Cal Ripken Jr.	1.25	.90	.50
13 Ozzie Smith	1.00	.70	.40
14 Mike Schmidt	1.50	1.25	.60
15 Ryne Sandberg	2.00	1.50	.80

1989 Ralston Purina

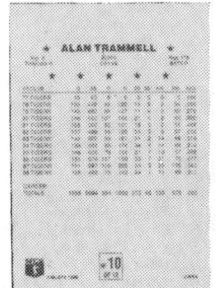

The Ralston Purina Co., in conjunction with Mike Schechter Associates, issued a 12-card "Superstars" set in 1989. As part of a late-spring and early-summer promotion, the standard-size cards were inserted, two per box, in specially-marked boxes of Crisp Crunch, Honey Nut O's, Fruit Rings and Frosted Flakes in most parts of the country. Ads on cereal boxes also offered complete sets through a mail-in offer. The fronts of the cards feature full-color player photos flanked by stars in all four corners. "Super Stars" appears at the top; the player's name and position are at the bottom. The backs include player stats and data, the card number and copyright line.

	MT	NR MT	EX
Complete Set:	9.00	6.75	3.50
Common Player:	.80	.60	.30
1 Ozzie Smith	.80	.60	.30
2 Andre Dawson	.80	.60	.30
3 Darryl Strawberry	1.00	.70	.40
4 Mike Schmidt	1.25	.90	.50
5 Orel Hershiser	.90	.70	.35
6 Tim Raines	.80	.60	.30
7 Roger Clemens	1.25	.90	.50
8 Kirby Puckett	1.00	.70	.40
9 George Brett	1.00	.70	.40
10 Alan Trammell	.80	.60	.30
11 Don Mattingly	1.75	1.25	.70
12 Jose Canseco	2.00	1.50	.80

1954 Red Heart Dog Food

This set of 33 cards was issued in three color-coded series by the Red Heart Dog Food Co. Card fronts feature hand-colored photos on either a blue, green or red background. The 11 red-background cards are scarcer than the 11-card blue or green series. Backs of the 2-5/8" by 3-3/4" cards contain biographical and statistical information along with a Red Heart ad. Each 11-card series was available via a mail-in offer.

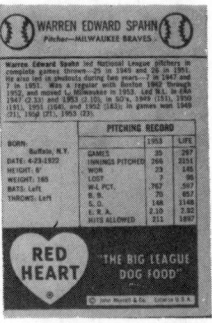

As late as the early 1970s, the company was still sending cards to collectors who requested them.

	NR MT	EX	VG
Complete Set:	2000.00	1000.00	600.00
Common Player:	25.00	12.50	7.50
(1) Richie Ashburn	40.00	20.00	12.00
(2) Frankie Baumholtz	30.00	15.00	9.00
(3) Gus Bell	25.00	12.50	7.50
(4) Billy Cox	30.00	15.00	9.00
(5) Alvin Dark	30.00	15.00	9.00
(6) Carl Erskine	35.00	17.50	10.50
(7) Ferris Fain	25.00	12.50	7.50
(8) Dee Fondy	25.00	12.50	7.50
(9) Nelson Fox	35.00	17.50	10.50
(10) Jim Gilliam	35.00	17.50	10.50
(11) Jim Hegan	30.00	15.00	9.00
(12) George Kell	35.00	17.50	10.50
(13) Ted Kluszewski	35.00	17.50	10.50
(14) Ralph Kiner	45.00	22.00	13.50
(15) Harvey Kuenn	30.00	15.00	9.00
(16) Bob Lemon	45.00	22.00	13.50
(17) Sherman Lollar	25.00	12.50	7.50
(18) Mickey Mantle	400.00	200.00	120.00
(19) Billy Martin	45.00	22.00	13.50
(20) Gil McDougald	35.00	17.50	10.50
(21) Roy McMillan	25.00	12.50	7.50
(22) Minnie Minoso	30.00	15.00	9.00
(23) Stan Musial	250.00	125.00	75.00
(24) Billy Pierce	30.00	15.00	9.00
(25) Al Rosen	35.00	17.50	10.50
(26) Hank Sauer	25.00	12.50	7.50
(27) Red Schoendienst	35.00	17.50	10.50
(28) Enos Slaughter	35.00	17.50	10.50
(29) Duke Snider	90.00	45.00	27.00
(30) Warren Spahn	60.00	30.00	18.00
(31) Sammy White	25.00	12.50	7.50
(32) Eddie Yost	25.00	12.50	7.50
(33) Gus Zernial	25.00	12.50	7.50

1982 Red Lobster Cubs

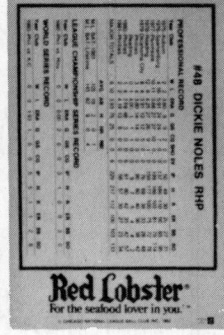

This 28-card set was co-sponsored by the team and a seafood restaurant chain for distribution at a 1982 Cubs promotional game. Card fronts are unbordered color pictures, with player name, number, position and a superimposed facsimile autograph. The set includes 25 players on the 2-1/4" by 3-1/2" cards, along with a card for manager Lee Elia, an unnumbered card for the coaching staff and a team picture. Card backs have complete player statistics and a Red Lobster ad.

		MT	NR MT	EX
Complete Set:		12.00	9.00	4.75
Common Player:		.20	.15	.08
1	Larry Bowa	.40	.30	.15
4	Lee Elia	.20	.15	.08
6	Keith Moreland	.40	.30	.15
7	Jody Davis	.40	.30	.15
10	Leon Durham	.40	.30	.15
15	Junior Kennedy	.20	.15	.08
17	Bump Wills	.20	.15	.08
18	Scot Thompson	.20	.15	.08
21	Jay Johnstone	.25	.20	.10
22	Bill Buckner	.40	.30	.15
23	Ryne Sandberg	3.00	2.25	1.25
24	Jerry Morales	.20	.15	.08
25	Gary Woods	.20	.15	.08
28	Steve Henderson	.20	.15	.08
29	Bob Molinaro	.20	.15	.08
31	Fergie Jenkins	1.00	.70	.40
33	Al Ripley	.20	.15	.08
34	Randy Martz	.20	.15	.08
36	Mike Proly	.20	.15	.08
37	Ken Kravec	.20	.15	.08
38	Willie Hernandez	.30	.25	.12
39	Bill Campbell	.20	.15	.08
41	Dick Tidrow	.20	.15	.08
46	Lee Smith	.50	.40	.20
47	Doug Bird	.20	.15	.08
48	Dickie Noles	.20	.15	.08
——	Team Photo	.20	.15	.08
——	Coaching Staff (Billy Connors, Tom Harmon, Gordy MacKenzie, John Vuckovich, Billy Williams)	.25	.20	.10

1952 Red Man Tobacco

This was the first national set of tobacco cards produced since the golden days of tobacco sets in the early part of the century. There are 52 cards in the set, with 25 top players and one manager from each league. Player selection was made by editor J.G. Taylor Spink of The Sporting News. Cards measure 3-1/2"by 4", including a 1/2" tab at the bottom of each card. These cards were redeemable for a free baseball cap from Red Man. Cards are harder to find with tabs intact, and thus more valuable in that form. Values quoted here are for cards with tabs. Cards with the tabs removed would be valued about 35-40 percent of the quoted figures. Card fronts are full color paintings of each player with biographical information inset in the portrait area. Card backs contain company advertising. Cards are numbered and dated only on the tabs.

		NR MT	EX	VG
Complete Set:		2000.00	1000.00	600.00
Common Player:		20.00	10.00	6.00
1A	Casey Stengel	55.00	27.00	16.50
1N	Leo Durocher	40.00	20.00	12.00

		NR MT	EX	VG
2A	Roberto Avila	20.00	10.00	6.00
2N	Richie Ashburn	35.00	17.50	10.50
3A	Larry "Yogi" Berra	80.00	40.00	24.00
3N	Ewell Blackwell	25.00	12.50	7.50
4A	Gil Coan	20.00	10.00	6.00
4N	Cliff Chambers	20.00	10.00	6.00
5A	Dom DiMaggio	30.00	15.00	9.00
5N	Murry Dickson	20.00	10.00	6.00
6A	Larry Doby	30.00	15.00	9.00
6N	Sid Gordon	20.00	10.00	6.00
7A	Ferris Fain	25.00	12.50	7.50
7N	Granny Hamner	20.00	10.00	6.00
8A	Bob Feller	80.00	40.00	24.00
8N	Jim Hearn	20.00	10.00	6.00
9A	Nelson Fox	35.00	17.50	10.50
9N	Monte Irvin	50.00	25.00	15.00
10A	Johnny Groth	20.00	10.00	6.00
10N	Larry Jansen	20.00	10.00	6.00
11A	Jim Hegan	20.00	10.00	6.00
11N	Willie Jones	20.00	10.00	6.00
12A	Eddie Joost	20.00	10.00	6.00
12N	Ralph Kiner	50.00	25.00	15.00
13A	George Kell	50.00	25.00	15.00
13N	Whitey Lockman	20.00	10.00	6.00
14A	Gil McDougald	30.00	15.00	9.00
14N	Sal Maglie	25.00	12.50	7.50
15A	Orestes Minoso	25.00	12.50	7.50
15N	Willie Mays	150.00	75.00	45.00
16A	Bill Pierce	25.00	12.50	7.50
16N	Stan Musial	150.00	75.00	45.00
17A	Bob Porterfield	20.00	10.00	6.00
17N	Pee Wee Reese	75.00	37.00	22.00
18A	Eddie Robinson	20.00	10.00	6.00
18N	Robin Roberts	50.00	25.00	15.00
19A	Saul Rogovin	20.00	10.00	6.00
19N	Al Schoendienst	30.00	15.00	9.00
20A	Bobby Shantz	25.00	12.50	7.50
20N	Enos Slaughter	50.00	25.00	15.00
21A	Vern Stephens	20.00	10.00	6.00
21N	Duke Snider	100.00	50.00	30.00
22A	Vic Wertz	20.00	10.00	6.00
22N	Warren Spahn	60.00	30.00	18.00
23A	Ted Williams	175.00	87.00	52.00
23N	Eddie Stanky	25.00	12.50	7.50
24A	Early Wynn	50.00	25.00	15.00
24N	Bobby Thomson	30.00	15.00	9.00
25A	Eddie Yost	20.00	10.00	6.00
25N	Earl Torgeson	20.00	10.00	6.00
26A	Gus Zernial	20.00	10.00	6.00
26N	Wes Westrum	20.00	10.00	6.00

1953 Red Man Tobacco

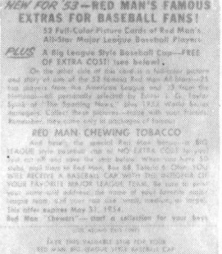

This was the chewing tobacco company's second annual set of 3-1/2" by 4" cards, including the tabs at the bottom of the cards. Formats for both the fronts and backs are similar to the '52 edition. The 1953 Red Man cards, however, include card numbers within the player biographical section, and the card backs are headlined "New for '53." Once again, cards with intact tabs (which were redeemable for a free cap) are more valuable. Prices below are for cards with tabs. Cards with tabs removed are worth about 35-40 percent of the stated values. Each league is represented by 25 players and a manager on the full-color cards, a total of 52.

		NR MT	EX	VG
Complete Set:		2300.00	1150.00	700.00
Common Player:		20.00	10.00	6.00
1A	Casey Stengel	55.00	27.00	16.50
1N	Charlie Dressen	25.00	12.50	7.50
2A	Hank Bauer	25.00	12.50	7.50
2N	Bobby Adams	20.00	10.00	6.00
3A	Larry "Yogi" Berra	80.00	40.00	24.00
3N	Richie Ashburn	35.00	17.50	10.50
4A	Walt Dropo	20.00	10.00	6.00
4N	Joe Black	25.00	12.50	7.50
5A	Nelson Fox	35.00	17.50	10.50
5N	Roy Campanella	80.00	40.00	24.00
6A	Jackie Jensen	25.00	12.50	7.50
6N	Ted Kluszewski	30.00	15.00	9.00
7A	Eddie Joost	20.00	10.00	6.00
7N	Whitey Lockman	20.00	10.00	6.00
8A	George Kell	50.00	25.00	15.00
8N	Sal Maglie	25.00	12.50	7.50
9A	Dale Mitchell	20.00	10.00	6.00
9N	Andy Pafko	25.00	12.50	7.50
10A	Phil Rizzuto	60.00	30.00	18.00
10N	Pee Wee Reese	75.00	37.00	22.00
11A	Eddie Robinson	20.00	10.00	6.00
11N	Robin Roberts	50.00	25.00	15.00
12A	Gene Woodling	25.00	12.50	7.50
12N	Al Schoendienst	30.00	15.00	9.00
13A	Gus Zernial	20.00	10.00	6.00
13N	Enos Slaughter	50.00	25.00	15.00
14A	Early Wynn	50.00	25.00	15.00
14N	Edwin "Duke" Snider	100.00	50.00	30.00
15A	Joe Dobson	20.00	10.00	6.00
15N	Ralph Kiner	50.00	25.00	15.00
16A	Billy Pierce	25.00	12.50	7.50
16N	Hank Sauer	20.00	10.00	6.00
17A	Bob Lemon	50.00	25.00	15.00
17N	Del Ennis	20.00	10.00	6.00
18A	Johnny Mize	50.00	25.00	15.00
18N	Granny Hamner	20.00	10.00	6.00
19A	Bob Porterfield	20.00	10.00	6.00
19N	Warren Spahn	60.00	30.00	18.00
20A	Bobby Shantz	25.00	12.50	7.50
20N	Wes Westrum	20.00	10.00	6.00
21A	"Mickey" Vernon	25.00	12.50	7.50
21N	Hoyt Wilhelm	50.00	25.00	15.00
22A	Dom DiMaggio	30.00	15.00	9.00
22N	Murry Dickson	20.00	10.00	6.00
23A	Gil McDougald	30.00	15.00	9.00
23N	Warren Hacker	20.00	10.00	6.00
24A	Al Rosen	30.00	15.00	9.00
24N	Gerry Staley	20.00	10.00	6.00
25A	Mel Parnell	20.00	10.00	6.00
25N	Bobby Thomson	25.00	12.50	7.50
26A	Roberto Avila	20.00	10.00	6.00
26N	Stan Musial	150.00	75.00	45.00

1954 Red Man Tobacco

In 1954, the Red Man set eliminated managers from the set, and issued only 25 player cards for each league. There are, however, four variations which bring the total set size to 54 full-color cards. Two cards exist for Gus Bell and Enos Slaughter, while American Leaguers George Kell, Sam Mele and Dave Philley are each shown with two different teams. Complete set prices quoted below do not include the scarcer of the variation pairs. Cards still measure 3-1/2" by 4" with tabs intact. Cards without tabs are

worth about 35-40 per cent of the values quoted below. Formats for the cards remain virtually unchanged, with card numbers included within the player information boxes as well as on the tabs.

		NR MT	EX	VG
Complete Set:		1800.00	900.00	550.00
Common Player:		20.00	10.00	6.00
1A	Bobby Avila	20.00	10.00	6.00
1N	Richie Ashburn	35.00	17.50	10.50
2A	Jim Busby	20.00	10.00	6.00
2N	Billy Cox	25.00	12.50	7.50
3A	Nelson Fox	35.00	17.50	10.50
3N	Del Crandall	25.00	12.50	7.50
4Aa	George Kell (Boston)	65.00	32.00	19.50
4Ab	George Kell (Chicago)	75.00	37.00	22.00
4N	Carl Erskine	30.00	15.00	9.00
5A	Sherman Lollar	20.00	10.00	6.00
5N	Monte Irvin	50.00	25.00	15.00
6Aa	Sam Mele (Baltimore)	50.00	25.00	15.00
6Ab	Sam Mele (Chicago)	75.00	37.00	22.00
6N	Ted Kluszewski	30.00	15.00	9.00
7A	Orestes Minoso	25.00	12.50	7.50
7N	Don Mueller	20.00	10.00	6.00
8A	Mel Parnell	20.00	10.00	6.00
8N	Andy Pafko	25.00	12.50	7.50
9Aa	Dave Philley (Cleveland)	50.00	25.00	15.00
9Ab	Dave Philley (Philadelphia)	75.00	37.00	22.00
9N	Del Rice	20.00	10.00	6.00
10A	Billy Pierce	25.00	12.50	7.50
10N	Al Schoendienst	30.00	15.00	9.00
11A	Jim Piersall	25.00	12.50	7.50
11N	Warren Spahn	60.00	30.00	18.00
12A	Al Rosen	30.00	15.00	9.00
12N	Curt Simmons	25.00	12.50	7.50
13A	"Mickey" Vernon	25.00	12.50	7.50
13N	Roy Campanella	80.00	40.00	24.00
14A	Sammy White	20.00	10.00	6.00
14N	Jim Gilliam	30.00	15.00	9.00
15A	Gene Woodling	25.00	12.50	7.50
15N	"Pee Wee" Reese	75.00	37.00	22.00
16A	Ed "Whitey" Ford	65.00	32.00	19.50
16N	Edwin "Duke" Snider	100.00	50.00	30.00
17A	Phil Rizzuto	60.00	30.00	18.00
17N	Rip Repulski	20.00	10.00	6.00
18A	Bob Porterfield	20.00	10.00	6.00
18N	Robin Roberts	50.00	25.00	15.00
19A	Al "Chico" Carrasquel	20.00	10.00	6.00
19Na	Enos Slaughter	90.00	45.00	27.00
19Nb	Gus Bell	90.00	45.00	27.00
20A	Larry "Yogi" Berra	80.00	40.00	24.00
20N	Johnny Logan	20.00	10.00	6.00
21A	Bob Lemon	50.00	25.00	15.00
21N	Johnny Antonelli	25.00	12.50	7.50
22A	Ferris Fain	25.00	12.50	7.50
22N	Gil Hodges	55.00	27.00	16.50
23A	Hank Bauer	25.00	12.50	7.50
23N	Eddie Mathews	55.00	27.00	16.50
24A	Jim Delsing	20.00	10.00	6.00
24N	Lew Burdette	30.00	15.00	9.00
25A	Gil McDougald	30.00	15.00	9.00
25N	Willie Mays	150.00	75.00	45.00

1955 Red Man Tobacco

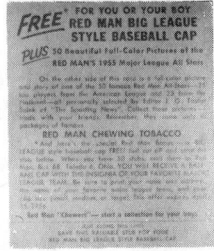

These 50 cards are quite similar to the 1954 edition, with card fronts virtually unchanged except for the data in the biographical box on the color picture area. This set of the 3-1/2" by 4" cards includes 25 players from each league, with no known variations. As with all Red Man sets, those cards complete with the redeemable tabs are more valuable. Values quoted below are for cards with tabs. Cards with the tabs removed are worth about 35-40 percent of those figures.

		NR MT	EX	VG
	Complete Set:	1500.00	750.00	450.00
	Common Player:	20.00	10.00	6.00
1A	Ray Boone	20.00	10.00	6.00
1N	Richie Ashburn	35.00	17.50	10.50
2A	Jim Busby	20.00	10.00	6.00
2N	Del Crandall	25.00	12.50	7.50
3A	Ed "Whitey" Ford	55.00	27.00	16.50
3N	Gil Hodges	65.00	32.00	19.50
4A	Nelson Fox	35.00	17.50	10.50
4N	Brooks Lawrence	20.00	10.00	6.00
5A	Bob Grim	20.00	10.00	6.00
5N	Johnny Logan	20.00	10.00	6.00
6A	Jack Harshman	20.00	10.00	6.00
6N	Sal Maglie	25.00	12.50	7.50
7A	Jim Hegan	20.00	10.00	6.00
7N	Willie Mays	150.00	75.00	45.00
8A	Bob Lemon	50.00	25.00	15.00
8N	Don Mueller	20.00	10.00	6.00
9A	Irv Noren	20.00	10.00	6.00
9N	Bill Sarni	20.00	10.00	6.00
10A	Bob Porterfield	20.00	10.00	6.00
10N	Warren Spahn	60.00	30.00	18.00
11A	Al Rosen	30.00	15.00	9.00
11N	Henry Thompson	20.00	10.00	6.00
12A	"Mickey" Vernon	25.00	12.50	7.50
12N	Hoyt Wilhelm	50.00	25.00	15.00
13A	Vic Wertz	20.00	10.00	6.00
13N	Johnny Antonelli	25.00	12.50	7.50
14A	Early Wynn	50.00	25.00	15.00
14N	Carl Erskine	30.00	15.00	9.00
15A	Bobby Avila	20.00	10.00	6.00
15N	Granny Hamner	20.00	10.00	6.00
16A	Larry "Yogi" Berra	80.00	40.00	24.00
16N	Ted Kluszewski	30.00	15.00	9.00
17A	Joe Coleman	20.00	10.00	6.00
17N	Pee Wee Reese	75.00	37.00	22.00
18A	Larry Doby	30.00	15.00	9.00
18N	Al Schoendienst	30.00	15.00	9.00
19A	Jackie Jensen	25.00	12.50	7.50
19N	Duke Snider	100.00	50.00	30.00
20A	Pete Runnels	20.00	10.00	6.00
20N	Frank Thomas	20.00	10.00	6.00
21A	Jim Piersall	25.00	12.50	7.50
21N	Ray Jablonski	20.00	10.00	6.00
22A	Hank Bauer	25.00	12.50	7.50
22N	James "Dusty" Rhodes	20.00	10.00	6.00
23A	"Chico" Carrasquel	20.00	10.00	6.00
23N	Gus Bell	20.00	10.00	6.00
24A	Orestes Minoso	25.00	12.50	7.50
24N	Curt Simmons	25.00	12.50	7.50
25A	Sandy Consuegra	20.00	10.00	6.00
25N	Marvin Grissom	20.00	10.00	6.00

1988 Revco

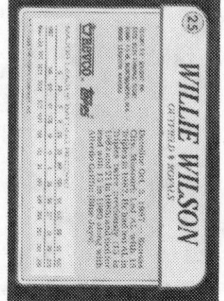

This super-glossy boxed set of 33 standard-size cards was produced by Topps for exclusive distribution by Revco stores east of the Mississippi

River. Card fronts feature a large blue Revco logo in the upper left corner opposite a yellow and black boxed "Topps League Leader" label. Player photos are framed in black and orange with a diagonal player name banner in the lower right corner that lists the player's name, team and position on white, orange and gold stripes. The numbered card backs are horizontal, printed in red and black on white stock and include the player name, followed by personal biographical data, batting/pitching stats and a brief career summary.

		MT	NR MT	EX
	Complete Set:	6.00	4.50	2.50
	Common Player:	.05	.04	.02
1	Tony Gwynn	.25	.20	.10
2	Andre Dawson	.15	.11	.06
3	Vince Coleman	.15	.11	.06
4	Jack Clark	.15	.11	.06
5	Tim Raines	.25	.20	.10
6	Tim Wallach	.10	.08	.04
7	Juan Samuel	.10	.08	.04
8	Nolan Ryan	.40	.30	.15
9	Rick Sutcliffe	.10	.08	.04
10	Kent Tekulve	.05	.04	.02
11	Steve Bedrosian	.10	.08	.04
12	Orel Hershiser	.10	.08	.04
13	Rick Rueschel	.07	.05	.03
14	Fernando Valenzuela	.20	.15	.08
15	Bob Welch	.10	.08	.04
16	Wade Boggs	.80	.60	.30
17	Mark McGwire	.80	.60	.30
18	George Bell	.20	.15	.08
19	Harold Reynolds	.05	.04	.02
20	Paul Molitor	.12	.09	.05
21	Kirby Puckett	.25	.20	.10
22	Kevin Seitzer	.30	.25	.12
23	Brian Downing	.05	.04	.02
24	Dwight Evans	.10	.08	.04
25	Willie Wilson	.07	.05	.03
26	Danny Tartabull	.12	.09	.05
27	Jimmy Key	.07	.05	.03
28	Roger Clemens	.40	.30	.15
29	Dave Stewart	.25	.20	.10
30	Mark Eichhorn	.05	.04	.02
31	Tom Henke	.05	.04	.02
32	Charlie Hough	.05	.04	.02
33	Mark Langston	.10	.08	.04

1988 Rite Aid

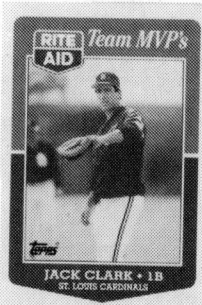
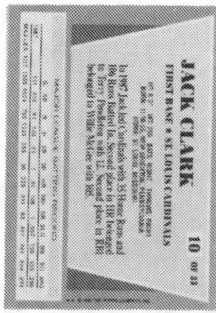

This premiere edition was produced by Topps for distribution by Rite Aid drug and discount stores in the Eastern United States. The boxed set includes 33 standard-size full-color cards with at least one card for each major league team. Four cards in the set highlight MVP's from the 1987 season. Card fronts have white borders and carry a yellow "Team MVP's" header above the player photo which is outlined in red and blue. A large Rite Aid logo appears upper left; the players name appears bottom center. The numbered card backs are black on blue and white card stock in a horizontal layout containing the player name, biography and statistics.

		MT	NR MT	EX
Complete Set:		4.00	3.00	1.50
Common Player:		.05	.04	.02

1	Dale Murphy	.20	.15	.08
2	Andre Dawson	.20	.15	.08
3	Eric Davis	.50	.40	.20
4	Mike Scott	.10	.08	.04
5	Pedro Guerrero	.15	.11	.06
6	Tim Raines	.25	.20	.10
7	Darryl Strawberry	.40	.30	.15
8	Mike Schmidt	.30	.25	.12
9	Mike Dunne	.05	.04	.02
10	Jack Clark	.15	.11	.06
11	Tony Gwynn	.25	.20	.10
12	Will Clark	.30	.25	.12
13	Cal Ripken	.30	.25	.12
14	Wade Boggs	.80	.60	.30
15	Wally Joyner	.30	.25	.12
16	Harold Baines	.12	.09	.05
17	Joe Carter	.12	.09	.05
18	Alan Trammell	.15	.11	.06
19	Kevin Seitzer	.30	.25	.12
20	Paul Molitor	.12	.09	.05
21	Kirby Puckett	.25	.20	.10
22	Don Mattingly	1.00	.70	.40
23	Mark McGwire	.80	.60	.30
24	Alvin Davis	.10	.08	.04
25	Ruben Sierra	.20	.15	.08
26	George Bell	.20	.15	.08
27	Jack Morris	.12	.09	.05
28	Jeff Reardon	.07	.05	.03
29	John Tudor	.07	.05	.03
30	Rick Rueschel	.07	.05	.03
31	Gary Gaetti	.12	.09	.05
32	Jeffrey Leonard	.05	.04	.02
33	Frank Viola	.12	.09	.05

1955 Rodeo Meats Athletics

Cloyd Boyer

Hey Kids —

This set of 2-1/2" by 3-1/2" color cards was issued by a local meat company to commemorate the first year of the Athletics in Kansas City. There are 38 different players included in the set, with nine players known to apppear in two different variations for a total of 47 cards in the set. Most variations are in background colors, although Bobby Shantz is also listed incorrectly as "Schantz" on one variation. The cards are unnumbered, with the Rodeo logo and player name on the fronts, and an ad for a scrapbook album listed on the backs.

		NR MT	EX	VG
Complete Set:		4000.00	2000.00	1200.
Common Player:		70.00	35.00	21.00

(1)	Joe Astroth	70.00	35.00	21.00
(2)	Harold Bevan	100.00	50.00	30.00
(3)	Charles Bishop	100.00	50.00	30.00
(4)	Don Bollweg	100.00	50.00	30.00
(5)	Lou Boudreau	200.00	100.00	60.00
(6)	Cloyd Boyer (blue background)	100.00	50.00	30.00
(7)	Cloyd Boyer (pink background)	70.00	35.00	21.00
(8)	Ed Burtschy	100.00	50.00	30.00
(9)	Art Ceccarelli	70.00	35.00	21.00
(10)	Joe DeMaestri (pea green background)	100.00	50.00	30.00
(11)	Joe DeMaestri (light green background)	70.00	35.00	21.00

		NR MT	EX	VG
(12)	Art Ditmar	70.00	35.00	21.00
(13)	John Dixon	100.00	50.00	30.00
(14)	Jim Finigan	70.00	35.00	21.00
(15)	Marion Fricano	100.00	50.00	30.00
(16)	John Gray	100.00	50.00	30.00
(17)	Tom Gorman	70.00	35.00	21.00
(18)	Ray Herbert	70.00	35.00	21.00
(19)	Forest "Spook" Jacobs (Forrest)	100.00	50.00	30.00
(20)	Alex Kellner	100.00	50.00	30.00
(21)	Harry Kraft (Craft)	70.00	35.00	21.00
(22)	Jack Littrell	70.00	35.00	21.00
(23)	Hector Lopez	80.00	40.00	24.00
(24)	Oscar Melillo	70.00	35.00	21.00
(25)	Arnold Portocarrero (purple background)	100.00	50.00	30.00
(26)	Arnold Portocarrero (grey background)	70.00	35.00	21.00
(27)	Vic Power (pink background)	125.00	62.00	37.00
(28)	Vic Power (yellow background)	80.00	40.00	24.00
(29)	Vic Raschi	100.00	50.00	30.00
(30)	Bill Renna (dark pink background)	100.00	50.00	30.00
(31)	Bill Renna (light pink background)	70.00	35.00	21.00
(32)	Al Robertson	100.00	50.00	30.00
(33)	Johnny Sain	125.00	62.00	37.00
(34a)	Bobby Schantz (incorrect spelling)	200.00	100.00	60.00
(34b)	Bobby Shantz (correct spelling)	125.00	62.00	37.00
(35)	Wilmer Shantz (orange background)	100.00	50.00	30.00
(36)	Wilmer Shantz (purple background)	70.00	35.00	21.00
(37)	Harry Simpson	70.00	35.00	21.00
(38)	Enos Slaughter	300.00	150.00	90.00
(39)	Lou Sleater	70.00	35.00	21.00
(40)	George Susce	70.00	35.00	21.00
(41)	Bob Trice	100.00	50.00	30.00
(42)	Elmer Valo (yellow background)	100.00	50.00	30.00
(43)	Elmer Valo (green background)	70.00	35.00	21.00
(44)	Bill Wilson (yellow background)	100.00	50.00	30.00
(45)	Bill Wilson (purple background)	70.00	35.00	21.00
(46)	Gus Zernial	80.00	40.00	24.00

1956 Rodeo Meats Athletics

Gus Zernial

Hey Kids...

Rodeo Meats issued another Kansas City Athletics set in 1956, but this one was a much smaller 13-card set. The 2-1/2" by 3-1/2" cards are again unnumbered, with the player name and Rodeo logo on the fronts. Card backs feature some of the same graphics and copy as the 1955 cards, but the album offer is omitted. The full-color cards were only available in packages of Rodeo hot dogs.

		NR MT	EX	VG
Complete Set:		1000.00	500.00	300.00
Common Player:		70.00	35.00	21.00

(1)	Joe Astroth	70.00	35.00	21.00
(2)	Lou Boudreau	200.00	100.00	60.00
(3)	Joe DeMaestri	70.00	35.00	21.00
(4)	Art Ditmar	70.00	35.00	21.00
(5)	Jim Finigan	70.00	35.00	21.00
(6)	Hector Lopez	80.00	40.00	24.00

		NR MT	EX	VG
(7)	Vic Power	80.00	40.00	24.00
(8)	Bobby Shantz	125.00	62.00	37.00
(9)	Harry Simpson	70.00	35.00	21.00
(10)	Enos Slaughter	200.00	100.00	60.00
(11)	Elmer Valo	70.00	35.00	21.00
(12)	Gus Zernial	80.00	40.00	24.00

1970 Rold Gold Pretzels

The 1970 Rold Gold Pretzels set of 15 cards honors the "Greatest Players Ever" in the first 100 years of baseball as chosen by the Baseball Writers of America. The cards, which measure 2-1/4" by 3-1/2" in size, feature a simulated 3-D effect. The set was re-released in 1972 by Kellogg's in packages of Danish-Go-Rounds. Rold Gold cards can be differentiated from the Kellogg's cards of 1972 by the 1970 copyright date found on the card reverse.

		NR MT	EX	VG
	Complete Set:	40.00	20.00	12.00
	Common Player:	1.00	.50	.30
1	Walter Johnson	2.50	1.25	.70
2	Rogers Hornsby	1.50	.70	.45
3	John McGraw	1.00	.50	.30
4	Mickey Cochrane	1.00	.50	.30
5	George Sisler	1.00	.50	.30
6	Babe Ruth	10.00	5.00	3.00
7	Robert "Lefty" Grove	1.50	.70	.45
8	Harold "Pie" Traynor	1.00	.50	.30
9	Honus Wagner	1.75	.90	.50
10	Eddie Collins	1.00	.50	.30
11	Tris Speaker	1.50	.70	.45
12	Cy Young	1.00	.50	.30
13	Lou Gehrig	6.00	3.00	1.75
14	Babe Ruth	10.00	5.00	3.00
15	Ty Cobb	6.00	3.00	1.75

1950 Royal Desserts

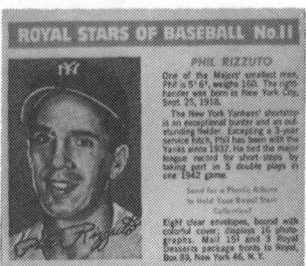

This set of 24 cards was issued one per box on the backs of various Royal Dessert products over a period of three years. The basic set contains 24 players, however a number of variations create the much

higher total for the set. In 1950, Royal issued cards with two different tints - black and white with red, or blue and white with red. Over the next two years, various sentences of the cards' biographies were updated up to three times in some cases. Some players from the set left the majors after 1950 and others were apparently never updated, but the 23 biography updates that do exist, added to the original 24 cards issued in 1950, give the set a total of 47 cards. The 2-1/2" by 3-1/2" cards are blank-backed with personal and playing biographies alongside the card front photos.

		NR MT	EX	VG
	Complete Set:	900.00	450.00	270.00
	Common Player:	20.00	10.00	6.00
1a	Stan Musial (2nd paragraph begins "Musial's 207...")	125.00	62.00	37.00
1b	Stan Musial (2nd paragraph begins "Musial batted...")	125.00	62.00	37.00
2a	Pee Wee Reese (2nd paragraph begins "Pee Wee's...")	70.00	35.00	21.00
2b	Pee Wee Reese (2nd paragraph begins "Captain...")	70.00	35.00	21.00
3a	George Kell (2nd paragraph ends "...in 1945, '46.")	35.00	17.50	10.50
3b	George Kell (2nd paragraph ends "...two base hits, 56.")	35.00	17.50	10.50
4a	Dom DiMaggio (2nd paragraph ends "...during 1947.")	30.00	15.00	9.00
4b	Dom DiMaggio (2nd paragraph ends "...with 11.")	30.00	15.00	9.00
5a	Warren Spahn (2nd paragraph ends "...shutouts 7.")	50.00	25.00	15.00
5b	Warren Spahn (2nd paragraph ends "...with 191.")	50.00	25.00	15.00
6a	Andy Pafko (2nd paragraph ends "...7 games.")	25.00	12.50	7.50
6b	Andy Pafko (2nd paragraph ends "...National League.")	25.00	12.50	7.50
6c	Andy Pafko (2nd paragraph ends "...weighs 190.")	25.00	12.50	7.50
7a	Andy Seminick (2nd paragraph ends "...as outfield.")	20.00	10.00	6.00
7b	Andy Seminick (2nd paragraph ends "...since 1916.")	20.00	10.00	6.00
7c	Andy Seminick (2nd paragraph ends "...in the outfield.")	20.00	10.00	6.00
7d	Andy Seminick (2nd paragraph ends "...right handed.")	20.00	10.00	6.00
8a	Lou Brissie (2nd paragraph ends "...when pitching.")	20.00	10.00	6.00
8b	Lou Brissie (2nd paragraph ends "...weighs 215.")	20.00	10.00	6.00
9a	Ewell Blackwell (2nd paragraph begins "Despite recent illness...")	25.00	12.50	7.50
9b	Ewell Blackwell (2nd paragraph begins "Blackwell's...")	25.00	12.50	7.50
10a	Bobby Thomson (2nd paragraph begins "In 1949...")	25.00	12.50	7.50
10b	Bobby Thomson (2nd paragraph begins "Thomson is...")	25.00	12.50	7.50
11a	Phil Rizzuto (2nd paragraph ends "...one 1942 game.")	60.00	30.00	18.00
11b	Phil Rizzuto (2nd paragraph ends "...Most Valuable Player.")	60.00	30.00	18.00
12	Tommy Henrich	30.00	15.00	9.00
13	Joe Gordon	25.00	12.50	7.50
14a	Ray Scarborough (Senators)	20.00	10.00	6.00
14b	Ray Scarborough (White Sox, 2nd paragraph ends "...military service.")	20.00	10.00	6.00
14c	Ray Scarborough (White Sox, 2nd paragraph ends "...the season.")	20.00	10.00	6.00
14d	Ray Scarborough (Red Sox)	20.00	10.00	6.00
15a	Stan Rojek (Pirates)	20.00	10.00	6.00
15b	Stan Rojek (Browns)	20.00	10.00	6.00
16	Luke Appling	30.00	15.00	9.00
17	Willard Marshall	20.00	10.00	6.00
18	Alvin Dark	30.00	15.00	9.00
19a	Dick Sisler (2nd paragraph ends "...service record.")	20.00	10.00	6.00
19b	Dick Sisler (2nd paragraph ends "...National League flag.")	20.00	10.00	6.00
19c	Dick Sisler (2nd paragraph ends "...Nov. 2, 1920.")	20.00	10.00	6.00
19d	Dick Sisler (2nd paragraph ends "...from '46 to '48.")	20.00	10.00	6.00
20	Johnny Ostrowski	20.00	10.00	6.00

		NR MT	EX	VG
21a	Virgil Trucks (2nd paragraph ends "...in military service.")	25.00	12.50	7.50
21b	Virgil Trucks (2nd paragraph ends "...that year.")	25.00	12.50	7.50
21c	Virgil Trucks (2nd paragraph ends "...for military service.")	25.00	12.50	7.50
22	Eddie Robinson	20.00	10.00	6.00
23	Nanny Fernandez	20.00	10.00	6.00
24	Ferris Fain	25.00	12.50	7.50

		NR MT	EX	VG
(1)	Ewell Blackwell	18.00	9.00	5.50
(2)	Leland V. Brissie Jr.	15.00	7.50	4.50
(3)	Alvin Dark	18.00	9.00	5.50
(4)	Dom DiMaggio	25.00	12.50	7.50
(5)	Ferris Fain	15.00	7.50	4.50
(6)	George Kell	28.00	14.00	8.50
(7)	Stan Musial	75.00	37.00	22.00
(8)	Andy Pafko	18.00	9.00	5.50
(9)	Pee Wee Reese	35.00	17.50	10.50
(10)	Phil Rizzuto	35.00	17.50	10.50
(11)	Eddie Robinson	15.00	7.50	4.50
(12)	Ray Scarborough	15.00	7.50	4.50
(13)	Andy Seminick	15.00	7.50	4.50
(14)	Dick Sisler	15.00	7.50	4.50
(15)	Warren Spahn	35.00	17.50	10.50
(16)	Bobby Thomson	25.00	12.50	7.50

The 25 most valuable baseball cards
(From The Standard Catalog of Baseball Cards, 2nd Edition)

1. 1909-1911 T206 Honus Wagner $200,000
2. 1909-1911 T206 Joe Doyle (N.Y. Natl., hands above head) $30,000
3. 1933 Goudey Napoleon (Larry) Lajoie $30,000
4. 1932 U.S. Caramel Charles (Lindy) Lindstrom $25,000
5. 1909-1911 T206 Eddie Plank $25,000
6. 1909-1911 Sherry Magie $15,000
7. 1909-1911 E90-1 American Caramel Mike Mitchell $10,000
8. 1951 Topps Current All-Stars Robin Roberts $9,500
9. 1952 Topps Mickey Mantle $8,900
10. 1951 Topps Current All-Stars Eddie Stanky $8,500
11. 1951 Topps Current All-Stars Jim Konstanty $8,500
12. 1909-1911 E90-1 American Caramel Shoeless Joe Jackson $7,500
13. 1909-1911 T206 Ray Demmitt (St. Louis) $7,500
14. 1912 T207 Irving Lewis $7,500
15. 1911 T3 Ty Cobb $6,500
16. 1912 T207 Louis Lowdermilk $5,500
17. 1933 Goudey Babe Ruth #53 ..... $5,200
18. 1933 Goudey Babe Ruth #181 ..... $4,500
19. 1933 Goudey Babe Ruth #149 ..... $4,500
20. 1951 Bowman Mickey Mantle $4,500
21. 1933 Goudey Babe Ruth #144 ..... $4,400
22. 1911 T205 Ty Cobb $4,000
23. 1934 Goudey Lou Gehrig $3,100
24. 1954 Bowman Ted Williams $3,000
25. 1933 DeLong Lou Gehrig $3,000

1952 Royal Desserts

This set, issued as a premium by Royal Desserts in 1952, consists of 16 unnumbered black and white cards, each measuring 5" by 7". The cards include the inscription "To A Royal Fan" along with the player's facsimile autograph.

	NR MT	EX	VG
Complete Set:	400.00	200.00	120.00
Common Player:	15.00	7.50	4.50

1988 Score

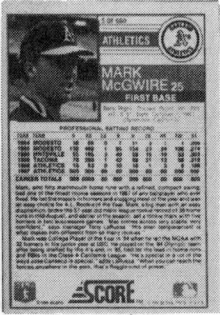

A fifth member joined the group of nationally distributed baseball cards in 1988. Titled "Score," the new cards are characterized by extremely sharp and excellent full-color photography and printing. Card backs are full-color also and carry a player head-shot, along with a brief biography and player personal and statistical information. The 660 cards in the set each measure 2-1/2" by 3-1/2" in size. The fronts come with one of six different border colors - blue, red, green, purple, orange and gold - which are equally divided at 110 cards per color. The Score set was produced by Major League Marketing, the same company that markets the "triple-action" Sportflics card sets.

	MT	NR MT	EX
Complete Set:	25.00	20.00	10.00
Common Player:	.04	.03	.02
1	Don Mattingly	1.50	1.25	.60
2	Wade Boggs	.60	.45	.25
3	Tim Raines	.20	.15	.08
4	Andre Dawson	.15	.11	.06
5	Mark McGwire	1.25	.90	.50
6	Kevin Seitzer	.60	.45	.25
7	Wally Joyner	.35	.25	.14
8	Jesse Barfield	.10	.08	.04
9	Pedro Guerrero	.15	.11	.06
10	Eric Davis	.60	.45	.25
11	George Brett	.30	.25	.12
12	Ozzie Smith	.12	.09	.05
13	Rickey Henderson	.25	.20	.10
14	Jim Rice	.20	.15	.08
15	*Matt Nokes*	.30	.25	.12
16	Mike Schmidt	.40	.30	.15
17	Dave Parker	.12	.09	.05
18	Eddie Murray	.25	.20	.10
19	Andres Galarraga	.12	.09	.05
20	Tony Fernandez	.10	.08	.04

		MT	NR MT	EX
21	Kevin McReynolds	.12	.09	.05
22	B.J. Surhoff	.10	.08	.04
23	Pat Tabler	.06	.05	.02
24	Kirby Puckett	.25	.20	.10
25	Benny Santiago	.35	.25	.14
26	Ryne Sandberg	.20	.15	.08
27	Kelly Downs	.08	.06	.03
28	Jose Cruz	.06	.05	.02
29	Pete O'Brien	.06	.05	.02
30	Mark Langston	.10	.08	.04
31	Lee Smith	.08	.06	.03
32	Juan Samuel	.10	.08	.04
33	Kevin Bass	.06	.05	.02
34	R.J. Reynolds	.04	.03	.02
35	Steve Sax	.12	.09	.05
36	John Kruk	.08	.06	.03
37	Alan Trammell	.15	.11	.06
38	Chris Bosio	.06	.05	.02
39	Brook Jacoby	.08	.06	.03
40	Willie McGee	.10	.08	.04
41	Dave Magadan	.10	.08	.04
42	Fred Lynn	.10	.08	.04
43	Kent Hrbek	.12	.09	.05
44	Brian Downing	.06	.05	.02
45	Jose Canseco	1.75	1.25	.70
46	Jim Presley	.08	.06	.03
47	Mike Stanley	.06	.05	.02
48	Tony Pena	.06	.05	.02
49	David Cone	.80	.60	.30
50	Rick Sutcliffe	.08	.06	.03
51	Doug Drabek	.10	.08	.04
52	Bill Doran	.06	.05	.02
53	Mike Scioscia	.06	.05	.02
54	Candy Maldonado	.06	.05	.02
55	Dave Winfield	.20	.15	.08
56	Lou Whitaker	.20	.15	.08
57	Tom Henke	.06	.05	.02
58	Ken Gerhart	.06	.05	.02
59	Glenn Braggs	.08	.06	.03
60	Julio Franco	.08	.06	.03
61	Charlie Leibrandt	.06	.05	.02
62	Gary Gaetti	.10	.08	.04
63	Bob Boone	.06	.05	.02
64	Luis Polonia	.20	.15	.08
65	Dwight Evans	.10	.08	.04
66	Phil Bradley	.08	.06	.03
67	Mike Boddicker	.06	.05	.02
68	Vince Coleman	.15	.11	.06
69	Howard Johnson	.08	.06	.03
70	Tim Wallach	.08	.06	.03
71	Keith Moreland	.06	.05	.02
72	Barry Larkin	.20	.15	.08
73	Alan Ashby	.04	.03	.02
74	Rick Rhoden	.06	.05	.02
75	Darrell Evans	.08	.06	.03
76	Dave Stieb	.08	.06	.03
77	Dan Plesac	.08	.06	.03
78	Will Clark	1.25	.90	.50
79	Frank White	.06	.05	.02
80	Joe Carter	.10	.08	.04
81	Mike Witt	.06	.05	.02
82	Terry Steinbach	.10	.08	.04
83	Alvin Davis	.10	.08	.04
84	Tom Herr	.06	.05	.02
85	Vance Law	.06	.05	.02
86	Kal Daniels	.15	.11	.06
87	Rick Honeycutt	.04	.03	.02
88	Alfredo Griffin	.06	.05	.02
89	Bret Saberhagen	.20	.15	.08
90	Bert Blyleven	.10	.08	.04
91	Jeff Reardon	.08	.06	.03
92	Cory Snyder	.15	.11	.06
93	Greg Walker	.06	.05	.02
94	Joe Magrane	.40	.30	.15
95	Rob Deer	.06	.05	.02
96	Ray Knight	.06	.05	.02
97	Casey Candaele	.04	.03	.02
98	John Cerutti	.06	.05	.02
99	Buddy Bell	.08	.06	.03
100	Jack Clark	.12	.09	.05
101	Eric Bell	.06	.05	.02
102	Willie Wilson	.08	.06	.03
103	Dave Schmidt	.04	.03	.02
104	Dennis Eckersley	.10	.08	.04
105	Don Sutton	.12	.09	.05
106	Danny Tartabull	.15	.11	.06
107	Fred McGriff	1.00	.70	.40
108	Les Straker	.15	.11	.06
109	Lloyd Moseby	.06	.05	.02
110	Roger Clemens	.50	.40	.20
111	Glenn Hubbard	.04	.03	.02
112	Ken Williams	.20	.15	.08

		MT	NR MT	EX
113	Ruben Sierra	.35	.25	.14
114	Stan Jefferson	.06	.05	.02
115	Milt Thompson	.04	.03	.02
116	Bobby Bonilla	.12	.09	.05
117	Wayne Tolleson	.04	.03	.02
118	Matt Williams	2.00	1.50	.80
119	Chet Lemon	.06	.05	.02
120	Dale Sveum	.06	.05	.02
121	Dennis Boyd	.06	.05	.02
122	Brett Butler	.06	.05	.02
123	Terry Kennedy	.06	.05	.02
124	Jack Howell	.06	.05	.02
125	Curt Young	.06	.05	.02
126a	Dale Valle (first name incorrect)	.25	.20	.10
126b	Dave Valle (correct spelling)	.06	.05	.02
127	Curt Wilkerson	.04	.03	.02
128	Tim Teufel	.04	.03	.02
129	Ozzie Virgil	.04	.03	.02
130	Brian Fisher	.06	.05	.02
131	Lance Parrish	.12	.09	.05
132	Tom Browning	.08	.06	.03
133a	Larry Anderson (incorrect spelling)	.25	.20	.10
133b	Larry Andersen (correct spelling)	.06	.05	.02
134a	Bob Brenley (incorrect spelling)	.25	.20	.10
134b	Bob Brenly (correct spelling)	.06	.05	.02
135	Mike Marshall	.10	.08	.04
136	Gerald Perry	.08	.06	.03
137	Bobby Meacham	.04	.03	.02
138	Larry Herndon	.04	.03	.02
139	Fred Manrique	.12	.09	.05
140	Charlie Hough	.06	.05	.02
141	Ron Darling	.10	.08	.04
142	Herm Winningham	.04	.03	.02
143	Mike Diaz	.06	.05	.02
144	Mike Jackson	.15	.11	.06
145	Denny Walling	.04	.03	.02
146	Rob Thompson	.06	.05	.02
147	Franklin Stubbs	.06	.05	.02
148	Albert Hall	.04	.03	.02
149	Bobby Witt	.08	.06	.03
150	Lance McCullers	.06	.05	.02
151	Scott Bradley	.04	.03	.02
152	Mark McLemore	.04	.03	.02
153	Tim Laudner	.04	.03	.02
154	Greg Swindell	.15	.11	.06
155	Marty Barrett	.06	.05	.02
156	Mike Heath	.04	.03	.02
157	Gary Ward	.06	.05	.02
158a	Lee Mazilli (incorrect spelling)	.25	.20	.10
158b	Lee Mazzilli (correct spelling)	.08	.06	.03
159	Tom Foley	.04	.03	.02
160	Robin Yount	.30	.25	.12
161	Steve Bedrosian	.10	.08	.04
162	Bob Walk	.04	.03	.02
163	Nick Esasky	.06	.05	.02
164	Ken Caminiti	.25	.20	.10
165	Jose Uribe	.04	.03	.02
166	Dave Anderson	.04	.03	.02
167	Ed Whitson	.04	.03	.02
168	Ernie Whitt	.06	.05	.02
169	Cecil Cooper	.08	.06	.03
170	Mike Pagliarulo	.08	.06	.03
171	Pat Sheridan	.04	.03	.02
172	Chris Bando	.04	.03	.02
173	Lee Lacy	.04	.03	.02
174	Steve Lombardozzi	.04	.03	.02
175	Mike Greenwell	1.25	.90	.50
176	Greg Minton	.04	.03	.02
177	Moose Haas	.04	.03	.02
178	Mike Kingery	.04	.03	.02
179	Greg Harris	.04	.03	.02
180	Bo Jackson	1.50	1.25	.70
181	Carmelo Martinez	.06	.05	.02
182	Alex Trevino	.04	.03	.02
183	Ron Oester	.04	.03	.02
184	Danny Darwin	.04	.03	.02
185	Mike Krukow	.06	.05	.02
186	Rafael Palmeiro	.35	.25	.14
187	Tim Burke	.04	.03	.02
188	Roger McDowell	.08	.06	.03
189	Garry Templeton	.06	.05	.02
190	Terry Pendleton	.06	.05	.02
191	Larry Parrish	.06	.05	.02
192	Rey Quinones	.04	.03	.02
193	Joaquin Andujar	.06	.05	.02
194	Tom Brunansky	.08	.06	.03
195	Donnie Moore	.04	.03	.02
196	Dan Pasqua	.08	.06	.03
197	Jim Gantner	.04	.03	.02
198	Mark Eichhorn	.06	.05	.02
199	John Grubb	.04	.03	.02

#	Player	MT	NR MT	EX
200	Bill Ripken	.20	.15	.08
201	Sam Horn	.30	.25	.12
202	Todd Worrell	.08	.06	.03
203	Terry Leach	.04	.03	.02
204	Garth Iorg	.04	.03	.02
205	Brian Dayett	.04	.03	.02
206	Bo Diaz	.06	.05	.02
207	Craig Reynolds	.04	.03	.02
208	Brian Holton	.08	.06	.03
209	Marvelle Wynne (Marvell)	.04	.03	.02
210	Dave Concepcion	.06	.05	.02
211	Mike Davis	.06	.05	.02
212	Devon White	.15	.11	.06
213	Mickey Brantley	.04	.03	.02
214	Greg Gagne	.04	.03	.02
215	Oddibe McDowell	.06	.05	.02
216	Jimmy Key	.08	.06	.03
217	Dave Bergman	.04	.03	.02
218	Calvin Schiraldi	.04	.03	.02
219	Larry Sheets	.06	.05	.02
220	Mike Easler	.06	.05	.02
221	Kurt Stillwell	.08	.06	.03
222	Chuck Jackson	.15	.11	.06
223	Dave Martinez	.08	.06	.03
224	Tim Leary	.06	.05	.02
225	Steve Garvey	.20	.15	.08
226	Greg Mathews	.06	.05	.02
227	Doug Sisk	.04	.03	.02
228	Dave Henderson	.08	.06	.03
229	Jimmy Dwyer	.04	.03	.02
230	Larry Owen	.04	.03	.02
231	Andre Thornton	.06	.05	.02
232	Mark Salas	.04	.03	.02
233	Tom Brookens	.04	.03	.02
234	Greg Brock	.06	.05	.02
235	Rance Mulliniks	.04	.03	.02
236	Bob Brower	.06	.05	.02
237	Joe Niekro	.06	.05	.02
238	Scott Bankhead	.04	.03	.02
239	Doug DeCinces	.06	.05	.02
240	Tommy John	.12	.09	.05
241	Rich Gedman	.06	.05	.02
242	Ted Power	.04	.03	.02
243	Dave Meads	.12	.09	.05
244	Jim Sundberg	.06	.05	.02
245	Ken Oberkfell	.04	.03	.02
246	Jimmy Jones	.08	.06	.03
247	Ken Landreaux	.04	.03	.02
248	Jose Oquendo	.04	.03	.02
249	John Mitchell	.15	.11	.06
250	Don Baylor	.08	.06	.03
251	Scott Fletcher	.06	.05	.02
252	Al Newman	.04	.03	.02
253	Carney Lansford	.08	.06	.03
254	Johnny Ray	.06	.05	.02
255	Gary Pettis	.04	.03	.02
256	Ken Phelps	.06	.05	.02
257	Rick Leach	.04	.03	.02
258	Tim Stoddard	.04	.03	.02
259	Ed Romero	.04	.03	.02
260	Sid Bream	.06	.05	.02
261a	Tom Neidenfuer (incorrect spelling)	.25	.20	.10
261b	Tom Niedenfuer (correct spelling)	.06	.05	.02
262	Rick Dempsey	.06	.05	.02
263	Lonnie Smith	.06	.05	.02
264	Bob Forsch	.06	.05	.02
265	Barry Bonds	.10	.08	.04
266	Willie Randolph	.06	.05	.02
267	Mike Ramsey	.04	.03	.02
268	Don Slaught	.04	.03	.02
269	Mickey Tettleton	.04	.03	.02
270	Jerry Reuss	.06	.05	.02
271	Marc Sullivan	.04	.03	.02
272	Jim Morrison	.04	.03	.02
273	Steve Balboni	.06	.05	.02
274	Dick Schofield	.04	.03	.02
275	John Tudor	.08	.06	.03
276	Gene Larkin	.20	.15	.08
277	Harold Reynolds	.06	.05	.02
278	Jerry Browne	.06	.05	.02
279	Willie Upshaw	.06	.05	.02
280	Ted Higuera	.08	.06	.03
281	Terry McGriff	.04	.03	.02
282	Terry Puhl	.04	.03	.02
283	Mark Wasinger	.12	.09	.05
284	Luis Salazar	.04	.03	.02
285	Ted Simmons	.08	.06	.03
286	John Shelby	.04	.03	.02
287	John Smiley	.30	.25	.12
288	Curt Ford	.04	.03	.02
289	Steve Crawford	.04	.03	.02
290	Dan Quisenberry	.06	.05	.02
291	Alan Wiggins	.04	.03	.02
292	Randy Bush	.04	.03	.02
293	John Candelaria	.06	.05	.02
294	Tony Phillips	.04	.03	.02
295	Mike Morgan	.04	.03	.02
296	Bill Wegman	.04	.03	.02
297a	Terry Franconia (incorrect spelling)	.25	.20	.10
297b	Terry Francona (correct spelling)	.06	.05	.02
298	Mickey Hatcher	.04	.03	.02
299	Andres Thomas	.06	.05	.02
300	Bob Stanley	.04	.03	.02
301	Alfredo Pedrique	.12	.09	.05
302	Jim Lindeman	.06	.05	.02
303	Wally Backman	.06	.05	.02
304	Paul O'Neill	.06	.05	.02
305	Hubie Brooks	.08	.06	.03
306	Steve Buechele	.04	.03	.02
307	Bobby Thigpen	.08	.06	.03
308	George Hendrick	.06	.05	.02
309	John Moses	.04	.03	.02
310	Ron Guidry	.12	.09	.05
311	Bill Schroeder	.04	.03	.02
312	Jose Nunez	.20	.15	.08
313	Bud Black	.04	.03	.02
314	Joe Sambito	.04	.03	.02
315	Scott McGregor	.06	.05	.02
316	Rafael Santana	.04	.03	.02
317	Frank Williams	.04	.03	.02
318	Mike Fitzgerald	.04	.03	.02
319	Rick Mahler	.04	.03	.02
320	Jim Gott	.04	.03	.02
321	Mariano Duncan	.04	.03	.02
322	Jose Guzman	.06	.05	.02
323	Lee Guetterman	.04	.03	.02
324	Dan Gladden	.04	.03	.02
325	Gary Carter	.15	.11	.06
326	Tracy Jones	.10	.08	.04
327	Floyd Youmans	.04	.03	.02
328	Bill Dawley	.04	.03	.02
329	Paul Noce	.10	.08	.04
330	Angel Salazar	.04	.03	.02
331	Goose Gossage	.12	.09	.05
332	George Frazier	.04	.03	.02
333	Ruppert Jones	.04	.03	.02
334	Billy Jo Robidoux	.04	.03	.02
335	Mike Scott	.10	.08	.04
336	Randy Myers	.10	.08	.04
337	Bob Sebra	.04	.03	.02
338	Eric Show	.06	.05	.02
339	Mitch Williams	.06	.05	.02
340	Paul Molitor	.10	.08	.04
341	Gus Polidor	.04	.03	.02
342	Steve Trout	.04	.03	.02
343	Jerry Don Gleaton	.04	.03	.02
344	Bob Knepper	.06	.05	.02
345	Mitch Webster	.06	.05	.02
346	John Morris	.04	.03	.02
347	Andy Hawkins	.04	.03	.02
348	Dave Leiper	.04	.03	.02
349	Ernest Riles	.04	.03	.02
350	Dwight Gooden	.40	.30	.15
351	Dave Righetti	.12	.09	.05
352	Pat Dodson	.04	.03	.02
353	John Habyan	.04	.03	.02
354	Jim Deshaies	.06	.05	.02
355	Butch Wynegar	.04	.03	.02
356	Bryn Smith	.04	.03	.02
357	Matt Young	.04	.03	.02
358	Tom Pagnozzi	.12	.09	.05
359	Floyd Rayford	.04	.03	.02
360	Darryl Strawberry	.30	.25	.12
361	Sal Butera	.04	.03	.02
362	Domingo Ramos	.04	.03	.02
363	Chris Brown	.06	.05	.02
364	Jose Gonzalez	.04	.03	.02
365	Dave Smith	.06	.05	.02
366	Andy McGaffigan	.04	.03	.02
367	Stan Javier	.04	.03	.02
368	Henry Cotto	.04	.03	.02
369	Mike Birkbeck	.06	.05	.02
370	Len Dykstra	.08	.06	.03
371	Dave Collins	.06	.05	.02
372	Spike Owen	.04	.03	.02
373	Geno Petralli	.04	.03	.02
374	Ron Karkovice	.04	.03	.02
375	Shane Rawley	.06	.05	.02
376	DeWayne Buice	.15	.11	.06
377	Bill Pecota	.15	.11	.06

	MT	NR MT	EX
378 Leon Durham	.06	.05	.02
379 Ed Olwine	.04	.03	.02
380 Bruce Hurst	.08	.06	.03
381 Bob McClure	.04	.03	.02
382 Mark Thurmond	.04	.03	.02
383 Buddy Biancalana	.04	.03	.02
384 Tim Conroy	.04	.03	.02
385 Tony Gwynn	.25	.20	.10
386 Greg Gross	.04	.03	.02
387 *Barry Lyons*	.12	.09	.05
388 Mike Felder	.04	.03	.02
389 Pat Clements	.04	.03	.02
390 Ken Griffey	.06	.05	.02
391 Mark Davis	.04	.03	.02
392 Jose Rijo	.06	.05	.02
393 Mike Young	.04	.03	.02
394 Willie Fraser	.06	.05	.02
395 Dion James	.06	.05	.02
396 *Steve Shields*	.12	.09	.05
397 Randy St. Claire	.04	.03	.02
398 Danny Jackson	.12	.09	.05
399 Cecil Fielder	.60	.45	.25
400 Keith Hernandez	.15	.11	.06
401 Don Carman	.06	.05	.02
402 *Chuck Crim*	.12	.09	.05
403 Rob Woodward	.04	.03	.02
404 Junior Ortiz	.04	.03	.02
405 Glenn Wilson	.06	.05	.02
406 Ken Howell	.04	.03	.02
407 Jeff Kunkel	.04	.03	.02
408 Jeff Reed	.04	.03	.02
409 Chris James	.10	.08	.04
410 Zane Smith	.06	.05	.02
411 Ken Dixon	.04	.03	.02
412 Ricky Horton	.06	.05	.02
413 Frank DiPino	.04	.03	.02
414 *Shane Mack*	.15	.11	.06
415 Danny Cox	.06	.05	.02
416 Andy Van Slyke	.10	.08	.04
417 Danny Heep	.04	.03	.02
418 John Cangelosi	.04	.03	.02
419a John Christiansen (incorrect spelling)			
	.25	.20	.10
419b John Christensen (correct spelling)	.06	.05	.02
420 *Joey Cora*	.12	.09	.05
421 Mike LaValliere	.06	.05	.02
422 Kelly Gruber	.04	.03	.02
423 Bruce Benedict	.04	.03	.02
424 Len Matuszek	.04	.03	.02
425 Kent Tekulve	.06	.05	.02
426 Rafael Ramirez	.04	.03	.02
427 Mike Flanagan	.06	.05	.02
428 Mike Gallego	.04	.03	.02
429 Juan Castillo	.04	.03	.02
430 Neal Heaton	.04	.03	.02
431 Phil Garner	.04	.03	.02
432 *Mike Dunne*	.20	.15	.08
433 Wallace Johnson	.04	.03	.02
434 Jack O'Connor	.04	.03	.02
435 Steve Jeltz	.04	.03	.02
436 *Donnell Nixon*	.15	.11	.06
437 Jack Lazorko	.04	.03	.02
438 *Keith Comstock*	.12	.09	.05
439 Jeff Robinson	.04	.03	.02
440 Graig Nettles	.08	.06	.03
441 Mel Hall	.06	.05	.02
442 *Gerald Young*	.30	.25	.12
443 Gary Redus	.04	.03	.02
444 Charlie Moore	.04	.03	.02
445 Bill Madlock	.08	.06	.03
446 Mark Clear	.04	.03	.02
447 Greg Booker	.04	.03	.02
448 Rick Schu	.04	.03	.02
449 Ron Kittle	.06	.05	.02
450 Dale Murphy	.30	.25	.12
451 Bob Dernier	.04	.03	.02
452 Dale Mohorcic	.06	.05	.02
453 Rafael Belliard	.04	.03	.02
454 Charlie Puleo	.04	.03	.02
455 Dwayne Murphy	.06	.05	.02
456 Jim Eisenreich	.04	.03	.02
457 David Palmer	.04	.03	.02
458 Dave Stewart	.08	.06	.03
459 Pascual Perez	.06	.05	.02
460 Glenn Davis	.12	.09	.05
461 Dan Petry	.06	.05	.02
462 Jim Winn	.04	.03	.02
463 Darrell Miller	.04	.03	.02
464 Mike Moore	.04	.03	.02
465 Mike LaCoss	.04	.03	.02
466 Steve Farr	.04	.03	.02

	MT	NR MT	EX
467 Jerry Mumphrey	.04	.03	.02
468 Kevin Gross	.06	.05	.02
469 Bruce Bochy	.04	.03	.02
470 Orel Hershiser	.20	.15	.08
471 Eric King	.06	.05	.02
472 *Ellis Burks*	1.50	1.25	.60
473 Darren Daulton	.04	.03	.02
474 Mookie Wilson	.06	.05	.02
475 Frank Viola	.12	.09	.05
476 Ron Robinson	.04	.03	.02
477 Bob Melvin	.04	.03	.02
478 Jeff Musselman	.06	.05	.02
479 Charlie Kerfeld	.04	.03	.02
480 Richard Dotson	.06	.05	.02
481 Kevin Mitchell	.70	.50	.30
482 Gary Roenicke	.04	.03	.02
483 Tim Flannery	.04	.03	.02
484 Rich Yett	.04	.03	.02
485 Pete Incaviglia	.12	.09	.05
486 Rick Cerone	.04	.03	.02
487 Tony Armas	.06	.05	.02
488 Jerry Reed	.04	.03	.02
489 Davey Lopes	.06	.05	.02
490 Frank Tanana	.06	.05	.02
491 Mike Loynd	.04	.03	.02
492 Bruce Ruffin	.06	.05	.02
493 Chris Speier	.04	.03	.02
494 Tom Hume	.04	.03	.02
495 Jesse Orosco	.06	.05	.02
496 *Robby Wine, Jr.*	.12	.09	.05
497 *Jeff Montgomery*	.20	.15	.08
498 Jeff Dedmon	.04	.03	.02
499 Luis Aguayo	.04	.03	.02
500 Reggie Jackson (1968-75 Oakland Athletics)	.20	.15	.08
501 Reggie Jackson (1976 Baltimore Orioles)	.20	.15	.08
502 Reggie Jackson (1977-81 New York Yankees)	.20	.15	.08
503 Reggie Jackson (1982-86 California Angels)	.20	.15	.08
504 Reggie Jackson (1987 Oakland Athletics)	.20	.15	.08
505 Billy Hatcher	.06	.05	.02
506 Ed Lynch	.04	.03	.02
507 Willie Hernandez	.06	.05	.02
508 Jose DeLeon	.06	.05	.02
509 Joel Youngblood	.04	.03	.02
510 Bob Welch	.08	.06	.03
511 Steve Ontiveros	.04	.03	.02
512 Randy Ready	.04	.03	.02
513 Juan Nieves	.06	.05	.02
514 Jeff Russell	.04	.03	.02
515 Von Hayes	.06	.05	.02
516 Mark Gubicza	.10	.08	.04
517 Ken Dayley	.04	.03	.02
518 Don Aase	.04	.03	.02
519 Rick Reuschel	.08	.06	.03
520 *Mike Henneman*	.25	.20	.10
521 Rick Aguilera	.04	.03	.02
522 Jay Howell	.06	.05	.02
523 Ed Correa	.04	.03	.02
524 Manny Trillo	.06	.05	.02
525 Kirk Gibson	.15	.11	.06
526 *Wally Ritchie*	.12	.09	.05
527 Al Nipper	.04	.03	.02
528 Atlee Hammaker	.04	.03	.02
529 Shawon Dunston	.08	.06	.03
530 Jim Clancy	.06	.05	.02
531 Tom Paciorek	.04	.03	.02
532 Joel Skinner	.04	.03	.02
533 Scott Garrelts	.04	.03	.02
534 Tom O'Malley	.04	.03	.02
535 John Franco	.08	.06	.03
536 *Paul Kilgus*	.20	.15	.08
537 Darrell Porter	.06	.05	.02
538 Walt Terrell	.06	.05	.02
539 *Bill Long*	.15	.11	.06
540 George Bell	.20	.15	.08
541 Jeff Sellers	.06	.05	.02
542 *Joe Boever*	.12	.09	.05
543 Steve Howe	.06	.05	.02
544 Scott Sanderson	.04	.03	.02
545 Jack Morris	.15	.11	.06
546 *Todd Benzinger*	.30	.25	.12
547 Steve Henderson	.04	.03	.02
548 Eddie Milner	.04	.03	.02
549 *Jeff Robinson*	.25	.20	.10
550 Cal Ripken, Jr.	.25	.20	.10
551 Jody Davis	.06	.05	.02
552 Kirk McCaskill	.06	.05	.02

		MT	NR MT	EX
553	Craig Lefferts	.04	.03	.02
554	Darnell Coles	.06	.05	.02
555	Phil Niekro	.15	.11	.06
556	Mike Aldrete	.06	.05	.02
557	Pat Perry	.04	.03	.02
558	Juan Agosto	.04	.03	.02
559	Rob Murphy	.06	.05	.02
560	Dennis Rasmussen	.08	.06	.03
561	Manny Lee	.04	.03	.02
562	*Jeff Blauser*	.20	.15	.08
563	Bob Ojeda	.06	.05	.02
564	Dave Dravecky	.06	.05	.02
565	Gene Garber	.04	.03	.02
566	Ron Roenicke	.04	.03	.02
567	*Tommy Hinzo*	.12	.09	.05
568	*Eric Nolte*	.12	.09	.05
569	Ed Hearn	.04	.03	.02
570	*Mark Davidson*	.12	.09	.05
571	*Jim Walewander*	.12	.09	.05
572	Donnie Hill	.04	.03	.02
573	Jamie Moyer	.06	.05	.02
574	Ken Schrom	.04	.03	.02
575	Nolan Ryan	.50	.40	.20
576	Jim Acker	.04	.03	.02
577	Jamie Quirk	.04	.03	.02
578	*Jay Aldrich*	.10	.08	.04
579	Claudell Washington	.06	.05	.02
580	Jeff Leonard	.06	.05	.02
581	Carmen Castillo	.04	.03	.02
582	Daryl Boston	.04	.03	.02
583	*Jeff DeWillis*	.15	.11	.06
584	*John Marzano*	.20	.15	.08
585	Bill Gullickson	.06	.05	.02
586	Andy Allanson	.08	.06	.03
587	Lee Tunnell	.04	.03	.02
588	Gene Nelson	.04	.03	.02
589	Dave LaPoint	.06	.05	.02
590	Harold Baines	.10	.08	.04
591	Bill Buckner	.08	.06	.03
592	Carlton Fisk	.20	.15	.08
593	Rick Manning	.04	.03	.02
594	*Doug Jones*	.35	.25	.14
595	Tom Candiotti	.04	.03	.02
596	Steve Lake	.04	.03	.02
597	*Jose Lind*	.25	.20	.10
598	*Ross Jones*	.12	.09	.05
599	Gary Matthews	.06	.05	.02
600	Fernando Valezuela	.15	.11	.06
601	Dennis Martinez	.06	.05	.02
602	*Les Lancaster*	.15	.11	.06
603	Ozzie Guillen	.06	.05	.02
604	Tony Bernazard	.04	.03	.02
605	Chili Davis	.06	.05	.02
606	Roy Smalley	.04	.03	.02
607	Ivan Calderon	.08	.06	.03
608	Jay Tibbs	.04	.03	.02
609	Guy Hoffman	.04	.03	.02
610	Doyle Alexander	.06	.05	.02
611	Mike Bielecki	.04	.03	.02
612	*Shawn Hillegas*	.15	.11	.06
613	Keith Atherton	.04	.03	.02
614	Eric Plunk	.04	.03	.02
615	Sid Fernandez	.08	.06	.03
616	Dennis Lamp	.04	.03	.02
617	Dave Engle	.04	.03	.02
618	Harry Spilman	.04	.03	.02
619	Don Robinson	.06	.05	.02
620	John Farrell	.30	.25	.12
621	*Nelson Liriano*	.15	.11	.06
622	Floyd Bannister	.06	.05	.02
623	Rookie Prospect (*Randy Milligan*)	1.00	.70	.40
624	Rookie Prospect (*Kevin Elster*)	.25	.20	.10
625	Rookie Prospect (*Jody Reed*)	.60	.45	.25
626	Rookie Prospect (*Shawn Abner*)	.20	.15	.08
627	Rookie Prospect (*Kirt Manwaring*)	.30	.25	.12
628	Rookie Prospect (*Pete Stanicek*)	.20	.15	.08
629	Rookie Prospect (*Rob Ducey*)	.12	.09	.05
630	Rookie Prospect (*Steve Kiefer*)	.04	.03	.02
631	Rookie Prospect (*Gary Thurman*)	.25	.20	.10
632	Rookie Prospect (*Darrel Akerfelds*)	.12	.09	.05
633	Rookie Prospect (*Dave Clark*)	.10	.08	.04
634	Rookie Prospect (*Roberto Kelly*)	1.00	.70	.40
635	Rookie Prospect (*Keith Hughes*)	.15	.11	.06
636	Rookie Prospect (*John Davis*)	.15	.11	.06
637	Rookie Prospect (*Mike Devereaux*)	.30	.25	.12
638	Rookie Prospect (*Tom Glavine*)	.35	.25	.14
639	Rookie Prospect (*Keith Miller*)	.25	.20	.10
640	Rookie Prospect (*Chris Gwynn*)	.20	.15	.08
641	Rookie Prospect (*Tim Crews*)	.15	.11	.06
642	Rookie Prospect (*Mackey Sasser*)	.20	.15	.08
643	Rookie Prospect (*Vicente Palacios*)	.15	.11	.06

		MT	NR MT	EX
644	Rookie Prospect (Kevin Romine)	.06	.05	.02
645	Rookie Prospect (*Gregg Jefferies*)	3.00	2.25	1.25
646	Rookie Prospect (*Jeff Treadway*)	.35	.25	.14
647	Rookie Prospect (*Ronnie Gant*)	2.00	1.50	.80
648	Rookie Sluggers (Mark McGwire, Matt Nokes)	.30	.25	.12
649	Speed and Power (Eric Davis, Tim Raines)	.25	.20	.10
650	Game Breakers (Jack Clark, Don Mattingly)	.60	.45	.25
651	Super Shortstops (Tony Fernandez, Cal Ripken, Jr., Alan Trammell)	.15	.11	.06
652	1987 Highlights (Vince Coleman)	.08	.06	.03
653	1987 Highlights (Kirby Puckett)	.12	.09	.05
654	1987 Highlights (Benito Santiago)	.10	.08	.04
655	1987 Highlights (Juan Nieves)	.06	.05	.02
656	1987 Highlights (Steve Bedrosian)	.06	.05	.02
657	1987 Highlights (Mike Schmidt)	.15	.11	.06
658	1987 Highlights (Don Mattingly)	.60	.45	.25
659	1987 Highlights (Mark McGwire)	.40	.30	.15
660	1987 Highlights (Paul Molitor)	.08	.06	.03

1988 Score Box Panels

This 18-card set, produced by Major League Marketing and manufactured by Optigraphics, is the premiere box-bottom set issued under the Score trademark. The set features 1987 major league All-star players in full-color action poses, framed by a white border. A "1987 All-Star" banner (red or purple) curves above an orange player name block beneath the player photo. Card backs are printed in red, blue, gold and black and carry the card number, player name and position and league logo. Six colorful "Great Moments in Baseball" trivia cards are also included in this set. Each trivia card highlights an historical event at a famous ballpark.

		MT	NR MT	EX
	Complete Panel Set:	8.00	6.00	3.25
	Complete Singles Set:	3.00	2.25	1.25
	Common Panel:	1.50	1.25	.60
	Common Single Player:	.15	.11	.06
	Panel	1.50	1.25	.60
1	Terry Kennedy	.15	.11	.06
3	Willie Randolph	.15	.11	.06
15	Eric Davis	.50	.40	.20
	Panel	2.00	1.50	.80
3	Don Mattingly	.90	.70	.35
5	Cal Ripken, Jr.	.35	.25	.14
11	Jack Clark	.25	.20	.10
	Panel	2.00	1.50	.80
4	Wade Boggs	.60	.45	.25
9	Bret Saberhagen	.20	.15	.08
12	Ryne Sandberg	.60	.45	.25
	Panel	1.50	1.25	.60
6	George Bell	.25	.20	.10
13	Mike Schmidt	.35	.25	.14
18	Mike Scott	.15	.11	.06
	Panel	2.00	1.50	.80
7	Rickey Henderson	.60	.45	.25
16	Andre Dawson	.25	.20	.10
17	Darryl Strawberry	.40	.30	.15
	Panel	1.50	1.25	.60
8	Dave Winfield	.25	.20	.10
10	Gary Carter	.20	.15	.08

		MT	NR MT	EX
14	Ozzie Smith	.15	.11	.06

1988 Score Traded

 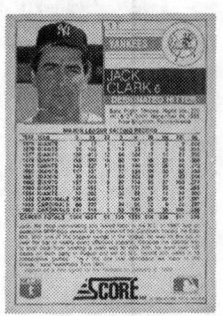

This 110-card set featuring new rookies and traded veterans is similar in design to the 1988 Score set, except for a change in border color. Individual standard-size player cards (2-1/2" by 3-1/2") feature a bright orange border framing full-figure action photos highlighted by a thin white outline. The player name (in white) is centered in the bottom margin, flanked by three yellow stars lower left and a yellow Score logo lower right. The backs carry full-color player close-ups on a cream-colored background, followed by card number, team name and logo, player personal information and a purple stats chart that lists year-by-year and major league totals. A brief player profile follows the stats chart and, on some cards, information is included about the player's trade or acquisition. The update set also includes 10 Magic Motion 3-D trivia cards.

		MT	NR MT	EX
Complete Set:		60.00	45.00	25.00
Common Player:		.08	.06	.03
1T	Jack Clark	.20	.15	.08
2T	Danny Jackson	.20	.15	.08
3T	Brett Butler	.10	.08	.04
4T	Kurt Stillwell	.12	.09	.05
5T	Tom Brunansky	.15	.11	.06
6T	Dennis Lamp	.08	.06	.03
7T	Jose DeLeon	.10	.08	.04
8T	Tom Herr	.12	.09	.05
9T	Keith Moreland	.10	.08	.04
10T	Kirk Gibson	.20	.15	.08
11T	Bud Black	.08	.06	.03
12T	Rafael Ramirez	.08	.06	.03
13T	Luis Salazar	.08	.06	.03
14T	Goose Gossage	.15	.11	.06
15T	Bob Welch	.15	.11	.06
16T	Vance Law	.10	.08	.04
17T	Ray Knight	.10	.08	.04
18T	Dan Quisenberry	.10	.08	.04
19T	Don Slaught	.08	.06	.03
20T	Lee Smith	.12	.09	.05
21T	Rick Cerone	.08	.06	.03
22T	Pat Tabler	.10	.08	.04
23T	Larry McWilliams	.08	.06	.03
24T	Rick Horton	.10	.08	.04
25T	Graig Nettles	.12	.09	.05
26T	Dan Petry	.10	.08	.04
27T	Joe Rijo	.10	.08	.04
28T	Chili Davis	.10	.08	.04
29T	Dickie Thon	.10	.08	.04
30T	Mackey Sasser(FC)	.15	.11	.06
31T	Mickey Tettleton	.08	.06	.03
32T	Rick Dempsey	.08	.06	.03
33T	Ron Hassey	.08	.06	.03
34T	Phil Bradley	.12	.09	.05
35T	Jay Howell	.10	.08	.04
36T	Bill Buckner	.12	.09	.05
37T	Alfredo Griffin	.10	.08	.04
38T	Gary Pettis	.08	.06	.03
39T	Calvin Schiraldi	.08	.06	.03
40T	John Candelaria	.10	.08	.04

		MT	NR MT	EX
41T	Joe Orsulak	.08	.06	.03
42T	Willie Upshaw	.10	.08	.04
43T	Herm Winningham	.08	.06	.03
44T	Ron Kittle	.12	.09	.05
45T	Bob Dernier	.08	.06	.03
46T	Steve Balboni	.10	.08	.04
47T	Steve Shields	.08	.06	.03
48T	Henry Cotto	.08	.06	.03
49T	Dave Henderson	.10	.08	.04
50T	Dave Parker	.15	.11	.06
51T	Mike Young	.08	.06	.03
52T	Mark Salas	.08	.06	.03
53T	Mike Davis	.08	.06	.03
54T	Rafael Santana	.08	.06	.03
55T	Don Baylor	.15	.11	.06
56T	Dan Pasqua	.12	.09	.05
57T	Ernest Riles	.08	.06	.03
58T	Glenn Hubbard	.08	.06	.03
59T	Mike Smithson	.08	.06	.03
60T	Richard Dotson	.10	.08	.04
61T	Jerry Reuss	.10	.08	.04
62T	Mike Jackson	.10	.08	.04
63T	Floyd Bannister	.10	.08	.04
64T	Jesse Orosco	.10	.08	.04
65T	Larry Parrish	.10	.08	.04
66T	Jeff Bittiger(FC)	.20	.15	.08
67T	Ray Hayward(FC)	.10	.08	.04
68T	Ricky Jordan(FC)	1.50	1.25	.60
69T	Tommy Gregg(FC)	.12	.09	.05
70T	Brady Anderson(FC)	.50	.40	.20
71T	Jeff Montgomery	.08	.06	.03
72T	Darryl Hamilton(FC)	.35	.25	.14
73T	Cecil Espy(FC)	.10	.08	.04
74T	Greg Briley(FC)	1.75	1.25	.70
75T	Joey Meyer(FC)	.20	.15	.08
76T	Mike Macfarlane(FC)	.25	.20	.10
77T	Oswald Peraza(FC)	.20	.15	.08
78T	Jack Armstrong(FC)	2.00	1.50	.80
79T	Don Heinkel(FC)	.20	.15	.08
80T	Mark Grace(FC)	25.00	18.00	9.00
81T	Steve Curry(FC)	.20	.15	.08
82T	Damon Berryhill(FC)	.70	.50	.30
83T	Steve Ellsworth(FC)	.20	.15	.08
84T	Pete Smith(FC)	.12	.09	.05
85T	Jack McDowell	.60	.45	.25
86T	Rob Dibble(FC)	2.00	1.50	.80
87T	Brian Harvey(FC)	.70	.50	.30
88T	John Dopson(FC)	.25	.20	.10
89T	Dave Gallagher(FC)	.25	.20	.10
90T	Todd Stottlemyre(FC)	.80	.60	.30
91T	Mike Schooler(FC)	1.00	.70	.40
92T	Don Gordon(FC)	.08	.06	.03
93T	Sil Campusano(FC)	.25	.20	.10
94T	Jeff Pico(FC)	.25	.20	.10
95T	Jay Buhner(FC)	.60	.45	.25
96T	Nelson Santovenia(FC)	.35	.25	.14
97T	Al Leiter(FC)	.30	.25	.12
98T	Luis Alicea(FC)	.20	.15	.08
99T	Pat Borders(FC)	.25	.20	.10
100T	Chris Sabo(FC)	8.00	6.00	3.25
101T	Tim Belcher(FC)	1.25	.90	.50
102T	Walt Weiss(FC)	2.75	2.00	1.00
103T	Craig Biggio(FC)	3.50	2.75	1.50
104T	Don August(FC)	.25	.20	.10
105T	Roberto Alomar(FC)	8.00	6.00	3.25
106T	Todd Burns(FC)	.30	.25	.12
107T	John Costello(FC)	.20	.15	.08
108T	Melido Perez(FC)	.60	.45	.25
109T	Darrin Jackson(FC)	.12	.09	.05
110T	Orestes Destrade(FC)	.15	.11	.06

1988 Score
Young Superstar - Series I

This 40-card standard-size set (2-1/2" by 3-1/2" cards) from Optigraphics was divided into five separate 8-card sets. Similar to the company's regular issue, these cards are distinguished by excellent full-color photography on both front and back. The glossy player photos, with team logo in the lower right corner, are centered on a white background and framed by a vivid blue and green border. A player name banner beneath the photo includes the name, position and uniform number. The card backs feature ful-color player closeups beneath

a hot pink player name/Score logo banner. Hot pink also frames the personal stats (in green), career stats (in black) and career biography (in blue). The backs also include quotes from well-known baseball authorities discussing player performance. This set was distributed via a write-in offer printed on 1988 Score 17-card package wrappers.

		MT	NR MT	EX
Complete Set:		9.00	6.75	3.50
Common Player:		.10	.08	.04
1	Mark McGwire	1.25	.90	.50
2	Benito Santiago	.30	.25	.12
3	Sam Horn	.25	.20	.10
4	Chris Bosio	.10	.08	.04
5	Matt Nokes	.25	.20	.10
6	Ken Williams	.15	.11	.06
7	Dion James	.10	.08	.04
8	B.J. Surhoff	.25	.20	.10
9	Joe Margrane	.20	.15	.08
10	Kevin Seitzer	.40	.30	.15
11	Stanley Jefferson	.10	.08	.04
12	Devon White	.30	.25	.12
13	Nelson Liriano	.15	.11	.06
14	Chris James	.25	.20	.10
15	Mike Henneman	.15	.11	.06
16	Terry Steinbach	.20	.15	.08
17	John Kruk	.25	.20	.10
18	Matt Williams	.60	.45	.25
19	Kelly Downs	.15	.11	.06
20	Bill Ripken	.15	.11	.06
21	Ozzie Guillen	.10	.08	.04
22	Luis Polonia	.15	.11	.06
23	Dave Magadan	.40	.30	.15
24	Mike Greenwell	.80	.60	.30
25	Will Clark	.50	.40	.20
26	Mike Dunne	.20	.15	.08
27	Wally Joyner	.50	.40	.20
28	Robby Thompson	.10	.08	.04
29	Ken Caminiti	.20	.15	.08
30	Jose Canseco	2.00	1.50	.80
31	Todd Benzinger	.30	.25	.12
32	Pete Incaviglia	.20	.15	.08
33	John Farrell	.20	.15	.08
34	Casey Candaele	.10	.08	.04
35	Mike Aldrete	.10	.08	.04
36	Ruben Sierra	.40	.30	.15
37	Ellis Burks	1.00	.70	.40
38	Tracy Jones	.20	.15	.08
39	Kal Daniels	.30	.25	.12
40	Cory Snyder	.30	.25	.12

1988 Score
Young Superstar - Series II

This set of 40 standard-size cards (2-1/2" by 3-1/2") and five Magic trivia cards is part of a double series issued by Score. Each series is divided into five smaller sets of eight baseball cards and one trivia card. The design on both series is similar, except for border color. Series I has blue and green borders. Series II has red and blue borders framing full-color player photos with the player name and

team logo printed beneath the photo. The card backs carry full-color head shots and stats in a variety of colors. Young Superstar series were offered via a write-in offer on the backs of 1988 Score card package wrappers. For each 8-card subset, collectors were instructed to send two Score wrappers and $1. Complete sets were offered by a number of hobby dealers nationwide.

		MT	NR MT	EX
Complete Set:		8.00	6.00	3.25
Common Player:		.10	.08	.04
1	Don Mattingly	1.50	1.25	.60
2	Glenn Braggs	.15	.11	.06
3	Dwight Gooden	.70	.50	.30
4	Jose Lind	.25	.20	.10
5	Danny Tartabull	.30	.25	.12
6	Tony Fernandez	.15	.11	.06
7	Julio Franco	.15	.11	.06
8	Andres Galarraga	.30	.25	.12
9	Bobby Bonilla	.40	.30	.15
10	Eric Davis	.70	.50	.30
11	Gerald Young	.25	.20	.10
12	Barry Bonds	.40	.30	.15
13	Jerry Browne	.10	.08	.04
14	Jeff Blauser	.15	.11	.06
15	Mickey Brantley	.10	.08	.04
16	Floyd Youmans	.10	.08	.04
17	Bret Saberhagen	.25	.20	.10
18	Shawon Dunston	.20	.15	.08
19	Len Dykstra	.15	.11	.06
20	Darryl Strawberry	.70	.50	.30
21	Rick Aguilera	.10	.08	.04
22	Ivan Calderon	.10	.08	.04
23	Roger Clemens	.70	.50	.30
24	Vince Coleman	.30	.25	.12
25	Gary Thurman	.25	.20	.10
26	Jeff Treadway	.25	.20	.10
27	Oddibe McDowell	.10	.08	.04
28	Fred McGriff	.40	.30	.15
29	Mark McLemore	.10	.08	.04
30	Jeff Musselman	.10	.08	.04
31	Mitch Williams	.10	.08	.04
32	Dan Plesac	.15	.11	.06
33	Juan Nieves	.10	.08	.04
34	Barry Larkin	.30	.25	.12
35	Greg Mathews	.15	.11	.06
36	Shane Mack	.10	.08	.04
37	Scott Bankhead	.10	.08	.04
38	Eric Bell	.10	.08	.04
39	Greg Swindell	.25	.20	.10
40	Kevin Elster	.20	.15	.08

A player's name in *italic* indicates a rookie card. An (FC) indicates a player's first card for that particular card company.

1989 Score

This set of 660 cards plus 56 Magic Motion trivia cards is the second annual basic issue from Score. Full-color player photos highlight 651 individual players and 9 season highlights, including the first Wrigley Field night game. Action photos are framed by thin brightly colored borders (green, cyan blue, purple, orange, red, royal blue) with a baseball diamond logo/player name beneath the photo. Full-color player close-ups (1-5/16" by 1-5/8") are

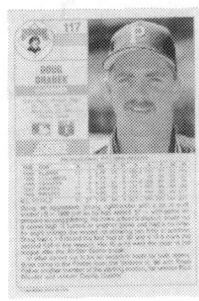

printed on the pastel-colored backs, along with the card number, personal information, stats and career highlights. The cards measure 2-1/2" by 3-1/2" in size.

	MT	NR MT	EX
Complete Set:	25.00	20.00	10.00
Common Player:	.03	.02	.01

		MT	NR MT	EX
1	Jose Canseco	1.25	.90	.50
2	Andre Dawson	.15	.11	.06
3	Mark McGwire	.60	.45	.25
4	Benny Santiago	.12	.09	.05
5	Rick Reuschel	.08	.06	.03
6	Fred McGriff	.35	.25	.14
7	Kal Daniels	.12	.09	.05
8	Gary Gaetti	.12	.09	.05
9	Ellis Burks	.50	.40	.20
10	Darryl Strawberry	.35	.25	.14
11	Julio Franco	.08	.06	.03
12	Lloyd Moseby	.06	.05	.02
13	*Jeff Pico*	.20	.15	.08
14	Johnny Ray	.06	.05	.02
15	Cal Ripken, Jr.	.30	.25	.12
16	Dick Schofield	.03	.02	.01
17	Mel Hall	.06	.05	.02
18	Bill Ripken	.06	.05	.02
19	Brook Jacoby	.08	.06	.03
20	Kirby Puckett	.35	.25	.14
21	Bill Doran	.06	.05	.02
22	Pete O'Brien	.06	.05	.02
23	Matt Nokes	.15	.11	.06
24	Brian Fisher	.06	.05	.02
25	Jack Clark	.12	.09	.05
26	Gary Pettis	.03	.02	.01
27	Dave Valle	.03	.02	.01
28	Willie Wilson	.08	.06	.03
29	Curt Young	.06	.05	.02
30	Dale Murphy	.30	.25	.12
31	Barry Larkin	.10	.08	.04
32	Dave Stewart	.08	.06	.03
33	Mike LaValliere	.06	.05	.02
34	Glen Hubbard	.03	.02	.01
35	Ryne Sandberg	.20	.15	.08
36	Tony Pena	.06	.05	.02
37	Greg Walker	.06	.05	.02
38	Von Hayes	.08	.06	.03
39	Kevin Mitchell	.40	.30	.15
40	Tim Raines	.25	.20	.10
41	Keith Hernandez	.20	.15	.08
42	Keith Moreland	.06	.05	.02
43	Ruben Sierra	.30	.25	.12
44	Chet Lemon	.06	.05	.02
45	Willie Randolph	.06	.05	.02
46	Andy Allanson	.03	.02	.01
47	Candy Maldonado	.06	.05	.02
48	Sid Bream	.06	.05	.02
49	Denny Walling	.03	.02	.01
50	Dave Winfield	.25	.20	.10
51	Alvin Davis	.10	.08	.04
52	Cory Snyder	.15	.11	.06
53	Hubie Brooks	.08	.06	.03
54	Chili Davis	.06	.05	.02
55	Kevin Seitzer	.25	.20	.10
56	Jose Uribe	.03	.02	.01
57	Tony Fernandez	.10	.08	.04
58	Tim Teufel	.03	.02	.01
59	Oddibe McDowell	.06	.05	.02
60	Les Lancaster	.06	.05	.02
61	Billy Hatcher	.06	.05	.02
62	Dan Gladden	.03	.02	.01

		MT	NR MT	EX
63	Marty Barrett	.06	.05	.02
64	Nick Esasky	.06	.05	.02
65	Wally Joyner	.20	.15	.08
66	Mike Greenwell	.60	.45	.25
67	Ken Williams	.06	.05	.02
68	Bob Horner	.08	.06	.03
69	Steve Sax	.12	.09	.05
70	Rickey Henderson	.30	.25	.12
71	Mitch Webster	.06	.05	.02
72	Rob Deer	.06	.05	.02
73	Jim Presley	.06	.05	.02
74	Albert Hall	.03	.02	.01
75a	George Brett ("...game's top hitters at 33..." on back)	.70	.50	.25
75b	George Brett ("...game's top hitters at 35..." on back)	.30	.25	.12
76	Brian Downing	.06	.05	.02
77	Dave Martinez	.06	.05	.02
78	Scott Fletcher	.06	.05	.02
79	Phil Bradley	.08	.06	.03
80	Ozzie Smith	.12	.09	.05
81	Larry Sheets	.06	.05	.02
82	Mike Aldrete	.06	.05	.02
83	Darnell Coles	.06	.05	.02
84	Len Dykstra	.08	.06	.03
85	Jim Rice	.20	.15	.08
86	Jeff Treadway	.10	.08	.04
87	Jose Lind	.08	.06	.03
88	Willie McGee	.10	.08	.04
89	Mickey Brantley	.03	.02	.01
90	Tony Gwynn	.30	.25	.12
91	R.J. Reynolds	.03	.02	.01
92	Milt Thompson	.03	.02	.01
93	Kevin McReynolds	.12	.09	.05
94	Eddie Murray	.25	.20	.10
95	Lance Parrish	.12	.09	.05
96	Ron Kittle	.06	.05	.02
97	Gerald Young	.10	.08	.04
98	Ernie Whitt	.06	.05	.02
99	Jeff Reed	.03	.02	.01
100	Don Mattingly	1.25	.90	.50
101	Gerald Perry	.08	.06	.03
102	Vance Law	.06	.05	.02
103	John Shelby	.03	.02	.01
104	*Chris Sabo*	1.25	.90	.50
105	Danny Tartabull	.15	.11	.06
106	Glenn Wilson	.06	.05	.02
107	Mark Davidson	.06	.05	.02
108	Dave Parker	.10	.08	.04
109	Eric Davis	.35	.25	.14
110	Alan Trammell	.15	.11	.06
111	Ozzie Virgil	.03	.02	.01
112	Frank Tanana	.06	.05	.02
113	Rafael Ramirez	.03	.02	.01
114	Dennis Martinez	.06	.05	.02
115	Jose DeLeon	.06	.05	.02
116	Bob Ojeda	.06	.05	.02
117	Doug Drabek	.06	.05	.02
118	Andy Hawkins	.03	.02	.01
119	Greg Maddux(FC)	.10	.08	.04
120	Cecil Fielder (photo on back reversed)	.90	.70	.35
121	Mike Scioscia	.06	.05	.02
122	Dan Petry	.06	.05	.02
123	Terry Kennedy	.06	.05	.02
124	Kelly Downs	.08	.06	.03
125a	Greg Gross (first name incorrect on card back)	.20	.15	.08
125b	Greg Gross (first name correct on card back)	.08	.06	.03
126	Fred Lynn	.10	.08	.04
127	Barry Bonds	.10	.08	.04
128	Harold Baines	.10	.08	.04
129	Doyle Alexander	.06	.05	.02
130	Kevin Elster	.08	.06	.03
131	Mike Heath	.03	.02	.01
132	Teddy Higuera	.08	.06	.03
133	Charlie Leibrandt	.06	.05	.02
134	Tim Laudner	.03	.02	.01
135a	Ray Knight (photo reversed)	.60	.45	.25
135b	Ray Knight (correct photo)	.08	.06	.03
136	Howard Johnson	.08	.06	.03
137	Terry Pendleton	.08	.06	.03
138	Andy McGaffigan	.03	.02	.01
139	Ken Oberkfell	.03	.02	.01
140	Butch Wynegar	.03	.02	.01
141	Rob Murphy	.03	.02	.01
142	*Rich Renteria*(FC)	.12	.09	.05
143	Jose Guzman	.08	.06	.03
144	Andres Galarraga	.12	.09	.05
145	Rick Horton	.06	.05	.02

		MT	NR MT	EX
146	Frank DiPino	.03	.02	.01
147	Glenn Braggs	.06	.05	.02
148	John Kruk	.06	.05	.02
149	Mike Schmidt	.35	.25	.14
150	Lee Smith	.08	.06	.03
151	Robin Yount	.25	.20	.10
152	Mark Eichhorn	.06	.05	.02
153	DeWayne Buice	.04	.03	.02
154	B.J. Surhoff	.08	.06	.03
155	Vince Coleman	.12	.09	.05
156	Tony Phillips	.03	.02	.01
157	Willie Fraser	.03	.02	.01
158	Lance McCullers	.06	.05	.02
159	Greg Gagne	.03	.02	.01
160	Jesse Barfield	.08	.06	.03
161	Mark Langston	.08	.06	.03
162	Kurt Stillwell	.06	.05	.02
163	Dion James	.03	.02	.01
164	Glenn Davis	.12	.09	.05
165	Walt Weiss	.40	.30	.15
166	Dave Concepcion	.08	.06	.03
167	Alfredo Griffin	.06	.05	.02
168	*Don Heinkel*	.15	.11	.06
169	Luis Rivera(FC)	.03	.02	.01
170	Shane Rawley	.06	.05	.02
171	Darrell Evans	.08	.06	.03
172	Robby Thompson	.06	.05	.02
173	Jody Davis	.06	.05	.02
174	Andy Van Slyke	.12	.09	.05
175	Wade Boggs ("And his .364 career BA..."			
	on back)	.70	.50	.30
176	Garry Templeton	.06	.05	.02
177	Gary Redus	.03	.02	.01
178	Craig Lefferts	.03	.02	.01
179	Carney Lansford	.06	.05	.02
180	Ron Darling	.10	.08	.04
181	Kirk McCaskill	.06	.05	.02
182	Tony Armas	.06	.05	.02
183	Steve Farr	.03	.02	.01
184	Tom Brunansky	.10	.08	.04
185	*Bryan Harvey*	.20	.15	.08
186	Mike Marshall	.10	.08	.04
187	Bo Diaz	.06	.05	.02
188	Willie Upshaw	.06	.05	.02
189	Mike Pagliarulo	.08	.06	.03
190	Mike Krukow	.06	.05	.02
191	Tommy Herr	.06	.05	.02
192	Jim Pankovits	.03	.02	.01
193	Dwight Evans	.10	.08	.04
194	Kelly Gruber	.03	.02	.01
195	Bobby Bonilla	.20	.15	.08
196	Wallace Johnson	.03	.02	.01
197	Dave Stieb	.08	.06	.03
198	*Pat Borders*	.20	.15	.08
199	Rafael Palmeiro	.12	.09	.05
200	Doc Gooden	.40	.30	.15
201	Pete Incaviglia	.08	.06	.03
202	Chris James	.08	.06	.03
203	Marvell Wynne	.03	.02	.01
204	Pat Sheridan	.03	.02	.01
205	Don Baylor	.08	.06	.03
206	Paul O'Neill	.03	.02	.01
207	Pete Smith	.08	.06	.03
208	Mark McLemore	.03	.02	.01
209	Henry Cotto	.03	.02	.01
210	Kirk Gibson	.15	.11	.06
211	Claudell Washington	.06	.05	.02
212	Randy Bush	.03	.02	.01
213	Joe Carter	.10	.08	.04
214	Bill Buckner	.08	.06	.03
215	Bert Blyleven (year of birth is 1957)			
		.25	.20	.10
216	Brett Butler	.06	.05	.02
217	Lee Mazzilli	.06	.05	.02
218	Spike Owen	.03	.02	.01
219	Bill Swift	.03	.02	.01
220	Tim Wallach	.08	.06	.03
221	David Cone	.30	.25	.12
222	Don Carman	.06	.05	.02
223	Rich Gossage	.10	.08	.04
224	Bob Walk	.03	.02	.01
225	Dave Righetti	.10	.08	.04
226	Kevin Bass	.06	.05	.02
227	Kevin Gross	.06	.05	.02
228	Tim Burke	.03	.02	.01
229	Rick Mahler	.03	.02	.01
230	Lou Whitaker	.15	.11	.06
231	*Luis Alicea*	.15	.11	.06
232	Roberto Alomar	.40	.30	.15
233	Bob Boone	.06	.05	.02
234	Dickie Thon	.03	.02	.01

		MT	NR MT	EX
235	Shawon Dunston	.08	.06	.03
236	Pete Stanicek	.08	.06	.03
237	*Craig Biggio*	.40	.30	.15
238	Dennis Boyd	.06	.05	.02
239	Tom Candiotti	.03	.02	.01
240	Gary Carter	.15	.11	.06
241	Mike Stanley	.03	.02	.01
242	Ken Phelps	.06	.05	.02
243	Chris Bosio	.03	.02	.01
244	Les Straker	.06	.05	.02
245	Dave Smith	.06	.05	.02
246	John Candelaria	.06	.05	.02
247	Joe Orsulak	.03	.02	.01
248	Storm Davis	.08	.06	.03
249	Floyd Bannister	.06	.05	.02
250	Jack Morris	.12	.09	.05
251	Bret Saberhagen	.12	.09	.05
252	Tom Niedenfuer	.06	.05	.02
253	Neal Heaton	.03	.02	.01
254	Eric Show	.06	.05	.02
255	Juan Samuel	.10	.08	.04
256	Dale Sveum	.06	.05	.02
257	Jim Gott	.03	.02	.01
258	Scott Garrelts	.03	.02	.01
259	Larry McWilliams	.03	.02	.01
260	Steve Bedrosian	.08	.06	.03
261	Jack Howell	.06	.05	.02
262	Jay Tibbs	.03	.02	.01
263	Jamie Moyer	.03	.02	.01
264	Doug Sisk	.03	.02	.01
265	Todd Worrell	.08	.06	.03
266	John Farrell	.08	.06	.03
267	Dave Collins	.06	.05	.02
268	Sid Fernandez	.08	.06	.03
269	Tom Brookens	.03	.02	.01
270	Shane Mack	.06	.05	.02
271	Paul Kilgus	.08	.06	.03
272	Chuck Crim	.03	.02	.01
273	Bob Knepper	.06	.05	.02
274	Mike Moore	.03	.02	.01
275	Guillermo Hernandez	.06	.05	.02
276	Dennis Eckersley	.10	.08	.04
277	Graig Nettles	.10	.08	.04
278	Rich Dotson	.06	.05	.02
279	Larry Herndon	.03	.02	.01
280	Gene Larkin	.08	.06	.03
281	Roger McDowell	.08	.06	.03
282	Greg Swindell	.10	.08	.04
283	Juan Agosto	.03	.02	.01
284	Jeff Robinson	.06	.05	.02
285	Mike Dunne	.08	.06	.03
286	Greg Mathews	.06	.05	.02
287	Kent Tekulve	.06	.05	.02
288	Jerry Mumphrey	.03	.02	.01
289	Jack McDowell	.08	.06	.03
290	Frank Viola	.12	.09	.05
291	Mark Gubicza	.08	.06	.03
292	Dave Schmidt	.03	.02	.01
293	Mike Henneman	.08	.06	.03
294	Jimmy Jones	.03	.02	.01
295	Charlie Hough	.06	.05	.02
296	Rafael Santana	.03	.02	.01
297	Chris Speier	.03	.02	.01
298	Mike Witt	.06	.05	.02
299	Pascual Perez	.06	.05	.02
300	Nolan Ryan	.35	.25	.14
301	Mitch Williams	.06	.05	.02
302	Mookie Wilson	.06	.05	.02
303	Mackey Sasser	.06	.05	.02
304	John Cerutti	.06	.05	.02
305	Jeff Reardon	.08	.06	.03
306	Randy Myers	.08	.06	.03
307	Greg Brock	.06	.05	.02
308	Bob Welch	.08	.06	.03
309	Jeff Robinson	.12	.09	.05
310	Harold Reynolds	.06	.05	.02
311	Jim Walewander	.03	.02	.01
312	Dave Magadan	.08	.06	.03
313	Jim Gantner	.03	.02	.01
314	Walt Terrell	.06	.05	.02
315	Wally Backman	.06	.05	.02
316	Luis Salazar	.03	.02	.01
317	Rick Rhoden	.06	.05	.02
318	Tom Henke	.06	.05	.02
319	*Mike Macfarlane*	.20	.15	.08
320	Dan Plesac	.08	.06	.03
321	Calvin Schiraldi	.03	.02	.01
322	Stan Javier	.03	.02	.01
323	Devon White	.10	.08	.04
324	Scott Bradley	.03	.02	.01
325	Bruce Hurst	.08	.06	.03

	MT	NR MT	EX			MT	NR MT	EX
326	Manny Lee	.03	.02	.01	416	Rick Honeycutt	.03	.02	.01
327	Rick Aguilera	.03	.02	.01	417	Greg Booker	.03	.02	.01
328	Bruce Ruffin	.03	.02	.01	418	Tim Belcher	.08	.06	.03
329	Ed Whitson	.03	.02	.01	419	Don August	.08	.06	.03
330	Bo Jackson	.40	.30	.15	420	Dale Mohorcic	.03	.02	.01
331	Ivan Calderon	.06	.05	.02	421	Steve Lombardozzi	.03	.02	.01
332	Mickey Hatcher	.03	.02	.01	422	Atlee Hammaker	.03	.02	.01
333	Barry Jones(FC)	.03	.02	.01	423	Jerry Don Gleaton	.03	.02	.01
334	Ron Hassey	.03	.02	.01	424	Scott Bailes(FC)	.03	.02	.01
335	Bill Wegman	.03	.02	.01	425	Bruce Sutter	.08	.06	.03
336	Damon Berryhill	.15	.11	.06	426	Randy Ready	.03	.02	.01
337	Steve Ontiverso	.03	.02	.01	427	Jerry Reed	.03	.02	.01
338	Dan Pasqua	.08	.06	.03	428	Bryn Smith	.03	.02	.01
339	Bill Pecota	.06	.05	.02	429	Tim Leary	.06	.05	.02
340	Greg Cadaret	.06	.05	.02	430	Mark Clear	.03	.02	.01
341	Scott Bankhead	.03	.02	.01	431	Terry Leach	.03	.02	.01
342	Ron Guidry	.12	.09	.05	432	John Moses	.03	.02	.01
343	Danny Heep	.03	.02	.01	433	Ozzie Guillen	.06	.05	.02
344	Bob Brower	.03	.02	.01	434	Gene Nelson	.03	.02	.01
345	Rich Gedman	.06	.05	.02	435	Gary Ward	.06	.05	.02
346	*Nelson Santovenia*	.20	.15	.08	436	Luis Aguayo	.03	.02	.01
347	George Bell	.20	.15	.08	437	Fernando Valenzuela	.15	.11	.06
348	Ted Power	.03	.02	.01	438	Jeff Russell	.03	.02	.01
349	Mark Grant	.03	.02	.01	439	Cecilio Guante	.03	.02	.01
350a	Roger Clemens (778 Wins)	1.00	.70	.40	440	Don Robinson	.03	.02	.01
350b	Roger Clemens (78 Wins)	.40	.30	.15	441	Rick Anderson(FC)	.03	.02	.01
351	Bill Long	.06	.05	.02	442	Tom Glavine	.08	.06	.03
352	Jay Bell(FC)	.06	.05	.02	443	Daryl Boston	.03	.02	.01
353	Steve Balboni	.06	.05	.02	444	Joe Price	.03	.02	.01
354	Bob Kipper	.03	.02	.01	445	Stewart Cliburn	.03	.02	.01
355	Steve Jeltz	.03	.02	.01	446	Manny Trillo	.03	.02	.01
356	Jesse Orosco	.06	.05	.02	447	Joel Skinner	.03	.02	.01
357	Bob Dernier	.03	.02	.01	448	Charlie Puleo	.03	.02	.01
358	Mickey Tettleton	.03	.02	.01	449	Carlton Fisk	.12	.09	.05
359	Duane Ward(FC)	.03	.02	.01	450	Will Clark	.50	.40	.20
360	Darrin Jackson(FC)	.08	.06	.03	451	Otis Nixon	.03	.02	.01
361	Rey Quinones	.03	.02	.01	452	Rick Schu	.03	.02	.01
362	Mark Grace	1.00	.70	.40	453	Todd Stottlemyre	.15	.11	.06
363	Steve Lake	.03	.02	.01	454	Tim Birtsas	.03	.02	.01
364	Pat Perry	.03	.02	.01	455	*Dave Gallagher*	.20	.15	.08
365	Terry Steinbach	.08	.06	.03	456	Barry Lyons	.03	.02	.01
366	Alan Ashby	.03	.02	.01	457	Fred Manrique	.06	.05	.02
367	Jeff Montgomery	.06	.05	.02	458	Ernest Riles	.03	.02	.01
368	Steve Buechele	.03	.02	.01	459	*Doug Jennings*(FC)	.20	.15	.08
369	Chris Brown	.06	.05	.02	460	Joe Magrane	.08	.06	.03
370	Orel Hershiser	.20	.15	.08	461	Jamie Quirk	.03	.02	.01
371	Todd Benzinger	.10	.08	.04	462	*Jack Armstrong*	.40	.30	.15
372	Ron Gant	.15	.11	.06	463	Bobby Witt	.08	.06	.03
373	Paul Assenmacher(FC)	.03	.02	.01	464	Keith Miller	.06	.05	.02
374	Joey Meyer	.08	.06	.03	465	*Todd Burns*	.30	.25	.12
375	Neil Allen	.03	.02	.01	466	*John Dopson*	.20	.15	.08
376	Mike Davis	.06	.05	.02	467	Rich Yett	.03	.02	.01
377	Jeff Parrett(FC)	.08	.06	.03	468	Craig Reynolds	.03	.02	.01
378	Jay Howell	.06	.05	.02	469	Dave Bergman	.03	.02	.01
379	Rafael Belliard	.03	.02	.01	470	Rex Hudler	.03	.02	.01
380	Luis Polonia	.06	.05	.02	471	Eric King	.03	.02	.01
381	Keith Atherton	.03	.02	.01	472	Joaquin Andujar	.06	.05	.02
382	Kent Hrbek	.15	.11	.06	473	*Sil Campusano*	.20	.15	.08
383	Bob Stanley	.03	.02	.01	474	Terry Mulholland(FC)	.03	.02	.01
384	Dave LaPoint	.06	.05	.02	475	Mike Flanagan	.06	.05	.02
385	Rance Mulliniks	.03	.02	.01	476	Greg Harris	.03	.02	.01
386	Melido Perez	.08	.06	.03	477	Tommy John	.10	.08	.04
387	Doug Jones	.10	.08	.04	478	Dave Anderson	.03	.02	.01
388	Steve Lyons	.03	.02	.01	479	Fred Toliver	.03	.02	.01
389	Alejandro Pena	.06	.05	.02	480	Jimmy Key	.08	.06	.03
390	Frank White	.06	.05	.02	481	Donell Nixon	.03	.02	.01
391	Pat Tabler	.06	.05	.02	482	Mark Portugal(FC)	.03	.02	.01
392	Eric Plunk(FC)	.03	.02	.01	483	Tom Pagnozzi	.06	.05	.02
393	Mike Maddux(FC)	.03	.02	.01	484	Jeff Kunkel	.03	.02	.01
394	Allan Anderson(FC)	.06	.05	.02	485	Frank Williams	.03	.02	.01
395	Bob Brenly	.03	.02	.01	486	Jody Reed	.10	.08	.04
396	Rick Cerone	.03	.02	.01	487	Roberto Kelly	.25	.20	.10
397	Scott Terry(FC)	.08	.06	.03	488	Shawn Hillegas	.06	.05	.02
398	Mike Jackson	.06	.05	.02	489	Jerry Reuss	.06	.05	.02
399	Bobby Thigpen	.08	.06	.03	490	Mark Davis	.03	.02	.01
400	Don Sutton	.12	.09	.05	491	Jeff Sellers	.03	.02	.01
401	Cecil Espy	.06	.05	.02	492	Zane Smith	.06	.05	.02
402	Junior Ortiz	.03	.02	.01	493	Al Newman(FC)	.03	.02	.01
403	Mike Smithson	.03	.02	.01	494	Mike Young	.03	.02	.01
404	Bud Black	.03	.02	.01	495	Larry Parrish	.06	.05	.02
405	Tom Foley	.03	.02	.01	496	Herm Winningham	.03	.02	.01
406	Andres Thomas	.06	.05	.02	497	Carmen Castillo	.03	.02	.01
407	Rick Sutcliffe	.08	.06	.03	498	Joe Hesketh	.03	.02	.01
408	Brian Harper	.03	.02	.01	499	Darrell Miller	.03	.02	.01
409	John Smiley	.10	.08	.04	500	Mike LaCoss	.03	.02	.01
410	Juan Nieves	.06	.05	.02	501	Charlie Lea	.03	.02	.01
411	Shawn Abner	.08	.06	.03	502	Bruce Benedict	.03	.02	.01
412	Wes Gardner(FC)	.06	.05	.02	503	Chuck Finley(FC)	.03	.02	.01
413	Darren Daulton	.03	.02	.01	504	Brad Wellman(FC)	.03	.02	.01
414	Juan Berenguer	.03	.02	.01	505	Tim Crews	.06	.05	.02
415	Charles Hudson	.03	.02	.01	506	Ken Gerhart	.06	.05	.02

		MT	NR MT	EX
507	Brian Holton (Born: Jan. 25, 1965 Denver, CO)	.20	.15	.08
508	Dennis Lamp	.03	.02	.01
509	Bobby Meacham (1984 Games is 099)	.20	.15	.08
510	Tracy Jones	.08	.06	.03
511	Mike Fitzgerald	.03	.02	.01
512	*Jeff Bittiger*	.12	.09	.05
513	Tim Flannery	.03	.02	.01
514	Ray Hayward(FC)	.03	.02	.01
515	Dave Leiper	.03	.02	.01
516	Rod Scurry	.03	.02	.01
517	Carmelo Martinez	.03	.02	.01
518	Curtis Wilkerson	.03	.02	.01
519	Stan Jefferson	.03	.02	.01
520	Dan Quisenberry	.06	.05	.02
521	Lloyd McClendon(FC)	.03	.02	.01
522	Steve Trout	.03	.02	.01
523	Larry Andersen	.03	.02	.01
524	Don Aase	.03	.02	.01
525	Bob Forsch	.06	.05	.02
526	Geno Petralli	.03	.02	.01
527	Angel Salazar	.03	.02	.01
528	*Mike Schooler*	.20	.15	.08
529	Jose Oquendo	.03	.02	.01
530	Jay Buhner	.10	.08	.04
531	Tom Bolton(FC)	.06	.05	.02
532	Al Nipper	.03	.02	.01
533	Dave Henderson	.08	.06	.03
534	*John Costello*(FC)	.20	.15	.08
535	Donnie Moore	.03	.02	.01
536	Mike Laga	.03	.02	.01
537	Mike Gallego	.03	.02	.01
538	Jim Clancy	.06	.05	.02
539	Joel Youngblood	.03	.02	.01
540	Rick Leach	.03	.02	.01
541	Kevin Romine	.03	.02	.01
542	Mark Salas	.03	.02	.01
543	Greg Minton	.03	.02	.01
544	Dave Palmer	.03	.02	.01
545	Dwayne Murphy	.06	.05	.02
546	Jim Deshaies	.03	.02	.01
547	Don Gordon(FC)	.03	.02	.01
548	*Ricky Jordan*	.50	.40	.20
549	Mike Boddicker	.06	.05	.02
550	Mike Scott	.10	.08	.04
551	Jeff Ballard(FC)	.08	.06	.03
552a	Jose Rijo (uniform number #24 on card back)	.20	.15	.08
552b	Jose Rijo (uniform number #27 on card back)	.08	.06	.03
553	Danny Darwin	.03	.02	.01
554	Tom Browning	.08	.06	.03
555	Danny Jackson	.12	.09	.05
556	Rick Dempsey	.06	.05	.02
557	Jeffrey Leonard	.06	.05	.02
558	Jeff Musselman	.06	.05	.02
559	Ron Robinson	.03	.02	.01
560	John Tudor	.08	.06	.03
561	Don Slaught	.03	.02	.01
562	Dennis Rasmussen	.08	.06	.03
563	*Brady Anderson*	.30	.25	.12
564	Pedro Guerrero	.12	.09	.05
565	Paul Molitor	.12	.09	.05
566	*Terry Clark*(FC)	.15	.11	.06
567	Terry Puhl	.03	.02	.01
568	Mike Campbell(FC)	.08	.06	.03
569	Paul Mirabella	.03	.02	.01
570	Jeff Hamilton(FC)	.06	.05	.02
571	*Oswald Peraza*	.20	.15	.08
572	Bob McClure	.03	.02	.01
573	*Jose Bautista*(FC)	.15	.11	.06
574	Alex Trevino	.03	.02	.01
575	John Franco	.08	.06	.03
576	*Mark Parent*(FC)	.15	.11	.06
577	Nelson Liriano	.06	.05	.02
578	Steve Shields	.03	.02	.01
579	Odell Jones	.03	.02	.01
580	Al Leiter	.20	.15	.08
581	Dave Stapleton(FC)	.06	.05	.02
582	1988 World Series (Jose Canseco, Kirk Gibson, Orel Hershiser, Dave Stewart)	.20	.15	.08
583	Donnie Hill	.03	.02	.01
584	Chuck Jackson	.06	.05	.02
585	Rene Gonzales(FC)	.06	.05	.02
586	Tracy Woodson(FC)	.08	.06	.03
587	Jim Adduci(FC)	.03	.02	.01
588	Mario Soto	.06	.05	.02
589	Jeff Blauser	.08	.06	.03
590	Jim Traber	.06	.05	.02
591	Jon Perlman(FC)	.03	.02	.01

		MT	NR MT	EX
592	Mark Williamson(FC)	.06	.05	.02
593	Dave Meads	.03	.02	.01
594	Jim Eisenreich	.03	.02	.01
595	*Paul Gibson*(FC)	.15	.11	.06
596	Mike Birkbeck	.03	.02	.01
597	Terry Francona	.03	.02	.01
598	Paul Zuvella(FC)	.03	.02	.01
599	Franklin Stubbs	.03	.02	.01
600	Gregg Jefferies	1.50	1.25	.60
601	John Cangelosi	.03	.02	.01
602	Mike Sharperson(FC)	.03	.02	.01
603	Mike Diaz	.06	.05	.02
604	*Gary Varsho*(FC)	.20	.15	.08
605	*Terry Blocker*(FC)	.12	.09	.05
606	Charlie O'Brien(FC)	.03	.02	.01
607	Jim Eppard(FC)	.08	.06	.03
608	John Davis	.03	.02	.01
609	Ken Griffey, Sr.	.08	.06	.03
610	Buddy Bell	.06	.05	.02
611	Ted Simmons	.08	.06	.03
612	Matt Williams	.10	.08	.04
613	Danny Cox	.06	.05	.02
614	Al Pedrique	.03	.02	.01
615	Ron Oester	.03	.02	.01
616	*John Smoltz*(FC)	.70	.50	.30
617	Bob Melvin	.03	.02	.01
618	*Rob Dibble*	.60	.45	.25
619	Kirt Manwaring	.10	.08	.04
620	1989 Rookie (Felix Fermin)(FC)	.06	.05	.02
621	1989 Rookie *(Doug Dascenzo)*(FC)	.25	.20	.10
622	1989 Rookie *(Bill Brennan)*(FC)	.20	.15	.08
623	1989 Rookie *(Carlos Quintana)*(FC)	.40	.30	.15
624	1989 Rookie *(Mike Harkey)*(FC)	.50	.40	.20
625	1989 Rookie *(Gary Sheffield)*(FC)	2.00	1.50	.80
626	1989 Rookie (Tom Prince)(FC)	.08	.06	.03
627	1989 Rookie *(Steve Searcy)*(FC)	.25	.20	.10
628	1989 Rookie *(Charlie Hayes)*(FC)	.25	.20	.10
629	1989 Rookie *(Felix Jose)*(FC)	.50	.40	.20
630	1989 Rookie *(Sandy Alomar)*(FC)	1.50	1.25	.60
631	1989 Rookie *(Derek Lilliquist)*(FC)	.40	.30	.15
632	1989 Rookie *(Geronimo Berroa)*(FC)	.06	.05	.02
633	1989 Rookie *(Luis Medina)*(FC)	.25	.20	.10
634	1989 Rookie *(Tom Gordon)*(FC)	.80	.60	.30
635	1989 Rookie *(Ramon Martinez)*(FC)	2.00	1.50	.80
636	1989 Rookie *(Craig Worthington)*(FC)	.35	.25	.12
637	1989 Rookie (Edgar Martinez)(FC)	.35	.25	.14
638	1989 Rookie *(Chad Krueter)*(FC)	.20	.15	.08
639	1989 Rookie *(Ron Jones)*(FC)	.30	.25	.12
640	1989 Rookie *(Van Snider)*(FC)	.20	.15	.08
641	1989 Rookie *(Lance Blankenship)*(FC)	.25	.20	.10
642	1989 Rookie *(Dwight Smith)*(FC)	.80	.60	.30
643	1989 Rookie *(Cameron Drew)*(FC)	.20	.15	.08
644	1989 Rookie *(Jerald Clark)*(FC)	.20	.15	.08
645	1989 Rookie *(Randy Johnson)*(FC)	.50	.40	.20
646	1989 Rookie *(Norm Charlton)*(FC)	.20	.15	.08
647	1989 Rookie *(Todd Frohwirth)*(FC)	.08	.06	.03
648	1989 Rookie *(Luis de los Santos)*(FC)	.20	.15	.08
649	1989 Rookie *(Tim Jones)*(FC)	.15	.11	.06
650	1989 Rookie *(Dave West)*(FC)	.40	.30	.15
651	1989 Rookie *(Bob Milacki)*(FC)	.25	.20	.10
652	1988 Highlight (Wrigley Field)	.06	.05	.02
653	1988 Highlight (Orel Hershiser)	.10	.08	.04
654a	1988 Highlight (Wade Boggs) ("...sixth consecutive seaason..." on back)	2.00	1.50	.80
654b	1988 Highlight (Wade Boggs) ("...sixth consecutive season..." on back)	.30	.25	.12
655	1988 Highlight (Jose Canseco)	.60	.45	.25
656	1988 Highlight (Doug Jones)	.06	.05	.02
657	1988 Highlight (Rickey Henderson)	.12	.09	.05
658	1988 Highlight (Tom Browning)	.06	.05	.02
659	1988 Highlight (Mike Greenwell)	.30	.25	.12
660	1988 Highlight (A.L. Win Streak)	.06	.05	.02

1989 Score Traded

Score issued its second consecutive traded set in 1989 to supplement and update its regular set. The 110-card traded set features the same basic card design as the regular 1989 Score set. The set consists of rookies and traded players pictured with correct teams. The set was sold by hobby dealers

in a special box that included an assortment of "Magic Motion" trivia cards.

	MT	NR MT	EX
Complete Set:	13.00	9.75	5.25
Common Player:	.06	.05	.02

		MT	NR MT	EX
1T	Rafael Palmeiro	.10	.08	.04
2T	Nolan Ryan	1.50	1.25	.60
3T	Jack Clark	.10	.08	.04
4T	Dave LaPoint	.06	.05	.02
5T	Mike Moore	.08	.06	.03
6T	Pete O'Brien	.06	.05	.02
7T	Jeffrey Leonard	.06	.05	.02
8T	Rob Murphy	.06	.05	.02
9T	Tom Herr	.06	.05	.02
10T	Claudell Washington	.06	.05	.02
11T	Mike Pagliarulo	.06	.05	.02
12T	Steve Lake	.06	.05	.02
13T	Spike Owen	.06	.05	.02
14T	Andy Hawkins	.06	.05	.02
15T	Todd Benzinger	.06	.05	.03
16T	Mookie Wilson	.06	.05	.03
17T	Bert Blyleven	.08	.06	.03
18T	Jeff Treadway	.06	.05	.02
19T	Bruce Hurst	.08	.06	.03
20T	Steve Sax	.12	.09	.05
21T	Juan Samuel	.06	.05	.02
22T	Jesse Barfield	.06	.05	.02
23T	Carmelo Castillo	.06	.05	.02
24T	Terry Leach	.06	.05	.02
25T	Mark Langston	.12	.09	.05
26T	Eric King	.06	.05	.02
27T	Steve Balboni	.06	.05	.02
28T	Len Dykstra	.06	.05	.02
29T	Keith Moreland	.06	.05	.02
30T	Terry Kennedy	.06	.05	.02
31T	Eddie Murray	.12	.09	.05
32T	Mitch Williams	.10	.08	.04
33T	Jeff Parrett	.06	.05	.02
34T	Wally Backman	.06	.05	.02
35T	Julio Franco	.10	.08	.04
36T	Lance Parrish	.06	.05	.02
37T	Nick Esasky	.06	.05	.02
38T	Luis Polonia	.06	.05	.02
39T	Kevin Gross	.06	.05	.02
40T	John Dopson	.06	.05	.02
41T	Willie Randolph	.08	.06	.03
42T	Jim Clancy	.06	.05	.02
43T	Tracy Jones	.06	.05	.02
44T	Phil Bradley	.06	.05	.02
45T	Milt Thompson	.06	.05	.02
46T	Chris James	.06	.05	.02
47T	Scott Fletcher	.06	.05	.02
48T	Kal Daniels	.08	.06	.03
49T	Steve Bedrosian	.06	.05	.02
50T	Rickey Henderson	.50	.40	.20
51T	Dion James	.06	.05	.02
52T	Tim Leary	.06	.05	.02
53T	Roger McDowell	.06	.05	.02
54T	Mel Hall	.06	.05	.02
55T	Dickie Thon	.06	.05	.02
56T	Zane Smith	.06	.05	.02
57T	Danny Heep	.06	.05	.02
58T	Bob McClure	.06	.05	.02
59T	Brian Holton	.06	.05	.02
60T	Randy Ready	.06	.05	.02
61T	Bob Melvin	.06	.05	.02
62T	Harold Baines	.08	.06	.03
63T	Lance McCullers	.06	.05	.02
64T	Jody Davis	.06	.05	.02

		MT	NR MT	EX
65T	Darrell Evans	.06	.05	.02
66T	Joel Youngblood	.08	.06	.03
67T	Frank Viola	.08	.06	.03
68T	Mike Aldrete	.06	.05	.02
69T	Greg Cadaret	.06	.05	.02
70T	John Kruk	.06	.05	.02
71T	Pat Sheridan	.06	.05	.02
72T	Oddibe McDowell	.06	.05	.02
73T	Tom Brookens	.06	.05	.02
74T	Bob Boone	.08	.06	.03
75T	Walt Terrell	.06	.05	.02
76T	Joel Skinner	.06	.05	.02
77T	Randy Johnson	.10	.08	.04
78T	Felix Fermin	.06	.05	.03
79T	Rick Mahler	.06	.05	.03
80T	Rich Dotson	.06	.05	.03
81T	Cris Carpenter(FC)	.20	.15	.08
82T	Bill Spiers(FC)	.35	.25	.14
83T	Junior Felix(FC)	1.25	.90	.50
84T	Joe Girardi(FC)	.30	.25	.12
85T	Jerome Walton(FC)	1.75	1.25	.70
86T	Greg Litton(FC)	.25	.20	.10
87T	Greg Harris(FC)	.20	.15	.08
88T	Jim Abbott(FC)	1.25	.90	.50
89T	Kevin Brown(FC)	.30	.25	.12
90T	John Wetteland(FC)	.50	.40	.20
91T	Gary Wayne(FC)	.20	.15	.08
92T	Rich Monteleone(FC)	.25	.20	.10
93T	Bob Geren(FC)	.30	.25	.12
94T	Clay Parker(FC)	.20	.15	.08
95T	Steve Finley(FC)	.35	.25	.14
96T	Gregg Olson(FC)	.80	.60	.30
97T	Ken Patterson(FC)	.15	.11	.06
98T	Ken Hill(FC)	.20	.15	.08
99T	Scott Scudder(FC)	.35	.25	.14
100T	Ken Griffey, Jr.(FC)	7.00	5.25	2.75
101T	Jeff Brantley(FC)	.25	.20	.10
102T	Donn Pall(FC)	.15	.11	.06
103T	Carlos Martinez(FC)	.30	.25	.12
104T	Joe Oliver(FC)	.40	.30	.15
105T	Omar Vizquel(FC)	.25	.20	.10
106T	Joey Belle(FC)	.30	.25	.12
107T	Kenny Rogers(FC)	.20	.15	.08
108T	Mark Carreon(FC)	.15	.11	.06
109T	Rolando Roomes(FC)	.20	.15	.08
110T	Pete Harnsisch(FC)	.20	.15	.08

1989 Score Young Superstar-Series I

This standard-size card set (2-1/2" by 3-1/2") displays full-color action photos with a high gloss finish. The card fronts feature a red and blue border surrounding the photo with the team logo in the lower right. A red band beneath the photo provided the setting for the player ID including name, position, and team number. The flip side features a red "Young Superstar" headline above a close-up photo. Above the headline, appears the player's personal information and statistics in orange and black ink respectively. The top of the flip side highlights the player's name and the Score logo in white within a purple band. To the right of the close-up photo a condensed scouting report and career highlights are revealed. The card number and related logos appear on the bottom portion. Five trivia cards featuring "A "ear to Remember" accompanied the series. Each trivia card relates to a highlight from the past 56 years. This set was distributed via a write-in offer with Score card wrappers.

		MT	NR MT	EX
Complete Set:		9.00	6.75	3.50
Common Player:		.10	.08	.04
1	Gregg Jefferies	.80	.60	.30
2	Jody Reed	.10	.08	.04
3	Mark Grace	.40	.30	.15
4	Dave Gallagher	.15	.11	.06
5	Bo Jackson	1.25	.90	.50
6	Jay Buhner	.10	.08	.04
7	Melido Perez	.10	.08	.04
8	Bobby Witt	.10	.08	.04
9	David Cone	.15	.11	.06
10	Chris Sabo	.15	.11	.06
11	Pat Borders	.10	.08	.04
12	Mark Grant	.10	.08	.04
13	Mike Macfarlane	.10	.08	.04
14	Mike Jackson	.10	.08	.04
15	Ricky Jordan	.30	.25	.12
16	Ron Gant	.10	.08	.04
17	Al Leiter	.10	.08	.04
18	Jeff Parrett	.10	.08	.04
19	Pete Smith	.10	.08	.04
20	Walt Weiss	.15	.11	.06
21	Doug Drabek	.12	.09	.05
22	Kirt Manwaring	.15	.11	.06
23	Keith Miller	.10	.08	.04
24	Damon Berryhill	.12	.09	.05
25	Gary Sheffield	.80	.60	.30
26	Brady Anderson	.20	.15	.08
27	Mitch Williams	.15	.11	.06
28	Roberto Alomar	.30	.25	.12
29	Bobby Thigpen	.12	.09	.05
30	Bryan Harvey	.10	.08	.04
31	Jose Rijo	.15	.11	.06
32	Dave West	.35	.25	.12
33	Joey Meyer	.10	.08	.04
34	Allan Anderson	.12	.09	.05
35	Rafael Palmeiro	.20	.15	.08
36	Tim Belcher	.30	.25	.12
37	John Smiley	.15	.11	.06
38	Mackey Sasser	.10	.08	.04
39	Greg Maddux	.30	.25	.12
40	Ramon Martinez	1.00	.70	.40
41	Randy Myers	.12	.09	.05
42	Scott Bankhead	.15	.11	.06

1989 Score Young Superstar-Series II

Score followed up with a second series of Young Superstars in 1989. The second series also included 42 cards and featured the same design as the first series. The set was also distributed via a write-in offer with Score card wrappers.

		MT	NR MT	EX
Complete Set:		6.00	4.50	2.50
Common Player:		.10	.08	.04
1	Sandy Alomar	.80	.60	.30
2	Tom Gordon	.60	.45	.25
3	Ron Jones	.30	.25	.12

		MT	NR MT	EX
4	Todd Burns	.10	.08	.04
5	Paul O'Neill	.10	.08	.04
6	Gene Larkin	.10	.08	.04
7	Eric King	.10	.08	.04
8	Jeff Robinson	.10	.08	.04
9	Bill Wegman	.10	.08	.04
10	Cecil Espy	.12	.09	.05
11	Jose Guzman	.10	.08	.04
12	Kelly Gruber	.20	.15	.08
13	Duane Ward	.10	.08	.04
14	Mark Gubicza	.25	.20	.10
15	Norm Charlton	.20	.15	.08
16	Jose Oquendo	.10	.08	.04
17	Geronimo Berroa	.15	.11	.06
18	Dwight Smith	.50	.40	.20
19	Lance McCullers	.10	.08	.04
20	Jimmy Jones	.10	.08	.04
21	Craig Worthington	.25	.20	.10
22	Mike Devereaux	.12	.09	.05
23	Bob Milacki	.15	.11	.06
24	Dale Sveum	.10	.08	.04
25	Carlos Quintana	.20	.15	.08
26	Luis Medina	.15	.11	.06
27	Steve Searcy	.15	.11	.06
28	Don August	.10	.08	.04
29	Shawn Hillegas	.10	.08	.04
30	Mike Campbell	.10	.08	.04
31	Mike Harkey	.25	.20	.10
32	Randy Johnson	.20	.15	.08
33	Craig Biggio	.35	.25	.12
34	Mike Schooler	.12	.09	.05
35	Andres Thomas	.10	.08	.04
36	Van Snider	.20	.15	.08
37	Cameron Drew	.15	.11	.06
38	Kevin Mitchell	.70	.50	.30
39	Lance Johnson	.15	.11	.06
40	Chad Kreuter	.20	.15	.08
41	Danny Jackson	.10	.08	.04
42	Kurt Stillwell	.10	.08	.04

1989 Score Rising Star

Similar in design to the Score Superstar set, this 100-card set showcased a host of rookies including Gary Sheffield and Gregg Jefferies. The full-color action photos are surrounded by a bright blue border with a green inner highlight line. The Score logo appears in the upper left in green and white. The player's name, position and team are found at the bottom. The flip sides display a full-color close-up of the player above his name and career highlights. The card number and player's rookie year are featured to the right. A "Rising Star" headline highlights the top border. Like the "Score Superstar" the Score "Rising Star" set was marketed as a combination with a related magazine. "1988-89 Baseball's 100 Hottest Rookies" accompanies the set which also includes six Magic Motion baseball trivia cards featuring "Rookies to Remember." The magazine/card sets were available at a select group of retailers.

		MT	NR MT	EX
Complete Set:		10.00	7.50	4.00
Common Player:		.07	.05	.03
1	Gregg Jefferies	.80	.60	.30
2	Vicente Palacios	.15	.11	.06
3	Cameron Drew	.10	.08	.04

		MT	NR MT	EX
4	Doug Dascenzo	.12	.09	.05
5	Luis Medina	.12	.09	.05
6	Craig Worthington	.20	.15	.08
7	Rob Ducey	.08	.06	.04
8	Hal Morris	.60	.45	.25
9	Bill Brennan	.07	.05	.03
10	Gary Sheffield	.80	.60	.30
11	Mike Devereaux	.10	.08	.04
12	Hensley Meulens	.40	.30	.15
13	Carlos Quintana	.20	.15	.08
14	Todd Frohwirth	.07	.05	.03
15	Scott Lusader	.09	.07	.04
16	Mark Carreon	.15	.11	.06
17	Torey Lovullo	.20	.15	.08
18	Randy Velarde	.12	.09	.05
19	Billy Bean	.09	.07	.04
20	Lance Blankenship	.15	.11	.06
21	Chris Gwynn	.15	.11	.06
22	Felix Jose	.20	.15	.08
23	Derek Lilliquist	.20	.15	.08
24	Gary Thurman	.07	.05	.03
25	Ron Jones	.20	.15	.08
26	Dave Justice	.40	.30	.15
27	Johnny Paredes	.08	.06	.03
28	Tim Jones	.10	.08	.04
29	Jose Gonzalez	.10	.08	.04
30	Geronimo Berroa	.15	.11	.06
31	Trevor Wilson	.12	.09	.05
32	Morris Madden	.30	.25	.12
33	Lance Johnson	.15	.11	.06
34	Marvin Freeman	.07	.05	.03
35	Jose Cecena	.07	.05	.03
36	Jim Corsi	.07	.05	.03
37	Rolando Roomes	.25	.20	.10
38	Scott Medvin	.07	.05	.03
39	Charlie Hayes	.20	.15	.08
40	Edgar Martinez	.15	.11	.06
41	Van Snider	.20	.15	.08
42	John Fishel	.07	.05	.02
43	Bruce Fields	.07	.05	.03
44	Darryl Hamilton	.09	.07	.04
45	Tom Prince	.09	.07	.03
46	Kirt Manwaring	.20	.15	.08
47	Steve Searcy	.12	.09	.05
48	Mike Harkey	.20	.15	.08
49	German Gonzalez	.07	.05	.03
50	Tony Perezchica	.07	.05	.03
51	Chad Kreuter	.15	.11	.06
52	Luis de los Santos	.10	.08	.04
53	Steve Curry	.07	.05	.03
54	Greg Bailey	.30	.25	.12
55	Ramon Martinez	.30	.25	.12
56	Ron Tingley	.07	.05	.03
57	Randy Kramer	.07	.05	.03
58	Alex Madrid	.07	.05	.03
59	Kevin Reimer	.15	.11	.06
60	Dave Otto	.07	.05	.03
61	Ken Patterson	.07	.05	.03
62	Keith Miller	.10	.08	.04
63	Randy Johnson	.10	.08	.04
64	Dwight Smith	.40	.30	.15
65	Eric Yelding	.20	.15	.08
66	Bob Geren	.40	.30	.15
67	Shane Turner	.25	.20	.10
68	Tom Gordon	.70	.50	.30
69	Jeff Huson	.30	.25	.12
70	Marty Brown	.25	.20	.10
71	Nelson Santovenia	.20	.15	.08
72	Roberto Alomar	.20	.15	.08
73	Mike Schooler	.15	.11	.06
74	Pete Smith	.10	.08	.04
75	John Costello	.07	.05	.03
76	Chris Sabo	.20	.15	.08
77	Damon Berryhill	.09	.07	.04
78	Mark Grace	.60	.45	.25
79	Melido Perez	.07	.05	.03
80	Al Leiter	.07	.05	.03
81	Todd Stottlemyre	.20	.15	.08
82	Mackey Sasser	.07	.05	.03
83	Don August	.07	.05	.03
84	Jeff Treadway	.07	.05	.03
85	Jody Reed	.09	.07	.05
86	Mike Campbell	.07	.05	.03
87	Ron Gant	.09	.07	.04
88	Ricky Jordan	.30	.25	.12
89	Terry Clark	.07	.05	.03
90	Roberto Kelly	.20	.15	.08
91	Pat Borders	.20	.15	.08
92	Bryan Harvey	.20	.15	.08
93	Joey Meyer	.20	.15	.08
94	Tim Belcher	.25	.20	.10
95	Walt Weiss	.15	.11	.06

		MT	NR MT	EX
96	Dave Gallagher	.15	.11	.06
97	Mike Macfarlane	.07	.05	.03
98	Craig Biggio	.30	.25	.12
99	Jack Armstrong	.15	.11	.06
100	Todd Burns	.07	.05	.03

1989 Score Superstar

This 100-card set features full-color action photos of baseball's superstars, and also includes six Magic Motion "Rookies to Remember" baseball trivia cards. The card fronts contain a bright red border with a blue line inside highlighting the photo. The Score logo appears in the bottom left corner. The player ID is displayed in unique fashion using overlapping triangles in white, green, and yellow. The flip side features a full-color player close-up directly beneath a bright red "Superstar" headline. The set was marketed along with the magazine "1989 Baseball's 100 Hottest Players". The magazine/card set combo was available at select retailers.

		MT	NR MT	EX
Complete Set:		9.00	6.75	3.50
Common Player:		.06	.05	.02
1	Jose Canseco	1.00	.70	.40
2	David Cone	.15	.11	.06
3	Dave Winfield	.15	.11	.06
4	George Brett	.15	.11	.06
5	Frank Viola	.09	.07	.05
6	Cory Snyder	.06	.05	.02
7	Alan Trammell	.09	.07	.04
8	Dwight Evans	.09	.07	.04
9	Tim Leary	.06	.05	.03
10	Don Mattingly	.80	.60	.30
11	Kirby Puckett	.30	.25	.12
12	Carney Lansford	.06	.05	.02
13	Dennis Martinez	.06	.05	.02
14	Kent Hrbek	.10	.08	.04
15	Doc Gooden	.30	.25	.12
16	Dennis Eckersley	.08	.06	.03
17	Kevin Seitzer	.08	.06	.03
18	Lee Smith	.06	.05	.02
19	Danny Tartabull	.15	.11	.06
20	Gerald Perry	.06	.05	.02
21	Gary Gaetti	.10	.08	.04
22	Rick Reuschel	.08	.06	.03
23	Keith Hernandez	.08	.06	.03
24	Jeff Reardon	.06	.05	.02
25	Mark McGwire	.80	.60	.30
26	Juan Samuel	.06	.05	.02
27	Jack Clark	.06	.05	.02
28	Robin Yount	.15	.11	.06
29	Steve Bedrosian	.06	.05	.02
30	Kirk Gibson	.08	.06	.03
31	Barry Bonds	.08	.06	.03
32	Dan Plesac	.06	.05	.02
33	Steve Sax	.06	.05	.02
34	Jeff Robinson	.06	.05	.02
35	Orel Hershiser	.10	.08	.04
36	Julio Franco	.08	.06	.03
37	Dave Righetti	.06	.05	.02
38	Bob Knepper	.06	.05	.02
39	Carlton Fisk	.08	.06	.03
41	Doug Jones	.06	.05	.02
42	Bobby Bonilla	.20	.15	.08
43	Ellis Burks	.30	.25	.12

		MT	NR MT	EX
44	Pedro Guerrero	.15	.11	.06
45	Rickey Henderson	.25	.20	.12
46	Glenn Davis	.10	.08	.04
47	Benny Santiago	.15	.11	.06
48	Greg Maddux	.20	.15	.08
49	Teddy Higuera	.06	.05	.02
50	Darryl Strawberry	.30	.25	.12
51	Mike Scott	.08	.06	.03
52	Mike Henneman	.06	.05	.02
53	Eric Davis	.35	.25	.12
54	Paul Molitor	.09	.07	.04
55	Rafael Palmeiro	.06	.05	.02
56	Joe Carter	.09	.07	.05
57	Ryne Sandberg	.15	.11	.06
58	Tony Fernandez	.08	.06	.03
59	Barry Larkin	.10	.08	.04
60	Ozzie Guillen	.06	.05	.02
61	Tom Browning	.06	.05	.02
62	Mark Davis	.08	.06	.03
63	Tom Henke	.06	.05	.02
64	Nolan Ryan	.60	.45	.25
65	Fred McGriff	.30	.25	.12
66	Dale Murphy	.10	.08	.06
67	Mark Langston	.10	.08	.06
68	Bobby Thigpen	.06	.05	.02
69	Mark Gubicza	.08	.06	.03
70	Mike Greenwell	.50	.40	.20
71	Ron Darling	.06	.05	.02
72	Gerald Young	.06	.05	.02
73	Wally Joyner	.10	.08	.04
74	Andres Galarraga	.10	.08	.04
75	Danny Jackson	.06	.05	.02
76	Mike Schmidt	.25	.20	.10
77	Cal Ripken, Jr.	.15	.11	.06
78	Alvin Davis	.08	.06	.03
79	Bruce Hurst	.06	.05	.02
80	Andre Dawson	.12	.09	.05
81	Bob Boone	.06	.05	.02
82	Harold Reynolds	.06	.05	.02
83	Eddie Murray	.06	.05	.02
84	Robby Thompson	.06	.05	.02
85	Will Clark	.80	.60	.30
86	Vince Coleman	.09	.07	.04
87	Doug Drabek	.06	.05	.02
88	Ozzie Smith	.08	.06	.03
89	Bob Welch	.06	.05	.02
90	Roger Clemens	.25	.20	.10
91	George Bell	.08	.06	.03
92	Andy Van Slyke	.08	.06	.03
93	Willie McGee	.06	.05	.02
94	Todd Worrell	.06	.05	.02
95	Tim Raines	.06	.05	.02
96	Kevin McReynolds	.10	.08	.04
97	John Franco	.06	.05	.02
98	Jim Gott	.06	.05	.02
99	Johnny Ray	.06	.05	.02
100	Wade Boggs	.80	.60	.30

1989 Score Yankees

This 33-card New York Yankee team set was produced by Score as an in-stadium promotion in 1989 and was distributed to fans attending the July 29 game at Yankee Stadium. The standard-size cards include a full-color player photo with a line drawing of the famous Yankee Stadium facade running along the top of the card. The player's name, "New York Yankees" and position appear below the photo. A second full-color photo is included on the back of the

card, along with stats, data and a brief player profile. The set includes a special Thurman Munson commemorative card.

		MT	NR MT	EX
	Complete Set:	7.00	5.25	2.75
	Common Player:	.15	.11	.06
1	Don Mattingly	1.75	1.25	.70
2	Steve Sax	.30	.25	.12
3	Alvaro Espinoza	.25	.20	.10
4	Luis Polonia	.20	.15	.08
5	Jesse Barfield	.25	.20	.10
6	Dave Righetti	.25	.20	.10
7	Dave Winfield	.30	.25	.12
8	John Candelaria	.15	.11	.06
9	Wayne Tolleson	.15	.11	.06
10	Ken Phelps	.15	.11	.06
11	Rafael Santana	.15	.11	.06
12	Don Slaught	.15	.11	.06
13	Mike Pagliarulo	.20	.15	.08
14	Lance McCullers	.15	.11	.06
15	Dave LaPoint	.15	.11	.06
16	Dale Mohorcic	.15	.11	.06
17	Steve Balboni	.15	.11	.06
18	Roberto Kelly	.50	.40	.20
19	Andy Hawkins	.25	.20	.10
20	Mel Hall	.20	.15	.08
21	Tom Brookens	.15	.11	.06
22	Deion Sanders	.70	.50	.30
23	Richard Dotson	.15	.11	.06
24	Lee Guetterman	.15	.11	.06
25	Bob Geren	.30	.25	.12
26	Jimmy Jones	.15	.11	.06
27	Chuck Cary	.15	.11	.06
28	Ron Guidry	.25	.20	.10
29	Hal Morris	.50	.40	.20
30	Clay Parker	.25	.20	.10
31	Dallas Green	.20	.15	.08
32	Thurman Munson	.70	.50	.30
33	Sponsor Card	.15	.11	.06

1990 Score

The regular Score set increased to 704 cards in 1990. Included were a series of cards picturing first-round draft picks, an expanded subset of rookie cards, four World Series specials, five Highlight cards, and a 13-card "Dream Team" series featuring the game's top players pictured on old tobacco-style cards. For the first time in a Score set, team logos are displayed on the card fronts in the lower right corner. Card backs again include a full-color portrait photo with player data. A one-paragraph write-up of each player was again provided by former Sports Illustrated editor Les Woodcock. The Score set was again distributed with "Magic Motion" trivia cards, this year using "Baseball's Most Valuable Players" as its theme.

		MT	NR MT	EX
	Complete Set:	25.00	20.00	10.00
	Common Player:	.04	.03	.02
1	Don Mattingly	.80	.60	.30
2	Cal Ripken, Jr.	.25	.20	.10

#	Player	MT	NR MT	EX
3	Dwight Evans	.08	.06	.03
4	Barry Bonds	.12	.09	.05
5	Kevin McReynolds	.12	.09	.05
6	Ozzie Guillen	.05	.04	.02
7	Terry Kennedy	.04	.03	.02
8	Bryan Harvey	.06	.05	.02
9	Alan Trammell	.09	.07	.04
10	Cory Snyder	.09	.07	.04
11	Jody Reed	.05	.04	.02
12	Roberto Alomar	.20	.15	.08
13	Pedro Guerrero	.09	.07	.04
14	Gary Redus	.04	.03	.02
15	Marty Barrett	.05	.04	.02
16	Ricky Jordan	.35	.25	.12
17	Joe Magrane	.07	.05	.03
18	Sid Fernandez	.07	.05	.03
19	Rich Dotson	.04	.03	.02
20	Jack Clark	.09	.07	.04
21	Bob Walk	.05	.04	.02
22	Ron Karkovice	.04	.03	.02
23	Lenny Harris(FC)	.10	.07	.04
24	Phil Bradley	.06	.05	.02
25	Andres Galarraga	.15	.11	.06
26	Brian Downing	.06	.05	.02
27	Dave Martinez	.06	.05	.02
28	Eric King	.04	.03	.02
29	Barry Lyons	.04	.03	.02
30	Dave Schmidt	.04	.03	.02
31	Mike Boddicker	.06	.05	.04
32	Tom Foley	.04	.03	.02
33	Brady Anderson	.07	.05	.03
34	Jim Presley	.05	.04	.02
35	Lance Parrish	.06	.05	.02
36	Von Hayes	.09	.07	.03
37	Lee Smith	.06	.05	.02
38	Herm Winningham	.04	.03	.02
39	Alejandro Pena	.04	.03	.02
40	Mike Scott	.09	.07	.04
41	Joe Orsulak	.04	.03	.02
42	Rafael Ramirez	.05	.04	.02
43	Gerald Young	.05	.04	.02
44	Dick Schofield	.05	.04	.02
45	Dave Smith	.06	.05	.02
46	Dave Magadan	.07	.05	.03
47	Dennis Martinez	.06	.05	.02
48	Greg Minton	.04	.03	.02
49	Milt Thompson	.04	.03	.02
50	Orel Hershiser	.12	.09	.05
51	Bip Roberts(FC)	.09	.07	.04
52	Jerry Browne	.09	.07	.04
53	Bob Ojeda	.05	.04	.02
54	Fernando Valenzuela	.09	.07	.04
55	Matt Nokes	.09	.07	.04
56	Brook Jacoby	.08	.06	.03
57	Frank Tanana	.05	.04	.02
58	Scott Fletcher	.05	.04	.02
59	Ron Oester	.05	.04	.02
60	Bob Boone	.08	.06	.03
61	Dan Gladden	.08	.06	.03
62	Darnell Coles	.04	.03	.02
63	Gregg Olson	.25	.20	.10
64	Todd Burns	.05	.04	.02
65	Todd Benzinger	.07	.05	.03
66	Dale Murphy	.12	.09	.05
67	Mike Flanagan	.06	.05	.02
68	Jose Oquendo	.06	.05	.02
69	Cecil Espy	.08	.06	.03
70	Chris Sabo	.10	.07	.04
71	Shane Rawley	.05	.04	.02
72	Tom Brunansky	.08	.06	.03
73	Vance Law	.05	.04	.02
74	B.J. Surhoff	.08	.06	.03
75	Lou Whitaker	.09	.07	.04
76	Ken Caminiti	.09	.07	.04
77	Nelson Liriano	.04	.03	.02
78	Tommy Gregg	.09	.07	.04
79	Don Slaught	.05	.04	.02
80	Eddie Murray	.12	.09	.05
81	Joe Boever	.08	.06	.02
82	Charlie Leibrandt	.06	.05	.02
83	Jose Lind	.06	.05	.02
84	Tony Phillips	.05	.04	.02
85	Mitch Webster	.04	.03	.02
86	Dan Plesac	.07	.05	.02
87	Rick Mahler	.05	.04	.02
88	Steve Lyons	.05	.04	.02
89	Tony Fernandez	.09	.07	.04
90	Ryne Sandberg	.20	.15	.08
91	Nick Esasky	.09	.07	.04
92	Luis Salazar	.04	.03	.02
93	Pete Incaviglia	.08	.06	.03
94	Ivan Calderon	.06	.05	.02
95	Jeff Treadway	.06	.05	.02
96	Kurt Stillwell	.06	.05.	.02
97	Gary Sheffield	.50	.40	.20
98	Jeffrey Leonard	.07	.05	.03
99	Andres Thomas	.05	.04	.02
100	Roberto Kelly	.15	.11	.06
101	Alvaro Espinoza(FC)	.15	.11	.06
102	Greg Gagne	.05	.04	.02
103	John Farrell	.05	.04	.02
104	Willie Wilson	.05	.04	.02
105	Glenn Braggs	.08	.06	.03
106	Chet Lemon	.06	.05	.02
107	Jamie Moyer	.06	.05	.02
108	Chuck Crim	.04	.03	.02
109	Dave Valle	.04	.03	.02
110	Walt Weiss	.10	.07	.04
111	Larry Sheets	.04	.03	.02
112	Don Robinson	.05	.04	.02
113	Danny Heep	.04	.03	.02
114	Carmelo Martinez	.06	.05	.02
115	Dave Gallagher	.08	.06	.03
116	Mike LaValliere	.05	.04	.02
117	Bob McClure	.04	.03	.02
118	Rene Gonzales	.04	.03	.02
119	Mark Parent	.05	.04	.02
120	Wally Joyner	.15	.11	.06
121	Mark Gubicza	.09	.07	.04
122	Tony Pena	.08	.06	.03
123	Carmen Castillo	.04	.03	.02
124	Howard Johnson	.20	.15	.08
125	Steve Sax	.10	.08	.04
126	Tim Belcher	.10	.08	.04
127	Tim Burke	.06	.05	.02
128	Al Newman	.04	.03	.02
129	Dennis Rasmussen	.05	.04	.02
130	Doug Jones	.06	.05	.02
131	Fred Lynn	.09	.07	.04
132	Jeff Hamilton	.06	.05	.02
133	German Gonzalez	.05	.04	.02
134	John Morris	.05	.04	.02
135	Dave Parker	.10	.08	.04
136	Gary Pettis	.05	.04	.02
137	Dennis Boyd	.07	.05	.02
138	Candy Maldonado	.06	.05	.02
139	Rick Cerone	.04	.03	.02
140	George Brett	.15	.11	.06
141	Dave Clark	.05	.04	.02
142	Dickie Thon	.05	.04	.02
143	Junior Ortiz	.04	.03	.02
144	Don August	.06	.05	.02
145	Gary Gaetti	.10	.08	.04
146	Kirt Manwaring	.12	.09	.05
147	Jeff Reed	.04	.03	.02
148	Jose Alvarez(FC)	.08	.06	.03
149	Mike Schooler	.08	.06	.03
150	Mark Grace	.30	.25	.12
151	Geronimo Berroa	.08	.06	.03
152	Barry Jones	.04	.03	.02
153	Geno Petralli	.05	.04	.02
154	Jim Deshaies	.08	.06	.03
155	Barry Larkin	.15	.11	.06
156	Alfredo Griffin	.05	.04	.02
157	Tom Henke	.06	.05	.02
158	Mike Jeffcoat(FC)	.05	.04	.02
159	Bob Welch	.09	.07	.04
160	Julio Franco	.10	.08	.04
161	Henry Cotto	.04	.03	.02
162	Terry Steinbach	.10	.08	.04
163	Damon Berryhill	.08	.06	.03
164	Tim Crews	.04	.03	.02
165	Tom Browning	.09	.07	.04
166	Frd Manrique	.04	.03	.02
167	Harold Reynolds	.09	.07	.04
168	Ron Hassey	.05	.04	.02
169	Shawon Dunston	.08	.06	.03
170	Bobby Bonilla	.15	.11	.06
171	Tom Herr	.07	.05	.03
172	Mike Heath	.04	.03	.02
173	Rich Gedman	.05	.04	.02
174	Bill Ripken	.05	.04	.02
175	Pete O'Brien	.07	.05	.03
176a	Lloyd McClendon (uniform number 1 on back)	3.00	2.25	1.25
176b	Lloyd McClendon (uniform number 10 on back)	.20	.15	.08
177	Brian Holton	.05	.04	.02
178	Jeff Blauser	.05	.04	.02
179	Jim Eisenreich	.05	.04	.02
180	Bert Blyleven	.09	.07	.04
181	Rob Murphy	.05	.04	.02

		MT	NR MT	EX
182	Bill Doran	.07	.05	.03
183	Curt Ford	.04	.03	.02
184	Mike Henneman	.06	.05	.02
185	Eric Davis	.30	.25	.12
186	Lance McCullers	.06	.05	.03
187	*Steve Davis*(FC)	.25	.20	.10
188	Bill Wegman	.05	.04	.02
189	Brian Harper	.06	.05	.02
190	Mike Moore	.09	.07	.04
191	Dale Mohorcic	.04	.03	.02
192	Tim Wallach	.09	.07	.04
193	Keith Hernandez	.09	.07	.04
194	Dave Righetti	.07	.05	.03
195a	Bret Saberhagen ("joke" on card back)			
		.25	.20	.10
195b	Bret Saberhagen ("joker" on card back)			
		.60	.45	.25
196	Paul Kilgus	.04	.03	.02
197	Bud Black	.05	.04	.02
198	Juan Samuel	.09	.07	.04
199	Kevin Seitzer	.15	.11	.06
200	Darryl Strawberry	.30	.25	.12
201	Dave Steib	.09	.07	.04
202	Charlie Hough	.06	.05	.02
203	Jack Morris	.08	.06	.03
204	Rance Mulliniks	.04	.03	.02
205	Alvin Davis	.10	.08	.04
206	Jack Howell	.06	.05	.02
207	Ken Patterson(FC)	.06	.05	.02
208	Terry Pendleton	.09	.07	.03
209	Craig Lefferts	.06	.05	.02
210	Kevin Brown(FC)	.10	.08	.04
211	Dan Petry	.04	.03	.02
212	Dave Leiper	.06	.05	.02
213	Daryl Boston	.04	.03	.02
214	Kevin Hickey(FC)	.08	.06	.03
215	Mike Krukow	.06	.05	.02
216	Terry Francona	.04	.03	.02
217	Kirk McCaskill	.08	.06	.03
218	Scott Bailes	.05	.04	.02
219	Bob Forsch	.04	.03	.02
220	Mike Aldrete	.05	.04	.02
221	Steve Buechele	.06	.05	.02
222	Jesse Barfield	.09	.07	.05
223	Juan Berenguer	.06	.05	.02
224	Andy McGaffigan	.06	.05	.02
225	Pete Smith	.09	.07	.04
226	Mike Witt	.06	.05	.02
227	Jay Howell	.08	.06	.03
228	Scott Bradley	.05	.04	.02
229	*Jerome Walton*	.80	.60	.30
230	Greg Swindell	.15	.11	.06
231	Atlee Hammaker	.04	.03	.02
232	Mike Devereaux	.09	.07	.04
233	Ken Hill	.09	.07	.04
234	Craig Worthington	.15	.11	.06
235	Scott Terry	.08	.06	.03
236	Brett Butler	.09	.07	.04
237	Doyle Alexander	.07	.05	.03
238	Dave Anderson	.04	.03	.02
239	Bob Milacki	.10	.08	.04
240	Dwight Smith	.50	.40	.20
241	Otis Nixon	.04	.03	.02
242	Pat Tabler	.06	.05	.02
243	Derek Lilliquist	.12	.09	.05
244	Danny Tartabull	.15	.11	.06
245	Wade Boggs	.30	.25	.12
246	Scott Garrelts	.08	.06	.03
247	Spike Owen	.04	.03	.02
248	Norm Charlton	.12	.09	.05
249	Gerald Perry	.06	.05	.02
250	Nolan Ryan	.50	.40	.20
251	Kevin Gross	.07	.05	.03
252	Randy Milligan	.07	.05	.03
253	Mike LaCoss	.05	.04	.02
254	Dave Bergman	.04	.03	.02
255	Tony Gwynn	.35	.25	.12
256	Felix Fermin	.04	.03	.02
257	Greg Harris	.10	.08	.04
258	*Junior Felix*	.40	.30	.15
259	Mark Davis	.09	.07	.04
260	Vince Coleman	.15	.11	.06
261	Paul Gibson	.10	.08	.04
262	Mitch Williams	.10	.08	.04
263	Jeff Russell	.08	.06	.03
264	*Omar Vizquel*	.10	.07	.04
265	Andre Dawson	.12	.09	.05
266	Storm Davis	.08	.06	.03
267	Guillermo Hernandez	.04	.03	.02
268	Mike Felder	.05	.04	.02
269	Tom Candiotti	.05	.04	.02
270	Bruce Hurst	.09	.07	.04
271	Fred McGriff	.30	.25	.12
272	Glenn Davis	.15	.11	.60
273	John Franco	.09	.07	.04
274	Rich Yett	.04	.03	.02
275	Craig Biggio	.15	.11	.06
276	Gene Larkin	.05	.04	.02
277	Rob Dibble	.15	.11	.06
278	Randy Bush	.05	.04	.02
279	Kevin Bass	.08	.06	.03
280a	Bo Jackson ("Watham" on card back)			
		1.00	.70	.40
280b	Bo Jackson ("Wathan" on card back)			
		1.75	1.25	.70
281	Wally Backman	.06	.05	.02
282	Larry Andersen	.04	.03	.02
283	Chris Bosio	.09	.07	.04
284	Juan Agosto	.04	.03	.02
285	Ozzie Smith	.10	.08	.04
286	George Bell	.10	.08	.04
287	Rex Hudler	.05	.04	.02
288	Pat Borders	.10	.08	.04
289	Danny Jackson	.07	.05	.03
290	Carlton Fisk	.09	.07	.04
291	Tracy Jones	.05	.04	.02
292	Allan Anderson	.07	.05	.03
293	Johnny Ray	.07	.05	.03
294	Lee Guetterman	.04	.03	.02
295	Paul O'Neill	.09	.07	.05
296	Carney Lansford	.08	.06	.03
297	Tom Brookens	.04	.03	.02
298	Claudell Washington	.08	.06	.03
299	Hubie Brooks	.08	.06	.03
300	Will Clark	.80	.60	.30
301	*Kenny Rogers*	.20	.15	.08
302	Darrell Evans	.07	.05	.03
303	Greg Briley	.25	.20	.10
304	Donn Pall	.09	.07	.04
305	Teddy Higuera	.09	.07	.04
306	Dan Pasqua	.07	.05	.02
307	Dave Winfield	.15	.11	.06
308	Dennis Powell	.04	.03	.02
309	Jose DeLeon	.08	.06	.03
310	Roger Clemens	.25	.20	.10
311	Melido Perez	.09	.07	.04
312	Devon White	.09	.07	.04
313	Doc Gooden	.25	.20	.10
314	*Carlos Martinez*	.20	.15	.08
315	Dennis Eckersley	.10	.08	.04
316	Clay Parker	.12	.09	.05
317	Rick Honeycutt	.05	.04	.02
318	Tim Laudner	.05	.04	.02
319	Joe Carter	.10	.08	.04
320	Robin Yount	.20	.15	.08
321	Felix Jose	.15	.11	.06
322	Mickey Tettleton	.09	.07	.04
323	Mike Gallego	.04	.03	.02
324	Edgar Martinez	.09	.07	.04
325	Dave Henderson	.09	.07	.04
326	Chili Davis	.09	.07	.04
327	Steve Balboni	.05	.04	.02
328	Jody Davis	.04	.03	.02
329	Shawn Hillegas	.04	.03	.02
330	Jim Abbott	.70	.50	.30
331	John Dopson	.10	.08	.04
332	Mark Williamson	.04	.03	.02
333	Jeff Robinson	.08	.06	.03
334	John Smiley	.09	.07	.04
335	Bobby Thigpen	.07	.05	.03
336	Garry Templeton	.05	.04	.02
337	Marvell Wynne	.05	.04	.02
338a	Ken Griffey, Sr. (uniform number 25 on card back)			
		.40	.30	.15
338b	Ken Griffey, Sr. (uniform number 30 on card back)			
		5.00	3.75	2.00
339	*Steve Finley*	.25	.20	.10
340	Ellis Burks	.25	.20	.10
341	Frank Williams	.04	.03	.02
342	Mike Morgan	.05	.04	.02
343	Kevin Mitchell	.35	.25	.12
344	Joel Youngblood	.04	.03	.02
345	Mike Greenwell	.50	.40	.20
346	Glenn Wilson	.05	.04	.02
347	John Costello	.05	.04	.02
348	Wes Gardner	.04	.03	.02
349	Jeff Ballard	.09	.07	.04
350	Mark Thurmond	.04	.03	.02
351	Randy Myers	.07	.05	.03
352	Shawn Abner	.07	.05	.03
353	Jesse Orosco	.04	.03	.02
354	Greg Walker	.05	.04	.02

		MT	NR MT	EX
355	Pete Harnisch	.15	.11	.06
356	Steve Farr	.05	.04	.02
357	Dave LaPoint	.05	.04	.02
358	Willie Fraser	.05	.04	.02
359	Mickey Hatcher	.04	.03	.02
360	Rickey Henderson	.30	.25	.12
361	Mike Fitzgerald	.04	.03	.02
362	Bill Schroeder	.04	.03	.02
363	Mark Carreon	.10	.08	.04
364	Ron Jones	.10	.08	.04
365	Jeff Montgomery	.06	.05	.02
366	Bill Krueger(FC)	.04	.03	.02
367	John Cangelosi	.04	.03	.02
368	Jose Gonzalez	.10	.08	.04
369	*Greg Hibbard*(FC)	.30	.25	.12
370	John Smoltz	.15	.11	.06
371	*Jeff Brantley*	.15	.11	.06
372	Frank White	.08	.06	.03
373	Ed Whitson	.06	.05	.02
374	Willie McGee	.09	.07	.04
375	Jose Canseco	.70	.50	.30
376	Randy Ready	.04	.03	.02
377	Don Aase	.04	.03	.02
378	Tony Armas	.05	.04	.02
379	Steve Bedrosian	.07	.05	.03
380	Chuck Finley	.07	.05	.03
381	Kent Hrbek	.12	.09	.05
382	Jim Gantner	.06	.05	.02
383	Mel Hall	.06	.05	.02
384	Mike Marshall	.07	.05	.03
385	Mark McGwire	.70	.50	.30
386	Wayne Tolleson	.04	.03	.02
387	Brian Holton	.05	.04	.02
388	*John Wetteland*	.30	.25	.12
389	Darren Daulton	.04	.03	.02
390	Rob Deer	.07	.05	.03
391	John Moses	.04	.03	.02
392	Todd Worrell	.07	.05	.03
393	Chuck Cary(FC)	.10	.08	.04
394	Stan Javier	.05	.04	.02
395	Willie Randolph	.09	.07	.04
396	Bill Buckner	.06	.05	.02
397	Robby Thompson	.07	.05	.02
398	Mike Scioscia	.07	.05	.03
399	Lonnie Smith	.09	.07	.04
400	Kirby Puckett	.40	.30	.15
401	Mark Langston	.15	.11	.06
402	Danny Darwin	.04	.03	.02
403	Greg Maddux	.15	.11	.06
404	Lloyd Moseby	.07	.05	.02
405	Rafael Palmeiro	.09	.07	.04
406	Chad Kreuter	.10	.08	.04
407	Jimmy Key	.09	.07	.05
408	Tim Birtsas	.04	.03	.02
409	Tim Raines	.10	.08	.04
410	Dave Stewart	.09	.07	.04
411	*Eric Yelding*(FC)	.30	.25	.12
412	*Kent Anderson*(FC)	.20	.15	.08
413	Les Lancaster	.05	.04	.02
414	Rick Dempsey	.04	.03	.02
415	Randy Johnson	.10	.08	.04
416	Gary Carter	.07	.05	.03
417	Rolando Roomes	.15	.11	.06
418	Dan Schatzeder	.04	.03	.02
419	Bryn Smith	.07	.05	.03
420	Ruben Sierra	.20	.15	.08
421	Steve Jeltz	.04	.03	.02
422	Ken Oberkfell	.04	.03	.02
423	Sid Bream	.04	.03	.02
424	Jim Clancy	.04	.03	.02
425	Kelly Gruber	.09	.07	.04
426	Rick Leach	.04	.03	.02
427	Lenny Dykstra	.07	.05	.03
428	Jeff Pico	.06	.05	.02
429	John Cerutti	.06	.05	.02
430	David Cone	.15	.11	.06
431	Jeff Kunkel	.04	.03	.02
432	Luis Aquino	.05	.04	.02
433	Ernie Whitt	.05	.04	.02
434	Bo Diaz	.05	.04	.02
435	Steve Lake	.04	.03	.02
436	Pat Perry	.04	.03	.02
437	Mike Davis	.05	.04	.02
438	Cecilio Guante	.04	.03	.02
439	Duane Ward	.04	.03	.02
440	Andy Van Slyke	.10	.08	.04
441	Gene Nelson	.04	.03	.02
442	Luis Polonia	.06	.05	.02
443	Kevin Elster	.06	.05	.02
444	Keith Moreland	.06	.05	.02
445	Roger McDowell	.06	.05	.02
446	Ron Darling	.08	.06	.03
447	Ernest Riles	.04	.03	.02
448	Mookie Wilson	.08	.06	.03
449a	*Bill Spiers* (66 missing for year of birth)	1.25	.90	.50
449b	*Bill Spiers* (1966 for birth year)	1.00	.70	.40
450	Rick Sutcliffe	.07	.05	.03
451	Nelson Santovenia	.10	.08	.04
452	Andy Allanson	.04	.03	.02
453	Bob Melvin	.04	.03	.02
454	Benny Santiago	.12	.09	.05
455	Jose Uribe	.05	.04	.02
456	Bill Landrum(FC)	.08	.06	.03
457	Bobby Witt	.07	.05	.03
458	Kevin Romine	.07	.05	.03
459	Lee Mazzilli	.04	.03	.02
460	Paul Molitor	.10	.08	.04
461	Ramon Martinez(FC)	.80	.60	.30
462	Frank DiPino	.04	.03	.02
463	Walt Terrell	.06	.05	.02
464	*Bob Geren*	.30	.25	.12
465	Rick Reuchel	.09	.07	.04
466	Mark Grant	.06	.05	.02
467	John Kruk	.07	.05	.03
468	Gregg Jefferies	.60	.45	.25
469	R.J. Reynolds	.04	.03	.02
470	Harold Baines	.09	.07	.04
471	Dennis Lamp	.04	.03	.02
472	Tom Gordon	.35	.25	.12
473	Terry Puhl	.04	.03	.02
474	Curtis Wilkerson	.04	.03	.02
475	Dan Quisenberry	.05	.04	.02
476	Oddibe McDowell	.07	.05	.03
477	Zane Smith	.04	.03	.02
478	Franklin Stubbs	.04	.03	.02
479	Wallace Johnson	.04	.03	.02
480	Jay Tibbs	.04	.03	.02
481	Tom Glavine	.09	.07	.03
482	Manny Lee	.05	.04	.02
483	Joe Hesketh	.04	.03	.02
484	Mike Bielecki	.07	.05	.03
485	Greg Brock	.06	.05	.02
486	Pascual Perez	.06	.05	.02
487	Kirk Gibson	.09	.07	.04
488	Scott Sanderson	.05	.04	.02
489	Domingo Ramos	.04	.03	.02
490	Kal Daniels	.10	.08	.04
491a	David Wells (Reverse negative on back photo)	4.00	3.00	1.50
491b	David Wells (Corrected)	.05	.04	.02
492	Jerry Reed	.04	.03	.02
493	Eric Show	.06	.05	.02
494	Mike Pagliarulo	.06	.05	.02
495	Ron Robinson	.05	.04	.02
496	Brad Komminsk	.04	.03	.02
497	*Greg Litton*	.25	.20	.10
498	Chris James	.07	.05	.02
499	Luis Quinones(FC)	.05	.04	.02
500	Frank Viola	.10	.08	.04
501	Tim Teufel	.05	.04	.02
502	Terry Leach	.04	.03	.02
503	Matt Williams	.20	.15	.08
504	Tim Leary	.06	.05	.02
505	Doug Drabek	.06	.05	.02
506	Mariano Duncan	.06	.05	.02
507	Charlie Hayes	.10	.08	.04
508	*Joey Belle*	.30	.25	.12
509	Pat Sheridan	.05	.04	.02
510	Mackey Sasser	.05	.04	.02
511	Jose Rijo	.09	.07	.04
512	Mike Smithson	.04	.03	.02
513	Gary Ward	.04	.03	.02
514	Dion James	.06	.05	.02
515	Jim Gott	.06	.05	.02
516	Drew Hall(FC)	.07	.05	.03
517	Doug Bair	.04	.03	.02
518	*Scott Scudder*	.20	.15	.08
519	Rick Aguilera	.06	.05	.02
520	Rafael Belliard	.05	.04	.02
521	Jay Buhner	.10	.08	.04
522	Jeff Reardon	.06	.05	.02
523	Steve Rosenberg(FC)	.09	.07	.04
524	Randy Velarde(FC)	.09	.07	.04
525	Jeff Musselman	.09	.07	.04
526	Bill Long	.06	.05	.02
527	*Gary Wayne*	.10	.08	.04
528	*Dave Johnson*(FC)	.15	.11	.06
529	Ron Kittle	.08	.06	.03
530	Erik Hanson(FC)	.20	.15	.08
531	Steve Wilson(FC)	.20	.15	.08
532	Joey Meyer	.04	.03	.02

#	Player	MT	NR MT	EX
533	Curt Young	.04	.03	.02
534	Kelly Downs	.06	.05	.02
535	Joe Girardi	.20	.15	.08
536	Lance Blankenship	.09	.07	.04
537	Greg Mathews	.05	.04	.02
538	Donell Nixon	.04	.03	.02
539	Mark Knudson(FC)	.09	.07	.04
540	*Jeff Wetherby*(FC)	.30	.25	.12
541	Darrin Jackson	.04	.03	.02
542	Terry Mulholland	.09	.07	.03
543	Eric Hetzel(FC)	.15	.11	.06
544	*Rick Reed*(FC)	.25	.20	.10
545	Dennis Cook(FC)	.20	.15	.08
546	Mike Jackson	.05	.04	.02
547	Brian Fisher	.06	.05	.02
548	*Gene Harris*(FC)	.20	.15	.08
549	Jeff King(FC)	.20	.15	.08
550	Dave Dravecky (Salute)	.10	.08	.04
551	Randy Kutcher(FC)	.08	.06	.03
552	Mark Portugal	.06	.05	.02
553	*Jim Corsi*(FC)	.12	.09	.05
554	Todd Stottlemyre	.12	.09	.05
555	Scott Bankhead	.09	.07	.04
556	Ken Dayley	.05	.04	.02
557	*Rick Wrona*(FC)	.25	.20	.10
558	Sammy Sosa(FC)	.35	.25	.14
559	Keith Miller	.08	.06	.03
560	Ken Griffey Jr.	3.00	2.25	1.25
561a	Ryne Sandberg (No Errors- 3B Position designation)	10.00	7.50	4.00
561b	Ryne Sandberg (No Errors- No position designation)	.50	.40	.20
562	Billy Hatcher	.06	.05	.02
563	Jay Bell(FC)	.09	.07	.04
564	*Jack Daugherty*(FC)	.30	.25	.12
565	*Rich Monteleone*	.20	.15	.08
566	Bo Jackson (All-Star MVP)	.60	.45	.25
567	*Tony Fossas*(FC)	.10	.08	.04
568	*Roy Smith*(FC)	.15	.11	.06
569	*Jaime Navarro*(FC)	.35	.25	.14
570	Lance Johnson(FC)	.15	.11	.06
571	*Mike Dyer*(FC)	.25	.20	.10
572	*Kevin Ritz*(FC)	.20	.15	.08
573	Dave West	.15	.11	.06
574	*Gary Mielke*(FC)	.25	.20	.10
575	Scott Lusader(FC)	.09	.07	.04
576	*Joe Oliver*	.30	.25	.12
577	Sandy Alomar, Jr.	.60	.45	.25
578	Andy Benes(FC)	.80	.60	.30
579	Tim Jones	.07	.05	.03
580	*Randy McCament*(FC)	.25	.20	10.00
581	Curt Schilling(FC)	.15	.11	.06
582	*John Orton*(FC)	.25	.20	.10
583a	*Milt Cuyler* (played in 998 games)(FC)	1.75	1.25	.70
583b	*Milt Cuyler* (played in 98 games)(FC)	.40	.30	.15
584	*Eric Anthony*(FC)	1.00	.70	.40
585	*Greg Vaughn*(FC)	.60	.45	.25
586	*Deion Sanders*(FC)	.50	.40	.20
587	Jose DeJesus(FC)	.15	.11	.06
588	*Chip Hale*(FC)	.30	.25	.12
589	John Olerud(FC)	2.50	2.00	1.00
590	*Steve Olin*(FC)	.35	.25	.12
591	Marquis Grissom(FC)	.60	.45	.25
592	Moises Alou(FC)	.50	.40	.20
593	Mark Lemke(FC)	.10	.08	.04
594	Dean Palmer(FC)	.30	.25	.12
595	Robin Ventura(FC)	.70	.50	.30
596	Tino Martinez(FC)	.90	.70	.35
597	*Mike Huff*(FC)	.25	.20	.10
598	Scott Hemond(FC)	.25	.20	.10
599	*Wally Whitehurst*(FC)	.20	.15	.08
600	*Todd Zeile*(FC)	.80	.60	.30
601	Glenallen Hill(FC)	.35	.25	.14
602	Hal Morris(FC)	.15	.11	.06
603	Juan Bell(FC)	.15	.11	.06
604	*Bobby Rose*(FC)	.25	.20	.10
605	Matt Merullo(FC)	.20	.15	.08
606	Kevin Maas(FC)	3.25	2.50	1.25
607	*Randy Nosek*(FC)	.25	.20	.10
608	*Billy Bates*(FC)	.20	.15	.08
609	*Mike Stanton*(FC)	.25	.20	.10
610	*Goose Gozzo*(FC)	.30	.25	.12
611	*Charles Nagy*(FC)	.25	.20	.10
612	*Scott Coolbaugh*(FC)	.30	.25	.12
613	Jose Vizcaino(FC)	.35	.25	.12
614	*Greg Smith*(FC)	.20	.15	.08
615	Jeff Huson(FC)	.25	.20	.10
616	*Mickey Weston*(FC)	.20	.15	.08
617	*John Pawlowski*(FC)	.20	.15	.08
618	*Joe Skalski*(FC)	.20	.15	.08
619	*Bernie Williams*(FC)	.50	.40	.20
620	*Shawn Holman*(FC)	.25	.20	.10
621	*Gary Eave*(FC)	.25	.20	.10
622	*Darrin Fletcher*(FC)	.25	.20	.10
623	*Pat Combs*(FC)	.30	.25	.12
624	*Mike Blowers*(FC)	.30	.25	.12
625	*Kevin Appier*(FC)	.30	.25	.12
626	*Pat Austin*(FC)	.30	.25	.12
627	*Kelly Mann*(FC)	.40	.30	.15
628	*Matt Kinzer*(FC)	.25	.20	.10
629	*Chris Hammond*(FC)	.25	.20	.10
630	*Dean Wilkins*(FC)	.25	.20	.10
631	*Larry Walker*(FC)	.25	.20	.10
632	*Blaine Beatty*(FC)	.25	.20	.10
633	Tom Barrett(FC)	.12	.09	.05
634	*Stan Belinda*(FC)	.35	.25	.14
635	*Tex Smith*(FC)	.25	.20	.10
636	Hensley Meulens(FC)	.40	.30	.15
637	*Juan Gonzalez*(FC)	2.00	1.50	.80
638	*Lenny Webster*(FC)	.25	.20	.10
639	*Mark Gardner*(FC)	.35	.25	.14
640	*Tommy Greene*(FC)	.25	.20	.10
641	*Mike Hartley*(FC)	.25	.20	.10
642	*Phil Stephenson*(FC)	.15	.11	.06
643	*Kevin Mmahat*(FC)	.15	.11	.06
644	*Ed Whited*(FC)	.15	.11	.06
645	*Delino DeShields*(FC)	1.00	.70	.40
646	Kevin Blankenship(FC)	.15	.11	.06
647	*Paul Sorrento*(FC)	.40	.30	.15
648	*Mike Roesler*(FC)	.25	.20	.12
649	*Jason Grimsley*(FC)	.25	.20	.10
650	Dave Justice(FC)	3.50	2.75	1.50
651	*Scott Cooper*(FC)	.25	.20	.10
652	Dave Eiland(FC)	.15	.11	.06
653	*Mike Munoz*(FC)	.25	.20	.10
654	*Jeff Fischer*(FC)	.25	.20	.10
655	*Terry Jorgenson*(FC)	.20	.15	.08
656	George Canale(FC)	.40	.30	.15
657	*Brian DuBois*(FC)	.40	.30	.15
658	Carlos Quintana	.10	.08	.04
659	Luis De los santos	.10	.08	.04
660	Jerald Clark	.10	.08	.04
661	#1 Draft Pick *(Donald Harris)*(FC)	.30	.25	.12
662	#1 Draft Pick *(Paul Coleman)*(FC)	.40	.30	.15
663	#1 Draft Pick *(Frank Thomas)*(FC)	4.00	3.00	1.50
664	#1 Draft Pick *(Brent Mayne)*(FC)	.40	.30	.15
665	#1 Draft Pick *(Eddie Zosky)*(FC)	.20	.15	.08
666	#1 Draft Pick *(Steve Hosey)*(FC)	.20	.15	.08
667	#1 Draft Pick *(Scott Bryant)*(FC)	.20	.15	.08
668	#1 Draft Pick *(Tom Goodwin)*(FC)	.40	.30	.15
669	#1 Draft Pick *(Cal Eldred)*(FC)	.20	.15	.08
670	#1 Draft Pick *(Earl Cunningham)*(FC)	.50	.40	.20
671	#1 Draft Pick *(Alan Zinter)*(FC)	.25	.20	.10
672	#1 Draft Pick *(Chuck Knoblauch)*(FC)	.25	.20	.10
673	#1 Draft Pick *(Kyle Abbott)*(FC)	.25	.20	.10
674	#1 Draft Pick *(Roger Salkeld)*(FC)	.30	.25	.12
675	#1 Draft Pick *(Maurice Vaughn)*(FC)	1.00	.70	.40
676	#1 Draft Pick *(Kiki Jones)*(FC)	.25	.20	.10
677	#1 Draft Pick *(Tyler Houston)*(FC)	.40	.30	.15
678	#1 Draft Pick *(Jeff Jackson)*(FC)	.40	.30	.15
679	#1 Draft Pick *(Greg Gohr)* (#1 Draft Pick)(FC)	.25	.20	.10
680	#1 Draft Pick *(Ben McDonald)* (#1 Draft Pick)(FC)	2.50	2.00	1.00
681	#1 Draft Pick *(Greg Blosser)* (#1 Draft Pick)(FC)	.30	.25	.12
682	#1 Draft Pick *(Willie Green)* (#1 Draft Pick)(FC)	.25	.20	.10
683	Dream Team (Wade Boggs)	.20	.15	.08
684	Dream Team (Will Clark)	.20	.15	.08
685	Dream Team (Tony Gwynn)	.20	.15	.08
686	Dream Team (Rickey Henderson)	.20	.15	.08
687	Dream Team (Bo Jackson)	.60	.45	.25
688	Dream Team (Mark Langston)	.20	.15	.11
689	Dream Team (Barry Larkin)	.20	.15	.11
690	Dream Team (Kirby Puckett)	.20	.15	.11
691	Dream Team (Ryne Sandberg)	.20	.15	.11
692	Dream Team (Mike Scott)	.20	.15	.11
693	Dream Team (Terry Steinbach)	.20	.15	.11
694	Dream Team (Bobby Thigpen)	.20	.15	.11
695	Dream Team (Mitch Williams)	.20	.15	.11
696	5000 K (Nolan Ryan)	.50	.40	.20
697	FB/BB NIKE (Bo Jackson)	8.00	6.00	3.25
698	ALCS MVP (Rickey Henderson)	.25	.20	.10
699	NLCS MVP (Will Clark)	.35	.25	.14
700	World Series 1,2	.30	.25	.12

	MT	NR MT	EX
701 Candlestick	.30	.25	.12
702 World Series Game 3	.30	.25	.12
703 World Series Wrap-up	.30	.25	.12
704 200 Hit (Wade Boggs)	.25	.20	.10
—— A. Bartlett Giamatti (Bonus-Dream Team)			
	3.50	2.75	1.50
—— Pat Combs (Bonus-Dream Team)	.30	.25	.12
—— Todd Zeile (Bonus-Dream Team)	.60	.45	.25
—— Luis de los Santos (Bonus-Dream Team)			
	.30	.25	.12
—— Mark Lemke (Bonus-Dream Team)	.30	.25	.12
—— Robin Ventura (Bonus-Dream Team)			
	.60	.45	.25
—— Jeff Huson (Bonus-Dream Team)	.30	.25	.12
—— Greg Vaughn (Bonus-Dream Team)	.60	.45	.25
—— Marquis Grissom (Bonus-Dream Team)			
	.50	.40	.20
—— Eric Anthony (Bonus-Dream Team)	.60	.45	.25

1990 Score Rising Stars

For the second consecutive year Score produced a 100-card "Rising Stars" set. The 1990 Score Rising Stars were made available as a boxed set and were also marketed with a related magazine like the 1989 issue. Magic Motion trivia cards featuring past MVP's accompany the card set. The cards feature full-color action photos on the front and posed shots on the flip sides.

	MT	NR MT	EX
Complete Set:	12.00	9.00	4.75
Common Player:	.08	.06	.03
1 Tom Gordon	.25	.20	.10
2 Jerome Walton	.40	.30	.15
3 Ken Griffey, Jr.	1.50	1.25	.60
4 Dwight Smith	.25	.20	.10
5 Jim Abbott	.25	.20	.10
6 Todd Zeile	.40	.30	.15
7 Donn Pall	.08	.06	.03
8 Rick Reed	.08	.06	.03
9 Joey Belle	.15	.11	.06
10 Gregg Jefferies	.35	.25	.14
11 Kevin Ritz	.10	.08	.04
12 Charlie Hayes	.15	.11	.06
13 Kevin Appier	.30	.25	.12
14 Jeff Huson	.15	.11	.06
15 Gary Wayne	.08	.06	.03
16 Eric Yelding	.15	.11	.06
17 Clay Parker	.08	.06	.03
18 Junior Felix	.30	.25	.12
19 Derek Lilliquist	.08	.06	.03
20 Gary Sheffield	.30	.25	.12
21 Craig Worthington	.08	.06	.03
22 Jeff Brantley	.10	.08	.04
23 Eric Hetzel	.10	.08	.04
24 Greg Harris	.08	.06	.03
25 John Wetteland	.20	.15	.08
26 Joe Oliver	.15	.11	.06
27 Kevin Maas	.80	.60	.30
28 Kevin Brown	.10	.08	.04
29 Mike Stanton	.15	.11	.06
30 Greg Vaughn	.40	.30	.15
31 Ron Jones	.08	.06	.03
32 Gregg Olson	.20	.15	.08
33 Joe Girardi	.10	.08	.04
34 Ken Hill	.08	.06	.03

	MT	NR MT	EX
35 Sammy Sosa	.35	.25	.14
36 Geronimo Berroa	.08	.06	.03
37 Omar Vizquel	.10	.08	.04
38 Dean Palmer	.10	.08	.04
39 John Olerud	1.50	1.25	.60
40 Deion Sanders	.25	.20	.10
41 Randy Kramer	.08	.06	.03
42 Scott Lusader	.08	.06	.03
43 Dave Johnson	.08	.06	.03
44 Jeff Wetherby	.08	.06	.03
45 Eric Anthony	.40	.30	.15
46 Kenny Rogers	.10	.08	.04
47 Matt Winters	.08	.06	.03
48 Goose Gozzo	.10	.08	.04
49 Carlos Quintana	.15	.11	.06
50 Bob Geren	.10	.08	.04
51 Chad Kreuter	.08	.06	.03
52 Randy Johnson	.10	.08	.04
53 Hensley Meulens	.15	.11	.06
54 Gene Harris	.10	.08	.04
55 Bill Spiers	.10	.08	.04
56 Kelly Mann	.15	.11	.06
57 Tom McCarthy	.08	.06	.03
58 Steve Finley	.10	.08	.04
59 Ramon Martinez	.50	.40	.20
60 Greg Briley	.08	.06	.03
61 Jack Daugherty	.10	.08	.04
62 Tim Jones	.08	.06	.03
63 Doug Strange	.08	.06	.03
64 John Orton	.08	.06	.03
65 Scott Scudder	.15	.11	.06
66 Mark Gardner	.20	.15	.08
67 Mark Carreon	.08	.06	.03
68 Bob Milacki	.08	.06	.03
69 Andy Benes	.10	.08	.04
70 Carlos Martinez	.10	.08	.04
71 Jeff King	.10	.08	.04
72 Brad Arnsberg	.08	.06	.03
73 Rick Wrona	.08	.06	.03
74 Cris Carpenter	.08	.06	.03
75 Dennis Cook	.08	.06	.03
76 Pete Harnisch	.10	.08	.04
77 Greg Hibbard	.15	.11	.06
78 Ed Whited	.08	.06	.03
79 Scott Coolbaugh	.15	.11	.06
80 Billy Bates	.08	.06	.03
81 German Gonzalez	.08	.06	.03
82 Lance Blankenship	.08	.06	.03
83 Lenny Harris	.10	.08	.04
84 Milt Cuyler	.20	.15	.08
85 Erik Hanson	.20	.15	.08
86 Kent Anderson	.08	.06	.03
87 Hal Morris	.40	.30	.15
88 Mike Brumley	.08	.06	.03
89 Ken Patterson	.08	.06	.03
90 Mike Devereaux	.08	.06	.03
91 Greg Litton	.10	.08	.04
92 Rolando Roomes	.08	.06	.03
93 Ben McDonald	1.50	1.25	.60
94 Curt Schilling	.10	.08	.04
95 Jose DeJesus	.15	.11	.06
96 Robin Ventura	.30	.25	.12
97 Steve Searcy	.08	.06	.03
98 Chip Hale	.10	.08	.04
99 Marquis Grissom	.40	.30	.15
100 Luis de los Santos	.10	.08	.04

1990 Score Superstar

100 of the game's top players are featured in this

set. The card fronts feature full-color action photos and are similar in style to the past Score Superstar set. The set was marketed as a boxed set and with a special magazine devoted to baseball's 100 hottest players. Each set includes a series of Magic Motion cards honoring past MVP winners. The player cards measure 2-1/2" by 3-1/2" in size.

		MT	NR MT	EX
	Complete Set:	9.00	6.75	3.50
	Common Player:	.08	.06	.03
1	Kirby Puckett	.30	.25	.12
2	Steve Sax	.10	.08	.04
3	Tony Gwynn	.15	.11	.06
4	Willie Randolph	.08	.06	.03
5	Jose Canseco	.70	.50	.30
6	Ozzie Smith	.10	.08	.04
7	Rick Reuschel	.08	.06	.03
8	Bill Doran	.08	.06	.03
9	Mickey Tettleton	.08	.06	.03
10	Don Mattingly	.50	.40	.20
11	Greg Swindell	.08	.06	.03
12	Bert Blyleven	.10	.08	.04
13	Dave Stewart	.15	.11	.06
14	Andres Galarraga	.10	.08	.04
15	Darryl Strawberry	.30	.25	.12
16	Ellis Burks	.20	.15	.08
17	Paul O'Neill	.08	.06	.03
18	Bruce Hurst	.08	.06	.03
19	Dave Smith	.08	.06	.03
20	Carney Lansford	.08	.06	.03
21	Robby Thompson	.08	.06	.03
22	Gary Gaetti	.10	.08	.04
23	Jeff Russell	.08	.06	.03
24	Chuck Finley	.10	.08	.04
25	Mark McGwire	.35	.25	.14
26	Alvin Davis	.10	.08	.04
27	George Bell	.10	.08	.04
28	Cory Snyder	.08	.06	.03
29	Keith Hernandez	.08	.06	.03
30	Will Clark	.40	.30	.15
31	Steve Bedrosian	.08	.06	.03
32	Ryne Sandberg	.40	.30	.15
33	Tom Browning	.08	.06	.03
34	Tim Burke	.08	.06	.03
35	John Smoltz	.10	.08	.04
36	Phil Bradley	.08	.06	.03
37	Bobby Bonilla	.15	.11	.06
38	Kirk McCaskill	.08	.06	.03
39	Dave Righetti	.10	.08	.04
40	Bo Jackson	.70	.50	.30
41	Alan Trammell	.10	.08	.04
42	Mike Moore	.08	.06	.03
43	Harold Reynolds	.08	.06	.03
44	Nolan Ryan	.50	.40	.20
45	Fred McGriff	.25	.20	.10
46	Brian Downing	.08	.06	.03
47	Brett Butler	.08	.06	.03
48	Mike Scioscia	.08	.06	.03
49	John Franco	.08	.06	.03
50	Kevin Mitchell	.30	.25	.12
51	Mark Davis	.08	.06	.03
52	Glenn Davis	.15	.11	.06
53	Barry Bonds	.20	.15	.08
54	Dwight Evans	.10	.08	.04
55	Terry Steinbach	.08	.06	.03
56	Dave Gallagher	.08	.06	.03
57	Roberto Kelly	.10	.08	.04
58	Rafael Palmeiro	.10	.08	.04
59	Joe Carter	.10	.08	.04
60	Mark Grace	.20	.15	.08
61	Pedro Guerrero	.10	.08	.04
62	Von Hayes	.08	.06	.03
63	Benny Santiago	.15	.11	.06
64	Dale Murphy	.10	.08	.04
65	John Smiley	.08	.06	.03
66	Cal Ripken, Jr.	.15	.11	.06
67	Mike Greenwell	.25	.20	.10
68	Devon White	.08	.06	.03
69	Ed Whitson	.08	.06	.03
70	Carlton Fisk	.15	.11	.06
71	Lou Whitaker	.10	.08	.04
72	Danny Tartabull	.10	.08	.04
73	Vince Coleman	.10	.08	.04
74	Andre Dawson	.15	.11	.06
75	Tim Raines	.10	.08	.04
76	George Brett	.15	.11	.06
77	Tom Herr	.08	.06	.03
78	Andy Van Slyke	.10	.08	.04

		MT	NR MT	EX
79	Roger Clemens	.30	.25	.12
80	Wade Boggs	.30	.25	.12
81	Wally Joyner	.10	.08	.04
82	Lonnie Smith	.08	.06	.03
83	Howard Johnson	.15	.11	.06
84	Julio Franco	.15	.11	.06
85	Ruben Sierra	.20	.15	.08
86	Dan Plesac	.08	.06	.03
87	Bobby Thigpen	.15	.11	.06
88	Kevin Seitzer	.10	.08	.04
89	Dave Steib	.10	.08	.04
90	Rickey Henderson	.30	.25	.12
91	Jeffrey Leonard	.08	.06	.03
92	Robin Yount	.15	.11	.06
93	Mitch Williams	.10	.08	.04
94	Orel Hershiser	.20	.15	.08
95	Eric Davis	.25	.20	.10
96	Mark Langston	.10	.08	.04
97	Mike Scott	.08	.06	.03
98	Paul Molitor	.10	.08	.04
99	Doc Gooden	.25	.20	.10
100	Kevin Bass	.08	.06	.03

1990 Score Traded

This 110-card set features players with new teams as well as 1990 Major League rookies. The cards feature full-color action photos framed in yellow with an orange border. The player's name and position appear in green print below the photo. The team logo is displayed next to the player's name. The card backs feature posed player photos and follow the style of the regular 1990 Score issue. The cards are numbered 1T-110T. Young hockey phenom Eric Lindros is featured trying out for the Toronto Blue Jays.

		MT	NR MT	EX
	Complete Set:	13.00	9.75	5.25
	Common Player:	.06	.05	.02
1T	Dave Winfield	.15	.11	.06
2T	Kevin Bass	.06	.05	.02
3T	Nick Esasky	.06	.05	.02
4T	Mitch Webster	.06	.05	.02
5T	Pascual Perez	.06	.05	.02
6T	Gary Pettis	.06	.05	.02
7T	Tony Pena	.08	.06	.03
8T	Candy Maldonado	.08	.06	.03
9T	Cecil Fielder	.60	.45	.25
10T	Carmelo Martinez	.06	.05	.02
11T	Mark Langston	.08	.06	.03
12T	Dave Parker	.15	.11	.06
13T	Don Slaught	.06	.05	.02
14T	Tony Phillips	.06	.05	.02
15T	John Franco	.08	.06	.03
16T	Randy Myers	.08	.06	.03
17T	Jeff Reardon	.08	.06	.03
18T	Sandy Alomar, Jr.	.30	.25	.12
19T	Joe Carter	.10	.08	.04
20T	Fred Lynn	.06	.05	.02
21T	Storm Davis	.06	.05	.02
22T	Craig Lefferts	.06	.05	.02
23T	Pete O'Brien	.06	.05	.02
24T	Dennis Boyd	.06	.05	.02
25T	Lloyd Moseby	.06	.05	.02
26T	Mark Davis	.06	.05	.02
27T	Tim Leary	.06	.05	.02

		MT	NR MT	EX
28T	Gerald Perry	.06	.05	.02
29T	Don Aase	.06	.05	.02
30T	Ernie Whitt	.06	.05	.02
31T	Dale Murphy	.10	.08	.04
32T	Alejandro Pena	.06	.05	.02
33T	Juan Samuel	.08	.06	.03
34T	Hubie Brooks	.08	.06	.03
35T	Gary Carter	.10	.08	.04
36T	Jim Presley	.06	.05	.02
37T	Wally Backman	.06	.05	.02
38T	Matt Nokes	.06	.05	.02
39T	Dan Petry	.06	.05	.02
40T	Franklin Stubbs	.06	.05	.02
41T	Jeff Huson	.15	.11	.06
42T	Billy Hatcher	.06	.05	.02
43T	Terry Leach	.06	.05	.02
44T	Phil Bradley	.06	.05	.02
45T	Claudell Washington	.06	.05	.02
46T	Luis Polonia	.06	.05	.02
47T	Daryl Boston	.06	.05	.02
48T	Lee Smith	.08	.06	.03
49T	Tom Brunansky	.08	.06	.03
50T	Mike Witt	.06	.05	.02
51T	Willie Randolph	.08	.06	.03
52T	Stan Javier	.06	.05	.02
53T	Brad Komminsk	.06	.05	.02
54T	John Candelaria	.06	.05	.02
55T	Bryn Smith	.06	.05	.02
56T	Glenn Braggs	.06	.05	.02
57T	Keith Hernandez	.08	.06	.03
58T	Ken Oberkfell	.06	.05	.02
59T	Steve Jeltz	.06	.05	.02
60T	Chris James	.06	.05	.02
61T	Scott Sanderson	.06	.05	.02
62T	Bill Long	.06	.05	.02
63T	Rick Cerone	.06	.05	.02
64T	Scott Bailes	.06	.05	.02
65T	Larry Sheets	.06	.05	.02
66T	Junior Ortiz	.06	.05	.02
67T	Francisco Cabrera(FC)	.20	.15	.08
68T	Gary DiSarcina(FC)	.20	.15	.08
69T	Greg Olson(FC)	.20	.15	.08
70T	Beau Allred(FC)	.20	.15	.11
71T	Oscar Azocar(FC)	.50	.40	.20
72T	Kent Mercker(FC)	.25	.20	.10
73T	John Burkett(FC)	.35	.25	.14
74T	Carlos Baerga(FC)	.50	.40	.20
75T	Dave Hollins(FC)	.30	.25	.12
76T	Todd Hundley(FC)	.20	.15	.08
77T	Rick Parker(FC)	.15	.11	.06
78T	Steve Cummings(FC)	.15	.11	.06
79T	Bill Sampen(FC)	.25	.20	.10
80T	Jerry Kutzler(FC)	.15	.11	.06
81T	Derek Bell(FC)	.25	.20	.10
82T	Kevin Tapani(FC)	.35	.25	.14
83T	Jim Leyritz(FC)	.40	.30	.15
84T	Ray Lankford(FC)	1.25	.90	.50
85T	Wayne Edwards(FC)	.15	.11	.06
86T	Frank Thomas(FC)	2.00	1.50	.80
87T	Tim Naehring(FC)	.40	.30	.15
88T	Willie Blair(FC)	.15	.11	.06
89T	Alan Mills(FC)	.25	.20	.10
90T	Scott Radinsky(FC)	.25	.20	.10
91T	Howard Farmer(FC)	.25	.20	.10
92T	Julio Machado(FC)	.15	.11	.06
93T	Rafael Valdez(FC)	.15	.11	.06
94T	Shawn Boskie(FC)	.25	.20	.10
95T	David Segui(FC)	.50	.40	.20
96T	Chris Hoiles(FC)	.30	.25	.12
97T	D.J. Dozier(FC)	.60	.45	.25
98T	Hector Villanueva(FC)	.35	.25	.14
99T	Eric Gunderson(FC)	.35	.25	.14
100T	Eric Lindros(FC)	1.75	1.25	.70
101T	Dave Otto(FC)	.12	.09	.05
102T	Dana Kiecker(FC)	.20	.15	.08
103T	Tim Drummond(FC)	.15	.11	.06
104T	Mickey Pina(FC)	.35	.25	.14
105T	Craig Grebeck(FC)	.20	.15	.08
106T	Bernard Gilkey(FC)	.25	.20	.10
107T	Tim Layana(FC)	.25	.20	.10
108T	Scott Chiamparino(FC)	.30	.25	.12
109T	Steve Avery(FC)	.40	.30	.15
110T	Terry Shumpert(FC)	.30	.25	.12

Definitions for grading conditions are located in the introduction section at the front of this book.

1991 Score Series I

Score introduced a two series format in 1991. The first series includes cards 1-441. Score cards once again feature multiple border colors within the set, several subsets (Master Blaster, K-Man, Highlights and Rifleman), full-color action photos on the front, posed photos on the flip side. Score eliminated providing the player's uniform number on the 1991 cards. Card number 441 of Series I features a Jose Canseco Vanity Fair photo. All of the 1991 Dream Team cards feature this style. The 1991 Score set when complete with Series II will mark its biggest issue. Rookie prospects and #1 Draft Picks highlight the 1991 Score set. The second series was due for release in February of 1991.

		MT	NR MT	EX
Complete Set:		15.00	11.00	6.00
Common Player:		.04	.03	.02
1	Jose Canseco	.35	.25	.14
2	Ken Griffey, Jr.	.70	.50	.30
3	Ryne Sandberg	.20	.15	.08
4	Nolan Ryan	.25	.20	.10
5	Bo Jackson	.35	.25	.14
6	Bret Saberhagen	.12	.09	.05
7	Will Clark	.20	.15	.08
8	Ellis Burks	.15	.11	.06
9	Joe Carter	.15	.11	.06
10	Rickey Henderson	.25	.20	.10
11	Ozzie Guillen	.10	.08	.04
12	Wade Boggs	.20	.15	.08
13	Jerome Walton	.15	.11	.06
14	John Franco	.10	.08	.04
15	Ricky Jordan	.08	.06	.03
16	Wally Backman	.04	.03	.02
17	Rob Dibble	.15	.11	.06
18	Glenn Braggs	.05	.04	.02
19	Cory Snyder	.10	.08	.04
20	Kal Daniels	.10	.08	.04
21	Mark Langston	.10	.08	.04
22	Kevin Gross	.06	.05	.02
23	Don Mattingly	.25	.20	.10
24	Dave Righetti	.08	.06	.03
25	Roberto Alomar	.15	.11	.06
26	Robby Thompson	.06	.05	.02
27	Jack McDowell	.08	.06	.03
28	Bip Roberts	.08	.06	.03
29	Jay Howell	.05	.04	.02
30	Dave Steib	.08	.06	.03
31	Johnny Ray	.04	.03	.02
32	Steve Sax	.10	.08	.04
33	Terry Mulholland	.08	.06	.03
34	Lee Guetterman	.04	.03	.02
35	Tim Raines	.12	.09	.05
36	Scott Fletcher	.04	.03	.02
37	Lance Parrish	.08	.06	.03
38	Tony Phillips	.05	.04	.02
39	Todd Stottlemyre	.06	.05	.02
40	Alan Trammell	.12	.09	.05
41	Todd Burns	.04	.03	.02
42	Mookie Wilson	.06	.05	.02
43	Chris Bosio	.05	.04	.02
44	Jeffrey Leonard	.06	.05	.02
45	Doug Jones	.08	.06	.03
46	Mike Scott	.08	.06	.03
47	Andy Hawkins	.05	.04	.02
48	Harold Reynolds	.08	.06	.03

		MT	NR MT	EX			MT	NR MT	EX
49	Paul Molitor	.12	.09	.05	141	Charlie Hough	.05	.04	.02
50	John Farrell	.05	.04	.02	142	Mike Henneman	.06	.05	.02
51	Danny Darwin	.06	.05	.02	143	Jeff Montgomery	.06	.05	.02
52	Jeff Blauser	.04	.03	.02	144	Lenny Harris	.06	.05	.02
53	John Tudor	.05	.04	.02	145	Bruce Hurst	.06	.05	.02
54	Milt Thompson	.04	.03	.02	146	Eric Anthony	.15	.11	.06
55	Dave Justice	.50	.40	.20	147	Paul Assenmacher	.04	.03	.02
56	Greg Olson	.12	.09	.05	148	Jesse Barfield	.06	.05	.02
57	Willie Blair	.12	.09	.05	149	Carlos Quintana	.08	.06	.03
58	Rick Parker	.10	.08	.04	150	Dave Stewart	.12	.09	.05
59	Shawn Boskie	.15	.11	.06	151	Roy Smith	.04	.03	.02
60	Kevin Tapani	.10	.08	.04	152	Paul Gibson	.04	.03	.02
61	Dave Hollins	.15	.11	.06	153	Mickey Hatcher	.04	.03	.02
62	Scott Radinsky	.12	.09	.05	154	Jim Eisenreich	.04	.03	.02
63	Francisco Cabrera	.10	.08	.04	155	Kenny Rogers	.06	.05	.02
64	Tim Layana	.15	.11	.06	156	Dave Schmidt	.04	.03	.02
65	Jim Leyritz	.20	.15	.08	157	Lance Johnson	.06	.05	.02
66	Wayne Edwards	.08	.06	.03	158	Dave West	.05	.04	.02
67	Lee Stevens(FC)	.15	.11	.06	159	Steve Balboni	.04	.03	.02
68	Bill Sampen	.15	.11	.06	160	Jeff Brantley	.08	.06	.03
69	Craig Grebeck	.10	.08	.04	161	Craig Biggio	.06	.05	.02
70	John Burkett	.15	.11	.06	162	Brook Jacoby	.06	.05	.02
71	Hector Villanueva	.15	.11	.06	163	Dan Gladden	.05	.04	.02
72	Oscar Azocar	.15	.11	.06	164	Jeff Reardon	.08	.06	.03
73	Alan Mills	.15	.11	.06	165	Mark Carreon	.05	.04	.02
74	Carlos Baerga	.25	.20	.10	166	Mel Hall	.05	.04	.02
75	Charles Nagy	.08	.06	.03	167	Gary Mielke	.06	.05	.02
76	Tim Drummond	.08	.06	.03	168	Cecil Fielder	.25	.20	.10
77	Dana Kiecker	.15	.11	.06	169	Darrin Jackson	.04	.03	.02
78	Tom Edens(FC)	.10	.08	.04	170	Rick Aguilera	.06	.05	.02
79	Kent Mercker	.10	.08	.04	171	Walt Weiss	.06	.05	.02
80	Steve Avery	.15	.11	.06	172	Steve Farr	.05	.04	.02
81	Lee Smith	.08	.06	.03	173	Jody Reed	.06	.05	.02
82	Dave Martinez	.05	.04	.02	174	Mike Jeffcoat	.04	.03	.02
83	Dave Winfield	.12	.09	.05	175	Mark Grace	.15	.11	.06
84	Bill Spiers	.06	.05	.02	176	Larry Sheets	.04	.03	.02
85	Dan Pasqua	.05	.04	.02	177	Bill Gullickson	.05	.04	.02
86	Randy Milligan	.06	.05	.02	178	Chris Gwynn	.06	.05	.02
87	Tracy Jones	.04	.03	.02	179	Melido Perez	.06	.05	.02
88	Greg Myers(FC)	.06	.05	.02	180	Sid Fernandez	.08	.06	.03
89	Keith Hernandez	.06	.05	.02	181	Tim Burke	.06	.05	.02
90	Todd Benzinger	.06	.05	.02	182	Gary Pettis	.05	.04	.02
91	Mike Jackson	.05	.04	.02	183	Rob Murphy	.04	.03	.02
92	Mike Stanley	.04	.03	.02	184	Craig Lefferts	.06	.05	.02
93	Candy Maldonado	.06	.05	.02	185	Howard Johnson	.10	.08	.04
94	John Kruk	.05	.04	.02	186	Ken Caminiti	.05	.04	.02
95	Cal Ripken,Jr.	.15	.11	.06	187	Tim Belcher	.06	.05	.02
96	Willie Fraser	.04	.03	.02	188	Greg Cadaret	.04	.03	.02
97	Mike Felder	.04	.03	.02	189	Matt Williams	.15	.11	.06
98	Bill Landrum	.05	.04	.02	190	Dave Magadan	.08	.06	.03
99	Chuck Crim	.04	.03	.02	191	Geno Petralli	.04	.03	.02
100	Chuck Finley	.08	.06	.03	192	Jeff Robinson	.05	.04	.02
101	Kirt Manwaring	.06	.05	.02	193	Jim Deshaies	.05	.04	.02
102	Jaime Navarro	.08	.06	.03	194	Willie Randolph	.06	.05	.02
103	Dickie Thon	.04	.03	.02	195	George Bell	.10	.08	.04
104	Brian Downing	.05	.04	.02	196	Hubie Brooks	.10	.08	.04
105	Jim Abbott	.12	.09	.05	197	Tom Gordon	.10	.08	.04
106	Tom Brookens	.04	.03	.02	198	Mike Fitzgerald	.04	.03	.02
107	Darryl Hamilton	.06	.05	.02	199	Mike Pagliarulo	.05	.04	.02
108	Bryan Harvey	.06	.05	.02	200	Kirby Puckett	.15	.11	.06
109	Greg Harris	.04	.03	.02	201	Shawon Dunston	.08	.06	.03
110	Greg Swindell	.08	.06	.03	202	Dennis Boyd	.05	.04	.02
111	Juan Berenguer	.04	.03	.02	203	Junior Felix	.08	.06	.03
112	Mike Heath	.04	.03	.02	204	Alejandro Pena	.04	.03	.02
113	Scott Bradley	.04	.03	.02	205	Pete Smith	.05	.04	.02
114	Jack Morris	.08	.06	.03	206	Tom Glavine	.06	.05	.02
115	Barry Jones	.05	.04	.02	207	Luis Salazar	.04	.03	.02
116	Kevin Romine	.04	.03	.02	208	John Smoltz	.08	.06	.03
117	Garry Templeton	.05	.04	.02	209	Doug Dascenzo	.05	.04	.02
118	Scott Sanderson	.05	.04	.02	210	Tim Wallach	.08	.06	.03
119	Roberto Kelly	.08	.06	.03	211	Greg Gagne	.05	.04	.02
120	George Brett	.15	.11	.06	212	Mark Gubicza	.08	.06	.03
121	Oddibe McDowell	.05	.04	.02	213	Mark Parent	.04	.03	.02
122	Jim Acker	.04	.03	.02	214	Ken Oberkfell	.04	.03	.02
123	Bill Swift	.05	.04	.02	215	Gary Carter	.08	.06	.03
124	Eric King	.05	.04	.02	216	Rafael Palmeiro	.10	.08	.04
125	Jay Buhner	.06	.05	.02	217	Tom Niedenfuer	.04	.03	.02
126	Matt Young	.04	.03	.02	218	Dave LaPoint	.05	.04	.02
127	Alvaro Espinoza	.05	.04	.02	219	Jeff Treadway	.05	.04	.02
128	Greg Hibbard	.08	.06	.03	220	Mitch Williams	.06	.05	.02
129	Jeff Robinson	.05	.04	.02	221	Jose DeLeon	.05	.04	.02
130	Mike Greenwell	.15	.11	.06	222	Mike LaValliere	.05	.04	.02
131	Dion James	.04	.03	.02	223	Darrel Akerfelds	.04	.03	.02
132	Donn Pall	.04	.03	.02	224	Kent Anderson	.05	.04	.02
133	Lloyd Moseby	.06	.05	.02	225	Dwight Evans	.08	.06	.03
134	Randy Velarde	.04	.03	.02	226	Gary Redus	.04	.03	.02
135	Allan Anderson	.05	.04	.02	227	Paul O'Neill	.06	.05	.02
136	Mark Davis	.06	.05	.02	228	Marty Barrett	.05	.04	.02
137	Eric Davis	.20	.15	.08	229	Tom Browning	.06	.05	.02
138	Phil Stephenson	.04	.03	.02	230	Terry Pendleton	.06	.05	.02
139	Felix Fermin	.04	.03	.02	231	Jack Armstrong	.08	.06	.03
140	Pedro Guerrero	.08	.06	.03					

#	Player	MT	NR MT	EX		#	Player	MT	NR MT	EX
232	Mike Boddicker	.06	.05	.02		323	Jay Bell	.06	.05	.02
233	Neal Heaton	.05	.04	.02		324	Mark McGwire	.20	.15	.08
234	Marquis Grissom	.10	.08	.04		325	Gary Gaetti	.10	.08	.04
235	Bert Blyleven	.08	.06	.03		326	Jeff Pico	.04	.03	.02
236	Curt Young	.05	.04	.02		327	Kevin McReynolds	.08	.06	.03
237	Don Carman	.05	.04	.02		328	Frank Tanana	.05	.04	.02
238	Charlie Hayes	.06	.05	.02		329	Eric Yelding	.06	.05	.02
239	Mark Knudson	.04	.03	.02		330	Barry Bonds	.20	.15	.08
240	Todd Zeile	.20	.15	.08		331	Brian McRae(FC)	.70	.50	.30
241	Larry Walker	.10	.08	.04		332	Pedro Munoz(FC)	.20	.15	.08
242	Jerald Clark	.06	.05	.02		333	Daryl Irvine(FC)	.20	.15	.08
243	Jeff Ballard	.05	.04	.02		334	Chris Hoiles	.15	.11	.06
244	Jeff King	.06	.05	.02		335	Thomas Howard(FC)	.20	.15	.08
245	Tom Brunansky	.08	.06	.03		336	Jeff Schulz(FC)	.20	.15	.08
246	Darren Daulton	.06	.05	.02		337	Jeff Manto(FC)	.15	.11	.06
247	Scott Terry	.04	.03	.02		338	Beau Allred	.10	.08	.04
248	Rob Deer	.06	.05	.02		339	Mike Bordick(FC)	.15	.11	.06
249	Brady Anderson	.04	.03	.02		340	Todd Hundley	.15	.11	.06
250	Lenny Dykstra	.08	.06	.03		341	Jim Vatcher(FC)	.15	.11	.06
251	Greg Harris	.06	.05	.02		342	Luis Sojo(FC)	.10	.08	.04
252	Mike Hartley	.08	.06	.03		343	Jose Offerman(FC)	.25	.20	.10
253	Joey Cora	.04	.03	.02		344	Pete Coachman(FC)	.25	.20	.10
254	Ivan Calderon	.08	.06	.03		345	Mike Benjamin(FC)	.10	.08	.04
255	Ted Power	.04	.03	.02		346	Ozzie Canseco(FC)	.25	.20	.10
256	Sammy Sosa	.15	.11	.06		347	Tim McIntosh(FC)	.15	.11	.06
257	Steve Buechele	.05	.04	.02		348	Phil Plantier(FC)	.50	.40	.20
258	Mike Devereaux	.05	.04	.02		349	Terry Shumpert	.15	.11	.06
259	Brad Komminsk	.04	.03	.02		350	Darren Lewis(FC)	.35	.25	.14
260	Teddy Higuera	.08	.06	.03		351	David Walsh(FC)	.20	.15	.08
261	Shawn Abner	.05	.04	.02		352	Scott Chiamparino	.15	.11	.06
262	Dave Valle	.05	.04	.02		353	Julio Valera(FC)	.15	.11	.06
263	Jeff Huson	.06	.05	.02		354	Anthony Telford(FC)	.20	.15	.08
264	Edgar Martinez	.06	.05	.02		355	Kevin Wickander(FC)	.10	.08	.04
265	Carlton Fisk	.10	.08	.04		356	Tim Naehring	.20	.15	.08
266	Steve Finley	.06	.05	.02		357	Jim Poole(FC)	.20	.15	.08
267	John Wetteland	.06	.05	.02		358	Mark Whiten(FC)	.25	.20	.10
268	Kevin Appier	.08	.06	.03		359	Terry Wells(FC)	.20	.15	.08
269	Steve Lyons	.04	.03	.02		360	Rafael Valdez	.10	.08	.04
270	Mickey Tettleton	.05	.04	.02		361	Mel Stottlemyre(FC)	.15	.11	.06
271	Luis Rivera	.04	.03	.02		362	David Segui	.20	.15	.08
272	Steve Jeltz	.04	.03	.02		363	Paul Abbott	.15	.11	.06
273	R.J. Reynolds	.04	.03	.02		364	Steve Howard(FC)	.15	.11	.06
274	Carlos Martinez	.05	.04	.02		365	Karl Rhodes(FC)	.15	.11	.06
275	Dan Plesac	.06	.05	.02		366	Rafael Novoa(FC)	.15	.11	.06
276	Mike Morgan	.04	.03	.02		367	Joe Grahe(FC)	.15	.11	.06
277	Jeff Russell	.06	.05	.02		368	Darren Reed(FC)	.20	.15	.08
278	Pete Incaviglia	.06	.05	.02		369	Jeff McKnight(FC)	.10	.08	.04
279	Kevin Seitzer	.08	.06	.03		370	Scott Leius(FC)	.10	.08	.04
280	Bobby Thigpen	.08	.06	.03		371	Mark Dewey(FC)	.20	.15	.08
281	Stan Javier	.04	.03	.02		372	Mark Lee(FC)	.20	.15	.08
282	Henry Cotto	.04	.03	.02		373	Rosario Rodriguez(FC)	.15	.11	.06
283	Gary Wayne	.05	.04	.02		374	Chuck McElroy(FC)	.10	.08	.04
284	Shane Mack	.05	.04	.02		375	Mike Bell(FC)	.15	.11	.06
285	Brian Holman	.06	.05	.02		376	Mickey Morandini(FC)	.10	.08	.04
286	Gerald Perry	.05	.04	.02		377	Bill Haselman(FC)	.20	.15	.08
287	Steve Crawford	.04	.03	.02		378	Dave Pavlas(FC)	.15	.11	.06
288	Nelson Liriano	.04	.03	.02		379	Derrick May(FC)	.40	.30	.15
289	Don Aase	.04	.03	.02		380	Jeromy Burnitz (#1 Draft Pick)(FC)	.50	.40	.20
290	Randy Johnson	.06	.05	.02		381	Donald Peters (#1 Draft Pick)(FC)	.40	.30	.15
291	Harold Baines	.08	.06	.03		382	Alex Fernandez (#1 Draft Pick)(FC)	1.25	.90	.50
292	Kent Hrbek	.08	.06	.03		383	Michael Mussina (#1 Draft Pick)(FC)	.40	.30	.15
293	Les Lancaster	.04	.03	.02		384	Daniel Smith (#1 Draft Pick)(FC)	.35	.25	.14
294	Jeff Musselman	.04	.03	.02		385	Lance Dickson (#1 Draft Pick)(FC)	.40	.30	.15
295	Kurt Stillwell	.06	.05	.02		386	Carl Everett (#1 Draft Pick)(FC)	.50	.40	.20
296	Stan Belinda	.06	.05	.02		387	Thomas Nevers (#1 Draft Pick)(FC)	.40	.30	.15
297	Lou Whitaker	.08	.06	.03		388	Adam Hyzdu (#1 Draft Pick)	.40	.30	.15
298	Glenn Wilson	.05	.04	.02		389	Todd Van Poppel (#1 Draft Pick)(FC)	2.00	1.50	.80
299	Omar Vizquel	.04	.03	.02		390	Rondell White (#1 Draft Pick)(FC)	.40	.30	.15
300	Ramon Martinez	.20	.15	.08		391	Marc Newfield (#1 Draft Pick)(FC)	.40	.30	.15
301	Dwight Smith	.06	.05	.02		392	Julio Franco (AS)	.10	.08	.04
302	Tim Crews	.04	.03	.02		393	Wade Boggs (AS)	.20	.15	.08
303	Lance Blankenship	.05	.04	.02		394	Ozzie Guillen (AS)	.10	.08	.04
304	Sid Bream	.06	.05	.02		395	Cecil Fielder (AS)	.20	.15	.08
305	Rafael Ramirez	.04	.03	.02		396	Ken Griffey,Jr. (AS)	.30	.25	.12
306	Steve Wilson	.06	.05	.02		397	Rickey Henderson (AS)	.20	.15	.08
307	Mackey Sasser	.06	.05	.02		398	Jose Canseco (AS)	.30	.25	.12
308	Franklin Stubbs	.06	.05	.02		399	Roger Clemens (AS)	.15	.11	.06
309	Jack Daugherty	.06	.05	.02		400	Sandy Alomar,Jr. (AS)	.10	.08	.04
310	Eddie Murray	.10	.08	.04		401	Bobby Thigpen (AS)	.10	.08	.04
311	Bob Welch	.08	.06	.03		402	Bobby Bonilla (Master Blaster)	.10	.08	.04
312	Brian Harper	.06	.05	.02		403	Eric Davis (Master Blaster)	.10	.08	.04
313	Lance McCullers	.04	.03	.02		404	Fred McGriff (Master Blaster)	.10	.08	.04
314	Dave Smith	.06	.05	.02		405	Glenn Davis (Master Blaster)	.10	.08	.04
315	Bobby Bonilla	.15	.11	.06		406	Kevin Mitchell (Master Blaster)	.10	.08	.04
316	Jerry Don Gleaton	.04	.03	.02		407	Rob Dibble (K-Man)	.10	.08	.04
317	Greg Maddux	.08	.06	.03		408	Ramon Martinez (K-Man)	.15	.11	.06
318	Keith Miller	.05	.04	.03						
319	Mark Portugal	.04	.03	.02						
320	Robin Ventura	.08	.06	.03						
321	Bob Ojeda	.04	.03	.02						
322	Mike Harkey	.08	.06	.03						

		MT	NR MT	EX
409	David Cone (K-Man)	.10	.08	.04
410	Bobby Witt (K-Man)	.10	.08	.04
411	Mark Langston (K-Man)	.10	.08	.04
412	Bo Jackson (Rifleman)	.30	.25	.12
413	Shawon Dunston (Rifleman)	.10	.08	.04
414	Jesse Barfield (Rifleman)	.08	.06	.03
415	Ken Caminiti (Rifleman)	.08	.06	.03
416	Benito Santiago (Rifleman)	.10	.08	.04
417	Nolan Ryan (Highlight)	.30	.25	.12
418	Bobby Thigpen (Highlight)	.10	.08	.04
419	Ramon Martinez (Highlight)	.15	.11	.06
420	Bo Jackson (Highlight)	.20	.15	.08
421	Carlton Fisk (Highlight)	.10	.08	.04
422	Jimmy Key	.06	.05	.02
423	Junior Noboa(FC)	.05	.04	.02
424	Al Newman	.04	.03	.02
425	Pat Borders	.05	.04	.02
426	Von Hayes	.08	.06	.03
427	Tim Teufel	.04	.03	.02
428	Eric Plunk	.04	.03	.02
429	John Moses	.04	.03	.02
430	Mike Witt	.05	.04	.02
431	Otis Nixon	.04	.03	.02
432	Tony Fernandez	.08	.06	.03
433	Rance Mulliniks	.04	.03	.02
434	Dan Petry	.04	.03	.02
435	Bob Geren	.05	.04	.02
436	Steve Frey(FC)	.06	.05	.02
437	Jamie Moyer	.05	.04	.02
438	Junior Ortiz	.04	.03	.02
439	Tom O'Malley	.04	.03	.02
440	Pat Combs	.06	.05	.02
441	Jose Canseco (Dream Team)	1.50	1.25	.60

1991 Score Rising Star

Marketed along with "1990-91 "Baseball's Hottest Rookies" magazine, this 100-card set features top rookies and young players such as Alex Fernandez and Frank Thomas. The cards are similar in design to the Score Superstar set. The magazine/card sets were available to a select group of retailers.

		MT	NR MT	EX
Complete Set:		10.00	7.50	4.00
Common Player:		.08	.06	.03
1	Sandy Alomar, Jr.	.15	.11	.06
2	Tom Edens	.08	.06	.03
3	Terry Shumpert	.15	.11	.06
4	Shawn Boskie	.20	.15	.08
5	Steve Avery	.15	.11	.06
6	Deion Sanders	.10	.08	.04
7	John Burkett	.10	.08	.04
8	Stan Belinda	.08	.06	.03
9	Thomas Howard	.15	.11	.06
10	Wayne Edwards	.08	.06	.03
11	Rick Parker	.08	.06	.03
12	Randy Veres	.08	.06	.03
13	Alex Cole	.15	.11	.06
14	Scott Chaimparino	.10	.08	.04
15	Greg Olson	.08	.06	.03
16	Jose DeJesus	.10	.08	.04
17	Mike Blowers	.08	.06	.03
18	Jeff Huson	.08	.06	.03
19	Willie Blair	.10	.08	.04
20	Howard Farmer	.10	.08	.04
21	Larry Walker	.15	.11	.06

		MT	NR MT	EX
22	Scott Hemond	.08	.06	.03
23	Mel Stottlemyre	.10	.08	.04
24	Mark Whiten	.25	.20	.10
25	Jeff Schulz	.10	.08	.04
26	Gary Disarcina	.08	.06	.03
27	George Canale	.08	.06	.03
28	Dean Palmer	.10	.08	.04
29	Jim Leyritz	.20	.15	.08
30	Carlos Baerga	.20	.15	.08
31	Rafael Valdez	.15	.11	.06
32	Derek Bell	.20	.15	.08
33	Francisco Cabrera	.08	.06	.03
34	Chris Hoiles	.20	.15	.08
35	Craig Grebeck	.08	.06	.03
36	Scott Coolbaugh	.08	.06	.03
37	Kevin Wickander	.10	.08	.04
38	Marquis Grissom	.15	.11	.06
39	Chip Hale	.08	.06	.03
40	Kevin Maas	.50	.40	.20
41	Juan Gonzalez	.60	.45	.25
42	Eric Anthony	.25	.20	.10
43	Luis Sojo	.10	.08	.04
44	Paul Sorrento	.08	.06	.03
45	Dave Justice	.60	.45	.25
46	Oscar Azocar	.08	.06	.03
47	Charles Nagy	.08	.06	.03
48	Robin Ventura	.20	.15	.08
49	Reggie Harris	.15	.11	.06
50	Ben McDonald	.50	.40	.20
51	Hector Villanueva	.15	.11	.06
52	Kevin Tapani	.15	.11	.06
53	Brian Bohanon	.08	.06	.03
54	Tim Layana	.10	.08	.04
55	Delino DeShields	.25	.20	.10
56	Beau Allred	.08	.06	.03
57	Eric Gunderson	.20	.15	.08
58	Kent Mercker	.10	.08	.04
59	Juan Bell	.10	.08	.04
60	Glenallen Hill	.10	.08	.04
61	David Segui	.30	.25	.12
62	Alan Mills	.15	.11	.06
63	Mike Harkey	.15	.11	.06
64	Bill Sampen	.15	.11	.06
65	Greg Vaughn	.20	.15	.08
66	Alex Fernandez	1.00	.70	.40
67	Mike Hartley	.08	.06	.03
68	Travis Fryman	.40	.30	.15
69	Dave Rohde	.10	.08	.04
70	Tom Lampkin	.08	.06	.03
71	Mark Gardner	.15	.11	.06
72	Pat Combs	.10	.08	.04
73	Kevin Appier	.15	.11	.06
74	Mike Fetters	.08	.06	.03
75	Greg Myers	.08	.06	.03
76	Steve Searcy	.08	.06	.03
77	Tim Naehring	.25	.20	.10
78	Frank Thomas	1.00	.70	.40
79	Todd Hundley	.10	.08	.04
80	Ed Vosburg	.15	.11	.06
81	Todd Zeile	.20	.15	.08
82	Lee Stevens	.10	.08	.04
83	Scott Radinsky	.10	.08	.04
84	Hensley Meulens	.10	.08	.04
85	Brian DuBois	.08	.06	.03
86	Steve Olin	.08	.06	.03
87	Julio Machado	.10	.08	.04
88	Jose Vizcaino	.10	.08	.04
89	Mark Lemke	.08	.06	.03
90	Felix Jose	.10	.08	.04
91	Wally Whitehurst	.08	.06	.03
92	Dana Kiecker	.10	.08	.04
93	Mike Munoz	.08	.06	.03
94	Adam Peterson	.08	.06	.03
95	Tim Drummond	.08	.06	.03
96	Dave Hollins	.10	.08	.04
97	Craig Wilson	.10	.08	.04
98	Hal Morris	.20	.15	.08
99	Jose Offerman	.30	.25	.12
100	John Olerud	.30	.25	.12

1991 Score Superstar

This 100-card set features full-color action photos on the card fronts and posed shots on the flip sides. The set was marketed along with the magazine "1991 Baseball's Hottest Players". The cards feature red, white, and blue borders and display the player's name and position below the photo on the card front.

KEN GRIFFEY, JR.
CENTER FIELD

The backs contain brief career highlights of the player. The magazine/card set combo was available to select retailers.

		MT	NR MT	EX
	Complete Set:	10.00	7.50	4.00
	Common Player:	.08	.06	.03
1	Jose Canseco	.30	.25	.12
2	Bo Jackson	.30	.25	.12
3	Wade Boggs	.15	.11	.06
4	Will Clark	.20	.15	.08
5	Ken Griffey, Jr.	.50	.40	.20
6	Doug Drabek	.10	.08	.04
7	Kirby Puckett	.15	.11	.06
8	Joe Orsulak	.08	.06	.03
9	Eric Davis	.15	.11	.06
10	Rickey Henderson	.20	.15	.08
11	Lenny Dykstra	.10	.08	.04
12	Ruben Sierra	.10	.08	.04
13	Paul Molitor	.10	.08	.04
14	Ron Gant	.15	.11	.06
15	Ozzie Guillen	.10	.08	.04
16	Ramon Martinez	.20	.15	.08
17	Edgar Martinez	.08	.06	.03
18	Ozzie Smith	.10	.08	.04
19	Charlie Hayes	.08	.06	.03
20	Barry Larkin	.15	.11	.06
21	Cal Ripken, Jr.	.15	.11	.06
22	Andy Van Slyke	.10	.08	.04
23	Don Mattingly	.25	.20	.10
24	Dave Stewart	.15	.11	.06
25	Nolan Ryan	.20	.15	.08
26	Barry Bonds	.20	.15	.08
27	Gregg Olson	.10	.08	.04
28	Chris Sabo	.10	.08	.04
29	John Franco	.10	.08	.04
30	Gary Sheffield	.20	.15	.08
31	Jeff Treadway	.08	.06	.03
32	Tom Browning	.08	.06	.03
33	Jose Lind	.08	.06	.03
34	Dave Magadan	.10	.08	.04
35	Dale Murphy	.10	.08	.04
36	Tom Candiotti	.08	.06	.03
37	Willie McGee	.10	.08	.04
38	Robin Yount	.15	.11	.06
39	Mark McGwire	.20	.15	.08
40	George Bell	.10	.08	.04
41	Carlton Fisk	.10	.08	.04
42	Bobby Bonilla	.10	.08	.04
43	Randy Milligan	.08	.06	.03
44	Dave Parker	.15	.11	.06
45	Shawon Dunston	.10	.08	.04
46	Brian Harper	.08	.06	.03
47	John Tudor	.08	.06	.03
48	Ellis Burks	.15	.11	.06
49	Bob Welch	.10	.08	.04
50	Roger Clemens	.20	.15	.08
51	Mike Henneman	.08	.06	.03
52	Eddie Murray	.15	.11	.06
53	Kal Daniels	.10	.08	.04
54	Doug Jones	.10	.08	.04
55	Craig Biggio	.10	.08	.04
56	Rafael Palmeiro	.15	.11	.06
57	Wally Joyner	.10	.08	.04
58	Tim Wallach	.10	.08	.04
59	Bret Saberhagen	.15	.11	.06
60	Ryne Sandberg	.20	.15	.08
61	Benito Santiago	.10	.08	.04
62	Darryl Strawberry	.20	.15	.08
63	Alan Trammell	.10	.08	.04

		MT	NR MT	EX
64	Kelly Gruber	.15	.11	.06
65	Dwight Gooden	.20	.15	.08
66	Dave Winfield	.10	.08	.04
67	Rick Aguilera	.08	.06	.03
68	Dave Righetti	.10	.08	.04
69	Jim Abbott	.10	.08	.04
70	Frank Viola	.15	.11	.06
71	Fred McGriff	.20	.15	.08
72	Steve Sax	.10	.08	.04
73	Dennis Eckersley	.15	.11	.06
74	Cory Snyder	.08	.06	.03
75	Mackey Sasser	.08	.06	.03
76	Candy Maldonado	.10	.08	.04
77	Matt Williams	.15	.11	.06
78	Kent Hrbek	.10	.08	.04
79	Randy Myers	.10	.08	.04
80	Gregg Jefferies	.20	.15	.08
81	Joe Carter	.10	.08	.04
82	Mike Greenwell	.15	.11	.06
83	Jack Armstrong	.10	.08	.04
84	Julio Franco	.10	.08	.04
85	George Brett	.15	.11	.06
86	Howard Johnson	.10	.08	.04
87	Andre Dawson	.15	.11	.06
88	Cecil Fielder	.25	.20	.10
89	Tim Raines	.10	.08	.04
90	Chuck Finley	.10	.08	.04
91	Mark Grace	.15	.11	.06
92	Brook Jacoby	.10	.08	.04
93	Dave Steib	.10	.08	.04
94	Tony Gwynn	.15	.11	.06
95	Bobby Thigpen	.10	.08	.04
96	Roberto Kelly	.10	.08	.04
97	Kevin Seitzer	.10	.08	.04
98	Kevin Mitchell	.15	.11	.06
99	Dwight Evans	.10	.08	.04
100	Roberto Alomar	.10	.08	.04

1989 Scoremasters

This unique 42-card boxed set from Score was reproduced from original artwork done by sports artist Jeffrey Rubin. The paintings are reproduced on a standard-size, white, glossy stock, and the set includes the top stars of the game, including four key rookies (Walton, Gordon, Jefferies and Griffey Jr.).

		MT	NR MT	EX
	Complete Set:	13.00	9.75	5.25
	Common Player:	.20	.15	.08
1	Bo Jackson	1.00	.70	.40
2	Jerome Walton	.70	.50	.30
3	Cal Ripken, Jr.	.35	.25	.12
4	Mike Scott	.20	.15	.08
5	Nolan Ryan	1.00	.70	.40
6	Don Mattingly	1.25	.90	.50
7	Tom Gordon	1.00	.70	.40
8	Jack Morris	.20	.15	.08
9	Carlton Fisk	.30	.25	.12
10	Will Clark	1.00	.70	.40
11	George Brett	.40	.30	.15
12	Kevin Mitchell	.40	.30	.15
13	Mark Langston	.30	.25	.12
14	Dave Stewart	.20	.15	.08
15	Dale Murphy	.25	.20	.10
16	Gary Gaetti	.20	.15	.08

		MT	NR MT	EX
17	Wade Boggs	.50	.40	.20
18	Eric Davis	.70	.50	.30
19	Kirby Puckett	.70	.50	.30
20	Roger Clemens	.50	.40	.20
21	Orel Hershiser	.30	.25	.12
22	Mark Grace	.50	.40	.20
23	Ryne Sandberg	.35	.25	.12
24	Barry Larkin	.20	.15	.08
25	Ellis Burks	.40	.30	.15
26	Doc Gooden	.40	.30	.15
27	Ozzie Smith	.25	.20	.10
28	Andre Dawson	.20	.15	.08
29	Julio Franco	.20	.15	.08
30	Ken Griffey, Jr.	1.50	1.25	.60
31	Ruben Sierra	.30	.25	.12
32	Mark McGwire	.80	.60	.30
33	Andres Galarraga	.20	.15	.08
34	Joe Carter	.30	.25	.12
35	Vince Coleman	.20	.15	.08
36	Mike Greenwell	.50	.40	.20
37	Tony Gwynn	.40	.30	.15
38	Andy Van Slyke	.20	.15	.08
39	Gregg Jefferies	1.00	.70	.40
40	Jose Canseco	1.00	.70	.40
41	Dave Winfield	.20	.15	.08
42	Darryl Strawberry	.40	.30	.15

1985 7-11 Twins

The Minnesota Twins, in co-operation with 7-Eleven and the Fire Marshall's Association, issued this set of 13 baseball fire safety cards. The card fronts feature full-color pictures of Twins players. A fire safety tip and short player history appear on the back. The cards were given out at all 7-Eleven stores in the state and at the Twins June 3 baseball game. Each fan received one baseball card with a poster which told how to collect the other cards in the set. Twelve cards feature players and the 13th card has an artist's rendering of Twins players on the front and a checklist of the set on the back. A group of 50,000 cards was distributed to fifth graders throughout the state by the fire departments.

		MT	NR MT	EX
	Complete Set:	7.00	5.25	2.75
	Common Player:	.20	.15	.08
1	Kirby Puckett	2.00	1.50	.80
2	Frank Viola	1.00	.70	.40
3	Mickey Hatcher	.20	.15	.08
4	Kent Hrbek	1.25	.90	.50
5	John Butcher	.20	.15	.08
6	Roy Smalley	.20	.15	.08
7	Tom Brunansky	.80	.60	.30
8	Ron Davis	.20	.15	.08
9	Gary Gaetti	1.00	.70	.40
10	Tim Teufel	.30	.25	.12
11	Mike Smithson	.20	.15	.08
12	Tim Laudner	.30	.25	.12
----	Checklist	.10	.08	.04

NOTE: A card number in parentheses ( ) indicates the set is unnumbered.

1984 7-Up Cubs

 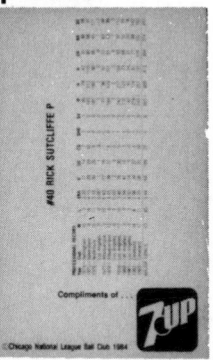

The Chicago Cubs and 7-Up issued this 28-card set featuring full-color game-action photos on a 2-1/4" by 3-1/2" borderless front. The backs have the player's stats and personal information. This was the third consecutive year the Cubs issued this type of set as a giveaway at a "Baseball Card Day" promotional game.

		MT	NR MT	EX
	Complete Set:	12.00	9.00	4.75
	Common Player:	.20	.15	.08
1	Larry Bowa	.40	.30	.15
6	Keith Moreland	.40	.30	.15
7	Jody Davis	.40	.30	.15
10	Leon Durham	.40	.30	.15
11	Ron Cey	.40	.30	.15
15	Ron Hassey	.20	.15	.08
18	Richie Hebner	.20	.15	.08
19	Dave Owen	.20	.15	.08
20	Bob Dernier	.20	.15	.08
21	Jay Johnstone	.25	.20	.10
23	Ryne Sandberg	3.00	2.25	1.25
24	Scott Sanderson	.25	.20	.10
25	Gary Woods	.20	.15	.08
27	Thad Bosley	.20	.15	.08
28	Henry Cotto	.30	.25	.12
34	Steve Trout	.25	.20	.10
36	Gary Matthews	.40	.30	.15
39	George Frazier	.20	.15	.08
40	Rick Sutcliffe	.80	.60	.30
41	Warren Brusstar	.20	.15	.08
42	Rich Bordi	.20	.15	.08
43	Dennis Eckersley	.80	.60	.30
44	Dick Ruthven	.20	.15	.08
46	Lee Smith	.50	.40	.20
47	Rick Reuschel	.50	.40	.20
49	Tim Stoddard	.20	.15	.08
----	Jim Frey	.20	.15	.08
----	Cubs Coaches (Ruben Amaro, Billy Connors, Johnny Oates, John Vukovich, Don Zimmer)	.20	.15	.08

1985 7-Up Cubs

This was the second year a Chicago Cubs card set

was released with 7-Up as the sponsor. The set has 28 unnumbered cards in the standard 2-1/2" by 3-1/2" size. They were distributed to fans attending the Cubs game on August 14 at Wrigley Field. They feature full-color game-action photos of the players. Card backs contain the player's professional stats.

		MT	NR MT	EX
Complete Set:		8.00	6.00	3.25
Common Player:		.10	.08	.04
1	Larry Bowa	.25	.20	.10
6	Keith Moreland	.30	.25	.12
7	Jody Davis	.30	.25	.12
10	Leon Durham	.30	.25	.12
11	Ron Cey	.30	.25	.12
15	Davey Lopes	.25	.20	.10
16	Steve Lake	.10	.08	.04
18	Richie Hebner	.10	.08	.04
20	Bob Dernier	.10	.08	.04
21	Scott Sanderson	.15	.11	.06
22	Billy Hatcher	.30	.25	.12
23	Ryne Sandberg	3.00	2.25	1.25
24	Brian Dayett	.10	.08	.04
25	Gary Woods	.10	.08	.04
27	Thad Bosley	.10	.08	.04
28	Chris Speier	.10	.08	.04
31	Ray Fontenot	.10	.08	.04
34	Steve Trout	.20	.15	.08
36	Gary Matthews	.30	.25	.12
39	George Frazier	.10	.08	.04
40	Rick Sutcliffe	.70	.50	.30
41	Warren Brusstar	.10	.08	.04
42	Lary Sorensen	.10	.08	.04
43	Dennis Eckersley	.80	.60	.30
44	Dick Ruthven	.10	.08	.04
46	Lee Smith	.35	.25	.14
----	Jim Frey	.10	.08	.04
----	Coaching Staff (Ruben Amaro, Billy Connors, Johnny Oates, John Vukovich, Don Zimmer)	.10	.08	.04

1984 Smokey Bear Dodgers

Unlike the California Angels and San Diego Padres sets issued in conjunction with the Forestry Service in 1984, the Los Angeles Dodgers set contains only three players, pictured on much larger 5" by 7" cards. Ken Landreaux, Tom Niedenfuer and Steve Sax (plus a Smokey the Bear card) are pictured on the cards. Each player is pictured in a forest scene on the full-color fronts. Backs of the unnumbered cards have brief biographical information and lifetime statistics. The cards were distributed at a Dodgers home game.

		MT	NR MT	EX
Complete Set:		10.00	7.50	4.00
Common Player:		2.50	2.00	1.00
(1)	Ken Landreaux	2.50	2.00	1.00
(2)	Tom Niedenfuer	2.50	2.00	1.00
(3)	Steve Sax	5.00	3.75	2.00
(4)	Smokey Bear	.50	.40	.20

1984 Smokey Bear Angels

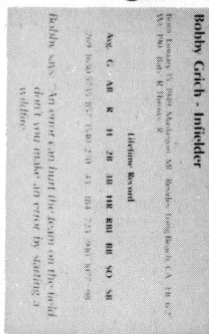

This 32-card set was distributed at a June home game to fans 14 and under. Cards measure 2-1/2" by 3-1/2". The full-color card fronts list the player name along with the team logo and Forestry service logos commemorating the 40th birthday of Smokey the the Bear. The black and white card backs list tips for preventing forest fires.

		MT	NR MT	EX
Complete Set:		8.00	6.00	3.25
Common Player:		.20	.15	.08
(1)	Don Aase	.20	.15	.08
(2)	Juan Beniquez	.20	.15	.08
(3)	Bob Boone	.30	.25	.12
(4)	Rick Burleson	.30	.25	.12
(5)	Rod Carew	1.00	.70	.40
(6)	John Curtis	.20	.15	.08
(7)	Doug DeCinces	.30	.25	.12
(8)	Brian Downing	.30	.25	.12
(9)	Ken Forsch	.20	.15	.08
(10)	Bobby Grich	.30	.25	.12
(11)	Reggie Jackson	1.25	.90	.50
(12)	Ron Jackson	.20	.15	.08
(13)	Tommy John	.60	.45	.25
(14)	Curt Kaufman	.20	.15	.08
(15)	Bruce Kison	.20	.15	.08
(16)	Frank LaCorte	.20	.15	.08
(17)	Fred Lynn	.60	.45	.25
(18)	John McNamara	.20	.15	.08
(19)	Jerry Narron	.20	.15	.08
(20)	Gary Pettis	.40	.30	.15
(21)	Robert Picciolo	.20	.15	.08
(22)	Ron Romanick	.20	.15	.08
(23)	Luis Sanchez	.20	.15	.08
(24)	Dick Schofield	.30	.25	.12
(25)	Daryl Sconiers	.20	.15	.08
(26)	Jim Slaton	.20	.15	.08
(27)	Ellis Valentine	.20	.15	.08
(28)	Robert Wilfong	.20	.15	.08
(29)	Mike Witt	.50	.40	.20
(30)	Geoff Zahn	.20	.15	.08
----	Forestry Dept. Logo Card	.10	.08	.04
----	Smokey Logo Card	.10	.08	.04

1984 Smokey Bear Jackson Mets In Majors

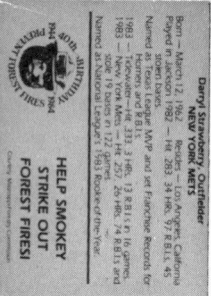

This set, issued in conjunction with the Mississippi Forestry Commission, features big leaguers who played for the Mets' Double-A farm club. The fifteen 3" by 4" cards have a black and white portrait photo on the front with the name, position and major league team shown in blue. A Smokey the Bear logo is also included. Card backs feature player information and career highlights.

	MT	NR MT	EX
Complete Set:	60.00	45.00	25.00
Common Player:	1.00	.70	.40

		MT	NR MT	EX
(1)	Neil Allen	1.00	.70	.40
(2)	Wally Backman	2.00	1.50	.80
(3)	Hubie Brooks	3.00	2.25	1.25
(4)	Jody Davis	2.00	1.50	.80
(5)	Brian Giles	1.00	.70	.40
(6)	Dave Johnson	2.00	1.50	.80
(7)	Tim Leary	2.00	1.50	.80
(8)	Lee Mazzilli	2.00	1.50	.80
(9)	Jesse Orosco	2.00	1.50	.80
(10)	Jeff Reardon	3.00	2.25	1.25
(11)	Doug Sisk	1.00	.70	.40
(12)	Darryl Strawberry	20.00	15.00	8.00
(13)	Mookie Wilson	4.00	3.00	1.50
(14)	Marvel Wynne (Marvell)	2.00	1.50	.80
(15)	Ned Yost	1.00	.70	.40

1984 Smokey Bear Padres

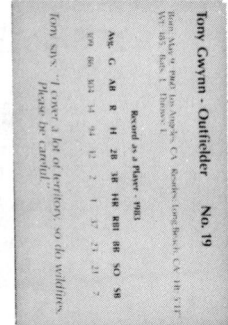

This set of 28 full-color cards is very similar in format to the Angels set of the same year. San Diego Padres players are posed in photos with Smokey the Bear. Forestry Department and team logos are also pictured on the card fronts. The Padres cards feature players, coaches, broadcasters and the Famous Chicken, all posing with Smokey. The backs of the cards which were distributed at a Padres home game, offer brief player information and a fire prevention tip.

	MT	NR MT	EX
Complete Set:	10.00	7.50	4.00
Common Player:	.25	.20	.10

		MT	NR MT	EX
1	Garry Templeton	.40	.30	.15
2	Alan Wiggins	.25	.20	.10
4	Luis Salazar	.25	.20	.10
6	Steve Garvey	1.25	.90	.50
7	Kurt Bevacqua	.25	.20	.10
10	Doug Gwosdz	.25	.20	.10
11	Tim Flannery	.25	.20	.10
16	Terry Kennedy	.40	.30	.15
18	Kevin McReynolds	1.25	.90	.50
19	Tony Gwynn	1.50	1.25	.60
20	Bobby Brown	.25	.20	.10
30	Eric Show	.50	.40	.20
31	Ed Whitson	.25	.20	.10
35	Luis DeLeon	.25	.20	.10
38	Mark Thurmond	.25	.20	.10
42	Sid Monge	.25	.20	.10
43	Dave Dravecky	.40	.30	.15
48	Tim Lollar	.25	.20	.10
------	Smokey Logo Card	.25	.20	.10
------	The Chicken (mascot)	.40	.30	.15

		MT	NR MT	EX
------	Dave Campbell (broadcaster)	.25	.20	.10
------	Jerry Coleman (broadcaster)	.25	.20	.10
------	Harry Dunlop (coach)	.25	.20	.10
------	Harold (Doug) Harvey (umpire)	.25	.20	.10
------	Jack Krol (coach)	.25	.20	.10
------	Jack McKeon (vice-president)	.25	.20	.10
------	Norm Sherry (coach)	.25	.20	.10
------	Ozzie Virgil (coach)	.25	.20	.10
------	Dick Williams (manager)	.25	.20	.10

1985 Smokey Bear Angels

The California Forestry Service and the California Angels gave this full-color set of oversized baseball cards to fans attending the July 14 game at Anaheim Stadium. The 24 cards feature player photos on the fronts with their last name at the top of the cards above the picture. On the card bottoms are the logos for Smokey Bear, the Angels, the State Forestry Service and the U.S. Forestry Service. The cards measure 4-1/4" by 6". On the card backs, printed in black and white, are personal data, limited playing stats and a wildfire safety tip from Smokey the Bear.

	MT	NR MT	EX
Complete Set:	7.00	5.25	2.75
Complete Set:	.20	.15	.08

		MT	NR MT	EX
1	Mike Witt	.50	.40	.20
2	Reggie Jackson	1.25	.90	.50
3	Bob Boone	.30	.25	.12
4	Mike Brown	.20	.15	.08
5	Rod Carew	1.00	.70	.40
6	Doug DeCinces	.30	.25	.12
7	Brian Downing	.30	.25	.12
8	Ken Forsch	.20	.15	.08
9	Gary Pettis	.20	.15	.08
10	Jerry Narron	.20	.15	.08
11	Ron Romanick	.20	.15	.08
12	Bobby Grich	.30	.25	.12
13	Dick Schofield	.30	.25	.12
14	Juan Beniquez	.20	.15	.08
15	Geoff Zahn	.20	.15	.08
16	Luis Sanchez	.20	.15	.08
17	Jim Slaton	.20	.15	.08
18	Doug Corbett	.20	.15	.08
19	Ruppert Jones	.20	.15	.08
20	Rob Wilfong	.20	.15	.08
21	Donnie Moore	.20	.15	.08
22	Pat Clements	.20	.15	.08
23	Tommy John	.60	.45	.25
24	Gene Mauch	.30	.25	.12

1986 Smokey Bear Angels

The California Angels, in conjuction with the Forestry Service, issued this 24-card set of Wildfire Prevention baseball cards. The cards measure 4-1/4" by 6" and offer a full-color front with the player's picture placed in an oval frame. The card backs have player stats with a drawing and slogan for fire prevention. The sets were given out on August 9th at the Angels game in Anaheim Stadium.

		MT	NR MT	EX
Complete Set:		8.00	6.00	3.25
Common Player:		.20	.15	.08

1	Mike Witt	.50	.40	.20
2	Reggie Jackson	1.25	.90	.50
3	Bob Boone	.30	.25	.12
4	Don Sutton	.60	.45	.25
5	Kirk McCaskill	.50	.40	.20
6	Doug DeCinces	.30	.25	.12
7	Brian Downing	.30	.25	.12
8	Doug Corbett	.20	.15	.08
9	Gary Pettis	.20	.15	.08
10	Jerry Narron	.20	.15	.08
11	Ron Romanick	.20	.15	.08
12	Bobby Grich	.30	.25	.12
13	Dick Schofield	.30	.25	.12
14	George Hendrick	.30	.25	.12
15	Rick Burleson	.30	.25	.12
16	John Candelaria	.30	.25	.12
17	Jim Slaton	.20	.15	.08
18	Darrell Miller	.30	.25	.12
19	Ruppert Jones	.20	.15	.08
20	Rob Wilfong	.20	.15	.08
21	Donnie Moore	.20	.15	.08
22	Wally Joyner	2.50	2.00	1.00
23	Terry Forster	.30	.25	.12
24	Gene Mauch	.30	.25	.12

1987 Smokey Bear

The U.S. Forestry Service and Major League Baseball united in an effort to promote National Smokey the Bear Day. Two perforated sheets of baseball cards, one each for the American and National Leagues, were produced by the Forestry Service. The sheet of American Leaguers measures 18" by 24" and contains 16 full-color cards. The National League sheet measures 20" by 18" and contains 15 cards. Each individual card is 4" by 6" and contains a fire prevention tip on the back. An average number of 25,000 sets was sent to all teams.

	MT	NR MT	EX
Complete Set:	8.00	6.00	3.25
Common Player:	.20	.15	.08

1A	Jose Canseco	1.50	1.25	.60
1N	Steve Sax	.40	.30	.15
2A	Dennis "Oil Can" Boyd	.20	.15	.08
2Na	Dale Murphy (shirttail out)	5.00	3.75	2.00
2Nb	Dale Murphy (shirttail in)	.80	.60	.30
3A	John Candelaria	.20	.15	.08
3Na	Jody Davis (standing)	3.50	2.75	1.50
3Nb	Jody Davis (kneeling)	.25	.20	.10
4A	Harold Baines	.30	.25	.12
4N	Bill Gullickson	.20	.15	.08
5A	Joe Carter	.30	.25	.12
5N	Mike Scott	.30	.25	.12
6A	Jack Morris	.40	.30	.15
6N	Roger McDowell	.25	.20	.10
7A	Buddy Biancalana	.20	.15	.08
7N	Steve Bedrosian	.30	.25	.12
8A	Kirby Puckett	.70	.50	.30
8N	Johnny Ray	.25	.20	.10
9A	Mike Pagliarulo	.25	.20	.10
9N	Ozzie Smith	.30	.25	.12
10A	Larry Sheets	.25	.20	.10
10N	Steve Garvey	.60	.45	.25
11A	Mike Moore	.20	.15	.08
11N	Smokey Bear Logo Card	.05	.04	.02
12A	Charlie Hough	.20	.15	.08
12N	Mike Krukow	.20	.15	.08
13A	Smokey Bear Logo Card	.05	.04	.02
13N	Smokey Bear	.05	.04	.02
14A	Tom Henke	.20	.15	.08
14N	Mike Fitzgerald	.20	.15	.08
15A	Jim Gantner	.20	.15	.08
15N	National League Logo Card	.05	.04	.02
16A	American League Logo Card	.05	.04	.02

1987 Smokey Bear A's

The 1987 Smokey Bear A's set is not comparable to any other Smokey Bear issue produced in 1987 or before. The 12 cards in the set are bound together in a book titled "Smokey Bear's Fire Prevention Color-Grams." The Color-Gram cards feature two cards in one. A near-standard size (2-1/2" by 3-3/4") black and white card is attached to a large perforated (3-3/4" by 6") card, also black and white. The large card, which has a postcard back, features a caricature photo of the player and is intended to be colored and then mailed. The card backs contain personal and statistical information and carry a Smokey the Bear cartoon message. The books were distributed at an Oakland A's game during the 1987 season.

		MT	NR MT	EX
Complete Book:		6.00	4.50	2.50
Complete Singles Set:		3.00	2.25	1.25
Common Single Player:		.15	.11	.06

(1)	Joaquin Andujar	.20	.15	.08
(2)	Jose Canseco	1.50	1.25	.60
(3)	Mike Davis	.25	.20	.10
(4)	Alfredo Griffin	.25	.20	.10
(5)	Moose Haas	.15	.11	.06
(6)	Jay Howell	.25	.20	.10
(7)	Reggie Jackson	.80	.60	.30
(8)	Carney Lansford	.30	.25	.12
(9)	Dwayne Murphy	.25	.20	.10
(10)	Tony Phillips	.15	.11	.06

		MT	NR MT	EX
(11)	Dave Stewart	.40	.30	.15
(12)	Curt Young	.30	.25	.12

1987 Smokey Bear Angels

A 24-card set featuring the California Angels and produced by the U.S. Forestry Service was distributed to 25,000 fans in attendance at Anaheim Stadium on August 1st. The full-color cards measure 4" x 6". The card fronts carry a unique design with baseballs and bats framing the player photo. Only the player's last name is given on the card fronts. The backs contain the player's name, position and personal statistics along with a Smokey Bear cartoon and a fire prevention tip.

		MT	NR MT	EX
	Complete Set:	8.00	6.00	3.25
	Common Player:	.20	.15	.08
1	John Candelaria	.30	.25	.12
2	Don Sutton	.60	.45	.25
3	Mike Witt	.50	.40	.20
4	Gary Lucas	.20	.15	.08
5	Kirk McCaskill	.30	.25	.12
6	Chuck Finley	.30	.25	.12
7	Willie Fraser	.30	.25	.12
8	Donnie Moore	.20	.15	.08
9	Urbano Lugo	.20	.15	.08
10	Butch Wynegar	.25	.20	.10
11	Darrell Miller	.20	.15	.08
12	Wally Joyner	2.00	1.50	.80
13	Mark McLemore	.20	.15	.08
14	Mark Ryal	.20	.15	.08
15	Dick Schofield	.25	.20	.10
16	Jack Howell	.30	.25	.12
17	Doug DeCinces	.30	.25	.12
18	Gus Polidor	.20	.15	.08
19	Brian Downing	.30	.25	.12
20	Gary Pettis	.20	.15	.08
21	Ruppert Jones	.20	.15	.08
22	George Hendrick	.25	.20	.10
23	Devon White	1.25	.90	.50
----	Smokey Bear Logo Card/Checklist	.10	.08	.04

1987 Smokey Bear Cardinals

Approximately 25,000 fans in attendance at Busch Stadium on August 24th received a 25-card set featuring the St. Louis Cardinals. Produced by the U.S. Forestry Service, the cards measure 4" by 6". The card fronts feature a full-color photo set inside an oval frame. Only the player's last name appears on the front. The card reverse carries the player's name, position and personal data plus a Smokey Bear cartoon with a fire prevention message.

		MT	NR MT	EX
	Complete Set:	8.00	6.00	3.25
	Common Player:	.20	.15	.08
1	Ray Soff	.20	.15	.08
2	Todd Worrell	.50	.40	.20
3	John Tudor	.35	.25	.14
4	Pat Perry	.20	.15	.08
5	Rick Horton	.20	.15	.08
6	Dan Cox	.30	.25	.12
7	Bob Forsch	.30	.25	.12
8	Greg Mathews	.40	.30	.15
9	Bill Dawley	.20	.15	.08
10	Steve Lake	.20	.15	.08
11	Tony Pena	.30	.25	.12
12	Tom Pagnozzi	.30	.25	.12
13	Jack Clark	.80	.60	.30
14	Jim Lindeman	.35	.25	.14
15	Mike Laga	.20	.15	.08
16	Terry Pendleton	.40	.30	.15
17	Ozzie Smith	.80	.60	.30
18	Jose Oquendo	.20	.15	.08
19	Tom Lawless	.20	.15	.08
20	Tom Herr	.30	.25	.12
21	Curt Ford	.20	.15	.08
22	Willie McGee	.70	.50	.30
23	Tito Landrum	.20	.15	.08
24	Vince Coleman	.80	.60	.30
25	Whitey Herzog	.30	.25	.12

1987 Smokey Bear Dodgers

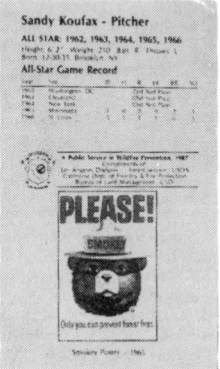

The 40-card Smokey Bear Dodgers set features "25 Years of Dodger All-Stars." The cards, which measure 2-1/2" by 3-3/4", were given out to fans 14 years of age and younger at the September 18th game at Dodgers Stadium. The card fronts contain full-color photos set in the shape of Dodger Stadium and have attractive silver borders. The backs carry the player's All-Star Game record plus a fire prevention message. Many of the photos used in the set were from team-issued picture packs sold by the Dodgers in the past.

		MT	NR MT	EX
	Complete Set:	10.00	7.50	4.00
	Common Player:	.20	.15	.08
(1)	Walt Alston	.40	.30	.15
(2)	Dusty Baker	.25	.20	.10
(3)	Jim Brewer	.20	.15	.08
(4)	Ron Cey	.30	.25	.12
(5)	Tommy Davis	.25	.20	.10
(6)	Willie Davis	.25	.20	.10
(7)	Don Drysdale	.80	.60	.30
(8)	Steve Garvey	.80	.60	.30

		MT	NR MT	EX
(9)	Bill Grabarkewitz	.20	.15	.08
(10)	Pedro Guerrero	.50	.40	.20
(11)	Tom Haller	.20	.15	.08
(12)	Orel Hershiser	.60	.45	.25
(13)	Burt Hooton	.20	.15	.08
(14)	Steve Howe	.20	.15	.08
(15)	Tommy John	.50	.40	.20
(16)	Sandy Koufax	1.25	.90	.50
(17)	Tom Lasorda	.30	.25	.12
(18)	Jim Lefebvre	.20	.15	.08
(19)	Davey Lopes	.25	.20	.10
(20)	Mike Marshall (outfielder)	.40	.30	.15
(21)	Mike Marshall (pitcher)	.25	.20	.10
(22)	Andy Messersmith	.20	.15	.08
(23)	Rick Monday	.25	.20	.10
(24)	Manny Mota	.25	.20	.10
(25)	Claude Osteen	.20	.15	.08
(26)	Johnny Podres	.30	.25	.12
(27)	Phil Regan	.20	.15	.08
(28)	Jerry Reuss	.25	.20	.10
(29)	Rick Rhoden	.25	.20	.10
(30)	John Roseboro	.25	.20	.10
(31)	Bill Russell	.25	.20	.10
(32)	Steve Sax	.40	.30	.15
(33)	Bill Singer	.20	.15	.08
(34)	Reggie Smith	.25	.20	.10
(35)	Don Sutton	.60	.45	.25
(36)	Fernando Valenzuela	.70	.50	.30
(37)	Bob Welch	.30	.25	.12
(38)	Maury Wills	.40	.30	.15
(39)	Jim Wynn	.20	.15	.08
(40)	Logo Card/Checklist	.10	.08	.04

		MT	NR MT	EX
17	Ruben Sierra	1.50	1.25	.60
18	Larry Parrish	.50	.40	.20
19	Bobby Valentine	.40	.30	.15
20	Tom House	.30	.25	.12
21	Tom Robson	.30	.25	.12
22	Edwin Correa	.40	.30	.15
23	Mike Stanley	.60	.45	.25
24	Joe Ferguson	.30	.25	.12
25	Art Howe	.30	.25	.12
26	Bob Brower	.50	.40	.20
27	Mike Loynd	.50	.40	.20
28	Curtis Wilkerson	.30	.25	.12
29	Tim Foli	.30	.25	.12
30	Dave Oliver	.30	.25	.12
31	Jerry Browne	.50	.40	.20
32	Jeff Russell	.30	.25	.12

1988 Smokey Bear Angels

This set includes 25 borderless full-color cards (2-1/2" by 3-1/2") that are highlighted by a thin white inset outline on the card fronts. The player name, team logo and a Smokey Bear picture logo appear in the lower right corner. The backs are black and white and include personal information and a large cartoon-style fire prevention logo. The set also includes a team logo checklist card. Part of the U.S. Forest Service fire prevention campaign, the cards were distributed in three separate in-stadium giveaways during August and September, 1988 games.

		MT	NR MT	EX
Complete Set:		10.00	7.50	4.00
Common Player:		.30	.25	.12
1	Cookie Rojas	.30	.25	.12
2	Johnny Ray	.40	.30	.15
3	Jack Howell	.40	.30	.15
4	Mike Witt	.50	.40	.20
5	Tony Armas	.40	.30	.15
6	Gus Polidor	.30	.25	.12
7	DeWayne Buice	.40	.30	.15
8	Dan Petry	.40	.30	.15
9	Bob Boone	.40	.30	.15
10	Chili Davis	.40	.30	.15
11	Greg Minton	.30	.25	.12
12	Kirk McCaskill	.40	.30	.15
13	Devon White	.80	.60	.30
14	Willie Fraser	.30	.25	.12
15	Chuck Finley	.30	.25	.12
16	Dick Schofield	.30	.25	.12
17	Wally Joyner	1.50	1.25	.60
18	Brian Downing	.40	.30	.15
19	Stewart Cliburn	.30	.25	.12
20	Donnie Moore	.30	.25	.12
21	Bryan Harvey	.40	.30	.15
22	Mark McLemore	.30	.25	.12
23	Butch Wynegar	.30	.25	.12
24	George Hendrick	.40	.30	.15
-----	Team Logo/Checklist	.30	.25	.12

1987 Smokey Bear Rangers

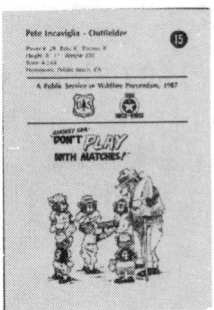

The 1987 Smokey Bear Rangers set is made up of 32 full-color cards. Co-sponsored by the Texas Rangers, U.S. Forest Service and Texas Forest Service, the set was given out to fans at special promotions at Arlington Stadium. The cards measure 4-1/4" by 6" and feature full-color photos on the fronts. The backs contain brief player personal information, along with the card number and a Smokey the Bear message. Cards of Mike Mason and Tom Paciorek were withdrawn from the sets given out by the Rangers and are quite scarce.

		MT	NR MT	EX
Complete Set:		70.00	52.00	27.00
Common Player:		.30	.25	.12
1	Charlie Hough	.60	.45	.25
2	Greg Harris	.30	.25	.12
3	Jose Guzman	.60	.45	.25
4	Mike Mason	25.00	20.00	10.00
5	Dale Mohorcic	.50	.40	.20
6	Bobby Witt	.80	.60	.30
7	Mitch Williams	.50	.40	.20
8	Geno Petralli	.30	.25	.12
9	Don Slaught	.30	.25	.12
10	Darrell Porter	.30	.25	.12
11	Steve Beuchele	.40	.30	.15
12	Pete O'Brien	.60	.45	.25
13	Scott Fletcher	.40	.30	.15
14	Tom Paciorek	25.00	20.00	10.00
15	Pete Incaviglia	1.00	.70	.40
16	Oddibe McDowell	.60	.45	.25

NOTE: A card number in parentheses ( ) indicates the set is unnumbered.

1988 Smokey Bear Cardinals

This set of 25 oversized (3" by 5") cards features full-color action photos that fill the entire card fronts. A thin white line frames the player photo. The player name, team logo and Smokey Bear picture logo are printed in the lower right corner. The black and white cards backs contain player information and a Smokey Bear fire prevention cartoon. The card sets were distributed to young St. Louis fans as part of a Forest Service fire prevention campaign. The National Association of State Foresters co-sponsored this set.

		MT	NR MT	EX
	Complete Set:	10.00	7.50	4.00
	Common Player:	.20	.15	.08
1	Whitey Herzog	.30	.25	.12
2	Danny Cox	.30	.25	.12
3	Ken Dayley	.20	.15	.08
4	Jose DeLeon	.30	.25	.12
5	Bob Forsch	.30	.25	.12
6	Joe Magrane	.50	.40	.20
7	Greg Mathews	.30	.25	.12
8	Scott Terry	.20	.15	.08
9	John Tudor	.35	.25	.14
10	Todd Worrell	.50	.40	.20
11	Steve Lake	.20	.15	.08
12	Tom Pagnozzi	.20	.15	.08
13	Tony Pena	.30	.25	.12
14	Bob Horner	.35	.25	.14
15	Tom Lawless	.20	.15	.08
16	Jose Oquendo	.20	.15	.08
17	Terry Pendleton	.40	.30	.15
18	Ozzie Smith	.80	.60	.30
19	Vince Coleman	.80	.60	.30
20	Curt Ford	.20	.15	.08
21	Willie McGee	.70	.50	.30
22	Larry McWilliams	.20	.15	.08
23	Steve Peters	.30	.25	.12
24	Luis Alicea	.30	.25	.12
25	Tom Brunansky	.50	.40	.20

1988 Smokey Bear Dodgers

Record-breaking Dodgers from the past three decades are featured on this 32-card perforated

sheet. Individual cards measure 2-1/2" by 4" and are printed on a light blue background in a design similar to the 1987 Smokey Bear Dodgers All-Star set. The black and white card backs contain the player name, a brief summary of the player's record-breaking performance and a reproduction of one of a number of Smokey Bear fire prevention posters printed during the 1950s through the 1980s. The sheets were distributed to fans in Dodger Stadium. Sponsors the Piedmont brand of the Liggett & Meyers Tobacco Co., the stamps include the Forest Service, California Dept. of Forestry and the Bureau of Land Management.

		MT	NR MT	EX
	Complete Set:	10.00	7.50	4.00
	Common Player:	.20	.15	.08
1	Walter Alston	.40	.30	.15
2	John Roseboro	.25	.20	.10
3	Frank Howard	.40	.30	.15
4	Sandy Koufax	1.25	.90	.50
5	Manny Mota	.25	.20	.10
6	Record Pitchers (Sandy Koufax, Jerry Reuss, Bill Singer)	.70	.50	.30
7	Maury Wills	.40	.30	.15
8	Tommy Davis	.25	.20	.10
9	Phil Regan	.20	.15	.08
10	Wes Parker	.20	.15	.08
11	Don Drysdale	.80	.60	.30
12	Willie Davis	.25	.20	.10
13	Bill Russell	.25	.20	.10
14	Jim Brewer	.20	.15	.08
15	Record Fielders (Ron Cey, Steve Garvey, Davey Lopes, Bill Russell)	.50	.40	.20
16	Mike Marshall (pitcher)	.25	.20	.10
17	Steve Garvey	.80	.60	.30
18	Davey Lopes	.25	.20	.10
19	Burt Hooton	.20	.15	.08
20	Jim Wynn	.20	.15	.08
21	Record Hitters (Dusty Baker, Ron Cey, Steve Garvey, Reggie Smith)	.50	.40	.20
22	Dusty Baker	.25	.20	.10
23	Tom Lasorda	.30	.25	.12
24	Fernando Valenzuela	.70	.50	.30
25	Steve Sax	.40	.30	.15
26	Dodger Stadium	.20	.15	.08
27	Ron Cey	.30	.25	.12
28	Pedro Guerrero	.50	.40	.20
29	Mike Marshall (outfielder)	.40	.30	.15
30	Don Sutton	.60	.45	.25
----	Logo Card/Checklist	.20	.15	.08
----	Smokey Bear	.20	.15	.08

1988 Smokey Bear Padres

This 33-card oversized (3" by 5") set was produced in conjunction with the U.S. Forest Service as a fire prevention campaign promotion. A full-color player photo, framed by a thin white line, fills the card face. The player number and position and Smokey Bear logo appear lower right. The black and white card backs are printed in horizontal postcard format, with player info and a Smokey Bear cartoon on the left half of the card back. The set was available for purchase at the Padres Gift Shop. Cards of Candy Sierra and Larry Bowa were not released by the

Padres and are quite rare. The complete set price does not include the two rare cards.

		MT	NR MT	EX
Complete Set:		12.00	9.00	4.75
Common Player:		.30	.25	.12
(1)	Shawn Abner	.50	.40	.20
(2)	Roberto Alomar	1.25	.90	.50
(3)	Sandy Alomar	.30	.25	.12
(4)	Greg Booker	.30	.25	.12
(5)	Larry Bowa	10.00	7.50	4.00
(6)	Chris Brown	.40	.30	.15
(7)	Mark Davis	.30	.25	.12
(8)	Pat Dobson	.30	.25	.12
(9)	Tim Flannery	.30	.25	.12
(10)	Mark Grant	.30	.25	.12
(11)	Tony Gwynn	1.50	1.25	.60
(12)	Andy Hawkins	.50	.40	.20
(13)	Stan Jefferson	.30	.25	.12
(14)	Jimmy Jones	.30	.25	.12
(15)	John Kruk	.80	.60	.30
(16)	Dave Leiper	.30	.25	.12
(17)	Shane Mack	.40	.30	.15
(18)	Carmelo Martinez	.40	.30	.15
(19)	Lance McCullers	.40	.30	.15
(20)	Keith Moreland	.40	.30	.15
(21)	Eric Nolte	.40	.30	.15
(22)	Amos Otis	.30	.25	.12
(23)	Mark Parent	.40	.30	.15
(24)	Randy Ready	.30	.25	.12
(25)	Greg Riddoch	.30	.25	.12
(26)	Benito Santiago	.80	.60	.30
(27)	Eric Show	.50	.40	.20
(28)	Candy Sierra	10.00	7.50	4.00
(29)	Denny Sommers	.30	.25	.12
(30)	Garry Templeton	.40	.30	.15
(31)	Dickie Thon	.40	.30	.15
(32)	Ed Whitson	.30	.25	.12
(33)	Marvell Wynne	.30	.25	.12

1988 Smokey Bear Rangers

This 21-card oversized (3-1/2" by 5") set was distributed to Rangers' fans at Smokey Bear Game Day on August 7th. The card fronts feature full-color action photos framed in an oval blue and red border on a white background. A nameplate above the photo identifies the player and a "Wildfire Prevention" logo is printed beneath the photo. Rangers (left) and Smokey (right) logos fill the upper corners of the card face. The card backs are black and white and include player info., U.S. and Texas Forest Service logos, and fire prevention tips.

		MT	NR MT	EX
Complete Set:		9.00	6.75	3.50
Common Player:		.30	.25	.12
1	Tom O'Malley	.30	.25	.12
2	Pete O'Brien	.50	.40	.20
3	Geno Petralli	.30	.25	.12
4	Pete Incaviglia	.70	.50	.30
5	Oddibe McDowell	.50	.40	.20
6	Dale Mohorcic	.30	.25	.12
7	Bobby Witt	.60	.45	.25
8	Bobby Valentine	.40	.30	.15

		MT	NR MT	EX
9	Ruben Sierra	1.00	.70	.40
10	Scott Fletcher	.40	.30	.15
11	Mike Stanley	.40	.30	.15
12	Steve Buechele	.40	.30	.15
13	Charlie Hough	.50	.40	.20
14	Larry Parrish	.40	.30	.15
15	Jerry Browne	.30	.25	.12
16	Bob Brower	.30	.25	.12
17	Jeff Russell	.30	.25	.12
18	Edwin Correa	.30	.25	.12
19	Mitch Williams	.40	.30	.15
20	Jose Guzman	.40	.30	.15
21	Curtis Wilkerson	.30	.25	.12

1988 Smokey Bear Royals

This 28-card set featuring full-color player caricatures by K.K. Goodale was produced for an in-stadium promotion on August 14, 1988. The 3" by 5" cards depict players, manager and coaches in action poses against a white background with a Royals logo upper left, opposite the Smokey Bear logo. The backs are black and white and contain brief player data and a Smokey cartoon.

		MT	NR MT	EX
Complete Set:		12.00	9.00	4.75
Common Player:		.20	.15	.08
1	John Wathan	.30	.25	.12
2	Royals Coaches (Frank Funk, Adrian Garrett, Mike Lum, Ed Napolean, Bob Schaefer, Jim Schaefer)	.20	.15	.08
3	Willie Wilson	.40	.30	.15
4	Danny Tartabull	.70	.50	.30
5	Bo Jackson	1.50	1.25	.60
6	Gary Thurman	.40	.30	.15
7	Jerry Don Gleaton	.20	.15	.08
8	Floyd Bannister	.30	.25	.12
9	Buddy Black	.20	.15	.08
10	Steve Farr	.20	.15	.08
11	Gene Garber	.20	.15	.08
12	Mark Gubicza	.50	.40	.20
13	Charlie Liebrandt	.30	.25	.12
14	Ted Power	.20	.15	.08
15	Dan Quisenberry	.30	.25	.12
16	Bret Saberhagen	.70	.50	.30
17	Mike Macfarlane	.30	.25	.12
18	Scotti Madison	.30	.25	.12
19	Jamie Quirk	.20	.15	.08
20	George Brett	1.25	.90	.50
21	Kevin Seitzer	.80	.60	.30
22	Bill Pecota	.20	.15	.08
23	Kurt Stillwell	.35	.25	.14
24	Brad Wellman	.20	.15	.08
25	Frank White	.30	.25	.12
26	Jim Eisenreich	.20	.15	.08
27	Smokey Bear	.20	.15	.08
----	Checklist	.20	.15	.08

Definitions for grading conditions are located in the introduction section at the front of this book.

1988 Smokey Bear Twins

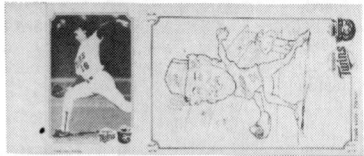

This 8-1/4" by 3-3/4" booklet contains a dozen postcards called Color-Grams featuring caricatures (suitable for coloring) of star players from the Minnesota Twins. Postcards are attached along a perforated edge to a baseball card-size stub with a black and white photo of the featured player. The backs of the postcards include the player name and personal information. The card stubs include the same information, along with a fire prevention tip. Twins Color-Grams were produced as a public service by the U.S. Forest Service and Dept. of Agriculture and were distributed to fans at the Metrodome.

		MT	NR MT	EX
Complete Set:		12.00	.50	.30
Common Player:		.70	.50	.30
(1)	Bert Blyleven	1.00	.50	.30
(2)	Randy Bush	.70	.50	.30
(3)	Gary Gaetti	1.50	.50	.30
(4)	Greg Gagne	.70	.50	.30
(5)	Dan Gladden	.70	.50	.30
(6)	Kent Hrbek	1.75	.50	.30
(7)	Gene Larkin	.70	.50	.30
(8)	Tim Laudner	.70	.50	.30
(9)	Al Newman	.70	.50	.30
(10)	Kirby Puckett	2.00	.50	.30
(11)	Jeff Reardon	1.00	.50	.30
(12)	Frank Viola	1.75	.50	.30

1989 Smokey Bear Angels All-Stars

The U.S. Forest Service, in conjunction with the California Angels, issued a 20-card set of "Angels All-Stars" in 1989. The standard-size cards are printed on a silver background and the player photos are bordered in red. Beneath the photo a banner stretches across homeplate, reading "Angels All-Stars," along with the player's name and position, which are flanked by Smokey Bear on the left and the Angels 1989 All-Star Game logo on the right. Card

backs highlight the player's career with the Angels and include an illustrated fire prevention tip.

		MT	NR MT	EX
Complete Set:		6.00	4.50	2.50
Common Player:		.20	.15	.08
1	Bill Rigney	.20	.15	.08
2	Dean Chance	.20	.15	.08
3	Jim Fregosi	.40	.30	.15
4	Bobby Knoop	.40	.30	.15
5	Don Mincher	.20	.15	.08
6	Clyde Wright	.20	.15	.08
7	Nolan Ryan	1.00	.70	.40
8	Frank Robinson	.80	.60	.30
9	Frank Tanana	.20	.15	.08
10	Rod Carew	.50	.40	.20
11	Bobby Grich	.20	.15	.08
12	Brian Downing	.20	.15	.08
13	Don Baylor	.35	.25	.14
14	Fred Lynn	.20	.15	.08
15	Reggie Jackson	.70	.50	.30
16	Doug DeCinces	.20	.15	.08
17	Bob Boone	.20	.15	.08
18	Wally Joyner	.60	.45	.25
19	Mike Witt	.20	.15	.08
20	Johnny Ray	.20	.15	.08

1989 Smokey Bear Cardinals

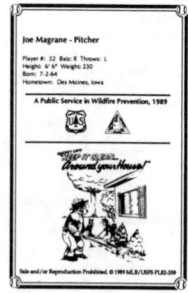

This 25-card set featuring action player photos was issued by the U.S. Forest Service to promote fire safety. The cards measure 4" by 6" and include the player's name, team logo and a small picture of Smokey Bear beneath the player photo.

		MT	NR MT	EX
Complete Set:		10.00	7.50	4.00
Common Player:		.20	.15	.08
(1)	Tom Brunansky	.50	.40	.20
(2)	Cris Carpenter	.50	.40	.20
(3)	Vince Coleman	.80	.60	.30
(4)	John Costello	.30	.25	.12
(5)	Ken Dayley	.20	.15	.08
(6)	Jose DeLeon	.35	.25	.14
(7)	Frank DiPino	.20	.15	.08
(8)	Whitey Herzog	.30	.25	.12
(9)	Ken Hill	.80	.60	.30
(10)	Pedro Guerrero	.80	.60	.30
(11)	Tim Jones	.30	.25	.12
(12)	Jim Lindeman	.20	.15	.08
(13)	Joe Magrane	.50	.40	.20
(14)	Willie McGee	.50	.40	.20
(15)	John Morris	.30	.25	.12
(16)	Jose Oquendo	.30	.25	.12
(17)	Tom Pagnozzi	.20	.15	.08
(18)	Tony Pena	.30	.25	.12
(19)	Terry Pendleton	.30	.25	.12
(20)	Dan Quisenberry	.20	.15	.08
(21)	Ozzie Smith	.80	.60	.30
(22)	Scott Terry	.30	.25	.12
(23)	Milt Thompson	.30	.25	.12
(24)	Denny Walling	.20	.15	.11
(25)	Todd Worrell	.50	.40	.20

A player's name in *italic* indicates a rookie card. An (FC) indicates a player's first card for that particular card company.

1990 Smokey Bear Angels

This 20-card set was released by the U.S. Forestry Service in conjunction with the California Angels. The sets were distributed at a 1990 Angels home game. (May 27) The cards feature full-color action photos surrounded by metallic looking silver borders. Both California Angels and Smokey Bear logos appear on the fronts. Card backs contain player data and a cartoon Smokey Bear message urging the prevention of forest fires.

		MT	NR MT	EX
Complete Set:		5.00	3.75	2.00
Common Player:		.20	.15	.08
1	Jim Abbott	.50	.40	.20
2	Bert Blyleven	.40	.30	.15
3	Chili Davis	.30	.25	.12
4	Brian Downing	.20	.15	.08
5	Chuck Finley	.30	.25	.12
6	Willie Fraser	.20	.15	.08
7	Bryan Harvey	.30	.25	.12
8	Jack Howell	.20	.15	.08
9	Wally Joyner	.40	.30	.15
10	Mark Langston	.30	.25	.12
11	Kirk McCaskill	.25	.20	.10
12	Mark McLemore	.20	.15	.08
13	Lance Parrish	.30	.25	.12
14	Johnny Ray	.20	.15	.08
15	Dick Schofield	.20	.15	.08
16	Mike Witt	.20	.15	.08
17	Claudell Washington	.20	.15	.08
18	Devon White	.20	.15	.08
19	Scott Bailes	.20	.15	.08
20	Bob McClure	.20	.15	.08

1986 Sportflics

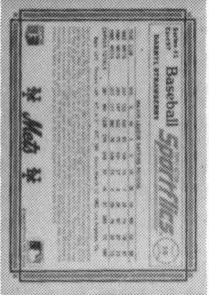

The premiere issue from Sportflics was distributed nationally by Amurol Division of Wrigley Gum Company. These high quality, three-phase "Magic Motion" cards depict three different photos per card, with each visible separately as the card is tilted. The 1986 issue features 200 full-color baseball cards plus 133 trivia cards. The cards come in the standard 2-1/2" by 3-1/2" size with the backs containing

player stats and personal information. There are three different types of picture cards: 1) Tri-Star cards - 50 cards feature three players on one card; 2) Big Six cards - 10 cards which have six players in special categories; and 3) the Big Twelve card of 12 World Series players from the Kansas City Royals. The trivia cards are 1-3/4" by 2" and do not have player photos.

		MT	NR MT	EX
Complete Set:		40.00	30.00	16.00
Common Player:		.10	.08	.04
1	George Brett	1.00	.70	.40
2	Don Mattingly	4.00	3.00	1.50
3	Wade Boggs	2.00	1.50	.80
4	Eddie Murray	.60	.45	.25
5	Dale Murphy	1.00	.70	.40
6	Rickey Henderson	1.50	1.25	.60
7	Harold Baines	.20	.15	.08
8	Cal Ripken, Jr.	.60	.45	.25
9	Orel Hershiser	.40	.30	.15
10	Bret Saberhagen	.30	.25	.12
11	Tim Raines	.40	.30	.15
12	Fernando Valenzuela	.30	.25	.12
13	Tony Gwynn	.60	.45	.25
14	Pedro Guerrero	.25	.20	.10
15	Keith Hernandez	.35	.25	.14
16	Ernest Riles	.20	.15	.08
17	Jim Rice	.30	.25	.12
18	Ron Guidry	.25	.20	.10
19	Willie McGee	.25	.20	.10
20	Ryne Sandberg	1.75	1.25	.70
21	Kirk Gibson	.35	.25	.14
22	Ozzie Guillen	.30	.25	.12
23	Dave Parker	.25	.20	.10
24	Vince Coleman	1.50	1.25	.60
25	Tom Seaver	.40	.30	.15
26	Brett Butler	.10	.08	.04
27	Steve Carlton	.40	.30	.15
28	Gary Carter	.35	.25	.14
29	Cecil Cooper	.15	.11	.06
30	Jose Cruz	.10	.08	.04
31	Alvin Davis	.20	.15	.08
32	Dwight Evans	.15	.11	.06
33	Julio Franco	.15	.11	.06
34	Damaso Garcia	.10	.08	.04
35	Steve Garvey	.40	.30	.15
36	Kent Hrbek	.25	.20	.10
37	Reggie Jackson	.50	.40	.20
38	Fred Lynn	.20	.15	.08
39	Paul Molitor	.15	.11	.06
40	Jim Presley	.15	.11	.06
41	Dave Righetti	.20	.15	.08
42a	Robin Yount (Yankees logo on back)	2.00	1.50	.80
42b	Robin Yount (Brewers logo on back)	.60	.45	.25
43	Nolan Ryan	2.00	1.50	.80
44	Mike Schmidt	1.25	.90	.50
45	Lee Smith	.10	.08	.04
46	Rick Sutcliffe	.15	.11	.06
47	Bruce Sutter	.15	.11	.06
48	Lou Whitaker	.20	.15	.08
49	Dave Winfield	.50	.40	.20
50	Pete Rose	1.50	1.25	.60
51	National League MVPs (Steve Garvey, Pete Rose, Ryne Sandberg)	.70	.50	.30
52	Slugging Stars (Harold Baines, George Brett, Jim Rice)	.35	.25	.14
53	No-Hitters (Phil Niekro, Jerry Reuss, Mike Witt)	.15	.11	.06
54	Big Hitters (Don Mattingly, Cal Ripken, Jr., Robin Yount)	1.25	.90	.50
55	Bullpen Aces (Goose Gossage, Dan Quisenberry, Lee Smith)	.10	.08	.04
56	Rookies of the Year (Pete Rose, Steve Sax, Darryl Strawberry)	.80	.60	.30
57	American League MVPs (Don Baylor, Reggie Jackson, Cal Ripken, Jr.)	.35	.25	.14
58	Repeat Batting Champs (Bill Madlock, Dave Parker, Pete Rose)	.60	.45	.25
59	Cy Young Winners (Mike Flanagan, Ron Guidry, LaMarr Hoyt)	.10	.08	.04
60	Double Award Winners (Tom Seaver, Rick Sutcliffe, Fernando Valenzuela)	.20	.15	.08
61	Home Run Champs (Tony Armas, Reggie Jackson, Jim Rice)	.25	.20	.10
62	National League MVPs (Keith Hernandez, Dale Murphy, Mike Schmidt)	.50	.40	.20
63	American League MVPs (George Brett, Fred Lynn, Robin Yount)	.30	.25	.12

#	Player / Subject	MT	NR MT	EX
64	Comeback Players (Bert Blyleven, John Denny, Jerry Koosman)	.10	.08	.04
65	Cy Young Relievers (Rollie Fingers, Willie Hernandez, Bruce Sutter)	.15	.11	.06
66	Rookies Of The Year (Andre Dawson, Bob Horner, Gary Matthews)	.15	.11	.06
67	Rookies Of The Year (Carlton Fisk, Ron Kittle, Tom Seaver)	.15	.11	.06
68	Home Run Champs (George Foster, Dave Kingman, Mike Schmidt)	.30	.25	.12
69	Double Award Winners (Rod Carew, Cal Ripken, Jr., Pete Rose)	.70	.50	.30
70	Cy Young Winners (Steve Carlton, Tom Seaver, Rick Sutcliffe)	.25	.20	.10
71	Top Sluggers (Reggie Jackson, Fred Lynn, Robin Yount)	.30	.25	.12
72	Rookies of the Year (Dave Righetti, Rick Sutcliffe, Fernando Valenzuela)	.15	.11	.06
73	Rookies Of The Year (Fred Lynn, Eddie Murray, Cal Ripken, Jr.)	.25	.20	.10
74	Rookies Of The Year (Rod Carew, Alvin Davis, Lou Whitaker)	.20	.15	.08
75	Batting Champs (Wade Boggs, Carney Lansford, Don Mattingly)	1.50	1.25	.60
76	Jesse Barfield	.20	.15	.08
77	Phil Bradley	.15	.11	.06
78	Chris Brown	.25	.20	.10
79	Tom Browning	.30	.25	.12
80	Tom Brunansky	.15	.11	.06
81	Bill Buckner	.10	.08	.04
82	Chili Davis	.10	.08	.04
83	Mike Davis	.10	.08	.04
84	Rich Gedman	.10	.08	.04
85	Willie Hernandez	.10	.08	.04
86	Ron Kittle	.10	.08	.04
87	Lee Lacy	.10	.08	.04
88	Bill Madlock	.15	.11	.06
89	Mike Marshall	.15	.11	.06
90	Keith Moreland	.10	.08	.04
91	Graig Nettles	.15	.11	.06
92	Lance Parrish	.20	.15	.08
93	Kirby Puckett	2.00	1.50	.80
94	Juan Samuel	.20	.15	.08
95	Steve Sax	.20	.15	.08
96	Dave Stieb	.10	.08	.04
97	Darryl Strawberry	1.25	.90	.50
98	Willie Upshaw	.10	.08	.04
99	Frank Viola	.20	.15	.08
100	Dwight Gooden	1.50	1.25	.60
101	Joaquin Andujar	.10	.08	.04
102	George Bell	.40	.30	.15
103	Bert Blyleven	.15	.11	.06
104	Mike Boddicker	.10	.08	.04
105	Britt Burns	.10	.08	.04
106	Rod Carew	.40	.30	.15
107	Jack Clark	.25	.20	.10
108	Danny Cox	.10	.08	.04
109	Ron Darling	.15	.11	.06
110	Andre Dawson	.25	.20	.10
111	Leon Durham	.10	.08	.04
112	Tony Fernandez	.15	.11	.06
113	Tom Herr	.10	.08	.04
114	Teddy Higuera	.80	.60	.30
115	Bob Horner	.15	.11	.06
116	Dave Kingman	.15	.11	.06
117	Jack Morris	.20	.15	.08
118	Dan Quisenberry	.10	.08	.04
119	Jeff Reardon	.15	.11	.06
120	Bryn Smith	.10	.08	.04
121	Ozzie Smith	.25	.20	.10
122	John Tudor	.15	.11	.06
123	Tim Wallach	.15	.11	.06
124	Willie Wilson	.15	.11	.06
125	Carlton Fisk	.25	.20	.10
126	RBI Sluggers (Gary Carter, George Foster, Al Oliver)	.15	.11	.06
127	Run Scorers (Keith Hernandez, Tim Raines, Ryne Sandberg)	.25	.20	.10
128	Run Scorers (Paul Molitor, Cal Ripken, Jr., Willie Wilson)	.20	.15	.08
129	No-Hitters (John Candelaria, Dennis Eckersley, Bob Forsch)	.10	.08	.04
130	World Series MVPs (Ron Cey, Rollie Fingers, Pete Rose)	.50	.40	.20
131	All-Star Game MVPs (Dave Concepcion, George Foster, Bill Madlock)	.10	.08	.04
132	Cy Young Winners (Vida Blue, John Denny, Fernando Valenzuela)	.15	.11	.06
133	Comeback Players (Doyle Alexander, Joaquin Andujar, Richard Dotson)	.10	.08	.04
134	Big Winners (John Denny, Tom Seaver, Rick Sutcliffe)	.15	.11	.06
135	Veteran Pitchers (Phil Niekro, Tom Seaver, Don Sutton)	.25	.20	.10
136	Rookies Of The Year (Vince Coleman, Dwight Gooden, Alfredo Griffin)	.80	.60	.30
137	All-Star Game MVPs (Gary Carter, Steve Garvey, Fred Lynn)	.20	.15	.08
138	Veteran Hitters (Tony Perez, Pete Rose, Rusty Staub)	.50	.40	.20
139	Power Hitters (George Foster, Jim Rice, Mike Schmidt)	.30	.25	.12
140	Batting Champs (Bill Buckner, Tony Gwynn, Al Oliver)	.20	.15	.08
141	No-Hitters (Jack Morris, Dave Righetti, Nolan Ryan)	.20	.15	.08
142	No-Hitters (Vida Blue, Bert Blyleven, Tom Seaver)	.15	.11	.06
143	Strikeout Kings (Dwight Gooden, Nolan Ryan, Fernando Valenzuela)	1.25	.90	.50
144	Base Stealers (Dave Lopes, Tim Raines, Willie Wilson)	.15	.11	.06
145	RBI Sluggers (Tony Armas, Cecil Cooper, Eddie Murray)	.15	.11	.06
146	American League MVPs (Rod Carew, Rollie Fingers, Jim Rice)	.25	.20	.10
147	World Series MVPs (Rick Dempsey, Reggie Jackson, Alan Trammell)	.25	.20	.10
148	World Series MVPs (Pedro Guerrero, Darrell Porter, Mike Schmidt)	.20	.15	.08
149	ERA Leaders (Mike Boddicker, Ron Guidry, Rick Sutcliffe)	.10	.08	.04
150	Comeback Players (Reggie Jackson, Dave Kingman, Fred Lynn)	.20	.15	.08
151	Buddy Bell	.15	.11	.06
152	Dennis Boyd	.10	.08	.04
153	Dave Concepcion	.15	.11	.06
154	Brian Downing	.10	.08	.04
155	Shawon Dunston	.15	.11	.06
156	John Franco	.15	.11	.06
157	Scott Garrelts	.10	.08	.04
158	Bob James	.10	.08	.04
159	Charlie Leibrandt	.10	.08	.04
160	Oddibe McDowell	.30	.25	.12
161	Roger McDowell	.50	.40	.20
162	Mike Moore	.10	.08	.04
163	Phil Niekro	.25	.20	.10
164	Al Oliver	.15	.11	.06
165	Tony Pena	.10	.08	.04
166	Ted Power	.10	.08	.04
167	Mike Scioscia	.10	.08	.04
168	Mario Soto	.10	.08	.04
169	Bob Stanley	.10	.08	.04
170	Garry Templeton	.10	.08	.04
171	Andre Thornton	.10	.08	.04
172	Alan Trammell	.30	.25	.12
173	Doug DeCinces	.10	.08	.04
174	Greg Walker	.10	.08	.04
175	Don Sutton	.25	.20	.10
176	1985 Award Winners (Vince Coleman, Dwight Gooden, Ozzie Guillen, Don Mattingly, Wille McGee, Bret Saberhagen)	1.25	.90	.50
177	1985 Hot Rookies (Stewart Cliburn, Brian Fisher, Joe Hesketh, Joe Orsulak, Mark Salas, Larry Sheets)	.40	.30	.15
178	Future Stars (Jose Canseco, Mark Funderburk, Mike Greenwell, Steve Lombardozzi, Billy Joe Robidoux, Dan Tartabull)	18.00	13.50	7.25
179	1985 Gold Glovers (George Brett, Ron Guidry, Keith Hernandez, Don Mattingly, Willie McGee, Dale Murphy)	1.25	.90	.50
180	Active .300 Hitters (Wade Boggs, George Brett, Rod Carew, Cecil Cooper, Don Mattingly, Willie Wilson)	1.25	.90	.50
181	Active .300 Hitters (Pedro Guerrero, Tony Gwynn, Keith Hernandez, Bill Madlock, Dave Parker, Pete Rose)	.70	.50	.30
182	1985 Milestones (Rod Carew, Phil Niekro, Pete Rose, Nolan Ryan, Tom Seaver, Matt Tallman)	1.50	1.25	.60
183	1985 Triple Crown (Wade Boggs, Darrell Evans, Don Mattingly, Willie McGee, Dale Murphy, Dave Parker)	1.25	.90	.50
184	1985 Highlights (Wade Boggs, Dwight Gooden, Rickey Henderson, Don Mattingly, Willie McGee, John Tudor)	1.50	1.25	.60
185	1985 20-Game Winners (Joaquin Andujar, Tom Browning, Dwight Gooden, Ron Guidry, Bret Saberhagen, John Tudor)	.60	.45	.25
186	Kansas City Royals (Steve Balboni, George Brett, Dane Iorg, Danny Jackson, Charlie Leibrandt, Darryl Motley, Dan Quisenberry, Bret Saberhagen, Lonnie Smith, Jim Sundberg, Frank White, Willie Wilson)	.40	.30	.15

		MT	NR MT	EX
187	Hubie Brooks	.10	.08	.04
188	Glenn Davis	.60	.45	.25
189	Darrell Evans	.10	.08	.04
190	Rich Gossage	.15	.11	.06
191	Andy Hawkins	.10	.08	.04
192	Jay Howell	.10	.08	.04
193	LaMarr Hoyt	.10	.08	.04
194	Davey Lopes	.10	.08	.04
195	Mike Scott	.20	.15	.08
196	Ted Simmons	.15	.11	.06
197	Gary Ward	.10	.08	.04
198	Bob Welch	.15	.11	.06
199	Mike Young	.10	.08	.04
200	Buddy Biancalana	.10	.08	.04

1986 Sportflics Decade Greats

This set, produced by Sportflics, features outstanding players, by position, from the 1930s to the 1980s by decades. The card fronts are printed in sepia-toned photos or full-color with the Sportflics three-phase "Magic Motion" animation. The complete set contains 75 cards with 59 single player cards and 16 multi-player cards. Biographies appear on the card backs which are printed in full-color and color-coded by decade. The set was distributed only through hobby dealers and is in the popular 2-1/2" by 3-1/2" size.

		MT	NR MT	EX
	Complete Set:	14.00	10.50	5.50
	Common Player:	.15	.11	.06
1	Babe Ruth	2.50	2.00	1.00
2	Jimmie Foxx	.40	.30	.15
3	Lefty Grove	.30	.25	.12
4	Hank Greenberg	.30	.25	.12
5	Al Simmons	.15	.11	.06
6	Carl Hubbell	.30	.25	.12
7	Joe Cronin	.25	.20	.10
8	Mel Ott	.30	.25	.12
9	Lefty Gomez	.30	.25	.12
10	Lou Gehrig	1.50	1.25	.60
11	Pie Traynor	.15	.11	.06
12	Charlie Gehringer	.30	.25	.12
13	Catchers (Mickey Cochrane, Bill Dickey, Gabby Hartnett)	.30	.25	.12
14	Pitchers (Dizzy Dean, Paul Derringer, Red Ruffing)	.30	.25	.12
15	Outfielders (Earl Averill, Joe Medwick, Paul Waner)	.15	.11	.06
16	Bob Feller	.60	.45	.25
17	Lou Boudreau	.15	.11	.06
18	Enos Slaughter	.25	.20	.10
19	Hal Newhouser	.15	.11	.06
20	Joe DiMaggio	1.50	1.25	.60
21	Pee Wee Reese	.40	.30	.15
22	Phil Rizzuto	.30	.25	.12
23	Ernie Lombardi	.15	.11	.06
24	Infielders (Joe Cronin, George Kell, Johnny Mize)	.15	.11	.06
25	Ted Williams	1.25	.90	.50
26	Mickey Mantle	3.00	2.25	1.25
27	Warren Spahn	.30	.25	.12
28	Jackie Robinson	1.00	.70	.40
29	Ernie Banks	.30	.25	.12
30	Stan Musial	1.00	.70	.40

		MT	NR MT	EX
31	Yogi Berra	.60	.45	.25
32	Duke Snider	.70	.50	.30
33	Roy Campanella	.70	.50	.30
34	Eddie Mathews	.30	.25	.12
35	Ralph Kiner	.30	.25	.12
36	Early Wynn	.25	.20	.10
37	Double Play Duo (Luis Aparicio, Nellie Fox)	.25	.20	.10
38	First Basemen (Gil Hodges, Ted Kluszewski, Mickey Vernon)	.25	.20	.10
40	Henry Aaron	1.00	.70	.40
41	Frank Robinson	.30	.25	.12
42	Bob Gibson	.30	.25	.12
43	Roberto Clemente	1.00	.70	.40
44	Whitey Ford	.40	.30	.15
45	Brooks Robinson	.50	.40	.20
46	Juan Marichal	.25	.20	.10
47	Carl Yastrzemski	1.00	.70	.40
48	First Basemen (Orlando Cepeda, Harmon Killebrew, Willie McCovey)	.30	.25	.12
49	Catchers (Bill Freehan, Elston Howard, Joe Torre)	.15	.11	.06
50	Willie Mays	1.00	.70	.40
51	Outfielders (Al Kaline, Tony Oliva, Billy Williams)	.30	.25	.12
52	Tom Seaver	.60	.45	.25
53	Reggie Jackson	.70	.50	.30
54	Steve Carlton	.40	.30	.15
55	Mike Schmidt	.70	.50	.30
56	Joe Morgan	.25	.20	.10
57	Jim Rice	.40	.30	.15
58	Jim Palmer	.30	.25	.12
59	Lou Brock	.30	.25	.12
60	Pete Rose	1.25	.90	.50
61	Steve Garvey	.40	.30	.15
62	Catchers (Carlton Fisk, Thurman Munson, Ted Simmons)	.25	.20	.10
63	Pitchers (Vida Blue, Catfish Hunter, Nolan Ryan)	.30	.25	.12
64	George Brett	.80	.60	.30
65	Don Mattingly	2.25	1.75	.90
66	Fernando Valenzuela	.30	.25	.12
67	Dale Murphy	.80	.60	.30
68	Wade Boggs	1.50	1.25	.60
69	Rickey Henderson	.60	.45	.25
70	Eddie Murray	.60	.45	.25
71	Ron Guidry	.25	.20	.10
72	Catchers (Gary Carter, Lance Parrish, Tony Pena)	.30	.25	.12
73	Infielders (Cal Ripken, Jr., Lou Whitaker, Robin Yount)	.30	.25	.12
74	Outfielders (Pedro Guerrero, Tim Raines, Dave Winfield)	.30	.25	.12
75	Dwight Gooden	1.00	.70	.40

1986 Sportflics Rookies

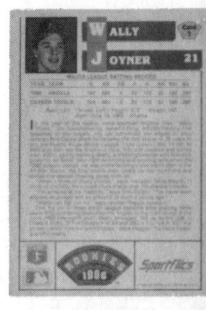

The 1986 Rookies set issued by Sportflics offers 50 cards and features 47 individual rookie players. In addition, there are two Tri-Star cards; one highlights former Rookies of the Year and the other features three prominent players. There is one "Big Six" card featuring six superstars. The full-color photos on the 2-1/2" by 3-1/2" cards use Sportflics three-phase "Magic Motion" animation. The set was packaged in an attractive collector box which also contained 34 trivia cards that measure 1-3/4" by 2". The set was distributed only by hobby dealers.

		MT	NR MT	EX
	Complete Set:	20.00	15.00	8.00
	Common Player:	.20	.15	.08
1	John Kruk	.80	.60	.30
2	Edwin Correa	.20	.15	.08
3	Pete Incaviglia	.50	.40	.20
4	Dale Sveum	.30	.25	.12
5	Juan Nieves	.30	.25	.12
6	Will Clark	3.50	2.75	1.50
7	Wally Joyner	2.50	2.00	1.00
8	Lance McCullers	.20	.15	.08
9	Scott Bailes	.20	.15	.08
10	Dan Plesac	.40	.30	.15
11	Jose Canseco	4.00	3.00	1.50
12	Bobby Witt	.40	.30	.15
13	Barry Bonds	.70	.50	.30
14	Andres Thomas	.20	.15	.08
15	Jim Deshaies	.30	.25	.12
16	Ruben Sierra	2.00	1.50	.80
17	Steve Lombardozzi	.20	.15	.08
18	Cory Snyder	.50	.40	.20
19	Reggie Williams	.20	.15	.08
20	Mitch Williams	.20	.15	.08
21	Glenn Braggs	.30	.25	.12
22	Danny Tartabull	.80	.60	.30
23	Charlie Kerfeld	.20	.15	.08
24	Paul Assenmacher	.20	.15	.08
25	Robby Thompson	.30	.25	.12
26	Bobby Bonilla	.70	.50	.30
27	Andres Galarraga	.70	.50	.30
28	Billy Jo Robidoux	.20	.15	.08
29	Bruce Ruffin	.30	.25	.12
30	Greg Swindell	.60	.45	.25
31	John Cangelosi	.20	.15	.08
32	Jim Traber	.20	.15	.08
33	Russ Morman	.20	.15	.08
34	Barry Larkin	.60	.45	.25
35	Todd Worrell	.50	.40	.20
36	John Cerutti	.20	.15	.08
37	Mike Kingery	.20	.15	.08
38	Mark Eichhorn	.20	.15	.08
39	Scott Bankhead	.20	.15	.08
40	Bo Jackson	2.00	1.50	.80
41	Greg Mathews	.30	.25	.12
42	Eric King	.20	.15	.08
43	Kal Daniels	.80	.60	.30
44	Calvin Schiraldi	.20	.15	.08
45	Mickey Brantley	.20	.15	.08
46	Outstanding Rookie Seasons (Fred Lynn, Willie Mays, Pete Rose)	.80	.60	.30
47	Outstanding Rookie Seasons (Dwight Gooden, Tom Seaver, Fernando Valenzuela)	.80	.60	.30
48	Outstanding Rookie Seasons (Eddie Murray, Dave Righetti, Cal Ripken, Jr., Steve Sax, Darryl Strawberry, Lou Whitaker)	.60	.45	.25
49	Kevin Mitchell	2.00	1.50	.80
50	Mike Diaz	.20	.15	.08

1987 Sportflics

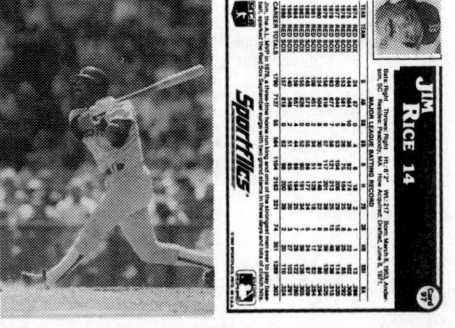

For its second season in the national baseball card market, Sportflics' basic issue was again a 200-card set of 2-1/2" by 3-1/2" "Magic Motion" cards, which offer three different photos on the same card, each visible in turn as the card is moved from top to bottom or side to side. Besides single-player cards, the '87 Sportflics set includes several three- and six-player cards, though not as many as in the 1986 set. The card backs feature a small player portrait photo on the single-player cards, an innovation for 1987.

		MT	NR MT	EX
	Complete Set:	35.00	27.50	15.00
	Common Player:	.10	.08	.04
1	Don Mattingly	3.00	2.25	1.25
2	Wade Boggs	1.25	.90	.50
3	Dale Murphy	.50	.40	.20
4	Rickey Henderson	1.00	.70	.40
5	George Brett	.70	.50	.30
6	Eddie Murray	.50	.40	.20
7	Kirby Puckett	.90	.70	.35
8	Ryne Sandberg	1.00	.70	.40
9	Cal Ripken Jr.	.50	.40	.20
10	Roger Clemens	1.50	1.25	.60
11	Ted Higuera	.15	.11	.06
12	Steve Sax	.20	.15	.08
13	Chris Brown	.10	.08	.04
14	Jesse Barfield	.15	.11	.06
15	Kent Hrbek	.20	.15	.08
16	Robin Yount	.30	.25	.12
17	Glenn Davis	.25	.20	.10
18	Hubie Brooks	.10	.08	.04
19	Mike Scott	.15	.11	.06
20	Darryl Strawberry	.70	.50	.30
21	Alvin Davis	.15	.11	.06
22	Eric Davis	1.00	.70	.40
23	Danny Tartabull	.30	.25	.12
24a	Cory Snyder (Pat Tabler photo on back (facing front), 3/4 swing on front)	2.50	2.00	1.00
24b	Cory Snyder (Pat Tabler photo on back (facing front), 1/4 swing on front)	2.50	2.00	1.00
24c	Cory Snyder (Snyder photo on back (facing to side))	1.50	1.25	.60
25	Pete Rose	1.25	.90	.50
26	Wally Joyner	1.50	1.25	.60
27	Pedro Guerrero	.20	.15	.08
28	Tom Seaver	.30	.25	.12
29	Bob Knepper	.10	.08	.04
30	Mike Schmidt	.80	.60	.30
31	Tony Gwynn	.50	.40	.20
32	Don Slaught	.10	.08	.04
33	Todd Worrell	.30	.25	.12
34	Tim Raines	.40	.30	.15
35	Dave Parker	.20	.15	.08
36	Bob Ojeda	.10	.08	.04
37	Pete Incaviglia	.50	.40	.20
38	Bruce Hurst	.15	.11	.06
39	Bobby Witt	.40	.30	.15
40	Steve Garvey	.40	.30	.15
41	Dave Winfield	.40	.30	.15
42	Jose Cruz	.10	.08	.04
43	Orel Hershiser	.40	.30	.15
44	Reggie Jackson	.50	.40	.20
45	Chili Davis	.10	.08	.04
46	Robby Thompson	.30	.25	.12
47	Dennis Boyd	.10	.08	.04
48	Kirk Gibson	.30	.25	.12
49	Fred Lynn	.20	.15	.08
50	Gary Carter	.30	.25	.12
51	George Bell	.40	.30	.15
52	Pete O'Brien	.10	.08	.04
53	Ron Darling	.15	.11	.06
54	Paul Molitor	.15	.11	.06
55	Mike Pagliarulo	.15	.11	.06
56	Mike Boddicker	.10	.08	.04
57	Dave Righetti	.20	.15	.08
58	Len Dykstra(FC)	.15	.11	.06
59	Mike Witt	.10	.08	.04
60	Tony Bernazard	.10	.08	.04
61	John Kruk	.30	.25	.12
62	Mike Krukow	.10	.08	.04
63	Sid Fernandez	.15	.11	.06
64	Gary Gaetti	.20	.15	.08
65	Vince Coleman	.30	.25	.12
66	Pat Tabler	.10	.08	.04
67	Mike Scioscia	.10	.08	.04
68	Scott Garrelts	.10	.08	.04
69	Brett Butler	.10	.08	.04
70	Bill Buckner	.10	.08	.04
71a	Dennis Rasmussen (John Montefusco photo on back)	.25	.20	.10
71b	Dennis Rasmussen (Rasmussen photo on back)	.15	.11	.06
72	Tim Wallach	.15	.11	.06
73	Bob Horner	.15	.11	.06

		MT	NR MT	EX
74	Willie McGee	.15	.11	.06
75	American League First Basemen (Wally Joyner, Don Mattingly, Eddie Murray)	1.50	1.25	.60
76	Jesse Orosco	.10	.08	.04
77	National League Relief Pitchers (Jeff Reardon, Dave Smith, Todd Worrell)	.15	.11	.06
78	Candy Maldonado	.10	.08	.04
79	National League Shortstops (Hubie Brooks, Shawon Dunston, Ozzie Smith)	.15	.11	.06
80	American League Left Fielders (George Bell, Jose Canseco, Jim Rice)	1.50	1.25	.60
81	Bert Blyleven	.15	.11	.06
82	Mike Marshall	.15	.11	.06
83	Ron Guidry	.20	.15	.08
84	Julio Franco	.15	.11	.06
85	Willie Wilson	.15	.11	.06
86	Lee Lacy	.10	.08	.04
87	Jack Morris	.20	.15	.08
88	Ray Knight	.10	.08	.04
89	Phil Bradley	.15	.11	.06
90	Jose Canseco	3.00	2.25	1.25
91	Gary Ward	.10	.08	.04
92	Mike Easler	.10	.08	.04
93	Tony Pena	.10	.08	.04
94	Dave Smith	.10	.08	.04
95	Will Clark	3.50	2.75	1.50
96	Lloyd Moseby	.10	.08	.04
97	Jim Rice	.40	.30	.15
98	Shawon Dunston	.15	.11	.06
99	Don Sutton	.25	.20	.10
100	Dwight Gooden	1.00	.70	.40
101	Lance Parrish	.20	.15	.08
102	Mark Langston	.15	.11	.06
103	Floyd Youmans	.10	.08	.04
104	Lee Smith	.10	.08	.04
105	Willie Hernandez	.10	.08	.04
106	Doug DeCinces	.10	.08	.04
107	Ken Schrom	.10	.08	.04
108	Don Carman	.10	.08	.04
109	Brook Jacoby	.15	.11	.06
110	Steve Bedrosian	.15	.11	.06
111	American League Pitchers (Roger Clemens, Teddy Higuera, Jack Morris)	.50	.40	.20
112	American League Second Basemen (Marty Barrett, Tony Bernazard, Lou Whitaker)	.10	.08	.04
113	American League Shortstops (Tony Fernandez, Scott Fletcher, Cal Ripken)	.25	.20	.10
114	American League Third Basemen (Wade Boggs, George Brett, Gary Gaetti)	.80	.60	.30
115	National League Third Basemen (Chris Brown, Mike Schmidt, Tim Wallach)	.35	.25	.14
116	National League Second Basemen (Bill Doran, Johnny Ray, Ryne Sandberg)	.15	.11	.06
117	National League Right Fielders (Kevin Bass, Tony Gwynn, Dave Parker)	.25	.20	.10
118	Hot Rookie Prospects (David Clark, Pat Dodson, Ty Gainey, Phil Lombardi, Benito Santiago, Terry Steinbach)	1.75	1.25	.70
119	1986 Season Highlights (Dave Righetti, Mike Scott, Fernando Valenzuela)	.15	.11	.06
120	National League Pitchers (Dwight Gooden, Mike Scott, Fernando Valenzuela)	.40	.30	.15
121	Johnny Ray	.10	.08	.04
122	Keith Moreland	.10	.08	.04
123	Juan Samuel	.15	.11	.06
124	Wally Backman	.10	.08	.04
125	Nolan Ryan	2.00	1.50	.80
126	Greg Harris	.10	.08	.04
127	Kirk McCaskill	.10	.08	.04
128	Dwight Evans	.15	.11	.06
129	Rick Rhoden	.10	.08	.04
130	Bill Madlock	.15	.11	.06
131	Oddibe McDowell	.10	.08	.04
132	Darrell Evans	.10	.08	.04
133	Keith Hernandez	.30	.25	.12
134	Tom Brunansky	.15	.11	.06
135	Kevin McReynolds	.20	.15	.08
136	Scott Fletcher	.10	.08	.04
137	Lou Whitaker	.20	.15	.08
138	Carney Lansford	.10	.08	.04
139	Andre Dawson	.25	.20	.10
140	Carlton Fisk	.20	.15	.08
141	Buddy Bell	.15	.11	.06
142	Ozzie Smith	.20	.15	.08
143	Dan Pasqua	.15	.11	.06
144	Kevin Mitchell	1.50	1.25	.60

		MT	NR MT	EX
145	Bret Saberhagen	.25	.20	.10
146	Charlie Kerfeld	.10	.08	.04
147	Phil Niekro	.25	.20	.10
148	John Candelaria	.10	.08	.04
149	Rich Gedman	.10	.08	.04
150	Fernando Valenzuela	.30	.25	.12
151	National League Catchers (Gary Carter, Tony Pena, Mike Scioscia)	.15	.11	.06
152	National League Left Fielders (Vince Coleman, Jose Cruz, Tim Raines)	.20	.15	.08
153	American League Right Fielders (Harold Baines, Jesse Barfield, Dave Winfield)	.25	.20	.10
154	American League Catchers (Rich Gedman, Lance Parrish, Don Slaught)	.10	.08	.04
155	National League Center Fielders (Eric Davis, Kevin McReynolds, Dale Murphy)	.70	.50	.30
156	1986 Season Highlights (Jim Deshaies, Mike Schmidt, Don Sutton)	.30	.25	.12
157	American League Speedburners (John Cangelosi, Rickey Henderson, Gary Pettis)	.25	.20	.10
158	Hot Rookie Prospects (Randy Asadoor, Casey Candaele, Dave Cochrane, Rafael Palmeiro, Tim Pyznarski, Kevin Seitzer)	1.50	1.25	.60
159	The Best of the Best (Roger Clemens, Dwight Gooden, Rickey Henderson, Don Mattingly, Dale Murphy, Eddie Murray)	1.25	.90	.50
160	Roger McDowell	.15	.11	.06
161	Brian Downing	.10	.08	.04
162	Bill Doran	.10	.08	.04
163	Don Baylor	.15	.11	.06
164	Alfredo Griffin	.10	.08	.04
165	Don Aase	.10	.08	.04
166	Glenn Wilson	.10	.08	.04
167	Dan Quisenberry	.10	.08	.04
168	Frank White	.10	.08	.04
169	Cecil Cooper	.15	.11	.06
170	Jody Davis	.10	.08	.04
171	Harold Baines	.20	.15	.08
172	Rob Deer	.10	.08	.04
173	John Tudor	.15	.11	.06
174	Larry Parrish	.10	.08	.04
175	Kevin Bass	.10	.08	.04
176	Joe Carter	.15	.11	.06
177	Mitch Webster	.10	.08	.04
178	Dave Kingman	.15	.11	.06
179	Jim Presley	.15	.11	.06
180	Mel Hall	.10	.08	.04
181	Shane Rawley	.10	.08	.04
182	Marty Barrett	.10	.08	.04
183	Damaso Garcia	.10	.08	.04
184	Bobby Grich	.10	.08	.04
185	Leon Durham	.10	.08	.04
186	Ozzie Guillen	.10	.08	.04
187	Tony Fernandez	.15	.11	.06
188	Alan Trammell	.30	.25	.12
189	Jim Clancy	.10	.08	.04
190	Bo Jackson	4.00	3.00	1.50
191	Bob Forsch	.10	.08	.04
192	John Franco	.10	.08	.04
193	Von Hayes	.10	.08	.04
194	American League Relief Pitchers (Don Aase, Mark Eichhorn, Dave Righetti)	.10	.08	.04
195	National League First Basemen (Will Clark, Glenn Davis, Keith Hernandez)	1.00	.70	.40
196	1986 Season Highlights (Roger Clemens, Joe Cowley, Bob Horner)	.35	.25	.14
197	The Best of the Best (Wade Boggs, George Brett, Hubie Brooks, Tony Gwynn, Tim Raines, Ryne Sandberg)	.80	.60	.30
198	American League Center Fielders (Rickey Henderson, Fred Lynn, Kirby Puckett)	.25	.20	.10
199	National League Speedburners (Vince Coleman, Eric Davis, Tim Raines)	.50	.40	.20
200	Steve Carlton	.40	.30	.15

1987 Sportflics Rookie Discs

The 1987 Sportflics Rookie Discs set consists of seven discs which measure 4" in diameter. The front of the discs offer three "Magic Motion" photos in full color, encompassed by a blue border. The disc backs are printed in red, blue, yellow and green and include the team logo, player statistics, player biography and

the disc number. The set was issued with Cooperstown Timeless Trivia Cards.

		MT	NR MT	EX
	Complete Set:	20.00	15.00	8.00
	Common Player:	1.00	.70	.40
1	Casey Candaele	1.00	.70	.40
2	Mark McGwire	4.00	3.00	1.50
3	Kevin Seitzer	3.00	2.25	1.25
4	Joe Magrane	2.00	1.50	.80
5	Benito Santiago	2.50	2.00	1.00
6	Dave Magadan	2.00	1.50	.80
7	Devon White	2.50	2.00	1.00

1987 Sportflics Rookie Prospects

The 1987 Sportflics Rookie Prospects set consists of 10 cards that are the standard 2-1/2" by 3-1/2" size. The card fronts feature Sportflics' "Magic Motion" process. Card backs contain a player photo plus a short biography and player personal and statistical information. The set was offered in two separately wrapped mylar packs of five cards to hobby dealers purchasing cases of Sportflics' Team Preview set. Twenty-four packs of "Rookie Prospects" cards were included with each case.

		MT	NR MT	EX
	Complete Set:	8.00	6.00	3.25
	Common Player:	.50	.40	.20
1	Terry Steinbach	1.00	.70	.40
2	Rafael Palmeiro	1.50	1.25	.60
3	Dave Magadan	1.25	.90	.50
4	Marvin Freeman	.50	.40	.20
5	Brick Smith	.50	.40	.20
6	B.J. Surhoff	1.00	.70	.40
7	John Smiley	.50	.40	.20
8	Alonzo Powell	.50	.40	.20
9	Benny Santiago	1.50	1.25	.60
10	Devon White	1.00	.70	.40

1987 Sportflics Rookies

The 1987 Sportflics Rookies set was issued in two series of 25 cards. The first was released in July with the second series following in October. The cards, which are the standard 2-1/2" by 3-1/2", feature Sportflics' special "Magic Motion" process. The card fronts contain a full-color photo and present three different pictures, depending on how the card is held. The backs also contain a full-color photo along with player statistics and a biography.

		MT	NR MT	EX
	Complete Set:	15.00	11.00	6.00
	Common Player:	.20	.15	.08
1	Eric Bell	.20	.15	.08
2	Chris Bosio	.20	.15	.08
3	Bob Brower	.20	.15	.08
4	Jerry Browne	.20	.15	.08
5	Ellis Burks	1.50	1.25	.60
6	Casey Candaele	.20	.15	.08
7	Joey Cora	.20	.15	.08
8	Ken Gerhart	.30	.25	.12
9	Mike Greenwell	2.00	1.50	.80
10	Stan Jefferson	.20	.15	.08
11	Dave Magadan	.70	.50	.30
12	Joe Magrane	.40	.30	.15
13	Fred McGriff	.80	.60	.30
14	Mark McGwire	2.00	1.50	.80
15	Mark McLemore	.20	.15	.08
16	Jeff Musselman	.20	.15	.08
17	Matt Nokes	.40	.30	.15
18	Paul O'Neill	.20	.15	.08
19	Luis Polonia	.20	.15	.08
20	Benny Santiago	.80	.60	.30
21	Kevin Seitzer	.80	.60	.30
22	Terry Steinbach	.30	.25	.12
23	B.J. Surhoff	.70	.50	.30
24	Devon White	.40	.30	.15
25	Matt Williams	.70	.50	.30
26	DeWayne Buice	.20	.15	.08
27	Willie Fraser	.20	.15	.08
28	Bill Ripken	.30	.25	.12
29	Mike Henneman	.30	.25	.12
30	Shawn Hillegas	.20	.15	.08
31	Shane Mack	.20	.15	.08
32	Rafael Palmeiro	.70	.50	.30
33	Mike Jackson	.20	.15	.08
34	Gene Larkin	.20	.15	.08
35	Jimmy Jones	.20	.15	.08
36	Gerald Young	.40	.30	.15
37	Ken Caminiti	.20	.15	.08
38	Sam Horn	.60	.45	.25
39	David Cone	1.00	.70	.40
40	Mike Dunne	.50	.40	.20
41	Ken Williams	.30	.25	.12
42	John Morris	.20	.15	.08
43	Jim Lindeman	.30	.25	.12
44	Todd Benzinger	.70	.50	.30
45	Mike Stanley	.30	.25	.12
46	Les Straker	.20	.15	.08
47	Jeff Robinson	.50	.40	.20
48	Jeff Blauser	.30	.25	.12
49	John Marzano	.30	.25	.12
50	Keith Miller	.30	.25	.12

1987 Sportflics Superstar Discs

Released in three series of six discs and numbered 1 through 18, the 1987 Sportflics Superstar Disc set features the special "Magic Motion" process. Each disc, which measures 4-1/2" in diameter, contains three different player photos, depending which way it is tilted. A red border, containing eleven stars, with the player's name and uniform number, surrounds the photo. The backs have a turquoise border which carries the words "Superstar Disc Collector Series." The backs also include the team logo, player statistics, player biography and the disc number. The discs were issued with eighteen 1-3/4" by 2-1/2" Cooperstown Timeless Trivia Cards.

		MT	NR MT	EX
Complete Set:		65.00	49.00	26.00
Common Player:		2.00	1.50	.80
1	Jose Canseco	6.00	4.50	2.50
2	Mike Scott	2.00	1.50	.80
3	Ryne Sandberg	3.00	2.25	1.25
4	Mike Schmidt	3.75	2.75	1.50
5	Dale Murphy	2.50	2.00	1.00
6	Fernando Valenzuela	2.50	2.00	1.00
7	Tony Gwynn	3.50	2.75	1.50
8	Cal Ripken	3.50	2.75	1.50
9	Gary Carter	2.75	2.00	1.00
10	Cory Snyder	2.75	2.00	1.00
11	Kirby Puckett	3.00	2.25	1.25
12	George Brett	3.75	2.75	1.50
13	Keith Hernandez	2.00	1.50	.80
14	Rickey Henderson	4.00	3.00	1.50
15	Tim Raines	2.75	2.00	1.00
16	Bo Jackson	4.00	3.00	1.50
17	Pete Rose	4.00	3.00	1.50
18	Eric Davis	3.75	2.75	1.50

1987 Sportflics Team Preview

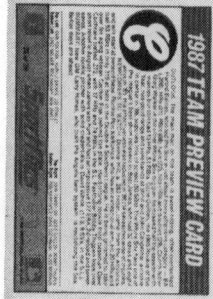

The 1987 Sportflics Team Preview set appeared to be a good idea, but never caught on with collectors. The intent of the set is to provide a pre-season look at each of the 26 major league clubs. The card backs contain three categories of the team preview: Outlook, Newcomers to Watch and Summary. Using the "Magic Motion" process, 12 different players are featured on the card fronts. Four of the different player photos can be made visible at once. The cards, which measure 2-1/2" by 3-1/2", were issued with team logo/trivia cards in a specially designed box.

		MT	NR MT	EX
Complete Set:		10.00	7.50	4.00
Common Team:		.40	.30	.15
1	Texas Rangers (Scott Fletcher, Greg Harris, Charlie Hough, Pete Incaviglia, Mike Loynd, Oddibe McDowell, Pete O'Brien, Larry Parrish, Ruben Sierra, Don Slaught, Mitch Williams, Bobby Witt)	.50	.40	.20
2	New York Mets (Wally Backman, Gary Carter, Ron Darling, Lenny Dykstra, Sid Fernandez, Dwight Gooden, Keith Hernandez, Dave Magadan, Kevin McReynolds, Randy Myers, Bob Ojeda, Darryl Strawberry)	.70	.50	.30
3	Cleveland Indians (Tony Bernazard, Brett Butler, Tom Candiotti, Joe Carter, Julio Franco, Mel Hall, Brook Jacoby, Phil Niekro, Ken Schrom, Cory Snyder, Greg Swindell, Pat Tabler)	.50	.40	.20
4	Cincinnati Reds (Buddy Bell, Tom Browning, Kal Daniels, Eric Davis, John Franco, Bill Gullickson, Tracy Jones, Barry Larkin, Rob Murphy, Paul O'Neill, Dave Parker, Pete Rose)	.60	.45	.25
5	Toronto Blue Jays (Jesse Barfield, George Bell, John Cerutti, Mark Eichhorn, Tony Fernandez, Tom Henke, Glenallen Hill, Jimmy Key, Fred McGriff, Lloyd Moseby, Dave Stieb, Willie Upshaw)	.50	.40	.20
6	Philadelphia Phillies (Steve Bedrosian, Don Carman, Marvin Freeman, Kevin Gross, Von Hayes, Shane Rawley, Bruce Ruffin, Juan Samuel, Mike Schmidt, Kent Tekulve, Milt Thompson, Glenn Wilson)	.50	.40	.20
7	New York Yankees (Rickey Henderson, Phil Lombardi, Don Mattingly, Mike Pagliarulo, Dan Pasqua, Willie Randolph, Dennis Rasmussen, Rick Rhoden, Dave Righetti, Joel Skinner, Bob Tewksbury, Dave Winfield)	.80	.60	.30
8	Houston Astros (Kevin Bass, Jose Cruz, Glenn Davis, Jim Deshaies, Bill Doran, Ty Gainey, Charlie Kerfeld, Bob Knepper, Nolan Ryan, Mike Scott, Dave Smith, Robby Wine)	.40	.30	.15
9	Boston Red Sox (Marty Barrett, Don Baylor, Wade Boggs, Dennis Boyd, Roger Clemens, Pat Dodson, Dwight Evans, Mike Greenwell, Dave Henderson, Bruce Hurst, Jim Rice, Calvin Schiraldi)	.60	.45	.25
10	San Francisco Giants (Bob Brenly, Chris Brown, Will Clark, Chili Davis, Kelly Downs, Scott Garrelts, Mark Grant, Mike Krukow, Jeff Leonard, Candy Maldonado, Terry Mulholland, Robby Thompson)	.50	.40	.20
11	California Angels (John Candelaria, Doug DeCinces, Brian Downing, Ruppert Jones, Wally Joyner, Kirk McCaskill, Darrell Miller, Donnie Moore, Gary Pettis, Don Sutton, Devon White, Mike Witt)	.50	.40	.20
12	St. Louis Cardinals (Jack Clark, Vince Coleman, Danny Cox, Bob Forsch, Tom Herr, Joe Magrane, Willie McGee, Terry Pendleton, Ozzie Smith, John Tudor, Andy Van Slyke, Todd Worrell)	.60	.45	.25
13	Kansas City Royals (George Brett, Mark Gubicza, Bo Jackson, Charlie Leibrandt, Hal McRae, Dan Quisenberry, Bret Saberhagen, Kevin Seitzer, Lonnie Smith, Danny Tartabull, Frank White, Willie Wilson)	.50	.40	.20
14	Los Angeles Dodgers (Ralph Bryant, Mariano Duncan, Jose Gonzalez, Pedro Guerrero, Orel Hershiser, Mike Marshall, Steve Sax, Mike Scioscia, Franklin Stubbs, Fernando Valenzuela, Reggie Williams, Matt Young)	.50	.40	.20
15	Detroit Tigers (Darnell Coles, Darrell Evans, Kirk Gibson, Willie Hernandez, Eric King, Chet Lemon, Dwight Lowry, Jack Morris, Dan Petry, Frank Tanana, Alan Trammell, Lou Whitaker)	.60	.45	.25

		MT	NR MT	EX
16	San Diego Padres (Randy Asadoor, Steve Garvey, Tony Gwynn, Andy Hawkins, Jim Jones, John Kruk, Craig Lefferts, Shane Mack, Lance McCullers, Kevin Mitchell, Benny Santiago, Ed Wojna)	.50	.40	.20
17	Minnesota Twins (Bert Blyleven, Tom Brunansky, Gary Gaetti, Greg Gagne, Kent Hrbek, Joe Klink, Steve Lombardozzi, Kirby Puckett, Jeff Reardon, Mark Salas, Roy Smalley, Frank Viola)	.60	.45	.25
18	Pittsburgh Pirates (Barry Bonds, Bobby Bonilla, Sid Bream, Mike Diaz, Brian Fisher, Jim Morrison, Joe Orsulak, Bob Patterson, Tony Pena, Johnny Ray, R.J. Reynolds, John Smiley)	.50	.40	.20
19	Milwaukee Brewers (Glenn Braggs, Rob Deer, Teddy Higuera, Paul Molitor, Juan Nieves, Dan Plesac, Tim Pyznarski, Ernest Riles, Billy Jo Robidoux, B.J. Surhoff, Dale Sveum, Robin Yount)	.50	.40	.20
20	Montreal Expos (Hubie Brooks, Tim Burke, Casey Candaele, Dave Collins, Mike Fitzgerald, Andres Galarraga, Billy Moore, Alonzo Powell, Randy St. Claire, Tim Wallach, Mitch Webster, Floyd Youmans)	.50	.40	.20
21	Baltimore Orioles (Don Aase, Eric Bell, Mike Boddicker, Ken Gerhardt, Terry Kennedy, Ray Knight, Lee Lacy, Fred Lynn, Eddie Murray, Cal Ripken, Jr., Larry Sheets, Jim Traber)	.50	.40	.20
22	Chicago Cubs (Jody Davis, Shawon Dunston, Leon Durham, Dennis Eckersley, Greg Maddux, Dave Martinez, Keith Moreland, Jerry Mumphrey, Rafael Palmeiro, Ryne Sandberg, Scott Sanderson, Lee Smith)	.40	.30	.15
23	Oakland Athletics (Jose Canseco, Mike Davis, Alfredo Griffin, Reggie Jackson, Carney Lansford, Mark McGwire, Dwayne Murphy, Rob Nelson, Tony Phillips, Jose Rijo, Terry Steinbach, Curt Young)	.70	.50	.30
24	Atlanta Braves (Paul Assenmacher, Gene Garber, Tom Glavine, Ken Griffey, Glenn Hubbard, Dion James, Rick Mahler, Dale Murphy, Ken Oberkfell, David Palmer, Zane Smith, Andres Thomas)	.50	.40	.20
25	Seattle Mariners (Scott Bankhead, Phil Bradley, Scott Bradley, Mickey Brantley, Alvin Davis, Steve Fireovid, Mark Langston, Mike Moore, Donell Nixon, Ken Phelps, Jim Presley, Dave Valle)	.40	.30	.15
26	Chicago White Sox (Harold Baines, John Cangelosi, Dave Cochrane, Joe Cowley, Carlton Fisk, Ozzie Guillen, Ron Hassey, Bob James, Ron Karkovice, Russ Mormon, Bobby Thigpen, Greg Walker)	.40	.30	.15

1988 Sportflics

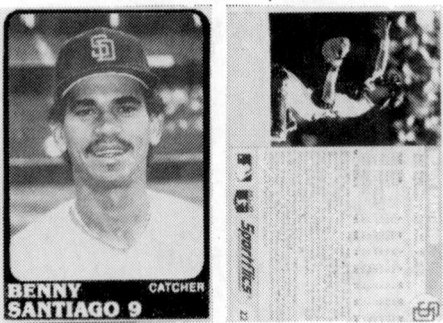

BENNY SANTIAGO 9   CATCHER

The design of the 1988 Sportflics set differs greatly from the previous two years. Besides increasing the number of cards in the set to 225, Sportflics included the player name, team and uniform number on the card front. The triple-action color photos are surrounded by a red border. The backs are re-designed, also. Full-color action photos, plus extensive statistics and informative biographies are utilized. Three highlights cards and three rookie

prospects card are included in the set. The cards are the standard 2-1/2" by 3-1/2".

		MT	NR MT	EX
Complete Set:		35.00	27.50	15.00
Common Player:		.10	.08	.04
1	Don Mattingly	2.00	1.50	.80
2	Tim Raines	.35	.25	.14
3	Andre Dawson	.25	.20	.10
4	George Bell	.30	.25	.12
5	Joe Carter	.15	.11	.06
6	Matt Nokes	.50	.40	.20
7	Dave Winfield	.35	.25	.14
8	Kirby Puckett	.50	.40	.20
9	Will Clark	2.00	1.50	.80
10	Eric Davis	.70	.50	.30
11	Rickey Henderson	.50	.40	.20
12	Ryne Sandberg	.25	.20	.10
13	Jesse Barfield	.15	.11	.06
14	Ozzie Guillen	.10	.08	.04
15	Bret Saberhagen	.20	.15	.08
16	Tony Gwynn	.40	.30	.15
17	Kevin Seitzer	.50	.40	.20
18	Jack Clark	.20	.15	.08
19	Danny Tartabull	.30	.25	.12
20	Ted Higuera	.15	.11	.06
21	Charlie Leibrandt, Jr.	.10	.08	.04
22	Benny Santiago	.50	.40	.20
23	Fred Lynn	.15	.11	.06
24	Rob Thompson	.10	.08	.04
25	Alan Trammell	.25	.20	.10
26	Tony Fernandez	.15	.11	.06
27	Rick Sutcliffe	.15	.11	.06
28	Gary Carter	.25	.20	.10
29	Cory Snyder	.30	.25	.12
30	Lou Whitaker	.20	.15	.08
31	Keith Hernandez	.25	.20	.10
32	Mike Witt	.10	.08	.04
33	Harold Baines	.15	.11	.06
34	Robin Yount	.25	.20	.10
35	Mike Schmidt	.80	.60	.30
36	Dion James	.10	.08	.04
37	Tom Candiotti	.10	.08	.04
38	Tracy Jones	.15	.11	.06
39	Nolan Ryan	1.00	.70	.40
40	Fernando Valenzuela	.25	.20	.10
41	Vance Law	.10	.08	.04
42	Roger McDowell	.10	.08	.04
43	Carlton Fisk	.15	.11	.06
44	Scott Garrelts	.10	.08	.04
45	Lee Guetterman	.10	.08	.04
46	Mark Langston	.15	.11	.06
47	Willie Randolph	.10	.08	.04
48	Bill Doran	.10	.08	.04
49	Larry Parrish	.10	.08	.04
50	Wade Boggs	1.25	.90	.50
51	Shane Rawley	.10	.08	.04
52	Alvin Davis	.15	.11	.06
53	Jeff Reardon	.15	.11	.06
54	Jim Presley	.10	.08	.04
55	Kevin Bass	.10	.08	.04
56	Kevin McReynolds	.20	.15	.08
57	B.J. Surhoff	.15	.11	.06
58	Julio Franco	.15	.11	.06
59	Eddie Murray	.40	.30	.15
60	Jody Davis	.10	.08	.04
61	Todd Worrell	.15	.11	.06
62	Von Hayes	.10	.08	.04
63	Billy Hatcher	.10	.08	.04
64	John Kruk	.15	.11	.06
65	Tom Henke	.10	.08	.04
66	Mike Scott	.15	.11	.06
67	Vince Coleman	.20	.15	.08
68	Ozzie Smith	.20	.15	.08
69	Ken Williams	.20	.15	.08
70	Steve Bedrosian	.15	.11	.06
71	Luis Polonia	.20	.15	.08
72	Brook Jacoby	.15	.11	.06
73	Ron Darling	.15	.11	.06
74	Lloyd Moseby	.10	.08	.04
75	Wally Joyner	.40	.30	.15
76	Dan Quisenberry	.10	.08	.04
77	Scott Fletcher	.10	.08	.04
78	Kirk McCaskill	.10	.08	.04
79	Paul Molitor	.15	.11	.06
80	Mike Aldrete	.10	.08	.04
81	Neal Heaton	.10	.08	.04
82	Jeffrey Leonard	.10	.08	.04
83	Dave Magadan	.15	.11	.06
84	Danny Cox	.10	.08	.04

		MT	NR MT	EX
85	Lance McCullers	.10	.08	.04
86	Jay Howell	.10	.08	.04
87	Charlie Hough	.10	.08	.04
88	Gene Garber	.10	.08	.04
89	Jesse Orosco	.10	.08	.04
90	Don Robinson	.10	.08	.04
91	Willie McGee	.15	.11	.06
92	Bert Blyleven	.15	.11	.06
93	Phil Bradley	.15	.11	.06
94	Terry Kennedy	.10	.08	.04
95	Kent Hrbek	.20	.15	.08
96	Juan Samuel	.15	.11	.06
97	Pedro Guerrero	.20	.15	.08
98	Sid Bream	.10	.08	.04
99	Devon White	.30	.25	.12
100	Mark McGwire	1.25	.90	.50
101	Dave Parker	.15	.11	.06
102	Glenn Davis	.20	.15	.08
103	Greg Walker	.10	.08	.04
104	Rick Rhoden	.10	.08	.04
105	Mitch Webster	.10	.08	.04
106	Lenny Dykstra	.10	.08	.04
107	Gene Larkin	.15	.11	.06
108	Floyd Youmans	.10	.08	.04
109	Andy Van Slyke	.15	.11	.06
110	Mike Scioscia	.10	.08	.04
111	Kirk Gibson	.25	.20	.10
112	Kal Daniels	.30	.25	.12
113	Ruben Sierra	.50	.40	.20
114	Sam Horn	.30	.25	.12
115	Ray Knight	.10	.08	.04
116	Jimmy Key	.10	.08	.04
117	Bo Diaz	.10	.08	.04
118	Mike Greenwell	1.00	.70	.40
119	Barry Bonds	.50	.40	.20
120	Reggie Jackson	.40	.30	.15
121	Mike Pagliarulo	.15	.11	.06
122	Tommy John	.20	.15	.08
123	Bill Madlock	.15	.11	.06
124	Ken Caminiti	.30	.25	.12
125	Gary Ward	.10	.08	.04
126	Candy Maldonado	.10	.08	.04
127	Harold Reynolds	.10	.08	.04
128	Joe Magrane	.30	.25	.12
129	Mike Henneman	.25	.20	.10
130	Jim Gantner	.10	.08	.04
131	Bobby Bonilla	.15	.11	.06
132	John Farrell	.30	.25	.12
133	Frank Tanana	.10	.08	.04
134	Zane Smith	.10	.08	.04
135	Dave Righetti	.20	.15	.08
136	Rick Reuschel	.10	.08	.04
137	Dwight Evans	.15	.11	.06
138	Howard Johnson	.10	.08	.04
139	Terry Leach	.10	.08	.04
140	Casey Candaele	.10	.08	.04
141	Tom Herr	.10	.08	.04
142	Tony Pena	.10	.08	.04
143	Lance Parrish	.20	.15	.08
144	Ellis Burks	1.25	.90	.50
145	Pete O'Brien	.10	.08	.04
146	Mike Boddicker	.10	.08	.04
147	Buddy Bell	.10	.08	.04
148	Bo Jackson	2.00	1.50	.80
149	Frank White	.10	.08	.04
150	George Brett	.60	.45	.25
151	Tim Wallach	.10	.08	.04
152	Cal Ripken, Jr.	.40	.30	.15
153	Brett Butler	.10	.08	.04
154	Gary Gaetti	.15	.11	.06
155	Darryl Strawberry	.60	.45	.25
156	Alfredo Griffin	.10	.08	.04
157	Marty Barrett	.10	.08	.04
158	Jim Rice	.30	.25	.12
159	Terry Pendleton	.10	.08	.04
160	Orel Hershiser	.35	.25	.14
161	Larry Sheets	.10	.08	.04
162	Dave Stewart	.10	.08	.04
163	Shawon Dunston	.15	.11	.06
164	Keith Moreland	.10	.08	.04
165	Ken Oberkfell	.10	.08	.04
166	Ivan Calderon	.10	.08	.04
167	Bob Welch	.15	.11	.06
168	Fred McGriff	.40	.30	.15
169	Pete Incaviglia	.15	.11	.06
170	Dale Murphy	.60	.45	.25
171	Mike Dunne	.25	.20	.10
172	Chili Davis	.10	.08	.04
173	Milt Thompson	.10	.08	.04
174	Terry Steinbach	.15	.11	.06
175	Oddibe McDowell	.10	.08	.04

		MT	NR MT	EX
176	Jack Morris	.20	.15	.08
177	Sid Fernandez	.15	.11	.06
178	Ken Griffey	.10	.08	.04
179	Lee Smith	.10	.08	.04
180	1987 Highlights (Juan Nieves, Kirby Puckett, Mike Schmidt)	.25	.20	.10
181	Brian Downing	.10	.08	.04
182	Andres Galarraga	.20	.15	.08
183	Rob Deer	.10	.08	.04
184	Greg Brock	.10	.08	.04
185	Doug DeCinces	.10	.08	.04
186	Johnny Ray	.10	.08	.04
187	Hubie Brooks	.10	.08	.04
188	Darrell Evans	.10	.08	.04
189	Mel Hall	.10	.08	.04
190	Jim Deshaies	.10	.08	.04
191	Dan Plesac	.15	.11	.06
192	Willie Wilson	.15	.11	.06
193	Mike LaValliere	.10	.08	.04
194	Tom Brunansky	.15	.11	.06
195	John Franco	.15	.11	.06
196	Frank Viola	.20	.15	.08
197	Bruce Hurst	.10	.08	.04
198	John Tudor	.10	.08	.04
199	Bob Forsch	.10	.08	.04
200	Dwight Gooden	.60	.45	.25
201	Jose Canseco	2.00	1.50	.80
202	Carney Lansford	.10	.08	.04
203	Kelly Downs	.10	.08	.04
204	Glenn Wilson	.10	.08	.04
205	Pat Tabler	.10	.08	.04
206	Mike Davis	.10	.08	.04
207	Roger Clemens	.80	.60	.30
208	Dave Smith	.10	.08	.04
209	Curt Young	.10	.08	.04
210	Mark Eichhorn	.10	.08	.04
211	Juan Nieves	.10	.08	.04
212	Bob Boone	.10	.08	.04
213	Don Sutton	.20	.15	.08
214	Willie Upshaw	.10	.08	.04
215	Jim Clancy	.10	.08	.04
216	Bill Ripken	.25	.20	.10
217	Ozzie Virgil	.10	.08	.04
218	Dave Concepcion	.10	.08	.04
219	Alan Ashby	.10	.08	.04
220	Mike Marshall	.15	.11	.06
221	1987 Highlights (Vince Coleman, Mark McGwire, Paul Molitor)	.50	.40	.20
222	1987 Highlights (Steve Bedrosian, Don Mattingly, Benito Santiago)	.80	.60	.30
223	Hot Rookie Prospects (Shawn Abner, Jay Buhner, Gary Thurman)	.40	.30	.15
224	Hot Rookie Prospects (Tim Crews, John Davis, Vincente Palacios)	.30	.25	.12
225	Hot Rookie Prospects (Keith Miller, Jody Reed, Jeff Treadway)	.50	.40	.20

1988 Sportflics Gamewinners

This set of 25 standard-size cards (2-1/2" by 3-1/2"), featuring star players in the Sportflics patented 3-D Magic Motion design, was issued by Weiser Card Co. of Plainsboro, N.J., for use as a youth organizational fundraiser. (Weiser's president is former Yankees outfielder Bobby Murcer.) A limited number of sets was produced for test marketing in the Northwestern U.S., with plans for a 1989 set to be marketed nationwide. A green-and-yellow

Gamewinners logo banner spans the upper border of the cards face, with a matching player name (with uniform number and position) below the full-color triple photo. The card backs carry large full-color player photos (1-3/4" by 1-3/4"), along with stats, personal information and career high-lights.

	MT	NR MT	EX
Complete Set:	10.00	7.50	4.00
Common Player:	.20	.15	.08

		MT	NR MT	EX
1	Don Mattingly	2.50	2.00	1.00
2	Mark McGwire	1.00	.70	.40
3	Wade Boggs	1.50	1.25	.60
4	Will Clark	.60	.45	.25
5	Eric Davis	.80	.60	.30
6	Willie Randolph	.20	.15	.08
7	Dave Winfield	.50	.40	.20
8	Rickey Henderson	.60	.45	.25
9	Dwight Gooden	.80	.60	.30
10	Benny Santiago	.40	.30	.15
11	Keith Hernandez	.40	.30	.15
12	Juan Samuel	.30	.25	.12
13	Kevin Seitzer	.60	.45	.25
14	Gary Carter	.50	.40	.20
15	Darryl Strawberry	.80	.60	.30
16	Rick Rhoden	.20	.15	.08
17	Howard Johnson	.20	.15	.08
18	Matt Nokes	.50	.40	.20
19	Dave Righetti	.30	.25	.12
20	Roger Clemens	.80	.60	.30
21	Mike Schmidt	.70	.50	.30
22	Kevin McReynolds	.30	.25	.12
23	Mike Pagliarulo	.20	.15	.08
24	Kevin Elster	.20	.15	.08
25	Jack Clark	.30	.25	.12

1989 Sportflics

This basic issue includes 225 standard-size player cards (2-1/2" by 3-1/2") and 153 trivia cards, all featuring the patented Magic Motion design. A 5-card sub-set of triple photo cards called "Tri-Star" features a mix of veterans and rookies. The card fronts feature a white outer border and double color inner border in one of six color schemes (i.e. red, blue, purple). The inner border color changes when the card is tilted and the bottom border carries a double stripe of colors. The player name appears in the top border, player postition and uniform number appear, alternately, in the bottom border. The card backs contain crisp 1-7/8" by 1-3/4" player action shots, along with personal information, stats and career highlights. "The Unforgettables" trivia cards in this set salute members of the Hall of Fame.

	MT	NR MT	EX
Complete Set:	40.00	30.00	15.00
Common Player:	.10	.08	.04

		MT	NR MT	EX
1	Jose Canseco	1.75	1.25	.70
2	Wally Joyner	.40	.30	.15
3	Roger Clemens	.60	.45	.25
4	Greg Swindell	.15	.11	.06
5	Jack Morris	.20	.15	.08
6	Mickey Brantley	.10	.08	.04

		MT	NR MT	EX
7	Jim Presley	.15	.11	.06
8	Pete O'Brien	.10	.08	.04
9	Jesse Barfield	.15	.11	.06
10	Frank Viola	.20	.15	.08
11	Kevin Bass	.10	.08	.04
12	Glenn Wilson	.10	.08	.04
13	Chris Sabo	1.00	.70	.40
14	Fred McGriff	.50	.40	.20
15	Mark Grace	1.25	.90	.50
16	Devon White	.20	.15	.08
17	Juan Samuel	.15	.11	.06
18	Lou Whitaker	.25	.20	.10
19	Greg Walker	.10	.08	.04
20	Roberto Alomar	.50	.40	.20
21	Mike Schmidt	.60	.45	.25
22	Benny Santiago	.25	.20	.10
23	Dave Stewart	.10	.08	.04
24	Dave Winfield	.35	.25	.14
25	George Bell	.30	.25	.12
26	Jack Clark	.20	.15	.08
27	Doug Drabek	.10	.08	.04
28	Ron Gant	.15	.11	.06
29	Glenn Braggs	.10	.08	.04
30	Rafael Palmeiro	.20	.15	.08
31	Brett Butler	.10	.08	.04
32	Ron Darling	.15	.11	.06
33	Alvin Davis	.15	.11	.06
34	Bob Walk	.10	.08	.04
35	Dave Stieb	.15	.11	.06
36	Orel Hershiser	.40	.30	.15
37	John Farrell	.15	.11	.06
38	Doug Jones	.10	.08	.04
39	Kelly Downs	.10	.08	.04
40	Bob Boone	.10	.08	.04
41	Gary Sheffield	2.25	1.75	.90
42	Doug Dascenzo	.30	.25	.12
43	Chad Krueter	.20	.15	.08
44	Ricky Jordan	1.75	1.25	.70
45	Dave West	.70	.50	.30
46	Danny Tartabull	.30	.25	.12
47	Teddy Higuera	.15	.11	.06
48	Gary Gaetti	.15	.11	.06
49	Dave Parker	.15	.11	.06
50	Don Mattingly	3.00	2.25	1.25
51	David Cone	.25	.20	.10
52	Kal Daniels	.25	.20	.10
53	Carney Lansford	.10	.08	.04
54	Mike Marshall	.15	.11	.06
55	Kevin Seitzer	.30	.25	.12
56	Mike Henneman	.10	.08	.04
57	Bill Doran	.10	.08	.04
58	Steve Sax	.20	.15	.08
59	Lance Parrish	.15	.11	.06
60	Keith Hernandez	.25	.20	.10
61	Jose Uribe	.10	.08	.04
62	Jose Lind	.15	.11	.06
63	Steve Bedrosian	.15	.11	.06
64	George Brett	.60	.45	.25
65	Kirk Gibson	.25	.20	.10
66	Cal Ripken, Jr.	.50	.40	.20
67	Mitch Webster	.10	.08	.04
68	Fred Lynn	.15	.11	.06
69	Eric Davis	.60	.45	.25
70	Bo Jackson	.70	.50	.30
71	Kevin Elster	.15	.11	.06
72	Rick Reuschel	.10	.08	.04
73	Tim Burke	.10	.08	.04
74	Mark Davis	.10	.08	.04
75	Claudell Washington	.10	.08	.04
76	Lance McCullers	.10	.08	.04
77	Mike Moore	.10	.08	.04
78	Robby Thompson	.10	.08	.04
79	Roger McDowell	.10	.08	.04
80	Danny Jackson	.15	.11	.06
81	Tim Leary	.10	.08	.04
82	Bobby Witt	.15	.11	.06
83	Jim Gott	.10	.08	.04
84	Andy Hawkins	.10	.08	.04
85	Ozzie Guillen	.10	.08	.04
86	John Tudor	.15	.11	.06
87	Todd Burns	.25	.20	.10
88	Dave Gallagher	.25	.20	.10
89	Jay Buhner	.15	.11	.06
90	Gregg Jefferies	2.00	1.50	.80
91	Bob Welch	.15	.11	.06
92	Charlie Hough	.10	.08	.04
93	Tony Fernandez	.15	.11	.06
94	Ozzie Virgil	.10	.08	.04
95	Andre Dawson	.25	.20	.10
96	Hubie Brooks	.10	.08	.04
97	Kevin McReynolds	.20	.15	.08
98	Mike LaValliere	.10	.08	.04

		MT	NR MT	EX
99	Terry Pendleton	.10	.08	.04
100	Wade Boggs	1.75	1.25	.70
101	Dennis Eckersley	.15	.11	.06
102	Mark Gubicza	.15	.11	.06
103	Frank Tanana	.10	.08	.04
104	Joe Carter	.15	.11	.06
105	Ozzie Smith	.20	.15	.08
106	Dennis Martinez	.10	.08	.04
107	Jeff Treadway	.15	.11	.06
108	Greg Maddux	.15	.11	.06
109	Bret Saberhagen	.20	.15	.08
110	Dale Murphy	.60	.45	.25
111	Rob Deer	.10	.08	.04
112	Pete Incaviglia	.15	.11	.06
113	Vince Coleman	.20	.15	.08
114	Tim Wallach	.15	.11	.06
115	Nolan Ryan	.60	.45	.25
116	Walt Weiss	.35	.25	.14
117	Brian Downing	.10	.08	.04
118	Melido Perez	.15	.11	.06
119	Terry Steinbach	.15	.11	.06
120	Mike Scott	.15	.11	.06
121	Tim Belcher	.15	.11	.06
122	Mike Boddicker	.10	.08	.04
123	Len Dykstra	.10	.08	.04
124	Fernando Valenzuela	.25	.20	.10
125	Gerald Young	.15	.11	.06
126	Tom Henke	.10	.08	.04
127	Dave Henderson	.10	.08	.04
128	Dan Plesac	.15	.11	.06
129	Chili Davis	.10	.08	.04
130	Bryan Harvey	.25	.20	.10
131	Don August	.15	.11	.06
132	Mike Harkey	.50	.40	.20
133	Luis Polonia	.10	.08	.04
134	Craig Worthington	.35	.25	.14
135	Joey Meyer	.15	.11	.06
136	Barry Larkin	.25	.20	.10
137	Glenn Davis	.20	.15	.08
138	Mike Scioscia	.10	.08	.04
139	Andres Galarraga	.20	.15	.08
140	Doc Gooden	.60	.45	.25
141	Keith Moreland	.10	.08	.04
142	Kevin Mitchell	.10	.08	.04
143	Mike Greenwell	.80	.60	.30
144	Mel Hall	.10	.08	.04
145	Rickey Henderson	.50	.40	.20
146	Barry Bonds	.20	.15	.08
147	Eddie Murray	.40	.30	.15
148	Lee Smith	.10	.08	.04
149	Julio Franco	.15	.11	.06
150	Tim Raines	.35	.25	.14
151	Mitch Williams	.10	.08	.04
152	Tim Laudner	.10	.08	.04
153	Mike Pagliarulo	.15	.11	.06
154	Floyd Bannister	.10	.08	.04
155	Gary Carter	.25	.20	.10
156	Kirby Puckett	.40	.30	.15
157	Harold Baines	.20	.15	.08
158	Dave Righetti	.20	.15	.08
159	Mark Langston	.15	.11	.06
160	Tony Gwynn	.50	.40	.20
161	Tom Brunansky	.15	.11	.06
162	Vance Law	.10	.08	.04
163	Kelly Gruber	.10	.08	.04
164	Gerald Perry	.15	.11	.06
165	Harold Reynolds	.10	.08	.04
166	Andy Van Slyke	.15	.11	.06
167	Jimmy Key	.15	.11	.06
168	Jeff Reardon	.15	.11	.06
169	Milt Thompson	.10	.08	.04
170	Will Clark	.80	.60	.30
171	Chet Lemon	.10	.08	.04
172	Pat Tabler	.10	.08	.04
173	Jim Rice	.30	.25	.12
174	Billy Hatcher	.10	.08	.04
175	Bruce Hurst	.15	.11	.06
176	John Franco	.15	.11	.06
177	Van Snider	.25	.20	.10
178	Ron Jones	.35	.25	.14
179	Jerald Clark	.30	.25	.12
180	Tom Browning	.15	.11	.06
181	Von Hayes	.10	.08	.04
182	Bobby Bonilla	.15	.11	.06
183	Todd Worrell	.15	.11	.06
184	John Kruk	.15	.11	.06
185	Scott Fletcher	.10	.08	.04
186	Willie Wilson	.15	.11	.06
187	Jody Davis	.10	.08	.04
188	Kent Hrbek	.20	.15	.08
189	Ruben Sierra	.35	.25	.14

		MT	NR MT	EX
190	Shawon Dunston	.15	.11	.06
191	Ellis Burks	.70	.50	.30
192	Brook Jacoby	.15	.11	.06
193	Jeff Robinson	.15	.11	.06
194	Rich Dotson	.10	.08	.04
195	Johnny Ray	.10	.08	.04
196	Cory Snyder	.25	.20	.10
197	Mike Witt	.10	.08	.04
198	Marty Barrett	.10	.08	.04
199	Robin Yount	.30	.25	.12
200	Mark McGwire	1.00	.70	.40
201	Ryne Sandberg	.30	.25	.12
202	John Candelaria	.10	.08	.04
203	Matt Nokes	.20	.15	.08
204	Dwight Evans	.15	.11	.06
205	Darryl Strawberry	.60	.45	.25
206	Willie McGee	.15	.11	.06
207	Bobby Thigpen	.15	.11	.06
208	B.J. Surhoff	.15	.11	.06
209	Paul Molitor	.15	.11	.06
210	Jody Reed	.15	.11	.06
211	Doyle Alexander	.10	.08	.04
212	Dennis Rasmussen	.15	.11	.06
213	Kevin Gross	.10	.08	.04
214	Kirk McCaskill	.10	.08	.04
215	Alan Trammell	.30	.25	.12
216	Damon Berryhill	.15	.11	.06
217	Rick Sutcliffe	.15	.11	.06
218	Don Slaught	.10	.08	.04
219	Carlton Fisk	.30	.25	.12
220	Allan Anderson	.10	.08	.04
221	1988 Highlights (Wade Boggs, Jose Canseco, Mike Greenwell)	1.50	1.25	.60
222	1988 Highlights (Tom Browning, Dennis Eckersley, Orel Hershiser)	.25	.20	.10
223	Hot Rookie Prospects (Sandy Alomar, Gregg Jefferies, Gary Sheffield)	2.00	1.50	.80
224	Hot Rookie Prospects (Randy Johnson, Ramon Martinez, Bob Milacki)	.60	.45	.25
225	Hot Rookie Prospects (Geronimo Berroa, Cameron Drew, Ron Jones)	.35	.25	.14

1990 Sportflics

The Sportflics set for 1990 again contained 225 cards. The cards feature the unique "Magic Motion" effect which displays either of two different photos depending on how the card is tilted. (Previous years' sets had used three photos per card.) The two-photo "Magic Motion" sequence is designed to depict sequential game-action, showing a batter following through on his swing, a pitcher completing his motion, etc. Sportflics also added a moving red and yellow "marquee" border on the cards to compliment the animation effect. The player's name, which appears below the animation, remains stationary. The set includes 19 special rookie cards. The backs contain a color player photo, team logo, player information and stats. The cards were distributed in non-transparent mylar packs with small MVP trivia cards.

		MT	NR MT	EX
Complete Set:		35.00	25.00	14.00
Common Player:		.10	.08	.04
1	Kevin Mitchell	.40	.30	.15
2	Wade Boggs	1.00	.70	.40

#	Player	MT	NR MT	EX
3	Cory Snyder	.10	.08	.04
4	Paul O'Neill	.10	.08	.04
5	Will Clark	1.00	.70	.40
6	Tony Fernandez	.10	.08	.04
7	Ken Griffey, Jr.	3.00	2.25	1.25
8	Nolan Ryan	.60	.45	.25
9	Rafael Palmeiro	.10	.08	.04
10	Jesse Barfield	.10	.08	.04
11	Kirby Puckett	.40	.30	.15
12	Steve Sax	.10	.08	.04
13	Fred McGriff	.40	.30	.15
14	Gregg Jefferies	1.50	1.25	.06
15	Mark Grace	.90	.70	.35
16	Devon White	.10	.08	.04
17	Juan Samuel	.15	.11	.06
18	Robin Yount	.25	.20	.10
19	Glenn Davis	.10	.08	.04
20	Jeffrey Leonard	.10	.08	.04
21	Chili Davis	.10	.08	.04
22	Craig Biggio	.70	.50	.30
23	Jose Canseco	1.50	1.25	.70
24	Derek Lilliquist	.30	.25	.12
25	Chris Bosio	.10	.08	.04
26	Dave Steib	.10	.08	.04
27	Bobby Thigpen	.10	.08	.04
28	Jack Clark	.10	.08	.04
29	Kevin Ritz	.30	.25	.12
30	Tom Gordon	.80	.60	.30
31	Bryan Harvey	.10	.08	.04
32	Jim Deshaies	.10	.08	.04
33	Terry Steinbach	.15	.11	.06
34	Tom Glavine	.15	.11	.06
35	Bob Welch	.10	.08	.04
36	Charlie Hayes	.20	.15	.08
37	Jeff Reardon	.10	.08	.04
38	Joe Orsulak	.10	.08	.04
39	Scott Garrelts	.10	.08	.04
40	Bob Boone	.10	.08	.04
41	Scott Bankhead	.10	.08	.04
42	Tom Henke	.10	.08	.04
43	Greg Briley	.40	.30	.15
44	Teddy Higuera	.10	.08	.04
45	Pat Borders	.10	.08	.04
46	Kevin Seitzer	.15	.11	.06
47	Bruce Hurst	.15	.11	.06
48	Ozzie Guillen	.10	.08	.04
49	Wally Joyner	.50	.40	.20
50	Mike Greenwell	.40	.30	.15
51	Gary Gaetti	.12	.09	.05
52	Gary Sheffield	1.00	.70	.40
53	Dennis Martinez	.10	.08	.04
54	Ryne Sanberg	.20	.15	.08
55	Mike Scott	.12	.09	.05
56	Todd Benzinger	.10	.08	.04
57	Kelly Gruber	.15	.11	.06
58	Jose Lind	.10	.08	.04
59	Allan Anderson	.10	.08	.04
60	Robby Thompson	.10	.08	.04
61	John Smoltz	.30	.25	.12
62	Mark Davis	.12	.09	.05
63	Tom Herr	.10	.08	.06
64	Randy Johnson	.20	.15	.08
65	Lonnie Smith	.10	.08	.04
66	Pedro Guerrero	.15	.11	.06
67	Jerome Walton	1.00	.70	.40
68	Ramon Martinez	.60	.45	.25
69	Tim Raines	.12	.09	.05
70	Matt Williams	.20	.15	.08
71	Joe Oliver	.35	.25	.12
72	Nick Esasky	.12	.09	.05
73	Kevin Brown	.25	.20	.10
74	Walt Weiss	.12	.09	.05
75	Roger McDowell	.10	.08	.04
76	Jose DeLeon	.10	.08	.04
77	Brian Downing	.10	.08	.04
78	Jay Howell	.10	.08	.04
79	Jose Uribe	.10	.08	.04
80	Ellis Burks	.50	.40	.20
81	Sammy Sosa	.50	.40	.20
82	Johnny Ray	.50	.40	.20
83	Danny Darwin	.10	.08	.04
84	Carney Lansford	.12	.09	.05
85	Jose Oquendo	.10	.08	.04
86	John Cerutti	.10	.08	.04
87	Dave Winfield	.15	.11	.08
88	Dave Righetti	.10	.08	.04
89	Danny Jackson	.10	.08	.04
90	Andy Benes	.70	.50	.30
91	Tom Browning	.10	.08	.04
92	Pete O'Brien	.10	.08	.04
93	Roberto Alomar	.15	.11	.06
94	Bret Saberhagen	.15	.11	.06
95	Phil Bradley	.10	.08	.04
96	Doug Jones	.10	.08	.04
97	Eric Davis	.80	.60	.30
98	Tony Gwynn	.40	.30	.15
99	Jim Abbott	.70	.50	.30
100	Cal Ripken, Jr.	.15	.11	.06
101	Andy Van Slyke	.12	.09	.05
102	Dan Plesac	.10	.08	.04
103	Lou Whitaker	.10	.08	.04
104	Steve Bedrosian	.10	.08	.04
105	Dave Gallagher	.10	.08	.04
106	Keith Hernandez	.10	.08	.04
107	Duane Ward	.10	.08	.04
108	Andre Dawson	.15	.11	.08
109	Howard Johnson	.20	.15	.08
110	Mark Langston	.12	.09	.05
111	Jerry Browne	.10	.08	.04
112	Alvin Davis	.10	.08	.04
113	Sid Fernandez	.10	.08	.04
114	Mike Devereaux	.10	.08	.04
115	Benny Santiago	.12	.09	.05
116	Bip Roberts	.10	.08	.04
117	Craig Worthington	.15	.11	.06
118	Kevin Elster	.10	.08	.04
119	Harold Reynolds	.10	.08	.04
120	Joe Carter	.15	.11	.04
121	Brian Harper	.10	.08	.04
122	Frank Viola	.15	.11	.06
123	Jeff Ballard	.10	.08	.04
124	John Kruk	.10	.08	.04
125	Harold Baines	.10	.08	.04
126	Tom Candiotti	.10	.08	.04
127	Kevin McReynolds	.15	.11	.06
128	Mookie Wilson	.10	.08	.04
129	Danny Tartabull	.12	.09	.05
130	Craig Lefferts	.10	.08	.04
131	Jose DeJesus	.15	.11	.06
132	John Orton	.30	.20	.10
133	Curt Schilling	.20	.15	.08
134	Marquis Grissom	1.00	.70	.40
135	Greg Vaughn	1.00	.70	.40
136	Brett Butler	.10	.08	.04
137	Rob Deer	.10	.08	.04
138	John Franco	.10	.08	.04
139	Keith Moreland	.10	.08	.04
140	Dave Smith	.10	.08	.04
141	Mark McGwire	.60	.45	.25
142	Vince Coleman	.15	.11	.06
143	Barry Bonds	.15	.11	.06
144	Mike Henneman	.10	.08	.04
145	Doc Gooden	.30	.25	.12
146	Darryl Strawberry	.30	.25	.12
147	Von Hayes	.10	.08	.04
148	Andres Galarraga	.12	.09	.05
149	Roger Clemens	.25	.20	.10
150	Don Mattingly	1.00	.70	.40
151	Joe Magrane	.10	.08	.04
152	Dwight Smith	.60	.45	.25
153	Ricky Jordan	.30	.25	.12
154	Alan Trammell	.10	.08	.04
155	Brook Jacoby	.10	.08	.04
156	Lenny Dykstra	.10	.08	.04
157	Mike LaValliere	.10	.08	.04
158	Julio Franco	.12	.09	.05
159	Joey Belle	.80	.60	.30
160	Barry Larkin	.15	.11	.06
161	Rick Reuschel	.10	.08	.04
162	Nelson Santovenia	.10	.08	.04
163	Mike Scioscia	.10	.08	.04
164	Damon Berryhill	.10	.08	.04
165	Todd Worrell	.10	.08	.04
166	Jim Eisenreich	.10	.08	.04
167	Ivan Calderon	.10	.08	.04
168	Goose Gozzo	.25	.20	.10
169	Kirk McCaskill	.10	.08	.04
170	Dennis Eckersley	.10	.08	.04
171	Mickey Tettleton	.12	.09	.05
172	Chuck Finley	.10	.08	.04
173	Dave Magadan	.10	.08	.04
174	Terry Pendleton	.10	.08	.04
175	Willie Randolph	.10	.08	.04
176	Jeff Huson	.25	.20	.10
177	Todd Zeile	1.25	.90	.50
178	Steve Olin	.40	.30	.15
179	Eric Anthony	1.00	.70	.40
180	Scott Coolbaugh	.50	.40	.20
181	Rick Sutcliffe	.10	.08	.04
182	Tim Wallach	.10	.08	.04
183	Paul Molitor	.12	.09	.05
184	Roberto Kelly	.12	.09	.05
185	Mike Moore	.10	.08	.04

		MT	NR MT	EX
186	Junior Felix	.70	.50	.30
187	Mike Schooler	.10	.08	.04
188	Ruben Sierra	.30	.25	.12
189	Dale Murphy	.12	.09	.05
190	Dan Gladden	.10	.08	.04
191	John Smiley	.10	.08	.04
192	Jeff Russell	.10	.08	.04
193	Bert Blyleven	.10	.08	.04
194	Dave Stewart	.12	.09	.05
195	Bobby Bonilla	.12	.09	.05
196	Mitch Williams	.10	.08	.04
197	Orel Hershiser	.20	.15	.08
198	Kevin Bass	.10	.08	.04
199	Tim Burke	.10	.08	.04
200	Bo Jackson	1.25	.90	.50
201	David Cone	.12	.09	.05
202	Gary Pettis	.10	.08	.04
203	Kent Hrbek	.10	.08	.04
204	Carlton Fisk	.10	.08	.04
205	Bob Geren	.30	.25	.12
206	Bill Spiers	.40	.30	.15
207	Oddibe McDowell	.10	.08	.04
208	Rickey Henderson	.30	.25	.12
209	Ken Caminiti	.10	.08	.04
210	Devon White	.10	.08	.04
211	Greg Maddux	.15	.11	.06
212	Ed Whitson	.10	.08	.04
213	Carlos Martinez	.25	.20	.10
214	George Brett	.25	.20	.10
215	Gregg Olson	.50	.40	.20
216	Kenny Rogers	.20	.15	.08
217	Dwight Evans	.10	.08	.04
218	Pat Tabler	.10	.08	.04
219	Jeff Treadway	.10	.08	.04
220	Scott Fletcher	.10	.08	.04
221	Deion Sanders	.70	.50	.30
222	Robin Ventura	.70	.50	.30
223	Chip Hale	.50	.40	.20
224	Tommy Greene	.40	.30	.15
225	Dean Palmer	.40	.30	.15

1953 Stahl-Meyer Franks

These nine cards, issued in packages of hot dogs by a New York area meat company, feature three players from each of the New York teams of the day - Dodgers Giants and Yankees. Cards in the set measure 3-1/4" by 4-1/2". The card fronts in this unnumbered set feature color photos with player name and facsimile autograph. The backs list both biographical and statistical information on half the card and a ticket offer promotion on the other half. The card corners are cut diagonally, although some cards (apparently cut from sheets) with square corners have been seen. Cards are white-bordered.

		NR MT	EX	VG
Complete Set:		4000.00	2000.00	1200.
Common Player:		125.00	62.00	37.00
(1)	Hank Bauer	150.00	75.00	45.00
(2)	Roy Campanella	500.00	250.00	150.00
(3)	Gil Hodges	275.00	137.00	82.00
(4)	Monte Irvin	200.00	100.00	60.00
(5)	Whitey Lockman	125.00	62.00	37.00
(6)	Mickey Mantle	1800.00	900.00	540.00
(7)	Phil Rizzuto	275.00	137.00	82.00

		NR MT	EX	VG
(8)	Duke Snider	500.00	250.00	150.00
(9)	Bobby Thompson	150.00	75.00	45.00

1954 Stahl-Meyer Franks

The 1954 set of Stahl-Meyer Franks was increased to 12 cards which retained the 3-1/4" by 4-1/2" size. The most prominent addition to the '54 set was New York Giants slugger Willie Mays. The card fronts are identical in format to the previous year's set. However, the backs are different as they are designed on a vertical format. The backs also contain an advertisement for a "Johnny Stahl-Meyer Baseball Kit." The cards in the set are unnumbered.

		NR MT	EX	VG
Complete Set:		5500.00	2750.00	1575.
Common Player:		125.00	62.00	37.00
(1)	Hank Bauer	150.00	75.00	45.00
(2)	Carl Erskine	150.00	75.00	45.00
(3)	Gil Hodges	300.00	150.00	90.00
(4)	Monte Irvin	225.00	112.00	67.00
(5)	Whitey Lockman	125.00	62.00	37.00
(6)	Gil McDougald	150.00	75.00	45.00
(7)	Mickey Mantle	2000.00	1000.00	600.00
(8)	Willie Mays	1000.00	500.00	300.00
(9)	Don Mueller	125.00	62.00	37.00
(10)	Don Newcombe	150.00	75.00	45.00
(11)	Phil Rizzuto	300.00	150.00	90.00
(12)	Duke Snider	525.00	262.00	157.00

1955 Stahl-Meyer Franks

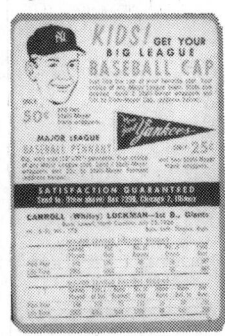

Eleven of the 12 players in the 1955 set are the same as those featured in 1954. The exception is the New York Giants Dusty Rhodes, who replaced Willie Mays on the 3-1/4" by 4-1/2" cards. The card fronts are again full-color photos bordered in yellow with diagonal corners, and four players from each of the three New York teams are featured. The backs offer a new promotion, with a drawing of Mickey Mantle and advertisements selling pennants and caps. Player statistics are still included on the vertical card backs. The cards in the set are unnumbered.

		NR MT	EX	VG
Complete Set:		4300.00	2150.00	1290.
Common Player:		125.00	62.00	37.00
(1)	Hank Bauer	150.00	75.00	45.00
(2)	Carl Erskine	150.00	75.00	45.00
(3)	Gil Hodges	300.00	150.00	90.00
(4)	Monte Irvin	200.00	100.00	60.00
(5)	Whitey Lockman	125.00	62.00	37.00
(6)	Mickey Mantle	2000.00	1000.00	600.00
(7)	Gil McDougald	150.00	75.00	45.00
(8)	Don Mueller	125.00	62.00	37.00
(9)	Don Newcombe	150.00	75.00	45.00
(10)	Jim Rhodes	125.00	62.00	37.00
(11)	Phil Rizzuto	300.00	150.00	90.00
(12)	Duke Snider	525.00	262.00	157.00

1983 Stuart Expos

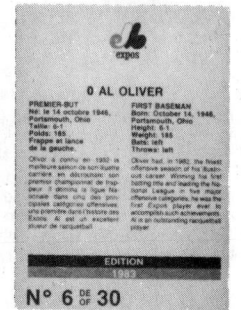

This set of Montreal Expos players and coaches was issued by a Montreal area baking company for inclusion in packages of snack cakes. The 30 cards feature full-color player photos, with the player name, number and team logo also on the card fronts. The backs list brief player biographies in both English and French. Twenty-five players are pictured on the 2-1/2" by 3-1/2" cards.

		MT	NR MT	EX
Complete Set:		12.00	9.00	4.75
Common Player:		.25	.20	.10
1	Bill Virdon	.25	.20	.10
2	Woodie Fryman	.25	.20	.10
3	Vern Rapp	.25	.20	.10
4	Andre Dawson	2.00	1.50	.80
5	Jeff Reardon	.70	.50	.30
6	Al Oliver	.50	.40	.20
7	Doug Flynn	.25	.20	.10
8	Gary Carter	1.00	.70	.40
9	Tim Raines	1.50	1.25	.60
10	Steve Rogers	.30	.25	.12
11	Billy DeMars	.25	.20	.10
12	Tim Wallach	1.00	.70	.40
13	Galen Cisco	.25	.20	.10
14	Terry Francona	.25	.20	.10
15	Bill Gullickson	.25	.20	.10
16	Ray Burris	.25	.20	.10
17	Scott Sanderson	.35	.25	.14
18	Warren Cromartie	.25	.20	.10
19	Jerry White	.25	.20	.10
20	Bobby Ramos	.25	.20	.10
21	Jim Wohlford	.25	.20	.10
22	Dan Schatzeder	.25	.20	.10
23	Charlie Lea	.25	.20	.10
24	Bryan Little	.25	.20	.10
25	Mel Wright	.25	.20	.10
26	Tim Blackwell	.25	.20	.10
27	Chris Speier	.25	.20	.10
28	Randy Lerch	.25	.20	.10
29	Bryn Smith	.35	.25	.14
30	Brad Mills	.25	.20	.10

Definitions for grading conditions are located in the introduction section at the front of this book.

1984 Stuart Expos

For the second year in a row, Stuart Cakes issued a full-color card set of the Montreal Expos. The 2-1/2" by 3-1/2" cards again list the player name and number along with the team and company logos on the card fronts. The backs are bilingual with biographical information in both English and French. The 40-card set was issued in two series. Card numbers 21-40, issued late in the summer, are more difficult to find than the first 20 cards. The 40 cards include players, the manager, coaches and team mascot.

		MT	NR MT	EX
Complete Set:		40.00	30.00	15.00
Common Player: 1-20		.25	.20	.10
Common Player: 21-40		.50	.40	.20
1	Youppi! (mascot)	.25	.20	.10
2	Bill Virdon	.25	.20	.10
3	Billy DeMars	.25	.20	.10
4	Galen Cisco	.25	.20	.10
5	Russ Nixon	.25	.20	.10
6	Felipe Alou	.25	.20	.10
7	Dan Schatzeder	.25	.20	.10
8	Charlie Lea	.25	.20	.10
9	Bobby Ramos	.25	.20	.10
10	Bob James	.25	.20	.10
11	Andre Dawson	1.25	.90	.50
12	Gary Lucas	.25	.20	.10
13	Jeff Reardon	.50	.40	.20
14	Tim Wallach	1.00	.70	.40
15	Gary Carter	1.25	.90	.50
16	Bill Gullickson	.25	.20	.10
17	Pete Rose	4.00	3.00	1.50
18	Terry Francona	.25	.20	.10
19	Steve Rogers	.30	.25	.12
20	Tim Raines	1.50	1.25	.60
21	Bryn Smith	.50	.40	.20
22	Greg Harris	.50	.40	.20
23	David Palmer	.50	.40	.20
24	Jim Wohlford	.50	.40	.20
25	Miguel Dilone	.50	.40	.20
26	Mike Stenhouse	.50	.40	.20
27	Chris Speier	.50	.40	.20
28	Derrel Thomas	.50	.40	.20
29	Doug Flynn	.50	.40	.20
30	Bryan Little	.50	.40	.20
31	Argenis Salazar	.50	.40	.20
32	Mike Fuentes	.50	.40	.20
33	Joe Kerrigan	.50	.40	.20
34	Andy McGaffigan	.45	.35	.20
35	Fred Breining	.50	.40	.20
36	Expos 1983 All-Stars (Gary Carter, Andre Dawson, Tim Raines, Steve Rogers)	1.50	1.25	.60
37	Co-Players Of The Year (Andre Dawson, Tim Raines)	1.50	1.25	.60
38	Expos' Coaching Staff (Felipe Alou, Galen Cisco, Billy DeMars, Joe Kerrigan, Russ Nixon, Bill Virdon)	.50	.40	.20
39	Team Photo	.50	.40	.20
40	Checklist	.50	.40	.20

NOTE: A card number in parentheses ( ) indicates the set is unnumbered.

1987 Stuart

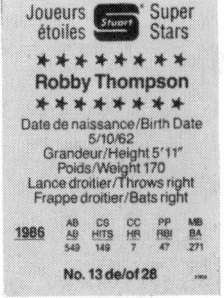

Twenty-eight four-part folding panels make up the 1987 Stuart Super Stars set, which was issued only in Canada. Three player cards and a sweepstakes entry form card comprise each panel. All 26 major league teams are included with the Montreal Expos and Toronto Blue Jays being represented twice. The cards, which are full color and measure 2-1/2" by 3-1/2", are written in both English and French. The card backs contain the player's previous year's statistics. All team insignias have been airbrushed away.

	MT	NR MT	EX
Complete Panel Set:	50.00	37.00	20.00
Complete Singles Set:	20.00	15.00	8.00
Common Panel:	.80	.60	.30
Common Single Player:	.10	.08	.04
Panel (New York Mets)	4.00	3.00	1.50
1a Gary Carter	.50	.40	.20
1b Keith Hernandez	.40	.30	.15
1c Darryl Strawberry	.60	.45	.25
Panel (Atlanta Braves)	2.25	1.75	.90
2a Bruce Benedict	.10	.08	.04
2b Ken Griffey	.15	.11	.06
2c Dale Murphy	.60	.45	.25
Panel (Chicago Cubs)	1.50	1.25	.60
3a Jody Davis	.15	.11	.06
3b Andre Dawson	.30	.25	.12
3c Leon Durham	.15	.11	.06
Panel (Cincinnati Reds)	2.50	2.00	1.00
4a Buddy Bell	.15	.11	.06
4b Eric Davis	.60	.45	.25
4c Dave Parker	.25	.20	.10
Panel (Houston Astros)	2.25	1.75	.90
5a Glenn Davis	.25	.20	.10
5b Nolan Ryan	.70	.50	.30
5c Mike Scott	.25	.20	.10
Panel (Los Angeles Dodgers)	2.25	1.75	.90
6a Pedro Guerrero	.25	.20	.10
6b Mike Marshall	.20	.15	.08
6c Fernando Valenzuela	.40	.30	.15
Panel (Montreal Expos)	1.75	1.25	.70
7a Tim Raines	.40	.30	.15
7b Tim Wallach	.20	.15	.08
7c Mitch Webster	.10	.08	.04
Panel (Montreal Expos)	.80	.60	.30
8a Hubie Brooks	.15	.11	.06
8b Bryn Smith	.10	.08	.04
8c Floyd Youmans	.10	.08	.04
Panel (Philadelphia Phillies)	2.25	1.75	.90
9a Shane Rawley	.10	.08	.04
9b Juan Samuel	.20	.15	.08
9c Mike Schmidt	.80	.60	.30
Panel (Pittsburgh Pirates)	.80	.60	.30
10a Jim Morrison	.10	.08	.04
10b Johnny Ray	.15	.11	.06
10c R.J. Reynolds	.10	.08	.04
Panel (St. Louis Cardinals)	2.00	1.50	.80
11a Jack Clark	.25	.20	.10
11b Vince Coleman	.30	.25	.12
11c Ozzie Smith	.25	.20	.10
Panel (San Diego Padres)	3.00	2.25	1.25
12a Steve Garvey	.50	.40	.20
12b Tony Gwynn	.50	.40	.20
12c John Kruk	.20	.15	.08
Panel (San Francisco Giants)	.80	.60	.30

	MT	NR MT	EX
13a Chili Davis	.10	.08	.04
13b Jeffrey Leonard	.10	.08	.04
13c Robbie Thompson	.10	.08	.04
Panel (Baltimore Orioles)	3.00	2.25	1.25
14a Fred Lynn	.25	.20	.10
14b Eddie Murray	.50	.40	.20
14c Cal Ripken	.50	.40	.20
Panel (Boston Red Sox)	4.00	3.00	1.50
15a Don Baylor	.15	.11	.06
15b Wade Boggs	.80	.60	.30
15c Roger Clemens	.60	.45	.25
Panel	2.50	2.00	1.00
16a Doug DeCinces	.10	.08	.04
16b Wally Joyner	.80	.60	.30
16c Mike Witt	.10	.08	.04
Panel (Chicago White Sox)	1.50	1.25	.60
17a Harold Baines	.20	.15	.08
17b Carlton Fisk	.25	.20	.10
17c Ozzie Guillen	.15	.11	.06
Panel (Cleveland Indians)	1.00	.70	.40
18a Joe Carter	.20	.15	.08
18b Julio Franco	.15	.11	.06
18c Pat Tabler	.10	.08	.04
Panel (Detroit Tigers)	2.50	2.00	1.00
19a Kirk Gibson	.40	.30	.15
19b Jack Morris	.25	.20	.10
19c Alan Trammell	.40	.30	.15
Panel (Kansas City Royals)	2.50	2.00	1.00
20a George Brett	.60	.45	.25
20b Bret Saberhagen	.30	.25	.12
20c Willie Wilson	.15	.11	.06
Panel (Milwaukee Brewers)	2.00	1.50	.80
21a Cecil Cooper	.15	.11	.06
21b Paul Molitor	.20	.15	.08
21c Robin Yount	.40	.30	.15
Panel (Minnesota Twins)	2.50	2.00	1.00
22a Tom Brunansky	.20	.15	.08
22b Kent Hrbek	.30	.25	.12
22c Kirby Puckett	.50	.40	.20
Panel (New York Yankees)	5.00	3.75	2.00
23a Rickey Henderson	.50	.40	.20
23b Don Mattingly	1.00	.70	.40
23c Dave Winfield	.50	.40	.20
Panel (Oakland A's)	2.75	2.00	1.00
24a Jose Canseco	.90	.70	.35
24b Alfredo Griffin	.10	.08	.04
24c Carney Lansford	.10	.08	.04
Panel 25 (Seattle Mariners)	1.50	1.25	.60
25a Phil Bradley	.15	.11	.06
25b Alvin Davis	.20	.15	.08
25c Mark Langston	.20	.15	.08
Panel (Texas Rangers)	1.50	1.25	.60
26a Pete Incaviglia	.30	.25	.12
26b Pete O'Brien	.10	.08	.04
26c Larry Parrish	.10	.08	.04
Panel (Toronto Blue Jays)	2.25	1.75	.90
27a Jesse Barfield	.20	.15	.08
27b George Bell	.40	.30	.15
27c Tony Fernandez	.20	.15	.08
Panel (Toronto Blue Jays)	.80	.60	.30
28a Lloyd Moseby	.10	.08	.04
28b Dave Stieb	.15	.11	.06
28c Ernie Whitt	.10	.08	.04

1962 Sugardale Weiners

The Sugardale Meats set of black and white cards measure 5-1/8" by 3-3/4". The 22-card set includes 18 Cleveland Indians and four Pittsburgh Pirates players. The Indians cards are numbered from 1-19 with card number 6 not issued. The Pirates cards are lettered from A to D. The card fronts contain a relatively small player photo, with biographical information and Sugardale logo. The backs are printed in red and offer playing tips and another company logo. Card number 10 (Bob Nieman) is considerably more scarce than other cards in the set.

		NR MT	EX	VG
Complete Set:		2000.00	1000.00	600.00
Common Player:		40.00	20.00	12.00
A	Dick Groat	70.00	35.00	21.00
B	Roberto Clemente	500.00	300.00	150.00
C	Don Hoak	55.00	27.00	16.50
D	Dick Stuart	55.00	27.00	16.50
1	Barry Latman	40.00	20.00	12.00
2	Gary Bell	45.00	22.00	13.50
3	Dick Donovan	40.00	20.00	12.00
4	Frank Funk	40.00	20.00	12.00
5	Jim Perry	60.00	30.00	18.00
6	Not issued			
7	Johnny Romano	40.00	20.00	12.00
8	Ty Cline	40.00	20.00	12.00
9	Tito Francona	45.00	22.00	13.50
10	Bob Nieman	300.00	150.00	90.00
11	Willie Kirkland	40.00	20.00	12.00
12	Woodie Held	45.00	22.00	13.50
13	Jerry Kindall	40.00	20.00	12.00
14	Bubba Phillips	40.00	20.00	12.00
15	Mel Harder	45.00	22.00	13.50
16	Salty Parker	40.00	20.00	12.00
17	Ray Katt	40.00	20.00	12.00
18	Mel McGaha	40.00	20.00	12.00
19	Pedro Ramos	40.00	20.00	12.00

		NR MT	EX	VG
6	Not issued			
7	Johnny Romano	40.00	20.00	12.00
8	Mike De La Hoz	40.00	20.00	12.00
9	Tito Francona	45.00	22.00	13.50
10	Gene Green	40.00	20.00	12.00
11	Willie Kirkland	40.00	20.00	12.00
12	Woodie Held	45.00	22.00	13.50
13	Jerry Kindall	40.00	20.00	12.00
14	Max Alvis	45.00	22.00	13.50
15	Mel Harder	45.00	22.00	13.50
16	George Strickland	40.00	20.00	12.00
17	Elmer Valo	40.00	20.00	12.00
18	Birdie Tebbetts	45.00	22.00	13.50
19	Pedro Ramos	40.00	20.00	12.00
20	Al Luplow	40.00	20.00	12.00
21	Not issued			
22	Not issued			
23	Jim Grant	45.00	22.00	13.50
24	Victor Davalillo	45.00	22.00	13.50
25	Jerry Walker	40.00	20.00	12.00
26	Sam McDowell	60.00	30.00	18.00
27	Fred Whitfield	40.00	20.00	12.00
28	Jack Kralick	40.00	20.00	12.00
29	Not issued			
30	Not issued			
31	Not issued			
32	Not issued			
33	Bob Allen	40.00	20.00	12.00

1984 Tastykake Phillies

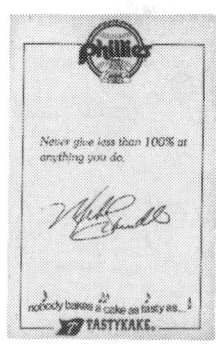

This 40-card regional set featuring the Philadelphia Phillies was issued as a promotion by Tastykake in 1984 and was distributed as a complete set to fans attending the April 21st game at Philadelphia's Veterans Stadium. The large (3-1/2" by 5-1/4") full-color cards have a white border surrounding the photo with "Phillies" at the top and the player's name at the bottom. A 1984 Phillies copyright line appears in the lower left corner. The backs display facsimile autographs, a brief inspirational message and the Tastykake and Phillies logos. The set includes special cards featuring the club's broadcasters, manager and coaches, a team photo, logo/checklist card and two action photos of Mike Schmidt and Steve Carlton, labeled "Future Hall of Famers".

		MT	NR MT	EX
Complete Set:		10.00	7.50	4.00
Common Player:		.20	.15	.08
(1)	Luis Aguayo	.20	.15	.08
(2)	Larry Andersen	.20	.15	.08
(3)	Dave Bristol	.20	.15	.08
(4)	Marty Bystrom	.20	.15	.08
(5)	Bill Campbell	.20	.15	.08
(6)	Steve Carlton	2.00	1.50	.80
(7)	Future Hall of Famer (Steve Carlton)			
		1.50	1.25	.60
(8)	Don Carman	.60	.45	.25
(9)	Tim Corcoran	.20	.15	.08
(10)	Ivan DeJesus	.20	.15	.08

1963 Sugardale Weiners

Sugardale Meats again featured Cleveland and Pittsburgh players in its 1963 set, which grew to 31 cards. The black and white cards again measure 5-1/8" by 3-3/4", and consist of 28 Indians and five Pirates players. Card formats are virtually identical to the 1962 cards, with the only real difference being the information included in the player biographies. The cards are numbered 1-38, with numbers 6, 21, 22 and 29-32 not issued. Cards for Bob Skinner (#35) and Jim Perry (#5) are scarce as these two players were traded during the season and their cards withdrawn from distribution. The red card backs again offer playing tips.

		NR MT	EX	VG
Complete Set:		2000.00	1000.00	600.00
A	Don Cardwell	40.00	20.00	12.00
B	Robert R. Skinner	125.00	62.00	37.00
C	Donald B. Schwall	40.00	20.00	12.00
D	Jim Pagliaroni	40.00	20.00	12.00
E	Dick Schofield	45.00	22.00	13.50
1	Barry Latman	40.00	20.00	12.00
2	Gary Bell	45.00	22.00	13.50
3	Dick Donovan	40.00	20.00	12.00
4	Joe Adcock	60.00	30.00	18.00
5	Jim Perry	150.00	75.00	45.00

		MT	NR MT	EX
(11)	John Denny	.25	.20	.10
(12)	Bo Diaz	.25	.20	.10
(13)	John Felske	.20	.15	.08
(14)	Kiko Garcia	.20	.15	.08
(15)	Tony Ghelfi	.20	.15	.08
(16)	Greg Gross	.20	.15	.08
(17)	Kevin Gross	.50	.40	.20
(18)	Von Hayes	.70	.50	.30
(19)	Al Holland	.20	.15	.08
(20)	Charles Hudson	.35	.25	.14
(21)	Deron Johnson	.20	.15	.08
(22)	Jerry Koosman	.25	.20	.10
(23)	Joe Lefebvre	.20	.15	.08
(24)	Sixto Lezcano	.20	.15	.08
(25)	Garry Maddox	.25	.20	.10
(26)	Len Matuszek	.20	.15	.08
(27)	Tug McGraw	.40	.30	.15
(28)	Claude Osteen	.20	.15	.08
(29)	Paul Owens	.20	.15	.08
(30)	John Russell	.30	.25	.12
(31)	Mike Ryan	.20	.15	.08
(32)	Juan Samuel	.60	.45	.25
(33)	Mike Schmidt	3.00	2.25	1.25
(34)	Future Hall of Famer (Mike Schmidt)	2.00	1.00	.60
(35)	Jeff Stone	.25	.20	.10
(36)	Ozzie Virgil	.25	.20	.10
(37)	Dave Wehrmeister	.20	.15	.08
(38)	Glenn Wilson	.25	.20	.10
(39)	John Wockenfuss	.20	.15	.08
(40)	Phillie Phanatic	.20	.15	.08
(41)	Phillies Broadcasters (Richie Ashburn, Harry Kalas, Andy Musser, Chris Wheeler)	.25	.20	.10
(42)	Veterans Stadium	.20	.15	.08
(43)	Team Photo	.20	.15	.08
(44)	Checklist	.20	.15	.08

		MT	NR MT	EX
9	Phillies Pitchers (Larry Andersen, Bill Campbell, Steve Carlton, Don Carman, John Denny, Kevin Gross, Al Holland, Charles Hudson, Jerry Koosman, Shane Rawley, Pat Zachry)	.30	.25	.12
10	Phillies Catchers (Darren Daulton, Bo Diaz, Ozzie Virgil)	.20	.15	.08
11	Phillies Infielders (Luis Aguayo, Ivan De Jesus, Steve Jeltz, John Russell, Juan Samuel, Mike Schmidt)	.50	.40	.20
12	Phillies Outfielders (Tim Corcoran, Greg Gross, Von Hayes, Jeff Stone, Glenn Wilson)	.25	.20	.10
13	Larry Andersen	.20	.15	.08
14	Steve Carlton	2.00	1.50	.80
15	Don Carman	.60	.45	.25
16	John Denny	.20	.15	.08
17	Tony Ghelfi	.30	.25	.12
18	Kevin Gross	.20	.15	.08
19	Al Holland	.25	.20	.10
20	Charles Hudson	.25	.20	.10
21	Jerry Koosman	.30	.25	.12
22	Shane Rawley	.20	.15	.08
23	Pat Zachry	.20	.15	.08
24	Darren Daulton	.25	.20	.10
25	Bo Diaz	.25	.20	.10
26	Ozzie Virgil	.20	.15	.08
27	John Wockenfuss	.20	.15	.08
28	Luis Aguayo	.20	.15	.08
29	Kiko Garcia	.20	.15	.08
30	Steve Jeltz	.20	.15	.08
31	John Russell	.30	.25	.12
32	Juan Samuel	.60	.45	.25
33	Mike Schmidt	3.00	2.25	1.25
34	Tim Corcoran	.20	.15	.08
35	Greg Gross	.20	.15	.08
36	Von Hayes	.60	.45	.25
37	Joe Lefebvre	.20	.15	.08
38	Garry Maddox	.25	.20	.10
40	Glenn Wilson	.25	.20	.10
41	Future Phillies (Ramon Caraballo, Mike Diaz)	.50	.40	.20
42	Future Phillies (Rodger Cole, Mike Maddux)	.50	.40	.20
43	Future Phillies (Chris James, Rick Schu)	1.00	.70	.40
44	Future Phillies (Ken Jackson, Francisco Melendez)	.25	.20	.10
45	Future Phillies (Rocky Childress, Randy Salava)	.25	.20	.10
46	Future Phillies (Ralph Citarella, Rich Surhoff)	.25	.20	.10
47	Team Photo	.20	.15	.08

1985 Tastykake Phillies

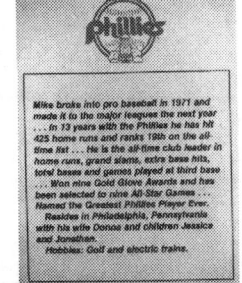

#20   MIKE SCHMIDT   3B

This regional set of Phillies cards, sponsored by Tastykake, was given away at a stadium promotion on April 21st at Philadelphia's Veterans Stadium. The 47 full-color cards measure a large 3" by 5" and are numbered according to the player's uniform number. In addition to player's from the 1985 Phillies roster, the set includes the manager, coaches, group photos, and cards of 14 promising minor leaguers in the club's farm system. The full-color cards are printed on a white, glossy stock and surrrounded by a white border. The player's uniform number, name and position appear below, with a 1985 Phillies copyright in the lower right corner. The backs of the cards display the Phillies and Tastykake logos at the top and bottom respectively, with player information in the center.

	MT	NR MT	EX
Complete Set:	12.00	9.00	4.75
Common Player:	.20	.15	.08

		MT	NR MT	EX
1	Checklist	.20	.15	.08
2	John Felske	.20	.15	.08
3	Dave Bristol	.20	.15	.08
4	Lee Elia	.20	.15	.08
5	Claude Osteen	.20	.15	.08
6	Mike Ryan	.20	.15	.08
7	Del Unser	.20	.15	.08
8	Phillies Coaching Staff (Dave Bristol, Lee Elia, John Felske, Hank King, Claude Osteen, Mike Ryan, Del Unser)	.20	.15	.08

1986 Tastykake Phillies

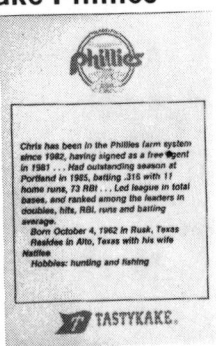

#26   CHRIS JAMES   OF

The 1986 Tastykake Phillies set consists of 49 cards that measure 3-1/2" by 5-1/4" in size. The cards were given away at the Phillies' annual baseball card day promotion. The card fronts feature a full-color photo along with the player's name, uniform number and position. The card backs are printed in red and black and carry a brief player biography. Five cards commemorating past Phillies' pennants were included in the set.

	MT	NR MT	EX
Complete Set:	12.00	9.00	4.75

		MT	NR MT	EX
Common Player:		.15	.11	.06
2	Jim Davenport	.15	.11	.06
3	Claude Osteen	.15	.11	.06
4	Lee Elia	.15	.11	.06
5	Mike Ryan	.15	.11	.06
6	John Russell	.20	.15	.08
7	John Felske	.15	.11	.06
8	Juan Samuel	.50	.40	.20
9	Von Hayes	.50	.40	.20
10	Darren Daulton	.15	.11	.06
11	Tom Foley	.15	.11	.06
12	Glenn Wilson	.20	.15	.08
14	Jeff Stone	.15	.11	.06
15	Rick Schu	.20	.15	.08
16	Luis Aguayo	.15	.11	.06
20	Mike Schmidt	2.00	1.50	.80
21	Greg Gross	.15	.11	.06
22	Gary Redus	.15	.11	.06
23	Joe Lefebvre	.15	.11	.06
24	Milt Thompson	.30	.25	.12
25	Del Unser	.15	.11	.06
26	Chris James	1.00	.70	.40
27	Kent Tekulve	.20	.15	.08
28	Shane Rawley	.25	.20	.10
29	Ronn Reynolds	.15	.11	.06
30	Steve Jeltz	.15	.11	.06
31	Garry Maddox	.25	.20	.10
32	Steve Carlton	1.50	1.25	.60
33	Dave Shipanoff	.15	.11	.06
35	Randy Lerch	.15	.11	.06
36	Robin Roberts	.60	.45	.25
39	Dave Rucker	.15	.11	.06
40	Steve Bedrosian	.40	.30	.15
41	Tom Hume	.15	.11	.06
42	Don Carman	.50	.40	.20
43	Fred Toliver	.20	.15	.08
46	Kevin Gross	.30	.25	.12
47	Larry Andersen	.15	.11	.06
48	Dave Stewart	.50	.40	.20
49	Charles Hudson	.20	.15	.08
50	Rocky Childress	.20	.15	.08
----	Future Phillies (Ramon Caraballo, Joe Cipolloni)	.20	.15	.08
----	Future Phillies (Arturo Gonzalez, Mike Maddux)	.40	.30	.15
----	Future Phillies (Ricky Jordan, Francisco Melendez)	3.00	2.25	1.25
----	Future Phillies (Randy Day, Kevin Ward)	.20	.15	.08
----	The 1915 Phillies	.15	.11	.06
----	The 1950 Phillies	.15	.11	.06
----	The 1980 Phillies	.15	.11	.06
----	The 1983 Phillies	.15	.11	.06
----	June 11, 1985 - A Night To Remember	.15	.11	.06

available for $4 via a mail-in offer to the Phillies ball club.

		MT	NR MT	EX
Complete Set:		10.00	7.50	4.00
Common Player:		.15	.11	.06
6	John Russell	.15	.11	.06
7	John Felske	.15	.11	.06
8	Juan Samuel	.50	.40	.20
10	Darren Daulton	.15	.11	.06
11	Greg Legg	.20	.15	.08
12	Glenn Wilson	.20	.15	.08
13	Lance Parrish	.50	.40	.20
14	Jeff Stone	.15	.11	.06
15	Rick Schu	.15	.11	.06
16	Luis Aguayo	.15	.11	.06
17	Ron Roenicke	.15	.11	.06
18	Chris James	1.00	.70	.40
20	Mike Schmidt	2.00	1.50	.80
21	Greg Gross	.15	.11	.06
23	Joe Cipolloni	.20	.15	.08
24	Milt Thompson	.20	.15	.08
27	Kent Tekulve	.20	.15	.08
28	Shane Rawley	.25	.20	.10
29	Ronn Reynolds	.15	.11	.06
30	Steve Jeltz	.15	.11	.06
33	Mike Jackson	.40	.30	.15
34	Mike Easler	.20	.15	.08
35	Dan Schatzeder	.15	.11	.06
37	Ken Dowell	.20	.15	.08
38	Jim Olander	.20	.15	.08
39a	Joe Cowley	.15	.11	.06
39b	Bob Scanlan	.20	.15	.08
40	Steve Bedrosian	.40	.30	.15
41	Tom Hume	.15	.11	.06
42	Don Carman	.30	.25	.12
43	Freddie Toliver	.15	.11	.06
44	Mike Maddux	.30	.25	.12
45	Greg Jelks	.40	.30	.15
46	Kevin Gross	.25	.20	.10
47	Bruce Ruffin	.40	.30	.15
48	Marvin Freeman	.30	.25	.12
49	Len Watts	.20	.15	.08
50	Tom Newell	.20	.15	.08
51	Ken Jackson	.30	.25	.12
52	Todd Frohwirth	.30	.25	.12
58	Doug Bair	.15	.11	.06
----	Shawn Burton, Rick Lundblade	.20	.15	.08
----	Jeff Kaye, Darren Loy	.20	.15	.08
----	Phillies Coaches (Jim Davenport, Lee Elia, Claude Osteen, Mike Ryan, Del Unser)	.15	.11	.06
----	Phillie Phanatic	.15	.11	.06
----	Team Photo	.15	.11	.06

1987 Tastykake Phillies

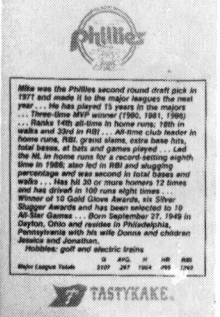

#20   MIKE SCHMIDT   3B

A 46-card set featuring the Philadelphia Phillies and sponsored by Tastykake was given out to fans present at Veterans Stadium for the Phillies' April 12th baseball card day promotion. The cards measure 3-1/2" by 5-1/4" with fronts that feature a full-color player photo framed with a white border. The player's number, name and position appear below the photo. Card backs are printed in red and black and contain a brief biography. The set was

1988 Tastykake Phillies

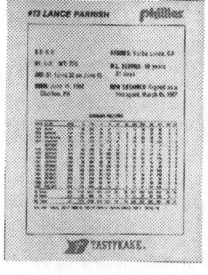

#13 LANCE PARRISH   CATCHER

This 39-card set was co-produced by Tastykake and the Phillies. The semi-glossy oversize cards, 4-7/8" by 6-1/4", feature full-color action photos with white borders. The coaching staff, young player prospects, the team mascot and a full team photo are included in the set. The card backs carry personal data and career stats in black letters, with the Phillies and Tastykake logos in red. Card numbers correspond to player uniform numbers. The cards were available upon request from individual players and were not made available as a set. Nine cards (#'s

4, 6, 7, 11, 15 Gutierrez, 16 Bowa, 17, 33 and Broadcasters) were added later in the year. These cards have blank backs.

		MT	NR MT	EX
	Complete Set:	12.00	9.00	4.75
	Common Player:	.15	.11	.06
4a	Lee Elia (vertical format)	.15	.11	.06
4b	Lee Elia (horizontal format)	.15	.11	.06
6	John Russell	.15	.11	.06
7	John Vukovich	.15	.11	.06
8	Juan Samuel	.50	.40	.20
9	Von Hayes	.35	.25	.14
10	Darren Daulton	.15	.11	.06
11	Keith Miller	.40	.30	.15
13	Lance Parrish	.50	.40	.20
15a	Bill Almon	.15	.11	.06
15b	Jackie Gutierrez	.15	.11	.06
16a	Luis Aguayo	.15	.11	.06
16b	Larry Bowa	.20	.15	.08
17	Ricky Jordan	1.50	1.25	.60
18	Chris James	.40	.30	.15
19	Mike Young	.15	.11	.06
20	Mike Schmidt	2.00	1.50	.80
21	Greg Gross	.15	.11	.06
22	Bob Dernier	.15	.11	.06
24	Milt Thompson	.20	.15	.08
27	Kent Tekulve	.25	.20	.10
28	Shane Rawley	.25	.20	.10
29	Phil Bradley	.50	.40	.20
30	Steve Jeltz	.15	.11	.06
31	Jeff Calhoun	.15	.11	.06
33	Greg Harris	.15	.11	.06
38	Wally Ritchie	.25	.20	.10
40	Steve Bedrosian	.35	.25	.14
42	Don Carman	.25	.20	.10
44	Mike Maddux	.25	.20	.10
45	David Palmer	.15	.11	.06
46	Kevin Gross	.25	.20	.10
47	Bruce Ruffin	.20	.15	.08
52	Todd Frohwirth	.20	.15	.08
-----	Coaching Staff (Dave Bristol, Claude Osteen, Mike Ryan, Tony Taylor, Del Unser, John Vukovich)	.15	.11	.06
-----	Phillies Prospects (Tom Barrett, Brad Brink, Steve DeAngelis, Ron Jones, Keith Miller, Brad Moore, Howard Nichols, Shane Turner)	.40	.30	.15
-----	Phillie Phanatic	.15	.11	.06
-----	Team Photo	.15	.11	.06
-----	Broadcasters (Richie Ashburn, Harry Kalas, Garry Maddox, Andy Musser, Chris Wheeler)	.15	.11	.06

1989 Tastykake Phillies

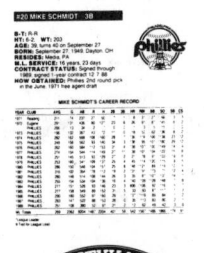

These oversize (approximately 4" by 6") cards feature very nice borderless action photos of the Philadelphia Phillies. The 36-card set was sponsored by Tastykake (whose logo appears on the bottom of the card backs) and was given to fans attending the May 13 Phillies game as a stadium promotion. The backs include player information and complete stats.

		MT	NR MT	EX
	Complete Set:	15.00	11.00	6.00
	Common Player:	.15	.11	.06
2	Larry Bowa	.15	.11	.06
3	Darold Knowles	.15	.11	.06
4a	Lenny Dykstra	.25	.20	.10
4b	Denis Menke	.15	.11	.06
5	Mike Ryan	.15	.11	.06
6	Dwayne Murphy	.15	.11	.06
7	John Vuckovich	.15	.11	.06
8a	Juan Samuel	.50	.40	.20
8b	Charlie Hayes	.25	.20	.10
9	Von Hayes	.35	.25	.12
10	Darren Daulton	.15	.11	.06
11	John Kruk	.25	.20	.10
12	Tony Taylor	.15	.11	.06
13	Roger McDowell	.25	.20	.10
15	Floyd Youmans	.15	.11	.06
16	Nick Leyva	.20	.15	.08
17	Ricky Jordan	.70	.50	.30
18	Jim Adduci (Update Card)	.25	.20	.10
19	Tom Nieto	.15	.11	.06
20	Mike Schmidt	1.00	.70	.40
21	Dickie Thon	.15	.11	.06
22	Bob Dernier	.15	.11	.06
23	Randy Ready (Update Card)	.25	.20	.10
24	Curt Ford	.15	.11	.06
25	Steve Lake	.15	.11	.06
26	Chris James	.80	.60	.30
27	Randy O'Neal	.15	.11	.06
28	Tom Herr	.30	.25	.12
30	Steve Jeltz	.15	.11	.06
31	Mark Ryal	.25	.20	.15
33	Greg Harris	.15	.11	.06
34	Alex Madrid	.20	.15	.08
35	Eric Bullock (Update Card)	.25	.20	.10
39	Dennis Cook (Update Card)	.25	.20	.10
40	Steve Bedrosian	.35	.25	.12
41	Steve Ontiveros	.20	.15	.08
42	Don Carman	.20	.15	.08
43	Ken Howell	.15	.11	.06
44	Mike Maddux	.25	.20	.10
45	Terry Mulholland (Update Card)	.25	.20	.10
46	Larry McWilliams	.15	.11	.06
47	Bruce Ruffin	.30	.25	.12
49	Jeff Parrett	.30	.25	.12
52	Todd Frohwirth	.20	.15	.08
-----	Sponsor Card	.15	.11	.06

1986 Texas Gold Ice Cream Reds

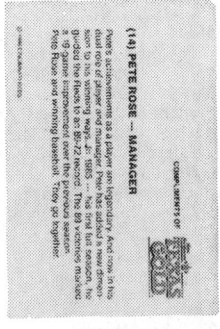

One of the last regional baseball card sets produced during the 1986 season was a 28-card team set sponsored by a Cincinnati-area ice cream company and given to fans attending a September 19th game. Photos on the 2-1/2" by 3-1/2" cards are game-action shots, and include three different cards of playing manager Pete Rose. The set is also notable for the inclusion of first cards of some of the Reds' young stars.

		MT	NR MT	EX
	Complete Set:	25.00	20.00	10.00
	Common Player:	.25	.20	.10

		MT	NR MT	EX
6	Bo Diaz	.35	.25	.14
9	Max Venable	.25	.20	.10
11	Kurt Stillwell	.80	.60	.30
12	Nick Esasky	.60	.45	.25
13	Dave Concepcion	.50	.40	.20
14a	Pete Rose (commemorative)	2.00	1.50	.80
14b	Pete Rose (infield)	2.00	1.50	.80
14c	Pete Rose (manager)	2.00	1.50	.80
16	Ron Oester	.25	.20	.10
20	Eddie Milner	.25	.20	.10
22	Sal Butera	.25	.20	.10
24	Tony Perez	.70	.50	.30
25	Buddy Bell	.35	.25	.14
28	Kal Daniels	1.50	1.25	.60
29	Tracy Jones	.80	.60	.30
31	John Franco	.80	.60	.30
32	Tom Browning	.60	.45	.25
33	Ron Robinson	.35	.25	.14
34	Bill Gullickson	.25	.20	.10
36	Mario Soto	.35	.25	.14
39	Dave Parker	1.00	.70	.40
40	John Denny	.25	.20	.10
44	Eric Davis	3.00	2.25	1.25
45	Chris Welsh	.25	.20	.10
48	Ted Power	.25	.20	.10
49	Joe Price	.25	.20	.10
----	Coaches Card (Scott Breeden, Billy DeMars, Tommy Helms, Bruce Kimm, Jim Lett, George Scherger)	.25	.20	.10
----	Logo/Coupon Card	.10	.08	.04

1983 Thorn Apple Valley Cubs

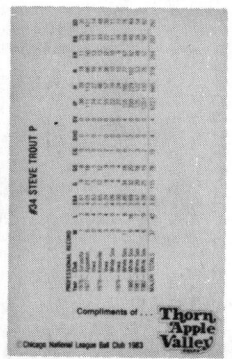

This set of 27 cards was issued in conjuction with a "Baseball Card Day" promotion at Wrigley Field in 1983. Thorn Apple Valley was the meat company which produced the hot dogs sold at the ballpark. The cards feature borderless color photos with the player's name, uniform number (also the card's number in the checklist) and an abbreviation for their position. Card backs feature annual statistics. Of the 27 cards, which measure 2-1/4" by 3-1/2", 25 feature players, one is a team card, and one features the manager and coaches.

		MT	NR MT	EX
Complete Set:		12.00	9.00	4.75
Common Player:		.20	.15	.08
1	Larry Bowa	.40	.30	.15
6	Keith Moreland	.40	.30	.15
7	Jody Davis	.40	.30	.15
10	Leon Durham	.40	.30	.15
11	Ron Cey	.40	.30	.15
16	Steve Lake	.20	.15	.08
20	Thad Bosley	.20	.15	.08
21	Jay Johnstone	.25	.20	.10
22	Bill Buckner	.40	.30	.15
23	Ryne Sandberg	3.00	2.25	1.25
24	Jerry Morales	.20	.15	.08
25	Gary Woods	.20	.15	.08
27	Mel Hall	.30	.25	.12
29	Tom Veryzer	.20	.15	.08
30	Chuck Rainey	.20	.15	.08
31	Fergie Jenkins	.70	.50	.30
32	Craig Lefferts	.30	.25	.12
33	Joe Carter	2.50	2.00	1.00

		MT	NR MT	EX
34	Steve Trout	.25	.20	.10
36	Mike Proly	.20	.15	.08
39	Bill Campbell	.20	.15	.08
41	Warren Brusstar	.20	.15	.08
44	Dick Ruthven	.20	.15	.08
46	Lee Smith	.50	.40	.20
48	Dickie Noles	.20	.15	.08
----	Coaching Staff (Ruben Amaro, Billy Connors, Duffy Dyer, Lee Elia, Fred Koenig, John Vukovich)	.20	.15	.08
----	Team Photo	.20	.15	.08

1948 Topps Magic Photos

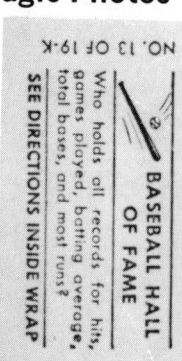

The first Topps baseball cards appeared as a subset of 19 cards from an issue of 252 "Magic Photos." The set takes its name from the self-developing nature of the cards. The cards were blank on the front when first taken from the wrapper. By spitting on the wrapper and holding it to the card while exposing it to light the black and white photo appeared. Measuring 7/8" by 1-1/2," the cards are very similar to Topps 1956 "Hocus Focus" issue.

		NR MT	EX	VG
Complete Set:		750.00	375.00	225.00
Common Player:		10.00	5.00	3.00
1	Lou Boudreau	20.00	10.00	6.00
2	Cleveland Indians	10.00	5.00	3.00
3	Bob Eliott	15.00	7.50	4.50
4	Cleveland Indians 4-3	10.00	5.00	3.00
5	Cleveland Indians 4-1 (Lou Boudreau Scoring)	20.00	10.00	6.00
6	"Babe" Ruth 714	150.00	75.00	45.00
7	Tris Speaker 793	25.00	12.50	7.50
8	Rogers Hornsby	50.00	25.00	15.00
9	Connie Mack	40.00	20.00	12.00
10	Christy Mathewson	50.00	25.00	15.00
11	Hans Wagner	50.00	25.00	15.00
12	Grover Alexander	30.00	15.00	9.00
13	Ty Cobb	100.00	50.00	30.00
14	Lou Gehrig	100.00	50.00	30.00
15	Walter Johnson	50.00	25.00	15.00
16	Cy Young	30.00	15.00	9.00
17	George Sisler 257	20.00	10.00	6.00
18	Tinker and Evers	20.00	10.00	6.00
19	Third Base Cleveland Indians	10.00	5.00	3.00

1951 Topps Blue Backs

Sold two cards in a package with a piece of candy for 1¢, the Topps Blue Backs are more scarce then their Red Back counterparts. The 2" by 2-5/8" cards carry a black and white player photograph on a red, white, yellow and green background along with the player's name and other information including their 1950 record on the front. The back is printed in blue on a white background. The 52-card set has varied baseball situations on them, making the playing of a rather elementary game of baseball possible. Although scarce, Blue Backs were printed on thick cardboard and have survived quite well over the

years. There are, however, few stars (Johnny Mize and Enos Slaughter are two) in the set. Despite being a Topps product, Blue Backs do not currently enjoy great popularity.

		NR MT	EX	VG
	Complete Set:	1900.00	950.00	575.00
	Common Player:	30.00	15.00	9.00
1	Eddie Yost	30.00	15.00	9.00
2	Henry (Hank) Majeski	30.00	15.00	9.00
3	Richie Ashburn	50.00	25.00	15.00
4	Del Ennis	30.00	15.00	9.00
5	Johnny Pesky	25.00	12.50	7.50
6	Albert (Red) Schoendienst	35.00	17.50	10.50
7	Gerald Staley	30.00	15.00	9.00
8	Dick Sisler	30.00	15.00	9.00
9	Johnny Sain	35.00	17.50	10.50
10	Joe Page	30.00	15.00	9.00
11	Johnny Groth	30.00	15.00	9.00
12	Sam Jethroe	30.00	15.00	9.00
13	James (Mickey) Vernon	25.00	12.50	7.50
14	George Munger	30.00	15.00	9.00
15	Eddie Joost	30.00	15.00	9.00
16	Murry Dickson	30.00	15.00	9.00
17	Roy Smalley	30.00	15.00	9.00
18	Ned Garver	30.00	15.00	9.00
19	Phil Masi	30.00	15.00	9.00
20	Ralph Branca	30.00	15.00	9.00
21	Billy Johnson	30.00	15.00	9.00
22	Bob Kuzava	30.00	15.00	9.00
23	Paul (Dizzy) Trout	30.00	15.00	9.00
24	Sherman Lollar	30.00	15.00	9.00
25	Sam Mele	30.00	15.00	9.00
26	Chico Carresquel (Carrasquel)	30.00	15.00	9.00
27	Andy Pafko	25.00	12.50	7.50
28	Harry (The Cat) Brecheen	30.00	15.00	9.00
29	Granville Hamner	30.00	15.00	9.00
30	Enos (Country) Slaughter	60.00	30.00	18.00
31	Lou Brissie	30.00	15.00	9.00
32	Bob Elliott	30.00	15.00	9.00
33	Don Lenhardt	30.00	15.00	9.00
34	Earl Torgeson	30.00	15.00	9.00
35	Tommy Byrne	30.00	15.00	9.00
36	Cliff Fannin	30.00	15.00	9.00
37	Bobby Doerr	55.00	27.00	16.50
38	Irv Noren	30.00	15.00	9.00
39	Ed Lopat	30.00	15.00	9.00
40	Vic Wertz	25.00	12.50	7.50
41	Johnny Schmitz	30.00	15.00	9.00
42	Bruce Edwards	30.00	15.00	9.00
43	Willie (Puddin' Head) Jones	30.00	15.00	9.00
44	Johnny Wyrostek	30.00	15.00	9.00
45	Bill Pierce	25.00	12.50	7.50
46	Gerry Priddy	30.00	15.00	9.00
47	Herman Wehmeier	30.00	15.00	9.00
48	Billy Cox	30.00	15.00	9.00
49	Henry (Hank) Sauer	30.00	15.00	9.00
50	Johnny Mize	60.00	30.00	18.00
51	Eddie Waitkus	30.00	15.00	9.00
52	Sam Chapman	30.00	15.00	9.00

1951 Topps Red Backs

Like the Blue Backs, the Topps Red Backs which were sold at the same time, came two to a package for 1¢. Their black and white photographs appear on

a red, white, blue and yellow background. The back printing is red on white. Their 2" by 2-5/8" size is the same as Blue Backs. Also identical is the set size (52 cards) and the game situations to be found on the fronts of the cards, for use in playing a card game of baseball. Red Backs are more common than the Blue Backs by virtue of a recent discovery of a large hoard of unopened boxes.

		NR MT	EX	VG
	Complete Set:	750.00	375.00	230.00
	Common Player:	9.00	4.50	2.75
1	Larry (Yogi) Berra	75.00	38.00	23.50
2	Sid Gordon	5.00	2.50	1.50
3	Ferris Fain	9.00	4.50	2.75
4	Verne Stephens (Vern)	9.00	4.50	2.75
5	Phil Rizzuto	25.00	12.50	7.50
6	Allie Reynolds	10.00	5.00	3.00
7	Howie Pollet	5.00	2.50	1.50
8	Early Wynn	25.00	12.50	7.50
9	Roy Sievers	9.00	4.50	2.75
10	Mel Parnell	9.00	4.50	2.75
11	Gene Hermanski	5.00	2.50	1.50
12	Jim Hegan	5.00	2.50	1.50
13	Dale Mitchell	5.00	2.50	1.50
14	Wayne Terwilliger	5.00	2.50	1.50
15	Ralph Kiner	25.00	12.50	7.50
16	Preacher Roe	8.00	4.00	2.50
17	Dave Bell	8.00	4.00	2.50
18	Gerry Coleman	8.00	4.00	2.50
19	Dick Kokos	5.00	2.50	1.50
20	Dominick DiMaggio (Dominic)	10.00	5.00	3.00
21	Larry Jansen	5.00	2.50	1.50
22	Bob Feller	25.00	12.50	7.50
23	Ray Boone	9.00	4.50	2.75
24	Hank Bauer	10.00	5.00	3.00
25	Cliff Chambers	5.00	2.50	1.50
26	Luke Easter	9.00	4.50	2.75
27	Wally Westlake	5.00	2.50	1.50
28	Elmer Valo	5.00	2.50	1.50
29	Bob Kennedy	5.00	2.50	1.50
30	Warren Spahn	25.00	12.50	7.50
31	Gil Hodges	25.00	12.50	7.50
32	Henry Thompson	5.00	2.50	1.50
33	William Werle	5.00	2.50	1.50
34	Grady Hatton	5.00	2.50	1.50
35	Al Rosen	10.00	5.00	3.00
36a	Gus Zernial (Chicago in bio)	20.00	10.00	6.00
36b	Gus Zernial (Philadelphia in bio)	12.00	6.00	3.50
37	Wes Westrum	9.00	4.50	2.75
38	Ed (Duke) Snider	60.00	30.00	17.50
39	Ted Kluszewski	10.00	5.00	3.00
40	Mike Garcia	9.00	4.50	2.75
41	Whitey Lockman	5.00	2.50	1.50
42	Ray Scarborough	5.00	2.50	1.50
43	Maurice McDermott	5.00	2.50	1.50
44	Sid Hudson	5.00	2.50	1.50
45	Andy Seminick	5.00	2.50	1.50
46	Billy Goodman	5.00	2.50	1.50
47	Tommy Glaviano	5.00	2.50	1.50
48	Eddie Stanky	9.00	4.50	2.75
49	Al Zarilla	5.00	2.50	1.50
50	Monte Irvin	25.00	12.50	7.50
51	Eddie Robinson	5.00	2.50	1.50
52a	Tommy Holmes (Boston in bio)	20.00	10.00	6.00
52b	Tommy Holmes (Hartford in bio)	20.00	10.00	6.00

1951 Topps
Connie Mack's All-Stars

A set of die-cut, 2-1/16" by 5-1/4" cards, all eleven players are Hall of Famers. The cards feature a black and white photograph of the player printed on a red background with a red, white, blue, yellow and black plaque underneath. Like the "Current All-Stars," with which they were issued, the background could be removed making it possible for the card to stand up. This practice, however, resulted in the card's mutilation and lowers its condition in the eyes of today's collectors. Connie Mack All-Stars are scarce today and, despite being relatively expensive, retain a certain popularity as one of Topps first issues.

		NR MT	EX	VG
Complete Set:		9500.00	4500.00	1950.
Common Player:		350.00	150.00	60.00
(1)	Grover Cleveland Alexander	550.00	275.00	100.00
(2)	Gordon Stanley Cochrane	400.00	175.00	75.00
(3)	Edward Trowbridge Collins	350.00	150.00	60.00
(4)	James J. Collins	350.00	150.00	60.00
(5)	Henry Louis Gehrig	2000.00	1000.00	350.00
(6)	Walter Johnson	750.00	325.00	150.00
(7)	Connie Mack	400.00	175.00	75.00
(8)	Christopher Mathewson	750.00	325.00	135.00
(9)	George Herman Ruth	2250.00	1150.00	450.00
(10)	Tristram Speaker	575.00	275.00	100.00
(11)	John Peter Wagner	500.00	225.00	100.00

1951 Topps Current All-Stars

The Topps Current All-Stars are very similar to the Connie Mack All-Stars of the same year. The 2-1/16 by 5-1/4" cards have a black and white photograph on a red die-cut background. Most of the background could be folded over or removed so that the card would stand up. A plaque at the base carries brief biographical information. The set was to contain 11 cards, but only eight were actually issued in gum packs. Those of Jim Konstanty, Robin Roberts and Eddie Stanky were not released and are very rare. A big problem with the set is that if the card was used as it was intended it was folded and, thus, damaged from a collector's viewpoint. That makes top quality examples of any players difficult to find and quite expensive.

		NR MT	EX	VG
Complete Set:		40000.00	20000.00	8500.
Common Player:		500.00	250.00	100.00
(1)	Lawrence (Yogi) Berra	1500.00	750.00	450.00
(2)	Lawrence Eugene Doby	750.00	375.00	150.00
(3)	Walter Dropo	750.00	375.00	150.00
(4)	Walter (Hoot) Evers	500.00	250.00	100.00
(5)	George Clyde Kell	1000.00	500.00	200.00
(6)	Ralph McPherran Kiner	1075.00	525.00	200.00
(7)	James Casimir Konstanty	8500.00	4250.00	2000.
(8)	Robert G. Lemon	1075.00	525.00	200.00
(9)	Phillip Rizzuto	1200.00	600.00	225.00
(10)	Robin Evan Roberts	9500.00	4750.00	2250.
(11)	Edward Raymond Stanky	8500.00	4250.00	2000.

1951 Topps Teams

An innovative issue for 1951, the Topps team cards were a nine-card set, 5-1/4" by 2-1/16," which carried a black and white picture of a major league team surrounded by a yellow border on the front. The back identifies team members with red printing on white cardboard. There are two versions of each card, with and without the date "1950" in the banner that carries the team name. Undated versions are valued slightly higher than the cards with dates. Strangely only nine teams were issued. Scarcity varies, with the Cardinals and Red Sox being the most difficult to obtain. The complete set price does not include the scarcer variations.

		NR MT	EX	VG
Complete Set:		4500.00	2200.00	975.00
Common Team:		150.00	70.00	30.00
(1a)	Boston Red Sox (1950)	250.00	100.00	50.00
(1b)	Boston Red Sox (without 1950)	300.00	125.00	60.00
(2a)	Brooklyn Dodgers (1950)	300.00	125.00	60.00
(2b)	Brooklyn Dodgers (without 1950)	350.00	150.00	70.00
(3a)	Chicago White Sox (1950)	150.00	75.00	45.00
(3b)	Chicago White Sox (without 1950)	200.00	85.00	40.00
(4a)	Cincinnati Reds (1950)	150.00	70.00	30.00
(4b)	Cincinnati Reds (without 1950)	200.00	85.00	40.00
(5a)	New York Giants (1950)	250.00	100.00	50.00
(5b)	New York Giants (without 1950)	300.00	125.00	60.00
(6a)	Philadelphia Athletics (1950)	150.00	70.00	30.00
(6b)	Philadelphia Athletics (without 1950)	200.00	85.00	40.00
(7a)	Philadelphia Phillies (1950)	150.00	70.00	30.00
(7b)	Philadelphia Phillies (without 1950)	200.00	85.00	40.00
(8a)	St. Louis Cardinals (1950)	150.00	70.00	40.00
(8b)	St. Louis Cardinals (without 1950)	200.00	85.00	40.00
(9a)	Washington Senators (1950)	150.00	70.00	30.00
(9b)	Washington Senators (without 1950)	200.00	85.00	40.00

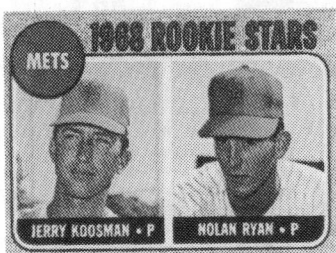

1952 Topps

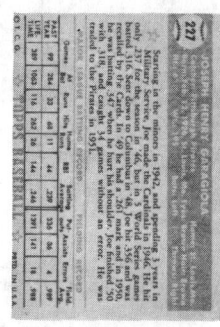

At 407 cards, the 1952 Topps set was the largest set of its day, both in number of cards and physical dimensions of the cards. Cards are 2-5/8" by 3-3/4" with a hand-colored black and white photo on front. Major baseball card innovations presented in the set include the first-ever use of color team logos as part of the design, and the inclusion of stats for the previous season and overall career on the backs. A major variety in the set is that first 80 cards can be found with backs printed entirely in black or black and red. Backs entirely in black command a $10-15 premium. Card numbers 311-407 were printed in limited supplies and are extremely rare.

	NR MT	EX	VG
Complete Set:	40000.00	16000.00	8000.
Common Player: 1-80	50.00	30.00	15.00
Common Player: 81-250	20.00	7.50	3.00
Common Player: 251-280	40.00	16.00	6.00
Common Player: 281-300	45.00	23.00	13.50
Common Player: 301-310	40.00	12.00	6.00
Common Player: 311-407	150.00	75.00	45.00

#	Player	NR MT	EX	VG
1	Andy Pafko	1200.00	150.00	25.00
2	*James E. Runnels*	80.00	20.00	6.00
3	Hank Thompson	55.00	15.00	5.50
4	Don Lenhardt	55.00	15.00	5.50
5	Larry Jansen	55.00	15.00	5.50
6	Grady Hatton	55.00	15.00	5.50
7	Wayne Terwilliger	60.00	16.00	6.00
8	Fred Marsh	55.00	15.00	5.50
9	Bobby Hogue	65.00	18.00	6.50
10	Al Rosen	80.00	24.00	8.00
11	Phil Rizzuto	175.00	45.00	15.00
12	Monty Basgall	55.00	15.00	5.50
13	Johnny Wyrostek	55.00	15.00	5.50
14	Bob Elliott	55.00	15.00	5.50
15	Johnny Pesky	60.00	16.00	6.00
16	Gene Hermanski	55.00	15.00	5.50
17	Jim Hegan	55.00	15.00	5.50
18	Merrill Combs	55.00	15.00	5.50
19	Johnny Bucha	55.00	15.00	5.50
20	*Billy Loes*	110.00	55.00	32.00
21	Ferris Fain	60.00	16.00	6.00
22	Dom DiMaggio	80.00	20.00	8.00
23	Billy Goodman	55.00	15.00	5.50
24	Luke Easter	60.00	16.00	6.00
25	Johnny Groth	55.00	15.00	5.50
26	Monty Irvin	90.00	27.00	9.00
27	Sam Jethroe	55.00	15.00	5.50
28	Jerry Priddy	55.00	15.00	5.50
29	Ted Kluszewski	80.00	24.00	8.00
30	Mel Parnell	60.00	16.00	6.00
31	Gus Zernial	60.00	16.00	6.00
32	Eddie Robinson	55.00	15.00	5.50
33	Warren Spahn	225.00	112.00	67.00
34	Elmer Valo	55.00	15.00	5.50
35	Hank Sauer	60.00	16.00	6.00
36	Gil Hodges	150.00	75.00	45.00
37	Duke Snider	250.00	100.00	63.00
38	Wally Westlake	55.00	15.00	5.50
39	"Dizzy" Trout	60.00	16.00	6.00
40	Irv Noren	55.00	15.00	5.50
41	Bob Wellman	55.00	15.00	5.50
42	Lou Kretlow	55.00	15.00	5.50
43	Ray Scarborough	55.00	15.00	5.50
44	Con Dempsey	55.00	15.00	5.50

#	Player	NR MT	EX	VG
45	Eddie Joost	55.00	15.00	5.50
46	Gordon Goldsberry	55.00	15.00	5.50
47	Willie Jones	55.00	15.00	5.50
48a	Joe Page (Johnny Sain bio)	225.00	68.00	23.00
48b	Joe Page (correct bio)	80.00	24.00	8.00
49a	Johnny Sain (Joe Page bio)	225.00	68.00	23.00
49b	Johnny Sain (correct bio)	80.00	24.00	8.00
50	Marv Rickert	55.00	15.00	5.50
51	Jim Russell	60.00	16.00	6.00
52	Don Mueller	55.00	15.00	5.50
53	Chris Van Cuyk	60.00	16.00	6.00
54	Leo Kiely	55.00	15.00	5.50
55	Ray Boone	60.00	16.00	6.00
56	Tommy Glaviano	55.00	15.00	5.50
57	Ed Lopat	80.00	24.00	8.00
58	Bob Mahoney	55.00	15.00	5.50
59	Robin Roberts	125.00	38.00	12.50
60	Sid Hudson	55.00	15.00	5.50
61	"Tookie" Gilbert	55.00	15.00	5.50
62	Chuck Stobbs	55.00	15.00	5.50
63	Howie Pollet	55.00	15.00	5.50
64	Roy Sievers	65.00	18.00	6.50
65	Enos Slaughter	125.00	56.00	35.00
66	"Preacher" Roe	100.00	50.00	30.00
67	Allie Reynolds	90.00	27.00	12.00
68	Cliff Chambers	55.00	15.00	5.50
69	Virgil Stallcup	55.00	15.00	5.50
70	Al Zarilla	55.00	15.00	5.50
71	Tom Upton	55.00	15.00	5.50
72	Karl Olson	55.00	15.00	5.50
73	William Werle	55.00	15.00	5.50
74	Andy Hansen	55.00	15.00	5.50
75	Wes Westrum	60.00	16.00	6.00
76	Eddie Stanky	65.00	18.00	6.50
77	Bob Kennedy	55.00	15.00	5.50
78	Ellis Kinder	55.00	15.00	5.50
79	Gerald Staley	55.00	15.00	5.50
80	Herman Wehmeier	55.00	15.00	5.50
81	Vernon Law	25.00	11.00	6.25
82	Duane Pillette	20.00	9.00	5.00
83	Billy Johnson	20.00	9.00	5.00
84	Vern Stephens	20.00	9.00	5.00
85	Bob Kuzava	30.00	13.50	7.50
86	Ted Gray	20.00	9.00	5.00
87	Dale Coogan	20.00	9.00	5.00
88	Bob Feller	125.00	56.00	35.00
89	Johnny Lipon	20.00	9.00	5.00
90	Mickey Grasso	20.00	9.00	5.00
91	Al Schoendienst	75.00	38.00	23.00
92	Dale Mitchell	20.00	9.00	5.00
93	Al Sima	20.00	9.00	5.00
94	Sam Mele	20.00	9.00	5.00
95	Ken Holcombe	20.00	9.00	5.00
96	Willard Marshall	20.00	9.00	5.00
97	Earl Torgeson	20.00	9.00	5.00
98	Bill Pierce	25.00	11.00	6.25
99	Gene Woodling	40.00	18.00	10.00
100	Del Rice	20.00	9.00	5.00
101	Max Lanier	20.00	9.00	5.00
102	Bill Kennedy	20.00	9.00	5.00
103	Cliff Mapes	20.00	9.00	5.00
104	Don Kolloway	20.00	9.00	5.00
105	John Pramesa	20.00	9.00	5.00
106	Mickey Vernon	25.00	11.00	6.25
107	Connie Ryan	20.00	9.00	5.00
108	Jim Konstanty	25.00	11.00	6.25
109	Ted Wilks	20.00	9.00	5.00
110	Dutch Leonard	20.00	9.00	5.00
111	Harry Lowrey	20.00	9.00	5.00
112	Henry Majeski	20.00	9.00	5.00
113	Dick Sisler	20.00	9.00	5.00
114	Willard Ramsdell	20.00	9.00	5.00
115	George Munger	20.00	9.00	5.00
116	Carl Scheib	20.00	9.00	5.00
117	Sherman Lollar	25.00	11.00	6.25
118	Ken Raffensberger	20.00	9.00	5.00
119	Maurice McDermott	20.00	9.00	5.00
120	Bob Chakales	20.00	9.00	5.00
121	Gus Niarhos	20.00	9.00	5.00
122	Jack Jensen	70.00	35.00	21.00
123	Eddie Yost	25.00	11.00	6.25
124	Monte Kennedy	20.00	9.00	5.00
125	Bill Rigney	25.00	11.00	6.25
126	Fred Hutchinson	25.00	11.00	6.25
127	Paul Minner	20.00	9.00	5.00
128	Don Bollweg	30.00	13.50	7.50
129	Johnny Mize	70.00	35.00	21.00
130	Sheldon Jones	20.00	9.00	5.00
131	Morrie Martin	20.00	9.00	5.00
132	Clyde Kluttz	20.00	9.00	5.00
133	Al Widmar	20.00	9.00	5.00

#	Player	NR MT	EX	VG
134	Joe Tipton	20.00	9.00	5.00
135	Dixie Howell	20.00	9.00	5.00
136	Johnny Schmitz	25.00	11.00	6.25
137	*Roy McMillan*	25.00	11.00	6.25
138	Bill MacDonald	20.00	9.00	5.00
139	Ken Wood	20.00	9.00	5.00
140	John Antonelli	25.00	11.00	6.25
141	Clint Hartung	20.00	9.00	5.00
142	Harry Perkowski	20.00	9.00	5.00
143	Les Moss	20.00	9.00	5.00
144	Ed Blake	20.00	9.00	5.00
145	Joe Haynes	20.00	9.00	5.00
146	Frank House	20.00	9.00	5.00
147	Bob Young	20.00	9.00	5.00
148	Johnny Klippstein	20.00	9.00	5.00
149	Dick Kryhoski	20.00	9.00	5.00
150	Ted Beard	20.00	9.00	5.00
151	Wally Post	20.00	9.00	5.00
152	Al Evans	20.00	9.00	5.00
153	Bob Rush	20.00	9.00	5.00
154	Joe Muir	20.00	9.00	5.00
155	Frank Overmire	30.00	13.50	7.50
156	Frank Hiller	20.00	9.00	5.00
157	Bob Usher	20.00	9.00	5.00
158	Eddie Waitkus	20.00	9.00	5.00
159	Saul Rogovin	20.00	9.00	5.00
160	Owen Friend	20.00	9.00	5.00
161	Bud Byerly	20.00	9.00	5.00
162	Del Crandall	25.00	11.00	6.25
163	Stan Rojek	20.00	9.00	5.00
164	Walt Dubiel	20.00	9.00	5.00
165	Eddie Kazak	20.00	9.00	5.00
166	Paul LaPalme	20.00	9.00	5.00
167	Bill Howerton	20.00	9.00	5.00
168	Charlie Silvera	30.00	13.50	7.50
169	Howie Judson	20.00	9.00	5.00
170	Gus Bell	25.00	11.00	6.25
171	Ed Erautt	20.00	9.00	5.00
172	Eddie Miksis	20.00	9.00	5.00
173	Roy Smalley	20.00	9.00	5.00
174	Clarence Marshall	20.00	9.00	5.00
175	*Billy Martin*	300.00	150.00	90.00
176	Hank Edwards	20.00	9.00	5.00
177	Bill Wight	20.00	9.00	5.00
178	Cass Michaels	20.00	9.00	5.00
179	Frank Smith	20.00	9.00	5.00
180	*Charley Maxwell*	25.00	11.00	6.25
181	Bob Swift	20.00	9.00	5.00
182	Billy Hitchcock	20.00	9.00	5.00
183	Erv Dusak	20.00	9.00	5.00
184	Bob Ramazzotti	20.00	9.00	5.00
185	Bill Nicholson	20.00	9.00	5.00
186	Walt Masterson	20.00	9.00	5.00
187	Bob Miller	20.00	9.00	5.00
188	Clarence Podbielan	25.00	11.00	6.25
189	Pete Reiser	25.00	11.00	6.25
190	Don Johnson	20.00	9.00	5.00
191	Yogi Berra	375.00	187.00	112.00
192	Myron Ginsberg	20.00	9.00	5.00
193	Harry Simpson	20.00	9.00	5.00
194	Joe Hatten	20.00	9.00	5.00
195	*Orestes Minoso*	70.00	35.00	20.00
196	Solly Hemus	20.00	9.00	5.00
197	George Strickland	20.00	9.00	5.00
198	Phil Haugstad	25.00	11.00	6.25
199	George Zuverink	20.00	9.00	5.00
200	Ralph Houk	50.00	23.00	12.50
201	Alex Kellner	20.00	9.00	5.00
202	Joe Collins	30.00	13.50	7.50
203	Curt Simmons	25.00	11.00	6.25
204	Ron Northey	20.00	9.00	5.00
205	Clyde King	25.00	11.00	6.25
206	Joe Ostrowski	30.00	13.50	7.50
207	Mickey Harris	20.00	9.00	5.00
208	Marlin Stuart	20.00	9.00	5.00
209	Howie Fox	20.00	9.00	5.00
210	Dick Fowler	20.00	9.00	5.00
211	Ray Coleman	20.00	9.00	5.00
212	Ned Garver	20.00	9.00	5.00
213	Nippy Jones	20.00	9.00	5.00
214	Johnny Hopp	30.00	13.50	7.50
215	Hank Bauer	40.00	18.00	10.00
216	Richie Ashburn	60.00	30.00	18.00
217	George Stirnweiss	20.00	9.00	5.00
218	Clyde McCullough	20.00	9.00	5.00
219	Bobby Shantz	25.00	11.00	6.25
220	Joe Presko	20.00	9.00	5.00
221	Granny Hamner	20.00	9.00	5.00
222	"Hoot" Evers	20.00	9.00	5.00
223	Del Ennis	25.00	11.00	6.25
224	Bruce Edwards	20.00	9.00	5.00
225	Frank Baumholtz	20.00	9.00	5.00
226	Dave Philley	25.00	11.00	6.25
227	Joe Garagiola	125.00	62.00	37.00
228	Al Brazle	20.00	9.00	5.00
229	Gene Bearden	20.00	9.00	5.00
230	Matt Batts	20.00	9.00	5.00
231	Sam Zoldak	20.00	9.00	5.00
232	Billy Cox	30.00	13.50	7.50
233	*Bob Friend*	25.00	11.00	6.25
234	Steve Souchock	20.00	9.00	5.00
235	Walt Dropo	25.00	11.00	6.25
236	Ed Fitz Gerald	20.00	9.00	5.00
237	Jerry Coleman	30.00	13.50	7.50
238	Art Houtteman	20.00	9.00	5.00
239	Rocky Bridges	25.00	11.00	6.25
240	Jack Phillips	20.00	9.00	5.00
241	Tommy Byrne	20.00	9.00	5.00
242	Tom Poholsky	20.00	9.00	5.00
243	Larry Doby	40.00	16.00	9.00
244	Vic Wertz	25.00	11.00	6.25
245	Sherry Robertson	20.00	9.00	5.00
246	George Kell	50.00	23.00	12.50
247	Randy Gumpert	20.00	9.00	5.00
248	Frank Shea	20.00	9.00	5.00
249	Bobby Adams	20.00	9.00	5.00
250	Carl Erskine	50.00	30.00	15.00
251	Chico Carrasquel	40.00	16.00	6.00
252	Vern Bickford	40.00	16.00	6.00
253	Johnny Berardino	50.00	18.00	7.50
254	Joe Dobson	40.00	16.00	6.00
255	Clyde Vollmer	40.00	16.00	6.00
256	Pete Suder	40.00	16.00	6.00
257	Bobby Avila	40.00	16.00	6.00
258	Steve Gromek	40.00	16.00	6.00
259	Bob Addis	40.00	16.00	6.00
260	Pete Castiglione	40.00	16.00	6.00
261	Willie Mays	1200.00	600.00	350.00
262	Virgil Trucks	45.00	18.00	6.75
263	Harry Brecheen	45.00	18.00	6.75
264	Roy Hartsfield	40.00	16.00	6.00
265	Chuck Diering	40.00	16.00	6.00
266	Murry Dickson	40.00	16.00	6.00
267	Sid Gordon	40.00	16.00	6.00
268	Bob Lemon	200.00	100.00	60.00
269	Willard Nixon	40.00	16.00	6.00
270	Lou Brissie	40.00	16.00	6.00
271	Jim Delsing	40.00	16.00	6.00
272	Mike Garcia	45.00	18.00	6.75
273	Erv Palica	45.00	18.00	6.75
274	Ralph Branca	60.00	25.00	9.00
275	Pat Mullin	40.00	16.00	6.00
276	Jim Wilson	40.00	16.00	6.00
277	Early Wynn	150.00	75.00	45.00
278	Al Clark	40.00	16.00	6.00
279	Ed Stewart	40.00	16.00	6.00
280	Cloyd Boyer	40.00	16.00	6.00
281	Tommy Brown	50.00	20.00	7.50
282	Birdie Tebbetts	50.00	20.00	7.50
283	Phil Masi	50.00	20.00	7.50
284	Hank Arft	50.00	20.00	7.50
285	Cliff Fannin	50.00	20.00	7.50
286	Joe DeMaestri	50.00	20.00	7.50
287	Steve Bilko	50.00	20.00	7.50
288	Chet Nichols	50.00	20.00	7.50
289	Tommy Holmes	55.00	25.00	8.25
290	Joe Astroth	50.00	20.00	7.50
291	Gil Coan	50.00	20.00	7.50
292	Floyd Baker	50.00	20.00	7.50
293	Sibby Sisti	50.00	20.00	7.50
294	Walker Cooper	50.00	20.00	7.50
295	Phil Cavarretta	55.00	22.00	8.25
296	"Red" Rolfe	50.00	20.00	7.50
297	Andy Seminick	50.00	20.00	7.50
298	Bob Ross	50.00	20.00	7.50
299	Ray Murray	50.00	20.00	7.50
300	Barney McCosky	50.00	20.00	7.50
301	Bob Porterfield	40.00	16.00	6.00
302	Max Surkont	40.00	16.00	6.00
303	Harry Dorish	40.00	16.00	6.00
304	Sam Dente	40.00	16.00	6.00
305	Paul Richards	45.00	18.00	6.75
306	Lou Sleator	40.00	16.00	6.00
307	Frank Campos	40.00	16.00	6.00
308	Luis Aloma	40.00	16.00	6.00
309	Jim Busby	40.00	16.00	6.00
310	George Metkovich	40.00	16.00	6.00
311	Mickey Mantle	9000.00	4500.00	2750.
312	Jackie Robinson	875.00	435.00	245.00
313	Bobby Thomson	150.00	75.00	45.00
314	Roy Campanella	1400.00	700.00	375.00
315	Leo Durocher	250.00	100.00	63.00

		NR MT	EX	VG
316	Davey Williams	150.00	75.00	45.00
317	Connie Marrero	150.00	75.00	45.00
318	Hal Gregg	150.00	75.00	45.00
319	Al Walker	150.00	75.00	45.00
320	John Rutherford	150.00	75.00	45.00
321	*Joe Black*	225.00	90.00	56.00
322	Randy Jackson	150.00	75.00	45.00
323	Bubba Church	150.00	75.00	45.00
324	Warren Hacker	150.00	75.00	45.00
325	Bill Serena	150.00	75.00	45.00
326	George Shuba	150.00	75.00	45.00
327	Archie Wilson	150.00	75.00	45.00
328	Bob Borkowski	150.00	75.00	45.00
329	Ivan Delock	150.00	75.00	45.00
330	Turk Lown	150.00	75.00	45.00
331	Tom Morgan	160.00	80.00	48.00
332	Tony Bartirome	150.00	75.00	45.00
333	Pee Wee Reese	750.00	375.00	230.00
334	Wilmer Mizell	150.00	75.00	45.00
335	Ted Lepcio	150.00	75.00	45.00
336	Dave Koslo	150.00	75.00	45.00
337	Jim Hearn	150.00	75.00	45.00
338	Sal Yvars	150.00	75.00	45.00
339	Russ Meyer	150.00	75.00	45.00
340	Bob Hooper	150.00	75.00	45.00
341	Hal Jeffcoat	150.00	75.00	45.00
342	*Clem Labine*	200.00	90.00	52.00
343	Dick Gernert	150.00	75.00	45.00
344	Ewell Blackwell	160.00	80.00	48.00
345	Sam White	150.00	75.00	45.00
346	George Spencer	150.00	75.00	45.00
347	Joe Adcock	200.00	100.00	60.00
348	Bob Kelly	150.00	75.00	45.00
349	Bob Cain	150.00	75.00	45.00
350	Cal Abrams	150.00	75.00	45.00
351	Al Dark	200.00	90.00	52.00
352	Karl Drews	150.00	75.00	45.00
353	Bob Del Greco	150.00	75.00	45.00
354	Fred Hatfield	150.00	75.00	45.00
355	Bobby Morgan	150.00	75.00	45.00
356	Toby Atwell	150.00	75.00	45.00
357	Smoky Burgess	175.00	90.00	48.00
358	John Kucab	150.00	75.00	45.00
359	Dee Fondy	150.00	75.00	45.00
360	George Crowe	150.00	75.00	45.00
361	Bill Posedel	150.00	75.00	45.00
362	Ken Heintzelman	150.00	75.00	45.00
363	Dick Rozek	150.00	75.00	45.00
364	Clyde Sukeforth	150.00	75.00	45.00
365	"Cookie" Lavagetto	150.00	75.00	45.00
366	Dave Madison	150.00	75.00	45.00
367	Bob Thorpe	150.00	75.00	45.00
368	Ed Wright	150.00	75.00	45.00
369	*Dick Groat*	250.00	125.00	60.00
370	Billy Hoeft	150.00	75.00	45.00
371	Bob Hofman	150.00	75.00	45.00
372	*Gil McDougald*	250.00	120.00	67.00
373	Jim Turner	160.00	80.00	48.00
374	Al Benton	150.00	75.00	45.00
375	Jack Merson	150.00	75.00	45.00
376	Faye Throneberry	150.00	75.00	45.00
377	Chuck Dressen	175.00	90.00	52.00
378	Les Fusselman	150.00	75.00	45.00
379	Joe Rossi	150.00	75.00	45.00
380	Clem Koshorek	150.00	75.00	45.00
381	Milton Stock	150.00	75.00	45.00
382	Sam Jones	150.00	75.00	45.00
383	Del Wilber	150.00	75.00	45.00
384	Frank Crosetti	250.00	125.00	67.00
385	Herman Franks	150.00	75.00	45.00
386	Eddie Yuhas	150.00	75.00	45.00
387	Billy Meyer	150.00	75.00	45.00
388	Bob Chipman	150.00	75.00	45.00
389	Ben Wade	150.00	75.00	45.00
390	Glenn Nelson	150.00	75.00	45.00
391	Ben Chapman (photo actually Sam Chapman)	150.00	75.00	45.00
392	*Hoyt Wilhelm*	400.00	190.00	112.00
393	Ebba St. Claire	150.00	75.00	45.00
394	Billy Herman	200.00	90.00	52.00
395	Jake Pitler	150.00	75.00	45.00
396	*Dick Williams*	225.00	112.00	68.00
397	Forrest Main	150.00	75.00	45.00
398	Hal Rice	150.00	75.00	45.00
399	Jim Fridley	150.00	75.00	45.00
400	Bill Dickey	500.00	225.00	135.00
401	Bob Schultz	150.00	75.00	45.00
402	Earl Harrist	150.00	75.00	45.00
403	Bill Miller	160.00	80.00	48.00
404	Dick Brodowski	150.00	75.00	45.00
405	Eddie Pellagrini	150.00	75.00	45.00

		NR MT	EX	VG
406	*Joe Nuxhall*	175.00	87.00	52.00
407	*Ed Mathews*	2000.00	1000.00	600.00

1953 Topps

The 1953 Topps set reflects the company's continuing legal battles with Bowman. The set, originally intended to consist of 280 cards, is lacking six numbers (#'s 253, 261, 267, 268, 271 and 275) which probably represent players whose contracts were lost to the competition. The 2-5/8" by 3-3/4" cards feature painted player pictures. A color team logo appears at a bottom panel (red for American Leaugue and black for National.) Card backs contain the first baseball trivia questions along with brief statistics and player biographies. In the red panel at the top which lists the player's personal data, cards from the 2nd Series (#'s 86-165 plus 10, 44, 61, 72 and 81) can be found with that data printed in either black or white, black being the scarcer variety. Card numbers 221-280 are the scarce high numbers.

	NR MT	EX	VG
Complete Set:	12000.00	6000.00	3600.
Common Player Singleprint: 1-165	25.00	12.50	7.50
Common Player: 1-165	20.00	10.00	6.00
Common Player: 166-220	18.00	9.00	5.50
Common Player Singleprint: 221-280	90.00	45.00	27.00
Common Player: 221-280	45.00	23.00	13.50

		NR MT	EX	VG
1	Jackie Robinson	600.00	240.00	150.00
2	Luke Easter	25.00	12.50	7.50
3	George Crowe	25.00	12.50	7.50
4	Ben Wade	25.00	12.50	7.50
5	Joe Dobson	25.00	12.50	7.50
6	Sam Jones	25.00	12.50	7.50
7	Bob Borkowski	20.00	10.00	6.00
8	Clem Koshorek	20.00	10.00	6.00
9	Joe Collins	30.00	15.00	9.00
10	Smoky Burgess	30.00	15.00	9.00
11	Sal Yvars	25.00	12.50	7.50
12	Howie Judson	20.00	10.00	6.00
13	Connie Marrero	20.00	10.00	6.00
14	Clem Labine	25.00	12.50	7.50
15	Bobo Newsom	25.00	12.50	7.50
16	Harry Lowrey	20.00	10.00	6.00
17	Billy Hitchcock	25.00	12.50	7.50
18	Ted Lepcio	20.00	10.00	6.00
19	Mel Parnell	20.00	10.00	6.00
20	Hank Thompson	25.00	12.50	7.50
21	Billy Johnson	25.00	12.50	7.50
22	Howie Fox	20.00	10.00	6.00
23	Toby Atwell	20.00	10.00	6.00
24	Ferris Fain	25.00	12.50	7.50
25	Ray Boone	25.00	12.50	7.50
26	Dale Mitchell	20.00	10.00	6.00
27	Roy Campanella	200.00	80.00	50.00
28	Eddie Pellagrini	25.00	12.50	7.50
29	Hal Jeffcoat	25.00	12.50	7.50
30	Willard Nixon	25.00	12.50	7.50
31	Ewell Blackwell	40.00	20.00	12.00
32	Clyde Vollmer	25.00	12.50	7.50
33	Bob Kennedy	20.00	10.00	6.00
34	George Shuba	25.00	12.50	7.50
35	Irv Noren	25.00	12.50	7.50
36	Johnny Groth	20.00	10.00	6.00
37	Ed Mathews	100.00	50.00	30.00

		NR MT	EX	VG			NR MT	EX	VG
38	Jim Hearn	20.00	10.00	6.00	131	Harry Byrd	20.00	10.00	6.00
39	Eddie Miksis	25.00	12.50	7.50	132	Tom Morgan	25.00	12.50	7.50
40	John Lipon	25.00	12.50	7.50	133	Gil Coan	20.00	10.00	6.00
41	Enos Slaughter	90.00	45.00	27.00	134	Rube Walker	25.00	12.50	7.50
42	Gus Zernial	20.00	10.00	6.00	135	Al Rosen	35.00	17.50	10.50
43	Gil McDougald	40.00	20.00	12.00	136	Ken Heintzelman	20.00	10.00	6.00
44	Ellis Kinder	30.00	15.00	9.00	137	John Rutherford	25.00	12.50	7.50
45	Grady Hatton	20.00	10.00	6.00	138	George Kell	60.00	30.00	18.00
46	Johnny Klippstein	20.00	10.00	6.00	139	Sammy White	20.00	10.00	6.00
47	Bubba Church	20.00	10.00	6.00	140	Tommy Glaviano	20.00	10.00	6.00
48	Bob Del Greco	20.00	10.00	6.00	141	Allie Reynolds	35.00	17.50	10.50
49	Faye Throneberry	20.00	10.00	6.00	142	Vic Wertz	25.00	12.50	7.50
50	Chuck Dressen	25.00	12.50	7.50	143	Billy Pierce	25.00	12.50	7.50
51	Frank Campos	20.00	10.00	6.00	144	Bob Schultz	20.00	10.00	6.00
52	Ted Gray	20.00	10.00	6.00	145	Harry Dorish	20.00	10.00	6.00
53	Sherman Lollar	20.00	10.00	6.00	146	Granville Hamner	20.00	10.00	6.00
54	Bob Feller	100.00	50.00	30.00	147	Warren Spahn	110.00	50.00	28.00
55	Maurice McDermott	20.00	10.00	6.00	148	Mickey Grasso	20.00	10.00	6.00
56	Gerald Staley	20.00	10.00	6.00	149	Dom DiMaggio	25.00	12.50	7.50
57	Carl Scheib	25.00	12.50	7.50	150	Harry Simpson	20.00	10.00	6.00
58	George Metkovich	25.00	12.50	7.50	151	Hoyt Wilhelm	60.00	30.00	18.00
59	Karl Drews	20.00	10.00	6.00	152	Bob Adams	20.00	10.00	6.00
60	Cloyd Boyer	20.00	10.00	6.00	153	Andy Seminick	20.00	10.00	6.00
61	Early Wynn	85.00	42.00	25.00	154	Dick Groat	25.00	12.50	7.50
62	Monte Irvin	40.00	20.00	12.00	155	Dutch Leonard	20.00	10.00	6.00
63	Gus Niarhos	20.00	10.00	6.00	156	Jim Rivera	20.00	10.00	6.00
64	Dave Philley	25.00	12.50	7.50	157	Bob Addis	20.00	10.00	6.00
65	Earl Harrist	25.00	12.50	7.50	158	*John Logan*	25.00	12.50	7.50
66	Orestes Minoso	30.00	15.00	9.00	159	Wayne Terwilliger	20.00	10.00	6.00
67	Roy Sievers	25.00	12.50	7.50	160	Bob Young	20.00	10.00	6.00
68	Del Rice	25.00	12.50	7.50	161	Vern Bickford	20.00	10.00	6.00
69	Dick Brodowski	25.00	12.50	7.50	162	Ted Kluszewski	35.00	17.50	10.50
70	Ed Yuhas	25.00	12.50	7.50	163	Fred Hatfield	20.00	10.00	6.00
71	Tony Bartirome	25.00	12.50	7.50	164	Frank Shea	20.00	10.00	6.00
72	Fred Hutchinson	25.00	12.50	7.50	165	Billy Hoeft	20.00	10.00	6.00
73	Eddie Robinson	25.00	12.50	7.50	166	Bill Hunter	18.00	9.00	5.50
74	Joe Rossi	25.00	12.50	7.50	167	Art Schult	20.00	10.00	6.00
75	Mike Garcia	25.00	12.50	7.50	168	Willard Schmidt	18.00	9.00	5.50
76	Pee Wee Reese	150.00	75.00	45.00	169	Dizzy Trout	20.00	10.00	6.00
77	John Mize	75.00	37.00	22.00	170	Bill Werle	18.00	9.00	5.50
78	Al Schoendienst	65.00	33.00	20.00	171	Bill Glynn	18.00	9.00	5.50
79	Johnny Wyrostek	25.00	12.50	7.50	172	Rip Repulski	18.00	9.00	5.50
80	Jim Hegan	25.00	12.50	7.50	173	Preston Ward	18.00	9.00	5.50
82	Mickey Mantle	2000.00	1000.00	600.00	174	Billy Loes	20.00	10.00	6.00
83	Howie Pollet	25.00	12.50	7.50	175	Ron Kline	18.00	9.00	5.50
84	Bob Hooper	20.00	10.00	6.00	176	*Don Hoak*	20.00	10.00	6.00
85	Bobby Morgan	25.00	12.50	7.50	177	Jim Dyck	18.00	9.00	5.50
86	Billy Martin	90.00	45.00	27.50	178	Jim Waugh	18.00	9.00	5.50
87	Ed Lopat	35.00	17.50	10.50	179	Gene Hermanski	18.00	9.00	5.50
88	Willie Jones	20.00	10.00	6.00	180	Virgil Stallcup	18.00	9.00	5.50
89	Chuck Stobbs	20.00	10.00	6.00	181	Al Zarilla	18.00	9.00	5.50
90	Hank Edwards	20.00	10.00	6.00	182	Bob Hofman	18.00	9.00	5.50
91	Ebba St. Claire	20.00	10.00	6.00	183	*Stu Miller*	20.00	10.00	6.00
92	Paul Minner	20.00	10.00	6.00	184	*Hal Brown*	20.00	10.00	6.00
93	Hal Rice	20.00	10.00	6.00	185	Jim Pendleton	18.00	9.00	5.50
94	William Kennedy	20.00	10.00	6.00	186	Charlie Bishop	18.00	9.00	5.50
95	Willard Marshall	20.00	10.00	6.00	187	Jim Fridley	18.00	9.00	5.50
96	Virgil Trucks	25.00	12.50	7.50	188	*Andy Carey*	20.00	10.00	6.00
97	Don Kolloway	20.00	10.00	6.00	189	Ray Jablonski	18.00	9.00	5.50
98	Cal Abrams	20.00	10.00	6.00	190	Dixie Walker	20.00	10.00	6.00
99	Dave Madison	20.00	10.00	6.00	191	Ralph Kiner	50.00	25.00	15.00
100	Bill Miller	25.00	12.50	7.50	192	Wally Westlake	18.00	9.00	5.50
101	Ted Wilks	20.00	10.00	6.00	193	Mike Clark	18.00	9.00	5.50
102	Connie Ryan	20.00	10.00	6.00	194	Eddie Kazak	18.00	9.00	5.50
103	Joe Astroth	20.00	10.00	6.00	195	Ed McGhee	18.00	9.00	5.50
104	Yogi Berra	200.00	100.00	60.00	196	Bob Keegan	18.00	9.00	5.50
105	Joe Nuxhall	25.00	12.50	7.50	197	Del Crandall	20.00	10.00	6.00
106	Johnny Antonelli	25.00	12.50	7.50	198	Forrest Main	18.00	9.00	5.50
107	Danny O'Connell	20.00	10.00	6.00	199	Marion Fricano	18.00	9.00	5.50
108	Bob Porterfield	20.00	10.00	6.00	200	Gordon Goldsberry	18.00	9.00	5.50
109	Alvin Dark	30.00	15.00	9.00	201	Paul LaPalme	18.00	9.00	5.50
110	Herman Wehmeier	20.00	10.00	6.00	202	Carl Sawatski	18.00	9.00	5.50
111	Hank Sauer	16.00	8.00	4.75	203	Cliff Fannin	18.00	9.00	5.50
112	Ned Garver	20.00	10.00	6.00	204	Dick Bokelmann	18.00	9.00	5.50
113	Jerry Priddy	20.00	10.00	6.00	205	Vern Benson	18.00	9.00	5.50
114	Phil Rizzuto	90.00	45.00	27.00	206	*Ed Bailey*	20.00	10.00	6.00
115	George Spencer	20.00	10.00	6.00	207	Whitey Ford	125.00	62.00	37.00
116	Frank Smith	20.00	10.00	6.00	208	Jim Wilson	18.00	9.00	5.50
117	Sid Gordon	20.00	10.00	6.00	209	Jim Greengrass	18.00	9.00	5.50
118	Gus Bell	16.00	8.00	4.75	210	*Bob Cerv*	20.00	10.00	6.00
119	John Sain	40.00	20.00	12.00	211	J.W. Porter	18.00	9.00	5.50
120	Davey Williams	20.00	10.00	6.00	212	Jack Dittmer	18.00	9.00	5.50
121	Walt Dropo	20.00	10.00	6.00	213	Ray Scarborough	20.00	10.00	6.00
122	Elmer Valo	20.00	10.00	6.00	214	Bill Bruton	20.00	10.00	6.00
123	Tommy Byrne	20.00	10.00	6.00	215	*Gene Conley*	20.00	10.00	6.00
124	Sibby Sisti	20.00	10.00	6.00	216	Jim Hughes	20.00	10.00	6.00
125	Dick Williams	25.00	12.50	7.50	217	Murray Wall	18.00	9.00	5.50
126	Bill Connelly	20.00	10.00	6.00	218	Les Fusselman	18.00	9.00	5.50
127	Clint Courtney	20.00	10.00	6.00	219	Pete Runnels (photo actually Don Johnson)	20.00	10.00	6.00
128	Wilmer Mizell	20.00	10.00	6.00					
129	Keith Thomas	20.00	10.00	6.00	220	Satchell Paige	400.00	200.00	120.00
130	Turk Lown	20.00	10.00	6.00					

		NR MT	EX	VG
221	Bob Milliken	90.00	45.00	27.00
222	Vic Janowicz	45.00	23.00	13.50
223	John O'Brien	45.00	23.00	13.50
224	Lou Sleater	45.00	23.00	13.50
225	Bobby Shantz	60.00	30.00	18.00
226	Ed Erautt	90.00	45.00	27.00
227	Morris Martin	45.00	23.00	13.50
228	Hal Newhouser	100.00	45.00	27.00
229	Rocky Krsnich	90.00	45.00	27.00
230	Johnny Lindell	45.00	23.00	13.50
231	Solly Hemus	45.00	23.00	13.50
232	Dick Kokos	90.00	45.00	27.00
233	Al Aber	90.00	45.00	27.00
234	Ray Murray	45.00	23.00	13.50
235	John Hetki	45.00	23.00	13.50
236	Harry Perkowski	90.00	45.00	27.00
237	Clarence Podbielan	45.00	23.00	13.50
238	Cal Hogue	45.00	23.00	13.50
239	Jim Delsing	90.00	45.00	27.00
240	Freddie Marsh	45.00	23.00	13.50
241	Al Sima	45.00	23.00	13.50
242	Charlie Silvera	90.00	45.00	27.00
243	Carlos Bernier	45.00	23.00	13.50
244	Willie Mays	1600.00	800.00	475.00
245	Bill Norman	90.00	45.00	27.00
246	Roy Face	90.00	45.00	27.00
247	Mike Sandlock	45.00	23.00	13.50
248	Gene Stephens	45.00	23.00	13.50
249	Ed O'Brien	45.00	23.00	13.50
250	Bob Wilson	90.00	45.00	27.00
251	Sid Hudson	90.00	45.00	27.00
252	Henry Foiles	90.00	45.00	27.00
253	Not Issued			
254	Preacher Roe	80.00	40.00	24.00
255	Dixie Howell	90.00	45.00	27.00
256	Les Peden	90.00	45.00	27.00
257	Bob Boyd	90.00	45.00	27.00
258	Jim Gilliam	350.00	175.00	105.00
259	Roy McMillan	90.00	45.00	27.00
260	Sam Calderone	90.00	45.00	27.00
261	Not Issued			
262	Bob Oldis	90.00	45.00	27.00
263	John Podres	300.00	150.00	90.00
264	Gene Woodling	60.00	30.00	18.00
265	Jackie Jensen	150.00	75.00	45.00
266	Bob Cain	90.00	45.00	27.00
267	Not Issued			
268	Not Issued			
269	Duane Pillette	90.00	45.00	27.00
270	Vern Stephens	90.00	45.00	27.00
271	Not Issued			
272	Bill Antonello	90.00	45.00	27.00
273	Harvey Haddix	125.00	62.00	37.00
274	John Riddle	90.00	45.00	27.00
275	Not Issued			
276	Ken Raffensberger	45.00	23.00	13.50
277	Don Lund	90.00	45.00	27.00
278	Willie Miranda	90.00	45.00	27.00
279	Joe Coleman	45.00	23.00	13.50
280	Milt Bolling	500.00	175.00	75.00

1954 Topps

The first issue to use two player pictures on the front, the 1954 Topps set is very popular today. Solid color backgrounds frame both color head- and-shoulders and black and white action pictures of the player. The player's name, position, team and team logo appear at the top. Backs include an "Inside Baseball" cartoon regarding the player as well as statistics and biography. The 250-card, 2-5/8" by 3-3/4", set includes manager and coaches cards, and the first use of two players together on a modern card; the players were, appropriately, the O'Brien twins.

		NR MT	EX	VG
Complete Set:		7500.00	3750.00	2250.00
Common Player: 1-50		15.00	7.50	4.50
Common Player: 51-75		35.00	17.50	10.50
Common Player: 76-250		15.00	7.50	4.50
1	Ted Williams	600.00	150.00	90.00
2	Gus Zernial	15.00	7.50	4.50
3	Monte Irvin	30.00	15.00	9.00
4	Hank Sauer	35.00	17.50	10.50
5	Ed Lopat	20.00	10.00	6.00
6	Pete Runnels	15.00	7.50	4.50
7	Ted Kluszewski	35.00	17.50	10.50
8	Bobby Young	15.00	7.50	4.50
9	Harvey Haddix	15.00	7.50	4.50
10	Jackie Robinson	300.00	150.00	90.00
11	Paul Smith	15.00	7.50	4.50
12	Del Crandall	15.00	7.50	4.50
13	Billy Martin	70.00	35.00	20.00
14	Preacher Roe	80.00	40.00	24.00
15	Al Rosen	20.00	10.00	6.00
16	Vic Janowicz	15.00	7.50	4.50
17	Phil Rizzuto	80.00	40.00	25.00
18	Walt Dropo	15.00	7.50	4.50
19	Johnny Lipon	15.00	7.50	4.50
20	Warren Spahn	100.00	50.00	30.00
21	Bobby Shantz	15.00	7.50	4.50
22	Jim Greengrass	15.00	7.50	4.50
23	Luke Easter	15.00	7.50	4.50
24	Granny Hamner	15.00	7.50	4.50
25	Harvey Kuenn	30.00	15.00	9.00
26	Ray Jablonski	15.00	7.50	4.50
27	Ferris Fain	15.00	7.50	4.50
28	Paul Minner	15.00	7.50	4.50
29	Jim Hegan	15.00	7.50	4.50
30	Ed Mathews	80.00	40.00	25.00
31	Johnny Klippstein	15.00	7.50	4.50
32	Duke Snider	125.00	56.00	35.00
33	Johnny Schmitz	15.00	7.50	4.50
34	Jim Rivera	15.00	7.50	4.50
35	Junior Gilliam	35.00	17.50	10.50
36	Hoyt Wilhelm	45.00	23.00	13.50
37	Whitey Ford	100.00	50.00	30.00
38	Eddie Stanky	15.00	7.50	4.50
39	Sherm Lollar	15.00	7.50	4.50
40	Mel Parnell	15.00	7.50	4.50
41	Willie Jones	15.00	7.50	4.50
42	Don Mueller	15.00	7.50	4.50
43	Dick Groat	15.00	7.50	4.50
44	Ned Garver	15.00	7.50	4.50
45	Richie Ashburn	30.00	15.00	9.00
46	Ken Raffensberger	15.00	7.50	4.50
47	Ellis Kinder	15.00	7.50	4.50
48	Billy Hunter	15.00	7.50	4.50
49	Ray Murray	15.00	7.50	4.50
50	Yogi Berra	250.00	125.00	75.00
51	Johnny Lindell	35.00	17.50	10.50
52	Vic Power	35.00	17.50	10.50
53	Jack Dittmer	35.00	17.50	10.50
54	Vern Stephens	35.00	17.50	10.50
55	Phil Cavarretta	25.00	12.50	7.50
56	Willie Miranda	35.00	17.50	10.50
57	Luis Aloma	35.00	17.50	10.50
58	Bob Wilson	35.00	17.50	10.50
59	Gene Conley	25.00	12.50	7.50
60	Frank Baumholtz	35.00	17.50	10.50
61	Bob Cain	35.00	17.50	10.50
62	Eddie Robinson	35.00	17.50	10.50
63	Johnny Pesky	25.00	12.50	7.50
64	Hank Thompson	35.00	17.50	10.50
65	Bob Swift	35.00	17.50	10.50
66	Ted Lepcio	35.00	17.50	10.50
67	Jim Willis	35.00	17.50	10.50
68	Sammy Calderone	35.00	17.50	10.50
69	Bud Podbielan	35.00	17.50	10.50
70	Larry Doby	45.00	23.00	13.50
71	Frank Smith	35.00	17.50	10.50
72	Preston Ward	35.00	17.50	10.50
73	Wayne Terwilliger	35.00	17.50	10.50
74	Bill Taylor	35.00	17.50	10.50
75	Fred Haney	35.00	17.50	10.50
76	Bob Scheffing	15.00	7.50	4.50
77	Ray Boone	15.00	7.50	4.50
78	Ted Kazanski	15.00	7.50	4.50

		NR MT	EX	VG
79	Andy Pafko	15.00	7.50	4.50
80	Jackie Jensen	15.00	7.50	4.50
81	Dave Hoskins	15.00	7.50	4.50
82	Milt Bolling	15.00	7.50	4.50
83	Joe Collins	15.00	7.50	4.50
84	Dick Cole	15.00	7.50	4.50
85	*Bob Turley*	15.00	7.50	4.50
86	Billy Herman	35.00	17.50	10.50
87	Roy Face	15.00	7.50	4.50
88	Matt Batts	15.00	7.50	4.50
89	Howie Pollet	15.00	7.50	4.50
90	Willie Mays	350.00	175.00	105.00
91	Bob Oldis	15.00	7.50	4.50
92	Wally Westlake	15.00	7.50	4.50
93	Sid Hudson	15.00	7.50	4.50
94	*Ernie Banks*	650.00	325.00	200.00
95	Hal Rice	15.00	7.50	4.50
96	Charlie Silvera	15.00	7.50	4.50
97	Jerry Lane	15.00	7.50	4.50
98	Joe Black	15.00	7.50	4.50
99	Bob Hofman	15.00	7.50	4.50
100	Bob Keegan	15.00	7.50	4.50
101	Gene Woodling	35.00	17.50	10.50
102	Gil Hodges	70.00	35.00	21.00
103	*Jim Lemon*	15.00	7.50	4.50
104	Mike Sandlock	15.00	7.50	4.50
105	Andy Carey	15.00	7.50	4.50
106	Dick Kokos	15.00	7.50	4.50
107	Duane Pillette	15.00	7.50	4.50
108	Thornton Kipper	15.00	7.50	4.50
109	Bill Bruton	15.00	7.50	4.50
110	Harry Dorish	15.00	7.50	4.50
111	Jim Delsing	15.00	7.50	4.50
112	Bill Renna	15.00	7.50	4.50
113	Bob Boyd	15.00	7.50	4.50
114	Dean Stone	15.00	7.50	4.50
115	"Rip" Repulski	15.00	7.50	4.50
116	Steve Bilko	15.00	7.50	4.50
117	Solly Hemus	15.00	7.50	4.50
118	Carl Scheib	15.00	7.50	4.50
119	Johnny Antonelli	15.00	7.50	4.50
120	Roy McMillan	15.00	7.50	4.50
121	Clem Labine	15.00	7.50	4.50
122	Johnny Logan	15.00	7.50	4.50
123	Bobby Adams	15.00	7.50	4.50
124	Marion Fricano	15.00	7.50	4.50
125	Harry Perkowski	15.00	7.50	4.50
126	Ben Wade	15.00	7.50	4.50
127	Steve O'Neill	15.00	7.50	4.50
128	*Henry Aaron*	1500.00	750.00	450.00
129	Forrest Jacobs	15.00	7.50	4.50
130	Hank Bauer	35.00	17.50	10.50
131	Reno Bertoia	15.00	7.50	4.50
132	*Tom Lasorda*	175.00	87.00	50.00
133	Del Baker	15.00	7.50	4.50
134	Cal Hogue	15.00	7.50	4.50
135	Joe Presko	15.00	7.50	4.50
136	Connie Ryan	15.00	7.50	4.50
137	*Wally Moon*	15.00	7.50	4.50
138	Bob Borkowski	15.00	7.50	4.50
139	Ed & Johnny O'Brien	35.00	17.50	10.50
140	Tom Wright	15.00	7.50	4.50
141	*Joe Jay*	15.00	7.50	4.50
142	Tom Poholsky	15.00	7.50	4.50
143	Rollie Hemsley	15.00	7.50	4.50
144	Bill Werle	15.00	7.50	4.50
145	Elmer Valo	15.00	7.50	4.50
146	Don Johnson	15.00	7.50	4.50
147	John Riddle	15.00	7.50	4.50
148	Bob Trice	15.00	7.50	4.50
149	Jim Robertson	15.00	7.50	4.50
150	Dick Kryhoski	15.00	7.50	4.50
151	Alex Grammas	15.00	7.50	4.50
152	Mike Blyzka	15.00	7.50	4.50
153	"Rube" Walker	15.00	7.50	4.50
154	Mike Fornieles	15.00	7.50	4.50
155	Bob Kennedy	15.00	7.50	4.50
156	Joe Coleman	15.00	7.50	4.50
157	Don Lenhardt	15.00	7.50	4.50
158	"Peanuts" Lowrey	15.00	7.50	4.50
159	Dave Philley	15.00	7.50	4.50
160	"Red" Kress	15.00	7.50	4.50
161	John Hetki	15.00	7.50	4.50
162	Herman Wehmeier	15.00	7.50	4.50
163	Frank House	15.00	7.50	4.50
164	Stu Miller	15.00	7.50	4.50
165	Jim Pendleton	15.00	7.50	4.50
166	Johnny Podres	35.00	17.50	10.50
167	Don Lund	15.00	7.50	4.50
168	Morrie Martin	15.00	7.50	4.50
169	Jim Hughes	15.00	7.50	4.50

		NR MT	EX	VG
170	*Jim Rhodes*	15.00	7.50	4.50
171	Leo Kiely	15.00	7.50	4.50
172	Hal Brown	15.00	7.50	4.50
173	Jack Harshman	15.00	7.50	4.50
174	Tom Qualters	15.00	7.50	4.50
175	Frank Leja	15.00	7.50	4.50
176	Bob Keely	15.00	7.50	4.50
177	Bob Milliken	15.00	7.50	4.50
178	Bill Gynn (Glynn)	15.00	7.50	4.50
179	Gair Allie	15.00	7.50	4.50
180	Wes Westrum	15.00	7.50	4.50
181	Mel Roach	15.00	7.50	4.50
182	Chuck Harmon	15.00	7.50	4.50
183	Earle Combs	35.00	17.50	10.50
184	Ed Bailey	15.00	7.50	4.50
185	Chuck Stobbs	15.00	7.50	4.50
186	Karl Olson	15.00	7.50	4.50
187	"Heinie" Manush	35.00	17.50	10.50
188	Dave Jolly	15.00	7.50	4.50
189	Bob Ross	15.00	7.50	4.50
190	Ray Herbert	15.00	7.50	4.50
191	*Dick Schofield*	15.00	7.50	4.50
192	"Cot" Deal	15.00	7.50	4.50
193	Johnny Hopp	15.00	7.50	4.50
194	Bill Sarni	15.00	7.50	4.50
195	Bill Consolo	15.00	7.50	4.50
196	Stan Jok	15.00	7.50	4.50
197	"Schoolboy" Rowe	15.00	7.50	4.50
198	Carl Sawatski	15.00	7.50	4.50
199	"Rocky" Nelson	15.00	7.50	4.50
200	Larry Jansen	15.00	7.50	4.50
201	*Al Kaline*	650.00	330.00	200.00
202	*Bob Purkey*	15.00	7.50	4.50
203	Harry Brecheen	15.00	7.50	4.50
204	Angel Scull	15.00	7.50	4.50
205	Johnny Sain	35.00	17.50	10.50
206	Ray Crone	15.00	7.50	4.50
207	Tom Oliver	15.00	7.50	4.50
208	Grady Hatton	15.00	7.50	4.50
209	Charlie Thompson	15.00	7.50	4.50
210	*Bob Buhl*	15.00	7.50	4.50
211	Don Hoak	15.00	7.50	4.50
212	Mickey Micelotta	15.00	7.50	4.50
213	John Fitzpatrick	15.00	7.50	4.50
214	Arnold Portocarrero	15.00	7.50	4.50
215	Ed McGhee	15.00	7.50	4.50
216	Al Sima	15.00	7.50	4.50
217	Paul Schreiber	15.00	7.50	4.50
218	Fred Marsh	15.00	7.50	4.50
219	Charlie Kress	15.00	7.50	4.50
220	Ruben Gomez	15.00	7.50	4.50
221	Dick Brodowski	15.00	7.50	4.50
222	Bill Wilson	15.00	7.50	4.50
223	Joe Haynes	15.00	7.50	4.50
224	Dick Weik	15.00	7.50	4.50
225	Don Liddle	15.00	7.50	4.50
226	Jehosie Heard	15.00	7.50	4.50
227	Buster Mills	15.00	7.50	4.50
228	Gene Hermanski	15.00	7.50	4.50
229	Bob Talbot	15.00	7.50	4.50
230	Bob Kuzava	15.00	7.50	4.50
231	Roy Smalley	15.00	7.50	4.50
232	Lou Limmer	15.00	7.50	4.50
233	Augie Galan	15.00	7.50	4.50
234	*Jerry Lynch*	15.00	7.50	4.50
235	Vern Law	15.00	7.50	4.50
236	Paul Penson	15.00	7.50	4.50
237	Mike Ryba	15.00	7.50	4.50
238	Al Aber	15.00	7.50	4.50
239	*Bill Skowron*	60.00	30.00	18.00
240	Sam Mele	15.00	7.50	4.50
241	Bob Miller	15.00	7.50	4.50
242	Curt Roberts	15.00	7.50	4.50
243	Ray Blades	15.00	7.50	4.50
244	Leroy Wheat	15.00	7.50	4.50
245	Roy Sievers	15.00	7.50	4.50
246	Howie Fox	15.00	7.50	4.50
247	Eddie Mayo	15.00	7.50	4.50
248	*Al Smith*	15.00	7.50	4.50
249	Wilmer Mizell	15.00	7.50	4.50
250	Ted Williams	625.00	125.00	55.00

1955 Topps

The 1955 Topps set is numerically the smallest of the regular issue Topps sets. The 3-3/4" by 2-5/8" cards mark the first time that Topps used a horizontal format. While that format was new, the design was

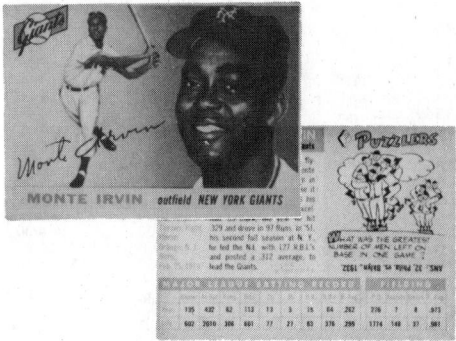

MONTE IRVIN outfield NEW YORK GIANTS

not; they are very similar to the 1954 cards to the point many pictures appeared in both years. Although it was slated for a 210-card set, the 1955 Topps set turned out to be only 206 cards with numbers 175, 186, 203 and 209 never being released. The scarce high numbers in this set begin with #161.

	NR MT	EX	VG
Complete Set:	5750.00	2875.00	1700.
Common Player: 1-150	6.00	3.00	1.75
Common Player: 151-160	15.00	7.50	4.50
Common Player: 161-210	20.00	10.00	6.00

#	Player	NR MT	EX	VG
1	"Dusty" Rhodes	50.00	15.00	9.00
2	Ted Williams	400.00	160.00	100.00
3	Art Fowler	6.00	3.00	1.75
4	Al Kaline	175.00	87.00	50.00
5	Jim Gilliam	10.00	5.00	3.00
6	Stan Hack	6.00	3.00	1.75
7	Jim Hegan	6.00	3.00	1.75
8	Hal Smith	6.00	3.00	1.75
9	Bob Miller	6.00	3.00	1.75
10	Bob Keegan	6.00	3.00	1.75
11	Ferris Fain	6.00	3.00	1.75
12	"Jake" Thies	6.00	3.00	1.75
13	Fred Marsh	6.00	3.00	1.75
14	Jim Finigan	6.00	3.00	1.75
15	Jim Pendleton	6.00	3.00	1.75
16	Roy Sievers	15.00	7.50	4.50
17	Bobby Hofman	6.00	3.00	1.75
18	Russ Kemmerer	6.00	3.00	1.75
19	Billy Herman	15.00	7.50	4.50
20	Andy Carey	9.00	4.50	2.75
21	Alex Grammas	6.00	3.00	1.75
22	Bill Skowron	12.00	6.00	3.50
23	Jack Parks	6.00	3.00	1.75
24	Hal Newhouser	6.00	3.00	1.75
25	Johnny Podres	20.00	10.00	6.00
26	Dick Groat	15.00	7.50	4.50
27	Billy Gardner	6.00	3.00	1.75
28	Ernie Banks	175.00	87.00	52.00
29	Herman Wehmeier	6.00	3.00	1.75
30	Vic Power	6.00	3.00	1.75
31	Warren Spahn	60.00	30.00	18.00
32	Ed McGhee	6.00	3.00	1.75
33	Tom Qualters	6.00	3.00	1.75
34	Wayne Terwilliger	6.00	3.00	1.75
35	Dave Jolly	6.00	3.00	1.75
36	Leo Kiely	6.00	3.00	1.75
37	Joe Cunningham	15.00	7.50	4.50
38	Bob Turley	12.00	6.00	3.50
39	Bill Glynn	6.00	3.00	1.75
40	Don Hoak	15.00	7.50	4.50
41	Chuck Stobbs	6.00	3.00	1.75
42	"Windy" McCall	6.00	3.00	1.75
43	Harvey Haddix	6.00	3.00	1.75
44	"Corky" Valentine	6.00	3.00	1.75
45	Hank Sauer	6.00	3.00	1.75
46	Ted Kazanski	6.00	3.00	1.75
47	Hank Aaron	350.00	175.00	105.00
48	Bob Kennedy	6.00	3.00	1.75
49	J.W. Porter	6.00	3.00	1.75
50	Jackie Robinson	225.00	100.00	60.00
51	Jim Hughes	6.00	3.00	1.75
52	Bill Tremel	6.00	3.00	1.75
53	Bill Taylor	6.00	3.00	1.75
54	Lou Limmer	6.00	3.00	1.75
55	"Rip" Repulski	6.00	3.00	1.75
56	Ray Jablonski	6.00	3.00	1.75
57	Billy O'Dell	6.00	3.00	1.75

#	Player	NR MT	EX	VG
58	Jim Rivera	6.00	3.00	1.75
59	Gair Allie	6.00	3.00	1.75
60	Dean Stone	6.00	3.00	1.75
61	"Spook" Jacobs	6.00	3.00	1.75
62	Thornton Kipper	6.00	3.00	1.75
63	Joe Collins	9.00	4.50	2.75
64	Gus Triandos	15.00	7.50	4.50
65	Ray Boone	6.00	3.00	1.75
66	Ron Jackson	6.00	3.00	1.75
67	Wally Moon	6.00	3.00	1.75
68	Jim Davis	6.00	3.00	1.75
69	Ed Bailey	6.00	3.00	1.75
70	Al Rosen	12.00	6.00	3.50
71	Ruben Gomez	6.00	3.00	1.75
72	Karl Olson	6.00	3.00	1.75
73	Jack Shepard	6.00	3.00	1.75
74	Bob Borkowski	6.00	3.00	1.75
75	Sandy Amoros	6.00	3.00	1.75
76	Howie Pollet	6.00	3.00	1.75
77	Arnold Portocarrero	6.00	3.00	1.75
78	Gordon Jones	6.00	3.00	1.75
79	Danny Schell	6.00	3.00	1.75
80	Bob Grim	9.00	4.50	2.75
81	Gene Conley	6.00	3.00	1.75
82	Chuck Harmon	6.00	3.00	1.75
83	Tom Brewer	6.00	3.00	1.75
84	Camilo Pascual	15.00	7.50	4.50
85	Don Mossi	15.00	7.50	4.50
86	Bill Wilson	6.00	3.00	1.75
87	Frank House	6.00	3.00	1.75
88	Bob Skinner	15.00	7.50	4.50
89	Joe Frazier	6.00	3.00	1.75
90	Karl Spooner	9.00	4.50	2.75
91	Milt Bolling	6.00	3.00	1.75
92	Don Zimmer	30.00	15.00	9.00
93	Steve Bilko	6.00	3.00	1.75
94	Reno Bertoia	6.00	3.00	1.75
95	Preston Ward	6.00	3.00	1.75
96	Charlie Bishop	6.00	3.00	1.75
97	Carlos Paula	6.00	3.00	1.75
98	Johnny Riddle	6.00	3.00	1.75
99	Frank Leja	9.00	4.50	2.75
100	Monte Irvin	25.00	12.50	7.50
101	Johnny Gray	6.00	3.00	1.75
102	Wally Westlake	6.00	3.00	1.75
103	Charlie White	6.00	3.00	1.75
104	Jack Harshman	6.00	3.00	1.75
105	Chuck Diering	6.00	3.00	1.75
106	Frank Sullivan	6.00	3.00	1.75
107	Curt Roberts	6.00	3.00	1.75
108	"Rube" Walker	6.00	3.00	1.75
109	Ed Lopat	12.00	6.00	3.50
110	Gus Zernial	6.00	3.00	1.75
111	Bob Milliken	6.00	3.00	1.75
112	Nelson King	6.00	3.00	1.75
113	Harry Brecheen	6.00	3.00	1.75
114	Lou Ortiz	6.00	3.00	1.75
115	Ellis Kinder	6.00	3.00	1.75
116	Tom Hurd	6.00	3.00	1.75
117	Mel Roach	6.00	3.00	1.75
118	Bob Purkey	6.00	3.00	1.75
119	Bob Lennon	6.00	3.00	1.75
120	Ted Kluszewski	20.00	10.00	6.00
121	Bill Renna	6.00	3.00	1.75
122	Carl Sawatski	6.00	3.00	1.75
123	Sandy Koufax	800.00	400.00	250.00
124	Harmon Killebrew	300.00	150.00	90.00
125	Ken Boyer	40.00	20.00	12.00
126	Dick Hall	6.00	3.00	1.75
127	Dale Long	6.00	3.00	1.75
128	Ted Lepcio	6.00	3.00	1.75
129	Elvin Tappe	6.00	3.00	1.75
130	Mayo Smith	6.00	3.00	1.75
131	Grady Hatton	6.00	3.00	1.75
132	Bob Trice	6.00	3.00	1.75
133	Dave Hoskins	6.00	3.00	1.75
134	Joe Jay	6.00	3.00	1.75
135	Johnny O'Brien	6.00	3.00	1.75
136	"Bunky" Stewart	6.00	3.00	1.75
137	Harry Elliott	6.00	3.00	1.75
138	Ray Herbert	6.00	3.00	1.75
139	Steve Kraly	9.00	4.50	2.75
140	Mel Parnell	6.00	3.00	1.75
141	Tom Wright	6.00	3.00	1.75
142	Jerry Lynch	6.00	3.00	1.75
143	Dick Schofield	6.00	3.00	1.75
144	Joe Amalfitano	6.00	3.00	1.75
145	Elmer Valo	6.00	3.00	1.75
146	Dick Donovan	6.00	3.00	1.75
147	Laurin Pepper	6.00	3.00	1.75
148	Hal Brown	6.00	3.00	1.75

		NR MT	EX	VG
149	Ray Crone	6.00	3.00	1.75
150	Mike Higgins	6.00	3.00	1.75
151	"Red" Kress	15.00	7.50	4.50
152	*Harry Agganis*	75.00	38.00	23.00
153	"Bud" Podbielan	15.00	7.50	4.50
154	Willie Miranda	15.00	7.50	4.50
155	Ed Mathews	80.00	40.00	24.00
156	Joe Black	20.00	10.00	6.00
157	Bob Miller	15.00	7.50	4.50
158	Tom Carroll	20.00	10.00	6.00
159	Johnny Schmitz	15.00	7.50	4.50
160	Ray Narleski	15.00	7.50	4.50
161	*Chuck Tanner*	25.00	12.50	7.50
162	Joe Coleman	20.00	10.00	6.00
163	Faye Throneberry	20.00	10.00	6.00
164	*Roberto Clemente*	1200.00	600.00	350.00
165	Don Johnson	20.00	10.00	6.00
166	Hank Bauer	30.00	15.00	9.00
167	Tom Casagrande	20.00	10.00	6.00
168	Duane Pillette	20.00	10.00	6.00
169	Bob Oldis	20.00	10.00	6.00
170	Jim Pearce	20.00	10.00	6.00
171	Dick Brodowski	20.00	10.00	6.00
172	Frank Baumholtz	20.00	10.00	6.00
173	Bob Kline	20.00	10.00	6.00
174	Rudy Minarcin	20.00	10.00	6.00
175	Not Issued			
176	Norm Zauchin	20.00	10.00	6.00
177	Jim Robertson	20.00	10.00	6.00
178	Bobby Adams	20.00	10.00	6.00
179	Jim Bolger	20.00	10.00	6.00
180	Clem Labine	20.00	10.00	6.00
181	Roy McMillan	20.00	10.00	6.00
182	Humberto Robinson	20.00	10.00	6.00
183	Tony Jacobs	20.00	10.00	6.00
184	Harry Perkowski	20.00	10.00	6.00
185	Don Ferrarese	20.00	10.00	6.00
186	Not Issued			
187	Gil Hodges	125.00	62.00	40.00
188	Charlie Silvera	20.00	10.00	6.00
189	Phil Rizzuto	125.00	56.00	35.00
190	Gene Woodling	20.00	10.00	6.00
191	Ed Stanky	20.00	10.00	6.00
192	Jim Delsing	20.00	10.00	6.00
193	Johnny Sain	35.00	17.50	10.50
194	Willie Mays	500.00	250.00	150.00
195	Ed Roebuck	20.00	10.00	6.00
196	Gale Wade	20.00	10.00	6.00
197	Al Smith	20.00	10.00	6.00
198	Yogi Berra	225.00	100.00	60.00
199	Bert Hamric	20.00	10.00	6.00
200	Jack Jensen	40.00	20.00	12.00
201	Sherm Lollar	20.00	10.00	6.00
202	Jim Owens	20.00	10.00	6.00
203	Not Issued			
204	Frank Smith	20.00	10.00	6.00
205	Gene Freese	20.00	10.00	6.00
206	Pete Daley	20.00	10.00	6.00
207	Bill Consolo	20.00	10.00	6.00
208	Ray Moore	20.00	10.00	6.00
209	Not Issued			
210	Duke Snider	500.00	125.00	75.00

1955 Topps Doubleheaders

This set is a throwback to the 1911 T201 Mecca Double Folders. The cards were perforated allowing them to be folded. Open, there is a color painting of a player set against a ballpark background. When folded, a different stadium and player appears, although both share the same lower legs and feet. Back gives abbreviated career histories. Placed side by side in reverse numerical order, the backgrounds form a continuous stadium scene. When open, the cards measure 2-1/16" by 4-7/8." The 66 cards in the set mean 132 total players, all of whom also appeared in the lower number regular 1955 Topps set.

		NR MT	EX	VG
Complete Set:		3500.00	1750.00	1050.
Common Player:		25.00	12.50	7.50
1	Al Rosen			
2	Chuck Diering	25.00	12.50	7.50
3	Monte Irvin			
4	Russ Kemmerer	25.00	12.50	7.50
5	Ted Kazanski			
6	Gordon Jones	25.00	12.50	7.50
7	Bill Taylor			
8	Billy O'Dell	25.00	12.50	7.50
9	J.W. Porter			
10	Thornton Kipper	25.00	12.50	7.50
11	Curt Roberts			
12	Arnie Portocarrero	25.00	12.50	7.50
13	Wally Westlake			
14	Frank House	25.00	12.50	7.50
15	"Rube" Walker			
16	Lou Limmer	25.00	12.50	7.50
17	Dean Stone			
18	Charlie White	25.00	12.50	7.50
19	Karl Spooner			
20	Jim Hughes	25.00	12.50	7.50
21	Bill Skowron			
22	Frank Sullivan	25.00	12.50	7.50
23	Jack Shepard			
24	Stan Hack	25.00	12.50	7.50
25	Jackie Robinson			
26	Don Hoak	275.00	137.00	80.00
27	"Dusty" Rhodes			
28	Jim Davis	25.00	12.50	7.50
29	Vic Power			
30	Ed Bailey	25.00	12.50	7.50
31	Howie Pollet			
32	Ernie Banks	150.00	75.00	45.00
33	Jim Pendleton			
34	Gene Conley	25.00	12.50	7.50
35	Karl Olson	25.00	12.50	7.50
36	Andy Carey	25.00	12.50	7.50
37	Wally Moon	25.00	12.50	7.50
38	Joe Cunningham	25.00	12.50	7.50
39	Fred Marsh			
40	"Jake" Thies	25.00	12.50	7.50
41	Ed Lopat			
42	Harvey Haddix	25.00	12.50	7.50
43	Leo Kiely			
44	Chuck Stobbs	25.00	12.50	7.50
45	Al Kaline			
46	"Corky" Valentine	300.00	150.00	90.00
47	"Spook" Jacobs			
48	Johnny Gray	25.00	12.50	7.50
49	Ron Jackson			
50	Jim Finigan	25.00	12.50	7.50
51	Ray Jablonski			
52	Bob Keegan	25.00	12.50	7.50
53	Billy Herman			
54	Sandy Amoros	25.00	12.50	7.50
55	Chuck Harmon			
56	Bob Skinner	25.00	12.50	7.50
57	Dick Hall			
58	Bob Grim	25.00	12.50	7.50
59	Billy Glynn			
60	Bob Miller	25.00	12.50	7.50
61	Billy Gardner			
62	John Hetki	25.00	12.50	7.50
63	Bob Borkowski			
64	Bob Turley	25.00	12.50	7.50
65	Joe Collins			
66	Jack Harshman	25.00	12.50	7.50
67	Jim Hegan			
68	Jack Parks	25.00	12.50	7.50
69	Ted Williams			
70	Hal Smith	300.00	150.00	90.00
71	Gair Allie			
72	Grady Hatton	25.00	12.50	7.50
73	Jerry Lynch			
74	Harry Brecheen	25.00	12.50	7.50
75	Tom Wright			
76	"Bunky" Stewart	25.00	12.50	7.50

		NR MT	EX	VG
77	Dave Hoskins			
78	Ed McGhee	25.00	12.50	7.50
79	Roy Sievers			
80	Art Fowler	25.00	12.50	7.50
81	Danny Schell			
82	Gus Triandos	25.00	12.50	7.50
83	Joe Frazier			
84	Don Mossi	25.00	12.50	7.50
85	Elmer Valo			
86	Hal Brown	25.00	12.50	7.50
87	Bob Kennedy			
88	"Windy" McCall	25.00	12.50	7.50
89	Ruben Gomez			
90	Jim Rivera	25.00	12.50	7.50
91	Lou Ortiz			
92	Milt Bolling	25.00	12.50	7.50
93	Carl Sawatski			
94	Elvin Tappe	25.00	12.50	7.50
95	Dave Jolly			
96	Bobby Hofman	25.00	12.50	7.50
97	Preston Ward			
98	Don Zimmer	25.00	12.50	7.50
99	Bill Renna			
100	Dick Groat	25.00	12.50	7.50
101	Bill Wilson			
102	Bill Tremel	25.00	12.50	7.50
103	Hank Sauer			
104	Camilo Pascual	25.00	12.50	7.50
105	Hank Aaron			
106	Ray Herbert	450.00	225.00	135.00
107	Alex Grammas			
108	Tom Qualters	25.00	12.50	7.50
109	Hal Newhouser			
110	Charlie Bishop	25.00	12.50	7.50
111	Harmon Killebrew			
112	John Podres	250.00	125.00	75.00
113	Ray Boone			
114	Bob Purkey	25.00	12.50	7.50
115	Dale Long			
116	Ferris Fain	25.00	12.50	7.50
117	Steve Bilko			
118	Bob Milliken	25.00	12.50	7.50
119	Mel Parnell			
120	Tom Hurd	25.00	12.50	7.50
121	Ted Kluszewski			
122	Jim Owens	25.00	12.50	7.50
123	Gus Zernial			
124	Bob Trice	25.00	12.50	7.50
125	"Rip" Repulski			
126	Ted Lepcio	25.00	12.50	7.50
127	Warren Spahn			
128	Tom Brewer	200.00	100.00	60.00
129	Jim Gilliam			
130	Ellis Kinder	25.00	12.50	7.50
131	Herm Wehmeier			
132	Wayne Terwilliger	25.00	12.50	7.50

1956 Topps

This 340-card set is quite similar in design to the 1955 Topps set, again using both a portrait and an "action" picture. Some portraits are the same as those used in 1955 (and even 1954). Innovations found in the 1956 Topps set of 2-5/8" by 3-3/4" cards include team cards introduced as part of a regular set. Additionally, there are two unnumbered checklist cards (the complete set price quoted below does not include the checklist cards). Finally, there

are cards of the two league presidents, William Harridge and Warren Giles. On the backs, a three-panel cartoon depicts big moments from the player's career while biographical information appears above the cartoon and the statistics below. Card backs for numbers 1-180 can be found with either white or grey cardboard. Some dealers charge a premium for grey backs (#'s 1-100) and white backs (#'s 101-180).

		NR MT	EX	VG
Complete Set:		6000.00	3000.00	1750.
Common Player: 1-100		7.00	3.50	2.00
Common Player: 101-180		10.00	5.00	3.00
Common Player: 181-260		15.00	7.50	4.50
Common Player: 261-340		10.00	5.00	3.00
1	William Harridge	125.00	25.00	3.75
2	Warren Giles	11.00	5.50	3.25
3	Elmer Valo	7.00	3.50	2.00
4	Carlos Paula	7.00	3.50	2.00
5	Ted Williams	350.00	175.00	105.00
6	Ray Boone	10.00	5.00	3.00
7	Ron Negray	7.00	3.50	2.00
8	Walter Alston	30.00	15.00	9.00
9	Ruben Gomez	7.00	3.50	2.00
10	Warren Spahn	70.00	35.00	20.00
11a	Cubs Team (with date)	40.00	20.00	12.00
11b	Cubs Team (no date, name centered)	11.00	5.50	3.25
11c	Cubs Team (no date, name at left)	12.00	6.00	3.50
12	Andy Carey	10.00	5.00	3.00
13	Roy Face	10.00	5.00	3.00
14	Ken Boyer	12.00	6.00	3.50
15	Ernie Banks	75.00	38.00	23.00
16	*Hector Lopez*	10.00	5.00	3.00
17	Gene Conley	10.00	5.00	3.00
18	Dick Donovan	7.00	3.50	2.00
19	Chuck Diering	7.00	3.50	2.00
20	Al Kaline	80.00	40.00	24.00
21	Joe Collins	10.00	5.00	3.00
22	Jim Finigan	7.00	3.50	2.00
23	Freddie Marsh	7.00	3.50	2.00
24	Dick Groat	10.00	5.00	3.00
25	Ted Kluszewski	15.00	7.50	4.50
26	Grady Hatton	7.00	3.50	2.00
27	Nelson Burbrink	7.00	3.50	2.00
28	Bobby Hofman	7.00	3.50	2.00
29	Jack Harshman	7.00	3.50	2.00
30	Jackie Robinson	150.00	60.00	38.00
31	Hank Aaron	200.00	100.00	60.00
32	Frank House	7.00	3.50	2.00
33	Roberto Clemente	300.00	150.00	90.00
34	Tom Brewer	7.00	3.50	2.00
35	Al Rosen	11.00	5.50	3.25
36	Rudy Minarcin	7.00	3.50	2.00
37	Alex Grammas	7.00	3.50	2.00
38	Bob Kennedy	7.00	3.50	2.00
39	Don Mossi	10.00	5.00	3.00
40	Bob Turley	11.00	5.50	3.25
41	Hank Sauer	7.00	3.50	2.00
42	Sandy Amoros	10.00	5.00	3.00
43	Ray Moore	7.00	3.50	2.00
44	"Windy" McCall	7.00	3.50	2.00
45	Gus Zernial	10.00	5.00	3.00
46	Gene Freese	7.00	3.50	2.00
47	Art Fowler	7.00	3.50	2.00
48	Jim Hegan	7.00	3.50	2.00
49	*Pedro Ramos*	10.00	5.00	3.00
50	"Dusty" Rhodes	10.00	5.00	3.00
51	Ernie Oravetz	7.00	3.50	2.00
52	Bob Grim	10.00	5.00	3.00
53	Arnold Portocarrero	7.00	3.50	2.00
54	Bob Keegan	7.00	3.50	2.00
55	Wally Moon	10.00	5.00	3.00
56	Dale Long	10.00	5.00	3.00
57	"Duke" Maas	7.00	3.50	2.00
58	Ed Roebuck	10.00	5.00	3.00
59	Jose Santiago	7.00	3.50	2.00
60	Mayo Smith	7.00	3.50	2.00
61	Bill Skowron	11.00	5.50	3.25
62	Hal Smith	7.00	3.50	2.00
63	*Roger Craig*	25.00	12.50	7.50
64	Luis Arroyo	7.00	3.50	2.00
65	Johnny O'Brien	7.00	3.50	2.00
66	Bob Speake	7.00	3.50	2.00
67	Vic Power	7.00	3.50	2.00
68	Chuck Stobbs	7.00	3.50	2.00
69	Chuck Tanner	10.00	5.00	3.00

		NR MT	EX	VG			NR MT	EX	VG
70	Jim Rivera	7.00	3.50	2.00	141	Joe Frazier	10.00	5.00	3.00
71	Frank Sullivan	7.00	3.50	2.00	142	Gene Baker	10.00	5.00	3.00
72a	Phillies Team (with date)	40.00	20.00	12.00	143	Jim Piersall	10.00	5.00	3.00
72b	Phillies Team (no date, name centered)				144	Leroy Powell	10.00	5.00	3.00
		11.00	5.50	3.25	145	Gil Hodges	45.00	23.00	13.50
72c	Philadelphia Phillies (no date, name at				146	Senators Team	11.00	5.50	3.25
left)		12.00	6.00	3.50	147	Earl Torgeson	10.00	5.00	3.00
73	Wayne Terwilliger	7.00	3.50	2.00	148	Alvin Dark	10.00	5.00	3.00
74	Jim King	7.00	3.50	2.00	149	"Dixie" Howell	10.00	5.00	3.00
75	Roy Sievers	10.00	5.00	3.00	150	"Duke" Snider	100.00	45.00	27.00
76	Ray Crone	7.00	3.50	2.00	151	"Spook" Jacobs	10.00	5.00	3.00
77	Harvey Haddix	10.00	5.00	3.00	152	Billy Hoeft	10.00	5.00	3.00
78	Herman Wehmeier	7.00	3.50	2.00	153	Frank Thomas	10.00	5.00	3.00
79	Sandy Koufax	300.00	150.00	90.00	154	Dave Pope	10.00	5.00	3.00
80	Gus Triandos	10.00	5.00	3.00	155	Harvey Kuenn	11.00	5.50	3.25
81	Wally Westlake	7.00	3.50	2.00	156	Wes Westrum	10.00	5.00	3.00
82	Bill Renna	7.00	3.50	2.00	157	Dick Brodowski	10.00	5.00	3.00
83	Karl Spooner	10.00	5.00	3.00	158	Wally Post	10.00	5.00	3.00
84	"Babe" Birrer	7.00	3.50	2.00	159	Clint Courtney	10.00	5.00	3.00
85a	Indians Team (with date)	40.00	20.00	12.00	160	Billy Pierce	11.00	5.50	3.25
85b	Indians Team (no date, name centered)				161	Joe DeMaestri	10.00	5.00	3.00
		11.00	5.50	3.25	162	"Gus" Bell	10.00	5.00	3.00
85c	Indians Team (no date, name at left)				163	Gene Woodling	10.00	5.00	3.00
		12.00	6.00	3.50	164	Harmon Killebrew	110.00	55.00	33.00
86	Ray Jablonski	7.00	3.50	2.00	165	"Red" Schoendienst	25.00	12.50	7.50
87	Dean Stone	7.00	3.50	2.00	166	Dodgers Team	200.00	100.00	60.00
88	Johnny Kucks	10.00	5.00	3.00	167	Harry Dorish	10.00	5.00	3.00
89	Norm Zauchin	7.00	3.50	2.00	168	Sammy White	10.00	5.00	3.00
90a	Redlegs Team (with date)	40.00	20.00	12.00	169	Bob Nelson	10.00	5.00	3.00
90b	Redlegs Team (no date, name centered)				170	Bill Virdon	11.00	5.50	3.25
		11.00	5.50	3.25	171	Jim Wilson	10.00	5.00	3.00
90c	Redlegs Team (no date, name at left)				172	*Frank Torre*	10.00	5.00	3.00
		12.00	6.00	3.50	173	Johnny Podres	15.00	7.50	4.50
91	Gail Harris	7.00	3.50	2.00	174	Glen Gorbous	10.00	5.00	3.00
92	"Red" Wilson	7.00	3.50	2.00	175	Del Crandall	11.00	5.50	3.25
93	George Susce, Jr.	7.00	3.50	2.00	176	Alex Kellner	10.00	5.00	3.00
94	Ronnie Kline	7.00	3.50	2.00	177	Hank Bauer	15.00	7.50	4.50
95a	Braves Team (with date)	40.00	20.00	12.00	178	Joe Black	10.00	5.00	3.00
95b	Braves Team (no date, name centered)				179	Harry Chiti	10.00	5.00	3.00
		11.00	5.50	3.25	180	Robin Roberts	25.00	12.50	7.50
95c	Braves Team (no date, name at left)				181	Billy Martin	80.00	40.00	25.00
		12.00	6.00	3.50	182	Paul Minner	15.00	7.50	4.50
96	Bill Tremel	7.00	3.50	2.00	183	Stan Lopata	15.00	7.50	4.50
97	Jerry Lynch	7.00	3.50	2.00	184	Don Bessent	15.00	7.50	4.50
98	Camilo Pascual	10.00	5.00	3.00	185	Bill Bruton	15.00	7.50	4.50
99	Don Zimmer	11.00	5.50	3.25	186	Ron Jackson	15.00	7.50	4.50
100a	Orioles Team (with date)	40.00	20.00	12.00	187	Early Wynn	30.00	15.00	9.00
100b	Orioles Team (no date, name centered)				188	White Sox Team	15.00	7.50	4.50
		11.00	5.50	3.25	189	Ned Garver	15.00	7.50	4.50
100c	Orioles Team (no date, name at left)				190	Carl Furillo	20.00	10.00	6.00
		12.00	6.00	3.50	191	Frank Lary	15.00	7.50	4.50
101	Roy Campanella	100.00	45.00	27.00	192	"Smoky" Burgess	15.00	7.50	4.50
102	Jim Davis	10.00	5.00	3.00	193	Wilmer Mizell	15.00	7.50	4.50
103	Willie Miranda	10.00	5.00	3.00	194	Monte Irvin	30.00	15.00	9.00
104	Bob Lennon	10.00	5.00	3.00	195	George Kell	30.00	15.00	9.00
105	Al Smith	10.00	5.00	3.00	196	Tom Poholsky	15.00	7.50	4.50
106	Joe Astroth	10.00	5.00	3.00	197	Granny Hamner	15.00	7.50	4.50
107	Ed Mathews	35.00	17.50	10.50	198	Ed Fitzgerald (Fitz Gerald)	15.00	7.50	4.50
108	Laurin Pepper	10.00	5.00	3.00	199	Hank Thompson	15.00	7.50	4.50
109	Enos Slaughter	25.00	12.50	7.50	200	Bob Feller	90.00	45.00	27.00
110	Yogi Berra	125.00	56.00	35.00	201	"Rip" Repulski	15.00	7.50	4.50
111	Red Sox Team	10.00	5.00	3.00	202	Jim Hearn	15.00	7.50	4.50
112	Dee Fondy	10.00	5.00	3.00	203	Bill Tuttle	15.00	7.50	4.50
113	Phil Rizzuto	50.00	25.00	15.00	204	Art Swanson	15.00	7.50	4.50
114	Jim Owens	10.00	5.00	3.00	205	"Whitey" Lockman	15.00	7.50	4.50
115	Jackie Jensen	10.00	5.00	3.00	206	Erv Palica	15.00	7.50	4.50
116	Eddie O'Brien	10.00	5.00	3.00	207	Jim Small	15.00	7.50	4.50
117	Virgil Trucks	10.00	5.00	3.00	208	Elston Howard	25.00	12.50	7.50
118	"Nellie" Fox	20.00	10.00	6.00	209	Max Surkont	15.00	7.50	4.50
119	*Larry Jackson*	10.00	5.00	3.00	210	Mike Garcia	15.00	7.50	4.50
120	Richie Ashburn	30.00	15.00	9.00	211	Murry Dickson	15.00	7.50	4.50
121	Pirates Team	11.00	5.50	3.25	212	Johnny Temple	15.00	7.50	4.50
122	Willard Nixon	10.00	5.00	3.00	213	Tigers Team	25.00	12.50	7.50
123	Roy McMillan	10.00	5.00	3.00	214	Bob Rush	15.00	7.50	4.50
124	Don Kaiser	10.00	5.00	3.00	215	Tommy Byrne	15.00	7.50	4.50
125	"Minnie" Minoso	15.00	7.50	4.50	216	Jerry Schoonmaker	15.00	7.50	4.50
126	Jim Brady	10.00	5.00	3.00	217	Billy Klaus	15.00	7.50	4.50
127	Willie Jones	10.00	5.00	3.00	218	Joe Nuxall (Nuxhall)	15.00	7.50	4.50
128	Eddie Yost	10.00	5.00	3.00	219	Lew Burdette	15.00	7.50	4.50
129	"Jake" Martin	10.00	5.00	3.00	220	Del Ennis	15.00	7.50	4.50
130	Willie Mays	225.00	90.00	56.00	221	Bob Friend	15.00	7.50	4.50
131	Bob Roselli	10.00	5.00	3.00	222	Dave Philley	15.00	7.50	4.50
132	Bobby Avila	10.00	5.00	3.00	223	Randy Jackson	15.00	7.50	4.50
133	Ray Narleski	10.00	5.00	3.00	224	"Bud" Podbielan	15.00	7.50	4.50
134	Cardinals Team	11.00	5.50	3.25	225	Gil McDougald	20.00	10.00	6.00
135	Mickey Mantle	750.00	375.00	225.00	226	Giants Team	50.00	30.00	15.00
136	Johnny Logan	10.00	5.00	3.00	227	Russ Meyer	15.00	7.50	4.50
137	Al Silvera	10.00	5.00	3.00	228	"Mickey" Vernon	15.00	7.50	4.50
138	Johnny Antonelli	10.00	5.00	3.00	229	Harry Brecheen	15.00	7.50	4.50
139	Tommy Carroll	10.00	5.00	3.00	230	"Chico" Carrasquel	15.00	7.50	4.50
140	*Herb Score*	20.00	10.00	6.00	231	Bob Hale	15.00	7.50	4.50

		NR MT	EX	VG
232	"Toby" Atwell	15.00	7.50	4.50
233	Carl Erskine	20.00	10.00	6.00
234	"Pete" Runnels	15.00	7.50	4.50
235	Don Newcombe	18.00	9.00	5.50
236	Athletics Team	15.00	7.50	4.50
237	Jose Valdivielso	15.00	7.50	4.50
238	Walt Dropo	15.00	7.50	4.50
239	Harry Simpson	15.00	7.50	4.50
240	"Whitey" Ford	100.00	50.00	30.00
241	Don Mueller	15.00	7.50	4.50
242	Hershell Freeman	15.00	7.50	4.50
243	Sherm Lollar	15.00	7.50	4.50
244	Bob Buhl	15.00	7.50	4.50
245	Billy Goodman	15.00	7.50	4.50
246	Tom Gorman	15.00	7.50	4.50
247	Bill Sarni	15.00	7.50	4.50
248	Bob Porterfield	15.00	7.50	4.50
249	Johnny Klippstein	15.00	7.50	4.50
250	Larry Doby	15.00	7.50	4.50
251	Yankees Team	225.00	112.00	67.00
252	Vernon Law	15.00	7.50	4.50
253	Irv Noren	15.00	7.50	4.50
254	George Crowe	15.00	7.50	4.50
255	Bob Lemon	25.00	12.50	7.50
256	Tom Hurd	15.00	7.50	4.50
257	Bobby Thomson	15.00	7.50	4.50
258	Art Ditmar	15.00	7.50	4.50
259	Sam Jones	15.00	7.50	4.50
260	"Pee Wee" Reese	90.00	45.00	27.00
261	Bobby Shantz	10.00	5.00	3.00
262	Howie Pollet	10.00	5.00	3.00
263	Bob Miller	10.00	5.00	3.00
264	Ray Monzant	10.00	5.00	3.00
265	Sandy Consuegra	10.00	5.00	3.00
266	Don Ferrarese	10.00	5.00	3.00
267	Bob Nieman	10.00	5.00	3.00
268	Dale Mitchell	10.00	5.00	3.00
269	Jack Meyer	10.00	5.00	3.00
270	Billy Loes	10.00	5.00	3.00
271	Foster Castleman	10.00	5.00	3.00
272	Danny O'Connell	10.00	5.00	3.00
273	Walker Cooper	10.00	5.00	3.00
274	Frank Baumholtz	10.00	5.00	3.00
275	Jim Greengrass	10.00	5.00	3.00
276	George Zuverink	10.00	5.00	3.00
277	Daryl Spencer	10.00	5.00	3.00
278	Chet Nichols	10.00	5.00	3.00
279	Johnny Groth	10.00	5.00	3.00
280	Jim Gilliam	10.00	5.00	3.00
281	Art Houtteman	10.00	5.00	3.00
282	Warren Hacker	10.00	5.00	3.00
283	Hal Smith	10.00	5.00	3.00
284	Ike Delock	10.00	5.00	3.00
285	Eddie Miksis	10.00	5.00	3.00
286	Bill Wight	10.00	5.00	3.00
287	Bobby Adams	10.00	5.00	3.00
288	Bob Cerv	20.00	10.00	6.00
289	Hal Jeffcoat	10.00	5.00	3.00
290	Curt Simmons	10.00	5.00	3.00
291	Frank Kellert	10.00	5.00	3.00
292	Luis Aparicio	125.00	62.00	37.00
293	Stu Miller	10.00	5.00	3.00
294	Ernie Johnson	10.00	5.00	3.00
295	Clem Labine	10.00	5.00	3.00
296	Andy Seminick	10.00	5.00	3.00
297	Bob Skinner	10.00	5.00	3.00
298	Johnny Schmitz	10.00	5.00	3.00
299	Charley Neal	15.00	7.50	4.50
300	Vic Wertz	10.00	5.00	3.00
301	Marv Grissom	10.00	5.00	3.00
302	Eddie Robinson	11.00	5.50	3.25
303	Jim Dyck	10.00	5.00	3.00
304	Frank Malzone	10.00	5.00	3.00
305	Brooks Lawrence	10.00	5.00	3.00
306	Curt Roberts	10.00	5.00	3.00
307	Hoyt Wilhelm	35.00	17.50	10.50
308	"Chuck" Harmon	10.00	5.00	3.00
309	Don Blasingame	10.00	5.00	3.00
310	Steve Gromek	10.00	5.00	3.00
311	Hal Naragon	10.00	5.00	3.00
312	Andy Pafko	10.00	5.00	3.00
313	Gene Stephens	10.00	5.00	3.00
314	Hobie Landrith	10.00	5.00	3.00
315	Milt Bolling	10.00	5.00	3.00
316	Jerry Coleman	10.00	5.00	3.00
317	Al Aber	10.00	5.00	3.00
318	Fred Hatfield	10.00	5.00	3.00
319	Jack Crimian	10.00	5.00	3.00
320	Joe Adcock	15.00	7.50	4.50
321	Jim Konstanty	11.00	5.50	3.25
322	Karl Olson	10.00	5.00	3.00

		NR MT	EX	VG
323	Willard Schmidt	10.00	5.00	3.00
324	"Rocky" Bridges	10.00	5.00	3.00
325	Don Liddle	10.00	5.00	3.00
326	Connie Johnson	10.00	5.00	3.00
327	Bob Wiesler	10.00	5.00	3.00
328	Preston Ward	10.00	5.00	3.00
329	Lou Berberet	10.00	5.00	3.00
330	Jim Busby	10.00	5.00	3.00
331	Dick Hall	10.00	5.00	3.00
332	Don Larsen	25.00	12.50	7.50
333	Rube Walker	10.00	5.00	3.00
334	Bob Miller	10.00	5.00	3.00
335	Don Hoak	10.00	5.00	3.00
336	Ellis Kinder	10.00	5.00	3.00
337	Bobby Morgan	10.00	5.00	3.00
338	Jim Delsing	10.00	5.00	3.00
339	Rance Pless	10.00	5.00	3.00
340	Mickey McDermott	30.00	15.00	9.00
----	Checklist 1/3	225.00	90.00	56.00
----	Checklist 2/4	225.00	90.00	56.00

1956 Topps Hocus Focus Large

These sets are a direct descendant of the 1948 Topps Magic Photo" issue. Again, the baseball players were part of a larger overall series covering several topical areas. There are two distinct issues of Hocus Focus cards in 1956. The "large" cards, measuring 1" by 1-5/8," consists of 18 players. The "small" cards, 7/8 by 1-3/8," state on the back that they are a series of 23, though only 13 are known. Besides players on the cards themselves, the easiest way to distinguish Hocus Focus cards of 1956 from the Magic Photos of 1948 is to remember that the 1956 cards actually have the words "Hocus Focus" on the back. The photos on these cards were developed by wetting the cards surface and exposing to light. Prices below are for cards with well-developed pictures. Cards with poorly developed photos are worth significantly less.

		NR MT	EX	VG
Complete Set:		525.00	262.00	157.00
Common Player:		12.00	6.00	3.50
1	Dick Groat	25.00	12.50	7.50
2	Ed Lopat	25.00	12.50	7.50
3	Hank Sauer	12.00	6.00	3.50
4	"Dusty" Rhodes	12.00	6.00	3.50
5	Ted Williams	125.00	62.00	37.00
6	Harvey Haddix	12.00	6.00	3.50
7	Ray Boone	12.00	6.00	3.50
8	Al Rosen	25.00	12.50	7.50
9	Mayo Smith	12.00	6.00	3.50
10	Warren Spahn	70.00	35.00	21.00
11	Jim Rivera	12.00	6.00	3.50
12	Ted Kluszewski	25.00	12.50	7.50
13	Gus Zernial	12.00	6.00	3.50
14	Jackie Robinson	125.00	62.00	37.00
15	Hal Smith	12.00	6.00	3.50
16	Johnny Schmitz	12.00	6.00	3.50
17	"Spook" Jacobs	12.00	6.00	3.50
18	Mel Parnell	12.00	6.00	3.50

1956 Topps Pins

One of Topps first specialty issues, the 60-pin set of ballplayers issued in 1956 contains a high percentage of big-name stars which, combined with the scarcity of the pins, makes collecting a complete set extremely challenging. Compounding the situation is the fact that some pins are seen far less often than others, though the reason is unknown. Chuck Stobbs, Hector Lopez and Chuck Diering are unaccountably scarce. Measuring 1-1/8" in diameter, the pins utilize the same portraits found on 1956 Topps baseball cards. The photos are set against a solid color background.

		NR MT	EX	VG
Complete Set:		2500.00	1250.00	750.00
Common Player:		15.00	7.50	4.50
(1)	Hank Aaron	100.00	50.00	30.00
(2)	Sandy Amoros	15.00	7.50	4.50
(3)	Luis Arroyo	15.00	7.50	4.50
(4)	Ernie Banks	50.00	25.00	15.00
(5)	Yogi Berra	70.00	35.00	21.00
(6)	Joe Black	15.00	7.50	4.50
(7)	Ray Boone	15.00	7.50	4.50
(8)	Ken Boyer	20.00	10.00	6.00
(9)	Joe Collins	15.00	7.50	4.50
(10)	Gene Conley	15.00	7.50	4.50
(11)	Chuck Diering	225.00	112.00	67.00
(12)	Dick Donovan	15.00	7.50	4.50
(13)	Jim Finigan	15.00	7.50	4.50
(14)	Art Fowler	15.00	7.50	4.50
(15)	Ruben Gomez	15.00	7.50	4.50
(16)	Dick Groat	20.00	10.00	6.00
(17)	Harvey Haddix	15.00	7.50	4.50
(18)	Jack Harshman	15.00	7.50	4.50
(19)	Grady Hatton	15.00	7.50	4.50
(20)	Jim Hegan	15.00	7.50	4.50
(21)	Gil Hodges	40.00	20.00	12.00
(22)	Bobby Hofman	15.00	7.50	4.50
(23)	Frank House	15.00	7.50	4.50
(24)	Jackie Jensen	20.00	10.00	6.00
(25)	Al Kaline	60.00	30.00	18.00
(26)	Bob Kennedy	15.00	7.50	4.50
(27)	Ted Kluszewski	25.00	12.50	7.50
(28)	Dale Long	15.00	7.50	4.50
(29)	Hector Lopez	200.00	100.00	60.00
(30)	Ed Mathews	40.00	20.00	12.00
(31)	Willie Mays	100.00	50.00	30.00
(32)	Roy McMillan	15.00	7.50	4.50
(33)	Willie Miranda	15.00	7.50	4.50
(34)	Wally Moon	15.00	7.50	4.50
(35)	Don Mossi	15.00	7.50	4.50
(36)	Ron Negray	15.00	7.50	4.50
(37)	Johnny O'Brien	15.00	7.50	4.50
(38)	Carlos Paula	15.00	7.50	4.50
(39)	Vic Power	15.00	7.50	4.50
(40)	Jim Rivera	15.00	7.50	4.50
(41)	Phil Rizzuto	40.00	20.00	12.00
(42)	Jackie Robinson	100.00	50.00	30.00
(43)	Al Rosen	25.00	12.50	7.50
(44)	Hank Sauer	15.00	7.50	4.50
(45)	Roy Sievers	15.00	7.50	4.50
(46)	Bill Skowron	20.00	10.00	6.00
(47)	Al Smith	15.00	7.50	4.50
(48)	Hal Smith	15.00	7.50	4.50
(49)	Mayo Smith	15.00	7.50	4.50
(50)	Duke Snider	70.00	35.00	21.00

		NR MT	EX	VG
(51)	Warren Spahn	50.00	25.00	15.00
(52)	Karl Spooner	15.00	7.50	4.50
(53)	Chuck Stobbs	175.00	87.00	52.00
(54)	Frank Sullivan	15.00	7.50	4.50
(55)	Bill Tremel	15.00	7.50	4.50
(56)	Gus Triandos	15.00	7.50	4.50
(57)	Bob Turley	20.00	10.00	6.00
(58)	Herman Wehmeier	15.00	7.50	4.50
(59)	Ted Williams	110.00	55.00	33.00
(60)	Gus Zernial	15.00	7.50	4.50

1957 Topps

For 1957, Topps reduced the size of its cards to the now-standard 2-1/2" by 3-1/2." Set size was increased to 407 cards. Another change came in the form of the use of real color photographs as opposed to the hand-colored black and whites of previous years. For the first time since 1954, there were also cards with more than one player. The two, "Dodger Sluggers" and "Yankees' Power Hitters" began a trend toward the increased use of mulitple-player cards. Another first-time innovation, found on the backs, is complete players statistics. The scarce cards in the set are not the highest numbers, but rather numbers 265-352. Four unnumbered checklist cards were issued along with the set. They are quite expensive and are not included in the complete set prices quoted below.

		NR MT	EX	VG
Complete Set:		7000.00	3500.00	2000.
Common Player: 1-264		5.00	2.50	1.50
Common Player: 265-352		15.00	7.50	4.50
Common Player: 353-407		5.00	2.50	1.50
1	Ted Williams	425.00	100.00	38.00
2	Yogi Berra	150.00	70.00	45.00
3	Dale Long	5.00	2.50	1.50
4	Johnny Logan	5.00	2.50	1.50
5	Sal Maglie	8.00	4.00	2.50
6	Hector Lopez	5.00	2.50	1.50
7	Luis Aparicio	30.00	15.00	9.00
8	Don Mossi	5.00	2.50	1.50
9	Johnny Temple	5.00	2.50	1.50
10	Willie Mays	200.00	80.00	50.00
11	George Zuverink	5.00	2.50	1.50
12	Dick Groat	6.00	3.00	1.75
13	Wally Burnette	5.00	2.50	1.50
14	Bob Nieman	5.00	2.50	1.50
15	Robin Roberts	20.00	10.00	6.00
16	Walt Moryn	5.00	2.50	1.50
17	Billy Gardner	5.00	2.50	1.50
18	Don Drysdale	200.00	80.00	50.00
19	Bob Wilson	5.00	2.50	1.50
20	Hank Aaron (photo reversed)	225.00	125.00	70.00
21	Frank Sullivan	5.00	2.50	1.50
22	Jerry Snyder (photo actually Ed Fitz Gerald)	5.00	2.50	1.50
23	Sherm Lollar	5.00	2.50	1.50
24	Bill Mazeroski	35.00	17.50	10.50
25	Whitey Ford	50.00	25.00	15.00
26	Bob Boyd	5.00	2.50	1.50
27	Ted Kazanski	5.00	2.50	1.50
28	Gene Conley	5.00	2.50	1.50
29	Whitey Herzog	25.00	12.50	7.50
30	Pee Wee Reese	50.00	30.00	15.00

		NR MT	EX	VG				NR MT	EX	VG
31	Ron Northey	5.00	2.50	1.50		122	Ken Boyer	8.00	4.00	2.50
32	Hersh Freeman	5.00	2.50	1.50		123	Steve Ridzik	5.00	2.50	1.50
33	Jim Small	5.00	2.50	1.50		124	Dave Philley	5.00	2.50	1.50
34	Tom Sturdivant	6.00	3.00	1.75		125	Al Kaline	60.00	30.00	18.00
35	*Frank Robinson*	300.00	150.00	90.00		126	Bob Wiesler	5.00	2.50	1.50
36	Bob Grim	6.00	3.00	1.75		127	Bob Buhl	5.00	2.50	1.50
37	Frank Torre	5.00	2.50	1.50		128	Ed Bailey	5.00	2.50	1.50
38	Nellie Fox	12.00	6.00	3.50		129	Saul Rogovin	5.00	2.50	1.50
39	Al Worthington	5.00	2.50	1.50		130	Don Newcombe	10.00	5.00	3.00
40	Early Wynn	18.00	9.00	5.50		131	Milt Bolling	5.00	2.50	1.50
41	Hal Smith	5.00	2.50	1.50		132	Art Ditmar	6.00	3.00	1.75
42	Dee Fondy	5.00	2.50	1.50		133	Del Crandall	6.00	3.00	1.75
43	Connie Johnson	5.00	2.50	1.50		134	Don Kaiser	5.00	2.50	1.50
44	Joe DeMaestri	5.00	2.50	1.50		135	Bill Skowron	12.00	6.00	3.50
45	Carl Furillo	9.00	4.50	2.75		136	Jim Hegan	5.00	2.50	1.50
46	Bob Miller	5.00	2.50	1.50		137	Bob Rush	5.00	2.50	1.50
47	Don Blasingame	5.00	2.50	1.50		138	Minnie Minoso	8.00	4.00	2.50
48	Bill Bruton	5.00	2.50	1.50		139	Lou Kretlow	5.00	2.50	1.50
49	Daryl Spencer	5.00	2.50	1.50		140	Frank Thomas	5.00	2.50	1.50
50	Herb Score	6.00	3.00	1.75		141	Al Aber	5.00	2.50	1.50
51	Clint Courtney	5.00	2.50	1.50		142	Charley Thompson	5.00	2.50	1.50
52	Lee Walls	5.00	2.50	1.50		143	Andy Pafko	6.00	3.00	1.75
53	Clem Labine	6.00	3.00	1.75		144	Ray Narleski	5.00	2.50	1.50
54	Elmer Valo	5.00	2.50	1.50		145	Al Smith	5.00	2.50	1.50
55	Ernie Banks	70.00	35.00	21.00		146	Don Ferrarese	5.00	2.50	1.50
56	Dave Sisler	5.00	2.50	1.50		147	Al Walker	6.00	3.00	1.75
57	Jim Lemon	5.00	2.50	1.50		148	Don Mueller	5.00	2.50	1.50
58	Ruben Gomez	5.00	2.50	1.50		149	Bob Kennedy	5.00	2.50	1.50
59	Dick Williams	6.00	3.00	1.75		150	Bob Friend	6.00	3.00	1.75
60	Billy Hoeft	5.00	2.50	1.50		151	Willie Miranda	5.00	2.50	1.50
61	Dusty Rhodes	5.00	2.50	1.50		152	Jack Harshman	5.00	2.50	1.50
62	Billy Martin	50.00	25.00	15.00		153	Karl Olson	5.00	2.50	1.50
63	Ike Delock	5.00	2.50	1.50		154	Red Schoendienst	20.00	10.00	6.00
64	Pete Runnels	6.00	3.00	1.75		155	Jim Brosnan	5.00	2.50	1.50
65	Wally Moon	5.00	2.50	1.50		156	Gus Triandos	5.00	2.50	1.50
66	Brooks Lawrence	5.00	2.50	1.50		157	Wally Post	5.00	2.50	1.50
67	Chico Carrasquel	5.00	2.50	1.50		158	Curt Simmons	6.00	3.00	1.75
68	Ray Crone	5.00	2.50	1.50		159	Solly Drake	5.00	2.50	1.50
69	Roy McMillan	5.00	2.50	1.50		160	Billy Pierce	6.00	3.00	1.75
70	Richie Ashburn	15.00	7.50	4.50		161	Pirates Team	8.00	4.00	2.50
71	Murry Dickson	5.00	2.50	1.50		162	Jack Meyer	5.00	2.50	1.50
72	Bill Tuttle	5.00	2.50	1.50		163	Sammy White	5.00	2.50	1.50
73	George Crowe	5.00	2.50	1.50		164	Tommy Carroll	6.00	3.00	1.75
74	Vito Valentinetti	5.00	2.50	1.50		165	Ted Kluszewski	18.00	9.00	5.50
75	Jim Piersall	6.00	3.00	1.75		166	Roy Face	6.00	3.00	1.75
76	Bob Clemente	200.00	80.00	50.00		167	Vic Power	5.00	2.50	1.50
77	Paul Foytack	5.00	2.50	1.50		168	Frank Lary	6.00	3.00	1.75
78	Vic Wertz	6.00	3.00	1.75		169	Herb Plews	5.00	2.50	1.50
79	*Lindy McDaniel*	6.00	3.00	1.75		170	Duke Snider	85.00	42.00	25.00
80	Gil Hodges	50.00	30.00	15.00		171	Red Sox Team	9.00	4.50	2.75
81	Herm Wehmeier	5.00	2.50	1.50		172	Gene Woodling	6.00	3.00	1.75
82	Elston Howard	15.00	7.50	4.50		173	Roger Craig	8.00	4.00	2.50
83	Lou Skizas	5.00	2.50	1.50		174	Willie Jones	5.00	2.50	1.50
84	Moe Drabowsky	5.00	2.50	1.50		175	Don Larsen	8.00	4.00	2.50
85	Larry Doby	8.00	4.00	2.50		176	Gene Baker	5.00	2.50	1.50
86	Bill Sarni	5.00	2.50	1.50		177	Eddie Yost	5.00	2.50	1.50
87	Tom Gorman	5.00	2.50	1.50		178	Don Bessent	5.00	2.50	1.50
88	Harvey Kuenn	6.00	3.00	1.75		179	Ernie Oravetz	5.00	2.50	1.50
89	Roy Sievers	5.00	2.50	1.50		180	Gus Bell	5.00	2.50	1.50
90	Warren Spahn	80.00	40.00	25.00		181	Dick Donovan	5.00	2.50	1.50
91	Mack Burk	5.00	2.50	1.50		182	Hobie Landrith	5.00	2.50	1.50
92	Mickey Vernon	6.00	3.00	1.75		183	Cubs Team	8.00	4.00	2.50
93	Hal Jeffcoat	5.00	2.50	1.50		184	*Tito Francona*	6.00	3.00	1.75
94	Bobby Del Greco	5.00	2.50	1.50		185	Johnny Kucks	6.00	3.00	1.75
95	Mickey Mantle	650.00	250.00	175.00		186	Jim King	5.00	2.50	1.50
96	*Hank Aguirre*	6.00	3.00	1.75		187	Virgil Trucks	5.00	2.50	1.50
97	Yankees Team	30.00	15.00	9.00		188	Felix Mantilla	5.00	2.50	1.50
98	Al Dark	8.00	4.00	2.50		189	Willard Nixon	5.00	2.50	1.50
99	Bob Keegan	5.00	2.50	1.50		190	Randy Jackson	5.00	2.50	1.50
100	League Presidents (Warren Giles, William Harridge)	6.00	3.00	1.75		191	Joe Margoneri	5.00	2.50	1.50
101	Chuck Stobbs	5.00	2.50	1.50		192	Jerry Coleman	6.00	3.00	1.75
102	Ray Boone	5.00	2.50	1.50		193	Del Rice	5.00	2.50	1.50
103	Joe Nuxhall	6.00	3.00	1.75		194	Hal Brown	5.00	2.50	1.50
104	Hank Foiles	5.00	2.50	1.50		195	Bobby Avila	5.00	2.50	1.50
105	Johnny Antonelli	6.00	3.00	1.75		196	Larry Jackson	5.00	2.50	1.50
106	Ray Moore	5.00	2.50	1.50		197	Hank Sauer	5.00	2.50	1.50
107	Jim Rivera	5.00	2.50	1.50		198	Tigers Team	9.00	4.50	2.75
108	Tommy Byrne	6.00	3.00	1.75		199	Vernon Law	6.00	3.00	1.75
109	Hank Thompson	5.00	2.50	1.50		200	Gil McDougald	12.00	6.00	3.50
110	Bill Virdon	6.00	3.00	1.75		201	Sandy Amoros	5.00	2.50	1.50
111	Hal Smith	5.00	2.50	1.50		202	Dick Gernert	5.00	2.50	1.50
112	Tom Brewer	5.00	2.50	1.50		203	Hoyt Wilhelm	18.00	9.00	5.50
113	Wilmer Mizell	5.00	2.50	1.50		204	Athletics Team	8.00	4.00	2.50
114	Braves Team	10.00	5.00	3.00		205	Charley Maxwell	5.00	2.50	1.50
115	Jim Gilliam	8.00	4.00	2.50		206	Willard Schmidt	5.00	2.50	1.50
116	Mike Fornieles	5.00	2.50	1.50		207	Billy Hunter	5.00	2.50	1.50
117	Joe Adcock	6.00	3.00	1.75		208	Lew Burdette	6.00	3.00	1.75
118	Bob Porterfield	5.00	2.50	1.50		209	Bob Skinner	5.00	2.50	1.50
119	Stan Lopata	5.00	2.50	1.50		210	Roy Campanella	80.00	40.00	24.00
120	Bob Lemon	18.00	9.00	5.50		211	Camilo Pascual	5.00	2.50	1.50
121	*Cletis Boyer*	15.00	7.50	4.50		212	*Rocco Colavito*	70.00	35.00	21.00

		NR MT	EX	VG			NR MT	EX	VG
213	Les Moss	5.00	2.50	1.50	304	Joe Cunningham	18.00	9.00	5.50
214	Phillies Team	8.00	4.00	2.50	305	Chico Fernandez	15.00	7.50	4.50
215	Enos Slaughter	20.00	10.00	6.00	306	Darrell Johnson	18.00	9.00	5.50
216	Marv Grissom	5.00	2.50	1.50	307	Jack Phillips	15.00	7.50	4.50
217	Gene Stephens	5.00	2.50	1.50	308	Dick Hall	15.00	7.50	4.50
218	Ray Jablonski	5.00	2.50	1.50	309	Jim Busby	15.00	7.50	4.50
219	Tom Acker	5.00	2.50	1.50	310	Max Surkont	15.00	7.50	4.50
220	Jackie Jensen	6.00	3.00	1.75	311	Al Pilarcik	15.00	7.50	4.50
221	Dixie Howell	5.00	2.50	1.50	312	*Tony Kubek*	125.00	62.00	37.00
222	Alex Grammas	5.00	2.50	1.50	313	Mel Parnell	18.00	9.00	5.50
223	Frank House	5.00	2.50	1.50	314	Ed Bouchee	15.00	7.50	4.50
224	Marv Blaylock	5.00	2.50	1.50	315	Lou Berberet	15.00	7.50	4.50
225	Harry Simpson	5.00	2.50	1.50	316	Billy O'Dell	15.00	7.50	4.50
226	Preston Ward	5.00	2.50	1.50	317	Giants Team	40.00	20.00	12.00
227	Jerry Staley	5.00	2.50	1.50	318	Mickey McDermott	15.00	7.50	4.50
228	Smoky Burgess	6.00	3.00	1.75	319	Gino Cimoli	18.00	9.00	5.50
229	George Susce	5.00	2.50	1.50	320	Neil Chrisley	15.00	7.50	4.50
230	George Kell	18.00	9.00	5.50	321	Red Murff	15.00	7.50	4.50
231	Solly Hemus	5.00	2.50	1.50	322	Redlegs Team	40.00	20.00	12.00
232	Whitey Lockman	5.00	2.50	1.50	323	Wes Westrum	18.00	9.00	5.50
233	Art Fowler	5.00	2.50	1.50	324	Dodgers Team	90.00	45.00	27.00
234	Dick Cole	5.00	2.50	1.50	325	Frank Bolling	15.00	7.50	4.50
235	Tom Poholsky	5.00	2.50	1.50	326	Pedro Ramos	15.00	7.50	4.50
236	Joe Ginsberg	5.00	2.50	1.50	327	Jim Pendleton	15.00	7.50	4.50
237	Foster Castleman	5.00	2.50	1.50	328	*Brooks Robinson*	350.00	175.00	105.00
238	Eddie Robinson	5.00	2.50	1.50	329	White Sox Team	25.00	12.50	7.50
239	Tom Morgan	5.00	2.50	1.50	330	Jim Wilson	15.00	7.50	4.50
240	Hank Bauer	10.00	5.00	3.00	331	Ray Katt	15.00	7.50	4.50
241	Joe Lonnett	5.00	2.50	1.50	332	Bob Bowman	15.00	7.50	4.50
242	Charley Neal	5.00	2.50	1.50	333	Ernie Johnson	15.00	7.50	4.50
243	Cardinals Team	8.00	4.00	2.50	334	Jerry Schoonmaker	15.00	7.50	4.50
244	Billy Loes	5.00	2.50	1.50	335	Granny Hamner	15.00	7.50	4.50
245	Rip Repulski	5.00	2.50	1.50	336	*Haywood Sullivan*	18.00	9.00	5.50
246	Jose Valdivielso	5.00	2.50	1.50	337	Rene Valdes	18.00	9.00	5.50
247	Turk Lown	5.00	2.50	1.50	338	*Jim Bunning*	100.00	50.00	30.00
248	Jim Finigan	5.00	2.50	1.50	339	Bob Speake	15.00	7.50	4.50
249	Dave Pope	5.00	2.50	1.50	340	Bill Wight	15.00	7.50	4.50
250	Ed Mathews	30.00	15.00	9.00	341	Don Gross	15.00	7.50	4.50
251	Orioles Team	8.00	4.00	2.50	342	Gene Mauch	20.00	10.00	6.00
252	Carl Erskine	10.00	5.00	3.00	343	Taylor Phillips	15.00	7.50	4.50
253	Gus Zernial	5.00	2.50	1.50	344	Paul LaPalme	15.00	7.50	4.50
254	Ron Negray	5.00	2.50	1.50	345	Paul Smith	15.00	7.50	4.50
255	Charlie Silvera	5.00	2.50	1.50	346	Dick Littlefield	15.00	7.50	4.50
256	Ronnie Kline	5.00	2.50	1.50	347	Hal Naragon	15.00	7.50	4.50
257	Walt Dropo	5.00	2.50	1.50	348	Jim Hearn	15.00	7.50	4.50
258	Steve Gromek	5.00	2.50	1.50	349	Nelson King	15.00	7.50	4.50
259	Eddie O'Brien	5.00	2.50	1.50	350	Eddie Miksis	15.00	7.50	4.50
260	Del Ennis	5.00	2.50	1.50	351	Dave Hillman	15.00	7.50	4.50
261	Bob Chakales	5.00	2.50	1.50	352	Ellis Kinder	15.00	7.50	4.50
262	Bobby Thomson	6.00	3.00	1.75	353	Cal Neeman	5.00	2.50	1.50
263	George Strickland	5.00	2.50	1.50	354	Rip Coleman	5.00	2.50	1.50
264	Bob Turley	8.00	4.00	2.50	355	Frank Malzone	5.00	2.50	1.50
265	Harvey Haddix	20.00	10.00	6.00	356	Faye Throneberry	5.00	2.50	1.50
266	Ken Kuhn	15.00	7.50	4.50	357	Earl Torgeson	5.00	2.50	1.50
267	Danny Kravitz	15.00	7.50	4.50	358	Jerry Lynch	5.00	2.50	1.50
268	Jackie Collum	15.00	7.50	4.50	359	Tom Cheney	5.00	2.50	1.50
269	Bob Cerv	15.00	7.50	4.50	360	Johnny Groth	5.00	2.50	1.50
270	Senators Team	25.00	12.50	7.50	361	Curt Barclay	5.00	2.50	1.50
271	Danny O'Connell	15.00	7.50	4.50	362	Roman Mejias	5.00	2.50	1.50
272	Bobby Shantz	25.00	12.50	7.50	363	Eddie Kasko	5.00	2.50	1.50
273	Jim Davis	15.00	7.50	4.50	364	Cal McLish	5.00	2.50	1.50
274	Don Hoak	18.00	9.00	5.50	365	Ossie Virgil	5.00	2.50	1.50
275	Indians Team	25.00	12.50	7.50	366	Ken Lehman	5.00	2.50	1.50
276	Jim Pyburn	15.00	7.50	4.50	367	Ed Fitz Gerald	5.00	2.50	1.50
277	Johnny Podres	50.00	25.00	15.00	368	Bob Purkey	5.00	2.50	1.50
278	Fred Hatfield	15.00	7.50	4.50	369	Milt Graff	5.00	2.50	1.50
279	Bob Thurman	15.00	7.50	4.50	370	Warren Hacker	5.00	2.50	1.50
280	Alex Kellner	15.00	7.50	4.50	371	Bob Lennon	5.00	2.50	1.50
281	Gail Harris	15.00	7.50	4.50	372	Norm Zauchin	5.00	2.50	1.50
282	Jack Dittmer	15.00	7.50	4.50	373	Pete Whisenant	5.00	2.50	1.50
283	*Wes Covington*	18.00	9.00	5.50	374	Don Cardwell	5.00	2.50	1.50
284	Don Zimmer	20.00	10.00	6.00	375	*Jim Landis*	6.00	3.00	1.75
285	Ned Garver	15.00	7.50	4.50	376	Don Elston	5.00	2.50	1.50
286	*Bobby Richardson*	100.00	50.00	30.00	377	Andre Rodgers	5.00	2.50	1.50
287	Sam Jones	15.00	7.50	4.50	378	Elmer Singleton	5.00	2.50	1.50
288	Ted Lepcio	15.00	7.50	4.50	379	Don Lee	5.00	2.50	1.50
289	Jim Bolger	15.00	7.50	4.50	380	Walker Cooper	5.00	2.50	1.50
290	Andy Carey	18.00	9.00	5.50	381	Dean Stone	5.00	2.50	1.50
291	Windy McCall	15.00	7.50	4.50	382	Jim Brideweser	5.00	2.50	1.50
292	Billy Klaus	15.00	7.50	4.50	383	*Juan Pizarro*	6.00	3.00	1.75
293	Ted Abernathy	15.00	7.50	4.50	384	Bobby Gene Smith	5.00	2.50	1.50
294	Rocky Bridges	15.00	7.50	4.50	385	Art Houtteman	5.00	2.50	1.50
295	Joe Collins	18.00	9.00	5.50	386	Lyle Luttrell	5.00	2.50	1.50
296	Johnny Klippstein	15.00	7.50	4.50	387	*Jack Sanford*	6.00	3.00	1.75
297	Jack Crimian	15.00	7.50	4.50	388	Pete Daley	5.00	2.50	1.50
298	Irv Noren	15.00	7.50	4.50	389	Dave Jolly	5.00	2.50	1.50
299	Chuck Harmon	15.00	7.50	4.50	390	Reno Bertoia	5.00	2.50	1.50
300	Mike Garcia	18.00	9.00	5.50	391	*Ralph Terry*	8.00	4.00	2.50
301	Sam Esposito	15.00	7.50	4.50	392	Chuck Tanner	6.00	3.00	1.75
302	Sandy Koufax	400.00	200.00	120.00	393	Raul Sanchez	5.00	2.50	1.50
303	Billy Goodman	15.00	7.50	4.50	394	Luis Arroyo	5.00	2.50	1.50

		NR MT	EX	VG
395	Bubba Phillips	5.00	2.50	1.50
396	Casey Wise	5.00	2.50	1.50
397	Roy Smalley	5.00	2.50	1.50
398	Al Cicotte	6.00	3.00	1.75
399	Billy Consolo	5.00	2.50	1.50
400	Dodgers' Sluggers (Roy Campanella, Carl Furillo, Gil Hodges, Duke Snider)	150.00	60.00	38.00
401	*Earl Battey*	6.00	3.00	1.75
402	Jim Pisoni	5.00	2.50	1.50
403	Dick Hyde	5.00	2.50	1.50
404	Harry Anderson	5.00	2.50	1.50
405	Duke Maas	5.00	2.50	1.50
406	Bob Hale	5.00	2.50	1.50
407	Yankees' Power Hitters (Yogi Berra, Mickey Mantle)	350.00	140.00	88.00
---a	Checklist Series 1-2 (Big Blony ad on back)	125.00	56.00	35.00
---b	Checklist Series 1-2 (Bazooka ad on back)	125.00	56.00	35.00
---a	Checklist Series 2-3 (Big Blony ad on back)	175.00	70.00	44.00
---b	Checklist Series 2-3 (Bazooka ad on back)	175.00	70.00	44.00
---a	Checklist Series 3-4 (Big Blony ad on back)	350.00	140.00	88.00
---b	Checklist Series 3-4 (Bazooka ad on back)	350.00	140.00	88.00
---a	Checklist Series 4-5 (Big Blony ad on back)	450.00	225.00	135.00
---b	Checklist Series 4-5 (Bazooka ad on back)	450.00	225.00	135.00
----	Contest Card (Saturday, May 4th)	15.00	7.50	4.50
----	Contest Card (Saturday, May 25th)	15.00	7.50	4.50
----	Contest Card (Saturday, June 22nd)	15.00	7.50	4.50
----	Contest Card (Friday, July 19)	15.00	7.50	4.50
----	Lucky Penny Insert Card	15.00	7.50	4.50

1958 Topps

Topps continued to expand its set size in 1958 with the release of a 494-card set. One card (#145) was not issued after Ed Bouchee was suspended from baseball. Cards retained the 2-1/2" by 3-1/2" size. There are a number of variations, including yellow or white lettering on 33 cards between numbers 2-108 (higher priced yellow letter variations checklisted below are not included in the complete sets prices). The number of multiple-player cards was increased. A major innovation is the addition of 20 "All-Star" cards. For the first time, checklists were incorporated into the numbered series, as the backs of team cards.

		NR MT	EX	VG
Complete Set:		4000.00	2000.00	1200.
Common Player: 1-110		5.00	2.50	1.50
Common Player: 111-440		2.50	1.25	.70
Common Player: 441-495		2.00	1.00	.60
1	Ted Williams	375.00	80.00	35.00
2a	Bob Lemon (yellow team letters)	35.00	17.50	10.50
2b	Bob Lemon (white team letters)	15.00	7.50	4.50
3	Alex Kellner	5.00	2.50	1.50
4	Hank Foiles	5.00	2.50	1.50

		NR MT	EX	VG
5	Willie Mays	150.00	75.00	45.00
6	George Zuverink	5.00	2.50	1.50
7	Dale Long	5.00	2.50	1.50
8a	Eddie Kasko (yellow name letters)	20.00	10.00	6.00
8b	Eddie Kasko (white name letters)	5.00	2.50	1.50
9	Hank Bauer	9.00	4.50	2.75
10	Lou Burdette	8.00	4.00	2.50
11a	Jim Rivera (yellow team letters)	20.00	10.00	6.00
11b	Jim Rivera (white team letters)	5.00	2.50	1.50
12	George Crowe	5.00	2.50	1.50
13a	Billy Hoeft (yellow name letters)	20.00	10.00	6.00
13b	Billy Hoeft (white name, orange triangle by foot)	6.00	3.00	1.75
13c	Billy Hoeft (white name, red triangle by foot)	5.00	2.50	1.50
14	Rip Repulski	5.00	2.50	1.50
15	Jim Lemon	5.00	2.50	1.50
16	Charley Neal	5.00	2.50	1.50
17	Felix Mantilla	5.00	2.50	1.50
18	Frank Sullivan	5.00	2.50	1.50
19	Giants Team/Checklist 1-88	10.00	5.00	3.00
20a	Gil McDougald (yellow name letters)	25.00	12.50	7.50
20b	Gil McDougald (white name letters)	9.00	4.50	2.75
21	Curt Barclay	5.00	2.50	1.50
22	Hal Naragon	5.00	2.50	1.50
23a	Bill Tuttle (yellow name letters)	20.00	10.00	6.00
23b	Bill Tuttle (white name letters)	5.00	2.50	1.50
24a	Hobie Landrith (yellow name letters)	20.00	10.00	6.00
24b	Hobie Landrith (white name letters)	5.00	2.50	1.50
25	Don Drysdale	40.00	20.00	12.00
26	Ron Jackson	5.00	2.50	1.50
27	Bud Freeman	5.00	2.50	1.50
28	Jim Busby	5.00	2.50	1.50
29	Ted Lepcio	5.00	2.50	1.50
30a	Hank Aaron (yellow name letters)	350.00	140.00	88.00
30b	Hank Aaron (white name letters)	150.00	60.00	38.00
31	Tex Clevenger	5.00	2.50	1.50
32a	J.W. Porter (yellow name letters)	20.00	10.00	6.00
32b	J.W. Porter (white name letters)	5.00	2.50	1.50
33a	Cal Neeman (yellow team letters)	20.00	10.00	6.00
33b	Cal Neeman (white team letters)	5.00	2.50	1.50
34	Bob Thurman	5.00	2.50	1.50
35a	Don Mossi (yellow name letters)	20.00	10.00	6.00
35b	Don Mossi (white name letters)	5.00	2.50	1.50
36	Ted Kazanski	5.00	2.50	1.50
37	*Mike McCormick* (photo actually Ray Monzant)	6.00	3.00	1.75
38	Dick Gernert	5.00	2.50	1.50
39	Bob Martyn	5.00	2.50	1.50
40	George Kell	12.00	6.00	3.50
41	Dave Hillman	5.00	2.50	1.50
42	*John Roseboro*	6.00	3.00	1.75
43	Sal Maglie	8.00	4.00	2.50
44	Senators Team/Checklist 1-88	10.00	5.00	3.00
45	Dick Groat	6.00	3.00	1.75
46a	Lou Sleater (yellow name letters)	20.00	10.00	6.00
46b	Lou Sleater (white name letters)	5.00	2.50	1.50
47	*Roger Maris*	400.00	200.00	125.00
48	Chuck Harmon	5.00	2.50	1.50
49	Smoky Burgess	6.00	3.00	1.75
50a	Billy Pierce (yellow team letters)	20.00	10.00	6.00
50b	Billy Pierce (white team letters)	6.00	3.00	1.75
51	Del Rice	5.00	2.50	1.50
52a	Bob Clemente (yellow team letters)	250.00	100.00	63.00
52b	Bob Clemente (white team letters)	200.00	100.00	60.00
53a	Morrie Martin (yellow name letters)	20.00	10.00	6.00
53b	Morrie Martin (white name letters)	5.00	2.50	1.50
54	*Norm Siebern*	7.00	3.50	2.00
55	Chico Carrasquel	5.00	2.50	1.50
56	Bill Fischer	5.00	2.50	1.50
57a	Tim Thompson (yellow name letters)	20.00	10.00	6.00
57b	Tim Thompson (white name letters)	5.00	2.50	1.50
58a	Art Schult (yellow team letters)	20.00	10.00	6.00
58b	Art Schult (white team letters)	5.00	2.50	1.50
59	Dave Sisler	5.00	2.50	1.50

	NR MT	EX	VG
60a Del Ennis (yellow name letters)	20.00	10.00	6.00
60b Del Ennis (white name letters)	5.00	2.50	1.50
61a Darrell Johnson (yellow name letters)	20.00	10.00	6.00
61b Darrell Johnson (white name letters)	6.00	3.00	1.75
62 Joe DeMaestri	5.00	2.50	1.50
63 Joe Nuxhall	6.00	3.00	1.75
64 Joe Lonnett	5.00	2.50	1.50
65a Von McDaniel (yellow name letters)	20.00	10.00	6.00
65b Von McDaniel (white name letters)	5.00	2.50	1.50
66 Lee Walls	5.00	2.50	1.50
67 Joe Ginsberg	5.00	2.50	1.50
68 Daryl Spencer	5.00	2.50	1.50
69 Wally Burnette	5.00	2.50	1.50
70a Al Kaline (yellow name letters)	200.00	80.00	50.00
70b Al Kaline (white name letters)	75.00	38.00	23.00
71 Dodgers Team/Checklist 1-88	20.00	10.00	6.00
72 Bud Byerly	5.00	2.50	1.50
73 Pete Daley	5.00	2.50	1.50
74 Roy Face	6.00	3.00	1.75
75 Gus Bell	5.00	2.50	1.50
76a Dick Farrell (yellow team letters)	20.00	10.00	6.00
76b Dick Farrell (white team letters)	5.00	2.50	1.50
77a Don Zimmer (yellow team letters)	20.00	10.00	6.00
77b Don Zimmer (white team letters)	6.00	3.00	1.75
78a Ernie Johnson (yellow name letters)	20.00	10.00	6.00
78b Ernie Johnson (white name letters)	5.00	2.50	1.50
79a Dick Williams (yellow team letters)	20.00	10.00	6.00
79b Dick Williams (white team letters)	6.00	3.00	1.75
80 Dick Drott	5.00	2.50	1.50
81a *Steve Boros* (yellow team letters)	20.00	10.00	6.00
81b *Steve Boros* (white team letters)	5.00	2.50	1.50
82 Ronnie Kline	5.00	2.50	1.50
83 Bob Hazle	5.00	2.50	1.50
84 Billy O'Dell	5.00	2.50	1.50
85a Luis Aparicio (yellow team letters)	50.00	25.00	15.00
85b Luis Aparicio (white team letters)	20.00	10.00	6.00
86 Valmy Thomas	5.00	2.50	1.50
87 Johnny Kucks	6.00	3.00	1.75
88 Duke Snider	60.00	30.00	18.00
89 Billy Klaus	5.00	2.50	1.50
90 Robin Roberts	15.00	7.50	4.50
91 Chuck Tanner	6.00	3.00	1.75
92a Clint Courtney (yellow name letters)	20.00	10.00	6.00
92b Clint Courtney (white name letters)	5.00	2.50	1.50
93 Sandy Amoros	5.00	2.50	1.50
94 Bob Skinner	5.00	2.50	1.50
95 Frank Bolling	5.00	2.50	1.50
96 Joe Durham	5.00	2.50	1.50
97a Larry Jackson (yellow name letters)	20.00	10.00	6.00
97b Larry Jackson (white name letters)	5.00	2.50	1.50
98a Billy Hunter (yellow name letters)	20.00	10.00	6.00
98b Billy Hunter (white name letters)	5.00	2.50	1.50
99 Bobby Adams	5.00	2.50	1.50
100a Early Wynn (yellow team letters)	30.00	15.00	9.00
100b Early Wynn (white team letters)	15.00	7.50	4.50
101a Bobby Richardson (yellow name letters)	30.00	15.00	9.00
101b Bobby Richardson (white name letters)	10.00	5.00	3.00
102 George Strickland	5.00	2.50	1.50
103 Jerry Lynch	5.00	2.50	1.50
104 Jim Pendleton	5.00	2.50	1.50
105 Billy Gardner	5.00	2.50	1.50
106 Dick Schofield	5.00	2.50	1.50
107 Ossie Virgil	5.00	2.50	1.50
108a Jim Landis (yellow team letters)	20.00	10.00	6.00
108b Jim Landis (white team letters)	5.00	2.50	1.50
109 Herb Plews	5.00	2.50	1.50
110 Johnny Logan	5.00	2.50	1.50
111 Stu Miller	2.50	1.25	.70
112 Gus Zernial	2.75	1.50	.80
113 Jerry Walker	2.50	1.25	.70
114 Irv Noren	2.50	1.25	.70
115 Jim Bunning	15.00	7.50	4.50

	NR MT	EX	VG
116 Dave Philley	2.75	1.50	.80
117 Frank Torre	2.50	1.25	.70
118 Harvey Haddix	2.50	1.25	.70
119 Harry Chiti	2.50	1.25	.70
120 Johnny Podres	5.00	2.50	1.50
121 Eddie Miksis	2.50	1.25	.70
122 Walt Moryn	2.50	1.25	.70
123 Dick Tomanek	2.50	1.25	.70
124 Bobby Usher	2.50	1.25	.70
125 Al Dark	3.75	2.00	1.25
126 Stan Palys	2.50	1.25	.70
127 Tom Sturdivant	3.75	2.00	1.25
128 *Willie Kirkland*	2.75	1.50	.80
129 Jim Derrington	2.50	1.25	.70
130 Jackie Jensen	3.75	2.00	1.25
131 Bob Henrich	2.50	1.25	.70
132 Vernon Law	3.25	1.75	1.00
133 Russ Nixon	2.50	1.25	.70
134 Phillies Team/Checklist 89-176	8.00	4.00	2.50
135 Mike Drabowsky	2.50	1.25	.70
136 Jim Finigan	2.50	1.25	.70
137 Russ Kemmerer	2.50	1.25	.70
138 Earl Torgeson	2.50	1.25	.70
139 George Brunet	2.50	1.25	.70
140 Wes Covington	2.75	1.50	.80
141 Ken Lehman	2.50	1.25	.70
142 Enos Slaughter	20.00	10.00	6.00
143 Billy Muffett	2.50	1.25	.70
144 Bobby Morgan	2.50	1.25	.70
145 Not Issued			
146 Dick Gray	2.50	1.25	.70
147 *Don McMahon*	3.25	1.75	1.00
148 Billy Consolo	2.50	1.25	.70
149 Tom Acker	2.50	1.25	.70
150 Mickey Mantle	500.00	225.00	140.00
151 Buddy Pritchard	2.50	1.25	.70
152 Johnny Antonelli	3.25	1.75	1.00
153 Les Moss	2.50	1.25	.70
154 Harry Byrd	2.50	1.25	.70
155 Hector Lopez	2.50	1.25	.70
156 Dick Hyde	2.50	1.25	.70
157 Dee Fondy	2.50	1.25	.70
158 Indians Team/Checklist 177-264	7.00	3.50	2.00
159 Taylor Phillips	2.50	1.25	.70
160 Don Hoak	2.75	1.50	.80
161 Don Larsen	6.00	3.00	1.75
162 Gil Hodges	18.00	9.00	5.50
163 Jim Wilson	2.50	1.25	.70
164 Bob Taylor	2.50	1.25	.70
165 Bob Nieman	2.50	1.25	.70
166 Danny O'Connell	2.50	1.25	.70
167 Frank Baumann	2.50	1.25	.70
168 Joe Cunningham	2.75	1.50	.80
169 Ralph Terry	2.75	1.50	.80
170 Vic Wertz	3.25	1.75	1.00
171 Harry Anderson	2.50	1.25	.70
172 Don Gross	2.50	1.25	.70
173 Eddie Yost	2.75	1.50	.80
174 A's Team/Checklist 89-176	8.00	4.00	2.50
175 *Marv Throneberry*	10.00	5.00	3.00
176 Bob Buhl	2.75	1.50	.80
177 Al Smith	2.50	1.25	.70
178 Ted Kluszewski	5.00	2.50	1.50
179 Willy Miranda	2.50	1.25	.70
180 Lindy McDaniel	2.50	1.25	.70
181 Willie Jones	2.50	1.25	.70
182 Joe Caffie	2.50	1.25	.70
183 Dave Jolly	2.50	1.25	.70
184 Elvin Tappe	2.50	1.25	.70
185 Ray Boone	2.75	1.50	.80
186 Jack Meyer	2.50	1.25	.70
187 Sandy Koufax	125.00	62.00	40.00
188 Milt Bolling (photo actually Lou Berberet)	2.50	1.25	.70
189 George Susce	2.50	1.25	.70
190 Red Schoendienst	15.00	7.50	4.50
191 Art Ceccarelli	2.50	1.25	.70
192 Milt Graff	2.50	1.25	.70
193 *Jerry Lumpe*	5.00	2.50	1.50
194 Roger Craig	3.25	1.75	1.00
195 Whitey Lockman	2.50	1.25	.70
196 Mike Garcia	2.75	1.50	.80
197 Haywood Sullivan	2.75	1.50	.80
198 Bill Virdon	3.25	1.75	1.00
199 Don Blasingame	2.50	1.25	.70
200 Bob Keegan	2.50	1.25	.70
201 Jim Bolger	2.50	1.25	.70
202 *Woody Held*	3.25	1.75	1.00
203 Al Walker	2.50	1.25	.70
204 Leo Kiely	2.50	1.25	.70
205 Johnny Temple	2.50	1.25	.70

#	Player	NR MT	EX	VG
206	Bob Shaw	3.25	1.75	1.00
207	Solly Hemus	2.50	1.25	.70
208	Cal McLish	2.50	1.25	.70
209	Bob Anderson	2.50	1.25	.70
210	Wally Moon	2.75	1.50	.80
211	Pete Burnside	2.50	1.25	.70
212	Bubba Phillips	2.50	1.25	.70
213	Red Wilson	2.50	1.25	.70
214	Willard Schmidt	2.50	1.25	.70
215	Jim Gilliam	5.00	2.50	1.50
216	Cards Team/Checklist 177-264	7.00	3.50	2.00
217	Jack Harshman	2.50	1.25	.70
218	Dick Rand	2.50	1.25	.70
219	Camilo Pascual	2.75	1.50	.80
220	Tom Brewer	2.50	1.25	.70
221	Jerry Kindall	2.50	1.25	.70
222	Bud Daley	2.50	1.25	.70
223	Andy Pafko	3.25	1.75	1.00
224	Bob Grim	3.75	2.00	1.25
225	Billy Goodman	2.50	1.25	.70
226	Bob Smith (photo actually Bobby Gene Smith)	2.50	1.25	.70
227	Gene Stephens	2.50	1.25	.70
228	Duke Maas	2.50	1.25	.70
229	Frank Zupo	2.50	1.25	.70
230	Richie Ashburn	8.00	4.00	2.50
231	Lloyd Merritt	2.50	1.25	.70
232	Reno Bertoia	2.50	1.25	.70
233	Mickey Vernon	2.75	1.50	.80
234	Carl Sawatski	2.50	1.25	.70
235	Tom Gorman	2.50	1.25	.70
236	Ed Fitz Gerald	2.50	1.25	.70
237	Bill Wight	2.50	1.25	.70
238	Bill Mazeroski	7.00	3.50	2.00
239	Chuck Stobbs	2.50	1.25	.70
240	Moose Skowron	7.00	3.50	2.00
241	Dick Littlefield	2.50	1.25	.70
242	Johnny Klippstein	2.50	1.25	.70
243	Larry Raines	2.50	1.25	.70
244	*Don Demeter*	2.75	1.50	.80
245	*Frank Lary*	2.75	1.50	.80
246	Yankees Team/Checklist 177-264	35.00	17.50	10.50
247	Casey Wise	2.50	1.25	.70
248	Herm Wehmeier	2.50	1.25	.70
249	Ray Moore	2.50	1.25	.70
250	Roy Sievers	3.25	1.75	1.00
251	Warren Hacker	2.50	1.25	.70
252	Bob Trowbridge	2.50	1.25	.70
253	Don Mueller	2.50	1.25	.70
254	Alex Grammas	2.50	1.25	.70
255	Bob Turley	5.00	2.50	1.50
256	White Sox Team/Checklist 265-352	8.00	4.00	2.50
257	Hal Smith	2.50	1.25	.70
258	Carl Erskine	5.00	2.50	1.50
259	Al Pilarcik	2.50	1.25	.70
260	Frank Malzone	2.75	1.50	.80
261	Turk Lown	2.50	1.25	.70
262	Johnny Groth	2.50	1.25	.70
263	Eddie Bressoud	2.75	1.50	.80
264	Jack Sanford	2.75	1.50	.80
265	Pete Runnels	2.75	1.50	.80
266	Connie Johnson	2.50	1.25	.70
267	Sherm Lollar	2.75	1.50	.80
268	Granny Hamner	2.50	1.25	.70
269	Paul Smith	2.50	1.25	.70
270	Warren Spahn	35.00	17.50	10.50
271	Billy Martin	10.00	5.00	3.00
272	Ray Crone	2.50	1.25	.70
273	Hal Smith	2.50	1.25	.70
274	Rocky Bridges	2.50	1.25	.70
275	Elston Howard	8.00	4.00	2.50
276	Bobby Avila	2.50	1.25	.70
277	Virgil Trucks	2.75	1.50	.80
278	Mack Burk	2.50	1.25	.70
279	Bob Boyd	2.50	1.25	.70
280	Jim Piersall	3.25	1.75	1.00
281	Sam Taylor	2.50	1.25	.70
282	Paul Foytack	2.50	1.25	.70
283	Ray Shearer	2.50	1.25	.70
284	Ray Katt	2.50	1.25	.70
285	Frank Robinson	65.00	33.00	20.00
286	Gino Cimoli	2.50	1.25	.70
287	Sam Jones	2.50	1.25	.70
288	Harmon Killebrew	50.00	30.00	15.00
289	Series Hurling Rivals (Lou Burdette, Bobby Shantz)	4.00	2.00	1.25
290	Dick Donovan	2.50	1.25	.70
291	Don Landrum	2.50	1.25	.70
292	Ned Garver	2.50	1.25	.70
293	Gene Freese	2.50	1.25	.70
294	Hal Jeffcoat	2.50	1.25	.70
295	Minnie Minoso	4.00	2.00	1.25
296	*Ryne Duren*	8.00	4.00	2.50
297	Don Buddin	2.50	1.25	.70
298	Jim Hearn	2.50	1.25	.70
299	Harry Simpson	3.75	2.00	1.25
300	League Presidents (Warren Giles, William Harridge)	3.75	2.00	1.25
301	Randy Jackson	2.50	1.25	.70
302	Mike Baxes	2.50	1.25	.70
303	Neil Chrisley	2.50	1.25	.70
304	Tigers' Big Bats (Al Kaline, Harvey Kuenn)	8.00	4.00	2.50
305	Clem Labine	2.75	1.50	.80
306	Whammy Douglas	2.50	1.25	.70
307	Brooks Robinson	70.00	35.00	20.00
308	Paul Giel	2.50	1.25	.70
309	Gail Harris	2.50	1.25	.70
310	Ernie Banks	50.00	25.00	15.00
311	Bob Purkey	2.50	1.25	.70
312	Red Sox Team/Checklist 353-440	8.00	4.00	2.50
313	Bob Rush	2.50	1.25	.70
314	Dodgers' Boss & Power (Walter Alston, Duke Snider)	15.00	7.50	4.50
315	Bob Friend	3.25	1.75	1.00
316	Tito Francona	2.75	1.50	.80
317	*Albie Pearson*	3.25	1.75	1.00
318	Frank House	2.50	1.25	.70
319	Lou Skizas	2.50	1.25	.70
320	Whitey Ford	35.00	17.50	10.50
321	Sluggers Supreme (Ted Kluszewski, Ted Williams)	20.00	10.00	6.00
322	Harding Peterson	2.50	1.25	.70
323	Elmer Valo	2.50	1.25	.70
324	Hoyt Wilhelm	15.00	7.50	4.50
325	Joe Adcock	3.25	1.75	1.00
326	Bob Miller	2.50	1.25	.70
327	Cubs Team/Checklist 265-352	8.00	4.00	2.50
328	Ike Delock	2.50	1.25	.70
329	Bob Cerv	2.50	1.25	.70
330	Ed Bailey	2.50	1.25	.70
331	Pedro Ramos	2.50	1.25	.70
332	Jim King	2.50	1.25	.70
333	Andy Carey	3.75	2.00	1.25
334	Mound Aces (Bob Friend, Billy Pierce)	3.25	1.75	1.00
335	Ruben Gomez	2.50	1.25	.70
336	Bert Hamric	2.50	1.25	.70
337	Hank Aguirre	2.50	1.25	.70
338	Walt Dropo	2.75	1.50	.80
339	Fred Hatfield	2.50	1.25	.70
340	Don Newcombe	6.00	3.00	1.75
341	Pirates Team/Checklist 265-352	8.00	4.00	2.50
342	Jim Brosnan	2.75	1.50	.80
343	*Orlando Cepeda*	50.00	25.00	15.00
344	Bob Porterfield	2.50	1.25	.70
345	Jim Hegan	2.50	1.25	.70
346	Steve Bilko	2.50	1.25	.70
347	Don Rudolph	2.50	1.25	.70
348	Chico Fernandez	2.50	1.25	.70
349	Murry Dickson	2.50	1.25	.70
350	Ken Boyer	5.00	2.50	1.50
351	Braves' Fence Busters (Hank Aaron, Joe Adcock, Del Crandall, Ed Mathews)	20.00	10.00	6.00
352	Herb Score	3.75	2.00	1.25
353	Stan Lopata	2.50	1.25	.70
354	Art Ditmar	3.75	2.00	1.25
355	Bill Bruton	2.75	1.50	.80
356	Bob Malkmus	2.50	1.25	.70
357	Danny McDevitt	2.50	1.25	.70
358	Gene Baker	2.50	1.25	.70
359	Billy Loes	2.50	1.25	.70
360	Roy McMillan	2.50	1.25	.70
361	Mike Fornieles	2.50	1.25	.70
362	Ray Jablonski	2.50	1.25	.70
363	Don Elston	2.50	1.25	.70
364	Earl Battey	2.75	1.50	.80
365	Tom Morgan	2.50	1.25	.70
366	Gene Green	2.50	1.25	.70
367	Jack Urban	2.50	1.25	.70
368	Rocky Colavito	10.00	5.00	3.00
369	Ralph Lumenti	2.50	1.25	.70
370	Yogi Berra	80.00	40.00	25.00
371	Marty Keough	2.50	1.25	.70
372	Don Cardwell	2.50	1.25	.70
373	Joe Pignatano	2.50	1.25	.70
374	Brooks Lawrence	2.50	1.25	.70
375	Pee Wee Reese	50.00	30.00	15.00
376	Charley Rabe	2.50	1.25	.70

		NR MT	EX	VG
377a	Braves Team (alphabetical checklist on back)	9.00	4.50	2.75
377b	Braves Team (numerical checklist on back)	60.00	30.00	18.00
378	Hank Sauer	2.75	1.50	.80
379	Ray Herbert	2.50	1.25	.70
380	Charley Maxwell	2.50	1.25	.70
381	Hal Brown	2.50	1.25	.70
382	Al Cicotte	3.75	2.00	1.25
383	Lou Berberet	2.50	1.25	.70
384	John Goryl	2.50	1.25	.70
385	Wilmer Mizell	2.50	1.25	.70
386	Birdie's Young Sluggers (Ed Bailey, Frank Robinson, Birdie Tebbetts)	7.00	3.50	2.00
387	Wally Post	2.50	1.25	.70
388	Billy Moran	2.50	1.25	.70
389	Bill Taylor	2.50	1.25	.70
390	Del Crandall	3.25	1.75	1.00
391	Dave Melton	2.50	1.25	.70
392	Bennie Daniels	2.50	1.25	.70
393	Tony Kubek	15.00	7.50	4.50
394	Jim Grant	3.25	1.75	1.00
395	Willard Nixon	2.50	1.25	.70
396	Dutch Dotterer	2.50	1.25	.70
397a	Tigers Team (alphabetical checklist on back)	9.00	4.50	2.75
397b	Tigers Team (numerical checklist on back)	60.00	30.00	18.00
398	Gene Woodling	2.75	1.50	.80
399	Marv Grissom	2.50	1.25	.70
400	Nellie Fox	8.00	4.00	2.50
401	Don Bessent	2.50	1.25	.70
402	Bobby Gene Smith	2.50	1.25	.70
403	Steve Korcheck	2.50	1.25	.70
404	Curt Simmons	3.25	1.75	1.00
405	Ken Aspromonte	2.50	1.25	.70
406	Vic Power	2.50	1.25	.70
407	Carlton Willey	2.50	1.25	.70
408a	Orioles Team (alphabetical checklist on back)	8.00	4.00	2.50
408b	Orioles Team (numerical checklist on back)	60.00	30.00	18.00
409	Frank Thomas	2.50	1.25	.70
410	Murray Wall	2.50	1.25	.70
411	Tony Taylor	2.75	1.50	.80
412	Jerry Staley	2.50	1.25	.70
413	Jim Davenport	2.75	1.50	.80
414	Sammy White	2.50	1.25	.70
415	Bob Bowman	2.50	1.25	.70
416	Foster Castleman	2.50	1.25	.70
417	Carl Furillo	6.00	3.00	1.75
418	World Series Batting Foes (Hank Aaron, Mickey Mantle)	100.00	45.00	27.00
419	Bobby Shantz	4.50	2.25	1.25
420	Vada Pinson	18.00	9.00	5.50
421	Dixie Howell	2.50	1.25	.70
422	Norm Zauchin	2.50	1.25	.70
423	Phil Clark	2.50	1.25	.70
424	Larry Doby	4.00	2.00	1.25
425	Sam Esposito	2.50	1.25	.70
426	Johnny O'Brien	2.50	1.25	.70
427	Al Worthington	2.50	1.25	.70
428a	Redlegs Team (alphabetical checklist on back)	8.00	4.00	2.50
428b	Redlegs Team (numerical checklist on back)	50.00	25.00	15.00
429	Gus Triandos	2.75	1.50	.80
430	Bobby Thomson	3.25	1.75	1.00
431	Gene Conley	2.75	1.50	.80
432	John Powers	2.50	1.25	.70
433	Pancho Herrera	2.50	1.25	.70
434	Harvey Kuenn	3.25	1.75	1.00
435	Ed Roebuck	2.50	1.25	.70
436	Rival Fence Busters (Willie Mays, Duke Snider)	50.00	25.00	15.00
437	Bob Speake	2.50	1.25	.70
438	Whitey Herzog	3.75	2.00	1.25
439	Ray Narleski	2.50	1.25	.70
440	Ed Mathews	30.00	15.00	9.00
441	Jim Marshall	2.00	1.00	.60
442	Phil Paine	2.00	1.00	.60
443	Billy Harrell	4.50	2.25	1.25
444	Danny Kravitz	2.00	1.00	.60
445	Bob Smith	2.00	1.00	.60
446	Carroll Hardy	4.50	2.25	1.25
447	Ray Monzant	2.00	1.00	.60
448	Charlie Lau	2.75	1.50	.80
449	Gene Fodge	2.00	1.00	.60
450	Preston Ward	4.50	2.25	1.25
451	Joe Taylor	2.00	1.00	.60
452	Roman Mejias	2.00	1.00	.60

		NR MT	EX	VG
453	Tom Qualters	2.00	1.00	.60
454	Harry Hanebrink	2.00	1.00	.60
455	Hal Griggs	2.00	1.00	.60
456	Dick Brown	2.00	1.00	.60
457	Milt Pappas	2.75	1.50	.80
458	Julio Becquer	2.00	1.00	.60
459	Ron Blackburn	2.00	1.00	.60
460	Chuck Essegian	2.00	1.00	.60
461	Ed Mayer	2.00	1.00	.60
462	Gary Geiger	4.50	2.25	1.25
463	Vito Valentinetti	2.00	1.00	.60
464	Curt Flood	12.00	6.00	3.50
465	Arnie Portocarrero	2.00	1.00	.60
466	Pete Whisenant	2.00	1.00	.60
467	Glen Hobbie	2.00	1.00	.60
468	Bob Schmidt	2.00	1.00	.60
469	Don Ferrarese	2.00	1.00	.60
470	R.C. Stevens	2.00	1.00	.60
471	Lenny Green	2.00	1.00	.60
472	Joe Jay	2.00	1.00	.60
473	Bill Renna	2.00	1.00	.60
474	Roman Semproch	2.00	1.00	.60
475	All-Star Managers (Fred Haney, Casey Stengel)	15.00	7.50	4.50
476	Stan Musial AS	25.00	12.50	7.50
477	Bill Skowron AS	4.00	2.00	1.25
478	Johnny Temple AS	2.50	1.25	.70
479	Nellie Fox AS	5.00	2.50	1.50
480	Eddie Mathews AS	10.00	5.00	3.00
481	Frank Malzone AS	2.50	1.25	.70
482	Ernie Banks AS	15.00	7.50	4.50
483	Luis Aparicio AS	8.00	4.00	2.50
484	Frank Robinson AS	12.00	6.00	3.50
485	Ted Williams AS	40.00	20.00	12.00
486	Willie Mays AS	30.00	15.00	9.00
487	Mickey Mantle AS	60.00	30.00	18.00
488	Hank Aaron AS	30.00	15.00	9.00
489	Jackie Jensen AS	3.25	1.75	1.00
490	Ed Bailey AS	2.50	1.25	.70
491	Sherm Lollar AS	2.50	1.25	.70
492	Bob Friend AS	3.25	1.75	1.00
493	Bob Turley AS	3.75	2.00	1.25
494	Warren Spahn AS	15.00	7.50	4.50
495	Herb Score AS	6.00	2.00	1.00
----	Contest Card (All-Star Game, July 8)	15.00	7.50	4.50
----	Felt Emblems Insert Card	15.00	7.50	4.50

1959 Topps

 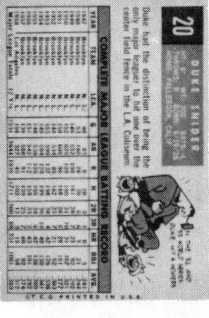

These 2-1/2" by 3-1/2" cards have a round photograph at the center of the front with a solid-color background and white border. A facsimile autograph is found across the photo. The 572-card set marks the largest set issued to that time. Card numbers below 507 have red and green printing with the card number in white in a green box. On high number cards beginning with #507, the printing is black and red and the card number is in a black box. Specialty cards include multiple-player cards, team cards with checklists, "All-Star" cards, highlights from previous season, and 31 "Rookie Stars." There is also a card of the commissioner, Ford Frick, and one Roy Campanella in a wheelchair. A handful of cards can be found with and without lines added to the biographies on back indicating trades or demotions; those without the added lines are considerably more rare and valuable and are not included in the complete set price. Card numbers 199-286 can be found with either white or grey backs, with the grey stock being the less common.

		NR MT	EX	VG
Complete Set:		4000.00	2000.00	1200.
Common Player: 1-110		4.00	2.00	1.25
Common Player: 111-506		2.50	1.25	.70
Common Player: 507-572		10.00	5.00	3.00
1	Ford Frick	60.00	3.75	1.50
2	Eddie Yost	5.00	2.00	1.25
3	Don McMahon	4.00	2.00	1.25
4	Albie Pearson	4.00	2.00	1.25
5	Dick Donovan	4.00	2.00	1.25
6	Alex Grammas	4.00	2.00	1.25
7	Al Pilarcik	4.00	2.00	1.25
8	Phillies Team/Checklist 1-88	12.00	6.00	3.50
9	Paul Giel	4.00	2.00	1.25
10	Mickey Mantle	350.00	140.00	88.00
11	Billy Hunter	4.00	2.00	1.25
12	Vern Law	5.00	2.50	1.50
13	Dick Gernert	4.00	2.00	1.25
14	Pete Whisenant	4.00	2.00	1.25
15	Dick Drott	4.00	2.00	1.25
16	Joe Pignatano	4.00	2.00	1.25
17	Danny's All-Stars (Ted Kluszewski, Danny Murtaugh, Frank Thomas)	5.00	2.50	1.50
18	Jack Urban	4.00	2.00	1.25
19	Ed Bressoud	4.00	2.00	1.25
20	Duke Snider	50.00	25.00	15.00
21	Connie Johnson	4.00	2.00	1.25
22	Al Smith	4.00	2.00	1.25
23	Murry Dickson	5.00	2.50	1.50
24	Red Wilson	4.00	2.00	1.25
25	Don Hoak	4.50	2.25	1.25
26	Chuck Stobbs	4.00	2.00	1.25
27	Andy Pafko	4.50	2.25	1.25
28	Red Worthington	4.00	2.00	1.25
29	Jim Bolger	4.00	2.00	1.25
30	Nellie Fox	10.00	5.00	3.00
31	Ken Lehman	4.00	2.00	1.25
32	Don Buddin	4.00	2.00	1.25
33	Ed Fitz Gerald	4.00	2.00	1.25
34	Pitchers Beware (Al Kaline, Charlie Maxwell)	9.00	4.50	2.75
35	Ted Kluszewski	7.00	3.50	2.00
36	Hank Aguirre	4.00	2.00	1.25
37	Gene Green	4.00	2.00	1.25
38	Morrie Martin	4.00	2.00	1.25
39	Ed Bouchee	4.00	2.00	1.25
40	Warren Spahn	40.00	20.00	12.00
41	Bob Martyn	4.00	2.00	1.25
42	Murray Wall	4.00	2.00	1.25
43	Steve Bilko	4.00	2.00	1.25
44	Vito Valentinetti	4.00	2.00	1.25
45	Andy Carey	5.00	2.50	1.50
46	Bill Henry	4.00	2.00	1.25
47	Jim Finigan	4.00	2.00	1.25
48	Orioles Team/Checklist 1-88	10.00	5.00	3.00
49	Bill Hall	4.00	2.00	1.25
50	Willie Mays	125.00	56.00	35.00
51	Rip Coleman	4.00	2.00	1.25
52	Coot Veal	4.00	2.00	1.25
53	Stan Williams	4.00	2.00	1.25
54	Mel Roach	4.00	2.00	1.25
55	Tom Brewer	4.00	2.00	1.25
56	Carl Sawatski	4.00	2.00	1.25
57	Al Cicotte	4.00	2.00	1.25
58	Eddie Miksis	4.00	2.00	1.25
59	Irv Noren	4.00	2.00	1.25
60	Bob Turley	6.00	3.00	1.75
61	Dick Brown	4.00	2.00	1.25
62	Tony Taylor	4.00	2.00	1.25
63	Jim Hearn	4.00	2.00	1.25
64	Joe DeMaestri	4.00	2.00	1.25
65	Frank Torre	4.00	2.00	1.25
66	Joe Ginsberg	4.00	2.00	1.25
67	Brooks Lawrence	4.00	2.00	1.25
68	Dick Schofield	4.00	2.00	1.25
69	Giants Team/Checklist 89-176	12.00	6.00	3.50
70	Harvey Kuenn	5.00	2.50	1.50
71	Don Bessent	4.00	2.00	1.25
72	Bill Renna	4.00	2.00	1.25
73	Ron Jackson	4.00	2.00	1.25
74	Directing the Power (Cookie Lavagetto, Jim Lemon, Roy Sievers)	4.50	2.25	1.25
75	Sam Jones	4.00	2.00	1.25
76	Bobby Richardson	9.00	4.50	2.75
77	John Goryl	4.00	2.00	1.25

		NR MT	EX	VG
78	Pedro Ramos	4.00	2.00	1.25
79	Harry Chiti	4.00	2.00	1.25
80	Minnie Minoso	5.00	2.50	1.50
81	Hal Jeffcoat	4.00	2.00	1.25
82	Bob Boyd	4.00	2.00	1.25
83	Bob Smith	4.00	2.00	1.25
84	Reno Bertoia	4.00	2.00	1.25
85	Harry Anderson	4.00	2.00	1.25
86	Bob Keegan	4.00	2.00	1.25
87	Danny O'Connell	4.00	2.00	1.25
88	Herb Score	4.50	2.25	1.25
89	Billy Gardner	4.00	2.00	1.25
90	Bill Skowron	8.00	4.00	2.50
91	Herb Moford	4.00	2.00	1.25
92	Dave Philley	4.00	2.00	1.25
93	Julio Becquer	4.00	2.00	1.25
94	W. Sox Team/Checklist 89-176	15.00	7.50	4.50
95	Carl Willey	4.00	2.00	1.25
96	Lou Berberet	4.00	2.00	1.25
97	Jerry Lynch	4.00	2.00	1.25
98	Arnie Portocarrero	4.00	2.00	1.25
99	Ted Kazanski	4.00	2.00	1.25
100	Bob Cerv	4.00	2.00	1.25
101	Alex Kellner	4.00	2.00	1.25
102	*Felipe Alou*	8.00	4.00	2.50
103	Billy Goodman	4.00	2.00	1.25
104	Del Rice	4.00	2.00	1.25
105	Lee Walls	4.00	2.00	1.25
106	Hal Woodeshick	4.00	2.00	1.25
107	Norm Larker	4.00	2.00	1.25
108	Zack Monroe	5.00	2.50	1.50
109	Bob Schmidt	4.00	2.00	1.25
110	George Witt	4.00	2.00	1.25
111	Redlegs Team/Checklist 89-176	8.00	4.00	2.50
112	Billy Consolo	2.50	1.25	.70
113	Taylor Phillips	2.50	1.25	.70
114	Earl Battey	2.75	1.50	.80
115	Mickey Vernon	2.75	1.50	.80
116	*Bob Allison*	5.00	2.50	1.50
117	*John Blanchard*	3.25	1.75	1.00
118	John Buzhardt	2.50	1.25	.70
119	*John Callison*	5.00	2.50	1.50
120	Chuck Coles	2.50	1.25	.70
121	Bob Conley	2.50	1.25	.70
122	Bennie Daniels	2.50	1.25	.70
123	Don Dillard	2.50	1.25	.70
124	Dan Dobbek	2.50	1.25	.70
125	*Ron Fairly*	3.50	1.75	1.00
126	Eddie Haas	2.50	1.25	.70
127	Kent Hadley	2.50	1.25	.70
128	Bob Hartman	2.50	1.25	.70
129	Frank Herrera	2.50	1.25	.70
130	Lou Jackson	2.50	1.25	.70
131	*Deron Johnson*	3.25	1.75	1.00
132	Don Lee	2.50	1.25	.70
133	*Bob Lillis*	2.75	1.50	.70
134	Jim McDaniel	2.50	1.25	.70
135	Gene Oliver	2.50	1.25	.70
136	*Jim O'Toole*	2.75	1.50	.80
137	Dick Ricketts	2.50	1.25	.70
138	John Romano	2.50	1.25	.70
139	Ed Sadowski	2.50	1.25	.70
140	Charlie Secrest	2.50	1.25	.70
141	Joe Shipley	2.50	1.25	.70
142	Dick Stigman	2.50	1.25	.70
143	Willie Tasby	2.50	1.25	.70
144	Jerry Walker	2.50	1.25	.70
145	Dom Zanni	2.50	1.25	.70
146	Jerry Zimmerman	2.50	1.25	.70
147	Cub's Clubbers (Ernie Banks, Dale Long, Walt Moryn)	9.00	4.50	2.75
148	Mike McCormick	2.75	1.50	.80
149	Jim Bunning	8.00	4.00	2.50
150	Stan Musial	125.00	62.00	37.00
151	Bob Malkmus	2.50	1.25	.70
152	Johnny Klippstein	2.50	1.25	.70
153	Jim Marshall	2.50	1.25	.70
154	Ray Herbert	2.50	1.25	.70
155	Enos Slaughter	15.00	7.50	4.50
156	Ace Hurlers (Billy Pierce, Robin Roberts)	3.50	1.75	1.00
157	Felix Mantilla	2.50	1.25	.70
158	Walt Dropo	2.75	1.50	.80
159	Bob Shaw	2.50	1.25	.70
160	Dick Groat	3.00	1.50	.90
161	Frank Baumann	2.50	1.25	.70
162	Bobby G. Smith	2.50	1.25	.70
163	Sandy Koufax	125.00	56.00	35.00
164	Johnny Groth	2.50	1.25	.70
165	Bill Bruton	2.75	1.50	.80
166	Destruction Crew (Rocky Colavito, Larry Doby, Minnie Minoso)	3.25	1.75	1.00

		NR MT	EX	VG
167	Duke Maas	3.00	1.50	.90
168	Carroll Hardy	2.50	1.25	.70
169	Ted Abernathy	2.50	1.25	.70
170	Gene Woodling	2.75	1.50	.80
171	Willard Schmidt	2.50	1.25	.70
172	A's Team/Checklist 177-242	7.00	3.50	2.00
173	*Bill Monbouquette*	2.75	1.50	.80
174	Jim Pendleton	2.50	1.25	.70
175	Dick Farrell	2.50	1.25	.70
176	Preston Ward	2.50	1.25	.70
177	Johnny Briggs	2.50	1.25	.70
178	Ruben Amaro	2.50	1.25	.70
179	Don Rudolph	2.50	1.25	.70
180	Yogi Berra	60.00	30.00	18.00
181	Bob Porterfield	2.50	1.25	.70
182	Milt Graff	2.50	1.25	.70
183	Stu Miller	2.50	1.25	.70
184	Harvey Haddix	2.75	1.50	.80
185	Jim Busby	2.50	1.25	.70
186	Mudcat Grant	2.75	1.50	.80
187	Bubba Phillips	2.50	1.25	.70
188	Juan Pizarro	2.50	1.25	.70
189	Neil Chrisley	2.50	1.25	.70
190	Bill Virdon	2.75	1.50	.80
191	Russ Kemmerer	2.50	1.25	.70
192	Charley Beamon	2.50	1.25	.70
193	Sammy Taylor	2.50	1.25	.70
194	Jim Brosnan	2.75	1.50	.80
195	Rip Repulski	2.50	1.25	.70
196	Billy Moran	2.50	1.25	.70
197	Ray Semproch	2.50	1.25	.70
198	Jim Davenport	2.50	1.25	.70
199	Leo Kiely	2.50	1.25	.70
200	Warren Giles	2.75	1.50	.80
201	Tom Acker	2.50	1.25	.70
202	Roger Maris	125.00	56.00	35.00
203	Ozzie Virgil	2.50	1.25	.70
204	Casey Wise	2.50	1.25	.70
205	Don Larsen	7.00	3.50	2.00
206	Carl Furillo	5.00	2.50	1.50
207	George Strickland	2.50	1.25	.70
208	Willie Jones	2.50	1.25	.70
209	Lenny Green	2.50	1.25	.70
210	Ed Bailey	2.50	1.25	.70
211	Bob Blaylock	2.50	1.25	.70
212	Fence Busters (Hank Aaron, Eddie Mathews)	50.00	25.00	15.00
213	Jim Rivera	2.50	1.25	.70
214	Marcelino Solis	2.50	1.25	.70
215	Jim Lemon	2.50	1.25	.70
216	Andre Rodgers	2.50	1.25	.70
217	Carl Erskine	4.00	2.00	1.25
218	Roman Mejias	2.50	1.25	.70
219	George Zuverink	2.50	1.25	.70
220	Frank Malzone	2.75	1.50	.80
221	Bob Bowman	2.50	1.25	.70
222	Bobby Shantz	3.50	1.75	1.00
223	Cards Team/Checklist 265-352	7.00	3.50	2.00
224	*Claude Osteen*	3.00	1.50	.90
225	Johnny Logan	2.75	1.50	.80
226	Art Ceccarelli	2.50	1.25	.70
227	Hal Smith	2.50	1.25	.70
228	Don Gross	2.50	1.25	.70
229	Vic Power	2.50	1.25	.70
230	Bill Fischer	2.50	1.25	.70
231	Ellis Burton	2.50	1.25	.70
232	Eddie Kasko	2.50	1.25	.70
233	Paul Foytack	2.50	1.25	.70
234	Chuck Tanner	3.00	1.50	.90
235	Valmy Thomas	2.50	1.25	.70
236	Ted Bowsfield	2.50	1.25	.70
237	Run Preventers (Gil McDougald, Bobby Richardson, Bob Turley)	4.00	2.00	1.25
238	Gene Baker	2.50	1.25	.70
239	Bob Trowbridge	2.50	1.25	.70
240	Hank Bauer	7.00	3.50	2.00
241	Billy Muffett	2.50	1.25	.70
242	Ron Samford	2.50	1.25	.70
243	Marv Grissom	2.50	1.25	.70
244	Dick Gray	2.50	1.25	.70
245	Ned Garver	2.50	1.25	.70
246	J.W. Porter	2.50	1.25	.70
247	Don Ferrarese	2.50	1.25	.70
248	Red Sox Team/Checklist 177-264	8.00	4.00	2.50
249	Bobby Adams	2.50	1.25	.70
250	Billy O'Dell	2.50	1.25	.70
251	Cletis Boyer	4.50	2.25	1.25
252	Ray Boone	2.75	1.50	.80
253	Seth Morehead	2.50	1.25	.70
254	Zeke Bella	2.50	1.25	.70

		NR MT	EX	VG
255	Del Ennis	2.75	1.50	.80
256	Jerry Davie	2.50	1.25	.70
257	*Leon Wagner*	3.00	1.50	.90
258	Fred Kipp	2.50	1.25	.70
259	Jim Pisoni	2.50	1.25	.70
260	Early Wynn	15.00	7.50	4.50
261	Gene Stephens	2.50	1.25	.70
262	Hitters' Foes (Don Drysdale, Clem Labine, Johnny Podres)	8.00	4.00	2.50
263	Buddy Daley	2.50	1.25	.70
264	Chico Carrasquel	2.50	1.25	.70
265	Ron Kline	2.50	1.25	.70
266	Woody Held	2.75	1.50	.80
267	John Romonosky	2.50	1.25	.70
268	Tito Francona	2.75	1.50	.80
269	Jack Meyer	2.50	1.25	.70
270	Gil Hodges	18.00	9.00	5.50
271	*Orlando Pena*	2.75	1.50	.80
272	Jerry Lumpe	3.25	1.75	1.00
273	Joe Jay	2.50	1.25	.70
274	Jerry Kindall	2.50	1.25	.70
275	Jack Sanford	2.50	1.25	.70
276	Pete Daley	2.50	1.25	.70
277	Turk Lown	2.50	1.25	.70
278	Chuck Essegian	2.50	1.25	.70
279	Ernie Johnson	2.50	1.25	.70
280	Frank Bolling	2.50	1.25	.70
281	Walt Craddock	2.50	1.25	.70
282	R.C. Stevens	2.50	1.25	.70
283	Russ Heman	2.50	1.25	.70
284	Steve Korcheck	2.50	1.25	.70
285	Joe Cunningham	2.75	1.50	.80
286	Dean Stone	2.50	1.25	.70
287	Don Zimmer	2.75	1.50	.80
288	Dutch Dotterer	2.50	1.25	.70
289	Johnny Kucks	3.00	1.50	.90
290	Wes Covington	2.75	1.50	.80
291	Pitching Partners (Camilo Pascual, Pedro Ramos)	2.75	1.50	.80
292	Dick Williams	2.75	1.50	.80
293	Ray Moore	2.50	1.25	.70
294	Hank Foiles	2.50	1.25	.70
295	Billy Martin	15.00	7.50	4.50
296	*Ernie Broglio*	2.75	1.50	.80
297	*Jackie Brandt*	2.75	1.50	.80
298	Tex Clevenger	2.50	1.25	.70
299	Billy Klaus	2.50	1.25	.70
300	Richie Ashburn	12.00	6.00	3.50
301	Earl Averill	2.50	1.25	.70
302	Don Mossi	2.75	1.50	.80
303	Marty Keough	2.50	1.25	.70
304	Cubs Team/Checklist 265-352	7.00	3.50	2.00
305	Curt Raydon	2.50	1.25	.70
306	Jim Gilliam	5.00	2.50	1.50
307	Curt Barclay	2.50	1.25	.70
308	Norm Siebern	3.50	1.75	1.00
309	Sal Maglie	3.00	1.50	.90
310	Luis Aparicio	15.00	7.50	4.50
311	Norm Zauchin	2.50	1.25	.70
312	Don Newcombe	4.50	2.25	1.25
313	Frank House	2.50	1.25	.70
314	Don Cardwell	2.50	1.25	.70
315	Joe Adcock	3.00	1.50	.90
316a	Ralph Lumenti (without option statement)	80.00	40.00	24.00
316b	Ralph Lumenti (with option statement)	2.50	1.25	.70
317	N.L. Hitting Kings (Richie Ashburn, Willie Mays)	15.00	7.50	4.50
318	Rocky Bridges	2.50	1.25	.70
319	Dave Hillman	2.50	1.25	.70
320	Bob Skinner	2.75	1.50	.80
321a	Bob Giallombardo (without option statement)	80.00	40.00	24.00
321b	Bob Giallombardo (with option statement)	2.50	1.25	.70
322a	Harry Hanebrink (without trade statement)	65.00	33.00	18.00
322b	Harry Hanebrink (with trade statement)	2.50	1.25	.70
323	Frank Sullivan	2.50	1.25	.70
324	Don Demeter	2.50	1.25	.70
325	Ken Boyer	5.00	2.50	1.50
326	Marv Throneberry	4.00	2.00	1.25
327	*Gary Bell*	2.75	1.50	.80
328	Lou Skizas	2.50	1.25	.70
329	Tigers Team/Checklist 353-429	8.00	4.00	2.50
330	Gus Triandos	2.75	1.50	.80
331	Steve Boros	2.75	1.50	.80
332	Ray Monzant	2.50	1.25	.70
333	Harry Simpson	2.50	1.25	.70

#	Player	NR MT	EX	VG
334	Glen Hobbie	2.50	1.25	.70
335	Johnny Temple	2.50	1.25	.70
336a	Billy Loes (without trade statement)	65.00	33.00	18.00
336b	Billy Loes (with trade statement)	2.50	1.25	.70
337	George Crowe	2.50	1.25	.70
338	*George Anderson*	20.00	10.00	6.00
339	Roy Face	3.00	1.50	.90
340	Roy Sievers	2.75	1.50	.80
341	Tom Qualters	2.50	1.25	.70
342	Ray Jablonski	2.50	1.25	.70
343	Billy Hoeft	2.50	1.25	.70
344	Russ Nixon	2.50	1.25	.70
345	Gil McDougald	8.00	4.00	2.50
346	Batter Bafflers (Tom Brewer, Dave Sisler)	2.75	1.50	.80
347	Bob Buhl	2.75	1.50	.80
348	Ted Lepcio	2.50	1.25	.70
349	Hoyt Wilhelm	15.00	7.50	4.50
350	Ernie Banks	60.00	30.00	18.00
351	Earl Torgeson	2.50	1.25	.70
352	Robin Roberts	15.00	7.50	4.50
353	Curt Flood	3.00	1.50	.90
354	Pete Burnside	2.50	1.25	.70
355	Jim Piersall	3.00	1.50	.90
356	Bob Mabe	2.50	1.25	.70
357	*Dick Stuart*	4.50	2.25	1.25
358	Ralph Terry	2.75	1.50	.80
359	*Bill White*	18.00	9.00	5.50
360	Al Kaline	50.00	25.00	15.00
361	Willard Nixon	2.50	1.25	.70
362a	Dolan Nichols (without option statement)	80.00	40.00	24.00
362b	Dolan Nichols (with option statement)	2.50	1.25	.70
363	Bobby Avila	2.50	1.25	.70
364	Danny McDevitt	2.50	1.25	.70
365	Gus Bell	2.75	1.50	.80
366	Humberto Robinson	2.50	1.25	.70
367	Cal Neeman	2.50	1.25	.70
368	Don Mueller	2.50	1.25	.70
369	Dick Tomanek	2.50	1.25	.70
370	Pete Runnels	2.75	1.50	.80
371	Dick Brodowski	2.50	1.25	.70
372	Jim Hegan	2.50	1.25	.70
373	Herb Plews	2.50	1.25	.70
374	Art Ditmar	3.00	1.50	.90
375	Bob Nieman	2.50	1.25	.70
376	Hal Naragon	2.50	1.25	.70
377	Johnny Antonelli	2.75	1.50	.80
378	Gail Harris	2.50	1.25	.70
379	Bob Miller	2.50	1.25	.70
380	Hank Aaron	125.00	56.00	35.00
381	Mike Baxes	2.50	1.25	.70
382	Curt Simmons	2.75	1.50	.80
383	Words of Wisdom (Don Larsen, Casey Stengel)	5.00	2.50	1.50
384	Dave Sisler	2.50	1.25	.70
385	Sherm Lollar	2.75	1.50	.80
386	Jim Delsing	2.50	1.25	.70
387	Don Drysdale	30.00	15.00	9.00
388	Bob Will	2.50	1.25	.70
389	Joe Nuxhall	2.75	1.50	.80
390	Orlando Cepeda	12.00	6.00	3.50
391	Milt Pappas	2.75	1.50	.80
392	Whitey Herzog	4.50	2.25	1.25
393	Frank Lary	2.75	1.50	.80
394	Randy Jackson	2.50	1.25	.70
395	Elston Howard	7.00	3.50	2.00
396	Bob Rush	2.50	1.25	.70
397	Senators Team/Checklist 430-495	7.00	3.50	2.00
398	Wally Post	2.50	1.25	.70
399	Larry Jackson	2.50	1.25	.70
400	Jackie Jensen	4.00	2.00	1.25
401	Ron Blackburn	2.50	1.25	.70
402	Hector Lopez	2.50	1.25	.70
403	Clem Labine	2.75	1.50	.80
404	Hank Sauer	2.75	1.50	.80
405	Roy McMillan	2.50	1.25	.70
406	Solly Drake	2.50	1.25	.70
407	Moe Drabowsky	2.50	1.25	.70
408	Keystone Combo (Luis Aparicio, Nellie Fox)	7.00	3.50	2.00
409	Gus Zernial	2.75	1.50	.80
410	Billy Pierce	2.75	1.50	.80
411	Whitey Lockman	2.50	1.25	.70
412	Stan Lopata	2.50	1.25	.70
413	Camillo Pascual (Camilo)	2.75	1.50	.80
414	Dale Long	2.75	1.50	.80
415	Bill Mazeroski	3.50	1.75	1.00
416	Haywood Sullivan	2.50	1.25	.70
417	Virgil Trucks	3.00	1.50	.90
418	Gino Cimoli	2.50	1.25	.70
419	Braves Team/Checklist 353-429	8.00	4.00	2.50
420	Rocco Colavito	7.00	3.50	2.00
421	Herm Wehmeier	2.50	1.25	.70
422	Hobie Landrith	2.50	1.25	.70
423	Bob Grim	2.50	1.25	.70
424	Ken Aspromonte	2.50	1.25	.70
425	Del Crandall	2.75	1.50	.80
426	Jerry Staley	2.50	1.25	.70
427	Charlie Neal	2.50	1.25	.70
428	Buc Hill Aces (Roy Face, Bob Friend, Ron Kline, Vern Law)	3.25	1.75	1.00
429	Bobby Thomson	2.75	1.50	.80
430	Whitey Ford	30.00	15.00	9.00
431	Whammy Douglas	2.50	1.25	.70
432	Smoky Burgess	3.00	1.50	.90
433	Billy Harrell	2.50	1.25	.70
434	Hal Griggs	2.50	1.25	.70
435	Frank Robinson	60.00	30.00	18.00
436	Granny Hamner	2.50	1.25	.70
437	Ike Delock	2.50	1.25	.70
438	Sam Esposito	2.50	1.25	.70
439	Brooks Robinson	35.00	17.50	10.50
440	Lou Burdette	8.00	4.00	2.50
441	John Roseboro	2.75	1.50	.80
442	Ray Narleski	2.50	1.25	.70
443	Daryl Spencer	2.50	1.25	.70
444	*Ronnie Hansen*	2.75	1.50	.80
445	Cal McLish	2.50	1.25	.70
446	Rocky Nelson	2.50	1.25	.70
447	Bob Anderson	2.50	1.25	.70
448	Vada Pinson	4.00	2.00	1.25
449	Tom Gorman	2.50	1.25	.70
450	Ed Mathews	30.00	15.00	9.00
451	Jimmy Constable	2.50	1.25	.70
452	Chico Fernandez	2.50	1.25	.70
453	Les Moss	2.50	1.25	.70
454	Phil Clark	2.50	1.25	.70
455	Larry Doby	3.25	1.75	1.00
456	Jerry Casale	2.50	1.25	.70
457	Dodgers Team/Checklist 430-495	12.00	6.00	3.50
458	Gordon Jones	2.50	1.25	.70
459	Bill Tuttle	2.50	1.25	.70
460	Bob Friend	2.75	1.50	.80
461	Mantle Hits 42nd Homer For Crown	30.00	15.00	9.00
462	Colavito's Great Catch Saves Game	3.00	1.50	.90
463	Kaline Becomes Youngest Bat Champ	8.00	4.00	2.50
464	Mays' Catch Makes Series History	15.00	7.50	4.50
465	Sievers Sets Homer Mark	2.75	1.50	.80
466	Pierce All Star Starter	2.75	1.50	.80
467	Aaron Clubs World Series Homer	15.00	7.50	4.50
468	Snider's Play Brings L.A. Victory	9.00	4.50	2.75
469	Hustler Banks Wins M.V.P. Award	8.00	4.00	2.50
470	Musial Raps Out 3,000th Hit	12.00	6.00	3.50
471	Tom Sturdivant	3.00	1.50	.90
472	Gene Freese	2.50	1.25	.70
473	Mike Fornieles	2.50	1.25	.70
474	Moe Thacker	2.50	1.25	.70
475	Jack Harshman	2.50	1.25	.70
476	Indians Team/Checklist 496-572	7.00	3.50	2.00
477	Barry Latman	2.50	1.25	.70
478	Bob Clemente	70.00	35.00	21.00
479	Lindy McDaniel	2.50	1.25	.70
480	Red Schoendienst	12.00	6.00	3.50
481	Charley Maxwell	2.50	1.25	.70
482	Russ Meyer	2.50	1.25	.70
483	Clint Courtney	2.50	1.25	.70
484	Willie Kirkland	2.50	1.25	.70
485	Ryne Duren	3.50	1.75	1.00
486	Sammy White	2.50	1.25	.70
487	Hal Brown	2.50	1.25	.70
488	Walt Moryn	2.50	1.25	.70
489	John C. Powers	2.50	1.25	.70
490	Frank Thomas	2.50	1.25	.70
491	Don Blasingame	2.50	1.25	.70
492	Gene Conley	2.75	1.50	.80
493	Jim Landis	2.50	1.25	.70
494	Don Pavletich	2.50	1.25	.70
495	Johnny Podres	4.00	2.00	1.25
496	Wayne Terwilliger	2.50	1.25	.70
497	Hal R. Smith	2.50	1.25	.70
498	Dick Hyde	2.50	1.25	.70
499	Johnny O'Brien	2.50	1.25	.70
500	Vic Wertz	2.75	1.50	.80

		NR MT	EX	VG
501	Bobby Tiefenauer	2.50	1.25	.70
502	Al Dark	3.25	1.75	1.00
503	Jim Owens	2.50	1.25	.70
504	Ossie Alvarez	2.50	1.25	.70
505	Tony Kubek	8.00	4.00	2.50
506	Bob Purkey	2.50	1.25	.70
507	Bob Hale	10.00	5.00	3.00
508	Art Fowler	10.00	5.00	3.00
509	*Norm Cash*	30.00	15.00	9.00
510	Yankees Team/Checklist 496-572			
		45.00	22.00	13.50
511	George Susce	10.00	5.00	3.00
512	George Altman	10.00	5.00	3.00
513	Tom Carroll	10.00	5.00	3.00
514	*Bob Gibson*	350.00	175.00	105.00
515	Harmon Killebrew	110.00	50.00	28.00
516	Mike Garcia	11.00	5.50	3.25
517	Joe Koppe	10.00	5.00	3.00
518	*Mike Cueller (Cuellar)*	15.00	7.50	4.50
519	Infield Power (Dick Gernert, Frank Malzone, Pete Runnels)	12.00	6.00	3.50
520	Don Elston	10.00	5.00	3.00
521	Gary Geiger	10.00	5.00	3.00
522	Gene Snyder	10.00	5.00	3.00
523	Harry Bright	10.00	5.00	3.00
524	Larry Osborne	10.00	5.00	3.00
525	Jim Coates	11.00	5.50	3.25
526	Bob Speake	10.00	5.00	3.00
527	Solly Hemus	10.00	5.00	3.00
528	Pirates Team/Checklist 496-572			
		25.00	12.50	7.50
529	*George Bamberger*	11.00	5.50	3.25
530	Wally Moon	11.00	5.50	3.25
531	Ray Webster	10.00	5.00	3.00
532	Mark Freeman	10.00	5.00	3.00
533	Darrell Johnson	11.00	5.50	3.25
534	Faye Throneberry	10.00	5.00	3.00
535	Ruben Gomez	10.00	5.00	3.00
536	Dan Kravitz	10.00	5.00	3.00
537	Rodolfo Arias	10.00	5.00	3.00
538	Chick King	10.00	5.00	3.00
539	Gary Blaylock	10.00	5.00	3.00
540	Willy Miranda	10.00	5.00	3.00
541	Bob Thurman	10.00	5.00	3.00
542	*Jim Perry*	15.00	7.50	4.50
543	Corsair Outfield Trio (Bob Clemente, Bob Skinner, Bill Virdon)	35.00	17.50	10.50
544	Lee Tate	10.00	5.00	3.00
545	Tom Morgan	10.00	5.00	3.00
546	Al Schroll	10.00	5.00	3.00
547	Jim Baxes	10.00	5.00	3.00
548	Elmer Singleton	10.00	5.00	3.00
549	Howie Nunn	10.00	5.00	3.00
550	Roy Campanella	125.00	62.00	37.00
551	Fred Haney AS	11.00	5.50	3.25
552	Casey Stengel AS	30.00	15.00	9.00
553	Orlando Cepeda AS	12.00	6.00	3.50
554	Bill Skowron AS	12.00	6.00	3.50
555	Bill Mazeroski AS	12.00	6.00	3.50
556	Nellie Fox AS	15.00	7.50	4.50
557	Ken Boyer AS	12.00	6.00	3.50
558	Frank Malzone AS	11.00	5.50	3.25
559	Ernie Banks AS	30.00	15.00	9.00
560	Luis Aparicio AS	20.00	10.00	6.00
561	Hank Aaron AS	125.00	62.00	37.00
562	Al Kaline AS	35.00	17.50	10.50
563	Willie Mays AS	125.00	62.00	37.00
564	Mickey Mantle AS	200.00	100.00	60.00
565	Wes Covington AS	11.00	5.50	3.25
566	Roy Sievers AS	11.00	5.50	3.25
567	Del Crandall AS	11.00	5.50	3.25
568	Gus Triandos AS	11.00	5.50	3.25
569	Bob Friend AS	11.00	5.50	3.25
570	Bob Turley AS	11.00	5.50	3.25
571	Warren Spahn AS	40.00	20.00	12.00
572	Billy Pierce AS	15.00	6.00	3.25
----	Elect Your Favorite Rookie Insert (paper stock, September 29 date on back)	15.00	7.50	4.50
----	Felt Pennants Insert (paper stock)			
		15.00	7.50	4.50

1960 Topps

In 1960, Topps returned to a horizontal format (3-1/2" by 2-1/2") with a color portrait and a black and white "action" photograph on the front. The backs returned to the use of just the previous year and lifetime statistics along with a cartoon and short

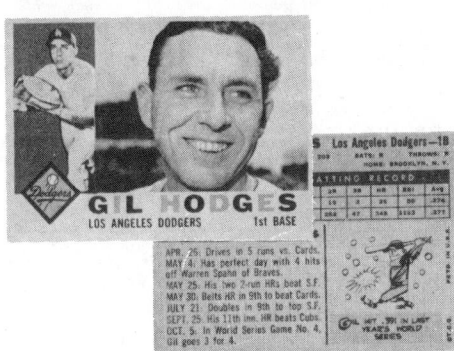

career summary or previous season highlights. Specialty cards in the 572-card set are multi-player cards, managers and coaches cards, and highlights of the 1959 World Series. Two groups of rookie cards are included. The first are numbers 117-148, which are the Sport Magazine rookies. The second group is called "Topps All-Star Rookies." Finally, there is a continuation of the All-Star cards to close out the set in the scarcer high numbers. Card #'s 375-440 can be found with backs printed on either white or grey cardboard, with the white stock being the less common.

		NR MT	EX	VG
Complete Set:		3400.00	1700.00	1020.
Common Player: 1-286		1.50	.70	.45
Common Player: 287-440		1.75	.90	.50
Common Player: 441-506		3.50	1.75	1.00
Common Player: 507-572		8.00	4.00	2.50
1	Early Wynn	35.00	10.00	5.00
2	Roman Mejias	2.25	.70	.45
3	Joe Adcock	2.25	1.25	.70
4	Bob Purkey	1.50	.70	.45
5	Wally Moon	1.75	.90	.50
6	Lou Berberet	1.50	.70	.45
7	Master & Mentor (Willie Mays, Bill Rigney)	8.00	4.00	2.50
8	Bud Daley	1.50	.70	.45
9	Faye Throneberry	1.50	.70	.45
10	Ernie Banks	40.00	20.00	12.00
11	Norm Siebern	1.75	.90	.50
12	Milt Pappas	1.75	.90	.50
13	Wally Post	1.50	.70	.45
14	Jim Grant	1.50	.70	.45
15	Pete Runnels	1.75	.90	.50
16	Ernie Broglio	1.50	.70	.45
17	Johnny Callison	1.75	.90	.50
18	Dodgers Team/Checklist 1-88	10.00	5.00	3.00
19	Felix Mantilla	1.50	.70	.45
20	Roy Face	2.00	1.00	.60
21	Dutch Dotterer	1.50	.70	.45
22	Rocky Bridges	1.50	.70	.45
23	Eddie Fisher	1.50	.70	.45
24	Dick Gray	1.50	.70	.45
25	Roy Sievers	3.50	1.75	1.00
26	Wayne Terwilliger	1.50	.70	.45
27	Dick Drott	1.50	.70	.45
28	Brooks Robinson	50.00	25.00	15.00
29	Clem Labine	1.75	.90	.50
30	Tito Francona	1.75	.90	.50
31	Sammy Esposito	1.50	.70	.45
32	Sophomore Stalwarts (Jim O'Toole, Vada Pinson)	3.50	1.75	1.00
33	Tom Morgan	1.50	.70	.45
34	George Anderson	2.50	1.25	.70
35	Whitey Ford	25.00	12.50	7.50
36	Russ Nixon	1.50	.70	.45
37	Bill Bruton	1.75	.90	.50
38	Jerry Casale	1.50	.70	.45
39	Earl Averill	1.50	.70	.45
40	Joe Cunningham	1.75	.90	.50
41	Barry Latman	1.50	.70	.45
42	Hobie Landrith	1.50	.70	.45
43	Senators Team/Checklist 1-88	6.00	3.00	1.75
44	Bobby Locke	1.50	.70	.45
45	Roy McMillan	1.50	.70	.45
46	Jack Fisher	1.50	.70	.45
47	Don Zimmer	2.25	1.25	.70

#	Name	NR MT	EX	VG
48	Hal Smith	1.50	.70	.45
49	Curt Raydon	1.50	.70	.45
50	Al Kaline	25.00	12.50	7.50
51	Jim Coates	2.00	1.00	.60
52	Dave Philley	1.50	.70	.45
53	Jackie Brandt	1.50	.70	.45
54	Mike Fornieles	1.50	.70	.45
55	Bill Mazeroski	3.00	1.50	.90
56	Steve Korcheck	1.50	.70	.45
57	Win - Savers (Turk Lown, Gerry Staley)	1.75	.90	.50
58	Gino Cimoli	1.50	.70	.45
59	Juan Pizarro	1.50	.70	.45
60	Gus Triandos	1.75	.90	.50
61	Eddie Kasko	1.50	.70	.45
62	Roger Craig	2.25	1.25	.70
63	George Strickland	1.50	.70	.45
64	Jack Meyer	1.50	.70	.45
65	Elston Howard	6.00	3.00	1.75
66	Bob Trowbridge	1.50	.70	.45
67	Jose Pagan	1.75	.90	.50
68	Dave Hillman	1.50	.70	.45
69	Billy Goodman	1.50	.70	.45
70	Lou Burdette	3.25	1.75	1.00
71	Marty Keough	1.50	.70	.45
72	Tigers Team/Checklist 89-176	8.00	4.00	2.50
73	Bob Gibson	40.00	20.00	12.00
74	Walt Moryn	1.50	.70	.45
75	Vic Power	1.50	.70	.45
76	Bill Fischer	1.50	.70	.45
77	Hank Foiles	1.50	.70	.45
78	Bob Grim	1.50	.70	.45
79	Walt Dropo	1.75	.90	.50
80	Johnny Antonelli	2.00	1.00	.60
81	Russ Snyder	1.50	.70	.45
82	Ruben Gomez	1.50	.70	.45
83	Tony Kubek	4.50	2.25	1.25
84	Hal Smith	1.50	.70	.45
85	Frank Lary	1.75	.90	.50
86	Dick Gernert	1.50	.70	.45
87	John Romonosky	1.50	.70	.45
88	John Roseboro	1.75	.90	.50
89	Hal Brown	1.50	.70	.45
90	Bobby Avila	1.50	.70	.45
91	Bennie Daniels	1.50	.70	.45
92	Whitey Herzog	3.25	1.75	1.00
93	Art Schult	1.50	.70	.45
94	Leo Kiely	1.50	.70	.45
95	Frank Thomas	1.50	.70	.45
96	Ralph Terry	2.50	1.25	.70
97	Ted Lepcio	1.50	.70	.45
98	Gordon Jones	1.50	.70	.45
99	Lenny Green	1.50	.70	.45
100	Nellie Fox	7.00	3.50	2.00
101	Bob Miller	1.50	.70	.45
102	Kent Hadley	2.00	1.00	.60
103	Dick Farrell	1.50	.70	.45
104	Dick Schofield	1.50	.70	.45
105	Larry Sherry	1.50	.70	.45
106	Billy Gardner	1.50	.70	.45
107	Carl Willey	1.50	.70	.45
108	Pete Daley	1.50	.70	.45
109	Cletis Boyer	3.00	1.50	.90
110	Cal McLish	1.50	.70	.45
111	Vic Wertz	1.75	.90	.50
112	Jack Harshman	1.50	.70	.45
113	Bob Skinner	1.50	.70	.45
114	Ken Aspromonte	1.50	.70	.45
115	Fork & Knuckler (Roy Face, Hoyt Wilhelm)	4.00	2.00	1.25
116	Jim Rivera	1.50	.70	.45
117	Tom Borland	1.50	.70	.45
118	Bob Bruce	1.50	.70	.45
119	Chico Cardenas	1.75	.90	.50
120	Duke Carmel	1.50	.70	.45
121	Camilo Carreon	1.50	.70	.45
122	Don Dillard	1.50	.70	.45
123	Dan Dobbek	1.50	.70	.45
124	Jim Donohue	1.50	.70	.45
125	Dick Ellsworth	1.75	.90	.50
126	Chuck Estrada	1.75	.90	.50
127	Ronnie Hansen	1.50	.70	.45
128	Bill Harris	1.50	.70	.45
129	Bob Hartman	1.50	.70	.45
130	Frank Herrera	1.50	.70	.45
131	Ed Hobaugh	1.50	.70	.45
132	Frank Howard	10.00	5.00	3.00
133	Manuel Javier	2.00	1.00	.60
134	Deron Johnson	2.00	1.00	.60
135	Ken Johnson	1.50	.70	.45
136	Jim Kaat	25.00	12.50	7.50
137	Lou Klimchock	1.50	.70	.45
138	Art Mahaffey	1.75	.90	.50
139	Carl Mathias	1.50	.70	.45
140	Julio Navarro	1.50	.70	.45
141	Jim Proctor	1.50	.70	.45
142	Bill Short	2.00	1.00	.60
143	Al Spangler	1.50	.70	.45
144	Al Stieglitz	1.50	.70	.45
145	Jim Umbricht	1.50	.70	.45
146	Ted Wieand	1.50	.70	.45
147	Bob Will	1.50	.70	.45
148	Carl Yastrzemski	350.00	140.00	88.00
149	Bob Nieman	1.50	.70	.45
150	Billy Pierce	2.25	1.25	.70
151	Giants Team/Checklist 177-264	6.00	3.00	1.75
152	Gail Harris	1.50	.70	.45
153	Bobby Thomson	2.00	1.00	.60
154	Jim Davenport	1.50	.70	.45
155	Charlie Neal	1.50	.70	.45
156	Art Ceccarelli	1.50	.70	.45
157	Rocky Nelson	1.50	.70	.45
158	Wes Covington	1.50	.70	.45
159	Jim Piersall	2.00	1.00	.60
160	Rival All Stars (Ken Boyer, Mickey Mantle)	30.00	15.00	9.00
161	Ray Narleski	1.50	.70	.45
162	Sammy Taylor	1.50	.70	.45
163	Hector Lopez	2.00	1.00	.60
164	Reds Team/Checklist 89-176	7.00	3.50	2.00
165	Jack Sanford	1.50	.70	.45
166	Chuck Essegian	1.50	.70	.45
167	Valmy Thomas	1.50	.70	.45
168	Alex Grammas	1.50	.70	.45
169	Jake Striker	1.50	.70	.45
170	Del Crandall	2.00	1.00	.60
171	Johnny Groth	1.50	.70	.45
172	Willie Kirkland	1.50	.70	.45
173	Billy Martin	9.00	4.50	2.75
174	Indians Team/Checklist 89-176	6.00	3.00	1.75
175	Pedro Ramos	1.50	.70	.45
176	Vada Pinson	3.25	1.75	1.00
177	Johnny Kucks	1.50	.70	.45
178	Woody Held	1.50	.70	.45
179	Rip Coleman	1.50	.70	.45
180	Harry Simpson	1.50	.70	.45
181	Billy Loes	1.50	.70	.45
182	Glen Hobbie	1.50	.70	.45
183	Eli Grba	2.00	1.00	.60
184	Gary Geiger	1.50	.70	.45
185	Jim Owens	1.50	.70	.45
186	Dave Sisler	1.50	.70	.45
187	Jay Hook	1.50	.70	.45
188	Dick Williams	2.00	1.00	.60
189	Don McMahon	1.50	.70	.45
190	Gene Woodling	1.75	.90	.50
191	Johnny Klippstein	1.50	.70	.45
192	Danny O'Connell	1.50	.70	.45
193	Dick Hyde	1.50	.70	.45
194	Bobby Gene Smith	1.50	.70	.45
195	Lindy McDaniel	1.50	.70	.45
196	Andy Carey	2.00	1.00	.60
197	Ron Kline	1.50	.70	.45
198	Jerry Lynch	1.50	.70	.45
199	Dick Donovan	1.50	.70	.45
200	Willie Mays	100.00	50.00	30.00
201	Larry Osborne	1.50	.70	.45
202	Fred Kipp	1.50	.70	.45
203	Sammy White	1.50	.70	.45
204	Ryne Duren	2.50	1.25	.70
205	Johnny Logan	1.75	.90	.50
206	Claude Osteen	1.75	.90	.50
207	Bob Boyd	1.50	.70	.45
208	White Sox Team/Checklist 177-264	6.00	3.00	1.75
209	Ron Blackburn	1.50	.70	.45
210	Harmon Killebrew	25.00	12.50	7.50
211	Taylor Phillips	1.50	.70	.45
212	Walt Alston	6.00	3.00	1.75
213	Chuck Dressen	1.75	.90	.50
214	Jimmie Dykes	1.50	.70	.45
215	Bob Elliott	1.75	.90	.50
216	Joe Gordon	1.75	.90	.50
217	Charley Grimm	1.75	.90	.50
218	Solly Hemus	1.50	.70	.45
219	Fred Hutchinson	1.75	.90	.50
220	Billy Jurges	1.50	.70	.45
221	Cookie Lavagetto	1.50	.70	.45
222	Al Lopez	5.00	2.50	1.50
223	Danny Murtaugh	1.75	.90	.50
224	Paul Richards	1.75	.90	.50
225	Bill Rigney	1.50	.70	.45

		NR MT	EX	VG
226	Eddie Sawyer	1.50	.70	.45
227	Casey Stengel	18.00	9.00	5.50
228	Ernie Johnson	1.50	.70	.45
229	Joe Morgan	1.50	.70	.45
230	Mound Magicians (Bob Buhl, Lou Burdette, Warren Spahn)	6.00	3.00	1.75
231	Hal Naragon	1.50	.70	.45
232	Jim Busby	1.50	.70	.45
233	Don Elston	1.50	.70	.45
234	Don Demeter	1.50	.70	.45
235	Gus Bell	1.75	.90	.50
236	Dick Ricketts	1.50	.70	.45
237	Elmer Valo	2.00	1.00	.60
238	Danny Kravitz	1.50	.70	.45
239	Joe Shipley	1.50	.70	.45
240	Luis Aparicio	10.00	5.00	3.00
241	Albie Pearson	1.50	.70	.45
242	Cards Team/Checklist 265-352	6.00	3.00	1.75
243	Bubba Phillips	1.50	.70	.45
244	Hal Griggs	1.50	.70	.45
245	Eddie Yost	1.75	.90	.50
246	Lee Maye	1.50	.70	.45
247	Gil McDougald	4.50	2.25	1.25
248	Del Rice	1.50	.70	.45
249	*Earl Wilson*	1.75	.90	.50
250	Stan Musial	100.00	50.00	30.00
251	Bobby Malkmus	1.50	.70	.45
252	Ray Herbert	1.50	.70	.45
253	Eddie Bressoud	1.50	.70	.45
254	Arnie Portocarrero	1.50	.70	.45
255	Jim Gilliam	3.25	1.75	1.00
256	Dick Brown	1.50	.70	.45
257	Gordy Coleman	1.50	.70	.45
258	Dick Groat	4.00	2.00	1.25
259	George Altman	1.50	.70	.45
260	Power Plus (Rocky Colavito, Tito Francona)	3.00	1.50	.90
261	Pete Burnside	1.50	.70	.45
262	Hank Bauer	2.00	1.00	.60
263	Darrell Johnson	1.50	.70	.45
264	Robin Roberts	15.00	7.50	4.50
265	Rip Repulski	1.50	.70	.45
266	Joe Jay	1.50	.70	.45
267	Jim Marshall	1.50	.70	.45
268	Al Worthington	1.50	.70	.45
269	Gene Green	1.50	.70	.45
270	Bob Turley	3.25	1.75	1.00
271	Julio Becquer	1.50	.70	.45
272	Fred Green	1.50	.70	.45
273	Neil Chrisley	1.50	.70	.45
274	Tom Acker	1.50	.70	.45
275	Curt Flood	3.00	1.50	.90
276	Ken McBride	1.50	.70	.45
277	Harry Bright	1.50	.70	.45
278	Stan Williams	1.50	.70	.45
279	Chuck Tanner	2.50	1.25	.70
280	Frank Sullivan	1.50	.70	.45
281	Ray Boone	1.75	.90	.50
282	Joe Nuxhall	2.00	1.00	.60
283	John Blanchard	2.75	1.50	.80
284	Don Gross	1.50	.70	.45
285	Harry Anderson	1.50	.70	.45
286	Ray Semproch	1.50	.70	.45
287	Felipe Alou	2.50	1.25	.70
288	Bob Mabe	1.75	.90	.50
289	Willie Jones	1.75	.90	.50
290	Jerry Lumpe	2.00	1.00	.60
291	Bob Keegan	1.75	.90	.50
292	Dodger Backstops (Joe Pignatano, John Roseboro)	2.00	1.00	.60
293	Gene Conley	2.00	1.00	.60
294	Tony Taylor	1.50	.70	.45
295	Gil Hodges	18.00	9.00	5.50
296	Nelson Chittum	1.75	.90	.50
297	Reno Bertoia	1.75	.90	.50
298	George Witt	1.75	.90	.50
299	Earl Torgeson	1.75	.90	.50
300	Hank Aaron	125.00	56.00	35.00
301	Jerry Davie	1.75	.90	.50
302	Phillies Team/Checklist 353-429	7.00	3.50	2.00
303	Billy O'Dell	1.75	.90	.50
304	Joe Ginsberg	1.75	.90	.50
305	Richie Ashburn	7.00	3.50	2.00
306	Frank Baumann	1.75	.90	.50
307	Gene Oliver	1.75	.90	.50
308	Dick Hall	1.75	.90	.50
309	Bob Hale	1.75	.90	.50
310	Frank Malzone	2.00	1.00	.60
311	Raul Sanchez	1.75	.90	.50
312	Charlie Lau	2.00	1.00	.60
313	Turk Lown	1.75	.90	.50

		NR MT	EX	VG
314	Chico Fernandez	1.75	.90	.50
315	Bobby Shantz	3.25	1.75	1.00
316	*Willie McCovey*	200.00	100.00	60.00
317	Pumpsie Green	1.75	.90	.50
318	Jim Baxes	1.75	.90	.50
319	Joe Koppe	1.75	.90	.50
320	Bob Allison	2.25	1.25	.70
321	Ron Fairly	2.00	1.00	.60
322	Willie Tasby	1.75	.90	.50
323	Johnny Romano	1.75	.90	.50
324	Jim Perry	2.50	1.25	.70
325	Jim O'Toole	2.00	1.00	.60
326	Bob Clemente	80.00	40.00	25.00
327	*Ray Sadecki*	2.25	1.25	.70
328	Earl Battey	2.00	1.00	.60
329	Zack Monroe	2.25	1.25	.70
330	Harvey Kuenn	3.00	1.50	.90
331	Henry Mason	1.75	.90	.50
332	Yankees Team/Checklist 265-352	20.00	10.00	6.00
333	Danny McDevitt	1.75	.90	.50
334	Ted Abernathy	1.75	.90	.50
335	Red Schoendienst	10.00	5.00	3.00
336	Ike Delock	1.75	.90	.50
337	Cal Neeman	1.75	.90	.50
338	Ray Monzant	1.75	.90	.50
339	Harry Chiti	1.75	.90	.50
340	Harvey Haddix	2.25	1.25	.70
341	Carroll Hardy	1.75	.90	.50
342	Casey Wise	1.75	.90	.50
343	Sandy Koufax	90.00	45.00	27.00
344	Clint Courtney	1.75	.90	.50
345	Don Newcombe	2.50	1.25	.70
346	J.C. Martin (photo actually Gary Peters)	1.75	.90	.50
347	Ed Bouchee	1.75	.90	.50
348	Barry Shetrone	1.75	.90	.50
349	Moe Drabowsky	1.75	.90	.50
350	Mickey Mantle	350.00	140.00	88.00
351	Don Nottebart	1.75	.90	.50
352	Cincy Clouters (Gus Bell, Jerry Lynch, Frank Robinson)	5.00	2.50	1.50
353	Don Larsen	2.25	1.25	.70
354	Bob Lillis	1.75	.90	.50
355	Bill White	3.00	1.50	.90
356	Joe Amalfitano	1.75	.90	.50
357	Al Schroll	1.75	.90	.50
358	Joe DeMaestri	2.25	1.25	.70
359	Buddy Gilbert	1.75	.90	.50
360	Herb Score	2.50	1.25	.70
361	Bob Oldis	1.75	.90	.50
362	Russ Kemmerer	1.75	.90	.50
363	Gene Stephens	1.75	.90	.50
364	Paul Foytack	1.75	.90	.50
365	Minnie Minoso	3.00	1.50	.90
366	*Dallas Green*	3.25	1.75	1.00
367	Bill Tuttle	1.75	.90	.50
368	Daryl Spencer	1.75	.90	.50
369	Billy Hoeft	1.75	.90	.50
370	Bill Skowron	6.00	3.00	1.75
371	Bud Byerly	1.75	.90	.50
372	Frank House	1.75	.90	.50
373	Don Hoak	2.00	1.00	.60
374	Bob Buhl	2.00	1.00	.60
375	Dale Long	2.00	1.00	.60
376	Johnny Briggs	1.75	.90	.50
377	Roger Maris	90.00	45.00	27.00
378	Stu Miller	1.75	.90	.50
379	Red Wilson	1.75	.90	.50
380	Bob Shaw	1.75	.90	.50
381	Braves Team/Checklist 353-429	7.00	3.50	2.00
382	Ted Bowsfield	1.75	.90	.50
383	Leon Wagner	1.75	.90	.50
384	Don Cardwell	1.75	.90	.50
385	World Series Game 1 (Neal Steals Second)	3.50	1.75	1.00
386	World Series Game 2 (Neal Belts 2nd Homer)	3.50	1.75	1.00
387	World Series Game 3 (Furillo Breaks Up Game)	3.50	1.75	1.00
388	World Series Game 4 (Hodges' Winning Homer)	3.75	2.00	1.25
389	World Series Game 5 (Luis Swipes Base)	3.75	2.00	1.25
390	World Series Game 6 (Scrambling After Ball)	3.50	1.75	1.00
391	World Series Summary (The Champs Celebrate)	3.50	1.75	1.00
392	Tex Clevenger	1.75	.90	.50
393	Smoky Burgess	2.50	1.25	.70
394	Norm Larker	1.75	.90	.50

	NR MT	EX	VG
395 Hoyt Wilhelm	15.00	7.50	4.50
396 Steve Bilko	1.75	.90	.50
397 Don Blasingame	1.75	.90	.50
398 Mike Cuellar	2.25	1.25	.70
399 Young Hill Stars (Jack Fisher, Milt Pappas, Jerry Walker)	2.25	1.25	.70
400 Rocky Colavito	6.00	3.00	1.75
401 Bob Duliba	1.75	.90	.50
402 Dick Stuart	2.00	1.00	.60
403 Ed Sadowski	1.75	.90	.50
404 Bob Rush	1.75	.90	.50
405 Bobby Richardson	6.00	3.00	1.75
406 Billy Klaus	1.75	.90	.50
407 *Gary Peters* (photo actually J.C. Martin)	2.25	1.25	.70
408 Carl Furillo	4.00	2.00	1.25
409 Ron Samford	1.75	.90	.50
410 Sam Jones	1.75	.90	.50
411 Ed Bailey	1.75	.90	.50
412 Bob Anderson	1.75	.90	.50
413 A's Team/Checklist 430-495	7.00	3.50	2.00
414 Don Williams	1.75	.90	.50
415 Bob Cerv	1.75	.90	.50
416 Humberto Robinson	1.75	.90	.50
417 Chuck Cottier	1.75	.90	.50
418 Don Mossi	2.00	1.00	.60
419 George Crowe	1.75	.90	.50
420 Ed Mathews	25.00	12.50	7.50
421 Duke Maas	2.25	1.25	.70
422 Johnny Powers	1.75	.90	.50
423 Ed Fitz Gerald	1.75	.90	.50
424 Pete Whisenant	1.75	.90	.50
425 Johnny Podres	3.00	1.50	.90
426 Ron Jackson	1.75	.90	.50
427 Al Grunwald	1.75	.90	.50
428 Al Smith	1.75	.90	.50
429 American League Kings (Nellie Fox, Harvey Kuenn)	2.25	1.25	.70
430 Art Ditmar	2.00	1.00	.60
431 Andre Rodgers	1.75	.90	.50
432 Chuck Stobbs	1.75	.90	.50
433 Irv Noren	1.75	.90	.50
434 Brooks Lawrence	1.75	.90	.50
435 Gene Freese	1.75	.90	.50
436 Marv Throneberry	2.25	1.25	.70
437 Bob Friend	2.50	1.25	.70
438 Jim Coker	1.75	.90	.50
439 Tom Brewer	1.75	.90	.50
440 Jim Lemon	2.00	1.00	.60
441 Gary Bell	3.50	1.75	1.00
442 Joe Pignatano	3.50	1.75	1.00
443 Charlie Maxwell	3.50	1.75	1.00
444 Jerry Kindall	3.50	1.75	1.00
445 Warren Spahn	35.00	17.50	10.50
446 Ellis Burton	3.50	1.75	1.00
447 Ray Moore	3.50	1.75	1.00
448 *Jim Gentile*	4.00	2.00	1.25
449 Jim Brosnan	3.75	2.00	1.25
450 Orlando Cepeda	8.00	4.00	2.50
451 Curt Simmons	4.00	2.00	1.25
452 Ray Webster	3.50	1.75	1.00
453 Vern Law	4.50	2.25	1.25
454 Hal Woodeshick	3.50	1.75	1.00
455 Orioles Coaches (Harry Brecheen, Lum Harris, Eddie Robinson)	3.75	2.00	1.25
456 Red Sox Coaches (Del Baker, Billy Herman, Sal Maglie, Rudy York)	4.00	2.00	1.25
457 Cubs Coaches (Lou Klein, Charlie Root, Elvin Tappe)	3.75	2.00	1.25
458 White Sox Coaches (Ray Berres, Johnny Cooney, Tony Cuccinello, Don Gutteridge)	3.75	2.00	1.25
459 Reds Coaches (Cot Deal, Wally Moses, Reggie Otero)	3.75	2.00	1.25
460 Indians Coaches (Mel Harder, Red Kress, Bob Lemon, Jo-Jo White)	4.00	2.00	1.25
461 Tigers Coaches (Luke Appling, Tom Ferrick, Billy Hitchcock)	4.00	2.00	1.25
462 A's Coaches (Walker Cooper, Fred Fitzsimmons, Don Heffner)	3.75	2.00	1.25
463 Dodgers Coaches (Joe Becker, Bobby Bragan, Greg Mulleavy, Pete Reiser)	4.00	2.00	1.25
464 Braves Coaches (George Myatt, Andy Pafko, Bob Scheffing, Whitlow Wyatt)	3.75	2.00	1.25
465 Yankees Coaches (Frank Crosetti, Bill Dickey, Ralph Houk, Ed Lopat)	7.00	3.50	2.00
466 Phillies Coaches (Dick Carter, Andy Cohen, Ken Silvestri)	3.75	2.00	1.25
467 Pirates Coaches (Bill Burwell, Sam Narron, Frank Oceak, Mickey Vernon)	4.00	2.00	1.25

	NR MT	EX	VG
468 Cardinals Coaches (Ray Katt, Johnny Keane, Howie Pollet, Harry Walker)	3.75	2.00	1.25
469 Giants Coaches (Salty Parker, Bill Posedel, Wes Westrum)	3.75	2.00	1.25
470 Senators Coaches (Ellis Clary, Sam Mele, Bob Swift)	3.75	2.00	1.25
471 Ned Garver	3.50	1.75	1.00
472 Al Dark	4.50	2.25	1.25
473 Al Cicotte	3.50	1.75	1.00
474 Haywood Sullivan	3.75	2.00	1.25
475 Don Drysdale	30.00	15.00	9.00
476 Lou Johnson	3.50	1.75	1.00
477 Don Ferrarese	3.50	1.75	1.00
478 Frank Torre	3.50	1.75	1.00
479 Georges Maranda	3.50	1.75	1.00
480 Yogi Berra	50.00	25.00	15.00
481 Wes Stock	3.50	1.75	1.00
482 Frank Bolling	3.50	1.75	1.00
483 Camilo Pascual	3.75	2.00	1.25
484 Pirates Team/Checklist 430-495	15.00	7.50	4.50
485 Ken Boyer	4.50	2.25	1.25
486 Bobby Del Greco	3.50	1.75	1.00
487 Tom Sturdivant	3.50	1.75	1.00
488 Norm Cash	5.00	2.50	1.50
489 Steve Ridzik	3.50	1.75	1.00
490 Frank Robinson	40.00	20.00	12.00
491 Mel Roach	3.50	1.75	1.00
492 Larry Jackson	3.50	1.75	1.00
493 Duke Snider	40.00	20.00	12.00
494 Orioles Team/Checklist 496-572	7.00	3.50	2.00
495 Sherm Lollar	2.00	1.00	.60
496 Bill Virdon	4.00	2.00	1.25
497 John Tsitouris	3.50	1.75	1.00
498 Al Pilarcik	3.50	1.75	1.00
499 Johnny James	4.00	2.00	1.25
500 Johnny Temple	3.50	1.75	1.00
501 Bob Schmidt	3.50	1.75	1.00
502 Jim Bunning	8.00	4.00	2.50
503 Don Lee	3.50	1.75	1.00
504 Seth Morehead	3.50	1.75	1.00
505 Ted Kluszewski	5.00	2.50	1.50
506 Lee Walls	3.50	1.75	1.00
507 Dick Stigman	8.00	4.00	2.50
508 Billy Consolo	8.00	4.00	2.50
509 *Tommy Davis*	18.00	9.00	5.50
510 Jerry Staley	8.00	4.00	2.50
511 Ken Walters	8.00	4.00	2.50
512 Joe Gibbon	8.00	4.00	2.50
513 Cubs Team/Checklist 496-572	25.00	12.50	7.50
514 *Steve Barber*	9.00	4.50	2.75
515 Stan Lopata	8.00	4.00	2.50
516 Marty Kutyna	8.00	4.00	2.50
517 Charley James	8.00	4.00	2.50
518 *Tony Gonzalez*	9.00	4.50	2.75
519 Ed Roebuck	8.00	4.00	2.50
520 Don Buddin	8.00	4.00	2.50
521 Mike Lee	8.00	4.00	2.50
522 Ken Hunt	9.00	4.50	2.75
523 *Clay Dalrymple*	9.00	4.50	2.75
524 Bill Henry	8.00	4.00	2.50
525 Marv Breeding	8.00	4.00	2.50
526 Paul Giel	8.00	4.00	2.50
527 Jose Valdivielso	8.00	4.00	2.50
528 Ben Johnson	8.00	4.00	2.50
529 Norm Sherry	8.00	4.00	2.50
530 Mike McCormick	9.00	4.50	2.75
531 Sandy Amoros	8.00	4.00	2.50
532 Mike Garcia	10.00	5.00	3.00
533 Lu Clinton	8.00	4.00	2.50
534 Ken MacKenzie	8.00	4.00	2.50
535 Whitey Lockman	8.00	4.00	2.50
536 Wynn Hawkins	8.00	4.00	2.50
537 Red Sox Team/Checklist 496-572	25.00	12.50	7.50
538 Frank Barnes	8.00	4.00	2.50
539 Gene Baker	8.00	4.00	2.50
540 Jerry Walker	8.00	4.00	2.50
541 Tony Curry	8.00	4.00	2.50
542 Ken Hamlin	8.00	4.00	2.50
543 Elio Chacon	8.00	4.00	2.50
544 Bill Monbouquette	9.00	4.50	2.75
545 Carl Sawatski	8.00	4.00	2.50
546 Hank Aguirre	8.00	4.00	2.50
547 *Bob Aspromonte*	9.00	4.50	2.75
548 *Don Mincher*	9.00	4.50	2.75
549 John Buzhardt	8.00	4.00	2.50
550 Jim Landis	8.00	4.00	2.50
551 Ed Rakow	8.00	4.00	2.50
552 Walt Bond	8.00	4.00	2.50
553 Bill Skowron AS	12.00	6.00	3.50

		NR MT	EX	VG
554	Willie McCovey AS	45.00	22.00	13.50
555	Nellie Fox AS	15.00	7.50	4.50
556	Charlie Neal AS	9.00	4.50	2.75
557	Frank Malzone AS	9.00	4.50	2.75
558	Eddie Mathews AS	25.00	12.50	7.50
559	Luis Aparicio AS	18.00	9.00	5.50
560	Ernie Banks AS	40.00	20.00	12.00
561	Al Kaline AS	40.00	20.00	12.00
562	Joe Cunningham AS	9.00	4.50	2.75
563	Mickey Mantle AS	175.00	87.00	50.00
564	Willie Mays AS	85.00	42.00	25.00
565	Roger Maris AS	100.00	45.00	27.00
566	Hank Aaron AS	100.00	45.00	27.00
567	Sherm Lollar AS	9.00	4.50	2.75
568	Del Crandall AS	9.00	4.50	2.75
569	Camilo Pascual AS	9.00	4.50	2.75
570	Don Drysdale AS	30.00	15.00	9.00
571	Billy Pierce AS	9.00	4.50	2.75
572	Johnny Antonelli AS	15.00	5.00	2.75
----	Elect Your Favorite Rookie Insert (paper stock, no date on back)	15.00	7.50	4.50
----	Hot Iron Transfer Insert (paper stock)	15.00	7.50	4.50

1960 Topps Baseball Tattoos

Probably the least popular of all Topps products among parents and teachers, the Topps Tattoos were delightful little items on the reverse of the wrappers of Topps "Tattoo Bubble Gum." The entire wrapper was 1-9/16" by 3-1/2." The happy owner simply moistened his skin and applied the back of the wrapper to the wet spot. Presto, out came a "tattoo" in color (although often blurred by running colors). The set offered 96 tattoo possibilities of which 55 were players, 16 teams, 15 action shots and 10 autographed balls. Surviving specimens are very rare today.

		NR MT	EX	VG
	Complete Set:	675.00	337.00	202.00
	Common Player:	3.00	1.50	.90
(1)	Hank Aaron	25.00	12.50	7.50
(2)	Bob Allison	5.00	2.50	1.50
(3)	John Antonelli	5.00	2.50	1.50
(4)	Richie Ashburn	7.00	3.50	2.00
(5)	Ernie Banks	15.00	7.50	4.50
(6)	Yogi Berra	18.00	9.00	5.50
(7)	Lew Burdette	6.00	3.00	1.75
(8)	Orlando Cepeda	7.00	3.50	2.00
(9)	Rocky Colavito	6.00	3.00	1.75
(10)	Joe Cunningham	3.00	1.50	.90
(11)	Buddy Daley	3.00	1.50	.90
(12)	Don Drysdale	12.00	6.00	3.50
(13)	Ryne Duren	5.00	2.50	1.50
(14)	Roy Face	5.00	2.50	1.50
(15)	Whitey Ford	15.00	7.50	4.50
(16)	Nellie Fox	7.00	3.50	2.00
(17)	Tito Francona	3.00	1.50	.90
(18)	Gene Freese	3.00	1.50	.90
(19)	Jim Gilliam	6.00	3.00	1.75
(20)	Dick Groat	6.00	3.00	1.75
(21)	Ray Herbert	3.00	1.50	.90
(22)	Glen Hobbie	3.00	1.50	.90
(23)	Jackie Jensen	6.00	3.00	1.75
(24)	Sam Jones	3.00	1.50	.90

		NR MT	EX	VG
(25)	Al Kaline	15.00	7.50	4.50
(26)	Harmon Killebrew	12.00	6.00	3.50
(27)	Harvy Kuenn (Harvey)	6.00	3.00	1.75
(28)	Frank Lary	3.00	1.50	.90
(29)	Vernon Law	5.00	2.50	1.50
(30)	Frank Malzone	3.00	1.50	.90
(31)	Mickey Mantle	75.00	37.00	22.00
(32)	Roger Maris	15.00	7.50	4.50
(33)	Ed Mathews	12.00	6.00	3.50
(34)	Willie Mays	25.00	12.50	7.50
(35)	Cal Mclish	3.00	1.50	.90
(36)	Wally Moon	5.00	2.50	1.50
(37)	Walt Moryn	3.00	1.50	.90
(38)	Don Mossi	3.00	1.50	.90
(39)	Stan Musial	25.00	12.50	7.50
(40)	Charlie Neal	3.00	1.50	.90
(41)	Don Newcombe	5.00	2.50	1.50
(42)	Milt Pappas	5.00	2.50	1.50
(43)	Camilo Pascual	5.00	2.50	1.50
(44)	Billie Pierce (Billy)	5.00	2.50	1.50
(45)	Robin Roberts	12.00	6.00	3.50
(46)	Frank Robinson	15.00	7.50	4.50
(47)	Pete Runnels	5.00	2.50	1.50
(48)	Herb Score	5.00	2.50	1.50
(49)	Warren Spahn	12.00	6.00	3.50
(50)	Johnny Temple	3.00	1.50	.90
(51)	Gus Triandos	3.00	1.50	.90
(52)	Jerry Walker	3.00	1.50	.90
(53)	Bill White	5.00	2.50	1.50
(54)	Gene Woodling	5.00	2.50	1.50
(55)	Early Wynn	12.00	6.00	3.50
(56)	Chicago Cubs Logo	3.00	1.50	.90
(57)	Cincinnati Reds Logo	3.00	1.50	.90
(58)	Los Angeles Dodgers Logo	3.00	1.50	.90
(59)	Milwaukee Braves Logo	3.00	1.50	.90
(60)	Philadelphia Phillies Logo	3.00	1.50	.90
(61)	Pittsburgh Pirates Logo	5.00	2.50	1.50
(62)	San Francisco Giants Logo	3.00	1.50	.90
(63)	St. Louis Cardinals Logo	3.00	1.50	.90
(64)	Baltimore Orioles Logo	3.00	1.50	.90
(65)	Boston Red Sox Logo	3.00	1.50	.90
(66)	Chicago White Sox Logo	3.00	1.50	.90
(67)	Cleveland Indians Logo	3.00	1.50	.90
(68)	Detroit Tigers Logo	3.00	1.50	.90
(69)	Kansas City Athletics Logo	3.00	1.50	.90
(70)	New York Yankees Logo	6.00	3.00	1.75
(71)	Washington Senators Logo	3.00	1.50	.90
(72)	Autograph (Richie Ashburn)	3.00	1.50	.90
(73)	Autograph (Rocky Colavito)	3.00	1.50	.90
(74)	Autograph (Roy Face)	3.00	1.50	.90
(75)	Autograph (Jackie Jensen)	3.00	1.50	.90
(76)	Autograph (Harmon Killebrew)	5.00	2.50	1.50
(77)	Autograph (Mickey Mantle)	25.00	12.50	7.50
(78)	Autograph (Willie Mays)	10.00	5.00	3.00
(79)	Autograph (Stan Musial)	10.00	5.00	3.00
(80)	Autograph (Billy Pierce)	3.00	1.50	.90
(81)	Autograph (Jerry Walker)	3.00	1.50	.90
(82)	Run-Down	3.00	1.50	.90
(83)	Out At First	3.00	1.50	.90
(84)	The Final Word	3.00	1.50	.90
(85)	Twisting Foul	3.00	1.50	.90
(86)	Out At Home	3.00	1.50	.90
(87)	Circus Catch	3.00	1.50	.90
(88)	Great Catch	3.00	1.50	.90
(89)	Stolen Base	3.00	1.50	.90
(90)	Grand Slam Homer	3.00	1.50	.90
(91)	Double Play	3.00	1.50	.90
(92)	Right-Handed Follow-Thru (no caption)	3.00	1.50	.90
(93)	Right-Handed High Leg Kick (no caption)	3.00	1.50	.90
(94)	Left-Handed Pitcher (no caption)	3.00	1.50	.90
(95)	Right-Handed Batter (no caption)	3.00	1.50	.90
(96)	Left-Handed Batter (no caption)	3.00	1.50	.90

1961 Topps

Except for some of the specialty cards, Topps returned to a vertical format with their 1961 cards. The set is numbered through 598, however only 587 cards were printed. No numbers 426, 587 and 588 were issued. Two cards numbered 463 exist (one a Braves team card and one a player card of Jack Fisher). Actually, the Braves team card is checklisted as #426. Designs for 1961 are basically large color portraits; the backs return to extensive statistics. A three-panel cartoon highlighting the player's career

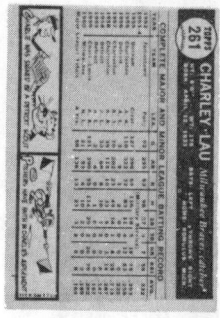

appears on the card backs. Innovations include numbered checklists, cards for statistical leaders, and 10 "Baseball Thrills" cards. The scarce high numbers are card numbers 523-589.

		NR MT	EX	VG
	Complete Set:	4800.00	2400.00	1450.
	Common Player: 1-370	1.00	.50	.30
	Common Player: 371-522	1.50	.70	.45
	Common Player: 523-589	20.00	10.00	6.00
1	Dick Groat	12.00	2.00	.70
2	Roger Maris	175.00	87.00	52.00
3	John Buzhardt	1.00	.50	.30
4	Lenny Green	1.00	.50	.30
5	Johnny Romano	1.00	.50	.30
6	Ed Roebuck	1.00	.50	.30
7	White Sox Team	2.50	1.25	.70
8	Dick Williams	1.50	.70	.45
9	Bob Purkey	1.00	.50	.30
10	Brooks Robinson	30.00	15.00	9.00
11	Curt Simmons	1.25	.60	.40
12	Moe Thacker	1.00	.50	.30
13	Chuck Cottier	1.00	.50	.30
14	Don Mossi	1.25	.60	.40
15	Willie Kirkland	1.00	.50	.30
16	Billy Muffett	1.00	.50	.30
17	Checklist 1-88	5.00	2.50	1.50
18	Jim Grant	1.00	.50	.30
19	Cletis Boyer	2.25	1.25	.70
20	Robin Roberts	10.00	5.00	3.00
21	Zorro Versalles	2.00	1.00	.60
22	Clem Labine	1.25	.60	.40
23	Don Demeter	1.00	.50	.30
24	Ken Johnson	1.00	.50	.30
25	Red's Heavy Artillery (Gus Bell, Vada Pinson, Frank Robinson)	6.00	3.00	1.75
26	Wes Stock	1.00	.50	.30
27	Jerry Kindall	1.00	.50	.30
28	Hector Lopez	1.50	.70	.45
29	Don Nottebart	1.00	.50	.30
30	Nellie Fox	6.00	3.00	1.75
31	Bob Schmidt	1.00	.50	.30
32	Ray Sadecki	1.00	.50	.30
33	Gary Geiger	1.00	.50	.30
34	Wynn Hawkins	1.00	.50	.30
35	Ron Santo	20.00	10.00	6.00
36	Jack Kralick	1.00	.50	.30
37	Charlie Maxwell	1.00	.50	.30
38	Bob Lillis	1.00	.50	.30
39	Leo Posada	1.00	.50	.30
40	Bob Turley	2.50	1.25	.70
41	N.L. Batting Leaders (Bob Clemente, Dick Groat, Norm Larker, Willie Mays)	4.00	2.00	1.25
42	A.L. Batting Leaders (Minnie Minoso, Pete Runnels, Bill Skowron, Al Smith)	2.50	1.25	.70
43	N.L. Home Run Leaders (Hank Aaron, Ernie Banks, Ken Boyer, Eddie Mathews)	4.00	2.00	1.25
44	A.L. Home Run Leaders (Rocky Colavito, Jim Lemon, Mickey Mantle, Roger Maris)	15.00	7.50	4.50
45	N.L. E.R.A. Leaders (Ernie Broglio, Don Drysdale, Bob Friend, Mike McCormick, Stan Williams)	3.25	1.75	1.00
46	A.L. E.R.A. Leaders (Frank Baumann, Hal Brown, Jim Bunning, Art Ditmar)	2.50	1.25	.70
47	N.L. Pitching Leaders (Ernie Broglio, Lou Burdette, Vern Law, Warren Spahn)	3.25	1.75	1.00
48	A.L. Pitching Leaders (Bud Daley, Art Ditmar, Chuck Estrada, Frank Lary, Milt Pappas, Jim Perry)	2.50	1.25	.70
49	N.L. Strikeout Leaders (Ernie Broglio, Don Drysdale, Sam Jones, Sandy Koufax)	4.00	2.00	1.25
50	A.L. Strikeout Leaders (Jim Bunning, Frank Lary, Pedro Ramos, Early Wynn)	3.00	1.50	.90
51	Tigers Team	3.50	1.75	1.00
52	George Crowe	1.00	.50	.30
53	Russ Nixon	1.00	.50	.30
54	Earl Francis	1.00	.50	.30
55	Jim Davenport	1.00	.50	.30
56	Russ Kemmerer	1.00	.50	.30
57	Marv Throneberry	1.75	.90	.50
58	Joe Schaffernoth	1.00	.50	.30
59	Jim Woods	1.00	.50	.30
60	Woodie Held	1.00	.50	.30
61	Ron Piche	1.00	.50	.30
62	Al Pilarcik	1.00	.50	.30
63	Jim Kaat	8.00	4.00	2.50
64	Alex Grammas	1.00	.50	.30
65	Ted Kluszewski	4.00	2.00	1.25
66	Bill Henry	1.00	.50	.30
67	Ossie Virgil	1.00	.50	.30
68	Deron Johnson	1.50	.70	.45
69	Earl Wilson	1.00	.50	.30
70	Bill Virdon	2.00	1.00	.60
71	Jerry Adair	1.25	.60	.40
72	Stu Miller	1.00	.50	.30
73	Al Spangler	1.00	.50	.30
74	Joe Pignatano	1.00	.50	.30
75	Lindy Shows Larry (Larry Jackson, Lindy McDaniel)	1.50	.70	.45
76	Harry Anderson	1.00	.50	.30
77	Dick Stigman	1.00	.50	.30
78	Lee Walls	1.00	.50	.30
79	Joe Ginsberg	1.00	.50	.30
80	Harmon Killebrew	18.00	9.00	5.50
81	Tracy Stallard	1.00	.50	.30
82	Joe Christopher	1.00	.50	.30
83	Bob Bruce	1.00	.50	.30
84	Lee Maye	1.00	.50	.30
85	Jerry Walker	1.00	.50	.30
86	Dodgers Team	3.50	1.75	1.00
87	Joe Amalfitano	1.00	.50	.30
88	Richie Ashburn	6.00	3.00	1.75
89	Billy Martin	6.00	3.00	1.75
90	Jerry Staley	1.00	.50	.30
91	Walt Moryn	1.00	.50	.30
92	Hal Naragon	1.00	.50	.30
93	Tony Gonzalez	1.00	.50	.30
94	Johnny Kucks	1.00	.50	.30
95	Norm Cash	3.50	1.75	1.00
96	Billy O'Dell	1.00	.50	.30
97	Jerry Lynch	1.00	.50	.30
98a	Checklist 89-176 (word "Checklist" in red on front)	7.00	3.50	2.00
98b	Checklist 89-176 ("Checklist" in yellow, 98 on back in black)	5.00	2.50	1.50
98c	Checklist 89-176 ("Checklist" in yellow, 98 on back in white)	7.00	3.50	2.00
99	Don Buddin	1.00	.50	.30
100	Harvey Haddix	1.50	.70	.45
101	Bubba Phillips	1.00	.50	.30
102	Gene Stephens	1.00	.50	.30
103	Ruben Amaro	1.00	.50	.30
104	John Blanchard	1.50	.70	.45
105	Carl Willey	1.00	.50	.30
106	Whitey Herzog	2.25	1.25	.70
107	Seth Morehead	1.00	.50	.30
108	Dan Dobbek	1.00	.50	.30
109	Johnny Podres	2.25	1.25	.70
110	Vada Pinson	3.00	1.50	.90
111	Jack Meyer	1.00	.50	.30
112	Chico Fernandez	1.00	.50	.30
113	Mike Fornieles	1.00	.50	.30
114	Hobie Landrith	1.00	.50	.30
115	Johnny Antonelli	1.25	.60	.40
116	Joe DeMaestri	1.50	.70	.45
117	Dale Long	1.25	.60	.40
118	Chris Cannizzaro	1.00	.50	.30
119	A's Big Armor (Hank Bauer, Jerry Lumpe, Norm Siebern)	1.50	.70	.45
120	Ed Mathews	15.00	7.50	4.50
121	Eli Grba	1.00	.50	.30
122	Cubs Team	2.50	1.25	.70
123	Billy Gardner	1.00	.50	.30
124	J.C. Martin	1.00	.50	.30
125	Steve Barber	1.00	.50	.30
126	Dick Stuart	1.25	.60	.40
127	Ron Kline	1.00	.50	.30
128	Rip Repulski	1.00	.50	.30
129	Ed Hobaugh	1.00	.50	.30
130	Norm Larker	1.00	.50	.30

		NR MT	EX	VG
131	Paul Richards	1.25	.60	.40
132	Al Lopez	3.00	1.50	.90
133	Ralph Houk	3.00	1.50	.90
134	Mickey Vernon	1.25	.60	.40
135	Fred Hutchinson	1.25	.60	.40
136	Walt Alston	4.00	2.00	1.25
137	Chuck Dressen	1.25	.60	.40
138	Danny Murtaugh	1.25	.60	.40
139	Solly Hemus	1.00	.50	.30
140	Gus Triandos	1.25	.60	.40
141	*Billy Williams*	110.00	55.00	32.00
142	Luis Arroyo	1.50	.70	.45
143	Russ Snyder	1.00	.50	.30
144	Jim Coker	1.00	.50	.30
145	Bob Buhl	1.25	.60	.40
146	Marty Keough	1.00	.50	.30
147	Ed Rakow	1.00	.50	.30
148	Julian Javier	1.25	.60	.40
149	Bob Oldis	1.00	.50	.30
150	Willie Mays	100.00	50.00	30.00
151	Jim Donohue	1.00	.50	.30
152	Earl Torgeson	1.00	.50	.30
153	Don Lee	1.00	.50	.30
154	Bobby Del Greco	1.00	.50	.30
155	Johnny Temple	1.00	.50	.30
156	Ken Hunt	1.00	.50	.30
157	Cal McLish	1.00	.50	.30
158	Pete Daley	1.00	.50	.30
159	Orioles Team	2.50	1.25	.70
160	Whitey Ford	25.00	12.50	7.50
161	Sherman Jones (photo actually Eddie Fisher)	1.00	.50	.30
162	Jay Hook	1.00	.50	.30
163	Ed Sadowski	1.00	.50	.30
164	Felix Mantilla	1.00	.50	.30
165	Gino Cimoli	1.00	.50	.30
166	Danny Kravitz	1.00	.50	.30
167	Giants Team	2.50	1.25	.70
168	Tommy Davis	3.00	1.50	.90
169	Don Elston	1.00	.50	.30
170	Al Smith	1.00	.50	.30
171	Paul Foytack	1.00	.50	.30
172	Don Dillard	1.00	.50	.30
173	Beantown Bombers (Jackie Jensen, Frank Malzone, Vic Wertz)	2.00	1.00	.60
174	Ray Semproch	1.00	.50	.30
175	Gene Freese	1.00	.50	.30
176	Ken Aspromonte	1.00	.50	.30
177	Don Larsen	1.50	.70	.45
178	Bob Nieman	1.00	.50	.30
179	Joe Koppe	1.00	.50	.30
180	Bobby Richardson	5.00	2.50	1.50
181	Fred Green	1.00	.50	.30
182	Dave Nicholson	1.00	.50	.30
183	Andre Rodgers	1.00	.50	.30
184	Steve Bilko	1.00	.50	.30
185	Herb Score	1.50	.70	.45
186	Elmer Valo	1.00	.50	.30
187	Billy Klaus	1.00	.50	.30
188	Jim Marshall	1.00	.50	.30
189	Checklist 177-264	5.00	2.50	1.50
190	Stan Williams	1.00	.50	.30
191	Mike de la Hoz	1.00	.50	.30
192	Dick Brown	1.00	.50	.30
193	Gene Conley	1.25	.60	.40
194	Gordy Coleman	1.00	.50	.30
195	Jerry Casale	1.00	.50	.30
196	Ed Bouchee	1.00	.50	.30
197	Dick Hall	1.00	.50	.30
198	Carl Sawatski	1.00	.50	.30
199	Bob Boyd	1.00	.50	.30
200	Warren Spahn	25.00	12.50	7.50
201	Pete Whisenant	1.00	.50	.30
202	Al Neiger	1.00	.50	.30
203	Eddie Bressoud	1.00	.50	.30
204	Bob Skinner	1.25	.60	.40
205	Bill Pierce	1.75	.90	.50
206	Gene Green	1.00	.50	.30
207	Dodger Southpaws (Sandy Koufax, Johnny Podres)	15.00	7.50	4.50
208	Larry Osborne	1.00	.50	.30
209	Ken McBride	1.00	.50	.30
210	Pete Runnels	1.25	.60	.40
211	Bob Gibson	20.00	10.00	6.00
212	Haywood Sullivan	1.25	.60	.40
213	*Bill Stafford*	2.00	1.00	.60
214	Danny Murphy	1.00	.50	.30
215	Gus Bell	1.25	.60	.40
216	Ted Bowsfield	1.00	.50	.30
217	Mel Roach	1.00	.50	.30
218	Hal Brown	1.00	.50	.30

		NR MT	EX	VG
219	Gene Mauch	2.50	1.25	.70
220	Al Dark	1.25	.60	.40
221	Mike Higgins	1.00	.50	.30
222	Jimmie Dykes	1.00	.50	.30
223	Bob Scheffing	1.00	.50	.30
224	Joe Gordon	1.25	.60	.40
225	Bill Rigney	1.00	.50	.30
226	Harry Lavagetto	1.00	.50	.30
227	Juan Pizarro	1.00	.50	.30
228	Yankees Team	10.00	5.00	3.00
229	Rudy Hernandez	1.00	.50	.30
230	Don Hoak	1.25	.60	.40
231	Dick Drott	1.00	.50	.30
232	Bill White	1.50	.70	.45
233	Joe Jay	1.00	.50	.30
234	Ted Lepcio	1.00	.50	.30
235	Camilo Pascual	1.25	.60	.40
236	Don Gile	1.00	.50	.30
237	Billy Loes	1.00	.50	.30
238	Jim Gilliam	2.50	1.25	.70
239	Dave Sisler	1.00	.50	.30
240	Ron Hansen	1.00	.50	.30
241	Al Cicotte	1.00	.50	.30
242	Hal W. Smith	1.00	.50	.30
243	Frank Lary	1.25	.60	.40
244	Chico Cardenas	1.25	.60	.40
245	Joe Adcock	2.00	1.00	.60
246	Bob Davis	1.00	.50	.30
247	Billy Goodman	1.00	.50	.30
248	Ed Keegan	1.00	.50	.30
249	Reds Team	4.00	2.00	1.25
250	Buc Hill Aces (Roy Face, Vern Law)	2.00	1.00	.60
251	Bill Bruton	1.00	.50	.30
252	Bill Short	1.50	.70	.45
253	Sammy Taylor	1.00	.50	.30
254	Ted Sadowski	1.00	.50	.30
255	Vic Power	1.00	.50	.30
256	Billy Hoeft	1.00	.50	.30
257	Carroll Hardy	1.00	.50	.30
258	Jack Sanford	1.00	.50	.30
259	John Schaive	1.00	.50	.30
260	Don Drysdale	15.00	7.50	4.50
261	Charlie Lau	1.25	.60	.40
262	Tony Curry	1.00	.50	.30
263	Ken Hamlin	1.00	.50	.30
264	Glen Hobbie	1.00	.50	.30
265	Tony Kubek	5.00	2.50	1.50
266	Lindy McDaniel	1.00	.50	.30
267	Norm Siebern	1.25	.60	.40
268	Ike DeLock (Delock)	1.00	.50	.30
269	Harry Chiti	1.00	.50	.30
270	Bob Friend	1.50	.70	.45
271	Jim Landis	1.00	.50	.30
272	Tom Morgan	1.00	.50	.30
273	Checklist 265-352	5.00	2.50	1.50
274	Gary Bell	1.00	.50	.30
275	Gene Woodling	1.25	.60	.40
276	Ray Rippelmeyer	1.00	.50	.30
277	Hank Foiles	1.00	.50	.30
278	Don McMahon	1.00	.50	.30
279	Jose Pagan	1.00	.50	.30
280	Frank Howard	2.50	1.25	.70
281	Frank Sullivan	1.00	.50	.30
282	Faye Throneberry	1.00	.50	.30
283	Bob Anderson	1.00	.50	.30
284	Dick Gernert	1.00	.50	.30
285	Sherm Lollar	1.25	.60	.40
286	George Witt	1.00	.50	.30
287	Carl Yastrzemski	175.00	70.00	44.00
288	Albie Pearson	1.00	.50	.30
289	Ray Moore	1.00	.50	.30
290	Stan Musial	65.00	33.00	20.00
291	Tex Clevenger	1.00	.50	.30
292	Jim Baumer	1.00	.50	.30
293	Tom Sturdivant	1.00	.50	.30
294	Don Blasingame	1.00	.50	.30
295	Milt Pappas	1.25	.60	.40
296	Wes Covington	1.00	.50	.30
297	Athletics Team	2.50	1.25	.70
298	Jim Golden	1.00	.50	.30
299	Clay Dalrymple	1.00	.50	.30
300	Mickey Mantle	300.00	150.00	90.00
301	Chet Nichols	1.00	.50	.30
302	Al Heist	1.00	.50	.30
303	Gary Peters	1.25	.60	.40
304	Rocky Nelson	1.00	.50	.30
305	Mike McCormick	1.25	.60	.40
306	World Series Game 1 (Virdon Saves Game)	3.50	1.75	1.00
307	World Series Game 2 (Mantle Slams 2 Homers)	20.00	10.00	6.00

		NR MT	EX	VG
308	World Series Game 3 (Richardson Is Hero)	4.00	2.00	1.25
309	World Series Game 4 (Cimoli Is Safe In Crucial Play)	3.00	1.50	.90
310	World Series Game 5 (Face Saves the Day)	3.50	1.75	1.00
311	World Series Game 6 (Ford Pitches Second Shutout)	5.00	2.50	1.50
312	World Series Game 7 (Mazeroski's Homer Wins It!)	5.00	2.50	1.50
313	World Series Summary (The Winners Celebrate)	3.00	1.50	.90
314	Bob Miller	1.00	.50	.30
315	Earl Battey	1.25	.60	.40
316	Bobby Gene Smith	1.00	.50	.30
317	*Jim Brewer*	1.25	.60	.40
318	Danny O'Connell	1.00	.50	.30
319	Valmy Thomas	1.00	.50	.30
320	Lou Burdette	2.50	1.25	.70
321	Marv Breeding	1.00	.50	.30
322	Bill Kunkel	1.00	.50	.30
323	Sammy Esposito	1.00	.50	.30
324	Hank Aguirre	1.00	.50	.30
325	Wally Moon	1.25	.60	.40
326	Dave Hillman	1.00	.50	.30
327	*Matty Alou*	4.00	2.00	1.25
328	Jim O'Toole	1.00	.50	.30
329	Julio Becquer	1.00	.50	.30
330	Rocky Colavito	3.00	1.50	.90
331	Ned Garver	1.00	.50	.30
332	Dutch Dotterer (photo actually Tommy Dotterer)	1.00	.50	.30
333	Fritz Brickell	1.50	.70	.45
334	Walt Bond	1.00	.50	.30
335	Frank Bolling	1.00	.50	.30
336	Don Mincher	1.25	.60	.40
337	Al's Aces (Al Lopez, Herb Score, Early Wynn)	3.50	1.75	1.00
338	Don Landrum	1.00	.50	.30
339	Gene Baker	1.00	.50	.30
340	Vic Wertz	1.25	.60	.40
341	Jim Owens	1.00	.50	.30
342	Clint Courtney	1.00	.50	.30
343	Earl Robinson	1.00	.50	.30
344	Sandy Koufax	80.00	40.00	24.00
345	Jim Piersall	2.00	1.00	.60
346	Howie Nunn	1.00	.50	.30
347	Cardinals Team	2.50	1.25	.70
348	Steve Boros	1.00	.50	.30
349	Danny McDevitt	1.50	.70	.45
350	Ernie Banks	30.00	15.00	9.00
351	Jim King	1.00	.50	.30
352	Bob Shaw	1.00	.50	.30
353	Howie Bedell	1.00	.50	.30
354	Billy Harrell	1.00	.50	.30
355	Bob Allison	1.25	.60	.40
356	Ryne Duren	2.25	1.25	.70
357	Daryl Spencer	1.00	.50	.30
358	Earl Averill	1.00	.50	.30
359	Dallas Green	1.25	.60	.40
360	Frank Robinson	30.00	15.00	9.00
361a	Checklist 353-429 ("Topps Baseball" in black on front)	5.00	2.50	1.50
361b	Checklist 353-429 ("Topps Baseball" in yellow)	6.00	3.00	1.75
362	Frank Funk	1.00	.50	.30
363	John Roseboro	1.25	.60	.40
364	Moe Drabowsky	1.00	.50	.30
365	Jerry Lumpe	1.25	.60	.40
366	Eddie Fisher	1.00	.50	.30
367	Jim Rivera	1.00	.50	.30
368	Bennie Daniels	1.00	.50	.30
369	Dave Philley	1.25	.60	.40
370	Roy Face	2.00	1.00	.60
371	Bill Skowron	5.00	2.50	1.50
372	Bob Hendley	1.50	.70	.45
373	Red Sox Team	5.00	2.50	1.50
374	Paul Giel	1.50	.70	.45
375	Ken Boyer	4.00	2.00	1.25
376	Mike Roarke	1.50	.70	.45
377	Ruben Gomez	1.50	.70	.45
378	Wally Post	1.50	.70	.45
379	Bobby Shantz	2.50	1.25	.70
380	Minnie Minoso	3.00	1.50	.90
381	Dave Wickersham	1.50	.70	.45
382	Frank Thomas	1.50	.70	.45
383	Frisco First Liners (Mike McCormick, Billy O'Dell, Jack Sanford)	2.00	1.00	.60
384	Chuck Essegian	1.50	.70	.45
385	Jim Perry	2.50	1.25	.70
386	Joe Hicks	1.50	.70	.45

		NR MT	EX	VG
387	Duke Maas	2.50	1.25	.70
388	Bob Clemente	80.00	40.00	25.00
389	Ralph Terry	3.00	1.50	.90
390	Del Crandall	2.50	1.25	.70
391	Winston Brown	1.50	.70	.45
392	Reno Bertoia	1.50	.70	.45
393	Batter Bafflers (Don Cardwell, Glen Hobbie)	1.75	.90	.50
394	Ken Walters	1.50	.70	.45
395	Chuck Estrada	1.50	.70	.45
396	Bob Aspromonte	1.50	.70	.45
397	Hal Woodeshick	1.50	.70	.45
398	Hank Bauer	2.50	1.25	.70
399	Cliff Cook	1.50	.70	.45
400	Vern Law	2.50	1.25	.70
401	Babe Ruth Hits 60th Homer	15.00	7.50	4.50
402	Larsen Pitches Perfect Game	10.00	5.00	3.00
403	Brooklyn-Boston Play 26-Inning Tie	2.00	1.00	.60
404	Hornsby Tops N.L. With .424 Average	3.50	1.75	1.00
405	Gehrig Benched After 2,130 Games	12.00	6.00	3.50
406	Mantle Blasts 565 ft. Home Run	30.00	15.00	9.00
407	Jack Chesbro Wins 41st Game	2.50	1.25	.70
408	Mathewson Strikes Out 267 Batters	3.50	1.75	1.00
409	Johnson Hurls 3rd Shutout in 4 Days	4.00	2.00	1.25
410	Haddix Pitches 12 Perfect Innings	2.50	1.25	.70
411	Tony Taylor	1.50	.70	.45
412	Larry Sherry	1.50	.70	.45
413	Eddie Yost	1.75	.90	.50
414	Dick Donovan	1.50	.70	.45
415	Hank Aaron	100.00	50.00	30.00
416	*Dick Howser*	8.00	4.00	2.50
417	Juan Marichal	125.00	62.00	37.00
418	Ed Bailey	1.50	.70	.45
419	Tom Borland	1.50	.70	.45
420	Ernie Broglio	1.50	.70	.45
421	Ty Cline	1.50	.70	.45
422	Bud Daley	1.50	.70	.45
423	Charlie Neal	1.50	.70	.45
424	Turk Lown	1.50	.70	.45
425	Yogi Berra	60.00	30.00	18.00
426	Not Issued			
427	Dick Ellsworth	1.50	.70	.45
428	Ray Barker	1.50	.70	.45
429	Al Kaline	35.00	17.50	10.50
430	Bill Mazeroski	3.50	1.75	1.00
431	Chuck Stobbs	1.50	.70	.45
432	Coot Veal	1.50	.70	.45
433	Art Mahaffey	1.50	.70	.45
434	Tom Brewer	1.50	.70	.45
435	Orlando Cepeda	7.00	3.50	2.00
436	*Jim Maloney*	2.50	1.25	.70
437a	Checklist 430-506 (#440 is Louis Aparicio)	6.00	3.00	1.75
437b	Checklist 430-506 (#440 is Luis Aparicio)	6.50	3.25	2.00
438	Curt Flood	2.50	1.25	.70
439	*Phil Regan*	1.75	.90	.50
440	Luis Aparicio	12.00	6.00	3.50
441	Dick Bertell	1.50	.70	.45
442	Gordon Jones	1.50	.70	.45
443	Duke Snider	35.00	17.50	10.50
444	Joe Nuxhall	1.75	.90	.50
445	Frank Malzone	1.75	.90	.50
446	Bob "Hawk" Taylor	1.50	.70	.45
447	Harry Bright	1.50	.70	.45
448	Del Rice	1.50	.70	.45
449	*Bobby Bolin*	1.75	.90	.50
450	Jim Lemon	1.50	.70	.45
451	Power For Ernie (Ernie Broglio, Daryl Spencer, Bill White)	1.75	.90	.50
452	Bob Allen	1.50	.70	.45
453	Dick Schofield	1.50	.70	.45
454	Pumpsie Green	1.50	.70	.45
455	Early Wynn	15.00	7.50	4.50
456	Hal Bevan	1.50	.70	.45
457	Johnny James	1.50	.70	.45
458	Willie Tasby	1.50	.70	.45
459	Terry Fox	1.50	.70	.45
460	Gil Hodges	18.00	9.00	5.50
461	Smoky Burgess	2.50	1.25	.70
462	Lou Klimchock	1.50	.70	.45
463a	Braves Team (should be card #426)	4.00	2.00	1.25
463b	Jack Fisher	1.75	.90	.50
464	*Leroy Thomas*	1.50	.70	.45
465	Roy McMillan	1.50	.70	.45

		NR MT	EX	VG
466	Ron Moeller	1.50	.70	.45
467	Indians Team	3.50	1.75	1.00
468	Johnny Callison	1.75	.90	.50
469	Ralph Lumenti	1.50	.70	.45
470	Roy Sievers	1.75	.90	.50
471	Phil Rizzuto MVP	8.00	4.00	2.50
472	Yogi Berra MVP	25.00	12.50	7.50
473	Bobby Shantz MVP	3.50	1.75	1.00
474	Al Rosen MVP	3.50	1.75	1.00
475	Mickey Mantle MVP	90.00	45.00	27.00
476	Jackie Jensen MVP	3.50	1.75	1.00
477	Nellie Fox MVP	4.00	2.00	1.25
478	Roger Maris MVP	30.00	15.00	9.00
479	Jim Konstanty MVP	2.50	1.25	.70
480	Roy Campanella MVP	20.00	10.00	6.00
481	Hank Sauer MVP	2.50	1.25	.70
482	Willie Mays MVP	30.00	15.00	9.00
483	Don Newcombe MVP	3.50	1.75	1.00
484	Hank Aaron MVP	30.00	15.00	9.00
485	Ernie Banks MVP	20.00	10.00	6.00
486	Dick Groat MVP	3.50	1.75	1.00
487	Gene Oliver	1.50	.70	.45
488	Joe McClain	1.50	.70	.45
489	Walt Dropo	1.75	.90	.50
490	Jim Bunning	8.00	4.00	2.50
491	Phillies Team	3.50	1.75	1.00
492	Ron Fairly	1.75	.90	.50
493	Don Zimmer	2.00	1.00	.60
494	Tom Cheney	1.50	.70	.45
495	Elston Howard	6.00	3.00	1.75
496	Ken MacKenzie	1.50	.70	.45
497	Willie Jones	1.50	.70	.45
498	Ray Herbert	1.50	.70	.45
499	Chuck Schilling	1.50	.70	.45
500	Harvey Kuenn	3.00	1.50	.90
501	John DeMerit	1.50	.70	.45
502	Clarence Coleman	1.50	.70	.45
503	Tito Francona	1.75	.90	.50
504	Billy Consolo	1.50	.70	.45
505	Red Schoendienst	8.00	4.00	2.50
506	*Willie Davis*	8.00	4.00	2.50
507	Pete Burnside	1.50	.70	.45
508	Rocky Bridges	1.50	.70	.45
509	Camilo Carreon	1.50	.70	.45
510	Art Ditmar	2.50	1.25	.70
511	Joe Morgan	1.50	.70	.45
512	Bob Will	1.50	.70	.45
513	Jim Brosnan	1.75	.90	.50
514	Jake Wood	1.50	.70	.45
515	Jackie Brandt	1.50	.70	.45
516	Checklist 507-587	6.00	3.00	1.75
517	Willie McCovey	50.00	25.00	15.00
518	Andy Carey	1.50	.70	.45
519	Jim Pagliaroni	1.50	.70	.45
520	Joe Cunningham	1.75	.90	.50
521	Brother Battery (Larry Sherry, Norm Sherry)	2.00	1.00	.60
522	Dick Farrell	1.50	.70	.45
523	Joe Gibbon	20.00	10.00	6.00
524	Johnny Logan	22.00	11.00	6.50
525	*Ron Perranoski*	22.00	11.00	6.50
526	R.C. Stevens	20.00	10.00	6.00
527	Gene Leek	20.00	10.00	6.00
528	Pedro Ramos	20.00	10.00	6.00
529	Bob Roselli	20.00	10.00	6.00
530	Bobby Malkmus	20.00	10.00	6.00
531	Jim Coates	22.00	11.00	6.50
532	Bob Hale	20.00	10.00	6.00
533	Jack Curtis	20.00	10.00	6.00
534	Eddie Kasko	20.00	10.00	6.00
535	Larry Jackson	20.00	10.00	6.00
536	Bill Tuttle	20.00	10.00	6.00
537	Bobby Locke	20.00	10.00	6.00
538	Chuck Hiller	20.00	10.00	6.00
539	Johnny Klippstein	20.00	10.00	6.00
540	Jackie Jensen	30.00	15.00	9.00
541	Roland Sheldon	22.00	11.00	6.50
542	Twins Team	40.00	20.00	12.00
543	Roger Craig	35.00	17.50	10.50
544	George Thomas	20.00	10.00	6.00
545	Hoyt Wilhelm	55.00	28.00	16.50
546	Marty Kutyna	20.00	10.00	6.00
547	Leon Wagner	22.00	11.00	6.50
548	Ted Wills	20.00	10.00	6.00
549	Hal R. Smith	20.00	10.00	6.00
550	Frank Baumann	20.00	10.00	6.00
551	George Altman	20.00	10.00	6.00
552	Jim Archer	20.00	10.00	6.00
553	Bill Fischer	20.00	10.00	6.00
554	Pirates Team	35.00	17.50	10.50
555	Sam Jones	20.00	10.00	6.00

		NR MT	EX	VG
556	Ken R. Hunt	20.00	10.00	6.00
557	Jose Valdivielso	20.00	10.00	6.00
558	Don Ferrarese	20.00	10.00	6.00
559	Jim Gentile	22.00	11.00	6.50
560	Barry Latman	20.00	10.00	6.00
561	Charley James	20.00	10.00	6.00
562	Bill Monbouquette	22.00	11.00	6.50
563	Bob Cerv	22.00	11.00	6.50
564	Don Cardwell	20.00	10.00	6.00
565	Felipe Alou	25.00	12.50	7.50
566	Paul Richards AS	25.00	12.50	7.50
567	Danny Murtaugh AS	25.00	12.50	7.50
568	Bill Skowron AS	35.00	17.50	10.50
569	Frank Herrera AS	25.00	12.50	7.50
570	Nellie Fox AS	40.00	20.00	12.00
571	Bill Mazeroski AS	35.00	17.50	10.50
572	Brooks Robinson AS	80.00	40.00	24.00
573	Ken Boyer AS	35.00	17.50	10.50
574	Luis Aparicio AS	45.00	23.00	13.50
575	Ernie Banks AS	75.00	38.00	23.00
576	Roger Maris AS	90.00	45.00	27.00
577	Hank Aaron AS	150.00	75.00	45.00
578	Mickey Mantle AS	450.00	225.00	135.00
579	Willie Mays AS	150.00	75.00	45.00
580	Al Kaline AS	75.00	38.00	23.00
581	Frank Robinson AS	75.00	38.00	23.00
582	Earl Battey AS	25.00	12.50	7.50
583	Del Crandall AS	30.00	15.00	9.00
584	Jim Perry AS	30.00	15.00	9.00
585	Bob Friend AS	30.00	15.00	9.00
586	Whitey Ford AS	75.00	38.00	23.00
587	Not Issued			
588	Not Issued			
589	Warren Spahn AS	125.00	56.00	35.00

1961 Topps Dice Game

One of the more obscure Topps test issues that may have never actually been issued is the 1961 Topps Dice Game. Eighteen black and white cards, each measuring 2-1/2" by 3-1/2" in size, comprise the set. Interestingly, there are no identifying marks, such as copyrights or trademarks, to indicate the set was produced by Topps. The card backs contain various baseball plays that occur when a certain pitch is called and a specific number of the dice is rolled.

		NR MT	EX	VG
Complete Set:		7200.00	3600.00	2150.
Common Player:		100.00	50.00	30.00
(1)	Earl Battey	100.00	50.00	30.00
(2)	Del Crandall	100.00	50.00	30.00
(3)	Jim Davenport	100.00	50.00	30.00
(4)	Don Drysdale	350.00	175.00	105.00
(5)	Dick Groat	150.00	75.00	45.00
(6)	Al Kaline	600.00	300.00	175.00
(7)	Tony Kubek	150.00	75.00	45.00
(8)	Mickey Mantle	2500.00	1250.00	750.00
(9)	Willie Mays	1000.00	500.00	300.00
(10)	Bill Mazeroski	150.00	75.00	45.00
(11)	Stan Musial	800.00	400.00	240.00
(12)	Camilo Pascual	100.00	50.00	30.00
(13)	Bobby Richardson	150.00	75.00	45.00
(14)	Brooks Robinson	400.00	200.00	120.00
(15)	Frank Robinson	350.00	175.00	105.00
(16)	Norm Siebern	100.00	50.00	30.00
(17)	Leon Wagner	100.00	50.00	30.00

		NR MT	EX	VG
(18)	Bill White	100.00	50.00	30.00

1961 Topps Magic Rub-Offs

Not too different in concept from the tattoos of the previous year, the Topps Magic Rub-Off was designed to leave impressions of team themes or individual players when properly applied. Measuring 2-1/16" by 3-1/16," the Magic Rub-Off was not designed specifically for application to the owner's skin. The set of 36 Rub-Offs seems to almost be a tongue-in-cheek product as the team themes were a far cry from official logos, and the players seem to have been included for their nicknames. Among the players (one representing each team) the best known and most valuable are Yogi Berra and Ernie Banks.

		NR MT	EX	VG
	Complete Set:	85.00	42.00	25.00
	Common Player:	1.00	.50	.30
(1)	Baltimore Orioles Pennant	1.00	.50	.30
(2)	Ernie "Bingo" Banks	12.00	6.00	3.50
(3)	Yogi Berra	20.00	10.00	6.00
(4)	Boston Red Sox Pennant	1.00	.50	.30
(5)	Jackie "Ozark" Brandt	1.25	.60	.40
(6)	Jim "Professor" Brosnan	1.25	.60	.40
(7)	Chicago Cubs Pennant	1.00	.50	.30
(8)	Chicago White Sox Pennant	1.00	.50	.30
(9)	Cincinnati Red Legs Pennant	1.00	.50	.30
(10)	Cleveland Indians Pennant	1.00	.50	.30
(11)	Detroit Tigers Pennant	1.25	.60	.40
(12)	Henry "Dutch" Dotterer	1.25	.60	.40
(13)	Joe "Flash" Gordon	1.50	.70	.45
(14)	Harvey "The Kitten" Haddix	1.50	.70	.45
(15)	Frank "Pancho" Hererra	1.25	.60	.40
(16)	Frank "Tower" Howard	3.50	1.75	1.00
(17)	"Sad" Sam Jones	1.25	.60	.40
(18)	Kansas City Athletics Pennant	1.00	.50	.30
(19)	Los Angeles Angels Pennant	1.00	.50	.30
(20)	Los Angeles Dodgers Pennant	1.25	.60	.40
(21)	Omar "Turk" Lown	1.25	.60	.40
(22)	Billy "The Kid" Martin	8.00	4.00	2.50
(23)	Duane "Duke" Mass (Maas)	1.25	.60	.40
(24)	Charlie "Paw Paw" Maxwell	1.25	.60	.40
(25)	Milwaukee Braves Pennant	1.00	.50	.30
(26)	Minnesota Twins Pennant	1.00	.50	.30
(27)	"Farmer" Ray Moore	1.00	.50	.30
(28)	Walt "Moose" Moryn	1.00	.50	.30
(29)	New York Yankees Pennant	2.50	1.25	.70
(30)	Philadelphia Phillies Pennant	1.00	.50	.30
(31)	Pittsburgh Pirates Pennant	1.00	.50	.30
(32)	John "Honey" Romano	1.25	.60	.40
(33)	"Pistol Pete" Runnels	1.50	.70	.45
(34)	St. Louis Cardinals Pennant	1.00	.50	.30
(35)	San Francisco Giants Pennant	1.00	.50	.30
(36)	Washington Senators Pennant	1.00	.50	.30

1961 Topps Stamps

Issued as an added insert to 1961 Topps wax packs these 1-3/8" by 1-3/16" stamps were desigend to be collected and placed in an album which could be bought for an additional 10¢. Packs of

cards contained two stamps. There are 208 stamps in a complete set which depict 207 different players (Al Kaline appears twice). There are 104 players on brown stamps and 104 on green. While there are many Hall of Famers on the stamps, prices remain low because there is relatively little interest in what is a non-card set.

		NR MT	EX	VG
	Complete Set:	225.00	112.00	70.00
	Stamp Album:	35.00	17.50	10.50
	Common Player:	.40	.20	.12
(1)	Hank Aaron	10.00	5.00	3.00
(2)	Joe Adcock	.50	.25	.15
(3)	Hank Aguirre	.40	.20	.12
(4)	Bob Allison	.50	.25	.15
(5)	George Altman	.40	.20	.12
(6)	Bob Anderson	.40	.20	.12
(7)	Johnny Antonelli	.50	.25	.15
(8)	Luis Aparicio	1.50	.70	.45
(9)	Luis Arroyo	.50	.25	.15
(10)	Richie Ashburn	.80	.40	.25
(11)	Ken Aspromonte	.40	.20	.12
(12)	Ed Bailey	.40	.20	.12
(13)	Ernie Banks	6.00	3.00	1.75
(14)	Steve Barber	.40	.20	.12
(15)	Earl Battey	.50	.25	.15
(16)	Hank Bauer	.50	.25	.15
(17)	Gus Bell	.50	.25	.15
(18)	Yogi Berra	5.00	2.50	1.50
(19)	Reno Bertoia	.40	.20	.12
(20)	John Blanchard	.50	.25	.15
(21)	Don Blasingame	.40	.20	.12
(22)	Frank Bolling	.40	.20	.12
(23)	Steve Boros	.40	.20	.12
(24)	Ed Bouchee	.40	.20	.12
(25)	Bob Boyd	.40	.20	.12
(26)	Cletis Boyer	.50	.25	.15
(27)	Ken Boyer	.50	.25	.15
(28)	Jackie Brandt	.40	.20	.12
(29)	Marv Breeding	.40	.20	.12
(30)	Eddie Bressoud	.40	.20	.12
(31)	Jim Brewer	.40	.20	.12
(32)	Tom Brewer	.40	.20	.12
(33)	Jim Brosnan	.50	.25	.15
(34)	Bill Bruton	.40	.20	.12
(35)	Bob Buhl	.50	.25	.15
(36)	Jim Bunning	1.00	.50	.30
(37)	Smoky Burgess	.50	.25	.15
(38)	John Buzhardt	.40	.20	.12
(39)	Johnny Callison	.50	.25	.15
(40)	Chico Cardenas	.40	.20	.12
(41)	Andy Carey	.40	.20	.12
(42)	Jerry Casale	.40	.20	.12
(43)	Norm Cash	.50	.25	.15
(44)	Orlando Cepeda	1.25	.60	.40
(45)	Bob Cerv	.40	.20	.12
(46)	Harry Chiti	.40	.20	.12
(47)	Gene Conley	.50	.25	.15
(48)	Wes Covington	.40	.20	.12
(49)	Del Crandall	.50	.25	.15
(50)	Tony Curry	.40	.20	.12
(51)	Bud Daley	.40	.20	.12
(52)	Pete Daley	.40	.20	.12
(53)	Clay Dalrymple	.40	.20	.12
(54)	Jim Davenport	.40	.20	.12
(55)	Tommy Davis	.50	.25	.15
(56)	Bobby Del Greco	.40	.20	.12
(57)	Ike Delock	.40	.20	.12

		NR MT	EX	VG
(58)	Art Ditmar	.50	.25	.15
(59)	Dick Donovan	.40	.20	.12
(60)	Don Drysdale	6.00	3.00	1.75
(61)	Dick Ellsworth	.40	.20	.12
(62)	Don Elston	.40	.20	.12
(63)	Chuck Estrada	.40	.20	.12
(64)	Roy Face	.50	.25	.15
(65)	Dick Farrell	.40	.20	.12
(66)	Chico Fernandez	.40	.20	.12
(67)	Curt Flood	.50	.25	.15
(68)	Whitey Ford	4.00	2.00	1.25
(69)	Tito Francona	.40	.20	.12
(70)	Gene Freese	.40	.20	.12
(71)	Bob Friend	.50	.25	.15
(72)	Billy Gardner	.40	.20	.12
(73)	Ned Garver	.40	.20	.12
(74)	Gary Geiger	.40	.20	.12
(75)	Jim Gentile	.40	.20	.12
(76)	Dick Gernert	.40	.20	.12
(77)	Tony Gonzalez	.40	.20	.12
(78)	Alex Grammas	.40	.20	.12
(79)	Jim Grant	.40	.20	.12
(80)	Dick Groat	.50	.25	.15
(81)	Dick Hall	.40	.20	.12
(82)	Ron Hansen	.40	.20	.12
(83)	Bob Hartman	.40	.20	.12
(84)	Woodie Held	.40	.20	.12
(85)	Ray Herbert	.40	.20	.12
(86)	Frank Herrera	.40	.20	.12
(87)	Whitey Herzog	.50	.25	.15
(88)	Don Hoak	.50	.25	.15
(89)	Elston Howard	.80	.40	.25
(90)	Frank Howard	.50	.25	.15
(91)	Ken Hunt	.40	.20	.12
(92)	Larry Jackson	.40	.20	.12
(93)	Julian Javier	.40	.20	.12
(94)	Joe Jay	.40	.20	.12
(95)	Jackie Jensen	.50	.25	.15
(96)	Jim Kaat	1.00	.50	.30
(97a)	Al Kaline (green)	7.00	3.50	2.00
(97b)	Al Kaline (brown)	7.00	3.50	2.00
(98)	Eddie Kasko	.40	.20	.12
(99)	Russ Kemmerer	.40	.20	.12
(100)	Harmon Killebrew	5.00	2.50	1.50
(101)	Billy Klaus	.40	.20	.12
(102)	Ron Kline	.40	.20	.12
(103)	Johnny Klippstein	.40	.20	.12
(104)	Ted Kluszewski	.40	.20	.12
(105)	Tony Kubek	.80	.40	.25
(106)	Harvey Kuenn	.50	.25	.15
(107)	Jim Landis	.40	.20	.12
(108)	Hobie Landrith	.40	.20	.12
(109)	Norm Larker	.40	.20	.12
(110)	Frank Lary	.40	.20	.12
(111)	Barry Latman	.40	.20	.12
(112)	Vern Law	.50	.25	.15
(113)	Jim Lemon	.40	.20	.12
(114)	Sherm Lollar	.50	.25	.15
(115)	Dale Long	.50	.25	.15
(116)	Jerry Lumpe	.40	.20	.12
(117)	Jerry Lynch	.40	.20	.12
(118)	Art Mahaffey	.40	.20	.12
(119)	Frank Malzone	.40	.20	.12
(120)	Felix Mantilla	.40	.20	.12
(121)	Mickey Mantle	50.00	25.00	15.00
(122)	Juan Marichal	5.00	2.50	1.50
(123)	Roger Maris	12.00	6.00	3.50
(124)	Billy Martin	1.00	.50	.30
(125)	J.C. Martin	.40	.20	.12
(126)	Ed Mathews	3.00	1.50	.90
(127)	Charlie Maxwell	.40	.20	.12
(128)	Willie Mays	7.00	3.50	2.00
(129)	Bill Mazeroski	.50	.25	.15
(130)	Mike McCormick	.40	.20	.12
(131)	Willie McCovey	3.00	1.50	.90
(132)	Lindy McDaniel	.40	.20	.12
(133)	Roy McMillan	.40	.20	.12
(134)	Minnie Minoso	.50	.25	.15
(135)	Bill Monbouquette	.40	.20	.12
(136)	Wally Moon	.50	.25	.15
(137)	Stan Musial	7.00	3.50	2.00
(138)	Charlie Neal	.40	.20	.12
(139)	Rocky Nelson	.40	.20	.12
(140)	Russ Nixon	.40	.20	.12
(141)	Billy O'Dell	.40	.20	.12
(142)	Jim O'Toole	.40	.20	.12
(143)	Milt Pappas	.50	.25	.15
(144)	Camilo Pascual	.50	.25	.15
(145)	Jim Perry	.50	.25	.15
(146)	Bubba Phillips	.40	.20	.12
(147)	Bill Pierce	.50	.25	.15

		NR MT	EX	VG
(148)	Jim Piersall	.50	.25	.15
(149)	Vada Pinson	.50	.25	.15
(150)	Johnny Podres	.50	.25	.15
(151)	Wally Post	.40	.20	.12
(152)	Vic Powers (Power)	.40	.20	.12
(153)	Pedro Ramos	.40	.20	.12
(154)	Robin Roberts	1.50	.70	.45
(155)	Brooks Robinson	3.75	2.00	1.25
(156)	Frank Robinson	3.50	1.75	1.00
(157)	Ed Roebuck	.40	.20	.12
(158)	John Romano	.40	.20	.12
(159)	John Roseboro	.50	.25	.15
(160)	Pete Runnels	.50	.25	.15
(161)	Ed Sadowski	.40	.20	.12
(162)	Jack Sanford	.40	.20	.12
(163)	Ron Santo	.50	.25	.15
(164)	Ray Semproch	.40	.20	.12
(165)	Bobby Shantz	.50	.25	.15
(166)	Bob Shaw	.40	.20	.12
(167)	Larry Sherry	.40	.20	.12
(168)	Norm Siebern	.40	.20	.12
(169)	Roy Sievers	.50	.25	.15
(170)	Curt Simmons	.50	.25	.15
(171)	Dave Sisler	.40	.20	.12
(172)	Bob Skinner	.40	.20	.12
(173)	Al Smith	.40	.20	.12
(174)	Hal Smith	.40	.20	.12
(175)	Hal Smith	.40	.20	.12
(176)	Duke Snider	3.75	2.00	1.25
(177)	Warren Spahn	3.00	1.50	.90
(178)	Daryl Spencer	.40	.20	.12
(179)	Bill Stafford	.50	.25	.15
(180)	Jerry Staley	.40	.20	.12
(181)	Gene Stephens	.40	.20	.12
(182)	Chuck Stobbs	.40	.20	.12
(183)	Dick Stuart	.50	.25	.15
(184)	Willie Tasby	.40	.20	.12
(185)	Sammy Taylor	.40	.20	.12
(186)	Tony Taylor	.40	.20	.12
(187)	Johnny Temple	.40	.20	.12
(188)	Marv Throneberry	.50	.25	.15
(189)	Gus Triandos	.50	.25	.15
(190)	Bob Turley	.50	.25	.15
(191)	Bill Tuttle	.40	.20	.12
(192)	Zorro Versalles	.40	.20	.12
(193)	Bill Virdon	.50	.25	.15
(194)	Lee Walls	.40	.20	.12
(195)	Vic Wertz	.50	.25	.15
(196)	Pete Whisenant	.40	.20	.12
(197)	Bill White	.50	.25	.15
(198)	Hoyt Wilhelm	1.50	.70	.45
(199)	Bob Will	.40	.20	.12
(200)	Carl Willey	.40	.20	.12
(201)	Billy Williams	2.50	1.25	.70
(202)	Dick Williams	.50	.25	.15
(203)	Stan Williams	.40	.20	.12
(204)	Gene Woodling	.50	.25	.15
(205)	Early Wynn	2.00	1.00	.60
(206)	Carl Yastrzemski	12.00	6.00	3.50
(207)	Eddie Yost	.40	.20	.12

1962 Topps

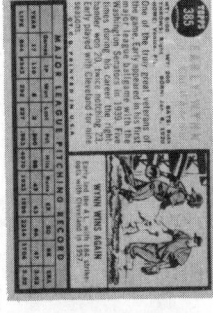

The 1962 Topps set established another plateau for set size with 598 cards. The 2-1/2" by 3-1/2" cards feature a photograph set against a woodgrain background. The lower righthand corner has been made to look like it is curling away. Many established specialty cards dot the set including statistical leaders, multi-player cards, team cards, checklists, World Series cards and All-Stars. Of note is that 1962 was the first year of the multi-player rookie card. There is a 9-card "In Action" subset and a 10-card run of special Babe Ruth cards. Photo variations of several cards in the 2nd Series (#'s 110-196) exist. All cards in the 2nd Series can be found with two distinct printing variations, an early printing with the cards containing a very noticeable greenish tint, having been corrected to clear photos in subsequent print runs. The complete set price in the checklist that follows does not include the higher-priced variations.

		NR MT	EX	VG
Complete Set:		4000.00	1800.00	1000.
Common Player: 1-370		1.50	.70	.40
Common Player: 371-522		2.50	1.25	.60
Common Player: 523-598		12.00	5.50	3.00
1	Roger Maris	250.00	45.00	27.00
2	Jim Brosnan	1.75	.60	.30
3	Pete Runnels	1.50	.70	.40
4	John DeMerit	2.00	.90	.50
5	Sandy Koufax	100.00	50.00	30.00
6	Marv Breeding	1.50	.70	.40
7	Frank Thomas	2.00	.90	.50
8	Ray Herbert	1.50	.70	.40
9	Jim Davenport	1.50	.70	.40
10	Bob Clemente	90.00	40.00	25.00
11	Tom Morgan	1.50	.70	.40
12	Harry Craft	1.50	.70	.40
13	Dick Howser	1.75	.80	.45
14	Bill White	1.50	.70	.40
15	Dick Donovan	1.50	.70	.40
16	Darrell Johnson	1.50	.70	.40
17	Johnny Callison	1.75	.80	.45
18	Managers' Dream (Mickey Mantle, Willie Mays)	100.00	50.00	30.00
19	*Ray Washburn*	1.50	.70	.40
20	Rocky Colavito	3.00	1.25	.70
21	Jim Kaat	4.00	1.75	1.00
22a	Checklist 1-88 (numbers 121 - 176 on back)	5.00	2.25	1.25
22b	Checklist 1-88 (numbers 33-88 on back)	4.00	1.75	1.00
23	Norm Larker	1.50	.70	.40
24	Tigers Team	3.50	1.50	.90
25	Ernie Banks	30.00	15.00	9.00
26	Chris Cannizzaro	2.00	.90	.50
27	Chuck Cottier	1.50	.70	.40
28	Minnie Minoso	2.50	1.25	.60
29	Casey Stengel	15.00	6.75	3.75
30	Ed Mathews	12.00	5.50	3.00
31	*Tom Tresh*	7.00	3.25	1.75
32	John Roseboro	1.75	.80	.45
33	Don Larsen	1.75	.80	.45
34	Johnny Temple	1.50	.70	.40
35	*Don Schwall*	1.75	.80	.45
36	Don Leppert	1.50	.70	.40
37	Tribe Hill Trio (Barry Latman, Jim Perry, Dick Stigman)	1.75	.80	.45
38	Gene Stephens	1.50	.70	.40
39	Joe Koppe	1.50	.70	.40
40	Orlando Cepeda	5.00	2.25	1.25
41	Cliff Cook	1.50	.70	.40
42	Jim King	1.50	.70	.40
43	Dodgers Team	3.50	1.50	.90
44	Don Taussig	1.50	.70	.40
45	Brooks Robinson	30.00	12.50	7.50
46	*Jack Baldschun*	1.50	.70	.40
47	Bob Will	1.50	.70	.40
48	Ralph Terry	2.50	1.25	.60
49	Hal Jones	1.50	.70	.40
50	Stan Musial	75.00	29.00	16.00
51	A.L. Batting Leaders (Norm Cash, Elston Howard, Al Kaline, Jim Piersall)	3.00	1.25	.70
52	N.L. Batting Leaders (Ken Boyer, Bob Clemente, Wally Moon, Vada Pinson)	3.50	1.50	.90
53	A.L. Home Run Leaders (Jim Gentile, Harmon Killebrew, Mickey Mantle, Roger Maris)	20.00	9.00	5.50
54	N.L. Home Run Leaders (Orlando Cepeda, Willie Mays, Frank Robinson)	3.50	1.50	.90
55	A.L. E.R.A. Leaders (Dick Donovan, Don Mossi, Milt Pappas, Bill Stafford)	2.50	1.25	.60
56	N.L. E.R.A. Leaders (Mike McCormick, Jim O'Toole, Curt Simmons, Warren Spahn)	3.00	1.25	.70
57	A.L. Win Leaders (Steve Barber, Jim Bunning, Whitey Ford, Frank Lary)	3.00	1.25	.70
58	N.L. Win Leaders (Joe Jay, Jim O'Toole, Warren Spahn)	3.00	1.25	.70
59	A.L. Strikeout Leaders (Jim Bunning, Whitey Ford, Camilo Pascual, Juan Pizzaro)	3.00	1.25	.70
60	N.L. Strikeout Leaders (Don Drysdale, Sandy Koufax, Jim O'Toole, Stan Williams)	3.50	1.50	.90
61	Cardinals Team	2.50	1.25	.60
62	Steve Boros	1.50	.70	.40
63	*Tony Cloninger*	2.00	.90	.50
64	Russ Snyder	1.50	.70	.40
65	Bobby Richardson	6.00	2.75	1.50
66	Cuno Barragon (Barragan)	1.50	.70	.40
67	Harvey Haddix	1.75	.80	.45
68	Ken L. Hunt	1.50	.70	.40
69	Phil Ortega	1.50	.70	.40
70	Harmon Killebrew	15.00	6.75	3.75
71	Dick LeMay	1.50	.70	.40
72	Bob's Pupils (Steve Boros, Bob Scheffing, Jake Wood)	1.75	.80	.45
73	Nellie Fox	7.00	3.25	1.75
74	Bob Lillis	1.50	.70	.40
75	Milt Pappas	1.75	.80	.45
76	Howie Bedell	1.50	.70	.40
77	Tony Taylor	1.50	.70	.40
78	Gene Green	1.50	.70	.40
79	Ed Hobaugh	1.50	.70	.40
80	Vada Pinson	2.50	1.25	.60
81	Jim Pagliaroni	1.50	.70	.40
82	Deron Johnson	1.50	.70	.40
83	Larry Jackson	1.50	.70	.40
84	Lenny Green	1.50	.70	.40
85	Gil Hodges	12.00	6.00	3.50
86	*Donn Clendenon*	1.75	.80	.45
87	Mike Roarke	1.50	.70	.40
88	Ralph Houk	2.50	1.25	.60
89	Barney Schultz	1.50	.70	.40
90	Jim Piersall	2.00	.90	.50
91	J.C. Martin	1.50	.70	.40
92	Sam Jones	1.50	.70	.40
93	John Blanchard	2.00	.90	.50
94	Jay Hook	2.00	.90	.50
95	Don Hoak	1.75	.80	.45
96	Eli Grba	1.50	.70	.40
97	Tito Francona	1.50	.70	.40
98	Checklist 89-176	4.00	1.75	1.00
99	*John Powell*	15.00	6.75	4.00
100	Warren Spahn	30.00	12.50	7.50
101	Carroll Hardy	1.50	.70	.40
102	Al Schroll	1.50	.70	.40
103	Don Blasingame	1.50	.70	.40
104	Ted Savage	1.50	.70	.40
105	Don Mossi	1.50	.70	.40
106	Carl Sawatski	1.50	.70	.40
107	Mike McCormick	1.50	.70	.40
108	Willie Davis	2.50	1.25	.60
109	Bob Shaw	1.50	.70	.40
110	Bill Skowron	5.00	2.25	1.25
111	Dallas Green	1.75	.80	.45
112	Hank Foiles	1.50	.70	.40
113	White Sox Team	2.50	1.25	.60
114	Howie Koplitz	1.50	.70	.40
115	Bob Skinner	1.50	.70	.40
116	Herb Score	2.00	.90	.50
117	Gary Geiger	1.50	.70	.40
118	Julian Javier	1.50	.70	.40
119	Danny Murphy	1.50	.70	.40
120	Bob Purkey	1.50	.70	.40
121	Billy Hitchcock	1.50	.70	.40
122	Norm Bass	1.50	.70	.40
123	Mike de la Hoz	1.50	.70	.40
124	Bill Pleis	1.50	.70	.40
125	Gene Woodling	1.75	.80	.45
126	Al Cicotte	1.50	.70	.40
127	Pride of the A's (Hank Bauer, Jerry Lumpe, Norm Siebern)	1.75	.80	.45
128	Art Fowler	1.50	.70	.40
129a	Lee Walls (facing left)	15.00	7.50	4.50
129b	Lee Walls (facing right)	1.50	.70	.40
130	Frank Bolling	1.50	.70	.40
131	*Pete Richert*	1.75	.80	.45
132a	Angels Team (with inset photos)	10.00	4.50	2.50
132b	Angels Team (without inset photos)	3.00	1.25	.70
133	Felipe Alou	1.75	.80	.45
134a	Billy Hoeft (green sky in background)	15.00	7.50	4.50
134b	Billy Hoeft (blue sky in background)	1.50	.70	.40

		NR MT	EX	VG
135	Babe As A Boy	7.00	3.25	1.75
136	Babe Joins Yanks	7.00	3.25	1.75
137	Babe and Mgr. Huggins	7.00	3.25	1.75
138	The Famous Slugger	7.00	3.25	1.75
139a	Hal Reniff (pitching)	40.00	20.00	12.00
139b	Hal Reniff (portrait)	18.00	9.00	5.50
139c	Babe Hits 60	10.00	4.00	2.50
140	Gehrig and Ruth	9.00	4.00	2.25
141	Twilight Years	7.00	3.25	1.75
142	Coaching for the Dodgers	7.00	3.25	1.75
143	Greatest Sports Hero	7.00	3.25	1.75
144	Farewell Speech	7.00	3.25	1.75
145	Barry Latman	1.50	.70	.40
146	Don Demeter	1.50	.70	.40
147a	Bill Kunkel (pitching)	15.00	7.50	4.50
147b	Bill Kunkel (portrait)	1.50	.70	.40
148	Wally Post	1.50	.70	.40
149	Bob Duliba	1.50	.70	.40
150	Al Kaline	25.00	12.50	7.50
151	Johnny Klippstein	1.50	.70	.40
152	Mickey Vernon	1.50	.70	.40
153	Pumpsie Green	1.50	.70	.40
154	Lee Thomas	1.50	.70	.40
155	Stu Miller	1.50	.70	.40
156	Merritt Ranew	1.50	.70	.40
157	Wes Covington	1.50	.70	.40
158	Braves Team	3.00	1.25	.70
159	Hal Reniff	2.00	.90	.50
160	Dick Stuart	1.50	.70	.40
161	Frank Baumann	1.50	.70	.40
162	Sammy Drake	2.00	.90	.50
163	Hot Corner Guardians (Cletis Boyer, Billy Gardner)	3.00	1.25	.70
164	Hal Naragon	1.50	.70	.40
165	Jackie Brandt	1.50	.70	.40
166	Don Lee	1.50	.70	.40
167	*Tim McCarver*	18.00	7.50	4.50
168	Leo Posada	1.50	.70	.40
169	Bob Cerv	2.00	.90	.50
170	Ron Santo	3.50	1.50	.90
171	Dave Sisler	1.50	.70	.40
172	Fred Hutchinson	1.50	.70	.40
173	Chico Fernandez	1.50	.70	.40
174a	Carl Willey (with cap)	15.00	7.50	4.50
174b	Carl Willey (no cap)	1.50	.70	.40
175	Frank Howard	3.00	1.25	.70
176a	Eddie Yost (batting)	15.00	7.50	4.50
176b	Eddie Yost (portrait)	1.50	.70	.40
177	Bobby Shantz	1.75	.80	.45
178	Camilo Carreon	1.50	.70	.40
179	Tom Sturdivant	1.50	.70	.40
180	Bob Allison	1.75	.80	.45
181	Paul Brown	1.50	.70	.40
182	Bob Nieman	1.50	.70	.40
183	Roger Craig	3.00	1.25	.70
184	Haywood Sullivan	1.50	.70	.40
185	Roland Sheldon	2.00	.90	.50
186	Mack Jones	1.50	.70	.40
187	Gene Conley	1.50	.70	.40
188	Chuck Hiller	1.50	.70	.40
189	Dick Hall	1.50	.70	.40
190a	Wally Moon (with cap)	9.00	4.00	2.25
190b	Wally Moon (no cap)	1.75	.80	.45
191	Jim Brewer	1.50	.70	.40
192a	Checklist 177-264 (192 is Check List, 3)	6.00	2.75	1.50
192b	Checklist 177-264 (192 is Check List 3)	4.00	1.75	1.00
193	Eddie Kasko	1.50	.70	.40
194	*Dean Chance*	3.00	1.25	.70
195	Joe Cunningham	1.50	.70	.40
196	Terry Fox	1.50	.70	.40
197	Daryl Spencer	1.50	.70	.40
198	Johnny Keane	1.50	.70	.40
199	*Gaylord Perry*	150.00	60.00	38.50
200	Mickey Mantle	450.00	200.00	125.00
201	Ike Delock	1.50	.70	.40
202	Carl Warwick	1.50	.70	.40
203	Jack Fisher	1.50	.70	.40
204	Johnny Weekly	1.50	.70	.40
205	Gene Freese	1.50	.70	.40
206	Senators Team	2.50	1.25	.60
207	Pete Burnside	1.50	.70	.40
208	Billy Martin	6.00	2.75	1.50
209	*Jim Fregosi*	5.00	2.25	1.25
210	Roy Face	2.00	.90	.50
211	Midway Masters (Frank Bolling, Roy McMillan)	1.75	.80	.45
212	Jim Owens	1.50	.70	.40
213	Richie Ashburn	6.00	2.75	1.50
214	Dom Zanni	1.50	.70	.40

		NR MT	EX	VG
215	Woody Held	1.50	.70	.40
216	Ron Kline	1.50	.70	.40
217	Walt Alston	4.00	1.75	1.00
218	*Joe Torre*	15.00	6.00	3.50
219	*Al Downing*	4.00	1.75	1.00
220	Roy Sievers	1.75	.80	.45
221	Bill Short	1.50	.70	.40
222	Jerry Zimmerman	1.50	.70	.40
223	Alex Grammas	1.50	.70	.40
224	Don Rudolph	1.50	.70	.40
225	Frank Malzone	1.50	.70	.40
226	Giants Team	4.00	1.75	1.00
227	Bobby Tiefenauer	1.50	.70	.40
228	Dale Long	1.50	.70	.40
229	Jesus McFarlane	1.50	.70	.40
230	Camilo Pascual	1.75	.80	.45
231	Ernie Bowman	1.50	.70	.40
232	World Series Game 1 (Yanks Win Opener)	3.00	1.25	.70
233	World Series Game 2 (Jay Ties It Up)	3.00	1.25	.70
234	World Series Game 3 (Maris Wins It In The 9th)	8.00	3.50	2.00
235	World Series Game 4 (Ford Sets New Mark)	7.00	3.25	1.75
236	World Series Game 5 (Yanks Crush Reds In Finale)	3.00	1.25	.70
237	World Series Summary (The Winners Celebrate)	3.00	1.25	.70
238	Norm Sherry	1.50	.70	.40
239	Cecil Butler	1.50	.70	.40
240	George Altman	1.50	.70	.40
241	Johnny Kucks	1.50	.70	.40
242	Mel McGaha	1.50	.70	.40
243	Robin Roberts	12.00	5.50	3.00
244	Don Gile	1.50	.70	.40
245	Ron Hansen	1.50	.70	.40
246	Art Ditmar	1.50	.70	.40
247	Joe Pignatano	1.50	.70	.40
248	Bob Aspromonte	1.50	.70	.40
249	Ed Keegan	1.50	.70	.40
250	Norm Cash	3.00	1.25	.70
251	Yankees Team	12.00	5.50	3.50
252	Earl Francis	1.50	.70	.40
253	Harry Chiti	1.50	.70	.40
254	Gordon Windhorn	1.50	.70	.40
255	Juan Pizarro	1.50	.70	.40
256	Elio Chacon	2.00	.90	.50
257	Jack Spring	1.50	.70	.40
258	Marty Keough	1.50	.70	.40
259	Lou Klimchock	1.50	.70	.40
260	Bill Pierce	2.00	.90	.50
261	George Alusik	1.50	.70	.40
262	Bob Schmidt	1.50	.70	.40
263	The Right Pitch (Joe Jay, Bob Purkey, Jim Turner)	1.75	.80	.45
264	Dick Ellsworth	1.50	.70	.40
265	Joe Adcock	2.00	.90	.50
266	John Anderson	1.50	.70	.40
267	Dan Dobbek	1.50	.70	.40
268	Ken McBride	1.50	.70	.40
269	Bob Oldis	1.50	.70	.40
270	Dick Groat	2.00	.90	.50
271	Ray Rippelmeyer	1.50	.70	.40
272	Earl Robinson	1.50	.70	.40
273	Gary Bell	1.50	.70	.40
274	Sammy Taylor	1.50	.70	.40
275	Norm Siebern	1.50	.70	.40
276	Hal Kostad	1.50	.70	.40
277	Checklist 265-352	4.00	1.75	1.00
278	Ken Johnson	1.50	.70	.40
279	Hobie Landrith	2.00	.90	.50
280	Johnny Podres	2.50	1.25	.60
281	*Jake Gibbs*	2.25	1.00	.60
282	Dave Hillman	1.50	.70	.40
283	Charlie Smith	1.50	.70	.40
284	Ruben Amaro	1.50	.70	.40
285	Curt Simmons	2.00	.90	.50
286	Al Lopez	3.00	1.25	.70
287	George Witt	1.50	.70	.40
288	Billy Williams	25.00	12.50	7.50
289	Mike Krsnich	1.50	.70	.40
290	Jim Gentile	1.50	.70	.40
291	Hal Stowe	2.00	.90	.50
292	Jerry Kindall	1.50	.70	.40
293	Bob Miller	2.00	.90	.50
294	Phillies Team	2.50	1.25	.60
295	Vern Law	2.00	.90	.50
296	Ken Hamlin	1.50	.70	.40
297	Ron Perranoski	1.50	.70	.40
298	Bill Tuttle	1.50	.70	.40

		NR MT	EX	VG
299	*Don Wert*	1.50	.70	.40
300	Willie Mays	150.00	60.00	38.00
301	Galen Cisco	1.50	.70	.40
302	*John Edwards*	1.50	.70	.40
303	Frank Torre	1.50	.70	.40
304	Dick Farrell	1.50	.70	.40
305	Jerry Lumpe	1.50	.70	.40
306	Redbird Rippers (Larry Jackson, Lindy McDaniel)	1.75	.80	.45
307	Jim Grant	1.50	.70	.40
308	Neil Chrisley	2.00	.90	.50
309	Moe Morhardt	1.50	.70	.40
310	Whitey Ford	25.00	12.50	7.50
311	Kubek Makes The Double Play	3.50	1.50	.90
312	Spahn Shows No-Hit Form	7.00	3.50	2.00
313	Maris Blasts 61st	15.00	6.75	3.75
314	Colavito's Power	3.50	1.50	.90
315	Ford Tosses A Curve	6.00	2.75	1.50
316	Killebrew Sends One Into Orbit	5.00	2.25	1.25
317	Musial Plays 21st Season	12.00	5.50	3.00
318	The Switch Hitter Connects (Mickey Mantle)	40.00	16.00	9.00
319	McCormick Shows His Stuff	1.75	.80	.45
320	Hank Aaron	150.00	60.00	38.00
321	Lee Stange	1.50	.70	.40
322	Al Dark	1.75	.80	.45
323	Don Landrum	1.50	.70	.40
324	Joe McClain	1.50	.70	.40
325	Luis Aparicio	15.00	7.50	4.50
326	Tom Parsons	1.50	.70	.40
327	Ozzie Virgil	1.50	.70	.40
328	Ken Walters	1.50	.70	.40
329	Bob Bolin	1.50	.70	.40
330	Johnny Romano	1.50	.70	.40
331	Moe Drabowsky	1.50	.70	.40
332	Don Buddin	1.50	.70	.40
333	Frank Cipriani	1.50	.70	.40
334	Red Sox Team	3.50	1.50	.90
335	Bill Bruton	1.50	.70	.40
336	Billy Muffett	1.50	.70	.40
337	Jim Marshall	2.00	.90	.50
338	Billy Gardner	2.25	1.00	.60
339	Jose Valdivielso	1.50	.70	.40
340	Don Drysdale	30.00	15.00	9.00
341	Mike Hershberger	1.50	.70	.40
342	Ed Rakow	1.50	.70	.40
343	Albie Pearson	1.50	.70	.40
344	Ed Bauta	1.50	.70	.40
345	Chuck Schilling	1.50	.70	.40
346	Jack Kralick	1.50	.70	.40
347	Chuck Hinton	1.50	.70	.40
348	Larry Burright	1.50	.70	.40
349	Paul Foytack	1.50	.70	.40
350	Frank Robinson	40.00	18.00	12.00
351	Braves' Backstops (Del Crandall, Joe Torre)	3.00	1.25	.70
352	Frank Sullivan	1.50	.70	.40
353	Bill Mazeroski	3.50	1.50	.90
354	Roman Mejias	1.50	.70	.40
355	Steve Barber	1.50	.70	.40
356	Tom Haller	1.75	.80	.45
357	Jerry Walker	1.50	.70	.40
358	Tommy Davis	2.50	1.25	.60
359	Bobby Locke	1.50	.70	.40
360	Yogi Berra	80.00	35.00	20.00
361	Bob Hendley	1.50	.70	.40
362	Ty Cline	1.50	.70	.40
363	Bob Roselli	1.50	.70	.40
364	Ken Hunt	1.50	.70	.40
365	Charley Neal	2.00	.90	.50
366	Phil Regan	1.50	.70	.40
367	Checklist 353-429	4.00	1.75	1.00
368	Bob Tillman	1.50	.70	.40
369	Ted Bowsfield	1.50	.70	.40
370	Ken Boyer	4.00	1.75	1.00
371	Earl Battey	2.75	1.25	.70
372	Jack Curtis	2.50	1.25	.60
373	Al Heist	2.50	1.25	.60
374	Gene Mauch	2.75	1.25	.70
375	Ron Fairly	2.75	1.25	.70
376	Bud Daley	3.00	1.25	.70
377	Johnny Orsino	2.50	1.25	.60
378	Bennie Daniels	2.50	1.25	.60
379	Chuck Essegian	2.50	1.25	.60
380	Lou Burdette	4.00	1.75	1.00
381	Chico Cardenas	2.50	1.25	.60
382	Dick Williams	3.50	1.50	.90
383	Ray Sadecki	2.50	1.25	.60
384	Athletics Team	3.50	1.50	.90
385	Early Wynn	20.00	10.00	6.00
386	Don Mincher	2.50	1.25	.60

		NR MT	EX	VG
387	Lou Brock	125.00	56.00	35.00
388	Ryne Duren	2.75	1.25	.70
389	Smoky Burgess	3.00	1.25	.70
390	Orlando Cepeda AS	5.00	2.25	1.25
391	Bill Mazeroski AS	3.50	1.50	.90
392	Ken Boyer AS	3.50	1.50	.90
393	Roy McMillan AS	2.75	1.25	.70
394	Hank Aaron AS	30.00	15.00	9.00
395	Willie Mays AS	30.00	15.00	9.00
396	Frank Robinson AS	12.00	5.50	3.00
397	John Roseboro AS	2.75	1.25	.70
398	Don Drysdale AS	10.00	4.50	2.50
399	Warren Spahn AS	10.00	4.50	2.50
400	Elston Howard	7.00	3.25	1.75
401	AL & NL Homer Kings (Orlando Cepeda, Roger Maris)	20.00	9.00	5.00
402	Gino Cimoli	2.50	1.25	.60
403	Chet Nichols	2.50	1.25	.60
404	Tim Harkness	2.50	1.25	.60
405	Jim Perry	3.00	1.25	.70
406	Bob Taylor	2.50	1.25	.60
407	Hank Aguirre	2.50	1.25	.60
408	Gus Bell	3.00	1.25	.70
409	Pirates Team	3.50	1.50	.90
410	Al Smith	2.50	1.25	.60
411	Danny O'Connell	2.50	1.25	.60
412	Charlie James	2.50	1.25	.60
413	Matty Alou	3.50	1.50	.90
414	Joe Gaines	2.50	1.25	.60
415	Bill Virdon	3.50	1.50	.90
416	Bob Scheffing	2.50	1.25	.60
417	Joe Azcue	2.50	1.25	.60
418	Andy Carey	2.50	1.25	.60
419	Bob Bruce	2.50	1.25	.60
420	Gus Triandos	2.75	1.25	.70
421	Ken MacKenzie	3.00	1.25	.60
422	Steve Bilko	2.50	1.25	.60
423	Rival League Relief Aces (Roy Face, Hoyt Wilhelm)	5.00	2.25	1.25
424	Al McBean	2.50	1.25	.60
425	Carl Yastrzemski	200.00	80.00	50.00
426	Bob Farley	2.50	1.25	.60
427	Jake Wood	2.50	1.25	.60
428	Joe Hicks	2.50	1.25	.60
429	Bill O'Dell	2.50	1.25	.60
430	Tony Kubek	7.00	3.25	1.75
431	*Bob Rodgers*	3.00	1.25	.70
432	Jim Pendleton	2.50	1.25	.60
433	Jim Archer	2.50	1.25	.60
434	Clay Dalrymple	2.50	1.25	.60
435	Larry Sherry	2.50	1.25	.60
436	Felix Mantilla	3.00	1.25	.70
437	Ray Moore	2.50	1.25	.60
438	Dick Brown	2.50	1.25	.60
439	Jerry Buchek	2.50	1.25	.60
440	Joe Jay	2.50	1.25	.60
441	Checklist 430-506	5.00	2.25	1.25
442	Wes Stock	2.50	1.25	.60
443	Del Crandall	3.50	1.50	.90
444	Ted Wills	2.50	1.25	.60
445	Vic Power	2.50	1.25	.60
446	Don Elston	2.50	1.25	.60
447	Willie Kirkland	2.50	1.25	.60
448	Joe Gibbon	2.50	1.25	.60
449	Jerry Adair	2.50	1.25	.60
450	Jim O'Toole	2.50	1.25	.60
451	*Jose Tartabull*	2.75	1.25	.70
452	Earl Averill	2.50	1.25	.60
453	Cal McLish	2.50	1.25	.60
454	Floyd Robinson	2.50	1.25	.60
455	Luis Arroyo	3.00	1.25	.70
456	Joe Amalfitano	2.50	1.25	.60
457	Lou Clinton	2.50	1.25	.60
458a	Bob Buhl ("M" on cap)	2.75	1.25	.70
458b	Bob Buhl (plain cap)	60.00	30.00	18.00
459	Ed Bailey	2.50	1.25	.60
460	Jim Bunning	8.00	3.50	2.00
461	*Ken Hubbs*	8.00	3.50	2.00
462a	Willie Tasby ("W" on cap)	2.50	1.25	.60
462b	Willie Tasby (plain cap)	60.00	30.00	18.00
463	Hank Bauer	3.00	1.25	.70
464	*Al Jackson*	3.50	1.50	.90
465	Reds Team	4.00	1.75	1.00
466	Norm Cash AS	4.00	1.75	1.00
467	Chuck Schilling AS	3.00	1.25	.70
468	Brooks Robinson AS	12.00	5.50	3.00
469	Luis Aparicio AS	8.00	3.50	2.00
470	Al Kaline AS	10.00	4.50	2.50
471	Mickey Mantle AS	65.00	29.00	16.00
472	Rocky Colavito AS	5.00	2.25	1.25
473	Elston Howard AS	5.00	2.25	1.25

		NR MT	EX	VG
474	Frank Lary AS	3.00	1.25	.70
475	Whitey Ford AS	10.00	4.50	2.50
476	Orioles Team	3.50	1.50	.90
477	Andre Rodgers	2.50	1.25	.60
478	Don Zimmer	3.50	1.50	.90
479	*Joel Horlen*	2.75	1.25	.70
480	Harvey Kuenn	3.50	1.50	.90
481	Vic Wertz	2.75	1.25	.70
482	Sam Mele	2.50	1.25	.60
483	Don McMahon	2.50	1.25	.60
484	Dick Schofield	2.50	1.25	.60
485	Pedro Ramos	2.50	1.25	.60
486	Jim Gilliam	4.00	1.75	1.00
487	Jerry Lynch	2.50	1.25	.60
488	Hal Brown	2.50	1.25	.60
489	Julio Gotay	2.50	1.25	.60
490	Clete Boyer	4.00	1.75	1.00
491	Leon Wagner	2.50	1.25	.60
492	Hal Smith	2.50	1.25	.60
493	Danny McDevitt	2.50	1.25	.60
494	Sammy White	2.50	1.25	.60
495	Don Cardwell	2.50	1.25	.60
496	Wayne Causey	2.50	1.25	.60
497	Ed Bouchee	3.00	1.25	.70
498	Jim Donohue	2.50	1.25	.60
499	Zoilo Versalles	2.75	1.25	.70
500	Duke Snider	30.00	13.50	7.50
501	Claude Osteen	2.75	1.25	.70
502	Hector Lopez	3.00	1.25	.70
503	Danny Murtaugh	2.75	1.25	.70
504	Eddie Bressoud	2.50	1.25	.60
505	Juan Marichal	25.00	11.00	6.25
506	Charley Maxwell	2.50	1.25	.60
507	Ernie Broglio	2.50	1.25	.60
508	Gordy Coleman	2.50	1.25	.60
509	*Dave Giusti*	2.75	1.25	.70
510	Jim Lemon	2.50	1.25	.60
511	Bubba Phillips	2.50	1.25	.60
512	Mike Fornieles	2.50	1.25	.60
513	Whitey Herzog	4.00	1.75	1.00
514	Sherm Lollar	2.75	1.25	.70
515	Stan Williams	2.50	1.25	.60
516	Checklist 507-598	8.00	3.50	2.00
517	Dave Wickersham	2.50	1.25	.60
518	Lee Maye	2.50	1.25	.60
519	Bob Johnson	2.50	1.25	.60
520	Bob Friend	3.00	1.25	.70
521	Jacke Davis	2.50	1.25	.60
522	Lindy McDaniel	2.50	1.25	.60
523	Russ Nixon	12.00	5.50	3.00
524	Howie Nunn	12.00	5.50	3.00
525	George Thomas	12.00	5.50	3.00
526	Hal Woodeshick	12.00	5.50	3.00
527	*Dick McAuliffe*	15.00	5.00	2.75
528	Turk Lown	12.00	5.50	3.00
529	John Schaive	12.00	5.50	3.00
530	Bob Gibson	200.00	90.00	55.00
531	Bobby G. Smith	12.00	5.50	3.00
532	Dick Stigman	12.00	5.50	3.00
533	Charley Lau	13.00	5.75	3.25
534	Tony Gonzalez	12.00	5.50	3.00
535	Ed Roebuck	12.00	5.50	3.00
536	Dick Gernert	12.00	5.50	3.00
537	Indians Team	15.00	6.75	3.75
538	Jack Sanford	12.00	5.50	3.00
539	Billy Moran	12.00	5.50	3.00
540	Jim Landis	12.00	5.50	3.00
541	Don Nottebart	12.00	5.50	3.00
542	Dave Philley	12.00	5.50	3.00
543	Bob Allen	12.00	5.50	3.00
544	Willie McCovey	150.00	60.00	38.00
545	Hoyt Wilhelm	55.00	25.00	14.00
546	Moe Thacker	12.00	5.50	3.00
547	Don Ferrarese	12.00	5.50	3.00
548	Bobby Del Greco	12.00	5.50	3.00
549	Bill Rigney	12.00	5.50	3.00
550	Art Mahaffey	12.00	5.50	3.00
551	Harry Bright	12.00	5.50	3.00
552	Cubs Team	15.00	6.75	3.75
553	Jim Coates	15.00	6.75	3.75
554	Bubba Morton	12.00	5.50	3.00
555	John Buzhardt	12.00	5.50	3.00
556	Al Spangler	12.00	5.50	3.00
557	Bob Anderson	12.00	5.50	3.00
558	John Goryl	12.00	5.50	3.00
559	Mike Higgins	12.00	5.50	3.00
560	Chuck Estrada	12.00	5.50	3.00
561	Gene Oliver	12.00	5.50	3.00
562	Bill Henry	12.00	5.50	3.00
563	Ken Aspromonte	12.00	5.50	3.00
564	Bob Grim	12.00	5.50	3.00
565	Jose Pagan	12.00	5.50	3.00
566	Marty Kutyna	12.00	5.50	3.00
567	Tracy Stallard	12.00	5.50	3.00
568	Jim Golden	12.00	5.50	3.00
569	Ed Sadowski	12.00	5.50	3.00
570	Bill Stafford	15.00	6.75	3.75
571	Billy Klaus	12.00	5.50	3.00
572	Bob Miller	13.00	5.75	3.25
573	Johnny Logan	13.00	5.75	3.25
574	Dean Stone	12.00	5.50	3.00
575	Red Schoendienst	25.00	11.25	6.25
576	Russ Kemmerer	12.00	5.50	3.00
577	Dave Nicholson	12.00	5.50	3.00
578	Jim Duffalo	12.00	5.50	3.00
579	Jim Schaffer	12.00	5.50	3.00
580	Bill Monbouquette	13.00	5.75	3.25
581	Mel Roach	12.00	5.50	3.00
582	Ron Piche	12.00	5.50	3.00
583	Larry Osborne	12.00	5.50	3.00
584	Twins Team	15.00	6.75	3.75
585	Glen Hobbie	12.00	5.50	3.00
586	Sammy Esposito	12.00	5.50	3.00
587	Frank Funk	12.00	5.50	3.00
588	Birdie Tebbetts	12.00	5.50	3.00
589	Bob Turley	18.00	8.00	4.50
590	Curt Flood	18.00	8.00	4.50
591	Rookie Parade Pitchers (Sam McDowell, Ron Nischwitz, Art Quirk, *Dick Radatz*, *Ron Taylor*)	35.00	15.50	8.75
592	Rookie Parade Pitchers (*Bo Belinsky*, Joe Bonikowski, *Jim Bouton*, Dan Pfister, Dave Stenhouse)	45.00	20.00	11.25
593	Rookie Parade Pitchers (Craig Anderson, *Jack Hamilton*, Jack Lamabe, Bob Moorhead, *Bob Veale*)	25.00	11.25	6.25
594	Rookie Parade Catchers (Doug Camilli, *Doc Edwards*, Don Pavletich, Ken Retzer, *Bob Uecker*)	125.00	56.00	35.00
595	Rookie Parade Infielders (*Ed Charles*, Marlin Coughtry, Bob Sadowski, Felix Torres)	25.00	11.25	6.25
596	Rookie Parade Infielders (*Bernie Allen*, Phil Linz, Joe Pepitone, Rich Rollins)	70.00	30.00	15.00
597	Rookie Parade Infielders (Rod Kanehl, Jim McKnight, *Denis Menke*, Amado Samuel)	25.00	11.25	6.25
598	Rookie Parade Outfielders (Howie Goss, *Jim Hickman*, Manny Jimenez, Al Luplow, Ed Olivares)	60.00	25.00	12.00

1962 Topps Baseball Bucks

Issued in their own 1¢ package, the 1962 Topps "Baseball Bucks" were another in the growing list of specialty Topps items. The 96 Baseball Bucks in the set measure 4-1/8" by 1-3/4," and were designed to look vaguely like dollar bills. The center player portrait has a banner underneath with the player's name. His home park is shown on the right and there is some biographical information on the left. The back features a large denomination, with the player's league and team logo on either side.

	NR MT	EX	VG
Complete Set:	700.00	350.00	210.00
Common Player:	2.00	1.00	.60

		NR MT	EX	VG
(1)	Hank Aaron	30.00	15.00	9.00
(2)	Joe Adcock	3.00	1.50	.90
(3)	George Altman	2.00	1.00	.60
(4)	Jim Archer	2.00	1.00	.60
(5)	Richie Ashburn	5.00	2.50	1.50
(6)	Ernie Banks	20.00	10.00	8.00
(7)	Earl Battey	2.50	1.25	.70
(8)	Gus Bell	2.50	1.25	.70
(9)	Yogi Berra	18.00	9.00	5.50
(10)	Ken Boyer	3.00	1.50	.90
(11)	Jackie Brandt	2.00	1.00	.60
(12)	Jim Bunning	4.00	2.00	1.25
(13)	Lou Burdette	3.00	1.50	.90
(14)	Don Cardwell	2.00	1.00	.60
(15)	Norm Cash	3.00	1.50	.90
(16)	Orlando Cepeda	4.50	2.25	1.25
(17)	Bob Clemente	40.00	20.00	12.50
(18)	Rocky Colavito	3.00	1.50	.90
(19)	Chuck Cottier	2.00	1.00	.60
(20)	Roger Craig	2.50	1.25	.70
(21)	Bennie Daniels	2.00	1.00	.60
(22)	Don Demeter	2.00	1.00	.60
(23)	Don Drysdale	15.00	7.50	4.50
(24)	Chuck Estrada	2.00	1.00	.60
(25)	Dick Farrell	2.00	1.00	.60
(26)	Whitey Ford	12.00	6.00	3.50
(27)	Nellie Fox	4.00	2.00	1.25
(28)	Tito Francona	2.00	1.00	.60
(29)	Bob Friend	2.50	1.25	.70
(30)	Jim Gentile	2.00	1.00	.60
(31)	Dick Gernert	2.00	1.00	.60
(32)	Lenny Green	2.00	1.00	.60
(33)	Dick Groat	3.00	1.50	.90
(34)	Woody Held	2.00	1.00	.60
(35)	Don Hoak	2.50	1.25	.70
(36)	Gil Hodges	10.00	5.00	3.00
(37)	Frank Howard	3.00	1.50	.90
(38)	Elston Howard	4.00	2.00	1.25
(39)	Dick Howser	3.00	1.50	.90
(40)	Ken Hunt	2.00	1.00	.60
(41)	Larry Jackson	2.00	1.00	.60
(42)	Joe Jay	4.00	2.00	1.25
(43)	Al Kaline	12.00	6.00	3.50
(44)	Harmon Killebrew	12.00	6.00	3.50
(45)	Sandy Koufax	35.00	17.50	10.50
(46)	Harvey Kuenn	4.00	2.00	1.25
(47)	Jim Landis	2.00	1.00	.60
(48)	Norm Larker	2.00	1.00	.60
(49)	Frank Lary	2.00	1.00	.60
(50)	Jerry Lumpe	2.00	1.00	.60
(51)	Art Mahaffey	2.00	1.00	.60
(52)	Frank Malzone	2.00	1.00	.60
(53)	Felix Mantilla	2.50	1.25	.70
(54)	Mickey Mantle	125.00	62.00	37.00
(55)	Roger Maris	12.00	6.00	3.50
(56)	Ed Mathews	10.00	5.00	3.00
(57)	Willie Mays	35.00	17.50	10.50
(58)	Ken McBride	2.00	1.00	.60
(59)	Mike McCormick	2.00	1.00	.60
(60)	Minnie Minoso	4.00	2.00	1.25
(61)	Wally Moon	2.50	1.25	.70
(62)	Stu Miller	2.00	1.00	.60
(63)	Stan Musial	30.00	15.00	9.00
(64)	Danny O'Connell	2.00	1.00	.60
(65)	Jim O'Toole	4.00	2.00	1.25
(66)	Camilo Pascual	2.50	1.25	.70
(67)	Jim Perry	3.00	1.50	.90
(68)	Jimmy Piersall	4.00	2.00	1.25
(69)	Vada Pinson	6.00	3.00	1.75
(70)	Juan Pizarro	2.00	1.00	.60
(71)	Johnny Podres	3.00	1.50	.90
(72)	Vic Power	2.00	1.00	.60
(73)	Bob Purkey	12.00	6.00	3.50
(74)	Pedro Ramos	2.00	1.00	.60
(75)	Brooks Robinson	15.00	7.50	4.50
(76)	Floyd Robinson	2.00	1.00	.60
(77)	Frank Robinson	15.00	7.50	4.50
(78)	Johnny Romano	2.00	1.00	.60
(79)	Pete Runnels	2.50	1.25	.70
(80)	Don Schwall	2.00	1.00	.60
(81)	Bobby Shantz	3.00	1.50	.90
(82)	Norm Siebern	2.00	1.00	.60
(83)	Roy Sievers	2.50	1.25	.70
(84)	Hal (W.) Smith	2.00	1.00	.60
(85)	Warren Spahn	10.00	5.00	3.00
(86)	Dick Stuart	2.50	1.25	.70
(87)	Tony Taylor	2.00	1.00	.60
(88)	Lee Thomas	2.00	1.00	.60
(89)	Gus Triandos	2.50	1.25	.70
(90)	Leon Wagner	2.00	1.00	.60
(91)	Jerry Walker	2.00	1.00	.60
(92)	Bill White	2.50	1.25	.70

		NR MT	EX	VG
(93)	Billy Williams	9.00	4.50	2.75
(94)	Gene Woodling	2.50	1.25	.70
(95)	Early Wynn	9.00	4.50	2.75
(96)	Carl Yastrzemski	30.00	15.00	9.00

1962 Topps Stamps

CARL YASTRZEMSKI
BOST. RED SOX   OUTFIELD

An artistic improvement over the somewhat drab Topps stamps of the previous year, the 1962 stamps, 1-3/8" by 1-7/8," had color player photographs set on red or yellow backgrounds. As in 1961, they were issued in two-stamp panels as insert with Topps baseball cards. A change from 1961 was the inclusion of team emblems in the set. A complete set consists of 201 stamps; Roy Sievers was originally portrayed on the wrong team - Athletics - and was later corrected to the Phillies.

		NR MT	EX	VG
Complete Set:		220.00	110.00	67.00
Stamp Album:		35.00	17.50	10.50
Common Player:		.25	.13	.08
(1)	Hank Aaron	10.00	5.00	3.00
(2)	Jerry Adair	.25	.13	.08
(3)	Joe Adcock	.35	.20	.11
(4)	Bob Allison	.30	.15	.09
(5)	Felipe Alou	.35	.20	.11
(6)	George Altman	.25	.13	.08
(7)	Joe Amalfitano	.25	.13	.08
(8)	Ruben Amaro	.25	.13	.08
(9)	Luis Aparicio	1.50	.70	.45
(10)	Jim Archer	.25	.13	.08
(11)	Bob Aspromonte	.25	.13	.08
(12)	Ed Bailey	.25	.13	.08
(13)	Jack Baldschun	.25	.13	.08
(14)	Ernie Banks	6.00	3.00	1.75
(15)	Earl Battey	.30	.15	.09
(16)	Gus Bell	.35	.20	.11
(17)	Yogi Berra	5.00	2.50	1.50
(18)	Dick Bertell	.25	.13	.08
(19)	Steve Bilko	.25	.13	.08
(20)	Frank Bolling	.25	.13	.08
(21)	Steve Boros	.25	.13	.08
(22)	Ted Bowsfield	.25	.13	.08
(23)	Clete Boyer	.35	.20	.11
(24)	Ken Boyer	.50	.25	.15
(25)	Jackie Brandt	.25	.13	.08
(26)	Bill Bruton	.25	.13	.08
(27)	Jim Bunning	1.00	.50	.30
(28)	Lou Burdette	.35	.20	.11
(29)	Smoky Burgess	.30	.15	.09
(30)	Johnny Callizon (Callison)	.30	.15	.09
(31)	Don Cardwell	.25	.13	.08
(32)	Camilo Carreon	.25	.13	.08
(33)	Norm Cash	.50	.25	.15
(34)	Orlando Cepeda	1.00	.50	.30
(35)	Bob Clemente	15.00	7.50	4.50
(36)	Ty Cline	.25	.13	.08
(37)	Rocky Colavito	.80	.40	.25
(38)	Gordon Coleman	.25	.13	.08
(39)	Chuck Cottier	.25	.13	.08
(40)	Roger Craig	.35	.20	.11
(41)	Del Crandall	.35	.20	.11
(42)	Pete Daley	.25	.13	.08
(43)	Clay Dalrymple	.25	.13	.08
(44)	Bennie Daniels	.25	.13	.08

		NR MT	EX	VG
(45)	Jim Davenport	.25	.13	.08
(46)	Don Demeter	.25	.13	.08
(47)	Dick Donovan	.25	.13	.08
(48)	Don Drysdale	7.00	3.50	2.00
(49)	John Edwards	.25	.13	.08
(50)	Dick Ellsworth	.25	.13	.08
(51)	Chuck Estrada	.25	.13	.08
(52)	Roy Face	.35	.20	.11
(53)	Ron Fairly	.30	.15	.09
(54)	Dick Farrell	.25	.13	.08
(55)	Whitey Ford	5.00	2.50	1.50
(56)	Mike Fornieles	.25	.13	.08
(57)	Nellie Fox	.80	.40	.25
(58)	Tito Francona	.25	.13	.08
(59)	Gene Freese	.25	.13	.08
(60)	Bob Friend	.35	.20	.11
(61)	Gary Geiger	.25	.13	.08
(62)	Jim Gentile	.25	.13	.08
(63)	Tony Gonzalez	.25	.13	.08
(64)	Lenny Green	.25	.13	.08
(65)	Dick Groat	.35	.20	.11
(66)	Ron Hansen	.25	.13	.08
(67)	Al Heist	.25	.13	.08
(68)	Woody Held	.25	.13	.08
(69)	Ray Herbert	.25	.13	.08
(70)	Chuck Hinton	.25	.13	.08
(71)	Don Hoak	.30	.15	.09
(72)	Glen Hobbie	.25	.13	.08
(73)	Gil Hodges	5.00	2.50	1.50
(74)	Jay Hook	.35	.20	.11
(75)	Elston Howard	.80	.40	.25
(76)	Frank Howard	.50	.25	.15
(77)	Dick Howser	.35	.20	.11
(78)	Ken Hunt	.25	.13	.08
(79)	Larry Jackson	.25	.13	.08
(80)	Julian Javier	.25	.13	.08
(81)	Joe Jay	.25	.13	.08
(82)	Bob Johnson	.25	.13	.08
(83)	Sam Jones	.25	.13	.08
(84)	Al Kaline	7.00	3.50	2.00
(85)	Eddie Kasko	.25	.13	.08
(86)	Harmon Killebrew	5.00	2.50	1.50
(87)	Sandy Koufax	10.00	5.00	3.00
(88)	Jack Kralick	.25	.13	.08
(89)	Tony Kubek	.80	.40	.25
(90)	Harvey Kuenn	.50	.25	.15
(91)	Jim Landis	.25	.13	.08
(92)	Hobie Landrith	.35	.20	.11
(93)	Frank Lary	.25	.13	.08
(94)	Barry Latman	.25	.13	.08
(95)	Jerry Lumpe	.25	.13	.08
(96)	Art Mahaffey	.25	.13	.08
(97)	Frank Malzone	.25	.13	.08
(98)	Felix Mantilla	.35	.20	.11
(99)	Mickey Mantle	45.00	22.00	13.50
(100)	Juan Marichal	2.00	1.00	.60
(101)	Roger Maris	5.00	2.50	1.50
(102)	J.C. Martin	.25	.13	.08
(103)	Ed Mathews	3.00	1.50	.90
(104)	Willie Mays	7.00	3.50	2.00
(105)	Bill Mazeroski	.50	.25	.15
(106)	Ken McBride	.25	.13	.08
(107)	Tim McCarver	.50	.25	.15
(108)	Joe McClain	.25	.13	.08
(109)	Mike McCormick	.25	.13	.08
(110)	Lindy McDaniel	.25	.13	.08
(111)	Roy McMillan	.25	.13	.08
(112)	Bob L. Miller	.35	.20	.11
(113)	Stu Miller	.25	.13	.08
(114)	Minnie Minoso	.50	.25	.15
(115)	Bill Monbouquette	.25	.13	.08
(116)	Wally Moon	.30	.15	.09
(117)	Don Mossi	.30	.15	.09
(118)	Stan Musial	7.00	3.50	2.00
(119)	Russ Nixon	.25	.13	.08
(120)	Danny O'Connell	.25	.13	.08
(121)	Jim O'Toole	.25	.13	.08
(122)	Milt Pappas	.30	.15	.09
(123)	Camilo Pascual	.30	.15	.09
(124)	Albie Pearson	.25	.13	.08
(125)	Jim Perry	.35	.20	.11
(126)	Bubba Phillips	.25	.13	.08
(127)	Jimmy Piersall	.35	.20	.11
(128)	Vada Pinson	.50	.25	.15
(129)	Juan Pizarro	.25	.13	.08
(130)	Johnny Podres	.35	.20	.11
(131)	Leo Posada	.25	.13	.08
(132)	Vic Power	.25	.13	.08
(133)	Bob Purkey	.25	.13	.08
(134)	Pedro Ramos	.25	.13	.08
(135)	Bobby Richardson	.80	.40	.25

		NR MT	EX	VG
(136)	Brooks Robinson	3.75	2.00	1.25
(137)	Floyd Robinson	.25	.13	.08
(138)	Frank Robinson	3.50	1.75	1.00
(139)	Bob Rodgers	.30	.15	.09
(140)	Johnny Romano	.25	.13	.08
(141)	John Roseboro	.30	.15	.09
(142)	Pete Runnels	.30	.15	.09
(143)	Ray Sadecki	.25	.13	.08
(144)	Ron Santo	.35	.20	.11
(145)	Chuck Schilling	.25	.13	.08
(146)	Barney Schultz	.25	.13	.08
(147)	Don Schwall	.25	.13	.08
(148)	Bobby Shantz	.35	.20	.11
(149)	Bob Shaw	.25	.13	.08
(150)	Norm Siebern	.25	.13	.08
(151a)	Roy Sievers (Kansas City)	1.00	.50	.30
(151b)	Roy Sievers (Philadelphia)	.30	.15	.09
(152)	Bill Skowron	.50	.25	.15
(153)	Hal (W.) Smith	.25	.13	.08
(154)	Duke Snider	3.75	2.00	1.25
(155)	Warren Spahn	3.00	1.50	.90
(156)	Al Spangler	.25	.13	.08
(157)	Daryl Spencer	.25	.13	.08
(158)	Gene Stephens	.25	.13	.08
(159)	Dick Stuart	.30	.15	.09
(160)	Haywood Sullivan	.25	.13	.08
(161)	Tony Taylor	.25	.13	.08
(162)	George Thomas	.25	.13	.08
(163)	Lee Thomas	.25	.13	.08
(164)	Bob Tiefenauer	.25	.13	.08
(165)	Joe Torre	.50	.25	.15
(166)	Gus Triandos	.30	.15	.09
(167)	Bill Tuttle	.25	.13	.08
(168)	Zoilo Versalles	.25	.13	.08
(169)	Bill Virdon	.35	.20	.11
(170)	Leon Wagner	.25	.13	.08
(171)	Jerry Walker	.25	.13	.08
(172)	Lee Walls	.25	.13	.08
(173)	Bill White	.30	.15	.09
(174)	Hoyt Wilhelm	1.50	.70	.45
(175)	Billy Williams	2.00	1.00	.60
(176)	Jake Wood	.25	.13	.08
(177)	Gene Woodling	.35	.20	.11
(178)	Early Wynn	2.00	1.00	.60
(179)	Carl Yastrzemski	12.00	6.00	3.50
(180)	Don Zimmer	.35	.20	.11
(181)	Baltimore Orioles Logo	.25	.13	.08
(182)	Boston Red Sox Logo	.25	.13	.08
(183)	Chicago Cubs Logo	.25	.13	.08
(184)	Chicago White Sox Logo	.25	.13	.08
(185)	Cincinnati Reds Logo	.25	.13	.08
(186)	Cleveland Indians Logo	.25	.13	.08
(187)	Detroit Tigers Logo	.25	.13	.08
(188)	Houston Colts Logo	.25	.13	.08
(189)	Kansas City Athletics Logo	.25	.13	.08
(190)	Los Angeles Angels Logo	.25	.13	.08
(191)	Los Angeles Dodgers Logo	.25	.13	.08
(192)	Milwaukee Braves Logo	.25	.13	.08
(193)	Minnesota Twins Logo	.25	.13	.08
(194)	New York Mets Logo	.35	.20	.11
(195)	New York Yankees Logo	.35	.20	.11
(196)	Philadelphia Phillies Logo	.25	.13	.08
(197)	Pittsburgh Pirates Logo	.25	.13	.08
(198)	St. Louis Cardinals Logo	.25	.13	.08
(199)	San Francisco Giants Logo	.25	.13	.08
(200)	Washington Senators Logo	.25	.13	.08

Wrong backs, blank backs

Collectors occasionally find recent (1980s) cards which have wrong backs (player on front doesn't match bio/stats on back) or blank backs. Such cards result from mistakes in the printing process. They aren't very popular with collectors, so they have little, if any, premium value. Most collectors feel they are merely damaged cards and value them lower than correctly printed specimens. The only exception seems to be currently hot superstars or rookie cards, for which a few collectors are willing to pay premiums.

1963 Topps

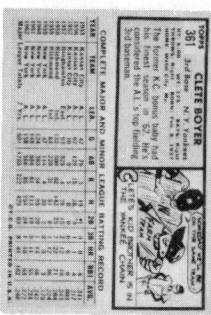

Although the number of cards dropped to 576, the 1963 Topps set is among the most popular of the 1960s. A color photo dominates the 2-1/2" by 3-1/2" card, but a colored circle at the bottom carries a black and white portrait as well. A colored band gives the player's name, team and position. The backs again feature career statistics and a cartoon, career summary and brief biographical details. The set is somewhat unlike those immediately preceding it in that there are fewer specialty cards. The major groupings are statistical leaders, World Series highlights and rookies. It is one rookie which makes the set special - Pete Rose. As one of most avidly sought cards in history and a high-numbered card at that, the Rose rookie card accounts for much of the value of a complete set.

	NR MT	EX	VG
Complete Set:	4000.00	2000.00	1250.
Common Player: 1-283	.70	.35	.20
Common Player: 284-446	2.00	1.00	.60
Common Player: 447-506	8.00	4.00	2.50
Common Player: 507-576	5.00	2.50	1.50

		NR MT	EX	VG
1	N.L. Batting Leaders (Hank Aaron, Tommy Davis, Stan Musial, Frank Robinson, Bill White)	40.00	6.00	3.50
2	A.L. Batting Leaders (Chuck Hinton, Mickey Mantle, Floyd Robinson, Pete Runnels, Norm Siebern)	15.00	7.50	4.50
3	N.L. Home Run Leaders (Hank Aaron, Ernie Banks, Orlando Cepeda, Willie Mays, Frank Robinson)	12.00	6.00	3.50
4	A.L. Home Run Leaders (Norm Cash, Rocky Colavito, Jim Gentile, Harmon Killebrew, Roger Maris, Leon Wagner)	4.00	2.00	1.25
5	N.L. E.R.A. Leaders (Don Drysdale, Bob Gibson, Sandy Koufax, Bob Purkey, Bob Shaw)	4.00	2.00	1.25
6	A.L. E.R.A. Leaders (Hank Aguirre, Dean Chance, Eddie Fisher, Whitey Ford, Robin Roberts)	3.50	1.75	1.00
7	N.L. Pitching Leaders (Don Drysdale, Joe Jay, Art Mahaffey, Billy O'Dell, Bob Purkey, Jack Sanford)	3.50	1.75	1.00
8	A.L. Pitching Leaders (Jim Bunning, Dick Donovan, Ray Herbert, Camilo Pascual, Ralph Terry)	3.00	1.50	.90
9	N.L. Strikeout Leaders (Don Drysdale, Dick Farrell, Bob Gibson, Sandy Koufax, Billy O'Dell)	4.00	2.00	1.25
10	A.L. Strikeout Leaders (Jim Bunning, Jim Kaat, Camilo Pascual, Juan Pizarro, Ralph Terry)	3.00	1.50	.90
11	Lee Walls	.70	.35	.20
12	Steve Barber	.70	.35	.20
13	Phillies Team	2.25	1.25	.70
14	Pedro Ramos	.70	.35	.20
15	Ken Hubbs	2.00	1.00	.60
16	Al Smith	.70	.35	.20
17	Ryne Duren	1.00	.50	.30
18	Buc Blasters (Smoky Burgess, Bob Clemente, Bob Skinner, Dick Stuart)	8.00	4.00	2.50
19	Pete Burnside	.70	.35	.20
20	Tony Kubek	5.00	2.50	1.50

		NR MT	EX	V
21	Marty Keough	.70	.35	.20
22	Curt Simmons	1.00	.50	.30
23	Ed Lopat	1.25	.60	.40
24	Bob Bruce	.70	.35	.20
25	Al Kaline	25.00	12.50	7.50
26	Ray Moore	.70	.35	.20
27	Choo Choo Coleman	1.25	.60	.40
28	Mike Fornieles	.70	.35	.20
29a	1962 Rookie Stars (John Boozer, Ray Culp, Sammy Ellis, Jesse Gonder)	5.00	2.50	1.50
29b	1963 Rookie Stars (John Boozer, Ray Culp, Sammy Ellis, Jesse Gonder)	1.25	.60	.40
30	Harvey Kuenn	1.50	.70	.45
31	Cal Koonce	.70	.35	.20
32	Tony Gonzalez	.70	.35	.20
33	Bo Belinsky	2.00	1.00	.60
34	Dick Schofield	.70	.35	.20
35	John Buzhardt	.70	.35	.20
36	Jerry Kindall	.70	.35	.20
37	Jerry Lynch	.70	.35	.20
38	Bud Daley	1.25	.60	.40
39	Angels Team	2.25	1.25	.70
40	Vic Power	.70	.35	.20
41	Charlie Lau	1.00	.50	.20
42	Stan Williams	1.25	.60	.40
43	Veteran Masters (Casey Stengel, Gene Woodling)	4.00	2.00	1.25
44	Terry Fox	.70	.35	.20
45	Bob Aspromonte	.70	.35	.20
46	Tommie Aaron	1.25	.60	.40
47	Don Lock	.70	.35	.20
48	Birdie Tebbetts	.70	.35	.20
49	Dal Maxvill	1.25	.60	.40
50	Bill Pierce	1.25	.60	.40
51	George Alusik	.70	.35	.20
52	Chuck Schilling	.70	.35	.20
53	Joe Moeller	.70	.35	.20
54a	1962 Rookie Stars (Jack Cullen, Dave DeBusschere, Harry Fanok, Nelson Mathews)	8.00	4.00	2.50
54b	1963 Rookie Stars (Jack Cullen, Dave DeBusschere, Harry Fanok, Nelson Mathews)	4.00	2.00	2.50
55	Bill Virdon	1.50	.70	.45
56	Dennis Bennett	.70	.35	.20
57	Billy Moran	.70	.35	.20
58	Bob Will	.70	.35	.20
59	Craig Anderson	1.00	.50	.30
60	Elston Howard	6.00	3.00	1.75
61	Ernie Bowman	.70	.35	.20
62	Bob Hendley	.70	.35	.20
63	Reds Team	2.50	1.25	.70
64	Dick McAuliffe	.90	.45	.25
65	Jackie Brandt	.70	.35	.20
66	Mike Joyce	.70	.35	.20
67	Ed Charles	.70	.35	.20
68	Friendly Foes (Gil Hodges, Duke Snider)	6.50	3.25	2.00
69	Bud Zipfel	.70	.35	.20
70	Jim O'Toole	.70	.35	.20
71	Bobby Wine	.90	.45	.25
72	Johnny Romano	.70	.35	.20
73	Bobby Bragan	.90	.45	.25
74	Denver Lemaster	.90	.45	.25
75	Bob Allison	1.25	.60	.40
76	Earl Wilson	.70	.35	.20
77	Al Spangler	.70	.35	.20
78	Marv Throneberry	3.50	1.75	1.00
79	Checklist 1-88	2.50	1.25	.70
80	Jim Gilliam	3.00	1.50	.90
81	Jimmie Schaffer	.70	.35	.20
82	Ed Rakow	.70	.35	.20
83	Charley James	.70	.35	.20
84	Ron Kline	.70	.35	.20
85	Tom Haller	.90	.45	.25
86	Charley Maxwell	.70	.35	.20
87	Bob Veale	.90	.45	.25
88	Ron Hansen	.70	.35	.20
89	Dick Stigman	.70	.35	.20
90	Gordy Coleman	.70	.35	.20
91	Dallas Green	.90	.45	.25
92	Hector Lopez	1.25	.60	.40
93	Galen Cisco	.90	.45	.25
94	Bob Schmidt	.70	.35	.20
95	Larry Jackson	.70	.35	.20
96	Lou Clinton	.70	.35	.20
97	Bob Duliba	.70	.35	.20
98	George Thomas	.70	.35	.20
99	Jim Umbricht	.70	.35	.20
100	Joe Cunningham	.90	.45	.25
101	Joe Gibbon	.70	.35	.20

 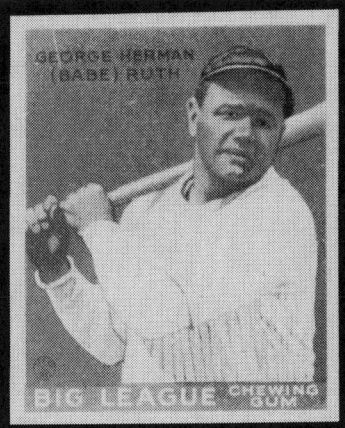 

		NR MT	EX	VG
102a	Checklist 89-176 ("Checklist" in red on front)	3.00	1.50	.90
102b	Checklist 89-176 ("Checklist" in white)	6.00	3.00	1.75
103	Chuck Essegian	.70	.35	.20
104	Lew Krausse	.70	.35	.20
105	Ron Fairly	.90	.45	.25
106	Bob Bolin	.70	.35	.20
107	Jim Hickman	1.00	.50	.30
108	Hoyt Wilhelm	9.00	4.50	2.75
109	Lee Maye	.70	.35	.20
110	Rich Rollins	.90	.45	.25
111	Al Jackson	1.00	.50	.30
112	Dick Brown	.70	.35	.20
113	Don Landrum (photo actally Ron Santo)	.90	.45	.25
114	Dan Osinski	.70	.35	.20
115	Carl Yastrzemski	80.00	40.00	25.00
116	Jim Brosnan	.90	.45	.25
117	Jacke Davis	.70	.35	.20
118	Sherm Lollar	.90	.45	.25
119	Bob Lillis	.70	.35	.20
120	Roger Maris	50.00	25.00	15.00
121	Jim Hannan	.70	.35	.20
122	Julio Gotay	.70	.35	.20
123	Frank Howard	2.50	1.25	.70
124	Dick Howser	1.50	.70	.45
125	Robin Roberts	6.00	3.00	1.75
126	Bob Uecker	30.00	15.00	9.00
127	Bill Tuttle	.70	.35	.20
128	Matty Alou	.90	.45	.25
129	Gary Bell	.70	.35	.20
130	Dick Groat	1.50	.70	.45
131	Senators Team	2.25	1.25	.70
132	Jack Hamilton	.70	.35	.20
133	Gene Freese	.70	.35	.20
134	Bob Scheffing	.70	.35	.20
135	Richie Ashburn	4.50	2.25	1.25
136	Ike Delock	.70	.35	.20
137	Mack Jones	.70	.35	.20
138	Pride of N.L. (Willie Mays, Stan Musial)	30.00	15.00	9.00
139	Earl Averill	.70	.35	.20
140	Frank Lary	.90	.45	.25
141	Manny Mota	4.00	2.00	1.25
142	World Series Game 1 (Yanks' Ford Wins Series Opener)	3.50	1.75	1.00
143	World Series Game 2 (Sanford Flashes Shutout Magic)	2.25	1.25	.70
144	World Series Game 3 (Maris Sparks Yankee Rally)	4.00	2.00	1.25
145	World Series Game 4 (Hiller Blasts Grand Slammer)	2.25	1.25	.70
146	World Series Game 5 (Tresh's Homer Defeats Giants)	3.00	1.50	.90
147	World Series Game 6 (Pierce Stars In 3 Hit Victory)	3.00	1.50	.90
148	World Series Game 7 (Yanks Celebrate As Terry Wins)	3.00	1.50	.90
149	Marv Breeding	.70	.35	.20
150	Johnny Podres	2.00	1.00	.60
151	Pirates Team	2.25	1.25	.70
152	Ron Nischwitz	.70	.35	.20
153	Hal Smith	.70	.35	.20
154	Walt Alston	3.00	1.50	.90
155	Bill Stafford	1.25	.60	.40
156	Roy McMillan	.70	.35	.20
157	Diego Segui	.90	.45	.25
158	1963 Rookie Stars (Rogelio Alvarez, Tommy Harper, Dave Roberts, Bob Saverine)	.90	.45	.25
159	Jim Pagliaroni	.70	.35	.20
160	Juan Pizarro	.70	.35	.20
161	Frank Torre	.70	.35	.20
162	Twins Team	2.25	1.25	.70
163	Don Larsen	1.25	.60	.40
164	Bubba Morton	.70	.35	.20
165	Jim Kaat	5.00	2.50	1.50
166	Johnny Keane	.70	.35	.20
167	Jim Fregosi	1.50	.70	.45
168	Russ Nixon	.70	.35	.20
169	1963 Rookie Stars (Dick Egan, Julio Navarro, Gaylord Perry, Tommie Sisk)	18.00	9.00	5.50
170	Joe Adcock	1.50	.70	.45
171	Steve Hamilton	.70	.35	.20
172	Gene Oliver	.70	.35	.20
173	Bomber's Best (Mickey Mantle, Bobby Richardson, Tom Tresh)	45.00	23.00	13.50
174	Larry Burright	1.00	.50	.30
175	Bob Buhl	.90	.45	.25
176	Jim King	.70	.35	.20
177	Bubba Phillips	.70	.35	.20
178	Johnny Edwards	.70	.35	.20
179	Ron Piche	.70	.35	.20
180	Bill Skowron	1.50	.70	.45
181	Sammy Esposito	.70	.35	.20
182	Albie Pearson	.70	.35	.20
183	Joe Pepitone	4.00	2.00	1.25
184	Vern Law	1.25	.60	.40
185	Chuck Hiller	.70	.35	.20
186	Jerry Zimmerman	.70	.35	.20
187	Willie Kirkland	.70	.35	.20
188	Eddie Bressoud	.70	.35	.20
189	Dave Giusti	.70	.35	.20
190	Minnie Minoso	1.50	.70	.45
191	Checklist 177-264	3.00	1.50	.90
192	Clay Dalrymple	.70	.35	.20
193	Andre Rodgers	.70	.35	.20
194	Joe Nuxhall	.90	.45	.25
195	Manny Jimenez	.70	.35	.20
196	Doug Camilli	.70	.35	.20
197	Roger Craig	2.00	1.00	.60
198	Lenny Green	.70	.35	.20
199	Joe Amalfitano	.70	.35	.20
200	Mickey Mantle	350.00	175.00	105.00
201	Cecil Butler	.70	.35	.20
202	Red Sox Team	2.50	1.25	.70
203	Chico Cardenas	.70	.35	.20
204	Don Nottebart	.70	.35	.20
205	Luis Aparicio	10.00	5.00	3.00
206	Ray Washburn	.70	.35	.20
207	Ken Hunt	.70	.35	.20
208	1963 Rookie Stars (Ron Herbel, John Miller, Ron Taylor, Wally Wolf)	.70	.35	.20
209	Hobie Landrith	.70	.35	.20
210	Sandy Koufax	125.00	56.00	35.00
211	Fred Whitfield	.70	.35	.20
212	Glen Hobbie	.70	.35	.20
213	Billy Hitchcock	.70	.35	.20
214	Orlando Pena	.70	.35	.20
215	Bob Skinner	.90	.45	.25
216	Gene Conley	.90	.45	.25
217	Joe Christopher	1.00	.50	.30
218	Tiger Twirlers (Jim Bunning, Frank Lary, Don Mossi)	2.00	1.00	.60
219	Chuck Cottier	.70	.35	.20
220	Camilo Pascual	.90	.45	.25
221	Cookie Rojas	.90	.45	.25
222	Cubs Team	2.25	1.25	.70
223	Eddie Fisher	.70	.35	.20
224	Mike Roarke	.70	.35	.20
225	Joe Jay	.70	.35	.20
226	Julian Javier	.90	.45	.25
227	Jim Grant	.70	.35	.20
228	1963 Rookie Stars (Max Alvis, Bob Bailey, Ed Kranepool, Pedro Oliva)	30.00	15.00	9.00
229	Willie Davis	1.50	.70	.45
230	Pete Runnels	.90	.45	.25
231	Eli Grba (photo actually Ryne Duren)	.90	.45	.25
232	Frank Malzone	.90	.45	.25
233	Casey Stengel	12.00	6.00	3.50
234	Dave Nicholson	.70	.35	.20
235	Billy O'Dell	.70	.35	.20
236	Bill Bryan	.70	.35	.20
237	Jim Coates	1.25	.60	.40
238	Lou Johnson	.70	.35	.20
239	Harvey Haddix	.90	.45	.25
240	Rocky Colavito	3.00	1.50	.90
241	Billy Smith	.70	.35	.20
242	Power Plus (Hank Aaron, Ernie Banks)	35.00	17.50	10.50
243	Don Leppert	.70	.35	.20
244	John Tsitouris	.70	.35	.20
245	Gil Hodges	12.00	6.00	3.50
246	Lee Stange	.70	.35	.20
247	Yankees Team	8.00	4.00	2.50
248	Tito Francona	.90	.45	.25
249	Leo Burke	.70	.35	.20
250	Stan Musial	100.00	45.00	27.00
251	Jack Lamabe	.70	.35	.20
252	Ron Santo	2.00	1.00	.60
253	1963 Rookie Stars (Len Gabrielson, Pete Jernigan, Deacon Jones, John Wojcik)	.70	.35	.20
254	Mike Hershberger	.70	.35	.20
255	Bob Shaw	.70	.35	.20
256	Jerry Lumpe	.90	.45	.25
257	Hank Aguirre	.70	.35	.20
258	Alvin Dark	.90	.45	.25
259	Johnny Logan	.90	.45	.25
260	Jim Gentile	.90	.45	.25

		NR MT	EX	VG
261	Bob Miller	.70	.35	.20
262	Ellis Burton	.70	.35	.20
263	Dave Stenhouse	.70	.35	.20
264	Phil Linz	1.50	.70	.45
265	Vada Pinson	2.50	1.25	.70
266	Bob Allen	.70	.35	.20
267	Carl Sawatski	.70	.35	.20
268	Don Demeter	.70	.35	.20
269	Don Mincher	.90	.45	.25
270	Felipe Alou	.90	.45	.25
271	Dean Stone	.70	.35	.20
272	Danny Murphy	.70	.35	.20
273	Sammy Taylor	1.00	.50	.30
274	Checklist 265-352	3.00	1.50	.90
275	Ed Mathews	15.00	7.50	4.50
276	Barry Shetrone	.70	.35	.20
277	Dick Farrell	.70	.35	.20
278	Chico Fernandez	.70	.35	.20
279	Wally Moon	.90	.45	.25
280	Bob Rodgers	.90	.45	.25
281	Tom Sturdivant	.70	.35	.20
282	Bob Del Greco	.70	.35	.20
283	Roy Sievers	.90	.45	.25
284	Dave Sisler	2.00	1.00	.60
285	Dick Stuart	2.25	1.25	.70
286	Stu Miller	2.00	1.00	.60
287	Dick Bertell	2.00	1.00	.60
288	White Sox Team	3.50	1.75	1.00
289	Hal Brown	2.75	1.50	.80
290	Bill White	2.25	1.25	.70
291	Don Rudolph	2.00	1.00	.60
292	Pumpsie Green	2.25	1.25	.70
293	Bill Pleis	2.00	1.00	.60
294	Bill Rigney	2.00	1.00	.60
295	Ed Roebuck	2.00	1.00	.60
296	Doc Edwards	2.25	1.25	.70
297	Jim Golden	2.00	1.00	.60
298	Don Dillard	2.00	1.00	.60
299	1963 Rookie Stars (Tom Butters, Bob Dustal, Dave Morehead, Dan Schneider)	2.00	1.00	.60
300	Willie Mays	125.00	56.00	35.00
301	Bill Fischer	2.00	1.00	.60
302	Whitey Herzog	3.50	1.75	1.00
303	Earl Francis	2.00	1.00	.60
304	Harry Bright	2.00	1.00	.60
305	Don Hoak	2.25	1.25	.70
306	Star Receivers (Earl Battey, Elston Howard)	3.50	1.75	1.00
307	Chet Nichols	2.00	1.00	.60
308	Camilo Carreon	2.00	1.00	.60
309	Jim Brewer	2.00	1.00	.60
310	Tommy Davis	3.00	1.50	.90
311	Joe McClain	2.00	1.00	.60
312	Colt .45s Team	9.00	4.50	2.75
313	Ernie Broglio	2.00	1.00	.60
314	John Goryl	2.00	1.00	.60
315	Ralph Terry	3.00	1.50	.90
316	Norm Sherry	1.25	.60	.40
317	Sam McDowell	3.00	1.50	.90
318	Gene Mauch	2.25	1.25	.70
319	Joe Gaines	2.00	1.00	.60
320	Warren Spahn	40.00	20.00	12.50
321	Gino Cimoli	2.00	1.00	.60
322	Bob Turley	2.25	1.25	.70
323	Bill Mazeroski	3.50	1.75	1.00
324	1963 Rookie Stars (Vic Davalillo, Phil Roof, Pete Ward, George Williams)	2.50	1.25	.70
325	Jack Sanford	2.00	1.00	.60
326	Hank Foiles	2.00	1.00	.60
327	Paul Foytack	2.00	1.00	.60
328	Dick Williams	2.75	1.50	.80
329	Lindy McDaniel	2.00	1.00	.60
330	Chuck Hinton	2.00	1.00	.60
331	Series Foes (Bill Pierce, Bill Stafford)	3.00	1.50	.90
332	Joel Horlen	2.00	1.00	.60
333	Carl Warwick	2.00	1.00	.60
334	Wynn Hawkins	2.25	1.25	.70
335	Leon Wagner	2.25	1.25	.70
336	Ed Bauta	2.00	1.00	.60
337	Dodgers Team	8.00	4.00	2.50
338	Russ Kemmerer	2.00	1.00	.60
339	Ted Bowsfield	2.00	1.00	.60
340	Yogi Berra	80.00	40.00	25.00
341	Jack Baldschun	2.00	1.00	.60
342	Gene Woodling	2.50	1.25	.70
343	Johnny Pesky	2.25	1.25	.70
344	Don Schwall	2.00	1.00	.60
345	Brooks Robinson	30.00	15.00	9.00
346	Billy Hoeft	2.00	1.00	.60
347	Joe Torre	4.50	2.25	1.25
348	Vic Wertz	2.25	1.25	.70
349	Zoilo Versalles	2.25	1.25	.70
350	Bob Purkey	2.00	1.00	.60
351	Al Luplow	2.00	1.00	.60
352	Ken Johnson	2.00	1.00	.60
353	Billy Williams	20.00	10.00	6.00
354	Dom Zanni	2.00	1.00	.60
355	Dean Chance	2.25	1.25	.70
356	John Schaive	2.00	1.00	.60
357	George Altman	2.00	1.00	.60
358	Milt Pappas	2.25	1.25	.70
359	Haywood Sullivan	2.25	1.25	.70
360	Don Drysdale	40.00	20.00	12.50
361	Clete Boyer	3.50	1.75	1.00
362	Checklist 353-429	4.00	2.00	1.25
363	Dick Radatz	2.25	1.25	.70
364	Howie Goss	2.00	1.00	.60
365	Jim Bunning	8.00	4.00	2.50
366	Tony Taylor	2.00	1.00	.60
367	Tony Cloninger	2.25	1.25	.70
368	Ed Bailey	2.00	1.00	.60
369	Jim Lemon	2.00	1.00	.60
370	Dick Donovan	2.00	1.00	.60
371	Rod Kanehl	2.25	1.25	.70
372	Don Lee	2.00	1.00	.60
373	Jim Campbell	2.00	1.00	.60
374	Claude Osteen	2.25	1.25	.70
375	Ken Boyer	4.00	2.00	1.25
376	Johnnie Wyatt	2.00	1.00	.60
377	Orioles Team	3.50	1.75	1.00
378	Bill Henry	2.00	1.00	.60
379	Bob Anderson	2.00	1.00	.60
380	Ernie Banks	40.00	20.00	12.00
381	Frank Baumann	2.00	1.00	.60
382	Ralph Houk	3.50	1.75	1.00
383	Pete Richert	2.00	1.00	.60
384	Bob Tillman	2.00	1.00	.60
385	Art Mahaffey	2.00	1.00	.60
386	1963 Rookie Stars (John Bateman, Larry Bearnarth, Ed Kirkpatrick, Garry Roggenburk)	2.25	1.25	.70
387	Al McBean	2.00	1.00	.60
388	Jim Davenport	2.00	1.00	.60
389	Frank Sullivan	2.00	1.00	.60
390	Hank Aaron	125.00	56.00	35.00
391	Bill Dailey	2.00	1.00	.60
392	Tribe Thumpers (Tito Francona, Johnny Romano)	2.25	1.25	.70
393	Ken MacKenzie	2.25	1.25	.70
394	Tim McCarver	4.00	2.00	1.25
395	Don McMahon	2.00	1.00	.60
396	Joe Koppe	2.00	1.00	.60
397	Athletics Team	3.50	1.75	1.00
398	Boog Powell	7.00	3.50	2.00
399	Dick Ellsworth	2.00	1.00	.60
400	Frank Robinson	45.00	23.00	13.50
401	Jim Bouton	8.00	4.00	2.50
402	Mickey Vernon	2.25	1.25	.70
403	Ron Perranoski	2.25	1.25	.70
404	Bob Oldis	2.00	1.00	.60
405	Floyd Robinson	2.00	1.00	.60
406	Howie Koplitz	2.00	1.00	.60
407	1963 Rookie Stars (Larry Elliot, Frank Kostro, Chico Ruiz, Dick Simpson)	2.00	1.00	.60
408	Billy Gardner	2.00	1.00	.60
409	Roy Face	2.75	1.50	.80
410	Earl Battey	2.25	1.25	.70
411	Jim Constable	2.00	1.00	.60
412	Dodgers' Big Three (Don Drysdale, Sandy Koufax, Johnny Podres)	25.00	12.50	7.50
413	Jerry Walker	2.00	1.00	.60
414	Ty Cline	2.00	1.00	.60
415	Bob Gibson	30.00	15.00	9.00
416	Alex Grammas	2.00	1.00	.60
417	Giants Team	3.50	1.75	1.00
418	Johnny Orsino	2.00	1.00	.60
419	Tracy Stallard	2.25	1.25	.70
420	Bobby Richardson	8.00	4.00	2.50
421	Tom Morgan	2.00	1.00	.60
422	Fred Hutchinson	2.25	1.25	.70
423	Ed Hobaugh	2.00	1.00	.60
424	Charley Smith	2.00	1.00	.60
425	Smoky Burgess	2.50	1.25	.70
426	Barry Latman	2.00	1.00	.60
427	Bernie Allen	2.00	1.00	.60
428	Carl Boles	2.00	1.00	.60
429	Lou Burdette	3.00	1.50	.90
430	Norm Siebern	2.25	1.25	.70
431a	Checklist 430-506 ("Checklist" in black on front)	4.50	2.25	1.25

		NR MT	EX	VG
431b	Checklist 430-506 ("Checklist" in white)			
		7.00	3.50	2.00
432	Roman Mejias	2.00	1.00	.60
433	Denis Menke	2.25	1.25	.70
434	Johnny Callison	2.50	1.25	.70
435	Woody Held	2.00	1.00	.60
436	Tim Harkness	2.25	1.25	.70
437	Bill Bruton	2.00	1.00	.60
438	Wes Stock	2.00	1.00	.60
439	Don Zimmer	2.75	1.50	.80
440	Juan Marichal	20.00	10.00	6.00
441	Lee Thomas	2.00	1.00	.60
442	J.C. Hartman	2.00	1.00	.60
443	Jim Piersall	2.75	1.50	.80
444	Jim Maloney	2.25	1.25	.70
445	Norm Cash	3.00	1.50	.90
446	Whitey Ford	30.00	15.00	9.00
447	Felix Mantilla	8.00	4.00	2.50
448	Jack Kralick	8.00	4.00	2.50
449	Jose Tartabull	8.00	4.00	2.50
450	Bob Friend	9.00	4.50	2.75
451	Indians Team	10.00	5.00	3.00
452	Barney Schultz	8.00	4.00	2.50
453	Jake Wood	8.00	4.00	2.50
454a	Art Fowler (card # on orange background)			
		10.00	5.00	3.00
454b	Art Fowler (card # on white background)			
		8.00	4.00	2.50
455	Ruben Amaro	8.00	4.00	2.50
456	Jim Coker	8.00	4.00	2.50
457	Tex Clevenger	9.00	4.50	2.75
458	Al Lopez	11.00	5.50	3.25
459	Dick LeMay	8.00	4.00	2.50
460	Del Crandall	9.00	4.50	2.75
461	Norm Bass	8.00	4.00	2.50
462	Wally Post	8.00	4.00	2.50
463	Joe Schaffernoth	8.00	4.00	2.50
464	Ken Aspromonte	8.00	4.00	2.50
465	Chuck Estrada	8.00	4.00	2.50
466	1963 Rookie Stars (Bill Freehan, Tony Martinez, Nate Oliver, Jerry Robinson)			
		25.00	12.50	7.50
467	Phil Ortega	8.00	4.00	2.50
468	Carroll Hardy	8.00	4.00	2.50
469	Jay Hook	9.00	4.50	2.75
470	Tom Tresh	20.00	10.00	6.00
471	Ken Retzer	8.00	4.00	2.50
472	Lou Brock	125.00	62.00	37.00
473	Mets Team	100.00	50.00	30.00
474	Jack Fisher	8.00	4.00	2.50
475	Gus Triandos	8.00	4.00	2.50
476	Frank Funk	8.00	4.00	2.50
477	Donn Clendenon	9.00	4.50	2.75
478	Paul Brown	8.00	4.00	2.50
479	Ed Brinkman	9.00	4.50	2.75
480	Bill Monbouquette	9.00	4.50	2.75
481	Bob Taylor	8.00	4.00	2.50
482	Felix Torres	8.00	4.00	2.50
483	Jim Owens	8.00	4.00	2.50
484	Dale Long	9.00	4.50	2.75
485	Jim Landis	8.00	4.00	2.50
486	Ray Sadecki	8.00	4.00	2.50
487	John Roseboro	9.00	4.50	2.75
488	Jerry Adair	8.00	4.00	2.50
489	Paul Toth	8.00	4.00	2.50
490	Willie McCovey	90.00	45.00	27.00
491	Harry Craft	8.00	4.00	2.50
492	Dave Wickersham	8.00	4.00	2.50
493	Walt Bond	8.00	4.00	2.50
494	Phil Regan	8.00	4.00	2.50
495	Frank Thomas	9.00	4.50	2.75
496	1963 Rookie Stars (Carl Bouldin, Steve Dalkowski, Fred Newman, Jack Smith)			
		9.00	4.50	2.75
497	Bennie Daniels	8.00	4.00	2.50
498	Eddie Kasko	8.00	4.00	2.50
499	J.C. Martin	8.00	4.00	2.50
500	Harmon Killebrew	90.00	45.00	27.00
501	Joe Azcue	8.00	4.00	2.50
502	Daryl Spencer	8.00	4.00	2.50
503	Braves Team	10.00	5.00	3.00
504	Bob Johnson	8.00	4.00	2.50
505	Curt Flood	12.00	6.00	3.50
506	Gene Green	9.00	4.50	2.75
507	Roland Sheldon	6.00	3.00	1.75
508	Ted Savage	5.00	2.50	1.50
509a	Checklist 507-576 (copyright centered)			
		15.00	7.50	4.50
509b	Checklist 509-576 (copyright to right)			
		12.00	6.00	3.50
510	Ken McBride	5.00	2.50	1.50

		NR MT	EX	VG
511	Charlie Neal	5.50	2.75	1.75
512	Cal McLish	5.00	2.50	1.50
513	Gary Geiger	5.00	2.50	1.50
514	Larry Osborne	5.00	2.50	1.50
515	Don Elston	5.00	2.50	1.50
516	Purnal Goldy	5.00	2.50	1.50
517	Hal Woodeshick	5.00	2.50	1.50
518	Don Blasingame	5.00	2.50	1.50
519	Claude Raymond	5.00	2.50	1.50
520	Orlando Cepeda	15.00	7.50	4.50
521	Dan Pfister	5.00	2.50	1.50
522	1963 Rookie Stars (Mel Nelson, Gary Peters, Art Quirk, Jim Roland)	5.50	2.75	1.75
523	Bill Kunkel	6.00	3.00	1.75
524	Cardinals Team	8.00	4.00	2.50
525	Nellie Fox	12.00	6.00	3.50
526	Dick Hall	5.00	2.50	1.50
527	Ed Sadowski	5.00	2.50	1.50
528	Carl Willey	5.50	2.75	1.75
529	Wes Covington	5.00	2.50	1.50
530	Don Mossi	5.50	2.75	1.75
531	Sam Mele	5.00	2.50	1.50
532	Steve Boros	5.00	2.50	1.50
533	Bobby Shantz	6.00	3.00	1.75
534	Ken Walters	5.00	2.50	1.50
535	Jim Perry	6.00	3.00	1.75
536	Norm Larker	5.00	2.50	1.50
537	1963 Rookie Stars (Pedro Gonzalez, Ken McMullen, Pete Rose, Al Weis)	600.00	240.00	150.00
538	George Brunet	5.00	2.50	1.50
539	Wayne Causey	5.00	2.50	1.50
540	Bob Clemente	175.00	87.00	52.00
541	Ron Moeller	5.00	2.50	1.50
542	Lou Klimchock	5.00	2.50	1.50
543	Russ Snyder	5.00	2.50	1.50
544	1963 Rookie Stars (Duke Carmel, Bill Haas, Dick Phillips, Rusty Staub)	30.00	15.00	9.00
545	Jose Pagan	5.00	2.50	1.50
546	Hal Reniff	6.00	3.00	1.75
547	Gus Bell	5.50	2.75	1.75
548	Tom Satriano	5.00	2.50	1.50
549	1963 Rookie Stars (Marcelino Lopez, Pete Lovrich, Elmo Plaskett, Paul Ratliff)	5.50	2.75	1.75
550	Duke Snider	70.00	35.00	20.00
551	Billy Klaus	5.00	2.50	1.50
552	Tigers Team	12.00	6.00	3.50
553	1963 Rookie Stars (Brock Davis, Jim Gosger, John Herrnstein, Willie Stargell)	275.00	137.00	82.00
554	Hank Fischer	5.00	2.50	1.50
555	John Blanchard	6.00	3.00	1.75
556	Al Worthington	5.00	2.50	1.50
557	Cuno Barragan	5.00	2.50	1.50
558	1963 Rookie Stars (Bill Faul, Ron Hunt, Bob Lipski, Al Moran)	6.00	3.00	1.75
559	Danny Murtaugh	5.50	2.75	1.75
560	Ray Herbert	5.00	2.50	1.50
561	Mike de la Hoz	5.00	2.50	1.50
562	1963 Rookie Stars (Randy Cardinal, Dave McNally, Don Rowe, Ken Rowe)	9.00	4.50	2.75
563	Mike McCormick	5.50	2.75	1.75
564	George Banks	5.00	2.50	1.50
565	Larry Sherry	5.00	2.50	1.50
566	Cliff Cook	5.50	2.75	1.75
567	Jim Duffalo	5.00	2.50	1.50
568	Bob Sadowski	5.00	2.50	1.50
569	Luis Arroyo	6.00	3.00	1.75
570	Frank Bolling	5.00	2.50	1.50
571	Johnny Klippstein	5.00	2.50	1.50
572	Jack Spring	5.00	2.50	1.50
573	Coot Veal	5.00	2.50	1.50
574	Hal Kolstad	5.00	2.50	1.50
575	Don Cardwell	5.50	2.50	1.50
576	Johnny Temple	8.00	2.50	1.25

1963 Topps Peel-Offs

Measuring 1-1/4" by 2-3/4," Topps Peel-Offs were an insert with 1963 Topps baseball cards. There are 46 players in the unnumbered set, each pictured in a color photo inside an oval with the player's name, team and position in a band below. The back of the Peel-Off is removable, leaving a sticky surface that made the Peel-Off a popular decorative item among youngsters of the day. Naturally, that makes them quite scarce today, but as a non-card Topps issue, demand is not particularly strong.

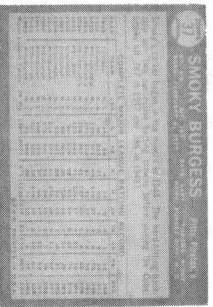

	NR MT	EX	VG
Complete Set:	175.00	87.00	52.00
Common Player:	1.00	.50	.30
(1) Hank Aaron	10.00	5.00	3.00
(2) Luis Aparicio	3.00	1.50	.90
(3) Richie Ashburn	2.00	1.00	.60
(4) Bob Aspromonte	1.00	.50	.30
(5) Ernie Banks	5.00	2.50	1.50
(6) Ken Boyer	1.50	.70	.45
(7) Jim Bunning	1.75	.90	.50
(8) Johnny Callison	1.25	.60	.40
(9) Orlando Cepeda	1.75	.90	.50
(10) Bob Clemente	8.00	4.00	2.50
(11) Rocky Colavito	1.75	.90	.50
(12) Tommy Davis	1.50	.70	.45
(13) Dick Donovan	1.00	.50	.30
(14) Don Drysdale	4.00	2.00	1.25
(15) Dick Farrell	1.00	.50	.30
(16) Jim Gentile	1.00	.50	.30
(17) Ray Herbert	1.00	.50	.30
(18) Chuck Hinton	1.00	.50	.30
(19) Ken Hubbs	1.50	.70	.45
(20) Al Jackson	1.00	.50	.30
(21) Al Kaline	5.00	2.50	1.50
(22) Harmon Killebrew	5.00	2.50	1.50
(23) Sandy Koufax	8.00	4.00	2.50
(24) Jerry Lumpe	1.00	.50	.30
(25) Art Mahaffey	1.00	.50	.30
(26) Mickey Mantle	50.00	25.00	15.00
(27) Willie Mays	10.00	5.00	3.00
(28) Bill Mazeroski	1.50	.70	.45
(29) Bill Monbouquette	1.00	.50	.30
(30) Stan Musial	10.00	5.00	3.00
(31) Camilo Pascual	1.25	.60	.40
(32) Bob Purkey	1.00	.50	.30
(33) Bobby Richardson	1.75	.90	.50
(34) Brooks Robinson	6.00	3.00	1.75
(35) Floyd Robinson	1.00	.50	.30
(36) Frank Robinson	5.00	2.50	1.50
(37) Bob Rodgers	1.00	.50	.30
(38) Johnny Romano	1.00	.50	.30
(39) Jack Sanford	1.00	.50	.30
(40) Norm Siebern	1.00	.50	.30
(41) Warren Spahn	5.00	2.50	1.50
(42) Dave Stenhouse	1.00	.50	.30
(43) Ralph Terry	1.25	.60	.40
(44) Lee Thomas	1.00	.50	.30
(45) Bill White	1.25	.60	.40
(46) Carl Yastrzemski	12.00	6.00	3.50

1964 Topps

The 1964 Topps set is a 587-card issue of 2-1/2" by 3-1/2" cards which is considered by many as being among the company's best efforts. Card fronts feature a large color photo which blends into a top panel which contains the team name, while a panel below the picture carries the player's name and position. An interesting innovation on the back is a baseball quiz question which required the rubbing of a white panel to reveal the answer. As in 1963, specialty cards remained modest in number with a 12-card set of statistical leaders, a few multi-player cards, rookies and World Series highlights. An interesting card is an "In Memoriam" card for Ken Hubbs who was killed in an airplane crash.

	NR MT	EX	VG
Complete Set:	2500.00	1250.00	750.00
Common Player: 1-370	.70	.35	.20
Common Player: 371-522	1.00	.50	.30
Common Player: 523-587	4.00	2.00	1.25
1 N.L. E.R.A. Leaders (Dick Ellsworth, Bob Friend, Sandy Koufax)	10.00	3.00	1.50
2 A.L. E.R.A. Leaders (Camilo Pascual, Gary Peters, Juan Pizarro)	3.00	1.50	.90
3 N.L. Pitching Leaders (Sandy Koufax, Jim Maloney, Juan Marichal, Warren Spahn)	5.00	2.50	1.50
4a A.L. Pitching Leaders (Jim Bouton, Whitey Ford, Camilo Pascual) (apostrophe after "Pitching" on back)	5.00	2.50	1.50
4b A.L. Pitching Leaders (Jim Bouton, Whitey Ford, Camilo Pascual) (no apostrophe)	3.50	1.75	1.00
5 N.L. Strikeout Leaders (Don Drysdale, Sandy Koufax, Jim Maloney)	4.00	2.00	1.25
6 A.L. Strikeout Leaders (Jim Bunning, Camilo Pascual, Dick Stigman)	3.00	1.50	.90
7 N.L. Batting Leaders (Hank Aaron, Bob Clemente, Tommy Davis, Dick Groat)	5.00	2.50	1.50
8 A.L. Batting Leaders (Al Kaline, Rich Rollins, Carl Yastrzemski)	5.00	2.50	1.50
9 N.L. Home Run Leaders (Hank Aaron, Orlando Cepeda, Willie Mays, Willie McCovey)	5.00	2.50	1.50
10 A.L. Home Run Leaders (Bob Allison, Harmon Killebrew, Dick Stuart)	3.50	1.75	1.00
11 N.L. R.B.I. Leaders (Hank Aaron, Ken Boyer, Bill White)	4.50	2.25	1.25
12 A.L. R.B.I. Leaders (Al Kaline, Harmon Killebrew, Dick Stuart)	4.50	2.25	1.25
13 Hoyt Wilhelm	8.00	4.00	2.50
14 Dodgers Rookies (Dick Nen, Nick Willhite)	.70	.35	.20
15 Zoilo Versalles	.80	.40	.25
16 John Boozer	.70	.35	.20
17 Willie Kirkland	.70	.35	.20
18 Billy O'Dell	.70	.35	.20
19 Don Wert	.70	.35	.20
20 Bob Friend	1.25	.60	.40
21 Yogi Berra	30.00	15.00	9.00
22 Jerry Adair	.70	.35	.20
23 Chris Zachary	.70	.35	.20
24 Carl Sawatski	.70	.35	.20
25 Bill Monbouquette	.80	.40	.25
26 Gino Cimoli	.70	.35	.20
27 Mets Team	3.50	1.75	1.00
28 Claude Osteen	.80	.40	.25
29 Lou Brock	30.00	15.00	9.00
30 Ron Perranoski	.80	.40	.25
31 Dave Nicholson	.70	.35	.20
32 Dean Chance	1.25	.60	.40
33 Reds Rookies (Sammy Ellis, Mel Queen)	.80	.40	.25
34 Jim Perry	1.25	.60	.40
35 Ed Mathews	15.00	7.50	4.50
36 Hal Reniff	1.00	.50	.30
37 Smoky Burgess	1.25	.60	.40
38 *Jim Wynn*	1.50	.70	.45
39 Hank Aguirre	.70	.35	.20
40 Dick Groat	1.50	.70	.45
41 Friendly Foes (Willie McCovey, Leon Wagner)	3.00	1.50	.90

		NR MT	EX	VG
42	Moe Drabowsky	.70	.35	.20
43	Roy Sievers	.90	.45	.25
44	Duke Carmel	.80	.40	.25
45	Milt Pappas	.90	.45	.25
46	Ed Brinkman	.80	.40	.25
47	Giants Rookies (*Jesus Alou*, Ron Herbel)			
		1.25	.60	.40
48	Bob Perry	.70	.35	.20
49	Bill Henry	.70	.35	.20
50	Mickey Mantle	200.00	80.00	50.00
51	Pete Richert	.70	.35	.20
52	Chuck Hinton	.70	.35	.20
53	Denis Menke	.70	.35	.20
54	Sam Mele	.70	.35	.20
55	Ernie Banks	25.00	12.50	7.50
56	Hal Brown	.70	.35	.20
57	Tim Harkness	.80	.40	.25
58	Don Demeter	.70	.35	.20
59	Ernie Broglio	.70	.35	.20
60	Frank Malzone	.80	.40	.25
61	Angel Backstops (Bob Rodgers, Ed Sadowski)			
		.80	.40	.25
62	Ted Savage	.70	.35	.20
63	Johnny Orsino	.70	.35	.20
64	Ted Abernathy	.70	.35	.20
65	Felipe Alou	1.25	.60	.40
66	Eddie Fisher	.70	.35	.20
67	Tigers Team	3.50	1.75	1.00
68	Willie Davis	1.50	.70	.45
69	Clete Boyer	1.50	.70	.45
70	Joe Torre	2.50	1.25	.70
71	Jack Spring	.70	.35	.20
72	Chico Cardenas	.70	.35	.20
73	*Jimmie Hall*	.80	.40	.25
74	Pirates Rookies (Tom Butters, Bob Priddy)			
		.70	.35	.20
75	Wayne Causey	.70	.35	.20
76	Checklist 1-88	3.00	1.50	.90
77	Jerry Walker	.70	.35	.20
78	Merritt Ranew	.70	.35	.20
79	Bob Heffner	.70	.35	.20
80	Vada Pinson	2.50	1.25	.70
81	All-Star Vets (Nellie Fox, Harmon Killebrew)			
		4.00	2.00	1.25
82	Jim Davenport	.70	.35	.20
83	Gus Triandos	.80	.40	.25
84	Carl Willey	.80	.40	.25
85	Pete Ward	.80	.40	.25
86	Al Downing	1.50	.70	.45
87	Cardinals Team	4.00	2.00	1.25
88	John Roseboro	.80	.40	.25
89	Boog Powell	2.50	1.25	.70
90	Earl Battey	.80	.40	.25
91	Bob Bailey	.80	.40	.25
92	Steve Ridzik	.70	.35	.20
93	Gary Geiger	.70	.35	.20
94	Braves Rookies (Jim Britton, Larry Maxie)			
		.70	.35	.20
95	George Altman	.80	.40	.25
96	Bob Buhl	.80	.40	.25
97	Jim Fregosi	1.25	.60	.40
98	Bill Bruton	.70	.35	.20
99	Al Stanek	.70	.35	.20
100	Elston Howard	5.00	2.50	1.50
101	Walt Alston	3.00	1.50	.90
102	Checklist 89-176	3.00	1.50	.90
103	Curt Flood	2.00	1.00	.60
104	Art Mahaffey	.70	.35	.20
105	Woody Held	.70	.35	.20
106	Joe Nuxhall	.80	.40	.25
107	White Sox Rookies (Bruce Howard, Frank Kreutzer)			
		.70	.35	.20
108	John Wyatt	.70	.35	.20
109	Rusty Staub	5.00	2.50	1.50
110	Albie Pearson	.70	.35	.20
111	Don Elston	.70	.35	.20
112	Bob Tillman	.70	.35	.20
113	Grover Powell	.80	.40	.25
114	Don Lock	.70	.35	.20
115	Frank Bolling	.70	.35	.20
116	Twins Rookies (Tony Oliva, Jay Ward)			
		4.00	2.00	1.25
117	Earl Francis	.70	.35	.20
118	John Blanchard	1.00	.50	.30
119	Gary Kolb	.70	.35	.20
120	Don Drysdale	15.00	7.50	4.50
121	Pete Runnels	.80	.40	.25
122	Don McMahon	.70	.35	.20
123	Jose Pagan	.70	.35	.20
124	Orlando Pena	.70	.35	.20
125	Pete Rose	150.00	75.00	45.00

		NR MT	EX	VG
126	Russ Snyder	.70	.35	.20
127	Angels Rookies (Aubrey Gatewood, Dick Simpson)			
		.70	.35	.20
128	*Mickey Lolich*	10.00	5.00	3.00
129	Amado Samuel	.80	.40	.25
130	Gary Peters	.80	.40	.25
131	Steve Boros	.80	.40	.25
132	Braves Team	2.25	1.25	.70
133	Jim Grant	.70	.35	.20
134	Don Zimmer	1.50	.70	.45
135	Johnny Callison	1.50	.70	.45
136	World Series Game 1 (Koufax Strikes Out 15)			
		5.00	2.50	1.50
137	World Series Game 2 (Davis Sparks Rally)			
		2.50	1.25	.70
138	World Series Game 3 (L.A. Takes 3rd Straight)			
		2.50	1.25	.70
139	World Series Game 4 (Sealing Yanks' Doom)			
		2.50	1.25	.70
140	World Series Summary (The Dodgers Celebrate)			
		2.50	1.25	.70
141	Danny Murtaugh	.80	.40	.25
142	John Bateman	.70	.35	.20
143	Bubba Phillips	.70	.35	.20
144	Al Worthington	.70	.35	.20
145	Norm Siebern	.80	.40	.25
146	Indians Rookies (Bob Chance, *Tommy John*)			
		60.00	30.00	18.00
147	Ray Sadecki	.70	.35	.20
148	J.C. Martin	.70	.35	.20
149	Paul Foytack	.70	.35	.20
150	Willie Mays	70.00	35.00	21.00
151	Athletics Team	2.25	1.25	.70
152	Denver Lemaster	.70	.35	.20
153	Dick Williams	1.50	.70	.45
154	Dick Tracewski	.70	.35	.20
155	Duke Snider	25.00	12.50	7.50
156	Bill Dailey	.70	.35	.20
157	Gene Mauch	.90	.45	.25
158	Ken Johnson	.70	.35	.20
159	Charlie Dees	.70	.35	.20
160	Ken Boyer	4.00	2.00	1.25
161	Dave McNally	1.25	.60	.40
162	Hitting Area (Vada Pinson, Dick Sisler)			
		.80	.40	.25
163	Donn Clendenon	1.00	.50	.30
164	Bud Daley	1.00	.50	.30
165	Jerry Lumpe	.80	.40	.25
166	Marty Keough	.70	.35	.20
167	Senators Rookies (Mike Brumley, *Lou Piniella*)			
		20.00	10.00	6.00
168	Al Weis	.70	.35	.20
169	Del Crandall	1.25	.60	.40
170	Dick Radatz	.80	.40	.25
171	Ty Cline	.70	.35	.20
172	Indians Team	2.25	1.25	.70
173	Ryne Duren	.90	.45	.25
174	Doc Edwards	.80	.40	.25
175	Billy Williams	10.00	5.00	3.00
176	Tracy Stallard	.80	.40	.25
177	Harmon Killebrew	12.00	6.00	3.50
178	Hank Bauer	.90	.45	.25
179	Carl Warwick	.70	.35	.20
180	Tommy Davis	1.50	.70	.45
181	Dave Wickersham	.70	.35	.20
182	Sox Sockers (Chuck Schilling, Carl Yastrzemski)			
		7.00	3.50	2.00
183	Ron Taylor	.70	.35	.20
184	Al Luplow	.70	.35	.20
185	Jim O'Toole	.70	.35	.20
186	Roman Mejias	.70	.35	.20
187	Ed Roebuck	.70	.35	.20
188	Checklist 177-264	3.00	1.50	.90
189	Bob Hendley	.70	.35	.20
190	Bobby Richardson	4.50	2.25	1.25
191	Clay Dalrymple	.70	.35	.20
192	Cubs Rookies (John Boccabella, Billy Cowan)			
		.70	.35	.20
193	Jerry Lynch	.70	.35	.20
194	John Goryl	.70	.35	.20
195	Floyd Robinson	.70	.35	.20
196	Jim Gentile	.80	.40	.25
197	Frank Lary	.80	.40	.25
198	Len Gabrielson	.70	.35	.20
199	Joe Azcue	.70	.35	.20
200	Sandy Koufax	80.00	40.00	25.00
201	Orioles Rookies (Sam Bowens, *Wally Bunker*)			
		.80	.40	.25
202	Galen Cisco	.80	.40	.25
203	John Kennedy	.70	.35	.20
204	Matty Alou	.90	.45	.25

		NR MT	EX	VG
205	Nellie Fox	4.00	2.00	1.25
206	Steve Hamilton	1.00	.50	.30
207	Fred Hutchinson	.80	.40	.25
208	Wes Covington	.70	.35	.20
209	Bob Allen	.70	.35	.20
210	Carl Yastrzemski	80.00	40.00	25.00
211	Jim Coker	.70	.35	.20
212	Pete Lovrich	.70	.35	.20
213	Angels Team	2.25	1.25	.70
214	Ken McMullen	.80	.40	.25
215	Ray Herbert	.70	.35	.20
216	Mike de la Hoz	.70	.35	.20
217	Jim King	.70	.35	.20
218	Hank Fischer	.70	.35	.20
219	Young Aces (Jim Bouton, Al Downing)	2.00	1.00	.60
220	Dick Ellsworth	.70	.35	.20
221	Bob Saverine	.70	.35	.20
222	Bill Pierce	.90	.45	.25
223	George Banks	.70	.35	.20
224	Tommie Sisk	.70	.35	.20
225	Roger Maris	45.00	23.00	13.50
226	Colts Rookies (Gerald Grote, Larry Yellen)	1.25	.60	.40
227	Barry Latman	.70	.35	.20
228	Felix Mantilla	.70	.35	.20
229	Charley Lau	.80	.40	.25
230	Brooks Robinson	20.00	10.00	6.00
231	Dick Calmus	.70	.35	.20
232	Al Lopez	3.00	1.50	.90
233	Hal Smith	.70	.35	.20
234	Gary Bell	.70	.35	.20
235	Ron Hunt	.80	.40	.25
236	Bill Faul	.70	.35	.20
237	Cubs Team	2.25	1.25	.70
238	Roy McMillan	.70	.35	.20
239	Herm Starrette	.70	.35	.20
240	Bill White	1.50	.70	.45
241	Jim Owens	.70	.35	.20
242	Harvey Kuenn	1.50	.70	.45
243	Phillies Rookies (Richie Allen, John Herrnstein)	8.00	4.00	2.50
244	*Tony LaRussa*	12.00	6.00	3.50
245	Dick Stigman	.70	.35	.20
246	Manny Mota	1.25	.60	.40
247	Dave DeBusschere	2.00	1.00	.60
248	Johnny Pesky	.80	.40	.25
249	Doug Camilli	.70	.35	.20
250	Al Kaline	18.00	9.00	5.50
251	Choo Choo Coleman	.80	.40	.25
252	Ken Aspromonte	.70	.35	.20
253	Wally Post	.70	.35	.20
254	Don Hoak	.80	.40	.25
255	Lee Thomas	.70	.35	.20
256	Johnny Weekly	.70	.35	.20
257	Giants Team	2.25	1.25	.70
258	Garry Roggenburk	.70	.35	.20
259	Harry Bright	1.00	.50	.30
260	Frank Robinson	18.00	9.00	5.50
261	Jim Hannan	.70	.35	.20
262	Cardinals Rookie Stars (Harry Fanok, *Mike Shannon*)	1.50	.70	.45
263	Chuck Estrada	.70	.35	.20
264	Jim Landis	.70	.35	.20
265	Jim Bunning	5.00	2.50	1.50
266	Gene Freese	.70	.35	.20
267	*Wilbur Wood*	1.50	.70	.45
268	Bill's Got It (Danny Murtaugh, Bill Virdon)	.90	.45	.25
269	Ellis Burton	.70	.35	.20
270	Rich Rollins	.70	.35	.20
271	Bob Sadowski	.70	.35	.20
272	Jake Wood	.70	.35	.20
273	Mel Nelson	.70	.35	.20
274	Checklist 265-352	3.00	1.50	.90
275	John Tsitouris	.70	.35	.20
276	Jose Tartabull	.70	.35	.20
277	Ken Retzer	.70	.35	.20
278	Bobby Shantz	1.50	.70	.45
279	Joe Koppe	.70	.35	.20
280	Juan Marichal	10.00	5.00	3.00
281	Yankees Rookies (Jake Gibbs, Tom Metcalf)	1.00	.50	.30
282	Bob Bruce	.70	.35	.20
283	*Tommy McCraw*	.80	.40	.25
284	Dick Schofield	.70	.35	.20
285	Robin Roberts	10.00	5.00	3.00
286	Don Landrum	.70	.35	.20
287	Red Sox Rookies (*Tony Conigliaro*, Bill Spanswick)	18.00	9.00	5.50
288	Al Moran	.80	.40	.25
289	Frank Funk	.70	.35	.20
290	Bob Allison	.90	.45	.25
291	Phil Ortega	.70	.35	.20
292	Mike Roarke	.70	.35	.20
293	Phillies Team	2.25	1.25	.70
294	Ken Hunt	.70	.35	.20
295	Roger Craig	1.50	.70	.45
296	Ed Kirkpatrick	.70	.35	.20
297	Ken MacKenzie	.70	.35	.20
298	Harry Craft	.70	.35	.20
299	Bill Stafford	1.00	.50	.30
300	Hank Aaron	90.00	45.00	27.00
301	Larry Brown	.70	.35	.20
302	Dan Pfister	.70	.35	.20
303	Jim Campbell	.70	.35	.20
304	Bob Johnson	.70	.35	.20
305	Jack Lamabe	.70	.35	.20
306	Giant Gunners (Orlando Cepeda, Willie Mays)	12.00	6.00	3.50
307	Joe Gibbon	.70	.35	.20
308	Gene Stephens	.70	.35	.20
309	Paul Toth	.70	.35	.20
310	Jim Gilliam	3.00	1.50	.90
311	Tom Brown	.70	.35	.20
312	Tigers Rookies (Fritz Fisher, Fred Gladding)	.70	.35	.20
313	Chuck Hiller	.70	.35	.20
314	Jerry Buchek	.70	.35	.20
315	Bo Belinsky	.90	.45	.25
316	Gene Oliver	.70	.35	.20
317	Al Smith	.70	.35	.20
318	Twins Team	2.25	1.25	.70
319	Paul Brown	.70	.35	.20
320	Rocky Colavito	3.00	1.50	.90
321	Bob Lillis	.70	.35	.20
322	George Brunet	.70	.35	.20
323	John Buzhardt	.70	.35	.20
324	Casey Stengel	12.00	6.00	3.50
325	Hector Lopez	1.00	.50	.30
326	Ron Brand	.70	.35	.20
327	Don Blasingame	.70	.35	.20
328	Bob Shaw	.70	.35	.20
329	Russ Nixon	.70	.35	.20
330	Tommy Harper	.80	.40	.25
331	A.L. Bombers (Norm Cash, Al Kaline, Mickey Mantle, Roger Maris)	60.00	30.00	18.00
332	Ray Washburn	.70	.35	.20
333	Billy Moran	.70	.35	.20
334	Lew Krausse	.70	.35	.20
335	Don Mossi	.80	.40	.25
336	Andre Rodgers	.70	.35	.20
337	Dodgers Rookies (*Al Ferrara, Jeff Torborg*)	.80	.40	.25
338	Jack Kralick	.70	.35	.20
339	Walt Bond	.70	.35	.20
340	Joe Cunningham	.80	.40	.25
341	Jim Roland	.70	.35	.20
342	Willie Stargell	25.00	12.50	7.50
343	Senators Team	2.25	1.25	.70
344	Phil Linz	1.00	.50	.30
345	Frank Thomas	.80	.40	.25
346	Joe Jay	.70	.35	.20
347	Bobby Wine	.80	.40	.25
348	Ed Lopat	.90	.45	.25
349	Art Fowler	.70	.35	.20
350	Willie McCovey	20.00	10.00	6.00
351	Dan Schneider	.70	.35	.20
352	Eddie Bressoud	.70	.35	.20
353	Wally Moon	.90	.45	.25
354	Dave Giusti	.70	.35	.20
355	Vic Power	.70	.35	.20
356	Reds Rookies (Bill McCool, Chico Ruiz)	.70	.35	.20
357	Charley James	.70	.35	.20
358	Ron Kline	.70	.35	.20
359	Jim Schaffer	.70	.35	.20
360	Joe Pepitone	2.50	1.25	.70
361	Jay Hook	.80	.40	.25
362	Checklist 353-429	3.00	1.50	.90
363	Dick McAuliffe	.80	.40	.25
364	Joe Gaines	.70	.35	.20
365	Cal McLish	.70	.35	.20
366	Nelson Mathews	.70	.35	.20
367	Fred Whitfield	.70	.35	.20
368	White Sox Rookies (Fritz Ackley, *Don Buford*)	.90	.45	.25
369	Jerry Zimmerman	.70	.35	.20
370	Hal Woodeshick	.70	.35	.20
371	Frank Howard	3.00	1.50	.90
372	Howie Koplitz	1.00	.50	.30
373	Pirates Team	3.00	1.50	.90

		NR MT	EX	VG
374	Bobby Bolin	1.00	.50	.30
375	Ron Santo	2.50	1.25	.70
376	Dave Morehead	1.00	.50	.30
377	Bob Skinner	1.00	.50	.30
378	Braves Rookies (Jack Smith, *Woody Woodward*)	1.25	.60	.40
379	Tony Gonzalez	1.00	.50	.30
380	Whitey Ford	25.00	12.50	7.50
381	Bob Taylor	1.25	.60	.40
382	Wes Stock	1.00	.50	.30
383	Bill Rigney	1.00	.50	.30
384	Ron Hansen	1.00	.50	.30
385	Curt Simmons	1.25	.60	.40
386	Lenny Green	1.00	.50	.30
387	Terry Fox	1.00	.50	.30
388	Athletics Rookies (John O'Donoghue, George Williams)	1.00	.50	.30
389	Jim Umbricht	1.00	.50	.30
390	Orlando Cepeda	6.00	3.00	1.75
391	Sam McDowell	1.25	.60	.40
392	Jim Pagliaroni	1.00	.50	.30
393	Casey Teaches (Ed Kranepool, Casey Stengel)	5.00	2.50	1.50
394	Bob Miller	1.00	.50	.30
395	Tom Tresh	3.00	1.50	.90
396	Dennis Bennett	1.00	.50	.30
397	Chuck Cottier	1.00	.50	.30
398	Mets Rookies (Bill Haas, Dick Smith)	1.25	.60	.40
399	Jackie Brandt	1.00	.50	.30
400	Warren Spahn	25.00	12.50	7.50
401	Charlie Maxwell	1.00	.50	.30
402	Tom Sturdivant	1.00	.50	.30
403	Reds Team	3.50	1.75	1.00
404	Tony Martinez	1.00	.50	.30
405	Ken McBride	1.00	.50	.30
406	Al Spangler	1.00	.50	.30
407	Bill Freehan	2.00	1.00	.60
408	Cubs Rookies (Fred Burdette, Jim Stewart)	1.00	.50	.30
409	Bill Fischer	1.00	.50	.30
410	Dick Stuart	1.25	.60	.40
411	Lee Walls	1.00	.50	.30
412	Ray Culp	1.00	.50	.30
413	Johnny Keane	1.00	.50	.30
414	Jack Sanford	1.00	.50	.30
415	Tony Kubek	5.00	2.50	1.50
416	Lee Maye	1.00	.50	.30
417	Don Cardwell	1.00	.50	.30
418	Orioles Rookies (*Darold Knowles*, Les Narum)	1.25	.60	.40
419	*Ken Harrelson*	3.00	1.50	.90
420	Jim Maloney	1.25	.60	.40
421	Camilo Carreon	1.00	.50	.30
422	Jack Fisher	1.25	.60	.40
423	Tops In NL (Hank Aaron, Willie Mays)	80.00	40.00	25.00
424	Dick Bertell	1.00	.50	.30
425	Norm Cash	2.50	1.25	.70
426	Bob Rodgers	1.25	.60	.40
427	Don Rudolph	1.00	.50	.30
428	Red Sox Rookies (Archie Skeen, Pete Smith)	1.00	.50	.30
429	Tim McCarver	3.00	1.50	.90
430	Juan Pizarro	1.00	.50	.30
431	George Alusik	1.00	.50	.30
432	Ruben Amaro	1.00	.50	.30
433	Yankees Team	10.00	5.00	3.00
434	Don Nottebart	1.00	.50	.30
435	Vic Davalillo	1.00	.50	.30
436	Charlie Neal	1.00	.50	.30
437	Ed Bailey	1.00	.50	.30
438	Checklist 430-506	4.00	2.00	1.25
439	Harvey Haddix	1.50	.70	.45
440	Bob Clemente	80.00	40.00	24.00
441	Bob Duliba	1.00	.50	.30
442	Pumpsie Green	1.25	.60	.40
443	Chuck Dressen	1.25	.60	.40
444	Larry Jackson	1.00	.50	.30
445	Bill Skowron	2.50	1.25	.70
446	Julian Javier	1.25	.60	.40
447	Ted Bowsfield	1.00	.50	.30
448	Cookie Rojas	1.25	.60	.40
449	Deron Johnson	1.00	.50	.30
450	Steve Barber	1.00	.50	.30
451	Joe Amalfitano	1.00	.50	.30
452	Giants Rookies (Gil Garrido, *Jim Hart*)	1.25	.60	.40
453	Frank Baumann	1.00	.50	.30
454	Tommie Aaron	1.25	.60	.40
455	Bernie Allen	1.00	.50	.30

		NR MT	EX	VG
456	Dodgers Rookies (Wes Parker, John Werhas)	2.00	1.00	.60
457	Jesse Gonder	1.25	.60	.40
458	Ralph Terry	2.00	1.00	.60
459	Red Sox Rookies (Pete Charton, Dalton Jones)	1.00	.50	.30
460	Bob Gibson	20.00	10.00	6.00
461	George Thomas	1.00	.50	.30
462	Birdie Tebbetts	1.00	.50	.30
463	Don Leppert	1.00	.50	.30
464	Dallas Green	1.25	.60	.40
465	Mike Hershberger	1.00	.50	.30
466	Athletics Rookies (Dick Green, Aurelio Monteagudo)	1.25	.60	.40
467	Bob Aspromonte	1.00	.50	.30
468	Gaylord Perry	25.00	12.50	7.50
469	Cubs Rookies (Fred Norman, Sterling Slaughter)	1.00	.50	.30
470	Jim Bouton	3.00	1.50	.90
471	*Gates Brown*	1.25	.60	.40
472	Vern Law	1.50	.70	.45
473	Orioles Team	3.00	1.50	.90
474	Larry Sherry	1.00	.50	.30
475	Ed Charles	1.00	.50	.30
476	Braves Rookies (*Rico Carty*, Dick Kelley)	1.25	.60	.40
477	Mike Joyce	.90	.45	.25
478	Dick Howser	2.00	1.00	.60
479	Cardinals Rookies (Dave Bakenhaster, Johnny Lewis)	1.00	.50	.30
480	Bob Purkey	1.00	.50	.30
481	Chuck Schilling	1.00	.50	.30
482	Phillies Rookies (*John Briggs, Danny Cater*)	1.25	.60	.40
483	Fred Valentine	1.00	.50	.30
484	Bill Pleis	1.00	.50	.30
485	Tom Haller	1.25	.60	.40
486	Bob Kennedy	1.00	.50	.30
487	Mike McCormick	1.25	.60	.40
488	Yankees Rookies (Bob Meyer, Pete Mikkelsen)	1.50	.70	.45
489	Julio Navarro	1.00	.50	.30
490	Ron Fairly	1.50	.70	.45
491	Ed Rakow	1.00	.50	.30
492	Colts Rookies (Jim Beauchamp, Mike White)	1.00	.50	.30
493	Don Lee	1.00	.50	.30
494	Al Jackson	1.25	.60	.40
495	Bill Virdon	2.00	1.00	.60
496	White Sox Team	3.00	1.50	.90
497	Jeoff Long	1.00	.50	.30
498	Dave Stenhouse	1.00	.50	.30
499	Indians Rookies (Chico Salmon, Gordon Seyfried)	1.00	.50	.30
500	Camilo Pascual	1.25	.60	.40
501	Bob Veale	1.25	.60	.40
502	Angels Rookies (*Bobby Knoop*, Bob Lee)	1.25	.60	.40
503	Earl Wilson	1.00	.50	.30
504	Claude Raymond	1.00	.50	.30
505	Stan Williams	1.50	.70	.45
506	Bobby Bragan	1.25	.60	.40
507	John Edwards	1.00	.50	.30
508	Diego Segui	1.00	.50	.30
509	Pirates Rookies (Gene Alley, Orlando McFarlane)	1.25	.60	.40
510	Lindy McDaniel	1.00	.50	.30
511	Lou Jackson	1.00	.50	.30
512	Tigers Rookies (*Willie Horton, Joe Sparma*)	3.00	1.50	.90
513	Don Larsen	1.50	.70	.45
514	Jim Hickman	1.25	.60	.40
515	Johnny Romano	1.00	.50	.30
516	Twins Rookies (Jerry Arrigo, Dwight Siebler)	1.00	.50	.30
517a	Checklist 507-587 (wrong numbering on back)	7.00	3.50	2.00
517b	Checklist 507-587 (correct numbering on back)	4.50	2.25	1.25
518	Carl Bouldin	1.00	.50	.30
519	Charlie Smith	1.25	.60	.40
520	Jack Baldschun	1.00	.50	.30
521	Tom Satriano	1.00	.50	.30
522	Bobby Tiefenauer	1.00	.50	.30
523	Lou Burdette	6.00	3.00	1.75
524	Reds Rookies (Jim Dickson, Bobby Klaus)	4.00	2.00	1.25
525	Al McBean	4.00	2.00	1.25
526	Lou Clinton	4.00	2.00	1.25
527	Larry Bearnarth	4.50	2.25	1.25
528	Athletics Rookies (Dave Duncan, Tom Reynolds)	4.50	2.25	1.25

		NR MT	EX	VG
529	Al Dark	4.50	2.25	1.25
530	Leon Wagner	4.50	2.25	1.25
531	Dodgers Team	8.00	4.00	2.50
532	Twins Rookies (Bud Bloomfield, Joe Nossek)	4.00	2.00	1.25
533	Johnny Klippstein	4.00	2.00	1.25
534	Gus Bell	4.50	2.25	1.25
535	Phil Regan	4.00	2.00	1.25
536	Mets Rookies (Larry Elliot, John Stephenson)	4.50	2.25	1.25
537	Dan Osinski	4.00	2.00	1.25
538	Minnie Minoso	8.00	4.00	2.50
539	Roy Face	5.00	2.50	1.50
540	Luis Aparicio	15.00	7.50	4.50
541	Braves Rookies (*Phil Niekro*, Phil Roof)	150.00	60.00	38.00
542	Don Mincher	4.50	2.25	1.25
543	Bob Uecker	75.00	38.00	23.00
544	Colts Rookies (Steve Hertz, Joe Hoerner)	4.00	2.00	1.25
545	Max Alvis	4.50	2.25	1.25
546	Joe Christopher	4.50	2.25	1.25
547	Gil Hodges	12.00	6.00	3.50
548	N.L. Rookies (Wayne Schurr, Paul Speckenbach)	4.00	2.00	1.25
549	Joe Moeller	4.00	2.00	1.25
550	Ken Hubbs	10.00	5.00	3.00
551	Billy Hoeft	4.00	2.00	1.25
552	Indians Rookies (Tom Kelley, *Sonny Siebert*)	4.50	2.25	1.25
553	Jim Brewer	4.00	2.00	1.25
554	Hank Foiles	4.00	2.00	1.25
555	Lee Stange	4.00	2.00	1.25
556	Mets Rookies (Steve Dillon, Ron Locke)	4.50	2.25	1.25
557	Leo Burke	4.00	2.00	1.25
558	Don Schwall	4.00	2.00	1.25
559	Dick Phillips	4.00	2.00	1.25
560	Dick Farrell	4.00	2.00	1.25
561	Phillies Rookies (Dave Bennett, *Rick Wise*)	4.50	2.25	1.25
562	Pedro Ramos	4.00	2.00	1.25
563	Dal Maxvill	4.50	2.25	1.25
564	A.L. Rookies (Joe McCabe, Jerry McNertney)	4.00	2.00	1.25
565	Stu Miller	4.00	2.00	1.25
566	Ed Kranepool	5.00	2.50	1.50
567	Jim Kaat	12.00	6.00	3.50
568	N.L. Rookies (Phil Gagliano, Cap Peterson)	4.00	2.00	1.25
569	Fred Newman	4.00	2.00	1.25
570	Bill Mazeroski	8.00	4.00	2.50
571	Gene Conley	3.50	1.75	1.00
572	A.L. Rookies (Dick Egan, Dave Gray)	4.00	2.00	1.25
573	Jim Duffalo	4.00	2.00	1.25
574	Manny Jimenez	4.00	2.00	1.25
575	Tony Cloninger	4.50	2.25	1.25
576	Mets Rookies (Jerry Hinsley, Bill Wakefield)	4.50	2.25	1.25
577	Gordy Coleman	4.00	2.00	1.25
578	Glen Hobbie	4.00	2.00	1.25
579	Red Sox Team	6.00	3.00	1.75
580	Johnny Podres	6.00	3.00	1.75
581	Yankees Rookies (Pedro Gonzalez, Archie Moore)	5.00	2.50	1.50
582	Rod Kanehl	4.50	2.25	1.25
583	Tito Francona	4.50	2.25	1.25
584	Joel Horlen	4.00	2.00	1.25
585	Tony Taylor	4.00	2.00	1.25
586	Jim Piersall	6.00	3.00	1.75
587	Bennie Daniels	8.00	2.50	1.25

1964 Topps Coins

The 164 metal coins in this set were issued by Topps as inserts in the company's baseball card wax packs. The series is divided into two principal types, 120 "regular" coins and 44 All-Star coins. The 1-1/2" diameter coins feature a full-color background for the player photos in the "regular" series, while the players in the All-Star series are featured against plain red or blue backgrounds. There are two variations each of the Mantle, Causey and Hinton coins among the All-Star subset.

		NR MT	EX	VG
Complete Set:		700.00	350.00	210.00
Common Player:		1.00	.50	.30
1	Don Zimmer	1.00	.50	.30
2	Jim Wynn	1.00	.50	.30
3	Johnny Orsino	1.00	.50	.30
4	Jim Bouton	1.25	.60	.40
5	Dick Groat	1.25	.60	.40
6	Leon Wagner	1.00	.50	.30
7	Frank Malzone	1.00	.50	.30
8	Steve Barber	1.00	.50	.30
9	Johnny Romano	1.00	.50	.30
10	Tom Tresh	1.25	.60	.40
11	Felipe Alou	1.00	.50	.30
12	Dick Stuart	1.00	.50	.30
13	Claude Osteen	1.00	.50	.30
14	Juan Pizarro	1.00	.50	.30
15	Donn Clendenon	1.00	.50	.30
16	Jimmie Hall	1.00	.50	.30
17	Larry Jackson	1.00	.50	.30
18	Brooks Robinson	12.00	6.00	3.50
19	Bob Allison	1.00	.50	.30
20	Ed Roebuck	1.00	.50	.30
21	Pete Ward	1.00	.50	.30
22	Willie McCovey	8.00	4.00	2.50
23	Elston Howard	1.50	.70	.45
24	Diego Segui	1.00	.50	.30
25	Ken Boyer	1.50	.70	.45
26	Carl Yastrzemski	20.00	10.00	6.00
27	Bill Mazeroski	1.50	.70	.45
28	Jerry Lumpe	1.00	.50	.30
29	Woody Held	1.00	.50	.30
30	Dick Radatz	1.00	.50	.30
31	Luis Aparicio	5.00	2.50	1.50
32	Dave Nicholson	1.00	.50	.30
33	Ed Mathews	8.00	4.00	2.50
34	Don Drysdale	10.00	5.00	3.00
35	Ray Culp	1.00	.50	.30
36	Juan Marichal	8.00	4.00	2.50
37	Frank Robinson	8.00	4.00	2.50
38	Chuck Hinton	1.00	.50	.30
39	Floyd Robinson	1.00	.50	.30
40	Tommy Harper	1.00	.50	.30
41	Ron Hansen	1.00	.50	.30
42	Ernie Banks	10.00	5.00	3.00
43	Jesse Gonder	1.00	.50	.30
44	Billy Williams	7.00	3.50	2.00
45	Vada Pinson	1.50	.70	.45
46	Rocky Colavito	1.50	.70	.45
47	Bill Monbouquette	1.00	.50	.30
48	Max Alvis	1.00	.50	.30
49	Norm Siebern	1.00	.50	.30
50	John Callison	1.00	.50	.30
51	Rich Rollins	1.00	.50	.30
52	Ken McBride	1.00	.50	.30
53	Don Lock	1.00	.50	.30
54	Ron Fairly	1.00	.50	.30
55	Bob Clemente	20.00	10.00	6.00
56	Dick Ellsworth	1.00	.50	.30
57	Tommy Davis	1.25	.60	.40
58	Tony Gonzalez	1.00	.50	.30
59	Bob Gibson	10.00	5.00	3.00
60	Jim Maloney	1.00	.50	.30
61	Frank Howard	1.50	.70	.45
62	Jim Pagliaroni	1.00	.50	.30
63	Orlando Cepeda	2.00	1.00	.60
64	Ron Perranoski	1.00	.50	.30
65	Curt Flood	1.25	.60	.40
66	Al McBean	1.00	.50	.30
67	Dean Chance	1.00	.50	.30
68	Ron Santo	1.25	.60	.40
69	Jack Baldschun	1.00	.50	.30
70	Milt Pappas	1.00	.50	.30
71	Gary Peters	1.00	.50	.30
72	Bobby Richardson	1.50	.70	.45
73	Lee Thomas	1.00	.50	.30
74	Hank Aguirre	1.00	.50	.30
75	Carl Willey	1.00	.50	.30

		NR MT	EX	VG
76	Camilo Pascual	1.00	.50	.30
77	Bob Friend	1.00	.50	.30
78	Bill White	1.00	.50	.30
79	Norm Cash	1.25	.60	.40
80	Willie Mays	18.00	9.00	5.50
81	Duke Carmel	1.00	.50	.30
82	Pete Rose	25.00	12.50	7.50
83	Hank Aaron	20.00	10.00	6.00
84	Bob Aspromonte	1.00	.50	.30
85	Jim O'Toole	1.00	.50	.30
86	Vic Davalillo	1.00	.50	.30
87	Bill Freehan	1.00	.50	.30
88	Warren Spahn	8.00	4.00	2.50
89	Ron Hunt	1.00	.50	.30
90	Denis Menke	1.00	.50	.30
91	Turk Farrell	1.00	.50	.30
92	Jim Hickman	1.00	.50	.30
93	Jim Bunning	2.00	1.00	.60
94	Bob Hendley	1.00	.50	.30
95	Ernie Broglio	1.00	.50	.30
96	Rusty Staub	1.50	.70	.45
97	Lou Brock	8.00	4.00	2.50
98	Jim Fregosi	1.00	.50	.30
99	Jim Grant	1.00	.50	.30
100	Al Kaline	15.00	7.50	4.50
101	Earl Battey	1.00	.50	.30
102	Wayne Causey	1.00	.50	.30
103	Chuck Schilling	1.00	.50	.30
104	Boog Powell	1.50	.70	.45
105	Dave Wickersham	1.00	.50	.30
106	Sandy Koufax	15.00	7.50	4.50
107	John Bateman	1.00	.50	.30
108	Ed Brinkman	1.00	.50	.30
109	Al Downing	1.00	.50	.30
110	Joe Azcue	1.00	.50	.30
111	Albie Pearson	1.00	.50	.30
112	Harmon Killebrew	10.00	5.00	3.00
113	Tony Taylor	1.00	.50	.30
114	Alvin Jackson	1.00	.50	.30
115	Billy O'Dell	1.00	.50	.30
116	Don Demeter	1.00	.50	.30
117	Ed Charles	1.00	.50	.30
118	Joe Torre	1.50	.70	.45
119	Don Nottebart	1.00	.50	.30
120	Mickey Mantle	40.00	20.00	12.00
121	Joe Pepitone	1.25	.60	.40
122	Dick Stuart	1.00	.50	.30
123	Bobby Richardson	1.50	.70	.45
124	Jerry Lumpe	1.00	.50	.30
125	Brooks Robinson	10.00	5.00	3.00
126	Frank Malzone	1.00	.50	.30
127	Luis Aparicio	5.00	2.50	1.50
128	Jim Fregosi	1.00	.50	.30
129	Al Kaline	15.00	7.50	4.50
130	Leon Wagner	1.00	.50	.30
131a	Mickey Mantle (batting lefthanded)			
		45.00	23.00	13.50
131b	Mickey Mantle (batting righthanded)			
		45.00	23.00	13.50
132	Albie Pearson	1.00	.50	.30
133	Harmon Killebrew	10.00	5.00	3.00
134	Carl Yastrzemski	20.00	10.00	6.00
135	Elston Howard	1.50	.70	.45
136	Earl Battey	1.00	.50	.30
137	Camilo Pascual	1.00	.50	.30
138	Jim Bouton	1.25	.60	.40
139	Whitey Ford	8.00	4.00	2.50
140	Gary Peters	1.00	.50	.30
141	Bill White	1.00	.50	.30
142	Orlando Cepeda	2.00	1.00	.60
143	Bill Mazeroski	1.50	.70	.45
144	Tony Taylor	1.00	.50	.30
145	Ken Boyer	1.50	.70	.45
146	Ron Santo	1.25	.60	.40
147	Dick Groat	1.25	.60	.40
148	Roy McMillan	1.00	.50	.30
149	Hank Aaron	18.00	9.00	4.50
150	Bob Clemente	20.00	10.00	6.00
151	Willie Mays	18.00	9.00	5.50
152	Vada Pinson	1.50	.70	.45
153	Tommy Davis	1.25	.60	.40
154	Frank Robinson	8.00	4.00	2.50
155	Joe Torre	1.50	.70	.45
156	Tim McCarver	1.25	.60	.40
157	Juan Marichal	7.00	3.50	2.00
158	Jim Maloney	1.00	.50	.30
159	Sandy Koufax	15.00	7.50	4.50
160	Warren Spahn	8.00	4.00	2.50
161a	Wayne Causey (N.L. on back)	15.00	7.50	4.50
161b	Wayne Causey (A.L. on back)	1.00	.50	.30
162a	Chuck Hinton (N.L. on back)	15.00	7.50	4.50

		NR MT	EX	VG
162b	Chuck Hinton (A.L. on back)	1.00	.50	.30
163	Bob Aspromonte	1.00	.50	.30
164	Ron Hunt	1.00	.50	.30

1964 Topps Giants

Measuring 3-1/8" by 5-1/4" the Topps Giants were the company's first postcard-size issue. The cards feature large color photographs surrounded by white borders with a white baseball containing the player's name, position and team. Card backs carry another photo of the player surrounded by a newspaper-style explanation of the depicted career highlight. The 60-card set contains primarily stars which means it's an excellent place to find inexpensive cards of Hall of Famers. The '64 Giants were not printed in equal quantity and seven of the cards, including Sandy Koufax and Willie Mays, are significantly scarcer than the remainder of the set.

		NR MT	EX	VG
Complete Set:		90.00	45.00	27.00
Common Player:		.12	.06	.04
1	Gary Peters	.12	.06	.04
2	Ken Johnson	.12	.06	.04
3	Sandy Koufax	15.00	7.50	4.50
4	Bob Bailey	.12	.06	.04
5	Milt Pappas	.25	.13	.08
6	Ron Hunt	.12	.06	.04
7	Whitey Ford	1.75	.90	.50
8	Roy McMillan	.12	.06	.04
9	Rocky Colavito	.40	.20	.12
10	Jim Bunning	.50	.25	.15
11	Bob Clemente	5.00	2.50	1.50
12	Al Kaline	3.00	1.50	.90
13	Nellie Fox	.60	.30	.20
14	Tony Gonzalez	.12	.06	.04
15	Jim Gentile	.12	.06	.04
16	Dean Chance	.12	.06	.04
17	Dick Ellsworth	.12	.06	.04
18	Jim Fregosi	.25	.13	.08
19	Dick Groat	.40	.20	.12
20	Chuck Hinton	.12	.06	.04
21	Elston Howard	.50	.25	.15
22	Dick Farrell	.12	.06	.04
23	Albie Pearson	.12	.06	.04
24	Frank Howard	.50	.25	.15
25	Mickey Mantle	15.00	7.50	4.50
26	Joe Torre	.40	.20	.12
27	Ed Brinkman	.12	.06	.04
28	Bob Friend	4.00	2.00	1.25
29	Frank Robinson	1.75	.90	.50
30	Bill Freehan	.25	.13	.08
31	Warren Spahn	1.25	.60	.40
32	Camilo Pascual	.12	.06	.04
33	Pete Ward	.12	.06	.04
34	Jim Maloney	.12	.06	.04
35	Dave Wickersham	.12	.06	.04
36	Johnny Callison	.25	.13	.08
37	Juan Marichal	3.00	1.50	.90
38	Harmon Killebrew	3.00	1.50	.90
39	Luis Aparicio	1.25	.60	.40
40	Dick Radatz	.12	.06	.04
41	Bob Gibson	3.00	1.50	.90
42	Dick Stuart	4.00	2.00	1.25
43	Tommy Davis	.40	.20	.12

		NR MT	EX	VG
44	Tony Oliva	.50	.25	.15
45	Wayne Causey	4.00	2.00	1.25
46	Max Alvis	.12	.06	.04
47	Galen Cisco	4.00	2.00	1.25
48	Carl Yastrzemski	3.00	1.50	.90
49	Hank Aaron	5.00	2.50	1.50
50	Brooks Robinson	3.00	1.50	.90
51	Willie Mays	15.00	7.50	4.50
52	Billy Williams	1.25	.60	.40
53	Juan Pizarro	.12	.06	.04
54	Leon Wagner	.12	.06	.04
55	Orlando Cepeda	.70	.35	.20
56	Vada Pinson	.50	.25	.15
57	Ken Boyer	.60	.30	.20
58	Ron Santo	.40	.20	.12
59	John Romano	.12	.06	.04
60	Bill Skowron	4.00	2.00	1.25

		NR MT	EX	VG
(31)	Woody Held	3.50	1.75	1.00
(32)	Chuck Hinton	3.50	1.75	1.00
(33)	Elston Howard	7.00	3.50	2.00
(34)	Frank Howard	25.00	12.50	7.50
(35)	Ron Hunt	3.50	1.75	1.00
(36)	Al Jackson	3.50	1.75	1.00
(37)	Ken Johnson	3.50	1.75	1.00
(38)	Al Kaline	40.00	20.00	12.00
(39)	Harmon Killebrew	40.00	20.00	12.00
(40)	Sandy Koufax	40.00	20.00	12.00
(41)	Don Lock	20.00	10.00	6.00
(42)	Jerry Lumpe	20.00	10.00	6.00
(43)	Jim Maloney	3.50	1.75	1.00
(44)	Frank Malzone	3.50	1.75	1.00
(45)	Mickey Mantle	350.00	175.00	105.00
(46)	Juan Marichal	100.00	50.00	30.00
(47)	Ed Mathews	100.00	50.00	30.00
(48)	Willie Mays	90.00	45.00	27.00
(49)	Bill Mazeroski	6.00	3.00	1.75
(50)	Ken McBride	3.50	1.75	1.00
(51)	Willie McCovey	100.00	50.00	30.00
(52)	Claude Osteen	3.50	1.75	1.00
(53)	Jim O'Toole	3.50	1.75	1.00
(54)	Camilo Pascual	3.50	1.75	1.00
(55)	Albie Pearson	20.00	10.00	6.00
(56)	Gary Peters	3.50	1.75	1.00
(57)	Vada Pinson	6.00	3.00	1.75
(58)	Juan Pizarro	3.50	1.75	1.00
(59)	Boog Powell	6.00	3.00	1.75
(60)	Bobby Richardson	7.00	3.50	2.00
(61)	Brooks Robinson	50.00	25.00	15.00
(62)	Floyd Robinson	3.50	1.75	1.00
(63)	Frank Robinson	40.00	20.00	12.00
(64)	Ed Roebuck	20.00	10.00	6.00
(65)	Rich Rollins	3.50	1.75	1.00
(66)	Johnny Romano	3.50	1.75	1.00
(67)	Ron Santo	25.00	12.50	7.50
(68)	Norm Siebern	3.50	1.75	1.00
(69)	Warren Spahn	100.00	50.00	30.00
(70)	Dick Stuart	20.00	10.00	6.00
(71)	Lee Thomas	3.50	1.75	1.00
(72)	Joe Torre	7.00	3.50	2.00
(73)	Pete Ward	3.50	1.75	1.00
(74)	Bill White	20.00	10.00	6.00
(75)	Billy Williams	100.00	50.00	30.00
(76)	Hal Woodeshick	20.00	10.00	6.00
(77)	Carl Yastrzemski	350.00	175.00	105.00

1964 Topps Stand-Ups

These 2-1/2" by 3-1/2" cards were the first since the All-Star sets of 1951 to be die-cut. This made it possible for a folded card to stand on display. The 77-cards in the set feature color photographs of the player with yellow and green backgrounds. Directions for folding are on the yellow top background, and when folded only the green background remains. Of the 77 cards, 55 were double-printed while 22 were single-printed, making them twice as scarce. Included in the single-printed group are Warren Spahn, Don Drysdale, Juan Marichal, Willie McCovey and Carl Yastrzemski.

		NR MT	EX	VG
Complete Set:		2400.00	1200.00	720.00
Common Player:		3.50	1.75	1.00
(1)	Hank Aaron	90.00	45.00	27.00
(2)	Hank Aguirre	3.50	1.75	1.00
(3)	George Altman	3.50	1.75	1.00
(4)	Max Alvis	3.50	1.75	1.00
(5)	Bob Aspromonte	3.50	1.75	1.00
(6)	Jack Baldschun	20.00	10.00	6.00
(7)	Ernie Banks	40.00	20.00	12.00
(8)	Steve Barber	3.50	1.75	1.00
(9)	Earl Battey	3.50	1.75	1.00
(10)	Ken Boyer	6.00	3.00	1.75
(11)	Ernie Broglio	3.50	1.75	1.00
(12)	Johnny Callison	4.00	2.00	1.25
(13)	Norm Cash	25.00	12.50	7.50
(14)	Wayne Causey	3.50	1.75	1.00
(15)	Orlando Cepeda	8.00	4.00	2.50
(16)	Ed Charles	3.50	1.75	1.00
(17)	Bob Clemente	55.00	27.00	16.50
(18)	Donn Clendenon	20.00	10.00	6.00
(19)	Rocky Colavito	6.00	3.00	1.75
(20)	Ray Culp	20.00	10.00	6.00
(21)	Tommy Davis	6.00	3.00	1.75
(22)	Don Drysdale	100.00	50.00	30.00
(23)	Dick Ellsworth	3.50	1.75	1.00
(24)	Dick Farrell	3.50	1.75	1.00
(25)	Jim Fregosi	4.00	2.00	1.25
(26)	Bob Friend	4.00	2.00	1.25
(27)	Jim Gentile	3.50	1.75	1.00
(28)	Jesse Gonder	20.00	10.00	6.00
(29)	Tony Gonzalez	20.00	10.00	6.00
(30)	Dick Groat	6.00	3.00	1.75

1965 Topps

The 1965 Topps set features a large color photograph of the player which was surrounded by a colored, round-cornered frame and a white border. The bottom of the 2-1/2" by 3-1/2" cards include a pennant with a color team logo and name over the left side of a rectangle which features the player's name and position. Backs feature statistics and, if space allowed, a cartoon and headline about the player. There are no multi-player cards in the 1965 set other than the usual team cards and World Series highlights. Rookie cards include team, as well as league groupings from two to four players per card. Also present in the 598-card set are statistical leaders.

	NR MT	EX	VG
Complete Set:	3500.00	1750.00	1050.

		NR MT	EX	VG
	Common Player: 1-198	.70	.35	.20
	Common Player: 199-446	.90	.45	.25
	Common Player: 447-522	1.25	.60	.40
	Common Player: 523-598	4.00	2.00	1.25
1	A.L. Batting Leaders (Elston Howard, Tony Oliva, Brooks Robinson)	8.00	3.00	1.25
2	N.L. Batting Leaders (Hank Aaron, Rico Carty, Bob Clemente)	5.00	2.50	1.50
3	A.L. Home Run Leaders (Harmon Killebrew, Mickey Mantle, Boog Powell)	15.00	7.50	4.50
4	N.L. Home Run Leaders (Johnny Callison, Orlando Cepeda, Jim Hart, Willie Mays, Billy Williams)	4.50	2.25	1.25
5	A.L. RBI Leaders (Harmon Killebrew, Mickey Mantle, Brooks Robinson, Dick Stuart)	15.00	7.50	4.50
6	N.L. RBI Leaders (Ken Boyer, Willie Mays, Ron Santo)	4.50	2.25	1.25
7	A.L. ERA Leaders (Dean Chance, Joel Horlen)	2.50	1.25	.70
8	N.L. ERA Leaders (Don Drysdale, Sandy Koufax)	4.50	2.25	1.25
9	A.L. Pitching Leaders (Wally Bunker, Dean Chance, Gary Peters, Juan Pizarro, Dave Wickersham)	4.00	2.00	1.25
10	N.L. Pitching Leaders (Larry Jackson, Juan Marichal, Ray Sadecki)	3.50	1.75	1.00
11	A.L. Strikeout Leaders (Dean Chance, Al Downing, Camilo Pascual)	2.50	1.25	.70
12	N.L. Strikeout Leaders (Don Drysdale, Bob Gibson, Bob Veale)	3.50	1.75	1.00
13	Pedro Ramos	1.00	.50	.30
14	Len Gabrielson	.70	.35	.20
15	Robin Roberts	8.00	4.00	2.50
16	Astros Rookies (Sonny Jackson, Joe Morgan)	200.00	100.00	60.00
17	Johnny Romano	.70	.35	.20
18	Bill McCool	.70	.35	.20
19	Gates Brown	.80	.40	.25
20	Jim Bunning	4.00	2.00	1.25
21	Don Blasingame	.70	.35	.20
22	Charlie Smith	.80	.40	.25
23	Bob Tiefenauer	.70	.35	.20
24	Twins Team	4.00	2.00	1.25
25	Al McBean	.70	.35	.20
26	Bobby Knoop	.70	.35	.20
27	Dick Bertell	.70	.35	.20
28	Barney Schultz	.70	.35	.20
29	Felix Mantilla	.70	.35	.20
30	Jim Bouton	2.50	1.25	.70
31	Mike White	.70	.35	.20
32	Herman Franks	.70	.35	.20
33	Jackie Brandt	.70	.35	.20
34	Cal Koonce	.70	.35	.20
35	Ed Charles	.70	.35	.20
36	Bobby Wine	.80	.40	.25
37	Fred Gladding	.70	.35	.20
38	Jim King	.70	.35	.20
39	Gerry Arrigo	.70	.35	.20
40	Frank Howard	2.50	1.25	.70
41	White Sox Rookies (Bruce Howard, Marv Staehle)	.70	.35	.20
42	Earl Wilson	.70	.35	.20
43	Mike Shannon	.80	.40	.25
44	Wade Blasingame	.70	.35	.20
45	Roy McMillan	.80	.40	.25
46	Bob Lee	.70	.35	.20
47	Tommy Harper	.80	.40	.25
48	Claude Raymond	.80	.40	.25
49	Orioles Rookies (Curt Blefary, John Miller)	.90	.45	.25
50	Juan Marichal	8.00	4.00	2.50
51	Billy Bryan	.70	.35	.20
52	Ed Roebuck	.70	.35	.20
53	Dick McAuliffe	.80	.40	.25
54	Joe Gibbon	.70	.35	.20
55	Tony Conigliaro	2.50	1.25	.70
56	Ron Kline	.70	.35	.20
57	Cardinals Team	2.25	1.25	.70
58	Fred Talbot	.70	.35	.20
59	Nate Oliver	.70	.35	.20
60	Jim O'Toole	.70	.35	.20
61	Chris Cannizzaro	.80	.40	.25
62	Jim Katt (Kaat)	5.00	2.50	1.50
63	Ty Cline	.70	.35	.20
64	Lou Burdette	2.00	1.00	.60
65	Tony Kubek	4.50	2.25	1.25
66	Bill Rigney	.70	.35	.20
67	Harvey Haddix	.90	.45	.25

		NR MT	EX	VG
68	Del Crandall	.90	.45	.25
69	Bill Virdon	1.25	.60	.40
70	Bill Skowron	1.25	.60	.40
71	John O'Donoghue	.70	.35	.20
72	Tony Gonzalez	.70	.35	.20
73	Dennis Ribant	.80	.40	.25
74	Red Sox Rookies (Rico Petrocelli, Jerry Stephenson)	2.50	1.25	.70
75	Deron Johnson	.70	.35	.20
76	Sam McDowell	.90	.45	.25
77	Doug Camilli	.70	.35	.20
78	Dal Maxvill	.80	.40	.25
79a	Checklist 1-88 (61 is C. Cannizzaro)	3.00	1.50	.90
79b	Checklist 1-88 (61 is Cannizzaro)	5.00	2.50	1.50
80	Turk Farrell	.70	.35	.20
81	Don Buford	.80	.40	.25
82	Braves Rookies (Santos Alomar, John Braun)	.80	.40	.25
83	George Thomas	.70	.35	.20
84	Ron Herbel	.70	.35	.20
85	Willie Smith	.70	.35	.20
86	Les Narum	.70	.35	.20
87	Nelson Mathews	.70	.35	.20
88	Jack Lamabe	.70	.35	.20
89	Mike Hershberger	.70	.35	.20
90	Rich Rollins	.70	.35	.20
91	Cubs Team	2.25	1.25	.70
92	Dick Howser	1.25	.60	.40
93	Jack Fisher	.80	.40	.25
94	Charlie Lau	.90	.45	.25
95	Bill Mazeroski	2.50	1.25	.70
96	Sonny Siebert	.80	.40	.25
97	Pedro Gonzalez	1.00	.50	.30
98	Bob Miller	.70	.35	.20
99	Gil Hodges	6.00	3.00	1.75
100	Ken Boyer	2.50	1.25	.70
101	Fred Newman	.70	.35	.20
102	Steve Boros	.80	.40	.25
103	Harvey Kuenn	1.25	.60	.40
104	Checklist 89-176	3.00	1.50	.90
105	Chico Salmon	.70	.35	.20
106	Gene Oliver	.70	.35	.20
107	Phillies Rookies (Pat Corrales, Costen Shockley)	2.00	1.00	.60
108	Don Mincher	.80	.40	.25
109	Walt Bond	.70	.35	.20
110	Ron Santo	1.50	.70	.45
111	Lee Thomas	.70	.35	.20
112	Derrell Griffith	.70	.35	.20
113	Steve Barber	.70	.35	.20
114	Jim Hickman	.90	.45	.25
115	Bobby Richardson	4.50	2.25	1.25
116	Cardinals Rookies (Dave Dowling, Bob Tolan)	1.25	.60	.40
117	Wes Stock	.70	.35	.20
118	Hal Lanier	1.50	.70	.45
119	John Kennedy	.70	.35	.20
120	Frank Robinson	30.00	15.00	9.00
121	Gene Alley	.80	.40	.25
122	Bill Pleis	.70	.35	.20
123	Frank Thomas	.70	.35	.20
124	Tom Satriano	.70	.35	.20
125	Juan Pizarro	.70	.35	.20
126	Dodgers Team	4.00	2.00	1.25
127	Frank Lary	.80	.40	.25
128	Vic Davalillo	.80	.40	.25
129	Bennie Daniels	.70	.35	.20
130	Al Kaline	25.00	12.50	7.50
131	Johnny Keane	1.50	.70	.45
132	World Series Game 1 (Cards Take Opener)	2.50	1.25	.70
133	World Series Game 2 (Stottlemyre Wins)	3.00	1.50	.90
134	World Series Game 3 (Mantle's Clutch HR)	18.00	9.00	5.50
135	World Series Game 4 (Boyer's Grand Slam)	2.50	1.25	.70
136	World Series Game 5 (10th Inning Triumph)	2.50	1.25	.70
137	World Series Game 6 (Bouton Wins Again)	3.00	1.50	.90
138	World Series Game 7 (Gibson Wins Finale)	3.50	1.75	1.00
139	World Series Summary (The Cards Celebrate)	2.50	1.25	.70
140	Dean Chance	.80	.40	.25
141	Charlie James	.70	.35	.20
142	Bill Monbouquette	.80	.40	.25
143	Pirates Rookies (John Gelnar, Jerry May)	.70	.35	.20

#	Player	NR MT	EX	VG
144	Ed Kranepool	.90	.45	.25
145	*Luis Tiant*	8.00	4.00	2.50
146	Ron Hansen	.70	.35	.20
147	Dennis Bennett	.70	.35	.20
148	Willie Kirkland	.70	.35	.20
149	Wayne Schurr	.70	.35	.20
150	Brooks Robinson	20.00	10.00	6.00
151	Athletics Team	2.25	1.25	.70
152	Phil Ortega	.70	.35	.20
153	Norm Cash	2.00	1.00	.60
154	Bob Humphreys	.70	.35	.20
155	Roger Maris	40.00	20.00	12.00
156	Bob Sadowski	.70	.35	.20
157	Zoilo Versalles	1.50	.70	.45
158	Dick Sisler	.70	.35	.20
159	Jim Duffalo	.70	.35	.20
160	Bob Clemente	75.00	38.00	23.00
161	Frank Baumann	.70	.35	.20
162	Russ Nixon	.70	.35	.20
163	John Briggs	.70	.35	.20
164	Al Spangler	.70	.35	.20
165	Dick Ellsworth	.70	.35	.20
166	Indians Rookies (*Tommie Agee*, George Culver)	1.50	.70	.45
167	Bill Wakefield	.80	.40	.25
168	Dick Green	.80	.40	.25
169	Dave Vineyard	.70	.35	.20
170	Hank Aaron	75.00	38.00	23.00
171	Jim Roland	.70	.35	.20
172	Jim Piersall	1.50	.70	.45
173	Tigers Team	3.25	1.75	1.00
174	Joe Jay	.70	.35	.20
175	Bob Aspromonte	.70	.35	.20
176	Willie McCovey	18.00	9.00	5.50
177	Pete Mikkelsen	1.00	.50	.30
178	Dalton Jones	.70	.35	.20
179	Hal Woodeshick	.70	.35	.20
180	Bob Allison	1.25	.60	.40
181	Senators Rookies (Don Loun, Joe McCabe)	.70	.35	.20
182	Mike de la Hoz	.70	.35	.20
183	Dave Nicholson	.70	.35	.20
184	John Boozer	.70	.35	.20
185	Max Alvis	.70	.35	.20
186	Billy Cowan	.70	.35	.20
187	Casey Stengel	18.00	9.00	5.00
188	Sam Bowens	.70	.35	.20
189	Checklist 177-264	3.00	1.50	.90
190	Bill White	1.25	.60	.40
191	Phil Regan	.70	.35	.20
192	Jim Coker	.70	.35	.20
193	Gaylord Perry	12.00	6.00	3.50
194	Angels Rookies (Bill Kelso, *Rick Reichardt*)	.80	.40	.25
195	Bob Veale	.80	.40	.25
196	Ron Fairly	.80	.40	.25
197	Diego Segui	.70	.35	.20
198	Smoky Burgess	1.25	.60	.40
199	Bob Heffner	.90	.45	.25
200	Joe Torre	2.50	1.25	.70
201	Twins Rookies (*Cesar Tovar*, Sandy Valdespino)	1.00	.50	.30
202	Leo Burke	.90	.45	.25
203	Dallas Green	1.25	.60	.40
204	Russ Snyder	.90	.45	.25
205	Warren Spahn	20.00	10.00	6.00
206	Willie Horton	1.25	.60	.40
207	Pete Rose	150.00	60.00	38.00
208	Tommy John	10.00	5.00	3.00
209	Pirates Team	2.50	1.25	.70
210	Jim Fregosi	1.50	.70	.45
211	Steve Ridzik	.90	.45	.25
212	Ron Brand	.90	.45	.25
213	Jim Davenport	.90	.45	.25
214	Bob Purkey	.90	.45	.25
215	Pete Ward	.90	.45	.25
216	Al Worthington	.90	.45	.25
217	Walt Alston	3.50	1.75	1.00
218	Dick Schofield	.90	.45	.25
219	Bob Meyer	.90	.45	.25
220	Billy Williams	10.00	5.00	3.00
221	John Tsitouris	.90	.45	.25
222	Bob Tillman	.90	.45	.25
223	Dan Osinski	.90	.45	.25
224	Bob Chance	.90	.45	.25
225	Bo Belinsky	1.00	.50	.30
226	Yankees Rookies (Jake Gibbs, Elvio Jimenez)	1.50	.70	.45
227	Bobby Klaus	1.00	.50	.30
228	Jack Sanford	.90	.45	.25
229	Lou Clinton	.90	.45	.25
230	Ray Sadecki	.90	.45	.25
231	Jerry Adair	.90	.45	.25
232	*Steve Blass*	1.00	.50	.30
233	Don Zimmer	1.50	.70	.45
234	White Sox Team	4.00	2.00	1.25
235	Chuck Hinton	.90	.45	.25
236	*Dennis McLain*	15.00	7.50	4.50
237	Bernie Allen	.90	.45	.25
238	Joe Moeller	.90	.45	.25
239	Doc Edwards	1.00	.50	.30
240	Bob Bruce	.90	.45	.25
241	Mack Jones	.90	.45	.25
242	George Brunet	.90	.45	.25
243	Reds Rookies (Ted Davidson, *Tommy Helms*)	1.00	.50	.30
244	Lindy McDaniel	.90	.45	.25
245	Joe Pepitone	3.00	1.50	.90
246	Tom Butters	.90	.45	.25
247	Wally Moon	1.00	.50	.30
248	Gus Triandos	1.00	.50	.30
249	Dave McNally	1.25	.60	.40
250	Willie Mays	100.00	50.00	30.00
251	Billy Herman	2.00	1.00	.60
252	Pete Richert	.90	.45	.25
253	Danny Cater	1.00	.50	.30
254	Roland Sheldon	1.50	.70	.45
255	Camilo Pascual	1.00	.50	.30
256	Tito Francona	1.00	.50	.30
257	Jim Wynn	1.25	.60	.40
258	Larry Bearnarth	1.00	.50	.30
259	Tigers Rookies (*Jim Northrup, Ray Oyler*)	1.25	.60	.40
260	Don Drysdale	15.00	7.50	4.50
261	Duke Carmel	1.50	.70	.45
262	Bud Daley	.90	.45	.25
263	Marty Keough	.90	.45	.25
264	Bob Buhl	1.00	.50	.30
265	Jim Pagliaroni	.90	.45	.25
266	*Bert Campaneris*	4.00	2.00	1.25
267	Senators Team	2.50	1.25	.70
268	Ken McBride	.90	.45	.25
269	Frank Bolling	.90	.45	.25
270	Milt Pappas	1.00	.50	.30
271	Don Wert	.90	.45	.25
272	Chuck Schilling	.90	.45	.25
273	Checklist 265-352	3.25	1.75	1.00
274	Lum Harris	.90	.45	.25
275	Dick Groat	1.75	.90	.50
276	Hoyt Wilhelm	10.00	5.00	3.00
277	Johnny Lewis	1.00	.50	.30
278	Ken Retzer	.90	.45	.25
279	Dick Tracewski	.90	.45	.25
280	Dick Stuart	1.00	.50	.30
281	Bill Stafford	1.50	.70	.45
282	Giants Rookies (Dick Estelle, *Masanori Murakami*)	1.25	.60	.40
283	Fred Whitfield	.90	.45	.25
284	Nick Willhite	.90	.45	.25
285	Ron Hunt	1.00	.50	.30
286	Athletics Rookies (Jim Dickson, Aurelio Monteagudo)	.90	.45	.25
287	Gary Kolb	.90	.45	.25
288	Jack Hamilton	.90	.45	.25
289	Gordy Coleman	.90	.45	.25
290	Wally Bunker	.90	.45	.25
291	Jerry Lynch	.90	.45	.25
292	Larry Yellen	.90	.45	.25
293	Angels Team	2.50	1.25	.70
294	Tim McCarver	2.75	1.50	.80
295	Dick Radatz	1.00	.50	.30
296	Tony Taylor	.90	.45	.25
297	Dave DeBusschere	3.50	1.75	1.00
298	Jim Stewart	.90	.45	.25
299	Jerry Zimmerman	.90	.45	.25
300	Sandy Koufax	100.00	50.00	30.00
301	Birdie Tebbetts	.90	.45	.25
302	Al Stanek	.90	.45	.25
303	Johnny Orsino	.90	.45	.25
304	Dave Stenhouse	.90	.45	.25
305	Rico Carty	1.50	.70	.45
306	Bubba Phillips	.90	.45	.25
307	Barry Latman	.90	.45	.25
308	Mets Rookies (*Cleon Jones*, Tom Parsons)	1.25	.60	.40
309	Steve Hamilton	1.50	.70	.45
310	Johnny Callison	1.25	.60	.40
311	Orlando Pena	.90	.45	.25
312	Joe Nuxhall	1.00	.50	.30
313	Jimmie Schaffer	.90	.45	.25
314	Sterling Slaughter	.90	.45	.25
315	Frank Malzone	1.00	.50	.30

		NR MT	EX	VG
316	Reds Team	2.75	1.50	.80
317	Don McMahon	.90	.45	.25
318	Matty Alou	1.00	.50	.30
319	Ken McMullen	.90	.45	.25
320	Bob Gibson	18.00	9.00	5.50
321	Rusty Staub	3.50	1.75	1.00
322	Rick Wise	1.00	.50	.30
323	Hank Bauer	1.00	.50	.30
324	Bobby Locke	.90	.45	.25
325	Donn Clendenon	1.00	.50	.30
326	Dwight Siebler	.90	.45	.25
327	Denis Menke	.90	.45	.25
328	Eddie Fisher	.90	.45	.25
329	Hawk Taylor	1.00	.50	.30
330	Whitey Ford	18.00	9.00	5.50
331	Dodgers Rookies (Al Ferrara, John Purdin)			
		1.00	.50	.30
332	Ted Abernathy	.90	.45	.25
333	Tommie Reynolds	.90	.45	.25
334	Vic Roznovsky	.90	.45	.25
335	Mickey Lolich	3.50	1.75	1.00
336	Woody Held	.90	.45	.25
337	Mike Cuellar	1.50	.70	.45
338	Phillies Team	2.50	1.25	.70
339	Ryne Duren	1.00	.50	.30
340	Tony Oliva	3.50	1.75	1.00
341	Bobby Bolin	.90	.45	.25
342	Bob Rodgers	1.00	.50	.30
343	Mike McCormick	1.00	.50	.30
344	Wes Parker	1.00	.50	.30
345	Floyd Robinson	.90	.45	.25
346	Bobby Bragan	1.00	.50	.30
347	Roy Face	1.50	.70	.45
348	George Banks	.90	.45	.25
349	Larry Miller	1.00	.50	.30
350	Mickey Mantle	350.00	140.00	88.00
351	Jim Perry	1.25	.60	.40
352	Alex Johnson	1.00	.50	.30
353	Jerry Lumpe	1.00	.50	.30
354	Cubs Rookies (Billy Ott, Jack Warner)			
		.90	.45	.25
355	Vada Pinson	2.50	1.25	.70
356	Bill Spanswick	.90	.45	.25
357	Carl Warwick	.90	.45	.25
358	Albie Pearson	.90	.45	.25
359	Ken Johnson	.90	.45	.25
360	Orlando Cepeda	5.00	2.50	1.50
361	Checklist 353-429	3.25	1.75	1.00
362	Don Schwall	.90	.45	.25
363	Bob Johnson	.90	.45	.25
364	Galen Cisco	1.00	.50	.30
365	Jim Gentile	1.00	.50	.30
366	Dan Schneider	.90	.45	.25
367	Leon Wagner	1.00	.50	.30
368	White Sox Rookies (Ken Berry, Joel Gibson)			
		1.00	.50	.30
369	Phil Linz	1.50	.70	.45
370	Tommy Davis	1.50	.70	.45
371	Frank Kreutzer	.90	.45	.25
372	Clay Dalrymple	.90	.45	.25
373	Curt Simmons	1.00	.50	.30
374	Angels Rookies (Jose Cardenal, Dick Simpson)			
		1.00	.50	.30
375	Dave Wickersham	.90	.45	.25
376	Jim Landis	.90	.45	.25
377	Willie Stargell	25.00	12.50	7.50
378	Chuck Estrada	.90	.45	.25
379	Giants Team	2.50	1.25	.70
380	Rocky Colavito	3.00	1.50	.90
381	Al Jackson	1.00	.50	.30
382	J.C. Martin	.90	.45	.25
383	Felipe Alou	1.00	.50	.30
384	Johnny Klippstein	.90	.45	.25
385	Carl Yastrzemski	100.00	50.00	30.00
386	Cubs Rookies (Paul Jaeckel, Fred Norman)			
		.90	.45	.25
387	Johnny Podres	2.00	1.00	.60
388	John Blanchard	1.50	.70	.45
389	Don Larsen	1.25	.60	.40
390	Bill Freehan	1.25	.60	.40
391	Mel McGaha	.90	.45	.25
392	Bob Friend	1.50	.70	.45
393	Ed Kirkpatrick	.90	.45	.25
394	Jim Hannan	.90	.45	.25
395	Jim Hart	1.00	.50	.30
396	Frank Bertaina	.90	.45	.25
397	Jerry Buchek	.90	.45	.25
398	Reds Rookies (Dan Neville, Art Shamsky)			
		1.00	.50	.30
399	Ray Herbert	.90	.45	.25
400	Harmon Killebrew	15.00	7.50	4.50

		NR MT	EX	VG
401	Carl Willey	1.00	.50	.30
402	Joe Amalfitano	.90	.45	.25
403	Red Sox Team	3.00	1.50	.90
404	Stan Williams	.90	.45	.25
405	John Roseboro	1.00	.50	.30
406	Ralph Terry	1.00	.50	.30
407	Lee Maye	.90	.45	.25
408	Larry Sherry	.90	.45	.25
409	Astros Rookies (Jim Beauchamp, Larry Dierker)			
		1.00	.50	.30
410	Luis Aparicio	9.00	4.50	2.75
411	Roger Craig	2.00	1.00	.60
412	Bob Bailey	.90	.45	.25
413	Hal Reniff	1.50	.70	.45
414	Al Lopez	3.00	1.50	.90
415	Curt Flood	1.50	.70	.45
416	Jim Brewer	.90	.45	.25
417	Ed Brinkman	1.00	.50	.30
418	Johnny Edwards	.90	.45	.25
419	Ruben Amaro	.90	.45	.25
420	Larry Jackson	.90	.45	.25
421	Twins Rookies (Gary Dotter, Jay Ward)			
		.90	.45	.25
422	Aubrey Gatewood	.90	.45	.25
423	Jesse Gonder	1.00	.50	.30
424	Gary Bell	.90	.45	.25
425	Wayne Causey	.90	.45	.25
426	Braves Team	2.50	1.25	.70
427	Bob Saverine	.90	.45	.25
428	Bob Shaw	.90	.45	.25
429	Don Demeter	.90	.45	.25
430	Gary Peters	1.00	.50	.30
431	Cardinals Rookies (Nelson Briles, Wayne Spiezio)			
		1.00	.50	.30
432	Jim Grant	1.00	.50	.30
433	John Bateman	.90	.45	.25
434	Dave Morehead	.90	.45	.25
435	Willie Davis	1.50	.70	.45
436	Don Elston	.90	.45	.25
437	Chico Cardenas	.90	.45	.25
438	Harry Walker	1.00	.50	.30
439	Moe Drabowsky	.90	.45	.25
440	Tom Tresh	2.50	1.25	.70
441	Denver Lemaster	.90	.45	.25
442	Vic Power	.90	.45	.25
443	Checklist 430-506	3.25	1.75	1.00
444	Bob Hendley	.90	.45	.25
445	Don Lock	.90	.45	.25
446	Art Mahaffey	.90	.45	.25
447	Julian Javier	1.25	.60	.40
448	Lee Stange	1.25	.60	.40
449	Mets Rookies (Jerry Hinsley, Gary Kroll)			
		1.50	.70	.45
450	Elston Howard	5.00	2.50	1.50
451	Jim Owens	1.25	.60	.40
452	Gary Geiger	1.25	.60	.40
453	Dodgers Rookies (Willie Crawford, John Werhas)			
		1.50	.70	.45
454	Ed Rakow	1.25	.60	.40
455	Norm Siebern	1.50	.70	.40
456	Bill Henry	1.25	.60	.40
457	Bob Kennedy	1.25	.60	.40
458	John Buzhardt	1.25	.60	.40
459	Frank Kostro	1.25	.60	.40
460	Richie Allen	6.00	3.00	1.75
461	Braves Rookies (Clay Carroll, Phil Niekro)			
		35.00	17.50	10.50
462	Lew Krausse (photo actually Pete Lovrich)			
		1.25	.60	.40
463	Manny Mota	1.50	.70	.45
464	Ron Piche	1.25	.60	.40
465	Tom Haller	1.25	.60	.40
466	Senators Rookies (Pete Craig, Dick Nen)			
		1.25	.60	.40
467	Ray Washburn	1.25	.60	.40
468	Larry Brown	1.25	.60	.40
469	Don Nottebart	1.25	.60	.40
470	Yogi Berra	50.00	30.00	15.00
471	Billy Hoeft	1.25	.60	.40
472	Don Pavletich	1.25	.60	.40
473	Orioles Rookies (Paul Blair, Dave Johnson)			
		10.00	5.00	3.00
474	Cookie Rojas	1.25	.60	.40
475	Clete Boyer	3.00	1.50	.90
476	Billy O'Dell	1.25	.60	.40
477	Cardinals Rookies (Fritz Ackley, Steve Carlton)			
		400.00	200.00	120.00
478	Wilbur Wood	1.00	.50	.30
479	Ken Harrelson	2.50	1.25	.70
480	Joel Horlen	1.25	.60	.40
481	Indians Team	3.00	1.50	.90

		NR MT	EX	VG
482	Bob Priddy	1.25	.60	.40
483	George Smith	1.25	.60	.40
484	Ron Perranoski	1.50	.70	.45
485	Nellie Fox	6.00	3.00	1.75
486	Angels Rookies (Tom Egan, Pat Rogan)	1.25	.60	.40
487	Woody Woodward	1.50	.70	.45
488	Ted Wills	1.25	.60	.40
489	Gene Mauch	1.50	.70	.45
490	Earl Battey	1.50	.70	.45
491	Tracy Stallard	1.25	.60	.40
492	Gene Freese	1.25	.60	.40
493	Tigers Rookies (Bruce Brubaker, Bill Roman)	1.25	.60	.40
494	Jay Ritchie	1.25	.60	.40
495	Joe Christopher	1.50	.70	.45
496	Joe Cunningham	1.25	.60	.40
497	Giants Rookies (*Ken Henderson*, Jack Hiatt)	1.50	.70	.45
498	Gene Stephens	1.25	.60	.40
499	Stu Miller	1.25	.60	.40
500	Ed Mathews	25.00	12.50	7.50
501	Indians Rookies (Ralph Gagliano, Jim Rittwage)	1.25	.60	.40
502	Don Cardwell	1.25	.60	.40
503	Phil Gagliano	1.25	.60	.40
504	Jerry Grote	1.50	.70	.45
505	Ray Culp	1.25	.60	.40
506	Sam Mele	1.25	.60	.40
507	Sammy Ellis	1.25	.60	.40
508a	Checklist 507-598 (large print on front)	6.00	3.00	1.75
508b	Checklist 507-598 (small print on front)	4.00	2.00	1.25
509	Red Sox Rookies (Bob Guindon, Gerry Vezendy)	1.25	.60	.40
510	Ernie Banks	60.00	30.00	18.00
511	Ron Locke	1.50	.70	.45
512	Cap Peterson	1.25	.60	.40
513	Yankees Team	9.00	4.50	2.75
514	Joe Azcue	1.25	.60	.40
515	Vern Law	2.00	1.00	.60
516	Al Weis	1.25	.60	.40
517	Angels Rookies (Paul Schaal, Jack Warner)	1.25	.60	.40
518	Ken Rowe	1.25	.60	.40
519	Bob Uecker	45.00	22.00	13.50
520	Tony Cloninger	1.50	.70	.45
521	Phillies Rookies (Dave Bennett, Morrie Stevens)	1.25	.60	.40
522	Hank Aguirre	1.25	.60	.40
523	Mike Brumley	4.00	2.00	1.25
524	Dave Giusti	4.00	2.00	1.25
525	Eddie Bressoud	4.00	2.00	1.25
526	Athletics Rookies (*Jim Hunter, Rene Lachemann, Skip Lockwood, Johnny Odom*)	150.00	75.00	45.00
527	Jeff Torborg	4.50	2.25	1.25
528	George Altman	4.00	2.00	1.25
529	Jerry Fosnow	4.00	2.00	1.25
530	Jim Maloney	4.50	2.25	1.25
531	Chuck Hiller	4.00	2.00	1.25
532	Hector Lopez	5.00	2.50	1.50
533	Mets Rookies (Jim Bethke, *Tug McGraw*, Dan Napolean, *Ron Swoboda*)	18.00	9.00	5.50
534	John Herrnstein	4.00	2.00	1.25
535	Jack Kralick	4.00	2.00	1.25
536	Andre Rodgers	4.00	2.00	1.25
537	Angels Rookies (Marcelino Lopez, *Rudy May*, Phil Roof)	5.00	2.50	1.50
538	Chuck Dressen	4.50	2.25	1.25
539	Herm Starrette	4.00	2.00	1.25
540	Lou Brock	40.00	20.00	12.00
541	White Sox Rookies (Greg Bollo, Bob Locker)	4.00	2.00	1.25
542	Lou Klimchock	4.00	2.00	1.25
543	Ed Connolly	4.00	2.00	1.25
544	Howie Reed	4.00	2.00	1.25
545	Jesus Alou	4.50	2.25	1.25
546	Indians Rookies (Ray Barker, Bill Davis, Mike Hedlund, Floyd Weaver)	4.00	2.00	1.25
547	Jake Wood	4.00	2.00	1.25
548	Dick Stigman	4.00	2.00	1.25
549	Cubs Rookies (*Glenn Beckert*, Roberto Pena)	5.00	2.50	1.50
550	*Mel Stottlemyre*	20.00	10.00	6.00
551	Mets Team	12.00	6.00	3.50
552	Julio Gotay	4.00	2.00	1.25
553	Astros Rookies (Dan Coombs, Jack McClure, Gene Ratliff)	4.00	2.00	1.25
554	Chico Ruiz	4.00	2.00	1.25

		NR MT	EX	VG
555	Jack Baldschun	4.00	2.00	1.25
556	Red Schoendienst	10.00	5.00	3.00
557	Jose Santiago	4.00	2.00	1.25
558	Tommie Sisk	4.00	2.00	1.25
559	Ed Bailey	4.00	2.00	1.25
560	Boog Powell	8.00	4.00	2.50
561	Dodgers Rookies (Dennis Daboll, *Mike Kekich, Jim Lefebvre*, Hector Valle)	6.00	3.00	1.75
562	Billy Moran	4.00	2.00	1.25
563	Julio Navarro	4.00	2.00	1.25
564	Mel Nelson	4.00	2.00	1.25
565	Ernie Broglio	4.00	2.00	1.25
566	Yankees Rookies (Gil Blanco, Art Lopez, Ross Moschitto)	5.00	2.50	1.50
567	Tommie Aaron	4.50	2.25	1.25
568	Ron Taylor	4.00	2.00	1.25
569	Gino Cimoli	4.50	2.25	1.25
570	Claude Osteen	4.00	2.00	1.25
571	Ossie Virgil	4.00	2.00	1.25
572	Orioles Team	6.00	3.00	1.75
573	Red Sox Rookies (*Jim Lonborg*, Gerry Moses, Mike Ryan, Bill Schlesinger)	10.00	5.00	3.00
574	Roy Sievers	4.50	2.25	1.25
575	Jose Pagan	4.00	2.00	1.25
576	Terry Fox	4.00	2.00	1.25
577	A.L. Rookies (Jim Buschhorn, Darold Knowles, Richie Scheinblum)	4.00	2.00	1.25
578	Camilo Carreon	4.00	2.00	1.25
579	Dick Smith	4.00	2.00	1.25
580	Jimmie Hall	4.00	2.00	1.25
581	N.L. Rookies (Kevin Collins, *Tony Perez*, Dave Ricketts)	80.00	40.00	24.00
582	Bob Schmidt	5.00	2.50	1.50
583	Wes Covington	4.00	2.00	1.25
584	Harry Bright	4.00	2.00	1.25
585	Hank Fischer	4.00	2.00	1.25
586	Tommy McCraw	4.00	2.00	1.25
587	Joe Sparma	4.00	2.00	1.25
588	Lenny Green	4.00	2.00	1.25
589	Giants Rookies (Frank Linzy, Bob Schroder)	4.00	2.00	1.25
590	Johnnie Wyatt	4.00	2.00	1.25
591	Bob Skinner	4.50	2.25	1.25
592	Frank Bork	4.00	2.00	1.25
593	Tigers Rookies (Jackie Moore, John Sullivan)	4.00	2.00	1.25
594	Joe Gaines	4.00	2.00	1.25
595	Don Lee	4.00	2.00	1.25
596	Don Landrum	4.00	2.00	1.25
597	Twins Rookies (Joe Nossek, Dick Reese, John Sevcik)	4.50	2.00	1.25
598	Al Downing	10.00	3.00	1.75

1965 Topps Embossed

Inserted in regular packs, the 2-1/8" by 3-1/2" Topps Embossed cards are one of the more fascinating issues of the company. The fronts feature an embossed profile portrait on gold foil-like cardboard (some collectors report finding the cards with silver cardboard). The player's name, team and position are below the portrait - which is good, because most of the embossed portraits are otherwise unrecognizeable. There is a gold border with American players framed in blue and National Leaguers in red. The set contains 72 cards divided equally between the leagues. The set provides an inexpensive way to add some interesting cards to a collection. Being special cards, many stars appear in the set.

		NR MT	EX	VG
Complete Set:		90.00	45.00	27.00
Common Player:		.50	.25	.15
1	Carl Yastrzemski	5.00	2.50	1.50
2	Ron Fairly	.50	.25	.15
3	Max Alvis	.50	.25	.15
4	Jim Ray Hart	.50	.25	.15
5	Bill Skowron	.60	.30	.20
6	Ed Kranepool	.50	.25	.15
7	Tim McCarver	.60	.30	.20
8	Sandy Koufax	5.00	2.50	1.50
9	Donn Clendenon	.50	.25	.15
10	John Romano	.50	.25	.15
11	Mickey Mantle	15.00	7.50	4.50
12	Joe Torre	.70	.35	.20
13	Al Kaline	5.00	2.50	1.50
14	Al McBean	.50	.25	.15
15	Don Drysdale	1.50	.70	.45
16	Brooks Robinson	2.00	1.00	.60
17	Jim Bunning	1.00	.50	.30
18	Gary Peters	.50	.25	.15
19	Bob Clemente	5.00	2.50	1.50
20	Milt Pappas	.50	.25	.15
21	Wayne Causey	.50	.25	.15
22	Frank Robinson	2.00	1.00	.60
23	Bill Mazeroski	.60	.30	.20
24	Diego Segui	.50	.25	.15
25	Jim Bouton	.60	.30	.20
26	Ed Mathews	1.50	.70	.45
27	Willie Mays	6.00	3.00	1.75
28	Ron Santo	.60	.30	.20
29	Boog Powell	.60	.30	.20
30	Ken McBride	.50	.25	.15
31	Leon Wagner	.50	.25	.15
32	John Callison	.50	.25	.15
33	Zoilo Versalles	.50	.25	.15
34	Jack Baldschun	.50	.25	.15
35	Ron Hunt	.50	.25	.15
36	Richie Allen	.70	.35	.20
37	Frank Malzone	.50	.25	.15
38	Bob Allison	.50	.25	.15
39	Jim Fregosi	.60	.30	.20
40	Billy Williams	1.50	.70	.45
41	Bill Freehan	.50	.25	.15
42	Vada Pinson	.70	.35	.20
43	Bill White	.50	.25	.15
44	Roy McMillan	.50	.25	.15
45	Orlando Cepeda	1.00	.50	.30
46	Rocky Colavito	.70	.35	.20
47	Ken Boyer	.70	.35	.20
48	Dick Radatz	.50	.25	.15
49	Tommy Davis	.60	.30	.20
50	Walt Bond	.50	.25	.15
51	John Orsino	.50	.25	.15
52	Joe Christopher	.50	.25	.15
53	Al Spangler	.50	.25	.15
54	Jim King	.50	.25	.15
55	Mickey Lolich	.70	.35	.20
56	Harmon Killebrew	2.00	1.00	.60
57	Bob Shaw	.50	.25	.15
58	Ernie Banks	4.00	2.00	1.25
59	Hank Aaron	5.00	2.50	1.50
60	Chuck Hinton	.50	.25	.15
61	Bob Aspromonte	.50	.25	.15
62	Lee Maye	.50	.25	.15
63	Joe Cunningham	.50	.25	.15
64	Pete Ward	.50	.25	.15
65	Bobby Richardson	1.00	.50	.30
66	Dean Chance	.50	.25	.15
67	Dick Ellsworth	.50	.25	.15
68	Jim Maloney	.50	.25	.15
69	Bob Gibson	1.50	.70	.45
70	Earl Battey	.50	.25	.15
71	Tony Kubek	1.00	.50	.30
72	Jack Kralick	.50	.25	.15

1965 Topps Transfers

Issued as strips of three players each as inserts in 1965, the Topps Transfers were 2" by 3" portraits of players. The transfers have blue or red bands at the top and bottom with the team name and position in the top band and the player's name in the bottom. As is so often the case, the superstars in the transfer set can be quite expensive, but like many of Topps non-card products, the transfers are neither terribly expensive or popular today.

		NR MT	EX	VG
Complete Set:		225.00	112.00	67.00
Common Player:		.60	.30	.20
(1)	Hank Aaron	15.00	7.50	4.50
(2)	Richie Allen	.80	.40	.25
(3)	Bob Allison	.70	.35	.20
(4)	Max Alvis	.60	.30	.20
(5)	Luis Aparicio	2.50	1.25	.70
(6)	Bob Aspromonte	.60	.30	.20
(7)	Walt Bond	.60	.30	.20
(8)	Jim Bouton	.80	.40	.25
(9)	Ken Boyer	.80	.40	.25
(10)	Jim Bunning	1.00	.50	.30
(11)	John Callison	.70	.35	.20
(12)	Rico Carty	.70	.35	.20
(13)	Wayne Causey	.60	.30	.20
(14)	Orlando Cepeda	1.00	.50	.30
(15)	Bob Chance	.60	.30	.20
(16)	Dean Chance	.60	.30	.20
(17)	Joe Christopher	.60	.30	.20
(18)	Bob Clemente	15.00	7.50	4.50
(19)	Rocky Colavito	.80	.40	.25
(20)	Tony Conigliaro	.70	.35	.20
(21)	Tommy Davis	.80	.40	.25
(22)	Don Drysdale	4.00	2.00	1.25
(23)	Bill Freehan	.70	.35	.20
(24)	Jim Fregosi	.70	.35	.20
(25)	Bob Gibson	4.00	2.00	1.25
(26)	Dick Groat	.70	.35	.20
(27)	Tom Haller	.60	.30	.20
(28)	Chuck Hinton	.60	.30	.20
(29)	Elston Howard	1.00	.50	.30
(30)	Ron Hunt	.60	.30	.20
(31)	Al Jackson	.60	.30	.20
(32)	Al Kaline	5.00	2.50	1.50
(33)	Harmon Killebrew	5.00	2.50	1.50
(34)	Jim King	.60	.30	.20
(35)	Ron Kline	.60	.30	.20
(36)	Bobby Knoop	.60	.30	.20
(37)	Sandy Koufax	10.00	5.00	3.00
(38)	Ed Kranepool	.60	.30	.20
(39)	Jim Maloney	.60	.30	.20
(40)	Mickey Mantle	60.00	30.00	18.00
(41)	Juan Marichal	4.00	2.00	1.25
(42)	Lee Maye	.60	.30	.20
(43)	Willie Mays	15.00	7.50	4.50
(44)	Bill Mazeroski	.80	.40	.25
(45)	Tony Oliva	.80	.40	.25
(46)	Jim O'Toole	.60	.30	.20
(47)	Milt Pappas	.70	.35	.20
(48)	Camilo Pascual	.70	.35	.20
(49)	Gary Peters	.60	.30	.20
(50)	Vada Pinson	.80	.40	.25
(51)	Juan Pizarro	.60	.30	.20
(52)	Boog Powell	.80	.40	.25
(53)	Dick Radatz	.60	.30	.20
(54)	Bobby Richardson	1.00	.50	.30
(55)	Brooks Robinson	6.00	3.00	1.75
(56)	Frank Robinson	5.00	2.50	1.50
(57)	Bob Rodgers	.70	.35	.20
(58)	John Roseboro	.70	.35	.20
(59)	Ron Santo	.80	.40	.25
(60)	Diego Segui	.60	.30	.20
(61)	Bill Skowron	.70	.35	.20
(62)	Al Spangler	.60	.30	.20

		NR MT	EX	VG
(63)	Dick Stuart	.70	.35	.20
(64)	Luis Tiant	.80	.40	.25
(65)	Joe Torre	.80	.40	.25
(66)	Bob Veale	.60	.30	.20
(67)	Leon Wagner	.60	.30	.20
(68)	Pete Ward	.60	.30	.20
(69)	Bill White	.70	.35	.20
(70)	Dave Wickersham	.60	.30	.20
(71)	Billy Williams	3.00	1.50	.90
(72)	Carl Yastrzemski	25.00	12.50	7.50

1966 Topps

 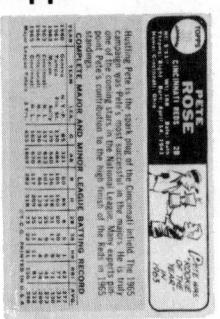

In 1966, Topps produced another 598-card set. The 2-1/2" by 3-1/2" cards feature the almost traditional color photograph with a diagonal strip in the upper left-hand corner carrying the team name. A band at the bottom carries the player's name and position. Multi-player cards returned in 1966 after having had a year's hiatus. The statistical leader cards feature the categorical leader and two runners-up. Most team managers have cards as well. The 1966 set features a handful of cards found with without a notice of the player's sale or trade to another team. Cards without the notice bring higher prices not included in the complete set prices below.

		NR MT	EX	VG
Complete Set:		4500.00	2250.00	1350.
Common Player: 1-110		.60	.30	.20
Common Player: 111-446		.70	.35	.20
Common Player: 447-522		3.50	1.75	1.00
Common Player Singleprint: 523-598		20.00	10.00	6.00
Common Player: 523-598		15.00	7.50	4.50

		NR MT	EX	VG
1	Willie Mays	200.00	50.00	18.00
2	Ted Abernathy	.80	.30	.20
3	Sam Mele	.60	.30	.20
4	Ray Culp	.60	.30	.20
5	Jim Fregosi	1.00	.50	.30
6	Chuck Schilling	.60	.30	.20
7	Tracy Stallard	.60	.30	.20
8	Floyd Robinson	.60	.30	.20
9	Clete Boyer	1.50	.70	.45
10	Tony Cloninger	.70	.35	.20
11	Senators Rookies (Brant Alyea, Pete Craig)	.60	.30	.20
12	John Tsitouris	.60	.30	.20
13	Lou Johnson	.60	.30	.20
14	Norm Siebern	.70	.35	.20
15	Vern Law	1.00	.50	.30
16	Larry Brown	.70	.35	.20
17	Johnny Stephenson	.70	.35	.20
18	Roland Sheldon	.60	.30	.20
19	Giants Team	2.00	1.00	.60
20	Willie Horton	.80	.40	.25
21	Don Nottebart	.60	.30	.20
22	Joe Nossek	.60	.30	.20
23	Jack Sanford	.60	.30	.20
24	Don Kessinger	1.25	.60	.40
25	Pete Ward	.60	.30	.20
26	Ray Sadecki	.60	.30	.20
27	Orioles Rookies (Andy Etchebarren, Darold Knowles)	.70	.35	.20
28	Phil Niekro	10.00	5.00	3.00
29	Mike Brumley	.60	.30	.20

		NR MT	EX	VG
30	Pete Rose	60.00	30.00	18.00
31	Jack Cullen	.80	.40	.25
32	Adolfo Phillips	.60	.30	.20
33	Jim Pagliaroni	.60	.30	.20
34	Checklist 1-88	2.00	1.00	.60
35	Ron Swoboda	.80	.40	.25
36	Jim Hunter	25.00	12.50	7.50
37	Billy Herman	1.50	.70	.45
38	Ron Nischwitz	.60	.30	.20
39	Ken Henderson	.60	.30	.20
40	Jim Grant	.60	.30	.20
41	Don LeJohn	.60	.30	.20
42	Aubrey Gatewood	.60	.30	.20
43	Don Landrum	.60	.30	.20
44	Indians Rookies (Bill Davis, Tom Kelley)	.60	.30	.20
45	Jim Gentile	.70	.35	.20
46	Howie Koplitz	.60	.30	.20
47	J.C. Martin	.60	.30	.20
48	Paul Blair	.80	.40	.25
49	Woody Woodward	.70	.35	.20
50	Mickey Mantle	175.00	70.00	44.00
51	Gordon Richardson	.70	.35	.20
52	Power Plus (Johnny Callison, Wes Covington)	1.00	.50	.30
53	Bob Duliba	.60	.30	.20
54	Jose Pagan	.60	.30	.20
55	Ken Harrelson	1.50	.70	.45
56	Sandy Valdespino	.60	.30	.20
57	Jim Lefebvre	.70	.35	.20
58	Dave Wickersham	.60	.30	.20
59	Reds Team	2.25	1.25	.70
60	Curt Flood	1.50	.70	.45
61	Bob Bolin	.60	.30	.20
62a	Merritt Ranew (no sold statement)	15.00	7.50	4.50
62b	Merritt Ranew (with sold statement)	.60	.30	.20
63	Jim Stewart	.60	.30	.20
64	Bob Bruce	.60	.30	.20
65	Leon Wagner	.70	.35	.20
66	Al Weis	.60	.30	.20
67	Mets Rookies (Cleon Jones, Dick Selma)	.80	.40	.25
68	Hal Reniff	.80	.40	.25
69	Ken Hamlin	.60	.30	.20
70	Carl Yastrzemski	60.00	30.00	18.00
71	Frank Carpin	.60	.30	.20
72	Tony Perez	10.00	5.00	3.00
73	Jerry Zimmerman	.60	.30	.20
74	Don Mossi	.70	.35	.20
75	Tommy Davis	1.50	.70	.45
76	Red Schoendienst	1.50	.70	.45
77	Johnny Orsino	.60	.30	.20
78	Frank Linzy	.60	.30	.20
79	Joe Pepitone	2.00	1.00	.60
80	Richie Allen	2.50	1.25	.70
81	Ray Oyler	.60	.30	.20
82	Bob Hendley	.60	.30	.20
83	Albie Pearson	.60	.30	.20
84	Braves Rookies (Jim Beauchamp, Dick Kelley)	.60	.30	.20
85	Eddie Fisher	.60	.30	.20
86	John Bateman	.60	.30	.20
87	Dan Napoleon	.70	.35	.20
88	Fred Whitfield	.60	.30	.20
89	Ted Davidson	.60	.30	.20
90	Luis Aparicio	9.00	4.50	2.75
91a	Bob Uecker (no trade statement)	80.00	40.00	24.00
91b	Bob Uecker (with trade statement)	15.00	7.50	4.50
92	Yankees Team	4.00	2.00	1.25
93	Jim Lonborg	1.00	.50	.30
94	Matty Alou	1.00	.50	.30
95	Pete Richert	.60	.30	.20
96	Felipe Alou	1.00	.50	.30
97	Jim Merritt	.60	.30	.20
98	Don Demeter	.60	.30	.20
99	Buc Belters (Donn Clendenon, Willie Stargell)	3.50	1.75	1.00
100	Sandy Koufax	80.00	40.00	24.00
101a	Checklist 89-176 (115 is Spahn)	7.00	3.50	2.00
101b	Checklist 89-176 (115 is Henry)	3.00	1.50	.90
102	Ed Kirkpatrick	.60	.30	.20
103a	Dick Groat (no trade statement)	20.00	10.00	6.00
103b	Dick Groat (with trade statement)	1.50	.70	.45
104a	Alex Johnson (no trade statement)	15.00	7.50	4.50
104b	Alex Johnson (with trade statement)	.70	.35	.20

		NR MT	EX	VG
105	Milt Pappas	.70	.35	.20
106	Rusty Staub	2.50	1.25	.70
107	Athletics Rookies (Larry Stahl, Ron Tompkins)	.60	.30	.20
108	Bobby Klaus	.70	.35	.20
109	Ralph Terry	.70	.35	.20
110	Ernie Banks	25.00	12.50	7.50
111	Gary Peters	.80	.40	.25
112	Manny Mota	.90	.45	.25
113	Hank Aguirre	.70	.35	.20
114	Jim Gosger	.70	.35	.20
115	Bill Henry	.70	.35	.20
116	Walt Alston	2.50	1.25	.70
117	Jake Gibbs	1.00	.50	.30
118	Mike McCormick	.80	.40	.25
119	Art Shamsky	.70	.35	.20
120	Harmon Killebrew	15.00	7.50	4.50
121	Ray Herbert	.70	.35	.20
122	Joe Gaines	.70	.35	.20
123	Pirates Rookies (Frank Bork, Jerry May)	.70	.35	.20
124	Tug McGraw	3.00	1.50	.90
125	Lou Brock	20.00	10.00	6.00
126	*Jim Palmer*	300.00	150.00	90.00
127	Ken Berry	.70	.35	.20
128	Jim Landis	.70	.35	.20
129	Jack Kralick	.70	.35	.20
130	Joe Torre	2.25	1.25	.70
131	Angels Team	2.25	1.25	.70
132	Orlando Cepeda	5.00	2.50	1.50
133	Don McMahon	.70	.35	.20
134	Wes Parker	.80	.40	.25
135	Dave Morehead	.70	.35	.20
136	Woody Held	.70	.35	.20
137	Pat Corrales	1.00	.50	.30
138	Roger Repoz	1.00	.50	.30
139	Cubs Rookies (Byron Browne, Don Young)	.70	.35	.20
140	Jim Maloney	.80	.40	.25
141	Tom McCraw	.70	.35	.20
142	Don Dennis	.70	.35	.20
143	Jose Tartabull	.70	.35	.20
144	Don Schwall	.70	.35	.20
145	Bill Freehan	.90	.45	.25
146	George Altman	.70	.35	.20
147	Lum Harris	.70	.35	.20
148	Bob Johnson	.70	.35	.20
149	Dick Nen	.70	.35	.20
150	Rocky Colavito	2.50	1.25	.70
151	Gary Wagner	.70	.35	.20
152	Frank Malzone	.80	.40	.25
153	Rico Carty	1.50	.70	.45
154	Chuck Hiller	.80	.40	.25
155	Marcelino Lopez	.70	.35	.20
156	DP Combo (Hal Lanier, Dick Schofield)	1.00	.50	.30
157	Rene Lachemann	.80	.40	.25
158	Jim Brewer	.70	.35	.20
159	Chico Ruiz	.70	.35	.20
160	Whitey Ford	20.00	10.00	6.00
161	Jerry Lumpe	.80	.40	.25
162	Lee Maye	.70	.35	.20
163	Tito Francona	.80	.40	.25
164	White Sox Rookies (Tommie Agee, Marv Staehle)	.90	.45	.25
165	Don Lock	.70	.35	.20
166	Chris Krug	.70	.35	.20
167	Boog Powell	2.50	1.25	.70
168	Dan Osinski	.70	.35	.20
169	Duke Sims	.70	.35	.20
170	Cookie Rojas	.70	.35	.20
171	Nick Willhite	.70	.35	.20
172	Mets Team	3.00	1.50	.90
173	Al Spangler	.70	.35	.20
174	Ron Taylor	.70	.35	.20
175	Bert Campaneris	1.50	.70	.45
176	Jim Davenport	.70	.35	.20
177	Hector Lopez	1.00	.50	.30
178	Bob Tillman	.70	.35	.20
179	Cardinals Rookies (Dennis Aust, Bob Tolan)	.80	.40	.25
180	Vada Pinson	2.50	1.25	.70
181	Al Worthington	.70	.35	.20
182	Jerry Lynch	.70	.35	.20
183a	Checklist 177-264 (large print on front)	2.50	1.25	.70
183b	Checklist 177-264 (small print on front)	4.00	2.00	1.25
184	Denis Menke	.70	.35	.20
185	Bob Buhl	.80	.40	.25
186	Ruben Amaro	1.00	.50	.30

		NR MT	EX	VG
187	Chuck Dressen	.80	.40	.25
188	Al Luplow	.80	.40	.25
189	John Roseboro	.90	.45	.25
190	Jimmie Hall	.70	.35	.20
191	Darrell Sutherland	.80	.40	.25
192	Vic Power	.70	.35	.20
193	Dave McNally	1.00	.50	.30
194	Senators Team	2.25	1.25	.70
195	Joe Morgan	40.00	20.00	12.00
196	Don Pavletich	.70	.35	.20
197	Sonny Siebert	.80	.40	.25
198	*Mickey Stanley*	1.00	.50	.30
199	Chisox Clubbers (Floyd Robinson, Johnny Romano, Bill Skowron)	1.00	.50	.30
200	Ed Mathews	10.00	5.00	3.00
201	Jim Dickson	.70	.35	.20
202	Clay Dalrymple	.70	.35	.20
203	Jose Santiago	.70	.35	.20
204	Cubs Team	2.25	1.25	.70
205	Tom Tresh	2.00	1.00	.60
206	Alvin Jackson	.70	.35	.20
207	Frank Quilici	.70	.35	.20
208	Bob Miller	.70	.35	.20
209	Tigers Rookies (Fritz Fisher, *John Hiller*)	1.25	.60	.40
210	Bill Mazeroski	2.50	1.25	.70
211	Frank Kreutzer	.70	.35	.20
212	Ed Kranepool	1.00	.50	.30
213	Fred Newman	.70	.35	.20
214	Tommy Harper	.80	.40	.25
215	N.L. Batting Leaders (Hank Aaron, Bob Clemente, Willie Mays)	8.00	4.00	2.50
216	A.L. Batting Leaders (Vic Davalillo, Tony Oliva, Carl Yastrzemski)	4.00	2.00	1.25
217	N.L. Home Run Leaders (Willie Mays, Willie McCovey, Billy Williams)	5.00	2.50	1.50
218	A.L. Home Run Leaders (Norm Cash, Tony Conigliaro, Willie Horton)	2.50	1.25	.70
219	N.L. RBI Leaders (Deron Johnson, Willie Mays, Frank Robinson)	4.00	2.00	1.25
220	A.L. RBI Leaders (Rocky Colavito, Willie Horton, Tony Oliva)	2.50	1.25	.70
221	N.L. ERA Leaders (Sandy Koufax, Vern Law, Juan Marichal)	4.00	2.00	1.25
222	A.L. ERA Leaders (Eddie Fisher, Sam McDowell, Sonny Siebert)	2.50	1.25	.70
223	N.L. Pitching Leaders (Tony Cloninger, Don Drysdale, Sandy Koufax)	4.00	2.00	1.25
224	A.L. Pitching Leaders (Jim Grant, Jim Kaat, Mel Stottlemyre)	3.00	1.50	.90
225	N.L. Strikeout Leaders (Bob Gibson, Sandy Koufax, Bob Veale)	4.00	2.00	1.25
226	A.L. Strikeout Leaders (Mickey Lolich, Sam McDowell, Denny McLain, Sonny Siebert)	2.50	1.25	.70
227	Russ Nixon	.70	.35	.20
228	Larry Dierker	.80	.40	.25
229	Hank Bauer	.80	.40	.25
230	Johnny Callison	1.25	.60	.40
231	Floyd Weaver	.70	.35	.20
232	Glenn Beckert	1.00	.50	.30
233	Dom Zanni	.70	.35	.20
234	Yankees Rookies (Rich Beck, *Roy White*)	3.50	1.75	1.00
235	Don Cardwell	.70	.35	.20
236	Mike Hershberger	.70	.35	.20
237	Billy O'Dell	.70	.35	.20
238	Dodgers Team	3.50	1.75	1.00
239	Orlando Pena	.70	.35	.20
240	Earl Battey	.80	.40	.25
241	Dennis Ribant	.80	.40	.25
242	Jesus Alou	.80	.40	.25
243	Nelson Briles	.80	.40	.25
244	Astros Rookies (Chuck Harrison, Sonny Jackson)	.70	.35	.20
245	John Buzhardt	.70	.35	.20
246	Ed Bailey	.70	.35	.20
247	Carl Warwick	.70	.35	.20
248	Pete Mikkelsen	.70	.35	.20
249	Bill Rigney	.70	.35	.20
250	Sam Ellis	.70	.35	.20
251	Ed Brinkman	.80	.40	.25
252	Denver Lemaster	.70	.35	.20
253	Don Wert	.70	.35	.20
254	Phillies Rookies (*Ferguson Jenkins*, Bill Sorrell)	60.00	30.00	18.00
255	Willie Stargell	15.00	7.50	4.50
256	Lew Krausse	.70	.35	.20
257	Jeff Torborg	.80	.40	.25
258	Dave Giusti	.70	.35	.20
259	Red Sox Team	2.50	1.25	.70

		NR MT	EX	VG
260	Bob Shaw	.70	.35	.20
261	Ron Hansen	.70	.35	.20
262	Jack Hamilton	.80	.40	.25
263	Tom Egan	.70	.35	.20
264	Twins Rookies (Andy Kosco, Ted Uhlaender)	.70	.35	.20
265	Stu Miller	.70	.35	.20
266	Pedro Gonzalez	.70	.35	.20
267	Joe Sparma	.70	.35	.20
268	John Blanchard	.70	.35	.20
269	Don Heffner	.70	.35	.20
270	Claude Osteen	.90	.45	.25
271	Hal Lanier	1.00	.50	.30
272	Jack Baldschun	.70	.35	.20
273	Astro Aces (Bob Aspromonte, Rusty Staub)	1.50	.70	.45
274	Buster Narum	.70	.35	.20
275	Tim McCarver	2.50	1.25	.70
276	Jim Bouton	2.50	1.25	.70
277	George Thomas	.70	.35	.20
278	Calvin Koonce	.70	.35	.20
279a	Checklist 265-352 (player's cap black)	4.00	2.00	1.25
279b	Checklist 265-352 (player's cap red)	3.00	1.50	.90
280	Bobby Knoop	.70	.35	.20
281	Bruce Howard	.70	.35	.20
282	Johnny Lewis	.80	.40	.25
283	Jim Perry	1.00	.50	.30
284	Bobby Wine	.80	.40	.25
285	Luis Tiant	2.50	1.25	.70
286	Gary Geiger	.70	.35	.20
287	Jack Aker	.70	.35	.20
288	Dodgers Rookies (Bill Singer, Don Sutton)	125.00	56.00	35.00
289	Larry Sherry	.80	.40	.25
290	Ron Santo	2.00	1.00	.60
291	Moe Drabowsky	.70	.35	.20
292	Jim Coker	.70	.35	.20
293	Mike Shannon	.80	.40	.25
294	Steve Ridzik	.70	.35	.20
295	Jim Hart	.80	.40	.25
296	Johnny Keane	1.25	.60	.40
297	Jim Owens	.70	.35	.20
298	Rico Petrocelli	1.25	.60	.40
299	Lou Burdette	2.00	1.00	.60
300	Bob Clemente	70.00	35.00	20.00
301	Greg Bollo	.70	.35	.20
302	Ernie Bowman	.80	.40	.25
303	Indians Team	2.25	1.25	.70
304	John Herrnstein	.70	.35	.20
305	Camilo Pascual	.90	.45	.25
306	Ty Cline	.70	.35	.20
307	Clay Carroll	.80	.40	.25
308	Tom Haller	.80	.40	.25
309	Diego Segui	.70	.35	.20
310	Frank Robinson	35.00	17.50	10.50
311	Reds Rookies (Tommy Helms, Dick Simpson)	.90	.45	.25
312	Bob Saverine	.70	.35	.20
313	Chris Zachary	.70	.35	.20
314	Hector Valle	.70	.35	.20
315	Norm Cash	2.00	1.00	.60
316	Jack Fisher	.80	.40	.25
317	Dalton Jones	.70	.35	.20
318	Harry Walker	.80	.40	.25
319	Gene Freese	.70	.35	.20
320	Bob Gibson	15.00	7.50	4.50
321	Rick Reichardt	.70	.35	.20
322	Bill Faul	.70	.35	.20
323	Ray Barker	1.00	.50	.30
324	John Boozer	.70	.35	.20
325	Vic Davalillo	.80	.40	.25
326	Braves Team	2.25	1.25	.70
327	Bernie Allen	.70	.35	.20
328	Jerry Grote	.90	.45	.25
329	Pete Charton	.70	.35	.20
330	Ron Fairly	.90	.45	.25
331	Ron Herbel	.70	.35	.20
332	Billy Bryan	.70	.35	.20
333	Senators Rookies (Joe Coleman, Jim French)	.90	.45	.25
334	Marty Keough	.70	.35	.20
335	Juan Pizarro	.70	.35	.20
336	Gene Alley	.80	.40	.25
337	Fred Gladding	.70	.35	.20
338	Dal Maxvill	.80	.40	.25
339	Del Crandall	1.00	.50	.30
340	Dean Chance	.80	.40	.25
341	Wes Westrum	.90	.45	.25
342	Bob Humphreys	.70	.35	.20
343	Joe Christopher	.70	.35	.20
344	Steve Blass	.80	.40	.25
345	Bob Allison	1.00	.50	.30
346	Mike de la Hoz	.70	.35	.20
347	Phil Regan	.70	.35	.20
348	Orioles Team	3.50	1.75	1.00
349	Cap Peterson	.70	.35	.20
350	Mel Stottlemyre	3.00	1.50	.90
351	Fred Valentine	.70	.35	.20
352	Bob Aspromonte	.70	.35	.20
353	Al McBean	.70	.35	.20
354	Smoky Burgess	1.00	.50	.30
355	Wade Blasingame	.70	.35	.20
356	Red Sox Rookies (Owen Johnson, Ken Sanders)	.70	.35	.20
357	Gerry Arrigo	.70	.35	.20
358	Charlie Smith	.70	.35	.20
359	Johnny Briggs	.70	.35	.20
360	Ron Hunt	.90	.45	.25
361	Tom Satriano	.70	.35	.20
362	Gates Brown	.70	.35	.20
363	Checklist 353-429	3.00	1.50	.90
364	Nate Oliver	.70	.35	.20
365	Roger Maris	75.00	38.00	23.00
366	Wayne Causey	.70	.35	.20
367	Mel Nelson	.70	.35	.20
368	Charlie Lau	.90	.45	.25
369	Jim King	.70	.35	.20
370	Chico Cardenas	.70	.35	.20
371	Lee Stange	.70	.35	.20
372	Harvey Kuenn	1.50	.70	.45
373	Giants Rookies (Dick Estelle, Jack Hiatt)	.70	.35	.20
374	Bob Locker	.70	.35	.20
375	Donn Clendenon	.80	.40	.25
376	Paul Schaal	.70	.35	.20
377	Turk Farrell	.70	.35	.20
378	Dick Tracewski	.70	.35	.20
379	Cardinals Team	2.25	1.25	.70
380	Tony Conigliaro	2.00	1.00	.60
381	Hank Fischer	.70	.35	.20
382	Phil Roof	.70	.35	.20
383	Jackie Brandt	.70	.35	.20
384	Al Downing	1.50	.70	.45
385	Ken Boyer	2.50	1.25	.70
386	Gil Hodges	6.00	3.00	1.75
387	Howie Reed	.70	.35	.20
388	Don Mincher	.80	.40	.25
389	Jim O'Toole	.70	.35	.20
390	Brooks Robinson	15.00	7.50	4.50
391	Chuck Hinton	.70	.35	.20
392	Cubs Rookies (Bill Hands, Randy Hundley)	.90	.45	.25
393	George Brunet	.70	.35	.20
394	Ron Brand	.70	.35	.20
395	Len Gabrielson	.70	.35	.20
396	Jerry Stephenson	.70	.35	.20
397	Bill White	1.00	.50	.30
398	Danny Cater	.70	.35	.20
399	Ray Washburn	.70	.35	.20
400	Zoilo Versalles	.80	.40	.25
401	Ken McMullen	.70	.35	.20
402	Jim Hickman	.90	.45	.25
403	Fred Talbot	.70	.35	.20
404	Pirates Team	2.25	1.25	.70
405	Elston Howard	4.00	2.00	1.25
406	Joe Jay	.70	.35	.20
407	John Kennedy	.70	.35	.20
408	Lee Thomas	.70	.35	.20
409	Billy Hoeft	.70	.35	.20
410	Al Kaline	18.00	9.00	5.50
411	Gene Mauch	.90	.45	.25
412	Sam Bowens	.70	.35	.20
413	John Romano	.70	.35	.20
414	Dan Coombs	.70	.35	.20
415	Max Alvis	.70	.35	.20
416	Phil Ortega	.70	.35	.20
417	Angels Rookies (Jim McGlothlin, Ed Sukla)	.70	.35	.20
418	Phil Gagliano	.70	.35	.20
419	Mike Ryan	.70	.35	.20
420	Juan Marichal	8.00	4.00	2.50
421	Roy McMillan	.80	.40	.25
422	Ed Charles	.70	.35	.20
423	Ernie Broglio	.70	.35	.20
424	Reds Rookies (Lee May, Darrell Osteen)	2.25	1.25	.70
425	Bob Veale	.80	.40	.25
426	White Sox Team	2.25	1.25	.70
427	John Miller	.70	.35	.20
428	Sandy Alomar	.70	.35	.20

		NR MT	EX	VG
429	Bill Monbouquette	.80	.40	.25
430	Don Drysdale	12.00	6.00	3.50
431	Walt Bond	.70	.35	.20
432	Bob Heffner	.70	.35	.20
433	Alvin Dark	.80	.40	.25
434	Willie Kirkland	.70	.35	.20
435	Jim Bunning	6.00	3.00	1.75
436	Julian Javier	.70	.35	.20
437	Al Stanek	.70	.35	.20
438	Willie Smith	.70	.35	.20
439	Pedro Ramos	1.00	.50	.30
440	Deron Johnson	.70	.35	.20
441	Tommie Sisk	.70	.35	.20
442	Orioles Rookies (Ed Barnowski, Eddie Watt)	.70	.35	.20
443	Bill Wakefield	.80	.40	.25
444a	Checklist 430-506 (456 is R. Sox Rookies)	3.00	1.50	.90
444b	Checklist 430-506 (456 is Red Sox Rookies)	5.00	2.50	1.50
445	Jim Kaat	5.00	2.50	1.50
446	Mack Jones	.70	.35	.20
447	Dick Ellsworth (photo actually Ken Hubbs)	3.50	1.75	1.00
448	Eddie Stanky	3.75	2.00	1.25
449	Joe Moeller	3.50	1.75	1.00
450	Tony Oliva	7.00	3.50	2.00
451	Barry Latman	3.50	1.75	1.00
452	Joe Azcue	3.50	1.75	1.00
453	Ron Kline	3.50	1.75	1.00
454	Jerry Buchek	3.50	1.75	1.00
455	Mickey Lolich	6.00	3.00	1.75
456	Red Sox Rookies (Darrell Brandon, Joe Foy)	3.50	1.75	1.00
457	Joe Gibbon	3.50	1.75	1.00
458	Manny Jiminez (Jimenez)	3.50	1.75	1.00
459	Bill McCool	3.50	1.75	1.00
460	Curt Blefary	3.50	1.75	1.00
461	Roy Face	6.00	3.00	1.75
462	Bob Rodgers	2.50	1.25	.70
463	Phillies Team	6.00	3.00	1.75
464	Larry Bearnarth	3.75	2.00	1.25
465	Don Buford	3.75	2.00	1.25
466	Ken Johnson	3.50	1.75	1.00
467	Vic Roznovsky	3.50	1.75	1.00
468	Johnny Podres	6.00	3.00	1.75
469	Yankees Rookies (*Bobby Murcer*, Dooley Womack)	15.00	7.50	4.50
470	Sam McDowell	4.00	2.00	1.25
471	Bob Skinner	3.50	1.75	1.00
472	Terry Fox	3.50	1.75	1.00
473	Rich Rollins	3.50	1.75	1.00
474	Dick Schofield	3.50	1.75	1.00
475	Dick Radatz	3.75	2.00	1.25
476	Bobby Bragan	3.75	2.00	1.25
477	Steve Barber	3.50	1.75	1.00
478	Tony Gonzalez	3.50	1.75	1.00
479	Jim Hannan	3.50	1.75	1.00
480	Dick Stuart	3.75	2.00	1.25
481	Bob Lee	3.50	1.75	1.00
482	Cubs Rookies (John Boccabella, Dave Dowling)	3.50	1.75	1.00
483	Joe Nuxhall	3.75	2.00	1.25
484	Wes Covington	3.50	1.75	1.00
485	Bob Bailey	3.50	1.75	1.00
486	Tommy John	15.00	7.50	4.50
487	Al Ferrara	3.50	1.75	1.00
488	George Banks	3.50	1.75	1.00
489	Curt Simmons	3.75	2.00	1.25
490	Bobby Richardson	12.00	6.00	3.50
491	Dennis Bennett	3.50	1.75	1.00
492	Athletics Team	5.00	2.50	1.50
493	Johnny Klippstein	3.50	1.75	1.00
494	Gordon Coleman	3.50	1.75	1.00
495	Dick McAuliffe	3.75	2.00	1.25
496	Lindy McDaniel	3.50	1.75	1.00
497	Chris Cannizzaro	3.50	1.75	1.00
498	Pirates Rookies (*Woody Fryman*, Luke Walker)	4.00	2.00	1.25
499	Wally Bunker	3.50	1.75	1.00
500	Hank Aaron	80.00	40.00	24.00
501	John O'Donoghue	3.50	1.75	1.00
502	Lenny Green	3.50	1.75	1.00
503	Steve Hamilton	3.75	2.00	1.25
504	Grady Hatton	3.50	1.75	1.00
505	Jose Cardenal	3.50	1.75	1.00
506	Bo Belinsky	3.75	2.00	1.25
507	John Edwards	3.50	1.75	1.00
508	*Steve Hargan*	3.75	2.00	1.25
509	Jake Wood	3.50	1.75	1.00
510	Hoyt Wilhelm	15.00	7.50	4.50

		NR MT	EX	VG
511	Giants Rookies (Bob Barton, *Tito Fuentes*)	3.75	2.00	1.25
512	Dick Stigman	3.50	1.75	1.00
513	Camilo Carreon	3.50	1.75	1.00
514	Hal Woodeshick	3.50	1.75	1.00
515	Frank Howard	7.00	3.50	2.00
516	Eddie Bressoud	2.00	1.00	.60
517a	Checklist 507-598 (529 is W. Sox Rookies)	9.00	4.50	2.75
517b	Checklist 506-598 (529 is White Sox Rookies)	10.00	5.00	3.00
518	Braves Rookies (Herb Hippauf, Arnie Umbach)	3.50	1.75	1.00
519	Bob Friend	6.00	3.00	1.75
520	Jim Wynn	4.00	2.00	1.25
521	John Wyatt	3.50	1.75	1.00
522	Phil Linz	3.50	1.75	1.00
523	Bob Sadowski	15.00	7.50	4.50
524	Giants Rookies (Ollie Brown, Don Mason)	20.00	10.00	6.00
525	Gary Bell	15.00	7.50	4.50
526	Twins Team	50.00	25.00	15.00
527	Julio Navarro	15.00	7.50	4.50
528	Jesse Gonder	20.00	10.00	6.00
529	White Sox Rookies (*Lee Elia*, Dennis Higgins, Bill Voss)	18.00	9.00	5.50
530	Robin Roberts	35.00	17.50	10.50
531	Joe Cunningham	15.00	7.50	4.50
532	Aurelio Monteagudo	15.00	7.50	4.50
533	Jerry Adair	15.00	7.50	4.50
534	Mets Rookies (Dave Eilers, Rob Gardner)	18.00	9.00	5.50
535	Willie Davis	25.00	12.50	7.50
536	Dick Egan	15.00	7.50	4.50
537	Herman Franks	15.00	7.50	4.50
538	Bob Allen	15.00	7.50	4.50
539	Astros Rookies (Bill Heath, Carroll Sembera)	15.00	7.50	4.50
540	Denny McLain	35.00	17.50	10.50
541	Gene Oliver	15.00	7.50	4.50
542	George Smith	15.00	7.50	4.50
543	Roger Craig	20.00	10.00	6.00
544	Cardinals Rookies (Joe Hoerner, George Kernek, Jimmy Williams)	20.00	10.00	6.00
545	Dick Green	20.00	10.00	6.00
546	Dwight Siebler	15.00	7.50	4.50
547	*Horace Clarke*	20.00	10.00	6.00
548	Gary Kroll	20.00	10.00	6.00
549	Senators Rookies (Al Closter, Casey Cox)	15.00	7.50	4.50
550	Willie McCovey	95.00	45.00	27.00
551	Bob Purkey	20.00	10.00	6.00
552	Birdie Tebbetts	15.00	7.50	4.50
553	Major League Rookies (Pat Garrett, Jackie Warner)	15.00	7.50	4.50
554	Jim Northrup	18.00	9.00	5.50
555	Ron Perranoski	18.00	9.00	5.50
556	Mel Queen	20.00	10.00	6.00
557	Felix Mantilla	15.00	7.50	4.50
558	Red Sox Rookies (Guido Grilli, Pete Magrini, *George Scott*)	20.00	10.00	6.00
559	Roberto Pena	15.00	7.50	4.50
560	Joel Horlen	15.00	7.50	4.50
561	Choo Choo Coleman	20.00	10.00	6.00
562	Russ Snyder	15.00	7.50	4.50
563	Twins Rookies (Pete Cimino, Cesar Tovar)	18.00	9.00	5.50
564	Bob Chance	15.00	7.50	4.50
565	Jimmy Piersall	30.00	15.00	9.00
566	Mike Cuellar	18.00	9.00	5.50
567	Dick Howser	20.00	10.00	6.00
568	Athletics Rookies (Paul Lindblad, Ron Stone)	15.00	7.50	4.50
569	Orlando McFarlane	15.00	7.50	4.50
570	Art Mahaffey	20.00	10.00	6.00
571	Dave Roberts	15.00	7.50	4.50
572	Bob Priddy	15.00	7.50	4.50
573	Derrell Griffith	15.00	7.50	4.50
574	Mets Rookies (Bill Hepler, Bill Murphy)	18.00	9.00	5.50
575	Earl Wilson	15.00	7.50	4.50
576	Dave Nicholson	20.00	10.00	6.00
577	Jack Lamabe	15.00	7.50	4.50
578	Chi Chi Olivo	15.00	7.50	4.50
579	Orioles Rookies (Frank Bertaina, Gene Brabender, Dave Johnson)	20.00	10.00	6.00
580	Billy Williams	70.00	35.00	21.00
581	Tony Martinez	15.00	7.50	4.50
582	Garry Roggenburk	15.00	7.50	4.50
583	Tigers Team	100.00	45.00	27.00
584	Yankees Rookies (Frank Fernandez, *Fritz Peterson*)	18.00	9.00	5.50

		NR MT	EX	VG
585	Tony Taylor	15.00	7.50	4.50
586	Claude Raymond	15.00	7.50	4.50
587	Dick Bertell	15.00	7.50	4.50
588	Athletics Rookies (Chuck Dobson, Ken Suarez)	15.00	7.50	4.50
589	Lou Klimchock	18.00	9.00	5.50
590	Bill Skowron	35.00	17.50	10.50
591	N.L. Rookies (*Grant Jackson*, Bart Shirley)	20.00	10.00	6.00
592	Andre Rodgers	15.00	7.50	4.50
593	Doug Camilli	20.00	10.00	6.00
594	Chico Salmon	15.00	7.50	4.50
595	Larry Jackson	15.00	7.50	4.50
596	Astros Rookies (*Nate Colbert*, Greg Sims)	18.00	9.00	5.50
597	John Sullivan	15.00	7.50	4.50
598	Gaylord Perry	350.00	150.00	90.00

1966 Topps Rub-Offs

Returning to a concept last tried in 1961, Topps tried an expanded version of Rub-Offs in 1966. Measuring 2-1/16" by 3," the Rub-Offs are in vertical format for the 100 players and horizontal for the 20 team pennants. The player Rub-Offs feature a color photo.

		NR MT	EX	VG
Complete Set:		225.00	112.00	67.00
Common Player:		.60	.30	.20
(1)	Hank Aaron	8.00	4.00	2.50
(2)	Jerry Adair	.60	.30	.20
(3)	Richie Allen	1.00	.50	.30
(4)	Jesus Alou	.60	.30	.20
(5)	Max Alvis	.60	.30	.20
(6)	Bob Aspromonte	.60	.30	.20
(7)	Ernie Banks	3.50	1.75	1.00
(8)	Earl Battey	.70	.35	.20
(9)	Curt Blefary	.60	.30	.20
(10)	Ken Boyer	1.00	.50	.30
(11)	Bob Bruce	.60	.30	.20
(12)	Jim Bunning	1.50	.70	.45
(13)	Johnny Callison	.70	.35	.20
(14)	Bert Campaneris	.70	.35	.20
(15)	Jose Cardenal	.60	.30	.20
(16)	Dean Chance	.60	.30	.20
(17)	Ed Charles	.60	.30	.20
(18)	Bob Clemente	7.00	3.50	2.00
(19)	Tony Cloninger	.60	.30	.20
(20)	Rocky Colavito	1.00	.50	.30
(21)	Tony Conigliaro	1.00	.50	.30
(22)	Vic Davalillo	.60	.30	.20
(23)	Willie Davis	.70	.35	.20
(24)	Don Drysdale	3.00	1.50	.90
(25)	Sammy Ellis	.60	.30	.20
(26)	Dick Ellsworth	.60	.30	.20
(27)	Ron Fairly	.70	.35	.20
(28)	Dick Farrell	.60	.30	.20
(29)	Eddie Fisher	.60	.30	.20
(30)	Jack Fisher	.60	.30	.20
(31)	Curt Flood	.70	.35	.20
(32)	Whitey Ford	3.50	1.75	1.00
(33)	Bill Freehan	.70	.35	.20
(34)	Jim Fregosi	.70	.35	.20
(35)	Bob Gibson	3.00	1.50	.90
(36)	Jim Grant	.60	.30	.20
(37)	Jimmie Hall	.60	.30	.20

		NR MT	EX	VG
(38)	Ken Harrelson	.70	.35	.20
(39)	Jim Hart	.60	.30	.20
(40)	Joel Horlen	.60	.30	.20
(41)	Willie Horton	.70	.35	.20
(42)	Frank Howard	1.00	.50	.30
(43)	Deron Johnson	.60	.30	.20
(44)	Al Kaline	4.00	2.00	1.25
(45)	Harmon Killebrew	4.00	2.00	1.25
(46)	Bobby Knoop	.60	.30	.20
(47)	Sandy Koufax	7.00	3.50	2.00
(48)	Ed Kranepool	.60	.30	.20
(49)	Gary Kroll	.60	.30	.20
(50)	Don Landrum	.60	.30	.20
(51)	Vernon Law	.70	.35	.20
(52)	Johnny Lewis	.60	.30	.20
(53)	Don Lock	.60	.30	.20
(54)	Mickey Lolich	1.00	.50	.30
(55)	Jim Maloney	.60	.30	.20
(56)	Felix Mantilla	.60	.30	.20
(57)	Mickey Mantle	40.00	20.00	12.00
(58)	Juan Marichal	3.00	1.50	.90
(59)	Ed Mathews	3.00	1.50	.90
(60)	Willie Mays	8.00	4.00	2.50
(61)	Bill Mazeroski	1.00	.50	.30
(62)	Dick McAuliffe	.60	.30	.20
(63)	Tim McCarver	.70	.35	.20
(64)	Willie McCovey	3.00	1.50	.90
(65)	Sammy McDowell	.70	.35	.20
(66)	Ken McMullen	.60	.30	.20
(67)	Denis Menke	.60	.30	.20
(68)	Bill Monbouquette	.60	.30	.20
(69)	Joe Morgan	2.00	1.00	.60
(70)	Fred Newman	.60	.30	.20
(71)	John O'Donoghue	.60	.30	.20
(72)	Tony Oliva	1.00	.50	.30
(73)	Johnny Orsino	.60	.30	.20
(74)	Phil Ortega	.60	.30	.20
(75)	Milt Pappas	.70	.35	.20
(76)	Dick Radatz	.60	.30	.20
(77)	Bobby Richardson	1.50	.70	.45
(78)	Pete Richert	.60	.30	.20
(79)	Brooks Robinson	4.00	2.00	1.25
(80)	Floyd Robinson	.60	.30	.20
(81)	Frank Robinson	3.50	1.75	1.00
(82)	Cookie Rojas	.60	.30	.20
(83)	Pete Rose	20.00	10.00	6.00
(84)	John Roseboro	.60	.30	.20
(85)	Ron Santo	1.00	.50	.30
(86)	Bill Skowron	.70	.35	.20
(87)	Willie Stargell	3.00	1.50	.90
(88)	Mel Stottlemyre	.70	.35	.20
(89)	Dick Stuart	.60	.30	.20
(90)	Ron Swoboda	.60	.30	.20
(91)	Fred Talbot	.60	.30	.20
(92)	Ralph Terry	.60	.30	.20
(93)	Joe Torre	1.00	.50	.30
(94)	Tom Tresh	.70	.35	.20
(95)	Bob Veale	.60	.30	.20
(96)	Pete Ward	.60	.30	.20
(97)	Bill White	.70	.35	.20
(98)	Billy Williams	2.00	1.00	.60
(99)	Jim Wynn	.70	.35	.20
(100)	Carl Yastrzemski	12.00	6.00	3.50
(101)	Angels Pennant	.60	.30	.20
(102)	Astros Pennant	.60	.30	.20
(103)	Athletics Pennant	.60	.30	.20
(104)	Braves Pennant	.60	.30	.20
(105)	Cards Pennant	.60	.30	.20
(106)	Cubs Pennant	.60	.30	.20
(107)	Dodgers Pennant	.60	.30	.20
(108)	Giants Pennant	.60	.30	.20
(109)	Indians Pennant	.60	.30	.20
(110)	Mets Pennant	.60	.30	.20
(111)	Orioles Pennant	.60	.30	.20
(112)	Phillies Pennant	.60	.30	.20
(113)	Pirates Pennant	.60	.30	.20
(114)	Red Sox Pennant	.60	.30	.20
(115)	Reds Pennant	.60	.30	.20
(116)	Senators Pennant	.60	.30	.20
(117)	Tigers Pennant	.60	.30	.20
(118)	Twins Pennant	.60	.30	.20
(119)	White Sox Pennant	.60	.30	.20
(120)	Yankees Pennant	.60	.30	.20

A player's name in *italic* type indicates a rookie card. An (FC) indicates a player's first card for that particular card company.

1967 Topps

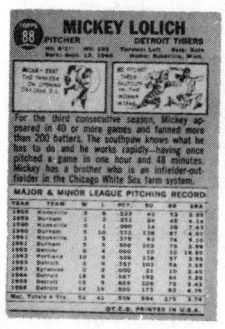

This 609-card set of 2-1/2" by 3-1/2" cards marked the largest set up to that time for Topps. Card fronts feature large color photographs bordered by white. The player's name and position are printed at the top with the team at the bottom. Across the front of the card with the exception of #254 (Milt Pappas) there is a facsimile autograph. The backs were the first to be done vertically, although they continued to carry familiar statistical and biographical information. The only subsets are statistical leaders and World Series highlights. Rookie cards are done by team or league with two players per card. The high numbers (#'s 534-609) in '67 are quite scarce, and while it is known that some are even scarcer, by virtue of having been short-printed in relation to the rest of the series, there is no general agreement on which cards are involved.

	NR MT	EX	VG
Complete Set:	5000.00	2500.00	1500.
Common Player: 1-110	.60	.30	.20
Common Player: 111-370	.70	.35	.20
Common Player: 371-457	.80	.40	.25
Common Player: 458-533	3.00	1.50	.90
Common Player: 534-609	5.00	2.50	1.50

		NR MT	EX	VG
1	The Champs (Hank Bauer, Brooks Robinson, Frank Robinson)	15.00	7.50	4.50
2	Jack Hamilton	.80	.40	.25
3	Duke Sims	.60	.30	.20
4	Hal Lanier	.80	.40	.25
5	Whitey Ford	12.00	6.00	3.50
6	Dick Simpson	.60	.30	.20
7	Don McMahon	.60	.30	.20
8	Chuck Harrison	.60	.30	.20
9	Ron Hansen	.60	.30	.20
10	Matty Alou	.80	.40	.25
11	Barry Moore	.60	.30	.20
12	Dodgers Rookies (Jimmy Campanis, Bill Singer)	.70	.35	.20
13	Joe Sparma	.60	.30	.20
14	Phil Linz	.60	.30	.20
15	Earl Battey	.70	.35	.20
16	Bill Hands	.60	.30	.20
17	Jim Gosger	.60	.30	.20
18	Gene Oliver	.60	.30	.20
19	Jim McGlothlin	.60	.30	.20
20	Orlando Cepeda	4.00	2.00	1.25
21	Dave Bristol	.60	.30	.20
22	Gene Brabender	.60	.30	.20
23	Larry Elliot	.70	.35	.20
24	Bob Allen	.60	.30	.20
25	Elston Howard	3.00	1.50	.90
26a	Bob Priddy (no trade statement)	8.00	4.00	2.50
26b	Bob Priddy (with trade statement)	.60	.30	.20
27	Bob Saverine	.60	.30	.20
28	Barry Latman	.60	.30	.20
29	Tommy McCraw	.60	.30	.20
30	Al Kaline	20.00	10.00	6.00
31	Jim Brewer	.60	.30	.20
32	Bob Bailey	.60	.30	.20
33	Athletics Rookies (Sal Bando, Randy Schwartz)	1.75	.90	.50
34	Pete Cimino	.60	.30	.20
35	Rico Carty	1.00	.50	.30
36	Bob Tillman	.60	.30	.20

		NR MT	EX	VG
37	Rick Wise	.70	.35	.20
38	Bob Johnson	.60	.30	.20
39	Curt Simmons	.80	.40	.25
40	Rick Reichardt	.60	.30	.20
41	Joe Hoerner	.60	.30	.20
42	Mets Team	3.00	1.50	.90
43	Chico Salmon	.60	.30	.20
44	Joe Nuxhall	.80	.40	.25
45	Roger Maris	40.00	20.00	12.00
46	Lindy McDaniel	.60	.30	.20
47	Ken McMullen	.60	.30	.20
48	Bill Freehan	.80	.40	.25
49	Roy Face	1.25	.60	.40
50	Tony Oliva	2.50	1.25	.70
51	Astros Rookies (Dave Adlesh, Wes Bales)	.60	.30	.20
52	Dennis Higgins	.60	.30	.20
53	Clay Dalrymple	.60	.30	.20
54	Dick Green	.60	.30	.20
55	Don Drysdale	12.00	6.00	3.50
56	Jose Tartabull	.60	.30	.20
57	Pat Jarvis	.70	.35	.20
58	Paul Schaal	.60	.30	.20
59	Ralph Terry	.80	.40	.25
60	Luis Aparicio	5.00	2.50	1.50
61	Gordy Coleman	.60	.30	.20
62	Checklist 1-109 (Frank Robinson)	3.00	1.50	.90
63	Cards' Clubbers (Lou Brock, Curt Flood)	4.50	2.25	1.25
64	Fred Valentine	.60	.30	.20
65	Tom Haller	.70	.35	.20
66	Manny Mota	.80	.40	.25
67	Ken Berry	.60	.30	.20
68	Bob Buhl	.70	.35	.20
69	Vic Davalillo	.70	.35	.20
70	Ron Santo	1.75	.90	.50
71	Camilo Pascual	.70	.35	.20
72	Tigers Rookies (George Korince, John Matchick)	.60	.30	.20
73	Rusty Staub	2.50	1.25	.70
74	Wes Stock	.60	.30	.20
75	George Scott	1.00	.50	.20
76	Jim Barbieri	.60	.30	.20
77	Dooley Womack	.80	.40	.25
78	Pat Corrales	1.00	.50	.30
79	Bubba Morton	.60	.30	.20
80	Jim Maloney	.70	.35	.20
81	Eddie Stanky	.70	.35	.20
82	Steve Barber	.60	.30	.20
83	Ollie Brown	.60	.30	.20
84	Tommie Sisk	.60	.30	.20
85	Johnny Callison	1.00	.50	.20
86a	Mike McCormick (no trade statement)	9.00	4.50	2.75
86b	Mike McCormick (with trade statement)	.70	.35	.20
87	George Altman	.60	.30	.20
88	Mickey Lolich	2.25	1.25	.70
89	Felix Millan	.80	.40	.25
90	Jim Nash	.60	.30	.20
91	Johnny Lewis	.70	.35	.20
92	Ray Washburn	.60	.30	.20
93	Yankees Rookies (Stan Bahnsen, Bobby Murcer)	2.50	1.25	.70
94	Ron Fairly	.80	.40	.25
95	Sonny Siebert	.70	.35	.20
96	Art Shamsky	.60	.30	.20
97	Mike Cuellar	.80	.40	.25
98	Rich Rollins	.60	.30	.20
99	Lee Stange	.60	.30	.20
100	Frank Robinson	20.00	10.00	6.00
101	Ken Johnson	.60	.30	.20
102	Phillies Team	2.00	1.00	.60
103a	Checklist 110-196 (Mickey Mantle) (170 is D McAuliffe)	8.00	4.00	2.50
103b	Checklist 110-196 (Mickey Mantle) (170 is D. McAuliffe)	6.00	3.00	1.75
104	Minnie Rojas	.60	.30	.20
105	Ken Boyer	2.00	1.00	.60
106	Randy Hundley	.70	.35	.20
107	Joel Horlen	.60	.30	.20
108	Alex Johnson	.60	.30	.20
109	Tribe Thumpers (Rocky Colavito, Leon Wagner)	1.50	.70	.45
110	Jack Aker	.60	.30	.20
111	John Kennedy	.70	.35	.20
112	Dave Wickersham	.70	.35	.20
113	Dave Nicholson	.70	.35	.20
114	Jack Baldschun	.70	.35	.20
115	Paul Casanova	.70	.35	.20
116	Herman Franks	.70	.35	.20

		NR MT	EX	VG
117	Darrell Brandon	.70	.35	.20
118	Bernie Allen	.70	.35	.20
119	Wade Blasingame	.70	.35	.20
120	Floyd Robinson	.70	.35	.20
121	Ed Bressoud	.80	.40	.25
122	George Brunet	.70	.35	.20
123	Pirates Rookies (Jim Price, Luke Walker)			
		.70	.35	.20
124	Jim Stewart	.70	.35	.20
125	Moe Drabowsky	.70	.35	.20
126	Tony Taylor	.70	.35	.20
127	John O'Donoghue	.70	.35	.20
128	Ed Spiezio	.70	.35	.20
129	Phil Roof	.70	.35	.20
130	Phil Regan	.70	.35	.20
131	Yankees Team	4.00	2.00	1.25
132	Ozzie Virgil	.70	.35	.20
133	Ron Kline	.70	.35	.20
134	Gates Brown	.70	.35	.20
135	Deron Johnson	.70	.35	.20
136	Carroll Sembera	.70	.35	.20
137	Twins Rookies (Ron Clark, Jim Ollom)			
		.70	.35	.20
138	Dick Kelley	.70	.35	.20
139	Dalton Jones	.70	.35	.20
140	Willie Stargell	20.00	10.00	6.00
141	John Miller	.70	.35	.20
142	Jackie Brandt	.70	.35	.20
143	Sox Sockers (Don Buford, Pete Ward)			
		.80	.40	.25
144	Bill Hepler	.80	.40	.25
145	Larry Brown	.70	.35	.20
146	Steve Carlton	90.00	45.00	27.00
147	Tom Egan	.70	.35	.20
148	Adolfo Phillips	.70	.35	.20
149	Joe Moeller	.70	.35	.20
150	Mickey Mantle	200.00	80.00	50.00
151	World Series Game 1 (Moe Mows Down 11)			
		2.00	1.00	.60
152	World Series Game 2 (Palmer Blanks Dodgers)			
		3.50	1.75	1.00
153	World Series Game 3 (Blair's Homer Defeats L.A.)			
		2.00	1.00	.60
154	World Series Game 4 (Orioles Win 4th Straight)			
		2.00	1.00	.60
155	World Series Summary (The Winners Celebrate)			
		2.00	1.00	.60
156	Ron Herbel	.70	.35	.20
157	Danny Cater	.70	.35	.20
158	Jimmy Coker	.70	.35	.20
159	Bruce Howard	.70	.35	.20
160	Willie Davis	1.25	.60	.40
161	Dick Williams	1.25	.60	.40
162	Billy O'Dell	.70	.35	.20
163	Vic Roznovsky	.70	.35	.20
164	Dwight Siebler	.70	.35	.20
165	Cleon Jones	.80	.40	.25
166	Ed Mathews	10.00	5.00	3.00
167	Senators Rookies (Joe Coleman, Tim Cullen)			
		.80	.40	.25
168	Ray Culp	.70	.35	.20
169	Horace Clarke	1.00	.50	.30
170	Dick McAuliffe	.80	.40	.25
171	Calvin Koonce	.70	.35	.20
172	Bill Heath	.70	.35	.20
173	Cardinals Team	2.00	1.00	.60
174	Dick Radatz	.80	.40	.25
175	Bobby Knoop	.70	.35	.20
176	Sammy Ellis	.70	.35	.20
177	Tito Fuentes	.70	.35	.20
178	John Buzhardt	.70	.35	.20
179	Braves Rookies (Cecil Upshaw, Chas. Vaughn)			
		.70	.35	.20
180	Curt Blefary	.70	.35	.20
181	Terry Fox	.70	.35	.20
182	Ed Charles	.70	.35	.20
183	Jim Pagliaroni	.70	.35	.20
184	George Thomas	.70	.35	.20
185	*Ken Holtzman*	2.75	1.50	.80
186	Mets Maulers (Ed Kranepool, Ron Swoboda)			
		1.50	.70	.45
187	Pedro Ramos	.70	.35	.20
188	Ken Harrelson	1.50	.70	.45
189	Chuck Hinton	.70	.35	.20
190	Turk Farrell	.70	.35	.20
191a	Checklist 197-283 (Willie Mays) (214 is Dick Kelley)			
		5.00	2.50	1.50
191b	Checklist 197-283 (Willie Mays) (214 is Tom Kelley)			
		4.00	2.00	1.25
192	Fred Gladding	.70	.35	.20
193	Jose Cardenal	.80	.40	.25
194	Bob Allison	.90	.45	.25
195	Al Jackson	.70	.35	.20
196	Johnny Romano	.70	.35	.20
197	Ron Perranoski	.80	.40	.25
198	Chuck Hiller	.80	.40	.25
199	Billy Hitchcock	.70	.35	.20
200	Willie Mays	75.00	38.00	23.00
201	Hal Reniff	1.00	.50	.30
202	Johnny Edwards	.70	.35	.20
203	Al McBean	.70	.35	.20
204	Orioles Rookies *(Mike Epstein, Tom Phoebus)*	.90	.45	.25
205	Dick Groat	1.50	.70	.45
206	Dennis Bennett	.70	.35	.20
207	John Orsino	.70	.35	.20
208	Jack Lamabe	.70	.35	.20
209	Joe Nossek	.70	.35	.20
210	Bob Gibson	15.00	7.50	4.50
211	Twins Team	2.00	1.00	.60
212	Chris Zachary	.70	.35	.20
213	*Jay Johnstone*	1.75	.90	.50
214	Tom Kelley	.70	.35	.20
215	Ernie Banks	18.00	9.00	5.50
216	Bengal Belters (Norm Cash, Al Kaline)			
		3.50	1.75	1.00
217	Rob Gardner	.80	.40	.25
218	Wes Parker	.80	.40	.25
219	Clay Carroll	.80	.40	.25
220	Jim Hart	.80	.40	.25
221	Woody Fryman	.80	.40	.25
222	Reds Rookies (Lee May, Darrell Osteen)			
		1.00	.50	.30
223	Mike Ryan	.70	.35	.20
224	Walt Bond	.70	.35	.20
225	Mel Stottlemyre	2.25	1.25	.70
226	Julian Javier	.80	.40	.25
227	Paul Lindblad	.70	.35	.20
228	Gil Hodges	5.00	2.50	1.50
229	Larry Jackson	.70	.35	.20
230	Boog Powell	2.50	1.25	.70
231	John Bateman	.70	.35	.20
232	Don Buford	.80	.40	.25
233	A.L. ERA Leaders (Steve Hargan, Joel Horlen, Gary Peters)			
		2.00	1.00	.60
234	N.L. ERA Leaders (Mike Cuellar, Sandy Koufax, Juan Marichal)			
		4.00	2.00	1.25
235	A.L. Pitching Leaders (Jim Kaat, Denny McLain, Earl Wilson)			
		2.50	1.25	.70
236	N.L. Pitching Leaders (Bob Gibson, Sandy Koufax, Juan Marichal, Gaylord Perry)			
		5.00	2.50	1.50
237	A.L. Strikeout Leaders (Jim Kaat, Sam McDowell, Earl Wilson)			
		2.50	1.25	.70
238	N.L. Strikeout Leaders (Jim Bunning, Sandy Koufax, Bob Veale)			
		4.00	2.00	1.25
239	AL 1966 Batting Leaders (Al Kaline, Tony Oliva, Frank Robinson)			
		4.00	2.00	1.25
240	N.L. Batting Leaders (Felipe Alou, Matty Alou, Rico Carty)			
		2.00	1.00	.60
241	A.L. RBI Leaders (Harmon Killebrew, Boog Powell, Frank Robinson)			
		3.50	1.75	1.00
242	N.L. RBI Leaders (Hank Aaron, Richie Allen, Bob Clemente)			
		5.00	2.50	1.50
243	A.L. Home Run Leaders (Harmon Killebrew, Boog Powell, Frank Robinson)			
		3.50	1.75	1.00
244	N.L. Home Run Leaders (Hank Aaron, Richie Allen, Willie Mays)			
		5.00	2.50	1.50
245	Curt Flood	1.50	.70	.45
246	Jim Perry	1.00	.50	.30
247	Jerry Lumpe	.80	.40	.25
248	Gene Mauch	.80	.40	.25
249	Nick Willhite	.70	.35	.20
250	Hank Aaron	75.00	38.00	23.00
251	Woody Held	.70	.35	.20
252	Bob Bolin	.70	.35	.20
253	Indians Rookies (Bill Davis, Gus Gil)	.70	.35	.20
254	Milt Pappas	.80	.40	.25
255	Frank Howard	2.50	1.25	.70
256	Bob Hendley	.70	.35	.20
257	Charley Smith	1.00	.50	.30
258	Lee Maye	.70	.35	.20
259	Don Dennis	.70	.35	.20
260	Jim Lefebvre	.80	.40	.25
261	John Wyatt	.70	.35	.20
262	Athletics Team	2.00	1.00	.60
263	Hank Aguirre	.70	.35	.20
264	Ron Swoboda	.80	.40	.25
265	Lou Burdette	1.50	.70	.45
266	Pitt Power (Donn Clendenon, Willie Stargell)			
		3.50	1.75	1.00

#	Player	NR MT	EX	VG
267	Don Schwall	.70	.35	.20
268	John Briggs	.70	.35	.20
269	Don Nottebart	.70	.35	.20
270	Zoilo Versalles	.80	.40	.25
271	Eddie Watt	.70	.35	.20
272	Cubs Rookies (Bill Connors, Dave Dowling)	.70	.35	.20
273	Dick Lines	.70	.35	.20
274	Bob Aspromonte	.70	.35	.20
275	Fred Whitfield	.70	.35	.20
276	Bruce Brubaker	.70	.35	.20
277	Steve Whitaker	1.00	.50	.30
278	Checklist 284-370 (Jim Kaat)	3.00	1.50	.90
279	Frank Linzy	.70	.35	.20
280	Tony Conigliaro	2.00	1.00	.60
281	Bob Rodgers	.70	.35	.20
282	Johnny Odom	.80	.40	.25
283	Gene Alley	.80	.40	.25
284	Johnny Podres	3.00	1.50	.90
285	Lou Brock	15.00	7.50	4.50
286	Wayne Causey	.70	.35	.20
287	Mets Rookies (Greg Goossen, Bart Shirley)	.80	.40	.25
288	Denver Lemaster	.70	.35	.20
289	Tom Tresh	1.75	.90	.50
290	Bill White	1.00	.50	.30
291	Jim Hannan	.70	.35	.20
292	Don Pavletich	.70	.35	.20
293	Ed Kirkpatrick	.70	.35	.20
294	Walt Alston	3.25	1.75	1.00
295	Sam McDowell	1.00	.50	.30
296	Glenn Beckert	.80	.40	.25
297	Dave Morehead	.70	.35	.20
298	Ron Davis	.70	.35	.20
299	Norm Siebern	.80	.40	.25
300	Jim Kaat	4.50	2.25	1.25
301	Jesse Gonder	.70	.35	.20
302	Orioles Team	2.00	1.00	.60
303	Gil Blanco	.70	.35	.20
304	Phil Gagliano	.70	.35	.20
305	Earl Wilson	.70	.35	.20
306	Bud Harrelson	1.75	.90	.50
307	Jim Beauchamp	.70	.35	.20
308	Al Downing	1.25	.60	.40
309	Hurlers Beware (Richie Allen, Johnny Callison)	2.00	1.00	.60
310	Gary Peters	.80	.40	.25
311	Ed Brinkman	.80	.40	.25
312	Don Mincher	.80	.40	.25
313	Bob Lee	.70	.35	.20
314	Red Sox Rookies (Mike Andrews, Reggie Smith)	3.00	1.50	.90
315	Billy Williams	8.00	4.00	2.50
316	Jack Kralick	.70	.35	.20
317	Cesar Tovar	.70	.35	.20
318	Dave Giusti	.70	.35	.20
319	Paul Blair	.80	.40	.25
320	Gaylord Perry	10.00	5.00	3.00
321	Mayo Smith	.70	.35	.20
322	Jose Pagan	.70	.35	.20
323	Mike Hershberger	.70	.35	.20
324	Hal Woodeshick	.70	.35	.20
325	Chico Cardenas	.70	.35	.20
326	Bob Uecker	20.00	10.00	6.00
327	Angels Team	2.00	1.00	.60
328	Clete Boyer	.90	.45	.25
329	Charlie Lau	.80	.40	.25
330	Claude Osteen	.80	.40	.25
331	Joe Foy	.70	.35	.20
332	Jesus Alou	.70	.35	.20
333	Ferguson Jenkins	10.00	5.00	3.00
334	Twin Terrors (Bob Allison, Harmon Killebrew)	3.50	1.75	1.00
335	Bob Veale	.80	.40	.25
336	Joe Azcue	.70	.35	.20
337	Joe Morgan	25.00	12.50	7.50
338	Bob Locker	.70	.35	.20
339	Chico Ruiz	.70	.35	.20
340	Joe Pepitone	2.00	1.00	.60
341	Giants Rookies (Dick Dietz, Bill Sorrell)	.80	.40	.25
342	Hank Fischer	.70	.35	.20
343	Tom Satriano	.70	.35	.20
344	Ossie Chavarria	.70	.35	.20
345	Stu Miller	.70	.35	.20
346	Jim Hickman	.80	.40	.25
347	Grady Hatton	.70	.35	.20
348	Tug McGraw	2.25	1.25	.70
349	Bob Chance	.70	.35	.20
350	Joe Torre	2.00	1.00	.60
351	Vern Law	1.25	.60	.40
352	Ray Oyler	.70	.35	.20
353	Bill McCool	.70	.35	.20
354	Cubs Team	2.00	1.00	.60
355	Carl Yastrzemski	90.00	45.00	27.00
356	Larry Jaster	.70	.35	.20
357	Bill Skowron	1.50	.70	.45
358	Ruben Amaro	1.00	.50	.30
359	Dick Ellsworth	.70	.35	.20
360	Leon Wagner	.80	.40	.25
361	Checklist 371-457 (Bob Clemente)	4.50	2.25	1.25
362	Darold Knowles	.70	.35	.20
363	Dave Johnson	2.00	1.00	.60
364	Claude Raymond	.70	.35	.20
365	John Roseboro	.80	.40	.25
366	Andy Kosco	.70	.35	.20
367	Angels Rookies (Bill Kelso, Don Wallace)	.70	.35	.20
368	Jack Hiatt	.70	.35	.20
369	Jim Hunter	12.00	6.00	3.50
370	Tommy Davis	1.50	.70	.45
371	Jim Lonborg	1.50	.70	.45
372	Mike de la Hoz	.80	.40	.25
373	White Sox Rookies (Duane Josephson, Fred Klages)	.80	.40	.25
374	Mel Queen	.80	.40	.25
375	Jake Gibbs	1.00	.50	.30
376	Don Lock	.80	.40	.25
377	Luis Tiant	2.25	1.25	.70
378	Tigers Team	3.00	1.50	.90
379	Jerry May	.80	.40	.25
380	Dean Chance	.90	.45	.25
381	Dick Schofield	.80	.40	.25
382	Dave McNally	1.00	.50	.30
383	Ken Henderson	.80	.40	.25
384	Cardinals Rookies (Jim Cosman, Dick Hughes)	.80	.40	.25
385	Jim Fregosi	1.25	.60	.40
386	Dick Selma	.90	.45	.25
387	Cap Peterson	.80	.40	.25
388	Arnold Earley	.80	.40	.25
389	Al Dark	.90	.45	.25
390	Jim Wynn	1.00	.50	.30
391	Wilbur Wood	.90	.45	.25
392	Tommy Harper	.90	.45	.25
393	Jim Bouton	2.25	1.25	.70
394	Jake Wood	.80	.40	.25
395	Chris Short	1.00	.50	.30
396	Atlanta Aces (Tony Cloninger, Denis Menke)	1.00	.50	.30
397	Willie Smith	.80	.40	.25
398	Jeff Torborg	.90	.45	.25
399	Al Worthington	.80	.40	.25
400	Bob Clemente	70.00	35.00	21.00
401	Jim Coates	.80	.40	.25
402	Phillies Rookies (Grant Jackson, Billy Wilson)	.80	.40	.25
403	Dick Nen	.80	.40	.25
404	Nelson Briles	.90	.45	.25
405	Russ Snyder	.80	.40	.25
406	Lee Elia	.90	.45	.25
407	Reds Team	2.50	1.25	.70
408	Jim Northrup	.90	.45	.25
409	Ray Sadecki	.80	.40	.25
410	Lou Johnson	.80	.40	.25
411	Dick Howser	1.50	.70	.45
412	Astros Rookies (Norm Miller, Doug Rader)	1.00	.50	.30
413	Jerry Grote	.90	.45	.25
414	Casey Cox	.80	.40	.25
415	Sonny Jackson	.80	.40	.25
416	Roger Repoz	.80	.40	.25
417	Bob Bruce	.80	.40	.25
418	Sam Mele	.80	.40	.25
419	Don Kessinger	.90	.45	.25
420	Denny McLain	3.00	1.50	.90
421	Dal Maxvill	.90	.45	.25
422	Hoyt Wilhelm	8.00	4.00	2.50
423	Fence Busters (Willie Mays, Willie McCovey)	12.00	6.00	3.50
424	Pedro Gonzalez	.80	.40	.25
425	Pete Mikkelsen	.80	.40	.25
426	Lou Clinton	1.00	.50	.30
427	Ruben Gomez	.80	.40	.25
428	Dodgers Rookies (Tom Hutton, Gene Michael)	1.00	.50	.30
429	Garry Roggenburk	.80	.40	.25
430	Pete Rose	75.00	37.00	22.00
431	Ted Uhlaender	.80	.40	.25
432	Jimmie Hall	.80	.40	.25
433	Al Luplow	.90	.45	.25

		NR MT	EX	VG
434	Eddie Fisher	.80	.40	.25
435	Mack Jones	.80	.40	.25
436	Pete Ward	.80	.40	.25
437	Senators Team	2.25	1.25	.70
438	Chuck Dobson	.80	.40	.25
439	Byron Browne	.80	.40	.25
440	Steve Hargan	.80	.40	.25
441	Jim Davenport	.80	.40	.25
442	Yankees Rookies (Bill Robinson, Joe Verbanic)	1.25	.60	.40
443	Tito Francona	.90	.45	.25
444	George Smith	.80	.40	.25
445	Don Sutton	15.00	7.50	4.50
446	Russ Nixon	.80	.40	.25
447	Bo Belinsky	1.00	.50	.30
448	Harry Walker	.90	.45	.25
449	Orlando Pena	.80	.40	.25
450	Richie Allen	3.00	1.50	.90
451	Fred Newman	.80	.40	.25
452	Ed Kranepool	1.00	.50	.30
453	Aurelio Monteagudo	.80	.40	.25
454a	Checklist 458-533 (Juan Marichal) (left ear shows)	5.00	2.50	1.50
454b	Checklist 458-533 (Juan Marichal) (no left ear)	2.00	1.25	
455	Tommie Agee	.70	.35	.20
456	Phil Niekro	7.00	3.50	2.00
457	Andy Etchebarren	.80	.40	.25
458	Lee Thomas	3.00	1.50	.90
459	Senators Rookies (Dick Bosman, Pete Craig)	3.75	2.00	1.25
460	Harmon Killebrew	55.00	28.00	16.50
461	Bob Miller	3.00	1.50	.90
462	Bob Barton	3.00	1.50	.90
463	Tribe Hill Aces (Sam McDowell, Sonny Siebert)	4.00	2.00	1.25
464	Dan Coombs	3.00	1.50	.90
465	Willie Horton	3.75	2.00	1.25
466	Bobby Wine	3.00	1.50	.90
467	Jim O'Toole	3.00	1.50	.90
468	Ralph Houk	4.50	2.25	1.25
469	Len Gabrielson	3.00	1.50	.90
470	Bob Shaw	3.00	1.50	.90
471	Rene Lachemann	3.00	1.50	.90
472	Pirates Rookies (John Gelnar, George Spriggs)	3.00	1.50	.90
473	Jose Santiago	3.00	1.50	.90
474	Bob Tolan	3.75	2.00	1.25
475	Jim Palmer	100.00	50.00	30.00
476	Tony Perez	70.00	35.00	20.00
477	Braves Team	4.75	2.50	1.50
478	Bob Humphreys	3.00	1.50	.90
479	Gary Bell	3.00	1.50	.90
480	Willie McCovey	30.00	15.00	9.00
481	Leo Durocher	4.50	2.25	1.25
482	Bill Monbouquette	3.75	2.00	1.25
483	Jim Landis	3.00	1.50	.90
484	Jerry Adair	3.00	1.50	.90
485	Tim McCarver	4.50	2.25	1.25
486	Twins Rookies (Rich Reese, Bill Whitby)	3.00	1.50	.90
487	Tom Reynolds	3.00	1.50	.90
488	Gerry Arrigo	3.00	1.50	.90
489	Doug Clemens	3.00	1.50	.90
490	Tony Cloninger	3.75	2.00	1.25
491	Sam Bowens	3.00	1.50	.90
492	Pirates Team	4.75	2.50	1.50
493	Phil Ortega	3.00	1.50	.90
494	Bill Rigney	3.00	1.50	.90
495	Fritz Peterson	4.00	2.00	1.25
496	Orlando McFarlane	3.00	1.50	.90
497	Ron Campbell	3.00	1.50	.90
498	Larry Dierker	3.75	2.00	1.25
499	Indians Rookies (George Culver, Jose Vidal)	3.00	1.50	.90
500	Juan Marichal	15.00	7.50	4.50
501	Jerry Zimmerman	3.00	1.50	.90
502	Derrell Griffith	3.00	1.50	.90
503	Dodgers Team	5.00	2.50	1.50
504	Orlando Martinez	3.00	1.50	.90
505	Tommy Helms	3.00	1.50	.90
506	Smoky Burgess	4.00	2.00	1.25
507	Orioles Rookies (Ed Barnowski, Larry Haney)	3.00	1.50	.90
508	Dick Hall	3.00	1.50	.90
509	Jim King	3.00	1.50	.90
510	Bill Mazeroski	4.50	2.25	1.25
511	Don Wert	3.00	1.50	.90
512	Red Schoendienst	6.00	3.00	1.75
513	Marcelino Lopez	3.00	1.50	.90
514	John Werhas	3.00	1.50	.90

		NR MT	EX	VG
515	Bert Campaneris	4.00	2.00	1.25
516	Giants Team	4.75	2.50	1.50
517	Fred Talbot	3.75	2.00	1.25
518	Denis Menke	3.00	1.50	.90
519	Ted Davidson	3.00	1.50	.90
520	Max Alvis	3.00	1.50	.90
521	Bird Bombers (Curt Blefary, Boog Powell)	4.50	2.25	1.25
522	John Stephenson	3.00	1.50	.90
523	Jim Merritt	3.00	1.50	.90
524	Felix Mantilla	3.00	1.50	.90
525	Ron Hunt	3.75	2.00	1.25
526	Tigers Rookies (Pat Dobson, George Korince)	3.75	2.00	1.25
527	Dennis Ribant	3.00	1.50	.90
528	Rico Petrocelli	3.75	2.00	1.25
529	Gary Wagner	3.00	1.50	.90
530	Felipe Alou	4.00	2.00	1.25
531	Checklist 534-609 (Brooks Robinson)	5.00	2.50	1.50
532	Jim Hicks	3.00	1.50	.90
533	Jack Fisher	3.00	1.50	.90
534	Hank Bauer	8.00	4.00	2.50
535	Donn Clendenon	6.00	3.00	1.75
536	Cubs Rookies (Joe Niekro, Paul Popovich)	30.00	15.00	9.00
537	Chuck Estrada	5.00	2.50	1.50
538	J.C. Martin	8.00	4.00	2.50
539	Dick Egan	5.00	2.50	1.50
540	Norm Cash	25.00	12.50	7.50
541	Joe Gibbon	8.00	4.00	2.50
542	Athletics Rookies (Rick Monday, Tony Pierce)	12.00	6.00	3.50
543	Dan Schneider	8.00	4.00	2.50
544	Indians Team	12.00	6.00	3.50
545	Jim Grant	8.00	4.00	2.50
546	Woody Woodward	8.00	4.00	2.50
547	Red Sox Rookies (Russ Gibson, Bill Rohr)	8.00	4.00	2.50
548	Tony Gonzalez	5.00	2.50	1.50
549	Jack Sanford	12.00	6.00	3.50
550	Vada Pinson	6.00	3.00	1.75
551	Doug Camilli	5.00	2.50	1.50
552	Ted Savage	5.00	2.50	1.50
553	Yankees Rookies (Mike Hegan, Thad Tillotson)	15.00	7.50	4.50
554	Andre Rodgers	5.00	2.50	1.50
555	Don Cardwell	8.00	4.00	2.50
556	Al Weis	5.00	2.50	1.50
557	Al Ferrara	12.00	6.00	3.50
558	Orioles Rookies (Mark Belanger, Bill Dillman)	25.00	12.50	7.50
559	Dick Tracewski	5.00	2.50	1.50
560	Jim Bunning	40.00	20.00	12.00
561	Sandy Alomar	8.00	4.00	2.50
562	Steve Blass	6.00	3.00	1.75
563	Joe Adcock	18.00	9.00	5.50
564	Astros Rookies (Alonzo Harris, Aaron Pointer)	8.00	4.00	2.50
565	Lew Krausse	8.00	4.00	2.50
566	Gary Geiger	5.00	2.50	1.50
567	Steve Hamilton	8.00	4.00	2.50
568	John Sullivan	8.00	4.00	2.50
569	A.L. Rookies (Hank Allen, Rod Carew)	450.00	225.00	135.00
570	Maury Wills	75.00	37.00	22.00
571	Larry Sherry	12.00	6.00	3.50
572	Don Demeter	12.00	6.00	3.50
573	White Sox Team	15.00	7.50	4.50
574	Jerry Buchek	12.00	6.00	3.50
575	Dave Boswell	12.00	6.00	3.50
576	N.L. Rookies (Norm Gigon, Ramon Hernandez)	18.00	9.00	5.50
577	Bill Short	8.00	4.00	2.50
578	John Boccabella	8.00	4.00	2.50
579	Bill Henry	8.00	4.00	2.50
580	Rocky Colavito	70.00	35.00	21.00
581	Mets Rookies (Bill Denehy, Tom Seaver)	1500.00	750.00	450.00
582	Jim Owens	5.00	2.50	1.50
583	Ray Barker	8.00	4.00	2.50
584	Jim Piersall	18.00	9.00	5.50
585	Wally Bunker	8.00	4.00	2.50
586	Manny Jimenez	8.00	4.00	2.50
587	N.L. Rookies (Don Shaw, Gary Sutherland)	15.00	7.50	4.50
588	Johnny Klippstein	5.00	2.50	1.50
589	Dave Ricketts	5.00	2.50	1.50
590	Pete Richert	8.00	4.00	2.50
591	Ty Cline	5.00	2.50	1.50
592	N.L. Rookies (Jim Shellenback, Ron Willis)	7.00	3.50	2.00

		NR MT	EX	VG
593	Wes Westrum	8.00	4.00	2.50
594	Dan Osinski	8.00	4.00	2.50
595	Cookie Rojas	5.00	2.50	1.50
596	Galen Cisco	5.00	2.50	1.50
597	Ted Abernathy	5.00	2.50	1.50
598	White Sox Rookies (Ed Stroud, Walt Williams)	7.00	3.50	2.00
599	Bob Duliba	5.00	2.50	1.50
600	Brooks Robinson	200.00	100.00	60.00
601	Bill Bryan	8.00	4.00	2.50
602	Juan Pizarro	8.00	4.00	2.50
603	Athletics Rookies (Tim Talton, Ramon Webster)	8.00	4.00	2.50
604	Red Sox Team	90.00	45.00	27.00
605	Mike Shannon	6.00	3.00	1.75
606	Ron Taylor	8.00	4.00	2.50
607	Mickey Stanley	6.00	3.00	1.75
608	Cubs Rookies (Rich Nye, John Upham)	6.00	3.00	1.75
609	Tommy John	100.00	50.00	30.00

1967 Topps Pin-Ups

The 5" by 7" "All Star Pin-ups" were inserts to regular 1967 Topps baseball cards. They feature a full color picture with the player's name, position and team in a circle on the lower left side of the front. The numbered set consists of 32 players (generally big names). Even so, they are rather inexpensive. Because the large paper pin-ups had to be folded several times to fit into the wax packs, they are almost never found in true "Mint" condition.

		NR MT	EX	VG
Complete Set:		60.00	30.00	18.00
Common Player:		.25	.13	.08
1	Boog Powell	.40	.20	.12
2	Bert Campaneris	.30	.15	.09
3	Brooks Robinson	3.00	1.50	.90
4	Tommie Agee	.25	.13	.08
5	Carl Yastrzemski	3.50	1.75	1.00
6	Mickey Mantle	12.00	6.00	3.50
7	Frank Howard	.50	.25	.15
8	Sam McDowell	.25	.13	.08
9	Orlando Cepeda	.60	.30	.20
10	Chico Cardenas	.25	.13	.08
11	Bob Clemente	5.00	2.50	1.50
12	Willie Mays	5.00	2.50	1.50
13	Cleon Jones	.25	.13	.08
14	John Callison	.25	.13	.08
15	Hank Aaron	5.00	2.50	1.50
16	Don Drysdale	3.00	1.50	.90
17	Bobby Knoop	.25	.13	.08
18	Tony Oliva	.50	.25	.15
19	Frank Robinson	2.00	1.00	.60
20	Denny McLain	.50	.25	.15
21	Al Kaline	5.00	2.50	1.50
22	Joe Pepitone	.40	.20	.12
23	Harmon Killebrew	5.00	2.50	1.50
24	Leon Wagner	.25	.13	.08
25	Joe Morgan	5.00	2.50	1.50
26	Ron Santo	.40	.20	.12
27	Joe Torre	.60	.30	.20
28	Juan Marichal	2.00	1.00	.60
29	Matty Alou	.25	.13	.08
30	Felipe Alou	.25	.13	.08
31	Ron Hunt	.25	.13	.08

		NR MT	EX	VG
32	Willie McCovey	2.00	1.00	.60

1967 Topps Stand-Ups

Never actually issued, no more than a handful of each of these rare test issues has made their way into the hobby market. Designed so that the color photo of the player's head could be popped out of the black background, and the top folded over to create a stand-up display, examples of these 3-1/8" by 5-1/4" cards can be found either die-cut around the portrait or without the cutting. Blank-backed, there are 24 cards in the set, numbered on the front at bottom left. The cards are popular with advanced superstar collectors.

		NR MT	EX	VG
Complete Set:		6750.00	3375.00	2025.
Common Player:		65.00	32.00	19.50
1	Pete Rose	700.00	350.00	210.00
2	Gary Peters	65.00	32.00	19.50
3	Frank Robinson	200.00	100.00	60.00
4	Jim Lonborg	65.00	32.00	19.50
5	Ron Swoboda	65.00	32.00	19.50
6	Harmon Killebrew	200.00	100.00	60.00
7	Bob Clemente	800.00	400.00	240.00
8	Mickey Mantle	1500.00	750.00	450.00
9	Jim Fregosi	75.00	37.00	22.00
10	Al Kaline	300.00	150.00	90.00
11	Don Drysdale	250.00	125.00	75.00
12	Dean Chance	65.00	32.00	19.50
13	Orlando Cepeda	75.00	37.00	22.00
14	Tim McCarver	75.00	37.00	22.00
15	Frank Howard	75.00	37.00	22.00
16	Max Alvis	65.00	32.00	19.50
17	Rusty Staub	75.00	37.00	22.00
18	Richie Allen	75.00	37.00	22.00
19	Willie Mays	600.00	300.00	175.00
20	Hank Aaron	600.00	300.00	175.00
21	Carl Yastrzemski	600.00	300.00	180.00
22	Ron Santo	75.00	37.00	22.00
23	Jim Hunter	200.00	100.00	60.00
24	Jim Wynn	65.00	32.00	19.50

1967 Topps Stickers Pirates

Considered a "test" issue, this 33-sticker set of 2-1/2" by 3-1/2" stickers is very similar to the Red Sox stickers which were produced the same year. Player stickers have a color picture (often just the player's head) and the player's name in large "comic book" letters. Besides the players, there are other topics such as "I Love the Pirates," "Bob Clemente for Mayor," and a number of similar sentiments. The stickers have blank backs and are rather scarce.

		NR MT	EX	VG
Complete Set:		250.00	125.00	75.00
Common Player:		3.00	1.50	.90
1	Gene Alley	5.00	2.50	1.50
2	Matty Alou	7.00	3.50	2.00
3	Dennis Ribant	3.00	1.50	.90
4	Steve Blass	5.00	2.50	1.50
5	Juan Pizarro	3.00	1.50	.90
6	Bob Clemente	75.00	38.00	23.00
7	Donn Clendenon	5.00	2.50	1.50
8	Roy Face	7.00	3.50	2.00
9	Woody Fryman	3.00	1.50	.90
10	Jesse Gonder	3.00	1.50	.90
11	Vern Law	7.00	3.50	2.00
12	Al McBean	3.00	1.50	.90
13	Jerry May	3.00	1.50	.90
14	Bill Mazeroski	12.00	6.00	3.50
15	Pete Mikkelsen	3.00	1.50	.90
16	Manny Mota	5.00	2.50	1.50
17	Billy O'Dell	3.00	1.50	.90
18	Jose Pagan	3.00	1.50	.90
19	Jim Pagliaroni	3.00	1.50	.90
20	Johnny Pesky	3.00	1.50	.90
21	Tommie Sisk	3.00	1.50	.90
22	Willie Stargell	40.00	20.00	12.50
23	Bob Veale	5.00	2.50	1.50
24	Harry Walker	3.00	1.50	.90
25	I Love The Pirates	3.00	1.50	.90
26	Let's Go Pirates	3.00	1.50	.90
27	Bob Clemente For Mayor	35.00	17.50	10.50
28	National League Batting Champion (Matty Alou)	4.00	2.00	1.25
29	Happiness Is A Pirate Win	3.00	1.50	.90
30	Donn Clendenon Is My Hero	4.00	2.00	1.25
31	Pirates' Home Run Champion (Willie Stargell)	15.00	7.50	4.50
32	Pirates Logo	3.00	1.50	.90
33	Pirates Pennant	3.00	1.50	.90

1967 Topps Stickers Red Sox

Like the 1967 Pirates Stickers, the Red Sox Stickers were part of the same test procedure. The Red Sox Stickers have the same 2-1/2" by 3-1/2" dimensions, color picture and large player's name on the front. A set is complete at 33 stickers. The majority are players, but themes such as "Let's Go Red Sox" are also included.

		NR MT	EX	VG
Complete Set:		225.00	112.00	67.00
Common Player:		3.00	1.50	.90
1	Dennis Bennett	3.00	1.50	.90
2	Darrell Brandon	3.00	1.50	.90
3	Tony Conigliaro	15.00	7.50	4.50

		NR MT	EX	VG
4	Don Demeter	3.00	1.50	.90
5	Hank Fischer	3.00	1.50	.90
6	Joe Foy	3.00	1.50	.90
7	Mike Andrews	3.00	1.50	.90
8	Dalton Jones	3.00	1.50	.90
9	Jim Lonborg	9.00	4.50	2.75
10	Don McMahon	3.00	1.50	.90
11	Dave Morehead	3.00	1.50	.90
12	George Smith	3.00	1.50	.90
13	Rico Petrocelli	6.00	3.00	1.75
14	Mike Ryan	3.00	1.50	.90
15	Jose Santiago	3.00	1.50	.90
16	George Scott	6.00	3.00	1.75
17	Sal Maglie	5.00	2.50	1.50
18	Reggie Smith	10.00	5.00	3.00
19	Lee Stange	3.00	1.50	.90
20	Jerry Stephenson	3.00	1.50	.90
21	Jose Tartabull	3.00	1.50	.90
22	George Thomas	3.00	1.50	.90
23	Bob Tillman	3.00	1.50	.90
24	Johnnie Wyatt	3.00	1.50	.90
25	Carl Yastrzemski	75.00	37.00	22.00
26	Dick Williams	6.00	3.00	1.75
27	I Love The Red Sox	3.00	1.50	.90
28	Let's Go Red Sox	3.00	1.50	.90
29	Carl Yastrzemski For Mayor	35.00	17.50	10.50
30	Tony Conigliaro Is My Hero	7.00	3.50	2.00
31	Happiness Is A Boston Win	3.00	1.50	.90
32	Red Sox Logo	3.00	1.50	.90
33	Red Sox Pennant	3.00	1.50	.90

1968 Topps

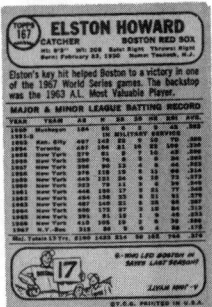

In 1968, Topps returned to a 598-card set of 2-1/2" by 3-1/2" cards. It is not, however, more of the same by way of appearance as the cards feature a color photograph on a background of what appears to be a burlap fabric. The player's name is below the photo but on the unusual background. A colored circle on the lower right carries the team and position. Backs were also changed. While retaining the vertical format introduced the previous year, with stats in the middle and cartoon at the bottom. The set features many of the old favorite subsets, including statistical leaders, World Series highlights, multi-player cards, checklists, rookie cards and the return of All-Star cards.

		NR MT	EX	VG
Complete Set:		2600.00	1300.00	750.00
Common Player: 1-533		.60	.30	.20
Common Player: 534-598		1.00	.50	.30
1	N.L. Batting Leaders (Matty Alou, Bob Clemente, Tony Gonzalez)	8.00	2.00	1.00
2	A.L. Batting Leaders (Al Kaline, Frank Robinson, Carl Yastrzemski)	4.00	2.00	1.25
3	N.L. RBI Leaders (Hank Aaron, Orlando Cepeda, Bob Clemente)	4.00	2.00	1.25
4	A.L. RBI Leaders (Harmon Killebrew, Frank Robinson, Carl Yastrzemski)	4.00	2.00	1.25
5	N.L. Home Run Leaders (Hank Aaron, Willie McCovey, Ron Santo, Jim Wynn)	4.00	2.00	1.25
6	A.L. Home Run Leaders (Frank Howard, Harmon Killebrew, Carl Yastrzemski)	4.00	2.00	1.25
7	N.L. ERA Leaders (Jim Bunning, Phil Niekro, Chris Short)	2.50	1.25	.70

		NR MT	EX	VG
8	A.L. ERA Leaders (Joe Horlen, Gary Peters, Sonny Siebert)	1.50	.70	.45
9	N.L. Pitching Leaders (Jim Bunning, Ferguson Jenkins, Mike McCormick, Claude Osteen)	2.50	1.25	.70
10a	A.L. Pitching Leaders (Dean Chance, Jim Lonborg, Earl Wilson) ("Lonberg" on back)	3.50	1.75	1.00
10b	A.L. Pitching Leaders (Dean Chance, Jim Lonborg, Earl Wilson) ("Lonberg" on back)	1.50	.70	.45
11	N.L. Strikeout Leaders (Jim Bunning, Ferguson Jenkins, Gaylord Perry)	3.00	1.50	.90
12	A.L. Strikeout Leaders (Dean Chance, Jim Lonborg, Sam McDowell)	1.50	.70	.45
13	Chuck Hartenstein	.60	.30	.20
14	Jerry McNertney	.60	.30	.20
15	Ron Hunt	.70	.35	.20
16	Indians Rookies (Lou Piniella, Richie Scheinblum)	2.50	1.25	.70
17	Dick Hall	.60	.30	.20
18	Mike Hershberger	.60	.30	.20
19	Juan Pizarro	.60	.30	.20
20	Brooks Robinson	15.00	7.50	4.50
21	Ron Davis	.60	.30	.20
22	Pat Dobson	.70	.35	.20
23	Chico Cardenas	.60	.30	.20
24	Bobby Locke	.60	.30	.20
25	Julian Javier	.70	.35	.20
26	Darrell Brandon	.60	.30	.20
27	Gil Hodges	6.00	3.00	1.75
28	Ted Uhlaender	.60	.30	.20
29	Joe Verbanic	.90	.45	.25
30	Joe Torre	2.00	1.00	.60
31	Ed Stroud	.60	.30	.20
32	Joe Gibbon	.60	.30	.20
33	Pete Ward	.60	.30	.20
34	Al Ferrara	.60	.30	.20
35	Steve Hargan	.60	.30	.20
36	Pirates Rookies (Bob Moose, *Bob Robertson*)	.90	.45	.25
37	Billy Williams	7.00	3.50	2.00
38	Tony Pierce	.60	.30	.20
39	Cookie Rojas	.60	.30	.20
40	Denny McLain	3.75	2.00	1.25
41	Julio Gotay	.60	.30	.20
42	Larry Haney	.60	.30	.20
43	Gary Bell	.60	.30	.20
44	Frank Kostro	.60	.30	.20
45	Tom Seaver	200.00	100.00	60.00
46	Dave Ricketts	.60	.30	.20
47	Ralph Houk	1.75	.90	.50
48	Ted Davidson	.60	.30	.20
49a	Ed Brinkman (yellow team letters)	60.00	30.00	18.00
49b	Ed Brinkman (white team letters)	.70	.35	.20
50	Willie Mays	50.00	25.00	15.00
51	Bob Locker	.60	.30	.20
52	Hawk Taylor	.60	.30	.20
53	Gene Alley	.70	.35	.20
54	Stan Williams	.60	.30	.20
55	Felipe Alou	1.00	.50	.30
56	Orioles Rookies (Dave Leonhard, Dave May)	.60	.30	.20
57	Dan Schneider	.60	.30	.20
58	Ed Mathews	9.00	4.50	2.75
59	Don Lock	.60	.30	.20
60	Ken Holtzman	1.00	.50	.30
61	Reggie Smith	1.50	.70	.45
62	Chuck Dobson	.60	.30	.20
63	Dick Kenworthy	.70	.35	.20
64	Jim Merritt	.60	.30	.20
65	John Roseboro	.90	.45	.25
66a	Casey Cox (yellow team letters)	60.00	30.00	18.00
66b	Casey Cox (white team letters)	.60	.30	.20
67	Checklist 1-109 (Jim Kaat)	3.00	1.50	.90
68	Ron Willis	.60	.30	.20
69	Tom Tresh	1.75	.90	.50
70	Bob Veale	.70	.35	.20
71	Vern Fuller	.60	.30	.20
72	Tommy John	5.00	2.50	1.50
73	Jim Hart	.70	.35	.20
74	Milt Pappas	.90	.45	.25
75	Don Mincher	.70	.35	.20
76	Braves Rookies (Jim Britton, *Ron Reed*)	1.00	.50	.30
77	*Don Wilson*	.90	.45	.25
78	Jim Northrup	.70	.35	.20
79	Ted Kubiak	.60	.30	.20
80	Rod Carew	125.00	62.00	37.00
81	Larry Jackson	.60	.30	.20
82	Sam Bowens	.60	.30	.20

		NR MT	EX	VG
83	John Stephenson	.60	.30	.20
84	Bob Tolan	.70	.35	.20
85	Gaylord Perry	8.00	4.00	2.50
86	Willie Stargell	8.00	4.00	2.50
87	Dick Williams	1.00	.50	.30
88	Phil Regan	.60	.30	.20
89	Jake Gibbs	.90	.45	.25
90	Vada Pinson	2.00	1.00	.60
91	Jim Ollom	.60	.30	.20
92	Ed Kranepool	.90	.45	.25
93	Tony Cloninger	.70	.35	.20
94	Lee Maye	.60	.30	.20
95	Bob Aspromonte	.60	.30	.20
96	Senators Rookies (Frank Coggins, Dick Nold)	.60	.30	.20
97	Tom Phoebus	.60	.30	.20
98	Gary Sutherland	.60	.30	.20
99	Rocky Colavito	2.25	1.25	.70
100	Bob Gibson	10.00	5.00	3.00
101	Glenn Beckert	.90	.45	.25
102	Jose Cardenal	.70	.35	.25
103	Don Sutton	6.00	3.00	1.75
104	Dick Dietz	.60	.30	.20
105	Al Downing	1.25	.60	.40
106	Dalton Jones	.60	.30	.20
107	Checklist 110-196 (Juan Marichal)	3.50	1.75	1.00
108	Don Pavletich	.60	.30	.20
109	Bert Campaneris	1.00	.50	.30
110	Hank Aaron	40.00	20.00	12.00
111	Rich Reese	.60	.30	.20
112	Woody Fryman	.70	.35	.20
113	Tigers Rookies (Tom Matchick, Daryl Patterson)	.60	.30	.20
114	Ron Swoboda	.90	.45	.25
115	Sam McDowell	.90	.45	.25
116	Ken McMullen	.60	.30	.20
117	Larry Jaster	.60	.30	.20
118	Mark Belanger	1.00	.50	.30
119	Ted Savage	.60	.30	.20
120	Mel Stottlemyre	2.00	1.00	.60
121	Jimmie Hall	.60	.30	.20
122	Gene Mauch	.90	.45	.25
123	Jose Santiago	.60	.30	.20
124	Nate Oliver	.60	.30	.20
125	Joe Horlen	.60	.30	.20
126	Bobby Etheridge	.60	.30	.20
127	Paul Lindblad	.60	.30	.20
128	Astros Rookies (Tom Dukes, Alonzo Harris)	.60	.30	.20
129	Mickey Stanley	.70	.35	.20
130	Tony Perez	5.00	2.50	1.50
131	Frank Bertaina	.60	.30	.20
132	Bud Harrelson	1.00	.50	.30
133	Fred Whitfield	.60	.30	.20
134	Pat Jarvis	.60	.30	.20
135	Paul Blair	.70	.35	.20
136	Randy Hundley	.60	.30	.20
137	Twins Team	2.00	1.00	.60
138	Ruben Amaro	.90	.45	.25
139	Chris Short	.90	.45	.25
140	Tony Conigliaro	1.50	.70	.45
141	Dal Maxvill	.70	.35	.20
142	White Sox Rookies (Buddy Bradford, Bill Voss)	.60	.30	.20
143	Pete Cimino	.60	.30	.20
144	Joe Morgan	15.00	7.50	4.50
145	Don Drysdale	8.00	4.00	2.50
146	Sal Bando	1.00	.50	.30
147	Frank Linzy	.60	.30	.20
148	Dave Bristol	.60	.30	.20
149	Bob Saverine	.60	.30	.20
150	Bob Clemente	40.00	20.00	12.00
151	World Series Game 1 (Brock Socks 4-Hits In Opener)	3.50	1.75	1.00
152	World Series Game 2 (Yaz Smashes Two Homers)	5.00	2.50	1.50
153	World Series Game 3 (Briles Cools Off Boston)	2.00	1.00	.60
154	World Series Game 4 (Gibson Hurls Shutout!)	3.50	1.75	1.00
155	World Series Game 5 (Lonborg Wins Again!)	2.50	1.25	.70
156	World Series Game 6 (Petrocelli Socks Two Homers)	2.50	1.25	.70
157	World Series Game 7 (St. Louis Wins It!)	2.00	1.00	.60
158	World Series Summary (The Cardinals Celebrate!)	2.00	1.00	.60
159	Don Kessinger	.90	.45	.25
160	Earl Wilson	.70	.35	.20

	NR MT	EX	VG
161 Norm Miller	.60	.30	.20
162 Cardinals Rookies (Hal Gilson, *Mike Torrez*)	1.00	.50	.30
163 Gene Brabender	.60	.30	.20
164 Ramon Webster	.60	.30	.20
165 Tony Oliva	2.50	1.25	.70
166 Claude Raymond	.60	.30	.20
167 Elston Howard	3.00	1.50	.90
168 Dodgers Team	2.50	1.25	.70
169 Bob Bolin	.60	.30	.20
170 Jim Fregosi	1.00	.50	.30
171 Don Nottebart	.60	.30	.20
172 Walt Williams	.60	.30	.20
173 John Boozer	.60	.30	.20
174 Bob Tillman	.60	.30	.20
175 Maury Wills	3.50	1.75	1.00
176 Bob Allen	.60	.30	.20
177 Mets Rookies (*Jerry Koosman, Nolan Ryan*)	1400.00	700.00	425.00
178 Don Wert	.70	.35	.20
179 Bill Stoneman	.60	.30	.20
180 Curt Flood	1.50	.70	.45
181 Jerry Zimmerman	.60	.30	.20
182 Dave Giusti	.60	.30	.20
183 Bob Kennedy	.60	.30	.20
184 Lou Johnson	.60	.30	.20
185 Tom Haller	.70	.35	.20
186 Eddie Watt	.60	.30	.20
187 Sonny Jackson	.60	.30	.20
188 Cap Peterson	.60	.30	.20
189 Bill Landis	.60	.30	.20
190 Bill White	1.00	.50	.30
191 Dan Frisella	.70	.35	.20
192a Checklist 197-283 (Carl Yastrzemski) ("To increase the..." on back)	4.50	2.25	1.25
192b Checklist 197-283 (Carl Yastrzemski) ("To increase your..." on back)	6.00	3.00	1.75
193 Jack Hamilton	.60	.30	.20
194 Don Buford	.70	.35	.20
195 Joe Pepitone	2.00	1.00	.60
196 Gary Nolan	.60	.30	.20
197 Larry Brown	.60	.30	.20
198 Roy Face	1.25	.60	.40
199 A's Rookies (Darrell Osteen, Roberto Rodriguez)	.60	.30	.20
200 Orlando Cepeda	4.00	2.00	1.25
201 *Mike Marshall*	1.75	.90	.50
202 Adolfo Phillips	.60	.30	.20
203 Dick Kelley	.60	.30	.20
204 Andy Etchebarren	.60	.30	.20
205 Juan Marichal	8.00	4.00	2.50
206 Cal Ermer	.60	.30	.20
207 Carroll Sembera	.60	.30	.20
208 Willie Davis	1.00	.50	.30
209 Tim Cullen	.60	.30	.20
210 Gary Peters	.70	.35	.20
211 J.C. Martin	.70	.35	.20
212 Dave Morehead	.60	.30	.20
213 Chico Ruiz	.60	.30	.20
214 Yankees Rookies (Stan Bahnsen, Frank Fernandez)	1.00	.50	.30
215 Jim Bunning	4.50	2.25	1.25
216 Bubba Morton	.60	.30	.20
217 Turk Farrell	.60	.30	.20
218 Ken Suarez	.60	.30	.20
219 Rob Gardner	.60	.30	.20
220 Harmon Killebrew	9.00	4.50	2.75
221 Braves Team	2.00	1.00	.60
222 Jim Hardin	.60	.30	.20
223 Ollie Brown	.60	.30	.20
224 Jack Aker	.60	.30	.20
225 Richie Allen	2.25	1.25	.70
226 Jimmie Price	.60	.30	.20
227 Joe Hoerner	.60	.30	.20
228 Dodgers Rookies (*Jack Billingham*, Jim Fairey)	.80	.40	.25
229 Fred Klages	.60	.30	.20
230 Pete Rose	50.00	25.00	15.00
231 Dave Baldwin	.60	.30	.20
232 Denis Menke	.60	.30	.20
233 George Scott	.90	.45	.25
234 Bill Monbouquette	.90	.45	.25
235 Ron Santo	1.50	.70	.45
236 Tug McGraw	1.75	.90	.50
237 Alvin Dark	.90	.45	.25
238 Tom Satriano	.60	.30	.20
239 Bill Henry	.60	.30	.20
240 Al Kaline	10.00	5.00	3.00
241 Felix Millan	.70	.35	.20
242 Moe Drabowsky	.60	.30	.20
243 Rich Rollins	.60	.30	.20
244 John Donaldson	.60	.30	.20
245 Tony Gonzalez	.60	.30	.20
246 Fritz Peterson	1.00	.50	.30
247 Red Rookies (*Johnny Bench*, Ron Tompkins)	300.00	120.00	75.00
248 Fred Valentine	.60	.30	.20
249 Bill Singer	.80	.40	.25
250 Carl Yastrzemski	35.00	17.50	10.50
251 *Manny Sanguillen*	1.25	.60	.40
252 Angels Team	2.00	1.00	.60
253 Dick Hughes	.60	.30	.20
254 Cleon Jones	.90	.45	.25
255 Dean Chance	.70	.35	.20
256 Norm Cash	2.00	1.00	.60
257 Phil Niekro	5.00	2.50	1.50
258 Cubs Rookies (Jose Arcia, Bill Schlesinger)	.60	.30	.20
259 Ken Boyer	1.75	.90	.50
260 Jim Wynn	.90	.45	.25
261 Dave Duncan	.60	.30	.20
262 Rick Wise	.70	.35	.20
263 Horace Clarke	.90	.45	.25
264 Ted Abernathy	.60	.30	.20
265 Tommy Davis	1.50	.70	.45
266 Paul Popovich	.60	.30	.20
267 Herman Franks	.60	.30	.20
268 Bob Humphreys	.60	.30	.20
269 Bob Tiefenauer	.60	.30	.20
270 Matty Alou	1.00	.50	.30
271 Bobby Knoop	.60	.30	.20
272 Ray Culp	.60	.30	.20
273 Dave Johnson	1.75	.90	.50
274 Mike Cuellar	.90	.45	.25
275 Tim McCarver	1.75	.90	.50
276 Jim Roland	.60	.30	.20
277 Jerry Buchek	.70	.35	.20
278a Checklist 284-370 (Orlando Cepeda) (copyright at right)	3.00	1.50	.90
278b Checklist 284-370 (Orlando Cepeda) (copyright at left)	5.00	2.50	1.50
279 Bill Hands	.60	.30	.20
280 Mickey Mantle	200.00	100.00	60.00
281 Jim Campanis	.60	.30	.20
282 Rick Monday	1.25	.60	.40
283 Mel Queen	.60	.30	.20
284 John Briggs	.60	.30	.20
285 Dick McAuliffe	.80	.40	.25
286 Cecil Upshaw	.60	.30	.20
287 White Sox Rookies (Mickey Abarbanel, Cisco Carlos)	.60	.30	.20
288 Dave Wickersham	.60	.30	.20
289 Woody Held	.60	.30	.20
290 Willie McCovey	8.00	4.00	2.50
291 Dick Lines	.60	.30	.20
292 Art Shamsky	.80	.40	.25
293 Bruce Howard	.60	.30	.20
294 Red Schoendienst	1.50	.70	.45
295 Sonny Siebert	.60	.30	.20
296 Byron Browne	.60	.30	.20
297 Russ Gibson	.60	.30	.20
298 Jim Brewer	.60	.30	.20
299 Gene Michael	1.00	.50	.30
300 Rusty Staub	2.00	1.00	.60
301 Twins Rookies (George Mitterwald, Rick Renick)	.60	.30	.20
302 Gerry Arrigo	.60	.30	.20
303 Dick Green	.60	.30	.20
304 Sandy Valdespino	.60	.30	.20
305 Minnie Rojas	.60	.30	.20
306 Mike Ryan	.60	.30	.20
307 John Hiller	.90	.45	.25
308 Pirates Team	2.00	1.00	.60
309 Ken Henderson	.60	.30	.20
310 Luis Aparicio	5.00	2.50	1.50
311 Jack Lamabe	.60	.30	.20
312 Curt Blefary	.60	.30	.20
313 Al Weis	.70	.35	.20
314 Red Sox Rookies (Bill Rohr, George Spriggs)	.60	.30	.20
315 Zoilo Versalles	.70	.35	.20
316 Steve Barber	.90	.45	.25
317 Ron Brand	.60	.30	.20
318 Chico Salmon	.60	.30	.20
319 George Culver	.60	.30	.20
320 Frank Howard	2.00	1.00	.60
321 Leo Durocher	2.25	1.25	.70
322 Dave Boswell	.70	.35	.20
323 Deron Johnson	.60	.30	.20
324 Jim Nash	.60	.30	.20
325 Manny Mota	.90	.45	.25
326 Dennis Ribant	.60	.30	.20

		NR MT	EX	VG
327	Tony Taylor	.60	.30	.20
328	Angels Rookies (Chuck Vinson, Jim Weaver)	.60	.30	.20
329	Duane Josephson	.60	.30	.20
330	Roger Maris	40.00	20.00	12.00
331	Dan Osinski	.60	.30	.20
332	Doug Rader	.70	.35	.20
333	Ron Herbel	.60	.30	.20
334	Orioles Team	2.00	1.00	.60
335	Bob Allison	1.00	.50	.30
336	John Purdin	.60	.30	.20
337	Bill Robinson	.90	.45	.25
338	Bob Johnson	.60	.30	.20
339	Rich Nye	.60	.30	.20
340	Max Alvis	.60	.30	.20
341	Jim Lemon	.60	.30	.20
342	Ken Johnson	.60	.30	.20
343	Jim Gosger	.60	.30	.20
344	Donn Clendenon	.70	.35	.20
345	Bob Hendley	.70	.35	.20
346	Jerry Adair	.60	.30	.20
347	George Brunet	.60	.30	.20
348	Phillies Rookies (Larry Colton, Dick Thoenen)	.60	.30	.20
349	Ed Spiezio	.60	.30	.20
350	Hoyt Wilhelm	6.00	3.00	1.75
351	Bob Barton	.60	.30	.20
352	Jackie Hernandez	.60	.30	.20
353	Mack Jones	.60	.30	.20
354	Pete Richert	.60	.30	.20
355	Ernie Banks	15.00	7.50	4.50
356	Checklist 371-457 (Ken Holtzman)	2.50	1.25	.70
357	Len Gabrielson	.60	.30	.20
358	Mike Epstein	.70	.35	.20
359	Joe Moeller	.60	.30	.20
360	Willie Horton	.90	.45	.25
361	Harmon Killebrew AS	5.00	2.50	1.50
362	Orlando Cepeda AS	2.75	1.50	.80
363	Rod Carew AS	10.00	5.00	3.00
364	Joe Morgan AS	3.00	1.50	.90
365	Brooks Robinson AS	6.00	3.00	1.75
366	Ron Santo AS	1.75	.90	.50
367	Jim Fregosi AS	1.00	.50	.30
368	Gene Alley AS	1.00	.50	.30
369	Carl Yastrzemski AS	15.00	7.50	4.50
370	Hank Aaron AS	15.00	7.50	4.50
371	Tony Oliva AS	2.00	1.00	.60
372	Lou Brock AS	5.00	2.50	1.50
373	Frank Robinson AS	5.00	2.50	1.50
374	Bob Clemente AS	15.00	7.50	4.50
375	Bill Freehan AS	1.00	.50	.30
376	Tim McCarver AS	1.50	.70	.45
377	Joe Horlen AS	1.00	.50	.30
378	Bob Gibson AS	5.00	2.50	1.50
379	Gary Peters AS	1.00	.50	.30
380	Ken Holtzman AS	1.00	.50	.30
381	Boog Powell	2.50	1.25	.70
382	Ramon Hernandez	.60	.30	.20
383	Steve Whitaker	.90	.45	.25
384	Reds Rookies (Bill Henry, *Hal McRae*)	6.00	3.00	1.75
385	Jim Hunter	10.00	5.00	3.00
386	Greg Goossen	.70	.35	.20
387	Joe Foy	.60	.30	.20
388	Ray Washburn	.60	.30	.20
389	Jay Johnstone	.90	.45	.25
390	Bill Mazeroski	1.75	.90	.50
391	Bob Priddy	.60	.30	.20
392	Grady Hatton	.60	.30	.20
393	Jim Perry	1.00	.50	.30
394	Tommie Aaron	.90	.45	.25
395	Camilo Pascual	.90	.45	.25
396	Bobby Wine	.60	.30	.20
397	Vic Davalillo	.70	.35	.20
398	Jim Grant	.60	.30	.20
399	Ray Oyler	.70	.35	.20
400a	Mike McCormick (white team letters)	40.00	20.00	12.00
400b	Mike McCormick (yellow team letters)	.70	.35	.20
401	Mets Team	3.25	1.75	1.00
402	Mike Hegan	1.00	.50	.30
403	John Buzhardt	.60	.30	.20
404	Floyd Robinson	.60	.30	.20
405	Tommy Helms	.70	.35	.20
406	Dick Ellsworth	.60	.30	.20
407	Gary Kolb	.60	.30	.20
408	Steve Carlton	70.00	35.00	21.00
409	Orioles Rookies (Frank Peters, Ron Stone)	.60	.30	.20
410	Ferguson Jenkins	3.50	1.75	1.00
411	Ron Hansen	.60	.30	.20
412	Clay Carroll	.70	.35	.20
413	Tommy McCraw	.60	.30	.20
414	Mickey Lolich	2.75	1.50	.80
415	Johnny Callison	1.00	.50	.30
416	Bill Rigney	.60	.30	.20
417	Willie Crawford	.60	.30	.20
418	Eddie Fisher	.60	.30	.20
419	Jack Hiatt	.60	.30	.20
420	Cesar Tovar	.60	.30	.20
421	Ron Taylor	.70	.35	.20
422	Rene Lachemann	.60	.30	.20
423	Fred Gladding	.60	.30	.20
424	White Sox Team	2.00	1.00	.60
425	Jim Maloney	.70	.35	.20
426	Hank Allen	.60	.30	.20
427	Dick Calmus	.60	.30	.20
428	Vic Roznovsky	.60	.30	.20
429	Tommie Sisk	.60	.30	.20
430	Rico Petrocelli	.90	.45	.25
431	Dooley Womack	.90	.45	.25
432	Indians Rookies (Bill Davis, Jose Vidal)	.60	.30	.20
433	Bob Rodgers	.90	.45	.25
434	Ricardo Joseph	.60	.30	.20
435	Ron Perranoski	.70	.35	.20
436	Hal Lanier	.90	.45	.25
437	Don Cardwell	.70	.35	.20
438	Lee Thomas	.60	.30	.20
439	Luman Harris	.60	.30	.20
440	Claude Osteen	.90	.45	.25
441	Alex Johnson	.60	.30	.20
442	Dick Bosman	.60	.30	.20
443	Joe Azcue	.60	.30	.20
444	Jack Fisher	.60	.30	.20
445	Mike Shannon	.70	.35	.20
446	Ron Kline	.60	.30	.20
447	Tigers Rookies (George Korince, Fred Lasher)	.60	.30	.20
448	Gary Wagner	.60	.30	.20
449	Gene Oliver	.60	.30	.20
450	Jim Kaat	6.00	3.00	1.75
451	Al Spangler	.60	.30	.20
452	Jesus Alou	.70	.35	.20
453	Sammy Ellis	.60	.30	.20
454	Checklist 458-533 (Frank Robinson)	4.00	2.00	1.25
455	Rico Carty	1.00	.50	.30
456	John O'Donoghue	.60	.30	.20
457	Jim Lefebvre	.70	.35	.20
458	Lew Krausse	.60	.30	.20
459	Dick Simpson	.60	.30	.20
460	Jim Lonborg	1.00	.50	.30
461	Chuck Hiller	.60	.30	.20
462	Barry Moore	.60	.30	.20
463	Jimmie Schaffer	.60	.30	.20
464	Don McMahon	.60	.30	.20
465	Tommie Agee	.90	.45	.25
466	Bill Dillman	.60	.30	.20
467	Dick Howser	1.50	.70	.45
468	Larry Sherry	.60	.30	.20
469	Ty Cline	.60	.30	.20
470	Bill Freehan	1.00	.50	.30
471	Orlando Pena	.60	.30	.20
472	Walt Alston	2.50	1.25	.70
473	Al Worthington	.60	.30	.20
474	Paul Schaal	.60	.30	.20
475	Joe Niekro	2.25	1.25	.70
476	Woody Woodward	.70	.35	.20
477	Phillies Team	2.00	1.00	.60
478	Dave McNally	1.00	.50	.30
479	Phil Gagliano	.60	.30	.20
480	Manager's Dream (Chico Cardenas, Bob Clemente, Tony Oliva)	15.00	7.50	4.50
481	John Wyatt	.60	.30	.20
482	Jose Pagan	.60	.30	.20
483	Darold Knowles	.60	.30	.20
484	Phil Roof	.60	.30	.20
485	Ken Berry	.60	.30	.20
486	Cal Koonce	.70	.35	.20
487	Lee May	1.25	.60	.40
488	Dick Tracewski	.60	.30	.20
489	Wally Bunker	.60	.30	.20
490	Super Stars (Harmon Killebrew, Mickey Mantle, Willie Mays)	80.00	40.00	24.00
491	Denny Lemaster	.60	.30	.20
492	Jeff Torborg	.70	.35	.20
493	Jim McGlothlin	.60	.30	.20
494	Ray Sadecki	.60	.30	.20
495	Leon Wagner	.70	.35	.20

		NR MT	EX	VG
496	Steve Hamilton	.90	.45	.25
497	Cards Team	3.50	1.75	1.00
498	Bill Bryan	.60	.30	.20
499	Steve Blass	.70	.35	.20
500	Frank Robinson	10.00	5.00	3.00
501	John Odom	.70	.35	.20
502	Mike Andrews	.60	.30	.20
503	Al Jackson	.70	.35	.20
504	Russ Snyder	.60	.30	.20
505	Joe Sparma	.70	.35	.20
506	Clarence Jones	.60	.30	.20
507	Wade Blasingame	.60	.30	.20
508	Duke Sims	.60	.30	.20
509	Dennis Higgins	.60	.30	.20
510	Ron Fairly	.90	.45	.25
511	Bill Kelso	.60	.30	.20
512	Grant Jackson	.60	.30	.20
513	Hank Bauer	.90	.45	.25
514	Al McBean	.60	.30	.20
515	Russ Nixon	.60	.30	.20
516	Pete Mikkelsen	.60	.30	.20
517	Diego Segui	.60	.30	.20
518a	Checklist 534-598 (Clete Boyer) (539 is Maj. L. Rookies)	3.00	1.50	.90
518b	Checklist 534-598 (Clete Boyer) (539 is Amer. L. Rookies)	5.00	2.50	1.50
519	Jerry Stephenson	.60	.30	.20
520	Lou Brock	18.00	9.00	5.50
521	Don Shaw	.70	.35	.20
522	Wayne Causey	.60	.30	.20
523	John Tsitouris	.60	.30	.20
524	Andy Kosco	.90	.45	.25
525	Jim Davenport	.60	.30	.20
526	Bill Denehy	.60	.30	.20
527	Tito Francona	.70	.35	.20
528	Tigers Team	25.00	12.50	7.50
529	Bruce Von Hoff	.60	.30	.20
530	Bird Belters (Brooks Robinson, Frank Robinson)	7.00	3.50	2.00
531	Chuck Hinton	.60	.30	.20
532	Luis Tiant	1.75	.90	.50
533	Wes Parker	.90	.45	.25
534	Bob Miller	1.00	.50	.30
535	Danny Cater	1.00	.50	.30
536	Bill Short	1.25	.60	.40
537	Norm Siebern	1.00	.50	.30
538	Manny Jimenez	1.00	.50	.30
539	Major League Rookies (Mike Ferraro, Jim Ray)	1.25	.60	.40
540	Nelson Briles	1.00	.50	.30
541	Sandy Alomar	1.00	.50	.30
542	John Boccabella	1.00	.50	.30
543	Bob Lee	1.00	.50	.30
544	Mayo Smith	1.25	.60	.40
545	Lindy McDaniel	1.00	.50	.30
546	Roy White	2.50	1.25	.70
547	Dan Coombs	1.00	.50	.30
548	Bernie Allen	1.00	.50	.30
549	Orioles Rookies (Curt Motton, Roger Nelson)	1.00	.50	.30
550	Clete Boyer	1.25	.60	.40
551	Darrell Sutherland	1.00	.50	.30
552	Ed Kirkpatrick	1.00	.50	.30
553	Hank Aguirre	1.00	.50	.30
554	A's Team	3.00	1.50	.90
555	Jose Tartabull	1.00	.50	.30
556	Dick Selma	1.25	.60	.40
557	Frank Quilici	1.00	.50	.30
558	Jim Edwards	1.00	.50	.30
559	Pirates Rookies (Carl Taylor, Luke Walker)	1.00	.50	.30
560	Paul Casanova	1.00	.50	.30
561	Lee Elia	1.00	.50	.30
562	Jim Bouton	2.50	1.25	.70
563	Ed Charles	1.25	.60	.40
564	Eddie Stanky	1.25	.60	.40
565	Larry Dierker	1.25	.60	.40
566	Ken Harrelson	2.00	1.00	.60
567	Clay Dalrymple	1.00	.50	.30
568	Willie Smith	1.00	.50	.30
569	N.L. Rookies (Ivan Murrell, Les Rohr)	1.25	.60	.40
570	Rick Reichardt	1.00	.50	.30
571	Tony LaRussa	1.75	.90	.50
572	Don Bosch	1.25	.60	.40
573	Joe Coleman	1.25	.60	.40
574	Reds Team	3.00	1.50	.90
575	Jim Palmer	50.00	25.00	15.00
576	Dave Adlesh	1.00	.50	.30
577	Fred Talbot	1.25	.60	.40
578	Orlando Martinez	1.00	.50	.30

		NR MT	EX	VG
579	N.L. Rookies (Larry Hisle, Mike Lum)	1.75	.90	.50
580	Bob Bailey	1.00	.50	.30
581	Garry Roggenburk	1.00	.50	.30
582	Jerry Grote	1.25	.60	.40
583	Gates Brown	1.25	.60	.40
584	Larry Shepard	1.00	.50	.30
585	Wilbur Wood	1.25	.60	.40
586	Jim Pagliaroni	1.00	.50	.30
587	Roger Repoz	1.00	.50	.30
588	Dick Schofield	1.00	.50	.30
589	Twins Rookies (Ron Clark, Moe Ogier)	1.00	.50	.30
590	Tommy Harper	1.25	.60	.40
591	Dick Nen	1.00	.50	.30
592	John Bateman	1.00	.50	.30
593	Lee Stange	1.00	.50	.30
594	Phil Linz	1.25	.60	.40
595	Phil Ortega	1.00	.50	.30
596	Charlie Smith	1.25	.60	.40
597	Bill McCool	1.00	.50	.30
598	Jerry May	2.00	.60	.30

1968 Topps
Action All-Star Stickers

Still another of the many Topps test issues of the late 1960s, the Action All-Star stickers were sold in a strip of three, with bubblegum, for 10¢. The strip is comprised of three 3-1/4" by 5-1/4" panels, perforated at the joints for separation. The central panel which is numbered, contains a large color picture of a star player. The top and bottom panels contains smaller pictures of three players each. While there are 16 numbered center panels, only 12 of them are different; panels 13-16 show players previously used. Similarly, the triple-player panels at top and bottom of stickers 13-16 repeat panels from #'s 1-4. Prices below are for stickers which have all three panels still joined. Individual panels are priced signicantly lower.

		NR MT	EX	VG
	Complete Set:	1300.00	650.00	390.00
	Common Player:	18.00	9.00	5.50
1	Orlando Cepeda, Joe Horlen, Al Kaline, Bill Mazeroski, Claude Osteen, Mel Stottlemyre, Carl Yastrzemski	100.00	50.00	30.00
2	Don Drysdale, Harmon Killebrew, Mike McCormick, Tom Phoebus, George Scott, Ron Swoboda, Pete Ward	30.00	15.00	9.00
3	Hank Aaron, Paul Casanova, Jim Maloney, Joe Pepitone, Rick Reichardt, Frank Robinson, Tom Seaver	35.00	17.50	10.50
4	Bob Aspromonte, Johnny Callison, Dean Chance, Jim Lefebvre, Jim Lonborg, Frank Robinson, Ron Santo	25.00	12.50	7.50
5	Bert Campaneris, Al Downing, Willie Horton, Ed Kranepool, Willie Mays, Pete Rose, Ron Santo	200.00	100.00	60.00
6	Max Alvis, Ernie Banks, Al Kaline, Tim McCarver, Rusty Staub, Walt Williams, Carl Yastrzemski	70.00	35.00	21.00
7	Rod Carew, Tony Gonzalez, Steve Hargan, Mickey Mantle, Willie McCovey, Rick Monday, Billy Williams	300.00	150.00	90.00

		NR MT	EX	VG
8	Clete Boyer, Jim Bunning, Tony Conigliaro, Mike Cuellar, Joe Horlen, Ken McMullen, Don Mincher	18.00	9.00	5.50
9	Orlando Cepeda, Bob Clemente, Jim Fregosi, Harmon Killebrew, Willie Mays, Chris Short, Earl Wilson	20.00		12.00
10	Hank Aaron, Bob Gibson, Bud Harrelson, Jim Hunter, Mickey Mantle, Gary Peters, Vada Pinson	100.00	50.00	30.00
11	Don Drysdale, Bill Freehan, Frank Howard, Ferguson Jenkins, Tony Oliva, Bob Veale, Jim Wynn	30.00	15.00	9.00
12	Richie Allen, Bob Clemente, Sam McDowell, Jim McGlothlin, Tony Perez, Brooks Robinson, Joe Torre	100.00	50.00	30.00
13	Dean Chance, Don Drysdale, Jim Lefebvre, Tom Phoebus, Frank Robinson, George Scott, Carl Yastrzemski	100.00	50.00	30.00
14	Paul Casanova, Orlando Cepeda, Joe Horlen, Harmon Killebrew, Bill Mazeroski, Rick Reichardt, Tom Seaver	35.00	17.50	10.50
15	Bob Aspromonte, Johnny Callison, Jim Lonborg, Mike McCormick, Frank Robinson, Ron Swoboda, Pete Ward	30.00	15.00	9.00
16	Hank Aaron, Al Kaline, Jim Maloney, Claude Osteen, Joe Pepitone, Ron Santo, Mel Stottlemyre	30.00	15.00	9.00

1968 Topps Discs

One of the scarcest of all Topps collectibles, this 28-player set was apparently a never-completed test issue. These full-color, cardboard discs, which measure approximately 2-1/8" in diameter, were apparently intended to be made into a "pin" set, but for some reason, production was never completed and no actual "pins" are known to exist. Uncut sheets of the player discs have been found, however. The discs include a player portrait photo with the name beneath and the city and team nickname along the sides. The set includes eight Hall of Famers.

		NR MT	EX	VG
	Complete Set:	3500.00	1750.00	1050.
	Common Player:	35.00	17.50	10.50
(1)	Hank Aaron	250.00	125.00	75.00
(2)	Richie Allen	60.00	30.00	18.00
(3)	Gene Alley	35.00	17.50	10.50
(4)	Rod Carew	300.00	150.00	90.00
(5)	Orlando Cepeda	60.00	30.00	18.00
(6)	Dean Chance	35.00	17.50	10.50
(7)	Bob Clemente	350.00	175.00	100.00
(8)	Tommy Davis	35.00	17.50	10.50
(9)	Bill Freehan	35.00	17.50	10.50
(10)	Jim Fregosi	35.00	17.50	10.50
(11)	Steve Hargan	35.00	17.50	10.50
(12)	Frank Howard	60.00	30.00	18.00
(13)	Al Kaline	200.00	100.00	60.00
(14)	Harmon Killebrew	150.00	75.00	45.00
(15)	Mickey Mantle	600.00	300.00	175.00
(16)	Willie Mays	300.00	150.00	90.00
(17)	Mike McCormick	35.00	17.50	10.50
(18)	Rick Monday	35.00	17.50	10.50
(19)	Claude Osteen	35.00	17.50	10.50
(20)	Gary Peters	35.00	17.50	10.50
(21)	Brooks Robinson	200.00	100.00	60.00
(22)	Frank Robinson	150.00	75.00	45.00

		NR MT	EX	VG
(23)	Pete Rose	400.00	200.00	125.00
(24)	Ron Santo	60.00	30.00	18.00
(25)	Rusty Staub	60.00	30.00	18.00
(26)	Joe Torre	60.00	30.00	18.00
(27)	Carl Yastrzemski	150.00	75.00	45.00
(28)	Bob Veale	35.00	17.50	10.50

1968 Topps Game

A throwback to the Red and Blue Back sets of 1951, the 33-cards in the 1968 Topps Game set, inserted into packs of regular '68 Topps cards or purchases as a complete boxed set, enable the owner to play a game of baseball based on the game situations on each card. Also on the 2-1/4" by 3-1/4" cards were a color photograph of a player and his facsimile autograph. One redeeming social value of the set (assuming you're not mesmerized by the game) is that it affords an inexpensive way to get big-name cards as the set is loaded with stars, but not at all popular with collectors.

		NR MT	EX	VG
	Complete Set:	55.00	27.00	16.50
	Common Player:	.30	.15	.09
1	Mateo Alou	.50	.25	.15
2	Mickey Mantle	15.00	7.50	4.50
3	Carl Yastrzemski	3.25	1.75	1.00
4	Henry Aaron	3.00	1.50	.90
5	Harmon Killebrew	1.75	.90	.50
6	Roberto Clemente	3.00	1.50	.90
7	Frank Robinson	1.75	.90	.50
8	Willie Mays	3.00	1.50	.90
9	Brooks Robinson	2.00	1.00	.60
10	Tommy Davis	.50	.25	.15
11	Bill Freehan	.50	.25	.15
12	Claude Osteen	.40	.20	.12
13	Gary Peters	.30	.15	.09
14	Jim Lonborg	.40	.20	.12
15	Steve Hargan	.30	.15	.09
16	Dean Chance	.40	.20	.12
17	Mike McCormick	.30	.15	.09
18	Tim McCarver	.60	.30	.20
19	Ron Santo	.60	.30	.20
20	Tony Gonzalez	.30	.15	.09
21	Frank Howard	.70	.35	.20
22	George Scott	.40	.20	.12
23	Rich Allen	.70	.35	.20
24	Jim Wynn	.40	.20	.12
25	Gene Alley	.40	.20	.12
26	Rick Monday	.40	.20	.12
27	Al Kaline	2.00	1.00	.60
28	Rusty Staub	.70	.35	.20
29	Rod Carew	2.75	1.50	.80
30	Pete Rose	7.50	3.75	2.25
31	Joe Torre	.70	.35	.20
32	Orlando Cepeda	1.00	.50	.30
33	Jim Fregosi	.50	.25	.15

NOTE: A card number in parentheses ( ) indicates the set is unnumbered.

1968 Topps Plaks

Among the scarcest of the Topps test issues of the late 1960s, the "All Star Baseball Plaks" were plastic busts of two dozen stars of the era which came packaged like model airplane parts. The busts had to be snapped off a sprue and could be inserted into a base which carried the player's name. Packed with the plastic plaks was one of two checklist cards which featured six color photos per side. The 2-1/8" by 4" checklist cards are popular with superstar collectors and are considerably easier to find today than the actual plaks.

		NR MT	EX	VG
Complete Set:		2300.00	1150.00	690.00
Common Player:		20.00	10.00	6.00
1	Max Alvis	20.00	10.00	6.00
2	Frank Howard	30.00	15.00	9.00
3	Dean Chance	20.00	10.00	6.00
4	Jim Hunter	50.00	25.00	15.00
5	Jim Fregosi	25.00	12.50	7.50
6	Al Kaline	60.00	30.00	18.00
7	Harmon Killebrew	60.00	30.00	18.00
8	Gary Peters	20.00	10.00	6.00
9	Jim Lonborg	20.00	10.00	6.00
10	Frank Robinson	60.00	30.00	18.00
11	Mickey Mantle	800.00	400.00	240.00
12	Carl Yastrzemski	175.00	87.00	52.00
13	Hank Aaron	100.00	50.00	30.00
14	Bob Clemente	100.00	50.00	30.00
15	Richie Allen	30.00	15.00	9.00
16	Tommy Davis	25.00	12.50	7.50
17	Orlando Cepeda	30.00	15.00	9.00
18	Don Drysdale	50.00	25.00	15.00
19	Willie Mays	100.00	50.00	30.00
20	Rusty Staub	30.00	15.00	9.00
21	Tim McCarver	30.00	15.00	9.00
22	Pete Rose	250.00	125.00	75.00
23	Ron Santo	30.00	15.00	9.00
24	Jim Wynn	20.00	10.00	6.00
---	Checklist Card 1-12	250.00	125.00	75.00
---	Checklist Card 13-24	250.00	125.00	75.00

A player's name in *italic* indicates a rookie card. An (FC) indicates a player's first card for that particular card company.

1968 Topps Posters

Yet another innovation from the creative minds at

Topps appeared in 1968; a set of color player posters. Measuring 9-3/4" by 18-1/8," each poster was sold separately with its own piece of gum, rather than as an insert. The posters feature a large color photograph with a star at the bottom containing the player's name, position and team. There are 24 different posters which were folded numerous times to fit into the package they were sold in.

		NR MT	EX	VG
Complete Set:		325.00	162.00	97.00
Common Player:		3.00	1.50	.90
1	Dean Chance	3.00	1.50	.90
2	Max Alvis	3.00	1.50	.90
3	Frank Howard	8.00	4.00	2.50
4	Jim Fregosi	7.00	3.50	2.00
5	Jim Hunter	12.00	6.00	3.50
6	Bob Clemente	25.00	12.50	7.50
7	Don Drysdale	12.00	6.00	3.50
8	Jim Wynn	3.00	1.50	.90
9	Al Kaline	25.00	12.50	7.50
10	Harmon Killebrew	20.00	10.00	6.00
11	Jim Lonborg	3.00	1.50	.90
12	Orlando Cepeda	8.00	4.00	2.50
13	Gary Peters	3.00	1.50	.90
14	Hank Aaron	25.00	12.50	7.50
15	Richie Allen	8.00	4.00	2.50
16	Carl Yastrzemski	20.00	10.00	6.00
17	Ron Swoboda	3.00	1.50	.90
18	Mickey Mantle	50.00	25.00	15.00
19	Tim McCarver	7.00	3.50	2.00
20	Willie Mays	25.00	12.50	7.50
21	Ron Santo	7.00	3.50	2.00
22	Rusty Staub	7.00	3.50	2.00
23	Pete Rose	40.00	20.00	12.00
24	Frank Robinson	15.00	7.50	4.50

1968 Topps 3-D

These are very rare pioneer issues on the part of Topps. The cards measure 2-1/4" by 3-1/2" and were specially printed to simulate a three-dimensional effect. Backgrounds are a purposely blurred stadium scene, in front of which was a normally sharp color player photograph. The outer layer is a thin coating of ribbed plastic. The special process gives the picture the illusion of depth when the card is moved or tilted. As this was done two years before Kellogg's began its 3-D cards, this 12-card test issue really was breaking new ground. Unfortunately, production and distribution were limited making the cards very tough to find.

		NR MT	EX	VG
Complete Set:		9000.00	4500.00	2500.
Common Player:		350.00	175.00	105.00
(1)	Bob Clemente	2500.00	1250.00	750.00
(2)	Willie Davis	400.00	200.00	125.00
(3)	Ron Fairly	400.00	200.00	125.00
(4)	Curt Flood	400.00	200.00	125.00
(5)	Jim Lonborg	400.00	200.00	125.00
(6)	Jim Maloney	350.00	175.00	105.00
(7)	Tony Perez	600.00	300.00	175.00
(8)	Boog Powell	500.00	250.00	150.00

		NR MT	EX	VG
(9)	Bill Robinson	350.00	175.00	105.00
(10)	Rusty Staub	450.00	230.00	135.00
(11)	Mel Stottlemyre	400.00	200.00	120.00
(12)	Ron Swoboda	350.00	175.00	105.00

1969 Topps

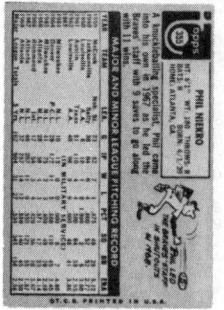

The 1969 Topps set broke yet another record for quantity as the issue is officially a whopping 664 cards. With substantial numbers of variations, the number of possible cards runs closer to 700. The design of the 2-1/2" by 3-1/2" cards in the set feature a color photo with the team name printed in block letters underneath. A circle contains the player's name and position. Card backs returned to a horizontal format. Despite the size of the set, it contains no teamcards. It does, however, have multi-player cards, All-Stars, statistical leaders, and World Series highlights. Most significant among the varieties are white and yellow letter cards from the run of #'s 440-511. The complete set prices below do not include the scarcer and more expensive "white letter" variations.

	NR MT	EX	VG
Complete Set:	2000.00	1000.00	600.00
Common Player: 1-218	.40	.20	.12
Common Player: 219-327	.90	.45	.25
Common Player: 328-512	.40	.20	.12
Common Player: 513-664	.70	.35	.20

		NR MT	EX	VG
1	A.L. Batting Leaders (Danny Cater, Tony Oliva, Carl Yastrzemski)	7.00	2.00	1.00
2	N.L. Batting Leaders (Felipe Alou, Matty Alou, Pete Rose)	4.00	2.00	1.25
3	A.L. RBI Leaders (Ken Harrelson, Frank Howard, Jim Northrup)	2.00	1.00	.60
4	N.L. RBI Leaders (Willie McCovey, Ron Santo, Billy Williams)	3.50	1.75	1.00
5	A.L. Home Run Leaders (Ken Harrelson, Willie Horton, Frank Howard)	2.00	1.00	.60
6	N.L. Home Run Leaders (Richie Allen, Ernie Banks, Willie McCovey)	3.50	1.75	1.00
7	A.L. ERA Leaders (Sam McDowell, Dave McNally, Luis Tiant)	2.00	1.00	.60
8	N.L. ERA Leaders (Bobby Bolin, Bob Gibson, Bob Veale)	3.00	1.50	.90
9	A.L. Pitching Leaders (Denny McLain, Dave McNally, Mel Stottlemyre, Luis Tiant)	2.00	1.00	.60
10	N.L. Pitching Leaders (Bob Gibson, Fergie Jenkins, Juan Marichal)	3.50	1.75	1.00
11	A.L. Strikeout Leaders (Sam McDowell, Denny McLain, Luis Tiant)	2.00	1.00	.60
12	N.L. Strikeout Leaders (Bob Gibson, Fergie Jenkins, Bill Singer)	3.00	1.50	.90
13	Mickey Stanley	.50	.25	.15
14	Al McBean	.40	.20	.12
15	Boog Powell	2.50	1.25	.70
16	Giants Rookies (Cesar Gutierrez, Rich Robertson)	.40	.20	.12
17	Mike Marshall	1.25	.60	.40
18	Dick Schofield	.40	.20	.12
19	Ken Suarez	.40	.20	.12
20	Ernie Banks	15.00	7.50	4.50
21	Jose Santiago	.40	.20	.12
22	Jesus Alou	.50	.25	.15

		NR MT	EX	VG
23	Lew Krausse	.40	.20	.12
24	Walt Alston	3.00	1.50	.90
25	Roy White	1.25	.60	.40
26	Clay Carroll	.50	.25	.15
27	Bernie Allen	.40	.20	.12
28	Mike Ryan	.40	.20	.12
29	Dave Morehead	.40	.20	.12
30	Bob Allison	1.00	.50	.30
31	Mets Rookies (Gary Gentry, Amos Otis)	1.25	.60	.40
32	Sammy Ellis	.40	.20	.12
33	Wayne Causey	.40	.20	.12
34	Gary Peters	.50	.25	.15
35	Joe Morgan	15.00	7.50	4.50
36	Luke Walker	.40	.20	.12
37	Curt Motton	.40	.20	.12
38	Zoilo Versalles	.50	.25	.15
39	Dick Hughes	.40	.20	.12
40	Mayo Smith	.40	.20	.12
41	Bob Barton	.40	.20	.12
42	Tommy Harper	1.00	.50	.30
43	Joe Niekro	1.25	.60	.40
44	Danny Cater	.40	.20	.12
45	Maury Wills	2.50	1.25	.70
46	Fritz Peterson	1.00	.50	.30
47a	Paul Popovich (emblem visible thru airbrush)	4.00	2.00	1.25
47b	Paul Popovich (helmet emblem completely airbrushed)	.40	.20	.12
48	Brant Alyea	.40	.20	.12
49a	Royals Rookies (Steve Jones, Eliseo Rodriquez) (Rodriquez on front)	6.00	3.00	1.75
49b	Royals Rookies (Steve Jones, Eliseo Rodriquez) (Rodriguez on front)	.40	.20	.12
50	Bob Clemente	40.00	20.00	12.00
51	Woody Fryman	.50	.25	.15
52	Mike Andrews	.40	.20	.12
53	Sonny Jackson	.40	.20	.12
54	Cisco Carlos	.40	.20	.12
55	Jerry Grote	1.00	.50	.30
56	Rich Reese	.40	.20	.12
57	Checklist 1-109 (Denny McLain)	3.00	1.50	.90
58	Fred Gladding	.40	.20	.12
59	Jay Johnstone	.70	.35	.20
60	Nelson Briles	.40	.20	.12
61	Jimmie Hall	.40	.20	.12
62	Chico Salmon	.80	.40	.25
63	Jim Hickman	.50	.25	.15
64	Bill Monbouquette	.50	.25	.15
65	Willie Davis	1.00	.50	.30
66	Orioles Rookies (Mike Adamson, Merv Rettenmund)	.70	.35	.20
67	Bill Stoneman	.40	.20	.12
68	Dave Duncan	.40	.20	.12
69	Steve Hamilton	.70	.35	.20
70	Tommy Helms	.50	.25	.15
71	Steve Whitaker	.40	.20	.12
72	Ron Taylor	.60	.30	.20
73	Johnny Briggs	.40	.20	.12
74	Preston Gomez	.40	.20	.12
75	Luis Aparicio	5.00	2.50	1.50
76	Norm Miller	.40	.20	.12
77a	Ron Perranoski (LA visible thru airbrush)	4.50	2.25	1.25
77b	Ron Perranoski (cap emblem completely airbrushed)	.50	.25	.15
78	Tom Satriano	.40	.20	.12
79	Milt Pappas	.70	.35	.20
80	Norm Cash	1.75	.90	.50
81	Mel Queen	.40	.20	.12
82	Pirates Rookies (Rich Hebner, Al Oliver)	9.00	4.50	2.75
83	Mike Ferraro	.80	.40	.25
84	Bob Humphreys	.40	.20	.12
85	Lou Brock	15.00	7.50	4.50
86	Pete Richert	.40	.20	.12
87	Horace Clarke	.70	.35	.20
88	Rich Nye	.40	.20	.12
89	Russ Gibson	.40	.20	.12
90	Jerry Koosman	2.50	1.25	.70
91	Al Dark	.70	.35	.20
92	Jack Billingham	.50	.25	.15
93	Joe Foy	.40	.20	.12
94	Hank Aguirre	.40	.20	.12
95	Johnny Bench	150.00	60.00	38.00
96	Denver Lemaster	.40	.20	.12
97	Buddy Bradford	.40	.20	.12
98	Dave Giusti	.40	.20	.12
99a	Twins Rookies (Danny Morris, Graig Nettles) (black loop above "Twins")	20.00	10.00	6.00
99b	Twins Rookies (Danny Morris, Graig Nettles) (no black loop)	12.00	6.00	3.50

		NR MT	EX	VG
100	Hank Aaron	50.00	25.00	15.00
101	Daryl Patterson	.40	.20	.12
102	Jim Davenport	.40	.20	.12
103	Roger Repoz	.40	.20	.12
104	Steve Blass	.50	.25	.15
105	Rick Monday	.80	.40	.25
106	Jim Hannan	.40	.20	.12
107a	Checklist 110-218 (Bob Gibson) (161 is Jim Purdin)	3.00	1.50	.90
107b	Checklist 110-218 (Bob Gibson) (161 is John Purdin)	6.00	3.00	1.75
108	Tony Taylor	.40	.20	.12
109	Jim Lonborg	.80	.40	.25
110	Mike Shannon	.50	.25	.15
111	Johnny Morris	.80	.40	.25
112	J.C. Martin	.70	.35	.20
113	Dave May	.40	.20	.12
114	Yankees Rookies (Alan Closter, John Cumberland)	.70	.35	.20
115	Bill Hands	.40	.20	.12
116	Chuck Harrison	.40	.20	.12
117	Jim Fairey	.40	.20	.12
118	Stan Williams	.40	.20	.12
119	Doug Rader	.50	.25	.15
120	Pete Rose	35.00	17.50	10.50
121	Joe Grzenda	.40	.20	.12
122	Ron Fairly	.80	.40	.25
123	Wilbur Wood	.80	.40	.25
124	Hank Bauer	.80	.40	.25
125	Ray Sadecki	.40	.20	.12
126	Dick Tracewski	.40	.20	.12
127	Kevin Collins	.60	.30	.20
128	Tommie Aaron	.70	.35	.20
129	Bill McCool	.40	.20	.12
130	Carl Yastrzemski	25.00	12.50	7.50
131	Chris Cannizzaro	.40	.20	.12
132	Dave Baldwin	.40	.20	.12
133	Johnny Callison	1.00	.50	.30
134	Jim Weaver	.40	.20	.12
135	Tommy Davis	1.50	.70	.45
136	Cards Rookies (Steve Huntz, Mike Torrez)	.50	.25	.15
137	Wally Bunker	.40	.20	.12
138	John Bateman	.40	.20	.12
139	Andy Kosco	.40	.20	.12
140	Jim Lefebvre	.50	.25	.15
141	Bill Dillman	.40	.20	.12
142	Woody Woodward	.50	.25	.15
143	Joe Nossek	.40	.20	.12
144	Bob Hendley	.60	.30	.20
145	Max Alvis	.50	.25	.15
146	Jim Perry	1.00	.50	.30
147	Leo Durocher	2.25	1.25	.70
148	Lee Stange	.40	.20	.12
149	Ollie Brown	.40	.20	.12
150	Denny McLain	3.00	1.50	.90
151a	Clay Dalrymple (Phillies)	7.00	3.50	2.00
151b	Clay Dalrymple (Orioles)	.40	.20	.12
152	Tommie Sisk	.40	.20	.12
153	Ed Brinkman	.50	.25	.15
154	Jim Britton	.40	.20	.12
155	Pete Ward	.40	.20	.12
156	Astros Rookies (Hal Gilson, Leon McFadden)	.40	.20	.12
157	Bob Rodgers	.70	.35	.20
158	Joe Gibbon	.40	.20	.12
159	Jerry Adair	.40	.20	.12
160	Vada Pinson	2.00	1.00	.60
161	John Purdin	.40	.20	.12
162	World Series Game 1 (Gibson Fans 17; Sets New Record)	3.50	1.75	1.00
163	World Series Game 2 (Tiger Homers Deck The Cards)	2.50	1.25	.70
164	World Series Game 3 (McCarver's Homer Puts St. Louis Ahead)	2.50	1.25	.70
165	World Series Game 4 (Brock's Lead-Off Homer Starts Cards' Romp)	3.50	1.75	1.00
166	World Series Game 5 (Kaline's Key Hit Sparks Tiger Rally)	3.50	1.75	1.00
167	World Series Game 6 (Tiger 10-Run Inning Ties Mark)	2.50	1.25	.70
168	World Series Game 7 (Lolich Series Hero, Outduels Gibson)	2.75	1.50	.80
169	World Series Summary (Tigers Celebrate Their Victory)	2.50	1.25	.70
170	Frank Howard	2.00	1.00	.60
171	Glenn Beckert	.80	.40	.25
172	Jerry Stephenson	.40	.20	.12
173	White Sox Rookies (Bob Christian, Gerry Nyman)	.40	.20	.12
174	Grant Jackson	.40	.20	.12

		NR MT	EX	VG
175	Jim Bunning	4.00	2.00	1.25
176	Joe Azcue	.40	.20	.12
177	Ron Reed	.50	.25	.15
178	Ray Oyler	.80	.40	.25
179	Don Pavletich	.40	.20	.12
180	Willie Horton	.80	.40	.25
181	Mel Nelson	.40	.20	.12
182	Bill Rigney	.40	.20	.12
183	Don Shaw	.40	.20	.12
184	Roberto Pena	.40	.20	.12
185	Tom Phoebus	.40	.20	.12
186	John Edwards	.40	.20	.12
187	Leon Wagner	.50	.25	.15
188	Rick Wise	.50	.25	.15
189	Red Sox Rookies (Joe Lahoud, John Thibdeau)	.40	.20	.12
190	Willie Mays	50.00	25.00	15.00
191	Lindy McDaniel	.70	.35	.20
192	Jose Pagan	.40	.20	.12
193	Don Cardwell	.70	.35	.20
194	Ted Uhlaender	.40	.20	.12
195	John Odom	.50	.25	.15
196	Lum Harris	.40	.20	.12
197	Dick Selma	.40	.20	.12
198	Willie Smith	.40	.20	.12
199	Jim French	.40	.20	.12
200	Bob Gibson	12.00	6.00	3.50
201	Russ Snyder	.40	.20	.12
202	Don Wilson	.40	.20	.12
203	Dave Johnson	1.50	.70	.45
204	Jack Hiatt	.40	.20	.12
205	Rick Reichardt	.40	.20	.12
206	Phillies Rookies (Larry Hisle, Barry Lersch)	.80	.40	.25
207	Roy Face	1.25	.60	.40
208a	Donn Clendenon (Expos)	7.00	3.50	2.00
208b	Donn Clendenon (Houston)	.50	.25	.15
209	Larry Haney (photo reversed)	.80	.40	.25
210	Felix Millan	.40	.20	.12
211	Galen Cisco	.40	.20	.12
212	Tom Tresh	1.25	.60	.40
213	Gerry Arrigo	.40	.20	.12
214	Checklist 219-327	2.50	1.25	.70
215	Rico Petrocelli	.80	.40	.25
216	Don Sutton	4.00	2.00	1.25
217	John Donaldson	.40	.20	.12
218	John Roseboro	.60	.30	.20
219	*Freddie Patek*	1.25	.60	.40
220	Sam McDowell	1.25	.60	.40
221	Art Shamsky	1.00	.50	.30
222	Duane Josephson	.90	.45	.25
223	Tom Dukes	.90	.45	.25
224	Angels Rookies (Bill Harrelson, Steve Kealey)	.90	.45	.25
225	Don Kessinger	1.00	.50	.30
226	Bruce Howard	.90	.45	.25
227	Frank Johnson	.90	.45	.25
228	Dave Leonhard	.90	.45	.25
229	Don Lock	.90	.45	.25
230	Rusty Staub	2.50	1.25	.70
231	Pat Dobson	1.00	.50	.30
232	Dave Ricketts	.90	.45	.25
233	Steve Barber	1.00	.50	.30
234	Dave Bristol	.90	.45	.25
235	Jim Hunter	10.00	5.00	3.00
236	Manny Mota	1.00	.50	.30
237	*Bobby Cox*	1.50	.70	.45
238	Ken Johnson	.90	.45	.25
239	Bob Taylor	.90	.45	.25
240	Ken Harrelson	2.00	1.00	.60
241	Jim Brewer	.90	.45	.25
242	Frank Kostro	.90	.45	.25
243	Ron Kline	.90	.45	.25
244	Indians Rookies (*Ray Fosse*, George Woodson)	1.25	.60	.40
245	Ed Charles	1.00	.50	.30
246	Joe Coleman	1.00	.50	.30
247	Gene Oliver	.90	.45	.25
248	Bob Priddy	.90	.45	.25
249	Ed Spiezio	.90	.45	.25
250	Frank Robinson	18.00	9.00	5.50
251	Ron Herbel	.90	.45	.25
252	Chuck Cottier	.90	.45	.25
253	Jerry Johnson	.90	.45	.25
254	Joe Schultz	1.00	.50	.30
255	Steve Carlton	40.00	20.00	12.00
256	Gates Brown	.90	.45	.25
257	Jim Ray	.90	.45	.25
258	Jackie Hernandez	.90	.45	.25
259	Bill Short	.90	.45	.25
260	*Reggie Jackson*	500.00	250.00	150.00

#	Player	NR MT	EX	VG
261	Bob Johnson	.90	.45	.25
262	Mike Kekich	1.00	.50	.30
263	Jerry May	.90	.45	.25
264	Bill Landis	.90	.45	.25
265	Chico Cardenas	.90	.45	.25
266	Dodgers Rookies (Alan Foster, Tom Hutton)	.90	.45	.25
267	Vicente Romo	.90	.45	.25
268	Al Spangler	.90	.45	.25
269	Al Weis	1.00	.50	.30
270	Mickey Lolich	3.50	1.75	1.00
271	Larry Stahl	.90	.45	.25
272	Ed Stroud	.90	.45	.25
273	Ron Willis	.90	.45	.25
274	Clyde King	.90	.45	.25
275	Vic Davalillo	.90	.45	.25
276	Gary Wagner	.90	.45	.25
277	*Rod Hendricks*	.90	.45	.25
278	Gary Geiger	.90	.45	.25
279	Roger Nelson	.90	.45	.25
280	Alex Johnson	.90	.45	.25
281	Ted Kubiak	.90	.45	.25
282	Pat Jarvis	.90	.45	.25
283	Sandy Alomar	.90	.45	.25
284	Expos Rookies (Jerry Robertson, Mike Wegener)	.90	.45	.25
285	Don Mincher	1.00	.50	.30
286	*Dock Ellis*	1.25	.60	.40
287	Jose Tartabull	.90	.45	.25
288	Ken Holtzman	1.00	.50	.30
289	Bart Shirley	.90	.45	.25
290	Jim Kaat	4.50	2.25	1.25
291	Vern Fuller	.90	.45	.25
292	Al Downing	1.25	.60	.40
293	Dick Dietz	.90	.45	.25
294	Jim Lemon	.90	.45	.25
295	Tony Perez	4.50	2.25	1.25
296	*Andy Messersmith*	1.25	.60	.40
297	Deron Johnson	.90	.45	.25
298	Dave Nicholson	.90	.45	.25
299	Mark Belanger	1.00	.50	.30
300	Felipe Alou	1.25	.60	.40
301	Darrell Brandon	.90	.45	.25
302	Jim Pagliaroni	.90	.45	.25
303	Cal Koonce	1.00	.50	.30
304	Padres Rookies (Bill Davis, *Clarence Gaston*)	1.00	.50	.30
305	Dick McAuliffe	1.00	.50	.30
306	Jim Grant	.90	.45	.25
307	Gary Kolb	.90	.45	.25
308	Wade Blasingame	.90	.45	.25
309	Walt Williams	.90	.45	.25
310	Tom Haller	1.00	.50	.30
311	*Sparky Lyle*	4.00	2.00	1.25
312	Lee Elia	.90	.45	.25
313	Bill Robinson	1.00	.50	.30
314	Checklist 328-425 (Don Drysdale)	3.50	1.75	1.00
315	Eddie Fisher	.90	.45	.25
316	Hal Lanier	1.00	.50	.30
317	Bruce Look	.90	.45	.25
318	Jack Fisher	.90	.45	.25
319	Ken McMullen	.90	.45	.25
320	Dal Maxvill	1.00	.50	.30
321	Jim McAndrew	1.00	.50	.30
322	Jose Vidal	1.00	.50	.30
323	Larry Miller	.90	.45	.25
324	Tigers Rookies (Les Cain, Dave Campbell)	.90	.45	.25
325	Jose Cardenal	1.00	.50	.30
326	Gary Sutherland	.90	.45	.25
327	Willie Crawford	.90	.45	.25
328	Joe Horlen	.40	.20	.12
329	Rick Joseph	.40	.20	.12
330	Tony Conigliaro	1.50	.70	.45
331	Braves Rookies (Gil Garrido, *Tom House*)	.50	.25	.15
332	Fred Talbot	.80	.40	.25
333	Ivan Murrell	.40	.20	.12
334	Phil Roof	.40	.20	.12
335	Bill Mazeroski	1.75	.90	.50
336	Jim Roland	.40	.20	.12
337	Marty Martinez	.40	.20	.12
338	*Del Unser*	.50	.25	.15
339	Reds Rookies (Steve Mingori, Jose Pena)	.40	.20	.12
340	Dave McNally	.80	.40	.25
341	Dave Adlesh	.40	.20	.12
342	Bubba Morton	.40	.20	.12
343	Dan Frisella	.70	.35	.20
344	Tom Matchick	.40	.20	.12
345	Frank Linzy	.40	.20	.12

#	Player	NR MT	EX	V
346	Wayne Comer	.80	.40	.2
347	Randy Hundley	.40	.20	.1
348	Steve Hargan	.40	.20	.1
349	Dick Williams	.80	.40	.2
350	Richie Allen	2.00	1.00	.6
351	Carroll Sembera	.40	.20	.1
352	Paul Schaal	.40	.20	.1
353	Jeff Torborg	.50	.25	.1
354	Nate Oliver	.80	.40	.2
355	Phil Niekro	10.00	5.00	3.0
356	Frank Quilici	.40	.20	.1
357	Carl Taylor	.40	.20	.1
358	Athletics Rookies (George Lauzerique, Roberto Rodriguez)	.40	.20	.1
359	Dick Kelley	.40	.20	.1
360	Jim Wynn	.80	.40	.2
361	Gary Holman	.40	.20	.1
362	Jim Maloney	.50	.25	.1
363	Russ Nixon	.40	.20	.1
364	Tommie Agee	.80	.40	.2
365	Jim Fregosi	1.00	.50	.3
366	Bo Belinsky	1.00	.50	.3
367	Lou Johnson	.40	.20	.1
368	Vic Roznovsky	.40	.20	.1
369	Bob Skinner	.40	.20	.1
370	Juan Marichal	7.00	3.50	2.0
371	Sal Bando	.80	.40	.2
372	Adolfo Phillips	.40	.20	.1
373	Fred Lasher	.40	.20	.1
374	Bob Tillman	.40	.20	.1
375	Harmon Killebrew	12.00	6.00	3.5
376	Royals Rookies (Mike Fiore, *Jim Rooker*)	.50	.25	.1
377	Gary Bell	.80	.40	.2
378	Jose Herrera	.40	.20	.1
379	Ken Boyer	1.75	.90	.5
380	Stan Bahnsen	.80	.40	.2
381	Ed Kranepool	.80	.40	.2
382	Pat Corrales	.80	.40	.2
383	Casey Cox	.40	.20	.1
384	Larry Shepard	.40	.20	.1
385	Orlando Cepeda	3.50	1.75	1.0
386	Jim McGlothlin	.40	.20	.1
387	Bobby Klaus	.40	.20	.1
388	Tom McCraw	.40	.20	.1
389	Dan Coombs	.40	.20	.1
390	Bill Freehan	.70	.35	.2
391	Ray Culp	.40	.20	.1
392	Bob Burda	.40	.20	.1
393	Gene Grabender	.40	.20	.1
394	Pilots Rookies (Lou Piniella, Marv Staehle)	3.00	1.50	.9
395	Chris Short	.60	.30	.2
396	Jim Campanis	.40	.20	.1
397	Chuck Dobson	.40	.20	.1
398	Tito Francona	.50	.25	.1
399	Bob Bailey	.40	.20	.1
400	Don Drysdale	8.00	4.00	2.5
401	Jake Gibbs	.80	.40	.2
402	Ken Boswell	.70	.35	.2
403	Bob Miller	.40	.20	.1
404	Cubs Rookies (Vic LaRose, Gary Ross)	.40	.20	.1
405	Lee May	1.00	.50	.3
406	Phil Ortega	.40	.20	.1
407	Tom Egan	.40	.20	.1
408	Nate Colbert	.40	.20	.1
409	Bob Moose	.40	.20	.1
410	Al Kaline	12.00	6.00	3.5
411	Larry Dierker	.50	.25	.1
412	Checklist 426-512 (Mickey Mantle)	7.00	3.50	2.0
413	Roland Sheldon	.80	.40	.2
414	Duke Sims	.40	.20	.1
415	Ray Washburn	.40	.20	.1
416	Willie McCovey AS	3.50	1.75	1.0
417	Ken Harrelson AS	1.00	.50	.3
418	Tommy Helms AS	.70	.35	.2
419	Rod Carew AS	6.00	3.00	1.7
420	Ron Santo AS	1.00	.50	.3
421	Brooks Robinson AS	4.00	2.00	1.2
422	Don Kessinger AS	.70	.35	.2
423	Bert Campaneris AS	.80	.40	.2
424	Pete Rose AS	12.00	6.00	3.5
425	Carl Yastrzemski AS	6.00	3.00	1.7
426	Curt Flood AS	1.00	.50	.3
427	Tony Oliva AS	1.50	.70	.4
428	Lou Brock AS	3.50	1.75	1.0
429	Willie Horton AS	.80	.40	.2
430	Johnny Bench AS	10.00	5.00	3.0
431	Bill Freehan AS	.70	.35	.2

#	Card	NR MT	EX	VG
432	Bob Gibson AS	3.50	1.75	1.00
433	Denny McLain AS	1.50	.70	.45
434	Jerry Koosman AS	1.00	.50	.30
435	Sam McDowell AS	.80	.40	.25
436	Gene Alley	.70	.35	.20
437	Luis Alcaraz	.40	.20	.12
438	Gary Waslewski	.40	.20	.12
439	White Sox Rookies (Ed Herrmann, Dan Lazar)	.40	.20	.12
440a	Willie McCovey (last name in white)	90.00	45.00	27.00
440b	Willie McCovey (last name in yellow)	20.00	10.00	6.00
441a	Dennis Higgins (last name in white)	10.00	5.00	3.00
441b	Dennis Higgins (last name in yellow)	.40	.20	.12
442	Ty Cline	.40	.20	.12
443	Don Wert	.40	.20	.12
444a	Joe Moeller (last name in white)	10.00	5.00	3.00
444b	Joe Moeller (last name in yellow)	.40	.20	.12
445	Bobby Knoop	.40	.20	.12
446	Claude Raymond	.40	.20	.12
447a	Ralph Houk (last name in white)	15.00	7.50	4.50
447b	Ralph Houk (last name in yellow)	1.50	.70	.45
448	Bob Tolan	.50	.25	.15
449	Paul Lindblad	.40	.20	.12
450	Billy Williams	6.00	3.00	1.75
451a	Rich Rollins (first name in white)	10.00	5.00	3.00
451b	Rich Rollins (first name in yellow)	.80	.40	.25
452a	Al Ferrara (first name in white)	10.00	5.00	3.00
452b	Al Ferrara (first name in yellow)	.40	.20	.12
453	Mike Cuellar	.80	.40	.25
454a	Phillies Rookies (Larry Colton, *Don Money*) (names in white)	10.00	5.00	3.00
454b	Phillies Rookies (Larry Colton, *Don Money*) (names in yellow)	.80	.40	.25
455	Sonny Siebert	.40	.20	.12
456	Bud Harrelson	1.00	.50	.30
457	Dalton Jones	.40	.20	.12
458	Curt Blefary	.40	.20	.12
459	Dave Boswell	.40	.20	.12
460	Joe Torre	1.75	.90	.50
461a	Mike Epstein (last name in white)	10.00	5.00	3.00
461b	Mike Epstein (last name in yellow)	.50	.25	.15
462	Red Schoendienst	1.50	.70	.45
463	Dennis Ribant	.40	.20	.12
464a	Dave Marshall (last name in white)	10.00	5.00	3.00
464b	Dave Marshall (last name in yellow)	.40	.20	.12
465	Tommy John	4.50	2.25	1.25
466	John Boccabella	.40	.20	.12
467	Tom Reynolds	.40	.20	.12
468a	Pirates Rookies (Bruce Dal Canton, Bob Robertson) (names in white)	10.00	5.00	3.00
468b	Pirates Rookies (Bruce Dal Canton, Bob Robertson) (names in yellow)	.50	.25	.15
469	Chico Ruiz	.40	.20	.12
470a	Mel Stottlemyre (last name in white)	15.00	7.50	4.50
470b	Mel Stottlemyre (last name in yellow)	1.50	.70	.45
471a	Ted Savage (last name in white)	10.00	5.00	3.00
471b	Ted Savage (last name in yellow)	.40	.20	.12
472	Jim Price	.40	.20	.12
473a	Jose Arcia (first name in white)	10.00	5.00	3.00
473b	Jose Arcia (first name in yellow)	.40	.20	.12
474	Tom Murphy	.40	.20	.12
475	Tim McCarver	1.50	.70	.45
476a	Red Sox Rookies (Ken Brett, *Gerry Moses*) (names in white)	10.00	5.00	3.00
476b	Red Sox Rookies (Ken Brett, *Gerry Moses*) (names in yellow)	.50	.25	.15
477	Jeff James	.40	.20	.12
478	Don Buford	.60	.30	.20
479	Richie Scheinblum	.40	.20	.12
480	Tom Seaver	90.00	45.00	27.00
481	*Bill Melton*	.80	.40	.25
482a	Jim Gosger (first name in white)	10.00	5.00	3.00
482b	Jim Gosger (first name in yellow)	.80	.40	.25
483	Ted Abernathy	.40	.20	.12
484	Joe Gordon	.50	.25	.15
485a	Gaylord Perry (last name in white)	75.00	38.00	23.00
485b	Gaylord Perry (last name in yellow)	10.00	5.00	3.00
486a	Paul Casanova (last name in white)	10.00	5.00	3.00
486b	Paul Casanova (last name in yellow)	.40	.20	.12
487	Denis Menke	.40	.20	.12
488	Joe Sparma	.40	.20	.12
489	Clete Boyer	.80	.40	.25
490	Matty Alou	1.00	.50	.30
491a	Twins Rookies (Jerry Crider, George Mitterwald) (names in white)	10.00	5.00	3.00
491b	Twins Rookies (Jerry Crider, George Mitterwald) (names in yellow)	.40	.20	.12
492	Tony Cloninger	.50	.25	.15
493a	Wes Parker (last name in white)	10.00	5.00	3.00
493b	Wes Parker (last name in yellow)	.70	.35	.20
494	Ken Berry	.40	.20	.12
495	Bert Campaneris	1.25	.60	.40
496	Larry Jaster	.40	.20	.12
497	Julian Javier	.40	.20	.12
498	Juan Pizarro	.40	.20	.12
499	Astros Rookies (Don Bryant, Steve Shea)	.40	.20	.12
500a	Mickey Mantle (last name in white)	475.00	190.00	119.00
500b	Mickey Mantle (last name in yellow)	175.00	70.00	44.00
501a	Tony Gonzalez (first name in white)	10.00	5.00	3.00
501b	Tony Gonzalez (first name in yellow)	.40	.20	.12
502	Minnie Rojas	.40	.20	.12
503	Larry Brown	.40	.20	.12
504	Checklist 513-588 (Brooks Robinson)	4.00	2.00	1.25
505a	Bobby Bolin (last name in white)	10.00	5.00	3.00
505b	Bobby Bolin (last name in yellow)	.40	.20	.12
506	Paul Blair	.50	.25	.15
507	Cookie Rojas	.40	.20	.12
508	Moe Drabowsky	.40	.20	.12
509	Manny Sanguillen	.50	.25	.15
510	Rod Carew	60.00	30.00	18.00
511a	Diego Segui (first name in white)	10.00	5.00	3.00
511b	Diego Segui (first name in yellow)	.80	.40	.25
512	Cleon Jones	.80	.40	.25
513	Camilo Pascual	.90	.45	.25
514	Mike Lum	.70	.35	.20
515	Dick Green	.70	.35	.20
516	Earl Weaver	3.50	1.75	1.00
517	Mike McCormick	.80	.40	.25
518	Fred Whitfield	.70	.35	.20
519	Yankees Rookies (Len Boehmer, Gerry Kenney)	1.00	.50	.30
520	Bob Veale	.80	.40	.25
521	George Thomas	.70	.35	.20
522	Joe Hoerner	.70	.35	.20
523	Bob Chance	.70	.35	.20
524	Expos Rookies (Jose Laboy, Floyd Wicker)	.70	.35	.20
525	Earl Wilson	.70	.35	.20
526	Hector Torres	.70	.35	.20
527	Al Lopez	3.00	1.50	.90
528	Claude Osteen	.90	.45	.25
529	Ed Kirkpatrick	.70	.35	.20
530	Cesar Tovar	.70	.35	.20
531	Dick Farrell	.70	.35	.20
532	Bird Hill Aces (Mike Cuellar, Jim Hardin, Dave McNally, Tom Phoebus)	1.50	.70	.45
533	Nolan Ryan	375.00	187.00	112.00
534	Jerry McNertney	.90	.45	.25
535	Phil Regan	.70	.35	.20
536	Padres Rookies (Danny Breeden, *Dave Roberts*)	.80	.40	.25
537	Mike Paul	.70	.35	.20
538	Charlie Smith	.70	.35	.20
539	Ted Shows How (Mike Epstein, Ted Williams)	3.25	1.75	1.00
540	Curt Flood	1.50	.70	.45
541	Joe Verbanic	1.00	.50	.30
542	Bob Aspromonte	.70	.35	.20
543	Fred Newman	.70	.35	.20
544	Tigers Rookies (Mike Kilkenny, Ron Woods)	.70	.35	.20
545	Willie Stargell	10.00	5.00	3.00
546	Jim Nash	.70	.35	.20
547	Billy Martin	5.00	2.50	1.50
548	Bob Locker	.70	.35	.20
549	Ron Brand	.70	.35	.20
550	Brooks Robinson	15.00	7.50	4.50
551	Wayne Granger	.70	.35	.20
552	Dodgers Rookies (*Ted Sizemore, Bill Sudakis*)	.80	.40	.25
553	Ron Davis	.70	.35	.20
554	Frank Bertaina	.70	.35	.20
555	Jim Hart	.80	.40	.25
556	A's Stars (Sal Bando, Bert Campaneris, Danny Cater)	1.50	.70	.45

		NR MT	EX	VG
557	Frank Fernandez	1.00	.50	.30
558	*Tom Burgmeier*	.80	.40	.25
559	Cards Rookies (Joe Hague, Jim Hicks)			
		.70	.35	.20
560	Luis Tiant	1.50	.70	.45
561	Ron Clark	.70	.35	.20
562	Bob Watson	1.00	.50	.30
563	Marty Pattin	.90	.45	.25
564	Gil Hodges	6.00	3.00	1.75
565	Hoyt Wilhelm	6.00	3.00	1.75
566	Ron Hansen	.70	.35	.20
567	Pirates Rookies (Elvio Jimenez, Jim Shellenback)	.70	.35	.20
568	Cecil Upshaw	.70	.35	.20
569	Billy Harris	.70	.35	.20
570	Ron Santo	1.75	.90	.50
571	Cap Peterson	.70	.35	.20
572	Giants Heroes (Juan Marichal, Willie McCovey)	7.00	3.50	2.00
573	Jim Palmer	30.00	15.00	9.00
574	George Scott	.90	.45	.25
575	Bill Singer	.80	.40	.25
576	Phillies Rookies (Ron Stone, Bill Wilson)	.70	.35	.20
577	Mike Hegan	1.00	.50	.30
578	Don Bosch	.70	.35	.20
579	*Dave Nelson*	.80	.40	.25
580	Jim Northrup	.80	.40	.25
581	Gary Nolan	.70	.35	.20
582a	Checklist 589-664 (Tony Oliva) (red circle on back)	3.50	1.75	1.00
582b	Checklist 589-664 (Tony Oliva) (white circle on back)	2.50	1.25	.70
583	*Clyde Wright*	.80	.40	.25
584	Don Mason	.70	.35	.20
585	Ron Swoboda	.90	.45	.25
586	Tim Cullen	.70	.35	.20
587	*Joe Rudi*	1.75	.90	.50
588	Bill White	1.00	.50	.30
589	Joe Pepitone	2.00	1.00	.60
590	Rico Carty	1.00	.50	.30
591	Mike Hedlund	.70	.35	.20
592	Padres Rookies (Rafael Robles, Al Santorini)	.70	.35	.20
593	Don Nottebart	.70	.35	.20
594	Dooley Womack	.70	.35	.20
595	Lee Maye	.70	.35	.20
596	Chuck Hartenstein	.70	.35	.20
597	A.L. Rookies (Larry Burchart, *Rollie Fingers*, Bob Floyd)	80.00	40.00	25.00
598	Ruben Amaro	.70	.35	.20
599	John Boozer	.70	.35	.20
600	Tony Oliva	2.25	1.25	.70
601	Tug McGraw	2.00	1.00	.60
602	Cubs Rookies (Alec Distaso, Jim Qualls, Don Young)	.70	.35	.20
603	Joe Keough	.70	.35	.20
604	Bobby Etheridge	.70	.35	.20
605	Dick Ellsworth	.70	.35	.20
606	Gene Mauch	.90	.45	.25
607	Dick Bosman	.70	.35	.20
608	Dick Simpson	1.00	.50	.30
609	Phil Gagliano	.70	.35	.20
610	Jim Hardin	.70	.35	.20
611	Braves Rookies (Bob Didier, Walt Hriniak, Gary Neibauer)	.70	.35	.20
612	Jack Aker	1.00	.50	.30
613	Jim Beauchamp	.70	.35	.20
614	Astros Rookies (Tom Griffin, Skip Guinn)	.70	.35	.20
615	Len Gabrielson	.70	.35	.20
616	Don McMahon	.70	.35	.20
617	Jesse Gonder	.70	.35	.20
618	Ramon Webster	.70	.35	.20
619	Royals Rookies (Bill Butler, *Pat Kelly*, Juan Rios)	.80	.40	.25
620	Dean Chance	.80	.40	.25
621	Bill Voss	.70	.35	.20
622	Dan Osinski	.70	.35	.20
623	Hank Allen	.70	.35	.20
624	N.L. Rookies (Darrel Chaney, Duffy Dyer, Terry Harmon)	.80	.40	.25
625	Mack Jones	.70	.35	.20
626	Gene Michael	1.00	.50	.30
627	George Stone	.70	.35	.20
628	Red Sox Rookies (*Bill Conigliaro*, Syd O'Brien, Fred Wenz)	.90	.45	.25
629	Jack Hamilton	.70	.35	.20
630	*Bobby Bonds*	15.00	7.50	4.50
631	John Kennedy	.90	.45	.25
632	Jon Warden	.70	.35	.20

		NR MT	EX	VG
633	Harry Walker	.80	.40	.25
634	Andy Etchebarren	.70	.35	.20
635	George Culver	.70	.35	.20
636	Woodie Held	.70	.35	.20
637	Padres Rookies (Jerry DaVanon, *Clay Kirby*, Frank Reberger)	.80	.40	.25
638	Ed Sprague	.70	.35	.20
639	Barry Moore	.70	.35	.20
640	Fergie Jenkins	5.00	2.50	1.50
641	N.L. Rookies (Bobby Darwin, Tommy Dean, John Miller)	.70	.35	.20
642	John Hiller	.80	.40	.25
643	Billy Cowan	1.00	.50	.30
644	Chuck Hinton	.70	.35	.20
645	George Brunet	.70	.35	.20
646	Expos Rookies (Dan McGinn, *Carl Morton*)	.90	.45	.25
647	Dave Wickersham	.70	.35	.20
648	Bobby Wine	.70	.35	.20
649	Al Jackson	.90	.45	.25
650	Ted Williams	9.00	4.50	2.75
651	Gus Gil	.90	.45	.25
652	Eddie Watt	.70	.35	.20
653	*Aurelio Rodriguez* (photo actually batboy Leonard Garcia)	1.50	.70	.45
654	White Sox Rookies (*Carlos May*, Rich Morales, Don Secrist)	.90	.45	.25
655	Mike Hershberger	.70	.35	.20
656	Dan Schneider	.70	.35	.20
657	Bobby Murcer	2.25	1.25	.70
658	A.L. Rookies (Bill Burbach, Tom Hall, Jim Miles)	1.00	.50	.30
659	Johnny Podres	1.75	.90	.50
660	Reggie Smith	1.75	.90	.50
661	Jim Merritt	.70	.35	.20
662	Royals Rookies (Dick Drago, Bob Oliver, George Spriggs)	.80	.40	.25
663	Dick Radatz	.90	.45	.25
664	Ron Hunt	2.00	.50	.25

1969 Topps Decals

Designed as an insert for 1969 regular issue card packs, these decals are virtually identical in format to the '69 cards. The 48 decals in the set measure 1" by 2-1/2," although they are mounted on white paper backing which measures 1-3/4" by 2-1/8."

		NR MT	EX	VG
Complete Set:		350.00	175.00	105.00
Common Player:		4.00	2.00	1.25
(1)	Hank Aaron	40.00	20.00	12.00
(2)	Richie Allen	4.00	2.00	1.25
(3)	Felipe Alou	4.00	2.00	1.25
(4)	Matty Alou	4.00	2.00	1.25
(5)	Luis Aparicio	4.50	2.25	1.25
(6)	Bob Clemente	50.00	25.00	15.00
(7)	Donn Clendenon	4.00	2.00	1.25
(8)	Tommy Davis	4.00	2.00	1.25
(9)	Don Drysdale	7.00	3.50	2.00
(10)	Joe Foy	4.00	2.00	1.25
(11)	Jim Fregosi	4.00	2.00	1.25
(12)	Bob Gibson	7.00	3.50	2.00
(13)	Tony Gonzalez	4.00	2.00	1.25
(14)	Tom Haller	4.00	2.00	1.25
(15)	Ken Harrelson	4.00	2.00	1.25
(16)	Tommy Helms	4.00	2.00	1.25

		NR MT	EX	VG
17)	Willie Horton	4.00	2.00	1.25
18)	Frank Howard	4.00	2.00	1.25
19)	Reggie Jackson	100.00	50.00	30.00
20)	Fergie Jenkins	6.00	3.00	1.75
21)	Harmon Killebrew	6.00	3.00	1.75
22)	Jerry Koosman	4.00	2.00	1.25
23)	Mickey Mantle	75.00	38.00	23.00
24)	Willie Mays	35.00	17.50	10.50
25)	Tim McCarver	4.00	2.00	1.25
26)	Willie McCovey	7.00	3.50	2.00
27)	Sam McDowell	4.00	2.00	1.25
28)	Denny McLain	4.00	2.00	1.25
29)	Dave McNally	4.00	2.00	1.25
30)	Don Mincher	4.00	2.00	1.25
31)	Rick Monday	4.00	2.00	1.25
32)	Tony Oliva	4.00	2.00	1.25
33)	Camilo Pascual	4.00	2.00	1.25
34)	Rick Reichardt	4.00	2.00	1.25
35)	Pete Rose	25.00	12.50	7.50
36)	Frank Robinson	7.00	3.50	2.00
37)	Ron Santo	4.00	2.00	1.25
38)	Dick Selma	4.00	2.00	1.25
39)	Tom Seaver	50.00	25.00	15.00
40)	Chris Short	4.00	2.00	1.25
41)	Rusty Staub	4.00	2.00	1.25
42)	Mel Stottlemyre	4.00	2.00	1.25
43)	Luis Tiant	4.00	2.00	1.25
44)	Pete Ward	4.00	2.00	1.25
45)	Hoyt Wilhelm	6.00	3.00	1.75
46)	Maury Wills	4.00	2.00	1.25
47)	Jim Wynn	4.00	2.00	1.25
48)	Carl Yastrzemski	30.00	15.00	9.00

1969 Topps Deckle Edge

These 2-1/4" by 3-1/4" inch cards take their name from their interesting borders which have a scalloped effect. The fronts have a black and white picture of the player along with a blue facsimile autograph. Backs have the player's name and the card number in light blue ink in a small box at the bottom of the card. Technically, there are only 33 numbered cards, but there are actually 35 possible players; both Jim Wynn and Hoyt Wilhelm cards are found as #11 while cards of Joe Foy and Rusty Staub can be found as #22. Many of the players in the set are stars.

		NR MT	EX	VG
	Complete Set:	100.00	50.00	30.00
	Common Player:	1.00	.50	.30
	Brooks Robinson	15.00	7.50	4.50
	Boog Powell	1.00	.50	.30
	Ken Harrelson	1.00	.50	.30
	Carl Yastrzemski	15.00	7.50	4.50
	Jim Fregosi	1.00	.50	.30
	Luis Aparicio	1.25	.60	.40
	Luis Tiant	1.00	.50	.30
	Denny McLain	1.00	.50	.30
	Willie Horton	1.00	.50	.30
0	Bill Freehan	1.00	.50	.30
1a	Hoyt Wilhelm	10.00	5.00	3.00
1b	Jim Wynn	10.00	5.00	3.00
2	Rod Carew	15.00	7.50	4.50
3	Mel Stottlemyre	1.00	.50	.30
4	Rick Monday	1.00	.50	.30
5	Tommy Davis	1.00	.50	.30

		NR MT	EX	VG
16	Frank Howard	1.00	.50	.30
17	Felipe Alou	1.00	.50	.30
18	Don Kessinger	1.00	.50	.30
19	Ron Santo	1.00	.50	.30
20	Tommy Helms	1.00	.50	.30
21	Pete Rose	10.00	5.00	3.00
22a	Rusty Staub	2.25	1.25	.70
22b	Joe Foy	7.00	3.50	2.00
23	Tom Haller	1.00	.50	.30
24	Maury Wills	1.00	.50	.30
25	Jerry Koosman	1.00	.50	.30
26	Richie Allen	1.00	.50	.30
27	Bob Clemente	15.00	7.50	4.50
28	Curt Flood	1.00	.50	.30
29	Bob Gibson	10.00	5.00	3.00
30	Al Ferrara	1.00	.50	.30
31	Willie McCovey	10.00	5.00	3.00
32	Juan Marichal	7.00	3.50	2.00
33	Willie Mays, Willie Mays	15.00	7.50	4.50

1969 Topps 4-On-1 Mini Stickers

Another in the long line of Topps test issues, the 4-on-1s are 2-1/2" by 3-1/2" cards with blank backs featuring a quartet of miniature stickers in the design of the same cards from the 1969 Topps regular set. There are 25 different cards, for a total of 100 different stickers. As they are not common, Mint cards bring fairly strong prices on today's market. As the set was drawn from the 3rd Series of the regular cards, it includes some rookie stickers and World Series highlight stickers.

		NR MT	EX	VG
	Complete Set:	950.00	475.00	285.00
	Common Player:	15.00	7.50	4.50
(1)	Jerry Adair, Willie Mays, Johnny Morris, Don Wilson	100.00	50.00	30.00
(2)	Tommie Aaron, Jim Britton, Donn Clendenon, Woody Woodward	15.00	7.50	4.50
(3)	World Series Game 4, Tommy Davis, Don Pavletich, Vada Pinson	20.00	10.00	6.00
(4)	Max Alvis, Glenn Beckert, Ron Fairly, Rick Wise	15.00	7.50	4.50
(5)	Johnny Callison, Jim French, Lum Harris, Dick Selma	15.00	7.50	4.50
(6)	World Series Game 3, Bob Gibson, Larry Haney, Rick Reichardt	40.00	20.00	12.00
(7)	Houston Rookie Stars, Wally Bunker, Don Cardwell, Joe Gibbon	15.00	7.50	4.50
(8)	Ollie Brown, Jim Bunning, Andy Kosco, Ron Reed	20.00	10.00	6.00
(9)	Bill Dillman, Jim Lefebvre, John Purdin, John Roseboro	15.00	7.50	4.50
(10)	Bill Hands, Chuck Harrison, Lindy McDaniel, Felix Millan	15.00	7.50	4.50
(11)	Jack Hiatt, Dave Johnson, Mel Nelson, Tommie Sisk	18.00	9.00	5.50
(12)	Clay Dalrymple, Leo Durocher, John Odom, Wilbur Wood	18.00	9.00	5.50
(13)	Hank Bauer, Kevin Collins, Ray Oyler, Russ Snyder	15.00	7.50	4.50
(14)	Red Sox Rookie Stars, World Series Game 7, Gerry Arrigo, Jim Perry	18.00	9.00	5.50

	NR MT	EX	VG
(15) World Series Game 2, Bill McCool, Roberto Pena, Doug Rader	15.00	7.50	4.50
(16) Ed Brinkman, Roy Face, Willie Horton, Bob Rodgers	18.00	9.00	5.50
(17) Dave Baldwin, J.C. Martin, Dave May, Ray Sadecki	15.00	7.50	4.50
(18) World Series Game 1, Jose Pagan, Tom Phoebus, Mike Shannon	15.00	7.50	4.50
(19) Pete Rose, Lee Stange, Don Sutton, Ted Uhlaender	275.00	137.00	82.00
(20) Joe Grzenda, Frank Howard, Dick Tracewski, Jim Weaver	20.00	10.00	6.00
(21) White Sox Rookie Stars, Joe Azcue, Grant Jackson, Denny McLain	20.00	10.00	6.00
(22) John Edwards, Jim Fairey, Phillies Rookies, Stan Williams	15.00	7.50	4.50
(23) World Series Summary, John Bateman, Willie Smith, Leon Wagner	15.00	7.50	4.50
(24) World Series Game 5, Yankees Rookies, Chris Cannizzaro, Bob Hendley	15.00	7.50	4.50
(25) Cardinals Rookie Stars, Joe Nossek, Rico Petrocelli, Carl Yastrzemski	175.00	87.00	52.00

1969 Topps Stamps

Topps continued to refine its efforts at baseball stamps in 1969 with the release of 240 player stamps, each measuring 1" by 1-7/16." Each stamp jsd s color photo along with the player's name, position and team. Unlike prior stamp issues, the 1969 stamps have 24 separate albums (one per team). The stamps were issued in strips of 12.

	NR MT	EX	VG
Complete Sheet Set:	250.00	125.00	75.00
Common Sheet:	1.25	.60	.40
Complete Stamp Album Set:	14.00	7.00	4.25
Single Stamp Album:	.50	.25	.15

	NR MT	EX	VG
(1) Tommie Agee, Sandy Alomar, Jose Cardenal, Dean Chance, Joe Foy, Jim Grant, Don Kessinger, Mickey Mantle, Jerry May, Bob Rodgers, Cookie Rojas, Gary Sutherland	18.00	9.00	5.50
(2) Jesus Alou, Mike Andrews, Larry Brown, Moe Drabowsky, Alex Johnson, Lew Krausse, Jim Lefebvre, Dal Maxvill, John Odom, Claude Osteen, Rick Reichardt, Luis Tiant	1.50	.70	.45
(3) Hank Aaron, Matty Alou, Max Alvis, Nelson Briles, Eddie Fisher, Bud Harrelson, Willie Horton, Randy Hundley, Larry Jaster, Jim Kaat, Gary Peters, Pete Ward	7.00	3.50	2.00
(4) Don Buford, John Callison, Tommy Davis, Jackie Hernandez, Fergie Jenkins, Lee May, Denny McLain, Bob Oliver, Roberto Pena, Tony Perez, Joe Torre, Tom Tresh	3.00	1.50	.90
(5) Jim Bunning, Dean Chance, Joe Foy, Sonny Jackson, Don Kessinger, Rick Monday, Gaylord Perry, Roger Repoz, Cookie Rojas, Mel Stottlemyre, Leon Wagner, Jim Wynn	3.00	1.50	.90
(6) Felipe Alou, Gerry Arrigo, Bob Aspromonte, Gary Bell, Clay Dalrymple, Jim Fregosi, Tony Gonzalez, Duane Josephson, Dick McAuliffe, Tony Oliva, Brooks Robinson, Willie Stargell	6.00	3.00	1.75
(7) Steve Barber, Donn Clendenon, Joe Coleman, Vic Davalillo, Russ Gibson, Jerry Grote, Tom Haller, Andy Kosco, Willie McCovey, Don Mincher, Joe Morgan, Don			

	NR MT	EX	VG
Wilson	4.00	2.00	1.25
(8) George Brunet, Don Buford, John Callison, Danny Cater, Tommy Davis, Willie Davis, John Edwards, Jim Hart, Mickey Lolich, Willie Mays, Roberto Pena, Mickey Stanley	7.00	3.50	2.00
(9) Ernie Banks, Glenn Beckert, Ken Berry, Horace Clarke, Bob Clemente, Larry Dierker, Len Gabrielson, Jake Gibbs, Jerry Koosman, Sam McDowell, Tom Satriano, Bill Singer	3.50	1.75	1.00
(10) Gene Alley, Lou Brock, Larry Brown, Moe Drabowsky, Frank Howard, Tommie John, Roger Nelson, Claude Osteen, Phil Regan, Rick Reichardt, Tony Taylor, Roy White	4.00	2.00	1.25
(11) Bob Allison, John Bateman, Don Drysdale, Dave Johnson, Harmon Killebrew, Jim Maloney, Bill Mazeroski, Gerry McNertney, Ron Perranoski, Rico Petrocelli, Pete Rose, Billy Williams	18.00	9.00	5.50
(12) Bernie Allen, Jose Arcia, Stan Bahnsen, Sal Bando, Jim Davenport, Tito Francona, Dick Green, Ron Hunt, Mack Jones, Vada Pinson, George Scott, Don Wert	1.50	.70	.45
(13) Gerry Arrigo, Bob Aspromonte, Joe Azcue, Curt Blefary, Orlando Cepeda, Bill Freehan, Jim Fregosi, Dave Giusti, Duane Josephson, Tim McCarver, Jose Santiago, Bob Tolan	2.00	1.00	.60
(14) Jerry Adair, Johnny Bench, Clete Boyer, John Briggs, Bert Campaneris, Woody Fryman, Ron Kline, Bobby Knoop, Ken McMullen, Adolfo Phillips, John Roseboro, Tom Seaver	7.00	3.50	2.00
(15) Norm Cash, Ron Fairly, Bob Gibson, Bill Hands, Cleon Jones, Al Kaline, Paul Schaal, Mike Shannon, Duke Sims, Reggie Smith, Steve Whitaker, Carl Yastrzemski	12.00	6.00	3.50
(16) Steve Barber, Paul Casanova, Dick Dietz, Russ Gibson, Jerry Grote, Tom Haller, Ed Kranepool, Juan Marichal, Denis Menke, Jim Nash, Bill Robinson, Frank Robinson	4.00	2.00	1.25
(17) Bobby Bolin, Ollie Brown, Rod Carew, Mike Epstein, Bud Harrelson, Larry Jaster, Dave McNally, Willie Norton, Milt Pappas, Gary Peters, Paul Popovich, Stan Williams	6.00	3.00	1.75
(18) Ted Abernathy, Bob Allison, Ed Brinkman, Don Drysdale, Jim Hardin, Julian Javier, Hal Lanier, Jim McGlothlin, Ron Perranoski, Rich Rollins, Ron Santo, Billy Williams	3.00	1.50	.90
(19) Richie Allen, Luis Aparicio, Wally Bunker, Curt Flood, Ken Harrelson, Jim Hunter, Denver Lemaster, Felix Millan, Jim Northrop (Northrup), Art Shamsky, Larry Stahl, Ted Uhlaender	3.00	1.50	.90
(20) Bob Bailey, Johnny Bench, Woody Fryman, Jim Hannan, Ron Kline, Al McBean, Camilo Pascual, Joe Pepitone, Doug Rader, Ron Reed, John Roseboro, Sonny Siebert	3.00	1.50	.90
(21) Jack Aker, Tommy Harper, Tommy Helms, Dennis Higgins, Jim Hunter, Don Lock, Lee Maye, Felix Millan, Jim Northrop (Northrup), Larry Stahl, Don Sutton, Zoilo Versalles	3.00	1.50	.90
(22) Norm Cash, Ed Charles, Joe Horlen, Pat Jarvis, Jim Lonborg, Manny Mota, Boog Powell, Dick Selma, Mike Shannon, Duke Sims, Steve Whitaker, Hoyt Wilhelm	3.00	1.50	.90
(23) Bernie Allen, Ray Culp, Al Ferrara, Tito Francona, Dick Green, Ron Hunt, Ray Oyler, Tom Phoebus, Rusty Staub, Bob Veale, Maury Wills, Wilbur Wood	2.00	1.00	.60
(24) Ernie Banks, Mark Belanger, Steve Blass, Horace Clarke, Bob Clemente, Larry Dierker, Dave Duncan, Chico Salmon, Chris Short, Ron Swoboda, Cesar Tovar, Rick Wise	3.50	1.75	1.00

1969 Topps Super

These 2-1/4" by 3-1/4" cards are not the bigger "Super" cards which would be seen in following years. Rather, what enabled Topps to dub them "Super Baseball Cards" is their high-gloss finish which enhances the bright color photograph used on their

		NR MT	EX	VG
54	Chris Short	25.00	12.50	7.50
55	Cookie Rojas	25.00	12.50	7.50
56	Mateo Alou	25.00	12.50	7.50
57	Steve Blass	25.00	12.50	7.50
58	Roberto Clemente	700.00	350.00	210.00
59	Curt Flood	25.00	12.50	7.50
60	Robert Gibson	90.00	45.00	27.00
61	Tim McCarver	25.00	12.50	7.50
62	Dick Selma	25.00	12.50	7.50
63	Ollie Brown	25.00	12.50	7.50
64	Juan Marichal	90.00	45.00	27.00
65	Willie Mays	500.00	250.00	150.00
66	Willie McCovey	90.00	45.00	27.00

1969 Topps Team Posters

fronts. The only other design element on the front is a facsimile autograph. The backs contain a box at the the bottom which carries the player's name, team, position, a copyright line and the card number. Another unusual feature is that the cards have rounded corners. The 66-card set saw limited production, meaning supplies are tight today. Considering the quality of the cards and the fact that many big names are represented, it's easy to understand why the set is quite expensive and desirable.

		NR MT	EX	VG
Complete Set:		6000.00	3000.00	1800.
Common Player:		25.00	12.50	7.50
1	Dave McNally	25.00	12.50	7.50
2	Frank Robinson	350.00	175.00	105.00
3	Brooks Robinson	350.00	175.00	105.00
4	Ken Harrelson	25.00	12.50	7.50
5	Carl Yastrzemski	700.00	350.00	210.00
6	Ray Culp	25.00	12.50	7.50
7	James Fregosi	25.00	12.50	7.50
8	Rick Reichardt	25.00	12.50	7.50
9	V. Davalillo	25.00	12.50	7.50
10	Luis Aparicio	35.00	17.50	10.50
11	Pete Ward	25.00	12.50	7.50
12	Joe Horlen	25.00	12.50	7.50
13	Luis Tiant	25.00	12.50	7.50
14	Sam McDowell	25.00	12.50	7.50
15	Jose Cardenal	25.00	12.50	7.50
16	Willie Horton	25.00	12.50	7.50
17	Denny McLain	25.00	12.50	7.50
18	Bill Freehan	25.00	12.50	7.50
19	Harmon Killebrew	275.00	137.00	82.00
20	Tony Oliva	25.00	12.50	7.50
21	Dean Chance	25.00	12.50	7.50
22	Joe Foy	25.00	12.50	7.50
23	Roger Nelson	25.00	12.50	7.50
24	Mickey Mantle	1500.00	750.00	450.00
25	Mel Stottlemyre	25.00	12.50	7.50
26	Roy White	25.00	12.50	7.50
27	Rick Monday	25.00	12.50	7.50
28	Reginald Jackson	750.00	375.00	225.00
29	Dagoberto Campaneris	25.00	12.50	7.50
30	Frank Howard	25.00	12.50	7.50
31	Camilo Pascual	25.00	12.50	7.50
32	Tommy Davis	25.00	12.50	7.50
33	Don Mincher	25.00	12.50	7.50
34	Henry Aaron	500.00	250.00	150.00
35	Felipe Rojas Alou	25.00	12.50	7.50
36	Joseph Torre	25.00	12.50	7.50
37	Fergie Jenkins	25.00	12.50	7.50
38	Ronald Santo	25.00	12.50	7.50
39	Billy Williams	40.00	20.00	12.00
40	Tommy Helms	25.00	12.50	7.50
41	Pete Rose	500.00	250.00	150.00
42	Joe Morgan	275.00	137.00	82.00
43	Jim Wynn	25.00	12.50	7.50
44	Curt Blefary	25.00	12.50	7.50
45	Willie Davis	25.00	12.50	7.50
46	Donald Drysdale	275.00	137.00	82.00
47	Tom Haller	25.00	12.50	7.50
48	Rusty Staub	25.00	12.50	7.50
49	Maurice Wills	25.00	12.50	7.50
50	Cleon Jones	25.00	12.50	7.50
51	Jerry Koosman	25.00	12.50	7.50
52	Tom Seaver	700.00	350.00	210.00
53	Rich Allen	25.00	12.50	7.50

Picking up where the 1968 posters left off, the 1969 poster is larger at about 12" by 20." The posters, 24 in number like the previous year, are very different in style. Each has a team focus with a large pennant carrying the team name, along with nine or ten photos of players. Each of the photos carries a name and a facsimile autograph. Unfortunately, the bigger size of 1969 posters meant they had to be folded to fit in their packages as was the case in 1968. That means that collectors today will have a tough job finding them without fairly heavy creases from the folding.

		NR MT	EX	VG
Complete Set:		900.00	450.00	270.00
Common Poster:		17.00	8.50	5.00
1	Detroit Tigers (Norm Cash, Bill Freehan, Willie Horton, Al Kaline, Mickey Lolich, Dick McAuliffe, Denny McLain, Jim Northrup, Mickey Stanley, Don Wert, Earl Wilson)	40.00	20.00	12.00
2	Atlanta Braves (Hank Aaron, Felipe Alou, Clete Boyer, Rico Carty, Tito Francona, Sonny Jackson, Pat Jarvis, Felix Millan, Phil Niekro, Milt Pappas, Joe Torre)	40.00	20.00	12.00
3	Boston Red Sox (Mike Andrews, Tony Conigliaro, Ray Culp, Russ Gibson, Ken Harrelson, Jim Lonborg, Rico Petrocelli, Jose Santiago, George Scott, Reggie Smith, Carl Yastrzemski)	60.00	30.00	18.00
4	Chicago Cubs (Ernie Banks, Glenn Beckert, Bill Hands, Jim Hickman, Ken Holtzman, Randy Hundley, Fergie Jenkins, Don Kessinger, Adolfo Phillips, Ron Santo, Billy Williams)	35.00	17.50	10.50
5	Baltimore Orioles (Mark Belanger, Paul Blair, Don Buford, Andy Etchebarren, Jim Hardin, Dave Johnson, Dave McNally, Tom Phoebus, Boog Powell, Brooks Robinson, Frank Robinson)	50.00	25.00	15.00
6	Houston Astros (Curt Blefary, Donn Clendenon, Larry Dierker, John Edwards, Denny Lemaster, Denis Menke, Norm Miller, Joe Morgan, Doug Rader, Don Wilson, Jim Wynn)	17.00	8.50	5.00
7	Kansas City Royals (Jerry Adair, Wally Bunker, Mike Fiore, Joe Foy, Jackie Hernandez, Pat Kelly, Dave Morehead, Roger Nelson, Dave Nicholson, Eliseo Rodriguez, Steve Whitaker)	17.00	8.50	5.00

	NR MT	EX	VG

8 Philadelphia Phillies (Richie Allen, Johnny Callison, Woody Fryman, Larry Hisle, Don Money, Cookie Rojas, Mike Ryan, Chris Short, Tony Taylor, Bill White, Rick Wise)
17.00 8.50 5.00

9 Seattle Pilots (Jack Aker, Steve Barber, Gary Bell, Tommy Davis, Jim Gosger, Tommy Harper, Gerry McNertney, Don Mincher, Ray Oyler, Rich Rollins, Chico Salmon) 35.00 17.50 10.50

10 Montreal Expos (Bob Bailey, John Bateman, Jack Billingham, Jim Grant, Larry Jaster, Mack Jones, Manny Mota, Rusty Staub, Gary Sutherland, Jim Williams, Maury Wills)
17.00 8.50 5.00

11 Chicago White Sox (Sandy Alomar, Luis Aparicio, Ken Berry, Buddy Bradford, Joe Horlen, Tommy John, Duane Josephson, Tom McCraw, Bill Melton, Pete Ward, Wilbur Wood)
17.00 8.50 5.00

12 San Diego Padres (Jose Arcia, Danny Breeden, Ollie Brown, Bill Davis, Ron Davis, Tony Gonzalez, Dick Kelley, Al McBean, Roberto Pena, Dick Selma, Ed Spiezio)
17.00 8.50 5.00

13 Cleveland Indians (Max Alvis, Joe Azcue, Jose Cardenal, Vern Fuller, Lou Johnson, Sam McDowell, Sonny Siebert, Duke Sims, Russ Snyder, Luis Tiant, Zoilo Versalles)
17.00 8.50 5.00

14 San Francisco Giants (Bobby Bolin, Jim Davenport, Dick Dietz, Jim Hart, Ron Hunt, Hal Lanier, Juan Marichal, Willie Mays, Willie McCovey, Gaylord Perry, Charlie Smith)
40.00 20.00 12.00

15 Minnesota Twins (Bob Allison, Chico Cardenas, Rod Carew, Dean Chance, Jim Kaat, Harmon Killebrew, Tony Oliva, Jim Perry, John Roseboro, Cesar Tovar, Ted Uhlaender)
40.00 20.00 12.00

16 Pittsburgh Pirates (Gene Alley, Matty Alou, Steve Blass, Jim Bunning, Bob Clemente, Rich Hebner, Jerry May, Bill Mazeroski, Bob Robertson, Willie Stargell, Bob Veale)
40.00 20.00 12.00

17 California Angels (Ruben Amaro, George Brunet, Bob Chance, Vic Davalillo, Jim Fregosi, Bobby Knoop, Jim McGlothlin, Rick Reichardt, Roger Repoz, Bob Rodgers, Hoyt Wilhelm) 20.00 10.00 6.00

18 St. Louis Cardinals (Nelson Briles, Lou Brock, Orlando Cepeda, Curt Flood, Bob Gibson, Julian Javier, Dal Maxvill, Tim McCarver, Vada Pinson, Mike Shannon, Ray Washburn) 35.00 17.50 10.50

19 New York Yankees (Stan Bahnsen, Horace Clarke, Bobby Cox, Jake Gibbs, Mickey Mantle, Joe Pepitone, Fritz Peterson, Bill Robinson, Mel Stottlemyre, Tom Tresh, Roy White) 90.00 45.00 27.00

20 Cincinnati Reds (Gerry Arrigo, Johnny Bench, Tommy Helms, Alex Johnson, Jim Maloney, Lee May, Gary Nolan, Tony Perez, Pete Rose, Bob Tolan, Woody Woodward)
90.00 45.00 27.00

21 Oakland Athletics (Sal Bando, Bert Campaneris, Danny Cater, Dick Green, Mike Hershberger, Jim Hunter, Reggie Jackson, Rick Monday, Jim Nash, John Odom, Jim Pagliaroni) 60.00 30.00 18.00

22 Los Angeles Dodgers (Willie Crawford, Willie Davis, Don Drysdale, Ron Fairly, Tom Haller, Andy Kosco, Jim Lefebvre, Claude Osteen, Paul Popovich, Bill Singer, Bill Sudakis) 35.00 17.50 10.50

23 Washington Senators (Bernie Allen, Brant Alyea, Ed Brinkman, Paul Casanova, Joe Coleman, Mike Epstein, Jim Hannan, Frank Howard, Ken McMullen, Camilo Pascual, Del Unser) 17.00 8.50 5.00

24 New York Mets (Tommie Agee, Ken Boswell, Ed Charles, Jerry Grote, Bud Harrelson, Cleon Jones, Jerry Koosman, Ed Kranepool, Jim McAndrew, Tom Seaver, Ron Swoboda) 100.00 50.00 30.00

NOTE: A card number in parentheses ( ) indicates the set is unnumbered.

1970 Topps

 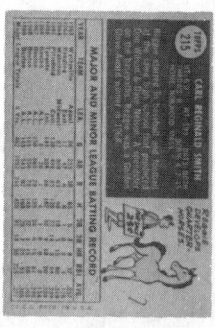

Topps established another set size record by coming out with 720 cards in 1970. The 2-1/2" by 3-1/2" cards have a color photo with a thin white frame. The photo have the player's team overprinted at the top, while the player's name in script and his position are at the bottom. A gray border surrounds the front. Card backs follows the normal design pattern, although they are more readable than some issues of the past. Team cards returned and were joined with many of the usual specialty cards. The World Series highlights were joined by cards with playoff highlights. Statistical leaders and All-Stars are also included in the set. High-numbered cards provide the most expensive cards in the set.

		NR MT	EX	VG
	Complete Set:	1500.00	750.00	450.00
	Common Player: 1-546	.30	.15	.09
	Common Player: 547-633	.80	.40	.25
	Common Player: 634-720	2.00	1.00	.60
1	World Champions (Mets Team)	10.00	3.00	1.00
2	Diego Segui	.60	.30	.20
3	Darrel Chaney	.30	.15	.09
4	Tom Egan	.30	.15	.09
5	Wes Parker	.40	.20	.12
6	Grant Jackson	.30	.15	.09
7	Indians Rookies (Gary Boyd, Russ Nagelson)	.30	.15	.09
8	Jose Martinez	.30	.15	.09
9	Checklist 1-132	2.50	1.25	.70
10	Carl Yastrzemski	40.00	20.00	12.00
11	Nate Colbert	.30	.15	.09
12	John Hiller	.40	.20	.12
13	Jack Hiatt	.30	.15	.09
14	Hank Allen	.30	.15	.09
15	Larry Dierker	.40	.20	.12
16	Charlie Metro	.30	.15	.09
17	Hoyt Wilhelm	4.00	2.00	1.25
18	Carlos May	.50	.25	.15
19	John Boccabella	.30	.15	.09
20	Dave McNally	.60	.30	.20
21	Athletics Rookies (Vida Blue, Gene Tenace)	3.00	1.50	.90
22	Ray Washburn	.30	.15	.09
23	Bill Robinson	.50	.25	.15
24	Dick Selma	.30	.15	.09
25	Cesar Tovar	.30	.15	.09
26	Tug McGraw	1.25	.60	.40
27	Chuck Hinton	.30	.15	.09
28	Billy Wilson	.30	.15	.09
29	Sandy Alomar	.30	.15	.09
30	Matty Alou	.80	.40	.25
31	Marty Pattin	.50	.25	.15
32	Harry Walker	.40	.20	.12
33	Don Wert	.30	.15	.09
34	Willie Crawford	.30	.15	.09
35	Joe Horlen	.30	.15	.09
36	Reds Rookies (Danny Breeden, Bernie Carbo)	.50	.25	.15
37	Dick Drago	.30	.15	.09
38	Mack Jones	.30	.15	.09
39	Mike Nagy	.30	.15	.09
40	Rich Allen	1.50	.70	.45
41	George Lauzerique	.30	.15	.09
42	Tito Fuentes	.30	.15	.09
43	Jack Aker	.50	.25	.15

		NR MT	EX	VG
44	Roberto Pena	.30	.15	.09
45	Dave Johnson	1.00	.50	.30
46	Ken Rudolph	.30	.15	.09
47	Bob Miller	.30	.15	.09
48	Gill Garrido (Gil)	.30	.15	.09
49	Tim Cullen	.30	.15	.09
50	Tommie Agee	.40	.20	.12
51	Bob Christian	.30	.15	.09
52	Bruce Dal Canton	.30	.15	.09
53	John Kennedy	.50	.25	.15
54	Jeff Torborg	.40	.20	.12
55	John Odom	.40	.20	.12
56	Phillies Rookies (Joe Lis, Scott Reid)			
		.30	.15	.09
57	Pat Kelly	.30	.15	.09
58	Dave Marshall	.30	.15	.09
59	Dick Ellsworth	.30	.15	.09
60	Jim Wynn	.60	.30	.20
61	N.L. Batting Leaders (Bob Clemente, Cleon Jones, Pete Rose)	5.00	2.50	1.50
62	A.L. Batting Leaders (Rod Carew, Tony Oliva, Reggie Smith)	2.50	1.25	.70
63	N.L. RBI Leaders (Willie McCovey, Tony Perez, Ron Santo)	2.50	1.25	.70
64	A.L. RBI Leaders (Reggie Jackson, Harmon Killebrew, Boog Powell)	2.50	1.25	.70
65	N.L. Home Run Leaders (Hank Aaron, Lee May, Willie McCovey)	3.00	1.50	.90
66	A.L. Home Run Leaders (Frank Howard, Reggie Jackson, Harmon Killebrew)	2.50	1.25	.70
67	N.L. ERA Leaders (Steve Carlton, Bob Gibson, Juan Marichal)	3.00	1.50	.90
68	A.L. ERA Leaders (Dick Bosman, Mike Cuellar, Jim Palmer)	2.00	1.00	.60
69	N.L. Pitching Leaders (Fergie Jenkins, Juan Marichal, Phil Niekro, Tom Seaver)	2.50	1.25	.70
70	A.L. Pitching Leaders (Dave Boswell, Mike Cuellar, Dennis McLain, Dave McNally, Jim Perry, Mel Stottlemyre)	2.00	1.00	.60
71	N.L. Strikeout Leaders (Bob Gibson, Fergie Jenkins, Bill Singer)	2.50	1.25	.70
72	A.L. Strikeout Leaders (Mickey Lolich, Sam McDowell, Andy Messersmith)	2.00	1.00	.60
73	Wayne Granger	.30	.15	.09
74	Angels Rookies (Greg Washburn, Wally Wolf)	.30	.15	.09
75	Jim Kaat	2.50	1.25	.70
76	Carl Taylor	.30	.15	.09
77	Frank Linzy	.30	.15	.09
78	Joe Lahoud	.30	.15	.09
79	Clay Kirby	.30	.15	.09
80	Don Kessinger	.40	.20	.12
81	Dave May	.30	.15	.09
82	Frank Fernandez	.50	.25	.15
83	Don Cardwell	.30	.15	.09
84	Paul Casanova	.30	.15	.09
85	Max Alvis	.30	.15	.09
86	Lum Harris	.30	.15	.09
87	Steve Renko	.30	.15	.09
88	Pilots Rookies (Dick Baney, Miguel Fuentes)	.50	.25	.15
89	Juan Rios	.30	.15	.09
90	Tim McCarver	1.00	.50	.30
91	Rich Morales	.30	.15	.09
92	George Culver	.30	.15	.09
93	Rick Renick	.30	.15	.09
94	Fred Patek	.40	.20	.12
95	Earl Wilson	.30	.15	.09
96	Cards Rookies (Leron Lee, *Jerry Reuss*)	2.00	1.00	.60
97	Joe Moeller	.30	.15	.09
98	Gates Brown	.30	.15	.09
99	Bobby Pfeil	.30	.15	.09
100	Mel Stottlemyre	1.00	.50	.30
101	Bobby Floyd	.30	.15	.09
102	Joe Rudi	.80	.40	.25
103	Frank Reberger	.30	.15	.09
104	Gerry Moses	.30	.15	.09
105	Tony Gonzalez	.30	.15	.09
106	Darold Knowles	.30	.15	.09
107	Bobby Etheridge	.30	.15	.09
108	Tom Burgmeier	.40	.20	.12
109	Expos Rookies (Garry Jestadt, Carl Morton)	.40	.20	.12
110	Bob Moose	.30	.15	.09
111	Mike Hegan	.50	.25	.15
112	Dave Nelson	.30	.15	.09
113	Jim Ray	.30	.15	.09
114	Gene Michael	.60	.30	.20
115	Alex Johnson	.40	.20	.12
116	Sparky Lyle	1.00	.50	.30

		NR MT	EX	VG
117	Don Young	.30	.15	.09
118	George Mitterwald	.30	.15	.09
119	Chuck Taylor	.30	.15	.09
120	Sal Bando	.80	.40	.25
121	Orioles Rookies (Fred Beene, *Terry Crowley*)	.40	.20	.12
122	George Stone	.30	.15	.09
123	Don Gutteridge	.30	.15	.09
124	Larry Jaster	.30	.15	.09
125	Deron Johnson	.30	.15	.09
126	Marty Martinez	.30	.15	.09
127	Joe Coleman	.40	.20	.12
128a	Checklist 133-263 (226 is R Perranoski)	3.00	1.50	.90
128b	Checklist 133-263 (226 is R. Perranoski)	2.50	1.25	.70
129	Jimmie Price	.30	.15	.09
130	Ollie Brown	.30	.15	.09
131	Dodgers Rookies (Ray Lamb, Bob Stinson)	.30	.15	.09
132	Jim McGlothlin	.30	.15	.09
133	Clay Carroll	.40	.20	.12
134	Danny Walton	.50	.25	.15
135	Dick Dietz	.30	.15	.09
136	Steve Hargan	.30	.15	.09
137	Art Shamsky	.30	.15	.09
138	Joe Foy	.30	.15	.09
139	Rich Nye	.30	.15	.09
140	Reggie Jackson	125.00	62.00	37.00
141	Pirates Rookies (Dave Cash, Johnny Jeter)	.50	.25	.15
142	Fritz Peterson	.50	.25	.15
143	Phil Gagliano	.30	.15	.09
144	Ray Culp	.30	.15	.09
145	Rico Carty	.80	.40	.25
146	Danny Murphy	.30	.15	.09
147	Angel Hermoso	.30	.15	.09
148	Earl Weaver	1.25	.60	.40
149	Billy Champion	.30	.15	.09
150	Harmon Killebrew	6.00	3.00	1.75
151	Dave Roberts	.30	.15	.09
152	Ike Brown	.30	.15	.09
153	Gary Gentry	.30	.15	.09
154	Senators Rookies (Jan Dukes, Jim Miles)	.30	.15	.09
155	Denis Menke	.30	.15	.09
156	Eddie Fisher	.30	.15	.09
157	Manny Mota	.50	.25	.15
158	Jerry McNertney	.50	.25	.15
159	Tommy Helms	.40	.20	.12
160	Phil Niekro	3.50	1.75	1.00
161	Richie Scheinblum	.30	.15	.09
162	Jerry Johnson	.30	.15	.09
163	Syd O'Brien	.30	.15	.09
164	Ty Cline	.30	.15	.09
165	Ed Kirkpatrick	.30	.15	.09
166	Al Oliver	2.00	1.00	.60
167	Bill Burbach	.50	.25	.15
168	Dave Watkins	.30	.15	.09
169	Tom Hall	.30	.15	.09
170	Billy Williams	4.50	2.25	1.25
171	Jim Nash	.30	.15	.09
172	Braves Rookies (*Ralph Garr*, Garry Hill)	1.00	.50	.30
173	Jim Hicks	.30	.15	.09
174	Ted Sizemore	.30	.15	.09
175	Dick Bosman	.30	.15	.09
176	Jim Hart	.40	.20	.12
177	Jim Northrup	.40	.20	.12
178	Denny Lemaster	.30	.15	.09
179	Ivan Murrell	.30	.15	.09
180	Tommy John	2.75	1.50	.80
181	Sparky Anderson	1.25	.60	.40
182	Dick Hall	.30	.15	.09
183	Jerry Grote	.40	.20	.12
184	Ray Fosse	.40	.20	.12
185	Don Mincher	.50	.25	.15
186	Rick Joseph	.30	.15	.09
187	Mike Hedlund	.30	.15	.09
188	Manny Sanguillen	.40	.20	.12
189	Yankees Rookies (Dave McDonald, *Thurman Munson*)	100.00	50.00	30.00
190	Joe Torre	1.25	.60	.40
191	Vicente Romo	.30	.15	.09
192	Jim Qualls	.30	.15	.09
193	Mike Wegener	.30	.15	.09
194	Chuck Manuel	.30	.15	.09
195	N.L. Playoff Game 1 (Seaver Wins Opener!)	3.00	1.50	.90
196	N.L. Playoff Game 2 (Mets Show Muscle!)	1.75	.90	.50

		NR MT	EX	VG
197	N.L. Playoff Game 3 (Ryan Saves The Day!)	6.00	3.00	1.75
198	N.L. Playoffs Summary (We're Number One!)	1.75	.90	.50
199	A.L. Playoff Game 1 (Orioles Win A Squeaker!)	1.50	.70	.45
200	A.L. Playoff Game 2 (Powell Scores Winning Run!)	1.75	.90	.50
201	A.L. Playoff Game 3 (Birds Wrap It Up!)	1.50	.70	.45
202	A.L. Playoffs Summary (Sweep Twins In Three!)	1.50	.70	.45
203	Rudy May	.40	.20	.12
204	Len Gabrielson	.30	.15	.09
205	Bert Campaneris	.80	.40	.25
206	Clete Boyer	.40	.20	.12
207	Tigers Rookies (Norman McRae, Bob Reed)	.30	.15	.09
208	Fred Gladding	.30	.15	.09
209	Ken Suarez	.30	.15	.09
210	Juan Marichal	8.00	4.00	2.50
211	Ted Williams	7.00	3.50	2.00
212	Al Santorini	.30	.15	.09
213	Andy Etchebarren	.30	.15	.09
214	Ken Boswell	.30	.15	.09
215	Reggie Smith	.60	.30	.20
216	Chuck Hartenstein	.30	.15	.09
217	Ron Hansen	.30	.15	.09
218	Ron Stone	.30	.15	.09
219	Jerry Kenney	.50	.25	.15
220	Steve Carlton	20.00	10.00	6.00
221	Ron Brand	.30	.15	.09
222	Jim Rooker	.30	.15	.09
223	Nate Oliver	.30	.15	.09
224	Steve Barber	.50	.25	.15
225	Lee May	.60	.30	.20
226	Ron Perranoski	.40	.20	.12
227	Astros Rookies (John Mayberry, Bob Watkins)	1.00	.50	.30
228	Aurelio Rodriguez	.40	.20	.12
229	Rich Robertson	.30	.15	.09
230	Brooks Robinson	10.00	5.00	3.00
231	Luis Tiant	1.25	.60	.40
232	Bob Didier	.30	.15	.09
233	Lew Krausse	.30	.15	.09
234	Tommy Dean	.30	.15	.09
235	Mike Epstein	.40	.20	.12
236	Bob Veale	.40	.20	.12
237	Russ Gibson	.30	.15	.09
238	Jose Laboy	.30	.15	.09
239	Ken Berry	.30	.15	.09
240	Fergie Jenkins	2.50	1.25	.70
241	Royals Rookies (Al Fitzmorris, Scott Northey)	.30	.15	.09
242	Walter Alston	1.75	.90	.50
243	Joe Sparma	.30	.15	.09
244a	Checklist 264-372 (red bat on front)	3.00	1.50	.90
244b	Checklist 264-372 (brown bat on front)	2.50	1.25	.70
245	Leo Cardenas	.30	.15	.09
246	Jim McAndrew	.30	.15	.09
247	Lou Klimchock	.30	.15	.09
248	Jesus Alou	.40	.20	.12
249	Bob Locker	.50	.25	.15
250	Willie McCovey	6.00	3.00	1.75
251	Dick Schofield	.30	.15	.09
252	Lowell Palmer	.30	.15	.09
253	Ron Woods	.50	.25	.15
254	Camilo Pascual	.50	.25	.15
255	Jim Spencer	.50	.25	.15
256	Vic Davalillo	.40	.20	.12
257	Dennis Higgins	.30	.15	.09
258	Paul Popovich	.30	.15	.09
259	Tommie Reynolds	.30	.15	.09
260	Claude Osteen	.50	.25	.15
261	Curt Motton	.30	.15	.09
262	Padres Rookies (Jerry Morales, Jim Williams)	.30	.15	.09
263	Duane Josephson	.30	.15	.09
264	Rich Hebner	.40	.20	.12
265	Randy Hundley	.30	.15	.09
266	Wally Bunker	.30	.15	.09
267	Twins Rookies (Herman Hill, Paul Ratliff)	.30	.15	.09
268	Claude Raymond	.30	.15	.09
269	Cesar Gutierrez	.30	.15	.09
270	Chris Short	.40	.20	.12
271	Greg Goossen	.50	.25	.15
272	Hector Torres	.30	.15	.09
273	Ralph Houk	1.00	.50	.30

		NR MT	EX	VG
274	Gerry Arrigo	.30	.15	.09
275	Duke Sims	.30	.15	.09
276	Ron Hunt	.40	.20	.12
277	Paul Doyle	.30	.15	.09
278	Tommie Aaron	.50	.25	.15
279	Bill Lee	.50	.25	.15
280	Donn Clendenon	.40	.20	.12
281	Casey Cox	.30	.15	.09
282	Steve Huntz	.30	.15	.09
283	Angel Bravo	.30	.15	.09
284	Jack Baldschun	.30	.15	.09
285	Paul Blair	.40	.20	.12
286	Dodgers Rookies (Bill Buckner, Jack Jenkins)	6.00	3.00	1.75
287	Fred Talbot	.30	.15	.09
288	Larry Hisle	.40	.20	.12
289	Gene Brabender	.50	.25	.15
290	Rod Carew	50.00	25.00	15.00
291	Leo Durocher	1.25	.60	.40
292	Eddie Leon	.30	.15	.09
293	Bob Bailey	.30	.15	.09
294	Jose Azcue	.30	.15	.09
295	Cecil Upshaw	.30	.15	.09
296	Woody Woodward	.40	.20	.12
297	Curt Blefary	.50	.25	.15
298	Ken Henderson	.30	.15	.09
299	Buddy Bradford	.30	.15	.09
300	Tom Seaver	80.00	40.00	25.00
301	Chico Salmon	.30	.15	.09
302	Jeff James	.30	.15	.09
303	Brant Alyea	.30	.15	.09
304	Bill Russell	1.50	.70	.45
305	World Series Game 1 (Buford Belts Leadoff Homer!)	1.75	.90	.50
306	World Series Game 2 (Clendenon's Homer Breaks Ice!)	1.75	.90	.50
307	World Series Game 3 (Agee's Catch Saves The Day!)	1.75	.90	.50
308	World Series Game 4 (Martin's Bunt Ends Deadlock!)	1.75	.90	.50
309	World Series Game 5 (Koosman Shuts The Door!)	1.75	.90	.50
310	World Series Summary (Mets Whoop It Up!)	1.75	.90	.50
311	Dick Green	.30	.15	.09
312	Mike Torrez	.40	.20	.12
313	Mayo Smith	.30	.15	.09
314	Bill McCool	.30	.15	.09
315	Luis Aparicio	4.50	2.25	1.25
316	Skip Guinn	.30	.15	.09
317	Red Sox Rookies (Luis Alvarado, Billy Conigliaro)	.40	.20	.12
318	Willie Smith	.30	.15	.09
319	Clayton Dalrymple	.30	.15	.09
320	Jim Maloney	.40	.20	.12
321	Lou Piniella	1.50	.70	.45
322	Luke Walker	.30	.15	.09
323	Wayne Comer	.50	.25	.15
324	Tony Taylor	.30	.15	.09
325	Dave Boswell	.30	.15	.09
326	Bill Voss	.30	.15	.09
327	Hal King	.30	.15	.09
328	George Brunet	.30	.15	.09
329	Chris Cannizzaro	.30	.15	.09
330	Lou Brock	6.00	3.00	1.75
331	Chuck Dobson	.30	.15	.09
332	Bobby Wine	.30	.15	.09
333	Bobby Murcer	1.25	.60	.40
334	Phil Regan	.30	.15	.09
335	Bill Freehan	.40	.20	.12
336	Del Unser	.30	.15	.09
337	Mike McCormick	.40	.20	.12
338	Paul Schaal	.30	.15	.09
339	Johnny Edwards	.30	.15	.09
340	Tony Conigliaro	1.25	.60	.40
341	Bill Sudakis	.30	.15	.09
342	Wilbur Wood	.40	.20	.12
343a	Checklist 373-459 (red bat on front)	3.50	1.75	1.00
343b	Checklist 373-459 (brown bat on front)	3.00	1.50	.90
344	Marcelino Lopez	.30	.15	.09
345	Al Ferrara	.30	.15	.09
346	Red Schoendienst	1.25	.60	.40
347	Russ Snyder	.30	.15	.09
348	Mets Rookies (Jesse Hudson, Mike Jorgensen)	.40	.20	.12
349	Steve Hamilton	.50	.25	.15
350	Roberto Clemente	40.00	20.00	12.00
351	Tom Murphy	.30	.15	.09
352	Bob Barton	.30	.15	.09

		NR MT	EX	VG
353	Stan Williams	.30	.15	.09
354	Amos Otis	.50	.25	.15
355	Doug Rader	.30	.15	.09
356	Fred Lasher	.30	.15	.09
357	Bob Burda	.30	.15	.09
358	*Pedro Borbon*	.40	.20	.12
359	Phil Roof	.50	.25	.15
360	Curt Flood	1.00	.50	.30
361	Ray Jarvis	.30	.15	.09
362	Joe Hague	.30	.15	.09
363	Tom Shopay	.30	.15	.09
364	Dan McGinn	.30	.15	.09
365	Zoilo Versalles	.40	.20	.12
366	Barry Moore	.30	.15	.09
367	Mike Lum	.30	.15	.09
368	Ed Herrmann	.30	.15	.09
369	Alan Foster	.30	.15	.09
370	Tommy Harper	.70	.35	.20
371	Rod Gaspar	.30	.15	.09
372	Dave Giusti	.30	.15	.09
373	Roy White	1.00	.50	.30
374	Tommie Sisk	.30	.15	.09
375	Johnny Callison	.80	.40	.25
376	Lefty Phillips	.30	.15	.09
377	Bill Butler	.30	.15	.09
378	Jim Davenport	.30	.15	.09
379	Tom Tischinski	.30	.15	.09
380	Tony Perez	3.00	1.50	.90
381	Athletics Rookies (Bobby Brooks, Mike Olivo)	.30	.15	.09
382	Jack DiLauro	.30	.15	.09
383	Mickey Stanley	.40	.20	.12
384	Gary Neibauer	.30	.15	.09
385	George Scott	.40	.20	.12
386	Bill Dillman	.30	.15	.09
387	Orioles Team	1.50	.70	.45
388	Byron Browne	.30	.15	.09
389	Jim Shellenback	.30	.15	.09
390	Willie Davis	.80	.40	.25
391	Larry Brown	.30	.15	.09
392	Walt Hriniak	.30	.15	.09
393	John Gelnar	.50	.25	.15
394	Gil Hodges	4.00	2.00	1.25
395	Walt Williams	.30	.15	.09
396	Steve Blass	.40	.20	.12
397	Roger Repoz	.30	.15	.09
398	Bill Stoneman	.30	.15	.09
399	Yankees Team	2.00	1.00	.60
400	Denny McLain	1.50	.70	.45
401	Giants Rookies (John Harrell, Bernie Williams)	.30	.15	.09
402	Ellie Rodriguez	.30	.15	.09
403	Jim Bunning	3.25	1.75	1.00
404	Rich Reese	.30	.15	.09
405	Bill Hands	.30	.15	.09
406	Mike Andrews	.30	.15	.09
407	Bob Watson	.40	.20	.12
408	Paul Lindblad	.30	.15	.09
409	Bob Tolan	.40	.20	.12
410	Boog Powell	2.00	1.00	.60
411	Dodgers Team	1.50	.70	.45
412	Larry Burchart	.30	.15	.09
413	Sonny Jackson	.30	.15	.09
414	Paul Edmondson	.30	.15	.09
415	Julian Javier	.30	.15	.09
416	Joe Verbanic	.50	.25	.15
417	John Bateman	.30	.15	.09
418	John Donaldson	.50	.25	.15
419	Ron Taylor	.30	.15	.09
420	Ken McMullen	.30	.15	.09
421	Pat Dobson	.40	.20	.12
422	Royals Team	1.25	.60	.40
423	Jerry May	.30	.15	.09
424	Mike Kilkenny	.30	.15	.09
425	Bobby Bonds	1.25	.60	.40
426	Bill Rigney	.30	.15	.09
427	Fred Norman	.30	.15	.09
428	Don Buford	.40	.20	.12
429	Cubs Rookies (Randy Bobb, Jim Cosman)	.30	.15	.09
430	Andy Messersmith	.50	.25	.15
431	Ron Swoboda	.40	.20	.12
432a	Checklist 460-546 ("Baseball" on front in yellow)	4.00	2.00	1.25
432b	Checklist 460-546 ("Baseball" on front in white)	2.50	1.25	.70
433	Ron Bryant	.30	.15	.09
434	Felipe Alou	.70	.35	.20
435	Nelson Briles	.30	.15	.09
436	Phillies Team	1.25	.60	.40
437	Danny Cater	.50	.25	.15

		NR MT	EX	VG
438	Pat Jarvis	.30	.15	.09
439	Lee Maye	.30	.15	.09
440	Bill Mazeroski	1.00	.50	.30
441	John O'Donoghue	.50	.25	.15
442	Gene Mauch	.70	.35	.20
443	Al Jackson	.30	.15	.09
444	White Sox Rookies (Bill Farmer, John Matias)	.30	.15	.09
445	Vada Pinson	1.25	.60	.40
446	*Billy Grabarkewitz*	.40	.20	.12
447	Lee Stange	.30	.15	.09
448	Astros Team	1.25	.60	.40
449	Jim Palmer	15.00	7.50	4.50
450	Willie McCovey AS	3.50	1.75	1.00
451	Boog Powell AS	1.00	.50	.30
452	Felix Millan AS	.50	.25	.15
453	Rod Carew AS	4.00	2.00	1.25
454	Ron Santo AS	.80	.40	.25
455	Brooks Robinson AS	3.50	1.75	1.00
456	Don Kessinger AS	.50	.25	.15
457	Rico Petrocelli AS	.50	.25	.15
458	Pete Rose AS	8.00	4.00	2.50
459	Reggie Jackson AS	8.00	4.00	2.50
460	Matty Alou AS	.70	.35	.20
461	Carl Yastrzemski AS	5.00	2.50	1.50
462	Hank Aaron AS	5.50	2.75	1.75
463	Frank Robinson AS	3.50	1.75	1.00
464	Johnny Bench AS	10.00	5.00	3.00
465	Bill Freehan AS	.50	.25	.15
466	Juan Marichal AS	2.75	1.50	.80
467	Denny McLain AS	.80	.40	.25
468	Jerry Koosman AS	.60	.30	.20
469	Sam McDowell AS	.60	.30	.20
470	Willie Stargell	7.00	3.50	2.00
471	Chris Zachary	.30	.15	.09
472	Braves Team	1.25	.60	.40
473	Don Bryant	.50	.25	.15
474	Dick Kelley	.30	.15	.09
475	Dick McAuliffe	.40	.20	.12
476	Don Shaw	.30	.15	.09
477	Orioles Rookies (Roger Freed, Al Severinsen)	.30	.15	.09
478	Bob Heise	.30	.15	.09
479	Dick Woodson	.30	.15	.09
480	Glenn Beckert	.40	.20	.12
481	Jose Tartabull	.30	.15	.09
482	Tom Hilgendorf	.30	.15	.09
483	Gail Hopkins	.30	.15	.09
484	Gary Nolan	.30	.15	.09
485	Jay Johnstone	.50	.25	.15
486	Terry Harmon	.30	.15	.09
487	Cisco Carlos	.30	.15	.09
488	J.C. Martin	.30	.15	.09
489	Eddie Kasko	.30	.15	.09
490	Bill Singer	.40	.20	.12
491	Graig Nettles	4.00	2.00	1.25
492	Astros Rookies (Keith Lampard, Scipio Spinks)	.30	.15	.09
493	Lindy McDaniel	.50	.25	.15
494	Larry Stahl	.30	.15	.09
495	Dave Morehead	.30	.15	.09
496	Steve Whitaker	.30	.15	.09
497	Eddie Watt	.30	.15	.09
498	Al Weis	.30	.15	.09
499	Skip Lockwood	.50	.25	.15
500	Hank Aaron	40.00	20.00	12.00
501	White Sox Team	1.25	.60	.40
502	Rollie Fingers	15.00	7.50	4.50
503	Dal Maxvill	.40	.20	.12
504	Don Pavletich	.30	:15	.09
505	Ken Holtzman	.40	.20	.12
506	Ed Stroud	.30	.15	.09
507	Pat Corrales	.50	.25	.15
508	Joe Niekro	.70	.35	.20
509	Expos Team	1.25	.60	.40
510	Tony Oliva	1.75	.90	.50
511	Joe Hoerner	.30	.15	.09
512	Billy Harris	.30	.15	.09
513	Preston Gomez	.30	.15	.09
514	Steve Hovley	.50	.25	.15
515	Don Wilson	.30	.15	.09
516	Yankees Rookies (John Ellis, Jim Lyttle)	.50	.25	.15
517	Joe Gibbon	.30	.15	.09
518	Bill Melton	.40	.20	.12
519	Don McMahon	.30	.15	.09
520	Willie Horton	.70	.35	.20
521	Cal Koonce	.30	.15	.09
522	Angels Team	1.25	.60	.40
523	Jose Pena	.30	.15	.09
524	Alvin Dark	.60	.30	.20

		NR MT	EX	VG
525	Jerry Adair	.30	.15	.09
526	Ron Herbel	.30	.15	.09
527	Don Bosch	.30	.15	.09
528	Elrod Hendricks	.30	.15	.09
529	Bob Aspromonte	.30	.15	.09
530	Bob Gibson	8.00	4.00	2.50
531	Ron Clark	.30	.15	.09
532	Danny Murtaugh	.50	.25	.15
533	Buzz Stephen	.50	.25	.15
534	Twins Team	1.50	.70	.45
535	Andy Kosco	.30	.15	.09
536	Mike Kekich	.50	.25	.15
537	Joe Morgan	12.00	6.00	3.50
538	Bob Humphreys	.30	.15	.09
539	Phillies Rookies (*Larry Bowa*, Dennis Doyle)	3.00	1.50	.90
540	Gary Peters	.40	.20	.12
541	Bill Heath	.30	.15	.09
542a	Checklist 547-633 (grey bat on front)	3.50	1.75	1.00
542b	Checklist 547-633 (brown bat on front)	2.50	1.25	.70
543	Clyde Wright	.30	.15	.09
544	Reds Team	1.25	.60	.40
545	Ken Harrelson	1.25	.60	.40
546	Ron Reed	.40	.20	.12
547	Rick Monday	1.00	.50	.30
548	Howie Reed	.80	.40	.25
549	Cardinals Team	1.75	.90	.50
550	Frank Howard	2.25	1.25	.70
551	Dock Ellis	.90	.45	.25
552	Royals Rookies (Don O'Riley, Dennis Paepke, Fred Rico)	.80	.40	.25
553	Jim Lefebvre	.90	.45	.25
554	Tom Timmermann	.80	.40	.25
555	Orlando Cepeda	3.25	1.75	1.00
556	Dave Bristol	.90	.45	.25
557	Ed Kranepool	1.00	.50	.30
558	Vern Fuller	.80	.40	.25
559	Tommy Davis	1.25	.60	.40
560	Gaylord Perry	7.00	3.50	2.00
561	Tom McCraw	.80	.40	.25
562	Ted Abernathy	.80	.40	.25
563	Red Sox Team	2.00	1.00	.60
564	Johnny Briggs	.80	.40	.25
565	Jim Hunter	7.00	3.50	2.00
566	Gene Alley	.90	.45	.25
567	Bob Oliver	.80	.40	.25
568	Stan Bahnsen	.90	.45	.25
569	Cookie Rojas	.80	.40	.25
570	Jim Fregosi	1.00	.50	.30
571	Jim Brewer	.80	.40	.25
572	Frank Quilici	.80	.40	.25
573	Padres Rookies (Mike Corkins, Rafael Robles, Ron Slocum)	.80	.40	.25
574	Bobby Bolin	.90	.45	.25
575	Cleon Jones	.90	.45	.25
576	Milt Pappas	.90	.45	.25
577	Bernie Allen	.80	.40	.25
578	Tom Griffin	.80	.40	.25
579	Tigers Team	2.25	1.25	.70
580	Pete Rose	75.00	37.00	22.00
581	Tom Satriano	.80	.40	.25
582	Mike Paul	.80	.40	.25
583	Hal Lanier	.90	.45	.25
584	Al Downing	.90	.45	.25
585	Rusty Staub	2.00	1.00	.60
586	Rickey Clark	.80	.40	.25
587	Jose Arcia	.80	.40	.25
588a	Checklist 634-720 (666 is Adolpho Phillips)	4.50	2.25	1.25
588b	Checklist 634-720 (666 is Adolfo Phillips)	3.00	1.50	.90
589	Joe Keough	.80	.40	.25
590	Mike Cuellar	.90	.45	.25
591	Mike Ryan	.80	.40	.25
592	Daryl Patterson	.80	.40	.25
593	Cubs Team	1.75	.90	.50
594	Jake Gibbs	.90	.45	.25
595	Maury Wills	2.50	1.25	.70
596	Mike Hershberger	.90	.45	.25
597	Sonny Siebert	.80	.40	.25
598	Joe Pepitone	1.25	.60	.40
599	Senators Rookies (Gene Martin, Dick Stelmaszek, Dick Such)	.80	.40	.25
600	Willie Mays	50.00	25.00	15.00
601	Pete Richert	.80	.40	.25
602	Ted Savage	.80	.40	.25
603	Ray Oyler	.80	.40	.25
604	Clarence Gaston	.80	.40	.25
605	Rick Wise	.90	.45	.25

		NR MT	EX	VG
606	Chico Ruiz	.80	.40	.25
607	Gary Waslewski	.80	.40	.25
608	Pirates Team	1.75	.90	.50
609	*Buck Martinez*	.90	.45	.25
610	Jerry Koosman	1.25	.60	.40
611	Norm Cash	1.50	.70	.45
612	Jim Hickman	.90	.45	.25
613	Dave Baldwin	.90	.45	.25
614	Mike Shannon	.90	.45	.25
615	Mark Belanger	.90	.45	.25
616	Jim Merritt	.80	.40	.25
617	Jim French	.80	.40	.25
618	Billy Wynne	.80	.40	.25
619	Norm Miller	.80	.40	.25
620	Jim Perry	1.00	.50	.30
621	Braves Rookies (*Darrell Evans*, Rick Kester, Mike McQueen)	15.00	7.50	4.50
622	Don Sutton	7.00	3.50	2.00
623	Horace Clarke	.90	.45	.25
624	Clyde King	.80	.40	.25
625	Dean Chance	.90	.45	.25
626	Dave Ricketts	.80	.40	.25
627	Gary Wagner	.80	.40	.25
628	Wayne Garrett	.80	.40	.25
629	Merv Rettenmund	.90	.45	.25
630	Ernie Banks	20.00	10.00	6.00
631	Athletics Team	1.75	.90	.50
632	Gary Sutherland	.80	.40	.25
633	Roger Nelson	.80	.40	.25
634	Bud Harrelson	2.25	1.25	.70
635	Bob Allison	2.25	1.25	.70
636	Jim Stewart	2.00	1.00	.60
637	Indians Team	3.00	1.50	.90
638	Frank Bertaina	2.00	1.00	.60
639	Dave Campbell	2.00	1.00	.60
640	Al Kaline	30.00	15.00	9.00
641	Al McBean	2.00	1.00	.60
642	Angels Rookies (Greg Garrett, Gordon Lund, Jarvis Tatum)	2.00	1.00	.60
643	Jose Pagan	2.00	1.00	.60
644	Gerry Nyman	2.00	1.00	.60
645	Don Money	2.00	1.00	.60
646	Jim Britton	2.00	1.00	.60
647	Tom Matchick	2.00	1.00	.60
648	Larry Haney	2.00	1.00	.60
649	Jimmie Hall	2.00	1.00	.60
650	Sam McDowell	2.50	1.25	.70
651	Jim Gosger	2.00	1.00	.60
652	Rich Rollins	2.25	1.25	.70
653	Moe Drabowsky	2.00	1.00	.60
654	N.L. Rookies (Boots Day, *Oscar Gamble*, Angel Mangual)	2.50	1.25	.70
655	John Roseboro	2.25	1.25	.70
656	Jim Hardin	2.00	1.00	.60
657	Padres Team	4.00	2.00	1.25
658	Ken Tatum	2.00	1.00	.60
659	Pete Ward	2.25	1.25	.70
660	Johnny Bench	150.00	60.00	38.00
661	Jerry Robertson	2.00	1.00	.60
662	Frank Lucchesi	2.00	1.00	.60
663	Tito Francona	2.25	1.25	.70
664	Bob Robertson	2.00	1.00	.60
665	Jim Lonborg	2.25	1.25	.70
666	Adolfo Phillips	2.00	1.00	.60
667	Bob Meyer	2.25	1.25	.70
668	Bob Tillman	2.00	1.00	.60
669	White Sox Rookies (Bart Johnson, Dan Lazar, Mickey Scott)	2.00	1.00	.60
670	Ron Santo	3.25	1.75	1.00
671	Jim Campanis	2.00	1.00	.60
672	Leon McFadden	2.00	1.00	.60
673	Ted Uhlaender	2.00	1.00	.60
674	Dave Leonhard	2.00	1.00	.60
675	Jose Cardenal	2.25	1.25	.70
676	Senators Team	3.25	1.75	1.00
677	Woodie Fryman	2.25	1.25	.70
678	Dave Duncan	2.00	1.00	.60
679	Ray Sadecki	2.00	1.00	.60
680	Rico Petrocelli	2.25	1.25	.70
681	Bob Garibaldi	2.00	1.00	.60
682	Dalton Jones	2.00	1.00	.60
683	Reds Rookies (Vern Geishert, Hal McRae, Wayne Simpson)	2.75	1.50	.80
684	Jack Fisher	2.00	1.00	.60
685	Tom Haller	2.25	1.25	.70
686	Jackie Hernandez	2.00	1.00	.60
687	Bob Priddy	2.00	1.00	.60
688	Ted Kubiak	2.25	1.25	.70
689	Frank Tepedino	2.25	1.25	.70
690	Ron Fairly	2.25	1.25	.70
691	Joe Grzenda	2.00	1.00	.60

		NR MT	EX	VG
692	Duffy Dyer	2.00	1.00	.60
693	Bob Johnson	2.00	1.00	.60
694	Gary Ross	2.00	1.00	.60
695	Bobby Knoop	2.00	1.00	.60
696	Giants Team	3.25	1.75	1.00
697	Jim Hannan	2.00	1.00	.60
698	Tom Tresh	2.75	1.50	.80
699	Hank Aguirre	2.00	1.00	.60
700	Frank Robinson	40.00	20.00	12.00
701	Jack Billingham	2.00	1.00	.60
702	A.L. Rookies (Bob Johnson, Ron Klimkowski, Bill Zepp)	2.25	1.25	.70
703	Lou Marone	2.00	1.00	.60
704	Frank Baker	2.00	1.00	.60
705	Tony Cloninger	2.25	1.25	.70
706	John McNamara	2.50	1.25	.70
707	Kevin Collins	2.00	1.00	.60
708	Jose Santiago	2.00	1.00	.60
709	Mike Fiore	2.00	1.00	.60
710	Felix Millan	2.00	1.00	.60
711	Ed Brinkman	2.25	1.25	.70
712	Nolan Ryan	350.00	175.00	105.00
713	Pilots Team	12.00	6.00	3.50
714	Al Spangler	2.00	1.00	.60
715	Mickey Lolich	5.00	2.50	1.50
716	Cards Rookies (Sal Campisi, *Reggie Cleveland*, Santiago Guzman)	2.25	1.25	.70
717	Tom Phoebus	2.00	1.00	.60
718	Ed Spiezio	2.00	1.00	.60
719	Jim Roland	2.25	.90	.50
720	Rick Reichardt	4.00	1.00	.50

1970 Topps Candy Lids

The 1970 Topps Candy Lids are a test issue that was utilized again in 1973. The set is made up of 24 lids that measure 1-7/8" in diameter and were the tops of small 1.1 oz. tubs of "Baseball Stars Candy." Unlike the 1973 versions, the 1970 lids have no border surrounding the full-color photos. Frank Howard, Tom Seaver and Carl Yastrzemski photos are found on the bottom (inside) of the candy lid.

		NR MT	EX	VG
	Complete Set:	2000.00	1000.00	600.00
	Common Player:	30.00	15.00	9.00
(1)	Hank Aaron	200.00	100.00	60.00
(2)	Rich Allen	50.00	25.00	15.00
(3)	Luis Aparicio	80.00	40.00	24.00
(4)	Johnny Bench	200.00	100.00	60.00
(5)	Ollie Brown	30.00	15.00	9.00
(6)	Willie Davis	30.00	15.00	9.00
(7)	Jim Fregosi	30.00	15.00	9.00
(8)	Mike Hegan	30.00	15.00	9.00
(9)	Frank Howard	50.00	25.00	15.00
(10)	Reggie Jackson	200.00	100.00	60.00
(11)	Fergie Jenkins	60.00	30.00	18.00
(12)	Harmon Killebrew	100.00	50.00	30.00
(13)	Juan Marichal	100.00	50.00	30.00
(14)	Bill Mazeroski	50.00	25.00	15.00
(15)	Tim McCarver	50.00	25.00	15.00
(16)	Sam McDowell	30.00	15.00	9.00
(17)	Denny McLain	50.00	25.00	15.00
(18)	Lou Piniella	50.00	25.00	15.00
(19)	Frank Robinson	100.00	50.00	30.00
(20)	Tom Seaver	175.00	87.00	52.00
(21)	Rusty Staub	50.00	25.00	15.00
(22)	Mel Stottlemyre	50.00	25.00	15.00
(23)	Jim Wynn	30.00	15.00	9.00
(24)	Carl Yastrzemski	150.00	75.00	45.00

1970 Topps Posters

Helping to ease a price increase, Topps included extremely fragile 8-11/16" by 9-5/8" posters in packs of regular cards. The posters feature color portraits and a smaller black and white "action" pose as well as the player's name, team and position at the top. Although there are Hall of Famers in the 24-poster set, all the top names are not represented. Once again, due to folding, heavy creases are a fact of life for today's collector.

		NR MT	EX	VG
	Complete Set:	25.00	12.50	7.50
	Common Player:	.40	.20	.12
1	Joe Horlen	.40	.20	.12
2	Phil Niekro	1.50	.70	.45
3	Willie Davis	.50	.25	.15
4	Lou Brock	2.00	1.00	.60
5	Ron Santo	.60	.30	.20
6	Ken Harrelson	.50	.25	.15
7	Willie McCovey	2.00	1.00	.60
8	Rick Wise	.40	.20	.12
9	Andy Messersmith	.40	.20	.12
10	Ron Fairly	.50	.25	.15
11	Johnny Bench	3.25	1.75	1.00
12	Frank Robinson	2.50	1.25	.70
13	Tommie Agee	.40	.20	.12
14	Roy White	.50	.25	.15
15	Larry Dierker	.40	.20	.12
16	Rod Carew	3.00	1.50	.90
17	Don Mincher	.40	.20	.12
18	Ollie Brown	.40	.20	.12
19	Ed Kirkpatrick	.40	.20	.12
20	Reggie Smith	.50	.25	.15
21	Bob Clemente	5.00	2.50	1.50
22	Frank Howard	.60	.30	.20
23	Bert Campaneris	.50	.25	.15
24	Denny McLain	.60	.30	.20

1970 Topps Scratch-Offs

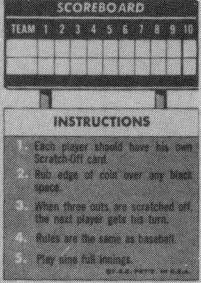

Needing inserts, and having not given up on the idea of a game which could be played with baseball cards, Topps provided a new game - the baseball scratch-off. The set consists of 24 cards. Unfolded, they measure 3-3/8" by 5," and reveal a baseball game of sorts which was played by rubbing the black ink off playing squares which then determined the "action." Fronts of the cards have a player picture as "captain," while backs have instructions and a scoreboard. Inserts with white centers are from 1970 while those with red centers are from 1971.

		NR MT	EX	VG
Complete Set:		20.00	10.00	6.00
Common Player:		.30	.15	.09
(1)	Hank Aaron	2.00	1.00	.60
(2)	Rich Allen	.50	.25	.15
(3)	Luis Aparicio	1.00	.50	.30
(4)	Sal Bando	.30	.15	.09
(5)	Glenn Beckert	.30	.15	.09
(6)	Dick Bosman	.30	.15	.09
(7)	Nate Colbert	.30	.15	.09
(8)	Mike Hegan	.30	.15	.09
(9)	Mack Jones	.30	.15	.09
(10)	Al Kaline	1.50	.70	.45
(11)	Harmon Killebrew	1.50	.70	.45
(12)	Juan Marichal	1.25	.60	.40
(13)	Tim McCarver	.40	.20	.12
(14)	Sam McDowell	.30	.15	.09
(15)	Claude Osteen	.30	.15	.09
(16)	Tony Perez	.60	.30	.20
(17)	Lou Piniella	.40	.20	.12
(18)	Boog Powell	.50	.25	.15
(19)	Tom Seaver	2.00	1.00	.60
(20)	Jim Spencer	.30	.15	.09
(21)	Willie Stargell	1.25	.60	.40
(22)	Mel Stottlemyre	.30	.15	.09
(23)	Jim Wynn	.30	.15	.09
(24)	Carl Yastrzemski	2.25	1.25	.70

1970 Topps Story Booklets

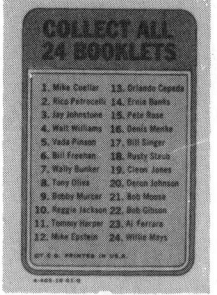

Measuring 2-1/2" by 3-7/16," the Topps Story Booklet was a 1970 regular pack insert. The booklet feature a photo, title and booklet number on the "cover." Inside are six pages of comic book story. The backs give a checklist of other available booklets. Not every star had a booklet as the set is only 24 in number.

		NR MT	EX	VG
Complete Set:		30.00	15.00	9.00
Common Player:		.30	.15	.09
1	Mike Cuellar	.40	.20	.12
2	Rico Petrocelli	.40	.20	.12
3	Jay Johnstone	.40	.20	.12
4	Walt Williams	.30	.15	.09
5	Vada Pinson	.50	.25	.15
6	Bill Freehan	.40	.20	.12
7	Wally Bunker	.30	.15	.09
8	Tony Oliva	.50	.25	.15
9	Bobby Murcer	.40	.20	.12
10	Reggie Jackson	5.00	2.50	1.50
11	Tommy Harper	.30	.15	.09

		NR MT	EX	VG
12	Mike Epstein	.30	.15	.09
13	Orlando Cepeda	.90	.45	.25
14	Ernie Banks	3.00	1.50	.90
15	Pete Rose	8.00	4.00	2.50
16	Denis Menke	.30	.15	.09
17	Bill Singer	.30	.15	.09
18	Rusty Staub	.50	.25	.15
19	Cleon Jones	.30	.15	.09
20	Deron Johnson	.30	.15	.09
21	Bob Moose	.30	.15	.09
22	Bob Gibson	4.00	2.00	1.25
23	Al Ferrara	.30	.15	.09
24	Willie Mays	7.00	3.50	2.00

1970 Topps Super

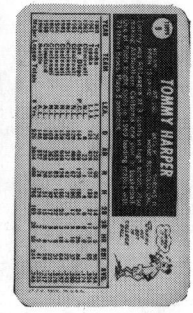

Representing a refinement of the concept begun in 1969, the 1970 Topps Supers had a new 3-1/8" by 5-1/4" postcard size. Printed on heavy stock with rounded corners, card fronts feature a borderless color photograph and facsimile autograph. Card backs are simply an enlarged back from the player's regular 1970 Topps card. The Topps Supers set numbers 42 cards. Probably due to the press sheet configuration eight of the 42 had smaller printings. The most elusive is card #38 (Boog Powell). The set was more widely produced than was the case in 1969, meaning collectors stand a much better chance of affording it.

		NR MT	EX	VG
Complete Set:		250.00	125.00	75.00
Common Player:		.75	.40	.25
1	Claude Osteen	3.00	1.50	.90
2	Sal Bando	3.50	1.75	1.00
3	Luis Aparicio	2.50	1.25	.70
4	Harmon Killebrew	4.00	2.00	1.25
5	Tom Seaver	25.00	12.50	7.50
6	Larry Dierker	.90	.45	.25
7	Bill Freehan	1.00	.50	.30
8	Johnny Bench	15.00	7.50	4.50
9	Tommy Harper	.90	.45	.25
10	Sam McDowell	1.00	.50	.30
11	Louis Brock	4.00	2.00	1.25
12	Roberto Clemente	15.00	7.50	4.50
13	Willie McCovey	4.00	2.00	1.25
14	Rico Petrocelli	.90	.45	.25
15	Philip Niekro	2.25	1.25	.70
16	Frank Howard	1.50	.70	.45
17	Denny McLain	1.25	.60	.40
18	Willie Mays	15.00	7.50	4.50
19	Wilver Stargell	3.50	1.75	1.00
20	Joe Horlen	.90	.45	.25
21	Ronald Santo	1.00	.50	.30
22	Dick Bosman	.90	.45	.25
23	Tim McCarver	1.00	.50	.30
24	Henry Aaron	15.00	7.50	4.50
25	Andy Messersmith	.90	.45	.25
26	Tony Oliva	1.25	.60	.40
27	Mel Stottlemyre	1.00	.50	.30
28	Reginald M. Jackson	18.00	9.00	5.50
29	Carl Yastrzemski	12.00	6.00	3.50
30	James Fregosi	1.00	.50	.30
31	Vada Pinson	1.25	.60	.40
32	Lou Piniella	1.25	.60	.40
33	Robert Gibson	4.00	2.00	1.25

		NR MT	EX	VG
34	Pete Rose	25.00	12.50	7.50
35	Jim Wynn	1.00	.50	.30
36	Ollie Brown	3.00	1.50	.90
37	Frank Robinson	18.00	9.00	5.50
38	John "Boog" Powell	60.00	30.00	18.00
39	Willie Davis	3.50	1.75	1.00
40	Billy Williams	12.00	6.00	3.50
41	Rusty Staub	1.25	.60	.40
42	Tommie Agee	.90	.45	.25

1971 Topps Baseball Tattoos

Topps once again produced baseball tattoos in 1971. This time, the tattoos came in a variety of sizes, shapes and themes. The sheets of tattoos measure 3-1/2" by 14-1/4." Each sheet contains an assortment of tattoos in two sizes, 1-3/4" by 2-3/8," or 1-3/16" by 1-3/4." There are players, facsimile autographed baseballs, team pennants and assorted baseball cartoon figures carried on the 16 different sheets. Listings below are for complete sheets; with the exception of the biggest-name stars, individual tattoos have little or no collector value.

		NR MT	EX	VG
	Complete Sheet Set:	175.00	87.00	52.00
	Common Sheet:	4.00	2.00	1.25
1	Brooks Robinson Autograph, Montreal Expos Pennant, San Francisco Giants Pennant, Sal Bando, Dick Bosman, Nate Colbert, Cleon Jones, Juan Marichal, B. Robinson	10.00	5.00	3.00
2	Boston Red Sox Pennant, Carl Yastrzemski Autograph, New York Mets Pennant, Glenn Beckert, Tommy Harper, Ken Henderson, Fritz Peterson, Bob Robertson, C. Yastrzemski	18.00	9.00	5.50
3	Jim Fregosi Autograph, New York Yankees Pennant, Philadelphia Phillies Pennant ector value., Orlando Cepeda, Jim Fregosi, Randy Hundley, Reggie Jackson, Jerry Koosman, Jim Palmer	15.00	7.50	4.50
4	Kansas City Royals Pennant, Oakland Athletics Pennant, Sam McDowell Autograph, Dick Dietz, C. Gaston, Dave Johnson, Sam McDowell, Gary Nolan, Amos Otis	3.50	1.75	1.00
5	Al Kaline Autograph, Atlanta Braves Pennant, L.A. Dodgers Pennant, B. Grabarkewitz, Al Kaline, Lee May, Tom Murphy, Vada Pinson, M. Sanguillen	10.00	5.00	3.00
6	Chicago Cubs Pennant, Cincinnati Reds Pennant, Harmon Killebrew Autograph, Luis Aparicio, Paul Blair, C. Cannizzaro, D. Clendenon, Larry Dieker, H. Killebrew	10.00	5.00	3.00
7	Boog Powell Autograph, Cleveland Indians Pennant, Milwaukee Brewers Pennant, Rich Allen, B. Campaneris, Don Money, Boog Powell, Ted Savage, Rusty Staub	5.00	2.50	1.50
8	Chicago White Sox Pennant, Frank Howard Autograph, San Diego Padres Pennant, Leo Cardenas, Bill Hands, Frank Howard, Wes Parker, Reggie Smith, W. Stargell	5.00	2.50	1.50
9	Detroit Tigers Pennant, Henry Aaron Autograph, Hank Aaron, Tommy Agee, Jim Hunter, Dick McAuliffe, Tony Perez, Lou Piniella	15.00	7.50	4.50

		NR MT	EX	VG
10	Baltimore Orioles Pennant, Fergie Jenkins Autograph, R. Clemente, T. Conigliaro, Fergie Jenkins, T. Munson, Gary Peters, Joe Torre	12.00	6.00	3.50
11	Johnny Bench Autograph, Washington Senators Pennant, Johnny Bench, Rico Carty, B. Mazeroski, Bob Oliver, R. Petrocelli, F. Robinson	10.00	5.00	3.00
12	Billy Williams Autograph, Houston Astros Pennant, Bill Freehan, Dave McNally, Felix Millan, M. Stottlemyre, Bob Tolan, Billy Williams	6.00	3.00	1.75
13	Pittsburgh Pirates Pennant, Willie McCovey Autograph, Ray Culp, Bud Harrelson, Mickey Lolich, W. McCovey, Ron Santo, Roy White	9.00	4.50	2.75
14	Minnesota Twins Pennant, Tom Seaver Autograph, Bill Melton, Jim Perry, Pete Rose, Tom Seaver, Maury Wills, Clyde Wright	25.00	12.50	7.50
15	Robert Gibson Autograph, St. Louis Cardinals Pennant, Rod Carew, Bob Gibson, Alex Johnson, Don Kessinger, Jim Merritt, Rick Monday	9.00	4.50	2.75
16	California Angels Pennant, Willie Mays Autograph, Larry Bowa, Mike Cuellar, Ray Fosse, Willie Mays, Carl Morton, Tony Oliva	15.00	7.50	4.50

1971 Topps

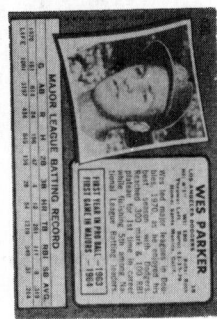

In 1971, Topps again increased the size of its set to 752 cards. These well-liked cards, measuring 2-1/2" by 3-1/2," feature a large color photo which has a thin white frame. Above the picture, in the card's overall black border, is the player's name, team and position. A facsimile autograph completes the front. Backs feature a major change as a black and white "snapshot" of the player appears. Abbreviated statistics, a line giving the player's first pro and major league games and a short biography complete the back of these innovative cards. Specialty cards in this issue are limited. There are statistical leaders as well as World Series and playoff highlights. High numbered cards #644-752 are scarce.

		NR MT	EX	VG
	Complete Set:	1500.00	750.00	425.00
	Common Player: 1-523	.35	.20	.11
	Common Player: 524-643	.80	.40	.25
	Common Player: 644-752	2.25	1.25	.70
1	World Champions (Orioles Team)	5.00	1.25	.60
2	Dock Ellis	.50	.20	.12
3	Dick McAuliffe	.40	.20	.12
4	Vic Davalillo	.40	.20	.12
5	Thurman Munson	35.00	17.50	10.50
6	Ed Spiezio	.35	.20	.11
7	Jim Holt	.35	.20	.11
8	Mike McQueen	.35	.20	.11
9	George Scott	.50	.25	.15
10	Claude Osteen	.50	.25	.15
11	*Elliott Maddox*	.50	.25	.15
12	Johnny Callison	.60	.30	.20
13	White Sox Rookies (Charlie Brinkman, Dick Moloney)	.35	.20	.11
14	*Dave Concepcion*	7.00	3.50	2.00

No.	Player	NR MT	EX	VG
15	Andy Messersmith	.40	.20	.12
16	*Ken Singleton*	1.75	.90	.50
17	Billy Sorrell	.35	.20	.11
18	Norm Miller	.35	.20	.11
19	Skip Pitlock	.35	.20	.11
20	Reggie Jackson	50.00	25.00	15.00
21	Dan McGinn	.35	.20	.11
22	Phil Roof	.35	.20	.11
23	Oscar Gamble	.40	.20	.12
24	Rich Hand	.35	.20	.11
25	Clarence Gaston	.35	.20	.11
26	*Bert Blyleven*	60.00	30.00	18.00
27	Pirates Rookies (Fred Cambria, Gene Clines)	.35	.20	.11
28	Ron Klimkowski	.40	.20	.12
29	Don Buford	.40	.20	.12
30	Phil Niekro	3.25	1.75	1.00
31	Eddie Kasko	.35	.20	.11
32	Jerry DaVanon	.35	.20	.11
33	Del Unser	.35	.20	.11
34	Sandy Vance	.35	.20	.11
35	Lou Piniella	1.25	.60	.40
36	Dean Chance	.40	.20	.12
37	Rich McKinney	.35	.20	.11
38	*Jim Colborn*	.40	.20	.12
39	Tigers Rookies (Gene Lamont, *Lerrin LaGrow*)	.40	.20	.12
40	Lee May	.60	.30	.20
41	Rick Austin	.35	.20	.11
42	Boots Day	.35	.20	.11
43	Steve Kealey	.35	.20	.11
44	Johnny Edwards	.35	.20	.11
45	Jim Hunter	5.00	2.50	1.50
46	Dave Campbell	.35	.20	.11
47	Johnny Jeter	.35	.20	.11
48	Dave Baldwin	.35	.20	.11
49	Don Money	.40	.20	.12
50	Willie McCovey	6.00	3.00	1.75
51	Steve Kline	.40	.20	.12
52	Braves Rookies (Oscar Brown, *Earl Williams*)	.40	.20	.12
53	Paul Blair	.40	.20	.12
54	Checklist 1-132	2.50	1.25	.70
55	Steve Carlton	25.00	12.50	7.50
56	Duane Josephson	.35	.20	.11
57	Von Joshua	.35	.20	.11
58	Bill Lee	.40	.20	.12
59	Gene Mauch	.60	.30	.20
60	Dick Bosman	.35	.20	.11
61	A.L. Batting Leaders (Alex Johnson, Tony Oliva, Carl Yastrzemski)	2.25	1.25	.70
62	N.L. Batting Leaders (Rico Carty, Manny Sanguillen, Joe Torre)	1.25	.60	.40
63	A.L. RBI Leaders (Tony Conigliaro, Frank Howard, Boog Powell)	1.25	.60	.40
64	N.L. RBI Leaders (Johnny Bench, Tony Perez, Billy Williams)	2.25	1.25	.70
65	A.L. Home Run Leaders (Frank Howard, Harmon Killebrew, Carl Yastrzemski)	2.25	1.25	.70
66	N.L. Home Run Leaders (Johnny Bench, Tony Perez, Billy Williams)	2.25	1.25	.70
67	A.L. ERA Leaders (Jim Palmer, Diego Segui, Clyde Wright)	1.25	.60	.40
68	N.L. ERA Leaders (Tom Seaver, Wayne Simpson, Luke Walker)	1.50	.70	.45
69	A.L. Pitching Leaders (Mike Cuellar, Dave McNally, Jim Perry)	1.25	.60	.40
70	N.L. Pitching Leaders (Bob Gibson, Fergie Jenkins, Gaylord Perry)	2.00	1.00	.60
71	A.L. Strikeout Leaders (Bob Johnson, Mickey Lolich, Sam McDowell)	1.25	.60	.40
72	N.L. Strikeout Leaders (Bob Gibson, Fergie Jenkins, Tom Seaver)	2.25	1.25	.70
73	George Brunet	.35	.20	.11
74	Twins Rookies (Pete Hamm, Jim Nettles)	.35	.20	.11
75	Gary Nolan	.35	.20	.11
76	Ted Savage	.35	.20	.11
77	Mike Compton	.35	.20	.11
78	Jim Spencer	.40	.20	.12
79	Wade Blasingame	.35	.20	.11
80	Bill Melton	.40	.20	.12
81	Felix Millan	.35	.20	.11
82	Casey Cox	.35	.20	.11
83	Mets Rookies (Randy Bobb, *Tim Foli*)	.50	.25	.15
84	Marcel Lachemann	.35	.20	.11
85	Billy Grabarkewitz	.35	.20	.11
86	Mike Kilkenny	.35	.20	.11
87	Jack Heidemann	.35	.20	.11
88	Hal King	.35	.20	.11
89	Ken Brett	.35	.20	.11
90	Joe Pepitone	.70	.35	.20
91	Bob Lemon	1.25	.60	.40
92	Fred Wenz	.35	.20	.11
93	Senators Rookies (Norm McRae, Denny Riddleberger)	.35	.20	.11
94	Don Hahn	.35	.20	.11
95	Luis Tiant	1.50	.70	.45
96	Joe Hague	.35	.20	.11
97	Floyd Wicker	.35	.20	.11
98	Joe Decker	.35	.20	.11
99	Mark Belanger	.40	.20	.12
100	Pete Rose	45.00	23.00	13.50
101	Les Cain	.35	.20	.11
102	Astros Rookies (*Ken Forsch*, Larry Howard)	.50	.25	.15
103	Rich Severson	.35	.20	.11
104	Dan Frisella	.35	.20	.11
105	Tony Conigliaro	1.25	.60	.40
106	Tom Dukes	.35	.20	.11
107	Roy Foster	.35	.20	.11
108	John Cumberland	.35	.20	.11
109	Steve Hovley	.35	.20	.11
110	Bill Mazeroski	1.25	.60	.40
111	Yankees Rookies (Loyd Colson, Bobby Mitchell)	.40	.20	.12
112	Manny Mota	.60	.30	.20
113	Jerry Crider	.35	.20	.11
114	Billy Conigliaro	.40	.20	.12
115	Donn Clendenon	.40	.20	.12
116	Ken Sanders	.35	.20	.11
117	*Ted Simmons*	12.00	6.00	3.50
118	Cookie Rojas	.35	.20	.11
119	Frank Lucchesi	.35	.20	.11
120	Willie Horton	.60	.30	.20
121	1971 Rookie Stars (Jim Dunegan, Roe Skidmore)	.35	.20	.11
122	Eddie Watt	.35	.20	.11
123a	Checklist 133-263 (card # on right, orange helmet)	2.50	1.25	.70
123b	Checklist 133-263 (card # on right, red helmet)	2.50	1.25	.70
123c	Checklist 133-263 (card # centered)	3.50	1.75	1.00
124	*Don Gullett*	.70	.35	.20
125	Ray Fosse	.35	.20	.11
126	Danny Coombs	.35	.20	.11
127	*Danny Thompson*	.40	.20	.12
128	Frank Johnson	.35	.20	.11
129	Aurelio Monteagudo	.35	.20	.11
130	Denis Menke	.35	.20	.11
131	Curt Blefary	.40	.20	.12
132	Jose Laboy	.35	.20	.11
133	Mickey Lolich	1.25	.60	.40
134	Jose Arcia	.35	.20	.11
135	Rick Monday	.50	.25	.15
136	Duffy Dyer	.35	.20	.11
137	Marcelino Lopez	.35	.20	.11
138	Phillies Rookies (Joe Lis, *Willie Montanez*)	.50	.25	.15
139	Paul Casanova	.35	.20	.11
140	Gaylord Perry	4.00	2.00	1.25
141	Frank Quilici	.35	.20	.11
142	Mack Jones	.35	.20	.11
143	Steve Blass	.40	.20	.12
144	Jackie Hernandez	.35	.20	.11
145	Bill Singer	.40	.20	.12
146	Ralph Houk	.80	.40	.25
147	Bob Priddy	.35	.20	.11
148	John Mayberry	.50	.25	.15
149	Mike Hershberger	.35	.20	.11
150	Sam McDowell	.70	.35	.20
151	Tommy Davis	.70	.35	.20
152	Angels Rookies (Lloyd Allen, Winston Llenas)	.35	.20	.11
153	Gary Ross	.35	.20	.11
154	Cesar Gutierrez	.35	.20	.11
155	Ken Henderson	.35	.20	.11
156	Bart Johnson	.35	.20	.11
157	Bob Bailey	.35	.20	.11
158	Jerry Reuss	1.00	.50	.30
159	Jarvis Tatum	.35	.20	.11
160	Tom Seaver	30.00	15.00	9.00
161	Coins Checklist	2.50	1.25	.70
162	Jack Billingham	.35	.20	.11
163	Buck Martinez	.35	.20	.11
164	Reds Rookies (Frank Duffy, *Milt Wilcox*)	.60	.30	.20
165	Cesar Tovar	.35	.20	.11
166	Joe Hoerner	.35	.20	.11
167	Tom Grieve	.35	.20	.11

	NR MT	EX	VG
168 Bruce Dal Canton	.35	.20	.11
169 Ed Herrmann	.35	.20	.11
170 Mike Cuellar	.60	.30	.20
171 Bobby Wine	.35	.20	.11
172 Duke Sims	.35	.20	.11
173 Gil Garrido	.35	.20	.11
174 *Dave LaRoche*	.50	.25	.15
175 Jim Hickman	.40	.20	.12
176 Red Sox Rookies (Doug Griffin, Bob Montgomery)	.35	.20	.11
177 Hal McRae	.70	.35	.20
178 Dave Duncan	.35	.20	.11
179 Mike Corkins	.35	.20	.11
180 Al Kaline	12.00	6.00	3.50
181 Hal Lanier	.60	.30	.20
182 Al Downing	.40	.20	.12
183 Gil Hodges	4.00	2.00	1.25
184 Stan Bahnsen	.50	.25	.15
185 Julian Javier	.40	.20	.12
186 Bob Spence	.35	.20	.11
187 Ted Abernathy	.35	.20	.11
188 Dodgers Rookies (Mike Strahler, *Bob Valentine*)	1.75	.90	.50
189 George Mitterwald	.35	.20	.11
190 Bob Tolan	.40	.20	.12
191 Mike Andrews	.35	.20	.11
192 Billy Wilson	.35	.20	.11
193 *Bob Grich*	1.75	.90	.50
194 Mike Lum	.35	.20	.11
195 A.L. Playoff Game 1 (Powell Muscles Twins!)	1.25	.60	.40
196 A.L. Playoff Game 2 (McNally Makes It Two Straight!)	1.25	.60	.40
197 A.L. Playoff Game 3 (Palmer Mows 'Em Down!)	1.75	.90	.50
198 A.L. Playoffs Summary (A Team Effort!)	1.25	.60	.40
199 N.L. Playoff Game 1 (Cline Pinch-Triple Decides It!)	1.25	.60	.40
200 N.L. Playoff Game 2 (Tolan Scores For Third Time!)	1.25	.60	.40
201 N.L. Playoff Game 3 (Cline Scores Winning Run!)	1.25	.60	.40
202 N.L. Playoffs Summary (World Series Bound!)	1.25	.60	.40
203 *Larry Gura*	.70	.35	.20
204 Brewers Rookies (George Kopacz, Bernie Smith)	.35	.20	.11
205 Gerry Moses	.35	.20	.11
206a Checklist 264-393 (orange helmet)	2.50	1.25	.70
206b Checklist 264-393 (red helmet)	2.50	1.25	.70
207 Alan Foster	.35	.20	.11
208 Billy Martin	1.75	.90	.50
209 Steve Renko	.35	.20	.11
210 Rod Carew	30.00	15.00	9.00
211 Phil Hennigan	.35	.20	.11
212 Rich Hebner	.40	.20	.12
213 Frank Baker	.40	.20	.12
214 Al Ferrara	.35	.20	.11
215 Diego Segui	.35	.20	.11
216 Cards Rookies (Reggie Cleveland, Luis Melendez)	.35	.20	.11
217 Ed Stroud	.35	.20	.11
218 Tony Cloninger	.40	.20	.12
219 Elrod Hendricks	.35	.20	.11
220 Ron Santo	.80	.40	.25
221 Dave Morehead	.35	.20	.11
222 Bob Watson	.40	.20	.12
223 Cecil Upshaw	.35	.20	.11
224 Alan Gallagher	.35	.20	.11
225 Gary Peters	.40	.20	.12
226 Bill Russell	.60	.30	.20
227 Floyd Weaver	.35	.20	.11
228 Wayne Garrett	.35	.20	.11
229 Jim Hannan	.35	.20	.11
230 Willie Stargell	8.00	4.00	2.50
231 Indians Rookies (Vince Colbert, *John Lowenstein*)	.50	.25	.15
232 John Strohmayer	.35	.20	.11
233 Larry Bowa	1.75	.90	.50
234 Jim Lyttle	.40	.20	.12
235 Nate Colbert	.35	.20	.11
236 Bob Humphreys	.35	.20	.11
237 *Cesar Cedeno*	1.50	.70	.45
238 Chuck Dobson	.35	.20	.11
239 Red Schoendienst	1.00	.50	.30
240 Clyde Wright	.35	.20	.11
241 Dave Nelson	.35	.20	.11
242 Jim Ray	.35	.20	.11
243 Carlos May	.40	.20	.12
244 Bob Tillman	.35	.20	.11
245 Jim Kaat	2.50	1.25	.70
246 Tony Taylor	.35	.20	.11
247 Royals Rookies (Jerry Cram, *Paul Splittorff*)	.70	.35	.20
248 Hoyt Wilhelm	3.75	2.00	1.25
249 Chico Salmon	.35	.20	.11
250 Johnny Bench	40.00	20.00	12.00
251 Frank Reberger	.35	.20	.11
252 Eddie Leon	.35	.20	.11
253 Bill Sudakis	.35	.20	.11
254 Cal Koonce	.35	.20	.11
255 Bob Robertson	.35	.20	.11
256 Tony Gonzalez	.35	.20	.11
257 Nelson Briles	.35	.20	.11
258 Dick Green	.35	.20	.11
259 Dave Marshall	.35	.20	.11
260 Tommy Harper	.40	.20	.12
261 Darold Knowles	.35	.20	.11
262 Padres Rookies (Dave Robinson, Jim Williams)	.35	.20	.11
263 John Ellis	.40	.20	.12
264 Joe Morgan	10.00	5.00	3.00
265 Jim Northrup	.40	.20	.12
266 Bill Stoneman	.35	.20	.11
267 Rich Morales	.35	.20	.11
268 Phillies Team	1.25	.60	.40
269 Gail Hopkins	.35	.20	.11
270 Rico Carty	.70	.35	.20
271 Bill Zepp	.35	.20	.11
272 Tommy Helms	.40	.20	.12
273 Pete Richert	.35	.20	.11
274 Ron Slocum	.35	.20	.11
275 Vada Pinson	1.25	.60	.40
276 Giants Rookies (Mike Davison, *George Foster*)	4.00	2.00	1.25
277 Gary Waslewski	.40	.20	.12
278 Jerry Grote	.50	.25	.15
279 Lefty Phillips	.35	.20	.11
280 Fergie Jenkins	3.00	1.50	.90
281 Danny Walton	.35	.20	.11
282 Jose Pagan	.35	.20	.11
283 Dick Such	.35	.20	.11
284 Jim Gosger	.35	.20	.11
285 Sal Bando	.60	.30	.20
286 Jerry McNertney	.35	.20	.11
287 Mike Fiore	.35	.20	.11
288 Joe Moeller	.35	.20	.11
289 White Sox Team	1.25	.60	.40
290 Tony Oliva	1.50	.70	.45
291 George Culver	.35	.20	.11
292 Jay Johnstone	.60	.30	.20
293 Pat Corrales	.50	.25	.15
294 Steve Dunning	.35	.20	.11
295 Bobby Bonds	1.25	.60	.40
296 Tom Timmermann	.35	.20	.11
297 Johnny Briggs	.35	.20	.11
298 Jim Nelson	.35	.20	.11
299 Ed Kirkpatrick	.35	.20	.11
300 Brooks Robinson	12.00	6.00	3.50
301 Earl Wilson	.35	.20	.11
302 Phil Gagliano	.35	.20	.11
303 Lindy McDaniel	.40	.20	.12
304 Ron Brand	.35	.20	.11
305 Reggie Smith	.60	.30	.20
306 Jim Nash	.35	.20	.11
307 Don Wert	.35	.20	.11
308 Cards Team	1.25	.60	.40
309 Dick Ellsworth	.35	.20	.11
310 Tommie Agee	.40	.20	.12
311 Lee Stange	.35	.20	.11
312 Harry Walker	.40	.20	.12
313 Tom Hall	.35	.20	.11
314 Jeff Torborg	.40	.20	.12
315 Ron Fairly	.50	.25	.15
316 Fred Scherman	.35	.20	.11
317 Athletics Rookies (Jim Driscoll, Angel Mangual)	.35	.20	.11
318 Rudy May	.40	.20	.12
319 Ty Cline	.35	.20	.11
320 Dave McNally	.50	.25	.15
321 Tom Matchick	.35	.20	.11
322 Jim Beauchamp	.35	.20	.11
323 Billy Champion	.35	.20	.11
324 Graig Nettles	2.50	1.25	.70
325 Juan Marichal	5.00	2.50	1.50
326 Richie Scheinblum	.35	.20	.11
327 World Series Game 1 (Powell Homers To Opposite Field!)	1.25	.60	.40
328 World Series Game 2 (Buford Goes 2-For 4!)	1.25	.60	.40

		NR MT	EX	VG
329	World Series Game 3 (F. Robinson Shows Muscle!)	2.00	1.00	.60
330	World Series Game 4 (Reds Stay Alive!)	1.25	.60	.40
331	World Series Game 5 (B. Robinson Commits Robbery!)	2.00	1.00	.60
332	World Series Summary (Clinching Performance!)	1.25	.60	.40
333	Clay Kirby	.35	.20	.11
334	Roberto Pena	.35	.20	.11
335	Jerry Koosman	1.00	.50	.30
336	Tigers Team	1.75	.90	.50
337	Jesus Alou	.40	.20	.12
338	Gene Tenace	.50	.25	.15
339	Wayne Simpson	.35	.20	.11
340	Rico Petrocelli	.50	.25	.15
341	*Steve Garvey*	80.00	40.00	25.00
342	Frank Tepedino	.40	.20	.12
343	Pirates Rookies (Ed Acosta, *Milt May*)	.40	.20	.12
344	Ellie Rodriguez	.35	.20	.11
345	Joe Horlen	.35	.20	.11
346	Lum Harris	.35	.20	.11
347	Ted Uhlaender	.35	.20	.11
348	Fred Norman	.35	.20	.11
349	Rich Reese	.35	.20	.11
350	Billy Williams	4.50	2.25	1.25
351	Jim Shellenback	.35	.20	.11
352	Denny Doyle	.35	.20	.11
353	Carl Taylor	.35	.20	.11
354	Don McMahon	.35	.20	.11
355	Bud Harrelson	.40	.20	.12
356	Bob Locker	.35	.20	.11
357	Reds Team	1.25	.60	.40
358	Danny Cater	.40	.20	.12
359	Ron Reed	.40	.20	.12
360	Jim Fregosi	.80	.40	.25
361	Don Sutton	3.50	1.75	1.00
362	Orioles Rookies (Mike Adamson, Roger Freed)	.35	.20	.11
363	Mike Nagy	.35	.20	.11
364	Tommy Dean	.35	.20	.11
365	Bob Johnson	.35	.20	.11
366	Ron Stone	.35	.20	.11
367	Dalton Jones	.35	.20	.11
368	Bob Veale	.40	.20	.12
369a	Checklist 394-523 (orange helmet)	2.50	1.25	.70
369b	Checklist 394-523 (red helmet, black line above ear)	2.50	1.25	.70
369c	Checklist 394-523 (red helmet, no line)	2.50	1.25	.70
370	Joe Torre	2.25	1.25	.70
371	Jack Hiatt	.35	.20	.11
372	Lew Krausse	.35	.20	.11
373	Tom McCraw	.35	.20	.11
374	Clete Boyer	.50	.25	.15
375	Steve Hargan	.35	.20	.11
376	Expos Rookies (Clyde Mashore, Ernie McAnally)	.35	.20	.11
377	Greg Garrett	.35	.20	.11
378	Tito Fuentes	.35	.20	.11
379	Wayne Granger	.35	.20	.11
380	Ted Williams	5.00	2.50	1.50
381	Fred Gladding	.35	.20	.11
382	Jake Gibbs	.40	.20	.12
383	Rod Gaspar	.35	.20	.11
384	Rollie Fingers	4.00	2.00	1.25
385	Maury Wills	1.25	.60	.40
386	Red Sox Team	1.50	.70	.45
387	Ron Herbel	.35	.20	.11
388	Al Oliver	1.75	.90	.50
389	Ed Brinkman	.40	.20	.12
390	Glenn Beckert	.50	.25	.15
391	Twins Rookies (Steve Brye, Cotton Nash)	.35	.20	.11
392	Grant Jackson	.35	.20	.11
393	Merv Rettenmund	.40	.20	.12
394	Clay Carroll	.40	.20	.12
395	Roy White	.70	.35	.20
396	Dick Schofield	.35	.20	.11
397	Alvin Dark	.50	.25	.15
398	Howie Reed	.35	.20	.11
399	Jim French	.35	.20	.11
400	Hank Aaron	30.00	15.00	9.00
401	Tom Murphy	.35	.20	.11
402	Dodgers Team	1.50	.70	.45
403	Joe Coleman	.40	.20	.12
404	Astros Rookies (Buddy Harris, Roger Metzger)	.35	.20	.11
405	Leo Cardenas	.35	.20	.11

		NR MT	EX	VG
406	Ray Sadecki	.35	.20	.11
407	Joe Rudi	.60	.30	.20
408	Rafael Robles	.35	.20	.11
409	Don Pavletich	.35	.20	.11
410	Ken Holtzman	.40	.20	.12
411	George Spriggs	.35	.20	.11
412	Jerry Johnson	.35	.20	.11
413	Pat Kelly	.35	.20	.11
414	Woodie Fryman	.40	.20	.12
415	Mike Hegan	.35	.20	.11
416	Gene Alley	.40	.20	.12
417	Dick Hall	.35	.20	.11
418	Adolfo Phillips	.35	.20	.11
419	Ron Hansen	.40	.20	.12
420	Jim Merritt	.35	.20	.11
421	John Stephenson	.35	.20	.11
422	Frank Bertaina	.35	.20	.11
423	Tigers Rookies (Tim Marting, Dennis Saunders)	.35	.20	.11
424	Roberto Rodriguez (Rodriguez)	.35	.20	.11
425	Doug Rader	.35	.20	.11
426	Chris Cannizzaro	.35	.20	.11
427	Bernie Allen	.35	.20	.11
428	Jim McAndrew	.35	.20	.11
429	Chuck Hinton	.35	.20	.11
430	Wes Parker	.40	.20	.12
431	Tom Burgmeier	.35	.20	.11
432	Bob Didier	.35	.20	.11
433	Skip Lockwood	.35	.20	.11
434	Gary Sutherland	.35	.20	.11
435	Jose Cardenal	.40	.20	.12
436	Wilbur Wood	.50	.25	.15
437	Danny Murtaugh	.40	.20	.12
438	Mike McCormick	.50	.25	.15
439	Phillies Rookies (*Greg Luzinski*, Scott Reid)	2.00	1.00	.60
440	Bert Campaneris	.70	.35	.20
441	Milt Pappas	.40	.20	.12
442	Angels Team	1.25	.60	.40
443	Rich Robertson	.35	.20	.11
444	Jimmie Price	.35	.20	.11
445	Art Shamsky	.35	.20	.11
446	Bobby Bolin	.35	.20	.11
447	*Cesar Geronimo*	.60	.30	.20
448	Dave Roberts	.35	.20	.11
449	Brant Alyea	.35	.20	.11
450	Bob Gibson	8.00	4.00	2.50
451	Joe Keough	.35	.20	.11
452	John Boccabella	.35	.20	.11
453	Terry Crowley	.35	.20	.11
454	Mike Paul	.35	.20	.11
455	Don Kessinger	.40	.20	.12
456	Bob Meyer	.35	.20	.11
457	Willie Smith	.35	.20	.11
458	White Sox Rookies (Dave Lemonds, Ron Lolich)	.35	.20	.11
459	Jim Lefebvre	.40	.20	.12
460	Fritz Peterson	.50	.25	.15
461	Jim Hart	.40	.20	.12
462	Senators Team	1.50	.70	.45
463	Tom Kelley	.35	.20	.11
464	Aurelio Rodriguez	.40	.20	.12
465	Tim McCarver	.80	.40	.25
466	Ken Berry	.35	.20	.11
467	Al Santorini	.35	.20	.11
468	Frank Fernandez	.35	.20	.11
469	Bob Aspromonte	.35	.20	.11
470	Bob Oliver	.35	.20	.11
471	Tom Griffin	.35	.20	.11
472	Ken Rudolph	.35	.20	.11
473	Gary Wagner	.35	.20	.11
474	Jim Fairey	.35	.20	.11
475	Ron Perranoski	.40	.20	.12
476	Dal Maxvill	.40	.20	.12
477	Earl Weaver	1.00	.50	.30
478	Bernie Carbo	.40	.20	.12
479	Dennis Higgins	.35	.20	.11
480	Manny Sanguillen	.40	.20	.12
481	Daryl Patterson	.35	.20	.11
482	Padres Team	1.25	.60	.40
483	Gene Michael	.50	.25	.15
484	Don Wilson	.35	.20	.11
485	Ken McMullen	.35	.20	.11
486	Steve Huntz	.35	.20	.11
487	Paul Schaal	.35	.20	.11
488	Jerry Stephenson	.35	.20	.11
489	Luis Alvarado	.35	.20	.11
490	Deron Johnson	.35	.20	.11
491	Jim Hardin	.35	.20	.11
492	Ken Boswell	.35	.20	.11
493	Dave May	.35	.20	.11

	NR MT	EX	VG
494 Braves Rookies (Ralph Garr, Rick Kester)			
	.50	.25	.15
495 Felipe Alou	.60	.30	.20
496 Woody Woodward	.40	.20	.12
497 Horacio Pina	.35	.20	.11
498 John Kennedy	.35	.20	.11
499 Checklist 524-643	2.50	1.25	.70
500 Jim Perry	.60	.30	.20
501 Andy Etchebarren	.35	.20	.11
502 Cubs Team	1.25	.60	.40
503 Gates Brown	.35	.20	.11
504 Ken Wright	.35	.20	.11
505 Ollie Brown	.35	.20	.11
506 Bobby Knoop	.35	.20	.11
507 George Stone	.35	.20	.11
508 Roger Repoz	.35	.20	.11
509 Jim Grant	.35	.20	.11
510 Ken Harrelson	1.25	.60	.40
511 Chris Short	.40	.20	.12
512 Red Sox Rookies (Mike Garman, Dick Mills)			
	.35	.20	.11
513 Nolan Ryan	125.00	62.00	37.00
514 Ron Woods	.40	.20	.12
515 Carl Morton	.35	.20	.11
516 Ted Kubiak	.35	.20	.11
517 Charlie Fox	.35	.20	.11
518 Joe Grzenda	.35	.20	.11
519 Willie Crawford	.35	.20	.11
520 Tommy John	3.00	1.50	.90
521 Leron Lee	.35	.20	.11
522 Twins Team	1.25	.60	.40
523 John Odom	.40	.20	.12
524 Mickey Stanley	.90	.45	.25
525 Ernie Banks	25.00	12.50	7.50
526 Ray Jarvis	.80	.40	.25
527 Cleon Jones	.90	.45	.25
528 Wally Bunker	.80	.40	.25
529 N.L. Rookies (Bill Buckner, Enzo Hernandez, Marty Perez)	4.00	2.00	1.25
530 Carl Yastrzemski	50.00	25.00	15.00
531 Mike Torrez	.90	.45	.25
532 Bill Rigney	.80	.40	.25
533 Mike Ryan	.80	.40	.25
534 Luke Walker	.80	.40	.25
535 Curt Flood	1.75	.90	.50
536 Claude Raymond	.80	.40	.25
537 Tom Egan	.80	.40	.25
538 Angel Bravo	.80	.40	.25
539 Larry Brown	.80	.40	.25
540 Larry Dierker	.90	.45	.25
541 Bob Burda	.80	.40	.25
542 Bob Miller	.80	.40	.25
543 Yankees Team	2.75	1.50	.80
544 Vida Blue	2.50	1.25	.70
545 Dick Dietz	.80	.40	.25
546 John Matias	.80	.40	.25
547 Pat Dobson	.90	.45	.25
548 Don Mason	.80	.40	.25
549 Jim Brewer	.80	.40	.25
550 Harmon Killebrew	15.00	7.50	4.50
551 Frank Linzy	.80	.40	.25
552 Buddy Bradford	.80	.40	.25
553 Kevin Collins	.80	.40	.25
554 Lowell Palmer	.80	.40	.25
555 Walt Williams	.80	.40	.25
556 Jim McGlothlin	.80	.40	.25
557 Tom Satriano	.80	.40	.25
558 Hector Torres	.80	.40	.25
559 A.L. Rookies (Terry Cox, Bill Gogolewski, Gary Jones)	.90	.45	.25
560 Rusty Staub	2.25	1.25	.70
561 Syd O'Brien	.80	.40	.25
562 Dave Giusti	.80	.40	.25
563 Giants Team	2.00	1.00	.60
564 Al Fitzmorris	.80	.40	.25
565 Jim Wynn	1.00	.50	.30
566 Tim Cullen	.80	.40	.25
567 Walt Alston	2.50	1.25	.70
568 Sal Campisi	.80	.40	.25
569 Ivan Murrell	.80	.40	.25
570 Jim Palmer	25.00	12.50	7.50
571 Ted Sizemore	.80	.40	.25
572 Jerry Kenney	.90	.45	.25
573 Ed Kranepool	1.00	.50	.30
574 Jim Bunning	4.00	2.00	1.25
575 Bill Freehan	1.00	.50	.30
576 Cubs Rookies (Brock Davis, Adrian Garrett, Garry Jestadt)	.80	.40	.25
577 Jim Lonborg	1.00	.50	.30
578 Ron Hunt	.90	.45	.25
579 Marty Pattin	.80	.40	.25

	NR MT	EX	VG
580 Tony Perez	4.00	2.00	1.25
581 Roger Nelson	.80	.40	.25
582 Dave Cash	.80	.40	.25
583 Ron Cook	.80	.40	.25
584 Indians Team	2.00	1.00	.60
585 Willie Davis	2.25	1.25	.70
586 Dick Woodson	.80	.40	.25
587 Sonny Jackson	.80	.40	.25
588 Tom Bradley	.80	.40	.25
589 Bob Barton	.80	.40	.25
590 Alex Johnson	.80	.40	.25
591 Jackie Brown	.80	.40	.25
592 Randy Hundley	.80	.40	.25
593 Jack Aker	.90	.45	.25
594 Cards Rookies (Bob Chlupsa, *Al Hrabosky*, Bob Stinson)	2.25	1.25	.70
595 Dave Johnson	1.75	.90	.50
596 Mike Jorgensen	.80	.40	.25
597 Ken Suarez	.80	.40	.25
598 Rick Wise	.90	.45	.25
599 Norm Cash	2.00	1.00	.60
600 Willie Mays	60.00	30.00	18.00
601 Ken Tatum	.80	.40	.25
602 Marty Martinez	.80	.40	.25
603 Pirates Team	3.00	1.50	.90
604 John Gelnar	.80	.40	.25
605 Orlando Cepeda	3.25	1.75	1.00
606 Chuck Taylor	.80	.40	.25
607 Paul Ratliff	.80	.40	.25
608 Mike Wegener	.80	.40	.25
609 Leo Durocher	2.25	1.25	.70
610 Amos Otis	1.00	.50	.30
611 Tom Phoebus	.80	.40	.25
612 Indians Rookies (Lou Camilli, Ted Ford, Steve Mingori)	.80	.40	.25
613 Pedro Borbon	.90	.45	.25
614 Billy Cowan	.80	.40	.25
615 Mel Stottlemyre	1.75	.90	.50
616 Larry Hisle	.90	.45	.25
617 Clay Dalrymple	.80	.40	.25
618 Tug McGraw	2.25	1.25	.70
619a Checklist 644-752 (no copyright on back)			
	4.50	2.25	1.25
619b Checklist 644-752 (with copyright, no wavy line on helmet brim)	3.00	1.50	.90
619c Checklist 644-752 (with copyright, wavy line on helmet brim)	3.00	1.50	.90
620 Frank Howard	2.25	1.25	.70
621 Ron Bryant	.80	.40	.25
622 Joe Lahoud	.80	.40	.25
623 Pat Jarvis	.80	.40	.25
624 Athletics Team	2.00	1.00	.60
625 Lou Brock	10.00	5.00	3.00
626 Freddie Patek	.90	.45	.25
627 Steve Hamilton	.80	.40	.25
628 John Bateman	.80	.40	.25
629 John Hiller	.90	.45	.25
630 Roberto Clemente	25.00	12.50	7.50
631 Eddie Fisher	.80	.40	.25
632 Darrel Chaney	.80	.40	.25
633 A.L. Rookies (Bobby Brooks, Pete Koegel, Scott Northey)	.80	.40	.25
634 Phil Regan	.80	.40	.25
635 Bobby Murcer	2.00	1.00	.60
636 Denny Lemaster	.80	.40	.25
637 Dave Bristol	.80	.40	.25
638 Stan Williams	.80	.40	.25
639 Tom Haller	.90	.45	.25
640 Frank Robinson	25.00	12.50	7.50
641 Mets Team	3.50	1.75	1.00
642 Jim Roland	.80	.40	.25
643 Rick Reichardt	.80	.40	.25
644 Jim Stewart	2.25	1.25	.70
645 Jim Maloney	2.50	1.25	.70
646 Bobby Floyd	2.25	1.25	.70
647 Juan Pizarro	2.25	1.25	.70
648 Mets Rookies (Rich Folkers, Ted Martinez, *Jon Matlack*)	3.50	1.75	1.00
649 Sparky Lyle	3.00	1.50	.90
650 Rich Allen	9.00	4.50	2.75
651 Jerry Robertson	2.25	1.25	.70
652 Braves Team	3.25	1.75	1.00
653 Russ Snyder	2.25	1.25	.70
654 Don Shaw	2.25	1.25	.70
655 Mike Epstein	2.50	1.25	.70
656 Gerry Nyman	2.25	1.25	.70
657 Jose Azcue	2.25	1.25	.70
658 Paul Lindblad	2.25	1.25	.70
659 Byron Browne	2.25	1.25	.70
660 Ray Culp	2.25	1.25	.70
661 Chuck Tanner	3.00	1.50	.90

		NR MT	EX	VG
662	Mike Hedlund	2.25	1.25	.70
663	Marv Staehle	2.25	1.25	.70
664	Major League Rookies (Archie Reynolds, Bob Reynolds, Ken Reynolds)	2.25	1.25	.70
665	Ron Swoboda	2.25	1.25	.70
666	Gene Brabender	2.25	1.25	.70
667	Pete Ward	2.50	1.25	.70
668	Gary Neibauer	2.25	1.25	.70
669	Ike Brown	2.25	1.25	.70
670	Bill Hands	2.25	1.25	.70
671	Bill Voss	2.25	1.25	.70
672	Ed Crosby	2.25	1.25	.70
673	Gerry Janeski	2.25	1.25	.70
674	Expos Team	3.25	1.75	1.00
675	Dave Boswell	2.25	1.25	.70
676	Tommie Reynolds	2.25	1.25	.70
677	Jack DiLauro	2.25	1.25	.70
678	George Thomas	2.25	1.25	.70
679	Don O'Riley	2.25	1.25	.70
680	Don Mincher	2.50	1.25	.70
681	Bill Butler	2.25	1.25	.70
682	Terry Harmon	2.25	1.25	.70
683	Bill Burbach	2.50	1.25	.70
684	Curt Motton	2.25	1.25	.70
685	Moe Drabowsky	2.25	1.25	.70
686	Chico Ruiz	2.25	1.25	.70
687	Ron Taylor	2.25	1.25	.70
688	Sparky Anderson	3.50	1.75	1.00
689	Frank Baker	2.25	1.25	.70
690	Bob Moose	2.25	1.25	.70
691	Bob Heise	2.25	1.25	.70
692	A.L. Rookies (Hal Haydel, Rogelio Moret, Wayne Twitchell)	2.25	1.25	.70
693	Jose Pena	2.25	1.25	.70
694	Rick Renick	2.25	1.25	.70
695	Joe Niekro	3.25	1.75	1.00
696	Jerry Morales	2.25	1.25	.70
697	Rickey Clark	2.25	1.25	.70
698	Brewers Team	3.50	1.75	1.00
699	Jim Britton	2.25	1.25	.70
700	Boog Powell	4.00	2.00	1.25
701	Bob Garibaldi	2.25	1.25	.70
702	Milt Ramirez	2.25	1.25	.70
703	Mike Kekich	2.50	1.25	.70
704	J.C. Martin	2.25	1.25	.70
705	Dick Selma	2.25	1.25	.70
706	Joe Foy	2.25	1.25	.70
707	Fred Lasher	2.25	1.25	.70
708	Russ Nagelson	2.25	1.25	.70
709	Major League Rookies (Dusty Baker, Don Baylor, Tom Paciorek)	40.00	20.00	12.00
710	Sonny Siebert	2.25	1.25	.70
711	Larry Stahl	2.25	1.25	.70
712	Jose Martinez	2.25	1.25	.70
713	Mike Marshall	2.75	1.50	.80
714	Dick Williams	2.75	1.50	.80
715	Horace Clarke	2.50	1.25	.70
716	Dave Leonhard	2.25	1.25	.70
717	Tommie Aaron	2.50	1.25	.70
718	Billy Wynne	2.25	1.25	.70
719	Jerry May	2.25	1.25	.70
720	Matty Alou	2.75	1.50	.80
721	John Morris	2.25	1.25	.70
722	Astros Team	3.25	1.75	1.00
723	Vicente Romo	2.25	1.25	.70
724	Tom Tischinski	2.25	1.25	.70
725	Gary Gentry	2.25	1.25	.70
726	Paul Popovich	2.25	1.25	.70
727	Ray Lamb	2.25	1.25	.70
728	N.L. Rookies (Keith Lampard, Wayne Redmond, Bernie Williams)	2.25	1.25	.70
729	Dick Billings	2.25	1.25	.70
730	Jim Rooker	2.25	1.25	.70
731	Jim Qualls	2.25	1.25	.70
732	Bob Reed	2.25	1.25	.70
733	Lee Maye	2.25	1.25	.70
734	Rob Gardner	2.50	1.25	.70
735	Mike Shannon	2.50	1.25	.70
736	Mel Queen	2.25	1.25	.70
737	Preston Gomez	2.25	1.25	.70
738	Russ Gibson	2.25	1.25	.70
739	Barry Lersch	2.25	1.25	.70
740	Luis Aparicio	15.00	7.50	4.50
741	Skip Guinn	2.25	1.25	.70
742	Royals Team	3.25	1.75	1.00
743	John O'Donoghue	2.25	1.25	.70
744	Chuck Manuel	2.25	1.25	.70
745	Sandy Alomar	2.25	1.25	.70
746	Andy Kosco	2.25	1.25	.70
747	N.L. Rookies (Balor Moore, Al Severinsen, Scipio Spinks)	2.25	1.25	.70

		NR MT	EX	VG
748	John Purdin	2.25	1.25	.70
749	Ken Szotkiewicz	2.25	1.25	.70
750	Denny McLain	6.00	3.00	1.75
751	Al Weis	2.50	1.25	.70
752	Dick Drago	3.75	1.25	.70

1971 Topps Coins

Measuring 1-1/2" in diameter, the latest edition of the Topps coins was a 153-piece set. The coins feature a color photograph surrounded by a colored band on the front. The band carries the player's name, team, position and several stars. Backs have a short biography, the coin number and encouragement to collect the entire set. Back colors differ, with #'s 1-51 having a brass back, #'s 52-102 chrome backs, and the rest have blue backs. Most of the stars of the period are included in the set.

		NR MT	EX	VG
Complete Set:		400.00	200.00	120.00
Common Player:		.90	.45	.25
1	Clarence Gaston	.90	.45	.25
2	Dave Johnson	1.25	.60	.40
3	Jim Bunning	2.00	1.00	.60
4	Jim Spencer	.90	.45	.25
5	Felix Millan	.90	.45	.25
6	Gerry Moses	.90	.45	.25
7	Fergie Jenkins	2.00	1.00	.60
8	Felipe Alou	1.00	.50	.30
9	Jim McGlothlin	.90	.45	.25
10	Dick McAuliffe	.90	.45	.25
11	Joe Torre	1.50	.70	.45
12	Jim Perry	1.25	.60	.40
13	Bobby Bonds	1.25	.60	.40
14	Danny Cater	.90	.45	.25
15	Bill Mazeroski	1.50	.70	.45
16	Luis Aparicio	5.00	2.50	1.50
17	Doug Rader	.90	.45	.25
18	Vada Pinson	1.50	.70	.45
19	John Bateman	.90	.45	.25
20	Lew Krausse	.90	.45	.25
21	Billy Grabarkewitz	.90	.45	.25
22	Frank Howard	1.50	.70	.45
23	Jerry Koosman	1.25	.60	.40
24	Rod Carew	8.00	4.00	2.50
25	Al Ferrara	.90	.45	.25
26	Dave McNally	1.00	.50	.30
27	Jim Hickman	.90	.45	.25
28	Sandy Alomar	.90	.45	.25
29	Lee May	1.00	.50	.30
30	Rico Petrocelli	1.00	.50	.30
31	Don Money	.90	.45	.25
32	Jim Rooker	.90	.45	.25
33	Dick Dietz	.90	.45	.25
34	Roy White	1.00	.50	.30
35	Carl Morton	.90	.45	.25
36	Walt Williams	.90	.45	.25
37	Phil Niekro	3.25	1.75	1.00
38	Bill Freehan	1.00	.50	.30
39	Julian Javier	.90	.45	.25
40	Rick Monday	1.00	.50	.30
41	Don Wilson	.90	.45	.25
42	Ray Fosse	.90	.45	.25
43	Art Shamsky	.90	.45	.25
44	Ted Savage	.90	.45	.25

		NR MT	EX	VG
45	Claude Osteen	1.00	.50	.30
46	Ed Brinkman	.90	.45	.25
47	Matty Alou	1.00	.50	.30
48	Bob Oliver	.90	.45	.25
49	Danny Coombs	.90	.45	.25
50	Frank Robinson	7.00	3.50	2.00
51	Randy Hundley	.90	.45	.25
52	Cesar Tovar	.90	.45	.25
53	Wayne Simpson	.90	.45	.25
54	Bobby Murcer	1.25	.60	.40
55	Tony Taylor	.90	.45	.25
56	Tommy John	2.50	1.25	.70
57	Willie McCovey	7.00	3.50	2.00
58	Carl Yastrzemski	15.00	7.50	4.50
59	Bob Bailey	.90	.45	.25
60	Clyde Wright	.90	.45	.25
61	Orlando Cepeda	2.00	1.00	.60
62	Al Kaline	7.00	3.50	2.00
63	Bob Gibson	7.00	3.50	2.00
64	Bert Campaneris	1.25	.60	.40
65	Ted Sizemore	.90	.45	.25
66	Duke Sims	.90	.45	.25
67	Bud Harrelson	.90	.45	.25
68	Jerry McNertney	.90	.45	.25
69	Jim Wynn	1.00	.50	.30
70	Dick Bosman	.90	.45	.25
71	Roberto Clemente	15.00	7.50	4.50
72	Rich Reese	.90	.45	.25
73	Gaylord Perry	4.00	2.00	1.25
74	Boog Powell	1.50	.70	.45
75	Billy Williams	5.00	2.50	1.50
76	Bill Melton	.90	.45	.25
77	Nate Colbert	.90	.45	.25
78	Reggie Smith	1.25	.60	.40
79	Deron Johnson	.90	.45	.25
80	Jim Hunter	5.00	2.50	1.50
81	Bob Tolan	.90	.45	.25
82	Jim Northrup	.90	.45	.25
83	Ron Fairly	1.00	.50	.30
84	Alex Johnson	.90	.45	.25
85	Pat Jarvis	.90	.45	.25
86	Sam McDowell	1.00	.50	.30
87	Lou Brock	7.00	3.50	2.00
88	Danny Walton	.90	.45	.25
89	Denis Menke	.90	.45	.25
90	Jim Palmer	7.00	3.50	2.00
91	Tommie Agee	.90	.45	.25
92	Duane Josephson	.90	.45	.25
93	Willie Davis	1.00	.50	.30
94	Mel Stottlemyre	1.00	.50	.30
95	Ron Santo	1.25	.60	.40
96	Amos Otis	1.00	.50	.30
97	Ken Henderson	.90	.45	.25
98	George Scott	1.00	.50	.30
99	Dock Ellis	.90	.45	.25
100	Harmon Killebrew	7.00	3.50	2.00
101	Pete Rose	30.00	15.00	9.00
102	Rick Reichardt	.90	.45	.25
103	Cleon Jones	.90	.45	.25
104	Ron Perranoski	.90	.45	.25
105	Tony Perez	2.50	1.25	.70
106	Mickey Lolich	1.25	.60	.40
107	Tim McCarver	1.25	.60	.40
108	Reggie Jackson	12.00	6.00	3.50
109	Chris Cannizzaro	.90	.45	.25
110	Steve Hargan	.90	.45	.25
111	Rusty Staub	2.50	1.25	.70
112	Andy Messersmith	1.00	.50	.30
113	Rico Carty	1.25	.60	.40
114	Brooks Robinson	7.00	3.50	2.00
115	Steve Carlton	7.00	3.50	2.00
116	Mike Hegan	.90	.45	.25
117	Joe Morgan	4.50	2.25	1.25
118	Thurman Munson	5.00	2.50	1.50
119	Don Kessinger	1.00	.50	.30
120	Joe Horlen	.90	.45	.25
121	Wes Parker	1.00	.50	.30
122	Sonny Siebert	.90	.45	.25
123	Willie Stargell	5.00	2.50	1.50
124	Ellie Rodriguez	.90	.45	.25
125	Juan Marichal	5.00	2.50	1.50
126	Mike Epstein	.90	.45	.25
127	Tom Seaver	8.00	4.00	2.50
128	Tony Oliva	2.50	1.25	.70
129	Jim Merritt	.90	.45	.25
130	Willie Horton	1.00	.50	.30
131	Rick Wise	.90	.45	.25
132	Sal Bando	1.00	.50	.30
133	Ollie Brown	.90	.45	.25
134	Ken Harrelson	1.00	.50	.30
135	Mack Jones	.90	.45	.25

		NR MT	EX	VG
136	Jim Fregosi	1.00	.50	.30
137	Hank Aaron	15.00	7.50	4.50
138	Fritz Peterson	.90	.45	.25
139	Joe Hague	.90	.45	.25
140	Tommy Harper	.90	.45	.25
141	Larry Dierker	.90	.45	.25
142	Tony Conigliaro	1.50	.70	.45
143	Glenn Beckert	1.00	.50	.30
144	Carlos May	.90	.45	.25
145	Don Sutton	3.25	1.75	1.00
146	Paul Casanova	.90	.45	.25
147	Bob Moose	.90	.45	.25
148	Leo Cardenas	.90	.45	.25
149	Johnny Bench	8.00	4.00	2.50
150	Mike Cuellar	1.00	.50	.30
151	Donn Clendenon	.90	.45	.25
152	Lou Piniella	1.25	.60	.40
153	Willie Mays	15.00	7.50	4.50

1971 Topps Greatest Moments

This 55-card set features a great moment from the careers of top players at the time. The front of the 2-1/2" by 4-3/4" cards features a portrait photo of the player at the left and deckle-edge action photo at the right. There is a small headline on the white border of the action photo. The player's name and "One of Baseball's Greatest Moments" along with a black border complete the front. The back features a detail from the front photo and the story of the event. The newspaper style presentation includes the name of real newspapers. Relatively scarce, virtually every card in this set is a star or at least an above-average player.

		NR MT	EX	VG
Complete Set:		1550.00	775.00	465.00
Common Player:		4.00	2.00	1.25
1	Thurman Munson	60.00	30.00	18.00
2	Hoyt Wilhelm	30.00	15.00	9.00
3	Rico Carty	15.00	7.50	4.50
4	Carl Morton	4.00	2.00	1.25
5	Sal Bando	5.00	2.50	1.50
6	Bert Campaneris	5.00	2.50	1.50
7	Jim Kaat	20.00	10.00	6.00
8	Harmon Killebrew	60.00	30.00	18.00
9	Brooks Robinson	75.00	37.00	22.00
10	Jim Perry	15.00	7.50	4.50
11	Tony Oliva	20.00	10.00	6.00
12	Vada Pinson	20.00	10.00	6.00
13	Johnny Bench	175.00	87.00	52.00
14	Tony Perez	25.00	12.50	7.50
15	Pete Rose	90.00	45.00	27.00
16	Jim Fregosi	4.00	2.00	1.25
17	Alex Johnson	4.00	2.00	1.25
18	Clyde Wright	4.00	2.00	1.25
19	Al Kaline	25.00	12.50	7.50
20	Denny McLain	20.00	10.00	6.00
21	Jim Northrup	15.00	7.50	4.50
22	Bill Freehan	15.00	7.50	4.50
23	Mickey Lolich	20.00	10.00	6.00
24	Bob Gibson	18.00	9.00	5.50
25	Tim McCarver	5.00	2.50	1.50
26	Orlando Cepeda	7.00	3.50	2.00
27	Lou Brock	18.00	9.00	5.50
28	Nate Colbert	4.00	2.00	1.25

		NR MT	EX	VG
29	Maury Wills	20.00	10.00	6.00
30	Wes Parker	15.00	7.50	4.50
31	Jim Wynn	15.00	7.50	4.50
32	Larry Dierker	15.00	7.50	4.50
33	Bill Melton	15.00	7.50	4.50
34	Joe Morgan	40.00	20.00	12.00
35	Rusty Staub	20.00	10.00	6.00
36	Ernie Banks	25.00	12.50	7.50
37	Billy Williams	50.00	25.00	15.00
38	Lou Piniella	20.00	10.00	6.00
39	Rico Petrocelli	4.00	2.00	1.25
40	Carl Yastrzemski	60.00	30.00	18.00
41	Willie Mays	45.00	22.00	13.50
42	Tommy Harper	15.00	7.50	4.50
43	Jim Bunning	7.00	3.50	2.00
44	Fritz Peterson	15.00	7.50	4.50
45	Roy White	15.00	7.50	4.50
46	Bobby Murcer	15.00	7.50	4.50
47	Reggie Jackson	250.00	125.00	75.00
48	Frank Howard	20.00	10.00	6.00
49	Dick Bosman	15.00	7.50	4.50
50	Sam McDowell	4.00	2.00	1.25
51	Luis Aparicio	12.00	6.00	3.50
52	Willie McCovey	15.00	7.50	4.50
53	Joe Pepitone	15.00	7.50	4.50
54	Jerry Grote	15.00	7.50	4.50
55	Bud Harrelson	15.00	7.50	4.50

1971 Topps Super

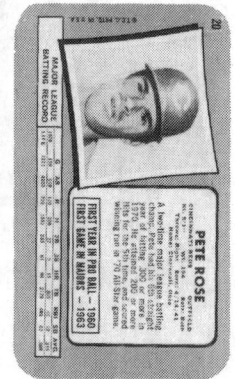

Topps continued to produce its special oversized cards in 1971. The cards, measuring 3-1/8" by 5-1/4," carry a large color photograph with a facsimile autograph on the front. Backs are basically enlargements of the player's regular Topps card. The set size was enlarged to 63 cards in 1971, so there are no short-printed cards as in 1970. Again, Topps included almost every major star who was active at the time, so the set of oversized cards with rounded corners remains an interesting source for those seeking the big names of the era.

		NR MT	EX	VG
Complete Set:		200.00	100.00	60.00
Common Player:		.80	.40	.25
1	Reggie Smith	1.00	.50	.30
2	Gaylord Perry	3.00	1.50	.90
3	Ted Savage	.80	.40	.25
4	Donn Clendenon	.80	.40	.25
5	John "Boog" Powell	1.25	.60	.40
6	Tony Perez	1.75	.90	.50
7	Dick Bosman	.80	.40	.25
8	Alex Johnson	.80	.40	.25
9	Rusty Staub	1.25	.60	.40
10	Mel Stottlemyre	1.00	.50	.30
11	Tony Oliva	1.50	.70	.45
12	Bill Freehan	1.00	.50	.30
13	Fritz Peterson	.80	.40	.25
14	Wes Parker	.80	.40	.25
15	Cesar Cedeno	1.25	.60	.40
16	Sam McDowell	1.00	.50	.30
17	Frank Howard	1.50	.70	.45
18	Dave McNally	1.00	.50	.30
19	Rico Petrocelli	.80	.40	.25
20	Pete Rose	25.00	12.50	7.50
21	Luke Walker	.80	.40	.25

		NR MT	EX	VG
22	Nate Colbert	.80	.40	.25
23	Luis Aparicio	2.50	1.25	.70
24	Jim Perry	1.00	.50	.30
25	Louis Brock	4.50	2.25	1.25
26	Roy White	1.00	.50	.30
27	Claude Osteen	.80	.40	.25
28	Carl W. Morton	.80	.40	.25
29	Ricardo A. Jacabo Carty	1.00	.50	.30
30	Larry Dierker	.80	.40	.25
31	Dagoberto Campaneris	1.00	.50	.30
32	Johnny Bench	8.00	4.00	2.50
33	Felix Millan	.80	.40	.25
34	Tim McCarver	1.25	.60	.40
35	Ronald Santo	1.25	.60	.40
36	Tommie Agee	.80	.40	.25
37	Roberto Clemente	10.00	5.00	3.00
38	Reggie Jackson	15.00	7.50	4.50
39	Clyde Wright	.80	.40	.25
40	Rich Allen	1.50	.70	.45
41	Curt Flood	1.25	.60	.40
42	Fergie Jenkins	1.75	.90	.50
43	Willie Stargell	3.00	1.50	.90
44	Henry Aaron	10.00	5.00	3.00
45	Amos Otis	1.00	.50	.30
46	Willie McCovey	4.50	2.25	1.25
47	William Melton	.80	.40	.25
48	Robert Gibson	3.50	1.75	1.00
49	Carl Yastrzemski	15.00	7.50	4.50
50	Glenn Beckert	1.00	.50	.30
51	Ray Fosse	.80	.40	.25
52	Clarence Gaston	.80	.40	.25
53	Tom Seaver	8.00	4.00	2.50
54	Al Kaline	6.00	3.00	1.75
55	Jim Northrup	.80	.40	.25
56	Willie Mays	10.00	5.00	3.00
57	Sal Bando	1.00	.50	.30
58	Deron Johnson	.80	.40	.25
59	Brooks Robinson	7.00	3.50	2.00
60	Harmon Killebrew	6.00	3.00	1.75
61	Joseph Torre	1.75	.90	.50
62	Lou Piniella	1.25	.60	.40
63	Tommy Harper	.80	.40	.25

1972 Topps

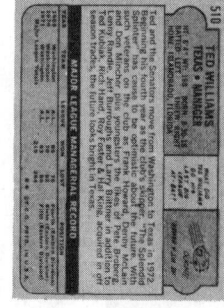

The largest Topps issue of its time appeared in 1972, with the set size reaching the 787 mark. The 2-1/2" by 3-1/2" cards are something special as well. Their fronts have a color photo which is shaped into an arch and surrounded by two different color borders, all of which is inside the overall white border. The player's name is in a white panel below the picture while the team name is above the picture in what might best be described as "superhero" type in a variety of colors. No mention of the player's position appears on the front. Cards backs are tame by comparison, featuring statistics and a trivia question. The set features a record number of specialty card including more than six dozen "In Action" (shown as "IA" in checklists below) cards featuring action shots of popular players. There are the usual statistical leaders, playoff and World Series highlights. Other innovations are 16 "Boyhood Photo" cards which depict scrapbook black and white photos of 1972's top players, and a group of cards depicting the trophies which comprise baseball's major awards. Finally, a group of seven "Traded"

cards was included which feature a large "Traded" across the front of the card.

	NR MT	EX	VG
Complete Set:	1400.00	700.00	420.00
Common Player: 1-394	.25	.13	.08
Common Player: 395-525	.30	.15	.09
Common Player: 526-656	.70	.35	.20
Common Player: 657-787	2.25	1.25	.70

#	Player	NR MT	EX	VG
1	World Champions (Pirates Team)	4.00	.75	.45
2	Ray Culp	.25	.13	.08
3	Bob Tolan	.30	.15	.09
4	Checklist 1-132	2.25	1.25	.70
5	John Bateman	.25	.13	.08
6	Fred Scherman	.25	.13	.08
7	Enzo Hernandez	.25	.13	.08
8	Ron Swoboda	.30	.15	.09
9	Stan Williams	.25	.13	.08
10	Amos Otis	.40	.20	.12
11	Bobby Valentine	.60	.30	.20
12	Jose Cardenal	.30	.15	.09
13	Joe Grzenda	.25	.13	.08
14	Phillies Rookiess (Mike Anderson, Pete Koegel, Wayne Twitchell)	.25	.13	.08
15	Walt Williams	.25	.13	.08
16	Mike Jorgensen	.25	.13	.08
17	Dave Duncan	.25	.13	.08
18a	Juan Pizarro (green under "C" and "S")	3.50	1.75	1.00
18b	Juan Pizarro (yellow under "C" and "S")	.25	.13	.08
19	Billy Cowan	.25	.13	.08
20	Don Wilson	.25	.13	.08
21	Braves Team	.90	.45	.25
22	Rob Gardner	.30	.15	.09
23	Ted Kubiak	.25	.13	.08
24	Ted Ford	.25	.13	.08
25	Bill Singer	.30	.15	.09
26	Andy Etchebarren	.25	.13	.08
27	Bob Johnson	.25	.13	.08
28	Twins Rookies (Steve Brye, Bob Gebhard, Hal Haydel)	.25	.13	.08
29a	Bill Bonham (green under "C" and "S")	3.50	1.75	1.00
29b	Bill Bonham (yellow under "C" and "S")	.30	.15	.09
30	Rico Petrocelli	.50	.25	.15
31	Cleon Jones	.30	.15	.09
32	Cleon Jones IA	.30	.15	.09
33	Billy Martin	1.50	.70	.45
34	Billy Martin IA	.80	.40	.25
35	Jerry Johnson	.25	.13	.08
36	Jerry Johnson IA	.25	.13	.08
37	Carl Yastrzemski	12.00	6.00	3.50
38	Carl Yastrzemski IA	8.00	4.00	2.50
39	Bob Barton	.25	.13	.08
40	Bob Barton IA	.25	.13	.08
41	Tommy Davis	.60	.30	.20
42	Tommy Davis IA	.30	.15	.09
43	Rick Wise	.30	.15	.09
44	Rick Wise IA	.25	.13	.08
45a	Glenn Beckert (green under "C" and "S")	3.50	1.75	1.00
45b	Glenn Beckert (yellow under "C" and "S")	.40	.20	.12
46	Glenn Beckert IA	.30	.15	.09
47	John Ellis	.30	.15	.09
48	John Ellis IA	.30	.15	.09
49	Willie Mays	25.00	12.50	7.50
50	Willie Mays IA	10.00	5.00	3.00
51	Harmon Killebrew	4.00	2.00	1.25
52	Harmon Killebrew IA	2.00	1.00	.60
53	Bud Harrelson	.40	.20	.12
54	Bud Harrelson IA	.30	.15	.09
55	Clyde Wright	.25	.13	.08
56	Rich Chiles	.25	.13	.08
57	Bob Oliver	.25	.13	.08
58	Ernie McAnally	.25	.13	.08
59	Fred Stanley	.40	.20	.12
60	Manny Sanguillen	.30	.15	.09
61	Cubs Rookies (Gene Hiser, Burt Hooton, Earl Stephenson)	1.00	.50	.30
62	Angel Mangual	.25	.13	.08
63	Duke Sims	.25	.13	.08
64	Pete Broberg	.25	.13	.08
65	Cesar Cedeno	.80	.40	.25
66	Ray Corbin	.25	.13	.08
67	Red Schoendienst	.80	.40	.25
68	Jim York	.25	.13	.08
69	Roger Freed	.25	.13	.08
70	Mike Cuellar	.50	.25	.15
71	Angels Team	.90	.45	.25
72	Bruce Kison	.80	.40	.25
73	Steve Huntz	.25	.13	.08
74	Cecil Upshaw	.25	.13	.08
75	Bert Campaneris	.60	.30	.20
76	Don Carrithers	.25	.13	.08
77	Ron Theobald	.25	.13	.08
78	Steve Arlin	.25	.13	.08
79	Red Sox Rookies (Cecil Cooper, Carlton Fisk, Mike Garman)	150.00	75.00	45.00
80	Tony Perez	2.00	1.00	.60
81	Mike Hedlund	.25	.13	.08
82	Ron Woods	.25	.13	.08
83	Dalton Jones	.25	.13	.08
84	Vince Colbert	.25	.13	.08
85	N.L. Batting Leaders (Glenn Beckert, Ralph Garr, Joe Torre)	1.25	.60	.40
86	A.L. Batting Leaders (Bobby Murcer, Tony Oliva, Merv Rettenmund)	1.25	.60	.40
87	N.L. RBI Leaders (Hank Aaron, Willie Stargell, Joe Torre)	2.25	1.25	.70
88	A.L. RBI Leaders (Harmon Killebrew, Frank Robinson, Reggie Smith)	2.25	1.25	.70
89	N.L. Home Run Leaders (Hank Aaron, Lee May, Willie Stargell)	2.25	1.25	.70
90	A.L. Home Run Leaders (Norm Cash, Reggie Jackson, Bill Melton)	1.75	.90	.50
91	N.L. ERA Leaders (Dave Roberts, Tom Seaver, Don Wilson)	1.75	.90	.50
92	A.L. ERA Leaders (Vida Blue, Jim Palmer, Wilbur Wood)	1.50	.70	.45
93	N.L. Pitching Leaders (Steve Carlton, Al Downing, Fergie Jenkins, Tom Seaver)	2.00	1.00	.60
94	A.L. Pitching Leaders (Vida Blue, Mickey Lolich, Wilbur Wood)	1.25	.60	.40
95	N.L. Strikeout Leaders (Fergie Jenkins, Tom Seaver, Bill Stoneman)	1.75	.90	.50
96	A.L. Strikeout Leaders (Vida Blue, Joe Coleman, Mickey Lolich)	1.25	.60	.40
97	Tom Kelley	.25	.13	.08
98	Chuck Tanner	.50	.25	.15
99	Ross Grimsley	.60	.30	.20
100	Frank Robinson	4.00	2.00	1.25
101	Astros Rookies (Ray Busse, Bill Grief, J.R. Richard)	1.00	.50	.30
102	Lloyd Allen	.25	.13	.08
103	Checklist 133-263	2.25	1.25	.70
104	Toby Harrah	1.00	.50	.30
105	Gary Gentry	.25	.13	.08
106	Brewers Team	.90	.45	.25
107	Jose Cruz	1.75	.90	.50
108	Gary Waslewski	.30	.15	.09
109	Jerry May	.25	.13	.08
110	Ron Hunt	.30	.15	.09
111	Jim Grant	.25	.13	.08
112	Greg Luzinski	.80	.40	.25
113	Rogelio Moret	.25	.13	.08
114	Bill Buckner	1.25	.60	.40
115	Jim Fregosi	.70	.35	.20
116	Ed Farmer	.30	.15	.09
117a	Cleo James (green under "C" and "S")	3.50	1.75	1.00
117b	Cleo James (yellow under "C" and "S")	.25	.13	.08
118	Skip Lockwood	.25	.13	.08
119	Marty Perez	.25	.13	.08
120	Bill Freehan	.60	.30	.20
121	Ed Sprague	.25	.13	.08
122	Larry Biittner	.25	.13	.08
123	Ed Acosta	.25	.13	.08
124	Yankees (Alan Closter, Roger Hambright, Rusty Torres)	.30	.15	.09
125	Dave Cash	.25	.13	.08
126	Bart Johnson	.25	.13	.08
127	Duffy Dyer	.25	.13	.08
128	Eddie Watt	.25	.13	.08
129	Charlie Fox	.25	.13	.08
130	Bob Gibson	5.00	2.50	1.50
131	Jim Nettles	.25	.13	.08
132	Joe Morgan	5.00	2.50	1.50
133	Joe Keough	.25	.13	.08
134	Carl Morton	.25	.13	.08
135	Vada Pinson	.80	.40	.25
136	Darrel Chaney	.25	.13	.08
137	Dick Williams	.50	.25	.15
138	Mike Kekich	.30	.15	.09
139	Tim McCarver	.80	.40	.25
140	Pat Dobson	.30	.15	.09
141	Mets Rookies (Buzz Capra, Jon Matlack, Leroy Stanton)	.40	.20	.12

#		NR MT	EX	VG
142	*Chris Chambliss*	1.25	.60	.40
143	Garry Jestadt	.25	.13	.08
144	Marty Pattin	.25	.13	.08
145	Don Kessinger	.40	.20	.12
146	Steve Kealey	.25	.13	.08
147	*Dave Kingman*	3.50	1.75	1.00
148	Dick Billings	.25	.13	.08
149	Gary Neibauer	.25	.13	.08
150	Norm Cash	.70	.35	.20
151	Jim Brewer	.25	.13	.08
152	Gene Clines	.25	.13	.08
153	Rick Auerbach	.25	.13	.08
154	Ted Simmons	1.50	.70	.45
155	Larry Dierker	.30	.15	.09
156	Twins Team	.90	.45	.25
157	Don Gullett	.40	.20	.12
158	Jerry Kenney	.30	.15	.09
159	John Boccabella	.25	.13	.08
160	Andy Messersmith	.40	.20	.12
161	Brock Davis	.25	.13	.08
162	Brewers Rookies (Jerry Bell, *Darrell Porter*, Bob Reynolds) (Bell & Porter photos transposed)	1.00	.50	.30
163	Tug McGraw	.80	.40	.25
164	Tug McGraw IA	.40	.20	.12
165	*Chris Speier*	.80	.40	.25
166	Chris Speier IA	.40	.20	.12
167	Deron Johnson	.25	.13	.08
168	Deron Johnson IA	.25	.13	.08
169	Vida Blue	.80	.40	.25
170	Vida Blue IA	.40	.20	.12
171	Darrell Evans	1.50	.70	.45
172	Darrell Evans IA	.80	.40	.25
173	Clay Kirby	.25	.13	.08
174	Clay Kirby IA	.25	.13	.08
175	Tom Haller	.30	.15	.09
176	Tom Haller IA	.25	.13	.08
177	Paul Schaal	.25	.13	.08
178	Paul Schaal IA	.25	.13	.08
179	Dock Ellis	.30	.15	.09
180	Dock Ellis IA	.25	.13	.08
181	Ed Kranepool	.40	.20	.12
182	Ed Kranepool IA	.30	.15	.09
183	Bill Melton	.30	.15	.09
184	Bill Melton IA	.25	.13	.08
185	Ron Bryant	.25	.13	.08
186	Ron Bryant IA	.25	.13	.08
187	Gates Brown	.25	.13	.08
188	Frank Lucchesi	.25	.13	.08
189	Gene Tenace	.40	.20	.12
190	Dave Giusti	.25	.13	.08
191	*Jeff Burroughs*	.80	.40	.25
192	Cubs Team	.90	.45	.25
193	*Kurt Bevacqua*	.40	.20	.12
194	Fred Norman	.25	.13	.08
195	Orlando Cepeda	2.00	1.00	.60
196	Mel Queen	.25	.13	.08
197	Johnny Briggs	.25	.13	.08
198	Dodgers Rookies (*Charlie Hough*, Bob O'Brien, Mike Strahler)	2.25	1.25	.70
199	Mike Fiore	.25	.13	.08
200	Lou Brock	4.00	2.00	1.25
201	Phil Roof	.25	.13	.08
202	Scipio Spinks	.25	.13	.08
203	*Ron Blomberg*	.50	.25	.15
204	Tommy Helms	.25	.13	.08
205	Dick Drago	.25	.13	.08
206	Dal Maxvill	.30	.15	.09
207	Tom Egan	.25	.13	.08
208	Milt Pappas	.40	.20	.12
209	Joe Rudi	.60	.30	.20
210	Denny McLain	1.25	.60	.40
211	Gary Sutherland	.25	.13	.08
212	Grant Jackson	.25	.13	.08
213	Angels Rookies (Art Kusnyer, Billy Parker, Tom Silverio)	.25	.13	.08
214	Mike McQueen	.25	.13	.08
215	Alex Johnson	.25	.13	.08
216	Joe Niekro	.50	.25	.15
217	Roger Metzger	.25	.13	.08
218	Eddie Kasko	.25	.13	.08
219	*Rennie Stennett*	.40	.20	.12
220	Jim Perry	.60	.30	.20
221	N.L. Playoffs (Bucs Champs!)	1.25	.60	.40
222	A.L. Playoffs (Orioles Champs!)	1.25	.60	.40
223	World Series Game 1	1.25	.60	.40
224	World Series Game 2	1.25	.60	.40
225	World Series Game 3	1.25	.60	.40
226	World Series Game 4	1.50	.70	.45
227	World Series Game 5	1.25	.60	.40
228	World Series Game 6	1.25	.60	.40
229	World Series Game 7	1.25	.60	.40
230	World Series Summary (Series Celebration)	1.25	.60	.40
231	Casey Cox	.25	.13	.08
232	Giants Rookies (Chris Arnold, Jim Barr, Dave Rader)	.30	.15	.09
233	Jay Johnstone	.40	.20	.12
234	Ron Taylor	.25	.13	.08
235	Merv Rettenmund	.30	.15	.09
236	Jim McGlothlin	.25	.13	.08
237	Yankees Team	1.25	.60	.40
238	Leron Lee	.25	.13	.08
239	Tom Timmermann	.25	.13	.08
240	Rich Allen	1.75	.90	.50
241	Rollie Fingers	4.00	2.00	1.25
242	Don Mincher	.30	.15	.09
243	Frank Linzy	.25	.13	.08
244	Steve Braun	.25	.13	.08
245	Tommie Agee	.30	.15	.09
246	Tom Burgmeier	.25	.13	.08
247	Milt May	.25	.13	.08
248	Tom Bradley	.25	.13	.08
249	Harry Walker	.30	.15	.09
250	Boog Powell	1.25	.60	.40
251a	Checklist 264-394 (small print on front)	2.25	1.25	.70
251b	Checklist 264-394 (large print on front)	2.25	1.25	.70
252	Ken Reynolds	.25	.13	.08
253	Sandy Alomar	.25	.13	.08
254	Boots Day	.25	.13	.08
255	Jim Lonborg	.40	.20	.12
256	George Foster	1.50	.70	.45
257	Tigers Rookies (Jim Foor, Tim Hosley, Paul Jata)	.25	.13	.08
258	Randy Hundley	.25	.13	.08
259	Sparky Lyle	.70	.35	.20
260	Ralph Garr	.40	.20	.12
261	Steve Mingori	.25	.13	.08
262	Padres Team	.90	.45	.25
263	Felipe Alou	.50	.25	.15
264	Tommy John	2.00	1.00	.60
265	Wes Parker	.30	.15	.09
266	Bobby Bolin	.25	.13	.08
267	Dave Concepcion	1.75	.90	.50
268	A's Rookies (Dwain Anderson, Chris Floethe)	.25	.13	.08
269	Don Hahn	.25	.13	.08
270	Jim Palmer	12.00	6.00	3.50
271	Ken Rudolph	.25	.13	.08
272	*Mickey Rivers*	1.00	.50	.30
273	Bobby Floyd	.25	.13	.08
274	Al Severinsen	.25	.13	.08
275	Cesar Tovar	.25	.13	.08
276	Gene Mauch	.50	.25	.15
277	Elliott Maddox	.30	.15	.09
278	Dennis Higgins	.25	.13	.08
279	Larry Brown	.25	.13	.08
280	Willie McCovey	4.00	2.00	1.25
281	Bill Parsons	.25	.13	.08
282	Astros Team	.90	.45	.25
283	Darrell Brandon	.25	.13	.08
284	Ike Brown	.25	.13	.08
285	Gaylord Perry	4.00	2.00	1.25
286	Gene Alley	.30	.15	.09
287	Jim Hardin	.30	.15	.09
288	Johnny Jeter	.25	.13	.08
289	Syd O'Brien	.25	.13	.08
290	Sonny Siebert	.25	.13	.08
291	Hal McRae	.60	.30	.20
292	Hal McRae IA	.30	.15	.09
293	Danny Frisella	.25	.13	.08
294	Danny Frisella IA	.25	.13	.08
295	Dick Dietz	.25	.13	.08
296	Dick Dietz IA	.25	.13	.08
297	Claude Osteen	.40	.20	.12
298	Claude Osteen IA	.30	.15	.09
299	Hank Aaron	20.00	10.00	6.00
300	Hank Aaron IA	8.00	4.00	2.50
301	George Mitterwald	.25	.13	.08
302	George Mitterwald IA	.25	.13	.08
303	Joe Pepitone	.50	.25	.15
304	Joe Pepitone IA	.30	.15	.09
305	Ken Boswell	.25	.13	.08
306	Ken Boswell IA	.25	.13	.08
307	Steve Renko	.25	.13	.08
308	Steve Renko IA	.25	.13	.08
309	Roberto Clemente	20.00	10.00	6.00
310	Roberto Clemente IA	6.00	3.00	1.75
311	Clay Carroll	.30	.15	.09
312	Clay Carroll IA	.25	.13	.08

		NR MT	EX	VG
313	Luis Aparicio	3.00	1.50	.90
314	Luis Aparicio IA	1.50	.70	.45
315	Paul Splittorff	.30	.15	.09
316	Cardinals Rookies (Jim Bibby, Santiago Guzman, Jorge Roque)	.50	.25	.15
317	Rich Hand	.25	.13	.08
318	Sonny Jackson	.25	.13	.08
319	Aurelio Rodriguez	.30	.15	.09
320	Steve Blass	.30	.15	.09
321	Joe Lahoud	.25	.13	.08
322	Jose Pena	.25	.13	.08
323	Earl Weaver	.80	.40	.25
324	Mike Ryan	.25	.13	.08
325	Mel Stottlemyre	.80	.40	.25
326	Pat Kelly	.25	.13	.08
327	Steve Stone	1.00	.50	.30
328	Red Sox Team	1.00	.50	.30
329	Roy Foster	.25	.13	.08
330	Jim Hunter	3.50	1.75	1.00
331	Stan Swanson	.25	.13	.08
332	Buck Martinez	.25	.13	.08
333	Steve Barber	.25	.13	.08
334	Rangers Rookies (Bill Fahey, Jim Mason, Tom Ragland)	.25	.13	.08
335	Bill Hands	.25	.13	.08
336	Marty Martinez	.25	.13	.08
337	Mike Kilkenny	.25	.13	.08
338	Bob Grich	.70	.35	.20
339	Ron Cook	.25	.13	.08
340	Roy White	.70	.35	.20
341	Boyhood Photo (Joe Torre)	.50	.25	.15
342	Boyhood Photo (Wilbur Wood)	.40	.20	.12
343	Boyhood Photo (Willie Stargell)	1.50	.70	.45
344	Boyhood Photo (Dave McNally)	.40	.20	.12
345	Boyhood Photo (Rick Wise)	.30	.15	.09
346	Boyhood Photo (Jim Fregosi)	.40	.20	.12
347	Boyhood Photo (Tom Seaver)	2.00	1.00	.60
348	Boyhood Photo (Sal Bando)	.40	.20	.12
349	Al Fitzmorris	.25	.13	.08
350	Frank Howard	1.25	.60	.40
351	Braves Rookies (Jimmy Britton, Tom House, Rick Kester)	.25	.13	.08
352	Dave LaRoche	.30	.15	.09
353	Art Shamsky	.25	.13	.08
354	Tom Murphy	.25	.13	.08
355	Bob Watson	.30	.15	.09
356	Gerry Moses	.25	.13	.08
357	Woodie Fryman	.30	.15	.09
358	Sparky Anderson	.70	.35	.20
359	Don Pavletich	.25	.13	.08
360	Dave Roberts	.25	.13	.08
361	Mike Andrews	.25	.13	.08
362	Mets Team	1.25	.60	.40
363	Ron Klimkowski	.25	.13	.08
364	Johnny Callison	.50	.25	.15
365	Dick Bosman	.25	.13	.08
366	Jimmy Rosario	.25	.13	.08
367	Ron Perranoski	.30	.15	.09
368	Danny Thompson	.30	.15	.09
369	Jim Lefebvre	.30	.15	.09
370	Don Buford	.30	.15	.09
371	Denny Lemaster	.25	.13	.08
372	Royals Rookies (Lance Clemons, Monty Montgomery)	.25	.13	.08
373	John Mayberry	.40	.20	.12
374	Jack Heidemann	.25	.13	.08
375	Reggie Cleveland	.25	.13	.08
376	Andy Kosco	.25	.13	.08
377	Terry Harmon	.25	.13	.08
378	Checklist 395-525	2.25	1.25	.70
379	Ken Berry	.25	.13	.08
380	Earl Williams	.30	.15	.09
381	White Sox Team	.90	.45	.25
382	Joe Gibbon	.25	.13	.08
383	Brant Alyea	.25	.13	.08
384	Dave Campbell	.25	.13	.08
385	Mickey Stanley	.30	.15	.09
386	Jim Colborn	.25	.13	.08
387	Horace Clarke	.30	.15	.09
388	Charlie Williams	.25	.13	.08
389	Bill Rigney	.25	.13	.08
390	Willie Davis	.50	.25	.15
391	Ken Sanders	.25	.13	.08
392	Pirates Rookies (Fred Cambria, Richie Zisk)	.70	.35	.20
393	Curt Motton	.25	.13	.08
394	Ken Forsch	.30	.15	.09
395	Matty Alou	.60	.30	.20
396	Paul Lindblad	.30	.15	.09
397	Phillies Team	.90	.45	.25
398	Larry Hisle	.40	.20	.12
399	Milt Wilcox	.40	.20	.12
400	Tony Oliva	1.50	.70	.45
401	Jim Nash	.30	.15	.09
402	Bobby Heise	.30	.15	.09
403	John Cumberland	.30	.15	.09
404	Jeff Torborg	.40	.20	.12
405	Ron Fairly	.50	.25	.15
406	George Hendrick	1.00	.50	.30
407	Chuck Taylor	.30	.15	.09
408	Jim Northrup	.40	.20	.12
409	Frank Baker	.40	.20	.12
410	Fergie Jenkins	3.00	1.50	.90
411	Bob Montgomery	.30	.15	.09
412	Dick Kelley	.30	.15	.09
413	White Sox Rookies (Don Eddy, Dave Lemonds)	.30	.15	.09
414	Bob Miller	.30	.15	.09
415	Cookie Rojas	.30	.15	.09
416	Johnny Edwards	.30	.15	.09
417	Tom Hall	.30	.15	.09
418	Tom Shopay	.30	.15	.09
419	Jim Spencer	.30	.15	.09
420	Steve Carlton	15.00	7.50	4.50
421	Ellie Rodriguez	.30	.15	.09
422	Ray Lamb	.30	.15	.09
423	Oscar Gamble	.40	.20	.12
424	Bill Gogolewski	.30	.15	.09
425	Ken Singleton	.70	.35	.20
426	Ken Singleton IA	.40	.20	.12
427	Tito Fuentes	.30	.15	.09
428	Tito Fuentes IA	.30	.15	.09
429	Bob Robertson	.30	.15	.09
430	Bob Robertson IA	.30	.15	.09
431	Clarence Gaston	.30	.15	.09
432	Clarence Gaston IA	.30	.15	.09
433	Johnny Bench	30.00	15.00	9.00
434	Johnny Bench IA	10.00	5.00	3.00
435	Reggie Jackson	30.00	15.00	9.00
436	Reggie Jackson IA	10.00	5.00	3.00
437	Maury Wills	1.50	.70	.45
438	Maury Wills IA	.70	.35	.20
439	Billy Williams	3.50	1.75	1.00
440	Billy Williams IA	1.75	.90	.50
441	Thurman Munson	15.00	7.50	4.50
442	Thurman Munson IA	8.00	4.00	2.50
443	Ken Henderson	.30	.15	.09
444	Ken Henderson IA	.30	.15	.09
445	Tom Seaver	25.00	12.50	7.50
446	Tom Seaver IA	9.00	4.50	2.75
447	Willie Stargell	4.00	2.00	1.25
448	Willie Stargell IA	2.00	1.00	.60
449	Bob Lemon	.90	.45	.25
450	Mickey Lolich	1.25	.60	.40
451	Tony LaRussa	.60	.30	.20
452	Ed Herrmann	.30	.15	.09
453	Barry Lersch	.30	.15	.09
454	A's Team	2.00	1.00	.60
455	Tommy Harper	.40	.20	.12
456	Mark Belanger	.40	.20	.12
457	Padres Rookies (Darcy Fast, Mike Ivie, Derrel Thomas)	.40	.20	.12
458	Aurelio Monteagudo	.30	.15	.09
459	Rick Renick	.30	.15	.09
460	Al Downing	.40	.20	.12
461	Tim Cullen	.30	.15	.09
462	Rickey Clark	.30	.15	.09
463	Bernie Carbo	.30	.15	.09
464	Jim Roland	.30	.15	.09
465	Gil Hodges	3.00	1.50	.90
466	Norm Miller	.30	.15	.09
467	Steve Kline	.40	.20	.12
468	Richie Scheinblum	.30	.15	.09
469	Ron Herbel	.30	.15	.09
470	Ray Fosse	.30	.15	.09
471	Luke Walker	.30	.15	.09
472	Phil Gagliano	.30	.15	.09
473	Dan McGinn	.30	.15	.09
474	Orioles Rookies (Don Baylor, Roric Harrison, Johnny Oates)	2.50	1.25	.70
475	Gary Nolan	.30	.15	.09
476	Lee Richard	.30	.15	.09
477	Tom Phoebus	.30	.15	.09
478a	Checklist 526-656 (small print on front)	2.25	1.25	.70
478b	Checklist 526-656 (large printing on front)	2.25	1.25	.70
479	Don Shaw	.30	.15	.09
480	Lee May	.60	.30	.20
481	Billy Conigliaro	.30	.15	.09
482	Joe Hoerner	.30	.15	.09
483	Ken Suarez	.30	.15	.09

		NR MT	EX	VG
484	Lum Harris	.30	.15	.09
485	Phil Regan	.30	.15	.09
486	John Lowenstein	.30	.15	.09
487	Tigers Team	1.50	.70	.45
488	Mike Nagy	.30	.15	.09
489	Expos Rookies (Terry Humphrey, Keith Lampard)	.30	.15	.09
490	Dave McNally	.50	.25	.15
491	Boyhood Photo (Lou Piniella)	.60	.30	.20
492	Boyhood Photo (Mel Stottlemyre)	.40	.20	.12
493	Boyhood Photo (Bob Bailey)	.30	.15	.09
494	Boyhood Photo (Willie Horton)	.40	.20	.12
495	Boyhood Photo (Bill Melton)	.30	.15	.09
496	Boyhood Photo (Bud Harrelson)	.40	.20	.12
497	Boyhood Photo (Jim Perry)	.40	.20	.12
498	Boyhood Photo (Brooks Robinson)	2.00	1.00	.60
499	Vicente Romo	.30	.15	.09
500	Joe Torre	1.25	.60	.40
501	Pete Hamm	.30	.15	.09
502	Jackie Hernandez	.30	.15	.09
503	Gary Peters	.30	.15	.09
504	Ed Spiezio	.30	.15	.09
505	Mike Marshall	.50	.25	.15
506	Indians Rookies (Terry Ley, Jim Moyer, Dick Tidrow)	.60	.30	.20
507	Fred Gladding	.30	.15	.09
508	Ellie Hendricks	.30	.15	.09
509	Don McMahon	.30	.15	.09
510	Ted Williams	5.00	2.50	1.50
511	Tony Taylor	.30	.15	.09
512	Paul Popovich	.30	.15	.09
513	Lindy McDaniel	.40	.20	.12
514	Ted Sizemore	.30	.15	.09
515	Bert Blyleven	8.00	4.00	2.50
516	Oscar Brown	.30	.15	.09
517	Ken Brett	.40	.20	.12
518	Wayne Garrett	.30	.15	.09
519	Ted Abernathy	.30	.15	.09
520	Larry Bowa	1.25	.60	.40
521	Alan Foster	.30	.15	.09
522	Dodgers Team	1.25	.60	.40
523	Chuck Dobson	.30	.15	.09
524	Reds Rookies (Ed Armbrister, Mel Behney)	.30	.15	.09
525	Carlos May	.40	.20	.12
526	Bob Bailey	.70	.35	.20
527	Dave Leonhard	.70	.35	.20
528	Ron Stone	.70	.35	.20
529	Dave Nelson	.70	.35	.20
530	Don Sutton	3.50	1.75	1.00
531	Freddie Patek	.70	.35	.20
532	Fred Kendall	.70	.35	.20
533	Ralph Houk	1.25	.60	.40
534	Jim Hickman	.80	.40	.25
535	Ed Brinkman	.80	.40	.25
536	Doug Rader	.70	.35	.20
537	Bob Locker	.70	.35	.20
538	Charlie Sands	.70	.35	.20
539	Terry Forster	1.25	.60	.40
540	Felix Millan	.70	.35	.20
541	Roger Repoz	.70	.35	.20
542	Jack Billingham	.70	.35	.20
543	Duane Josephson	.70	.35	.20
544	Ted Martinez	.70	.35	.20
545	Wayne Granger	.70	.35	.20
546	Joe Hague	.70	.35	.20
547	Indians Team	1.50	.70	.45
548	Frank Reberger	.70	.35	.20
549	Dave May	.70	.35	.20
550	Brooks Robinson	15.00	7.50	4.50
551	Ollie Brown	.70	.35	.20
552	Ollie Brown IA	.70	.35	.20
553	Wilbur Wood	.90	.45	.25
554	Wilbur Wood IA	.80	.40	.25
555	Ron Santo	1.50	.70	.45
556	Ron Santo IA	.80	.40	.25
557	John Odom	.70	.35	.20
558	John Odom IA	.70	.35	.20
559	Pete Rose	60.00	30.00	18.00
560	Pete Rose IA	30.00	15.00	9.00
561	Leo Cardenas	.70	.35	.20
562	Leo Cardenas IA	.70	.35	.20
563	Ray Sadecki	.70	.35	.20
564	Ray Sadecki IA	.70	.35	.20
565	Reggie Smith	.90	.45	.25
566	Reggie Smith IA	.80	.40	.25
567	Juan Marichal	6.00	3.00	1.75
568	Juan Marichal IA	3.00	1.50	.90
569	Ed Kirkpatrick	.70	.35	.20
570	Ed Kirkpatrick IA	.70	.35	.20

		NR MT	EX	VG
571	Nate Colbert	.70	.35	.20
572	Nate Colbert IA	.70	.35	.20
573	Fritz Peterson	.80	.40	.25
574	Fritz Peterson IA	.80	.40	.25
575	Al Oliver	2.00	1.00	.60
576	Leo Durocher	1.25	.60	.40
577	Mike Paul	.70	.35	.20
578	Billy Grabarkewitz	.70	.35	.20
579	Doyle Alexander	2.75	1.50	.80
580	Lou Piniella	1.75	.90	.50
581	Wade Blasingame	.70	.35	.20
582	Expos Team	2.25	1.25	.70
583	Darold Knowles	.70	.35	.20
584	Jerry McNertney	.70	.35	.20
585	George Scott	.80	.40	.25
586	Denis Menke	.70	.35	.20
587	Billy Wilson	.70	.35	.20
588	Jim Holt	.70	.35	.20
589	Hal Lanier	1.00	.50	.30
590	Graig Nettles	2.50	1.25	.70
591	Paul Casanova	.70	.35	.20
592	Lew Krausse	.70	.35	.20
593	Rich Morales	.70	.35	.20
594	Jim Beauchamp	.70	.35	.20
595	Nolan Ryan	125.00	62.00	37.00
596	Manny Mota	.90	.45	.25
597	Jim Magnuson	.80	.40	.25
598	Hal King	.70	.35	.20
599	Billy Champion	.70	.35	.20
600	Al Kaline	12.00	6.00	3.50
601	George Stone	.70	.35	.20
602	Dave Bristol	.70	.35	.20
603	Jim Ray	.70	.35	.20
604a	Checklist 657-787 (copyright on right)	3.50	1.75	1.00
604b	Checklist 657-787 (copyright on left)	5.00	2.50	1.50
605	Nelson Briles	.70	.35	.20
606	Luis Melendez	.70	.35	.20
607	Frank Duffy	.70	.35	.20
608	Mike Corkins	.70	.35	.20
609	Tom Grieve	.70	.35	.20
610	Bill Stoneman	.70	.35	.20
611	Rich Reese	.70	.35	.20
612	Joe Decker	.70	.35	.20
613	Mike Ferraro	.70	.35	.20
614	Ted Uhlaender	.70	.35	.20
615	Steve Hargan	.70	.35	.20
616	Joe Ferguson	.80	.40	.25
617	Royals Team	2.25	1.25	.70
618	Rich Robertson	.70	.35	.20
619	Rich McKinney	.80	.40	.25
620	Phil Niekro	4.50	2.25	1.25
621	Commissioners Award	.90	.45	.25
622	MVP Award	.90	.45	.25
623	Cy Young Award	.90	.45	.25
624	Minor League Player Of The Year Award	.90	.45	.25
625	Rookie Of The Year Award	.90	.45	.25
626	Babe Ruth Award	1.00	.50	.30
627	Moe Drabowsky	.70	.35	.20
628	Terry Crowley	.70	.35	.20
629	Paul Doyle	.70	.35	.20
630	Rich Hebner	.80	.40	.25
631	John Strohmayer	.70	.35	.20
632	Mike Hegan	.70	.35	.20
633	Jack Hiatt	.70	.35	.20
634	Dick Woodson	.70	.35	.20
635	Don Money	.80	.40	.25
636	Bill Lee	.90	.45	.25
637	Preston Gomez	.70	.35	.20
638	Ken Wright	.70	.35	.20
639	J.C. Martin	.70	.35	.20
640	Joe Coleman	.80	.40	.25
641	Mike Lum	.70	.35	.20
642	Denny Riddleberger	.70	.35	.20
643	Russ Gibson	.70	.35	.20
644	Bernie Allen	.80	.40	.25
645	Jim Maloney	.80	.40	.25
646	Chico Salmon	.70	.35	.20
647	Bob Moose	.70	.35	.20
648	Jim Lyttle	.70	.35	.20
649	Pete Richert	.70	.35	.20
650	Sal Bando	1.00	.50	.30
651	Reds Team	2.00	1.00	.60
652	Marcelino Lopez	.70	.35	.20
653	Jim Fairey	.70	.35	.20
654	Horacio Pina	.70	.35	.20
655	Jerry Grote	.80	.40	.25
656	Rudy May	.80	.40	.25
657	Bobby Wine	2.25	1.25	.70

		NR MT	EX	VG
658	Steve Dunning	2.25	1.25	.70
659	Bob Aspromonte	2.25	1.25	.70
660	Paul Blair	2.50	1.25	.70
661	Bill Virdon	2.50	1.25	.70
662	Stan Bahnsen	2.50	1.25	.70
663	Fran Healy	2.25	1.25	.70
664	Bobby Knoop	2.25	1.25	.70
665	Chris Short	2.50	1.25	.70
666	Hector Torres	2.25	1.25	.70
667	Ray Newman	2.25	1.25	.70
668	Rangers Team	3.25	1.75	1.00
669	Willie Crawford	2.25	1.25	.70
670	Ken Holtzman	2.75	1.50	.80
671	Donn Clendenon	2.50	1.25	.70
672	Archie Reynolds	2.25	1.25	.70
673	Dave Marshall	2.25	1.25	.70
674	John Kennedy	2.25	1.25	.70
675	Pat Jarvis	2.25	1.25	.70
676	Danny Cater	2.25	1.25	.70
677	Ivan Murrell	2.25	1.25	.70
678	Steve Luebber	2.25	1.25	.70
679	Astros Rookies (Bob Fenwick, Bob Stinson)	2.25	1.25	.70
680	Dave Johnson	3.50	1.75	1.00
681	Bobby Pfeil	2.25	1.25	.70
682	Mike McCormick	2.50	1.25	.70
683	Steve Hovley	2.25	1.25	.70
684	Hal Breeden	2.25	1.25	.70
685	Joe Horlen	2.25	1.25	.70
686	Steve Garvey	55.00	28.00	16.50
687	Del Unser	2.25	1.25	.70
688	Cardinals Team	3.25	1.75	1.00
689	Eddie Fisher	2.25	1.25	.70
690	Willie Montanez	2.50	1.25	.70
691	Curt Blefary	2.25	1.25	.70
692	Curt Blefary IA	2.25	1.25	.70
693	Alan Gallagher	2.25	1.25	.70
694	Alan Gallagher IA	2.25	1.25	.70
695	Rod Carew	70.00	35.00	21.00
696	Rod Carew IA	30.00	15.00	9.00
697	Jerry Koosman	4.50	2.25	1.25
698	Jerry Koosman IA	2.50	1.25	.70
699	Bobby Murcer	4.00	2.00	1.25
700	Bobby Murcer IA	2.50	1.25	.70
701	Jose Pagan	2.25	1.25	.70
702	Jose Pagan IA	2.25	1.25	.70
703	Doug Griffin	2.25	1.25	.70
704	Doug Griffin IA	2.25	1.25	.70
705	Pat Corrales	2.50	1.25	.70
706	Pat Corrales IA	2.25	1.25	.70
707	Tim Foli	2.25	1.25	.70
708	Tim Foli IA	2.25	1.25	.70
709	Jim Kaat	6.50	3.25	2.00
710	Jim Kaat IA	3.25	1.75	1.00
711	Bobby Bonds	6.00	3.00	1.75
712	Bobby Bonds IA	2.50	1.25	.70
713	Gene Michael	2.50	1.25	.70
714	Gene Michael IA	2.50	1.25	.70
715	Mike Epstein	2.50	1.25	.70
716	Jesus Alou	2.50	1.25	.70
717	Bruce Dal Canton	2.25	1.25	.70
718	Del Rice	2.25	1.25	.70
719	Cesar Geronimo	2.50	1.25	.70
720	Sam McDowell	3.00	1.50	.90
721	Eddie Leon	2.25	1.25	.70
722	Bill Sudakis	2.25	1.25	.70
723	Al Santorini	2.25	1.25	.70
724	A.L. Rookies (John Curtis, Rich Hinton, Mickey Scott)	2.50	1.25	.70
725	Dick McAuliffe	2.50	1.25	.70
726	Dick Selma	2.25	1.25	.70
727	Jose Laboy	2.25	1.25	.70
728	Gail Hopkins	2.25	1.25	.70
729	Bob Veale	2.50	1.25	.70
730	Rick Monday	2.75	1.50	.80
731	Orioles Team	3.25	1.75	1.00
732	George Culver	2.25	1.25	.70
733	Jim Hart	2.50	1.25	.70
734	Bob Burda	2.25	1.25	.70
735	Diego Segui	2.25	1.25	.70
736	Bill Russell	3.00	1.50	.90
737	*Lenny Randle*	2.50	1.25	.70
738	Jim Merritt	2.25	1.25	.70
739	Don Mason	2.25	1.25	.70
740	Rico Carty	3.25	1.75	1.00
741	Major League Rookies (Tom Hutton, *Rick Miller, John Milner*)	2.50	1.25	.70
742	Jim Rooker	2.25	1.25	.70
743	Cesar Gutierrez	2.25	1.25	.70
744	*Jim Slaton*	2.50	1.25	.70
745	Julian Javier	2.25	1.25	.70

		NR MT	EX	VG
746	Lowell Palmer	2.25	1.25	.70
747	Jim Stewart	2.25	1.25	.70
748	Phil Hennigan	2.25	1.25	.70
749	Walter Alston	5.00	2.50	1.50
750	Willie Horton	2.75	1.50	.80
751	Steve Carlton Traded	30.00	15.00	9.00
752	Joe Morgan Traded	25.00	12.50	7.50
753	Denny McLain Traded	6.00	3.00	1.75
754	Frank Robinson Traded	18.00	9.00	5.50
755	Jim Fregosi Traded	2.75	1.50	.80
756	Rick Wise Traded	2.50	1.25	.70
757	Jose Cardenal Traded	2.50	1.25	.70
758	Gil Garrido	2.25	1.25	.70
759	Chris Cannizzaro	2.25	1.25	.70
760	Bill Mazeroski	3.75	2.00	1.25
761	Major League Rookies (*Ron Cey, Ben Oglivie, Bernie Williams*)	12.00	6.00	3.50
762	Wayne Simpson	2.25	1.25	.70
763	Ron Hansen	2.25	1.25	.70
764	Dusty Baker	3.00	1.50	.90
765	Ken McMullen	2.25	1.25	.70
766	Steve Hamilton	2.25	1.25	.70
767	Tom McCraw	2.25	1.25	.70
768	Denny Doyle	2.25	1.25	.70
769	Jack Aker	2.50	1.25	.70
770	Jim Wynn	2.75	1.50	.80
771	Giants Team	3.25	1.75	1.00
772	Ken Tatum	2.25	1.25	.70
773	Ron Brand	2.25	1.25	.70
774	Luis Alvarado	2.25	1.25	.70
775	Jerry Reuss	3.50	1.75	1.00
776	Bill Voss	2.25	1.25	.70
777	Hoyt Wilhelm	15.00	7.50	4.50
778	Twins Rookies (Vic Albury, *Rick Dempsey, Jim Strickland*)	3.25	1.75	1.00
779	Tony Cloninger	2.50	1.25	.70
780	Dick Green	2.25	1.25	.70
781	Jim McAndrew	2.25	1.25	.70
782	Larry Stahl	2.25	1.25	.70
783	Les Cain	2.25	1.25	.70
784	Ken Aspromonte	2.25	1.25	.70
785	Vic Davalillo	2.25	1.25	.70
786	Chuck Brinkman	2.50	1.25	.70
787	Ron Reed	4.50	1.25	.70

1972 Topps Cloth Stickers

Despite the fact they were never actually issued, examples of this test issue can readily be found within the hobby. The set of 33 contains stickers with designs identical to cards found in three contiguous rows of a regular Topps card sheet that year; thus the inclusion of a meaningless checklist card. Sometimes found in complete 33-sticker strips, individual stickers nominally measure 2-1/2" by 3-1/2," though dimensions vary according to the care with which they were cut. Stickers are unnumbered and blank-backed, and do not contain glue.

		NR MT	EX	VG
Complete Set:		200.00	100.00	60.00
Common Player:		3.00	1.50	.90
(1)	Hank Aaron	50.00	25.00	15.00
(2)	Luis Aparicio IA	10.00	5.00	3.00
(3)	Ike Brown	3.00	1.50	.90
(4)	Johnny Callison	5.00	2.50	1.50

		NR MT	EX	VG
(5)	Checklist 264-319	3.00	1.50	.90
(6)	Roberto Clemente IA	25.00	12.50	7.50
(7)	Dave Concepcion	8.00	4.00	2.50
(8)	Ron Cook	3.00	1.50	.90
(9)	Willie Davis	5.00	2.50	1.50
(10)	Al Fitzmorris	3.00	1.50	.90
(11)	Bobby Floyd	3.00	1.50	.90
(12)	Roy Foster	3.00	1.50	.90
(13)	Jim Fregosi Boyhood Photo	4.00	2.00	1.25
(14)	Danny Frisella IA	3.00	1.50	.90
(15)	Woody Fryman	3.50	1.75	1.00
(16)	Terry Harmon	3.00	1.50	.90
(17)	Frank Howard	7.00	3.50	2.00
(18)	Ron Klimkowski	3.00	1.50	.90
(19)	Joe Lahoud	3.00	1.50	.90
(20)	Jim Lefebvre	3.50	1.75	1.00
(21)	Elliott Maddox	3.00	1.50	.90
(22)	Marty Martinez	3.00	1.50	.90
(23)	Willie McCovey	25.00	12.50	7.50
(24)	Hal McRae	6.00	3.00	1.75
(25)	Syd O'Brien	3.00	1.50	.90
(26)	Red Sox Team	4.00	2.00	1.25
(27)	Aurelio Rodriguez	3.50	1.75	1.00
(28)	Al Severinsen	3.00	1.50	.90
(29)	Art Shamsky	3.00	1.50	.90
(30)	Steve Stone	4.00	2.00	1.25
(31)	Stan Swanson	3.00	1.50	.90
(32)	Bob Watson	3.50	1.75	1.00
(33)	Roy White	6.00	3.00	1.75

1972 Topps Posters

Issued as a separate set, rather than as a wax pack insert, the twenty-four 9-7/16" by 18" posters of 1972 feature a borderless full-color picture on the front with the player's name, team and position. Printed on very thin paper, the posters, as happened with earlier issues, were folded for packaging, causing large creases which cannot be removed. Even so, they are good display items for they feature many of stars of the period.

		NR MT	EX	VG
Complete Set:		300.00	150.00	90.00
Common Player:		5.00	2.50	1.50
1	Dave McNally	5.00	2.50	1.50
2	Carl Yastrzemski	30.00	15.00	9.00
3	Bill Melton	5.00	2.50	1.50
4	Ray Fosse	5.00	2.50	1.50
5	Mickey Lolich	6.00	3.00	1.75
6	Amos Otis	5.00	2.50	1.50
7	Tony Oliva	6.00	3.00	1.75
8	Vida Blue	6.00	3.00	1.75
9	Hank Aaron	20.00	10.00	6.00
10	Fergie Jenkins	8.00	4.00	2.50
11	Pete Rose	50.00	25.00	15.00
12	Willie Davis	6.00	3.00	1.75
13	Tom Seaver	20.00	10.00	6.00
14	Rick Wise	5.00	2.50	1.50
15	Willie Stargell	12.00	6.00	3.50
16	Joe Torre	7.00	3.50	2.00
17	Willie Mays	20.00	10.00	6.00
18	Andy Messersmith	5.00	2.50	1.50
19	Wilbur Wood	5.00	2.50	1.50
20	Harmon Killebrew	15.00	7.50	4.50
21	Billy Williams	12.00	6.00	3.50
22	Bud Harrelson	5.00	2.50	1.50

		NR MT	EX	VG
23	Roberto Clemente	20.00	10.00	6.00
24	Willie McCovey	15.00	7.50	4.50

1973 Topps

 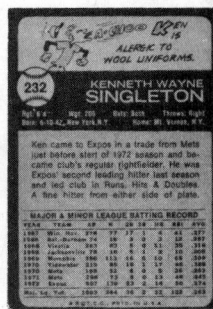

Topps cut back to 660 cards in 1973. The set is interesting for it marks the last time cards were issued by series, a procedure which had produced many a scarce high number card over the years. These 2-1/2" by 3-1/2" cards have a color photo, accented by a silhouette of a player on the front, indicative of his position. Card backs are vertical for the first time since 1968, with the usual statistical and biographical information. Specialty cards begin with card number 1, which depicted Ruth, Mays and Aaron as the all-time home run leaders. It was followed by statistical leaders, although there also were additional all-time leader cards. Also present are playoff and World Series highlights. From the age-and-youth department, the 1973 Topps set has coaches and managers as well as more "Boyhood Photos."

		NR MT	EX	VG
Complete Set:		1000.00	450.00	275.00
Common Player: 1-396		.25	.13	.08
Common Player: 397-528		.40	.20	.12
Common Player: 529-660		1.25	.60	.40
1	All Time Home Run Leaders (Hank Aaron, Willie Mays, Babe Ruth)	20.00	10.00	6.00
2	Rich Hebner	.30	.15	.09
3	Jim Lonborg	.40	.20	.12
4	John Milner	.25	.13	.08
5	Ed Brinkman	.30	.15	.09
6	Mac Scarce	.25	.13	.08
7	Rangers Team	.90	.45	.25
8	Tom Hall	.25	.13	.08
9	Johnny Oates	.25	.13	.08
10	Don Sutton	2.00	1.00	.60
11	Chris Chambliss	.70	.35	.20
12a	Padres Mgr./Coaches (Dave Garcia, Johnny Podres, Bob Skinner, Whitey Wietelmann, Don Zimmer) (Coaches background brown)	.50	.25	.15
12b	Padres Mgr./Coaches (Dave Garcia, Johnny Podres, Bob Skinner, Whitey Wietelmann, Don Zimmer) (Coaches background orange)	.40	.20	.12
13	George Hendrick	.70	.35	.20
14	Sonny Siebert	.25	.13	.08
15	Ralph Garr	.30	.15	.09
16	Steve Braun	.25	.13	.08
17	Fred Gladding	.25	.13	.08
18	Leroy Stanton	.25	.13	.08
19	Tim Foli	.25	.13	.08
20a	Stan Bahnsen (small gap in left border)	.50	.25	.15
20b	Stan Bahnsen (no gap)	.25	.13	.08
21	Randy Hundley	.25	.13	.08
22	Ted Abernathy	.25	.13	.08
23	Dave Kingman	1.25	.60	.40
24	Al Santorini	.25	.13	.08
25	Roy White	.40	.20	.12
26	Pirates Team	.90	.45	.25
27	Bill Gogolewski	.25	.13	.08
28	Hal McRae	.50	.25	.15

		NR MT	EX	VG
9	Tony Taylor	.25	.13	.08
0	Tug McGraw	.60	.30	.20
1	*Buddy Bell*	4.00	2.00	1.25
2	Fred Norman	.25	.13	.08
3	Jim Breazeale	.25	.13	.08
4	Pat Dobson	.30	.15	.09
5	Willie Davis	.50	.25	.15
6	Steve Barber	.25	.13	.08
7	Bill Robinson	.25	.13	.08
8	Mike Epstein	.30	.15	.09
9	Dave Roberts	.25	.13	.08
0	Reggie Smith	.50	.25	.15
1	Tom Walker	.25	.13	.08
2	Mike Andrews	.25	.13	.08
3	Randy Moffitt	.30	.15	.09
4	Rick Monday	.40	.20	.12
5	Ellie Rodriguez (photo actually Paul Ratliff)	.25	.13	.08
6	Lindy McDaniel	.30	.15	.09
7	Luis Melendez	.25	.13	.08
8	Paul Splittorff	.30	.15	.09
9a	Twins Mgr./Coaches (Vern Morgan, Frank Quilici, Bob Rodgers, Ralph Rowe, Al Worthington) (Coaches background brown)	.50	.25	.15
9b	Twins Mgr./Coaches (Vern Morgan, Frank Quilici, Bob Rodgers, Ralph Rowe, Al Worthington) (Coaches background orange)	.30	.15	.09
0	Roberto Clemente	25.00	12.50	7.50
1	Chuck Seelbach	.25	.13	.08
2	Denis Menke	.25	.13	.08
3	Steve Dunning	.25	.13	.08
4	Checklist 1-132	2.00	1.00	.60
5	Jon Matlack	.40	.20	.12
6	Merv Rettenmund	.30	.15	.09
7	Derrel Thomas	.25	.13	.08
8	Mike Paul	.25	.13	.08
9	*Steve Yeager*	.60	.30	.20
0	Ken Holtzman	.40	.20	.12
1	Batting Leaders (Rod Carew, Billy Williams)	1.75	.90	.50
2	Home Run Leaders (Dick Allen, Johnny Bench)	1.50	.70	.45
3	Runs Batted In Leaders (Dick Allen, Johnny Bench)	1.50	.70	.45
4	Stolen Base Leaders (Lou Brock, Bert Campaneris)	1.25	.60	.40
5	Earned Run Average Leaders (Steve Carlton, Luis Tiant)	1.25	.60	.40
6	Victory Leaders (Steve Carlton, Gaylord Perry, Wilbur Wood)	1.25	.60	.40
7	Strikeout Leaders (Steve Carlton, Nolan Ryan)	2.50	1.25	.70
8	Leading Firemen (Clay Carroll, Sparky Lyle)	.80	.40	.25
9	Phil Gagliano	.25	.13	.08
0	Milt Pappas	.40	.20	.12
1	Johnny Briggs	.25	.13	.08
2	Ron Reed	.30	.15	.09
3	Ed Herrmann	.25	.13	.08
4	Billy Champion	.25	.13	.08
5	Vada Pinson	.80	.40	.25
6	Doug Rader	.25	.13	.08
7	Mike Torrez	.30	.15	.09
8	Richie Scheinblum	.25	.13	.08
9	Jim Willoughby	.25	.13	.08
0	Tony Oliva	1.25	.60	.40
1a	Cubs Mgr./Coaches (Hank Aguirre, Ernie Banks, Larry Jansen, Whitey Lockman, Pete Reiser) (trees in Coaches background)	.70	.35	.20
1b	Cubs Mgr./Coaches (Hank Aguirre, Ernie Banks, Larry Jansen, Whitey Lockman, Pete Reiser) (orange, solid background)	.50	.25	.15
2	Fritz Peterson	.30	.15	.09
3	Leron Lee	.25	.13	.08
4	Rollie Fingers	3.00	1.50	.90
5	Ted Simmons	1.25	.60	.40
6	Tom McCraw	.25	.13	.08
7	Ken Boswell	.25	.13	.08
8	Mickey Stanley	.30	.15	.09
9	Jack Billingham	.25	.13	.08
0	Brooks Robinson	5.00	2.50	1.50
1	Dodgers Team	1.00	.50	.30
2	Jerry Bell	.25	.13	.08
3	Jesus Alou	.30	.15	.09
4	Dick Billings	.25	.13	.08
5	Steve Blass	.30	.15	.09
6	Doug Griffin	.25	.13	.08
7	Willie Montanez	.30	.15	.09
8	Dick Woodson	.25	.13	.08
9	Carl Taylor	.25	.13	.08

		NR MT	EX	VG
100	Hank Aaron	20.00	10.00	6.00
101	Ken Henderson	.25	.13	.08
102	Rudy May	.30	.15	.09
103	Celerino Sanchez	.30	.15	.09
104	Reggie Cleveland	.25	.13	.08
105	Carlos May	.30	.15	.09
106	Terry Humphrey	.25	.13	.08
107	Phil Hennigan	.25	.13	.08
108	Bill Russell	.40	.20	.12
109	Doyle Alexander	1.00	.50	.30
110	Bob Watson	.30	.15	.09
111	Dave Nelson	.25	.13	.08
112	Gary Ross	.25	.13	.08
113	Jerry Grote	.30	.15	.09
114	Lynn McGlothen	.25	.13	.08
115	Ron Santo	.80	.40	.25
116a	Yankees Mgr./Coaches (Jim Hegan, Ralph Houk, Elston Howard, Dick Howser, Jim Turner) (Coaches background brown)	1.00	.50	.30
116b	Yankees Mgr./Coaches (Jim Hegan, Ralph Houk, Elston Howard, Dick Howser, Jim Turner) (Coaches background orange)	.70	.35	.20
117	Ramon Hernandez	.25	.13	.08
118	John Mayberry	.40	.20	.12
119	Larry Bowa	.80	.40	.25
120	Joe Coleman	.30	.15	.09
121	Dave Rader	.25	.13	.08
122	Jim Strickland	.25	.13	.08
123	Sandy Alomar	.25	.13	.08
124	Jim Hardin	.25	.13	.08
125	Ron Fairly	.40	.20	.12
126	Jim Brewer	.25	.13	.08
127	Brewers Team	.90	.45	.25
128	Ted Sizemore	.25	.13	.08
129	Terry Forster	.40	.20	.12
130	Pete Rose	20.00	10.00	6.00
131a	Red Sox Mgr./Coaches (Doug Camilli, Eddie Kasko, Don Lenhardt, Eddie Popowski, Lee Stange) (Coaches background brown)	.50	.25	.15
131b	Red Sox Mgr./Coaches (Doug Camilli, Eddie Kasko, Don Lenhardt, Eddie Popowski, Lee Stange) (Coaches background orange)	.30	.15	.09
132	Matty Alou	.60	.30	.20
133	Dave Roberts	.25	.13	.08
134	Milt Wilcox	.30	.15	.09
135	Lee May	.50	.25	.15
136a	Orioles Mgr./Coaches (George Bamberger, Jim Frey, Billy Hunter, George Staller, Earl Weaver) (Coaches background brown)	1.00	.50	.30
136b	Orioles Mgr./Coaches (George Bamberger, Jim Frey, Billy Hunter, George Staller, Earl Weaver) (Coaches background orange)	.70	.35	.20
137	Jim Beauchamp	.25	.13	.08
138	Horacio Pina	.25	.13	.08
139	Carmen Fanzone	.25	.13	.08
140	Lou Piniella	.80	.40	.25
141	Bruce Kison	.30	.15	.09
142	Thurman Munson	8.00	4.00	2.50
143	John Curtis	.25	.13	.08
144	Marty Perez	.25	.13	.08
145	Bobby Bonds	.70	.35	.20
146	Woodie Fryman	.30	.15	.09
147	Mike Anderson	.25	.13	.08
148	*Dave Goltz*	.60	.30	.20
149	Ron Hunt	.30	.15	.09
150	Wilbur Wood	.40	.20	.12
151	Wes Parker	.30	.15	.09
152	Dave May	.25	.13	.08
153	Al Hrabosky	.40	.20	.12
154	Jeff Torborg	.30	.15	.09
155	Sal Bando	.70	.35	.20
156	Cesar Geronimo	.30	.15	.09
157	Denny Riddleberger	.25	.13	.08
158	Astros Team	.90	.45	.25
159	Clarence Gaston	.25	.13	.08
160	Jim Palmer	8.00	4.00	2.50
161	Ted Martinez	.25	.13	.08
162	Pete Broberg	.25	.13	.08
163	Vic Davalillo	.30	.15	.09
164	Monty Montgomery	.25	.13	.08
165	Luis Aparicio	2.75	1.50	.80
166	Terry Harmon	.25	.13	.08
167	Steve Stone	.50	.25	.15
168	Jim Northrup	.30	.15	.09
169	Ron Schueler	.25	.13	.08

		NR MT	EX	VG
170	Harmon Killebrew	3.50	1.75	1.00
171	Bernie Carbo	.25	.13	.08
172	Steve Kline	.30	.15	.09
173	Hal Breeden	.25	.13	.08
174	*Rich Gossage*	9.00	4.50	2.75
175	Frank Robinson	5.00	2.50	1.50
176	Chuck Taylor	.25	.13	.08
177	Bill Plummer	.25	.13	.08
178	Don Rose	.25	.13	.08
179a	A's Mgr./Coaches (Jerry Adair, Vern Hoscheit, Irv Noren, Wes Stock, Dick Williams) (Coaches background brown)	.80	.40	.25
179b	A's Mgr./Coaches (Jerry Adair, Vern Hoscheit, Irv Noren, Wes Stock, Dick Williams) (Coaches background orange)	.50	.25	.15
180	Fergie Jenkins	1.50	.70	.45
181	Jack Brohamer	.25	.13	.08
182	*Mike Caldwell*	.50	.25	.15
183	Don Buford	.30	.15	.09
184	Jerry Koosman	.50	.25	.15
185	Jim Wynn	.40	.20	.12
186	Bill Fahey	.25	.13	.08
187	Luke Walker	.25	.13	.08
188	Cookie Rojas	.25	.13	.08
189	Greg Luzinski	.70	.35	.20
190	Bob Gibson	3.50	1.75	1.00
191	Tigers Team	1.25	.60	.40
192	Pat Jarvis	.25	.13	.08
193	Carlton Fisk	30.00	15.00	9.00
194	*Jorge Orta*	.50	.25	.15
195	Clay Carroll	.30	.15	.09
196	Ken McMullen	.25	.13	.08
197	Ed Goodson	.25	.13	.08
198	Horace Clarke	.30	.15	.09
199	Bert Blyleven	1.50	.70	.45
200	Billy Williams	2.75	1.50	.80
201	A.L. Playoffs (Hendrick Scores Winning Run.)	1.00	.50	.30
202	N.L. Playoffs (Foster's Run Decides It.)	1.00	.50	.30
203	World Series Game 1 (Tenace The Menace.)	1.00	.50	.30
204	World Series Game 2 (A's Make It Two Straight.)	1.00	.50	.30
205	World Series Game 3 (Reds Win Squeeker.)	1.00	.50	.30
206	World Series Game 4 (Tenace Singles In Ninth.)	1.00	.50	.30
207	World Series Game 5 (Odom Out At Plate.)	1.00	.50	.30
208	World Series Game 6 (Reds' Slugging Ties Series.)	1.00	.50	.30
209	World Series Game 7 (Campy Starts Winning Rally.)	1.00	.50	.30
210	World Series Summary (World Champions.)	1.00	.50	.30
211	Balor Moore	.25	.13	.08
212	Joe Lahoud	.25	.13	.08
213	Steve Garvey	15.00	7.50	4.50
214	Dave Hamilton	.25	.13	.08
215	Dusty Baker	.50	.25	.15
216	Toby Harrah	.40	.20	.12
217	Don Wilson	.25	.13	.08
218	Aurelio Rodriguez	.30	.15	.09
219	Cardinals Team	.90	.45	.25
220	Nolan Ryan	50.00	25.00	15.00
221	Fred Kendall	.25	.13	.08
222	Rob Gardner	.25	.13	.08
223	Bud Harrelson	.30	.15	.09
224	Bill Lee	.30	.15	.09
225	Al Oliver	1.25	.60	.40
226	Ray Fosse	.25	.13	.08
227	Wayne Twitchell	.25	.13	.08
228	Bobby Darwin	.25	.13	.08
229	Roric Harrison	.25	.13	.08
230	Joe Morgan	5.00	2.50	1.50
231	Bill Parsons	.25	.13	.08
232	Ken Singleton	.40	.20	.12
233	Ed Kirkpatrick	.25	.13	.08
234	*Bill North*	.50	.25	.15
235	Jim Hunter	3.00	1.50	.90
236	Tito Fuentes	.25	.13	.08
237a	Braves Mgr./Coaches (Lew Burdette, Jim Busby, Roy Hartsfield, Eddie Mathews, Ken Silvestri) (Coaches background brown)	1.25	.60	.40
237b	Braves Mgr./Coaches (Lew Burdette, Jim Busby, Roy Hartsfield, Eddie Mathews, Ken Silvestri) (Coaches background orange)	1.00	.50	.30
238	Tony Muser	.25	.13	.08
239	Pete Richert	.25	.13	.08
240	Bobby Murcer	.60	.30	.20
241	Dwain Anderson	.25	.13	.08
242	George Culver	.25	.13	.08
243	Angels Team	.90	.45	.25
244	Ed Acosta	.25	.13	.08
245	Carl Yastrzemski	15.00	7.50	4.50
246	Ken Sanders	.25	.13	.08
247	Del Unser	.25	.13	.08
248	Jerry Johnson	.25	.13	.08
249	Larry Biittner	.25	.13	.08
250	Manny Sanguillen	.30	.15	.09
251	Roger Nelson	.25	.13	.08
252a	Giants Mgr./Coaches (Joe Amalfitano, Charlie Fox, Andy Gilbert, Don McMahon, John McNamara) (Coaches background brown)	.50	.25	.15
252b	Giants Mgr./Coaches (Joe Amalfitano, Charlie Fox, Andy Gilbert, Don McMahon, John McNamara) (Coaches background orange)	.30	.15	.09
253	Mark Belanger	.30	.15	.09
254	Bill Stoneman	.25	.13	.08
255	Reggie Jackson	25.00	12.50	7.50
256	Chris Zachary	.25	.13	.08
257a	Mets Mgr./Coaches (Yogi Berra, Roy McMillan, Joe Pignatano, Rube Walker, Eddie Yost) (Coaches background brown)	1.50	.70	.45
257b	Mets Mgr./Coaches (Yogi Berra, Roy McMillan, Joe Pignatano, Rube Walker, Eddie Yost) (Coaches background orange)	1.25	.60	.40
258	Tommy John	1.75	.90	.50
259	Jim Holt	.25	.13	.08
260	Gary Nolan	.25	.13	.08
261	Pat Kelly	.25	.13	.08
262	Jack Aker	.25	.13	.08
263	George Scott	.30	.15	.09
264	Checklist 133-264	2.00	1.00	.60
265	Gene Michael	.40	.20	.12
266	Mike Lum	.25	.13	.08
267	Lloyd Allen	.25	.13	.08
268	Jerry Morales	.25	.13	.08
269	Tim McCarver	.70	.35	.20
270	Luis Tiant	.80	.40	.25
271	Tom Hutton	.25	.13	.08
272	Ed Farmer	.25	.13	.08
273	Chris Speier	.30	.15	.09
274	Darold Knowles	.25	.13	.08
275	Tony Perez	1.25	.60	.40
276	Joe Lovitto	.25	.13	.08
277	Bob Miller	.25	.13	.08
278	Orioles Team	.90	.45	.25
279	Mike Strahler	.25	.13	.08
280	Al Kaline	5.00	2.50	1.50
281	Mike Jorgensen	.25	.13	.08
282	Steve Hovley	.25	.13	.08
283	Ray Sadecki	.25	.13	.08
284	Glenn Borgmann	.25	.13	.08
285	Don Kessinger	.30	.15	.09
286	Frank Linzy	.25	.13	.08
287	Eddie Leon	.25	.13	.08
288	Gary Gentry	.25	.13	.08
289	Bob Oliver	.25	.13	.08
290	Cesar Cedeno	.40	.20	.12
291	Rogelio Moret	.25	.13	.08
292	Jose Cruz	.80	.40	.25
293	Bernie Allen	.30	.15	.09
294	Steve Arlin	.25	.13	.08
295	Bert Campaneris	.60	.30	.20
296	Reds Mgr./Coaches (Sparky Anderson, Alex Grammas, Ted Kluszewski, George Scherger, Larry Shepard)	.70	.35	.20
297	Walt Williams	.25	.13	.08
298	Ron Bryant	.25	.13	.08
299	Ted Ford	.25	.13	.08
300	Steve Carlton	18.00	9.00	5.50
301	Billy Grabarkewitz	.25	.13	.08
302	Terry Crowley	.25	.13	.08
303	Nelson Briles	.25	.13	.08
304	Duke Sims	.25	.13	.08
305	Willie Mays	25.00	12.50	7.50
306	Tom Burgmeier	.25	.13	.08
307	Boots Day	.25	.13	.08
308	Skip Lockwood	.25	.13	.08
309	Paul Popovich	.25	.13	.08
310	Dick Allen	.80	.40	.25
311	Joe Decker	.25	.13	.08
312	Oscar Brown	.25	.13	.08
313	Jim Ray	.25	.13	.08
314	Ron Swoboda	.30	.15	.09

	NR MT	EX	VG
315 John Odom	.30	.15	.09
316 Padres Team	.90	.45	.25
317 Danny Cater	.25	.13	.08
318 Jim McGlothlin	.25	.13	.08
319 Jim Spencer	.25	.13	.08
320 Lou Brock	3.50	1.75	1.00
321 Rich Hinton	.25	.13	.08
322 *Garry Maddox*	.80	.40	.25
323 Tigers Mgr./Coaches (Art Fowler, Billy Martin, Joe Schultz, Charlie Silvera, Dick Tracewski)	1.00	.50	.30
324 Al Downing	.30	.15	.09
325 Boog Powell	1.00	.50	.30
326 Darrell Brandon	.25	.13	.08
327 John Lowenstein	.25	.13	.08
328 Bill Bonham	.25	.13	.08
329 Ed Kranepool	.30	.15	.09
330 Rod Carew	15.00	7.50	4.50
331 Carl Morton	.25	.13	.08
332 *John Felske*	.30	.15	.09
333 Gene Clines	.25	.13	.08
334 Freddie Patek	.25	.13	.08
335 Bob Tolan	.30	.15	.09
336 Tom Bradley	.25	.13	.08
337 Dave Duncan	.25	.13	.08
338 Checklist 265-396	2.00	1.00	.60
339 Dick Tidrow	.30	.15	.09
340 Nate Colbert	.30	.15	.09
341 Boyhood Photo (Jim Palmer)	1.25	.60	.40
342 Boyhood Photo (Sam McDowell)	.40	.20	.12
343 Boyhood Photo (Bobby Murcer)	.40	.20	.12
344 Boyhood Photo (Jim Hunter)	1.25	.60	.40
345 Boyhood Photo (Chris Speier)	.30	.15	.09
346 Boyhood Photo (Gaylord Perry)	1.25	.60	.40
347 Royals Team	.90	.45	.25
348 Rennie Stennett	.30	.15	.09
349 Dick McAuliffe	.30	.15	.09
350 Tom Seaver	25.00	12.50	7.50
351 Jimmy Stewart	.25	.13	.08
352 *Don Stanhouse*	.40	.20	.12
353 Steve Brye	.25	.13	.08
354 Billy Parker	.25	.13	.08
355 Mike Marshall	.40	.20	.12
356 White Sox Mgr./Coaches (Joe Lonnett, Jim Mahoney, Al Monchak, Johnny Sain, Chuck Tanner)	.50	.25	.15
357 Ross Grimsley	.30	.15	.09
358 Jim Nettles	.25	.13	.08
359 Cecil Upshaw	.25	.13	.08
360 Joe Rudi (photo actually Gene Tenace)	.40	.20	.12
361 Fran Healy	.25	.13	.08
362 Eddie Watt	.25	.13	.08
363 Jackie Hernandez	.25	.13	.08
364 Rick Wise	.30	.15	.09
365 Rico Petrocelli	.40	.20	.12
366 Brock Davis	.25	.13	.08
367 Burt Hooton	.40	.20	.12
368 Bill Buckner	.70	.35	.20
369 Lerrin LaGrow	.25	.13	.08
370 Willie Stargell	3.50	1.75	1.00
371 Mike Kekich	.30	.15	.09
372 Oscar Gamble	.30	.15	.09
373 Clyde Wright	.25	.13	.08
374 Darrell Evans	.70	.35	.20
375 Larry Dierker	.30	.15	.09
376 Frank Duffy	.25	.13	.08
377 Expos Mgr./Coaches (Dave Bristol, Larry Doby, Gene Mauch, Cal McLish, Jerry Zimmerman)	.50	.25	.15
378 Lenny Randle	.25	.13	.08
379 Cy Acosta	.25	.13	.08
380 Johnny Bench	20.00	10.00	6.00
381 Vicente Romo	.25	.13	.08
382 Mike Hegan	.25	.13	.08
383 Diego Segui	.25	.13	.08
384 Don Baylor	1.00	.50	.30
385 Jim Perry	.50	.25	.15
386 Don Money	.30	.15	.09
387 Jim Barr	.25	.13	.08
388 Ben Oglivie	.50	.25	.15
389 Mets Team	1.75	.90	.50
390 Mickey Lolich	.70	.35	.20
391 *Lee Lacy*	.80	.40	.25
392 Dick Drago	.25	.13	.08
393 Jose Cardenal	.30	.15	.09
394 Sparky Lyle	.70	.35	.20
395 Roger Metzger	.25	.13	.08
396 Grant Jackson	.25	.13	.08
397 Dave Cash	.40	.20	.12
398 Rich Hand	.40	.20	.12

	NR MT	EX	VG
399 George Foster	1.50	.70	.45
400 Gaylord Perry	3.00	1.50	.90
401 Clyde Mashore	.40	.20	.12
402 Jack Hiatt	.40	.20	.12
403 Sonny Jackson	.40	.20	.12
404 Chuck Brinkman	.40	.20	.12
405 Cesar Tovar	.40	.20	.12
406 Paul Lindblad	.40	.20	.12
407 Felix Millan	.40	.20	.12
408 Jim Colborn	.40	.20	.12
409 Ivan Murrell	.40	.20	.12
410 Willie McCovey	5.00	2.50	1.50
411 Ray Corbin	.40	.20	.12
412 Manny Mota	.60	.30	.20
413 Tom Timmermann	.40	.20	.12
414 Ken Rudolph	.40	.20	.12
415 Marty Pattin	.40	.20	.12
416 Paul Schaal	.40	.20	.12
417 Scipio Spinks	.40	.20	.12
418 Bobby Grich	.60	.30	.20
419 Casey Cox	.50	.25	.15
420 Tommie Agee	.50	.25	.15
421 Angels Mgr./Coaches (Tom Morgan, Salty Parker, Jimmie Reese, John Roseboro, Bobby Winkles)	.40	.20	.12
422 Bob Robertson	.40	.20	.12
423 Johnny Jeter	.40	.20	.12
424 Denny Doyle	.40	.20	.12
425 Alex Johnson	.40	.20	.12
426 Dave LaRoche	.40	.20	.12
427 Rick Auerbach	.40	.20	.12
428 Wayne Simpson	.40	.20	.12
429 Jim Fairey	.40	.20	.12
430 Vida Blue	.80	.40	.25
431 Gerry Moses	.50	.25	.15
432 Dan Frisella	.40	.20	.12
433 Willie Horton	.60	.30	.20
434 Giants Team	1.00	.50	.30
435 Rico Carty	.60	.30	.20
436 Jim McAndrew	.40	.20	.12
437 John Kennedy	.40	.20	.12
438 Enzo Hernandez	.40	.20	.12
439 Eddie Fisher	.40	.20	.12
440 Glenn Beckert	.50	.25	.15
441 Gail Hopkins	.40	.20	.12
442 Dick Dietz	.40	.20	.12
443 Danny Thompson	.50	.25	.15
444 Ken Brett	.50	.25	.15
445 Ken Berry	.40	.20	.12
446 Jerry Reuss	.60	.30	.20
447 Joe Hague	.40	.20	.12
448 John Hiller	.50	.25	.15
449a Indians Mgr./Coaches (Ken Aspromonte, Rocky Colavito, Joe Lutz, Warren Spahn) (Spahn's ear pointed)	.50	.25	.15
449b Indians Mgr./Coaches (Ken Aspromonte, Rocky Colavito, Joe Lutz, Warren Spahn) (Spahn's ear round)	.80	.40	.25
450 Joe Torre	1.00	.50	.30
451 John Vukovich	.40	.20	.12
452 Paul Casanova	.40	.20	.12
453 Checklist 397-528	2.25	1.25	.70
454 Tom Haller	.50	.25	.15
455 Bill Melton	.50	.25	.15
456 Dick Green	.40	.20	.12
457 John Strohmayer	.40	.20	.12
458 Jim Mason	.40	.20	.12
459 Jimmy Howarth	.40	.20	.12
460 Bill Freehan	.60	.30	.20
461 Mike Corkins	.40	.20	.12
462 Ron Blomberg	.50	.25	.15
463 Ken Tatum	.40	.20	.12
464 Cubs Team	1.00	.50	.30
465 Dave Giusti	.40	.20	.12
466 Jose Arcia	.40	.20	.12
467 Mike Ryan	.40	.20	.12
468 Tom Griffin	.40	.20	.12
469 Dan Monzon	.40	.20	.12
470 Mike Cuellar	.60	.30	.20
471 Hit Leader (Ty Cobb)	3.00	1.50	.90
472 Grand Slam Leader (Lou Gehrig)	3.00	1.50	.90
473 Total Base Leader (Hank Aaron)	3.00	1.50	.90
474 R.B.I. Leader (Babe Ruth)	5.00	2.50	1.50
475 Batting Leader (Ty Cobb)	3.00	1.50	.90
476 Shutout Leader (Walter Johnson)	1.25	.60	.40
477 Victory Leader (Cy Young)	1.25	.60	.40
478 Strikeout Leader (Walter Johnson)	1.25	.60	.40
479 Hal Lanier	.60	.30	.20
480 Juan Marichal	3.50	1.75	1.00
481 White Sox Team	1.25	.60	.40

#	Player	NR MT	EX	VG
482	*Rick Reuschel*	6.00	3.00	1.75
483	Dal Maxvill	.50	.25	.15
484	Ernie McAnally	.40	.20	.12
485	Norm Cash	.80	.40	.25
486a	Phillies Mgr./Coaches (Carroll Berringer, Billy DeMars, Danny Ozark, Ray Rippelmeyer, Bobby Wine) (Coaches background brown red)	.70	.35	.20
486b	Phillies Mgr./Coaches (Carroll Beringer, Billy DeMars, Danny Ozark, Ray Rippelmeyer, Bobby Wine) (Coaches background orange)	.50	.25	.15
487	Bruce Dal Canton	.40	.20	.12
488	Dave Campbell	.40	.20	.12
489	Jeff Burroughs	.60	.30	.20
490	Claude Osteen	.60	.30	.20
491	Bob Montgomery	.40	.20	.12
492	Pedro Borbon	.40	.20	.12
493	Duffy Dyer	.40	.20	.12
494	Rich Morales	.40	.20	.12
495	Tommy Helms	.40	.20	.12
496	Ray Lamb	.40	.20	.12
497	Cardinals Mgr./Coaches (Vern Benson, George Kissell, Red Schoendienst, Barney Schultz)	.90	.45	.25
498	Graig Nettles	2.50	1.25	.70
499	Bob Moose	.40	.20	.12
500	A's Team	1.75	.90	.50
501	Larry Gura	.50	.25	.15
502	Bobby Valentine	.60	.30	.20
503	Phil Niekro	3.00	1.50	.90
504	Earl Williams	.40	.20	.12
505	Bob Bailey	.40	.20	.12
506	Bart Johnson	.40	.20	.12
507	Darrel Chaney	.40	.20	.12
508	Gates Brown	.40	.20	.12
509	Jim Nash	.40	.20	.12
510	Amos Otis	.60	.30	.20
511	Sam McDowell	.60	.30	.20
512	Dalton Jones	.40	.20	.12
513	Dave Marshall	.40	.20	.12
514	Jerry Kenney	.40	.20	.12
515	Andy Messersmith	.50	.25	.15
516	Danny Walton	.40	.20	.12
517a	Pirates Mgr./Coaches (Don Leppert, Bill Mazeroski, Dave Ricketts, Bill Virdon, Mel Wright) (Coaches background brown)	1.00	.50	.30
517b	Pirates Mgr./Coaches (Don Leppert, Bill Mazeroski, Dave Ricketts, Bill Virdon, Mel Wright) (Coaches background orange)	.50	.25	.15
518	Bob Veale	.50	.25	.15
519	John Edwards	.40	.20	.12
520	Mel Stottlemyre	.60	.30	.20
521	Braves Team	1.00	.50	.30
522	Leo Cardenas	.40	.20	.12
523	Wayne Granger	.40	.20	.12
524	Gene Tenace	.40	.20	.12
525	Jim Fregosi	.70	.35	.20
526	Ollie Brown	.40	.20	.12
527	Dan McGinn	.40	.20	.12
528	Paul Blair	.50	.25	.15
529	Milt May	1.25	.60	.40
530	Jim Kaat	3.25	1.75	1.00
531	Ron Woods	1.25	.60	.40
532	Steve Mingori	1.25	.60	.40
533	Larry Stahl	1.25	.60	.40
534	Dave Lemonds	1.25	.60	.40
535	John Callison	1.50	.70	.45
536	Phillies Team	2.50	1.25	.70
537	Bill Slayback	1.25	.60	.40
538	Jim Hart	1.50	.70	.45
539	Tom Murphy	1.25	.60	.40
540	Cleon Jones	1.50	.70	.45
541	Bob Bolin	1.25	.60	.40
542	Pat Corrales	1.50	.70	.45
543	Alan Foster	1.25	.60	.40
544	Von Joshua	1.25	.60	.40
545	Orlando Cepeda	3.25	1.75	1.00
546	Jim York	1.25	.60	.40
547	Bobby Heise	1.25	.60	.40
548	Don Durham	1.25	.60	.40
549	Rangers Mgr./Coaches (Chuck Estrada, Whitey Herzog, Chuck Hiller, Jackie Moore)	2.00	1.00	.60
550	Dave Johnson	2.75	1.50	.80
551	Mike Kilkenny	1.25	.60	.40
552	J.C. Martin	1.25	.60	.40
553	Mickey Scott	1.25	.60	.40
554	Dave Concepcion	2.50	1.25	.70
555	Bill Hands	1.25	.60	.40
556	Yankees Team	4.00	2.00	1.25
557	Bernie Williams	1.25	.60	.40
558	Jerry May	1.25	.60	.40
559	Barry Lersch	1.25	.60	.40
560	Frank Howard	2.25	1.25	.70
561	Jim Geddes	1.25	.60	.40
562	Wayne Garrett	1.25	.60	.40
563	Larry Haney	1.25	.60	.40
564	Mike Thompson	1.25	.60	.40
565	Jim Hickman	1.50	.70	.45
566	Lew Krausse	1.25	.60	.40
567	Bob Fenwick	1.25	.60	.40
568	Ray Newman	1.25	.60	.40
569	Dodgers Mgr./Coaches (Red Adams, Walt Alston, Monty Basgall, Jim Gillam, Tom Lasorda)	3.00	1.50	.90
570	Bill Singer	1.50	.70	.45
571	Rusty Torres	1.25	.60	.40
572	Gary Sutherland	1.25	.60	.40
573	Fred Beene	1.50	.70	.45
574	Bob Didier	1.25	.60	.40
575	Dock Ellis	1.50	.70	.45
576	Expos Team	2.50	1.25	.70
577	Eric Soderholm	1.50	.70	.45
578	Ken Wright	1.25	.60	.40
579	Tom Grieve	1.25	.60	.40
580	Joe Pepitone	2.00	1.00	.60
581	Steve Kealey	1.25	.60	.40
582	Darrell Porter	1.75	.90	.50
583	Bill Greif	1.25	.60	.40
584	Chris Arnold	1.25	.60	.40
585	Joe Niekro	2.00	1.00	.60
586	Bill Sudakis	1.50	.70	.45
587	Rich McKinney	1.25	.60	.40
588	Checklist 529-660	10.00	5.00	3.00
589	Ken Forsch	1.50	.70	.45
590	Deron Johnson	1.25	.60	.40
591	Mike Hedlund	1.25	.60	.40
592	John Boccabella	1.25	.60	.40
593	Royals Mgr./Coaches (Galen Cisco, Harry Dunlop, Charlie Lau, Jack McKeon)	1.50	.70	.45
594	Vic Harris	1.25	.60	.40
595	Don Gullett	1.50	.70	.45
596	Red Sox Team	2.75	1.50	.80
597	Mickey Rivers	1.75	.90	.50
598	Phil Roof	1.25	.60	.40
599	Ed Crosby	1.25	.60	.40
600	Dave McNally	1.75	.90	.50
601	Rookie Catchers (George Pena, Sergio Robles, Rick Stelmaszek)	1.25	.60	.40
602	Rookie Pitchers (Mel Behney, Ralph Garcia, *Doug Rau*)	1.50	.70	.45
603	Rookie Third Basemen (Terry Hughes, Bill McNulty, *Ken Reitz*)	1.50	.70	.45
604	Rookie Pitchers (Jesse Jefferson, Dennis O'Toole, Bob Strampe)	1.25	.60	.40
605	Rookie First Basemen (Pat Bourque, *Enos Cabell*, Gonzalo Marquez)	1.75	.90	.50
606	Rookie Outfielders (*Gary Matthews*, Tom Paciorek, Jorge Roque)	2.25	1.25	.70
607	Rookie Shortstops (Ray Busse, Pepe Frias, Mario Guerrero)	1.25	.60	.40
608	Rookie Pitchers (*Steve Busby*, Dick Colpaert, *George Medich*)	1.50	.70	.45
609	Rookie Second Basemen (Larvell Blanks, Pedro Garcia, *Dave Lopes*)	3.00	1.50	.90
610	Rookie Pitchers (Jimmy Freeman, Charlie Hough, Hank Webb)	1.75	.90	.50
611	Rookie Outfielders (Rich Coggins, Jim Wohlford, Richie Zisk)	1.50	.70	.45
612	Rookie Pitchers (Steve Lawson, Bob Reynolds, Brent Strom)	1.25	.60	.40
613	Rookie Catchers (*Bob Boone*, Mike Ivie, Skip Jutze)	30.00	15.00	9.00
614	Rookie Outfielders (Alonza Bumbry, *Dwight Evans*, Charlie Spikes)	70.00	35.00	21.00
615	Rookie Third Basemen (Ron Cey, John Hilton, *Mike Schmidt*)	450.00	225.00	135.00
616	Rookie Pitchers (Norm Angelini, Steve Blateric, Mike Garman)	1.50	.70	.45
617	Rich Chiles	1.25	.60	.40
618	Andy Etchebarren	1.25	.60	.40
619	Billy Wilson	1.25	.60	.40
620	Tommy Harper	1.50	.70	.45
621	Joe Ferguson	1.25	.60	.40
622	Larry Hisle	1.50	.70	.45
623	Steve Renko	1.25	.60	.40
624	Astros Mgr./Coaches (Leo Durocher, Preston Gomez, Grady Hatton, Hub Kittle, Jim Owens)	2.25	1.25	.70
625	Angel Mangual	1.25	.60	.40

		NR MT	EX	VG
626	Bob Barton	1.25	.60	.40
627	Luis Alvarado	1.25	.60	.40
628	Jim Slaton	1.50	.70	.45
629	Indians Team	2.50	1.25	.70
630	Denny McLain	3.00	1.50	.90
631	Tom Matchick	1.25	.60	.40
632	Dick Selma	1.25	.60	.40
633	Ike Brown	1.25	.60	.40
634	Alan Closter	1.50	.70	.45
635	Gene Alley	1.50	.70	.45
636	Rick Clark	1.25	.60	.40
637	Norm Niller	1.25	.60	.40
638	Ken Reynolds	1.25	.60	.40
639	Willie Crawford	1.25	.60	.40
640	Dick Bosman	1.25	.60	.40
641	Reds Team	2.75	1.50	.80
642	Jose Laboy	1.25	.60	.40
643	Al Fitzmorris	1.25	.60	.40
644	Jack Heidemann	1.25	.60	.40
645	Bob Locker	1.25	.60	.40
646	Brewers Mgr./Coaches (Del Crandall, Harvey Kuenn, Joe Nossek, Bob Shaw, Jim Walton)	1.75	.90	.50
647	George Stone	1.25	.60	.40
648	Tom Egan	1.25	.60	.40
649	Rich Folkers	1.25	.60	.40
650	Felipe Alou	1.75	.90	.50
651	Don Carrithers	1.25	.60	.40
652	Ted Kubiak	1.25	.60	.40
653	Joe Hoerner	1.25	.60	.40
654	Twins Team	2.50	1.25	.70
655	Clay Kirby	1.25	.60	.40
656	John Ellis	1.25	.60	.40
657	Bob Johnson	1.25	.60	.40
658	Elliott Maddox	1.50	.70	.45
659	Jose Pagan	1.50	.70	.45
660	Fred Scherman	2.25	.70	.45

		NR MT	EX	VG
(17)	Ray Fosse	2.00	1.00	.60
(18)	Bill Freehan	3.00	1.50	.90
(19)	Bob Gibson	15.00	7.50	4.50
(20)	Bud Harrelson	2.00	1.00	.60
(21)	Jim Hunter	12.00	6.00	3.50
(22)	Reggie Jackson	25.00	12.50	7.50
(23)	Fergie Jenkins	7.00	3.50	2.00
(24)	Al Kaline	15.00	7.50	4.50
(25)	Harmon Killebrew	15.00	7.50	4.50
(26)	Clay Kirby	2.00	1.00	.60
(27)	Mickey Lolich	4.00	2.00	1.25
(28)	Greg Luzinski	3.00	1.50	.90
(29)	Mike Marshall	2.00	1.00	.60
(30)	Lee May	2.00	1.00	.60
(31)	John Mayberry	2.00	1.00	.60
(32)	Willie Mays	30.00	15.00	9.00
(33)	Willie McCovey	15.00	7.50	4.50
(34)	Thurman Munson	15.00	7.50	4.50
(35)	Bobby Murcer	3.00	1.50	.90
(36)	Gary Nolan	2.00	1.00	.60
(37)	Amos Otis	2.00	1.00	.60
(38)	Jim Palmer	12.00	6.00	3.50
(39)	Gaylord Perry	12.00	6.00	3.50
(40)	Lou Piniella	3.00	1.50	.90
(41)	Brooks Robinson	18.00	9.00	5.50
(42)	Frank Robinson	15.00	7.50	4.50
(43)	Ellie Rodriguez	2.00	1.00	.60
(44)	Pete Rose	65.00	32.00	19.50
(45)	Nolan Ryan	18.00	9.00	5.50
(46)	Manny Sanguillen	2.00	1.00	.60
(47)	George Scott	2.00	1.00	.60
(48)	Tom Seaver	20.00	10.00	6.00
(49)	Chris Speier	2.00	1.00	.60
(50)	Willie Stargell	15.00	7.50	4.50
(51)	Don Sutton	12.00	6.00	3.50
(52)	Joe Torre	4.00	2.00	1.25
(53)	Billy Williams	12.00	6.00	3.50
(54)	Wilbur Wood	2.00	1.00	.60
(55)	Carl Yastrzemski	25.00	12.50	7.50

1973 Topps Candy Lids

A bit out of the ordinary, the Topps Candy Lids were the top of a product called "Baseball Stars Bubble Gum." The bottom (inside) of the lids carry a color photo of a player with a ribbon which contains the name, position and team. The lids are 1-7/8" in diameter. A total of 55 different lids were made, featuring most of the stars of the day.

		NR MT	EX	VG
Complete Set:		450.00	225.00	135.00
Common Player:		2.00	1.00	.60
(1)	Hank Aaron	30.00	15.00	9.00
(2)	Dick Allen	4.00	2.00	1.25
(3)	Dusty Baker	2.00	1.00	.60
(4)	Sal Bando	3.00	1.50	.90
(5)	Johnny Bench	20.00	10.00	6.00
(6)	Bobby Bonds	3.00	1.50	.90
(7)	Dick Bosman	2.00	1.00	.60
(8)	Lou Brock	15.00	7.50	4.50
(9)	Rod Carew	20.00	10.00	6.00
(10)	Steve Carlton	20.00	10.00	6.00
(11)	Nate Colbert	2.00	1.00	.60
(12)	Willie Davis	3.00	1.50	.90
(13)	Larry Dierker	2.00	1.00	.60
(14)	Mike Epstein	2.00	1.00	.60
(15)	Carlton Fisk	7.00	3.50	2.00
(16)	Tim Foli	2.00	1.00	.60

1973 Topps Comics

Strictly a test issue, if ever publicly distributed at all (most are found without any folding which would have occurred had they actually been used to wrap a piece of bubblegum), the 24 players in the 1973 Topps Comics issue appear on 4-5/8" by 3-7/16" waxed paper wrappers. The inside of the wrapper combines a color photo and facsimile autograph with a comic-style presentation of the player's career highlights. The Comics share a checklist with the 1973 Topps Pin-Ups, virtually all star players.

		NR MT	EX	VG
Complete Set:		3000.00	1500.00	900.00
Common Player:		70.00	35.00	21.00
(1)	Hank Aaron	200.00	100.00	60.00
(2)	Dick Allen	80.00	40.00	24.00
(3)	Johnny Bench	150.00	75.00	45.00
(4)	Steve Carlton	125.00	62.00	37.00
(5)	Nate Colbert	70.00	35.00	21.00
(6)	Willie Davis	80.00	40.00	24.00
(7)	Mike Epstein	70.00	35.00	21.00
(8)	Reggie Jackson	200.00	100.00	60.00
(9)	Harmon Killebrew	125.00	62.00	37.00
(10)	Mickey Lolich	80.00	40.00	24.00

		NR MT	EX	VG
(11)	Mike Marshall	70.00	35.00	21.00
(12)	Lee May	70.00	35.00	21.00
(13)	Willie McCovey	125.00	62.00	37.00
(14)	Bobby Murcer	80.00	40.00	24.00
(15)	Gaylord Perry	100.00	50.00	30.00
(16)	Lou Piniella	80.00	40.00	24.00
(17)	Brooks Robinson	125.00	62.00	37.00
(18)	Nolan Ryan	125.00	62.00	37.00
(19)	George Scott	70.00	35.00	21.00
(20)	Tom Seaver	150.00	75.00	45.00
(21)	Willie Stargell	100.00	50.00	30.00
(22)	Joe Torre	80.00	40.00	24.00
(23)	Billy Williams	100.00	50.00	30.00
(24)	Carl Yastrzemski	250.00	125.00	75.00

1973 Topps Pin-Ups

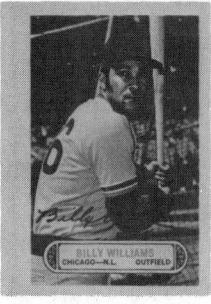

Another test issue of 1973, the 24 Topps Pin-Ups include the same basic format and the same checklist of star-caliber players as the Comics test issue of the same year. The 3-7/16" by 4-5/8" Pin-Ups are actually the inside of a wrapper for a piece of bubblegum. The color player photo features a decorative lozenge inserted at bottom with the player's name, team and position. There is also a facsimile autograph. Curiously, neither the Pin-Ups nor the Comics of 1973 bear team logos on the players' caps.

		NR MT	EX	VG
Complete Set:		1250.00	625.00	375.00
Common Player:		30.00	15.00	9.00
(1)	Hank Aaron	90.00	45.00	27.00
(2)	Dick Allen	35.00	17.50	10.50
(3)	Johnny Bench	70.00	35.00	21.00
(4)	Steve Carlton	60.00	30.00	18.00
(5)	Nate Colbert	30.00	15.00	9.00
(6)	Willie Davis	35.00	17.50	10.50
(7)	Mike Epstein	30.00	15.00	9.00
(8)	Reggie Jackson	90.00	45.00	27.00
(9)	Harmon Killebrew	50.00	25.00	15.00
(10)	Mickey Lolich	35.00	17.50	10.50
(11)	Mike Marshall	30.00	15.00	9.00
(12)	Lee May	30.00	15.00	9.00
(13)	Willie McCovey	50.00	25.00	15.00
(14)	Bobby Murcer	35.00	17.50	10.50
(15)	Gaylord Perry	45.00	22.00	13.50
(16)	Lou Piniella	35.00	17.50	10.50
(17)	Brooks Robinson	55.00	27.00	16.50
(18)	Nolan Ryan	55.00	27.00	16.50
(19)	George Scott	30.00	15.00	9.00
(20)	Tom Seaver	75.00	37.00	22.00
(21)	Willie Stargell	45.00	22.00	13.50
(22)	Joe Torre	35.00	17.50	10.50
(23)	Billy Williams	45.00	22.00	13.50
(24)	Carl Yastrzemski	110.00	55.00	33.00

1973 Topps Team Checklists

This is a 24-card unnumbered set of 2-1/2" by 3-1/2" cards that is generally believed to have been included with the high-numbered series in 1973, while also being made available in a mail-in offer. The front of the cards have the team name at the top and a

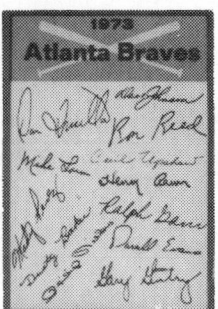
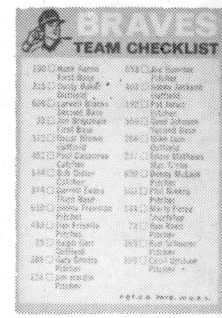

white panel with various facsimile autographs takes up the rest of the space except for a blue border. Backs feature the team name and checklist. Relatively scarce, these somewhat mysterious cards are not included by many in their collections despite their obvious relationship to the regular set.

		NR MT	EX	VG
Complete Set:		75.00	37.00	22.00
Common Checklist:		3.00	1.50	.90
(1)	Atlanta Braves	3.00	1.50	.90
(2)	Baltimore Orioles	3.00	1.50	.90
(3)	Boston Red Sox	3.00	1.50	.90
(4)	California Angels	3.00	1.50	.90
(5)	Chicago Cubs	3.00	1.50	.90
(6)	Chicago White Sox	3.00	1.50	.90
(7)	Cincinnati Reds	3.00	1.50	.90
(8)	Cleveland Indians	3.00	1.50	.90
(9)	Detroit Tigers	3.50	1.75	1.00
(10)	Houston Astros	3.00	1.50	.90
(11)	Kansas City Royals	3.00	1.50	.90
(12)	Los Angeles Dodgers	3.00	1.50	.90
(13)	Milwaukee Brewers	3.00	1.50	.90
(14)	Minnesota Twins	3.00	1.50	.90
(15)	Montreal Expos	3.00	1.50	.90
(16)	New York Mets	3.50	1.75	1.00
(17)	New York Yankees	3.50	1.75	1.00
(18)	Oakland A's	3.50	1.75	1.00
(19)	Philadelphia Phillies	3.00	1.50	.90
(20)	Pittsburgh Pirates	3.00	1.50	.90
(21)	St. Louis Cardinals	3.00	1.50	.90
(22)	San Diego Padres	3.00	1.50	.90
(23)	San Francisco Giants	3.00	1.50	.90
(24)	Texas Rangers	3.00	1.50	.90

1974 Topps

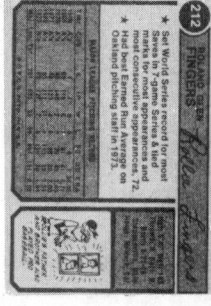

Issued all at once at the beginning of the year, rather than by series throughout the baseball season as had been done since 1952, this 660-card '74 Topps set features a famous group of error cards. At the time the cards were printed, it was uncertain whether the San Diego Padres would move to Washington, D.C., and by the time a decision was made some Padres cards had appeared with a "Washington, Nat'l League" designation on the front. A total of 15 cards were affected, and those with the

Washington designation bring prices well in excess of regular cards of the same players (the Washington variations are not included in the complete set prices quoted below). The 2-1/2" by 3-1/2" cards feature color photos (frequently game-action shots) along with the player's name, team and position. Specialty cards abound, starting with a Hank Aaron tribute and running through the usual managers, statistical leaders, playoff and World Series highlights, multi-player rookie cards and All-Stars.

		NR MT	EX	VG
	Complete Set:	450.00	230.00	135.00
	Common Player:	.20	.10	.06
1	Hank Aaron	30.00	15.00	9.00
2	Aaron Special 1954-57	3.00	1.50	.90
3	Aaron Special 1958-61	3.00	1.50	.90
4	Aaron Special 1962-65	3.00	1.50	.90
5	Aaron Special 1966-69	3.00	1.50	.90
6	Aaron Special 1970-73	3.00	1.50	.90
7	Jim Hunter	3.00	1.50	.90
8	George Theodore	.20	.10	.06
9	Mickey Lolich	.60	.30	.20
10	Johnny Bench	15.00	7.50	4.50
11	Jim Bibby	.25	.13	.08
12	Dave May	.20	.10	.06
13	Tom Hilgendorf	.20	.10	.06
14	Paul Popovich	.20	.10	.06
15	Joe Torre	.80	.40	.25
16	Orioles Team	.80	.40	.25
17	Doug Bird	.20	.10	.06
18	Gary Thomasson	.20	.10	.06
19	Gerry Moses	.25	.13	.08
20	Nolan Ryan	40.00	20.00	12.00
21	Bob Gallagher	.20	.10	.06
22	Cy Acosta	.20	.10	.06
23	Craig Robinson	.20	.10	.06
24	John Hiller	.25	.13	.08
25	Ken Singleton	.30	.15	.09
26	*Bill Campbell*	.40	.20	.12
27	George Scott	.30	.15	.09
28	Manny Sanguillen	.25	.13	.08
29	Phil Niekro	2.00	1.00	.60
30	Bobby Bonds	.50	.25	.15
31	Astros Mgr./Coaches (Roger Craig, Preston Gomez, Grady Hatton, Hub Kittle, Bob Lillis)	.20	.10	.06
32a	John Grubb (Washington)	3.50	1.75	1.00
32b	John Grubb (San Diego)	.25	.13	.08
33	Don Newhauser	.20	.10	.06
34	Andy Kosco	.20	.10	.06
35	Gaylord Perry	6.00	3.00	1.75
36	Cardinals Team	.80	.40	.25
37	Dave Sells	.20	.10	.06
38	Don Kessinger	.25	.13	.08
39	Ken Suarez	.20	.10	.06
40	Jim Palmer	5.00	2.50	1.50
41	Bobby Floyd	.20	.10	.06
42	Claude Osteen	.30	.15	.09
43	Jim Wynn	.30	.15	.09
44	Mel Stottlemyre	.40	.20	.12
45	Dave Johnson	.70	.35	.20
46	Pat Kelly	.20	.10	.06
47	*Dick Ruthven*	.25	.13	.08
48	Dick Sharon	.20	.10	.06
49	Steve Renko	.20	.10	.06
50	Rod Carew	12.00	6.00	3.50
51	Bobby Heise	.20	.10	.06
52	Al Oliver	1.00	.50	.30
53a	Fred Kendall (Washington)	3.50	1.75	1.00
53b	Fred Kendall (San Diego)	.25	.13	.08
54	*Elias Sosa*	.25	.13	.08
55	Frank Robinson	3.50	1.75	1.00
56	Mets Team	1.00	.50	.30
57	Darold Knowles	.20	.10	.06
58	Charlie Spikes	.20	.10	.06
59	Ross Grimsley	.25	.13	.08
60	Lou Brock	3.50	1.75	1.00
61	Luis Aparicio	2.50	1.25	.70
62	Bob Locker	.20	.10	.06
63	Bill Sudakis	.20	.10	.06
64	Doug Rau	.20	.10	.06
65	Amos Otis	.30	.15	.09
66	Sparky Lyle	.50	.25	.15
67	Tommy Helms	.20	.10	.06
68	Grant Jackson	.20	.10	.06
69	Del Unser	.20	.10	.06
70	Dick Allen	.80	.40	.25

		NR MT	EX	VG
71	Danny Frisella	.20	.10	.06
72	Aurleio Rodriguez	.25	.13	.08
73	Mike Marshall	.70	.35	.20
74	Twins Team	.80	.40	.25
75	Jim Colborn	.20	.10	.06
76	Mickey Rivers	.30	.15	.09
77a	Rich Troedson (Washington)	3.50	1.75	1.00
77b	Rich Troedson (San Diego)	.25	.13	.08
78	Giants Mgr./Coaches (Joe Amalfitano, Charlie Fox, Andy Gilbert, Don McMahon, John McNamara)	.20	.10	.06
79	Gene Tenace	.30	.15	.09
80	Tom Seaver	7.00	3.50	2.00
81	Frank Duffy	.20	.10	.06
82	Dave Giusti	.20	.10	.06
83	Orlando Cepeda	1.00	.50	.30
84	Rick Wise	.25	.13	.08
85	Joe Morgan	5.00	2.50	1.50
86	Joe Ferguson	.20	.10	.06
87	Fergie Jenkins	2.00	1.00	.60
88	Freddie Patek	.20	.10	.06
89	Jackie Brown	.20	.10	.06
90	Bobby Murcer	.40	.20	.12
91	Ken Forsch	.25	.13	.08
92	Paul Blair	.25	.13	.08
93	Rod Gilbreath	.20	.10	.06
94	Tigers Team	.90	.45	.25
95	Steve Carlton	7.00	3.50	2.00
96	*Jerry Hairston*	.40	.20	.12
97	Bob Bailey	.20	.10	.06
98	Bert Blyleven	1.00	.50	.30
99	Brewers Mgr./Coaches (Del Crandall, Harvey Kuenn, Joe Nossek, Jim Walton, Al Widmar)	.25	.13	.08
100	Willie Stargell	3.00	1.50	.90
101	Bobby Valentine	.30	.15	.09
102a	Bill Greif (Washington)	3.50	1.75	1.00
102b	Bill Greif (San Diego)	.25	.13	.08
103	Sal Bando	.40	.20	.12
104	Ron Bryant	.20	.10	.06
105	Carlton Fisk	10.00	5.00	3.00
106	Harry Parker	.20	.10	.06
107	Alex Johnson	.20	.10	.06
108	Al Hrabosky	.25	.13	.08
109	Bob Grich	.40	.20	.12
110	Billy Williams	2.75	1.50	.80
111	Clay Carroll	.25	.13	.08
112	Dave Lopes	.40	.20	.12
113	Dick Drago	.20	.10	.06
114	Angels Team	.80	.40	.25
115	Willie Horton	.30	.15	.09
116	Jerry Reuss	.30	.15	.09
117	Ron Blomberg	.25	.13	.08
118	Bill Lee	.25	.13	.08
119	Phillies Mgr./Coaches (Carroll Beringer, Bill DeMars, Danny Ozark, Ray Ripplemeyer, Bobby Wine)	.25	.13	.08
120	Wilbur Wood	.30	.15	.09
121	Larry Lintz	.20	.10	.06
122	Jim Holt	.20	.10	.06
123	Nelson Briles	.20	.10	.06
124	Bob Coluccio	.20	.10	.06
125a	Nate Colbert (Washington)	3.50	1.75	1.00
125b	Nate Colbert (San Diego)	.30	.15	.09
126	Checklist 1-132	1.50	.70	.45
127	Tom Paciorek	.25	.13	.08
128	John Ellis	.20	.10	.06
129	Chris Speier	.25	.13	.08
130	Reggie Jackson	20.00	10.00	6.00
131	Bob Boone	.50	.25	.15
132	Felix Millan	.20	.10	.06
133	*David Clyde*	.30	.15	.09
134	Denis Menke	.20	.10	.06
135	Roy White	.40	.20	.12
136	Rick Reuschel	.80	.40	.25
137	Al Bumbry	.25	.13	.08
138	Ed Brinkman	.25	.13	.08
139	Aurelio Monteagudo	.20	.10	.06
140	Darrell Evans	.60	.30	.20
141	Pat Bourque	.20	.10	.06
142	Pedro Garcia	.20	.10	.06
143	Dick Woodson	.20	.10	.06
144	Dodgers Mgr./Coaches (Red Adams, Walter Alston, Monty Basgall, Jim Gilliam, Tom Lasorda)	1.25	.60	.40
145	Dock Ellis	.25	.13	.08
146	Ron Fairly	.30	.15	.09
147	Bart Johnson	.20	.10	.06
148a	Dave Hilton (Washington)	3.50	1.75	1.00
148b	Dave Hilton (San Diego)	.25	.13	.08
149	Mac Scarce	.20	.10	.06

		NR MT	EX	VG
150	John Mayberry	.30	.15	.09
151	Diego Segui	.20	.10	.06
152	Oscar Gamble	.30	.15	.09
153	Jon Matlack	.30	.15	.09
154	Astros Team	.80	.40	.25
155	Bert Campaneris	.40	.20	.12
156	Randy Moffitt	.20	.10	.06
157	Vic Harris	.20	.10	.06
158	Jack Billingham	.20	.10	.06
159	Jim Ray Hart	.25	.13	.08
160	Brooks Robinson	3.50	1.75	1.00
161	*Ray Burris*	.40	.20	.12
162	Bill Freehan	.40	.20	.12
163	Ken Berry	.20	.10	.06
164	Tom House	.20	.10	.06
165	Willie Davis	.40	.20	.12
166	Royals Mgr./Coaches (Galen Cisco, Harry Dunlop, Charlie Lau, Jack McKeon)	.25	.13	.08
167	Luis Tiant	.50	.25	.15
168	Danny Thompson	.25	.13	.08
169	*Steve Rogers*	.70	.35	.20
170	Bill Melton	.25	.13	.08
171	Eduardo Rodriguez	.20	.10	.06
172	Gene Clines	.20	.10	.06
173a	*Randy Jones* (Washington)	4.00	2.00	1.25
173b	*Randy Jones* (San Diego)	.40	.20	.12
174	Bill Robinson	.20	.10	.06
175	Reggie Cleveland	.20	.10	.06
176	John Lowenstein	.20	.10	.06
177	Dave Roberts	.20	.10	.06
178	Garry Maddox	.40	.20	.12
179	Mets Mgr./Coaches (Yogi Berra, Roy McMillan, Joe Pignatano, Rube Walker, Eddie Yost)	1.25	.60	.40
180	Ken Holtzman	.30	.15	.09
181	Cesar Geronimo	.25	.13	.08
182	Lindy McDaniel	.25	.13	.08
183	Johnny Oates	.20	.10	.06
184	Rangers Team	.80	.40	.25
185	Jose Cardenal	.25	.13	.08
186	Fred Scherman	.20	.10	.06
187	Don Baylor	.70	.35	.20
188	Rudy Meoli	.20	.10	.06
189	Jim Brewer	.20	.10	.06
190	Tony Oliva	.80	.40	.25
191	Al Fitzmorris	.20	.10	.06
192	Mario Guerrero	.20	.10	.06
193	Tom Walker	.20	.10	.06
194	Darrell Porter	.30	.15	.09
195	Carlos May	.25	.13	.08
196	Jim Fregosi	.40	.20	.12
197a	Vicente Romo (Washington)	3.50	1.75	1.00
197b	Vicente Romo (San Diego)	.25	.13	.08
198	Dave Cash	.20	.10	.06
199	Mike Kekich	.20	.10	.06
200	Cesar Cedeno	.40	.20	.12
201	Batting Leaders (Rod Carew, Pete Rose)	4.00	2.00	1.25
202	Home Run Leaders (Reggie Jackson, Willie Stargell)	2.00	1.00	.60
203	Runs Batted In Leaders (Reggie Jackson, Willie Stargell)	2.00	1.00	.60
204	Stolen Base Leaders (Lou Brock, Tommy Harper)	1.25	.60	.40
205	Victory Leaders (Ron Bryant, Wilbur Wood)	.50	.25	.15
206	Earned Run Average Leaders (Jim Palmer, Tom Seaver)	2.00	1.00	.60
207	Strikeout Leaders (Nolan Ryan, Tom Seaver)	2.00	1.00	.60
208	Leading Firemen (John Hiller, Mike Marshall)	.50	.25	.15
209	Ted Sizemore	.20	.10	.06
210	Bill Singer	.25	.13	.08
211	Cubs Team	.80	.40	.25
212	Rollie Fingers	4.00	2.00	1.25
213	Dave Rader	.20	.10	.06
214	Billy Grabarkewitz	.20	.10	.06
215	Al Kaline	3.50	1.75	1.00
216	Ray Sadecki	.20	.10	.06
217	Tim Foli	.20	.10	.06
218	Johnny Briggs	.20	.10	.06
219	Doug Griffin	.20	.10	.06
220	Don Sutton	2.00	1.00	.60
221	White Sox Mgr./Coaches (Joe Lonnett, Jim Mahoney, Alex Monchak, Johnny Sain, Chuck Tanner)	.30	.15	.09
222	Ramon Hernandez	.20	.10	.06
223	Jeff Burroughs	.50	.25	.15
224	Roger Metzger	.20	.10	.06
225	Paul Splittorff	.25	.13	.08

		NR MT	EX	VG
226a	Washington Nat'l. Team	6.00	3.00	1.75
226b	Padres Team	1.00	.50	.30
227	Mike Lum	.20	.10	.06
228	Ted Kubiak	.20	.10	.06
229	Fritz Peterson	.30	.15	.09
230	Tony Perez	1.25	.60	.40
231	Dick Tidrow	.20	.10	.06
232	Steve Brye	.20	.10	.06
233	Jim Barr	.20	.10	.06
234	John Milner	.20	.10	.06
235	Dave McNally	.30	.15	.09
236	Cardinals Mgr./Coaches (Vern Benson, George Kissell, Johnny Lewis, Red Schoendienst, Barney Schultz)	.40	.20	.12
237	Ken Brett	.25	.13	.08
238	Fran Healy	.20	.10	.06
239	Bill Russell	.30	.15	.09
240	Joe Coleman	.25	.13	.08
241a	Glenn Beckert (Washington)	4.00	2.00	1.25
241b	Glenn Beckert (San Diego)	.30	.15	.09
242	Bill Gogolewski	.20	.10	.06
243	Bob Oliver	.20	.10	.06
244	Carl Morton	.20	.10	.06
245	Cleon Jones	.25	.13	.08
246	A's Team	1.25	.60	.40
247	Rick Miller	.20	.10	.06
248	Tom Hall	.20	.10	.06
249	George Mitterwald	.20	.10	.06
250a	Willie McCovey (Washington)	25.00	12.50	7.50
250b	Willie McCovey (San Diego)	4.00	2.00	1.25
251	Graig Nettles	1.50	.70	.45
252	*Dave Parker*	50.00	25.00	15.00
253	John Boccabella	.20	.10	.06
254	Stan Bahnsen	.20	.10	.06
255	Larry Bowa	.40	.20	.12
256	Tom Griffin	.20	.10	.06
257	Buddy Bell	1.25	.60	.40
258	Jerry Morales	.20	.10	.06
259	Bob Reynolds	.20	.10	.06
260	Ted Simmons	.80	.40	.25
261	Jerry Bell	.20	.10	.06
262	Ed Kirkpatrick	.20	.10	.06
263	Checklist 133-264	1.50	.70	.45
264	Joe Rudi	.40	.20	.12
265	Tug McGraw	.60	.30	.20
266	Jim Northrup	.25	.13	.08
267	Andy Messersmith	.30	.15	.09
268	Tom Grieve	.20	.10	.06
269	Bob Johnson	.20	.10	.06
270	Ron Santo	.50	.25	.15
271	Bill Hands	.20	.10	.06
272	Paul Casanova	.20	.10	.06
273	Checklist 265-396	1.50	.70	.45
274	Fred Beene	.25	.13	.08
275	Ron Hunt	.25	.13	.08
276	Angels Mgr./Coaches (Tom Morgan, Salty Parker, Jimmie Reese, John Roseboro, Bobby Winkles)	.20	.10	.06
277	Gary Nolan	.20	.10	.06
278	Cookie Rojas	.20	.10	.06
279	Jim Crawford	.20	.10	.06
280	Carl Yastrzemski	12.00	6.00	3.50
281	Giants Team	.80	.40	.25
282	Doyle Alexander	.40	.20	.12
283	Mike Schmidt	125.00	62.00	37.00
284	Dave Duncan	.20	.10	.06
285	Reggie Smith	.40	.20	.12
286	Tony Muser	.20	.10	.06
287	Clay Kirby	.20	.10	.06
288	*Gorman Thomas*	2.00	1.00	.60
289	Rick Auerbach	.20	.10	.06
290	Vida Blue	.60	.30	.20
291	Don Hahn	.20	.10	.06
292	Chuck Seelbach	.20	.10	.06
293	Milt May	.20	.10	.06
294	Steve Foucault	.20	.10	.06
295	Rick Monday	.30	.15	.09
296	Ray Corbin	.20	.10	.06
297	Hal Breeden	.20	.10	.06
298	Roric Harrison	.20	.10	.06
299	Gene Michael	.30	.15	.09
300	Pete Rose	15.00	7.50	4.50
301	Bob Montgomery	.20	.10	.06
302	Rudy May	.25	.13	.08
303	George Hendrick	.30	.15	.09
304	Don Wilson	.20	.10	.06
305	Tito Fuentes	.20	.10	.06
306	Orioles Mgr./Coaches (George Bamberger, Jim Frey, Billy Hunter, George Staller, Earl Weaver)	.70	.35	.20
307	Luis Melendez	.20	.10	.06

		NR MT	EX	VG
308	Bruce Dal Canton	.20	.10	.06
309a	Dave Roberts (Washington)	3.50	1.75	1.00
309b	Dave Roberts (San Diego)	.25	.13	.08
310	Terry Forster	.30	.15	.09
311	Jerry Grote	.25	.13	.08
312	Deron Johnson	.20	.10	.06
313	Berry Lersch	.20	.10	.06
314	Brewers Team	.80	.40	.25
315	Ron Cey	.60	.30	.20
316	Jim Perry	.40	.20	.12
317	Richie Zisk	.30	.15	.09
318	Jim Merritt	.20	.10	.06
319	Randy Hundley	.20	.10	.06
320	Dusty Baker	.40	.20	.12
321	Steve Braun	.20	.10	.06
322	Ernie McAnally	.20	.10	.06
323	Richie Scheinblum	.20	.10	.06
324	Steve Kline	.25	.13	.08
325	Tommy Harper	.25	.13	.08
326	Reds Mgr./Coaches (Sparky Anderson, Alex Grammas, Ted Kluszewski, George Scherger, Larry Shepard)	.50	.25	.15
327	Tom Timmermann	.20	.10	.06
328	Skip Jutze	.20	.10	.06
329	Mark Belanger	.30	.15	.09
330	Juan Marichal	2.75	1.50	.80
331	All Star Catchers (Johnny Bench, Carlton Fisk)	2.00	1.00	.60
332	All Star First Basemen (Hank Aaron, Dick Allen)	2.00	1.00	.60
333	All Star Second Basemen (Rod Carew, Joe Morgan)	2.00	1.00	.60
334	All Star Third Basemen (Brooks Robinson, Ron Santo)	1.25	.60	.40
335	All Star Shortstops (Bert Campaneris, Chris Speier)	.40	.20	.12
336	All Star Left Fielders (Bobby Murcer, Pete Rose)	2.50	1.25	.70
337	All Star Center Fielders (Cesar Cedeno, Amos Otis)	.40	.20	.12
338	All Star Right Fielders (Reggie Jackson, Billy Williams)	2.00	1.00	.60
339	All Star Pitchers (Jim Hunter, Rick Wise)	.80	.40	.25
340	Thurman Munson	6.00	3.00	1.75
341	Dan Driessen	.80	.40	.25
342	Jim Lonborg	.30	.15	.09
343	Royals Team	.80	.40	.25
344	Mike Caldwell	.25	.13	.08
345	Bill North	.25	.13	.08
346	Ron Reed	.25	.13	.08
347	Sandy Alomar	.20	.10	.06
348	Pete Richert	.20	.10	.06
349	John Vukovich	.20	.10	.06
350	Bob Gibson	2.75	1.50	.80
351	Dwight Evans	3.50	1.75	1.00
352	Bill Stoneman	.20	.10	.06
353	Rich Coggins	.20	.10	.06
354	Cubs Mgr./Coaches (Hank Aguirre, Whitey Lockman, Jim Marshall, J.C. Martin, Al Spangler)	.20	.10	.06
355	Dave Nelson	.20	.10	.06
356	Jerry Koosman	.40	.20	.12
357	Buddy Bradford	.20	.10	.06
358	Dal Maxvill	.25	.13	.08
359	Brent Strom	.20	.10	.06
360	Greg Luzinski	.70	.35	.20
361	Don Carrithers	.20	.10	.06
362	Hal King	.20	.10	.06
363	Yankees Team	1.25	.60	.40
364a	Clarence Gaston (Washington)	3.50	1.75	1.00
364b	Clarence Gaston (San Diego)	.25	.13	.08
365	Steve Busby	.25	.13	.08
366	Larry Hisle	.25	.13	.08
367	Norm Cash	.50	.25	.15
368	Manny Mota	.40	.20	.12
369	Paul Lindblad	.20	.10	.06
370	Bob Watson	.25	.13	.08
371	Jim Slaton	.20	.10	.06
372	Ken Reitz	.20	.10	.06
373	John Curtis	.20	.10	.06
374	Marty Perez	.20	.10	.06
375	Earl Williams	.20	.10	.06
376	Jorge Orta	.25	.13	.08
377	Ron Woods	.20	.10	.06
378	Burt Hooton	.30	.15	.09
379	Rangers Mgr./Coaches (Art Fowler, Frank Lucchesi, Billy Martin, Jackie Moore, Charlie Silvera)	.80	.40	.25
380	Bud Harrelson	.25	.13	.08
381	Charlie Sands	.20	.10	.06

		NR MT	EX	VG
382	Bob Moose	.20	.10	.06
383	Phillies Team	.80	.40	.25
384	Chris Chambliss	.40	.20	.12
385	Don Gullett	.25	.13	.08
386	Gary Matthews	.60	.30	.20
387a	Rich Morales (Washington)	3.50	1.75	1.00
387b	Rich Morales (San Diego)	.25	.13	.08
388	Phil Roof	.20	.10	.06
389	Gates Brown	.20	.10	.06
390	Lou Piniella	.70	.35	.20
391	Billy Champion	.20	.10	.06
392	Dick Green	.20	.10	.06
393	Orlando Pena	.20	.10	.06
394	Ken Henderson	.20	.10	.06
395	Doug Rader	.20	.10	.06
396	Tommy Davis	.40	.20	.12
397	George Stone	.20	.10	.06
398	Duke Sims	.25	.13	.08
399	Mike Paul	.20	.10	.06
400	Harmon Killebrew	4.00	2.00	1.25
401	Elliott Maddox	.20	.10	.06
402	Jim Rooker	.20	.10	.06
403	Red Sox Mgr./Coaches (Don Bryant, Darrell Johnson, Eddie Popowski, Lee Stange, Don Zimmer)	.25	.13	.08
404	Jim Howarth	.20	.10	.06
405	Ellie Rodriguez	.20	.10	.06
406	Steve Arlin	.20	.10	.06
407	Jim Wohlford	.20	.10	.06
408	Charlie Hough	.40	.20	.12
409	Ike Brown	.20	.10	.06
410	Pedro Borbon	.20	.10	.06
411	Frank Baker	.20	.10	.06
412	Chuck Taylor	.20	.10	.06
413	Don Money	.25	.13	.08
414	Checklist 397-528	1.50	.70	.45
415	Gary Gentry	.20	.10	.06
416	White Sox Team	.80	.40	.25
417	Rich Folkers	.20	.10	.06
418	Walt Williams	.20	.10	.06
419	Wayne Twitchell	.20	.10	.06
420	Ray Fosse	.20	.10	.06
421	Dan Fife	.20	.10	.06
422	Gonzalo Marquez	.20	.10	.06
423	Fred Stanley	.25	.13	.08
424	Jim Beauchamp	.20	.10	.06
425	Pete Broberg	.20	.10	.06
426	Rennie Stennett	.20	.10	.06
427	Bobby Bolin	.20	.10	.06
428	Gary Sutherland	.20	.10	.06
429	Dick Lange	.20	.10	.06
430	Matty Alou	.40	.20	.12
431	Gene Garber	.50	.25	.15
432	Chris Arnold	.20	.10	.06
433	Lerrin LaGrow	.20	.10	.06
434	Ken McMullen	.20	.10	.06
435	Dave Concepcion	.70	.35	.20
436	Don Hood	.20	.10	.06
437	Jim Lyttle	.20	.10	.06
438	Ed Herrmann	.20	.10	.06
439	Norm Miller	.20	.10	.06
440	Jim Kaat	1.25	.60	.40
441	Tom Ragland	.20	.10	.06
442	Alan Foster	.20	.10	.06
443	Tom Hutton	.20	.10	.06
444	Vic Davalillo	.25	.13	.08
445	George Medich	.30	.15	.09
446	Len Randle	.20	.10	.06
447	Twins Mgr./Coaches (Vern Morgan, Frank Quilici, Bob Rodgers, Ralph Rowe)	.20	.10	.06
448	Ron Hodges	.20	.10	.06
449	Tom McCraw	.20	.10	.06
450	Rich Hebner	.25	.13	.08
451	Tommy John	1.50	.70	.45
452	Gene Hiser	.20	.10	.06
453	Balor Moore	.20	.10	.06
454	Kurt Bevacqua	.20	.10	.06
455	Tom Bradley	.20	.10	.06
456	Dave Winfield	50.00	30.00	15.00
457	Chuck Goggin	.20	.10	.06
458	Jim Ray	.20	.10	.06
459	Reds Team	.90	.45	.25
460	Boog Powell	.90	.45	.25
461	John Odom	.25	.13	.08
462	Luis Alvarado	.20	.10	.06
463	Pat Dobson	.30	.15	.09
464	Jose Cruz	.80	.40	.25
465	Dick Bosman	.20	.10	.06
466	Dick Billings	.20	.10	.06
467	Winston Llenas	.20	.10	.06
468	Pepe Frias	.20	.10	.06

		NR MT	EX	VG
469	Joe Decker	.20	.10	.06
470	A.L. Playoffs	2.00	1.00	.60
471	N.L. Playoffs	.80	.40	.25
472	World Series Game 1	.80	.40	.25
473	World Series Game 2	2.00	1.00	.60
474	World Series Game 3	.80	.40	.25
475	World Series Game 4	.80	.40	.25
476	World Series Game 5	.80	.40	.25
477	World Series Game 6	2.00	1.00	.60
478	World Series Game 7	.80	.40	.25
479	World Series Summary	.80	.40	.25
480	Willie Crawford	.20	.10	.06
481	Jerry Terrell	.20	.10	.06
482	Bob Didier	.20	.10	.06
483	Braves Team	.80	.40	.25
484	Carmen Fanzone	.20	.10	.06
485	Felipe Alou	.40	.20	.12
486	Steve Stone	.40	.20	.12
487	Ted Martinez	.20	.10	.06
488	Andy Etchebarren	.20	.10	.06
489	Pirates Mgr./Coaches (Don Leppert, Bill Mazeroski, Danny Murtaugh, Don Osborn, Bob Skinner)	.30	.15	.09
490	Vada Pinson	.70	.35	.20
491	Roger Nelson	.20	.10	.06
492	Mike Rogodzinski	.20	.10	.06
493	Joe Hoerner	.20	.10	.06
494	Ed Goodson	.20	.10	.06
495	Dick McAuliffe	.25	.13	.08
496	Tom Murphy	.20	.10	.06
497	Bobby Mitchell	.20	.10	.06
498	Pat Corrales	.40	.20	.12
499	Rusty Torres	.20	.10	.06
500	Lee May	.40	.20	.12
501	Eddie Leon	.20	.10	.06
502	Dave LaRoche	.20	.10	.06
503	Eric Soderholm	.20	.10	.06
504	Joe Niekro	.40	.20	.12
505	Bill Buckner	.50	.25	.15
506	Ed Farmer	.20	.10	.06
507	Larry Stahl	.20	.10	.06
508	Expos Team	.80	.40	.25
509	Jesse Jefferson	.20	.10	.06
510	Wayne Garrett	.20	.10	.06
511	Toby Harrah	.30	.15	.09
512	Joe Lahoud	.20	.10	.06
513	Jim Campanis	.20	.10	.06
514	Paul Schaal	.20	.10	.06
515	Willie Montanez	.25	.13	.08
516	Horacio Pina	.20	.10	.06
517	Mike Hegan	.25	.13	.08
518	Derrel Thomas	.20	.10	.06
519	Bill Sharp	.20	.10	.06
520	Tim McCarver	.60	.30	.20
521	Indians Mgr./Coaches (Ken Aspromonte, Clay Bryant, Tony Pacheco)	.20	.10	.06
522	J.R. Richard	.30	.15	.09
523	Cecil Cooper	1.50	.70	.45
524	Bill Plummer	.20	.10	.06
525	Clyde Wright	.20	.10	.06
526	Frank Tepedino	.20	.10	.06
527	Bobby Darwin	.20	.10	.06
528	Bill Bonham	.20	.10	.06
529	Horace Clarke	.25	.13	.08
530	Mickey Stanley	.25	.13	.08
531	Expos Mgr./Coaches (Dave Bristol, Larry Doby, Gene Mauch, Cal McLish, Jerry Zimmerman)	.40	.20	.12
532	Skip Lockwood	.20	.10	.06
533	Mike Phillips	.20	.10	.06
534	Eddie Watt	.20	.10	.06
535	Bob Tolan	.25	.13	.08
536	Duffy Dyer	.20	.10	.06
537	Steve Mingori	.20	.10	.06
538	Cesar Tovar	.20	.10	.06
539	Lloyd Allen	.20	.10	.06
540	Bob Robertson	.20	.10	.06
541	Indians Team	.80	.40	.25
542	Rich Gossage	2.00	1.00	.60
543	Danny Cater	.20	.10	.06
544	Ron Schueler	.20	.10	.06
545	Billy Conigliaro	.20	.10	.06
546	Mike Corkins	.20	.10	.06
547	Glenn Borgmann	.20	.10	.06
548	Sonny Siebert	.20	.10	.06
549	Mike Jorgensen	.20	.10	.06
550	Sam McDowell	.40	.20	.12
551	Von Joshua	.20	.10	.06
552	Denny Doyle	.20	.10	.06
553	Jim Willoughby	.20	.10	.06
554	Tim Johnson	.20	.10	.06

		NR MT	EX	VG
555	Woodie Fryman	.25	.13	.08
556	Dave Campbell	.20	.10	.06
557	Jim McGlothlin	.20	.10	.06
558	Bill Fahey	.20	.10	.06
559	Darrel Chaney	.20	.10	.06
560	Mike Cuellar	.40	.20	.12
561	Ed Kranepool	.30	.15	.09
562	Jack Aker	.20	.10	.06
563	Hal McRae	.40	.20	.12
564	Mike Ryan	.20	.10	.06
565	Milt Wilcox	.25	.13	.08
566	Jackie Hernandez	.20	.10	.06
567	Red Sox Team	.90	.45	.25
568	Mike Torrez	.25	.13	.08
569	Rick Dempsey	.40	.20	.12
570	Ralph Garr	.30	.15	.09
571	Rich Hand	.20	.10	.06
572	Enzo Hernandez	.20	.10	.06
573	Mike Adams	.20	.10	.06
574	Bill Parsons	.20	.10	.06
575	Steve Garvey	12.00	6.00	3.50
576	Scipio Spinks	.20	.10	.06
577	Mike Sadek	.20	.10	.06
578	Ralph Houk	.40	.20	.12
579	Cecil Upshaw	.20	.10	.06
580	Jim Spencer	.20	.10	.06
581	Fred Norman	.20	.10	.06
582	*Bucky Dent*	.90	.45	.25
583	Marty Pattin	.20	.10	.06
584	Ken Rudolph	.20	.10	.06
585	Merv Rettenmund	.25	.13	.08
586	Jack Brohamer	.20	.10	.06
587	*Larry Christenson*	.25	.13	.08
588	Hal Lanier	.40	.20	.12
589	Boots Day	.20	.10	.06
590	Rogelio Moret	.20	.10	.06
591	Sonny Jackson	.20	.10	.06
592	Ed Bane	.20	.10	.06
593	Steve Yeager	.25	.13	.08
594	Leroy Stanton	.20	.10	.06
595	Steve Blass	.25	.13	.08
596	Rookie Pitchers (*Wayne Garland*, Fred Holdsworth, *Mark Littell*, Dick Pole)	.30	.15	.09
597	Rookie Shortstops (Dave Chalk, John Gamble, Pete Mackanin, *Manny Trillo*)	.80	.40	.25
598	Rookie Outfielders (Dave Augustine, *Ken Griffey*, Steve Ontiveros, Jim Tyrone)	15.00	7.50	4.50
599a	Rookie Pitchers (Ron Diorio, Dave Freisleben, Frank Riccelli, Greg Shanahan) (Freisleben- Washington)	.80	.40	.25
599b	Rookie Pitchers (Ron Diorio, Dave Freisleben, Frank Riccelli, Greg Shanahan) (Freisleben- San Diego large print)	3.50	1.75	1.00
599c	Rookie Pitchers (Ron Diorio, Dave Freisleben, Frank Riccelli, Greg Shanahan) (Freisleben- San Diego small print)	6.00	3.00	1.75
600	Rookie Infielders (Ron Cash, Jim Cox, *Bill Madlock*, Reggie Sanders)	2.25	1.25	.70
601	Rookie Outfielders (Ed Armbrister, Rich Bladt, *Brian Downing, Bake McBride*)	2.00	1.00	.60
602	Rookie Pitchers (Glenn Abbott, Rick Henninger, Craig Swan, Dan Vossler)	.20	.10	.06
603	Rookie Catchers (Barry Foote, Tom Lundstedt, *Charlie Moore*, Sergio Robles)	.30	.15	.09
604	Rookie Infielders (Terry Hughes, John Knox, *Andy Thornton, Frank White*)	5.00	2.50	1.50
605	Rookie Pitchers (Vic Albury, Ken Frailing, Kevin Kobel, *Frank Tanana*)	2.00	1.00	.60
606	Rookie Outfielders (Jim Fuller, Wilbur Howard, Tommy Smith, Otto Velez)	.25	.13	.08
607	Rookie Shortstops (Leo Foster, Tom Heintzelman, Dave Rosello, *Frank Taveras*)	.25	.13	.08
608a	Rookie Pitchers (Bob Apodaca, Dick Baney, John D'Acquisto, Mike Wallace)	2.50	1.25	.70
608b	Rookie Pitchers (Bob Apodaca, Dick Baney, John D'Acquisto, Mike Wallace)	.25	.13	.08
609	Rico Petrocelli	.30	.15	.09
610	Dave Kingman	.90	.45	.25
611	Rick Stelmaszek	.20	.10	.06
612	Luke Walker	.20	.10	.06
613	Dan Monzon	.20	.10	.06
614	Adrian Devine	.20	.10	.06
615	Johnny Jeter	.20	.10	.06
616	Larry Gura	.25	.13	.08
617	Ted Ford	.20	.10	.06
618	Jim Mason	.20	.10	.06

		NR MT	EX	VG
619	Mike Anderson	.20	.10	.06
620	Al Downing	.25	.13	.08
621	Bernie Carbo	.20	.10	.06
622	Phil Gagliano	.20	.10	.06
623	Celerino Sanchez	.25	.13	.08
624	Bob Miller	.20	.10	.06
625	Ollie Brown	.20	.10	.06
626	Pirates Team	.80	.40	.25
627	Carl Taylor	.20	.10	.06
628	Ivan Murrell	.20	.10	.06
629	Rusty Staub	.70	.35	.20
630	Tommie Agee	.25	.13	.08
631	Steve Barber	.20	.10	.06
632	George Culver	.20	.10	.06
633	Dave Hamilton	.20	.10	.06
634	Braves Mgr./Coaches (Jim Busby, Eddie Mathews, Connie Ryan, Ken Silvestri, Herm Starrette)	.90	.45	.25
635	John Edwards	.20	.10	.06
636	Dave Goltz	.25	.13	.08
637	Checklist 529-660	1.50	.70	.45
638	Ken Sanders	.20	.10	.06
639	Joe Lovitto	.20	.10	.06
640	Milt Pappas	.40	.20	.12
641	Chuck Brinkman	.20	.10	.06
642	Terry Harmon	.20	.10	.06
643	Dodgers Team	.90	.45	.25
644	Wayne Granger	.25	.13	.08
645	Ken Boswell	.20	.10	.06
646	George Foster	1.25	.60	.40
647	*Juan Beniquez*	.70	.35	.20
648	Terry Crowley	.20	.10	.06
649	Fernando Gonzalez	.20	.10	.06
650	Mike Epstein	.20	.10	.06
651	Leron Lee	.20	.10	.06
652	Gail Hopkins	.20	.10	.06
653	Bob Stinson	.20	.10	.06
654a	Jesus Alou (no position listed)	5.00	2.50	1.50
654b	Jesus Alou (Outfield)	.40	.20	.12
655	Mike Tyson	.20	.10	.06
656	Adrian Garrett	.20	.10	.06
657	Jim Shellenback	.20	.10	.06
658	Lee Lacy	.30	.15	.09
659	Joe Lis	.20	.10	.06
660	Larry Dierker	.50	.15	.09

1974 Topps Deckle Edge

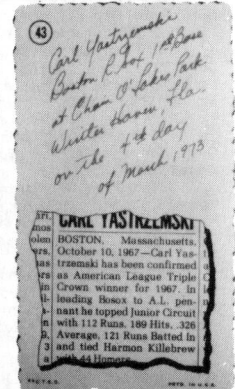

These borderless 2-7/8" by 5" cards feature a black and white photograph with a facsimile autograph on the front. The backs have in handwritten script the player's name, team, position and the date and location of the picture. Below is a mock newspaper clipping providing a detail from the player's career. The cards take their names from their specially cut edges which give them a scalloped appearance. The 72-card set was a test issue and received rather limited distribution.

		NR MT	EX	VG
Complete Set:		2000.00	1000.00	600.00
Common Player:		10.00	5.00	3.00
1	Amos Otis	10.00	5.00	3.00
2	Darrell Evans	15.00	7.50	4.50
3	Robert Gibson	50.00	25.00	15.00
4	David Nelson	10.00	5.00	3.00

		NR MT	EX	VG
5	Steven N. Carlton	80.00	40.00	25.00
6	Jim "Catfish" Hunter	40.00	20.00	12.00
7	Thurman Munson	50.00	25.00	15.00
8	Bob Grich	15.00	7.50	4.50
9	Tom Seaver	100.00	50.00	30.00
10	Ted L. Simmons	20.00	10.00	6.00
11	Robert J. Valentine	10.00	5.00	3.00
12	Don Sutton	25.00	12.50	7.50
13	Wilbur Wood	10.00	5.00	3.00
14	Douglas Lee Rader	10.00	5.00	3.00
15	Chris Chambliss	10.00	5.00	3.00
16	Pete Rose	200.00	100.00	60.00
17	John F. Hiller	10.00	5.00	3.00
18	Burt Hooton	10.00	5.00	3.00
19	Tim Foli	10.00	5.00	3.00
20	Louis Brock	60.00	30.00	20.00
21	Ron Bryant	10.00	5.00	3.00
22	Manuel Sanguillen	10.00	5.00	3.00
23	Bobby Tolan	10.00	5.00	3.00
24	Greg Luzinski	15.00	7.50	4.50
25	Brooks Robinson	60.00	30.00	18.00
26	Felix Millan	10.00	5.00	3.00
27	Luis Tiant	15.00	7.50	4.50
28	Willie McCovey	60.00	30.00	20.00
29	Chris Speier	10.00	5.00	3.00
30	George Scott	10.00	5.00	3.00
31	Willie Stargell	50.00	25.00	15.00
32	Rod Carew	100.00	50.00	30.00
33	Leslie Charles Spikes	10.00	5.00	3.00
34	Nate Colbert	10.00	5.00	3.00
35	Richie Hebner	10.00	5.00	3.00
36	Bobby Lee Bonds	15.00	7.50	4.50
37	Buddy Bell	15.00	7.50	4.50
38	Claude Osteen	10.00	5.00	3.00
39	Richard A. Allen	15.00	7.50	4.50
40	Bill Russell	10.00	5.00	3.00
41	Nolan Ryan	175.00	87.00	52.00
42	Willie Davis	15.00	7.50	4.50
43	Carl Yastrzemski	125.00	62.00	37.00
44	Jonathon T. Matlack	10.00	5.00	3.00
45	Jim Palmer	30.00	15.00	9.00
46	Dagoberto Campaneris	15.00	7.50	4.50
47	Bert Blyleven	20.00	10.00	6.00
48	Jeff Burroughs	10.00	5.00	3.00
49	James W. Colborn	10.00	5.00	3.00
50	Dave Johnson	15.00	7.50	4.50
51	John Mayberry	10.00	5.00	3.00
52	Don Kessinger	10.00	5.00	3.00
53	Joseph H. Coleman	10.00	5.00	3.00
54	Tony Perez	20.00	10.00	6.00
55	Jose Cardenal	10.00	5.00	3.00
56	Paul Splittorff	10.00	5.00	3.00
57	Henry Aaron	150.00	75.00	45.00
58	David May	10.00	5.00	3.00
59	Fergie Jenkins	30.00	15.00	9.00
60	Ron Blomberg	10.00	5.00	3.00
61	Reggie Jackson	150.00	75.00	45.00
62	Tony Oliva	15.00	7.50	4.50
63	Bobby Ray Murcer	15.00	7.50	4.50
64	Carlton Fisk	20.00	10.00	6.00
65	Stephen Rogers	10.00	5.00	3.00
66	Frank Robinson	40.00	20.00	12.00
67	Joe Ferguson	10.00	5.00	3.00
68	Bill Melton	10.00	5.00	3.00
69	Robert Watson	10.00	5.00	3.00
70	Larry Bowa	15.00	7.50	4.50
71	Johnny Bench	90.00	45.00	27.00
72	Willie Horton	10.00	5.00	3.00

1974 Topps Puzzles

One of many test issues by Topps in the mid-1970s,

the 12-player jigsaw puzzle set was an innovation which never caught on with collectors. The 40-piece puzzles (4-3/4" by 7-1/2") feature color photos with a decorative lozenge at bottom naming the player, team and position. The puzzles came in individual wrappers.

		NR MT	EX	VG
Complete Set:		600.00	300.00	200.00
Common Player:		12.00	6.00	3.50
(1)	Hank Aaron	80.00	40.00	25.00
(2)	Dick Allen	12.00	6.00	3.50
(3)	Johnny Bench	75.00	38.00	23.00
(4)	Bobby Bonds	12.00	6.00	3.50
(5)	Bob Gibson	35.00	17.50	10.50
(6)	Reggie Jackson	60.00	30.00	18.00
(7)	Bobby Murcer	12.00	6.00	3.50
(8)	Jim Palmer	50.00	25.00	15.00
(9)	Nolan Ryan	80.00	40.00	24.00
(10)	Tom Seaver	80.00	40.00	24.00
(11)	Willie Stargell	30.00	15.00	9.00
(12)	Carl Yastrzemski	70.00	35.00	21.00

1974 Topps Stamps

Topps continued to market baseball stamps in 1974 through the release of 240 unnumbered stamps featuring color player portraits. The player's name, team and position are found in an oval at the bottom of the 1" by 1-1/2" stamps. The stamps, sold separately rather than issued as an insert, came in strips of six which were then pasted in an appropriate team album designed to hold 10 stamps.

		NR MT	EX	VG
Complete Sheet Set:		100.00	50.00	30.00
Common Sheet:		1.00	.50	.30
Complete Stamp Album Set:		75.00	37.00	22.00
Single Stamp Album:		2.50	1.25	.70

(1)   Hank Aaron, Luis Aparicio, Bob Bailey, Johnny Bench, Ron Blomberg, Bob Boone, Lou Brock, Bud Harrelson, Randy Jones, Dave Rader, Nolan Ryan, Joe Torre   6.00   3.00   1.75

(2)   Buddy Bell, Steve Braun, Jerry Grote, Tommy Helms, Bill Lee, Mike Lum, Dave May, Brooks Robinson, Bill Russell, Del Unser, Wilbur Wood, Carl Yastrzemski   10.00   5.00   3.00

(3)   Jerry Bell, Jerry Bell, Jim Colborn, Toby Harrah, Ken Henderson, John Hiller, Randy Hundley, Don Kessinger, Jerry Koosman, Dave Lopes, Felix Millan, Thurman Munson, Ted Simmons   3.50   1.75   1.00

(4)   Jerry Bell, Bill Buckner, Jim Colborn, Ken Henderson, Don Kessinger, Felix Millan, George Mitterwald, Dave Roberts, Ted Simmons, Jim Slaton, Charlie Spikes, Paul Splittorff   1.00   .50   .30

(5)   Glenn Beckert, Jim Bibby, Bill Buckner, Jim Lonborg, George Mitterwald, Dave Parker, Dave Roberts, Jim Slaton, Reggie Smith, Charlie Spikes, Paul Splittorff, Bob Watson   3.50   1.75   1.00

(6)   Paul Blair, Bobby Bonds, Ed Brinkman, Norm Cash, Mike Epstein, Tommy Harper, Mike Marshall, Phil Niekro, Cookie Rojas, George Scott, Mel Stottlemyre, Jim Wynn   3.50   1.75   1.00

	NR MT	EX	VG

(7)   Jack Billingham, Reggie Cleveland, Bobby Darwin, Dave Duncan, Tim Foli, Ed Goodson, Cleon Jones, Mickey Lolich, George Medich, John Milner, Rick Monday, Bobby Murcer   1.00   .50   .30

(8)   Steve Carlton, Orlando Cepeda, Joe Decker, Reggie Jackson, Dave Johnson, John Mayberry, Bill Melton, Roger Metzger, Dave Nelson, Jerry Reuss, Jim Spencer, Bobby Valentine   6.00   3.00   1.75

(9)   Dan Driessen, Pedro Garcia, Grant Jackson, Al Kaline, Clay Kirby, Carlos May, Willie Montanez, Rogelio Moret, Jim Palmer, Doug Rader, J. R. Richard, Frank Robinson   3.50   1.75   1.00

(10)   Pedro Garcia, Ralph Garr, Wayne Garrett, Ron Hunt, Al Kaline, Fred Kendall, Carlos May, Jim Palmer, Doug Rader, Frank Robinson, Rick Wise, Richie Zisk   3.50   1.75   1.00

(11)   Dusty Baker, Larry Bowa, Steve Busby, Chris Chambliss, Dock Ellis, Cesar Geronimo, Fran Healy, Deron Johnson, Jorge Orta, Joe Rudi, Mickey Stanley, Rennie Stennett   3.50   1.75   1.00

(12)   Bob Coluccio, Ray Corbin, John Ellis, Oscar Gamble, Dave Giusti, Bill Greif, Alex Johnson, Mike Jorgensen, Andy Messersmith, Elias Sosa, Willie Stargell   3.50   1.75   1.00

(13)   Ron Bryant, Nate Colbert, Jose Cruz, Dan Driessen, Billy Grabarkewitz, Don Gullett, Willie Horton, Grant Jackson, Clay Kirby, Willie Montanez, Rogelio Moret, J. R. Richard   1.00   .50   .30

(14)   Carlton Fisk, Bill Freehan, Bobby Grich, Vic Harris, George Hendrick, Ed Herrmann, Jim Holt, Ken Holtzman, Fergie Jenkins, Lou Piniella, Steve Rogers, Ken Singleton   3.50   1.75   1.00

(15)   Stan Bahnsen, Sal Bando, Mark Belanger, David Clyde, Willie Crawford, Burt Hooton, Jon Matlack, Tim McCarver, Joe Morgan, Gene Tenace, Dick Tidrow, Dave Winfield   5.00   2.50   1.50

(16)   Hank Aaron, Stan Bahnsen, Bob Bailey, Johnny Bench, Bob Boone, Joe Matlack, Tim McCarver, Joe Morgan, Dave Rader, Gene Tenace, Dick Tidrow, Joe Torre   5.00   2.50   1.50

(17)   John Boccabella, Frank Duffy, Darrell Evans, Sparky Lyle, Lee May, Don Money, Bill North, Ted Sizemore, Chris Speier, Wayne Twitchell, Billy Williams, Earl Williams   1.00   .50   .30

(18)   John Boccabella, Bobby Darwin, Frank Duffy, Dave Duncan, Tim Foli, Cleon Jones, Mickey Lolich, Sparky Lyle, Lee May, Rick Monday, Bill North, Billy Williams   1.00   .50   .30

(19)   Don Baylor, Vida Blue, Tom Bradley, Jose Cardenal, Ron Cey, Greg Luzinski, Johnny Oates, Tony Oliva, Al Oliver, Tony Perez, Darrell Porter, Roy White   3.50   1.75   1.00

(20)   Pedro Borbon, Rod Carew, Roric Harrison, Jim Hunter, Ed Kirkpatrick, Garry Maddox, Gene Michael, Rick Miller, Claude Osteen, Amos Otis, Rich Reuschel, Mike Tyson   5.00   2.50   1.50

(21)   Sandy Alomar, Bert Campaneris, Tommy Davis, Joe Ferguson, Tito Fuentes, Jerry Morales, Carl Morton, Gaylord Perry, Vada Pinson, Dave Roberts, Ellie Rodriguez   3.50   1.75   1.00

(22)   Dick Allen, Jeff Burroughs, Joe Coleman, Terry Forster, Bob Gibson, Harmon Killebrew, Tug McGraw, Bob Oliver, Steve Renko, Pete Rose, Luis Tiant, Otto Velez   13.00   6.50   4.00

(23)   Johnny Briggs, Willie Davis, Jim Fregosi, Rich Hebner, Pat Kelly, Dave Kingman, Willie McCovey, Graig Nettles, Freddie Patek, Marty Pattin, Manny Sanguillen, Richie Scheinblum   5.00   2.50   1.50

(24)   Bert Blyleven, Nelson Briles, Cesar Cedeno, Ron Fairly, Johnny Grubb, Dave McNally, Aurelio Rodriguez, Ron Santo, Tom Seaver, Bill Singer, Bill Sudakis, Don Sutton   6.00   3.00   1.75

A player's name in *italic* type indicates a rookie card. An (FC) indicates a player's first card for that particular card company.

1974 Topps Team Checklists

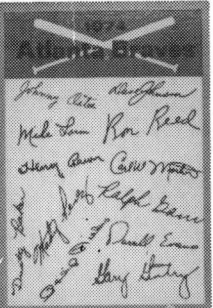

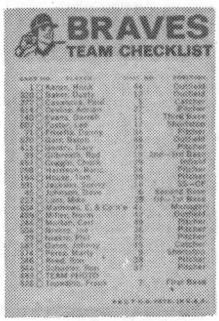

This set is a repeat of the 1973 mystery set in the form of 24 unnumbered 2-1/2" by 3-1/2" checklist cards. As with the 1973 set, the 1974s feature a team name on the front at the top with a white panel and a number of facsimile autographs below. Backs feature the team name and a checklist. The big difference between the 1973 and 1974 checklists is that the 1973s have blue borders while the 1974s have a red border. The 1974s were inserted into packages of the regular issue Topps cards.

		NR MT	EX	VG
Complete Set:		12.00	6.00	3.50
Common Checklist:		.50	.25	.15
(1)	Atlanta Braves	.50	.25	.15
(2)	Baltimore Orioles	.50	.25	.15
(3)	Boston Red Sox	.50	.25	.15
(4)	California Angels	.50	.25	.15
(5)	Chicago Cubs	.50	.25	.15
(6)	Chicago White Sox	.50	.25	.15
(7)	Cincinnati Reds	.50	.25	.15
(8)	Cleveland Indians	.50	.25	.15
(9)	Detroit Tigers	.50	.25	.15
(10)	Houston Astros	.50	.25	.15
(11)	Kansas City Royals	.50	.25	.15
(12)	Los Angeles Dodgers	.50	.25	.15
(13)	Milwaukee Brewers	.50	.25	.15
(14)	Minnesota Twins	.50	.25	.15
(15)	Montreal Expos	.50	.25	.15
(16)	New York Mets	.50	.25	.15
(17)	New York Yankees	.50	.25	.15
(18)	Oakland A's	.50	.25	.15
(19)	Philadelphia Phillies	.50	.25	.15
(20)	Pittsburgh Pirates	.50	.25	.15
(21)	St. Louis Cardinals	.50	.25	.15
(22)	San Diego Padres	.50	.25	.15
(23)	San Francisco Giants	.50	.25	.15
(24)	Texas Rangers	.50	.25	.15

1974 Topps Traded

Appearing late in the season, these 2-1/2" by 3-1/2" cards are basically the same as the regular issue Topps cards. The major change was that a big

red panel with the word "Traded" was added below the player photo. Backs feature a "Baseball News" newspaper which contains the details of the trade. Card numbers correspond to the player's regular card number in 1974 except that the suffix "T" is added after the number. The set consists of 43 player cards and a checklist. In most cases, Topps did not obtain pictures of the players in their new uniforms. Instead the Topps artists simply provided the needed changes to existing photos.

		NR MT	EX	VG
Complete Set:		8.00	4.00	2.50
Common Player:		.12	.06	.04
23T	Craig Robinson	.12	.06	.04
42T	Claude Osteen	.15	.08	.05
43T	Jim Wynn	.20	.10	.06
51T	Bobby Heise	.12	.06	.04
59T	Ross Grimsley	.15	.08	.05
62T	Bob Locker	.12	.06	.04
63T	Bill Sudakis	.12	.06	.04
73T	Mike Marshall	.20	.10	.06
123T	Nelson Briles	.12	.06	.04
139T	Aurelio Monteagudo	.12	.06	.04
151T	Diego Segui	.12	.06	.04
165T	Willie Davis	.20	.10	.06
175T	Reggie Cleveland	.12	.06	.04
182T	Lindy McDaniel	.12	.06	.04
186T	Fred Scherman	.12	.06	.04
249T	George Mitterwald	.12	.06	.04
262T	Ed Kirkpatrick	.12	.06	.04
269T	Bob Johnson	.12	.06	.04
270T	Ron Santo	.30	.15	.09
313T	Barry Lersch	.12	.06	.04
319T	Randy Hundley	.12	.06	.04
330T	Juan Marichal	1.25	.60	.40
348T	Pete Richert	.12	.06	.04
373T	John Curtis	.12	.06	.04
390T	Lou Piniella	.50	.25	.15
428T	Gary Sutherland	.12	.06	.04
454T	Kurt Bevacqua	.12	.06	.04
458T	Jim Ray	.12	.06	.04
485T	Felipe Alou	.20	.10	.06
486T	Steve Stone	.20	.10	.06
496T	Tom Murphy	.12	.06	.04
516T	Horacio Pina	.12	.06	.04
534T	Eddie Watt	.12	.06	.04
538T	Cesar Tovar	.12	.06	.04
544T	Ron Schueler	.12	.06	.04
579T	Cecil Upshaw	.12	.06	.04
585T	Merv Rettenmund	.15	.08	.05
612T	Luke Walker	.12	.06	.04
616T	Larry Gura	.15	.08	.05
618T	Jim Mason	.12	.06	.04
630T	Tommie Agee	.15	.08	.05
648T	Terry Crowley	.12	.06	.04
649T	Fernando Gonzalez	.12	.06	.04
-----	Traded Checklist	.70	.35	.20

1975 Topps

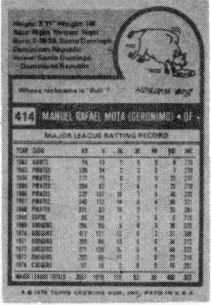

This year Topps produced another 660-card set, one which collectors either seem to like or despise. The 2-1/2" by 3-1/2" cards have a color photo which is framed by a round-cornered white frame. Around that is an eye-catching two-color border in bright colors. The team name appears at the top in bright letters while the player name is at the bottom and his position a baseball at the lower right. A facsimile autograph runs across the picture. The card backs are vertical feature normal statistical and biographical information along with a trivia quiz. Specialty cards include a new 24-card series on MVP winners going back to 1951. Other specialty cards include statistical leaders and post-season highlights. The real highlight of the set, however, are the rookie cards which include their numbers such names as George Brett, Gary Carter, Robin Yount, Jim Rice, Keith Hernandez and Fred Lynn. While the set was released at one time, card numbers 1-132 were printed in somewhat shorter supply than the remainder of the issue.

	NR MT	EX	VG
Complete Set:	750.00	375.00	225.00
Common Player: 1-132	.30	.15	.09
Common Player: 133-660	.20	.10	.06
Complete Mini Set:	1400.00	700.00	400.00
Common Mini Player:	.40	.20	.12

		NR MT	EX	VG
1	'74 Highlights (Hank Aaron)	35.00	17.50	10.50
2	'74 Highlights (Lou Brock)	2.00	1.00	.60
3	'74 Highlights (Bob Gibson)	1.75	.90	.50
4	'74 Highlights (Al Kaline)	1.75	.90	.50
5	'74 Highlights (Nolan Ryan)	6.00	3.00	1.75
6	'74 Highlights (Mike Marshall)	.40	.20	.12
7	'74 Highlights (Dick Bosman, Steve Busby, Nolan Ryan)	1.00	.50	.30
8	Rogelio Moret	.30	.15	.09
9	Frank Tepedino	.30	.15	.09
10	Willie Davis	.35	.20	.11
11	Bill Melton	.35	.20	.11
12	David Clyde	.35	.20	.11
13	Gene Locklear	.30	.15	.09
14	Milt Wilcox	.35	.20	.11
15	Jose Cardenal	.35	.20	.11
16	Frank Tanana	.40	.20	.12
17	Dave Concepcion	.60	.30	.20
18	Tigers Team (Ralph Houk)	.90	.45	.25
19	Jerry Koosman	.40	.20	.12
20	Thurman Munson	6.00	3.00	1.75
21	Rollie Fingers	4.00	2.00	1.25
22	Dave Cash	.30	.15	.09
23	Bill Russell	.35	.20	.11
24	Al Fitzmorris	.30	.15	.09
25	Lee May	.40	.20	.12
26	Dave McNally	.35	.20	.11
27	Ken Reitz	.30	.15	.09
28	Tom Murphy	.30	.15	.09
29	Dave Parker	15.00	7.50	4.50
30	Bert Blyleven	1.00	.50	.30
31	Dave Rader	.30	.15	.09
32	Reggie Cleveland	.30	.15	.09
33	Dusty Baker	.40	.20	.12
34	Steve Renko	.30	.15	.09
35	Ron Santo	.50	.25	.15
36	Joe Lovitto	.30	.15	.09
37	Dave Freisleben	.30	.15	.09
38	Buddy Bell	.80	.40	.25
39	Andy Thornton	.70	.35	.20
40	Bill Singer	.35	.20	.11
41	Cesar Geronimo	.35	.20	.11
42	Joe Coleman	.35	.20	.11
43	Cleon Jones	.35	.20	.11
44	Pat Dobson	.35	.20	.11
45	Joe Rudi	.40	.20	.12
46	Phillies Team (Danny Ozark)	.80	.40	.25
47	Tommy John	1.25	.60	.40
48	Freddie Patek	.30	.15	.09
49	Larry Dierker	.30	.15	.09
50	Brooks Robinson	5.00	2.50	1.50
51	Bob Forsch	.80	.40	.25
52	Darrell Porter	.35	.20	.11
53	Dave Giusti	.30	.15	.09
54	Eric Soderholm	.30	.15	.09
55	Bobby Bonds	.50	.25	.15
56	Rick Wise	.35	.20	.11
57	Dave Johnson	.80	.40	.25
58	Chuck Taylor	.30	.15	.09
59	Ken Henderson	.30	.15	.09
60	Fergie Jenkins	1.25	.60	.40
61	Dave Winfield	15.00	7.50	4.50
62	Fritz Peterson	.30	.15	.09
63	Steve Swisher	.30	.15	.09
64	Dave Chalk	.30	.15	.09
65	Don Gullett	.35	.20	.11

		NR MT	EX	VG
66	Willie Horton	.35	.20	.11
67	Tug McGraw	.50	.25	.15
68	Ron Blomberg	.35	.20	.11
69	John Odom	.35	.20	.11
70	Mike Schmidt	75.00	38.00	23.00
71	Charlie Hough	.35	.20	.11
72	Royals Team (Jack McKeon)	.80	.40	.25
73	J.R. Richard	.35	.20	.11
74	Mark Belanger	.35	.20	.11
75	Ted Simmons	.70	.35	.20
76	Ed Sprague	.30	.15	.09
77	Richie Zisk	.35	.20	.11
78	Ray Corbin	.30	.15	.09
79	Gary Matthews	.40	.20	.12
80	Carlton Fisk	8.00	4.00	2.50
81	Ron Reed	.35	.20	.11
82	Pat Kelly	.30	.15	.09
83	Jim Merritt	.30	.15	.09
84	Enzo Hernandez	.30	.15	.09
85	Bill Bonham	.30	.15	.09
86	Joe Lis	.30	.15	.09
87	George Foster	1.25	.60	.40
88	Tom Egan	.30	.15	.09
89	Jim Ray	.30	.15	.09
90	Rusty Staub	.60	.30	.20
91	Dick Green	.30	.15	.09
92	Cecil Upshaw	.35	.20	.11
93	Dave Lopes	.40	.20	.12
94	Jim Lonborg	.35	.20	.11
95	John Mayberry	.35	.20	.11
96	Mike Cosgrove	.30	.15	.09
97	Earl Williams	.30	.15	.09
98	Rich Folkers	.30	.15	.09
99	Mike Hegan	.30	.15	.09
100	Willie Stargell	2.50	1.25	.70
101	Expos Team (Gene Mauch)	.80	.40	.25
102	Joe Decker	.30	.15	.09
103	Rick Miller	.30	.15	.09
104	Bill Madlock	1.25	.60	.40
105	Buzz Capra	.30	.15	.09
106	*Mike Hargrove*	.40	.20	.12
107	Jim Barr	.30	.15	.09
108	Tom Hall	.30	.15	.09
109	George Hendrick	.35	.20	.11
110	Wilbur Wood	.35	.20	.11
111	Wayne Garrett	.30	.15	.09
112	Larry Hardy	.30	.15	.09
113	Elliott Maddox	.35	.20	.11
114	Dick Lange	.30	.15	.09
115	Joe Ferguson	.30	.15	.09
116	Lerrin LaGrow	.30	.15	.09
117	Orioles Team (Earl Weaver)	.90	.45	.25
118	Mike Anderson	.30	.15	.09
119	Tommy Helms	.30	.15	.09
120	Steve Busby (photo actually Fran Healy)	.35	.20	.11
121	Bill North	.30	.15	.09
122	Al Hrabosky	.35	.20	.11
123	Johnny Briggs	.30	.15	.09
124	Jerry Reuss	.40	.20	.12
125	Ken Singleton	.40	.20	.12
126	Checklist 1-132	1.50	.70	.45
127	Glen Borgmann	.30	.15	.09
128	Bill Lee	.35	.20	.11
129	Rick Monday	.35	.20	.11
130	Phil Niekro	2.00	1.00	.60
131	Toby Harrah	.35	.20	.11
132	Randy Moffitt	.30	.15	.09
133	Dan Driessen	.30	.15	.09
134	Ron Hodges	.20	.10	.06
135	Charlie Spikes	.20	.10	.06
136	Jim Mason	.25	.13	.08
137	Terry Forster	.30	.15	.09
138	Del Unser	.20	.10	.06
139	Horacio Pina	.20	.10	.06
140	Steve Garvey	6.00	3.00	1.75
141	Mickey Stanley	.25	.13	.08
142	Bob Reynolds	.20	.10	.06
143	*Cliff Johnson*	.40	.20	.12
144	Jim Wohlford	.20	.10	.06
145	Ken Holtzman	.30	.15	.09
146	Padres Team (John McNamara)	.80	.40	.25
147	Pedro Garcia	.20	.10	.06
148	Jim Rooker	.20	.10	.06
149	Tim Foli	.20	.10	.06
150	Bob Gibson	2.50	1.25	.70
151	Steve Brye	.20	.10	.06
152	Mario Guerrero	.20	.10	.06
153	Rick Reuschel	.40	.20	.12
154	Mike Lum	.20	.10	.06
155	Jim Bibby	.20	.10	.06

		NR MT	EX	VG
156	Dave Kingman	.90	.45	.25
157	Pedro Borbon	.20	.10	.06
158	Jerry Grote	.25	.13	.08
159	Steve Arlin	.20	.10	.06
160	Graig Nettles	1.50	.70	.45
161	Stan Bahnsen	.20	.10	.06
162	Willie Montanez	.20	.10	.06
163	Jim Brewer	.20	.10	.06
164	Mickey Rivers	.25	.13	.08
165	Doug Rader	.20	.10	.06
166	Woodie Fryman	.25	.13	.08
167	Rich Coggins	.20	.10	.06
168	Bill Greif	.20	.10	.06
169	Cookie Rojas	.20	.10	.06
170	Bert Campaneris	.40	.20	.12
171	Ed Kirkpatrick	.20	.10	.06
172	Red Sox Team (Darrell Johnson)	1.25	.60	.40
173	Steve Rogers	.30	.15	.09
174	Bake McBride	.25	.13	.08
175	Don Money	.25	.13	.08
176	Burt Hooton	.30	.15	.09
177	Vic Correll	.20	.10	.06
178	Cesar Tovar	.20	.10	.06
179	Tom Bradley	.20	.10	.06
180	Joe Morgan	6.00	3.00	1.75
181	Fred Beene	.20	.10	.06
182	Don Hahn	.20	.10	.06
183	Mel Stottlemyre	.40	.20	.12
184	Jorge Orta	.20	.10	.06
185	Steve Carlton	15.00	7.50	4.50
186	Willie Crawford	.20	.10	.06
187	Denny Doyle	.20	.10	.06
188	Tom Griffin	.20	.10	.06
189	1951 - MVPs (Larry (Yogi) Berra, Roy Campanella)	1.50	.70	.45
190	1952 - MVPs (Hank Sauer, Bobby Shantz)	.40	.20	.12
191	1953 - MVPs (Roy Campanella, Al Rosen)	.90	.45	.25
192	1954 - MVPs (Yogi Berra, Willie Mays)	1.50	.70	.45
193	1955 - MVPs (Yogi Berra, Roy Campanella)	1.50	.70	.45
194	1956 - MVPs (Mickey Mantle, Don Newcombe)	12.00	6.00	3.50
195	1957 - MVPs (Hank Aaron, Mickey Mantle)	12.00	6.00	3.50
196	1958 - MVPs (Ernie Banks, Jackie Jensen)	.90	.45	.25
197	1959 - MVPs (Ernie Banks, Nellie Fox)	.90	.45	.25
198	1960 - MVPs (Dick Groat, Roger Maris)	1.25	.60	.40
199	1961 - MVPs (Roger Maris, Frank Robinson)	1.50	.70	.45
200	1962 - MVPs (Mickey Mantle, Maury Wills)	12.00	6.00	3.50
201	1963 - MVPs (Elston Howard, Sandy Koufax)	1.50	.70	.45
202	1964 - MVPs (Ken Boyer, Brooks Robinson)	1.25	.60	.40
203	1965 - MVPs (Willie Mays. Zoilo Versalles)	1.25	.60	.40
204	1966 - MVPs (Bob Clemente, Frank Robinson)	1.50	.70	.45
205	1967 - MVPs (Orlando Cepeda, Carl Yastrzemski)	1.25	.60	.40
206	1968 - MVPs (Bob Gibson, Denny McLain)	1.25	.60	.40
207	1969 - MVPs (Harmon Killebrew, Willie McCovey)	1.50	.70	.45
208	1970 - MVPs (Johnny Bench, Boog Powell)	1.25	.60	.40
209	1971 - MVPs (Vida Blue, Joe Torre)	.50	.25	.15
210	1972 - MVPs (Rich Allen, Johnny Bench)	1.25	.60	.40
211	1973 - MVPs (Reggie Jackson, Pete Rose)	4.00	2.00	1.25
212	1974 - MVPs (Jeff Burroughs, Steve Garvey)	.90	.45	.25
213	Oscar Gamble	.25	.13	.08
214	Harry Parker	.20	.10	.06
215	Bobby Valentine	.30	.15	.09
216	Giants Team (Wes Westrum)	.80	.40	.25
217	Lou Piniella	.70	.35	.20
218	Jerry Johnson	.20	.10	.06
219	Ed Herrmann	.20	.10	.06
220	Don Sutton	1.50	.70	.45
221	Aurelio Rodriguez (Rodriguez)	.25	.13	.08
222	Dan Spillner	.20	.10	.06
223	*Robin Yount*	200.00	100.00	60.00

		NR MT	EX	VG
224	Ramon Hernandez	.20	.10	.06
225	Bob Grich	.40	.20	.12
226	Bill Campbell	.25	.13	.08
227	Bob Watson	.25	.13	.08
228	*George Brett*	200.00	100.00	60.00
229	Barry Foote	.20	.10	.06
230	Jim Hunter	2.00	1.00	.60
231	Mike Tyson	.20	.10	.06
232	Diego Segui	.20	.10	.06
233	Billy Grabarkewitz	.20	.10	.06
234	Tom Grieve	.20	.10	.06
235	Jack Billingham	.20	.10	.06
236	Angels Team (Dick Williams)	.80	.40	.25
237	Carl Morton	.20	.10	.06
238	Dave Duncan	.20	.10	.06
239	George Stone	.20	.10	.06
240	Garry Maddox	.25	.13	.08
241	Dick Tidrow	.25	.13	.08
242	Jay Johnstone	.25	.13	.08
243	Jim Kaat	1.25	.60	.40
244	Bill Buckner	.50	.25	.15
245	Mickey Lolich	.50	.25	.15
246	Cardinals Team (Red Schoendienst)	.80	.40	.25
247	Enos Cabell	.25	.13	.08
248	Randy Jones	.25	.13	.08
249	Danny Thompson	.25	.13	.08
250	Ken Brett	.25	.13	.08
251	Fran Healy	.20	.10	.06
252	Fred Scherman	.20	.10	.06
253	Jesus Alou	.25	.13	.08
254	Mike Torrez	.25	.13	.08
255	Dwight Evans	5.00	2.50	1.50
256	Billy Champion	.20	.10	.06
257	Checklist 133-264	1.50	.70	.45
258	Dave LaRoche	.20	.10	.06
259	Len Randle	.20	.10	.06
260	Johnny Bench	10.00	5.00	3.00
261	Andy Hassler	.20	.10	.06
262	Rowland Office	.20	.10	.06
263	Jim Perry	.40	.20	.12
264	John Milner	.20	.10	.06
265	Ron Bryant	.20	.10	.06
266	Sandy Alomar	.25	.13	.08
267	Dick Ruthven	.20	.10	.06
268	Hal McRae	.40	.20	.12
269	Doug Rau	.20	.10	.06
270	Ron Fairly	.30	.15	.09
271	Jerry Moses	.20	.10	.06
272	Lynn McGlothen	.20	.10	.06
273	Steve Braun	.20	.10	.06
274	Vicente Romo	.20	.10	.06
275	Paul Blair	.25	.13	.08
276	White Sox Team (Chuck Tanner)	.80	.40	.25
277	Frank Taveras	.20	.10	.06
278	Paul Lindblad	.20	.10	.06
279	Milt May	.20	.10	.06
280	Carl Yastrzemski	10.00	5.00	3.00
281	Jim Slaton	.20	.10	.06
282	Jerry Morales	.20	.10	.06
283	Steve Foucault	.20	.10	.06
284	Ken Griffey	.70	.35	.20
285	Ellie Rodriguez	.20	.10	.06
286	Mike Jorgensen	.20	.10	.06
287	Roric Harrison	.20	.10	.06
288	Bruce Ellingsen	.20	.10	.06
289	Ken Rudolph	.20	.10	.06
290	Jon Matlack	.25	.13	.08
291	Bill Sudakis	.25	.13	.08
292	Ron Schueler	.20	.10	.06
293	Dick Sharon	.20	.10	.06
294	*Geoff Zahn*	.40	.20	.12
295	Vada Pinson	.60	.30	.20
296	Alan Foster	.20	.10	.06
297	Craig Kusick	.20	.10	.06
298	Johnny Grubb	.20	.10	.06
299	Bucky Dent	.40	.20	.12
300	Reggie Jackson	15.00	7.50	4.50
301	Dave Roberts	.20	.10	.06
302	*Rick Burleson*	.50	.25	.15
303	Grant Jackson	.20	.10	.06
304	Pirates Team (Danny Murtaugh)	.80	.40	.25
305	Jim Colborn	.20	.10	.06
306	Batting Leaders (Rod Carew, Ralph Garr)	.80	.40	.25
307	Home Run Leaders (Dick Allen, Mike Schmidt)	.90	.45	.25
308	Runs Batted In Leaders (Johnny Bench, Jeff Burroughs)	.90	.45	.25
309	Stolen Base Leaders (Lou Brock, Bill North)	.80	.40	.25

	NR MT	EX	VG
310 Victory Leaders (Jim Hunter, Fergie Jenkins, Andy Messersmith, Phil Niekro)	.80	.40	.25
311 Earned Run Average Leaders (Buzz Capra, Jim Hunter)	.50	.25	.15
312 Strikeout Leaders (Steve Carlton, Nolan Ryan)	2.50	1.25	.70
313 Leading Firemen (Terry Forster, Mike Marshall)	.50	.25	.15
314 Buck Martinez	.20	.10	.06
315 Don Kessinger	.25	.13	.08
316 Jackie Brown	.20	.10	.06
317 Joe Lahoud	.20	.10	.06
318 Ernie McAnally	.20	.10	.06
319 Johnny Oates	.20	.10	.06
320 Pete Rose	18.00	9.00	5.50
321 Rudy May	.25	.13	.08
322 Ed Goodson	.20	.10	.06
323 Fred Holdsworth	.20	.10	.06
324 Ed Kranepool	.30	.15	.09
325 Tony Oliva	.80	.40	.25
326 Wayne Twitchell	.20	.10	.06
327 Jerry Hairston	.20	.10	.06
328 Sonny Siebert	.20	.10	.06
329 Ted Kubiak	.20	.10	.06
330 Mike Marshall	.30	.15	.09
331 Indians Team (Frank Robinson)	.90	.45	.25
332 Fred Kendall	.20	.10	.06
333 Dick Drago	.20	.10	.06
334 *Greg Scott*	.30	.15	.09
335 Jim Palmer	6.00	3.00	1.75
336 Rennie Stennett	.20	.10	.06
337 Kevin Kobel	.20	.10	.06
338 Rick Stelmaszek	.20	.10	.06
339 Jim Fregosi	.40	.20	.12
340 Paul Splittorff	.25	.13	.08
341 Hal Breeden	.20	.10	.06
342 Leroy Stanton	.20	.10	.06
343 Danny Frisella	.20	.10	.06
344 Ben Oglivie	.30	.15	.09
345 Clay Carroll	.25	.13	.08
346 Bobby Darwin	.20	.10	.06
347 Mike Caldwell	.20	.10	.06
348 Tony Muser	.20	.10	.06
349 Ray Sadecki	.20	.10	.06
350 Bobby Murcer	.40	.20	.12
351 Bob Boone	.40	.20	.12
352 Darold Knowles	.20	.10	.06
353 Luis Melendez	.20	.10	.06
354 Dick Bosman	.20	.10	.06
355 Chris Cannizzaro	.20	.10	.06
356 Rico Petrocelli	.30	.15	.09
357 Ken Forsch	.25	.13	.08
358 Al Bumbry	.25	.13	.08
359 Paul Popovich	.20	.10	.06
360 George Scott	.30	.15	.09
361 Dodgers Team (Walter Alston)	1.00	.50	.30
362 Steve Hargan	.20	.10	.06
363 Carmen Fanzone	.20	.10	.06
364 Doug Bird	.20	.10	.06
365 Bob Bailey	.20	.10	.06
366 Ken Sanders	.20	.10	.06
367 Craig Robinson	.20	.10	.06
368 Vic Albury	.20	.10	.06
369 Merv Rettenmund	.20	.10	.06
370 Tom Seaver	15.00	7.50	4.50
371 Gates Brown	.20	.10	.06
372 John D'Acquisto	.20	.10	.06
373 Bill Sharp	.20	.10	.06
374 Eddie Watt	.20	.10	.06
375 Roy White	.40	.20	.12
376 Steve Yeager	.20	.10	.06
377 Tom Hilgendorf	.20	.10	.06
378 Derrel Thomas	.20	.10	.06
379 Bernie Carbo	.20	.10	.06
380 Sal Bando	.40	.20	.12
381 John Curtis	.20	.10	.06
382 Don Baylor	.60	.30	.20
383 Jim York	.20	.10	.06
384 Brewers Team (Del Crandall)	.80	.40	.25
385 Dock Ellis	.25	.13	.08
386 Checklist 265-396	1.50	.70	.45
387 Jim Spencer	.20	.10	.06
388 Steve Stone	.30	.15	.09
389 Tony Solaita	.20	.10	.06
390 Ron Cey	.40	.20	.12
391 Don DeMola	.20	.10	.06
392 Bruce Bochte	.40	.20	.12
393 Gary Gentry	.20	.10	.06
394 Larvell Blanks	.20	.10	.06
395 Bud Harrelson	.25	.13	.08

	NR MT	EX	VG
396 Fred Norman	.20	.10	.06
397 Bill Freehan	.40	.20	.12
398 Elias Sosa	.20	.10	.06
399 Terry Harmon	.20	.10	.06
400 Dick Allen	.80	.40	.25
401 Mike Wallace	.25	.13	.08
402 Bob Tolan	.25	.13	.08
403 Tom Buskey	.20	.10	.06
404 Ted Sizemore	.20	.10	.06
405 John Montague	.20	.10	.06
406 Bob Gallagher	.20	.10	.06
407 *Herb Washington*	.30	.15	.09
408 Clyde Wright	.20	.10	.06
409 Bob Robertson	.20	.10	.06
410 Mike Cueller (Cuellar)	.40	.20	.12
411 George Mitterwald	.20	.10	.06
412 Bill Hands	.20	.10	.06
413 Marty Pattin	.20	.10	.06
414 Manny Mota	.30	.15	.09
415 John Hiller	.25	.13	.08
416 Larry Lintz	.20	.10	.06
417 Skip Lockwood	.20	.10	.06
418 Leo Foster	.20	.10	.06
419 Dave Goltz	.25	.13	.08
420 Larry Bowa	.40	.20	.12
421 Mets Team (Yogi Berra)	1.00	.50	.30
422 Brian Downing	.30	.15	.09
423 Clay Kirby	.20	.10	.06
424 John Lowenstein	.20	.10	.06
425 Tito Fuentes	.20	.10	.06
426 George Medich	.25	.13	.08
427 Clarence Gaston	.20	.10	.06
428 Dave Hamilton	.20	.10	.06
429 *Jim Dwyer*	.30	.15	.09
430 Luis Tiant	.50	.25	.15
431 Rod Gilbreath	.20	.10	.06
432 Ken Berry	.20	.10	.06
433 Larry Demery	.20	.10	.06
434 Bob Locker	.20	.10	.06
435 Dave Nelson	.20	.10	.06
436 Ken Frailing	.20	.10	.06
437 *Al Cowens*	.40	.20	.12
438 Don Carrithers	.20	.10	.06
439 Ed Brinkman	.25	.13	.08
440 Andy Messersmith	.30	.15	.09
441 Bobby Heise	.20	.10	.06
442 Maximino Leon	.20	.10	.06
443 Twins Team (Frank Quilici)	.80	.40	.25
444 Gene Garber	.25	.13	.08
445 Felix Millan	.20	.10	.06
446 Bart Johnson	.20	.10	.06
447 Terry Crowley	.20	.10	.06
448 Frank Duffy	.20	.10	.06
449 Charlie Williams	.20	.10	.06
450 Willie McCovey	3.00	1.50	.90
451 Rick Dempsey	.40	.20	.12
452 Angel Mangual	.20	.10	.06
453 Claude Osteen	.30	.15	.09
454 Doug Griffin	.20	.10	.06
455 Don Wilson	.20	.10	.06
456 Bob Coluccio	.20	.10	.06
457 Mario Mendoza	.20	.10	.06
458 Ross Grimsley	.25	.13	.08
459 A.L. Championships	.80	.40	.25
460 N.L. Championships	.80	.40	.25
461 World Series Game 1	1.50	.70	.45
462 World Series Game 2	.80	.40	.25
463 World Series Game 3	1.00	.50	.30
464 World Series Game 4	.80	.40	.25
465 World Series Game 5	.80	.40	.25
466 World Series Summary	.80	.40	.25
467 Ed Halicki	.20	.10	.06
468 Bobby Mitchell	.20	.10	.06
469 Tom Dettore	.20	.10	.06
470 Jeff Burroughs	.30	.15	.09
471 Bob Stinson	.20	.10	.06
472 Bruce Dal Canton	.20	.10	.06
473 Ken McMullen	.20	.10	.06
474 Luke Walker	.20	.10	.06
475 Darrell Evans	.60	.30	.20
476 *Ed Figueroa*	.30	.15	.09
477 Tom Hutton	.20	.10	.06
478 Tom Burgmeier	.20	.10	.06
479 Ken Boswell	.20	.10	.06
480 Carlos May	.25	.13	.08
481 *Will McEnaney*	.30	.15	.09
482 Tom McCraw	.20	.10	.06
483 Steve Ontiveros	.20	.10	.06
484 Glenn Beckert	.30	.15	.09
485 Sparky Lyle	.40	.20	.12
486 Ray Fosse	.20	.10	.06

		NR MT	EX	VG
487	Astros Team (Preston Gomez)	.80	.40	.25
488	Bill Travers	.20	.10	.06
489	Cecil Cooper	1.00	.50	.30
490	Reggie Smith	.30	.15	.09
491	Doyle Alexander	.40	.20	.12
492	Rich Hebner	.25	.13	.08
493	Don Stanhouse	.20	.10	.06
494	Pete LaCock	.25	.13	.08
495	Nelson Briles	.20	.10	.06
496	Pepe Frias	.20	.10	.06
497	Jim Nettles	.20	.10	.06
498	Al Downing	.25	.13	.08
499	Marty Perez	.20	.10	.06
500	Nolan Ryan	40.00	20.00	12.00
501	Bill Robinson	.20	.10	.06
502	Pat Bourque	.20	.10	.06
503	Fred Stanley	.25	.13	.08
504	Buddy Bradford	.20	.10	.06
505	Chris Speier	.25	.13	.08
506	Leron Lee	.20	.10	.06
507	Tom Carroll	.20	.10	.06
508	Bob Hansen	.20	.10	.06
509	Dave Hilton	.20	.10	.06
510	Vida Blue	.50	.25	.15
511	Rangers Team (Billy Martin)	.90	.45	.25
512	Larry Milbourne	.20	.10	.06
513	Dick Pole	.20	.10	.06
514	Jose Cruz	.50	.25	.15
515	Manny Sanguillen	.25	.13	.08
516	Don Hood	.20	.10	.06
517	Checklist 397-528	1.25	.60	.40
518	Leo Cardenas	.20	.10	.06
519	Jim Todd	.20	.10	.06
520	Amos Otis	.30	.15	.09
521	Dennis Blair	.20	.10	.06
522	Gary Sutherland	.20	.10	.06
523	Tom Paciorek	.25	.13	.08
524	John Doherty	.20	.10	.06
525	Tom House	.20	.10	.06
526	Larry Hisle	.25	.13	.08
527	Mac Scarce	.20	.10	.06
528	Eddie Leon	.20	.10	.06
529	Gary Thomasson	.20	.10	.06
530	Gaylord Perry	2.25	1.25	.70
531	Reds Team (Sparky Anderson)	.90	.45	.25
532	Gorman Thomas	.60	.30	.20
533	Rudy Meoli	.20	.10	.06
534	Alex Johnson	.25	.13	.08
535	Gene Tenace	.25	.13	.08
536	Bob Moose	.20	.10	.06
537	Tommy Harper	.25	.13	.08
538	Duffy Dyer	.20	.10	.06
539	Jesse Jefferson	.20	.10	.06
540	Lou Brock	3.00	1.50	.90
541	Roger Metzger	.20	.10	.06
542	Pete Broberg	.20	.10	.06
543	Larry Biittner	.20	.10	.06
544	Steve Mingori	.20	.10	.06
545	Billy Williams	2.25	1.25	.70
546	John Knox	.20	.10	.06
547	Von Joshua	.20	.10	.06
548	Charlie Sands	.20	.10	.06
549	Bill Butler	.20	.10	.06
550	Ralph Garr	.25	.13	.08
551	Larry Christenson	.20	.10	.06
552	Jack Brohamer	.20	.10	.06
553	John Boccabella	.20	.10	.06
554	Rich Gossage	1.25	.60	.40
555	Al Oliver	.80	.40	.25
556	Tim Johnson	.20	.10	.06
557	Larry Gura	.25	.13	.08
558	Dave Roberts	.20	.10	.06
559	Bob Montgomery	.20	.10	.06
560	Tony Perez	1.00	.50	.30
561	A's Team (Alvin Dark)	.90	.45	.25
562	Gary Nolan	.20	.10	.06
563	Wilbur Howard	.20	.10	.06
564	Tommy Davis	.40	.20	.12
565	Joe Torre	.70	.35	.20
566	Ray Burris	.20	.10	.06
567	Jim Sundberg	.70	.35	.20
568	Dale Murray	.20	.10	.06
569	Frank White	.40	.20	.12
570	Jim Wynn	.30	.15	.09
571	Dave Lemanczyk	.20	.10	.06
572	Roger Nelson	.20	.10	.06
573	Orlando Pena	.20	.10	.06
574	Tony Taylor	.20	.10	.06
575	Gene Clines	.20	.10	.06
576	Phil Roof	.20	.10	.06
577	John Morris	.20	.10	.06

		NR MT	EX	VG
578	Dave Tomlin	.20	.10	.06
579	Skip Pitlock	.20	.10	.06
580	Frank Robinson	3.00	1.50	.90
581	Darrel Chaney	.20	.10	.06
582	Eduardo Rodriguez	.20	.10	.06
583	Andy Etchebarren	.20	.10	.06
584	Mike Garman	.20	.10	.06
585	Chris Chambliss	.40	.20	.12
586	Tim McCarver	.60	.30	.20
587	Chris Ward	.20	.10	.06
588	Rick Auerbach	.20	.10	.06
589	Braves Team (Clyde King)	.80	.40	.25
590	Cesar Cedeno	.40	.20	.12
591	Glenn Abbott	.20	.10	.06
592	Balor Moore	.20	.10	.06
593	Gene Lamont	.20	.10	.06
594	Jim Fuller	.20	.10	.06
595	Joe Niekro	.40	.20	.12
596	Ollie Brown	.20	.10	.06
597	Winston Llenas	.20	.10	.06
598	Bruce Kison	.20	.10	.06
599	Nate Colbert	.20	.10	.06
600	Rod Carew	7.00	3.50	2.00
601	Juan Beniquez	.30	.15	.09
602	John Vukovich	.20	.10	.06
603	Lew Krausse	.20	.10	.06
604	Oscar Zamora	.20	.10	.06
605	John Ellis	.20	.10	.06
606	Bruce Miller	.20	.10	.06
607	Jim Holt	.20	.10	.06
608	Gene Michael	.30	.15	.09
609	Ellie Hendricks	.20	.10	.06
610	Ron Hunt	.25	.13	.08
611	Yankees Team (Bill Virdon)	1.25	.60	.40
612	Terry Hughes	.20	.10	.06
613	Bill Parsons	.20	.10	.06
614	Rookie Pitchers (Jack Kucek, Dyar Miller, Vern Ruhle, Paul Siebert)	.20	.10	.06
615	Rookie Pitchers (Pat Darcy, Dennis Leonard, Tom Underwood, Hank Webb)	.60	.30	.20
616	Rookie Outfielders (Dave Augustine, Pepe Mangual, Jim Rice, John Scott)	30.00	15.00	9.00
617	Rookie Infielders (Mike Cubbage, Doug DeCinces, Reggie Sanders, Manny Trillo)	1.25	.60	.40
618	Rookie Pitchers (Jamie Easterly, Tom Johnson, Scott McGregor, Rick Rhoden)	2.25	1.25	.70
619	Rookie Outfielders (Benny Ayala, Nyls Nyman, Tommy Smith, Jerry Turner)	.20	.10	.06
620	Rookie Catchers-Outfielders (Gary Carter, Marc Hill, Danny Meyer, Leon Roberts)	35.00	17.50	10.50
621	Rookie Pitchers (John Denny, Rawly Eastwick, Jim Kern, Juan Veintidos)	.60	.30	.20
622	Rookie Outfielders (Ed Armbrister, Fred Lynn, Tom Poquette, Terry Whitfield)	12.00	6.00	3.50
623	Rookie Infielders (Phil Garner, Keith Hernandez, Bob Sheldon, Tom Veryzer)	20.00	10.00	6.00
624	Rookie Pitchers (Doug Konieczny, Gary Lavelle, Jim Otten, Eddie Solomon)	.30	.15	.09
625	Boog Powell	.70	.35	.20
626	Larry Haney	.20	.10	.06
627	Tom Walker	.20	.10	.06
628	Ron LeFlore	.80	.40	.25
629	Joe Hoerner	.20	.10	.06
630	Greg Luzinski	.70	.35	.20
631	Lee Lacy	.25	.13	.08
632	Morris Nettles	.20	.10	.06
633	Paul Casanova	.20	.10	.06
634	Cy Acosta	.20	.10	.06
635	Chuck Dobson	.20	.10	.06
636	Charlie Moore	.25	.13	.08
637	Ted Martinez	.20	.10	.06
638	Cubs Team (Jim Marshall)	.80	.40	.25
639	Steve Kline	.20	.10	.06
640	Harmon Killebrew	3.50	1.75	1.00
641	Jim Northrup	.25	.13	.08
642	Mike Phillips	.20	.10	.06
643	Brent Strom	.20	.10	.06
644	Bill Fahey	.20	.10	.06
645	Danny Cater	.20	.10	.06
646	Checklist 529-660	1.50	.70	.45
647	Claudell Washington	2.50	1.25	.70
648	Dave Pagan	.25	.13	.08
649	Jack Heidemann	.20	.10	.06
650	Dave May	.20	.10	.06
651	John Morlan	.20	.10	.06

		NR MT	EX	VG
652	Lindy McDaniel	.20	.10	.06
653	Lee Richards	.20	.10	.06
654	Jerry Terrell	.20	.10	.06
655	Rico Carty	.40	.20	.12
656	Bill Plummer	.20	.10	.06
657	Bob Oliver	.20	.10	.06
658	Vic Harris	.20	.10	.06
659	Bob Apodaca	.20	.10	.06
660	Hank Aaron	30.00	15.00	9.00

1975 Topps Mini

 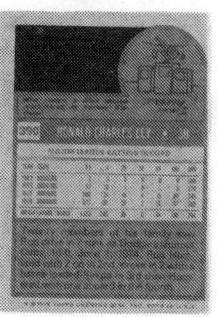

One of the most popular Topps sets of the 1970s is really a test issue. The Topps Minis measure 2-1/4" by 3-1/8," exactly 20" smaller than the regular card size. Other than their size, the Minis are in every way the same as the regular cards. The experiment primarily took place in parts of Michigan and the West Coast, where the Minis were snapped up quickly by collectors.

		NR MT	EX	VG
Complete Set:		1200.00	600.00	350.00
Common Player:		.40	.20	.12
1	'74 Highlights (Hank Aaron)	25.00	12.50	7.50
2	'74 Highlights (Lou Brock)	3.50	1.75	1.00
3	'74 Highlights (Bob Gibson)	3.25	1.75	1.00
4	'74 Highlights (Al Kaline)	3.25	1.75	1.00
5	'74 Highlights (Nolan Ryan)	3.25	1.75	1.00
6	'74 Highlights (Mike Marshall)	.60	.30	.20
7	'74 Highlights (Dick Bosman, Steve Busby, Nolan Ryan)	1.50	.70	.45
8	Rogelio Moret	.40	.20	.12
9	Frank Tepedino	.40	.20	.12
10	Willie Davis	.60	.30	.20
11	Bill Melton	.40	.20	.12
12	David Clyde	.40	.20	.12
13	Gene Locklear	.40	.20	.12
14	Milt Wilcox	.40	.20	.12
15	Jose Cardenal	.40	.20	.12
16	Frank Tanana	.60	.30	.20
17	Dave Concepcion	.90	.45	.25
18	Tigers Team (Ralph Houk)	1.25	.60	.40
19	Jerry Koosman	.40	.20	.12
20	Thurman Munson	10.00	5.00	3.00
21	Rollie Fingers	3.00	1.50	.90
22	Dave Cash	.40	.20	.12
23	Bill Russell	.60	.30	.20
24	Al Fitzmorris	.40	.20	.12
25	Lee May	.60	.30	.20
26	Dave McNally	.60	.30	.20
27	Ken Reitz	.40	.20	.12
28	Tom Murphy	.40	.20	.12
29	Dave Parker	10.00	5.00	3.00
30	Bert Blyleven	2.00	1.00	.60
31	Dave Rader	.40	.20	.12
32	Reggie Cleveland	.40	.20	.12
33	Dusty Baker	.60	.30	.20
34	Steve Renko	.40	.20	.12
35	Ron Santo	.80	.40	.25
36	Joe Lovitto	.40	.20	.12
37	Dave Freisleben	.40	.20	.12
38	Buddy Bell	1.50	.70	.45
39	Andy Thornton	1.00	.50	.30
40	Bill Singer	.40	.20	.12
41	Cesar Geronimo	.40	.20	.12
42	Joe Coleman	.40	.20	.12

		NR MT	EX	VG
43	Cleon Jones	.40	.20	.12
44	Pat Dobson	.40	.20	.12
45	Joe Rudi	.60	.30	.20
46	Phillies Team (Danny Ozark)	1.25	.60	.40
47	Tommy John	2.50	1.25	.70
48	Freddie Patek	.40	.20	.12
49	Larry Dierker	.40	.20	.12
50	Brooks Robinson	7.00	3.50	2.00
51	Bob Forsch	1.25	.60	.40
52	Darrell Porter	.60	.30	.20
53	Dave Giusti	.40	.20	.12
54	Eric Soderholm	.40	.20	.12
55	Bobby Bonds	.80	.40	.25
56	Rick Wise	.60	.30	.20
57	Dave Johnson	1.25	.60	.40
58	Chuck Taylor	.40	.20	.12
59	Ken Henderson	.40	.20	.12
60	Fergie Jenkins	1.75	.90	.50
61	Dave Winfield	20.00	10.00	6.00
62	Fritz Peterson	.40	.20	.12
63	Steve Swisher	.40	.20	.12
64	Dave Chalk	.40	.20	.12
65	Don Gullett	.40	.20	.12
66	Willie Horton	.60	.30	.20
67	Tug McGraw	.80	.40	.25
68	Ron Blomberg	.40	.20	.12
69	John Odom	.40	.20	.12
70	Mike Schmidt	80.00	40.00	25.00
71	Charlie Hough	.60	.30	.20
72	Royals Team (Jack McKeon)	1.25	.60	.40
73	J.R. Richard	.60	.30	.20
74	Mark Belanger	.60	.30	.20
75	Ted Simmons	1.00	.50	.30
76	Ed Sprague	.40	.20	.12
77	Richie Zisk	.60	.30	.20
78	Ray Corbin	.40	.20	.12
79	Gary Matthews	.60	.30	.20
80	Carlton Fisk	7.00	3.50	2.00
81	Ron Reed	.40	.20	.12
82	Pat Kelly	.40	.20	.12
83	Jim Merritt	.40	.20	.12
84	Enzo Hernandez	.40	.20	.12
85	Bill Bonham	.40	.20	.12
86	Joe Lis	.40	.20	.12
87	George Foster	1.75	.90	.50
88	Tom Egan	.40	.20	.12
89	Jim Ray	.40	.20	.12
90	Rusty Staub	.90	.45	.25
91	Dick Green	.40	.20	.12
92	Cecil Upshaw	.40	.20	.12
93	Dave Lopes	.60	.30	.20
94	Jim Lonborg	.40	.20	.12
95	John Mayberry	.40	.20	.12
96	Mike Cosgrove	.40	.20	.12
97	Earl Williams	.40	.20	.12
98	Rich Folkers	.40	.20	.12
99	Mike Hegan	.40	.20	.12
100	Willie Stargell	7.00	3.50	2.00
101	Expos Team (Gene Mauch)	1.25	.60	.40
102	Joe Decker	.40	.20	.12
103	Rick Miller	.40	.20	.12
104	Bill Madlock	2.00	1.00	.60
105	Buzz Capra	.40	.20	.12
106	Mike Hargrove	.60	.30	.20
107	Jim Barr	.40	.20	.12
108	Tom Hall	.40	.20	.12
109	George Hendrick	.40	.20	.12
110	Wilbur Wood	.40	.20	.12
111	Wayne Garrett	.40	.20	.12
112	Larry Hardy	.40	.20	.12
113	Elliott Maddox	.40	.20	.12
114	Dick Lange	.40	.20	.12
115	Joe Ferguson	.40	.20	.12
116	Lerrin LaGrow	.40	.20	.12
117	Orioles Team (Earl Weaver)	1.25	.60	.40
118	Mike Anderson	.40	.20	.12
119	Tommy Helms	.40	.20	.12
120	Steve Busby (photo actually Fran Healy)	.40	.20	.12
121	Bill North	.40	.20	.12
122	Al Hrabosky	.40	.20	.12
123	Johnny Briggs	.40	.20	.12
124	Jerry Reuss	.60	.30	.20
125	Ken Singleton	.60	.30	.20
126	Checklist 1-132	2.25	1.25	.70
127	Glen Borgmann	.40	.20	.12
128	Bill Lee	.60	.30	.20
129	Rick Monday	.60	.30	.20
130	Phil Niekro	4.00	2.00	1.25
131	Toby Harrah	.40	.20	.12
132	Randy Moffitt	.40	.20	.12

#	Name	NR MT	EX	VG
133	Dan Driessen	.60	.30	.20
134	Ron Hodges	.40	.20	.12
135	Charlie Spikes	.40	.20	.12
136	Jim Mason	.40	.20	.12
137	Terry Forster	.40	.20	.12
138	Del Unser	.40	.20	.12
139	Horacio Pina	.40	.20	.12
140	Steve Garvey	12.00	6.00	3.50
141	Mickey Stanley	.40	.20	.12
142	Bob Reynolds	.40	.20	.12
143	Cliff Johnson	.40	.20	.12
144	Jim Wohlford	.40	.20	.12
145	Ken Holtzman	.60	.30	.20
146	Padres Team (John McNamara)	1.25	.60	.40
147	Pedro Garcia	.40	.20	.12
148	Jim Rooker	.40	.20	.12
149	Tim Foli	.40	.20	.12
150	Bob Gibson	7.00	3.50	2.00
151	Steve Brye	.40	.20	.12
152	Mario Guerrero	.40	.20	.12
153	Rick Reuschel	.60	.30	.20
154	Mike Lum	.40	.20	.12
155	Jim Bibby	.40	.20	.12
156	Dave Kingman	1.50	.70	.45
157	Pedro Borbon	.40	.20	.12
158	Jerry Grote	.40	.20	.12
159	Steve Arlin	.40	.20	.12
160	Graig Nettles	2.25	1.25	.70
161	Stan Bahnsen	.40	.20	.12
162	Willie Montanez	.40	.20	.12
163	Jim Brewer	.40	.20	.12
164	Mickey Rivers	.60	.30	.20
165	Doug Rader	.40	.20	.12
166	Woodie Fryman	.40	.20	.12
167	Rich Coggins	.40	.20	.12
168	Bill Greif	.40	.20	.12
169	Cookie Rojas	.40	.20	.12
170	Bert Campaneris	.60	.30	.20
171	Ed Kirkpatrick	.40	.20	.12
172	Red Sox Team (Darrell Johnson)	1.25	.60	.40
173	Steve Rogers	.40	.20	.12
174	Bake McBride	.40	.20	.12
175	Don Money	.40	.20	.12
176	Burt Hooton	.40	.20	.12
177	Vic Correll	.40	.20	.12
178	Cesar Tovar	.40	.20	.12
179	Tom Bradley	.40	.20	.12
180	Joe Morgan	10.00	5.00	3.00
181	Fred Beene	.40	.20	.12
182	Don Hahn	.40	.20	.12
183	Mel Stottlemyre	.60	.30	.20
184	Jorge Orta	.40	.20	.12
185	Steve Carlton	20.00	10.00	6.00
186	Willie Crawford	.40	.20	.12
187	Denny Doyle	.40	.20	.12
188	Tom Griffin	.40	.20	.12
189	1951-MVPs (Larry (Yogi) Berra, Roy Campanella)	2.25	1.25	.70
190	1952-MVPs (Hank Sauer, Bobby Shantz)	.60	.30	.20
191	1953-MVPs (Roy Campanella, Al Rosen)	1.25	.60	.40
192	1954-MVPs (Yogi Berra, Willie Mays)	2.25	1.25	.70
193	1955-MVPs (Yogi Berra, Roy Campanella)	2.25	1.25	.70
194	1956-MVPs (Mickey Mantle, Don Newcombe)	9.00	4.50	2.75
195	1957-MVPs (Hank Aaron, Mickey Mantle)	10.00	5.00	3.00
196	1958-MVPs (Ernie Banks, Jackie Jensen)	1.25	.60	.40
197	1959-MVPs (Ernie Banks, Nellie Fox)	1.25	.60	.40
198	1960-MVPs (Dick Groat, Roger Maris)	1.75	.90	.50
199	1961-MVPs (Roger Maris, Frank Robinson)	2.25	1.25	.70
200	1962-MVPs (Mickey Mantle, Maury Wills)	9.00	4.50	2.75
201	1963-MVPs (Elston Howard, Sandy Koufax)	2.25	1.25	.70
202	1964-MVPs (Ken Boyer, Brooks Robinson)	1.75	.90	.50
203	1965-MVPs (Willie Mays, Zoilo Versalles)	1.75	.90	.50
204	1966-MVPs (Bob Clemente, Frank Robinson)	2.25	1.25	.70
205	1967-MVPs (Orlando Cepeda, Carl Yastrzemski)	1.75	.90	.50
206	1968-MVPs (Bob Gibson, Denny McLain)	1.75	.90	.50
207	1969-MVPs (Harmon Killebrew, Willie McCovey)	2.25	1.25	.70
208	1970-MVPs (Johnny Bench, Boog Powell)	1.75	.90	.50
209	1971-MVPs (Vida Blue, Joe Torre)	.80	.40	.25
210	1972-MVPs (Rich Allen, Johnny Bench)	1.75	.90	.50
211	1973-MVPs (Reggie Jackson, Pete Rose)	7.00	3.50	2.00
212	1974-MVPs (Jeff Burroughs, Steve Garvey)	1.25	.60	.40
213	Oscar Gamble	.40	.20	.12
214	Harry Parker	.40	.20	.12
215	Bobby Valentine	.40	.20	.12
216	Giants Team (Wes Westrum)	1.25	.60	.40
217	Lou Piniella	.80	.40	.25
218	Jerry Johnson	.40	.20	.12
219	Ed Herrmann	.40	.20	.12
220	Don Sutton	3.00	1.50	.90
221	Aurelio Rodriquez (Rodriguez)	.40	.20	.12
222	Dan Spillner	.40	.20	.12
223	Robin Yount	200.00	100.00	60.00
224	Ramon Hernandez	.40	.20	.12
225	Bob Grich	.60	.30	.20
226	Bill Campbell	.40	.20	.12
227	Bob Watson	.40	.20	.12
228	George Brett	150.00	75.00	45.00
229	Barry Foote	.40	.20	.12
230	Jim Hunter	4.00	2.00	1.25
231	Mike Tyson	.40	.20	.12
232	Diego Segui	.40	.20	.12
233	Billy Grabarkewitz	.40	.20	.12
234	Tom Grieve	.40	.20	.12
235	Jack Billingham	.40	.20	.12
236	Angels Team (Dick Williams)	1.25	.60	.40
237	Carl Morton	.40	.20	.12
238	Dave Duncan	.40	.20	.12
239	George Stone	.40	.20	.12
240	Garry Maddox	.60	.30	.20
241	Dick Tidrow	.40	.20	.12
242	Jay Johnstone	.60	.30	.20
243	Jim Kaat	2.00	1.00	.60
244	Bill Buckner	.80	.40	.25
245	Mickey Lolich	.80	.40	.25
246	Cardinals Team (Red Schoendienst)	1.25	.60	.40
247	Enos Cabell	.40	.20	.12
248	Randy Jones	.40	.20	.12
249	Danny Thompson	.40	.20	.12
250	Ken Brett	.40	.20	.12
251	Fran Healy	.40	.20	.12
252	Fred Scherman	.40	.20	.12
253	Jesus Alou	.40	.20	.12
254	Mike Torrez	.40	.20	.12
255	Dwight Evans	2.25	1.25	.70
256	Billy Champion	.40	.20	.12
257	Checklist 133-264	2.25	1.25	.70
258	Dave LaRoche	.40	.20	.12
259	Len Randle	.40	.20	.12
260	Johnny Bench	15.00	7.50	4.50
261	Andy Hassler	.40	.20	.12
262	Rowland Office	.40	.20	.12
263	Jim Perry	.60	.30	.20
264	John Milner	.40	.20	.12
265	Ron Bryant	.40	.20	.12
266	Sandy Alomar	.40	.20	.12
267	Dick Ruthven	.40	.20	.12
268	Hal McRae	.60	.30	.20
269	Doug Rau	.40	.20	.12
270	Ron Fairly	.60	.30	.20
271	Jerry Moses	.40	.20	.12
272	Lynn McGlothen	.40	.20	.12
273	Steve Braun	.40	.20	.12
274	Vicente Romo	.40	.20	.12
275	Paul Blair	.60	.30	.20
276	White Sox Team (Chuck Tanner)	1.25	.60	.40
277	Frank Taveras	.40	.20	.12
278	Paul Lindblad	.40	.20	.12
279	Milt May	.40	.20	.12
280	Carl Yastrzemski	15.00	7.50	4.50
281	Jim Slaton	.40	.20	.12
282	Jerry Morales	.40	.20	.12
283	Steve Foucault	.40	.20	.12
284	Ken Griffey	1.00	.50	.30
285	Ellie Rodriguez	.40	.20	.12
286	Mike Jorgensen	.40	.20	.12
287	Roric Harrison	.40	.20	.12
288	Bruce Ellingsen	.40	.20	.12
289	Ken Rudolph	.40	.20	.12
290	Jon Matlack	.40	.20	.12
291	Bill Sudakis	.40	.20	.12

		NR MT	EX	VG
292	Ron Schueler	.40	.20	.12
293	Dick Sharon	.40	.20	.12
294	Geoff Zahn	.40	.20	.12
295	Vada Pinson	.90	.45	.25
296	Alan Foster	.40	.20	.12
297	Craig Kusick	.40	.20	.12
298	Johnny Grubb	.40	.20	.12
299	Bucky Dent	.60	.30	.20
300	Reggie Jackson	20.00	10.00	6.00
301	Dave Roberts	.40	.20	.12
302	Rick Burleson	.80	.40	.25
303	Grant Jackson	.40	.20	.12
304	Pirates Team (Danny Murtaugh)	1.25	.60	.40
305	Jim Colborn	.40	.20	.12
306	Batting Leaders (Rod Carew, Ralph Garr)	1.25	.60	.40
307	Home Run Leaders (Dick Allen, Mike Schmidt)	1.25	.60	.40
308	Runs Batted In Leaders (Johnny Bench, Jeff Burroughs)	1.25	.60	.40
309	Stole Base Leaders (Lou Brock, Bill North)	1.25	.60	.40
310	Victory Leaders (Jim Hunter, Fergie Jenkins, Andy Messersmith, Phil Niekro)	1.25	.60	.40
311	Earned Run Average Leaders (Buzz Capra, Jim Hunter)	.80	.40	.25
312	Strikeout Leaders (Steve Carlton, Nolan Ryan)	2.50	1.25	.70
313	Leading Firemen (Terry Forster, Mike Marshall)	.80	.40	.25
314	Buck Martinez	.40	.20	.12
315	Don Kessinger	.40	.20	.12
316	Jackie Brown	.40	.20	.12
317	Joe Lahoud	.40	.20	.12
318	Ernie McAnally	.40	.20	.12
319	Johnny Oates	.40	.20	.12
320	Pete Rose	40.00	20.00	12.00
321	Rudy May	.40	.20	.12
322	Ed Goodson	.40	.20	.12
323	Fred Holdsworth	.40	.20	.12
324	Ed Kranepool	.40	.20	.12
325	Tony Oliva	1.25	.60	.40
326	Wayne Twitchell	.40	.20	.12
327	Jerry Hairston	.40	.20	.12
328	Sonny Siebert	.40	.20	.12
329	Ted Kubiak	.40	.20	.12
330	Mike Marshall	.60	.30	.20
331	Indians Team (Frank Robinson)	1.25	.60	.40
332	Fred Kendall	.40	.20	.12
333	Dick Drago	.40	.20	.12
334	Greg Gross	.40	.20	.12
335	Jim Palmer	15.00	7.50	4.50
336	Rennie Stennett	.40	.20	.12
337	Kevin Kobel	.40	.20	.12
338	Rick Stelmaszek	.40	.20	.12
339	Jim Fregosi	.60	.30	.20
340	Paul Splittorff	.40	.20	.12
341	Hal Breeden	.40	.20	.12
342	Leroy Stanton	.40	.20	.12
343	Danny Frisella	.40	.20	.12
344	Ben Oglivie	.60	.30	.20
345	Clay Carroll	.40	.20	.12
346	Bobby Darwin	.40	.20	.12
347	Mike Caldwell	.40	.20	.12
348	Tony Muser	.40	.20	.12
349	Ray Sadecki	.40	.20	.12
350	Bobby Murcer	.60	.30	.20
351	Bob Boone	.60	.30	.20
352	Darold Knowles	.40	.20	.12
353	Luis Melendez	.40	.20	.12
354	Dick Bosman	.40	.20	.12
355	Chris Cannizzaro	.40	.20	.12
356	Rico Petrocelli	.40	.20	.12
357	Ken Forsch	.40	.20	.12
358	Al Bumbry	.40	.20	.12
359	Paul Popovich	.40	.20	.12
360	George Scott	.40	.20	.12
361	Dodgers Team (Walter Alston)	1.50	.70	.45
362	Steve Hargan	.40	.20	.12
363	Carmen Fanzone	.40	.20	.12
364	Doug Bird	.40	.20	.12
365	Bob Bailey	.40	.20	.12
366	Ken Sanders	.40	.20	.12
367	Craig Robinson	.40	.20	.12
368	Vic Albury	.40	.20	.12
369	Merv Rettenmund	.40	.20	.12
370	Tom Seaver	25.00	12.50	7.50
371	Gates Brown	.40	.20	.12
372	John D'Acquisto	.40	.20	.12
373	Bill Sharp	.40	.20	.12

		NR MT	EX	VG
374	Eddie Watt	.40	.20	.12
375	Roy White	.60	.30	.20
376	Steve Yeager	.40	.20	.12
377	Tom Hilgendorf	.40	.20	.12
378	Derrel Thomas	.40	.20	.12
379	Bernie Carbo	.40	.20	.12
380	Sal Bando	.60	.30	.20
381	John Curtis	.40	.20	.12
382	Don Baylor	.90	.45	.25
383	Jim York	.40	.20	.12
384	Brewers Team (Del Crandall)	1.25	.60	.40
385	Dock Ellis	.40	.20	.12
386	Checklist 265-396	2.25	1.25	.70
387	Jim Spencer	.40	.20	.12
388	Steve Stone	.60	.30	.20
389	Tony Solaita	.40	.20	.12
390	Ron Cey	.60	.30	.20
391	Don DeMola	.40	.20	.12
392	Bruce Bochte	.40	.20	.12
393	Gary Gentry	.40	.20	.12
394	Larvell Blanks	.40	.20	.12
395	Bud Harrelson	.40	.20	.12
396	Fred Norman	.40	.20	.12
397	Bill Freehan	.60	.30	.20
398	Elias Sosa	.40	.20	.12
399	Terry Harmon	.40	.20	.12
400	Dick Allen	1.25	.60	.40
401	Mike Wallace	.40	.20	.12
402	Bob Tolan	.40	.20	.12
403	Tom Buskey	.40	.20	.12
404	Ted Sizemore	.40	.20	.12
405	John Montague	.40	.20	.12
406	Bob Gallagher	.40	.20	.12
407	Herb Washington	.40	.20	.12
408	Clyde Wright	.40	.20	.12
409	Bob Robertson	.40	.20	.12
410	Mike Cueller (Cuellar)	.60	.30	.20
411	George Mitterwald	.40	.20	.12
412	Bill Hands	.40	.20	.12
413	Marty Pattin	.40	.20	.12
414	Manny Mota	.60	.30	.20
415	John Hiller	.40	.20	.12
416	Larry Lintz	.40	.20	.12
417	Skip Lockwood	.40	.20	.12
418	Leo Foster	.40	.20	.12
419	Dave Goltz	.40	.20	.12
420	Larry Bowa	.60	.30	.20
421	Mets Team (Yogi Berra)	1.50	.70	.45
422	Brian Downing	.60	.30	.20
423	Clay Kirby	.40	.20	.12
424	John Lowenstein	.40	.20	.12
425	Tito Fuentes	.40	.20	.12
426	George Medich	.40	.20	.12
427	Clarence Gaston	.40	.20	.12
428	Dave Hamilton	.40	.20	.12
429	Jim Dwyer	.40	.20	.12
430	Luis Tiant	.80	.40	.25
431	Rod Gilbreath	.40	.20	.12
432	Ken Berry	.40	.20	.12
433	Larry Demery	.40	.20	.12
434	Bob Locker	.40	.20	.12
435	Dave Nelson	.40	.20	.12
436	Ken Frailing	.40	.20	.12
437	Al Cowens	.40	.20	.12
438	Don Carrithers	.40	.20	.12
439	Ed Brinkman	.40	.20	.12
440	Andy Messersmith	.60	.30	.20
441	Bobby Heise	.40	.20	.12
442	Maximino Leon	.40	.20	.12
443	Twins Team (Frank Quilici)	1.25	.60	.40
444	Gene Garber	.40	.20	.12
445	Felix Millan	.40	.20	.12
446	Bart Johnson	.40	.20	.12
447	Terry Crowley	.40	.20	.12
448	Frank Duffy	.40	.20	.12
449	Charlie Williams	.40	.20	.12
450	Willie McCovey	7.00	3.50	2.00
451	Rick Dempsey	.60	.30	.20
452	Angel Mangual	.40	.20	.12
453	Claude Osteen	.40	.20	.12
454	Doug Griffin	.40	.20	.12
455	Don Wilson	.40	.20	.12
456	Bob Coluccio	.40	.20	.12
457	Mario Mendoza	.40	.20	.12
458	Ross Grimsley	.40	.20	.12
459	A.L. Championships	1.25	.60	.40
460	N.L. Championships	1.25	.60	.40
461	World Series Game 1	2.25	1.25	.70
462	World Series Game 2	1.50	.70	.45
463	World Series Game 3	1.50	.70	.45
464	World Series Game 4	1.25	.60	.40

	NR MT	EX	VG
465 World Series Game 5	1.25	.60	.40
466 World Series Summary	1.25	.60	.40
467 Ed Halicki	.40	.20	.12
468 Bobby Mitchell	.40	.20	.12
469 Tom Dettore	.40	.20	.12
470 Jeff Burroughs	.40	.20	.12
471 Bob Stinson	.40	.20	.12
472 Bruce Dal Canton	.40	.20	.12
473 Ken McMullen	.40	.20	.12
474 Luke Walker	.40	.20	.12
475 Darrell Evans	.90	.45	.25
476 Ed Figueroa	.40	.20	.12
477 Tom Hutton	.40	.20	.12
478 Tom Burgmeier	.40	.20	.12
479 Ken Boswell	.40	.20	.12
480 Carlos May	.40	.20	.12
481 Will McEnaney	.40	.20	.12
482 Tom McCraw	.40	.20	.12
483 Steve Ontiveros	.40	.20	.12
484 Glenn Beckert	.40	.20	.12
485 Sparky Lyle	.60	.30	.20
486 Ray Fosse	.40	.20	.12
487 Astros Team (Preston Gomez)	1.25	.60	.40
488 Bill Travers	.40	.20	.12
489 Cecil Cooper	1.50	.70	.45
490 Reggie Smith	.60	.30	.20
491 Doyle Alexander	.60	.30	.20
492 Rich Hebner	.40	.20	.12
493 Doug Stanhouse	.40	.20	.12
494 Pete LaCock	.40	.20	.12
495 Nelson Briles	.40	.20	.12
496 Pepe Frias	.40	.20	.12
497 Jim Nettles	.40	.20	.12
498 Al Downing	.40	.20	.12
499 Marty Perez	.40	.20	.12
500 Nolan Ryan	40.00	20.00	12.00
501 Bill Robinson	.40	.20	.12
502 Pat Bourque	.40	.20	.12
503 Fred Stanley	.40	.20	.12
504 Buddy Bradford	.40	.20	.12
505 Chris Speier	.40	.20	.12
506 Leron Lee	.40	.20	.12
507 Tom Carroll	.40	.20	.12
508 Bob Hansen	.40	.20	.12
509 Dave Hilton	.40	.20	.12
510 Vida Blue	.80	.40	.25
511 Rangers Team (Billy Martin)	1.25	.60	.40
512 Larry Milbourne	.40	.20	.12
513 Dick Pole	.40	.20	.12
514 Jose Cruz	.80	.40	.25
515 Manny Sanguillen	.40	.20	.12
516 Don Hood	.40	.20	.12
517 Checklist 397-528	2.25	1.25	.70
518 Leo Cardenas	.40	.20	.12
519 Jim Todd	.40	.20	.12
520 Amos Otis	.40	.20	.12
521 Dennis Blair	.40	.20	.12
522 Gary Sutherland	.40	.20	.12
523 Tom Paciorek	.40	.20	.12
524 John Doherty	.40	.20	.12
525 Tom House	.40	.20	.12
526 Larry Hisle	.40	.20	.12
527 Mac Scarce	.40	.20	.12
528 Eddie Leon	.40	.20	.12
529 Gary Thomasson	.40	.20	.12
530 Gaylord Perry	6.00	3.00	1.75
531 Reds Team (Sparky Anderson)	1.25	.60	.40
532 Gorman Thomas	.80	.40	.25
533 Rudy Meoli	.40	.20	.12
534 Alex Johnson	.40	.20	.12
535 Gene Tenace	.40	.20	.12
536 Bob Moose	.40	.20	.12
537 Tommy Harper	.40	.20	.12
538 Duffy Dyer	.40	.20	.12
539 Jesse Jefferson	.40	.20	.12
540 Lou Brock	7.00	3.50	2.00
541 Roger Metzger	.40	.20	.12
542 Pete Broberg	.40	.20	.12
543 Larry Biittner	.40	.20	.12
544 Steve Mingori	.40	.20	.12
545 Billy Williams	6.00	3.00	1.75
546 John Knox	.40	.20	.12
547 Von Joshua	.40	.20	.12
548 Charlie Sands	.40	.20	.12
549 Bill Butler	.40	.20	.12
550 Ralph Garr	.40	.20	.12
551 Larry Christenson	.40	.20	.12
552 Jack Brohamer	.40	.20	.12
553 John Boccabella	.40	.20	.12
554 Rich Gossage	1.75	.90	.50
555 Al Oliver	1.25	.60	.40

	NR MT	EX	VG
556 Tim Johnson	.40	.20	.12
557 Larry Gura	.40	.20	.12
558 Dave Roberts	.40	.20	.12
559 Bob Montgomery	.40	.20	.12
560 Tony Perez	1.25	.60	.40
561 A's Team (Alvin Dark)	1.25	.60	.40
562 Gary Nolan	.40	.20	.12
563 Wilbur Howard	.40	.20	.12
564 Tommy Davis	.60	.30	.20
565 Joe Torre	1.00	.50	.30
566 Ray Burris	.40	.20	.12
567 Jim Sundberg	1.00	.50	.30
568 Dale Murray	.40	.20	.12
569 Frank White	.60	.30	.20
570 Jim Wynn	.60	.30	.20
571 Dave Lemanczyk	.40	.20	.12
572 Roger Nelson	.40	.20	.12
573 Orlando Pena	.40	.20	.12
574 Tony Taylor	.40	.20	.12
575 Gene Clines	.40	.20	.12
576 Phil Roof	.40	.20	.12
577 John Morris	.40	.20	.12
578 Dave Tomlin	.40	.20	.12
579 Skip Pitlock	.40	.20	.12
580 Frank Robinson	7.00	3.50	2.00
581 Darrel Chaney	.40	.20	.12
582 Eduardo Rodriguez	.40	.20	.12
583 Andy Etchebarren	.40	.20	.12
584 Mike Garman	.40	.20	.12
585 Chris Chambliss	.60	.30	.20
586 Tim McCarver	.90	.45	.25
587 Chris Ward	.40	.20	.12
588 Rick Auerbach	.40	.20	.12
589 Braves Team (Clyde King)	1.25	.60	.40
590 Cesar Cedeno	.60	.30	.20
591 Glenn Abbott	.40	.20	.12
592 Balor Moore	.40	.20	.12
593 Gene Lamont	.40	.20	.12
594 Jim Fuller	.40	.20	.12
595 Joe Niekro	.60	.30	.20
596 Ollie Brown	.40	.20	.12
597 Winston Llenas	.40	.20	.12
598 Bruce Kison	.40	.20	.12
599 Nate Colbert	.40	.20	.12
600 Rod Carew	18.00	9.00	5.50
601 Juan Beniquez	.40	.20	.12
602 John Vukovich	.40	.20	.12
603 Lew Krausse	.40	.20	.12
604 Oscar Zamora	.40	.20	.12
605 John Ellis	.40	.20	.12
606 Bruce Miller	.40	.20	.12
607 Jim Holt	.40	.20	.12
608 Gene Michael	.40	.20	.12
609 Ellie Hendricks	.40	.20	.12
610 Ron Hunt	.40	.20	.12
611 Yankees Team (Bill Virdon)	1.75	.90	.50
612 Terry Hughes	.40	.20	.12
613 Bill Parsons	.40	.20	.12
614 Rookie Pitchers (Jack Kucek, Dyar Miller, Vern Ruhle, Paul Siebert)	.40	.20	.12
615 Rookie Pitchers (Pat Darcy, Dennis Leonard, Tom Underwood, Hank Webb)	.90	.45	.25
616 Rookie Outfielders (Dave Augustine, Pepe Mangual, Jim Rice, John Scott)	50.00	25.00	15.00
617 Rookie Infielders (Mike Cubbage, Doug DeCinces, Reggie Sanders, Manny Trillo)	2.50	1.25	.70
618 Rookie Pitchers (Jamie Easterly, Tom Johnson, Scott McGregor, Rick Rhoden)	5.00	2.50	1.50
619 Rookie Outfielders (Benny Ayala, Nyls Nyman, Tommy Smith, Jerry Turner)	.40	.20	.12
620 Rookie Catchers-Outfielders (Gary Carter, Marc Hill, Danny Meyer, Leon Roberts)	50.00	25.00	15.00
621 Rookie Pitchers (John Denny, Rawly Eastwick, Jim Kern, Juan Veintidos)	.90	.45	.25
622 Rookie Outfielders (Ed Armbrister, Fred Lynn, Tom Poquette, Terry Whitfield)	15.00	7.50	4.50
623 Rookie Infielders (Phil Garner, Keith Hernandez, Bob Sheldon, Tom Veryzer)	40.00	20.00	12.00
624 Rookie Pitchers (Doug Konieczny, Gary Lavelle, Jim Otten, Eddie Solomon)	.40	.20	.12
625 Boog Powell	1.00	.50	.30
626 Larry Haney	.40	.20	.12
627 Tom Walker	.40	.20	.12
628 Ron LeFlore	1.25	.60	.40
629 Joe Hoerner	.40	.20	.12

		NR MT	EX	VG
630	Greg Luzinski	1.00	.50	.30
631	Lee Lacy	.40	.20	.12
632	Morris Nettles	.40	.20	.12
633	Paul Casanova	.40	.20	.12
634	Cy Acosta	.40	.20	.12
635	Chuck Dobson	.40	.20	.12
636	Charlie Moore	.40	.20	.12
637	Ted Martinez	.40	.20	.12
638	Cubs Team (Jim Marshall)	1.25	.60	.40
639	Steve Kline	.40	.20	.12
640	Harmon Killebrew	6.00	3.00	1.75
641	Jim Northrup	.40	.20	.12
642	Mike Phillips	.40	.20	.12
643	Brent Strom	.40	.20	.12
644	Bill Fahey	.40	.20	.12
645	Danny Cater	.40	.20	.12
646	Checklist 529-660	2.25	1.25	.70
647	Claudell Washington	2.50	1.25	.70
648	Dave Pagan	.40	.20	.12
649	Jack Heidemann	.40	.20	.12
650	Dave May	.40	.20	.12
651	John Morlan	.40	.20	.12
652	Lindy McDaniel	.40	.20	.12
653	Lee Richards	.40	.20	.12
654	Jerry Terrell	.40	.20	.12
655	Rico Carty	.60	.30	.20
656	Bill Plummer	.40	.20	.12
657	Bob Oliver	.40	.20	.12
658	Vic Harris	.40	.20	.12
659	Bob Apodaca	.40	.20	.12
660	Hank Aaron	35.00	17.50	10.50

1976 Topps

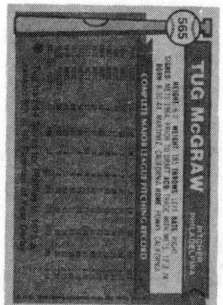

These 2-1/2" by 3-1/2" cards begin a design trend for Topps. The focus was more on the photo quality than in past years with a corresponding trend toward simplicity in the borders. The front of the cards has the player's name and team in two strips while his position is in the lower left corner under a drawing of a player representing that position. The backs have a bat and ball with the card number on the left; statistics and personal information and career highlights on the right. The 660-card set features a number of specialty sets including record-setting performances, statistical leaders, playoff and World Series highlights, the Sporting News All-Time All-Stars and father and son combinations.

		NR MT	EX	VG
Complete Set:		400.00	200.00	125.00
Common Player:		.15	.08	.05
1	'75 Record Breaker (Hank Aaron)	12.00	6.00	3.50
2	'75 Record Breaker (Bobby Bonds)	.40	.20	.12
3	'75 Record Breaker (Mickey Lolich)	.35	.20	.11
4	'75 Record Breaker (Dave Lopes)	.35	.20	.11
5	'75 Record Breaker (Tom Seaver)	1.50	.70	.45
6	'75 Record Breaker (Rennie Stennett)	.30	.15	.09
7	Jim Umbarger	.15	.08	.05
8	Tito Fuentes	.15	.08	.05
9	Paul Lindblad	.15	.08	.05
10	Lou Brock	3.00	1.50	.90
11	Jim Hughes	.15	.08	.05

		NR MT	EX	VG
12	Richie Zisk	.20	.10	.06
13	Johnny Wockenfuss	.15	.08	.05
14	Gene Garber	.20	.10	.06
15	George Scott	.25	.13	.08
16	Bob Apodaca	.15	.08	.05
17	Yankees Team (Billy Martin)	1.25	.60	.40
18	Dale Murray	.15	.08	.05
19	George Brett	40.00	20.00	12.00
20	Bob Watson	.20	.10	.06
21	Dave LaRoche	.15	.08	.05
22	Bill Russell	.20	.10	.06
23	Brian Downing	.25	.13	.08
24	Cesar Geronimo	.20	.10	.06
25	Mike Torrez	.20	.10	.06
26	Andy Thornton	.25	.13	.08
27	Ed Figueroa	.15	.08	.05
28	Dusty Baker	.25	.13	.08
29	Rick Burleson	.30	.15	.09
30	*John Montefusco*	.35	.20	.11
31	Len Randle	.15	.08	.05
32	Danny Frisella	.15	.08	.05
33	Bill North	.15	.08	.05
34	Mike Garman	.15	.08	.05
35	Tony Oliva	.60	.30	.20
36	Frank Taveras	.15	.08	.05
37	John Hiller	.20	.10	.06
38	Garry Maddox	.20	.10	.06
39	Pete Broberg	.15	.08	.05
40	Dave Kingman	.80	.40	.25
41	*Tippy Martinez*	.40	.20	.12
42	Barry Foote	.15	.08	.05
43	Paul Splittorff	.20	.10	.06
44	Doug Rader	.15	.08	.05
45	Boog Powell	.60	.30	.20
46	Dodgers Team (Walter Alston)	1.00	.50	.30
47	Jesse Jefferson	.15	.08	.05
48	Dave Concepcion	.40	.20	.12
49	Dave Duncan	.15	.08	.05
50	Fred Lynn	2.00	1.00	.60
51	Ray Burris	.15	.08	.05
52	Dave Chalk	.15	.08	.05
53	Mike Beard	.15	.08	.05
54	Dave Rader	.15	.08	.05
55	Gaylord Perry	2.00	1.00	.60
56	Bob Tolan	.20	.10	.06
57	Phil Garner	.30	.15	.09
58	Ron Reed	.20	.10	.06
59	Larry Hisle	.20	.10	.06
60	Jerry Reuss	.30	.15	.09
61	Ron LeFlore	.30	.15	.09
62	Johnny Oates	.15	.08	.05
63	Bobby Darwin	.15	.08	.05
64	Jerry Koosman	.30	.15	.09
65	Chris Chambliss	.30	.15	.09
66	Father & Son (Buddy Bell, Gus Bell)	.50	.25	.15
67	Father & Son (Bob Boone, Ray Boone)	.40	.20	.12
68	Father & Son (Joe Coleman, Joe Coleman, Jr.)	.20	.10	.06
69	Father & Son (Jim Hegan, Mike Hegan)	.20	.10	.06
70	Father & Son (Roy Smalley, Roy Smalley, Jr.)	.25	.13	.08
71	Steve Rogers	.20	.10	.06
72	Hal McRae	.25	.13	.08
73	Orioles Team (Earl Weaver)	.80	.40	.25
74	Oscar Gamble	.20	.10	.06
75	Larry Dierker	.20	.10	.06
76	Willie Crawford	.15	.08	.05
77	Pedro Borbon	.15	.08	.05
78	Cecil Cooper	1.00	.50	.30
79	Jerry Morales	.15	.08	.05
80	Jim Kaat	.90	.45	.25
81	Darrell Evans	.50	.25	.15
82	Von Joshua	.15	.08	.05
83	Jim Spencer	.15	.08	.05
84	Brent Strom	.15	.08	.05
85	Mickey Rivers	.25	.13	.08
86	Mike Tyson	.15	.08	.05
87	Tom Burgmeier	.15	.08	.05
88	Duffy Dyer	.15	.08	.05
89	Vern Ruhle	.15	.08	.05
90	Sal Bando	.30	.15	.09
91	Tom Hutton	.15	.08	.05
92	Eduardo Rodriguez	.15	.08	.05
93	Mike Phillips	.15	.08	.05
94	Jim Dwyer	.30	.15	.09
95	Brooks Robinson	2.75	1.50	.80
96	Doug Bird	.15	.08	.05
97	Wilbur Howard	.15	.08	.05

		NR MT	EX	VG
98	*Dennis Eckersley*	20.00	10.00	6.00
99	Lee Lacy	.20	.10	.06
100	Jim Hunter	3.00	1.50	.90
101	Pete LaCock	.15	.08	.05
102	Jim Willoughby	.15	.08	.05
103	Biff Pocoroba	.15	.08	.05
104	Reds Team (Sparky Anderson)	.90	.45	.25
105	Gary Lavelle	.15	.08	.05
106	Tom Grieve	.15	.08	.05
107	Dave Roberts	.15	.08	.05
108	Don Kirkwood	.15	.08	.05
109	Larry Lintz	.15	.08	.05
110	Carlos May	.20	.10	.06
111	Danny Thompson	.20	.10	.06
112	*Kent Tekulve*	.80	.40	.25
113	Gary Sutherland	.15	.08	.05
114	Jay Johnstone	.25	.13	.08
115	Ken Holtzman	.25	.13	.08
116	Charlie Moore	.15	.08	.05
117	Mike Jorgensen	.15	.08	.05
118	Red Sox Team (Darrell Johnson)	.90	.45	.25
119	Checklist 1-132	1.25	.60	.40
120	Rusty Staub	.35	.20	.11
121	Tony Solaita	.15	.08	.05
122	Mike Cosgrove	.15	.08	.05
123	Walt Williams	.20	.10	.06
124	Doug Rau	.15	.08	.05
125	Don Baylor	.50	.25	.15
126	Tom Dettore	.15	.08	.05
127	Larvell Blanks	.15	.08	.05
128	Ken Griffey	.35	.20	.11
129	Andy Etchebarren	.15	.08	.05
130	Luis Tiant	.40	.20	.12
131	Bill Stein	.25	.13	.08
132	Don Hood	.15	.08	.05
133	Gary Matthews	.25	.13	.08
134	Mike Ivie	.15	.08	.05
135	Bake McBride	.20	.10	.06
136	Dave Goltz	.20	.10	.06
137	Bill Robinson	.15	.08	.05
138	Lerrin LaGrow	.15	.08	.05
139	Gorman Thomas	.35	.20	.11
140	Vida Blue	.40	.20	.12
141	*Larry Parrish*	.80	.40	.25
142	Dick Drago	.15	.08	.05
143	Jerry Grote	.20	.10	.06
144	Al Fitzmorris	.15	.08	.05
145	Larry Bowa	.35	.20	.11
146	George Medich	.20	.10	.06
147	Astros Team (Bill Virdon)	.80	.40	.25
148	Stan Thomas	.15	.08	.05
149	Tommy Davis	.30	.15	.09
150	Steve Garvey	4.50	2.25	1.25
151	Bill Bonham	.15	.08	.05
152	Leroy Stanton	.15	.08	.05
153	Buzz Capra	.15	.08	.05
154	Bucky Dent	.30	.15	.09
155	Jack Billingham	.15	.08	.05
156	Rico Carty	.25	.13	.08
157	Mike Caldwell	.15	.08	.05
158	Ken Reitz	.15	.08	.05
159	Jerry Terrell	.15	.08	.05
160	Dave Winfield	6.00	3.00	1.75
161	Bruce Kison	.15	.08	.05
162	Jack Pierce	.15	.08	.05
163	Jim Slaton	.15	.08	.05
164	Pepe Mangual	.15	.08	.05
165	Gene Tenace	.20	.10	.06
166	Skip Lockwood	.15	.08	.05
167	Freddie Patek	.15	.08	.05
168	Tom Hilgendorf	.15	.08	.05
169	Graig Nettles	1.00	.50	.30
170	Rick Wise	.20	.10	.06
171	Greg Gross	.15	.08	.05
172	Rangers Team (Frank Lucchesi)	.80	.40	.25
173	Steve Swisher	.15	.08	.05
174	Charlie Hough	.25	.13	.08
175	Ken Singleton	.30	.15	.09
176	Dick Lange	.15	.08	.05
177	Marty Perez	.15	.08	.05
178	Tom Buskey	.15	.08	.05
179	George Foster	1.00	.50	.30
180	Rich Gossage	1.25	.60	.40
181	Willie Montanez	.20	.10	.06
182	Harry Rasmussen	.15	.08	.05
183	Steve Braun	.15	.08	.05
184	Bill Greif	.15	.08	.05
185	Dave Parker	3.75	1.75	1.00
186	Tom Walker	.15	.08	.05
187	Pedro Garcia	.15	.08	.05
188	Fred Scherman	.15	.08	.05
189	Claudell Washington	.40	.20	.12
190	Jon Matlack	.25	.13	.08
191	N.L. Batting Leaders (Bill Madlock, Manny Sanguillen, Ted Simmons)	.60	.30	.20
192	A.L. Batting Leaders (Rod Carew, Fred Lynn, Thurman Munson)	1.50	.70	.45
193	N.L. Home Run Leaders (Dave Kingman, Greg Luzinski, Mike Schmidt)	1.25	.60	.40
194	A.L. Home Run Leaders (Reggie Jackson, John Mayberry, George Scott)	1.25	.60	.40
195	N.L. Runs Batted In Ldrs. (Johnny Bench, Greg Luzinski, Tony Perez)	1.25	.60	.40
196	A.L. Runs Batted In Ldrs. (Fred Lynn, John Mayberry, George Scott)	.60	.30	.20
197	N.L. Stolen Base Leaders (Lou Brock, Dave Lopes, Joe Morgan)	.90	.45	.25
198	A.L. Stolen Base Leaders (Amos Otis, Mickey Rivers, Claudell Washington)	.50	.25	.15
199	N.L. Victory Leaders (Randy Jones, Andy Messersmith, Tom Seaver)	.80	.40	.25
200	A.L. Victory Leaders (Vida Blue, Jim Hunter, Jim Palmer)	.90	.45	.25
201	N.L. Earned Run Avg. Ldrs. (Randy Jones, Andy Messersmith, Tom Seaver)	.80	.40	.25
202	A.L. Earned Run Avg. Ldrs. (Dennis Eckersley, Jim Hunter, Jim Palmer)	.90	.45	.25
203	N.L. Strikeout Leaders (Andy Messersmith, John Montefusco, Tom Seaver)	.80	.40	.25
204	A.L. Strikeout Leaders (Bert Blyleven, Gaylord Perry, Frank Tanana)	.70	.35	.20
205	Major League Leading Firemen (Rich Gossage, Al Hrabosky)	.50	.25	.15
206	Manny Trillo	.20	.10	.06
207	Andy Hassler	.15	.08	.05
208	Mike Lum	.15	.08	.05
209	Alan Ashby	.35	.20	.11
210	Lee May	.25	.13	.08
211	Clay Carroll	.20	.10	.06
212	Pat Kelly	.15	.08	.05
213	Dave Heaverlo	.15	.08	.05
214	Eric Soderholm	.15	.08	.05
215	Reggie Smith	.25	.13	.08
216	Expos Team (Karl Kuehl)	.80	.40	.25
217	Dave Freisleben	.15	.08	.05
218	John Knox	.15	.08	.05
219	Tom Murphy	.15	.08	.05
220	Manny Sanguillen	.20	.10	.06
221	Jim Todd	.15	.08	.05
222	Wayne Garrett	.15	.08	.05
223	Ollie Brown	.15	.08	.05
224	Jim York	.15	.08	.05
225	Roy White	.25	.13	.08
226	Jim Sundberg	.25	.13	.08
227	Oscar Zamora	.15	.08	.05
228	John Hale	.15	.08	.05
229	*Jerry Remy*	.30	.15	.09
230	Carl Yastrzemski	8.00	4.00	2.50
231	Tom House	.15	.08	.05
232	Frank Duffy	.15	.08	.05
233	Grant Jackson	.15	.08	.05
234	Mike Sadek	.15	.08	.05
235	Bert Blyleven	1.00	.50	.30
236	Royals Team (Whitey Herzog)	.80	.40	.25
237	Dave Hamilton	.15	.08	.05
238	Larry Biittner	.15	.08	.05
239	John Curtis	.15	.08	.05
240	Pete Rose	15.00	7.50	4.50
241	Hector Torres	.15	.08	.05
242	Dan Meyer	.15	.08	.05
243	Jim Rooker	.15	.08	.05
244	Bill Sharp	.15	.08	.05
245	Felix Millan	.15	.08	.05
246	Cesar Tovar	.15	.08	.05
247	Terry Harmon	.15	.08	.05
248	Dick Tidrow	.20	.10	.06
249	Cliff Johnson	.20	.10	.06
250	Fergie Jenkins	1.00	.50	.30
251	Rick Monday	.30	.15	.09
252	Tim Nordbrook	.15	.08	.05
253	Bill Buckner	.50	.25	.15
254	Rudy Meoli	.15	.08	.05
255	Fritz Peterson	.15	.08	.05
256	Rowland Office	.15	.08	.05
257	Ross Grimsley	.20	.10	.06
258	Nyls Nyman	.15	.08	.05
259	Darrel Chaney	.15	.08	.05
260	Steve Busby	.20	.10	.06
261	Gary Thomasson	.15	.08	.05
262	Checklist 133-264	1.50	.70	.45
263	*Lyman Bostock*	.80	.40	.25

		NR MT	EX	VG			NR MT	EX	VG
264	Steve Renko	.15	.08	.05	352	Dave Giusti	.15	.08	.05
265	Willie Davis	.30	.15	.09	353	*Sixto Lezcano*	.30	.15	.09
266	Alan Foster	.15	.08	.05	354	Ron Blomberg	.20	.10	.06
267	Aurelio Rodriguez	.20	.10	.06	355	Steve Carlton	5.00	2.50	1.50
268	Del Unser	.15	.08	.05	356	Ted Martinez	.15	.08	.05
269	Rick Austin	.15	.08	.05	357	Ken Forsch	.20	.10	.06
270	Willie Stargell	3.00	1.50	.90	358	Buddy Bell	.50	.25	.15
271	Jim Lonborg	.20	.10	.06	359	Rick Reuschel	.30	.15	.09
272	Rick Dempsey	.25	.13	.08	360	Jeff Burroughs	.20	.10	.06
273	Joe Niekro	.30	.15	.09	361	Tigers Team (Ralph Houk)	1.00	.50	.30
274	Tommy Harper	.20	.10	.06	362	Will McEnaney	.15	.08	.05
275	*Rick Manning*	.40	.20	.12	363	*Dave Collins*	.40	.20	.12
276	Mickey Scott	.15	.08	.05	364	Elias Sosa	.15	.08	.05
277	Cubs Team (Jim Marshall)	.80	.40	.25	365	Carlton Fisk	6.00	3.00	1.75
278	Bernie Carbo	.15	.08	.05	366	Bobby Valentine	.30	.15	.09
279	Roy Howell	.15	.08	.05	367	Bruce Miller	.15	.08	.05
280	Burt Hooton	.20	.10	.06	368	Wilbur Wood	.25	.13	.08
281	Dave May	.15	.08	.05	369	Frank White	.30	.15	.09
282	Dan Osborn	.15	.08	.05	370	Ron Cey	.40	.20	.12
283	Merv Rettenmund	.15	.08	.05	371	Ellie Hendricks	.15	.08	.05
284	Steve Ontiveros	.15	.08	.05	372	Rick Baldwin	.15	.08	.05
285	Mike Cuellar	.25	.13	.08	373	Johnny Briggs	.15	.08	.05
286	Jim Wohlford	.15	.08	.05	374	Dan Warthen	.15	.08	.05
287	Pete Mackanin	.15	.08	.05	375	Ron Fairly	.25	.13	.08
288	Bill Campbell	.15	.08	.05	376	Rich Hebner	.20	.10	.06
289	Enzo Hernandez	.15	.08	.05	377	Mike Hegan	.15	.08	.05
290	Ted Simmons	.60	.30	.20	378	Steve Stone	.25	.13	.08
291	Ken Sanders	.15	.08	.05	379	Ken Boswell	.15	.08	.05
292	Leon Roberts	.15	.08	.05	380	Bobby Bonds	.35	.20	.11
293	Bill Castro	.15	.08	.05	381	Denny Doyle	.15	.08	.05
294	Ed Kirkpatrick	.15	.08	.05	382	Matt Alexander	.15	.08	.05
295	Dave Cash	.15	.08	.05	383	John Ellis	.15	.08	.05
296	Pat Dobson	.20	.10	.06	384	Phillies Team (Danny Ozark)	.80	.40	.25
297	Roger Metzger	.15	.08	.05	385	Mickey Lolich	.40	.20	.12
298	Dick Bosman	.15	.08	.05	386	Ed Goodson	.15	.08	.05
299	Champ Summers	.15	.08	.05	387	Mike Miley	.15	.08	.05
300	Johnny Bench	6.00	3.00	1.75	388	Stan Perzanowski	.15	.08	.05
301	Jackie Brown	.15	.08	.05	389	Glenn Adams	.15	.08	.05
302	Rick Miller	.15	.08	.05	390	Don Gullett	.20	.10	.06
303	Steve Foucault	.15	.08	.05	391	Jerry Hairston	.15	.08	.05
304	Angels Team (Dick Williams)	.80	.40	.25	392	Checklist 265-396	1.50	.70	.45
305	Andy Messersmith	.25	.13	.08	393	Paul Mitchell	.15	.08	.05
306	Rod Gilbreath	.15	.08	.05	394	Fran Healy	.15	.08	.05
307	Al Bumbry	.20	.10	.06	395	Jim Wynn	.30	.15	.09
308	Jim Barr	.15	.08	.05	396	Bill Lee	.20	.10	.06
309	Bill Melton	.20	.10	.06	397	Tim Foli	.15	.08	.05
310	Randy Jones	.30	.15	.09	398	Dave Tomlin	.15	.08	.05
311	Cookie Rojas	.15	.08	.05	399	Luis Melendez	.15	.08	.05
312	Don Carrithers	.15	.08	.05	400	Rod Carew	5.00	2.50	1.50
313	*Dan Ford*	.25	.13	.08	401	Ken Brett	.20	.10	.06
314	Ed Kranepool	.25	.13	.08	402	Don Money	.20	.10	.06
315	Al Hrabosky	.20	.10	.06	403	Geoff Zahn	.20	.10	.06
316	Robin Yount	40.00	20.00	12.00	404	Enos Cabell	.20	.10	.06
317	*John Candelaria*	1.75	.90	.50	405	Rollie Fingers	5.00	2.50	1.50
318	Bob Boone	.30	.15	.09	406	Ed Herrmann	.20	.10	.06
319	Larry Gura	.20	.10	.06	407	Tom Underwood	.15	.08	.05
320	Willie Horton	.25	.13	.08	408	Charlie Spikes	.15	.08	.05
321	Jose Cruz	.35	.20	.11	409	Dave Lemanczyk	.15	.08	.05
322	Glenn Abbott	.15	.08	.05	410	Ralph Garr	.20	.10	.06
323	Rob Sperring	.15	.08	.05	411	Bill Singer	.20	.10	.06
324	Jim Bibby	.15	.08	.05	412	Toby Harrah	.25	.13	.08
325	Tony Perez	.80	.40	.25	413	Pete Varney	.15	.08	.05
326	Dick Pole	.15	.08	.05	414	Wayne Garland	.15	.08	.05
327	Dave Moates	.15	.08	.05	415	Vada Pinson	.50	.25	.15
328	Carl Morton	.15	.08	.05	416	Tommy John	1.25	.60	.40
329	Joe Ferguson	.15	.08	.05	417	Gene Clines	.15	.08	.05
330	Nolan Ryan	30.00	15.00	9.00	418	Jose Morales	.15	.08	.05
331	Padres Team (John McNamara)	.80	.40	.25	419	Reggie Cleveland	.15	.08	.05
332	Charlie Williams	.15	.08	.05	420	Joe Morgan	5.00	2.50	1.50
333	Bob Coluccio	.15	.08	.05	421	A's Team	.80	.40	.25
334	Dennis Leonard	.25	.13	.08	422	Johnny Grubb	.15	.08	.05
335	Bob Grich	.25	.13	.08	423	Ed Halicki	.15	.08	.05
336	Vic Albury	.15	.08	.05	424	Phil Roof	.15	.08	.05
337	Bud Harrelson	.20	.10	.06	425	Rennie Stennett	.15	.08	.05
338	Bob Bailey	.15	.08	.05	426	Bob Forsch	.25	.13	.08
339	John Denny	.25	.13	.08	427	Kurt Bevacqua	.15	.08	.05
340	Jim Rice	8.00	4.00	2.50	428	Jim Crawford	.15	.08	.05
341	All Time All-Stars (Lou Gehrig)	3.00	1.50	.90	429	Fred Stanley	.20	.10	.06
342	All Time All-Stars (Rogers Hornsby)	1.25	.60	.40	430	Jose Cardenal	.20	.10	.06
343	All Time All-Stars (Pie Traynor)	.80	.40	.25	431	Dick Ruthven	.15	.08	.05
344	All Time All-Stars (Honus Wagner)	1.25	.60	.40	432	Tom Veryzer	.15	.08	.05
345	All Time All-Stars (Babe Ruth)	5.00	2.50	1.50	433	Rick Waits	.15	.08	.05
346	All Time All-Stars (Ty Cobb)	3.00	1.50	.90	434	Morris Nettles	.15	.08	.05
347	All Time All-Stars (Ted Williams)	3.00	1.50	.90	435	Phil Niekro	2.00	1.00	.60
348	All Time All-Stars (Mickey Cochrane)	.80	.40	.25	436	Bill Fahey	.15	.08	.05
349	All Time All-Stars (Walter Johnson)	1.25	.60	.40	437	Terry Forster	.25	.13	.08
350	All Time All-Stars (Lefty Grove)	1.00	.50	.30	438	Doug DeCinces	.50	.25	.15
351	Randy Hundley	.15	.08	.05	439	Rick Rhoden	.60	.30	.20
					440	John Mayberry	.25	.13	.08
					441	Gary Carter	10.00	5.00	3.00
					442	Hank Webb	.15	.08	.05

		NR MT	EX	VG
443	Giants Team	.80	.40	.25
444	Gary Nolan	.15	.08	.05
445	Rico Petrocelli	.25	.13	.08
446	Larry Haney	.15	.08	.05
447	Gene Locklear	.15	.08	.05
448	Tom Johnson	.15	.08	.05
449	Bob Robertson	.15	.08	.05
450	Jim Palmer	5.00	2.50	1.50
451	Buddy Bradford	.15	.08	.05
452	Tom Hausman	.15	.08	.05
453	Lou Piniella	.60	.30	.20
454	Tom Griffin	.15	.08	.05
455	Dick Allen	.50	.25	.15
456	Joe Coleman	.20	.10	.06
457	Ed Crosby	.15	.08	.05
458	Earl Williams	.15	.08	.05
459	Jim Brewer	.15	.08	.05
460	Cesar Cedeno	.30	.15	.09
461	NL & AL Championships	.80	.40	.25
462	1975 World Series	.80	.40	.25
463	Steve Hargan	.15	.08	.05
464	Ken Henderson	.15	.08	.05
465	Mike Marshall	.30	.15	.09
466	Bob Stinson	.15	.08	.05
467	Woodie Fryman	.20	.10	.06
468	Jesus Alou	.20	.10	.06
469	Rawly Eastwick	.15	.08	.05
470	Bobby Murcer	.35	.20	.11
471	Jim Burton	.15	.08	.05
472	Bob Davis	.15	.08	.05
473	Paul Blair	.20	.10	.06
474	Ray Corbin	.15	.08	.05
475	Joe Rudi	.30	.15	.09
476	Bob Moose	.15	.08	.05
477	Indians Team (Frank Robinson)	.80	.40	.25
478	Lynn McGlothen	.15	.08	.05
479	Bobby Mitchell	.15	.08	.05
480	Mike Schmidt	30.00	15.00	9.00
481	Rudy May	.20	.10	.06
482	Tim Hosley	.15	.08	.05
483	Mickey Stanley	.20	.10	.06
484	Eric Raich	.15	.08	.05
485	Mike Hargrove	.20	.10	.06
486	Bruce Dal Canton	.15	.08	.05
487	Leron Lee	.15	.08	.05
488	Claude Osteen	.20	.10	.06
489	Skip Jutze	.15	.08	.05
490	Frank Tanana	.30	.15	.09
491	Terry Crowley	.15	.08	.05
492	Marty Pattin	.15	.08	.05
493	Derrel Thomas	.15	.08	.05
494	Craig Swan	.15	.08	.05
495	Nate Colbert	.15	.08	.05
496	Juan Beniquez	.20	.10	.06
497	Joe McIntosh	.15	.08	.05
498	Glenn Borgmann	.15	.08	.05
499	Mario Guerrero	.15	.08	.05
500	Reggie Jackson	15.00	7.50	4.50
501	Billy Champion	.15	.08	.05
502	Tim McCarver	.50	.25	.15
503	Elliott Maddox	.20	.10	.06
504	Pirates Team (Danny Murtaugh)	.80	.40	.25
505	Mark Belanger	.20	.10	.06
506	George Mitterwald	.15	.08	.05
507	Ray Bare	.15	.08	.05
508	*Duane Kuiper*	.20	.10	.06
509	Bill Hands	.15	.08	.05
510	Amos Otis	.25	.13	.08
511	Jamie Easterly	.15	.08	.05
512	Ellie Rodriguez	.15	.08	.05
513	Bart Johnson	.15	.08	.05
514	Dan Driessen	.30	.15	.09
515	Steve Yeager	.15	.08	.05
516	Wayne Granger	.15	.08	.05
517	John Milner	.15	.08	.05
518	*Doug Flynn*	.20	.10	.06
519	Steve Brye	.15	.08	.05
520	Willie McCovey	2.50	1.25	.70
521	Jim Colborn	.15	.08	.05
522	Ted Sizemore	.15	.08	.05
523	Bob Montgomery	.15	.08	.05
524	Pete Falcone	.15	.08	.05
525	Billy Williams	2.25	1.25	.70
526	Checklist 397-528	1.50	.70	.45
527	Mike Anderson	.15	.08	.05
528	Dock Ellis	.20	.10	.06
529	Deron Johnson	.15	.08	.05
530	Don Sutton	1.50	.70	.45
531	Mets Team (Joe Frazier)	.90	.45	.25
532	Milt May	.15	.08	.05
533	Lee Richard	.15	.08	.05

		NR MT	EX	VG
534	Stan Bahnsen	.15	.08	.05
535	Dave Nelson	.15	.08	.05
536	Mike Thompson	.15	.08	.05
537	Tony Muser	.15	.08	.05
538	Pat Darcy	.15	.08	.05
539	John Balaz	.15	.08	.05
540	Bill Freehan	.25	.13	.08
541	Steve Mingori	.15	.08	.05
542	Keith Hernandez	6.00	3.00	1.75
543	Wayne Twitchell	.15	.08	.05
544	Pepe Frias	.15	.08	.05
545	Sparky Lyle	.35	.20	.11
546	Dave Rosello	.15	.08	.05
547	Roric Harrison	.15	.08	.05
548	Manny Mota	.25	.13	.08
549	Randy Tate	.15	.08	.05
550	Hank Aaron	15.00	7.50	4.50
551	Jerry DaVanon	.15	.08	.05
552	Terry Humphrey	.15	.08	.05
553	Randy Moffitt	.15	.08	.05
554	Ray Fosse	.15	.08	.05
555	Dyar Miller	.15	.08	.05
556	Twins Team (Gene Mauch)	.80	.40	.25
557	Dan Spillner	.15	.08	.05
558	Clarence Gaston	.15	.08	.05
559	Clyde Wright	.15	.08	.05
560	Jorge Orta	.15	.08	.05
561	Tom Carroll	.15	.08	.05
562	Adrian Garrett	.15	.08	.05
563	Larry Demery	.15	.08	.05
564	Bubble Gum Blowing Champ (Kurt Bevacqua)	.30	.15	.09
565	Tug McGraw	.35	.20	.11
566	Ken McMullen	.15	.08	.05
567	George Stone	.15	.08	.05
568	Rob Andrews	.15	.08	.05
569	Nelson Briles	.15	.08	.05
570	George Hendrick	.20	.10	.06
571	Don DeMola	.15	.08	.05
572	Rich Coggins	.20	.10	.06
573	Bill Travers	.15	.08	.05
574	Don Kessinger	.20	.10	.06
575	Dwight Evans	3.00	1.50	.90
576	Maximino Leon	.15	.08	.05
577	Marc Hill	.15	.08	.05
578	Ted Kubiak	.15	.08	.05
579	Clay Kirby	.15	.08	.05
580	Bert Campaneris	.30	.15	.09
581	Cardinals Team (Red Schoendienst)	.80	.40	.25
582	Mike Kekich	.15	.08	.05
583	Tommy Helms	.15	.08	.05
584	Stan Wall	.15	.08	.05
585	Joe Torre	.50	.25	.15
586	Ron Schueler	.15	.08	.05
587	Leo Cardenas	.15	.08	.05
588	Kevin Kobel	.15	.08	.05
589	Rookie Pitchers (Santo Alcala, *Mike Flanagan*, Joe Pactwa, Pablo Torrealba)	1.00	.50	.30
590	Rookie Outfielders (Henry Cruz, Chet Lemon, *Ellis Valentine*, Terry Whitfield)	1.00	.50	.30
591	Rookie Pitchers (Steve Grilli, Craig Mitchell, Jose Sosa, George Throop)	.15	.08	.05
592	Rookie Infielders (Dave McKay, *Willie Randolph*, Jerry Royster, Roy Staiger)	5.00	2.50	1.50
593	Rookie Pitchers (Larry Anderson, Ken Crosby, Mark Littell, *Butch Metzger*)	.25	.13	.08
594	Rookie Catchers & Outfielders (Andy Merchant, Ed Ott, Royle Stillman, Jerry White)	.15	.08	.05
595	Rookie Pitchers (Steve Barr, Art DeFilippis, Randy Lerch, Sid Monge)	.15	.08	.05
596	Rookie Infielders (Lamar Johnson, *Johnny LeMaster*, Jerry Manuel, *Craig Reynolds*)	.35	.20	.11
597	Rookie Pitchers (*Don Aase*, Jack Kucek, Frank LaCorte, Mike Pazik)	.50	.25	.15
598	Rookie Outfielders (Hector Cruz, *Jamie Quirk*, Jerry Turner, Joe Wallis)	.20	.10	.06
599	Rookie Pitchers (Rob Dressler, *Ron Guidry*, Bob McClure, Pat Zachry)	10.00	5.00	3.00
600	Tom Seaver	12.00	6.00	3.50
601	Ken Rudolph	.15	.08	.05
602	Doug Konieczny	.15	.08	.05
603	Jim Holt	.15	.08	.05
604	Joe Lovitto	.15	.08	.05
605	Al Downing	.20	.10	.06
606	Brewers Team (Alex Grammas)	.80	.40	.25

		NR MT	EX	VG
607	Rich Hinton	.15	.08	.05
608	Vic Correll	.15	.08	.05
609	Fred Norman	.15	.08	.05
610	Greg Luzinski	.40	.20	.12
611	Rich Folkers	.15	.08	.05
612	Joe Lahoud	.15	.08	.05
613	Tim Johnson	.15	.08	.05
614	Fernando Arroyo	.15	.08	.05
615	Mike Cubbage	.15	.08	.05
616	Buck Martinez	.15	.08	.05
617	Darold Knowles	.15	.08	.05
618	Jack Brohamer	.15	.08	.05
619	Bill Butler	.15	.08	.05
620	Al Oliver	.70	.35	.20
621	Tom Hall	.15	.08	.05
622	Rick Auerbach	.15	.08	.05
623	Bob Allietta	.15	.08	.05
624	Tony Taylor	.15	.08	.05
625	J.R. Richard	.25	.13	.08
626	Bob Sheldon	.15	.08	.05
627	Bill Plummer	.15	.08	.05
628	John D'Acquisto	.15	.08	.05
629	Sandy Alomar	.20	.10	.06
630	Chris Speier	.20	.10	.06
631	Braves Team (Dave Bristol)	.80	.40	.25
632	Rogelio Moret	.15	.08	.05
633	*John Stearns*	.30	.15	.09
634	Larry Christenson	.15	.08	.05
635	Jim Fregosi	.25	.13	.08
636	Joe Decker	.15	.08	.05
637	Bruce Bochte	.20	.10	.06
638	Doyle Alexander	.30	.15	.09
639	Fred Kendall	.15	.08	.05
640	Bill Madlock	1.00	.50	.30
641	Tom Paciorek	.20	.10	.06
642	Dennis Blair	.15	.08	.05
643	Checklist 529-660	1.50	.70	.45
644	Tom Bradley	.15	.08	.05
645	Darrell Porter	.20	.10	.06
646	John Lowenstein	.15	.08	.05
648	Al Cowens	.20	.10	.06
649	Dave Roberts	.15	.08	.05
650	Thurman Munson	7.00	3.50	2.00
651	John Odom	.20	.10	.06
652	Ed Armbrister	.15	.08	.05
653	*Mike Norris*	.30	.15	.09
654	Doug Griffin	.15	.08	.05
655	Mike Vail	.15	.08	.05
656	White Sox Team (Chuck Tanner)	.80	.40	.25
657	*Roy Smalley*	.40	.20	.12
658	Jerry Johnson	.15	.08	.05
659	Ben Oglivie	.25	.13	.08
660	Dave Lopes	.60	.13	.08

		NR MT	EX	VG
Complete Set:		10.00	5.00	3.00
Common Player:		.15	.08	.05
27T	Ed Figueroa	.20	.10	.06
28T	Dusty Baker	.35	.20	.11
44T	Doug Rader	.15	.08	.05
58T	Ron Reed	.20	.10	.06
74T	Oscar Gamble	.25	.13	.08
80T	Jim Kaat	.60	.30	.20
83T	Jim Spencer	.15	.08	.05
85T	Mickey Rivers	.30	.15	.09
99T	Lee Lacy	.20	.10	.06
120T	Rusty Staub	.50	.25	.15
127T	Larvell Blanks	.15	.08	.05
146T	George Medich	.15	.08	.05
158T	Ken Reitz	.15	.08	.05
208T	Mike Lum	.15	.08	.05
211T	Clay Carroll	.20	.10	.06
231T	Tom House	.15	.08	.05
250T	Fergie Jenkins	1.00	.50	.30
259T	Darrel Chaney	.15	.08	.05
292T	Leon Roberts	.15	.08	.05
296T	Pat Dobson	.20	.10	.06
309T	Bill Melton	.20	.10	.06
338T	Bob Bailey	.15	.08	.05
380T	Bobby Bonds	.35	.20	.11
383T	John Ellis	.15	.08	.05
385T	Mickey Lolich	.50	.25	.15
401T	Ken Brett	.20	.10	.06
410T	Ralph Garr	.20	.10	.06
411T	Bill Singer	.20	.10	.06
428T	Jim Crawford	.15	.08	.05
434T	Morris Nettles	.15	.08	.05
464T	Ken Henderson	.15	.08	.05
497T	Joe McIntosh	.15	.08	.05
524T	Pete Falcone	.15	.08	.05
527T	Mike Anderson	.15	.08	.05
528T	Dock Ellis	.20	.10	.06
532T	Milt May	.15	.08	.05
554T	Ray Fosse	.15	.08	.05
579T	Clay Kirby	.15	.08	.05
583T	Tommy Helms	.15	.08	.05
592T	Willie Randolph	1.00	.50	.30
618T	Jack Brohamer	.15	.08	.05
632T	Rogelio Moret	.15	.08	.05
649T	Dave Roberts	.15	.08	.05
----	Traded Checklist	.80	.40	.25

1976 Topps Traded

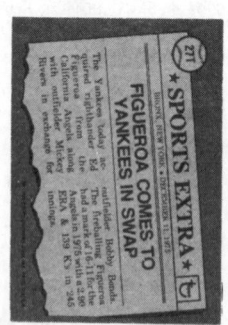

Similar to the Topps Traded set of 1974, the 2-1/2" by 3-1/2" cards feature photos of players traded after the printing deadline. The style of the cards is essentially the same as the regular issue but with a large "Sports Extra" headline announcing the trade and its date. The backs continue in newspaper style to detail the specifics of the trade. There are 43 player cards and one checklist in the set. Numbers remain the same as the player's regular card, with the addition of a "T" suffix.

1977 Topps

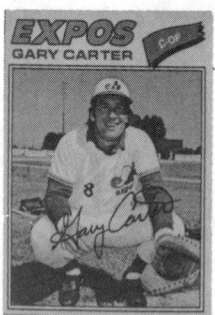
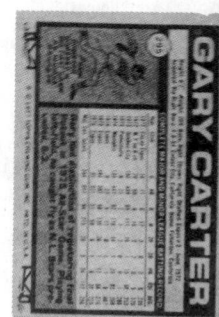

The 1977 Topps Set is a 660-card effort featuring front designs dominated by a color photograph on which there is a facsimile autograph. Above the picture are the player's name, team and position. The backs of the 2-1/2" by 3-1/2" cards include personal and career statistics along with newspaper-style highlights and a cartoon. Specialty cards include statistical leaders, record performances, a new "Turn Back The Clock" feature which highlighted great past moments and a "Big League Brothers" feature.

		NR MT	EX	VG
Complete Set:		375.00	200.00	120.00
Common Player:		.15	.08	.05
1	Batting Leaders (George Brett, Bill Madlock)	2.50	.70	.45
2	Home Run Leaders (Graig Nettles, Mike Schmidt)	1.25	.60	.40

		NR MT	EX	VG
3	Runs Batted In Leaders (George Foster, Lee May)	.50	.25	.15
4	Stolen Base Leaders (Dave Lopes, Bill North)	.30	.15	.09
5	Victory Leaders (Randy Jones, Jim Palmer)	.80	.40	.25
6	Strikeout Leaders (Nolan Ryan, Tom Seaver)	3.00	1.50	.90
7	Earned Run Avg. Ldrs. (John Denny, Mark Fidrych)	.30	.15	.09
8	Leading Firemen (Bill Campbell, Rawly Eastwick)	.30	.15	.09
9	Doug Rader	.15	.08	.05
10	Reggie Jackson	10.00	5.00	3.00
11	Rob Dressler	.15	.08	.05
12	Larry Haney	.15	.08	.05
13	Luis Gomez	.15	.08	.05
14	Tommy Smith	.15	.08	.05
15	Don Gullett	.20	.10	.06
16	Bob Jones	.15	.08	.05
17	Steve Stone	.25	.13	.08
18	Indians Team (Frank Robinson)	.80	.40	.25
19	John D'Acquisto	.15	.08	.05
20	Graig Nettles	.90	.45	.25
21	Ken Forsch	.20	.10	.06
22	Bill Freehan	.25	.13	.08
23	Dan Driessen	.25	.13	.08
24	Carl Morton	.15	.08	.05
25	Dwight Evans	2.50	1.25	.70
26	Ray Sadecki	.15	.08	.05
27	Bill Buckner	.35	.20	.11
28	Woodie Fryman	.20	.10	.06
29	Bucky Dent	.25	.13	.08
30	Greg Luzinski	.40	.20	.12
31	Jim Todd	.15	.08	.05
32	Checklist 1-132	1.25	.60	.40
33	Wayne Garland	.15	.08	.05
34	Angels Team (Norm Sherry)	.70	.35	.20
35	Rennie Stennett	.15	.08	.05
36	John Ellis	.15	.08	.05
37	Steve Hargan	.15	.08	.05
38	Craig Kusick	.15	.08	.05
39	Tom Griffin	.15	.08	.05
40	Bobby Murcer	.30	.15	.09
41	Jim Kern	.15	.08	.05
42	Jose Cruz	.30	.15	.09
43	Ray Bare	.15	.08	.05
44	Bud Harrelson	.20	.10	.06
45	Rawly Eastwick	.15	.08	.05
46	Buck Martinez	.15	.08	.05
47	Lynn McGlothen	.15	.08	.05
48	Tom Paciorek	.15	.08	.05
49	Grant Jackson	.15	.08	.05
50	Ron Cey	.35	.20	.11
51	Brewers Team (Alex Grammas)	.70	.35	.20
52	Ellis Valentine	.20	.10	.06
53	Paul Mitchell	.15	.08	.05
54	Sandy Alomar	.20	.10	.06
55	Jeff Burroughs	.25	.13	.08
56	Rudy May	.20	.10	.06
57	Marc Hill	.15	.08	.05
58	Chet Lemon	.30	.15	.09
59	Larry Christenson	.15	.08	.05
60	Jim Rice	4.50	2.25	1.25
61	Manny Sanguillen	.15	.08	.05
62	Eric Raich	.15	.08	.05
63	Tito Fuentes	.15	.08	.05
64	Larry Biittner	.15	.08	.05
65	Skip Lockwood	.15	.08	.05
66	Roy Smalley	.20	.10	.06
67	*Joaquin Andujar*	.60	.30	.20
68	Bruce Bochte	.20	.10	.06
69	Jim Crawford	.15	.08	.05
70	Johnny Bench	7.00	3.50	2.00
71	Dock Ellis	.20	.10	.06
72	Mike Anderson	.15	.08	.05
73	Charlie Williams	.15	.08	.05
74	A's Team (Jack McKeon)	.70	.35	.20
75	Dennis Leonard	.20	.10	.06
76	Tim Foli	.15	.08	.05
77	Dyar Miller	.15	.08	.05
78	Bob Davis	.15	.08	.05
79	Don Money	.15	.08	.05
80	Andy Messersmith	.25	.13	.08
81	Juan Beniquez	.20	.10	.06
82	Jim Rooker	.15	.08	.05
83	Kevin Bell	.15	.08	.05
84	Ollie Brown	.15	.08	.05
85	Duane Kuiper	.15	.08	.05
86	Pat Zachry	.15	.08	.05
87	Glenn Borgmann	.15	.08	.05
88	Stan Wall	.15	.08	.05

		NR MT	EX	VG
89	*Butch Hobson*	.20	.10	.06
90	Cesar Cedeno	.30	.15	.09
91	John Verhoeven	.15	.08	.05
92	Dave Rosello	.15	.08	.05
93	Tom Poquette	.15	.08	.05
94	Craig Swan	.15	.08	.05
95	Keith Hernandez	3.00	1.50	.90
96	Lou Piniella	.40	.20	.12
97	Dave Heaverlo	.15	.08	.05
98	Milt May	.15	.08	.05
99	Tom Hausman	.15	.08	.05
100	Joe Morgan	5.00	2.50	1.50
101	Dick Bosman	.15	.08	.05
102	Jose Morales	.15	.08	.05
103	Mike Bacsik	.15	.08	.05
104	*Omar Moreno*	.25	.13	.08
105	Steve Yeager	.15	.08	.05
106	Mike Flanagan	.35	.20	.11
107	Bill Melton	.20	.10	.06
108	Alan Foster	.15	.08	.05
109	Jorge Orta	.15	.08	.05
110	Steve Carlton	6.00	3.00	1.75
111	Rico Petrocelli	.25	.13	.08
112	Bill Greif	.15	.08	.05
113	Blue Jays Mgr./Coaches (Roy Hartsfield, Don Leppert, Bob Miller, Jackie Moore, Harry Warner)	.25	.13	.08
114	Bruce Dal Canton	.15	.08	.05
115	Rick Manning	.20	.10	.06
116	Joe Niekro	.30	.15	.09
117	Frank White	.25	.13	.08
118	Rick Jones	.15	.08	.05
119	John Stearns	.20	.10	.06
120	Rod Carew	8.00	4.00	2.50
121	Gary Nolan	.15	.08	.05
122	Ben Oglivie	.20	.10	.06
123	Fred Stanley	.20	.10	.06
124	George Mitterwald	.15	.08	.05
125	Bill Travers	.15	.08	.05
126	Rod Gilbreath	.15	.08	.05
127	Ron Fairly	.25	.13	.08
128	Tommy John	1.25	.60	.40
129	Mike Sadek	.15	.08	.05
130	Al Oliver	.60	.30	.20
131	Orlando Ramirez	.15	.08	.05
132	Chip Lang	.15	.08	.05
133	Ralph Garr	.20	.10	.06
134	Padres Team (John McNamara)	.70	.35	.20
135	Mark Belanger	.20	.10	.06
136	*Jerry Mumphrey*	.40	.20	.12
137	Jeff Terpko	.15	.08	.05
138	Bob Stinson	.15	.08	.05
139	Fred Norman	.15	.08	.05
140	Mike Schmidt	25.00	12.50	7.50
141	Mark Littell	.15	.08	.05
142	Steve Dillard	.15	.08	.05
143	Ed Herrmann	.15	.08	.05
144	*Bruce Sutter*	2.00	1.00	.70
145	Tom Veryzer	.15	.08	.05
146	Dusty Baker	.25	.13	.08
147	Jackie Brown	.15	.08	.05
148	Fran Healy	.20	.10	.06
149	Mike Cubbage	.15	.08	.05
150	Tom Seaver	10.00	5.00	3.00
151	Johnnie LeMaster	.15	.08	.05
152	Gaylord Perry	2.00	1.00	.60
153	Ron Jackson	.15	.08	.05
154	Dave Giusti	.15	.08	.05
155	Joe Rudi	.25	.13	.08
156	Pete Mackanin	.15	.08	.05
157	Ken Brett	.20	.10	.06
158	Ted Kubiak	.15	.08	.05
159	Bernie Carbo	.15	.08	.05
160	Will McEnaney	.15	.08	.05
161	*Garry Templeton*	.80	.40	.25
162	Mike Cuellar	.25	.13	.08
163	Dave Hilton	.15	.08	.05
164	Tug McGraw	.35	.20	.11
165	Jim Wynn	.25	.13	.08
166	Bill Campbell	.15	.08	.05
167	Rich Hebner	.15	.08	.05
168	Charlie Spikes	.15	.08	.05
169	Darold Knowles	.15	.08	.05
170	Thurman Munson	5.00	2.50	1.50
171	Ken Sanders	.15	.08	.05
172	John Milner	.15	.08	.05
173	Chuck Scrivener	.15	.08	.05
174	Nelson Briles	.15	.08	.05
175	*Butch Wynegar*	.40	.20	.12
176	Bob Robertson	.15	.08	.05
177	Bart Johnson	.15	.08	.05

		NR MT	EX	VG
178	Bombo Rivera	.15	.08	.05
179	Paul Hartzell	.15	.08	.05
180	Dave Lopes	.25	.13	.08
181	Ken McMullen	.15	.08	.05
182	Dan Spillner	.15	.08	.05
183	Cardinals Team (Vern Rapp)	.70	.35	.20
184	Bo McLaughlin	.15	.08	.05
185	Sixto Lezcano	.20	.10	.06
186	Doug Flynn	.15	.08	.05
187	Dick Pole	.15	.08	.05
188	Bob Tolan	.20	.10	.06
189	Rick Dempsey	.20	.10	.06
190	Ray Burris	.15	.08	.05
191	Doug Griffin	.15	.08	.05
192	Clarence Gaston	.15	.08	.05
193	Larry Gura	.15	.08	.05
194	Gary Matthews	.25	.13	.08
195	Ed Figueroa	.20	.10	.06
196	Len Randle	.15	.08	.05
197	Ed Ott	.15	.08	.05
198	Wilbur Wood	.20	.10	.06
199	Pepe Frias	.15	.08	.05
200	Frank Tanana	.30	.15	.09
201	Ed Kranepool	.25	.13	.08
202	Tom Johnson	.15	.08	.05
203	Ed Armbrister	.15	.08	.05
204	Jeff Newman	.15	.08	.05
205	Pete Falcone	.15	.08	.05
206	Boog Powell	.50	.25	.15
207	Glenn Abbott	.15	.08	.05
208	Checklist 133-264	1.25	.60	.40
209	Rob Andrews	.15	.08	.05
210	Fred Lynn	1.50	.70	.45
211	Giants Team (Joe Altobelli)	.70	.35	.20
212	Jim Mason	.15	.08	.05
213	Maximino Leon	.15	.08	.05
214	Darrell Porter	.20	.10	.06
215	Butch Metzger	.15	.08	.05
216	Doug DeCinces	.25	.13	.08
217	Tom Underwood	.15	.08	.05
218	John Wathan	.60	.30	.20
219	Joe Coleman	.20	.10	.06
220	Chris Chambliss	.30	.15	.09
221	Bob Bailey	.15	.08	.05
222	Francisco Barrios	.15	.08	.05
223	Earl Williams	.15	.08	.05
224	Rusty Torres	.15	.08	.05
225	Bob Apodaca	.15	.08	.05
226	Leroy Stanton	.15	.08	.05
227	Joe Sambito	.25	.13	.08
228	Twins Team (Gene Mauch)	.80	.40	.25
229	Don Kessinger	.20	.10	.06
230	Vida Blue	.40	.20	.12
231	Record Breaker (George Brett)	3.00	1.50	.90
232	Record Breaker (Minnie Minoso)	.35	.20	.11
233	Record Breaker (Jose Morales)	.20	.10	.06
234	Record Breaker (Nolan Ryan)	6.00	3.00	1.75
235	Cecil Cooper	.60	.30	.20
236	Tom Buskey	.15	.08	.05
237	Gene Clines	.15	.08	.05
238	Tippy Martinez	.15	.08	.05
239	Bill Plummer	.15	.08	.05
240	Ron LeFlore	.25	.13	.08
241	Dave Tomlin	.15	.08	.05
242	Ken Henderson	.15	.08	.05
243	Ron Reed	.20	.10	.06
244	John Mayberry	.20	.10	.06
245	Rick Rhoden	.30	.15	.09
246	Mike Vail	.15	.08	.05
247	Chris Knapp	.15	.08	.05
248	Wilbur Howard	.15	.08	.05
249	Pete Redfern	.15	.08	.05
250	Bill Madlock	.40	.20	.12
251	Tony Muser	.15	.08	.05
252	Dale Murray	.15	.08	.05
253	John Hale	.15	.08	.05
254	Doyle Alexander	.30	.15	.09
255	George Scott	.20	.10	.06
256	Joe Hoerner	.15	.08	.05
257	Mike Miley	.15	.08	.05
258	Luis Tiant	.35	.20	.11
259	Mets Team (Joe Frazier)	.80	.40	.25
260	J.R. Richard	.25	.13	.08
261	Phil Garner	.20	.10	.06
262	Al Cowens	.15	.08	.05
263	Mike Marshall	.25	.13	.08
264	Tom Hutton	.15	.08	.05
265	Mark Fidrych	.70	.35	.20
266	Derrel Thomas	.15	.08	.05
267	Ray Fosse	.15	.08	.05
268	Rick Sawyer	.15	.08	.05

		NR MT	EX	VG
269	Joe Lis	.15	.08	.05
270	Dave Parker	5.00	2.50	1.50
271	Terry Forster	.20	.10	.06
272	Lee Lacy	.15	.08	.05
273	Eric Soderholm	.15	.08	.05
274	Don Stanhouse	.15	.08	.05
275	Mike Hargrove	.20	.10	.06
276	A.L. Championship (Chambliss' Dramatic Homer Decides It)	.70	.35	.20
277	N.L. Championship (Reds Sweep Phillies 3 In Row)	.70	.35	.20
278	Danny Frisella	.15	.08	.05
279	Joe Wallis	.15	.08	.05
280	Jim Hunter	2.00	1.00	.60
281	Roy Staiger	.15	.08	.05
282	Sid Monge	.15	.08	.05
283	Jerry DaVanon	.15	.08	.05
284	Mike Norris	.20	.10	.06
285	Brooks Robinson	2.50	1.25	.70
286	Johnny Grubb	.15	.08	.05
287	Reds Team (Sparky Anderson)	.80	.40	.25
288	Bob Montgomery	.15	.08	.05
289	Gene Garber	.20	.10	.06
290	Amos Otis	.20	.10	.06
291	Jason Thompson	.35	.20	.11
292	Rogelio Moret	.15	.08	.05
293	Jack Brohamer	.15	.08	.05
294	George Medich	.15	.08	.05
295	Gary Carter	6.00	3.00	1.75
296	Don Hood	.15	.08	.05
297	Ken Reitz	.15	.08	.05
298	Charlie Hough	.25	.13	.08
299	Otto Velez	.15	.08	.05
300	Jerry Koosman	.30	.15	.09
301	Toby Harrah	.20	.10	.06
302	Mike Garman	.15	.08	.05
303	Gene Tenace	.20	.10	.06
304	Jim Hughes	.15	.08	.05
305	Mickey Rivers	.25	.13	.08
306	Rick Waits	.15	.08	.05
307	Gary Sutherland	.15	.08	.05
308	Gene Pentz	.15	.08	.05
309	Red Sox Team (Don Zimmer)	.80	.40	.25
310	Larry Bowa	.30	.15	.09
311	Vern Ruhle	.15	.08	.05
312	Rob Belloir	.15	.08	.05
313	Paul Blair	.20	.10	.06
314	Steve Mingori	.15	.08	.05
315	Dave Chalk	.15	.08	.05
316	Steve Rogers	.20	.10	.06
317	Kurt Bevacqua	.15	.08	.05
318	Duffy Dyer	.15	.08	.05
319	Rich Gossage	.90	.45	.25
320	Ken Griffey	.30	.15	.09
321	Dave Goltz	.20	.10	.06
322	Bill Russell	.20	.10	.06
323	Larry Lintz	.15	.08	.05
324	John Curtis	.15	.08	.05
325	Mike Ivie	.15	.08	.05
326	Jesse Jefferson	.15	.08	.05
327	Astros Team (Bill Virdon)	.70	.35	.20
328	Tommy Boggs	.15	.08	.05
329	Ron Hodges	.15	.08	.05
330	George Hendrick	.20	.10	.06
331	Jim Colborn	.15	.08	.05
332	Elliott Maddox	.20	.10	.06
333	Paul Reuschel	.15	.08	.05
334	Bill Stein	.15	.08	.05
335	Bill Robinson	.15	.08	.05
336	Denny Doyle	.15	.08	.05
337	Ron Schueler	.15	.08	.05
338	Dave Duncan	.15	.08	.05
339	Adrian Devine	.15	.08	.05
340	Hal McRae	.30	.15	.09
341	Joe Kerrigan	.15	.08	.05
342	Jerry Remy	.15	.08	.05
343	Ed Halicki	.15	.08	.05
344	Brian Downing	.25	.13	.08
345	Reggie Smith	.25	.13	.08
346	Bill Singer	.20	.10	.06
347	George Foster	1.25	.60	.40
348	Brent Strom	.15	.08	.05
349	Jim Holt	.15	.08	.05
350	Larry Dierker	.20	.10	.06
351	Jim Sundberg	.20	.10	.06
352	Mike Phillips	.15	.08	.05
353	Stan Thomas	.15	.08	.05
354	Pirates Team (Chuck Tanner)	.80	.40	.25
355	Lou Brock	2.25	1.25	.70
356	Checklist 265-396	1.25	.60	.40
357	Tim McCarver	.40	.20	.12

#	Player	NR MT	EX	VG
358	Tom House	.15	.08	.05
359	Willie Randolph	.80	.40	.25
360	Rick Monday	.25	.13	.08
361	Eduardo Rodriguez	.15	.08	.05
362	Tommy Davis	.30	.15	.09
363	Dave Roberts	.15	.08	.05
364	Vic Correll	.15	.08	.05
365	Mike Torrez	.20	.10	.06
366	Ted Sizemore	.15	.08	.05
367	Dave Hamilton	.15	.08	.05
368	Mike Jorgensen	.15	.08	.05
369	Terry Humphrey	.15	.08	.05
370	John Montefusco	.20	.10	.06
371	Royals Team (Whitey Herzog)	.80	.40	.25
372	Rich Folkers	.15	.08	.05
373	Bert Campaneris	.30	.15	.09
374	Kent Tekulve	.30	.15	.09
375	Larry Hisle	.20	.10	.06
376	Nino Espinosa	.15	.08	.05
377	Dave McKay	.15	.08	.05
378	Jim Umbarger	.15	.08	.05
379	Larry Cox	.15	.08	.05
380	Lee May	.25	.13	.08
381	Bob Forsch	.20	.10	.06
382	Charlie Moore	.15	.08	.05
383	Stan Bahnsen	.15	.08	.05
384	Darrel Chaney	.15	.08	.05
385	Dave LaRoche	.15	.08	.05
386	Manny Mota	.25	.13	.08
387	Yankees Team (Billy Martin)	1.25	.60	.40
388	Terry Harmon	.15	.08	.05
389	Ken Kravec	.15	.08	.05
390	Dave Winfield	4.00	2.00	1.25
391	Dan Warthen	.15	.08	.05
392	Phil Roof	.15	.08	.05
393	John Lowenstein	.15	.08	.05
394	Bill Laxton	.15	.08	.05
395	Manny Trillo	.20	.10	.06
396	Tom Murphy	.15	.08	.05
397	Larry Herndon	.40	.20	.12
398	Tom Burgmeier	.15	.08	.05
399	Bruce Boisclair	.15	.08	.05
400	Steve Garvey	5.00	2.50	1.50
401	Mickey Scott	.15	.08	.05
402	Tommy Helms	.15	.08	.05
403	Tom Grieve	.15	.08	.05
404	Eric Rasmussen	.15	.08	.05
405	Claudell Washington	.25	.13	.08
406	Tim Johnson	.15	.08	.05
407	Dave Freisleben	.15	.08	.05
408	Cesar Tovar	.15	.08	.05
409	Pete Broberg	.15	.08	.05
410	Willie Montanez	.15	.08	.05
411	World Series Games 1 & 2	.70	.35	.20
412	World Series Games 3 & 4	.70	.35	.20
413	World Series Summary	.70	.35	.20
414	Tommy Harper	.20	.10	.06
415	Jay Johnstone	.20	.10	.06
416	Chuck Hartenstein	.15	.08	.05
417	Wayne Garrett	.15	.08	.05
418	White Sox Team (Bob Lemon)	.80	.40	.25
419	Steve Swisher	.15	.08	.05
420	Rusty Staub	.35	.20	.11
421	Doug Rau	.15	.08	.05
422	Freddie Patek	.15	.08	.05
423	Gary Lavelle	.15	.08	.05
424	Steve Brye	.15	.08	.05
425	Joe Torre	.40	.20	.12
426	Dick Drago	.15	.08	.05
427	Dave Rader	.15	.08	.05
428	Rangers Team (Frank Lucchesi)	.70	.35	.20
429	Ken Boswell	.15	.08	.05
430	Fergie Jenkins	1.25	.60	.40
431	Dave Collins	.25	.13	.08
432	Buzz Capra	.15	.08	.05
433	Turn Back The Clock (Nate Colbert)	.20	.10	.06
434	Turn Back The Clock (Carl Yastrzemski)	2.00	1.00	.60
435	Turn Back The Clock (Maury Wills)	.35	.20	.11
436	Turn Back The Clock (Bob Keegan)	.20	.10	.06
437	Turn Back The Clock (Ralph Kiner)	.50	.25	.15
438	Marty Perez	.15	.08	.05
439	Gorman Thomas	.30	.15	.09
440	Jon Matlack	.20	.10	.06
441	Larvell Blanks	.15	.08	.05
442	Braves Team (Dave Bristol)	.70	.35	.20
443	Lamar Johnson	.15	.08	.05
444	Wayne Twitchell	.15	.08	.05
445	Ken Singleton	.25	.13	.08
446	Bill Bonham	.15	.08	.05
447	Jerry Turner	.15	.08	.05
448	Ellie Rodriguez	.15	.08	.05
449	Al Fitzmorris	.15	.08	.05
450	Pete Rose	9.00	4.50	2.75
451	Checklist 397-528	1.25	.60	.40
452	Mike Caldwell	.15	.08	.05
453	Pedro Garcia	.15	.08	.05
454	Andy Etchebarren	.15	.08	.05
455	Rick Wise	.20	.10	.06
456	Leon Roberts	.15	.08	.05
457	Steve Luebber	.15	.08	.05
458	Leo Foster	.15	.08	.05
459	Steve Foucault	.15	.08	.05
460	Willie Stargell	2.50	1.25	.70
461	Dick Tidrow	.20	.10	.06
462	Don Baylor	.35	.20	.11
463	Jamie Quirk	.15	.08	.05
464	Randy Moffitt	.15	.08	.05
465	Rico Carty	.25	.13	.08
466	Fred Holdsworth	.15	.08	.05
467	Phillies Team (Danny Ozark)	.70	.35	.20
468	Ramon Hernandez	.15	.08	.05
469	Pat Kelly	.15	.08	.05
470	Ted Simmons	.60	.30	.20
471	Del Unser	.15	.08	.05
472	Rookie Pitchers (Don Aase, Bob McClure, Gil Patterson, Dave Wehrmeister)	.25	.13	.08
473	Rookie Outfielders (Andre Dawson, Gene Richards, John Scott, Denny Walling)	45.00	23.00	13.50
474	Rookie Shortstops (Bob Bailor, Kiko Garcia, Craig Reynolds, Alex Taveras)	.15	.08	.05
475	Rookie Pitchers (Chris Batton, Rick Camp, Scott McGregor, Manny Sarmiento)	.30	.15	.09
476	Rookie Catchers (Gary Alexander, Rick Cerone, Dale Murphy, Kevin Pasley)	60.00	30.00	18.00
477	Rookie Infielders (Doug Ault, Rich Dauer, Orlando Gonzalez, Phil Mankowski)	.25	.13	.08
478	Rookie Pitchers (Jim Gideon, Leon Hooten, Dave Johnson, Mark Lemongello)	.15	.08	.05
479	Rookie Outfielders (Brian Asselstine, Wayne Gross, Sam Mejias, Alvis Woods)	.25	.13	.08
480	Carl Yastrzemski	5.00	2.50	1.50
481	Roger Metzger	.15	.08	.05
482	Tony Solaita	.15	.08	.05
483	Richie Zisk	.20	.10	.06
484	Burt Hooton	.20	.10	.06
485	Roy White	.30	.15	.09
486	Ed Bane	.15	.08	.05
487	Rookie Pitchers (Larry Anderson, Ed Glynn, Joe Henderson, Greg Terlecky)	.15	.08	.05
488	Rookie Outfielders (Jack Clark, Ruppert Jones, Lee Mazzilli, Dan Thomas)	20.00	10.00	6.00
489	Rookie Pitchers (Len Barker, Randy Lerch, Greg Minton, Mike Overy)	.40	.20	.12
490	Rookie Shortstops (Billy Almon, Mickey Klutts, Tommy McMillan, Mark Wagner)	.25	.13	.08
491	Rookie Pitchers (Mike Dupree, Denny Martinez, Craig Mitchell, Bob Sykes)	2.00	1.00	.60
492	Rookie Outfielders (Tony Armas, Steve Kemp, Carlos Lopez, Gary Woods)	1.00	.50	.30
493	Rookie Pitchers (Mike Krukow, Jim Otten, Gary Wheelock, Mike Willis)	.70	.35	.20
494	Rookie Infielders (Juan Bernhardt, Mike Champion, Jim Gantner, Bump Wills)	.50	.25	.15
495	Al Hrabosky	.20	.10	.06
496	Gary Thomasson	.15	.08	.05
497	Clay Carroll	.20	.10	.06
498	Sal Bando	.25	.13	.08
499	Pablo Torrealba	.15	.08	.05
500	Dave Kingman	.60	.30	.20
501	Jim Bibby	.15	.08	.05
502	Randy Hundley	.15	.08	.05
503	Bill Lee	.20	.10	.06
504	Dodgers Team (Tom Lasorda)	1.00	.50	.30
505	Oscar Gamble	.20	.10	.06
506	Steve Grilli	.15	.08	.05
507	Mike Hegan	.15	.08	.05
508	Dave Pagan	.15	.08	.05
509	Cookie Rojas	.15	.08	.05
510	John Candelaria	.80	.40	.25
511	Bill Fahey	.15	.08	.05
512	Jack Billingham	.15	.08	.05
513	Jerry Terrell	.15	.08	.05
514	Cliff Johnson	.15	.08	.05
515	Chris Speier	.15	.08	.05

		NR MT	EX	VG
516	Bake McBride	.15	.08	.05
517	*Pete Vuckovich*	.50	.25	.15
518	Cubs Team (Herman Franks)	.70	.35	.20
519	Don Kirkwood	.15	.08	.05
520	Garry Maddox	.20	.10	.06
521	Bob Grich	.25	.13	.08
522	Enzo Hernandez	.15	.08	.05
523	Rollie Fingers	5.00	2.50	1.50
524	Rowland Office	.15	.08	.05
525	Dennis Eckersley	5.00	2.50	1.50
526	Larry Parrish	.35	.20	.11
527	Dan Meyer	.15	.08	.05
528	Bill Castro	.15	.08	.05
529	Jim Essian	.15	.08	.05
530	Rick Reuschel	.30	.15	.09
531	Lyman Bostock	.25	.13	.08
532	Jim Willoughby	.15	.08	.05
533	Mickey Stanley	.20	.10	.06
534	Paul Splittorff	.20	.10	.06
535	Cesar Geronimo	.20	.10	.06
536	Vic Albury	.15	.08	.05
537	Dave Roberts	.15	.08	.05
538	Frank Taveras	.15	.08	.05
539	Mike Wallace	.15	.08	.05
540	Bob Watson	.20	.10	.06
541	John Denny	.15	.08	.05
542	Frank Duffy	.15	.08	.05
543	Ron Blomberg	.20	.10	.06
544	Gary Ross	.15	.08	.05
545	Bob Boone	.25	.13	.08
546	Orioles Team (Earl Weaver)	.80	.40	.25
547	Willie McCovey	2.75	1.50	.80
548	*Joel Youngblood*	.30	.15	.09
549	Jerry Royster	.15	.08	.05
550	Randy Jones	.20	.10	.06
551	Bill North	.15	.08	.05
552	Pepe Mangual	.15	.08	.05
553	Jack Heidemann	.15	.08	.05
554	Bruce Kimm	.15	.08	.05
555	Dan Ford	.20	.10	.06
556	Doug Bird	.15	.08	.05
557	Jerry White	.15	.08	.05
558	Elias Sosa	.15	.08	.05
559	Alan Bannister	.15	.08	.05
560	Dave Concepcion	.35	.20	.11
561	Pete LaCock	.15	.08	.05
562	Checklist 529-660	1.25	.60	.40
563	Bruce Kison	.15	.08	.05
564	Alan Ashby	.20	.10	.06
565	Mickey Lolich	.50	.25	.15
566	Rick Miller	.15	.08	.05
567	Enos Cabell	.20	.10	.06
568	Carlos May	.20	.10	.06
569	Jim Lonborg	.20	.10	.06
570	Bobby Bonds	.35	.20	.11
571	Darrell Evans	.40	.20	.12
572	Ross Grimsley	.20	.10	.06
573	Joe Ferguson	.15	.08	.05
574	Aurelio Rodriguez	.20	.10	.06
575	Dick Ruthven	.15	.08	.05
576	Fred Kendall	.15	.08	.05
577	Jerry Augustine	.15	.08	.05
578	Bob Randall	.15	.08	.05
579	Don Carrithers	.15	.08	.05
580	George Brett	25.00	12.50	7.50
581	Pedro Borbon	.15	.08	.05
582	Ed Kirkpatrick	.15	.08	.05
583	Paul Lindblad	.15	.08	.05
584	Ed Goodson	.15	.08	.05
585	Rick Burleson	.20	.10	.06
586	Steve Renko	.15	.08	.05
587	Rick Baldwin	.15	.08	.05
588	Dave Moates	.15	.08	.05
589	Mike Cosgrove	.15	.08	.05
590	Buddy Bell	.30	.15	.09
591	Chris Arnold	.15	.08	.05
592	Dan Briggs	.15	.08	.05
593	Dennis Blair	.15	.08	.05
594	Biff Pocoroba	.15	.08	.05
595	John Hiller	.20	.10	.06
596	*Jerry Martin*	.25	.13	.08
597	Mariners Mgr./Coaches (Don Bryant, Jim Busby, Darrell Johnson, Vada Pinson, Wes Stock)	.25	.13	.08
598	Sparky Lyle	.35	.20	.11
599	Mike Tyson	.15	.08	.05
600	Jim Palmer	5.00	2.50	1.50
601	Mike Lum	.15	.08	.05
602	Andy Hassler	.15	.08	.05
603	Willie Davis	.25	.13	.08
604	Jim Slaton	.15	.08	.05

		NR MT	EX	VG
605	Felix Millan	.15	.08	.05
606	Steve Braun	.15	.08	.05
607	Larry Demery	.15	.08	.05
608	Roy Howell	.15	.08	.05
609	Jim Barr	.15	.08	.05
610	Jose Cardenal	.20	.10	.06
611	Dave Lemanczyk	.15	.08	.05
612	Barry Foote	.15	.08	.05
613	Reggie Cleveland	.15	.08	.05
614	Greg Gross	.15	.08	.05
615	Phil Niekro	2.00	1.00	.60
616	Tommy Sandt	.15	.08	.05
617	Bobby Darwin	.15	.08	.05
618	Pat Dobson	.20	.10	.06
619	Johnny Oates	.15	.08	.05
620	Don Sutton	1.50	.70	.45
621	Tigers Team (Ralph Houk)	.80	.40	.25
622	Jim Wohlford	.15	.08	.05
623	Jack Kucek	.15	.08	.05
624	Hector Cruz	.15	.08	.05
625	Ken Holtzman	.25	.13	.08
626	Al Bumbry	.20	.10	.06
627	Bob Myrick	.15	.08	.05
628	Mario Guerrero	.15	.08	.05
629	Bobby Valentine	.25	.13	.08
630	Bert Blyleven	1.25	.60	.40
631	Big League Brothers (George Brett, Ken Brett)	1.75	.90	.50
632	Big League Brothers (Bob Forsch, Ken Forsch)	.30	.15	.09
633	Big League Brothers (Carlos May, Lee May)	.30	.15	.09
634	Big League Brothers (Paul Reuschel, Rick Reuschel) (names switched)	.30	.15	.09
635	Robin Yount	25.00	12.50	7.50
636	Santo Alcala	.15	.08	.05
637	Alex Johnson	.15	.08	.05
638	Jim Kaat	.80	.40	.25
639	Jerry Morales	.15	.08	.05
640	Carlton Fisk	5.00	2.50	1.50
641	Dan Larson	.15	.08	.05
642	Willie Crawford	.15	.08	.05
643	Mike Pazik	.15	.08	.05
644	Matt Alexander	.15	.08	.05
645	Jerry Reuss	.25	.13	.08
646	Andres Mora	.15	.08	.05
647	Expos Team (Dick Williams)	.80	.40	.25
648	Jim Spencer	.15	.08	.05
649	Dave Cash	.15	.08	.05
650	Nolan Ryan	30.00	15.00	9.00
651	Von Joshua	.15	.08	.05
652	Tom Walker	.15	.08	.05
653	Diego Segui	.15	.08	.05
654	Ron Pruitt	.15	.08	.05
655	Tony Perez	.80	.40	.25
656	Ron Guidry	2.75	1.50	.80
657	Mick Kelleher	.15	.08	.05
658	Marty Pattin	.15	.08	.05
659	Merv Rettenmund	.15	.08	.05
660	Willie Horton	.40	.13	.08

1977 Topps Cloth Stickers

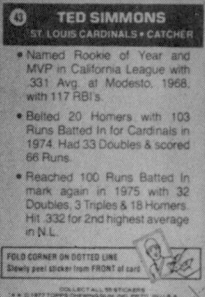

One of the few Topps specialty issues of the late 1970s, the 73-piece set of cloth stickers issued in 1977 includes 55 player stickers and 18 puzzle cards which could be joined to form a photo of the American League or National League All-Star teams. Issued as a separate issue, the 2-1/2" by 3-1/2"

stickers have a paper backing which could be removed to allow the cloth to be adhered to a jacket, notebook, etc.

		NR MT	EX	VG
	Complete Set:	250.00	125.00	75.00
	Common Player:	.20	.10	.06
1	Alan Ashby	.20	.10	.06
2	Buddy Bell	1.00	.50	.30
3	Johnny Bench	5.00	2.50	1.50
4	Vida Blue	.50	.25	.15
5	Bert Blyleven	1.00	.50	.30
6	Steve Braun	.50	.25	.15
7	George Brett	15.00	7.50	4.50
8	Lou Brock	6.00	3.00	1.75
9	Jose Cardenal	.20	.10	.06
10	Rod Carew	15.00	7.50	4.50
11	Steve Carlton	12.00	6.00	3.50
12	Dave Cash	.20	.10	.06
13	Cesar Cedeno	1.00	.50	.30
14	Ron Cey	.50	.25	.15
15	Mark Fidrych	.50	.25	.15
16	Dan Ford	.20	.10	.06
17	Wayne Garland	.20	.10	.06
18	Ralph Garr	.20	.10	.06
19	Steve Garvey	4.00	2.00	1.25
20	Mike Hargrove	.20	.10	.06
21	Jim Hunter	6.00	3.00	1.75
22	Reggie Jackson	12.00	6.00	3.50
23	Randy Jones	.20	.10	.06
24	Dave Kingman	1.00	.50	.30
25	Bill Madlock	.70	.35	.20
26	Lee May	.50	.25	.15
27	John Mayberry	.20	.10	.06
28	Andy Messersmith	.20	.10	.06
29	Willie Montanez	.20	.10	.06
30	John Montefusco	.50	.25	.15
31	Joe Morgan	6.00	3.00	1.75
32	Thurman Munson	6.00	3.00	1.75
33	Bobby Murcer	.50	.25	.15
34	Al Oliver	1.25	.60	.40
35	Dave Pagan	.20	.10	.06
36	Jim Palmer	15.00	7.50	4.50
37	Tony Perez	.70	.35	.20
38	Pete Rose	30.00	15.00	9.00
39	Joe Rudi	.50	.25	.15
40	Nolan Ryan	40.00	20.00	12.00
41	Mike Schmidt	30.00	15.00	9.00
42	Tom Seaver	25.00	12.50	7.50
43	Ted Simmons	.70	.35	.20
44	Bill Singer	.20	.10	.06
45	Willie Stargell	1.50	.70	.45
46	Rusty Staub	.50	.25	.15
47	Don Sutton	1.25	.60	.40
48	Luis Tiant	.70	.35	.20
49	Bill Travers	.20	.10	.06
50	Claudell Washington	.50	.25	.15
51	Bob Watson	.20	.10	.06
52	Dave Winfield	6.00	3.00	1.75
53	Carl Yastrzemski	4.50	2.25	1.25
54	Robin Yount	25.00	12.50	7.50
55	Richie Zisk	.20	.10	.06

1978 Topps

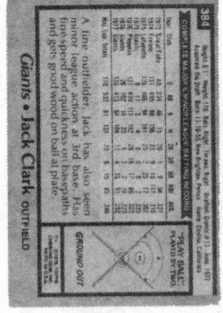

JACK CLARK

At 726 cards, this was the largest issue from Topps since 1972. In design, the color player photo is slightly larger than usual, with the player's name and team at the bottom. In the upper right-hand corner of the 2-1/2" by 3-1/2" cards there is a small white baseball with the player's position. Most of the starting All-Stars from the previous year had a red, white and blue shield instead of the baseball. Backs feature statistics and a baseball situation which made a card game of baseball possible. Specialty cards include baseball records, statistical leaders and the World Series and playoffs. As one row of cards per sheet had to be double-printed to accommodate the 726-card set size, some cards are more common, yet that seems to have no serious impact on their prices.

		NR MT	EX	VG
	Complete Set:	325.00	162.00	100.00
	Common Player:	.12	.06	.04
1	Record Breaker (Lou Brock)	2.00	.45	.25
2	Record Breaker (Sparky Lyle)	.25	.13	.08
3	Record Breaker (Willie McCovey)	.70	.35	.20
4	Record Breaker (Brooks Robinson)	.90	.45	.25
5	Record Breaker (Pete Rose)	2.00	1.00	.60
6	Record Breaker (Nolan Ryan)	4.00	2.00	1.25
7	Record Breaker (Reggie Jackson)	1.50	.70	.45
8	Mike Sadek	.12	.06	.04
9	Doug DeCinces	.25	.13	.08
10	Phil Niekro	2.00	1.00	.60
11	Rick Manning	.12	.06	.04
12	Don Aase	.20	.10	.06
13	Art Howe	.12	.06	.04
14	Lerrin LaGrow	.12	.06	.04
15	Tony Perez	.25	.13	.08
16	Roy White	.25	.13	.08
17	Mike Krukow	.25	.13	.08
18	Bob Grich	.25	.13	.08
19	Darrell Porter	.20	.10	.06
20	Pete Rose	3.50	1.75	1.00
21	Steve Kemp	.25	.13	.08
22	Charlie Hough	.20	.10	.06
23	Bump Wills	.12	.06	.04
24	Don Money	.12	.06	.04
25	Jon Matlack	.20	.10	.06
26	Rich Hebner	.12	.06	.04
27	Geoff Zahn	.12	.06	.04
28	Ed Ott	.12	.06	.04
29	Bob Lacey	.12	.06	.04
30	George Hendrick	.20	.10	.06
31	Glenn Abbott	.12	.06	.04
32	Garry Templeton	.30	.15	.09
33	Dave Lemanczyk	.12	.06	.04
34	Willie McCovey	2.00	1.00	.60
35	Sparky Lyle	.30	.15	.09
36	*Eddie Murray*	45.00	23.00	13.50
37	Rick Waits	.12	.06	.04
38	Willie Montanez	.12	.06	.04
39	*Floyd Bannister*	1.00	.50	.30
40	Carl Yastrzemski	5.00	2.50	1.50
41	Burt Hooton	.20	.10	.06
42	Jorge Orta	.12	.06	.04
43	Bill Atkinson	.12	.06	.04
44	Toby Harrah	.20	.10	.06
45	Mark Fidrych	.25	.13	.08
46	Al Cowens	.12	.06	.04
47	Jack Billingham	.12	.06	.04
48	Don Baylor	.35	.20	.11
49	Ed Kranepool	.20	.10	.06
50	Rick Reuschel	.40	.20	.12
51	Charlie Moore	.12	.06	.04
52	Jim Lonborg	.20	.10	.06
53	Phil Garner	.12	.06	.04
54	Tom Johnson	.12	.06	.04
55	Mitchell Page	.12	.06	.04
56	Randy Jones	.20	.10	.06
57	Dan Meyer	.12	.06	.04
58	Bob Forsch	.20	.10	.06
59	Otto Velez	.12	.06	.04
60	Thurman Munson	3.00	1.50	.90
61	Larvell Blanks	.12	.06	.04
62	Jim Barr	.12	.06	.04
63	Don Zimmer	.20	.10	.06
64	Gene Pentz	.12	.06	.04
65	Ken Singleton	.25	.13	.08
66	White Sox Team	.50	.25	.15
67	Claudell Washington	.25	.13	.08
68	Steve Foucault	.12	.06	.04
69	Mike Vail	.12	.06	.04
70	Rich Gossage	1.00	.50	.30
71	Terry Humphrey	.12	.06	.04

		NR MT	EX	VG
72	Andre Dawson	15.00	7.50	4.50
73	Andy Hassler	.12	.06	.04
74	Checklist 1-121	.90	.45	.25
75	Dick Ruthven	.12	.06	.04
76	Steve Ontiveros	.12	.06	.04
77	Ed Kirkpatrick	.12	.06	.04
78	Pablo Torrealba	.12	.06	.04
79	Darrell Johnson	.12	.06	.04
80	Ken Griffey	.25	.13	.08
81	Pete Redfern	.12	.06	.04
82	Giants Team	.50	.25	.15
83	Bob Montgomery	.12	.06	.04
84	Kent Tekulve	.25	.13	.08
85	Ron Fairly	.20	.10	.06
86	Dave Tomlin	.12	.06	.04
87	John Lowenstein	.12	.06	.04
88	Mike Phillips	.12	.06	.04
89	Ken Clay	.20	.10	.06
90	Larry Bowa	.30	.15	.09
91	Oscar Zamora	.12	.06	.04
92	Adrian Devine	.12	.06	.04
93	Bobby Cox	.12	.06	.04
94	Chuck Scrivener	.12	.06	.04
95	Jamie Quirk	.12	.06	.04
96	Orioles Team	.50	.25	.15
97	Stan Bahnsen	.12	.06	.04
98	Jim Essian	.12	.06	.04
99	*Willie Hernandez*	.70	.35	.20
100	George Brett	12.00	6.00	3.50
101	Sid Monge	.12	.06	.04
102	Matt Alexander	.12	.06	.04
103	Tom Murphy	.12	.06	.04
104	Lee Lacy	.12	.06	.04
105	Reggie Cleveland	.12	.06	.04
106	Bill Plummer	.12	.06	.04
107	Ed Halicki	.12	.06	.04
108	Von Joshua	.12	.06	.04
109	Joe Torre	.30	.15	.09
110	Richie Zisk	.20	.10	.06
111	Mike Tyson	.12	.06	.04
112	Astros Team	.50	.25	.15
113	Don Carrithers	.12	.06	.04
114	Paul Blair	.20	.10	.06
115	Gary Nolan	.12	.06	.04
116	Tucker Ashford	.12	.06	.04
117	John Montague	.12	.06	.04
118	Terry Harmon	.12	.06	.04
119	Denny Martinez	.25	.13	.08
120	Gary Carter	5.00	2.50	1.50
121	Alvis Woods	.12	.06	.04
122	Dennis Eckersley	3.00	1.50	.90
123	Manny Trillo	.20	.10	.06
124	*Dave Rozema*	.25	.13	.08
125	George Scott	.20	.10	.06
126	Paul Moskau	.12	.06	.04
127	Chet Lemon	.20	.10	.06
128	Bill Russell	.20	.10	.06
129	Jim Colborn	.12	.06	.04
130	Jeff Burroughs	.20	.10	.06
131	Bert Blyleven	.90	.45	.25
132	Enos Cabell	.20	.10	.06
133	Jerry Augustine	.12	.06	.04
134	*Steve Henderson*	.25	.13	.08
135	Ron Guidry	.70	.35	.20
136	Ted Sizemore	.12	.06	.04
137	Craig Kusick	.12	.06	.04
138	Larry Demery	.12	.06	.04
139	Wayne Gross	.12	.06	.04
140	Rollie Fingers	3.00	1.50	.90
141	Ruppert Jones	.20	.10	.06
142	John Montefusco	.20	.10	.06
143	Keith Hernandez	2.50	1.25	.70
144	Jesse Jefferson	.12	.06	.04
145	Rick Monday	.20	.10	.06
146	Doyle Alexander	.30	.15	.09
147	Lee Mazzilli	.25	.13	.08
148	Andre Thornton	.25	.13	.08
149	Dale Murray	.12	.06	.04
150	Bobby Bonds	.35	.20	.11
151	Milt Wilcox	.12	.06	.04
152	*Ivan DeJesus*	.20	.10	.06
153	Steve Stone	.25	.13	.08
154	Cecil Cooper	.20	.10	.06
155	Butch Hobson	.12	.06	.04
156	Andy Messersmith	.20	.10	.06
157	Pete LaCock	.12	.06	.04
158	Joaquin Andujar	.25	.13	.08
159	Lou Piniella	.35	.20	.11
160	Jim Palmer	5.00	2.50	1.50
161	Bob Boone	.25	.13	.08
162	Paul Thormodsgard	.12	.06	.04

		NR MT	EX	VG
163	Bill North	.12	.06	.04
164	Bob Owchinko	.12	.06	.04
165	Rennie Stennett	.12	.06	.04
166	Carlos Lopez	.12	.06	.04
167	Tim Foli	.12	.06	.04
168	Reggie Smith	.25	.13	.08
169	Jerry Johnson	.12	.06	.04
170	Lou Brock	2.00	1.00	.60
171	Pat Zachry	.12	.06	.04
172	Mike Hargrove	.20	.10	.06
173	Robin Yount	15.00	7.50	4.50
174	Wayne Garland	.12	.06	.04
175	Jerry Morales	.12	.06	.04
176	Milt May	.12	.06	.04
177	Gene Garber	.12	.06	.04
178	Dave Chalk	.12	.06	.04
179	Dick Tidrow	.20	.10	.06
180	Dave Concepcion	.35	.20	.11
181	Ken Forsch	.20	.10	.06
182	Jim Spencer	.12	.06	.04
183	Doug Bird	.12	.06	.04
184	Checklist 122-242	.90	.45	.25
185	Ellis Valentine	.20	.10	.06
186	*Bob Stanley*	.25	.13	.08
187	Jerry Royster	.12	.06	.04
188	Al Bumbry	.20	.10	.06
189	Tom Lasorda	.30	.15	.09
190	John Candelaria	.25	.13	.08
191	Rodney Scott	.12	.06	.04
192	Padres Team	.50	.25	.15
193	Rich Chiles	.12	.06	.04
194	Derrel Thomas	.12	.06	.04
195	Larry Dierker	.20	.10	.06
196	Bob Bailor	.12	.06	.04
197	Nino Espinosa	.12	.06	.04
198	Ron Pruitt	.12	.06	.04
199	Craig Reynolds	.12	.06	.04
200	Reggie Jackson	10.00	5.00	3.00
201	Batting Leaders (Rod Carew, Dave Parker)	.80	.40	.25
202	Home Run Leaders (George Foster, Jim Rice)	.25	.13	.08
203	Runs Batted In Ldrs. (George Foster, Larry Hisle)	.25	.13	.08
204	Stolen Base Leaders (Freddie Patek, Frank Taveras)	.12	.06	.04
205	Victory Leaders (Steve Carlton, Dave Goltz, Dennis Leonard, Jim Palmer)	.60	.30	.20
206	Strikeout Leaders (Phil Niekro, Nolan Ryan)	.35	.20	.11
207	Earned Run Avg. Ldrs. (John Candelaria, Frank Tanana)	.12	.06	.04
208	Leading Firemen (Bill Campbell, Rollie Fingers)	.35	.20	.11
209	Dock Ellis	.12	.06	.04
210	Jose Cardenal	.12	.06	.04
211	Earl Weaver	.20	.10	.06
212	Mike Caldwell	.12	.06	.04
213	Alan Bannister	.12	.06	.04
214	Angels Team	.50	.25	.15
215	Darrell Evans	.35	.20	.11
216	Mike Paxton	.12	.06	.04
217	Rod Gilbreath	.12	.06	.04
218	Marty Pattin	.12	.06	.04
219	Mike Cubbage	.12	.06	.04
220	Pedro Borbon	.12	.06	.04
221	Chris Speier	.20	.10	.06
222	Jerry Martin	.12	.06	.04
223	Bruce Kison	.12	.06	.04
224	Jerry Tabb	.12	.06	.04
225	Don Gullett	.12	.06	.04
226	Joe Ferguson	.12	.06	.04
227	Al Fitzmorris	.12	.06	.04
228	Manny Mota	.12	.06	.04
229	Leo Foster	.12	.06	.04
230	Al Hrabosky	.20	.10	.06
231	Wayne Nordhagen	.12	.06	.04
232	Mickey Stanley	.20	.10	.06
233	Dick Pole	.12	.06	.04
234	Herman Franks	.12	.06	.04
235	Tim McCarver	.35	.20	.11
236	Terry Whitfield	.12	.06	.04
237	Rich Dauer	.12	.06	.04
238	Juan Beniquez	.20	.10	.06
239	Dyar Miller	.12	.06	.04
240	Gene Tenace	.20	.10	.06
241	Pete Vuckovich	.20	.10	.06
242	Barry Bonnell	.12	.06	.04
243	Bob McClure	.12	.06	.04
244	Expos Team	.20	.10	.06
245	Rick Burleson	.20	.10	.06

		NR MT	EX	VG
246	Dan Driessen	.20	.10	.06
247	Larry Christenson	.12	.06	.04
248	Frank White	.12	.06	.04
249	Dave Goltz	.12	.06	.04
250	Graig Nettles	.30	.15	.09
251	Don Kirkwood	.12	.06	.04
252	Steve Swisher	.12	.06	.04
253	Jim Kern	.12	.06	.04
254	Dave Collins	.20	.10	.06
255	Jerry Reuss	.20	.10	.06
256	Joe Altobelli	.12	.06	.04
257	Hector Cruz	.12	.06	.04
258	John Hiller	.20	.10	.06
259	Dodgers Team	.80	.40	.25
260	Bert Campaneris	.25	.13	.08
261	Tim Hosley	.12	.06	.04
262	Rudy May	.12	.06	.04
263	Danny Walton	.12	.06	.04
264	Jamie Easterly	.12	.06	.04
265	Sal Bando	.12	.06	.04
266	*Bob Shirley*	.20	.10	.06
267	Doug Ault	.12	.06	.04
268	Gil Flores	.12	.06	.04
269	Wayne Twitchell	.12	.06	.04
270	Carlton Fisk	5.00	2.50	1.50
271	Randy Lerch	.12	.06	.04
272	Royle Stillman	.12	.06	.04
273	Fred Norman	.12	.06	.04
274	Freddie Patek	.12	.06	.04
275	Dan Ford	.12	.06	.04
276	Bill Bonham	.12	.06	.04
277	Bruce Boisclair	.12	.06	.04
278	Enrique Romo	.12	.06	.04
279	Bill Virdon	.20	.10	.06
280	Buddy Bell	.30	.15	.09
281	Eric Rasmussen	.12	.06	.04
282	Yankees Team	1.00	.50	.30
283	Omar Moreno	.12	.06	.04
284	Randy Moffitt	.12	.06	.04
285	Steve Yeager	.12	.06	.04
286	Ben Oglivie	.20	.10	.06
287	Kiko Garcia	.12	.06	.04
288	Dave Hamilton	.12	.06	.04
289	Checklist 243-363	.90	.45	.25
290	Willie Horton	.20	.10	.06
291	Gary Ross	.12	.06	.04
292	Gene Richard	.12	.06	.04
293	Mike Willis	.12	.06	.04
294	Larry Parrish	.25	.13	.08
295	Bill Lee	.20	.10	.06
296	Biff Pocoroba	.12	.06	.04
297	Warren Brusstar	.12	.06	.04
298	Tony Armas	.25	.13	.08
299	Whitey Herzog	.30	.15	.09
300	Joe Morgan	5.00	2.50	1.50
301	Buddy Schultz	.12	.06	.04
302	Cubs Team	.50	.25	.15
303	Sam Hinds	.12	.06	.04
304	John Milner	.12	.06	.04
305	Rico Carty	.20	.10	.06
306	Joe Niekro	.25	.13	.08
307	Glenn Borgmann	.12	.06	.04
308	Jim Rooker	.12	.06	.04
309	Cliff Johnson	.20	.10	.06
310	Don Sutton	3.00	1.50	.90
311	Jose Baez	.12	.06	.04
312	Greg Minton	.12	.06	.04
313	Andy Etchebarren	.12	.06	.04
314	Paul Lindblad	.12	.06	.04
315	Mark Belanger	.20	.10	.06
316	Henry Cruz	.12	.06	.04
317	Dave Johnson	.30	.15	.09
318	Tom Griffin	.12	.06	.04
319	Alan Ashby	.12	.06	.04
320	Fred Lynn	.90	.45	.25
321	Santo Alcala	.12	.06	.04
322	Tom Paciorek	.12	.06	.04
323	Jim Fregosi	.12	.06	.04
324	Vern Rapp	.12	.06	.04
325	Bruce Sutter	.50	.25	.15
326	Mike Lum	.12	.06	.04
327	Rick Langford	.12	.06	.04
328	Brewers Team	.50	.25	.15
329	John Verhoeven	.12	.06	.04
330	Bob Watson	.20	.10	.06
331	Mark Littell	.12	.06	.04
332	Duane Kuiper	.12	.06	.04
333	Jim Todd	.12	.06	.04
334	John Stearns	.12	.06	.04
335	Bucky Dent	.30	.15	.09
336	Steve Busby	.20	.10	.06

		NR MT	EX	VG
337	Tom Grieve	.12	.06	.04
338	Dave Heaverlo	.12	.06	.04
339	Mario Guerrero	.12	.06	.04
340	Bake McBride	.12	.06	.04
341	Mike Flanagan	.25	.13	.08
342	Aurelio Rodriguez	.20	.10	.06
343	John Wathan	.12	.06	.04
344	Sam Ewing	.12	.06	.04
345	Luis Tiant	.35	.20	.11
346	Larry Biittner	.12	.06	.04
347	Terry Forster	.20	.10	.06
348	Del Unser	.12	.06	.04
349	Rick Camp	.12	.06	.04
350	Steve Garvey	5.00	2.50	1.50
351	Jeff Torborg	.20	.10	.06
352	Tony Scott	.12	.06	.04
353	Doug Bair	.12	.06	.04
354	Cesar Geronimo	.20	.10	.06
355	Bill Travers	.12	.06	.04
356	Mets Team	.70	.35	.20
357	Tom Poquette	.12	.06	.04
358	Mark Lemongello	.12	.06	.04
359	Marc Hill	.12	.06	.04
360	Mike Schmidt	15.00	7.50	4.50
361	Chris Knapp	.12	.06	.04
362	Dave May	.12	.06	.04
363	Bob Randall	.12	.06	.04
364	Jerry Turner	.12	.06	.04
365	Ed Figueroa	.20	.10	.06
366	Larry Milbourne	.12	.06	.04
367	Rick Dempsey	.20	.10	.06
368	Balor Moore	.12	.06	.04
369	Tim Nordbrook	.12	.06	.04
370	Rusty Staub	.30	.15	.09
371	Ray Burris	.12	.06	.04
372	Brian Asselstine	.12	.06	.04
373	Jim Willoughby	.12	.06	.04
374	Jose Morales	.12	.06	.04
375	Tommy John	.90	.45	.25
376	Jim Wohlford	.12	.06	.04
377	Manny Sarmiento	.12	.06	.04
378	Bobby Winkles	.12	.06	.04
379	Skip Lockwood	.12	.06	.04
380	Ted Simmons	.40	.20	.12
381	Phillies Team	.70	.35	.20
382	Joe Lahoud	.12	.06	.04
383	Mario Mendoza	.12	.06	.04
384	Jack Clark	5.00	2.50	1.50
385	Tito Fuentes	.12	.06	.04
386	Bob Gorinski	.12	.06	.04
387	Ken Holtzman	.25	.13	.08
388	Bill Fahey	.12	.06	.04
389	Julio Gonzalez	.12	.06	.04
390	Oscar Gamble	.20	.10	.06
391	Larry Haney	.12	.06	.04
392	Billy Almon	.12	.06	.04
393	Tippy Martinez	.12	.06	.04
394	Roy Howell	.12	.06	.04
395	Jim Hughes	.12	.06	.04
396	Bob Stinson	.12	.06	.04
397	Greg Gross	.12	.06	.04
398	Don Hood	.12	.06	.04
399	Pete Mackanin	.12	.06	.04
400	Nolan Ryan	20.00	10.00	6.00
401	Sparky Anderson	.30	.15	.09
402	Dave Campbell	.12	.06	.04
403	Bud Harrelson	.20	.10	.06
404	Tigers Team	.60	.30	.20
405	Rawly Eastwick	.12	.06	.04
406	Mike Jorgensen	.12	.06	.04
407	Odell Jones	.12	.06	.04
408	Joe Zdeb	.12	.06	.04
409	Ron Schueler	.12	.06	.04
410	Bill Madlock	.50	.25	.15
411	A.L. Championships (Yankees Rally To Defeat Royals)	.70	.35	.20
412	N.L. Championships (Dodgers Overpower Phillies In Four)	.50	.25	.15
413	World Series (Reggie & Yankees Reign Supreme)	1.25	.60	.40
414	Darold Knowles	.12	.06	.04
415	Ray Fosse	.12	.06	.04
416	Jack Brohamer	.12	.06	.04
417	Mike Garman	.12	.06	.04
418	Tony Muser	.12	.06	.04
419	Jerry Garvin	.12	.06	.04
420	Greg Luzinski	.35	.20	.11
421	Junior Moore	.12	.06	.04
422	Steve Braun	.12	.06	.04
423	Dave Rosello	.12	.06	.04
424	Red Sox Team	.70	.35	.20

		NR MT	EX	VG
425	Steve Rogers	.12	.06	.04
426	Fred Kendall	.12	.06	.04
427	*Mario Soto*	.40	.20	.12
428	Joel Youngblood	.20	.10	.06
429	Mike Barlow	.12	.06	.04
430	Al Oliver	.40	.20	.12
431	Butch Metzger	.12	.06	.04
432	Terry Bulling	.12	.06	.04
433	Fernando Gonzalez	.12	.06	.04
434	Mike Norris	.12	.06	.04
435	Checklist 364-484	.90	.45	.25
436	Vic Harris	.12	.06	.04
437	Bo McLaughlin	.12	.06	.04
438	John Ellis	.12	.06	.04
439	Ken Kravec	.12	.06	.04
440	Dave Lopes	.25	.13	.08
441	Larry Gura	.12	.06	.04
442	Elliott Maddox	.12	.06	.04
443	Darrel Chaney	.12	.06	.04
444	Roy Hartsfield	.12	.06	.04
445	Mike Ivie	.12	.06	.04
446	Tug McGraw	.35	.20	.11
447	Leroy Stanton	.12	.06	.04
448	Bill Castro	.12	.06	.04
449	Tim Blackwell	.12	.06	.04
450	Tom Seaver	6.00	3.00	1.75
451	Twins Team	.50	.25	.15
452	Jerry Mumphrey	.20	.10	.06
453	Doug Flynn	.12	.06	.04
454	Dave LaRoche	.12	.06	.04
455	Bill Robinson	.12	.06	.04
456	Vern Ruhle	.12	.06	.04
457	Bob Bailey	.12	.06	.04
458	Jeff Newman	.12	.06	.04
459	Charlie Spikes	.12	.06	.04
460	Jim Hunter	3.00	1.50	.90
461	Rob Andrews	.12	.06	.04
462	Rogelio Moret	.12	.06	.04
463	Kevin Bell	.12	.06	.04
464	Jerry Grote	.20	.10	.06
465	Hal McRae	.30	.15	.09
466	Dennis Blair	.12	.06	.04
467	Alvin Dark	.20	.10	.06
468	*Warren Cromartie*	.20	.10	.06
469	Rick Cerone	.20	.10	.06
470	J.R. Richard	.25	.13	.08
471	Roy Smalley	.20	.10	.06
472	Ron Reed	.20	.10	.06
473	Bill Buckner	.30	.15	.09
474	Jim Slaton	.12	.06	.04
475	Gary Matthews	.20	.10	.06
476	Bill Stein	.12	.06	.04
477	Doug Capilla	.12	.06	.04
478	Jerry Remy	.12	.06	.04
479	Cardinals Team	.50	.25	.15
480	Ron LeFlore	.25	.13	.08
481	Jackson Todd	.12	.06	.04
482	Rick Miller	.12	.06	.04
483	Ken Macha	.12	.06	.04
484	Jim Norris	.12	.06	.04
485	Chris Chambliss	.30	.15	.09
486	John Curtis	.12	.06	.04
487	Jim Tyrone	.12	.06	.04
488	Dan Spillner	.12	.06	.04
489	Rudy Meoli	.12	.06	.04
490	Amos Otis	.20	.10	.06
491	Scott McGregor	.20	.10	.06
492	Jim Sundberg	.20	.10	.06
493	Steve Renko	.12	.06	.04
494	Chuck Tanner	.20	.10	.06
495	Dave Cash	.12	.06	.04
496	*Jim Clancy*	.30	.15	.09
497	Glenn Adams	.12	.06	.04
498	Joe Sambito	.12	.06	.04
499	Mariners Team	.50	.25	.15
500	George Foster	.70	.35	.20
501	Dave Roberts	.12	.06	.04
502	Pat Rockett	.12	.06	.04
503	Ike Hampton	.12	.06	.04
504	Roger Freed	.12	.06	.04
505	Felix Millan	.12	.06	.04
506	Ron Blomberg	.12	.06	.04
507	Willie Crawford	.12	.06	.04
508	Johnny Oates	.12	.06	.04
509	Brent Strom	.12	.06	.04
510	Willie Stargell	5.00	2.50	1.50
511	Frank Duffy	.12	.06	.04
512	Larry Herndon	.20	.10	.06
513	Barry Foote	.12	.06	.04
514	Rob Sperring	.12	.06	.04
515	Tim Corcoran	.12	.06	.04
516	Gary Beare	.12	.06	.04
517	Andres Mora	.12	.06	.04
518	Tommy Boggs	.12	.06	.04
519	Brian Downing	.25	.13	.08
520	Larry Hisle	.20	.10	.06
521	Steve Staggs	.12	.06	.04
522	Dick Williams	.20	.10	.06
523	*Donnie Moore*	.25	.13	.08
524	Bernie Carbo	.12	.06	.04
525	Jerry Terrell	.12	.06	.04
526	Reds Team	.60	.30	.20
527	Vic Correll	.12	.06	.04
528	Rob Picciolo	.12	.06	.04
529	Paul Hartzell	.12	.06	.04
530	Dave Winfield	5.00	2.50	1.50
531	Tom Underwood	.12	.06	.04
532	Skip Jutze	.12	.06	.04
533	Sandy Alomar	.12	.06	.04
534	Wilbur Howard	.12	.06	.04
535	Checklist 485-605	.90	.45	.25
536	Roric Harrison	.12	.06	.04
537	Bruce Bochte	.20	.10	.06
538	Johnnie LeMaster	.12	.06	.04
539	Vic Davalillo	.12	.06	.04
540	Steve Carlton	5.00	2.50	1.50
541	Larry Cox	.12	.06	.04
542	Tim Johnson	.12	.06	.04
543	Larry Harlow	.12	.06	.04
544	Len Randle	.12	.06	.04
545	Bill Campbell	.12	.06	.04
546	Ted Martinez	.12	.06	.04
547	John Scott	.12	.06	.04
548	Billy Hunter	.12	.06	.04
549	Joe Kerrigan	.12	.06	.04
550	John Mayberry	.20	.10	.06
551	Braves Team	.50	.25	.15
552	Francisco Barrios	.12	.06	.04
553	*Terry Puhl*	.35	.20	.11
554	Joe Coleman	.20	.10	.06
555	Butch Wynegar	.20	.10	.06
556	Ed Armbrister	.12	.06	.04
557	Tony Solaita	.12	.06	.04
558	Paul Mitchell	.12	.06	.04
559	Phil Mankowski	.12	.06	.04
560	Dave Parker	5.00	2.50	1.50
561	Charlie Williams	.12	.06	.04
562	Glenn Burke	.12	.06	.04
563	Dave Rader	.12	.06	.04
564	Mick Kelleher	.12	.06	.04
565	Jerry Koosman	.25	.13	.08
566	Merv Rettenmund	.12	.06	.04
567	Dick Drago	.12	.06	.04
568	Tom Hutton	.12	.06	.04
569	*Lary Sorensen*	.20	.10	.06
570	Dave Kingman	.60	.30	.20
571	Buck Martinez	.12	.06	.04
572	Rick Wise	.20	.10	.06
573	Luis Gomez	.12	.06	.04
574	Bob Lemon	.30	.15	.09
575	Pat Dobson	.20	.10	.06
576	Sam Mejias	.12	.06	.04
577	A's Team	.50	.25	.15
578	Buzz Capra	.12	.06	.04
579	*Rance Mulliniks*	.35	.20	.11
580	Rod Carew	6.00	3.00	1.75
581	Lynn McGlothen	.12	.06	.04
582	Fran Healy	.20	.10	.06
583	George Medich	.12	.06	.04
584	John Hale	.12	.06	.04
585	Woodie Fryman	.12	.06	.04
586	Ed Goodson	.12	.06	.04
587	John Urrea	.12	.06	.04
588	Jim Mason	.12	.06	.04
589	*Bob Knepper*	1.00	.50	.30
590	Bobby Murcer	.30	.15	.09
591	George Zeber	.20	.10	.06
592	Bob Apodaca	.12	.06	.04
593	Dave Skaggs	.12	.06	.04
594	Dave Freisleben	.12	.06	.04
595	Sixto Lezcano	.12	.06	.04
596	Gary Wheelock	.12	.06	.04
597	Steve Dillard	.12	.06	.04
598	Eddie Solomon	.12	.06	.04
599	Gary Woods	.12	.06	.04
600	Frank Tanana	.25	.13	.08
601	Gene Mauch	.25	.13	.08
602	Eric Soderholm	.12	.06	.04
603	Will McEnaney	.12	.06	.04
604	Earl Williams	.12	.06	.04
605	Rick Rhoden	.25	.13	.08
606	Pirates Team	.50	.25	.15

		NR MT	EX	VG
607	Fernando Arroyo	.12	.06	.04
608	Johnny Grubb	.12	.06	.04
609	John Denny	.12	.06	.04
610	Garry Maddox	.20	.10	.06
611	Pat Scanlon	.12	.06	.04
612	Ken Henderson	.12	.06	.04
613	Marty Perez	.12	.06	.04
614	Joe Wallis	.12	.06	.04
615	Clay Carroll	.20	.10	.06
616	Pat Kelly	.12	.06	.04
617	Joe Nolan	.12	.06	.04
618	Tommy Helms	.12	.06	.04
619	*Thad Bosley*	.20	.10	.06
620	Willie Randolph	.30	.15	.09
621	Craig Swan	.12	.06	.04
622	Champ Summers	.12	.06	.04
623	Eduardo Rodriguez	.12	.06	.04
624	Gary Alexander	.12	.06	.04
625	Jose Cruz	.25	.13	.08
626	Blue Jays Team	.25	.13	.08
627	Dave Johnson	.12	.06	.04
628	Ralph Garr	.20	.10	.06
629	Don Stanhouse	.12	.06	.04
630	Ron Cey	.25	.13	.08
631	Danny Ozark	.20	.10	.06
632	Rowland Office	.12	.06	.04
633	Tom Veryzer	.12	.06	.04
634	Len Barker	.20	.10	.06
635	Joe Rudi	.25	.13	.08
636	Jim Bibby	.12	.06	.04
637	Duffy Dyer	.12	.06	.04
638	Paul Splittorff	.20	.10	.06
639	Gene Clines	.12	.06	.04
640	Lee May	.12	.06	.04
641	Doug Rau	.12	.06	.04
642	Denny Doyle	.12	.06	.04
643	Tom House	.12	.06	.04
644	Jim Dwyer	.12	.06	.04
645	Mike Torrez	.20	.10	.06
646	Rick Auerbach	.12	.06	.04
647	Steve Dunning	.12	.06	.04
648	Gary Thomasson	.12	.06	.04
649	*Moose Haas*	.25	.13	.08
650	Cesar Cedeno	.25	.13	.08
651	Doug Rader	.12	.06	.04
652	Checklist 606-726	.90	.45	.25
653	Ron Hodges	.12	.06	.04
654	Pepe Frias	.12	.06	.04
655	Lyman Bostock	.20	.10	.06
656	Dave Garcia	.12	.06	.04
657	Bombo Rivera	.12	.06	.04
658	Manny Sanguillen	.12	.06	.04
659	Rangers Team	.50	.25	.15
660	Jason Thompson	.20	.10	.06
661	Grant Jackson	.12	.06	.04
662	Paul Dade	.12	.06	.04
663	Paul Reuschel	.12	.06	.04
664	Fred Stanley	.20	.10	.06
665	Dennis Leonard	.20	.10	.06
666	Billy Smith	.12	.06	.04
667	Jeff Byrd	.12	.06	.04
668	Dusty Baker	.25	.13	.08
669	Pete Falcone	.12	.06	.04
670	Jim Rice	3.50	1.75	1.00
671	Gary Lavelle	.12	.06	.04
672	Don Kessinger	.20	.10	.06
673	Steve Brye	.12	.06	.04
674	*Ray Knight*	1.25	.60	.40
675	Jay Johnstone	.20	.10	.06
676	Bob Myrick	.12	.06	.04
677	Ed Herrmann	.12	.06	.04
678	Tom Burgmeier	.12	.06	.04
679	Wayne Garrett	.12	.06	.04
680	Vida Blue	.30	.15	.09
681	Rob Belloir	.12	.06	.04
682	Ken Brett	.20	.10	.06
683	Mike Champion	.12	.06	.04
684	Ralph Houk	.20	.10	.06
685	Frank Taveras	.12	.06	.04
686	Gaylord Perry	2.00	1.00	.60
687	*Julio Cruz*	.25	.13	.08
688	George Mitterwald	.12	.06	.04
689	Indians Team	.50	.25	.15
690	Mickey Rivers	.25	.13	.08
691	Ross Grimsley	.20	.10	.06
692	Ken Reitz	.12	.06	.04
693	Lamar Johnson	.12	.06	.04
694	Elias Sosa	.12	.06	.04
695	Dwight Evans	2.00	1.00	.60
696	Steve Mingori	.12	.06	.04
697	Roger Metzger	.12	.06	.04

		NR MT	EX	VG
698	Juan Bernhardt	.12	.06	.04
699	Jackie Brown	.12	.06	.04
700	Johnny Bench	5.00	2.50	1.50
701	Rookie Pitchers (*Tom Hume*, Larry Landreth, *Steve McCatty*, Bruce Taylor)	.25	.13	.08
702	Rookie Catchers (Bill Nahorodny, Kevin Pasley, Rick Sweet, Don Werner)	.12	.06	.04
703	Rookie Pitchers (*Larry Andersen*, Tim Jones, Mickey Mahler, *Jack Morris*)	6.00	3.00	1.75
704	Rookie 2nd Basemen (Garth Iorg, Dave Oliver, Sam Perlozzo, *Lou Whitaker*)	20.00	10.00	6.00
705	Rookie Outfielders (*Dave Bergman*, Miguel Dilone, Clint Hurdle, Willie Norwood)	.25	.13	.08
706	Rookie 1st Basemen (Wayne Cage, Ted Cox, *Pat Putnam*, Dave Revering)	.20	.10	.06
707	Rookie Shortstops (Mickey Klutts, *Paul Molitor*, Alan Trammell, U.L. Washington)	50.00	25.00	15.00
708	Rookie Catchers (*Bo Diaz*, Dale Murphy, *Lance Parrish, Ernie Whitt*)	30.00	15.00	9.00
709	Rookie Pitchers (Steve Burke, Matt Keough, Lance Rautzhan, *Dan Schatzeder*)	.20	.10	.06
710	Rookie Outfielders (Dell Alston, Rick Bosetti, *Mike Easler*, Keith Smith)	.50	.25	.15
711	Rookie Pitchers (Cardell Camper, Dennis Lamp, Craig Mitchell, Roy Thomas)	.12	.06	.04
712	Bobby Valentine	.25	.13	.08
713	Bob Davis	.12	.06	.04
714	Mike Anderson	.12	.06	.04
715	Jim Kaat	.60	.30	.20
716	Clarence Gaston	.12	.06	.04
717	Nelson Briles	.12	.06	.04
718	Ron Jackson	.12	.06	.04
719	Randy Elliott	.12	.06	.04
720	Fergie Jenkins	1.00	.50	.30
721	Billy Martin	2.00	1.00	.60
722	Pete Broberg	.12	.06	.04
723	Johnny Wockenfuss	.12	.06	.04
724	Royals Team	.70	.35	.20
725	Kurt Bevacqua	.12	.06	.04
726	Wilbur Wood	.40	.10	.06

1979 Topps

 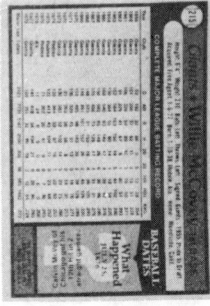

The size of this issue remained the same as in 1978 with 726 cards making their appearance. Actually, the 2-1/2" by 3-1/2" cards have a relatively minor design change from the previous year. The large color photo still dominates the front, with the player's name, team and position below it. The baseball with the player's position was moved to the lower left and the position replaced by a Topps logo. On the back, the printing color was changed and the game situation was replaced by a quiz called "Baseball Dates". Specialty cards include statistical leaders, major league records set during the season and eight cards devoted to career records. For the first time, rookies were arranged by teams under the heading of "Prospects."

	NR MT	EX	VG
Complete Set:	250.00	125.00	75.00
Common Player:	.12	.06	.04

#	Player	NR MT	EX	VG
1	Batting Leaders (Rod Carew, Dave Parker)	2.00	1.00	.60
2	Home Run Leaders (George Foster, Jim Rice)	.50	.25	.15
3	Runs Batted In Leaders (George Foster, Jim Rice)	.50	.25	.15
4	Stolen Base Leaders (Ron LeFlore, Omar Moreno)	.25	.13	.08
5	Victory Leaders (Ron Guidry, Gaylord Perry)	.50	.25	.15
6	Strikeout Leaders (J.R. Richard, Nolan Ryan)	.50	.25	.15
7	Earned Run Avg. Leaders (Ron Guidry, Craig Swan)	.25	.13	.08
8	Leading Firemen (Rollie Fingers, Rich Gossage)	.40	.20	.12
9	Dave Campbell	.12	.06	.04
10	Lee May	.20	.10	.06
11	Marc Hill	.12	.06	.04
12	Dick Drago	.12	.06	.04
13	Paul Dade	.12	.06	.04
14	Rafael Landestoy	.12	.06	.04
15	Ross Grimsley	.20	.10	.06
16	Fred Stanley	.20	.10	.06
17	Donnie Moore	.20	.10	.06
18	Tony Solaita	.12	.06	.04
19	Larry Gura	.12	.06	.04
20	Joe Morgan	.40	.20	.12
21	Kevin Kobel	.12	.06	.04
22	Mike Jorgensen	.12	.06	.04
23	Terry Forster	.20	.10	.06
24	Paul Molitor	4.00	2.00	1.25
25	Steve Carlton	4.00	2.00	1.25
26	Jamie Quirk	.12	.06	.04
27	Dave Goltz	.20	.10	.06
28	Steve Brye	.12	.06	.04
29	Rick Langford	.12	.06	.04
30	Dave Winfield	2.50	1.25	.70
31	Tom House	.12	.06	.04
32	Jerry Mumphrey	.12	.06	.04
33	Dave Rozema	.12	.06	.04
34	Rob Andrews	.12	.06	.04
35	Ed Figueroa	.20	.10	.06
36	Alan Ashby	.12	.06	.04
37	Joe Kerrigan	.12	.06	.04
38	Bernie Carbo	.12	.06	.04
39	Dale Murphy	8.00	4.00	2.50
40	Dennis Eckersley	2.00	1.00	.60
41	Twins Team (Gene Mauch)	.50	.25	.15
42	Ron Blomberg	.12	.06	.04
43	Wayne Twitchell	.12	.06	.04
44	Kurt Bevacqua	.12	.06	.04
45	Al Hrabosky	.20	.10	.06
46	Ron Hodges	.12	.06	.04
47	Fred Norman	.12	.06	.04
48	Merv Rettenmund	.12	.06	.04
49	Vern Ruhle	.12	.06	.04
50	Steve Garvey	1.25	.60	.40
51	Ray Fosse	.12	.06	.04
52	Randy Lerch	.12	.06	.04
53	Mick Kelleher	.12	.06	.04
54	Dell Alston	.12	.06	.04
55	Willie Stargell	2.00	1.00	.60
56	John Hale	.12	.06	.04
57	Eric Rasmussen	.12	.06	.04
58	Bob Randall	.12	.06	.04
59	John Denny	.12	.06	.04
60	Mickey Rivers	.20	.10	.06
61	Bo Diaz	.20	.10	.06
62	Randy Moffitt	.12	.06	.04
63	Jack Brohamer	.12	.06	.04
64	Tom Underwood	.12	.06	.04
65	Mark Belanger	.20	.10	.06
66	Tigers Team (Les Moss)	.60	.30	.20
67	Jim Mason	.12	.06	.04
68	Joe Niekro	.12	.06	.04
69	Elliott Maddox	.12	.06	.04
70	John Candelaria	.25	.13	.08
71	Brian Downing	.20	.10	.06
72	Steve Mingori	.12	.06	.04
73	Ken Henderson	.12	.06	.04
74	Shane Rawley	.30	.15	.09
75	Steve Yeager	.12	.06	.04
76	Warren Cromartie	.12	.06	.04
77	Dan Briggs	.12	.06	.04
78	Elias Sosa	.12	.06	.04
79	Ted Cox	.12	.06	.04
80	Jason Thompson	.20	.10	.06
81	Roger Erickson	.12	.06	.04
82	Mets Team (Joe Torre)	.60	.30	.20
83	Fred Kendall	.12	.06	.04
84	Greg Minton	.12	.06	.04
85	Gary Matthews	.20	.10	.06
86	Rodney Scott	.12	.06	.04
87	Pete Falcone	.12	.06	.04
88	Bob Molinaro	.12	.06	.04
89	Dick Tidrow	.20	.10	.06
90	Bob Boone	.25	.13	.08
91	Terry Crowley	.12	.06	.04
92	Jim Bibby	.12	.06	.04
93	Phil Mankowski	.12	.06	.04
94	Len Barker	.12	.06	.04
95	Robin Yount	12.00	6.00	3.50
96	Indians Team (Jeff Torborg)	.50	.25	.15
97	Sam Mejias	.12	.06	.04
98	Ray Burris	.12	.06	.04
99	John Wathan	.20	.10	.06
100	Tom Seaver	4.00	2.00	1.25
101	Roy Howell	.12	.06	.04
102	Mike Anderson	.12	.06	.04
103	Jim Todd	.12	.06	.04
104	Johnny Oates	.12	.06	.04
105	Rick Camp	.12	.06	.04
106	Frank Duffy	.12	.06	.04
107	Jesus Alou	.20	.10	.06
108	Eduardo Rodriguez	.12	.06	.04
109	Joel Youngblood	.12	.06	.04
110	Vida Blue	.30	.15	.09
111	Roger Freed	.12	.06	.04
112	Phillies Team (Danny Ozark)	.50	.25	.15
113	Pete Redfern	.12	.06	.04
114	Cliff Johnson	.20	.10	.06
115	Nolan Ryan	15.00	7.50	4.50
116	Ozzie Smith	45.00	23.00	13.50
117	Grant Jackson	.12	.06	.04
118	Bud Harrelson	.20	.10	.06
119	Don Stanhouse	.12	.06	.04
120	Jim Sundberg	.20	.10	.06
121	Checklist 1-121	.25	.13	.08
122	Mike Paxton	.12	.06	.04
123	Lou Whitaker	3.00	1.50	.90
124	Dan Schatzeder	.12	.06	.04
125	Rick Burleson	.20	.10	.06
126	Doug Bair	.12	.06	.04
127	Thad Bosley	.12	.06	.04
128	Ted Martinez	.12	.06	.04
129	Marty Pattin	.12	.06	.04
130	Bob Watson	.12	.06	.04
131	Jim Clancy	.25	.13	.08
132	Rowland Office	.12	.06	.04
133	Bill Castro	.12	.06	.04
134	Alan Bannister	.12	.06	.04
135	Bobby Murcer	.25	.13	.08
136	Jim Kaat	.60	.30	.20
137	Larry Wolfe	.12	.06	.04
138	Mark Lee	.12	.06	.04
139	Luis Pujols	.12	.06	.04
140	Don Gullett	.20	.10	.06
141	Tom Paciorek	.12	.06	.04
142	Charlie Williams	.12	.06	.04
143	Tony Scott	.12	.06	.04
144	Sandy Alomar	.12	.06	.04
145	Rick Rhoden	.25	.13	.08
146	Duane Kuiper	.12	.06	.04
147	Dave Hamilton	.12	.06	.04
148	Bruce Boisclair	.12	.06	.04
149	Manny Sarmiento	.12	.06	.04
150	Wayne Cage	.12	.06	.04
151	John Hiller	.20	.10	.06
152	Rick Cerone	.20	.10	.06
153	Dennis Lamp	.12	.06	.04
154	Jim Gantner	.12	.06	.04
155	Dwight Evans	1.00	.50	.30
156	Buddy Solomon	.12	.06	.04
157	U.L. Washington	.12	.06	.04
158	Joe Sambito	.12	.06	.04
159	Roy White	.25	.13	.08
160	Mike Flanagan	.30	.15	.09
161	Barry Foote	.12	.06	.04
162	Tom Johnson	.12	.06	.04
163	Glenn Burke	.12	.06	.04
164	Mickey Lolich	.40	.20	.12
165	Frank Taveras	.12	.06	.04
166	Leon Roberts	.12	.06	.04
167	Roger Metzger	.12	.06	.04
168	Dave Freisleben	.12	.06	.04
169	Bill Nahorodny	.12	.06	.04
170	Don Sutton	1.25	.60	.40
171	Gene Clines	.12	.06	.04
172	Mike Bruhert	.12	.06	.04
173	John Lowenstein	.12	.06	.04
174	Rick Auerbach	.12	.06	.04
175	George Hendrick	.20	.10	.06

		NR MT	EX	VG
176	Aurelio Rodriguez	.20	.10	.06
177	Ron Reed	.20	.10	.06
178	Alvis Woods	.12	.06	.04
179	Jim Beattie	.12	.06	.04
180	Larry Hisle	.20	.10	.06
181	Mike Garman	.12	.06	.04
182	Tim Johnson	.12	.06	.04
183	Paul Splittorff	.20	.10	.06
184	Darrel Chaney	.12	.06	.04
185	Mike Torrez	.20	.10	.06
186	Eric Soderholm	.12	.06	.04
187	Mark Lemongello	.12	.06	.04
188	Pat Kelly	.12	.06	.04
189	*Eddie Whitson*	.50	.25	.15
190	Ron Cey	.25	.13	.08
191	Mike Norris	.12	.06	.04
192	Cardinals Team (Ken Boyer)	.50	.25	.15
193	Glenn Adams	.12	.06	.04
194	Randy Jones	.20	.10	.06
195	Bill Madlock	.40	.20	.12
196	Steve Kemp	.12	.06	.04
197	Bob Apodaca	.12	.06	.04
198	Johnny Grubb	.12	.06	.04
199	Larry Milbourne	.12	.06	.04
200	Johnny Bench	2.00	1.00	.60
201	Record Breaker (Mike Edwards)	.12	.06	.04
202	Record Breaker (Ron Guidry)	.35	.20	.11
203	Record Breaker (J.R. Richard)	.20	.10	.06
204	Record Breaker (Pete Rose)	1.50	.70	.45
205	Record Breaker (John Stearns)	.12	.06	.04
206	Record Breaker (Sammy Stewart)	.12	.06	.04
207	Dave Lemanczyk	.12	.06	.04
208	Clarence Gaston	.12	.06	.04
209	Reggie Cleveland	.12	.06	.04
210	Larry Bowa	.30	.15	.09
211	Denny Martinez	.20	.10	.06
212	*Carney Lansford*	8.00	4.00	2.50
213	Bill Travers	.12	.06	.04
214	Red Sox Team (Don Zimmer)	.60	.30	.20
215	Willie McCovey	1.50	.70	.45
216	Wilbur Wood	.20	.10	.06
217	Steve Dillard	.12	.06	.04
218	Dennis Leonard	.20	.10	.06
219	Roy Smalley	.20	.10	.06
220	Cesar Geronimo	.20	.10	.06
221	Jesse Jefferson	.12	.06	.04
222	Bob Beall	.12	.06	.04
223	Kent Tekulve	.25	.13	.08
224	Dave Revering	.12	.06	.04
225	Rich Gossage	.70	.35	.20
226	Ron Pruitt	.12	.06	.04
227	Steve Stone	.20	.10	.06
228	Vic Davalillo	.12	.06	.04
229	Doug Flynn	.12	.06	.04
230	Bob Forsch	.20	.10	.06
231	Johnny Wockenfuss	.12	.06	.04
232	Jimmy Sexton	.12	.06	.04
233	Paul Mitchell	.12	.06	.04
234	Toby Harrah	.20	.10	.06
235	Steve Rogers	.20	.10	.06
236	Jim Dwyer	.12	.06	.04
237	Billy Smith	.12	.06	.04
238	Balor Moore	.12	.06	.04
239	Willie Horton	.20	.10	.06
240	Rick Reuschel	.25	.13	.08
241	Checklist 122-242	.25	.13	.08
242	Pablo Torrealba	.12	.06	.04
243	Buck Martinez	.12	.06	.04
244	Pirates Team (Chuck Tanner)	.80	.40	.25
245	Jeff Burroughs	.20	.10	.06
246	Darrell Jackson	.12	.06	.04
247	Tucker Ashford	.12	.06	.04
248	Pete LaCock	.12	.06	.04
249	Paul Thormodsgard	.12	.06	.04
250	Willie Randolph	.30	.15	.09
251	Jack Morris	2.00	1.00	.60
252	Bob Stinson	.12	.06	.04
253	Rick Wise	.20	.10	.06
254	Luis Gomez	.12	.06	.04
255	Tommy John	.80	.40	.25
256	Mike Sadek	.12	.06	.04
257	Adrian Devine	.12	.06	.04
258	Mike Phillips	.12	.06	.04
259	Reds Team (Sparky Anderson)	.60	.30	.20
260	Richie Zisk	.20	.10	.06
261	Mario Guerrero	.12	.06	.04
262	Nelson Briles	.12	.06	.04
263	Oscar Gamble	.20	.10	.06
264	*Don Robinson*	.50	.25	.15
265	Don Money	.12	.06	.04
266	Jim Willoughby	.12	.06	.04

		NR MT	EX	VG
267	Joe Rudi	.20	.10	.06
268	Julio Gonzalez	.12	.06	.04
269	Woodie Fryman	.20	.10	.06
270	Butch Hobson	.12	.06	.04
271	Rawly Eastwick	.12	.06	.04
272	Tim Corcoran	.12	.06	.04
273	Jerry Terrell	.12	.06	.04
274	Willie Norwood	.12	.06	.04
275	Junior Moore	.12	.06	.04
276	Jim Colborn	.12	.06	.04
277	Tom Grieve	.12	.06	.04
278	Andy Messersmith	.25	.13	.08
279	Jerry Grote	.12	.06	.04
280	Andre Thornton	.25	.13	.08
281	Vic Correll	.12	.06	.04
282	Blue Jays Team (Roy Hartsfield)	.50	.25	.15
283	Ken Kravec	.12	.06	.04
284	Johnnie LeMaster	.12	.06	.04
285	Bobby Bonds	.30	.15	.09
286	Duffy Dyer	.12	.06	.04
287	Andres Mora	.12	.06	.04
288	Milt Wilcox	.20	.10	.06
289	Jose Cruz	.25	.13	.08
290	Dave Lopes	.25	.13	.08
291	Tom Griffin	.12	.06	.04
292	Don Reynolds	.12	.06	.04
293	Jerry Garvin	.12	.06	.04
294	Pepe Frias	.12	.06	.04
295	Mitchell Page	.12	.06	.04
296	Preston Hanna	.12	.06	.04
297	Ted Sizemore	.12	.06	.04
298	Rich Gale	.12	.06	.04
299	Steve Ontiveros	.12	.06	.04
300	Rod Carew	5.00	2.50	1.50
301	Tom Hume	.12	.06	.04
302	Braves Team (Bobby Cox)	.50	.25	.15
303	Lary Sorensen	.12	.06	.04
304	Steve Swisher	.12	.06	.04
305	Willie Montanez	.12	.06	.04
306	Floyd Bannister	.30	.15	.09
307	Larvell Blanks	.12	.06	.04
308	Bert Blyleven	.60	.30	.20
309	Ralph Garr	.20	.10	.06
310	Thurman Munson	5.00	2.50	1.50
311	Gary Lavelle	.12	.06	.04
312	Bob Robertson	.12	.06	.04
313	Dyar Miller	.12	.06	.04
314	Larry Harlow	.12	.06	.04
315	Jon Matlack	.20	.10	.06
316	Milt May	.12	.06	.04
317	Jose Cardenal	.12	.06	.04
318	*Bob Welch*	15.00	7.50	4.50
319	Wayne Garrett	.12	.06	.04
320	Carl Yastrzemski	2.50	1.25	.70
321	Gaylord Perry	2.00	1.00	.60
322	Danny Goodwin	.12	.06	.04
323	Lynn McGlothen	.12	.06	.04
324	Mike Tyson	.12	.06	.04
325	Cecil Cooper	.40	.20	.12
326	Pedro Borbon	.12	.06	.04
327	Art Howe	.12	.06	.04
328	A's Team (Jack McKeon)	.50	.25	.15
329	Joe Coleman	.20	.10	.06
330	George Brett	10.00	5.00	3.00
331	Mickey Mahler	.12	.06	.04
332	Gary Alexander	.12	.06	.04
333	Chet Lemon	.20	.10	.06
334	Craig Swan	.12	.06	.04
335	Chris Chambliss	.25	.13	.08
336	Bobby Thompson	.12	.06	.04
337	John Montague	.12	.06	.04
338	Vic Harris	.12	.06	.04
339	Ron Jackson	.12	.06	.04
340	Jim Palmer	5.00	2.50	1.50
341	*Willie Upshaw*	.40	.20	.12
342	Dave Roberts	.12	.06	.04
343	Ed Glynn	.12	.06	.04
344	Jerry Royster	.12	.06	.04
345	Tug McGraw	.30	.15	.09
346	Bill Buckner	.30	.15	.09
347	Doug Rau	.12	.06	.04
348	Andre Dawson	5.00	2.50	1.50
349	Jim Wright	.12	.06	.04
350	Garry Templeton	.20	.10	.06
351	Wayne Nordhagen	.12	.06	.04
352	Steve Renko	.12	.06	.04
353	Checklist 243-363	.60	.30	.20
354	Bill Bonham	.12	.06	.04
355	Lee Mazzilli	.20	.10	.06
356	Giants Team (Joe Altobelli)	.50	.25	.15
357	Jerry Augustine	.12	.06	.04

		NR MT	EX	VG
358	Alan Trammell	4.00	2.00	1.25
359	Dan Spillner	.12	.06	.04
360	Amos Otis	.20	.10	.06
361	Tom Dixon	.12	.06	.04
362	Mike Cubbage	.12	.06	.04
363	Craig Skok	.12	.06	.04
364	Gene Richards	.12	.06	.04
365	Sparky Lyle	.30	.15	.09
366	Juan Bernhardt	.12	.06	.04
367	Dave Skaggs	.12	.06	.04
368	Don Aase	.20	.10	.06
369a	Bump Wills (Blue Jays)	3.00	1.50	.90
369b	Bump Wills (Rangers)	3.50	1.75	1.00
370	Dave Kingman	.35	.20	.11
371	Jeff Holly	.12	.06	.04
372	Lamar Johnson	.12	.06	.04
373	Lance Rautzhan	.12	.06	.04
374	Ed Herrmann	.12	.06	.04
375	Bill Campbell	.12	.06	.04
376	Gorman Thomas	.25	.13	.08
377	Paul Moskau	.12	.06	.04
378	Rob Picciolo	.12	.06	.04
379	Dale Murray	.12	.06	.04
380	John Mayberry	.20	.10	.06
381	Astros Team (Bill Virdon)	.50	.25	.15
382	Jerry Martin	.12	.06	.04
383	Phil Garner	.20	.10	.06
384	Tommy Boggs	.12	.06	.04
385	Dan Ford	.12	.06	.04
386	Francisco Barrios	.12	.06	.04
387	Gary Thomasson	.12	.06	.04
388	Jack Billingham	.12	.06	.04
389	Joe Zdeb	.12	.06	.04
390	Rollie Fingers	3.00	1.50	.90
391	Al Oliver	.40	.20	.12
392	Doug Ault	.12	.06	.04
393	Scott McGregor	.20	.10	.06
394	Randy Stein	.12	.06	.04
395	Dave Cash	.12	.06	.04
396	Bill Plummer	.12	.06	.04
397	Sergio Ferrer	.12	.06	.04
398	Ivan DeJesus	.12	.06	.04
399	David Clyde	.12	.06	.04
400	Jim Rice	2.50	1.25	.70
401	Ray Knight	.25	.13	.08
402	Paul Hartzell	.12	.06	.04
403	Tim Foli	.12	.06	.04
404	White Sox Team (Don Kessinger)	.50	.25	.15
405	Butch Wynegar	.20	.10	.06
406	Joe Wallis	.12	.06	.04
407	Pete Vuckovich	.20	.10	.06
408	Charlie Moore	.12	.06	.04
409	*Willie Wilson*	1.50	.70	.45
410	Darrell Evans	.30	.15	.09
411	Hits Record Holders (Ty Cobb, George Sisler)	.70	.35	.20
412	Runs Batted In Record Holders (Hank Aaron, Hack Wilson)	.70	.35	.20
413	Home Run Record Holders (Hank Aaron, Roger Maris)	1.00	.50	.30
414	Batting Avg. Record Holders (Ty Cobb, Roger Hornsby)	.70	.35	.20
415	Stolen Bases Record Holders (Lou Brock)	.70	.35	.20
416	Wins Record Holders (Jack Chesbro, Cy Young)	.40	.20	.12
417	Strikeouts Record Holders (Walter Johnson, Nolan Ryan)	.40	.20	.12
418	Earned Run Avg. Record Holders (Walter Johnson, Dutch Leonard)	.20	.10	.06
419	Dick Ruthven	.12	.06	.04
420	Ken Griffey	.25	.13	.08
421	Doug DeCinces	.25	.13	.08
422	Ruppert Jones	.12	.06	.04
423	Bob Montgomery	.12	.06	.04
424	Angels Team (Jim Fregosi)	.60	.30	.20
425	Rick Manning	.12	.06	.04
426	Chris Speier	.20	.10	.06
427	Andy Replogle	.12	.06	.04
428	Bobby Valentine	.25	.13	.08
429	John Urrea	.12	.06	.04
430	Dave Parker	3.00	1.50	.90
431	Glenn Borgmann	.12	.06	.04
432	Dave Heaverlo	.12	.06	.04
433	Larry Biittner	.12	.06	.04
434	Ken Clay	.20	.10	.06
435	Gene Tenace	.20	.10	.06
436	Hector Cruz	.12	.06	.04
437	Rick Williams	.12	.06	.04
438	Horace Speed	.12	.06	.04
439	Frank White	.25	.13	.08
440	Rusty Staub	.30	.15	.09
441	Lee Lacy	.12	.06	.04
442	Doyle Alexander	.25	.13	.08
443	Bruce Bochte	.12	.06	.04
444	*Aurelio Lopez*	.20	.10	.06
445	Steve Henderson	.12	.06	.04
446	Jim Lonborg	.20	.10	.06
447	Manny Sanguillen	.12	.06	.04
448	Moose Haas	.12	.06	.04
449	Bombo Rivera	.12	.06	.04
450	Dave Concepcion	.30	.15	.09
451	Royals Team (Whitey Herzog)	.50	.25	.15
452	Jerry Morales	.12	.06	.04
453	Chris Knapp	.12	.06	.04
454	Len Randle	.12	.06	.04
455	Bill Lee	.12	.06	.04
456	Chuck Baker	.12	.06	.04
457	Bruce Sutter	.50	.25	.15
458	Jim Essian	.12	.06	.04
459	Sid Monge	.12	.06	.04
460	Graig Nettles	.50	.25	.15
461	Jim Barr	.12	.06	.04
462	Otto Velez	.12	.06	.04
463	Steve Comer	.12	.06	.04
464	Joe Nolan	.12	.06	.04
465	Reggie Smith	.25	.13	.08
466	Mark Littell	.12	.06	.04
467	Don Kessinger	.12	.06	.04
468	Stan Bahnsen	.12	.06	.04
469	Lance Parrish	3.00	1.50	.90
470	Garry Maddox	.12	.06	.04
471	Joaquin Andujar	.20	.10	.06
472	Craig Kusick	.12	.06	.04
473	Dave Roberts	.12	.06	.04
474	Dick Davis	.12	.06	.04
475	Dan Driessen	.20	.10	.06
476	Tom Poquette	.12	.06	.04
477	Bob Grich	.25	.13	.08
478	Juan Beniquez	.12	.06	.04
479	Padres Team (Roger Craig)	.50	.25	.15
480	Fred Lynn	.70	.35	.20
481	Skip Lockwood	.12	.06	.04
482	Craig Reynolds	.12	.06	.04
483	Checklist 364-484	.25	.13	.08
484	Rick Waits	.12	.06	.04
485	Bucky Dent	.25	.13	.08
486	Bob Knepper	.25	.13	.08
487	Miguel Dilone	.12	.06	.04
488	Bob Owchinko	.12	.06	.04
489	Larry Cox (photo actually Dave Rader)	.12	.06	.04
490	Al Cowens	.12	.06	.04
491	Tippy Martinez	.12	.06	.04
492	Bob Bailor	.12	.06	.04
493	Larry Christenson	.12	.06	.04
494	Jerry White	.12	.06	.04
495	Tony Perez	.60	.30	.04
496	Barry Bonnell	.12	.06	.04
497	Glenn Abbott	.12	.06	.04
498	Rich Chiles	.12	.06	.04
499	Rangers Team (Pat Corrales)	.50	.25	.15
500	Ron Guidry	.90	.45	.25
501	Junior Kennedy	.12	.06	.04
502	Steve Braun	.12	.06	.04
503	Terry Humphrey	.12	.06	.04
504	*Larry McWilliams*	.20	.10	.06
505	Ed Kranepool	.20	.10	.06
506	John D'Acquisto	.12	.06	.04
507	Tony Armas	.20	.10	.06
508	Charlie Hough	.20	.10	.06
509	Mario Mendoza	.12	.06	.04
510	Ted Simmons	.40	.20	.12
511	Paul Reuschel	.12	.06	.04
512	Jack Clark	1.50	.70	.45
513	Dave Johnson	.30	.15	.09
514	Mike Proly	.12	.06	.04
515	Enos Cabell	.12	.06	.04
516	Champ Summers	.12	.06	.04
517	Al Bumbry	.20	.10	.06
518	Jim Umbarger	.12	.06	.04
519	Ben Oglivie	.20	.10	.06
520	Gary Carter	5.00	2.50	1.50
521	Sam Ewing	.12	.06	.04
522	Ken Holtzman	.20	.10	.06
523	John Milner	.12	.06	.04
524	Tom Burgmeier	.12	.06	.04
525	Freddie Patek	.12	.06	.04
526	Dodgers Team (Tom Lasorda)	.60	.30	.20
527	Lerrin LaGrow	.12	.06	.04
528	Wayne Gross	.12	.06	.04
529	Brian Asselstine	.12	.06	.04

		NR MT	EX	VG
530	Frank Tanana	.25	.13	.08
531	Fernando Gonzalez	.12	.06	.04
532	Buddy Schultz	.12	.06	.04
533	Leroy Stanton	.12	.06	.04
534	Ken Forsch	.12	.06	.04
535	Ellis Valentine	.12	.06	.04
536	Jerry Reuss	.20	.10	.06
537	Tom Veryzer	.12	.06	.04
538	Mike Ivie	.12	.06	.04
539	John Ellis	.12	.06	.04
540	Greg Luzinski	.30	.15	.09
541	Jim Slaton	.12	.06	.04
542	Rick Bosetti	.12	.06	.04
543	Kiko Garcia	.12	.06	.04
544	Fergie Jenkins	.40	.20	.12
545	John Stearns	.12	.06	.04
546	Bill Russell	.20	.10	.06
547	Clint Hurdle	.12	.06	.04
548	Enrique Romo	.12	.06	.04
549	Bob Bailey	.12	.06	.04
550	Sal Bando	.20	.10	.06
551	Cubs Team (Herman Franks)	.50	.25	.15
552	Jose Morales	.12	.06	.04
553	Denny Walling	.12	.06	.04
554	Matt Keough	.12	.06	.04
555	Biff Pocoroba	.12	.06	.04
556	Mike Lum	.12	.06	.04
557	Ken Brett	.20	.10	.06
558	Jay Johnstone	.20	.10	.06
559	Greg Pryor	.12	.06	.04
560	John Montefusco	.12	.06	.04
561	Ed Ott	.12	.06	.04
562	Dusty Baker	.25	.13	.08
563	Roy Thomas	.12	.06	.04
564	Jerry Turner	.12	.06	.04
565	Rico Carty	.25	.13	.08
566	Nino Espinosa	.12	.06	.04
567	Rich Hebner	.12	.06	.04
568	Carlos Lopez	.12	.06	.04
569	Bob Sykes	.12	.06	.04
570	Cesar Cedeno	.25	.13	.08
571	Darrell Porter	.20	.10	.06
572	Rod Gilbreath	.12	.06	.04
573	Jim Kern	.12	.06	.04
574	Claudell Washington	.20	.10	.06
575	Luis Tiant	.30	.15	.09
576	Mike Parrott	.12	.06	.04
577	Brewers Team (George Bamberger)			
		.50	.25	.15
578	Pete Broberg	.12	.06	.04
579	Greg Gross	.12	.06	.04
580	Ron Fairly	.20	.10	.06
581	Darold Knowles	.12	.06	.04
582	Paul Blair	.20	.10	.06
583	Julio Cruz	.12	.06	.04
584	Jim Rooker	.12	.06	.04
585	Hal McRae	.25	.13	.08
586	*Bob Horner*	.90	.45	.25
587	Ken Reitz	.12	.06	.04
588	Tom Murphy	.12	.06	.04
589	Terry Whitfield	.12	.06	.04
590	J.R. Richard	.20	.10	.06
591	Mike Hargrove	.20	.10	.06
592	Mike Krukow	.20	.10	.06
593	Rick Dempsey	.20	.10	.06
594	Bob Shirley	.12	.06	.04
595	Phil Niekro	1.25	.60	.40
596	Jim Wohlford	.12	.06	.04
597	Bob Stanley	.20	.10	.06
598	Mark Wagner	.12	.06	.04
599	Jim Spencer	.20	.10	.06
600	George Foster	.60	.30	.20
601	Dave LaRoche	.12	.06	.04
602	Checklist 485-605	.60	.30	.20
603	Rudy May	.12	.06	.04
604	Jeff Newman	.12	.06	.04
605	Rick Monday	.12	.06	.04
606	Expos Team (Dick Williams)	.50	.25	.15
607	Omar Moreno	.12	.06	.04
608	Dave McKay	.12	.06	.04
609	Silvio Martinez	.12	.06	.04
610	Mike Schmidt	12.00	6.00	3.50
611	Jim Norris	.12	.06	.04
612	*Rick Honeycutt*	.30	.15	.09
613	Mike Edwards	.12	.06	.04
614	Willie Hernandez	.20	.10	.06
615	Ken Singleton	.20	.10	.06
616	Billy Almon	.12	.06	.04
617	Terry Puhl	.12	.06	.04
618	Jerry Remy	.12	.06	.04
619	*Ken Landreaux*	.25	.13	.08

		NR MT	EX	VG
620	Bert Campaneris	.25	.13	.08
621	Pat Zachry	.12	.06	.04
622	Dave Collins	.20	.10	.06
623	Bob McClure	.12	.06	.04
624	Larry Herndon	.20	.10	.06
625	Mark Fidrych	.25	.13	.08
626	Yankees Team (Bob Lemon)	.80	.40	.25
627	Gary Serum	.12	.06	.04
628	Del Unser	.12	.06	.04
629	Gene Garber	.12	.06	.04
630	Bake McBride	.12	.06	.04
631	Jorge Orta	.12	.06	.04
632	Don Kirkwood	.12	.06	.04
633	Rob Wilfong	.12	.06	.04
634	Paul Lindblad	.20	.10	.06
635	Don Baylor	.50	.25	.15
636	Wayne Garland	.12	.06	.04
637	Bill Robinson	.12	.06	.04
638	Al Fitzmorris	.12	.06	.04
639	Manny Trillo	.20	.10	.06
640	Eddie Murray	12.00	6.00	3.50
641	*Bobby Castillo*	.12	.06	.04
642	Wilbur Howard	.12	.06	.04
643	Tom Hausman	.12	.06	.04
644	Manny Mota	.20	.10	.06
645	George Scott	.12	.06	.04
646	Rick Sweet	.12	.06	.04
647	Bob Lacey	.12	.06	.04
648	Lou Piniella	.35	.20	.11
649	John Curtis	.12	.06	.04
650	Pete Rose	4.50	2.25	1.25
651	Mike Caldwell	.12	.06	.04
652	Stan Papi	.12	.06	.04
653	Warren Brusstar	.12	.06	.04
654	Rick Miller	.12	.06	.04
655	Jerry Koosman	.30	.15	.09
656	Hosken Powell	.12	.06	.04
657	George Medich	.12	.06	.04
658	Taylor Duncan	.12	.06	.04
659	Mariners Team (Darrell Johnson)	.50	.25	.15
660	Ron LeFlore	.12	.06	.04
661	Bruce Kison	.12	.06	.04
662	Kevin Bell	.12	.06	.04
663	Mike Vail	.12	.06	.04
664	Doug Bird	.12	.06	.04
665	Lou Brock	1.50	.70	.45
666	Rich Dauer	.12	.06	.04
667	Don Hood	.12	.06	.04
668	Bill North	.12	.06	.04
669	Checklist 606-726	.60	.30	.20
670	Jim Hunter	1.25	.60	.40
671	Joe Ferguson	.12	.06	.04
672	Ed Halicki	.12	.06	.04
673	Tom Hutton	.12	.06	.04
674	Dave Tomlin	.12	.06	.04
675	Tim McCarver	.30	.15	.09
676	Johnny Sutton	.12	.06	.04
677	Larry Parrish	.25	.13	.08
678	Geoff Zahn	.12	.06	.04
679	Derrel Thomas	.12	.06	.04
680	Carlton Fisk	2.00	1.00	.60
681	*John Henry Johnson*	.12	.06	.04
682	Dave Chalk	.12	.06	.04
683	Dan Meyer	.12	.06	.04
684	Jamie Easterly	.12	.06	.04
685	Sixto Lezcano	.12	.06	.04
686	Ron Schueler	.12	.06	.04
687	Rennie Stennett	.12	.06	.04
688	Mike Willis	.12	.06	.04
689	Orioles Team (Earl Weaver)	.70	.35	.20
690	Buddy Bell	.12	.06	.04
691	Dock Ellis	.12	.06	.04
692	Mickey Stanley	.20	.10	.06
693	Dave Rader	.12	.06	.04
694	Burt Hooton	.20	.10	.06
695	Keith Hernandez	2.00	1.00	.60
696	Andy Hassler	.12	.06	.04
697	Dave Bergman	.12	.06	.04
698	Bill Stein	.12	.06	.04
699	Hal Dues	.12	.06	.04
700	Reggie Jackson	7.00	3.50	2.00
701	Orioles Prospects (Mark Corey, John Flinn, *Sammy Stewart*)	.20	.10	.06
702	Red Sox Prospects (Joel Finch, Garry Hancock, Allen Ripley)	.12	.06	.04
703	Angels Prospects (Jim Anderson, Dave Frost, Bob Slater)	.12	.06	.04
704	White Sox Prospects (Ross Baumgarten, Mike Colbern, *Mike Squires*)	.20	.10	.06
705	Indians Prospects (*Alfredo Griffin*, Tim Norrid, Dave Oliver)	.70	.35	.20

		NR MT	EX	VG
706	Tigers Prospects (Dave Stegman, Dave Tobik, Kip Young) .12		.06	.04
707	Royals Prospects (Randy Bass, Jim Gaudet, Randy Yost) .12		.06	.04
708	Brewers Prospects *(Kevin Bass, Eddie Romero, Ned Yost)* 1.25		.60	.40
709	Twins Prospects (Sam Perlozzo, Rick Sofield, Kevin Stanfield) .12		.06	.04
710	Yankees Prospects (Brian Doyle, *Mike Heath*, Dave Rajsich) .30		.15	.09
711	A's Prospects *(Dwayne Murphy*, Bruce Robinson, Alan Wirth) .50		.25	.15
712	Mariners Prospects (Bud Anderson, Greg Biercevicz, Byron McLaughlin) .12		.06	.04
713	Rangers Prospects *(Danny Darwin*, Pat Putnam, *Billy Sample).70*		.35	.20
714	Blue Jays Prospects (Victor Cruz, Pat Kelly, Ernie Whitt) .20		.10	.06
715	Braves Prospects *(Bruce Benedict*, Glenn Hubbard, Larry Whisenton) .40		.20	.12
716	Cubs Prospects (Dave Geisel, Karl Pagel, Scot Thompson) .12		.06	.04
717	Reds Prospects *(Mike LaCoss, Ron Oester, Harry Spilman)* .40		.20	.12
718	Astros Prospects (Bruce Bochy, Mike Fischlin, Don Pisker) .12		.06	.04
719	Dodgers Prospects *(Pedro Guerrero, Rudy Law, Joe Simpson)* 10.00		5.00	3.00
720	Expos Prospects (Jerry Fry, Jerry Pirtle, Scott Sanderson) .30		.15	.09
721	Mets Prospects *(Juan Berenguer*, Dwight Bernard, Dan Norman) .30		.15	.09
722	Phillies Prospects *(Jim Morrison, Lonnie Smith*, Jim Wright) 3.00		1.50	.90
723	Pirates Prospects *(Dale Berra, Eugenio Cotes, Ben Wiltbank)* .20		.10	.06
724	Cardinals Prospects (Tom Bruno, *George Frazier, Terry Kennedy)* .50		.25	.15
725	Padres Prospects (Jim Beswick, Steve Mura, Broderick Perkins) .12		.06	.04
726	Giants Prospects (Greg Johnston, Joe Strain, John Tamargo) .25		.06	.04

1979 Topps Comics

Issued as the 3" by 3-3/4" wax wrapper for a piece of bubblegum, this "test" issue was bought up in great quantities by speculators and remains rather common. It is also inexpensive, because the comic-style player representations were not popular with collectors. The set is complete at 33 pieces.

		NR MT	EX	VG
Complete Set:		8.00	4.00	2.50
Common Player:		.10	.05	.03
1	Eddie Murray	.40	.20	.12
2	Jim Rice	.30	.15	.09
3	Carl Yastrzemski	.60	.30	.20
4	Nolan Ryan	.30	.15	.09
5	Chet Lemon	.10	.05	.03
6	Andre Thornton	.10	.05	.03
7	Rusty Staub	.15	.08	.05
8	Ron LeFlore	.10	.05	.03
9	George Brett	.50	.25	.15
10	Larry Hisle	.10	.05	.03
11	Rod Carew	.35	.20	.11
12	Reggie Jackson	.40	.20	.12

		NR MT	EX	VG
13	Ron Guidry	.20	.10	.06
14	Mitchell Page	.10	.05	.03
15	Leon Roberts	.10	.05	.03
16	Al Oliver	.15	.08	.05
17	John Mayberry	.10	.05	.03
18	Bob Horner	.20	.10	.06
19	Phil Niekro	.25	.13	.08
20	Dave Kingman	.15	.08	.05
21	John Bench	.40	.20	.12
22	Tom Seaver	.40	.20	.12
23	J.R. Richard	.10	.05	.03
24	Steve Garvey	.35	.20	.11
25	Reggie Smith	.15	.08	.05
26	Ross Grimsley	.10	.05	.03
27	Craig Swan	.10	.05	.03
28	Pete Rose	.90	.45	.25
29	Dave Parker	.20	.10	.06
30	Ted Simmons	.15	.08	.05
31	Dave Winfield	.30	.15	.09
32	Jack Clark	.20	.10	.06
33	Vida Blue	.15	.08	.05

1980 Topps

 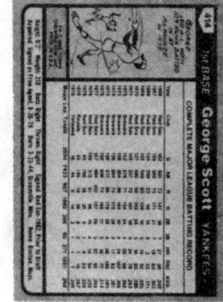

Again numbering 726 cards measuring 2-1/2" by 3-1/2", Topps did make some design changes in 1980. Fronts have the usual color picture with a facsimile autograph. The player's name appears above the picture, while his position is on a pennant at the upper left and his team on another pennant in the lower right. Backs no longer feature games, returning instead to statistics, personal information, a few headlines and a cartoon about the player. Specialty cards include statistical leaders, and previous season highlights. Many rookies again appear in team threesomes.

		NR MT	EX	VG
Complete Set:		300.00	150.00	90.00
Common Player:		.12	.06	.04
1	1979 Highlights (Lou Brock, Carl Yastrzemski)	1.50	.70	.45
2	1979 Highlights (Willie McCovey)	.80	.40	.25
3	1979 Highlights (Manny Mota)	.20	.10	.06
4	1979 Highlights (Pete Rose)	2.00	1.00	.60
5	1979 Highlights (Garry Templeton)	.20	.10	.06
6	1979 Highlights (Del Unser)	.12	.06	.04
7	Mike Lum	.12	.06	.04
8	Craig Swan	.12	.06	.04
9	Steve Braun	.12	.06	.04
10	Denny Martinez	.20	.10	.06
11	Jimmy Sexton	.12	:06	.04
12	John Curtis	.12	.06	.04
13	Ron Pruitt	.12	.06	.04
14	Dave Cash	.12	.06	.04
15	Bill Campbell	.12	.06	.04
16	Jerry Narron	.20	.10	.06
17	Bruce Sutter	.35	.25	.14
18	Ron Jackson	.12	.06	.04
19	Balor Moore	.12	.06	.04
20	Dan Ford	.12	.06	.04
21	Manny Sarmiento	.12	.06	.04
22	Pat Putnam	.12	.06	.04
23	Derrel Thomas	.12	.06	.04
24	Jim Slaton	.12	.06	.04
25	Lee Mazzilli	.20	.10	.06

		NR MT	EX	VG
26	Marty Pattin	.12	.06	.04
27	Del Unser	.12	.06	.04
28	Bruce Kison	.12	.06	.04
29	Mark Wagner	.12	.06	.04
30	Vida Blue	.30	.15	.09
31	Jay Johnstone	.20	.10	.06
32	Julio Cruz	.12	.06	.04
33	Tony Scott	.12	.06	.04
34	Jeff Newman	.12	.06	.04
35	Luis Tiant	.30	.15	.09
36	Rusty Torres	.12	.06	.04
37	Kiko Garcia	.12	.06	.04
38	Dan Spillner	.12	.06	.04
39	Rowland Office	.12	.06	.04
40	Carlton Fisk	4.00	2.00	1.25
41	Rangers Team (Pat Corrales)	.50	.25	.15
42	*Dave Palmer*	.40	.20	.12
43	Bombo Rivera	.12	.06	.04
44	Bill Fahey	.12	.06	.04
45	Frank White	.25	.13	.08
46	Rico Carty	.20	.10	.06
47	Bill Bonham	.12	.06	.04
48	Rick Miller	.12	.06	.04
49	Mario Guerrero	.12	.06	.04
50	J.R. Richard	.20	.10	.06
51	Joe Ferguson	.12	.06	.04
52	Warren Brusstar	.12	.06	.04
53	Ben Oglivie	.20	.10	.06
54	Dennis Lamp	.12	.06	.04
55	Bill Madlock	.40	.20	.12
56	Bobby Valentine	.20	.10	.06
57	Pete Vuckovich	.20	.10	.06
58	Doug Flynn	.12	.06	.04
59	Eddy Putman	.12	.06	.04
60	Bucky Dent	.25	.13	.08
61	Gary Serum	.12	.06	.04
62	Mike Ivie	.12	.06	.04
63	Bob Stanley	.20	.10	.06
64	Joe Nolan	.12	.06	.04
65	Al Bumbry	.20	.10	.06
66	Royals Team (Jim Frey)	.60	.30	.20
67	Doyle Alexander	.25	.13	.08
68	Larry Harlow	.12	.06	.04
69	Rick Williams	.12	.06	.04
70	Gary Carter	4.00	2.00	1.25
71	John Milner	.12	.06	.04
72	Fred Howard	.12	.06	.04
73	Dave Collins	.20	.10	.06
74	Sid Monge	.12	.06	.04
75	Bill Russell	.20	.10	.06
76	John Stearns	.12	.06	.04
77	*Dave Stieb*	10.00	5.00	3.00
78	Ruppert Jones	.12	.06	.04
79	Bob Owchinko	.12	.06	.04
80	Ron LeFlore	.20	.10	.06
81	Ted Sizemore	.12	.06	.04
82	Astros Team (Bill Virdon)	.50	.25	.15
83	*Steve Trout*	.30	.15	.09
84	Gary Lavelle	.12	.06	.04
85	Ted Simmons	.40	.20	.12
86	Dave Hamilton	.12	.06	.04
87	Pepe Frias	.12	.06	.04
88	Ken Landreaux	.20	.10	.06
89	Don Hood	.20	.10	.06
90	Manny Trillo	.20	.10	.06
91	Rick Dempsey	.20	.10	.06
92	Rick Rhoden	.25	.13	.08
93	Dave Roberts	.12	.06	.04
94	*Neil Allen*	.30	.15	.09
95	Cecil Cooper	.35	.20	.11
96	A's Team (Jim Marshall)	.50	.25	.15
97	Bill Lee	.20	.10	.06
98	Jerry Terrell	.12	.06	.04
99	Victor Cruz	.12	.06	.04
100	Johnny Bench	3.00	1.50	.90
101	Aurelio Lopez	.12	.06	.04
102	Rich Dauer	.12	.06	.04
103	*Bill Caudill*	.20	.10	.06
104	Manny Mota	.20	.10	.06
105	Frank Tanana	.20	.10	.06
106	*Jeff Leonard*	2.00	1.00	.60
107	Francisco Barrios	.12	.06	.04
108	Bob Horner	.40	.30	.15
109	Bill Travers	.12	.06	.04
110	Fred Lynn	.35	.20	.11
111	Bob Knepper	.20	.10	.06
112	White Sox Team (Tony LaRussa)	.50	.25	.15
113	Geoff Zahn	.12	.06	.04
114	Juan Beniquez	.12	.06	.04
115	Sparky Lyle	.25	.13	.08
116	Larry Cox	.12	.06	.04

		NR MT	EX	VG
117	Dock Ellis	.12	.06	.04
118	Phil Garner	.20	.10	.06
119	Sammy Stewart	.12	.06	.04
120	Greg Luzinski	.30	.15	.09
121	Checklist 1-121	.50	.25	.15
122	Dave Rosello	.12	.06	.04
123	Lynn Jones	.12	.06	.04
124	Dave Lemanczyk	.12	.06	.04
125	Tony Perez	.50	.25	.15
126	Dave Tomlin	.12	.06	.04
127	Gary Thomasson	.12	.06	.04
128	Tom Burgmeier	.12	.06	.04
129	Craig Reynolds	.12	.06	.04
130	Amos Otis	.20	.10	.06
131	Paul Mitchell	.12	.06	.04
132	Biff Pocoroba	.12	.06	.04
133	Jerry Turner	.12	.06	.04
134	Matt Keough	.12	.06	.04
135	Bill Buckner	.30	.15	.09
136	Dick Ruthven	.12	.06	.04
137	*John Castino*	.20	.10	.06
138	Ross Baumgarten	.12	.06	.04
139	*Dane Iorg*	.20	.10	.06
140	Rich Gossage	.60	.30	.20
141	Gary Alexander	.12	.06	.04
142	Phil Huffman	.12	.06	.04
143	Bruce Bochte	.12	.06	.04
144	Steve Comer	.12	.06	.04
145	Darrell Evans	.30	.15	.09
146	Bob Welch	.90	.45	.25
147	Terry Puhl	.12	.06	.04
148	Manny Sanguillen	.12	.06	.04
149	Tom Hume	.12	.06	.04
150	Jason Thompson	.20	.10	.06
151	Tom Hausman	.12	.06	.04
152	John Fulgham	.12	.06	.04
153	Tim Blackwell	.12	.06	.04
154	Lary Sorensen	.12	.06	.04
155	Jerry Remy	.12	.06	.04
156	Tony Brizzolara	.12	.06	.04
157	Willie Wilson	.20	.10	.06
158	Rob Picciolo	.12	.06	.04
159	Ken Clay	.20	.10	.06
160	Eddie Murray	6.00	3.00	1.75
161	Larry Christenson	.12	.06	.04
162	Bob Randall	.12	.06	.04
163	Steve Swisher	.12	.06	.04
164	Greg Pryor	.12	.06	.04
165	Omar Moreno	.12	.06	.04
166	Glenn Abbott	.12	.06	.04
167	Jack Clark	1.00	.50	.30
168	Rick Waits	.12	.06	.04
169	Luis Gomez	.12	.06	.04
170	Burt Hooton	.20	.10	.06
171	Fernando Gonzalez	.12	.06	.04
172	Ron Hodges	.12	.06	.04
173	John Henry Johnson	.12	.06	.04
174	Ray Knight	.20	.10	.06
175	Rick Reuschel	.25	.13	.08
176	Champ Summers	.12	.06	.04
177	Dave Heaverlo	.12	.06	.04
178	Tim McCarver	.30	.15	.09
179	*Ron Davis*	.20	.10	.06
180	Warren Cromartie	.12	.06	.04
181	Moose Haas	.12	.06	.04
182	Ken Reitz	.12	.06	.04
183	Jim Anderson	.12	.06	.04
184	Steve Renko	.12	.06	.04
185	Hal McRae	.25	.13	.08
186	Junior Moore	.12	.06	.04
187	Alan Ashby	.12	.06	.04
188	Terry Crowley	.12	.06	.04
189	Kevin Kobel	.12	.06	.04
190	Buddy Bell	.25	.13	.08
191	Ted Martinez	.12	.06	.04
192	Braves Team (Bobby Cox)	.50	.25	.15
193	Dave Goltz	.20	.10	.06
194	Mike Easler	.20	.10	.06
195	John Montefusco	.20	.10	.06
196	Lance Parrish	1.50	.70	.45
197	Byron McLaughlin	.12	.06	.04
198	Dell Alston	.12	.06	.04
199	Mike LaCoss	.20	.10	.06
200	Jim Rice	2.00	1.00	.60
201	Batting Leaders (Keith Hernandez, Fred Lynn)	.50	.25	.15
202	Home Run Leaders (Dave Kingman, Gorman Thomas)	.25	.13	.08
203	Runs Batted In Leaders (Don Baylor, Dave Winfield)	.50	.25	.15
204	Stolen Base Leaders (Omar Moreno, Willie Wilson)	.20	.10	.06

		NR MT	EX	VG
205	Victory Leaders (Mike Flanagan, Joe Niekro, Phil Niekro)	.40	.20	.12
206	Strikeout Leaders (J.R. Richard, Nolan Ryan)	.50	.25	.15
207	Earned Run Avg. Leaders (Ron Guidry, J.R. Richard)	.25	.13	.08
208	Wayne Cage	.12	.06	.04
209	Von Joshua	.12	.06	.04
210	Steve Carlton	7.00	3.50	2.00
211	Dave Skaggs	.12	.06	.04
212	Dave Roberts	.12	.06	.04
213	Mike Jorgensen	.12	.06	.04
214	Angels Team (Jim Fregosi)	.50	.25	.15
215	Sixto Lezcano	.12	.06	.04
216	Phil Mankowski	.12	.06	.04
217	Ed Halicki	.12	.06	.04
218	Jose Morales	.12	.06	.04
219	Steve Mingori	.12	.06	.04
220	Dave Concepcion	.30	.15	.09
221	Joe Cannon	.12	.06	.04
222	*Ron Hassey*	.35	.20	.11
223	Bob Sykes	.12	.06	.04
224	Willie Montanez	.12	.06	.04
225	Lou Piniella	.30	.15	.09
226	Bill Stein	.12	.06	.04
227	Len Barker	.12	.06	.04
228	Johnny Oates	.12	.06	.04
229	Jim Bibby	.12	.06	.04
230	Dave Winfield	2.00	1.00	.60
231	Steve McCatty	.12	.06	.04
232	Alan Trammell	4.00	2.00	1.25
233	LaRue Washington	.12	.06	.04
234	Vern Ruhle	.12	.06	.04
235	Andre Dawson	4.00	2.00	1.25
236	Marc Hill	.12	.06	.04
237	Scott McGregor	.20	.10	.06
238	Rob Wilfong	.12	.06	.04
239	Don Aase	.12	.06	.04
240	Dave Kingman	.40	.20	.12
241	Checklist 122-242	.50	.25	.15
242	Lamar Johnson	.12	.06	.04
243	Jerry Augustine	.12	.06	.04
244	Cardinals Team (Ken Boyer)	.50	.25	.15
245	Phil Niekro	3.00	1.50	.90
246	Tim Foli	.12	.06	.04
247	Frank Riccelli	.12	.06	.04
248	Jamie Quirk	.12	.06	.04
249	Jim Clancy	.20	.10	.06
250	Jim Kaat	.50	.25	.15
251	Kip Young	.12	.06	.04
252	Ted Cox	.12	.06	.04
253	John Montague	.12	.06	.04
254	Paul Dade	.12	.06	.04
255	Dusty Baker	.12	.06	.04
256	Roger Erickson	.12	.06	.04
257	Larry Herndon	.20	.10	.06
258	Paul Moskau	.12	.06	.04
259	Mets Team (Joe Torre)	.60	.30	.20
260	Al Oliver	.35	.20	.11
261	Dave Chalk	.12	.06	.04
262	Benny Ayala	.12	.06	.04
263	Dave LaRoche	.12	.06	.04
264	Bill Robinson	.12	.06	.04
265	Robin Yount	8.00	4.00	2.50
266	Bernie Carbo	.12	.06	.04
267	Dan Schatzeder	.12	.06	.04
268	Rafael Landestoy	.12	.06	.04
269	Dave Tobik	.12	.06	.04
270	Mike Schmidt	6.00	3.00	1.75
271	Dick Drago	.12	.06	.04
272	Ralph Garr	.20	.10	.06
273	Eduardo Rodriguez	.12	.06	.04
274	Dale Murphy	5.50	2.75	1.75
275	Jerry Koosman	.25	.13	.08
276	Tom Veryzer	.12	.06	.04
277	Rick Bosetti	.12	.06	.04
278	Jim Spencer	.20	.10	.06
279	Rob Andrews	.12	.06	.04
280	Gaylord Perry	3.00	1.50	.90
281	Paul Blair	.20	.10	.06
282	Mariners Team (Darrell Johnson)	.50	.25	.15
283	John Ellis	.12	.06	.04
284	Larry Murray	.12	.06	.04
285	Don Baylor	.35	.20	.11
286	Darold Knowles	.12	.06	.04
287	John Lowenstein	.12	.06	.04
288	Dave Rozema	.12	.06	.04
289	Bruce Bochy	.12	.06	.04
290	Steve Garvey	2.00	1.00	.60
291	Randy Scarbery	.12	.06	.04
292	Dale Berra	.12	.06	.04

		NR MT	EX	VG
293	Elias Sosa	.12	.06	.04
294	Charlie Spikes	.12	.06	.04
295	Larry Gura	.12	.06	.04
296	Dave Rader	.12	.06	.04
297	Tim Johnson	.12	.06	.04
298	Ken Holtzman	.20	.10	.06
299	Steve Henderson	.12	.06	.04
300	Ron Guidry	.70	.35	.20
301	Mike Edwards	.12	.06	.04
302	Dodgers Team (Tom Lasorda)	.60	.30	.20
303	Bill Castro	.12	.06	.04
304	Butch Wynegar	.20	.10	.06
305	Randy Jones	.20	.10	.06
306	Denny Walling	.12	.06	.04
307	Rick Honeycutt	.20	.10	.06
308	Mike Hargrove	.20	.10	.06
309	Larry McWilliams	.12	.06	.04
310	Dave Parker	2.00	1.00	.60
311	Roger Metzger	.12	.06	.04
312	Mike Barlow	.12	.06	.04
313	Johnny Grubb	.12	.06	.04
314	*Tim Stoddard*	.20	.10	.06
315	Steve Kemp	.25	.13	.08
316	Bob Lacey	.12	.06	.04
317	Mike Anderson	.12	.06	.04
318	Jerry Reuss	.20	.10	.06
319	Chris Speier	.12	.06	.04
320	Dennis Eckersley	1.25	.60	.40
321	Keith Hernandez	1.50	.70	.45
322	Claudell Washington	.20	.10	.06
323	Mick Kelleher	.12	.06	.04
324	Tom Underwood	.12	.06	.04
325	Dan Driessen	.20	.10	.06
326	Bo McLaughlin	.12	.06	.04
327	Ray Fosse	.12	.06	.04
328	Twins Team (Gene Mauch)	.50	.25	.15
329	Bert Roberge	.12	.06	.04
330	Al Cowens	.12	.06	.04
331	Rich Hebner	.12	.06	.04
332	Enrique Romo	.12	.06	.04
333	Jim Norris	.12	.06	.04
334	Jim Beattie	.20	.10	.06
335	Willie McCovey	1.50	.70	.45
336	George Medich	.12	.06	.04
337	Carney Lansford	.30	.15	.09
338	Johnny Wockenfuss	.12	.06	.04
339	John D'Acquisto	.12	.06	.04
340	Ken Singleton	.20	.10	.06
341	Jim Essian	.12	.06	.04
342	Odell Jones	.12	.06	.04
343	Mike Vail	.12	.06	.04
344	Randy Lerch	.12	.06	.04
345	Larry Parrish	.20	.10	.06
346	Buddy Solomon	.12	.06	.04
347	*Harry Chappas*	.20	.10	.06
348	Checklist 243-363	.50	.25	.15
349	Jack Brohamer	.12	.06	.04
350	George Hendrick	.20	.10	.06
351	Bob Davis	.12	.06	.04
352	Dan Briggs	.12	.06	.04
353	Andy Hassler	.12	.06	.04
354	Rick Auerbach	.12	.06	.04
355	Gary Matthews	.20	.10	.06
356	Padres Team (Jerry Coleman)	.50	.25	.15
357	Bob McClure	.12	.06	.04
358	Lou Whitaker	1.25	.60	.40
359	Randy Moffitt	.12	.06	.04
360	Darrell Porter	.12	.06	.04
361	Wayne Garland	.12	.06	.04
362	Danny Goodwin	.12	.06	.04
363	Wayne Gross	.12	.06	.04
364	Ray Burris	.12	.06	.04
365	Bobby Murcer	.25	.13	.08
366	Rob Dressler	.12	.06	.04
367	Billy Smith	.12	.06	.04
368	*Willie Aikens*	.20	.10	.06
369	Jim Kern	.12	.06	.04
370	Cesar Cedeno	.25	.13	.08
371	Jack Morris	1.00	.50	.30
372	Joel Youngblood	.12	.06	.04
373	*Dan Petry*	.30	.15	.09
374	Jim Gantner	.20	.10	.06
375	Ross Grimsley	.12	.06	.04
376	Gary Allenson	.12	.06	.04
377	Junior Kennedy	.12	.06	.04
378	Jerry Mumphrey	.12	.06	.04
379	Kevin Bell	.12	.06	.04
380	Garry Maddox	.20	.10	.06
381	Cubs Team (Preston Gomez)	.50	.25	.15
382	Dave Freisleben	.12	.06	.04
383	Ed Ott	.12	.06	.04

		NR MT	EX	VG			NR MT	EX	VG
384	Joey McLaughlin	.12	.06	.04	474	Steve Busby	.12	.06	.04
385	Enos Cabell	.12	.06	.04	475	Cesar Geronimo	.12	.06	.04
386	Darrell Jackson	.12	.06	.04	476	Bob Shirley	.12	.06	.04
387a	Fred Stanley (name in red)	.20	.10	.06	477	Buck Martinez	.12	.06	.04
387b	Fred Stanley (name in yellow)	3.00	1.50	.90	478	Gil Flores	.12	.06	.04
388	Mike Paxton	.12	.06	.04	479	Expos Team (Dick Williams)	.50	.25	.15
389	Pete LaCock	.12	.06	.04	480	Bob Watson	.20	.10	.06
390	Fergie Jenkins	.40	.20	.12	481	Tom Paciorek	.12	.06	.04
391	Tony Armas	.12	.06	.04	482	*Rickey Henderson*	200.00	100.00	60.00
392	Milt Wilcox	.12	.06	.04	483	Bo Diaz	.20	.10	.06
393	Ozzie Smith	8.00	4.00	2.50	484	Checklist 364-484	.50	.25	.15
394	Reggie Cleveland	.12	.06	.04	485	Mickey Rivers	.20	.10	.06
395	Ellis Valentine	.12	.06	.04	486	Mike Tyson	.12	.06	.04
396	Dan Meyer	.12	.06	.04	487	Wayne Nordhagen	.12	.06	.04
397	Roy Thomas	.12	.06	.04	488	Roy Howell	.12	.06	.04
398	Barry Foote	.12	.06	.04	489	Preston Hanna	.12	.06	.04
399	Mike Proly	.12	.06	.04	490	Lee May	.20	.10	.06
400	George Foster	.50	.25	.15	491	Steve Mura	.12	.06	.04
401	Pete Falcone	.12	.06	.04	492	Todd Cruz	.12	.06	.04
402	Merv Rettenmund	.12	.06	.04	493	Jerry Martin	.12	.06	.04
403	Pete Redfern	.12	.06	.04	494	Craig Minetto	.12	.06	.04
404	Orioles Team (Earl Weaver)	.60	.30	.20	495	Bake McBride	.12	.06	.04
405	Dwight Evans	.60	.30	.20	496	Silvio Martinez	.12	.06	.04
406	Paul Molitor	1.50	.70	.45	497	Jim Mason	.12	.06	.04
407	Tony Solaita	.12	.06	.04	498	Danny Darwin	.20	.10	.06
408	Bill North	.12	.06	.04	499	Giants Team (Dave Bristol)	.50	.25	.15
409	Paul Splittorff	.20	.10	.06	500	Tom Seaver	2.00	1.00	.60
410	Bobby Bonds	.25	.13	.08	501	Rennie Stennett	.12	.06	.04
411	Frank LaCorte	.12	.06	.04	502	Rich Wortham	.12	.06	.04
412	Thad Bosley	.12	.06	.04	503	Mike Cubbage	.12	.06	.04
413	Allen Ripley	.12	.06	.04	504	Gene Garber	.12	.06	.04
414	George Scott	.20	.10	.06	505	Bert Campaneris	.20	.10	.06
415	Bill Atkinson	.12	.06	.04	506	Tom Buskey	.12	.06	.04
416	*Tom Brookens*	.35	.20	.11	507	Leon Roberts	.12	.06	.04
417	Craig Chamberlain	.12	.06	.04	508	U.L. Washington	.12	.06	.04
418	Roger Freed	.12	.06	.04	509	Ed Glynn	.12	.06	.04
419	Vic Correll	.12	.06	.04	510	Ron Cey	.25	.13	.08
420	Butch Hobson	.12	.06	.04	511	Eric Wilkins	.12	.06	.04
421	Doug Bird	.12	.06	.04	512	Jose Cardenal	.12	.06	.04
422	Larry Milbourne	.12	.06	.04	513	Tom Dixon	.12	.06	.04
423	Dave Frost	.12	.06	.04	514	Steve Ontiveros	.12	.06	.04
424	Yankees Team (Dick Howser)	.70	.35	.20	515	Mike Caldwell	.12	.06	.04
425	Mark Belanger	.20	.10	.06	516	Hector Cruz	.12	.06	.04
426	Grant Jackson	.12	.06	.04	517	Don Stanhouse	.12	.06	.04
427	Tom Hutton	.12	.06	.04	518	Nelson Norman	.12	.06	.04
428	Pat Zachry	.12	.06	.04	519	Steve Nicosia	.12	.06	.04
429	Duane Kuiper	.12	.06	.04	520	Steve Rogers	.20	.10	.06
430	Larry Hisle	.12	.06	.04	521	Ken Brett	.12	.06	.04
431	Mike Krukow	.20	.10	.06	522	Jim Morrison	.12	.06	.04
432	Willie Norwood	.12	.06	.04	523	Ken Henderson	.12	.06	.04
433	Rich Gale	.12	.06	.04	524	Jim Wright	.12	.06	.04
434	Johnnie LeMaster	.12	.06	.04	525	Clint Hurdle	.12	.06	.04
435	Don Gullett	.20	.10	.06	526	Phillies Team (Dallas Green)	.70	.35	.20
436	Billy Almon	.12	.06	.04	527	Doug Rau	.12	.06	.04
437	Joe Niekro	.20	.10	.06	528	Adrian Devine	.12	.06	.04
438	Dave Revering	.12	.06	.04	529	Jim Barr	.12	.06	.04
439	Mike Phillips	.12	.06	.04	530	Jim Sundberg	.12	.06	.04
440	Don Sutton	1.00	.50	.30	531	Eric Rasmussen	.12	.06	.04
441	Eric Soderholm	.12	.06	.04	532	Willie Horton	.20	.10	.06
442	Jorge Orta	.12	.06	.04	533	Checklist 485-605	.50	.25	.15
443	Mike Parrott	.12	.06	.04	534	Andre Thornton	.25	.13	.08
444	Alvis Woods	.12	.06	.04	535	Bob Forsch	.20	.10	.06
445	Mark Fidrych	.20	.10	.06	536	Lee Lacy	.12	.06	.04
446	Duffy Dyer	.12	.06	.04	537	*Alex Trevino*	.20	.10	.06
447	Nino Espinosa	.12	.06	.04	538	Joe Strain	.12	.06	.04
448	Jim Wohlford	.12	.06	.04	539	Rudy May	.12	.06	.04
449	Doug Bair	.12	.06	.04	540	Pete Rose	4.00	2.00	1.25
450	George Brett	8.00	4.00	2.50	541	Miguel Dilone	.12	.06	.04
451	Indians Team (Dave Garcia)	.50	.25	.15	542	Joe Coleman	.12	.06	.04
452	Steve Dillard	.12	.06	.04	543	Pat Kelly	.12	.06	.04
453	Mike Bacsik	.12	.06	.04	544	*Rick Sutcliffe*	3.25	1.75	1.00
454	Tom Donohue	.12	.06	.04	545	Jeff Burroughs	.20	.10	.06
455	Mike Torrez	.20	.10	.06	546	Rick Langford	.12	.06	.04
456	Frank Taveras	.12	.06	.04	547	John Wathan	.20	.10	.06
457	Bert Blyleven	.50	.25	.15	548	Dave Rajsich	.12	.06	.04
458	Billy Sample	.12	.06	.04	549	Larry Wolfe	.12	.06	.04
459	Mickey Lolich	.12	.06	.04	550	Ken Griffey	.25	.13	.08
460	Willie Randolph	.25	.13	.08	551	Pirates Team (Chuck Tanner)	.50	.25	.15
461	Dwayne Murphy	.20	.10	.06	552	Bill Nahorodny	.12	.06	.04
462	Mike Sadek	.12	.06	.04	553	Dick Davis	.12	.06	.04
463	Jerry Royster	.12	.06	.04	554	Art Howe	.12	.06	.04
464	John Denny	.12	.06	.04	555	Ed Figueroa	.20	.10	.06
465	Rick Monday	.20	.10	.06	556	Joe Rudi	.20	.10	.06
466	Mike Squires	.12	.06	.04	557	Mark Lee	.12	.06	.04
467	Jesse Jefferson	.12	.06	.04	558	Alfredo Griffin	.25	.13	.08
468	Aurelio Rodriguez	.20	.10	.06	559	Dale Murray	.12	.06	.04
469	Randy Niemann	.12	.06	.04	560	Dave Lopes	.25	.13	.08
470	Bob Boone	.20	.10	.06	561	Eddie Whitson	.20	.10	.06
471	Hosken Powell	.12	.06	.04	562	Joe Wallis	.12	.06	.04
472	Willie Hernandez	.20	.10	.06	563	Will McEnaney	.12	.06	.04
473	Bump Wills	.12	.06	.04	564	Rick Manning	.12	.06	.04

	NR MT	EX	VG
565 Dennis Leonard	.20	.10	.06
566 Bud Harrelson	.20	.10	.06
567 Skip Lockwood	.12	.06	.04
568 *Gary Roenicke*	.25	.13	.08
569 Terry Kennedy	.25	.13	.08
570 Roy Smalley	.20	.10	.06
571 Joe Sambito	.12	.06	.04
572 Jerry Morales	.12	.06	.04
573 Kent Tekulve	.20	.10	.06
574 Scot Thompson	.12	.06	.04
575 Ken Kravec	.12	.06	.04
576 Jim Dwyer	.12	.06	.04
577 Blue Jays Team (Bobby Mattick)	.50	.25	.15
578 Scott Sanderson	.20	.10	.06
579 Charlie Moore	.12	.06	.04
580 Nolan Ryan	12.00	6.00	3.50
581 Bob Bailor	.12	.06	.04
582 Brian Doyle	.20	.10	.06
583 Bob Stinson	.12	.06	.04
584 Kurt Bevacqua	.12	.06	.04
585 Al Hrabosky	.20	.10	.06
586 Mitchell Page	.12	.06	.04
587 Garry Templeton	.20	.10	.06
588 Greg Minton	.12	.06	.04
589 Chet Lemon	.20	.10	.06
590 Jim Palmer	5.00	2.50	1.50
591 Rick Cerone	.12	.06	.04
592 Jon Matlack	.20	.10	.06
593 Jesus Alou	.12	.06	.04
594 Dick Tidrow	.12	.06	.04
595 Don Money	.12	.06	.04
596 Rick Matula	.12	.06	.04
597 Tom Poquette	.12	.06	.04
598 Fred Kendall	.12	.06	.04
599 Mike Norris	.12	.06	.04
600 Reggie Jackson	7.00	3.50	2.00
601 Buddy Schultz	.12	.06	.04
602 Brian Downing	.20	.10	.06
603 Jack Billingham	.12	.06	.04
604 Glenn Adams	.12	.06	.04
605 Terry Forster	.20	.10	.06
606 Reds Team (John McNamara)	.50	.25	.15
607 Woodie Fryman	.20	.10	.06
608 Alan Bannister	.12	.06	.04
609 Ron Reed	.20	.10	.06
610 Willie Stargell	1.50	.70	.45
611 Jerry Garvin	.12	.06	.04
612 Cliff Johnson	.20	.10	.06
613 Randy Stein	.12	.06	.04
614 John Hiller	.20	.10	.06
615 Doug DeCinces	.20	.10	.06
616 Gene Richards	.12	.06	.04
617 Joaquin Andujar	.20	.10	.06
618 Bob Montgomery	.12	.06	.04
619 Sergio Ferrer	.12	.06	.04
620 Richie Zisk	.20	.10	.06
621 Bob Grich	.20	.10	.06
622 Mario Soto	.20	.10	.06
623 Gorman Thomas	.20	.10	.06
624 Lerrin LaGrow	.12	.06	.04
625 Chris Chambliss	.25	.13	.08
626 Tigers Team (Sparky Anderson)	.60	.30	.20
627 Pedro Borbon	.12	.06	.04
628 Doug Capilla	.12	.06	.04
629 Jim Todd	.12	.06	.04
630 Larry Bowa	.25	.13	.08
631 Mark Littell	.12	.06	.04
632 Barry Bonnell	.12	.06	.04
633 Bob Apodaca	.12	.06	.04
634 Glenn Borgmann	.12	.06	.04
635 John Candelaria	.20	.10	.06
636 Toby Harrah	.20	.10	.06
637 Joe Simpson	.12	.06	.04
638 *Mark Clear*	.20	.10	.06
639 Larry Biittner	.12	.06	.04
640 Mike Flanagan	.25	.13	.08
641 Ed Kranepool	.20	.10	.06
642 Ken Forsch	.12	.06	.04
643 John Mayberry	.20	.10	.06
644 Charlie Hough	.20	.10	.06
645 Rick Burleson	.20	.10	.06
646 Checklist 606-726	.50	.25	.15
647 Milt May	.12	.06	.04
648 Roy White	.20	.10	.06
649 Tom Griffin	.12	.06	.04
650 Joe Morgan	5.00	2.50	1.50
651 Rollie Fingers	.50	.25	.15
652 Mario Mendoza	.12	.06	.04
653 Stan Bahnsen	.12	.06	.04
654 Bruce Boisclair	.12	.06	.04
655 Tug McGraw	.25	.13	.08

	NR MT	EX	VG
656 Larvell Blanks	.12	.06	.04
657 Dave Edwards	.12	.06	.04
658 Chris Knapp	.12	.06	.04
659 Brewers Team (George Bamberger)	.50	.25	.15
660 Rusty Staub	.30	.15	.09
661 Orioles Future Stars (Mark Corey, Dave Ford, Wayne Krenchicki)	.12	.06	.04
662 Red Sox Future Stars (Joel Finch, Mike O'Berry, Chuck Rainey)	.12	.06	.04
663 Angels Future Stars (Ralph Botting, Bob Clark, *Dickie Thon*)	.30	.15	.09
664 White Sox Future Stars (Mike Colbern, *Guy Hoffman*, Dewey Robinson)	.20	.10	.06
665 Indians Future Stars (Larry Andersen, Bobby Cuellar, Sandy Wihtol)	.12	.06	.04
666 Tigers Future Stars (Mike Chris, Al Greene, Bruce Robbins)	.12	.06	.04
667 Royals Future Stars (Renie Martin, Bill Paschall, *Dan Quisenberry*)	1.00	.50	.30
668 Brewers Future Stars (Danny Boitano, Willie Mueller, Lenn Sakata)	.12	.06	.04
669 Twins Future Stars (Dan Graham, Rick Sofield, *Gary Ward*)	.35	.20	.11
670 Yankees Future Stars (Bobby Brown, Brad Gulden, Darryl Jones)	.20	.10	.06
671 A's Future Stars (Derek Bryant, Brian Kingman, *Mike Morgan*)	.20	.10	.06
672 Mariners Future Stars (Charlie Beamon, Rodney Craig, Rafael Vasquez)	.12	.06	.04
673 Rangers Future Stars (Brian Allard, Jerry Don Gleaton, Greg Mahlberg)	.12	.06	.04
674 Blue Jays Future Stars (Butch Edge, Pat Kelly, Ted Wilborn)	.12	.06	.04
675 Braves Future Stars (Bruce Benedict, Larry Bradford, Eddie Miller)	.12	.06	.04
676 Cubs Future Stars (Dave Geisel, Steve Macko, Karl Pagel)	.12	.06	.04
677 Reds Future Stars (Art DeFreites, *Frank Pastore*, Harry Spilman)	.12	.06	.04
678 Astros Future Stars (Reggie Baldwin, Alan Knicely, *Pete Ladd*)	.12	.06	.04
679 Dodgers Future Stars (Joe Beckwith, *Mickey Hatcher*, Dave Patterson)	.50	.25	.15
680 Expos Future Stars (*Tony Bernazard*, Randy Miller, John Tamargo)	.20	.10	.06
681 Mets Future Stars (Dan Norman, *Jesse Orosco, Mike Scott*)	10.00	5.00	3.00
682 Phillies Future Stars (Ramon Aviles, *Dickie Noles*, Kevin Saucier)	.20	.10	.06
683 Pirates Future Stars (Dorian Boyland, Alberto Lois, Harry Saferight)	.12	.06	.04
684 Cardinals Future Stars (George Frazier, *Tom Herr*, Dan O'Brien)	1.25	.60	.40
685 Padres Future Stars (Tim Flannery, Brian Greer, Jim Wilhelm)	.12	.06	.04
686 Giants Future Stars (Greg Johnston, Dennis Littlejohn, Phil Nastu)	.12	.06	.04
687 Mike Heath	.12	.06	.04
688 Steve Stone	.20	.10	.06
689 Red Sox Team (Don Zimmer)	.60	.30	.20
690 Tommy John	.60	.30	.20
691 Ivan DeJesus	.12	.06	.04
692 Rawly Eastwick	.12	.06	.04
693 Craig Kusick	.12	.06	.04
694 Jim Rooker	.12	.06	.04
695 Reggie Smith	.20	.10	.06
696 Julio Gonzalez	.12	.06	.04
697 David Clyde	.12	.06	.04
698 Oscar Gamble	.20	.10	.06
699 Floyd Bannister	.20	.10	.06
700 Rod Carew	6.00	3.00	1.75
701 *Ken Oberkfell*	.30	.15	.09
702 Ed Farmer	.12	.06	.04
703 Otto Velez	.12	.06	.04
704 Gene Tenace	.20	.10	.06
705 Freddie Patek	.12	.06	.04
706 Tippy Martinez	.12	.06	.04
707 Elliott Maddox	.12	.06	.04
708 Bob Tolan	.12	.06	.04
709 Pat Underwood	.12	.06	.04
710 Graig Nettles	.35	.20	.11
711 Bob Galasso	.12	.06	.04
712 Rodney Scott	.12	.06	.04
713 Terry Whitfield	.12	.06	.04
714 Fred Norman	.12	.06	.04
715 Sal Bando	.20	.10	.06
716 Lynn McGlothen	.12	.06	.04
717 Mickey Klutts	.12	.06	.04
718 Greg Gross	.12	.06	.04
719 Don Robinson	.20	.10	.06

		NR MT	EX	VG
720	Carl Yastrzemski	1.25	.60	.40
721	Paul Hartzell	.12	.06	.04
722	Jose Cruz	.20	.10	.06
723	Shane Rawley	.20	.10	.06
724	Jerry White	.12	.06	.04
725	Rick Wise	.20	.10	.06
726	Steve Yeager	.20	.06	.04

1980 Topps
Superstar 5X7 Photos

DAVEY LOPES
Los Angeles Dodgers
SECOND BASE

In actuality, these cards measure 4-7/8" by 6-7/8". These were another Topps "test" issue that was bought out almost entirely by investors. The 60 cards have a color photo on the front and a blue ink facsimile autograph. Backs have the player's name, team position and card number. The issue was printed on different cardboard stocks, with the first on thick cardboard with a white back and the second on thinner cardboard with a gray back. Prices below are for the more common gray backs; white backs are valued about three times these figures shown. The issue was distributed in selected geographical areas, but they were hoarded quickly. Those who hoarded them still probably have much of their supply as the set has never taken off, despite the presence of many big-name stars.

		NR MT	EX	VG
Complete Set:		9.00	4.50	2.75
Common Player:		.10	.05	.03
1	Willie Stargell	.30	.15	.09
2	Mike Schmidt	.30	.15	.09
3	Johnny Bench	.50	.25	.15
4	Jim Palmer	.35	.20	.11
5	Jim Rice	.40	.20	.12
6	Reggie Jackson	.25	.13	.08
7	Ron Guidry	.20	.10	.06
8	Lee Mazzilli	.10	.05	.03
9	Don Baylor	.15	.08	.05
10	Fred Lynn	.20	.10	.06
11	Ken Singleton	.10	.05	.03
12	Rod Carew	.25	.13	.08
13	Steve Garvey	.25	.13	.08
14	George Brett	.30	.15	.09
15	Tom Seaver	.40	.20	.12
16	Dave Kingman	.15	.08	.05
17	Dave Parker	.10	.05	.03
18	Dave Winfield	.40	.20	.12
19	Pete Rose	1.00	.50	.30
20	Nolan Ryan	1.00	.50	.30
21	Graig Nettles	.15	.08	.05
22	Carl Yastrzemski	.60	.30	.20
23	Tommy John	.25	.13	.08
24	George Foster	.15	.08	.05
25	James Rodney Richard	.10	.05	.03
26	Keith Hernandez	.30	.15	.09
27	Bob Horner	.15	.08	.05
28	Eddie Murray	.40	.20	.12
29	Steve Kemp	.10	.05	.03
30	Gorman Thomas	.10	.05	.03
31	Sixto Lezcano	.10	.05	.03
32	Bruce Sutter	.15	.08	.05
33	Cecil Cooper	.15	.08	.05

		NR MT	EX	VG
34	Larry Bowa	.10	.05	.03
35	Al Oliver	.15	.08	.05
36	Ted Simmons	.15	.08	.05
37	Garry Templeton	.10	.05	.03
38	Jerry Koosman	.10	.05	.03
39	Darrell Porter	.10	.05	.03
40	Roy Smalley	.10	.05	.03
41	Craig Swan	.10	.05	.03
42	Jason Thompson	.10	.05	.03
43	Andre Thornton	.10	.05	.03
44	Rick Manning	.10	.05	.03
45	Kent Tekulve	.10	.05	.03
46	Phil Niekro	.30	.15	.09
47	Buddy Bell	.15	.08	.05
48	Randy Jones	.10	.05	.03
49	Brian Downing	.10	.05	.03
50	Amos Otis	.10	.05	.03
51	Rick Bosetti	.10	.05	.03
52	Gary Carter	.40	.20	.12
53	Larry Parrish	.15	.08	.05
54	Jack Clark	.20	.10	.06
55	Bruce Bochte	.10	.05	.03
56	Cesar Cedeno	.15	.08	.05
57	Chet Lemon	.10	.05	.03
58	Dave Revering	.10	.05	.03
59	Vida Blue	.15	.08	.05
60	Davey Lopes	.15	.08	.05

1981 Topps

 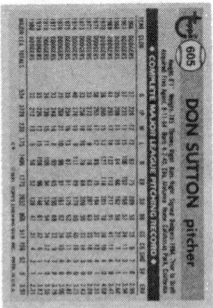

This is another 726-card set of 2-1/2" by 3-1/2" cards from Topps. The cards have the usual color photo with all cards from the same team sharing the same color borders. The player's name appears under the photo with his team and position appearing on a baseball cap at the lower left. The Topps logo returned in a small baseball in the lower right corner. Card backs include the usual stats along with a headline and a cartoon if there was room. Specialty cards include previous season record-breakers, highlights of the playoffs and World Series, along with the final appearance of team cards.

		MT	NR MT	EX
Complete Set:		125.00	87.00	52.00
Common Player:		.08	.06	.03
1	Batting Leaders (George Brett, Bill Buckner)	1.00	.70	.40
2	Home Run Leaders (Reggie Jackson, Ben Oglivie, Mike Schmidt)	.40	.30	.15
3	Runs Batted In Leaders (Cecil Cooper, Mike Schmidt)	.30	.25	.12
4	Stolen Base Leaders (Rickey Henderson, Ron LeFlore)	.25	.20	.10
5	Victory Leaders (Steve Carlton, Steve Stone)	.20	.15	.08
6	Strikeout Leaders (Len Barker, Steve Carlton)	.20	.15	.08
7	Earned Run Avg. Leaders (Rudy May, Don Sutton)	.15	.11	.06
8	Leading Firemen (Rollie Fingers, Tom Hume, Dan Quisenberry)	.10	.08	.04
9	Pete LaCock	.08	.06	.03
10	Mike Flanagan	.12	.09	.05
11	Jim Wohlford	.08	.06	.03
12	Mark Clear	.08	.06	.03

		MT	NR MT	EX
13	*Joe Charboneau*	.15	.11	.06
14	*John Tudor*	1.75	1.25	.70
15	Larry Parrish	.15	.11	.06
16	Ron Davis	.10	.08	.04
17	Cliff Johnson	.08	.06	.03
18	Glenn Adams	.08	.06	.03
19	Jim Clancy	.12	.09	.05
20	Jeff Burroughs	.10	.08	.04
21	Ron Oester	.08	.06	.03
22	Danny Darwin	.08	.06	.03
23	Alex Trevino	.08	.06	.03
24	Don Stanhouse	.08	.06	.03
25	Sixto Lezcano	.08	.06	.03
26	U.L. Washington	.08	.06	.03
27	Champ Summers	.08	.06	.03
28	Enrique Romo	.08	.06	.03
29	Gene Tenace	.10	.08	.04
30	Jack Clark	.50	.40	.20
31	Checklist 1-121	.08	.06	.03
32	Ken Oberkfell	.08	.06	.03
33	Rick Honeycutt	.08	.06	.03
34	Aurelio Rodriguez	.10	.08	.04
35	Mitchell Page	.08	.06	.03
36	Ed Farmer	.08	.06	.03
37	Gary Roenicke	.08	.06	.03
38	Win Remmerswaal	.08	.06	.03
39	Tom Veryzer	.08	.06	.03
40	Tug McGraw	.20	.15	.08
41	Rangers Future Stars (Bob Babcock, John Butcher, Jerry Don Gleaton)	.10	.08	.04
42	Jerry White	.08	.06	.03
43	Jose Morales	.08	.06	.03
44	Larry McWilliams	.08	.06	.03
45	Enos Cabell	.08	.06	.03
46	Rick Bosetti	.08	.06	.03
47	Ken Brett	.10	.08	.04
48	Dave Skaggs	.08	.06	.03
49	Bob Shirley	.08	.06	.03
50	Dave Lopes	.12	.09	.05
51	Bill Robinson	.08	.06	.03
52	Hector Cruz	.08	.06	.03
53	Kevin Saucier	.08	.06	.03
54	Ivan DeJesus	.08	.06	.03
55	Mike Norris	.08	.06	.03
56	Buck Martinez	.08	.06	.03
57	Dave Roberts	.08	.06	.03
58	Joel Youngblood	.08	.06	.03
59	Dan Petry	.12	.09	.05
60	Willie Randolph	.15	.11	.06
61	Butch Wynegar	.08	.06	.03
62	Joe Pettini	.08	.06	.03
63	Steve Renko	.08	.06	.03
64	Brian Asselstine	.08	.06	.03
65	Scott McGregor	.10	.08	.04
66	Royals Future Stars (Manny Castillo, Tim Ireland, Mike Jones)	.08	.06	.03
67	Ken Kravec	.08	.06	.03
68	Matt Alexander	.08	.06	.03
69	Ed Halicki	.08	.06	.03
70	Al Oliver	.15	.11	.06
71	Hal Dues	.08	.06	.03
72	Barry Evans	.08	.06	.03
73	Doug Bair	.08	.06	.03
74	Mike Hargrove	.08	.06	.03
75	Reggie Smith	.15	.11	.06
76	Mario Mendoza	.08	.06	.03
77	Mike Barlow	.08	.06	.03
78	Steve Dillard	.08	.06	.03
79	Bruce Robbins	.08	.06	.03
80	Rusty Staub	.15	.11	.06
81	Dave Stapleton	.08	.06	.03
82	Astros Future Stars (Danny Heep, Alan Knicely, Bobby Sprowl)	.08	.06	.03
83	Mike Proly	.08	.06	.03
84	Johnnie LeMaster	.08	.06	.03
85	Mike Caldwell	.08	.06	.03
86	Wayne Gross	.08	.06	.03
87	Rick Camp	.08	.06	.03
88	Joe Lefebvre	.08	.06	.03
89	Darrell Jackson	.08	.06	.03
90	Bake McBride	.08	.06	.03
91	Tim Stoddard	.08	.06	.03
92	Mike Easler	.10	.08	.04
93	Ed Glynn	.08	.06	.03
94	Harry Spilman	.08	.06	.03
95	Jim Sundberg	.10	.08	.04
96	A's Future Stars (Dave Beard, *Ernie Camacho*, Pat Dempsey)	.12	.09	.05
97	Chris Speier	.08	.06	.03
98	Clint Hurdle	.08	.06	.03
99	Eric Wilkins	.08	.06	.03

		MT	NR MT	EX
100	Rod Carew	3.00	2.25	1.25
101	Benny Ayala	.08	.06	.03
102	Dave Tobik	.08	.06	.03
103	Jerry Martin	.08	.06	.03
104	Terry Forster	.10	.08	.04
105	Jose Cruz	.15	.11	.06
106	Don Money	.08	.06	.03
107	Rich Wortham	.08	.06	.03
108	Bruce Benedict	.08	.06	.03
109	Mike Scott	1.00	.70	.40
110	Carl Yastrzemski	2.00	1.50	.80
111	Greg Minton	.08	.06	.03
112	White Sox Future Stars (Rusty Kuntz, Fran Mullins, Leo Sutherland)	.08	.06	.03
113	Mike Phillips	.08	.06	.03
114	Tom Underwood	.08	.06	.03
115	Roy Smalley	.08	.06	.03
116	Joe Simpson	.08	.06	.03
117	Pete Falcone	.08	.06	.03
118	Kurt Bevacqua	.08	.06	.03
119	Tippy Martinez	.08	.06	.03
120	Larry Bowa	.20	.15	.08
121	Larry Harlow	.08	.06	.03
122	John Denny	.08	.06	.03
123	Al Cowens	.08	.06	.03
124	Jerry Garvin	.08	.06	.03
125	Andre Dawson	1.75	1.25	.70
126	*Charlie Leibrandt*	.50	.40	.20
127	Rudy Law	.08	.06	.03
128	Gary Allenson	.08	.06	.03
129	Art Howe	.08	.06	.03
130	Larry Gura	.08	.06	.03
131	*Keith Moreland*	.45	.35	.20
132	Tommy Boggs	.08	.06	.03
133	Jeff Cox	.08	.06	.03
134	Steve Mura	.08	.06	.03
135	Gorman Thomas	.12	.09	.05
136	Doug Capilla	.08	.06	.03
137	Hosken Powell	.08	.06	.03
138	*Rich Dotson*	.30	.25	.12
139	Oscar Gamble	.10	.08	.04
140	Bob Forsch	.10	.08	.04
141	Miguel Dilone	.08	.06	.03
142	Jackson Todd	.08	.06	.03
143	Dan Meyer	.08	.06	.03
144	Allen Ripley	.08	.06	.03
145	Mickey Rivers	.10	.08	.04
146	Bobby Castillo	.08	.06	.03
147	Dale Berra	.08	.06	.03
148	Randy Niemann	.08	.06	.03
149	Joe Nolan	.08	.06	.03
150	Mark Fidrych	.12	.09	.05
151	Claudell Washington	.12	.09	.05
152	John Urrea	.08	.06	.03
153	Tom Poquette	.08	.06	.03
154	Rick Langford	.08	.06	.03
155	Chris Chambliss	.12	.09	.05
156	Bob McClure	.08	.06	.03
157	John Wathan	.12	.09	.05
158	Fergie Jenkins	.30	.25	.12
159	Brian Doyle	.08	.06	.03
160	Garry Maddox	.12	.09	.05
161	Dan Graham	.08	.06	.03
162	Doug Corbett	.08	.06	.03
163	Billy Almon	.08	.06	.03
164	*Lamarr Hoyt (LaMarr)*	.20	.15	.08
165	Tony Scott	.08	.06	.03
166	Floyd Bannister	.12	.09	.05
167	Terry Whitfield	.08	.06	.03
168	Don Robinson	.08	.06	.03
169	John Mayberry	.10	.08	.04
170	Ross Grimsley	.08	.06	.03
171	Gene Richards	.08	.06	.03
172	Gary Woods	.08	.06	.03
173	Bump Wills	.08	.06	.03
174	Doug Rau	.08	.06	.03
175	Dave Collins	.10	.08	.04
176	Mike Krukow	.10	.08	.04
177	Rick Peters	.08	.06	.03
178	Jim Essian	.08	.06	.03
179	Rudy May	.08	.06	.03
180	Pete Rose	3.25	2.50	1.25
181	Elias Sosa	.08	.06	.03
182	Bob Grich	.15	.11	.06
183	Dick Davis	.08	.06	.03
184	Jim Dwyer	.08	.06	.03
185	Dennis Leonard	.10	.08	.04
186	Wayne Nordhagen	.08	.06	.03
187	Mike Parrott	.08	.06	.03
188	Doug DeCinces	.15	.11	.06
189	Craig Swan	.08	.06	.03

		MT	NR MT	EX
190	Cesar Cedeno	.15	.11	.06
191	Rick Sutcliffe	.40	.30	.15
192	Braves Future Stars (Terry Harper, Ed Miller, Rafael Ramirez)	.25	.20	.10
193	Pete Vuckovich	.10	.08	.04
194	Rod Scurry	.10	.08	.04
195	Rich Murray	.08	.06	.03
196	Duffy Dyer	.08	.06	.03
197	Jim Kern	.08	.06	.03
198	Jerry Dybzinski	.08	.06	.03
199	Chuck Rainey	.08	.06	.03
200	George Foster	.25	.20	.10
201	Record Breaker (Johnny Bench)	.40	.30	.15
202	Record Breaker (Steve Carlton)	.40	.30	.15
203	Record Breaker (Bill Gullickson)	.08	.06	.03
204	Record Breaker (Ron LeFlore, Rodney Scott)	.10	.08	.04
205	Record Breaker (Pete Rose)	.80	.60	.30
206	Record Breaker (Mike Schmidt)	.50	.40	.20
207	Record Breaker (Ozzie Smith)	.20	.15	.08
208	Record Breaker (Willie Wilson)	.20	.15	.08
209	Dickie Thon	.10	.08	.04
210	Jim Palmer	2.00	1.50	.80
211	Derrel Thomas	.08	.06	.03
212	Steve Nicosia	.08	.06	.03
213	Al Holland	.10	.08	.04
214	Angels Future Stars (Ralph Botting, Jim Dorsey, John Harris)	.08	.06	.03
215	Larry Hisle	.10	.08	.04
216	John Henry Johnson	.08	.06	.03
217	Rich Hebner	.08	.06	.03
218	Paul Splittorff	.08	.06	.03
219	Ken Landreaux	.08	.06	.03
220	Tom Seaver	3.00	2.25	1.25
221	Bob Davis	.08	.06	.03
222	Jorge Orta	.08	.06	.03
223	Roy Lee Jackson	.08	.06	.03
224	Pat Zachry	.08	.06	.03
225	Ruppert Jones	.08	.06	.03
226	Manny Sanguillen	.08	.06	.03
227	Fred Martinez	.08	.06	.03
228	Tom Paciorek	.08	.06	.03
229	Rollie Fingers	1.50	1.25	.60
230	George Hendrick	.10	.08	.04
231	Joe Beckwith	.08	.06	.03
232	Mickey Klutts	.08	.06	.03
233	Skip Lockwood	.08	.06	.03
234	Lou Whitaker	.60	.45	.25
235	Scott Sanderson	.08	.06	.03
236	Mike Ivie	.08	.06	.03
237	Charlie Moore	.08	.06	.03
238	Willie Hernandez	.12	.09	.05
239	Rick Miller	.08	.06	.03
240	Nolan Ryan	6.00	4.50	2.50
241	Checklist 122-242	.08	.06	.03
242	Chet Lemon	.10	.08	.04
243	Sal Butera	.08	.06	.03
244	Cardinals Future Stars (Tito Landrum, Al Olmsted, Andy Rincon)	.15	.11	.06
245	Ed Figueroa	.08	.06	.03
246	Ed Ott	.08	.06	.03
247	Glenn Hubbard	.10	.08	.04
248	Joey McLaughlin	.08	.06	.03
249	Larry Cox	.08	.06	.03
250	Ron Guidry	.50	.40	.20
251	Tom Brookens	.10	.08	.04
252	Victor Cruz	.08	.06	.03
253	Dave Bergman	.08	.06	.03
254	Ozzie Smith	3.00	2.25	1.25
255	Mark Littell	.08	.06	.03
256	Bombo Rivera	.08	.06	.03
257	Rennie Stennett	.08	.06	.03
258	Joe Price	.12	.09	.05
259	Mets Future Stars (Juan Berenguer, Hubie Brooks, Mookie Wilson)	2.50	2.00	1.00
260	Ron Cey	.15	.11	.06
261	Rickey Henderson	35.00	27.00	15.00
262	Sammy Stewart	.08	.06	.03
263	Brian Downing	.12	.09	.05
264	Jim Norris	.08	.06	.03
265	John Candelaria	.12	.09	.05
266	Tom Herr	.15	.11	.06
267	Stan Bahnsen	.08	.06	.03
268	Jerry Royster	.08	.06	.03
269	Ken Forsch	.08	.06	.03
270	Greg Luzinski	.20	.15	.08
271	Bill Castro	.08	.06	.03
272	Bruce Kimm	.08	.06	.03
273	Stan Papi	.08	.06	.03
274	Craig Chamberlain	.08	.06	.03
275	Dwight Evans	.25	.20	.10
276	Dan Spillner	.08	.06	.03
277	Alfredo Griffin	.12	.09	.05
278	Rick Sofield	.08	.06	.03
279	Bob Knepper	.12	.09	.05
280	Ken Griffey	.15	.11	.06
281	Fred Stanley	.08	.06	.03
282	Mariners Future Stars (Rick Anderson, Greg Biercevicz, Rodney Craig)	.08	.06	.03
283	Billy Sample	.08	.06	.03
284	Brian Kingman	.08	.06	.03
285	Jerry Turner	.08	.06	.03
286	Dave Frost	.08	.06	.03
287	Lenn Sakata	.08	.06	.03
288	Bob Clark	.08	.06	.03
289	Mickey Hatcher	.10	.08	.04
290	Bob Boone	.08	.06	.03
291	Aurelio Lopez	.08	.06	.03
292	Mike Squires	.08	.06	.03
293	Charlie Lea	.15	.11	.06
294	Mike Tyson	.08	.06	.03
295	Hal McRae	.15	.11	.06
296	Bill Nahorodny	.08	.06	.03
297	Bob Bailor	.08	.06	.03
298	Buddy Solomon	.08	.06	.03
299	Elliott Maddox	.08	.06	.03
300	Paul Molitor	.40	.30	.15
301	Matt Keough	.08	.06	.03
302	Dodgers Future Stars (Jack Perconte, Mike Scioscia, Fernando Valenzuela)	7.00	5.25	2.75
303	Johnny Oates	.08	.06	.03
304	John Castino	.08	.06	.03
305	Ken Clay	.08	.06	.03
306	Juan Beniquez	.08	.06	.03
307	Gene Garber	.08	.06	.03
308	Rick Manning	.08	.06	.03
309	Luis Salazar	.20	.15	.08
310	Vida Blue	.08	.06	.03
311	Freddie Patek	.08	.06	.03
312	Rick Rhoden	.12	.09	.05
313	Luis Pujols	.08	.06	.03
314	Rich Dauer	.08	.06	.03
315	Kirk Gibson	6.00	4.50	2.50
316	Craig Minetto	.08	.06	.03
317	Lonnie Smith	.10	.08	.04
318	Steve Yeager	.08	.06	.03
319	Rowland Office	.08	.06	.03
320	Tom Burgmeier	.08	.06	.03
321	Leon Durham	.25	.20	.10
322	Neil Allen	.10	.08	.04
323	Jim Morrison	.08	.06	.03
324	Mike Willis	.08	.06	.03
325	Ray Knight	.12	.09	.05
326	Biff Pocoroba	.08	.06	.03
327	Moose Haas	.08	.06	.03
328	Twins Future Stars (Dave Engle, Greg Johnston, Gary Ward)	.12	.09	.05
329	Joaquin Andujar	.12	.09	.05
330	Frank White	.12	.09	.05
331	Dennis Lamp	.08	.06	.03
332	Lee Lacy	.08	.06	.03
333	Sid Monge	.08	.06	.03
334	Dane Iorg	.08	.06	.03
335	Rick Cerone	.08	.06	.03
336	Eddie Whitson	.08	.06	.03
337	Lynn Jones	.08	.06	.03
338	Checklist 243-363	.25	.20	.10
339	John Ellis	.08	.06	.03
340	Bruce Kison	.08	.06	.03
341	Dwayne Murphy	.10	.08	.04
342	Eric Rasmussen	.08	.06	.03
343	Frank Taveras	.08	.06	.03
344	Byron McLaughlin	.08	.06	.03
345	Warren Cromartie	.08	.06	.03
346	Larry Christenson	.08	.06	.03
347	Harold Baines	4.00	3.00	1.50
348	Bob Sykes	.08	.06	.03
349	Glenn Hoffman	.08	.06	.03
350	J.R. Richard	.12	.09	.05
351	Otto Velez	.08	.06	.03
352	Dick Tidrow	.08	.06	.03
353	Terry Kennedy	.12	.09	.05
354	Mario Soto	.10	.08	.04
355	Bob Horner	.25	.20	.10
356	Padres Future Stars (George Stablein, Craig Stimac, Tom Tellmann)	.08	.06	.03
357	Jim Slaton	.08	.06	.03
358	Mark Wagner	.08	.06	.03
359	Tom Hausman	.08	.06	.03
360	Willie Wilson	.30	.25	.12
361	Joe Strain	.08	.06	.03

	MT	NR MT	EX
362 Bo Diaz	.10	.08	.04
363 Geoff Zahn	.08	.06	.03
364 *Mike Davis*	.35	.25	.14
365 Graig Nettles	.12	.09	.05
366 Mike Ramsey	.08	.06	.03
367 Denny Martinez	.10	.08	.04
368 Leon Roberts	.08	.06	.03
369 Frank Tanana	.12	.09	.05
370 Dave Winfield	1.00	.70	.40
371 Charlie Hough	.15	.11	.06
372 Jay Johnstone	.10	.08	.04
373 Pat Underwood	.08	.06	.03
374 Tom Hutton	.08	.06	.03
375 Dave Concepcion	.20	.15	.08
376 Ron Reed	.08	.06	.03
377 Jerry Morales	.08	.06	.03
378 Dave Rader	.08	.06	.03
379 Lary Sorensen	.08	.06	.03
380 Willie Stargell	1.00	.70	.40
381 Cubs Future Stars (Carlos Lezcano, Steve Macko, Randy Martz)	.08	.06	.03
382 *Paul Mirabella*(FC)	.12	.09	.05
383 Eric Soderholm	.08	.06	.03
384 Mike Sadek	.08	.06	.03
385 Joe Sambito	.08	.06	.03
386 Dave Edwards	.08	.06	.03
387 Phil Niekro	1.50	1.25	.60
388 Andre Thornton	.12	.09	.05
389 Marty Pattin	.08	.06	.03
390 Cesar Geronimo	.08	.06	.03
391 Dave Lemanczyk	.08	.06	.03
392 Lance Parrish	.70	.50	.30
393 Broderick Perkins	.08	.06	.03
394 Woodie Fryman	.10	.08	.04
395 Scot Thompson	.08	.06	.03
396 Bill Campbell	.08	.06	.03
397 Julio Cruz	.08	.06	.03
398 Ross Baumgarten	.08	.06	.03
399 Orioles Future Stars (*Mike Boddicker,* Mark Corey, *Floyd Rayford*)	2.00	1.50	.80
400 Reggie Jackson	2.00	1.50	.80
401 A.L. Championships (Royals Sweep Yankees)	.50	.40	.20
402 N.L. Championships (Phillies Squeak Past Astros)	.40	.30	.15
403 World Series (Phillies Beat Royals In 6)	.25	.20	.10
404 World Series Summary (Phillies Win First World Series)	.25	.20	.10
405 Nino Espinosa	.08	.06	.03
406 Dickie Noles	.08	.06	.03
407 Ernie Whitt	.10	.08	.04
408 Fernando Arroyo	.08	.06	.03
409 Larry Herndon	.10	.08	.04
410 Bert Campaneris	.12	.09	.05
411 Terry Puhl	.08	.06	.03
412 *Britt Burns*	.12	.09	.05
413 Tony Bernazard	.08	.06	.03
414 John Pacella	.08	.06	.03
415 Ben Oglivie	.10	.08	.04
416 Gary Alexander	.08	.06	.03
417 Dan Schatzeder	.08	.06	.03
418 Bobby Brown	.08	.06	.03
419 Tom Hume	.08	.06	.03
420 Keith Hernandez	.80	.60	.30
421 Bob Stanley	.08	.06	.03
422 Dan Ford	.08	.06	.03
423 Shane Rawley	.15	.11	.06
424 Yankees Future Stars (Tim Lollar, Bruce Robinson, Dennis Werth)	.08	.06	.03
425 Al Bumbry	.10	.08	.04
426 Warren Brusstar	.08	.06	.03
427 John D'Acquisto	.08	.06	.03
428 John Stearns	.08	.06	.03
429 Mick Kelleher	.08	.06	.03
430 Jim Bibby	.08	.06	.03
431 Dave Roberts	.08	.06	.03
432 Len Barker	.10	.08	.04
433 Rance Mulliniks	.08	.06	.03
434 Roger Erickson	.08	.06	.03
435 Jim Spencer	.08	.06	.03
436 Gary Lucas	.08	.06	.03
437 Mike Heath	.08	.06	.03
438 John Montefusco	.10	.08	.04
439 Denny Walling	.08	.06	.03
440 Jerry Reuss	.12	.09	.05
441 Ken Reitz	.08	.06	.03
442 Ron Pruitt	.08	.06	.03
443 Jim Beattie	.08	.06	.03
444 Garth Iorg	.08	.06	.03
445 Ellis Valentine	.08	.06	.03

	MT	NR MT	EX
446 Checklist 364-484	.25	.20	.10
447 Junior Kennedy	.08	.06	.03
448 Tim Corcoran	.08	.06	.03
449 Paul Mitchell	.08	.06	.03
450 Dave Kingman	.10	.08	.04
451 Indians Future Stars (Chris Bando, Tom Brennan, Sandy Wihtol)	.12	.09	.05
452 Renie Martin	.08	.06	.03
453 Rob Wilfong	.08	.06	.03
454 Andy Hassler	.08	.06	.03
455 Rick Burleson	.10	.08	.04
456 *Jeff Reardon*	1.25	.90	.50
457 Mike Lum	.08	.06	.03
458 Randy Jones	.10	.08	.04
459 Greg Gross	.08	.06	.03
460 Rich Gossage	.40	.30	.15
461 Dave McKay	.08	.06	.03
462 Jack Brohamer	.08	.06	.03
463 Milt May	.08	.06	.03
464 Adrian Devine	.08	.06	.03
465 Bill Russell	.12	.09	.05
466 Bob Molinaro	.08	.06	.03
467 Dave Stieb	.80	.60	.30
468 Johnny Wockenfuss	.08	.06	.03
469 Jeff Leonard	.20	.15	.08
470 Manny Trillo	.10	.08	.04
471 Mike Vail	.08	.06	.03
472 Dyar Miller	.08	.06	.03
473 Jose Cardenal	.08	.06	.03
474 Mike LaCoss	.08	.06	.03
475 Buddy Bell	.15	.11	.06
476 Jerry Koosman	.15	.11	.06
477 Luis Gomez	.08	.06	.03
478 Juan Eichelberger	.08	.06	.03
479 Expos Future Stars (Bobby Pate, *Tim Raines*, Roberto Ramos)	9.00	6.75	3.50
480 Carlton Fisk	.80	.60	.30
481 Bob Lacey	.08	.06	.03
482 Jim Gantner	.10	.08	.04
483 Mike Griffin	.08	.06	.03
484 Max Venable	.08	.06	.03
485 Garry Templeton	.12	.09	.05
486 Marc Hill	.08	.06	.03
487 Dewey Robinson	.08	.06	.03
488 *Damaso Garcia*	.12	.09	.05
489 John Littlefield (photo actually Mark Riggins)	.08	.06	.03
490 Eddie Murray	3.00	2.25	1.25
491 Gordy Pladson	.08	.06	.03
492 Barry Foote	.08	.06	.03
493 Dan Quisenberry	.20	.15	.08
494 *Bob Walk*	.50	.40	.20
495 Dusty Baker	.12	.09	.05
496 Paul Dade	.08	.06	.03
497 Fred Norman	.08	.06	.03
498 Pat Putnam	.08	.06	.03
499 Frank Pastore	.08	.06	.03
500 Jim Rice	1.00	.70	.40
501 Tim Foli	.08	.06	.03
502 Giants Future Stars (Chris Bourjos, Al Hargesheimer, Mike Rowland)	.08	.06	.03
503 Steve McCatty	.08	.06	.03
504 Dale Murphy	2.50	2.00	1.00
505 Jason Thompson	.08	.06	.03
506 Phil Huffman	.08	.06	.03
507 Jamie Quirk	.08	.06	.03
508 Rob Dressler	.08	.06	.03
509 Pete Mackanin	.08	.06	.03
510 Lee Mazzilli	.10	.08	.04
511 Wayne Garland	.08	.06	.03
512 Gary Thomasson	.08	.06	.03
513 Frank LaCorte	.08	.06	.03
514 George Riley	.08	.06	.03
515 Robin Yount	4.00	3.00	1.50
516 Doug Bird	.08	.06	.03
517 Richie Zisk	.10	.08	.04
518 Grant Jackson	.08	.06	.03
519 John Tamargo	.08	.06	.03
520 Steve Stone	.12	.09	.05
521 Sam Mejias	.08	.06	.03
522 Mike Colbern	.08	.06	.03
523 John Fulgham	.08	.06	.03
524 Willie Aikens	.08	.06	.03
525 Mike Torrez	.10	.08	.04
526 Phillies Future Stars (Marty Bystrom, Jay Loviglio, Jim Wright)	.08	.06	.03
527 Danny Goodwin	.08	.06	.03
528 Gary Matthews	.12	.09	.05
529 Dave LaRoche	.08	.06	.03
530 Steve Garvey	1.25	.90	.50
531 John Curtis	.08	.06	.03

		MT	NR MT	EX
532	Bill Stein	.08	.06	.03
533	Jesus Figueroa	.08	.06	.03
534	*Dave Smith*	.40	.30	.15
535	Omar Moreno	.08	.06	.03
536	Bob Owchinko	.08	.06	.03
537	Ron Hodges	.08	.06	.03
538	Tom Griffin	.08	.06	.03
539	Rodney Scott	.08	.06	.03
540	Mike Schmidt	5.00	3.75	2.00
541	Steve Swisher	.08	.06	.03
542	Larry Bradford	.08	.06	.03
543	Terry Crowley	.08	.06	.03
544	Rich Gale	.08	.06	.03
545	Johnny Grubb	.08	.06	.03
546	Paul Moskau	.08	.06	.03
547	Mario Guerrero	.08	.06	.03
548	Dave Goltz	.10	.08	.04
549	Jerry Remy	.08	.06	.03
550	Tommy John	.50	.40	.20
551	Pirates Future Stars *(Vance Law, Tony Pena, Pascual Perez)*	2.50	2.00	1.00
552	Steve Trout	.08	.06	.03
553	Tim Blackwell	.08	.06	.03
554	Bert Blyleven	.25	.20	.10
555	Cecil Cooper	.20	.15	.08
556	Jerry Mumphrey	.08	.06	.03
557	Chris Knapp	.08	.06	.03
558	Barry Bonnell	.08	.06	.03
559	Willie Montanez	.08	.06	.03
560	Joe Morgan	.70	.50	.30
561	Dennis Littlejohn	.08	.06	.03
562	Checklist 485-605	.25	.20	.10
563	Jim Kaat	.30	.25	.12
564	Ron Hassey	.08	.06	.03
565	Burt Hooton	.10	.08	.04
566	Del Unser	.08	.06	.03
567	Mark Bomback	.08	.06	.03
568	Dave Revering	.08	.06	.03
569	Al Williams	.08	.06	.03
570	Ken Singleton	.12	.09	.05
571	Todd Cruz	.08	.06	.03
572	Jack Morris	.60	.45	.25
573	Phil Garner	.10	.08	.04
574	Bill Caudill	.08	.06	.03
575	Tony Perez	.35	.25	.14
576	Reggie Cleveland	.08	.06	.03
577	Blue Jays Future Stars *(Luis Leal, Brian Milner, Ken Schrom)*	.20	.15	.08
578	*Bill Gullickson*	.20	.15	.08
579	Tim Flannery	.08	.06	.03
580	Don Baylor	.15	.11	.06
581	Roy Howell	.08	.06	.03
582	Gaylord Perry	.70	.50	.30
583	Larry Milbourne	.08	.06	.03
584	Randy Lerch	.08	.06	.03
585	Amos Otis	.10	.08	.04
586	Silvio Martinez	.08	.06	.03
587	Jeff Newman	.08	.06	.03
588	Gary Lavelle	.08	.06	.03
589	Lamar Johnson	.08	.06	.03
590	Bruce Sutter	.25	.20	.10
591	John Lowenstein	.08	.06	.03
592	Steve Comer	.08	.06	.03
593	Steve Kemp	.12	.09	.05
594	Preston Hanna	.08	.06	.03
595	Butch Hobson	.08	.06	.03
596	Jerry Augustine	.08	.06	.03
597	Rafael Landestoy	.08	.06	.03
598	George Vukovich	.08	.06	.03
599	Dennis Kinney	.08	.06	.03
600	Johnny Bench	1.50	1.25	.60
601	Don Aase	.08	.06	.03
602	Bobby Murcer	.15	.11	.06
603	John Verhoeven	.08	.06	.03
604	Rob Picciolo	.08	.06	.03
605	Don Sutton	.70	.50	.30
606	Reds Future Stars *(Bruce Berenyi, Geoff Combe, Paul Householder)*	.08	.06	.03
607	Dave Palmer	.08	.06	.03
608	Greg Pryor	.08	.06	.03
609	Lynn McGlothen	.08	.06	.03
610	Darrell Porter	.10	.08	.04
611	Rick Matula	.08	.06	.03
612	Duane Kuiper	.08	.06	.03
613	Jim Anderson	.08	.06	.03
614	Dave Rozema	.08	.06	.03
615	Rick Dempsey	.12	.09	.05
616	Rick Wise	.10	.08	.04
617	Craig Reynolds	.08	.06	.03
618	John Milner	.08	.06	.03
619	Steve Henderson	.08	.06	.03

		MT	NR MT	EX
620	Dennis Eckersley	.80	.60	.30
621	Tom Donohue	.08	.06	.03
622	Randy Moffitt	.08	.06	.03
623	Sal Bando	.12	.09	.05
624	Bob Welch	.70	.50	.30
625	Bill Buckner	.15	.11	.06
626	Tigers Future Stars (Dave Steffen, Jerry Ujdur, Roger Weaver)	.08	.06	.03
627	Luis Tiant	.20	.15	.08
628	Vic Correll	.08	.06	.03
629	Tony Armas	.12	.09	.05
630	Steve Carlton	1.25	.90	.50
631	Ron Jackson	.08	.06	.03
632	Alan Bannister	.08	.06	.03
633	Bill Lee	.10	.08	.04
634	Doug Flynn	.08	.06	.03
635	Bobby Bonds	.15	.11	.06
636	Al Hrabosky	.10	.08	.04
637	Jerry Narron	.08	.06	.03
638	Checklist 606	.25	.20	.10
639	Carney Lansford	.15	.11	.06
640	Dave Parker	.60	.45	.25
641	Mark Belanger	.10	.08	.04
642	Vern Ruhle	.08	.06	.03
643	*Lloyd Moseby*	1.25	.90	.50
644	Ramon Aviles	.08	.06	.03
645	Rick Reuschel	.15	.11	.06
646	Marvis Foley	.08	.06	.03
647	Dick Drago	.08	.06	.03
648	Darrell Evans	.25	.20	.10
649	Manny Sarmiento	.08	.06	.03
650	Bucky Dent	.12	.09	.05
651	Pedro Guerrero	1.25	.90	.50
652	John Montague	.08	.06	.03
653	Bill Fahey	.08	.06	.03
654	Ray Burris	.08	.06	.03
655	Dan Driessen	.12	.09	.05
656	Jon Matlack	.10	.08	.04
657	Mike Cubbage	.08	.06	.03
658	Milt Wilcox	.08	.06	.03
659	Brewers Future Stars (John Flinn, Ed Romero, Ned Yost)	.08	.06	.03
660	Gary Carter	1.00	.70	.40
661	Orioles Team (Earl Weaver)	.30	.25	.12
662	Red Sox Team (Ralph Houk)	.30	.25	.12
663	Angels Team (Jim Fregosi)	.25	.20	.10
664	White Sox Team (Tony LaRussa)	.25	.20	.10
665	Indians Team (Dave Garcia)	.25	.20	.10
666	Tigers Team (Sparky Anderson)	.30	.25	.12
667	Royals Team (Jim Frey)	.25	.20	.10
668	Brewers Team (Bob Rodgers)	.25	.20	.10
669	Twins Team (John Goryl)	.25	.20	.10
670	Yankees Team (Gene Michael)	.35	.25	.14
671	A's Team (Billy Martin)	.30	.25	.12
672	Mariners Team (Maury Wills)	.25	.20	.10
673	Rangers Team (Don Zimmer)	.25	.20	.10
674	Blue Jays Team (Bobby Mattick)	.25	.20	.10
675	Braves Team (Bobby Cox)	.25	.20	.10
676	Cubs Team (Joe Amalfitano)	.25	.20	.10
677	Reds Team (John McNamara)	.25	.20	.10
678	Astros Team (Bill Virdon)	.25	.20	.10
679	Dodgers Team (Tom Lasorda)	.35	.25	.14
680	Expos Team (Dick Williams)	.25	.20	.10
681	Mets Team (Joe Torre)	.30	.25	.12
682	Phillies Team (Dallas Green)	.25	.20	.10
683	Pirates Team (Chuck Tanner)	.25	.20	.10
684	Cardinals Team (Whitey Herzog)	.30	.25	.12
685	Padres Team (Frank Howard)	.25	.20	.10
686	Giants Team (Dave Bristol)	.25	.20	.10
687	Jeff Jones	.08	.06	.03
688	Kiko Garcia	.08	.06	.03
689	Red Sox Future Stars *(Bruce Hurst,* Keith MacWhorter, *Reid Nichols)*	2.50	2.00	1.00
690	Bob Watson	.10	.08	.04
691	Dick Ruthven	.08	.06	.03
692	Lenny Randle	.08	.06	.03
693	*Steve Howe*	.20	.15	.08
694	Bud Harrelson	.08	.06	.03
695	Kent Tekulve	.10	.08	.04
696	Alan Ashby	.08	.06	.03
697	Rick Waits	.08	.06	.03
698	Mike Jorgensen	.08	.06	.03
699	Glenn Abbott	.08	.06	.03
700	George Brett	4.00	3.00	1.50
701	Joe Rudi	.12	.09	.05
702	George Medich	.08	.06	.03
703	Alvis Woods	.08	.06	.03
704	Bill Travers	.08	.06	.03
705	Ted Simmons	.25	.20	.10
706	Dave Ford	.08	.06	.03
707	Dave Cash	.08	.06	.03

		MT	NR MT	EX
708	Doyle Alexander	.12	.09	.05
709	Alan Trammell	.30	.25	.12
710	Ron LeFlore	.08	.06	.03
711	Joe Ferguson	.08	.06	.03
712	Bill Bonham	.08	.06	.03
713	Bill North	.08	.06	.03
714	Pete Redfern	.08	.06	.03
715	Bill Madlock	.25	.20	.10
716	Glenn Borgmann	.08	.06	.03
717	Jim Barr	.08	.06	.03
718	Larry Biittner	.08	.06	.03
719	Sparky Lyle	.12	.09	.05
720	Fred Lynn	.35	.25	.14
721	Toby Harrah	.10	.08	.04
722	Joe Niekro	.20	.15	.08
723	Bruce Bochte	.08	.06	.03
724	Lou Piniella	.20	.15	.08
725	Steve Rogers	.10	.08	.04
726	Rick Monday	.15	.11	.06

1981 Topps
Home Team 5 X 7 Photos

Once again testing the popularity of large cards, Topps issued 4-7/8" by 6-7/8" cards in two different sets. The Home Team cards feature a large color photo, facsimile autograph and white border on the front. Backs have the player's name, team, position and a checklist at the bottom. The 102 cards were sold in limited areas corresponding to the teams' geographic home. It was also possible to order the whole set by mail. Eleven teams are involved in the issue, with the number of players from each team ranging from 6 to 12. Although it is an attractive set featuring many stars, ready availability and many collectors' aversion to large cards keep prices relatively low today.

		MT	NR MT	EX
Complete Set:		40.00	30.00	16.00
Common Player:		.20	.15	.08
(1)	Dusty Baker	.25	.20	.10
(2)	Don Baylor	.40	.30	.15
(3)	Rick Burleson	.20	.15	.08
(4)	Rod Carew	.90	.70	.35
(5)	Ron Cey	.30	.25	.12
(6)	Steve Garvey	.90	.70	.35
(7)	Bobby Grich	.30	.25	.12
(8)	Butch Hobson	.20	.15	.08
(9)	Burt Hooton	.20	.15	.08
(10)	Steve Howe	.20	.15	.08
(11)	Dave Lopes	.25	.20	.10
(12)	Fred Lynn	.50	.40	.20
(13)	Rick Monday	.25	.20	.10
(14)	Jerry Reuss	.25	.20	.10
(15)	Bill Russell	.25	.20	.10
(16)	Reggie Smith	.30	.25	.12
(17)	Bob Welch	.40	.30	.15
(18)	Steve Yeager	.20	.15	.08
(19)	Buddy Bell	.30	.25	.12
(20)	Cesar Cedeno	.30	.25	.12
(21)	Jose Cruz	.30	.25	.12
(22)	Art Howe	.20	.15	.08
(23)	Jon Matlack	.20	.15	.08
(24)	Al Oliver	.40	.30	.15

		MT	NR MT	EX
(25)	Terry Puhl	.20	.15	.08
(26)	Mickey Rivers	.25	.20	.10
(27)	Nolan Ryan	.70	.50	.30
(28)	Jim Sundberg	.25	.20	.10
(29)	Don Sutton	.60	.45	.25
(30)	Bump Wills	.20	.15	.08
(31)	Tim Blackwell	.20	.15	.08
(32)	Bill Buckner	.40	.30	.15
(33)	Britt Burns	.20	.15	.08
(34)	Ivan DeJesus	.20	.15	.08
(35)	Rich Dotson	.25	.20	.10
(36)	Leon Durham	.25	.20	.10
(37)	Ed Farmer	.20	.15	.08
(38)	Lamar Johnson	.20	.15	.08
(39)	Dave Kingman	.40	.30	.15
(40)	Mike Krukow	.25	.20	.10
(41)	Ron LeFlore	.25	.20	.10
(42)	Chet Lemon	.25	.20	.10
(43)	Bob Molinaro	.20	.15	.08
(44)	Jim Morrison	.20	.15	.08
(45)	Wayne Nordhagen	.20	.15	.08
(46)	Ken Reitz	.20	.15	.08
(47)	Rick Reuschel	.30	.25	.12
(48)	Mike Tyson	.20	.15	.08
(49)	Neil Allen	.20	.15	.08
(50)	Rick Cerone	.20	.15	.08
(51)	Bucky Dent	.25	.20	.10
(52)	Doug Flynn	.20	.15	.08
(53)	Rich Gossage	.60	.45	.25
(54)	Ron Guidry	.60	.45	.25
(55)	Reggie Jackson	.90	.70	.35
(56)	Tommy John	.50	.40	.20
(57)	Ruppert Jones	.20	.15	.08
(58)	Rudy May	.20	.15	.08
(59)	Lee Mazzilli	.25	.20	.10
(60)	Graig Nettles	.40	.30	.15
(61)	Willie Randolph	.30	.25	.12
(62)	Rusty Staub	.40	.30	.15
(63)	Frank Taveras	.20	.15	.08
(64)	Alex Trevino	.20	.15	.08
(65)	Bob Watson	.25	.20	.10
(66)	Dave Winfield	.90	.70	.35
(67)	Bob Boone	.25	.20	.10
(68)	Larry Bowa	.40	.30	.15
(69)	Steve Carlton	.70	.50	.30
(70)	Greg Luzinski	.40	.30	.15
(71)	Garry Maddox	.25	.20	.10
(72)	Bake McBride	.20	.15	.08
(73)	Tug McGraw	.40	.30	.15
(74)	Pete Rose	1.75	1.25	.70
(75)	Dick Ruthven	.20	.15	.08
(76)	Mike Schmidt	.90	.70	.35
(77)	Manny Trillo	.25	.20	.10
(78)	Del Unser	.20	.15	.08
(79)	Tom Burgmeier	.20	.15	.08
(80)	Dennis Eckersley	.40	.30	.15
(81)	Dwight Evans	.50	.40	.20
(82)	Carlton Fisk	.60	.45	.25
(83)	Glenn Hoffman	.20	.15	.08
(84)	Carney Lansford	.30	.25	.12
(85)	Tony Perez	.50	.40	.20
(86)	Jim Rice	.70	.50	.30
(87)	Bob Stanley	.20	.15	.08
(88)	Dave Stapleton	.20	.15	.08
(89)	Frank Tanana	.25	.20	.10
(90)	Carl Yastrzemski	1.25	.90	.50
(91)	Johnny Bench	.90	.70	.35
(92)	Dave Collins	.25	.20	.10
(93)	Dave Concepcion	.40	.30	.15
(94)	Dan Driessen	.25	.20	.10
(95)	George Foster	.50	.40	.20
(96)	Ken Griffey	.30	.25	.12
(97)	Tom Hume	.20	.15	.08
(98)	Ray Knight	.25	.20	.10
(99)	Joe Nolan	.20	.15	.08
(100)	Ron Oester	.20	.15	.08
(101)	Tom Seaver	.70	.50	.30
(102)	Mario Soto	.25	.20	.10

1981 Topps
National 5X7 Photos

This set is the other half of Topps' efforts with large cards in 1981. Measuring 4-7/8" by 6-7/8", the National photo issue was limited to 15 cards. They were sold in areas not covered by the Home Team sets and feature ten cards which carry the same

TED SIMMONS
Milwaukee Brewers
CATCHER

photos as found in the Home Team set, but with no checklist on the backs. Five cards are unique to the National set: George Brett, Cecil Cooper, Jim Palmer, Dave Parker and Ted Simmons. With their wide distribution and a limited demand, there are currently plenty of these cards to meet the demand, thus keeping prices fairly low.

	MT	NR MT	EX
Complete Set:	8.00	6.00	3.25
Common Player:	.30	.25	.12

		MT	NR MT	EX
(1)	Buddy Bell	.30	.25	.12
(2)	Johnny Bench	.60	.45	.25
(3)	George Brett	.90	.70	.35
(4)	Rod Carew	.60	.45	.25
(5)	Cecil Cooper	.40	.30	.15
(6)	Steve Garvey	.70	.50	.30
(7)	Rich Gossage	.40	.30	.15
(8)	Reggie Jackson	.70	.50	.30
(9)	Jim Palmer	.70	.50	.30
(10)	Dave Parker	.60	.45	.25
(11)	Jim Rice	.50	.40	.20
(12)	Pete Rose	1.25	.90	.50
(13)	Mike Schmidt	.70	.50	.30
(14)	Tom Seaver	.60	.45	.25
(15)	Ted Simmons	.50	.40	.20

1981 Topps Scratchoffs

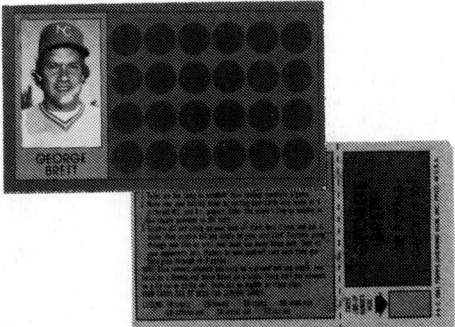

Sold as a separate issue with bubble gum, this 108-card set was issued in three-card panels that measure 3-1/4" by 5-1/4". Each individual card measures 1-13/16" by 3-1/4" and contains a small player photo alongside a series of black dots designed to be scratched off as part of a baseball game. Cards of National League players have a green backgrounds, while American League players have a red background. While there are 108 different players in the set, there are 144 possible combinations. An intact panel of three cards is valued approximately 20-25 percent more the sum of the individual cards.

	MT	NR MT	EX
Complete Set:	4.00	3.00	1.50
Common Player:	.02	.02	.01

		NR MT	EX	VG
1	George Brett	.12	.09	.05
2	Cecil Cooper	.04	.03	.02
3	Reggie Jackson	.12	.09	.05
4	Al Oliver	.04	.03	.02
5	Fred Lynn	.06	.05	.02
6	Tony Armas	.02	.02	.01
7	Ben Oglivie	.02	.02	.01
8	Tony Perez	.06	.05	.02
9	Eddie Murray	.10	.08	.04
10	Robin Yount	.08	.06	.03
11	Steve Kemp	.04	.03	.02
12	Joe Charboneau	.04	.03	.02
13	Jim Rice	.10	.08	.04
14	Lance Parrish	.08	.06	.03
15	John Mayberry	.02	.02	.01
16	Richie Zisk	.02	.02	.01
17	Ken Singleton	.04	.03	.02
18	Rod Carew	.10	.08	.04
19	Rick Manning	.02	.02	.01
20	Willie Wilson	.04	.03	.02
21	Buddy Bell	.04	.03	.02
22	Dave Revering	.02	.02	.01
23	Tom Paciorek	.02	.02	.01
24	Champ Summers	.02	.02	.01
25	Carney Lansford	.04	.03	.02
26	Lamar Johnson	.02	.02	.01
27	Willie Aikens	.02	.02	.01
28	Rick Cerone	.02	.02	.01
29	Al Bumbry	.02	.02	.01
30	Bruce Bochte	.02	.02	.01
31	Mickey Rivers	.02	.02	.01
32	Mike Hargrove	.02	.02	.01
33	John Castino	.02	.02	.01
34	Chet Lemon	.04	.03	.02
35	Paul Molitor	.06	.05	.02
36	Willie Randolph	.04	.03	.02
37	Rick Burleson	.02	.02	.01
38	Alan Trammell	.08	.06	.03
39	Rickey Henderson	.10	.08	.04
40	Dan Meyer	.02	.02	.01
41	Ken Landreaux	.02	.02	.01
42	Damaso Garcia	.02	.02	.01
43	Roy Smalley	.02	.02	.01
44	Otto Velez	.02	.02	.01
45	Sixto Lezcano	.02	.02	.01
46	Toby Harrah	.04	.03	.02
47	Frank White	.04	.03	.02
48	Dave Stapleton	.02	.02	.01
49	Steve Stone	.04	.03	.02
50	Jim Palmer	.08	.06	.03
51	Larry Gura	.02	.02	.01
52	Tommy John	.06	.05	.02
53	Mike Norris	.02	.02	.01
54	Ed Farmer	.02	.02	.01
55	Bill Buckner	.04	.03	.02
56	Steve Garvey	.10	.08	.04
57	Reggie Smith	.04	.03	.02
58	Bake McBride	.02	.02	.01
59	Dave Parker	.06	.05	.02
60	Mike Schmidt	.12	.09	.05
61	Bob Horner	.04	.03	.02
62	Pete Rose	.20	.15	.08
63	Ted Simmons	.06	.05	.02
64	Johnny Bench	.12	.09	.05
65	George Foster	.06	.05	.02
66	Gary Carter	.10	.08	.04
67	Keith Hernandez	.08	.06	.03
68	Ozzie Smith	.06	.05	.02
69	Dave Kingman	.06	.05	.02
70	Jack Clark	.06	.05	.02
71	Dusty Baker	.04	.03	.02
72	Dale Murphy	.12	.09	.05
73	Ron Cey	.04	.03	.02
74	Greg Luzinski	.04	.03	.02
75	Lee Mazzilli	.02	.02	.01
76	Gary Matthews	.04	.03	.02
77	Cesar Cedeno	.04	.03	.02
78	Warren Cromartie	.02	.02	.01
79	Steve Henderson	.02	.02	.01
80	Ellis Valentine	.02	.02	.01
81	Mike Easler	.02	.02	.01
82	Garry Templeton	.04	.03	.02
83	Jose Cruz	.04	.03	.02
84	Dave Collins	.02	.02	.01
85	George Hendrick	.02	.02	.01
86	Gene Richards	.02	.02	.01
87	Terry Whitfield	.02	.02	.01
88	Terry Puhl	.02	.02	.01
89	Larry Parrish	.04	.03	.02
90	Andre Dawson	.08	.06	.03
91	Ken Griffey	.04	.03	.02
92	Dave Lopes	.02	.02	.01

		MT	NR MT	EX
93	Doug Flynn	.02	.02	.01
94	Ivan DeJesus	.02	.02	.01
95	Dave Concepcion	.04	.03	.02
96	John Stearns	.02	.02	.01
97	Jerry Mumphrey	.02	.02	.01
98	Jerry Martin	.02	.02	.01
99	Art Howe	.02	.02	.01
100	Omar Moreno	.02	.02	.01
101	Ken Reitz	.02	.02	.01
102	Phil Garner	.02	.02	.01
103	Jerry Reuss	.04	.03	.02
104	Steve Carlton	.10	.08	.04
105	Jim Bibby	.02	.02	.01
106	Steve Rogers	.02	.02	.01
107	Tom Seaver	.10	.08	.04
108	Vida Blue	.04	.03	.02

1981 Topps Traded

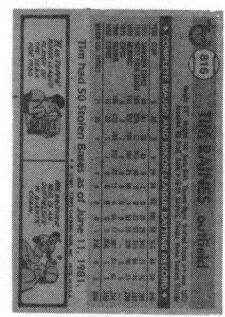

The 132 cards in this extension set are numbered from 727 to 858, technically making them a high-numbered series of the regular Topps set. The set was not packaged in gum packs, but rather placed in a specially designed red box and sold through baseball card dealers only. While many complained about the method, the fact remains, even at higher prices, the set has done well for its owners as it features not only mid-season trades, but also single-player rookie cards of some of the hottest prospects. The cards measure 2-1/2" by 3-1/2".

		MT	NR MT	EX
Complete Set:		30.00	22.00	12.00
Common Player:		.10	.08	.04

		MT	NR MT	EX
727	Danny Ainge(FC)	.50	.40	.20
728	Doyle Alexander	.20	.15	.08
729	Gary Alexander	.10	.08	.04
730	Billy Almon	.10	.08	.04
731	Joaquin Andujar	.15	.11	.06
732	Bob Bailor	.10	.08	.04
733	Juan Beniquez	.10	.08	.04
734	Dave Bergman	.10	.08	.04
735	Tony Bernazard	.10	.08	.04
736	Larry Biittner	.10	.08	.04
737	Doug Bird	.10	.08	.04
738	Bert Blyleven	1.00	.70	.40
739	Mark Bomback	.10	.08	.04
740	Bobby Bonds	.20	.15	.08
741	Rick Bosetti	.10	.08	.04
742	Hubie Brooks	1.25	.90	.50
743	Rick Burleson	.15	.11	.06
744	Ray Burris	.10	.08	.04
745	Jeff Burroughs	.15	.11	.06
746	Enos Cabell	.10	.08	.04
747	Ken Clay	.10	.08	.04
748	Mark Clear	.10	.08	.04
749	Larry Cox	.10	.08	.04
750	Hector Cruz	.10	.08	.04
751	Victor Cruz	.10	.08	.04
752	Mike Cubbage	.10	.08	.04
753	Dick Davis	.10	.08	.04
754	Brian Doyle	.10	.08	.04
755	Dick Drago	.10	.08	.04
756	Leon Durham	.25	.20	.10
757	Jim Dwyer	.10	.08	.04
758	Dave Edwards	.10	.08	.04

		MT	NR MT	EX
759	Jim Essian	.10	.08	.04
760	Bill Fahey	.10	.08	.04
761	Rollie Fingers	1.50	1.25	.60
762	Carlton Fisk	4.00	3.00	1.50
763	Barry Foote	.10	.08	.04
764	Ken Forsch	.10	.08	.04
765	Kiko Garcia	.10	.08	.04
766	Cesar Geronimo	.10	.08	.04
767	Gary Gray	.10	.08	.04
768	Mickey Hatcher	.15	.11	.06
769	Steve Henderson	.10	.08	.04
770	Marc Hill	.10	.08	.04
771	Butch Hobson	.10	.08	.04
772	Rick Honeycutt	.10	.08	.04
773	Roy Howell	.10	.08	.04
774	Mike Ivie	.10	.08	.04
775	Roy Lee Jackson	.10	.08	.04
776	Cliff Johnson	.10	.08	.04
777	Randy Jones	.15	.11	.06
778	Ruppert Jones	.10	.08	.04
779	Mick Kelleher	.10	.08	.04
780	Terry Kennedy	.20	.15	.08
781	Dave Kingman	.40	.30	.15
782	Bob Knepper	.15	.11	.06
783	Ken Kravec	.10	.08	.04
784	Bob Lacey	.10	.08	.04
785	Dennis Lamp	.10	.08	.04
786	Rafael Landestoy	.10	.08	.04
787	Ken Landreaux	.10	.08	.04
788	Carney Lansford	.20	.15	.08
789	Dave LaRoche	.10	.08	.04
790	Joe Lefebvre	.10	.08	.04
791	Ron LeFlore	.15	.11	.06
792	Randy Lerch	.10	.08	.04
793	Sixto Lezcano	.10	.08	.04
794	John Littlefield	.10	.08	.04
795	Mike Lum	.10	.08	.04
796	Greg Luzinski	.25	.20	.10
797	Fred Lynn	.50	.40	.20
798	Jerry Martin	.10	.08	.04
799	Buck Martinez	.10	.08	.04
800	Gary Matthews	.20	.15	.08
801	Mario Mendoza	.10	.08	.04
802	Larry Milbourne	.10	.08	.04
803	Rick Miller	.10	.08	.04
804	John Montefusco	.10	.08	.04
805	Jerry Morales	.10	.08	.04
806	Jose Morales	.10	.08	.04
807	Joe Morgan	2.00	1.50	.80
808	Jerry Mumphrey	.10	.08	.04
809	Gene Nelson(FC)	.30	.25	.12
810	Ed Ott	.10	.08	.04
811	Bob Owchinko	.10	.08	.04
812	Gaylord Perry	1.25	.90	.50
813	Mike Phillips	.10	.08	.04
814	Darrell Porter	.15	.11	.06
815	Mike Proly	.10	.08	.04
816	Tim Raines	8.00	6.00	3.25
817	Lenny Randle	.10	.08	.04
818	Doug Rau	.10	.08	.04
819	Jeff Reardon	.80	.60	.30
820	Ken Reitz	.10	.08	.04
821	Steve Renko	.10	.08	.04
822	Rick Reuschel	.25	.20	.10
823	Dave Revering	.10	.08	.04
824	Dave Roberts	.10	.08	.04
825	Leon Roberts	.10	.08	.04
826	Joe Rudi	.20	.15	.08
827	Kevin Saucier	.10	.08	.04
828	Tony Scott	.10	.08	.04
829	Bob Shirley	.10	.08	.04
830	Ted Simmons	.40	.30	.15
831	Lary Sorensen	.10	.08	.04
832	Jim Spencer	.10	.08	.04
833	Harry Spilman	.10	.08	.04
834	Fred Stanley	.10	.08	.04
835	Rusty Staub	.30	.25	.12
836	Bill Stein	.10	.08	.04
837	Joe Strain	.10	.08	.04
838	Bruce Sutter	.50	.40	.20
839	Don Sutton	1.25	.90	.50
840	Steve Swisher	.10	.08	.04
841	Frank Tanana	.20	.15	.08
842	Gene Tenace	.15	.11	.06
843	Jason Thompson	.10	.08	.04
844	Dickie Thon	.15	.11	.06
845	Bill Travers	.10	.08	.04
846	Tom Underwood	.10	.08	.04
847	John Urrea	.10	.08	.04
848	Mike Vail	.10	.08	.04
849	Ellis Valentine	.10	.08	.04

		MT	NR MT	EX
850	Fernando Valenzuela	5.00	3.75	2.00
851	Pete Vuckovich	.15	.11	.06
852	Mark Wagner	.10	.08	.04
853	Bob Walk	.50	.40	.20
854	Claudell Washington	.15	.11	.06
855	Dave Winfield	3.00	2.25	1.25
856	Geoff Zahn	.10	.08	.04
857	Richie Zisk	.15	.11	.06
858	Checklist 727-858	.10	.08	.04

1982 Topps

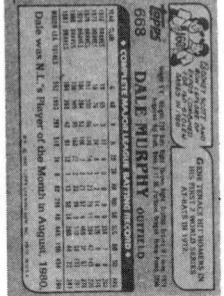

At 792 cards, this was the largest issue produced up to that time, eliminating the need for double-printed cards. The 2-1/2" by 3-1/2" cards feature a front color photo with a pair of stripes down the left side. Under the player's photo are found his name, team and position. A facsimile autograph runs across the front of the picture. Specialty cards include great performances of the previous season, All-Stars, statistical leaders and "In Action" cards (indicated by "IA" in listings below). Managers and hitting/pitching leaders have cards, while rookies are shown as "Future Stars" on group cards.

		MT	NR MT	EX
	Complete Set:	90.00	65.00	35.00
	Common Player:	.08	.06	.03
1	1981 Highlight (Steve Carlton)	.50	.40	.20
2	1981 Highlight (Ron Davis)	.08	.06	.03
3	1981 Highlight (Tim Raines)	.30	.25	.12
4	1981 Highlight (Pete Rose)	.70	.50	.30
5	1981 Highlight (Nolan Ryan)	.30	.25	.12
6	1981 Highlight (Fernando Valenzuela)	.30	.25	.12
7	Scott Sanderson	.08	.06	.03
8	Rich Dauer	.08	.06	.03
9	Ron Guidry	.35	.25	.14
10	Ron Guidry IA	.15	.11	.06
11	Gary Alexander	.08	.06	.03
12	Moose Haas	.08	.06	.03
13	Lamar Johnson	.08	.06	.03
14	Steve Howe	.10	.08	.04
15	Ellis Valentine	.08	.06	.03
16	Steve Comer	.08	.06	.03
17	Darrell Evans	.25	.20	.10
18	Fernando Arroyo	.08	.06	.03
19	Ernie Whitt	.10	.08	.04
20	Garry Maddox	.12	.09	.05
21	Orioles Future Stars (Bob Bonner, *Cal Ripken*, Jeff Schneider)	25.00	18.00	10.00
22	Jim Beattie	.08	.06	.03
23	Willie Hernandez	.10	.08	.04
24	Dave Frost	.08	.06	.03
25	Jerry Remy	.08	.06	.03
26	Jorge Orta	.08	.06	.03
27	Tom Herr	.12	.09	.05
28	John Urrea	.08	.06	.03
29	Dwayne Murphy	.10	.08	.04
30	Tom Seaver	1.00	.70	.40
31	Tom Seaver IA	.30	.25	.12
32	Gene Garber	.08	.06	.03
33	Jerry Morales	.08	.06	.03
34	Joe Sambito	.08	.06	.03
35	Willie Aikens	.08	.06	.03
36	Rangers Batting & Pitching Ldrs. (George Medich, Al Oliver)	.12	.09	.05

		MT	NR MT	EX
37	Dan Graham	.08	.06	.03
38	Charlie Lea	.08	.06	.03
39	Lou Whitaker	.40	.30	.15
40	Dave Parker	.35	.25	.14
41	Dave Parker IA	.15	.11	.06
42	Rick Sofield	.08	.06	.03
43	Mike Cubbage	.08	.06	.03
44	Britt Burns	.08	.06	.03
45	Rick Cerone	.08	.06	.03
46	Jerry Augustine	.08	.06	.03
47	Jeff Leonard	.15	.11	.06
48	Bobby Castillo	.08	.06	.03
49	Alvis Woods	.08	.06	.03
50	Buddy Bell	.15	.11	.06
51	Cubs Future Stars (Jay Howell, Carlos Lezcano, Ty Waller)	.40	.30	.15
52	Larry Andersen	.08	.06	.03
53	Greg Gross	.08	.06	.03
54	Ron Hassey	.08	.06	.03
55	Rick Burleson	.10	.08	.04
56	Mark Littell	.08	.06	.03
57	Craig Reynolds	.08	.06	.03
58	John D'Acquisto	.08	.06	.03
59	Rich Gedman(FC)	.50	.40	.20
60	Tony Armas	.12	.09	.05
61	Tommy Boggs	.08	.06	.03
62	Mike Tyson	.08	.06	.03
63	Mario Soto	.10	.08	.04
64	Lynn Jones	.08	.06	.03
65	Terry Kennedy	.12	.09	.05
66	Astros Batting & Pitching Ldrs. (Art Howe, Nolan Ryan)	.25	.20	.10
67	Rich Gale	.08	.06	.03
68	Roy Howell	.08	.06	.03
69	Al Williams	.08	.06	.03
70	Tim Raines	1.75	1.25	.70
71	Roy Lee Jackson	.08	.06	.03
72	Rick Auerbach	.08	.06	.03
73	Buddy Solomon	.08	.06	.03
74	Bob Clark	.08	.06	.03
75	Tommy John	.30	.25	.12
76	Greg Pryor	.08	.06	.03
77	Miguel Dilone	.08	.06	.03
78	George Medich	.08	.06	.03
79	Bob Bailor	.08	.06	.03
80	Jim Palmer	1.00	.70	.40
81	Jim Palmer IA	.30	.25	.12
82	Bob Welch	.20	.15	.08
83	Yankees Future Stars (Steve Balboni, Andy McGaffigan, Andre Robertson)(FC)	.50	.40	.20
84	Rennie Stennett	.08	.06	.03
85	Lynn McGlothen	.08	.06	.03
86	Dane Iorg	.08	.06	.03
87	Matt Keough	.08	.06	.03
88	Biff Pocoroba	.08	.06	.03
89	Steve Henderson	.08	.06	.03
90	Nolan Ryan	4.00	3.00	1.50
91	Carney Lansford	.12	.09	.05
92	Brad Havens	.08	.06	.03
93	Larry Hisle	.10	.08	.04
94	Andy Hassler	.08	.06	.03
95	Ozzie Smith	.80	.60	.30
96	Royals Batting & Pitching Ldrs. (George Brett, Larry Gura)	.35	.25	.14
97	Paul Moskau	.08	.06	.03
98	Terry Bulling	.08	.06	.03
99	Barry Bonnell	.08	.06	.03
100	Mike Schmidt	2.50	2.00	1.00
101	Mike Schmidt IA	.70	.50	.30
102	Dan Briggs	.08	.06	.03
103	Bob Lacey	.08	.06	.03
104	Rance Mulliniks	.08	.06	.03
105	Kirk Gibson	1.25	.90	.50
106	Enrique Romo	.08	.06	.03
107	Wayne Krenchicki	.08	.06	.03
108	Bob Sykes	.08	.06	.03
109	Dave Revering	.08	.06	.03
110	Carlton Fisk	.50	.40	.20
111	Carlton Fisk IA	.15	.11	.06
112	Billy Sample	.08	.06	.03
113	Steve McCatty	.08	.06	.03
114	Ken Landreaux	.08	.06	.03
115	Gaylord Perry	.40	.30	.15
116	Jim Wohlford	.08	.06	.03
117	Rawly Eastwick	.08	.06	.03
118	Expos Future Stars (Terry Francona, Brad Mills, Bryn Smith)(FC)	.25	.20	.10
119	Joe Pittman	.08	.06	.03
120	Gary Lucas	.08	.06	.03
121	Ed Lynch	.08	.06	.03
122	Jamie Easterly	.08	.06	.03

	MT	NR MT	EX
123 Danny Goodwin	.08	.06	.03
124 Reid Nichols	.08	.06	.03
125 Danny Ainge	.20	.15	.08
126 Braves Batting & Pitching Ldrs. (Rick Mahler, Claudell Washington)	.10	.08	.04
127 Lonnie Smith	.10	.08	.04
128 Frank Pastore	.08	.06	.03
129 Checklist 1-132	.12	.09	.05
130 Julio Cruz	.08	.06	.03
131 Stan Bahnsen	.08	.06	.03
132 Lee May	.10	.08	.04
133 Pat Underwood	.08	.06	.03
134 Dan Ford	.08	.06	.03
135 Andy Rincon	.08	.06	.03
136 Lenn Sakata	.08	.06	.03
137 George Cappuzzello	.08	.06	.03
138 Tony Pena	.20	.15	.08
139 Jeff Jones	.08	.06	.03
140 Ron LeFlore	.10	.08	.04
141 Indians Future Stars (Chris Bando, Tom Brennan, *Von Hayes*)(FC)	2.00	1.50	.80
142 Dave LaRoche	.08	.06	.03
143 Mookie Wilson	.12	.09	.05
144 Fred Breining	.08	.06	.03
145 Bob Horner	.20	.15	.08
146 Mike Griffin	.08	.06	.03
147 Denny Walling	.08	.06	.03
148 Mickey Klutts	.08	.06	.03
149 Pat Putnam	.08	.06	.03
150 Ted Simmons	.20	.15	.08
151 Dave Edwards	.08	.06	.03
152 Ramon Aviles	.08	.06	.03
153 Roger Erickson	.08	.06	.03
154 Dennis Werth	.08	.06	.03
155 Otto Velez	.08	.06	.03
156 A's Batting & Pitching Ldrs. (Rickey Henderson, Steve McCatty)	.25	.20	.10
157 Steve Crawford	.08	.06	.03
158 Brian Downing	.12	.09	.05
159 Larry Biittner	.08	.06	.03
160 Luis Tiant	.15	.11	.06
161 Batting Leaders (Carney Lansford, Bill Madlock)	.20	.15	.08
162 Home Run Leaders (Tony Armas, Dwight Evans, Bobby Grich, Eddie Murray, Mike Schmidt)	.35	.25	.14
163 Runs Batted In Leaders (Eddie Murray, Mike Schmidt)	.40	.30	.15
164 Stolen Base Leaders (Rickey Henderson, Tim Raines)	.35	.25	.14
165 Victory Leaders (Denny Martinez, Steve McCatty, Jack Morris, Tom Seaver, Pete Vuckovich)	.20	.15	.08
166 Strikeout Leaders (Len Barker, Fernando Valenzuela)	.20	.15	.08
167 Earned Run Avg. Leaders (Steve McCatty, Nolan Ryan)	.20	.15	.08
168 Leading Relievers (Rollie Fingers, Bruce Sutter)	.20	.15	.08
169 Charlie Leibrandt	.12	.09	.05
170 Jim Bibby	.08	.06	.03
171 Giants Future Stars (*Bob Brenly, Chili Davis*, Bob Tufts)	1.25	.90	.50
172 Bill Gullickson	.10	.08	.04
173 Jamie Quirk	.08	.06	.03
174 Dave Ford	.08	.06	.03
175 Jerry Mumphrey	.08	.06	.03
176 Dewey Robinson	.08	.06	.03
177 John Ellis	.08	.06	.03
178 Dyar Miller	.08	.06	.03
179 Steve Garvey	.80	.60	.30
180 Steve Garvey IA	.40	.30	.15
181 Silvio Martinez	.08	.06	.03
182 Larry Herndon	.10	.08	.04
183 Mike Proly	.08	.06	.03
184 Mick Kelleher	.08	.06	.03
185 Phil Niekro	.50	.40	.20
186 Cardinals Batting & Pitching Ldrs. (Bob Forsch, Keith Hernandez)	.25	.20	.10
187 Jeff Newman	.08	.06	.03
188 Randy Martz	.08	.06	.03
189 Glenn Hoffman	.08	.06	.03
190 J.R. Richard	.12	.09	.05
191 *Tim Wallach*(FC)	3.50	2.75	1.50
192 Broderick Perkins	.08	.06	.03
193 Darrell Jackson	.08	.06	.03
194 Mike Vail	.08	.06	.03
195 Paul Molitor	.35	.25	.14
196 Willie Upshaw	.12	.09	.05
197 Shane Rawley	.15	.11	.06
198 Chris Speier	.08	.06	.03
199 Don Aase	.08	.06	.03
200 George Brett	2.00	1.50	.80
201 George Brett IA	1.00	.70	.40
202 Rick Manning	.08	.06	.03
203 Blue Jays Future Stars (*Jesse Barfield*, Brian Milner, Boomer Wells)	3.00	2.25	1.25
204 Gary Roenicke	.08	.06	.03
205 Neil Allen	.08	.06	.03
206 Tony Bernazard	.08	.06	.03
207 Rod Scurry	.08	.06	.03
208 Bobby Murcer	.15	.11	.06
209 Gary Lavelle	.08	.06	.03
210 Keith Hernandez	.60	.45	.25
211 Dan Petry	.10	.08	.04
212 Mario Mendoza	.08	.06	.03
213 *Dave Stewart*(FC)	12.00	9.00	4.75
214 Brian Asselstine	.08	.06	.03
215 Mike Krukow	.10	.08	.04
216 White Sox Batting & Pitching Ldrs. (Dennis Lamp, Chet Lemon)	.10	.08	.04
217 Bo McLaughlin	.08	.06	.03
218 Dave Roberts	.08	.06	.03
219 John Curtis	.08	.06	.03
220 Manny Trillo	.10	.08	.04
221 Jim Slaton	.08	.06	.03
222 Butch Wynegar	.08	.06	.03
223 Lloyd Moseby	.20	.15	.08
224 Bruce Bochte	.08	.06	.03
225 Mike Torrez	.10	.08	.04
226 Checklist 133-264	.12	.09	.05
227 Ray Burris	.08	.06	.03
228 Sam Mejias	.08	.06	.03
229 Geoff Zahn	.08	.06	.03
230 Willie Wilson	.20	.15	.08
231 Phillies Future Stars (*Mark Davis, Bob Dernier, Ozzie Virgil*)(FC)	1.50	1.25	.60
232 Terry Crowley	.08	.06	.03
233 Duane Kuiper	.08	.06	.03
234 Ron Hodges	.08	.06	.03
235 Mike Easler	.10	.08	.04
236 John Martin	.08	.06	.03
237 Rusty Kuntz	.08	.06	.03
238 Kevin Saucier	.08	.06	.03
239 Jon Matlack	.10	.08	.04
240 Bucky Dent	.12	.09	.05
241 Bucky Dent IA	.10	.08	.04
242 Milt May	.08	.06	.03
243 Bob Owchinko	.08	.06	.03
244 Rufino Linares	.08	.06	.03
245 Ken Reitz	.08	.06	.03
246 Mets Batting & Pitching Ldrs. (Hubie Brooks, Mike Scott)	.20	.15	.08
247 Pedro Guerrero	.90	.70	.35
248 Frank LaCorte	.08	.06	.03
249 Tim Flannery	.08	.06	.03
250 Tug McGraw	.15	.11	.06
251 Fred Lynn	.30	.25	.12
252 Fred Lynn IA	.15	.11	.06
253 Chuck Baker	.08	.06	.03
254 *Jorge Bell*(FC)	9.00	6.75	3.50
255 Tony Perez	.30	.25	.12
256 Tony Perez IA	.15	.11	.06
257 Larry Harlow	.08	.06	.03
258 Bo Diaz	.10	.08	.04
259 Rodney Scott	.08	.06	.03
260 Bruce Sutter	.20	.15	.08
261 Tigers Future Stars (Howard Bailey, Marty Castillo, Dave Rucker)	.08	.06	.03
262 Doug Bair	.08	.06	.03
263 Victor Cruz	.08	.06	.03
264 Dan Quisenberry	.20	.15	.08
265 Al Bumbry	.10	.08	.04
266 Rick Leach	.15	.11	.06
267 Kurt Bevacqua	.08	.06	.03
268 Rickey Keeton	.08	.06	.03
269 Jim Essian	.08	.06	.03
270 Rusty Staub	.15	.11	.06
271 Larry Bradford	.08	.06	.03
272 Bump Wills	.08	.06	.03
273 Doug Bird	.08	.06	.03
274 *Bob Ojeda*(FC)	.70	.50	.30
275 Bob Watson	.10	.08	.04
276 Angels Batting & Pitching Ldrs. (Rod Carew, Ken Forsch)	.25	.20	.10
277 Terry Puhl	.08	.06	.03
278 John Littlefield	.08	.06	.03
279 Bill Russell	.10	.08	.04
280 Ben Oglivie	.10	.08	.04
281 John Verhoeven	.08	.06	.03
282 Ken Macha	.08	.06	.03
283 Brian Allard	.08	.06	.03

		MT	NR MT	EX
284	Bob Grich	.15	.11	.06
285	Sparky Lyle	.12	.09	.05
286	Bill Fahey	.08	.06	.03
287	Alan Bannister	.08	.06	.03
288	Garry Templeton	.12	.09	.05
289	Bob Stanley	.08	.06	.03
290	Ken Singleton	.12	.09	.05
291	Pirates Future Stars (Vance Law, Bob Long, *Johnny Ray*)(FC)	1.00	.70	.40
292	Dave Palmer	.08	.06	.03
293	Rob Picciolo	.08	.06	.03
294	Mike LaCoss	.08	.06	.03
295	Jason Thompson	.08	.06	.03
296	Bob Walk	.12	.09	.05
297	Clint Hurdle	.08	.06	.03
298	Danny Darwin	.08	.06	.03
299	Steve Trout	.08	.06	.03
300	Reggie Jackson	1.00	.70	.40
301	Reggie Jackson IA	.50	.40	.20
302	Doug Flynn	.08	.06	.03
303	Bill Caudill	.08	.06	.03
304	Johnnie LeMaster	.08	.06	.03
305	Don Sutton	.50	.40	.20
306	Don Sutton IA	.25	.20	.10
307	Randy Bass	.08	.06	.03
308	Charlie Moore	.08	.06	.03
309	Pete Redfern	.08	.06	.03
310	Mike Hargrove	.08	.06	.03
311	Dodgers Batting & Pitching Leaders (Dusty Baker, Burt Hooton)	.12	.09	.05
312	Lenny Randle	.08	.06	.03
313	John Harris	.08	.06	.03
314	Buck Martinez	.08	.06	.03
315	Burt Hooton	.10	.08	.04
316	Steve Braun	.08	.06	.03
317	Dick Ruthven	.08	.06	.03
318	Mike Heath	.08	.06	.03
319	Dave Rozema	.08	.06	.03
320	Chris Chambliss	.10	.08	.04
321	Chris Chambliss IA	.10	.08	.04
322	Garry Hancock	.08	.06	.03
323	Bill Lee	.10	.08	.04
324	Steve Dillard	.08	.06	.03
325	Jose Cruz	.15	.11	.06
326	Pete Falcone	.08	.06	.03
327	Joe Nolan	.08	.06	.03
328	Ed Farmer	.08	.06	.03
329	U.L. Washington	.08	.06	.03
330	Rick Wise	.10	.08	.04
331	Benny Ayala	.08	.06	.03
332	Don Robinson	.10	.08	.04
333	Brewers Future Stars (*Frank DiPino, Marshall Edwards, Chuck Porter*)	.12	.09	.05
334	Aurelio Rodriguez	.10	.08	.04
335	Jim Sundberg	.10	.08	.04
336	Mariners Batting & Pitching Ldrs. (Glenn Abbott, Tom Paciorek)	.10	.08	.04
337	Pete Rose AS	.80	.60	.30
338	Dave Lopes AS	.12	.09	.05
339	Mike Schmidt AS	.60	.45	.25
340	Dave Concepcion AS	.12	.09	.05
341	Andre Dawson AS	.25	.20	.10
342a	George Foster AS (no autograph)	2.25	1.75	.90
342b	George Foster AS (autograph on front)	.40	.30	.15
343	Dave Parker AS	.20	.15	.08
344	Gary Carter AS	.35	.25	.14
345	Fernando Valenzuela AS	.35	.25	.14
346	Tom Seaver AS	.35	.25	.14
347	Bruce Sutter AS	.12	.09	.05
348	Derrel Thomas	.08	.06	.03
349	George Frazier	.08	.06	.03
350	Thad Bosley	.08	.06	.03
351	Reds Future Stars (Scott Brown, Geoff Combe, Paul Householder)	.08	.06	.03
352	Dick Davis	.08	.06	.03
353	Jack O'Connor	.08	.06	.03
354	Roberto Ramos	.08	.06	.03
355	Dwight Evans	.25	.20	.10
356	Denny Lewallyn	.08	.06	.03
357	Butch Hobson	.08	.06	.03
358	Mike Parrott	.08	.06	.03
359	Jim Dwyer	.08	.06	.03
360	Len Barker	.10	.08	.04
361	Rafael Landestoy	.08	.06	.03
362	Jim Wright	.08	.06	.03
363	Bob Molinaro	.08	.06	.03
364	Doyle Alexander	.12	.09	.05
365	Bill Madlock	.20	.15	.08
366	Padres Batting & Pitching Ldrs. (Juan Eichelberger, Luis Salazar)	.10	.08	.04

		MT	NR MT	EX
367	Jim Kaat	.25	.20	.10
368	Alex Trevino	.08	.06	.03
369	Champ Summers	.08	.06	.03
370	Mike Norris	.08	.06	.03
371	Jerry Don Gleaton	.08	.06	.03
372	Luis Gomez	.08	.06	.03
373	*Gene Nelson*	.15	.11	.06
374	Tim Blackwell	.08	.06	.03
375	Dusty Baker	.12	.09	.05
376	Chris Welsh	.08	.06	.03
377	Kiko Garcia	.08	.06	.03
378	Mike Caldwell	.08	.06	.03
379	Rob Wilfong	.08	.06	.03
380	Dave Stieb	.25	.20	.10
381	Red Sox Future Stars (Bruce Hurst, Dave Schmidt, Julio Valdez)	.25	.20	.10
382	Joe Simpson	.08	.06	.03
383a	Pascual Perez (no position on front)	35.00	26.00	14.00
383b	Pascual Perez (position on front)	.12	.09	.05
384	Keith Moreland	.12	.09	.05
385	Ken Forsch	.08	.06	.03
386	Jerry White	.08	.06	.03
387	Tom Veryzer	.08	.06	.03
388	Joe Rudi	.12	.09	.05
389	George Vukovich	.08	.06	.03
390	Eddie Murray	1.25	.90	.50
391	Dave Tobik	.08	.06	.03
392	Rick Bosetti	.08	.06	.03
393	Al Hrabosky	.10	.08	.04
394	Checklist 265-396	.12	.09	.05
395	Omar Moreno	.08	.06	.03
396	Twins Batting & Pitching Ldrs. (Fernando Arroyo, John Castino)	.10	.08	.04
397	Ken Brett	.10	.08	.04
398	Mike Squires	.08	.06	.03
399	Pat Zachry	.08	.06	.03
400	Johnny Bench	1.00	.70	.40
401	Johnny Bench IA	.40	.30	.15
402	Bill Stein	.08	.06	.03
403	Jim Tracy	.08	.06	.03
404	Dickie Thon	.10	.08	.04
405	Rick Reuschel	.15	.11	.06
406	Al Holland	.08	.06	.03
407	Danny Boone	.08	.06	.03
408	Ed Romero	.08	.06	.03
409	Don Cooper	.08	.06	.03
410	Ron Cey	.15	.11	.06
411	Ron Cey IA	.10	.08	.04
412	Luis Leal	.08	.06	.03
413	Dan Meyer	.08	.06	.03
414	Elias Sosa	.08	.06	.03
415	Don Baylor	.15	.11	.06
416	Marty Bystrom	.08	.06	.03
417	Pat Kelly	.08	.06	.03
418	Rangers Future Stars (John Butcher, Bobby Johnson, *Dave Schmidt*)(FC)	.20	.15	.08
419	Steve Stone	.12	.09	.05
420	George Hendrick	.10	.08	.04
421	Mark Clear	.08	.06	.03
422	Cliff Johnson	.08	.06	.03
423	Stan Papi	.08	.06	.03
424	Bruce Benedict	.08	.06	.03
425	John Candelaria	.12	.09	.05
426	Orioles Batting & Pitching Ldrs. (Eddie Murray, Sammy Stewart)	.35	.25	.14
427	Ron Oester	.08	.06	.03
428	Lamarr Hoyt (LaMarr)	.08	.06	.03
429	John Wathan	.10	.08	.04
430	Vida Blue	.15	.11	.06
431	Vida Blue IA	.10	.08	.04
432	Mike Scott	.25	.20	.10
433	Alan Ashby	.08	.06	.03
434	Joe Lefebvre	.08	.06	.03
435	Robin Yount	2.00	1.50	.80
436	Joe Strain	.08	.06	.03
437	Juan Berenguer	.08	.06	.03
438	Pete Mackanin	.08	.06	.03
439	*Dave Righetti*(FC)	2.50	2.00	1.00
440	Jeff Burroughs	.10	.08	.04
441	Astros Future Stars (Danny Heep, Billy Smith, Bobby Sprowl)	.08	.06	.03
442	Bruce Kison	.08	.06	.03
443	Mark Wagner	.08	.06	.03
444	Terry Forster	.10	.08	.04
445	Larry Parrish	.12	.09	.05
446	Wayne Garland	.08	.06	.03
447	Darrell Porter	.10	.08	.04
448	Darrell Porter IA	.10	.08	.04
449	*Luis Aguayo*(FC)	.12	.09	.05
450	Jack Morris	.50	.40	.20

		MT	NR MT	EX
451	Ed Miller	.08	.06	.03
452	Lee Smith(FC)	1.25	.90	.50
453	Art Howe	.08	.06	.03
454	Rick Langford	.08	.06	.03
455	Tom Burgmeier	.08	.06	.03
456	Cubs Batting & Pitching Ldrs. (Bill Buckner, Randy Martz)	.15	.11	.06
457	Tim Stoddard	.08	.06	.03
458	Willie Montanez	.08	.06	.03
459	Bruce Berenyi	.08	.06	.03
460	Jack Clark	.30	.25	.12
461	Rich Dotson	.12	.09	.05
462	Dave Chalk	.08	.06	.03
463	Jim Kern	.08	.06	.03
464	Juan Bonilla	.08	.06	.03
465	Lee Mazzilli	.10	.08	.04
466	Randy Lerch	.08	.06	.03
467	Mickey Hatcher	.10	.08	.04
468	Floyd Bannister	.12	.09	.05
469	Ed Ott	.08	.06	.03
470	John Mayberry	.10	.08	.04
471	Royals Future Stars (Atlee Hammaker, Mike Jones, Darryl Motley)	.25	.20	.10
472	Oscar Gamble	.10	.08	.04
473	Mike Stanton	.08	.06	.03
474	Ken Oberkfell	.08	.06	.03
475	Alan Trammell	.50	.40	.20
476	Brian Kingman	.08	.06	.03
477	Steve Yeager	.08	.06	.03
478	Ray Searage	.08	.06	.03
479	Rowland Office	.08	.06	.03
480	Steve Carlton	.80	.60	.30
481	Steve Carlton IA	.40	.30	.15
482	Glenn Hubbard	.10	.08	.04
483	Gary Woods	.08	.06	.03
484	Ivan DeJesus	.08	.06	.03
485	Kent Tekulve	.10	.08	.04
486	Yankees Batting & Pitching Ldrs. (Tommy John, Jerry Mumphrey)	.20	.15	.08
487	Bob McClure	.08	.06	.03
488	Ron Jackson	.08	.06	.03
489	Rick Dempsey	.10	.08	.04
490	Dennis Eckersley	.20	.15	.08
491	Checklist 397-528	.12	.09	.05
492	Joe Price	.08	.06	.03
493	Chet Lemon	.10	.08	.04
494	Hubie Brooks	.20	.15	.08
495	Dennis Leonard	.10	.08	.04
496	Johnny Grubb	.08	.06	.03
497	Jim Anderson	.08	.06	.03
498	Dave Bergman	.08	.06	.03
499	Paul Mirabella	.08	.06	.03
500	Rod Carew	.80	.60	.30
501	Rod Carew IA	.40	.30	.15
502	Braves Future Stars (Steve Bedrosian, Brett Butler, Larry Owen)	2.50	2.00	1.00
503	Julio Gonzalez	.08	.06	.03
504	Rick Peters	.08	.06	.03
505	Graig Nettles	.25	.20	.10
506	Graig Nettles IA	.12	.09	.05
507	Terry Harper	.08	.06	.03
508	Jody Davis(FC)	.40	.30	.15
509	Harry Spilman	.08	.06	.03
510	Fernando Valenzuela	1.50	1.25	.60
511	Ruppert Jones	.08	.06	.03
512	Jerry Dybzinski	.08	.06	.03
513	Rick Rhoden	.12	.09	.05
514	Joe Ferguson	.08	.06	.03
515	Larry Bowa	.20	.15	.08
516	Larry Bowa IA	.12	.09	.05
517	Mark Brouhard	.08	.06	.03
518	Garth Iorg	.08	.06	.03
519	Glenn Adams	.08	.06	.03
520	Mike Flanagan	.12	.09	.05
521	Billy Almon	.08	.06	.03
522	Chuck Rainey	.08	.06	.03
523	Gary Gray	.08	.06	.03
524	Tom Hausman	.08	.06	.03
525	Ray Knight	.12	.09	.05
526	Expos Batting & Pitching Ldrs. (Warren Cromartie, Bill Gullickson)	.10	.08	.04
527	John Henry Johnson	.08	.06	.03
528	Matt Alexander	.08	.06	.03
529	Allen Ripley	.08	.06	.03
530	Dickie Noles	.08	.06	.03
531	A's Future Stars (Rich Bordi, Mark Budaska, Kelvin Moore)	.08	.06	.03
532	Toby Harrah	.10	.08	.04
533	Joaquin Andujar	.10	.08	.04
534	Dave McKay	.08	.06	.03
535	Lance Parrish	.50	.40	.20

		MT	NR MT	EX
536	Rafael Ramirez	.10	.08	.04
537	Doug Capilla	.08	.06	.03
538	Lou Piniella	.15	.11	.06
539	Vern Ruhle	.08	.06	.03
540	Andre Dawson	1.00	.70	.40
541	Barry Evans	.08	.06	.03
542	Ned Yost	.08	.06	.03
543	Bill Robinson	.08	.06	.03
544	Larry Christenson	.08	.06	.03
545	Reggie Smith	.15	.11	.06
546	Reggie Smith IA	.10	.08	.04
547	Rod Carew AS	.35	.25	.14
548	Willie Randolph AS	.12	.09	.05
549	George Brett AS	.60	.45	.25
550	Bucky Dent AS	.12	.09	.05
551	Reggie Jackson AS	.50	.40	.20
552	Ken Singleton AS	.12	.09	.05
553	Dave Winfield AS	.40	.30	.15
554	Carlton Fisk AS	.20	.15	.08
555	Scott McGregor AS	.12	.09	.05
556	Jack Morris AS	.20	.15	.08
557	Rich Gossage AS	.20	.15	.08
558	John Tudor	.30	.25	.12
559	Indians Batting & Pitching Ldrs. (Bert Blyleven, Mike Hargrove)	.15	.11	.06
560	Doug Corbett	.08	.06	.03
561	Cardinals Future Stars (Glenn Brummer, Luis DeLeon, Gene Roof)	.08	.06	.03
562	Mike O'Berry	.08	.06	.03
563	Ross Baumgarten	.08	.06	.03
564	Doug DeCinces	.15	.11	.06
565	Jackson Todd	.08	.06	.03
566	Mike Jorgensen	.08	.06	.03
567	Bob Babcock	.08	.06	.03
568	Joe Pettini	.08	.06	.03
569	Willie Randolph	.15	.11	.06
570	Willie Randolph IA	.10	.08	.04
571	Glenn Abbott	.08	.06	.03
572	Juan Beniquez	.08	.06	.03
573	Rick Waits	.08	.06	.03
574	Mike Ramsey	.08	.06	.03
575	Al Cowens	.08	.06	.03
576	Giants Batting & Pitching Ldrs. (Vida Blue, Milt May)	.15	.11	.06
577	Rick Monday	.12	.09	.05
578	Shooty Babitt	.08	.06	.03
579	Rick Mahler(FC)	.30	.25	.12
580	Bobby Bonds	.15	.11	.06
581	Ron Reed	.08	.06	.03
582	Luis Pujols	.08	.06	.03
583	Tippy Martinez	.08	.06	.03
584	Hosken Powell	.08	.06	.03
585	Rollie Fingers	.30	.25	.12
586	Rollie Fingers IA	.15	.11	.06
587	Tim Lollar	.08	.06	.03
588	Dale Berra	.08	.06	.03
589	Dave Stapleton	.08	.06	.03
590	Al Oliver	.20	.15	.08
591	Al Oliver IA	.10	.08	.04
592	Craig Swan	.08	.06	.03
593	Billy Smith	.08	.06	.03
594	Renie Martin	.08	.06	.03
595	Dave Collins	.10	.08	.04
596	Damaso Garcia	.08	.06	.03
597	Wayne Nordhagen	.08	.06	.03
598	Bob Galasso	.08	.06	.03
599	White Sox Future Stars (Jay Loviglio, Reggie Patterson, Leo Sutherland)	.08	.06	.03
600	Dave Winfield	.60	.45	.25
601	Sid Monge	.08	.06	.03
602	Freddie Patek	.08	.06	.03
603	Rich Hebner	.08	.06	.03
604	Orlando Sanchez	.08	.06	.03
605	Steve Rogers	.10	.08	.04
606	Blue Jays Batting & Pitching Ldrs. (John Mayberry, Dave Stieb)	.15	.11	.06
607	Leon Durham	.10	.08	.04
608	Jerry Royster	.08	.06	.03
609	Rick Sutcliffe	.25	.20	.10
610	Rickey Henderson	8.00	6.00	3.25
611	Joe Niekro	.20	.15	.08
612	Gary Ward	.10	.08	.04
613	Jim Gantner	.10	.08	.04
614	Juan Eichelberger	.08	.06	.03
615	Bob Boone	.12	.09	.05
616	Bob Boone IA	.10	.08	.04
617	Scott McGregor	.10	.08	.04
618	Tim Foli	.08	.06	.03
619	Bill Campbell	.08	.06	.03
620	Ken Griffey	.15	.11	.06
621	Ken Griffey IA	.10	.08	.04

		MT	NR MT	EX
622	Dennis Lamp	.08	.06	.03
623	Mets Future Stars (Ron Gardenhire, *Terry Leach*, Tim Leary)(FC)	.70	.50	.30
624	Fergie Jenkins	.25	.20	.10
625	Hal McRae	.15	.11	.06
626	Randy Jones	.10	.08	.04
627	Enos Cabell	.08	.06	.03
628	Bill Travers	.08	.06	.03
629	Johnny Wockenfuss	.08	.06	.03
630	Joe Charboneau	.10	.08	.04
631	Gene Tenace	.10	.08	.04
632	Bryan Clark	.08	.06	.03
633	Mitchell Page	.08	.06	.03
634	Checklist 529-660	.12	.09	.05
635	Ron Davis	.10	.08	.04
636	Phillies Batting & Pitching Ldrs. (Steve Carlton, Pete Rose)	.50	.40	.20
637	Rick Camp	.08	.06	.03
638	John Milner	.08	.06	.03
639	Ken Kravec	.08	.06	.03
640	Cesar Cedeno	.15	.11	.06
641	Steve Mura	.08	.06	.03
642	Mike Scioscia	.10	.08	.04
643	Pete Vuckovich	.10	.08	.04
644	John Castino	.08	.06	.03
645	Frank White	.12	.09	.05
646	Frank White IA	.10	.08	.04
647	Warren Brusstar	.08	.06	.03
648	Jose Morales	.08	.06	.03
649	Ken Clay	.08	.06	.03
650	Carl Yastrzemski	1.25	.90	.50
651	Carl Yastrzemski IA	.60	.45	.25
652	Steve Nicosia	.08	.06	.03
653	Angels Future Stars (*Tom Brunansky*, Luis Sanchez, Daryl Sconiers)	2.50	2.00	1.00
654	Jim Morrison	.08	.06	.03
655	Joel Youngblood	.08	.06	.03
656	Eddie Whitson	.08	.06	.03
657	Tom Poquette	.08	.06	.03
658	Tito Landrum	.08	.06	.03
659	Fred Martinez	.08	.06	.03
660	Dave Concepcion	.15	.11	.06
661	Dave Concepcion IA	.10	.08	.04
662	Luis Salazar	.08	.06	.03
663	Hector Cruz	.08	.06	.03
664	Dan Spillner	.08	.06	.03
665	Jim Clancy	.12	.09	.05
666	Tigers Batting & Pitching Ldrs. (Steve Kemp, Dan Petry)	.15	.11	.06
667	Jeff Reardon	.25	.20	.10
668	Dale Murphy	2.00	1.50	.80
669	Larry Milbourne	.08	.06	.03
670	Steve Kemp	.12	.09	.05
671	Mike Davis	.10	.08	.04
672	Bob Knepper	.12	.09	.05
673	Keith Drumright	.08	.06	.03
674	Dave Goltz	.10	.08	.04
675	Cecil Cooper	.20	.15	.08
676	Sal Butera	.08	.06	.03
677	Alfredo Griffin	.12	.09	.05
678	Tom Paciorek	.08	.06	.03
679	Sammy Stewart	.08	.06	.03
680	Gary Matthews	.12	.09	.05
681	Dodgers Future Stars (*Mike Marshall*, Ron Roenicke, *Steve Sax*)(FC)	4.00	3.00	1.50
682	Jesse Jefferson	.08	.06	.03
683	Phil Garner	.10	.08	.04
684	Harold Baines	.70	.50	.30
685	Bert Blyleven	.20	.15	.08
686	Gary Allenson	.08	.06	.03
687	Greg Minton	.08	.06	.03
688	Leon Roberts	.08	.06	.03
689	Lary Sorensen	.08	.06	.03
690	Dave Kingman	.20	.15	.08
691	Dan Schatzeder	.08	.06	.03
692	Wayne Gross	.08	.06	.03
693	Cesar Geronimo	.08	.06	.03
694	Dave Wehrmeister	.08	.06	.03
695	Warren Cromartie	.08	.06	.03
696	Pirates Batting & Pitching Ldrs. (Bill Madlock, Buddy Solomon)	.15	.11	.06
697	John Montefusco	.08	.06	.03
698	Tony Scott	.08	.06	.03
699	Dick Tidrow	.08	.06	.03
700	George Foster	.25	.20	.10
701	George Foster IA	.12	.09	.05
702	Steve Renko	.08	.06	.03
703	Brewers Batting & Pitching Ldrs. (Cecil Cooper, Pete Vuckovich)	.15	.11	.06
704	Mickey Rivers	.10	.08	.04
705	Mickey Rivers IA	.10	.08	.04

		MT	NR MT	EX
706	Barry Foote	.08	.06	.03
707	Mark Bomback	.08	.06	.03
708	Gene Richards	.08	.06	.03
709	Don Money	.08	.06	.03
710	Jerry Reuss	.12	.09	.05
711	Mariners Future Stars (Dave Edler, *Dave Henderson*, Reggie Walton)	2.00	1.50	.80
712	Denny Martinez	.10	.08	.04
713	Del Unser	.08	.06	.03
714	Jerry Koosman	.12	.09	.05
715	Willie Stargell	.70	.50	.30
716	Willie Stargell IA	.30	.25	.12
717	Rick Miller	.08	.06	.03
718	Charlie Hough	.12	.09	.05
719	Jerry Narron	.08	.06	.03
720	Greg Luzinski	.20	.15	.08
721	Greg Luzinski IA	.12	.09	.05
722	Jerry Martin	.08	.06	.03
723	Junior Kennedy	.08	.06	.03
724	Dave Rosello	.08	.06	.03
725	Amos Otis	.10	.08	.04
726	Amos Otis IA	.10	.08	.04
727	Sixto Lezcano	.08	.06	.03
728	Aurelio Lopez	.08	.06	.03
729	Jim Spencer	.08	.06	.03
730	Gary Carter	.70	.50	.30
731	Padres Future Stars (Mike Armstrong, Doug Gwosdz, Fred Kuhaulua)	.08	.06	.03
732	Mike Lum	.08	.06	.03
733	Larry McWilliams	.08	.06	.03
734	Mike Ivie	.08	.06	.03
735	Rudy May	.08	.06	.03
736	Jerry Turner	.08	.06	.03
737	Reggie Cleveland	.08	.06	.03
738	Dave Engle	.08	.06	.03
739	Joey McLaughlin	.08	.06	.03
740	Dave Lopes	.12	.09	.05
741	Dave Lopes IA	.10	.08	.04
742	Dick Drago	.08	.06	.03
743	John Stearns	.08	.06	.03
744	*Mike Witt*(FC)	.80	.60	.30
745	Bake McBride	.08	.06	.03
746	Andre Thornton	.12	.09	.05
747	John Lowenstein	.08	.06	.03
748	Marc Hill	.08	.06	.03
749	Bob Shirley	.08	.06	.03
750	Jim Rice	.90	.70	.35
751	Rick Honeycutt	.08	.06	.03
752	Lee Lacy	.08	.06	.03
753	Tom Brookens	.08	.06	.03
754	Joe Morgan	.50	.40	.20
755	Joe Morgan IA	.20	.15	.08
756	Reds Batting & Pitching Ldrs. (Ken Griffey, Tom Seaver)	.30	.25	.12
757	Tom Underwood	.08	.06	.03
758	Claudell Washington	.12	.09	.05
759	Paul Splittorff	.08	.06	.03
760	Bill Buckner	.15	.11	.06
761	Dave Smith	.12	.09	.05
762	Mike Phillips	.08	.06	.03
763	Tom Hume	.08	.06	.03
764	Steve Swisher	.08	.06	.03
765	Gorman Thomas	.12	.09	.05
766	Twins Future Stars (Lenny Faedo, *Kent Hrbek*, Tim Laudner)(FC)	6.00	4.50	2.50
767	Roy Smalley	.08	.06	.03
768	Jerry Garvin	.08	.06	.03
769	Richie Zisk	.10	.08	.04
770	Rich Gossage	.35	.25	.14
771	Rich Gossage IA	.15	.11	.06
772	Bert Campaneris	.12	.09	.05
773	John Denny	.08	.06	.03
774	Jay Johnstone	.10	.08	.04
775	Bob Forsch	.10	.08	.04
776	Mark Belanger	.10	.08	.04
777	Tom Griffin	.08	.06	.03
778	Kevin Hickey	.08	.06	.03
779	Grant Jackson	.08	.06	.03
780	Pete Rose	2.25	1.75	.90
781	Pete Rose IA	1.00	.70	.40
782	Frank Taveras	.08	.06	.03
783	*Greg Harris*(FC)	.15	.11	.06
784	Milt Wilcox	.08	.06	.03
785	Dan Driessen	.10	.08	.04
786	Red Sox Batting & Pitching Ldrs. (Carney Lansford, Mike Torrez)	.12	.09	.05
787	Fred Stanley	.08	.06	.03
788	Woodie Fryman	.10	.08	.04
789	Checklist 661-792	.12	.09	.05
790	Larry Gura	.08	.06	.03
791	Bobby Brown	.08	.06	.03

		MT	NR MT	EX
792	Frank Tanana	.12	.09	.05

1982 Topps Traded

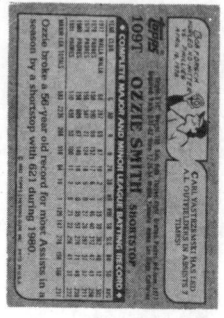

Topps released its second straight 132-card Traded set in September of 1982. Again, the 2-1/2" by 3-1/2" cards feature not only players who had been traded during the season, but also promising rookies who were given their first individual cards. The cards follow the basic design of the regular issues, but have their backs printed in red rather than the regular-issue green. As in 1981, the cards were not available in normal retail outlets and could only be purchased through regular baseball card dealers. Unlike the previous year, the cards are numbered 1-132 with the letter "T" following the number.

		MT	NR MT	EX
Complete Set:		50.00	37.00	20.00
Common Player:		.10	.08	.04
1T	Doyle Alexander	.20	.15	.08
2T	Jesse Barfield	2.00	1.50	.80
3T	Ross Baumgarten	.10	.08	.04
4T	Steve Bedrosian	.80	.60	.30
5T	Mark Belanger	.15	.11	.06
6T	Kurt Bevacqua	.10	.08	.04
7T	Tim Blackwell	.10	.08	.04
8T	Vida Blue	.25	.20	.10
9T	Bob Boone	.20	.15	.08
10T	Larry Bowa	.25	.20	.10
11T	Dan Briggs	.10	.08	.04
12T	Bobby Brown	.10	.08	.04
13T	Tom Brunansky	1.75	1.25	.70
14T	Jeff Burroughs	.15	.11	.06
15T	Enos Cabell	.10	.08	.04
16T	Bill Campbell	.10	.08	.04
17T	Bobby Castillo	.10	.08	.04
18T	Bill Caudill	.10	.08	.04
19T	Cesar Cedeno	.20	.15	.08
20T	Dave Collins	.15	.11	.06
21T	Doug Corbett	.10	.08	.04
22T	Al Cowens	.10	.08	.04
23T	Chili Davis	1.50	1.25	.60
24T	Dick Davis	.10	.08	.04
25T	Ron Davis	.10	.08	.04
26T	Doug DeCinces	.20	.15	.08
27T	Ivan DeJesus	.10	.08	.04
28T	Bob Dernier	.20	.15	.08
29T	Bo Diaz	.15	.11	.06
30T	Roger Erickson	.10	.08	.04
31T	Jim Essian	.10	.08	.04
32T	Ed Farmer	.10	.08	.04
33T	Doug Flynn	.10	.08	.04
34T	Tim Foli	.10	.08	.04
35T	Dan Ford	.10	.08	.04
36T	George Foster	.40	.30	.15
37T	Dave Frost	.10	.08	.04
38T	Rich Gale	.10	.08	.04
39T	Ron Gardenhire	.10	.08	.04
40T	Ken Griffey	.25	.20	.10
41T	Greg Harris	.15	.11	.06
42T	Von Hayes	1.50	1.25	.60
43T	Larry Herndon	.15	.11	.06
44T	Kent Hrbek	6.00	4.50	2.50
45T	Mike Ivie	.10	.08	.04
46T	Grant Jackson	.10	.08	.04

		MT	NR MT	EX
47T	Reggie Jackson	5.00	3.75	2.00
48T	Ron Jackson	.10	.08	.04
49T	Fergie Jenkins	.40	.30	.15
50T	Lamar Johnson	.10	.08	.04
51T	Randy Johnson	.10	.08	.04
52T	Jay Johnstone	.15	.11	.06
53T	Mick Kelleher	.10	.08	.04
54T	Steve Kemp	.15	.11	.06
55T	Junior Kennedy	.10	.08	.04
56T	Jim Kern	.10	.08	.04
57T	Ray Knight	.20	.15	.08
58T	Wayne Krenchicki	.10	.08	.04
59T	Mike Krukow	.15	.11	.06
60T	Duane Kuiper	.10	.08	.04
61T	Mike LaCoss	.10	.08	.04
62T	Chet Lemon	.15	.11	.06
63T	Sixto Lezcano	.10	.08	.04
64T	Dave Lopes	.15	.11	.06
65T	Jerry Martin	.10	.08	.04
66T	Renie Martin	.10	.08	.04
67T	John Mayberry	.15	.11	.06
68T	Lee Mazzilli	.15	.11	.06
69T	Bake McBride	.10	.08	.04
70T	Dan Meyer	.10	.08	.04
71T	Larry Milbourne	.10	.08	.04
72T	Eddie Milner(FC)	.20	.15	.08
73T	Sid Monge	.10	.08	.04
74T	Jose Morales	.10	.08	.04
75T	Keith Moreland	.20	.15	.08
76T	John Montefusco	.10	.08	.04
77T	Jim Morrison	.10	.08	.04
78T	Rance Mulliniks	.10	.08	.04
79T	Steve Mura	.10	.08	.04
80T	Gene Nelson	.10	.08	.04
81T	Joe Nolan	.10	.08	.04
82T	Dickie Noles	.10	.08	.04
83T	Al Oliver	.30	.25	.12
84T	Jorge Orta	.10	.08	.04
85T	Tom Paciorek	.10	.08	.04
86T	Larry Parrish	.20	.15	.08
87T	Jack Perconte	.10	.08	.04
88T	Gaylord Perry	1.75	1.25	.70
89T	Rob Picciolo	.10	.08	.04
90T	Joe Pittman	.10	.08	.04
91T	Hosken Powell	.10	.08	.04
92T	Mike Proly	.10	.08	.04
93T	Greg Pryor	.10	.08	.04
94T	Charlie Puleo(FC)	.15	.11	.06
95T	Shane Rawley	.20	.15	.08
96T	Johnny Ray	.80	.60	.30
97T	Dave Revering	.10	.08	.04
98T	Cal Ripken	25.00	20.00	10.00
99T	Allen Ripley	.10	.08	.04
100T	Bill Robinson	.10	.08	.04
101T	Aurelio Rodriguez	.15	.11	.06
102T	Joe Rudi	.20	.15	.08
103T	Steve Sax	5.00	3.75	2.00
104T	Dan Schatzeder	.10	.08	.04
105T	Bob Shirley	.10	.08	.04
106T	Eric Show(FC)	.50	.40	.20
107T	Roy Smalley	.15	.11	.06
108T	Lonnie Smith	.15	.11	.06
109T	Ozzie Smith	7.00	5.25	2.75
110T	Reggie Smith	.20	.15	.08
111T	Lary Sorensen	.10	.08	.04
112T	Elias Sosa	.10	.08	.04
113T	Mike Stanton	.10	.08	.04
114T	Steve Stroughter	.10	.08	.04
115T	Champ Summers	.10	.08	.04
116T	Rick Sutcliffe	.50	.40	.20
117T	Frank Tanana	.20	.15	.08
118T	Frank Taveras	.10	.08	.04
119T	Garry Templeton	.20	.15	.08
120T	Alex Trevino	.10	.08	.04
121T	Jerry Turner	.10	.08	.04
122T	Ed Vande Berg(FC)	.15	.11	.06
123T	Tom Veryzer	.10	.08	.04
124T	Ron Washington	.10	.08	.04
125T	Bob Watson	.15	.11	.06
126T	Dennis Werth	.10	.08	.04
127T	Eddie Whitson	.15	.11	.06
128T	Rob Wilfong	.10	.08	.04
129T	Bump Wills	.10	.08	.04
130T	Gary Woods	.10	.08	.04
131T	Butch Wynegar	.15	.11	.06
132T	Checklist 1-132	.10	.08	.04

NOTE: A card number in parentheses ( ) indicates the set is unnumbered.

1983 Topps

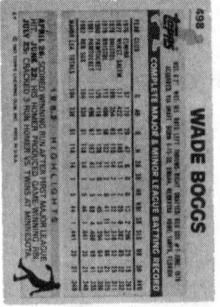

The 1983 Topps set totals 792 cards. Missing among the regular 2-1/2" by 3-1/2" cards are some form of future stars cards, as Topps was saving them for the now-established late season "Traded" set. The 1983 cards carry a large color photo as well as a smaller color photo on the front, quite similar in design to the 1963 set. Team colors frame the card, which, at the bottom, have the player's name, position and team. At the upper right-hand corner is a Topps Logo. The backs are horizontal and include statistics, personal information and 1982 highlights. Specialty cards include record-breaking performances, league leaders, All-Stars, numbered checklists "Team Leaders" and "Super Veteran" cards which are horizontal with a current and first-season picture of the honored player.

		MT	NR MT	EX
Complete Set:		125.00	87.00	52.00
Common Player:		.08	.06	.03
1	Record Breaker (Tony Armas)	.12	.09	.05
2	Record Breaker (Rickey Henderson)	.50	.40	.20
3	Record Breaker (Greg Minton)	.08	.06	.03
4	Record Breaker (Lance Parrish)	.20	.15	.08
5	Record Breaker (Manny Trillo)	.08	.06	.03
6	Record Breaker (John Wathan)	.08	.06	.03
7	Gene Richards	.08	.06	.03
8	Steve Balboni	.10	.08	.04
9	Joey McLaughlin	.08	.06	.03
10	Gorman Thomas	.12	.09	.05
11	Billy Gardner	.08	.06	.03
12	Paul Mirabella	.08	.06	.03
13	Larry Herndon	.10	.08	.04
14	Frank LaCorte	.08	.06	.03
15	Ron Cey	.15	.11	.06
16	George Vukovich	.08	.06	.03
17	Kent Tekulve	.10	.08	.04
18	Super Veteran (Kent Tekulve)	.10	.08	.04
19	Oscar Gamble	.10	.08	.04
20	Carlton Fisk	.60	.45	.25
21	Orioles Batting & Pitching Ldrs. (Eddie Murray, Jim Palmer)	.35	.25	.14
22	Randy Martz	.08	.06	.03
23	Mike Heath	.08	.06	.03
24	Steve Mura	.08	.06	.03
25	Hal McRae	.15	.11	.06
26	Jerry Royster	.08	.06	.03
27	Doug Corbett	.08	.06	.03
28	Bruce Bochte	.08	.06	.03
29	Randy Jones	.10	.08	.04
30	Jim Rice	.70	.50	.30
31	Bill Gullickson	.08	.06	.03
32	Dave Bergman	.08	.06	.03
33	Jack O'Connor	.08	.06	.03
34	Paul Householder	.08	.06	.03
35	Rollie Fingers	.30	.25	.12
36	Super Veteran (Rollie Fingers)	.15	.11	.06
37	Darrell Johnson	.08	.06	.03
38	Tim Flannery	.08	.06	.03
39	Terry Puhl	.08	.06	.03
40	Fernando Valenzuela	.50	.40	.20
41	Jerry Turner	.08	.06	.03
42	Dale Murray	.08	.06	.03
43	Bob Dernier	.08	.06	.03
44	Don Robinson	.10	.08	.04
45	John Mayberry	.10	.08	.04
46	Richard Dotson	.12	.09	.05
47	Dave McKay	.08	.06	.03
48	Lary Sorensen	.08	.06	.03
49	Willie McGee(FC)	4.00	3.00	1.50
50	Bob Horner	.20	.15	.08
51	Cubs Batting & Pitching Ldrs. (Leon Durham, Fergie Jenkins)	.15	.11	.06
52	Onix Concepcion(FC)	.08	.06	.03
53	Mike Witt	.30	.25	.12
54	Jim Maler	.08	.06	.03
55	Mookie Wilson	.12	.09	.05
56	Chuck Rainey	.08	.06	.03
57	Tim Blackwell	.08	.06	.03
58	Al Holland	.08	.06	.03
59	Benny Ayala	.08	.06	.03
60	Johnny Bench	.60	.45	.25
61	Super Veteran (Johnny Bench)	.30	.25	.12
62	Bob McClure	.08	.06	.03
63	Rick Monday	.12	.09	.05
64	Bill Stein	.08	.06	.03
65	Jack Morris	.35	.25	.14
66	Bob Lillis	.08	.06	.03
67	Sal Butera	.08	.06	.03
68	Eric Show	.30	.25	.12
69	Lee Lacy	.08	.06	.03
70	Steve Carlton	.60	.45	.25
71	Super Veteran (Steve Carlton)	.30	.25	.12
72	Tom Paciorek	.08	.06	.03
73	Allen Ripley	.08	.06	.03
74	Julio Gonzalez	.08	.06	.03
75	Amos Otis	.10	.08	.04
76	Rick Mahler	.12	.09	.05
77	Hosken Powell	.08	.06	.03
78	Bill Caudill	.08	.06	.03
79	Mick Kelleher	.08	.06	.03
80	George Foster	.20	.15	.08
81	Yankees Batting & Pitching Ldrs. (Jerry Mumphrey, Dave Righetti)	.15	.11	.06
82	Bruce Hurst	.15	.11	.06
83	Ryne Sandberg(FC)	45.00	33.00	17.00
84	Milt May	.08	.06	.03
85	Ken Singleton	.12	.09	.05
86	Tom Hume	.08	.06	.03
87	Joe Rudi	.12	.09	.05
88	Jim Gantner	.10	.08	.04
89	Leon Roberts	.08	.06	.03
90	Jerry Reuss	.12	.09	.05
91	Larry Milbourne	.08	.06	.03
92	Mike LaCoss	.08	.06	.03
93	John Castino	.08	.06	.03
94	Dave Edwards	.08	.06	.03
95	Alan Trammell	.50	.40	.20
96	Dick Howser	.08	.06	.03
97	Ross Baumgarten	.08	.06	.03
98	Vance Law	.10	.08	.04
99	Dickie Noles	.08	.06	.03
100	Pete Rose	1.75	1.25	.70
101	Super Veteran (Pete Rose)	.80	.60	.30
102	Dave Beard	.08	.06	.03
103	Darrell Porter	.10	.08	.04
104	Bob Walk	.08	.06	.03
105	Don Baylor	.15	.11	.06
106	Gene Nelson	.08	.06	.03
107	Mike Jorgensen	.08	.06	.03
108	Glenn Hoffman	.08	.06	.03
109	Luis Leal	.08	.06	.03
110	Ken Griffey	.15	.11	.06
111	Expos Batting & Pitching Ldrs. (Al Oliver, Steve Rogers)	.15	.11	.06
112	Bob Shirley	.08	.06	.03
113	Ron Roenicke	.08	.06	.03
114	Jim Slaton	.08	.06	.03
115	Chili Davis	.20	.15	.08
116	Dave Schmidt	.10	.08	.04
117	Alan Knicely	.08	.06	.03
118	Chris Welsh	.08	.06	.03
119	Tom Brookens	.08	.06	.03
120	Len Barker	.10	.08	.04
121	Mickey Hatcher	.10	.08	.04
122	Jimmy Smith	.08	.06	.03
123	George Frazier	.08	.06	.03
124	Marc Hill	.08	.06	.03
125	Leon Durham	.10	.08	.04
126	Joe Torre	.10	.08	.04
127	Preston Hanna	.08	.06	.03
128	Mike Ramsey	.08	.06	.03
129	Checklist 1-132	.12	.09	.05
130	Dave Stieb	.20	.15	.08
131	Ed Ott	.08	.06	.03

	MT	NR MT	EX
132 Todd Cruz	.08	.06	.03
133 Jim Barr	.08	.06	.03
134 Hubie Brooks	.15	.11	.06
135 Dwight Evans	.25	.20	.10
136 Willie Aikens	.08	.06	.03
137 Woodie Fryman	.10	.08	.04
138 Rick Dempsey	.10	.08	.04
139 Bruce Berenyi	.08	.06	.03
140 Willie Randolph	.12	.09	.05
141 Indians Batting & Pitching Ldrs. (Toby Harrah, Rick Sutcliffe)	.12	.09	.05
142 Mike Caldwell	.08	.06	.03
143 Joe Pettini	.08	.06	.03
144 Mark Wagner	.08	.06	.03
145 Don Sutton	.40	.30	.15
146 Super Veteran (Don Sutton)	.20	.15	.08
147 Rick Leach	.08	.06	.03
148 Dave Roberts	.08	.06	.03
149 Johnny Ray	.15	.11	.06
150 Bruce Sutter	.20	.15	.08
151 Super Veteran (Bruce Sutter)	.12	.09	.05
152 Jay Johnstone	.10	.08	.04
153 Jerry Koosman	.12	.09	.05
154 Johnnie LeMaster	.08	.06	.03
155 Dan Quisenberry	.20	.15	.08
156 Billy Martin	.12	.09	.05
157 Steve Bedrosian	.25	.20	.10
158 Rob Wilfong	.08	.06	.03
159 Mike Stanton	.08	.06	.03
160 Dave Kingman	.20	.15	.08
161 Super Veteran (Dave Kingman)	.10	.08	.04
162 Mark Clear	.08	.06	.03
163 Cal Ripken	5.00	3.75	2.00
164 Dave Palmer	.08	.06	.03
165 Dan Driessen	.10	.08	.04
166 John Pacella	.08	.06	.03
167 Mark Brouhard	.08	.06	.03
168 Juan Eichelberger	.08	.06	.03
169 Doug Flynn	.08	.06	.03
170 Steve Howe	.10	.08	.04
171 Giants Batting & Pitching Ldrs. (Bill Laskey, Joe Morgan)	.15	.11	.06
172 Vern Ruhle	.08	.06	.03
173 Jim Morrison	.08	.06	.03
174 Jerry Ujdur	.08	.06	.03
175 Bo Diaz	.10	.08	.04
176 Dave Righetti	.35	.25	.14
177 Harold Baines	.25	.20	.10
178 Luis Tiant	.15	.11	.06
179 Super Veteran (Luis Tiant)	.10	.08	.04
180 Rickey Henderson	6.00	4.50	2.50
181 Terry Felton	.08	.06	.03
182 Mike Fischlin	.08	.06	.03
183 *Ed Vande Berg*	.12	.09	.05
184 Bob Clark	.08	.06	.03
185 Tim Lollar	.08	.06	.03
186 Whitey Herzog	.10	.08	.04
187 Terry Leach	.12	.09	.05
188 Rick Miller	.08	.06	.03
189 Dan Schatzeder	.08	.06	.03
190 Cecil Cooper	.20	.15	.08
191 Joe Price	.08	.06	.03
192 Floyd Rayford	.08	.06	.03
193 Harry Spilman	.08	.06	.03
194 Cesar Geronimo	.08	.06	.03
195 Bob Stoddard	.08	.06	.03
196 Bill Fahey	.08	.06	.03
197 *Jim Eisenreich*(FC)	.15	.11	.06
198 Kiko Garcia	.08	.06	.03
199 Marty Bystrom	.08	.06	.03
200 Rod Carew	.70	.50	.30
201 Super Veteran (Rod Carew)	.35	.25	.14
202 Blue Jays Batting & Pitching Ldrs. (Damaso Garcia, Dave Stieb)	.12	.09	.05
203 Mike Morgan	.15	.11	.06
204 Junior Kennedy	.08	.06	.03
205 Dave Parker	.40	.30	.15
206 Ken Oberkfell	.08	.06	.03
207 Rick Camp	.08	.06	.03
208 Dan Meyer	.08	.06	.03
209 *Mike Moore*(FC)	2.00	1.50	.70
210 Jack Clark	.30	.25	.12
211 John Denny	.08	.06	.03
212 John Stearns	.08	.06	.03
213 Tom Burgmeier	.08	.06	.03
214 Jerry White	.08	.06	.03
215 Mario Soto	.10	.08	.04
216 Tony LaRussa	.10	.08	.04
217 Tim Stoddard	.08	.06	.03
218 Roy Howell	.08	.06	.03
219 Mike Armstrong	.08	.06	.03

	MT	NR MT	EX
220 Dusty Baker	.12	.09	.05
221 Joe Niekro	.15	.11	.06
222 Damaso Garcia	.08	.06	.03
223 John Montefusco	.08	.06	.03
224 Mickey Rivers	.10	.08	.04
225 Enos Cabell	.08	.06	.03
226 Enrique Romo	.08	.06	.03
227 Chris Bando	.08	.06	.03
228 Joaquin Andujar	.10	.08	.04
229 Phillies Batting & Pitching Ldrs. (Steve Carlton, Bo Diaz)	.20	.15	.08
230 Fergie Jenkins	.25	.20	.10
231 Super Veteran (Fergie Jenkins)	.12	.09	.05
232 Tom Brunansky	.30	.25	.12
233 Wayne Gross	.08	.06	.03
234 Larry Andersen	.08	.06	.03
235 Claudell Washington	.10	.08	.04
236 Steve Renko	.08	.06	.03
237 Dan Norman	.08	.06	.03
238 *Bud Black*(FC)	.25	.20	.10
239 Dave Stapleton	.08	.06	.03
240 Rich Gossage	.30	.25	.12
241 Super Veteran (Rich Gossage)	.15	.11	.06
242 Joe Nolan	.08	.06	.03
243 Duane Walker	.08	.06	.03
244 Dwight Bernard	.08	.06	.03
245 Steve Sax	.35	.25	.14
246 George Bamberger	.08	.06	.03
247 Dave Smith	.12	.09	.05
248 Bake McBride	.08	.06	.03
249 Checklist 133-264	.12	.09	.05
250 Bill Buckner	.15	.11	.06
251 *Alan Wiggins*(FC)	.08	.06	.03
252 Luis Aguayo	.08	.06	.03
253 Larry McWilliams	.08	.06	.03
254 Rick Cerone	.08	.06	.03
255 Gene Garber	.08	.06	.03
256 Super Veteran (Gene Garber)	.08	.06	.03
257 Jesse Barfield	.50	.40	.20
258 Manny Castillo	.08	.06	.03
259 Jeff Jones	.08	.06	.03
260 Steve Kemp	.12	.09	.05
261 Tigers Batting & Pitching Ldrs. (Larry Herndon, Dan Petry)	.10	.08	.04
262 Ron Jackson	.08	.06	.03
263 Renie Martin	.08	.06	.03
264 Jamie Quirk	.08	.06	.03
265 Joel Youngblood	.08	.06	.03
266 Paul Boris	.08	.06	.03
267 Terry Francona	.08	.06	.03
268 *Storm Davis*(FC)	.70	.50	.30
269 Ron Oester	.08	.06	.03
270 Dennis Eckersley	.20	.15	.08
271 Ed Romero	.08	.06	.03
272 Frank Tanana	.12	.09	.05
273 Mark Belanger	.10	.08	.04
274 Terry Kennedy	.12	.09	.05
275 Ray Knight	.12	.09	.05
276 Gene Mauch	.10	.08	.04
277 Rance Mulliniks	.08	.06	.03
278 Kevin Hickey	.08	.06	.03
279 Greg Gross	.08	.06	.03
280 Bert Blyleven	.20	.15	.08
281 Andre Robertson	.08	.06	.03
282 Reggie Smith	.12	.09	.05
283 Super Veteran (Reggie Smith)	.10	.08	.04
284 Jeff Lahti	.08	.06	.03
285 Lance Parrish	.40	.30	.15
286 Rick Langford	.08	.06	.03
287 Bobby Brown	.08	.06	.03
288 *Joe Cowley*(FC)	.12	.09	.05
289 Jerry Dybzinski	.08	.06	.03
290 Jeff Reardon	.15	.11	.06
291 Pirates Batting & Pitching Ldrs. (John Candelaria, Bill Madlock)	.15	.11	.06
292 Craig Swan	.08	.06	.03
293 Glenn Gulliver	.08	.06	.03
294 Dave Engle	.08	.06	.03
295 Jerry Remy	.08	.06	.03
296 Greg Harris	.08	.06	.03
297 Ned Yost	.08	.06	.03
298 Floyd Chiffer	.08	.06	.03
299 George Wright	.08	.06	.03
300 Mike Schmidt	2.25	1.75	.90
301 Super Veteran (Mike Schmidt)	.60	.45	.25
302 Ernie Whitt	.10	.08	.04
303 Miguel Dilone	.08	.06	.03
304 Dave Rucker	.08	.06	.03
305 Larry Bowa	.15	.11	.06
306 Tom Lasorda	.12	.09	.05
307 Lou Piniella	.15	.11	.06

		MT	NR MT	EX
308	Jesus Vega	.08	.06	.03
309	Jeff Leonard	.12	.09	.05
310	Greg Luzinski	.15	.11	.06
311	Glenn Brummer	.08	.06	.03
312	Brian Kingman	.08	.06	.03
313	Gary Gray	.08	.06	.03
314	Ken Dayley(FC)	.15	.11	.06
315	Rick Burleson	.10	.08	.04
316	Paul Splittorff	.08	.06	.03
317	Gary Rajsich	.08	.06	.03
318	John Tudor	.15	.11	.06
319	Lenn Sakata	.08	.06	.03
320	Steve Rogers	.10	.08	.04
321	Brewers Batting & Pitching Ldrs. (Pete Vuckovich, Robin Yount)	.20	.15	.08
322	Dave Van Gorder	.08	.06	.03
323	Luis DeLeon	.08	.06	.03
324	Mike Marshall	.30	.25	.12
325	Von Hayes	.20	.15	.08
326	Garth Iorg	.08	.06	.03
327	Bobby Castillo	.08	.06	.03
328	Craig Reynolds	.08	.06	.03
329	Randy Niemann	.08	.06	.03
330	Buddy Bell	.15	.11	.06
331	Mike Krukow	.10	.08	.04
332	Glenn Wilson(FC)	.30	.25	.12
333	Dave LaRoche	.08	.06	.03
334	Super Veteran (Dave LaRoche)	.08	.06	.03
335	Steve Henderson	.08	.06	.03
336	Rene Lachemann	.08	.06	.03
337	Tito Landrum	.08	.06	.03
338	Bob Owchinko	.08	.06	.03
339	Terry Harper	.08	.06	.03
340	Larry Gura	.08	.06	.03
341	Doug DeCinces	.15	.11	.06
342	Atlee Hammaker	.10	.08	.04
343	Bob Bailor	.08	.06	.03
344	Roger LaFrancois	.08	.06	.03
345	Jim Clancy	.10	.08	.04
346	Joe Pittman	.08	.06	.03
347	Sammy Stewart	.08	.06	.03
348	Alan Bannister	.08	.06	.03
349	Checklist 265-396	.12	.09	.05
350	Robin Yount	1.50	1.25	.60
351	Reds Batting & Pitching Ldrs. (Cesar Cedeno, Mario Soto)	.12	.09	.05
352	Mike Scioscia	.10	.08	.04
353	Steve Comer	.08	.06	.03
354	Randy Johnson	.08	.06	.03
355	Jim Bibby	.08	.06	.03
356	Gary Woods	.08	.06	.03
357	Len Matuszek(FC)	.08	.06	.03
358	Jerry Garvin	.08	.06	.03
359	Dave Collins	.10	.08	.04
360	Nolan Ryan	4.00	3.00	1.50
361	Super Veteran (Nolan Ryan)	.30	.25	.12
362	Bill Almon	.08	.06	.03
363	John Stuper(FC)	.08	.06	.03
364	Brett Butler	.20	.15	.08
365	Dave Lopes	.12	.09	.05
366	Dick Williams	.08	.06	.03
367	Bud Anderson	.08	.06	.03
368	Richie Zisk	.10	.08	.04
369	Jesse Orosco	.15	.11	.06
370	Gary Carter	.50	.40	.20
371	Mike Richardt	.08	.06	.03
372	Terry Crowley	.08	.06	.03
373	Kevin Saucier	.08	.06	.03
374	Wayne Krenchicki	.08	.06	.03
375	Pete Vuckovich	.10	.08	.04
376	Ken Landreaux	.08	.06	.03
377	Lee May	.10	.08	.04
378	Super Veteran (Lee May)	.10	.08	.04
379	Guy Sularz	.08	.06	.03
380	Ron Davis	.08	.06	.03
381	Red Sox Batting & Pitching Ldrs. (Jim Rice, Bob Stanley)	.25	.20	.10
382	Bob Knepper	.12	.09	.05
383	Ozzie Virgil	.10	.08	.04
384	Dave Dravecky(FC)	1.25	.90	.50
385	Mike Easler	.10	.08	.04
386	Rod Carew AS	.35	.25	.14
387	Bob Grich AS	.10	.08	.04
388	George Brett AS	.50	.40	.20
389	Robin Yount AS	.25	.20	.10
390	Reggie Jackson AS	.50	.40	.20
391	Rickey Henderson AS	.70	.50	.30
392	Fred Lynn AS	.15	.11	.06
393	Carlton Fisk AS	.15	.11	.06
394	Pete Vuckovich AS	.10	.08	.04
395	Larry Gura AS	.08	.06	.03
396	Dan Quisenberry AS	.12	.09	.05
397	Pete Rose AS	.70	.50	.30
398	Manny Trillo AS	.10	.08	.04
399	Mike Schmidt AS	.60	.45	.25
400	Dave Concepcion AS	.12	.09	.05
401	Dale Murphy AS	.70	.50	.30
402	Andre Dawson AS	.20	.15	.08
403	Tim Raines AS	.35	.25	.14
404	Gary Carter AS	.35	.25	.14
405	Steve Rogers AS	.10	.08	.04
406	Steve Carlton AS	.35	.25	.14
407	Bruce Sutter AS	.12	.09	.05
408	Rudy May	.08	.06	.03
409	Marvis Foley	.08	.06	.03
410	Phil Niekro	.40	.30	.15
411	Super Veteran (Phil Niekro)	.20	.15	.08
412	Rangers Batting & Pitching Ldrs. (Buddy Bell, Charlie Hough)	.15	.11	.06
413	Matt Keough	.08	.06	.03
414	Julio Cruz	.08	.06	.03
415	Bob Forsch	.10	.08	.04
416	Joe Ferguson	.08	.06	.03
417	Tom Hausman	.08	.06	.03
418	Greg Pryor	.08	.06	.03
419	Steve Crawford	.08	.06	.03
420	Al Oliver	.20	.15	.08
421	Super Veteran (Al Oliver)	.12	.09	.05
422	George Cappuzzello	.08	.06	.03
423	Tom Lawless(FC)	.10	.08	.04
424	Jerry Augustine	.08	.06	.03
425	Pedro Guerrero	.35	.25	.14
426	Earl Weaver	.10	.08	.04
427	Roy Lee Jackson	.08	.06	.03
428	Champ Summers	.08	.06	.03
429	Eddie Whitson	.08	.06	.03
430	Kirk Gibson	.50	.40	.20
431	Gary Gaetti(FC)	5.00	3.75	2.00
432	Porfirio Altamirano	.08	.06	.03
433	Dale Berra	.08	.06	.03
434	Dennis Lamp	.08	.06	.03
435	Tony Armas	.12	.09	.05
436	Bill Campbell	.08	.06	.03
437	Rick Sweet	.08	.06	.03
438	Dave LaPoint(FC)	.40	.30	.15
439	Rafael Ramirez	.08	.06	.03
440	Ron Guidry	.30	.25	.12
441	Astros Batting & Pitching Ldrs. (Ray Knight, Joe Niekro)	.12	.09	.05
442	Brian Downing	.12	.09	.05
443	Don Hood	.08	.06	.03
444	Wally Backman(FC)	.25	.20	.10
445	Mike Flanagan	.12	.09	.05
446	Reid Nichols	.08	.06	.03
447	Bryn Smith	.10	.08	.04
448	Darrell Evans	.20	.15	.08
449	Eddie Milner	.12	.09	.05
450	Ted Simmons	.20	.15	.08
451	Super Veteran (Ted Simmons)	.12	.09	.05
452	Lloyd Moseby	.15	.11	.06
453	Lamar Johnson	.08	.06	.03
454	Bob Welch	.15	.11	.06
455	Sixto Lezcano	.08	.06	.03
456	Lee Elia	.08	.06	.03
457	Milt Wilcox	.08	.06	.03
458	Ron Washington	.08	.06	.03
459	Ed Farmer	.08	.06	.03
460	Roy Smalley	.08	.06	.03
461	Steve Trout	.08	.06	.03
462	Steve Nicosia	.08	.06	.03
463	Gaylord Perry	.40	.30	.15
464	Super Veteran (Gaylord Perry)	.20	.15	.08
465	Lonnie Smith	.10	.08	.04
466	Tom Underwood	.08	.06	.03
467	Rufino Linares	.08	.06	.03
468	Dave Goltz	.10	.08	.04
469	Ron Gardenhire	.08	.06	.03
470	Greg Minton	.08	.06	.03
471	Royals Batting & Pitching Ldrs. (Vida Blue, Willie Wilson)	.15	.11	.06
472	Gary Allenson	.08	.06	.03
473	John Lowenstein	.08	.06	.03
474	Ray Burris	.08	.06	.03
475	Cesar Cedeno	.12	.09	.05
476	Rob Picciolo	.08	.06	.03
477	Tom Niedenfuer(FC)	.15	.11	.06
478	Phil Garner	.10	.08	.04
479	Charlie Hough	.12	.09	.05
480	Toby Harrah	.10	.08	.04
481	Scot Thompson	.08	.06	.03
482	Tony Gwynn(FC)	20.00	15.00	8.00
483	Lynn Jones	.08	.06	.03

	MT	NR MT	EX
484 Dick Ruthven	.08	.06	.03
485 Omar Moreno	.08	.06	.03
486 Clyde King	.08	.06	.03
487 Jerry Hairston	.08	.06	.03
488 Alfredo Griffin	.10	.08	.04
489 Tom Herr	.12	.09	.05
490 Jim Palmer	.50	.40	.20
491 Super Veteran (Jim Palmer)	.20	.15	.08
492 Paul Serna	.08	.06	.03
493 Steve McCatty	.08	.06	.03
494 Bob Brenly	.10	.08	.04
495 Warren Cromartie	.08	.06	.03
496 Tom Veryzer	.08	.06	.03
497 Rick Sutcliffe	.20	.15	.08
498 *Wade Boggs* (FC)	35.00	27.00	15.00
499 Jeff Little	.10	.08	.04
500 Reggie Jackson	.70	.50	.30
501 Super Veteran (Reggie Jackson)	.35	.25	.14
502 Braves Batting & Pitching Ldrs. (Dale Murphy, Phil Niekro)	.50	.40	.20
503 Moose Haas	.08	.06	.03
504 Don Werner	.08	.06	.03
505 Garry Templeton	.12	.09	.05
506 *Jim Gott* (FC)	.25	.20	.10
507 Tony Scott	.08	.06	.03
508 Tom Filer	.15	.11	.06
509 Lou Whitaker	.40	.30	.20
510 Tug McGraw	.15	.11	.06
511 Super Veteran (Tug McGraw)	.10	.08	.04
512 Doyle Alexander	.12	.09	.05
513 Fred Stanley	.08	.06	.03
514 Rudy Law	.08	.06	.03
515 Gene Tenace	.10	.08	.04
516 Bill Virdon	.08	.06	.03
517 Gary Ward	.10	.08	.04
518 Bill Laskey	.08	.06	.03
519 Terry Bulling	.08	.06	.03
520 Fred Lynn	.25	.20	.10
521 Bruce Benedict	.08	.06	.03
522 Pat Zachry	.08	.06	.03
523 Carney Lansford	.12	.09	.05
524 Tom Brennan	.08	.06	.03
525 Frank White	.12	.09	.05
526 Checklist 397-528	.12	.09	.05
527 Larry Biittner	.08	.06	.03
528 Jamie Easterly	.08	.06	.03
529 Tim Laudner	.10	.08	.04
530 Eddie Murray	.80	.60	.30
531 Athletics Batting & Pitching Ldrs. (Rickey Henderson, Rick Langford)	.30	.25	.12
532 Dave Stewart	2.00	1.50	.80
533 Luis Salazar	.08	.06	.03
534 John Butcher	.08	.06	.03
535 Manny Trillo	.10	.08	.04
536 Johnny Wockenfuss	.08	.06	.03
537 Rod Scurry	.08	.06	.03
538 Danny Heep	.08	.06	.03
539 Roger Erickson	.08	.06	.03
540 Ozzie Smith	.30	.25	.12
541 Britt Burns	.08	.06	.03
542 Jody Davis	.12	.09	.05
543 Alan Fowlkes	.08	.06	.03
544 Larry Whisenton	.08	.06	.03
545 Floyd Bannister	.12	.09	.05
546 Dave Garcia	.08	.06	.03
547 Geoff Zahn	.08	.06	.03
548 Brian Giles	.08	.06	.03
549 *Charlie Puleo*	.15	.11	.06
550 Carl Yastrzemski	1.00	.70	.40
551 Super Veteran (Carl Yastrzemski)	.40	.30	.15
552 Tim Wallach	.30	.25	.12
553 Denny Martinez	.10	.08	.04
554 Mike Vail	.08	.06	.03
555 Steve Yeager	.08	.06	.03
556 Willie Upshaw	.10	.08	.04
557 Rick Honeycutt	.08	.06	.03
558 Dickie Thon	.10	.08	.04
559 Pete Redfern	.08	.06	.03
560 Ron LeFlore	.10	.08	.04
561 Cardinals Batting & Pitching Ldrs. (Joaquin Andujar, Lonnie Smith)	.12	.09	.05
562 Dave Rozema	.08	.06	.03
563 Juan Bonilla	.08	.06	.03
564 Sid Monge	.08	.06	.03
565 Bucky Dent	.12	.09	.05
566 Manny Sarmiento	.08	.06	.03
567 Joe Simpson	.08	.06	.03
568 Willie Hernandez	.12	.09	.05
569 Jack Perconte	.08	.06	.03
570 Vida Blue	.15	.11	.06
571 Mickey Klutts	.08	.06	.03

	MT	NR MT	EX
572 Bob Watson	.10	.08	.04
573 Andy Hassler	.08	.06	.03
574 Glenn Adams	.08	.06	.03
575 Neil Allen	.08	.06	.03
576 Frank Robinson	.12	.09	.05
577 Luis Aponte	.08	.06	.03
578 David Green	.08	.06	.03
579 Rich Dauer	.08	.06	.03
580 Tom Seaver	1.00	.70	.40
581 Super Veteran (Tom Seaver)	.30	.25	.12
582 Marshall Edwards	.08	.06	.03
583 Terry Forster	.10	.08	.04
584 Dave Hostetler	.08	.06	.03
585 Jose Cruz	.15	.11	.06
586 *Frank Viola* (FC)	10.00	7.50	4.00
587 Ivan DeJesus	.08	.06	.03
588 Pat Underwood	.08	.06	.03
589 Alvis Woods	.08	.06	.03
590 Tony Pena	.12	.09	.05
591 White Sox Batting & Pitching Ldrs. (LaMarr Hoyt, Greg Luzinski)	.15	.11	.06
592 Shane Rawley	.12	.09	.05
593 Broderick Perkins	.08	.06	.03
594 Eric Rasmussen	.08	.06	.03
595 Tim Raines	.50	.40	.20
596 Randy Johnson	.08	.06	.03
597 Mike Proly	.08	.06	.03
598 Dwayne Murphy	.10	.08	.04
599 Don Aase	.08	.06	.03
600 George Brett	1.00	.70	.40
601 Ed Lynch	.08	.06	.03
602 Rich Gedman	.12	.09	.05
603 Joe Morgan	.40	.30	.15
604 Super Veteran (Joe Morgan)	.15	.11	.06
605 Gary Roenicke	.08	.06	.03
606 Bobby Cox	.08	.06	.03
607 Charlie Leibrandt	.10	.08	.04
608 Don Money	.08	.06	.03
609 Danny Darwin	.08	.06	.03
610 Steve Garvey	.70	.50	.30
611 Bert Roberge	.08	.06	.03
612 Steve Swisher	.08	.06	.03
613 Mike Ivie	.08	.06	.03
614 Ed Glynn	.08	.06	.03
615 Garry Maddox	.12	.09	.05
616 Bill Nahorodny	.08	.06	.03
617 Butch Wynegar	.08	.06	.03
618 LaMarr Hoyt	.08	.06	.03
619 Keith Moreland	.10	.08	.04
620 Mike Norris	.08	.06	.03
621 Mets Batting & Pitching Ldrs. (Craig Swan, Mookie Wilson)	.12	.09	.05
622 Dave Edler	.08	.06	.03
623 Luis Sanchez	.08	.06	.03
624 Glenn Hubbard	.10	.08	.04
625 Ken Forsch	.08	.06	.03
626 Jerry Martin	.08	.06	.03
627 Doug Bair	.08	.06	.03
628 Julio Valdez	.08	.06	.03
629 Charlie Lea	.08	.06	.03
630 Paul Molitor	.30	.25	.12
631 Tippy Martinez	.08	.06	.03
632 Alex Trevino	.08	.06	.03
633 Vicente Romo	.08	.06	.03
634 Max Venable	.08	.06	.03
635 Graig Nettles	.20	.15	.08
636 Super Veteran (Graig Nettles)	.12	.09	.05
637 Pat Corrales	.08	.06	.03
638 Dan Petry	.10	.08	.04
639 Art Howe	.08	.06	.03
640 Andre Thornton	.12	.09	.05
641 Billy Sample	.08	.06	.03
642 Checklist 529-660	.12	.09	.05
643 Bump Wills	.08	.06	.03
644 Joe Lefebvre	.08	.06	.03
645 Bill Madlock	.15	.11	.06
646 Jim Essian	.08	.06	.03
647 Bobby Mitchell	.08	.06	.03
648 Jeff Burroughs	.10	.08	.04
649 Tommy Boggs	.08	.06	.03
650 George Hendrick	.10	.08	.04
651 Angels Batting & Pitching Ldrs. (Rod Carew, Mike Witt)	.30	.25	.12
652 Butch Hobson	.08	.06	.03
653 Ellis Valentine	.08	.06	.03
654 Bob Ojeda	.15	.11	.06
655 Al Bumbry	.10	.08	.04
656 Dave Frost	.08	.06	.03
657 Mike Gates	.08	.06	.03
658 Frank Pastore	.08	.06	.03
659 Charlie Moore	.08	.06	.03

		MT	NR MT	EX
560	Mike Hargrove	.08	.06	.03
561	Bill Russell	.10	.08	.04
562	Joe Sambito	.08	.06	.03
563	Tom O'Malley	.08	.06	.03
564	Bob Molinaro	.08	.06	.03
565	Jim Sundberg	.10	.08	.04
566	Sparky Anderson	.12	.09	.05
567	Dick Davis	.08	.06	.03
568	Larry Christenson	.08	.06	.03
569	Mike Squires	.08	.06	.03
570	Jerry Mumphrey	.08	.06	.03
571	Lenny Faedo	.08	.06	.03
572	Jim Kaat	.20	.15	.08
573	Super Veteran (Jim Kaat)	.12	.09	.05
574	Kurt Bevacqua	.08	.06	.03
575	Jim Beattie	.08	.06	.03
576	Biff Pocoroba	.08	.06	.03
577	Dave Revering	.08	.06	.03
578	Juan Beniquez	.08	.06	.03
579	Mike Scott	.20	.15	.08
580	Andre Dawson	.80	.60	.30
581	Dodgers Batting & Pitching Ldrs. (Pedro Guerrero, Fernando Valenzuela)	.25	.20	.10
582	Bob Stanley	.08	.06	.03
583	Dan Ford	.08	.06	.03
584	Rafael Landestoy	.08	.06	.03
585	Lee Mazzilli	.10	.08	.04
586	Randy Lerch	.08	.06	.03
587	U.L. Washington	.08	.06	.03
588	Jim Wohlford	.08	.06	.03
589	Ron Hassey	.08	.06	.03
590	Kent Hrbek	.70	.50	.30
591	Dave Tobik	.08	.06	.03
592	Denny Walling	.08	.06	.03
593	Sparky Lyle	.12	.09	.05
594	Super Veteran (Sparky Lyle)	.10	.08	.04
595	Ruppert Jones	.08	.06	.03
596	Chuck Tanner	.08	.06	.03
597	Barry Foote	.08	.06	.03
598	Tony Bernazard	.08	.06	.03
599	Lee Smith	.20	.15	.08
700	Keith Hernandez	.50	.40	.20
701	Batting Leaders (Al Oliver, Willie Wilson)	.15	.11	.06
702	Home Run Leaders (Reggie Jackson, Dave Kingman, Gorman Thomas)	.25	.20	.10
703	Runs Batted In Leaders (Hal McRae, Dale Murphy, Al Oliver)	.35	.25	.14
704	Stolen Base Leaders (Rickey Henderson, Tim Raines)	.35	.25	.14
705	Victory Leaders (Steve Carlton, LaMarr Hoyt)	.20	.15	.08
706	Strikeout Leaders (Floyd Bannister, Steve Carlton)	.20	.15	.08
707	Earned Run Average Leaders (Steve Rogers, Rick Sutcliffe)	.12	.09	.05
708	Leading Firemen (Dan Quisenberry, Bruce Sutter)	.15	.11	.06
709	Jimmy Sexton	.08	.06	.03
710	Willie Wilson	.20	.15	.08
711	Mariners Batting & Pitching Ldrs. (Jim Beattie, Bruce Bochte)	.12	.09	.05
712	Bruce Kison	.08	.06	.03
713	Ron Hodges	.08	.06	.03
714	Wayne Nordhagen	.08	.06	.03
715	Tony Perez	.25	.20	.10
716	Super Veteran (Tony Perez)	.12	.09	.05
717	Scott Sanderson	.08	.06	.03
718	Jim Dwyer	.08	.06	.03
719	Rich Gale	.08	.06	.03
720	Dave Concepcion	.15	.11	.06
721	John Martin	.08	.06	.03
722	Jorge Orta	.08	.06	.03
723	Randy Moffitt	.08	.06	.03
724	Johnny Grubb	.08	.06	.03
725	Dan Spillner	.08	.06	.03
726	Harvey Kuenn	.10	.08	.04
727	Chet Lemon	.10	.08	.04
728	Ron Reed	.08	.06	.03
729	Jerry Morales	.08	.06	.03
730	Jason Thompson	.08	.06	.03
731	Al Williams	.08	.06	.03
732	Dave Henderson	.15	.11	.06
733	Buck Martinez	.08	.06	.03
734	Steve Braun	.08	.06	.03
735	Tommy John	.25	.20	.10
736	Super Veteran (Tommy John)	.12	.09	.05
737	Mitchell Page	.08	.06	.03
738	Tim Foli	.08	.06	.03
739	Rick Ownbey	.08	.06	.03
740	Rusty Staub	.15	.11	.06

		MT	NR MT	EX
741	Super Veteran (Rusty Staub)	.10	.08	.04
742	Padres Batting & Pitching Ldrs. (Terry Kennedy, Tim Lollar)	.12	.09	.05
743	Mike Torrez	.10	.08	.04
744	Brad Mills	.08	.06	.03
745	Scott McGregor	.10	.08	.04
746	John Wathan	.10	.08	.04
747	Fred Breining	.08	.06	.03
748	Derrel Thomas	.08	.06	.03
749	Jon Matlack	.10	.08	.04
750	Ben Oglivie	.10	.08	.04
751	Brad Havens	.08	.06	.03
752	Luis Pujols	.08	.06	.03
753	Elias Sosa	.08	.06	.03
754	Bill Robinson	.08	.06	.03
755	John Candelaria	.12	.09	.05
756	Russ Nixon	.08	.06	.03
757	Rick Manning	.08	.06	.03
758	Aurelio Rodriguez	.10	.08	.04
759	Doug Bird	.08	.06	.03
760	Dale Murphy	1.50	1.25	.60
761	Gary Lucas	.08	.06	.03
762	Cliff Johnson	.08	.06	.03
763	Al Cowens	.08	.06	.03
764	Pete Falcone	.08	.06	.03
765	Bob Boone	.12	.09	.05
766	Barry Bonnell	.08	.06	.03
767	Duane Kuiper	.08	.06	.03
768	Chris Speier	.08	.06	.03
769	Checklist 661-792	.12	.09	.05
770	Dave Winfield	.50	.40	.20
771	Twins Batting & Pitching Ldrs. (Bobby Castillo, Kent Hrbek)	.20	.15	.08
772	Jim Kern	.08	.06	.03
773	Larry Hisle	.10	.08	.04
774	Alan Ashby	.08	.06	.03
775	Burt Hooton	.10	.08	.04
776	Larry Parrish	.12	.09	.05
777	John Curtis	.08	.06	.03
778	Rich Hebner	.08	.06	.03
779	Rick Waits	.08	.06	.03
780	Gary Matthews	.12	.09	.05
781	Rick Rhoden	.12	.09	.05
782	Bobby Murcer	.12	.09	.05
783	Super Veteran (Bobby Murcer)	.10	.08	.04
784	Jeff Newman	.08	.06	.03
785	Dennis Leonard	.10	.08	.04
786	Ralph Houk	.10	.08	.04
787	Dick Tidrow	.08	.06	.03
788	Dane Iorg	.08	.06	.03
789	Bryan Clark	.08	.06	.03
790	Bob Grich	.12	.09	.05
791	Gary Lavelle	.08	.06	.03
792	Chris Chambliss	.10	.08	.04

1983 Topps All-Star Glossy Set Of 40

This set was a "consolation prize" in a scratch-off contest in regular packs of 1983 cards. The 2-1/2" by 3-1/2" cards have a large color photo surrounded by a yellow frame on the front. In very small type on a white border is printed the player's name. Backs carry the player's name, team, position and the card number along with a Topps identification. A major feature is that the surface of the front is glossy, which most collectors find very attractive. With many top stars, the set is a popular one, but the price has not moved too far above the issue price.

		MT	NR MT	EX
Complete Set:		13.00	9.75	5.25
Common Player:		.15	.11	.06
1	Carl Yastrzemski	1.00	.70	.40
2	Mookie Wilson	.15	.11	.06
3	Andre Thornton	.15	.11	.06
4	Keith Hernandez	.40	.30	.15
5	Robin Yount	.40	.30	.15
6	Terry Kennedy	.15	.11	.06
7	Dave Winfield	.60	.45	.25
8	Mike Schmidt	1.00	.70	.40
9	Buddy Bell	.20	.15	.08
10	Fernando Valenzuela	.50	.40	.20
11	Rich Gossage	.25	.20	.10
12	Bob Horner	.20	.15	.08
13	Toby Harrah	.15	.11	.06
14	Pete Rose	1.25	.90	.50
15	Cecil Cooper	.20	.15	.08
16	Dale Murphy	1.00	.70	.40
17	Carlton Fisk	.30	.25	.12
18	Ray Knight	.15	.11	.06
19	Jim Palmer	.40	.30	.15
20	Gary Carter	.50	.40	.20
21	Richard Zisk	.15	.11	.06
22	Dusty Baker	.15	.11	.06
23	Willie Wilson	.20	.15	.08
24	Bill Buckner	.15	.11	.06
25	Dave Stieb	.20	.15	.08
26	Bill Madlock	.20	.15	.08
27	Lance Parrish	.30	.25	.12
28	Nolan Ryan	1.00	.70	.40
29	Rod Carew	.60	.45	.25
30	Al Oliver	.20	.15	.08
31	George Brett	1.00	.70	.40
32	Jack Clark	.25	.20	.10
33	Rickey Henderson	.70	.50	.30
34	Dave Concepcion	.20	.15	.08
35	Kent Hrbek	.30	.25	.12
36	Steve Carlton	.50	.40	.20
37	Eddie Murray	.60	.45	.25
38	Ruppert Jones	.15	.11	.06
39	Reggie Jackson	.70	.50	.30
40	Bruce Sutter	.20	.15	.08

1983 Topps Foldouts

Another Topps test issue, these 3-1/2" by 5-5/16" cards were printed in booklets like souvenier postcards. Each of the booklets have a theme of currently playing statistical leaders in a specific category such as home runs. The cards feature a color player photo on each side. A black strip at the bottom gives the player's name, position and team along with statistics in the particular category. A facsimile autograph crosses the photograph. Booklets carry nine cards, with eight having players on both sides and one doubling as the back cover, for a total of 17 cards per booklet. There are 85 cards in the set, although some players appear in more than one category. Naturally, most of the players pictured are stars. Even so, the set is a problem as it seems to be most valuable when complete and unseparated, so the cards are difficult to display.

		MT	NR MT	EX
Complete Set:		8.00	6.00	3.25
Common Folder:		1.00	.70	.40

1	Pitching Leaders (Vida Blue, Bert Blyleven, Steve Carlton, Fergie Jenkins, Tommy John, Jim Kaat, Jerry Koosman, Joe Niekro, Phil Niekro, Jim Palmer, Gaylord Perry, Jerry Reuss, Nolan Ryan, Tom Seaver, Paul Splittorff, Don Sutton, Mike Torrez)			
		1.75	1.25	.70
2	Home Run Leaders (Johnny Bench, Ron Cey, Darrell Evans, George Foster, Reggie Jackson, Dave Kingman, Greg Luzinski, John Mayberry, Rick Monday, Joe Morgan, Bobby Murcer, Graig Nettles, Tony Perez, Jim Rice, Mike Schmidt, Rusty Staub, Carl Yastrzemski)			
		2.50	2.00	1.00
3	Batting Leaders (George Brett, Rod Carew, Cecil Cooper, Steve Garvey, Ken Griffey, Pedro Guerrero, Keith Hernandez, Dane Iorg, Fred Lynn, Bill Madlock, Bake McBride, Al Oliver, Dave Parker, Jim Rice, Pete Rose, Lonnie Smith, Willie Wilson)			
		2.50	2.00	1.00
4	Relief Aces (Tom Burgmeier, Bill Campbell, Ed Farmer, Rollie Fingers, Terry Forster, Gene Garber, Rich Gossage, Jim Kern, Gary Lavelle, Tug McGraw, Greg Minton, Randy Moffitt, Dan Quisenberry, Ron Reed, Elias Sosa, Bruce Sutter, Kent Tekulve)			
		1.00	.70	.40
5	Stolen Base Leaders (Don Baylor, Larry Bowa, Al Bumbry, Rod Carew, Cesar Cedeno, Dave Concepcion, Jose Cruz, Julio Cruz, Rickey Henderson, Ron LeFlore, Davey Lopes, Garry Maddox, Omar Moreno, Joe Morgan, Amos Otis, Mickey Rivers, Willie Wilson)			
		1.00	.70	.40

1983 Topps Traded

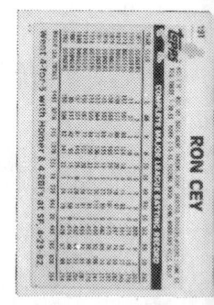

These 2-1/2" by 3-1/2" cards mark a continuation of the traded set introduced in 1981. The 132 cards retain the basic design of the year's regular issue, with their numbering being 1-132 with the "T" suffix. Cards in the set include traded players, new managers and promising rookies. Sold only through dealers, the set was in heavy demand as it contained the first cards of Darryl Strawberry, Ron Kittle, Julio Franco and Mel Hall. While some of those cards were very hot in 1983, it seems likely that some of the rookies may not live up to their initial promise.

		MT	NR MT	EX
Complete Set:		100.00	75.00	40.00
Common Player:		.10	.08	.04
1T	Neil Allen	.10	.08	.04
2T	Bill Almon	.10	.08	.04
3T	Joe Altobelli	.10	.08	.04
4T	Tony Armas	.20	.15	.08
5T	Doug Bair	.10	.08	.04
6T	Steve Baker	.10	.08	.04
7T	Floyd Bannister	.20	.15	.08
8T	Don Baylor	.30	.25	.12

		MT	NR MT	EX
9T	Tony Bernazard	.10	.08	.04
10T	Larry Biittner	.10	.08	.04
11T	Dann Bilardello	.10	.08	.04
12T	Doug Bird	.10	.08	.04
13T	Steve Boros	.10	.08	.04
14T	Greg Brock(FC)	.30	.25	.12
15T	Mike Brown	.10	.08	.04
16T	Tom Burgmeier	.10	.08	.04
17T	Randy Bush(FC)	.20	.15	.08
18T	Bert Campaneris	.20	.15	.08
19T	Ron Cey	.25	.20	.10
20T	Chris Codiroli(FC)	.15	.11	.06
21T	Dave Collins	.15	.11	.06
22T	Terry Crowley	.10	.08	.04
23T	Julio Cruz	.10	.08	.04
24T	Mike Davis	.15	.11	.06
25T	Frank DiPino	.10	.08	.04
26T	Bill Doran(FC)	2.50	2.00	1.00
27T	Jerry Dybzinski	.10	.08	.04
28T	Jamie Easterly	.10	.08	.04
29T	Juan Eichelberger	.10	.08	.04
30T	Jim Essian	.10	.08	.04
31T	Pete Falcone	.10	.08	.04
32T	Mike Ferraro	.10	.08	.04
33T	Terry Forster	.15	.11	.06
34T	Julio Franco(FC)	5.00	3.75	2.00
35T	Rich Gale	.10	.08	.04
36T	Kiko Garcia	.10	.08	.04
37T	Steve Garvey	1.50	1.25	.60
38T	Johnny Grubb	.10	.08	.04
39T	Mel Hall(FC)	.90	.70	.35
40T	Von Hayes	.90	.70	.35
41T	Danny Heep	.10	.08	.04
42T	Steve Henderson	.10	.08	.04
43T	Keith Hernandez	1.00	.70	.40
44T	Leo Hernandez	.10	.08	.04
45T	Willie Hernandez	.25	.20	.10
46T	Al Holland	.10	.08	.04
47T	Frank Howard	.15	.11	.06
48T	Bobby Johnson	.10	.08	.04
49T	Cliff Johnson	.10	.08	.04
50T	Odell Jones	.10	.08	.04
51T	Mike Jorgensen	.10	.08	.04
52T	Bob Kearney	.10	.08	.04
53T	Steve Kemp	.15	.11	.06
54T	Matt Keough	.10	.08	.04
55T	Ron Kittle(FC)	1.00	.70	.40
56T	Mickey Klutts	.10	.08	.04
57T	Alan Knicely	.10	.08	.04
58T	Mike Krukow	.15	.11	.06
59T	Rafael Landestoy	.10	.08	.04
60T	Carney Lansford	.25	.20	.10
61T	Joe Lefebvre	.10	.08	.04
62T	Bryan Little	.10	.08	.04
63T	Aurelio Lopez	.10	.08	.04
64T	Mike Madden	.10	.08	.04
65T	Rick Manning	.10	.08	.04
66T	Billy Martin	.20	.15	.08
67T	Lee Mazzilli	.15	.11	.06
68T	Andy McGaffigan	.10	.08	.04
69T	Craig McMurtry(FC)	.20	.15	.08
70T	John McNamara	.10	.08	.04
71T	Orlando Mercado	.10	.08	.04
72T	Larry Milbourne	.10	.08	.04
73T	Randy Moffitt	.10	.08	.04
74T	Sid Monge	.10	.08	.04
75T	Jose Morales	.10	.08	.04
76T	Omar Moreno	.10	.08	.04
77T	Joe Morgan	2.00	1.50	.80
78T	Mike Morgan	.10	.08	.04
79T	Dale Murray	.10	.08	.04
80T	Jeff Newman	.10	.08	.04
81T	Pete O'Brien(FC)	1.00	.70	.40
82T	Jorge Orta	.10	.08	.04
83T	Alejandro Pena(FC)	.60	.45	.25
84T	Pascual Perez	.20	.15	.08
85T	Tony Perez	.60	.45	.25
86T	Broderick Perkins	.10	.08	.04
87T	Tony Phillips(FC)	.20	.15	.08
88T	Charlie Puleo	.10	.08	.04
89T	Pat Putnam	.10	.08	.04
90T	Jamie Quirk	.10	.08	.04
91T	Doug Rader	.10	.08	.04
92T	Chuck Rainey	.10	.08	.04
93T	Bobby Ramos	.10	.08	.04
94T	Gary Redus(FC)	.40	.30	.15
95T	Steve Renko	.10	.08	.04
96T	Leon Roberts	.10	.08	.04
97T	Aurelio Rodriguez	.15	.11	.06
98T	Dick Ruthven	.10	.08	.04
99T	Daryl Sconiers	.10	.08	.04

		MT	NR MT	EX
100T	Mike Scott	.50	.40	.20
101T	Tom Seaver	4.00	3.00	1.50
102T	John Shelby(FC)	.40	.30	.15
103T	Bob Shirley	.10	.08	.04
104T	Joe Simpson	.10	.08	.04
105T	Doug Sisk(FC)	.15	.11	.06
106T	Mike Smithson(FC)	.20	.15	.08
107T	Elias Sosa	.10	.08	.04
108T	Darryl Strawberry(FC)	80.00	60.00	33.00
109T	Tom Tellmann	.10	.08	.04
110T	Gene Tenace	.15	.11	.06
111T	Gorman Thomas	.25	.20	.10
112T	Dick Tidrow	.10	.08	.04
113T	Dave Tobik	.10	.08	.04
114T	Wayne Tolleson(FC)	.20	.15	.08
115T	Mike Torrez	.15	.11	.06
116T	Manny Trillo	.15	.11	.06
117T	Steve Trout	.10	.08	.04
118T	Lee Tunnell(FC)	.15	.11	.06
119T	Mike Vail	.10	.08	.04
120T	Ellis Valentine	.10	.08	.04
121T	Tom Veryzer	.10	.08	.04
122T	George Vukovich	.10	.08	.04
123T	Rick Waits	.10	.08	.04
124T	Greg Walker(FC)	.40	.30	.15
125T	Chris Welsh	.10	.08	.04
126T	Len Whitehouse	.10	.08	.04
127T	Eddie Whitson	.15	.11	.06
128T	Jim Wohlford	.10	.08	.04
129T	Matt Young(FC)	.20	.15	.08
130T	Joel Youngblood	.10	.08	.04
131T	Pat Zachry	.10	.08	.04
132T	Checklist 1-132	.10	.08	.04

1984 Topps

 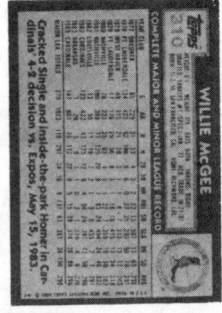

Another 792-card regular set from Topps. For the second straight year, the 2-1/2" by 3-1/2" cards featured a color action photo on the front along with a small portrait photo in the lower left. The team name runs in big letters down the left side, while the player's name and position runs under the large action photo. In the upper right-hand corner is the Topps logo. Backs have a team logo in the upper right corner, along with statistics, personal information and a few highlights. The backs have an unusual and hard-to-read red and purple coloring. Specialty cards include past season highlights, team leaders, major league statistical leaders, All-Stars, active career leaders and numbered checklists. Again, promising rookies were saved for the traded set. Late in 1984, Topps introduced a specially boxed "Tiffany" edition of the 1984 set, with the cards printed on white cardboard with a glossy finish. A total of 10,000 sets were produced. Prices for Tiffany edition superstars can run from six to eight times the value of the "regular" edition, while common cards sell in the 40¢ range.

		MT	NR MT	EX
Complete Set:		110.00	83.00	45.00
Common Player:		.08	.06	.03
1	1983 Highlight (Steve Carlton)	.30	.25	.12
2	1983 Highlight (Rickey Henderson)	.30	.25	.12
3	1983 Highlight (Dan Quisenberry)	.10	.08	.04

		MT	NR MT	EX
4	1983 Highlight (Steve Carlton, Gaylord Perry, Nolan Ryan)	.30	.25	.12
5	1983 Highlight (Bob Forsch, Dave Righetti, Mike Warren)	.15	.11	.06
6	1983 Highlight (Johnny Bench, Gaylord Perry, Carl Yastrzemski)	.40	.30	.15
7	Gary Lucas	.08	.06	.03
8	*Don Mattingly*(FC)	30.00	23.00	12.00
9	Jim Gott	.10	.08	.04
10	Robin Yount	1.00	.70	.40
11	Twins Batting & Pitching Leaders (Kent Hrbek, Ken Schrom)	.20	.15	.08
12	Billy Sample	.08	.06	.03
13	Scott Holman	.08	.06	.03
14	Tom Brookens	.08	.06	.03
15	Burt Hooton	.10	.08	.04
16	Omar Moreno	.08	.06	.03
17	John Denny	.08	.06	.03
18	Dale Berra	.08	.06	.03
19	*Ray Fontenot*(FC)	.10	.08	.04
20	Greg Luzinski	.12	.09	.05
21	Joe Altobelli	.08	.06	.03
22	Bryan Clark	.08	.06	.03
23	Keith Moreland	.10	.08	.04
24	John Martin	.08	.06	.03
25	Glenn Hubbard	.10	.08	.04
26	Bud Black	.10	.08	.04
27	Daryl Sconiers	.08	.06	.03
28	Frank Viola	1.00	.70	.40
29	Danny Heep	.08	.06	.03
30	Wade Boggs	6.00	4.50	2.50
31	Andy McGaffigan	.08	.06	.03
32	Bobby Ramos	.08	.06	.03
33	Tom Burgmeier	.08	.06	.03
34	Eddie Milner	.08	.06	.03
35	Don Sutton	.30	.25	.12
36	Denny Walling	.08	.06	.03
37	Rangers Batting & Pitching Leaders (Buddy Bell, Rick Honeycutt)	.12	.09	.05
38	Luis DeLeon	.08	.06	.03
39	Garth Iorg	.08	.06	.03
40	Dusty Baker	.12	.09	.05
41	Tony Bernazard	.08	.06	.03
42	Johnny Grubb	.08	.06	.03
43	Ron Reed	.10	.08	.04
44	Jim Morrison	.08	.06	.03
45	Jerry Mumphrey	.08	.06	.03
46	Ray Smith	.08	.06	.03
47	Rudy Law	.08	.06	.03
48	Julio Franco(FC)	1.75	1.25	.70
49	John Stuper	.08	.06	.03
50	Chris Chambliss	.10	.08	.04
51	Jim Frey	.08	.06	.03
52	Paul Splittorff	.08	.06	.03
53	Juan Beniquez	.08	.06	.03
54	Jesse Orosco	.10	.08	.04
55	Dave Concepcion	.15	.11	.06
56	Gary Allenson	.08	.06	.03
57	Dan Schatzeder	.08	.06	.03
58	Max Venable	.08	.06	.03
59	Sammy Stewart	.08	.06	.03
60	Paul Molitor	.20	.15	.08
61	*Chris Codiroli*	.10	.08	.04
62	Dave Hostetler	.08	.06	.03
63	Ed Vande Berg	.08	.06	.03
64	Mike Scioscia	.08	.06	.03
65	Kirk Gibson	.40	.30	.15
66	Astros Batting & Pitching Leaders (Jose Cruz, Nolan Ryan)	.25	.20	.10
67	Gary Ward	.10	.08	.04
68	Luis Salazar	.08	.06	.03
69	Rod Scurry	.08	.06	.03
70	Gary Matthews	.12	.09	.05
71	Leo Hernandez	.08	.06	.03
72	Mike Squires	.08	.06	.03
73	Jody Davis	.10	.08	.04
74	Jerry Martin	.08	.06	.03
75	Bob Forsch	.10	.08	.04
76	Alfredo Griffin	.10	.08	.04
77	Brett Butler	.10	.08	.04
78	Mike Torrez	.10	.08	.04
79	Rob Wilfong	.08	.06	.03
80	Steve Rogers	.10	.08	.04
81	Billy Martin	.12	.09	.05
82	Doug Bird	.08	.06	.03
83	Richie Zisk	.10	.08	.04
84	Lenny Faedo	.08	.06	.03
85	Atlee Hammaker	.08	.06	.03
86	*John Shelby*(FC)	.25	.20	.10
87	Frank Pastore	.08	.06	.03
88	Rob Picciolo	.08	.06	.03
89	*Mike Smithson*(FC)	.15	.11	.06

		MT	NR MT	EX
90	Pedro Guerrero	.35	.25	.14
91	Dan Spillner	.08	.06	.03
92	Lloyd Moseby	.12	.09	.05
93	Bob Knepper	.10	.08	.04
94	Mario Ramirez	.08	.06	.03
95	Aurelio Lopez	.08	.06	.03
96	Royals Batting & Pitching Leaders (Larry Gura, Hal McRae)	.10	.08	.04
97	LaMarr Hoyt	.08	.06	.03
98	Steve Nicosia	.08	.06	.03
99	*Craig Lefferts*(FC)	.20	.15	.08
100	Reggie Jackson	.60	.45	.25
101	Porfirio Altamirano	.08	.06	.03
102	Ken Oberkfell	.08	.06	.03
103	Dwayne Murphy	.10	.08	.04
104	Ken Dayley	.08	.06	.03
105	Tony Armas	.12	.09	.05
106	Tim Stoddard	.08	.06	.03
107	Ned Yost	.08	.06	.03
108	Randy Moffitt	.08	.06	.03
109	Brad Wellman	.08	.06	.03
110	Ron Guidry	.30	.25	.12
111	Bill Virdon	.08	.06	.03
112	Tom Niedenfuer	.10	.08	.03
113	Kelly Paris	.08	.06	.03
114	Checklist 1-132	.08	.06	.03
115	Andre Thornton	.12	.09	.05
116	George Bjorkman	.08	.06	.03
117	Tom Veryzer	.08	.06	.03
118	Charlie Hough	.12	.09	.05
119	Johnny Wockenfuss	.08	.06	.03
120	Keith Hernandez	.40	.30	.15
121	*Pat Sheridan*(FC)	.15	.11	.06
122	Cecilio Guante(FC)	.10	.08	.04
123	Butch Wynegar	.08	.06	.03
124	Damaso Garcia	.08	.06	.03
125	Britt Burns	.08	.06	.03
126	Braves Batting & Pitching Leaders (Craig McMurtry, Dale Murphy)	.25	.20	.10
127	Mike Madden	.08	.06	.03
128	Rick Manning	.08	.06	.03
129	Bill Laskey	.08	.06	.03
130	Ozzie Smith	.20	.15	.08
131	Batting Leaders (Wade Boggs, Bill Madlock)	.50	.40	.20
132	Home Run Leaders (Jim Rice, Mike Schmidt)	.50	.40	.20
133	Runs Batted In Leaders (Cecil Cooper, Dale Murphy, Jim Rice)	.40	.30	.15
134	Stolen Base Leaders (Rickey Henderson, Tim Raines)	.30	.25	.12
135	Victory Leaders (John Denny, LaMarr Hoyt)	.10	.08	.04
136	Strikeout Leaders (Steve Carlton, Jack Morris)	.25	.20	.10
137	Earned Run Average Leaders (Atlee Hammaker, Rick Honeycutt)	.10	.08	.04
138	Leading Firemen (Al Holland, Dan Quisenberry)	.12	.09	.05
139	Bert Campaneris	.12	.09	.05
140	Storm Davis	.12	.09	.05
141	Pat Corrales	.08	.06	.03
142	Rich Gale	.08	.06	.03
143	Jose Morales	.08	.06	.03
144	Brian Harper	.08	.06	.03
145	Gary Lavelle	.08	.06	.03
146	Ed Romero	.08	.06	.03
147	Dan Petry	.10	.08	.04
148	Joe Lefebvre	.08	.06	.03
149	Jon Matlack	.10	.08	.04
150	Dale Murphy	1.00	.70	.40
151	Steve Trout	.08	.06	.03
152	Glenn Brummer	.08	.06	.03
153	Dick Tidrow	.08	.06	.03
154	Dave Henderson	.12	.09	.05
155	Frank White	.12	.09	.05
156	Athletics Batting & Pitching Leaders (Tim Conroy, Rickey Henderson)	.25	.20	.10
157	Gary Gaetti	.70	.50	.30
158	John Curtis	.08	.06	.03
159	Darryl Cias	.08	.06	.03
160	Mario Soto	.10	.08	.04
161	*Junior Ortiz*(FC)	.10	.08	.04
162	Bob Ojeda	.12	.09	.05
163	Lorenzo Gray	.08	.06	.03
164	Scott Sanderson	.08	.06	.03
165	Ken Singleton	.12	.09	.05
166	Jamie Nelson	.08	.06	.03
167	Marshall Edwards	.08	.06	.03
168	Juan Bonilla	.08	.06	.03
169	Larry Parrish	.12	.09	.05

		MT	NR MT	EX
170	Jerry Reuss	.12	.09	.05
171	Frank Robinson	.12	.09	.05
172	Frank DiPino	.08	.06	.03
173	*Marvell Wynne*(FC)	.20	.15	.08
174	Juan Berenguer	.08	.06	.03
175	Graig Nettles	.20	.15	.08
176	Lee Smith	.15	.11	.06
177	Jerry Hairston	.08	.06	.03
178	Bill Krueger	.08	.06	.03
179	Buck Martinez	.08	.06	.03
180	Manny Trillo	.10	.08	.04
181	Roy Thomas	.08	.06	.03
182	*Darryl Strawberry*	18.00	13.50	7.25
183	Al Williams	.08	.06	.03
184	Mike O'Berry	.08	.06	.03
185	Sixto Lezcano	.08	.06	.03
186	Cardinals Batting & Pitching Leaders			
	(Lonnie Smith, John Stuper)	.10	.08	.04
187	Luis Aponte	.08	.06	.03
188	Bryan Little	.08	.06	.03
189	*Tim Conroy*(FC)	.12	.09	.05
190	Ben Oglivie	.10	.08	.04
191	Mike Boddicker	.12	.09	.05
192	*Nick Esasky*(FC)	.90	.70	.35
193	Darrell Brown	.08	.06	.03
194	Domingo Ramos	.08	.06	.03
195	Jack Morris	.30	.25	.12
196	Don Slaught(FC)	.12	.09	.05
197	Garry Hancock	.08	.06	.03
198	*Bill Doran*	.80	.60	.30
199	Willie Hernandez	.12	.09	.05
200	Andre Dawson	.35	.25	.14
201	Bruce Kison	.08	.06	.03
202	Bobby Cox	.08	.06	.03
203	Matt Keough	.08	.06	.03
204	*Bobby Meacham*(FC)	.15	.11	.06
205	Greg Minton	.08	.06	.03
206	*Andy Van Slyke*(FC)	3.00	2.25	1.25
207	Donnie Moore	.08	.06	.03
208	*Jose Oquendo*(FC)	.15	.11	.06
209	Manny Sarmiento	.08	.06	.03
210	Joe Morgan	.30	.25	.12
211	Rick Sweet	.08	.06	.03
212	Broderick Perkins	.08	.06	.03
213	Bruce Hurst	.15	.11	.06
214	Paul Householder	.08	.06	.03
215	Tippy Martinez	.08	.06	.03
216	White Sox Batting & Pitching Leaders			
	(Richard Dotson, Carlton Fisk)	.15	.11	.06
217	Alan Ashby	.08	.06	.03
218	Rick Waits	.08	.06	.03
219	Joe Simpson	.08	.06	.03
220	Fernando Valenzuela	.40	.30	.15
221	Cliff Johnson	.08	.06	.03
222	Rick Honeycutt	.08	.06	.03
223	Wayne Krenchicki	.08	.06	.03
224	Sid Monge	.08	.06	.03
225	Lee Mazzilli	.10	.08	.04
226	Juan Eichelberger	.08	.06	.03
227	Steve Braun	.08	.06	.03
228	John Rabb	.08	.06	.03
229	Paul Owens	.08	.06	.03
230	Rickey Henderson	4.00	3.00	1.50
231	Gary Woods	.08	.06	.03
232	Tim Wallach	.15	.11	.06
233	Checklist 133-264	.08	.06	.03
234	Rafael Ramirez	.08	.06	.03
235	*Matt Young*	.15	.11	.06
236	Ellis Valentine	.08	.06	.03
237	John Castino	.08	.06	.03
238	Reid Nichols	.08	.06	.03
239	Jay Howell	.10	.08	.04
240	Eddie Murray	.60	.45	.25
241	Billy Almon	.08	.06	.03
242	Alex Trevino	.08	.06	.03
243	Pete Ladd	.08	.06	.03
244	Candy Maldonado(FC)	.50	.40	.20
245	Rick Sutcliffe	.15	.11	.06
246	Mets Batting & Pitching Leaders (Tom			
	Seaver, Mookie Wilson)	.25	.20	.10
247	Onix Concepcion	.08	.06	.03
248	*Bill Dawley*(FC)	.10	.08	.04
249	Jay Johnstone	.10	.08	.04
250	Bill Madlock	.12	.09	.05
251	Tony Gwynn	3.00	2.25	1.25
252	Larry Christenson	.08	.06	.03
253	Jim Wohlford	.08	.06	.03
254	Shane Rawley	.12	.09	.05
255	Bruce Benedict	.08	.06	.03
256	Dave Geisel	.08	.06	.03
257	Julio Cruz	.08	.06	.03

		MT	NR MT	EX
258	Luis Sanchez	.08	.06	.03
259	Sparky Anderson	.12	.09	.05
260	Scott McGregor	.10	.08	.04
261	Bobby Brown	.08	.06	.03
262	*Tom Candiotti*(FC)	.25	.20	.10
263	Jack Fimple	.08	.06	.03
264	Doug Frobel	.08	.06	.03
265	*Donnie Hill*(FC)	.15	.11	.06
266	Steve Lubratich	.08	.06	.03
267	*Carmelo Martinez*(FC)	.25	.20	.10
268	Jack O'Connor	.08	.06	.03
269	Aurelio Rodriguez	.10	.08	.04
270	*Jeff Russell*(FC)	.20	.15	.08
271	Moose Haas	.08	.06	.03
272	Rick Dempsey	.10	.08	.04
273	Charlie Puleo	.08	.06	.03
274	Rick Monday	.10	.08	.04
275	Len Matuszek	.08	.06	.03
276	Angels Batting & Pitching Leaders (Rod			
	Carew, Geoff Zahn)	.20	.15	.08
277	Eddie Whitson	.08	.06	.03
278	Jorge Bell	1.00	.70	.40
279	Ivan DeJesus	.08	.06	.03
280	Floyd Bannister	.12	.09	.05
281	Larry Milbourne	.08	.06	.03
282	Jim Barr	.08	.06	.03
283	Larry Biittner	.08	.06	.03
284	Howard Bailey	.08	.06	.03
285	Darrell Porter	.10	.08	.04
286	Lary Sorensen	.08	.06	.03
287	Warren Cromartie	.08	.06	.03
288	Jim Beattie	.08	.06	.03
289	Randy Johnson	.08	.06	.03
290	Dave Dravecky	.10	.08	.04
291	Chuck Tanner	.08	.06	.03
292	Tony Scott	.08	.06	.03
293	Ed Lynch	.08	.06	.03
294	U.L. Washington	.08	.06	.03
295	Mike Flanagan	.12	.09	.05
296	Jeff Newman	.08	.06	.03
297	Bruce Berenyi	.08	.06	.03
298	Jim Gantner	.10	.08	.04
299	John Butcher	.08	.06	.03
300	Pete Rose	1.50	1.25	.60
301	Frank LaCorte	.08	.06	.03
302	Barry Bonnell	.08	.06	.03
303	Marty Castillo	.08	.06	.03
304	Warren Brusstar	.08	.06	.03
305	Roy Smalley	.08	.06	.03
306	Dodgers Batting & Pitching Leaders			
	(Pedro Guerrero, Bob Welch)	.15	.11	.06
307	Bobby Mitchell	.08	.06	.03
308	Ron Hassey	.08	.06	.03
309	*Tony Phillips*	.15	.11	.06
310	Willie McGee	.35	.25	.14
311	Jerry Koosman	.12	.09	.05
312	Jorge Orta	.08	.06	.03
313	Mike Jorgensen	.08	.06	.03
314	Orlando Mercado	.08	.06	.03
315	Bob Grich	.12	.09	.05
316	Mark Bradley	.08	.06	.03
317	Greg Pryor	.08	.06	.03
318	Bill Gullickson	.08	.06	.03
319	Al Bumbry	.10	.08	.04
320	Bob Stanley	.08	.06	.03
321	Harvey Kuenn	.10	.08	.04
322	Ken Schrom	.08	.06	.03
323	Alan Knicely	.08	.06	.03
324	*Alejandro Pena*	.30	.25	.12
325	Darrell Evans	.15	.11	.06
326	Bob Kearney	.08	.06	.03
327	Ruppert Jones	.08	.06	.03
328	Vern Ruhle	.08	.06	.03
329	Pat Tabler(FC)	.20	.15	.08
330	John Candelaria	.12	.09	.05
331	Bucky Dent	.12	.09	.05
332	*Kevin Gross*(FC)	.35	.25	.14
333	Larry Herndon	.10	.08	.04
334	Chuck Rainey	.08	.06	.03
335	Don Baylor	.15	.11	.06
336	Mariners Batting & Pitching Leaders (Pat			
	Putnam, Matt Young)	.10	.08	.04
337	Kevin Hagen	.08	.06	.03
338	Mike Warren	.08	.06	.03
339	Roy Lee Jackson	.08	.06	.03
340	Hal McRae	.12	.09	.05
341	Dave Tobik	.08	.06	.03
342	Tim Foli	.08	.06	.03
343	Mark Davis	.08	.06	.03
344	Rick Miller	.08	.06	.03
345	Kent Hrbek	.40	.30	.15

	MT	NR MT	EX
346 Kurt Bevacqua	.08	.06	.03
347 Allan Ramirez	.08	.06	.03
348 Toby Harrah	.10	.08	.04
349 Bob Gibson	.08	.06	.03
350 George Foster	.20	.15	.08
351 Russ Nixon	.08	.06	.03
352 Dave Stewart	.90	.70	.50
353 Jim Anderson	.08	.06	.03
354 Jeff Burroughs	.10	.08	.04
355 Jason Thompson	.08	.06	.03
356 Glenn Abbott	.08	.06	.03
357 Ron Cey	.12	.09	.05
358 Bob Dernier	.08	.06	.03
359 *Jim Acker*(FC)	.12	.09	.05
360 Willie Randolph	.12	.09	.05
361 Dave Smith	.10	.08	.04
362 David Green	.08	.06	.03
363 Tim Laudner	.08	.06	.03
364 Scott Fletcher(FC)	.15	.11	.06
365 Steve Bedrosian	.12	.09	.05
366 Padres Batting & Pitching Leaders (Dave Dravecky, Terry Kennedy)	.12	.09	.05
367 Jamie Easterly	.08	.06	.03
368 Hubie Brooks	.15	.11	.06
369 Steve McCatty	.08	.06	.03
370 Tim Raines	.40	.30	.15
371 Dave Gumpert	.08	.06	.03
372 Gary Roenicke	.08	.06	.03
373 Bill Scherrer	.08	.06	.03
374 Don Money	.08	.06	.03
375 Dennis Leonard	.10	.08	.04
376 *Dave Anderson*(FC)	.15	.11	.06
377 Danny Darwin	.08	.06	.03
378 Bob Brenly	.08	.06	.03
379 Checklist 265-396	.08	.06	.03
380 Steve Garvey	.50	.40	.20
381 Ralph Houk	.10	.08	.04
382 Chris Nyman	.08	.06	.03
383 Terry Puhl	.08	.06	.03
384 *Lee Tunnell*	.10	.08	.04
385 Tony Perez	.20	.15	.08
386 George Hendrick AS	.10	.08	.04
387 Johnny Ray AS	.12	.09	.05
388 Mike Schmidt AS	.35	.25	.14
389 Ozzie Smith AS	.15	.11	.06
390 Tim Raines AS	.25	.20	.10
391 Dale Murphy AS	.40	.30	.15
392 Andre Dawson AS	.20	.15	.08
393 Gary Carter AS	.30	.25	.12
394 Steve Rogers AS	.10	.08	.04
395 Steve Carlton AS	.25	.20	.10
396. Jesse Orosco AS	.10	.08	.04
397 Eddie Murray AS	.35	.25	.14
398 Lou Whitaker AS	.20	.15	.08
399 George Brett AS	.35	.25	.14
400 Cal Ripken AS	.35	.25	.14
401 Jim Rice AS	.30	.25	.12
402 Dave Winfield AS	.30	.25	.12
403 Lloyd Moseby AS	.12	.09	.05
404 Ted Simmons AS	.15	.11	.06
405 LaMarr Hoyt AS	.10	.08	.04
406 Ron Guidry AS	.20	.15	.08
407 Dan Quisenberry AS	.12	.09	.05
408 Lou Piniella	.15	.11	.06
409 *Juan Agosto*(FC)	.15	.11	.06
410 Claudell Washington	.10	.08	.04
411 Houston Jimenez	.08	.06	.03
412 Doug Rader	.08	.06	.03
413 *Spike Owen*(FC)	.20	.15	.08
414 Mitchell Page	.08	.06	.03
415 Tommy John	.25	.20	.10
416 Dane Iorg	.08	.06	.03
417 Mike Armstrong	.08	.06	.03
418 Ron Hodges	.08	.06	.03
419 John Henry Johnson	.08	.06	.03
420 Cecil Cooper	.15	.11	.06
421 Charlie Lea	.08	.06	.03
422 Jose Cruz	.12	.09	.05
423 Mike Morgan	.08	.06	.03
424 Dann Bilardello	.08	.06	.03
425 Steve Howe	.10	.08	.04
426 Orioles Batting & Pitching Leaders (Mike Boddicker, Cal Ripken)	.25	.20	.10
427 Rick Leach	.08	.06	.03
428 Fred Breining	.08	.06	.03
429 *Randy Bush*	.15	.11	.06
430 Rusty Staub	.12	.09	.05
431 Chris Bando	.08	.06	.03
432 *Charlie Hudson*(FC)	.20	.15	.08
433 Rich Hebner	.08	.06	.03
434 Harold Baines	.25	.20	.10

	MT	NR MT	EX
435 Neil Allen	.08	.06	.03
436 Rick Peters	.08	.06	.03
437 Mike Proly	.08	.06	.03
438 Biff Pocoroba	.08	.06	.03
439 Bob Stoddard	.08	.06	.03
440 Steve Kemp	.10	.08	.04
441 Bob Lillis	.08	.06	.03
442 Byron McLaughlin	.08	.06	.03
443 Benny Ayala	.08	.06	.03
444 Steve Renko	.08	.06	.03
445 Jerry Remy	.08	.06	.03
446 Luis Pujols	.08	.06	.03
447 Tom Brunansky	.20	.15	.08
448 Ben Hayes	.08	.06	.03
449 Joe Pettini	.08	.06	.03
450 Gary Carter	.40	.30	.15
451 Bob Jones	.08	.06	.03
452 Chuck Porter	.08	.06	.03
453 Willie Upshaw	.10	.08	.04
454 Joe Beckwith	.08	.06	.03
455 Terry Kennedy	.10	.08	.04
456 Cubs Batting & Pitching Leaders (Fergie Jenkins, Keith Moreland)	.15	.11	.06
457 Dave Rozema	.08	.06	.03
458 Kiko Garcia	.08	.06	.03
459 Kevin Hickey	.08	.06	.03
460 Dave Winfield	.40	.30	.15
461 Jim Maler	.08	.06	.03
462 Lee Lacy	.08	.06	.03
463 Dave Engle	.08	.06	.03
464 Jeff Jones	.08	.06	.03
465 Mookie Wilson	.12	.09	.05
466 Gene Garber	.08	.06	.03
467 Mike Ramsey	.08	.06	.03
468 Geoff Zahn	.08	.06	.03
469 Tom O'Malley	.08	.06	.03
470 Nolan Ryan	3.00	2.25	1.25
471 Dick Howser	.08	.06	.03
472 Mike Brown	.08	.06	.03
473 Jim Dwyer	.08	.06	.03
474 Greg Bargar	.08	.06	.03
475 *Gary Redus*	.25	.20	.10
476 Tom Tellmann	.08	.06	.03
477 Rafael Landestoy	.08	.06	.03
478 Alan Bannister	.08	.06	.03
479 Frank Tanana	.12	.09	.05
480 Ron Kittle(FC)	.40	.30	.15
481 *Mark Thurmond*(FC)	.10	.08	.04
482 Enos Cabell	.08	.06	.03
483 Fergie Jenkins	.20	.15	.08
484 Ozzie Virgil	.08	.06	.03
485 Rick Rhoden	.12	.09	.05
486 Yankees Batting & Pitching Leaders (Don Baylor, Ron Guidry)	.15	.11	.06
487 Ricky Adams	.08	.06	.03
488 Jesse Barfield	.25	.20	.10
489 Dave Von Ohlen	.08	.06	.03
490 Cal Ripken	.60	.45	.25
491 Bobby Castillo	.08	.06	.03
492 Tucker Ashford	.08	.06	.03
493 Mike Norris	.08	.06	.03
494 Chili Davis	.12	.09	.05
495 Rollie Fingers	.25	.20	.10
496 Terry Francona	.08	.06	.03
497 Bud Anderson	.08	.06	.03
498 Rich Gedman	.10	.08	.04
499 Mike Witt	.15	.11	.06
500 George Brett	1.00	.70	.40
501 Steve Henderson	.08	.06	.03
502 Joe Torre	.08	.06	.03
503 Elias Sosa	.08	.06	.03
504 Mickey Rivers	.10	.08	.04
505 Pete Vuckovich	.10	.08	.04
506 Ernie Whitt	.10	.08	.04
507 Mike LaCoss	.08	.06	.03
508 Mel Hall	.20	.15	.08
509 Brad Havens	.08	.06	.03
510 Alan Trammell	.40	.30	.15
511 Marty Bystrom	.08	.06	.03
512 Oscar Gamble	.10	.08	.04
513 Dave Beard	.08	.06	.03
514 Floyd Rayford	.08	.06	.03
515 Gorman Thomas	.10	.08	.04
516 Expos Batting & Pitching Leaders (Charlie Lea, Al Oliver)	.12	.09	.05
517 John Moses	.12	.09	.05
518 *Greg Walker*	.45	.35	.20
519 Ron Davis	.08	.06	.03
520 Bob Boone	.10	.08	.04
521 Pete Falcone	.08	.06	.03
522 Dave Bergman	.08	.06	.03

#	Player	MT	NR MT	EX
523	Glenn Hoffman	.08	.06	.03
524	Carlos Diaz	.08	.06	.03
525	Willie Wilson	.15	.11	.06
526	Ron Oester	.08	.06	.03
527	Checklist 397-528	.08	.06	.03
528	Mark Brouhard	.08	.06	.03
529	*Keith Atherton*(FC)	.20	.15	.08
530	Dan Ford	.08	.06	.03
531	Steve Boros	.08	.06	.03
532	Eric Show	.12	.09	.05
533	Ken Landreaux	.08	.06	.03
534	*Pete O'Brien*	.70	.50	.30
535	Bo Diaz	.10	.08	.04
536	Doug Bair	.08	.06	.03
537	Johnny Ray	.12	.09	.05
538	Kevin Bass	.15	.11	.06
539	George Frazier	.08	.06	.03
540	George Hendrick	.10	.08	.04
541	Dennis Lamp	.08	.06	.03
542	Duane Kuiper	.08	.06	.03
543	*Craig McMurtry*	.12	.09	.05
544	Cesar Geronimo	.08	.06	.03
545	Bill Buckner	.15	.11	.06
546	Indians Batting & Pitching Leaders (Mike Hargrove, Lary Sorensen)	.10	.08	.04
547	Mike Moore	.10	.08	.04
548	Ron Jackson	.08	.06	.03
549	*Walt Terrell*	.50	.40	.20
550	Jim Rice	.40	.30	.15
551	Scott Ullger	.08	.06	.03
552	Ray Burris	.08	.06	.03
553	Joe Nolan	.08	.06	.03
554	Ted Power(FC)	.12	.09	.05
555	Greg Brock	.15	.11	.06
556	Joey McLaughlin	.08	.06	.03
557	Wayne Tolleson	.10	.08	.04
558	Mike Davis	.10	.08	.04
559	Mike Scott	.20	.15	.08
560	Carlton Fisk	.30	.25	.12
561	Whitey Herzog	.10	.08	.04
562	Manny Castillo	.08	.06	.03
563	Glenn Wilson	.10	.08	.04
564	Al Holland	.08	.06	.03
565	Leon Durham	.10	.08	.04
566	Jim Bibby	.08	.06	.03
567	Mike Heath	.08	.06	.03
568	Pete Filson	.08	.06	.03
569	Bake McBride	.08	.06	.03
570	Dan Quisenberry	.12	.09	.05
571	Bruce Bochy	.08	.06	.03
572	Jerry Royster	.08	.06	.03
573	Dave Kingman	.15	.11	.06
574	Brian Downing	.12	.09	.05
575	Jim Clancy	.10	.08	.04
576	Giants Batting & Pitching Leaders (Atlee Hammaker, Jeff Leonard)	.10	.08	.04
577	Mark Clear	.08	.06	.03
578	Lenn Sakata	.08	.06	.03
579	Bob James	.08	.06	.03
580	Lonnie Smith	.10	.08	.04
581	*Jose DeLeon*(FC)	.60	.45	.25
582	Bob McClure	.08	.06	.03
583	Derrel Thomas	.08	.06	.03
584	Dave Schmidt	.08	.06	.03
585	Dan Driessen	.10	.08	.04
586	Joe Niekro	.15	.11	.06
587	Von Hayes	.15	.11	.06
588	Milt Wilcox	.08	.06	.03
589	Mike Easler	.10	.08	.04
590	Dave Stieb	.15	.11	.06
591	Tony LaRussa	.10	.08	.04
592	Andre Robertson	.08	.06	.03
593	Jeff Lahti	.08	.06	.03
594	Gene Richards	.08	.06	.03
595	Jeff Reardon	.15	.11	.06
596	Ryne Sandberg	7.00	5.25	2.75
597	Rick Camp	.08	.06	.03
598	Rusty Kuntz	.08	.06	.03
599	*Doug Sisk*	.10	.08	.04
600	Rod Carew	.50	.40	.20
601	John Tudor	.12	.09	.05
602	John Wathan	.10	.08	.04
603	Renie Martin	.08	.06	.03
604	John Lowenstein	.08	.06	.03
605	Mike Caldwell	.08	.06	.03
606	Blue Jays Batting & Pitching Leaders (Lloyd Moseby, Dave Stieb)	.15	.11	.06
607	Tom Hume	.08	.06	.03
608	Bobby Johnson	.08	.06	.03
609	Dan Meyer	.08	.06	.03
610	Steve Sax	.20	.15	.08
611	Chet Lemon	.10	.08	.04
612	Harry Spilman	.08	.06	.03
613	Greg Gross	.08	.06	.03
614	Len Barker	.10	.08	.04
615	Garry Templeton	.12	.09	.05
616	Don Robinson	.10	.08	.04
617	Rick Cerone	.08	.06	.03
618	Dickie Noles	.08	.06	.03
619	Jerry Dybzinski	.08	.06	.03
620	Al Oliver	.20	.15	.08
621	Frank Howard	.10	.08	.04
622	Al Cowens	.08	.06	.03
623	Ron Washington	.08	.06	.03
624	Terry Harper	.08	.06	.03
625	Larry Gura	.10	.08	.04
626	Bob Clark	.08	.06	.03
627	Dave LaPoint	.10	.08	.04
628	Ed Jurak	.08	.06	.03
629	Rick Langford	.08	.06	.03
630	Ted Simmons	.15	.11	.06
631	Denny Martinez	.10	.08	.04
632	Tom Foley	.08	.06	.03
633	Mike Krukow	.10	.08	.04
634	Mike Marshall	.15	.11	.06
635	Dave Righetti	.25	.20	.10
636	Pat Putnam	.08	.06	.03
637	Phillies Batting & Pitching Leaders (John Denny, Gary Matthews)	.10	.08	.04
638	George Vukovich	.08	.06	.03
639	Rick Lysander	.08	.06	.03
640	Lance Parrish	.35	.25	.14
641	Mike Richardt	.08	.06	.03
642	Tom Underwood	.08	.06	.03
643	Mike Brown	.08	.06	.03
644	Tim Lollar	.08	.06	.03
645	Tony Pena	.12	.09	.05
646	Checklist 529-660	.08	.06	.03
647	Ron Roenicke	.08	.06	.03
648	Len Whitehouse	.08	.06	.03
649	Tom Herr	.12	.09	.05
650	Phil Niekro	.30	.25	.12
651	John McNamara	.08	.06	.03
652	Rudy May	.08	.06	.03
653	Dave Stapleton	.08	.06	.03
654	Bob Bailor	.08	.06	.03
655	Amos Otis	.10	.08	.04
656	Bryn Smith	.08	.06	.03
657	Thad Bosley	.08	.06	.03
658	Jerry Augustine	.08	.06	.03
659	Duane Walker	.08	.06	.03
660	Ray Knight	.12	.09	.05
661	Steve Yeager	.08	.06	.03
662	Tom Brennan	.08	.06	.03
663	Johnnie LeMaster	.08	.06	.03
664	Dave Stegman	.08	.06	.03
665	Buddy Bell	.15	.11	.06
666	Tigers Batting & Pitching Leaders (Jack Morris, Lou Whitaker)	.15	.11	.06
667	Vance Law	.10	.08	.04
668	Larry McWilliams	.08	.06	.03
669	Dave Lopes	.10	.08	.04
670	Rich Gossage	.25	.20	.10
671	Jamie Quirk	.08	.06	.03
672	Ricky Nelson	.08	.06	.03
673	Mike Walters	.08	.06	.03
674	Tim Flannery	.08	.06	.03
675	Pascual Perez	.10	.08	.04
676	Brian Giles	.08	.06	.03
677	Doyle Alexander	.12	.09	.05
678	Chris Speier	.08	.06	.03
679	Art Howe	.08	.06	.03
680	Fred Lynn	.25	.20	.10
681	Tom Lasorda	.12	.09	.05
682	Dan Morogiello	.08	.06	.03
683	*Marty Barrett*(FC)	.60	.45	.25
684	Bob Shirley	.08	.06	.03
685	Willie Aikens	.08	.06	.03
686	Joe Price	.08	.06	.03
687	Roy Howell	.08	.06	.03
688	George Wright	.08	.06	.03
689	Mike Fischlin	.08	.06	.03
690	Jack Clark	.25	.20	.10
691	*Steve Lake*(FC)	.10	.08	.04
692	Dickie Thon	.10	.08	.04
693	Alan Wiggins	.08	.06	.03
694	Mike Stanton	.08	.06	.03
695	Lou Whitaker	.40	.30	.15
696	Pirates Batting & Pitching Leaders (Bill Madlock, Rick Rhoden)	.15	.11	.06
697	Dale Murray	.08	.06	.03
698	Marc Hill	.08	.06	.03

		MT	NR MT	EX
699	Dave Rucker	.08	.06	.03
700	Mike Schmidt	1.25	.90	.50
701	NL Active Career Batting Leaders (Bill Madlock, Dave Parker, Pete Rose)	.35	.25	.14
702	NL Active Career Hit Leaders (Tony Perez, Pete Rose, Rusty Staub)	.35	.25	.14
703	NL Active Career Home Run Leaders (Dave Kingman, Tony Perez, Mike Schmidt)	.30	.25	.12
704	NL Active Career RBI Leaders (Al Oliver, Tony Perez, Rusty Staub)	.15	.11	.06
705	NL Active Career Stolen Bases Leaders (Larry Bowa, Cesar Cedeno, Joe Morgan)	.12	.09	.05
706	NL Active Career Victory Leaders (Steve Carlton, Fergie Jenkins, Tom Seaver)	.30	.25	.12
707	NL Active Career Strikeout Leaders (Steve Carlton, Nolan Ryan, Tom Seaver)	.35	.25	.14
708	NL Active Career ERA Leaders (Steve Carlton, Steve Rogers, Tom Seaver)	.25	.20	.10
709	NL Active Career Save Leaders (Gene Garber, Tug McGraw, Bruce Sutter)	.12	.09	.05
710	AL Active Career Batting Leaders (George Brett, Rod Carew, Cecil Cooper)	.30	.25	.12
711	AL Active Career Hit Leaders (Bert Campaneris, Rod Carew, Reggie Jackson)	.30	.25	.12
712	AL Active Career Home Run Leaders (Reggie Jackson, Greg Luzinski, Graig Nettles)	.20	.15	.08
713	AL Active Career RBI Leaders (Reggie Jackson, Graig Nettles, Ted Simmons)	.20	.15	.08
714	AL Active Career Stolen Bases Leaders (Bert Campaneris, Dave Lopes, Omar Moreno)	.10	.08	.04
715	AL Active Career Victory Leaders (Tommy John, Jim Palmer, Don Sutton)	.25	.20	.10
716	AL Active Strikeout Leaders (Bert Blyleven, Jerry Koosman, Don Sutton)	.15	.11	.06
717	AL Active Career ERA Leaders (Rollie Fingers, Ron Guidry, Jim Palmer)	.15	.11	.06
718	AL Active Career Save Leaders (Rollie Fingers, Rich Gossage, Dan Quisenberry)	.15	.11	.06
719	Andy Hassler	.08	.06	.03
720	Dwight Evans	.20	.15	.08
721	Del Crandall	.08	.06	.03
722	Bob Welch	.15	.11	.06
723	Rich Dauer	.08	.06	.03
724	Eric Rasmussen	.08	.06	.03
725	Cesar Cedeno	.12	.09	.05
726	Brewers Batting & Pitching Leaders (Moose Haas, Ted Simmons)	.12	.09	.05
727	Joel Youngblood	.08	.06	.03
728	Tug McGraw	.12	.09	.05
729	Gene Tenace	.10	.08	.04
730	Bruce Sutter	.20	.15	.08
731	Lynn Jones	.08	.06	.03
732	Terry Crowley	.08	.06	.03
733	Dave Collins	.10	.08	.04
734	Odell Jones	.08	.06	.03
735	Rick Burleson	.10	.08	.04
736	Dick Ruthven	.08	.06	.03
737	Jim Essian	.08	.06	.03
738	*Bill Schroeder*(FC)	.20	.15	.08
739	Bob Watson	.10	.08	.04
740	Tom Seaver	.70	.50	.30
741	Wayne Gross	.08	.06	.03
742	Dick Williams	.08	.06	.03
743	Don Hood	.08	.06	.03
744	Jamie Allen	.08	.06	.03
745	Dennis Eckersley	.15	.11	.06
746	Mickey Hatcher	.10	.08	.04
747	Pat Zachry	.08	.06	.03
748	Jeff Leonard	.12	.09	.05
749	Doug Flynn	.08	.06	.03
750	Jim Palmer	.60	.45	.25
751	Charlie Moore	.08	.06	.03
752	Phil Garner	.10	.08	.04
753	Doug Gwosdz	.08	.06	.03
754	Kent Tekulve	.10	.08	.04
755	Garry Maddox	.10	.08	.04
756	Reds Batting & Pitching Leaders (Ron Oester, Mario Soto)	.10	.08	.04
757	Larry Bowa	.15	.11	.06
758	Bill Stein	.08	.06	.03
759	Richard Dotson	.12	.09	.05
760	Bob Horner	.15	.11	.06
761	John Montefusco	.08	.06	.03
762	Rance Mulliniks	.08	.06	.03

		MT	NR MT	EX
763	Craig Swan	.08	.06	.03
764	Mike Hargrove	.08	.06	.03
765	Ken Forsch	.08	.06	.03
766	Mike Vail	.08	.06	.03
767	Carney Lansford	.12	.09	.05
768	Champ Summers	.08	.06	.03
769	Bill Caudill	.08	.06	.03
770	Ken Griffey	.12	.09	.05
771	Billy Gardner	.08	.06	.03
772	Jim Slaton	.08	.06	.03
773	Todd Cruz	.08	.06	.03
774	Tom Gorman	.08	.06	.03
775	Dave Parker	.30	.25	.12
776	Craig Reynolds	.08	.06	.03
777	Tom Paciorek	.08	.06	.03
778	*Andy Hawkins*(FC)	.40	.30	.15
779	Jim Sundberg	.10	.08	.04
780	Steve Carlton	.50	.40	.20
781	Checklist 661-792	.08	.06	.03
782	Steve Balboni	.10	.08	.04
783	Luis Leal	.08	.06	.03
784	Leon Roberts	.08	.06	.03
785	Joaquin Andujar	.10	.08	.04
786	Red Sox Batting & Pitching Leaders (Wade Boggs, Bob Ojeda)	.40	.30	.15
787	Bill Campbell	.08	.06	.03
788	Milt May	.08	.06	.03
789	Bert Blyleven	.20	.15	.08
790	Doug DeCinces	.12	.09	.05
791	Terry Forster	.10	.08	.04
792	Bill Russell	.10	.08	.04

1984 Topps All-Star Glossy Set Of 22

These 2-1/2" by 3-1/2" cards were a result of the success of Topps' efforts the previous year with glossy cards on a mail-in basis. A 22-card set, the cards are divided evenly between the two leagues. Each All-Star Game starter for both leagues, the managers and the honorary team captains have an All-Star Glossy card. The cards feature a large color photo on the front with an All-Star banner across the top and the league emblem in the lower left. The player's name and position appear below the photo. Backs have a name, team, position and card number along with the phrase "1983 All-Star Game Commemorative Set". The '84 Glossy All-Stars were distributed one card per pack in Topps rack packs that year.

		MT	NR MT	EX
Complete Set:		6.00	4.50	2.50
Common Player:		.20	.15	.08
1	Harvey Kuenn	.20	.15	.08
2	Rod Carew	.50	.40	.20
3	Manny Trillo	.20	.15	.08
4	George Brett	.80	.60	.30
5	Robin Yount	.40	.30	.15
6	Jim Rice	.50	.40	.20
7	Fred Lynn	.25	.20	.10
8	Dave Winfield	.50	.40	.20
9	Ted Simmons	.25	.20	.10
10	Dave Stieb	.25	.20	.10

		MT	NR MT	EX
11	Carl Yastrzemski	.80	.60	.30
12	Whitey Herzog	.20	.15	.08
13	Al Oliver	.25	.20	.10
14	Steve Sax	.30	.25	.12
15	Mike Schmidt	.80	.60	.30
16	Ozzie Smith	.30	.25	.12
17	Tim Raines	.50	.40	.20
18	Andre Dawson	.35	.25	.14
19	Dale Murphy	.80	.60	.30
20	Gary Carter	.50	.40	.20
21	Mario Soto	.20	.15	.08
22	Johnny Bench	.60	.45	.25

		MT	NR MT	EX
37	Tim Raines	.50	.40	.20
38	Dan Quisenberry	.15	.11	.06
39	Mike Schmidt	1.00	.70	.40
40	Carlton Fisk	.30	.25	.12

1984 Topps All-Star
Glossy Set Of 40

For the second straight year in 1984, Topps produced a 40-card All-Star "Collector's Edition" set as a "consolation prize" for its sweepstakes game. By collecting game cards and sending them in with a bit of cash, the collector could receive one of eight different five-card series. As the previous year, the 2-1/2" by 3-1/2" cards feature a nearly full-frame color photo on its glossy finish front. Backs are printed in red and blue.

		MT	NR MT	EX
	Complete Set:	16.00	12.00	6.50
	Common Player:	.15	.11	.06
1	Pete Rose	1.25	.90	.50
2	Lance Parrish	.30	.25	.12
3	Steve Rogers	.15	.11	.06
4	Eddie Murray	.60	.45	.25
5	Johnny Ray	.20	.15	.08
6	Rickey Henderson	.70	.50	.30
7	Atlee Hammaker	.15	.11	.06
8	Wade Boggs	3.00	2.25	1.25
9	Gary Carter	.50	.40	.20
10	Jack Morris	.30	.25	.12
11	Darrell Evans	.20	.15	.08
12	George Brett	1.00	.70	.40
13	Bob Horner	.20	.15	.08
14	Ron Guidry	.30	.25	.12
15	Nolan Ryan	.50	.40	.20
16	Dave Winfield	.60	.45	.25
17	Ozzie Smith	.25	.20	.10
18	Ted Simmons	.20	.15	.08
19	Bill Madlock	.20	.15	.08
20	Tony Armas	.15	.11	.06
21	Al Oliver	.20	.15	.08
22	Jim Rice	.50	.40	.20
23	George Hendrick	.15	.11	.06
24	Dave Stieb	.20	.15	.08
25	Pedro Guerrero	.25	.20	.10
26	Rod Carew	.60	.45	.25
27	Steve Carlton	.50	.40	.20
28	Dave Righetti	.30	.25	.12
29	Darryl Strawberry	3.00	2.25	1.25
30	Lou Whitaker	.30	.25	.12
31	Dale Murphy	1.00	.70	.40
32	LaMarr Hoyt	.15	.11	.06
33	Jesse Orosco	.15	.11	.06
34	Cecil Cooper	.20	.15	.08
35	Andre Dawson	.35	.25	.14
36	Robin Yount	.40	.30	.15

1984 Topps
Gallery of Immortals

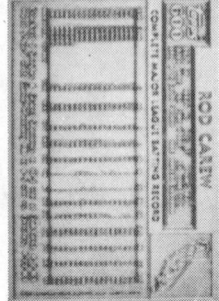

The Gallery of Immortals set of aluminum, bronze and silver replicas was the first miniature set of 12 from Topps and the start of an annual tradition (in 1985, the name was changed to Gallery of Champions) .Each mini is an exact replica (one-quarter scale) of the featured player's official Topps baseball card card, both front and back, in minute detail. The bronze and silver sets include a dozen three-dimensional raised metal cards packaged in a velvet-lined case that bears the title of the set in gold-embossed letters. A certificate of authenticity is included with each set. A Tom Seaver pewter metal mini-card was given as a premium to dealers who purchased bronze and silver sets (value $75). A Darryl Strawberry bronze was given as a premium to dealers who purchased cases of the 1984 Topps Traded sets (value $12). Additionally, a Steve Carlton bronze was issued as a premium in 1983 to dealers who purchased 1983 Topps Traded sets (value $50).

		MT	NR MT	EX
	Complete Aluminum Set:	30.00	22.00	12.00
	Complete Bronze Set:	175.00	131.00	70.00
	Complete Silver Set:	600.00	450.00	240.00
(1a)	George Brett (aluminum)	1.50	1.25	.60
(1b)	George Brett (bronze)	15.00	11.00	6.00
(1c)	George Brett (silver)	80.00	60.00	32.00
(2a)	Rod Carew (aluminum)	1.50	1.25	.60
(2b)	Rod Carew (bronze)	12.50	9.50	5.00
(2c)	Rod Carew (silver)	50.00	37.00	20.00
(3a)	Steve Carlton (aluminum)	1.50	1.25	.60
(3b)	Steve Carlton (bronze)	12.50	9.50	5.00
(3c)	Steve Carlton (silver)	50.00	37.00	20.00
(4a)	Rollie Fingers (aluminum)	1.25	.90	.50
(4b)	Rollie Fingers (bronze)	10.00	7.50	4.00
(4c)	Rollie Fingers (silver)	20.00	15.00	8.00
(5a)	Steve Garvey (aluminum)	1.50	1.25	.60
(5b)	Steve Garvey (bronze)	12.50	9.50	5.00
(5c)	Steve Garvey (silver)	50.00	37.00	20.00
(6a)	Reggie Jackson (aluminum)	1.50	1.25	.60
(6b)	Reggie Jackson (bronze)	15.00	11.00	6.00
(6c)	Reggie Jackson (silver)	80.00	60.00	32.00
(7a)	Joe Morgan (aluminum)	1.25	.90	.50
(7b)	Joe Morgan (bronze)	10.00	7.50	4.00
(7c)	Joe Morgan (silver)	20.00	15.00	8.00
(8a)	Jim Palmer (aluminum)	1.25	.90	.50
(8b)	Jim Palmer (bronze)	10.00	7.50	4.00
(8c)	Jim Palmer (silver)	20.00	15.00	8.00
(9a)	Pete Rose (aluminum)	2.50	2.00	1.00
(9b)	Pete Rose (bronze)	25.00	18.50	10.00
(9c)	Pete Rose (silver)	110.00	82.00	44.00
(10a)	Nolan Ryan (aluminum)	1.50	1.25	.60
(10b)	Nolan Ryan (bronze)	12.50	9.50	5.00
(10c)	Nolan Ryan (silver)	80.00	60.00	33.00
(11a)	Mike Schmidt (aluminum)	1.50	1.25	.60
(11b)	Mike Schmidt (bronze)	15.00	11.00	6.00

		MT	NR MT	EX
(11c)	Mike Schmidt (silver)	80.00	60.00	32.00
(12a)	Tom Seaver (aluminum)	1.50	1.25	.60
(12b)	Tom Seaver (bronze)	12.50	9.50	5.00
(12c)	Tom Seaver (silver)	50.00	37.00	20.00

1984 Topps Rub Downs

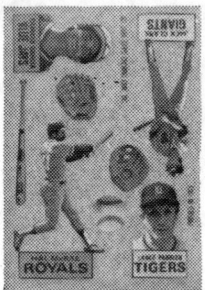

This set, produced by Topps in 1984, consists of 32 "Rub Down" sheets featuring 112 different players. Each sheet measures 2-3/8" by 3-15/16" and includes small, color baseball player figures along with bats, balls and gloves. The pictures can be transferred to another surface by rubbing the paper backing. The sheets, which were sold as a separate issue, are somewhat reminiscent of earlier tattoo sets issued by Topps. The sheets are not numbered.

		MT	NR MT	EX
Complete Set:		9.00	6.75	3.50
Common Player:		.10	.08	.04
(1)	Tony Armas, Harold Baines, Lonnie Smith	.10	.08	.04
(2)	Don Baylor, George Hendrick, Ron Kittle, Johnnie LeMaster	.10	.08	.04
(3)	Buddy Bell, Ray Knight, Lloyd Moseby	.10	.08	.04
(4)	Bruce Benedict, Atlee Hammaker, Frank White	.10	.08	.04
(5)	Wade Boggs, Rick Dempsey, Keith Hernandez	.60	.45	.25
(6)	George Brett, Andre Dawson, Paul Molitor, Alan Wiggins	.40	.30	.15
(7)	Tom Brunansky, Pedro Guerrero, Darryl Strawberry	.40	.30	.15
(8)	Bill Buckner, Rich Gossage, Dave Stieb, Rick Sutcliffe	.15	.11	.06
(9)	Rod Carew, Carlton Fisk, Johnny Ray, Matt Young	.25	.20	.10
(10)	Steve Carlton, Bob Horner, Dan Quisenberry	.25	.20	.10
(11)	Gary Carter, Phil Garner, Ron Guidry	.25	.20	.10
(12)	Ron Cey, Steve Kemp, Greg Luzinski, Kent Tekulve	.10	.08	.04
(13)	Chris Chambliss, Dwight Evans, Julio Franco	.15	.11	.06
(14)	Jack Clark, Damaso Garcia, Hal McRae, Lance Parrish	.20	.15	.08
(15)	Dave Concepcion, Cecil Cooper, Fred Lynn, Jesse Orosco	.15	.11	.06
(16)	Jose Cruz, Gary Matthews, Jack Morris, Jim Rice	.20	.15	.08
(17)	Ron Davis, Kent Hrbek, Tom Seaver	.25	.20	.10
(18)	John Denny, Carney Lansford, Mario Soto, Lou Whitaker	.10	.08	.04
(19)	Leon Durham, Dave Lopes, Steve Sax	.15	.11	.06
(20)	George Foster, Gary Gaetti, Bobby Grich, Gary Redus	.15	.11	.06
(21)	Steve Garvey, Bill Russell, Jerry REmy, George Wright	.20	.15	.08
(22)	Moose Haas, Bruce Sutter, Dickie Thon, Andre Thornton	.10	.08	.04
(23)	Toby Harrah, Pat Putnam, Tim Raines, Mike Schmidt	.30	.25	.12
(24)	Rickey Henderson, Dave Righetti, Pete Rose	.70	.50	.30
(25)	Steve Henderson, Bill Madlock, Alan Trammell	.20	.15	.08
(26)	LaMarr Hoyt, Larry Parrish, Nolan Ryan	.25	.20	.10
(27)	Reggie Jackson, Eric Show, Jason Thompson	.30	.25	.12
(28)	Tommy John, Terry Kennedy, Eddie Murray, Ozzie Smith	.25	.20	.10
(29)	Jeff Leonard, Dale Murphy, Ken Singleton, Dave Winfield	.30	.25	.12
(30)	Craig McMurtry, Cal Ripken, Steve Rogers, Willie Upshaw	.25	.20	.10
(31)	Ben Oglivie, Jim Palmer, Darrell Porter	.20	.15	.08
(32)	Tony Pena, Fernando Valenzuela, Robin Yount	.20	.15	.08

1984 Topps Super

 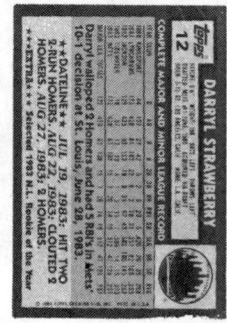

The next installment in Topps' continuing production of large-format cards, these 4-7/8" by 6-7/8" cards were sold in cellophane packs with a complete set being 30 cards. Other than their size and the change in card number on the back, there is nothing to distinguish the Supers from the regular 1984 Topps cards of the same players. One plus is that the players are all big name stars, and are likely to remain in demand.

		MT	NR MT	EX
Complete Set:		12.00	9.00	4.75
Common Player:		.20	.15	.08
1	Cal Ripken	.70	.50	.30
2	Dale Murphy	.90	.70	.35
3	LaMarr Hoyt	.20	.15	.08
4	John Denny	.20	.15	.08
5	Jim Rice	.50	.40	.20
6	Mike Schmidt	.90	.70	.35
7	Wade Boggs	1.25	.90	.50
8	Bill Madlock	.20	.15	.08
9	Dan Quisenberry	.20	.15	.08
10	Al Holland	.20	.15	.08
11	Ron Kittle	.20	.15	.08
12	Darryl Strawberry	1.25	.90	.50
13	George Brett	.90	.70	.35
14	Bill Buckner	.25	.20	.10
15	Carlton Fisk	.30	.25	.12
16	Steve Carlton	.50	.40	.20
17	Ron Guidry	.35	.25	.14
18	Gary Carter	.50	.40	.20
19	Rickey Henderson	1.00	.70	.40
20	Andre Dawson	.35	.25	.14
21	Reggie Jackson	.60	.45	.25
22	Steve Garvey	.50	.40	.20
23	Fred Lynn	.30	.25	.12
24	Pedro Guerrero	.25	.20	.10
25	Eddie Murray	.60	.45	.25
26	Keith Hernandez	.50	.40	.20
27	Dave Winfield	.50	.40	.20
28	Nolan Ryan	1.00	.70	.40
29	Robin Yount	.40	.30	.15
30	Fernando Valenzuela	.40	.30	.15

NOTE: A card number in parentheses ( ) indicates the set is unnumbered.

1984 Topps Traded

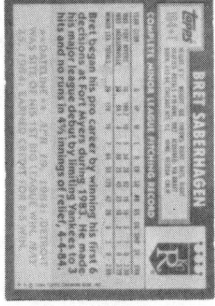

The popular Topps Traded set returned for its fourth year in 1984 with another 132-card set. The 2-1/2" by 3-1/2" cards have an identical design to the regular Topps cards except that the back cardboard is white and the card numbers carry a "T" suffix. As before, the set was sold only through hobby dealers. Also as before, players who changed teams, new managers and promising rookies are included in the set. The presence of several promising young rookies in especially high demand from investors and speculators had made this one of the most expensive Topps issues of recent years. A glossy-finish "Tiffany" version of the set was also issued, valued at four to five times the price of the normal Traded cards.

	MT	NR MT	EX
Complete Set:	110.00	82.00	45.00
Common Player:	.10	.08	.04

		MT	NR MT	EX
1T	Willie Aikens	.10	.08	.04
2T	Luis Aponte	.10	.08	.04
3T	Mike Armstrong	.10	.08	.04
4T	Bob Bailor	.10	.08	.04
5T	Dusty Baker	.20	.15	.08
6T	Steve Balboni	.20	.15	.08
7T	Alan Bannister	.10	.08	.04
8T	Dave Beard	.10	.08	.04
9T	Joe Beckwith	.10	.08	.04
10T	Bruce Berenyi	.10	.08	.04
11T	Dave Bergman	.10	.08	.04
12T	Tony Bernazard	.10	.08	.04
13T	Yogi Berra	.20	.15	.08
14T	Barry Bonnell	.10	.08	.04
15T	Phil Bradley(FC)	1.75	1.25	.70
16T	Fred Breining	.10	.08	.04
17T	Bill Buckner	.25	.20	.10
18T	Ray Burris	.10	.08	.04
19T	John Butcher	.10	.08	.04
20T	Brett Butler	.20	.15	.08
21T	Enos Cabell	.10	.08	.04
22T	Bill Campbell	.10	.08	.04
23T	Bill Caudill	.10	.08	.04
24T	Bob Clark	.10	.08	.04
25T	Bryan Clark	.10	.08	.04
26T	Jaime Cocanower	.10	.08	.04
27T	Ron Darling(FC)	4.00	3.00	1.50
28T	Alvin Davis(FC)	7.00	5.25	2.75
29T	Ken Dayley	.10	.08	.04
30T	Jeff Dedmon(FC)	.15	.11	.06
31T	Bob Dernier	.10	.08	.04
32T	Carlos Diaz	.10	.08	.04
33T	Mike Easler	.15	.11	.06
34T	Dennis Eckersley	.30	.25	.12
35T	Jim Essian	.10	.08	.04
36T	Darrell Evans	.25	.20	.10
37T	Mike Fitzgerald(FC)	.15	.11	.06
38T	Tim Foli	.10	.08	.04
39T	George Frazier	.10	.08	.04
40T	Rich Gale	.10	.08	.04
41T	Barbaro Garbey	.15	.11	.06
42T	Dwight Gooden(FC)	45.00	34.00	18.00
43T	Rich Gossage	.40	.30	.15
44T	Wayne Gross	.10	.08	.04
45T	Mark Gubicza(FC)	4.00	3.00	1.50
46T	Jackie Gutierrez	.10	.08	.04
47T	Mel Hall	.20	.15	.08
48T	Toby Harrah	.15	.11	.06

		MT	NR MT	EX
49T	Ron Hassey	.10	.08	.04
50T	Rich Hebner	.10	.08	.04
51T	Willie Hernandez	.30	.25	.12
52T	Ricky Horton(FC)	.40	.30	.15
53T	Art Howe	.10	.08	.04
54T	Dane Iorg	.10	.08	.04
55T	Brook Jacoby(FC)	2.50	2.00	1.00
56T	Mike Jeffcoat(FC)	.15	.11	.06
57T	Dave Johnson	.15	.11	.06
58T	Lynn Jones	.10	.08	.04
59T	Ruppert Jones	.10	.08	.04
60T	Mike Jorgensen	.10	.08	.04
61T	Bob Kearney	.10	.08	.04
62T	Jimmy Key(FC)	3.00	2.25	1.25
63T	Dave Kingman	.40	.30	.15
64T	Jerry Koosman	.25	.20	.10
65T	Wayne Krenchicki	.10	.08	.04
66T	Rusty Kuntz	.10	.08	.04
67T	Rene Lachemann	.10	.08	.04
68T	Frank LaCorte	.10	.08	.04
69T	Dennis Lamp	.10	.08	.04
70T	Mark Langston(FC)	12.00	9.00	4.75
71T	Rick Leach	.10	.08	.04
72T	Craig Lefferts	.15	.11	.06
73T	Gary Lucas	.10	.08	.04
74T	Jerry Martin	.10	.08	.04
75T	Carmelo Martinez	.25	.20	.10
76T	Mike Mason(FC)	.15	.11	.06
77T	Gary Matthews	.25	.20	.10
78T	Andy McGaffigan	.10	.08	.04
79T	Larry Milbourne	.10	.08	.04
80T	Sid Monge	.10	.08	.04
81T	Jackie Moore	.10	.08	.04
82T	Joe Morgan	1.50	1.25	.60
83T	Graig Nettles	.50	.40	.20
84T	Phil Niekro	1.00	.70	.40
85T	Ken Oberkfell	.10	.08	.04
86T	Mike O'Berry	.10	.08	.04
87T	Al Oliver	.30	.25	.12
88T	Jorge Orta	.10	.08	.04
89T	Amos Otis	.15	.11	.06
90T	Dave Parker	2.00	1.50	.80
91T	Tony Perez	.60	.45	.25
92T	Gerald Perry(FC)	1.25	.90	.50
93T	Gary Pettis(FC)	.25	.20	.10
94T	Rob Picciolo	.10	.08	.04
95T	Vern Rapp	.10	.08	.04
96T	Floyd Rayford	.10	.08	.04
97T	Randy Ready(FC)	.25	.20	.10
98T	Ron Reed	.15	.11	.06
99T	Gene Richards	.10	.08	.04
100T	Jose Rijo(FC)	4.00	3.00	1.50
101T	Jeff Robinson(FC)	.50	.40	.20
102T	Ron Romanick(FC)	.20	.15	.08
103T	Pete Rose	7.00	5.25	2.75
104T	Bret Saberhagen(FC)	20.00	15.00	8.00
105T	Juan Samuel(FC)	2.00	1.50	.80
106T	Scott Sanderson	.10	.08	.04
107T	Dick Schofield(FC)	.35	.25	.14
108T	Tom Seaver	3.75	2.75	1.50
109T	Jim Slaton	.10	.08	.04
110T	Mike Smithson	.10	.08	.04
111T	Lary Sorensen	.10	.08	.04
112T	Tim Stoddard	.10	.08	.04
113T	Champ Summers	.10	.08	.04
114T	Jim Sundberg	.15	.11	.06
115T	Rick Sutcliffe	.50	.40	.20
116T	Craig Swan	.10	.08	.04
117T	Tim Teufel(FC)	.30	.25	.12
118T	Derrel Thomas	.10	.08	.04
119T	Gorman Thomas	.25	.20	.10
120T	Alex Trevino	.10	.08	.04
121T	Manny Trillo	.15	.11	.06
122T	John Tudor	.25	.20	.10
123T	Tom Underwood	.10	.08	.04
124T	Mike Vail	.10	.08	.04
125T	Tom Waddell	.10	.08	.04
126T	Gary Ward	.10	.08	.04
127T	Curt Wilkerson	.10	.08	.04
128T	Frank Williams(FC)	.25	.20	.10
129T	Glenn Wilson	.20	.15	.08
130T	Johnny Wockenfuss	.10	.08	.04
131T	Ned Yost	.10	.08	.04
132T	Checklist 1-132	.10	.08	.04

Definitions for grading conditions are located in the introduction section at the front of this book.

1985 Topps

 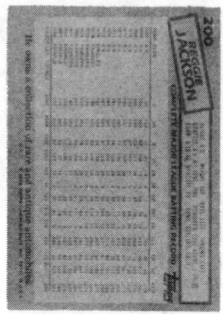

Holding the line at 792 cards, Topps did initiate some major design changes in its 2-1/2" by 3-1/2" cards in 1985. The use of two photos on the front was discontinued in favor of one large color photo. The Topps logo appears in the upper left-hand corner. At the bottom runs a diagonal rectangular box with the team name. It joins a team logo, and below that point runs the player's position and name. The backs feature statistics, biographical information and a trivia question. Some interesting specialty sets were introduced in 1985, including the revival of the father/son theme from 1976, a subset of the 1984 U.S. Olympic Baseball Team members and a set featuring #1 draft choices since the inception of the baseball draft in 1965. Again in 1985, a glossy-finish "Tiffany" edition of the regular set was produced, though the number was cut back to 5,000 sets. Values range from four times regular value for common cards to five-six times for high-demand stars and rookie cards.

		MT	NR MT	EX
Complete Set:		100.00	75.00	40.00
Common Player:		.06	.05	.02
1	Record Breaker (Carlton Fisk)	.15	.11	.06
2	Record Breaker (Steve Garvey)	.20	.15	.08
3	Record Breaker (Dwight Gooden)	1.00	.70	.40
4	Record Breaker (Cliff Johnson)	.08	.06	.03
5	Record Breaker (Joe Morgan)	.15	.11	.06
6	Record Breaker (Pete Rose)	.60	.45	.25
7	Record Breaker (Nolan Ryan)	.30	.25	.12
8	Record Breaker (Juan Samuel)(FC)	.20	.15	.08
9	Record Breaker (Bruce Sutter)	.12	.09	.05
10	Record Breaker (Don Sutton)	.20	.15	.08
11	Ralph Houk	.08	.06	.03
12	Dave Lopes	.08	.06	.03
13	Tim Lollar	.06	.05	.02
14	Chris Bando	.06	.05	.02
15	Jerry Koosman	.10	.08	.04
16	Bobby Meacham	.06	.05	.02
17	Mike Scott	.15	.11	.06
18	Mickey Hatcher	.06	.05	.02
19	George Frazier	.06	.05	.02
20	Chet Lemon	.08	.06	.03
21	Lee Tunnell	.06	.05	.02
22	Duane Kuiper	.06	.05	.02
23	*Bret Saberhagen*	6.00	4.50	2.50
24	Jesse Barfield	.25	.20	.10
25	Steve Bedrosian	.12	.09	.05
26	Roy Smalley	.06	.05	.02
27	Bruce Berenyi	.06	.05	.02
28	Dann Bilardello	.06	.05	.02
29	Odell Jones	.06	.05	.02
30	Cal Ripken	.50	.40	.20
31	Terry Whitfield	.06	.05	.02
32	Chuck Porter	.06	.05	.02
33	Tito Landrum	.06	.05	.02
34	Ed Nunez(FC)	.08	.06	.03
35	Graig Nettles	.15	.11	.06
36	Fred Breining	.06	.05	.02
37	Reid Nichols	.06	.05	.02
38	Jackie Moore	.06	.05	.02
39	Johnny Wockenfuss	.06	.05	.02
40	Phil Niekro	.25	.20	.10

		MT	NR MT	EX
41	Mike Fischlin	.06	.05	.02
42	Luis Sanchez	.06	.05	.02
43	Andre David	.06	.05	.02
44	Dickie Thon	.08	.06	.03
45	Greg Minton	.06	.05	.02
46	Gary Woods	.06	.05	.02
47	Dave Rozema	.06	.05	.02
48	Tony Fernandez(FC)	1.25	.90	.50
49	Butch Davis	.06	.05	.02
50	John Candelaria	.10	.08	.04
51	Bob Watson	.08	.06	.03
52	Jerry Dybzinski	.06	.05	.02
53	Tom Gorman	.06	.05	.02
54	Cesar Cedeno	.10	.08	.04
55	Frank Tanana	.10	.08	.04
56	Jim Dwyer	.06	.05	.02
57	Pat Zachry	.06	.05	.02
58	Orlando Mercado	.06	.05	.02
59	Rick Waits	.06	.05	.02
60	George Hendrick	.08	.06	.03
61	Curt Kaufman	.06	.05	.02
62	Mike Ramsey	.06	.05	.02
63	Steve McCatty	.06	.05	.02
64	*Mark Bailey*(FC)	.10	.08	.04
65	Bill Buckner	.12	.09	.05
66	Dick Williams	.06	.05	.02
67	*Rafael Santana*(FC)	.20	.15	.08
68	Von Hayes	.10	.08	.04
69	*Jim Winn*(FC)	.10	.08	.04
70	Don Baylor	.12	.09	.05
71	Tim Laudner	.06	.05	.02
72	Rick Sutcliffe	.12	.09	.05
73	Rusty Kuntz	.06	.05	.02
74	Mike Krukow	.08	.06	.03
75	Willie Upshaw	.08	.06	.03
76	Alan Bannister	.06	.05	.02
77	Joe Beckwith	.06	.05	.02
78	Scott Fletcher	.08	.06	.03
79	Rick Mahler	.06	.05	.02
80	Keith Hernandez	.30	.25	.12
81	Lenn Sakata	.06	.05	.02
82	Joe Price	.06	.05	.02
83	Charlie Moore	.06	.05	.02
84	Spike Owen	.08	.06	.03
85	Mike Marshall	.15	.11	.06
86	Don Aase	.06	.05	.02
87	David Green	.06	.05	.02
88	Bryn Smith	.06	.05	.02
89	Jackie Gutierrez	.06	.05	.02
90	Rich Gossage	.20	.15	.08
91	Jeff Burroughs	.08	.06	.03
92	Paul Owens	.06	.05	.02
93	*Don Schulze*(FC)	.10	.08	.04
94	Toby Harrah	.08	.06	.03
95	Jose Cruz	.10	.08	.04
96	Johnny Ray	.12	.09	.05
97	Pete Filson	.06	.05	.02
98	Steve Lake	.06	.05	.02
99	Milt Wilcox	.06	.05	.02
100	George Brett	.50	.40	.20
101	Jim Acker	.06	.05	.02
102	Tommy Dunbar	.06	.05	.02
103	Randy Lerch	.06	.05	.02
104	Mike Fitzgerald	.08	.06	.03
105	Ron Kittle	.10	.08	.04
106	Pascual Perez	.08	.06	.03
107	Tom Foley	.06	.05	.02
108	Darnell Coles(FC)	.15	.11	.06
109	Gary Roenicke	.06	.05	.02
110	Alejandro Pena	.08	.06	.03
111	Doug DeCinces	.10	.08	.04
112	Tom Tellmann	.06	.05	.02
113	Tom Herr	.10	.08	.04
114	Bob James	.06	.05	.02
115	Rickey Henderson	2.00	1.50	.80
116	Dennis Boyd(FC)	.15	.11	.06
117	Greg Gross	.06	.05	.02
118	Eric Show	.08	.06	.03
119	Pat Corrales	.06	.05	.02
120	Steve Kemp	.08	.06	.03
121	Checklist 1-132	.06	.05	.02
122	Tom Brunansky	.12	.09	.05
123	Dave Smith	.08	.06	.03
124	Rich Hebner	.06	.05	.02
125	Kent Tekulve	.08	.06	.03
126	Ruppert Jones	.06	.05	.02
127	*Mark Gubicza*	1.25	.90	.50
128	Ernie Whitt	.08	.06	.03
129	Gene Garber	.06	.05	.02
130	Al Oliver	.12	.09	.05
131	Father - Son (Buddy Bell, Gus Bell)	.12	.09	.05
132	Father - Son (Dale Berra, Yogi Berra)	.20	.15	.08

		MT	NR MT	EX
133	Father - Son (Bob Boone, Ray Boone)			
		.12	.09	.05
134	Father - Son (Terry Francona, Tito Francona)			
		.08	.06	.03
135	Father - Son (Bob Kennedy, Terry Kennedy)			
		.08	.06	.03
136	Father - Son (Bill Kunkel, Jeff Kunkel)(FC)			
		.08	.06	.03
137	Father - Son (Vance Law, Vern Law)			
		.10	.08	.04
138	Father - Son (Dick Schofield, Dick Schofield)			
		.08	.06	.03
139	Father - Son (Bob Skinner, Joel Skinner)			
		.08	.06	.03
140	Father - Son (Roy Smalley, Roy Smalley)			
		.08	.06	.03
141	Father - Son (Dave Stenhouse, Mike Stenhouse)			
		.08	.06	.03
142	Father - Son (Dizzy Trout, Steve Trout)			
		.08	.06	.03
143	Father - Son (Ossie Virgil, Ozzie Virgil)			
		.08	.06	.03
144	Ron Gardenhire	.06	.05	.02
145	*Alvin Davis*	2.00	1.50	.80
146	Gary Redus	.08	.06	.03
147	Bill Swaggerty	.06	.05	.02
148	Steve Yeager	.06	.05	.02
149	Dickie Noles	.06	.05	.02
150	Jim Rice	.35	.25	.14
151	Moose Haas	.06	.05	.02
152	Steve Braun	.06	.05	.02
153	Frank LaCorte	.06	.05	.02
154	Argenis Salazar(FC)	.06	.05	.02
155	Yogi Berra	.12	.09	.05
156	Craig Reynolds	.06	.05	.02
157	Tug McGraw	.10	.08	.04
158	Pat Tabler	.08	.06	.03
159	Carlos Diaz	.06	.05	.02
160	Lance Parrish	.25	.20	.10
161	Ken Schrom	.06	.05	.02
162	*Benny Distefano*(FC)	.10	.08	.04
163	Dennis Eckersley	.12	.09	.05
164	Jorge Orta	.06	.05	.02
165	Dusty Baker	.08	.06	.03
166	Keith Atherton	.06	.05	.02
167	Rufino Linares	.06	.05	.02
168	Garth Iorg	.06	.05	.02
169	Dan Spillner	.06	.05	.02
170	George Foster	.15	.11	.06
171	Bill Stein	.06	.05	.02
172	Jack Perconte	.06	.05	.02
173	Mike Young(FC)	.12	.09	.05
174	Rick Honeycutt	.06	.05	.02
175	Dave Parker	.25	.20	.10
176	Bill Schroeder	.06	.05	.02
177	Dave Von Ohlen	.06	.05	.02
178	Miguel Dilone	.06	.05	.02
179	Tommy John	.20	.15	.08
180	Dave Winfield	.35	.25	.14
181	*Roger Clemens*(FC)	13.00	9.75	5.25
182	Tim Flannery	.06	.05	.02
183	Larry McWilliams	.06	.05	.02
184	Carmen Castillo(FC)	.10	.08	.04
185	Al Holland	.06	.05	.02
186	Bob Lillis	.06	.05	.02
187	Mike Walters	.06	.05	.02
188	Greg Pryor	.06	.05	.02
189	Warren Brusstar	.06	.05	.02
190	Rusty Staub	.12	.09	.05
191	Steve Nicosia	.08	.06	.03
192	Howard Johnson(FC)	4.00	3.00	1.50
193	*Jimmy Key*	1.00	.70	.40
194	Dave Stegman	.06	.05	.02
195	Glenn Hubbard	.06	.05	.02
196	Pete O'Brien	.12	.09	.05
197	Mike Warren	.06	.05	.02
198	Eddie Milner	.06	.05	.02
199	Denny Martinez	.08	.06	.03
200	Reggie Jackson	.40	.30	.15
201	Burt Hooton	.08	.06	.03
202	Gorman Thomas	.10	.08	.04
203	Bob McClure	.06	.05	.02
204	Art Howe	.06	.05	.02
205	Steve Rogers	.08	.06	.03
206	Phil Garner	.08	.06	.03
207	Mark Clear	.06	.05	.02
208	Champ Summers	.06	.05	.02
209	Bill Campbell	.06	.05	.02
210	Gary Matthews	.10	.08	.04
211	Clay Christiansen	.06	.05	.02
212	George Vukovich	.06	.05	.02

		MT	NR MT	EX
213	Billy Gardner	.06	.05	.02
214	John Tudor	.10	.08	.04
215	Bob Brenly	.06	.05	.02
216	Jerry Don Gleaton	.06	.05	.02
217	Leon Roberts	.06	.05	.02
218	Doyle Alexander	.10	.08	.04
219	Gerald Perry	.35	.25	.14
220	Fred Lynn	.20	.15	.08
221	Ron Reed	.06	.05	.02
222	Hubie Brooks	.10	.08	.04
223	Tom Hume	.06	.05	.02
224	Al Cowens	.06	.05	.02
225	Mike Boddicker	.10	.08	.04
226	Juan Beniquez	.06	.05	.02
227	Danny Darwin	.06	.05	.02
228	Dion James(FC)	.20	.15	.08
229	Dave LaPoint	.08	.06	.03
230	Gary Carter	.35	.25	.14
231	Dwayne Murphy	.08	.06	.03
232	Dave Beard	.06	.05	.02
233	Ed Jurak	.06	.05	.02
234	Jerry Narron	.06	.05	.02
235	Garry Maddox	.10	.08	.04
236	Mark Thurmond	.06	.05	.02
237	Julio Franco	.50	.40	.20
238	*Jose Rijo*	1.00	.70	.40
239	Tim Teufel	.12	.09	.05
240	Dave Stieb	.12	.09	.05
241	Jim Frey	.06	.05	.02
242	Greg Harris	.06	.05	.02
243	Barbaro Garbey	.10	.08	.04
244	Mike Jones	.06	.05	.02
245	Chili Davis	.10	.08	.04
246	Mike Norris	.06	.05	.02
247	Wayne Tolleson	.06	.05	.02
248	Terry Forster	.08	.06	.03
249	Harold Baines	.15	.11	.06
250	Jesse Orosco	.08	.06	.03
251	Brad Gulden	.06	.05	.02
252	Dan Ford	.06	.05	.02
253	*Sid Bream*(FC)	.40	.30	.15
254	Pete Vuckovich	.08	.06	.03
255	Lonnie Smith	.08	.06	.03
256	Mike Stanton	.06	.05	.02
257	Brian Little (Bryan)	.06	.05	.02
258	Mike Brown	.06	.05	.02
259	Gary Allenson	.06	.05	.02
260	Dave Righetti	.20	.15	.08
261	Checklist 133-264	.06	.05	.02
262	*Greg Booker*(FC)	.12	.09	.05
263	Mel Hall	.08	.06	.03
264	Joe Sambito	.06	.05	.02
265	Juan Samuel(FC)	.50	.40	.20
266	Frank Viola	.20	.15	.08
267	*Henry Cotto*(FC)	.15	.11	.06
268	Chuck Tanner	.06	.05	.02
269	*Doug Baker*(FC)	.10	.08	.04
270	Dan Quisenberry	.10	.08	.04
271	1968 #1 Draft Pick (Tim Foli)	.08	.06	.03
272	1969 #1 Draft Pick (Jeff Burroughs)			
		.08	.06	.03
273	1974 #1 Draft Pick (Bill Almon)	.08	.06	.03
274	1976 #1 Draft Pick (Floyd Bannister)			
		.10	.08	.04
275	1977 #1 Draft Pick (Harold Baines)			
		.15	.11	.06
276	1978 #1 Draft Pick (Bob Horner)	.15	.11	.06
277	1979 #1 Draft Pick (Al Chambers)	.08	.06	.03
278	1980 #1 Draft Pick (Darryl Strawberry)			
		1.25	.90	.50
279	1981 #1 Draft Pick (Mike Moore)(FC)			
		.20	.15	.08
280	1982 #1 Draft Pick (*Shawon Dunston*)(FC)			
		3.00	2.25	1.25
281	1983 #1 Draft Pick (Tim Belcher)(FC)			
		1.50	1.25	.60
282	1984 #1 Draft Pick (*Shawn Abner*)(FC)			
		.60	.45	.25
283	Fran Mullins	.06	.05	.02
284	Marty Bystrom	.06	.05	.02
285	Dan Driessen	.08	.06	.03
286	Rudy Law	.06	.05	.02
287	Walt Terrell	.08	.06	.03
288	*Jeff Kunkel*(FC)	.10	.08	.04
289	Tom Underwood	.06	.05	.02
290	Cecil Cooper	.12	.09	.05
291	Bob Welch	.12	.09	.05
292	Brad Komminsk(FC)	.08	.06	.03
293	Curt Young(FC)	.35	.25	.14
294	*Tom Nieto*(FC)	.10	.08	.04
295	Joe Niekro	.10	.08	.04

		MT	NR MT	EX
296	Ricky Nelson	.06	.05	.02
297	Gary Lucas	.06	.05	.02
298	Marty Barrett	.15	.11	.06
299	Andy Hawkins	.08	.06	.03
300	Rod Carew	.40	.30	.15
301	John Montefusco	.06	.05	.02
302	Tim Corcoran	.06	.05	.02
303	*Mike Jeffcoat*	.08	.06	.03
304	Gary Gaetti	.25	.20	.10
305	Dale Berra	.06	.05	.02
306	Rick Reuschel	.10	.08	.04
307	Sparky Anderson	.08	.06	.03
308	John Wathan	.08	.06	.03
309	Mike Witt	.12	.09	.05
310	Manny Trillo	.08	.06	.03
311	Jim Gott	.06	.05	.02
312	Marc Hill	.06	.05	.02
313	Dave Schmidt	.06	.05	.02
314	Ron Oester	.06	.05	.02
315	Doug Sisk	.06	.05	.02
316	John Lowenstein	.06	.05	.02
317	*Jack Lazorko*(FC)	.10	.08	.04
318	Ted Simmons	.12	.09	.05
319	Jeff Jones	.06	.05	.02
320	Dale Murphy	.60	.45	.25
321	*Ricky Horton*	.30	.25	.12
322	Dave Stapleton	.06	.05	.02
323	Andy McGaffigan	.06	.05	.02
324	Bruce Bochy	.06	.05	.02
325	John Denny	.06	.05	.02
326	Kevin Bass	.10	.08	.04
327	Brook Jacoby	.30	.25	.12
328	Bob Shirley	.06	.05	.02
329	Ron Washington	.06	.05	.02
330	Leon Durham	.08	.06	.03
331	Bill Laskey	.06	.05	.02
332	Brian Harper	.06	.05	.02
333	Willie Hernandez	.08	.06	.03
334	Dick Howser	.06	.05	.02
335	Bruce Benedict	.06	.05	.02
336	Rance Mulliniks	.06	.05	.02
337	Billy Sample	.06	.05	.02
338	Britt Burns	.06	.05	.02
339	Danny Heep	.06	.05	.02
340	Robin Yount	.60	.45	.25
341	Floyd Rayford	.06	.05	.02
342	Ted Power	.06	.05	.02
343	Bill Russell	.08	.06	.03
344	Dave Henderson	.10	.08	.04
345	Charlie Lea	.06	.05	.02
346	*Terry Pendleton*(FC)	.70	.50	.30
347	Rick Langford	.06	.05	.02
348	Bob Boone	.08	.06	.03
349	Domingo Ramos	.06	.05	.02
350	Wade Boggs	3.50	2.75	1.50
351	Juan Agosto	.06	.05	.02
352	Joe Morgan	.30	.25	.12
353	Julio Solano	.06	.05	.02
354	Andre Robertson	.06	.05	.02
355	Bert Blyleven	.12	.09	.05
356	Dave Meier	.06	.05	.02
357	Rich Bordi	.06	.05	.02
358	Tony Pena	.10	.08	.04
359	Pat Sheridan	.06	.05	.02
360	Steve Carlton	.40	.30	.15
361	Alfredo Griffin	.08	.06	.03
362	Craig McMurtry	.06	.05	.02
363	Ron Hodges	.06	.05	.02
364	Richard Dotson	.10	.08	.04
365	Danny Ozark	.06	.05	.02
366	Todd Cruz	.06	.05	.02
367	Keefe Cato	.06	.05	.02
368	Dave Bergman	.06	.05	.02
369	*R.J. Reynolds*(FC)	.25	.20	.10
370	Bruce Sutter	.12	.09	.05
371	Mickey Rivers	.08	.06	.03
372	Roy Howell	.06	.05	.02
373	Mike Moore	.06	.05	.02
374	Brian Downing	.10	.08	.04
375	Jeff Reardon	.12	.09	.05
376	Jeff Newman	.06	.05	.02
377	Checklist 265-396	.06	.05	.02
378	Alan Wiggins	.06	.05	.02
379	Charles Hudson	.08	.06	.03
380	Ken Griffey	.10	.08	.04
381	Roy Smith	.06	.05	.02
382	Denny Walling	.06	.05	.02
383	Rick Lysander	.06	.05	.02
384	Jody Davis	.10	.08	.04
385	Jose DeLeon	.08	.06	.03
386	*Dan Gladden*(FC)	.30	.25	.12

		MT	NR MT	EX
387	*Buddy Biancalana*(FC)	.12	.09	.05
388	Bert Roberge	.06	.05	.02
389	1984 United States Baseball Team (Rod Dedeaux)	.06	.05	.02
390	1984 United States Baseball Team (Sid Akins)(FC)	.10	.08	.04
391	1984 United States Baseball Team (Flavio Alfaro)	.06	.05	.02
392	1984 United States Baseball Team (Don August)(FC)	.20	.15	.08
393	1984 United States Baseball Team (Scott Bankhead)(FC)	.70	.50	.30
394	1984 United States Baseball Team (Bob Caffrey)(FC)	.08	.06	.03
395	1984 United States Baseball Team (Mike Dunne)(FC)	.25	.20	.10
396	1984 United States Baseball Team (Gary Green)(FC)	.08	.06	.03
397	1984 United States Baseball Team (John Hoover)	.06	.05	.02
398	1984 United States Baseball Team (Shane Mack)(FC)	.40	.30	.15
399	1984 United States Baseball Team (John Marzano)(FC)	.25	.20	.10
400	1984 United States Baseball Team (Oddibe McDowell)(FC)	.80	.60	.30
401	1984 United States Baseball Team (Mark McGwire)(FC)	18.00	13.50	7.25
402	1984 United States Baseball Team (Pat Pacillo)(FC)	.20	.15	.08
403	1984 United States Baseball Team (Cory Snyder)(FC)	3.00	2.25	1.25
404	1984 United States Baseball Team (Billy Swift)(FC)	.30	.25	.12
405	Tom Veryzer	.06	.05	.02
406	Len Whitehouse	.06	.05	.02
407	Bobby Ramos	.06	.05	.02
408	Sid Monge	.06	.05	.02
409	Brad Wellman	.06	.05	.02
410	Bob Horner	.15	.11	.06
411	Bobby Cox	.06	.05	.02
412	Bud Black	.06	.05	.02
413	Vance Law	.08	.06	.03
414	Gary Ward	.08	.06	.03
415	Ron Darling	1.00	.70	.40
416	Wayne Gross	.06	.05	.02
417	*John Franco*(FC)	1.50	1.25	.70
418	Ken Landreaux	.06	.05	.02
419	Mike Caldwell	.06	.05	.02
420	Andre Dawson	.30	.25	.12
421	Dave Rucker	.06	.05	.02
422	Carney Lansford	.10	.08	.04
423	Barry Bonnell	.06	.05	.02
424	*Al Nipper*(FC)	.15	.11	.06
425	Mike Hargrove	.06	.05	.02
426	Verne Ruhle	.06	.05	.02
427	Mario Ramirez	.06	.05	.02
428	Larry Andersen	.06	.05	.02
429	Rick Cerone	.06	.05	.02
430	Ron Davis	.06	.05	.02
431	U.L. Washington	.06	.05	.02
432	Thad Bosley	.06	.05	.02
433	Jim Morrison	.06	.05	.02
434	Gene Richards	.06	.05	.02
435	Dan Petry	.08	.06	.03
436	Willie Aikens	.06	.05	.02
437	Al Jones	.06	.05	.02
438	Joe Torre	.08	.06	.03
439	Junior Ortiz	.06	.05	.02
440	Fernando Valenzuela	.30	.25	.12
441	Duane Walker	.06	.05	.02
442	Ken Forsch	.06	.05	.02
443	George Wright	.06	.05	.02
444	Tony Phillips	.06	.05	.02
445	Tippy Martinez	.06	.05	.02
446	Jim Sundberg	.08	.06	.03
447	Jeff Lahti	.06	.05	.02
448	Derrel Thomas	.06	.05	.02
449	*Phil Bradley*	.80	.60	.30
450	Steve Garvey	.40	.30	.15
451	Bruce Hurst	.12	.09	.05
452	John Castino	.06	.05	.02
453	Tom Waddell	.06	.05	.02
454	Glenn Wilson	.08	.06	.03
455	Bob Knepper	.08	.06	.03
456	Tim Foli	.06	.05	.02
457	Cecilio Guante	.06	.05	.02
458	Randy Johnson	.06	.05	.02
459	Charlie Leibrandt	.08	.06	.03
460	Ryne Sandberg	2.00	1.50	.80
461	Marty Castillo	.06	.05	.02

		MT	NR MT	EX
462	Gary Lavelle	.06	.05	.02
463	Dave Collins	.08	.06	.03
464	Mike Mason(FC)	.10	.08	.04
465	Bob Grich	.10	.08	.04
466	Tony LaRussa	.08	.06	.03
467	Ed Lynch	.06	.05	.02
468	Wayne Krenchicki	.06	.05	.02
469	Sammy Stewart	.06	.05	.02
470	Steve Sax	.20	.15	.08
471	Pete Ladd	.06	.05	.02
472	Jim Essian	.06	.05	.02
473	Tim Wallach	.12	.09	.05
474	Kurt Kepshire	.06	.05	.02
475	Andre Thornton	.10	.08	.04
476	Jeff Stone(FC)	.12	.09	.05
477	Bob Ojeda	.10	.08	.04
478	Kurt Bevacqua	.06	.05	.02
479	Mike Madden	.06	.05	.02
480	Lou Whitaker	.30	.25	.12
481	Dale Murray	.06	.05	.02
482	Harry Spilman	.06	.05	.02
483	Mike Smithson	.06	.05	.02
484	Larry Bowa	.10	.08	.04
485	Matt Young	.06	.05	.02
486	Steve Balboni	.08	.06	.03
487	Frank Williams	.15	.11	.06
488	Joel Skinner(FC)	.08	.06	.03
489	Bryan Clark	.06	.05	.02
490	Jason Thompson	.06	.05	.02
491	Rick Camp	.06	.05	.02
492	Dave Johnson	.08	.06	.03
493	Orel Hershiser(FC)	6.00	4.50	2.50
494	Rich Dauer	.06	.05	.02
495	Mario Soto	.08	.06	.03
496	Donnie Scott	.06	.05	.02
497	Gary Pettis	.15	.11	.06
498	Ed Romero	.06	.05	.02
499	Danny Cox(FC)	.20	.20	.10
500	Mike Schmidt	.60	.45	.25
501	Dan Schatzeder	.06	.05	.02
502	Rick Miller	.06	.05	.02
503	Tim Conroy	.06	.05	.02
504	Jerry Willard	.06	.05	.02
505	Jim Beattie	.06	.05	.02
506	Franklin Stubbs(FC)	.40	.30	.15
507	Ray Fontenot	.06	.05	.02
508	John Shelby	.08	.06	.03
509	Milt May	.06	.05	.02
510	Kent Hrbek	.25	.20	.10
511	Lee Smith	.10	.08	.04
512	Tom Brookens	.06	.05	.02
513	Lynn Jones	.06	.05	.02
514	Jeff Cornell	.06	.05	.02
515	Dave Concepcion	.12	.09	.05
516	Roy Lee Jackson	.06	.05	.02
517	Jerry Martin	.06	.05	.02
518	Chris Chambliss	.08	.06	.03
519	Doug Rader	.06	.05	.02
520	LaMarr Hoyt	.06	.05	.02
521	Rick Dempsey	.08	.06	.03
522	Paul Molitor	.15	.11	.06
523	Candy Maldonado	.10	.08	.04
524	Rob Wilfong	.06	.05	.02
525	Darrell Porter	.08	.06	.03
526	Dave Palmer	.06	.05	.02
527	Checklist 397-528	.06	.05	.02
528	Bill Krueger	.06	.05	.02
529	Rich Gedman	.10	.08	.04
530	Dave Dravecky	.08	.06	.03
531	Joe Lefebvre	.06	.05	.02
532	Frank DiPino	.06	.05	.02
533	Tony Bernazard	.06	.05	.02
534	Brian Dayett(FC)	.06	.05	.02
535	Pat Putnam	.06	.05	.02
536	Kirby Puckett(FC)	15.00	11.00	6.00
537	Don Robinson	.08	.06	.03
538	Keith Moreland	.08	.06	.03
539	Aurelio Lopez	.06	.05	.02
540	Claudell Washington	.08	.06	.03
541	Mark Davis	.06	.05	.02
542	Don Slaught	.06	.05	.02
543	Mike Squires	.06	.05	.02
544	Bruce Kison	.06	.05	.02
545	Lloyd Moseby	.10	.08	.04
546	Brent Gaff	.06	.05	.02
547	Pete Rose	.60	.45	.25
548	Larry Parrish	.10	.08	.04
549	Mike Scioscia	.08	.06	.03
550	Scott McGregor	.08	.06	.03
551	Andy Van Slyke	.35	.25	.14
552	Chris Codiroli	.06	.05	.02
553	Bob Clark	.06	.05	.02
554	Doug Flynn	.06	.05	.02
555	Bob Stanley	.06	.05	.02
556	Sixto Lezcano	.06	.05	.02
557	Len Barker	.08	.06	.03
558	Carmelo Martinez	.08	.06	.03
559	Jay Howell	.08	.06	.03
560	Bill Madlock	.12	.09	.05
561	Darryl Motley	.06	.05	.02
562	Houston Jimenez	.06	.05	.02
563	Dick Ruthven	.06	.05	.02
564	Alan Ashby	.06	.05	.02
565	Kirk Gibson	.35	.25	.14
566	Ed Vande Berg	.06	.05	.02
567	Joel Youngblood	.06	.05	.02
568	Cliff Johnson	.06	.05	.02
569	Ken Oberkfell	.06	.05	.02
570	Darryl Strawberry	4.00	3.00	1.50
571	Charlie Hough	.08	.06	.03
572	Tom Paciorek	.06	.05	.02
573	Jay Tibbs(FC)	.15	.11	.06
574	Joe Altobelli	.06	.05	.02
575	Pedro Guerrero	.25	.20	.10
576	Jaime Cocanower	.06	.05	.02
577	Chris Speier	.06	.05	.02
578	Terry Francona	.06	.05	.02
579	Ron Romanick	.10	.08	.04
580	Dwight Evans	.12	.09	.05
581	Mark Wagner	.06	.05	.02
582	Ken Phelps(FC)	.20	.15	.08
583	Bobby Brown	.06	.05	.02
584	Kevin Gross	.10	.08	.04
585	Butch Wynegar	.06	.05	.02
586	Bill Scherrer	.06	.05	.02
587	Doug Frobel	.06	.05	.02
588	Bobby Castillo	.06	.05	.02
589	Bob Dernier	.06	.05	.02
590	Ray-Knight	.10	.08	.04
591	Larry Herndon	.08	.06	.03
592	Jeff Robinson	.30	.25	.12
593	Rick Leach	.06	.05	.02
594	Curt Wilkerson(FC)	.08	.06	.03
595	Larry Gura	.06	.05	.02
596	Jerry Hairston	.06	.05	.02
597	Brad Lesley	.06	.05	.02
598	Jose Oquendo	.06	.05	.02
599	Storm Davis	.10	.08	.04
600	Pete Rose	1.00	.70	.40
601	Tom Lasorda	.10	.08	.04
602	Jeff Dedmon	.12	.09	.05
603	Rick Manning	.06	.05	.02
604	Daryl Sconiers	.06	.05	.02
605	Ozzie Smith	.15	.11	.06
606	Rich Gale	.06	.05	.02
607	Bill Almon	.06	.05	.02
608	Craig Lefferts	.08	.06	.03
609	Broderick Perkins	.06	.05	.02
610	Jack Morris	.25	.20	.10
611	Ozzie Virgil	.06	.05	.02
612	Mike Armstrong	.06	.05	.02
613	Terry Puhl	.06	.05	.02
614	Al Williams	.06	.05	.02
615	Marvell Wynne	.06	.05	.02
616	Scott Sanderson	.06	.05	.02
617	Willie Wilson	.12	.09	.05
618	Pete Falcone	.06	.05	.02
619	Jeff Leonard	.10	.08	.04
620	Dwight Gooden	9.00	6.75	3.50
621	Marvis Foley	.06	.05	.02
622	Luis Leal	.06	.05	.02
623	Greg Walker	.12	.09	.05
624	Benny Ayala	.06	.05	.02
625	Mark Langston	2.25	1.75	.90
626	German Rivera	.06	.05	.02
627	Eric Davis(FC)	15.00	11.00	6.00
628	Rene Lachemann	.06	.05	.02
629	Dick Schofield	.12	.09	.05
630	Tim Raines	.35	.25	.14
631	Bob Forsch	.08	.06	.03
632	Bruce Bochte	.06	.05	.02
633	Glenn Hoffman	.06	.05	.02
634	Bill Dawley	.06	.05	.02
635	Terry Kennedy	.08	.06	.03
636	Shane Rawley	.10	.08	.04
637	Brett Butler	.08	.06	.03
638	Mike Pagliarulo(FC)	.80	.60	.30
639	Ed Hodge	.06	.05	.02
640	Steve Henderson	.06	.05	.02
641	Rod Scurry	.06	.05	.02
642	Dave Owen	.06	.05	.02
643	Johnny Grubb	.06	.05	.02

		MT	NR MT	EX
644	Mark Huismann(FC)	.06	.05	.02
645	Damaso Garcia	.06	.05	.02
646	Scot Thompson	.06	.05	.02
647	Rafael Ramirez	.06	.05	.02
648	Bob Jones	.06	.05	.02
649	Sid Fernandez(FC)	.90	.70	.35
650	Greg Luzinski	.10	.08	.04
651	Jeff Russell	.08	.06	.03
652	Joe Nolan	.06	.05	.02
653	Mark Brouhard	.06	.05	.02
654	Dave Anderson	.06	.05	.02
655	Joaquin Andujar	.08	.06	.03
656	Chuck Cottier	.06	.05	.02
657	Jim Slaton	.06	.05	.02
658	Mike Stenhouse	.06	.05	.02
659	Checklist 529-660	.06	.05	.02
660	Tony Gwynn	.80	.60	.30
661	Steve Crawford	.06	.05	.02
662	Mike Heath	.06	.05	.02
663	Luis Aguayo	.06	.05	.02
664	*Steve Farr*(FC)	.30	.25	.12
665	Don Mattingly	10.00	7.50	4.00
666	Mike LaCoss	.06	.05	.02
667	Dave Engle	.06	.05	.02
668	Steve Trout	.06	.05	.02
669	Lee Lacy	.06	.05	.02
670	Tom Seaver	.30	.25	.12
671	Dane Iorg	.06	.05	.02
672	Juan Berenguer	.06	.05	.02
673	Buck Martinez	.06	.05	.02
674	Atlee Hammaker	.06	.05	.02
675	Tony Perez	.15	.11	.06
676	*Albert Hall*(FC)	.15	.11	.06
677	Wally Backman	.08	.06	.03
678	Joey McLaughlin	.06	.05	.02
679	Bob Kearney	.06	.05	.02
680	Jerry Reuss	.08	.06	.03
681	Ben Oglivie	.08	.06	.03
682	Doug Corbett	.06	.05	.02
683	Whitey Herzog	.08	.06	.03
684	Bill Doran	.12	.09	.05
685	Bill Caudill	.06	.05	.02
686	Mike Easler	.08	.06	.03
687	Bill Gullickson	.06	.05	.02
688	Len Matuszek	.06	.05	.02
689	Luis DeLeon	.06	.05	.02
690	Alan Trammell	.35	.25	.14
691	Dennis Rasmussen(FC)	.30	.25	.12
692	Randy Bush	.06	.05	.02
693	Tim Stoddard	.06	.05	.02
694	Joe Carter(FC)	3.00	2.25	1.25
695	Rick Rhoden	.10	.08	.04
696	John Rabb	.06	.05	.02
697	Onix Concepcion	.06	.05	.02
698	Jorge Bell	.40	.30	.15
699	Donnie Moore	.06	.05	.02
700	Eddie Murray	.50	.40	.20
701	Eddie Murray AS	.30	.25	.12
702	Damaso Garcia AS	.08	.06	.03
703	George Brett AS	.35	.25	.14
704	Cal Ripken AS	.30	.25	.12
705	Dave Winfield AS	.20	.15	.08
706	Rickey Henderson AS	.30	.25	.12
707	Tony Armas AS	.08	.06	.03
708	Lance Parrish AS	.15	.11	.06
709	Mike Boddicker AS	.08	.06	.03
710	Frank Viola AS	.12	.09	.05
711	Dan Quisenberry AS	.10	.08	.04
712	Keith Hernandez AS	.20	.15	.08
713	Ryne Sandberg AS	.20	.15	.08
714	Mike Schmidt AS	.30	.25	.12
715	Ozzie Smith AS	.12	.09	.05
716	Dale Murphy AS	.35	.25	.14
717	Tony Gwynn AS	.35	.25	.14
718	Jeff Leonard AS	.10	.08	.04
719	Gary Carter AS	.20	.15	.08
720	Rick Sutcliffe AS	.12	.09	.05
721	Bob Knepper AS	.08	.06	.03
722	Bruce Sutter AS	.10	.08	.04
723	Dave Stewart	.12	.09	.05
724	Oscar Gamble	.08	.06	.03
725	Floyd Bannister	.10	.08	.04
726	Al Bumbry	.08	.06	.03
727	Frank Pastore	.06	.05	.02
728	Bob Bailor	.06	.05	.02
729	Don Sutton	.30	.25	.12
730	Dave Kingman	.15	.11	.06
731	Neil Allen	.06	.05	.02
732	John McNamara	.06	.05	.02
733	Tony Scott	.06	.05	.02
734	John Henry Johnson	.06	.05	.02

		MT	NR MT	EX
735	Garry Templeton	.08	.06	.03
736	Jerry Mumphrey	.06	.05	.02
737	Bo Diaz	.08	.06	.03
738	Omar Moreno	.06	.05	.02
739	Ernie Camacho	.06	.05	.02
740	Jack Clark	.20	.15	.08
741	John Butcher	.06	.05	.02
742	Ron Hassey	.06	.05	.02
743	Frank White	.10	.08	.04
744	Doug Bair	.06	.05	.02
745	Buddy Bell	.12	.09	.05
746	Jim Clancy	.08	.06	.03
747	Alex Trevino	.06	.05	.02
748	Lee Mazzilli	.08	.06	.03
749	Julio Cruz	.06	.05	.02
750	Rollie Fingers	.20	.15	.08
751	Kelvin Chapman	.06	.05	.02
752	Bob Owchinko	.06	.05	.02
753	Greg Brock	.08	.06	.03
754	Larry Milbourne	.06	.05	.02
755	Ken Singleton	.08	.06	.03
756	Rob Picciolo	.06	.05	.02
757	Willie McGee	.30	.25	.12
758	Ray Burris	.06	.05	.02
759	Jim Fanning	.06	.05	.02
760	Nolan Ryan	1.50	1.25	.60
761	Jerry Remy	.06	.05	.02
762	Eddie Whitson	.06	.05	.02
763	Kiko Garcia	.06	.05	.02
764	Jamie Easterly	.06	.05	.02
765	Willie Randolph	.10	.08	.04
766	Paul Mirabella	.06	.05	.02
767	Darrell Brown	.06	.05	.02
768	Ron Cey	.10	.08	.04
769	Joe Cowley	.06	.05	.02
770	Carlton Fisk	.40	.30	.15
771	Geoff Zahn	.06	.05	.02
772	Johnnie LeMaster	.06	.05	.02
773	Hal McRae	.10	.08	.04
774	Dennis Lamp	.06	.05	.02
775	Mookie Wilson	.10	.08	.04
776	Jerry Royster	.06	.05	.02
777	Ned Yost	.06	.05	.02
778	Mike Davis	.08	.06	.03
779	Nick Esasky	.08	.06	.03
780	Mike Flanagan	.10	.08	.04
781	Jim Gantner	.08	.06	.03
782	Tom Niedenfuer	.08	.06	.03
783	Mike Jorgensen	.06	.05	.02
784	Checklist 661-792	.06	.05	.02
785	Tony Armas	.10	.08	.04
786	Enos Cabell	.06	.05	.02
787	Jim Wohlford	.06	.05	.02
788	Steve Comer	.06	.05	.02
789	Luis Salazar	.06	.05	.02
790	Ron Guidry	.25	.20	.10
791	Ivan DeJesus	.06	.05	.02
792	Darrell Evans	.12	.09	.05

1985 Topps All-Star Glossy Set Of 22

This was the second straight year for this set of 22 cards featuring the starting players, the honorary captains and the managers in the All-Star Game. The set is virtually identical to that of the previous year in design with a color photo, All-Star banner, league emblem, and player's name and position on the front.

What makes the cards special is their high gloss finish. The cards were available as inserts in Topps rack packs. With their combination of attractive appearance and big-name stars, these 2-1/2" by 3-1/2" cards will probably continue to enjoy a great deal of popularity.

		MT	NR MT	EX
Complete Set:		7.00	5.25	2.75
Common Player:		.20	.15	.08
1	Paul Owens	.20	.15	.08
2	Steve Garvey	.50	.40	.20
3	Ryne Sandberg	.40	.30	.15
4	Mike Schmidt	.60	.45	.25
5	Ozzie Smith	.30	.25	.12
6	Tony Gwynn	.60	.45	.25
7	Dale Murphy	.80	.60	.30
8	Darryl Strawberry	1.00	.70	.40
9	Gary Carter	.50	.40	.20
10	Charlie Lea	.20	.15	.08
11	Willie McCovey	.40	.30	.15
12	Joe Altobelli	.20	.15	.08
13	Rod Carew	.50	.40	.20
14	Lou Whitaker	.30	.25	.12
15	George Brett	.80	.60	.30
16	Cal Ripken	.60	.45	.25
17	Dave Winfield	.50	.40	.20
18	Chet Lemon	.20	.15	.08
19	Reggie Jackson	.60	.45	.25
20	Lance Parrish	.30	.25	.12
21	Dave Stieb	.25	.20	.10
22	Hank Greenberg	.20	.15	.08

		MT	NR MT	EX
13	Keith Hernandez	.40	.30	.15
14	Dave Winfield	.60	.45	.25
15	Reggie Jackson	.70	.50	.30
16	Alan Trammell	.35	.25	.14
17	Bert Blyleven	.20	.15	.08
18	Tony Armas	.15	.11	.06
19	Rich Gossage	.25	.20	.10
20	Jose Cruz	.15	.11	.06
21	Ryne Sandberg	.40	.30	.15
22	Bruce Sutter	.20	.15	.08
23	Mike Schmidt	1.00	.70	.40
24	Cal Ripken	.70	.50	.30
25	Dan Petry	.15	.11	.06
26	Jack Morris	.30	.25	.12
27	Don Mattingly	3.50	2.75	1.50
28	Eddie Murray	.60	.45	.25
29	Tony Gwynn	.60	.45	.25
30	Charlie Lea	.15	.11	.06
31	Juan Samuel	.30	.25	.12
32	Phil Niekro	.35	.25	.14
33	Alejandro Pena	.15	.11	.06
34	Harold Baines	.25	.20	.10
35	Dan Quisenberry	.15	.11	.06
36	Gary Carter	.50	.40	.20
37	Mario Soto	.15	.11	.06
38	Dwight Gooden	2.50	2.00	1.00
39	Tom Brunansky	.20	.15	.08
40	Dave Stieb	.20	.15	.08

1985 Topps All-Star Glossy Set Of 40

Similar to previous years' glossy sets, the 1985 All-Star "Collector's Edition" glossy set of 40 could be obtained through the mail in eight five-card subsets. To obtain the 2-1/2" by 3-1/2" cards, collectors had to accumulate sweepstakes insert cards from Topps packs, and pay 75¢ postage and handling. Under the circumstances, the complete set of 40 cards was not inexpensive. They are however, rather attractive and popular cards, and the set size enabled Topps to include some players who didn't make their 22-card set.

		MT	NR MT	EX
Complete Set:		18.00	13.50	7.25
Common Player:		.15	.11	.06
1	Dale Murphy	1.00	.70	.40
2	Jesse Orosco	.15	.11	.06
3	Bob Brenly	.15	.11	.06
4	Mike Boddicker	.15	.11	.06
5	Dave Kingman	.25	.20	.10
6	Jim Rice	.50	.40	.20
7	Frank Viola	.30	.25	.12
8	Alvin Davis	.35	.25	.14
9	Rick Sutcliffe	.20	.15	.08
10	Pete Rose	1.25	.90	.50
11	Leon Durham	.15	.11	.06
12	Joaquin Andujar	.15	.11	.06

1985 Topps All-Time Record Holders

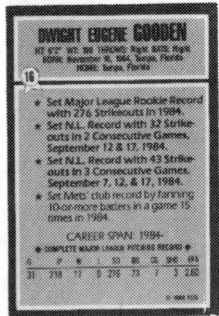

This 44-card boxed set was produced by Topps for the Woolworth's chain stores. Many hobbyists refer to this as the "Woolworth's" set, but that name does not appear anywhere on the cards. Featuring a combination of black and white and color photos of baseball record holders from all eras, the set is in the standard 2-1/2" by 3-1/2" format. Backs, printed in blue and orange, give career details and personal data. Because it combined old-timers with current players, the set did not achieve a great deal of collector popularity.

		MT	NR MT	EX
Complete Set:		6.00	4.50	2.50
Common Player:		.05	.04	.02
1	Hank Aaron	.25	.20	.10
2	Grover Alexander	.10	.08	.04
3	Ernie Banks	.12	.09	.05
4	Yogi Berra	.15	.11	.06
5	Lou Brock	.12	.09	.05
6	Steve Carlton	.12	.09	.05
7	Jack Chesbro	.07	.05	.03
8	Ty Cobb	.30	.25	.12
9	Sam Crawford	.07	.05	.03
10	Rollie Fingers	.07	.05	.03
11	Whitey Ford	.12	.09	.05
12	Johnny Frederick	.05	.04	.02
13	Frankie Frisch	.07	.05	.03
14	Lou Gehrig	.30	.25	.12
15	Jim Gentile	.05	.04	.02
16	Dwight Gooden	.60	.45	.25
17	Rickey Henderson	.15	.11	.06
18	Rogers Hornsby	.12	.09	.05

		MT	NR MT	EX
19	Frank Howard	.07	.05	.03
20	Cliff Johnson	.05	.04	.02
21	Walter Johnson	.15	.11	.06
22	Hub Leonard	.05	.04	.02
23	Mickey Mantle	1.00	.70	.40
24	Roger Maris	.12	.09	.05
25	Christy Mathewson	.12	.09	.05
26	Willie Mays	.20	.15	.08
27	Stan Musial	.20	.15	.08
28	Dan Quisenberry	.05	.04	.02
29	Frank Robinson	.12	.09	.05
30	Pete Rose	.40	.30	.15
31	Babe Ruth	.60	.45	.25
32	Nolan Ryan	.12	.09	.05
33	George Sisler	.10	.08	.04
34	Tris Speaker	.10	.08	.04
35	Ed Walsh	.07	.05	.03
36	Lloyd Waner	.07	.05	.03
37	Earl Webb	.05	.04	.02
38	Ted Williams	.30	.25	.12
39	Maury Wills	.07	.05	.03
40	Hack Wilson	.07	.05	.03
41	Owen Wilson	.05	.04	.02
42	Willie Wilson	.07	.05	.03
43	Rudy York	.05	.04	.02
44	Cy Young	.12	.09	.05

1985 Topps Gallery of Champions

 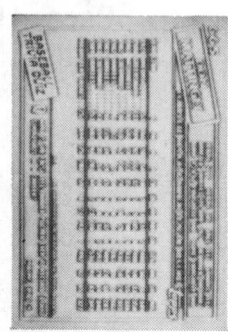

This second annual aluminum, bronze, and silver miniature issues honors 12 award winners from the previous season (MVP, Cy Young, Rookie of Year, Fireman, etc.). Each mini is an exact reproduction, at one-quarter scale of the player's official Topps baseball card, both front and back. The bronze and silver sets were issued in a specially-designed velvet-like case. Aluminum sets came cello-wrapped. A Dwight Gooden pewter replica was given as a premium to dealers who bought bronze and silver sets (value $75). A Pete Rose bronze was issued as a premium to dealers purchasing cases of 1985 Topps Traded sets (value $12).

		MT	NR MT	EX
Complete Aluminum Set:		30.00	22.00	12.00
Complete Bronze Set:		175.00	131.00	70.00
Complete Silver Set:		600.00	450.00	240.00
(1a)	Tony Armas (aluminum)	.70	.50	.30
(1b)	Tony Armas (bronze)	7.50	5.75	3.00
(1c)	Tony Armas (silver)	20.00	15.00	8.00
(2a)	Alvin Davis (aluminum)	1.00	.70	.40
(2b)	Alvin Davis (bronze)	10.00	7.50	4.00
(2c)	Alvin Davis (silver)	30.00	22.00	12.00
(3a)	Dwight Gooden (aluminum)	3.00	2.25	1.25
(3b)	Dwight Gooden (bronze)	25.00	18.50	10.00
(3c)	Dwight Gooden (silver)	125.00	94.00	50.00
(4a)	Tony Gwynn (aluminum)	1.25	.90	.50
(4b)	Tony Gwynn (bronze)	12.00	9.00	4.75
(4c)	Tony Gwynn (silver)	50.00	37.00	20.00
(5a)	Willie Hernandez (aluminum)	.70	.50	.30
(5b)	Willie Hernandez (bronze)	7.50	5.75	3.00
(5c)	Willie Hernandez (silver)	20.00	15.00	8.00
(6a)	Don Mattingly (aluminum)	8.00	6.00	3.25
(6b)	Don Mattingly (bronze)	50.00	37.00	20.00

		MT	NR MT	EX
(6c)	Don Mattingly (silver)	200.00	150.00	80.00
(7a)	Dale Murphy (aluminum)	1.50	1.25	.60
(7b)	Dale Murphy (bronze)	15.00	11.00	6.00
(7c)	Dale Murphy (silver)	80.00	60.00	32.00
(8a)	Dan Quisenberry (aluminum)	.70	.50	.30
(8b)	Dan Quisenberry (bronze)	7.50	5.75	3.00
(8c)	Dan Quisenberry (silver)	20.00	15.00	8.00
(9a)	Ryne Sandberg (aluminum)	1.25	.90	.50
(9b)	Ryne Sandberg (bronze)	12.50	9.50	5.00
(9c)	Ryne Sandberg (silver)	70.00	52.00	27.00
(10a)	Mike Schmidt (aluminum)	1.50	1.25	.60
(10b)	Mike Schmidt (bronze)	15.00	11.00	6.00
(10c)	Mike Schmidt (silver)	80.00	60.00	32.00
(11a)	Rick Sutcliffe (aluminum)	.70	.50	.30
(11b)	Rick Sutcliffe (bronze)	7.50	5.75	3.00
(11c)	Rick Sutcliffe (silver)	20.00	15.00	8.00
(12a)	Bruce Sutter (aluminum)	.70	.50	.30
(12b)	Bruce Sutter (bronze)	7.50	5.75	3.00
(12c)	Bruce Sutter (silver)	20.00	15.00	8.00

1985 Topps Rub Downs

Similar in size and design to the Rub Downs of the previous year, the 1985 set again consisted of 32 unnumbered sheets featuring 112 different players. The set was sold by Topps as a separate issue.

	MT	NR MT	EX
Complete Set:	8.00	6.00	3.25
Common Player:	.10	.08	.04
(1) Tony Armas, Harold Baines, Lonnie Smith	.10	.08	.04
(2) Don Baylor, George Hendrick, Ron Kittle, Johnnie LeMaster	.10	.08	.04
(3) Buddy Bell, Tony Gwynn, Lloyd Moseby	.25	.20	.10
(4) Bruce Benedict, Atlee Hammaker, Frank White	.10	.08	.04
(5) Mike Boddicker, Rod Carew, Carlton Fisk, Johnny Ray	.25	.20	.10
(6) Wade Boggs, Rick Dempsey, Keith Hernandez	.60	.45	.25
(7) George Brett, Andre Dawson, Paul Molitor, Alan Wiggins	.30	.25	.12
(8) Tom Brunansky, Pedro Guerrero, Darryl Strawberry	.40	.30	.15
(9) Bill Buckner, Tim Raines, Ryne Sandberg, Mike Schmidt	.30	.25	.12
(10) Steve Carlton, Bob Horner, Dan Quisenberry	.25	.20	.10
(11) Gary Carter, Phil Garner, Ron Guidry	.25	.20	.10
(12) Jack Clark, Damaso Garcia, Hal McRae, Lance Parrish	.20	.15	.08
(13) Dave Concepcion, Cecil Cooper, Fred Lynn, Jesse Orosco	.15	.11	.06
(14) Jose Cruz, Jack Morris, Jim Rice, Rick Sutcliffe	.20	.15	.08
(15) Alvin Davis, Steve Kemp, Greg Luzinski, Kent Tekulve	.20	.15	.08
(16) Ron Davis, Kent Hrbek, Juan Samuel	.20	.15	.08
(17) John Denny, Carney Lansford, Mario Soto, Lou Whitaker	.15	.11	.06
(18) Leon Durham, Willie Hernandez, Steve Sax	.15	.11	.06
(19) Dwight Evans, Julio Franco, Dwight Gooden	.40	.30	.15

		MT	NR MT	EX
(20)	George Foster, Gary Gaetti, Bobby Grich, Gary Redus	.15	.11	.06
(21)	Steve Garvey, Jerry Remy, Bill Russell, George Wright	.20	.15	.08
(22)	Kirk Gibson, Rich Gossage, Don Mattingly, Dave Stieb	.90	.70	.35
(23)	Moose Haas, Bruce Sutter, Dickie Thon, Andre Thornton	.10	.08	.04
(24)	Rickey Henderson, Dave Righetti, Pete Rose	.70	.50	.30
(25)	Steve Henderson, Bill Madlock, Alan Trammell	.15	.11	.06
(26)	LaMarr Hoyt, Larry Parrish, Nolan Ryan	.25	.20	.10
(27)	Reggie Jackson, Eric Show, Jason Thompson	.30	.25	.12
(28)	Terry Kennedy, Eddie Murray, Tom Seaver, Ozzie Smith	.25	.20	.10
(29)	Mark Langston, Ben Oglivie, Darrell Porter	.15	.11	.06
(30)	Jeff Leonard, Gary Matthews, Dale Murphy, Dave Winfield	.30	.25	.12
(31)	Craig McMurtry, Cal Ripken, Steve Rogers, Willie Upshaw	.25	.20	.10
(32)	Tony Pena, Fernando Valenzuela, Robin Yount	.20	.15	.08

		MT	NR MT	EX
27	Kirk Gibson	.35	.25	.14
28	Juan Samuel	.35	.25	.14
29	Reggie Jackson	.60	.45	.25
30	Darryl Strawberry	.90	.70	.35
31	Tom Seaver	.50	.40	.20
32	Pete Rose	1.25	.90	.50
33	Dwight Evans	.30	.25	.12
34	Jose Cruz	.20	.15	.08
35	Bert Blyleven	.25	.20	.10
36	Keith Hernandez	.50	.40	.20
37	Robin Yount	.40	.30	.15
38	Joaquin Andujar	.20	.15	.08
39	Lloyd Moseby	.20	.15	.08
40	Chili Davis	.20	.15	.08
41	Kent Hrbek	.35	.25	.14
42	Dave Parker	.30	.25	.12
43	Jack Morris	.35	.25	.14
44	Pedro Guerrero	.30	.25	.12
45	Mike Witt	.20	.15	.08
46	George Brett	.90	.70	.35
47	Ozzie Smith	.30	.25	.12
48	Cal Ripken	.70	.50	.30
49	Rich Gossage	.25	.20	.10
50	Jim Rice	.50	.40	.20
51	Harold Baines	.25	.20	.10
52	Fernando Valenzuela	.40	.30	.15
53	Buddy Bell	.25	.20	.10
54	Jesse Orosco	.20	.15	.08
55	Lance Parrish	.35	.25	.14
56	Jason Thompson	.20	.15	.08
57	Tom Brunansky	.25	.20	.10
58	Dave Righetti	.30	.25	.12
59	Dave Kingman	.25	.20	.10
60	Dave Winfield	.50	.40	.20

1985 Topps Super

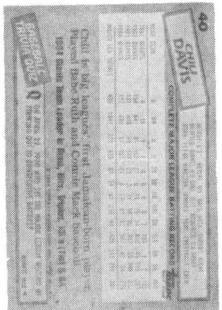

Still trying to sell collectors on the idea of jumbo-sized cards, Topps returned for a second year with its 4-7/8" by 6-7/8" "Super" set. In fact, the set size was doubled from the previous year, to 60 cards. The Supers are identical to the regular-issue 1985 cards of the same players, only the card numbers on back were changed. The cards were again sold three per pack for 50¢.

		MT	NR MT	EX
Complete Set:		14.00	10.50	5.50
Common Player:		.20	.15	.08
1	Ryne Sandberg	.50	.40	.20
2	Willie Hernandez	.20	.15	.08
3	Rick Sutcliffe	.25	.20	.10
4	Don Mattingly	2.25	1.75	.90
5	Tony Gwynn	.70	.50	.30
6	Alvin Davis	.35	.25	.14
7	Dwight Gooden	2.00	1.50	.80
8	Dan Quisenberry	.20	.15	.08
9	Bruce Sutter	.25	.20	.10
10	Tony Armas	.20	.15	.08
11	Dale Murphy	.90	.70	.35
12	Mike Schmidt	.90	.70	.35
13	Gary Carter	.50	.40	.20
14	Rickey Henderson	.70	.50	.30
15	Tim Raines	.50	.40	.20
16	Mike Boddicker	.20	.15	.08
17	Alejandro Pena	.20	.15	.08
18	Eddie Murray	.60	.45	.25
19	Gary Matthews	.20	.15	.08
20	Mark Langston	.30	.25	.12
21	Mario Soto	.20	.15	.08
22	Dave Stieb	.25	.20	.08
23	Nolan Ryan	.50	.40	.20
24	Steve Carlton	.50	.40	.20
25	Alan Trammell	.40	.30	.15
26	Steve Garvey	.50	.40	.20

1985 Topps 3-D

These 4-1/4" by 6" cards were something new. Printed on plastic, rather than paper, the player picture on the card is actually raised above the surface much like might be found on a relief map; a true 3-D baseball card. The plastic cards include the player's name, a Topps logo and card number across the top, and a team logo on the side. The backs are blank but have two peel-off adhesive strips so that the card may be attached to a flat surface. There are 30 cards in the set, the bulk of whom are stars.

		MT	NR MT	EX
Complete Set:		16.00	12.00	6.50
Common Player:		.20	.15	.08
1	Mike Schmidt	.90	.70	.35
2	Eddie Murray	.70	.50	.30
3	Dale Murphy	.90	.70	.35
4	George Brett	.90	.70	.35
5	Pete Rose	1.25	.90	.50
6	Jim Rice	.60	.45	.25
7	Ryne Sandberg	.50	.40	.20
8	Don Mattingly	2.50	2.00	1.00
9	Darryl Strawberry	.90	.70	.35
10	Rickey Henderson	.80	.60	.30
11	Keith Hernandez	.50	.40	.20
12	Dave Kingman	.20	.15	.08
13	Tony Gwynn	.80	.60	.30
14	Reggie Jackson	.70	.50	.30
15	Gary Carter	.60	.45	.25

		MT	NR MT	EX
16	Cal Ripken	.80	.60	.30
17	Tim Raines	.50	.40	.20
18	Dave Winfield	.60	.45	.25
19	Dwight Gooden	2.00	1.50	.80
20	Dave Stieb	.20	.15	.08
21	Fernando Valenzuela	.50	.40	.20
22	Mark Langston	.30	.25	.12
23	Bruce Sutter	.25	.20	.10
24	Dan Quisenberry	.20	.15	.08
25	Steve Carlton	.60	.45	.25
26	Mike Boddicker	.20	.15	.08
27	Goose Gossage	.30	.25	.12
28	Jack Morris	.40	.30	.15
29	Rick Sutcliffe	.25	.20	.10
30	Tom Seaver	.60	.45	.25

1985 Topps Traded

 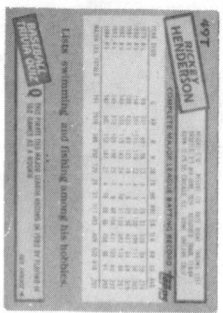

By 1985, the Topps Traded set had become a yearly feature, and Topps continued the tradition with another 132-card set. The 2-1/2" by 3-1/2" cards followed the pattern of being virtually identical in design to the regular cards issued by Topps. Sold only through established hobby dealers, the set features traded veterans and promising rookies. A glossy-finish "Tiffany" edition of the set is valued at four times normal Traded card value for commons, up to five or six times normal value for superstars and hot rookies.

		MT	NR MT	EX
Complete Set:		18.00	13.50	7.25
Common Player:		.10	.08	.04
1T	Don Aase	.10	.08	.04
2T	Bill Almon	.10	.08	.04
3T	Benny Ayala	.10	.08	.04
4T	Dusty Baker	.15	.11	.06
5T	George Bamberger	.10	.08	.04
6T	Dale Berra	.10	.08	.04
7T	Rich Bordi	.10	.08	.04
8T	Daryl Boston(FC)	.20	.15	.08
9T	Hubie Brooks	.25	.20	.10
10T	Chris Brown(FC)	.25	.20	.10
11T	Tom Browning(FC)	1.25	.90	.50
12T	Al Bumbry	.10	.08	.04
13T	Ray Burris	.10	.08	.04
14T	Jeff Burroughs	.15	.11	.06
15T	Bill Campbell	.10	.08	.04
16T	Don Carman(FC)	.40	.30	.15
17T	Gary Carter	.70	.50	.30
18T	Bobby Castillo	.10	.08	.04
19T	Bill Caudill	.10	.08	.04
20T	Rick Cerone	.10	.08	.04
21T	Bryan Clark	.10	.08	.04
22T	Jack Clark	.35	.25	.14
23T	Pat Clements(FC)	.20	.15	.08
24T	Vince Coleman(FC)	7.00	5.25	2.75
25T	Dave Collins	.15	.11	.06
26T	Danny Darwin	.15	.11	.06
27T	Jim Davenport	.10	.08	.04
28T	Jerry Davis	.10	.08	.04
29T	Brian Dayett	.10	.08	.04
30T	Ivan DeJesus	.10	.08	.04
31T	Ken Dixon	.10	.08	.04
32T	Mariano Duncan(FC)	.20	.15	.08
33T	John Felske	.10	.08	.04

		MT	NR MT	EX
34T	Mike Fitzgerald	.10	.08	.04
35T	Ray Fontenot	.10	.08	.04
36T	Greg Gagne(FC)	.35	.25	.14
37T	Oscar Gamble	.15	.11	.06
38T	Scott Garrelts(FC)	.50	.40	.20
39T	Bob Gibson	.10	.08	.04
40T	Jim Gott	.10	.08	.04
41T	David Green	.10	.08	.04
42T	Alfredo Griffin	.15	.11	.06
43T	Ozzie Guillen(FC)	3.00	2.25	1.25
44T	Eddie Haas	.10	.08	.04
45T	Terry Harper	.10	.08	.04
46T	Toby Harrah	.15	.11	.06
47T	Greg Harris	.10	.08	.04
48T	Ron Hassey	.10	.08	.04
49T	Rickey Henderson	3.00	2.25	1.25
50T	Steve Henderson	.10	.08	.04
51T	George Hendrick	.15	.11	.06
52T	Joe Hesketh(FC)	.20	.15	.08
53T	Teddy Higuera(FC)	2.25	1.75	.90
54T	Donnie Hill	.10	.08	.04
55T	Al Holland	.10	.08	.04
56T	Burt Hooton	.15	.11	.06
57T	Jay Howell	.15	.11	.06
58T	Ken Howell(FC)	.15	.11	.06
59T	LaMarr Hoyt	.10	.08	.04
60T	Tim Hulett(FC)	.15	.11	.06
61T	Bob James	.10	.08	.04
62T	Steve Jeltz(FC)	.15	.11	.06
63T	Cliff Johnson	.10	.08	.04
64T	Howard Johnson	2.00	1.50	.80
65T	Ruppert Jones	.10	.08	.04
66T	Steve Kemp	.15	.11	.06
67T	Bruce Kison	.10	.08	.04
68T	Alan Knicely	.10	.08	.04
69T	Mike LaCoss	.10	.08	.04
70T	Lee Lacy	.10	.08	.04
71T	Dave LaPoint	.20	.15	.08
72T	Gary Lavelle	.10	.08	.04
73T	Vance Law	.15	.11	.06
74T	Johnnie LeMaster	.10	.08	.04
75T	Sixto Lezcano	.10	.08	.04
76T	Tim Lollar	.10	.08	.04
77T	Fred Lynn	.30	.25	.12
78T	Billy Martin	.20	.15	.08
79T	Ron Mathis	.10	.08	.04
80T	Len Matuszek	.10	.08	.04
81T	Gene Mauch	.15	.11	.06
82T	Oddibe McDowell	.60	.45	.25
83T	Roger McDowell(FC)	.90	.70	.35
84T	John McNamara	.10	.08	.04
85T	Donnie Moore	.10	.08	.04
86T	Gene Nelson	.10	.08	.04
87T	Steve Nicosia	.10	.08	.04
88T	Al Oliver	.30	.25	.12
89T	Joe Orsulak(FC)	.20	.15	.08
90T	Rob Picciolo	.10	.08	.04
91T	Chris Pittaro	.10	.08	.04
92T	Jim Presley(FC)	1.00	.70	.40
93T	Rick Reuschel	.25	.20	.10
94T	Bert Roberge	.10	.08	.04
95T	Bob Rodgers	.10	.08	.04
96T	Jerry Royster	.10	.08	.04
97T	Dave Rozema	.10	.08	.04
98T	Dave Rucker	.10	.08	.04
99T	Vern Ruhle	.10	.08	.04
100T	Paul Runge(FC)	.15	.11	.06
101T	Mark Salas(FC)	.15	.11	.06
102T	Luis Salazar	.10	.08	.04
103T	Joe Sambito	.10	.08	.04
104T	Rick Schu(FC)	.20	.15	.08
105T	Donnie Scott	.10	.08	.04
106T	Larry Sheets(FC)	.50	.40	.20
107T	Don Slaught	.10	.08	.04
108T	Roy Smalley	.15	.11	.06
109T	Lonnie Smith	.15	.11	.06
110T	Nate Snell	.10	.08	.04
111T	Chris Speier	.10	.08	.04
112T	Mike Stenhouse	.10	.08	.04
113T	Tim Stoddard	.10	.08	.04
114T	Jim Sundberg	.15	.11	.06
115T	Bruce Sutter	.25	.20	.10
116T	Don Sutton	.60	.45	.25
117T	Kent Tekulve	.15	.11	.06
118T	Tom Tellmann	.10	.08	.04
119T	Walt Terrell	.15	.11	.06
120T	Mickey Tettleton(FC)	.80	.60	.30
121T	Derrel Thomas	.10	.08	.04
122T	Rich Thompson	.10	.08	.04
123T	Alex Trevino	.10	.08	.04
124T	John Tudor	.25	.20	.10

		MT	NR MT	EX
125T	Jose Uribe(FC)	.25	.20	.10
126T	Bobby Valentine	.10	.08	.04
127T	Dave Von Ohlen	.10	.08	.04
128T	U.L. Washington	.10	.08	.04
129T	Earl Weaver	.15	.11	.06
130T	Eddie Whitson	.10	.08	.04
131T	Herm Winningham(FC)	.20	.15	.08
132T	Checklist 1-132	.10	.08	.04

1986 Topps

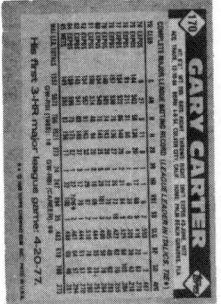

GARY CARTER

The 1986 Topps set consists of 792 cards. Fronts of the 2-1/2" by 3-1/2" cards feature color photos with the Topps logo in the upper right-hand corner while the player's position is in the lower left-hand corner. Above the picture is the team name, while below it is the player's name. The borders are a departure from previous practice, as the top 7/8" is black, while the remainder was white. There are no card numbers 51 and 171 in the set; the card that should have been #51, Bobby Wine, shares #57 with Bill Doran, while #171, Bob Rodgers, shares #141 with Chuck Cottier. Once again, a 5,000-set glossy-finish "Tiffany" edition was produced. Values are four to six times higher than the same card in the regular issue.

		MT	NR MT	EX
Complete Set:		40.00	30.00	15.00
Common Player:		.05	.04	.02
1	Pete Rose	.90	.70	.35
2	Rose Special 1963-66	.30	.25	.12
3	Rose Special 1967-70	.30	.25	.12
4	Rose Special 1971-74	.30	.25	.12
5	Rose Special 1975-78	.30	.25	.12
6	Rose Special 1979-82	.30	.25	.12
7	Rose Special 1983-85	.30	.25	.12
8	Dwayne Murphy	.07	.05	.03
9	Roy Smith	.05	.04	.02
10	Tony Gwynn	.40	.30	.15
11	Bob Ojeda	.07	.05	.03
12	Jose Uribe(FC)	.20	.15	.08
13	Bob Kearney	.05	.04	.02
14	Julio Cruz	.05	.04	.02
15	Eddie Whitson	.05	.04	.02
16	Rick Schu(FC)	.07	.05	.03
17	Mike Stenhouse	.05	.04	.02
18	Brent Gaff	.05	.04	.02
19	Rich Hebner	.05	.04	.02
20	Lou Whitaker	.25	.20	.10
21	George Bamberger	.05	.04	.02
22	Duane Walker	.05	.04	.02
23	Manny Lee(FC)	.15	.11	.06
24	Len Barker	.07	.05	.03
25	Willie Wilson	.12	.09	.05
26	Frank DiPino	.05	.04	.02
27	Ray Knight	.07	.05	.03
28	Eric Davis	2.50	2.00	1.00
29	Tony Phillips	.05	.04	.02
30	Eddie Murray	.40	.30	.15
31	Jamie Easterly	.05	.04	.02
32	Steve Yeager	.05	.04	.02
33	Jeff Lahti	.05	.04	.02
34	Ken Phelps(FC)	.07	.05	.03
35	Jeff Reardon	.12	.09	.05
36	Tigers Leaders (Lance Parrish)	.12	.09	.05

		MT	NR MT	EX
37	Mark Thurmond	.05	.04	.02
38	Glenn Hoffman	.05	.04	.02
39	Dave Rucker	.05	.04	.02
40	Ken Griffey	.10	.08	.04
41	Brad Wellman	.05	.04	.02
42	Geoff Zahn	.05	.04	.02
43	Dave Engle	.05	.04	.02
44	Lance McCullers(FC)	.25	.20	.10
45	Damaso Garcia	.05	.04	.02
46	Billy Hatcher(FC)	.20	.15	.08
47	Juan Berenguer	.05	.04	.02
48	Bill Almon	.05	.04	.02
49	Rick Manning	.05	.04	.02
50	Dan Quisenberry	.07	.05	.03
51	Not Issued			
52	Chris Welsh	.05	.04	.02
53	Len Dykstra(FC)	3.00	2.25	1.25
54	John Franco	.12	.09	.05
55	Fred Lynn	.15	.11	.06
56	Tom Niedenfuer	.07	.05	.03
57a	Bobby Wine	.05	.04	.02
57b	Bill Doran	.10	.08	.04
58	Bill Krueger	.05	.04	.02
59	Andre Thornton	.07	.05	.03
60	Dwight Evans	.12	.09	.05
61	Karl Best	.05	.04	.02
62	Bob Boone	.07	.05	.03
63	Ron Roenicke	.05	.04	.02
64	Floyd Bannister	.10	.08	.04
65	Dan Driessen	.07	.05	.03
66	Cardinals Leaders (Bob Forsch)	.07	.05	.03
67	Carmelo Martinez	.07	.05	.03
68	Ed Lynch	.05	.04	.02
69	Luis Aguayo	.05	.04	.02
70	Dave Winfield	.30	.25	.12
71	Ken Schrom	.05	.04	.02
72	Shawon Dunston	.20	.15	.08
73	Randy O'Neal(FC)	.07	.05	.03
74	Rance Mulliniks	.05	.04	.02
75	Jose DeLeon	.07	.05	.03
76	Dion James	.07	.05	.03
77	Charlie Leibrandt	.07	.05	.03
78	Bruce Benedict	.05	.04	.02
79	Dave Schmidt	.07	.05	.03
80	Darryl Strawberry	.70	.50	.30
81	Gene Mauch	.07	.05	.03
82	Tippy Martinez	.05	.04	.02
83	Phil Garner	.07	.05	.03
84	Curt Young	.07	.05	.03
85	Tony Perez	.15	.11	.06
86	Tom Waddell	.05	.04	.02
87	Candy Maldonado	.10	.08	.04
88	Tom Nieto	.05	.04	.02
89	Randy St. Claire(FC)	.07	.05	.03
90	Garry Templeton	.07	.05	.03
91	Steve Crawford	.05	.04	.02
92	Al Cowens	.05	.04	.02
93	Scot Thompson	.05	.04	.02
94	Rick Bordi	.05	.04	.02
95	Ozzie Virgil	.05	.04	.02
96	Blue Jay Leaders (Jim Clancy)	.07	.05	.03
97	Gary Gaetti	.20	.15	.08
98	Dick Ruthven	.05	.04	.02
99	Buddy Biancalana	.05	.04	.02
100	Nolan Ryan	.70	.50	.30
101	Dave Bergman	.05	.04	.02
102	Joe Orsulak	.15	.11	.06
103	Luis Salazar	.05	.04	.02
104	Sid Fernandez	.12	.09	.05
105	Gary Ward	.07	.05	.03
106	Ray Burris	.05	.04	.02
107	Rafael Ramirez	.05	.04	.02
108	Ted Power	.05	.04	.02
109	Len Matuszek	.05	.04	.02
110	Scott McGregor	.07	.05	.03
111	Roger Craig	.07	.05	.03
112	Bill Campbell	.05	.04	.02
113	U.L. Washington	.05	.04	.02
114	Mike Brown	.05	.04	.02
115	Jay Howell	.07	.05	.03
116	Brook Jacoby	.10	.08	.04
117	Bruce Kison	.05	.04	.02
118	Jerry Royster	.05	.04	.02
119	Barry Bonnell	.05	.04	.02
120	Steve Carlton	.30	.25	.12
121	Nelson Simmons	.05	.04	.02
122	Pete Filson	.05	.04	.02
123	Greg Walker	.10	.08	.04
124	Luis Sanchez	.05	.04	.02
125	Dave Lopes	.07	.05	.03
126	Mets Leaders (Mookie Wilson)	.07	.05	.03
127	Jack Howell(FC)	.30	.25	.12

#	Player	MT	NR MT	EX
128	John Wathan	.07	.05	.03
129	Jeff Dedmon(FC)	.05	.04	.02
130	Alan Trammell	.30	.25	.12
131	Checklist 1-132	.05	.04	.02
132	Razor Shines	.05	.04	.02
133	Andy McGaffigan	.05	.04	.02
134	Carney Lansford	.10	.08	.04
135	Joe Niekro	.10	.08	.04
136	Mike Hargrove	.05	.04	.02
137	Charlie Moore	.05	.04	.02
138	Mark Davis	.05	.04	.02
139	Daryl Boston	.10	.08	.04
140	John Candelaria	.10	.08	.04
141a	Bob Rodgers	.05	.04	.02
141b	Chuck Cottier	.05	.04	.02
142	Bob Jones	.05	.04	.02
143	Dave Van Gorder	.05	.04	.02
144	Doug Sisk	.05	.04	.02
145	Pedro Guerrero	.20	.15	.08
146	Jack Perconte	.05	.04	.02
147	Larry Sheets	.20	.15	.08
148	Mike Heath	.05	.04	.02
149	Brett Butler	.07	.05	.03
150	Joaquin Andujar	.07	.05	.03
151	Dave Stapleton	.05	.04	.02
152	Mike Morgan	.05	.04	.02
153	Ricky Adams	.05	.04	.02
154	Bert Roberge	.05	.04	.02
155	Bob Grich	.10	.08	.04
156	White Sox Leaders (Richard Dotson)	.07	.05	.03
157	Ron Hassey	.05	.04	.02
158	Derrel Thomas	.05	.04	.02
159	Orel Hershiser	1.00	.70	.40
160	Chet Lemon	.07	.05	.03
161	Lee Tunnell	.05	.04	.02
162	Greg Gagne	.10	.08	.04
163	Pete Ladd	.05	.04	.02
164	Steve Balboni	.07	.05	.03
165	Mike Davis	.07	.05	.03
166	Dickie Thon	.07	.05	.03
167	Zane Smith(FC)	.15	.11	.06
168	Jeff Burroughs	.07	.05	.03
169	George Wright	.05	.04	.02
170	Gary Carter	.25	.20	.10
171	Not Issued			
172	Jerry Reed	.05	.04	.02
173	Wayne Gross	.05	.04	.02
174	Brian Snyder	.05	.04	.02
175	Steve Sax	.15	.11	.06
176	Jay Tibbs	.05	.04	.02
177	Joel Youngblood	.05	.04	.02
178	Ivan DeJesus	.05	.04	.02
179	*Stu Cliburn*(FC)	.10	.08	.04
180	Don Mattingly	3.00	2.25	1.25
181	Al Nipper	.05	.04	.02
182	Bobby Brown	.05	.04	.02
183	Larry Andersen	.05	.04	.02
184	Tim Laudner	.05	.04	.02
185	Rollie Fingers	.20	.15	.08
186	Astros Leaders (Jose Cruz)	.07	.05	.03
187	Scott Fletcher	.07	.05	.03
188	Bob Dernier	.05	.04	.02
189	Mike Mason	.05	.04	.02
190	George Hendrick	.07	.05	.03
191	Wally Backman	.07	.05	.03
192	Milt Wilcox	.05	.04	.02
193	Daryl Sconiers	.05	.04	.02
194	Craig McMurtry	.05	.04	.02
195	Dave Concepcion	.12	.09	.05
196	Doyle Alexander	.10	.08	.04
197	Enos Cabell	.05	.04	.02
198	Ken Dixon	.05	.04	.02
199	Dick Howser	.05	.04	.02
200	Mike Schmidt	.50	.40	.20
201	Record Breaker (Vince Coleman)(FC)	.30	.25	.12
202	Record Breaker (Dwight Gooden)	.40	.30	.15
203	Record Breaker (Keith Hernandez)	.20	.15	.08
204	Record Breaker (Phil Niekro)	.15	.11	.06
205	Record Breaker (Tony Perez)	.10	.08	.04
206	Record Breaker (Pete Rose)	.50	.40	.20
207	Record Breaker (Fernando Valenzuela)	.20	.15	.08
208	Ramon Romero	.05	.04	.02
209	Randy Ready	.10	.08	.04
210	Calvin Schiraldi(FC)	.10	.08	.04
211	Ed Wojna	.05	.04	.02
212	Chris Speier	.05	.04	.02
213	Bob Shirley	.05	.04	.02
214	Randy Bush	.05	.04	.02
215	Frank White	.10	.08	.04
216	A's Leaders (Dwayne Murphy)	.07	.05	.03
217	Bill Scherrer	.05	.04	.02
218	Randy Hunt	.05	.04	.02
219	Dennis Lamp	.05	.04	.02
220	Bob Horner	.10	.08	.04
221	Dave Henderson	.10	.08	.04
222	Craig Gerber	.05	.04	.02
223	Atlee Hammaker	.05	.04	.02
224	Cesar Cedeno	.10	.08	.04
225	Ron Darling	.15	.11	.06
226	Lee Lacy	.05	.04	.02
227	Al Jones	.05	.04	.02
228	Tom Lawless	.05	.04	.02
229	Bill Gullickson	.05	.04	.02
230	Terry Kennedy	.07	.05	.03
231	Jim Frey	.05	.04	.02
232	Rick Rhoden	.10	.08	.04
233	Steve Lyons(FC)	.07	.05	.03
234	Doug Corbett	.05	.04	.02
235	Butch Wynegar	.05	.04	.02
236	Frank Eufemia	.05	.04	.02
237	Ted Simmons	.12	.09	.05
238	Larry Parrish	.10	.08	.04
239	Joel Skinner	.05	.04	.02
240	Tommy John	.20	.15	.08
241	Tony Fernandez	.20	.15	.08
242	Rich Thompson	.05	.04	.02
243	Johnny Grubb	.05	.04	.02
244	Craig Lefferts	.05	.04	.02
245	Jim Sundberg	.07	.05	.03
246	Phillies Leaders (Steve Carlton)	.15	.11	.06
247	Terry Harper	.05	.04	.02
248	Spike Owen	.05	.04	.02
249	Rob Deer(FC)	.40	.30	.15
250	Dwight Gooden	2.00	1.50	.80
251	Rich Dauer	.05	.04	.02
252	Bobby Castillo	.05	.04	.02
253	Dann Bilardello	.05	.04	.02
254	*Ozzie Guillen*	1.00	.70	.40
255	Tony Armas	.07	.05	.03
256	Kurt Kepshire	.05	.04	.02
257	Doug DeCinces	.10	.08	.04
258	*Tim Burke*(FC)	.25	.20	.10
259	Dan Pasqua(FC)	.20	.15	.08
260	Tony Pena	.10	.08	.04
261	Bobby Valentine	.05	.04	.02
262	Mario Ramirez	.05	.04	.02
263	Checklist 133-264	.05	.04	.02
264	*Darren Daulton*(FC)	.12	.09	.05
265	Ron Davis	.05	.04	.02
266	Keith Moreland	.07	.05	.03
267	Paul Molitor	.15	.11	.06
268	Mike Scott	.15	.11	.06
269	Dane Iorg	.05	.04	.02
270	Jack Morris	.20	.15	.08
271	Dave Collins	.07	.05	.03
272	Tim Tolman	.05	.04	.02
273	Jerry Willard	.05	.04	.02
274	Ron Gardenhire	.05	.04	.02
275	Charlie Hough	.08	.06	.03
276	Yankees Leaders (Willie Randolph)	.07	.05	.03
277	Jaime Cocanower	.05	.04	.02
278	Sixto Lezcano	.05	.04	.02
279	Al Pardo	.05	.04	.02
280	Tim Raines	.30	.25	.12
281	Steve Mura	.05	.04	.02
282	Jerry Mumphrey	.05	.04	.02
283	Mike Fischlin	.05	.04	.02
284	Brian Dayett	.05	.04	.02
285	Buddy Bell	.10	.08	.04
286	Luis DeLeon	.05	.04	.02
287	*John Christensen*(FC)	.10	.08	.04
288	Don Aase	.05	.04	.02
289	Johnnie LeMaster	.05	.04	.02
290	Carlton Fisk	.30	.25	.12
291	Tom Lasorda	.07	.05	.03
292	Chuck Porter	.05	.04	.02
293	Chris Chambliss	.07	.05	.03
294	Danny Cox	.10	.08	.04
295	Kirk Gibson	.30	.25	.12
296	Geno Petralli(FC)	.07	.05	.03
297	Tim Lollar	.05	.04	.02
298	Craig Reynolds	.05	.04	.02
299	Bryn Smith	.05	.04	.02
300	George Brett	.50	.40	.20
301	Dennis Rasmussen	.12	.09	.05
302	Greg Gross	.05	.04	.02
303	Curt Wardle	.05	.04	.02
304	*Mike Gallego*(FC)	.12	.09	.05
305	Phil Bradley	.15	.11	.06

		MT	NR MT	EX
306	Padres Leaders (Terry Kennedy)	.07	.05	.03
307	Dave Sax	.05	.04	.02
308	Ray Fontenot	.05	.04	.02
309	John Shelby	.05	.04	.02
310	Greg Minton	.05	.04	.02
311	Dick Schofield	.05	.04	.02
312	Tom Filer	.05	.04	.02
313	Joe DeSa	.05	.04	.02
314	Frank Pastore	.05	.04	.02
315	Mookie Wilson	.10	.08	.04
316	Sammy Khalifa	.05	.04	.02
317	Ed Romero	.05	.04	.02
318	Terry Whitfield	.05	.04	.02
319	Rick Camp	.05	.04	.02
320	Jim Rice	.30	.25	.12
321	Earl Weaver	.07	.05	.03
322	Bob Forsch	.07	.05	.03
323	Jerry Davis	.05	.04	.02
324	Dan Schatzeder	.05	.04	.02
325	Juan Beniquez	.05	.04	.02
326	Kent Tekulve	.07	.05	.03
327	Mike Pagliarulo	.20	.15	.08
328	Pete O'Brien	.10	.08	.04
329	Kirby Puckett	3.00	2.25	1.25
330	Rick Sutcliffe	.12	.09	.05
331	Alan Ashby	.05	.04	.02
332	Darryl Motley	.05	.04	.02
333	Tom Henke(FC)	.15	.11	.06
334	Ken Oberkfell	.05	.04	.02
335	Don Sutton	.25	.20	.10
336	Indians Leaders (Andre Thornton)	.07	.05	.03
337	Darnell Coles	.07	.05	.03
338	Jorge Bell	.25	.20	.10
339	Bruce Berenyi	.05	.04	.02
340	Cal Ripken	.40	.30	.15
341	Frank Williams	.05	.04	.02
342	Gary Redus	.05	.04	.02
343	Carlos Diaz	.05	.04	.02
344	Jim Wohlford	.05	.04	.02
345	Donnie Moore	.05	.04	.02
346	Bryan Little	.05	.04	.02
347	*Teddy Higuera*	1.00	.70	.40
348	Cliff Johnson	.05	.04	.02
349	Mark Clear	.05	.04	.02
350	Jack Clark	.20	.15	.08
351	Chuck Tanner	.05	.04	.02
352	Harry Spilman	.05	.04	.02
353	Keith Atherton	.05	.04	.02
354	Tony Bernazard	.05	.04	.02
355	Lee Smith	.10	.08	.04
356	Mickey Hatcher	.05	.04	.02
357	Ed Vande Berg	.05	.04	.02
358	Rick Dempsey	.07	.05	.03
359	Mike LaCoss	.05	.04	.02
360	Lloyd Moseby	.10	.08	.04
361	Shane Rawley	.10	.08	.04
362	Tom Paciorek	.05	.04	.02
363	Terry Forster	.07	.05	.03
364	Reid Nichols	.05	.04	.02
365	Mike Flanagan	.10	.08	.04
366	Reds Leaders (Dave Concepcion)	.07	.05	.03
367	Aurelio Lopez	.05	.04	.02
368	Greg Brock	.07	.05	.03
369	Al Holland	.05	.04	.02
370	*Vince Coleman*	1.50	1.25	.60
371	Bill Stein	.05	.04	.02
372	Ben Oglivie	.07	.05	.03
373	*Urbano Lugo*(FC)	.07	.05	.03
374	Terry Francona	.05	.04	.02
375	Rich Gedman	.10	.08	.04
376	Bill Dawley	.05	.04	.02
377	Joe Carter	.30	.25	.12
378	Bruce Bochte	.05	.04	.02
379	Bobby Meacham	.05	.04	.02
380	LaMarr Hoyt	.05	.04	.02
381	Ray Miller	.05	.04	.02
382	*Ivan Calderon*(FC)	1.00	.70	.40
383	*Chris Brown*	.20	.15	.08
384	Steve Trout	.05	.04	.02
385	Cecil Cooper	.10	.08	.04
386	*Cecil Fielder*(FC)	7.00	5.25	2.75
387	Steve Kemp	.07	.05	.03
388	Dickie Noles	.05	.04	.02
389	Glenn Davis(FC)	3.50	2.75	1.50
390	Tom Seaver	.40	.30	.15
391	Julio Franco	.10	.08	.04
392	John Russell(FC)	.10	.08	.04
393	Chris Pittaro	.05	.04	.02
394	Checklist 265-396	.05	.04	.02
395	Scott Garrelts	.07	.05	.03
396	Red Sox Leaders (Dwight Evans)	.07	.05	.03
397	*Steve Buechele*(FC)	.20	.15	.08
398	*Earnie Riles*(FC)	.15	.11	.06
399	Bill Swift	.12	.09	.05
400	Rod Carew	.30	.25	.12
401	Turn Back The Clock (Fernando Valenzuela)	.15	.11	.06
402	Turn Back The Clock (Tom Seaver)	.15	.11	.06
403	Turn Back The Clock (Willie Mays)	.20	.15	.08
404	Turn Back The Clock (Frank Robinson)	.15	.11	.06
405	Turn Back The Clock (Roger Maris)	.20	.15	.08
406	Scott Sanderson	.05	.04	.02
407	Sal Butera	.05	.04	.02
408	Dave Smith	.07	.05	.03
409	*Paul Runge*	.07	.05	.03
410	Dave Kingman	.15	.11	.06
411	Sparky Anderson	.07	.05	.03
412	Jim Clancy	.07	.05	.03
413	Tim Flannery	.05	.04	.02
414	Tom Gorman	.05	.04	.02
415	Hal McRae	.10	.08	.04
416	Denny Martinez	.07	.05	.03
417	R.J. Reynolds	.07	.05	.03
418	Alan Knicely	.05	.04	.02
419	Frank Wills	.05	.04	.02
420	Von Hayes	.10	.08	.04
421	Dave Palmer	.05	.04	.02
422	Mike Jorgensen	.05	.04	.02
423	Dan Spillner	.05	.04	.02
424	Rick Miller	.05	.04	.02
425	Larry McWilliams	.05	.04	.02
426	Brewers Leaders (Charlie Moore)	.07	.05	.03
427	Joe Cowley	.05	.04	.02
428	Max Venable	.05	.04	.02
429	Greg Booker	.05	.04	.02
430	Kent Hrbek	.20	.15	.08
431	George Frazier	.05	.04	.02
432	Mark Bailey	.05	.04	.02
433	Chris Codiroli	.05	.04	.02
434	Curt Wilkerson	.05	.04	.02
435	Bill Caudill	.05	.04	.02
436	Doug Flynn	.05	.04	.02
437	Rick Mahler	.05	.04	.02
438	Clint Hurdle	.05	.04	.02
439	Rick Honeycutt	.05	.04	.02
440	Alvin Davis	.30	.25	.12
441	Whitey Herzog	.07	.05	.03
442	Ron Robinson(FC)	.12	.09	.05
443	Bill Buckner	.10	.08	.04
444	Alex Trevino	.05	.04	.02
445	Bert Blyleven	.12	.09	.05
446	Lenn Sakata	.05	.04	.02
447	Jerry Don Gleaton	.05	.04	.02
448	*Herm Winningham*	.15	.11	.06
449	Rod Scurry	.05	.04	.02
450	Graig Nettles	.15	.11	.06
451	Mark Brown	.05	.04	.02
452	Bob Clark	.05	.04	.02
453	Steve Jeltz	.07	.05	.03
454	Burt Hooton	.07	.05	.03
455	Willie Randolph	.10	.08	.04
456	Braves Leaders (Dale Murphy)	.25	.20	.10
457	*Mickey Tettleton*	.60	.45	.25
458	Kevin Bass	.10	.08	.04
459	Luis Leal	.05	.04	.02
460	Leon Durham	.07	.05	.03
461	Walt Terrell	.07	.05	.03
462	Domingo Ramos	.05	.04	.02
463	Jim Gott	.05	.04	.02
464	Ruppert Jones	.07	.05	.03
465	Jesse Orosco	.07	.05	.03
466	Tom Foley	.05	.04	.02
467	Bob James	.05	.04	.02
468	Mike Scioscia	.07	.05	.03
469	Storm Davis	.10	.08	.04
470	Bill Madlock	.12	.09	.05
471	Bobby Cox	.05	.04	.02
472	Joe Hesketh	.07	.05	.03
473	Mark Brouhard	.05	.04	.02
474	John Tudor	.10	.08	.04
475	Juan Samuel	.12	.09	.05
476	Ron Mathis	.05	.04	.02
477	Mike Easler	.07	.05	.03
478	Andy Hawkins	.05	.04	.02
479	*Bob Melvin*(FC)	.12	.09	.05
480	*Oddibe McDowell*	.30	.25	.12
481	Scott Bradley(FC)	.10	.08	.04
482	Rick Lysander	.05	.04	.02
483	George Vukovich	.05	.04	.02
484	Donnie Hill	.05	.04	.02
485	Gary Matthews	.10	.08	.04

#	Player	MT	NR MT	EX
486	Angels Leaders (Bob Grich)	.07	.05	.03
487	Bret Saberhagen	.70	.50	.30
488	Lou Thornton	.05	.04	.02
489	Jim Winn	.05	.04	.02
490	Jeff Leonard	.07	.05	.03
491	Pascual Perez	.07	.05	.03
492	Kelvin Chapman	.05	.04	.02
493	Gene Nelson	.05	.04	.02
494	Gary Roenicke	.05	.04	.02
495	Mark Langston	.20	.15	.08
496	Jay Johnstone	.07	.05	.03
497	John Stuper	.05	.04	.02
498	Tito Landrum	.05	.04	.02
499	Bob Gibson	.05	.04	.02
500	Rickey Henderson	.70	.50	.30
501	Dave Johnson	.07	.05	.03
502	Glen Cook	.05	.04	.02
503	Mike Fitzgerald	.05	.04	.02
504	Denny Walling	.05	.04	.02
505	Jerry Koosman	.10	.08	.04
506	Bill Russell	.07	.05	.03
507	*Steve Ontiveros*(FC)	.12	.09	.05
508	Alan Wiggins	.05	.04	.02
509	Ernie Camacho	.05	.04	.02
510	Wade Boggs	2.00	1.50	.80
511	Ed Nunez	.05	.04	.02
512	Thad Bosley	.05	.04	.02
513	Ron Washington	.05	.04	.02
514	Mike Jones	.05	.04	.02
515	Darrell Evans	.12	.09	.05
516	Giants Leaders (Greg Minton)	.07	.05	.03
517	*Milt Thompson*(FC)	.25	.20	.10
518	Buck Martinez	.05	.04	.02
519	Danny Darwin	.05	.04	.02
520	Keith Hernandez	.30	.25	.12
521	Nate Snell	.05	.04	.02
522	Bob Bailor	.05	.04	.02
523	Joe Price	.05	.04	.02
524	Darrell Miller(FC)	.07	.05	.03
525	Marvell Wynne	.05	.04	.02
526	Charlie Lea	.05	.04	.02
527	Checklist 397-528	.05	.04	.02
528	Terry Pendleton	.15	.11	.06
529	Marc Sullivan	.05	.04	.02
530	Rich Gossage	.20	.15	.08
531	Tony LaRussa	.07	.05	.03
532	*Don Carman*	.25	.20	.10
533	Billy Sample	.05	.04	.02
534	Jeff Calhoun	.05	.04	.02
535	Toby Harrah	.07	.05	.03
536	Jose Rijo	.10	.08	.04
537	Mark Salas	.07	.05	.03
538	Dennis Eckersley	.12	.09	.05
539	Glenn Hubbard	.05	.04	.02
540	Dan Petry	.07	.05	.03
541	Jorge Orta	.05	.04	.02
542	Don Schulze	.05	.04	.02
543	Jerry Narron	.05	.04	.02
544	Eddie Milner	.05	.04	.02
545	Jimmy Key	.15	.11	.06
546	Mariners Leaders (Dave Henderson)	.07	.05	.03
547	*Roger McDowell*	.40	.30	.15
548	Mike Young	.05	.04	.02
549	Bob Welch	.12	.09	.05
550	Tom Herr	.10	.08	.04
551	Dave LaPoint	.07	.05	.03
552	Marc Hill	.05	.04	.02
553	Jim Morrison	.05	.04	.02
554	Paul Householder	.05	.04	.02
555	Hubie Brooks	.10	.08	.04
556	John Denny	.05	.04	.02
557	Gerald Perry	.12	.09	.05
558	Tim Stoddard	.05	.04	.02
559	Tommy Dunbar	.05	.04	.02
560	Dave Righetti	.20	.15	.08
561	Bob Lillis	.05	.04	.02
562	Joe Beckwith	.05	.04	.02
563	Alejandro Sanchez	.05	.04	.02
564	Warren Brusstar	.05	.04	.02
565	Tom Brunansky	.12	.09	.05
566	Alfredo Griffin	.07	.05	.03
567	Jeff Barkley	.05	.04	.02
568	Donnie Scott	.05	.04	.02
569	Jim Acker	.05	.04	.02
570	Rusty Staub	.10	.08	.04
571	Mike Jeffcoat	.05	.04	.02
572	Paul Zuvella	.05	.04	.02
573	Tom Hume	.05	.04	.02
574	Ron Kittle	.10	.08	.04
575	Mike Boddicker	.07	.05	.03
576	Expos Leaders (Andre Dawson)	.12	.09	.05
577	Jerry Reuss	.07	.05	.03
578	Lee Mazzilli	.07	.05	.03
579	Jim Slaton	.05	.04	.02
580	Willie McGee	.15	.11	.06
581	Bruce Hurst	.12	.09	.05
582	Jim Gantner	.07	.05	.03
583	Al Bumbry	.05	.04	.02
584	*Brian Fisher*(FC)	.30	.25	.12
585	Garry Maddox	.07	.05	.03
586	Greg Harris	.05	.04	.02
587	Rafael Santana	.05	.04	.02
588	Steve Lake	.05	.04	.02
589	Sid Bream	.10	.08	.04
590	Bob Knepper	.07	.05	.03
591	Jackie Moore	.05	.04	.02
592	Frank Tanana	.10	.08	.04
593	Jesse Barfield	.20	.15	.08
594	Chris Bando	.05	.04	.02
595	Dave Parker	.20	.15	.08
596	Onix Concepcion	.05	.04	.02
597	Sammy Stewart	.05	.04	.02
598	Jim Presley	.25	.20	.10
599	*Rick Aguilera*(FC)	.20	.15	.08
600	Dale Murphy	.50	.40	.20
601	Gary Lucas	.05	.04	.02
602	*Mariano Duncan*	.15	.11	.06
603	Bill Laskey	.05	.04	.02
604	Gary Pettis	.05	.04	.02
605	Dennis Boyd	.07	.05	.03
606	Royals Leaders (Hal McRae)	.07	.05	.03
607	Ken Dayley	.05	.04	.02
608	Bruce Bochy	.05	.04	.02
609	Barbaro Garbey	.05	.04	.02
610	Ron Guidry	.15	.11	.06
611	Gary Woods	.05	.04	.02
612	Richard Dotson	.10	.08	.04
613	Roy Smalley	.05	.04	.02
614	Rick Waits	.05	.04	.02
615	Johnny Ray	.10	.08	.04
616	Glenn Brummer	.05	.04	.02
617	Lonnie Smith	.07	.05	.03
618	Jim Pankovits	.05	.04	.02
619	Danny Heep	.05	.04	.02
620	Bruce Sutter	.12	.09	.05
621	John Felske	.05	.04	.02
622	Gary Lavelle	.05	.04	.02
623	Floyd Rayford	.05	.04	.02
624	Steve McCatty	.05	.04	.02
625	Bob Brenly	.05	.04	.02
626	Roy Thomas	.05	.04	.02
627	Ron Oester	.05	.04	.02
628	*Kirk McCaskill*(FC)	.35	.25	.14
629	*Mitch Webster*(FC)	.25	.20	.10
630	Fernando Valenzuela	.30	.25	.12
631	Steve Braun	.05	.04	.02
632	Dave Von Ohlen	.05	.04	.02
633	Jackie Gutierrez	.05	.04	.02
634	Roy Lee Jackson	.05	.04	.02
635	Jason Thompson	.05	.04	.02
636	Cubs Leaders (Lee Smith)	.07	.05	.03
637	Rudy Law	.05	.04	.02
638	John Butcher	.05	.04	.02
639	Bo Diaz	.07	.05	.03
640	Jose Cruz	.10	.08	.04
641	Wayne Tolleson	.05	.04	.02
642	Ray Searage	.05	.04	.02
643	Tom Brookens	.05	.04	.02
644	Mark Gubicza	.12	.09	.05
645	Dusty Baker	.07	.05	.03
646	Mike Moore	.05	.04	.02
647	Mel Hall	.07	.05	:03
648	Steve Bedrosian	.10	.08	.04
649	Ronn Reynolds	.05	.04	.02
650	Dave Stieb	.12	.09	.05
651	Billy Martin	.12	.09	.05
652	Tom Browning	.25	.20	.10
653	Jim Dwyer	.05	.04	.02
654	Ken Howell	.07	.05	.03
655	Manny Trillo	.07	.05	.03
656	Brian Harper	.05	.04	.02
657	Juan Agosto	.05	.04	.02
658	Rob Wilfong	.05	.04	.02
659	Checklist 529-660	.05	.04	.02
660	Steve Garvey	.30	.25	.12
661	Roger Clemens	3.00	2.25	1.25
662	Bill Schroeder	.05	.04	.02
663	Neil Allen	.05	.04	.02
664	Tim Corcoran	.05	.04	.02
665	Alejandro Pena	.07	.05	.03
666	Rangers Leaders (Charlie Hough)	.07	.05	.03

#		MT	NR MT	EX
667	Tim Teufel	.05	.04	.02
668	Cecilio Guante	.05	.04	.02
669	Ron Cey	.10	.08	.04
670	Willie Hernandez	.07	.05	.03
671	Lynn Jones	.05	.04	.02
672	Rob Picciolo	.05	.04	.02
673	Ernie Whitt	.07	.05	.03
674	Pat Tabler	.07	.05	.03
675	Claudell Washington	.07	.05	.03
676	Matt Young	.05	.04	.02
677	Nick Esasky	.07	.05	.03
678	Dan Gladden	.07	.05	.03
679	Britt Burns	.05	.04	.02
680	George Foster	.15	.11	.06
681	Dick Williams	.05	.04	.02
682	Junior Ortiz	.05	.04	.02
683	Andy Van Slyke	.15	.11	.06
684	Bob McClure	.05	.04	.02
685	Tim Wallach	.12	.09	.05
686	Jeff Stone	.05	.04	.02
687	Mike Trujillo	.05	.04	.02
688	Larry Herndon	.07	.05	.03
689	Dave Stewart	.12	.09	.05
690	Ryne Sandberg	.35	.25	.14
691	Mike Madden	.05	.04	.02
692	Dale Berra	.05	.04	.02
693	Tom Tellmann	.05	.04	.02
694	Garth Iorg	.05	.04	.02
695	Mike Smithson	.05	.04	.02
696	Dodgers Leaders (Bill Russell)	.07	.05	.03
697	Bud Black	.05	.04	.02
698	Brad Komminsk	.05	.04	.02
699	Pat Corrales	.05	.04	.02
700	Reggie Jackson	.35	.25	.14
701	Keith Hernandez AS	.15	.11	.06
702	Tom Herr AS	.07	.05	.03
703	Tim Wallach AS	.07	.05	.03
704	Ozzie Smith AS	.10	.08	.04
705	Dale Murphy AS	.30	.25	.12
706	Pedro Guerrero AS	.12	.09	.05
707	Willie McGee AS	.12	.09	.05
708	Gary Carter AS	.20	.15	.08
709	Dwight Gooden AS	.40	.30	.15
710	John Tudor AS	.07	.05	.03
711	Jeff Reardon AS	.07	.05	.03
712	Don Mattingly AS	.90	.70	.35
713	Damaso Garcia AS	.05	.04	.02
714	George Brett AS	.30	.25	.12
715	Cal Ripken AS	.25	.20	.10
716	Rickey Henderson AS	.25	.20	.10
717	Dave Winfield AS	.20	.15	.08
718	Jorge Bell AS	.20	.15	.08
719	Carlton Fisk AS	.12	.09	.05
720	Bret Saberhagen AS	.15	.11	.06
721	Ron Guidry AS	.10	.08	.04
722	Dan Quisenberry AS	.07	.05	.03
723	Marty Bystrom	.05	.04	.02
724	Tim Hulett	.07	.05	.03
725	Mario Soto	.07	.05	.03
726	Orioles Leaders (Rick Dempsey)	.07	.05	.03
727	David Green	.05	.04	.02
728	Mike Marshall	.12	.09	.05
729	Jim Beattie	.05	.04	.02
730	Ozzie Smith	.15	.11	.06
731	Don Robinson	.07	.05	.03
732	Floyd Youmans (FC)	.20	.15	.08
733	Ron Romanick	.05	.04	.02
734	Marty Barrett	.10	.08	.04
735	Dave Dravecky	.07	.05	.03
736	Glenn Wilson	.07	.05	.03
737	Pete Vuckovich	.07	.05	.03
738	Andre Robertson	.05	.04	.02
739	Dave Rozema	.05	.04	.02
740	Lance Parrish	.20	.15	.08
741	Pete Rose	.40	.30	.15
742	Frank Viola	.15	.11	.06
743	Pat Sheridan	.05	.04	.02
744	Lary Sorensen	.05	.04	.02
745	Willie Upshaw	.07	.05	.03
746	Denny Gonzalez	.05	.04	.02
747	Rick Cerone	.05	.04	.02
748	Steve Henderson	.05	.04	.02
749	Ed Jurak	.05	.04	.02
750	Gorman Thomas	.10	.08	.04
751	Howard Johnson	.12	.09	.05
752	Mike Krukow	.07	.05	.03
753	Dan Ford	.05	.04	.02
754	Pat Clements	.12	.09	.05
755	Harold Baines	.15	.11	.06
756	Pirates Leaders (Rick Rhoden)	.07	.05	.03
757	Darrell Porter	.07	.05	.03
758	Dave Anderson	.05	.04	.02
759	Moose Haas	.05	.04	.02
760	Andre Dawson	.20	.15	.08
761	Don Slaught	.05	.04	.02
762	Eric Show	.07	.05	.03
763	Terry Puhl	.05	.04	.02
764	Kevin Gross	.07	.05	.03
765	Don Baylor	.12	.09	.05
766	Rick Langford	.05	.04	.02
767	Jody Davis	.10	.08	.04
768	Vern Ruhle	.05	.04	.02
769	Harold Reynolds (FC)	.70	.50	.30
770	Vida Blue	.10	.08	.04
771	John McNamara	.05	.04	.02
772	Brian Downing	.07	.05	.03
773	Greg Pryor	.05	.04	.02
774	Terry Leach	.05	.04	.02
775	Al Oliver	.10	.08	.04
776	Gene Garber	.05	.04	.02
777	Wayne Krenchicki	.05	.04	.02
778	Jerry Hairston	.05	.04	.02
779	Rick Reuschel	.10	.08	.04
780	Robin Yount	.50	.40	.20
781	Joe Nolan	.05	.04	.02
782	Ken Landreaux	.05	.04	.02
783	Ricky Horton	.07	.05	.03
784	Alan Bannister	.05	.04	.02
785	Bob Stanley	.05	.04	.02
786	Twins Leaders (Mickey Hatcher)	.07	.05	.03
787	Vance Law	.07	.05	.03
788	Marty Castillo	.05	.04	.02
789	Kurt Bevacqua	.05	.04	.02
790	Phil Niekro	.25	.20	.10
791	Checklist 661-792	.05	.04	.02
792	Charles Hudson	.06	.05	.02

1986 Topps All-Star Glossy Set Of 22

As in previous years, Topps continued to make the popular glossy-surfaced cards as an insert in rack packs. The All-Star Glossy set of 22 2-1/2" by 3-1/2" cards shows little design change from previous years. Cards feature a front color photo and All-Star banner at the top. The bottom has the player's name and position. The set includes the All-Star starting teams as well as the managers and honorary captains.

		MT	NR MT	EX
Complete Set:		6.00	4.50	2.50
Common Player:		.20	.15	.08
1	Sparky Anderson	.20	.15	.08
2	Eddie Murray	.50	.40	.20
3	Lou Whitaker	.30	.25	.12
4	George Brett	.80	.60	.30
5	Cal Ripken	.60	.45	.25
6	Jim Rice	.50	.40	.20
7	Rickey Henderson	.60	.45	.25
8	Dave Winfield	.50	.40	.20
9	Carlton Fisk	.30	.25	.12
10	Jack Morris	.30	.25	.12
11	A.L. All-Star Team	.20	.15	.08
12	Dick Williams	.20	.15	.08
13	Steve Garvey	.50	.40	.20
14	Tom Herr	.20	.15	.08

		MT	NR MT	EX
15	Graig Nettles	.20	.15	.08
16	Ozzie Smith	.30	.25	.12
17	Tony Gwynn	.60	.45	.25
18	Dale Murphy	.80	.60	.30
19	Darryl Strawberry	.80	.60	.30
20	Terry Kennedy	.20	.15	.08
21	LaMarr Hoyt	.20	.15	.08
22	N.L. All-Star Team	.20	.15	.08

1986 Topps All-Star Glossy Set Of 60

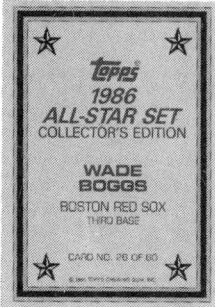

The Topps All-Star & Hot Prospects Glossy Set of 60 cards represents an expansion of a good idea. The 2-1/2" by 3-1/2" cards had a good following when they were limited to stars, but Topps realized that the addition of top young players would spice up the set even further, so in 1986 it was expanded from 40 to 60 cards. The cards themselves are basically all color glossy pictures with the player's name in very small print in the lower left-hand corner. To obtain the set, it was necessary to send $1 plus six special offer cards from wax packs to Topps for each series. At 60 cards, that meant the process had to be repeated six times as there were 10 cards in each series, making the set quite expensive from the outset.

		MT	NR MT	EX
Complete Set:		15.00	11.00	6.00
Common Player:		.15	.11	.06
1	Oddibe McDowell	.25	.20	.10
2	Reggie Jackson	.70	.50	.30
3	Fernando Valenzuela	.35	.25	.14
4	Jack Clark	.25	.20	.10
5	Rickey Henderson	.70	.50	.30
6	Steve Balboni	.15	.11	.06
7	Keith Hernandez	.40	.30	.15
8	Lance Parrish	.30	.25	.12
9	Willie McGee	.25	.20	.10
10	Chris Brown	.40	.30	.15
11	Darryl Strawberry	.90	.70	.35
12	Ron Guidry	.30	.25	.12
13	Dave Parker	.25	.20	.10
14	Cal Ripken	.70	.50	.30
15	Tim Raines	.50	.40	.20
16	Rod Carew	.60	.45	.25
17	Mike Schmidt	.90	.70	.35
18	George Brett	.90	.70	.35
19	Joe Hesketh	.15	.11	.06
20	Dan Pasqua	.20	.15	.08
21	Vince Coleman	1.00	.70	.40
22	Tom Seaver	.50	.40	.20
23	Gary Carter	.50	.40	.20
24	Orel Hershiser	.40	.30	.15
25	Pedro Guerrero	.30	.25	.12
26	Wade Boggs	1.25	.90	.50
27	Bret Saberhagen	.30	.25	.12
28	Carlton Fisk	.25	.20	.10
29	Kirk Gibson	.35	.25	.14
30	Brian Fisher	.20	.15	.08
31	Don Mattingly	3.00	2.25	1.25
32	Tom Herr	.15	.11	.06
33	Eddie Murray	.60	.45	.25
34	Ryne Sandberg	.40	.30	.15
35	Dan Quisenberry	.15	.11	.06

		MT	NR MT	EX
36	Jim Rice	.50	.40	.20
37	Dale Murphy	.90	.70	.35
38	Steve Garvey	.50	.40	.20
39	Roger McDowell	.25	.20	.10
40	Earnie Riles	.15	.11	.06
41	Dwight Gooden	1.25	.90	.50
42	Dave Winfield	.50	.40	.20
43	Dave Stieb	.20	.15	.08
44	Bob Horner	.20	.15	.08
45	Nolan Ryan	.50	.40	.20
46	Ozzie Smith	.25	.20	.10
47	Jorge Bell	.50	.40	.20
48	Gorman Thomas	.15	.11	.06
49	Tom Browning	.25	.20	.10
50	Larry Sheets	.20	.15	.08
51	Pete Rose	1.25	.90	.50
52	Brett Butler	.15	.11	.06
53	John Tudor	.20	.15	.08
54	Phil Bradley	.20	.15	.08
55	Jeff Reardon	.20	.15	.08
56	Rich Gossage	.25	.20	.10
57	Tony Gwynn	.60	.45	.25
58	Ozzie Guillen	.25	.20	.10
59	Glenn Davis	.35	.25	.14
60	Darrell Evans	.15	.11	.06

1986 Topps Box Panels

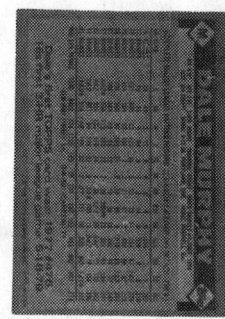

DALE MURPHY

Following the lead of Donruss, which introduced the concept in 1985, Topps produced special cards on the bottom panels of wax boxes. Individual cards measure 2-1/2" by 3-1/2", the same as regular cards. Design of the cards is virtually identical with regular '86 Topps, though the top border is in red, rather than black. The cards are lettered "A" through "P", rather than numbered on the back.

		MT	NR MT	EX
Complete Panel Set:		12.00	9.00	4.75
Complete Singles Set:		6.00	4.50	2.50
Common Panel:		2.00	1.50	.80
Common Single Player:		.15	.11	.06
	Panel	3.50	2.75	1.50
A	Jorge Bell	.20	.15	.08
B	Wade Boggs	.60	.45	.25
C	George Brett	.35	.25	.14
D	Vince Coleman	.35	.25	.14
	Panel	2.00	1.50	.80
E	Carlton Fisk	.15	.11	.06
F	Dwight Gooden	.40	.30	.15
G	Pedro Guerrero	.15	.11	.06
H	Ron Guidry	.15	.11	.06
	Panel	3.50	2.75	1.50
I	Reggie Jackson	.30	.25	.12
J	Don Mattingly	.90	.70	.35
K	Oddibe McDowell	.15	.11	.06
L	Willie McGee	.15	.11	.06
	Panel	3.00	2.25	1.25
M	Dale Murphy	.35	.25	.14
N	Pete Rose	.50	.40	.20
O	Bret Saberhagen	.15	.11	.06
P	Fernando Valenzuela	.20	.15	.08

NOTE: A card number in parentheses ( ) indicates the set is unnumbered.

1986 Topps
Gallery Of Champions

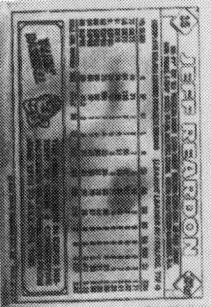

For the third consecutive year Topps issued 12 "metal mini-cards" as a dealer-ordering incentive. The metal replicas were minted 1/4-size (approximately 1-1/4" by 1-3/4") of the regular cards and come in silver, aluminum and bronze. The bronze and silver sets were issued in leather-like velvet-lined display cases. A bronze 1952 Topps Mickey Mantle was given as a premium for dealers purchasing 1986 Traded sets, while a pewter Don Mattingly was issued as a premium to those ordering the aluminum, bronze and silver sets. The Mantle bronze is valued at $12 and the Mattingly pewter at $100.

		MT	NR MT	EX
	Complete Aluminum Set:	30.00	22.00	12.00
	Complete Bronze Set:	175.00	131.00	70.00
	Complete Silver Set:	650.00	487.00	260.00
(1a)	Wade Boggs (aluminum)	3.00	2.25	1.25
(1b)	Wade Boggs (bronze)	25.00	18.50	10.00
(1c)	Wade Boggs (silver)	125.00	94.00	50.00
(2a)	Vince Coleman (aluminum)	1.25	.90	.50
(2b)	Vince Coleman (bronze)	12.00	9.00	4.75
(2c)	Vince Coleman (silver)	50.00	37.00	20.00
(3a)	Darrell Evans (aluminum)	.70	.50	.30
(3b)	Darrell Evans (bronze)	7.50	5.75	3.00
(3c)	Darrell Evans (silver)	20.00	15.00	8.00
(4a)	Dwight Gooden (aluminum)	2.00	1.50	.80
(4b)	Dwight Gooden (bronze)	20.00	15.00	8.00
(4c)	Dwight Gooden (silver)	100.00	75.00	40.00
(5a)	Ozzie Guillen (aluminum)	.70	.50	.30
(5b)	Ozzie Guillen (bronze)	7.50	5.75	3.00
(5c)	Ozzie Guillen (silver)	20.00	15.00	8.00
(6a)	Don Mattingly (aluminum)	8.00	6.00	3.25
(6b)	Don Mattingly (bronze)	50.00	37.00	20.00
(6c)	Don Mattingly (silver)	200.00	150.00	80.00
(7a)	Willie McGee (aluminum)	1.00	.70	.40
(7b)	Willie McGee (bronze)	10.00	7.50	4.00
(7c)	Willie McGee (silver)	30.00	22.00	12.00
(8a)	Dale Murphy (aluminum)	1.50	1.25	.60
(8b)	Dale Murphy (bronze)	15.00	11.00	6.00
(8c)	Dale Murphy (silver)	80.00	60.00	32.00
(9a)	Dan Quisenberry (aluminum)	.70	.50	.30
(9b)	Dan Quisenberry (bronze)	7.50	5.75	3.00
(9c)	Dan Quisenberry (silver)	20.00	15.00	8.00
(10a)	Jeff Reardon (aluminum)	.70	.50	.30
(10b)	Jeff Reardon (bronze)	7.50	5.75	3.00
(10c)	Jeff Reardon (silver)	20.00	15.00	8.00
(11a)	Pete Rose (aluminum)	2.50	2.00	1.00
(11b)	Pete Rose (bronze)	25.00	18.50	10.00
(11c)	Pete Rose (silver)	110.00	82.00	44.00
(12a)	Bret Saberhagen (aluminum)	1.00	.70	.40
(12b)	Bret Saberhagen (bronze)	10.00	7.50	4.00
(12c)	Bret Saberhagen (silver)	30.00	22.00	12.00

A baseball card history feature, definitions for grading conditions and tips on how to use this catalog are located in the introduction section at the front of this book.

1986 Topps
Mini League Leaders

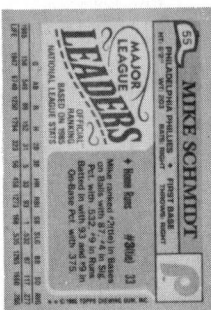

Topps had long experimented with bigger cards, but in 1986, they also decided to try smaller ones. These 2-1/8" by 2-15/16" cards feature top players in a number of categories. Sold in plastic packs as a regular Topps issue, the 66-card set is attractive as well as innovative. The cards feature color photos and a minimum of added information on the fronts where only the player's name and Topps logo appear. Backs limited information as well, but do feature whatever information was required to justify the player's inclusion in a set of league leaders.

		MT	NR MT	EX
	Complete Set:	8.00	6.00	3.25
	Common Player:	.09	.07	.04
1	Eddie Murray	.40	.30	.15
2	Cal Ripken	.40	.30	.15
3	Wade Boggs	.80	.60	.30
4	Dennis Boyd	.09	.07	.04
5	Dwight Evans	.15	.11	.06
6	Bruce Hurst	.15	.11	.06
7	Gary Pettis	.09	.07	.04
8	Harold Baines	.15	.11	.06
9	Floyd Bannister	.09	.07	.04
10	Britt Burns	.09	.07	.04
11	Carlton Fisk	.20	.15	.08
12	Brett Butler	.15	.11	.06
13	Darrell Evans	.15	.11	.06
14	Jack Morris	.25	.20	.10
15	Lance Parrish	.25	.20	.10
16	Walt Terrell	.09	.07	.04
17	Steve Balboni	.09	.07	.04
18	George Brett	.50	.40	.20
19	Charlie Leibrandt	.09	.07	.04
20	Bret Saberhagen	.20	.15	.08
21	Lonnie Smith	.09	.07	.04
22	Willie Wilson	.15	.11	.06
23	Bert Blyleven	.15	.11	.06
24	Mike Smithson	.09	.07	.04
25	Frank Viola	.20	.15	.08
26	Ron Guidry	.20	.15	.08
27	Rickey Henderson	.40	.30	.15
28	Don Mattingly	1.25	.90	.50
29	Dave Winfield	.30	.25	.12
30	Mike Moore	.09	.07	.04
31	Gorman Thomas	.09	.07	.04
32	Toby Harrah	.09	.07	.04
33	Charlie Hough	.09	.07	.04
34	Doyle Alexander	.09	.07	.04
35	Jimmy Key	.15	.11	.06
36	Dave Stieb	.15	.11	.06
37	Dale Murphy	.50	.40	.20
38	Keith Moreland	.09	.07	.04
39	Ryne Sandberg	.30	.25	.12
40	Tom Browning	.15	.11	.06
41	Dave Parker	.20	.15	.08
42	Mario Soto	.09	.07	.04
43	Nolan Ryan	.30	.25	.12
44	Pedro Guerrero	.20	.15	.08
45	Orel Hershiser	.30	.25	.12
46	Mike Scioscia	.09	.07	.04
47	Fernando Valenzuela	.25	.20	.10
48	Bob Welch	.15	.11	.06
49	Tim Raines	.30	.25	.12

		MT	NR MT	EX
50	Gary Carter	.30	.25	.12
51	Sid Fernandez	.15	.11	.06
52	Dwight Gooden	.70	.50	.30
53	Keith Hernandez	.25	.20	.10
54	Juan Samuel	.20	.15	.08
55	Mike Schmidt	.50	.40	.20
56	Glenn Wilson	.09	.07	.04
57	Rick Reuschel	.15	.11	.06
58	Joaquin Andujar	.09	.07	.04
59	Jack Clark	.20	.15	.08
60	Vince Coleman	.60	.45	.25
61	Danny Cox	.09	.07	.04
62	Tom Herr	.09	.07	.04
63	Willie McGee	.15	.11	.06
64	John Tudor	.15	.11	.06
65	Tony Gwynn	.40	.30	.15
66	Checklist	.09	.07	.04

1986 Topps Super

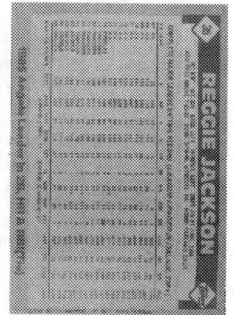

REGGIE JACKSON

A third year of oversize, 4-7/8" by 6-7/8", versions of Topps' regular issue cards saw the set once again hit the 60-card mark. Besides being four times the size of a normal card, the Supers differ only in the number on the back of the card.

		MT	NR MT	EX
Complete Set:		12.00	9.00	4.75
Common Player:		.20	.15	.08
1	Don Mattingly	2.25	1.75	.90
2	Willie McGee	.35	.25	.14
3	Bret Saberhagen	.35	.25	.14
4	Dwight Gooden	1.50	1.25	.60
5	Dan Quisenberry	.20	.15	.08
6	Jeff Reardon	.25	.20	.10
7	Ozzie Guillen	.25	.20	.10
8	Vince Coleman	.70	.50	.30
9	Harold Baines	.25	.20	.10
10	Jorge Bell	.50	.40	.20
11	Bert Blyleven	.25	.20	.10
12	Wade Boggs	1.25	.90	.50
13	Phil Bradley	.25	.20	.10
14	George Brett	.80	.60	.30
15	Hubie Brooks	.20	.15	.08
16	Tom Browning	.25	.20	.10
17	Bill Buckner	.20	.15	.08
18	Brett Butler	.20	.15	.08
19	Gary Carter	.50	.40	.20
20	Cecil Cooper	.25	.20	.10
21	Darrell Evans	.25	.20	.10
22	Dwight Evans	.20	.15	.08
23	Carlton Fisk	.30	.25	.12
24	Steve Garvey	.50	.40	.20
25	Kirk Gibson	.35	.25	.14
26	Rich Gossage	.25	.20	.10
27	Pedro Guerrero	.30	.25	.12
28	Ron Guidry	.30	.25	.12
29	Tony Gwynn	.70	.50	.30
30	Rickey Henderson	.70	.50	.30
31	Keith Hernandez	.50	.40	.20
32	Tom Herr	.20	.15	.08
33	Orel Hershiser	.50	.40	.20
34	Jay Howell	.20	.15	.08
35	Reggie Jackson	.60	.45	.25
36	Bob James	.20	.15	.08
37	Charlie Leibrandt	.20	.15	.08
38	Jack Morris	.35	.25	.14

		MT	NR MT	EX
39	Dale Murphy	.80	.60	.30
40	Eddie Murray	.60	.45	.25
41	Dave Parker	.35	.25	.14
42	Tim Raines	.50	.40	.20
43	Jim Rice	.50	.40	.20
44	Dave Righetti	.30	.25	.12
45	Cal Ripken	.70	.50	.30
46	Pete Rose	1.00	.70	.40
47	Nolan Ryan	.50	.40	.20
48	Ryne Sandberg	.50	.40	.20
49	Mike Schmidt	.80	.60	.30
50	Tom Seaver	.50	.40	.20
51	Bryn Smith	.20	.15	.08
52	Lee Smith	.20	.15	.08
53	Ozzie Smith	.30	.25	.12
54	Dave Stieb	.20	.15	.08
55	Darryl Strawberry	.80	.60	.30
56	Gorman Thomas	.20	.15	.08
57	John Tudor	.20	.15	.08
58	Fernando Valenzuela	.40	.30	.15
59	Willie Wilson	.25	.20	.10
60	Dave Winfield	.50	.40	.20

1986 Topps Super Star

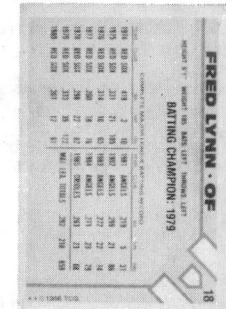

FRED LYNN ● OF

Labeled "Topps' Collector Series" in a red band at the top of the front, this set marked the second year of Topps' production of a special boxed set for the Woolworth chain of stores, though Woolworth's name does not appear anywhere on the card. The cards, which measure 2-1/2" by 3-1/2", feature a color photo with its lower right corner rolled up to reveal the words "Super Star" on a bright yellow border. The player's name appears in the lower left corner. The 66-card set features stars and retains a certain measure of popularity on that basis.

		MT	NR MT	EX
Complete Set:		7.00	5.25	2.75
Common Player:		.09	.07	.04
1	Tony Armas	.09	.07	.04
2	Don Baylor	.12	.09	.05
3	Wade Boggs	1.00	.70	.40
4	George Brett	.40	.30	.15
5	Bill Buckner	.09	.07	.04
6	Rod Carew	.30	.25	.12
7	Gary Carter	.30	.25	.12
8	Cecil Cooper	.12	.09	.05
9	Darrell Evans	.12	.09	.05
10	Dwight Evans	.15	.11	.05
11	George Foster	.12	.09	.05
12	Bobby Grich	.09	.07	.04
13	Tony Gwynn	.35	.25	.14
14	Keith Hernandez	.25	.20	.10
15	Reggie Jackson	.30	.25	.12
16	Dave Kingman	.12	.09	.05
17	Carney Lansford	.09	.07	.04
18	Fred Lynn	.12	.09	.05
19	Bill Madlock	.12	.09	.05
20	Don Mattingly	2.00	1.50	.80
21	Willie McGee	.20	.15	.08
22	Hal McRae	.09	.07	.04
23	Dale Murphy	.40	.30	.15
24	Eddie Murray	.35	.25	.14
25	Ben Oglivie	.09	.07	.04
26	Al Oliver	.12	.09	.05

		MT	NR MT	EX
27	Dave Parker	.20	.15	.08
28	Jim Rice	.30	.25	.12
29	Pete Rose	.90	.70	.35
30	Mike Schmidt	.40	.30	.15
31	Gorman Thomas	.09	.07	.04
32	Willie Wilson	.12	.09	.05
33	Dave Winfield	.30	.25	.12

1986 Topps Tattoos

Topps returned to tattoos in 1986, marketing a set of 24 different tattoo sheets. Each sheet of tattoos measures 3-7/16" by 14" and includes both player and smaller action tattoos. As the action tattoos were uniform and not of any particular player, they add little value to the sheet. The player tattoos measure 1-3/16" by 2-3/8". With 24 sheets, eight players per sheet, there are 192 players represented in the set. The sheets are numbered.

		MT	NR MT	EX
Complete Set:		6.00	4.50	2.50
Common Player:		.20	.15	.08
1	Julio Franco, Rich Gossage, Keith Hernandez, Charlie Leibrandt, Jack Perconte, Lee Smith, Dickie Thon, Dave Winfield	.25	.20	.10
2	Jesse Barfield, Shawon Dunston, Dennis Eckersley, Brian Fisher, Moose Haas, Mike Moore, Dale Murphy, Bret Saberhagen	.30	.25	.12
3	George Bell, Bob Brenly, Steve Carlton, Jose DeLeon, Bob Horner, Bob James, Dan Quisenberry, Andre Thornton	.25	.20	.10
4	Mike Davis, Leon Durham, Darrell Evans, Glenn Hubbard, Johnny Ray, Cal Ripken, Ted Simmons	.25	.20	.10
5	John Candelaria, Rick Dempsey, Steve Garvey, Ozzie Guillen, Gary Matthews, Jesse Orosco, Tony Pena	.25	.20	.10
6	Bruce Bochte, George Brett, Cecil Cooper, Sammy Khalifa, Ron Kittle, Scott McGregor, Pete Rose, Mookie Wilson	.45	.35	.20
7	John Franco, Carney Lansford, Don Mattingly, Graig Nettles, Rick Reuschel, Mike Schmidt, Larry Sheets, Don Sutton	.45	.35	.20
8	Cecilio Guante, Willie Hernandez, Mike Krukow, Fred Lynn, Phil Niekro, Ed Nunez, Ryne Sandberg, Pat Tabler	.25	.20	.10
9	Brett Butler, Chris Codiroli, Jim Gantner, Charlie Hough, Dave Parker, Rick Rhoden, Glenn Wilson, Robin Yount	.20	.15	.08
10	Tom Browning, Ron Darling, Von Hayes, Chet Lemon, Tom Seaver, Mike Smithson, Bruce Sutter, Alan Trammell	.25	.20	.10
11	Tony Armas, Jose Cruz, Jay Howell, Rick Mahler, Jack Morris, Rafael Ramirez, Dave Righetti, Mike Young	.20	.15	.08
12	Alvin Davis, Doug DeCinces, Andy Hawkins, Dennis Lamp, Keith Moreland, Jim Presley, Mario Soto, John Tudor	.20	.15	.08
13	Hubie Brooks, Jody Davis, Dwight Evans, Ron Hassey, Charles Hudson, Kirby Puckett, Jose Uribe	.20	.15	.08
14	Tony Bernazard, Phil Bradley, Bill Buckner, Brian Downing, Dan Driessen, Ron Guidry, LaMarr Hoyt, Garry Maddox	.20	.15	.08
15	Buddy Bell, Joe Carter, Tony Fernandez, Tito Landrum, Jeff Leonard, Hal McRae, Willie Randolph, Juan Samuel	.20	.15	.08
16	Dennis Boyd, Vince Coleman, Scott Garrelts, Alfredo Griffin, Donnie Moore, Tony Perez, Ozzie Smith, Frank White	.25	.20	.10
17	Rich Gedman, Kent Hrbek, Reggie Jackson, Mike Marshall, Terry Pendleton, Tim Raines, Mark Salas, Claudell Washington	.25	.20	.10
18	Chris Brown, Tom Brunansky, Glenn Davis, Ron Davis, Burt Hooton, Darryl Strawberry, Frank Viola, Tim Wallach	.30	.25	.12
19	Jack Clark, Bill Doran, Toby Harrah, Bill Madlock, Pete O'Brien, Larry Parrish, Mike Scioscia, Garry Templeton	.20	.15	.08
20	Gary Carter, Andre Dawson, Dwight Gooden, Orel Hershiser, Oddibe McDowell, Roger McDowell, Dwayne Murphy, Jim Rice	.40	.30	.15
21	Steve Balboni, Mike Easler, Charlie Lea, Lloyd Moseby, Steve Sax, Rick Sutcliffe, Gary Ward, Willie Wilson	.20	.15	.08
22	Wade Boggs, Dave Concepcion, Kirk Gibson, Tom Herr, Lance Parrish, Jeff Reardon, Bryn Smith, Gorman Thomas	.30	.25	.12
23	Carlton Fisk, Bob Grich, Pedro Guerrero, Willie McGee, Paul Molitor, Mike Scott, Dave Stieb, Lou Whitaker	.20	.15	.08
24	Bert Blyleven, Damaso Garcia, Phil Garner, Tony Gwynn, Rickey Henderson, Ben Oglivie, Nolan Ryan, Fernando Valenzuela	.30	.25	.12

1986 Topps Traded

 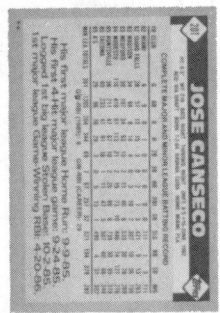

This 132-card set of 2-1/2" by 3-1/2" cards is one of the most popular sets of recent times. As always, the set features traded veterans, including such players as Phil Niekro and Tom Seaver. They are not, however, the reason for the excitement. The demand is there because of a better than usual crop of rookies who also appear in the sets. Among those are Jose Canseco, Wally Joyner, Pete Incaviglia, Todd Worrell, and the first card of Bo Jackson. As in the previous two years, a glossy-finish "Tiffany" edition of 5,000 Traded sets was produced. The "Tiffany" cards are worth four to six times the value of the regular Traded cards.

		MT	NR MT	EX
Complete Set:		35.00	26.00	14.00
Common Player:		.08	.06	.03
1T	Andy Allanson(FC)	.20	.15	.08
2T	Neil Allen	.08	.06	.03
3T	Joaquin Andujar	.10	.08	.04
4T	Paul Assenmacher(FC)	.20	.15	.08
5T	Scott Bailes(FC)	.20	.15	.08
6T	Don Baylor	.15	.11	.06
7T	Steve Bedrosian	.15	.11	.06
8T	Juan Beniquez	.08	.06	.03
9T	Juan Berenguer	.08	.06	.03
10T	Mike Bielecki(FC)	.50	.40	.20
11T	Barry Bonds(FC)	6.00	4.50	2.50
12T	Bobby Bonilla(FC)	5.00	3.75	2.00
13T	Juan Bonilla	.08	.06	.03
14T	Rich Bordi	.08	.06	.03
15T	Steve Boros	.08	.06	.03
16T	Rick Burleson	.10	.08	.04

		MT	NR MT	EX
17T	Bill Campbell	.08	.06	.03
18T	Tom Candiotti	.08	.06	.03
19T	John Cangelosi(FC)	.20	.15	.08
20T	Jose Canseco(FC)	10.00	7.50	4.00
21T	Carmen Castillo	.08	.06	.03
22T	Rick Cerone	.08	.06	.03
23T	John Cerutti(FC)	.20	.15	.08
24T	Will Clark(FC)	10.00	7.50	4.00
25T	Mark Clear	.08	.06	.03
26T	Darnell Coles	.12	.09	.05
27T	Dave Collins	.10	.08	.04
28T	Tim Conroy	.08	.06	.03
29T	Joe Cowley	.08	.06	.03
30T	Joel Davis(FC)	.12	.09	.05
31T	Rob Deer	.15	.11	.06
32T	John Denny	.08	.06	.03
33T	Mike Easler	.10	.08	.04
34T	Mark Eichhorn(FC)	.20	.15	.08
35T	Steve Farr	.08	.06	.03
36T	Scott Fletcher	.15	.11	.06
37T	Terry Forster	.10	.08	.04
38T	Terry Francona	.08	.06	.03
39T	Jim Fregosi	.08	.06	.03
40T	Andres Galarraga(FC)	1.75	1.25	.70
41T	Ken Griffey	.12	.09	.05
42T	Bill Gullickson	.08	.06	.03
43T	Jose Guzman(FC)	.35	.25	.14
44T	Moose Haas	.08	.06	.03
45T	Billy Hatcher	.20	.15	.08
46T	Mike Heath	.08	.06	.03
47T	Tom Hume	.08	.06	.03
48T	Pete Incaviglia(FC)	.50	.40	.20
49T	Dane Iorg	.08	.06	.03
50T	Bo Jackson(FC)	10.00	7.50	4.00
51T	Wally Joyner(FC)	1.75	1.25	.70
52T	Charlie Kerfeld(FC)	.15	.11	.06
53T	Eric King(FC)	.20	.15	.08
54T	Bob Kipper(FC)	.12	.09	.05
55T	Wayne Krenchicki	.08	.06	.03
56T	John Kruk(FC)	.40	.30	.15
57T	Mike LaCoss	.08	.06	.03
58T	Pete Ladd	.08	.06	.03
59T	Mike Laga	.08	.06	.03
60T	Hal Lanier	.08	.06	.03
61T	Dave LaPoint	.12	.09	.05
62T	Rudy Law	.08	.06	.03
63T	Rick Leach	.08	.06	.03
64T	Tim Leary	.08	.06	.03
65T	Dennis Leonard	.10	.08	.04
66T	Jim Leyland	.08	.06	.03
67T	Steve Lyons	.12	.09	.05
68T	Mickey Mahler	.08	.06	.03
69T	Candy Maldonado	.15	.11	.06
70T	Roger Mason(FC)	.10	.08	.04
71T	Bob McClure	.08	.06	.03
72T	Andy McGaffigan	.08	.06	.03
73T	Gene Michael	.08	.06	.03
74T	Kevin Mitchell(FC)	5.00	3.75	2.00
75T	Omar Moreno	.08	.06	.03
76T	Jerry Mumphrey	.08	.06	.03
77T	Phil Niekro	.40	.30	.15
78T	Randy Niemann	.08	.06	.03
79T	Juan Nieves(FC)	.25	.20	.10
80T	Otis Nixon(FC)	.12	.09	.05
81T	Bob Ojeda	.12	.09	.05
82T	Jose Oquendo	.08	.06	.03
83T	Tom Paciorek	.08	.06	.03
84T	Dave Palmer	.08	.06	.03
85T	Frank Pastore	.08	.06	.03
86T	Lou Piniella	.12	.09	.05
87T	Dan Plesac(FC)	.40	.30	.15
88T	Darrell Porter	.10	.08	.04
89T	Rey Quinones(FC)	.20	.15	.08
90T	Gary Redus	.10	.08	.04
91T	Bip Roberts	.08	.06	.03
92T	Billy Jo Robidoux(FC)	.15	.11	.06
93T	Jeff Robinson	.12	.09	.05
94T	Gary Roenicke	.08	.06	.03
95T	Ed Romero	.08	.06	.03
96T	Argenis Salazar	.08	.06	.03
97T	Joe Sambito	.08	.06	.03
98T	Billy Sample	.08	.06	.03
99T	Dave Schmidt	.08	.06	.03
100T	Ken Schrom	.08	.06	.03
101T	Tom Seaver	.60	.45	.25
102T	Ted Simmons	.20	.15	.08
103T	Sammy Stewart	.08	.06	.03
104T	Kurt Stillwell(FC)	.30	.25	.12
105T	Franklin Stubbs	.12	.09	.05
106T	Dale Sveum(FC)	.25	.20	.10
107T	Chuck Tanner	.08	.06	.03
108T	Danny Tartabull(FC)	.80	.60	.30

		MT	NR MT	EX
109T	Tim Teufel	.08	.06	.03
110T	Bob Tewksbury(FC)	.15	.11	.06
111T	Andres Thomas(FC)	.30	.25	.12
112T	Milt Thompson	.12	.09	.05
113T	Robby Thompson(FC)	.50	.40	.20
114T	Jay Tibbs	.08	.06	.03
115T	Wayne Tolleson	.08	.06	.03
116T	Alex Trevino	.08	.06	.03
117T	Manny Trillo	.10	.08	.04
118T	Ed Vande Berg	.08	.06	.03
119T	Ozzie Virgil	.08	.06	.03
120T	Bob Walk	.08	.06	.03
121T	Gene Walter(FC)	.12	.09	.05
122T	Claudell Washington	.12	.09	.05
123T	Bill Wegman(FC)	.20	.15	.08
124T	Dick Williams	.08	.06	.03
125T	Mitch Williams(FC)	.70	.50	.30
126T	Bobby Witt(FC)	1.00	.70	.40
127T	Todd Worrell(FC)	.60	.45	.25
128T	George Wright	.08	.06	.03
129T	Ricky Wright	.08	.06	.03
130T	Steve Yeager	.08	.06	.03
131T	Paul Zuvella	.08	.06	.03
132T	Checklist	.08	.06	.03

1986 Topps 3-D

This set is a second effort in the production of over-size (4-1/2" by 6") plastic cards on which the player figure is embossed. Cards were sold one per pack for approximately 50¢. The 30 players in the set are among the game's top stars. The embossed color photo is bordered at bottom by a strip of contrasting color on which the player name appears. At the top, a row of white baseballs each contain a letter of the team nickname. Backs have no printing, and contain two self-adhesive strips with which the cards can be attached to a hard surface.

		MT	NR MT	EX
Complete Set:		13.00	9.75	5.25
Common Player:		.20	.15	.08
1	Bert Blyleven	.30	.25	.12
2	Gary Carter	.60	.45	.25
3	Wade Boggs	1.25	.90	.50
4	Dwight Gooden	1.00	.70	.40
5	George Brett	.80	.60	.30
6	Rich Gossage	.30	.25	.12
7	Darrell Evans	.20	.15	.08
8	Pedro Guerrero	.30	.25	.12
9	Ron Guidry	.30	.25	.12
10	Keith Hernandez	.50	.40	.20
11	Rickey Henderson	.70	.50	.30
12	Orel Hershiser	.50	.40	.20
13	Reggie Jackson	.60	.45	.25
14	Willie McGee	.30	.25	.12
15	Don Mattingly	2.25	1.75	.90
16	Dale Murphy	.40	.30	.15
17	Jack Morris	.30	.25	.12
18	Dave Parker	.30	.25	.12
19	Eddie Murray	.60	.45	.25
20	Jeff Reardon	.30	.25	.12
21	Dan Quisenberry	.20	.15	.08
22	Pete Rose	1.00	.70	.40
23	Jim Rice	.50	.40	.20
24	Mike Schmidt	.80	.60	.30

		MT	NR MT	EX
25	Bret Saberhagen	.30	.25	.12
26	Darryl Strawberry	.80	.60	.30
27	Dave Stieb	.20	.15	.08
28	John Tudor	.20	.15	.08
29	Dave Winfield	.50	.40	.20
30	Fernando Valenzuela	.40	.30	.15

1987 Topps

 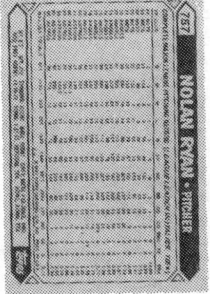

Many collectors feel that Topps' 1987 set of 792 card is a future classic. The 2-1/2" by 3-1/2" design is closely akin to the 1962 set in that the player photo is set against a woodgrain border. Instead of a rolling corner, as in 1962, the player photos in '87 feature a couple of clipped corners at top left and bottom right, where the team logo and player name appear. The player's position is not given on the front of the card. For the first time in several years, the trophy which designates members of Topps All-Star Rookie Team returned to the card design. As in the previous three years, Topps issued a glossy-finish "Tiffany" edition of their 792-card set. However, it was speculated that as many as 50,000 sets were produced as opposed to the 5,000 sets printed in 1985 and 1986. Because of the large print run, the values for the Tiffany cards are only 3-4 times higher than the same card in the regular issue.

		MT	NR MT	EX
Complete Set:		50.00	37.00	20.00
Common Player:		.05	.04	.02
1	Record Breaker (Roger Clemens)	.35	.25	.14
2	Record Breaker (Jim Deshaies)	.07	.05	.03
3	Record Breaker (Dwight Evans)	.07	.05	.03
4	Record Breaker (Dave Lopes)	.07	.05	.03
5	Record Breaker (Dave Righetti)	.07	.05	.03
6	Record Breaker (Ruben Sierra)	.25	.20	.10
7	Record Breaker (Todd Worrell)	.07	.05	.03
8	Terry Pendleton	.07	.05	.03
9	Jay Tibbs	.05	.04	.02
10	Cecil Cooper	.10	.08	.04
11	Indians Leaders (Jack Aker, Chris Bando, Phil Niekro)	.07	.05	.03
12	*Jeff Sellers*(FC)	.15	.11	.06
13	Nick Esasky	.07	.05	.03
14	Dave Stewart	.12	.09	.05
15	Claudell Washington	.07	.05	.03
16	Pat Clements	.05	.04	.02
17	Pete O'Brien	.10	.08	.04
18	Dick Howser	.05	.04	.02
19	Matt Young	.05	.04	.02
20	Gary Carter	.20	.15	.08
21	Mark Davis	.05	.04	.02
22	Doug DeCinces	.07	.05	.03
23	Lee Smith	.10	.08	.04
24	Tony Walker	.05	.04	.02
25	Bert Blyleven	.12	.09	.05
26	Greg Brock	.07	.05	.03
27	Joe Cowley	.05	.04	.02
28	Rick Dempsey	.07	.05	.03
29	Jimmy Key	.10	.08	.04
30	Tim Raines	.25	.20	.10
31	Braves Leaders (Glenn Hubbard, Rafael Ramirez)	.07	.05	.03
32	Tim Leary	.07	.05	.03

		MT	NR MT	EX
33	Andy Van Slyke	.12	.09	.05
34	Jose Rijo	.07	.05	.03
35	Sid Bream	.07	.05	.03
36	*Eric King*	.25	.20	.10
37	Marvell Wynne	.05	.04	.02
38	Dennis Leonard	.07	.05	.03
39	Marty Barrett	.07	.05	.03
40	Dave Righetti	.12	.09	.05
41	Bo Diaz	.07	.05	.03
42	Gary Redus	.05	.04	.02
43	Gene Michael	.05	.04	.02
44	Greg Harris	.05	.04	.02
45	Jim Presley	.10	.08	.04
46	Danny Gladden	.05	.04	.02
47	Dennis Powell	.07	.05	.03
48	Wally Backman	.07	.05	.03
49	Terry Harper	.05	.04	.02
50	Dave Smith	.07	.05	.03
51	Mel Hall	.07	.05	.03
52	Keith Atherton	.05	.04	.02
53	Ruppert Jones	.05	.04	.02
54	Bill Dawley	.05	.04	.02
55	Tim Wallach	.10	.08	.04
56	Brewers Leaders (Jamie Cocanower, Paul Molitor, Charlie Moore, Herm Starrette)	.07	.05	.03
57	*Scott Nielsen*(FC)	.10	.08	.04
58	Thad Bosley	.05	.04	.02
59	Ken Dayley	.05	.04	.02
60	Tony Pena	.07	.05	.03
61	*Bobby Thigpen*(FC)	1.00	.70	.40
62	Bobby Meacham	.05	.04	.02
63	Fred Toliver(FC)	.07	.05	.03
64	Harry Spilman	.05	.04	.02
65	Tom Browning	.10	.08	.04
66	Marc Sullivan	.05	.04	.02
67	Bill Swift	.05	.04	.02
68	Tony LaRussa	.07	.05	.03
69	Lonnie Smith	.07	.05	.03
70	Charlie Hough	.07	.05	.03
71	*Mike Aldrete*(FC)	.20	.15	.08
72	Walt Terrell	.07	.05	.03
73	Dave Anderson	.05	.04	.02
74	Dan Pasqua	.10	.08	.04
75	Ron Darling	.12	.09	.05
76	Rafael Ramirez	.05	.04	.02
77	Bryan Oelkers	.05	.04	.02
78	Tom Foley	.05	.04	.02
79	Juan Nieves	.10	.08	.04
80	*Wally Joyner*	.80	.60	.30
81	Padres Leaders (Andy Hawkins, Terry Kennedy)	.07	.05	.03
82	*Rob Murphy*(FC)	.15	.11	.06
83	Mike Davis	.07	.05	.03
84	Steve Lake	.05	.04	.02
85	Kevin Bass	.07	.05	.03
86	Nate Snell	.05	.04	.02
87	Mark Salas	.05	.04	.02
88	Ed Wojna	.05	.04	.02
89	Ozzie Guillen	.25	.20	.10
90	Dave Stieb	.10	.08	.04
91	Harold Reynolds	.10	.08	.04
92a	Urbano Lugo (no trademark on front)	.30	.25	.12
92b	Urbano Lugo (trademark on front)	.07	.05	.03
93	Jim Leyland	.05	.04	.02
94	Calvin Schiraldi	.05	.04	.02
95	Oddibe McDowell	.07	.05	.03
96	Frank Williams	.05	.04	.02
97	Glenn Wilson	.07	.05	.03
98	Bill Scherrer	.05	.04	.02
99	Darryl Motley	.05	.04	.02
100	Steve Garvey	.20	.15	.08
101	*Carl Willis*(FC)	.10	.08	.04
102	Paul Zuvella	.05	.04	.02
103	Rick Aguilera	.06	.05	.02
104	Billy Sample	.05	.04	.02
105	Floyd Youmans	.07	.05	.03
106	Blue Jays Leaders (George Bell, Willie Upshaw)	.07	.05	.03
107	John Butcher	.05	.04	.02
108	Jim Gantner (photo reversed)	.07	.05	.03
109	R.J. Reynolds	.05	.04	.02
110	John Tudor	.10	.08	.04
111	Alfredo Griffin	.07	.05	.03
112	Alan Ashby	.05	.04	.02
113	Neil Allen	.05	.04	.02
114	Billy Beane	.05	.04	.02
115	Donnie Moore	.05	.04	.02
116	Bill Russell	.07	.05	.03
117	Jim Beattie	.05	.04	.02

		MT	NR MT	EX
118	Bobby Valentine	.05	.04	.02
119	Ron Robinson	.05	.04	.02
120	Eddie Murray	.30	.25	.12
121	Kevin Romine(FC)	.12	.09	.05
122	Jim Clancy	.07	.05	.03
123	John Kruk	.35	.25	.14
124	Ray Fontenot	.05	.04	.02
125	Bob Brenly	.05	.04	.02
126	Mike Loynd(FC)	.15	.11	.06
127	Vance Law	.07	.05	.03
128	Checklist 1-132	.05	.04	.02
129	Rick Cerone	.05	.04	.02
130	Dwight Gooden	.80	.60	.30
131	Pirates Leaders (Sid Bream, Tony Pena)			
		.07	.05	.03
132	Paul Assenmacher	.15	.11	.06
133	Jose Oquendo	.05	.04	.02
134	Rich Yett(FC)	.12	.09	.05
135	Mike Easler	.07	.05	.03
136	Ron Romanick	.05	.04	.02
137	Jerry Willard	.05	.04	.02
138	Roy Lee Jackson	.05	.04	.02
139	Devon White(FC)	.50	.40	.20
140	Bret Saberhagen	.15	.11	.06
141	Herm Winningham	.05	.04	.02
142	Rick Sutcliffe	.10	.08	.04
143	Steve Boros	.05	.04	.02
144	Mike Scioscia	.07	.05	.03
145	Charlie Kerfeld	.07	.05	.03
146	Tracy Jones(FC)	.25	.20	.10
147	Randy Niemann	.05	.04	.02
148	Dave Collins	.07	.05	.03
149	Ray Searage	.05	.04	.02
150	Wade Boggs	1.00	.70	.40
151	Mike LaCoss	.05	.04	.02
152	Toby Harrah	.07	.05	.03
153	Duane Ward(FC)	.12	.09	.05
154	Tom O'Malley	.05	.04	.02
155	Eddie Whitson	.05	.04	.02
156	Mariners Leaders (Bob Kearney, Phil Regan, Matt Young)	.07	.05	.03
157	Danny Darwin	.05	.04	.02
158	Tim Teufel	.05	.04	.02
159	Ed Olwine	.05	.04	.02
160	Julio Franco	.10	.08	.04
161	Steve Ontiveros	.05	.04	.02
162	Mike LaValliere	.25	.20	.10
163	Kevin Gross	.07	.05	.03
164	Sammy Khalifa	.05	.04	.02
165	Jeff Reardon	.10	.08	.04
166	Bob Boone	.07	.05	.03
167	Jim Deshaies	.25	.20	.10
168	Lou Piniella	.07	.05	.03
169	Ron Washington	.05	.04	.02
170	Future Stars (Bo Jackson)	5.00	3.75	2.00
171	Chuck Cary(FC)	.10	.08	.04
172	Ron Oester	.05	.04	.02
173	Alex Trevino	.05	.04	.02
174	Henry Cotto	.05	.04	.02
175	Bob Stanley	.05	.04	.02
176	Steve Buechele	.07	.05	.03
177	Keith Moreland	.07	.05	.03
178	Cecil Fielder	1.75	1.25	.70
179	Bill Wegman	.10	.08	.04
180	Chris Brown	.07	.05	.03
181	Cardinals Leaders (Mike LaValliere, Ozzie Smith, Ray Soff)	.07	.05	.03
182	Lee Lacy	.05	.04	.02
183	Andy Hawkins	.05	.04	.02
184	Bobby Bonilla	3.00	2.25	1.25
185	Roger McDowell	.10	.08	.04
186	Bruce Benedict	.05	.04	.02
187	Mark Huismann	.05	.04	.02
188	Tony Phillips	.05	.04	.02
189	Joe Hesketh	.05	.04	.02
190	Jim Sundberg	.07	.05	.03
191	Charles Hudson	.05	.04	.02
192	Cory Snyder(FC)	.70	.50	.30
193	Roger Craig	.07	.05	.03
194	Kirk McCaskill	.07	.05	.03
195	Mike Pagliarulo	.10	.08	.04
196	Randy O'Neal	.05	.04	.02
197	Mark Bailey	.05	.04	.02
198	Lee Mazzilli	.07	.05	.03
199	Mariano Duncan	.05	.04	.02
200	Pete Rose	.60	.45	.25
201	John Cangelosi	.12	.09	.05
202	Ricky Wright	.05	.04	.02
203	Mike Kingery(FC)	.15	.11	.06
204	Sammy Stewart	.05	.04	.02
205	Graig Nettles	.10	.08	.04

		MT	NR MT	EX
206	Twins Leaders (Tim Laudner, Frank Viola)			
		.07	.05	.03
207	George Frazier	.05	.04	.02
208	John Shelby	.05	.04	.02
209	Rick Schu	.05	.04	.02
210	Lloyd Moseby	.07	.05	.03
211	John Morris(FC)	.07	.05	.03
212	Mike Fitzgerald	.05	.04	.02
213	Randy Myers(FC)	.50	.40	.20
214	Omar Moreno	.05	.04	.02
215	Mark Langston	.12	.09	.05
216	Future Stars (B.J. Surhoff)(FC)	.50	.40	.20
217	Chris Codiroli	.05	.04	.02
218	Sparky Anderson	.07	.05	.03
219	Cecilio Guante	.05	.04	.02
220	Joe Carter	.12	.09	.05
221	Vern Ruhle	.05	.04	.02
222	Denny Walling	.05	.04	.02
223	Charlie Leibrandt	.07	.05	.03
224	Wayne Tolleson	.05	.04	.02
225	Mike Smithson	.05	.04	.02
226	Max Venable	.05	.04	.02
227	Jamie Moyer(FC)	.20	.15	.08
228	Curt Wilkerson	.05	.04	.02
229	Mike Birkbeck(FC)	.15	.11	.06
230	Don Baylor	.10	.08	.04
231	Giants Leaders (Bob Brenly, Mike Krukow)	.07	.05	.03
232	Reggie Williams	.10	.08	.04
233	Russ Morman(FC)	.10	.08	.04
234	Pat Sheridan	.05	.04	.02
235	Alvin Davis	.10	.08	.04
236	Tommy John	.15	.11	.06
237	Jim Morrison	.05	.04	.02
238	Bill Krueger	.05	.04	.02
239	Juan Espino	.05	.04	.02
240	Steve Balboni	.07	.05	.03
241	Danny Heep	.05	.04	.02
242	Rick Mahler	.05	.04	.02
243	Whitey Herzog	.07	.05	.03
244	Dickie Noles	.05	.04	.02
245	Willie Upshaw	.07	.05	.03
246	Jim Dwyer	.05	.04	.02
247	Jeff Reed(FC)	.07	.05	.03
248	Gene Walter	.07	.05	.03
249	Jim Pankovits	.05	.04	.02
250	Teddy Higuera	.15	.11	.06
251	Rob Wilfong	.05	.04	.02
252	Denny Martinez	.05	.04	.02
253	Eddie Milner	.05	.04	.02
254	Bob Tewksbury	.12	.09	.05
255	Juan Samuel	.10	.08	.04
256	Royals Leaders (George Brett, Frank White)	.10	.08	.04
257	Bob Forsch	.07	.05	.03
258	Steve Yeager	.05	.04	.02
259	Mike Greenwell(FC)	2.75	2.00	1.00
260	Vida Blue	.07	.05	.03
261	Ruben Sierra(FC)	3.50	2.75	1.50
262	Jim Winn	.05	.04	.02
263	Stan Javier(FC)	.07	.05	.03
264	Checklist 133-264	.05	.04	.02
265	Darrell Evans	.10	.08	.04
266	Jeff Hamilton(FC)	.25	.20	.10
267	Howard Johnson	.10	.08	.04
268	Pat Corrales	.05	.04	.02
269	Cliff Speck	.05	.04	.02
270	Jody Davis	.07	.05	.03
271	Mike Brown	.05	.04	.02
272	Andres Galarraga	.70	.50	.30
273	Gene Nelson	.05	.04	.02
274	Jeff Hearron(FC)	.05	.04	.02
275	LaMarr Hoyt	.05	.04	.02
276	Jackie Gutierrez	.05	.04	.02
277	Juan Agosto	.05	.04	.02
278	Gary Pettis	.05	.04	.02
279	Dan Plesac	.30	.25	.12
280	Jeffrey Leonard	.07	.05	.03
281	Reds Leaders (Bo Diaz, Bill Gullickson, Pete Rose)	.10	.08	.04
282	Jeff Calhoun	.05	.04	.02
283	Doug Drabek(FC)	1.00	.70	.40
284	John Moses	.05	.04	.02
285	Dennis Boyd	.07	.05	.03
286	Mike Woodard(FC)	.07	.05	.03
287	Dave Von Ohlen	.05	.04	.02
288	Tito Landrum	.05	.04	.02
289	Bob Kipper	.07	.05	.03
290	Leon Durham	.07	.05	.03
291	Mitch Williams(FC)	.60	.45	.25
292	Franklin Stubbs	.07	.05	.03

		MT	NR MT	EX
293	Bob Rodgers	.05	.04	.02
294	Steve Jeltz	.05	.04	.02
295	Len Dykstra	.12	.09	.05
296	*Andres Thomas*	.25	.20	.10
297	Don Schulze	.05	.04	.02
298	Larry Herndon	.05	.04	.02
299	Joel Davis	.07	.05	.03
300	Reggie Jackson	.30	.25	.12
301	Luis Aquino(FC)	.10	.08	.04
302	Bill Schroeder	.05	.04	.02
303	Juan Berenguer	.05	.04	.02
304	Phil Garner	.05	.04	.02
305	John Franco	.10	.08	.04
306	Red Sox Leaders (Rich Gedman, John McNamara, Tom Seaver)	.07	.05	.03
307	*Lee Guetterman*(FC)	.15	.11	.06
308	Don Slaught	.05	.04	.02
309	Mike Young	.05	.04	.02
310	Frank Viola	.15	.11	.06
311	Turn Back The Clock (Rickey Henderson)	.10	.08	.04
312	Turn Back The Clock (Reggie Jackson)	.10	.08	.04
313	Turn Back The Clock (Roberto Clemente)	.15	.11	.06
314	Turn Back The Clock (Carl Yastrzemski)	.10	.08	.04
315	Turn Back The Clock (Maury Wills)	.07	.05	.03
316	Brian Fisher	.07	.05	.03
317	Clint Hurdle	.05	.04	.02
318	Jim Fregosi	.05	.04	.02
319	*Greg Swindell*(FC)	1.00	.70	.40
320	*Barry Bonds*	4.00	3.00	1.50
321	Mike Laga	.05	.04	.02
322	Chris Bando	.05	.04	.02
323	Al Newman	.07	.05	.03
324	Dave Palmer	.05	.04	.02
325	Garry Templeton	.07	.05	.03
326	Mark Gubicza	.10	.08	.04
327	*Dale Sveum*	.20	.15	.08
328	Bob Welch	.10	.08	.04
329	Ron Roenicke	.05	.04	.02
330	Mike Scott	.12	.09	.05
331	Mets Leaders (Gary Carter, Keith Hernandez, Dave Johnson, Darryl Strawberry)	.10	.08	.04
332	Joe Price	.05	.04	.02
333	Ken Phelps	.07	.05	.03
334	*Ed Correa*	.15	.11	.06
335	Candy Maldonado	.07	.05	.03
336	*Allan Anderson*(FC)	.25	.20	.10
337	Darrell Miller	.05	.04	.02
338	Tim Conroy	.05	.04	.02
339	Donnie Hill	.05	.04	.02
340	Roger Clemens	1.00	.70	.40
341	Mike Brown	.05	.04	.02
342	Bob James	.05	.04	.02
343	Hal Lanier	.05	.04	.02
344a	Joe Niekro (copyright outside yellow on back)	.30	.25	.12
344b	Joe Niekro (copyright inside yellow on back)	.07	.05	.03
345	Andre Dawson	.20	.15	.08
346	Shawon Dunston	.07	.05	.03
347	Mickey Brantley(FC)	.07	.05	.03
348	Carmelo Martinez	.07	.05	.03
349	Storm Davis	.10	.08	.04
350	Keith Hernandez	.20	.15	.08
351	Gene Garber	.05	.04	.02
352	Mike Felder(FC)	.07	.05	.03
353	Ernie Camacho	.05	.04	.02
354	Jamie Quirk	.05	.04	.02
355	Don Carman	.07	.05	.03
356	White Sox Leaders (Ed Brinkman, Julio Cruz)	.07	.05	.03
357	*Steve Fireovid*(FC)	.07	.05	.03
358	Sal Butera	.05	.04	.02
359	Doug Corbett	.05	.04	.02
360	Pedro Guerrero	.15	.11	.06
361	Mark Thurmond	.05	.04	.02
362	*Luis Quinones*(FC)	.12	.09	.05
363	Jose Guzman	.12	.09	.05
364	Randy Bush	.05	.04	.02
365	Rick Rhoden	.07	.05	.03
366	*Mark McGwire*	3.00	2.25	1.25
367	Jeff Lahti	.05	.04	.02
368	John McNamara	.05	.04	.02
369	Brian Dayett	.05	.04	.02
370	Fred Lynn	.15	.11	.06
371	*Mark Eichhorn*	.15	.11	.06
372	Jerry Mumphrey	.05	.04	.02
373	Jeff Dedmon	.05	.04	.02
374	Glenn Hoffman	.05	.04	.02
375	Ron Guidry	.12	.09	.05
376	Scott Bradley	.05	.04	.02
377	John Henry Johnson	.05	.04	.02
378	Rafael Santana	.05	.04	.02
379	John Russell	.05	.04	.02
380	Rich Gossage	.15	.11	.06
381	Expos Leaders (Mike Fitzgerald, Bob Rodgers)	.07	.05	.03
382	Rudy Law	.05	.04	.02
383	Ron Davis	.05	.04	.02
384	Johnny Grubb	.05	.04	.02
385	Orel Hershiser	.30	.25	.12
386	Dickie Thon	.07	.05	.03
387	*T.R. Bryden*(FC)	.10	.08	.04
388	Geno Petralli	.05	.04	.02
389	Jeff Robinson	.07	.05	.03
390	Gary Matthews	.07	.05	.03
391	Jay Howell	.07	.05	.03
392	Checklist 265-396	.05	.04	.02
393	Pete Rose	.40	.30	.15
394	Mike Bielecki	.07	.05	.03
395	Damaso Garcia	.05	.04	.02
396	Tim Lollar	.05	.04	.02
397	Greg Walker	.07	.05	.03
398	Brad Havens	.05	.04	.02
399	Curt Ford(FC)	.07	.05	.03
400	George Brett	.35	.25	.14
401	Billy Jo Robidoux	.07	.05	.03
402	Mike Trujillo	.05	.04	.02
403	Jerry Royster	.05	.04	.02
404	Doug Sisk	.05	.04	.02
405	Brook Jacoby	.10	.08	.04
406	Yankees Leaders (Rickey Henderson, Don Mattingly)	.15	.11	.06
407	Jim Acker	.05	.04	.02
408	John Mizerock	.05	.04	.02
409	Milt Thompson	.07	.05	.03
410	Fernando Valenzuela	.25	.20	.10
411	Darnell Coles	.07	.05	.03
412	Eric Davis	.90	.70	.35
413	Moose Haas	.05	.04	.02
414	Joe Orsulak	.05	.04	.02
415	*Bobby Witt*	.70	.50	.30
416	Tom Nieto	.05	.04	.02
417	Pat Perry(FC)	.07	.05	.03
418	Dick Williams	.05	.04	.02
419	*Mark Portugal*(FC)	.10	.08	.04
420	*Will Clark*	5.00	3.75	2.00
421	Jose DeLeon	.07	.05	.03
422	Jack Howell	.07	.05	.03
423	Jaime Cocanower	.05	.04	.02
424	Chris Speier	.05	.04	.02
425	Tom Seaver	.30	.25	.12
426	Floyd Rayford	.05	.04	.02
427	Ed Nunez	.05	.04	.02
428	Bruce Bochy	.05	.04	.02
429	Future Stars *(Tim Pyznarski)*(FC)	.10	.08	.04
430	Mike Schmidt	.40	.30	.15
431	Dodgers Leaders (Tom Niedenfuer, Ron Perranoski, Alex Trevino)	.07	.05	.03
432	Jim Slaton	.05	.04	.02
433	*Ed Hearn*(FC)	.10	.08	.04
434	Mike Fischlin	.05	.04	.02
435	Bruce Sutter	.12	.09	.05
436	*Andy Allanson*	.15	.11	.06
437	Ted Power	.05	.04	.02
438	*Kelly Downs*(FC)	.30	.25	.12
439	Karl Best	.05	.04	.02
440	Willie McGee	.10	.08	.04
441	*Dave Leiper*(FC)	.10	.08	.04
442	Mitch Webster	.07	.05	.03
443	John Felske	.05	.04	.02
444	Jeff Russell	.05	.04	.02
445	Dave Lopes	.07	.05	.03
446	*Chuck Finley*(FC)	.90	.70	.35
447	Bill Almon	.05	.04	.02
448	*Chris Bosio*(FC)	.25	.20	.10
449	Future Stars *(Pat Dodson)*(FC)	.10	.08	.04
450	Kirby Puckett	.30	.25	.12
451	Joe Sambito	.05	.04	.02
452	Dave Henderson	.10	.08	.04
453	*Scott Terry*(FC)	.12	.09	.05
454	Luis Salazar	.05	.04	.02
455	Mike Boddicker	.07	.05	.03
456	A's Leaders (Carney Lansford, Tony LaRussa, Mickey Tettleton, Dave Von Ohlen)	.07	.05	.03
457	Len Matuszek	.05	.04	.02
458	Kelly Gruber(FC)	1.25	.90	.50

#	Player	MT	NR MT	EX
459	Dennis Eckersley	.10	.08	.04
460	Darryl Strawberry	.35	.25	.14
461	Craig McMurtry	.05	.04	.02
462	Scott Fletcher	.07	.05	.03
463	Tom Candiotti	.05	.04	.02
464	Butch Wynegar	.05	.04	.02
465	Todd Worrell	.30	.25	.12
466	Kal Daniels(FC)	1.25	.90	.50
467	Randy St. Claire	.05	.04	.02
468	George Bamberger	.05	.04	.02
469	*Mike Diaz*(FC)	.15	.11	.06
470	Dave Dravecky	.07	.05	.03
471	Ronn Reynolds	.05	.04	.02
472	Bill Doran	.07	.05	.03
473	Steve Farr	.05	.04	.02
474	Jerry Narron	.05	.04	.02
475	Scott Garrelts	.05	.04	.02
476	Danny Tartabull	.90	.70	.35
477	Ken Howell	.05	.04	.02
478	Tim Laudner	.05	.04	.02
479	*Bob Sebra*(FC)	.10	.08	.04
480	Jim Rice	.25	.20	.10
481	Phillies Leaders (Von Hayes, Juan Samuel, Glenn Wilson)	.07	.05	.03
482	Daryl Boston	.05	.04	.02
483	Dwight Lowry	.05	.04	.02
484	Jim Traber(FC)	.15	.11	.06
485	Tony Fernandez	.10	.08	.04
486	Otis Nixon	.05	.04	.02
487	Dave Gumpert	.05	.04	.02
488	Ray Knight	.07	.05	.03
489	Bill Gullickson	.05	.04	.02
490	Dale Murphy	.40	.30	.15
491	*Ron Karkovice*(FC)	.10	.08	.04
492	Mike Heath	.05	.04	.02
493	Tom Lasorda	.07	.05	.03
494	*Barry Jones*(FC)	.12	.09	.05
495	Gorman Thomas	.10	.08	.04
496	Bruce Bochte	.05	.04	.02
497	*Dale Mohorcic*(FC)	.15	.11	.06
498	Bob Kearney	.05	.04	.02
499	*Bruce Ruffin*(FC)	.20	.15	.08
500	Don Mattingly	2.25	1.75	.90
501	Craig Lefferts	.05	.04	.02
502	Dick Schofield	.05	.04	.02
503	Larry Andersen	.05	.04	.02
504	Mickey Hatcher	.05	.04	.02
505	Bryn Smith	.05	.04	.02
506	Orioles Leaders (Rich Bordi, Rick Dempsey, Earl Weaver)	.07	.05	.03
507	Dave Stapleton	.05	.04	.02
508	*Scott Bankhead*	.25	.20	.10
509	Enos Cabell	.05	.04	.02
510	Tom Henke	.07	.05	.03
511	Steve Lyons	.05	.04	.02
512	*Dave Magadan*(FC)	.90	.70	.35
513	Carmen Castillo	.05	.04	.02
514	Orlando Mercado	.05	.04	.02
515	Willie Hernandez	.07	.05	.03
516	Ted Simmons	.10	.08	.04
517	Mario Soto	.07	.05	.03
518	Gene Mauch	.07	.05	.03
519	Curt Young	.07	.05	.03
520	Jack Clark	.15	.11	.06
521	Rick Reuschel	.10	.08	.04
522	Checklist 397-528	.05	.04	.02
523	Earnie Riles	.05	.04	.02
524	Bob Shirley	.05	.04	.02
525	Phil Bradley	.10	.08	.04
526	Roger Mason	.05	.04	.02
527	Jim Wohlford	.05	.04	.02
528	Ken Dixon	.05	.04	.02
529	*Alvaro Espinoza*(FC)	.07	.05	.03
530	Tony Gwynn	.35	.25	.14
531	Astros Leaders (Yogi Berra, Hal Lanier, Denis Menke, Gene Tenace)	.07	.05	.03
532	Jeff Stone	.05	.04	.02
533	Argenis Salazar	.05	.04	.02
534	Scott Sanderson	.05	.04	.02
535	Tony Armas	.07	.05	.03
536	*Terry Mulholland*(FC)	.10	.08	.04
537	Rance Mulliniks	.05	.04	.02
538	Tom Niedenfuer	.07	.05	.03
539	Reid Nichols	.05	.04	.02
540	Terry Kennedy	.07	.05	.03
541	*Rafael Belliard*(FC)	.10	.08	.04
542	Ricky Horton	.07	.05	.03
543	Dave Johnson	.07	.05	.03
544	Zane Smith	.07	.05	.03
545	Buddy Bell	.07	.05	.03
546	Mike Morgan	.05	.04	.02
547	Rob Deer	.10	.08	.04
548	*Bill Mooneyham*(FC)	.10	.08	.04
549	Bob Melvin	.05	.04	.02
550	*Pete Incaviglia*	.40	.30	.15
551	Frank Wills	.05	.04	.02
552	Larry Sheets	.07	.05	.03
553	*Mike Maddux*(FC)	.15	.11	.06
554	Buddy Biancalana	.05	.04	.02
555	Dennis Rasmussen	.10	.08	.04
556	Angels Leaders (Bob Boone, Marcel Lachemann, Mike Witt)	.07	.05	.03
557	*John Cerutti*	.15	.11	.06
558	Greg Gagne	.05	.04	.02
559	Lance McCullers	.07	.05	.03
560	Glenn Davis	.25	.20	.10
561	*Rey Quinones*	.15	.11	.06
562	*Bryan Clutterbuck*(FC)	.10	.08	.04
563	John Stefero	.05	.04	.02
564	Larry McWilliams	.05	.04	.02
565	Dusty Baker	.07	.05	.03
566	Tim Hulett	.05	.04	.02
567	*Greg Mathews*(FC)	.20	.15	.08
568	Earl Weaver	.07	.05	.03
569	Wade Rowdon(FC)	.07	.05	.03
570	Sid Fernandez	.10	.08	.04
571	Ozzie Virgil	.05	.04	.02
572	Pete Ladd	.05	.04	.02
573	Hal McRae	.07	.05	.03
574	Manny Lee	.05	.04	.02
575	Pat Tabler	.07	.05	.03
576	Frank Pastore	.05	.04	.02
577	Dann Bilardello	.05	.04	.02
578	Billy Hatcher	.07	.05	.03
579	Rick Burleson	.07	.05	.03
580	Mike Krukow	.07	.05	.03
581	Cubs Leaders (Ron Cey, Steve Trout)	.07	.05	.03
582	Bruce Berenyi	.05	.04	.02
583	Junior Ortiz	.05	.04	.02
584	Ron Kittle	.07	.05	.03
585	*Scott Bailes*	.15	.11	.06
586	Ben Oglivie	.07	.05	.03
587	Eric Plunk(FC)	.10	.08	.04
588	Wallace Johnson	.05	.04	.02
589	Steve Crawford	.05	.04	.02
590	Vince Coleman	.25	.20	.10
591	Spike Owen	.05	.04	.02
592	Chris Welsh	.05	.04	.02
593	Chuck Tanner	.05	.04	.02
594	Rick Anderson	.05	.04	.02
595	Keith Hernandez AS	.12	.09	.05
596	Steve Sax AS	.07	.05	.03
597	Mike Schmidt AS	.20	.15	.08
598	Ozzie Smith AS	.07	.05	.03
599	Tony Gwynn AS	.20	.15	.08
600	Dave Parker AS	.10	.08	.04
601	Darryl Strawberry AS	.20	.15	.08
602	Gary Carter AS	.15	.11	.06
603a	Dwight Gooden AS (no trademark on front)	.80	.60	.30
603b	Dwight Gooden AS (trademark on front)	.30	.25	.12
604	Fernando Valenzuela AS	.12	.09	.05
605	Todd Worrell AS	.10	.08	.04
606a	Don Mattingly AS (no trademark on front)	1.75	1.25	.70
606b	Don Mattingly AS (trademark on front)	.70	.50	.30
607	Tony Bernazard AS	.05	.04	.02
608	Wade Boggs AS	.40	.30	.15
609	Cal Ripken AS	.15	.11	.06
610	Jim Rice AS	.15	.11	.06
611	Kirby Puckett AS	.15	.11	.06
612	George Bell AS	.12	.09	.05
613	Lance Parrish AS	.10	.08	.04
614	Roger Clemens AS	.30	.25	.12
615	Teddy Higuera AS	.10	.08	.04
616	Dave Righetti AS	.10	.08	.04
617	Al Nipper	.05	.04	.02
618	Tom Kelly	.05	.04	.02
619	Jerry Reed	.05	.04	.02
620	Jose Canseco	6.00	4.50	2.50
621	Danny Cox	.07	.05	.03
622	*Glenn Braggs*(FC)	.40	.30	.15
623	*Kurt Stillwell*(FC)	.35	.25	.14
624	Tim Burke	.05	.04	.02
625	Mookie Wilson	.07	.05	.03
626	Joel Skinner	.05	.04	.02
627	Ken Oberkfell	.05	.04	.02
628	Bob Walk	.05	.04	.02
629	Larry Parrish	.07	.05	.03

		MT	NR MT	EX
630	John Candelaria	.07	.05	.03
631	Tigers Leaders (Sparky Anderson, Mike Heath, Willie Hernandez)	.07	.05	.03
632	Rob Woodward(FC)	.07	.05	.03
633	Jose Uribe	.07	.05	.03
634	Future Stars *(Rafael Palmeiro)*(FC)	1.25	.90	.50
635	Ken Schrom	.05	.04	.02
636	Darren Daulton	.05	.04	.02
637	Bip Roberts	.05	.04	.02
638	Rich Bordi	.05	.04	.02
639	Gerald Perry	.10	.08	.04
640	Mark Clear	.05	.04	.02
641	Domingo Ramos	.05	.04	.02
642	Al Pulido	.05	.04	.02
643	Ron Shepherd	.05	.04	.02
644	John Denny	.05	.04	.02
645	Dwight Evans	.12	.09	.05
646	Mike Mason	.05	.04	.02
647	Tom Lawless	.05	.04	.02
648	*Barry Larkin*	2.50	2.00	1.00
649	Mickey Tettleton	.05	.04	.02
650	Hubie Brooks	.07	.05	.03
651	Benny Distefano	.05	.04	.02
652	Terry Forster	.07	.05	.03
653	*Kevin Mitchell*	3.00	2.25	1.25
654	Checklist 529-660	.05	.04	.02
655	Jesse Barfield	.15	.11	.06
656	Rangers Leaders (Bobby Valentine, Rickey Wright)	.07	.05	.03
657	Tom Waddell	.05	.04	.02
658	*Robby Thompson*	.30	.25	.12
659	Aurelio Lopez	.05	.04	.02
660	Bob Horner	.10	.08	.04
661	Lou Whitaker	.15	.11	.06
662	Frank DiPino	.05	.04	.02
663	Cliff Johnson	.05	.04	.02
664	Mike Marshall	.10	.08	.04
665	Rod Scurry	.05	.04	.02
666	Von Hayes	.07	.05	.03
667	Ron Hassey	.05	.04	.02
668	Juan Bonilla	.05	.04	.02
669	Bud Black	.05	.04	.02
670	Jose Cruz	.07	.05	.03
671a	Ray Soff (no "D*" before copyright line)	.20	.15	.08
671b	Ray Soff ("D*" before copyright line)	.05	.04	.02
672	Chili Davis	.07	.05	.03
673	Don Sutton	.15	.11	.06
674	Bill Campbell	.05	.04	.02
675	Ed Romero	.05	.04	.02
676	Charlie Moore	.05	.04	.02
677	Bob Grich	.07	.05	.03
678	Carney Lansford	.07	.05	.03
679	Kent Hrbek	.15	.11	.06
680	Ryne Sandberg	.40	.30	.15
681	George Bell	.25	.20	.10
682	Jerry Reuss	.07	.05	.03
683	Gary Roenicke	.05	.04	.02
684	Kent Tekulve	.07	.05	.03
685	Jerry Hairston	.05	.04	.02
686	Doyle Alexander	.07	.05	.03
687	Alan Trammell	.25	.20	.10
688	Juan Beniquez	.05	.04	.02
689	Darrell Porter	.07	.05	.03
690	Dane Iorg	.05	.04	.02
691	Dave Parker	.15	.11	.06
692	Frank White	.07	.05	.03
693	Terry Puhl	.05	.04	.02
694	Phil Niekro	.20	.15	.08
695	Chico Walker	.05	.04	.02
696	Gary Lucas	.05	.04	.02
697	Ed Lynch	.05	.04	.02
698	Ernie Whitt	.07	.05	.03
699	Ken Landreaux	.05	.04	.02
700	Dave Bergman	.05	.04	.02
701	Willie Randolph	.07	.05	.03
702	Greg Gross	.05	.04	.02
703	Dave Schmidt	.05	.04	.02
704	Jesse Orosco	.07	.05	.03
705	Bruce Hurst	.10	.08	.04
706	Rick Manning	.05	.04	.02
707	Bob McClure	.05	.04	.02
708	Scott McGregor	.07	.05	.03
709	Dave Kingman	.10	.08	.04
710	Gary Gaetti	.15	.11	.06
711	Ken Griffey	.07	.05	.03
712	Don Robinson	.07	.05	.03
713	Tom Brookens	.05	.04	.02
714	Dan Quisenberry	.07	.05	.03

		MT	NR MT	EX
715	Bob Dernier	.05	.04	.02
716	Rick Leach	.05	.04	.02
717	Ed Vande Berg	.05	.04	.02
718	Steve Carlton	.25	.20	.10
719	Tom Hume	.05	.04	.02
720	Richard Dotson	.07	.05	.03
721	Tom Herr	.07	.05	.03
722	Bob Knepper	.07	.05	.03
723	Brett Butler	.07	.05	.03
724	Greg Minton	.05	.04	.02
725	George Hendrick	.07	.05	.03
726	Frank Tanana	.07	.05	.03
727	Mike Moore	.05	.04	.02
728	Tippy Martinez	.05	.04	.02
729	Tom Paciorek	.05	.04	.02
730	Eric Show	.07	.05	.03
731	Dave Concepcion	.10	.08	.04
732	Manny Trillo	.07	.05	.03
733	Bill Caudill	.05	.04	.02
734	Bill Madlock	.10	.08	.04
735	Rickey Henderson	.40	.30	.15
736	Steve Bedrosian	.10	.08	.04
737	Floyd Bannister	.07	.05	.03
738	Jorge Orta	.05	.04	.02
739	Chet Lemon	.07	.05	.03
740	Rich Gedman	.07	.05	.03
741	Paul Molitor	.12	.09	.05
742	Andy McGaffigan	.05	.04	.02
743	Dwayne Murphy	.07	.05	.03
744	Roy Smalley	.05	.04	.02
745	Glenn Hubbard	.05	.04	.02
746	Bob Ojeda	.07	.05	.03
747	Johnny Ray	.07	.05	.03
748	Mike Flanagan	.07	.05	.03
749	Ozzie Smith	.15	.11	.06
750	Steve Trout	.07	.05	.03
751	Garth Iorg	.05	.04	.02
752	Dan Petry	.07	.05	.03
753	Rick Honeycutt	.05	.04	.02
754	Dave LaPoint	.07	.05	.03
755	Luis Aguayo	.05	.04	.02
756	Carlton Fisk	.20	.15	.08
757	Nolan Ryan	.40	.30	.15
758	Tony Bernazard	.05	.04	.02
759	Joel Youngblood	.05	.04	.02
760	Mike Witt	.07	.05	.03
761	Greg Pryor	.05	.04	.02
762	Gary Ward	.07	.05	.03
763	Tim Flannery	.05	.04	.02
764	Bill Buckner	.07	.05	.03
765	Kirk Gibson	.20	.15	.08
766	Don Aase	.05	.04	.02
767	Ron Cey	.07	.05	.03
768	Dennis Lamp	.05	.04	.02
769	Steve Sax	.15	.11	.06
770	Dave Winfield	.25	.20	.10
771	Shane Rawley	.07	.05	.03
772	Harold Baines	.12	.09	.05
773	Robin Yount	.35	.25	.14
774	Wayne Krenchicki	.05	.04	.02
775	Joaquin Andujar	.07	.05	.03
776	Tom Brunansky	.10	.08	.04
777	Chris Chambliss	.07	.05	.03
778	Jack Morris	.20	.15	.08
779	Craig Reynolds	.05	.04	.02
780	Andre Thornton	.07	.05	.03
781	Atlee Hammaker	.05	.04	.02
782	Brian Downing	.07	.05	.03
783	Willie Wilson	.10	.08	.04
784	Cal Ripken	.30	.25	.12
785	Terry Francona	.05	.04	.02
786	Jimy Williams	.05	.04	.02
787	Alejandro Pena	.07	.05	.03
788	Tim Stoddard	.05	.04	.02
789	Dan Schatzeder	.05	.04	.02
790	Julio Cruz	.05	.04	.02
791	Lance Parrish	.15	.11	.06
792	Checklist 661-792	.05	.04	.02

1987 Topps All-Star Glossy Set Of 22

For the fourth consecutive year, Topps produced an All-Star Game commemorative set of 22 cards. The glossy cards, which measure 2-1/2" by 3-1/2", were included in rack packs. Using the same basic

card design as in previous efforts with a few minor changes, the 1987 edition features American and National League logos on the card fronts. Card #'s 1-12 feature representatives from the American League, while #'s 13-22 are National Leaguers.

		MT	NR MT	EX
	Complete Set:	5.00	3.75	2.00
	Common Player:	.15	.11	.06
1	Whitey Herzog	.15	.11	.06
2	Keith Hernandez	.40	.30	.15
3	Ryne Sandberg	.40	.30	.15
4	Mike Schmidt	.70	.50	.30
5	Ozzie Smith	.30	.25	.12
6	Tony Gwynn	.50	.40	.20
7	Dale Murphy	.50	.40	.20
8	Darryl Strawberry	.80	.60	.30
9	Gary Carter	.40	.30	.15
10	Dwight Gooden	.60	.45	.25
11	Fernando Valenzuela	.30	.25	.12
12	Dick Howser	.15	.11	.06
13	Wally Joyner	.70	.50	.30
14	Lou Whitaker	.30	.25	.12
15	Wade Boggs	.70	.50	.30
16	Cal Ripken	.50	.40	.20
17	Dave Winfield	.40	.30	.15
18	Rickey Henderson	.80	.60	.30
19	Kirby Puckett	.40	.30	.15
20	Lance Parrish	.30	.25	.12
21	Roger Clemens	.60	.45	.25
22	Teddy Higuera	.30	.25	.12

1987 Topps All-Star Glossy Set Of 60

Using the same design as the previous year, the 1987 Topps All-Star Glossy set includes 48 All-Star performers plus 12 potential superstars branded as "Hot Prospects". The card fronts are uncluttered, save the player's name found in very small print at the bottom. The set was available via a mail-in offer. Six subsets make up the 60-card set, with each subset being available for $1.00 plus six special offer cards that were found in wax packs.

		MT	NR MT	EX
	Complete Set:	14.00	10.50	5.50
	Common Player:	.15	.11	.06
1	Don Mattingly	3.50	2.75	1.50
2	Tony Gwynn	.60	.45	.25
3	Gary Gaetti	.25	.20	.10
4	Glenn Davis	.30	.25	.12
5	Roger Clemens	.70	.50	.30
6	Dale Murphy	.90	.70	.35
7	Lou Whitaker	.30	.25	.12
8	Roger McDowell	.15	.11	.06
9	Cory Snyder	.50	.40	.20
10	Todd Worrell	.20	.15	.08
11	Gary Carter	.50	.40	.20
12	Eddie Murray	.60	.45	.25
13	Bob Knepper	.15	.11	.06
14	Harold Baines	.20	.15	.08
15	Jeff Reardon	.20	.15	.08
16	Joe Carter	.25	.20	.10
17	Dave Parker	.25	.20	.10
18	Wade Boggs	1.25	.90	.50
19	Danny Tartabull	.35	.25	.14
20	Jim Deshaies	.20	.15	.08
21	Rickey Henderson	.70	.50	.30
22	Rob Deer	.15	.11	.06
23	Ozzie Smith	.25	.20	.10
24	Dave Righetti	.25	.20	.10
25	Kent Hrbek	.30	.25	.12
26	Keith Hernandez	.40	.30	.15
27	Don Baylor	.15	.11	.06
28	Mike Schmidt	.90	.70	.35
29	Pete Incaviglia	.50	.40	.20
30	Barry Bonds	.50	.40	.20
31	George Brett	.90	.70	.35
32	Darryl Strawberry	.90	.70	.35
33	Mike Witt	.15	.11	.06
34	Kevin Bass	.15	.11	.06
35	Jesse Barfield	.20	.15	.08
36	Bob Ojeda	.15	.11	.06
37	Cal Ripken	.70	.50	.30
38	Vince Coleman	.25	.20	.10
39	Wally Joyner	1.75	1.25	.70
40	Robby Thompson	.20	.15	.08
41	Pete Rose	1.25	.90	.50
42	Jim Rice	.50	.40	.20
43	Tony Bernazard	.15	.11	.06
44	Eric Davis	1.00	.70	.40
45	George Bell	.50	.40	.20
46	Hubie Brooks	.15	.11	.06
47	Jack Morris	.30	.25	.12
48	Tim Raines	.50	.40	.20
49	Mark Eichhorn	.20	.15	.08
50	Kevin Mitchell	.25	.20	.10
51	Dwight Gooden	.80	.60	.30
52	Doug DeCinces	.15	.11	.06
53	Fernando Valenzuela	.35	.25	.14
54	Reggie Jackson	.70	.50	.30
55	Johnny Ray	.15	.11	.06
56	Mike Pagliarulo	.20	.15	.08
57	Kirby Puckett	.50	.40	.20
58	Lance Parrish	.30	.25	.12
59	Jose Canseco	3.00	2.25	1.25
60	Greg Mathews	.25	.20	.10

1987 Topps Baseball Highlights

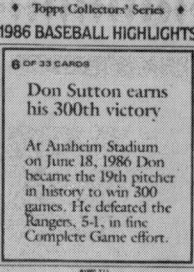

The "Baseball Highlights" boxed set of 33 cards was prepared by Topps for distribution at stores in the

Woolworth's chain. Each card measures 2-1/2" by 3-1/2" in size and features a memorable baseball event that occurred during the 1986 season. The glossy set sold for $1.99 in Woolworth's stores.

		MT	NR MT	EX
	Complete Set:	6.00	4.50	2.50
	Common Player:	.09	.07	.04
1	Steve Carlton	.30	.25	.12
2	Cecil Cooper	.12	.09	.05
3	Rickey Henderson	.50	.40	.20
4	Reggie Jackson	.30	.25	.12
5	Jim Rice	.25	.20	.10
6	Don Sutton	.20	.15	.08
7	Roger Clemens	.50	.40	.20
8	Mike Schmidt	.35	.25	.14
9	Jesse Barfield	.15	.11	.06
10	Wade Boggs	.70	.50	.30
11	Tim Raines	.30	.25	.12
12	Jose Canseco	1.00	.70	.40
13	Todd Worrell	.15	.11	.06
14	Dave Righetti	.15	.11	.06
15	Don Mattingly	1.25	.90	.50
16	Tony Gwynn	.35	.25	.14
17	Marty Barrett	.09	.07	.04
18	Mike Scott	.12	.09	.05
19	World Series Game #1 (Bruce Hurst)	.12	.09	.05
20	World Series Game #1 (Calvin Schiraldi)	.09	.07	.04
21	World Series Game #2 (Dwight Evans)	.12	.09	.05
22	World Series Game #2 (Dave Henderson)	.09	.07	.04
23	World Series Game #3 (Len Dykstra)	.12	.09	.05
24	World Series Game #3 (Bob Ojeda)	.09	.07	.04
25	World Series Game #4 (Gary Carter)	.30	.25	.12
26	World Series Game #4 (Ron Darling)	.15	.11	.06
27	Jim Rice	.30	.25	.12
28	Bruce Hurst	.09	.07	.04
29	World Series Game #6 (Darryl Strawberry)	.35	.25	.14
30	World Series Game #6 (Ray Knight)	.09	.07	.04
31	World Series Game #6 (Keith Hernandez)	.25	.20	.10
32	World Series Games #7 (Mets Celebrate)	.12	.09	.05
33	Ray Knight	.09	.07	.04

1987 Topps Box Panels

Offering baseball cards on retail boxes for a second straight year, Topps reduced the size of the cards to 2-1/8" by 3". Four different wax pack boxes were available, each featuring two cards that were placed on the sides of the boxes. The card fronts are identical in design to the regular issue cards. The backs are printed in blue and yellow and carry a commentary imitating a newspaper format. The cards are numbered A through H.

		MT	NR MT	EX
	Complete Panel Set:	5.00	3.75	2.00
	Complete Singles Set:	2.00	1.50	.80
	Common Panel:	.75	.60	.30
	Common Single Player:	.15	.11	.06
	Panel	1.25	.90	.50
A	Don Baylor	.15	.11	.06
B	Steve Carlton	.30	.25	.12
	Panel	.75	.60	.30
C	Ron Cey	.15	.11	.06
D	Cecil Cooper	.15	.11	.06
	Panel	1.75	1.25	.70
E	Rickey Henderson	.40	.30	.15
F	Jim Rice	.25	.20	.10
	Panel	1.25	.90	.50
G	Don Sutton	.20	.15	.08
H	Dave Winfield	.30	.25	.12

1987 Topps Gallery Of Champions

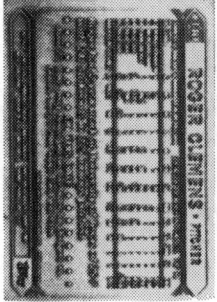

Designed as a tribute to the 1986 season's winners of baseball's most prestigious awards, the Gallery of Champions are metal "cards" that are one-quarter size replicas of the regular issue Topps cards. The bronze and silver sets were issued in leather-like velvet-lined display cases; the aluminum sets came cello-wrapped. Hobby dealers who purchased one bronze set or a 16-set case of aluminum "cards" received one free Jose Canseco pewter metal mini-card (value $60). The purchase of a silver set included five Canseco pewters. A 1953 Willie Mays bronze was given to dealers who brought cases of 1987 Topps Traded sets (value $10).

		MT	NR MT	EX
	Complete Aluminum Set:	30.00	22.00	12.00
	Complete Bronze Set:	175.00	131.00	70.00
	Complete Silver Set:	700.00	525.00	280.00
(1a)	Jesse Barfield (aluminum)	.70	.50	.30
(1b)	Jesse Barfield (bronze)	7.50	5.75	3.00
(1c)	Jesse Barfield (silver)	20.00	15.00	8.00
(2a)	Wade Boggs (aluminum)	3.00	2.25	1.25
(2b)	Wade Boggs (bronze)	25.00	18.50	10.00
(2c)	Wade Boggs (silver)	125.00	94.00	50.00
(3a)	Jose Canseco (aluminum)	3.00	2.25	1.25
(3b)	Jose Canseco (bronze)	25.00	18.50	10.00
(3c)	Jose Canseco (silver)	125.00	94.00	50.00
(4a)	Joe Carter (aluminum)	.70	.50	.30
(4b)	Joe Carter (bronze)	7.50	5.75	3.00
(4c)	Joe Carter (silver)	20.00	15.00	8.00
(5a)	Roger Clemens (aluminum)	2.00	1.50	.80
(5b)	Roger Clemens (bronze)	20.00	15.00	8.00
(5c)	Roger Clemens (silver)	90.00	67.00	36.00
(6a)	Tony Gwynn (aluminum)	1.25	.90	.50
(6b)	Tony Gwynn (bronze)	12.00	9.00	4.75
(6c)	Tony Gwynn (silver)	50.00	37.00	20.00
(7a)	Don Mattingly (aluminum)	8.00	6.00	3.25
(7b)	Don Mattingly (bronze)	50.00	37.00	20.00
(7c)	Don Mattingly (silver)	200.00	150.00	80.00
(8a)	Tim Raines (aluminum)	1.00	.70	.40
(8b)	Tim Raines (bronze)	10.00	7.50	4.00
(8c)	Tim Raines (silver)	30.00	22.00	12.00
(9a)	Dave Righetti (aluminum)	1.00	.70	.40
(9b)	Dave Righetti (bronze)	10.00	7.50	4.00

		MT	NR MT	EX
(9c)	Dave Righetti (silver)	30.00	22.00	12.00
(10a)	Mike Schmidt (aluminum)	1.50	1.25	.60
(10b)	Mike Schmidt (bronze)	15.00	11.00	6.00
(10c)	Mike Schmidt (silver)	80.00	60.00	32.00
(11a)	Mike Scott (aluminum)	.70	.50	.30
(11b)	Mike Scott (bronze)	7.50	5.75	3.00
(11c)	Mike Scott (silver)	20.00	15.00	8.00
(12a)	Todd Worrell (aluminum)	.70	.50	.30
(12b)	Todd Worrell (bronze)	10.00	7.50	4.00
(12c)	Todd Worrell (silver)	20.00	15.00	8.00

1987 Topps Glossy Rookies

The 1987 Topps Glossy Rookies set of 22 cards was introduced with Topps' new 100-card "Jumbo Packs". Intended for sale in supermarkets, the jumbo packs contained one glossy card. Measuring the standard 2-1/2" by 3-1/2" size, the special insert cards feature the top rookies from the previous season.

		MT	NR MT	EX
Complete Set:		12.00	9.00	4.75
Common Player:		.20	.15	.08
1	Andy Allanson	.20	.15	.08
2	John Cangelosi	.20	.15	.08
3	Jose Canseco	3.00	2.25	1.25
4	Will Clark	3.00	1.50	.90
5	Mark Eichhorn	.40	.30	.15
6	Pete Incaviglia	.70	.50	.30
7	Wally Joyner	1.00	.70	.40
8	Eric King	.30	.25	.12
9	Dave Magadan	.60	.45	.25
10	John Morris	.20	.15	.08
11	Juan Nieves	.40	.30	.15
12	Rafael Palmeiro	1.00	.70	.40
13	Billy Jo Robidoux	.20	.15	.08
14	Bruce Ruffin	.40	.30	.15
15	Ruben Sierra	1.25	.90	.50
16	Cory Snyder	.80	.60	.30
17	Kurt Stillwell	.60	.45	.25
18	Dale Sveum	.40	.30	.15
19	Danny Tartabull	.80	.60	.30
20	Andres Thomas	.40	.30	.15
21	Robby Thompson	.40	.30	.15
22	Todd Worrell	.40	.30	.15

1987 Topps Mini League Leaders

Returning for 1987, the Topps "Major League Leaders" set was increased in size from 66 to 76 cards. The 2-1/8" by 3" cards feature wood grain borders that encompass a white-bordered full-color photo. The card backs are printed in yellow, orange and brown and list the player's official ranking based on his 1986 American or National League statistics. The players featured are those who finished the top five in their leagues' various batting and pitching statistics. The cards were sold in plastic-wrapped packs, seven cards plus a game card per pack.

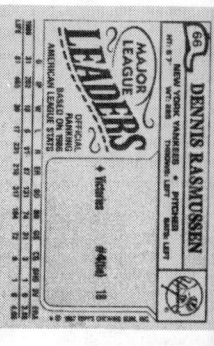

		MT	NR MT	EX
Complete Set:		8.00	6.00	3.25
Common Player:		.09	.07	.04
1	Bob Horner	.20	.15	.08
2	Dale Murphy	.50	.40	.20
3	Lee Smith	.09	.07	.04
4	Eric Davis	.60	.45	.25
5	John Franco	.15	.11	.06
6	Dave Parker	.20	.15	.08
7	Kevin Bass	.09	.07	.04
8	Glenn Davis	.20	.15	.08
9	Bill Doran	.15	.11	.06
10	Bob Knepper	.09	.07	.04
11	Mike Scott	.20	.15	.08
12	Dave Smith	.09	.07	.04
13	Mariano Duncan	.09	.07	.04
14	Orel Hershiser	.30	.25	.12
15	Steve Sax	.20	.15	.08
16	Fernando Valenzuela	.25	.20	.10
17	Tim Raines	.30	.25	.12
18	Jeff Reardon	.15	.11	.06
19	Floyd Youmans	.09	.07	.04
20	Gary Carter	.30	.25	.12
21	Ron Darling	.20	.15	.08
22	Sid Fernandez	.15	.11	.06
23	Dwight Gooden	.60	.45	.25
24	Keith Hernandez	.25	.20	.10
25	Bob Ojeda	.09	.07	.04
26	Darryl Strawberry	.50	.40	.20
27	Steve Bedrosian	.15	.11	.06
28	Von Hayes	.15	.11	.06
29	Juan Samuel	.20	.15	.08
30	Mike Schmidt	.50	.40	.20
31	Rick Rhoden	.09	.07	.04
32	Vince Coleman	.20	.15	.08
33	Danny Cox	.09	.07	.04
34	Todd Worrell	.15	.11	.06
35	Tony Gwynn	.40	.30	.15
36	Mike Krukow	.09	.07	.04
37	Candy Maldonado	.09	.07	.04
38	Don Aase	.09	.07	.04
39	Eddie Murray	.40	.30	.15
40	Cal Ripken	.40	.30	.15
41	Wade Boggs	.80	.60	.30
42	Roger Clemens	.60	.45	.25
43	Bruce Hurst	.15	.11	.06
44	Jim Rice	.30	.25	.12
45	Wally Joyner	.80	.60	.30
46	Donnie Moore	.09	.07	.04
47	Gary Pettis	.09	.07	.04
48	Mike Witt	.09	.07	.04
49	John Cangelosi	.09	.07	.04
50	Tom Candiotti	.09	.07	.04
51	Joe Carter	.20	.15	.08
52	Pat Tabler	.09	.07	.04
53	Kirk Gibson	.25	.20	.10
54	Willie Hernandez	.09	.07	.04
55	Jack Morris	.25	.20	.10
56	Alan Trammell	.30	.25	.12
57	George Brett	.50	.40	.20
58	Willie Wilson	.15	.11	.06
59	Rob Deer	.09	.07	.04
60	Teddy Higuera	.15	.11	.06
61	Bert Blyleven	.15	.11	.06
62	Gary Gaetti	.20	.15	.08
63	Kirby Puckett	.35	.25	.14
64	Rickey Henderson	.40	.30	.15
65	Don Mattingly	1.25	.90	.50
66	Dennis Rasmussen	.15	.11	.06
67	Dave Righetti	.20	.15	.08
68	Jose Canseco	1.00	.70	.40

		MT	NR MT	EX
69	Dave Kingman	.15	.11	.06
70	Phil Bradley	.15	.11	.06
71	Mark Langston	.15	.11	.06
72	Pete O'Brien	.09	.07	.04
73	Jesse Barfield	.15	.11	.06
74	George Bell	.25	.20	.10
75	Tony Fernandez	.15	.11	.06
76	Tom Henke	.09	.07	.04
77	Checklist	.09	.07	.04

1987 Topps Traded

 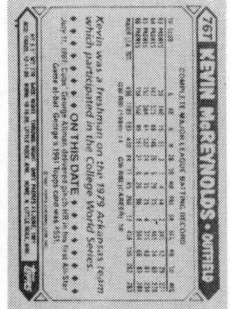

The Topps Traded set consists of 132 cards as have all Traded sets issued by Topps since 1981. The cards measure the standard 2 1/2" by 3 1/2" and are identical in design to the regular edition set. The purpose of the set is to update player trades and feature rookies not included in the regular issue. As they had done the previous three years, Topps produced a glossy-coated "Tiffany" edition of the Traded set. The Tiffany edition cards are valued at two to three times greater than the regular Traded cards.

		MT	NR MT	EX
	Complete Set:	13.00	9.75	5.25
	Common Player:	.06	.05	.02
1T	Bill Almon	.06	.05	.02
2T	Scott Bankhead	.08	.06	.03
3T	Eric Bell(FC)	.15	.11	.06
4T	Juan Beniquez	.06	.05	.02
5T	Juan Berenguer	.06	.05	.02
6T	Greg Booker	.06	.05	.02
7T	Thad Bosley	.06	.05	.02
8T	Larry Bowa	.10	.08	.04
9T	Greg Brock	.10	.08	.04
10T	Bob Brower(FC)	.15	.11	.06
11T	Jerry Browne(FC)	.30	.25	.12
12T	Ralph Bryant(FC)	.12	.09	.05
13T	DeWayne Buice(FC)	.15	.11	.06
14T	Ellis Burks(FC)	2.00	1.50	.80
15T	Ivan Calderon	.12	.09	.05
16T	Jeff Calhoun	.06	.05	.02
17T	Casey Candaele(FC)	.10	.08	.04
18T	John Cangelosi	.06	.05	.02
19T	Steve Carlton	.30	.25	.12
20T	Juan Castillo(FC)	.06	.05	.02
21T	Rick Cerone	.06	.05	.02
22T	Ron Cey	.10	.08	.04
23T	John Christensen	.06	.05	.02
24T	Dave Cone(FC)	1.25	.90	.50
25T	Chuck Crim(FC)	.15	.11	.06
26T	Storm Davis	.06	.05	.02
27T	Andre Dawson	.40	.30	.15
28T	Rick Dempsey	.08	.06	.03
29T	Doug Drabek	.50	.40	.20
30T	Mike Dunne	.30	.25	.12
31T	Dennis Eckersley	.20	.15	.08
32T	Lee Elia	.06	.05	.02
33T	Brian Fisher	.10	.08	.04
34T	Terry Francona	.06	.05	.02
35T	Willie Fraser(FC)	.15	.11	.06
36T	Billy Gardner	.06	.05	.02
37T	Ken Gerhart(FC)	.15	.11	.06
38T	Danny Gladden	.06	.05	.02
39T	Jim Gott	.06	.05	.02

		MT	NR MT	EX
40T	Cecilio Guante	.06	.05	.02
41T	Albert Hall	.06	.05	.02
42T	Terry Harper	.06	.05	.02
43T	Mickey Hatcher	.06	.05	.02
44T	Brad Havens	.06	.05	.02
45T	Neal Heaton	.06	.05	.02
46T	Mike Henneman(FC)	.30	.25	.12
47T	Donnie Hill	.06	.05	.02
48T	Guy Hoffman	.06	.05	.02
49T	Brian Holton(FC)	.15	.11	.06
50T	Charles Hudson	.06	.05	.02
51T	Danny Jackson(FC)	.30	.25	.12
52T	Reggie Jackson	.50	.40	.20
53T	Chris James(FC)	.40	.30	.15
54T	Dion James	.10	.08	.04
55T	Stan Jefferson(FC)	.20	.15	.08
56T	Joe Johnson(FC)	.08	.06	.03
57T	Terry Kennedy	.08	.06	.03
58T	Mike Kingery	.08	.06	.03
59T	Ray Knight	.10	.08	.04
60T	Gene Larkin(FC)	.30	.25	.12
61T	Mike LaValliere	.10	.08	.04
62T	Jack Lazorko	.06	.05	.02
63T	Terry Leach	.06	.05	.02
64T	Tim Leary	.06	.05	.02
65T	Jim Lindeman(FC)	.15	.11	.06
66T	Steve Lombardozzi(FC)	.06	.05	.02
67T	Bill Long(FC)	.20	.15	.08
68T	Barry Lyons(FC)	.15	.11	.06
69T	Shane Mack	.20	.15	.08
70T	Greg Maddux(FC)	.80	.60	.30
71T	Bill Madlock	.15	.11	.06
72T	Joe Magrane(FC)	.80	.60	.30
73T	Dave Martinez(FC)	.25	.20	.10
74T	Fred McGriff(FC)	2.00	1.50	.80
75T	Mark McLemore(FC)	.10	.08	.04
76T	Kevin McReynolds(FC)	.60	.45	.25
77T	Dave Meads(FC)	.15	.11	.06
78T	Eddie Milner	.06	.05	.02
79T	Greg Minton	.06	.05	.02
80T	John Mitchell(FC)	.15	.11	.06
81T	Kevin Mitchell	1.50	1.25	.60
82T	Charlie Moore	.06	.05	.02
83T	Jeff Musselman(FC)	.25	.20	.10
84T	Gene Nelson	.06	.05	.02
85T	Graig Nettles	.12	.09	.05
86T	Al Newman	.06	.05	.02
87T	Reid Nichols	.06	.05	.02
88T	Tom Niedenfuer	.08	.06	.03
89T	Joe Niekro	.10	.08	.04
90T	Tom Nieto	.06	.05	.02
91T	Matt Nokes(FC)	.40	.30	.15
92T	Dickie Noles	.06	.05	.02
93T	Pat Pacillo	.15	.11	.06
94T	Lance Parrish	.20	.15	.08
95T	Tony Pena	.10	.08	.04
96T	Luis Polonia(FC)	.30	.25	.12
97T	Randy Ready	.06	.05	.02
98T	Jeff Reardon	.12	.09	.05
99T	Gary Redus	.08	.06	.03
100T	Jeff Reed	.06	.05	.02
101T	Rick Rhoden	.10	.08	.04
102T	Cal Ripken, Sr.	.06	.05	.02
103T	Wally Ritchie(FC)	.15	.11	.06
104T	Jeff Robinson(FC)	.40	.30	.15
105T	Gary Roenicke	.06	.05	.02
106T	Jerry Royster	.06	.05	.02
107T	Mark Salas	.06	.05	.02
108T	Luis Salazar	.06	.05	.02
109T	Benny Santiago(FC)	1.25	.90	.50
110T	Dave Schmidt	.08	.06	.03
111T	Kevin Seitzer(FC)	.70	.50	.30
112T	John Shelby	.06	.05	.02
113T	Steve Shields(FC)	.08	.06	.03
114T	John Smiley(FC)	.40	.30	.15
115T	Chris Speier	.06	.05	.02
116T	Mike Stanley(FC)	.20	.15	.08
117T	Terry Steinbach(FC)	.60	.45	.25
118T	Les Straker(FC)	.20	.15	.08
119T	Jim Sundberg	.08	.06	.03
120T	Danny Tartabull	.35	.25	.14
121T	Tom Trebelhorn	.08	.06	.03
122T	Dave Valle(FC)	.12	.09	.05
123T	Ed Vande Berg	.06	.05	.02
124T	Andy Van Slyke	.20	.15	.08
125T	Gary Ward	.06	.05	.02
126T	Alan Wiggins	.06	.05	.02
127T	Bill Wilkinson(FC)	.15	.11	.06
128T	Frank Williams	.08	.06	.03
129T	Matt Williams(FC)	5.00	3.75	2.00
130T	Jim Winn	.06	.05	.02

		MT	NR MT	EX
131T	Matt Young	.06	.05	.02
132T	Checklist 1T-132T	.06	.05	.02

1988 Topps

 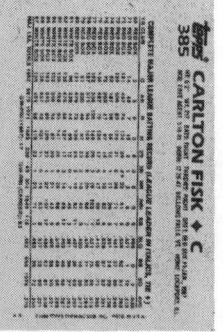

The 1988 Topps set features a clean, attractive design that should prove to be very popular with collectors for many years to come. The full-color player photo is surrounded by a thin yellow frame which is encompassed by a white border. The player's name appears in the lower right corner in a colored band which appears to wrap around the player photo. The player's team nickname is located in large letters at the top of the card. The Topps logo is placed in the lower left corner of the card. The card backs feature black print on orange and gray stock and includes the usual player personal and career statistics. Many of the cards contain a new feature entitled "This Way To The Clubhouse", which explains how the player joined his current team, be it by trade, free agency, etc. The 792-card set includes a number of special subsets including "Future Stars", "Turn Back The Clock", All-Star teams, All-Star rookie selections, and Record Breakers. All cards measure 2-1/2" by 3-1/2". For the fifth consecutive year, Topps issued a glossy "Tiffany" edition of its 792-card regular-issue set. The Tiffany cards have a value of 3-4 times greater than the same card in the regular issue. The Tiffany edition could be purchased by collectors directly from Topps for $99. The company placed ads for the Tiffany set in publications such as USA Today and The Sporting News.

		MT	NR MT	EX
Complete Set:		25.00	20.00	10.00
Common Player:		.04	.03	.02

1	'87 Record Breakers (Vince Coleman)	.08	.06	.03
2	'87 Record Breakers (Don Mattingly)	.60	.45	.25
3a	'87 Record Breakers (Mark McGwire) (white triangle by left foot)	.70	.50	.30
3b	'87 Record Breakers (Mark McGwire) (no triangle by left foot)	.50	.40	.20
4a	'87 Record Breakers (Eddie Murray) (no mention of record on front)	.10	.08	.04
4b	'87 Record Breakers (Eddie Murray) (record stated on card front)	1.25	.90	.50
5	'87 Record Breakers (Joe Niekro, Phil Niekro)	.10	.08	.04
6	'87 Record Breakers (Nolan Ryan)	.10	.08	.04
7	'87 Record Breakers (Benito Santiago)	.15	.11	.06
8	Kevin Elster(FC)	.25	.20	.10
9	Andy Hawkins	.04	.03	.02
10	Ryne Sandberg	.15	.11	.06
11	Mike Young	.04	.03	.02
12	Bill Schroeder	.04	.03	.02
13	Andres Thomas	.06	.05	.02
14	Sparky Anderson	.06	.05	.02
15	Chili Davis	.06	.05	.02
16	Kirk McCaskill	.06	.05	.02
17	Ron Oester	.04	.03	.02
18a	Al Leiter (no "NY" on shirt, photo actually Steve George)(FC)	.60	.45	.25
18b	Al Leiter ("NY" on shirt, correct photo)(FC)	.40	.30	.15
19	Mark Davidson(FC)	.12	.09	.05
20	Kevin Gross	.06	.05	.02
21	Red Sox Leaders (Wade Boggs, Spike Owen)	.15	.11	.06
22	Greg Swindell	.15	.11	.06
23	Ken Landreaux	.04	.03	.02
24	Jim Deshaies	.06	.05	.02
25	Andres Galarraga	.12	.09	.05
26	Mitch Williams	.06	.05	.02
27	R.J. Reynolds	.04	.03	.02
28	Jose Nunez(FC)	.20	.15	.08
29	Argenis Salazar	.04	.03	.02
30	Sid Fernandez	.08	.06	.03
31	Bruce Bochy	.04	.03	.02
32	Mike Morgan	.04	.03	.02
33	Rob Deer	.06	.05	.02
34	Ricky Horton	.06	.05	.02
35	Harold Baines	.10	.08	.04
36	Jamie Moyer	.06	.05	.02
37	Ed Romero	.04	.03	.02
38	Jeff Calhoun	.04	.03	.02
39	Gerald Perry	.08	.06	.03
40	Orel Hershiser	.20	.15	.08
41	Bob Melvin	.04	.03	.02
42	Bill Landrum(FC)	.10	.08	.04
43	Dick Schofield	.04	.03	.02
44	Lou Piniella	.06	.05	.02
45	Kent Hrbek	.12	.09	.05
46	Darnell Coles	.06	.05	.02
47	Joaquin Andujar	.06	.05	.02
48	Alan Ashby	.04	.03	.02
49	Dave Clark(FC)	.10	.08	.04
50	Hubie Brooks	.08	.06	.03
51	Orioles Leaders (Eddie Murray, Cal Ripken)	.12	.09	.05
52	Don Robinson	.06	.05	.02
53	Curt Wilkerson	.04	.03	.02
54	Jim Clancy	.06	.05	.02
55	Phil Bradley	.08	.06	.03
56	Ed Hearn	.04	.03	.02
57	Tim Crews(FC)	.15	.11	.06
58	Dave Magadan	.10	.08	.04
59	Danny Cox	.06	.05	.02
60	Rickey Henderson	.30	.25	.12
61	Mark Knudson(FC)	.10	.08	.04
62	Jeff Hamilton	.08	.06	.03
63	Jimmy Jones(FC)	.10	.08	.04
64	Ken Caminiti(FC)	.30	.25	.12
65	Leon Durham	.06	.05	.02
66	Shane Rawley	.06	.05	.02
67	Ken Oberkfell	.04	.03	.02
68	Dave Dravecky	.06	.05	.02
69	Mike Hart(FC)	.10	.08	.04
70	Roger Clemens	.50	.40	.20
71	Gary Pettis	.04	.03	.02
72	Dennis Eckersley	.10	.08	.04
73	Randy Bush	.04	.03	.02
74	Tom Lasorda	.06	.05	.02
75	Joe Carter	.10	.08	.04
76	Denny Martinez	.04	.03	.02
77	Tom O'Malley	.04	.03	.02
78	Dan Petry	.06	.05	.02
79	Ernie Whitt	.06	.05	.02
80	Mark Langston	.10	.08	.04
81	Reds Leaders (John Franco, Ron Robinson)	.06	.05	.02
82	Darrel Akerfelds(FC)	.12	.09	.05
83	Jose Oquendo	.04	.03	.02
84	Cecilio Guante	.04	.03	.02
85	Howard Johnson	.08	.06	.03
86	Ron Karkovice	.04	.03	.02
87	Mike Mason	.04	.03	.02
88	Earnie Riles	.04	.03	.02
89	Gary Thurman(FC)	.20	.15	.08
90	Dale Murphy	.30	.25	.12
91	Joey Cora(FC)	.12	.09	.05
92	Len Matuszek	.04	.03	.02
93	Bob Sebra	.04	.03	.02
94	Chuck Jackson(FC)	.15	.11	.06
95	Lance Parrish	.12	.09	.05
96	Todd Benzinger(FC)	.35	.25	.14
97	Scott Garrelts	.04	.03	.02
98	Rene Gonzales(FC)	.15	.11	.06
99	Chuck Finley	.06	.05	.02
100	Jack Clark	.12	.09	.05
101	Allan Anderson	.06	.05	.02
102	Barry Larkin	.35	.25	.14
103	Curt Young	.06	.05	.02
104	Dick Williams	.04	.03	.02
105	Jesse Orosco	.06	.05	.02
106	Jim Walewander(FC)	.12	.09	.05

		MT	NR MT	EX
107	Scott Bailes	.06	.05	.02
108	Steve Lyons	.04	.03	.02
109	Joel Skinner	.04	.03	.02
110	Teddy Higuera	.08	.06	.03
111	Expos Leaders (Hubie Brooks, Vance Law)			
		.06	.05	.02
112	*Les Lancaster*(FC)	.15	.11	.06
113	Kelly Gruber	.04	.03	.02
114	Jeff Russell	.04	.03	.02
115	Johnny Ray	.06	.05	.02
116	Jerry Don Gleaton	.04	.03	.02
117	*James Steels*(FC)	.10	.08	.04
118	Bob Welch	.08	.06	.03
119	*Robbie Wine*(FC)	.12	.09	.05
120	Kirby Puckett	.40	.30	.15
121	Checklist 1-132	.04	.03	.02
122	Tony Bernazard	.04	.03	.02
123	Tom Candiotti	.04	.03	.02
124	Ray Knight	.06	.05	.02
125	Bruce Hurst	.08	.06	.03
126	Steve Jeltz	.04	.03	.02
127	Jim Gott	.04	.03	.02
128	Johnny Grubb	.04	.03	.02
129	Greg Minton	.04	.03	.02
130	Buddy Bell	.08	.06	.03
131	Don Schulze	.04	.03	.02
132	Donnie Hill	.04	.03	.02
133	Greg Mathews	.06	.05	.02
134	Chuck Tanner	.04	.03	.02
135	Dennis Rasmussen	.08	.06	.03
136	Brian Dayett	.04	.03	.02
137	Chris Bosio	.06	.05	.02
138	Mitch Webster	.06	.05	.02
139	Jerry Browne	.06	.05	.02
140	Jesse Barfield	.10	.08	.04
141	Royals Leaders (George Brett, Bret Saberhagen)	.12	.09	.05
142	Andy Van Slyke	.10	.08	.04
143	Mickey Tettleton	.04	.03	.02
144	*Don Gordon*(FC)	.08	.06	.03
145	Bill Madlock	.08	.06	.03
146	*Donell Nixon*(FC)	.15	.11	.06
147	Bill Buckner	.08	.06	.03
148	Carmelo Martinez	.06	.05	.02
149	Ken Howell	.04	.03	.02
150	Eric Davis	.60	.45	.25
151	Bob Knepper	.06	.05	.02
152	*Jody Reed*(FC)	.50	.40	.20
153	John Habyan	.04	.03	.02
154	Jeff Stone	.04	.03	.02
155	Bruce Sutter	.10	.08	.04
156	Gary Matthews	.06	.05	.02
157	Atlee Hammaker	.04	.03	.02
158	Tim Hulett	.04	.03	.02
159	*Brad Arnsberg*(FC)	.12	.09	.05
160	Willie McGee	.10	.08	.04
161	Bryn Smith	.06	.05	.02
162	Mark McLemore	.06	.05	.02
163	Dale Mohorcic	.04	.03	.02
164	Dave Johnson	.06	.05	.02
165	Robin Yount	.20	.15	.08
166	*Rick Rodriguez*(FC)	.10	.08	.04
167	Rance Mulliniks	.04	.03	.02
168	Barry Jones	.04	.03	.02
169	*Ross Jones*(FC)	.12	.09	.05
170	Rich Gossage	.12	.09	.05
171	Cubs Leaders (Shawon Dunston, Manny Trillo)	.06	.05	.02
172	*Lloyd McClendon*(FC)	.10	.08	.04
173	Eric Plunk	.04	.03	.02
174	Phil Garner	.04	.03	.02
175	Kevin Bass	.06	.05	.02
176	Jeff Reed	.04	.03	.02
177	Frank Tanana	.06	.05	.02
178	Dwayne Henry (FC)	.06	.05	.02
179	Charlie Puleo	.04	.03	.02
180	Terry Kennedy	.06	.05	.02
181	Dave Cone	.80	.60	.30
182	Ken Phelps	.06	.05	.02
183	Tom Lawless	.04	.03	.02
184	Ivan Calderon	.08	.06	.03
185	Rick Rhoden	.06	.05	.02
186	Rafael Palmeiro	.35	.25	.14
187	Steve Kiefer(FC)	.06	.05	.02
188	John Russell	.04	.03	.02
189	*Wes Gardner*(FC)	.20	.15	.08
190	Candy Maldonado	.06	.05	.02
191	John Cerutti	.06	.05	.02
192	Devon White	.20	.15	.08
193	Brian Fisher	.06	.05	.02
194	Tom Kelly	.04	.03	.02

		MT	NR MT	EX
195	Dan Quisenberry	.06	.05	.02
196	Dave Engle	.04	.03	.02
197	Lance McCullers	.06	.05	.02
198	Franklin Stubbs	.06	.05	.02
199	*Dave Meads*	.12	.09	.05
200	Wade Boggs	.80	.60	.30
201	Rangers Leaders (Steve Buechele, Pete Incaviglia, Pete O'Brien, Bobby Valentine)	.06	.05	.02
202	Glenn Hoffman	.04	.03	.02
203	Fred Toliver	.04	.03	.02
204	Paul O'Neill(FC)	.12	.09	.05
205	*Nelson Liriano*(FC)	.20	.15	.08
206	Domingo Ramos	.04	.03	.02
207	*John Mitchell, John Mitchell*(FC)	.20	.15	.08
208	Steve Lake	.04	.03	.02
209	Richard Dotson	.06	.05	.02
210	Willie Randolph	.06	.05	.02
211	Frank DiPino	.04	.03	.02
212	Greg Brock	.06	.05	.02
213	Albert Hall	.04	.03	.02
214	Dave Schmidt	.04	.03	.02
215	Von Hayes	.06	.05	.02
216	Jerry Reuss	.06	.05	.02
217	Harry Spilman	.04	.03	.02
218	Dan Schatzeder	.04	.03	.02
219	Mike Stanley	.08	.06	.03
220	Tom Henke	.06	.05	.02
221	Rafael Belliard	.04	.03	.02
222	Steve Farr	.04	.03	.02
223	Stan Jefferson	.08	.06	.03
224	Tom Trebelhorn	.04	.03	.02
225	Mike Scioscia	.06	.05	.02
226	Dave Lopes	.06	.05	.02
227	Ed Correa	.04	.03	.02
228	Wallace Johnson	.04	.03	.02
229	Jeff Musselman	.08	.06	.03
230	Pat Tabler	.06	.05	.02
231	Pirates Leaders (Barry Bonds, Bobby Bonilla)	.10	.08	.04
232	Bob James	.04	.03	.02
233	Rafael Santana	.04	.03	.02
234	Ken Dayley	.04	.03	.02
235	Gary Ward	.06	.05	.02
236	Ted Power	.04	.03	.02
237	Mike Heath	.04	.03	.02
238	*Luis Polonia*	.20	.15	.08
239	Roy Smalley	.04	.03	.02
240	Lee Smith	.08	.06	.03
241	Damaso Garcia	.04	.03	.02
242	Tom Niedenfuer	.06	.05	.02
243	Mark Ryal(FC)	.04	.03	.02
244	Jeff Robinson	.04	.03	.02
245	Rich Gedman	.06	.05	.02
246	*Mike Campbell*(FC)	.20	.15	.08
247	Thad Bosley	.04	.03	.02
248	Storm Davis	.08	.06	.03
249	Mike Marshall	.10	.08	.04
250	Nolan Ryan	.50	.40	.20
251	Tom Foley	.04	.03	.02
252	Bob Brower	.06	.05	.02
253	Checklist 133-264	.04	.03	.02
254	Lee Elia	.04	.03	.02
255	Mookie Wilson	.06	.05	.02
256	Ken Schrom	.04	.03	.02
257	Jerry Royster	.04	.03	.02
258	Ed Nunez	.04	.03	.02
259	Ron Kittle	.06	.05	.02
260	Vince Coleman	.15	.11	.06
261	Giants Leaders (Will Clark, Candy Maldonado, Kevin Mitchell, Robby Thompson, Jose Uribe)	.10	.08	.04
262	Drew Hall(FC)	.12	.09	.05
263	Glenn Braggs	.08	.06	.03
264	*Les Straker*	.15	.11	.06
265	Bo Diaz	.06	.05	.02
266	Paul Assenmacher	.04	.03	.02
267	*Billy Bean*(FC)	.10	.08	.04
268	Bruce Ruffin	.06	.05	.02
269	*Ellis Burks*	1.25	.90	.50
270	Mike Witt	.06	.05	.02
271	Ken Gerhart	.06	.05	.02
272	Steve Ontiveros	.04	.03	.02
273	Garth Iorg	.04	.03	.02
274	Junior Ortiz	.04	.03	.02
275	Kevin Seitzer	.60	.45	.25
276	Luis Salazar	.04	.03	.02
277	Alejandro Pena	.06	.05	.02
278	Jose Cruz	.06	.05	.02
279	Randy St. Claire	.04	.03	.02

	MT	NR MT	EX
280 Pete Incaviglia	.12	.09	.05
281 Jerry Hairston	.04	.03	.02
282 Pat Perry	.04	.03	.02
283 Phil Lombardi(FC)	.06	.05	.02
284 Larry Bowa	.06	.05	.02
285 Jim Presley	.08	.06	.03
286 *Chuck Crim*	.12	.09	.05
287 Manny Trillo	.06	.05	.02
288 *Pat Pacillo*	.15	.11	.06
289 Dave Bergman	.04	.03	.02
290 Tony Fernandez	.10	.08	.04
291 Astros Leaders (Kevin Bass, Billy Hatcher)			
	.06	.05	.02
292 Carney Lansford	.08	.06	.03
293 *Doug Jones*(FC)	.35	.25	.14
294 *Al Pedrique*(FC)	.12	.09	.05
295 Bert Blyleven	.10	.08	.04
296 Floyd Rayford	.04	.03	.02
297 Zane Smith	.06	.05	.02
298 Milt Thompson	.04	.03	.02
299 Steve Crawford	.04	.03	.02
300 Don Mattingly	1.25	.90	.50
301 Bud Black	.04	.03	.02
302 Jose Uribe	.04	.03	.02
303 Eric Show	.06	.05	.02
304 George Hendrick	.06	.05	.02
305 Steve Sax	.12	.09	.05
306 Billy Hatcher	.06	.05	.02
307 Mike Trujillo	.04	.03	.02
308 Lee Mazzilli	.06	.05	.02
309 *Bill Long*	.15	.11	.06
310 Tom Herr	.06	.05	.02
311 Scott Sanderson	.04	.03	.02
312 Joey Meyer(FC)	.30	.25	.12
313 Bob McClure	.04	.03	.02
314 Jimy Williams	.04	.03	.02
315 Dave Parker	.12	.09	.05
316 Jose Rijo	.06	.05	.02
317 Tom Nieto	.04	.03	.02
318 Mel Hall	.06	.05	.02
319 Mike Loynd	.04	.03	.02
320 Alan Trammell	.15	.11	.06
321 White Sox Leaders (Harold Baines, Carlton Fisk)	.08	.06	.03
322 *Vicente Palacios*(FC)	.20	.15	.08
323 Rick Leach	.04	.03	.02
324 Danny Jackson	.20	.15	.08
325 Glenn Hubbard	.04	.03	.02
326 Al Nipper	.04	.03	.02
327 Larry Sheets	.06	.05	.02
328 *Greg Cadaret*(FC)	.15	.11	.06
329 Chris Speier	.04	.03	.02
330 Eddie Whitson	.04	.03	.02
331 Brian Downing	.06	.05	.02
332 Jerry Reed	.04	.03	.02
333 Wally Backman	.06	.05	.02
334 Dave LaPoint	.06	.05	.02
335 Claudell Washington	.06	.05	.02
336 Ed Lynch	.04	.03	.02
337 Jim Gantner	.04	.03	.02
338 Brian Holton	.08	.06	.03
339 Kurt Stillwell	.08	.06	.03
340 Jack Morris	.15	.11	.06
341 Carmen Castillo	.04	.03	.02
342 Larry Andersen	.04	.03	.02
343 Greg Gagne	.04	.03	.02
344 Tony LaRussa	.04	.03	.02
345 Scott Fletcher	.06	.05	.02
346 Vance Law	.06	.05	.02
347 Joe Johnson	.04	.03	.02
348 Jim Eisenreich	.04	.03	.02
349 Bob Walk	.04	.03	.02
350 Will Clark	1.00	.70	.40
351 Cardinals Leaders (Tony Pena, Red Schoendienst)	.06	.05	.02
352 *Billy Ripken*(FC)	.20	.15	.08
353 Ed Olwine	.04	.03	.02
354 Marc Sullivan	.04	.03	.02
355 Roger McDowell	.08	.06	.03
356 Luis Aguayo	.04	.03	.02
357 Floyd Bannister	.06	.05	.02
358 Rey Quinones	.04	.03	.02
359 Tim Stoddard	.04	.03	.02
360 Tony Gwynn	.25	.20	.10
361 Greg Maddux	.35	.25	.14
362 Juan Castillo	.04	.03	.02
363 Willie Fraser	.06	.05	.02
364 Nick Esasky	.06	.05	.02
365 Floyd Youmans	.04	.03	.02
366 Chet Lemon	.06	.05	.02
367 Tim Leary	.06	.05	.02
368 *Gerald Young*(FC)	.30	.25	.12
369 Greg Harris	.04	.03	.02
370 Jose Canseco	1.25	.90	.50
371 Joe Hesketh	.04	.03	.02
372 *Matt Williams*	2.00	1.50	.80
373 Checklist 265-396	.04	.03	.02
374 Doc Edwards	.04	.03	.02
375 Tom Brunansky	.08	.06	.03
376 *Bill Wilkinson*	.12	.09	.05
377 *Sam Horn*(FC)	.20	.15	.08
378 *Todd Frohwirth*(FC)	.15	.11	.06
379 Rafael Ramirez	.04	.03	.02
380 *Joe Magrane*	.40	.30	.15
381 Angels Leaders (Jack Howell, Wally Joyner)	.12	.09	.05
382 *Keith Miller*(FC)	.20	.15	.08
383 Eric Bell	.06	.05	.02
384 Neil Allen	.04	.03	.02
385 Carlton Fisk	.20	.15	.08
386 Don Mattingly AS	.40	.30	.15
387 Willie Randolph AS	.06	.05	.02
388 Wade Boggs AS	.35	.25	.14
389 Alan Trammell AS	.08	.06	.03
390 George Bell AS	.10	.08	.04
391 Kirby Puckett AS	.12	.09	.05
392 Dave Winfield AS	.12	.09	.05
393 Matt Nokes AS	.15	.11	.06
394 Roger Clemens AS	.15	.11	.06
395 Jimmy Key AS	.06	.05	.02
396 Tom Henke AS	.06	.05	.02
397 Jack Clark AS	.06	.05	.02
398 Juan Samuel AS	.06	.05	.02
399 Tim Wallach AS	.06	.05	.02
400 Ozzie Smith AS	.08	.06	.03
401 Andre Dawson AS	.10	.08	.04
402 Tony Gwynn AS	.15	.11	.06
403 Tim Raines AS	.12	.09	.05
404 Benny Santiago AS	.10	.08	.04
405 Dwight Gooden AS	.15	.11	.06
406 Shane Rawley AS	.06	.05	.02
407 Steve Bedrosian AS	.08	.06	.03
408 Dion James	.06	.05	.02
409 Joel McKeon(FC)	.04	.03	.02
410 Tony Pena	.06	.05	.02
411 Wayne Tolleson	.04	.03	.02
412 Randy Myers	.10	.08	.04
413 John Christensen	.04	.03	.02
414 John McNamara	.04	.03	.02
415 Don Carman	.06	.05	.02
416 Keith Moreland	.06	.05	.02
417 *Mark Ciardi*(FC)	.10	.08	.04
418 Joel Youngblood	.04	.03	.02
419 Scott McGregor	.06	.05	.02
420 Wally Joyner	.35	.25	.14
421 Ed Vande Berg	.04	.03	.02
422 Dave Concepcion	.06	.05	.02
423 *John Smiley*	.30	.25	.12
424 Dwayne Murphy	.06	.05	.02
425 Jeff Reardon	.08	.06	.03
426 Randy Ready	.04	.03	.02
427 *Paul Kilgus*(FC)	.20	.15	.08
428 John Shelby	.04	.03	.02
429 Tigers Leaders (Kirk Gibson, Alan Trammell)	.08	.06	.03
430 Glenn Davis	.12	.09	.05
431 Casey Candaele	.04	.03	.02
432 Mike Moore	.04	.03	.02
433 *Bill Pecota*(FC)	.15	.11	.06
434 Rick Aguilera	.04	.03	.02
435 Mike Pagliarulo	.08	.06	.03
436 Mike Bielecki	.04	.03	.02
437 *Fred Manrique*(FC)	.12	.09	.05
438 *Rob Ducey*(FC)	.12	.09	.05
439 Dave Martinez	.08	.06	.03
440 Steve Bedrosian	.10	.08	.04
441 Rick Manning	.04	.03	.02
442 *Tom Bolton*(FC)	.15	.11	.06
443 Ken Griffey	.06	.05	.02
444 Cal Ripken, Sr.	.04	.03	.02
445 Mike Krukow	.06	.05	.02
446 Doug DeCinces	.06	.05	.02
447 *Jeff Montgomery*(FC)	.30	.25	.12
448 Mike Davis	.06	.05	.02
449 *Jeff Robinson*	.25	.20	.10
450 Barry Bonds	.10	.08	.04
451 Keith Atherton	.04	.03	.02
452 Willie Wilson	.08	.06	.03
453 Dennis Powell	.04	.03	.02
454 Marvell Wynne	.04	.03	.02
455 *Shawn Hillegas*(FC)	.15	.11	.06
456 Dave Anderson	.04	.03	.02

#	Player	MT	NR MT	EX
457	Terry Leach	.04	.03	.02
458	Ron Hassey	.04	.03	.02
459	Yankees Leaders (Willie Randolph, Dave Winfield)	.08	.06	.03
460	Ozzie Smith	.12	.09	.05
461	Danny Darwin	.04	.03	.02
462	Don Slaught	.04	.03	.02
463	*Fred McGriff*	1.00	.70	.40
464	Jay Tibbs	.04	.03	.02
465	Paul Molitor	.10	.08	.04
466	Jerry Mumphrey	.04	.03	.02
467	Don Aase	.04	.03	.02
468	Darren Daulton	.04	.03	.02
469	Jeff Dedmon	.04	.03	.02
470	Dwight Evans	.10	.08	.04
471	Donnie Moore	.04	.03	.02
472	Robby Thompson	.06	.05	.02
473	Joe Niekro	.06	.05	.02
474	Tom Brookens	.04	.03	.02
475	Pete Rose	.20	.15	.08
476	Dave Stewart	.08	.06	.03
477	Jamie Quirk	.04	.03	.02
478	Sid Bream	.06	.05	.02
479	Brett Butler	.06	.05	.02
480	Dwight Gooden	.40	.30	.15
481	Mariano Duncan	.04	.03	.02
482	Mark Davis	.04	.03	.02
483	*Rod Booker*(FC)	.12	.09	.05
484	Pat Clements	.04	.03	.02
485	Harold Reynolds	.06	.05	.02
486	*Pat Keedy*(FC)	.10	.08	.04
487	Jim Pankovits	.04	.03	.02
488	Andy McGaffigan	.04	.03	.02
489	Dodgers Leaders (Pedro Guerrero, Fernando Valenzuela)	.08	.06	.03
490	Larry Parrish	.06	.05	.02
491	B.J. Surhoff	.10	.08	.04
492	Doyle Alexander	.06	.05	.02
493	Mike Greenwell	.70	.50	.30
494	*Wally Ritchie*	.12	.09	.05
495	Eddie Murray	.25	.20	.10
496	Guy Hoffman	.04	.03	.02
497	Kevin Mitchell	.30	.25	.12
498	Bob Boone	.06	.05	.02
499	Eric King	.06	.05	.02
500	Andre Dawson	.15	.11	.06
501	Tim Birtsas(FC)	.06	.05	.02
502	Danny Gladden	.04	.03	.02
503	*Junior Noboa*(FC)	.10	.08	.04
504	Bob Rodgers	.04	.03	.02
505	Willie Upshaw	.06	.05	.02
506	John Cangelosi	.04	.03	.02
507	Mark Gubicza	.10	.08	.04
508	Tim Teufel	.04	.03	.02
509	Bill Dawley	.04	.03	.02
510	Dave Winfield	.20	.15	.08
511	Joel Davis	.04	.03	.02
512	Alex Trevino	.04	.03	.02
513	Tim Flannery	.04	.03	.02
514	Pat Sheridan	.04	.03	.02
515	Juan Nieves	.06	.05	.02
516	Jim Sundberg	.06	.05	.02
517	Ron Robinson	.04	.03	.02
518	Greg Gross	.04	.03	.02
519	Mariners Leaders (Phil Bradley, Harold Reynolds)	.06	.05	.02
520	Dave Smith	.06	.05	.02
521	Jim Dwyer	.04	.03	.02
522	*Bob Patterson*(FC)	.12	.09	.05
523	Gary Roenicke	.04	.03	.02
524	Gary Lucas	.04	.03	.02
525	Marty Barrett	.06	.05	.02
526	Juan Berenguer	.04	.03	.02
527	Steve Henderson	.04	.03	.02
528a	Checklist 397-528 (#455 is Steve Carlton)	.40	.30	.15
528b	Checklist 397-528 (#455 is Shawn Hillegas)	.06	.05	.02
529	Tim Burke	.04	.03	.02
530	Gary Carter	.15	.11	.06
531	Rich Yett	.04	.03	.02
532	Mike Kingery	.04	.03	.02
533	*John Farrell*(FC)	.30	.25	.12
534	John Wathan	.06	.05	.02
535	Ron Guidry	.12	.09	.05
536	John Morris	.04	.03	.02
537	Steve Buechele	.04	.03	.02
538	Bill Wegman	.04	.03	.02
539	Mike LaValliere	.06	.05	.02
540	Bret Saberhagen	.25	.20	.10
541	Juan Beniquez	.04	.03	.02
542	*Paul Noce*(FC)	.10	.08	.04
543	Kent Tekulve	.06	.05	.02
544	Jim Traber	.06	.05	.02
545	Don Baylor	.08	.06	.03
546	John Candelaria	.06	.05	.02
547	*Felix Fermin*(FC)	.12	.09	.05
548	*Shane Mack*	.15	.11	.06
549	Braves Leaders (Ken Griffey, Dion James, Dale Murphy, Gerald Perry)	.08	.06	.03
550	Pedro Guerrero	.15	.11	.06
551	Terry Steinbach	.15	.11	.06
552	Mark Thurmond	.04	.03	.02
553	Tracy Jones	.10	.08	.04
554	Mike Smithson	.04	.03	.02
555	Brook Jacoby	.08	.06	.03
556	*Stan Clarke*(FC)	.12	.09	.05
557	Craig Reynolds	.04	.03	.02
558	Bob Ojeda	.06	.05	.02
559	*Ken Williams*(FC)	.20	.15	.08
560	Tim Wallach	.08	.06	.03
561	Rick Cerone	.04	.03	.02
562	Jim Lindeman	.10	.08	.04
563	Jose Guzman	.06	.05	.02
564	Frank Lucchesi	.04	.03	.02
565	Lloyd Moseby	.06	.05	.02
566	*Charlie O'Brien*(FC)	.12	.09	.05
567	Mike Diaz	.06	.05	.02
568	Chris Brown	.06	.05	.02
569	Charlie Leibrandt	.06	.05	.02
570	Jeffrey Leonard	.06	.05	.02
571	*Mark Williamson*(FC)	.12	.09	.05
572	Chris James	.15	.11	.06
573	Bob Stanley	.04	.03	.02
574	Graig Nettles	.08	.06	.03
575	Don Sutton	.12	.09	.05
576	*Tommy Hinzo*(FC)	.12	.09	.05
577	Tom Browning	.08	.06	.03
578	Gary Gaetti	.10	.08	.04
579	Mets Leaders (Gary Carter, Kevin McReynolds)	.08	.06	.03
580	Mark McGwire	.80	.60	.30
581	Tito Landrum	.04	.03	.02
582	*Mike Henneman*	.20	.15	.08
583	Dave Valle(FC)	.06	.05	.02
584	Steve Trout	.04	.03	.02
585	Ozzie Guillen	.06	.05	.02
586	Bob Forsch	.06	.05	.02
587	Terry Puhl	.04	.03	.02
588	*Jeff Parrett*(FC)	.20	.15	.08
589	Geno Petralli	.04	.03	.02
590	George Bell	.20	.15	.08
591	Doug Drabek	.06	.05	.02
592	Dale Sveum	.06	.05	.02
593	Bob Tewksbury	.04	.03	.02
594	Bobby Valentine	.04	.03	.02
595	Frank White	.06	.05	.02
596	John Kruk	.08	.06	.03
597	Gene Garber	.04	.03	.02
598	Lee Lacy	.04	.03	.02
599	Calvin Schiraldi	.04	.03	.02
600	Mike Schmidt	.40	.30	.15
601	Jack Lazorko	.04	.03	.02
602	Mike Aldrete	.06	.05	.02
603	Rob Murphy	.06	.05	.02
604	Chris Bando	.04	.03	.02
605	Kirk Gibson	.15	.11	.06
606	Moose Haas	.04	.03	.02
607	Mickey Hatcher	.04	.03	.02
608	Charlie Kerfeld	.04	.03	.02
609	Twins Leaders (Gary Gaetti, Kent Hrbek)	.08	.06	.03
610	Keith Hernandez	.15	.11	.06
611	Tommy John	.12	.09	.05
612	Curt Ford	.04	.03	.02
613	Bobby Thigpen	.08	.06	.03
614	Herm Winningham	.04	.03	.02
615	Jody Davis	.06	.05	.02
616	*Jay Aldrich*(FC)	.10	.08	.04
617	Oddibe McDowell	.06	.05	.02
618	Cecil Fielder	.60	.45	.25
619	*Mike Dunne*	.20	.15	.08
620	Cory Snyder	.15	.11	.06
621	Gene Nelson	.04	.03	.02
622	Kal Daniels	.15	.11	.06
623	Mike Flanagan	.06	.05	.02
624	Jim Leyland	.04	.03	.02
625	Frank Viola	.12	.09	.05
626	Glenn Wilson	.06	.05	.02
627	*Joe Boever*(FC)	.12	.09	.05
628	Dave Henderson	.08	.06	.03
629	Kelly Downs	.08	.06	.03

		MT	NR MT	EX
630	Darrell Evans	.08	.06	.03
631	Jack Howell	.06	.05	.02
632	*Steve Shields*	.12	.09	.05
633	*Barry Lyons*	.12	.09	.05
634	Jose DeLeon	.06	.05	.02
635	Terry Pendleton	.06	.05	.02
636	Charles Hudson	.04	.03	.02
637	*Jay Bell*(FC)	.25	.20	.10
638	Steve Balboni	.06	.05	.02
639	Brewers Leaders (Glenn Braggs, Tony Muser)	.06	.05	.02
640	Garry Templeton	.06	.05	.02
641	Rick Honeycutt	.04	.03	.02
642	Bob Dernier	.04	.03	.02
643	*Rocky Childress*(FC)	.12	.09	.05
644	Terry McGriff(FC)	.06	.05	.02
645	*Matt Nokes*	.30	.25	.12
646	Checklist 529-660	.04	.03	.02
647	Pascual Perez	.06	.05	.02
648	Al Newman	.04	.03	.02
649	*DeWayne Buice*	.15	.11	.06
650	Cal Ripken	.25	.20	.10
651	*Mike Jackson*(FC)	.15	.11	.06
652	Bruce Benedict	.04	.03	.02
653	Jeff Sellers	.06	.05	.02
654	Roger Craig	.06	.05	.02
655	Len Dykstra	.08	.06	.03
656	Lee Guetterman	.04	.03	.02
657	Gary Redus	.04	.03	.02
658	Tim Conroy	.04	.03	.02
659	Bobby Meacham	.04	.03	.02
660	Rick Reuschel	.08	.06	.03
661	Turn Back The Clock (Nolan Ryan)	.08	.06	.03
662	Turn Back The Clock (Jim Rice)	.08	.06	.03
663	Turn Back The Clock (Ron Blomberg)	.04	.03	.02
664	Turn Back The Clock (Bob Gibson)	.08	.06	.03
665	Turn Back The Clock (Stan Musial)	.12	.09	.05
666	Mario Soto	.06	.05	.02
667	Luis Quinones	.04	.03	.02
668	Walt Terrell	.06	.05	.02
669	Phillies Leaders (Lance Parrish, Mike Ryan)	.06	.05	.02
670	Dan Plesac	.08	.06	.03
671	Tim Laudner	.04	.03	.02
672	*John Davis*(FC)	.15	.11	.06
673	Tony Phillips	.04	.03	.02
674	Mike Fitzgerald	.04	.03	.02
675	Jim Rice	.20	.15	.08
676	Ken Dixon	.04	.03	.02
677	Eddie Milner	.04	.03	.02
678	Jim Acker	.04	.03	.02
679	Darrell Miller	.04	.03	.02
680	Charlie Hough	.06	.05	.02
681	Bobby Bonilla	.12	.09	.05
682	Jimmy Key	.08	.06	.03
683	Julio Franco	.08	.06	.03
684	Hal Lanier	.04	.03	.02
685	Ron Darling	.10	.08	.04
686	Terry Francona	.04	.03	.02
687	Mickey Brantley	.04	.03	.02
688	Jim Winn	.04	.03	.02
689	*Tom Pagnozzi*(FC)	.12	.09	.05
690	Jay Howell	.06	.05	.02
691	Dan Pasqua	.08	.06	.03
692	Mike Birkbeck	.06	.05	.02
693	Benny Santiago	.40	.30	.15
694	*Eric Nolte*(FC)	.12	.09	.05
695	Shawon Dunston	.08	.06	.03
696	Duane Ward	.04	.03	.02
697	Steve Lombardozzi	.08	.06	.03
698	Brad Havens	.04	.03	.02
699	Padres Leaders (Tony Gwynn, Benny Santiago)	.12	.09	.05
700	George Brett	.30	.25	.12
701	Sammy Stewart	.04	.03	.02
702	Mike Gallego	.04	.03	.02
703	Bob Brenly	.04	.03	.02
704	Dennis Boyd	.06	.05	.02
705	Juan Samuel	.10	.08	.04
706	Rick Mahler	.04	.03	.02
707	Fred Lynn	.10	.08	.04
708	Gus Polidor(FC)	.06	.05	.02
709	George Frazier	.04	.03	.02
710	Darryl Strawberry	.30	.25	.12
711	Bill Gullickson	.04	.03	.02
712	John Moses	.04	.03	.02
713	Willie Hernandez	.06	.05	.02
714	Jim Fregosi	.04	.03	.02
715	Todd Worrell	.08	.06	.03
716	Lenn Sakata	.04	.03	.02

		MT	NR MT	EX
717	Jay Baller(FC)	.06	.05	.02
718	Mike Felder	.04	.03	.02
719	Denny Walling	.04	.03	.02
720	Tim Raines	.20	.15	.08
721	Pete O'Brien	.06	.05	.02
722	Manny Lee	.04	.03	.02
723	Bob Kipper	.04	.03	.02
724	Danny Tartabull	.15	.11	.06
725	Mike Boddicker	.06	.05	.02
726	Alfredo Griffin	.06	.05	.02
727	Greg Booker	.04	.03	.02
728	Andy Allanson	.06	.05	.02
729	Blue Jays Leaders (George Bell, Fred McGriff)	.10	.08	.04
730	John Franco	.08	.06	.03
731	Rick Schu	.04	.03	.02
732	Dave Palmer	.04	.03	.02
733	Spike Owen	.04	.03	.02
734	Craig Lefferts	.04	.03	.02
735	Kevin McReynolds	.20	.15	.08
736	Matt Young	.04	.03	.02
737	Butch Wynegar	.04	.03	.02
738	Scott Bankhead	.04	.03	.02
739	Daryl Boston	.04	.03	.02
740	Rick Sutcliffe	.08	.06	.03
741	Mike Easler	.06	.05	.02
742	Mark Clear	.04	.03	.02
743	Larry Herndon	.04	.03	.02
744	Whitey Herzog	.06	.05	.02
745	Bill Doran	.06	.05	.02
746	*Gene Larkin*	.25	.20	.10
747	Bobby Witt	.08	.06	.03
748	Reid Nichols	.04	.03	.02
749	Mark Eichhorn	.06	.05	.02
750	Bo Jackson	1.25	.90	.50
751	Jim Morrison	.04	.03	.02
752	Mark Grant	.04	.03	.02
753	Danny Heep	.04	.03	.02
754	Mike LaCoss	.04	.03	.02
755	Ozzie Virgil	.04	.03	.02
756	Mike Maddux	.06	.05	.02
757	*John Marzano*	.15	.11	.06
758	*Eddie Williams*(FC)	.20	.15	.08
759	A's Leaders (Jose Canseco, Mark McGwire)	.40	.30	.15
760	Mike Scott	.10	.08	.04
761	Tony Armas	.06	.05	.02
762	Scott Bradley	.04	.03	.02
763	Doug Sisk	.04	.03	.02
764	Greg Walker	.06	.05	.02
765	Neal Heaton	.06	.05	.02
766	Henry Cotto	.04	.03	.02
767	*Jose Lind*(FC)	.25	.20	.10
768	Dickie Noles	.04	.03	.02
769	Cecil Cooper	.08	.06	.03
770	Lou Whitaker	.20	.15	.08
771	Ruben Sierra	.50	.40	.20
772	Sal Butera	.04	.03	.02
773	Frank Williams	.04	.03	.02
774	Gene Mauch	.06	.05	.02
775	Dave Stieb	.08	.06	.03
776	Checklist 661-792	.04	.03	.02
777	Lonnie Smith	.06	.05	.02
778a	Keith Comstock (white team letters)(FC)	6.00	4.50	2.50
778b	*Keith Comstock* (blue team letters)(FC)	.25	.20	.10
779	*Tom Glavine*(FC)	.35	.25	.14
780	Fernando Valenzuela	.15	.11	.06
781	*Keith Hughes*(FC)	.15	.11	.06
782	*Jeff Ballard*(FC)	.30	.25	.12
783	Ron Roenicke	.04	.03	.02
784	Joe Sambito	.04	.03	.02
785	Alvin Davis	.10	.08	.04
786	Joe Price	.04	.03	.02
787	Bill Almon	.04	.03	.02
788	Ray Searage	.04	.03	.02
789	Indians Leaders (Joe Carter, Cory Snyder)	.08	.06	.03
790	Dave Righetti	.12	.09	.05
791	Ted Simmons	.08	.06	.03
792	John Tudor	.08	.06	.03

A baseball card history feature, definitions for grading conditions and tips on how to use this catalog are located in the introduction section at the front of this book.

1988 Topps All-Star Glossy Set Of 22

The fifth edition of Topps' special All-Star inserts (22 cards) was included in the company's 1988 rack packs. The 1987 American and National League All-Star lineup, plus honorary captains Jim Hunter and Billy Williams, are featured on the standard-size All-Star inserts. The glossy full-color card fronts contain player photos centered between a red and yellow "1987 All-Star" logo printed across the card top and the player name (also red and yellow) which is printed across the bottom margin. A National or American League logo appears in the lower left corner. Card backs are printed in red and blue on a white background, with the title and All-Star logo emblem printed above the player name and card number.

$1.25, collectors received one of the six 10-card sets; 18 special offer cards and $7.50 earned the entire 60-card collection.

		MT	NR MT	EX
Complete Set:		4.00	3.00	1.50
Common Player:		.15	.11	.06
1	John McNamara	.15	.11	.06
2	Don Mattingly	1.00	.70	.40
3	Willie Randolph	.15	.11	.06
4	Wade Boggs	.80	.60	.30
5	Cal Ripken	.50	.40	.20
6	George Bell	.30	.25	.12
7	Rickey Henderson	.50	.40	.20
8	Dave Winfield	.40	.30	.15
9	Terry Kennedy	.15	.11	.06
10	Bret Saberhagen	.25	.20	.10
11	Jim Hunter	.25	.20	.10
12	Davey Johnson	.15	.11	.06
13	Jack Clark	.25	.20	.10
14	Ryne Sandberg	.40	.30	.15
15	Mike Schmidt	.60	.45	.25
16	Ozzie Smith	.25	.20	.10
17	Eric Davis	.60	.45	.25
18	Andre Dawson	.25	.20	.10
19	Darryl Strawberry	.60	.45	.25
20	Gary Carter	.40	.30	.15
21	Mike Scott	.15	.11	.06
22	Billy Williams	.25	.20	.10

1988 Topps All-Star Glossy Set Of 60

This standard-size collectors set includes 60 full-color glossy cards featuring All-Stars and Prospects in six separate 10-card sets. In 1986, Topps issued a similar set that included only All-Stars. Card fronts have a white border and a thin red line framing the player photo, with the player's name in the lower left corner. Card backs, in red and blue, include very basic player information (name, team and position), along with the card set logo and card number. Topps glossy collector sets were marketed via a special offer printed on a card packaged in all Topps wax packs. For six special offer cards and

		MT	NR MT	EX
Complete Set:		14.00	10.50	5.50
Common Player:		.15	.11	.06
1	Andre Dawson	.30	.25	.12
2	Jesse Barfield	.20	.15	.08
3	Mike Schmidt	.70	.50	.30
4	Ruben Sierra	.40	.30	.15
5	Mike Scott	.20	.15	.08
6	Cal Ripken	.70	.50	.30
7	Gary Carter	.50	.40	.20
8	Kent Hrbek	.30	.25	.12
9	Kevin Seitzer	.70	.50	.30
10	Mike Henneman	.25	.20	.10
11	Don Mattingly	2.00	1.50	.80
12	Tim Raines	.40	.30	.15
13	Roger Clemens	.80	.60	.30
14	Ryne Sandberg	.40	.30	.15
15	Tony Fernandez	.20	.15	.08
16	Eric Davis	.80	.60	.30
17	Jack Morris	.30	.25	.12
18	Tim Wallach	.20	.15	.08
19	Mike Dunne	.25	.20	.10
20	Mike Greenwell	1.00	.70	.40
21	Dwight Evans	.20	.15	.08
22	Darryl Strawberry	.80	.60	.30
23	Cory Snyder	.30	.25	.12
24	Pedro Guerrero	.25	.20	.10
25	Rickey Henderson	.60	.45	.25
26	Dale Murphy	.70	.50	.30
27	Kirby Puckett	.50	.40	.20
28	Steve Bedrosian	.20	.15	.08
29	Devon White	.25	.20	.10
30	Benny Santiago	.25	.20	.10
31	George Bell	.40	.30	.15
32	Keith Hernandez	.40	.30	.15
33	Dave Stewart	.15	.11	.06
34	Dave Parker	.25	.20	.10
35	Tom Henke	.15	.11	.06
36	Willie McGee	.20	.15	.08
37	Alan Trammell	.30	.25	.12
38	Tony Gwynn	.60	.45	.25
39	Mark McGwire	.80	.60	.30
40	Joe Magrane	.25	.20	.10
41	Jack Clark	.25	.20	.10
42	Willie Randolph	.15	.11	.06
43	Juan Samuel	.25	.20	.10
44	Joe Carter	.25	.20	.10
45	Shane Rawley	.15	.11	.06
46	Dave Winfield	.50	.40	.20
47	Ozzie Smith	.25	.20	.10
48	Wally Joyner	.70	.50	.30
49	B.J. Surhoff	.20	.15	.08
50	Ellis Burks	.80	.60	.30
51	Wade Boggs	.80	.60	.30
52	Howard Johnson	.20	.15	.08
53	George Brett	.70	.50	.30
54	Dwight Gooden	.80	.60	.30
55	Jose Canseco	2.00	1.50	.80
56	Lee Smith	.15	.11	.06
57	Paul Molitor	.20	.15	.08
58	Andres Galarraga	.30	.25	.12
59	Matt Nokes	.40	.30	.15
60	Casey Candaele	.15	.11	.06

1988 Topps American Baseball

This 88-card set, unlike Topps' United Kingdom football cards, was made available for distribution by U.S. hobby dealers. The cards were packaged in checklist-backed boxes with an American flag on the top flap. The 2-1/4" by 3" cards feature full-color player photos printed on white stock with a red line framing the photo. The team name, printed in individual team colors, intersects the red frame at the top of the card. A bright yellow name banner appears below the photo. Card backs have bright blue borders and cartoon-style horizontal layouts. The card number appears within a circle of red stars upper left, beside the player's name and team logo. A red banner containing the player career stats runs the length of the card back. The lower half of the flip side features a caricature of the player and a one-line caption. Below the cartoon, a short "Talkin' Baseball" paragraph provides elementary baseball information, obviously designed to acquaint soccer-playing European collectors with American baseball rules and terminology. A glossy edition of the set was issued and is valued at 2-3 times greater than the regular issue.

		MT	NR MT	EX
Complete Set:		9.00	6.75	3.50
Common Player:		.08	.06	.03
1	Harold Baines	.15	.11	.06
2	Steve Bedrosian	.10	.08	.04
3	George Bell	.25	.20	.10
4	Wade Boggs	.70	.50	.30
5	Barry Bonds	.20	.15	.08
6	Bob Boone	.08	.06	.03
7	George Brett	.40	.30	.15
8	Hubie Brooks	.08	.06	.03
9	Ivan Calderon	.10	.08	.04
10	Jose Canseco	1.25	.90	.50
11	Gary Carter	.30	.25	.12
12	Joe Carter	.15	.11	.06
13	Jack Clark	.20	.15	.08
14	Will Clark	.50	.40	.20
15	Roger Clemens	.60	.45	.25
16	Vince Coleman	.20	.15	.08
17	Alvin Davis	.15	.11	.06
18	Eric Davis	.70	.50	.30
19	Glenn Davis	.20	.15	.08
20	Andre Dawson	.25	.20	.10
21	Mike Dunne	.15	.11	.06
22	Dwight Evans	.10	.08	.04
23	Tony Fernandez	.15	.11	.06
24	John Franco	.10	.08	.04
25	Gary Gaetti	.20	.15	.08
26	Kirk Gibson	.25	.20	.10
27	Dwight Gooden	.60	.45	.25
28	Pedro Guerrero	.20	.15	.08
29	Tony Gwynn	.35	.25	.14
30	Billy Hatcher	.08	.06	.03
31	Rickey Henderson	.35	.25	.14
32	Tom Henke	.08	.06	.03
33	Keith Hernandez	.25	.20	.10
34	Orel Hershiser	.30	.25	.12
35	Teddy Higuera	.10	.08	.04
36	Charlie Hough	.08	.06	.03
37	Kent Hrbek	.25	.20	.10

		MT	NR MT	EX
38	Brook Jacoby	.10	.08	.04
39	Dion James	.08	.06	.03
40	Wally Joyner	.50	.40	.20
41	John Kruk	.15	.11	.06
42	Mark Langston	.15	.11	.06
43	Jeffrey Leonard	.08	.06	.03
44	Candy Maldonaldo	.08	.06	.03
45	Don Mattingly	1.25	.90	.50
46	Willie McGee	.15	.11	.06
47	Mark McGwire	.80	.60	.30
48	Kevin Mitchell	.08	.06	.03
49	Paul Molitor	.15	.11	.06
50	Jack Morris	.15	.11	.06
51	Lloyd Moseby	.10	.08	.04
52	Dale Murphy	.40	.30	.15
53	Eddie Murray	.30	.25	.12
54	Matt Nokes	.40	.30	.15
55	Dave Parker	.20	.15	.08
56	Larry Parrish	.08	.06	.03
57	Kirby Puckett	.35	.25	.14
58	Tim Raines	.30	.25	.12
59	Willie Randolph	.08	.06	.03
60	Harold Reynolds	.08	.06	.03
61	Cal Ripken	.35	.25	.14
62	Nolan Ryan	.80	.60	.30
63	Bret Saberhagen	.20	.15	.08
64	Juan Samuel	.15	.11	.06
65	Ryne Sandberg	.25	.20	.10
66	Benny Santiago	.15	.11	.06
67	Mike Schmidt	.40	.30	.15
68	Mike Scott	.10	.08	.04
69	Kevin Seitzer	.40	.30	.15
70	Larry Sheets	.08	.06	.03
71	Ruben Sierra	.15	.11	.06
72	Ozzie Smith	.15	.11	.06
73	Zane Smith	.08	.06	.03
74	Cory Snyder	.15	.11	.06
75	Dave Stewart	.10	.08	.04
76	Darryl Strawberry	.50	.40	.20
77	Rick Sutcliffe	.15	.11	.06
78	Danny Tartabull	.20	.15	.08
79	Alan Trammell	.25	.20	.10
80	Fernando Valenzuela	.20	.15	.08
81	Andy Van Slyke	.15	.11	.06
82	Frank Viola	.15	.11	.06
83	Greg Walker	.10	.08	.04
84	Tim Wallach	.10	.08	.04
85	Dave Winfield	.30	.25	.12
86	Mike Witt	.08	.06	.03
87	Robin Yount	.25	.20	.10
88	Checklist	.08	.06	.03

1988 Topps Big Baseball

1988 Topps Big Baseball cards (2-5/8" by 3-3/4") were issued in three series, 88 cards per series (a total set of 264 cards). Each series features current star players, sold in 7-card packages. The glossy cards are similar in format, both front and back, to the 1956 Topps 340-card set. Each card features a posed head shot and a close-up action photo on the front, framed by a wide white border and a dark blue inner border. A white outlines highlights the player closeup. The player's name appears below his head shot, in reversed type on a splash of color that fades from yellow to orange to red to pink. On the card back, the player's name is printed in large red letters across the top, ·followed by his team name and position in black. Personal info is printed in a red rectangle beside a Topps baseball logo bearing the card number. A triple cartoon strip, in full-color, illustrates career highlights, performance, personal background, etc. A red, white and blue statistics box (pitching, batting, fielding) is printed across the bottom.

		MT	NR MT	EX
Complete Set:		25.00	20.00	10.00
Common Player:		.05	.04	.02
1	Paul Molitor	.12	.09	.05
2	Milt Thompson	.05	.04	.02
3	Billy Hatcher	.05	.04	.02
4	Mike Witt	.05	.04	.02
5	Vince Coleman	.12	.09	.05
6	Dwight Evans	.10	.08	.04
7	Tim Wallach	.10	.08	.04
8	Alan Trammell	.15	.11	.06
9	Will Clark	.80	.60	.30
10	Jeff Reardon	.08	.06	.03
11	Dwight Gooden	.50	.40	.20
12	Benny Santiago	.12	.09	.05
13	Jose Canseco	1.25	.90	.50
14	Dale Murphy	.30	.25	.12
15	George Bell	.20	.15	.08
16	Ryne Sandberg	.20	.15	.08
17	Brook Jacoby	.08	.06	.03
18	Fernando Valenzuela	.15	.11	.06
19	Scott Fletcher	.05	.04	.02
20	Eric Davis	.60	.45	.25
21	Willie Wilson	.10	.08	.04
22	B.J. Surhoff	.10	.08	.04
23	Steve Bedrosian	.08	.06	.03
24	Dave Winfield	.25	.20	.10
25	Bobby Bonilla	.15	.11	.06
26	Larry Sheets	.08	.06	.03
27	Ozzie Guillen	.08	.06	.03
28	Checklist 1-88	.05	.04	.02
29	Nolan Ryan	.80	.60	.30
30	Bob Boone	.05	.04	.02
31	Tom Herr	.08	.06	.03
32	Wade Boggs	.90	.70	.35
33	Neal Heaton	.05	.04	.02
34	Doyle Alexander	.05	.04	.02
35	Candy Maldonado	.08	.06	.03
36	Kirby Puckett	.25	.20	.10
37	Gary Carter	.20	.15	.08
38	Lance McCullers	.08	.06	.03
39a	Terry Steinbach (black Topps logo on front)	.12	.09	.05
39b	Terry Steinbach (white Topps logo on front)	.12	.09	.05
40	Gerald Perry	.10	.08	.04
41	Tom Henke	.05	.04	.02
42	Leon Durham	.05	.04	.02
43	Cory Snyder	.12	.09	.05
44	Dale Sveum	.05	.04	.02
45	Lance Parrish	.12	.09	.05
46	Steve Sax	.12	.09	.05
47	Charlie Hough	.05	.04	.02
48	Kal Daniels	.15	.11	.06
49	Bo Jackson	1.00	.70	.40
50	Ron Guidry	.10	.08	.04
51	Bill Doran	.08	.06	.03
52	Wally Joyner	.40	.30	.15
53	Terry Pendleton	.08	.06	.03
54	Marty Barrett	.08	.06	.03
55	Andres Galarraga	.15	.11	.06
56	Larry Herndon	.05	.04	.02
57	Kevin Mitchell	.08	.06	.03
58	Greg Gagne	.05	.04	.02
59	Keith Hernandez	.15	.11	.06
60	John Kruk	.10	.08	.04
61	Mike LaValliere	.08	.06	.03
62	Cal Ripken	.30	.25	.12
63	Ivan Calderon	.08	.06	.03
64	Alvin Davis	.10	.08	.04
65	Luis Polonia	.08	.06	.03
66	Robin Yount	.20	.15	.08
67	Juan Samuel	.12	.09	.05
68	Andres Thomas	.05	.04	.02
69	Jeff Musselman	.05	.04	.02
70	Jerry Mumphrey	.05	.04	.02
71	Joe Carter	.12	.09	.05
72	Mike Scioscia	.05	.04	.02
73	Pete Incaviglia	.10	.08	.04

		MT	NR MT	EX
74	Barry Larkin	.15	.11	.06
75	Frank White	.08	.06	.03
76	Willie Randolph	.08	.06	.03
77	Kevin Bass	.05	.04	.02
78	Brian Downing	.08	.06	.03
79	Willie McGee	.10	.08	.04
80	Ellis Burks	.40	.30	.15
81	Hubie Brooks	.08	.06	.03
82	Darrell Evans	.08	.06	.03
83	Robby Thompson	.05	.04	.02
84	Kent Hrbek	.15	.11	.06
85	Ron Darling	.12	.09	.05
86	Stan Jefferson	.05	.04	.02
87	Teddy Higuera	.10	.08	.04
88	Mike Schmidt	.30	.25	.12
89	Barry Bonds	.15	.11	.06
90	Jim Presley	.08	.06	.03
91	Orel Hershiser	.25	.20	.10
92	Jesse Barfield	.10	.08	.04
93	Tom Candiotti	.05	.04	.02
94	Bret Saberhagen	.12	.09	.05
95	Jose Uribe	.05	.04	.02
96	Tom Browning	.10	.08	.04
97	Johnny Ray	.08	.06	.03
98	Mike Morgan	.05	.04	.02
100	Jim Sundberg	.05	.04	.02
101	Roger McDowell	.08	.06	.03
102	Randy Ready	.05	.04	.02
103	Mike Gallego	.05	.04	.02
104	Steve Buechele	.05	.04	.02
105	Greg Walker	.08	.06	.03
106	Jose Lind	.12	.09	.05
107	Steve Trout	.05	.04	.02
108	Rick Rhoden	.08	.06	.03
109	Jim Pankovits	.05	.04	.02
110	Ken Griffey	.08	.06	.03
111	Danny Cox	.08	.06	.03
112	Franklin Stubbs	.05	.04	.02
113	Lloyd Moseby	.08	.06	.03
114	Mel Hall	.08	.06	.03
115	Kevin Seitzer	.25	.20	.10
116	Tim Raines	.25	.20	.10
117	Juan Castillo	.05	.04	.02
118	Roger Clemens	.50	.40	.20
119	Mike Aldrete	.08	.06	.03
120	Mario Soto	.05	.04	.02
121	Jack Howell	.05	.04	.02
122	Rick Schu	.05	.04	.02
123	Jeff Robinson	.10	.08	.04
124	Doug Drabek	.08	.06	.03
125	Henry Cotto	.05	.04	.02
126	Checklist 89-176	.05	.04	.02
127	Gary Gaetti	.12	.09	.05
128	Rick Sutcliffe	.10	.08	.04
129	Howard Johnson	.08	.06	.03
130	Chris Brown	.08	.06	.03
131	Dave Henderson	.08	.06	.03
132	Curt Wilkerson	.05	.04	.02
133	Mike Marshall	.10	.08	.04
134	Kelly Gruber	.05	.04	.02
135	Julio Franco	.10	.08	.04
136	Kurt Stillwell	.12	.09	.05
137	Donnie Hill	.05	.04	.02
138	Mike Pagliarulo	.10	.08	.04
139	Von Hayes	.08	.06	.03
140	Mike Scott	.10	.08	.04
141	Bob Kipper	.05	.04	.02
142	Harold Reynolds	.08	.06	.03
143	Bob Brenly	.05	.04	.02
144	Dave Concepcion	.08	.06	.03
145	Devon White	.12	.09	.05
146	Jeff Stone	.05	.04	.02
147	Chet Lemon	.05	.04	.02
148	Ozzie Virgil	.05	.04	.02
149	Todd Worrell	.10	.08	.04
150	Mitch Webster	.05	.04	.02
151	Rob Deer	.08	.06	.03
152	Rich Gedman	.08	.06	.03
153	Andre Dawson	.15	.11	.06
154	Mike Davis	.05	.04	.02
155	Nelson Liriano	.08	.06	.03
156	Greg Swindell	.10	.08	.04
157	George Brett	.30	.25	.12
158	Kevin McReynolds	.15	.11	.06
159	Brian Fisher	.08	.06	.03
160	Mike Kingery	.05	.04	.02
161	Tony Gwynn	.25	.20	.10
162	Don Baylor	.10	.08	.04
163	Jerry Browne	.05	.04	.02
164	Dan Pasqua	.08	.06	.03
165	Rickey Henderson	.25	.20	.10

		MT	NR MT	EX
166	Brett Butler	.08	.06	.03
167	Nick Esasky	.05	.04	.02
168	Kirk McCaskill	.05	.04	.02
169	Fred Lynn	.10	.08	.04
170	Jack Morris	.12	.09	.05
171	Pedro Guerrero	.12	.09	.05
172	Dave Stieb	.10	.08	.04
173	Pat Tabler	.08	.06	.03
174	Floyd Bannister	.05	.04	.02
175	Rafael Belliard	.05	.04	.02
176	Mark Langston	.10	.08	.04
177	Greg Mathews	.08	.06	.03
178	Claudell Washington	.05	.04	.02
179	Mark McGwire	1.00	.70	.40
180	Bert Blyleven	.10	.08	.04
181	Jim Rice	.20	.15	.08
182	Mookie Wilson	.08	.06	.03
183	Willie Fraser	.05	.04	.02
184	Andy Van Slyke	.10	.08	.04
185	Matt Nokes	.10	.08	.04
186	Eddie Whitson	.05	.04	.02
187	Tony Fernandez	.10	.08	.04
188	Rick Reuschel	.08	.06	.03
189	Ken Phelps	.05	.04	.02
190	Juan Nieves	.08	.06	.03
191	Kirk Gibson	.20	.15	.08
192	Glenn Davis	.15	.11	.06
193	Zane Smith	.05	.04	.02
194	Jose DeLeon	.08	.06	.03
195	Gary Ward	.05	.04	.02
196	Pascual Perez	.05	.04	.02
197	Carlton Fisk	.12	.09	.05
198	Oddibe McDowell	.08	.06	.03
199	Mark Gubicza	.10	.08	.04
200	Glenn Hubbard	.05	.04	.02
201	Frank Viola	.15	.11	.06
202	Jody Reed	.12	.09	.05
203	Len Dykstra	.08	.06	.03
204	Dick Schofield	.05	.04	.02
205	Sid Bream	.05	.04	.02
206	Guillermo Hernandez	.05	.04	.02
207	Keith Moreland	.05	.04	.02
208	Mark Eichhorn	.05	.04	.02
209	Rene Gonzales	.08	.06	.03
210	Dave Valle	.05	.04	.02
211	Tom Brunansky	.10	.08	.04
212	Charles Hudson	.05	.04	.02
213	John Farrell	.10	.08	.04
214	Jeff Treadway	.12	.09	.05
215	Eddie Murray	.25	.20	.10
216	Checklist 177-264	.05	.04	.02
217	Greg Brock	.08	.06	.03
218	John Shelby	.05	.04	.02
219	Craig Reynolds	.05	.04	.02
220	Dion James	.05	.04	.02
221	Carney Lansford	.08	.06	.03
222	Juan Berenguer	.05	.04	.02
223	Luis Rivera	.08	.06	.03
224	Harold Baines	.12	.09	.05
225	Shawon Dunston	.08	.06	.03
226	Luis Aguayo	.05	.04	.02
227	Pete O'Brien	.08	.06	.03
228	Ozzie Smith	.12	.09	.05
229	Don Mattingly	1.50	1.25	.60
230	Danny Tartabull	.15	.11	.06
231	Andy Allanson	.05	.04	.02
232	John Franco	.08	.06	.03
233	Mike Greenwell	.80	.60	.30
234	Bob Ojeda	.08	.06	.03
235	Chili Davis	.08	.06	.03
236	Mike Dunne	.12	.09	.05
237	Jim Morrison	.05	.04	.02
238	Carmelo Martinez	.05	.04	.02
239	Ernie Whitt	.05	.04	.02
240	Scott Garrelts	.05	.04	.02
241	Mike Moore	.05	.04	.02
242	Dave Parker	.10	.08	.04
243	Tim Laudner	.05	.04	.02
244	Bill Wegman	.05	.04	.02
245	Bob Horner	.08	.06	.03
246	Rafael Santana	.05	.04	.02
247	Alfredo Griffin	.05	.04	.02
248	Mark Bailey	.05	.04	.02
249	Ron Gant	.12	.09	.05
250	Bryn Smith	.05	.04	.02
251	Lance Johnson	.10	.08	.04
252	Sam Horn	.10	.08	.04
253	Darryl Strawberry	.40	.30	.15
254	Chuck Finley	.05	.04	.02
255	Darnell Coles	.08	.06	.03
256	Mike Henneman	.10	.08	.04

		MT	NR MT	EX
257	Andy Hawkins	.08	.06	.03
258	Jim Clancy	.08	.06	.03
259	Atlee Hammaker	.05	.04	.02
260	Glenn Wilson	.05	.04	.02
261	Larry McWilliams	.05	.04	.02
262	Jack Clark	.12	.09	.05
263	Walt Weiss	.80	.60	.30
264	Gene Larkin	.08	.06	.03

1988 Topps Box Panels

After a one-year hiatus during which they appeared on the sides of Topps wax pack display boxes, Topps retail box cards returned to box bottoms in 1988. Topps first issued box-bottom cards in 1986, following the introduction of the concept by Donruss in 1985. Topps 1988 box-bottom series includes 16 standard-size baseball cards, four cards per each of four different display boxes. Card fronts follow the same design as the 1988 Topps basic issue; full-color player photos, framed in yellow, surrounded by a white border; diagonal player name lower right; team name in large letters at the top of the card front. Card backs are "numbered" A through P and are printed in black and orange.

		MT	NR MT	EX
Complete Panel Set:		7.00	5.25	2.75
Complete Singles Set:		3.00	2.25	1.25
Common Panel:		1.00	.70	.40
Common Single Player:		.08	.06	.03
	Panel	1.00	.70	.40
A	Don Baylor	.12	.09	.05
B	Steve Bedrosian	.12	.09	.05
C	Juan Beniquez	.08	.06	.03
D	Bob Boone	.08	.06	.03
	Panel	1.75	1.25	.70
E	Darrell Evans	.12	.09	.05
F	Tony Gwynn	.30	.25	.12
G	John Kruk	.15	.11	.06
H	Marvell Wynne	.08	.06	.03
	Panel	2.75	2.00	1.00
I	Joe Carter	.15	.11	.06
J	Eric Davis	.50	.40	.20
K	Howard Johnson	.12	.09	.05
L	Darryl Strawberry	.35	.25	.14
	Panel	2.50	2.00	1.00
M	Rickey Henderson	.50	.40	.20
N	Nolan Ryan	.35	.25	.14
O	Mike Schmidt	.08	.06	.03
P	Kent Tekulve	.08	.06	.03

1988 Topps Gallery Of Champions

These bronze replicas are exact reproductions at one-quarter scale of Topps official 1988 cards, both front and back. The set includes 12 three-dimensional raised metal cards packaged in a velvet-lined case that bears the title of the set in gold embossed letters. A deluxe limited edition of the set (1,000) was

produced in sterling silver and an economy version in aluminum. Topps first issued the metal mini-cards in 1984 (the initial set was called Gallery of Immortals). Since 1985, the metal cards have honored award-winning players from the previous season. A Mark McGwire pewter replica was given as a premium to dealers ordering the aluminum, bronze and silver sets ($50 value). The special pewter card is distinguished from the regular issue by a diagonal name banner in the lower right corner (regular) replicas have a rectangular name banner printer parallel to the lower edge of the card). A 1955 Topps Duke Snider bronze (value $10) was available to dealers purchasing cases of the 1988 Topps Traded sets.

		MT	NR MT	EX
Complete Aluminum Set:		20.00	15.00	8.00
Complete Bronze Set:		125.00	94.00	50.00
Complete Silver Set:		500.00	375.00	200.00
(1a)	Steve Bedrosian (aluminum)	.70	.50	.30
(1b)	Steve Bedrosian (bronze)	7.50	5.75	3.00
(1c)	Steve Bedrosian (silver)	20.00	15.00	8.00
(2a)	George Bell (aluminum)	1.00	.70	.40
(2b)	George Bell (bronze)	10.00	7.50	4.00
(2c)	George Bell (silver)	20.00	15.00	8.00
(3a)	Wade Boggs (aluminum)	3.00	2.25	1.25
(3b)	Wade Boggs (bronze)	25.00	18.50	10.00
(3c)	Wade Boggs (silver)	125.00	94.00	50.00
(4a)	Jack Clark (aluminum)	1.00	.70	.40
(4b)	Jack Clark (bronze)	10.00	7.50	4.00
(4c)	Jack Clark (silver)	20.00	15.00	8.00
(5a)	Roger Clemens (aluminum)	2.00	1.50	.80
(5b)	Roger Clemens (bronze)	20.00	15.00	8.00
(5c)	Roger Clemens (silver)	90.00	67.00	36.00
(6a)	Andre Dawson (aluminum)	1.00	.70	.40
(6b)	Andre Dawson (bronze)	10.00	7.50	4.00
(6c)	Andre Dawson (silver)	20.00	15.00	8.00
(7a)	Tony Gwynn (aluminum)	1.25	.90	.50
(7b)	Tony Gwynn (bronze)	12.00	9.00	4.75
(7c)	Tony Gwynn (silver)	50.00	37.00	20.00
(8a)	Mark Langston (aluminum)	.70	.50	.30
(8b)	Mark Langston (bronze)	7.50	5.75	3.00
(8c)	Mark Langston (silver)	20.00	15.00	8.00
(9a)	Mark McGwire (aluminum)	3.00	2.25	1.25
(9b)	Mark McGwire (bronze)	25.00	18.50	10.00
(9c)	Mark McGwire (silver)	125.00	94.00	50.00
(10a)	Dave Righetti (aluminum)	1.00	.70	.40
(10b)	Dave Righetti (bronze)	10.00	7.50	4.00
(10c)	Dave Righetti (silver)	20.00	15.00	8.00
(11a)	Nolan Ryan (aluminum)	1.00	.70	.40
(11b)	Nolan Ryan (bronze)	10.00	7.50	4.00
(11c)	Nolan Ryan (silver)	20.00	15.00	8.00
(12a)	Benny Santiago (aluminum)	1.00	.70	.40
(12b)	Benny Santiago (bronze)	10.00	7.50	4.00
(12c)	Benny Santiago (silver)	20.00	15.00	8.00

1988 Topps
Glossy Rookies

The Topps 1988 Rookies special insert cards follow the same basic design as the All-Star inserts. The set consists of 22 standard-size cards. Large, glossy

color player photos are printed on a white background below a red, yellow and blue "1987 Rookies" banner. A red and yellow player name appears beneath the photo. Red, white and blue card backs bear the title of the special insert set, the Rookies logo emblem, player name and card number.

		MT	NR MT	EX
Complete Set:		10.00	7.50	4.00
Common Player:		.20	.15	.08
1	Billy Ripken	.30	.25	.12
2	Ellis Burks	1.50	1.25	.60
3	Mike Greenwell	2.00	1.50	.80
4	DeWayne Buice	.20	.15	.08
5	Devon White	.40	.30	.15
6	Fred Manrique	.20	.15	.08
7	Mike Henneman	.40	.30	.15
8	Matt Nokes	.60	.45	.25
9	Kevin Seitzer	.80	.60	.30
10	B.J. Surhoff	.40	.30	.15
11	Casey Candaele	.20	.15	.08
12	Randy Myers	.60	.45	.25
13	Mark McGwire	1.50	1.25	.60
14	Luis Polonia	.25	.20	.10
15	Terry Steinbach	.40	.30	.15
16	Mike Dunne	.40	.30	.15
17	Al Pedrique	.20	.15	.08
18	Benny Santiago	.70	.50	.30
19	Kelly Downs	.40	.30	.15
20	Joe Magrane	.40	.30	.15
21	Jerry Browne	.20	.15	.08
22	Jeff Musselman	.25	.20	.10

1988 Topps
Mini League Leaders

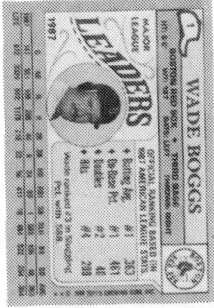

The third consecutive issue of Topps mini-cards (2-1/8" by 3") includes 77 cards spotlighting the top five ranked pitchers and batters. This set is unique in that it was the first time Topps included full-color player photos on both the front and back. Glossy action shots on the card fronts fade into a white border with a Topps logo in an upper corner. The player's name is printed in bold black letters beneath the photo. Horizontal reverses feature circular player photos on a blue and white background with the card number, player name, personal information, 1987 ranking and lifetime/1987 stats printed in red, black and yellow lettering.

		MT	NR MT	EX
	Complete Set:	8.00	6.00	3.25
	Common Player:	.09	.07	.04
1	Wade Boggs	.80	.60	.30
2	Roger Clemens	.60	.45	.25
3	Dwight Evans	.15	.11	.06
4	DeWayne Buice	.09	.07	.04
5	Brian Downing	.09	.07	.04
6	Wally Joyner	.60	.45	.25
7	Ivan Calderon	.15	.11	.06
8	Carlton Fisk	.20	.15	.08
9	Gary Redus	.09	.07	.04
10	Darrell Evans	.15	.11	.06
11	Jack Morris	.25	.20	.10
12	Alan Trammell	.30	.25	.12
13	Lou Whitaker	.20	.15	.08
14	Bret Saberhagen	.20	.15	.08
15	Kevin Seitzer	.50	.40	.20
16	Danny Tartabull	.25	.20	.10
17	Willie Wilson	.15	.11	.06
18	Teddy Higuera	.15	.11	.06
19	Paul Molitor	.20	.15	.08
20	Dan Plesac	.15	.11	.06
21	Robin Yount	.25	.20	.10
22	Kent Hrbek	.25	.20	.10
23	Kirby Puckett	.35	.25	.14
24	Jeff Reardon	.15	.11	.06
25	Frank Viola	.20	.15	.08
26	Rickey Henderson	.60	.45	.25
27	Don Mattingly	1.25	.90	.50
28	Willie Randolph	.15	.11	.06
29	Dave Righetti	.20	.15	.08
30	Jose Canseco	1.00	.70	.40
31	Mark McGwire	.90	.70	.35
32	Dave Stewart	.09	.07	.04
33	Phil Bradley	.15	.11	.06
34	Mark Langston	.15	.11	.06
35	Harold Reynolds	.09	.07	.04
36	Charlie Hough	.09	.07	.04
37	George Bell	.25	.20	.10
38	Tom Henke	.09	.07	.04
39	Jimmy Key	.15	.11	.06
40	Dion James	.09	.07	.04
41	Dale Murphy	.50	.40	.20
42	Zane Smith	.09	.07	.04
43	Andre Dawson	.25	.20	.10
44	Lee Smith	.09	.07	.04
45	Rick Sutcliffe	.15	.11	.06
46	Eric Davis	.60	.45	.25
47	John Franco	.15	.11	.06
48	Dave Parker	.20	.15	.08
49	Billy Hatcher	.09	.07	.04
50	Nolan Ryan	.60	.45	.25
51	Mike Scott	.20	.15	.08
52	Pedro Guerrero	.20	.15	.08
53	Orel Hershiser	.30	.25	.12
54	Fernando Valenzuela	.25	.20	.10
55	Bob Welch	.15	.11	.06
56	Andres Galarraga	.25	.20	.10
57	Tim Raines	.30	.25	.12
58	Tim Wallach	.15	.11	.06
59	Len Dykstra	.15	.11	.06
60	Dwight Gooden	.60	.45	.25
61	Howard Johnson	.15	.11	.06
62	Roger McDowell	.15	.11	.06
63	Darryl Strawberry	.50	.40	.20
64	Steve Bedrosian	.15	.11	.06
65	Shane Rawley	.09	.07	.04
66	Juan Samuel	.20	.15	.08
67	Mike Schmidt	.50	.40	.20
68	Mike Dunne	.15	.11	.06
69	Jack Clark	.25	.20	.10
70	Vince Coleman	.20	.15	.08
71	Willie McGee	.15	.11	.06
72	Ozzie Smith	.20	.15	.08
73	Todd Worrell	.15	.11	.06
74	Tony Gwynn	.40	.30	.15
75	John Kruk	.20	.15	.08
76	Rick Rueschel	.15	.11	.06
77	Checklist	.09	.07	.04

NOTE: A card number in parentheses ( ) indicates the set is unnumbered.

1988 Topps Traded

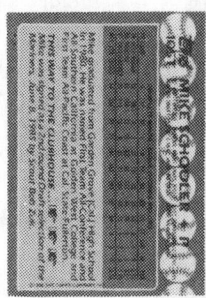

In addition to new players and traded veterans, 21 members of the U.S.A. Olympic Baseball team are showcased in this 132-card set, numbered 1T-132T. The standard-size (2-1/2" by 3-1/2") set follows the same design as the basic Topps issue - white borders, large full-color photos, team name (or U.S.A.) in large bold letters at the top of the card face, player name on a diagonal stripe across the lower right corner. Topps has issued its traded series each year since 1981 in boxed complete sets available through hobby dealers.

		MT	NR MT	EX
	Complete Set:	25.00	20.00	10.00
	Common Player:	.06	.05	.02
1T	Jim Abbott (U.S.A.)(FC)	5.00	3.75	2.00
2T	Juan Agosto	.06	.05	.02
3T	Luis Alicea(FC)	.15	.11	.06
4T	Roberto Alomar(FC)	2.00	1.50	.80
5T	Brady Anderson(FC)	.40	.30	.15
6T	Jack Armstrong(FC)	1.00	.70	.40
7T	Don August	.15	.11	.06
8T	Floyd Bannister	.08	.06	.03
9T	Bret Barberie (U.S.A.)(FC)	.30	.25	.12
10T	Jose Bautista(FC)	.15	.11	.06
11T	Don Baylor	.10	.08	.04
12T	Tim Belcher	.20	.15	.08
13T	Buddy Bell	.10	.08	.04
14T	Andy Benes (U.S.A.)(FC)	2.00	1.50	.80
15T	Damon Berryhill(FC)	.25	.20	.10
16T	Bud Black	.06	.05	.02
17T	Pat Borders(FC)	.20	.15	.08
18T	Phil Bradley	.10	.08	.04
19T	Jeff Branson (U.S.A.)(FC)	.20	.15	.08
20T	Tom Brunansky	.12	.09	.05
21T	Jay Buhner(FC)	.25	.20	.10
22T	Brett Butler	.08	.06	.03
23T	Jim Campanis (U.S.A.)(FC)	.20	.15	.08
24T	Sil Campusano(FC)	.25	.20	.10
25T	John Candelaria	.08	.06	.03
26T	Jose Cecena(FC)	.15	.11	.06
27T	Rick Cerone	.06	.05	.02
28T	Jack Clark	.15	.11	.06
29T	Kevin Coffman(FC)	.10	.08	.04
30T	Pat Combs (U.S.A.)(FC)	1.25	.90	.50
31T	Henry Cotto	.06	.05	.02
32T	Chili Davis	.08	.06	.03
33T	Mike Davis	.08	.06	.03
34T	Jose DeLeon	.08	.06	.03
35T	Richard Dotson	.10	.08	.04
36T	Cecil Espy(FC)	.08	.06	.03
37T	Tom Filer	.06	.05	.02
38T	Mike Fiore (U.S.A.)(FC)	.60	.45	.25
39T	Ron Gant(FC)	2.00	1.50	.80
40T	Kirk Gibson	.15	.11	.06
41T	Rich Gossage	.15	.11	.06
42T	Mark Grace(FC)	4.00	3.00	1.50
43T	Alfredo Griffin	.08	.06	.03
44T	Ty Griffin (U.S.A.)(FC)	1.00	.70	.40
45T	Bryan Harvey(FC)	.30	.25	.12
46T	Ron Hassey	.06	.05	.02
47T	Ray Hayward(FC)	.08	.06	.03
48T	Dave Henderson	.10	.08	.04
49T	Tom Herr	.10	.08	.04
50T	Bob Horner	.10	.08	.04
51T	Ricky Horton	.08	.06	.03

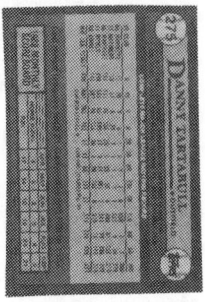

		MT	NR MT	EX
52T	Jay Howell	.08	.06	.03
53T	Glenn Hubbard	.06	.05	.02
54T	Jeff Innis(FC)	.15	.11	.06
55T	Danny Jackson	.15	.11	.06
56T	Darrin Jackson(FC)	.10	.08	.04
57T	Roberto Kelly(FC)	.60	.45	.25
58T	Ron Kittle	.10	.08	.04
59T	Ray Knight	.08	.06	.03
60T	Vance Law	.08	.06	.03
61T	Jeffrey Leonard	.08	.06	.03
62T	Mike Macfarlane(FC)	.20	.15	.08
63T	Scotti Madison(FC)	.15	.11	.06
64T	Kirt Manwaring(FC)	.20	.15	.08
65T	Mark Marquess (U.S.A.)	.06	.05	.02
66T	Tino Martinez (U.S.A.)(FC)	4.00	3.00	1.50
67T	Billy Masse (U.S.A.)(FC)	.40	.30	.15
68T	Jack McDowell(FC)	.20	.15	.08
69T	Jack McKeon	.06	.05	.02
70T	Larry McWilliams	.06	.05	.02
71T	Mickey Morandini (U.S.A.)(FC)	.50	.40	.20
72T	Keith Moreland	.08	.06	.03
73T	Mike Morgan	.06	.05	.02
74T	Charles Nagy (U.S.A.)(FC)	.40	.30	.15
75T	Al Nipper	.06	.05	.02
76T	Russ Nixon	.06	.05	.02
77T	Jesse Orosco	.08	.06	.03
78T	Joe Orsulak	.06	.05	.02
79T	Dave Palmer	.06	.05	.02
80T	Mark Parent(FC)	.20	.15	.08
81T	Dave Parker	.12	.09	.05
82T	Dan Pasqua	.10	.08	.04
83T	Melido Perez(FC)	.40	.30	.15
84T	Steve Peters(FC)	.15	.11	.06
85T	Dan Petry	.08	.06	.03
86T	Gary Pettis	.08	.06	.03
87T	Jeff Pico(FC)	.20	.15	.08
88T	Jim Poole (U.S.A.)(FC)	.20	.15	.08
89T	Ted Power	.06	.05	.02
90T	Rafael Ramirez	.06	.05	.02
91T	Dennis Rasmussen	.10	.08	.04
92T	Jose Rijo	.08	.06	.03
93T	Earnie Riles	.06	.05	.02
94T	Luis Rivera(FC)	.08	.06	.03
95T	Doug Robbins (U.S.A.)(FC)	.20	.15	.08
96T	Frank Robinson	.10	.08	.04
97T	Cookie Rojas	.06	.05	.02
98T	Chris Sabo(FC)	2.25	1.75	.90
99T	Mark Salas	.06	.05	.02
100T	Luis Salazar	.06	.05	.02
101T	Rafael Santana	.06	.05	.02
102T	Nelson Santovenia(FC)	.20	.15	.08
103T	Mackey Sasser(FC)	.10	.08	.04
104T	Calvin Schiraldi	.06	.05	.02
105T	Mike Schooler(FC)	.30	.25	.12
106T	Scott Servais (U.S.A.)(FC)	.20	.15	.08
107T	Dave Silvestri (U.S.A.)(FC)	.20	.15	.08
108T	Don Slaught	.06	.05	.02
109T	Joe Slusarski (U.S.A.)(FC)	.20	.15	.08
110T	Lee Smith	.10	.08	.04
111T	Pete Smith(FC)	.10	.08	.04
112T	Jim Snyder	.06	.05	.02
113T	Ed Sprague (U.S.A.)(FC)	.40	.30	.15
114T	Pete Stanicek(FC)	.15	.11	.06
115T	Kurt Stillwell	.10	.08	.04
116T	Todd Stottlemyre(FC)	.30	.25	.12
117T	Bill Swift	.06	.05	.02
118T	Pat Tabler	.08	.06	.03
119T	Scott Terry(FC)	.10	.08	.04
120T	Mickey Tettleton	.06	.05	.02
121T	Dickie Thon	.08	.06	.03
122T	Jeff Treadway(FC)	.20	.15	.08
123T	Willie Upshaw	.08	.06	.03
124T	Robin Ventura(FC)	2.00	1.50	.80
125T	Ron Washington	.06	.05	.02
126T	Walt Weiss(FC)	.70	.50	.30
127T	Bob Welch	.10	.08	.04
128T	David Wells(FC)	.08	.06	.03
129T	Glenn Wilson	.08	.06	.03
130T	Ted Wood (U.S.A.)(FC)	.40	.30	.15
131T	Don Zimmer	.06	.05	.02
132T	Checklist 1T-132T	.06	.05	.02

1989 Topps

Ten top young players who led the June 1988 draft picks are featured on "#1 Draft Pick" cards in this full-color basic set of 792 standard-size baseball cards. An additional five cards salute 1989 Future

Stars, 22 cards highlight All-Stars, seven contain Record Breakers, five are designated Turn Back The Clock, and six contain checklists. This set features the familiar white borders, but two inner photo corners (upper left and lower right) have been rounded off and the rectangular player name was replaced by a curved name banner in bright red or blue that leads to the team name in large script in the lower right corner. The card backs are printed in black on a red background and include personal information and complete minor and major league stats. Another new addition in this set is the special Monthly Scoreboard chart that lists monthly stats (April through September) in two of several categories (hits, run, home runs, stolen bases, RBIs, wins, strikeouts, games or saves).

		MT	NR MT	EX
Complete Set:		22.00	16.50	8.75
Common Player:		.03	.02	.01
1	Record Breaker (George Bell)	.08	.06	.03
2	Record Breaker (Wade Boggs)	.35	.25	.14
3	Record Breaker (Gary Carter)	.10	.08	.04
4	Record Breaker (Andre Dawson)	.08	.06	.03
5	Record Breaker (Orel Hershiser)	.10	.08	.04
6	Record Breaker (Doug Jones)	.06	.05	.02
7	Record Breaker (Kevin McReynolds)	.08	.06	.03
8	Dave Eiland(FC)	.20	.15	.08
9	Tim Teufel	.03	.02	.01
10	Andre Dawson	.15	.11	.06
11	Bruce Sutter	.08	.06	.03
12	Dale Sveum	.06	.05	.02
13	Doug Sisk	.03	.02	.01
14	Tom Kelly	.03	.02	.01
15	Robby Thompson	.06	.05	.02
16	Ron Robinson	.03	.02	.01
17	Brian Downing	.06	.05	.02
18	Rick Rhoden	.06	.05	.02
19	Greg Gagne	.03	.02	.01
20	Steve Bedrosian	.08	.06	.03
21	White Sox Leaders (Greg Walker)	.06	.05	.02
22	Tim Crews	.06	.05	.02
23	Mike Fitzgerald	.03	.02	.01
24	Larry Andersen	.03	.02	.01
25	Frank White	.06	.05	.02
26	Dale Mohorcic	.03	.02	.01
27	Orestes Destrade(FC)	.12	.09	.05
28	Mike Moore	.03	.02	.01
29	Kelly Gruber	.03	.02	.01
30	Doc Gooden	.40	.30	.15
31	Terry Francona	.03	.02	.01
32	Dennis Rasmussen	.08	.06	.03
33	B.J. Surhoff	.08	.06	.03
34	Ken Williams	.06	.05	.02
35	John Tudor	.08	.06	.03
36	Mitch Webster	.06	.05	.02
37	Bob Stanley	.03	.02	.01
38	Paul Runge	.03	.02	.01
39	Mike Maddux	.03	.02	.01
40	Steve Sax	.12	.09	.05
41	Terry Mulholland	.03	.02	.01
42	Jim Eppard(FC)	.08	.06	.03
43	Guillermo Hernandez	.06	.05	.02
44	Jim Snyder	.03	.02	.01
45	Kal Daniels	.12	.09	.05
46	Mark Portugal	.03	.02	.01
47	Carney Lansford	.06	.05	.02

		MT	NR MT	EX
48	Tim Burke	.03	.02	.01
49	*Craig Biggio*(FC)	.50	.40	.20
50	George Bell	.20	.15	.08
51	Angels Leaders (Mark McLemore)	.06	.05	.02
52	Bob Brenly	.03	.02	.01
53	Ruben Sierra	.30	.25	.12
54	Steve Trout	.03	.02	.01
55	Julio Franco	.08	.06	.03
56	Pat Tabler	.06	.05	.02
57	Alejandro Pena	.06	.05	.02
58	Lee Mazzilli	.06	.05	.02
59	Mark Davis	.03	.02	.01
60	Tom Brunansky	.10	.08	.04
61	Neil Allen	.03	.02	.01
62	Alfredo Griffin	.06	.05	.02
63	Mark Clear	.03	.02	.01
64	Alex Trevino	.03	.02	.01
65	Rick Reuschel	.08	.06	.03
66	Manny Trillo	.03	.02	.01
67	Dave Palmer	.03	.02	.01
68	Darrell Miller	.03	.02	.01
69	Jeff Ballard	.06	.05	.02
70	Mark McGwire	.60	.45	.25
71	Mike Boddicker	.06	.05	.02
72	John Moses	.03	.02	.01
73	Pascual Perez	.06	.05	.02
74	Nick Leyva	.03	.02	.01
75	Tom Henke	.06	.05	.02
76	*Terry Blocker*(FC)	.12	.09	.05
77	Doyle Alexander	.06	.05	.02
78	Jim Sundberg	.06	.05	.02
79	Scott Bankhead	.03	.02	.01
80	Cory Snyder	.15	.11	.06
81	Expos Leaders (Tim Raines)	.08	.06	.03
82	Dave Leiper	.03	.02	.01
83	Jeff Blauser(FC)	.15	.11	.06
84	#1 Draft Pick (Bill Bene)(FC)	.15	.11	.06
85	Kevin McReynolds	.12	.09	.05
86	Al Nipper	.03	.02	.01
87	Larry Owen	.03	.02	.01
88	*Darryl Hamilton*(FC)	.12	.09	.05
89	Dave LaPoint	.06	.05	.02
90	Vince Coleman	.12	.09	.05
91	Floyd Youmans	.03	.02	.01
92	Jeff Kunkel	.03	.02	.01
93	Ken Howell	.03	.02	.01
94	Chris Speier	.03	.02	.01
95	Gerald Young	.10	.08	.04
96	Rick Cerone	.03	.02	.01
97	Greg Mathews	.06	.05	.02
98	Larry Sheets	.06	.05	.02
99	*Sherman Corbett*(FC)	.12	.09	.05
100	Mike Schmidt	.35	.25	.14
101	Les Straker	.06	.05	.02
102	Mike Gallego	.03	.02	.01
103	Tim Birtsas	.03	.02	.01
104	Dallas Green	.03	.02	.01
105	Ron Darling	.10	.08	.04
106	Willie Upshaw	.06	.05	.02
107	Jose DeLeon	.06	.05	.02
108	Fred Manrique	.06	.05	.02
109	*Hipolito Pena*(FC)	.12	.09	.05
110	Paul Molitor	.12	.09	.05
111	Reds Leaders (Eric Davis)	.10	.08	.04
112	Jim Presley	.06	.05	.02
113	Lloyd Moseby	.06	.05	.02
114	Bob Kipper	.03	.02	.01
115	Jody Davis	.06	.05	.02
116	Jeff Montgomery	.06	.05	.02
117	Dave Anderson	.03	.02	.01
118	Checklist 1-132	.03	.02	.01
119	Terry Puhl	.03	.02	.01
120	Frank Viola	.12	.09	.05
121	Garry Templeton	.06	.05	.02
122	Lance Johnson(FC)	.10	.08	.04
123	Spike Owen	.03	.02	.01
124	Jim Traber	.06	.05	.02
125	Mike Krukow	.06	.05	.02
126	Sid Bream	.06	.05	.02
127	Walt Terrell	.06	.05	.02
128	Milt Thompson	.03	.02	.01
129	*Terry Clark*(FC)	.20	.15	.08
130	Gerald Perry	.08	.06	.03
131	Dave Otto(FC)	.08	.06	.03
132	Curt Ford	.03	.02	.01
133	Bill Long	.06	.05	.02
134	Don Zimmer	.03	.02	.01
135	Jose Rijo	.06	.05	.02
136	Joey Meyer	.08	.06	.03
137	Geno Petralli	.03	.02	.01
138	Wallace Johnson	.03	.02	.01
139	Mike Flanagan	.06	.05	.02

		MT	NR MT	EX
140	Shawon Dunston	.08	.06	.03
141	Indians Leaders (Brook Jacoby)	.06	.05	.02
142	Mike Diaz	.06	.05	.02
143	Mike Campbell	.08	.06	.03
144	Jay Bell	.06	.05	.02
145	Dave Stewart	.08	.06	.03
146	Gary Pettis	.03	.02	.01
147	DeWayne Buice	.03	.02	.01
148	Bill Pecota	.06	.05	.02
149	*Doug Dascenzo*(FC)	.25	.20	.10
150	Fernando Valenzuela	.15	.11	.06
151	Terry McGriff	.03	.02	.01
152	Mark Thurmond	.03	.02	.01
153	Jim Pankovits	.03	.02	.01
154	Don Carman	.06	.05	.02
155	Marty Barrett	.06	.05	.02
156	*Dave Gallagher*(FC)	.20	.15	.08
157	Tom Glavine	.08	.06	.03
158	Mike Aldrete	.06	.05	.02
159	Pat Clements	.03	.02	.01
160	Jeffrey Leonard	.06	.05	.02
161	#1 Draft Pick (Gregg Olson)(FC)	.80	.60	.30
162	John Davis	.03	.02	.01
163	Bob Forsch	.06	.05	.02
164	Hal Lanier	.03	.02	.01
165	Mike Dunne	.08	.06	.03
166	*Doug Jennings*(FC)	.20	.15	.08
167	Future Star (Steve Searcy)(FC)	.25	.20	.10
168	Willie Wilson	.08	.06	.03
169	Mike Jackson	.06	.05	.02
170	Tony Fernandez	.10	.08	.04
171	Braves Leaders (Andres Thomas)	.06	.05	.02
172	Frank Williams	.03	.02	.01
173	Mel Hall	.06	.05	.02
174	*Todd Burns*(FC)	.25	.20	.10
175	John Shelby	.03	.02	.01
176	Jeff Parrett	.08	.06	.03
177	#1 Draft Pick (Monty Fariss)(FC)	.35	.25	.14
178	Mark Grant	.03	.02	.01
179	Ozzie Virgil	.03	.02	.01
180	Mike Scott	.10	.08	.04
181	*Craig Worthington*(FC)	.40	.30	.15
182	Bob McClure	.03	.02	.01
183	Oddibe McDowell	.06	.05	.02
184	*John Costello*	.20	.15	.08
185	Claudell Washington	.06	.05	.02
186	Pat Perry	.03	.02	.01
187	Darren Daulton	.03	.02	.01
188	Dennis Lamp	.03	.02	.01
189	Kevin Mitchell	.50	.40	.20
190	Mike Witt	.06	.05	.02
191	*Sil Campusano*	.20	.15	.08
192	Paul Mirabella	.03	.02	.01
193	Sparky Anderson	.06	.05	.02
194	*Greg Harris*(FC)	.25	.20	.10
195	Ozzie Guillen	.06	.05	.02
196	Denny Walling	.03	.02	.01
197	Neal Heaton	.03	.02	.01
198	Danny Heep	.03	.02	.01
199	*Mike Schooler*	.30	.25	.12
200	George Brett	.30	.25	.12
201	Blue Jays Leaders (Kelly Gruber)	.06	.05	.02
202	*Brad Moore*(FC)	.12	.09	.05
203	Rob Ducey	.03	.02	.01
204	Brad Havens	.03	.02	.01
205	Dwight Evans	.10	.08	.04
206	Roberto Alomar	.50	.40	.20
207	Terry Leach	.03	.02	.01
208	Tom Pagnozzi	.06	.05	.02
209	*Jeff Bittiger*(FC)	.12	.09	.05
210	Dale Murphy	.30	.25	.12
211	Mike Pagliarulo	.08	.06	.03
212	Scott Sanderson	.03	.02	.01
213	Rene Gonzales	.06	.05	.02
214	Charlie O'Brien	.03	.02	.01
215	Kevin Gross	.06	.05	.02
216	Jack Howell	.06	.05	.02
217	Joe Price	.03	.02	.01
218	Mike LaValliere	.06	.05	.02
219	Jim Clancy	.06	.05	.02
220	Gary Gaetti	.12	.09	.05
221	Cecil Espy	.08	.06	.03
222	#1 Draft Pick (Mark Lewis)(FC)	.50	.40	.20
223	Jay Buhner	.10	.08	.04
224	Tony LaRussa	.06	.05	.02
225	*Ramon Martinez*(FC)	1.50	1.25	.60
226	Bill Doran	.06	.05	.02
227	John Farrell	.08	.06	.03
228	*Nelson Santovenia*	.25	.20	.10
229	Jimmy Key	.08	.06	.03
230	Ozzie Smith	.12	.09	.05

		MT	NR MT	EX
231	Padres Leaders (Roberto Alomar)	.10	.08	.04
232	Ricky Horton	.06	.05	.02
233	Future Star (Gregg Jefferies)(FC)	1.50	1.25	.60
234	Tom Browning	.08	.06	.03
235	John Kruk	.06	.05	.02
236	Charles Hudson	.03	.02	.01
237	Glenn Hubbard	.03	.02	.01
238	Eric King	.03	.02	.01
239	Tim Laudner	.03	.02	.01
240	Greg Maddux	.10	.08	.04
241	Brett Butler	.06	.05	.02
242	Ed Vande Berg	.03	.02	.01
243	Bob Boone	.06	.05	.02
244	Jim Acker	.03	.02	.01
245	Jim Rice	.20	.15	.08
246	Rey Quinones	.03	.02	.01
247	Shawn Hillegas	.06	.05	.02
248	Tony Phillips	.03	.02	.01
249	Tim Leary	.06	.05	.02
250	Cal Ripken	.30	.25	.12
251	*John Dopson*(FC)	.25	.20	.10
252	Billy Hatcher	.06	.05	.02
253	*Jose Alvarez*(FC)	.12	.09	.05
254	Tom LaSorda	.06	.05	.02
255	Ron Guidry	.12	.09	.05
256	Benny Santiago	.12	.09	.05
257	Rick Aguilera	.03	.02	.01
258	Checklist 133-264	.03	.02	.01
259	Larry McWilliams	.03	.02	.01
260	Dave Winfield	.25	.20	.10
261	Cardinals Leaders (Tom Brunansky)			
		.06	.05	.02
262	*Jeff Pico*	.20	.15	.08
263	Mike Felder	.03	.02	.01
264	*Rob Dibble*(FC)	.50	.40	.20
265	Kent Hrbek	.15	.11	.06
266	Luis Aquino	.03	.02	.01
267	Jeff Robinson	.06	.05	.02
268	Keith Miller	.06	.05	.02
269	Tom Bolton	.06	.05	.02
270	Wally Joyner	.20	.15	.08
271	Jay Tibbs	.03	.02	.01
272	Ron Hassey	.03	.02	.01
273	Jose Lind	.08	.06	.03
274	Mark Eichhorn	.06	.05	.02
275	Danny Tartabull	.15	.11	.06
276	Paul Kilgus	.08	.06	.03
277	Mike Davis	.06	.05	.02
278	Andy McGaffigan	.03	.02	.01
279	Scott Bradley	.03	.02	.01
280	Bob Knepper	.06	.05	.02
281	Gary Redus	.03	.02	.01
282	*Cris Carpenter*(FC)	.25	.20	.10
283	Andy Allanson	.03	.02	.01
284	Jim Leyland	.03	.02	.01
285	John Candelaria	.06	.05	.02
286	Darrin Jackson	.08	.06	.03
287	Juan Nieves	.06	.05	.02
288	Pat Sheridan	.03	.02	.01
289	Ernie Whitt	.06	.05	.02
290	John Franco	.08	.06	.03
291	Mets Leaders (Darryl Strawberry)	.12	.09	.05
292	*Jim Corsi*(FC)	.15	.11	.06
293	Glenn Wilson	.06	.05	.02
294	Juan Berenguer	.03	.02	.01
295	Scott Fletcher	.06	.05	.02
296	Ron Gant	.10	.08	.04
297	*Oswald Peraza*(FC)	.15	.11	.06
298	Chris James	.08	.06	.03
299	*Steve Ellsworth*(FC)	.12	.09	.05
300	Darryl Strawberry	.35	.25	.14
301	Charlie Leibrandt	.06	.05	.02
302	Gary Ward	.06	.05	.02
303	Felix Fermin	.06	.05	.02
304	Joel Youngblood	.03	.02	.01
305	Dave Smith	.06	.05	.02
306	Tracy Woodson(FC)	.10	.08	.04
307	Lance McCullers	.06	.05	.02
308	Ron Karkovice	.03	.02	.01
309	Mario Diaz(FC)	.10	.08	.04
310	Rafael Palmeiro	.20	.15	.08
311	Chris Bosio	.03	.02	.01
312	Tom Lawless	.03	.02	.01
313	Denny Martinez	.06	.05	.02
314	Bobby Valentine	.03	.02	.01
315	Greg Swindell	.10	.08	.04
316	Walt Weiss	.50	.40	.20
317	*Jack Armstrong*	.35	.25	.14
318	Gene Larkin	.08	.06	.03
319	Greg Booker	.03	.02	.01
320	Lou Whitaker	.15	.11	.06

		MT	NR MT	EX
321	Red Sox Leaders (Jody Reed)	.06	.05	.02
322	John Smiley	.10	.08	.04
323	Gary Thurman	.10	.08	.04
324	*Bob Milacki*(FC)	.25	.20	.10
325	Jesse Barfield	.08	.06	.03
326	Dennis Boyd	.06	.05	.02
327	*Mark Lemke*(FC)	.20	.15	.08
328	Rick Honeycutt	.03	.02	.01
329	Bob Melvin	.03	.02	.01
330	Eric Davis	.35	.25	.14
331	Curt Wilkerson	.03	.02	.01
332	Tony Armas	.06	.05	.02
333	Bob Ojeda	.06	.05	.02
334	Steve Lyons	.03	.02	.01
335	Dave Righetti	.10	.08	.04
336	Steve Balboni	.06	.05	.02
337	Calvin Schiraldi	.03	.02	.01
338	Jim Adduci(FC)	.06	.05	.02
339	Scott Bailes	.03	.02	.01
340	Kirk Gibson	.15	.11	.06
341	Jim Deshaies	.03	.02	.01
342	Tom Brookens	.03	.02	.01
343	Future Star *(Gary Sheffield)*(FC)	1.25	.90	.50
344	Tom Trebelhorn	.03	.02	.01
345	Charlie Hough	.06	.05	.02
346	Rex Hudler(FC)	.06	.05	.02
347	John Cerutti	.06	.05	.02
348	Ed Hearn	.03	.02	.01
349	*Ron Jones*(FC)	.30	.25	.12
350	Andy Van Slyke	.12	.09	.05
351	Giants Leaders (Bob Melvin)	.06	.05	.02
352	Rick Schu	.03	.02	.01
353	Marvell Wynne	.03	.02	.01
354	Larry Parrish	.06	.05	.02
355	Mark Langston	.08	.06	.03
356	Kevin Elster	.08	.06	.03
357	Jerry Reuss	.06	.05	.02
358	*Ricky Jordan*(FC)	.50	.40	.20
359	Tommy John	.10	.08	.04
360	Ryne Sandberg	.20	.15	.08
361	Kelly Downs	.08	.06	.03
362	Jack Lazorko	.03	.02	.01
363	Rich Yett	.03	.02	.01
364	Rob Deer	.06	.05	.02
365	Mike Henneman	.08	.06	.03
366	Herm Winningham	.03	.02	.01
367	*Johnny Paredes*(FC)	.20	.15	.08
368	Brian Holton	.06	.05	.02
369	Ken Caminiti	.06	.05	.02
370	Dennis Eckersley	.10	.08	.04
371	Manny Lee	.03	.02	.01
372	Craig Lefferts	.03	.02	.01
373	Tracy Jones	.08	.06	.03
374	John Wathan	.06	.05	.02
375	Terry Pendleton	.08	.06	.03
376	Steve Lombardozzi	.03	.02	.01
377	Mike Smithson	.03	.02	.01
378	Checklist 265-396	.03	.02	.01
379	Tim Flannery	.03	.02	.01
380	Rickey Henderson	.30	.25	.12
381	Orioles Leaders (Larry Sheets)	.06	.05	.02
382	*John Smoltz*(FC)	.60	.45	.25
383	Howard Johnson	.08	.06	.03
384	Mark Salas	.03	.02	.01
385	Von Hayes	.08	.06	.03
386	Andres Galarraga AS	.08	.06	.03
387	Ryne Sandberg AS	.10	.08	.04
388	Bobby Bonilla AS	.08	.06	.03
389	Ozzie Smith AS	.08	.06	.03
390	Darryl Strawberry AS	.15	.11	.06
391	Andre Dawson AS	.10	.08	.04
392	Andy Van Slyke AS	.08	.06	.03
393	Gary Carter AS	.10	.08	.04
394	Orel Hershiser AS	.12	.09	.05
395	Danny Jackson AS	.08	.06	.03
396	Kirk Gibson AS	.08	.06	.03
397	Don Mattingly AS	.60	.45	.25
398	Julio Franco AS	.06	.05	.02
399	Wade Boggs AS	.35	.25	.14
400	Alan Trammell AS	.08	.06	.03
401	Jose Canseco AS	.50	.40	.20
402	Mike Greenwell AS	.20	.15	.08
403	Kirby Puckett AS	.12	.09	.05
404	Bob Boone AS	.06	.05	.02
405	Roger Clemens AS	.15	.11	.06
406	Frank Viola AS	.08	.06	.03
407	Dave Winfield AS	.12	.09	.05
408	Greg Walker	.06	.05	.02
409	Ken Dayley	.03	.02	.01
410	Jack Clark	.12	.09	.05
411	Mitch Williams	.06	.05	.02

	MT	NR MT	EX			MT	NR MT	EX
412 Barry Lyons	.03	.02	.01	503 Al Newman	.03	.02	.01
413 Mike Kingery	.03	.02	.01	504 Bob Walk	.03	.02	.01
414 Jim Fregosi	.03	.02	.01	505 Pete Rose	.20	.15	.08
415 Rich Gossage	.10	.08	.04	506 Kirt Manwaring	.10	.08	.04
416 Fred Lynn	.10	.08	.04	507 Steve Farr	.03	.02	.01
417 Mike LaCoss	.03	.02	.01	508 Wally Backman	.06	.05	.02
418 Bob Dernier	.03	.02	.01	509 Bud Black	.03	.02	.01
419 Tom Filer	.03	.02	.01	510 Bob Horner	.08	.06	.03
420 Joe Carter	.10	.08	.04	511 Richard Dotson	.06	.05	.02
421 Kirk McCaskill	.06	.05	.02	512 Donnie Hill	.03	.02	.01
422 Bo Diaz	.06	.05	.02	513 Jesse Orosco	.06	.05	.02
423 Brian Fisher	.06	.05	.02	514 Chet Lemon	.06	.05	.02
424 Luis Polonia	.06	.05	.02	515 Barry Larkin	.20	.15	.08
425 Jay Howell	.06	.05	.02	516 Eddie Whitson	.03	.02	.01
426 Danny Gladden	.03	.02	.01	517 Greg Brock	.06	.05	.02
427 Eric Show	.06	.05	.02	518 Bruce Ruffin	.03	.02	.01
428 Craig Reynolds	.03	.02	.01	519 Yankees Leaders (Willie Randolph)	.03	.02	.01
429 Twins Leaders (Greg Gagne)	.06	.05	.02	520 Rick Sutcliffe	.08	.06	.03
430 Mark Gubicza	.08	.06	.03	521 Mickey Tettleton	.03	.02	.01
431 Luis Rivera	.06	.05	.02	522 *Randy Kramer*(FC)	.12	.09	.05
432 *Chad Kreuter*(FC)	.20	.15	.08	523 Andres Thomas	.06	.05	.02
433 Albert Hall	.03	.02	.01	524 Checklist 397-528	.03	.02	.01
434 *Ken Patterson*(FC)	.15	.11	.06	525 Chili Davis	.06	.05	.02
435 Len Dykstra	.08	.06	.03	526 Wes Gardner	.06	.05	.02
436 Bobby Meacham	.03	.02	.01	527 Dave Henderson	.08	.06	.03
437 #1 Draft Pick (*Andy Benes*)	1.25	.90	.50	528 *Luis Medina*(FC)	.25	.20	.10
438 Greg Gross	.03	.02	.01	529 Tom Foley	.03	.02	.01
439 Frank DiPino	.03	.02	.01	530 Nolan Ryan	.35	.25	.14
440 Bobby Bonilla	.10	.08	.04	531 *Dave Hengel*(FC)	.08	.06	.03
441 Jerry Reed	.03	.02	.01	532 Jerry Browne	.03	.02	.01
442 Jose Oquendo	.03	.02	.01	533 Andy Hawkins	.03	.02	.01
443 *Rod Nichols*(FC)	.15	.11	.06	534 Doc Edwards	.03	.02	.01
444 Moose Stubing	.03	.02	.01	535 Todd Worrell	.08	.06	.03
445 Matt Nokes	.15	.11	.06	536 Joel Skinner	.03	.02	.01
446 Rob Murphy	.03	.02	.01	537 Pete Smith	.08	.06	.03
447 Donell Nixon	.03	.02	.01	538 Juan Castillo	.03	.02	.01
448 Eric Plunk	.03	.02	.01	539 Barry Jones	.03	.02	.01
449 Carmelo Martinez	.03	.02	.01	540 Bo Jackson	.50	.40	.20
450 Roger Clemens	.40	.30	.15	541 Cecil Fielder	.25	.20	.10
451 Mark Davidson	.06	.05	.02	542 Todd Frohwirth	.06	.05	.02
452 *Israel Sanchez*	.12	.09	.05	543 Damon Berryhill	.15	.11	.06
453 *Tom Prince*(FC)	.08	.06	.03	544 Jeff Sellers	.03	.02	.01
454 Paul Assenmacher	.03	.02	.01	545 Mookie Wilson	.06	.05	.02
455 Johnny Ray	.06	.05	.02	546 Mark Williamson	.06	.05	.02
456 Tim Belcher	.08	.06	.03	547 Mark McLemore	.03	.02	.01
457 Mackey Sasser	.06	.05	.02	548 Bobby Witt	.08	.06	.03
458 *Donn Pall*(FC)	.20	.15	.08	549 Cubs Leaders (Jamie Moyer)	.03	.02	.01
459 Mariners Leaders (Dave Valle)	.06	.05	.02	550 Orel Hershiser	.20	.15	.08
460 Dave Stieb	.08	.06	.03	551 Randy Ready	.03	.02	.01
461 Buddy Bell	.06	.05	.02	552 Greg Cadaret	.06	.05	.02
462 Jose Guzman	.08	.06	.03	553 Luis Salazar	.03	.02	.01
463 Steve Lake	.03	.02	.01	554 Nick Esasky	.06	.05	.02
464 Bryn Smith	.03	.02	.01	555 Bert Blyleven	.10	.08	.04
465 Mark Grace	1.25	.90	.50	556 *Bruce Fields*(FC)	.06	.05	.02
466 Chuck Crim	.03	.02	.01	557 *Keith Miller*(FC)	.15	.11	.06
467 Jim Walewander	.03	.02	.01	558 Dan Pasqua	.08	.06	.03
468 Henry Cotto	.03	.02	.01	559 Juan Agosto	.03	.02	.01
469 *Jose Bautista*	.20	.15	.08	560 Rock Raines	.25	.20	.10
470 Lance Parrish	.12	.09	.05	561 Luis Aguayo	.03	.02	.01
471 *Steve Curry*(FC)	.20	.15	.08	562 Danny Cox	.06	.05	.02
472 Brian Harper	.03	.02	.01	563 Bill Schroeder	.03	.02	.01
473 Don Robinson	.03	.02	.01	564 Russ Nixon	.03	.02	.01
474 Bob Rodgers	.03	.02	.01	565 Jeff Russell	.03	.02	.01
475 Dave Parker	.10	.08	.04	566 Al Pedrique	.03	.02	.01
476 Jon Perlman(FC)	.06	.05	.02	567 David Wells	.08	.06	.03
477 Dick Schofield	.03	.02	.01	568 Mickey Brantley	.03	.02	.01
478 Doug Drabek	.06	.05	.02	569 *German Jimenez*(FC)	.08	.06	.03
479 *Mike Macfarlane*	.20	.15	.08	570 Tony Gwynn	.30	.25	.12
480 Keith Hernandez	.20	.15	.08	571 Billy Ripken	.06	.05	.02
481 Chris Brown	.06	.05	.02	572 Atlee Hammaker	.03	.02	.01
482 *Steve Peters*	.12	.09	.05	573 #1 Draft Pick (*Jim Abbott*)	1.25	.90	.50
483 Mickey Hatcher	.03	.02	.01	574 Dave Clark	.06	.05	.02
484 Steve Shields	.03	.02	.01	575 Juan Samuel	.10	.08	.04
485 Hubie Brooks	.08	.06	.03	576 Greg Minton	.03	.02	.01
486 Jack McDowell	.08	.06	.03	577 Randy Bush	.03	.02	.01
487 Scott Lusader(FC)	.08	.06	.03	578 John Morris	.03	.02	.01
488 Kevin Coffman	.06	.05	.02	579 Astros Leaders (Glenn Davis)	.08	.06	.03
489 Phillies Leaders (Mike Schmidt)	.12	.09	.05	580 Harold Reynolds	.06	.05	.02
490 *Chris Sabo*	1.00	.70	.40	581 Gene Nelson	.03	.02	.01
491 Mike Birkbeck	.03	.02	.01	582 Mike Marshall	.10	.08	.04
492 Alan Ashby	.03	.02	.01	583 *Paul Gibson*(FC)	.15	.11	.06
493 Todd Benzinger	.10	.08	.04	584 Randy Velarde(FC)	.10	.08	.04
494 Shane Rawley	.06	.05	.02	585 Harold Baines	.10	.08	.04
495 Candy Maldonado	.06	.05	.02	586 Joe Boever	.03	.02	.01
496 Dwayne Henry	.03	.02	.01	587 Mike Stanley	.03	.02	.01
497 Pete Stanicek	.12	.09	.05	588 *Luis Alicea*	.15	.11	.06
498 Dave Valle	.03	.02	.01	589 Dave Meads	.03	.02	.01
499 *Don Heinkel*(FC)	.15	.11	.06	590 Andres Galarraga	.12	.09	.05
500 Jose Canseco	1.00	.70	.40	591 Jeff Musselman	.06	.05	.02
501 Vance Law	.06	.05	.02	592 John Cangelosi	.03	.02	.01
502 Duane Ward	.03	.02	.01	593 Drew Hall	.10	.08	.04

		MT	NR MT	EX
594	Jimy Williams	.03	.02	.01
595	Teddy Higuera	.08	.06	.03
596	Kurt Stillwell	.06	.05	.02
597	*Terry Taylor*(FC)	.12	.09	.05
598	Ken Gerhart	.06	.05	.02
599	Tom Candiotti	.03	.02	.01
600	Wade Boggs	.90	.70	.35
601	Dave Dravecky	.06	.05	.02
602	Devon White	.10	.08	.04
603	Frank Tanana	.06	.05	.02
604	Paul O'Neill	.03	.02	.01
605a	Bob Welch (missing Complete Major League Pitching Record line)	2.50	2.00	1.00
605b	Bob Welch (contains Complete Major League Pitching Record line)	.08	.06	.03
606	Rick Dempsey	.06	.05	.02
607	#1 Draft Pick *(Willie Ansley)*(FC)	.50	.40	.20
608	Phil Bradley	.08	.06	.03
609	Tigers Leaders (Frank Tanana)	.06	.05	.02
610	Randy Myers	.08	.06	.03
611	Don Slaught	.03	.02	.01
612	Dan Quisenberry	.06	.05	.02
613	*Gary Varsho*(FC)	.20	.15	.08
614	Joe Hesketh	.03	.02	.01
615	Robin Yount	.25	.20	.10
616	*Steve Rosenberg*(FC)	.15	.11	.06
617	*Mark Parent*	.15	.11	.06
618	Rance Mulliniks	.03	.02	.01
619	Checklist 529-660	.03	.02	.01
620	Barry Bonds	.10	.08	.04
621	Rick Mahler	.03	.02	.01
622	Stan Javier	.03	.02	.01
623	Fred Toliver	.03	.02	.01
624	Jack McKeon	.03	.02	.01
625	Eddie Murray	.25	.20	.10
626	Jeff Reed	.03	.02	.01
627	Greg Harris	.03	.02	.01
628	Matt Williams	.10	.08	.04
629	Pete O'Brien	.06	.05	.02
630	Mike Greenwell	.50	.40	.20
631	Dave Bergman	.03	.02	.01
632	*Bryan Harvey*	.20	.15	.08
633	Daryl Boston	.03	.02	.01
634	Marvin Freeman(FC)	.08	.06	.03
635	Willie Randolph	.06	.05	.02
636	Bill Wilkinson	.06	.05	.02
637	Carmen Castillo	.03	.02	.01
638	Floyd Bannister	.06	.05	.02
639	Athletics Leaders (Walt Weiss)	.15	.11	.06
640	Willie McGee	.10	.08	.04
641	Curt Young	.06	.05	.02
642	Argenis Salazar	.03	.02	.01
643	*Louie Meadows*(FC)	.12	.09	.05
644	Lloyd McClendon	.03	.02	.01
645	Jack Morris	.12	.09	.05
646	Kevin Bass	.06	.05	.02
647	*Randy Johnson*(FC)	.50	.40	.20
648	Future Star *(Sandy Alomar)*(FC)	1.00	.70	.40
649	Stewart Cliburn	.03	.02	.01
650	Kirby Puckett	.25	.20	.10
651	Tom Niedenfuer	.06	.05	.02
652	Rich Gedman	.06	.05	.02
653	*Tommy Barrett*(FC)	.12	.09	.05
654	Whitey Herzog	.06	.05	.02
655	Dave Magadan	.08	.06	.03
656	Ivan Calderon	.06	.05	.02
657	Joe Magrane	.08	.06	.03
658	R.J. Reynolds	.03	.02	.01
659	Al Leiter	.15	.11	.06
660	Will Clark	.50	.40	.20
661	Turn Back The Clock (Dwight Gooden)	.20	.15	.08
662	Turn Back The Clock (Lou Brock)	.08	.06	.03
663	Turn Back The Clock (Hank Aaron)	.15	.11	.06
664	Turn Back The Clock (Gil Hodges)	.06	.05	.02
665	Turn Back The Clock (Tony Oliva)	.06	.05	.02
666	Randy St. Claire	.03	.02	.01
667	Dwayne Murphy	.06	.05	.02
668	Mike Bielecki	.03	.02	.01
669	Dodgers Leaders (Orel Hershiser)	.12	.09	.05
670	Kevin Seitzer	.25	.20	.10
671	Jim Gantner	.03	.02	.01
672	Allan Anderson	.06	.05	.02
673	Don Baylor	.08	.06	.03
674	Otis Nixon	.03	.02	.01
675	Bruce Hurst	.08	.06	.03
676	Ernie Riles	.03	.02	.01
677	Dave Schmidt	.03	.02	.01
678	Dion James	.03	.02	.01
679	Willie Fraser	.03	.02	.01
680	Gary Carter	.15	.11	.06

		MT	NR MT	EX
681	Jeff Robinson	.10	.08	.04
682	Rick Leach	.03	.02	.01
683	*Jose Cecena*	.15	.11	.06
684	Dave Johnson	.06	.05	.02
685	Jeff Treadway	.10	.08	.04
686	Scott Terry	.08	.06	.03
687	Alvin Davis	.10	.08	.04
688	Zane Smith	.06	.05	.02
689	Stan Jefferson	.03	.02	.01
690	Doug Jones	.10	.08	.04
691	Roberto Kelly	.25	.20	.10
692	Steve Ontiveros	.03	.02	.01
693	*Pat Borders*	.20	.15	.08
694	Les Lancaster	.06	.05	.02
695	Carlton Fisk	.20	.15	.08
696	Don August	.08	.06	.03
697	Franklin Stubbs	.03	.02	.01
698	Keith Atherton	.03	.02	.01
699	Pirates Leaders (Al Pedrique)	.06	.05	.02
700	Don Mattingly	.80	.60	.30
701	Storm Davis	.08	.06	.03
702	Jamie Quirk	.03	.02	.01
703	Scott Garrelts	.03	.02	.01
704	*Carlos Quintana*(FC)	.40	.30	.15
705	Terry Kennedy	.06	.05	.02
706	Pete Incaviglia	.08	.06	.03
707	Steve Jeltz	.03	.02	.01
708	Chuck Finley	.03	.02	.01
709	Tom Herr	.06	.05	.02
710	Dave Cone	.30	.25	.12
711	*Candy Sierra*(FC)	.12	.09	.05
712	Bill Swift	.03	.02	.01
713	#1 Draft Pick *(Ty Griffin)*	.70	.50	.25
714	Joe Morgan	.03	.02	.01
715	Tony Pena	.06	.05	.02
716	Wayne Tolleson	.03	.02	.01
717	Jamie Moyer	.03	.02	.01
718	Glenn Braggs	.06	.05	.02
719	Danny Darwin	.03	.02	.01
720	Tim Wallach	.08	.06	.03
721	*Ron Tingley*(FC)	.12	.09	.05
722	Todd Stottlemyre	.15	.11	.06
723	Rafael Belliard	.03	.02	.01
724	Jerry Don Gleaton	.03	.02	.01
725	Terry Steinbach	.08	.06	.03
726	Dickie Thon	.03	.02	.01
727	Joe Orsulak	.03	.02	.01
728	Charlie Puleo	.03	.02	.01
729	Rangers Leaders (Steve Buechele)	.06	.05	.02
730	Danny Jackson	.12	.09	.05
731	Mike Young	.03	.02	.01
732	Steve Buechele	.03	.02	.01
733	*Randy Bockus*(FC)	.06	.05	.02
734	Jody Reed	.10	.08	.04
735	Roger McDowell	.08	.06	.03
736	Jeff Hamilton	.06	.05	.02
737	*Norm Charlton*(FC)	.40	.30	.15
738	Darnell Coles	.06	.05	.02
739	Brook Jacoby	.08	.06	.03
740	Dan Plesac	.08	.06	.03
741	Ken Phelps	.06	.05	.02
742	Future Star *(Mike Harkey)*(FC)	.40	.30	.15
743	Mike Heath	.03	.02	.01
744	Roger Craig	.06	.05	.02
745	Fred McGriff	.40	.30	.15
746	*German Gonzalez*(FC)	.20	.15	.08
747	Wil Tejada(FC)	.06	.05	.02
748	Jimmy Jones	.03	.02	.01
749	Rafael Ramirez	.03	.02	.01
750	Bret Saberhagen	.12	.09	.05
751	Ken Oberkfell	.03	.02	.01
752	Jim Gott	.03	.02	.01
753	Jose Uribe	.03	.02	.01
754	Bob Brower	.03	.02	.01
755	Mike Scioscia	.06	.05	.02
756	*Scott Medvin*(FC)	.20	.15	.08
757	*Brady Anderson*	.30	.25	.12
758	Gene Walter	.03	.02	.01
759	Brewers Leaders (Rob Deer)	.06	.05	.02
760	Lee Smith	.08	.06	.03
761	*Dante Bichette*(FC)	.25	.20	.10
762	Bobby Thigpen	.08	.06	.03
763	Dave Martinez	.06	.05	.02
764	#1 Draft Pick *(Robin Ventura)*	1.00	.70	.40
765	Glenn Davis	.20	.15	.08
766	Cecilio Guante	.03	.02	.01
767	*Mike Capel*(FC)	.15	.11	.06
768	Bill Wegman	.03	.02	.01
769	Junior Ortiz	.03	.02	.01
770	Alan Trammell	.15	.11	.06
771	Ron Kittle	.06	.05	.02

		MT	NR MT	EX
772	Ron Oester	.03	.02	.01
773	Keith Moreland	.06	.05	.02
774	Frank Robinson	.08	.06	.03
775	Jeff Reardon	.08	.06	.03
776	Nelson Liriano	.06	.05	.02
777	Ted Power	.03	.02	.01
778	Bruce Benedict	.03	.02	.01
779	Craig McMurtry	.03	.02	.01
780	Pedro Guerrero	.12	.09	.05
781	*Greg Briley*(FC)	.70	.50	.30
782	Checklist 661-792	.03	.02	.01
783	*Trevor Wilson*(FC)	.15	.11	.06
784	#1 Draft Pick (*Steve Avery*)(FC)	.80	.60	.30
785	Ellis Burks	.50	.40	.20
786	Melido Perez	.08	.06	.03
787	*Dave West*(FC)	.30	.25	.12
788	Mike Morgan	.03	.02	.01
789	Royals Leaders (Bo Jackson)	.15	.11	.06
790	Sid Fernandez	.08	.06	.03
791	Jim Lindeman	.03	.02	.01
792	Rafael Santana	.03	.02	.01

1989 Topps All-Star Glossy Set Of 22

Bearing the same design and style of the past two years, Topps featured the top first-year players from the 1988 season in this glossy set. The full-color player photos appears beneath the "1988 Rookies" banner. The player's name is displayed beneath the photo. The flip side features the "1988 Rookies Commemorative Set" logo followed by the player's name, position, team, and card number. The glossy All-Stars are included in the Topps 1989 Jumbo Paks.

		MT	NR MT	EX
Complete Set:		3.50	2.75	1.50
Common Player:		.15	.11	.06
1	Roberto Alomar	.25	.20	.10
2	Brady Anderson	.20	.15	.08
3	Tim Belcher	.20	.15	.08
4	Damon Berryhill	.15	.11	.06
5	Jay Buhner	.20	.15	.11
6	Kevin Elster	.15	.11	.06
7	Cecil Espy	.15	.11	.06
8	Dave Gallagher	.15	.11	.06
9	Ron Gant	.15	.11	.06
10	Paul Gibson	.15	.11	.06
11	Mark Grace	.60	.45	.25
12	Darrin Jackson	.15	.11	.06
13	Gregg Jefferies	.70	.50	.30
14	Ricky Jordan	.50	.40	.20
15	Al Leiter	.15	.11	.06
16	Melido Perez	.15	.11	.06
17	Chris Sabo	.35	.25	.14
18	Nelson Santovenia	.20	.15	.08
19	Mackey Sasser			

Errors/variations

Collectors often wonder about errors found on cards, usually in the statistics or personal data on the card's back.

Such errors *add nothing* to the value of the card. The only time an error like this is likely to increase a card's value is if the manufacturer corrects the error in a later printing, thus creating two distinct variations. If enough collectors feel the variations are a desirable part of that issue, the value may increase. Whether the error version or the corrected card will have the greater value usually depends on relative scarcity. The more common version will almost always be worth less. So quite often, the error card can be worth less than the corrected version.

1989 Topps All-Star Glossy Set Of 60

For the seventh straight year Topps issued this "send-away" glossy set. Divided into six 10-card sets, it was available only by sending in special offer cards from the 1989 Topps wax packs. The 2-1/2" by 3-1/2" cards feature full-color photos bordered in white with a thin yellow frame. The player's name appears in small print in the lower right corner. Red-and-blue-printed flip sides provide basic information including player's name, team, and position. Any of the six 10-card sets were available for $1.25 and six special offer cards. The set was also made available in its complete 60-card set form for $7.50 and 18 special offer cards.

		MT	NR MT	EX
Complete Set:		10.00	7.50	4.00
Common Player:		.15	.11	.06
1	Kirby Puckett	.50	.40	.20
2	Eric Davis	.70	.50	.30
3	Joe Carter	.20	.15	.08
4	Andy Van Slyke	.20	.15	.08
5	Wade Boggs	.70	.50	.30
6	Dave Cone	.25	.20	.10
7	Kent Hrbek	.15	.11	.06
8	Darryl Strawberry	.70	.50	.30
9	Jay Buhner	.15	.11	.06
10	Ron Gant	.30	.25	.12
11	Will Clark	1.00	.70	.40
12	Jose Canseco	1.25	.90	.50
13	Juan Samuel	.15	.11	.06
14	George Brett	.25	.20	.10
15	Benny Santiago	.20	.15	.08
16	Dennis Eckersley	.15	.11	.06
17	Gary Carter	.15	.11	.06
18	Frank Viola	.20	.15	.08
19	Roberto Alomar	.30	.25	.12
20	Paul Gibson	.15	.11	.06
21	Dave Winfield	.20	.15	.08
22	Howard Johnson	.35	.25	.14
23	Roger Clemens	.40	.30	.15
24	Bobby Bonilla	.25	.20	.10
25	Alan Trammell	.20	.15	.08
26	Kevin McReynolds	.20	.15	.08
27	George Bell	.20	.15	.08
28	Bruce Hurst	.15	.11	.06
29	Mark Grace	.70	.50	.30
30	Tim Belcher	.20	.15	.08
31	Mike Greenwell	.70	.50	.30
32	Glenn Davis	.15	.11	.06
33	Gary Gaetti	.15	.11	.06
34	Ryne Sandberg	.70	.50	.30
35	Rickey Henderson	.70	.50	.30
36	Dwight Evans	.15	.11	.06
37	Doc Gooden	.50	.40	.20
38	Robin Yount	.25	.20	.10
39	Damon Berryhill	.15	.11	.06
40	Chris Sabo	.20	.15	.11
41	Mark McGwire	.70	.50	.30
42	Ozzie Smith	.25	.20	.10
43	Paul Molitor	.20	.15	.08
44	Andres Galarraga	.30	.25	.12
45	Dave Stewart	.15	.11	.06
46	Tom Browning	.15	.11	.06
47	Cal Ripken	.50	.40	.20
48	Orel Hershiser	.40	.30	.15

		MT	NR MT	EX
49	Dave Gallagher	.15	.11	.06
50	Walt Weiss	.20	.15	.08
51	Don Mattingly	1.50	1.25	.60
52	Tony Fernandez	.20	.15	.08
53	Rock Raines	.20	.15	.08
54	Jeff Reardon	.15	.11	.06
55	Kirk Gibson	.20	.15	.08
56	Jack Clark	.20	.15	.08
57	Danny Jackson	.15	.11	.06
58	Tony Gwynn	.60	.45	.25
59	Cecil Espy	.15	.11	.06
60	Jody Reed	.15	.11	.06

1989 Topps American Baseball

 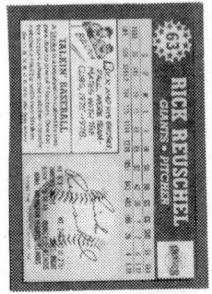

For the second consecutive year Topps released an 88-card set of baseball cards available in both the United States and the United Kingdom. The mini-sized cards (2-1/4" by 3") feature full-color photos on the card fronts. The cards are printed on white stock with a low gloss finish. The player action photo is outlined in red, white, and blue and framed in white. The card backs are printed horizontally and include a characterization cartoon along with biographical information and statistics. The cards are sold in packs of five cards with a stick of bubble gum.

		MT	NR MT	EX
Complete Set:		7.00	5.25	2.75
Common Player:		.08	.06	.03
1	Brady Anderson	.08	.06	.03
2	Harold Baines	.15	.11	.06
3	George Bell	.15	.11	.06
4	Wade Boggs	1.00	.70	.40
5	Barry Bonds	.20	.15	.08
6	Bobby Bonilla	.20	.15	.08
7	George Brett	.15	.11	.06
8	Hubie Brooks	.08	.06	.03
9	Tom Brunansky	.08	.06	.03
10	Jay Buhner	.08	.06	.03
11	Brett Butler	.08	.06	.03
12	Jose Canseco	1.25	.90	.50
13	Joe Carter	.15	.11	.06
14	Jack Clark	.08	.06	.03
15	Will Clark	.80	.60	.30
16	Roger Clemens	.30	.25	.12
17	Dave Cone	.08	.06	.03
18	Alvin Davis	.08	.06	.03
19	Eric Davis	.30	.25	.12
20	Glenn Davis	.08	.06	.03
21	Andre Dawson	.12	.09	.05
22	Bill Doran	.08	.06	.03
23	Dennis Eckersley	.08	.06	.03
24	Dwight Evans	.08	.06	.03
25	Tony Fernandez	.08	.06	.03
26	Carlton Fisk	.08	.06	.03
27	John Franco	.08	.06	.03
28	Andres Galarraga	.15	.11	.06
29	Ron Gant	.08	.06	.03
30	Kirk Gibson	.08	.06	.03
31	Doc Gooden	.25	.20	.10
32	Mike Greenwell	.50	.40	.20
33	Mark Gubicza	.08	.06	.03
34	Pedro Gurrero	.12	.09	.05
35	Ozzie Guillen	.08	.06	.03
36	Tony Gwynn	.15	.11	.06
37	Rickey Henderson	.15	.11	.06

		MT	NR MT	EX
38	Orel Hershiser	.15	.11	.06
39	Teddy Higuera	.08	.06	.03
40	Charlie Hough	.08	.06	.03
41	Kent Hrbek	.12	.09	.05
42	Bruce Hurst	.08	.06	.03
43	Bo Jackson	.50	.40	.20
44	Gregg Jefferies	.60	.45	.25
45	Ricky Jordan	.25	.20	.10
46	Wally Joyner	.15	.11	.06
47	Mark Langston	.12	.09	.05
48	Mike Marshall	.08	.06	.03
49	Don Mattingly	2.00	1.50	.80
50	Fred McGriff	.35	.25	.14
51	Mark McGwire	1.00	.70	.40
52	Kevin McReynolds	.15	.11	.06
53	Paul Molitor	.08	.06	.03
54	Jack Morris	.08	.06	.03
55	Dale Murphy	.15	.11	.06
56	Eddie Murray	.10	.08	.04
57	Pete O'Brien	.08	.06	.03
58	Rafael Palmeiro	.08	.06	.03
59	Gerald Perry	.08	.06	.03
60	Kirby Puckett	.30	.25	.12
61	Rock Raines	.08	.06	.03
62	Johnny Ray	.08	.06	.03
63	Rick Reuschel	.08	.06	.03
64	Cal Ripken	.15	.11	.06
65	Chris Sabo	.15	.11	.06
66	Juan Samuel	.08	.06	.03
67	Ryane Sandberg	.15	.11	.06
68	Benny Santiago	.15	.11	.06
69	Steve Sax	.08	.06	.03
70	Mike Schmidt	.20	.15	.11
71	Ruben Sierra	.20	.15	.11
72	Ozzie Smith	.15	.11	.06
73	Cory Snyder	.08	.06	.03
74	Dave Stewart	.08	.06	.03
75	Darryl Strawberry	.25	.20	.10
76	Greg Swindell	.15	.11	.06
77	Alan Trammell	.15	.11	.06
78	Fernando Valenzuela	.08	.06	.03
79	Andy Van Slyke	.20	.15	.08
80	Frank Viola	.20	.15	.08
81	Claudell Washington	.08	.06	.03
82	Walt Weiss	.08	.06	.03
83	Lou Whitaker	.08	.06	.03
84	Dave Winfield	.20	.15	.08
85	Mike Witt	.08	.06	.03
86	Gerald Young	.08	.06	.03
87	Robin Yount	.20	.15	.08
88	Checklist	.08	.06	.03

1989 Topps Big Baseball

Known by collectors as Topps "Big Baseball," the cards in this 330-card set measure 2-5/8" by 3-3/4" and are patterned after the 1956 Topps cards. The glossy card fronts are horizontally-designed and include two photos of each player, a posed head shot alongside an action photo. The backs include 1988 and career stats, but are dominated by a color cartoon featuring the player. The set was issued in three series of 110 cards each.

		MT	NR MT	EX
	Complete Set:	25.00	20.00	10.00
	Common Player:	.05	.04	.02
1	Orel Hershiser	.15	.11	.06
2	Harold Reynolds	.08	.06	.03
3	Jody Davis	.05	.04	.02
4	Greg Walker	.05	.04	.02
5	Barry Bonds	.08	.06	.03
6	Bret Saberhagen	.12	.09	.05
7	Johnny Ray	.05	.04	.02
8	Mike Fiore	.20	.15	.08
9	Juan Castillo	.05	.04	.02
10	Todd Burns	.05	.04	.02
11	Carmelo Martinez	.05	.04	.02
12	Geno Petralli	.05	.04	.02
13	Mel Hall	.05	.04	.02
14	Tom Browning	.08	.06	.03
15	Fred McGriff	.15	.11	.06
16	Kevin Elster	.05	.04	.02
17	Tim Leary	.05	.04	.02
18	Jim Rice	.05	.04	.02
19	Bret Barberie	.15	.11	.06
20	Jay Buhner	.05	.04	.02
21	Atlee Hammaker	.05	.04	.02
22	Lou Whitaker	.05	.04	.02
23	Paul Runge	.05	.04	.02
24	Carlton Fisk	.08	.06	.03
25	Jose Lind	.05	.04	.02
26	Mark Gubicza	.08	.06	.03
27	Billy Ripken	.05	.04	.02
28	Mike Pagliarulo	.05	.04	.02
29	Jim Deshaies	.05	.04	.02
30	Mark McLemore	.05	.04	.02
31	Scott Terry	.05	.04	.02
32	Franklin Stubbs	.05	.04	.02
33	Don August	.05	.04	.02
34	Mark McGwire	1.00	.70	.40
35	Eric Show	.05	.04	.02
36	Cecil Espy	.05	.04	.02
37	Ron Tingley	.05	.04	.02
38	Mickey Brantley	.05	.04	.02
39	Paul O'Neill	.05	.04	.02
40	Ed Sprague	.35	.25	.14
41	Len Dykstra	.05	.04	.02
42	Roger Clemens	.25	.20	.10
43	Ron Gant	.05	.04	.02
44	Dan Pasqua	.05	.04	.02
45	Jeff Robinson	.05	.04	.02
46	George Brett	.15	.11	.06
47	Bryn Smith	.05	.04	.02
48	Mike Marshall	.05	.04	.02
49	Doug Robbins	.15	.11	.06
50	Don Mattingly	1.50	1.25	.60
51	Mike Scott	.08	.06	.03
52	Steve Jeltz	.05	.04	.02
53	Dick Schofield	.05	.04	.02
54	Tom Brunansky	.08	.06	.03
55	Gary Sheffield	1.00	.70	.40
56	Dave Valle	.05	.04	.02
57	Carney Lansford	.08	.06	.03
58	Tony Gwynn	.15	.11	.06
59	Checklist	.05	.04	.02
60	Damon Berryhill	.05	.04	.02
61	Jack Morris	.05	.04	.02
62	Brett Butler	.05	.04	.02
63	Mickey Hatcher	.05	.04	.02
64	Bruce Sutter	.05	.04	.02
65	Robin Ventura	.80	.60	.30
66	Junior Ortiz	.05	.04	.02
67	Pat Tabler	.05	.04	.02
68	Greg Swindell	.08	.06	.03
69	Jeff Branson	.20	.15	.08
70	Manny Lee	.05	.04	.02
71	Dave Magadan	.05	.04	.02
72	Rich Gedman	.05	.04	.02
73	Rock Raines	.08	.06	.03
74	Mike Maddux	.05	.04	.02
75	Jim Presley	.05	.04	.02
76	Chuck Finley	.05	.04	.02
77	Jose Oquendo	.05	.04	.02
78	Rob Deer	.05	.04	.02
79	Jay Howell	.05	.04	.02
80	Terry Steinbach	.08	.06	.03
81	Eddie Whitson	.05	.04	.02
82	Ruben Sierra	.20	.15	.08
83	Bruce Benedict	.05	.04	.02
84	Fred Manrique	.05	.04	.02
85	John Smiley	.05	.04	.02
86	Mike Macfarlane	.05	.04	.02
87	Rene Gonzales	.05	.04	.02
88	Charles Hudson	.05	.04	.02
90	Les Straker	.05	.04	.02
91	Carmen Castillo	.05	.04	.02

		MT	NR MT	EX
92	Tracy Woodson	.05	.04	.02
93	Tino Martinez	.70	.50	.30
94	Herm Winningham	.05	.04	.02
95	Kelly Gruber	.05	.04	.02
96	Terry Leach	.05	.04	.02
97	Jody Reed	.05	.04	.02
98	Nelson Santovenia	.05	.04	.02
99	Tony Armas	.05	.04	.02
100	Greg Brock	.05	.04	.02
101	Dave Stewart	.05	.04	.02
102	Roberto Alomar	.08	.06	.03
103	Jim Sundberg	.05	.04	.02
104	Albert Hall	.05	.04	.02
105	Steve Lyons	.05	.04	.02
106	Sid Bream	.05	.04	.02
107	Danny Tartabull	.08	.06	.03
108	Rick Dempsey	.05	.04	.02
109	Rich Renteria	.05	.04	.02
110	Ozzie Smith	.08	.06	.03
111	Steve Sax	.08	.06	.03
112	Kelly Downs	.05	.04	.02
113	Larry Sheets	.05	.04	.02
114	Andy Benes	.50	.40	.20
115	Pete O'Brien	.05	.04	.02
116	Kevin McReynolds	.08	.06	.03
117	Juan Berenguer	.05	.04	.02
118	Billy Hatcher	.05	.04	.02
119	Rick Cerone	.05	.04	.02
120	Andre Dawson	.08	.06	.03
121	Storm Davis	.05	.04	.02
122	Devon White	.05	.04	.02
123	Alan Trammell	.08	.06	.03
124	Vince Coleman	.08	.06	.03
125	Al Leiter	.05	.04	.02
126	Dale Sveum	.05	.04	.02
127	Pete Incaviglia	.05	.04	.02
128	Dave Stieb	.08	.06	.03
129	Kevin Mitchell	.30	.25	.12
130	Dave Schmidt	.05	.04	.02
131	Gary Redus	.05	.04	.02
132	Ron Robinson	.05	.04	.02
133	Darnell Coles	.05	.04	.02
134	Benny Santiago	.08	.06	.03
135	John Farrell	.05	.04	.02
136	Willie Wilson	.05	.04	.02
137	Steve Bedrosian	.05	.04	.02
138	Don Slaught	.05	.04	.02
139	Darryl Strawberry	.25	.20	.10
140	Frank Viola	.10	.08	.04
141	Dave Silvestri	.20	.15	.08
142	Carlos Quintana	.05	.04	.02
143	Vance Law	.05	.04	.02
144	Dave Parker	.05	.04	.02
145	Tim Belcher	.05	.04	.02
146	Will Clark	.90	.70	.35
147	Mark Williamson	.05	.04	.02
148	Ozzie Guillen	.05	.04	.02
149	Kirk McCaskill	.05	.04	.02
150	Pat Sheridan	.05	.04	.02
151	Terry Pendleton	.05	.04	.02
152	Roberto Kelly	.05	.04	.02
153	Joey Meyer	.05	.04	.02
154	Mark Grant	.05	.04	.02
155	Joe Carter	.08	.06	.03
156	Steve Buechele	.05	.04	.02
157	Tony Fernandez	.08	.06	.03
158	Jeff Reed	.05	.04	.02
159	Bobby Bonilla	.08	.06	.03
160	Henry Cotto	.05	.04	.02
161	Kurt Stillwell	.05	.04	.02
162	Mickey Morandini	.25	.20	.10
163	Robby Thompson	.05	.04	.02
164	Rick Schu	.05	.04	.02
165	Stan Jefferson	.05	.04	.02
166	Ron Darling	.05	.04	.02
167	Kirby Puckett	.25	.20	.10
168	Bill Doran	.05	.04	.02
169	Dennis Lamp	.05	.04	.02
170	Ty Griffin	.60	.45	.25
171	Ron Hassey	.05	.04	.02
172	Dale Murphy	.08	.06	.03
173	Andres Galarraga	.08	.06	.03
174	Tim Flannery	.05	.04	.02
175	Cory Snyder	.05	.04	.02
176	Checklist	.05	.04	.02
177	Tommy Barrett	.05	.04	.02
178	Dan Petry	.05	.04	.02
179	Billy Masse	.20	.15	.08
180	Terry Kennedy	.05	.04	.02
181	Joe Orsulak	.05	.04	.02
182	Doyle Alexander	.05	.04	.02

	MT	NR MT	EX
183 Willie McGee	.05	.04	.02
184 Jim Gantner	.05	.04	.02
185 Keith Hernandez	.05	.04	.02
186 Greg Gagne	.05	.04	.02
187 Kevin Bass	.05	.04	.02
188 Mark Eichhorn	.05	.04	.02
189 Mark Grace	.25	.20	.10
190 Jose Canseco	1.00	.70	.40
191 Bobby Witt	.05	.04	.02
192 Rafael Santana	.05	.04	.02
193 Dwight Evans	.05	.04	.02
194 Greg Booker	.05	.04	.02
195 Brook Jacoby	.05	.04	.02
196 Rafael Belliard	.05	.04	.02
197 Candy Maldonado	.05	.04	.02
198 Mickey Tettleton	.08	.06	.03
199 Barry Larkin	.08	.06	.03
200 Frank White	.05	.04	.02
201 Wally Joyner	.15	.11	.06
202 Chet Lemon	.05	.04	.02
203 Joe Magrane	.05	.04	.02
204 Glenn Braggs	.05	.04	.02
205 Scott Fletcher	.05	.04	.02
206 Gary Ward	.05	.04	.02
207 Nelson Liriano	.05	.04	.02
208 Howard Johnson	.15	.11	.06
209 Kent Hrbek	.08	.06	.03
210 Ken Caminiti	.05	.04	.02
211 Mike Greenwell	.50	.40	.20
212 Ryne Sandberg	.25	.20	.10
213 Joe Slusarski	.25	.20	.10
214 Donnell Nixon	.05	.04	.02
215 Tim Wallach	.05	.04	.02
216 John Kruk	.05	.04	.02
217 Charles Nagy	.25	.20	.10
218 Alvin Davis	.08	.06	.03
219 Oswald Peraza	.05	.04	.02
220 Mike Schmidt	.30	.25	.12
221 Spike Owen	.05	.04	.02
222 Mike Smithson	.05	.04	.02
223 Dion James	.05	.04	.02
224 Ernie Whitt	.05	.04	.02
225 Mike Davis	.05	.04	.02
226 Gene Larkin	.05	.04	.02
227 Pat Combs	.50	.40	.20
228 Jack Howell	.05	.04	.02
229 Ron Oester	.05	.04	.02
230 Paul Gibson	.05	.04	.02
231 Mookie Wilson	.05	.04	.02
232 Glenn Hubbard	.05	.04	.02
233 Shawon Dunston	.05	.04	.02
234 Otis Nixon	.05	.04	.02
235 Melido Perez	.05	.04	.02
236 Jerry Browne	.05	.04	.02
237 Rick Rhoden	.05	.04	.02
238 Bo Jackson	.50	.40	.20
239 Randy Velarde	.05	.04	.02
240 Jack Clark	.05	.04	.02
241 Wade Boggs	.80	.60	.30
242 Lonnie Smith	.05	.04	.02
243 Mike Flanagan	.05	.04	.02
244 Willie Randolph	.05	.04	.02
245 Oddibe McDowell	.05	.04	.02
246 Ricky Jordan	.35	.25	.14
247 Greg Briley	.20	.15	.08
248 Rex Hudler	.05	.04	.02
249 Robin Yount	.20	.15	.08
250 Lance Parrish	.05	.04	.02
251 Chris Sabo	.20	.15	.08
252 Mike Henneman	.05	.04	.02
253 Gregg Jefferies	1.00	.70	.40
254 Curt Young	.05	.04	.02
255 Andy Van Slyke	.08	.06	.03
256 Rod Booker	.05	.04	.02
257 Rafael Palmeiro	.05	.04	.02
258 Jose Uribe	.05	.04	.02
259 Ellis Burks	.20	.15	.08
260 John Smoltz	.10	.08	.04
261 Tom Foley	.05	.04	.02
262 Lloyd Moseby	.05	.04	.02
263 Jim Poole	.15	.11	.06
264 Gary Gaetti	.08	.06	.03
265 Bob Dernier	.05	.04	.02
266 Harold Baines	.08	.06	.03
267 Tom Candiotti	.05	.04	.02
268 Rafael Ramirez	.05	.04	.02
269 Bob Boone	.05	.04	.02
270 Buddy Bell	.05	.04	.02
271 Rickey Henderson	.15	.11	.06
272 Willie Fraser	.05	.04	.02
273 Eric Davis	.25	.20	.10

	MT	NR MT	EX
274 Jeff Robinson	.05	.04	.02
275 Damaso Garcia	.05	.04	.02
276 Sid Fernandez	.05	.04	.02
277 Stan Javier	.05	.04	.02
278 Marty Barrett	.05	.04	.02
279 Gerald Perry	.05	.04	.02
280 Rob Ducey	.05	.04	.02
281 Mike Scioscia	.05	.04	.02
282 Randy Bush	.05	.04	.02
283 Tom Herr	.05	.04	.02
284 Glenn Wilson	.05	.04	.02
285 Pedro Guerrero	.10	.08	.04
286 Cal Ripken	.10	.08	.04
287 Randy Johnson	.15	.11	.06
288 Julio Franco	.08	.06	.03
289 Ivan Calderon	.05	.04	.02
290 Rich Yett	.05	.04	.02
291 Scott Servais	.20	.15	.08
292 Bill Pecota	.05	.04	.02
293 Ken Phelps	.05	.04	.02
294 Chili Davis	.05	.04	.02
295 Manny Trillo	.05	.04	.02
296 Mike Boddicker	.05	.04	.02
297 Geronimo Berroa	.05	.04	.02
298 Todd Stottlemyre	.05	.04	.02
299 Kirk Gibson	.05	.04	.02
300 Wally Backman	.05	.04	.02
301 Hubie Brooks	.05	.04	.02
302 Von Hayes	.05	.04	.02
303 Matt Nokes	.05	.04	.02
304 Doc Gooden	.20	.15	.08
305 Walt Weiss	.10	.08	.04
306 Mike LaValliere	.05	.04	.02
307 Cris Carpenter	.10	.08	.04
308 Ted Wood	.20	.15	.08
309 Jeff Russell	.05	.04	.02
310 Dave Gallagher	.05	.04	.02
311 Andy Allanson	.05	.04	.02
312 Craig Reynolds	.05	.04	.02
313 Kevin Seitzer	.08	.06	.03
314 Dave Winfield	.10	.08	.04
315 Andy McGaffigan	.05	.04	.02
316 Nick Esasky	.05	.04	.02
317 Jeff Blauser	.05	.04	.02
318 George Bell	.10	.08	.04
319 Eddie Murray	.10	.08	.04
320 Mark Davidson	.05	.04	.02
321 Juan Samuel	.05	.04	.02
322 Jim Abbott	.50	.40	.20
323 Kal Daniels	.05	.04	.02
324 Mike Brumley	.05	.04	.02
325 Gary Carter	.05	.04	.02
326 Dave Henderson	.05	.04	.02
327 Checklist	.05	.04	.02
328 Garry Templeton	.05	.04	.02
329 Pat Perry	.05	.04	.02
330 Paul Molitor	.08	.06	.03

1989 Topps Box Panels

GEORGE BRETT

Continuing its practice of printing baseball cards on the bottom panels of its wax pack boxes, Topps in 1989 issued a special 16-card set, printing four cards on each of four different box-bottom panels. The cards are identical in design to the regular 1989 Topps cards. They are designated by letter (from A through P) rather than by number.

		MT	NR MT	EX
	Complete Panel Set:	5.00	3.75	2.00
	Complete Singles Set:	2.00	1.50	.80
	Common Panel:	.50	.40	.20
	Common Single Player:	.08	.06	.03
	Panel	.50	.40	.20
A	George Brett	.25	.20	.10
B	Bill Buckner	.08	.06	.03
C	Darrell Evans	.08	.06	.03
D	Rich Gossage	.08	.06	.03
	Panel	1.00	.70	.40
E	Greg Gross	.08	.06	.03
F	Rickey Henderson	.30	.25	.12
G	Keith Hernandez	.15	.11	.06
H	Tom Lasorda	.08	.06	.03
	Panel	2.50	2.00	1.00
I	Jim Rice	.15	.11	.06
J	Cal Ripken	.35	.25	.14
K	Nolan Ryan	.50	.40	.20
L	Mike Schmidt	.25	.20	.10
	Panel	1.00	.70	.40
M	Bruce Sutter	.15	.11	.06
N	Don Sutton	.10	.08	.04
O	Kent Tekulve	.08	.06	.03
P	Dave Winfield	.25	.20	.10

1989 Topps Major League Debut

This 150-card set highlights the debut date of 1989 Major League rookies. Two checklist cards are also included in this boxed set. The checklist cards list the players in order of debut date, but the cards are numbered alphabetically. The card fronts resemble the 1990 Topps cards in style. A debut banner appears in an upper corner of the card. The flip sides are horizontal and are printed in black on yellow stock. An overview of the player's first game is provided on the card back. The set is packaged in an attractive red, blue, green and yellow collectors box. The set was available through select hobby dealers.

		MT	NR MT	EX
	Complete Set:	15.00	11.00	6.00
	Common Player:	.08	.06	.03
1	Jim Abbott	.30	.25	.12
2	Beau Allred	.15	.11	.06
3	Wilson Alvarez	.25	.20	.10
4	Kent Anderson	.08	.06	.03
5	Eric Anthony	.40	.30	.15
6	Kevin Appier	.25	.20	.10
7	Larry Arndt	.08	.06	.03
8	John Barfield	.08	.06	.03
9	Billy Bates	.08	.06	.03
10	Kevin Batiste	.10	.08	.04
11	Blaine Beatty	.20	.15	.08
12	Stan Belinda	.15	.11	.06
13	Juan Bell	.15	.11	.06
14	Joey Belle	.20	.15	.08
15	Andy Benes	.30	.25	.12
16	Mike Benjamin	.20	.15	.08
17	Geronimo Berroa	.08	.06	.03
18	Mike Blowers	.10	.08	.04
19	Brian Brady	.08	.06	.03

		MT	NR MT	EX
20	Francisco Cabrera	.25	.20	.10
21	George Canale	.08	.06	.03
22	Jose Cano	.08	.06	.03
23	Steve Carter	.10	.08	.04
24	Pat Combs	.30	.25	.12
25	Scott Coolbaugh	.15	.11	.06
26	Steve Cummings	.10	.08	.04
27	Pete Dalena	.08	.06	.03
28	Jeff Datz	.08	.06	.03
29	Bobby Davidson	.08	.06	.03
30	Drew Denson	.08	.06	.03
31	Gary DiSarcina	.20	.15	.08
32	Brian DuBois	.15	.11	.06
33	Mike Dyer	.10	.08	.04
34	Wayne Edwards	.10	.08	.04
35	Junior Felix	.30	.25	.12
36	Mike Fetters	.15	.11	.06
37	Steve Finley	.15	.11	.06
38	Darren Fletcher	.15	.11	.06
39	LaVel Freeman	.08	.06	.03
40	Steve Frey	.10	.08	.04
41	Mark Gardner	.20	.15	.08
42	Joe Girardi	.20	.15	.08
43	Juan Gonzalez	1.00	.70	.40
44	Goose Gozzo	.15	.11	.06
45	Tommy Greene	.15	.11	.06
46	Ken Griffey,Jr.	2.00	1.50	.80
47	Jason Grimsley	.20	.15	.08
48	Marquis Grissom	.40	.30	.15
49	Mark Guthrie	.10	.08	.04
50	Chip Hale	.08	.06	.03
51	John Hardy	.08	.06	.03
52	Gene Harris	.10	.08	.04
53	Mike Hartley	.10	.08	.04
54	Scott Hemond	.10	.08	.04
55	Xavier Hernandez	.10	.08	.04
56	Eric Hetzel	.15	.11	.06
57	Greg Hibbard	.25	.20	.10
58	Mark Higgins	.08	.06	.03
59	Glenallen Hill	.20	.15	.08
60	Chris Hoiles	.30	.25	.12
61	Shawn Holman	.10	.08	.04
62	Dann Howitt	.10	.08	.04
63	Mike Huff	.10	.08	.04
64	Terry Jorgenson	.10	.08	.04
65	Dave Justice	1.50	1.25	.60
66	Jeff King	.20	.15	.08
67	Matt Kinzer	.08	.06	.03
68	Joe Kraemer	.08	.06	.03
69	Marcus Lawton	.08	.06	.03
70	Derek Lilliquist	.15	.11	.06
71	Scott Little	.08	.06	.03
72	Greg Litton	.15	.11	.06
73	Rick Lueken	.10	.08	.04
74	Julio Machado	.15	.11	.06
75	Tom Magrann	.08	.06	.03
76	Kelly Mann	.20	.15	.08
77	Randy McCament	.08	.06	.03
78	Ben McDonald	1.00	.70	.40
79	Chuck McElroy	.20	.15	.08
80	Jeff McKnight	.10	.08	.04
81	Kent Mercker	.25	.20	.10
82	Matt Merullo	.08	.06	.03
83	Hensley Meulens	.15	.11	.06
84	Kevin Mmahat	.08	.06	.03
85	Mike Munoz	.08	.06	.03
86	Dan Murphy	.08	.06	.03
87	Jaime Navarro	.20	.15	.08
88	Randy Nosek	.10	.08	.04
89	John Olerud	1.25	.90	.50
90	Steve Olin	.10	.08	.04
91	Joe Oliver	.20	.15	.08
92	Francisco Oliveras	.10	.08	.04
93	Greg Olson	.15	.11	.06
94	John Orton	.10	.08	.04
95	Dean Palmer	.20	.15	.08
96	Ramon Pena	.08	.06	.03
97	Jeff Peterek	.08	.06	.03
98	Marty Pevey	.08	.06	.03
99	Rusty Richards	.08	.06	.03
100	Jeff Richardson	.08	.06	.03
101	Rob Richie	.08	.06	.03
102	Kevin Ritz	.10	.08	.04
103	Rosario Rodriguez	.25	.20	.10
104	Mike Roesler	.10	.08	.04
105	Kenny Rogers	.15	.11	.06
106	Bobby Rose	.20	.15	.08
107	Alex Sanchez	.15	.11	.06
108	Deion Sanders	.25	.20	.10
109	Jeff Schaefer	.08	.06	.03
110	Jeff Schulz	.10	.08	.04

		MT	NR MT	EX
111	Mike Schwabe	.10	.08	.04
112	Dick Scott	.08	.06	.03
113	Scott Scudder	.25	.20	.10
114	Rudy Seanez	.15	.11	.06
115	Joe Skalski	.08	.06	.03
116	Dwight Smith	.20	.15	.08
117	Greg Smith	.15	.11	.06
118	Mike Smith	.10	.08	.04
119	Paul Sorrento	.15	.11	.06
120	Sammy Sosa	.50	.40	.20
121	Billy Spiers	.15	.11	.06
122	Mike Stanton	.20	.15	.08
123	Phil Stephenson	.08	.06	.03
124	Doug Strange	.08	.06	.03
125	Russ Swan	.10	.08	.04
126	Kevin Tapani	.35	.25	.14
127	Stu Tate	.08	.06	.03
128	Greg Vaughn	.40	.30	.15
129	Robin Ventura	.25	.20	.10
130	Randy Veres	.08	.06	.03
131	Jose Vizcaino	.15	.11	.06
132	Omar Vizquel	.10	.08	.04
133	Larry Walker	.40	.30	.15
134	Jerome Walton	.50	.40	.20
135	Gary Wayne	.10	.08	.04
136	Lenny Webster	.10	.08	.04
137	Mickey Weston	.10	.08	.04
138	Jeff Wetherby	.08	.06	.03
139	John Wetteland	.25	.20	.10
140	Ed Whited	.08	.06	.03
141	Wally Whitehurst	.10	.08	.04
142	Kevin Wickander	.15	.11	.06
143	Dean Wilkins	.10	.08	.04
144	Dana Williams	.10	.08	.04
145	Paul Wilmet	.08	.06	.03
146	Craig Wilson	.15	.11	.06
147	Matt Winters	.08	.06	.03
148	Eric Yelding	.25	.20	.10
149	Clint Zavaras	.15	.11	.06
150	Todd Zeile	.50	.40	.20
——	Checklist (1 of 2)	.08	.06	.03
——	Checklist (2 of 2)	.08	.06	.03

1989 Topps
Mini League Leaders

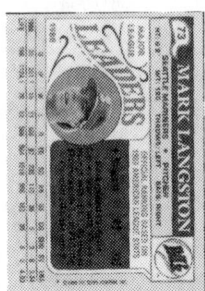

This 77-card set from Topps features baseball's statistical leaders from the 1988 season, and is referred to as a "mini" set because of the cards' small (2-1/8" by 3") size. The glossy cards feature action photos that have a soft focus on all edges. The player's team and name appear along the bottom of the card. The back features a head-shot of the player along with his 1988 season ranking and stats.

		MT	NR MT	EX
Complete Set:		7.00	5.25	2.75
Common Player:		.09	.07	.04
1	Dale Murphy	.35	.25	.14
2	Gerald Perry	.09	.07	.04
3	Andre Dawson	.20	.15	.08
4	Greg Maddux	.20	.15	.08
5	Rafael Palmeiro	.15	.11	.06
6	Tom Browning	.12	.09	.05
7	Kal Daniels	.15	.11	.06

		MT	NR MT	EX
8	Eric Davis	.60	.45	.25
9	John Franco	.09	.07	.04
10	Danny Jackson	.09	.07	.04
11	Barry Larkin	.15	.11	.06
12	Jose Rijo	.12	.09	.05
13	Chris Sabo	.20	.15	.08
14	Mike Scott	.09	.07	.04
15	Nolan Ryan	.50	.40	.20
16	Gerald Young	.09	.07	.04
17	Kirk Gibson	.12	.09	.05
18	Orel Hershiser	.25	.20	.10
19	Steve Sax	.12	.09	.05
20	John Tudor	.09	.07	.04
21	Hubie Brooks	.09	.07	.04
22	Andres Galarraga	.15	.11	.06
23	Otis Nixon	.09	.07	.04
24	Dave Cone	.15	.11	.06
25	Sid Fernandez	.12	.09	.05
26	Doc Gooden	.30	.25	.12
27	Kevin McReynolds	.20	.15	.08
28	Darryl Strawberry	.35	.25	.14
29	Juan Samuel	.09	.07	.04
30	Bobby Bonilla	.12	.09	.05
31	Sid Bream	.09	.07	.04
32	Andy Van Slyke	.12	.09	.05
33	Vince Coleman	.12	.09	.05
34	Jose DeLeon	.09	.07	.04
35	Joe Magrane	.12	.09	.05
36	Ozzie Smith	.12	.09	.05
37	Todd Worrell	.09	.07	.04
38	Tony Gwynn	.30	.25	.12
39	Brett Butler	.12	.09	.05
40	Will Clark	.80	.60	.30
41	Jim Gott	.09	.07	.04
42	Rick Reuschel	.12	.09	.05
43	Checklist	.09	.07	.04
44	Eddie Murray	.20	.15	.08
45	Wade Boggs	.80	.60	.30
46	Roger Clemens	.30	.25	.12
47	Dwight Evans	.12	.09	.05
48	Mike Greenwell	.70	.50	.30
49	Bruce Hurst	.12	.09	.05
50	Johnny Ray	.09	.07	.04
51	Doug Jones	.09	.07	.04
52	Greg Swindell	.15	.11	.06
53	Gary Pettis	.09	.07	.04
54	George Brett	.15	.11	.06
55	Mark Gubicza	.15	.11	.06
56	Willie Wilson	.09	.07	.04
57	Teddy Higuera	.12	.09	.05
58	Paul Molitor	.15	.11	.06
59	Robin Yount	.25	.20	.10
60	Allan Anderson	.09	.07	.04
61	Gary Gaetti	.12	.09	.04
62	Kirby Puckett	.40	.30	.15
63	Jeff Reardon	.09	.07	.04
64	Frank Viola	.12	.09	.05
65	Jack Clark	.12	.09	.05
66	Rickey Henderson	.25	.20	.10
67	Dave Winfield	.15	.11	.06
68	Jose Canseco	.80	.60	.30
69	Dennis Eckersley	.12	.09	.05
70	Mark McGwire	.80	.60	.30
71	Dave Stewart	.12	.09	.05
72	Alvin Davis	.12	.09	.05
73	Mark Langston	.12	.09	.05
74	Harold Reynolds	.12	.09	.05
75	George Bell	.15	.11	.06
76	Tony Fernandez	.15	.11	.06
77	Fred McGriff	.25	.20	.10

1990 Topps

The 1990 Topps set again included 792 cards, and sported a newly-designed front that featured six different color schemes. The set led off with a special four-card salute to Nolan Ryan, and other specials, including All-Stars, Number 1 Draft Picks, Record Breakers, manager cards, rookies, and "Turn Back the Clock" cards. The set also includes a special card commemorating A. Bartlett Giamatti, the late Baseball Commissioner. The backs are printed in black on a chartreuse background with the card number in the upper left corner. The set features 725

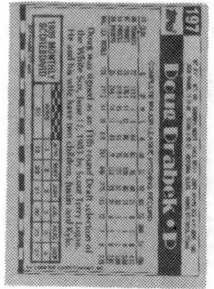

different individual player cards, the most ever, including 138 players making their first appearance in a regular Topps set.

		MT	NR MT	EX
	Complete Set:	25.00	20.00	10.00
	Common Player:	.03	.02	.01
1	Nolan Ryan	.35	.25	.14
2	Nolan Ryan (The Mets Years)	.20	.15	.08
3	Nolan Ryan (The Angels Years)	.20	.15	.08
4	Nolan Ryan (The Astros Years)	.20	.15	.08
5	Nolan Ryan (The Rangers)	.20	.15	.08
6	1989 Record Breaker (Vince Coleman)	.10	.08	.04
7	1989 Record Breaker (Rickey Henderson)	.20	.15	.08
8	1989 Record Breaker (Cal Ripken)	.15	.11	.06
9	Eric Plunk	.03	.02	.01
10	Barry Larkin	.15	.11	.06
11	Paul Gibson	.04	.03	.02
12	Joe Girardi(FC)	.15	.11	.06
13	Mark Williamson	.03	.02	.01
14	*Mike Fetters*(FC)	.20	.15	.08
15	Teddy Higuera	.06	.05	.02
16	*Kent Anderson*	.10	.08	.04
17	Kelly Downs	.05	.04	.02
18	Carlos Quintana	.09	.07	.04
19	Al Newman	.03	.02	.01
20	Mark Gubicza	.12	.09	.05
21	Jeff Torborg	.03	.02	.01
22	Bruce Ruffin	.03	.02	.01
23	Randy Velarde	.07	.05	.03
24	Joe Hesketh	.03	.02	.01
25	Willie Randolph	.08	.06	.03
26	Don Slaught	.03	.02	.01
27	Rick Leach	.03	.02	.01
28	Duane Ward	.04	.03	.02
29	John Cangelosi	.03	.02	.01
30	David Cone	.10	.08	.04
31	Henry Cotto	.03	.02	.01
32	John Farrell	.05	.04	.02
33	Greg Walker	.05	.04	.02
34	*Tony Fossas*(FC)	.07	.05	.03
35	Benito Santiago	.12	.09	.05
36	John Costello	.04	.03	.02
37	Domingo Ramos	.03	.02	.01
38	Wes Gardner	.04	.03	.02
39	Curt Ford	.04	.03	.02
40	Jay Howell	.06	.05	.02
41	Matt Williams	.15	.11	.06
42	Jeff Robinson	.05	.04	.02
43	Dante Bichette	.07	.05	.03
44	#1 Draft Pick *(Roger Salkeld)*(FC)	.30	.25	.12
45	Dave Parker	.09	.07	.04
46	Rob Dibble	.07	.05	.03
47	Brian Harper	.04	.03	.02
48	Zane Smith	.03	.02	.01
49	Tom Lawless	.03	.02	.01
50	Glenn Davis	.08	.06	.03
51	Doug Rader	.03	.02	.01
52	*Jack Daugherty*(FC)	.20	.15	.08
53	Mike LaCoss	.04	.03	.02
54	Joel Skinner	.04	.03	.02
55	Darrell Evans	.05	.04	.02
56	Franklin Stubbs	.04	.03	.02
57	*Greg Vaughn*(FC)	.60	.45	.25
58	Keith Miller	.10	.08	.04
59	Ted Power	.03	.02	.01
60	George Brett	.15	.11	.06
61	*Deion Sanders*	.40	.30	.15

		MT	NR MT	EX
62	Ramon Martinez	.10	.08	.04
63	Mike Pagliarulo	.04	.03	.02
64	Danny Darwin	.03	.02	.01
65	Devon White	.07	.05	.03
66	*Greg Litton*(FC)	.25	.20	.10
67	Scott Sanderson	.04	.03	.02
68	Dave Henderson	.06	.05	.02
69	Todd Frohwirth	.03	.02	.01
70	Mike Greenwell	.30	.25	.12
71	Allan Anderson	.05	.04	.02
72	*Jeff Huson*(FC)	.25	.20	.10
73	Bob Milacki	.05	.04	.02
74	#1 Draft Pick *(Jeff Jackson)*(FC)	.30	.25	.12
75	Doug Jones	.05	.04	.02
76	Dave Valle	.03	.02	.01
77	Dave Bergman	.03	.02	.01
78	Mike Flanagan	.04	.03	.02
79	Ron Kittle	.05	.04	.02
80	Jeff Russell	.05	.04	.02
81	Bob Rodgers	.03	.02	.01
82	Scott Terry	.04	.03	.02
83	Hensley Meulens	.30	.25	.12
84	Ray Searage	.03	.02	.01
85	Juan Samuel	.05	.04	.02
86	Paul Kilgus	.03	.02	.01
87	*Rick Luecken*(FC)	.15	.11	.06
88	Glenn Braggs	.05	.04	.02
89	*Clint Zavaras*(FC)	.15	.11	.06
90	Jack Clark	.06	.05	.02
91	*Steve Frey*(FC)	.20	.15	.08
92	Mike Stanley	.03	.02	.01
93	Shawn Hillegas	.03	.02	.01
94	Herm Winningham	.03	.02	.01
95	Todd Worrell	.05	.04	.02
96	Jody Reed	.04	.03	.02
97	Curt Schilling(FC)	.10	.08	.04
98	Jose Gonzalez(FC)	.10	.08	.04
99	*Rich Monteleone*(FC)	.15	.11	.06
100	Will Clark	.70	.50	.30
101	Shane Rawley	.04	.03	.02
102	Stan Javier	.04	.03	.02
103	Marvin Freeman	.09	.07	.04
104	Bob Knepper	.03	.02	.01
105	Randy Myers	.05	.04	.02
106	Charlie O'Brien	.03	.02	.01
107	Fred Lynn	.05	.04	.02
108	Rod Nichols	.04	.03	.02
109	Roberto Kelly	.08	.06	.03
110	Tommy Helms	.03	.02	.01
111	Ed Whited	.20	.15	.08
112	Glenn Wilson	.03	.02	.01
113	Manny Lee	.03	.02	.01
114	Mike Bielecki	.05	.04	.02
115	Tony Pena	.06	.05	.02
116	Floyd Bannister	.04	.03	.02
117	Mike Sharperson(FC)	.09	.07	.04
118	Erik Hanson	.10	.08	.04
119	Billy Hatcher	.04	.03	.02
120	John Franco	.05	.04	.02
121	Robin Ventura	.35	.25	.14
122	Shawn Abner	.03	.02	.01
123	Rich Gedman	.04	.03	.02
124	Dave Dravecky	.04	.03	.02
125	Kent Hrbek	.07	.05	.03
126	Randy Kramer	.03	.02	.01
127	Mike Devereaux	.06	.05	.02
128	Checklist 1-132	.03	.02	.01
129	Ron Jones	.10	.08	.04
130	Bert Blyleven	.05	.04	.02
131	Matt Nokes	.06	.05	.02
132	Lance Blankenship(FC)	.10	.08	.04
133	Ricky Horton	.03	.02	.01
134	#1 Draft Pick *(Earl Cunningham)*(FC)	.50	.40	.20
135	Dave Magadan	.05	.04	.02
136	Kevin Brown	.06	.05	.02
137	*Marty Pevey*(FC)	.15	.11	.06
138	Al Leiter	.04	.03	.02
139	Greg Brock	.04	.03	.02
140	Andre Dawson	.12	.09	.05
141	John Hart	.05	.04	.02
142	*Jeff Wetherby*(FC)	.20	.15	.08
143	Rafael Belliard	.03	.02	.01
144	Bud Black	.03	.02	.01
145	Terry Steinbach	.07	.05	.03
146	*Rob Richie*(FC)	.20	.15	.08
147	Chuck Finley	.04	.03	.02
148	Edgar Martinez(FC)	.09	.07	.04
149	Steve Farr	.04	.03	.02
150	Kirk Gibson	.09	.07	.04
151	Rick Mahler	.03	.02	.01

		MT	NR MT	EX			MT	NR MT	EX
152	Lonnie Smith	.05	.04	.02	243	Barry Jones	.03	.02	.01
153	Randy Milligan	.05	.04	.02	244	Bill Schroeder	.03	.02	.01
154	Mike Maddux	.05	.04	.02	245	Roger Clemens	.25	.20	.10
155	Ellis Burks	.25	.20	.10	246	Jim Eisenreich	.03	.02	.01
156	Ken Patterson	.04	.03	.02	247	Jerry Reed	.03	.02	.01
157	Craig Biggio	.15	.11	.06	248	Dave Anderson	.03	.02	.01
158	Craig Lefferts	.04	.03	.02	249	*Mike Smith*(FC)	.20	.15	.08
159	Mike Felder	.03	.02	.01	250	Jose Canseco	.70	.50	.30
160	Dave Righetti	.06	.05	.02	251	Jeff Blauser	.05	.04	.02
161	Harold Reynolds	.06	.05	.02	252	Otis Nixon	.03	.02	.01
162	*Todd Zeile*(FC)	.80	.60	.30	253	Mark Portugal	.03	.02	.01
163	Phil Bradley	.05	.04	.02	254	Francisco Cabrera	.25	.20	.10
164	#1 Draft Pick *(Jeff Juden)*(FC)	.35	.25	.14	255	Bobby Thigpen	.07	.05	.03
165	Walt Weiss	.08	.06	.03	256	Marvell Wynne	.03	.02	.01
166	Bobby Witt	.04	.03	.02	257	Jose DeLeon	.07	.05	.03
167	*Kevin Appier*(FC)	.35	.25	.14	258	Barry Lyons	.03	.02	.01
168	Jose Lind	.04	.03	.02	259	Lance McCullers	.05	.04	.02
169	Richard Dotson	.03	.02	.01	260	Eric Davis	.30	.25	.12
170	George Bell	.12	.09	.05	261	Whitey Herzog	.03	.02	.01
171	Russ Nixon	.03	.02	.01	262	Checklist 133-264	.03	.02	.01
172	Tom Lampkin(FC)	.10	.08	.04	263	*Mel Stottlemyre, Jr.*(FC)	.25	.20	.10
173	Tim Belcher	.12	.09	.05	264	Bryan Clutterbuck	.03	.02	.01
174	Jeff Kunkel	.03	.02	.01	265	Pete O'Brien	.06	.05	.02
175	Mike Moore	.07	.05	.02	266	German Gonzalez	.04	.03	.02
176	Luis Quinones	.03	.02	.01	267	Mark Davidson	.03	.02	.01
177	Mike Henneman	.05	.04	.02	268	Rob Murphy	.03	.02	.01
178	Chris James	.06	.05	.02	269	Dickie Thon	.03	.02	.01
179	Brian Holton	.04	.03	.02	270	Dave Stewart	.08	.06	.03
180	Rock Raines	.10	.08	.04	271	Chet Lemon	.05	.04	.02
181	Juan Agosto	.03	.02	.01	272	Bryan Harvey	.04	.03	.02
182	Mookie Wilson	.05	.04	.02	273	Bobby Bonilla	.15	.11	.06
183	Steve Lake	.03	.02	.01	274	*Goose Gozzo*(FC)	.20	.15	.08
184	Danny Cox	.04	.03	.02	275	Mickey Tettleton	.07	.05	.03
185	Ruben Sierra	.20	.15	.08	276	Gary Thurman	.03	.02	.01
186	Dave LaPoint	.03	.02	.01	277	*Lenny Harris*(FC)	.12	.09	.05
187	*Rick Wrona*(FC)	.12	.09	.05	278	Pascual Perez	.04	.03	.02
188	Mike Smithson	.03	.02	.01	279	Steve Buechele	.04	.03	.02
189	Dick Schofield	.04	.03	.02	280	Lou Whitaker	.07	.05	.03
190	Rick Reuschel	.06	.05	.02	281	Kevin Bass	.05	.04	.02
191	Pat Borders	.08	.06	.03	282	Derek Lilliquist	.10	.08	.04
192	Don August	.04	.03	.02	283	*Joey Belle*(FC)	.35	.25	.14
193	Andy Benes	.35	.25	.14	284	*Mark Gardner*(FC)	.30	.25	.12
194	Glenallen Hill(FC)	.25	.20	.10	285	Willie McGee	.06	.05	.02
195	Tim Burke	.05	.04	.02	286	Lee Guetterman	.03	.02	.01
196	Gerald Young	.04	.03	.02	287	Vance Law	.03	.02	.01
197	Doug Drabek	.07	.05	.03	288	Greg Briley	.15	.11	.06
198	Mike Marshall	.06	.05	.02	289	Norm Charlton	.10	.08	.04
199	*Sergio Valdez*(FC)	.20	.15	.08	290	Robin Yount	.20	.15	.08
200	Don Mattingly	.50	.40	.20	291	Dave Johnson	.03	.02	.01
201	Cito Gaston	.03	.02	.01	292	Jim Gott	.04	.03	.02
202	Mike Macfarlane	.03	.02	.01	293	Mike Gallego	.04	.03	.02
203	*Mike Roesler*(FC)	.15	.11	.06	294	Craig McMurtry	.03	.02	.01
204	Bob Dernier	.03	.02	.01	295	Fred McGriff	.25	.20	.10
205	Mark Davis	.09	.07	.04	296	Jeff Ballard	.07	.05	.03
206	Nick Esasky	.07	.05	.02	297	Tom Herr	.06	.05	.02
207	Bob Ojeda	.04	.03	.02	298	Danny Gladden	.05	.04	.02
208	Brook Jacoby	.04	.03	.02	299	Adam Peterson(FC)	.09	.07	.04
209	Greg Mathews	.04	.03	.02	300	Bo Jackson	.50	.40	.20
210	Ryne Sandberg	.20	.15	.08	301	Don Aase	.03	.02	.01
211	John Cerutti	.04	.03	.02	302	*Marcus Lawton*(FC)	.08	.06	.03
212	Joe Orsulak	.03	.02	.01	303	Rick Cerone	.03	.02	.01
213	Scott Bankhead	.05	.04	.02	304	Marty Clary(FC)	.08	.06	.03
214	Terry Francona	.03	.02	.01	305	Eddie Murray	.15	.11	.06
215	Kirk McCaskill	.04	.03	.02	306	Tom Niedenfuer	.03	.02	.01
216	Ricky Jordan	.20	.15	.08	307	Bip Roberts	.08	.06	.03
217	Don Robinson	.04	.03	.02	308	Jose Guzman	.05	.04	.02
218	Wally Backman	.04	.03	.02	309	*Eric Yelding*(FC)	.20	.15	.08
219	Donn Pall	.03	.02	.01	310	Steve Bedrosian	.05	.04	.02
220	Barry Bonds	.10	.08	.04	311	Dwight Smith	.90	.70	.35
221	*Gary Mielke*(FC)	.20	.15	.08	312	Dan Quisenberry	.05	.04	.02
222	Kurt Stillwell	.05	.04	.02	313	Gus Polidor	.03	.02	.01
223	Tommy Gregg	.06	.05	.02	314	#1 Draft Pick *(Donald Harris)*(FC)	.30	.25	.12
224	*Delino DeShields*(FC)	.80	.60	.30	315	Bruce Hurst	.06	.05	.02
225	Jim Deshaies	.05	.04	.02	316	Carney Lansford	.06	.05	.02
226	Mickey Hatcher	.03	.02	.01	317	*Mark Guthrie*(FC)	.20	.15	.08
227	*Kevin Tapani*(FC)	.30	.25	.12	318	Wallace Johnson	.03	.02	.01
228	Dave Martinez	.03	.02	.01	319	Dion James	.04	.03	.02
229	David Wells	.03	.02	.01	320	Dave Steib	.07	.05	.03
230	Keith Hernandez	.07	.05	.03	321	Joe Morgan	.03	.02	.01
231	Jack McKeon	.03	.02	.01	322	Junior Ortiz	.03	.02	.01
232	Darnell Coles	.04	.03	.02	323	Willie Wilson	.04	.03	.02
233	Ken Hill	.10	.08	.06	324	Pete Harnisch(FC)	.10	.08	.04
234	Mariano Duncan	.05	.04	.02	325	Robby Thompson	.06	.05	.02
235	Jeff Reardon	.04	.03	.02	326	*Tom McCarthy*(FC)	.10	.08	.04
236	Hal Morris(FC)	.10	.08	.06	327	Ken Williams	.03	.02	.01
237	*Kevin Ritz*(FC)	.20	.15	.08	328	Curt Young	.03	.02	.01
238	Felix Jose(FC)	.10	.08	.04	329	Oddibe McDowell	.06	.05	.02
239	Eric Show	.04	.03	.02	330	Ron Darling	.09	.07	.04
240	Mark Grace	.40	.30	.15	331	*Juan Gonzalez*(FC)	1.50	1.25	.60
241	Mike Krukow	.04	.03	.02	332	Paul O'Neill	.07	.05	.03
242	Fred Manrique	.03	.02	.01	333	Bill Wegman	.03	.02	.01

		MT	NR MT	EX			MT	NR MT	EX
334	Johnny Ray	.05	.04	.02	424	Jerry Reuss	.05	.04	.02
335	Andy Hawkins	.05	.04	.02	425	Bill Landrum	.05	.04	.02
336	Ken Griffey, Jr.	2.50	2.00	1.00	426	Jeff Hamilton	.05	.04	.02
337	Lloyd McClendon	.06	.05	.02	427	Carmem Castillo	.03	.02	.01
338	Dennis Lamp	.03	.02	.01	428	*Steve Davis*(FC)	.12	.09	.05
339	Dave Clark	.04	.03	.02	429	Tom Kelly	.03	.02	.01
340	Fernando Valenzuela	.06	.05	.02	430	Pete Incaviglia	.06	.05	.02
341	Tom Foley	.03	.02	.01	431	Randy Johnson	.10	.08	.04
342	Alex Trevino	.03	.02	.01	432	Damaso Garcia	.03	.02	.01
343	Frank Tanana	.04	.03	.02	433	*Steve Olin*(FC)	.12	.08	.04
344	*George Canale*(FC)	.25	.20	.10	434	Mark Carreon(FC)	.09	.07	.04
345	Harold Baines	.09	.07	.04	435	Kevin Seitzer	.09	.07	.04
346	Jim Presley	.04	.03	.02	436	Mel Hall	.05	.04	.02
347	Junior Felix	.40	.30	.15	437	Les Lancaster	.05	.04	.02
348	*Gary Wayne*(FC)	.12	.09	.05	438	Greg Myers(FC)	.10	.08	.04
349	*Steve Finley*(FC)	.30	.25	.12	439	Jeff Parrett	.06	.05	.02
350	Bret Saberhagen	.10	.08	.04	440	Alan Trammell	.09	.07	.04
351	Roger Craig	.03	.02	.01	441	Bob Kipper	.03	.02	.01
352	Bryn Smith	.05	.04	.02	442	Jerry Browne	.07	.05	.02
353	Sandy Alomar	.25	.20	.10	443	Cris Carpenter	.09	.07	.04
354	*Stan Belinda*(FC)	.20	.15	.08	444	*Kyle Abbott* (Number 1 Daft Pick)(FC)			
355	Marty Barrett	.05	.04	.02			.30	.25	.12
356	Randy Ready	.03	.02	.01	445	Danny Jackson	.05	.04	.02
357	Dave West	.20	.15	.08	446	Dan Pasqua	.05	.04	.02
358	Andres Thomas	.04	.03	.02	447	Atlee Hammaker	.03	.02	.01
359	Jimmy Jones	.03	.02	.01	448	Greg Gagne	.04	.03	.02
360	Paul Molitor	.09	.07	.04	449	Dennis Rasmussen	.04	.03	.02
361	*Randy McCament*(FC)	.25	.20	.10	450	Rickey Henderson	.20	.15	.08
362	Damon Berryhill	.06	.05	.02	451	Mark Lemke(FC)	.10	.08	.04
363	Dan Petry	.03	.02	.01	452	Luis de los Santos(FC)	.10	.08	.04
364	Rolando Roomes(FC)	.15	.11	.06	453	Jody Davis	.03	.02	.01
365	Ozzie Guillen	.05	.04	.02	454	Jeff King(FC)	.15	.11	.06
366	Mike Heath	.03	.02	.01	455	Jeffrey Leonard	.06	.05	.02
367	Mike Morgan	.03	.02	.01	456	Chris Gwynn(FC)	.09	.07	.03
368	Bill Doran	.06	.05	.02	457	Gregg Jefferies	.50	.40	.20
369	Todd Burns	.04	.03	.02	458	Bob McClure	.03	.02	.01
370	Tim Wallach	.07	.05	.03	459	Jim Lefebvre	.03	.02	.01
371	Jimmy Key	.08	.06	.03	460	Mike Scott	.09	.07	.03
372	Terry Kennedy	.03	.02	.01	461	*Carlos Martinez*(FC)	.25	.20	.10
373	Alvin Davis	.08	.06	.03	462	Denny Walling	.03	.02	.01
374	*Steve Cummings*(FC)	.20	.15	.08	463	Drew Hall	.03	.02	.01
375	Dwight Evans	.08	.06	.03	464	*Jerome Walton*	.70	.50	.30
376	Checklist 265-396	.03	.02	.01	465	Kevin Gross	.06	.05	.02
377	*Mickey Weston*(FC)	.20	.15	.08	466	Rance Mulliniks	.03	.02	.01
378	Luis Salazar	.03	.02	.01	467	Juan Nieves	.04	.03	.02
379	Steve Rosenberg	.03	.02	.01	468	Billy Ripken	.04	.03	.02
380	Dave Winfield	.15	.11	.06	469	John Kruk	.07	.05	.02
381	Frank Robinson	.03	.02	.01	470	Frank Viola	.09	.07	.04
382	Jeff Musselman	.03	.02	.01	471	Mike Brumley	.03	.02	.01
383	John Morris	.04	.03	.02	472	Jose Uribe	.04	.03	.02
384	*Pat Combs*	.50	.40	.20	473	Joe Price	.03	.02	.01
385	Fred McGriff AS	.20	.15	.08	474	Rich Thompson	.04	.03	.02
386	Julio Franco AS	.10	.08	.04	475	Bob Welch	.06	.05	.02
387	Wade Boggs AS	.20	.15	.08	476	Brad Komminsk	.03	.02	.02
388	Cal Ripken AS	.15	.11	.06	477	Willie Fraser	.03	.02	.01
389	Robin Yount AS	.20	.15	.08	478	Mike LaValliere	.04	.03	.02
390	Ruben Sierra AS	.20	.15	.08	479	Frank White	.06	.05	.02
391	Kirby Puckett AS	.20	.15	.08	480	Sid Fernandez	.09	.07	.04
392	Carlton Fisk AS	.08	.06	.03	481	Garry Templeton	.05	.04	.02
393	Bret Saberhagen AS	.10	.08	.04	482	*Steve Carter*(FC)	.20	.15	.08
394	Jeff Ballard AS	.08	.06	.03	483	Alejandro Pena	.04	.03	.02
395	Jeff Russell AS	.08	.06	.03	484	Mike Fitzgerald	.03	.02	.01
396	A. Bartlett Giamatti	.30	.25	.12	485	John Candelaria	.05	.04	.02
397	Will Clark AS	.25	.20	.10	486	Jeff Treadway	.05	.04	.02
398	Ryne Sandberg AS	.15	.11	.06	487	Steve Searcy	.05	.04	.02
399	Howard Johnson AS	.15	.11	.06	488	Ken Oberkfell	.03	.02	.01
400	Ozzie Smith AS	.10	.08	.04	489	Nick Leyva	.03	.02	.01
401	Kevin Mitchell AS	.20	.15	.08	490	Dan Plesac	.07	.05	.03
402	Eric Davis AS	.20	.15	.08	491	*Dave Cochrane*(FC)	.20	.15	.08
403	Tony Gwynn AS	.15	.11	.06	492	Ron Oester	.04	.03	.02
404	Craig Biggio AS	.15	.11	.06	493	*Jason Grimsley*(FC)	.25	.20	.10
405	Mike Scott AS	.08	.06	.03	494	Terry Puhl	.03	.02	.01
406	Joe Magrane AS	.08	.06	.03	495	Lee Smith	.06	.05	.02
407	Mark Davis AS	.08	.06	.03	496	Cecil Espy	.06	.05	.02
408	Trevor Wilson	.06	.05	.02	497	Dave Schmidt	.03	.02	.01
409	Tom Brunansky	.09	.07	.04	498	Rick Schu	.03	.02	.01
410	Joe Boever	.06	.05	.02	499	Bill Long	.04	.03	.02
411	Ken Phelps	.03	.02	.01	500	Kevin Mitchell	.35	.25	.14
412	Jamie Moyer	.04	.03	.02	501	Matt Young	.03	.02	.01
413	Brian DuBois(FC)	.20	.15	.08	502	Mitch Webster	.04	.03	.02
414	#1 Draft Pick (Frank Thomas)(FC)				503	Randy St. Claire	.03	.02	.01
		2.00	1.50	.80	504	Tom O'Malley	.03	.02	.01
415	Shawon Dunston	.06	.05	.02	505	Kelly Gruber	.08	.06	.03
416	*Dave Johnson*(FC)	.12	.09	.05	506	Tom Glavine	.10	.08	.04
417	Jim Gantner	.06	.05	.02	507	Gary Redus	.04	.03	.02
418	Tom Browning	.08	.06	.03	508	Terry Leach	.03	.02	.01
419	*Beau Allred*(FC)	.20	.15	.08	509	Tom Pagnozzi	.03	.02	.01
420	Carlton Fisk	.08	.06	.03	510	Doc Gooden	.25	.20	.10
421	Greg Minton	.03	.02	.01	511	Clay Parker	.07	.05	.03
422	Pat Sheridan	.03	.02	.01	512	Gary Pettis	.03	.02	.01
423	Fred Toliver	.03	.02	.01	513	Mark Eichhorn	.03	.02	.01

#	Name	MT	NR MT	EX
514	Andy Allanson	.03	.02	.01
515	Len Dykstra	.06	.05	.02
516	Tim Leary	.05	.04	.02
517	Roberto Alomar	.15	.11	.06
518	Bill Krueger	.03	.02	.01
519	Bucky Dent	.03	.02	.01
520	Mitch Williams	.09	.07	.03
521	Craig Worthington	.15	.11	.06
522	Mike Dunne	.04	.03	.02
523	Jay Bell	.03	.02	.01
524	Daryl Boston	.03	.02	.01
525	Wally Joyner	.20	.15	.08
526	Checklist 397-528	.03	.02	.01
527	Ron Hassey	.03	.02	.01
528	Kevin Wickander(FC)	.20	.15	.08
529	Greg Harris	.03	.02	.01
530	Mark Langston	.10	.08	.04
531	Ken Caminiti	.06	.05	.02
532	Cecilio Guante	.03	.02	.01
533	Tim Jones(FC)	.07	.05	.03
534	Louie Meadows	.07	.05	.03
535	John Smoltz	.15	.11	.06
536	Bob Geren	.15	.11	.06
537	Mark Grant	.03	.02	.01
538	Billy Spiers	.20	.15	.08
539	Neal Heaton	.03	.02	.01
540	Danny Tartabull	.09	.07	.03
541	Pat Perry	.03	.02	.01
542	Darren Daulton	.03	.02	.01
543	Nelson Liriano	.03	.02	.01
544	Dennis Boyd	.05	.04	.02
545	Kevin McReynolds	.09	.07	.04
546	Kevin Hickey	.05	.04	.02
547	Jack Howell	.05	.04	.02
548	Pat Clements	.03	.02	.01
549	Don Zimmer	.03	.02	.01
550	Julio Franco	.09	.07	.04
551	Tim Crews	.03	.02	.01
552	Mike Smith(FC)	.15	.11	.06
553	Scott Scudder(FC)	.20	.15	.11
554	Jay Buhner	.08	.06	.03
555	Jack Morris	.07	.05	.03
556	Gene Larkin	.03	.02	.01
557	Jeff Innis	.15	.11	.08
558	Rafael Ramirez	.04	.03	.02
559	Andy McGaffigan	.04	.03	.02
560	Steve Sax	.08	.06	.03
561	Ken Dayley	.03	.02	.01
562	Chad Kreuter	.10	.08	.04
563	Alex Sanchez	.10	.08	.04
564	#1 Draft Pick (Tyler Houston)(FC)	.50	.40	.20
565	Scott Fletcher	.05	.04	.02
566	Mark Knudson	.06	.05	.02
567	Ron Gant	.10	.08	.04
568	John Smiley	.07	.05	.03
569	Ivan Calderon	.05	.04	.02
570	Cal Ripken	.15	.11	.06
571	Brett Butler	.06	.05	.02
572	Greg Harris	.09	.07	.04
573	Danny Heep	.03	.02	.01
574	Bill Swift	.04	.03	.02
575	Lance Parrish	.07	.05	.03
576	Mike Dyer(FC)	.20	.15	.08
577	Charlie Hayes(FC)	.10	.08	.04
578	Joe Magrane	.09	.07	.04
579	Art Howe	.03	.02	.01
580	Joe Carter	.15	.11	.06
581	Ken Griffey	.05	.04	.02
582	Rick Honeycutt	.03	.02	.01
583	Bruce Benedict	.03	.02	.01
584	Phil Stephenson(FC)	.09	.07	.04
585	Kal Daniels	.10	.08	.04
586	Ed Nunez	.03	.02	.01
587	Lance Johnson	.08	.06	.03
588	Rick Rhoden	.03	.02	.01
589	Mike Aldrete	.03	.02	.01
590	Ozzie Smith	.10	.08	.04
591	Todd Stottlemyre	.08	.06	.03
592	R.J. Reynolds	.03	.02	.01
593	Scott Bradley	.03	.02	.01
594	Luis Sojo(FC)	.20	.15	.08
595	Greg Swindell	.10	.08	.04
596	Jose DeJesus(FC)	.10	.08	.04
597	Chris Bosio	.07	.05	.03
598	Brady Anderson	.05	.04	.02
599	Frank Williams	.03	.02	.01
600	Darryl Strawberry	.30	.15	.08
601	Luis Rivera	.04	.03	.02
602	Scott Garrelts	.07	.05	.03
603	Tony Armas	.03	.02	.01
604	Ron Robinson	.03	.02	.01
605	Mike Scioscia	.07	.05	.03
606	Storm Davis	.07	.05	.03
607	Steve Jeltz	.03	.02	.01
608	Eric Anthony(FC)	.70	.50	.30
609	Sparky Anderson	.03	.02	.01
610	Pedro Guerrero	.12	.09	.05
611	Walt Terrell	.05	.04	.02
612	Dave Gallagher	.07	.05	.02
613	Jeff Pico	.04	.03	.02
614	Nelson Santovenia	.09	.07	.04
615	Rob Deer	.07	.05	.03
616	Brian Holman	.10	.08	.04
617	Geronimo Berroa	.08	.06	.03
618	Eddie Whitson	.05	.04	.02
619	Rob Ducey	.08	.06	.03
620	Tony Castillo(FC)	.20	.15	.08
621	Melido Perez	.07	.05	.03
622	Sid Bream	.05	.04	.02
623	Jim Corsi	.05	.04	.02
624	Darrin Jackson	.04	.03	.02
625	Roger McDowell	.07	.05	.03
626	Bob Melvin	.03	.02	.01
627	Jose Rijo	.07	.05	.03
628	Candy Maldonado	.04	.03	.02
629	Eric Hetzel(FC)	.10	.08	.04
630	Gary Gaetti	.10	.08	.04
631	John Wetteland(FC)	.20	.15	.08
632	Scott Lusader	.06	.05	.02
633	Dennis Cook(FC)	.25	.20	.10
634	Luis Polonia	.06	.05	.02
635	Brian Downing	.06	.05	.02
636	Jesse Orosco	.03	.02	.01
637	Craig Reynolds	.03	.02	.01
638	Jeff Montgomery	.07	.05	.03
639	Tony LaRussa	.03	.02	.01
640	Rick Sutcliffe	.06	.05	.02
641	Doug Strange(FC)	.15	.11	.06
642	Jack Armstrong	.04	.03	.02
643	Alfredo Griffin	.04	.03	.02
644	Paul Assenmacher	.04	.03	.02
645	Jose Oquendo	.06	.05	.02
646	Checklist 529-660	.03	.02	.01
647	Rex Hudler	.03	.02	.01
648	Jim Clancy	.03	.02	.01
649	Dan Murphy(FC)	.15	.11	.06
650	Mike Witt	.06	.05	.02
651	Rafael Santana	.06	.05	.02
652	Mike Boddicker	.06	.05	.02
653	John Moses	.03	.02	.01
654	#1 Draft Pick (Paul Coleman)(FC)	.30	.25	.12
655	Gregg Olson	.30	.25	.12
656	Mackey Sasser	.05	.04	.02
657	Terry Mulholland	.06	.05	.02
658	Donell Nixon	.03	.02	.01
659	Greg Cadaret	.03	.02	.01
660	Vince Coleman	.10	.08	.04
661	Turn Back The Clock - 1985 (Dick Howser)	.07	.05	.03
662	Turn Back The Clock - 1980 (Mike Schmidt)	.07	.05	.03
663	Turn Back The Clock - 1975 (Fred Lynn)	.07	.05	.03
664	Turn Back The Clock - 1970 (Johnny Bench)	.07	.05	.03
665	Turn Back The Clock - 1965 (Sandy Koufax)	.07	.05	.03
666	Brian Fisher	.05	.04	.02
667	Curt Wilkerson	.03	.02	.01
668	Joe Oliver(FC)	.30	.25	.12
669	Tom Lasorda	.03	.02	.01
670	Dennis Eckersley	.09	.07	.04
671	Bob Boone	.09	.07	.04
672	Roy Smith	.03	.02	.01
673	Joey Meyer	.03	.02	.01
674	Spike Owen	.05	.04	.02
675	Jim Abbott	.70	.50	.30
676	Randy Kutcher(FC)	.07	.05	.03
677	Jay Tibbs	.03	.02	.01
678	Kirt Manwaring	.10	.08	.04
679	Gary Ward	.04	.03	.02
680	Howard Johnson	.15	.11	.06
681	Mike Schooler	.07	.05	.03
682	Dann Bilardello	.03	.02	.01
683	Kenny Rogers	.10	.08	.04
684	Julio Machado(FC)	.20	.15	.08
685	Tony Fernandez	.09	.07	.04
686	Carmelo Martinez	.06	.05	.02
687	Tim Birtsas	.03	.02	.01
688	Milt Thompson	.06	.05	.02
689	Rich Yett	.03	.02	.01
690	Mark McGwire	.50	.40	.20

		MT	NR MT	EX
		.03	.02	.01
		.50	.40	.20
	li	.03	.02	.01
	.7C)	.15	.11	.06
		.06	.05	.02
	Surhoff	.07	.05	.03
	Mike Davis	.03	.02	.01
	Omar Vizquel	.10	.08	.04
699	Jim Leyland	.03	.02	.01
700	Kirby Puckett	.25	.20	.10
701	*Bernie Williams*(FC)	.25	.20	.10
702	Tony Phillips	.04	.03	.02
703	*Jeff Brantley*	.12	.09	.05
704	Chip Hale(FC)	.20	.15	.08
705	Claudell Washington	.07	.05	.03
706	Geno Petralli	.03	.02	.01
707	Luis Aquino	.03	.02	.01
708	Larry Sheets	.03	.02	.01
709	Juan Berneguer	.03	.02	.01
710	Von Hayes	.09	.07	.04
711	Rick Aguilera	.05	.04	.02
712	Todd Benzinger	.09	.07	.04
713	*Tim Drummond*(FC)	.15	.11	.06
714	*Marquis Grissom*(FC)	.80	.60	.30
715	Greg Maddux	.15	.11	.06
716	Steve Balboni	.03	.02	.01
717	Ron Kakovice	.03	.02	.01
718	Gary Sheffield	.50	.40	.20
719	*Wally Whitehurst*(FC)	.15	.11	.06
720	Andres Galarraga	.15	.11	.06
721	Lee Mazzilli	.03	.02	.01
722	Felix Fermin	.03	.02	.01
723	Jeff Robinson	.05	.04	.02
724	Juan Bell(FC)	.10	.08	.04
725	Terry Pendleton	.07	.05	.03
726	Gene Nelson	.03	.02	.01
727	Pat Tabler	.05	.04	.02
728	Jim Acker	.03	.02	.01
729	Bobby Valentine	.03	.02	.01
730	Tony Gwynn	.20	.15	.08
731	Don Carman	.05	.04	.02
732	Ernie Riles	.03	.02	.01
733	John Dopson	.09	.07	.04
734	Kevin Elster	.06	.05	.02
735	Charlie Hough	.06	.05	.02
736	Rick Dempsey	.03	.02	.01
737	Chris Sabo	.15	.11	.06
738	*Gene Harris*	.10	.08	.04
739	Dale Sveum	.04	.03	.02
740	Jesse Barfield	.08	.06	.03
741	Steve Wilson	.10	.08	.04
742	Ernie Whitt	.05	.04	.02
743	Tom Candiotti	.05	.04	.02
744	*Kelly Mann*(FC)	.20	.15	.08
745	Hubie Brooks	.06	.05	.02
746	Dave Smith	.06	.05	.02
747	Randy Bush	.03	.02	.01
748	Doyle Alexander	.06	.05	.02
749	Mark Parent	.04	.03	.02
750	Dale Murphy	.10	.08	.04
751	Steve Lyons	.04	.03	.02
752	Tom Gordon	.50	.40	.20
753	Chris Speier	.03	.02	.01
754	Bob Walk	.05	.04	.02
755	Rafael Palmeiro	.08	.06	.03
756	Ken Howell	.03	.02	.01
757	*Larry Walker*(FC)	.30	.25	.12
758	Mark Thurmond	.03	.02	.01
759	Tom Trebelhorn	.03	.02	.01
760	Wade Boggs	.40	.30	.15
761	Mike Jackson	.05	.04	.02
762	Doug Dascenzo	.07	.05	.03
763	Denny Martinez	.07	.05	.03
764	Tim Teufel	.05	.04	.02
765	Chili Davis	.07	.05	.03
766	Brian Meyer(FC)	.10	.08	.04
767	Tracy Jones	.06	.05	.02
768	Chuck Crim	.04	.03	.02
769	*Greg Hibbard*(FC)	.30	.25	.12
770	Cory Snyder	.09	.07	.04
771	Pete Smith	.06	.05	.02
772	Jeff Reed	.03	.02	.01
773	Dave Leiper	.03	.02	.01
774	Ben McDonald(FC)	1.50	1.25	.60
775	Andy Van Slyke	.09	.07	.04
776	Charlie Leibrandt	.04	.03	.02
777	Tim Laudner	.03	.02	.01
778	Mike Jeffcoat	.03	.02	.01
779	Lloyd Moseby	.06	.05	.02
780	Orel Hershiser	.15	.11	.06
781	Mario Diaz	.03	.02	.01

		MT	NR MT	EX
782	Jose Alvarez	.03	.02	.01
783	Checklist 661-792	.03	.02	.01
784	Scott Bailes	.03	.02	.01
785	Jim Rice	.07	.05	.03
786	Eric King	.04	.03	.02
787	Rene Gonzales	.03	.02	.01
788	Frank DiPino	.03	.02	.01
789	John Wathan	.03	.02	.01
790	Gary Carter	.07	.05	.03
791	Alvaro Espinoza	.15	.11	.06
792	Gerald Perry	.06	.05	.02

1990 Topps All-Star Glossy Set of 22

One glossy All-Star card was included in each 1990 Topps rack pack. The cards measure 2-1/2" by 3-1/2" and feature a similar style to past glossy All-Star cards. Special cards of All-Star team captains Carl Yastrzemski and Don Drysdale are included in the set.

		MT	NR MT	EX
	Complete Set:	3.50	2.75	1.50
	Common Player:	.12	.09	.05
1	Tom Lasorda	.12	.09	.05
2	Will Clark	.35	.25	.14
3	Ryne Sandberg	.30	.25	.12
4	Howard Johnson	.15	.11	.06
5	Ozzie Smith	.15	.11	.06
6	Kevin Mitchell	.25	.20	.10
7	Eric Davis	.25	.20	.10
8	Tony Gwynn	.20	.15	.08
9	Benny Santiago	.15	.11	.06
10	Rick Rueschel	.12	.09	.05
11	Don Drysdale	.12	.09	.05
12	Tony LaRussa	.12	.09	.05
13	Mark McGwire	.30	.25	.12
14	Julio Franco	.15	.11	.06
15	Wade Boggs	.25	.20	.10
16	Cal Ripken	.20	.15	.08
17	Bo Jackson	.60	.45	.25
18	Kirby Puckett	.25	.20	.10
19	Ruben Sierra	.25	.20	.10
20	Terry Steinbach	.12	.09	.05
21	Dave Stewart	.15	.11	.06
22	Carl Yastrzemski	.15	.11	.06

1990 Topps All Star Glossy Set of 60

Sharp color photographs and a clutter-free design are features of the cards in this 60-card send away set. Topps initiated the redemption series in 1983 and increased the size of the set to 60 in 1986. Six special offer cards, which were included in Topps baseball wax packs, are necessary to obtain each of the six 10-card sets in the series.

		MT	NR MT	EX
	Complete Set:	9.00	6.75	3.50
	Common Player:	.10	.08	.04
1	Ryne Sandberg	.70	.50	.30
2	Nolan Ryan	.70	.50	.30
3	Glenn Davis	.15	.11	.06
4	Dave Stewart	.15	.11	.06
5	Barry Larkin	.15	.11	.06
6	Carney Lansford	.15	.11	.06
7	Darryl Strawberry	.60	.45	.25
8	Steve Sax	.15	.11	.06
9	Carlos Martinez	.10	.08	.04
10	Gary Sheffield	.40	.30	.15
11	Don Mattingly	.80	.60	.30
12	Mark Grace	.40	.30	.15
13	Bret Saberhagen	.20	.15	.08
14	Mike Scott	.10	.08	.04
15	Robin Yount	.20	.15	.08
16	Ozzie Smith	.15	.11	.06
17	Jeff Ballard	.10	.08	.04
18	Rick Reuschel	.10	.08	.04
19	Greg Briley	.10	.08	.04
20	Ken Griffey, Jr.	1.00	.70	.40
21	Kevin Mitchell	.30	.25	.12
22	Wade Boggs	.60	.45	.25
23	Doc Gooden	.50	.40	.20
24	George Bell	.15	.11	.06
25	Eric Davis	.40	.30	.15
26	Ruben Sierra	.25	.20	.10
27	Roberto Alomar	.20	.15	.08
28	Gary Gaetti	.15	.11	.06
29	Gregg Olson	.20	.15	.08
30	Tom Gordon	.20	.15	.08
31	Jose Canseco	.80	.60	.30
32	Pedro Guerrero	.15	.11	.06
33	Joe Carter	.15	.11	.06
34	Mike Scioscia	.10	.08	.04
35	Julio Franco	.15	.11	.06
36	Joe Magrane	.10	.08	.04
37	Rickey Henderson	.40	.30	.15
38	Rock Raines	.15	.11	.06
39	Jerome Walton	.35	.25	.14
40	Bob Geren	.10	.08	.04
41	Andre Dawson	.20	.15	.08
42	Mark McGwire	.60	.45	.25
43	Howard Johnson	.20	.15	.08
44	Bo Jackson	.80	.60	.30
45	Shawon Dunston	.20	.15	.08
46	Carlton Fisk	.20	.15	.08
47	Mitch Williams	.15	.11	.06
48	Kirby Puckett	.35	.25	.14
49	Craig Worthington	.10	.08	.04
50	Jim Abbott	.20	.15	.08
51	Cal Ripken	.25	.20	.10
52	Will Clark	.70	.50	.30
53	Dennis Eckersley	.20	.15	.08
54	Craig Biggio	.15	.11	.06
55	Fred McGriff	.20	.15	.08
56	Tony Gwynn	.20	.15	.08
57	Mickey Tettleton	.10	.08	.04
58	Mark Davis	.10	.08	.04
59	Omar Vizquel	.10	.08	.04
60	Gregg Jefferies	.30	.25	.12

1990 Topps Big Baseball

For the third consecutive year, Topps issued a 330-card set of the oversized cards (2-5/8" by 3-3/4"). The cards were issued in three 110-card series. The cards are reminiscent of Topps cards from the mid-1950s in that they feature players in portrait and action shots. The 1990 set has action photos in freeze frames. As in previous years, the cards are printed on white card stock with a glossy finish on the front. The card backs include 1989 and career hitting, fielding and pitching stats and a player cartoon.

		MT	NR MT	EX
	Complete Set:	22.00	16.50	8.75
	Common Player:	.05	.04	.02
1	Dwight Evans	.08	.06	.03
2	Kirby Puckett	.25	.20	.10
3	Kevin Gross	.06	.05	.02
4	Ron Hassey	.05	.04	.02
5	Lloyd McClendon	.05	.04	.02
6	Bo Jackson	1.00	.70	.40
7	Lonnie Smith	.06	.05	.02
8	Alvaro Espinoza	.06	.05	.02
9	Roberto Alomar	.15	.11	.06
10	Glenn Braggs	.06	.05	.02
11	David Cone	.10	.08	.04
12	Clauudell Washington	.05	.04	.02
13	Pedro Guerrero	.10	.08	.04
14	Todd Benzinger	.06	.05	.02
15	Jeff Russell	.06	.05	.02
16	Terry Kennedy	.05	.04	.02
17	Kelly Gruber	.15	.11	.06
18	Alfredo Griffin	.05	.04	.02
19	Mark Grace	.20	.15	.08
20	Dave Winfield	.12	.09	.05
21	Bret Saberhagen	.15	.11	.06
22	Roger Clemens	.30	.25	.12
23	Bob Walk	.05	.04	.02
24	Dave Magadan	.15	.11	.06
25	Spike Owen	.06	.05	.02
26	Jody Davis	.05	.04	.02
27	Kent Hrbek	.12	.09	.05
28	Mark McGwire	.50	.40	.20
29	Eddie Murray	.15	.11	.06
30	Paul O'Neill	.06	.05	.02
31	Jose DeLeon	.06	.05	.02
32	Steve Lyons	.05	.04	.02
33	Dan Plesac	.06	.05	.02
34	Jack Howell	.05	.04	.02
35	Greg Briley	.06	.05	.02
36	Andy Hawkins	.06	.05	.02
37	Cecil Espy	.05	.04	.02
38	Rick Sutcliffe	.08	.06	.03
39	Jack Clark	.12	.09	.05
40	Dale Murphy	.12	.09	.05
41	Mike Henneman	.06	.05	.02
42	Rick Honeycutt	.05	.04	.02
43	Willie Randolph	.06	.05	.02
44	Marty Barrett	.06	.05	.02
45	Willie Wilson	.06	.05	.02
46	Wallace Johnson	.05	.04	.02
47	Greg Brock	.06	.05	.02
48	Tom Browning	.06	.05	.02
49	Gerald Young	.05	.04	.02
50	Dennis Eckersley	.15	.11	.06
51	Scott Garrelts	.06	.05	.02
52	Gary Redus	.05	.04	.02
53	Al Newman	.05	.04	.02
54	Darryl Boston	.05	.04	.02
55	Ron Oester	.05	.04	.02
56	Danny Tartabull	.08	.06	.03
57	Gregg Jefferies	.30	.25	.12
58	Tom Foley	.05	.04	.02
59	Robin Yount	.20	.15	.08
60	Pat Borders	.06	.05	.02
61	Mike Greenwell	.30	.25	.12
62	Shawon Dunston	.10	.08	.04
63	Steve Buechele	.05	.04	.02
64	Dave Stewart	.12	.09	.05
65	Jose Oquendo	.05	.04	.02
66	Ron Gant	.20	.15	.08
67	Mike Scioscia	.06	.05	.02
68	Randy Velarde	.05	.04	.02

0 Topps Big Baseball

		MT	NR MT	EX
	...es	.06	.05	.02
		.08	.06	.03
		.06	.05	.02
		.25	.20	.10
		.05	.04	.02
	...eer	.06	.05	.02
	...yne Sandberg	.40	.30	.15
	Kevin Seitzer	.08	.06	.03
77	Wade Boggs	.50	.40	.20
78	Greg Gagne	.06	.05	.02
79	John Smiley	.06	.05	.02
80	Ivan Calderon	.08	.06	.03
81	Pete Incaviglia	.06	.05	.02
82	Orel Hershiser	.12	.09	.05
83	Carney Lansford	.08	.06	.03
84	Mike Fitzgerald	.05	.04	.02
85	Don Mattingly	.60	.45	.25
86	Chet Lemon	.06	.05	.02
87	Rolando Roomes	.05	.04	.02
88	Bill Spiers	.06	.05	.02
89	Pat Tabler	.06	.05	.02
90	Danny Heep	.05	.04	.02
91	Andre Dawson	.15	.11	.06
92	Randy Bush	.05	.04	.02
93	Tony Gwynn	.15	.11	.06
94	Tom Brunansky	.08	.06	.03
95	Johnny Ray	.06	.05	.02
96	Matt Williams	.15	.11	.06
97	Barry Lyons	.05	.04	.02
98	Jeff Hamilton	.05	.04	.02
99	Tom Glavine	.06	.05	.02
100	Ken Griffey,Sr.	.06	.05	.02
101	Tom Henke	.06	.05	.02
102	Dave Righetti	.08	.06	.03
103	Paul Molitor	.12	.09	.05
104	Mike LaValliere	.06	.05	.02
105	Frank White	.06	.05	.02
106	Bob Welch	.08	.06	.03
107	Ellis Burks	.25	.20	.10
108	Andres Galarraga	.08	.06	.03
109	Mitch Williams	.08	.06	.03
110	Checklist	.05	.04	.02
111	Craig Biggio	.08	.06	.03
112	Dave Steib	.08	.06	.03
113	Ron Darling	.06	.05	.02
114	Bert Blyleven	.10	.08	.04
115	Dickie Thon	.05	.04	.02
116	Carlos Martinez	.06	.05	.02
117	Jeff King	.06	.05	.02
118	Terry Steinbach	.06	.05	.02
119	Frank Tanana	.06	.05	.02
120	Mark Lemke	.06	.05	.02
121	Chris Sabo	.10	.08	.04
122	Glenn Davis	.15	.11	.06
123	Mel Hall	.06	.05	.02
124	Jim Gantner	.06	.05	.02
125	Benito Santiago	.10	.08	.04
126	Milt Thompson	.06	.05	.02
127	Rafael Palmeiro	.12	.09	.05
128	Barry Bonds	.20	.15	.08
129	Mike Bielecki	.06	.05	.02
130	Lou Whitaker	.10	.08	.04
131	Bob Ojeda	.05	.04	.02
132	Dion James	.05	.04	.02
133	Denny Martinez	.06	.05	.02
134	Fred McGriff	.20	.15	.08
135	Terry Pendleton	.06	.05	.02
136	Pat Combs	.10	.08	.04
137	Kevin Mitchell	.30	.25	.12
138	Marquis Grissom	.50	.40	.20
139	Chris Bosio	.06	.05	.02
140	Omar Vizquel	.05	.04	.02
141	Steve Sax	.10	.08	.04
142	Nelson Liriano	.05	.04	.02
143	Kevin Elster	.06	.05	.02
144	Dan Pasqua	.06	.05	.02
145	Dave Smith	.06	.05	.02
146	Craig Worthington	.06	.05	.02
147	Dan Gladden	.06	.05	.02
148	Oddibe McDowell	.05	.04	.02
149	Bip Roberts	.06	.05	.02
150	Randy Ready	.05	.04	.02
151	Dwight Smith	.10	.08	.04
152	Ed Whitson	.06	.05	.02
153	George Bell	.12	.09	.05
154	Tim Raines	.15	.11	.06
155	Sid Fernandez	.08	.06	.03
156	Henry Cotto	.05	.04	.02
157	Harold Baines	.12	.09	.05
158	Willie McGee	.10	.08	.04
159	Bill Doran	.06	.05	.02

		MT	NR MT	EX
160	Steve Balboni	.05	.04	.02
161	Pete Smith	.06	.05	.02
162	Frank Viola	.12	.09	.05
163	Gary Sheffield	.25	.20	.10
164	Bill Landrum	.06	.05	.02
165	Tony Fernandez	.08	.06	.03
166	Mike Heath	.05	.04	.02
167	Jody Reed	.08	.06	.03
168	Wally Joyner	.08	.06	.03
169	Robby Thompson	.06	.05	.02
170	Ken Caminiti	.06	.05	.02
171	Nolan Ryan	.40	.30	.15
172	Ricky Jordan	.08	.06	.03
173	Lance Blankenship	.05	.04	.02
174	Dwight Gooden	.30	.25	.12
175	Ruben Sierra	.20	.15	.08
176	Carlton Fisk	.15	.11	.06
177	Garry Templeton	.06	.05	.02
178	Mike Devereaux	.06	.05	.02
179	Mookie Wilson	.06	.05	.02
180	Jeff Blauser	.06	.05	.02
181	Scott Bradley	.05	.04	.02
182	Luis Salazar	.05	.04	.02
183	Rafael Ramirez	.06	.05	.02
184	Vince Coleman	.08	.06	.03
185	Doug Drabek	.10	.08	.04
186	Darryl Strawberry	.30	.25	.12
187	Tim Burke	.06	.05	.02
188	Jesse Barfield	.08	.06	.03
189	Barry Larkin	.15	.11	.06
190	Alan Trammell	.10	.08	.04
191	Steve Lake	.05	.04	.02
192	Derek Lilliquist	.06	.05	.02
193	Don Robinson	.06	.05	.02
194	Kevin McReynolds	.08	.06	.03
195	Melido Perez	.06	.05	.02
196	Jose Lind	.06	.05	.02
197	Eric Anthony	.50	.40	.20
198	B.J. Surhoff	.06	.05	.02
199	John Olerud	1.00	.70	.40
200	Mike Moore	.06	.05	.02
201	Mark Gubicza	.08	.06	.03
202	Phil Bradley	.06	.05	.02
203	Ozzie Smith	.12	.09	.05
204	Greg Maddux	.08	.06	.03
205	Julio Franco	.12	.09	.05
206	Tom Herr	.06	.05	.02
207	Scott Fletcher	.05	.04	.02
208	Bobby Bonilla	.15	.11	.06
209	Bob Geren	.06	.05	.02
210	Junior Felix	.20	.15	.08
211	Dick Schofield	.05	.04	.02
212	Jim Deshaies	.06	.05	.02
213	Jose Uribe	.06	.05	.02
214	John Kruk	.06	.05	.02
215	Ozzie Guillen	.08	.06	.03
216	Howard Johnson	.10	.08	.04
217	Andy Van Slyke	.08	.06	.03
218	Tim Laudner	.05	.04	.02
219	Manny Lee	.06	.05	.02
220	Checklist	.05	.04	.02
221	Cory Snyder	.08	.06	.02
222	Billy Hatcher	.06	.05	.02
223	Bud Black	.05	.04	.02
224	Will Clark	.40	.30	.15
225	Kevin Tapani	.20	.15	.08
226	Mike Pagliarulo	.06	.05	.02
227	Dave Parker	.12	.09	.05
228	Ben McDonald	1.00	.70	.40
229	Carlos Baerga	.50	.40	.20
230	Roger McDowell	.06	.05	.02
231	Delino DeShields	.50	.40	.20
232	Mark Langston	.10	.08	.04
233	Wally Backman	.06	.05	.02
234	Jim Eisenreich	.06	.05	.02
235	Mike Schooler	.06	.05	.02
236	Kevin Bass	.06	.05	.02
237	John Farrell	.05	.04	.02
238	Kal Daniels	.10	.08	.04
239	Tony Phillips	.06	.05	.02
240	Todd Stottlemyre	.06	.05	.02
241	Greg Olson	.15	.11	.06
242	Charlie Hough	.06	.05	.02
243	Mariano Duncan	.06	.05	.02
244	Billy Ripken	.05	.04	.02
245	Joe Carter	.12	.09	.05
246	Tim Belcher	.08	.06	.03
247	Roberto Kelly	.08	.06	.03
248	Candy Maldonado	.08	.06	.03
249	Mike Scott	.08	.06	.03
250	Ken Griffey,Jr.	1.25	.90	.50

		MT	NR MT	EX
251	Nick Esasky	.06	.05	.02
252	Tom Gordon	.15	.11	.06
253	John Tudor	.06	.05	.02
254	Gary Gaetti	.10	.08	.04
255	Neal Heaton	.06	.05	.02
256	Jerry Browne	.06	.05	.02
257	Joe Rijo	.06	.05	.02
258	Mike Boddicker	.06	.05	.02
259	Brett Butler	.06	.05	.02
260	Andy Benes	.10	.08	.04
261	Kevin Brown	.08	.06	.03
262	Hubie Brooks	.08	.06	.03
263	Randy Milligan	.06	.05	.02
264	John Franco	.10	.08	.04
265	Sandy Alomar	.30	.25	.12
266	Dave Valle	.06	.05	.02
267	Jerome Walton	.25	.20	.10
268	Bob Boone	.08	.06	.03
269	Ken Howell	.06	.05	.02
270	Jose Canseco	1.00	.70	.40
271	Joe Magrane	.08	.06	.03
272	Brian DuBois	.08	.06	.03
273	Carlos Quintana	.08	.06	.03
274	Lance Johnson	.06	.05	.02
275	Steve Bedrosian	.06	.05	.02
276	Brook Jacoby	.08	.06	.03
277	Fred Lynn	.06	.05	.02
278	Jeff Ballard	.06	.05	.02
279	Otis Nixon	.05	.04	.02
280	Chili Davis	.06	.05	.02
281	Joe Oliver	.12	.09	.05
282	Brian Holman	.08	.06	.03
283	Juan Samuel	.08	.06	.03
284	Rick Aguilera	.06	.05	.02
285	Jeff Reardon	.08	.06	.03
286	Sammy Sosa	.30	.25	.12
287	Carmelo Martinez	.06	.05	.02
288	Greg Swindell	.08	.06	.03
289	Erik Hanson	.15	.11	.06
290	Tony Pena	.08	.06	.03
291	Pascual Perez	.06	.05	.02
292	Rickey Henderson	.35	.25	.14
293	Kurt Stillwell	.06	.05	.02
294	Todd Zeile	.50	.40	.20
295	Bobby Thigpen	.10	.08	.04
296	Larry Walker	.30	.25	.12
297	Rob Murphy	.05	.04	.02
298	Mitch Webster	.05	.04	.02
299	Devon White	.06	.05	.02
300	Len Dykstra	.10	.08	.04
301	Keith Hernandez	.06	.05	.02
302	Gene Larkin	.06	.05	.02
303	Jeffrey Leonard	.06	.05	.02
304	Jim Presley	.06	.05	.02
305	Lloyd Moseby	.08	.06	.03
306	John Smoltz	.08	.06	.03
307	Sam Horn	.06	.05	.02
308	Greg Litton	.06	.05	.02
309	Dave Henderson	.08	.06	.03
310	Mark McLemore	.05	.04	.02
311	Gary Pettis	.06	.05	.02
312	Mark Davis	.05	.04	.02
313	Cecil Fielder	.50	.40	.20
314	Jack Armstrong	.08	.06	.03
315	Alvin Davis	.08	.06	.03
316	Doug Jones	.08	.06	.03
317	Eric Yelding	.08	.06	.03
318	Joe Orsulak	.06	.05	.02
319	Chuck Finley	.08	.06	.03
320	Glenn Wilson	.06	.05	.02
321	Harold Reynolds	.08	.06	.03
322	Teddy Higuera	.08	.06	.03
323	Lance Parrish	.08	.06	.03
324	Bruce Hurst	.06	.05	.02
325	Dave West	.06	.05	.02
326	Kirk Gibson	.10	.08	.04
327	Cal Ripken	.15	.11	.06
328	Rick Reuschel	.06	.05	.02
329	Jim Abbott	.15	.11	.06
330	Checklist	.05	.04	.02

1990 Topps Box Panels

This special 16-card set features four cards on four different box-bottom panels. The cards are identical in design to the regular 1990 Topps cards. The cards are designated by letter.

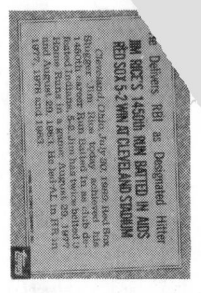

		MT	NR MT	EX
	Complete Panel Set:	4.00	3.00	1.50
	Complete Singles Set:	2.00	1.50	.80
	Common Panel:	.40	.30	.15
	Common Single Player:	.06	.05	.02
	Panel	.60	.45	.25
A	Wade Boggs	.25	.20	.10
B	George Brett	.20	.15	.08
C	Andre Dawson	.15	.11	.06
D	Darrell Evans	.06	.05	.02
	Panel	.60	.45	.25
E	Doc Gooden	.25	.20	.10
F	Rickey Henderson	.25	.20	.10
G	Tom Lasorda	.06	.05	.02
H	Fred Lynn	.06	.05	.02
	Panel	.40	.30	.15
I	Mark McGwire	.25	.20	.10
J	Dave Parker	.10	.08	.04
K	Jeff Reardon	.06	.05	.02
L	Rick Reuschel	.06	.05	.02
	Panel	.60	.45	.25
M	Jim Rice	.06	.05	.02
N	Cal Ripken	.10	.08	.04
O	Nolan Ryan	.25	.20	.10
P	Ryne Sandberg	.25	.20	.10

1990 Topps Traded

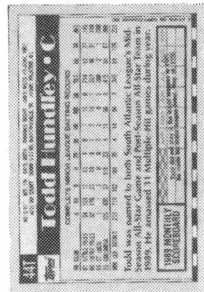

For the first time, Topps "Traded" series cards were made available nationwide in retail wax packs. The 132-card set was also sold in complete boxed form as it has been in recent years. The wax pack traded cards feature gray backs, while the boxed set cards feature white backs. The cards are numbered 1T-132T and showcase rookies, players who changed teams and new managers.

		MT	NR MT	EX
	Complete Set:	12.00	9.00	4.75
	Common Player:	.05	.04	.02
1T	Darrel Akerfelds	.05	.04	.02
2T	Sandy Alomar,Jr.	.30	.25	.12
3T	Brad Arnsberg	.05	.04	.02
4T	Steve Avery	.25	.20	.10
5T	Wally Backman	.05	.04	.02
6T	Carlos Baerga(FC)	.50	.40	.20

		MT	NR MT	EX
		.06	.05	.02
		.10	.08	.04
	(C)	.20	.15	.08
	(C)	.20	.15	.08
		.05	.04	.02
		.06	.05	.02
	aggs	.06	.05	.02
	...ie Brooks	.08	.06	.03
	Tom Brunansky	.08	.06	.03
16T	John Burkett(FC)	.30	.25	.12
17T	Casey Candaele	.05	.04	.02
18T	John Candelaria	.06	.05	.02
19T	Gary Carter	.10	.08	.04
20T	Joe Carter	.10	.08	.04
21T	Rick Cerone	.05	.04	.02
22T	Scott Coolbaugh(FC)	.20	.15	.08
23T	Bobby Cox	.05	.04	.02
24T	Mark Davis	.06	.05	.02
25T	Storm Davis	.06	.05	.02
26T	Edgar Diaz(FC)	.10	.08	.04
27T	Wayne Edwards(FC)	.20	.15	.08
28T	Mark Eichhorn	.05	.04	.02
29T	Scott Erickson(FC)	.25	.20	.10
30T	Nick Esasky	.06	.05	.02
31T	Cecil Fielder	.50	.40	.20
32T	John Franco	.08	.06	.03
33T	Travis Fryman(FC)	.80	.60	.30
34T	Bill Gullickson	.05	.04	.02
35T	Darryl Hamilton	.15	.11	.06
36T	Mike Harkey	.20	.15	.08
37T	Bud Harrelson	.05	.04	.02
38T	Billy Hatcher	.06	.05	.02
39T	Keith Hernandez	.08	.06	.03
40T	Joe Hesketh	.05	.04	.02
41T	Dave Hollins(FC)	.25	.20	.10
42T	Sam Horn	.08	.06	.03
43T	Steve Howard(FC)	.20	.15	.08
44T	Todd Hundley(FC)	.20	.15	.08
45T	Jeff Huson	.10	.08	.04
46T	Chris James	.05	.04	.02
47T	Stan Javier	.05	.04	.02
48T	Dave Justice(FC)	2.75	2.00	1.00
49T	Jeff Kaiser(FC)	.12	.09	.05
50T	Dana Kiecker(FC)	.20	.15	.08
51T	Joe Klink(FC)	.10	.08	.04
52T	Brent Knackert(FC)	.12	.09	.05
53T	Brad Komminsk	.05	.04	.02
54T	Mark Langston	.10	.08	.04
55T	Tim Layana(FC)	.25	.20	.10
56T	Rick Leach	.05	.04	.02
57T	Terry Leach	.05	.04	.02
58T	Tim Leary	.05	.04	.02
59T	Craig Lefferts	.05	.04	.02
60T	Charlie Leibrandt	.05	.04	.02
61T	Jim Leyritz(FC)	.30	.25	.12
62T	Fred Lynn	.06	.05	.02
63T	Kevin Maas(FC)	2.00	1.50	.80
64T	Shane Mack	.08	.06	.03
65T	Candy Maldonado	.06	.05	.02
66T	Fred Manrique	.05	.04	.02
67T	Mike Marshall	.05	.04	.02
68T	Carmelo Martinez	.05	.04	.02
69T	John Marzano	.06	.05	.02
70T	Ben McDonald	1.00	.70	.40
71T	Jack McDowell	.08	.06	.03
72T	John McNamara	.05	.04	.02
73T	Orlando Mercado	.05	.04	.02
74T	Stump Merrill	.05	.04	.02
75T	Alan Mills(FC)	.20	.15	.08
76T	Hal Morris	.35	.25	.14
77T	Lloyd Moseby	.06	.05	.02
78T	Randy Myers	.08	.06	.03
79T	Tim Naehring(FC)	.30	.25	.12
80T	Junior Noboa	.06	.05	.02
81T	Matt Nokes	.06	.05	.02
82T	Pete O'Brien	.05	.04	.02
83T	John Olerud(FC)	1.75	1.25	.70
84T	Greg Olson(FC)	.15	.11	.06
85T	Junior Ortiz	.05	.04	.02
86T	Dave Parker	.15	.11	.06
87T	Rick Parker(FC)	.15	.11	.06
88T	Bob Patterson	.05	.04	.02
89T	Alejandro Pena	.05	.04	.02
90T	Tony Pena	.08	.06	.03
91T	Pascual Perez	.05	.04	.02
92T	Gerald Perry	.05	.04	.02
93T	Dan Petry	.05	.04	.02
94T	Gary Pettis	.06	.05	.02
95T	Tony Phillips	.05	.04	.02
96T	Lou Pinella	.05	.04	.02
97T	Luis Polonia	.05	.04	.02

		MT	NR MT	EX
98T	Jim Presley	.06	.05	.02
99T	Scott Radinsky(FC)	.20	.15	.08
100T	Willie Randolph	.08	.06	.03
101T	Jeff Reardon	.08	.06	.03
102T	Greg Riddoch	.05	.04	.02
103T	Jeff Robinson	.05	.04	.02
104T	Ron Robinson	.05	.04	.02
105T	Kevin Romine	.05	.04	.02
106T	Scott Ruskin(FC)	.20	.15	.08
107T	John Russell	.05	.04	.02
108T	Bill Sampen(FC)	.20	.15	.08
109T	Juan Samuel	.08	.06	.03
110T	Scott Sanderson	.06	.05	.02
111T	Jack Savage(FC)	.10	.08	.04
112T	Dave Schmidt	.05	.04	.02
113T	Red Schoendienst	.05	.04	.02
114T	Terry Shumpert(FC)	.25	.20	.10
115T	Matt Sinatro	.05	.04	.02
116T	Don Slaught	.05	.04	.02
117T	Bryn Smith	.05	.04	.02
118T	Lee Smith	.08	.06	.03
119T	Paul Sorrento(FC)	.20	.15	.08
120T	Franklin Stubbs	.05	.04	.02
121T	Russ Swan(FC)	.20	.15	.08
122T	Bob Tewksbury	.05	.04	.02
123T	Wayne Tolleson	.05	.04	.02
124T	John Tudor	.06	.05	.02
125T	Randy Veres(FC)	.10	.08	.04
126T	Hector Villanueva(FC)	.30	.25	.12
127T	Mitch Webster	.05	.04	.02
128T	Ernie Whitt	.06	.05	.02
129T	Frank Wills	.06	.05	.02
130T	Dave Winfield	.15	.11	.06
131T	Matt Young	.05	.04	.02
132T	Checklist	.05	.04	.02

1991 Topps

 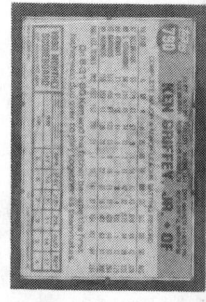

Topps celebrated its 40th anniversary in 1991 with the biggest promotional campaign in baseball card history. More than 300,000 vintage Topps cards (or certificates which can be redeemed for valuable older cards) produced from 1952 to present were randomly inserted in packs. Also a grand prize winner will receive one complete set from each year, and others will receive a single set from 1952-present. The 1991 Topps card fronts feature the "Topps 40 Years of Baseball" logo in the upper left corner. Card borders frame the player photos. All players of the same team have cards with the same frame/border colors. Both action and posed shots appear in full-color on the card fronts. The flip sides are printed horizontally and feature complete statistics. Record Breakers and other special cards were once again included in the set. The cards measure 2-1/2" by 3-1/2". Several cards feature horizontal fronts.

		MT	NR MT	EX
Complete Set:		22.00	16.50	8.75
Common Player:		.03	.02	.01
1	Nolan Ryan	.30	.25	.12
2	Record Breaker (George Brett)	.08	.06	.03
3	Record Breaker (Carlton Fisk)	.08	.06	.03
4	Record Breaker (Kevin Maas)	.10	.08	.04
5	Record Breaker (Cal Ripken)	.08	.04	.02

#	Player	MT	NR MT	EX
	Record Breaker (Nolan Ryan)	.20	.15	.08
	Record Breaker (Ryne Sandberg)	.10	.08	.04
	Record Breaker (Bobby Thigpen)	.08	.06	.03
10	Darrin Fletcher(FC)	.10	.08	.04
	Gregg Olson	.08	.06	.03
11	Roberto Kelly	.08	.06	.03
12	Paul Assenmacher	.04	.03	.02
13	Mariano Duncan	.06	.05	.02
14	Dennis Lamp	.03	.02	.01
15	Von Hayes	.08	.06	.03
16	Mike Heath	.04	.03	.02
17	Jeff Brantley	.06	.05	.02
18	Nelson Liriano	.03	.02	.01
19	Jeff Robinson	.04	.03	.02
20	Pedro Guerrero	.08	.06	.03
21	Joe Morgan	.03	.02	.01
22	Storm Davis	.06	.05	.02
23	Jim Gantner	.04	.03	.02
24	Dave Martinez	.05	.04	.02
25	Tim Belcher	.08	.06	.03
26	Luis Sojo	.06	.05	.02
27	Bobby Witt	.08	.06	.03
28	Alvaro Espinoza	.05	.04	.02
29	Bob Walk	.03	.02	.01
30	Gregg Jefferies	.15	.11	.06
31	Colby Ward(FC)	.15	.11	.06
32	Mike Simms(FC)	.15	.11	.06
33	Barry Jones	.05	.04	.02
34	Atlee Hammaker	.03	.02	.01
35	Greg Maddux	.08	.06	.03
36	Donnie Hill	.03	.02	.01
37	Tom Bolton	.05	.04	.02
38	Scott Bradley	.03	.02	.01
39	Jim Neidlinger(FC)	.20	.15	.08
40	Kevin Mitchell	.20	.15	.08
41	Ken Dayley	.04	.03	.02
42	Chris Hoiles(FC)	.25	.20	.10
43	Roger McDowell	.06	.05	.02
44	Mike Felder	.04	.03	.02
45	Chris Sabo	.10	.08	.04
46	Tim Drummond	.06	.05	.02
47	Brook Jacoby	.06	.05	.02
48	Dennis Boyd	.05	.04	.02
49	Pat Borders	.05	.04	.02
50	Bob Welch	.08	.06	.03
51	Art Howe	.03	.02	.01
52	Francisco Oliveras(FC)	.10	.08	.04
53	Mike Sahrperson	.06	.05	.02
54	Gary Mielke	.05	.04	.02
55	Jeffrey Leonard	.05	.04	.02
56	Jeff Parrett	.04	.03	.02
57	Jack Howell	.04	.03	.02
58	Mel Stottlemyre	.08	.06	.03
59	Eric Yelding	.06	.05	.02
60	Frank Viola	.12	.09	.05
61	Stan Javier	.04	.03	.02
62	Lee Guetterman	.03	.02	.01
63	Milt Thompson	.04	.03	.02
64	Tom Herr	.05	.04	.02
65	Bruce Hurst	.06	.05	.02
66	Terry Kennedy	.03	.02	.01
67	Rick Honeycutt	.03	.02	.01
68	Gary Sheffield	.15	.11	.06
69	Steve Wilson	.06	.05	.02
70	Ellis Burks	.15	.11	.06
71	Jim Acker	.03	.02	.01
72	Junior Ortiz	.03	.02	.01
73	Craig Worthington	.06	.05	.02
74	#1 Draft Pick (Shane Andrews)(FC)	.30	.25	.12
75	Jack Morris	.08	.06	.03
76	Jerry Browne	.05	.04	.02
77	Drew Hall	.03	.02	.01
78	Geno Petralli	.03	.02	.01
79	Frank Thomas	.50	.40	.20
80	Fernando Valenzuela	.08	.06	.03
81	Cito Gaston	.03	.02	.01
82	Tom Glavine	.05	.04	.02
83	Daryl Boston	.03	.02	.01
84	Bob McClure	.03	.02	.01
85	Jesse Barfield	.08	.06	.03
86	Les Lancaster	.04	.03	.02
87	Tracy Jones	.03	.02	.01
88	Bob Tewksbury	.04	.03	.02
89	Darren Daulton	.06	.05	.02
90	Danny Tartabull	.08	.06	.03
91	Greg Colbrunn(FC)	.15	.11	.06
92	Danny Jackson	.06	.05	.02
93	Ivan Calderon	.08	.06	.03
94	John Dopson	.05	.04	.02
95	Paul Molitor	.10	.08	.04

#	Player	MT	NR MT	EX
96	Trevor Wilson	.04	.03	.02
97	Brady Anderson	.04	.03	.02
98	Sergio Valdez	.05	.04	.02
99	Chris Gwynn	.05	.04	.02
100	Don Mattingly	.30	.25	.12
101	Rob Ducey	.04	.03	.02
102	Gene Larkin	.06	.05	.02
103	#1 Draft Pick (Tim Costo)(FC)	.50	.40	.20
104	Don Robinson	.04	.03	.02
105	Keith Miller	.05	.04	.02
106	Ed Nunez	.03	.02	.01
107	Luis Polonia	.04	.03	.02
108	Matt Young	.04	.03	.02
109	Greg Riddoch	.03	.02	.01
110	Tom Henke	.06	.05	.02
111	Andres Thomas	.03	.02	.01
112	Frank DiPino	.03	.02	.01
113	#1 Draft Pick (Carl Everett)(FC)	.35	.25	.14
114	Lance Dickson(FC)	.40	.30	.15
115	Hubie Brooks	.08	.06	.03
116	Mark Davis	.05	.04	.02
117	Dion James	.03	.02	.01
118	Tom Edens(FC)	.10	.08	.04
119	Carl Nichols(FC)	.05	.04	.02
120	Joe Carter	.08	.06	.03
121	Eric King	.05	.04	.02
122	Paul O'Neill	.06	.05	.02
123	Greg Harris	.05	.04	.02
124	Randy Bush	.04	.03	.02
125	Steve Bedrosian	.06	.05	.02
126	Bernard Gilkey(FC)	.25	.20	.10
127	Joe Price	.03	.02	.01
128	Travis Fryman	.50	.40	.20
129	Mark Eichhorn	.03	.02	.01
130	Ozzie Smith	.08	.06	.03
131	Checklist 1	.03	.02	.01
132	Jamie Quirk	.03	.02	.01
133	Greg Briley	.08	.06	.03
134	Kevin Elster	.04	.03	.02
135	Jerome Walton	.08	.06	.03
136	Dave Schmidt	.03	.02	.01
137	Randy Ready	.03	.02	.01
138	Jamie Moyer	.04	.03	.02
139	Jeff Treadway	.05	.04	.02
140	Fred McGriff	.10	.08	.04
141	Nick Leyva	.03	.02	.01
142	Curtis Wilkerson	.04	.03	.02
143	John Smiley	.04	.03	.02
144	Dave Henderson	.06	.05	.02
145	Lou Whitaker	.08	.06	.03
146	Dan Plesac	.06	.05	.02
147	Carlos Baerga	.20	.15	.08
148	Rey Palacios	.04	.03	.02
149	Al Osuna(FC)	.15	.11	.06
150	Cal Ripken	.12	.09	.05
151	Tom Browning	.06	.05	.02
152	Mickey Hatcher	.04	.03	.02
153	Bryan Harvey	.06	.05	.02
154	Jay Buhner	.06	.05	.02
155	Dwight Evans	.08	.06	.03
156	Carlos Martinez	.06	.05	.02
157	John Smoltz	.08	.06	.03
158	Jose Uribe	.04	.03	.02
159	Joe Boever	.03	.02	.01
160	Vince Coleman	.08	.06	.03
161	Tim Leary	.04	.03	.02
162	Ozzie Canseco(FC)	.25	.20	.10
163	Dave Johnson	.04	.03	.02
164	Edgar Diaz	.05	.04	.02
165	Sandy Alomar	.15	.11	.06
166	Harold Baines	.08	.06	.03
167	Randy Tomlin(FC)	.15	.11	.06
168	John Olerud	.60	.45	.25
169	Luis Aquino	.04	.03	.02
170	Carlton Fisk	.10	.08	.04
171	Tony LaRussa	.04	.03	.02
172	Pete Incaviglia	.06	.05	.02
173	Jason Grimsley	.06	.05	.02
174	Ken Caminiti	.05	.04	.02
175	Jack Armstrong	.08	.06	.03
176	John Orton(FC)	.06	.05	.02
177	Reggie Harris(FC)	.15	.11	.06
178	Dave Valle	.04	.03	.02
179	Pete Harnisch	.06	.05	.02
180	Tony Gwynn	.12	.09	.05
181	Duane Ward	.04	.03	.02
182	Junior Noboa	.04	.03	.02
183	Clay Parker	.04	.03	.02
184	Gary Green	.10	.08	.04
185	Joe Magrane	.06	.05	.02
186	Rod Booker	.03	.02	.01

		MT	NR MT	EX
187	Greg Cadaret	.03	.02	.01
188	Damon Berryhill	.06	.05	.02
189	Daryl Irvine(FC)	.15	.11	.06
190	Matt Williams	.15	.11	.06
191	Willie Blair	.10	.08	.04
192	Rob Deer	.06	.05	.02
193	Felix Fermin	.03	.02	.01
194	Xavier Hernandez(FC)	.08	.06	.03
195	Wally Joyner	.10	.08	.04
196	Jim Vatcher(FC)	.15	.11	.06
197	Chris Nabholz(FC)	.20	.15	.08
198	R.J. Reynolds	.04	.03	.02
199	Mike Hartley(FC)	.20	.15	.08
200	Darryl Strawberry	.20	.15	.08
201	Tom Kelly	.03	.02	.01
202	Jim Leyritz	.15	.11	.06
203	Gene Harris	.05	.04	.02
204	Herm Winningham	.04	.03	.02
205	Mike Perez(FC)	.15	.11	.06
206	Carlos Quintana	.08	.06	.03
207	Gary Wayne	.05	.04	.02
208	Willie Wilson	.06	.05	.02
209	Ken Howell	.05	.04	.02
210	Lance Parrish	.08	.06	.03
211	Brian Barnes(FC)	.15	.11	.06
212	Steve Finley	.06	.05	.02
213	Frank Wills	.06	.05	.02
214	Joe Girardi	.06	.05	.02
215	Dave Smith	.06	.05	.02
216	Greg Gagne	.04	.03	.02
217	Chris Bosio	.05	.04	.02
218	Rick Parker	.03	.02	.01
219	Jack McDowell	.06	.05	.02
220	Tim Wallach	.08	.06	.03
221	Don Slaught	.04	.03	.02
222	Brian McRae(FC)	.50	.40	.20
223	Allan Anderson	.04	.03	.02
224	Juan Gonzalez	.25	.20	.10
225	Randy Johnson	.06	.05	.02
226	Alfredo Griffin	.04	.03	.02
227	Steve Avery	.15	.11	.06
228	Rex Hudler	.04	.03	.02
229	Rance Mulliniks	.03	.02	.01
230	Sid Fernandez	.08	.06	.03
231	Doug Rader	.03	.02	.01
232	Len Dykstra	.08	.06	.03
233	Al Leiter	.03	.02	.01
234	Scott Erickson	.20	.15	.08
235	Dave Parker	.10	.08	.04
236	Frank Tanana	.06	.05	.02
237	Rick Cerone	.03	.02	.01
238	Mike Dunne	.03	.02	.01
239	Darren Lewis(FC)	.30	.25	.12
240	Mike Scott	.08	.06	.03
241	Dave Clark	.04	.03	.02
242	Mike LaCoss	.03	.02	.01
243	Lance Johnson	.06	.05	.02
244	Mike Jeffcoat	.03	.02	.01
245	Kal Daniels	.08	.06	.03
246	Kevin Wickander	.05	.04	.02
247	Jody Reed	.08	.06	.03
248	Tom Gordon	.08	.06	.03
249	Bob Melvin	.03	.02	.01
250	Dennis Eckersley	.10	.08	.04
251	Mark Lemke	.05	.04	.02
252	Mel Rojas(FC)	.15	.11	.06
253	Garry Templeton	.04	.03	.02
254	Shawn Boskie	.15	.11	.06
255	Brian Downing	.05	.04	.02
256	Greg Hibbard	.08	.06	.03
257	Tom O'Malley	.03	.02	.01
258	Chris Hammond(FC)	.15	.11	.06
259	Hensley Meulens	.08	.06	.03
260	Harold Reynolds	.06	.05	.02
261	Bud Harrelson	.03	.02	.01
262	Tim Jones	.04	.03	.02
263	Checklist 2	.03	.02	.01
264	Dave Hollins	.15	.11	.06
265	Mark Gubicza	.06	.05	.02
266	Carmen Castillo	.03	.02	.01
267	Mark Knudson	.03	.02	.01
268	Tom Brookens	.04	.03	.02
269	Joe Hesketh	.03	.02	.01
270	Mark McGwire	.25	.20	.10
271	Omar Olivares(FC)	.15	.11	.06
272	Jeff King	.06	.05	.02
273	Johnny Ray	.05	.04	.02
274	Ken Williams	.03	.02	.01
275	Alan Trammell	.10	.08	.04
276	Bill Swift	.05	.04	.02
277	Scott Coolbaugh	.06	.05	.02

		MT	NR MT	EX
278	Alex Fernandez(FC)	1.00	.70	.40
279	Jose Gonzalez	.04	.03	.02
280	Bret Saberhagen	.08	.06	.03
281	Larry Sheets	.04	.03	.02
282	Don Carman	.04	.03	.02
283	Marquis Grissom	.10	.08	.04
284	Bill Spiers	.06	.05	.02
285	Jim Abbott	.10	.08	.04
286	Ken Oberkfell	.04	.03	.02
287	Mark Grant	.03	.02	.01
288	Derrick May(FC)	.40	.30	.15
289	Tim Birtsas	.03	.02	.01
290	Steve Sax	.08	.06	.03
291	John Wathan	.03	.02	.01
292	Bud Black	.04	.03	.02
293	Jay Bell	.06	.05	.02
294	Mike Moore	.06	.05	.02
295	Rafael Palmeiro	.08	.06	.03
296	Mark Williamson	.04	.03	.02
297	Manny Lee	.04	.03	.02
298	Omar Vizquel	.04	.03	.02
299	Scott Radinsky	.15	.11	.06
300	Kirby Puckett	.15	.11	.06
301	Steve Farr	.04	.03	.02
302	Tim Teufel	.03	.02	.01
303	Mike Boddicker	.06	.05	.02
304	Kevin Reimer(FC)	.10	.08	.04
305	Mike Scioscia	.06	.05	.02
306	Lonnie Smith	.06	.05	.02
307	Andy Benes	.08	.06	.03
308	Tom Pagnozzi	.04	.03	.02
309	Norm Charlton	.08	.06	.03
310	Gary Carter	.08	.06	.03
311	Jeff Pico	.03	.02	.01
312	Charlie Hayes	.06	.05	.02
313	Ron Robinson	.06	.05	.02
314	Gary Pettis	.04	.03	.02
315	Roberto Alomar	.10	.08	.04
316	Gene Nelson	.03	.02	.01
317	Mike Fitzgerald	.03	.02	.01
318	Rick Aguilera	.06	.05	.02
319	Jeff McKnight(FC)	.05	.04	.02
320	Tony Fernandez	.08	.06	.03
321	Bob Rodgers	.03	.02	.01
322	Terry Shumpert	.20	.15	.08
323	Cory Snyder	.08	.06	.03
324	Ron Kittle	.08	.06	.03
325	Brett Butler	.06	.05	.02
326	Ken Patterson	.04	.03	.02
327	Ron Hassey	.03	.02	.01
328	Walt Terrell	.04	.03	.02
329	Dave Justice	.80	.60	.30
330	Doc Gooden	.20	.15	.08
331	Eric Anthony	.10	.08	.04
332	Kenny Rogers	.06	.05	.02
333	#1 Draft Pick (Chipper Jones)(FC)	.50	.40	.20
334	Todd Benzinger	.05	.04	.02
335	Mitch Williams	.08	.06	.03
336	Matt Nokes	.06	.05	.02
337	Keith Comstock	.03	.02	.01
338	Luis Rivera	.04	.03	.02
339	Larry Walker	.08	.06	.03
340	Ramon Martinez	.15	.11	.06
341	John Moses	.03	.02	.01
342	Mickey Morandini	.15	.11	.06
343	Jose Oquendo	.04	.03	.02
344	Jeff Russell	.06	.05	.02
345	Jose DeJesus	.06	.05	.02
346	Jesse Orosco	.04	.03	.02
347	Greg Vaughn	.10	.08	.04
348	Todd Stottlemyre	.06	.05	.02
349	Dave Gallagher	.04	.03	.02
350	Glenn Davis	.12	.09	.05
351	Joe Torre	.03	.02	.01
352	Frank White	.06	.05	.02
353	Tony Castillo	.05	.04	.02
354	Sid Bream	.05	.04	.02
355	Chili Davis	.06	.05	.02
356	Mike Marshall	.06	.05	.02
357	Jack Savage	.10	.08	.04
358	Mark Parent	.03	.02	.01
359	Chuck Cary	.04	.03	.02
360	Rock Raines	.15	.11	.06
361	Scott Garrelts	.05	.04	.02
362	Hector Villanueva	.15	.11	.06
363	Rick Mahler	.04	.03	.02
364	Dan Pasqua	.06	.05	.02
365	Mike Schooler	.06	.05	.02
366	Checklist 3	.03	.02	.01
367	Dave Walsh(FC)	.15	.11	.06
368	Felix Jose	.06	.05	.02

	MT	NR MT	EX			MT	NR MT	EX
369 Steve Searcy	.06	.05	.02	460 Dave Steib	.08	.06	.03
370 Kelly Gruber	.12	.09	.05	461 Robin Ventura	.08	.06	.03
371 Jeff Montgomery	.06	.05	.02	462 Steve Frey	.06	.05	.02
372 Spike Owen	.05	.04	.02	463 Dwight Smith	.06	.05	.02
373 Darrin Jackson	.04	.03	.02	464 Steve Buechele	.04	.03	.02
374 *Larry Casian*(FC)	.15	.11	.06	465 Ken Griffey	.05	.04	.02
375 Tony Pena	.06	.05	.02	466 Charles Nagy(FC)	.10	.08	.04
376 Mike Harkey	.08	.06	.03	467 Dennis Cook	.06	.05	.02
377 Rene Gonzales	.03	.02	.01	468 Tim Hulett	.04	.03	.02
378 *Wilson Alvarez*(FC)	.20	.15	.08	469 Chet Lemon	.05	.04	.02
379 Randy Velarde	.04	.03	.02	470 Howard Johnson	.10	.08	.04
380 Willie McGee	.08	.06	.03	471 #1 Draft Pick *(Mike Lieberthal)*(FC)			
381 Jose Lind	.05	.04	.02		.35	.25	.14
382 Mackey Sasser	.05	.04	.02	472 Kirt Manwaring	.05	.04	.02
383 Pete Smith	.06	.05	.02	473 Curt Young	.04	.03	.02
384 Gerald Perry	.05	.04	.02	474 *Phil Plantier*(FC)	.50	.40	.20
385 Mickey Tettleton	.05	.04	.02	475 Teddy Higuera	.08	.06	.03
386 Cecil Fielder (AS)	.10	.08	.04	476 Glenn Wilson	.05	.04	.02
387 Julio Franco (AS)	.08	.06	.03	477 Mike Fetters	.06	.05	.02
388 Kelly Gruber (AS)	.08	.06	.03	478 Kurt Stillwell	.05	.04	.02
389 Alan Trammell (AS)	.06	.05	.02	479 Bob Patterson	.03	.02	.01
390 Jose Canseco (AS)	.10	.08	.04	480 Dave Magadan	.10	.08	.04
391 Rickey Henderson (AS)	.10	.08	.04	481 Eddie Whitson	.05	.04	.02
392 Ken Griffey,Jr. (AS)	.15	.11	.06	482 Tino Martinez	.40	.30	.15
393 Carlton Fisk (AS)	.08	.06	.03	483 Mike Aldrete	.04	.03	.02
394 Bob Welch (AS)	.06	.05	.02	484 Dave LaPoint	.04	.03	.02
395 Chuck Finley (AS)	.06	.05	.02	485 Terry Pendleton	.06	.05	.02
396 Bobby Thigpen (AS)	.08	.06	.03	486 Tommy Greene(FC)	.10	.08	.04
397 Eddie Murray (AS)	.08	.06	.03	487 Rafael Belliard	.03	.02	.01
398 Ryne Sandberg (AS)	.10	.08	.04	488 Jeff Manto(FC)	.15	.11	.06
399 Matt Williams (AS)	.08	.06	.03	489 Bobby Valentine	.03	.02	.01
400 Barry Larkin (AS)	.08	.06	.03	490 Kirk Gibson	.08	.06	.03
401 Barry Bonds (AS)	.10	.08	.04	491 #1 Draft Pick *(Kurt Miller)*(FC)	.30	.25	.12
402 Darryl Strawberry (AS)	.10	.08	.04	492 Ernie Whitt	.05	.04	.02
403 Bobby Bonilla (AS)	.10	.08	.04	493 Jose Rijo	.08	.06	.03
404 Mike Scoscia (AS)	.06	.05	.02	494 Chris James	.06	.05	.02
405 Doug Drabek (AS)	.08	.06	.03	495 Charlie Hough	.04	.03	.02
406 Frank Viola (AS)	.08	.06	.03	496 Marty Barrett	.05	.04	.02
407 John Franco (AS)	.06	.05	.02	497 Ben McDonald	.30	.25	.12
408 Ernie Riles	.04	.03	.02	498 Mark Salas	.03	.02	.01
409 Mike Stanley	.03	.02	.01	499 Melido Perez	.06	.05	.02
410 Dave Righetti	.08	.06	.03	500 Will Clark	.30	.25	.12
411 Lance Blankenship	.04	.03	.02	501 Mike Bielecki	.05	.04	.02
412 Dave Bergman	.03	.02	.01	502 Carney Lansford	.06	.05	.02
413 Terry Mulholland	.06	.05	.02	503 Roy Smith	.04	.03	.02
414 Sammy Sosa	.15	.11	.06	504 *Julio Valera*(FC)	.15	.11	.06
415 Rick Sutcliffe	.08	.06	.03	505 Chuck Finley	.08	.06	.03
416 Randy Milligan	.06	.05	.02	506 Darnell Coles	.04	.03	.02
417 Bill Krueger	.03	.02	.01	507 Steve Jeltz	.03	.02	.01
418 Nick Esasky	.06	.05	.02	508 *Mike York*(FC)	.15	.11	.06
419 Jeff Reed	.03	.02	.01	509 Glenallen Hill	.06	.05	.02
420 Bobby Thigpen	.08	.06	.03	510 John Franco	.08	.06	.03
421 Alex Cole(FC)	.30	.25	.12	511 Steve Balboni	.03	.02	.01
422 Rick Rueschel	.06	.05	.02	512 Jose Mesa(FC)	.05	.04	.02
423 Rafael Ramirez	.04	.03	.02	513 Jerald Clark	.05	.04	.02
424 Calvin Schiraldi	.03	.02	.01	514 Mike Stanton	.08	.06	.03
425 Andy Van Slyke	.08	.06	.03	515 Alvin Davis	.08	.06	.03
426 *Joe Grahe*(FC)	.15	.11	.06	516 *Karl Rhodes*(FC)	.15	.11	.06
427 Rick Dempsey	.03	.02	.01	517 Joe Oliver	.06	.05	.02
428 *John Barfield*(FC)	.10	.08	.04	518 Cris Carpenter	.05	.04	.02
429 Stump Merrill	.03	.02	.01	519 Sparky Anderson	.04	.03	.02
430 Gary Gaetti	.08	.06	.03	520 Mark Grace	.15	.11	.06
431 Paul Gibson	.03	.02	.01	521 Joe Orsulak	.05	.04	.02
432 Delino DeShields	.15	.11	.06	522 Stan Belinda	.06	.05	.02
433 Pat Tabler	.04	.03	.02	523 *Rodney McCray*(FC)	.15	.11	.06
434 Julio Machado(FC)	.10	.08	.04	524 Darrel Akerfelds	.04	.03	.02
435 Kevin Maas	.60	.45	.25	525 Willie Randolph	.06	.05	.02
436 Scott Bankhead	.05	.04	.02	526 Moises Alou(FC)	.15	.11	.06
437 Doug Dascenzo	.04	.03	.02	527 Checklist 4	.03	.02	.01
438 Vicente Palacios	.05	.04	.02	528 Denny Martinez	.06	.05	.02
439 Dickie Thon	.03	.02	.01	529 #1 Daraft Pick *(Mark Newfield)*(FC)			
440 George Bell	.08	.06	.03		.30	.25	.12
441 Zane Smith	.04	.03	.02	530 Roger Clemens	.20	.15	.08
442 Charlie O'Brien	.04	.03	.02	531 *Dave Rhode*(FC)	.15	.11	.06
443 Jeff Innis	.05	.04	.02	532 Kirk McCaskill	.06	.05	.02
444 Glenn Braggs	.05	.04	.02	533 Oddibe McDowell	.05	.04	.02
445 Greg Swindell	.06	.05	.02	534 Mike Jackson	.04	.03	.02
446 *Craig Grebeck*(FC)	.15	.11	.06	535 Ruben Sierra	.15	.11	.06
447 John Burkett	.12	.09	.05	536 Mike Witt	.04	.03	.02
448 Craig Lefferts	.05	.04	.02	537 Mike LaValliere	.05	.04	.02
449 Juan Berenguer	.03	.02	.01	538 Bip Roberts	.05	.04	.02
450 Wade Boggs	.15	.11	.06	539 Scott Terry	.03	.02	.01
451 Neal Heaton	.05	.04	.02	540 George Brett	.12	.09	.05
452 Bill Schroeder	.03	.02	.01	541 Domingo Ramos	.03	.02	.01
453 Lenny Harris	.05	.04	.02	542 Rob Murphy	.03	.02	.01
454 Kevin Appier	.08	.06	.03	543 Junior Felix	.08	.06	.03
455 Walt Weiss	.06	.05	.02	544 Alejandro Pena	.03	.02	.01
456 Charlie Leibrandt	.05	.04	.02	545 Dale Murphy	.10	.08	.04
457 *Todd Hundley*	.12	.09	.05	546 Jeff Ballard	.05	.04	.02
458 Brian Holman	.06	.05	.02	547 Mike Pagliarulo	.04	.03	.02
459 Tom Trebelhorn	.03	.02	.01	548 Jaime Navarro	.15	.11	.06

		MT	NR MT	EX				MT	NR MT	EX
549	John McNamara	.03	.02	.01		640	Andre Dawson	.10	.08	.04
550	Eric Davis	.15	.11	.06		641	Mike Henneman	.06	.05	.02
551	Bob Kipper	.03	.02	.01		642	Hal Morris	.15	.11	.06
552	Jeff Hamilton	.04	.03	.02		643	Jim Presley	.06	.05	.02
553	*Joe Klink*	.10	.08	.04		644	Chuck Crim	.04	.03	.02
554	Brian Harper	.06	.05	.02		645	Juan Samuel	.06	.05	.02
555	*Turner Ward*(FC)	.20	.15	.08		646	*Andujar Cedeno*(FC)	.50	.40	.20
556	Gary Ward	.04	.03	.02		647	Mark Portugal	.04	.03	.02
557	Wally Whitehurst	.06	.05	.02		648	Lee Stevens(FC)	.15	.11	.06
558	Otis Nixon	.03	.02	.01		649	*Bill Sampen*	.15	.11	.06
559	Adam Peterson	.06	.05	.02		650	Jack Clark	.08	.06	.03
560	Greg Smith(FC)	.15	.11	.06		651	*Alan Mills*	.12	.09	.05
561	Tim McIntosh(FC)	.15	.11	.06		652	Kevin Romine	.03	.02	.01
562	Jeff Kunkel	.03	.02	.01		653	*Anthony Telford*(FC)	.20	.15	.08
563	*Brent Knackert*	.10	.08	.04		654	Paul Sorrento(FC)	.15	.11	.06
564	Dante Bichette	.08	.06	.03		655	Erik Hanson	.08	.06	.03
565	Craig Biggio	.08	.06	.03		656	Checklist 5	.03	.02	.01
566	*Craig Wilson*(FC)	.15	.11	.06		657	Mike Kingery	.03	.02	.01
567	Dwayne Henry	.03	.02	.01		658	*Scott Aldred*(FC)	.15	.11	.06
568	Ron Karkovice	.04	.03	.02		659	*Oscar Azocar*(FC)	.25	.20	.10
569	Curt Schilling	.05	.04	.02		660	Lee Smith	.06	.05	.02
570	Barry Bonds	.15	.11	.06		661	Steve Lake	.03	.02	.01
571	Pat Combs	.08	.06	.03		662	Rob Dibble	.08	.06	.03
572	Dave Anderson	.03	.02	.01		663	Greg Brock	.05	.04	.02
573	*Rich Rodriguez*(FC)	.15	.11	.06		664	John Farrell	.04	.03	.02
574	John Marzano	.04	.03	.02		665	Jim Leyland	.03	.02	.01
575	Robin Yount	.15	.11	.06		666	Danny Darwin	.06	.05	.02
576	Jeff Kaiser(FC)	.10	.08	.04		667	Kent Anderson	.04	.03	.02
577	Bill Doran	.06	.05	.02		668	Bill Long	.04	.03	.02
578	Dave West	.06	.05	.02		669	Lou Pinella	.04	.03	.02
579	Roger Craig	.03	.02	.01		670	Rickey Henderson	.35	.25	.14
580	Dave Stewart	.12	.09	.05		671	Andy McGaffigan	.03	.02	.01
581	Luis Quinones	.03	.02	.01		672	Shane Mack	.06	.05	.02
582	Marty Clary	.03	.02	.01		673	*Greg Olson*	.15	.11	.06
583	Tony Phillips	.04	.03	.02		674	Kevin Gross	.06	.05	.02
584	Kevin Brown	.06	.05	.02		675	Tom Brunansky	.08	.06	.03
585	Pete O'Brien	.04	.03	.02		676	*Scott Chiamparino*(FC)	.20	.15	.08
586	Fred Lynn	.05	.04	.02		677	Billy Ripken	.04	.03	.02
587	Jose Offerman(FC)	.40	.30	.15		678	Mark Davidson	.03	.02	.01
588	*Mark Whiten*(FC)	.25	.20	.10		679	Bill Bathe(FC)	.04	.03	.02
589	*Scott Ruskin*	.10	.08	.04		680	David Cone	.06	.05	.02
590	Eddie Murray	.12	.09	.05		681	*Jeff Schaefer*(FC)	.10	.08	.04
591	Ken Hill	.05	.04	.02		682	*Ray Lankford*(FC)	.60	.45	.25
592	B.J. Surhoff	.06	.05	.02		683	Derek Lilliquist	.05	.04	.02
593	*Mike Walker*(FC)	.15	.11	.06		684	Milt Cuyler(FC)	.15	.11	.06
594	*Rich Garces*(FC)	.15	.11	.06		685	Doug Drabek	.08	.06	.03
595	Bill Landrum	.05	.04	.02		686	Mike Gallego	.03	.02	.01
596	#1 Draft Pick *(Ronnie Walden)*(FC)	.30	.25	.12		687	John Cerutti	.03	.02	.01
597	Jerry Don Gleaton	.03	.02	.01		688	*Rosario Rodriguez*(FC)	.15	.11	.06
598	Sam Horn	.05	.04	.02		689	John Kruk	.06	.05	.02
599	Greg Myers	.04	.03	.02		690	Orel Hershiser	.10	.08	.04
600	Bo Jackson	.40	.30	.15		691	Mike Blowers	.10	.08	.04
601	Bob Ojeda	.04	.03	.02		692	*Efrain Valdez*(FC)	.15	.11	.06
602	Casey Candaele	.04	.03	.02		693	Francisco Cabrera	.08	.06	.03
603	*Wes Chamberlain*(FC)	.25	.20	.10		694	Randy Veres	.03	.02	.01
604	Billy Hatcher	.05	.04	.02		695	Kevin Seitzer	.08	.06	.03
605	Jeff Reardon	.08	.06	.03		696	Steve Olin	.05	.04	.02
606	Jim Gott	.04	.03	.02		697	Shawn Abner	.04	.03	.02
607	Edgar Martinez	.06	.05	.02		698	Mark Guthrie	.05	.04	.02
608	Todd Burns	.03	.02	.01		699	Jim Lefebvre	.03	.02	.01
609	Jeff Torborg	.03	.02	.01		700	Jose Canseco	.40	.30	.15
610	Andres Galarraga	.08	.06	.03		701	Pascual Perez	.05	.04	.02
611	Dave Eiland	.04	.03	.02		702	*Tim Naehring*	.20	.15	.08
612	Steve Lyons	.04	.03	.02		703	Juan Agosto	.03	.02	.01
613	Eric Show	.04	.03	.02		704	Devon White	.06	.05	.02
614	Luis Salazar	.04	.03	.02		705	Robby Thompson	.05	.04	.02
615	Bert Blyleven	.08	.06	.03		706	Brad Arnsberg	.04	.03	.02
616	Todd Zeile	.15	.11	.06		707	Jim Eisenreich	.04	.03	.02
617	Bill Wegman	.04	.03	.02		708	*John Mitchell*(FC)	.12	.09	.05
618	Sil Campusano	.04	.03	.02		709	Matt Sinatro	.03	.02	.01
619	David Wells	.04	.03	.02		710	Kent Hrbek	.08	.06	.03
620	Ozzie Guillen	.08	.06	.03		711	Gary Redus, Jose DeLeon	.05	.04	.02
621	Ted Power	.03	.02	.01		712	Ricky Jordan	.06	.05	.02
622	Jack Daugherty	.05	.04	.02		713	Scott Scudder	.08	.06	.03
623	Jeff Blauser	.04	.03	.02		714	Marvell Wynne	.04	.03	.02
624	Tom Candiotti	.04	.03	.02		715	Tim Burke	.06	.05	.02
625	Terry Steinbach	.06	.05	.02		716	Bob Geren	.06	.05	.02
626	Gerald Young	.03	.02	.01		717	Phil Bradley	.06	.05	.02
627	*Tim Layana*	.15	.11	.06		718	Steve Crawford	.03	.02	.01
628	Greg Litton	.05	.04	.02		719	Kevin McReynolds	.06	.05	.02
629	Wes Gardner	.04	.03	.02		720	Cecil Fielder	.20	.15	.08
630	Dave Winfield	.10	.08	.04		721	*Mark Lee*(FC)	.15	.11	.06
631	Mike Morgan	.04	.03	.02		722	Wally Backman	.04	.03	.02
632	Lloyd Moseby	.06	.05	.02		723	Candy Maldonado	.08	.06	.03
633	Kevin Tapani	.10	.08	.04		724	*David Segui*(FC)	.30	.25	.12
634	Henry Cotto	.03	.02	.01		725	Ron Gant	.12	.09	.05
635	Andy Hawkins	.04	.03	.02		726	Phil Stephenson	.04	.03	.02
636	Geronimo Pena(FC)	.15	.11	.06		727	Mookie Wilson	.06	.05	.02
637	Bruce Ruffin	.04	.03	.02		728	Scott Sanderson	.04	.03	.02
638	Mike Macfarlane	.04	.03	.02		729	Don Zimmer	.04	.03	.02
639	Frank Robinson	.05	.04	.02		730	Barry Larkin	.12	.09	.05

		MT	NR MT	EX
731	*Jeff Gray*(FC)	.15	.11	.06
732	Franklin Stubbs	.05	.04	.02
733	Kelly Downs	.04	.03	.02
734	John Russell	.03	.02	.01
735	Ron Darling	.06	.05	.02
736	Dick Schofield	.04	.03	.02
737	Tim Crews	.03	.02	.01
738	Mel Hall	.04	.03	.02
739	*Russ Swan*	.10	.08	.04
740	Ryne Sandberg	.20	.15	.08
741	Jimmy Key	.06	.05	.02
742	Tommy Gregg	.04	.03	.02
743	Bryn Smith	.04	.03	.02
744	Nelson Santovenia	.05	.04	.02
745	Doug Jones	.08	.06	.03
746	John Shelby	.03	.02	.01
747	Tony Fossas	.03	.02	.01
748	Al Newman	.03	.02	.01
749	Greg Harris	.04	.03	.02
750	Bobby Bonilla	.12	.09	.05
751	*Wayne Edwards*	.10	.08	.04
752	Kevin Bass	.05	.04	.02
753	*Paul Marak*(FC)	.15	.11	.06
754	Bill Pecota	.04	.03	.02
755	Mark Langston	.10	.08	.04
756	Jeff Huson	.05	.04	.02
757	Mark Gardner	.06	.05	.02
758	Mike Devereaux	.06	.05	.02
759	Bobby Cox	.03	.02	.01
760	Benny Santiago	.08	.06	.03
761	Larry Andersen	.04	.03	.02
762	Mitch Webster	.04	.03	.02
763	*Dana Kiecker*	.10	.08	.04
764	Mark Carreon	.05	.04	.02
765	Shawon Dunston	.08	.06	.03
766	Jeff Robinson	.05	.04	.02
767	#1 Draft Pick *(Dan Wilson)*(FC)	.30	.25	.12
768	Donn Pall	.04	.03	.02
769	*Tim Sherrill*(FC)	.15	.11	.06
770	Jay Howell	.06	.05	.02
772	Kent Mercker(FC)	.10	.08	.04
773	Tom Foley	.03	.02	.01
774	Dennis Rasmussen	.04	.03	.02
775	Julio Franco	.08	.06	.03
776	Brent Mayne(FC)	.15	.11	.06
777	John Candelaria	.05	.04	.02
778	Dan Gladden	.05	.04	.02
779	Carmelo Martinez	.04	.03	.02
780	Randy Myers	.08	.06	.03
781	Darryl Hamilton	.05	.04	.02
782	Jim Deshaies	.05	.04	.02
783	Joel Skinner	.03	.02	.01
784	Willie Fraser	.04	.03	.02
785	Scott Fletcher	.04	.03	.02
786	Eric Plunk	.03	.02	.01
787	Checklist 6	.03	.02	.01
788	Bob Milacki	.06	.05	.02
789	Tom Lasorda	.04	.03	.02
790	Ken Griffey,Jr.	.50	.40	.20
791	Mike Benjamin(FC)	.15	.11	.06
792	Mike Greenwell	.15	.11	.06

colorful, employing nine different colors including deep black borders. The backs, printed in blue and orange, contain career highlights and composite minor and major league statistics. The set was distributed in a specially designed box and sold for $1.99 in retail outlets.

		MT	NR MT	EX
Complete Set:		5.00	3.75	2.00
Common Player:		.09	.07	.04
1	Andy Allanson	.12	.09	.05
2	Paul Assenmacher	.12	.09	.05
3	Scott Bailes	.12	.09	.05
4	Barry Bonds	.30	.25	.12
5	Jose Canseco	1.50	1.25	.60
6	John Cerutti	.15	.11	.06
7	Will Clark	.90	.70	.35
8	Kal Daniels	.25	.20	.10
9	Jim Deshaies	.15	.11	.06
10	Mark Eichhorn	.12	.09	.05
11	Ed Hearn	.09	.07	.04
12	Pete Incaviglia	.40	.30	.15
13	Bo Jackson	.60	.45	.25
14	Wally Joyner	.60	.45	.25
15	Charlie Kerfeld	.09	.07	.04
16	Eric King	.12	.09	.05
17	John Kruk	.40	.30	.15
18	Barry Larkin	.30	.25	.12
19	Mike LaValliere	.15	.11	.06
20	Greg Mathews	.15	.11	.06
21	Kevin Mitchell	.20	.15	.08
22	Dan Plesac	.20	.15	.08
23	Bruce Ruffin	.15	.11	.06
24	Ruben Sierra	.50	.40	.20
25	Cory Snyder	.40	.30	.15
26	Kurt Stillwell	.20	.15	.08
27	Dale Sveum	.12	.09	.05
28	Danny Tartabull	.30	.25	.12
29	Andres Thomas	.15	.11	.06
30	Robby Thompson	.15	.11	.06
31	Jim Traber	.09	.07	.04
32	Mitch Williams	.15	.11	.06
33	Todd Worrell	.30	.25	.12

1988 Toys "R" Us Rookies

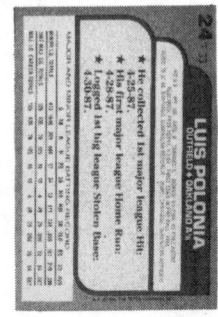

This 33-card boxed edition was produced by Topps for exclusive distribution at Toys "R" Us stores. The glossy standard-size cards spotlight rookies in both closeups and action photos on a bright blue background inlaid with yellow. The Toys "R" Us logo frames the top left corner, above a curving white banner that reads "Topps 1988 Collectors' Edition Rookies". A black Topps logo hugs the upper right-hand edge of the photo. The player name, red-lettered on a tube of yellow, frames the bottom. Card backs are horizontal, blue and pink on a bright pink background and include the player name, personal information and career highlights and stats.

1987 Toys "R" Us

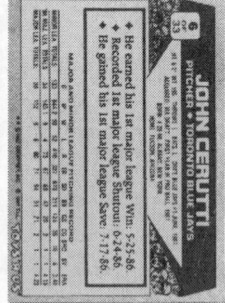

Marked as a collectors' edition set and titled "Baseball Rookies," the 1987 Toys "R" Us issue was produced by Topps for the toy store chain. The set is comprised of 33 glossy-coated cards, each measuring 2-1/2" by 3-1/2". The card fronts are very

	MT	NR MT	EX
Complete Set:	5.00	3.75	2.00
Common Player:	.09	.07	.04

		MT	NR MT	EX
1	Todd Benzinger	.20	.15	.08
2	Bob Brower	.09	.07	.04
3	Jerry Browne	.09	.07	.04
4	DeWayne Buice	.09	.07	.04
5	Ellis Burks	.70	.50	.30
6	Ken Caminiti	.12	.09	.05
7	Casey Candaele	.09	.07	.04
8	Dave Cone	.50	.40	.20
9	Kelly Downs	.20	.15	.08
10	Mike Dunne	.15	.11	.06
11	Ken Gerhart	.12	.09	.05
12	Mike Greenwell	.70	.50	.30
13	Mike Henneman	.12	.09	.05
14	Sam Horn	.20	.15	.08
15	Joe Magrane	.20	.15	.08
16	Fred Manrique	.12	.09	.05
17	John Marzano	.12	.09	.05
18	Fred McGriff	.15	.11	.06
19	Mark McGwire	1.00	.70	.40
20	Jeff Musselman	.12	.09	.05
21	Randy Myers	.20	.15	.08
22	Matt Nokes	.40	.30	.15
23	Al Pedrique	.12	.09	.05
24	Luis Polonia	.15	.11	.06
25	Billy Ripken	.25	.20	.10
26	Benny Santiago	.25	.20	.10
27	Kevin Seitzer	.70	.50	.30
28	John Smiley	.20	.15	.08
29	Mike Stanley	.09	.07	.04
30	Terry Steinbach	.20	.15	.08
31	B.J. Surhoff	.25	.20	.10
32	Bobby Thigpen	.12	.09	.05
33	Devon White	.25	.20	.10

		MT	NR MT	EX
18	Roberto Kelly	.25	.20	.10
19	Al Leiter	.09	.07	.04
20	Jack McDowell	.09	.07	.04
21	Melido Perez	.12	.09	.05
22	Jeff Pico	.09	.07	.04
23	Jody Reed	.12	.09	.05
24	Chris Sabo	.25	.20	.10
25	Nelson Santovenia	.15	.11	.06
26	Mackey Sasser	.09	.07	.04
27	Mike Schooler	.12	.09	.05
28	Gary Sheffield	.90	.70	.35
29	Pete Smith	.12	.09	.05
30	Pete Stanicek	.09	.07	.04
31	Jeff Treadway	.09	.07	.04
32	Walt Weiss	.25	.20	.10
33	Dave West	.35	.25	.14

1990 Toys "R" Us Rookies

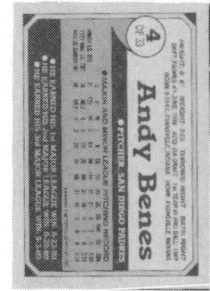

This 33-card set marks the fourth straigh year that Topps has produced a set to be sold exclusively at Toys "R" Us stores. The card fronts contain full- color photos of 1989 rookies. The flip sides are horizontal and provide both minor and major league totals. The complete set is packaged in a special box which features a checklist uon the back.

		MT	NR MT	EX
Complete Set:		4.00	3.00	1.50
Common Player:		.08	.06	.03
1	Jim Abbott	.15	.11	.06
2	Eric Anthony	.40	.30	.15
3	Joey Belle	.15	.11	.06
4	Andy Benes	.20	.15	.08
5	Greg Briley	.08	.06	.03
6	Kevin Brown	.10	.08	.04
7	Mark Carreon	.08	.06	.03
8	Mike Devereaux	.08	.06	.03
9	Junior Felix	.25	.20	.10
10	Mark Gardner	.15	.11	.06
11	Bob Geren	.08	.06	.03
12	Tom Gordon	.20	.15	.08
13	Ken Griffey,Jr.	1.00	.70	.40
14	Pete Harnisch	.10	.08	.04
15	Ken Hill	.08	.06	.03
16	Gregg Jefferies	.30	.25	.12
17	Derek Lilliquist	.08	.06	.03
18	Carlos Martinez	.10	.08	.04
19	Ramon Martinez	.60	.45	.25
20	Bob Milacki	.08	.06	.03
21	Gregg Olson	.15	.11	.06
22	Kenny Rogers	.10	.08	.04
23	Alex Sanchez	.10	.08	.04
24	Gary Sheffield	.30	.25	.12
25	Dwight Smith	.10	.08	.04
26	Billy Spiers	.08	.06	.03
27	Greg Vaughn	.40	.30	.15
28	Robin Ventura	.25	.20	.10
29	Jerome Walton	.40	.30	.15
30	Dave West	.08	.06	.03
31	John Wetteland	.15	.11	.06
32	Craig Worthington	.10	.08	.04
33	Todd Zeile	.40	.30	.15

1989 Toys "R" Us Rookies

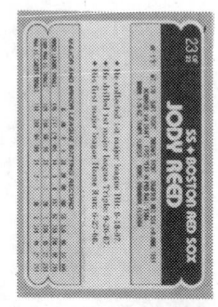

This glossy set of 33 top rookies was produced by Topps for the Toys 'R' Us chain and was sold in a special box. Each player's name and position appear below the full-color photo, while the Toys 'R' Us logo and "Topps 1989 Collector's Edition" appear along the top. Major and minor league stats are on the back. The set is numbered alphabetically.

		MT	NR MT	EX
Complete Set:		5.00	3.75	2.00
Common Player:		.09	.07	.04
1	Roberto Alomar	.20	.15	.08
2	Brady Anderson	.09	.07	.04
3	Tim Belcher	.20	.15	.08
4	Damon Berryhill	.12	.09	.05
5	Jay Buhner	.12	.09	.05
6	Sherman Corbett	.09	.07	.04
7	Kevin Elster	.12	.09	.05
8	Cecil Espy	.12	.09	.05
9	Dave Gallagher	.12	.09	.05
10	Ron Gant	.12	.09	.05
11	Paul Gibson	.09	.07	.04
12	Mark Grace	.90	.70	.35
13	Bryan Harvey	.12	.09	.05
14	Darrin Jackson	.09	.07	.04
15	Gregg Jefferies	.70	.50	.30
16	Ron Jones	.15	.11	.06
17	Ricky Jordan	.70	.50	.30

1969 Transogram

Produced by the Transogram toy company, the 2-1/2" by 3-1/2" cards were printed on the bottom of toy baseball player statue boxes. The cards feature a color photo of the player surrounded by a rounded white border. Below the photo is the player's name in red and his team and other personal details all printed in black. The overall background is yellow. The cards were designed to be cut off the box, but collectors prefer to find the box intact and better still, with the statue inside. Although the 60-card set features a lot of stars, and is fairly scarce, it does not have a lot of popularity today.

		NR MT	EX	VG
Complete Set:		600.00	300.00	180.00
Common Player:		.80	.40	.25
(1)	Hank Aaron	30.00	15.00	9.00
(2)	Richie Allen	4.00	2.00	1.25
(3)	Felipe Alou	3.00	1.50	.90
(4)	Matty Alou	3.00	1.50	.90
(5)	Luis Aparicio	15.00	7.50	4.50
(6)	Joe Azcue	2.00	1.00	.60
(7)	Ernie Banks	15.00	7.50	4.50
(8)	Lou Brock	20.00	10.00	6.00
(9)	John Callison	3.00	1.50	.90
(10)	Jose Cardenal	2.00	1.00	.60
(11)	Danny Cater	2.00	1.00	.60
(12)	Roberto Clemente	25.00	12.50	7.50
(13)	Willie Davis	1.00	.50	.30
(14)	Mike Epstein	2.00	1.00	.60
(15)	Jim Fregosi	1.00	.50	.30
(16)	Bob Gibson	8.00	4.00	2.50
(17)	Tom Haller	2.00	1.00	.60
(18)	Ken Harrelson	3.00	1.50	.90
(19)	Willie Horton	3.00	1.50	.90
(20)	Frank Howard	1.50	.70	.45
(21)	Tommy John	8.00	4.00	2.50
(22)	Al Kaline	15.00	7.50	4.50
(23)	Harmon Killebrew	15.00	7.50	4.50
(24)	Bobby Knoop	2.00	1.00	.60
(25)	Jerry Koosman	.80	.40	.25
(26)	Jim Lefebvre	2.00	1.00	.60
(27)	Mickey Mantle	125.00	62.00	37.00
(28)	Juan Marichal	8.00	4.00	2.50
(29)	Lee May	3.00	1.50	.90
(30)	Willie Mays	30.00	15.00	9.00
(31)	Bill Mazeroski	4.00	2.00	1.25
(32)	Tim McCarver	4.00	2.00	1.25
(33)	Willie McCovey	15.00	7.50	4.50
(34)	Denny McLain	1.50	.70	.45
(35)	Dave McNally	3.00	1.50	.90
(36)	Rick Monday	3.00	1.50	.90
(37)	Blue Moon Odom	.80	.40	.25
(38)	Tony Oliva	1.50	.70	.45
(39)	Camilo Pascual	3.00	1.50	.90
(40)	Tony Perez	7.00	3.50	2.00
(41)	Rico Petrocelli	1.00	.50	.30
(42)	Rick Reichardt	.80	.40	.25
(43)	Brooks Robinson	25.00	12.50	7.50
(44)	Frank Robinson	8.00	4.00	2.50
(45)	Cookie Rojas	2.00	1.00	.60
(46)	Pete Rose	30.00	15.00	9.00
(47)	Ron Santo	1.50	.70	.45
(48)	Tom Seaver	15.00	7.50	4.50
(49)	Rusty Staub	4.00	2.00	1.25
(50)	Mel Stottlemyre	1.00	.50	.30

		NR MT	EX	VG
(51)	Ron Swoboda	.80	.40	.25
(52)	Luis Tiant	3.00	1.50	.90
(53)	Joe Torre	4.00	2.00	1.25
(54)	Cesar Tovar	2.00	1.00	.60
(55)	Pete Ward	2.00	1.00	.60
(56)	Roy White	3.00	1.50	.90
(57)	Billy Williams	15.00	7.50	4.50
(58)	Don Wilson	2.00	1.00	.60
(59)	Jim Wynn	.80	.40	.25
(60)	Carl Yastrzemski	25.00	12.50	7.50

1970 Transogram

Like the 1969 cards, the 1970 Transogram cards were available on boxes of Transogram baseball statues. The cards are slightly larger at 2-9/16" by 3-1/2". The 30-card set has the same pictures as the 1969 set except for Joe Torre. All players in the '70 set were included in the '69 Transogram issue except for Reggie Jackson, Sam McDowell and Boog Powell. Three cards and three statues were part of each Transogram box in 1970. When available, most collectors prefer to find the cards as uncut panels of three, better yet, as complete boxes.

		NR MT	EX	VG
Complete Set:		300.00	150.00	90.00
Common Player:		.80	.40	.25
(1)	Hank Aaron	30.00	15.00	9.00
(2)	Ernie Banks	8.00	4.00	2.50
(3)	Roberto Clemente	25.00	12.50	6.00
(4)	Willie Davis	1.00	.50	.30
(5)	Jim Fregosi	1.00	.50	.30
(6)	Bob Gibson	8.00	4.00	2.50
(7)	Frank Howard	1.50	.70	.45
(8)	Reggie Jackson	40.00	20.00	12.00
(9)	Cleon Jones	.80	.40	.25
(10)	Al Kaline	13.00	6.50	4.00
(11)	Harmon Killebrew	13.00	6.50	4.00
(12)	Jerry Koosman	.80	.40	.25
(13)	Willie McCovey	13.00	6.50	4.00
(14)	Sam McDowell	3.00	1.50	.90
(15)	Denny McLain	1.50	.70	.45
(16)	Juan Marichal	8.00	4.00	2.50
(17)	Willie Mays	30.00	15.00	9.00
(18)	Blue Moon Odom	.80	.40	.25
(19)	Tony Oliva	1.50	.70	.45
(20)	Rico Petrocelli	1.00	.50	.30
(21)	Boog Powell	4.00	2.00	1.25
(22)	Rick Reichardt	.80	.40	.25
(23)	Frank Robinson	13.00	6.50	4.00
(24)	Pete Rose	30.00	15.00	9.00
(25)	Ron Santo	1.50	.70	.45
(26)	Tom Seaver	13.00	6.50	4.00
(27)	Mel Stottlemyre	1.00	.50	.30
(28)	Joe Torre	4.00	2.00	1.25
(29)	Jim Wynn	.80	.40	.25
(30)	Carl Yastrzemski	25.00	12.50	7.50

1970 Transogram Mets

JERRY KOOSMAN
PITCHER   NEW YORK METS
Ht: 6'2"   Wt: 205   Bats: Right   Throws: Left
Born: December 23, 1942   Home: Appleton, Minn.

The Transogram Mets set is a second set that the company produced in 1970. The cards are 2-9/16" by 3-1/2" and feature members of the World Champions Mets team. There are 15 cards in the set which retains the basic color picture with player's names in red and team, position and biographical details in a black format. As with the other Transogram sets, the cards are most valuable when they are still part of their original box with the statues. Values decrease for them if the cards are removed from the box. While the Mets set does not have the attraction of many Hall of Famers as was the case with the regular set, it does make a very nice item for the Mets team collector.

		NR MT	EX	VG
Complete Set:		150.00	75.00	45.00
Common Player:		.80	.40	.25
(1)	Tommie Agee	3.00	1.50	.90
(2)	Ken Boswell	2.00	1.00	.60
(3)	Donn Clendenon	3.00	1.50	.90
(4)	Gary Gentry	2.00	1.00	.60
(5)	Jerry Grote	3.00	1.50	.90
(6)	Bud Harrelson	3.00	1.50	.90
(7)	Cleon Jones	.80	.40	.25
(8)	Jerry Koosman	.80	.40	.25
(9)	Ed Kranepool	3.00	1.50	.90
(10)	Tug McGraw	7.00	3.50	2.00
(11)	Nolan Ryan	100.00	50.00	30.00
(12)	Art Shamsky	2.00	1.00	.60
(13)	Tom Seaver	25.00	12.50	7.50
(14)	Ron Swoboda	.80	.40	.25
(15)	Al Weis	2.00	1.00	.60

1983 True Value White Sox

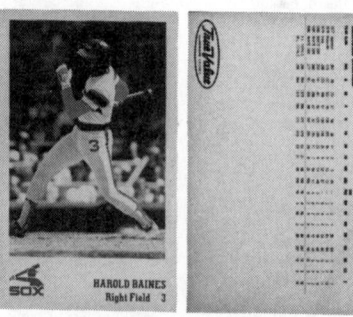

HAROLD BAINES
Right Field   3

Issued by the Chicago White Sox and True Value hardware stores, these 2-5/8" by 4-1/8" cards are a rather expensive and scarce regional set. The 23-card set was originally scheduled as part of a promotion in which cards were given out at special Tuesday night games. The idea was sound, but rainouts forced the cancellation of some games so

those scheduled cards were never given out. They were, however, smuggled out to hobby channels making it possible, although not easy, to assemble complete sets. The cards feature a large color photo with a wide white border. A red and blue White Sox logo is in the lower left corner, while the player's name, position and team number are in the lower right. Backs feature a True Value ad along with statistics. The three cards which were never given out through the normal channels are considered more scarce than the others. They are Marc Hill, Harold Baines and Salome Barojas.

		MT	NR MT	EX
Complete Set:		30.00	22.00	12.00
Common Player:		.40	.30	.15
1	Scott Fletcher	.60	.45	.25
2	Harold Baines	5.00	3.75	2.00
5	Vance Law	.50	.40	.20
7	Marc Hill	3.25	2.50	1.25
10	Tony LaRussa	.50	.40	.20
11	Rudy Law	.40	.30	.15
14	Tony Bernazard	.40	.30	.15
17	Jerry Hairston	.40	.30	.15
19	Greg Luzinski	1.00	.70	.40
24	Floyd Bannister	.60	.45	.25
25	Mike Squires	.40	.30	.15
30	Salome Barojas	3.25	2.50	1.25
31	LaMarr Hoyt	.50	.40	.20
34	Richard Dotson	.70	.50	.30
36	Jerry Koosman	.70	.50	.30
40	Britt Burns	.50	.40	.20
41	Dick Tidrow	.40	.30	.15
42	Ron Kittle	1.75	1.25	.70
44	Tom Paciorek	.40	.30	.15
45	Kevin Hickey	.40	.30	.15
53	Dennis Lamp	.40	.30	.15
67	Jim Kern	.40	.30	.15
72	Carlton Fisk	2.25	1.75	.90

1984 True Value White Sox

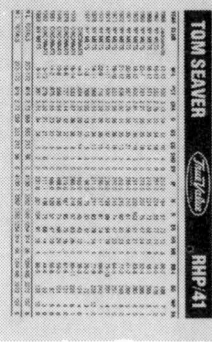

TOM SEAVER
Pitcher   41

True Value hardware stores and the Chicago White Sox gave their Tuesday night baseball card promotion at Comiskey Park another try in 1984. The cards measure 2-5/8" by 4-1/8" with 30 cards comprising the set. In addition to the players, there are cards for manager Tony LaRussa, the coaching staff, and former Sox greats Luis Aparicio and Minnie Minoso. Cards designs are very similar to the 1983 cards. As the cards were given out two at a time, it was very difficult to acquire a complete set. Additionally, as numbers available vary because of attendance, some cards are scarcer than others.

		MT	NR MT	EX
Complete Set:		25.00	18.50	10.00
Common Player:		.40	.30	.15
1	Scott Fletcher	.60	.45	.25
3	Harold Baines	2.25	1.75	.90
5	Vance Law	.50	.40	.20
7	Marc Hill	.40	.30	.15
8	Dave Stegman	.40	.30	.15
10	Tony LaRussa	.50	.40	.20
11	Rudy Law	.40	.30	.15

		MT	NR MT	EX
16	Julio Cruz	.40	.30	.15
17	Jerry Hairston	.40	.30	.15
19	Greg Luzinski	.90	.70	.35
20	Jerry Dybzinski	.40	.30	.15
24	Floyd Bannister	.60	.45	.25
25	Mike Squires	.40	.30	.15
27	Ron Reed	.40	.30	.15
29	Greg Walker	1.50	1.25	.60
30	Salome Barojas	.40	.30	.15
31	LaMarr Hoyt	.50	.40	.20
32	Tim Hulett	1.00	.70	.40
34	Richard Dotson	.70	.50	.30
40	Britt Burns	.40	.30	.15
41	Tom Seaver	4.00	3.00	1.50
42	Ron Kittle	1.00	.70	.40
44	Tom Paciorek	.40	.30	.15
50	Juan Agosto	.40	.30	.15
59	Tom Brennan	1.00	.70	.40
72	Carlton Fisk	2.00	1.50	.80
----	Minnie Minoso	2.00	1.50	.80
----	Luis Aparicio	2.00	1.50	.80
----	Nancy Faust (organist)	1.00	.70	.40
----	The Coaching Staff (Ed Brinkman, Dave Duncan, Art Kusnyer, Tony LaRussa, Jim Leyland, Dave Nelson, Joe Nossek)	.40	.30	.15

		MT	NR MT	EX
15	Bruce Sutter	.05	.04	.02
	Panel	1.00	.70	.40
16	Gary Carter	.15	.11	.06
17	George Brett	.20	.15	.08
18	Rick Sutcliffe	.05	.04	.02
	Panel	.40	.30	.15
19	Dave Stieb	.05	.04	.02
20	Buddy Bell	.05	.04	.02
21	Alvin Davis	.08	.06	.03
	Panel	.60	.45	.25
22	Cal Ripken, Jr.	.20	.15	.08
23	Bill Madlock	.05	.04	.02
24	Kent Hrbek	.10	.08	.04
	Panel	.50	.40	.20
25	Lou Whitaker	.08	.06	.03
26	Nolan Ryan	.15	.11	.06
27	Dwayne Murphy	.05	.04	.02
	Panel	2.00	1.50	.80
28	Mike Schmidt	.20	.15	.08
29	Andre Dawson	.10	.08	.04
30	Wade Boggs	.50	.40	.20

1986 True Value

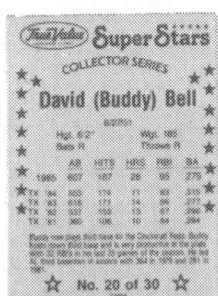

A 30-card set of 2-1/2" by 3-1/2" cards was available in three-card packets at True Value hardware stores with a purchase of $5 or more. Cards feature a photo enclosed by stars and a ball and bat at the bottom. The player's name and team are in the lower left while his position and a Major League Baseball logo are in the lower right. The True Value logo is in the upper left. Above the picture runs the phrase "Collector Series." Backs feature some personal information and brief 1985 statistics. Along with the player cards, the folders contained a sweepstakes card offering trips to post-season games and other prizes.

		MT	NR MT	EX
Complete Panel Set:		10.00	7.50	4.00
Complete Singles Set:		3.00	2.25	1.25
Common Panel:		.40	.30	.15
Common Single Player:		.05	.04	.02
	Panel	1.00	.70	.40
1	Pedro Guerrero	.08	.06	.03
2	Steve Garvey	.15	.11	.06
3	Eddie Murray	.20	.15	.08
	Panel	3.25	2.50	1.25
4	Pete Rose	.30	.25	.12
5	Don Mattingly	.80	.60	.30
6	Fernando Valenzuela	.10	.08	.04
	Panel	.60	.45	.25
7	Jim Rice	.15	.11	.06
8	Kirk Gibson	.10	.08	.04
9	Ozzie Smith	.08	.06	.03
	Panel	1.00	.70	.40
10	Dale Murphy	.20	.15	.08
11	Robin Yount	.10	.08	.04
12	Tom Seaver	.15	.11	.06
	Panel	.80	.60	.30
13	Reggie Jackson	.15	.11	.06
14	Ryne Sandberg	.10	.08	.04

1989 Upper Deck

Matt Williams

This premiere "Collector's Choice' issue from Upper Deck contains 700 cards (2-1/2" by 3-1/2") with full-color photos on both sides. The first 26 cards feature Star Rookies. The set also includes 26 special portrait cards with team checklist backs and seven numberical checklist cards (one for each 100 numbers). Team Checklist cards feature individual player portraits by artist Vernon Wells. Major 1988 award winners (Cy Young, Rookie of Year, MVP) are honored on 10 cards in the set, in addition to their individual player cards. There are also special cards for the Most Valuable Players in both League Championship series and the World Series. The card fronts feature head-and-shoulder poses framed by a white border. A vertical brown and green artist's rendition of the runner's lane that leads from home plate to first base is found along the right margin. The backs carry full-color action poses that fill the card back, except for a compact (yet complete) stats chart. A high-number series, cards 701-800, featuring rookies and traded players, was released in mid-season in foil packs mixed within the complete set, in boxed complete sets and in high number set boxes.

		MT	NR MT	EX
Complete Set: 1-700		70.00	52.00	27.00
Common Player: 1-700		.08	.06	.03
Complete Set: 1-800		90.00	67.00	35.00
Common Player: 701-800		.10	.08	.04
1	Star Rookie (Ken Griffey, Jr.)	30.00	22.00	12.50
2	Star Rookie (Luis Medina)	.30	.25	.12
3	Star Rookie (Tony Chance)	.20	.15	.08

		MT	NR MT	EX
4	Star Rookie (Dave Otto)	.08	.06	.03
5	Star Rookie (Sandy Alomar, Jr.)	5.00	3.75	2.00
6	Star Rookie (Rolando Roomes)	.40	.30	.15
7	Star Rookie (David West)	.40	.30	.15
8	Star Rookie (Cris Carpenter)	.30	.25	.12
9	Star Rookie (Gregg Jefferies)	4.00	3.00	1.50
10	Star Rookie (Doug Dascenzo)	.25	.20	.10
11	Star Rookie (Ron Jones)	.35	.25	.14
12	Star Rookie (Luis de los Santos)	.25	.20	.10
13a	Star Rookie (Gary Sheffield) (SS position on front is upside down)	6.00	4.50	2.50
13b	Star Rookie (Gary Sheffield) (SS position on front is correct)	4.00	3.00	1.50
14	Star Rookie (Mike Harkey)	1.00	.70	.40
15	Star Rookie (Lance Blankenship)	.25	.20	.10
16	Star Rookie (William Brennan)	.20	.15	.08
17	Star Rookie (John Smoltz)	1.00	.70	.40
18	Star Rookie (Ramon Martinez)	7.00	5.25	2.75
19	Star Rookie (Mark Lemke)	.20	.15	.08
20	Star Rookie (Juan Bell)	.35	.25	.12
21	Star Rookie (Rey Palacios)	.20	.15	.08
22	Star Rookie (Felix Jose)	.80	.60	.30
23	Star Rookie (Van Snider)	.25	.20	.10
24	Star Rookie (Dante Bichette)	.40	.30	.15
25	Star Rookie (Randy Johnson)	.70	.50	.30
26	Star Rookie (Carlos Quintana)	.90	.70	.35
27	Star Rookie Checklist 1-26	.08	.06	.03
28	Mike Schooler	.40	.30	.15
29	Randy St. Claire	.08	.06	.03
30	Jerald Clark	.25	.20	.10
31	Kevin Gross	.08	.06	.03
32	Dan Firova	.20	.15	.08
33	Jeff Calhoun	.08	.06	.03
34	Tommy Hinzo	.08	.06	.03
35	Ricky Jordan	.80	.60	.30
36	Larry Parrish	.08	.06	.03
37	Bret Saberhagen	.15	.11	.06
38	Mike Smithson	.08	.06	.03
39	Dave Dravecky	.08	.06	.03
40	Ed Romero	.08	.06	.03
41	Jeff Musselman	.08	.06	.03
42	Ed Hearn	.08	.06	.03
43	Rance Mulliniks	.08	.06	.03
44	Jim Eisenreich	.08	.06	.03
45	Sil Campusano	.20	.15	.08
46	Mike Krukow	.08	.06	.03
47	Paul Gibson	.20	.15	.08
48	Mike LaCoss	.08	.06	.03
49	Larry Herndon	.08	.06	.03
50	Scott Garrelts	.08	.06	.03
51	Dwayne Henry	.08	.06	.03
52	Jim Acker	.08	.06	.03
53	Steve Sax	.15	.11	.06
54	Pete O'Brien	.08	.06	.03
55	Paul Runge	.08	.06	.03
56	Rick Rhoden	.08	.06	.03
57	John Dopson	.25	.20	.10
58	Casey Candaele	.08	.06	.03
59	Dave Righetti	.12	.09	.05
60	Joe Hesketh	.08	.06	.03
61	Frank DiPino	.08	.06	.03
62	Tim Laudner	.08	.06	.03
63	Jamie Moyer	.08	.06	.03
64	Fred Toliver	.08	.06	.03
65	Mitch Webster	.08	.06	.03
66	John Tudor	.10	.08	.04
67	John Cangelosi	.08	.06	.03
68	Mike Devereaux	.15	.11	.06
69	Brian Fisher	.08	.06	.03
70	Mike Marshall	.12	.09	.05
71	Zane Smith	.08	.06	.03
72a	Brian Holton (ball not visible on card front, photo actually Shawn Hillegas)	2.00	1.50	.80
72b	Brian Holton (ball visible, correct photo)	.15	.11	.06
73	Jose Guzman	.10	.08	.04
74	Rick Mahler	.08	.06	.03
75	John Shelby	.08	.06	.03
76	Jim Deshaies	.08	.06	.03
77	Bobby Meacham	.08	.06	.03
78	Bryn Smith	.08	.06	.03
79	Joaquin Andujar	.08	.06	.03
80	Richard Dotson	.08	.06	.03
81	Charlie Lea	.08	.06	.03
82	Calvin Schiraldi	.08	.06	.03
83	Les Straker	.08	.06	.03
84	Les Lancaster	.08	.06	.03
85	Allan Anderson	.08	.06	.03
86	Junior Ortiz	.08	.06	.03
87	Jesse Orosco	.08	.06	.03
88	Felix Fermin	.08	.06	.03
89	Dave Anderson	.08	.06	.03

		MT	NR MT	EX
90	Rafael Belliard	.08	.06	.03
91	Franklin Stubbs	.08	.06	.03
92	Cecil Espy	.08	.06	.03
93	Albert Hall	.08	.06	.03
94	Tim Leary	.08	.06	.03
95	Mitch Williams	.08	.06	.03
96	Tracy Jones	.10	.08	.04
97	Danny Darwin	.08	.06	.03
98	Gary Ward	.08	.06	.03
99	Neal Heaton	.08	.06	.03
100	Jim Pankovits	.08	.06	.03
101	Bill Doran	.08	.06	.03
102	Tim Wallach	.10	.08	.04
103	Joe Magrane	.10	.08	.04
104	Ozzie Virgil	.08	.06	.03
105	Alvin Davis	.12	.09	.05
106	Tom Brookens	.08	.06	.03
107	Shawon Dunston	.10	.08	.04
108	Tracy Woodson	.10	.08	.04
109	Nelson Liriano	.08	.06	.03
110	Devon White	.12	.09	.05
111	Steve Balboni	.08	.06	.03
112	Buddy Bell	.08	.06	.03
113	German Jimenez	.08	.06	.03
114	Ken Dayley	.08	.06	.03
115	Andres Galarraga	.15	.11	.06
116	Mike Scioscia	.08	.06	.03
117	Gary Pettis	.08	.06	.03
118	Ernie Whitt	.08	.06	.03
119	Bob Boone	.08	.06	.03
120	Ryne Sandberg	.25	.20	.10
121	Bruce Benedict	.08	.06	.03
122	Hubie Brooks	.10	.08	.04
123	Mike Moore	.08	.06	.03
124	Wallace Johnson	.08	.06	.03
125	Bob Horner	.10	.08	.04
126	Chili Davis	.08	.06	.03
127	Manny Trillo	.08	.06	.03
128	Chet Lemon	.08	.06	.03
129	John Cerutti	.08	.06	.03
130	Orel Hershiser	.25	.20	.10
131	Terry Pendleton	.10	.08	.04
132	Jeff Blauser	.10	.08	.04
133	Mike Fitzgerald	.08	.06	.03
134	Henry Cotto	.08	.06	.03
135	Gerald Young	.12	.09	.05
136	Luis Salazar	.08	.06	.03
137	Alejandro Pena	.08	.06	.03
138	Jack Howell	.08	.06	.03
139	Tony Fernandez	.12	.09	.05
140	Mark Grace	1.75	1.25	.70
141	Ken Caminiti	.08	.06	.03
142	Mike Jackson	.08	.06	.03
143	Larry McWilliams	.08	.06	.03
144	Andres Thomas	.08	.06	.03
145	Nolan Ryan	2.00	1.50	.80
146	Mike Davis	.08	.06	.03
147	DeWayne Buice	.08	.06	.03
148	Jody Davis	.08	.06	.03
149	Jesse Barfield	.10	.08	.04
150	Matt Nokes	.20	.15	.08
151	Jerry Reuss	.08	.06	.03
152	Rick Cerone	.08	.06	.03
153	Storm Davis	.10	.08	.04
154	Marvell Wynne	.08	.06	.03
155	Will Clark	1.25	.90	.50
156	Luis Aguayo	.08	.06	.03
157	Willie Upshaw	.08	.06	.03
158	Randy Bush	.08	.06	.03
159	Ron Darling	.12	.09	.05
160	Kal Daniels	.15	.11	.06
161	Spike Owen	.08	.06	.03
162	Luis Polonia	.08	.06	.03
163	Kevin Mitchell	.50	.40	.20
164	Dave Gallagher	.25	.20	.10
165	Benito Santiago	.15	.11	.06
166	Greg Gagne	.08	.06	.03
167	Ken Phelps	.08	.06	.03
168	Sid Fernandez	.10	.08	.04
169	Bo Diaz	.08	.06	.03
170	Cory Snyder	.15	.11	.06
171	Eric Show	.08	.06	.03
172	Rob Thompson	.08	.06	.03
173	Marty Barrett	.08	.06	.03
174	Dave Henderson	.10	.08	.04
175	Ozzie Guillen	.08	.06	.03
176	Barry Lyons	.08	.06	.03
177	Kelvin Torve(FC)	.20	.15	.08
178	Don Slaught	.08	.06	.03
179	Steve Lombardozzi	.08	.06	.03
180	Chris Sabo	.80	.60	.30

		MT	NR MT	EX
181	Jose Uribe	.08	.06	.03
182	Shane Mack	.08	.06	.03
183	Ron Karkovice	.08	.06	.03
184	Todd Benzinger	.12	.09	.05
185	Dave Stewart	.10	.08	.04
186	Julio Franco	.10	.08	.04
187	Ron Robinson	.08	.06	.03
188	Wally Backman	.08	.06	.03
189	Randy Velarde	.08	.06	.03
190	Joe Carter	.12	.09	.05
191	Bob Welch	.10	.08	.04
192	Kelly Paris	.08	.06	.03
193	Chris Brown	.08	.06	.03
194	Rick Reuschel	.10	.08	.04
195	Roger Clemens	.50	.40	.20
196	Dave Concepcion	.10	.08	.04
197	Al Newman	.08	.06	.03
198	Brook Jacoby	.10	.08	.04
199	Mookie Wilson	.08	.06	.03
200	Don Mattingly	1.00	.70	.40
201	Dick Schofield	.08	.06	.03
202	Mark Gubicza	.10	.08	.04
203	Gary Gaetti	.15	.11	.06
204	Dan Pasqua	.10	.08	.04
205	Andre Dawson	.20	.15	.08
206	Chris Speier	.08	.06	.03
207	Kent Tekulve	.08	.06	.03
208	Rod Scurry	.08	.06	.03
209	Scott Bailes	.08	.06	.03
210	Rickey Henderson	.35	.25	.14
211	Harold Baines	.12	.09	.05
212	Tony Armas	.08	.06	.03
213	Kent Hrbek	.20	.15	.08
214	Darrin Jackson	.08	.06	.03
215	George Brett	.35	.25	.14
216	Rafael Santana	.08	.06	.03
217	Andy Allanson	.08	.06	.03
218	Brett Butler	.08	.06	.03
219	Steve Jeltz	.08	.06	.03
220	Jay Buhner	.10	.08	.04
221	Bo Jackson	1.75	1.25	.70
222	Angel Salazar	.08	.06	.03
223	Kirk McCaskill	.08	.06	.03
224	Steve Lyons	.08	.06	.03
225	Bert Blyleven	.10	.08	.04
226	Scott Bradley	.08	.06	.03
227	Bob Melvin	.08	.06	.03
228	Ron Kittle	.08	.06	.03
229	Phil Bradley	.10	.08	.04
230	Tommy John	.12	.09	.05
231	Greg Walker	.08	.06	.03
232	Juan Berenguer	.08	.06	.03
233	Pat Tabler	.08	.06	.03
234	*Terry Clark*	.20	.15	.08
235	Rafael Palmeiro	.25	.20	.10
236	Paul Zuvella	.08	.06	.03
237	Willie Randolph	.08	.06	.03
238	Bruce Fields	.08	.06	.03
239	Mike Aldrete	.08	.06	.03
240	Lance Parrish	.15	.11	.06
241	Greg Maddux	.12	.09	.05
242	John Moses	.08	.06	.03
243	Melido Perez	.10	.08	.04
244	Willie Wilson	.10	.08	.04
245	Mark McLemore	.08	.06	.03
246	Von Hayes	.10	.08	.04
247	Matt Williams	.12	.09	.05
248	John Candelaria	.08	.06	.03
249	Harold Reynolds	.08	.06	.03
250	Greg Swindell	.12	.09	.05
251	Juan Agosto	.08	.06	.03
252	Mike Felder	.08	.06	.03
253	Vince Coleman	.15	.11	.06
254	Larry Sheets	.08	.06	.03
255	George Bell	.25	.20	.10
256	Terry Steinbach	.10	.08	.04
257	*Jack Armstrong*	.60	.45	.25
258	Dickie Thon	.08	.06	.03
259	Ray Knight	.08	.06	.03
260	Darryl Strawberry	.40	.30	.15
261	Doug Sisk	.08	.06	.03
262	Alex Trevino	.08	.06	.03
263	Jeff Leonard	.08	.06	.03
264	Tom Henke	.08	.06	.03
265	Ozzie Smith	.15	.11	.06
266	Dave Bergman	.08	.06	.03
267	Tony Phillips	.08	.06	.03
268	Mark Davis	.08	.06	.03
269	Kevin Elster	.10	.08	.04
270	Barry Larkin	.20	.15	.08
271	Manny Lee	.08	.06	.03

		MT	NR MT	EX
272	Tom Brunansky	.12	.09	.05
273	*Craig Biggio*	.80	.60	.30
274	Jim Gantner	.08	.06	.03
275	Eddie Murray	.25	.20	.10
276	Jeff Reed	.08	.06	.03
277	Tim Teufel	.08	.06	.03
278	Rick Honeycutt	.08	.06	.03
279	Guillermo Hernandez	.08	.06	.03
280	John Kruk	.10	.08	.04
281	*Luis Alicea*	.20	.15	.08
282	Jim Clancy	.08	.06	.03
283	Billy Ripken	.08	.06	.03
284	Craig Reynolds	.08	.06	.03
285	Robin Yount	.35	.25	.14
286	Jimmy Jones	.08	.06	.03
287	Ron Oester	.08	.06	.03
288	Terry Leach	.08	.06	.03
289	Dennis Eckersley	.12	.09	.05
290	Alan Trammell	.20	.15	.08
291	Jimmy Key	.10	.08	.04
292	Chris Bosio	.08	.06	.03
293	Jose DeLeon	.08	.06	.03
294	Jim Traber	.08	.06	.03
295	Mike Scott	.12	.09	.05
296	Roger McDowell	.10	.08	.04
297	Garry Templeton	.08	.06	.03
298	Doyle Alexander	.08	.06	.03
299	Nick Esasky	.08	.06	.03
300	Mark McGwire	.70	.50	.30
301	*Darryl Hamilton*	.20	.15	.08
302	Dave Smith	.08	.06	.03
303	Rick Sutcliffe	.10	.08	.04
304	Dave Stapleton	.08	.06	.03
305	Alan Ashby	.08	.06	.03
306	Pedro Guerrero	.15	.11	.06
307	Ron Guidry	.12	.09	.05
308	Steve Farr	.08	.06	.03
309	Curt Ford	.08	.06	.03
310	Claudell Washington	.08	.06	.03
311	Tom Prince	.08	.06	.03
312	*Chad Kreuter*	.20	.15	.08
313	Ken Oberkfell	.08	.06	.03
314	Jerry Browne	.08	.06	.03
315	R.J. Reynolds	.08	.06	.03
316	Scott Bankhead	.08	.06	.03
317	Milt Thompson	.08	.06	.03
318	Mario Diaz	.10	.08	.04
319	Bruce Ruffin	.08	.06	.03
320	Dave Valle	.08	.06	.03
321a	*Gary Varsho* (batting righty on card back, photo actually Mike Bielecki)	2.00	1.50	.80
321b	*Gary Varsho* (batting lefty on card back, correct photo)	.30	.25	.12
322	Paul Mirabella	.08	.06	.03
323	Chuck Jackson	.08	.06	.03
324	Drew Hall	.10	.08	.04
325	Don August	.10	.08	.04
326	*Israel Sanchez*	.20	.15	.08
327	Denny Walling	.08	.06	.03
328	Joel Skinner	.08	.06	.03
329	Danny Tartabull	.20	.15	.08
330	Tony Pena	.08	.06	.03
331	Jim Sundberg	.08	.06	.03
332	Jeff Robinson	.12	.09	.05
333	Odibbe McDowell	.08	.06	.03
334	Jose Lind	.10	.08	.04
335	Paul Kilgus	.10	.08	.04
336	Juan Samuel	.12	.09	.05
337	Mike Campbell	.10	.08	.04
338	Mike Maddux	.08	.06	.03
339	Darnell Coles	.08	.06	.03
340	Bob Dernier	.08	.06	.03
341	Rafael Ramirez	.08	.06	.03
342	Scott Sanderson	.08	.06	.03
343	B.J. Surhoff	.10	.08	.04
344	Billy Hatcher	.08	.06	.03
345	Pat Perry	.08	.06	.03
346	Jack Clark	.15	.11	.06
347	Gary Thurman	.12	.09	.05
348	*Timmy Jones*	.20	.15	.08
349	Dave Winfield	.30	.25	.12
350	Frank White	.08	.06	.03
351	Dave Collins	.08	.06	.03
352	Jack Morris	.15	.11	.06
353	Eric Plunk	.08	.06	.03
354	Leon Durham	.08	.06	.03
355	Ivan DeJesus	.08	.06	.03
356	*Brian Holman*	.30	.25	.12
357a	Dale Murphy (photo on card front reversed)	100.00	75.00	40.00
357b	Dale Murphy (correct photo)	.35	.25	.14

		MT	NR MT	EX			MT	NR MT	EX
358	Mark Portugal	.08	.06	.03	449	Frank Williams	.08	.06	.03
359	Andy McGaffigan	.08	.06	.03	450	Don Aase	.08	.06	.03
360	Tom Glavine	.10	.08	.04	451	Lou Whitaker	.15	.11	.06
361	Keith Moreland	.08	.06	.03	452	Goose Gossage	.12	.09	.05
362	Todd Stottlemyre	.15	.11	.06	453	Ed Whitson	.08	.06	.03
363	Dave Leiper	.08	.06	.03	454	Jim Walewander	.08	.06	.03
364	Cecil Fielder	.80	.60	.30	455	Damon Berryhill	.12	.09	.05
365	Carmelo Martinez	.08	.06	.03	456	Tim Burke	.08	.06	.03
366	Dwight Evans	.10	.08	.04	457	Barry Jones	.08	.06	.03
367	Kevin McReynolds	.15	.11	.06	458	Joel Youngblood	.08	.06	.03
368	Rich Gedman	.08	.06	.03	459	Floyd Youmans	.08	.06	.03
369	Len Dykstra	.10	.08	.04	460	Mark Salas	.08	.06	.03
370	Jody Reed	.12	.09	.05	461	Jeff Russell	.08	.06	.03
371	Jose Canseco	1.50	1.25	.60	462	Darrell Miller	.08	.06	.03
372	Rob Murphy	.08	.06	.03	463	Jeff Kunkel	.08	.06	.03
373	Mike Henneman	.10	.08	.04	464	*Sherman Corbett*	.20	.15	.08
374	Walt Weiss	.40	.30	.15	465	Curtis Wilkerson	.08	.06	.03
375	*Rob Dibble*	.70	.50	.30	466	Bud Black	.08	.06	.03
376	Kirby Puckett	.30	.25	.12	467	Cal Ripken, Jr.	.35	.25	.14
377	Denny Martinez	.08	.06	.03	468	John Farrell	.10	.08	.04
378	Ron Gant	1.00	.70	.40	469	Terry Kennedy	.08	.06	.03
379	Brian Harper	.08	.06	.03	470	Tom Candiotti	.08	.06	.03
380	*Nelson Santovenia*	.20	.15	.08	471	Roberto Alomar	.80	.60	.30
381	Lloyd Moseby	.08	.06	.03	472	Jeff Robinson	.12	.09	.05
382	Lance McCullers	.08	.06	.03	473	Vance Law	.08	.06	.03
383	Dave Stieb	.10	.08	.04	474	Randy Ready	.08	.06	.03
384	Tony Gwynn	.30	.25	.12	475	Walt Terrell	.08	.06	.03
385	Mike Flanagan	.08	.06	.03	476	Kelly Downs	.10	.08	.04
386	Bob Ojeda	.08	.06	.03	477	*Johnny Paredes*	.20	.15	.08
387	Bruce Hurst	.10	.08	.04	478	Shawn Hillegas	.08	.06	.03
388	Dave Magadan	.10	.08	.04	479	Bob Brenly	.08	.06	.03
389	Wade Boggs	.80	.60	.30	480	Otis Nixon	.08	.06	.03
390	Gary Carter	.25	.20	.10	481	Johnny Ray	.08	.06	.03
391	Frank Tanana	.08	.06	.03	482	Geno Petralli	.08	.06	.03
392	Curt Young	.08	.06	.03	483	Stu Cliburn	.08	.06	.03
393	Jeff Treadway	.10	.08	.04	484	Pete Incaviglia	.10	.08	.04
394	Darrell Evans	.10	.08	.04	485	Brian Downing	.08	.06	.03
395	Glenn Hubbard	.08	.06	.03	486	Jeff Stone	.08	.06	.03
396	Chuck Cary	.08	.06	.03	487	Carmen Castillo	.08	.06	.03
397	Frank Viola	.15	.11	.06	488	Tom Niedenfuer	.08	.06	.03
398	Jeff Parrett	.10	.08	.04	489	Jay Bell	.08	.06	.03
399	*Terry Blocker*	.15	.11	.06	490	Rick Schu	.08	.06	.03
400	Dan Gladden	.08	.06	.03	491	*Jeff Pico*	.25	.20	.10
401	*Louie Meadows*	.20	.15	.08	492	*Mark Parent*	.20	.15	.08
402	Tim Raines	.25	.20	.10	493	Eric King	.08	.06	.03
403	Joey Meyer	.10	.08	.04	494	Al Nipper	.08	.06	.03
404	Larry Andersen	.08	.06	.03	495	Andy Hawkins	.08	.06	.03
405	Rex Hudler	.08	.06	.03	496	Daryl Boston	.08	.06	.03
406	Mike Schmidt	.80	.60	.30	497	Ernie Riles	.08	.06	.03
407	John Franco	.10	.08	.04	498	Pascual Perez	.08	.06	.03
408	*Brady Anderson*	.30	.25	.12	499	Bill Long	.08	.06	.03
409	Don Carman	.08	.06	.03	500	Kirt Manwaring	.10	.08	.04
410	Eric Davis	.40	.30	.15	501	Chuck Crim	.08	.06	.03
411	Bob Stanley	.08	.06	.03	502	Candy Maldonado	.08	.06	.03
412	Pete Smith	.10	.08	.04	503	Dennis Lamp	.08	.06	.03
413	Jim Rice	.25	.20	.10	504	Glenn Braggs	.08	.06	.03
414	Bruce Sutter	.10	.08	.04	505	Joe Price	.08	.06	.03
415	Oil Can Boyd	.08	.06	.03	506	Ken Williams	.08	.06	.03
416	Ruben Sierra	.40	.30	.15	507	Bill Pecota	.08	.06	.03
417	Mike LaValliere	.08	.06	.03	508	Rey Quinones	.08	.06	.03
418	Steve Buechele	.08	.06	.03	509	*Jeff Bittiger*	.15	.11	.06
419	Gary Redus	.08	.06	.03	510	Kevin Seitzer	.30	.25	.12
420	Scott Fletcher	.08	.06	.03	511	Steve Bedrosian	.10	.08	.04
421	Dale Sveum	.08	.06	.03	512	Todd Worrell	.10	.08	.04
422	Bob Knepper	.08	.06	.03	513	Chris James	.10	.08	.04
423	Luis Rivera	.08	.06	.03	514	Jose Oquendo	.08	.06	.03
424	Ted Higuera	.10	.08	.04	515	David Palmer	.08	.06	.03
425	Kevin Bass	.08	.06	.03	516	John Smiley	.12	.09	.05
426	Ken Gerhart	.08	.06	.03	517	Dave Clark	.08	.06	.03
427	Shane Rawley	.08	.06	.03	518	Mike Dunne	.10	.08	.04
428	Paul O'Neill	.08	.06	.03	519	Ron Washington	.08	.06	.03
429	Joe Orsulak	.08	.06	.03	520	Bob Kipper	.08	.06	.03
430	Jackie Gutierrez	.08	.06	.03	521	Lee Smith	.10	.08	.04
431	Gerald Perry	.10	.08	.04	522	Juan Castillo	.08	.06	.03
432	Mike Greenwell	.60	.45	.25	523	Don Robinson	.08	.06	.03
433	Jerry Royster	.08	.06	.03	524	Kevin Romine	.08	.06	.03
434	Ellis Burks	.60	.45	.25	525	Paul Molitor	.15	.11	.06
435	Ed Olwine	.08	.06	.03	526	Mark Langston	.10	.08	.04
436	Dave Rucker	.08	.06	.03	527	Donnie Hill	.08	.06	.03
437	Charlie Hough	.08	.06	.03	528	Larry Owen	.08	.06	.03
438	Bob Walk	.08	.06	.03	529	Jerry Reed	.08	.06	.03
439	Bob Brower	.08	.06	.03	530	Jack McDowell	.10	.08	.04
440	Barry Bonds	.12	.09	.05	531	Greg Mathews	.08	.06	.03
441	Tom Foley	.08	.06	.03	532	John Russell	.08	.06	.03
442	Rob Deer	.08	.06	.03	533	Don Quisenberry	.08	.06	.03
443	Glenn Davis	.15	.11	.06	534	Greg Gross	.08	.06	.03
444	Dave Martinez	.08	.06	.03	535	Danny Cox	.08	.06	.03
445	Bill Wegman	.08	.06	.03	536	Terry Francona	.08	.06	.03
446	Lloyd McClendon	.08	.06	.03	537	Andy Van Slyke	.15	.11	.06
447	Dave Schmidt	.08	.06	.03	538	Mel Hall	.08	.06	.03
448	Darren Daulton	.08	.06	.03	539	Jim Gott	.08	.06	.03

		MT	NR MT	EX
540	Doug Jones	.10	.08	.04
541	Criag Lefferts	.08	.06	.03
542	Mike Boddicker	.08	.06	.03
543	Greg Brock	.08	.06	.03
544	Atlee Hammaker	.08	.06	.03
545	Tom Bolton	.08	.06	.03
546	*Mike Macfarlane*	.20	.15	.08
547	*Rich Renteria*	.15	.11	.06
548	John Davis	.08	.06	.03
549	Floyd Bannister	.08	.06	.03
550	Mickey Brantley	.08	.06	.03
551	Duane Ward	.08	.06	.03
552	Dan Petry	.08	.06	.03
553	Mickey Tettleton	.08	.06	.03
554	Rick Leach	.08	.06	.03
555	Mike Witt	.08	.06	.03
556	Sid Bream	.08	.06	.03
557	Bobby Witt	.10	.08	.04
558	Tommy Herr	.08	.06	.03
559	Randy Milligan	.08	.06	.03
560	*Jose Cecena*	.20	.15	.08
561	Mackey Sasser	.08	.06	.03
562	Carney Lansford	.08	.06	.03
563	Rick Aguilera	.08	.06	.03
564	Ron Hassey	.08	.06	.03
565	Dwight Gooden	.50	.40	.20
566	Paul Assenmacher	.08	.06	.03
567	Neil Allen	.08	.06	.03
568	Jim Morrison	.08	.06	.03
569	Mike Pagliarulo	.10	.08	.04
570	Ted Simmons	.10	.08	.04
571	Mark Thurmond	.08	.06	.03
572	Fred McGriff	.40	.30	.15
573	Wally Joyner	.25	.20	.10
574	*Jose Bautista*	.20	.15	.08
575	Kelly Gruber	.08	.06	.03
576	Cecilio Guante	.08	.06	.03
577	Mark Davidson	.08	.06	.03
578	Bobby Bonilla	.12	.09	.05
579	Mike Stanley	.08	.06	.03
580	Gene Larkin	.10	.08	.04
581	Stan Javier	.08	.06	.03
582	Howard Johnson	.10	.08	.04
583a	Mike Gallego (photo on card back reversed)	1.50	1.25	.60
583b	Mike Gallego (correct photo)	.15	.11	.06
584	David Cone	.35	.25	.14
585	*Doug Jennings*	.20	.15	.08
586	Charlie Hudson	.08	.06	.03
587	Dion James	.08	.06	.03
588	Al Leiter	.15	.11	.06
589	Charlie Puleo	.08	.06	.03
590	Roberto Kelly	.25	.20	.10
591	Thad Bosley	.08	.06	.03
592	Pete Stanicek	.10	.08	.04
593	*Pat Borders*	.25	.20	.10
594	*Bryan Harvey*	.25	.20	.10
595	Jeff Ballard	.10	.08	.04
596	Jeff Reardon	.10	.08	.04
597	Doug Drabek	.08	.06	.03
598	Edwin Correa	.08	.06	.03
599	Keith Atherton	.08	.06	.03
600	Dave LaPoint	.08	.06	.03
601	Don Baylor	.10	.08	.04
602	Tom Pagnozzi	.08	.06	.03
603	Tim Flannery	.08	.06	.03
604	Gene Walter	.08	.06	.03
605	Dave Parker	.12	.09	.05
606	Mike Diaz	.08	.06	.03
607	Chris Gwynn	.10	.08	.04
608	Odell Jones	.08	.06	.03
609	Carlton Fisk	.15	.11	.06
610	Jay Howell	.08	.06	.03
611	Tim Crews	.08	.06	.03
612	Keith Hernandez	.20	.15	.08
613	Willie Fraser	.08	.06	.03
614	Jim Eppard	.08	.06	.03
615	Jeff Hamilton	.08	.06	.03
616	Kurt Stillwell	.08	.06	.03
617	Tom Browning	.10	.08	.04
618	Jeff Montgomery	.08	.06	.03
619	Jose Rijo	.08	.06	.03
620	Jamie Quirk	.08	.06	.03
621	Willie McGee	.12	.09	.05
622	Mark Grant	.08	.06	.03
623	Bill Swift	.08	.06	.03
624	Orlando Mercado	.08	.06	.03
625	*John Costello*	.20	.15	.08
626	Jose Gonzalez	.08	.06	.03
627a	Bill Schroeder (putting on shin guards on card back, photo actually Ronn Reynolds)	1.50	1.25	.60

		MT	NR MT	EX
627b	Bill Schroeder (arms crossed on card back, correct photo)	.15	.11	.06
628a	Fred Manrique (throwing on card back, photo actually Ozzie Guillen)	1.50	1.25	.60
628b	Fred Manrique (batting on card back, correct photo)	.15	.11	.06
629	Ricky Horton	.08	.06	.03
630	Dan Plesac	.10	.08	.04
631	Alfredo Griffin	.08	.06	.03
632	Chuck Finley	.08	.06	.03
633	Kirk Gibson	.20	.15	.08
634	Randy Myers	.10	.08	.04
635	Greg Minton	.08	.06	.03
636	Herm Winningham	.08	.06	.03
637	Charlie Leibrandt	.08	.06	.03
638	Tim Birtsas	.08	.06	.03
639	Bill Buckner	.10	.08	.04
640	Danny Jackson	.15	.11	.06
641	Greg Booker	.08	.06	.03
642	Jim Presley	.08	.06	.03
643	Gene Nelson	.08	.06	.03
644	Rod Booker	.08	.06	.03
645	Dennis Rasmussen	.10	.08	.04
646	Juan Nieves	.08	.06	.03
647	Bobby Thigpen	.10	.08	.04
648	Tim Belcher	.10	.08	.04
649	Mike Young	.08	.06	.03
650	Ivan Calderon	.08	.06	.03
651	*Oswaldo Peraza*	.20	.15	.08
652a	Pat Sheridan (no position on front)	30.00	22.00	12.00
652b	Pat Sheridan (position on front)	.08	.06	.03
653	Mike Morgan	.08	.06	.03
654	Mike Heath	.08	.06	.03
655	Jay Tibbs	.08	.06	.03
656	Fernando Valenzuela	.20	.15	.08
657	Lee Mazzilli	.08	.06	.03
658	Frank Viola	.08	.06	.03
659	Jose Canseco	.08	.06	.03
660	Walt Weiss	.08	.06	.03
661	Orel Hershiser	.08	.06	.03
662	Kirk Gibson	.08	.06	.03
663	Chris Sabo	.08	.06	.03
664	Dennis Eckersley	.08	.06	.03
665	Orel Hershiser	.08	.06	.03
666	Kirk Gibson	.08	.06	.03
667	Orel Hershiser	.08	.06	.03
668	Angels Checklist (Wally Joyner)	.08	.06	.03
669	Astros Checklist (Nolan Ryan)	.08	.06	.03
670	Athletics Checklist (Jose Canseco)	.08	.06	.03
671	Blue Jays Checklist (Fred McGriff)	.08	.06	.03
672	Braves Checklist (Dale Murphy)	.08	.06	.03
673	Brewers Checklist (Paul Molitor)	.08	.06	.03
674	Cardinals Checklist (Ozzie Smith)	.08	.06	.03
675	Cubs Checklist (Ryne Sandberg)	.08	.06	.03
676	Dodgers Checklist (Kirk Gibson)	.08	.06	.03
677	Expos Checklist (Andres Galarraga)	.08	.06	.03
678	Giants Checklist (Will Clark)	.08	.06	.03
679	Indians Checklist (Cory Snyder)	.08	.06	.03
680	Mariners Checklist (Alvin Davis)	.08	.06	.03
681	Mets Checklist (Darryl Strawberry)	.08	.06	.03
682	Orioles Checklist (Cal Ripken, Jr.)	.08	.06	.03
683	Padres Checklist (Tony Gwynn)	.08	.06	.03
684	Phillies Checklist (Mike Schmidt)	.08	.06	.03
685	Pirates Checklist (Andy Van Slyke)	.08	.06	.03
686	Rangers Checklist (Ruben Sierra)	.08	.06	.03
687	Red Sox Checklist (Wade Boggs)	.08	.06	.03
688	Reds Checklist (Eric Davis)	.08	.06	.03
689	Royals Checklist (George Brett)	.08	.06	.03
690	Tigers Checklist (Alan Trammell)	.08	.06	.03
691	Twins Checklist (Frank Viola)	.08	.06	.03
692	White Sox Checklist (Harold Baines)	.08	.06	.03
693	Yankees Checklist (Don Mattingly)	.08	.06	.03
694	Checklist 1-100	.08	.06	.03
695	Checklist 101-200	.08	.06	.03
696	Checklist 201-300	.08	.06	.03
697	Checklist 301-400	.08	.06	.03
698	Checklist 401-500	.08	.06	.03
699	Checklist 501-600	.08	.06	.03
700	Checklist 601-700	.08	.06	.03
701	Checklist 701-800	.20	.15	.08
702	Jessie Barfield	.10	.08	.04
703	Walt Terrell	.10	.08	.04
704	Dickie Thon	.10	.08	.04
705	Al Leiter	.10	.08	.04
706	Dave LaPoint	.10	.08	.04
707	Charlie Hayes(FC)	.15	.11	.06
708	Andy Hawkins	.10	.08	.04
709	Mickey Hatcher	.10	.08	.04

		MT	NR MT	EX
710	Lance McCullers	.10	.08	.04
711	Ron Kittle	.10	.08	.04
712	Bert Blyleven	.10	.08	.04
713	Rick Dempsey	.10	.08	.04
714	Ken Williams	.10	.08	.04
715	Steve Rosenberg(FC)	.15	.11	.06
716	Joe Skalski(FC)	.20	.15	.08
717	Spike Owen	.10	.08	.04
718	Todd Burns	.10	.08	.04
719	Kevin Gross	.10	.08	.04
720	Tommy Herr	.10	.08	.04
721	Rob Ducey	.10	.08	.04
722	Gary Green(FC)	.15	.11	.06
723	Gregg Olson(FC)	2.75	2.00	1.00
724	Greg Harris(FC)	.15	.11	.06
725	Craig Worthington(FC)	.50	.40	.20
726	Tom Howard(FC)	.35	.25	.14
727	Dale Mohorcic	.10	.08	.04
728	Rich Yett	.10	.08	.04
729	Mel Hall	.10	.08	.04
730	Floyd Youmans	.10	.08	.04
731	Lonnie Smith	.15	.11	.06
732	Wally Backman	.10	.08	.04
733	Trevor Wilson	.10	.08	.04
734	Jose Alvarez	.10	.08	.04
735	Bob Milacki(FC)	.15	.11	.06
736	Tom Gordon(FC)	2.00	1.50	.80
737	Wally Whitehurst(FC)	.25	.20	.10
738	Mike Aldrete	.10	.08	.04
739	Keith Miller	.10	.08	.04
740	Randy Milligan	.10	.08	.04
741	Jeff Parrett	.10	.08	.04
742	Steve Finley(FC)	.35	.25	.14
743	Junior Felix(FC)	2.00	1.50	.80
744	Pete Harnisch(FC)	.25	.20	.10
745	Bill Spiers(FC)	.50	.40	.20
746	Hensley Meulens(FC)	1.25	.90	.50
747	Juan Bell	.20	.15	.08
748	Steve Sax	.15	.11	.06
749	Phil Bradley	.10	.08	.04
750	Rey Quinones	.10	.08	.04
751	Tommy Gregg(FC)	.15	.11	.06
752	Kevin Brown(FC)	.10	.08	.04
753	Derek Lilliquist(FC)	.15	.11	.06
754	Todd Zeile(FC)	3.75	2.75	1.50
755	Jim Abbott(FC)	3.75	2.75	1.50
756	Ozzie Canseco(FC)	.70	.50	.30
757	Nick Esasky	.10	.08	.04
758	Mike Moore	.15	.11	.06
759	Rob Murphy	.10	.08	.04
760	Rick Mahler	.10	.08	.04
761	Fred Lynn	.10	.08	.04
762	Kevin Blankenship(FC)	.10	.08	.04
763	Eddie Murray	.15	.11	.06
764	Steve Searcy(FC)	.10	.08	.04
765	Jerome Walton(FC)	4.00	3.00	1.50
766	Erik Hanson(FC)	1.25	.90	.50
767	Bob Boone	.15	.11	.06
768	Edgar Martinez(FC)	.60	.45	.25
769	Jose DeJesus(FC)	.10	.08	.04
770	Greg Briley(FC)	1.00	.70	.40
771	Steve Peters(FC)	.10	.08	.04
772	Rafael Palmeiro	.15	.11	.06
773	Jack Clark	.15	.11	.06
774	Nolan Ryan	4.00	3.00	1.50
775	Lance Parrish	.10	.08	.04
776	Joe Girardi(FC)	.35	.25	.14
777	Willie Randolph	.10	.08	.04
778	Mitch Williams	.30	.25	.12
779	Dennis Cook(FC)	.40	.30	.15
780	Dwight Smith(FC)	1.50	1.25	.60
781	Lenny Harris(FC)	.40	.30	.15
782	Torey Lovullo(FC)	.15	.11	.06
783	Norm Charlton(FC)	.10	.08	.04
784	Chris Brown	.10	.08	.04
785	Todd Benzinger	.10	.08	.04
786	Shane Rawley	.10	.08	.04
787	Omar Vizquel(FC)	.25	.20	.10
788	LaVel Freeman(FC)	.25	.20	.10
789	Jeffrey Leonard	.10	.08	.04
790	Eddie Williams(FC)	.10	.08	.04
791	Jamie Moyer	.10	.08	.04
792	Bruce Hurst	.10	.08	.04
793	Julio Franco	.15	.11	.06
794	Claudell Washington	.10	.08	.04
795	Jody Davis	.10	.08	.04
796	Odibbe McDowell	.10	.08	.04
797	Paul Kilgus	.10	.08	.04
798	Tracy Jones	.10	.08	.04
799	Steve Wilson(FC)	.25	.20	.10
800	Pete O'Brien,			

1989 Upper Deck Promos

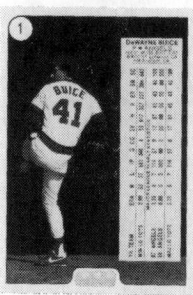

In 1988 Upper Deck produced a two card test set to be distributed as samples for the 1989 set. 18,000 of each card was produced. The cards were distributed to dealers at the 1988 National Sports Collectors Convention. Two other variations of the promo cards exist. Both variations involve differences in how the hologram was produced. 2,000-5,000 of one of the hologram variations exist, while less than 1,000 of the third variation exist. These sets are valued at $300 and $500 respectively. Joyner and Buice were selected for the promo cards because of a reported investment interest in Upper Deck. Joyner and Buice were not allowed to invest in the company due to their player status.

		MT	NR MT	EX
Complete Set:		150.00	110.00	60.00
Common Player:		50.00	37.00	20.00
1	DeWayne Buice	50.00	37.00	20.00
700	Wally Joyner	75.00	55.00	30.00

1990 Upper Deck

Following the success of its first issue, Upper Deck released another 800-card set in 1990. The cards contain full-color photos on both sides and are 2-1/2" by 3-1/2" in size. The artwork of Vernon Wells is featured on the front of all team checklist cards. The 1990 set also introduces two new Wells illustrations - a tribute to Mike Schmidt upon his retirement and one commemorating Nolan Ryan's 5,000 career strikeouts. The cards are similar in design to the 1989 issue. The Wade Boggs card depicts the Red Sox star in four stages of his batting swing via a quad-action photograph, much like the Jim Abbott card of 1989. The high- number series (701-800) was released as a boxed set, in factory sets and in wax packs at mid-season.

	MT	NR MT	EX
Complete Set: 1-700	40.00	30.00	15.00
Common Player: 1-700	.06	.05	.02
Complete Set: 1-800	50.00	37.00	20.00
Common Player: 701-800	.10	.08	.04

#	Player	MT	NR MT	EX
1	Star Rookie Checklist	.06	.05	.02
2	Randy Nosek(FC)	.15	.11	.06
3	Tom Dress(FC)	.15	.11	.06
4	Curt Young	.06	.05	.02
5	Angels Checklist	.06	.05	.02
6	Luis Salazar	.06	.05	.02
7	Phillies Checklist	.06	.05	.02
8	Jose Bautista	.08	.06	.03
9	Marquis Grissom(FC)	.70	.50	.30
10	Dodgers Checklist	.06	.05	.02
11	Rick Aguilera	.08	.06	.03
12	Padres Checklist	.06	.05	.02
13	Deion Sanders(FC)	.50	.40	.20
14	Marvell Wynne	.06	.05	.02
15	David West	.15	.11	.06
16	Pirates Checklist	.06	.05	.02
17	Sammy Sosa(FC)	.80	.60	.30
18	Yankees Checklist	.06	.05	.02
19	Jack Howell	.06	.05	.02
20	Mike Schmidt (Special Card)	1.00	.70	.40
21	Robin Ventura(FC)	.70	.50	.30
22	Brian Meyer(FC)	.20	.15	.08
23	Blaine Beatty(FC)	.20	.15	.08
24	Mariners Checklist	.06	.05	.02
25	Greg Vaughn(FC)	.70	.50	.30
26	Xavier Hernandez(FC)	.15	.11	.06
27	Jason Grimsley(FC)	.25	.20	.10
28	Eric Anthony(FC)	1.00	.70	.40
29	Expos Checklist	.06	.05	.02
30	David Wells	.06	.05	.02
31	Hal Morris(FC)	.70	.50	.30
32	Royals Checklist	.25	.20	.10
33	Kelly Mann(FC)	.15	.11	.06
34	Nolan Ryan (Special Card)	1.75	1.25	.70
35	Scott Service(FC)	.20	.15	.08
36	Athletics Checklist	.06	.05	.02
37	Tino Martinez(FC)	1.75	1.25	.70
38	Chili Davis	.09	.07	.04
39	Scott Sanderson	.06	.05	.02
40	Giants Checklist	.06	.05	.02
41	Tigers Checklist	.06	.05	.02
42	Scott Coolbaugh(FC)	.40	.30	.15
43	Jose Cano(FC)	.15	.11	.06
44	Jose Vizcaino(FC)	.40	.30	.15
45	Bob Hamelin(FC)	.70	.50	.30
46	Jose Offerman(FC)	1.50	1.25	.60
47	Kevin Blankenship	.10	.08	.04
48	Twins Checklist	.06	.05	.02
49	Tommy Greene(FC)	.50	.40	.20
50	Will Clark (Special Card)	.40	.30	.15
51	Rob Nelson(FC)	.09	.07	.04
52	Chris Hammond(FC)	.15	.11	.06
53	Indians Checklist	.06	.05	.02
54a	Ben McDonald (Orioles Logo)(FC)	30.00	22.00	12.00
54b	Ben McDonald (Rookies Logo)(FC)	3.00	2.25	1.25
55	Andy Benes(FC)	.30	.25	.12
56	John Olerud(FC)	4.00	3.00	1.50
57	Red Sox Checklist	.06	.05	.02
58	Tony Armas	.06	.05	.02
59	George Canale(FC)	.25	.20	.10
60a	Orioles Checklist (Jamie Weston)	4.00	3.00	1.50
60b	Orioles Checklist (Mickey Weston)	.08	.06	.03
61	Mike Stanton(FC)	.15	.11	.06
62	Mets Checklist	.06	.05	.02
63	Kent Mercker(FC)	.50	.40	.20
64	Francisco Cabrera(FC)	.30	.25	.20
65	Steve Avery(FC)	.60	.45	.25
66	Jose Canseco	.90	.70	.50
67	Matt Merullo(FC)	.15	.11	.06
68	Cardinals Checklist	.06	.05	.02
69	Ron Karkovice	.06	.05	.02
70	Kevin Maas(FC)	4.00	3.00	1.50
71	Dennis Cook	.10	.08	.04
72	Juan Gonzalez(FC)	3.00	2.25	1.25
73	Cubs Checklist	.06	.05	.02
74	Dean Palmer(FC)	.40	.30	.15
75	Bo Jackson (Special Card)	.80	.60	.30
76	Rob Richie(FC)	.20	.15	.08
77	Bobby Rose(FC)	.40	.30	.15
78	Brian DuBois(FC)	.15	.11	.06
79	White Sox Checklist	.06	.05	.02
80	Gene Nelson	.06	.05	.02
81	Bob McClure	.06	.05	.02
82	Rangers Checklist	.06	.05	.02
83	Greg Minton	.06	.05	.02
84	Braves Checklist	.06	.05	.02
85	Willie Fraser	.06	.05	.02
86	Neal Heaton	.06	.05	.02
87	Kevin Tapani(FC)	.30	.25	.12
88	Astros Checklist	.06	.05	.02
89a	Jim Gott (Incorrect Photo)	5.00	3.75	2.00
89b	Jim Gott (Photo of Gott)	.10	.08	.04
90	Lance Johnson(FC)	.09	.07	.04
91	Brewers Checklist	.06	.05	.02
92	Jeff Parrett	.08	.06	.03
93	Julio Machado(FC)	.25	.20	.10
94	Ron Jones	.10	.08	.04
95	Blue Jays Checklist	.06	.05	.02
96	Jerry Reuss	.06	.05	.02
97	Brian Fisher	.06	.05	.02
98	Kevin Ritz(FC)	.25	.20	.10
99	Reds Checklist	.06	.05	.02
100	Checklist 1-100	.06	.05	.02
101	Gerald Perry	.06	.05	.02
102	Kevin Appier(FC)	.30	.25	.12
103	Julio Franco	.10	.08	.04
104	Craig Biggio	.30	.25	.12
105	Bo Jackson	.90	.70	.35
106	Junior Felix	.70	.50	.30
107	Mike Harkey(FC)	.30	.25	.12
108	Fred McGriff	.25	.20	.10
109	Rick Sutcliffe	.08	.06	.03
110	Pete O'Brien	.08	.06	.03
111	Kelly Gruber	.10	.08	.04
112	Pat Borders	.10	.08	.04
113	Dwight Evans	.10	.08	.04
114	Dwight Gooden	.20	.15	.08
115	Kevin Batiste(FC)	.15	.11	.06
116	Eric Davis	.25	.20	.10
117	Kevin Mitchell	.40	.30	.15
118	Ron Oester	.06	.05	.02
119	Brett Butler	.09	.07	.04
120	Danny Jackson	.06	.05	.02
121	Tommy Gregg	.06	.05	.02
122	Ken Caminiti	.08	.06	.03
123	Kevin Brown	.10	.08	.04
124	George Brett	.15	.11	.06
125	Mike Scott	.10	.08	.04
126	Cory Snyder	.10	.08	.04
127	George Bell	.15	.11	.06
128	Mark Grace	.50	.40	.20
129	Devon White	.10	.08	.04
130	Tony Fernandez	.15	.11	.06
131	Dan Aase	.06	.05	.02
132	Rance Mulliniks	.06	.05	.02
133	Marty Barrett	.08	.06	.03
134	Nelson Liriano	.07	.05	.03
135	Mark Carreon(FC)	.15	.11	.06
136	Candy Maldonado	.06	.05	.02
137	Tim Birtsas	.06	.05	.02
138	Tom Brookens	.06	.05	.02
139	John Franco	.08	.06	.03
140	Mike LaCoss	.06	.05	.02
141	Jeff Treadway	.07	.05	.03
142	Pat Tabler	.07	.05	.03
143	Darrell Evans	.06	.05	.02
144	Rafael Ramirez	.06	.05	.02
145	Oddibe McDowell	.09	.07	.04
146	Brian Downing	.09	.07	.04
147	Curtis Wilkerson	.06	.05	.02
148	Ernie Whitt	.07	.05	.02
149	Bill Schroeder	.06	.05	.02
150	Domingo Ramos	.06	.05	.02
151	Rick Honeycutt	.06	.05	.02
152	Don Slaught	.06	.05	.02
153	Mitch Webster	.06	.05	.02
154	Tony Phillips	.07	.05	.02
155	Paul Kilgus	.06	.05	.02
156	Ken Griffey, Jr.	4.00	3.00	1.50

		MT	NR MT	EX
157	Gary Sheffield	.50	.40	.20
158	Wally Backman	.06	.05	.02
159	B.J. Surhoff	.08	.06	.03
160	Louie Meadows	.08	.06	.03
161	Paul O'Neill	.09	.07	.04
162	*Jeff McKnight*(FC)	.20	.15	.08
163	Alvaro Espinoza(FC)	.15	.11	.06
164	*Scott Scudder*(FC)	.20	.15	.08
165	Jeff Reed	.06	.05	.02
166	Gregg Jefferies	.60	.45	.25
167	Barry Larkin	.15	.11	.06
168	Gary Carter	.10	.08	.04
169	Robby Thompson	.09	.07	.04
170	Rolando Roomes	.15	.11	.06
171	Mark McGwire	.50	.40	.20
172	Steve Sax	.10	.08	.04
173	Mark Williamson	.06	.05	.02
174	Mitch Williams	.15	.11	.06
175	Brian Holton	.06	.05	.02
176	Rob Deer	.08	.06	.03
177	Tim Raines	.12	.09	.05
178	Mike Felder	.06	.05	.02
179	Harold Reynolds	.10	.08	.04
180	Terry Francona	.06	.05	.02
181	Chris Sabo	.15	.11	.06
182	Darryl Strawberry	.20	.15	.08
183	Willie Randolph	.10	.08	.04
184	Billy Ripken	.06	.05	.02
185	Mackey Sasser	.08	.06	.03
186	Todd Benzinger	.08	.06	.03
187	Kevin Elster	.07	.05	.03
188	Jose Uribe	.06	.05	.02
189	Tom Browning	.10	.08	.04
190	Keith Miller	.09	.07	.04
191	Don Mattingly	.80	.60	.30
192	Dave Parker	.12	.09	.05
193	Roberto Kelly	.12	.09	.05
194	Phil Bradley	.09	.07	.04
195	Ron Hassey	.07	.05	.03
196	Gerald Young	.06	.05	.02
197	Hubie Brooks	.08	.06	.03
198	Bill Doran	.09	.07	.04
199	Al Newman	.06	.05	.02
200	Checklist 101-200	.06	.05	.02
201	Terry Puhl	.06	.05	.02
202	Frank DiPino	.06	.05	.02
203	Jim Clancy	.06	.05	.02
204	Bob Ojeda	.07	.05	.03
205	Alex Trevino	.06	.05	.02
206	Dave Henderson	.10	.08	.04
207	Henry Cotto	.06	.05	.02
208	Rafael Belliard	.06	.05	.02
209	Stan Javier	.07	.05	.03
210	Jerry Reed	.06	.05	.02
211	Doug Dascenzo	.08	.06	.03
212	Andres Thomas	.07	.05	.03
213	Greg Maddux	.20	.15	.08
214	Mike Schooler	.09	.07	.04
215	Lonnie Smith	.09	.07	.04
216	Jose Rijo	.10	.08	.04
217	Greg Gagne	.08	.06	.03
218	Jim Gantner	.08	.06	.03
219	Allan Anderson	.09	.07	.04
220	Rick Mahler	.06	.05	.02
221	Jim Deshaies	.09	.07	.04
222	Keith Hernandez	.10	.08	.04
223	Vince Coleman	.12	.09	.05
224	David Cone	.20	.15	.08
225	Ozzie Smith	.20	.15	.08
226	Matt Nokes	.10	.08	.04
227	Barry Bonds	.10	.08	.04
228	Felix Jose	.10	.08	.04
229	Dennis Powell	.06	.05	.02
230	Mike Gallego	.06	.05	.02
231	Shawon Dunston	.09	.07	.04
232	Ron Gant	.10	.08	.04
233	*Omar Vizquel*	.10	.08	.04
234	Derek Lilliquist	.10	.08	.04
235	Erik Hanson	.10	.08	.04
236	Kirby Puckett	.50	.40	.20
237	*Bill Spiers*	.25	.20	.10
238	Dan Gladden	.07	.05	.03
239	Bryan Clutterbuck(FC)	.07	.05	.03
240	John Moses	.06	.05	.02
241	Ron Darling	.12	.09	.05
242	Joe Magrane	.12	.09	.05
243	Dave Magadan	.09	.07	.03
244	Pedro Guererro	.15	.11	.06
245	Glenn Davis	.10	.08	.04
246	Terry Steinbach	.12	.09	.05
247	Fred Lynn	.09	.07	.04

		MT	NR MT	EX
248	Gary Redus	.06	.05	.02
249	Kenny Williams	.06	.05	.02
250	Sid Bream	.06	.05	.02
251	Bob Welch	.08	.06	.03
252	Bill Buckner	.07	.05	.03
253	Carney Lansford	.09	.07	.04
254	Paul Molitor	.12	.09	.05
255	Jose DeJesus	.15	.11	.06
256	Orel Hershiser	.25	.20	.10
257	Tom Brunansky	.10	.08	.04
258	Mike Davis	.06	.05	.02
259	Jeff Ballard	.12	.09	.05
260	Scott Terry	.09	.07	.04
261	Sid Fernandez	.10	.08	.04
262	Mike Marshall	.08	.06	.03
263	Howard Johnson	.20	.15	.08
264	Kirk Gibson	.09	.07	.04
265	Kevin McReynolds	.15	.11	.06
266	Cal Ripken, Jr.	.15	.11	.06
267	Ozzie Guillen	.07	.05	.03
268	Jim Traber	.06	.05	.02
269	Bobby Thigpen	.09	.07	.04
270	Joe Orsulak	.06	.05	.02
271	Bob Boone	.09	.07	.04
272	Dave Stewart	.09	.07	.04
273	Tim Wallach	.09	.07	.04
274	Luis Aquino	.06	.05	.02
275	Mike Moore	.10	.08	.04
276	Tony Pena	.08	.06	.03
277	Eddie Murray	.15	.11	.06
278	Milt Thompson	.07	.05	.03
279	Alejandro Pena	.06	.05	.02
280	Ken Dayley	.06	.05	.02
281	Carmen Castillo	.06	.05	.02
282	Tom Henke	.08	.06	.03
283	Mickey Hatcher	.06	.05	.02
284	Roy Smith(FC)	.06	.05	.02
285	Manny Lee	.06	.05	.02
286	Dan Pasqua	.07	.05	.02
287	Larry Sheets	.06	.05	.02
288	Garry Templeton	.07	.05	.03
289	Eddie Williams	.07	.05	.03
290	Brady Anderson	.07	.05	.03
291	Spike Owen	.07	.05	.03
292	Storm Davis	.09	.07	.04
293	Chris Bosio	.09	.07	.04
294	Jim Eisenreich	.07	.05	.03
295	Don August	.07	.05	.03
296	Jeff Hamilton	.07	.05	.03
297	Mickey Tettleton	.10	.08	.04
298	Mike Scioscia	.09	.07	.04
299	Kevin Hickey(FC)	.06	.05	.02
300	Checklist 201-300	.06	.05	.02
301	Shawn Abner	.06	.05	.02
302	Kevin Bass	.08	.06	.03
303	Bip Roberts(FC)	.08	.06	.03
304	Joe Girardi	.10	.08	.04
305	Danny Darwin	.06	.05	.02
306	Mike Heath	.06	.05	.02
307	Mike Macfarlane	.06	.05	.02
308	Ed Whitson	.08	.06	.03
309	Tracy Jones	.07	.05	.02
310	Scott Fletcher	.07	.05	.02
311	Darnell Coles	.07	.05	.02
312	Mike Brumley	.06	.05	.02
313	Bill Swift	.06	.05	.02
314	Charlie Hough	.07	.05	.03
315	Jim Presley	.08	.06	.03
316	Luis Polonia	.07	.05	.03
317	Mike Morgan	.06	.05	.02
318	Lee Guetterman	.06	.05	.02
319	Jose Oquendo	.08	.06	.03
320	Wayne Tollenson	.06	.05	.02
321	Jody Reed	.07	.05	.03
322	Damon Berryhill	.09	.07	.04
323	Roger Clemens	.40	.30	.15
324	Ryne Sandberg	.15	.11	.06
325	Benito Santiago	.10	.08	.04
326	Bret Saberhagen	.15	.11	.06
327	Lou Whitaker	.10	.08	.04
328	Dave Gallagher	.10	.08	.04
329	Mike Pagliarulo	.07	.05	.03
330	Doyle Alexander	.07	.05	.03
331	Jeffrey Leonard	.09	.07	.04
332	Torey Lovullo	.20	.15	.08
333	Pete Incaviglia	.09	.07	.04
334	Rickey Henderson	.15	.11	.06
335	Rafael Palmeiro	.10	.08	.04
336	Ken Hill	.10	.08	.04
337	Dave Winfield	.12	.09	.05
338	Alfredo Griffin	.07	.05	.03

#	Player	MT	NR MT	EX
339	Andy Hawkins	.07	.05	.03
340	Ted Power	.06	.05	.02
341	Steve Wilson	.10	.08	.04
342	Jack Clark	.10	.08	.04
343	Ellis Burks	.25	.20	.10
344	Tony Gwynn	.20	.15	.08
345	*Jerome Walton*	.70	.50	.30
346	Roberto Alomar	.10	.08	.04
347	*Carlos Martinez*(FC)	.15	.11	.06
348	Chet Lemon	.07	.05	.03
349	Willie Wilson	.07	.05	.03
350	Greg Walker	.07	.05	.03
351	Tom Bolton	.06	.05	.02
352	German Gonzalez(FC)	.08	.06	.03
353	Harold Baines	.10	.08	.04
354	Mike Greenwell	.30	.25	.12
355	Ruben Sierra	.20	.15	.08
356	Anres Galarraga	.12	.09	.05
357	Andre Dawson	.15	.11	.06
358	*Jeff Brantley*(FC)	.10	.08	.04
359	Mike Bielecki	.08	.06	.03
360	Ken Oberkfell	.06	.05	.02
361	Kurt Stillwell	.07	.05	.03
362	Brian Holman	.09	.07	.04
363	Kevin Seitzer	.12	.09	.05
364	Alvin Davis	.15	.11	.06
365	Tom Gordon	.35	.25	.14
366	Bobby Bonilla	.10	.08	.04
367	Carlton Fisk	.10	.08	.04
368	*Steve Carter*(FC)	.15	.11	.06
369	Joel Skinner	.06	.05	.02
370	John Cangelosi	.06	.05	.02
371	Cecil Espy	.08	.06	.03
372	*Gary Wayne*(FC)	.25	.20	.10
373	Jim Rice	.08	.06	.03
374	*Mike Dyer*(FC)	.15	.11	.06
375	Joe Carter	.12	.09	.05
376	Dwight Smith	.35	.25	.14
377	*John Wetteland*(FC)	.25	.20	.10
378	Ernie Riles	.06	.05	.02
379	Otis Nixon	.06	.05	.02
380	Vance Law	.06	.05	.02
381	Dave Bergman	.06	.05	.02
382	Frank White	.07	.05	.03
383	Scott Bradley	.06	.05	.02
384	Israel Sanchez	.06	.05	.02
385	Gary Pettis	.06	.05	.02
386	Donn Pall(FC)	.06	.05	.02
387	John Smiley	.10	.08	.04
388	Tom Candiotti	.07	.05	.03
389	Junior Ortiz	.06	.05	.02
390	Steve Lyons	.06	.05	.02
391	Brian Harper	.06	.05	.02
392	Fred Manrique	.06	.05	.02
393	Lee Smith	.08	.06	.03
394	Jeff Kunkel	.06	.05	.02
395	Claudell Washington	.08	.06	.03
396	John Tudor	.07	.05	.03
397	Terry Kennedy	.07	.05	.03
398	Lloyd McClendon	.09	.07	.04
399	Craig Lefferts	.06	.05	.02
400	Checklist 301-400	.06	.05	.02
401	Keith Moreland	.06	.05	.02
402	Rich Gedman	.07	.05	.03
403	Jeff Robinson	.07	.05	.03
404	Randy Ready	.06	.05	.02
405	Rick Cerone	.06	.05	.02
406	Jeff Blauser	.07	.05	.03
407	Larry Andersen	.06	.05	.02
408	Joe Boever	.08	.06	.03
409	Felix Fermin	.06	.05	.02
410	Glenn Wilson	.06	.05	.02
411	Rex Hudler	.06	.05	.02
412	Mark Grant	.06	.05	.02
413	Dennis Martinez	.08	.06	.03
414	Darrin Jackson	.06	.05	.02
415	Mike Aldrete	.06	.05	.02
416	Roger McDowell	.09	.07	.04
417	Jeff Reardon	.10	.08	.04
418	Darren Daulton	.06	.05	.02
419	Tim Laudner	.08	.06	.03
420	Don Carman	.07	.05	.03
421	Lloyd Moseby	.09	.07	.04
422	Doug Drabek	.10	.08	.04
423	Lenny Harris	.09	.07	.04
424	Jose Lind	.07	.05	.03
425	*Dave Johnson*(FC)	.20	.15	.08
426	Jerry Browne	.09	.07	.04
427	*Eric Yelding*(FC)	.12	.09	.05
428	Brad Komminsk(FC)	.06	.05	.02
429	Jody Davis	.06	.05	.02

#	Player	MT	NR MT	EX
430	Mariano Duncan(FC)	.09	.07	.04
431	Mark Davis	.12	.09	.05
432	Nelson Santovenia	.10	.08	.04
433	Bruce Hurst	.10	.08	.04
434	*Jeff Huson*(FC)	.25	.20	.10
435	Chris James	.09	.07	.04
436	*Mark Guthrie*(FC)	.15	.11	.06
437	Charlie Hayes(FC)	.10	.08	.04
438	Shane Rawley	.08	.06	.03
439	Dickie Thon	.06	.05	.02
440	Juan Berenguer	.06	.05	.02
441	Kevin Romine	.06	.05	.02
442	Bill Landrum	.09	.07	.04
443	Todd Frohwirth	.07	.05	.03
444	Craig Worthington	.10	.08	.04
445	Fernando Valenzuela	.09	.07	.04
446	Joey Belle(FC)	.35	.25	.14
447	*Ed Whited*(FC)	.15	.11	.06
448	Dave Smith	.09	.07	.04
449	Dave Clark	.07	.05	.03
450	Juan Agosto	.06	.05	.02
451	Dave Valle	.06	.05	.02
452	Kent Hrbek	.15	.11	.06
453	Von Hayes	.10	.08	.04
454	Gary Gaetti	.15	.11	.06
455	Greg Briley	.20	.15	.08
456	Glenn Braggs	.08	.06	.03
457	Kirt Manwaring	.10	.08	.04
458	Mel Hall	.07	.05	.03
459	Brook Jacoby	.08	.06	.03
460	Pat Sheridan	.06	.05	.02
461	Rob Murphy	.06	.05	.02
462	Jimmy Key	.10	.08	.04
463	Nick Esasky	.10	.08	.04
464	Rob Ducey	.09	.07	.04
465	Carlos Quintana	.09	.07	.04
466	*Larry Walker*(FC)	.50	.40	.20
467	Todd Worrell	.10	.08	.04
468	Kevin Gross	.09	.07	.04
469	Terry Pendleton	.09	.07	.04
470	Dave Martinez	.07	.05	.02
471	Gene Larkin	.06	.05	.02
472	Len Dykstra	.09	.07	.04
473	Barry Lyons	.06	.05	.02
474	Terry Mulholland(FC)	.10	.08	.04
475	*Chip Hale*(FC)	.15	.11	.06
476	Jesse Barfield	.08	.06	.03
477	Dan Plesac	.09	.07	.04
478a	Scott Garrelts (Photo actually Bill Bathe)	3.00	2.25	1.25
478b	Scott Garrelts (Correct photo)	.10	.08	.04
479	Dave Righetti	.10	.08	.04
480	Gus Polidor(FC)	.06	.05	.02
481	Mookie Wilson	.09	.07	.04
482	Luis Rivera	.06	.05	.02
483	Mike Flanagan	.07	.05	.03
484	Dennis "Oil Can" Boyd	.07	.05	.03
485	John Cerutti	.07	.05	.03
486	John Costello	.07	.05	.03
487	Pascual Perez	.07	.05	.03
488	Tommy Herr	.09	.07	.04
489	Tom Foley	.06	.05	.02
490	Curt Ford	.06	.05	.02
491	Steve Lake	.06	.05	.02
492	Tim Teufel	.06	.05	.02
493	Randy Bush	.06	.05	.02
494	Mike Jackson	.06	.05	.02
495	Steve Jeltz	.06	.05	.02
496	Paul Gibson	.08	.06	.03
497	Steve Balboni	.06	.05	.02
498	Bud Black	.06	.05	.02
499	Dale Sveum	.06	.05	.02
500	Checklist 401-500	.06	.05	.02
501	Timmy Jones	.06	.05	.02
502	Mark Portugal	.06	.05	.02
503	Ivan Calderon	.07	.05	.03
504	Rick Rhoden	.06	.05	.02
505	Willie McGee	.09	.07	.04
506	Kirk McCaskill	.08	.06	.03
507	Dave LaPoint	.07	.05	.03
508	Jay Howell	.10	.08	.04
509	Johnny Ray	.08	.06	.03
510	Dave Anderson	.06	.05	.02
511	Chuck Crim	.06	.05	.02
512	Joe Hesketh	.06	.05	.02
513	Dennis Eckersley	.10	.08	.04
514	Greg Brock	.08	.06	.03
515	Tim Burke	.08	.06	.03
516	Frank Tanana	.07	.05	.03
517	Jay Bell	.07	.05	.03
518	Guillermo Hernandez	.07	.05	.03

#	Name	MT	NR MT	EX
519	Randy Kramer(FC)	.08	.06	.03
520	Charles Hudson	.06	.05	.02
521	Jim Corsi(FC)	.08	.06	.03
522	Steve Rosenberg	.08	.06	.03
523	Cris Carpenter	.10	.08	.04
524	*Matt Winters*(FC)	.12	.09	.05
525	Melido Perez	.08	.06	.03
526	Chris Gwynn	.08	.06	.03
527	Bert Blyleven	.09	.07	.04
528	Chuck Cary	.07	.05	.03
529	Daryl Boston	.06	.05	.02
530	Dale Mohorcic	.06	.05	.02
531	Geronimo Berroa(FC)	.09	.07	.04
532	Edgar Martinez	.09	.07	.04
533	Dale Murphy	.15	.11	.06
534	Jay Buhner	.09	.07	.04
535	John Smoltz	.15	.11	.06
536	Andy Van Slyke	.15	.11	.06
537	Mike Henneman	.09	.07	.04
538	Miguel Garcia(FC)	.07	.05	.03
539	Frank Williams	.06	.05	.02
540	R.J. Reynolds	.06	.05	.02
541	Shawn Hillegas	.06	.05	.02
542	Walt Weiss	.10	.08	.04
543	*Greg Hibbard*(FC)	.15	.11	.06
544	Nolan Ryan	1.00	.70	.40
545	*Todd Zeile*	1.25	.90	.50
546	Hensley Meulens	.20	.15	.08
547	Tim Belcher	.10	.08	.04
548	Mike Witt	.08	.06	.03
549	Greg Cadaret	.06	.05	.02
550	Franklin Stubbs	.06	.05	.02
551	*Tony Castillo*(FC)	.12	.09	.05
552	Jeff Robinson	.08	.06	.03
553	*Steve Olin*(FC)	.12	.09	.05
554	Alan Trammell	.10	.08	.04
555	Wade Boggs	.70	.50	.30
556	Will Clark	1.00	.70	.40
557	Jeff King(FC)	.10	.08	.04
558	Mike Fitzgerald	.06	.05	.02
559	Ken Howell	.06	.05	.02
560	Bob Kipper	.06	.05	.02
561	Scott Bankhead	.09	.07	.04
562a	*Jeff Innis* (Photo actually David West)(FC)	5.00	3.75	2.00
562b	*Jeff Innis* (Corrected)(FC)	.20	.15	.08
563	Randy Johnson	.10	.08	.04
564	*Wally Whithurst*	.10	.08	.04
565	*Gene Harris*(FC)	.10	.08	.04
566	Norm Charlton	.09	.07	.04
567	Robin Yount	.40	.30	.15
568	*Joe Oliver*(FC)	.35	.25	.14
569	Mark Parent	.07	.05	.03
570	John Farrell	.07	.05	.03
571	Tom Glavine	.10	.08	.04
572	Rod Nichols(FC)	.06	.05	.02
573	Jack Morris	.09	.07	.04
574	Greg Swindell	.12	.09	.05
575	Steve Searcy(FC)	.09	.07	.04
576	Ricky Jordan	.20	.15	.08
577	Matt Williams	.35	.25	.14
578	Mike LaValliere	.07	.05	.03
579	Bryn Smith	.08	.06	.03
580	Bruce Ruffin	.06	.05	.02
581	Randy Myers	.08	.06	.03
582	*Rick Wrona*(FC)	.15	.11	.06
583	Juan Samuel	.09	.07	.04
584	Les Lancaster	.07	.05	.03
585	Jeff Musselman	.07	.05	.03
586	Rob Dibble	.09	.07	.04
587	Eric Show	.07	.05	.03
588	Jesse Orosco	.06	.05	.02
589	Herm Winningham	.06	.05	.02
590	Andy Allanson	.06	.05	.02
591	Dion James	.06	.05	.02
592	Carmelo Martinez	.08	.06	.03
593	Luis Quinones(FC)	.08	.06	.03
594	Dennis Rasmussen	.08	.06	.03
595	Rich Yett	.06	.05	.02
596	Bob Walk	.08	.06	.03
597	Andy McGaffigan	.07	.05	.03
598	Billy Hatcher	.07	.05	.03
599	Bob Knepper	.06	.05	.02
600	Checklist 501-600	.06	.05	.02
601	Joey Cora(FC)	.10	.08	.04
602	*Steve Finley*	.15	.11	.06
603	Kal Daniels	.10	.08	.04
604	Gregg Olson	.30	.25	.12
605	Dave Steib	.09	.07	.04
606	*Kenny Rogers*(FC)	.15	.11	.06
607	Zane Smith	.06	.05	.02
608	*Bob Geren*(FC)	.25	.20	.10
609	Chad Kreuter	.10	.08	.04
610	Mike Smithson	.06	.05	.02
611	*Jeff Wetherby*(FC)	.15	.11	.06
612	*Gary Mielke*(FC)	.15	.11	.06
613	Pete Smith	.08	.06	.03
614	*Jack Daugherty*(FC)	.15	.11	.06
615	Lance McCullers	.08	.06	.03
616	Don Robinson	.06	.05	.02
617	Jose Guzman	.06	.05	.02
618	Steve Bedrosian	.08	.06	.03
619	Jamie Moyer	.06	.05	.02
620	Atlee Hammaker	.06	.05	.02
621	*Rick Luecken*(FC)	.15	.11	.06
622	Greg W. Harris	.09	.07	.04
623	Pete Harnisch	.10	.08	.04
624	Jerald Clark	.10	.08	.04
625	Jack McDowell	.07	.05	.03
626	Frank Viola	.12	.09	.05
627	Ted Higuera	.09	.07	.04
628	*Marty Pevey*(FC)	.15	.11	.06
629	Bill Wegman	.06	.05	.02
630	Eric Plunk	.06	.05	.02
631	Drew Hall	.06	.05	.02
632	Doug Jones	.08	.06	.03
633	Geno Petralli	.06	.05	.02
634	Jose Alvarez	.06	.05	.02
635	Bob Milacki(FC)	.10	.08	.04
636	Bobby Witt	.07	.05	.03
637	Trevor Wilson	.08	.06	.03
638	Jeff Russell	.08	.06	.03
639	Mike Krukow	.07	.05	.03
640	Rick Leach	.06	.05	.02
641	Dave Schmidt	.06	.05	.02
642	Terry Leach	.06	.05	.02
643	Calvin Schiraldi	.06	.05	.02
644	Bob Melvin	.06	.05	.02
645	Jim Abbott	.40	.30	.15
646	*Jaime Navarro*(FC)	.20	.15	.08
647	Mark Langston	.10	.08	.04
648	Juan Nieves	.08	.06	.03
649	Damaso Garcia	.06	.05	.02
650	Charlie O'Brien	.06	.05	.02
651	Eric King	.06	.05	.02
652	Mike Boddicker	.08	.06	.03
653	Duan Ward	.07	.05	.03
654	Bob Stanley	.06	.05	.02
655	Sandy Alomar, Jr.	.50	.40	.20
656	Danny Tartabull	.10	.08	.04
657	Randy McCament	.15	.11	.06
658	Charlie Leibrandt	.07	.05	.03
659	Dan Quisenberry	.07	.05	.03
660	Paul Assenmacher	.06	.05	.02
661	Walt Terrell	.07	.05	.03
662	Tim Leary	.07	.05	.03
663	Randy Milligan	.08	.06	.03
664	Bo Diaz	.06	.05	.02
665	Mark Lemke	.07	.05	.03
666	Jose Gonzalez	.08	.06	.03
667	Chuck Finley	.07	.05	.03
668	John Kruk	.08	.06	.03
669	Dick Schofield	.07	.05	.03
670	Tim Crews	.06	.05	.02
671	John Dopson	.09	.07	.04
672	*John Orton*(FC)	.15	.11	.06
673	Eric Hetzel(FC)	.10	.08	.04
674	Lance Parrish	.08	.06	.03
675	Ramon Martinez	.50	.40	.20
676	Mark Gubicza	.10	.08	.04
677	Greg Litton	.20	.15	.08
678	Greg Mathews	.07	.05	.03
679	Dave Dravecky	.07	.05	.03
680	Steve Farr	.07	.05	.03
681	Mike Devereaux	.09	.07	.04
682	Ken Griffey, Sr.	.08	.06	.03
683a	*Mickey Weston* (Jamie)(FC)	5.00	3.75	2.00
683b	*Mickey Weston* (corrected)(FC)	.30	.25	.12
684	Jack Armstrong	.07	.05	.03
685	Steve Buechele	.07	.05	.03
686	Bryan Harvey	.07	.05	.03
687	Lance Blankenship	.09	.07	.04
688	Dante Bichette	.09	.07	.04
689	Todd Burns	.09	.07	.04
690	Dan Petry	.06	.05	.02
691	*Kent Anderson*(FC)	.15	.11	.06
692	Todd Stottlemyre	.08	.06	.03
693	Wally Joyner	.15	.11	.06
694	Mike Rochford(FC)	.10	.08	.04
695	Floyd Bannister	.07	.05	.03
696	Rick Reuschel	.09	.07	.04
697	Jose DeLeon	.09	.07	.04

		MT	NR MT	EX
698	Jeff Montgomery	.08	.06	.03
699	Jeff Montgomery	.08	.06	.03
700a	Checklist 601-700 (Jamie Weston)			
		5.00	3.75	2.00
700b	Checklist 601-700 (Mickey Weston)			
		.10	.08	.04
701	Jim Gott	.10	.08	.04
702	"Rookie Threats" (Delino DeShields, Larry			
	Walker, Marquis Grissom)	1.00	.70	.40
703	Alejandro Pena	.10	.08	.04
704	Willie Randolph	.12	.09	.05
705	Tim Leary	.10	.08	.04
706	Chuck McElroy(FC)	.20	.15	.08
707	Gerald Perry	.10	.08	.04
708	Tom Brunansky	.12	.09	.05
709	John Franco	.15	.11	.06
710	Mark Davis	.10	.08	.04
711	Dave Justice(FC)	7.00	5.25	2.75
712	Storm Davis	.10	.08	.04
713	Scott Ruskin(FC)	.25	.20	.10
714	Glenn Braggs	.10	.08	.04
715	Kevin Bearse(FC)	.40	.30	.15
716	Jose Nunez(FC)	.15	.11	.06
717	Tim Layana(FC)	.30	.25	.12
718	Greg Myers(FC)	.12	.09	.05
719	Pete O'Brien	.10	.08	.04
720	John Candelaria	.10	.08	.04
721	Craig Grebeck(FC)	.25	.20	.10
722	Shawn Boskie(FC)	.30	.25	.12
723	Jim Leyritz(FC)	.40	.30	.15
724	Bill Sampen(FC)	.30	.25	.12
725	Scott Radinsky(FC)	.35	.25	.14
726	Todd Hundley(FC)	.30	.25	.12
727	Scott Hemond(FC)	.20	.15	.08
728	Lenny Webster(FC)	.25	.20	.10
729	Jeff Reardon	.12	.09	.05
730	Mitch Webster	.10	.08	.04
731	Brian Bohanon(FC)	.25	.20	.10
732	Rick Parker(FC)	.20	.15	.08
733	Terry Shumpert(FC)	.40	.30	.15
734a	6th No-Hitter (Nolan Ryan) (with 300 win			
	stripe)	4.00	3.00	1.50
734b	6th No-Hitter (Nolan Ryan) (without			
	stripe)	20.00	15.00	7.50
735	John Burkett(FC)	.40	.30	.15
736	Derrick May(FC)	1.25	.90	.50
737	Carlos Baerga(FC)	.50	.40	.20
738	Greg Smith(FC)	.15	.11	.06
739	Joe Kraemer(FC)	.15	.11	.06
740	Scott Sanderson	.10	.08	.04
741	Hector Villanueva(FC)	.40	.30	.15
742	Mike Fetters(FC)	.25	.20	.10
743	Mark Gardner(FC)	.30	.25	.12
744	Matt Nokes	.10	.08	.04
745	Dave Winfield	.20	.15	.08
746	Delino DeShields(FC)	2.00	1.50	.80
747	Dann Howitt(FC)	.20	.15	.08
748	Tony Pena	.12	.09	.05
749	Oil Can Boyd	.12	.09	.05
750	Mike Benjamin(FC)	.25	.20	.10
751	Alex Cole(FC)	1.00	.70	.40
752	Eric Gunderson(FC)	.40	.30	.15
753	Howard Farmer(FC)	.25	.20	.10
754	Joe Carter	.15	.11	.06
755	Ray Lankford(FC)	2.00	1.50	.80
756	Sandy Alomar,Jr.	.50	.40	.20
757	Alex Sanchez(FC)	.15	.11	.06
758	Nick Esasky	.10	.08	.04
759	Stan Belinda(FC)	.20	.15	.08
760	Jim Presley	.10	.08	.04
761	Gary DiSarcina(FC)	.20	.15	.08
762	Wayne Edwards(FC)	.20	.15	.08
763	Pat Combs(FC)	.20	.15	.08
764	Mickey Pina(FC)	.40	.30	.15
765	Wilson Alvarez(FC)	.35	.25	.14
766	Dave Parker	.15	.11	.06
767	Mike Blowers(FC)	.20	.15	.08
768	Tony Phillips	.10	.08	.04
769	Pascual Perez	.10	.08	.04
770	Gary Pettis	.10	.08	.04
771	Fred Lynn	.10	.08	.04
772	Mel Rojas(FC)	.20	.15	.08
773	David Segui(FC)	.60	.45	.25
774	Gary Carter	.15	.11	.06
775	Rafael Valdez(FC)	.15	.11	.06
776	Glenallen Hill(FC)	.15	.11	.06
777	Keith Hernandez	.12	.09	.05
778	Billy Hatcher	.12	.09	.05
779	Marty Clary(FC)	.10	.08	.04
780	Candy Maldonado	.12	.09	.05
781	Mike Marshall	.10	.08	.04

		MT	NR MT	EX
782	Billy Jo Robidoux(FC)	.10	.08	.04
783	Mark Langston	.12	.09	.05
784	Paul Sorrento(FC)	.25	.20	.10
785	Dave Hollins(FC)	.35	.25	.14
786	Cecil Fielder	.80	.60	.30
787	Matt Young	.10	.08	.04
788	Jeff Huson	.15	.11	.06
789	Lloyd Moseby	.12	.09	.05
790	Ron Kittle	.12	.09	.05
791	Hubie Brooks	.12	.09	.05
792	Craig Lefferts	.10	.08	.04
793	Kevin Bass	.10	.08	.04
794	Bryn Smith	.10	.08	.04
795	Juan Samuel	.12	.09	.05
796	Sam Horn(FC)	.15	.11	.06
797	Randy Myers	.12	.09	.05
798	Chris James	.10	.08	.04
799	Bill Gullickson	.10	.08	.04
800	Checklist 701-800	.10	.08	.04

1991 Upper Deck

115 rookies are included among the first 700 cards in the 1991 Upper Deck set. A 100-card high # series was once again planned for release in July or August. The 1991 Upper Deck cards feature high quality white stock and color photos on both the front and backs of the cards. A nine-card "Baseball Heroes" bonus set honoring Nolan Ryan, is among the many insert specials in the 1991 Upper Deck set. Others include a card of Chicago Bulls superstar Michael Jordan. Along with the Ryan bonus cards, 2,500 limited-edition cards personally autographed and numbered by Ryan will be randomly inserted. Upper Deck cards are packaged in tamper-proof foil packs. Each pack contains 15 cards and a 3-D team logo hologram sticker. The 1991 hologram stickers are full size.

		MT	NR MT	EX
	Complete Set:	40.00	30.00	15.00
	Common Player:	.05	.04	.02
1	Star Rookie Checklist	.05	.04	.02
2	Star Rookie *(Phil Plantier)*(FC)	.70	.50	.30
3	Star Rookie *(D.J. Dozier)*(FC)	.60	.45	.25
4	Star Rookie *(Dave Hansen)*(FC)	.20	.15	.08
5	Star Rookie *(Maurice Vaughn)*(FC)	.90	.70	.35
6	Star Rookie *(Leo Gomez)*(FC)	.60	.45	.25
7	Star Rookie *(Scott Aldred)*(FC)	.25	.20	.10
8	Star Rookie *(Scott Chiamparino)*(FC)	.30	.25	.12
9	Star Rookie *(Lance Dickson)*(FC)	.30	.25	.12
10	Star Rookie *(Sean Berry)*(FC)	.20	.15	.08
11	Star Rookie (Bernie Williams)(FC)	.20	.15	.08
12	Star Rookie (Brian Barnes)(FC)	.20	.15	.08
13	Star Rookie *(Narciso Elvira)*(FC)	.20	.15	.08
14	Star Rookie *(Mark Gardiner)*(FC)	.20	.15	.08
15	Star Rookie *(Greg Colbrunn)*(FC)	.20	.15	.08
16	Star Rookie *(Bernard Gilkey)*(FC)	.25	.20	.10
17	Star Rookie *(Mark Lewis)*(FC)	.30	.25	.12
18	Star Rookie *(Mickey Morandini)*(FC)	.15	.11	.06
19	Star Rookie *(Charles Nagy)*(FC)	.15	.11	.06
20	Star Rookie *(Geronimo Pena)*(FC)	.25	.20	.10
21	Star Rookie *(Henry Rodriguez)*(FC)	.50	.40	.20
22	Star Rookie *(Scott Cooper)*(FC)	.20	.15	.08
23	Star Rookie *(Andujar Cedeno)*(FC)	1.25	.90	.50
24	Star Rookie *(Eric Karros)*(FC)	.60	.45	.25
25	Star Rookie *(Steve Decker)*(FC)	.20	.15	.08
26	Star Rookie *(Kevin Belcher)*(FC)	.20	.15	.08
27	Star Rookie *(Jeff Conine)*(FC)	1.25	.90	.50
28	Oakland Athletics Checklist	.10	.08	.04
29	Chicago White Sox Checklist	.08	.06	.03
30	Texas Rangers Checklist	.08	.06	.03
31	California Angels Checklist	.08	.06	.03
32	Seattle Mariners Checklist	.10	.08	.04
33	Kansas City Royals Checklist	.10	.08	.04
34	Minnesota Twins Checklist	.08	.06	.03
35	Scott Leius(FC)	.10	.08	.04
36	Neal Heaton	.06	.05	.02
37	*Terry Lee*(FC)	.20	.15	.08
38	Gary Redus	.05	.04	.02
39	Barry Jones	.06	.05	.02
40	Chuck Knoblauch(FC)	.10	.08	.04
41	Larry Andersen	.05	.04	.02
43	Darryl Hamilton	.06	.05	.02
44	Toronto Blue Jays Checklist	.08	.06	.03
45	Detroit Tigers Checklist	.10	.08	.04

		MT	NR MT	EX
46	Cleveland Indians Checklist	.08	.06	.03
47	Baltimore Orioles Checklist	.08	.06	.03
48	Milwaukee Brewers Checklist	.08	.06	.03
49	New York Yankees Checklist	.08	.06	.03
50	Top Prospect Checklist	.05	.04	.02
51	Top Prospect (Kyle Abbott)(FC)	.25	.20	.10
52	Top Prospect (Jeff Juden)(FC)	.25	.20	.10
53	Top Prospect *(Todd Van Poppel)*(FC)	2.50	2.00	1.00
54	Top Prospect *(Steve Karsay)*(FC)	.40	.30	.15
55	Top Prospect *(Chipper Jones)*(FC)	.50	.40	.20
56	Top Prospect *(Chris Johnson)*(FC)	.25	.20	.10
57	Top Prospect *(John Ericks)*(FC)	.25	.20	.10
58	Top Prospect *(Gary Scott)*(FC)	.40	.30	.15
59	Top Prospect *(Kiki Jones)*(FC)	.35	.25	.14
60	Top Prospect *(Wilfredo Cordero)*(FC)	.25	.20	.10
61	Top Prospect *(Royce Clayton)*(FC)	.25	.20	.10
62	Top Prospect *(Tim Costo)*(FC)	.70	.50	.30
63	Top Prospect *(Roger Salkeld)*(FC)	.25	.20	.10
64	Top Prospect *(Brook Fordyce)*(FC)	.25	.20	.10
65	Top Prospect *(Mike Mussina)*(FC)	.70	.50	.30
66	Top Prospect *(Dave Staton)*(FC)	.60	.45	.25
67	Top Prospect *(Mike Lieberthal)*(FC)	.30	.25	.12
68	Top Prospect *(Kurt Miller)*(FC)	.30	.25	.12
69	Top Prospect *(Dan Peltier)*(FC)	.25	.20	.10
70	Top Prospect *(Greg Blosser)*(FC)	.40	.30	.15
71	Top Prospect *(Reggie Sanders)*(FC)	.25	.20	.10
72	Top Prospect (Brent Mayne)(FC)	.15	.11	.06
73	Top Prospect *(Rico Brogna)*(FC)	.35	.25	.14
74	Top Prospect *(Willie Banks)*(FC)	.35	.25	.14
75	Top Prospect *(Len Brutcher)*(FC)	.25	.20	.10
76	Top Prospect *(Pat Kelly)*(FC)	.25	.20	.10
77	Cincinnati Reds Checklist	.08	.06	.03
78	Los Angeles Dodgers Checklist	.08	.06	.03
79	San Francisco Giants Checklist	.08	.06	.03
80	San Diego Padres Checklist	.08	.06	.03
81	Houston Astros Checklist	.08	.06	.03
82	Atlanta Braves Checklist	.10	.08	.04
83	"Fielder's Feat"	.20	.15	.08
84	*Orlando Merced*(FC)	.10	.08	.04
85	Domingo Ramos	.05	.04	.02
86	Tom Bolton	.05	.04	.02
87	*Andres Santana*(FC)	.20	.15	.08
88	John Dopson	.05	.04	.02
89	Kenny Williams	.05	.04	.02
90	Marty Barrett	.06	.05	.02
91	Tom Pagnozzi	.06	.05	.02
92	Carmelo Martinez	.06	.05	.02
93	"Save Master"	.10	.08	.04
94	Pittsburgh Pirates Checklist	.10	.08	.04
95	New York Mets Checklist	.10	.08	.04
96	Montreal Expos Checklist	.08	.06	.03
97	Philadelphia Phillies Checklist	.08	.06	.03
98	St. Louis Cardinals Checklist	.08	.06	.03
99	Chicago Cubs Checklist	.10	.08	.04
100	Checklist 1-100	.05	.04	.02
101	Kevin Elster	.06	.05	.02
102	Tom Brookens	.05	.04	.02
103	Mackey Sasser	.08	.06	.03
104	Felix Fermin	.05	.04	.02
105	Kevin McReynolds	.12	.09	.04
106	Dave Steib	.12	.09	.05
107	Jeffrey Leonard	.06	.05	.02
108	Dave Henderson	.08	.06	.03
109	Sid Bream	.06	.05	.02
110	Henry Cotto	.05	.04	.02
111	Shawon Dunston	.12	.09	.04
112	Mariano Duncan	.08	.06	.03
113	Joe Girardi	.08	.06	.03
114	Billy Hatcher	.08	.06	.03
115	Greg Maddux	.12	.09	.04
116	Jerry Browne	.08	.06	.03
117	Juan Samuel	.08	.06	.03
118	Steve Olin	.06	.05	.02
119	Alfredo Griffin	.06	.05	.02
120	Mitch Webster	.06	.05	.02
121	Joel Skinner	.05	.04	.02
122	Frank Viola	.15	.11	.06
123	Cory Snyder	.10	.08	.04
124	Howard Johnson	.12	.09	.05
125	*Carlos Baerga*	.30	.25	.12
126	Tony Fernandez	.12	.09	.04
127	Dave Stewart	.15	.11	.06
128	Jay Buhner	.08	.06	.03
129	Mike LaValliere	.06	.05	.02
130	Scott Bradley	.05	.04	.02
131	Tony Phillips	.06	.05	.02
132	Ryne Sandberg	.20	.15	.08
133	Paul O'Neill	.08	.06	.03

    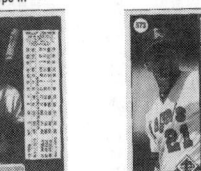 
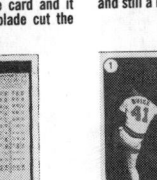       

		MT	NR MT	EX			MT	NR MT	EX
134	Mark Grace	.15	.11	.06	225	*Travis Fryman*(FC)	.80	.60	.30
135	Chris Sabo	.12	.09	.05	226	Joe Carter	.10	.08	.04
136	Ramon Martinez	.20	.15	.08	227	Julio Franco	.10	.08	.04
137	Brook Jacoby	.08	.06	.03	228	Craig Lefferts	.06	.05	.02
138	Candy Maldonado	.08	.06	.03	229	Gary Pettis	.06	.05	.02
139	Mike Scioscia	.08	.06	.03	230	Dennis Rasmussen	.06	.05	.02
140	Chris James	.08	.06	.03	231	Brian Downing	.06	.05	.02
141	Craig Worthington	.08	.06	.03	232	Carlos Quintana	.10	.08	.04
142	Manny Lee	.06	.05	.02	233	Gary Gaetti	.12	.09	.05
143	Tim Raines	.15	.11	.06	234	Mark Langston	.15	.11	.06
144	Sandy Alomar,Jr.	.15	.11	.06	235	Tim Wallach	.10	.08	.04
145	John Olerud	.60	.45	.25	236	Greg Swindell	.10	.08	.04
146	*Ozzie Canseco*	.15	.11	.06	237	Eddie Murray	.15	.11	.06
147	Pat Borders	.06	.05	.02	238	Jeff Manto(FC)	.15	.11	.06
148	Harold Reynolds	.10	.08	.04	239	Lenny Harris	.08	.06	.03
149	Tom Henke	.08	.06	.03	240	Jesse Orosco	.05	.04	.02
150	R.J. Reynolds	.05	.04	.02	241	Scott Lusader	.05	.04	.02
151	Mike Gallego	.05	.04	.02	242	Sid Fernandez	.08	.06	.03
152	Bobby Bonilla	.20	.15	.08	243	*Jim Leyritz*	.25	.20	.10
153	Terry Steinbach	.06	.05	.02	244	Cecil Fielder	.20	.15	.08
154	Barry Bonds	.20	.15	.08	245	Darryl Strawberry	.25	.20	.10
155	Jose Canseco	.50	.40	.20	246	Frank Thomas(FC)	2.00	1.50	.80
156	Gregg Jefferies	.15	.11	.06	247	Kevin Mitchell	.20	.15	.08
157	Matt Williams	.20	.15	.08	248	Lance Johnson	.06	.05	.02
158	Craig Biggio	.08	.06	.03	249	Rick Rueschel	.08	.06	.03
159	Daryl Boston	.05	.04	.02	250	Mark Portugal	.05	.04	.02
160	Ricky Jordan	.08	.06	.03	251	Derek Lilliquist	.06	.05	.02
161	Stan Belinda	.20	.15	.08	252	Brian Holman	.08	.06	.03
162	Ozzie Smith	.10	.08	.04	253	Rafael Valdez	.08	.06	.03
163	Tom Brunansky	.08	.06	.03	254	B.J. Surhoff	.06	.05	.02
164	Todd Zeile	.30	.25	.12	255	Tony Gwynn	.15	.11	.06
165	Mike Greenwell	.15	.11	.06	256	Andy Van Slyke	.12	.09	.05
166	Kal Daniels	.10	.08	.04	257	Todd Stottlemyre	.08	.06	.03
167	Kent Hrbek	.12	.09	.05	258	Jose Lind	.06	.05	.02
168	Franklin Stubbs	.06	.05	.02	259	Greg Myers	.06	.05	.02
169	Dick Schofield	.05	.04	.02	260	Jeff Ballard	.06	.05	.02
170	Junior Ortiz	.05	.04	.02	261	Bobby Thigpen	.08	.06	.03
171	*Hector Villanueva*	.30	.25	.12	262	*Jimmy Kremers*(FC)	.15	.11	.06
172	Dennis Eckersley	.15	.11	.06	263	Robin Ventura	.20	.15	.08
173	Mitch Williams	.08	.06	.03	264	John Smoltz	.10	.08	.04
174	Mark McGwire	.35	.25	.14	265	Sammy Sosa	.20	.15	.08
175	Fernando Valenzuela	.10	.08	.04	266	Gary Sheffield	.15	.11	.06
176	Gary Carter	.10	.08	.04	267	Lenny Dykstra	.10	.08	.04
177	Dave Magadan	.10	.08	.04	268	Bill Spiers	.06	.05	.02
178	Robby Thompson	.08	.06	.03	269	Charlie Hayes	.08	.06	.03
179	Bob Ojeda	.05	.04	.02	270	Brett Butler	.08	.06	.03
180	Ken Caminiti	.06	.05	.02	271	Bip Roberts	.08	.06	.03
181	Don Slaught	.05	.04	.02	272	Rob Deer	.06	.05	.02
182	Luis Rivera	.05	.04	.02	273	Fred Lynn	.08	.06	.03
183	Jay Bell	.06	.05	.02	274	Dave Parker	.15	.11	.06
184	Jody Reed	.08	.06	.03	275	Andy Benes	.10	.08	.04
185	Wally Backman	.06	.05	.02	276	Glenallen Hill	.08	.06	.03
186	Dave Martinez	.06	.05	.02	277	*Steve Howard*(FC)	.12	.09	.05
187	Luis Polonia	.05	.04	.02	278	Doug Drabek	.10	.08	.04
188	Shane Mack	.06	.05	.02	279	Joe Oliver	.08	.06	.03
189	Spike Owen	.06	.05	.02	280	Todd Benzinger	.06	.05	.02
190	Scott Bailes	.05	.04	.02	281	Eric King	.06	.05	.02
191	John Russell	.05	.04	.02	282	Jim Presley	.06	.05	.02
192	Walt Weiss	.08	.06	.03	283	Ken Patterson(FC)	.06	.05	.02
193	Jose Oquendo	.06	.05	.02	284	Jack Daugherty	.08	.06	.03
194	Carney Lansford	.08	.06	.03	285	Ivan Calderon	.10	.08	.04
195	Jeff Huson	.08	.06	.03	286	*Edgar Diaz*(FC)	.10	.08	.04
196	Keith Miller	.06	.05	.02	287	Kevin Bass	.08	.06	.03
197	Eric Yelding	.10	.08	.04	288	Don Carman	.06	.05	.02
198	Ron Darling	.06	.05	.02	289	Greg Brock	.06	.05	.02
199	John Kruk	.06	.05	.02	290	John Franco	.10	.08	.04
200	Checklist 101-200	.05	.04	.02	291	Joey Cora	.06	.05	.02
201	John Shelby	.05	.04	.02	292	Bill Wegman	.06	.05	.02
202	Bob Geren	.06	.05	.02	293	Eric Show	.06	.05	.02
203	Lance McCullers	.05	.04	.02	294	Scott Bankhead	.08	.06	.03
204	Alvaro Espinoza	.06	.05	.02	295	Garry Templeton	.06	.05	.02
205	Mark Salas	.05	.04	.02	296	Mickey Tettleton	.06	.05	.02
206	Mike Pagliarulo	.06	.05	.02	297	Luis Sojo(FC)	.15	.11	.06
207	Jose Uribe	.06	.05	.02	298	Jose Rijo	.08	.06	.03
208	Jim Deshaies	.06	.05	.02	299	Dave Johnson	.06	.05	.02
209	Ron Karkovice	.05	.04	.02	300	Checklist 201-300	.05	.04	.02
210	Rafael Ramirez	.06	.05	.02	301	Mark Grant	.05	.04	.02
211	Donnie Hill	.05	.04	.02	302	Pete Harnisch	.08	.06	.03
212	Brian Harper	.08	.06	.03	303	Greg Olson(FC)	.10	.08	.04
213	Jack Howell	.05	.04	.02	304	*Anthony Telford*(FC)	.35	.25	.14
214	Wes Gardner	.05	.04	.02	305	Lonnie Smith	.06	.05	.02
215	Tim Burke	.08	.06	.03	306	*Chris Hoiles*(FC)	.35	.25	.14
216	Doug Jones	.08	.06	.03	307	Bryn Smith	.06	.05	.02
217	Hubie Brooks	.10	.08	.04	308	Mike Devereaux	.06	.05	.02
218	Tom Candiotti	.06	.05	.02	309	Milt Thompson	.06	.05	.02
219	Gerald Perry	.06	.05	.02	310	Bob Melvin	.05	.04	.02
220	Jose DeLeon	.06	.05	.02	311	Luis Salazar	.05	.04	.02
221	Wally Whitehurst	.08	.06	.03	312	Ed Whitson	.06	.05	.02
222	*Alan Mills*(FC)	.15	.11	.06	313	Charlie Hough	.06	.05	.02
223	Alan Trammell	.12	.09	.05	314	Dave Clark	.05	.04	.02
224	Dwight Gooden	.25	.20	.10	315	*Eric Gunderson*	.25	.20	.10

		MT	NR MT	EX			MT	NR MT	EX
316	Dan Petry	.05	.04	.02	407	Bob Kipper	.05	.04	.02
317	Dante Bichette	.08	.06	.03	408	Darren Daulton	.08	.06	.03
318	Mike Heath	.05	.04	.02	409	Chuck Cary	.06	.05	.02
319	Damon Berryhill	.06	.05	.02	410	Bruce Ruffin	.06	.05	.02
320	Walt Terrell	.05	.04	.02	411	Juan Berenguer	.05	.04	.02
321	Scott Fletcher	.05	.04	.02	412	Gary Ward	.05	.04	.02
322	Dan Plesac	.08	.06	.03	413	Al Newman	.05	.04	.02
323	Jack McDowell	.08	.06	.03	414	Danny Jackson	.08	.06	.02
324	Paul Molitor	.12	.09	.05	415	Greg Gagne	.06	.05	.02
325	Ozzie Guillen	.10	.08	.04	416	Tom Herr	.06	.05	.02
326	Gregg Olson	.10	.08	.04	417	Jeff Parrett	.06	.05	.02
327	Pedro Guerrero	.10	.08	.04	418	Jeff Reardon	.08	.06	.03
328	Bob Milacki	.06	.05	.02	419	Mark Lemke	.06	.05	.02
329	John Tudor	.08	.06	.03	420	Charlie O'Brien	.05	.04	.02
330	Steve Finley	.08	.06	.03	421	Willie Randolph	.08	.06	.03
331	Jack Clark	.10	.08	.04	422	Steve Bedrosian	.08	.06	.03
332	Jerome Walton	.15	.11	.06	423	Mike Moore	.08	.06	.03
333	Andy Hawkins	.06	.05	.02	424	Jeff Brantley	.08	.06	.03
334	Derrick May	.20	.15	.08	425	Bob Welch	.10	.08	.04
335	Roberto Alomar	.10	.08	.04	426	Terry Mulholland	.08	.06	.03
336	Jack Morris	.08	.06	.03	427	Willie Blair(FC)	.15	.11	.06
337	Dave Winfield	.15	.11	.06	428	Darrin Fletcher(FC)	.10	.08	.04
338	Steve Searcy	.08	.06	.03	429	Mike Witt	.06	.05	.02
339	Chili Davis	.08	.06	.03	430	Joe Boever	.05	.04	.02
340	Larry Sheets	.06	.05	.02	431	Tom Gordon	.12	.09	.05
341	Ted Higuera	.08	.06	.03	432	Pedro Munoz(FC)	.20	.15	.08
342	David Segui	.30	.25	.12	433	Kevin Seitzer	.10	.08	.04
343	Greg Cadaret	.05	.04	.02	434	Kevin Tapani	.15	.11	.06
344	Robin Yount	.15	.11	.06	435	Bret Saberhagen	.12	.09	.05
345	Nolan Ryan	.30	.25	.12	436	Ellis Burks	.12	.09	.05
346	Ray Lankford	.50	.40	.20	437	Chuck Finley	.10	.08	.04
347	Cal Riken,Jr.	.15	.11	.06	438	Mike Boddicker	.08	.06	.03
348	Lee Smith	.08	.06	.03	439	Francisco Cabrera	.08	.06	.03
349	Brady Anderson	.05	.04	.02	440	Todd Hundley	.25	.20	.10
350	Frank DiPino	.05	.04	.02	441	Kelly Downs	.06	.05	.02
351	Hal Morris	.30	.25	.12	442	Dann Howitt(FC)	.15	.11	.06
352	Deion Sanders	.10	.08	.04	443	Scott Garrelts	.08	.06	.03
353	Barry Larkin	.10	.08	.04	444	Rickey Henderson	.30	.25	.12
354	Don Mattingly	.35	.25	.14	445	Will Clark	.40	.30	.15
355	Eric Davis	.20	.15	.08	446	Ben McDonald	.60	.45	.25
356	Jose Offerman	.30	.25	.12	447	Dale Murphy	.12	.09	.05
357	Mel Rojas	.12	.09	.05	448	Dave Righetti	.10	.08	.04
358	Rudy Seanez(FC)	.10	.08	.04	449	Dickie Thon	.05	.04	.02
359	Oil Can Boyd	.06	.05	.02	450	Ted Power	.05	.04	.02
360	Nelson Liriano	.05	.04	.02	451	Scott Coolbaugh	.08	.06	.03
361	Ron Gant	.15	.11	.06	452	Dwight Smith	.08	.06	.03
362	Howard Farmer	.15	.11	.06	453	Pete Incaviglia	.08	.06	.03
363	David Justice	1.00	.70	.40	454	Andre Dawson	.15	.11	.06
364	Delino DeShields	.30	.25	.12	455	Ruben Sierra	.20	.15	.08
365	Steve Avery	.25	.20	.10	456	Andres Galarraga	.10	.08	.04
366	David Cone	.12	.09	.05	457	Alvin Davis	.10	.08	.04
367	Iou Whitaker	.10	.08	.04	458	Tony Castillo	.06	.05	.02
368	Von Hayes	.10	.08	.04	459	Pete O'Brien	.06	.05	.02
369	Frank Tanana	.06	.05	.02	460	Charlie Leibrandt	.06	.05	.02
370	Tim Teufel	.05	.04	.02	461	Vince Coleman	.10	.08	.04
371	Randy Myers	.10	.08	.04	462	Steve Sax	.10	.08	.04
372	Roberto Kelly	.10	.08	.04	463	Omar Oliveras(FC)	.15	.11	.06
373	Jack Armstrong	.08	.06	.03	464	Oscar Azocar(FC)	.30	.25	.12
374	Kelly Gruber	.10	.08	.04	465	Joe Magrane	.08	.06	.03
375	Kevin Maas	.50	.40	.20	466	Karl Rhodes(FC)	.15	.11	.06
376	Randy Johnson	.10	.08	.04	467	Benito Santiago	.10	.08	.04
377	David West	.06	.05	.02	468	Joe Klink(FC)	.10	.08	.04
378	Brent Knackert(FC)	.12	.09	.05	469	Sil Campusano	.05	.04	.02
379	Rick Honeycutt	.05	.04	.02	470	Mark Parent	.05	.04	.02
380	Kevin Gross	.08	.06	.03	471	Shawn Boskie	.20	.15	.08
381	Tom Foley	.05	.04	.02	472	Kevin Brown	.10	.08	.04
382	Jeff Blauser	.06	.05	.02	473	Rick Sutcliffe	.08	.06	.03
383	Scott Ruskin	.15	.11	.06	474	Rafael Palmeiro	.12	.09	.05
384	Andres Thomas	.05	.04	.02	475	Mike Harkey	.10	.08	.04
385	Dennis Martinez	.08	.06	.03	476	Jaime Navarro	.15	.11	.06
386	Mike Henneman	.08	.06	.03	477	Marquis Grissom	.15	.11	.06
387	Felix Jose	.15	.11	.06	478	Marty Clary	.05	.04	.02
388	Alejandro Pena	.05	.04	.02	479	Greg Briley	.10	.08	.04
389	Chet Lemon	.06	.05	.02	480	Tom Glavine	.08	.06	.03
390	Craig Wilson(FC)	.10	.08	.04	481	Lee Guetterman	.05	.04	.02
391	Chuck Crim	.05	.04	.02	482	Rex Hudler	.06	.05	.02
392	Mel Hall	.06	.05	.02	483	Dave LaPoint	.06	.05	.02
393	Mark Knudson	.05	.04	.02	484	Terry Pendleton	.08	.06	.03
394	Norm Charlton	.08	.06	.03	485	Jesse Barfield	.08	.06	.03
395	Mike Felder	.05	.04	.02	486	Jose DeJesus	.08	.06	.03
396	Tim Layana	.15	.11	.06	487	Paul Abbott(FC)	.15	.11	.06
397	Steve Frey(FC)	.06	.05	.02	488	Ken Howell	.06	.05	.02
398	Bill Doran	.08	.06	.03	489	Greg W. Harris	.06	.05	.02
399	Dion James	.05	.04	.02	490	Roy Smith	.05	.04	.02
400	Checklist 301-400	.05	.04	.02	491	Paul Assenmacher	.05	.04	.02
401	Ron Hassey	.05	.04	.02	492	Geno Petralli	.05	.04	.02
402	Don Robinson	.06	.05	.02	493	Steve Wilson	.08	.06	.03
403	Gene Nelson	.05	.04	.02	494	Kevin Reimer(FC)	.08	.06	.03
404	Terry Kennedy	.05	.04	.02	495	Bill Long	.05	.04	.02
405	Todd Burns	.05	.04	.02	496	Mike Jackson	.06	.05	.02
406	Roger McDowell	.08	.06	.03	497	Oddibe McDowell	.06	.05	.02

		MT	NR MT	EX
498	Bill Swift	.06	.05	.02
499	Jeff Treadway	.06	.05	.02
500	Checklist 401-500	.05	.04	.02
501	Gene Larkin	.06	.05	.02
502	Bob Boone	.08	.06	.03
503	Allan Anderson	.06	.05	.02
504	Luis Aquino	.06	.05	.02
505	Mark Guthrie	.06	.05	.02
506	Joe Orsulak	.06	.05	.02
507	Dana Kiecker(FC)	.15	.11	.06
508	Dave Gallagher	.05	.04	.02
509	Greg W. Harris	.06	.05	.02
510	Mark Williamson	.05	.04	.02
511	Casey Candaele	.05	.04	.02
512	Mookie Wilson	.06	.05	.02
513	Dave Smith	.08	.06	.03
514	Chuck Carr(FC)	.15	.11	.06
515	Glenn Wilson	.06	.05	.02
516	Mike Fitzgerald	.05	.04	.02
517	Devon White	.08	.06	.03
518	Dave Hollins	.20	.15	.08
519	Mark Eichhorn	.05	.04	.02
520	Otis Nixon	.05	.04	.02
521	Terry Shumpert	.20	.15	.08
522	Scott Erickson(FC)	.30	.25	.12
523	Danny Tartabull	.10	.08	.04
524	Orel Hershiser	.15	.11	.06
525	George Brett	.15	.11	.06
526	Greg Vaughn	.20	.15	.08
527	Tim Naehring(FC)	.25	.20	.10
528	Curt Schilling(FC)	.06	.05	.02
529	Chris Bosio	.06	.05	.02
530	Sam Horn	.08	.06	.03
531	Mike Scott	.10	.08	.04
532	George Bell	.15	.11	.06
533	Eric Anthony	.25	.20	.10
534	Julio Valera(FC)	.15	.11	.06
535	Glenn Davis	.15	.11	.06
536	Larry Walker	.15	.11	.06
537	Pat Combs	.15	.11	.06
538	Chris Nabholz(FC)	.20	.15	.08
539	Kirk McCaskill	.08	.06	.03
540	Randy Ready	.05	.04	.02
541	Mark Gubicza	.10	.08	.04
542	Rick Aguilera	.08	.06	.03
543	Brian McRae(FC)	1.00	.70	.40
544	Kirby Puckett	.20	.15	.08
545	Bo Jackson	.70	.50	.30
546	Wade Boggs	.25	.20	.10
547	Tim McIntosh(FC)	.20	.15	.08
548	Randy Milligan	.08	.06	.03
549	Dwight Evans	.08	.06	.03
550	Billy Ripken	.05	.04	.02
551	Erik Hanson	.15	.11	.06
552	Lance Parrish	.10	.08	.04
553	Tino Martinez	.20	.15	.08
554	Jim Abbott	.15	.11	.06
555	Ken Griffey,Jr.	1.00	.70	.40
556	Milt Cuyler(FC)	.30	.25	.12
557	Mark Leonard(FC)	.20	.15	.08
558	Jay Howell	.08	.06	.03
559	Lloyd Moseby	.08	.06	.03
560	Chris Gwynn	.06	.05	.02
561	Mark Whiten(FC)	.35	.25	.14
562	Harold Baines	.10	.08	.04
563	Junior Felix	.15	.11	.06
564	Darren Lewis(FC)	.25	.20	.10
565	Fred McGriff	.15	.11	.06
566	Kevin Appier	.15	.11	.06
567	Luis Gonzalez(FC)	.20	.15	.08
568	Frank White	.08	.06	.03
569	Juan Agosto	.05	.04	.02
570	Mike Macfarlane	.06	.05	.02
571	Bert Blyleven	.10	.08	.04
572	Ken Griffey,Sr.	.10	.08	.04
573	Lee Stevens(FC)	.20	.15	.08
574	Edgar Martinez	.08	.06	.03
575	Wally Joyner	.10	.08	.04
576	Tim Belcher	.08	.06	.03
577	John Burkett	.10	.08	.04
578	Mike Morgan	.06	.05	.02
579	Paul Gibson	.05	.04	.02
580	Jose Vizcaino	.10	.08	.04
581	Duane Ward	.06	.05	.02
582	Scott Sanderson	.06	.05	.02
583	David Wells	.06	.05	.02
584	Willie McGee	.10	.08	.04
585	John Cerutti	.05	.04	.02
586	Danny Darwin	.08	.06	.03
587	Kurt Stillwell	.08	.06	.03
588	Rich Gedman	.05	.04	.02

		MT	NR MT	EX
589	Mark Davis	.08	.06	.03
590	Bill Gullickson	.06	.05	.03
591	Matt Young	.06	.05	.02
592	Bryan Harvey	.08	.06	.03
593	Omar Vizquel	.06	.05	.02
594	Scott Lewis(FC)	.15	.11	.06
595	Dave Valle	.06	.05	.02
596	Tim Crews	.05	.04	.02
597	Mike Bielecki	.06	.05	.02
598	Mike Sharperson	.06	.05	.02
599	Dave Bergman	.05	.04	.02
600	Checklist 501-600	.05	.04	.02
601	Steve Lyons	.06	.05	.02
602	Bruce Hurst	.08	.06	.03
603	Donn Pall	.05	.04	.02
604	Jim Vatcher(FC)	.15	.11	.06
605	Dan Pasqua	.06	.05	.02
606	Kenny Rogers	.08	.06	.03
607	Jeff Schulz(FC)	.15	.11	.06
608	Brad Arnsberg(FC)	.10	.08	.04
609	Willie Wilson	.08	.06	.03
610	Jamie Moyer	.06	.05	.02
611	Ron Oester	.05	.04	.02
612	Dennis Cook	.08	.06	.03
613	Rick Mahler	.05	.04	.02
614	Bill Landrum	.06	.05	.02
615	Scott Scudder	.15	.11	.06
616	Tom Edens(FC)	.08	.06	.03
617	"1917 Revisited"	.25	.20	.10
618	Jim Gantner	.06	.05	.02
619	Darrel Akerfelds(FC)	.06	.05	.02
620	Ron Robinson	.06	.05	.02
621	Scott Radinsky	.20	.15	.08
622	Pete Smith	.06	.05	.02
623	Melido Perez	.08	.06	.03
624	Jerald Clark	.06	.05	.02
625	Carlos Martinez	.08	.06	.03
626	Wes Chamberlain(FC)	.40	.30	.15
627	Bobby Witt	.08	.06	.03
628	Ken Dayley	.06	.05	.02
629	John Barfield(FC)	.10	.08	.04
630	Bob Tewksbury	.06	.05	.02
631	Glenn Braggs	.06	.05	.02
632	Jim Neidlinger(FC)	.20	.15	.08
633	Tom Browning	.08	.06	.03
634	Kirk Gibson	.12	.09	.05
635	Rob Dibble	.12	.09	.05
636	"Stolen Base Leaders"	.20	.15	.08
637	Jeff Montgomery	.08	.06	.03
638	Mike Schooler	.08	.06	.03
639	Storm Davis	.06	.05	.02
640	Rich Rodriguez(FC)	.15	.11	.06
641	Phil Bradley	.08	.06	.03
642	Kent Mercker	.15	.11	.06
643	Carlton Fisk	.12	.09	.05
644	Mike Bell(FC)	.20	.15	.08
645	Alex Fernandez(FC)	2.00	1.50	.80
646	Juan Gonzalez	.30	.25	.12
647	Ken Hill	.06	.05	.02
648	Jeff Russell	.08	.06	.03
649	Chuck Malone(FC)	.15	.11	.06
650	Steve Buechele	.06	.05	.02
651	Mike Benjamin	.15	.11	.06
652	Tony Pena	.08	.06	.03
653	Trevor Wilson	.08	.06	.03
654	Alex Cole	.30	.25	.12
655	Roger Clemens	.25	.20	.10
656	"The Bashing Years"	.25	.20	.10
657	Joe Grahe(FC)	.20	.15	.08
658	Jim Eisenreich	.06	.05	.02
659	Dan Gladden	.06	.05	.02
660	Steve Farr	.06	.05	.02
661	Bill Sampen	.20	.15	.08
662	Dave Rohde(FC)	.15	.11	.06
663	Mark Gardner	.20	.15	.08
664	Mike Simms(FC)	.25	.20	.10
665	Moises Alou(FC)	.15	.11	.06
666	Mickey Hatcher	.06	.05	.02
667	Jimmy Key	.08	.06	.03
668	John Wetteland	.10	.08	.04
669	John Smiley	.06	.05	.02
670	Jim Acker	.05	.04	.02
671	Pascual Perez	.06	.05	.02
672	Reggie Harris(FC)	.30	.25	.12
673	Matt Nokes	.08	.06	.03
674	Rafael Novoa(FC)	.15	.11	.06
675	Hensley Meulens	.10	.08	.04
676	Jeff M. Robinson	.06	.05	.02
677	"Ground Breaking"	.25	.20	.10
678	Johnny Ray	.06	.05	.02
679	Greg Hibbard	.10	.08	.04

		MT	NR MT	EX
680	Paul Sorrento	.20	.15	.08
681	Mike Marshall	.06	.05	.02
682	Jim Clancy	.05	.04	.02
683	Rob Murphy	.05	.04	.02
684	Dave Schmidt	.05	.04	.02
685	*Jeff Gray*(FC)	.15	.11	.06
686	Mike Hartley(FC)	.20	.15	.08
687	Jeff King	.08	.06	.03
688	Stan Javier	.06	.05	.02
689	Bob Walk	.06	.05	.02
690	Jim Gott	.06	.05	.02
691	Mike LaCoss	.05	.04	.02
692	John Farrell	.06	.05	.02
693	Tim Leary	.06	.05	.02
694	*Mike Walker*(FC)	.20	.15	.08
695	Eric Plunk	.05	.04	.02
696	Mike Fetters(FC)	.15	.11	.06
697	Wayne Edwards	.10	.08	.04
698	Tim Drummond(FC)	.15	.11	.06
699	Willie Fraser	.05	.04	.02
700	Checklist 601-700	.05	.04	.02

		MT	NR MT	EX
35	Jim Gott	.35	.25	.14
41	Mike Dunne	.30	.25	.12
43	Bill Landrum	.40	.30	.15
44	John Cangelosi	.25	.20	.10
49	Jeff Robinson	.35	.25	.12
52	Dorn Taylor	.60	.45	.25
54	Brian Fisher	.25	.20	.10
57	John Smiley	.50	.40	.20
----	Ray Miller, Tommy Sandt (31-37)	.20	.15	.08
----	Bruce Kimm (32-36)	.20	.15	.08
----	Gene Lamont (32-36)	.20	.15	.08
----	Milt May (39-45)	.20	.15	.08
----	Rich Donnelly (39-45)	.20	.15	.08

1950 W576
Callahan Hall Of Fame

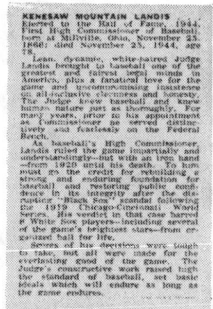

These cards, which feature drawings of Hall of Famers, were produced from 1950 through 1956 and sold by the Baseball Hall of Fame in Cooperstown. The cards measure 1-3/4" by 2-1/2" and include a detailed player biography on the back. When introduced in 1950 the set included all members of the Hall of Fame up to that time, and then new cards were added each year as more players were elected. Therefore, cards of players appearing in all previous editions are lesser in value than those players who appeared in just one or two years. When the set was discontinued in 1956 it consisted of 82 cards, which is now considered a complete set. The cards are not numbered and are listed here alphabetically.

		NR MT	EX	VG
Complete Set:		500.00	250.00	150.00
Common Player:		3.00	1.50	.90
(1)	Grover Alexander	6.00	3.00	1.75
(2)	"Cap" Anson	6.00	3.00	1.75
(3)	J. Franklin "Home Run" Baker	7.00	3.50	2.00
(4)	Edward G. Barrow	7.00	3.50	2.00
(5a)	Charles "Chief" Bender (different biography)	7.00	3.50	2.00
(5b)	Charles "Chief" Bender (different biography)	7.00	3.50	2.00
(6)	Roger Bresnahan	3.00	1.50	.90
(7)	Dan Brouthers	3.00	1.50	.90
(8)	Mordecai Brown	3.00	1.50	.90
(9)	Morgan G. Bulkeley	3.00	1.50	.90
(10)	Jesse Burkett	3.00	1.50	.90
(11)	Alexander Cartwright	3.00	1.50	.90
(12)	Henry Chadwick	3.00	1.50	.90
(13)	Frank Chance	3.00	1.50	.90
(14)	Albert B. Chandler	20.00	10.00	6.00
(15)	Jack Chesbro	3.00	1.50	.90
(16)	Fred Clarke	3.00	1.50	.90
(17)	Ty Cobb	30.00	15.00	9.00
(18a)	Mickey Cochran (name incorrect)	30.00	15.00	9.00
(18b)	Mickey Cochrane (name correct)	6.00	3.00	1.75
(19a)	Eddie Collins (different biography)	6.00	3.00	1.75
(19b)	Eddie Collins (different biography)	6.00	3.00	1.75

1989 Very Fine Pirates

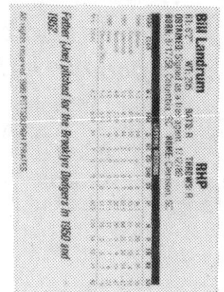

This 30-card set Pittsburgh Pirates team set was sponsored by Veryfine fruit juices, and was issued in the form of two uncut, perforated panels, each containing 15 standard-size cards. A third panel featured color action photographs. The panels were distributed in a stadium promotion to fans attending the April 23 Pirates game at Three Rivers Stadium. The cards display the Pirates traditional black and gold color scheme, and include the player's names and uniform number along the bottom. The "Veryfine" logo appears in the lower right corner. The backs include player data and complete stats.

		MT	NR MT	EX
Complete 3-Panel Set:		20.00	15.00	8.00
Complete Singles Card Set:		12.00	9.00	4.75
Common Player:		.20	.15	.08
0	Junior Ortiz	.20	.15	.08
2	Gary Redus	.30	.25	.12
3	Jay Bell	.30	.25	.12
5	Sid Bream	.30	.25	.12
6	Rafael Belliard	.25	.20	.10
10	Jim Leyland	.30	.25	.12
11	Glenn Wilson	.30	.25	.12
12	Mike La Valliere	.30	.25	.12
13	Jose Lind	.40	.30	.15
14	Ken Oberkfell	.25	.20	.10
15	Doug Drabek	.50	.40	.20
16	Bob Kipper	.20	.15	.08
17	Bob Walk	.25	.20	.10
18	Andy Van Slyke	1.00	.70	.40
23	R.J. Reynolds	.30	.25	.12
24	Barry Bonds	1.50	1.25	.60
25	Bobby Bonilla	1.50	1.25	.60
26	Neal Heaton	.30	.25	.12
30	Benny Distefano	.30	.25	.12

		NR MT	EX	VG
(20)	Jimmie Collins	3.00	1.50	.90
(21)	Charles A. Comiskey	3.00	1.50	.90
(22)	Tom Connolly	7.00	3.50	2.00
(23)	"Candy" Cummings	3.00	1.50	.90
(24)	Dizzy Dean	20.00	10.00	6.00
(25)	Ed Delahanty	3.00	1.50	.90
(26a)	Bill Dickey (different biography)	20.00	10.00	6.00
(26b)	Bill Dickey (different biography)	20.00	10.00	6.00
(27)	Joe DiMaggio	70.00	35.00	21.00
(28)	Hugh Duffy	3.00	1.50	.90
(29)	Johnny Evers	3.00	1.50	.90
(30)	Buck Ewing	3.00	1.50	.90
(31)	Jimmie Foxx	7.00	3.50	2.00
(32)	Frank Frisch	3.00	1.50	.90
(33)	Lou Gehrig	30.00	15.00	9.00
(34)	Charles Gehringer	3.00	1.50	.90
(35)	Clark Griffith	3.00	1.50	.90
(36)	Lefty Grove	6.00	3.00	1.75
(37)	Leo "Gabby" Hartnett	7.00	3.50	2.00
(38)	Harry Heilmann	3.00	1.50	.90
(39)	Rogers Hornsby	7.00	3.50	2.00
(40)	Carl Hubbell	6.00	3.00	1.75
(41)	Hughey Jennings	3.00	1.50	.90
(42)	Ban Johnson	3.00	1.50	.90
(43)	Walter Johnson	7.00	3.50	2.00
(44)	Willie Keeler	3.00	1.50	.90
(45)	Mike Kelly	3.00	1.50	.90
(46)	Bill Klem	7.00	3.50	2.00
(47)	Napoleon Lajoie	3.00	1.50	.90
(48)	Kenesaw M. Landis	3.00	1.50	.90
(49)	Ted Lyons	7.00	3.50	2.00
(50)	Connie Mack	7.00	3.50	2.00
(51)	Walter Maranville	7.00	3.50	2.00
(52)	Christy Mathewson	7.00	3.50	2.00
(53)	Tommy McCarthy	3.00	1.50	.90
(54)	Joe McGinnity	3.00	1.50	.90
(55)	John McGraw	6.00	3.00	1.75
(56)	Charles Nichols	3.00	1.50	.90
(57)	Jim O'Rourke	3.00	1.50	.90
(58)	Mel Ott	6.00	3.00	1.75
(59)	Herb Pennock	3.00	1.50	.90
(60)	Eddie Plank	3.00	1.50	.90
(61)	Charles Radbourne	3.00	1.50	.90
(62)	Wilbert Robinson	3.00	1.50	.90
(63)	Babe Ruth	70.00	35.00	21.00
(64)	Ray "Cracker" Schalk	7.00	3.50	2.00
(65)	Al Simmons	7.00	3.50	2.00
(66a)	George Sisler (different biography)			
		3.00	1.50	.90
(66b)	George Sisler (different biography)			
		3.00	1.50	.90
(67)	A. G. Spalding	3.00	1.50	.90
(68)	Tris Speaker	3.00	1.50	.90
(69)	Bill Terry	7.00	3.50	2.00
(70)	Joe Tinker	3.00	1.50	.90
(71)	"Pie" Traynor	3.00	1.50	.90
(72)	Clarence A. "Dizzy" Vance	7.00	3.50	2.00
(73)	Rube Waddell	3.00	1.50	.90
(74)	Hans Wagner	20.00	10.00	6.00
(75)	Bobby Wallace	7.00	3.50	2.00
(76)	Ed Walsh	3.00	1.50	.90
(77)	Paul Waner	6.00	3.00	1.75
(78)	George Wright	3.00	1.50	.90
(79)	Harry Wright	7.00	3.50	2.00
(80)	Cy Young	7.00	3.50	2.00
---a)	Museum Exterior View (different biography)	7.00	3.50	2.00
---b)	Museum Exterior View (different biography)	7.00	3.50	2.00
---a)	Museum Interior View (different biography)	7.00	3.50	2.00
---b)	Museum Interior View (different biography)	7.00	3.50	2.00

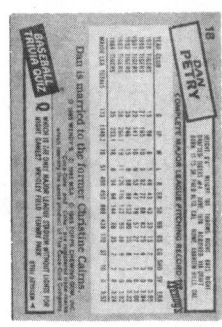

Michigan only.

		MT	NR MT	EX
Complete Set:		8.00	6.00	3.25
Common Player:		.15	.11	.06
1	Sparky Anderson	.30	.25	.12
2	Doug Bair	.15	.11	.06
3	Juan Berenguer	.15	.11	.06
4	Dave Bergman	.15	.11	.06
5	Tom Brookens	.15	.11	.06
6	Marty Castillo	.15	.11	.06
7	Darrell Evans	.40	.30	.15
8	Barbaro Garbey	.15	.11	.06
9	Kirk Gibson	1.00	.70	.40
10	Johnny Grubb	.15	.11	.06
11	Willie Hernandez	.25	.20	.10
12	Larry Herndon	.15	.11	.06
13	Rusty Kuntz	.15	.11	.06
14	Chet Lemon	.25	.20	.10
15	Aurelio Lopez	.15	.11	.06
16	Jack Morris	.80	.60	.30
17	Lance Parrish	.80	.60	.30
18	Dan Petry	.25	.20	.10
19	Bill Scherrer	.15	.11	.06
20	Alan Trammell	1.00	.70	.40
21	Lou Whitaker	.80	.60	.30
22	Milt Wilcox	.15	.11	.06

1954 Wilson Franks

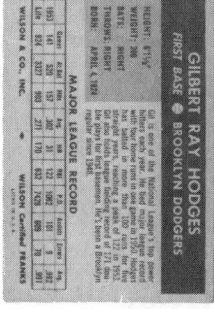

The 2-5/8" by 3-3/4" cards are among the most popular and difficult to find baseball card sets issued with hot dogs during the 1950s. The cards feature color-added photos on the front where the player's name, team and position appear at the top. The front also has a facsimile autograph and a color picture of a package of Wilson's frankfurters. The card backs feature personal information, a short career summary and 1953 and career statistics. The 20-card set includes players from a number of teams and was distributed nationally in the frankfurter packages. The problem with such distribution is that the cards are very tough to find without grease stains from the hot dogs.

1985 Wendy's Tigers

This 22-card set of cards measuring 2-1/2" by 3-1/2", which carry both Wendy's Hamburgers and Coca-Cola logos was produced by Topps. The cards feature a color photo with the player's team, name and position underneath the picture and the Wendy's logo in the lower left and Coke logo in the upper right. Backs are identical to 1985 Topps cards except they have different card numbers and are done in a red and black color scheme. Cards were distributed three to a pack along with a "Header" checklist in a cellophane package at selected Wendy's outlets in

		NR MT	EX	VG
Complete Set:		6500.00	3250.00	1950.
Common Player:		175.00	87.00	52.00
(1)	Roy Campanella	750.00	375.00	225.00
(2)	Del Ennis	175.00	87.00	52.00
(3)	Carl Erskine	200.00	100.00	60.00
(4)	Ferris Fain	175.00	87.00	52.00
(5)	Bob Feller	600.00	300.00	180.00
(6)	Nelson Fox	300.00	150.00	90.00
(7)	Johnny Groth	175.00	87.00	52.00
(8)	Stan Hack	175.00	87.00	52.00
(9)	Gil Hodges	500.00	250.00	150.00
(10)	Ray Jablonski	175.00	87.00	52.00
(11)	Harvey Kuenn	200.00	100.00	60.00
(12)	Roy McMillan	175.00	87.00	52.00
(13)	Andy Pafko	175.00	87.00	52.00
(14)	Paul Richards	175.00	87.00	52.00
(15)	Hank Sauer	175.00	87.00	52.00
(16)	Red Schoendienst	200.00	100.00	60.00
(17)	Enos Slaughter	400.00	200.00	120.00
(18)	Vern Stephens	175.00	87.00	52.00
(19)	Sammy White	175.00	87.00	52.00
(20)	Ted Williams	3000.00	1500.00	900.00

1988 Woolworth

 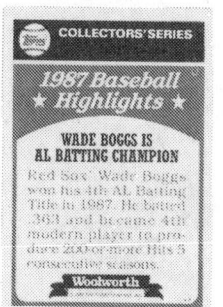

This 33-card boxed set was produced by Topps for exclusive distribution at Woolworth stores. The set includes 18 individual player cards and 15 World Series game action photo cards. World Series cards include two for each game of the Series, plus a card of 1987 Series MVP Frank Viola. Card front carry a Woolworth's Baseball Highlights heading on a red and yellow banner above the blue-bordered super glossy player photo. A white-lettered caption beneath the photo consists of either the player's name or a World Series game notation. Card backs are red, white and blue and contain the Topps logo, card number and "Collector's Series" label above a "1987 Baseball Highlights" logo and a brief description of the photo on the front.

		MT	NR MT	EX
Complete Set:		5.00	3.75	2.00
Common Player:		.09	.07	.04
1	Don Baylor	.12	.09	.05
2	Vince Coleman	.15	.11	.06
3	Darrell Evans	.12	.09	.05
4	Don Mattingly	.90	.70	.35
5	Eddie Murray	.30	.25	.12
6	Nolan Ryan	.30	.25	.12
7	Mike Schmidt	.35	.25	.14
8	Andre Dawson	.20	.15	.08
9	George Bell	.25	.20	.10
10	Steve Bedrosian	.12	.09	.05
11	Roger Clemens	.50	.40	.20
12	Tony Gwynn	.35	.25	.14
13	Wade Boggs	.70	.50	.30
14	Benny Santiago	.35	.25	.14
15	Mark McGwire	.80	.60	.30
16	Dave Righetti	.15	.11	.06
17	Jeffrey Leonard	.09	.07	.04
18	Gary Gaetti	.12	.09	.05
19	World Series Game #1 (Frank Viola)			
		.12	.09	.05
20	World Series Game #1 (Dan Gladden)			
		.09	.07	.04

		MT	NR MT	EX
21	World Series Game #2 (Bert Blyleven)			
		.12	.09	.05
22	World Series Game #2 (Gary Gaetti)			
		.12	.09	.05
23	World Series Game #3 (John Tudor)			
		.12	.09	.05
24	World Series Game #3 (Todd Worrell)			
		.12	.09	.05
25	World Series Game #4 (Tom Lawless)			
		.09	.07	.04
26	World Series Game #4 (Willie McGee)			
		.12	.09	.05
27	World Series Game #5 (Danny Cox)			
		.09	.07	.04
28	World Series Game #5 (Curt Ford)	.09	.07	.04
29	World Series Game #6 (Don Baylor)			
		.12	.09	.05
30	World Series Game #6 (Kent Hrbek)			
		.15	.11	.06
31	World Series Game #7 (Kirby Puckett)			
		.25	.20	.10
32	World Series Game #7 (Greg Gagne)			
		.09	.07	.04
33	World Series MVP (Frank Viola)	.12	.09	.05

1989 Woolworth

 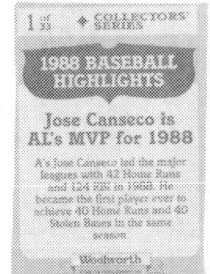

This 33-card set was produced by Topps for the Woolworth store chain and was sold in a special box with a checklist on the back. The glossy-coated cards commemorate the most memorable moments in baseball from the the 1988 season, and include the logo "Woolworth's Baseball Highlights" along the top. The player photos are framed in red, yellow and white and feature the player's name beneath the photo. The backs include a description of the various highlights. Orel Hershiser is pictured on four of the cards, and Jose Canseco appears on two.

		MT	NR MT	EX
Complete Set:		6.00	4.50	2.50
Common Player:		.09	.07	.04
1	Jose Canseco	1.25	.90	.50
2	Kirk Gibson	.15	.11	.06
3	Frank Viola	.15	.11	.06
4	Orel Hershiser	.15	.11	.06
5	Walt Weiss	.20	.15	.11
6	Chris Sabo	.20	.15	.11
7	George Bell	.15	.11	.06
8	Wade Boggs	1.00	.70	.40
9	Tom Browning	.12	.09	.05
10	Gary Carter	.12	.09	.05
11	Andre Dawson	.15	.11	.06
12	John Franco	.09	.07	.04
13	Randy Johnson	.15	.11	.06
14	Doug Jones	.09	.07	.04
15	Kevin McReynolds	.20	.15	.11
16	Gene Nelson	.09	.07	.04
17	Jeff Reardon	.09	.07	.04
18	Pat Tabler	.09	.07	.04
19	Tim Belcher	.25	.20	.10
20	Dennis Eckersley	.15	.11	.06
21	Orel Hershiser	.20	.15	.08
22	Gregg Jefferies	1.00	.70	.40
23	Jose Canseco	1.25	.90	.50

		MT	NR MT	EX
24	Kirk Gibson	.20	.15	.08
25	Orel Hershiser	.20	.15	.08
26	Mike Marshall	.09	.07	.04
27	Mark McGwire	.00	.70	.40
28	Rick Honeycutt	.09	.07	.04
29	Tim Belcher	.20	.15	.08
30	Jay Howell	.12	.09	.05
31	Mickey Hatcher	.09	.07	.04
32	Mike Davis	.09	.07	.04
33	Orel Hershiser	.15	.11	.06

1982 Zellers Expos

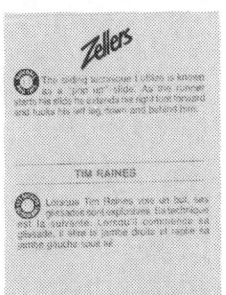

Produced and distributed by the Zellers department stores in Canada, this 60-card set was produced in the form of 20 three-card panels. The cards feature a photo of the player surrounded by rings and a yellow background. A red "Zellers" is above the photo and on either side of it are the words "Baseball Pro Tips" in English on the left and in French on the right. The player's name and the title of the playing tip are under the photo. Backs have the playing tip in both languages. Single cards measure 2-1/2" by 3-1/2" while the whole panel is 7-1/2" by 3-1/2". Although a number of stars are depicted, this set is not terribly popular as collectors do not generally like the playing tips idea. Total panels are worth more than separated cards.

		MT	NR MT	EX
Complete Set:		13.00	9.75	5.25
Common Player:		.40	.30	.15
1	Gary Carter (Catching Position)	1.00	.70	.40
2	Steve Rogers (Pitching Stance)	.50	.40	.20
3	Tim Raines (Sliding)	1.00	.70	.40
4	Andre Dawson (Batting Stance)	1.00	.70	.40
5	Terry Francona (Contact Hitting)	.40	.30	.15
6	Gary Carter (Fielding Pop Fouls)	1.00	.70	.40
7	Warren Cromartie (Fielding at First Base)			
		.40	.30	.15
8	Chris Speier (Fielding at Shortstop)			
		.40	.30	.15
9	Billy DeMars (Signals)	.40	.30	.15
10	Andre Dawson (Batting Stroke)	1.00	.70	.40
11	Terry Francona (Outfield Throws)	.40	.30	.15
12	Woodie Fryman (Holding the Runner-Left Handed)			
		.40	.30	.15
13	Gary Carter (Fielding Low Balls)	1.00	.70	.40
14	Andre Dawson (Playing Centerfield)			
		1.00	.70	.40
15	Bill Gullickson (The Slurve)	.50	.40	.20
16	Gary Carter (Catching Stance)	1.00	.70	.40
17	Scott Sanderson (Fielding as a Pitcher)			
		.40	.30	.15
18	Warren Cromartie (Handling Bad Throws)			
		.40	.30	.15
19	Gary Carter (Hitting Stride)	1.00	.70	.40
20	Ray Burris (Holding the Runner-Right Handed)	.40	.30	.15

1978 Zest Soap

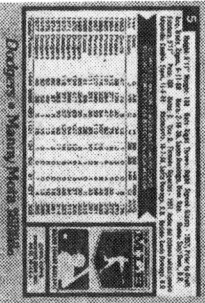

Produced by Topps for a Zest Soap promotion, the five cards in this set are almost identical to the regular 1978 Topps issue, except the backs are printed in both Spanish and English and the card numbers are different. The cards measure 2-1/2" by 3-1/2". Because of the player selection and the bilingual backs, it seems obvious that this set was aimed at the Hispanic community.

		NR MT	EX	VG
Complete Set:		6.00	3.00	1.75
Common Player:		.90	.45	.25
1	Joaquin Andujar	1.25	.60	.40
2	Bert Campaneris	1.50	.70	.45
3	Ed Figueroa	.90	.45	.25
4	Willie Montanez	.90	.45	.25
5	Manny Mota	1.50	.70	.45

Card Company Addresses

Bowman Co. — See Topps.

Donruss-Leaf — 2355 Waukegan Road, Bannockburn, IL 60015.

Fleer Corp. — 10th and Somerville, Philadelphia, PA 19141.

O-Pee-Chee Co. — P.O. Box 6306, London, Ontario, Canada N5W 5S1.

Score/Sportflics — 25 Ford Road, Westport, CT 06880.

Topps Gum Co. — 254 36th St., Brooklyn, NY 11232.

Upper Deck Co. — 23705 Via del Rio, Yorba Linda, CA 92686.

ALPHABETICAL
ROOKIE CARD CHECKLIST

A

Henry Aaron	1954 Topps #128
Tommie Aaron	1963 Topps #46
Don Aase	1976 Topps #597
Jim Abbott	1989 Topps #573
Kyle Abbott	1990 Score #673
Kyle Abbott	1990 Topps #444
Paul Abbott	1991 Upper Deck #487
Shawn Abner	1985 Topps #282
Johnny Abrego (RR)	1986 Donruss #32
Jim Acker	1984 Donruss #146
Jim Acker	1984 Fleer #145
Jim Acker	1984 Topps #359
Joe Adcock	1951 Bowman #323
Jim Adduci	1987 Donruss #495
Troy Afenir	1991 Fleer #1
Tommie Agee	1965 Topps #166
Harry Agganis	1955 Topps #152
Juan Agosto	1984 Donruss #208
Juan Agosto	1984 Fleer #50
Juan Agosto	1984 Topps #409
Luis Aguayo	1982 Donruss #622
Luis Aguayo	1982 Fleer #238
Luis Aguayo	1982 Topps #449
Rick Aguilera	1986 Donruss #441
Rick Aguilera	1986 Fleer #74
Rick Aguilera	1986 Topps #599
Hank Aguirre	1957 Topps #96
Willie Aikens	1980 Topps #368
Dan Ainge	1981 Fleer #418
Danny Ainge	1981 Donruss #569
Darrel Akerfelds	1988 Score #632
Darrel Akerfelds	1988 Topps #82
Scott Aldred	1991 Topps #658
Scott Aldred	1991 Upper Deck #7
Mike Aldrete	1987 Donruss #450
Mike Aldrete	1987 Fleer #264
Mike Aldrete	1987 Topps #71
Jay Aldrich	1988 Donruss #460
Jay Aldrich	1988 Fleer #155
Jay Aldrich	1988 Score #578
Jay Aldrich	1988 Topps #616
Doyle Alexander	1972 Topps #579
Gerald Alexander	1991 Fleer #278
Luis Alicea	1989 Donruss #466
Luis Alicea	1989 Fleer #443
Luis Alicea	1989 Score #231
Luis Alicea	1989 Topps #588
Luis Alicea	1989 Upper Deck #281
Andy Allanson	1987 Donruss #95
Andy Allanson	1987 Fleer #241
Andy Allanson	1987 Topps #436
Bernie Allen	1962 Topps #596
Neil Allen	1980 Topps #94
Richie Allen	1964 Topps #243
Rod Allen	1989 Fleer #397
Gene Alley	1964 Topps #509
Bob Allison	1959 Topps #116
Beau Allred	1990 Donruss #691
Beau Allred	1990 Fleer #419
Billy Almon	1977 Topps #490
Roberto Alomar	1988 Donruss #34
Sandy Alomar	1989 Score #630
Sandy Alomar	1989 Topps #648
Santos Alomar	1965 Topps #82
Sandy Alomar, Jr.	1989 Donruss #28
Sandy Alomar, Jr.	1989 Fleer #300
Sandy Alomar, Jr.	1989 Upper Deck #5
Felipe Alou	1959 Topps #102
Jesus Alou	1964 Topps #47
Matty Alou	1961 Topps #327
Moises Alou	1990 Fleer #650
Moises Alou	1990 Score #592
Jose Alvarez	1989 Donruss #405
Jose Alvarez	1989 Fleer #585
Jose Alvarez	1989 Topps #253
Wilson Alvarez	1991 Topps #378

Max Alvis	1963 Topps #228
Larry Andersen	1978 Topps #703
Allan Anderson	1987 Donruss #368
Allan Anderson	1987 Fleer #533
Allan Anderson	1987 Topps #336
Brady Anderson	1989 Donruss #519
Brady Anderson	1989 Fleer #606
Brady Anderson	1989 Score #563
Brady Anderson	1989 Topps #757
Brady Anderson	1989 Upper Deck #408
Dave Anderson	1984 Donruss #642
Dave Anderson	1984 Topps #376
George Anderson	1959 Topps #338
Kent Anderson	1990 Donruss #490
Kent Anderson	1990 Score #412
Kent Anderson	1990 Topps #16
Kent Anderson	1990 Upper Deck #691
Scott Anderson	1991 Fleer #225
Mike Andrews	1967 Topps #314
Shane Andrews	1991 Topps #74
Joaquin Andujar	1977 Topps #67
Willie Ansley	1989 Topps #607
Eric Anthony	1990 Donruss #34
Eric Anthony	1990 Fleer #222
Eric Anthony	1990 Score #584
Eric Anthony	1990 Topps #608
Eric Anthony	1990 Upper Deck #28
Johnny Antonelli	1950 Bowman #74
Luis Aparicio	1956 Topps #292
Kevin Appier	1990 Fleer #100
Kevin Appier	1990 Score #625
Kevin Appier	1990 Topps #167
Kevin Appier	1990 Upper Deck #102
Luis Aquino	1987 Donruss #655
Luis Aquino	1987 Topps #301
Tony Armas	1977 Topps #492
Jack Armstrong	1989 Donruss #493
Jack Armstrong	1989 Score #462
Jack Armstrong	1989 Topps #317
Jack Armstrong	1989 Upper Deck #257
Brad Arnsberg	1988 Fleer #202
Brad Arnsberg	1988 Score #159
Randy Asadoor	1987 Donruss #574
Randy Asadoor	1987 Fleer #650
Richie Ashburn	1949 Bowman #214
Bob Aspromonte	1960 Topps #547
Paul Assenmacher	1987 Donruss #290
Paul Assenmacher	1987 Fleer #511
Paul Assenmacher	1987 Topps #132
Keith Atherton	1984 Donruss #497
Keith Atherton	1984 Fleer #437
Keith Atherton	1984 Topps #529
Don August	1988 Donruss #602
Pat Austin	1990 Score #626
Steve Avery	1989 Topps #784
Roberto Avila	1951 Bowman #188
Oscar Azocar	1991 Donruss Series I #331
Oscar Azocar	1991 Fleer #655
Oscar Azocar	1991 Score Series I #72
Oscar Azocar	1991 Topps #659
Oscar Azocar	1991 Upper Deck #464

B

Wally Backman	1981 Fleer #336
Carlos Baerga	1991 Donruss Series I #274
Carlos Baerga	1991 Fleer #360
Carlos Baerga	1991 Score Series I #74
Carlos Baerga	1991 Topps #147
Carlos Baerga	1991 Upper Deck #125
Stan Bahnsen	1967 Topps #93
Scott Bailes	1987 Donruss #227
Scott Bailes	1987 Fleer #242
Scott Bailes	1987 Topps #585
Bob Bailey	1963 Topps #228
Ed Bailey	1953 Topps #206

Pat Borders .... 1989 Topps #693
Pat Borders .... 1989 Upper Deck #593
Mike Bordick .... 1991 Score Series I #339
Steve Boros .... 1958 Topps #81
Steve Boros .... 1958 Topps #81
Chris Bosio .... 1987 Donruss #478
Chris Bosio .... 1987 Fleer #338
Chris Bosio .... 1987 Topps #448
Shawn Boskie .... 1991 Donruss Series I #241
Shawn Boskie .... 1991 Fleer #416
Shawn Boskie .... 1991 Score Series I #59
Shawn Boskie .... 1991 Topps #254
Shawn Boskie .... 1991 Upper Deck #471
Thad Bosley .... 1978 Topps #619
Dick Bosman .... 1967 Topps #459
Lyman Bostock .... 1976 Topps #263
Daryl Boston (RR) .... 1985 Donruss #33
Dave Boswell .... 1967 Topps #575
Jim Bouton .... 1962 Topps #592
Larry Bowa .... 1970 Topps #539
Dennis Boyd .... 1984 Fleer #393
Dennis "Oil Can" Boyd .... 1984 Donruss #457
Cletis Boyer .... 1957 Topps #121
Ken Boyer .... 1955 Topps #125
Phil Bradley .... 1985 Donruss #631
Phil Bradley .... 1985 Fleer #486
Phil Bradley .... 1985 Topps #449
Scott Bradley (RR) .... 1985 Donruss #37
Glenn Braggs .... 1987 Donruss #337
Glenn Braggs .... 1987 Fleer #339
Glenn Braggs .... 1987 Topps #622
Jackie Brandt .... 1959 Topps #297
Jeff Brantley .... 1990 Donruss #466
Jeff Brantley .... 1990 Fleer #52
Jeff Brantley .... 1990 Score #371
Jeff Brantley .... 1990 Topps #703
Jeff Brantley .... 1990 Upper Deck #358
Mickey Brantley .... 1986 Fleer #651
Sid Bream .... 1985 Donruss #470
Sid Bream .... 1985 Topps #253
Bob Brenly .... 1982 Donruss #574
Bob Brenly .... 1982 Topps #171
Bill Brennan .... 1989 Score #622
William Brennan .... 1989 Donruss #589
William Brennan .... 1989 Upper Deck #16
George Brett .... 1975 Topps #228
Ken Brett .... 1969 Topps #476
Ken Brett .... 1969 Topps #476
Jim Brewer .... 1961 Topps #317
John Briggs .... 1964 Topps #482
Nelson Briles .... 1965 Topps #431
Greg Briley .... 1989 Topps #781
Ed Brinkman .... 1963 Topps #479
Greg Brock .... 1983 Donruss #579
Greg Brock .... 1983 Fleer #203
Ernie Broglio .... 1959 Topps #296
Rico Brogna .... 1991 Upper Deck #73
Tom Brookens .... 1980 Topps #416
Hubie Brooks .... 1981 Topps #259
Terry Bross .... 1990 Donruss #502
Bob Brower .... 1987 Donruss #651
Bobby Brown .... 1949 Bowman #19
Chris Brown .... 1986 Donruss #553
Chris Brown .... 1986 Fleer #535
Chris Brown .... 1986 Topps #383
Gates Brown .... 1964 Topps #471
Hal Brown .... 1953 Topps #184
Keith Brown .... 1989 Donruss #115
Keith Brown .... 1989 Fleer #154
Kevin Brown .... 1987 Donruss #627
Kevin Brown .... 1989 Fleer #641
Marty Brown .... 1989 Topps #645
Jerry Browne .... 1987 Fleer #647
Jerry Browne (RR) .... 1987 Donruss #41
Tom Browning .... 1985 Donruss #634
Mike Brumley .... 1988 Donruss #609
Tom Brunansky .... 1982 Topps #653
Len Brutcher .... 1991 Upper Deck #75
Bill Bruton .... 1953 Topps #214
Ralph Bryant .... 1987 Donruss #587
Ralph Bryant .... 1987 Fleer #649
Scott Bryant .... 1990 Score #667
T.R. Bryden .... 1987 Topps #387
Bill Buckner .... 1970 Topps #286
Steve Buechele .... 1986 Donruss #544
Steve Buechele .... 1986 Fleer #558
Steve Buechele .... 1986 Topps #397
Don Buford .... 1964 Topps #368
Bob Buhl .... 1954 Topps #210
Jay Buhner .... 1988 Donruss #545
DeWayne Buice .... 1988 Donruss #58
DeWayne Buice .... 1988 Fleer #487

DeWayne Buice .... 1988 Score #376
DeWayne Buice .... 1988 Topps #649
Eric Bullock .... 1989 Fleer #106
Alonza Bumbry .... 1973 Topps #614
Wally Bunker .... 1964 Topps #201
Jim Bunning .... 1957 Topps #338
Dave Burba .... 1991 Fleer #447
Lew Burdette .... 1952 Bowman #244
Forrest Burgess .... 1951 Bowman #317
Tom Burgmeier .... 1969 Topps #558
Tim Burke .... 1986 Donruss #421
Tim Burke .... 1986 Fleer #245
Tim Burke .... 1986 Topps #258
John Burkett .... 1988 Fleer #651
Ellis Burks .... 1988 Donruss #174
Ellis Burks .... 1988 Fleer #348
Ellis Burks .... 1988 Score #472
Ellis Burks .... 1988 Topps #269
Rick Burleson .... 1975 Topps #302
Jeromy Burnitz .... 1991 Score Series I #380
Britt Burns .... 1981 Donruss #279
Britt Burns .... 1981 Fleer #342
Britt Burns .... 1981 Fleer #342
Britt Burns .... 1981 Topps #412
Todd Burns .... 1989 Donruss #564
Todd Burns .... 1989 Fleer #3
Todd Burns .... 1989 Score #465
Todd Burns .... 1989 Topps #174
Ray Burris .... 1974 Topps #161
Jeff Burroughs .... 1972 Topps #191
Steve Busby .... 1973 Topps #608
Randy Bush .... 1984 Donruss #513
Randy Bush .... 1984 Fleer #558
Randy Bush .... 1984 Topps #429
Brett Butler .... 1982 Donruss #275
Brett Butler .... 1982 Topps #502
Randall Byers .... 1988 Donruss #605
Randell Byers (Randall) .... 1988 Fleer #653

C

Enos Cabell .... 1973 Topps #605
Francisco Cabrera .... 1990 Donruss #646
Francisco Cabrera .... 1990 Upper Deck #64
Greg Cadaret .... 1988 Donruss #528
Greg Cadaret .... 1988 Topps #328
Ivan Calderon .... 1986 Donruss #435
Ivan Calderon .... 1986 Fleer #462
Ivan Calderon .... 1986 Topps #382
Mike Caldwell .... 1973 Topps #182
John Callison .... 1959 Topps #119
Ernie Camacho .... 1981 Topps #96
Ken Caminiti .... 1988 Donruss #308
Ken Caminiti .... 1988 Fleer #441
Ken Caminiti .... 1988 Score #164
Ken Caminiti .... 1988 Topps #64
Roy Campanella .... 1949 Bowman #84
Bert Campaneris .... 1965 Topps #266
Bill Campbell .... 1974 Topps #26
Jim Campbell .... 1989 Fleer #646
Mike Campbell .... 1988 Donruss #30
Mike Campbell .... 1988 Fleer #372
Mike Campbell .... 1988 Topps #246
Sil Campusano .... 1989 Donruss #584
Sil Campusano .... 1989 Score #473
Sil Campusano .... 1989 Topps #191
Sil Campusano .... 1989 Upper Deck #45
George Canale .... 1990 Donruss #699
George Canale .... 1990 Fleer #641
George Canale .... 1990 Score #656
George Canale .... 1990 Topps #344
George Canale .... 1990 Upper Deck #59
Casey Candaele .... 1987 Donruss #549
John Candelaria .... 1976 Topps #317
Tom Candiotti .... 1984 Donruss #393
Tom Candiotti .... 1984 Fleer #197
Tom Candiotti .... 1984 Topps #262
John Cangelosi .... 1987 Donruss #162
John Cangelosi .... 1987 Fleer #489
John Cangelosi .... 1987 Topps #201
Jose Cano .... 1990 Upper Deck #43
Jose Canseco .... 1986 Fleer #649
Ozzie Canseco .... 1991 Score Series I #346
Ozzie Canseco .... 1991 Topps #162
Ozzie Canseco .... 1991 Upper Deck #146
Jose Canseco (RR) .... 1986 Donruss #39
Mike Capel .... 1989 Fleer #643
Mike Capel .... 1989 Topps #767
Nick Capra .... 1989 Topps #279
Bernie Carbo .... 1970 Topps #36
Jose Cardenal .... 1965 Topps #374
Chico Cardenas .... 1960 Topps #119

NOBODY BEATS OUR HAND

At The Dragon's Den, we realize that collectors don't want to gamble on the stores they visit. That's why we strive to carry the largest selection of stars, rookies, commons, sets and accessories in the East. Where else can you find eight large showcases crammed with the hottest stars and superstars of the past and present? Of course, we also have an extensive selection of common cards, as well as football, hockey and non-sport cards. And, we offer a large array of new and back issue comic books, posters, sports photos and games. Have something to sell? We're always buying quality sets and singles. Remember, at the Dragon's Den, the cards are always stacked in your favor.

Mail order on pre-advertised items only.

We buy, sell and trade.

THE DRAGON'S DEN

Baseball Cards, Comic Books, Games & More / OPEN EVERY DAY

914/793-4630 2614 Central Avenue Yonkers, NY 10710

Krause Publications
CUSTOMER SERVICE AWARD

Collector-only issues

Collectors may find some recent issues not included in this volume. In most cases these are illegal, unauthorized "collector-only" issues. Such cards often show nothing but the player's photo and his name on the front, and his name and perhaps a line or two of statistics on the back. The sets usually lack a manufacturer's name. They are often sold at shows and in shops, and frequently carry high price tags.

The cards *are not* legitimate issues. They can be printed and reprinted at will, so they lack any scarcity value.

Card company addresses

Collectors frequently want to know the addresses of the major baseball-card manufacturing companies. They are:

Topps Chewing Gum Co.
254 36th St.
Brooklyn, N.Y. 11232
Fleer Corp.
10th & Somerville
Philadelphia, Pa. 19141
Leaf-Donruss Co.
P.O. Box 2038
Memphis, Tenn. 38101
Sportflics/Score
Major League Marketing, Inc.
55 Ford Rd.
Westport, Ct. 06880
Upper Deck Co.
23705 Via Del Rio
Yorba Linda, CA 92686

Common Hobby Terms & Definitions

A

Airbrushing — An artist's technique used on baseball cards in which logos on uniforms or hats are altered or eliminated.

All-Star card (AS) — A card which denotes a player's selection to the previous year's All-Star Team.

Autographed card — Card which was personally autographed by the player depicted. Cards with facsimile signatures that are printed on many cards as part of the design, are not considered autographed cards.

Autograph guest — A current or former ball player or other celebrity who attends a card convention for the purpose of signing autographs for fans. Usually a fee is charged for the autograph, ranging from a few dollars to more than $30 for HOF players.

B

Baseball's Best — A set made by Donruss in 1988 and 1989. Also the name of a boxed set made by Fleer in 1987 and 1988, and the name of the set of insert cards made by *Baseball Cards* magazine in 1989 and 1990.

Bazooka cards — Cards issued with boxes of Bazooka Bubblegum (1959-1971, 1988-1990).

Big cards — Name for Topps' large, glossy-finish card issues produced in 1988-present. Cards reminiscent of Topps' cards from the 1950s.

Blank backs — A card that has a blank card back. Most collectors feel these cards are merely damaged, with a lower value than correctly-printed specimens, though some collectors will pay premiums on superstars or rookies.

Blanket — An early 20th-century collectible consisting of a square piece of felt or other fabric depicting a baseball player. Most popular are the 5" by 5" B-18 "blankets" from 1914, so-called because they were sometimes sewn together to form a blanket.

Blister pack — A blister pack is a method of card packaging in which cards are packaged in hard plastic on a cardboard backing, with three to four pockets of cards. Donruss (1987-present).

Borders — The portion of a card which surrounds the picture. They are usually white, but are sometimes other colors. Border condition is very important to the card's grade and value.

Bowman (B) — Sportscard manufacturer (1948-1955) bought out by Topps in 1956. Topps issued baseball sets under the Bowman name (1989-present).

Boxed sets — These are sets produced by one of the major card companies, usually in conjunction with a business, such as K-Mart or Walgreens. Boxed sets usually contain fewer than 60 cards, most of which are star players.

Box panel cards — Bonus cards which are featured on a panel of wax boxes of the major card companies. The idea was originated by Donruss in 1985. Complete sets range from four to 16 cards, and feature star players.

Brick — A "brick" of cards is any group of cards with similar characteristics, such as a 100-card brick of 1975 Topps cards. Bricks usually contain common cards.

Buy price — The price a dealer will to pay for cards or memorabilia.

Burger King cards (BK) — Cards issued in conjunction with Burger King (1977-1987).

C

Cabinet card — A large card from the 19th or early 20th centuries, usually issued on heavy cardboard.

Card lot — A "lot" of cards is the same card, such as a 1988 Topps Don Mattingly card, sold in a lot or "grouping" of five, 25, 50, 100 or whatever number of cards. A collector purchasing a "lot" of cards, gets the cards at a discounted price, as opposed to buying a single card. Example: a single Mattingly card costs $1, but 100 Mattingly cards cost $75 or 75-cents apiece.

Case — A sealed case containing wax boxes or other product units which card companies sell at wholesale to dealers or retail stores. For instance, a 1991 Topps "wax case" is made up of 20 "wax boxes."

Cello pack — A package of about 30 cards wrapped in a printed cellophane wrapper that allows you to see the top and bottom cards. There are usually 24 cello packs to a cello box, and 16 cello boxes to a cello case. Cello packs retail between for around $1. Issued by Topps, Fleer and Donruss.

Checklist (CL) — A list of every card in a particular set, usually with space allowing the collector to check whether or not he has the card. A checklist can appear on a card(s), in a book or elsewhere.

Classic cards — Baseball cards made by Game Time, Ltd., to go with its "Classic Baseball" trivia game (1987-present).

Coin — Can refer to an actual coin struck to commemorate an achievement made by a team or player; also, a collectible made soley from or with a combination of plastic, paper or metal, issued as a set, such as the 1988 Topps Coin set.

Collation — The act of putting cards in order, by hand or machine, usually numerically.

Collector issue — A set of cards produced primarily to be sold to collectors and not issued as a premium to be given away or sold with a commercial product.

Common card — A card which carries no premium value in a set. "Common" is a blunt way of saying the player depicted is not a star.

Convention — Also known as a "baseball card show" or "trading card show." A gathering of anywhere from one to 600 or more card dealers at a single location (convention center, hotel, school auditoriums or gymnasiums) for the purpose of buying, selling or trading cards.

Counterfeit cards — Cards made to look like original cards, and distributed with the intention of fooling a buyer. High-demand cards are the most likely to be counterfeited.

D

Dealer — A person who buys, sells and trades baseball cards and other memorabilia for profit. A dealer may be full-time, part-time, own a shop, operate a mail-order business from his home, deal at baseball card shows on weekends, or any combination of the above.

Die-cut card — A baseball card in which the player's outline has been partially separated from the background, enabling the card to be folded into a "stand-up" figure. Die-cut cards that have never been folded are worth more to collectors.

Disc — Circular-shaped card.

Donruss (D) — Baseball card manufacturer (1981-present).

Donruss Rookies (DR) — 56-card post-season set issued by Donruss which includes rookie players (1986-present). Sold exclusively through hobby dealers in separate box.

Double print (DP) — A card printed twice on the same sheet, making it twice as common as other cards on the sheet. Topps double-printed cards in virtually every set from 1952 to 1981. This was done to accomodate the year's set size on standard company printing sheets.

Drakes — Ohio-based bakery which made baseball cards in the 1950s, and again from 1981-1988.

E

Error — An error is usually found on card backs in the statistical or personal information, and sometimes on the card front (such as a reversed negative). If an error is not corrected, the error adds nothing to the value of the card. If the error is corrected, it is called a "variation" card.

Exhibit card — Postcard-size cards picturing baseball players and other celebrities and sold in penny-arcade machines. Exhibit cards were produced from the 1920s to the 1960s.

F

Factory set (F or FAC.) — A complete set collated (packaged) by the card producing company. Issued by all companies.

First card (FC) — Price guide designation which refers to the first appearance of a player in the major card sets.

Fleer (F) — Baseball card manufacturer (1959-1963, 1981-present).

Fleer Glossy Tin (FG) — Limited edition set produced by Fleer, which features the year's regular issue set in a high gloss finish and sold in a tin box (1987-present). Fleer Update sets also done in glossy style.

Fleer Update (FU) — 132-card post-season set from Fleer which includes players traded to other teams during the season, and rookies (1984-present). Sold exclusively through hobby dealers in its own separate box.

Food issue — A set of baseball cards or related memorabilia which was issued in conjunction with a food product, such as Post cereal or Hostess snack cakes.

G

Gallery of Champions — Trade name for a set of metallic reproductions of Topps cards made and sold by Topps from 1986-1988. The metals used were bronze, aluminum, pewter and silver.

Goudey — Baseball card manufacturer (1933-1936, 1938, 1941).

Grades — The physical state or condition of a card.

H

Hand collated set (H or HC) — A complete set put together by hand using cards from wax, cello, rack or vending boxes.

High-numbers — A term used to describe the final series in a particular set of cards. "High numbers" were generally produced in smaller quantities than other series and are, therefore, scarcer and more valuable.

Hall of Famer (HOFer) - A card picturing a member of the Baseball Hall of Fame, in Cooperstown, N.Y. Hall of Famer cards almost always command a premium over other cards.

Hartland statues — Wisconsin plastics company which produced, among other things, statues of baseball players in the late 1950s and early 1960s. Company reproduced the set in 1989 as Hartland's 25th Anniversary Commemorative Edition. Original statues very collectible.

I

In Action card (IA) — A card featuring a star player, designated with the words "In Action" on the card front. Most notably from the 1972 and 1982 Topps sets.

Inserts — A collectible included inside a regular pack of baseball cards to boost sales. Inserts have included posters, coins, stamps, tatoos, special cards, etc.

J

Jell-O cards — Cards sold as premiums with Jell-O packages (1962-1963).

K

Kellog's cards — Simulated three-dimensional cards given away in cereal boxes or via a mail-in offer (1970-1983).

Key cards — The most important (valuable) cards in a set, such as the Mickey Mantle card, a "key" card in the 1952 Topps set.

L

Last card — The final regular card issued for a player, such as Hank Aaron's "last" card was in the 1976 Topps set. No particular extra value is added for last cards.

Leaf-Donruss — Baseball cards produced by Donruss specifically for the Canadian market (1985-1988). Leaf issued its own set in 1990.

Legitimate issue — A card set issued as a premium with a commerical product to increase sales; not a "collector issue."

Letter of authenticity — A letter stating that a certain piece of memorabilia, like a uniform, is authentic.

Lithograph — A high-quality art print made in limited quantities.

M

MVP — Most Valuable Player award.

Mail-bid auction — An auction where bids are sent through the mail, with the highest bidder winning the merchandise.

Major set — A large, nationally-distributed set produced by a major card maker like Topps, Fleer, Donruss, Score, Sportflics or Upper Deck.

Megalot — A megalot describes a group of cards, usually 1,000 or more of the same player, purchased for investment or speculation.

Memorabilia — Refers to items other than cards, such as uniforms, bats, autographed baseballs, magazines, scorecards, pins, statues and the like.

Minis — Cards which resemble the regular issue cards in every way, except they are smaller in size. Most noteable are the 1975 Topps Minis.

Minor league cards — A card depicting a player from the minor leagues. Minor league sets are a fast-growing segment of the hobby.

Mother's cards — An Oakland, (Calif.)-based cookie company which produces popular high quality glossy finish regional sets (1982-present).

Multi-player card — A card picturing more than one player.

N

Non-sport card — A trading card or bubblegum card picturing a subject other than sports. Non-sports cards have depicted movie stars, television shows, moments in history and other subjects.

O

Obverse — The front of the card displaying the picture.

O-Pee-Chee (OPC) — Canadian card producing company (1965-present). O-Pee-Chee is Topps' official Canadian licensee, and O-Pee-Chee cards are almost identical to Topps' issues of the same year.

P

Panel — A strip of two or more uncut cards. Some card sets are issued in "panels."

Phone auction — An auction where bids for baseball cards or other memorabilia are taken over the phone, with the highest bidder getting the merchandise.

Plastic sheet — A polyethelyne or polyvinyl sheet designed to store baseball cards, the most common being the nine-pocket sheet (which fits today's standard-sized cards). The sheets have pre-punched holes on the left side which allows them to be placed in a three-ring binder.

Play Ball — Name of baseball cards produced by Gum, Inc., (1939-1941).

Police/Fire/Safety sets — Card sets sponsored by public law enforcement or fire fighting agencies and a major or minor league team. Card backs usually contain anti-drug messages, fire prevention tips or other safety messages.

Post cards — Cards sold as premiums on boxes of Post cereal (1960-1963, 1990).

Pre-rookie card — Name given to a major league player's minor league cards.

Price guide — A periodical or book which contains checklists of cards, sets and other memorabilia and their values in varying conditions.

Price on request (POR) — A dealer will advertise a card P.O.R. if he believes the card will fluctuate in price from the time he places his ad until the time the ad is seen by the public.

Promotional cards — Cards produced by the card companies which serve as a marketing tool for their upcoming cards. Promotional or "promo" cards are often sent to dealers to entice them to order cards. Promo cards have limited distribution and can be very expensive.

Proof card — A card produced by the card companies prior to printing their sets, which is "proofed" for errors, and checked for card design, photography, colors, statisical accuracy and so on. Proof cards are not distributed and a few of the older proof cards on the hobby market can be quite expensive.

PPD — Postage Paid.

R

Rack pack — A three-sectioned card package with about 14-16 cards per section. There are usually 24 rack packs to a rack box, and six rack boxes to a rack case. Topps, Fleer, Donruss, Score.

Rare — Difficult to obtain and limited in number. See "Scarce."

Rated Rookie (RR) — Donruss subset featuring young players the company feels are the top rookie players from a particular year (1984-present).

Record Breaker card (RB) — A special Topps card found in a regular issue set which commemorates a record-breaking performance by a player from the previous season.

Regional set — A card set distributed in one geographical area. Regional sets often depict players from one team.

Regular issue set — See "Major set."

Reprint cards — Cards reprinted to closely match original cards, made with the intention of allowing collectors to buy them as substitutes for cards they could not ever afford. Reprints are usually labled — but not always — "reprint."

Reverse — The back of a card.

Rookie card (R or RC) — The first appearance of a player in one of the major sets (Topps, Fleer, etc.), excluding update and traded sets. It may or may not be issued during the player's actual rookie season.

S

SASE — Self-Addressed Stamped Envelope.

Score (S or SC) — Brand name of sports cards (1988-present). Major League Marketing is the manufacturer.

Score Traded (ScTr) - 110-card post-season set issued by Score to include players traded during the season, as well as rookie players. Sold exclusively by hobby dealers in its own separate box.

Second-year card — The second card of a player issued in the major sets. Usually, a second-year card is the most expensive card of a player, next to the rookie card.

Sell price — The price a dealer sells a card.

Series — A group of cards that is part of a set, and was issued at one time. The term usually applied to Topps sets from 1952-1973, when sets were issued in various "series." Cards of different series are valued at different prices since some series are scarcer than others.

Set — A complete run of cards, including one number of each card issued by a particular manufacturer in a particular year; for example, a 1985 Fleer "set."

Set case — Companies sell their factory sets in sealed cases containing 8 to 16 sets per case, depending on the company. Issued by all major companies.

Skip-numbered — A set of cards not numbered in exact sequence. Some manufacturers have issued "skip-numbered" sets to trick collectors into buying more cards, looking for card numbers that didn't exist. Other sets became skip-numbered when one or more players were dropped from the set at the last minute and were not replaced with another.

Sleeve — A specially-designed, plastic wrapper used to house and protect individual baseball cards.

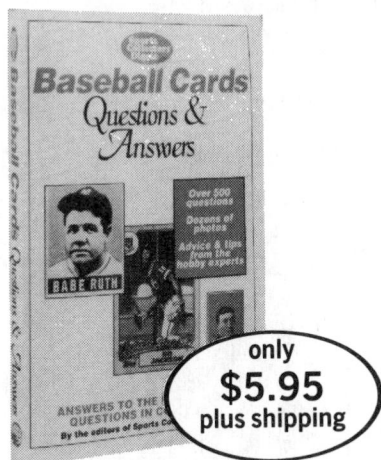
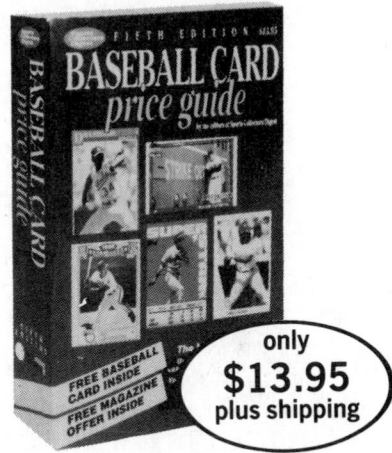

Special card — A card in a set that depicts something other than a single player; for example a checklist card, All-Star card, team card or leaders card.

Sportflics — Brand name of baseball cards (1986-present). Major League Marketing is the manufacturer.

SCD — *Sports Collectors Digest.*

Standard size card — A card which measures 2½" wide by 3½" tall. In 1957, Topps baseball cards were produced in the 2½" by 3½" size, which set the standard for modern baseball cards.

Star card — Card featuring a star player, but not one of "superstar" caliber. The term "minor star" may also be used to differentiate between levels of skill and popularity. In terms of value, "star" cards fall between "commons" and "superstars."

Starter lot — A group of cards from the same set, usually more than 100, which serves as a starting point for a hobbyist to begin putting a set together. Starter lots usually contain common players. Also known as a "starter set."

Starting Lineup — A line of plastic sports statues produced by Kenner (1988-present). Also, the name for a computer-based baseball game from Parker Brothers.

Sticker — An adhesive-backed baseball card. Stickers can be card-size or smaller. Topps, Fleer and Panini have issued major baseball sticker sets over the past years. Stickers are not overly popular with older collectors, though younger collectors seem to enjoy them.

Subset — A set of cards with the same theme within a larger set. Examples: Donruss Diamond Kings are a "subset" of the Donruss set; or Topps All-Star cards are a subset of the Topps set.

Super card — A designation referring to the physical size of a card. Generally, any card postcard-size or larger is referred to as a "super."

Superstar card — A card picturing a true "superstar," a player of Hall of Fame caliber, like Mike Schmidt.

Stock — Refers to the type of paper or cardboard used on a baseball card.

Swap Meet — Term used to describe early baseball card shows where most of the cards were traded between hobbyists.

T

Team card — Card which depicts an entire team.

Team set — A set which includes all cards relating to a certain team from a particular year, by a particular manufacturer.

Team issued set — A set produced to be sold or given away by a baseball team.

Test issue — A set of cards test-marketed on a small scale in a limited geographic areas of the country. Topps test-marketed a variety of items from the 1950s-1980s.

Tobacco cards — Cards issued in the late 19th and early 20th centuries as premiums with cigarettes or other tobacco products.

Topps (T) — Sports card company (1951-present).

Topps Tiffany (TTF) — Limited edition set produced by Topps, featuring the year's regular complete set in a high gloss finish (1984-present). Topps Traded sets also done in this style.

Topps Traded (TT or TTR) — 132-card post-season set which includes players traded to other teams during the year, as well as rookie players (1981-present). Sold mainly through hobby dealers.

Traded set — An auxiliary set of cards issued toward the end of the season to reflect trades made after the printing of the regular set. Also called "Update" sets, they may also include rookies not included in the regular set.

U

Uncut sheet — A full sheet of baseball cards that has never been cut into individual cards.

Upper Deck (UD) — Sportscard company (1989-present).

Upper Deck High Numbers (UDH) — 100-card set featuring players traded during the season, as well as rookie players. This set was sold through hobby dealers and in Upper Deck foil packs, similar to the way cards before 1974 were released.

V

Variation — A variation is the result of a card company correcting a previous mistake on a card, resulting in two or more variations of the same card. Some variations have increased in value, if they were produced in lesser quantities.

Vending box — Vending boxes contain 500 cards per box. There are 24 vending boxes per vending case, for a total of 12,000 cards. Topps.

W

Want list — A collector's or dealer's list of items he is wishing to buy. Often, a collector will send a dealer a "want" list, and the dealer will try to locate the items on the list.

Notes